Intermediate Accounting

Second Edition

Elizabeth A. Gordon
Fox School of Business, Temple University

Jana S. Raedy
Kenan-Flagler Business School, University of North Carolina at Chapel Hill

Alexander J. Sannella
Rutgers Business School, Rutgers University

Pearson

New York, NY

Vice President, Business, Economics, and UK Courseware: Donna Battista
Director of Portfolio Management: Adrienne D'Ambrosio
Specialist Portfolio Manager: Lacey Vitetta
Development Editor: Rebecca Caruso
Editorial Assistant: Elisa Marks
Vice President, Product Marketing: Roxanne McCarley
Senior Product Marketer: Tricia Murphy
Product Marketing Assistant: Marianela Silvestri
Manager of Field Marketing, Business Publishing: Adam Goldstein
Executive Field Marketing Manager: Nayke Popovich
Vice President, Production and Digital Studio, Arts and Business: Etain O'Dea
Director of Production, Business: Jeff Holcomb
Managing Producer, Business: Melissa Feimer
Content Producer: Emily Throne
Operations Specialist: Carol Melville
Design Lead: Kathryn Foot
Manager, Learning Tools: Brian Surette
Content Developer, Learning Tools: Sarah Peterson
Managing Producer, Digital Studio and GLP, Media Production and Development: Ashley Santora
Managing Producer, Digital Studio: Diane Lombardo
Digital Studio Producer: Mary Kate Murray
Digital Studio Producer: Alana Coles
Digital Content Team Lead: Noel Lotz
Digital Content Project Lead: Martha LaChance
Project Manager: Patty Donovan, SPi Global
Interior Design: Anthony Gemmellaro, Denise Hoffman, SPi Global
Cover Design: SPi Global
Cover Art: Excellent backgrounds/Shutterstock
Printer/Binder: LSC Communications, Inc./Courier Kendallville
Cover Printer: LSC Communications

Library of Congress Cataloging-in-Publication Data
Names: Gordon, Elizabeth A. (Associate professor), author. | Raedy, Jana Smith, author. | Sannella, Alexander John, author.
Title: Intermediate accounting / Elizabeth A. Gordon, Temple University, Jana S. Raedy, University of North Carolina at Chapel Hill, Alexander J. Sannella, Rutgers University.
Description: Second edition. | Hoboken, NJ : Pearson Education, [2019]
Identifiers: LCCN 2017050146 | ISBN 9780134730370 | ISBN 0134730372
Subjects: LCSH: Accounting.
Classification: LCC HF5636 .G67 2019 | DDC 657/.044—dc23
LC record
available at https://lccn.loc.gov/2017050146

4 2021

Pearson

ISBN 10: 0-13-473037-2
ISBN 13: 978-0-13-473037-0

For Paul, Andrew, Mary, and my parents
EAG

For Nicholas, Aidan, and Kevin
JSR

For Ayden Alexander and Chloe Mikenzie
AJS

About the Authors

Elizabeth A. Gordon, Ph.D., MBA, CPA

ELIZABETH A. GORDON IS ASSOCIATE PROFESSOR OF ACCOUNTING at the Fox School of Business at Temple University and a Merves Research Fellow. She received her doctorate from Columbia University, master's degree in business administration from Yale University, and bachelor's of science degree in accounting with highest distinction from Indiana University.

Dr. Gordon specializes in the areas of financial accounting and international financial reporting and investigates topics such as international financial reporting standards, corporate disclosure, executive compensation, related-party disclosures, and market development. Her research is published in top journals in her field including *Journal of Accounting Research*, *The Accounting Review*; *Review of Accounting Studies, Journal of Accounting, Auditing and Finance*; and *Journal of Accounting and Public Policy*. She serves as an editor of *Journal of International Financial Management and Accounting* and an associate editor of *Journal of International Accounting Research*. Dr. Gordon is a past president of the International Accounting Section of the American Accounting Association and serves as the vice president, finance and administration of the International Association for Accounting Education and Research.

Dr. Gordon has taught courses in financial accounting and international accounting at the graduate and undergraduate levels, receiving a number of teaching awards. She has coauthored accounting readings for the CFA Institute, integrating IFRS and U.S. GAAP. She was an auditor with PricewaterhouseCoopers, LLP, and interned at the U.S. Office of Management and Budget before entering academia. Dr. Gordon is a CPA in the State of Maryland. She has been on the faculty of the Graduate School of Business at the University of Chicago, the Rutgers Business School, and a visiting professor at the University of Pennsylvania.

Jana S. Raedy, Ph.D., CPA

JANA RAEDY IS ASSOCIATE PROFESSOR OF ACCOUNTING, associate dean of the Master of Accounting Program, and the Ernst & Young Scholar in Accounting at the Kenan-Flager Business School at the University of North Carolina at Chapel Hill. She received her bachelor of science and master of science degrees from the University of Kentucky and her doctorate from the Pennsylvania State University.

Dr. Raedy's research is primarily focused on issues in international financial reporting as well as areas in which financial reporting and taxation intersect. Her research is published in top journals such as *Journal of Accounting Research, Journal of Accounting and Economics, The Accounting Review, Contemporary Accounting Research*, and *Journal of the American Taxation Association*.

Dr. Raedy has taught a number of courses in financial reporting at the graduate level, including core financial reporting (both introductory and intermediate accounting), international financial reporting, and forensic accounting. For over 15 years, she has taught a self-developed course in applied financial accounting research with a heavy emphasis on judgment and decision making. During her academic career, she has received a number of different teaching awards. She currently is a team member of the Ernst & Young Academic Resource Center, which provides faculty nationwide with comprehensive teaching materials related to topics such as judgment, IFRS, and fair value.

Alexander J. Sannella, Ph.D., CPA

ALEXANDER J. SANNELLA IS CURRENTLY AN ASSOCIATE PROFESSOR of Accounting at the Rutgers Business School and is the Director of the MBA in Professional Accounting Program, Director of the Master of Accountancy in Professional Accounting and the Director of the Rutgers Business School Teaching Excellence Center. He earned a BBA in Finance and an MBA in Accounting from Iona College. He received his doctorate in accounting and finance from New York University and is a New York State Certified Public Accountant.

During his years at Rutgers Business School, Dr. Sannella has taught at both the graduate and undergraduate levels and served as Associate Dean of the Business School and Vice Chair of the Department of Accounting and Information Systems. Previously, Dr. Sannella served on the faculty of New York University as instructor of accounting at the Stern School of Business and as an Associate Professor of Accounting at Iona College's Hagan School of Business.

He has public accounting experience as an auditor for PricewaterhouseCoopers, LLP and KPMG, LLP. Dr. Sannella was also an independent consultant working on many projects with other public accounting firms, bankruptcy trustees, and leasing divisions of major insurance companies. He also served as a consultant to the Line of Business Program at the Federal Trade Commission in Washington.

Dr. Sannella has over 40 years of teaching experience at the university level and over 30 years of experience in developing and teaching commercial and investment bank training programs. His clients have included eight major investment banks and four of the world's largest commercial banks. His training programs include courses designed to train financial analysts and associates as well as special programs for sales and trading professionals.

The author of many scholarly journal articles and three books, Dr. Sannella's articles have focused on accounting education and market-based accounting research. His books focus on the effects of accounting alternatives on the judgment of analysts and other statement users. Many of the books' topics are included on training videos and CPE courses.

Dr. Sannella has been interviewed by several publications including the *Newark Star Ledger* and *NJ Biz*.

Brief Contents

Contents

*Multiple-Choice Questions Becker Professional Education

BECKER PROFESSIONAL EDUCATION®

CHAPTER 6

Statements of Financial Position and Cash Flows and the Annual Report 235

*Multiple-Choice Questions Becker Professional Education

BECKER PROFESSIONAL EDUCATION®

*Multiple-Choice Questions Becker Professional Education

BECKER PROFESSIONAL EDUCATION®

*Multiple-Choice Questions Becker Professional Education

BECKER PROFESSIONAL EDUCATION®

*Multiple-Choice Questions Becker Professional Education

*Multiple-Choice Questions Becker Professional Education

BECKER PROFESSIONAL EDUCATION®

*Multiple-Choice Questions Becker Professional Education

BECKER PROFESSIONAL EDUCATION®

*Multiple-Choice Questions Becker Professional Education

BECKER PROFESSIONAL EDUCATION

*Multiple-Choice Questions Becker Professional Education

BECKER PROFESSIONAL EDUCATION®

*Multiple-Choice Questions Becker Professional Education

BECKER PROFESSIONAL EDUCATION

CHAPTER 18

Accounting for Leases 1063

*Multiple-Choice Questions Becker Professional Education

BECKER PROFESSIONAL EDUCATION®

*Multiple-Choice Questions Becker Professional Education

*Multiple-Choice Questions Becker Professional Education

BECKER PROFESSIONAL EDUCATION

*Multiple-Choice Questions Becker Professional Education

BECKER PROFESSIONAL EDUCATION®

*Multiple-Choice Questions Becker Professional Education

BECKER PROFESSIONAL EDUCATION®

*Multiple-Choice Questions Becker Professional Education

BECKER PROFESSIONAL EDUCATION®

Preface

New to This Edition

Coverage of the Latest Standards

Students need to begin understanding and applying standard changes to critical topics such as revenue recognition and leasing as early as possible in their college curriculum to be prepared for the CPA exam and practice when they graduate. With this in mind, key second edition updates include:

- Chapter 10 incorporates ASU 2015-11, which changes the measurement of the market value for lower-of-cost-or-market computations to net realizable value for all firms except those using LIFO or RIM.
- Chapter 14 incorporates ASU 2015-03, which changes the accounting method for debt issue costs under U.S. GAAP and converges U.S. GAAP with IFRS. Debt issue costs are now netted with the debt, thus changing the effective interest rate.
- Chapter 16 is significantly altered to incorporate ASU 2016-01, ASU 2016-13, and changes to IFRS 9. The principal impact of these standards is to the subsequent measurement of equity investments and the impairment of debt investments.
- Chapter 17 incorporates ASU 2015-17, which simplifies the presentation of deferred tax assets and liabilities on the balance sheet. The deferred tax accounts are now reported only as noncurrent assets and liabilities.
- Chapter 18 is a new chapter that incorporates the entirely new lease standards, ASU 2016-02, and IFRS 16.
- Chapter 19 incorporates ASU 2016-09, which allows companies the option of reporting actual forfeitures in addition to the current method of estimated forfeitures.

Solving Teaching and Learning Challenges

Our textbook is based on the belief that success in today's business environment requires an intuitive understanding of financial reporting and the ability to interpret and apply changing standards. In a world where there are simply too many rules to memorize, a traditional rules-based teaching approach has become inefficient and inadequate. Our goals for this textbook are aligned with the American Accounting Association's Pathways Commission, which seeks to correct misperceptions about the mechanical nature of accounting and to shift focus to the importance of critical thinking by accounting decision makers, particularly when the business context and related accounting rules require judgment.

We seek to develop the judgment and decision-making skills that accountants require to critically evaluate financial accounting methods and the financial statements. Using the conceptual framework fundamentals as a guide throughout, we emphasize solving accounting problems by applying standards, understanding how business activities are reflected in the financial statements, and critically evaluating the trade-offs and assumptions of accounting methods.

Coverage Grounded in the Conceptual Principles

To apply what they learn in the classroom to their professional lives, students need a solid grounding in the conceptual principles of financial reporting and the economic concepts underlying accounting. Thus, we open the textbook with coverage of these foundational topics, including the conceptual framework. In each chapter, sections called "The Conceptual Framework Connection" guide discussions and analyses by explicitly laying out the relevant conceptual underpinnings. For example, in the chapter on long-term operating assets, we discuss the capitalization decision.

Focus on Judgment, Decision Making, and Critical-Thinking Skills

Increasingly, the accounting profession and business world are looking for well-trained professionals with strong problem-solving and critical-thinking skills.

Judgment

To prepare students for future careers, we highlight the various *judgments* involved in all major topics in the context of real-business situations. For example, in Chapter 3, we discuss the factors that Activision Blizzard, a leading provider of interactive game services, considered when applying revenue recognition rules to its new technology and virtual goods. Our goal is to develop students' critical-thinking skills in assessing the assumptions, choices, and judgments that managers make when analyzing and reporting the business activities of a company. For example, many rules govern impairments, but ultimately, reporting comes down to judgment related to issues such as the expectation of future cash flows. Future career success depends on students' understanding the importance and prominence of the many judgments that inform a final set of financial statements.

Real-World Business

We pair our focus on real business situations with meaningful *real-company examples*. We examine financial statements from several high-profile firms—such as Johnson & Johnson, Netflix, Tesla, Amazon, Snap, Facebook, General Electric, Ericsson, Target, Adidas, Nike, Novartis, Coca-Cola, Pepsi Bottling Group, Starbucks, Walmart, and Ford Motor Company—in examples throughout the book.

In addition, our *Practitioner Interviews* feature question-and-answer-style exchanges with leaders in the field that provide insights into topics from a practitioner perspective and timely viewpoints on the business impact of rapidly evolving standards. Interviews profile executives at major firms—the Big Four accounting firms and name-brand companies such as Microsoft—as well as members of standard-setting boards.

Problem-Solving Skills

We emphasize problem solving within the chapters with *worked examples* accompanying every important concept. The consistent problem-solving methodology utilizes a problem/solution format and highlights the logic guiding the process, fostering students' ability to tackle problems on their own.

A variety of *end-of-chapter exercises* revolves around judgment and decision making. We include short problems and time-intensive cases that emphasize building students' ability to read and interpret authoritative accounting literature.

Highlighting Key Differences between U.S. GAAP and IFRS Standards

The book's central focus and grounding for each topic is U.S. GAAP. When IFRS diverges, we address the key conceptual differences in separate sections, often working through examples that parallel the GAAP coverage and providing tables with side-by-side comparisons of the GAAP and IFRS standards. With the aim of preparing students to apply the latest standards, we highlight key differences between IFRS and U.S. GAAP as pertinent. Our approach allows the instructor flexibility in IFRS topics covered and the depth of coverage. End-of-chapter summaries recap the main points for each section and contrast the U.S. GAAP and IFRS standards.

Presenting both sets of standards is important because the business world now operates in a global setting. Given the large number of multinational firms and foreign subsidiaries in the United States and the mobility of the workforce across international borders, students need to understand both IFRS and U.S. GAAP.

Reassessment of Coverage

We give fresh consideration to the necessary and proper content of an intermediate textbook. Due to changes in the business world and in the authoritative accounting literature, some topics may warrant less coverage while others have gained importance. This focused reconsideration of topical coverage will set students on a trajectory for success in their accounting careers and on the CPA exam.

We have chosen to reassess coverage of topics based primarily on five criteria: (1) The topic is repeated elsewhere in the normal accounting curriculum, (2) the topic is industry specific, (3) the topic covers transactions/events that rarely occur, (4) the particular accounting method is not typically allowed under U.S. GAAP or IFRS, and (5) the topic covers transactions/events that do not commonly occur and the accounting treatment of the transaction is rule intensive.

By reassessing the coverage, we have made room for a number of topics not typically included in texts that have gained importance in the field (for example, tax contingencies, and revaluations of long-term operating assets under IFRS).

Get Students Ready . . .

Accounting Cycle Tutorial

Accessed through MyLab Accounting by computer, smartphone, or tablet, the Accounting Cycle Tutorial provides a refresher on the basics so students are ready for intermediate-level work. This updated version includes a new comprehensive problem.

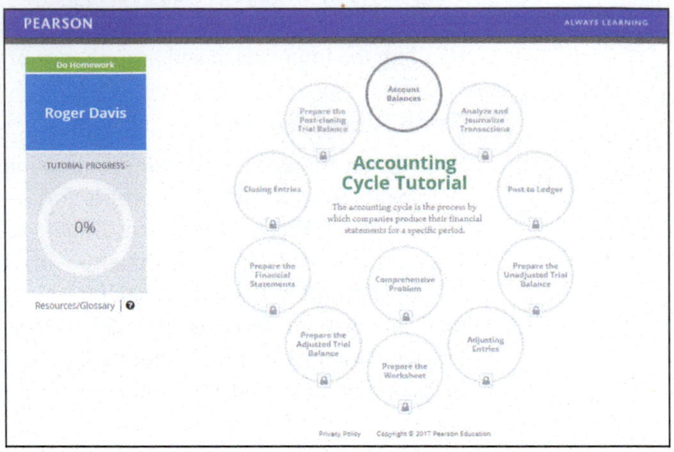

Time Value of Money Tutorial

The Time Value of Money Tutorial in MyLab ensures that students understand the basic theory and formulas of the TVM while helping test their ability to *apply* the TVM in the measurement of financial statement items. Students work through two sections. The first is to help them understand the theory using whichever method the instructor chooses (manually, through Excel, with tables, or via a calculator), and the second is to give students the opportunity to apply the theory by giving them a number of scenarios regarding each financial statement.

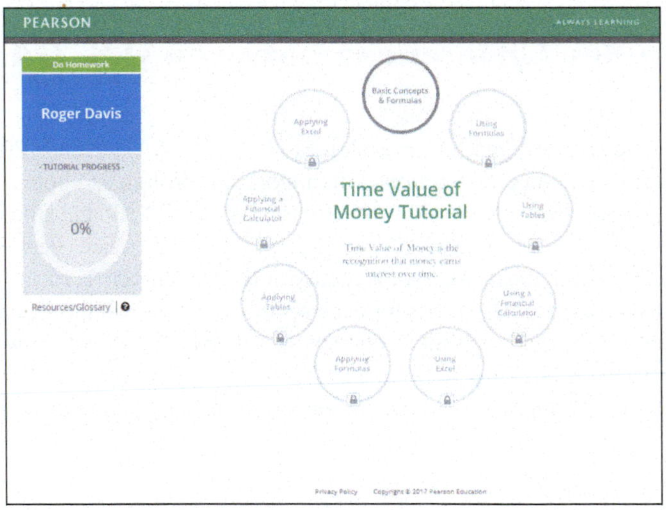

Worked Problem Videos

Worked Problem Videos provide step-by-step explanations of problems similar to those students will encounter in the text, helping them to understand how to arrive at the correct answers themselves.

Concept Overview Videos

Concept Overview Videos are short videos focusing on key concepts available in MyLab Accounting to further emphasize major concepts. These videos can be assigned as homework or used as part of a flipped classroom strategy.

To Be Decision Makers . . .

Conceptual Framework Connections

Each chapter guides students through discussions and analysis with a solid grounding in the conceptual framework fundamentals of reporting relevant, useful, timely, and understandable financial information.

THE CONCEPTUAL FRAMEWORK CONNECTION: Usefulness and Limitations of the Income Statements

The income statements provide useful information to financial statement users in three ways:

1. **Evaluate past performance.** Income statements enable financial statement users to evaluate the entity's past performance. By disclosing separate components of revenues and expenses, income statements provide useful information about the entity's overall past performance (i.e., the earnings) and identify the main factors that influence performance. Income statements provide confirmatory value, which is an aspect of relevant information. For example, investors are interested in whether companies meet or beat analysts' forecasts of net income as indicated by the statement of net income.
2. **Predict future performance.** Income statements have predictive value because they provide a basis for estimating future performance. Predictive value is an aspect of relevance. For example, a firm with a trend of earnings growth over the last 10 years may continue that growth in the future.
3. **Assess risks or uncertainties of achieving future cash flows.** Income statements provide information that is useful in assessing the risks or uncertainties of achieving future cash flows. Some items of income are more persistent in nature than others, making them strong indicators of future cash flows. For example, revenue from normal sales tends to persist from year to year. However, a gain from the sale of a specialized piece of equipment is

Emphasis on Judgment and Decision Making

Sections in each chapter identify key management decision points, and a unique full chapter dedicated to judgment and research identifies the assumptions, choices, and financial statement impacts from reporting business activities.

JUDGMENTS IN ACCOUNTING Inventory Costs

Judgment is crucial in determining the initial measurement of inventory. Deciding what costs to include in inventory is often subjective, as indicated by the Codification's statement that "although principles for the determination of inventory costs may be easily stated, their application . . . is difficult because of the variety of considerations in the allocation of costs and charges."[6] As a simple example, consider the requirement that companies capitalize freight-in costs into the inventory account whereas abnormal freight must be expensed. Deciding what freight cost is normal versus what is abnormal requires subjective judgment. For example, if an auto dealer pays freight for a shipment of vehicles delivered from the factory, it is a normal part of the dealer's business operations. In this case, the freight is considered part of the cost of inventory because it was reasonable and necessary to have the inventory in place and ready for sale. However, if sales begin to slow down and the dealer holds too much inventory, this inventory may have to be shipped to alternate locations. This additional freight may be considered abnormal and expensed because it is not a reasonable and necessary cost and does not represent a part of inventory value.

The decision to use the gross or net method of recording purchase discounts also affects the balance in the inventory account. In Example 10.4, the final balance in the inventory account is $4,960 using the gross method and $4,900 using the net method for the same three transactions. Thus, the inventory balance is impacted by management's choice of the method to account for the discount.

Worked Examples

Bolster students' problem-solving skills with model problem solutions for *every* important concept.

EXAMPLE 15.4 Common Stock Issue Costs

PROBLEM: Piper Products decided to raise additional financing by issuing common stock. The company received $4,000 in exchange for 1,000 shares of $1 par value common stock. Piper paid an underwriter $200 in stock issue costs. What is the necessary journal entry to record this transaction?

SOLUTION: The $200 of issue costs reduces Piper's cash received from the sale of the stock. Thus, it records the cash received at the net amount of $3,800, which is the $4,000 total proceeds less the $200 stock issue costs. The issue costs also reduce the additional paid-in capital in excess of par—common by $200. The journal entry follows.

Account	Current Year	
Cash	3,800	
Common Stock – $1 par		1,000
Additional Paid-in Capital in Excess of Par – Common		2,800

To Think Like Accountants . . .

Focus on Real-Company Financials

Disclosures and statements from well-known companies provide a connection to the application of accounting concepts and financial statement analysis.

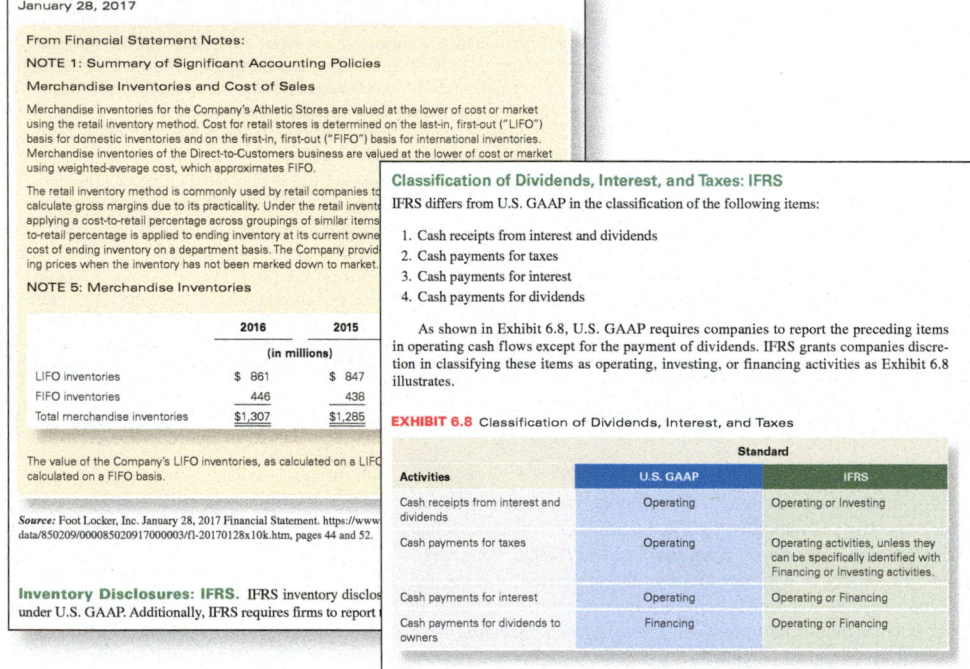

EXHIBIT 10.11 Inventory Disclosures, ***Foot Locker, Inc.***, Financial Statements, January 28, 2017

From Financial Statement Notes:

NOTE 1: Summary of Significant Accounting Policies

Merchandise Inventories and Cost of Sales

Merchandise inventories for the Company's Athletic Stores are valued at the lower of cost or market using the retail inventory method. Cost for retail stores is determined on the last-in, first-out ("LIFO") basis for domestic inventories and on the first-in, first-out ("FIFO") basis for international inventories. Merchandise inventories of the Direct-to-Customers business are valued at the lower of cost or market using weighted-average cost, which approximates FIFO.

The retail inventory method is commonly used by retail companies to calculate gross margins due to its practicality. Under the retail invent applying a cost-to-retail percentage across groupings of similar items to-retail percentage is applied to ending inventory at its current owne cost of ending inventory on a department basis. The Company provid ing prices when the inventory has not been marked down to market.

NOTE 5: Merchandise Inventories

	2016	2015
	(in millions)	
LIFO inventories	$ 861	$ 847
FIFO inventories	446	438
Total merchandise inventories	$1,307	$1,285

The value of the Company's LIFO inventories, as calculated on a LIF calculated on a FIFO basis.

Source: Foot Locker, Inc. January 28, 2017 Financial Statement. https://www data/850209/000085020917000003/fl-20170128x10k.htm, pages 44 and 52.

Inventory Disclosures: IFRS. IFRS inventory disclos under U.S. GAAP. Additionally, IFRS requires firms to report

Classification of Dividends, Interest, and Taxes: IFRS

IFRS differs from U.S. GAAP in the classification of the following items:

1. Cash receipts from interest and dividends
2. Cash payments for taxes
3. Cash payments for interest
4. Cash payments for dividends

As shown in Exhibit 6.8, U.S. GAAP requires companies to report the preceding items in operating cash flows except for the payment of dividends. IFRS grants companies discretion in classifying these items as operating, investing, or financing activities as Exhibit 6.8 illustrates.

EXHIBIT 6.8 Classification of Dividends, Interest, and Taxes

	Standard	
Activities	**U.S. GAAP**	**IFRS**
Cash receipts from interest and dividends	Operating	Operating or Investing
Cash payments for taxes	Operating	Operating activities, unless they can be specifically identified with Financing or Investing activities.
Cash payments for interest	Operating	Operating or Financing
Cash payments for dividends to owners	Financing	Operating or Financing

Key IFRS Differences

To prepare students for the global business world, IFRS material is highlighted in separate chapter sections. Side-by-side comparisons of GAAP and IFRS standards focus students on the key differences.

Interviews

Question-and-answer style exchanges with leaders in the field provide insight on topics from both standard-setter and practitioner perspectives and timely viewpoints on changing standards. Assign the new discussion questions to challenge students' understanding and critical-thinking skills.

Interview

BARBARA J. WIGHT

CHIEF FINANCIAL OFFICER TAYLOR GUITARS »

Barbara J. Wight

Barbara Wight is Chief Financial Officer at Taylor Guitars, an industry-leading guitar manufacturer whose instruments are played by leading musicians worldwide. She directs all financial, information technology, and legal affairs on behalf of the company and oversees various aspects of operations management, multinational manufacturing, acquisitions, and international compliance.

material market deliveries, it might want to use LIFO for materials subject to inflation and FIFO for materials whose pricing is stable or even in decline.

3 Describe the most common components included in the unit cost of inventory at Taylor.

Taylor states inventories at standard cost based on the expected raw material costs, labor, and overhead. Our primary raw material is wood.

At the beginning of each year, Taylor determines how many total labor hours it will need to build the forecasted number of guitars and allocates overhead (and labor) to each guitar based on the calculated overhead and labor rate. The overhead rate times the number of labor hours per guitar equals overhead applied to each guitar unit. Taylor drives production based on a hybrid model; we build to order and to a sales forecast of specific models to ensure that high-turnover models are in stock at all times.

4 What are the most significant judgments employed in the decision to write inventory down to market when applying the lower-of-cost-or-market rule?

From the First Day of Class and into Their Careers

Auto-Graded Excel Projects

Using proven, field-tested technology, MyLab Accounting's new auto-graded Excel Projects allow instructors to seamlessly integrate Excel content into their course without having to manually grade spreadsheets. Students have the opportunity to practice important accounting skills in Microsoft Excel, helping them to master key concepts and gain proficiency with Excel. Students simply download a spreadsheet, work live on an accounting problem in Excel, and then upload that file back into MyLab Accounting where they receive reports on their work that provide personalized, detailed feedback to pinpoint where they went wrong on any step of the problem.

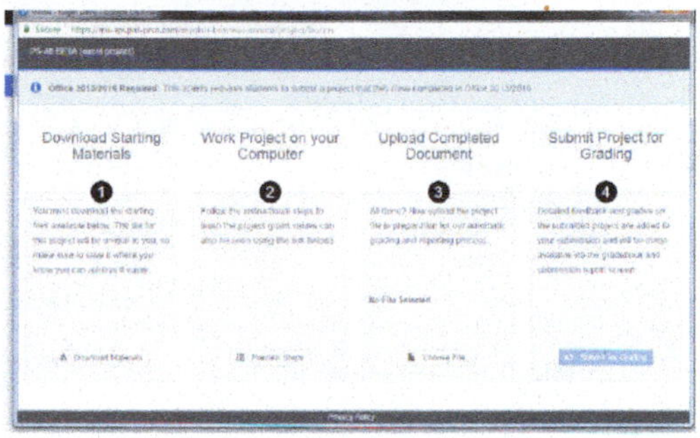

BECKER PROFESSIONAL EDUCATION®

Becker

Sample problems assignable in MyLab Accounting provide an introduction to the CPA Exam format and an opportunity for early practice with CPA exam style questions.

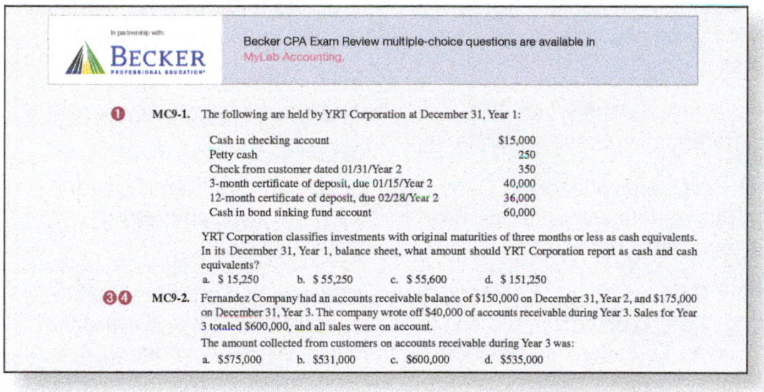

In partnership with: BECKER PROFESSIONAL EDUCATION

Becker CPA Exam Review multiple-choice questions are available in MyLab Accounting.

❶ **MC9-1.** The following are held by YRT Corporation at December 31, Year 1:

Cash in checking account	$15,000
Petty cash	250
Check from customer dated 01/31/Year 2	350
3-month certificate of deposit, due 01/15/Year 2	40,000
12-month certificate of deposit, due 02/28/Year 2	36,000
Cash in bond sinking fund account	60,000

YRT Corporation classifies investments with original maturities of three months or less as cash equivalents. In its December 31, Year 1, balance sheet, what amount should YRT Corporation report as cash and cash equivalents?

a. $ 15,250 b. $ 55,250 c. $ 55,600 d. $ 151,250

❸❹ **MC9-2.** Fernandez Company had an accounts receivable balance of $150,000 on December 31, Year 2, and $175,000 on December 31, Year 3. The company wrote off $40,000 of accounts receivable during Year 3. Sales for Year 3 totaled $600,000, and all sales were on account.

The amount collected from customers on accounts receivable during Year 3 was:

a. $575,000 b. $531,000 c. $600,000 d. $535,000

High-Quality and High-Quantity End-of-Chapter Exercises

Keyed to learning objectives, the items here progress in difficulty to test student understanding from the conceptual to multi-concept applied level.

Case exercises build students' ability to apply judgment-based analysis, read and interpret accounting literature, and analyze financial statements.

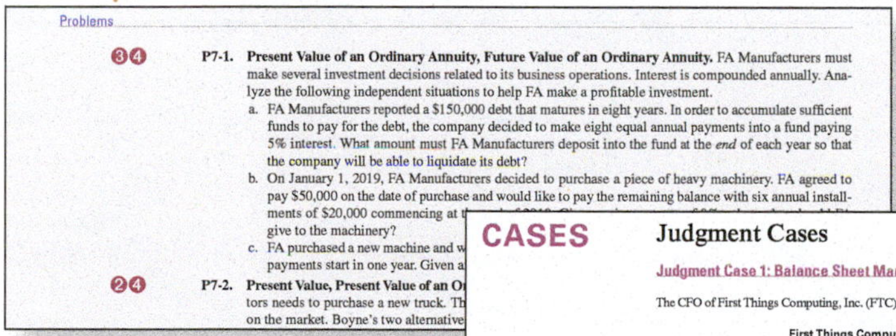

Problems

❸❹ **P7-1. Present Value of an Ordinary Annuity, Future Value of an Ordinary Annuity.** FA Manufacturers must make several investment decisions related to its business operations. Interest is compounded annually. Analyze the following independent situations to help FA make a profitable investment.

a. FA Manufacturers reported a $150,000 debt that matures in eight years. In order to accumulate sufficient funds to pay for the debt, the company decided to make eight equal annual payments into a fund paying 5% interest. What amount must FA Manufacturers deposit into the fund at the *end* of each year so that the company will be able to liquidate its debt?

b. On January 1, 2019, FA Manufacturers decided to purchase a piece of heavy machinery. FA agreed to pay $50,000 on the date of purchase and would like to pay the remaining balance with six annual installments of $20,000 commencing at t… give to the machinery?

c. FA purchased a new machine and w… payments start in one year. Given a…

❷❹ **P7-2. Present Value, Present Value of an O…** tors needs to purchase a new truck. Th… on the market. Boyne's two alternative…

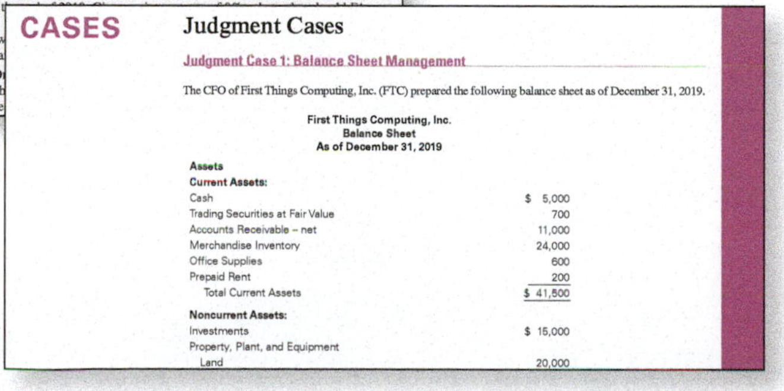

CASES

Judgment Cases

Judgment Case 1: Balance Sheet Management

The CFO of First Things Computing, Inc. (FTC) prepared the following balance sheet as of December 31, 2019.

First Things Computing, Inc.
Balance Sheet
As of December 31, 2019

Assets	
Current Assets:	
Cash	$ 5,000
Trading Securities at Fair Value	700
Accounts Receivable – net	11,000
Merchandise Inventory	24,000
Office Supplies	600
Prepaid Rent	200
Total Current Assets	$ 41,500
Noncurrent Assets:	
Investments	$ 15,000
Property, Plant, and Equipment	
Land	20,000

Instructor Teaching Resources

This program comes with the following teaching resources.

Supplements Available to Instructors at www.pearsonhighered.com/gordon	Supplement Features
Instructor's Manual	**Course Content**

Created in collaboration with
Mary Cline from Rock Valley College
Regan Garey from Lock Haven University
	• Tips for Taking Your Course from Traditional to Hybrid, Blended, or Online
	• Standard Syllabi for Intermediate Accounting–2-semester course
	• Standard Syllabi for Intermediate Accounting–3-semester course
	• "First Day of Class" student handouts include
	  • Student Walk-Through to Set Up MAL
	  • Tips on How to Get an A in This Class

	Chapter Content
	• Chapter Overview contains a brief synopsis and overview of each chapter. • Learning Objectives • Teaching Outline with Lecture Notes walks instructors through what material to cover and what examples to use when addressing certain items within the chapter. • IFRS Breakaways outline when IFRS diverges and addresses the key conceptual differences in these separate sections. • Student Supplement to Teaching Outline can be printed for (or emailed to) students. This outline will aid students in following the class and taking notes. • Assignment Grid indicates for each question, exercise, and problem the corresponding learning objective, the estimated completion time, and availability of Final Answer Questions and Worked Solutions in MyLab Accounting. • Suggestions for Class Activities are organized by learning objectives, allowing instructors to choose activities that fit with each day's discussions. • Model answers to Interview Discussion Questions • Guidance on Incorporating IFRS Material offers instructors direction on how to discuss the IFRS with their students.
Solutions Manual	
Created by the textbook authors	Contains solutions to all end-of-chapter questions, including short exercises, exercises, and problems

<table>
<tr><th>Supplements Available to Instructors at www.pearsonhighered.com/gordon</th><th>Supplement Features</th></tr>
<tr><th>Test Bank</th><th>Question Types</th></tr>
<tr><td>Created in collaboration with

Michael P. Griffin from University of Massachusetts Dartmouth

Kate Demarest from Carroll Community College</td><td>True/False and multiple-choice questions, essays, and problems make up more than 2,500 questions in this test bank. Most question types consist of both conceptual and computational problems, to ensure that students understand both the theory and the application. The Algorithmic test bank is available in MyLab Accounting. Most computational questions are formulated with an algorithm so that the same question is available with unique values. This offers instructors a greater pool of questions to select from and will help ensure that each student has a different test.

All questions include the following annotations:

• Difficulty level (1 for straight recall, 2 for some analysis, 3 for complex analysis)
• Type (multiple-choice and true/false questions, short-answer, essays, and problems)
• IFRS/GAAP indicator
• Learning Objective reference
• AACSB learning standard (Ethical Understanding and Reasoning; Analytical Thinking Skills; Information Technology; Diverse and Multicultural Work; Reflective Thinking; Application of Knowledge)</td></tr>
<tr><th>Computerized TestGen</th><th></th></tr>
<tr><td></td><td>TestGen allows instructors to:

• Customize, save, and generate classroom tests.
• Edit, add, or delete questions from the Test Item Files.
• Analyze test results.
• Organize a database of tests and student results.</td></tr>
<tr><th>PowerPoints</th><th></th></tr>
<tr><td>Created in collaboration with

Alisa Brink from Virginia Commonwealth University</td><td>Instructor PowerPoint Presentations mirror the organization of the text and include key exhibits, worked examples, and lecture notes. Instructors can download PowerPoint presentations that best match their teaching style.

• Lecture Support Only presentations consist of the chapter outline mirroring the text and include all main headings, key terms, key figures, and key tables.
• Worked Examples Only presentations consist of selected worked examples from the text for use as in-class demonstration problems.
• Combined presentations consist of both the lecture support and the examples organized to correspond to the text.

Modifying supplied PowerPoint presentations to correspond with classes can be a time-consuming task. To aid in this task, instructors can download a table of contents of the PowerPoint presentations. These documents will list the slide numbers for chapter content for quick removal of content that will not be covered in class.

Student PowerPoint Presentations are abridged versions of the Instructor PowerPoint Presentations and can be used as a study tool or note-taking tool for students.

The Image Library contains all image files from the text to assist instructors in modifying our supplied PowerPoint presentations or in creating their own PowerPoint presentations.</td></tr>
</table>

MyLab Accounting

For Students

http://www.pearson.com/mylab/accounting Online Homework and Assessment Manager

- Pearson eText
- Accounting Cycle Tutorial
- Time Value of Money Tutorial
- Worked Problem Videos
- Concept Overview Videos
- Auto-Graded Excel Projects
- Dynamic Study Modules
- Help Me Solve This
- Student PowerPoint Presentations
- Directed Reading Packets
- Study Plan
- Flash Cards

Reach Every Student with MyLab Accounting

MyLab Accounting is the teaching and learning platform that empowers you to reach every student. By combining trusted author content with digital tools and a flexible platform, MyLab personalizes the learning experience and improves results for each student.

Deliver Trusted Content

You deserve teaching materials that meet your own high standards for your course. That's why we partner with highly respected authors to develop interactive content and course-specific resources that you can trust—and that keep your students engaged.

Empower Each Learner

Each student learns at a different pace. Personalized learning pinpoints the precise areas where each student needs practice, giving all students the support they need—when and where they need it—to be successful.

Teach Your Course Your Way

Your course is unique. So whether you'd like to build your own assignments, teach multiple sections, or set prerequisites, MyLab Accounting gives you the flexibility to easily create your course to fit your needs.

Improve Student Results

When you teach with MyLab, student performance improves. That's why instructors have chosen MyLab for over 20 years, touching the lives of over 50 million students.

Acknowledgments

We are indebted to our colleagues for the time and expertise invested as manuscript reviewers, class testers, and focus group participants. We list all these contributors here but want to single out one group, our editorial board, for special notice. Their invaluable insights across the Intermediate I and Intermediate II chapters greatly improved the clarity, consistency, and accuracy of the textbook.

Brian Bratten, University of Kentucky
Alisa Brink, Virginia Commonwealth University
Terra Brown McGhee, University of Texas at Arlington
Nandini Chandar, Rider University
David DeBoskey, San Diego State University
Barbara Durham, University of Central Florida
Lisa Eiler, California State University, Fullerton
John Giles, North Carolina State University
Ying Huang, University of Louisville
Ronald Jastrzebski, University of Wisconsin–Whitewater
Kevin Melendrez, New Mexico State University
Joshua Neil, University of Colorado Boulder
Leslie Oakes, University of New Mexico
Denise Patterson, California State University, Fresno
Marietta Peytcheva, Lehigh University
Mary Ann Prater, Clemson University (Retired)
Rama Ramamurthy, Georgetown University
Randall Rentfro, The University of Tampa
Vic Stanton, Stanford University
Katherene Terrell, University of Central Oklahoma
John Trussel, The University of Tennessee at Chattanooga
Jan L. Williams, University of Baltimore
Yan Xiong, California State University, Sacramento

We are grateful for our colleagues' insights as well; we extend our sincere thanks to Steve Balsam, Brad Hendricks, Marco Malandra, Jonathon Reiter, Tanja Snively, and C. Daniel Stubbs. In addition, the following instructors gave their time to peer review and contribute to chapters:

Rebecca Adams, University of Virginia
Asher Albaz, Housatonic Community College
Daniel Ames, Illinois State University
Bridget Anakwe, Delaware State University
Matt Anderson, Michigan State University
Paul Ashcroft, Missouri State University
Eric Ball, Wake Tech Community College
Steven Balsam, Temple University
James Bannister, University of Hartford
Cheryl Bartlett, Central New Mexico Community College
Okera Bishop, Lone Star College, Kingwood
Kathleen Brenan, Ashland University
Anne Brooks, University of New Mexico
Kevin Brown, Wright State University
Stephen Brown, University of Maryland
Timothy Bryan, University of Southern Indiana
Jill Buchmann, Gateway Technical College
Charles Carslaw, University of Nevada, Reno
Deborah Carter, Coahoma Community College
Mary Ellen Carter, Boston College
Richard Cazier, The University of Texas at El Paso
Anna Cianci, Wake Forest University
Cheryl Clark, Point Park University
Dina Clark, Bloomsburg University of Pennsylvania
Mary Cline, Rock Valley College
Constance Crawford, Ramapo College of New Jersey
Cynthia Cuccia, University of Oklahoma
Marc Cussatt, Washington State University
Brent Daulton
Angela Davis, University of Oregon
David Dearman, University of Arkansas at Little Rock
Araya Debessay, University of Delaware
Kate Demarest, University of Baltimore
Michael Deschamps, Mira Costa College
David T. Doran, Pennsylvania State University
Nina Dorata, St. John's University
Tom Downen, Southern Illinois University
Joseph Dulin, University of Oklahoma
Dennis Elam, Texas A&M University–San Antonio
Desiree Elias, Florida International University
Gene Elrod, University of North Texas
Darlene Ely, Carroll Community College
James Emig, Villanova University
Ryan Enlow, University of Nevada, Las Vegas

Nancy Fan, California Polytechnic State University, Pomona
Patrick Fan, Virginia Tech
Magdy Farag, California Polytechnic State University, Pomona
Damon Fleming, San Diego State University
Marianne Fortuna, University of Georgia
Dan Fox, Boise State University
Micah Frankel, CSU East Bay
Mitchell Franklin, Syracuse University
Diane Franz, University of Toledo
Virginia Fullwood, Texas A&M University–Commerce
Regan Garey, Lock Haven University
Gregory Gaynor, University of Baltimore
Robin Gibson, Tri-County Community College
Lisa Gillespie, Loyola University Chicago
Hubert Glover, Drexel University
Giorgio Gotti, The University of Texas at El Paso
Pamela Graybeal, University of Central Florida
Amy Haas, Kingsborough Community College
Jan Hardesty, Pima Community College
Syed Hasan, George Mason University
Shanelle Hopkins, Carroll Community College
Susan Hughes, University of Vermont
Dave Hurtt, Baylor University
Mark Jackson, University of Nevada, Reno
Jeffrey Jones, College of Southern Nevada
Celina Jozsi, University of South Florida
John Karbens, Hawaii Pacific University
Mary Keener, The University of Tampa
Jerry Kreuze, Western Michigan University
Gaurav Kumar, University of Arkansas
Lisa Kutcher, Colorado State University
Jolene Lampton, Park University at Austin
Gerald Lander, University of South Florida
Ellen L. Landgraf, Loyola University Chicago
Nammy Lee, University of Virginia
Christy Lefevers, Catawba Valley Community College
Hui Lin, DePaul University
Ellen Lippman, University of Portland
Mary Loyland, University of North Dakota Bismarck
Ming Lu, Santa Monica College
James Lukawitz, University of Memphis
Marco Malandra, Temple University
Katie Maxwell, University of Arizona
Casey McNellis, University of Montana
Michelle Meckfessel, Case Western Reserve University
Linda Miller, Northeast Community College
Jose Miranda-Lopez, University of Tulsa
Joe Moran, College of DuPage
Laura Morgan, NHTI, Concord's Community College
Donald Minyard, University of Alabama
Volkan Muslu, University of Houston
Cory Ng, Temple University
Derek Oler, Texas Tech University
Kingsley Olibe, Kansas State University
Susan Pallas, Southeast Community College
Janet Papiernik, Indiana University–Purdue University Fort Wayne
Nancy Pasternack, University of Washington
Nori Pearson, Washington State University Pullman
Bonita Peterson Kramer, Montana State University
Marc Picconi, College of William and Mary
Catherine Plante, University of New Hampshire
Kristin Portz, St. Cloud State University
Richard Price, University of Oklahoma
Damian R. Prince, New Jersey City University
Lauren Psomostitis, North Seattle College
James Racic, Lakeland Community College
Raymond Reisig, Pace University
Cecile Roberti, Community College of Rhode Island
L. H. Rogero, University of Dayton
Eric Rothenburg, Kingsborough Community College
Brian Routh, University of Southern Indiana
Chris Ruderman, Linn-Benton Community College
Anwar Salimi, California Polytechnic State University, Pomona
Paul Schloemer, Ashland University
Kathleen Sevigny, Bridgewater State College
Marsha Shapiro, Park University
Praveen Sinha, California State University, Long Beach
Leonard Soffer, University of Chicago
Gregory Sommers, Southern Methodist University
Jalal Soroosh, Loyola University Maryland
Derinda Stiene, Caldwell Community College and Technical Institute
Stephen Strand, Southern Maine Community College
Joel Strong, St. Cloud State University
C. Daniel Stubbs, Rutgers University

Alan Styles, California State University San Marcos
Zane Swanson, University of Central Oklahoma
Robert Terrell, University of Central Oklahoma
Geoffrey Tickell, Indiana University of Pennsylvania
Paula Thomas, Middle Tennessee State University
Arindam Tripathy, University of Washington Tacoma
Norbert Tschakert, Salem State University
Frank Urbancic, University of South Alabama
Marcia Veit, University of Central Florida
Edward Walker, University of Central Oklahoma
Ping Wang, Pace University
Janis Weber, University of Louisiana at Monroe
Yan Xiong, California State University, Sacramento
Michael Yampuler, University of Houston
Shaokun Yu, Northern Illinois University

Instructors (and their students) who participated in our multiple class testing of select chapters and the corresponding key supplements follow.

Asher Albaz, Housatonic Community College
Bridget Anakwe, Delaware State University
Ira Bates, Florida Agricultural and Mechanical University
Alisa Brink, Virginia Commonwealth University
Steven Burris, Daley College
Cassandra Catlett, Carson–Newman University
Martha Cranford, Rowan Cabarrus Community College
Cynthia Cuccia, University of Oklahoma
Nina Dorata, St. John's University
Richard Ellison, Middlesex Community College
Anna Froman, Metro State University of Denver
Gregory Gaynor, University of Baltimore
Drew Goodson, Central Carolina Community College
Rita Grant, Grand Valley State University
Ying Huang, University of Louisville
Susan Hughes, University of Vermont
Christopher Jankiewicz, Howard Community College
Bill Jefferson, Metropolitan Community College
Christine Kuglin, Metropolitan State University of Denver
Jolene Lampton, Park University
Christa Land, Catawba Valley Community College
Hui Lin, DePaul University
Ellen Lippman, University of Portland
Stephani Mason, DePaul University
Tammy Metzke, Milwaukee Area Technical College
Linda Miller, Northeast Community College
Laura Morgan, New Hampshire Technical Institute
JT Norris, University of the Incarnate Word
Derek Oler, Texas Tech University
Kristen Reilly, Colorado State University
Jennifer Jones Rivers, University of Georgia
Melloney Simerly, Virginia Commonwealth University
Michelle Sotka, Howard Community College
Pamela Stuerke, University of Missouri–St. Louis
Robin Thomas, North Carolina State University
Michael Trendell, Governors State University
Joe Welker, Western Idaho Community College
Jan Williams, University of Baltimore

1 The Financial Reporting Environment

LEARNING OBJECTIVES

1. Define financial accounting and describe the demand for financial information, including the role of general-purpose financial statements, the information needs of financial statement users and other parties, and the factors that influence financial reporting.
2. Discuss the role of financial accounting standard setters in the United States and internationally.
3. Detail the standard-setting process.
4. Explain three recent trends in standard setting: principles-based, rules-based, and objectives-oriented standards; the asset/liability approach; and fair value measurements.

Introduction

WELL-DEVELOPED ACCOUNTING STANDARDS ENABLE WORLDWIDE capital markets to function effectively by providing credibility to published financial information used by investors, creditors, and others. Transparent financial information included in the financial statements allows these parties to make rational investment and credit decisions that direct capital to corporations that develop new products and technology, create employment, and encourage growth and development.

Andrew Burton/Getty Images

Consider ***Twitter, Inc.***, the social networking company, which raised capital of over $2.09 billion by issuing 80.5 million shares of stock in its initial public offering. Investors subsequently traded over 194 million shares of ***Twitter's*** stock valued at $8.2 billion during the first month after the initial public offering.[1] These investors based their decisions on the financial information provided by ***Twitter***. The capital provided by such investments fuels the overall economy and directs capital to its most productive uses.

Multiple factors in the overall accounting environment influence economic decisions at the firm level. For example, user groups such as investors and creditors impact the demand for accounting information and influence the standard-setting bodies. Financial reporting encompasses much more than the financial statements: Other key elements include the footnotes to the financial statements, the letter to the owners, management's discussion and analysis, the auditors' report, the management report, and press releases. Financial statement users rely on all categories of financial information to make rational economic decisions.

In this chapter, we first define *financial accounting* and discuss the demand and supply of financial information. We identify the economic entities that prepare financial information as well as the users of financial information. We then explore factors that shape accounting information. We also overview the historical development of the U.S. and international standard-setting bodies and discuss the standard-setting processes. We conclude the chapter with a review of recent trends in standard setting. «

[1]Twitter, Inc. is traded on the New York Stock Exchange. It made its initial public offering on November 7, 2013.

1 Define financial accounting and describe the demand for financial information, including the role of general-purpose financial statements, the information needs of financial statement users and other parties, and the factors that influence financial reporting.

Overview of Financial Reporting

Financial accounting is the process of identifying, measuring, and communicating financial information about an economic entity to various user groups within the legal, economic, political, and social environment. This definition contains four major elements:

1. Financial information
2. Economic entity
3. User groups
4. Legal, economic, political, and social environment

We will examine these elements in the following sections of the chapter.

Financial Information

Financial information falls into two categories: information that is or that is not governed by rules set forth by the accounting standard-setting bodies. Firms prepare the financial statements and the footnotes to the financial statements (also referred to as footnote disclosures) based on accounting standard setters' rules. In contrast, the letter to the owners, management's discussion and analysis, the auditors' report, the management report, and press releases are not governed by the accounting standard-setting bodies, although they are regulated to some degree by other authoritative bodies.[2]

Demand for Financial Information. The form, content, and extent that firms provide financial information is based on market participant demand. Financial accounting provides information that enables users to evaluate economic entities and make efficient resource allocation decisions based on the risks and returns of a particular investment. This process directs capital flows to their most productive uses. In this way, the demand for financial information is linked to the allocation of scarce resources, as illustrated in Exhibit 1.1.

EXHIBIT 1.1 Demand for Financial Information

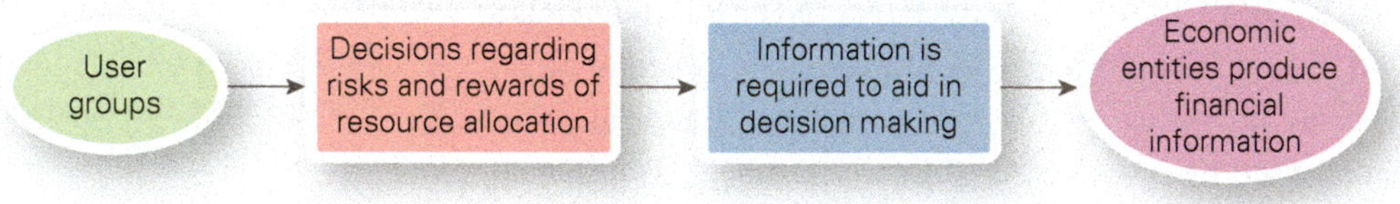

Capital is a scarce resource. How do investors and creditors make decisions regarding the amount of capital to invest in a given entity? Accountants report the economic performance and financial position of the firm so that potential debt and equity investors can adequately assess the risks and returns of investing in the entity. Similarly, lenders can use the financial statements to assess the potential for payment. For example, a bank limited in the number of loans that it can make would clearly prefer to lend to a business that has been profitable over the last five years rather than one that has not.

Transparent and complete financial statements aid investors in assessing the amounts and timing of future cash flows, as well as the uncertainty of cash flow realization. However, financial statement users should be aware that performance-based compensation can create an incentive for managers to strategically manage—or to misreport—financial statements. Compensating managers based upon reported net income provides a financial incentive to inflate net income. For example, when the Securities and Exchange Commission found that the ***Computer Sciences Corporation (CSC)*** committed accounting fraud that increased net earnings in 2010 and 2011,

[2]For a discussion of the financial statements and many of these other items, see Chapters 5 and 6.

CSC's CEO agreed to pay back $3.7 million of compensation he received based on the fraudulent earnings.[3] Financial accounting standards seek to limit this type of management behavior. Most managers faithfully report their financial statements, but it is important for standard setters and auditors to be aware of incentives to alter net income.

Sources of Financial Information. The financial reporting process generates a significant amount of financial information that yields the four basic financial statements, as well as the footnote disclosures. In the chapters that follow, we examine the theory, rationale, and principles underlying the four basic financial statements:

- The balance sheet (also referred to as the statement of financial position)
- The statement of comprehensive income[4]
- The statement of cash flows
- The statement of shareholders' equity

Published financial statements are called **general-purpose financial statements** because they provide information to a wide spectrum of user groups: investors, creditors, financial analysts, customers, employees, competitors, suppliers, unions, and government agencies. Although considered general purpose, most financial information is provided to satisfy users with limited ability or authority to obtain additional information, which includes investors and creditors. The **Financial Accounting Standards Board (FASB),** which is the body responsible for promulgating U.S. GAAP, identifies investors, lenders, and other creditors as the primary users of the financial statements.

Financial statements are the culmination of the financial reporting process. These financial statements, along with the accompanying footnote disclosures, are the primary source of publicly available financial information for investors and creditors. None of the other sources of financial information—such as management forecasts, press releases, and regulatory reports—provide as much information as the financial statements.

The term financial information includes more information than the financial statements. The financial statements include the four basic financial statements and the related footnotes. However, financial information also includes items such as:

- A letter to the shareholders
- A formal discussion and analysis of the firm by the management of the firm
- Management report
- Auditors' report
- Financial summary

Therefore, the general-purpose financial statements and the related footnotes are subsets of financial information. The financial statements and the footnotes are governed by U.S. GAAP, which may not always be the case for all components of financial information.[5]

Economic Entity

The second element in the definition of financial accounting involves the *economic entity* for which the financial statements and other financial information are presented. An **economic entity** is an organization or unit with activities that are separate from those of its owners and other entities. Financial information always relates to a particular economic entity. Economic entities can be corporations, partnerships, sole proprietorships, or governmental organizations. Also, economic

[3]https://www.sec.gov/news/pressrelease/2015-111.html

[4]Entities may report comprehensive income either in one combined statement or in two statements—the statement of net income and the statement of comprehensive income.

[5]We discuss these other types of financial information more extensively in Chapter 6.

entities may be privately held or publicly held.[6] If the entity is publicly held, then its equity can be bought and sold by external parties on stock exchanges.

The management of a particular economic entity prepares its financial information, including the financial statements. While the management of the entity may also use the financial information to some extent, they are better classified as preparers than users of financial information.[7]

Financial Statement User Groups

The third element in the financial accounting definition involves identifying the primary user groups that demand financial information. Some users employ accounting information to make economic decisions for their own benefit while other users employ accounting information to make economic decisions for the benefit of others or to assist others in making investment or credit decisions. Exhibit 1.2 lists the user groups.

EXHIBIT 1.2 User Groups

Users	Description
Equity Investors	Shareholders of the company
Creditors and Other Debt Investors	Entities including banks and other financial institutions that lend money to the company either through a private agreement or through a public debt offering
Competitors	Companies that produce the same service or product
Financial Analysts	Individuals employed at investment banks, commercial banks, and brokerage houses that use financial information to provide guidance to individuals and other entities in making investment and credit decisions
Employees and Labor Unions	Individuals that work for the company and the organizations that represent the employees' interests
Suppliers and Customers	Organizations that provide the necessary inputs for the products or services produced by the entity and companies or individuals that purchase the goods or services from the entity
Government Agencies	Agencies representing the government that are in charge of reviewing and/or regulating the company

Equity Investors. **Equity investors** are the shareholders of the company. That is, an equity investor purchases a percentage ownership of the company. Equity investors include individuals, other corporations, partnerships, mutual funds, pension plans, and other financial institutions that expect to receive a return on their investment either through dividends (i.e., distributions of cash or other assets to owners) or in the form of an increase in the price of their equity shares.

Equity investors use financial information to determine a company's ability to generate earnings and cash flow, as well as to make an assessment of the potential risks and returns of their investments. Equity investors also use financial information to assess the ability of the entity to pay dividends and to grow over time. Firm growth in earnings and cash flow are important for the investor to sell his or her investment at a gain.

[6]In this text book, we focus primarily on publicly traded entities. We use examples from the financial statements issued by manufacturing, retail, and service entities. We will not focus on financial statements from specialized industries such as insurance, banking, and other regulated industries.

[7]Managers of economic entities use accounting information for internal decision making as detailed in cost and managerial accounting courses.

Creditors and Other Debt Investors. **Creditors** and other debt investors are entities, including banks and other financial institutions, that lend money to the company. Debt can either be public or privately held. In the case of publicly traded debt, market participants invest in the entity's debt—specifically, the entity's bonds. In the case of privately held debt, companies obtain capital directly from lenders, such as commercial banks. Creditors typically receive a return on their investment in the form of interest income. However, in the case of public debt, they may also receive a return in the form of an increase in the price of the bonds.

Creditors use financial information to determine whether the principal and interest on their loans will likely be paid by debtors when due. Creditors are also concerned with the priority of claims against the assets of the debtor company. Some lenders have priority over others when determining the order of repayment. Finally, creditors can use financial information to assess the entity's current and future profitability and growth prospects.

Competitors. Competitors use financial information to determine their market position relative to the reporting entity. Companies analyze a competitor's financial information to identify its strategy and determine if it is possible to successfully compete with the company. An analysis of a competitor's financial information enables a financial statement user to identify that entity's objectives, assumptions, overall business strategy, and capabilities. For example, a pharmaceutical company would be interested in any increases in a rival's research and development expenses that could indicate new and competing products in the future.

Financial Analysts. **Financial analysts** employed at investment banks, commercial banks, and brokerage houses use financial information to provide guidance to individuals and other entities in making investment and credit decisions. Analysts use various techniques to estimate the value of an entity based on information obtained from the annual report and other publicly available information, as well as from interviews with company officers and outside industry or economic experts. Some financial analysts are equity analysts who follow an industry or certain companies and provide their opinions or recommendations on a regular basis. These reports result in a recommendation as to whether investors should buy or sell the stock of that company. For example, in the first quarter of 2017, there were 39 analyst recommendations issued for ***Twitter***—4 of which were buys, 27 were holds, and 8 were sells or underperforms.[8] Financial analysts act as market intermediaries in that they are trained to examine an extensive volume of financial data and reduce it to a manageable amount of information for use by investors.

Employees and Labor Unions. Employees and labor unions use financial statements to assess the economic performance and liquidity of entities employing members of the union. For example, the United Auto Workers represents employees in the automobile industry. Financial statement information can be useful during the negotiation of new labor agreements and compensation contracts.

Suppliers and Customers. Suppliers and customers use financial statements to determine a company's financial position. For suppliers, it is critically important to assess the company's ability to pay for goods and services provided. A company's financial condition indicates the quality of its products and its ability to honor warranties to potential customers. ***General Motors*** (***GM***) lost many prospective customers when it was in bankruptcy during the economic crisis of 2008. In this case, auto buyers were concerned that ***GM*** would not be in business long enough to fulfill its warranty obligation to its customers.

Government Agencies. Government agencies review the financial statements of publicly traded companies for a variety of reasons. For example, the U.S. Federal Trade Commission may review publicly available financial information to identify a potential monopoly or an entity in violation of antitrust laws.

[8]See http://www.nasdaq.com/symbol/twtr/recommendations

Other Parties Involved in the Preparation and Use of Financial Information

Another important group involved in the financial reporting process is the *preparers* themselves. **Financial statement preparers** are the companies that issue the financial statements.

In addition to preparers and users of the financial statements, other parties involved in the financial reporting process include:

- Auditors
- Accounting standard setters such as the Financial Accounting Standards Board and the *International Accounting Standards Board*
- Regulatory bodies such as the Securities and Exchange Commission and the Public Company Accounting Oversight Board
- Professional organizations such as the American Institute of Certified Public Accountants

Auditors can be *external* or *internal*. **External auditors** are independent of the company and are responsible for ensuring that management prepares and issues financial statements that comply with accounting standards and fairly present the financial position and economic performance of the company. Because external auditors are independent parties, they lend a significant amount of credibility to the financial statements. **Internal auditors** are employees of the company serving in an advisory role to management and providing information regarding the company's operations and proper functioning of its internal controls.

Accounting standard setters develop and promulgate accounting concepts, rules, and guidelines that provide information that is relevant and faithfully represents the economic performance and the financial position of the reporting entity. The Financial Accounting Standards Board (FASB), the primary standard setter in the United States, promulgates U.S. Generally Accepted Accounting Principles (U.S. GAAP). The **International Accounting Standards Board (IASB)** sets International Financial Reporting Standards (IFRS). We discuss the standard setters' role and the standard-setting process in more depth later in the chapter.

Regulatory bodies protect investors and oversee the accounting standard-setting process. In the United States, the U.S. Securities and Exchange Commission (SEC) regulates publicly traded companies.[9] Privately held companies are not required to comply with the SEC's regulations. The SEC gives the FASB the authority to issue U.S. GAAP. In addition, the SEC reviews the filings of public companies in the United States. The Public Company Accounting Oversight Board (PCAOB) sets auditing standards and oversees the audits of public companies in the United States.

Professional organizations such as the American Institute of Certified Public Accountants (AICPA) are also involved in the financial reporting process. The AICPA is the national professional association for Certified Public Accountants (CPAs) in the United States. The AICPA prepares and grades the Uniform CPA Examination. This organization also supports accounting professionals throughout their careers by providing training, professional skills development, and other resources.

Exhibit 1.3 summarizes the various groups involved in the financial reporting process.

Legal, Economic, Political, and Social Environment

Financial reporting takes place in a complex and dynamic world: Financial statement users' information needs change as business evolves. So, it is natural that environmental factors—legal, economic, political, and social—shape and influence the financial reporting process. The environment is the fourth element of the financial accounting definition. Financial accounting interacts with its environment in both a reactive and a proactive fashion.

Reactive Factors. Financial accounting reacts to pressure (lobbying) from various groups and changes in its environment. Accounting theories and procedures evolve to meet the dynamic changes and demands from the environment. For example, FASB made changes in the accounting

[9] A company is regulated by the SEC if it has either debt or equity that is publicly traded.

EXHIBIT 1.3 Parties Involved in the Financial Reporting Process in the United States

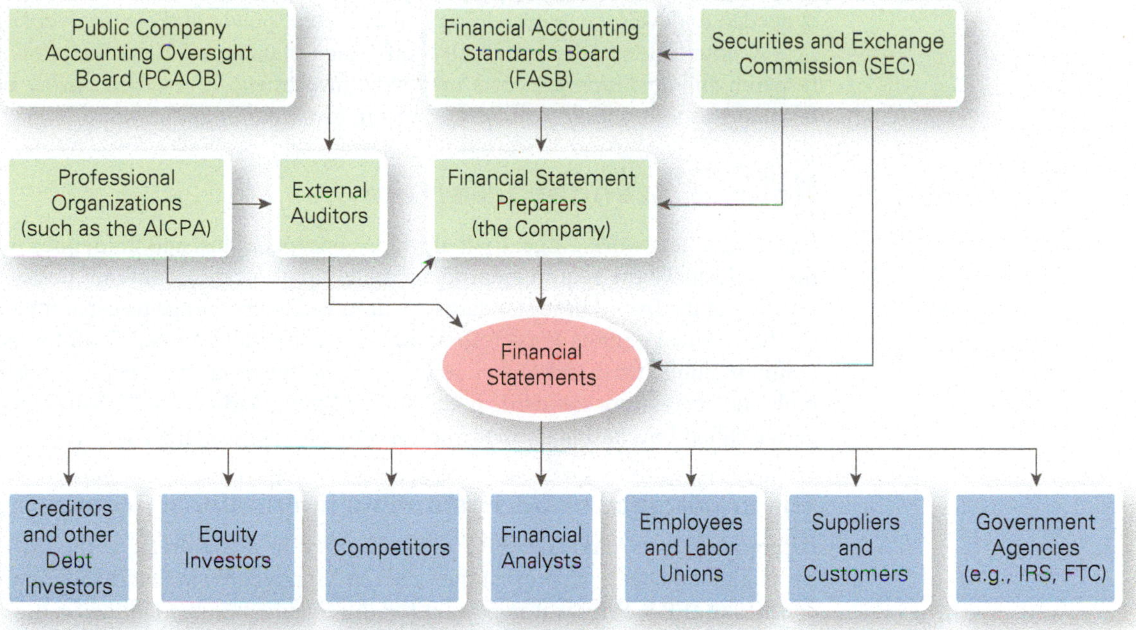

for off-balance sheet subsidiaries following the discovery of the massive fraud scheme at ***Enron*** in the early 2000s.

In addition, accounting conforms to economic conditions, legal standards, and social values. Today, accounting disclosures highlight a company's policies regarding pollution control, community service, and diversity in business. For example, in the letter to shareholders in ***Johnson & Johnson's*** 2015 annual report, CEO Alex Gorsky highlighted ***Johnson & Johnson's*** "legacy of caring through strategic partnerships," as shown in Exhibit 1.4.

EXHIBIT 1.4 ***Johnson & Johnson Company's*** 2015 Letter to the Shareholders Discussion of Corporate Philanthropy

> We understand the important role Johnson & Johnson plays in the world, and we continue to build on our 130-year legacy of caring through strategic philanthropy with hundreds of partner organizations worldwide. Our corporate philanthropy includes work with Operation Smile®—helping to provide safe surgeries for facial deformities in children; Save the Children®—providing care to tens of millions of children around the world in resource limited and crisis situations, including long-term support for Syrian refugees; and the Elizabeth Glaser Pediatric AIDS Foundation®—eliminating HIV infections in children around the world. We also partner with global health agencies and non-governmental organizations to battle some of the most deadly epidemics of our generation, like our commitment and partnership to rapidly develop a vaccine for Ebola. Through these commitments, we envision a world where everyone has the means to be healthy and can thrive. We are committed to using our capabilities, expertise, resources and partnerships to fulfill our role in making the world a better, healthier place for generations to come.

Source: Annual Report, 2015 Johnson and Johnson.

The development of accounting standards is also a political process that is heavily influenced by the various groups within the reporting environment. Lobby groups include investors, creditors, financial analysts, the financial community, academics, accounting organizations, and industry associations.

Proactive Factors. Financial accounting is proactive in that it can change or influence its environment by providing feedback information that is used by organizations and individuals to reshape the economy. Accounting information is used to efficiently allocate resources throughout the economy by directing capital flows to their most productive uses. For example, start-up capital is needed to develop new technology such as solar power and electric vehicles.

Accounting standards can also influence managerial behavior. For example, expensing research and development costs may slow investment in research during economic downturns because this accounting treatment results in lower earnings figures.

2 Discuss the role of financial accounting standard setters in the United States and internationally.

Role of Standard Setters

Standard setters work diligently to develop concepts, rules, and guidelines for financial reporting that will satisfy the requirement to accurately present the economic performance and financial position of the firm. These standards are designed to encourage transparent and truthful reporting. Publicly traded entities must follow the rules and guidelines set forth by the standard setters to maintain public trust and to ensure the efficient functioning of capital markets. The FASB promulgates accounting standards in the United States, and the IASB issues global accounting standards, called International Financial Reporting Standards (IFRS).

The Importance of Understanding International Accounting Standards

Although U.S. GAAP and IFRS are converged in many areas, some differences still remain. Throughout the text, we present the U.S. GAAP standards in detail and highlight pertinent differences with IFRS. Why is it important for an accountant in the United States to learn international accounting standards? There are several reasons:

- U.S. companies operate subsidiaries outside of the United States. Many of these subsidiaries report under IFRS in their home countries. Accountants must convert the subsidiaries' financial statements to U.S. GAAP when preparing consolidated financial statements. For example, ***Johnson & Johnson*** operates in over 60 countries throughout the world.
- Non-U.S. companies operate in the United States and prepare their financial statements using IFRS. Consequently, if you are working at or auditing an international firm, you will likely see IFRS. For example, ***GlaxoSmithKline*** is a worldwide pharmaceutical company based in the United Kingdom with 18% of its employees in the United States and a U.S. headquarters in Philadelphia.
- The SEC permits the use of IFRS-based financial statements by international companies with shares trading on U.S. stock exchanges.[10] U.S. accountants and auditors often assist these non-U.S. companies in preparing U.S. regulatory reports. As of September 2016, these companies represented a worldwide market capitalization in excess of $7 trillion across more than 500 companies.[11]
- The SEC promotes high-quality, globally accepted accounting standards. U.S. accountants and auditors need a working knowledge of IFRS to implement global standards in companies and perform audits.
- Many U.S. accountants now spend time working outside of the United States. IFRS is required or permitted in over 130 countries worldwide. Exhibit 1.5 presents a map that highlights the countries that require IFRS in red (as of May 2016).
- The accounting profession has determined that a working knowledge of IFRS is important for today's accountant. For example, the American Institute of Certified Public Accountants tests IFRS on the CPA exam.

To ensure that you are prepared to meet these challenges, we address both U.S. GAAP and IFRS in this text. We introduce accounting practices in the United States first. We then compare U.S. GAAP to IFRS in sections with green headings, focusing on similarities and differences. Where there are differences, we cover IFRS at the same level of detail as used for U.S. GAAP.

[10]The SEC eliminated the requirement that foreign issuers reconcile their financial statements from IFRS (or other accounting standards) to U.S. GAAP in 2007. To be clear, U.S. companies may not use IFRS in their financial statements. U.S. GAAP is required for U.S. companies.

[11]See Source: https://www.sec.gov/news/statement/white-2016-01-05.html

EXHIBIT 1.5 Global Usage of IFRS

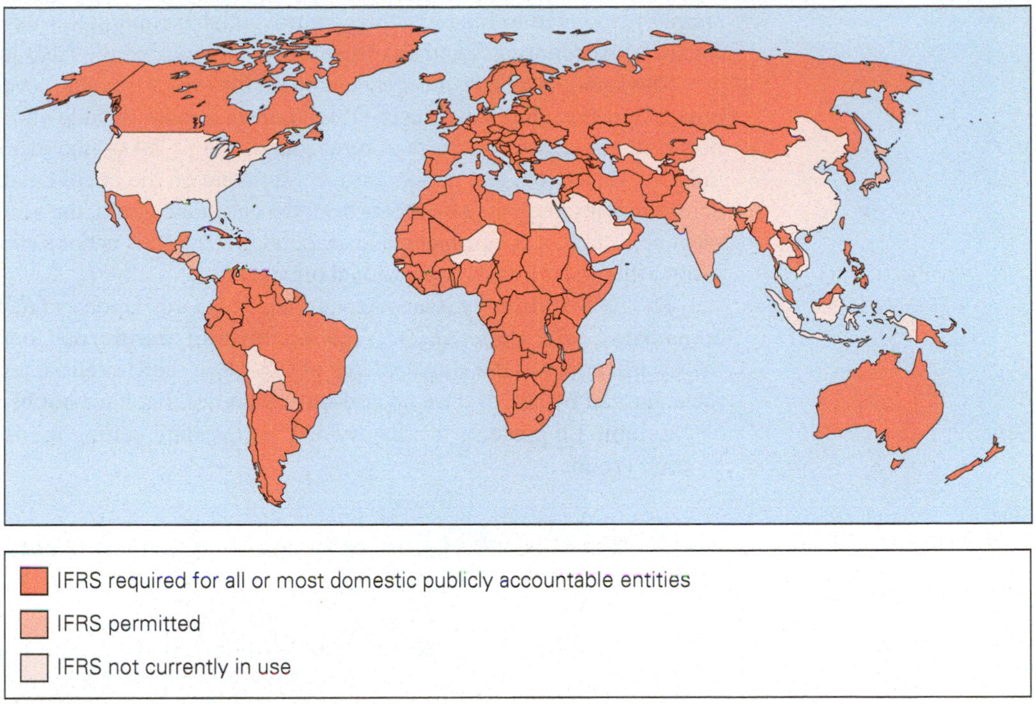

Source: Based on "The Global Financial Reporting Language," May 2016, IFRS Foundation table on p. 5. http://www.ifrs.org/Use-around-the-world/Documents/The-Global-Financial-Reporting-Language-May-2016.pdf

3 Detail the standard-setting process.

The Standard-Setting Process

We previously established that the FASB sets accounting standards in the United States and the IASB sets global accounting standards. The standard-setting processes are similar for the two Boards but there are some important differences that we will highlight.

Standard Setting

We begin with the history of U.S. standard setting, the structure of the standard-setting body, and the process of standard setting.

History of Standard Setting. U.S. financial reporting standard setting began with the 1934 Securities Exchange Act, which gave the SEC the power to promulgate accounting standards for all publicly traded firms. The SEC delegated its standard-setting power to the private sector, prompting the accounting profession to establish the first U.S. standard-setting board. The Committee on Accounting Procedures (CAP) was formed in 1939 as a subcommittee of the American Institute of Certified Public Accountants (AICPA) to reduce the number of accounting methods used in practice. Prior to the formation of the CAP, there were significant inconsistencies in the form and content of financial statements. For example, some companies would provide only a balance sheet while others would report only an income statement. During its tenure, the CAP produced 51 standards, referred to as Accounting Research Bulletins (ARBs or Bulletins).

The CAP accomplished its goal of reducing accounting alternatives and was replaced in 1959 by the Accounting Principles Board (APB). The APB, another subcommittee of the AICPA, issued pronouncements known as Opinions and Statements. The APB's primary objective was to respond to existing and emerging problems in financial reporting. The APB issued 31 APB Opinions and four APB Statements.

The APB was criticized for being slow to develop accounting standards and inactive on several controversial issues. The part-time board members were all CPAs still affiliated with their employers. As a result, board members were not viewed as independent. Further, the APB did not develop standards in anticipation of changes in the accounting environment. Rather, the Board simply responded to long-existing, controversial accounting issues. Due to these criticisms, the Financial Accounting Standards Board (FASB) replaced the APB in 1973.

The FASB is a more independent board than the APB. The seven members employed as full-time board members must sever all relationships with outside entities. In addition, board members of the FASB do not have to be accountants or CPAs—the members can join the board from industry, education, and public service. Members on the board have represented a broad range of constituencies, including members from the corporate world, the accounting profession, the investment community, government, and academia. The FASB is not a subcommittee of the AICPA and is not affiliated with any professional organization.

The FASB currently issues Accounting Standards Updates (ASUs) as part of the *Accounting Standards Codification* (ASC).[12] The **Accounting Standards Codification** (often referred to as the Codification) is the single source of GAAP in the United States and includes all pronouncements issued by any of the standard-setting bodies that have not been superseded.[13]

Exhibit 1.6 presents the history of U.S. standard setting as well as pronouncements issued by each group.

EXHIBIT 1.6 History of Accounting Standard Setting in the United States

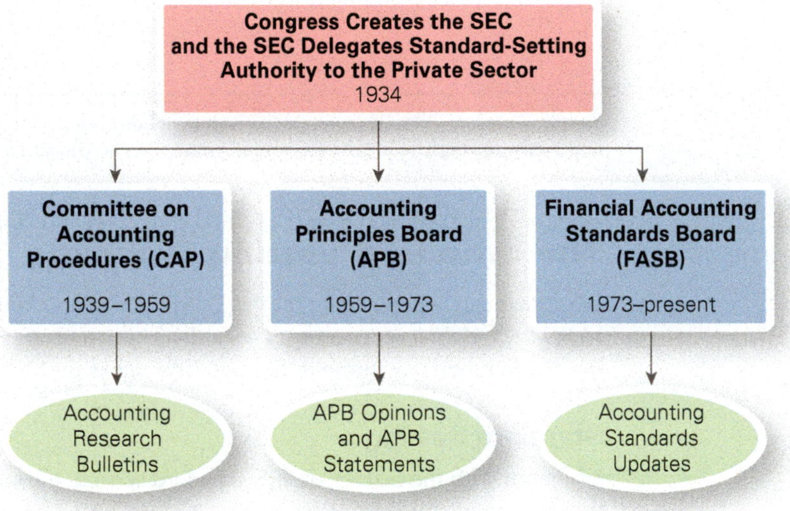

The Standard-Setting Structure. As illustrated by Exhibit 1.7, the FASB is part of a larger organizational structure that also includes the

- Financial Accounting Foundation (FAF)
- Governmental Accounting Standards Board (GASB)
- Financial Accounting Standards Advisory Council (FASAC)
- Governmental Accounting Standards Advisory Council (GASAC)
- Emerging Issues Task Force (EITF)
- Private Company Council (PCC)

The FAF is responsible for the oversight, administration, and finances of the FASB. The FAF obtains funds primarily through the Public Company Accounting Oversight Board (PCAOB), which assesses charges known as accounting support fees against issuers of equity securities based

[12]The primary pronouncements of the FASB were originally called Statements of Financial Accounting Standards (SFAS).

[13]We discuss the Codification in depth in Chapter 3.

EXHIBIT 1.7 Standard-Setting Organizational Structure in the United States

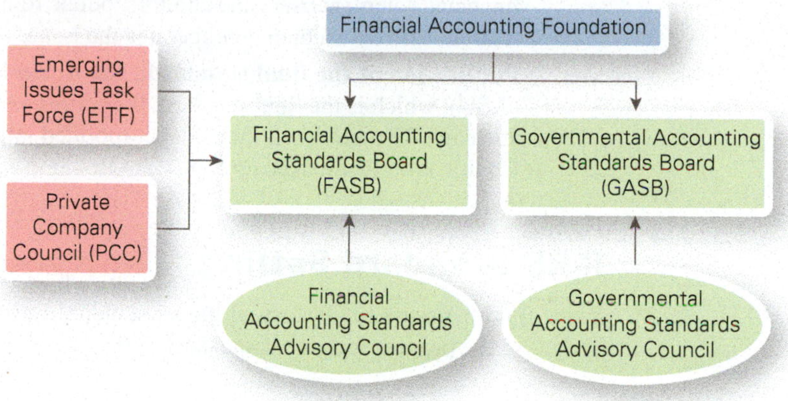

on their market capitalization.[14] Other sources of funds include publications, subscriptions, and contributions from state and local governments for the GASB.

The GASB sets standards for state and local governmental units. The FASAC exists to advise FASB on technical issues and the GASAC serves as an advisory board to the GASB.

The EITF was formed in 1984 to assist the FASB by addressing issues that are not as broad in scope as those found on the FASB's agenda. For example, EITF agenda items often include industry-specific issues. The EITF is made up of 13 representatives, including preparers, auditors, and financial statement users. The group reaches an EITF Consensus when three or fewer members object to a proposed position that has been exposed for public comment. Although the FASB members do not vote on the consensus at the EITF meetings, all consensus decisions must be approved by a majority of the FASB members before they become a part of U.S. GAAP.

In 2012, the PCC was established to set accounting standards for U.S private companies. Before this time, if a private company was required to present financial information according to U.S. GAAP, it followed the same rules as public companies with minor exceptions. Now the PCC is responsible for determining whether modifications to existing U.S. GAAP standards are warranted for private companies, and, if so, it has the responsibility of developing, deliberating, and voting on these modifications. However, the FASB retains the authority to make the final decision as to incorporating these changes into U.S. GAAP for private companies.

Standard-Setting Process. FASB follows a seven-step process to issue a final standard.[15]

Step 1: Identification of an issue. FASB identifies a financial reporting issue based on recommendations from analysts, government agencies, or other market participants.

Step 2: Decision to pursue. After consultation with FASB members and others as appropriate, the FASB Chairperson decides whether to add the issue to the technical agenda.

Step 3: Public meetings. Once added to the technical agenda, the Board holds public meetings where it deliberates the various issues identified by the FASB staff.

Step 4: Exposure Draft. The Board issues an Exposure Draft (ED), which is intended to solicit input from financial statement preparers, auditors, and users of the financial statements.[16]

---

[14]Market capitalization is the total value of a company's equity shares. It is equal to the market price per share multiplied by the total number of equity shares outstanding.

[15]See http://www.fasb.org/cs/ContentServer?site=FASB&c=Page&pagename=FASB%2FPage%2FSectionPage&cid=1176157307939.

[16]The Board may also issue a Discussion Paper to obtain input earlier in the project.

Step 5: Public roundtables. The Board may hold public roundtables to discuss the ED, if needed.

Step 6: Redeliberation. The FASB staff analyzes the comment letters received from preparers, financial statement users and auditors, public roundtable discussions, and any other information. The Board then redeliberates the issue.

Step 7: Publication of the final standard. The Board issues an Accounting Standards Update (ASU), which is the final standard. It requires a majority vote of the Board to issue a new standard. The ASU will then be incorporated into the body of the Accounting Standards Codification that makes up U.S. GAAP.

IFRS Standard Setting

We will now discuss the history of global standard setting, the structure of the standard-setting body, and the process for global standard setting.

History of Global Standard Setting: IFRS

Until recently, most countries established their own accounting standards. For instance, France, Germany, and Australia each had its own GAAP. The GAAP of each nation varied due to the country's specific needs for accounting information. Factors such as the country's sources of capital, its culture, tax laws, or other regulations influenced the development of their accounting standards. Given almost 200 countries in the world and almost as many sets of different GAAP standards, global investors and creditors struggled to compare accounting standards when analyzing companies and making investment and credit decisions.

Recognizing the need for comparable accounting information internationally, the professional accounting organizations from 10 countries formed the International Accounting Standards Committee (IASC) in 1973.[17] At that time, the IASC consisted of up to 16 part-time volunteer members setting International Accounting Standards (IAS). Companies in each country could adopt IAS on a voluntary basis. However, the IASC was criticized for allowing highly flexible accounting standards. As a result, most major developed countries continued to require the use of their own standards.

As global business relationships continued to grow, the need for a comparable and rigorous international set of accounting standards became apparent. In the 1990s, the IASC initiated an improvement project to develop a cohesive and uniform set of "core accounting standards" to meet the needs of investors in cross-border offerings and exchange listings. Shortly after this improvement project was completed, the International Organization of Securities Commissions (IOSCO) endorsed IAS for use in cross-border stock offerings and listings, allowing companies to report under IAS within their jurisdictions and on their exchanges.

Around the same time, the IASC began to recognize the limitations in its existing organizational structure. As a result, the International Accounting Standards Board (IASB) replaced the IASC in 2001. The IASB now promulgates standards called International Financial Reporting Standards (IFRS).

The IASB also developed a set of accounting standards to address the needs of private companies, called IFRS for small- and medium-sized entities (IFRS for SMEs). IFRS for SMEs is based on IFRS but eliminates certain costly reporting requirements that are designed to provide information to external financial statement users. IFRS for SMEs was developed because some countries require all public and private companies to prepare financial statements under IFRS. These countries can then allow private companies the option to use the less costly IFRS for SMEs.

[17]The original 10 countries were Australia, Canada, France, Germany, Japan, Mexico, the Netherlands, the United Kingdom, Ireland, and the United States. Other countries subsequently joined the committee.

Interview

DIRECTOR, AICPA

DANIEL J. NOLL »

Daniel J. Noll

Daniel J. Noll, Director of Accounting Standards at the American Institute of Certified Public Accountants, works with the Financial Reporting Executive Committee to develop AICPA positions on financial reporting matters. He also provides external financial reporting guidance and leads the AICPA's private company financial reporting efforts.

1 What is the role of effective financial reporting in enabling financial statement users to make rational economic decisions?

For users—the ultimate customers of financial reporting—financial statements are a critical information source for investing and lending decisions. Imagine you are the sole owner of the Bank of Your Town and are considering whether to loan money to a local business. Before parting with your cash, you would ask questions such as: How does the business's profit and cash flow look? Are the numbers the business provided trustworthy and developed using accounting practices consistent with how other businesses in the same industry report?

Useful and reliable financial statements allow investors and lenders to make smart capital allocation decisions. The notion of "efficient and effective" allocation of capital helps drive capitalist economies and societies to greater standards of living. An inefficient and wasteful allocation would reward poorly run entities until they ultimately flounder or go bust. Consequently, funding would not be available for well-run businesses that could grow, employ people, and improve their communities.

2 What is AICPA's general role in the accounting environment and the standard-setting process?

The AICPA is the world's largest member association representing the CPA profession, with more than 418,000 members in 143 countries, and a history of serving the public interest since 1887. AICPA members represent many areas of practice, including business and industry, public practice, government, education, and consulting. Student membership is free. The AICPA sets ethical standards for the profession and U.S. auditing standards for private companies; nonprofit organizations; and federal, state, and local governments. It develops and grades the Uniform CPA Examination, offers specialized credentials, builds the pipeline of future talent, and drives professional competency development to advance the vitality, relevance, and quality of the profession. The AICPA's Financial Reporting Executive Committee (FinREC) serves as the official voice on all GAAP matters, advocating for sound external financial reporting practices related to private and public companies, not-for-profit entities, and employee benefit plans.

3 What is AICPA's role in improving the effectiveness of financial reporting?

The AICPA routinely interacts with regulators, standard setters, and all participants in the financial reporting process to identify and solve issues and contribute to policy development. AICPA is not an accounting standard setter; rather, it identifies issues needing authoritative FASB resolution or weighs in publicly on what good accounting practices might be under various circumstances.

4 What are the key areas in which accounting professionals and financial statement users look to the AICPA for guidance?

The key areas related to GAAP as set by FASB are:

1. The AICPA's industry accounting and audit guides, although not GAAP, are often viewed as a bible for their particular industry. We help professionals understand and apply accounting standards to unique or significant transactions within their industries.
2. The AICPA's accounting and valuation guides, also not GAAP, help bridge any language barriers between accounting/auditing staff and valuation specialists when tackling complex fair value measurements.
3. The AICPA issued revenue recognition accounting guidance based on FASB's newly effective standard that replaced the prior industry-specific GAAP. Our new accounting guide helps upwards of 16 industries understand and apply the newly effective standard to their particular circumstances. Because every entity has revenue, and professionals have been challenged for many years to determine when to recognize it, companies, auditors, and regulators will give this standard front and center attention for many years to come.

Discussion Questions

1. Discuss the role that the AICPA will play in your accounting career as a student and when you join the profession.
2. How would you characterize the current relationship between the FASB and the AICPA?

Exhibit 1.8 presents the history of international accounting standard setting.

EXHIBIT 1.8 History of International Accounting Standard Setting

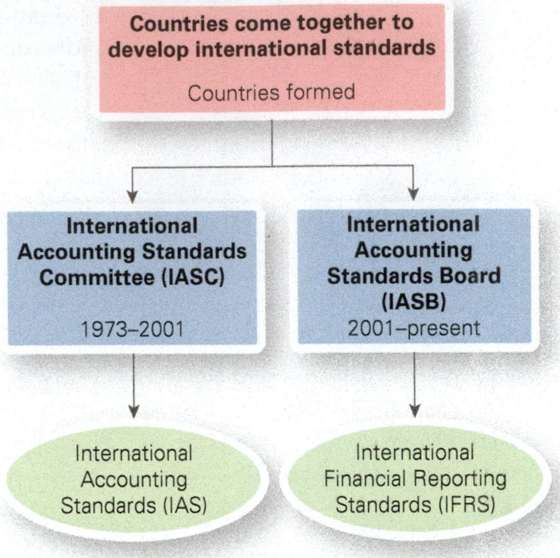

The Global Standard-Setting Structure: IFRS

As illustrated by Exhibit 1.9, the IASB is part of a larger organizational structure that also includes:

- The IFRS Foundation
- The Monitoring Board
- The IFRS Advisory Council
- The IFRS Interpretations Committee

The IFRS Foundation oversees the IASB and is responsible for financing the IASB's operations. Unlike funding for the FASB, the IASB relies on contributions from companies and other parties that have an interest in promoting international accounting standards. The Monitoring Board was formed in 2009 to enhance the public accountability of the IFRS Foundation while still allowing for independence in the standard-setting process.

The Monitoring Board oversees the IFRS Foundation, participates in nominating individuals to serve as foundation trustees, and approves appointments. The IFRS Advisory Council advises the IASB and the IFRS Foundation on many issues, including the IASB's agenda and the

EXHIBIT 1.9 International Accounting Organizational Structure

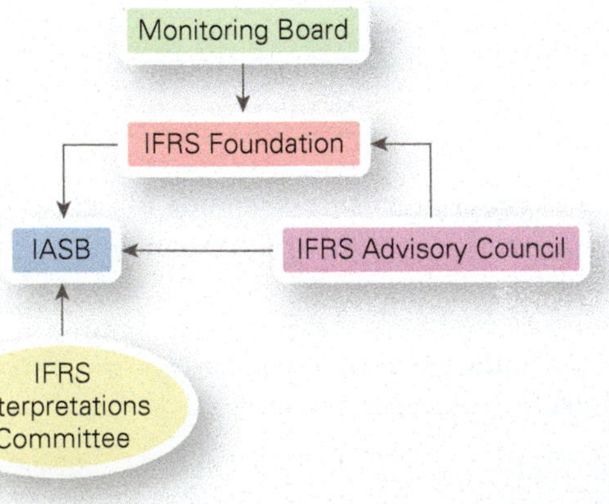

implementation of standards. The IFRS Interpretations Committee is the interpretative body of the IASB, similar to the EITF in the United States.

The IASB is composed of 14 members who are appointed by the IFRS Foundation's board of trustees. At least 11 members serve full time, and no more than 3 can be part-time members. To ensure broad and diverse international representation, the IASB is composed of:

- Four members from the Asia/Oceania region
- Four members from Europe
- Four members from the Americas
- One member from Africa
- One member appointed from any area, subject to maintaining overall geographical balance

The IFRS Interpretations Committee (IFRSIC) develops interpretations of standards that must be approved by the IASB. Whenever the need arises, the IFRS Interpretations Committee forms working groups, which are task forces for individual agenda projects. The IASB will also normally form working groups or other types of specialized advisory groups to advise on major projects; an example is the Emerging Economies Group.

Standard-Setting Process: IFRS

The IASB follows a similar process to the FASB's standard-setting process, so we discuss it only briefly here.

When a topic is identified, the Board considers the nature of the issues, seeks input from its constituents, and prepares an exposure draft. After receiving comments on the exposure draft, the IASB may modify the proposed standard before approving a final standard.

Unlike the FASB, the IASB is required to carry out a post-implementation review of each new standard or significant change to an existing standard. The review focuses on controversial issues identified during the development stage, unexpected costs, and implementation problems. This review is normally carried out up to two years after the new standard has been in effect.

Standard Setting as a Political Process

The issuance of new standards and changes in existing standards can have significant effects on an entity's reported net income. In turn, these income effects impact the flow of capital throughout the economy.

At the company level, managers have incentives to oppose changes in standards or new standards that reduce their company's reported net earnings. On the financial statement user level, a new standard or a change in existing standards should provide better and more transparent financial information that will assist users in making more effective investment and credit decisions.

Standard setters address the concerns of both the managers and financial statement users by employing the standard-setting processes we described in the previous section. These processes rely on the information gathered and opinions of users, managers, and auditors along with comments obtained from responses to exposure drafts and public roundtables. The standard-setting bodies analyze this information to gauge the economic consequences of the proposed standard and to assess the improvements in the quality of the financial information disseminated to the market. Standard setters address this trade-off between the income effects and the value of financial information, reaching a balance before issuing the final standard.

4 Explain three recent trends in standard setting: principles-based, rules-based, and objectives-oriented standards; the asset/liability approach; and fair value measurements.

Trends in Standard Setting

We conclude the chapter by introducing three current trends in standard setting, that we will explore further in later chapters:

- A move toward a less *rules-based* (or a more *principles-based*) system as found in International Financial Reporting Standards
- A move toward standards that are focused on the *asset/liability approach*
- A move toward measuring balance sheet items at *fair value* rather than historical cost

Rules- versus Principles-Based Standards

Both the U.S. GAAP and IFRS systems of accounting standards are based on principles and rules. A **principles-based standard** relies on theories, concepts, and principles of accounting that are linked to a well-developed theoretical framework. A **rules-based standard** contains specific, prescriptive procedures rather than relying on a consistent theoretical framework. For example, assume your parents tell you that you must maintain a GPA of at least 3.0 to receive a car at graduation. This is a rules-based standard. Now assume your parents tell you they will buy you a new car at graduation if you do well in school. This is an example of a principles-based standard. The SEC uses the term **objectives-oriented standard** to refer to a standard that is somewhere between a pure principles-based standard and a pure rules-based standard.[18]

Principles-Based Standards. Pure principles-based standards exhibit the following characteristics:

- Provide a clear discussion of the accounting objective related to the standard.
- Involve few, if any, exceptions.
- Involve no tests (referred to as **bright-line tests**) that require meeting a pre-established numerical threshold.[19]
- Provide insufficient guidance to implement the standard.
- Involve a significant amount of interpretation in application.

With pure principles-based standards, comparability across entities is often lost due to the extensive amount of preparer judgment required. In addition, preparers and auditors worry that regulators will not support the judgment used when reporting under a principles-based system, even judgments made honestly without intent to bias. Finally, the lack of application guidance can make it difficult to enforce principles-based reporting requirements in practice.

Rules-Based Standards. Unlike principles-based standards, rules-based standards may not relate to a consistent theoretical framework. In addition, pure rules-based standards:

- Contain numerous exceptions to the types of firms and industries that are covered by the standard.
- Contain numerous bright-line tests.
- Result in inconsistencies between standards.
- Contain detailed application guidance.
- Do not rely on extensive use of professional judgment.

As is the case with pure principles-based standards, pure rules-based standards also result in implementation problems. At times, reporting entities may circumvent rules and are therefore able to override the intent of the standard. A system of rules-based standards is difficult to interpret from a user perspective. Rules-based standards tend to result in an environment where financial reporting is viewed as an act of compliance rather than a process of disseminating transparent financial information to investors and creditors.

Objectives-Oriented Standards. An SEC report studying rules-based and principles-based standard setting indicated that an objectives-oriented standard is optimal.[20] Similar to principles-based standards, objectives-oriented standards are derived from and are consistent with

---

[18] See Study Pursuant to Section 108(d) of the Sarbanes-Oxley Act of 2002 on the Adoption by the United States Financial Reporting System of a Principles-Based Accounting System, U.S. Securities and Exchange Commission, July 2003 for a thorough discussion of principles and rules-based standards. The full text of the study is available at http://www.sec.gov/news/studies/principlesbasedstand.htm.

[19] For example, a rule specifying that a material item is 10% or more of net income is a bright-line test.

[20] Study Pursuant to Section 108(d) of the Sarbanes-Oxley Act of 2002 on the Adoption by the United States Financial Reporting System of a Principles-Based Accounting System, U.S. Securities and Exchange Commission, July 2003.

a high-quality theoretical framework and clearly stated accounting objectives. However, objectives-oriented standards include a sufficient level of rules to provide detail and structure, resulting in the consistent application of accounting standards across entities and across time. An objectives-oriented standard would minimize exceptions to a particular standard and reduce the number of bright-line tests used in its implementation. Many of the existing standards in both U.S. GAAP and IFRS qualify as objectives-oriented standards.

U.S. GAAP and IFRS: Rules versus Principles. Neither U.S. GAAP nor IFRS fits perfectly into a rules- or principles-based approach. The greatest difference between the two standards is that U.S. GAAP contains many more rules than does IFRS.[21] Although U.S. GAAP includes more rules than IFRS, it is not purely rules based. Similarly, IFRS is not purely principles based. Both U.S. GAAP and IFRS base standards on their respective *conceptual frameworks*, which we discuss in more detail in Chapter 2. Exhibit 1.10 shows the placement of U.S. GAAP and IFRS standards on the rules-based and principles-based continuum.

EXHIBIT 1.10 Rules versus Principles

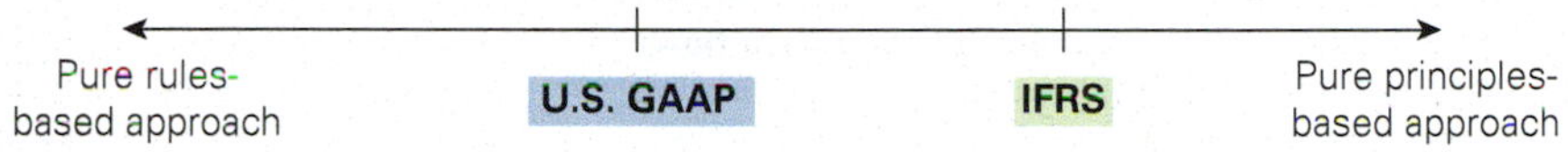

Asset/Liability Approach

The next trend relates to the interrelationship between the balance sheet and income statement. When a firm reports an event on the income statement, the transaction typically also changes a balance sheet account. For example, if a firm reports revenue, it also increases the balance in accounts receivable or cash.

Although the two financial statements are interrelated, which set of accounts is dominant—the revenues and expenses on the income statement or assets and liabilities on the balance sheet? For example, in a typical sales transaction, an accountant will increase accounts receivable and revenue. But how does the accountant decide whether to record the transaction?

1. Recording based on revenue recognition criteria involves an **income statement approach.**
2. Basing the decision on whether an economic resource is received and it meets the definition of an asset, such as accounts receivable, is an **asset/liability (balance sheet)** approach.

In FASB's early years, it tended to focus on an income statement approach. However, in recent years, it has shifted to the asset/liability approach.[22]

Fair Value Measurements

Another trend in standard setting is the movement toward the use of *fair value* measurements as a viable alternative to historical cost. **Fair value** is the amount at which an asset (or liability) could be bought (or incurred) or sold (or settled) in a current transaction between willing parties.[23] Twenty years ago, firms reported very few items on the balance sheet at fair value. Today, firms use fair values to measure some balance sheet accounts. For example, firms must report some investments in equity securities that have a readily determinable fair value and some investments in debt at fair value, as opposed to historical cost. We discuss fair value measurements more extensively in Chapter 2.

---

[21] It is likely that the considerable number of rules in U.S. GAAP were written in an attempt to protect preparers and auditors from potential, excessive litigation in the U.S. reporting environment.

[22] FASB, *Statement of Financial Accounting Standards No. 109*, "Accounting for Income Taxes" (Norwalk, CT: FASB, 1992), which is now codified as FASB ASC 740, *Income Taxes*, provides an example of the trend toward the use of the asset/liability approach. Prior to this standard, the profession employed an income statement approach when accounting for income taxes but now uses a balance sheet approach.

[23] See FASB ASC—Master Glossary.

Summary by Learning Objectives

In the following, we summarize the main points by learning objective. Throughout the chapter, we discuss the accounting and reporting of U.S. GAAP and IFRS side-by-side. The following table also highlights the major similarities and differences between the standards.

1 Define financial accounting and describe the demand for financial information, including the role of general-purpose financial statements, the information needs of financial statement users and other parties, and the factors that influence financial reporting.

Summary	Similarities and Differences between U.S. GAAP and IFRS
Financial accounting is the process of identifying, measuring, and communicating financial information about an economic entity to various user groups within the political, social, legal, and economic environment. Financial reporting aids investors, lenders, and other creditors in assessing the amounts and timing of future cash flows, as well as any uncertainty regarding those cash flows when making investment and credit decisions. General-purpose financial statements provide information to a wide spectrum of user groups: investors, creditors, financial analysts, insurance companies, unions, government agencies, and such. Financial statement users include equity investors, creditors, financial analysts, employees, labor unions, suppliers, debt investors, competitors, government agencies, and customers. Environmental factors such as legal, economic, political, or social factors impact the financial reporting process. Financial accounting is reactive when it reacts to pressure (lobbying) from various groups and changes in its environment. Financial accounting is proactive in that it can change or influence its environment by providing feedback information that is used by organizations and individuals to reshape the economy.	Similar under U.S. GAAP and IFRS.

2 Discuss the role of financial accounting standards setters in the United States and internationally.

Summary	Similarities and Differences between U.S. GAAP and IFRS
The Financial Accounting Standards Board (FASB) is the accounting standard setter in the United States. The International Accounting Standards Board (IASB) establishes International Financial Reporting Standards (IFRS).	➤ IFRS is required or permitted in over 130 countries worldwide. U.S. GAAP is required for U.S. companies.

Summary by Learning Objectives, continued

3 Detail the standard-setting process.

Summary	Similarities and Differences between U.S. GAAP and IFRS
In the United States, the Financial Accounting Standards Board (FASB) sets Generally Accepted Accounting Principles (GAAP). In setting standards, the FASB follows a seven-step process: Step 1: Identification of an issue. Step 2: Decision to pursue. Step 3: Public meetings. Step 4: Exposure Draft. Step 5: Public roundtables. Step 6: Redeliberation. Step 7: Publication of the final standard.	➤The International Accounting Standards Board (IASB) issues International Financial Reporting Standards (IFRS). The IASB has a similar process as the FASB, and it conducts a post-implementation review after an IFRS is issued.

4 Explain three recent trends in standard setting: principles-based, rules-based, and objectives-oriented standards; the asset/liability approach; and fair value measurements.

Summary	Similarities and Differences between U.S. GAAP and IFRS
Principles-based standards are standards consistent with a theoretical framework. Rules-based standards do not rely on a consistent theoretical framework but rather contain more specific, prescriptive rules. Objectives-oriented standards refer to standards that are somewhere between pure principles-based and pure rules-based. When deciding if a transaction should be recorded, the asset/liability approach bases the decision on whether an asset or liability should be reported on the balance sheet rather than if revenue or expenses should be recognized on the income statement. Fair value measurement, contrasted with historical cost, reports some items on the balance sheet at fair value.	➤We often think of U.S. GAAP as being more rules based than IFRS, but it is not purely rules based. Nor is IFRS purely principles based.

MyLab Accounting

Go to **http://www.pearson.com/mylab/accounting** for the following Questions, Brief Exercises, Exercises. They are available with immediate grading, explanations of correct and incorrect answers, and interactive media that acts as your own online tutor.

1 The Financial Reporting Environment

Questions

1 **Q1-1.** Which items are included in the definition of financial information? Is this concept synonymous with the term financial statements? Explain.

1 **Q1-2.** What is the purpose of generating financial statements and who are the primary users of this information?

1 **Q1-3.** How is the allocation of capital linked to the demand for financial reporting?

1 **Q1-4.** What are the roles and responsibilities of an external auditor?

2 **Q1-5.** What is the function of the accounting standard setters?

2 **Q1-6.** Can U.S. companies listed on U.S. stock exchanges use IFRS?

3 **Q1-7.** Who does the FASB consult in the standard-setting process?

1 3 **Q1-8.** Is the promulgation of financial accounting standards a political process? Explain.

4 **Q1-9.** How does a principles-based standard differ from a rules-based standard?

4 **Q1-10.** In recent years, what has been the FASB's approach to standard setting?

Brief Exercises

1 **BE1-1. General-Purpose Financial Statements.** Describe what is meant by the term "general-purpose financial statements." Discuss what group(s) benefit(s) from general-purpose financial statements.

1 **BE1-2. Financial Reporting Definition.** What is the definition of financial accounting?

1 **BE1-3. Financial Statement Users and Other Parties Involved in Financial Reporting.** Match the financial statement users and other parties involved in the use of and preparation of financial information with their role.

Financial Statement Users and Other Parties

____ Equity Investors

____ Creditors

____ Financial Analysts

____ Employees and Labor Unions

____ Suppliers and Customers

____ Government Agencies

____ Competitors

____ External Auditors

____ Internal Auditors

____ Regulatory Bodies

____ Professional Organizations

Role

1. Are banks and other financial institutions that lend money to the company.
2. Use financial statements to determine whether to conduct business or purchase products from a company.
3. Use financial information to determine their market position relative to the reporting entity and to attempt to identify future strategies of the reporting entity.
4. Are independent of the company and responsible for ensuring that management prepares and issues financial statements that comply with accounting standards and fairly present the financial position and economic performance of the company.
5. Use financial information to review and analyze reported results of the companies they cover and make investment recommendations.
6. Are employees of the company serving in an advisory role to management. They provide information to management regarding the company's operations and proper functioning of its internal controls.
7. Review the financial statements of publicly traded companies for a variety of reasons that are in the public interest.
8. Use financial information during negotiation of new labor agreements and compensation contracts.
9. Support accounting professionals throughout their careers by providing training, professional skills development, and other resources.
10. Are shareholders of the company.
11. Protect investors and oversee the accounting and auditing standard setting processes.

1 **BE1-4. Financial Statement Users.** Identify at least four different types of financial statement users and discuss why each would use the financial statements.

1 **BE1-5. Parties in the Financial Reporting Process.** Identify at least three types of parties in the financial reporting process and discuss why each would be interested in the financial statements.

1 **BE1-6. Economic Entity.** What is an economic entity?

3 **BE1-7. Standard-Setting Process.** Briefly explain how the financial statement preparers, users, and other interested parties are involved in the standard-setting process for U.S. GAAP.

3 **BE1-8. Standard-Setting Process.** What is the standard-setting process followed by FASB?

3 **BE1-9. FASB's Standard-Setting Process.** Order the steps in the Financial Accounting Standards Board's standard-setting process from 1 to 7.

______ The Board issues an Exposure Draft (ED), which is intended to solicit input.

______ After consultation with FASB members and others as appropriate, the FASB Chairperson decides whether to add the issue to the technical agenda.

______ The FASB staff analyzes the comment letters received, public roundtable discussions, and any other information. The Board then redeliberates the issue.

______ The Board may hold public roundtables to discuss the ED, if needed.

______ The Board issues an Accounting Standards Update (ASU), which is the final standard. It then incorporates the ASU into the Accounting Standards Codification that makes up U.S. GAAP.

______ A financial reporting issue is identified either by requests of financial statement users or by some other means.

______ The Board holds public meetings where it deliberates the various issues identified by the FASB staff.

3 **BE1-10. IASB's Standard-Setting Process.** What is the composition of the IASB's membership?

3 **BE1-11. SEC's Role.** What is the SEC's role in standard setting, both historically and currently?

4 **BE1-12. Characteristics of a Principles-Based or Rules-Based Accounting System.** Identify whether the items below are characteristics of a principles-based (P) or rules-based (R) accounting system:

______ Provides a clear discussion of the accounting objective related to the standard

______ Contains detailed application guidance

______ Contains numerous exceptions to the types of firms and industries that are covered

______ Involves no bright-line tests

______ Contains numerous bright-line tests

______ Involves a significant amount of interpretation in application

______ Involves few, if any, exceptions

______ Provides insufficient guidance to implement the standard

______ Would not rely on extensive use of professional judgment

______ Results in inconsistencies between standards

Exercises

1 **E1-1. Financial Accounting.** Define financial accounting and describe the four main elements in that definition.

1 **E1-2. Factors That Influence Financial Reporting.** Alicia O'Malley, a sociology major, is considering changing her major to accounting. Alicia is having some doubts because she fears that accounting and financial reporting are concerned only with numbers and are isolated from society. Convince Alicia to major in accounting by explaining how accounting interacts with its environment. In your answer, include a discussion of proactive and reactive factors.

2 **E1-3. Convergence of Accounting Standards, IFRS.** Vikram Patel, one of your friends from high school who is a finance major, is surprised that you are learning about international accounting. Explain why it is important for an accountant in the United States to learn International Financial Reporting Standards (IFRS).

3 **E1-4. History of Standard Setting in the United States.** Joe Choi, a history major, is considering transferring to your school of business to study accounting. Joe is having some doubts because he is uncertain if there is any room for history in accounting. Convince Joe to major in accounting by providing a history of standard setting in the United States. In your response, address the following items:

a. When did financial reporting standard setting begin in the United States?
b. Who had initial authority to set accounting standards?
c. Which organizations were delegated the authority to set standards? Comment on the types of standards issued and concerns with the standard-setting process under each organization.
d. Who currently sets accounting standards in the United States? What is the structure of the organization? What types of standards are issued?

4 **E1-5. Rules- versus Principles-Based Accounting.** Provide the key characteristics of rules-based standards and principles-based standards.

4 **E1-6. Asset/Liability Approach.** Consider the following comment: "Accounting standards have always focused on the asset/liability approach and still do today." Do you agree or disagree with this comment? Explain your answer.

4 **E1-7. Rules- versus Principles-Based Accounting.** Review the following statements and indicate if the statement is referring to a principles-based or a rules-based accounting standard.

Statement: An accountant will use a particular accounting standard only if . . .	Principles-Based or Rules-Based Accounting Standard
a. . . . the length of a contract covers substantially all of the useful life of a plant asset.	a. ______
b. . . . the number of new common shares a firm issues is equal to 20% of the previously outstanding shares.	b. ______
c. . . . a corporation owns over 50% of the voting shares of an affiliate company.	c. ______
d. . . . a corporation has the ability to control the operating and financing activities of an affiliate company.	d. ______
e. . . . it is more likely than not that a company's tax position will be sustained upon examination by the Internal Revenue Service.	e. ______
f. . . . the sum of the undiscounted future cash flows from the use of a plant asset is less than its carrying value.	f. ______

2 Financial Reporting Theory

LEARNING OBJECTIVES

1. Explain what a conceptual framework is and why it is important in accounting standard setting.
2. Define the objective of financial reporting.
3. Describe the qualitative characteristics of financial information, including the fundamental and enhancing characteristics of financial reporting.
4. Identify the elements of financial reporting.
5. Demonstrate an understanding of recognition and measurement in financial reporting including general recognition principles, revenue and expense recognition, and accrual accounting.
6. Explain the assumptions used in financial reporting.

Introduction

CHAPTER 1 PROVIDED A DETAILED DISCUSSION of the environment of financial accounting and the standard-setting process. Companies apply standards that are based on a *conceptual framework* that sets forth the theory of financial reporting.

Pichugin Dmitry/Shutterstock

Given diverse economic transactions, complex operating environments, and diverse industries, the standard setters require a logical and consistent basis for the development of the accounting standards. A conceptual framework provides a structure for developing new standards or revising existing standards. The framework ensures that standard setters develop all portions of the authoritative literature on a uniform basis that can be justified by a well-defined theoretical foundation. Companies then apply the authoritative literature in preparing their financial statements.

Consider two companies that generate revenues in different ways like ***Facebook, Inc.,*** the social media company, and ***Johnson & Johnson,*** the consumer healthcare, pharmaceutical, and medical device company. ***Facebook*** generates its revenues from advertising and fees for virtual currency and digital goods. ***Johnson & Johnson*** manufactures and sells a diverse range of healthcare products. Whereas ***Facebook*** primarily provides services and ***Johnson & Johnson*** manufactures and sells goods, both companies determine their costs associated with providing these services and goods based on the authoritative literature, which is grounded in the conceptual framework. Studying the conceptual framework of accounting will prepare you to understand the foundation of the guidance and associated financial reporting.

The conceptual framework defines the objective of financial reporting as providing financial information that is useful in making decisions about resource allocation. It identifies characteristics associated with high-quality financial information. The conceptual framework also defines the elements of the financial reporting system, such as assets and liabilities, and specifies the recognition and measurement criteria to be used in practice. Therefore, when investors and creditors analyze financial statements of companies such as ***Facebook*** or ***Johnson & Johnson***, they understand how the financial statements were prepared, what each financial statement contains, and what each line item on the statements represents.

We will discuss the purpose of a conceptual framework in the first part of this chapter. The FASB and the IASB currently have two separate conceptual frameworks, which are partially converged. The two boards have converged to the same objective of financial reporting and the same qualitative characteristics. Other areas such as elements and recognition, measurement, and the reporting entity are not converged. For these areas, we will discuss similarities and differences between U.S. GAAP and IFRS. «

1 Explain what a conceptual framework is and why it is important in accounting standard setting.

Overview of the Conceptual Framework

A **conceptual framework** sets forth theory, concepts, and principles to ensure that accounting standards are coherent and uniform. The conceptual framework states that a purpose of the conceptual framework is to assist standard setters in developing and revising accounting standards. However, the conceptual framework does not override accounting standards.

Conceptual Framework Components

In this chapter, we will examine the following conceptual framework components:

- Objective of financial reporting
- Characteristics associated with high-quality financial information
- Elements of the financial reporting system
- Recognition and measurement criteria

Throughout the rest of the text, we refer to this discussion of the conceptual framework. Sections in the text called "The Conceptual Framework Connection" provide a structure to guide our discussions and analyses by explicitly establishing the relevant conceptual underpinnings.

Exhibit 2.1 illustrates the relationship among the conceptual framework components. Specifically, the exhibit shows how the objective of financial reporting flows through to the qualitative characteristics, elements, measurement and recognition, and constraints, leading to financial standards for preparing financial statements. In this way, the financial statements are designed to meet the objective of financial reporting.

EXHIBIT 2.1 Conceptual Framework's Role in Standard Setting

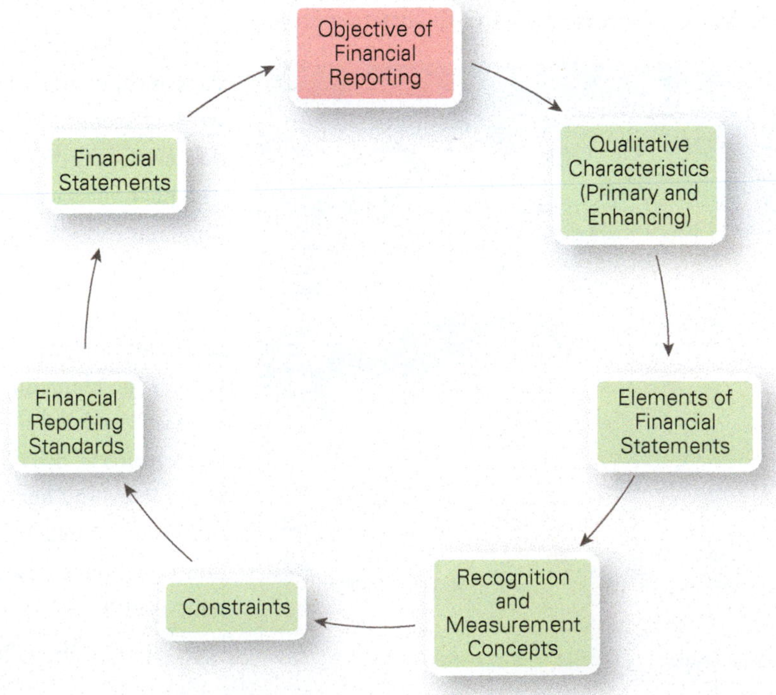

Exhibit 2.1 also illustrates the use of the conceptual framework in developing new standards and justifying existing standards. When developing new standards, the standard setters first determine if the proposed standard meets the objective of financial reporting. Next, the information provided by the new standard must possess the qualitative characteristics that make accounting information useful. The standard setters then consider the elements of the financial statements affected and the recognition and measurement concepts used to support the new standard. Before deciding to issue a new standard, the standard setters weigh constraints such as the cost and benefit of issuing the new standard, which may deter requiring the new standard. If the standard is issued, companies must disclose the changes in the financial statements.

The FASB is currently revising the conceptual framework. Exhibit 2.2 summarizes FASB's six-topic project initiated to revise its conceptual framework. The first topic on the objective of financial reporting and the qualitative characteristics has been completed. The FASB is currently working on Elements, Measurement, Presentation, and Disclosure. The other topic is inactive. At the current time, FASB and IASB are working independently on the conceptual framework.

EXHIBIT 2.2 FASB Conceptual Framework Project

Topic	Status
Topic 1: Objective and Qualitative Characteristics	Completed[1]
Topic 2: Elements	Active—No Exposure Draft Issued
Topic 3: Measurement	Active—No Exposure Draft Issued
Topic 4: Reporting Entity	Inactive
Topic 5: Presentation	Active—Exposure Draft Issued
Topic 6: Disclosure	Active—Exposure Draft Issued

Source: http://www.fasb.org/jsp/FASB/FASBContent_C/ProjectUpdatePage&cid=900000011090

Exhibit 2.3 provides a detailed overview of the current conceptual framework. In the following sections, we will discuss the concepts statements that comprise the current conceptual framework.

EXHIBIT 2.3 Overview of the Conceptual Framework

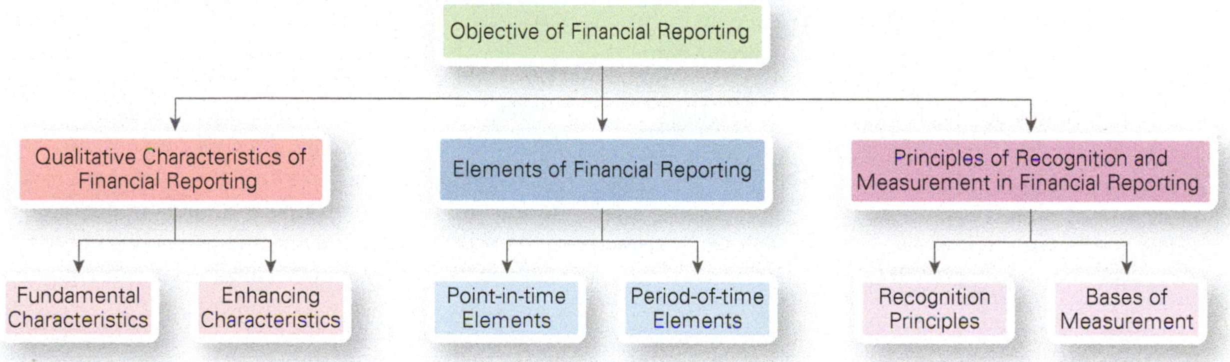

[1]The FASB issued *Statement of Financial Accounting Concepts No. 8*, "Conceptual Framework for Financial Reporting—Chapter 1, The Objective of General Purpose Financial Reporting and Chapter 3, Qualitative Characteristics of Useful Financial Information" (Norwalk, CT: Financial Accounting Foundation, 2010). *Statement of Financial Accounting Concepts Statement No. 8* superseded the sections of the existing conceptual framework covering the objective and qualitative characteristics of financial reporting. The IASB issued its own pronouncement, *Conceptual Framework for Financial Reporting* (London, UK: International Accounting Standards Board, 2010).

Interview

PAUL PACTER, FORMER MEMBER OF IASB »

Paul Pacter

Paul Pacter is a former member of the IASB. Prior to joining the Board, he served concurrently as its Director of Standards for Small- and Medium-sized Entities and also as Director in the Deloitte Touche Tohmatsu Global IFRS Office. Paul Pacter left the IASB in December, 2012.

1 How does a conceptual framework assist in the development of future accounting standards and reduce the possibility of non-comparable accounting treatments or creating conflicting accounting standards?

A common goal of the IASB and the FASB—and their constituents—is for their standards to be based on an agreed set of fundamental *concepts* rather than being a collection of current *practices*. Fundamental concepts start with agreement on the objective of financial reporting—who uses financial statements, for what kinds of decisions, and what information is relevant to those decisions? These concepts define the basic building blocks of a financial report (what is an asset, liability, income, and expense?) and the general principles for recognizing, measuring, and presenting them. A *conceptual framework* enables accounting standard setters to develop a high-quality and internally consistent body of standards, thereby ensuring that an entity's financial report meets the needs of users.

Without agreement on a conceptual framework, each IASB member would approach an accounting issue with his or her own personal conceptual framework. As board members changed, the underlying concepts would change, resulting in *ad hoc*, inconsistent, and possibly conflicting standards.

2 How effective is the current conceptual framework at assisting auditors and preparers of financial information in dealing with events and transactions not covered by a specific accounting pronouncement?

No matter how good a framework is, it will never be a machine where you input some accounting question and out comes a clear accounting answer. Developing and applying accounting standards consistent with the framework always requires judgment. The framework provides standard setters with guidance and direction to exercise those judgments. Although it gives some guidance to a preparer or auditor of financial statements, it is less useful to them.

The IASB has taken the conceptual framework to a higher level than FASB. IAS 8, our standard on accounting policies, sets out a hierarchy of accounting policies: To assert that you comply with IFRS, you must follow all our standards. If no standard directly addresses your accounting question, then you must develop a policy that results in the most relevant and reliable information, drawing an analogy with an existing standard. If you cannot do that, it is mandatory to look to the conceptual framework. So under IFRS, the conceptual framework becomes a part of the standards.

3 Why is knowledge of accounting important to be an effective businessperson, particularly in light of the recent global financial turmoil?

A business entity that raises capital from investors and creditors must be accountable to them, providing essential information about its performance, condition, and prospects through accurate and understandable financial accounting. It is also accountable to other constituents—vendors, employees, governments, and the community at large.

Capital providers want transparency. When they understand and have confidence in the financial figures, a company's ability to obtain the capital it needs—priced fairly relative to the risks that the capital provider assumes—improves. Ultimately, the economy in which it operates improves.

Accounting's role is to report faithfully and without bias the results of transactions and other economic events and conditions—both positive and negative—that affect a business entity. For example, obligations that meet the definition of a liability should be on the balance sheet. Impairments of assets that have already happened should be recognized as losses, even if there is cause for optimism that the situation may turn around.

4 What critical issues face the accounting profession today? What advice might you offer to future accountants?

The number one challenge for financial reporting is to stay relevant to the needs of investors, lenders, creditors, and other financial statement users. The information must be useful for capital allocation and pricing decisions. That is why governments and regulators require publicly traded companies (and often private companies as well) to publish accurate financial statements. We accountants must never lose sight of the important public interest in our work.

Discussion Questions

1. Discuss several components of the current conceptual framework that provide guidance and direction to accountants when exercising judgment.
2. Discuss the meaning of Paul Pacter's statement, "We accountants must never lose sight of the important public interest in our work."

Conceptual Framework: IFRS

The IASB's objective and qualitative characteristics are identical to U.S. GAAP. However, they differ in the descriptions of elements of financial reporting and principles of recognition and measurement in financial reporting. The IASB is also currently revising its framework.

❷ Define the objective of financial reporting.

The Objective of Financial Reporting

According to the conceptual framework, the objective of financial reporting is:

> To provide financial information about the reporting entity that is useful to existing and potential investors, lenders, and other creditors in making decisions about providing resources to the entity. Those decisions involve buying, selling, or holding equity and debt instruments and providing or settling loans and other forms of credit.[2]

The conceptual framework indicates that the primary users of financial information are the investors, lenders, and other creditors who cannot demand information from the entity.[3] For instance, if ***Bank of America*** extends credit to ***Johnson & Johnson***, the bank can demand any information needed to approve the loan. However, an individual investor in ***Johnson & Johnson's*** publicly traded debt usually cannot obtain additional information from the entity to help assess the amount, timing, and uncertainty of future cash flows. Investors also require financial information to form an opinion about a company's future cash flows and earnings—and many of the standard-setting board's decisions are based on this need.

❸ Describe the qualitative characteristics of financial information, including the fundamental and enhancing characteristics of financial reporting.

The Qualitative Characteristics of Financial Information

The objective of financial reporting is to provide useful information for decision making by investors, lenders, and other creditors. What characteristics make financial information useful? The conceptual framework divides the qualitative characteristics into *fundamental characteristics* and *enhancing characteristics*, and discusses the cost constraint on providing information.

Fundamental Characteristics

Fundamental characteristics are those basic characteristics that distinguish useful financial information from information that is not useful. The FASB identifies the two fundamental characteristics as *relevance* and *faithful representation.*

Relevance. Financial information is **relevant** if it is capable of making a difference in decision making by exhibiting the following attributes:

- Predictive value
- Confirmatory value
- Materiality

Information has **predictive value** if decision makers can use it as an input into processes that help forecast future outcomes. For example, companies report sales revenue each year. Financial statement users may use the prior year's revenues to predict future revenues. Both ***BMW*** and ***Porsche,*** German automobile manufacturers, reported sales increases in their earnings announcements for fiscal 2015. By highlighting the increase in sales, the companies implicitly benchmarked the current sales against past sales. The sales from prior years can then be useful to investors in forecasting future revenues in periods beyond 2015.

---

[2]From the FASB's *Concepts Statement No. 8*, Paragraph OB2, and the IASB's *Conceptual Framework for Financial Reporting*, Paragraph OB2.

[3]If the objective were to provide information to a different group (e.g., regulators), then the boards would arrive at different reporting requirements.

Information has **confirmatory value** if it provides feedback about prior evaluations. For example, financial statement users will often compare reported net income to prior earnings forecasts. Consider ***Johnson & Johnson,*** which beat or exceeded analysts' forecasted earnings per share in the fourth quarter of 2016, by reporting earnings per share of $1.58.

The concept of *materiality* also determines the relevance of information. Information is **material** if reporting it inaccurately or omitting it would affect financial statement users' decisions. The materiality of an item can depend on its size or nature. The conceptual framework does not specify a quantitative threshold for the materiality of an item nor does it identify the specific nature of items that would be considered material. Rather, whether an item is material depends on the company and its financial reporting. Preparers and auditors must use professional judgment to determine the materiality of an item.

As an example of materiality varying with size, consider a $5,000 loss incurred when a computer is damaged. For a small start-up consulting firm, the loss could be material—that is, it could affect a financial statement user's decision such as extending credit to the firm. For a large, profitable consulting firm, a $5,000 loss would likely be immaterial. The planned disposition of a major operating segment is an example of an item that is material by its nature. Even though there is no quantifiable amount that would be reported in the financial statements, not informing financial statement users of the planned disposition could affect their assessment of the company's future performance and their decisions about investing in or extending credit to the company.

Faithful Representation. The second qualitative characteristic, **faithful representation,** indicates whether financial information depicts the substance of an economic event in a manner that is

- Complete
- Neutral
- Free from error

The depiction of an economic event is considered **complete** if it includes all information—both descriptions and explanations—necessary for the financial statement user to understand the underlying economic event. For example, a company reports a balance of long-lived assets on its balance sheet. From this one amount, a financial statement user cannot fully understand the company's investment in its long-lived assets. A complete depiction of a company's long-lived assets includes a description of the nature of the assets, the balance by type, and a description of the depreciation method used for each type. For example, ***Johnson & Johnson*** reported $15,905 million of net property, plant, and equipment on its January 3, 2016, balance sheet, representing about 12% of its total assets. It presents its property, plant, and equipment in more depth in its footnotes to the financial statements to provide a more complete depiction of the company's property, plant, and equipment. In the footnote, ***Johnson & Johnson*** includes the amount of each major class of property, plant, and equipment such as the $22,511 million of machinery and equipment. After the table, ***Johnson & Johnson*** includes other information on its property, plant, and equipment such as the amounts of capitalized interest expense and depreciation expense. Exhibit 2.4 presents note 4 from ***Johnson & Johnson's*** 2015 annual report.

In its financial statement notes, ***Johnson & Johnson*** also states that its property, plant, and equipment are reported at cost. The company indicates that it depreciates plant and equipment using the straight-line method and provides estimated useful lives. Further, the company identifies and reports the historical costs of four different categories of property, plant, and equipment. ***Johnson & Johnson*** also reports the total accumulated depreciation on these assets.

Information is **neutral** if it is free from bias in both the selection and presentation of financial data. For example, assume that Haster Incorporated has three lawsuits pending at the end of the year. It discloses information only about the lawsuit that it expects to have a favorable outcome but not the two for which it expects unfavorable outcomes. This biased reporting does not faithfully represent the firm's financial position.

Information is reported **free from error** when there are no mistakes or omissions in the description of an event or in the process used to produce the financial information. However, the information need not be accurate in all respects. Specifically, firms report a significant amount of

EXHIBIT 2.4 ***Johnson & Johnson*** **Property, Plant and Equipment Note Excerpt, January 3, 2016, Financial Statements**

NOTE 4: Property, Plant and Equipment

At the end of 2015 and 2014, property, plant and equipment at cost and accumulated depreciation were:

(Dollars in Millions)	2015	2014
Land and land improvements	$ 780	$ 833
Buildings and building equipment	9,829	10,046
Machinery and equipment	22,511	22,206
Construction in progress	3,528	3,600
Total property, plant and equipment, gross	$ 36,648	$36,685
Less accumulated depreciation	(20,743)	(20,559)
Total property, plant and equipment, net	**$ 15,905**	**$16,126**

The Company capitalizes interest expense as part of the cost of construction of facilities and equipment. Interest expense capitalized in 2015, 2014, and 2013 was $102 million, $115 million, and $105 million, respectively.

Depreciation expense, including the amortization of capitalized interest in 2015, 2014, and 2013, was $2.5 billion, $2.5 billion, and $2.7 billion, respectively.

Upon retirement or other disposal of property, plant and equipment, the costs and related amounts of accumulated depreciation or amortization are eliminated from the asset and accumulated depreciation accounts, respectively. The difference, if any, between the net asset value and the proceeds are recorded in earnings.

Source: Annual Report, 2015 Johnson and Johnson

financial information based on estimates. For example, companies estimate the amount of receivables that will ultimately become uncollectible. Because the amount of uncollectible receivables is an estimate, the actual amount could be different.

Enhancing Characteristics

Even if information is relevant and representationally faithful, it may not be the most useful data available for decision making. The FASB identifies the following four **enhancing characteristics** that help distinguish more useful information from less useful information:

- Comparability
- Verifiability
- Timeliness
- Understandability

Comparability. Investors and creditors must be able to compare entities in making capital allocation decisions. **Comparability** allows financial statements users to identify and understand similarities and differences among several entities. Accounting standards often allow alternative methods, such as straight-line or accelerated depreciation, and require estimates, like the useful lives of long-lived assets. A company's financial information is useful if financial statement users can compare it with similar information from another company, companies in its industry, or to its prior year. For example, the requirement to disclose the useful lives of long-lived assets allows financial statement users to compare the aircraft fleets of ***American Airlines*** and ***Delta Airlines. American*** uses a 16- to 30-year useful life for its fleet whereas ***Delta*** uses a longer 20- to 32-year useful life.[4] The differing useful lives imply that ***American*** has aircraft with a shorter useful life and probably has different types of planes in its fleet than ***Delta.***

Verifiability. **Verifiability** means that a group of reasonably informed financial statement users are able to reach a consensus decision that reported information is a faithful representation of an underlying economic event. For example, two independent accountants would agree that a company owes $100,000 to a commercial bank by examining the loan agreement.

Timeliness. **Timely information** is available to financial statement users early enough to make a difference in decision making. In the United States, public companies prepare financial statements every quarter and annually. Imagine trying to make an investment decision if financial statements were issued only every five years: You would possess outdated information irrelevant to decision making in the current period. Generally, older information is less useful than more recent information.

Understandability. Information is **understandable** to reasonably informed financial statement users when financial statements classify, characterize, and clearly present all information. Because many companies are incredibly complex, it is very important to distill the vast amounts of financial data into a manageable report for users to read and understand. As an example of how financial statements are organized to aid understandability, companies separate current and noncurrent assets on their balance sheets. As a result, financial statement users can better understand a company's current and long-term resources.

We summarize the qualitative characteristics in Exhibit 2.5.

Cost Constraint

Providing all relevant and representationally faithful information available is costly. As a result, the conceptual framework stipulates that standard setters should compare the cost of requiring information to the benefits derived from presenting this information when developing accounting standards. Standard setters consider costs for both financial statement reporters and users.

A company consumes a significant amount of resources in collecting, processing, verifying, and communicating its financial results. New standards or significant revisions of existing standards require companies to increase training, update accounting systems, and renegotiate existing contracts based on updated accounting information. On the other hand, if the information required under a new standard is not provided to the users, they incur costs in obtaining or estimating that information on their own.

To illustrate, assume that standard setters are considering requiring that retail stores report the sales and operating profit generated by each store by month. This information may be useful to investors and financial analysts. However, the cost of providing such detailed store-by-store information every month can be greater than its benefits. As a result, the information will not be required.

4 Identify the elements of financial reporting.

Elements of Financial Reporting

The second phase of the conceptual framework project builds on the objective of financial reporting and characteristics of financial information. This section provides a discussion of the elements of financial reporting, which are the building blocks of the financial statements.

The two groups of elements are *point-in-time elements* and *period-of-time elements.*

1. **Point-in-time elements** represent resources, claims to resources, or interests in resources as of a specific point in time and appear on the balance sheet (statement of financial position). For example, accounts receivable and accounts payable are point-in-time elements.

[4]Sources: http://d1lge852tjjqow.cloudfront.net/CIK-0000027904/082dbd71-0d08-4ce4-b155-3f7bb2018395.pdf; http://phx.corporate-ir.net/phoenix.zhtml?c=117098&p=irol-reportsannual

EXHIBIT 2.5 Qualitative Characteristics of Financial Information

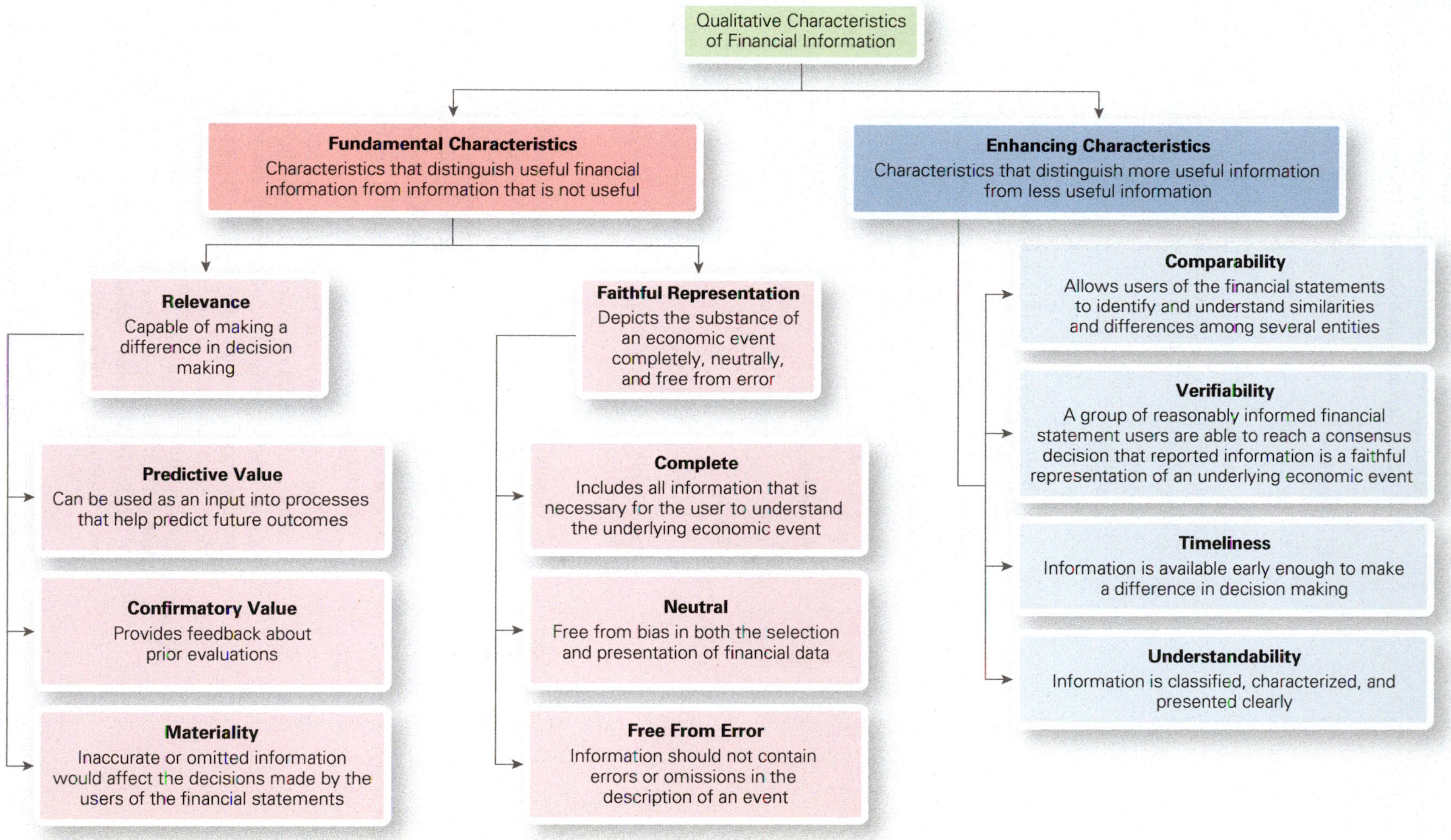

Qualitative Characteristics of Financial Information
Fundamental Characteristics
Characteristics that distinguish useful financial information from information that is not useful
Enhancing Characteristics
Characteristics that distinguish more useful information from less useful information
Relevance
Capable of making a difference in decision making
Predictive Value
Can be used as an input into processes that help predict future outcomes
Confirmatory Value
Provides feedback about prior evaluations
Materiality
Inaccurate or omitted information would affect the decisions made by the users of the financial statements
Faithful Representation
Depicts the substance of an economic event completely, neutrally, and free from error
Complete
Includes all information that is necessary for the user to understand the underlying economic event
Neutral
Free from bias in both the selection and presentation of financial data
Free From Error
Information should not contain errors or omissions in the description of an event
Comparability
Allows users of the financial statements to identify and understand similarities and differences among several entities
Verifiability
A group of reasonably informed financial statement users are able to reach a consensus decision that reported information is a faithful representation of an underlying economic event
Timeliness
Information is available early enough to make a difference in decision making
Understandability
Information is classified, characterized, and presented clearly

2. **Period-of-time elements** represent the results of events and circumstances that affect an entity during a period of time and appear on the income statement, statement of comprehensive income, or statement of shareholders' equity. Sales revenue, depreciation expense, and dividends declared are examples of period-of-time elements.

Elements

We begin by examining the point-in-time elements.

Point-in-Time Elements. U.S. GAAP identifies the three point-in-time elements, which represent resources, claims to resources, and interests in resources as of a point in time such as a specific balance sheet date. The point-in-time elements are:

1. Assets
2. Liabilities
3. Equity

Exhibit 2.6 presents the U.S. GAAP definitions of each element.

EXHIBIT 2.6 Definitions of Point-in-Time Elements

Element	Definition
Assets	Probable future economic benefits obtained or controlled by a particular entity as a result of past transactions or events
Liabilities	Probable future sacrifices of economic benefits arising from present obligations of a particular entity to transfer assets or provide services to other entities in the future as a result of past transactions or events
Equity	The net assets or residual interest in the assets of an entity that remains after deducting its liabilities.

Source: FASB, *Statement of Financial Accounting Concepts No. 6*, "Elements of Financial Statements," Paragraphs 25, 35, 49

Assets are probable future economic benefits resulting from some past event. In addition to the asset definition, U.S. GAAP identifies three enhancing characteristics of an asset:[5]

1. "It embodies a probable future benefit that involves a capacity, singly or in combination with other assets, to contribute directly or indirectly to future net cash inflows,
2. A particular entity can obtain the benefit and control others' access to it, and
3. The transaction or other event giving rise to the entity's right to or control of the benefit has already occurred."

The future economic benefit from an asset is the cash flows generated from its use. For instance, an account receivable is an asset because it generates cash upon collection. Controlling an asset means that no other entity can use or access it without permission. For example, another entity does not have the right to use another company's plant and equipment unless these assets are under a lease agreement. Finally, the asset arises out of an event or transaction that has already occurred. An account receivable usually arises when a completed sale transaction occurs.

U.S. GAAP defines **liabilities** as probable future sacrifices of economic benefits arising from present obligations of a particular entity to transfer assets or provide services to other entities in

[5]Financial Accounting Standards Board, *Statement of Financial Accounting Concepts No. 6*, "Elements of Financial Statements" (Stamford, CT: FASB, 1985), Paragraph 26.

the future as a result of past transactions or events. U.S. GAAP also identifies three characteristics that enhance the definition of a liability:[6]

1. "It embodies a present duty or responsibility to one or more other entities that entails settlement by probable future transfer or use of assets at a specified or determinable date, on occurrence of a specified event, or on demand,
2. The duty or responsibility obligates a particular entity, leaving it little or no discretion to avoid the future sacrifice, and
3. The transaction or other event obligating the entity has already happened."

These characteristics indicate that a liability will result in a future sacrifice, which can be the transfer of an asset such as cash or the use of an asset to fulfill the obligation. For example, salaries payable are a liability because the entity must pay its employees cash in the future in exchange for services they have already provided to the company.

Equity, or net assets, is the difference between assets and liabilities. This residual interest in a company's assets remains after the claims of creditors have been satisfied and therefore represents the ownership interest. The amount of equity is the cumulative result of investments by owners, comprehensive income, and distributions to owners.

Period-of-Time Elements. Period-of-time elements represent the results of events and circumstances that occur between two balance sheet dates. The point-in-time and period-of-time element groups interrelate or are said to articulate. Period-of-time elements will change point-in-time elements (i.e., assets, liabilities, and equity). For example, revenues will increase equity and expenses will decrease equity. Dividends declared will decrease equity. Another example is accounts receivable increasing when a sale is made on account. Salaries payable increases when employees have not yet been paid for work performed but equity is decreased.

In the conceptual framework, U.S. GAAP identifies seven period-of-time elements:

1. Investments by owners
2. Distributions to owners
3. Revenues
4. Gains
5. Expenses
6. Losses
7. Comprehensive income

The first two elements, investments by owners and distributions to owners, represent transactions with owners. Investments by owners include the issuance of stock. Dividends are an example of distributions to owners. The remaining five elements relate to business activities occurring during the period.

Revenues and expenses are changes in equity that arise in the ordinary course of business. Gains and losses also change equity but are not considered part of normal operations. For example, ***Target Corporation*** owns some of the stores it operates. ***Target*** records depreciation expense on the buildings as part of its operating income. Now assume that ***Target*** sold one of its stores. It would have a gain or loss on the sale measured as the difference between the sale proceeds and the building's carrying value. ***Target*** did not include the gain or loss in normal operations and it would not classify it as revenue or expense. Rather, it would recognize the amount as either a gain or loss on disposal.

Comprehensive income includes all changes in equity during a period except those resulting from investments by owners and distributions to owners. As a result, comprehensive income includes net income and other gains or losses currently not recognized on the traditional income statement. For example, if a company invests in certain debt securities and the fair value of these shares declines, the equity of the company decreases. The decline in equity is part of other

[6]FASB, *Statement of Financial Accounting Concepts No. 6*, "Elements of Financial Statements," Paragraph 36.

comprehensive income and may not be included on the traditional income statement.[7] The FASB's definition and summary of the period-of-time elements are in Exhibit 2.7.

EXHIBIT 2.7 Period-of-Time Elements

Element	Definition
Investments by Owners	Increases in equity of a particular business enterprise resulting from transfers to it from other entities of something valuable to obtain or increase ownership interests (or equity) in it. Assets are most commonly received as investments by owners, but that which is received may also include services or satisfaction or conversion of liabilities of the enterprise.
Distributions to Owners	Decreases in equity of a particular business enterprise resulting from transferring assets, rendering services, or incurring liabilities by the enterprise to owners. Distributions to owners decrease ownership interest (or equity) in an enterprise.
Revenues	Inflows or other enhancements of an entity's assets or settlements of its liabilities (or a combination of both) from delivering or producing goods, rendering services, or other activities that constitute the entity's ongoing major or central operations.
Gains	Increases in equity (net assets) from an entity's peripheral or incidental transactions and from all other transactions and other events and circumstances affecting the entity except those that result from revenues or investments by owners.
Expenses	Outflows or other consumption of assets or incurrences of liabilities (or a combination of both) from delivering or producing goods, rendering services, or carrying out other activities that constitute the entity's ongoing major or central operations.
Losses	Decreases in equity (net assets) from an entity's peripheral or incidental transactions and from all other transactions and other events and circumstances affecting the entity except those that result from expenses or distributions to owners.
Comprehensive Income	The change in equity of a business enterprise during a period from transactions and other events and circumstances from nonowner sources. It includes all changes in equity during a period except those resulting from investments by owners and distributions to owners.

Source: FASB, *Statement of Financial Accounting Concepts No. 6*, "Elements of Financial Statements"

Elements: IFRS

In this section, we discuss similarities and key differences in the elements under U.S. GAAP and IFRS.

Point-in-Time Elements. IFRS identifies the same three point-in-time elements as U.S. GAAP:

1. Assets
2. Liabilities
3. Equity

[7]We discuss the distinction between net income and comprehensive income in Chapter 5.

The definitions of these elements differ slightly in IFRS. Companies usually identify the same assets and liabilities under both U.S. GAAP and IFRS, however, so we do not explore the details of the IFRS definitions.[8]

Period-of-Time Elements. IFRS identifies four period-of-time elements:

1. Performance
2. Income (includes both revenues and gains)
3. Expenses (includes both expenses and losses)
4. Capital maintenance adjustments

IFRS explicitly identifies performance, or profit, as a separate element. In contrast, profit is the result of adding revenues and gains and subtracting expenses and losses under U.S. GAAP. Where U.S. GAAP identifies revenues and gains as separate elements, the income element in IFRS encompasses both revenues and gains as both increase equity. Similarly, where U.S. GAAP identifies expenses and losses as separate elements, the expense element under IFRS encompasses both expenses and losses as both decrease equity. Exhibit 2.8 illustrates the links between these definitions under U.S. GAAP and IFRS.

EXHIBIT 2.8 Links between Revenues, Gains, Income, Expenses, and Losses under U.S. GAAP and IFRS

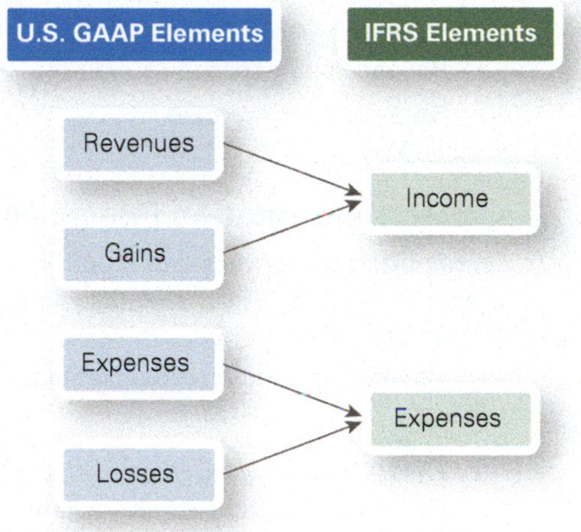

Unlike U.S. GAAP, IFRS determines capital maintenance adjustments from period to period. IFRS defines **capital maintenance adjustments** as restatements or revaluations of reported amounts of assets and liabilities that companies usually report in other comprehensive income. The concept of capital maintenance relates to how a company seeks to assess changes in its equity. Capital is maintained when the amount of equity in the current year is at least as much as it was in the prior year.[9] Because capital maintenance assesses changes in equity, it is linked to how profit is determined. There are two concepts of capital maintenance:

- *Financial capital maintenance*
- *Physical capital maintenance*

[8]One exception in assets and liabilities reported under U.S. GAAP and IFRS is related to the accounting for research and development costs. Under U.S. GAAP, companies expense all research and development costs. U.S. standard setters view the probable future economic benefits of research and development as so uncertain that research and development cannot be considered an asset. International standard setters also view research costs as uncertain and require companies to expense them under IFRS. However, companies can record development costs as an asset under IFRS when certain conditions are met. The difference in treating development costs as an asset is not due to a difference in the definition of an asset under U.S. GAAP and IFRS. Rather, it is attributable to differences in the interpretation of what is a probable future benefit. We discuss the accounting for research and development costs in Chapter 11.

[9]We exclude distributions to and contributions from owners during the period in determining whether capital has been maintained.

Under the concept of **financial capital maintenance,** capital is viewed as the financial amount, or money amount, invested in a company. A company earns profit only if the financial amount, or dollar amount, of the equity at the end of the period is higher than it was at the beginning of the period. For example, financial capital is maintained and a profit is earned when the ending balance of equity is $750,000 higher than the beginning balance.

Under the concept of **physical capital maintenance,** capital is viewed as the productive capacity of a company, such as units of output per day. A company earns a profit if its productive capacity is greater at the end of the period than it was at the beginning of the period. The concept of physical capital maintenance relies on current cost measurement and is consistent with the revaluation or restatement of long-lived operating assets and liabilities. For example, physical capital is maintained and a profit is earned when the output of goods produced is 200,000 units higher in the current year than in the prior year. IFRS allows a company to determine the concept of capital maintenance that is most appropriate for its business.

Finally, also note that unlike U.S. GAAP, IFRS does not treat transactions with the owners as separate elements.

5 Demonstrate an understanding of recognition and measurement in financial reporting, including general recognition principles, revenue and expense recognition, and accrual accounting.

Principles of Recognition and Measurement

The use of the accrual basis, rather than the cash basis, is a distinguishing feature of financial accounting. We discuss the underlying principles of accrual accounting in this section that include:

- General recognition
- Revenue and expense recognition
- Bases of measurement

General Recognition Principles

Recognition is the process of reporting an economic event in the financial statements. Recognized events are included in a line item on the financial statements as opposed to in the notes to the statements.[10]

Companies should recognize items when (and only when) they have met the following four criteria.

1. *The item meets the definition of one of the elements of the financial statements.* For example, before a company records an asset, the item must meet the definition of an asset.
2. *The item is measurable.* Events that are relevant to decision making are recognizable only if the firm can measure them. Consider an entity that has been sued. In the early stages of the lawsuit, it may not be possible to reliably estimate the amount of the potential obligation. Therefore, it does not report a liability on the balance sheet.
3. *The item must be reliable.* This notion is similar to the faithful representation characteristic discussed earlier in that reliable financial information depicts the substance of an economic event in a manner that is complete, neutral, and free from error.
4. *The item is relevant.* That is, it must allow financial statement users to make rational economic decisions.

An item could meet all four of the above criteria and still not be recognized due to the *cost-benefit constraint* or a *materiality threshold.* Similar to the cost constraint that standard setters apply when setting accounting standards, companies use the *cost-benefit constraint* when determining when to recognize an item in the financial statements. The **cost-benefit constraint** requires that the expected benefits from recognition exceed the costs of recognition. Reporting the individual wages and salaries for 2,500 employees worldwide in a company may be more useful

[10]FASB, *Statement of Financial Accounting Concepts No. 5*, "Recognition and Measurement in Financial Statements of Business Enterprises" (Stamford, CT: FASB, 1984), Paragraph 6.

in certain analyses than simply reporting total wage and salary expense on the income statement. However, the cost of providing that information will probably exceed its benefit.

The **materiality threshold** requires that an item be recognized in the financial statements if its omission or misstatement would significantly influence the judgment of a reasonably informed statement user. Materiality can apply to a numerical value or a nonquantifiable concern. For example, a company facing an antitrust violation has no amounts to report because the litigation is still in process. However, the firm must disclose the litigation to ensure its financial statements are transparent.

Revenue and Expense Recognition

The financial markets' emphasis on reported earnings makes revenue and expense recognition principles important. Recall from our earlier discussion that ***Johnson & Johnson*** beat analysts' forecasts in the fourth quarter of 2016. The ability to report earnings in line with or higher than forecasts can be critical to a company's stock price. The intent of the revenue and expense recognition principles is to recognize revenue and expenses in the appropriate time period.

The **revenue recognition principle** in the conceptual framework states that a company should recognize revenue when it is *realized* or *realizable* and *earned*:

1. An item is **realized** or **realizable** when a company exchanges a good or service for cash or claims to cash.
2. Revenues are considered **earned** when the seller has accomplished what it must do to be entitled to the revenues.[11,12]

A new revenue standard, which public companies can start adopting in 2017, is not completely aligned with the conceptual framework. That is, the new revenue standard indicates that the overarching principle of revenue recognition is the notion of the transfer of control of the goods or services. Five steps are applied to determine the timing and measurement of revenue:

1. Identify the contract with the customer.
2. Identify the separate performance obligations in the contract.
3. Determine the transaction price.
4. Allocate the transaction price to separate performance obligations.
5. Recognize revenue when each performance obligation is satisfied.

We expect that FASB will align the conceptual framework with the new standard when it rewrites the framework.

Expense recognition principles are used to determine the period when a company reports an expense on the income statement. Firms recognize expenses when:

1. The entity's economic benefits are consumed in the process of producing or delivering goods or rendering services.
2. An asset has experienced a reduced (or eliminated) future benefit, or when a liability has been incurred or increased, without an associated economic benefit.

Therefore, a company reports an expense when economic benefits are consumed. There are three main approaches to determine when to report an expense:

- Match with revenues
- Expense in period incurred
- Systematically allocate over periods of use

[11]See FASB's *Statement of Financial Accounting Concepts No. 5*, "Recognition and Measurement in Financial Statements of Business Enterprises," Paragraph 83 for a complete definition.

[12]Whereas FASB's *Statement of Financial Accounting Concepts No. 5* outlines requirements to recognize revenue, FASB's *Accounting Standards Update 2014-09*, "Revenue from Contracts with Customers" (Norwalk, CT: Financial Accounting Foundation, 2014) updates the guidance on when to recognize revenue.

The approach used depends on the type of expense. For example, some expenses—such as cost of goods sold—consume inventory when used and are matched with their related revenues. Specifically, firms match the cost of goods sold expense directly with the sales of inventory during the same period. Firms can also record expenses in the period in which they are incurred. For example, the salary of a staff accountant is recorded in the period worked. Finally, firms systematically allocate some expenses over the periods during which the related asset provides benefits. For example, a firm depreciates (i.e., expenses) a building over the periods that it will provide a benefit to the entity.

Commonly, firms reduce an asset or increase a liability when expected future cash flows change. For example, in the period that a company determines it can no longer sell certain inventory, it will record a loss on the income statement and write the inventory down on the balance sheet. Exhibit 2.9 summarizes these examples.

EXHIBIT 2.9 Examples of Expense Recognition

Income Statement Line Item	Related Balance Sheet Line Item	When to Recognize the Expense on the Income Statement	Approach to Recognize Expense
Cost of goods sold	Inventory	Upon sale of inventory	Match with revenue
Loss on inventory obsolescence	Inventory	When inventory value declines or becomes obsolete	Loss in period incurred
Supplies expense	Supplies	Upon use in operations and consumption of supplies	Expense in period incurred
Depreciation expense	Accumulated depreciation	Over time with use in production and consumption of future economic benefit	Systematically allocate over periods of use
Salary and wages expense	Salaries and wages payable	Recognize in the period services are performed	Expense in period incurred

Bases of Measurement

After a company determines that it should recognize an item, it has to measure the item.[13] For example, when a company purchases inventory from a supplier, it also incurs freight costs to have the inventory shipped to its stores. The company recognizes inventory as an asset. It measures the value of the inventory asset as the purchase price plus the freight costs and reports that amount on the balance sheet.

The initial measurement of elements in the financial statements and their subsequent measurement are both pertinent to financial reporting. U.S. GAAP identifies five measurement bases used in financial reporting.[14]

1. **Historical cost** is the amount of cash (or equivalent) that the firm paid to acquire the asset. In the case of a liability, historical cost is the amount of cash (or equivalent) that the firm received when it incurred the obligation. The historical cost of an asset may be adjusted for depreciation or amortization.
2. **Current cost** is the amount of cash (or equivalent) that would be required if the firm acquired the asset currently.
3. **Current market value** is the amount of cash (or equivalent) that the firm would receive by selling the asset in an orderly liquidation. Liabilities may also be measured at current market value.

[13]The information included in this section is currently under review. The FASB is developing a revised concepts statement on measurement. An exposure draft has not yet been issued.

[14]FASB, *Statement of Financial Accounting Concepts No. 5*, "Recognition and Measurement in Financial Statements of Business Enterprises," Paragraph 67.

4. **Net realizable value** is the amount of cash (or equivalent) to be received in exchange for an asset, less the direct costs of disposal. In the case of a liability, it is the amount of cash (or equivalent) expected to be paid to liquidate the obligation, including any direct costs of liquidation.
5. **Present value of future cash flows** results from discounting net cash flows the firm expects to receive on the exchange of an asset or to pay to liquidate a liability.[15]

The historical cost approach results in the general policy that firms initially record assets (and liabilities) at cost and maintain them at cost until selling, consuming, or otherwise disposing of them. Historical cost is the agreed-upon acquisition price arrived at objectively through an *arms-length transaction.* An **arms-length transaction** involves a buyer and seller who are independent and unrelated parties, each bargaining to maximize his or her own wealth. Although historical costs are unrelated to current market values, firms continue to use historical cost information for most assets and in most industries. The use of historical cost is justified because it is objective and subject to verification.

The current cost, current market value, net realizable value, and present value of future cash flows measurement bases are all consistent with fair value reporting.[16] There are times when fair value is observable, such as for a publicly traded equity security. When fair value is not directly observable—for example, an equity security that is not publicly traded—management uses judgment-based models to determine its fair value.

Fair Value Measurement and the Fair Value Hierarchy. The trend toward measuring financial assets and liabilities at fair value discussed in Chapter 1 impacts the amounts reported on the balance sheet. In order to improve user confidence in fair value measurements reported, the FASB requires disclosures that indicate the reliability of the inputs used in all fair value measures reported on the financial statements. This disclosure takes the form of a fair value hierarchy that provides three levels of reliability from the most to the least objective inputs used in the fair value measurement process.

Exhibit 2.10 presents the three levels of the fair value hierarchy.

EXHIBIT 2.10 Fair Value Hierarchy

Level	Inputs Used in the Measurement Process
Level 1	Quoted prices in active markets for an identical asset or liability. A publicly traded equity security is classified in this level.
Level 2	Inputs other than the quoted prices included in Level 1 that are observable for the asset or liability. For example, a building could be valued using a price per square foot obtained from transactions in a comparable building in a similar location.
Level 3	Unobservable inputs to value the asset or liability. For example, to measure the fair value of a private equity investment, a company might perform an analysis that relies on the present value of the expected future cash flows of that investment.

Source: FASB, *Statement of Financial Accounting Standards No. 157*, "Fair Value Measurement" (Norwalk, CT: FASB, 2006), Paragraphs 22–31

Ideally, companies would measure all financial assets and liabilities using Level 1 inputs, but that is not possible. Nonetheless, companies should use the highest level of reliability possible when determining fair values of financial assets or liabilities.

[15]Under U.S. GAAP, the present value measurement attribute is discussed in much greater length in the FASB's *Statement of Financial Accounting Concepts No. 7*, "Using Cash Flow Information and Present Value in Accounting Measurements" (Norwalk, CT: FASB, 2000).

[16]FASB, *Statement of Financial Accounting Concepts No. 7*, "Using Cash Flow Information and Present Value in Accounting Measurements," Paragraph 7.

The standard setters' decision as to whether a particular asset or liability should be measured at fair value often trades off the relevance of information provided with the ability of the information to be a faithful representation of the value of the asset or liability. For example, fair value is more relevant than historical cost, but it is typically a less faithful representation in terms of measuring the economic event than is historical cost.

However, U.S. companies generally do not report their nonfinancial assets such as equipment or land at market or appraisal values or adjust them for inflation. An exception is when an asset is impaired. For declines in fair value, firms are required to write down, or reduce, asset values.[17] In most industries, nonfinancial assets are not valued above initial cost.

Recognition and Measurement: IFRS

In this section, we discuss major differences in recognition and measurement between U.S. GAAP and IFRS.

General Recognition Principles. IFRS also has four recognition criteria. Notice that the first three recognition criteria are similar to U.S. GAAP:

1. The item meets the definition of one of the elements.
2. The item is measurable.
3. The measurement of the item must be reliable.
4. It is probable that future economic benefits will flow to or from the company.

To illustrate the fourth criterion, assume management determines it is probable that the company will collect an estimated amount of receivables, resulting in an economic benefit to the company. Management should not include any receivables unlikely to be collected as assets by establishing an allowance for uncollectible accounts. This fourth criterion is used instead of relevance under U.S. GAAP.

The IFRS cost-benefit constraint and materiality constraint are similar to U.S. GAAP. We summarize the U.S. GAAP and IFRS recognition criteria in Exhibit 2.11.

EXHIBIT 2.11 General Recognition Principles

U.S. GAAP	IFRS
An item is recognized in the financial statements if it is:	
An element of the financial statements	Similar under U.S. GAAP and IFRS
Measurable	Similar under U.S. GAAP and IFRS
Reliable	Similar under U.S. GAAP and IFRS
Relevant	Not included in IFRS
Not included in U.S. GAAP	Probable that any future economic benefit associated with the item will flow to or from the company
Recognition is subject to the:	
Cost-benefit constraint	Similar under U.S. GAAP and IFRS
Materiality constraint	Similar under U.S. GAAP and IFRS

Source: FASB, *Statement of Financial Accounting Concepts No. 5*, "Recognition and Measurement in Financial Statements of Business Enterprises" and IASB, *Conceptual Framework for Financial Reporting*

[17]We discuss accounting for long-lived asset write-downs, impairments, in Chapter 12.

Revenue and Expense Recognition. Under the current IFRS conceptual framework, firms recognize revenue when they meet both of the following criteria:

1. An increase in future economic benefits related to an increase in an asset or a decrease of a liability has occurred.
2. The revenue can be measured reliably.[18]

Similar to U.S. GAAP, the IASB's recently adopted new revenue standard is not completely aligned with the IFRS conceptual framework.[19] The IASB adopted the same new revenue standard as the FASB, applying the notion of the transfer of control of the goods or services for revenue recognition. We expect that IASB will align the conceptual framework with the new standard when it rewrites the framework.

Firms recognize expenses in the income statement when both of the following criteria are met:

1. A decrease in future economic benefits related to a decrease in an asset or an increase of a liability has occurred.
2. The expense can be measured reliably.[20]

Firms recognize expenses simultaneously with an increase in liabilities or a decrease in assets. For example, salaries payable is increased when a company recognizes salary expense. Unlike U.S. GAAP, IFRS does not use the matching approach for expense recognition.

Bases of Measurement. IFRS includes four of the five measurement bases used under U.S. GAAP. The four IFRS measurement bases are:

1. Historical cost
2. Current cost
3. Net realizable value
4. Present value of future cash flows

IFRS does not include current market value as a separate measurement basis. Rather, the view under IFRS is that current cost, net realizable value, and the present value of future cash flows are all current market value measures.

Cash versus Accrual Accounting

U.S. GAAP is based on *accrual accounting*. It follows that U.S. GAAP does not allow a *cash-basis system*.[21] To highlight the advantages of accrual accounting, we will begin by reviewing the cash-basis system.

Cash-Basis Accounting. Under the **cash basis,** firms recognize revenues only when they receive cash and recognize expenses only when they pay cash. Consequently, the cash basis measures cash receipts and disbursements but does not measure economic activity. Further, the cash basis enables firms to manipulate net income with the timing of cash flows. For example, a company using the cash basis could report higher net income by delaying payment of expenses until the next accounting period. Alternatively, to reduce reported earnings, a company could delay billing its customers until the next accounting period to ensure that it would not receive cash revenues in the current period.

---

[18] IASB, *Conceptual Framework for Financial Reporting*, Paragraph 4.47.

[19] IASB, *International Financial Reporting Standard 15*, "Revenue from Contracts with Customers" (London, UK: International Accounting Standards Board, 2014).

[20] IASB, *Conceptual Framework for Financial Reporting*, Paragraph 4.49.

[21] In U.S. GAAP, the mandate for accrual accounting is in the FASB's *Statement of Financial Accounting Concepts No. 6*, "Elements of Financial Statements" (Norwalk, CT: FASB, 1985), Paragraph 134. IFRS discusses accrual accounting in IASB, *Conceptual Framework for Financial Reporting*, Paragraphs OB17-19.

Accrual Accounting. Under the **accrual basis,** firms recognize revenues and expenses according to the principles we have discussed. When the firm receives or pays cash does not matter. Rather, the accrual basis seeks to report the underlying economics of each transaction on the company. In summary, the accrual basis of accounting recognizes revenues when control of a good or service passes to the customer and expenses when incurred. As a result, the major difference between cash and accrual accounting is the timing of revenue and expense recognition.

EXAMPLE 2.1

The Cash versus the Accrual Basis of Accounting

PROBLEM: Yards, Inc. mows lawns at a fee of $100 per month. In the current year, 200 customers prepaid for the four months in the summer, beginning on May 1. Yards received $80,000 of cash receipts ($100 per month × 200 customers × 4 months) in May. Yards, Inc. provided the required service for four months by mowing lawns throughout May, June, July, and August. During those months, the company incurred expenses of $10,000, $13,000, $12,000, and $10,000, respectively, and paid these expenses during the same month it consumed the economic benefit. Determine Yards Inc.'s net income for each month from May through August under both the cash and the accrual bases of accounting.

SOLUTION: Because Yards Inc. paid for the expenses in the same month it consumed the benefits, there is no difference in expense recognition between the cash basis and accrual basis. However, there is a difference in revenue recognition.

Under cash-basis accounting, Yards would recognize revenue of $80,000 in May because that is when it received cash. However, under the accrual basis, it would recognize revenue of $20,000 ($100 per yard × 200 yards) in each of the four months.

Thus, under both systems Yards will ultimately recognize $80,000 revenue, $45,000 in expenses, and $35,000 in net income. However, the timing of the revenue recognition differs, as illustrated in the following table.

	Revenue Recognition		Expense Recognition		Net Income (Loss)	
Month	**Cash Basis**	**Accrual Basis**	**Cash Basis**	**Accrual Basis**	**Cash Basis**	**Accrual Basis**
May	$80,000	$20,000	$10,000	$10,000	$70,000	$10,000
June	-0-	20,000	13,000	13,000	(13,000)	7,000
July	-0-	20,000	12,000	12,000	(12,000)	8,000
August	-0-	20,000	10,000	10,000	(10,000)	10,000
Totals	$80,000	$80,000	$45,000	$45,000	$35,000	$35,000

Note that the cash basis reports only cash receipts and disbursements but does not properly measure economic activity. Yards' cash-basis net income is overstated in May and understated in June, July, and August.

6 Explain the assumptions used in financial reporting.

Assumptions in Financial Reporting

We will now examine a number of underlying assumptions that are integral to the financial reporting process. The assumptions we discuss are:

- Going concern concept
- Business or economic entity concept
- Monetary unit assumption
- Periodicity assumption

U.S. GAAP does not directly state these four items as assumptions in the conceptual framework.[22] Yet, they are implicit in determining financial reporting standards.

Going Concern Concept

Many assumptions in the financial statements are based on long-term periods. How can a manager assert with certainty that a business will be viable in, say, 25 years? The **going concern concept** indicates that accountants will record transactions and prepare financial statements as if the entity will continue to operate for an indefinite period of time unless there is evidence to the contrary. That is, the entity will exist for a period of time long enough to carry out contemplated operations, utilize existing productive capacity, and liquidate outstanding obligations. This concept justifies accounting practices such as the long-term/short-term classifications on the balance sheet and the depreciation of buildings for as long as 40 years.

The going concern concept is also tied to the use of historical cost. A business planning to operate for an indefinite period of time will not sell productive assets. Consequently, market values are less relevant. If a business is in jeopardy of failing (e.g., bankruptcy), then the going concern assumption would not be valid. If the assumption is not applicable, accountants would measure assets and liabilities at the amount at which they expect to dispose of them, their liquidation values.

Business or Economic Entity Concept

The **business** or **economic entity concept** states that all transactions and events relate to the reporting entity and must be kept separate from the personal affairs of the owner, related businesses, and the owner's outside business interests. For example, Kyle Perry owns and operates several sporting goods shops called Perry's Sports. Perry's Sports is an economic entity separate from Kyle Perry. Perry's Sports owns its store buildings and reports them in the company's financial statements. Kyle Perry owns his house. The house is an asset of Kyle Perry and is not reported in the financial statements of Perry's Sports. Financial reporting for different entities must be separate and include disclosures describing transactions among related entities.

Monetary Unit Assumption

The **monetary unit assumption** stipulates that an entity measure and report its economic activities in dollars (or some other monetary unit). These dollars are assumed to remain relatively stable over time in terms of purchasing power. This assumption ignores any inflation or deflation experienced in the economy in which the entity operates. This assumption justifies adding dollars of different purchasing power on the balance sheet. For example, a company would add land purchased in the current period to the balance of land acquired in 1969.

Periodicity Assumption

The **periodicity assumption** specifies that an economic entity can divide its life into artificial time periods for the purpose of providing periodic reports on its economic activities. The periodicity assumption results in the need for accrual accounting because revenue and expenses must be reported in a given period under this assumption. In addition, the time periods used will vary depending on the demands of financial statement users. For example, the SEC currently requires quarterly financial statements for publicly traded firms. These statements use significant estimates and may be less representationally faithful than the annual report. However, quarterly statements are more timely (an enhancing characteristic) than reporting on an annual basis because timely information is more useful (relevant) in decision making.

Assumptions in Financial Reporting: IFRS

IFRS explicitly addresses the going concern assumption. The other assumptions are implicit in the standard-setting process.

[22]Another assumption, the *full disclosure principle*, states that accountants must report and disclose all information that can significantly affect the judgment of a reasonably informed financial statement user. The revisions to the conceptual framework added that financial information must be complete to be a faithful representation. Completeness, then, makes explicit the prior assumption of full disclosure.

Summary by Learning Objectives

In the following, we summarize the main points by learning objective. Throughout the chapter, we discuss the accounting and reporting of U.S. GAAP and IFRS side-by-side. The following table also highlights the major similarities and differences between the standards.

1 Explain what a conceptual framework is and why it is important in accounting standard setting.

Summary	Similarities and Differences between U.S. GAAP and IFRS
A conceptual framework sets forth the theory, concepts, and principles that underlie financial reporting. The FASB is working on a conceptual framework project divided into topics with the first one completed to date: 1. Objective and Qualitative Characteristics 2. Elements and Recognition 3. Measurement 4. Reporting Entity 5. Presentation 6. Disclosure.	Similar under U.S. GAAP and IFRS

2 Define the objective of financial reporting.

Summary	Similarities and Differences between U.S. GAAP and IFRS
The objective of financial reporting is to provide financial information that is useful to investors, lenders, and other creditors in making decisions about providing resources to an entity.	Similar under U.S. GAAP and IFRS

3 Describe the qualitative characteristics of financial information, including the fundamental and enhancing characteristics of financial reporting.

Summary	Similarities and Differences between U.S. GAAP and IFRS
Fundamental characteristics are relevance and faithful representation that distinguish useful financial reporting information from nonuseful information. Relevant information is capable of making a difference in decision making because • Of its predictive value: It can be used as an input into processes that help predict future outcomes. • Of its confirmatory value: It provides feedback about prior evaluations. • It is material: Reporting it inaccurately or omitting it would affect the decisions made by the financial statement users. Financial information is a faithful representation if it depicts the substance of an economic event • Completely, • Neutrally, and • Free from error. Enhancing characteristics distinguish more useful information from less useful information. There are four enhancing characteristics: • Comparability, • Verifiability, • Timeliness, and • Understandability.	Similar under U.S. GAAP and IFRS

Summary by Learning Objectives, continued

4 Identify the elements of financial reporting.

Summary	Similarities and Differences between U.S. GAAP and IFRS
There are two main groupings of elements: point-in-time and period-of-time. *U.S. GAAP Point-in-Time Elements:* Assets: Probable future economic benefits obtained or controlled by a particular entity as a result of past transactions or events Liabilities: Probable future sacrifices of economic benefits arising from present obligations of a particular entity to transfer assets or provide services to other entities in the future as a result of past transactions or events Equity: Or net assets, the residual interest in the assets of an entity that remains after deducting its liabilities *U.S. GAAP Period-of-Time Elements:* Investments by owners: Increases in an entity's equity resulting from transfers to it from other entities of something valuable to obtain or increase ownership interests (or equity) in the entity. Distributions to owners: Decreases in an entity's equity resulting from transferring assets, rendering services, or incurring liabilities to owners. Distributions to owners decrease ownership interest (or equity) in an enterprise. Revenues: Inflows or other enhancements of assets or settlements of liabilities (or a combination of both) from delivering or producing goods, rendering services, or other activities of the entity's ongoing major or central operations. Gains: Increases in an entity's equity from peripheral or incidental transactions and from all other transactions and other events and circumstances except those that result from revenues or investments by owners. Expenses: Outflows or other using up of assets or incurrences of liabilities (or a combination of both) from delivering or producing goods, rendering services, or carrying out other activities of the entity's ongoing major or central operations. Losses: Decreases in equity (net assets) from peripheral or incidental transactions of an entity and from all other transactions and other events and circumstances except those that result from expenses or distributions to owners. Comprehensive income: The change in equity of a business enterprise during a period from transactions and other events and circumstances from nonowner sources.	➤The point-in-time elements of financial reporting are defined slightly differently under U.S. GAAP and IFRS. In practice, though, IFRS and U.S. GAAP often lead to the same decisions on what is reported as an asset, liability, or equity for the items we discuss in the text. ➤The period-of-time elements are different under U.S. GAAP and IFRS. The only element in common is expenses, but it is defined differently under U.S. GAAP and IFRS. *IFRS Period-of-Time Elements:* 1. Performance: A separate element in IFRS. Under U.S. GAAP, profit is the result of adding revenues and gains and subtracting expenses and losses. 2. Income (both revenues and gains). 3. Expenses (both expenses and losses). 4. Capital maintenance adjustments: Restatements or revaluations of reported amounts of assets and liabilities.

Summary by Learning Objectives, continued

5 Demonstrate an understanding of recognition and measurement in financial reporting including general recognition principles, revenue and expense recognition, and accrual accounting.

Summary	Similarities and Differences between U.S. GAAP and IFRS
Recognition is the process of including an item as a line item in the financial statements of the entity. Under general recognition principles, an item is recognized in the financial statements if it is an element of the financial statements, measurable, reliable, and relevant. Recognition is subject to the cost-benefit constraint and materiality threshold constraint. In the FASB's conceptual framework, the revenue recognition principle states that revenue is recognized when it is 1. Realized or realizable. An item is considered realized or realizable when a good or service has been exchanged for cash or claims to cash. 2. Earned. Revenues are considered earned "when the entity has substantially accomplished what it must do to be entitled to the benefits represented by the revenues." New revenue recognition standards apply different guidance to recognize revenue—the notion of the transfer of control of goods or services to recognize revenue. Expense recognition involves the timing of when an expense is reported on the income statement. Expenses are recognized when 1. The entity's benefits are consumed in the process of producing or delivering goods or rendering services. 2. An asset has experienced a reduced (or eliminated) future benefit or when a liability has been incurred or increased without an associated economic benefit. There are three main approaches to determine when to report an expense: • Match with revenues • Expense in period incurred • Systematically allocate over periods of use	➤ IFRS differs from U.S. GAAP in how it defines when items are recognized and in revenue and expense recognition criteria. Under IFRS general recognition principles, an item is recognized in the financial statements if it is an element of the financial statements, measurable, reliable, and probable that any future economic benefit associated with the item will flow to or from the company. The IASB conceptual framework states that revenue is recognized when the following two criteria are met: 1. An increase in future economic benefits related to an increase in an asset or a decrease of a liability has arisen. 2. It can be measured reliably. Similar to U.S. GAAP, IFRS now uses the notion of a transfer of control of goods or services to recognize revenue. Expenses are recognized when: 1. A decrease in future economic benefits related to a decrease in an asset or an increase of a liability has arisen. 2. They can be measured reliably. IFRS does not recognize the matching approach.

6 Explain the assumptions used in financial reporting.

Summary	Similarities and Differences between U.S. GAAP and IFRS
Assumptions in financial reporting: • Going concern concept • Business or economic entity assumption • Monetary unit assumption • Periodicity assumption	➤ IFRS explicitly addresses the going concern assumption. The other assumptions are implicit in the standard-setting process.

MyLab Accounting

Go to **http://www.pearson.com/mylab/accounting** for the following Questions, Brief Exercises, Exercises. They are available with immediate grading, explanations of correct and incorrect answers, and interactive media that acts as your own online tutor.

2 Financial Reporting Theory

Questions

1 **Q2-1.** What is the conceptual framework for financial reporting?

1 **Q2-2.** Are the FASB and IASB conceptual frameworks fully converged? Explain.

1 **Q2-3.** Why is a conceptual framework of accounting necessary and justifiable?

2 **Q2-4.** Who are the primary financial statement user groups identified in the objective of financial reporting?

3 **Q2-5.** Explain the concept of relevance.

3 **Q2-6.** What are the attributes of relevance?

3 **Q2-7.** Explain the concept of materiality.

3 **Q2-8.** What is predictive value?

3 **Q2-9.** What is the difference between predictive value and confirmatory value?

3 **Q2-10.** When is financial information considered "understandable"?

4 **Q2-11.** What is the difference between a point-in-time element and a period-of-time element?

4 **Q2-12.** What are the elements of financial reporting and where are they reported?

4 **Q2-13.** What is the definition of an asset?

5 **Q2-14.** What is the recognition principle and when is an item considered recognized?

5 **Q2-15.** What is the revenue recognition principle and when is revenue considered recognized?

5 **Q2-16.** When are expenses recognized under U.S. GAAP?

5 Q2-17. When are expenses recognized under IFRS?

5 **Q2-18.** How are transactions recorded under accrual accounting?

5 **Q2-19.** Explain the historical cost concept.

6 **Q2-20.** Explain the going concern concept.

Brief Exercises

1 **BE2-1. Components of the Conceptual Framework.** List the components of the current conceptual framework.

2 **BE2-2. Users of Financial Information.** Describe the primary users of the financial statements according to the conceptual framework.

2 **BE2-3. Objective of Financial Reporting.** Explain the objective of financial reporting.

3 **BE2-4. Relevant and Faithful Representation.** Identify whether the following items are characteristics of information that are relevant (REL) or a faithful representation (FR):

______ Information that is neutral
______ Information that has decision-making implications because of its predictive value
______ Information that is complete
______ Information that is free from error
______ Information that has decision-making implications because of its confirmatory value

3 **BE2-5. Fundamental and Enhancing Characteristics.** Describe the fundamental characteristics of financial information. Explain the enhancing characteristics of financial reporting information.

3 **BE2-6. Faithful Representation.** Describe when financial information is a faithful representation.

3 **BE2-7. Costs and Benefits of Financial Reporting.** Explain the costs standard setters consider when comparing the cost of requiring information to the benefits to the users of having the information when setting a new standard.

3 5 **BE2-8. Historical Cost.** Discuss how well the historical cost concept satisfies the fundamental characteristics of relevance and faithful representation.

3 **BE2-9. Fundamental and Enhancing Characteristics.** Identify whether the following items are fundamental characteristics (FC) or enhancing characteristics (EC):

______ Comparable
______ Relevant
______ Timely
______ Understandable
______ Faithful representation
______ Verifiable

3 **BE2-10. Faithful Representation.** Match the component of a faithful representation to its definition:

Component of a Faithful Representation	Definition
1. Complete	A. Information is free from bias in both selection and presentation of financial data.
2. Neutral	B. Information should not contain errors or omissions in the description of the economic event and there are no errors in the process used to produce the financial information.
3. Free from error	C. Includes all information that is necessary for the user to understand the underlying economic event being depicted.

3 **BE2-11. Enhancing Characteristics.** Match the enhancing characteristic with its definition:

Enhancing Characteristic	Definition
______ 1. Comparability	A. Different knowledgeable parties could reach a consensus that a particular depiction is a faithful representation.
______ 2. Verifiability	B. Information is classified, characterized, and presented clearly.
______ 3. Timely	C. Users of the financial statements can identify and understand similarities and differences between different entities.
______ 4. Understandable	D. Information is available to financial statements users soon enough to be useful.

4 **BE2-12. Revenues and Gains.** Explain the difference between revenues and gains.

4 **BE2-13. Capital Maintenance Adjustments, IFRS.** Describe capital maintenance adjustments.

5 **BE2-14. Expense Recognition.** Discuss the three main approaches to recognizing expenses.

4 **BE2-15. Element Definitions.** Identify whether the following definitions relate to assets, liabilities, or equity.

Element	Definition
____________________	Probable future sacrifices of economic benefits arising from present obligations of a particular entity to transfer assets or provide services to other entities in the future as a result of past transactions or events.
____________________	The net assets are the residual interest in the assets of an entity that remains after deducting its liabilities.
____________________	Probable future economic benefits will be obtained or controlled by a particular entity as a result of past transactions or events.

4 **BE2-16. Element Definitions.** Match each element with its definition.

Element

______ 1. Gains

______ 2. Comprehensive income

______ 3. Losses

______ 4. Expenses

______ 5. Revenues

______ 6. Distributions to owners

______ 7. Investments by owners

Definition

A. Outflows or other consumption of assets or incurrences of liabilities (or a combination of both) from delivering or producing goods, rendering services, or carrying out other activities that constitute the entity's ongoing major or central operations.

B. Inflows or other enhancements of an entity's assets or settlements of its liabilities (or a combination of both) from delivering or producing goods, rendering services, or other activities that constitute the entity's ongoing major or central operations.

C. The change in equity of a business enterprise during a period from transactions and other events and circumstances from nonowner sources. It includes all changes in equity during a period except those resulting from investments by owners and distributions to owners.

D. Decreases in equity of a particular business enterprise resulting from transferring assets, rendering services, or incurring liabilities by the enterprise to owners. Distributions to owners decrease ownership interest (or equity) in an enterprise.

E. Increases in equity (net assets) from an entity's peripheral or incidental transactions and from all other transactions and other events and circumstances affecting the entity except those that result from revenues or investments by owners.

F. Decreases in equity (net assets) from an entity's peripheral or incidental transactions and from all other transactions and other events and circumstances affecting the entity except those that result from expenses or distributions to owners.

G. Increases in equity of a particular business enterprise resulting from transfers to it from other entities of something valuable to obtain or increase ownership interests (or equity) in it.

4 **BE2-17. Element Definitions, U.S. GAAP, IFRS.** Identify whether the following elements are elements under U.S. GAAP, IFRS, or both, and point-in-time or period-in-time elements.

Element	U.S. GAAP, IFRS, or Both	Point in Time or Period of Time
Investments by owners	______	______
Income	______	______
Losses	______	______
Liabilities	______	______
Equity	______	______
Comprehensive income	______	______
Assets	______	______
Gains	______	______
Capital maintenance adjustment	______	______
Expenses	______	______
Distributions to owners	______	______
Revenues	______	______
Performance	______	______

5 **BE2-18. Recognition, U.S. GAAP, IFRS.** Identify whether the following items are part of the general recognition principle under U.S. GAAP, IFRS, or both.

Item	U.S. GAAP, IFRS, or Both
Relevant	______
Subject to materiality constraint	______
An element of the financial statements	______
Probable that any future economic benefit associated with the item will flow to or from the company	______
Measurable	______
Reliable	______
Subject to cost-benefit constraint	______

5 **BE2-19. Measurement Bases.** Match the measurement basis with its definition.

Measurement Bases

______ 1. Historical cost
______ 2. Current cost
______ 3. Net realizable value
______ 4. Present value of future cash flows
______ 5. Current market value

Definition

A. Amount of cash (or equivalent) that would be required if the asset were acquired currently.

B. Amount of cash (or equivalent) that would be received by selling the asset in an orderly liquidation. Liabilities may also be measured at current market value.

C. Amount of cash (or equivalent) that is paid to acquire the asset. In the case of a liability, this measurement base is the amount of cash (or equivalent) that is received when the obligation was incurred. This measurement base may change over the life of the asset/liability if it is adjusted for depreciation or amortization.

D. Amount of cash (or equivalent) that is expected to be received in exchange for an asset less the direct costs of the disposal. In the case of a liability, it is the amount of cash (or equivalent) expected to be paid to liquidate the obligation, including any direct costs of liquidation.

E. Discounted net cash flows expected to be received on exchange of an asset, or paid out in the case of a liability.

5 **BE2-20. Cash versus Accrual Bases of Accounting.** The following events occurred at VG Consulting during the most recent month.

a. VG provided consulting services and billed clients $2,000.
b. VG collected $1,500 for consulting services performed in the prior month.
c. VG paid its monthly electric bill of $300.
d. Employees who worked for VG were not paid for services performed. Next month they will be paid $850.
e. VG collected fees of $700 for services to be performed in the following month.

For each event, determine the revenue or expense under the cash and accrual bases of accounting.

6 **BE2-21. Assumptions in Financial Reporting.** Indicate the assumption (going concern, business/economic entity, monetary unit, or periodicity) that best fits the following scenarios.

Scenario	Related Assumption
a. Monro Manufacturing requires that its division managers report to corporate headquarters on a monthly basis.	______
b. Rainbow Paints, Inc. owns 15% of New Eljam Company. Rainbow does not consolidate this affiliate company because it cannot control New Eljam's operations.	______
c. Financial analysts at Nelson Corporation use an infinite-growth assumption in building a model to value the company.	______
d. Factory buildings are reported on Jack Jones Warehousing Inc.'s balance sheet as the sum of the total cost of two plants; one of the plants was acquired in 1951 and the other was purchased in 2011.	______

Exercises

③ ⑤ ⑥ **E2-1. Conceptual Framework.** Noeleen Auto Mall, Ltd. recently completed an initial public offering (IPO) for $23,000,000 by listing its common shares on the New York Stock Exchange. Prior to its IPO, Noeleen was a privately held family business. As a public company, Noeleen faces increased reporting requirements, particularly those sanctioned by the Securities and Exchange Commission (SEC). Noeleen's Controller, Donald Lierni, was surprised to learn that a Form 10-Q was required to satisfy the company's first-quarter filing requirements with the SEC. Lierni lacked sufficient time to develop the "actual" numbers needed to prepare the report, meaning that he needed to make significant estimates before the 10-Q filing due date.

In addition, Noeleen now must satisfy a new group of financial statement users with additional information needs. Noeleen expended resources to meet the new reporting requirements and assess what information and disclosures to include/exclude from the financial reports. Lierni also learned that privately held companies are not subject to U.S. GAAP requirements like a publicly traded entity. That is, the company now must follow additional U.S. GAAP standards and is required to change several of its accounting methods. When considering his options, Lierni decides to take a "safe" approach and report the lowest income possible by adopting income-reducing standards. Here, the Controller proposes taking excessive write-downs for obsolete inventory and potentially impaired assets. He also decides to expense the cost of a significant investment in office equipment.

Finally, Noeleen created a separate legal entity to handle its auto financing, Benedict Arnold Credit Company, during the same year it went public. The separate entity is not consolidated with the primary financial statements. Lierni decides to keep this entity off of the balance sheet and does not see any need for disclosure of Noeleen's relationship with Benedict Arnold Credit.

Required »

Based on the information provided, list and explain the application of the relevant components of the conceptual framework of accounting. Identify seven issues and use the following table to present your solution.

Issue	Conceptual Framework
1. ______	1. ______
2. ______	2. ______
3. ______	3. ______
4. ______	4. ______
5. ______	5. ______
6. ______	6. ______
7. ______	7. ______

③ **E2-2. Qualitative Characteristics.** Referring to the qualitative characteristics of accounting information, indicate the fundamental characteristic (relevance or representationally faithful) and its related attribute (confirmatory value, completeness, materiality, neutrality, or predictive value) for each of the following uses of accounting information.

Use of Accounting Information	Fundamental Characteristic	Attribute
a. This year's reported earnings per share is $.50 below analysts' forecasts.	______	______
b. Potential creditors review a company's long-term liabilities footnote to determine that entity's ability to assume additional debt.	______	______
c. A corporation discloses both favorable and unfavorable tax settlements.	______	______
d. A company discloses the write-off of an accounts receivable. The receivable due from a major customer accounts for 35% of the company's current assets.	______	______
e. A financial analyst computes a company's five-year average cost of goods sold in order to forecast next year's gross profit margin.	______	______

3 **E2-3. Enhancing Characteristics.** Using the following table, match the enhancing characteristics (comparability, verifiability, timeliness, or understandability) with the following four scenarios. Also indicate if the enhancing characteristic is either satisfied or violated.

Scenario	Enhancing Characteristic	Satisfied or Violated
a. Auditors from two offices of a large public accounting firm agree on the measurement used for a client's plant assets.	__________	__________
b. The Later Than Sooner Company reports income only every two years.	__________	__________
c. Gladys Groceries reports its investments at cost while the other companies in the grocery industry use the fair value option to measure investments.	__________	__________
d. Grant Company engages in complex business transactions. These events are properly classified, characterized, presented clearly, and fully disclosed.	__________	__________

3 5 6 **E2-4. Concepts:** Determine the concept that is violated in each of the following cases:

a. Management examined registration and legal fees for a trademark, and determined that it should record a trademark for $5,000.
b. Katia Clothing, a U.S. GAAP reporter, purchased land five years ago and recently had it appraised for $65,000. The company reported this amount on its most recent balance sheet.
c. Edward McCormick owns two separate business: EMC Enterprises and Edward Associates. McCormick regularly pays the property taxes for EMC from the checking account of Edward Associates.
d. US Motors Inc. recently decided to recall 400,000 vehicles for a safety concern. US Motors did not report this information in its annual report.
e. Abare Company purchased new equipment for $2,500,000 and charged it to operating expenses on its most recent income statement.
f. Beeke Brothers Incorporated decided not to report its quarterly results to its shareholders.

1 3 4 5 6 **E2-5. Terms and Concepts.** Complete the following statements by identifying the appropriate term or concept.

a. A ________ sets forth theory, concepts, and principles to ensure that accounting standards are coherent and uniform.
b. Information has ______ if decision makers can use it as an input into processes that help forecast future outcomes.
c. ________ indicates whether financial information depicts the substance of an economic event in a manner that is complete, neutral, and free from error.
d. ________ allows financial statement users to identify and understand similarities and differences among several entities.
e. ___________ means that a group of reasonably informed financial statement users are able to reach a consensus decision that reported information is a faithful representation of an underlying economic event.
f. ___________ represent resources, claims to resources, or interests in resources as of a specific point in time and appear on the balance sheet (statement of financial position).
g. An ___________ involves a buyer and seller who are independent and unrelated parties, each bargaining to maximize his or her own wealth.
h. The ______ indicates that accountants will record transactions and prepare financial statements as if the entity will continue to operate for an indefinite period of time unless there is evidence to the contrary.
i. The ______ specifies that an economic entity can divide its life into artificial time periods for the purpose of providing periodic reports on its economic activities.
j. Financial information is _____ if it is capable of making a difference in decision making by exhibiting the following attributes: predictive value, confirmatory value, and materiality.

3 5 6 **E2-6. Concepts.** Review the following accounting practices and indicate whether you believe that the practice is correct or incorrect. Justify your answer with an accounting concept, principle, or assumption.

a. Citera Company, a large multinational corporation, expensed the acquisition of a $4,000 computer system.
b. Mason Manufacturing acquired a new metal stamping machine at a cost of $50,000. Mason will depreciate the asset over its 10-year useful life.

c. Gabriel Grocery Stores needed to overhaul one of its stores at a cost of $75,000. The company decided to expense this amount as repairs and maintenance.
d. Dina Design Studios charged the $600 cost of a new laptop for the owner's daughter to office equipment expense.
e. Walsh Water Services issues financial statements on both a quarterly and an annual basis to its shareholders.

5 **E2-7. Cash versus Accrual Bases of Accounting.** Top Notch Services was founded on January 2 and offers computer consulting and other technology-related services. During its first quarter of operations, the following events occurred:

a. In January, Top Notch provided and billed clients for $40,000 of consulting services. It was paid for these services in March.
b. In January, Top Notch collected $25,000 from clients for services provided during the month.
c. In February, Top Notch provided and billed clients for $45,000 of consulting services. It collected $12,000 in the current month and the remaining amount in March.
d. In March, Top Notch collected $34,000 from clients for services provided during the month and billed clients for an additional $21,000 for services provided.
e. Top Notch pays employees at the end of each month for service provided. Monthly payroll was $12,000, $13,000, and $15,000 in January, February, and March, respectively.
f. Top Notch pays its utility bills at the end of each month. Utility bills totaled $800, $850, and $1,000 in January, February, and March, respectively.
g. Top Notch hired an independent contractor who provided $1,200 of services in February. The contractor was paid in March.

Determine Top Notch's net income for each month from January through March under both the cash and the accrual bases of accounting. Explain any difference in total net income under cash versus accrual accounting for the three months.

5 **E2-8. Cash vs. Accrual.** You are provided the following information for the Del Campo Consulting Associates.

	2019	2018
Service revenue (accrual basis)	$250,000	$185,000
Cash collected from clients	80,000	97,000
Operating expenses:		
Salary expense (accrual basis)	12,000	16,500
Purchased supplies for cash	4,000	2,500
Purchased supplies on account	1,500	1,000
Depreciation expense	2,000	2,000
Rent paid in cash	7,000	3,000
Prepaid insurance	5,500	- 0-

Required:

Assume that all supplies purchased were used in operations in the year of purchase. Rental payments pertain to rental space used in the year of payment.

a. Prepare an income statement for Del Campo for 2019 and 2018 under both the cash and the accrual basis of accounting.
b. Compute operating cash flow for both years under cash and accrual bases.

Excel Project

Autograded Excel Project available in **MyLab Accounting**

3 Judgment and Applied Financial Accounting Research

LEARNING OBJECTIVES

1. Explain the importance and prevalence of judgment in the financial reporting process.
2. Discuss the role of accountants' assumptions and estimates and the related disclosures in the financial reporting process.
3. Identify obstacles to the use of sound judgment in preparing financial information and ways to overcome them.
4. Describe the types of authoritative literature and the literature hierarchy.
5. Outline and apply the steps in the applied financial accounting research process.

Introduction

ACCOUNTANTS USE *JUDGMENT* almost every day in their work when they evaluate facts to make a decision. For example, analyzing a business event and determining whether to record it or deciding whether to record a liability for pending litigation involves a great deal of judgment. Selecting and applying accounting methods—such as the choice of a cost-flow assumption (e.g., LIFO versus FIFO) in inventory valuation—and using assumptions and estimates in financial reporting also require judgment. Determining the provision for bad debts relies on the use of estimates. Financial statement preparers use the best information available to make these judgments, knowing business activities could change and there could be new information in the future.

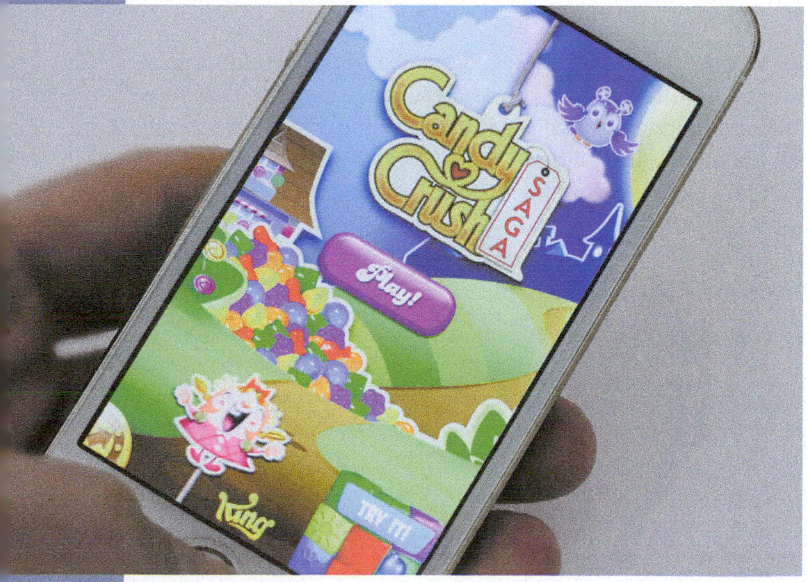

Blaize Pascall/Alamy Stock Images

Managers use judgment in preparing financial statements, making the best estimates at that time. Consider ***Activision Blizzard,*** a leading provider of interactive game services. ***Activision Blizzard*** users play games for free—yet, within these games, they can purchase virtual currency to obtain virtual goods to enhance their game-playing experience. For example, a Candy Crush player may purchase "gold bars." How does ***Activision Blizzard*** determine when the virtual goods are used and when to record revenues? Initially, ***Activision Blizzard*** records unearned revenue when players buy the virtual currency and virtual goods. ***Activision Blizzard*** recognizes revenue as the players use their virtual goods. Some virtual goods are consumable and used within days whereas others are durable and used over longer periods of time. ***Activision Blizzard*** relies on historical data in making judgments about when the virtual goods are used and when to record revenues. However, assumptions based on historical data can change rapidly in a young, growing, and dynamic market such as social game services. If ***Activision Blizzard*** revises assumptions based on new data, changes its product mix due to new game introductions, or modifies estimates used such as average playing periods, the amount of revenue recognized may differ significantly from one period to the next.

In this chapter, we identify areas in financial reporting that require judgment. We explore the assumptions and estimates disclosed in financial reports and highlight key judgment areas found in practice. We then discuss some obstacles to the use of good judgment and ways to overcome them. Because accountants are required to make judgments based on accounting standards and other authoritative literature, we explain the authoritative literature and its hierarchy in use for both U.S. GAAP and IFRS. We then outline the six steps used in the applied financial accounting research process. While the accounting standards differ, the use of judgment and the applied financial accounting research process are similar under U.S. GAAP and IFRS. «

1 Explain the importance and prevalence of judgment in the financial reporting process.

The Importance and Prevalence of Judgment in Financial Reporting

When first studying accounting, most students expect to encounter clear-cut methods and rules. In practice, accountants frequently use *judgment* to prepare and audit financial statements. **Judgment** is the process by which an accountant or manager reaches a decision in situations in which there are multiple alternatives.

Judgment and the Accountant

Accountants use judgment in several aspects of accounting and financial reporting, including researching and interpreting standards. Here, accountants seek answers to questions such as:

1. Should the company report a business event and, if so, when? For example, at times there are complexities involved in deciding when to recognize revenue. Specifically, should the company recognize revenue this year or defer it until future periods?
2. If the company decides to report a business event in the current period, then what is the appropriate financial reporting treatment? For example, there are multiple methods for reporting an investment in the equity of another company. Thus, when a company acquires that investment, accountants must decide which accounting method is most appropriate.
3. What amount(s) should the company report in the financial statements related to this business event? For example, when a company purchases inventory, there may be costs (such as freight costs) associated with that purchase other than the cost of the inventory itself. Accountants must determine what costs to include in the amount recorded as inventory.

Activision Blizzard, the social game service company, faced these types of questions when it started its business. In the new social media field, ***Activision Blizzard***, needed to grapple with how to apply revenue recognition rules developed years earlier to the way it delivers its virtual products.

Judgment: Use and Abuse

Accounting standards allow financial statement preparers to use judgment to report the substance of a transaction in the financial statements, within certain boundaries, in the manner that best reflects economic reality. The ability to apply judgment enhances the usefulness of the financial statements. Of course, management might also use this latitude to engage in *earnings management* behavior. **Earnings management** occurs when managers manipulate financial information and misrepresent the firm's financial position and performance.[1]

Judgment and Financial Statement Comparisons

Accounting standards afford management discretion in selecting accounting methods, applying those methods, and changing methods or estimates. This latitude can be problematic for users comparing the financial information reported by two firms in the same industry when each firm uses a different set of accounting methods or estimation techniques. In addition, the same firm may change its methods or estimation techniques over time. However, the flexibility afforded in the selection and application of accounting standards permits managers to choose those methods and assumptions that best reflect the economic reality of their transactions. Therefore, the

[1] We discuss earnings management in more depth in Chapter 5.

financial information provided and user decisions based on that information may be enhanced by not requiring all companies to use the same accounting methods.

For example, consider two firms in the same industry: One uses the *average-cost* inventory method and the other uses the *first-in, first-out* (FIFO) inventory costing method. The different inventory costing methods mean that the firms' financial statements will reflect different measurement bases for inventory. To compare the inventory balances as well as the cost of goods sold of these two firms, the investor will need to "undo" the effects of the inventory costing method choice. That is, a reasonably informed financial statement user would understand that ending inventory would be higher under FIFO than under average cost in a period of rising prices. Knowledge of the direction of the bias in the reported inventory valuation enables the financial statement user to interpret the results with ratio analysis and other financial statistics.

Accountants use their judgment to estimate and record economic events as accurately as possible. We highlight the use of judgment in each chapter in this text. We also include judgment cases in the end-of-chapter material to help develop your judgment and decision-making skills.

2 Discuss the role of accountants' assumptions and estimates and the related disclosures in the financial reporting process.

The Role of Assumptions and Estimates

After a manager or an accountant determines that a firm should report a business event in the financial statements, he or she often uses assumptions and estimates to answer the questions related to when to recognize the transaction, what accounting method to use, and what amount to record.

Assumptions and Estimates in the Financial Statements

Many amounts reported on the financial statements are based upon assumptions. For example:

1. Property, plant, and equipment are depreciated using a particular method (such as straight-line depreciation) that requires managers and accountants to make assumptions about the pattern of use.
2. Investments in another company are accounted for differently depending on how long management intends to hold the investment. Thus, managers and accountants must make assumptions about the duration of the investment.

Many of the balances reported on financial statements are estimates. Consider these two specific examples:

1. The value reported for property, plant, and equipment is net of accumulated depreciation. Depreciation is based upon estimates of the life and pattern of use of the depreciable assets.
2. Accounts receivable are reported on the balance sheet net of an allowance for those receivables that are not likely to be collected. However, the balance in the allowance account is an estimate as to how much of the accounts receivable balance might not be paid by customers.

It is important for financial statement preparers and users to understand the extensive use of assumptions and judgment in the financial statement preparation process.

Judgment-Related Disclosures

How does a financial statement user know where managers used judgment in the financial reporting process? Financial statement disclosures—specifically, the accounting policies footnote—provide this information. U.S. GAAP requires companies to disclose their significant accounting policies.

Accounting Policies Footnote. The accounting policies footnote outlining the portfolio of accounting choices is typically one of the first notes to the financial statements. In ***Johnson & Johnson's*** 2015 annual report, it listed accounting policy choices for 14 different areas: cash equivalents; investments; property, plant, and equipment and depreciation; revenue recognition; shipping and handling; inventories; intangible assets and goodwill; financial instruments; product liability; concentration of credit risk; research and development; advertising; income taxes; and net earnings per share. For example, ***Johnson & Johnson*** indicated that it reported inventory at the *lower-of-cost-or-market* and valued inventory using the *first-in, first-out* method. As another example, ***Johnson & Johnson*** disclosed that it reports property, plant, and equipment at cost, depreciating these assets using the *straight-line* method, and it also disclosed the lives that it uses to depreciate various groupings of assets. Toward the end of the disclosure, ***Johnson & Johnson*** also indicated that it uses estimates extensively in the preparation of financial information.

Industry Comparisons. Financial statement users rely on accounting policies footnote information to compare ***Johnson & Johnson*** to other firms in the industry. ***Johnson & Johnson's*** competitors include healthcare and pharmaceutical companies such as ***Pfizer Inc., GlaxoSmithKline plc,*** and ***AstraZeneca plc.*** Exhibit 3.1 illustrates the different methods, estimates, and assumptions that ***Johnson & Johnson*** and its competitors use in accounting for common items such as inventory and long-lived tangible assets. Notice that two of the companies—***Johnson & Johnson*** and ***Pfizer***—are U.S. GAAP reporters and that two report under IFRS—***GlaxoSmithKline*** and ***AstraZeneca.*** Next, two of the four companies use the first-in, first-out (FIFO) inventory cost flow assumption (***Johnson & Johnson*** and ***GlaxoSmithKline***), one uses average cost (***Pfizer***), and one uses a combination of FIFO and average cost (***AstraZeneca***). For depreciation of long-lived tangible assets, all four companies use the straight-line method. However, the asset categories and useful lives vary considerably among the companies and are influenced by management's judgment. For example, all four companies have a different range of useful lives for their buildings.[2]

In addition, the accounting policies footnote enables users to determine whether a company employs income-increasing or income-reducing accounting policies or methods. For example, a company using FIFO in a period of inflation will typically report lower cost of sales and higher gross profit than a company using LIFO.

EXHIBIT 3.1 Comparison of Accounting Methods, Estimates, and Assumptions for Inventory and Long-lived Tangible Assets

	Johnson & Johnson	Pfizer Inc.	GlaxoSmithKline plc	AstraZeneca plc
Reporting Standards	U.S. GAAP	U.S. GAAP	IFRS	IFRS
Inventory	FIFO	Average Cost	FIFO	FIFO and average cost
Long-lived Tangible Assets				
Depreciation Method	Straight-line	Straight-line	Straight-line	Straight-line
Useful lives by asset category:				
Building	20–30 years	33–50 years	20–50 years	10–50 years
Plant and equipment				3–15 years
Land and leasehold improvements	10–20 years		20–50 years or lease term	
Machinery and equipment	2–13 years	8–20 years	10–20 years	
Furniture, fixtures, and other		$3\text{–}12\frac{1}{2}$ years	3–10 years	

Sources: Based on Johnson & Johnson; Pfizer; GlaxoSmithKline; AstraZeneca

[2]Analysts and other financial statement users also employ various financial statement analysis techniques to understand a company's financial position and performance and compare it to other companies. We will discuss some of these techniques in Chapters 5 and 6 and apply them where appropriate throughout this text.

IFRS-Specific Disclosures. Our discussion of required disclosures of significant accounting policies thus far applies to both IFRS and U.S. GAAP. IFRS further requires that companies disclose additional information about the assumptions and estimates they made at the end of the reporting period.[3] For example, companies make estimates and assumptions regarding the amount of accounts receivable that will not be collectible. IFRS also requires that companies disclose the judgments (apart from those involving estimates and assumptions) that management has made in determining appropriate accounting treatments for amounts reported on the financial statements.[4] For example, companies will make judgments as to whether potential obligations are probable and thus should be reported as a liability. Companies also disclose if there is a significant risk that any amounts they reported will change in the coming year due to the underlying assumptions.[5]

In Exhibit 3.2, ***Telefonaktiebolaget LM Ericsson***, a Swedish technology, hardware, and equipment company and an IFRS reporter, stipulates in its second financial statement note that

EXHIBIT 3.2 Critical Accounting Estimates and Judgments Note Excerpt, ***Telefonaktiebolaget LM Ericsson***, December 31, 2015, Financial Statements

C2

CRITICAL ACCOUNTING ESTIMATES AND JUDGMENTS

The preparation of financial statements and application of accounting standards often involve management's judgment and the use of estimates and assumptions deemed to be reasonable at the time they are made. However, other results may be derived with different judgments or using different assumptions or estimates, and events may occur that could require a material adjustment to the carrying amount of the asset or liability affected. Following are the most important accounting policies subject to such judgments and the key sources of estimation uncertainty that the Company believes could have the most significant impact on the reported results and financial position.

The information in this note is grouped as per:

- Key sources of estimation uncertainty
- Judgments management has made in the process of applying the Company's accounting policies.

Revenue recognition

Key sources of estimation uncertainty

Examples of estimates of total contract revenue and cost that are necessary are the assessing of customer possibility to reach conditional purchase volumes triggering contractual discounts to be given to the customer, the impact on the Company revenue in relation to performance criteria and whether any loss provisions shall be made.

Judgments made in relation to accounting policies applied

Parts of the Company's sales are generated from large and complex customer contracts. Managerial judgment is applied regarding, among other aspects, conformance with acceptance criteria and if transfer of risks and rewards to the buyer has taken place to determine if revenue and costs should be recognized in the current period, degree of completion and the customer credit standing to assess whether payment is likely or not to justify revenue recognition.

Trade and customer finance receivables

Key sources of estimation uncertainty

The Company monitors the financial stability of its customers and the environment in which they operate to make estimates regarding the likelihood that the individual receivables will be paid. Total allowances for estimated losses as of December 31, 2015, were SEK 1.5 (1.5) billion or 2.0% (1.8%) of gross trade and customer finance receivables.

Credit risks for outstanding customer finance credits are regularly assessed as well, and allowances are recorded for estimated losses.

Continued

[3]See paragraphs 125–133 of IASC, *International Accounting Standard 1*, "Presentation of Financial Statements" (London, UK: International Accounting Standards Committee, 1975, Revised).

[4]See paragraphs 122–124 of IASC, *International Accounting Standard 1*, "Presentation of Financial Statements."

[5]In the United States, the SEC requires public companies to provide information in their annual regulatory filing, the 10-K, to supplement, not duplicate, the description of accounting policies in the footnotes to the financial statements. The discussion presents an analysis of the uncertainties involved in applying the accounting policies described in the footnote.

Inventory valuation

Key sources of estimation uncertainty

Inventories are valued at the lower of cost and net realizable value. Estimates are required in relation to forecasted sales volumes and inventory balances. In situations where excess inventory balances are identified, estimates of net realizable values for the excess volumes are made. Inventory allowances for estimated losses as of December 31, 2015, amounted to SEK 2.6 (3.3) billion or 8% (8%) of gross inventory.

Deferred taxes

Key sources of estimation uncertainty

Deferred tax assets and liabilities, are recognized for temporary differences and for tax loss carry-forwards. Deferred tax is recognized net of valuation allowances. The valuation of temporary differences and tax loss carry-forwards, is based on management's estimates of future taxable profits in different tax jurisdictions against which the temporary differences and loss carry-forwards may be utilized.

The largest amounts of tax loss carry-forwards are reported in Sweden, with an indefinite period of utilization (i.e. with no expiry date). For further detailed information, please refer to Note C8, "Taxes".

At December 31, 2015, the value of deferred tax assets amounted to SEK 13.2 (12.8) billion. The deferred tax assets related to loss carry-forwards are reported as non-current assets.

Accounting for income tax, value added tax, and other taxes

Key sources of estimation uncertainty

Accounting for these items is based upon evaluation of income-, value added- and other tax rules in all jurisdictions where we perform activities. The total complexity of rules related to taxes and the accounting for these require management's involvement in judgments regarding classification of transactions and in estimates of probable outcomes of claimed deductions and/or disputes.

Acquired intellectual property rights and other intangible assets, including goodwill

Key sources of estimation uncertainty

At initial recognition, future cash flows are estimated, to ensure that the initial carrying values do not exceed the expected discounted cash flows for the items of this type of assets. After initial recognition, impairment testing is performed whenever there is an indication of impairment, except in the case of goodwill for which impairment testing is performed at least once per year. Negative deviations in actual cash flows compared to estimated cash flows as well as new estimates that indicate lower future cash flows might result in recognition of impairment charges.

For further discussion on goodwill, see Note C1, "Significant accounting policies" and Note C10, "Intangible assets." Estimates related to acquired intangible assets are based on similar assumptions and risks as for goodwill.

At December 31, 2015, the amount of acquired intellectual property rights and other intangible assets amounted to SEK 50.4 (50.9) billion, including goodwill of SEK 41.1 (38.3) billion.

Judgments made in relation to accounting policies applied

At initial recognition and subsequent remeasurement, management judgments are made, both for key assumptions and regarding impairment indicators. In the purchase price allocation made for each acquisition, the purchase price shall be assigned to the identifiable assets, liabilities and contingent liabilities based on fair values for these assets. Any remaining excess value is reported as goodwill. This allocation requires management judgment as well as the definition of cash-generating units for impairment testing purposes. Other judgments might result in significantly different results and financial position in the future.

Provisions

Key sources of estimation uncertainty

Provisions mainly comprise amounts related to warranty, restructuring, contractual obligations and penalties to customers and estimated losses on customer contracts, risks associated with patent and other litigations, supplier or subcontractor claims and/or disputes, as well as provisions for unresolved income tax and value-added tax issues. The estimates related to the amounts of provisions for penalties, claims or losses receive special attention from the management. At December 31, 2015, provisions amounted to SEK 3.8 (4.4) billion. For further detailed information, see Note C18, "Provisions."

Judgments made in relation to accounting policies applied

Whether a present obligation is probable or not requires judgment. The nature and type of risks for these provisions differ and management's judgment is applied regarding the nature and extent of obligations in deciding if an outflow of resources is probable or not.

Contingent liabilities

Key sources of estimation uncertainty

As disclosed under "Provisions" there are uncertainties in the estimated amounts. The same type of uncertainty exists for contingent liabilities.

Continued

Judgments made in relation to accounting policies

As disclosed under Note C1, "Significant accounting policies" a potential obligation that is not likely to result in an economic outflow is classified as a contingent liability, with no impact on the Company's financial statements. However, should an obligation in a later period be deemed to be probable, then a provision shall be recognized, impacting the financial statements.

Pension and other post-employment benefits

Key sources of estimation uncertainty

Accounting for the costs of defined benefit pension plans and other applicable post-employment benefits is based on actuarial valuations, relying on key estimates for discount rates, future salary increases, employee turnover rates and mortality tables. The discount rate assumptions are based on rates for high-quality fixed-income investments with durations as close as possible to the Company's pension plans. As disclosed in note C1, "Significant accounting policies," the Company has in Sweden in periods up to the second quarter of 2015 estimated the discount rate for the Swedish pension liability based on the interest rates for Swedish covered bonds. Due to the development since then of the deepness of the Swedish covered bond market and the volatility in interest rates, the Company has decided to apply Swedish government bonds rate for this discounting for the fiscal year 2015. The rate applied is 2.1% (2.75%). At December 31, 2015, defined benefit obligations for pensions and other post-employment benefits amounted to SEK 78.1 (73.8) billion and fair value of plan assets to SEK 58.2 (56.9) billion. For more information on estimates and assumptions, see Note C17, "Post-employment benefits."

Foreign exchange risks

Key sources of estimation uncertainty

Foreign exchange risk impacts the financial results of the Company: see further disclosure in Note C20, "Financial risk management and financial instruments," under Foreign Exchange Risk.

Source: Ericsson, Financial Statements, December 31, 2015. https://www.ericsson.com/res/investors/docs/2015/ericsson-annual-report-2015-en.pdf, pages 69–70

the preparation of its financial statements often involves management's judgment and the use of assumptions and estimates. Notice the distinction between the uncertainty in making estimates in the first bullet point and the judgment management made in applying the accounting policies in the second bullet point. ***Ericsson's*** note continues to discuss 10 areas involving the use of estimates and assumptions, and 4 areas involving management's judgments in relation to accounting policies. The areas covered are trade and customer finance receivables; inventory valuation; deferred taxes; income tax, value-added tax, and other taxes; intellectual property rights and other intangible assets; provisions; contingent liabilities; pensions; and foreign exchange risks. For example, in the revenue recognition section, ***Ericsson*** explains that its managers made estimates in the amounts of provisions and the expected volume discounts and applied judgment in evaluating whether the firm could recognize revenue on its large and complex contracts. The section related to trade and customer finance receivables discloses that total allowances for uncollectible accounts were 2.0% of gross trade and customer finance receivables. As another example, ***Ericsson*** details that its allowance for inventory write-downs was 8% of gross inventory.

Key Judgment Areas in Practice

Based on an analysis of annual reports from 175 companies representing 19 industries and 48 countries, Exhibit 3.3 illustrates 14 major financial statement areas where managers use accounting estimates and judgments. For example, 40% of companies disclose that they use estimates and judgments in accounting for the allowance for uncollectible receivables. As we cover areas such as taxation, employee benefits, provisions, and revenue recognition throughout the textbook, we will highlight the need for judgment and present decision-making methods used to resolve complex accounting issues.[6]

[6]This data is based on a survey of companies reporting under IFRS. However, results would likely be very similar for companies reporting under U.S. GAAP.

EXHIBIT 3.3 Manager's Use of Accounting Estimates and Judgments under IFRS

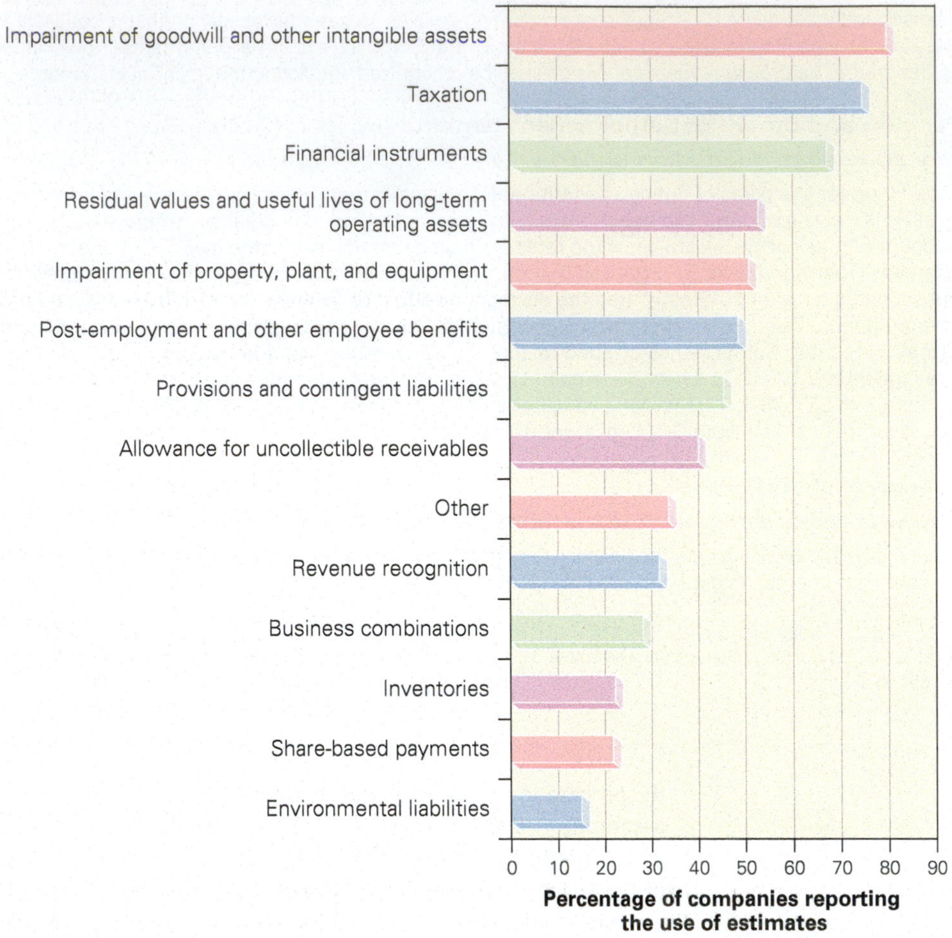

Source: AICPA, *IFRS Financial Statements: Best Practices in Presentation and Disclosure 2012/2013* (New York, NY: AICPA, 2012)

❸ Identify obstacles to the use of sound judgment in preparing financial information and ways to overcome them.

Judgment Obstacles in Preparing Financial Information

In preparing or auditing financial information, accountants face a number of potential impediments to the use of good judgment, such as:

- Factors that may influence management to intentionally bias their estimates.
- *Cognitive biases.*
- Complexity of the business environment and transactions.

An understanding and awareness of these obstacles prepares managers to overcome them in the financial reporting process as well as assists financial statement users in critically evaluating firm performance and condition.

Factors Influencing Management Behavior

Factors that influence management to intentionally bias estimates impede the use of good judgment. Areas of financial reporting that require significant judgment are particularly susceptible to management manipulation. For example, if management bonuses are tied to net income, management may have an incentive to bias reported income upward.

Analysts' forecasts may also influence management. Financial analysts use reported information to provide guidance to individuals and other entities in making investment and credit decisions. As part of this process, analysts release earnings forecasts. Because the stock price of a company tends to react negatively when actual earnings are less than this earnings forecast, management may have an incentive to bias earnings upward if it would otherwise miss the forecast.[7]

To minimize management bias, auditors exercise **professional skepticism,** which is "an attitude that includes a questioning mind and a critical assessment of audit evidence."[8] Auditors should not assume that management is dishonest—yet they should consider the possible incentives for management to bias information presented in the financial statements.[9]

Cognitive Biases

Cognitive biases can also impact the way accountants make judgments. **Cognitive biases** are systematic deviations from rationality, to which we are all subject, that can impact judgments on a day-to-day basis. We discuss some of the types of cognitive biases next, followed by techniques that are useful in reducing the impact of these biases.

Types of Cognitive Biases. Examples of cognitive biases are the *availability*, *overconfidence*, *confirmatory*, *groupthink*, and *anchoring* biases.

1. The **availability bias** is the tendency to use the data that is most readily available or most easily recalled to make a decision, as opposed to considering all relevant data. For example, if you were deciding which computer to buy, you might rely on your friend's advice instead of taking the time to research consumer reviews.
2. The **overconfidence bias** is the tendency to be more confident than your abilities and experience level would objectively warrant. For example, multiple research studies have asked study participants how confident they were in answers they provided to a set of questions. Research results repeatedly show that confidence systematically exceeds accuracy.
3. The **confirmatory bias** is when decision makers under-weight information that is not consistent with their initial beliefs. For example, if individuals have strong political beliefs, they may not adequately consider positions held by someone in another political party.
4. The **groupthink bias** is a phenomenon that occurs in situations where members of a group, in an attempt to avoid conflict, reach a consensus decision without considering all of the reasonable alternatives. For example, a group of students working on a case assignment may agree to a certain answer in order to avoid conflict with a dominant group member, even if everyone else in the group has not had a chance to express his or her views.
5. The **anchoring bias** occurs when the decision maker focuses on one piece of information (often the first piece of data encountered), weighting it more heavily than other pieces of information. For example, when you buy a used car, you may anchor on the sticker price of the car and not consider carefully enough what the car is really worth to you.

Techniques to Mitigate Cognitive Biases. To mitigate cognitive biases, accountants must be as objective as possible, which entails being free from any bias or other influences. The following techniques may prove helpful.

1. Be organized and methodical in the decision-making process. In our discussion of applied financial research later in the chapter, we outline steps in the research process that are also useful in solving a judgment-based problem objectively.
2. Generate alternatives, even when you think you have already arrived at the correct answer. Carefully consider each of these alternatives and reasons that it may be better than your initial assessment of the correct alternative.

---

[7] We discuss earnings management in more detail in Chapter 5.

[8] Public Company Accounting Oversight Board, *Staff Audit Practice Alert Number 10*, "Maintaining and Applying Professional Skepticism in Audits" (Washington, D.C.: Public Company Accounting Oversight Board, 2012).

[9] Professional skepticism is discussed more extensively in auditing courses.

3. Document your rationale about the alternatives. Often the process of documenting beliefs and thought processes—even if only in bullet format—challenges your thinking.
4. Delay your final judgment until you have gathered all of the facts and information and have considered all of the alternatives. This delay allows you to be more objective in your decision-making process.

Complexity of the Business Environment and Transactions

The increasing complexity of the business environment and related transactions also create an obstacle to the exercise of good judgment. Decisions related to complex transactions can often seem overwhelming, particularly to someone who is relatively new to the accounting profession. Even for experienced accountants, new issues arise all the time. For example, revenue recognition for virtual goods became a new accounting issue with the emergence of social media companies such as ***Activision Blizzard***. Also, proper exercise of judgment often requires a substantial amount of research of the authoritative literature.

In these cases, it is helpful to follow an organized process that allows the accountant to stay focused on the issue at hand and make well-informed decisions. That is, the accountant does not need to know every answer, but she does need to understand the steps involved in determining the most appropriate accounting treatment. We discuss this research process later in the chapter.

4 Describe the types of authoritative literature and the literature hierarchy.

Authoritative Literature Used in Applied Financial Accounting Research

Accountants undertake financial accounting research whenever they need information to determine the appropriate reporting treatment for a business transaction. In addition, accountants use financial accounting research whenever the analysis and interpretation of an economic event or accounting standard is not clear and thus requires judgment. Accounting standards may be unclear for three main reasons:

1. Judgment is involved because the standard setters allow for management discretion.
2. The issue is sufficiently complex that, although a single correct answer exists, it requires research to determine the correct answer.
3. There is simply no information in the accounting standards that directly provides guidance to resolve a specific reporting issue.

In these cases, accountants must *research* the authoritative literature and develop a recommended accounting treatment. **Research** is the systematic investigation into an issue. We will focus our discussion on applied research that requires critical-thinking skills, a knowledge base, thoroughness, and professional judgment. We begin our discussion with the content of the authoritative literature. The following section will then outline the steps to follow in the research process.

Authoritative Literature

As discussed in Chapter 1, U.S. standard setters have issued a number of different types of authoritative statements over the years that are part of U.S. GAAP. These standards include, but are not limited to, Accounting Research Bulletins of the Committee on Accounting Procedure, Accounting Principles Board Opinions, and Statements of Financial Accounting Standards of the FASB.

Due to the large volume of diverse and complex standards, the body of U.S. GAAP became difficult to use. In response to this problem, the FASB developed the Financial Accounting Standards Board Accounting Standards Codification (ASC), often referred to as the **Codification,** which groups and summarizes all current standards by topic. When the FASB issues a new pronouncement, it is referenced as an Accounting Standards Update (ASU). Once approved, ASUs are incorporated into the Codification.

EXHIBIT 3.4 Major Codification Topic Groupings

Topic	Numbering	Description
General Principles	1XX	Establishes the Codification as the authoritative source for U.S. GAAP.
Presentation	2XX	Covers items such as financial statements, interim reporting, and segment reporting.
Assets	3XX	Covers the accounting treatment for assets.
Liabilities	4XX	Covers the accounting treatment for liabilities.
Equity	5XX	Covers the accounting treatment for equity.
Revenue	6XX	Covers the accounting treatment for revenues.
Expenses	7XX	Covers the accounting treatment for expenses.
Broad Transactions	8XX	Includes items such as business combinations and consolidations, fair value measurements, financial instruments, and foreign currency matters.
Industry	9XX	Presents industry-specific guidance.

Codification Structure. The Codification is divided into topics, subtopics, sections, and paragraphs. Exhibit 3.4 presents the nine major topic groupings. The complete list of topics included in the Codification can be found in Appendix A.[10]

The number and type of subtopics vary depending on the main topic but are generally distinguished by accounting area or scope.[11] For example, the Codification breaks down the topic on intangibles into the various types of intangibles such as goodwill. Exhibit 3.5 presents the subtopics included under the topic of intangibles. Note that the topics will also cross-reference relevant industry topics. For example, Topic 350 includes Topic 908 *Airlines*.

EXHIBIT 3.5 Codification Subtopics for Topic 350 Intangibles—Goodwill and Other

Subtopic Number	Subtopic Description
10	Overall
20	Goodwill
30	General Intangibles Other Than Goodwill
40	Internal-Use Software
50	Website Development Costs
908	Airlines
920	Entertainment – Broadcasters
922	Entertainment – Cable Television
932	Extractive Activities – Oil and Gas
950	Financial Services – Title Plant
980	Regulated Operations
985	Software

[10]Access to the Codification is available to faculty and students for a minimal charge through the Academic Accounting Access program sponsored by the Financial Accounting Foundation (FAF), in a joint initiative with the American Accounting Association (AAA). See http://aaahq.org/fasb/access.cfm.

[11]Appendix A to this chapter presents the subtopics for Topic 350 – *Intangibles,* Topic 450 – *Contingencies*, and Topic 505 – *Equity*.

The sections under each subtopic are uniform throughout the Codification. For example, Section 25 is always recognition and Section 30 is always initial measurement. Appendix A presents the full set of sections included in the Codification.

As we discussed in Chapter 1, the SEC has the authority to promulgate accounting standards. For convenience, the Codification contains S sections written by the SEC (rather than the FASB). For example, S30 is a section that contains information about initial measurement issued by the SEC. All of the S sections refer to Section S99, which contains the actual text of the SEC documents. Accountants exercise caution when using S99 Sections: They do not represent the full breadth of SEC materials and may exclude the most recent information.

Accountants reference material from the Codification with a specific shorthand. To illustrate, consider the reference ASC 350-20–35-1. Exhibit 3.6 illustrates how to disaggregate a Codification reference.

EXHIBIT 3.6 Codification Reference

Reference	Title	Number
Topic	Intangibles – Goodwill and Other	350
Subtopic	Goodwill	20
Section	Subsequent Measurement	35
Paragraph		1

Example 3.1 illustrates the use of the Codification to locate information needed to resolve an accounting question.

EXAMPLE 3.1

Referencing the Codification

PROBLEM: You are the accountant for JC's Emporium. JC's has been sued and you have concluded that it must record a liability for the loss (a loss contingency). You are unsure what amount to report on the balance sheet. Using the "Structure of the U.S. GAAP Codification" in Appendix A, what are the best topic, subtopic, and sections to use to find this information in the Codification?

SOLUTION: Start in the Liabilities topic grouping—the 400s. In Appendix A, Contingencies are Topic 450. Within Topic 450, Subtopic 20 covers loss contingencies. Finally, because you are interested in how JC's should initially record this contingency, you will go to Section 30 – Initial Measurement. Thus, the information is most likely to be found in ASC 450-20-30.

The U.S. GAAP Hierarchy. When researching financial reporting issues, it is important to know the hierarchy of the literature. What if an accountant cannot find guidance for a transaction in the authoritative U.S. GAAP included in the Codification and SEC material? The accountant then must look elsewhere, as depicted by Level 3 in Exhibit 3.7's description of the levels used in the U.S. GAAP hierarchy.[12]

To illustrate the use of the hierarchy in practice, assume that an industry publication prescribes a particular accounting treatment, but a review of the Codification indicates that a different approach is more appropriate. In this case, the entity would be required to follow the Codification, which is the higher level of authority.

[12]The U.S. GAAP hierarchy is found in Paragraphs 1-3 of FASB ASC 105-10-5, *Generally Accepted Accounting Principles-Overall-Overview and Background.*

EXHIBIT 3.7 U.S. GAAP Hierarchy

Level	Literature Included
Level 1	The Codification and all SEC rules and interpretive releases. While the Codification applies to all entities that report under U.S. GAAP, the SEC materials only apply to publicly traded companies.
Level 2	Authoritative rules and principles from U.S. GAAP for similar transactions.
Level 3	Non-authoritative material such as the FASB Concepts Statements, IFRS, AICPA Issues Papers, Technical Information Services Inquiries and Replies included in AICPA Technical Practice Aids, pronouncements of professional associations or regulatory agencies, industry practice, and textbooks.

Authoritative Literature: IFRS

The IASB includes four categories of standards in IFRS, as listed here:

1. International Accounting Standards (IAS)
2. International Financial Reporting Standards (IFRS)
3. Standing Interpretations Committee (SIC) Interpretations
4. IFRS Interpretations Committee (IFRIC) Interpretations

Appendix B lists the IFRS standards and interpretations.

Hierarchy: IFRS. IFRS employs a four-level hierarchy to rank the authoritative support for its various accounting standards, as outlined in Exhibit 3.8.[13]

EXHIBIT 3.8 IFRS Hierarchy

Level	Literature Included
Level 1	IFRS standards and interpretations that specifically apply to a transaction, event, or condition.
Level 2	Authoritative rules from IFRS for similar and related transactions.
Level 3	The Conceptual Framework definitions, recognition criteria, and measurement concepts for assets, liabilities, income, and expenses.
Level 4	Recent pronouncements of other standard-setting bodies that use a similar Conceptual Framework to develop accounting standards, other accounting literature, and accepted industry practices, to the extent that they do not conflict with the sources in Levels 1 and 2.

When moving to Levels 2 and 3, IFRS addresses the need for management to use judgment in developing and applying accounting policies. Managers use their judgment to provide information that is relevant to the economic decision-making needs of users and is reliable. For information to be considered reliable in the financial statements, it must have the following characteristics:

1. Faithfully represents the financial position, financial performance, and cash flows of the entity.
2. Reflects the economic substance of transactions, other events and conditions, and not merely the legal form.
3. Is neutral (i.e., free from bias).
4. Is prudent (i.e., conservative).
5. Is complete in all material respects.[14]

[13]The IFRS hierarchy is found in IASC, *International Accounting Standard 8*, "Accounting Policies, Changes in Accounting Estimates and Errors" (London, UK: International Accounting Standards Committee, 1978, Revised), Paragraphs 7–12.
[14]Ibid., Paragraph 10.

ROBERT HERZ, CHAIRMAN, FASB (RETIRED) »

Robert Herz

Robert Herz was chairman of the Financial Accounting Standards Board (FASB) from July 2002 to September 2010. During his tenure, he actively promoted the creation of improved accounting standards and greater transparency in financial reporting. Prior to joining FASB, he was a senior partner with PricewaterhouseCoopers and was an original member of the International Accounting Standards Board.

1 How does the Codification enhance the FASB's mission, and what were the key factors that influenced FASB to create it?

FASB's mission is to issue and improve financial accounting and disclosure standards and to ensure that people can understand, use, and apply these standards. Prior to the Codification, U.S. GAAP accounting literature was extremely unwieldy, and users found it difficult to follow and comply with the standards. Codification greatly facilitated its usability. Before I joined the FASB, I had spoken and written about the need to deal with this issue. And once at FASB, I was in a position to address this issue. Together with FASB senior staff and board members, we developed a systematic reorganization of U.S. GAAP, in one place and with a rational structure. This was not a breakthrough concept; other bodies of literature and accounting standards in other countries are codified.

2 How does the Codification simplify accounting research for users?

Everybody in the financial reporting supply chain benefits from the Codification. Users range from managerial accountants who prepare accounting statements for their companies to auditors, investors, analysts who focus on accounting matters, litigation attorneys, SEC staff, and accounting instructors and their students. The Codification is also essential for accounting standards setters who issue proposals and revise standards. The Codification logically reorganized the official U.S. GAAP, resolving overlapping and conflicting U.S. GAAP requirements. No longer do users have to figure out which of maybe 30 documents might have pertinent parts of U.S. GAAP dealing with a particular subject. Functionalities such as keyword searches make it faster and easier for users to navigate U.S. GAAP to find all the relevant requirements of an issue.

3 Why was the Codification process so challenging?

The volume of accounting literature was high—and also came from many disconnected source documents in different formats. Larry Smith, FASB Director of Technical Application and Implementation Activities, Tom Hoey, the Codification project leader, and key staff developed a blueprint, timeline, and budget for the project. We then surveyed a broad range of users whose responses overwhelmingly supported the business case for Codification. With a green light from the FASB Board and the Trustees of the Financial Accounting Foundation and input from the SEC, we began to create the Codification.

This massive effort took about six years and included extensive reviews. Mappers sorted existing literature from FASB, AICPA, the SEC, and other organizations into 90 different Codification sections, each with many subtopics. Groups of authors compiled the literature and standardized its language. Everything was reviewed internally at the FASB and by external reviewers. A software developer built a state-of-the-art, Web-based, highly customized research platform for it. On July 1, 2009, after an 18-month trial period, the Codification became official and replaced existing U.S. GAAP.

4 What is the procedure for issuing changes to standards in the Codification?

After public due process procedures, the FASB issues a proposed Accounting Standards Update describing proposed modifications and how these would change the Codification. After carefully evaluating comments and other input and reanalyzing issues identified, a final standard is developed and published in the form of an Accounting Standards Update (ASU) that specifically updates or amends the relevant existing Codification sections. The ASU may also contain a discussion of the Board's Basis for Conclusions in developing the standard, as well as implementation guidance.

5 What accounting and reporting standards are not included in the Codification?

The Codification includes everything that is a U.S. GAAP requirement, as well as relevant SEC guidance. Some basic SEC reporting regulations such as Regulation SX are separately codified. The Codification doesn't cover International Financial Reporting Standards (IFRS).

6 What role has the Codification served in the ongoing convergence process?

Codifying U.S. GAAP literature has facilitated convergence with IFRS by making U.S. accounting requirements easier to access and compare with the corresponding international standards. That has helped the Boards in their deliberations of issues subject to convergence efforts.

Discussion Questions

1. Explain the way U.S. GAAP standards were structured prior to the Codification and indicate how the codification simplified research (provide examples).
2. Discuss the advantages and disadvantages of U.S. GAAP and IFRS convergence. What role has the Codification played?

Basis for Conclusions

The FASB includes a section in most of its pronouncements referred to as the **Basis for Conclusions** (BC), which are discussions of the Board's reasoning and thought processes used to create the standard. The BCs are not considered authoritative, but they are very useful in understanding the thought processes of the Board and thus the substance of the standard. The BCs are not included in the Codification but can be found in the Accounting Standards Updates or the Statements of Financial Accounting Standards themselves. Because of the richness of the material in the BCs, we include cases based on them in the end-of-chapter material.

Basis for Conclusions: IFRS. Unlike U.S. GAAP, the BCs are included directly in the International Accounting Standards and International Financial Reporting Standards.

5 Outline and apply the steps in the applied financial accounting research process.

Steps in the Applied Financial Accounting Research Process

Now that you are familiar with the form and content of the authoritative literature, we will outline the six steps used in the financial reporting research process. These steps are presented in Exhibit 3.9 and discussed more extensively below. Financial statement preparers as well as auditors can use this process.

EXHIBIT 3.9 Steps in the Financial Accounting Research Process

1. Establish and understand the facts.
2. Identify the issue: What is the research question?
3. Search the authoritative literature.
4. Evaluate the results of the search.
5. Develop conclusions.
6. Communicate the results of the research.

Step 1: Establish and Understand the Facts

The first step in the research process is to understand the facts involved in the business transaction. What exactly does the business transaction look like? What parties are involved and how? What are the stipulations specified in any relevant contract? What is the timing of the transaction(s)?

The way the facts are presented to the accountant will vary in practice. The facts may be conveyed to you in a concise and thorough manner. For example, your manager may explain the transaction to you at an audit team meeting or a client may email the information. Alternatively, you may need to spend a significant amount of time establishing the facts by talking to the parties involved or reading through documents.

Regardless of the manner in which the facts are initially presented, it is critical that the researcher thoroughly understand the business transaction. Misunderstood facts will often lead to incorrect conclusions.

Step 2: Identify the Issue: What is the Research Question?

After establishing the fact pattern associated with the business transaction, the researcher needs to identify the issue. That is, the researcher needs to determine the exact research question. For example, a research question might be, "Should ABC Company recognize the revenue associated with this business transaction in the current fiscal year or the next fiscal year?" Typically, the research question (or issue) can be articulated in just a few sentences.

Step 3: Search the Authoritative Literature

Searching the authoritative literature can take a considerable amount of time, depending on the specific research question, even for experienced accountants. Understanding the structure of the Codification is invaluable for completing this step. Because the Codification is organized by topic, the research typically begins by identifying the appropriate topic to examine. For example, when researching an issue related to inventory, begin with Topic 330 – *Inventory*. It is sometimes possible to refine the search further, depending on the nature of the research question. If your question related to inventory was an issue as to how to initially record an item of inventory, you would most likely begin at ASC 330-10-30 – *Inventory – Overall – Initial Measurement.*

When searching the authoritative literature, you will often see cross-references to other Codification topics. For example, if you were researching an issue related to disclosure requirements for inventory, you would start in ASC 330-10-50 – *Inventory – Overall – Disclosure*. However, paragraph 6 relates to disclosures of significant estimates and provides a cross-reference to ASC 275-10-50 – *Risks and Uncertainties – Overall – Disclosure*. Always check the applicability of cross-references to be certain that you have done a thorough search of the literature.

You should also be aware that the Codification includes a search engine. Thus, if you are unsure where to start your research or you are unsure whether you have found all of the appropriate literature, you may want to search for various terms within the Codification using the search engine.

Step 4: Evaluate the Results of the Search

After you have found all the relevant authoritative literature, take the time to read it thoroughly, keeping in mind that much of the language used is highly technical and complex.

You may find that after reading through the authoritative literature, you need to change or refine the research question. Thus, these steps can be an iterative process. In fact, sometimes you will discover that you need to obtain additional facts related to the business transaction and return to Step 1.

Step 5: Develop Conclusions

After assimilating the relevant literature, decide on the best financial reporting treatment. Sometimes, there is only one correct answer. In other cases, the answer may not exist in the literature, particularly in Level 1 of the hierarchy. Accountants use judgment to work down the levels of the hierarchy and sometimes have to utilize a similar transaction that is covered in the authoritative literature. Other times, there are multiple legitimate treatments found in the accounting standards. Accountants compare the various treatments and identify the alternative that will result in the most faithful representation of the economic event.

Step 6: Communicate the Results of the Research

After finishing the first five steps, the accountant documents and communicates the results of the research process. This documentation may be done in a variety of forms such as a memo to the file or a client letter. The information included depends upon the audience, but it will most likely include documentation from all of the preceding steps:

- The facts of the business transaction.
- The research question.
- The analysis of the issue (i.e., a summary of the authoritative literature).
- The recommendation.

When articulating your research and recommendation in written form, write clearly and concisely to address the research question and communicate all relevant information.

Applying the Research Process

Building research skills is critical to success in the accounting profession. The significant volume of accounting standards makes it impossible to commit them to memory. In addition, the business environment is constantly changing, requiring revisions of accounting standards. Nonetheless, professionals must be able to find the answers to technical accounting questions in order to function effectively on a day-to-day basis. Acquiring research skills takes a great deal of practice. To illustrate, let's take the case of deciding whether to capitalize or expense certain costs incurred during the production process (Example 3.2).

EXAMPLE 3.2

The Financial Reporting Research Process

PROBLEM: Tough Guy Enterprises, a U.S. GAAP reporter, manufactures high-quality jeans for little boys. The cost to produce one pair of jeans includes $10 of materials and $5 for labor. Tough Guy produced the following number of jeans over the past 5 years:

Year 1	5.0 million
Year 2	5.1 million
Year 3	4.9 million
Year 4	4.8 million
Year 5	5.2 million

Additional data are available for the current year (Year 6):

Number of jeans produced	4.2 million pairs
Variable production overhead	$6.3 million
Fixed production overhead	$5.0 million
General and administrative expenses	$1.0 million
Selling costs	$1 per pair of jeans
Cost of wasted material (spoilage)	$0.25 million

Search the Codification to determine how to record each type of cost. Write a memo to the file to communicate your results.

SOLUTION: We will follow the steps in the financial accounting research process.

1. Establish and understand the facts.

   The facts are straightforward, as captured in the problem statement. In real-world problems, the facts are typically more difficult to identify.

   Tough Guy Enterprises is a U.S. GAAP reporter that manufactures jeans. It produced the following number of jeans over the past five years:

Year 1	5.0 million
Year 2	5.1 million
Year 3	4.9 million
Year 4	4.8 million
Year 5	5.2 million

Continued

Additional facts for the current year or Year 6:

Material costs per pair	$10
Labor costs per pair	$5
Number of jeans produced	4.2 million
Variable production overhead	$6.3 million
Fixed production overhead	$5.0 million
General and administrative expenses	$1.0 million
Selling costs	$1 per pair of jeans
Cost of wasted material (spoilage)	$0.25 million

2. Identify the issue: What is the research question?

   The accounting issue is whether Tough Guy should record expenditures as an expense (expensed) or as an asset (capitalized as part of the cost of inventory) and included in cost of goods sold when the inventory is sold. As a result, the research question is: Which of these expenditures should Tough Guy allocate to inventory and which should it expense immediately?

3. Search the authoritative literature.

   We begin our search using Codification Topic 330 – *Inventory*. None of the industry subtopics is relevant (agriculture, airlines, contractors, entertainment, extractive activities, real estate, software). Next, we review the *Overall* subtopic, ASC 330-10. Because we are interested in the way Tough Guy will initially record inventory, we will use Section 30 – *Initial Measurement* of ASC 330-10.

4. Evaluate the results of the search.

   A thorough review of Section 30 identifies the relevant parts of the Codification to use in developing a conclusion, as summarized next.

Codification Reference	Standard
ASC 330-10-30-1	Inventory is typically stated at cost (i.e., the cost incurred to bring the inventory to its existing condition and location).
ASC 330-10-30-3	Variable production overhead costs are allocated to each unit of production on the basis of the actual use of the production facilities.
	The allocation of fixed production overhead is based on the normal capacity of the production facility.
	Normal capacity is the production expected to be achieved over a number of periods and under normal circumstances.
ASC 330-10-30-6	The actual level of production may be used if it approximates normal capacity.
	The amount of fixed overhead allocated to each unit of production should not be increased in periods of abnormally low production.
ASC 330-10-30-7	Unallocated overhead costs should be recognized in the period they are incurred.
	Wasted materials (spoilage) should be recognized in the period they are incurred.
ASC 330-10-30-8	General and administrative expenses are typically recognized as expenses if they are not clearly related to production.
	Selling costs are not included in inventory.

5. Develop conclusions.

The conclusions are clear in this case with one exception: fixed overhead allocation. The allocation of the fixed production overhead is more complex than the other costs. According to ASC 330-10-30-3, the allocation of fixed production overhead is based on the normal capacity of the production facility. Normal capacity is the production expected to be achieved over a number of periods and under normal circumstances. In this case, we estimate normal capacity at 5 million pairs of jeans per year, which is the average of the prior five years of production (5.0, 5.1, 4.9, 4.8, and 5.2 million). Thus, we would allocate $1 per pair of jeans to inventory (the fixed overhead of $5 million divided by the normal capacity of 5 million pairs of jeans). The total amount of fixed overhead allocated to inventory is $4.2 million ($1 per pair times 4.2 million pairs produced during the current year).

The following table lists the expenditures and their proper accounting treatment (expense versus capitalize).

Expenditure	Total Cost	Cost per Pair of Jeans (based on production of 4.2 M)	Cost Allocated to Inventory	Cost Allocated to Expense	Relevant ASC Reference
Cost of material	$42.00 M	$10.00	$ 42.00 M		ASC 330-10-30-1
Cost of labor	$21.00 M	$ 5.00	$ 21.00 M		ASC 330-10-30-1
Variable production overhead	$ 6.30 M	$ 1.50	$ 6.30 M ($1.50 × 4.2 M)		ASC 330-10-30-3
Fixed production overhead	$ 5.00 M	$ 1.00 to inventory; Remainder to expense	$ 4.20 M ($1.00 × 4.2 M)	$0.80 M ($5.0 M − $4.2 M)	ASC 330-10-30-3, ASC 330-10-30-6, ASC 330-10-30-7
General and administrative expenses	$ 1.00 M	$ 0.24		$1.00 M	ASC 330-10-30-8
Selling costs	$ 4.20 M	$ 1.00		$4.20 M	ASC 330-10-30-8
Wasted materials	$ 0.25 M	$ 0.06		$0.25 M	ASC 330-10-30-7
Totals	**$79.75 M**		**$73.5 M**	**$6.25 M**	

6. Communicate the results of the research.

The following memo to the file documents the results of the research.

MEMORANDUM TO THE FILE

TO: Client File – Tough Guy Enterprises

FROM: Jane Lawson

DATE: January 10, 2018

RE: Allocation of Costs Related to Inventory

Continued

FACTS

Tough Guy Enterprises manufactures jeans and is a U.S. GAAP reporter. The company produced 4.2 million pairs of jeans in the current year and the following number of jeans over the preceding five years:

Year 1	5.0 million
Year 2	5.1 million
Year 3	4.9 million
Year 4	4.8 million
Year 5	5.2 million

Tough Guy has incurred the following expenditures related to its jean production during the current year:

Material costs per pair	$10
Labor costs per pair	$5
Variable production overhead	$6.3 million
Fixed production overhead	$5.0 million
General and administrative expenses	$1.0 million
Selling costs	$1 per pair of jeans
Cost of wasted material (spoilage)	$0.25 million

ISSUE

Which of these expenditures should Tough Guy allocate to inventory and which should it expense immediately?

ANALYSIS

ASC 330-10-30-1 indicates that inventory is typically stated at cost (i.e., the cost incurred to bring the inventory to its existing condition and location).

ASC 330-10-30-3 states that variable production overhead costs are allocated to each unit of production on the basis of the actual use of the production facilities. The allocation of fixed production overhead is based on the normal capacity of the production facility where normal capacity is defined as the production expected to be achieved over a number of periods and under normal circumstances. ASC 330-10-30-6 allows the actual level of production to be used if it approximates normal capacity.

ASC 330-10-30-6 explains that the amount of fixed overhead allocated to each unit of production should not be increased in periods of abnormally low production.

ASC 330-10-30-7 requires that unallocated overhead costs be recognized in the period they are incurred and that wasted materials (spoilage) be recognized in the period they are incurred.

ASC 330-10-30-8 stipulates that general and administrative expenses should typically be recognized as expenses if they are not clearly related to production. Also, selling costs should not be included in inventory.

CONCLUSION

The conclusions are clear in this case with one exception: fixed overhead allocation. The allocation of the fixed production overhead is more complex than the other costs. According to ASC 330-10-30-3, the allocation of fixed production overhead is based on the normal capacity of the production facility. Normal capacity is the production expected to be achieved over a number of periods and under normal circumstances. In this case, we estimate normal capacity at 5 million pairs of jeans per year, which is the average of the prior five years of production (5.0, 5.1, 4.9, 4.8, and 5.2 million). Thus, we would allocate $1 per pair of jeans to inventory (the fixed overhead of $5 million divided by the normal capacity of 5 million pairs of jeans). The total amount of fixed overhead allocated to inventory is $4.2 million ($1 per pair times 4.2 million pairs produced during the current year).

In conclusion, Tough Guy should allocate $73.5 million to inventory and expense $6.25 million immediately. Specifics of this allocation are detailed in the following table.

Expenditure	Total Cost	Cost per Pair of Jeans (based on production of 4.2 M)	Cost Allocated to Inventory	Cost Allocated to Expense	Relevant ASC Reference
Cost of material	$42.00 M	$10.00	$42.00 M		ASC 330-10-30-1
Cost of labor	$21.00 M	$ 5.00	$21.00 M		ASC 330-10-30-1
Variable production overhead	$ 6.30 M	$ 1.50	$ 6.30 M ($1.50 × 4.2 M)		ASC 330-10-30-3
Fixed production overhead	$ 5.00 M	$ 1.00 to inventory; Remainder to expense	$ 4.20 M ($1.00 × 4.2 M)	$0.80 M ($5.0 M − $4.2 M)	ASC 330-10-30-3, ASC 330-10-30-6, ASC 330-10-30-7
General and administrative expenses	$ 1.00 M	$ 0.24		$1.00 M	ASC 330-10-30-8
Selling costs	$ 4.20 M	$ 1.00		$4.20 M	ASC 330-10-30-8
Wasted materials	$ 0.25 M	$ 0.06		$0.25 M	ASC 330-10-30-7
Totals	**$79.75 M**		**$ 73.5 M**	**$6.25 M**	

Financial research cases (referred to as Surfing the Standards cases) at the end of each chapter will guide you in developing and practicing your research skills.

Summary by Learning Objectives

Here we summarize the main points by learning objective. Throughout the chapter, we discuss the accounting and reporting of U.S. GAAP and IFRS side-by-side. The following table also highlights the major similarities and differences between the standards.

1 Explain the importance and prevalence of judgment in the financial reporting process.

Summary	Similarities and Differences between U.S. GAAP and IFRS
Judgment is the process by which a decision is reached in situations in which there are multiple alternatives. Managers make many judgments in financial reporting, including: 1. Whether to report a business event, and if so, when? 2. What is the appropriate financial reporting treatment? 3. What amount should be reported in the financial statements?	Similar under U.S. GAAP and IFRS.

Summary by Learning Objectives, continued

2 Discuss the role of accountants' assumptions and estimates and the related disclosures in the financial reporting process.

Summary	Similarities and Differences between U.S. GAAP and IFRS
Managers must make assumptions and estimates in selecting accounting methods and applying accounting standards. Companies report details about the accounting policies they use in one of the first footnotes to the financial statements.	➤ IFRS further requires that companies disclose additional information about the assumptions and estimates they made at the end of the reporting period. ➤ IFRS also requires that companies disclose the judgments (apart from those involving estimates and assumptions) that management has made in determining appropriate accounting treatments for amounts reported on the financial statements (in the process of applying the company's accounting policies).

3 Identify obstacles to the use of sound judgment in preparing financial information and ways to overcome them.

Summary	Similarities and Differences between U.S. GAAP and IFRS
Obstacles are potential impediments to the use of good judgment, including: • Factors that may influence management to intentionally bias their estimates. • Cognitive biases. • Increasing complexity of the business environment and transactions. To minimize cognitive bias, auditors exercise professional skepticism, which is "an attitude that includes a questioning mind and a critical assessment of audit evidence." Cognitive biases that impact the way accountants make judgments include: • Availability bias. • Overconfidence bias. • Confirmatory bias. • Groupthink bias. • Anchoring bias. Techniques to overcome biases include: • Be organized and methodical in the decision-making process. • Generate alternatives, even when you think you have already arrived at the correct answer. • Document your rationale about the alternatives. • Delay your final judgment until you have gathered all of the facts and information and have considered all of the alternatives.	Similar under U.S. GAAP and IFRS.

Summary by Learning Objectives, continued

4 Describe the types of authoritative literature and the literature hierarchy.

Summary	Similarities and Differences between U.S. GAAP and IFRS
When the appropriate financial reporting treatment for a business transaction is unclear, accountants must research the literature and develop a recommended accounting treatment. Research is the systematic investigation into an issue. The Financial Accounting Standards Board Accounting Standards Codification (FASB ASC) contains the authoritative U.S. GAAP literature. The U.S. GAAP hierarchy has three levels: **Level 1.** Codification and all SEC rules and interpretive releases. While the Codification applies to all entities that report under U.S. GAAP, the SEC materials only apply to publicly traded registrants. **Level 2.** Authoritative rules and principles from U.S. GAAP for similar transactions. **Level 3.** Other material such as the FASB Concepts Statements, IFRS, industry practice, and textbooks.	➤ The IFRS literature is comprised of: 1. International Financial Reporting Standards (IFRS). 2. International Accounting Standards (IAS). 3. IFRS Interpretations Committee (IFRIC) Interpretations. 4. Standing Interpretations Committee (SIC) Interpretations. The IFRS hierarchy has four levels: **Level 1.** IFRS standards and interpretations that specifically apply to a transaction, event, or condition. **Level 2.** Authoritative rules from IFRS for similar and related transactions. **Level 3.** The Conceptual Framework definitions, recognition criteria, and measurement concepts for assets, liabilities, income, and expenses. **Level 4.** Recent pronouncements of other standard-setting bodies that use a similar Conceptual Framework to develop accounting standards, other accounting literature and accepted industry practices, to the extent that these do not conflict with the sources in Levels 1 and 2.

5 Outline and apply the steps in the applied financial accounting research process.

Summary	Similarities and Differences between U.S. GAAP and IFRS
There are six steps in the financial accounting research process: 1. Establish and understand the facts. 2. Identify the issue: What is the research question? 3. Search the authoritative literature. 4. Evaluate the results of the search. 5. Develop conclusions. 6. Communicate the results of the research.	Similar under U.S. GAAP and IFRS.

MyLab Accounting

Go to **http://www.pearson.com/mylab/accounting** for the following Questions, Brief Exercises, Exercises, and Problems. They are available with immediate grading, explanations of correct and incorrect answers, and interactive media that acts as your own online tutor.

3 Judgment and Applied Financial Accounting Research

Questions

1 **Q3-1.** What is judgment and when is it used by accountants?

1 3 **Q3-2.** How can management create an impediment to the exercise of good judgment?

2 **Q3-3.** Does U.S. GAAP require that companies disclose information about the assumptions and estimates they make in their financial statements? Explain.

2 **Q3-4.** Does IFRS require that companies disclose information about the assumptions and estimates they make in their financial statements? Explain.

2 **Q3-5.** Does U.S. GAAP require that companies disclose their accounting policies? Explain.

2 **Q3-6.** Does IFRS require that companies disclose their accounting policies? Explain.

3 **Q3-7.** What is the difference between the availability and confirmatory biases?

3 **Q3-8.** What types of biases are individual decision makers subject to when exercising judgment in addressing accounting issues?

4 **Q3-9.** How does the Accounting Standards Codification make the body of U.S. GAAP easier to use?

4 **Q3-10.** What is the purpose of a literature hierarchy?

4 **Q3-11.** What is the Basis for Conclusions and where can they be found for U.S. GAAP?

4 **Q3-12.** What is the Basis for Conclusions and where can they be found for IFRS?

4 5 **Q3-13.** Explain how accountants and auditors use judgment as they prepare and audit financial statements.

4 5 **Q3-14.** What is research and when is financial accounting research required?

Brief Exercises

1 2 **BE3-1. Judgment in Accounting for Accounts Receivable.** Identify areas where managers make estimates and assumptions in accounting for accounts receivable.

1 2 **BE3-2. Judgment in Accounting for Plant and Equipment.** Identify areas where managers make estimates and assumptions in accounting for plant and equipment.

3 **BE3-3. Match Each Cognitive Bias Below with Its Description.**

Availability bias	a. A phenomenon that occurs in situations where members of a group, in an attempt to avoid conflict, reach a consensus decision without considering all of the reasonable alternatives.
Overconfidence bias	b. The tendency to be more confident than your abilities and experience level would objectively warrant.
Confirmatory bias	c. The tendency to use the data that is most readily available or most easily recalled to make a decision, as opposed to considering all relevant data.
Groupthink bias	d. The decision maker focuses on one piece of information, weighting it more heavily than other pieces of information.
Anchoring bias	e. A decision maker under-weights information that is not consistent with her initial beliefs.

3 **BE3-4. Techniques to Overcome Cognitive Biases.** Explain why it is important to understand cognitive biases in decision making. Identify at least three techniques used to mitigate cognitive biases in practice.

4 **BE3-5. Literature Hierarchy**. Put the three levels of the literature hierarchy for U.S. GAAP in correct order (use 1, 2, 3):

Level	Authoritative Literature
________	Authoritative rules and principles from U.S. GAAP for similar transactions.
________	Codification and all SEC rules and interpretive releases. Whereas the Codification applies to all entities that report under U.S. GAAP, the SEC materials apply only to publicly traded registrants.
________	Other material such as the FASB Concepts Statements, IFRS, industry practice, and textbooks.

4 **BE3-6. Literature Hierarchy**. Identify the level of the literature hierarchy for U.S. GAAP to which each item belongs.

Authoritative Literature	Level 1, 2, or 3?
a. Industry practice	________
b. FASB Concepts Statements	________
c. Codification	________
d. Textbooks	________
e. Authoritative rules and principles from U.S. GAAP for similar transactions	________
f. International Financial Reporting Standards (IFRS)	________
g. SEC rules and interpretive releases	________

4 **BE3-7. IFRS Literature Hierarchy.** Put the four levels of the IFRS literature hierarchy in correct order (use 1, 2, 3, 4):

Level	Authoritative Literature
________	Recent pronouncements of other standard-setting bodies that use a similar Conceptual Framework to develop accounting standards, other accounting literature, and accepted industry practices, to the extent that these do not conflict with the other sources in Levels 1 and 2.
________	IFRS standards and interpretations that specifically apply to a transaction, event, or condition.
________	The Conceptual Framework definitions, recognition criteria, and measurement concepts for assets, liabilities, income, and expenses.
________	Authoritative rules from IFRS for similar and related transactions.

4 5 A **BE3-8. Codification Research.** Referencing Appendix A, determine the topics, subtopics and sections of the Codification for the following balance sheet events.

Balance Sheet Event	Codification Reference
a. Inventory initial measurement	________
b. Application of the lower-of-cost-or-market rule for inventory	________
c. Accounts receivable initial measurement	________
d. Application of bad debt provision	________
e. Property, plant, and equipment, initial measurement	________
f. Depreciation	________

4 5 **BE3-9. Research Process.** Explain why research is important in accounting. Discuss the research process.

5 **BE3-10. Research Process**. Put the six steps of the research process in correct order (use 1–6).

Number	Step
________	Search the authoritative literature.
________	Communicate the results of the research.
________	Establish and understand the facts.
________	Evaluate the results of the search.
________	Identify the issue: What is the research question?
________	Develop conclusions.

Exercises

1 2 **E3-1. Accounting Policy Disclosures.** To compare entities in the same industry, it is important to determine the accounting methods used by each firm. Answer the following questions regarding accounting methods.

a. Where do firms provide information about their accounting methods?

b. Provide at least two examples of the accounting methods commonly covered in your first accounting course.

3 **E3-2. Cognitive Bias**. A team of accounting students is working on a case where they are required to assess a set of information to determine a company's allowance for bad debts. The students have many pieces of information to analyze, including:

- The company's allowance for bad debts has been 5% of its receivables for the last several years.
- This year, the company has strengthened its credit extension policy.
- The average time that an accounts receivable has been outstanding has increased from 40 to 50 days this year.
- The economy has weakened over the year, with a pending recession.

Following is part of the discussion at their first team meeting. Analyze the discussion and determine the type of cognitive bias most consistent with the statements made by each student, providing an explanation for your answer.

Discussion »

Tom initiated the discussion saying, "I have seen this kind of situation before when a company has to report a higher allowance than last year. Allowances are always increasing. "

Jennifer offered, "The first piece of information in the case is always the most important. The bad debts have historically been 5%. Therefore, the allowance has to be 5%."

Jake added, "As I look at the case, I keep coming back to the fact that the average time that an account receivable has been outstanding has increased by 10 days. In my view, this is the most important piece of information—the other facts don't matter."

Marina's view was, "Even though the economy has deteriorated, the historical data is always more important. The general trends in the economy are not relevant."

3 **E3-3. Cognitive Bias**. A team of accounting students is working on a case where they are required to assess a set of information to determine the useful life used to depreciate a company's machinery used to produce smart phone cases. The students have many pieces of information to analyze, including:

- The company has used a 20-year useful life for the last several years.
- The industry average useful life for similar equipment is 15 years.
- The company purchased the equipment 5 years ago.
- The demand for smart phone cases has increased over the last several years.
- This year, the company has explored purchasing new machinery using a more efficient technology to produce the cases. This equipment would have a useful life of about 10 years.
- The average time that a machine is down for repairs has increased from 3 days to 12 days per year.

Following is part of the discussion at their first team meeting. Analyze the discussion and determine the type of cognitive bias most consistent with the statements made by each student, providing an explanation for your answer.

Discussion »

Khalil initiated the discussion saying, "Information on what the other companies in the industry are using is what is relevant. The industry average is an aggregate of all the useful lives used and represents the best overall estimate. We need to use 15 years."

Ashanti's view was, "Even though the industry average is 15 years, the company's history is most important here. The company's history is the first piece of information presented because it is the most important. What another company is doing is just not relevant. So, we do not change the 20-year useful life."

Amanda asserted, "This is obvious. Of course, the answer is 10 years. Anyone can see that. All the facts support a 10-year useful life."

Joe suggested, "Amanda is convinced the answer is 10 years and is sure about it. Khalil wants 15 years. I am not sure what the answer is, but let's take the average of 12.5 years. Can we all agree to 12.5 years? We all should be happy with this answer."

4 5 A **E3-4. Authoritative Literature.** Provide the reference to the topic, subtopic and section in the Codification where you would most likely begin your research for the following areas.

a. Determine what amount to record upon acquisition of a receivable that you received when you sold services.

b. Resolve a question related to the way in which an airline company depreciates property, plant, and equipment.

c. Determine whether to recognize a contingent loss liability.

4 5 A **E3-5. Authoritative Literature.** Provide the reference to the Codification paragraph where you can find a listing of the items that should appear in other comprehensive income.

4 5 A **E3-6. Authoritative Literature.** To what entity types does ASC 330-10: *Inventory – Overall* not apply? Provide the Codification reference.

4 5 A **E3-7. Authoritative Literature.** How does FASB define cash equivalents? Provide the Codification reference.

4 5 A **E3-8. Authoritative Literature.** What is the objective of the statement of cash flows? Provide the Codification reference.

CASES

Judgment Cases

Judgment Case 1: Judgment and Estimation Uncertainty

Unlike U.S. GAAP, IFRS requires that an entity disclose (a) management's judgments with the most significant effect on the financial statements and (b) information about the major sources of estimation uncertainty that may result in a material adjustment to the carrying values of the entity's assets and liabilities. These disclosure requirements are included in IAS 1, *Presentation of Financial Statements*. Paragraph 122 contains the requirement related to judgments, and paragraph 125 contains the requirement related to estimation uncertainty.

Read paragraphs 122 through 133 and paragraph BC83 of IAS 1.

1. What are the two examples of judgments that could have a significant impact on the financial statements?
2. What are four examples of estimation uncertainty that could result in a material adjustment in future years?
3. Consider an entity that reports an asset at fair value when the fair value is based on recently observed market prices. If it is likely that this value might change significantly within the next year, should the entity disclose the estimation uncertainty? Explain your answer.

Judgment Case 2: Estimations on the Balance Sheet

Part 1: Read paragraph OB11 of Statement of Financial Accounting Concepts No. 8, *Conceptual Framework for Financial Reporting: Chapter 1, The Objective of General Purpose Financial Reporting*, and *Chapter 3, Qualitative Characteristics of Useful Financial Information*. What does FASB say about the degree to which the balance sheet is made up of estimates as opposed to exact depictions of the underlying economic position of the entity?

Part 2: The disclosures related to critical accounting estimates and judgments were previously seen in Exhibit 3.2 for ***Telefonaktiebolaget LM Ericsson (Ericsson)***. The balance sheets are presented on the following page. Focusing on ***Ericsson's*** assets, do you agree with the FASB's assessment about the degree to which the balance sheet is made up of estimates? Explain your answer.

TELEFONAKTIEBOLAGET LM ERICSSON

DECEMBER 31, 2015

CONSOLIDATED BALANCE SHEET

December 31, SEK million	Notes	2015	2014
Assets			
Non-current assets			
Intangible assets	C10, C26		
Capitalized development expenses		SEK 5,493	SEK 3,570
Goodwill		41,087	38,330
Intellectual property rights, brands and other intangible assets		9,316	12,534
Property, plant, and equipment	C11, C26, C27	15,901	13,341
Financial assets			
Equity in joint ventures and associated companies	C12	1,210	2,793
Other investments in shares and participations	C12	1,275	591
Customer finance, non-current	C12	1,739	1,932
Other financial assets, non-current	C12	5,634	5,900
Deferred tax assets	C8	13,183	12,778
		SEK 94,838	SEK 91,769
Current assets			
Inventories	C13	SEK 28,436	SEK 28,175
Trade receivables	C14	71,069	77,893
Customer finance, current	C14	2,041	2,289
Other current receivables	C15	21,709	21,273
Short-term investments	C20	26,046	31,171
Cash and cash equivalents	C25	40,224	40,988
		189,525	201,789
Total assets		**SEK 284,363**	**SEK 293,558**
Equity and liabilities			
Equity			
Stockholders' equity	C16	SEK146,525	SEK 144,306
Non-controlling interest in equity of subsidiaries		841	1,003
		SEK 147,366	SEK 145,309
Non-current liabilities			
Post-employment benefits	C17	SEK 22,664	SEK 20,385
Provisions, non-current	C18	176	202
Deferred tax liabilities	C8	2,472	3,177
Borrowings, non-current	C19, C20	22,744	21,864
Other non-current liabilities		1,851	1,797
		SEK49,907	SEK 47,425

Continued

CONSOLIDATED BALANCE SHEET

December 31, SEK million	Notes	2015	2014
Current liabilities			
Provisions, current	C18	SEK3,662	SEK 4,225
Borrowings, current	C19, C20	2,376	2,281
Trade payables	C22	22,389	24,473
Other current liabilities	C21	58,663	69,845
		87,090	100,824
Total equity and liabilities[1]		**SEK 284,363**	**SEK 293,558**

[1] Of which interest-bearing liabilities and post-employment benefits SEK 47,784 (44,530) million.

Source: Ericsson, Financial Statements, December 31, 2015. https://www.ericsson.com/res/investors/docs/2015/ericsson-annual-report-2015-en.pdf, page 58

Surfing the Standards Cases

Surfing the Standards Case 1: U.S. GAAP Hierarchy

The third level of the U.S. GAAP Hierarchy involves nonauthoritative materials such as textbooks. Read paragraph 3 of ASC 105-10-05, *Generally Accepted Accounting Principles – Overall – Overview and Background*. What examples of nonauthoritative sources does the FASB provide?

Surfing the Standards Case 2: Inventory Disclosures

Abtos Company is a U.S. manufacturer that is publicly traded. Abtos reports $12 million of inventory on its balance sheet. Inventory includes raw materials, work-in-process, and finished goods. Is Abtos required to disclose the amounts for each class of inventory, or can it simply report the total $12 million balance on its balance sheet? Provide Codification references to support your answer to this question.

Surfing the Standards Case 3: Research Expenditures

PharmY, Inc. is a U.S. GAAP reporter that is in the pharmaceutical industry. In the current year, PharmY incurred expenditures related to laboratory experiments designed to discover a new drug. The expenditures were as follows:

Laboratory equipment that will be used for this project only	$1,000,000
Materials that will be used for this project only	750,000
Wages for employees involved exclusively in the project	500,000

Search the Codification to determine how to record each type of cost. Write a memo to the file to communicate your results.

Basis for Conclusions Cases

Basis for Conclusions Case 1: Judgment and Estimation Uncertainty

Unlike U.S. GAAP, IFRS requires that an entity disclose (a) management's judgments with the most significant effect on the financial statements and (b) information about the major sources of estimation uncertainty that may result in a material adjustment to the carrying values of the entity's assets and liabilities. These disclosure requirements are included in *IAS 1*, "Presentation of Financial Statements." Paragraph 122 contains the requirement related to judgments and paragraph 125 contains the requirement related to estimation uncertainty.

Read paragraphs BC77 through BC84 in the basis for conclusions in IAS 1. What reasons did the Board give for requiring the disclosures about judgment? What reasons did the Board give for requiring the disclosures about estimation uncertainty?

Basis for Conclusions Case 2: Income Statement or Balance Sheet?

Certain transactions require a choice about which financial statement is more important—the income statement or the balance sheet. Read paragraphs BC1.31 and BC1.32 in the basis for conclusions of Statement of Financial Accounting Concepts No. 8, *Conceptual Framework for Financial Reporting: Chapter 1, The Objective of General Purpose Financial Reporting*, and *Chapter 3, Qualitative Characteristics of Useful Financial Information*.

a. The original portion of the U.S. GAAP conceptual framework that dealt with the objectives of financial reporting (Concepts Statement 1) has now been superseded. What opinion did it express related to the importance of these two financial statements?

b. What opinion did the original IFRS conceptual framework (the *Framework*) express related to the importance of these two financial statements?

c. What opinion does the new conceptual framework under U.S. GAAP express regarding the importance of these two financial statements?

APPENDIX A
Structure of U.S. GAAP Codification

Topics in the Codification

General Principles 1XX

105 Generally Accepted Accounting Principles

Presentation 2XX

205 Presentation of Financial Statements
210 Balance Sheet
215 Statement of Shareholders Equity
220 Comprehensive Income
225 Income Statement
230 Statement of Cash Flows
235 Notes to Financial Statements
250 Accounting Changes and Error Corrections
255 Changing Prices
260 Earnings per Share
270 Interim Reporting
272 Limited Liability Entities
274 Personal Financial Statements
275 Risks and Uncertainties
280 Segment Reporting

Assets 3XX

305 Cash and Cash Equivalents
310 Receivables
320 Investments–Debt and Equity Securities
321 Investments–Equity Securities
323 Investments–Equity Method and Joint Ventures
325 Investments–Other
326 Financial Instruments–Credit Losses
330 Inventory
340 Other Assets and Deferred Costs
350 Intangibles–Goodwill and Other
360 Property, Plant, and Equipment

Liabilities 4XX

405 Liabilities
410 Asset Retirement and Environmental Obligations
420 Exit or Disposal Cost Obligations
430 Deferred Revenue
440 Commitments
450 Contingencies

460 Guarantees
470 Debt
480 Distinguishing Liabilities from Equity

Equity 5XX
505 Equity

Revenue 6XX
605 Revenue Recognition
606 Revenue from Contracts with Customers
610 Other Income

Expenses 7XX
705 Cost of Sales and Services
710 Compensation–General
712 Compensation–Nonretirement Postemployment Benefits
715 Compensation–Retirement Benefits
718 Compensation–Stock Compensation
720 Other Expenses
730 Research and Development
740 Income Taxes

Broad Transactions 8XX
805 Business Combinations
808 Collaborative Arrangements
810 Consolidation
815 Derivatives and Hedging
820 Fair Value Measurements
825 Financial Instruments
830 Foreign Currency Matters
835 Interest
840 Leases
842 Leases
845 Nonmonetary Transactions
850 Related Party Disclosures
852 Reorganizations
853 Service Concession Arrangements
855 Subsequent Events
860 Transfers and Servicing

Industry 9XX
905 Agriculture
908 Airlines
910 Contractors–Construction
912 Contractors–Federal Government
915 Development Stage Entities
920 Entertainment–Broadcasters
922 Entertainment–Cable Television

924 Entertainment–Casinos
926 Entertainment–Films
928 Entertainment–Music
930 Extractive Activities–Mining
932 Extractive Activities–Oil and Gas
940 Financial Services–Broker and Dealers
942 Financial Services–Depository and Lending
944 Financial Services–Insurance
946 Financial Services–Investment Companies
948 Financial Services–Mortgage Banking
950 Financial Services–Title Plant
952 Franchisors
954 Health Care Entities
958 Not-for-Profit Entities
960 Plan Accounting–Defined Benefit Pension Plans
962 Plan Accounting–Defined Contribution Pension Plans
965 Plan Accounting–Health and Welfare Benefit Plans
970 Real Estate–General
972 Real Estate–Common Interest Realty Associations
974 Real Estate–Real Estate Investment Trusts
976 Real Estate–Retail Land
978 Real Estate–Time-Sharing Activities
980 Regulated Operations
985 Software
995 U.S. Steamship Entities

Selected Subtopics in the Codification (excluding industries)

Topic 350 – *Intangibles–Goodwill and Other*

Subtopic 10 Overall
Subtopic 20 Goodwill
Subtopic 30 General Intangibles Other than Goodwill
Subtopic 40 Internal-Use Software
Subtopic 50 Website Development Costs

Topic 450 – *Contingencies*

Subtopic 10 Overall
Subtopic 20 Loss Contingencies
Subtopic 30 Gain Contingencies

Topic 505 – *Equity*

Subtopic 10 Overall
Subtopic 20 Stock Dividends and Stock Splits
Subtopic 30 Treasury Stock
Subtopic 50 Equity-Based Payments to Non-Employees
Subtopic 60 Spinoffs and Reverse Spinoffs

Sections in the Codification

(where XXX is Topic and YY is Subtopic)

XXX-YY-00 Status
XXX-YY-05 Overview and Background
XXX-YY-10 Objectives
XXX-YY-15 Scope and Scope Exceptions
XXX-YY-20 Glossary
XXX-YY-25 Recognition
XXX-YY-30 Initial Measurement
XXX-YY-35 Subsequent Measurement
XXX-YY-40 Derecognition
XXX-YY-45 Other Presentation Matters
XXX-YY-50 Disclosure
XXX-YY-55 Implementation Guidance and Illustrations
XXX-YY-60 Relationships
XXX-YY-65 Transition and Open Effective Date Information
XXX-YY-70 Grandfathered Guidance
XXX-YY-75 XBRL Definitions
XXX-YY-S99 SEC Materials

APPENDIX B
IFRS Standards

IFRS Current Standards and Interpretations

International Accounting Standards (IASs)

- IAS 1 Presentation of Financial Statements
- IAS 2 Inventories
- IAS 7 Statement of Cash Flows
- IAS 8 Accounting Policies, Changes in Accounting Estimates and Errors
- IAS 10 Events after the Reporting Period
- IAS 12 Income Taxes
- IAS 16 Property, Plant, and Equipment
- IAS 19 Employee Benefits
- IAS 20 Accounting for Government Grants and Disclosure of Government Assistance
- IAS 21 The Effects of Changes in Foreign Exchange Rates
- IAS 23 Borrowing Costs
- IAS 24 Related Party Disclosures
- IAS 26 Accounting and Reporting by Retirement Benefit Plans
- IAS 27 Consolidated and Separate Financial Statements
- IAS 28 Investments in Associates
- IAS 29 Financial Reporting in Hyperinflationary Economies
- IAS 32 Financial Instruments: Presentation
- IAS 33 Earnings per Share

IAS 34 Interim Financial Reporting
IAS 36 Impairment of Assets
IAS 37 Provisions, Contingent Liabilities, and Contingent Assets
IAS 38 Intangible Assets
IAS 39 Financial Instruments: Recognition and Measurement
IAS 40 Investment Property
IAS 41 Agriculture

International Financial Reporting Standards (IFRSs)

IFRS 1 First-time Adoption of International Financial Reporting Standards
IFRS 2 Share-based Payment
IFRS 3 Business Combinations
IFRS 4 Insurance Contracts
IFRS 5 Non-current Assets Held for Sale and Discontinued Operations
IFRS 6 Exploration for and Evaluation of Mineral Resources
IFRS 7 Financial Instruments: Disclosures
IFRS 8 Operating Segments
IFRS 9 Financial Instruments
IFRS 10 Consolidated Financial Statements
IFRS 11 Joint Arrangements
IFRS 12 Disclosure of Interest in Other Entities
IFRS 13 Fair Value Measurement
IFRS 14 Regulatory Deferral Accounts
IFRS 15 Revenue from Contracts With Customers
IFRS 16 Leases

Standing Interpretations Committee (SIC) Interpretations

SIC 7 Introduction of the Euro
SIC 10 Government Assistance–No Specific Relation to Operating Activities
SIC 25 Income Taxes–Changes in the Tax Status of an Enterprise or its Shareholders
SIC 29 Service Concession Arrangements: Disclosures
SIC 32 Intangible Assets–Web Site Costs

IFRS Interpretations Committee (IFRIC) Interpretations

IFRIC 1 Changes in Existing Decommissioning, Restoration and Similar Liabilities
IFRIC 2 Members' Shares in Co-operative Entities and Similar Instruments
IFRIC 5 Rights to Interest Arising from Decommissioning, Restoration, and Environmental Rehabilitation Funds
IFRIC 6 Liabilities Arising from Participating in a Specific Market—Waste Electrical and Electronic Equipment
IFRIC 7 Applying the Restatement Approach under IAS 29, *Financial Reporting in Hyperinflationary Economies*
IFRIC 10 Interim Financial Reporting and Impairment
IFRIC 12 Service Concession Arrangements
IFRIC 14 IAS 19: The Limit on a Defined Benefit Asset, Minimum Funding Requirements, and Their Interaction
IFRIC 16 Hedges of a Net Investment in a Foreign Operation
IFRIC 17 Distributions of Non-cash Assets to Owners
IFRIC 19 Extinguishing Financial Liabilities with Equity Instruments
IFRIC 20 Stripping Costs in the Production Phase of a Surface Mine
IFRIC 21 Levies

4 Review of the Accounting Cycle

LEARNING OBJECTIVES

1. Describe the accounting cycle.
2. Explain transaction analysis, including the use of the accounting equation.
3. Illustrate journalizing transactions, including determining whether to debit or credit accounts.
4. Explain the importance of and show how to post journal entries to the general ledger.
5. Explain the importance of and illustrate the preparation of an unadjusted trial balance.
6. Discuss the need for adjusting journal entries and explain deferrals and accruals.
7. Explain the use of and illustrate the preparation of an adjusted trial balance.
8. Describe the preparation of the financial statements from the adjusted trial balance.
9. Explain the difference between permanent and temporary accounts and demonstrate the process of closing temporary accounts.
10. Explain the importance of and illustrate the preparation of a post-closing trial balance.

Darryl Brooks/Alamy Stock Photo

Introduction

COMPANIES SELL MERCHANDISE, purchase inventory, and compensate employees every day—and each individual event represents a *transaction*. Consider the retailer ***Target***. In its 1,792 U.S. stores, it reported sales of over $73 billion and employed over 390,000 people in fiscal year 2015. These statistics indicate the magnitude of ***Target's*** *transactions*. For example, if ***Target*** paid each employee weekly, there would be over 20 million paychecks issued in a year.

A company's accounting system tracks all the *transactions* that occur every day and ultimately aggregates and summarizes them in publicly available financial statements. The *accounting cycle* describes the process by which a company records *transactions* in its books and summarizes their effects in the financial statements.

In this chapter, we discuss the nine steps in the *accounting cycle*. The process starts with a transaction analysis to determine whether an economic event has occurred that changes assets, liabilities, or stockholders' equity. After making this determination, a company *journalizes* transactions and *posts* them to its ledger accounts. Next, the entity ensures numerical accuracy of the process by preparing a *trial balance*. Before preparing financial statements, a company determines whether adjustments are required to ensure that it has reported all economic events occurring in that period. Finally, it prepares the financial statements and closes all *temporary accounts*.

These steps ensure that every *transaction* flows to the financial statements, enabling investors, creditors, and other financial statement users to use the statements to analyze a company's financial position and economic performance. «

❶ Describe the accounting cycle.

The Accounting Cycle

The **accounting cycle** describes the process by which a company records business *transactions* and ultimately aggregates and summarizes them in the financial statements. As a roadmap for the chapter, Exhibit 4.1 presents the nine steps in the accounting cycle. The accounting cycle steps do not depend on the accounting standards being used: Whether a company uses U.S. GAAP or IFRS, the accounting cycle begins with analyzing transactions and ends with a post-closing trial balance.

EXHIBIT 4.1 The Accounting Cycle

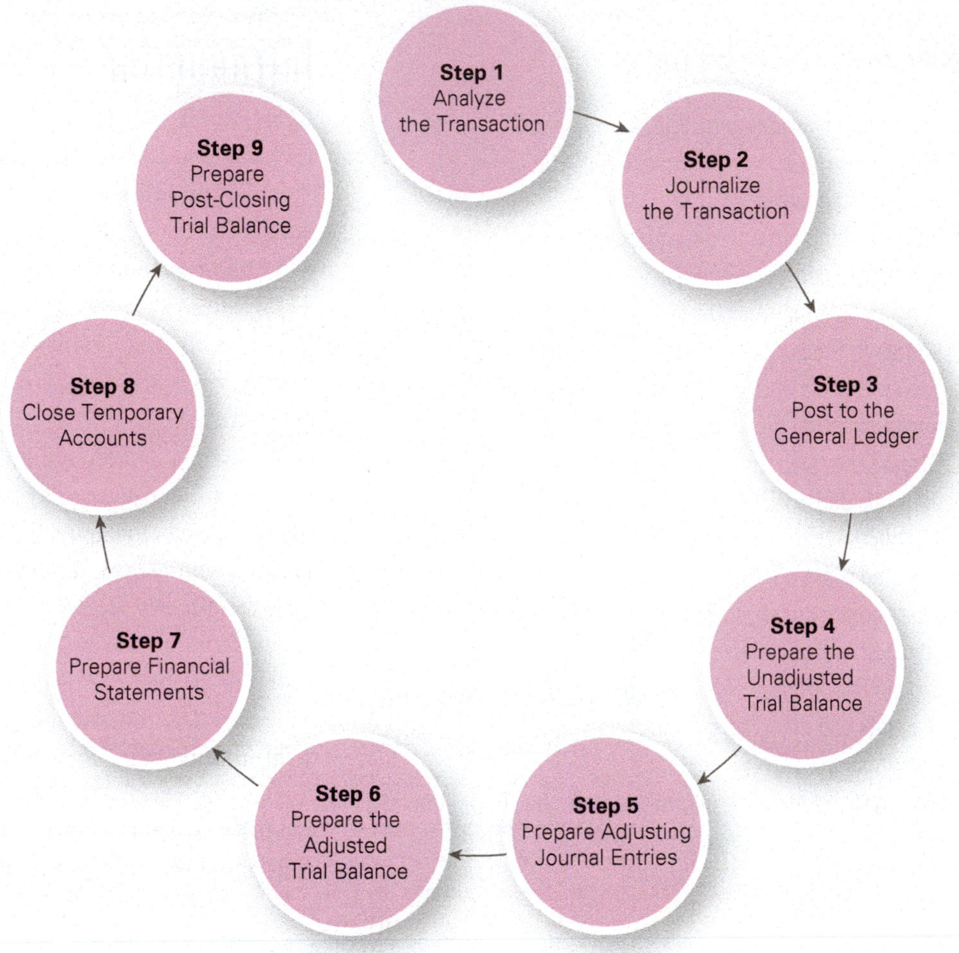

❷ Explain transaction analysis, including the use of the accounting equation.

Step 1: Analyze the Transaction

A **transaction** is an economic event that involves a change in an asset, a liability, or a stockholders' equity account that companies record in their accounting records. The *accounting equation* (also called the balance sheet equation) is initially used to analyze transactions. We begin this section by reviewing the accounting equation and then expand it to illustrate transaction analysis.

The Accounting Equation

The **accounting equation** illustrates the relationship among assets, liabilities, and stockholders' equity as follows:

$$\text{Assets} = \text{Liabilities} + \text{Stockholders' Equity} \qquad (4.1a)$$

Or, using abbreviations, this equation is:

$$A = L + E \quad (4.1b)$$

The accounting equation demonstrates that creditors and owners have claims to a company's assets. We review the definition of each element of the accounting equation in Exhibit 4.2, along with examples of each element.

EXHIBIT 4.2 Accounting Equation Definitions[1]

Element	Definition	Examples
Assets	Probable future economic benefits obtained or controlled by a particular entity as a result of past transactions or events.	Cash, receivables, inventory, buildings
Liabilities	Probable future sacrifices of economic benefits arising from present obligations of a particular entity to transfer assets or provide services to other entities in the future as a result of past transactions or events.	Accounts payable, salaries payable, notes payable, bonds payable
Stockholders' Equity	The net assets or residual interest in the assets of an entity that remains after deducting its liabilities.	Contributed capital, retained earnings, accumulated other comprehensive income

The fact that all transactions affect at least two accounts and that the accounting equation will always balance is referred to as the **double-entry system**. For example, if an asset increases, then there must be either a decrease in another asset, an increase in liabilities, or an increase in stockholders' equity.

An expanded version of the accounting equation includes the various components of stockholders' equity. Stockholders' equity in equation form is:

$$\begin{aligned}\text{Stockholders' Equity} = {} & \text{Contributed Capital} + \text{Ending Retained Earnings} \\ & + \text{Accumulated Other Comprehensive Income} \quad (4.2)\end{aligned}$$

Contributed capital consists primarily of owners' investments in the business. Accumulated other comprehensive income increases or decreases with other comprehensive income. Other comprehensive income is an additional component of comprehensive income. We introduce other comprehensive income and accumulated other comprehensive income now, due to its complexity, and we explore it in much more detail in future chapters.

Revenue and gains increase retained earnings, whereas expenses, losses, and distributions to owners (dividends) decrease retained earnings. We represent retained earnings in equation form as follows:

$$\begin{aligned}\text{Ending Retained Earnings} = {} & \text{Beginning Retained Earnings} + \text{Revenues} + \text{Gains} \\ & - \text{Expenses} - \text{Losses} - \text{Dividends Declared} \quad (4.3)\end{aligned}$$

When revenues and gains exceed expenses, losses, and dividends over time, retained earnings is positive. Retained earnings is negative when expenses, losses, and dividends exceed revenues and gains over time. A negative balance in retained earnings is called a **deficit**. We review definitions of each of these terms in Exhibit 4.3.

[1]U.S. GAAP definitions from FASB Concepts Statement No. 6, *Elements of Financial Statements*. IFRS definitions are nearly identical.

EXHIBIT 4.3 Expanded Accounting Equation Elements[2]

Element	Definition
Investments by Owners	Increases in equity of a particular business enterprise resulting from transfers to it from other entities of something valuable to obtain or increase ownership interests (or equity) in it. Assets are most commonly received as investments by owners, but that which is received may also include services or satisfaction of conversion of liabilities of the enterprise.
Distributions to Owners	Decreases in equity of a particular business enterprise resulting from transferring assets, rendering services, or incurring liabilities by the enterprise to owners. Distributions to owners decrease ownership interest (or equity) in an enterprise. Dividends are common distributions to owners.
Revenues	Inflows or other enhancements of an entity's assets or settlements of its liabilities (or a combination of both) from delivering or producing goods, rendering services, or other activities that constitute the entity's ongoing major or central operations.
Gains	Increases in equity (net assets) from an entity's peripheral or incidental transactions and from all other transactions and other events and circumstances affecting the entity except those that result from revenues or investments by owners.
Expenses	Outflows or other consumption of assets or incurrences of liabilities (or a combination of both) from delivering or producing goods, rendering services, or carrying out other activities that constitute the entity's ongoing major or central operations.
Losses	Decreases in equity (net assets) from an entity's peripheral or incidental transactions and from all other transactions and other events and circumstances affecting the entity except those that result from expenses or distributions to owners.

Exhibit 4.4 presents the components of stockholders' equity graphically. Consistent with Equation 4.2, stockholders' equity is comprised of contributed capital, ending retained earnings, and accumulated other comprehensive income. Also, ending retained earnings is equal to beginning retained earnings and is increased by net income and decreased by net losses and dividends. Net income (and net loss) is increased by revenues and gains and decreased by expenses and losses.

EXHIBIT 4.4 Components of Stockholders' Equity

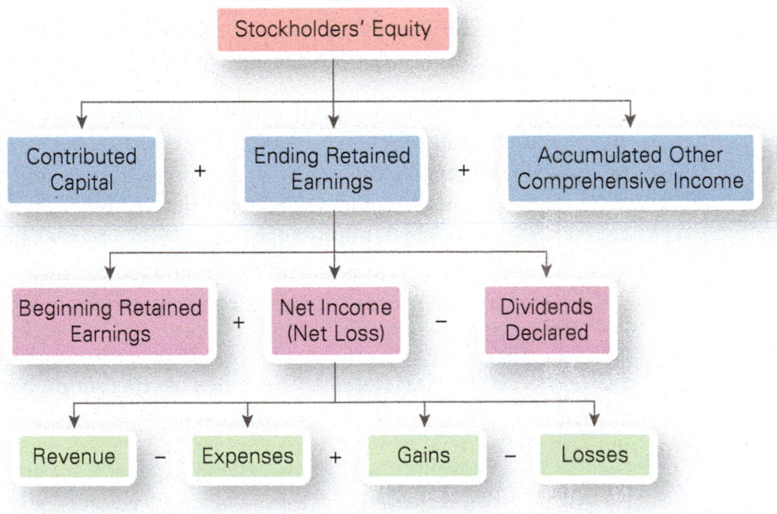

[2]U.S. GAAP definitions from FASB Concepts Statement No. 6, *Elements of Financial Statements*. IFRS definitions are somewhat different, as explained in Chapter 2, but these differences do not affect the explanations of the steps in the accounting cycle.

Given Equations 4.2 and 4.3, we expand the basic accounting equation to represent the elements of stockholders' equity as follows:

Assets	=	**Liabilities**	+	**Stockholders' Equity**										
Assets	=	Liabilities	+	Contributed Capital	+	***Ending Retained Earnings***							+	Accumulated Other Comprehensive Income
						Beginning Retained Earnings	+	Revenues and Gains	−	Expenses and Losses	−	Dividends Declared		

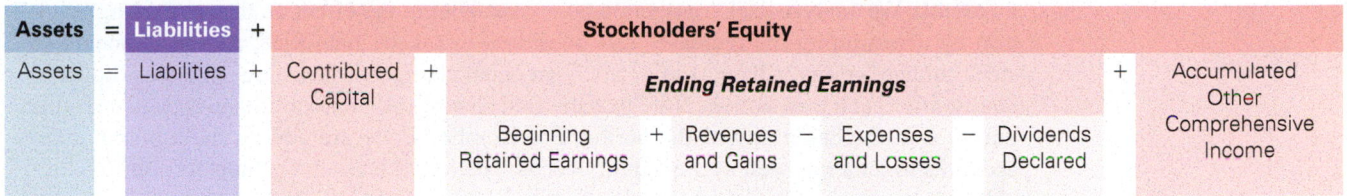

This expanded equation allows companies to analyze complex transactions.

EXAMPLE 4.1 Analysis of Transactions with the Expanded Accounting Equation

PROBLEM: Plush Service Corporation began 2018 with the following account balances.

Account	**Balance**	
Cash	$38,000	
Accounts Receivable	30,000	Total Noncash Assets = $100,000
Store Equipment	70,000	
Accounts Payable	3,000	
Legal Fees Payable	5,000	Total Liabilities = $38,000
Notes Payable	30,000	
Common Stock	60,000	
Retained Earnings	40,000	

The company engaged in the following transactions during 2018:

a. Issued an additional 10,000 shares of common stock on January 2. The stock was sold for $80,000, which equals the par value of the stock.
b. Purchased store equipment for $10,000 cash on January 3.
c. Provided services for cash of $35,000 on February 5.
d. Provided services on credit for $90,000 on February 10.
e. Received bill and paid utilities of $15,000 on February 15.
f. Sales employees worked and were paid sales salaries of $30,000 on March 1.
g. Incurred legal fees of $6,000 on April 10 but did not pay for these services.
h. Declared and paid dividends to stockholders of $2,000 on April 30.
i. Collected $25,000 for services to be provided over the coming year on June 30.
j. Paid $72,000 for a three-year insurance policy on July 10 with coverage beginning on August 1.
k. Paid $1,000 for a three-week equipment rental on September 10.
l. Collected $10,000 from the February 10 transaction on October 20.
m. Paid $1,000 of the amount owed for legal fees incurred on April 10 on November 18.

Continued

Assume that Plush Service is not subject to tax. Illustrate the effect of each transaction on the expanded accounting equation.

SOLUTION: We analyze each transaction below, explaining the effect on the accounting equation by determining the increases and decreases in assets, liabilities, and components of stockholders' equity. Changes in assets must equal changes in liabilities and stockholders' equity after each transaction. Note that the first row of the table on the next page contains balances at the beginning of the period. For simplicity, we are adding the noncash asset accounts together as well as the liability accounts. Noncash assets include accounts receivable and store equipment. Liabilities include accounts payable, legal fees payable, and notes payable.

TRANSACTIONS ANALYSIS

a. Plush received cash in exchange for equity. As a result, it will increase its assets and increase stockholders' equity through the contributed capital (common stock) account.

b. Because Plush paid cash to purchase store equipment. Store equipment increases and the asset cash decreases. This transaction changes the composition of the assets but not the total.

c. Because Plush received cash for services provided, it will increase its assets and will increase stockholders' equity through the service revenue account.

d. Plush provided services on account. Therefore, it will increase its noncash assets (for the receivable) and will also increase stockholders' equity through the service revenue account for services provided.

e. Because Plush used and paid for utilities, it will decrease the asset cash and decreases stockholders' equity by recognizing expenses.

f. Plush used and paid for the services of its employees, so it will decrease the asset cash and decrease stockholders' equity through expenses.

g. Because Plush incurred legal fees but did not yet pay for them, it will increase a liability and decrease stockholders' equity by recognizing expenses.

h. Plush declared and paid dividends. In this case, it will decrease the asset cash and decrease stockholders' equity due to the dividends declared.

i. Because Plush collected cash, it will increase the asset cash. However, Plush still owes services to the customer so it will also increase liabilities.

j. Plush acquired an asset (the benefit of an insurance policy) and paid cash. Thus, it will increase an asset, prepaid insurance, and decrease the asset cash.

k. Plush paid cash for an equipment rental. It will decrease the asset cash and increase an expense, thus decreasing equity.

l. Because Plush collected cash for amounts owed to the company, it will increase an asset, cash, and decrease another asset, accounts receivable.

m. Plush paid cash for amounts it owed for unpaid legal fees. The company will decrease the asset cash and decrease liabilities.

	Assets		= Liabilities	+ Stockholders' Equity					
					Ending Retained Earnings				
Ref	**Cash**	**Noncash Assets**	**Liabilities**	**Contributed Capital (Common Stock)**	**Beginning Retained Earnings**	**Revenues and Gains**	**Expenses and Losses**	**Dividends Declared**	**Acc. OCI***
Bal.	$38,000	$100,000	$38,000	$60,000	$40,000				
(a)	+80,000			+80,000					
(b)	−10,000	+10,000 Store Equipment							
(c)	+35,000					+35,000 Service Revenue			
(d)		+90,000 Accounts Receivable				+90,000 Service Revenue			
(e)	−15,000						−15,000 Utilities Expense		
(f)	−30,000						−30,000 Salaries Expense		
(g)			+6,000 Legal Fees Payable				−6,000 Legal Fees Expense		
(h)	−$2,000							−2,000 Dividends	
(i)	+25,000		+25,000 Unearned Service Revenues						
(j)	−72,000	+72,000 Prepaid Insurance							
(k)	−1,000						−1,000 Rental Expense		
(l)	+10,000	−10,000 Accounts Receivable							
(m)	−1,000		−1,000 Legal Fees Payable						
Bal.	$57,000	$262,000	= $68,000	$140,000	$40,000	$125,000	−$52,000	−$2,000	- 0-

Ending Retained Earnings = $111,000**

*Accumulated Other Comprehensive Income
**$40,000 + $125,000 − $52,000 − $2,000 = $111,000

❸ Illustrate journalizing transactions, including determining whether to debit or credit accounts.

Step 2: Journalize the Transactions

After analyzing the transaction, the second step in the accounting cycle is to *journalize* the transaction by formally recording the transaction in the accounting system. We will explain the journalization process, including the specific *accounts*, *debits* and *credits*, and *journal entries*.

Accounts

A company records each transaction in specific *accounts*, not just broad groupings such as assets and liabilities. An **account** is an individual record of increases and decreases in specific asset, liability, and stockholders' equity items. Exhibit 4.5 provides examples of asset, liability, and stockholders' equity accounts.

EXHIBIT 4.5 Account Examples

Account Type	Examples
Asset	Cash Accounts Receivable Inventory Prepaid Rent Building Equipment
Liability	Accounts Payable Wages Payable Notes Payable Bonds Payable
Stockholders' Equity	Common Stock Retained Earnings Sales Revenue Cost of Goods Sold Salary Expense Gain on Sale of Equipment Loss on Sale of Investments

A company's accounting system assigns each account a unique account number shown in the **chart of accounts**, a numerical listing of the account names and numbers that assists in locating the account in the ledger. The accounts are typically numbered in balance sheet order: assets, liabilities, equity, and the components of stockholders' equity including dividends, revenues, gains, expenses, and losses. Exhibit 4.6 presents a sample chart of accounts.

EXHIBIT 4.6 Sample Chart of Accounts

Assets
100 Cash 101 Accounts Receivable 102 Inventory 103 Prepaid Expenses 104 Office Supplies 150 Equipment 151 Accumulated Depreciation—Equipment 190 Other Assets
Liabilities
200 Accounts Payable 201 Tax Payable 202 Accrued Expenses Payable 210 Notes Payable
Stockholders' Equity
300 Common Stock 301 Retained Earnings 320 Dividends
Revenues
400 Sales Revenue
Expenses
500 Depreciation Expense 508 Wage Expense

Debits and Credits: A Review

Companies use *debits* and *credits* to *journalize* transactions. The terms *debit* and *credit* simply mean the left and the right side of an account, respectively—they do not imply increases or decreases. Conventions related to the type of account determine whether a debit or credit increases or decreases an account. Regardless of the accounts used to record the economic event, all transactions will result in debits being equal to credits. Just as assets equal liabilities plus stockholders' equity, debits always equal credits. This simple fact that debits equal credits forms the foundation of the double-entry system of accounting. Exhibit 4.7 presents the conventions for debits and credits in terms of increasing and decreasing accounts.

EXHIBIT 4.7 Debits and Credits

Account	Debits	Credits	Normal Balance*
Assets	Increase ↑	Decrease ↓	Debit
Liabilities	Decrease ↓	Increase ↑	Credit
Common Stock	Decrease ↓	Increase ↑	Credit
Retained Earnings	Decrease ↓	Increase ↑	Credit**
Accumulated Other Comprehensive Income	Decrease ↓	Increase ↑	Debit or Credit***
Dividends	Increase ↑	Decrease ↓	Debit
Revenues and Gains	Decrease ↓	Increase ↑	Credit
Expenses and Losses	Increase ↑	Decrease ↓	Debit

*The normal balance is the side of the account increase.

**The balance of retained earnings can be a debit when expenses, losses, and dividends exceed revenues and gains over time. A debit balance in retained earnings is called a deficit.

***Accumulated OCI will be a debit when cumulative OCI items net to a loss, or losses exceed gains. Accumulated OCI will be a credit when cumulative OCI items net to a gain, or gains exceed losses.

Asset accounts, such as cash and inventory, increase with a debit and decrease with a credit. When a company makes a sale of $400 and collects cash, it debits cash by $400. When a company pays employees, cash decreases, so it credits the cash account.

In general, liabilities and stockholders' equity increase with a credit and decrease with a debit. When a company purchases inventory on account, it credits accounts payable to reflect an increase in a liability. When the company pays its supplier the amount owed, it debits accounts payable to reflect a reduction in the liability.

Equity accounts, such as common stock and retained earnings, also increase with credits and decrease with debits. Revenues and gains are increases in equity, so these accounts will increase with credits. However, expenses and losses decrease equity, so they will increase with a debit. Similarly, dividends decrease equity so dividends also increase with debits.

The **normal balance** refers to the expected balance in an account, and it is the side that increases the value of the account. If an account increases with a debit, then its normal balance is a debit. Conversely, if an account increases by a credit, then its normal balance is a credit.

Journal Entries

Journalizing a transaction is the process of entering a transaction in the *general journal*. To journalize a transaction, companies prepare a **journal entry**, which contains the following elements in the common format:

a. The date the transaction occurred is in the first column.
b. Accounts debited are listed first and positioned at the left side. The dollar amount debited is placed in the debit column.
c. Accounts credited are recorded next and indented to the right a few spaces. The dollar amount credited is placed in the credit column.
d. A brief explanation is frequently included below the entry.

For example, Plush Service Corporation issued 10,000 shares of its common stock for $80,000 on January 2, 2018, as indicated by the following journal entry for this transaction.

Date	Account Titles and Explanations	Ref.	Debit	Credit
2018				
Jan 2	Cash		80,000	
	Common Stock			80,000
	(To record issuance of common stock)			

Companies initially record transactions in the *general journal*. The **general journal** presents transactions in chronological order with a column for the date, the account titles and explanations, reference number, debits, and credits. The column for the reference number is left blank until the entries are posted to the *general ledger* accounts, at which time the account number is included in the reference column. Because events are recorded in the general journal first, it is known as the book of original entry.

Using the general journal as the first record of the economic event has several advantages. The general journal maintains a complete record of the transaction and provides an explanation of the event when the transaction involves complex events. In addition, all economic events are listed in chronological order, facilitating the location and correction of errors.

In Example 4.2, we journalize the transactions from Example 4.1.

EXAMPLE 4.2 Journal Entries

PROBLEM: Consider the transactions for Plush Service Corporation from Example 4.1. Provide the journal entry for each transaction.

SOLUTION: We analyzed each transaction earlier. In the following journal entries, we indicate the increases and decreases in assets, liabilities, and stockholders' equity, the specific accounts affected, and whether the account is debited or credited.

		GENERAL JOURNAL		PAGE J1	
Trans*	Date	Account Titles and Explanations	Ref.	Debit	Credit
ⓐ	January 2	Cash		80,000	
		Common Stock			80,000
		(To record issuance of common stock)			
ⓑ	January 3	Store Equipment		10,000	
		Cash			10,000
		(To record purchase of store equipment)			
ⓒ	February 5	Cash		35,000	
		Service Revenue			35,000
		(To record services rendered)			
ⓓ	February 10	Accounts Receivable		90,000	
		Service Revenue			90,000
		(To record services rendered on account)			
ⓔ	February 15	Utilities Expense		15,000	
		Cash			15,000
		(To record payment for utilities)			

Trans*	Date	Account Titles and Explanations	Ref.	Debit	Credit
(f)	March 1	Salaries Expense		30,000	
		Cash			30,000
		(To record payment for salaries)			
(g)	April 10	Legal Fees Expense		6,000	
		Legal Fees Payable			6,000
		(To record incurrence of legal fees)			
(h)	April 30	Dividends		2,000	
		Cash			2,000
		(To record the declaration and payment for dividends)			
(i)	June 30	Cash		25,000	
		Unearned Service Revenue			25,000
		(To record receipt of payment for future services)			
(j)	July 10	Prepaid Insurance		72,000	
		Cash			72,000
		(To record payment for insurance)			
(k)	September 10	Rental Expense		1,000	
		Cash			1,000
		(To record payment for equipment rental)			
(l)	October 20	Cash		10,000	
		Accounts Receivable			10,000
		(To record the receipt of amounts due)			
(m)	November 18	Legal Fees Payable		1,000	
		Cash			1,000
		(To record the payment of amounts owed)			

**For reference only and not part of the recording process.*

4 Explain the importance of and show how to post journal entries to the general ledger.

Step 3: Post to the General Ledger

The next step in the accounting cycle is to *post* the journal entries to the *general ledger*. The **general ledger** contains all accounts maintained by the company with each account reflecting its increases, decreases, and balance. Each account is maintained in a single location for management analysis. An account has a debit balance if debits exceed credits, and a credit balance when credits are greater than debits. The account has a zero balance if debits equal credits.

Posting is the process of transferring information contained in journal entries to the individual ledger accounts. Each general ledger account has a column for the date, explanation, reference, debit, credit, and balance. The reference is the general journal page number.

The typical general ledger account has three money columns with the account balance determined after each journal entry is posted. The reference column, which contains the general journal page number, is completed when the event is posted from the journal to the ledger. For example, Exhibit 4.8 illustrates Plush Service Corporation's posting of the journal entry to the general ledger for the common stock issued on January 2, 2018. The balance in the cash account, No. 100, increases by $80,000 to $118,000. The balance in the common stock account, No. 300, also increases by $80,000 to $140,000. The reference column in the general ledger indicates the entry is from page J1 of the general journal.

EXHIBIT 4.8 Posting a Transaction from the General Journal to the General Ledger

GENERAL JOURNAL

PAGE J1

Date	Account Titles and Explanations	Ref.	Debit	Credit
2018				
Jan 2	Cash	100	80,000	
	Common Stock	300		80,000
	(To record issuance of common stock)			

GENERAL LEDGER

Cash — No. 100

Date	Explanation	Ref.	Debit	Credit	Balance
2018					
Balance					38,000
Jan 2	Issued common stock	J1	80,000		118,000

Common Stock — No. 300

Date	Explanation	Ref.	Debit	Credit	Balance
2018					
Balance					60,000
Jan 2	Issued common stock	J1		80,000	140,000

In Example 4.3, we post the journal entries made in Example 4.2.

EXAMPLE 4.3 Posting Journal Entries to the General Ledger

PROBLEM: Consider the transactions and beginning balances for Plush Service Corporation from Example 4.1. Post the journal entries from Example 4.2 to the general ledger.

SOLUTION:

GENERAL LEDGER

Cash — ***No. 100***

Date	Explanation	Ref.	Debit	Credit	Balance
2018					
Balance					38,000
Jan 2	Issued common stock		80,000		118,000
Jan 3	Purchased store equipment			10,000	108,000
Feb 5	Received cash for services provided		35,000		143,000
Feb 15	Paid for utilities			15,000	128,000
Mar 1	Paid salaries			30,000	98,000
Apr 30	Paid dividends			2,000	96,000
June 30	Received cash in advance of services		25,000		121,000
July 10	Paid insurance			72,000	49,000
Sept 10	Paid for equipment rental			1,000	48,000
Oct 20	Collected account receivable		10,000		58,000
Nov 18	Paid legal fees			1,000	57,000

Accounts Receivable — ***No. 101***

Date	Explanation	Ref.	Debit	Credit	Balance
2018					
Balance					30,000
Feb 10	Provided services on account		90,000		120,000
Oct 20	Collected account receivable			10,000	110,000

		Prepaid Insurance			No. 102
Date	**Explanation**	**Ref.**	**Debit**	**Credit**	**Balance**
2018					
July 10	Paid for insurance		72,000		72,000

		Store Equipment			No. 150
Date	**Explanation**	**Ref**	**Debit**	**Credit**	**Balance**
2018					
Balance					70,000
Jan 3	Purchased store equipment		10,000		80,000

		Accounts Payable			No. 200
Date	**Explanation**	**Ref.**	**Debit**	**Credit**	**Balance**
2018					
Balance					3,000

		Legal Fees Payable			No. 201
Date	**Explanation**	**Ref.**	**Debit**	**Credit**	**Balance**
2018					
Balance					5,000
Apr 10	Incurred legal expenses			6,000	11,000
Nov 18	Paid for legal fees		1,000		10,000

		Unearned Service Revenue			No. 202
Date	**Explanation**	**Ref.**	**Debit**	**Credit**	**Balance**
2018					
June 30	Received cash in advance of services			25,000	25,000

		Notes Payable			No. 210
Date	**Explanation**	**Ref.**	**Debit**	**Credit**	**Balance**
2018					
Balance					30,000

		Common Stock			No. 300
Date	**Explanation**	**Ref.**	**Debit**	**Credit**	**Balance**
2018					
Balance					60,000
Jan 2	Issued common stock			80,000	140,000

		Retained Earnings			No. 301
Date	**Explanation**	**Ref.**	**Debit**	**Credit**	**Balance**
2018					
Balance					40,000

Continued

	Dividends				No. 320
Date	**Explanation**	**Ref.**	**Debit**	**Credit**	**Balance**
2018					
April 30	Declared cash dividends		2,000		2,000

	Service Revenue				No. 400
Date	**Explanation**	**Ref.**	**Debit**	**Credit**	**Balance**
2018					
Feb 5	Provided services			35,000	35,000
Feb 10	Provided services on account			90,000	125,000

	Utilities Expense				No. 501
Date	**Explanation**	**Ref.**	**Debit**	**Credit**	**Balance**
2018					
Feb 15	Incurred utilities expense		15,000		15,000

	Salaries Expense				No. 502
Date	**Explanation**	**Ref.**	**Debit**	**Credit**	**Balance**
2018					
Mar 1	Incurred salaries expense		30,000		30,000

	Legal Fees Expense				No. 504
	Explanation	**Ref.**	**Debit**	**Credit**	**Balance**
2018					
Apr 10	Incurred legal fees expense		6,000		6,000

	Rental Expense				No. 506
Date	**Explanation**	**Ref.**	**Debit**	**Credit**	**Balance**
2018					
Sept 10	Incurred rental expense		1,000		1,000

The T-Account

We typically do not use the formal general ledger accounts when presenting illustrations in the text. Rather, we use a simplified version of the ledger accounts known as **t-accounts** with three main parts:

1. The account title,
2. A left (debit) side, and
3. A right (credit) side.

Exhibit 4.9 presents a sample t-account.

We will use the t-account rather than formal general ledger accounts for the remainder of the chapter.

EXHIBIT 4.9 T-Account

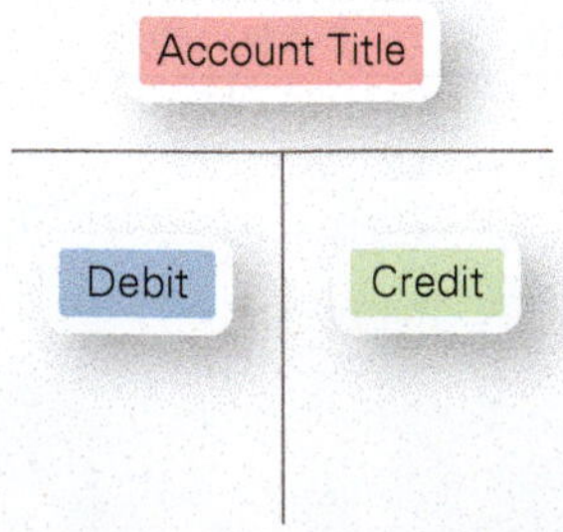

5 Explain the importance of and illustrate the preparation of an unadjusted trial balance.

Step 4: Prepare the Unadjusted Trial Balance

Throughout the accounting cycle, companies prepare several *trial balances*. A **trial balance** is a listing of the accounts and their ending debit or credit balances at a point in time. The accounts are listed with the balance sheet accounts first (assets, liabilities, and stockholders' equity), followed by dividends and the income statement accounts (revenues, gains, expenses, and losses).

The trial balance provides a check on the recording process by ensuring the equality of debits and credits; however, it does not prove the accuracy of the recording process. Debits can equal credits while numerous errors exist. For example, a trial balance will not reveal the following errors:

- A transaction that is not journalized.
- A correct journal entry that is not posted.
- An entry that is posted twice.
- The debiting or crediting of incorrect accounts.
- The debiting and crediting of incorrect dollar amounts.

After completing the posting process, the company prepares the **unadjusted trial balance**, an initial listing of all accounts and their debt or credit balances. Note that an unadjusted trial balance may not reflect all of a company's events and transactions because it has not made the *adjusting journal entries* at the time it prepares the unadjusted trial balance. For example, if equipment has not been depreciated throughout the accounting period, an adjusting entry to record depreciation in the current period will be recorded after the unadjusted trial balance is prepared. Example 4.4 illustrates preparing an unadjusted trial balance.

EXAMPLE 4.4

Unadjusted Trial Balance

PROBLEM: Using the information in Example 4.3, prepare an unadjusted trial balance for Plush Service Corporation.

SOLUTION: We take the ending balances in each of the accounts from the solution to Example 4.3 to prepare the trial balance, as presented here:

Plush Service Corporation
Unadjusted Trial Balance
At December 31, 2018

Account	Account #	Debit	Credit
Cash	100	$ 57,000	
Accounts Receivable	101	110,000	
Prepaid Insurance	102	72,000	
Store Equipment	150	80,000	
Accounts Payable	200		$ 3,000
Legal Fees Payable	201		10,000
Unearned Service Revenue	202		25,000
Notes Payable	210		30,000
Common Stock	300		140,000
Retained Earnings	301		40,000
Dividends	320	2,000	
Service Revenue	400		125,000
Utilities Expense	501	15,000	
Salaries Expense	502	30,000	
Legal Fees Expense	504	6,000	
Rental Expense	506	1,000	
Totals		$373,000	$373,000

6 Discuss the need for adjusting journal entries and explain deferrals and accruals.

Step 5: Prepare Adjusting Journal Entries

The unadjusted trial balance may not reflect all of a company's events and transactions because the *adjusting journal entries* have not been made. **Adjusting journal entries** are entries made to ensure that all revenues are recognized in the period when control of a good or service has passed to the customer, and all expenses are recognized in the period incurred. Adjusting journal entries are necessary because U.S. GAAP requires that financial information be reported using the *accrual basis* of accounting. The company prepares the *adjusted trial balance* after making all adjusting journal entries and posting these entries to the ledger accounts at the end of the reporting period. The **adjusted trial balance** is the listing of all accounts and their ending debit or credit balances after making the adjusting journal entries.

Cash versus Accrual Bases of Accounting

The *cash basis* of accounting is not acceptable for financial reporting under U.S. GAAP. Under the **cash basis**, companies recognize revenues only when cash is received and expenses only when cash is paid. This approach of revenue and expense recognition measures only cash receipts and disbursements but does not accurately measure the economic activity underlying cash receipts and payments.

Under the **accrual basis**, companies recognize revenues when control of a good or service has passed to the customer, regardless of when cash is received. Expenses are recognized when incurred, regardless of when cash is paid. Because U.S. GAAP requires the preparation of financial statements under the accrual basis and companies present these financial statements throughout the life of the firm, *adjusting journal entries* are needed at the end of each reporting period. Companies record adjusting journal entries (AJEs) to ensure that all economic events are properly reflected in the financial statements. Every AJE will impact one balance sheet account and one income statement account.

Adjusting journal entries involve accounting for both *deferrals* and *accruals*.

Deferrals

Deferrals occur when a company receives or pays cash before recognizing the revenue or expense in the financial statements. AJEs are required for both deferred expenses and deferred revenues.

Deferred Expenses. A **deferred expense** occurs when a company makes a cash payment before incurring an expense under accrual basis accounting. For example, paying rent on the first of the year for occupancy of a building during that year creates a deferred expense. The cash payment occurs on the first day of the year, but the expense is incurred ratably over the year. Thus, the company should not record the full amount of the expense until the end of the year. Deferred expenses are also referred to as **prepaid expenses**.

Companies record deferred expenses as assets until they are used or consumed in operations. Therefore, an adjusting journal entry for deferred expenses will cause a change in both an asset and an expense account as the asset is derecognized and the expense is recognized. Examples of deferred expenses include prepaid rent, prepaid insurance, supplies, and depreciation. Exhibit 4.10 illustrates this asset-expense relationship.

If the company does not adjust the prepaid expense, it will overstate assets and understate expenses. The adjusting journal entry results in a debit to an expense account and a credit to an asset account. It may be the case that the company initially records the cash payment as an expense, a scenario we discuss in Appendix A.

Depreciation and *amortization* are other types of deferred expenses. **Depreciation** is the systematic and rational allocation of the cost of a long-term operating asset to expense over the asset's expected useful life. **Amortization** is the systematic and rational allocation of the cost of an intangible asset to expense over the asset's expected useful life.

When a company purchases a long-term operating asset, it records the asset with a debit. As the company uses the asset over time, the company reports an expense on the income statement, debiting expense. It also reduces the carrying value of the asset by the same amount. In the case of depreciation, the credit to reduce the value of the asset is to an account referred to as accumulated depreciation. Accumulated depreciation is a **contra-asset account**, which is an asset account that has a normal credit balance. The contra-asset accumulated depreciation directly offsets the asset account, and the net value of the two accounts is the asset's net carrying value. In the case of amortization, the company may credit an accumulated amortization account or the intangible asset account directly.[3] Example 4.5 presents preparing an adjusting journal entry for a deferred expense.

EXHIBIT 4.10 Deferred Expenses

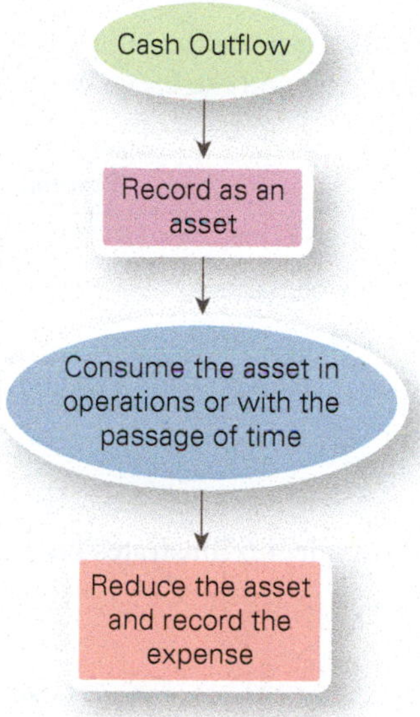

EXAMPLE 4.5

Deferred Expenses

PROBLEM: Plush Service Corporation paid $72,000 for a three-year insurance policy on July 10 with coverage beginning on August 1. As we saw in Example 4.2, on the date it purchased the insurance, Plush made the following journal entry:

Date	Account	Debit	Credit
July 10	Prepaid Insurance	72,000	
	Cash		72,000
	(To record payment for insurance)		

What adjusting journal entry is needed on December 31? Prepare the t-accounts for prepaid insurance and insurance expense both before and after the adjusting journal entry.

SOLUTION: The t-accounts for the prepaid insurance and insurance expense accounts would appear as follows on December 31 before Plush records the adjusting journal entry and posts to the t-accounts.

Prepaid Insurance

July 10	72,000	
	72,000	

Insurance Expense

0	
0	

Continued

[3]We discuss depreciation and amortization in more depth in Chapter 11.

On December 31, insurance expense is understated because Plush has received five months' insurance coverage and that portion of the coverage has expired. Prepaid insurance is overstated because there are only 31 of the 36 months of prepaid insurance remaining. In order to adjust the prepaid insurance account, Plush must prepare the following adjusting journal entry:

Date	Account	Debit	Credit
Dec 31	Insurance Expense ($72,000/36 mos.) × 5 mos.	10,000	
	Prepaid Insurance		10,000
	(To record expired insurance)		

After Plush posts the adjusting journal entry, the t-accounts will reflect the correct balances of the asset and the expense:

Prepaid Insurance

	Debit	Credit
July 10	72,000	
Unadjusted Balance	72,000	
AJE, Dec 31		10,000
Adjusted Balance	62,000	

Insurance Expense

	Debit	Credit
Unadjusted Balance	0	
AJE, Dec 31	10,000	
Adjusted Balance	10,000	

Example 4.6 illustrates recording depreciation expense.

EXAMPLE 4.6 Depreciation Expense

PROBLEM: Plush Service Corporation depreciates its store equipment at a rate of $8,000 per year. Provide the adjusting journal entry to record depreciation for the current year.

SOLUTION: Plush debits an expense account and credits accumulated depreciation for $8,000.

Date	Account	Debit	Credit
Dec 31	Depreciation Expense—Store Equipment	8,000	
	Accumulated Depreciation—Store Equipment		8,000
	(To record annual depreciation expense on equipment)		

Deferred Revenues. A **deferred revenue** occurs when a company receives cash before revenue should be recognized in the financial statements under accrual basis accounting. That is, deferred revenue represents cash that has been received before the occurrence of the underlying economic event that generates revenue. For example, a company receiving cash in advance for an online magazine subscription records deferred revenue. The cash receipt occurs on the first day of the year, but the revenue is recognized only when the magazine is made available for use (i.e., delivered) over the subscription period. Thus, the company should not record the full amount of the revenue until the product has been provided over the entire term of the subscription. Deferred revenues are also referred to as **unearned revenues** or **advance collections**.

Companies record unearned revenues as liabilities until control of a good or service passes to the customer. Therefore, an adjusting journal entry for unearned revenues will cause a change in both a liability and a revenue account as the liability is derecognized and the revenue is recognized. Examples of unearned revenues include advance collections of insurance, rent, and subscriptions. Exhibit 4.11 illustrates this liability-revenue relationship.

EXHIBIT 4.11 Deferred Revenues

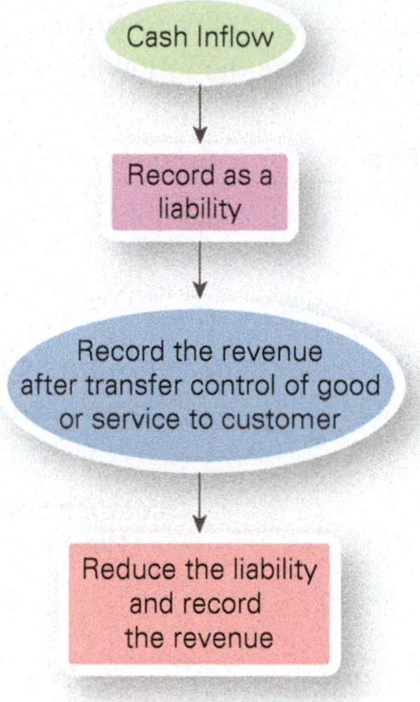

If the company does not adjust unearned revenue, it overstates liabilities and understates revenues. The adjusting journal entry results in a debit to a liability account and a credit to a revenue account. It may be the case that the company initially records the cash receipt as revenue, a scenario we discuss in Appendix A. Example 4.7 presents preparing an adjusting journal entry for a deferred revenue situation.

EXAMPLE 4.7 Deferred Revenues

PROBLEM: Plush Service Corporation collected $25,000 on June 30, 2018, for services to be provided over the next 12 months.

Plush estimated that 30% of the service fees collected in advance had been performed by the end of the year. As illustrated in Example 4.2, on the date it received the cash, Plush made the following journal entry to increase cash, an asset, and increase unearned service revenue, a liability:

Date	Account	Debit	Credit
June 30	Cash	25,000	
	Unearned Service Revenue		25,000
	(To record receipt of payment for future services)		

What adjusting journal entry is needed on December 31? Prepare the t-accounts for unearned service revenue and service revenue both before and after the adjusting journal entry.

SOLUTION: The t-accounts for the unearned service revenue and service revenue accounts would appear as follows on December 31 before Plush records the adjusting journal entry and posts it to the t-accounts.

	Unearned Service Revenue (Debit)	Unearned Service Revenue (Credit)	Service Revenue (Debit)	Service Revenue (Credit)	
June 30		25,000		35,000	Feb 5
				90,000	Feb 10
Dec 31		25,000		125,000	Dec 31

Continued

On December 31, service revenue is understated because a portion of the unearned revenue has now been performed. Plush determines that $7,500 should be recorded as service revenue (30% × $25,000). In order to adjust the unearned service revenue liability account, Plush must prepare the following adjusting journal entry:

Date	*Account*	*Debit*	*Credit*
Dec 31	Unearned Service Revenue	7,500	
	Service Revenue		7,500
	(To record revenue for services performed)		

After posting the adjusting journal entries, Plush's accounts will reflect the correct balances of the liability and the revenue.

Unearned Service Revenue

	Debit	Credit
June 30		25,000
Unadjusted Balance		25,000
AJE, Dec 31	7,500	
Adjusted Balance		17,500

Service Revenue

	Debit	Credit	
		35,000	Feb. 5
		90,000	Feb. 10
Unadjusted Balance		125,000	
AJE, Dec 31		7,500	
Adjusted Balance		132,500	

Accruals

Accruals occur when the economic event that gives rise to revenue or expenses occurs before the cash is received or paid. The two types of accruals are *accrued revenues* and *accrued expenses.*

Accrued Revenues. **Accrued revenues** occur when control of the good or service has passed to the customer but the seller has not yet received cash. For example, a wholesaler may deliver goods to a retailer on credit. In this case, there is an unrecorded asset (a receivable) and an unrecognized revenue. So, both assets and revenues are understated until the company makes an adjusting journal entry. Exhibit 4.12 presents this asset-revenue relationship.

EXHIBIT 4.12 Accrued Revenues

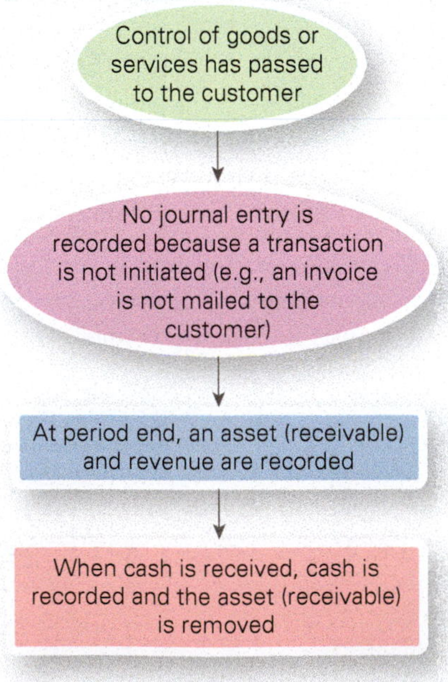

If the company does not adjust accrued revenue, then assets and revenues are both understated. The adjusting journal entry is needed to debit the asset account and credit the revenue account. Once the cash is received, the company debits cash and credits the asset (receivable) account.

EXAMPLE 4.8 Accrued Revenues

PROBLEM: On December 31, Plush Service Corporation received an invoice from a field technician indicating that services amounting to $35,000 had been provided but not yet billed to customers.

What adjusting journal entry is needed as of the end of the accounting period? Prepare the t-accounts for accounts receivable and service revenue earned both before and after the adjusting journal entry.

SOLUTION: Without the adjusting journal entry, Plush's assets and revenues are both understated. Currently, Plush has not prepared any journal entries related to this transaction.

Accounts Receivable

	Debit	Credit	
Bal.	30,000		
Feb 10	90,000		
		10,000	Oct 20
Unadjusted Bal. Dec 31	110,000		

Service Revenue

	Debit	Credit
Balance from Example 4.7		132,500
Unadjusted Bal. Dec 31		132,500

On December 31, an adjusting journal entry is required that will debit accounts receivable and credit service revenue.

Date	*Account*	*Debit*	*Credit*
Dec 31	Accounts Receivable	35,000	
	Service Revenue		35,000
	(To record revenue for services performed)		

Thus, at the end of the accounting period, the adjusted balances in these accounts are correct.

Accounts Receivable

	Debit	Credit	
Bal.	30,000		
Feb 10	90,000		
		10,000	Oct 20
Unadjusted Balance	110,000		
AJE, Dec 31	35,000		
Adjusted Balance	145,000		

Service Revenue

	Debit	Credit
Balance from Example 4.7		132,500
Unadjusted Balance		132,500
AJE, Dec 31		35,000
Adjusted Balance		167,500

Accrued Expenses. **Accrued expenses** occur when a company has incurred expenses but has not paid cash. For example, companies may incur an utility expense before a bill is received at the end of the month, and that amount remains unpaid at the end of the accounting period. Other common examples of accrued expenses are salaries and interest. In these cases, there is an unrecorded liability (a payable) and an unrecognized expense. The company understates both liabilities and expenses until it makes the adjusting journal entry. Exhibit 4.13 presents this liability-expense relationship.

EXHIBIT 4.13 Accrued Expenses

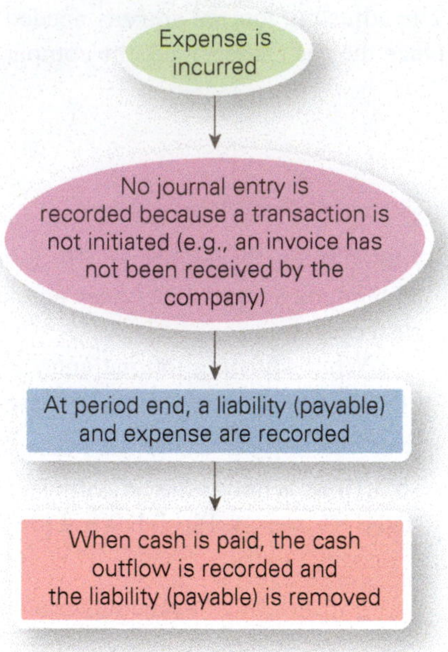

The adjusting journal entry debits the expense account and credits the liability account. Once cash is paid, the company debits the liability (payable) and credits cash.

EXAMPLE 4.9 Accrued Expenses

PROBLEM: Plush Service Corporation incurs salaries of $4,000 at the end of the year. The next payroll date is January 2 of the following year.

What adjusting journal entry is needed as of the end of the accounting period on December 31? Prepare the t-accounts for salaries payable and salaries expense both before and after the adjusting journal entry.

SOLUTION: Without the adjusting journal entry, Plush's liabilities and expenses are both understated. Currently, Plush has not prepared any journal entries related to this transaction.

	Salaries Payable	
		0
Unadjusted Balance		0

	Salaries Expense	
Mar 1	30,000	
Unadjusted Balance	30,000	

On December 31, an adjusting journal entry is required that will debit salaries expense and credit salaries payable.

Date	*Account*	*Debit*	*Credit*
Dec 31	Salaries Expense	4,000	
	Salaries Payable		4,000
	(To accrue salaries incurred)		

Thus, at the end of the accounting period, the adjusted balances in these accounts are correct.

	Salaries Payable	
		0
Unadjusted Balance		0
AJE, Dec 31		4,000
Adjusted Balance		4,000

	Salaries Expense	
Mar 1	30,000	
Unadjusted Balance	30,000	
AJE, Dec 31	4,000	
Adjusted Balance	34,000	

Exhibit 4.14 summarizes the different types of adjusting journal entries.

EXHIBIT 4.14 Summary of Adjusting Journal Entries

Adjustment	Need for Adjustment	Over/Understatement Prior to Adjustment	Adjusting Journal Entry
Deferred (Prepaid) Expense	Deferred cost originally recorded as an asset is now fully or partially used or expired.	Asset overstated Expense understated	Dr: Expense Cr: Asset
Deferred (Unearned) Revenue	Deferred revenues originally recorded as a liability are now recorded as revenue when transfer control of good or service to customer.	Liability overstated Revenue understated	Dr: Liability Cr: Revenue
Accrued Expense	Expenses incurred but unrecorded at the end of the accounting period.	Liability understated Expense understated	Dr: Expense Cr: Liability
Accrued Revenue	Revenues should be recorded but unrecorded at the end of the accounting period.	Asset understated Revenue understated	Dr: Asset Cr: Revenue

7 Explain the use of and illustrate the preparation of an adjusted trial balance.

Step 6: Prepare the Adjusted Trial Balance

Companies prepare *adjusted trial balances* after journalizing and posting all adjusting journal entries. Similar to the unadjusted trial balance, the *adjusted trial balance* lists all accounts and ending balances, including the accounts created during the adjustment process. Like the unadjusted trial balance, the adjusted trial balance ensures the equality of debits and credits after adjusting journal entries are made but cannot be used to prove the accuracy of the financial information included in the accounts. Note that the accounts included in the adjusted trial balance contain all the data needed to prepare the financial statements.

EXAMPLE 4.10

Adjusted Trial Balance

PROBLEM: Consider Plush Service Corporation from our prior examples. Prepare t-accounts that begin with the unadjusted balances from the unadjusted trial balance. Post the adjusting journal entries to the t-accounts and determine the adjusted balances. Prepare an adjusted trial balance at December 31, 2018.

SOLUTION:

Cash	Debit	Credit
Unadjusted Balance	57,000	
Adjusted Balance	57,000	

Accounts Receivable	Debit	Credit
Unadjusted Balance	110,000	
Ex. 4.8 Adjusting Entry	35,000	
Adjusted Balance	145,000	

Prepaid Insurance	Debit	Credit
Unadjusted Balance	72,000	
Ex. 4.5 Adjusting Entry		10,000
Adjusted Balance	62,000	

Store Equipment	Debit	Credit
Unadjusted Balance	80,000	
Adjusted Balance	80,000	

Accumulated Depreciation	Debit	Credit
Unadjusted Balance		0
Ex. 4.6 Adjusting Entry		8,000
Adjusted Balance		8,000

Accounts Payable	Debit	Credit
Unadjusted Balance		3,000
Adjusted Balance		3,000

Continued

Legal Fees Payable

	Debit	Credit
Unadjusted Balance		10,000
Adjusted Balance		10,000

Unearned Service Revenue

	Debit	Credit
Unadjusted Balance		25,000
Ex. 4.7 Adjusting Entry	7,500	
Adjusted Balance		17,500

Salaries Payable

	Debit	Credit
Unadjusted Balance		0
Ex. 4.9 Adjusting Entry		4,000
Adjusted Balance		4,000

Notes Payable

	Debit	Credit
Unadjusted Balance		30,000
Adjusted Balance		30,000

Common Stock

	Debit	Credit
Unadjusted Balance		140,000
Adjusted Balance		140,000

Retained Earnings

	Debit	Credit
Unadjusted Balance		40,000
Adjusted Balance		40,000

Dividends

	Debit	Credit
Unadjusted Balance	2,000	
Adjusted Balance	2,000	

Service Revenue

	Debit	Credit
Unadjusted Balance		125,000
Ex. 4.7 Adjusting Entry		7,500
Ex. 4.8 Adjusting Entry		35,000
Adjusted Balance		167,500

Utilities Expense

	Debit	Credit
Unadjusted Balance	15,000	
Adjusted Balance	15,000	

Salaries Expense

	Debit	Credit
Unadjusted Balance	30,000	
Ex. 4.9 Adjusting Entry	4,000	
Adjusted Balance	34,000	

Legal Fees Expense

	Debit	Credit
Unadjusted Balance	6,000	
Adjusted Balance	6,000	

Rental Expense

	Debit	Credit
Unadjusted Balance	1,000	
Adjusted Balance	1,000	

Insurance Expense

	Debit	Credit
Unadjusted Balance	0	
Ex. 4.5 Adjusting Entry	10,000	
Adjusted Balance	10,000	

Depreciation Expense—Store Equipment

	Debit	Credit
Unadjusted Balance	0	
Ex. 4.6 Adjusting Entry	8,000	
Adjusted Balance	8,000	

The adjusted trial balance for Plush Service Corporation is presented on the next page.

Plush Service Corporation
Adjusted Trial Balance
At December 31, 2018

Account	Account #	Debit	Credit
Cash	100	$ 57,000	
Accounts Receivable	101	145,000	
Prepaid Insurance	102	62,000	
Store Equipment	150	80,000	
Accumulated Depreciation—Store Equipment	151		$ 8,000
Accounts Payable	200		3,000
Legal Fees Payable	201		10,000
Unearned Service Revenue	202		17,500
Salaries Payable	204		4,000
Notes Payable	210		30,000
Common Stock	300		140,000
Retained Earnings	301		40,000
Dividends	320	2,000	
Service Revenue	400		167,500
Utilities Expense	501	15,000	
Salaries Expense	502	34,000	
Legal Fees Expense	504	6,000	
Rental Expense	506	1,000	
Insurance Expense	507	10,000	
Depreciation Expense—Store Equipment	508	8,000	
Totals		$420,000	$420,000

8 Describe the preparation of the financial statements from the adjusted trial balance.

Step 7: Prepare Financial Statements

After completing the adjusted trial balance, the company can prepare financial statements, a process we explore in depth in subsequent chapters. First, it prepares the statement of net income, which presents the financial results of operations, using the revenue and expense accounts.[4] Next, the company uses the resulting net income for the period, along with the equity accounts, to prepare the statement of stockholders' equity. The balance sheet includes all assets, liabilities, common stock, and the ending retained earnings balance obtained from the statement of stockholders' equity. The final step is preparing the statement of cash flows.[5]

Accountants occasionally use a worksheet to facilitate the preparation of the adjusting entries and financial statements (see Appendix B). Accountants may also use reversing entries as part of the accounting cycle (see Appendix C).

Exhibit 4.15 presents the sequence of financial statement preparation.

[4] We will not consider the statement of comprehensive income in this chapter. We will cover comprehensive income in depth in Chapter 5.

[5] The statement of cash flows is excluded from this illustration. We will discuss the statement of cash flows in subsequent chapters.

EXHIBIT 4.15 Sequence of Preparation of Financial Statements

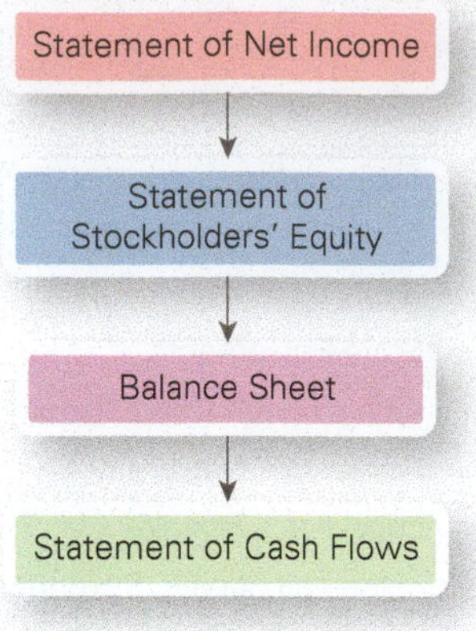

EXAMPLE 4.11 Financial Statements

PROBLEM: Using the adjusted trial balance for Plush Service Corporation in Example 4.10, prepare a statement of net income, a statement of stockholders' equity, and a balance sheet.

SOLUTION: The financial statements are presented here. We first identify the income statement accounts and include them on the statement of net income. Net income is computed as revenues less expenses.

Plush Service Corporation
Statement of Net Income
For the Year Ended December 31, 2018

Service Revenue		$167,500
Expenses:		
Salaries Expense	$34,000	
Utilities Expense	15,000	
Depreciation Expense–Store Equipment	8,000	
Legal Fees Expense	6,000	
Insurance Expense	10,000	
Rental Expense	1,000	
Total Expenses		(74,000)
NET INCOME		$ 93,500

Net income is needed to prepare the statement of stockholders' equity.

Plush Service Corporation
Statement of Stockholders' Equity
For the Year Ended December 31, 2018

	Common Stock	***Retained Earnings***	***Total Equity***
Balance, January 1, 2018	$ 60,000	$ 40,000	$100,000
Additional Stock Issue	80,000		80,000
Net Income		93,500	93,500
Dividends Declared		(2,000)	(2,000)
Balance, December 31, 2018	$140,000	$131,500	$271,500

Note that the ending retained earnings balance is $131,500. We use this balance in the balance sheet as follows. The other accounts are obtained directly from the adjusted trial balance.

Plush Service Corporation
Balance Sheet
At December 31, 2018

Assets		
Cash		$ 57,000
Accounts Receivable		145,000
Prepaid Insurance		62,000
Store Equipment	$80,000	
Accumulated Depreciation—Store Equipment	(8,000)	72,000
TOTAL ASSETS		$336,000
LIABILITIES AND STOCKHOLDERS' EQUITY		
Liabilities		
Accounts Payable		$ 3,000
Legal Fees Payable		10,000
Unearned Service Revenue		17,500
Salaries Payable		4,000
Notes Payable		30,000
TOTAL LIABILITIES		$ 64,500
Stockholders' Equity		
Common Stock		$140,000
Retained Earnings		131,500
TOTAL STOCKHOLDERS' EQUITY		$271,500
TOTAL LIABILITIES AND STOCKHOLDERS' EQUITY		$336,000

9 Explain the difference between permanent and temporary accounts and demonstrate the process of closing temporary accounts.

Step 8: Close Temporary Accounts

The next step in the accounting cycle requires *closing* all **temporary accounts**, which are all income statement accounts and dividends that must be reduced to a zero balance in order to report net income (or net loss) and dividends for the next accounting period. The temporary accounts begin the next period with a zero balance to ensure that prior-period revenues and expenses are not included in the computation of the next year's net income or loss. **Closing** is the process of bringing all temporary accounts to a zero balance.

In contrast to the income statement temporary accounts, the balance sheet consists of **permanent accounts**, which are accounts with cumulative balances carried forward period after period. Permanent accounts are not closed at the end of the period.

Closing each revenue and expense temporary account to retained earnings would involve a significant amount of detail flowing through the retained earnings account. To avoid this excessive detail in retained earnings, companies use another temporary account, income summary, to accumulate revenues and expenses and transfer the net value of the income summary to retained earnings in a single journal entry.

Four closing entries are required to close the temporary accounts.

1. Close out revenue and gain accounts: Debit all revenue and gain accounts and credit income summary for the total of the accounts debited.
2. Close out expense and loss accounts: Debit income summary for total expenses and losses and credit each expense and loss account for its balance.

3. Close out income summary account: Debit income summary and credit retained earnings for the amount of net income; conversely, credit income summary and debit retained earnings in the event of a net loss.
4. Close out the dividends account: Debit retained earnings and credit the dividends account for the year.

EXAMPLE 4.12

Closing Entries

PROBLEM: Consider Plush Service Corporation from the prior examples. Prepare the closing entries for Plush Service Corporation.

SOLUTION: We record each of the four closing entries. First, we debit the service revenue account and credit income summary. Second, we credit each of the expense accounts and debit the total amount to income summary. At this point, income summary will have a credit balance because revenues are greater than expenses and represent net income for the period. Third, we debit income summary for its balance (which, in this case, is net income as opposed to net loss) and credit retained earnings. Finally, we credit the dividends account for its balance and debit retained earnings. The closing entries on December 31 are presented here:

GENERAL JOURNAL **PAGE J4**

No.	*Account*	*Debit*	*Credit*
①	Service Revenue	167,500	
	Income Summary		167,500
	(To close revenue account)		
②	Income Summary	74,000	
	Salaries Expense		34,000
	Utilities Expense		15,000
	Depreciation Expense—Store Equipment		8,000
	Legal Fees Expense		6,000
	Insurance Expense		10,000
	Rental Expense		1,000
	(To close expense accounts)		
③	Income Summary	93,500	
	Retained Earnings		93,500
	(To close income summary)		
④	Retained Earnings	2,000	
	Dividends		2,000
	(To close dividends)		

Step 9: Prepare Post-Closing Trial Balance

10 Explain the importance of and illustrate the preparation of a post-closing trial balance.

After journalizing and posting all closing entries, the company prepares a *post-closing trial balance*. Similar to any trial balance, the objective of the *post-closing trial balance* is to prove the equality, not the accuracy, of the debits and credits related to the remaining accounts with non-zero balances. The **post-closing trial balance** contains only permanent balance sheet accounts because all temporary accounts were closed out and have zero balances.

EXAMPLE 4.13 Post-Closing Trial Balance

PROBLEM: Prepare the post-closing trial balance for Plush Service Corporation using the information provided in the prior examples.

SOLUTION: The post-closing trial balance only includes the permanent accounts because the temporary accounts have all been closed and now reflect zero balances. Plush updates the ending balance for retained earnings, a permanent account, to reflect the closing of all temporary accounts to retained earnings.

Plush Service Corporation
Post-Closing Trial Balance
At December 31, 2018

Account	*Account #*	*Debit*	*Credit*
Cash	100	$ 57,000	
Accounts Receivable	101	145,000	
Prepaid Insurance	102	62,000	
Store Equipment	150	80,000	
Accumulated Depreciation—Store Equipment	151		$ 8,000
Accounts Payable	200		3,000
Legal Fees Payable	201		10,000
Unearned Service Revenues	202		17,500
Salaries Payable	204		4,000
Notes Payable	210		30,000
Common Stock	300		140,000
Retained Earnings	301		131,500
Totals		$344,000	$344,000

Comprehensive Example

Example 4.14 provides a comprehensive example of the complete illustration of the accounting cycle.

EXAMPLE 4.14 Comprehensive Accounting Cycle Example

PROBLEM: The DS Wilson Company, which provides consulting services to major utility companies, was formed on January 2 of the current year. Transactions completed during the first year of operation are presented here.

January 2: Issued 600,000 shares of common stock for $10,000,000, which is the par value of the stock.

January 10: Acquired equipment in exchange for $2,000,000 cash and a $6,000,000 note payable. The note is due in 10 years.

February 1: Paid $24,000 for a business insurance policy covering the two-year period beginning on February 1.

February 22: Purchased $900,000 of supplies on account.

March 1: Paid wages of $185,600.

March 23: Billed $2,730,000 for services rendered on account.

April 1: Paid $100,000 of the amount due on the supplies purchased on February 22.

Continued

April 17:	Collected $210,000 of the outstanding accounts receivable.
May 1:	Paid wages of $200,400.
May 8:	Received bill and paid $98,200 for utilities.
May 24:	Paid $42,500 for sales commissions.
June 1:	Made the first payment on the note issued on January 10. The payment consisted of $60,000 of interest and $200,000 to be applied against the principal of the note.
June 16:	Billed customers for $560,000 of services rendered.
June 30:	Collected $300,000 on accounts receivable.
July 10:	Purchased $155,000 of supplies on account.
Aug 25:	Paid $160,000 for administrative expenses.
Sept 23:	Paid $30,000 for warehouse repairs.
October 1:	Paid wages of $90,000.
Nov 20:	Purchased supplies for $60,000 with cash.
Dec 15:	Collected $125,600 in advance for services to be provided in December and January of the following year.
Dec 30:	Declared and paid a $50,000 dividend to shareholders.

The chart of accounts used by DS Wilson is presented here

Chart of Accounts

Group	*Account #*	*Account Title*
100: Assets		
	101	Cash
	102	Accounts Receivable
	103	Supplies
	104	Prepaid Insurance
	110	Equipment
	112	Accumulated Depreciation—Equipment
200: Liabilities		
	201	Accounts Payable
	202	Unearned Service Revenue
	203	Wages Payable
	210	Interest Payable
	220	Notes Payable
300: Stockholders' Equity		
	301	Common Stock
	310	Retained Earnings
	320	Dividends
400: Revenues		
	401	Service Revenue
500: Expenses		
	501	Wage Expense
	502	Utilities Expense
	503	Selling Expense
	504	Administrative Expense
	505	Repairs Expense

Group	Account #	Account Title
	506	Insurance Expense
	507	Supplies Expense
	510	Depreciation Expense—Equipment
	520	Interest Expense
600: Other		
	601	Income Summary

a. Journalize the transactions for the year.
b. Post the journal entries to t-accounts.
c. Prepare an unadjusted trial balance as of December 31.
d. Journalize and post adjusting entries to t-accounts based on the following additional information.
   i. Eleven months of the insurance policy expired by the end of the year.
   ii. Depreciation for the equipment is $400,000.
   iii. The company provided a portion of the services related to the advance collection of December 15. The company recognized $70,000 as service revenue earned.
   iv. There are $500,000 of supplies on hand at the end of the year.
   v. An additional $170,000 of interest has accrued on the note by the end of the year.
   vi. Wilson accrued wages in the amount of $200,000.
e. Prepare an adjusted trial balance as of December 31.
f. Prepare a single-step income statement and statement of stockholders' equity for the current year and a classified balance sheet as of the end of the year.
g. Journalize and post closing entries.
h. Prepare a post-closing trial balance as of December 31.

SOLUTION

a. We first analyze each transaction and then present journal entries. Note that the reference numbers would not be added until the entries are posted.

January 2: Wilson will increase cash with a debit and increase common stock with a credit.

January 10: Wilson will increase equipment with a debit, decrease cash with a credit, and increase notes payable with a credit.

February 1: In the journal entry, Wilson will increase prepaid insurance with a debit and decrease cash with a credit.

February 22: Wilson will increase supplies with a debit and increase accounts payable with a credit.

March 1: Wilson will increase wage expense with a debit and decrease cash with a credit in the journal entry.

March 23: Wilson will increase accounts receivable with a debit and increase service revenue with a credit.

April 1: Wilson will decrease accounts payable with a debit of $100,000 and decrease cash with a credit of the same amount.

Continued

April 17:	Wilson will increase cash with a debit of $210,000 and decrease accounts receivable with a credit of the same amount.
May 1:	Wilson will increase wage expense with a debit and decrease cash with a credit.
May 8:	Wilson will increase utilities expense with a debit and decrease cash with a credit.
May 24:	Wilson will increase selling expense with a debit and decrease cash with a credit.
June 1:	Wilson will decrease the notes payable with a debit of $200,000, increase interest expense with debit of $60,000, and decrease cash with a credit of $260,000.
June 16:	Wilson will increase accounts receivable with a debit and increase service revenue with a credit.
June 30:	Wilson will increase cash with a debit and decrease accounts receivable with a credit.
July 10:	Wilson will increase supplies with a debit and increase accounts payable with a credit.
Aug 25:	Wilson will increase administrative expense with a debit and decrease cash with a credit.
Sept 23:	Wilson will increase repairs expense with a debit and decrease cash with a credit.
October 1:	Wilson will increase wage expense with a debit and decrease cash with a credit.
Nov 20:	Wilson will increase supplies with a debit and decrease cash with a credit.
Dec 15:	Wilson will increase cash with a debit and increase unearned service revenue with a credit.
Dec 30:	Wilson will increase dividends with a debit and decrease cash with a credit.

General Journal **Page J1**

Date	***Account Titles and Explanations***	***Ref.***	***Debit***	***Credit***
Current Year				
Jan 2	Cash	101	10,000,000	
	Common Stock	301		10,000,000
	(To record issuance of common stock)			
Jan 10	Equipment	110	8,000,000	
	Cash	101		2,000,000
	Notes Payable	220		6,000,000
	(To record purchase of equipment)			
Feb 1	Prepaid Insurance	104	24,000	
	Cash	101		24,000
	(To record payment for insurance)			
22	Supplies	103	900,000	
	Accounts Payable	201		900,000
	(To record purchase of supplies)			

General Journal — **Page J2**

Date	Account Titles and Explanations	Ref.	Debit	Credit
Current Year				
March 1	Wage expense	501	185,600	
	Cash	101		185,600
	(To record payment to employees)			
23	Accounts Receivable	102	2,730,000	
	Service Revenue	401		2,730,000
	(To record billings)			
April 1	Accounts Payable	201	100,000	
	Cash	101		100,000
	(To record payment for supplies)			
17	Cash	101	210,000	
	Accounts Receivable	102		210,000
	(To record collections from customers)			
May 1	Wage Expense	501	200,400	
	Cash	101		200,400
	(To record payment to employees)			
8	Utility Expense	502	98,200	
	Cash	101		98,200
	(To record payment for utilities)			
24	Selling Expense	503	42,500	
	Cash	101		42,500
	(To record payment for sales commissions)			
June 1	Notes Payable	220	200,000	
	Interest Expense	520	60,000	
	Cash	101		260,000
	(To record payment on note)			
16	Accounts Receivable	102	560,000	
	Service Revenue	401		560,000
	(To record customer billings)			
30	Cash	101	300,000	
	Accounts Receivable	102		300,000
	(To record collections from customer)			
July 10	Supplies	103	155,000	
	Accounts Payable	201		155,000
	(To record purchase of supplies)			
Aug 25	Administrative Expense	504	160,000	
	Cash	101		160,000
	(To record payment for administrative expenses)			

Continued

General Journal				Page J2
Date	*Account Titles and Explanations*	*Ref.*	*Debit*	*Credit*
Current Year				
Sept 23	Repairs Expense	505	30,000	
	Cash	101		30,000
	(To record payment for warehouse repairs)			
Oct 1	Wage Expense	501	90,000	
	Cash	101		90,000
	(To record payments to employees)			
Nov 20	Supplies	103	60,000	
	Cash	101		60,000
	(To record purchase of supplies)			
Dec 15	Cash	101	125,600	
	Unearned Service Revenue	202		125,600
	(To record collection of advance payments)			
30	Dividends	320	50,000	
	Cash	101		50,000
	(To record payment of dividends)			

b. The t-accounts are as follows:

Cash 101

	Debit	Credit
Jan 2	10,000,000	
10		2,000,000
Feb 1		24,000
March 1		185,600
April 1		100,000
17	210,000	
May 1		200,400
8		98,200
24		42,500
June 1		260,000
30	300,000	
Aug 25		160,000
Sept 23		30,000
Oct 1		90,000
Nov 20		60,000
Dec 15	125,600	
Dec 30		50,000
	7,334,900	

Accounts Receivable 102

	Debit	Credit
Mar 23	2,730,000	
Apr 17		210,000
June 16	560,000	
30		300,000
	2,780,000	

Supplies 103

Feb 22	900,000	
July 10	155,000	
Nov 20	60,000	
	1,115,000	

Prepaid Insurance 104

Feb 1	24,000	
	24,000	

Equipment 110

Jan 10	8,000,000	
	8,000,000	

Accumulated Depreciation—Equipment 112

		0
		0

Accounts Payable 201

Feb 22		900,000
April 1	100,000	
July 10		155,000
		955,000

Unearned Service Revenue 202

Dec 15		125,600
		125,600

Wages Payable 203

		0
		0

Interest Payable 210

		0
		0

Notes Payable 220

Jan 10		6,000,000
June 1	200,000	
		5,800,000

Common Stock 301

Jan 2		10,000,000
		10,000,000

Retained Earnings 310

		0
		0

Dividends 320

Dec 30	50,000	
	50,000	

Service Revenue 401

March 23		2,730,000
June 16		560,000
		3,290,000

Wage Expense 501

March 1	185,600	
May 1	200,400	
Oct 1	90,000	
	476,000	

Utilities Expense 502

May 8	98,200	
	98,200	

Selling Expense 503

May 24	42,500	
	42,500	

Continued

Administrative Expense 504

Aug 25	160,000	
	160,000	

Repairs Expense 505

Sept 23	30,000	
	30,000	

Insurance Expense 506

0	
0	

Supplies Expense 507

0	
0	

Depreciation Expense—Equipment 510

0	
0	

Interest Expense 520

June 1	60,000	
	60,000	

Income Summary 601

0	0

c. We prepare the unadjusted trial balance using the balances from the t-accounts in b. The unadjusted trial balance is as follows:

DS Wilson Company
Unadjusted Trial Balance
At December 31

Account	*Debit*	*Credit*
Cash	$ 7,334,900	
Accounts Receivable	2,780,000	
Supplies	1,115,000	
Prepaid Insurance	24,000	
Equipment	8,000,000	
Accounts Payable		$ 955,000
Unearned Service Revenue		125,600
Notes Payable		5,800,000
Common Stock		10,000,000
Retained Earnings		0
Dividends	50,000	
Service Revenue		3,290,000
Wage Expense	476,000	
Utilities Expense	98,200	
Selling Expense	42,500	
Administrative Expense	160,000	
Repairs Expense	30,000	
Interest Expense	60,000	
Totals	$20,170,600	$20,170,600

d. We analyze the additional information provided in order to prepare the adjusting entries.

i. On February 1, insurance was prepaid for 24 months. Policy begins on February 1. Because 11 months of the insurance policy have expired by the end of the year, Wilson will record 11 months of insurance expense with a debit and reduce prepaid insurance with a credit. The amount of insurance expense is $11,000, computed as follows:

$24,000 prepaid insurance/24 months = $1,000 per month
$1,000 per month × 11 months = $11,000

ii. Wilson will increase depreciation expense with a debit of $400,000 and increase accumulated depreciation with a credit for the same amount.

iii. Wilson will reduce its liability, unearned service revenue, with a debit of $70,000, and increase service revenue with a credit of $70,000.

iv. In the unadjusted trial balance, the balance of the supplies account is $1,115,000. However, at the end of the year, Wilson has $500,000 of supplies. Therefore, $615,000 of supplies must have been used.

$615,000 = $1,115,000 − $500,000

Wilson will increase supplies expense by $615,000 with a debit and decrease supplies with a credit for the same amount.

v. Wilson will increase interest expense by $170,000 with a debit and increase interest payable with a credit of the same amount.

vi. Wilson will increase wage expense with a debit and increase wages payable with a credit.

The adjusting entries are as follows:

GENERAL JOURNAL **PAGE J3**

Trans	*Date*	*Account Titles and Explanations*	*Ref*	*Debit*	*Credit*
(for example only)	**Current Year**	**Adjusting Entries**			
(i)	Dec 31	Insurance Expense	506	11,000	
		Prepaid Insurance	104		11,000
		(To record expired insurance)			
(ii)	31	Depreciation Expense—Equipment	510	400,000	
		Accumulated Depreciation—Equipment	112		400,000
		(To record depreciation on equipment)			
(iii)	31	Unearned Service Revenue	202	70,000	
		Service Revenue	401		70,000
		(To record revenue for services provided)			
(iv)	31	Supplies Expense	507	615,000	
		Supplies	103		615,000
		(To record supplies used)			
(v)	31	Interest Expense	520	170,000	
		Interest Payable	210		170,000
		(To record interest on note)			
(vi)	31	Wage Expense	501	200,000	
		Wages Payable	203		200,000
		(To record wages earned)			

Continued

The updated t-accounts, after adjusting journal entries, are as follows:

Cash 101

	Debit	Credit
Jan 2	10,000,000	
10		2,000,000
Feb 1		24,000
March 1		185,600
April 1		100,000
17	210,000	
May 1		200,400
8		98,200
24		42,500
June 1		260,000
30	300,000	
Aug 25		160,000
Sept 23		30,000
Oct 1		90,000
Nov 20		60,000
Dec 15	125,600	
Dec 30		50,000
	7,334,900	

Accounts Receivable 102

	Debit	Credit
Mar 23	2,730,000	
Apr 17		210,000
June 16	560,000	
30		300,000
	2,780,000	

Supplies 103

	Debit	Credit
Feb 22	900,000	
July 10	155,000	
Nov 20	60,000	
AJE		615,000
	500,000	

Prepaid Insurance 104

	Debit	Credit
Feb 1	24,000	
AJE		11,000
	13,000	

Equipment 110

	Debit	Credit
Jan 10	8,000,000	
	8,000,000	

Accumulated Depreciation—Equipment 112

	Debit	Credit
AJE		400,000
		400,000

Accounts Payable 201

	Debit	Credit
Feb 22		900,000
April 1	100,000	
July 10		155,000
		955,000

Unearned Service Revenue 202

	Debit	Credit
Dec 15		125,600
AJE	70,000	
		55,600

Wages Payable 203

	Debit	Credit
AJE		200,000
		200,000

Interest Payable 210

	Debit	Credit
AJE		170,000
		170,000

Notes Payable 220

	Debit	Credit
Jan 10		6,000,000
June 1	200,000	
		5,800,000

Common Stock 301

	Debit	Credit
Jan 2		10,000,000
		10,000,000

Retained Earnings 310

	Debit	Credit
	0	0
		0

Dividends 320

	Debit	Credit
Dec 30	50,000	
	50,000	

Service Revenue 401

	Debit	Credit
March 23		2,730,000
June 16		560,000
AJE		70,000
		3,360,000

Wage Expense 501

	Debit	Credit
March 1	185,600	
May 1	200,400	
Oct 1	90,000	
AJE	200,000	
	676,000	

Utilities Expense 502

	Debit	Credit
May 8	98,200	
	98,200	

Selling Expense 503

	Debit	Credit
May 24	42,500	
	42,500	

Administrative Expense 504

	Debit	Credit
Aug 25	160,000	
	160,000	

Repairs Expense 505

	Debit	Credit
Sept 23	30,000	
	30,000	

Insurance Expense 506

	Debit	Credit
AJE	11,000	
	11,000	

Supplies Expense 507

	Debit	Credit
AJE	615,000	
	615,000	

Depreciation Expense—Equipment 510

	Debit	Credit
AJE	400,000	
	400,000	

Interest Expense 520

	Debit	Credit
June 1	60,000	
AJE	170,000	
	230,000	

Income Summary 601

	Debit	Credit
	0	0

e. We use the balances from the updated t-accounts to prepare the adjusted trial balance.

DS Wilson Company
Adjusted Trial Balance
At December 31

Account	Debit	Credit
Cash	$ 7,334,900	
Accounts Receivable	2,780,000	
Supplies	500,000	
Prepaid Insurance	13,000	
Equipment	8,000,000	
Accumulated Depreciation—Equipment		$ 400,000
Accounts Payable		955,000
Unearned Service Revenue		55,600
Wages Payable		200,000
Interest Payable		170,000
Notes Payable		5,800,000
Common Stock		10,000,000
Retained Earnings, 1/1		0
Dividends	50,000	
Service Revenue		3,360,000
Wage Expense	676,000	
Utilities Expense	98,200	
Selling Expense	42,500	
Administrative Expense	160,000	
Repairs Expense	30,000	
Insurance Expense	11,000	
Interest Expense	230,000	
Supplies Expense	615,000	
Depreciation Expense—Equipment	400,000	
Totals	$20,940,600	$20,940,600

f. The financial statements are as follows:

DS Wilson Company
Statement of Net Income
For the Year Ended December 31

Revenues		
Service Revenues		$3,360,000
Expenses		
Wage Expense	$676,000	
Supplies Expense	615,000	
Depreciation Expense—Equipment	400,000	
Interest Expense	230,000	
Administrative Expense	160,000	
Utilities Expense	98,200	
Selling Expense	42,500	
Repair Expense	30,000	
Insurance Expense	11,000	
Total Expenses		(2,262,700)
Net Income		$ 1,097,300

DS Wilson Company
Statement of Stockholders' Equity
For the Year Ended December 31

	Common Stock	***Retained Earnings***	***Total Stockholders' Equity***
Balance, January 1	$ 0	$ 0	$ 0
Capital Investments	10,000,000		10,000,000
Net Income		1,097,300	1,097,300
Dividends Declared		(50,000)	(50,000)
Balance, December 31	$10,000,000	$1,047,300	$11,047,300

DS Wilson Company
Balance Sheet
As of December 31

ASSETS	
Current Assets:	
Cash	$ 7,334,900
Accounts Receivable	2,780,000
Supplies	500,000
Prepaid Insurance	13,000
Total Current Assets	$ 10,627,900
Noncurrent Assets:	
Equipment (less Accumulated Depreciation of $400,000)	$ 7,600,000
Total Noncurrent Assets	$ 7,600,000
TOTAL ASSETS	**$18,227,900**
LIABILITIES AND EQUITY	
Current Liabilities:	
Accounts Payable	$ 955,000
Unearned Service Revenue	55,600
Wages Payable	200,000
Interest Payable	170,000
Total Current Liabilities	$ 1,380,600
Noncurrent Liabilities:	
Notes Payable	$ 5,800,000
Total Noncurrent liabilities	$ 5,800,000
Total Liabilities	$ 7,180,600
Stockholders' Equity	
Common Stock	$10,000,000
Retained Earnings	1,047,300
Total Stockholders' Equity	$ 11,047,300
TOTAL LIABILITIES AND STOCKHOLDERS' EQUITY	**$ 18,227,900**

g. The closing entries for DS Wilson Company are presented next:

Date	Account Titles and Explanation	Ref.	Debit	Credit
Dec 31	Service Revenue	401	3,360,000	
	Income Summary	601		3,360,000
	(To close revenue account)			
31	Income Summary	601	2,262,700	
	Wage Expense	501		676,000
	Utilities Expense	502		98,200
	Selling Expense	503		42,500
	Administrative Expense	504		160,000
	Repairs Expense	505		30,000
	Insurance Expense	506		11,000
	Supplies Expense	507		615,000
	Depreciation Expense—Equipment	510		400,000
	Interest Expense	520		230,000
	(To close expense accounts)			
31	Income Summary	601	1,097,300	
	Retained Earnings	310		1,097,300
	(To close income summary account)			
31	Retained Earnings	310	50,000	
	Dividends	320		50,000
	(To close dividends account)			

h. The updated t-accounts, after closing entries (identified as CE), are as follows:

Cash 101

	Debit	Credit
Jan 2	10,000,000	
10		2,000,000
Feb 1		24,000
March 1		185,600
April 1		100,000
17	210,000	
May 1		200,400
8		98,200
24		42,500
June 1		260,000
30	300,000	
Aug 25		160,000
Sept 23		30,000
Oct 1		90,000
Nov 20		60,000
Dec 15	125,600	
Dec 30		50,000
	7,334,900	

Accounts Receivable 102

	Debit	Credit
Mar 23	2,730,000	
Apr 17		210,000
June 16	560,000	
30		300,000
	2,780,000	

Supplies 103

	Debit	Credit
Feb 22	900,000	
July 10	155,000	
Nov 20	60,000	
AJE		615,000
	500,000	

Prepaid Insurance 104

	Debit	Credit
Feb 1	24,000	
AJE		11,000
	13,000	

Equipment 110

	Debit	Credit
Jan 10	8,000,000	
	8,000,000	

Accumulated Depreciation—Equipment 112

	Debit	Credit
AJE		400,000
		400,000

Accounts Payable 201

	Debit	Credit
Feb 22		900,000
April 1	100,000	
July 10		155,000
		955,000

Unearned Service Revenue 202

	Debit	Credit
Dec 15		125,600
AJE	70,000	
		55,600

Wages Payable 203

	Debit	Credit
AJE		200,000
		200,000

Interest Payable 210

	Debit	Credit
AJE		170,000
		170,000

Notes Payable 220

	Debit	Credit
Jan 10		6,000,000
June 1	200,000	
		5,800,000

Common Stock 301

	Debit	Credit
Jan 2		10,000,000
		10,000,000

Retained Earnings 310

	Debit	Credit	
CE	50,000	1,097,300	CE
		1,047,300	

Dividends 320

	Debit	Credit	
Dec 30	50,000		
	50,000	50,000	CE

Service Revenue 401

	Debit	Credit
March 23		2,730,000
June 16		560,000
AJE		70,000
CE	3,360,000	3,360,000

Wage Expense 501

	Debit	Credit	
March 1	185,600		
May 1	200,400		
Oct 1	90,000		
AJE	200,000		
	676,000	676,000	CE

Utilities Expense 502

	Debit	Credit	
May 8	98,200		
	98,200	98,200	CE

Selling Expense 503

	Debit	Credit	
May 24	42,500		
	42,500	42,500	CE

Continued

Administrative Expense 504

Aug 25	160,000		
	160,000	160,000	CE

Repairs Expense 505

Sept 23	30,000		
	30,000	30,000	CE

Insurance Expense 506

AJE	11,000		
	11,000	11,000	CE

Supplies Expense 507

AJE	615,000		
	615,000	615,000	CE

Depreciation Expense—Equipment 510

AJE	400,000		
	400,000	400,000	CE

Interest Expense 520

June 1	60,000		
AJE	170,000		
	230,000	230,000	CE

Income Summary 601

CE	2,262,700	3,360,000	CE
CE	1,097,300	1,097,300	Balance

i. We present the post-closing trial balance for DS Wilson Company here.

DS Wilson Company
Post-Closing Trial Balance
At December 31

Account	***Debit***	***Credit***
Cash	$ 7,334,900	
Accounts Receivable	2,780,000	
Supplies	500,000	
Prepaid Insurance	13,000	
Equipment	8,000,000	
Accumulated Depreciation—Equipment		$ 400,000
Accounts Payable		955,000
Unearned Service Revenue		55,600
Wages Payable		200,000
Interest Payable		170,000
Notes Payable		5,800,000
Common Stock		10,000,000
Retained Earnings		1,047,300
Totals	$18,627,900	$18,627,900

Interview

JOHN FORISTALL, EXECUTIVE VICE PRESIDENT AND CHIEF FINANCIAL OFFICER SHOEBUY »

John Foristall

As executive vice president and chief financial officer of ShoeBuy, John Foristall oversees all aspects of corporate finance, including accounting and risk management, as well as other key operational areas including human resources and the company's warehouse operations, which is pivotal for the online retailer. Launched in 2000, ShoeBuy is the world's largest, most diverse shoe, clothing, and accessories shopping site, with billions of dollars of inventory available for sale.

1 How often does ShoeBuy create internal financial reports, and how does management use them?

As with most mature and growing businesses operating in a competitive landscape, ShoeBuy must understand its financial trajectory on a monthly—if not daily—basis. We use many daily and weekly reports and dashboards providing real-time data on key performance indicators to manage the business. We also create formal internal financial reports for management use monthly, quarterly, and annually. Management reviews these financials, accompanied by written commentaries, and discusses them monthly with the senior management team. Because we are a subsidiary of a public parent company, we also participate in the quarterly and annual public filing process.

On a macro level, we use our reports to gauge the financial performance and financial position of the company compared to previous periods and to our expectations (i.e., plan/forecast). These reports also drive accountability throughout the organization, providing a means to measure departmental performance. For example, at monthly financial reviews, the Merchandising team addresses the revenue performance of specific brands and footwear categories.

2 What are the most important adjusting entries made at the end of the accounting cycle and why?

The most significant end-of-cycle adjustment for ShoeBuy is an entry to estimate future customer returns. ShoeBuy provides a great customer experience by offering free shipping, both outbound and for returns. While ShoeBuy's return rate is well below the industry average, future returns can have a material impact on results, because our calendar-year reporting period coincides with our peak holiday season. Predicting January returns on sales from December (our biggest sale month) is a key component of ShoeBuy's year-end reporting process. Accurately estimating these returns requires historical data and trends—and given that ShoeBuy was founded more than 15 years ago, management can estimate this with a high degree of precision.

3 How do transactions flow through your accounting system?

ShoeBuy's key ecommerce transaction is the sale of product—footwear and related apparel. Online customers initiate purchase orders via ShoeBuy.com, triggering many entries as each order flows through our proprietary order fulfillment platform. We record the majority of our orders upon shipment and then recognize revenue and book the receivable. ShoeBuy's receivables are primarily from credit card providers that are paid within three to five days. Some ShoeBuy products ship directly from the footwear partner to the consumer (a drop-ship model), so shipment also triggers a payable to our footwear partners as well as an expense and a payable to various operational partners, such as shipping and marketing providers.

4 Are any adjusting entries reversed and if so, why?

At the beginning of any accounting period, ShoeBuy records and reverses certain entries made in the immediately preceding accounting period. They are used in situations where revenue or expenses were accrued in the preceding period to avoid double counting in the current period. Examples include our payroll accrual for unpaid wages and unshipped product ordered in the prior period.

5 What controls are in place to enhance the quality of the financial information generated by your accounting cycle?

First, we ensure proper segregation of duties and levels of review, ensuring that the Controller and CFO review and approve all journal entries and checks. We have very robust dashboards and scorecards allowing for detailed variance analysis to quickly alert us to results that differ from expectations. For example, we track revenue in a very granular fashion by using dashboards showing revenue by brand, by category, and even by marketing channel (e.g., did the customer come directly to ShoeBuy, via Google, or via an email promotion). We have standing meetings, such as our Monthly Financial Reviews, to discuss results and accountability with the senior management team. Last, ShoeBuy has monthly and quarterly calls with our parent company to discuss financial results as well as accounting and control updates.

Discussion Questions

1. John Foristall indicates that ShoeBuy's receivables are primarily from credit card sales. Discuss how the use of credit card sales impact cash flows relative to using open trade accounts receivable.
2. ShoeBuy uses reversing entries for events such as accrued payroll at year-end. How would the company's accounting be affected if reversing entries were not made for payroll?

Summary by Learning Objectives

In the following, we summarize the main points by learning objective. Throughout the chapter, we discuss the accounting and reporting of U.S. GAAP and IFRS. This table also highlights the major similarities and differences between the standards.

1 Describe the accounting cycle.

Summary	Similarities and Differences between U.S. GAAP and IFRS
The accounting cycle describes the process by which companies record business transactions in their books, which they ultimately aggregate and summarize in the financial statements.	Similar under U.S. GAAP and IFRS.

2 Explain transaction analysis, including the use of the accounting equation.

Summary	Similarities and Differences between U.S. GAAP and IFRS
A transaction is an economic event that involves a change in an asset, a liability, or stockholders' equity. The accounting equation assesses the effects of transactions on assets, liabilities, or stockholders' equity: Assets = Liabilities + Stockholders' Equity The expanded accounting equation includes income statement items and dividends: Assets = Liabilities + Contributed Capital + Accumulated Other Comprehensive Income + Beginning Retained Earnings − Dividends Declared + Revenues and Gains − Expenses and Losses A double-entry system is one in which all transactions affect at least two accounts and the accounting equation always holds.	Similar under U.S. GAAP and IFRS.

Summary by Learning Objectives, continued

❸ Illustrate journalizing transactions, including determining whether to debit or credit accounts.	
Summary	**Similarities and Differences between U.S. GAAP and IFRS**
Journalizing a transaction involves preparing a journal entry. The common format includes: a. The date the transaction occurred in first column. b. Accounts that are debited are listed first and positioned to the left side. c. Accounts that are credited are recorded next and indented to the right. d. A brief explanation below the entry. An account is an individual record of increases and decreases in specific asset, liability, and stockholders' equity items. The terms *debit* and *credit* mean left and right, respectively. Assets increase with a debit and decrease with a credit. Liability and equity accounts increase with a credit and decrease with a debit. Revenues and gains are increases in equity; these accounts will increase with credits. Expenses and losses decrease equity, so they increase with a debit. Similarly, dividends decrease equity, so they increase with debits. The normal balance of an account refers to its typical account balance—debit or credit.	Similar under U.S. GAAP and IFRS.

❹ Explain the importance of and show how to post journal entries to the general ledger.	
Summary	**Similarities and Differences between U.S. GAAP and IFRS**
Posting describes the transferring of information contained in journal entries to the individual ledger accounts. The general ledger contains all accounts maintained by the company—with each account reflecting its increases, decreases, and balance—in a single location for management analysis. The general ledger has a column for the date, explanation, reference, debit, credit, and balance. The reference is the general journal page number where the original journal entry occurred. T-accounts are used to depict the account. They have three main parts: a. The account title b. A left (debit) side c. A right (credit) side	Similar under U.S. GAAP and IFRS.

Summary by Learning Objectives, continued

5 Explain the importance of and illustrate the preparation of an unadjusted trial balance.

Summary	Similarities and Differences between U.S. GAAP and IFRS
A trial balance is a listing of the accounts and their ending debit or credit balances at a point in time. The balance sheet accounts are listed first (assets, liabilities, and equity), followed by dividends and the income statement accounts (revenues, gains, expenses, and losses). The trial balance provides a check on the recording process by ensuring the equality of debits and credits. The trial balance does not prove the accuracy of the recording process and will not reveal whether: • A transaction is not journalized. • A correct journal entry is not posted. • An entry is posted twice. • Incorrect accounts are used. • An entry is made using incorrect dollar amounts. An unadjusted trial balance may not reflect all of the events and circumstances of the company because the adjusting journal entries have not been made at the time the unadjusted trial balance is compiled.	Similar under U.S. GAAP and IFRS.

6 Discuss the need for adjusting journal entries and explain deferrals and accruals.

Summary	Similarities and Differences between U.S. GAAP and IFRS
Companies record adjusting journal entries (AJEs) at the end of each accounting period to ensure that the financial statements are presented under the accrual basis of accounting. Deferral AJEs occur when cash is received or paid before the revenue or expense is recognized in the financial statements. • A deferred expense occurs when a cash payment is made before an expense should appropriately be recognized in the financial statements under accrual basis accounting. • A deferred revenue occurs when cash is received before revenue should appropriately be recognized in the financial statements under accrual basis accounting. Accrual AJEs are created when the economic event that gives rise to accrual basis revenue or expense occurs before the cash is received or paid. • Accrued revenues occur when control of a good or service has passed to the customer, but cash has not yet been received. • Accrued expenses occur when expenses have been incurred, but cash has not yet been paid out.	Similar under U.S. GAAP and IFRS.

7 Explain the use of and illustrate the preparation of an adjusted trial balance.

Summary	Similarities and Differences between U.S. GAAP and IFRS
An adjusted trial balance reflects all of the events and circumstances of the company after it makes the adjusting journal entries to check that the amount of debits equals the amount of credits.	Similar under U.S. GAAP and IFRS.

Summary by Learning Objectives, continued

8 Describe the preparation of the financial statements from the adjusted trial balance.

Summary	Similarities and Differences between U.S. GAAP and IFRS
From the account balances in the adjusted trial balance, the company can prepare financial statements. • The income statement is prepared first, using the revenue, gains, losses, and expense accounts. • The resulting net income for the period, along with the equity accounts, is used to prepare the statement of stockholders' equity. • The balance sheet is prepared by including all assets, liabilities, common stock, and the ending retained earnings balance obtained from the statement of stockholders' equity.	➤ Differences in the income statement are illustrated in Chapter 5. Differences in the balance sheet are shown in Chapter 6.

9 Explain the difference between permanent and temporary accounts and demonstrate the process of closing temporary accounts.

Summary	Similarities and Differences between U.S. GAAP and IFRS
Income statement accounts and dividends are temporary accounts. These accounts must be reduced to a zero balance at the end of each period. Closing is the process of zeroing out temporary accounts. In addition to all of the income statement accounts, dividends is also a temporary account and must be closed. Permanent accounts are on the balance sheet. Permanent accounts are not closed at the end of the period. Four entries are required to close the temporary accounts: 1. Close out revenue and gain accounts: Debit each revenue and gain account and credit income summary for the total of the accounts debited. 2. Close out expense and loss accounts: Debit income summary for total of expenses and losses, and credit each expense and loss account for its balance. 3. Close out income summary account: Debit income summary and credit retained earnings for the amount of net income; conversely, credit income summary and debit retained earnings for the amount of any net loss. 4. Close out dividends account: Debit retained earnings and credit dividends for the period. The income summary account facilitates the closing process and is not included in the financial statements.	Similar under U.S. GAAP and IFRS.

10 Explain the importance of and illustrate the preparation of a post-closing trial balance.

Summary	Similarities and Differences between U.S. GAAP and IFRS
A post-closing trial balance is prepared after all closing entries have been journalized and posted. The post-closing trial balance proves the equality of the debits and credits. The post-closing trial balance contains only permanent (balance sheet) accounts, because all temporary accounts were closed out before preparation of the post-closing trial balance and will have zero balances.	Similar under U.S. GAAP and IFRS.

MyLab Accounting

Go to **http://www.pearson.com/mylab/accounting** for the following Questions, Multiple-Choice Questions, Brief Exercises, Exercises, and Problems. They are available with immediate grading, explanations of correct and incorrect answers, and interactive media that acts as your own online tutor.

4 Review of the Accounting Cycle

Questions

1 **Q4-1.** Describe the accounting cycle.

2 **Q4-2.** What is the accounting equation and what does it demonstrate?

2 **Q4-3.** What is equity? What are the three components of shareholders' equity? Explain each component.

2 **Q4-4.** When will retained earnings contain a positive balance? Negative balance?

2 **Q4-5.** Will all transactions have a dual effect on the accounting equation? Explain.

3 **Q4-6.** What do the terms *debit* and *credit* mean?

3 **Q4-7.** What is meant by the term *normal balance*? Provide the normal balance for assets, liabilities, and stockholders' equity.

3 **Q4-8.** Why is the general journal referred to as the "book of original entry"? How are transactions presented in the journal?

4 **Q4-9.** Are account balances found in the general ledger? Explain.

5 **Q4-10.** What is the purpose of an unadjusted trial balance?

6 **Q4-11.** Explain the difference between the accrual basis of accounting and the cash basis of accounting? Which basis is acceptable under U.S. GAAP? Explain.

6 **Q4-12.** Under the accrual basis of accounting, when do companies record deferrals and accruals?

6 **Q4-13.** Why are adjusting journal entries made? When do companies make these entries?

6 **Q4-14.** What is a deferred revenue? When will the full amount of the deferred revenue be recorded?

7 **Q4-15.** What is the purpose of the adjusted trial balance? What items are included in the adjusted trial balance?

7 8 **Q4-16.** Which statements can be prepared from the adjusted trial balance? What must be done before preparing the financial statements?

9 **Q4-17.** What are closing entries? Describe the four closing entries and their effects.

Multiple-Choice Questions

3 6 **MC4-1.** Jefferson, CPAs provides accounting services for a client at a flat contract rate of $10,000 a month. The terms of the contract include a required payment on the 15th day of each month for the prior month's accounting services. Assuming Jefferson, CPAs posts journal entries each month end, what is (are) the journal entry (entries) posted on December 31?

a. Cash	10,000	
Service Revenue		10,000
b. Cash	10,000	
Accounts Receivable		10,000
c. Accounts Receivable	5,000	
Cash	10,000	
Service Revenue		15,000
d. Cash	10,000	
Accounts Receivable		10,000
Accounts Receivable	10,000	
Service Revenue		10,000

6 **MC4-2.** Gates Accounting Services (GAS), a sole proprietorship, entered into a new 18-month office space contract on September 15, Year 1, paying the full $36,000 rent contract to the real estate company on that day (lease expiration March 15, Year 3). Assuming that GAS reports on a calendar year-end and that journal entries are posted on a quarterly basis (only), what adjusting journal entry (if any) would be made to the prepaid rent account prior to closing the December 31, Year 1, financial statements?

a. Debit prepaid rent $8,000.
b. Credit prepaid rent $6,000.
c. Credit prepaid rent $7,000.
d. No adjusting entry made.

6 **MC4-3.** Windy Harbor Boat Company pays its employees on a weekly basis each Friday. During the week ended Friday, January 3, Year 2, the company had a weekly payroll of $125,750. Assuming that the company is on a calendar basis, has a five-day workweek, and that daily wages are always the same, what adjusting journal entry (if any) would be made on December 31, Year 1?

a. Salary Expense	50,300	
Cash		50,300
b. Salary Expense	50,300	
Accrued Salaries Payable		50,300
c. Salary Expense	125,750	
Accrued Salaries Payable		125,750

d. No journal entry necessary.

6 **MC4-4.** State University sold all of its basketball tickets to its students for 15 home games on September 30 for $1,200,000 (basketball season starts November 1). Assuming the college basketball team played six home games prior to year-end, what adjusting journal entry (if any) is necessary on December 31, assuming the initial student ticket transactions were recorded on September 30?

a. Cash	480,000	
Basketball Revenue		480,000
b. Unearned Revenue	480,000	
Basketball Revenue		480,000
c. Unearned Revenue	720,000	
Student Receivables		720,000

d. No journal entry necessary.

6 **MC4-5.** During the fourth quarter ended December 31, Year 1, Lighting Fixtures Inc. (LFI) had average outstanding revolving bank loans of $1.2 million. Assume that the quarterly interest charges associated with these loans was $7,500. If LFI makes the interest payment to the banks on January 15, Year 2, what is the journal entry (if any) made by the company on December 31 to reflect this information?

a. Accrued Interest Payable	7,500	
Interest Expense		7,500
b. Interest Expense	7,500	
Accrued Interest Payable		7,500
c. Interest Expense	7,500	
Loans Payable		7,500

d. No journal entry necessary.

6 **MC4-6.** Sampson Manufacturing Company (SMC) has an empty warehouse that it rents out to a local beer distributor for a monthly rental fee of $6,000. Terms of the rental agreement include a 10-day payment grace period and an additional $200 monthly utility expense, necessary to maintain the beer distributor's products at the proper temperature, paid by SMC. Assuming that SMC records journal entries on a monthly basis and that it receives the December monthly rent payment on January 9, what is the adjusting journal entry (if any) made by SMC on December 31 (with December's $200 utility payment made on January 2)?

a. Rent Receivable	6, 000	
Rent Revenue		6,000

b.

Rent Receivable	5,800	
Utilities Expense	200	
Rent Revenue		6,000

c.

Rent Receivable	6,000	
Utilities Expense	200	
Rent Revenue		6,000
Utilities Payable		200

d. No journal entry necessary.

6 **MC4-7.** On July 15, Year 1, Southeastern University hired an associate professor for its Math Department at an annual (12-month) salary of $150,000. The salary is effective for its new school year, which commences August 16, and is payable in four quarterly calendar installments. Assuming that the university records journal entries on a monthly basis, what is the adjusting journal entry (if any) for August 31, Year 1?

a.

Salaries Expense	6,250	
Accrued Salaries Payable		6,250

b.

Salaries Payable	6,250	
Cash		6,250

c.

Salaries Expense	12,500	
Accrued Salaries Payable		12,500

d. No journal entry necessary.

6 **MC4-8.** Embree Corp. purchased a four-year insurance policy on May 1, Year 2, for $12,000, effective immediately. The company expensed the full cost of the policy in Year 2. The correct journal entry for Year 2 (ending December 31) will include a:

a. Debit to prepaid insurance of $10,000.
b. Credit to prepaid insurance of $9,000.
c. Debit to insurance expense of $3,000.
d. Credit to insurance expense of $2,000.

6 **MC4-9.** The Cougars football team sells season tickets in advance for $480 each. The season consists of 16 games. Half of these games are home games, and half of them are away games. For Year 3, the team has sold and collected payment for 10,000 season tickets. Through November 30, Year 3, six home games and five away games have been played. How much of the revenue collected in advance should be recognized on the income statement for the 11 months ended November 30, Year 3?

a. $1,800,000
b. $3,300,000
c. $3,600,000
d. $4,800,000

3 9 **MC4-10.** Choco-Delite Cookies Company (Choco) declared a $1,600,000 cash dividend on December 15, Year 2, payable to all stockholders on record the following month. On December 31, Year 2, the company completed a two-for-one stock split (*Note:* Prior to the split there were 2 million common shares outstanding with a par value of $2). If Choco had net income of $3,000,000 for Year 2, what is the *net* journal entry impact on the company's retained earnings account for December, assuming that Choco posts journal entries on a monthly basis and that temporary accounts are closed at year-end?

a. $3,400,000 credit (net)
b. $1,600,000 debit (net)
c. $3,000,000 credit (net)
d. $1,400,000 credit (net)

Brief Exercises

2 **BE4-1. Transaction Analysis.** At the beginning of the year, Buxton Builders purchased raw materials in the amount of $15,000 to produce goods to sell. Buxton paid cash. What is the effect of this transaction on the accounting equation?

2 **BE4-2. Transaction Analysis.** Florence's Floral Arrangements, Inc. had the following transactions in the month of January: The owners invested $100,000 (the par value of the stock) for 20,000 shares of common stock; the company purchased furniture for the florist shop in the amount of $12,000, which was put on a credit account with the vendor; and the company paid employees wages of $6,000 in cash. What is the effect of each of these transactions on the accounting equation?

3 **BE4-3. Journal Entries.** Using the information provided in BE4-2, prepare Florence's journal entries for the month of January. Omit explanations.

2 3 **BE4-4. Transaction Analysis; Journal Entries.** Cal's Computer Servicing, Inc., a service company that provides installation services for computer programs, had a service revenue transaction in the amount of $120,000 on May 31, 2018, with one customer. This customer chose to put the balance owed on its credit account with Cal's, and it will pay off the balance in the following month. What is the effect of the revenue transaction on the accounting equation? What is the journal entry for this transaction? Omit explanation.

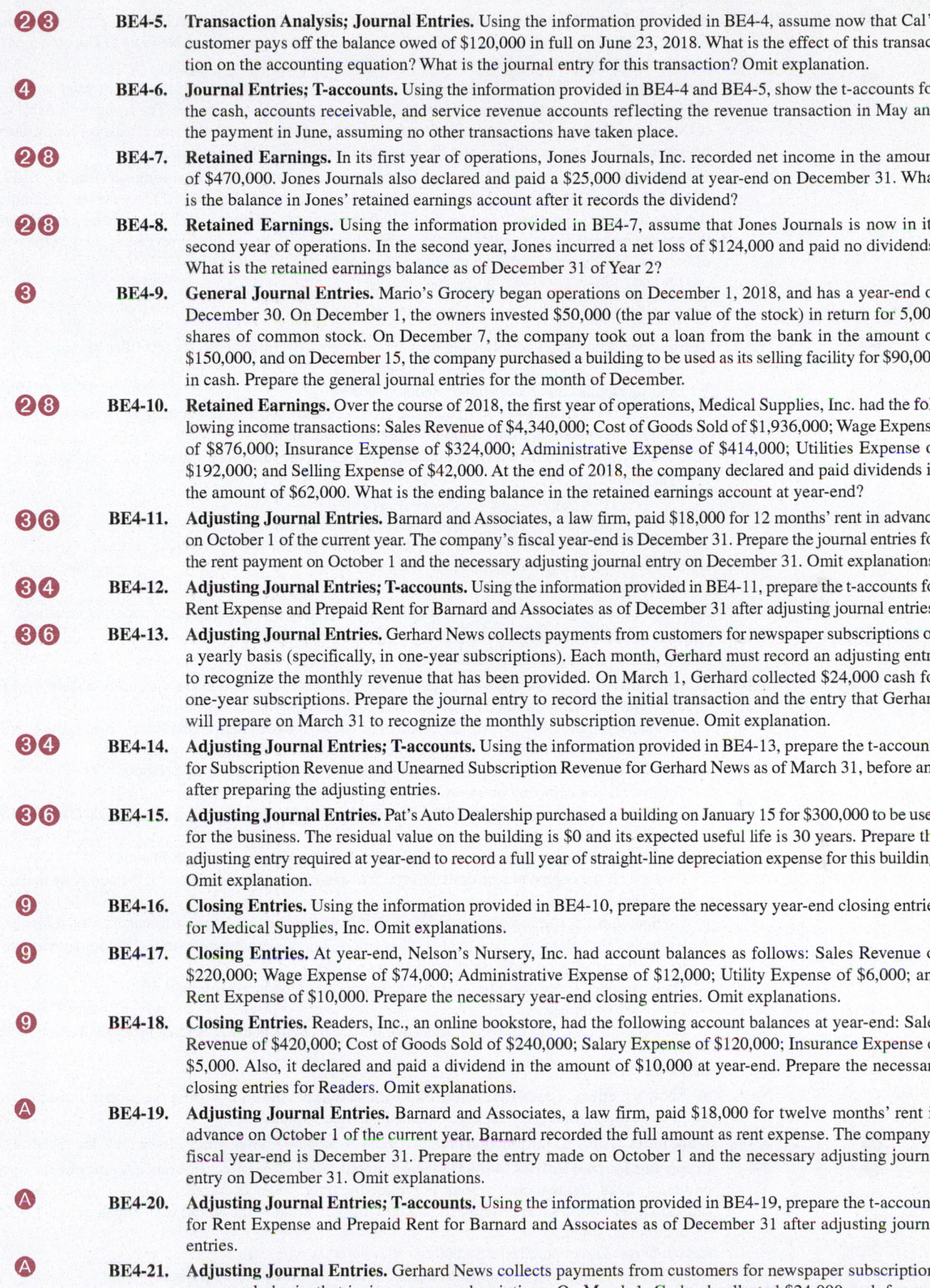

2 3 **BE4-5. Transaction Analysis; Journal Entries.** Using the information provided in BE4-4, assume now that Cal's customer pays off the balance owed of $120,000 in full on June 23, 2018. What is the effect of this transaction on the accounting equation? What is the journal entry for this transaction? Omit explanation.

4 **BE4-6. Journal Entries; T-accounts.** Using the information provided in BE4-4 and BE4-5, show the t-accounts for the cash, accounts receivable, and service revenue accounts reflecting the revenue transaction in May and the payment in June, assuming no other transactions have taken place.

2 8 **BE4-7. Retained Earnings.** In its first year of operations, Jones Journals, Inc. recorded net income in the amount of $470,000. Jones Journals also declared and paid a $25,000 dividend at year-end on December 31. What is the balance in Jones' retained earnings account after it records the dividend?

2 8 **BE4-8. Retained Earnings.** Using the information provided in BE4-7, assume that Jones Journals is now in its second year of operations. In the second year, Jones incurred a net loss of $124,000 and paid no dividends. What is the retained earnings balance as of December 31 of Year 2?

3 **BE4-9. General Journal Entries.** Mario's Grocery began operations on December 1, 2018, and has a year-end of December 30. On December 1, the owners invested $50,000 (the par value of the stock) in return for 5,000 shares of common stock. On December 7, the company took out a loan from the bank in the amount of $150,000, and on December 15, the company purchased a building to be used as its selling facility for $90,000 in cash. Prepare the general journal entries for the month of December.

2 8 **BE4-10. Retained Earnings.** Over the course of 2018, the first year of operations, Medical Supplies, Inc. had the following income transactions: Sales Revenue of $4,340,000; Cost of Goods Sold of $1,936,000; Wage Expense of $876,000; Insurance Expense of $324,000; Administrative Expense of $414,000; Utilities Expense of $192,000; and Selling Expense of $42,000. At the end of 2018, the company declared and paid dividends in the amount of $62,000. What is the ending balance in the retained earnings account at year-end?

3 6 **BE4-11. Adjusting Journal Entries.** Barnard and Associates, a law firm, paid $18,000 for 12 months' rent in advance on October 1 of the current year. The company's fiscal year-end is December 31. Prepare the journal entries for the rent payment on October 1 and the necessary adjusting journal entry on December 31. Omit explanations.

3 4 **BE4-12. Adjusting Journal Entries; T-accounts.** Using the information provided in BE4-11, prepare the t-accounts for Rent Expense and Prepaid Rent for Barnard and Associates as of December 31 after adjusting journal entries.

3 6 **BE4-13. Adjusting Journal Entries.** Gerhard News collects payments from customers for newspaper subscriptions on a yearly basis (specifically, in one-year subscriptions). Each month, Gerhard must record an adjusting entry to recognize the monthly revenue that has been provided. On March 1, Gerhard collected $24,000 cash for one-year subscriptions. Prepare the journal entry to record the initial transaction and the entry that Gerhard will prepare on March 31 to recognize the monthly subscription revenue. Omit explanation.

3 4 **BE4-14. Adjusting Journal Entries; T-accounts.** Using the information provided in BE4-13, prepare the t-accounts for Subscription Revenue and Unearned Subscription Revenue for Gerhard News as of March 31, before and after preparing the adjusting entries.

3 6 **BE4-15. Adjusting Journal Entries.** Pat's Auto Dealership purchased a building on January 15 for $300,000 to be used for the business. The residual value on the building is $0 and its expected useful life is 30 years. Prepare the adjusting entry required at year-end to record a full year of straight-line depreciation expense for this building. Omit explanation.

9 **BE4-16. Closing Entries.** Using the information provided in BE4-10, prepare the necessary year-end closing entries for Medical Supplies, Inc. Omit explanations.

9 **BE4-17. Closing Entries.** At year-end, Nelson's Nursery, Inc. had account balances as follows: Sales Revenue of $220,000; Wage Expense of $74,000; Administrative Expense of $12,000; Utility Expense of $6,000; and Rent Expense of $10,000. Prepare the necessary year-end closing entries. Omit explanations.

9 **BE4-18. Closing Entries.** Readers, Inc., an online bookstore, had the following account balances at year-end: Sales Revenue of $420,000; Cost of Goods Sold of $240,000; Salary Expense of $120,000; Insurance Expense of $5,000. Also, it declared and paid a dividend in the amount of $10,000 at year-end. Prepare the necessary closing entries for Readers. Omit explanations.

A **BE4-19. Adjusting Journal Entries.** Barnard and Associates, a law firm, paid $18,000 for twelve months' rent in advance on October 1 of the current year. Barnard recorded the full amount as rent expense. The company's fiscal year-end is December 31. Prepare the entry made on October 1 and the necessary adjusting journal entry on December 31. Omit explanations.

A **BE4-20. Adjusting Journal Entries; T-accounts.** Using the information provided in BE4-19, prepare the t-accounts for Rent Expense and Prepaid Rent for Barnard and Associates as of December 31 after adjusting journal entries.

A **BE4-21. Adjusting Journal Entries.** Gerhard News collects payments from customers for newspaper subscriptions on a yearly basis, that is, in one-year subscriptions. On March 1, Gerhard collected $24,000 cash for one-year subscriptions. Gerhard recorded the full amount as revenue. Prepare the entry made on March 1 and the necessary adjusting journal entry on December 31. Omit explanations.

A **BE4-22.** **Adjusting Journal Entries; T-accounts.** Using the information provided in BE4-21, prepare the t-accounts for Subscription Revenue and Unearned Subscription Revenue for Gerhard News as of December 31, before and after preparing adjusting entries.

C **BE4-23.** **Reversing Entries.** Thomas and Associates, a law firm, accrued $4,000 for four days of wages on December 31. On January 7, it paid two weeks of wages, totaling $10,000, to employees. The company's fiscal year-end is December 31. Prepare the journal entries for the accrued wages on December 31, the reversing entry at the beginning of the new fiscal year, and the payment on January 7. Omit explanations.

C **BE4-24.** **Reversing Entries.** Mueller Consulting is under contract to provide consulting services for $150,000 to Ames Computers. At the end of the current year, Mueller provided $30,000 of the services. It completes the services in the next year and receives the $150,000 payment on February 12. Prepare the journal entries for the service revenue recognized during the current year on December 31, the reversing entry at the beginning of the new fiscal year, and the payment on February 12. Omit explanations.

Exercises

2 **E4-1.** **Transaction Analysis.** The following transactions are taken from the books of Miller Manufacturing.

a. Bought office equipment with cash, $30,000.
b. Bought supplies on credit from a vendor, $15,000.
c. Sold goods for cash, $40,000 (ignore the inventory and cost of goods sold entry of this transaction).
d. Bought raw materials from a supplier on account, $22,000.
e. Sold goods to customers on account, $65,000 (ignore the inventory and cost of goods sold entry of this transaction).
f. Purchased raw materials by issuing a note payable, $14,000.
g. Paid cash toward note payable balance, $4,000.
h. Received cash from customer to apply to credit account balance, $3,000.
i. Paid for accounting and legal fees in cash, $5,000.
j. Paid salaries in cash, $12,000.

Show the effect of each transaction on assets, liabilities, and equity using the accounting equation.

3 **E4-2.** **Journal Entries.** Using the information given in E4-1, prepare the journal entry for each transaction for Miller Manufacturing. Omit explanations.

2 3 **E4-3.** **Transaction Analysis; Journal Entries.** Master Mind Games, Inc. is a new corporation started on January 1, 2018. The following transactions occurred during the first year of operations.

a. On January 1, the owners invested a total of $50,000 (the par value of the stock) to start the company. In exchange, the corporation issued the owners 5,000 shares of common stock.
b. On March 14, the company paid cash to purchase office equipment for $10,000.
c. On April 6, the company obtained a note from the bank for $100,000.
d. On May 31, salaries were accrued for time worked in May in the amount of $12,000. These salaries will be paid in June.
e. On June 15, the company paid cash to employees for salaries accrued on May 31.
f. On July 12, the company paid cash for legal fees associated with the startup of the company in the amount of $5,000.
g. On September 6, the company sold $32,000 of merchandise to a large customer. The customer paid cash for half of the transaction and put the other half on her credit account with the vendor (ignore the inventory and cost of goods sold entry of this transaction).
h. On November 1, the customer that purchased goods on September 6 paid off its credit account balance of $16,000 with cash.
i. On December 14, the company made a $10,000 cash payment towards its outstanding bank note balance.

Required »

a. Show the effect of each transaction on assets, liabilities, and equity using the accounting equation.
b. Prepare the journal entry for each transaction. Omit explanations.

4 **E4-4.** **T-accounts.** Using the information provided in E4-3, prepare Master Mind's t-accounts for each transaction.

3 **E4-5.** **Preparing Journal Entries in the General Journal.** The Dover Direct Insurance Agency began operations on June 1, 2018. In the month of June, the following transactions occurred:

June 2: Dover Direct's owner invested $80,000 (the par value of the stock) cash and acquired 4,000 shares of common stock.
June 8: Dover Direct purchased $8,000 of office supplies with cash.
June 15: Dover Direct paid employees $8,000 in cash for the biweekly payroll.
June 20: Dover Direct acquired new office furniture for $25,000. The company paid $10,000 in cash and financed the remainder by issuing a $15,000 note payable to the vendor.
June 22: Dover Direct collected $120,000 in sales revenue for the month, all of which was paid in cash.

Dover uses the following chart of accounts:

Assets

100 Cash
101 Accounts Receivable
102 Office Supplies
121 Furniture

Liabilities

200 Accounts Payable
210 Notes Payable

Stockholders' Equity

300 Common Stock

Revenues

400 Sales Revenue

Expenses

501 Wage Expense

Prepare the journal entries in the general journal format for Dover's transactions using appropriate account numbers. Assume the journal entries are posted to the ledger.

4 **E4-6. Posting to the General Ledger.** Using the information provided in E4-5, post Dover Direct Insurance Agency's journal entries to the general ledger for all relevant accounts for the month ended June 30, 2018. You do not need to provide explanations.

3 **E4-7. Preparing Journal Entries in the General Journal.** Cookies, Cakes & Crumbs Bakery (CC&C) ended its first year of operations on December 31, 2018. During 2018, the following transactions occurred:

January 10:	The owners of CC&C invested $200,000 (the par value of the stock) and acquired 20,000 shares of common stock.
March 15:	CC&C purchased equipment in the amount of $48,000 on credit account with the vendor.
April 12:	CC&C purchased supplies in the amount of $24,000 and paid cash.
May 31:	CC&C collected $82,000 in sales revenue for the month, all of which was paid in cash. Ignore Cost of Goods Sold.
June 15:	CC&C paid employees $22,000 in cash for wages.
July 31:	CC&C purchased supplies in the amount of $16,000 on credit account with the supplier.
September 30:	CC&C paid the balance due to the equipment vendor for the purchase made on March 15.
November 10:	CC&C paid the balance due to the supplier for the purchase made on July 31.
November 30:	CC&C recorded sales revenue in the amount of $216,000, half on credit and the other half paid in cash. Ignore Cost of Goods Sold.
December 20:	The customers who owed CC&C for the November 30 sales paid their balances in full with cash.

CC&C uses the following chart of accounts:

Assets

100 Cash
101 Accounts Receivable
102 Supplies
111 Equipment

Liabilities

200 Accounts Payable

Stockholders' Equity

300 Common Stock

Revenues

400 Sales Revenue

Expenses

503 Wage Expense

Prepare the journal entries in the general journal format for CC&C's transactions using appropriate account numbers. Assume the journal entries are posted to the ledger.

4 **E4-8. Preparing the T-accounts.** Using the information provided in E4-7, prepare CC&C's t-accounts for all relevant accounts for the year ended December 31, 2018. Post journal entries in E4-7 to the general ledger.

2 3 4 **E4-9. Transaction Analysis; Journal Entries and Posting to T-Accounts.** G&S Auto Body, Inc. started 2018 with the following balances:

Cash	$40,000
Accounts Receivable	100,000
Equipment	550,000
Accounts Payable	14,500
Salaries Payable	6,000
Notes Payable	108,000
Common Stock	235,000
Retained Earnings	326,500

The following transactions occurred during the current year:

a. On January 1, the owners invested a total of $150,000 (the par value of the stock) as an additional capital contribution. In exchange, the corporation issued the owners 50,000 shares of common stock.
b. On March 23, the company paid cash to purchase office equipment for $108,000.
c. On April 18, the company made a payment on the note due to a bank, $10,000.
d. On May 5, collected the balance of accounts receivable due from the prior year.
e. On May 31, salaries were accrued for time worked in May in the amount of $2,000. These salaries will be paid in June.
f. On June 30, the company paid cash to employees for salaries accrued on May 31 as well as the balance due from the prior year.
g. On July 8, the company paid cash for accounting fees in the amount of $6,000.
h. On September 6, the company performed repair work on a fleet of vehicles at a total charge of $76,000. The customer paid cash for half of the transaction and put the other half on its credit account with G&S.
i. On November 9, the customer who engaged G&S to do the repair work on September 6 paid off its account balance with cash.
j. On December 15, the company made a $10,000 cash payment to purchase parts and supplies (record in Parts and Supplies Inventory).

Required »

a. Show the effect of each transaction on assets, liabilities, and equity using the accounting equation.
b. Prepare the journal entry for each transaction. Omit explanations.
c. Post each journal entry to the t-accounts and determine the ending balances of each account at the end of the year.

2 3 4 **E4-10. Transaction Analysis; Journal Entries and Posting to T-Accounts.**
Hartman Housewares Company began the current year with the following account balances:

Cash	$70,000
Accounts Receivable	25,000
Supplies	5,000
Accounts Payable	28,000
Common Stock	32,000
Retained Earnings	40,000

The following transactions were completed during the current year.

a. Bought office equipment with cash, $10,000.
b. Bought supplies on credit from a vendor, $5,000.
c. Sold goods for cash, $12,000 (ignore the inventory and cost of goods sold entries of this transaction).
d. Bought raw materials from a supplier on account, $2,000.
e. Sold goods to customers on account, $6,000 (ignore the inventory and cost of goods sold entries of this transaction).
f. Purchased raw materials by issuing a note payable, $3,000.
g. Paid cash toward note payable balance, $500.

h. Received cash from customer to apply to credit account balance, $3,000.
i. Paid for accounting and legal fees in cash, $400.
j. Paid salaries in cash, $1,000.

Required:

a. Show the effect of each transaction on assets, liabilities, and equity using the accounting equation.
b. Prepare journal entries. Omit explanations.
c. Post each transaction to t-accounts.
d. Determine the ending balances for each account.

5 **E4-11. Preparing the Trial Balance.** Using the information provided in E4-6, prepare Dover Direct Insurance Agency's unadjusted trial balance at June 30, 2018.

6 **E4-12. Adjusting Journal Entries; T-accounts.** Fanatical Fashions, a department store, has the following unadjusted account balances as of December 31, 2018, the company's year-end:

- Cash: $3,230,000
- Accounts Receivable: $1,240,000
- Prepaid Insurance: $252,000
- Prepaid Rent: $480,000
- Buildings: $3,540,300
- Accumulated Depreciation—Buildings: $360,000
- Accounts Payable: $980,000
- Wages Payable: $420,000
- Note Payable: $360,000
- Common Stock: $1,000,000
- Sales Revenue: $7,450,300
- Wage Expense: $1,120,000
- Utilities Expense: $94,000
- Insurance Expense: $120,000
- Interest Expense: $234,000
- Rent Expense: $260,000
- Depreciation Expense—Buildings: $0

At year-end, Fanatical Fashions makes necessary adjusting journal entries to properly record revenues and expenses for the year. The following information applies to the adjusting journal entries:

- The prepaid insurance balance relates to a two-year insurance policy purchased in June that covers the period of July 1, 2018, to June 30, 2020.
- The prepaid rent balance relates to rent that was paid in January to cover the company's facilities for the current year.
- Wages for the year in the amount of $236,000 will be paid after year-end and have not yet been recorded.
- Fanatical purchased the buildings in the beginning of the year and depreciates on a yearly basis. It must record a full year of depreciation at the end of 2018. The buildings have no residual value, a 30-year estimated useful life, and will be depreciated on a straight-line basis.
- Fanatical has not yet recorded interest expense for 2018 on the note payable in the amount of $16,000.

Prepare the journal entries necessary to record the adjustments at year-end. Omit explanations..

7 **E4-13. Adjusted Trial Balance.** Using the information provided in E4-12, prepare an adjusted trial balance for Fanatical Fashions as of December 31, 2018.

6 **E4-14. Adjusting Journal Entries; T-Accounts.** MPS, Inc. has the following unadjusted account balances as of December 31, 2018, the company's year-end:

- Cash: $430,000
- Accounts Receivable: $2,000
- Prepaid Insurance: $14,000
- Prepaid Rent: $22,000
- Equipment: $60,000
- Accumulated Depreciation—Equipment: $0
- Accounts Payable: $10,000

- Common Stock: $16,000
- Sales Revenue: $823,100
- Wage Expense: $290,400
- Utilities Expense: $11,200
- Insurance Expense: $8,500
- Rent Expense: $11,000
- Depreciation Expense—Equipment: $0

At year-end, MPS makes adjusting journal entries to properly record revenues and expenses. The following information applies to the adjusting journal entries:

- The prepaid insurance balance relates to an insurance policy purchased on January 1, 2018, that covers the period of January 1, 2018, to December 31, 2018.
- The prepaid rent balance relates to rent paid in June 2018 to cover the period of July 1, 2018, to June 30, 2019.
- Wages for 2018 in the amount of $26,000 will be paid after year-end and have not yet been recorded.
- MPS purchased the equipment in the beginning of January 2018 and will depreciate it on a yearly basis. No depreciation has been recorded yet. The equipment has a useful life of 15 years, no residual value, and will be depreciated on a straight-line basis.

Prepare the journal entries necessary to record the adjustments at year-end. Omit explanations.

5 6 7 **E4-15. Unadjusted Trial Balance; Adjusted Trial Balance.** Using the information provided in E4-14:

Required »

a. Prepare an unadjusted trial balance for MPS, Inc. as of December 31, 2018.
b. Prepare an adjusted trial balance for MPS, Inc. as of December 31, 2018.

9 10 **E4-16. Closing Entries; Post-Closing Trial Balance.** Using the information provided in E4-14:

Required »

a. Prepare the necessary closing entries for MPS, Inc. at December 31, 2018. Omit explanations.
b. Prepare the post-closing trial balance for MPS, Inc. at December 31, 2018.

B **E4-17. Worksheet Preparation.** Using the information provided in E4-14, prepare a worksheet including the columns for the unadjusted trial balance, adjustments, the adjusted trial balance, income statement, and balance sheet.

6 7 **E4-18. Adjusting Journal Entries; Adjusted Trial Balance.** Magic Cleaning Services (MCS) has a fiscal year-end of December 31. It is the first year of operations. As of year-end, MCS has the following unadjusted trial balance:

Magic Cleaning Services
Unadjusted Trial Balance
At December 31

Account	Debit	Credit
Cash	$430,900	
Accounts Receivable	158,000	
Supplies	111,000	
Prepaid Rent	2,400	
Building	90,000	
Accounts Payable		$ 45,900
Unearned Service Revenue		98,000
Common Stock		100,000
Retained Earnings		0
Service Revenue		619,200
Wage Expense	48,600	
Utilities Expense	6,200	
Administrative Expense	16,000	
Totals	$863,100	$863,100

In addition, it has not adjusted for the following transactions:

- All of the prepaid rent expired by the end of the year.
- The building was purchased early this year and has a 30-year life with no residual value. Depreciation is to be recorded for a full year on a straight-line basis.
- The company provided a portion of the services related to an advance collection on December 20. It performed one-half of the services to be performed in the current year.
- Wages for the current year in the amount of $24,000 should be accrued and are set to be paid out to workers in January.

Required »

a. Journalize necessary adjusting journal entries. Omit explanations.
b. Prepare an adjusted trial balance as of December 31, 2018.

8 9 10 **E4-19. Preparing Financial Statements.** Using the adjusted trial balance for Magic Cleaning Services in E4-18, prepare a single-step income statement, a statement of shareholders' equity, and a balance sheet.

E4-20. Closing Entries; Post-Closing Trial Balance. Using the information provided in E4-18:

Required »

a. Prepare the necessary closing entries for Magic Cleaning Services at year-end. Omit explanations.
b. Prepare the post-closing trial balance for Magic Cleaning Services at year-end.

B **E4-21. Worksheet Preparation.** Using the information provided in E4-18, prepare a worksheet including the columns for the unadjusted trial balance, adjustments, the adjusted trial balance, income statement, and balance sheet.

9 **E4-22. Closing Entries.** Diane's Dairy Sales & Delivery finished its first year of operations on December 31, 2018. After adjusting journal entries, the company presented the following adjusted trial balance.

Diane's Dairy Sales & Delivery
Adjusted Trial Balance
At December 31

Account	Debit	Credit
Cash	$ 833,000	
Accounts Receivable	179,000	
Supplies	83,000	
Prepaid Insurance	13,000	
Prepaid Rent	30,000	
Equipment	350,000	
Accumulated Depreciation—Equipment		$ 30,000
Accounts Payable		150,500
Wages Payable		24,000
Unearned Revenue		12,000
Notes Payable, due 2019		80,000
Common Stock		1,000,000
Retained Earnings		0
Dividends	12,000	
Sales Revenue		1,000,500
Wage Expense	320,000	
Utility Expense	32,000	
Selling Expense	122,500	
Administrative Expense	192,500	
Insurance Expense	14,000	
Supplies Expense	85,000	
Depreciation Expense—Equipment	31,000	
Totals	$2,297,000	$2,297,000

Using this trial balance, prepare Diane's necessary entries to close out temporary accounts at year-end. Omit explanations.

8 **E4-23. Preparing Financial Statements.** Using the adjusted trial balance for Diane's Dairy Sales & Delivery in E4-22, prepare a single-step income statement, a statement of shareholders' equity, and a balance sheet.

10 **E4-24. Post-Closing Trial Balance.** Using the information in E4-22, prepare the post-closing trial balance for Diane's Dairy Sales & Delivery.

Problems

2 3 6 **P4-1. Transaction Analysis; Journal Entries; Adjusting Journal Entries.** Jester Entertainment Company began operations on January 1, 2018. The company had the following transactions in its first year of business:

- January 4: Owners invested $120,000 (the par value of the stock) in exchange for 20,000 shares of common stock.
- February 2: Jester took out a 10-year note payable in the amount of $80,000 to pay for operating expenses. Interest payments are due every six months, and the balance of the note will be paid off in a lump-sum in 10 years. The interest rate is 10% annually, that is, 5% every six months.
- February 16: Jester signed a rental lease for its operating facility and paid a year of rent up front in the amount of $60,000. The rental lease runs from March 1, 2018, through February 29, 2019.
- March 1: Jester purchased office supplies in the amount of $12,000 and paid in cash.
- March 12: Jester paid $18,000 cash for advertising expenses.
- April 1: Jester purchased a two-year insurance policy that runs from April 1, 2018, to March 31, 2020, in the amount of $40,000 and paid in full for the policy in cash.
- May 12: Jester negotiated a contract with a customer to provide entertainment services for a one-year period running from June 1, 2018, to May 31, 2019. The customer paid the contract in full on May 12 with cash in the amount of $64,000.
- June 16: Jester paid wages in the amount of $12,000 to employees in cash.
- July 20: Jester negotiated a contract with a customer to provide entertainment services for a six-month period running from September 1, 2018, to February 28, 2019. The customer paid the contract in full on July 20 with cash in the amount of $42,000.
- August 2: Jester paid cash in the amount of $4,000 for the first interest payment on the note payable taken out on February 2.
- August 18: Jester received and paid a utilities bill in the amount of $7,000 in cash.
- September 10: Jester paid wages in the amount of $28,000 in cash.
- October 1: Jester negotiated a contract with a customer to provide entertainment services for a one-year period running from October 1, 2018, to September 30, 2019, in the amount of $420,000. The customer paid the contract in full on October 1.
- November 14: Jester purchased office supplies in the amount of $26,000 on account with the vendor.
- December 6: Jester received an advertising bill for $22,000. The services were provided in 2018 and the bill will be paid in January.

Note: At year-end, Jester had $18,000 of office supplies remaining on hand.

Required »

a. Prepare the journal entries for the original transactions. Omit explanations.
b. Show the accounting equation effect of each of the original transactions.
c. Prepare any necessary year-end adjusting journal entries for these transactions.
d. Show the accounting equation effect of each of the adjusting journal entries.

2 3 6 **P4-2. Transaction Analysis; Journal Entries; Adjusting Journal Entries.** Branton Stores began operations on January 1, 2018. Branton had the following transactions in its first year of business:

- January 4: Owners invested $400,000 (the par value of the stock) in exchange for 40,000 shares of common stock.
- January 31: Branton purchased an office building for $320,000 and paid for the purchase with a note payable. Interest in the amount of $16,000 will be due annually on January 31 of each year, beginning in 2019.
- February 1: Branton rented out a portion of its office building to another company. The renter signed a rental lease for the period of February 1, 2018, to January 31, 2019, and paid the annual rent amount of $60,000 upfront in cash.
- March 1: Branton paid $12,000 cash for administrative expenses.

- March 28: Branton purchased supplies in the amount of $42,000 on account with the supplier.
- April 8: Branton purchased a one-year insurance policy that runs from May 1, 2018, to April 30, 2019, in the amount of $62,000 and paid for the policy in full in cash.
- May 1: Branton recorded sales revenue in the amount of $240,000 that was received in cash from customers. Ignore Cost of Goods Sold.
- July 6: Branton paid employees $34,000 in wages in cash.
- September 30: Branton recorded $320,000 in sales revenue. Of this amount, $200,000 was paid in cash and the remainder was on account. Ignore Cost of Goods Sold.
- October 31: Branton received a cash payment from a customer in the amount of $40,000 to be applied to its account balance related to the September 30 sale.
- November 15: Branton purchased supplies in the amount of $26,000 on account with the vendor.
- December 1: Branton recorded sales revenue in the amount of $222,000, all on credit. Ignore Cost of Goods Sold.
- December 22: Branton received a legal bill for $14,000, which it will pay when due in February 2019.

Note: Branton records straight-line depreciation on buildings, using a 32-year life and a salvage value of zero. At year-end, wages for 2018 in the amount of $86,000 are due to employees and will be paid in January 2019. Supplies in the amount of $6,000 remain on hand on December 31.

Required »

a. Prepare the journal entries for the transactions. Omit explanations.
b. Show the accounting equation effect of each of these transactions.
c. Prepare any necessary year-end adjusting journal entries for these transactions.
d. Show the accounting equation effect of each of the adjusting journal entries.

❸❹❺ **P4-3. Journal Entries; Post to the General Ledger; Prepare a Trial Balance.** Herman and Sons' Law Offices opened on January 1, 2018. During the first year of business, the company had the following transactions:

- January 2: The owners invested $250,000 (the par value of the stock) into the business and acquired 25,000 shares of common stock in return.
- January 15: Herman and Sons' bought an office building in the amount of $80,000. The company took out a long-term note from the bank to finance the purchase.
- February 12: Herman and Sons' billed clients for $60,000 of services performed.
- March 1: Herman and Sons' took out a two-year insurance policy, which it paid cash for in the amount of $22,000.
- March 10: Herman collected $20,000 from clients toward the outstanding accounts receivable balance.
- May 13: Herman received cash payments totaling $210,000 for legal services—$40,000 was for services previously billed to customers on February 12 and the remainder was for services provided in May not yet recorded.
- June 10: Herman purchased office supplies in the amount of $35,000, all on credit.
- July 15: Herman paid wages of $16,000 in cash to office staff workers.
- August 8: Herman paid off the $35,000 balance owed to a supplier for the purchase made on June 10.
- September 3: Herman and Sons' purchased $25,000 of office supplies in cash.
- September 20: The company paid $11,000 cash for utilities.
- October 1: Herman and Sons' paid wages in the amount of $24,000 to office workers.
- December 1: Herman and Sons' received cash payments from clients in the amount of $320,000 for services to be performed in the upcoming months.
- December 31: Herman declared and paid a $10,000 dividend.

The chart of accounts used by Herman and Sons' Law Offices is as follows:

Chart of Accounts

Group	Account #	Account Title
100: Assets		
	101	Cash
	102	Accounts Receivable
	103	Office Supplies
	104	Prepaid Insurance
	110	Building
	112	Accumulated Depreciation—Building

Chart of Accounts

Group	Account #	Account Title
200: Liabilities		
	201	Accounts Payable
	202	Unearned Service Revenue
	203	Wages Payable
	210	Interest Payable
	220	Notes Payable
300: Stockholders' Equity		
	301	Common Stock
	310	Retained Earnings
	320	Dividends
400: Revenues		
	401	Service Revenue
500: Expenses		
	501	Wage Expense
	502	Utilities Expense
	503	Selling Expense
	504	Administrative Expense
	505	Insurance Expense
	506	Supplies Expense
	510	Depreciation Expense—Building
	520	Interest Expense
600: Other		
	601	Income Summary

Required »

a. Journalize the transactions for the year. Omit explanations.
b. Post the journal entries to the general ledger.
c. Prepare an unadjusted trial balance as of December 31.

6 7 8 **P4-4. Preparing the Trial Balance; Adjusting Journal Entries; Preparing Financial Statements.** Using the information provided in P4-3, perform the following steps:

Required »

a. Journalize and post adjusting journal entries for Herman and Sons' based on the following additional information:
   - Of the cash payments received from customers on December 1, half of these services were performed in December and half relates to future services to be rendered in the following year.
   - Ten months of the insurance policy expired by the end of the year.
   - Depreciation for the full year should be recorded on the building purchased. The building has a 20-year life and no residual value. Depreciation will be recorded on a straight-line basis.
   - A total of $15,000 of office supplies remains on hand at the end of the year.
   - Interest expense in the amount of $7,000 should be accrued on the note payable.
   - Wages in the amount of $32,000 must be accrued at year-end to be paid in January.

b. Prepare an adjusted trial balance as of December 31.
c. Prepare a single-step income statement, a statement of shareholders' equity, and a balance sheet.

9 10 **P4-5. Closing Process.** Using the information in P4-3 and P4-4, perform the following steps for Herman and Sons':

Required »

a. Journalize and post the necessary closing entries at year-end. Omit explanations.
b. Prepare a post-closing trial balance as of December 31, 2018.

❸❹❺ **P4-6. Journal Entries; Post to the General Ledger; Prepare a Trial Balance.** Tides Tea Company began operations on January 1, 2018. During the first year of business, the company had the following transactions:

- January 18: The owners invested $200,000 (the par value of the stock) into the business and acquired 40,000 shares of common stock in return.
- February 1: Tides bought factory equipment in the amount of $45,000. The company took out a long-term note from the bank to finance the purchase.
- February 28: The company paid cash for rent to cover the 12-month period from March 1, 2018, through February 29, 2019, in the amount of $27,000.
- March 1: Tides purchased supplies in the amount of $28,000 on account.
- March 22: Tides recorded sales revenue in the amount of $120,000. Half of this amount was received in cash and half was paid on account. Ignore cost of goods sold.
- May 1: Tides received cash payments to pay off all the customer accounts.
- May 29: The company paid wages of $34,000 in cash.
- July 12: Tides recorded sales revenue in the amount of $180,000, all of which was paid in cash. Ignore cost of goods sold.
- July 31: Tides paid $3,200 cash for interest on the note taken out on February 1.
- August 8: Tides paid off the balance owed to a supplier for the purchase made on March 1.
- September 1: Tides paid $6,000 cash for utilities.
- October 14: Tides paid wages of $24,000 in cash.
- November 10: Tides recorded sales revenue in the amount of $218,000. One payment of $100,000 was received in cash; the remainder of this balance was sold on account. Ignore cost of goods sold.
- December 31: Tides declared and paid a $25,000 dividend.

The chart of accounts used by Tides Tea Company is as follows:

Chart of Accounts

Group	Account #	Account Title
100: Assets	101	Cash
	102	Accounts Receivable
	103	Supplies
	104	Prepaid Rent
	110	Equipment
	112	Accumulated Depreciation—Equipment
200: Liabilities	201	Accounts Payable
	203	Wages Payable
	210	Interest Payable
	220	Notes Payable
300: Equity	301	Common Stock
	310	Retained Earnings
	320	Dividends
400: Revenues	401	Sales Revenue
500: Expenses	501	Wage Expense
	502	Utilities Expense
	503	Rent Expense
	504	Administrative Expense
	505	Insurance Expense
	506	Supplies Expense
	510	Depreciation Expense—Equipment
	520	Interest Expense
600: Other	601	Income Summary

Required »

a. Journalize the transactions for the year. Omit explanations.
b. Post the journal entries to the general ledger.
c. Prepare an unadjusted trial balance as of December 31.

⑥⑦⑧ **P4-7. Preparing the Trial Balance; Adjusting Journal Entries; Preparing Financial Statements.** Using the information provided in P4-6, perform the following steps for Tides Tea Company:

Required »

a. Journalize and post adjusting journal entries based on the following additional information (omit explanations):
   - At December 31, interest in the amount of $2,600 has accrued on the note payable but has not yet been recorded. This amount will be paid on January 31, 2019.
   - The rent payment made on February 28 was for a 12-month lease covering March 1, 2018, to February 29, 2019.
   - Straight-line depreciation for the full year should be recorded on the equipment purchased on February 1. The equipment has a 15-year life and no residual value.
   - A total of $6,000 of supplies remains on hand at the end of the year.
   - Wage payments in the amount of $62,000 must be accrued at year-end.
   - On December 14, Tides received a utilities bill in the amount of $6,200 for the month of November that has not yet been recorded. The amount will be paid in January 2019.

b. Prepare an adjusted trial balance as of December 31.
c. Prepare an income statement, a statement of shareholders' equity, and a balance sheet.

②③④⑥⑦ **P4-8. Transaction Analysis; Journal Entries; Adjusting Journal Entries, Posting, Adjusted Trial Balance.** The post-closing trial balance for Heron Consulting Services, Inc. at December 31 of the prior year is presented here.

Heron Consulting Services, Inc.
Post-Closing Trial Balance
At December 31 (Prior Year)

Account	Debit	Credit
Cash	$1,000	
Accounts Receivable	800	
Supplies	150	
Prepaid Rent	300	
Building	6,500	
Accounts Payable		$ 750
Unearned Service Revenue		400
Common Stock		5,000
Retained Earnings		2,600
Service Revenue		0
Wage Expense	0	
Utilities Expense	0	
Administrative Expense	0	
Totals	$8,750	$8,750

The company reported the following transactions during the current year:

- January 2: Heron took out a 5%, 2-year note payable in the amount of $3,000 to pay for operating expenses. Interest is paid annually on January 1.
- February 1: Heron prepaid $600 for a one-year insurance policy. Policy begins February 1.
- March 1: Heron purchased office supplies for cash, $275.
- March 23: Heron paid $300 cash for advertising expenses.
- April 1: The existing balance of prepaid rent expired, so the company prepaid an additional $480 for a one-year lease on a warehouse.

- May 1: Heron signed a contract to perform consulting services and collected $550. Heron will not provide the services until next year.
- June 30: Heron paid wages in the amount of $200 to employees in cash.
- July 1: The company received $2,150 in cash for services rendered that day.
- August 8: Heron paid a utilities bill in the amount of $70 in cash.
- September 1: Heron paid wages in the amount of $80 in cash.
- October 1: Heron collected $250 of the accounts receivable balance.
- November 14: Heron purchased office equipment in the amount of $1,800 with cash. Heron will record $50 of depreciation on the equipment this year.
- December 6: Heron received a bill for $100 for deliveries made this year and will pay the bill next year.

Note: At year-end, Heron had $100 of supplies remaining on hand. Also, services pertaining to the beginning balance of unearned service revenue were performed during the year. Finally, Heron reports $500 of depreciation expense related to the buildings.

Required »

a. Show the accounting equation effect of each of the original transactions.
b. Prepare the journal entries for the original transactions. Omit explanations.
c. Prepare any necessary year-end adjusting journal entries for these transactions. Show the accounting equation effect of each of the adjusting journal entries.
d. Post all entries to the T-accounts.
e. Prepare the adjusted trial balance at the end of the year.

9 10 **P4-9. Closing Process.** Using the information in P4-6 and P4-7, perform the following steps for Tides Tea Company:

Required »

a. Journalize and post the necessary closing entries. Omit explanations.
b. Prepare a post-closing trial balance as of December 31.

9 10 **P4-10. Closing Process.** Sherlock Locksmiths, Inc. has the following adjusted trial balance for the year ended December 31, 2018.

Sherlock Locksmiths, Inc.
Adjusted Trial Balance
At December 31, 2018

Account	Debit	Credit
Cash	$1,734,900	
Accounts Receivable	778,000	
Supplies	250,000	
Prepaid Insurance	130,000	
Equipment	360,000	
Accumulated Depreciation—Equipment		$ 28,000
Accounts Payable		1,275,000
Unearned Service Revenue		39,600
Wages Payable		280,000
Interest Payable		60,000
Notes Payable		320,000
Common Stock		1,200,000
Retained Earnings		0
Dividends	12,000	
Service revenue		2,160,000
Wage Expense	1,276,000	
Utilities Expense	89,200	
Selling Expense	72,500	
Administrative Expense	182,000	
Repairs Expense	62,000	
Interest Expense	40,000	
Insurance Expense	121,000	
Supplies Expense	215,000	
Depreciation Expense—Equipment	40,000	
Totals	$5,362,600	$5,362,600

Required »

a. Journalize and post the necessary closing entries. Omit explanations.
b. Prepare a post-closing trial balance as of December 31.

③④⑤⑥ ⑦⑧⑨⑩ **P4-11. Transaction Analysis; Journal Entries, Posting, Unadjusted Trial Balance, Adjusting Journal Entries, Adjusted Trial Balance, Financial Statements, Closing Entries, Post-Closing Trial Balance.**

The Umbro Company, which is a fitness center, was formed on January 2 of the current year. Transactions completed during the first year of operation are presented below.

January 2:	Issued 900,000 shares of common stock for $15,000,000, which is the par value of the stock.
January 10:	Acquired equipment in exchange for $2,500,000 cash and a $6,000,000 note payable. The note is due in 10 years.
February 1:	Paid $36,000 for a business insurance policy covering the two-year period beginning on February 1.
February 22:	Purchased $930,000 of supplies on account.
March 1:	Paid wages of $194,600.
March 23:	Billed $2,820,000 for services rendered on account.
April 1:	Paid $130,000 of the amount due on the supplies purchased on February 22.
April 17:	Collected $190,000 of the outstanding accounts receivable.
May 1:	Paid wages of $209,400.
May 8:	Received bill and paid $96,700 for utilities.
May 24:	Paid $45,500 for sales commissions.
June 1:	Made the first payment on the note issued on January 10. The payment consisted of $50,000 of interest and $210,000 to be applied against the principal of the note.
June 16:	Billed customers for $680,000 of services rendered.
June 30:	Collected $450,000 on accounts receivable.
July 10:	Purchased $166,000 of supplies on account.
Aug 25:	Paid $150,000 for administrative expenses.
Sept 23:	Paid $35,000 for warehouse repairs.
October 1:	Paid wages of $100,000.
Nov 20:	Purchased supplies for $45,000 with cash.
Dec 15:	Collected $134,700 in advance for services to be provided in December and January of the following year.
Dec 30:	Declared and paid a $50,000 dividend to shareholders.

The chart of accounts used by the Umbro Company follows:

Chart of Accounts

Group	Account #	Account Title
100: Assets	101	Cash
	102	Accounts Receivable
	103	Supplies
	104	Prepaid Insurance
	110	Equipment
	112	Accumulated Depreciation—Equipment
200: Liabilities	201	Accounts Payable
	202	Unearned Service Revenue
	203	Wages Payable
	210	Interest Payable
	220	Notes Payable
300: Stockholders' Equity	301	Common Stock
	310	Retained Earnings
	320	Dividends
400: Revenues	401	Service Revenue

Chart of Accounts

Group	Account #	Account Title
500: Expenses	501	Wage Expense
	502	Utilities Expense
	503	Selling Expense
	504	Administrative Expense
	505	Repairs Expense
	506	Insurance Expense
	507	Supplies Expense
	510	Depreciation Expense—Equipment
	520	Interest Expense
600: Other	601	Income Summary

a. Journalize the transactions for the year.
b. Post the journal entries to t-accounts.
c. Prepare an unadjusted trial balance as of December 31.
d. Journalize and post adjusting entries to t-accounts based on the following additional information.
   i. Eleven months of the insurance policy expired by the end of the year.
   ii. Depreciation for the equipment is $420,000.
   iii. The company provided a portion of the services related to the advance collection of December 15. The company recognized $72,000 as service revenue for services performed.
   iv. There are $501,000 of supplies on hand at the end of the year.
   v. An additional $172,000 of interest has accrued on the note by the end of the year.
   vi. Umbro accrued wages in the amount of $240,000.
e. Prepare an adjusted trial balance as of December 31.
f. Prepare a single-step income statement and statement of stockholders' equity for the current year and a classified balance sheet as of the end of the year.
g. Journalize and post closing entries.
h. Prepare a post-closing trial balance as of December 31.

3 4 5 6 7 8 9 10 **P4-12. Transaction Analysis; Journal Entries, Posting, Unadjusted Trial Balance, Adjusting Journal Entries, Adjusted Trial Balance, Financial Statements, Closing Entries, Post-Closing Trial Balance.**

The Jiayin Li Corporation, which is a technology company, was formed on January 1 of the current year. Transactions completed during the first year of operation follow.

January 1:	Issued 1,000,000 shares of common stock for $15,000,000, which is the par value of the stock.
January 10:	Acquired equipment in exchange for $2,000,000 cash and a $5,000,000 note payable. The note is due in 10 years.
February 10:	Paid $48,000 for a business insurance policy covering the two-year period beginning on March 1.
February 14:	Purchased $900,000 of supplies on account.
March 1:	Paid wages of $195,000.
March 15:	Billed $2,500,000 for services rendered on account.
April 3:	Paid $125,000 of the amount due on the supplies purchased on February 14.
April 17:	Billed $2,000,000 for services rendered on account.
May 1:	Paid wages of $200,000.
May 7:	Collected $200,500 of the outstanding accounts receivable.
May 8:	Received bill and paid $96,500 for utilities.
May 24:	Paid $40,000 for sales commissions.
June 4:	Made the first payment on the note issued on January 10. The payment consisted of $50,000 of interest and $150,000 to be applied against the principal of the note.
June 18:	Billed customers for $646,000 of services rendered.
June 29:	Collected $450,000 on accounts receivable.
July 10:	Purchased $45,000 of supplies in cash.
Aug 25:	Paid $120,000 for administrative expenses.

Sept 23:	Paid $35,500 for warehouse repairs.
October 1:	Paid wages of $100,000.
Nov 23:	Purchased supplies for $500,000 on account.
Dec 19:	Collected $150,000 in advance for services to be provided in December and January of the following year.
Dec 30:	Declared and paid a $20,000 dividend to shareholders.

The chart of accounts used by Jiayin Li is presented here:

Chart of Accounts

Group	***Account #***	***Account Title***
100: Assets	101	Cash
	102	Accounts Receivable
	103	Supplies
	104	Prepaid Insurance
	110	Equipment
	112	Accumulated Depreciation—Equipment
200: Liabilities	201	Accounts Payable
	202	Unearned Service Revenue
	203	Wages Payable
	210	Interest Payable
	220	Notes Payable
300: Stockholders' Equity	301	Common Stock
	310	Retained Earnings
	320	Dividends
400: Revenues	401	Service Revenue
500: Expenses	501	Wage Expense
	502	Utilities Expense
	503	Selling Expense
	504	Administrative Expense
	505	Repairs Expense
	506	Insurance Expense
	510	Depreciation Expense—Equipment
	520	Interest Expense
600: Other	601	Income Summary

a. Journalize the transactions for the year.
b. Post the journal entries to t-accounts.
c. Prepare an unadjusted trial balance as of December 31.
d. Journalize and post adjusting entries to t-accounts based on the following additional information.
   i. Ten months of the insurance policy had expired by the end of the year.
   ii. Depreciation for the equipment is $380,000.
   iii. The company provided a portion of the services related to the advance collection of December 19. The company recognized $50,000 as service revenue for services performed.
   iv. An additional $160,000 of interest had accrued on the note by the end of the year.
   v. Jiayin Li Corporation accrued wages in the amount of $200,000.
e. Prepare an adjusted trial balance as of December 31.
f. Prepare a single-step income statement and statement of stockholders' equity for the current year and a classified balance sheet as of the end of the year.
g. Journalize and post closing entries.
h. Prepare a post-closing trial balance as of December 31.

Excel Project

Autograded Excel Project available in **MyLab Accounting**

APPENDIX A

Alternative Treatment of Deferred Revenues and Expenses

Depending on a company's accounting information system, prepaid expenses may initially be recorded as an expense instead of an asset. That is, the accounting information system could automatically debit all payments to insurers, landlords, and other payees to an expense account. Thus, if any prepaid amounts remain at the end of the year, assets are understated and expenses are overstated prior to the adjustment. In this case, the adjusting journal entry requires the creation of an asset for the unexpired portion of the prepaid asset and a reduction of the expense account for the same amount.

EXAMPLE 4A.1 Alternative Treatment of Prepaid Expenses

PROBLEM: FSU Corporation paid $3,000 on January 1 for a three-year insurance policy. The policy starts on January 1. FSU records all cash disbursements of this type by debiting an expense account as follows:

Date	*Account*	*Debit*	*Credit*
Jan 1	Insurance Expense	3,000	
	Cash		3,000
	(To record payment for insurance)		

Prepare the adjusting journal entry required on December 31.

SOLUTION: The insurance expense and prepaid insurance accounts would appear as follows on December 31 before any adjustment is made:

Insurance Expense

	Debit	Credit
January 1	3,000	
Dec 31 Bal.	3,000	

Prepaid Insurance

	Debit	Credit
January 1	0	
Dec 31 Bal.	0	

On December 31, insurance expense is overstated because only one year of insurance coverage has expired, not three. There are two years of prepaid insurance remaining, meaning that prepaid insurance, the asset, is understated. In order to adjust the insurance expense and the prepaid insurance accounts, FSU must record the following adjusting journal entry:

Date	*Account*	*Debit*	*Credit*
Dec 31	Prepaid Insurance	2,000	
	Insurance Expense		2,000
	(To record unexpired insurance)		

Continued

After FSU posts the adjusting journal entry, the accounts will reflect the correct balance for the asset and the expense.

Insurance Expense

January 1	3,000	
AJE		2,000
Dec 31 Bal.	1,000	

Prepaid Insurance

January 1	0	
AJE	2,000	
Dec 31 Bal.	2,000	

In addition, companies may initially record revenues collected in advance as revenue rather than crediting a liability account. Prior to the adjustment, revenues are overstated and liabilities are understated. The adjusting journal entry requires recording a liability for the unperformed portion and reducing the revenue account to properly reflect the amount performed at the end of the reporting period.

EXAMPLE 4A.2 Alternative Treatment of Unearned Revenue

PROBLEM: Nancy Frank Realty collected $100,000 in advance for a one-year lease on June 30 of the current year. One-half of the rent is earned by year-end, December 31.

On the date the rent was collected, Nancy Frank made the following journal entry.

Date	*Account*	*Debit*	*Credit*
June 30	Cash	100,000	
	Rent Revenue		100,000
	(To record advance collection)		

What adjusting journal entry is necessary on December 31?

SOLUTION: The rent revenue and unearned revenue accounts would appear as follows on December 31 before any adjustment is made:

Rent Revenue

June 30		100,000
Dec 31 Bal.		100,000

Unearned Rent Revenue

June 30		0
Dec 31 Bal.		0

On December 31, the revenue account is overstated and the liability account, unearned rent revenue, is understated because only one-half of the advance payment is performed at the

Continued

end of the year. To adjust the rent revenue account, Nancy Frank must prepare the following adjusting journal entry:

Date	Account	Debit	Credit
Dec 31	Rent Revenue	50,000	
	Unearned Rent Revenue (liability)		50,000
	(To record unearned rent revenue)		

After Nancy Frank posts the adjusting journal entries, the accounts will reflect the correct balances of the liability and revenue accounts.

Rent Revenue

	Debit	Credit
June 30		100,000
AJE	50,000	
Dec 31 Bal.		50,000

Unearned Rent Revenue

	Debit	Credit
June 30		0
AJE		50,000
Dec 31 Bal.		50,000

APPENDIX B

Using a Worksheet

A worksheet is a multiple-column form that may be used to simplify the adjustment process and the preparation of the financial statements. It includes columns for the account titles, the unadjusted trial balance, AJEs, adjusted trial balance, income statement, and balance sheet. Exhibit 4B.1 presents the standard form of the worksheet.

EXHIBIT 4B.1 Format of the Worksheet

	A	B	C	D	E	F	G	H	I	J	K
1	Account Title	Unadjusted Trial Balance		Adjustments		Adjusted Trial Balance		Income Statement		Balance Sheet	
2		Dr.	Cr.	Dr.	Cr.	Dr.	Cr.	Dr.	Cr.	Dr.	Cr.

The unadjusted trial balance and the adjusted trial balance columns reflect the account balances in the ledger at these two points in the accounting cycle. The adjustments column reflects the adjusting journal entries. After the worksheet has been completed, the income statement and balance sheet columns allow for the preparation of financial statements: The income statement is prepared from the income statement columns, and the statement of stockholders' equity and balance sheet are prepared from the balance sheet columns.

The steps in preparing a worksheet are as follows:

1. Prepare an unadjusted trial balance. Prepare the unadjusted trial balance directly on the worksheet—there is no need for a separate document.
2. Enter the adjusting journal entries in the adjustments columns. Note that the AJEs must also be recorded in the journal.
3. Compute the adjusted balances in the adjusted trial balance columns.
4. Place adjusted trial balance amounts in appropriate income statement and balance sheet columns.
5. Total the statement columns, compute the net income (or loss), and complete the worksheet.

A sample worksheet outlining the five steps is presented in Exhibit 4B.2.

EXHIBIT 4B.2 Sample Worksheet

	A	B	C	D	E	F	G	H	I	J	K
1		Unadjusted Trial Balance (STEP 1)		Adjustments (STEP 2)		Adjusted Trial Balance (STEP 3)		Income Statement (STEP 4)		Balance Sheet (STEP 4)	
2	**Account**	**Debit**	**Credit**	**Debit**	**Credit**	**Debit**	**Credit**	**Debit**	**Credit**	**Debit**	**Credit**
3	Cash										
4	Accounts Receivable										
5	Prepaid Insurance										
6	Machinery & Equipment										
7	Accumulated Depreciation—Machinery & Equipment										
8	Accounts Payable										
9	Wages Payable										
10	Common Stock										
11	Retained Earnings										
12	Dividends										
13	Fees Earned										
14	Wage Expense										
15	Rent Expense										
16	Depreciation Expense—Machinery & Equipment										
17	Insurance Expense										
18	Totals										
19	Net Income (Loss)										
20	Totals										

STEP 5 (rows 18–20)

Example 4B.1 illustrates worksheet preparation.

EXAMPLE 4B.1

Worksheet Preparation

PROBLEM: Enzo Educational Services provided the following unadjusted trial balance as of December 31 of the current year:

Enzo Educational Services
Unadjusted Trial Balance
At December 31

Account	Debit	Credit
Cash	$215,000	
Accounts Receivable	50,000	
Prepaid Insurance	40,000	
Machinery & Equipment	275,000	
Accumulated Depreciation—Machinery & Equipment		$ 27,500
Accounts Payable		24,000
Wages Payable		19,500
Common Stock		120,000
Retained Earnings		303,000
Dividends	9,000	
Fees Earned		200,000
Wage Expense	25,000	
Rent Expense	80,000	
Totals	$694,000	$694,000

In addition, note that:

a. Depreciation for the year is $27,500.
b. $8,000 of wages has accrued for the last pay period of the year to be paid on January 2.
c. The company rented equipment on account for $3,500 on December 15 and used the equipment for two weeks. The company has not recorded the event as of the date of the trial balance.
d. There should be $30,000 remaining in the prepaid insurance account.

Prepare the worksheet for Enzo Educational Services.

Enzo first enters the unadjusted trial balance on the worksheet, followed by the AJEs in the adjustments column. Enzo then computes the amounts for the adjusted trial balance. For example, the unadjusted balance for prepaid insurance is a debit of $40,000. An adjusting journal entry credits the account for $10,000, leaving a $30,000 debit adjusted balance.

Next, Enzo extends each amount from the adjusted trial balance to either the income statement or balance sheet columns. The income statement columns initially will not balance—the difference (revenues less expenses) is the net income or net loss for the period. Likewise, the balance sheet will not balance because the balance in retained earnings is the beginning balance, not the ending balance. Here as well, the difference between the debit and credit columns is the net income or net loss amount.

Continued

SOLUTION:

A	B	C	D	E	F	G	H	I	J	K
	Unadjusted Trial Balance (STEP 1)		Adjustments (STEP 2)		Adjusted Trial Balance (STEP 3)		Income Statement (STEP 4)		Balance Sheet (STEP 4)	
Account	**Debit**	**Credit**	**Debit**	**Credit**	**Debit**	**Credit**	**Debit**	**Credit**	**Debit**	**Credit**
Cash	215,000									
Accounts Receivable	50,000									
Prepaid Insurance	40,000			(d)10,000						
Machinery & Equipment	275,000									
Accumulated Depreciation—Machinery & Equipment		27,500		(a) 27,500						
Accounts Payable		24,000		(c) 3,500						
Wages Payable		19,500		(b) 8,000						
Common Stock		120,000								
Retained Earnings		303,000								
Dividends	9,000									
Fees Earned		200,000								
Wage Expense	25,000		(b) 8,000							
Rent Expense	80,000		(c) 3,500							
Depreciation Expense—Machinery & Equipment			(a) 27,500							
Insurance Expense			(d) 10,000							
Totals	694,000	694,000	49,000	49,000						
Net Income										

Letters (a) through (d) are used to cross-reference to the additional information provided in the illustration.

A	B	C	D	E	F	G	H	I	J	K
	Unadjusted Trial Balance (STEP 1)		Adjustments (STEP 2)		Adjusted Trial Balance (STEP 3)		Income Statement (STEP 4)		Balance Sheet (STEP 4)	
Account	**Debit**	**Credit**	**Debit**	**Credit**	**Debit**	**Credit**	**Debit**	**Credit**	**Debit**	**Credit**
Cash	215,000				215,000					
Accounts Receivable	50,000				50,000					
Prepaid Insurance	40,000			10,000	30,000					
Machinery & Equipment	275,000				275,000					
Accumulated Depreciation—Machinery & Equipment		27,500		27,500		55,000				
Accounts Payable		24,000		3,500		27,500				
Wages Payable		19,500		8,000		27,500				
Common Stock		120,000				120,000				
Retained Earnings		303,000				303,000				
Dividends	9,000				9,000					
Fees Earned		200,000				200,000				
Wage Expense	25,000		8,000		33,000					
Rent Expense	80,000		3,500		83,500					
Depreciation Expense—Machinery & Equipment			27,500		27,500					
Insurance Expense			10,000		10,000					
Totals	694,000	694,000	49,000	49,000	733,000	733,000				
Net Income										

Continued

A	B	C	D	E	F	G	H	I	J	K
	Unadjusted Trial Balance (STEP 1)		Adjustments (STEP 2)		Adjusted Trial Balance (STEP 3)		Income Statement (STEP 4)		Balance Sheet (STEP 4)	
Account	Debit	Credit	Debit	Credit	Debit	Credit	Debit	Credit	Debit	Credit
Cash	215,000				215,000				215,000	
Accounts Receivable	50,000				50,000				50,000	
Prepaid Insurance	40,000			10,000	30,000				30,000	
Machinery & Equipment	275,000				275,000				275,000	
Accumulated Depreciation—Machinery & Equipment		27,500		27,500		55,000				55,000
Accounts Payable		24,000		3,500		27,500				27,500
Wages Payable		19,500		8,000		27,500				27,500
Common Stock		120,000				120,000				120,000
Retained Earnings		303,000				303,000				303,000
Dividends	9,000				9,000				9,000	
Fees Earned		200,000				200,000		200,000		
Wage Expense	25,000		8,000		33,000		33,000			
Rent Expense	80,000		3,500		83,500		83,500			
Depreciation Expense—Machinery & Equipment			27,500		27,500		27,500			
Insurance Expense			10,000		10,000		10,000			
Totals	694,000	694,000	49,000	49,000	733,000	733,000	154,000	200,000	579,000	533,000
Net Income										

A	B	C	D	E	F	G	H	I	J	K
	Unadjusted Trial Balance (STEP 1)		Adjustments (STEP 2)		Adjusted Trial Balance (STEP 3)		Income Statement (STEP 4)		Balance Sheet (STEP 4)	
Account	**Debit**	**Credit**	**Debit**	**Credit**	**Debit**	**Credit**	**Debit**	**Credit**	**Debit**	**Credit**
Cash	215,000				215,000				215,000	
Accounts Receivable	50,000				50,000				50,000	
Prepaid Insurance	40,000			10,000	30,000				30,000	
Machinery & Equipment	275,000				275,000				275,000	
Accumulated Depreciation—Machinery & Equipment		27,500		27,500		55,000				55,000
Accounts Payable		24,000		3,500		27,500				27,500
Wages Payable		19,500		8,000		27,500				27,500
Common Stock		120,000				120,000				120,000
Retained Earnings		303,000				303,000				303,000
Dividends	9,000				9,000				9,000	
Fees Earned		200,000				200,000		200,000		
Wage Expense	25,000		8,000		33,000		33,000			
Rent Expense	80,000		3,500		83,500		83,500			
Depreciation Expense—Machinery & Equipment			27,500		27,500		27,500			
Insurance Expense			10,000		10,000		10,000			
Totals	694,000	694,000	49,000	49,000	733,000	733,000	154,000	200,000	579,000	533,000
Net Income							46,000			46,000
							200,000	200,000	579,000	579,000

STEP 5

APPENDIX C

Reversing Entries

Companies make **reversing entries** as an optional step in the accounting cycle at the beginning of the next accounting period to reverse the effects of the adjusting journal entries made in the previous period. Reversing entries simplify the recording of subsequent transactions related to the adjusting journal entries, and they typically apply to adjusting journal entries for accrued revenues and accrued expenses.

Because reversing entries are made in the accounting period following the period in which the adjusting journal entries were made, their use does not change the amounts reported in the previously issued financial statements.

EXAMPLE 4C.1 Reversing Entries

PROBLEM: EO Eleven, Inc. made the following adjusting journal entry on December 31, 2018, to accrue the first week, which is one-half of its bi-weekly $75,000 payroll:

Date	*Account*	*Debit*	*Credit*
Dec 31, 2018	Salary Expense	37,500	
	Salary Payable		37,500
	(To accrue salary expense)		

The related t-accounts follow:

Salary Expense

	Debit	Credit	
Dec 31, 2018	37,500		

Salary Payable

	Debit	Credit	
		37,500	Dec 31, 2018

The closing entry for the 2018 salary expense is presented here:

Date	*Account*	*Debit*	*Credit*
Dec 31, 2018	Income Summary	37,500	
	Salary Expense		37,500
	(To close salary expense)		

Salary Expense

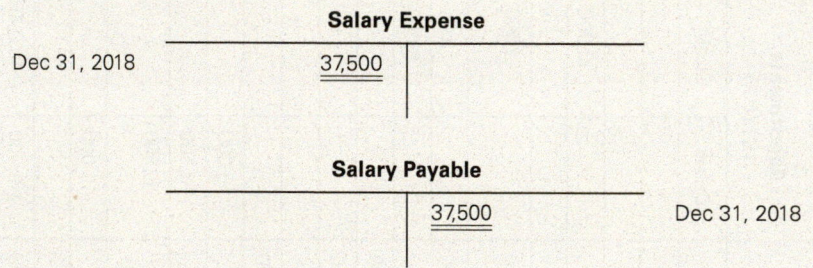

	Debit	Credit	
AJE, Dec 31, 2018	37,500		
		37,500	Dec 31, 2018
Balance	0		

What reversing entry will EO Eleven make related to this adjusting journal entry? What entry will EO Eleven make at the time of its next payroll on January 10? Provide t-accounts.

SOLUTION: On January 1, 2019, EO Eleven prepares the following reversing entry:

Date	*Account*	*Debit*	*Credit*
Jan 1, 2019	Salary Payable	37,500	
	Salary Expense		37,500
	(To reverse prior year's accrual)		

The t-accounts are as follows:

Salary Expense

		37,500	Jan 1, 2019

Salary Payable

		37,500	Dec 31, 2018
Jan 1, 2019	37,500		
		0	Bal.

At this point, EO Eleven can make its regular entry to record the January 10, 2019, biweekly payroll for $75,000 in the usual way. That is, the accounting information system does not have to be modified and it can process the regular payroll entry as follows:

Date	*Account*	*Debit*	*Credit*
Jan 10, 2019	Salary Expense	75,000	
	Cash		75,000
	(To record payment of salaries)		

The t-accounts are as follows:

Salary Expense

		37,500	Jan 1, 2019
Jan 10, 2019	75,000		
2019 Bal.	37,500		

Salary Payable

		37,500	Dec 31, 2018
Jan 1, 2019	37,500		
		0	Bal.

EO Eleven reports the correct expense of $37,500 for 2019.

5 Statements of Net Income and Comprehensive Income

LEARNING OBJECTIVES

1. Explain the difference between net income and comprehensive income; assess the usefulness and limitations of the income statements.
2. Define earnings quality, including permanent and transitory earnings and earnings management.
3. Identify the four primary elements on the statement of net income, and explain the nature and functional approaches to classifying items.
4. Explain the presentation of the statement of net income, including the multiple-step and single-step income statement formats.
5. Define income from continuing operations, including the components of operating income, non-operating income, and the income tax provision.
6. Demonstrate the accounting for a discontinued operation, including the criteria used to determine a discontinued operation and presentation on the statement of net income.
7. Describe the presentation of net income, noncontrolling interest, and earnings per share on the statement of net income.
8. Discuss the statement of comprehensive income.
9. Describe the components of and the reporting requirements for the statement of stockholders' equity.

Daniel2528/Shutterstock

Introduction

NET INCOME, REVENUES, AND GAINS less all expenses and losses, is one of the most important numbers companies report in the financial statements. It represents the return to the shareholders over a given time period—and, everything else being equal, shareholders prefer net income to a net loss. That is, investors prefer increased net income to no growth or decreased net income. In a survey of over 400 executives, 52% indicated that net income was the most important performance measure for a company.[1]

In analyzing a company, net income is an important measure of financial performance—but it represents only one view of a company's performance. Consider ***Kimberly-Clark Corporation***, the U.S.-based global manufacturer of personal care products, consumer tissues, and healthcare items with brands such as Kleenex, Scott, and Huggies. Its bottom-line net income increased to \$2,166 million in 2016, representing a \$1,153 million, or 114%, increase from the prior year.[2] Why would net income increase by over 100% in one year?

To obtain a complete picture of a company's financial performance, a company will often present steps, or subtotals, to get to net income. Let's consider ***Kimberly-Clark's*** gross profit and operating profit, steps to get to net income. During 2016,

[1] John Graham, Campbell Harvey, and Shiva Rajgopal, "The Economic Implications of Corporate Financial Reporting," *Journal of Accounting & Economics*, 2005, pp. 3–73.

[2] See Kimberly-Clark Corporation's annual report at http://www.cms.kimberly-clark.com/umbracoimages/UmbracoFileMedia/KMB-2016-10K_umbracoFile.pdf

Kimberly-Clark's gross profit, revenues less cost of goods sold, of $6,651 million increased only 0.4%, suggesting that ***Kimberly-Clark's*** manufacturing performance was relatively steady. However, ***Kimberly-Clark's*** operating income increased by $1,704 million, or 106%. Examining ***Kimberly-Clark's*** 2016 financial statements further, we find ***Kimberly-Clark*** reported a one-time expense in the prior year of $1,568 million primarily related to employee pension costs. This one-time expense depressed ***Kimberly-Clark's*** 2015 net income. In other words, ***Kimberly-Clark's*** 2016 net income figure looked much higher because its 2015 net income was unusually low due to a one-time expense. We will examine numerous measures of income—including net income, operating income, and gross profit—that include different aspects of performance and return to the shareholders.

In this chapter, we will discuss the reporting of income on the income statement and statement of comprehensive income. We begin with an overview and then cover specific presentation and format requirements, including the *single-step* and *multiple-step income statements.* Here, we will also discuss *discontinued operations.* Next, we will present important differences between U.S. GAAP and IFRS income statements. We then discuss the presentation of other comprehensive income and the statement of comprehensive income. We conclude by providing a discussion of the statement of stockholders' equity. «

1 Explain the difference between net income and comprehensive income; assess the usefulness and limitations of the income statements.

Overview of the Income Statements

The first step in our discussion of the income statements is outlining important terminology, the requirements for reporting the two components of *comprehensive income,* and the key advantages and limitations of the income statements. We first present U.S. GAAP requirements, and then discuss similarities and differences between U.S. GAAP and IFRS.

Income Statement Terminology

Comprehensive income is the change in a company's equity during a period of time resulting from transactions, events, and circumstances other than transactions with owners. For example, comprehensive income does not include new issues of shares or dividend distributions. Comprehensive income is composed of two parts: *net income* and *other comprehensive income.*

$$\text{Comprehensive income} = \text{Net income} + \text{Other Comprehensive Income}$$

1. **Net income** is a measure of financial performance resulting from the aggregation of revenues, expenses, gains, and losses that are not items of other comprehensive income. Net income is also referred to as net earnings.
2. **Other comprehensive income** (OCI) is composed of revenues, expenses, gains, and losses that are explicitly excluded from net income in specific accounting standards.[3] Standard setters specify that other comprehensive income includes unrealized gains and losses on an available-for-sale debt investment portfolio, unrealized gains and losses on cash flow hedges, foreign currency translation adjustments, and certain pension adjustments.[4]

[3]FASB ASC 220-10-20.

[4]FASB ASC 220-10-45-10A and IASC, *International Accounting Standard 1*, "Presentation of Financial Statements" (London, UK: International Accounting Standards Committee, 1975, Revised), Paragraph 7 (a)–(f) provide lists of items that should be included in OCI that we discuss in more detail later.

Reporting Income

Income statements are designed to reflect all components of comprehensive income by presenting an entity's financial performance and results of operations over a period of time. Entities may report comprehensive income in two ways:

- In one statement usually called the statement of comprehensive income, or
- In two consecutive statements: the statement of net income and the statement of comprehensive income.

The computation of net income and comprehensive income are the same under either alternative—only the format of the presentation differs. We will discuss both formats in depth later in this chapter. For consistency, we will refer to the financial statement(s) related to comprehensive income as the income statements throughout the rest of this chapter.

THE CONCEPTUAL FRAMEWORK CONNECTION: Usefulness and Limitations of the Income Statements

The income statements provide useful information to financial statement users in three ways:

1. **Evaluate past performance.** Income statements enable financial statement users to evaluate the entity's past performance. By disclosing separate components of revenues and expenses, income statements provide useful information about the entity's overall past performance (i.e., the earnings) and identify the main factors that influence performance. Income statements provide confirmatory value, which is an aspect of relevant information. For example, investors are interested in whether companies meet or beat analysts' forecasts of net income as indicated by the statement of net income.
2. **Predict future performance.** Income statements have predictive value because they provide a basis for estimating future performance. Predictive value is an aspect of relevance. For example, a firm with a trend of earnings growth over the last 10 years may continue that growth in the future.
3. **Assess risks or uncertainties of achieving future cash flows.** Income statements provide information that is useful in assessing the risks or uncertainties of achieving future cash flows. Some items of income are more persistent in nature than others, making them strong indicators of future cash flows. For example, revenue from normal sales tends to persist from year to year. However, a gain from the sale of a specialized piece of equipment is unlikely to reoccur in the following year.

While income statements are quite important to financial statement users, there are three main limitations. Income statements

1. **Exclude certain items.** Companies cannot measure certain revenues, expenses, gains, and losses reliably and therefore do not report them on the income statements. Unreliable information would result in financial statements that lack faithful representation, one of the fundamental qualitative characteristics identified in the conceptual framework. For example, assume an entity has been sued and a loss is likely. If the firm cannot reasonably estimate the loss, it would not report it on the income statement.
2. **Depend on accounting methods selected.** The measurement of income is dependent upon the accounting methods selected. For example, identical companies that purchase the same asset but depreciate that asset using different depreciation methods will report a different net income, resulting in reduced comparability.
3. **Require extensive judgment and estimation.** In general, allowing managers to use judgment when making accounting policy choices that best reflect the economic reality of a transaction will enhance the usefulness of the financial statements. However, due to significant subjectivity and estimation uncertainties involved in financial reporting, management can bias their judgments to enhance the entity's financial performance by manipulating revenues, gains, expenses, and losses. Even if management is not intentionally biasing reported earnings, different judgments will lead to different income numbers, resulting in reduced comparability.

② Define earnings quality, including permanent and transitory earnings and earnings management.

Earnings Quality

All the information included in the financial statements is important and useful for assessing a firm's financial position and performance—yet earnings is the single most important measure for financial statement users. Thus, preparers, auditors, regulators, and academics devote a considerable amount of time to focusing on *earnings quality.* **Earnings quality** captures the degree to which reported income provides financial statement users with useful information for predicting future firm performance.

We focus our discussion on two factors impacting earnings quality:

1. Earnings quality is dependent upon whether the components of earnings presented are *permanent* or *transitory* in nature.
2. Management will sometimes engage in earnings management by using the discretion afforded under the accounting standards to manipulate earnings to meet desired goals.

Permanent and Transitory Earnings

In assessing earnings quality, financial statement users gauge the portion of reported earnings that is *permanent* versus those that are *transitory.* **Permanent components of earnings** are likely to continue into the future. For example, earnings from sales revenue from regular customers are likely to continue into the future. **Transitory components of earnings** are unlikely to continue in the future. For example, gains or losses from the sale of equipment are usually transitory. Permanent earnings result in higher earnings quality whereas transitory earnings result in lower earnings quality.

The order of the income elements on the statement of net income guides financial statement users in distinguishing the permanent and transitory elements. Elements presented earlier in the statement of comprehensive income are typically more permanent than those included later in the statement. Exhibit 5.1 lists income statement line items commonly viewed as permanent and transitory.

EXHIBIT 5.1 Common Permanent and Transitory Items

Permanent	Transitory
• Sales • Cost of goods sold • Selling expenses • General and administrative expenses • Interest expense	• Gains and losses on disposal of long-lived assets • Impairment losses • Other unusual or infrequent items • Discontinued operations

Elements in OCI are often transitory in nature, such as unrealized gains and losses on investments that are held by the entity. Also, income that is included in special sections of the statement of net income such as income from discontinued items is typically transitory. Generally, they occur in one year and then do not reoccur in the foreseeable future.

Most elements presented in operating income are permanent in nature. For example, the salary expense related to an entity's sales force is likely to occur in every period for the foreseeable future. However, not all elements included in operating income are considered permanent. For example, discretionary expenses such as R&D expenses and training expenses are generally more transitory.

Given the issues and concerns with the usefulness of the income statement and earning quality, Appendix A introduces financial statement analysis as a technique for understanding and interpreting a company's performance. Appendix B extends the discussion of financial statement analysis to profitability analysis.

JUDGMENTS IN ACCOUNTING: Earnings Management

In addition to assessing the nature of the reported earnings, financial statement users should be aware of the possibility of earnings management, which lowers a firm's earnings quality.

Accounting standards allow managers to make judgments that affect the reported earnings number so that they can report the firm's financial position and performance in the most accurate and informative manner possible. A company's management understands the company's financial position and performance best. Thus, managers who are honest and have a desire to communicate accurate information to their stakeholders can do so.

However, some managers may use the areas of judgment inherent in financial reporting to manage earnings in an opportunistic—and sometimes fraudulent—fashion. For example, managers must determine which expenditures for equipment are material enough to record as an asset as opposed to an expense. They will likely expense a stapler but record a tractor as an asset. There is a gray area in this type of decision that provides an opportunity for earnings management. For example, should we expense a chair or record it as an asset? Of course, recording an asset for a material expenditure that the authoritative literature clearly designates as an expense constitutes fraud. Extreme forms of earnings management are fraudulent and thus illegal.

Motivation for Earnings Management. The flexibility in accounting standards gives management the ability to manipulate its reported earnings to meet company objectives. One of managers' overriding goals for the earnings presentation is to meet or exceed analysts' earnings forecasts. Financial analysts are trained to analyze a company, summarize relevant financial information for investors, and provide an opinion about whether investors should buy or sell stock in a company. In addition, financial analysts publish forecasts of a company's sales and earnings. If the company's actual earnings fall below this forecast, the market will most often react negatively, causing a drop in stock price.

For example, the share price of ***Nike Inc.*** declined about 7% when it released its sales for the second quarter of fiscal 2016 of $8.24 billion. Although this sales figure was a 6% increase from prior periods, the analysts' forecasts were $8.27 billion.[5] If ***Nike*** had reported sales higher than $8.27 billion, its share price likely would not have decreased. Thus, although it didn't do so, ***Nike*** had an incentive to manage revenues upward to beat analysts' forecasts.

Managers are also motivated to manage earnings to:

1. Beat benchmarks such as prior-quarter earnings or earnings from the same quarter of a prior year.
2. Avoid reporting a loss.
3. Present a firm's earnings as a smooth, upward trend.
4. Increase their own compensation when bonus plans are based on the net income (or stock price) of the firm.

In a survey of over 400 executives, 85.1% of those surveyed agreed that the earnings from the same quarter in the prior year is an important benchmark. In this same survey, 73.5% noted that analysts' forecasts were an important benchmark, and 65.2% indicated that avoiding a loss is important. Finally, 54.2% stated that earnings from the prior quarter is an important benchmark.[6]

In another study, researchers found evidence suggesting that 8% to 12% of companies that would have reported small earnings decreases instead exercised discretion in order to report small increases in earnings.[7] This same study found evidence suggesting that 30% to 44% of companies that would have reported a small loss instead exercised discretion in order to report a small profit.

Earnings Management Techniques. Managers employ earnings management techniques when actual earnings are either lower or higher than expected.

When low earnings are expected, the **big bath** earnings management technique involves increasing a net loss to allow the firm to show increased net income in the future. Managers can intentionally report very low or negative earnings in a period by accelerating the recognition of expenses into current-period earnings or deferring revenue recognition to the future reporting periods. This then allows them to report higher earnings in future periods than they would otherwise have reported because they have shifted expenses back to the prior period or shifted revenues to the future period.

[5] See http://fortune.com/2016/06/28/nike-shares-are-falling/

[6] John Graham, Campbell Harvey, and Shiva Rajgopal "The Economic Implications of Corporate Financial Reporting," *Journal of Accounting & Economics,* 2005, pp. 3–73.

[7] David Burgstahler and Ilia Dichev, "Earnings Management to Avoid Earnings Decreases and Losses," *Journal of Accounting & Economics,* 1997, pp. 99–126.

When earnings are higher than expected in the current period, managers may elect to reduce earnings to create *cookie jar reserves.* **Cookie jar reserves** are used in future periods to increase earnings as needed, possibly to exceed analysts' forecasts. For instance, managers could recognize an overstated warranty expense when earnings are high, thus increasing warranty expense and the warranty liability and reducing reported earnings. In later years, the managers have a sufficient warranty liability and may not need to increase the accrual. Therefore, management can report lower warranty expense and increase reported earnings in that period.

For example, let's assume that the management of Willens Retailers prepares an income statement for the year ended 2018 and realizes that earnings will exceed analysts' forecasts by $150,000. The company may choose to increase the estimate of warranty liability by an additional $125,000, thus increasing warranty expense by that amount. Willens will still exceed the analysts' forecasts, but only by $25,000. In future years, the company has $125,000 as a "reserve" to be used to increase income. Therefore, if management determines that the company is going to miss analysts' 2019 forecast by an amount less than or equal to $125,000, they can reduce their warranty liability, report little or no warranty expense, and thus increase net income.

Earnings Management in Practice. A survey of auditors provides a summary of the approaches management uses to manipulate earnings. The most common approach is through the manipulation of expenses and losses (52% of the occurrences of an earnings management attempt) followed by the manipulation of revenues (22% of the occurrences) and opportunities around business combinations (13%), as illustrated in Exhibit 5.2.[8]

EXHIBIT 5.2 Earnings Management Approaches Used in Practice

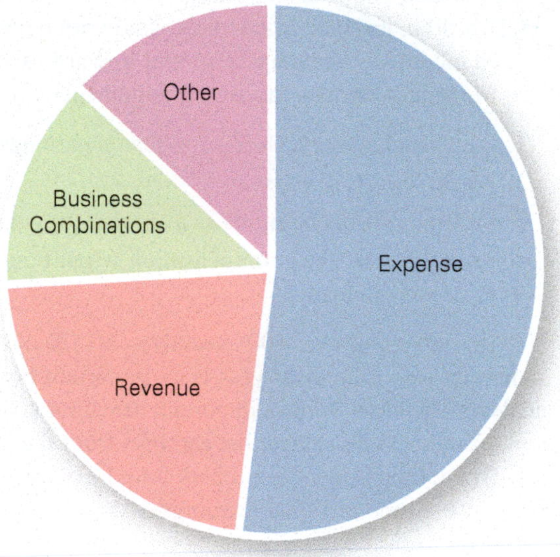

Statement of Net Income Elements and Classifications

3 Identify the four primary elements on the statement of net income, and explain the nature and functional approaches to classifying items.

We begin our in-depth discussion of the income statement with the statement of net income, first discussing the elements and then presenting the format of the statement of net income.

Statement of Net Income Elements

The statement of net income includes four primary elements: revenues, expenses, gains, and losses. We discussed these elements in Chapter 2, and repeat them in Exhibit 5.3 on the following page.

[8]Mark Nelson, John Elliott, and Robin Tarpley, "How Are Earnings Managed? Example from Auditors," *Accounting Horizons,* Supplement 2003, pp. 17–35.

EXHIBIT 5.3 Statement of Net Income Elements[9]

Element	Definition	Example
Revenues	Revenues are the inflows or other enhancements of an entity's assets. Revenues also include the settlements of liabilities from delivering or producing goods, rendering services, or other activities that constitute the entity's ongoing major or central operations.	A clothing retailer records revenue when it sells clothing to customers because this transaction is an inflow that occurs from its major operations.
Expenses	Expenses are the outflows or other consumption of assets or incurrences of liabilities from delivering or producing goods, rendering services, or carrying out other activities that constitute the entity's ongoing major or central operations.	A clothing retailer records the cost of the clothing that it sold as an expense because this transaction is an outflow related to its major operations.
Gains	Gains are increases in equity from an entity's peripheral or incidental transactions. Gains also arise from all other transactions and other events and circumstances affecting the entity, except those that result from revenues or investments by owners.	A clothing retailer sells some of its cash registers. If it sells the registers for more than their book value, then this transaction results in a gain. This inflow would only be classified as revenue if the retailer were in the business of selling cash registers.
Losses	Losses are decreases in equity from an entity's peripheral or incidental transactions. Losses also arise from all other transactions and other events and circumstances affecting the entity, except those that result from expenses or distributions to owners.	A clothing retailer would record a loss on the sale of an investment in government bonds if these securities are sold for a price less than their carrying amount. It would be an expense if the company were in the business of buying and selling government bonds.

Statement of Net Income Classifications

Managers make several decisions regarding the presentation, format, and the elements to include on the income statement, such as:

- Aggregating and summarizing accounts into financial statement components or line items.
- Grouping, or classifying, the components.
- Providing subtotals and totals.

For example, a company could have several accounts for salary and benefit expenses in its general ledger. Management may decide to aggregate salaries and benefits with selling and other expenses and summarize them in a line item on the income statement called, "Selling, General, and Administrative Expenses." Firms aggregate and summarize expenses by either *nature* or *function*. The **nature** approach refers to classification by the source of the expense such as:

- payroll costs,
- cost of raw materials used, or
- depreciation expense.

The **functional** approach refers to classification by the use of the expense such as:

- cost of goods sold (manufacturing or merchandising function),
- sales expenses (selling function), or
- administration expenses (administrative function).

The choice between the presentation by nature or function depends on factors such as the industry and company experience. Management selects the presentation that is faithfully representative and most relevant. U.S. GAAP allows firms to choose to group revenues and expenses either by the nature or functional approach. However, the SEC requires reporting by function. Companies using a functional presentation must include specific disclosures in the financial statement notes about the nature of the expenses.

[9]From FASB's Concept Statement No. 6, *Elements of Financial Statements*. IFRS's similar definitions are in the IASB's *Conceptual Framework for Financial Reporting* (London: International Accounting Standards Board, 2010).

4 Explain the presentation of the statement of net income, including the multiple-step and single-step income statement formats.

Statement of Net Income Presentation

There are two acceptable income statement formats:

- **Multiple-step income statement format**, which reports several critical subtotals before computing income from continuing operations (when discontinued operations included) and net income.
- **Single-step income statement format**, which combines all revenues and gains and all expenses and losses into single categories.

The multiple-step income statement format provides more useful information for evaluating and predicting performance than the single-step net income statement because a multiple-step format clearly separates key performance measures. Income statement elements are commonly grouped by and subtotaled into key performance measures. Key performance measures on the statement of net income include:

1. Gross profit
2. Operating income
3. Income before tax (income from continuing operations before tax when discontinued operations included)
4. Income from continuing operations (when discontinued operations included)
5. Net income
6. Earnings per share

These subtotals help financial statement users evaluate past performance, predict future performance, and assess risks or uncertainties of achieving future cash flows.

Because a multiple-step income statement clearly separates key performance measures, over 85% of U.S. companies use this format.[10] Therefore, we first focus our discussion on the multiple-step format and then describe the single-step format.

Multiple-Step Net Income Statement

The multiple-step income statement contains five common sections for reporting key performance measures. Exhibit 5.4 presents these five sections; we discuss each of these in more depth later in the chapter.

EXHIBIT 5.4 Five Common Sections of a Multiple-Step Net Income Statement

Section	Explanation
Operating Section	Reports the revenues and expenses related to the entity's principal operations. Also called major or central operations.
Non-Operating Section	Reports the revenues and expenses related to any secondary operations of the entity; also includes net financing costs (interest expense less interest income), unusual and/or infrequent items, and other gains and losses. Arises from peripheral or incidental transactions.
Income Tax Provision	Reports the income taxes related to continuing operations from all jurisdictions in which the entity operates (e.g., U.S. federal taxes, state taxes, and income taxes levied by foreign countries).
Discontinued Operations	Reports the results of operations for a component of an entity that has been disposed of by the end of the reporting period or that is held for sale at the end of the reporting period; also includes any gain or loss from the actual disposal of the component of the entity.
Net Income and Earnings per Share	Reports net income and several computations of the amount of earnings available to each shareholder in a company.

Exhibit 5.5 on the following page provides a sample multiple-step net income statement with the five sections highlighted by color as per Exhibit 5.4. The operating section is yellow and the non-operating section is green. The income tax provision is blue and discontinued operations is pink.

[10]Based on a survey reported in AICPA, *Accounting Trends and Techniques*—2010 (New York, NY: AICPA, 2010).

EXHIBIT 5.5 Multiple-Step Statement of Net Income

Puppini Products Statement of Net Income For the Year Ended December 31, 2018			
Sales	$234,800		
Less: Cost of Goods Sold	(65,000)		
Gross Profit		$169,800	← Key performance measure 1
Operating Expenses			
Selling Expenses:			
Selling Expenses and Salaries	$ 32,000		
Advertising Expense	14,000	(46,000)	
General and Administrative Expenses:			
Office Supplies Expense	$ 30,000		
Office Salaries Expense	10,000		
Depreciation Expense	5,000	(45,000)	
Operating Income		$ 78,800	← Key performance measure 2
Other Revenues and Gains			
Interest Income	$ 23,000		
Dividend Income	7,500		
Equity Investment Income	7,000		
Gain on Disposal of Plant Assets	4,700	42,200	
Other Expenses and Losses			
Interest Expense	$ (2,500)		
Loss on Asset Impairment	(1,500)		
Loss from Earthquake	(5,850)	(9,850)	
Income from Continuing Operations Before Tax		$ 111,150	← Key performance measure 3
Income Tax Expense		(33,650)	
Income from Continuing Operations		$ 77,500	← Key performance measure 4
Discontinued Operations			
Income from Operations of Discontinued Segment, net of tax of $3,500	$ 12,500		
Loss from Disposal of Discontinued Segment, net of tax of $3,000	(9,800)	2,700	
Net Income		$ 80,200	← Key performance measure 5
Earnings Per Share:			
Income from Continuing Operations		$1.94	
Income from Discontinued Operations		0.07	
Earnings Per Share		$2.01	← Key performance measure 6

Condensed Statement of Net Income

Companies use condensed income statements when a large number of line items limits the usefulness of the net income statement. That is, too much detail distracts the user from identifying key measures and relationships on the net income statement. Rather than present a cluttered income statement, many companies will provide a condensed income statement and disclose the details of significant revenues and expenses in the footnotes or supporting schedules.

Exhibit 5.6 on the following page presents a sample condensed, multiple-step statement of net income for Puppini Products.

EXHIBIT 5.6 Condensed Income Statement

Puppini Products Statement of Net Income For the Year Ended December 31, 2018			
Sales	$234,800		
Less: Cost of Goods Sold	(65,000)		
Gross Profit		$169,800	← Key performance measure 1
Operating Expenses			
Selling Expenses	$ 46,000		
General and Administrative Expenses	45,000		
Total Operating Expenses		(91,000)	
Operating Income		$ 78,800	← Key performance measure 2
Other Revenues/Gains and Expenses/Losses		32,350	
Income from Continuing Operations before Tax		$ 111,150	← Key performance measure 3
Income Tax Expense		(33,650)	
Income from Continuing Operations		$ 77,500	← Key performance measure 4
Discontinued Operations			
Income from Operations of Discontinued Segment, net of tax of $3,500	$ 12,500		
Loss from Disposal of Discontinued Segment, net of tax of $3,000	(9,800)	2,700	
Net Income		$ 80,200	← Key performance measure 5
Earnings Per Share:			
Income from Continuing Operations		$1.94	
Income from Discontinued Operations		0.07	
Earnings Per Share		$2.01	← Key performance measure 6

Exhibit 5.7 shows a sample footnote as an example of detailed footnotes or supplementary schedules needed to explain material income statement line items.

EXHIBIT 5.7 Footnote to Support Condensed Income Statement Line Items

Selling Expenses consist of the following:	
Selling Expenses and Salaries	$32,000
Advertising Expense	14,000
Total Selling Expenses	$46,000
General and Administrative Expenses consist of the following:	
Office Supplies Expense	$30,000
Office Salaries Expense	10,000
Depreciation Expense	5,000
Total General and Administrative Expenses	$45,000
Other Revenues/Gains and Expenses/Losses consist of the following:	
Interest Income	$23,000
Interest Expense	(2,500)
Dividend Income	7,500
Equity Investment Income	7,000
Gain on Disposal of Plant Assets	4,700
Loss on Asset Impairment	(1,500)
Loss from Earthquake	(5,850)
Total Other Revenues and Expenses	$32,350

Exhibit 5.8 presents the multiple-step income statement of ***Kimberly-Clark Corporation***. The multiple-step income statement includes gross profit, operating profit, and income before taxes and equity interests. The company includes a separate section to highlight its equity investment income (called share of net income of equity companies), which is about 6% of net income in 2016. Although ***Kimberly-Clark*** is a vast company, its income statement is very concisely presented.

EXHIBIT 5.8 Income Statement, ***Kimberly-Clark Corporation***, Financial Statement, December 31, 2016

Kimberly-Clark Corporation and Subsidiaries
Consolidated Income Statement

	Year Ended December 31		
(Millions of dollars, except per share amounts)	**2016**	**2015**	**2014**
Net Sales	$18,202	$18,591	$19,724
Cost of products sold	11,551	11,967	13,041
Gross Profit	6,651	6,624	6,683
Marketing, research and general expenses	3,326	3,443	3,709
Other (income) and expense, net	8	1,568	453
Operating Profit	3,317	1,613	2,521
Interest income	11	17	18
Interest expense	(319)	(295)	(284)
Income Before Income Taxes and Equity Interests	3,009	1,335	2,255
Provision for income taxes	(922)	(418)	(856)
Income Before Equity Interests	2,087	917	1,399
Share of net income of equity companies	132	149	146
Net Income from Continuing Operations	2,219	1,066	1,545
Income from discontinued operations, net of taxes			50
Net Income	2,219	1,066	1,595
Net income attributable to noncontrolling interests	(53)	(53)	(69)
Net Income Attributable to Kimberly-Clark Corporation	$ 2,166	$ 1,013	$ 1,526
Per Share Basis			
Net Income Attributable to Kimberly-Clark Corporation			
Basic			
Continuing operations	$ 6.03	$ 2.78	$ 3.94
Discontinued operations	-	-	0.13
Net income	$ 6.03	$ 2.78	$ 4.07
Diluted			
Continuing operations	$ 5.99	$ 2.77	$ 3.91
Discontinued operations	-	-	0.13
Net income	$ 5.99	$ 2.77	$ 4.04

Source: Kimberly-Clark Corporation's Annual report at http://www.cms.kimberly-clark.com/umbracoimages /UmbracoFileMedia/2016_AnnualReport_umbracoFile.pdf

Single-Step Statement of Net Income

Approximately 15% of reporting entities use a single-step format, which combines all revenues and gains and all expenses and losses into single categories.[11] Net income is arrived at in a "single step" by subtracting aggregate expenses and losses from aggregate revenues and gains. Exhibit 5.9 on the following page presents a sample single-step net income statement.

[11]Based on a survey reported in AICPA, *Accounting Trends and Techniques*—2010 (New York, NY: AICPA, 2010).

EXHIBIT 5.9 Single-Step Statement of Net Income

Puppini Products Statement of Net Income For the Year Ended December 31, 2018		
Revenues and Gains		
Sales	$234,800	
Interest Income	23,000	
Dividend Income	7,500	
Equity Investment Income	7,000	
Gain on Disposal of Plant Assets	4,700	
Total Revenues and Gains		$ 277,000
Expenses and Losses		
Cost of Goods Sold	$ 65,000	
Selling Expenses and Salaries	32,000	
Office Supplies Expense	30,000	
Advertising Expense	14,000	
Office Salaries Expense	10,000	
Depreciation Expense	5,000	
Interest Expense	2,500	
Loss on Asset Impairment	1,500	
Loss from Earthquake	5,850	
Income Tax Expense	33,650	
Total Expenses and Losses		199,500
Income from Continuing Operations		$ 77,500
Discontinued Operations		
Income from Operations of Discontinued Segment, net of tax of $3,500	$ 12,500	
Loss from Disposal of Discontinued Segment, net of tax of $3,000	(9,800)	2,700
Net Income		$ 80,200
Earnings per Share:		
Income from Continuing Operations		$ 1.94
Income from Discontinued Operations		0.07
Earnings per Share		$ 2.01

There are several drawbacks to the single-step format that limit the transparency of information for financial statement users:

- It combines revenues and gains and expenses and losses without classification.
- It does not separate operating and non-operating items.
- It does not classify expenses by function, such as selling expenses and general and administrative expenses.
- It does not identify key performance measures.

Exhibit 5.9 illustrates the shortcomings of the single-step format. Puppini combines operating and non-operating items. Specifically, total revenues and gains include sales revenue (operating) and interest income (non-operating revenue). The single-step statement also fails to separate items by function. For example, the cost of goods sold is a critical part of Puppini's manufacturing function, and sales salaries and advertising expenses are part of the selling function. Finally, Puppini's net income statement does not include key performance measures such as gross profit and operating income.[12]

[12]The information needed to compute these key measures are in fact included on a single-step net income statement. However, additional computations are required by the financial statement user to derive gross profit and operating income, resulting in added complexity for the average statement reader.

Statement of Net Income Presentation: IFRS

Whereas IFRS allows the single-step or multiple-step formats, IFRS requires that companies report the following line items on the income statement:

1. Revenue (Sales revenues are also called Turnover)
2. Finance costs
3. Share of income/loss of associates
4. Tax expense
5. After-tax profit or loss on discontinued operations
6. Net Income, also called Net Profit or Net Loss[13]

IFRS reporters present additional line items and subtotals that each company's management decides are relevant to financial statement users' understanding of its operating performance. So, these will vary by company. For example, ***Unilever Group***, a global Dutch consumer products and personal care company discussed later in Exhibit 5.11, does not report cost of goods sold on its income statement.

IIFRS also requires companies to disclose the following other items if they are not presented on the income statement:

- Write-downs of inventories or of property, plant, and equipment, as well as reversals
- Restructuring costs
- Disposals of property, plant, and equipment items
- Disposals of investments
- Discontinued operations
- Litigation settlements
- Other reversals of provisions[14]

If a company classifies expenses by function, it will disclose additional information on the nature of expenses, including depreciation and amortization expense and employee benefits expense.

Using IFRS requirements, Exhibit 5.10 formats the financial information and presents the income statement for Puppini Products (from Exhibits 5.6 and 5.7).[15] IFRS also requires line items or footnote disclosure for the gain on disposal of plant assets, $4,700, and the loss on asset impairment, ($1,500). Note the comments where IFRS requires certain line items and the similar key performance measures used under U.S. GAAP.

Exhibit 5.11 presents the IFRS income statement of ***Unilever Group***. Its income statement includes the required lines: turnover (revenue), finance costs, income from associates, taxation, and net profit. It reported no discontinued operations. The income statement does not report operating expenses, which is unusual. Rather, ***Unilever*** details operating expenses and gross profit in note 3 of the financial statements. The first table in note 3 provides the cost of goods sold and selling and administrative expenses not found on the income statement. The next table includes more detail on operating expense items. Observe that the final table classifies many of these expenses by their nature, such as staff costs and raw materials and goods purchased for resale.

Now that we have discussed the overall presentation of the statement of net income, we turn to a more extensive discussion of each section of the multiple-step statement of net income.

---

[13]See IASC, *International Accounting Standard 1*, "Presentation of Financial Statements," Paragraph 82.
[14]Ibid., Paragraph 98.
[15]In reformatting from U.S. GAAP to IFRS, we assume the amounts of all reported items are the same. In practice, the measurements could differ, as we will explain in subsequent chapters.

EXHIBIT 5.10 IFRS Income Statement (Based on Condensed Income Statement in Exhibit 5.6 and Footnote in Exhibit 5.7)

Puppini Products Statement of Profit and Loss For the Year Ended December 31, 2018			Comments
Sales	$234,800		Required under IFRS
Less: Cost of Goods Sold	(65,000)		
Gross Profit		$169,800	← Key performance measure
Operating Expenses			
Selling Expenses	$ 46,000		
General and Administrative Expenses	45,000		
Total Operating Expenses		(91,000)	
Operating Profit		$ 78,800	← Key performance measure
Finance Costs		(2,500)	Required under IFRS
Interest Income		23,000	
Income from Associates		7,000	Required under IFRS
Other Revenues/Gains and Expenses/Losses		4,850	This item includes dividend income of $7,500, gain on disposal of plant assets of $4,700, loss on asset impairment of $1,500, and loss from earthquake of $5,850.
Profit before Tax		$ 111,150	← Key performance measure
Income Tax Expense		(33,650)	Required under IFRS
Profit from Continuing Operations		$ 77,500	← Key performance measure
Discontinued Operations, Profit		2,700	Required under IFRS
Net Profit		$ 80,200	← Key performance measure; Required under IFRS Same under IFRS and U.S. GAAP
Earnings Per Share:			
Profit from Continuing Operations		$ 1.94	
Profit from Discontinued Operations		0.07	
Earnings Per Share		$ 2.01	← Key performance measure

5 Define income from continuing operations, including the components of operating income, non-operating income, and the income tax provision.

Income from Continuing Operations

In this section, we review several line items from a multiple-step income statement.

Income from continuing operations is income from portions of the business that are expected to continue into the future. Therefore, income from continuing operations does not include **discontinued operations**, which are portions of a company that have been disposed of or that are held for sale. Firms typically calculate income from continuing operations as the sum of three income statement items:

1. Operating income[16]
2. Non-operating items or non-operating revenues/gains and expenses/losses
3. Income tax provision

We discuss each of these items in the following sections.

[16] Operating income is often referred to as "earnings before interest and taxes" or EBIT.

EXHIBIT 5.11 Statement of Net Income and Notes, ***Unilever Group***, Financial Statements, December 31, 2016

Unilever Group
Consolidated Income Statement

CONSOLIDATED INCOME STATEMENT for the year ended 31 December	**Notes**	**€ million 2016**	**€ million 2015**	**€ million 2014**
Turnover	2	**52,713**	53,272	48,436
Operating profit	2	**7,801**	7,515	7,980
After (charging)/crediting non-core items	3	**(245)**	(350)	960
Net finance costs	5	**(563)**	(493)	(477)
Finance income		**115**	144	117
Finance costs		**(584)**	(516)	(500)
Pensions and similar obligations		**(94)**	(121)	(94)
Share of net profit/(loss) of joint ventures and associates	11	**127**	107	98
Other income/(loss) from non-current investments		**104**	91	45
Profit before taxation		**7,469**	7,220	7,646
Taxation	6A	**(1,922)**	(1,961)	(2,131)
Net profit		**5,547**	5,259	5,515
Attributable to:				
Non-controlling interests		**363**	350	344
Shareholders' equity		**5,184**	4,909	5,171
Combined earnings per share	7			
Basic earnings per share (€)		**1.83**	1.73	1.82
Diluted earnings per share (€)		**1.82**	1.72	1.79

NOTE 3: GROSS PROFIT AND OPERATING COSTS	**€ million 2016**	**€ million 2015**	**€ million 2014**
Turnover	**52,713**	53,272	48,436
Cost of sales	**(30,229)**	(30,808)	(28,387)
of which: Distribution costs	**(3,246)**	(3,358)	(3,079)
Gross profit	**22,484**	22,464	20,049
Selling and administrative expenses	**(14,683)**	(14,949)	(12,069)
of which: Brand and Marketing Investment	**(7,731)**	(8,003)	(7,166)
Research and Development	**(978)**	(1,005)	(955)
Operating profit	**7,801**	7,515	7,980

OTHER	**Notes**	**€ million 2016**	**€ million 2015**	**€ million 2014**
Other items within operating costs include:				
Staff costs	4A	**(6,523)**	(6,555)	(6,054)
Raw and packaging materials and goods purchased for resale		**(21,122)**	(21,543)	(19,816)
Amortisation of finite-life intangible assets and software	9	**(310)**	(273)	(180)
Depreciation of property, plant and equipment	10	**(1,154)**	(1,097)	(947)
Exchange gains/(losses):		**(209)**	(87)	12
On underlying transactions		**(28)**	(118)	15
On covering forward contracts		**(181)**	31	(3)
Lease rentals:		**(531)**	(534)	(535)
Minimum operating lease payments		**(536)**	(546)	(544)
Less: Sub-lease income relating to operating lease agreements		**5**	12	9

Source: See the ***Unilever Group's*** annual report at https://www.unilever.com/Images/unilever-annual-report-and-accounts-2016_tcm244-498880_en.pdf

Operating Income

Operating income includes revenues and expenses from the entity's principal operations. Exhibit 5.12 presents a typical operating income section of the income statement.

EXHIBIT 5.12 The Operating Section of the Statement of Net Income

Net Sales Revenue*
Less: Cost of Goods Sold
Gross Profit
Less: Selling Expenses
Less: General and Administrative Expenses
Operating Income

*Net Sales Revenue equals sales net of sales discounts and estimated returns and allowances.

Gross profit, net sales revenue less cost of goods sold, represents the amount of sales revenue available to cover operating and other expenses and contributes to overall net income that can potentially be distributed to shareholders. Financial statement users analyze the firm's gross profit to assess trends in profit margins.

Operating income is gross profit less all operating expenses (i.e., selling expenses and general and administrative expenses).[17] Operating income is a key financial performance measure because it:

1. Reflects the results of the core operations of the business.
2. Assists a financial statement user in comparing different firms' operations before considering sources of financing and their costs.
3. Provides a measure of income available to all outside stakeholders. The entity's stakeholders are the providers of capital (both debt and equity holders) and the government (through taxation).

Non-Operating Income

Non-operating income items include gains and losses along with revenues and expenses resulting from a company's peripheral activities. Non-operating income items are less useful than operating income items for predicting future earnings. Consequently, companies separate non-operating income items from the operating items on the statement of net income. For example, a gain or loss on the sale of a specialized piece of equipment is not likely to reoccur and is not part of the core operations of the business.

Specific non-operating items include interest revenue, interest expense, dividend revenue, and gains and items with an *unusual nature* and/or *infrequency in occurrence.* Items with an **unusual nature** are transactions or events possessing a high degree of abnormality and unrelated—or only remotely related—to the company's ordinary activities. Items that are **infrequent in occurrence** are transactions or events not reasonably expected to reoccur in the foreseeable future. If a gain or loss results from a transaction that is either unusual in nature and/or infrequent in occurrence, then companies report the event as a separate line item within income from continuing operations or disclose the item in the notes. Examples of transactions or events that are unusual or infrequent include:

- Restructuring charges.
- Losses on asset impairments.

[17] U.S. GAAP do not define operating income.

- Gains and losses on disposals of assets.
- Losses due to natural disasters such as an earthquake or hurricane.

Typically, companies sum operating income with the non-operating items to determine **income before tax**.

Income Tax Provision

The **income tax provision** reports the tax expense determined by considering the income tax effects of operating in all jurisdictions. Specifically, it includes U.S. federal, state, local, and foreign income taxes.

The income tax provision does not include other types of taxes. For example, payroll tax and property taxes are included in operating expenses. Also, note that companies report discontinued operations net of tax. Consequently, companies do not report the income tax expense associated with discontinued operations in the income tax provision.

Companies deduct the income tax provision from income before taxes to report **net income**. For many companies, net income is the final line on the income statement. As we address in the sections that follow, if companies report any discontinued operations, they include these gains, losses, and income following net income. As a result, income after the income tax provision is then called **income from continuing operations**, and the line item before income tax expense is called income from continuing operations before tax.

6 Demonstrate the accounting for a discontinued operation, including the criteria used to determine a discontinued operation and presentation on the statement of net income.

Discontinued Operations

Discontinued operations are portions of the business that a company has disposed of or is in the process of disposing of. The discontinued operations section of the statement of net income includes any income from *components of an entity* or a group of components of an entity that have been disposed of, abandoned during the reporting period, or are classified as held for sale as of the end of the reporting period.[18] We will identify the characteristics of discontinued operations before examining the reporting requirements.

Characteristics of a Discontinued Operation

A **component of an entity** has three main characteristics: It is (1) a portion of the entity (2) comprising operations and cash flows (3) that can be clearly distinguished, operationally and for financial reporting purposes, from the rest of the entity. A component of an entity can be:

- a reportable segment,
- an operating segment,
- a reporting unit,
- a subsidiary, or
- an asset group.

That is, a company must be able to separate the discontinued component's operations and cash flows from the continuing operations' earnings and cash flows. It should also be able to separately report discontinued operations in its financial statements.

After a company has determined that a portion of a business is a component of an entity or a group of components of an entity, the company must also demonstrate that the disposal represents a strategic shift that has or will have a major effect on the entity's operations and financial results. For example, the disposal of a major line of business would constitute a strategic shift that would have a major impact on the entity.

[18]A discontinued operation may also be composed of a business or nonprofit activity.

Discontinued Operations Reporting Requirements

Companies report income from discontinued operations and continuing operations separately. The separate reporting provides financial statement users with a measure of income from continuing operations, which is a preferred basis for predicting future performance. Clearly, a discontinued portion of a business will no longer generate future earnings and cash flows. Companies report three main types of income, gain, or loss under discontinued operations on the income statement:

1. Income or loss from operations of discontinued segment, unit or group, net of tax.
2. Loss on initial remeasurement of net assets held for sale to fair value less disposal costs, net of tax. In subsequent remeasurements, a loss or gain up to previously recognized losses can be reported.
3. Gain or loss on disposal of assets or disposal group(s) constituting the discontinued operation, net of tax.

Companies present the operating income, loss, or gain from the discontinued operation and income from continuing operations separately. If the company has *sold* the discontinued operation, it includes the operating income from the beginning of the reporting period to the date of disposal in the discontinued operations section of the statement of net income. If the company is *holding* the discontinued operation for sale as of the end of the reporting period, it presents the operating income from the entire reporting period in the discontinued operations section of the statement of net income. For example, assume a company earned $22 million of net income of which $3 million was from a loss on discontinued operations. The company would report income from continuing operations of $25 million and a $3 million loss from discontinued operations.

When a company decides to discontinue an operation, it remeasures the assets and liabilities of that operation to their fair values less selling costs if this amount is lower than their carrying value. Because the assets and liabilities are being held for sale, their value in the market is the most relevant value to financial statement users.

In the first period that the company remeasures the assets and liabilities of the operation, only a loss is permitted. If a write-down is necessary, the loss is equal to the difference between the book value of the net assets and their fair value net of selling costs. If the company writes down the net assets to fair value net of selling costs in one period and still holds the net assets in the next period, the company will report a gain in the subsequent period if the fair value net of selling costs increased. However, the write-up cannot result in a carrying value greater than the carrying value of the net assets before the write-down.[19]

When the company sells the discontinued operation, there could be a realized gain or loss on the sale. Companies present all amounts on the income statement related to discontinued operations *net of tax.* **Net of tax** means that the amount of income, gain, or loss, reported includes any income tax effects. As noted earlier, the income tax expense (or benefit) related to discontinued operations is not included in the tax provision related to continuing operations.

Companies are also required to disclose the following other income and expense items related to discontinued operations in the footnotes to the financial statements:

1. Pre-tax income (loss)
2. Pre-tax income (loss) attributable to the company's shareholders
3. Major line items to arrive at pre-tax income (loss) such as revenues and cost of sales, depreciation, and interest expense
4. Reconciliation of the major items making up the pre-tax profit (loss) disclosed in the notes to financial statements to the after-tax profit (loss) presented in the income statement
5. Carrying amounts of the major classes of assets and liabilities included as part of a discontinued operations and classified as held for sale
6. Gain or loss on remeasurement of net assets held for disposal

[19]See FASB ASC 205-20-45-3 and FASB ASC 360-10-35-40 for the related authoritative literature. Also, we discuss this issue in more detail in Chapter 12.

7. Reconciliation of the carrying amounts of major classes of assets and liabilities disclosed in the notes to financial statements to total assets and liabilities classified as held for sale on the balance sheet
8. Either total operating and investing cash flows related to the discontinued operation, or the depreciation, amortization, capital expenditures, and significant operating and investing non-cash items associated with the discontinued operation.

For example, ***General Electric's*** earnings included an after-tax loss of $954 million on discontinued operations of its financial services business in 2016.[20] Of this amount, $1,252 million was the after-tax loss on the disposal of the discontinued component.

EXAMPLE 5.1 Reporting Discontinued Operations When Company Is Holding the Discontinued Operation at the End of the Year

PROBLEM: ChooChoo, Inc. reported pre-tax income from all of its operations (including its toy car division) of $30 million for the year ended December 31, 2018. On August 1, 2018, ChooChoo committed to dispose of its toy car division. This division qualifies as a component of an entity that should be reported as a discontinued operation. The operating income related to this division for 2018 was $4 million. The carrying value of the toy car division exceeded the fair value less selling costs by $350,000. ChooChoo's income tax rate is 35% on all income. Prepare a partial statement of net income for ChooChoo for 2018, beginning with income from continuing operations before tax.

SOLUTION: Income from continuing operations before tax only relates to income from continuing operations; thus, ChooChoo would report $26 million, which is $30 million less the $4 million associated with the discontinued operation. Income tax is 35% of $26 million ($9.1 million).

ChooChoo should report $2.6 million of income from discontinued operations, which is the $4 million less tax expense of $1.4 million ($4 million × 35%). In addition, there is an after-tax remeasurement loss of $227,500, which is the total loss of $350,000 less the tax benefit of $122,500 ($350,000 × 35%).

ChooChoo, Inc.
Partial Statement of Net Income
For the Year Ended December 31, 2018

Income from Continuing Operations Before Tax	$26,000,000	
Income Tax Expense	(9,100,000)	
Income from Continuing Operations		$16,900,000
Discontinued Operations		
Income from Operations of Discontinued Operations, net of tax of $1,400,000	2,600,000	
Unrealized Loss on Remeasurement of Net Assets, net of tax of $122,500	(227,500)	
Income from Discontinued Operations		2,372,500
Net Income		$ 19,272,500

We now extend this example by assuming that ChooChoo sells the toy car division in the following year.

[20]See the General Electric Company's annual report at http://www.ge.com/ar2016/assets/pdf/GE_AR16.pdf

EXAMPLE 5.2 Reporting Discontinued Operations with Disposition during the Year

PROBLEM: ChooChoo has pre-tax profit from all operations in 2019 of $32 million. This amount includes a $5 million operating loss from the toy car division incurred between the beginning of the year and August 15, the disposal date of the division. The $32 million profit does not include a pre-tax gain on the sale of the toy car division of $2 million. Prepare a partial statement of net income for ChooChoo for 2019, beginning with income from continuing operations before tax.

SOLUTION: Income from continuing operations before tax relates only to income from continuing operations; thus, ChooChoo reports $37 million, which is $32 million with the $5 million loss associated with the discontinued operation added back in. Income tax is 35% of $37 million ($12.95 million).

ChooChoo reports two income classifications in the discontinued operation section:

1. An operating loss of $3.25 million, which is the $5 million loss less the tax benefit of $1.75 million ($5 million × 35%).
2. A gain from the disposal of $1.3 million, which is the $2 million pre-tax gain, less the associated tax expense of $0.7 million ($2 million × 35%).

ChooChoo, Inc.
Partial Statement of Net Income
For the Year Ended December 31, 2019

Income from Continuing Operations Before Tax	$ 37,000,000	
Income Tax Expense	(12,950,000)	
Income from Continuing Operations		$24,050,000
Discontinued Operations		
Loss from Operations of Discontinued Operations, net of tax benefit of $1,750,000	(3,250,000)	
Gain from Disposal of Discontinued Segment, net of tax of $700,000	1,300,000	
Loss on Discontinued Operations		(1,950,000)
Net Income		$22,100,000

After a company reports a component of an entity as a discontinued operation, it must separately report the results of operations of the discontinued component in the comparative statements of net income for all prior periods.[21]

Exhibit 5.13 illustrates ***General Electric Company's*** presentation of discontinued operations on the statement of net income and in additional footnote disclosures. The income from discontinued operations changed significantly over the three years presented with a loss of $954 million in 2016, a loss of $7,495 million in 2015, and income of $5,855 million in 2014.[22] In Note 2, ***General Electric*** provides more information about the portions of its businesses that it defined as discontinued operations, primarily its financial services businesses in GE Capital. The note further details the income related to the two classifications of total income or loss from discontinued operations: earnings or loss from discontinued operations, net of tax, and the gain or loss on disposal of the component, net of tax.

Companies often dispose of **individually significant operations**, operations that do not meet the definition of a discontinued operation. Because these disposals can be major and the amounts involved large, a company must disclose the pre-tax profit (loss) and the amount attributable to its shareholders.

[21] We discuss prior-period adjustments in Chapter 15. In addition to the impact on the net income statement, companies report assets that are classified as components of an entity held for sale separately on the balance sheet. We discuss this in detail in Chapter 12.

[22] See General Electric Company's annual report at http://www.ge.com/ar2016/assets/pdf/GE_AR16.pdf

EXHIBIT 5.13 Discontinued Operations, ***General Electric Company***, Financial Statements and Notes, December 31, 2016

Excerpt from Net Income Statement

General Electric Company and Consolidated Affiliates Statement of Earnings			
For the years ended December 31 (In millions; per-share amounts in dollars)	**2016**	**2015**	**2014**
EARNINGS FROM CONTINUING OPERATIONS	**$9,494**	$1,700	$9,490
Earnings (loss) from discontinued operations, net of taxes (Note 2)	**(954)**	(7,495)	5,855
NET EARNINGS	**$8,540**	($5,795)	$15,345

Excerpt from Note 2

Discontinued Operations

Discontinued operations primarily relate to our financial services businesses as a result of the GE Capital Exit Plan and include our Consumer business, most of our CLL business, our Real Estate business and our U.S. mortgage business (WMC). All of these operations were previously reported in the Capital segment. Results of operations, financial position and cash flows for these businesses are separately reported as discontinued operations for all periods presented.

(In millions)	**2016**	**2015**	**2014**
OPERATIONS			
Total revenues and other income (loss)	**$ 2,968**	$23,003	$31,136
Earnings (loss) from discontinued operations before income taxes	**$ (162)**	$ 887	$ 6,615
Benefit (provision) for income taxes	**460**	(791)	(776)
Earnings (loss) from discontinued operations, net of taxes	**$ 298**	**$ 96**	**$ 5,839**
DISPOSAL			
Gain (loss) on disposal before income taxes	**$ (750)**	$ (6,612)	$ 14
Benefit (provision) for income taxes[(a)]	**(502)**	(979)	1
Gain (loss) on disposal, net of taxes	**$ (1,252)**	$ (7,591)	$ 15
Earnings (loss) from discontinued operations, net of taxes[(b)(c)]	**$ (954)**	$ (7,495)	$ 5,854

[(a)] GE Capital's total tax benefit (provision) for discontinued operations and disposals included current tax benefit (provision) of $945 million, $(6,834) million and $(925) million for the years ended December 31, 2016, 2015 and 2014, respectively, including current U.S. Federal tax benefit (provision) of $1,224 million, $(6,245) million and $80 million for the years ended December 31, 2016, 2015 and 2014, respectively, and deferred tax benefit (provision) of $(988) million, $5,073 million and $154 million for the years ended December 31, 2016, 2015 and 2014, respectively.

[(b)] The sum of GE industrial earnings (loss) from discontinued operations, net of taxes, and GE Capital earnings (loss) from discontinued operations, net of taxes, after adjusting for earnings (loss) attributable to noncontrolling interests related to discontinued operations, is reported within GE industrial earnings (loss) from discontinued operations, net of taxes, on the Consolidated Statement of Earnings (Loss).

[(c)] Earnings (loss) from discontinued operations attributable to the Company, before income taxes, was $(911) million, $(6,038) million, and $6,472 million for the years ended December 31, 2016, 2015, and 2014, respectively.

***Source*:** Excerpt from General Electric Company's Financial Statements and Notes, December 31, 2013. See General Electric's annual report at http://www.ge.com/ar2013/assets/pdf/GE_AR13.pdf

Discontinued Operations: IFRS

We first describe the characteristics of discontinued operations under IFRS, noting differences with U.S. GAAP, and then outline the specific reporting requirements.

Characteristics of a Component of an Entity: IFRS. Similar to U.S. GAAP, IFRS defines a discontinued operation as a component of a company that it has either disposed of or classified as held for sale. However, IFRS defines a component of discontinued operations differently than U.S. GAAP. Specifically, IFRS requires that a discontinued operation represent a:

- Separate major line of business or geographical area of operations, or
- Subsidiary acquired exclusively with a view to resale.

Additionally, IFRS requires that the discontinued operation be part of a single, coordinated plan to dispose of a separate major line of business or geographical area of operations.[23]

EXAMPLE 5.3 IFRS Discontinued Operations

PROBLEM: Iron Horse Manufacturing Corporation, a maker of train engines and cars, is contemplating disposing of its Coach Car Company, which is one of its primary business segments. It plans to focus on engine manufacturing, where it has experienced significant growth. Iron Horse is considering the sale of Coach Car within the next 18 months but has not yet made a firm commitment. Would the disposal of Coach Car qualify as a discontinued operation under IFRS?

SOLUTION: The disposal of the Coach Car would not qualify as a discontinued operation under IFRS. Even though Coach Car meets the requirement of being a primary business segment, the discontinued operation is not a component of an entity held for sale and has not been disposed because Coach Car is not yet held for sale. It also appears that Iron Horse's management has not developed a plan to dispose of Coach Car.

Discontinued Operations Reporting Requirements: IFRS. IFRS income statement reporting is similar to U.S. GAAP. Disclosures under U.S. GAAP and IFRS differ, as noted in Exhibit 5.14.

EXHIBIT 5.14 Criteria and Reporting for Discontinued Operations: U.S. GAAP and IFRS

	U.S. GAAP	IFRS
Criteria for Determining a Discontinued Operation		
What is a discontinued operation?	Component of an entity held for sale or one that has been disposed.	Same as U.S. GAAP
What is the definition of a component of an entity?	1. A portion of the entity 2. comprising operations and cash flows 3. that can be clearly distinguished, operationally and for financial reporting purposes, from the rest of the entity.	1. Represents a separate major line of business or geographical area of operations or 2. A subsidiary acquired exclusively with a view to resale
Does the discontinued operation have to represent a strategic shift that has or will have a major impact on the entity?	Yes, it must represent a strategic shift.	Not a requirement under IFRS
Does the discontinued operation have to be part of a single coordinated disposal plan?	Not a requirement under U.S. GAAP	Yes, it must be part of a single, coordinated plan to dispose of a separate major line of business or geographical area of operations.

[23]IASB, *International Financial Reporting Standard 5,* "Non-current Assets Held for Sale and Discontinued Operations" (London, UK: International Accounting Standards Board, 2004, Revised), Paragraph 32.

	U.S. GAAP	IFRS
Reporting Requirements		
How is the discontinued operation reported on the income statement?	The operations and cash flows of the component have been or will be removed from the ongoing operations of the entity as a result of the disposal transaction.	Same as U.S. GAAP
What additional income statement disclosures related to discontinued operations are required?	- Pre-tax income (loss) - Pre-tax income (loss) attributable to the company's shareholders - Major line items to arrive at pre-tax income (loss) - Reconciliation of the major items making up the pre-tax profit (loss) disclosed in notes to the after-tax profit (loss) presented in the income statement - Carrying amounts of the major classes of assets and liabilities included in discontinued operations and classified as held for sale - Gain or loss on remeasurement of net assets held for disposal - Reconciliation of the carrying amounts of major classes of assets and liabilities disclosed in notes to total assets and liabilities classified as held for sale on the balance sheet - Either total operating and investing cash flows related to the discontinued operation, or the depreciation, amortization, capital expenditures, and significant operating and investing noncash items associated with the discontinued operation	- Revenues - Expenses - Income taxes on operations and income taxes on gains (losses) - Income taxes on gain (loss) on remeasurement related to discontinued operations - Pre-tax income (loss) - Gain (loss) on remeasurement for discontinued operations

IFRS reporters include any profit or loss related to discontinued operations on the income statement, net of taxes, on one line. Only one line is reported, and the amount reported is the sum of:

- Income or loss from discontinued operations, net of tax.
- Unrealized loss from remeasurement of net assets held for sale to lower of carrying value and fair value less disposal costs, net of tax.
- Realized gain or loss on disposal of assets or disposal group(s) constituting the discontinued operations, net of tax.

7 Describe the presentation of net income, noncontrolling interest, and earnings per share on the statement of net income.

Net Income, Noncontrolling Interest and Earnings per Share

Companies present net income on the income statement after discontinued operations. We discuss net income and two other items related to net income—*noncontrolling interest* and *earnings per share*—in this section.

Net income is the sum of the income from continuing operations and income, gains, or losses from discontinued operations. Companies commonly separate net income into net income attributable to their stockholders and net income attributable to the *noncontrolling interests.* Companies close net income attributable to their shareholders to retained earnings.

There is a **noncontrolling interest** when one company controls another company (e.g., a subsidiary) but owns less than 100% of its voting shares. The controlling company adds all of the subsidiary's income to its own because it controls the subsidiary's ability to generate income. However, because it does not own 100% of the subsidiary, the controlling company must identify the amount that is attributable to noncontrolling owners. The noncontrolling interest line item on the income statement represents the income attributable to the portion of a subsidiary owned by others.[24] The portion of income (loss) attributed to the noncontrolling interest is deducted (added) on the income statement to arrive at income attributed to the controlling interest.

Exhibit 5.8 shown previously presents the net income statement of ***Kimberly-Clark Corporation. Kimberly-Clark*** reported $2,219 million of net income in 2016.[25] Of this, $2,166 million is attributable to its shareholders and will be added to retained earnings, and $53 million is attributable to the noncontrolling interests.

Earnings per share represents the amount of earnings assigned to each outstanding share of the company's common stock. Companies report earnings per share for continuing operations, discontinued operations, and net income in a supplemental section of the income statement, directly below net income or loss for the period. Companies report earnings per share on both a basic and diluted basis.[26]

8 Discuss the statement of comprehensive income.

The Statement of Comprehensive Income

So far we have focused our discussion on the statement of net income, which does not include other comprehensive income (OCI). Companies may choose to report comprehensive income in one statement (usually called the statement of comprehensive income) or in two consecutive statements (the statement of net income and the statement of comprehensive income). The primary difference is whether a firm presents the income statement(s) on one page or two. In this section, we outline the elements presented and the format used for the statement of comprehensive income; note that these areas are consistent between the one- and two-statement alternatives.

Companies presenting in *two* statements are required to include the statement of comprehensive income immediately after the statement of net income (i.e., on the next page of the financial report). The statement of comprehensive income begins with net income and then presents the components of other comprehensive income, ultimately arriving at a figure for comprehensive income. Firms presenting *one* statement of comprehensive income combine the statement of net income with a presentation of OCI.

Statement of Comprehensive Income Elements

The Codification does not clearly define the concepts of net income versus OCI. However, U.S. GAAP provides a full list of the elements that should be included in OCI.[27] The key line items consist of:

1. Unrealized gains and losses from the available-for-sale portfolio of debt investment securities and derivatives classified as cash flow hedges.
2. Foreign currency translation gains and losses.
3. Unrecognized pension costs (benefits) from adjustments needed to bring the accounting pension asset or liability to the funded status of the pension plan.[28]

---

[24]We briefly discuss noncontrolling interest in this chapter because it is a common item reported on the income statement. The accounting for the ownership and control of other companies is commonly covered in advanced accounting courses.

[25]Source: Kimberly-Clark Corporation's Annual report at http://www.cms.kimberly-clark.com/umbracoimages/UmbracoFileMedia/KMB-2016-10K_umbracoFile.pdf

[26]We cover the computation of earnings per share in Chapter 20.

[27]The U.S. GAAP list is found in FASB ASC 220-10-45-10A.

[28]Unrealized gains and losses from available-for-sale investments are covered in Chapter 16. Derivatives and foreign currency translation gains and losses are typically covered in an advanced accounting course. Pensions are covered in Chapter 19.

The items reported as other comprehensive income typically have at least one of these three characteristics:

1. There is a low probability of cash realization in the short run.
2. These items are transitory components of income; excluding them from the income statement reduces earnings volatility.
3. The majority of these items are not part of the entity's normal operations.

Although not included in the net income statement, the disclosure of OCI items significantly improves the usefulness of the financial statements. For example, the disclosure of the unrealized gain or loss on available-for-sale investments can enhance an analyst's ability to understand how effectively a company is managing its investment portfolio. This information also assists the analyst in identifying potential realized gains or losses on future disposals of the investments. Similarly, OCI will provide information regarding future realized gains or losses from the sale of assets held by foreign subsidiaries or the liquidation of significant pension obligations.

Statement of Comprehensive Income Elements: IFRS

The presentation of the statement of comprehensive income is similar under U.S. GAAP and IFRS—but the line items can vary, depending on whether the standard setter allows certain items to go through OCI rather than net income.[29] In addition to the three items that go through other comprehensive income under U.S. GAAP, IFRS also allows companies to revalue long-lived assets and include the upward revaluations in OCI.

Statement of Comprehensive Income Format

We established that companies can present the elements of OCI in a separate statement or combined with the elements of net income into one statement. In the two-statement approach, companies first present the statement of net income, followed by a separate statement of comprehensive income. The statement of comprehensive income begins with net income and then presents the elements of OCI to arrive at comprehensive income for the period. In the one-statement approach, companies first present the elements of net income followed by the elements of OCI, netting to the comprehensive income for the period.

Companies may apply the tax effects to the OCI items in total or to each individual item comprising other comprehensive income. The majority of companies use the two-statement approach. With the two-statement approach, net income retains its emphasis as the primary income measure.

As we will discuss in Chapter 15, the standards require companies to report the accumulated balance of other comprehensive income in the stockholders' equity section of the balance sheet. The codification presents examples of the income statements under both approaches. We extend the Puppini Products income statement example from Exhibit 5.6 to include other comprehensive income. Exhibit 5.15 presents the two-statement approach, and Exhibit 5.16 presents the one-statement approach. Notice that net income and other comprehensive income are the same in both exhibits; only the presentation and formatting differ.

[29]The IFRS list of items in comprehensive income is found in IASC, *International Accounting Standard 1*, "Presentation of Financial Statements," Paragraph 7.

EXHIBIT 5.15 Statements of Net Income and Comprehensive Income: Two-Statement Approach

Puppini Products
Statement of Net Income
For the Year Ended December 31, 2018

Sales	$234,800	
Less: Cost of Goods Sold	(65,000)	
Gross Profit		$169,800
Operating Expenses:		
Selling Expenses	$ 46,000	
General and Administrative Expenses	45,000	
Total Operating Expenses		(91,000)
Operating Income		$ 78,800
Other Revenues/Gains and Expenses/Losses		32,350
Income from Continuing Operations before Tax		$ 111,150
Income Tax Expense		(33,650)
Income from Continuing Operations		$ 77,500
Discontinued Operations		
Income from Operations of Discontinued Segment, net of tax of $3,500	$ 12,500	
Loss from Disposal of Discontinued Segment, net of tax of $3,000	(9,800)	2,700
Net Income		$ 80,200
Earnings Per Share:		
Income from Continuing Operations		$1.94
Income from Discontinued Operations		0.07
Earnings Per Share		$2.01

Puppini Products
Statement of Comprehensive Income
For the Year Ended December 31, 2018

Net Income		$80,200
Other Comprehensive Income, Net of Tax		
Unrealized Gains in Available-for-Sale Securities:		
Unrealized holding gains arising during period	$ 6,300	
Less: reclassification adjustments for gains included in net income	(1,200)	5,100
Defined Benefit Pension Plans:		
Prior service cost arising during the period	$(1,400)	
Net loss arising during period	(750)	
Less: amortization of prior service cost included in net periodic pension costs	150	(2,000)
Foreign Currency Translation Adjustments		(5,400)
Other Comprehensive Income (Loss)		(2,300)
Comprehensive Income		$77,900

EXHIBIT 5.16 Statement of Comprehensive Income: One-Statement Approach

Puppini Products Statement of Comprehensive Income For the Year Ended December 31, 2018		
Sales	$ 234,800	
Less: Cost of Goods Sold	(65,000)	
Gross Profit		$ 169,800
Operating Expenses:		
Selling Expenses	$ 46,000	
General and Administrative Expenses	45,000	
Total Operating Expenses		(91,000)
Operating Income		$ 78,800
Other Revenues/Gains and Expenses/Losses		32,350
Income from Continuing Operations before Tax		$ 111,150
Income Tax Expense		(33,650)
Income from Continuing Operations		$ 77,500
Discontinued Operations		
Income from Operations of Discontinued Segment, Net of Tax of $3,500	$ 12,500	
Loss from Disposal of Discontinued Segment, Net of Tax of $3,000	(9,800)	2,700
Net Income		$ 80,200
Earnings per Share:		
Income from Continuing Operations		$1.94
Income from Discontinued Operations		0.07
Earnings per Share		$2.01
Other Comprehensive Income, Net of Tax		
Unrealized Gains in Available-for-Sale Securities:		
Unrealized holding gains arising during period	$ 6,300	
Less: reclassification adjustments for gains included in net income	(1,200)	$ 5,100
Defined Benefit Pension Plans:		
Prior service cost arising during the period	$ (1,400)	
Net loss arising during period	(750)	
Less: amortization of prior service cost included in net periodic pension costs	150	(2,000)
Foreign Currency Translation Adjustments		(5,400)
Other Comprehensive Income (Loss)		(2,300)
Comprehensive Income		$ 77,900

Exhibits 5.8 and 5.17 illustrate ***Kimberly-Clark's*** use of the two-statement approach. Note that its statement of comprehensive income begins with net income from its statement of net income in Exhibit 5.8. Two main other comprehensive income items in 2016 are $(107) million of loss from foreign currency translation adjustments and loss of $(113) million from postretirement adjustments. Each of these items is reported net of tax. In all years presented, ***Kimberly-Clark's*** comprehensive income attributable to stockholders was lower than its net income.

EXHIBIT 5.17 Statement of Comprehensive Income, ***Kimberly-Clark Corporation***, Financial Statement, December 31, 2016

Kimberly-Clark Corporation and Subsidiaries Consolidated Statement of Comprehensive Income			
	Year Ended December 31		
(Millions of dollars)	**2016**	**2015**	**2014**
Net Income	$ 2,219	$ 1,066	$ 1,595
Other Comprehensive Income (Loss), Net of Tax			
Unrealized currency translation adjustments	(107)	(922)	(835)
Employee postretirement benefits	(113)	942	(275)
Other	15	5	20
Total Other Comprehensive Income (Loss), Net of Tax	(205)	25	(1,090)
Comprehensive Income	2,014	1,091	505
Comprehensive income attributable to noncontrolling interests	(44)	(33)	(57)
Comprehensive Income Attributable to Kimberly-Clark Corporation	$ 1,970	$ 1,058	$ 448

Source: See Kimberly-Clark Corporation's Annual report at http://www.cms.kimberly-clark.com/umbracoimages/UmbracoFileMedia/2015_AnnualReport_umbracoFile.pdf

9 Describe the components of and the reporting requirements for the statement of stockholders' equity.

The Statement of Stockholders' Equity

The **statement of stockholders' equity** is a financial statement that summarizes the changes in stockholders' equity during a period and includes the following accounts:

1. Contributed capital accounts (e.g., common stock, preferred stock, and paid-in capital in excess of par) related to investments by owners
2. Retained earnings, including net income (loss) and distributions to owners
3. Accumulated other comprehensive income, also called reserves under IFRS[30]
4. Treasury stock
5. Noncontrolling interests

Although the balance sheet reports the final balances in each of these accounts, the statement of stockholders' equity provides an analysis of the changes in these accounts for the year.

Stockholders' Equity Requirements

Although U.S. GAAP does not require a statement of stockholders' equity, it is required by the SEC. Thus, U.S. non-public companies are not required to provide the statement of stockholders' equity with their financial statements. However, most non-public companies do include a statement of stockholders' equity on a voluntary basis.

Statement of Stockholders' Equity Accounts

In general, changes in contributed capital accounts are related to additional investments by equity investors and purchases and disposals of treasury stock by the entity. The net income (or loss) of the entity along with dividend declarations result in changes to the entity's retained earnings. Items included in other comprehensive income close into accumulated other comprehensive income.

[30] Chapter 15, "Accounting for Stockholders' Equity," discusses these accounts in detail.

GREG TIERNEY, VICE PRESIDENT, FINANCE, PLANNING & ANALYSIS AND CORPORATE CONTROLLER MILLERCOORS »

Greg Tierney

Greg Tierney is Chief Financial Officer at MillerCoors, the U.S. business unit of the Molson Coors Brewing Company. He is responsible for establishing strong financial management and commercial disciplines for the company and reporting financial performance to its shareholders. Prior to his current role, Greg served as MillerCoors' vice president of financial planning and corporate controller.

1 How is the income statement used in projecting future earnings and cash flows at MillerCoors?

We analyze our income statement line items to understand what trends drive our business performance. Being able to forecast drivers of performance—sales volumes, input costs, product mix, pricing, marketing investments, general and administrative spending—is key to projecting future earnings. Given that earnings are a significant component of cash flows, increases in net income drive higher operating cash flows. While, in general, strong earnings lead to strong cash flow, other items impact cash flow. Non-cash income statement items such as reserve adjustments, depreciation, or amortization do not impact the current period's cash flows, although capital expenditures do. If the company requires significant capital investment to generate earnings, such as building a new bottling plant, overall cash flow would be negatively impacted at the time of the addition, whereas the income statement will reflect the charge over time as the asset is depreciated. Working capital analysis is also critical for cash flow projections. For example, a significant lengthening of receivables (or days sales outstanding) could negatively impact operating cash flow in that period.

2 What are the most critical estimates used in measuring and reporting revenues and expenses at MillerCoors?

Revenue recognition at MillerCoors is fairly straightforward. We generally recognize revenue at the time of shipment, when the significant risks and rewards of ownership are transferred to the customer. Some expenses, however, require estimates and assumptions. Among the most significant are employee benefit-related assumptions such as pension and post-retirement medical expenses, as well as incentive compensation expenses where liabilities are tied to the attainment of performance targets. We also make estimates for inventory valuation related to obsolescence.

3 Describe the importance of separating income from continuing operations from other, nonrecurring items. Briefly discuss any nonrecurring items reported by MillerCoors in recent years.

Nonrecurring gains or losses that are infrequent and unusual by definition are not expected to recur. Separately reporting these items provides the financial statements reader with a clear perspective of the business's core operations and underlying performance. Similarly, removing income from discontinued operations allows the reader to understand the profitability of remaining business operations.

MillerCoors has reported several unusual and nonrecurring items. Recently, these included changes to employee benefit plans, as well as the impairment of intangible assets and material one-time charges related to the 2008 formation of MillerCoors as a joint venture between SABMiller and Molson Coors.

4 What primary factors affect earnings quality at MillerCoors?

Underlying business results, or ongoing activities, are the best measure of earnings quality. One-time events can skew earnings, either positively or negatively, on a period-by-period basis; however, these items are poor indicators of the core operations of the business. A one-time gain related to the sale of an asset or a one-time charge for restructuring will affect current-period earnings but has little bearing on future results. Adjusting for these items gives managers and the investment community a more accurate picture of how a company is performing and a better estimate of future performance. In external communications, we identify unusual items to give greater transparency and ensure that the analyst community understands the impact of these items.

5 How do the components of other comprehensive income affect the judgment of an informed financial statement user, and what common elements of comprehensive income does MillerCoors report?

Gains and losses appear in other comprehensive income (OCI) when they have not yet been realized in net income. This classification gives an understanding of the magnitude of charges that will have a future impact on earnings. MillerCoors reports pension and postretirement benefit gains and losses, as well as unrealized gains or losses on derivative instruments, as OCI.

Discussion Questions

1. Consider Greg Tierney's response to the second interview question in which he describes estimates used at MillerCoors LLC in preparation of the company's income statement. What other significant estimates impact the income statement?
2. Greg Tierney mentions that the other comprehensive income (OCI) classification assists users in understanding the magnitude of these charges and the future impact on earnings. Explain how OCI disclosures provide information about the future impact on earnings. «

Exhibit 5.18 illustrates the equity components changed by net income, comprehensive income, and transactions with owners. Net income increases retained earnings whereas net losses and dividends decrease retained earnings. Also, positive other comprehensive income will increase accumulated other comprehensive income, and negative other comprehensive income (loss) will decrease accumulated other comprehensive income. Finally, share issuances and the sale of treasury shares increase contributed capital, while share repurchases decrease it.

EXHIBIT 5.18 Income and Transactions with Owners in the Statement of Stockholders' Equity

Item		Component of Equity in Statement of Stockholders' Equity
Net Income (also called Net Profit or Net Loss)	Closes to	Retained Earnings
+/− Other Comprehensive Income	Closes to	Accumulated Other Comprehensive Income
= Comprehensive Income		
Dividends Declared	Closes to	Retained Earnings
Share Issuances or Repurchases	Accumulates in	Contributed Capital (or Retained Earnings for Certain Treasury Stock Transactions)

EXAMPLE 5.4 Computation of Stockholders' Equity

PROBLEM: Starling Corporation started the year on January 1 with the following balances in stockholders' equity on its balance sheet.

Retained earnings	$ 876,000
Common stock, $1 par (100,000 shares)	$ 100,000
Additional paid-in-capital	$ 342,000
Accumulated other comprehensive income	$ 17,000

It reported the following income items and transactions with owners during the current year:

Net loss	$ (29,000)
Dividends declared	$ 5,000
Issued 20,000 shares of common stock for $400,000	$ 400,000
Unrecognized pension costs, net of taxes	$ (12,000)
Unrealized gains on available-for-sale investments, net of taxes	$ 68,000
Foreign currency translation adjustments—loss, net of taxes	$ (34,000)

What is the amount of Starling's retained earnings, contributed capital, and accumulated other comprehensive income at the end of the year?

Use the following template to prepare a Statement of Stockholders' Equity and answer the questions.

	Common Stock	Additional Paid-in-Capital	Retained Earnings	Accumulated Other Comprehensive Income	Total
Balance, January 1	______	______	______	______	______
Net loss	______	______	______	______	______
Dividends Declared	______	______	______	______	______
Issuance of Common Stock	______	______	______	______	______
Other Comprehensive Income, net of taxes	______	______	______	______	______
Balance, December 31	______	______	______	______	______

SOLUTION: We first identify the component of stockholders' equity associated with each line item and transactions with owners.

Item	Component of Stockholders' Equity
Net loss	Retained Earnings
Dividends declared	Retained Earnings
Issued 20,000 shares of common stock for $400,000	Par value in Common Stock, Remaining amount in Additional Paid-in-Capital
Unrecognized pension costs, net of taxes	Other Comprehensive Income, then to Accumulated Other Comprehensive Income
Unrealized gains on available-for-sale investments, net of taxes	Other Comprehensive Income, then to Accumulated Other Comprehensive Income
Foreign currency translation adjustments—loss, net of taxes	Other Comprehensive Income, then to Accumulated Other Comprehensive Income

Next, we place the beginning balances in the template and add the income items and transactions with owners in the appropriate columns. We compute other comprehensive income as follows:

Unrecognized Pension Costs, net of taxes	$ (12,000)
Unrealized Gains on Available-for-sale Investments, net of taxes	68,000
Foreign Currency Translation Adjustments—Loss, net of taxes	(34,000)
Other Comprehensive Income, net of taxes	$ 22,000

Finally, we compute the totals across rows and down columns.

	Common Stock	Additional Paid-in-Capital	Retained Earnings	Accumulated Other Comprehensive Income	Total
Balance, January 1	$100,000	$342,000	$876,000	$17,000	$1,335,000
Net loss			(29,000)		(29,000)
Dividends Declared			(5,000)		(5,000)
Issuance of Common Stock	20,000	380,000			400,000
Other Comprehensive Income, net of taxes				22,000	22,000
Balance, December 31	$120,000	$722,000	$842,000	$39,000	$1,723,000

At the end of the year, retained earnings is $842,000, contributed capital is $842,000 ($120,000 + $722,000), and accumulated other comprehensive income is $39,000.

Exhibit 5.19 presents ***Kimberly-Clark's*** 2016 Statement of Stockholders' Equity. The first column reports the number of issued shares of common stock. The second column reports the dollar amount of common stock issued and the third the amount of additional paid-in-capital. The number of shares and dollar amount in treasury stock, which reduces equity, is in the next two columns. Retained earnings is in the sixth column, which increases with net income and decreases with dividends. The second-to-last column presents accumulated other comprehensive income. The last column represents the noncontrolling interests.

Stockholders' Equity Requirements: IFRS. Unlike U.S. GAAP, IFRS requires a statement of stockholders' equity.

EXHIBIT 5.19 Statement of Stockholders' Equity, ***Kimberly-Clark Corporation***, Financial Statements, December 31, 2016

Kimberly-Clark Corporation and Subsidiaries
Consolidated Statement of Stockholders' Equity

	Common Stock Issued		Additional Paid-in Capital	Treasury Stock		Retained Earnings	Accumulated Other Comprehensive Income (Loss)	Noncontrolling Interests
	Shares	Amount		Shares	Amount			
Balance at December 31, 2015	378,597	$ 473	$609	17,737	$(2,972)	$ 4,994	$(3,278)	$214
Net income in stockholders' equity	—	—	—	—	—	2,166	—	49
Other comprehensive income, net of tax	—	—	—	—	—	—	(196)	(8)
Stock-based awards exercised or vested	—	—	(14)	(1,906)	121	—	—	—
Income tax benefits on stock-based compensation	—	—	19	—	—	—	—	—
Shares repurchased	—	—	—	6,198	(778)	—	—	—
Recognition of stock-based compensation	—	—	77	—	—	—	—	—
Dividends declared	—	—	—	—	—	(1,322)	—	(36)
Other			6			(7)		
Balance at December 31, 2016	378,597	$ 473	$ 697	22,029	$ (3,629)	$ 5,831	$ (3,474)	$ 219

Source: Kimberly-Clark Corporation's Annual report at http://www.cms.kimberly-clark.com/umbracoimages/UmbracoFileMedia/2015_AnnualReport_umbracoFile.pdf

Summary by Learning Objectives

In the following, we summarize the main points by learning objective. Throughout the chapter, we discuss the accounting and reporting of U.S. GAAP and IFRS side-by-side. This table also highlights the major similarities and differences between the standards.

❶ Explain the difference between net income and comprehensive income; assess the usefulness and limitations of the income statements.

Summary	Similarities and Differences between U.S. GAAP and IFRS
Comprehensive income is the change in a company's equity during a period of time resulting from transactions and other events and circumstances from non-owner sources. Comprehensive income is the sum of net income and other comprehensive income. Net income is a measure of financial performance resulting from the aggregation of revenues, expenses, gains, and losses that are not items of other comprehensive income. Other comprehensive income (OCI) is revenues, expenses, gains, and losses that are explicitly excluded from net income in specific accounting standards. Advantages of the income statement include: 1. Provides confirmatory value. 2. Has predictive value. 3. Assesses the risks or uncertainties of achieving future cash flows. Disadvantages of the income statement include: 1. Certain revenues, expenses, gains, and losses that cannot be measured reliably are not reported on the income statements. 2. The measurement of income is dependent upon the accounting methods selected. 3. Even if management is not intentionally biasing the earnings figure, different judgments will lead to different income numbers, resulting in a lack of comparability.	Similar under U.S. GAAP and IFRS.

❷ Define earnings quality, including permanent and transitory earnings, and earnings management.

Summary	Similarities and Differences between U.S. GAAP and IFRS
Earnings quality captures the degree to which currently reported earnings provide financial statement users with information that is useful, particularly in predicting future firm performance. Permanent earnings are likely to continue into the future. Transitory earnings are not likely to continue into the future. Earnings management occurs when management uses the discretion afforded them under the accounting standards to inappropriately manipulate earnings to meet certain goals.	Similar under U.S. GAAP and IFRS.

Summary by Learning objectives, continued

❸ Identify the four primary elements on the statement of net income, and explain the nature and functional approaches to classifying items.

Summary	Similarities and Differences between U.S. GAAP and IFRS
The four primary elements included in the statement of net income are: • Revenues • Expenses (arranged by nature or function) • Gains • Losses The SEC requires presentation by function. U.S. GAAP allows presentation by either nature or function.	➤ Similar under U.S. GAAP and IFRS except that IFRS allows presentation by either nature or function.

❹ Explain the presentation of the statement of net income, including the multiple-step and single-step income statement formats.

Summary	Similarities and Differences between U.S. GAAP and IFRS
Two common income statement formats are: • Single-step income statement format that combines all revenues and gains and all expenses and losses into single categories • Multiple-step income statement format that reports several critical performance measures before computing income from continuing operations and net income, including: 1. Gross profit 2. Operating income 3. Income before tax (Income from continuing operations before tax when discontinued operations included) 4. Income from continuing operations (when discontinued operation is included) 5. Net income 6. Earnings per share	➤ IFRS allows multiple-step and single-step income statement formats but has additional requirements. IFRS requires certain line items to be reported on the income statement. • Revenue (Sales revenues are also called Turnover) • Finance costs • Share of income/loss of associates • Tax expense • After-tax profit or loss on discontinued operations • Net Income, also called Net Profit or Net Loss A company presents additional line items and subtotals relevant to understanding its financial performance. A company is required to disclose certain other items if they are not presented on the income statement.

❺ Define income from continuing operations, including the components of operating income, non-operating income, and the income tax provision.

Summary	Similarities and Differences between U.S. GAAP and IFRS
Net income from continuing operations is income from portions of the business that are expected to continue into the future. It is commonly presented as the sum of three income statement items: 1. **Operating income:** Revenues and expenses from the entity's principal operations. 2. **Non-operating income items:** Gains and losses along with revenues and expenses resulting from peripheral activities of the company including items with an unusual nature and/or are infrequent in occurrence. A transaction or event is unusual if it possesses a high degree of abnormality and is unrelated or only tangentially related to ordinary activities. A transaction or event is infrequent if it is not reasonably expected to reoccur in the foreseeable future. 3. **Income tax provision:** Reports the income tax expense associated with all income items included in income from continuing operations.	➤ Can be similar under IFRS formats but has additional requirements covered in LG6.

Summary by Learning objectives, continued

6 Demonstrate the accounting for a discontinued operation, including the criteria used to determine a discontinued operation and presentation on the statement of net income.

Summary	Similarities and Differences between U.S. GAAP and IFRS
Companies report discontinued operations for various income-related items associated with portions of the business that 1. have been disposed of, or 2. are in the process of being disposed of. A discontinued operation is a component or a group of components of an entity that is (1) a portion of the entity (2) comprising operations and cash flows (3) that can be clearly distinguished, operationally and for financial reporting purposes from the rest of the entity. The portion of the entity that is viewed as a component may be • a reportable segment • an operating segment • a reporting unit • a subsidiary • an asset group Companies must also demonstrate that the disposal represents a strategic shift that has or will have a major effect on the company's operations and financial results. Discontinued operations are reported net of taxes on the income statements. Companies report three main types of income, gain or loss under discontinued operations. For discontinued operations, companies disclose – Pre-tax income (loss) – Pre-tax income (loss) attributable to the company's shareholders – Major line items to arrive at pre-tax income (loss) – Reconciliation of the major items making up the pre-tax profit (loss) disclosed in notes to the after-tax profit (loss) presented in the income statement – Carrying amounts of the major classes of assets and liabilities included as part of discontinued operations and classified as held for sale – Gain or loss on remeasurement of net assets held for disposal – Reconciliation of the carrying amounts of major classes of assets and liabilities disclosed in notes to total assets and liabilities classified as held for sale on the balance sheet – Either total operating and investing cash flows related to the discontinued operation, or the depreciation, amortization, capital expenditures, and significant operating and investing noncash items associated with the discontinued operation For individually significant operations disposed of, companies disclose the pre-tax income (loss) and amount attributable to the company's shareholders.	➤ IFRS defines discontinued operations differently than U.S. GAAP: IFRS does not allow asset groups to be discontinued operations. A discontinued operation under IFRS could: (a) Represent a separate major line of business or geographical area of operations, or (b) Be a subsidiary acquired exclusively with the intention to resell. A discontinued operation should also be part of a single coordinated plan to dispose of a separate major line of business or geographical area of operations. The income statement presentation is similar under U.S. GAAP and IFRS with one exception; any income or loss from the operations and gain or loss on the sale or remeasurement must be summed for IFRS presentation. For discontinued operations, companies disclose – Revenues – Expenses – Income taxes on operations and income taxes on gains (losses) – Income taxes on gains and losses on remeasurement related to discontinued operations. – Pre-tax income (loss) – Gain (loss) on remeasurement for discontinued operations. No additional disclosures are required for those disposals not meeting the conditions to be reported as a discontinued operation.

Summary by Learning objectives, continued

7 Describe the presentation of net income, noncontrolling interest, and earnings per share on the statement of net income.

Summary	Similarities and Differences between U.S. GAAP and IFRS
Net income is presented after discontinued operations. Net income is separated into net income attributable to shareholders and net income attributable to the noncontrolling interests. There is a noncontrolling interest when one company controls another company but owns less than 100% of its voting shares. Earnings per share represents the amount of earnings assigned to each outstanding share of the company's common stock. Companies report earnings per share for income from continuing operations, discontinued operations, and net income in a supplemental section of the income statement directly below net income or loss for the period.	Similar under U.S. GAAP and IFRS.

8 Discuss the statement of comprehensive income.

Summary	Similarities and Differences between U.S. GAAP and IFRS
Companies have two choices in reporting comprehensive income: • In one statement, usually called the statement of comprehensive income, or • In two consecutive statements: the statement of net income and the statement of comprehensive income. OCI consists of: 1. Unrealized gains and losses from the available-for-sale portfolio of investment securities and derivatives classified as cash flow hedges. 2. Foreign currency translation gains and losses. 3. Unrecognized pension costs (benefits) from adjustments needed to bring the accounting pension asset or liability to the funded status of the pension plan. All OCI items must be shown net of tax. The tax effects can be applied to the OCI items in total or on each individual item comprising other comprehensive income.	Similar under U.S. GAAP and IFRS. ➤ OCI items will vary depending on the specific U.S. GAAP and IFRS accounting standards. For instance, IFRS allows the revaluation of long-lived assets and the effects of the upward revaluations are reported in OCI.

9 Describe the components of and the reporting requirements for the statement of stockholders' equity.

Summary	Similarities and Differences between U.S. GAAP and IFRS
The statement of stockholders' equity summarizes the changes in stockholders' equity, both by account and in total, during the period. The accounts summarized are: • Contributed capital accounts (common stock, treasury stock, preferred stock, and additional paid-in capital) • Retained earnings • Accumulated other comprehensive income • Noncontrolling interests A statement of stockholders' equity is not required under U.S. GAAP; however, the SEC requires a statement of stockholders' equity.	➤ Similar under U.S. GAAP and IFRS except a statement of stockholders' equity is required under IFRS.

MyLab Accounting

Go to **http://www.pearson.com/mylab/accounting** for the following Questions, Multiple-Choice Questions, Brief Exercises, Exercises, and Problems. They are available with immediate grading, explanations of correct and incorrect answers, and interactive media that acts as your own online tutor.

5 Statements of Net Income and Comprehensive Income

Questions

1 **Q5-1.** What are the three limitations of the income statement?

1 **Q5-2.** In what way is the income statement useful for financial statement users?

1 **Q5-3.** Can the terms *net income* and *comprehensive income* be used interchangeably? Explain.

2 **Q5-4.** What is meant by the term *earnings quality*?

2 **Q5-5.** What management behavior does the term *earnings management* describe?

2 **Q5-6.** What is the difference between permanent and transitory earnings?

3 **Q5-7.** Do entities report revenues, expenses, gains, and losses in net income or other comprehensive income? Explain.

3 **Q5-8.** Can entities combine cost of goods sold, payroll costs, and administrative expenses when aggregating and summarizing expenses by function on the income statement? Explain.

4 **Q5-9.** Explain the difference between a single-step and multiple-step income statement. Which statement is more transparent?

4 **Q5-10.** Is the presentation of the statement of net income under IFRS and U.S. GAAP identical? Explain.

4 **Q5-11.** What are the six key items to be reported on the statement of net income under IFRS? Must a company report operating income under IFRS?

5 **Q5-12.** Explain why operating income is an important measure of financial performance.

6 **Q5-13.** Does a business segment qualify as a discontinued operation? Explain.

6 **Q5-14.** If ***Procter & Gamble*** sells its Fabric Care and Home Care business segment, would it account for the sale as a discontinued operation? Explain.

7 **Q5-15.** What items are included in net income?

8 **Q5-16.** Are items of other comprehensive income included in the computation of net income? Explain.

8 **Q5-17.** What two choices must companies make when reporting comprehensive income?

8 **Q5-18.** Is the presentation of comprehensive income identical under IFRS and U.S. GAAP? Explain.

8 9 **Q5-19.** Can entities report other comprehensive income in the statement of stockholders' equity? Explain.

9 **Q5-20.** Are companies reporting under U.S. GAAP required to prepare a statement of stockholders' equity? Explain.

9 **Q5-21.** What accounts are summarized on the statement of stockholders' equity?

A **Q5-22.** What is financial statement analysis?

A **Q5-23.** Do auditors use financial statement analysis techniques? Explain.

A **Q5-24.** What are comparative financial statements and why are they useful?

A **Q5-25.** What is the difference between vertical and horizontal analysis?

B **Q5-26.** What defines a company's profitability?

B **Q5-27.** Explain the difference between return on equity and return on assets.

B **Q5-28.** How is a company's profit margin calculated?

Multiple-Choice Questions

1 **MC5-1.** Lyon Company has the following transactions in the current year. Assuming that all of the transactions are material, which of them will most likely have no effect on current year net income?

a. The sale of a factory building that was contributed by a shareholder in the prior year.
b. The settlement of litigation over an accident that occurred in the prior year but for which a loss had not previously been considered to be probable and reasonably estimable.
c. The determination that certain junk bonds purchased on a speculative basis several years previous were worthless.
d. The collection of a receivable from a customer whose account was written off in the prior year by a charge to the allowance for bad debts account.

2 **MC5-2.** Moore Furniture Inc., a public company, has experienced a consistent 5% increase in net income over the past three years. Moore's management team is under a lot of pressure from investors to maintain its earnings ratios. In order to do so, the CEO could manipulate net income in order to manage the earnings of the company. Which one of the following is *not* a method typically used to manage earnings?

a. Acquire a related business to allow management the opportunity to restructure transactions.
b. Move up the timing related to the launch of a new product that has a huge demand.
c. Engage in research and development projects to entice investors.
d. Recognize revenues prematurely from sales promotions with retailers.

4 **MC5-3.** Beach and Poole, CPA is reviewing income statement presentation with some interns that are working with the firm during the summer break. The interns were asked to list three things that were true about the multiple-step income statement. Choose the item below that is a true statement.

a. The multiple-step income statement lists gains and losses as part of income from normal operations.
b. The multiple-step income statement shows income or loss from operations *after* the gross margin and operating expenses lines but before other revenues and gains.
c. Freight out is classified as part of the inventory cost and moved to cost of goods sold when the item is purchased by a third party.
d. Gain/loss on the sale of equipment held for disposal from discontinued operations is included in the continuing operations section of the income statement.

5 **MC5-4.** Mission Flowers Company had the following transactions for the year ended December 31:

- Sales revenues of $775,000.
- Operating expenses of $550,000.
- Losses due to employee strike of $200,000. This was the first employee strike in the history of the company. Operating income of $100,000 from a subsidiary sold on November 1. The decision to dispose was made on February 28. The income was earned evenly over the 10 months ended October 31.
- The company's effective tax rate is 35%.

What amount should Mission Flowers report as income from continuing operations for the year ended December 31?

a. $33,750 b. $16,250 c. $81,250 d. $146,250

5 **MC5-5.** Allison Corporation's current year income from continuing operations before taxes was $1,000,000 before taking the following items into consideration:

- Depreciation was understated by $100,000.
- A strike by the employees of a supplier resulted in a loss of $200,000. This strike was the first such strike that Allison had encountered.
- The inventory at December 31 of the prior year was overstated by $300,000. The inventory at December 31 of the current year was correct.
- A flood in Allison's Houston facility destroyed equipment worth $500,000. The facility had just been rebuilt from damages that occurred in a flood in the prior year.

What was Allison's adjusted income from continuing operations before taxes?

a. $1,000,000 b. $900,000 c. $700,000 d. $500,000

6 **MC5-6.** On May 15, Year 1, Moran Inc. approved a plan to dispose of a component of its business. It is expected that the sale will occur on February 1, Year 2, at a selling price of $500,000, which was the current fair value of the component. During Year 1, disposal costs incurred by Moran totaled $15,000. The disposal of the component represents a strategic shift in the financial results for the entity. The component had actual or estimated operating losses as follows:

January 1 – May 14, Year 1	$130,000
May 15 – December 31, Year 1	50,000
January 1 – January 31, Year 2	15,000

The carrying amount of the component on May 15, Year 1 was $850,000.

Before income taxes, what amount should Moran report for discontinued operations in its Year 1 Income Statement?

a. $545,000 b. $365,000 c. $15,000 d. $380,000

8 **MC5-7.** Chili Co. had the following balances at December 31:

Foreign currency translation gain	$150,000
Unrealized loss on trading security	(35,000)
Net income	650,000
Loss on discontinued operations	(75,000)

The company's effective tax rate is 40%. What amount should Chili Co. report as comprehensive income for the year ended December 31?

a. $674,000 b. $719,000 c. $740,000 d. $800,000

8 **MC5-8.** Szuba Corporation reported the following transactions for the current year:

Sales	$500,000
Cost of goods sold	300,000
Operating expenses	100,000
Cash dividend	50,000
Unrealized gain on available-for-sale security	10,000
Unrealized gain on trading security	20,000

Ignoring income taxes, Szuba should report other comprehensive income of:

a. $80,000 b. $10,000 c. $60,000 d. $30,000

9 **MC5-9.** Glass Doors Inc. (GDI) is preparing the stockholders' equity section of their balance sheet. The following items occurred during the year. Which one of the following will *not* directly impact the stockholder's equity section of the balance sheet?

a. GDI owns securities classified as available for sale (AFS) with a cost basis of $376,000 and a fair value of $321,000. An unrealized loss was recorded of $55,000.
b. 100 shares of treasury stock were repurchased under the cost method for $7,500. The stock had a par value of $10.00 per share.
c. GDI sold 1,000 shares of common stock with a par value of $10 for $15,000.
d. GDI sold some old inventory for lower than originally paid.

Brief Exercises

1 **BE5-1. Advantages and Disadvantages of the Income Statement.** For each item in the following , identify whether it is an advantage or disadvantage of the income statement.

Item	Advantage/Disadvantage
1. Can be manipulated and managed.	______
2. Assesses risks or uncertainties of achieving future cash flows.	______
3. Depends on accounting methods selected.	______
4. Requires extensive judgment.	______
5. Predicts future performance.	______
6. Evaluates past performance.	______
7. Excludes certain items.	______

❶ **BE5-2. Advantages and Disadvantages of the Income Statement.** Match the description with the advantages and disadvantages of the income statements.

Advantage/Disadvantage	Description
1. Can be manipulated and managed.	a. The income statements provide confirmatory value.
2. Depends on accounting methods selected.	b. The income statements provide predictive value.
3. Predicts future performance.	c. Accounting policies determine amounts reported.
4. Evaluates past performance.	d. Items cannot be measured reliably and are therefore not reported on the income statements.
5. Excludes certain items.	e. Management can bias their judgments.

❶ **BE5-3. Advantages and Disadvantages of the Income Statement.** Match the item with the advantages and disadvantages of the income statements.

Item	Advantage/Disadvantage
1. Evaluates past performance.	a. The sale of a specialized piece of equipment is unlikely to reoccur in the following year.
2. Predicts future performance.	b. The income statements provide confirmatory value.
3. Assesses risks or uncertainties of achieving future cash flows.	c. Managers make estimates and assumptions.
4. Excludes certain items.	d. Investors expect past growth to continue.
5. Depends on accounting methods selected.	e. Managers manage earnings to meet analysts' forecasts.
6. Can be manipulated and managed.	f. Pending lawsuits may not be reported.
7. Requires extensive judgment.	g. Managers can choose from several inventory cost flow assumptions.

❷ **BE5-4.** Identify each of the earnings items as primarily permanent or transitory in nature.

Item	Permanent or Transitory?
Selling expenses	______
Sales salaries expense	______
Unrealized loss on available-for-sale bonds	______
Interest income	______
Depreciation expense	______
Amortization expense	______
Interest expense	______
Loss on asset impairment	______
Loss on sale of discontinued operations before tax	______
Gain due to flood damage	______
Sales	______
Gain on disposal of plant assets	______
Office supplies expense	______
Advertising expense	______
Office salaries expense	______
Gain on trading investments	______
Cost of goods sold	______

❹ **BE5-5. Income Statement Presentation.** Place the performance measures in the order in which they are commonly presented on the statement of net income.

- Earnings per Share
- Gross profit
- Income from Continuing Operations
- Net Income
- Operating Income

4 **BE5-6. Statement of Net Income Presentation, IFRS.** Which of the following items are required to be presented on an IFRS statement of net income?

Item	Yes/No?
Cost of Goods Sold	______
General and Administrative Expenses	______
Sales	______
Net Profit	______
Interest Expense	______
Gross Profit	______
Share of Income/Loss of Associates	______
Income Tax Expense	______
Operating Profit	______
Profit/Loss from Discontinued Operations, net of taxes	______
Profit from Continuing Operations	______

4 5 **BE5-7. Single-Step Statement of Net Income.** Carr Corporation provided the following partial-trial balance for the current year. Prepare a single-step income statement for the year ended December 31. Carr is subject to a 40% income tax rate.

Carr Corporation
Trial Balance (Selected Accounts)
For the Year Ended December 31

Account	Debit	Credit
Dividends	$ 1,345	
Sales		$123,750
Dividend Income		560
Interest Income		1,000
Gain on Disposal of Plant Assets		986
Unrealized Gain on Trading Investments		2,000
Cost of Goods Sold	45,678	
Office Supplies Expense	4,500	
Sales Salaries Expense	3,570	
Selling Expenses	12,000	
Accounting and Legal Fees—General Expense	800	
Advertising Expense	4,000	
Office Salaries Expense	6,780	
Depreciation Expense—General Expense	9,000	
Interest Expense	2,100	
Loss on Asset Impairment	1,840	

4 5 **BE5-8. Statement of Net Income, IFRS.** Using the information provided in BE5-7, prepare a statement of net income and additional disclosures that would meet IFRS requirements. Indicate items that IFRS requires be reported on the statement of net income. Use the condensed format.

4 5 **BE5-9. Multiple-Step Statement of Net Income.** Using the information provided in BE5-7, prepare a multiple-step income statement for the current year.

4 5 **BE5-10. Condensed Statement of Net Income.** Using the information provided in BE5-7, prepare a condensed, multiple-step income statement for the current year. Include supporting schedules.

6 **BE5-11. Discontinued Operations, IFRS.** Woorley Corporation needs to determine whether the disposal of its Tools Division qualifies as a discontinued operation. The Tools Division is one of Woorley's three major business segments. Its recent financial performance has been strong, yet Woorley believes that this segment will contract over the next three to five years. Woorley has developed a plan to dispose of the Tools Division and focus on its other two operating segments going forward. Does the disposal of the Tools Division qualify as a discontinued operation under IFRS?

6 **BE5-12. Discontinued Operations.** The Banks Corporation sold its credit subsidiary on December 31 of the current year at a gain of $237. See the following for the corporation's income statement before removing the discontinued subsidiary and before the inclusion of the gain on the sale of the subsidiary:

Banks Corporation
Statement of Net Income
For the Year Ended December 31

Sales	$ 10,000
Cost of Goods Sold	6,700
Gross Profit	$ 3,300
Selling, General, and Administrative Expenses	700
Depreciation and Amortization Expense	950
Income Before Tax	$ 1,650
Income Tax Expense (at 40%)	660
Net Income	$ 990

Prepare Banks Corporation's statement of net income for the current year reflecting the discontinued subsidiary, assuming that it met all of the necessary conditions to be reported as a discontinued operation. The discontinued subsidiary accounted for 20% of revenues and 15% of all operating expenses.

6 **BE5-13. Discontinued Operations.** Jojo, Inc. held a discontinued operation as of December 31, 2018. The operating loss from the discontinued operation was $500,000 for the period. As of December 31, 2018, the net assets of the discontinued operations had decreased in fair value by $272,000. Jojo's tax rate is 30%. Prepare the discontinued operations part of its income statement.

6 **BE5-14. Discontinued Operations.** Coftee Company committed to a plan on October 1 of the current year to discontinue its beverage segment. Income from operating the segment was $1,250,000 for January through September and $727,000 for October through November. Coftee sold the segment on November 30 for a loss of $168,000. Coftee's tax rate is 20%. Prepare the discontinued operations part of Coftee's income statement.

8 **BE5-15. Comprehensive Income Statement, One-statement Approach.** Steven Stores, Inc. provided the following statement of net income for the current year. All income is subject to a 40% income tax rate.

Steven Stores, Inc.
Statement of Net Income
For the Year Ended December 31

Sales	$12,000	
Less: Cost of Goods Sold	(4,000)	
Gross Profit		$ 8,000
Operating Expenses:		
Selling Expenses	$ 3,500	
General and Administrative Expenses	1,500	
Total Operating Expenses		(5,000)
Operating Income		$ 3,000
Income Tax Expense		(1,200)
Net Income		$ 1,800

The company also had $735 of unrealized holding gains on its available-for-sale investment portfolio. Prepare a statement of comprehensive income using the one-statement approach.

8 **BE5-16. Comprehensive Income Statement, Separate Statement Approach.** Using the information provided in BE5-15, report comprehensive income in a separate statement of comprehensive income.

9 **BE5-17. Computation of Retained Earnings.** Taxi Cabs, Inc. reported the following account balances on its balance sheet as of the beginning of the current year.

Retained Earnings	$1,250,000
Common Stock, $1 Par (200,000 Shares)	$ 200,000
Additional Paid-in-Capital in Excess of Par–Common	$ 775,000
Accumulated other Comprehensive Income	$ 345,000

It reported the following information for the current year:

Net Income	$140,000
Unrecognized Pension Costs	$ (67,000)
Dividends Declared	$ 10,000
Issued 50,000 Shares of Common Stock for $125,000	$125,000
Unrealized Losses on Available-for-Sale Investments	$(22,000)
Foreign Currency Translation Adjustments—Gain	$ 13,000

What is the balance in the retained earnings account at the end of the year?

9 **BE5-18. Computation of Contributed Capital.** Using the information from BE5-17 what is the amount of Taxi Cabs' contributed capital at the end of the year?

9 **BE5-19. Computation of Accumulated Other Comprehensive Income.** Using the information from BE5-17 what is the balance in the accumulated other comprehensive income account at the end of the year? Ignore taxes.

A **BE5-20. Horizontal Analyses.** Complete the following horizontal analyses of Dragonfly Corporation's income statement. What was the largest percentage increase in expenses? What was the largest percentage decrease in expenses? What would explain the changes?

(in millions)	**2019**	**2018**	**Change**	**Percent Change**
Sales	$ 63,762	$61,890	______	______
Cost of Goods Sold	33,092	30,096	______	______
Gross Profit	30,670	31,794	______	______
Selling, General, and Administrative Expenses	15,335	15,897	______	______
Research and Development Expense	7,052	7,844	______	______
Interest Expense	145	142	______	______
Earnings Before Provision for Taxes	8,138	7,911	______	______
Provision for Taxes	2,848	2,769	______	______
Net Income	$ 5,290	$ 5,142	______	______

A **BE5-21. Vertical Analyses.** Complete the following vertical analyses of Dragonfly Corporation's income statement. What line item is the largest percent of sales in 2019? How has it changed from 2018 to 2019?

			As of percent of sales	
(in millions)	**2019**	**2018**	**2019**	**2018**
Sales	$ 63,762	$ 61,890	______	______
Cost of Goods Sold	33,092	30,096	______	______
Gross Profit	30,670	31,794	______	______
Selling, General, and Administrative Expenses	15,335	15,897	______	______
Research and Development Expense	7,052	7,844	______	______
Interest Expense	145	142	______	______
Earnings Before Provision for Taxes	8,138	7,911	______	______
Provision for Taxes	2,848	2,769	______	______
Net Income	$ 5,290	$ 5,142	______	______

B **BE5-22. Ratio Analyses.** Green Grasshopper Incorporated is interested in assessing the following scenarios on its indicators of profitability. Solve each scenario independently.

a. Green Grasshopper has taken significant steps to decrease expenses and expects its net income to increase by $6 million to $54 million. If its profit margin is 7.5%, what will the profit margin be after considering the decreased expenses?
b. Green Grasshopper has taken significant steps to decrease expenses and expects its net income to increase by $6 million to $54 million. If its average total assets are $490 million, what will its return on assets be?

Exercises

4 5 6 **E5-1. Multiple-Step and Single-Step Statements of Net Income.**

The Tamer Tire Company provided the following partial trial balance for the current year ended December 31. The company is subject to a 40% income tax rate.

Tamer Tire Company
Trial Balance (Selected Accounts)
For the Year Ended December 31

Account	Debit	Credit
Dividends	$ 2,300	
Sales		$320,000
Interest Income		12,000
Dividend Income		8,000
Gain on Flood Damage		32,000
Gain on Disposal of Plant Assets		3,400
Unrealized Gain on Trading Investments		46,000
Cost of Goods Sold	64,000	
Office Supplies Expense	5,000	
Advertising Expense	10,000	
Office Salaries Expense	14,000	
Selling Expenses	36,000	
Accounting and Legal Fees—General	3,500	
Sales Salaries Expense	7,000	
Systems Consulting Fees—General	2,000	
Depreciation Expense—General	18,000	
Amortization Expense—General	11,000	
Interest Expense	4,500	
Loss on Asset Impairment	12,500	
Loss on Discontinued Operations—Before Tax	20,000	
Unrealized Loss on Available-for-Sale Bonds	5,600	

Required »

a. Prepare a single-step income statement.
b. Prepare a multiple-step income statement.

4 5 6 **E5-2. Condensed Statement of Net Income.** Using the trial balance provided in E5-1, prepare a condensed, multiple-step income statement with all supporting schedules.

4 5 6 **E5-3. Condensed Statement of Net Income.** Bradley Corporation provided the following account balances as of the end of the current year. The company is subject to a 40% income tax rate.

Bradley Corporation
Trial Balance (Selected Accounts)
For the Year Ended December 31

Account	**Debit**	**Credit**
Dividends	$13,200	
Sales		$1,245,890
Interest Income		6,700
Dividend Income		5,400
Unrealized Gain on Trading Securities		12,000
Gain on Disposal of Plant Assets		16,700
Gain on Flood Damage—Before Tax		18,700
Gain on Discontinued Operations—Before Tax		30,000
Cost of Goods Sold	65,000	
Sales Salaries Expense	32,500	
Office Supplies Expense	21,500	
Advertising Expense	79,500	
Office Salaries Expense	23,500	
Systems Consulting Fees—General	18,900	
Selling Expenses	75,000	
Accounting and Legal Fees—Administrative	34,500	
Depreciation Expense—General	89,750	
Amortization Expense—General	12,000	
Interest Expense	14,000	
Loss on Asset Impairment	58,900	
Unrealized Loss on Available-for-Sale Bonds	6,080	

Required »

a. Prepare a condensed, multiple-step statement of net income for the current year ended December 31.
b. Prepare a footnote containing the supporting schedules needed for the condensed statement of net income format.

4 5 6 **E5-4. Multiple-step and Single-Step Statements of Net Income.** Using the information provided in E5-3, prepare a single-step and a multiple-step statement of net income for Bradley Corporation.

4 5 6 **E5-5. Multiple-step Statement of Net Income.** The current year's statement of net income for Boley Boxes, Inc. in a single-step format follows.

Boley Boxes, Inc.
Income Statement
For the Year Ended December 31

Revenues and Gains		
Sales	$875,650	
Interest Income	325	
Dividend Income	780	
Gain on Sale of Investment Securities	4,300	
Unrealized Gain on Trading Securities	6,000	
Total Revenues and Gains		$887,055

Boley Boxes, Inc.
Income Statement
For the Year Ended December 31

Expenses and Losses		
Cost of Goods Sold	$ 45,000	
Selling Expenses	32,560	
Sales Salaries Expense	14,567	
Advertising Expense	16,400	
Depreciation Expense—General	2,500	
Amortization Expense—General	1,680	
Office Salaries Expense	19,400	
Office Supplies Expense	23,000	
Loss on Asset Impairment	3,450	
Legal Fees—General	2,150	
Accounting Fees—General	4,300	
Interest Expense	5,000	
Income Tax Expense at 40%*	286,819	
Total Expenses and Losses		(456,826)
Income from Continuing Operations		$430,229
Gain on Discontinued Operations—Net of tax		2,700
Net Income		$432,929

*40% × ($887,055 − $170,007) = 40% × $717,048 = $286,819.

Prepare Boley's income statement using a multiple-step format.

❹❺❻ **E5-6. Condensed Statement of Net Income.** Using the information provided in E5-5, prepare a condensed, multiple-step statement of net income for Boley Boxes, Inc. that includes all supporting schedules.

❹❺❻ **E5-7. Multiple-step Income Statement.** Ciara's Cookie Company provided the following accounts from its year-end trial balance.

Ciara's Cookie Company
Adjusted Trial Balance (Selected Accounts)
For the Current Year Ended

Account	Debit	Credit
Common Stock (no par): Beginning Balance		$ 456,000
Retained Earnings: Beginning Balance		1,200,950
Accumulated Other Comprehensive Income: Beginning Balance	$ 55,675	
Dividends	57,000	
Sales		1,200,895
Interest Income		3,400
Dividend Income		3,250
Gain on Disposal of Plant Assets		76,000
Unrealized Gain on Trading Securities		27,250
Gain on Sale of Discontinued Operations—Before Tax		56,780
Unrealized Gain on Available-for-Sale Bonds—Before Tax		3,500
Cost of Goods Sold	450,000	
Selling Expenses	37,450	
Office Salaries Expense	65,000	
Legal Fees—General	8,000	
Sales Salaries Expense	23,500	
Advertising Expense	21,500	

Ciara's Cookie Company
Adjusted Trial Balance (Selected Accounts)
For the Current Year Ended

Account	Debit	Credit
Office Supplies Expense	$54,800	
Accounting Fees—Administrative	10,425	
Amortization Expense—General	12,000	
Depreciation Expense—General	25,500	
Interest Expense	6,700	
Loss on Asset Impairment	9,050	

The company is subject to a 40% income tax rate.

Prepare a multiple-step income statement for the current year.

6 **E5-8. Discontinued Operations.** Elegant Homes Corporation provided the following statement of net income on December 31, 2018, before the disposal of a business segment. The income statement includes the results of operations of Elegant's mobile home division. The company made a commitment to dispose of the mobile home division on December 1, 2018.

Elegant Homes Corporation
Income Statement
For the Year Ended December 31, 2018

Sales	$500
Cost of Goods Sold	(120)
Gross Profit	$380
Selling Expenses	(80)
General and Administrative Expenses	(65)
Other Revenues and Expenses	(40)
Loss on Asset Impairment	(38)
Income Before Tax	$157
Income Tax Expense (at 40%)	(63)
Net Income	$ 94

The mobile home division accounts for 20% of sales, cost of goods sold, selling, and general and administrative expenses. Assume no gain or loss on remeasurement of the division.

Prepare the multiple-step income statement for 2018 only, assuming that Elegant sells the segment on December 31 at a $130 pretax loss. Round to the nearest dollar.

9 **E5-9. Prepare Statement of Stockholders' Equity.** Dane Products, Incorporated provided the following information for the current year ended December 31.

Retained Earnings, Beginning Balance	$520,000
Common Stock-no par: Beginning Balance	234,500
Net Income	89,500
Dividends Declared	(15,000)
Unrealized Gain on Available-for-Sale Debt Investments—Net of tax	11,000
New Issue of Common Stock	25,000
Accumulated Other Comprehensive Income (loss): Beginning Balance	(55,675)

Required »

Prepare a statement of stockholders' equity for the current year.

9 **E5-10. Prepare Statement of Stockholders' Equity.** Ciara's Cookie Company provided the following account balances from its year-end trial balance.

Ciara's Cookie Company
Trial Balance (Selected Accounts)
For the Current Year Ended December 31

Account	Debit	Credit
Retained Earnings, Beginning Balance		$1,200,950
Accumulated Other Comprehensive Income, Beginning Balance	$ 55,675	
Dividends	57,000	
Sales		1,200,895
Interest Income		3,400
Dividend Income		3,250
Gain on Sale of Property		6,789
Gain on Disposal of Plant Assets		76,000
Unrealized Gain on Trading Investments		27,250
Unrealized Gain on Available-for-Sale Bonds Before Tax		3,500
Gain on Sale of Discontinued Operations Before Tax		56,780
Cost of Goods Sold	450,000	
Selling Expenses	37,450	
Office Supplies Expense	54,800	
Amortization Expense	12,000	
Sales Salaries Expense	23,500	
Advertising Expense	21,500	
Office Salaries Expense	65,000	
Depreciation Expense	25,500	
Legal Fees	8,000	
Accounting Fees	10,425	
Interest Expense	6,700	
Loss on Asset Impairment	9,050	

During the year, Ciara issued no-par common stock. The proceeds of the new issue were $25,000. The company is subject to a 40% income tax rate. The beginning balance in common stock was $456,000.

Prepare a statement of stockholders' equity for the current year. *Note:* You will need to solve for net income using the given information. Round to the nearest dollar.

9 **E5-11. Prepare a Statement of Stockholders' Equity.** Bluebird Products, Inc. provided the following information from its current-year trial balance.

Bluebird Products, Inc.
Trial Balance (Partial)
For the Year Ended December 31

Account	Debit	Credit
Retained Earnings, Beginning Balance		$3,200,950
Accumulated Other Comprehensive Income, Beginning Balance		95,675
Dividends	$76,500	
Sales		2,200,000
Interest Income		34,500
Dividend Income		12,300
Gain on Disposal of Plant Assets		100,500
Unrealized Gain on Trading Investments		86,000
Unrealized Gain on Available-for-Sale Bonds Before Tax		45,600
Gain due to Flood Damage Before Tax		109,000

Bluebird Products, Inc.
Trial Balance (Partial)
For the Year Ended December 31

Account	Debit	Credit
Cost of Goods Sold	$750,000	
Selling Expenses	20,000	
Office Supplies Expense	123,500	
Amortization Expense	34,500	
Sales Salaries Expense	55,000	
Advertising Expense	68,900	
Office Salaries Expense	78,500	
Depreciation Expense	68,000	
Accounting and Legal Fees	10,425	
Systems Consulting Fees	44,550	
Interest Expense	23,750	
Loss on Asset Impairment	12,350	
Loss on Sale of Discontinued Operations Before Tax	90,000	

Bluebird issued $345,000 of no-par common stock on June 30 of the current year. The company is subject to a 40% income tax rate. The beginning balance in common stock was $1,456,000.

Prepare a statement of stockholders' equity for the year ended December 31. *Note:* You will need to solve for net income using the given information.

B **E5-12. Profitability Analyses.** Use the following excerpt from Dragonfly Corporation's balance sheet and its income statement to compute Dragonfly's profit margin and return on assets for 2018 and 2019. Comment on Dragonfly's profitability and changes in profitability from 2018 to 2019. Dragonfly's total assets at the end of 2017 were $157,534 million.

Assets (dollars in millions)	2019	2018
Current Assets		
Cash and Cash Equivalents	$ 13,420	$ 19,355
Marketable Securities	7,623	2,394
Accounts Receivable Trade, Net	22,120	20,872
Inventories	47,415	45,630
Prepaid Expenses and Other Receivables	1,312	1,264
Total Current Assets	91,890	89,515
Property, Plant, and Equipment, Net	67,045	65,762
Other Assets	3,773	3,770
Total Assets	$162,708	$159,047

(in millions)	2019	2018
Sales	$ 63,762	$ 61,890
Cost of Goods Sold	33,092	30,096
Gross Profit	30,670	31,794
Selling, General, and Administrative Expenses	15,335	15,897
Research and Development Expense	7,052	7,844
Interest Expense	145	142
Earnings Before Taxes	8,138	7,911
Income Tax Expense	2,848	2,769
Net Income	$ 5,290	$ 5,142

Problems

4 5 6 **P5-1. Multiple-Step and Single-Step Income Statement.** Bluebird Products, Inc. provided the following information from its current-year trial balance.

Bluebird Products, Inc.
Trial Balance (Partial)
For the Year Ended December 31

Account	Debit	Credit
Common Stock (no par)—Beginning Balance		$1,456,000
Retained Earnings—Beginning Balance		3,200,950
Accumulated Other Comprehensive Income—Beginning Balance		95,675
Dividends	$ 76,500	
Sales		2,200,000
Interest Income		34,500
Dividend Income		12,300
Gain on Disposal of Plant Assets		100,500
Unrealized Gain on Trading Securities		86,000
Unrealized Gain on Available-for-Sale Bonds		45,600
Cost of Goods Sold	750,000	
Selling Expenses	20,000	
Office Supplies Expense	123,500	
Sales Salaries Expense	55,000	
Advertising Expense	68,900	
Office Salaries Expense	78,500	
Accounting and Legal Fees—General	10,425	
Systems Consulting Fees—General	44,550	
Depreciation Expense—General	68,000	
Amortization Expense—General	34,500	
Interest Expense	23,750	
Loss on Discontinued Operations—Before Tax	90,000	
Loss on Asset Impairment	12,350	

Required »

a. Prepare a single-step income statement for the year ended December 31. The tax rate is 40%.
b. Prepare a multiple-step income statement for the year ended December 31.

4 5 6 **P5-2. Condensed Income Statement.** Using the information from P5-1, prepare a condensed, multiple-step income statement with all supporting disclosures.

4 5 6 **P5-3. Multiple-step, Single-step, and Condensed Statements of Net Income.** Right Angle Manufacturing Company provided the following information for the year ended December 31 for the current year.

Right Angle Manufacturing Company
Trial Balance (Partial)
For the Year Ended December 31

Account	Debit	Credit
Common Stock—Beginning Balance		$ 75,000
Retained Earnings—Beginning Balance		95,000
Accumulated Other Comprehensive Income—Beginning Balance	$3,400	
Dividends	500	
Sales		230,000
Dividend Income		200
Interest Income		680
Gain on Disposal of Plant Assets		1,000
Unrealized Gain on Trading Securities		$4,000
Cost of Goods Sold	$75,000	

Right Angle Manufacturing Company
Trial Balance (Partial)
For the Year Ended December 31

Account	Debit	Credit
Selling Expenses	1,450	
Advertising Expense	3,400	
Office Supplies Expense	1,250	
Sales Salaries Expense	145	
Office Salaries Expense	1,890	
Accounting and Legal Fees—Administrative	575	
Systems Consulting Fees—General	670	
Depreciation Expense—General	2,350	
Amortization Expense—General	3,000	
Interest Expense	890	
Loss on Asset Impairment	900	
Loss on Discontinued Operations—Before Tax	250	
Unrealized Loss on Available-for-Sale Bonds	780	

Required »

a. Prepare a single-step income statement for the current year. The tax rate is 40%.
b. Prepare a multiple-step income statement for the current year.
c. Prepare a condensed, multiple-step income statement for the current year and include all supporting schedules.

4 **P5-4. Statement of Net Income Presentation, IFRS.** Cardinal Manufacturing, Ltd., an IFRS reporter, provided the following information from its current-year trial balance.

Cardinal Manufacturing, Ltd.
Trial Balance (Partial)
For the Current Year Ended

Account	Debit	Credit
Common Stock (no par)—Beginning Balance		$3,876,000
Retained Earnings—Beginning Balance		2,720,000
Accumulated Other Comprehensive Income—Beginning Balance		85,675
Dividends	$ 58,500	
Sales		2,500,000
Interest Income		4,500
Income from Share of Associates		75,000
Gain on Disposal of Plant Assets		100,500
Gain on Flood Damage—Before Tax		56,000
Unrealized Gain on Available-for-Sale Bonds		45,600
Cost of Goods Sold	980,000	
Selling Expenses	20,000	
Office Supplies Expense	123,500	
Sales Salaries Expense	145,000	
Advertising Expense	68,900	
Office Salaries Expense	78,500	
Systems Consulting Fees—General	44,550	
Depreciation Expense—General	130,000	
Interest Expense	98,750	
Loss on Asset Impairment	9,350	
Loss on Discontinued Operations—Before Tax	140,000	

Required »

Prepare a statement of net income and additional disclosure that would meet IFRS presentation requirements. Indicate items IFRS requires to be reported on the income statement. The tax rate is 40%.

4 5 6 **P5-5. Income Statement Presentation, Classification, and Net of Tax.** Complete the following table by indicating:

1. The section of the income statement where the item should be included (e.g., operating, non-operating, discontinued operations), and
2. Whether the event is reported net of tax.

The first event is completed as a guide.

	Income Statement Classification	Reported Net of Tax?
Loss on disposal of equipment	*Non-operating*	*No*
Gain on sale of plant assets	______	____
Impairment loss	______	____
Loss on inventory write-off after government prohibition	______	____
Operating income	______	____
Unrealized loss on available-for-sale investments	______	____
Gain on disposal of expropriated land	______	____
Unrealized gain on trading securities	______	____
Operating income of discontinued division	______	____
Loss on inventory write-off due to obsolescence	______	____

6 **P5-6. Discontinued Operations.** Clockers, Inc. committed to sell a division on March 22, 2018. It sold the division on June 14, 2020. Income from operating this division was $3,240,000, $1,005,000, and $332,000 in 2018, 2019 and 2020, respectively. On December 31, 2018, the carrying value of the division was $10,000,000 and the fair value was $9,500,000. On December 31, 2019, the fair value of the division was $10,100,000 and the carrying value of the division was $10,000,000. The division was sold for $9,800,000 when the carrying value was $10,000,000. Prepare the discontinued operations section of the income statement for 2018 through 2020, assuming Clockers' income tax rate is 35%.

4 5 6 8 **P5-7. Multiple-step, Single-step, and Condensed Statements of Net Income. Statement of Comprehensive Income, Two-Statement Approach.** Delaney Products, Inc. provided the following information from its current-year trial balance.

Delaney Products, Inc.
Trial Balance (Partial)
For the Year Ended December 31

Account	Debit	Credit
Common Stock (no par)—Beginning Balance		$ 82,000
Retained Earnings—Beginning Balance		750,000
Accumulated Other Comprehensive Income—Beginning Balance		210,000
Dividends	$ 125	
Sales		400,000
Dividend Income		866
Interest Income		4,000
Gain on Disposal of Plant Assets		890
Unrealized Gain on Trading Securities		200
Cost of Goods Sold	25,000	
Selling Expenses	5,000	
Advertising Expense	7,000	
Office Salaries Expense	6,700	
Sales Salaries Expense	2,100	
Office Supplies Expense	2,000	
Accounting and Legal Fees—Administrative	300	
Systems Consulting Fees—Administrative	350	
Amortization Expense—Administrative	5,500	
Depreciation Expense—Administrative	8,250	
Interest Expense	900	
Unrealized Loss on Available-for-Sale Investments—Before Tax	933	
Loss on Asset Impairment	467	
Loss on Discontinued Operations—Before Tax	1,000	

Delaney issued $55,000 of common stock on October 1 of the current year. The company also repurchased $13,500 of its shares at the end of the reporting period. The company is subject to a 40% income tax rate.

Required »

a. Prepare an income statement for the current year using each reporting format (single-step, multiple-step, and condensed, multiple-step with supporting disclosures). Round to the nearest dollar.
b. Prepare a separate statement of comprehensive income for the current year.

8 **P5-8. Statement of Comprehensive Income, Single- and Two-Statement Approaches.** Tortarella Timber Company provided the following information for the current year:

1. Operating income amounted to $345,000.
2. The company sold investments in bonds at a pre-tax loss of $23,500.
3. Tortarella reported a $5,600 unrealized loss on an available-for-sale portfolio that is included in other comprehensive income.
4. The company reported a $12,000 unrealized gain on its trading portfolio, which is included in net income.
5. Tortarella committed to discontinue its retail lumber stores division on January 1 of the current year. The retail lumber stores meet the criteria to be presented as a discontinued operation. The retail lumber stores accounted for 15% of the company's operating income. The stores were operated all year.
6. The retail lumber stores division was sold at December 31 of the current year for a $16,850 pre-tax loss. There was no gain or loss on remeasurement on January 1.

The company is subject to a 30% income tax rate.

Required »

a. Prepare a single statement of comprehensive income beginning with operating income.
b. Prepare separate statements of net income and comprehensive income.

9 **P5-9. Prepare Statement of Stockholders' Equity.** Use the information in P5-3 for Right Angle Manufacturing Company and the following additional information provided to complete the requirements.

Right Angle issued $20,000 of no-par common stock in the current year. The company also repurchased $15,000 of its shares at the end of the reporting period. The company is subject to a 40% income tax rate. The beginning balance of common stock (no par) was $75,000.

Required »

a. Prepare a statement of stockholders' equity for the year ended December 31.
b. Prepare a partial balance sheet to show the ending balances in the stockholders' equity section.

A B **P5-10. Vertical Analyses, Profitability Analyses.** The Golden Fence Company and Stone Wall Corporation are competitors in manufacturing walls and fences. You are interested in comparing the two firms' profitability. Their income statements and other information follow.

(amounts in millions)	Golden Fence Company	Stone Wall Corporation
Sales	$ 987,236	$ 67,450
Cost of Goods Sold	678,626	43,370
Gross Profit	308,610	24,080
Selling, General, and Administrative Expenses	58,636	2,408
Other Operating Expenses	12,344	722
Interest Expense	24,689	193
Earnings Before Provision for Taxes	212,941	20,757
Provision for Taxes	74,529	7,265
Net Income	$ 138,412	$ 13,492
Average Total Assets	$1,258,287	$102,211
Average Stockholders' Equity	$ 654,309	$ 74,614

Golden Fence is the larger company based on sales and total assets, so you perform the following steps to compare and analyze the companies.

Required »

a. Prepare common-size income statements. Comment on differences in the relative size of each line item.
b. Compute profit margin, return on assets, and return on stockholders' equity. Which company appears more profitable?

Excel Project

Autograded Excel Project available in **MyLab Accounting**

CASES Judgment Cases

Judgment Case 1: Earnings Management

The CFO of First Things Computing, Inc. (FTC) prepared the following net income statement for the year ended December 31, 2019.

First Things Computing, Inc.
Statement of Net Income
For the Year Ended December 31, 2019

Revenues and Gains		
Sales	$234,800	
Interest Income	23,000	
Dividend Income	7,500	
Equity Investment Income	7,000	
Gain on Disposal of Plant Assets	4,700	
Total Revenues and Gains		$ 277,000
Expenses and Losses		
Cost of Goods Sold	$ 65,000	
Selling Expenses and Salaries	32,000	
Office Supplies Expense	30,000	
Advertising Expense	14,000	
Office Salaries Expense	10,000	
Depreciation Expense	5,000	
Interest Expense	2,500	
Loss on Asset Impairment	6,000	
Total Expense and Losses		164,500
Income before income taxes		112,500
Income Tax Expense		(39,375)
Net income from Continuing Operations		$ 73,125
Discontinued Operations		
Income from Operations of Discontinued Segment, Net of Tax of $6,730	$ 12,500	
Loss from Disposal of Discontinued Segment, Net of Tax of $5,277	(9,800)	2,700
Net Income		$ 75,825
Earnings per share:		
Income from Continuing Operations		$4.88
Income from Discontinued Operations		0.18
Earnings per share		$ 5.06

FTC had 15,000 common shares outstanding for the entire year. It had no preferred stock or dilutive securities. Thus, its earnings per share (EPS) is computed simply as earnings divided by shares outstanding. According to the current statement of net income, its EPS is $5.06 ($75,825 net income divided by 15,000 shares).

FTC records income tax expense at 35% of income from continuing operations before income taxes. The CFO will make the following adjustments before finalizing the financial statements:

1. FTC will need to record some amount of bad debt expense. The offset will be a reduction in accounts receivable. This adjustment is a matter of judgment and reasonable estimates range between $1,000 and $3,000.
2. FTC will need to write down its inventory (i.e., reduce the reported value of inventory). The offset will be to cost of goods sold. This adjustment is a matter of judgment and reasonable estimates range between $2,500 and $3,750.
3. FTC may need to record an impairment of property, plant, and equipment (PPE) (i.e., reduce the reported value of PPE). The offset will be an impairment loss reported on the statement of net income. This adjustment is a matter of judgment and reasonable estimates range between $0 and $5,000.
4. FTC may need to record an impairment of noncurrent investments (i.e., reduce the reported value of noncurrent investments). The offset will be an impairment loss reported on the statement of net income. This adjustment is a matter of judgment and reasonable estimates range between $250 and $750.

5. FTC may need to record a litigation contingency (i.e., it may need to record a liability for an unresolved lawsuit). The offset is to litigation expense. The lawsuit is expected to be settled in 2020. FTC's attorneys believe that they can provide a point estimate of the amount for which FTC will be liable. The estimate will either be $2,000 or $10,000.
6. FTC may need to reduce the reported amount of its deferred tax asset. The amount by which the asset needs to be reduced is highly judgmental and ranges from $0 to $5,000. The offset to this adjustment is income tax expense. (Thus, this adjustment impacts post-tax net income, but no pre-tax net income).
7. FTC currently has unearned revenue on its balance sheet of $5,400. However, up to $5,000 of this amount could possibly be recognized as revenue in 2019. However, this amount is a matter of judgment.

Required »

a. If FTC makes the most conservative choices for all these adjustments resulting in the lowest income number, what is the impact on net income and earnings per share?
b. If FTC makes the least conservative choices for all these adjustments by making the choices that will result in the highest income number, what is the impact on net income and earnings per share?
c. Do you think that the management of FTC will care very much about the choices related to these adjustments? Why or why not?

Financial Statement Analysis Cases

Financial Statement Analysis Case 1: Vertical Analyses of *Johnson & Johnson* and *Pfizer Inc.*

Pfizer Inc. is a US company that manufactures and distributes pharmaceutical and consumer healthcare products that are similar to those sold by ***Johnson & Johnson.*** Use the excerpts of ***Johnson & Johnson's*** and ***Pfizer's*** income statements to answer the following questions:

a. Compute each line item as a percentage of sales for both companies.
b. If sales are used as a measure of size, which company is larger?
c. Which company has a higher cost of goods sold relative to sales?
d. Which company has higher selling, general, and administrative expenses relative to sales?
e. Which company has higher research and development expenses relative to sales?
f. Which company has a higher income from continuing operations relative to sales? Comment on the difference or lack of difference given other relationships observed.
g. Which company has a higher profit margin? Comment on the difference between the two companies.

	Johnson & Johnson	Pfizer
*(amounts in millions)**	2016	2016
Net Sales	$71,890	$52,824
Cost of Goods Sold	21,685	12,329
Gross Profit	50,205	40,495
Selling, General, and Administrative Expenses	19,945	14,837
Research and Development Expenses	9,095	7,872
In-Process Research and Development	29	0
Amortization of Intangible Assets	-	4,056
Restructuring Charges, Net	491	1,724
Interest Expense	726	-
Interest Income	(368)	-
Other Expense (income), Net	484	3,655
Income from Continuing Operations Before Income Taxes	19,803	8,351
Income Tax Expense	3,263	1,123
Income from Continuing Operations	$16,540	$ 7,229
Income from Discontinued Operations, Net of Income Taxes		17
Net Income Before Noncontrolling Interests	$16,540	$ 7,246
Income Attributable to Noncontrolling Interests		31
Net Income	$ 16,540	$ 7,215

* The captions for some lines have been changed for consistency in comparing the two companies.
Sources: Johnson & Johnson and Pfizer income statements

Financial Statement Analysis Case 2: Profitability Analysis of *Johnson & Johnson* and *Pfizer Inc.*

Pfizer Inc. is a U.S. company that manufactures and distributes pharmaceutical and consumer healthcare products that are similar to those sold by ***Johnson & Johnson.*** In the following, we present ***Johnson & Johnson's*** profitability ratios computed in Example 5B.1 in the chapter appendix. Use these and the excerpts of ***Pfizer's*** income statements to answer the following questions:

a. If ***Johnson & Johnson's*** sales are $71,890 million in 2016, which company is larger using sales as a measure of size?
b. Compute ***Pfizer's*** profit margin in 2016 and 2015.
c. Compute ***Pfizer's*** return on assets in 2016 and 2015.
d. Compute ***Pfizer's*** return on equity in 2016 and 2015.
e. Compare ***Johnson & Johnson's*** and ***Pfizer's*** profit margins in 2016 and 2015.
f. Compare ***Johnson & Johnson's*** and ***Pfizer's*** return on assets in 2016 and 2015.
g. Compare ***Johnson & Johnson's*** and ***Pfizer's*** return on equity in 2016 and 2015.

Pfizer Inc. (all dollars in millions)

Balance Sheets (excerpts) **End of Year**	**2016**	**2015**	**2014**
Total assets	$171,615	$167,381	$167,566
Total stockholders' equity	$ 59,544	$64,720	$ 71,301
Statement of Earnings (excerpts) **For the year**	**2016**	**2015**	**2014**
Sales to customers	$52,824	$48,851	$49,605
Net earnings	$7,215	$6,960	$9,135

Johnson & Johnson (from Example 5B.1 in Appendix B)

Profitability Measure	**2016**	**2015**
Profit Margin	23.0%	22.0%
Return on Assets	12.0%	11.7%
Return on Equity	23.6%	21.9%

Sources: Johnson & Johnson and Pfizer income statements

Surfing the Standards Cases

Surfing the Standards Case 1: Interest Allocation to Discontinued Operations

Kimbro Concrete Companies is disposing of its blacktop segment this year and is reporting it as a discontinued operation on the statement of net income in the current year.

The ratio of consolidated debt to equity is uniform for all operations of the company. What is the minimum amount of interest that Kimbro Concrete can allocate to its discontinued operations? What is the maximum amount of interest that it can allocate to discontinued operations? Provide explanations of your calculations, including references to the codification.

The following information is available related to the net assets and debt of Kimbro Concrete. Interest expense for all debt is 7% of the principal balance.

Net Assets of Kimbro Concrete	$10,500,000
Net Assets of Blacktop Segment	$ 1,200,000

Debt of Kimbro Concrete:	Principal	Interest
Directly attributable to continuing operations	$ 500,000	$ 35,000
Required to be repaid upon disposal of the blacktop segment	100,000	7,000
Debt that will be assumed by the buyer of the blacktop segment	150,000	10,500
All other debt	1,250,000	87,500
TOTAL	$ 2,000,000	$140,000

Surfing the Standards Case 2: Amounts Paid by Shareholders for an Entity's Expenses

Moocher Company, a publicly traded company that has a December 31 year-end, manufactures and sells novelty toys. Recently, one of the toys that Moocher produced and sold was found to cause serious digestive problems for dogs that ate the toy. Accordingly, Moocher was sued by a group of consumers in May of the current year. Moocher didn't believe that it would lose the suit in a court ruling, but it did not want the bad publicity. Because Moocher did not have extensive cash reserves, the primary shareholder (55% owner) of Moocher transferred 40,000 shares to the plaintiffs to settle the case in December of the current year. The market value of the shares was $25 per share at the time of the transfer.

Does Moocher Company need to report anything in its annual financial statements for the current year related to this transaction?

Use the U.S. authoritative literature to support your conclusions.

Basis for Conclusions Cases

Basis for Conclusions Case 1: Presentation of the Tax Effects of Items Included in Other Comprehensive Income

Companies report all amounts related to other comprehensive income net of tax. *Net of tax* means that the amount of income (or loss) reported includes any income tax effects. Companies do not include the income tax expense (or benefit) related to items included in other comprehensive income in the income tax expense line item reported on the statement of income immediately following the net income before income tax line item.

Read paragraphs BC14 and BC15 of ASU 2011-05 – *Presentation of Comprehensive Income* and answer the following questions.

1. What are the requirements related to the presentation of the gross amounts, the net of tax amounts, and the tax impact of items include in OCI?
2. Did respondents to the exposure draft agree with this approach? Did any respondents disagree? If so, what were their concerns?
3. Why did the board make the decision that it did?

Basis for Conclusions Case 2: Reporting Other Comprehensive Income

Both U.S. GAAP and IFRS include the concept of comprehensive income. Comprehensive income is divided into net income and other comprehensive income. Read paragraphs 58 through 67 in SFAS No. 130 and paragraph BC49 through BC54 in IAS 1. Also read the discussion of the dissenting opinions in SFAS No. 130.

Required »

1. In theory, what four possible reporting methods for OCI could standard setters allow?
2. What are the pros and cons of these four possible methods of reporting OCI?
3. Which method of reporting OCI do you think is best? Explain why you prefer your chosen method.

APPENDIX A
Financial Statement Analysis

As discussed in Chapter 2, the objective of financial reporting is to provide financial information that investors and creditors can use to make rational resource allocation decisions. The annual report contains a significant amount of information about a company's financial performance and financial position for use in decision making. In this appendix, we discuss **financial statement analysis**, which provides the tools and techniques necessary to evaluate a company's performance over time, relative to certain benchmarks or compared to similar entities.

The Importance of Financial Statement Analysis

Financial statements should provide information that allows users to understand important relationships among financial statement line items and changes in them for a company over time. Consider the following scenarios:

1. Assume an auditor observes that accounts receivable is increasing as a percent of total assets. She may seek additional information such as whether sales are also increasing, collections are decreasing, or the firm has relaxed credit extension practices.
2. If the percentage of cost of goods sold to sales has increased, a company's manager would seek to determine the reason. Higher cost of sales percentages could be due to higher raw material costs.
3. Consider a bank reviewing a credit line application for a company. If the company's existing debt is high or its cash flows are decreasing, the bank would be concerned about its ability to repay the loan.

Horizontal Analysis and Vertical Analysis of Financial Statements

Johnson & Johnson's annual report includes balance sheets for the past two years and income and cash flow statements for a three-year period. Reporting results of operations, financial position, and cash flows for more than one year results in **comparative financial statements**. Companies issue comparative financial statements in order to provide financial information for more than one reporting period, thus allowing a user to compare the company on a year-to-year basis. Year-to-year changes in a company's financial position, operating performance, or cash flows can identify changes in activities, confirm projections, or identify trends to consider for the future.

Comparative financial statements can also be used to create *common-size financial statements*. **Common-size financial statements** measure each financial statement line item relative to some key amount or total. For example, to convert all income statement line items into a common-size percentage, divide each line by sales. Financial statement users can use common-size financial statements to compare a company to itself over time or to compare different firms of varying size.

There are two types of financial statement analyses: *vertical analysis* and *horizontal analysis*. Vertical analysis uses common-size financial statements. Horizontal analysis examines financial statements over time. In this section, we use horizontal and vertical analyses to compare one company to itself over time.

Horizontal Analysis

Horizontal analysis examines the percentage change in financial statement items from year to year. Horizontal analyses can provide information about increases or decreases in a company's income and expenses, which could indicate growth or a change in business strategy. For example, a company entering a new line of business could experience rapid sales growth or higher advertising costs. Example 5A.1 presents an illustration of a horizontal analysis for ***Johnson & Johnson.***

EXAMPLE 5A.1 Horizontal Analysis of *Johnson & Johnson's* 2015 and 2016 Income Statements

PROBLEM: Use the excerpts of ***Johnson & Johnson's*** income statements provided to answer the following questions about changes in line items from the income statement from 2015 to 2016.

a. Compute the difference in each line item from 2015 to 2016.
b. Using 2015 as a base year, determine the change and percentage change in each line item from 2015 to 2016.
c. Did sales to customers increase or decrease from 2015 to 2016?
d. Did net income increase or decrease from 2015 to 2016?
e. What line item(s) is (are) driving the differences between sales to customers and net income from 2015 to 2016?

Johnson & Johnson
Income Statements (excerpt)

(dollars in millions)	2016	2015
Sales to customers	$71,890	$70,074
Cost of products sold	21,685	21,536
Gross profit	50,205	48,538
Selling, marketing, and administrative expenses	19,945	21,203
Research and development expense	9,095	9,046
In-process research and development	29	224
Interest income	(368)	(128)
Interest expense, net of portion capitalized	726	552
Other (income) expense, net	484	(2,064)
Restructuring	491	509
Earnings before provision for taxes on income	19,803	19,196
Provision for taxes on income	3,263	3,787
Net earnings	$16,540	$15,409

Note: The line item in-process research and development is a loss that relates to asset write-off of in-process research and development assets acquired when Johnson & Johnson purchased other companies.
Source: Johnson & Johnson Company's 2015 and 2016 Income Statements. See the Johnson & Johnson Company annual report at http://files.shareholder.com/downloads/JNJ/3809936545x0xS200406-17-6/200406/filing.pdf

SOLUTION:

a. and b. The table on the next page computes the dollar difference from 2015 to 2016 and the percentage change by dividing the 2016 changes by the 2015 amounts.
c. Sales to customers increased by $1,816 million from 2015 to 2016. Sales increased by about 2.6%.
d. Net income increased by $1,131 million from 2015 to 2016. Net earnings increased by 7.3%.
e. The increase in net income is due primarily to an increase of $1,816 million in sales; a decrease in selling, marketing and administrative expense of $1,258 million; and a decrease in provision for taxes of $524 million.

(dollars in millions)	2016	2015	Change 2016–2015	Percent Change from 2015
Sales to customers	$71,890	$70,074	$1,816	2.6%
Cost of products sold	21,685	21,536	149	0.7%
Gross profit	50,205	48,538	1,667	3.4%
Selling, marketing, and administrative expenses	19,945	21,203	(1,258)	(5.9%)
Research and development expense	9,095	9,046	49	0.5%
In-process research and development	29	224	(195)	(87.1%)
Interest income	(368)	(128)	240	187.5%
Interest expense, net of portion capitalized	726	552	174	31.5%
Other (income) expense, net	484	(2,064)	2,548	(123.4%)
Restructuring	491	509	(18)	(3.5%)
Earnings before provision for taxes on income	19,803	19,196	607	3.2%
Provision for taxes on income	3,263	3,787	(524)	(13.8%)
Net earnings	$16,540	$15,409	$1,131	7.3%

Vertical Analysis

Vertical analysis expresses financial information in relation to some relevant total or amount within one year. On the income statement, each income statement line item is expressed as a proportion of sales. On the balance sheet, each item is expressed as a percent of total assets.[31]

EXAMPLE 5A.2 Vertical Analysis of *Johnson & Johnson's* 2015 and 2016 Income Statements

PROBLEM: Use the excerpts of ***Johnson & Johnson's*** income statements to answer the following questions about changes in sales from 2015 to 2016.

a. Compute each line item as a percentage of sales for 2015 and 2016.
b. Which line item makes up the largest proportion of sales in 2015 and 2016? (Keep in mind that some of the items like gross profit and earnings before provision for taxes on income are subtotals.)
c. Comment on any changes in the income and expenses as a percent of sales from 2015 and 2016.

(dollars in millions)	2016	2015
Sales to customers	$71,890	$70,074
Cost of products sold	21,685	21,536
Gross profit	50,205	48,538
Selling, marketing, and administrative expenses	19,945	21,203
Research and development expense	9,095	9,046
In-process research and development	29	224
Interest income	(368)	(128)
Interest expense, net of portion capitalized	726	552
Other (income) expense, net	484	(2,064)
Restructuring	491	509
Earnings before provision for taxes on income	19,803	19,196
Provision for taxes on income	3,263	3,787
Net earnings	$16,540	$15,409

Source: Johnson & Johnson Company's 2015 and 2016 Income Statements. See Johnson & Johnson Company's Annual Report at http://files.shareholder.com/downloads/JNJ/3809936545x0xS200406-17-6/200406/filing.pdf

[31] Sales and total assets do not have to be used as the denominator for vertical analyses. However, they are the most common bases used in practice.

SOLUTION:

(dollars in millions)	2016	2015	Percent of Sales 2016	Percent of Sales 2015
Sales to customers	$71,890	$70,074	100.0%	100.0%
Cost of products sold	21,685	21,536	30.2%	30.7%
Gross profit	50,205	48,538	69.8%	69.3%
Selling, marketing, and administrative expenses	19,945	21,203	27.7%	30.3%
Research and development expense	9,095	9,046	12.7%	12.9%
In-process research and development	29	224	0.0%	0.3%
Interest income	(368)	(128)	(0.5%)	(0.2%)
Interest expense, net of portion capitalized	726	552	1.0%	0.8%
Other (income) expense, net	484	(2,064)	0.7%	(2.9%)
Restructuring	491	509	0.7%	0.7%
Earnings before provision for taxes on income	19,803	19,196	27.5%	27.4%
Provision for taxes on income	3,263	3,787	4.5%	5.4%
Net earnings	$16,540	$15,409	23.0%	22.0%

a. The preceding table computes the percent of each line item to sales for 2015 and 2016. For example, net earnings of $16,540 million in 2016 is 23.0% of sales ($16,540 million divided by $71,890 million).

b. In 2016 and 2015, cost of products sold made up over 30.2% and 30.7% of sales in 2016 and 2015, respectively.

c. The percent of cost of products sold, research and development expense, in-process research and development expense, interest income, interest expense, and the provision for taxes on income to sales remains very similar from year to year with most items changing less than 1% of sales. Selling, marketing, and administrative expenses is a smaller percentage of sales in 2016 at 27.7% compared to 30.3% in 2015. Other (income) expense was negative in 2015 and (2.9%) of sales. In 2016, other (income) expense was positive and 0.7% of sales. It is a greater percentage of sales in 2015 when compared to 2016.

APPENDIX B
Profitability Analysis

Ratio analysis is one of the most common financial statement analysis tools. **Ratios** compute meaningful relationships between financial statement items useful in:

- Understanding a company over time.
- Comparing one company to another company.
- Benchmarking a company to an industry standard.

In this section, we introduce the most common ratios for profitability analyses.[32] In management's discussion and analysis of financial condition and results of operations, companies will often comment on the profitability using the ratios we discuss on the next page.[33]

[32] We will expand our coverage of ratios as we cover additional topics in later chapters.

[33] We present commonly used ratio definitions and computations. It is important to understand how each company defines its ratios because computations could vary.

Profitability

Profitability is a company's ability to generate a return for its shareholders based on the revenues or resources available. The "bottom-line" return to the shareholders is the company's net income. Profitability analysis allows a financial statement user to assess how well a company has performed and how much return it has generated relative to its revenues or resources. Three common measures of profitability are:

1. Profit margin
2. Return on assets
3. Return on equity

Profit Margin

Firms measure profitability as the percent of each dollar of sales that is available for distribution. The **profit margin** indicates the percent of each dollar of sales remaining after covering cost of sales and other business expenses. The profit margin is computed as net income divided by sales revenue:

$$\text{Profit Margin} = \frac{\text{Net Income}}{\text{Sales Revenue}} \tag{5B.1}$$

A higher profit margin indicates a higher return to shareholders.

Return on Assets

Firms also assess profitability based on how well a company is using its resources. The **return on assets ratio** measures the income generated for shareholders from each dollar of average total assets.

$$\text{Return on Assets} = \frac{\text{Net Income}}{\text{Average Total Assets}} \tag{5B.2}$$

Average total assets is used as the base in the denominator. A firm earns income over a period of time. However, total assets are measured at a point in time, the balance sheet date. To obtain a measure of the assets in use over the period in which income is earned, we take the average of total assets at the beginning and ending of the period. The assumption is that the firm earns net income evenly over the year on assets it employs. Average total assets is computed as:

$$\text{Average Total Assets} = \frac{\text{Beginning Total Assets} + \text{Ending Total Assets}}{2} \tag{5B.3}$$

Return on Equity Ratio

The **return on equity ratio** measures the return on shareholders' investment in the company. Return on equity is the amount of net income the company generates by using the equity provided by shareholders:

$$\text{Return on Equity} = \frac{\text{Net Income}}{\text{Average Stockholders' Equity}} \tag{5B.4}$$

Similar to using average total assets in return on assets, we use the average shareholders' equity as the base in the denominator. Again, the assumption is that the firm earns net income evenly over the year. Average shareholders' equity is computed as:

$$\text{Average Stockholders' Equity} = \frac{\text{Beginning Stockholders' Equity} + \text{Ending Stockholders' Equity}}{2} \tag{5B.5}$$

The various return ratios address the question of how well a company is using its resources. In contrast to the return on assets ratio, the return on equity is an indicator of a company's return to its shareholders.

When analyzing ratios based on net income, it is important to assess whether the income items are recurring or non-recurring. Recurring income items are better indicators of future performance and profitability than nonrecurring items. For example, a loss on discontinued operations is not expected to recur. In Example 5A.1, ***Johnson & Johnson*** reported losses on the restructuring of $491 million and $509 million in 2016 and 2015, respectively. Whereas a large company like ***Johnson & Johnson*** is expected to have these types of losses and expenses, the amounts can vary each year and may not recur.

EXAMPLE 5B.1

Profitability Analysis of *Johnson & Johnson's* 2015 and 2016

PROBLEM: Use the following information provided from the 2016 ***Johnson & Johnson*** annual report to compute the profit margin, return on assets, and return on equity for 2015 and 2016. What does each measure indicate about ***Johnson & Johnson's*** profitability? What do the measures taken together indicate about ***Johnson & Johnson's*** profitability?

(dollars in millions)

Balance Sheets (excerpts) **End of Year**	**2016**	**2015**	**2014**
Total assets	$141,208	$133,411	$130,358
Total stockholders' equity	$ 70,418	$ 69,752	$ 71,150
Statement of Earnings (excerpts) **For the Year**	**2016**	**2015**	**2014**
Sales to customers	$71,890	$70,074	$74,331
Net earnings	$16,540	$15,409	$16,323

Source: Johnson & Johnson Company's Annual Report at http://files.shareholder.com/downloads/JNJ/3809936545x0xS200406-17-6/200406/filing.pdf

SOLUTION: The table on the next page provides the computations of the profit margin, return on assets, and return on equity for 2016 and 2015.

Johnson & Johnson reported profit margins of 23.0% and 22.0% in 2016 and 2015, respectively. The results indicate that ***Johnson & Johnson*** is able to return 23.0 and 22.0 cents of each dollar of sales to its stockholders in 2016 and 2015, respectively. Its return on assets of 12.0% and 11.7% in 2016 and 2015, respectively, suggests that for each dollar invested in assets, the return is about $0.12 and $0.12 in 2016 and 2015, respectively. The return on equity of 23.6% and 21.9% in 2016 and 2015, respectively, indicates that for each dollar of equity invested, the return is about $0.24 and $0.22 in 2016 and 2015, respectively.

All profitability ratios are positive. All three ratios increased from 2015 to 2016. One reason for the increase is higher income in 2016; however, further analysis is required to determine the contributing factors. For example, an analyst could examine the income statement line items for any changes or unusual items. In this case, part of the increase in net income in 2016 is due to the lower selling, marketing, and administrative expenses. In addition, the denominator in two of the ratios is increasing, suggesting that ***Johnson & Johnson*** is able to increase overall profitability as a percentage of sales and total assets.

Profitability Measure	2016	2015
$\text{Profit Margin} = \frac{\text{Net Income}}{\text{Sales}}$	$\frac{\$16,540}{\$71,890} = 23.0\%$	$\frac{\$15,409}{\$70,074} = 22.0\%$
$\text{Return on Assets} = \frac{\text{Net Income}}{\text{Average Total Assets}}$	$\frac{\$16,540}{\$137,310} = 12.0\%$	$\frac{\$15,409}{\$131,885} = 11.7\%$
$\text{Average Total Assets} = \frac{\text{Beginning Total Assets + Ending Total Assets}}{2}$	$\frac{\$133,411 + 141,208}{2} = \$137,310$	$\frac{\$130,358 + 133,411}{2} = \$131,885$
$\text{Return on Equity} = \frac{\text{Net Income}}{\text{Average Stockholders' Equity}}$	$\frac{\$16,540}{\$70,085} = 23.6\%$	$\frac{\$15,409}{\$70,451} = 21.9\%$
$\text{Average Stockholders' Equity} = \frac{\text{Beginning Stockholders' Equity + Ending Stockholders' Equity}}{2}$	$\frac{\$69,752 + 70,418}{2} = \$70,085$	$\frac{\$71,150 + 69,752}{2} = \$70,451$

Exhibit 5B.1 summarizes profitability ratios, computations, desirable characteristics, and potential problems.

EXHIBIT 5B.1 Profitability Ratios

Ratios	Equation	Desirable Equation Characteristics	Potential Problems
$\text{Profit Margin} = \frac{\text{Net Income}}{\text{Sales}}$	(5B.1)	Higher ratio is preferred to lower.	Net income can include non-recurring items.
$\text{Return on Assets} = \frac{\text{Net Income}}{\text{Average Total Assets}}$	(5B.2)	Higher ratio is preferred to lower.	Net income can include non-recurring items.
Denominator:			
$\text{Average Total Assets} = \frac{\text{Beginning Total Assets + Ending Total Assets}}{2}$	(5B.3)		
$\text{Return on Equity} = \frac{\text{Net Income}}{\text{Average Stockholders' Equity}}$	(5B.4)	Higher ratio is preferred to lower.	Net income can include non-recurring items.
Denominator:			
$\text{Average Stockholders' Equity} = \frac{\text{(Beginning Stockholders' Equity + Ending Stockholders' Equity)}}{2}$	(5B.5)		

6 Statements of Financial Position and Cash Flows and the Annual Report

LEARNING OBJECTIVES

1. Discuss the usefulness and limitations of the statement of financial position, including its use in understanding liquidity, solvency, and financial flexibility.
2. Provide an overview of classifications on the statement of financial position for typical assets, liabilities, and stockholders' equity.
3. Explain the presentation of current and noncurrent assets and liabilities on the statement of financial position and name the common statement formats.
4. Explain the statement of cash flows and classify common business activities into operating, investing, and financing cash flows.
5. Explain the direct and indirect formats of the statement of cash flows.
6. Review the four primary financial statements and financial statement articulation.
7. Explain the purpose of the notes to the financial statements, including the summary of significant accounting policies, subsequent events, going concern uncertainties, and related-party transactions.
8. Identify and describe the typical content of an annual report.

marcelokrelling/Fotolia

Introduction

THE BALANCE SHEET, or statement of financial position, summarizes an entity's economic resources (assets), obligations (liabilities), and stockholders' equity. Financial statement users rely on the balance sheet information to help determine an entity's ability to generate future cash flows and to evaluate its exposure to risk. A strong balance sheet generally indicates a firm with solid financial health.

What makes a balance sheet strong? In simple terms, a strong balance sheet has limited obligations so that a company can make timely debt payments. A company with significant levels of debt may be at risk of defaulting on payments or even filing for bankruptcy when the economy is faltering or markets are weak. Declining sales and low cash flows make it difficult for a company to liquidate its debt when due.

Companies actively manage their levels of debt. To maximize shareholder return, companies seek to borrow at low interest rates and operate efficiently. Too much debt can drain a company's ability to grow when cash is used to make debt payments rather than to invest. Consider ***Zoe's Kitchen Inc.,*** a fast, casual restaurant chain that raised over $80 million in its 2014 initial public offering (IPO). ***Zoe's Kitchen*** planned to use about $50 million to "clean up" its balance sheet by paying off debt and allocating the remaining $30 million to support growth plans. With the cash raised from the IPO, ***Zoe's Kitchen*** was able to both lower its debt and fund future growth. The lower debt also frees up cash for investment that would have otherwise been used to pay principal and interest on the debt.

A healthy balance sheet, then, provides adequate cash and other assets for managing day-to-day operations, making timely debt payments, stimulating future growth, and funding any unexpected needs. The importance of cash management necessitates a separate financial statement, the *statement of cash flows*, to explain changes in cash.

In this chapter, we complete our look at the four basic financial statements by examining the *statement of financial position* and the *statement of cash flows*. (We addressed the statements of net income and comprehensive income and the statement of stockholders' equity in Chapter 5.) The discussion begins with an overview of the balance sheet, followed by an examination of the presentation of current and noncurrent assets and liabilities on the statement of financial position. We then introduce the statement of cash flows. We also discuss the differences between U.S. GAAP and IFRS regarding the form and content of the statement of financial position and the statement of cash flows.

Next, we examine how the four basic financial statements interrelate, or *articulate*, to provide comprehensive information on a company's operating performance and financial position. Financial reports also include the notes that accompany the financial statements, a key source of essential information regarding a company's accounting policies and further explain the amounts reported. The financial statements are usually part of a company's annual report to shareholders, which also includes additional disclosures that supplement and enhance the financial statements. We outline the components of the annual report using the ***Johnson & Johnson*** 2016 annual report. «

1 Discuss the usefulness and limitations of the statement of financial position, including its use in understanding liquidity, solvency, and financial flexibility.

The Statement of Financial Position

The **statement of financial position**, also called the **balance sheet**, lists an entity's assets, liabilities, and equity as of a specific point in time.[1] The balance sheet consists of permanent accounts with cumulative balances that the company carries forward period to period over the life of the firm. As noted in Chapter 4, permanent accounts are not closed at year-end.

THE CONCEPTUAL FRAMEWORK CONNECTION: Usefulness and Limitations of the Balance Sheet

The balance sheet provides critical information to financial statement users in three key areas. Specifically, the balance sheet:

1. Summarizes the economic resources and obligations that impact the entity's ability to generate future cash flows.
2. Is useful in assessing an entity's rate of return on its investments when examined in conjunction with the income statement.
3. Aids in assessing the risk associated with an entity by providing inputs for cash flow measures.

Three common cash flow measures based on balance sheet information are *liquidity, solvency,* and *financial flexibility.* **Liquidity** is a measure of an asset's nearness to cash—that is, how quickly the firm can convert assets into cash and pay liabilities with minimal risk of loss. Analyzing an entity's liquidity allows investors to determine whether it will have the resources needed to pay its currently maturing obligations, pay dividends, and/or buy back its own equity shares. Thus, the more liquid an entity, the lower the risk associated with that entity.

Solvency is a measure of a firm's long-term ability to pay its obligations as they mature. A firm with a high level of debt relative to its equity may have difficulty meeting the fixed payments associated with its debt and therefore is in a position of low solvency. We discuss various financial ratios that are used to measure liquidity and solvency in Appendix B.

[1] We use the terms statement of financial position and balance sheet interchangeably in this chapter.

Financial flexibility indicates an entity's ability to respond to unexpected needs and opportunities by taking actions that alter the amounts and timing of cash flows. For example, expanding into international markets may require additional debt financing. An entity with low levels of debt on its balance sheet can borrow the funds needed to finance this expansion. The greater an entity's financial flexibility, the lower its risk.

Whereas the statement of financial position provides a number of benefits, financial statement users also realize that the statement has certain limitations related to the following issues.

- Many of the accounts on the balance sheet are reported at historical cost as opposed to market values or liquidation values. For example, assume an entity purchased land 10 years ago for $1,000 that now has a market value of $10,000. The firm reports the asset on the balance sheet under U.S. GAAP at the historical cost of $1,000. In this way, relying on historical costs limits the relevance of information in the balance sheet.
- A number of assets and liabilities are not reported on the balance sheet. For example, assets such as human capital and a company's reputation for quality products will not be reported on the balance sheet.
- Many of the accounts reported on the balance sheet are based on estimates as opposed to determinable amounts. For example, the net realizable value of accounts receivable is based on the estimated amount of cash that the entity expects to collect.

❷ Provide an overview of classifications on the statement of financial position for typical assets, liabilities, and stockholders' equity.

Balance Sheet Classifications

The three primary classifications on the balance sheet are assets, liabilities, and stockholders' equity. The balance sheet utilizes sub-classifications within each of these broad groups that enhance the usefulness of the balance sheet by grouping the accounts according to characteristics such as nature, function, or size. One of the primary distinctions is *current* versus *noncurrent.* **Noncurrent assets** are resources that the firm expects to convert to cash, use, or consume in a period of more than one year or one operating cycle, whichever is longer. **Noncurrent liabilities** are obligations that are due after one year or one operating cycle, whichever is longer. Exhibit 6.1 presents the typical groupings used to subdivide these categories; we discuss each of these sub-classifications in more detail in the following pages.

EXHIBIT 6.1 Balance Sheet Classifications

Assets	Liabilities	Stockholders' equity
Current assets	Current liabilities	Contributed capital
Noncurrent assets	Noncurrent liabilities	
– Long-term investments		Retained earnings
– Property, plant, and equipment		Accumulated other comprehensive income
– Intangible assets		Noncontrolling interest
– Other assets		

Managers make several decisions related to how to report, or format, the classifications in Exhibit 6.1 on the balance sheet. The reporting options include:

- Aggregating and summarizing accounts into financial statement components or line items. For example, a company could have several accounts for property, plant, and equipment in its general ledger that it aggregates and summarizes in a single line item called "Property, plant, and equipment."
- Grouping or classifying the components. Specifically, assets and liabilities can be grouped or classified as current and noncurrent.
- Providing subtotals and totals. Subtotals often relate to how items are grouped.

Assets

As indicated in Exhibit 6.1, assets are generally subdivided on the balance sheet as *current assets; long-term investments; property, plant, and equipment; intangible assets;* and *other assets.*

Current Assets. **Current assets** are resources that the firm expects to convert to cash, to use, or to consume within one year or one *operating cycle*, whichever is longer. The **operating cycle** is the period of time from the acquisition of goods to the point at which the entity receives cash from the sale of the goods. For example, consider a clothing wholesaler whose operating cycle begins when it purchases clothing inventory. It will then sell the inventory to retailers on credit. The operating cycle is completed when the wholesaler receives payment from its customers.

Current assets primarily include:

- *Cash and cash equivalents.*
- *Short-term investments.*
- *Accounts receivable.*
- *Inventory.*
- *Prepaid expenses.*

Cash and cash equivalents include cash (coins, currency, and money orders) and cash equivalents (short-term, highly liquid investments acquired with three months or less to maturity). Cash equivalents include:

- Commercial paper (i.e., short-term loans receivable from high-quality corporations sold by commercial banks).
- Money market funds.
- U.S. Treasury bills.

For example, a three-year Treasury instrument acquired with two months to maturity is a cash equivalent.

Short-term investments not classified as cash equivalents are investments in debt or equity securities of other corporations or governmental entities that the entity has the ability and intent to sell within the next year or operating cycle, whichever is longer. For example, an entity would classify 100 shares of ***Microsoft*** that it intends to sell within the next year as a short-term investment.

Accounts receivable (also called trade receivables) are amounts owed to the entity resulting from the sale of goods or services to customers on credit. Accounts receivable arise in the normal course of a company's trade or business and do not require a formal written agreement.[2] Accounts receivable are measured net of an allowance for estimated bad debts and are classified as current assets because they are usually due within 30 to 60 days.

Inventory is tangible property that is either (a) held for sale in the ordinary course of business, (b) used as raw materials in the manufacturing process to produce finished goods to be sold in the ordinary course of business, or (c) held as supplies to be currently consumed when providing goods or services. For a retail or wholesale business, inventory includes all goods held for resale. In the case of a manufacturing company, inventory is made up of three components: raw materials, work-in-process, and finished goods. Inventory is classified as a current asset.

Prepaid expenses are assets that arise when expenses are paid before they are incurred. Common examples are prepaid rent and prepaid insurance. Prepaid expenses are typically considered current assets because the benefits associated with these prepayments are usually consumed within a year or operating cycle if longer. However, any portion of the associated benefit that extends beyond the upcoming year is classified as noncurrent in other assets.

Long-Term Investments. **Long-term investments** are noncurrent assets that are not used directly in the operations of the business. Examples are investments in debt and equity securities and investments in land and other property that are not used in operations. Long-term investments

[2] A *note receivable* is a receivable supported by a formal agreement that specifies payment terms.

are classified as noncurrent because management does not intend to convert them into cash within the next year (or operating cycle, if longer).

Property, Plant, and Equipment. **Property, plant, and equipment** are assets that are tangible, long-lived, and used in the production and sale of the company's goods and services. This balance sheet category includes items such as buildings, land, machinery and equipment, office furniture and equipment, and natural resources. With the exception of land (which is not depreciated), all property, plant, and equipment is reported on the balance sheet net of accumulated depreciation or depletion.

Intangible Assets. **Intangible assets** are assets that lack physical substance but have economic value due to the rights they confer upon the holder. This classification does not include financial assets. Common examples of intangible assets include trademarks, trade names, broadcast licenses, patents, copyrights, and franchises. Certain intangible assets are reported on the balance sheet net of accumulated amortization, but others are not subject to amortization. Intangible assets that have a definite or finite useful life are amortized whereas those that have an indefinite life are not amortized.[3]

Other Assets. This other assets category includes any noncurrent asset that does not fall into any of the primary balance sheet classifications. For example, long-term prepaid expenses and land held for resale may be classified as other assets.

Liabilities

Liabilities are generally classified on the balance sheet as either *current* or *noncurrent.* We discuss each next.

Current Liabilities. **Current liabilities** are obligations that the firm expects to liquidate through the use of current assets or the creation of other current liabilities. Current liabilities will typically be paid within one year or operating cycle, whichever is longer. Current liabilities commonly include:

- *Accounts payable.*
- *Short-term notes payable.*
- *Current maturities of long-term debt.*
- *Accrued liabilities.*
- *Unearned revenues.*

Accounts payable (also called trade payables) are obligations due to suppliers of goods or services incurred in the normal course of business operations. There is no formal, written agreement required for an accounts payable.[4] If customers pay on time, there is no interest on accounts payable. Accounts payable are classified as current liabilities because they are generally due within 30 to 60 days.

Short-term notes payable are formal, written promises to pay cash at a fixed maturity date in the future. The maturity date is within the next year or operating cycle, if longer. Notes payable will usually carry a fixed rate of interest but may have an interest rate of zero.[5]

Current maturities of long-term debt represent the portion of any long-term debt that is payable within the next year or operating cycle, if longer. However, this amount must be paid from current assets or result in the creation of other current liabilities in order to be classified as current. For example, if the maturity of the debt is extended or if the debt is replaced by equity or other long-term debt, the debt is classified as long term.

[3]We discuss depreciation and amortization in depth in Chapter 11.
[4]If a formal agreement exists, then the payable is classified as a note payable.
[5]We discuss these notes payable in Chapter 14.

Accrued liabilities represent expenses incurred by an entity that remain unpaid at the end of the accounting period. Accrued liabilities include items such as utilities payable, wages and salaries payable, interest payable, and taxes payable. These accounts will be paid within the next year or operating cycle, if longer. If the entity will not pay an accrued liability within the next year, it classifies it as a *long-term liability.*

Unearned revenues (sometimes referred to as deferred revenues) are liabilities resulting from advance collections of cash from a customer for goods or services to be provided in the future under existing sales or service contracts. The firm removes the liability from the balance sheet when it provides the goods or services to the customer. If the firm will not provide the goods or services associated with the unearned revenues to the customer within the next year (or operating cycle, if longer), it classifies the unearned revenue as a *long-term liability.*

Noncurrent Liabilities. Noncurrent liabilities are obligations an entity does not expect to satisfy within one year or operating cycle, whichever is longer. Noncurrent liabilities are not liquidated through the use of current assets or the creation of other current liabilities. Long-term notes payable, the long-term portion of capital lease obligations, bonds payable, and pension obligations are examples of noncurrent liabilities.

Stockholders' Equity

Stockholders' equity, also referred to as shareholders' equity and owners' equity, is generally separated into four major categories: *contributed capital, retained earnings, accumulated other comprehensive income,* and *noncontrolling interest.*[6]

Contributed Capital. Contributed capital (also called paid-in capital) primarily represents the amounts invested by shareholders. It includes the stock sold by the entity at face or *par value* and amounts received above *par value*, known as additional paid-in capital or paid-in capital in excess of par. The face or stated value on the share certificate is its **par value**, which is an arbitrary value that the organizers of the corporation place on the stock.[7]

Retained Earnings. Retained earnings are the cumulative earnings (losses) of the company that have not been distributed as dividends to shareholders.

Accumulated Other Comprehensive Income. Comprehensive income is the change in an entity's equity during the period resulting from transactions with nonowners. In other words, it includes all changes in equity during a period except those changes that result from investments and distributions to owners. Comprehensive income is the sum of net income and other comprehensive income. Other comprehensive income includes revenues, expenses, gains, and losses that are excluded from net income but included in comprehensive income.

Accumulated other comprehensive income (or loss) is the cumulative amount of other comprehensive income (or loss) over the life of the entity.[8]

Noncontrolling Interest. A **noncontrolling interest** exists when one company controls another company (e.g., a subsidiary) but owns less than 100% of its voting shares. The controlling company adds all of the subsidiary's assets and liabilities to its own balance sheet. However, because it does not own 100% of the voting shares, it must separate the amount that is owned by outside shareholders. The noncontrolling interest is the amount of the company's net assets owned by outside shareholders.[9] To illustrate, assume a parent company owns 90% of the voting shares of a subsidiary that reports $100 in assets and $40 in liabilities. The shareholders' equity (net assets) of the subsidiary is equal to $60 with $6 (10% × $60) of the net assets owned by the noncontrolling interest.

---

[6]We will expand our discussion of stockholders' equity in Chapter 15 to include transactions such as treasury stock and dividends.

[7]We discuss capital stock in greater detail in Chapter 15.

[8]IFRS uses the term *reserves* for accumulated other comprehensive income.

[9]The noncontrolling interest is a required classification in the stockholders' equity section of corporate balance sheets. The accounting for the ownership and control of other companies is covered in detail in advanced accounting courses.

IFRS Balance Sheet Classification

IFRS has additional requirements for the presentation of specific asset and liability line items.

Assets: IFRS. As an additional requirement, IFRS specifies that, at a minimum, companies report the following asset categories:[10]

- Cash and cash equivalents
- Trade and other receivables
- Investments accounted for using the equity method[11]
- Financial assets (other than those included in investments, receivables, and investment properties)
- Inventories
- Property, plant, and equipment
- Biological assets (i.e., living animals or plants)
- Investment properties
- Intangible assets
- Receivables related to current taxes
- Deferred-tax assets

Similar to U.S. GAAP, IFRS defines current assets as resources that the firm expects to convert to cash, use, or consume within one year or one operating cycle, whichever is longer. However, IFRS also requires that current assets be held primarily for trading or cash and cash equivalents (unless they are restricted for use).

Liabilities: IFRS. IFRS specifically requires that, at a minimum, companies report the following liabilities:[12]

- Trade and other payables
- Provisions (such as warranty liabilities and pension benefits)
- Financial liabilities (other than the above)
- Taxes payable
- Deferred tax liability

IFRS defines current liabilities similarly to U S. GAAP as obligations that the firm expects to liquidate through the use of current assets or the creation of other current liabilities that will typically be paid within one year or operating cycle, whichever is longer. In addition, IFRS specifies that current liabilities are obligations held primarily for trading and for which a company does not have the right to defer settling beyond the current year.

3 Explain the presentation of current and noncurrent assets and liabilities on the statement of financial position and name the common statement formats.

Balance Sheet Presentation and Format

Assets, liabilities, and equity are the key elements on corporate balance sheets. We now describe the balance sheet presentation and the two formats found in practice.

Asset Presentation

After grouping assets as current and noncurrent, companies make further classifications. Specifically, within current and noncurrent assets, companies list each asset in decreasing order of liquidity. Current assets precede noncurrent assets. The most liquid asset is first, followed by less liquid assets. Cash, the most liquid asset, is usually listed first, followed by short-term investments, receivables, and then other less liquid assets.

---

[10]This list is from IASC, *International Accounting Standard 1*, "Presentation of Financial Statements" (London, UK: International Accounting Standards Committee, Revised), Paragraph 54. Although the FASB does not require that any particular asset categories be reported, the SEC does have this requirement. See Regulation S-X Rule 5-02.

[11]We discuss these investments in detail in Chapter 16.

[12]This list is from IASC, *International Accounting Standard 1*, "Presentation of Financial Statements," Paragraph 54. Although FASB does not require that any particular liability categories be reported, the SEC does have this requirement. See Regulation S-X Rule 5-02.

Liabilities Presentation

Companies list liabilities in increasing order of maturity. That is, current liabilities are listed before long-term liabilities. Also, within each group, the individual liability accounts are listed in order of maturity. Thus, accounts payable is often the first liability listed on the balance sheet and is reported before the current portion of long-term debt.

Balance Sheet Format

There are two balance sheet formats:

1. The **account format** lists assets on the left side and liabilities and stockholders' equity on the right side of the statement.
2. The **report format** lists liabilities and stockholders' equity directly below assets on the same page.

Exhibit 6.2 presents a sample account format balance sheet for Breanne Baking Equipment Company. Exhibit 6.3 presents a sample report format balance sheet for the same company. Notice that there is no quantitative difference between these two formats: It is simply a matter of whether the liabilities and equity sections appear in a column beside the assets (the account format) or below the assets (the report format).

EXHIBIT 6.2 Account Form Balance Sheet

Breanne Baking Equipment Company
Balance Sheet
As of December 31, 2018

Assets			**Liabilities**	
Current Assets:			**Current Liabilities:**	
Cash		$ 5,000	Accounts Payable	$ 2,700
Trading Securities at fair value		700	Short-Term Notes Payable	1,000
Accounts Receivable – net		11,000	Current Portion of Long-Term Debt	300
Merchandise Inventory		24,000	Interest Payable	200
Office Supplies		600	Income Taxes Payable	1,500
Prepaid Rent		200	Unearned Revenue	400
Total Current Assets		$ 41,500	Total Current Liabilities	$ 6,100
Noncurrent Assets:			**Noncurrent Liabilities:**	
Long-Term Investments		$ 15,000	Notes Payable	$ 40,000
Property, Plant, and Equipment:			Bonds Payable	60,000
Land		$ 20,000	Total Noncurrent Liabilities	$100,000
Buildings	$ 90,000		Total Liabilities	$106,100
Less: Accumulated Depreciation	(10,000)	80,000	**Stockholders' Equity**	
Machinery and Equipment	$ 70,000		Common Stock–at par	$ 20,000
Less: Accumulated Depreciation	(62,000)	8,000	Additional Paid-in Capital	30,000
Property, Plant, and Equipment – net		$108,000	Retained Earnings	5,000
Intangible Assets: Franchise – net		$ 4,500	Accumulated Other Comprehensive Income	11,000
Other Assets		3,100	Total Stockholders' Equity	$ 66,000
Total Noncurrent Assets		$130,600	Total Liabilities and Stockholders' Equity	$172,100
Total Assets		$172,100		

EXHIBIT 6.3 Report Form Balance Sheet

Breanne Baking Equipment Company Balance Sheet At December 31, 2018		
Assets		
Current Assets:		
Cash		$ 5,000
Trading Securities at fair value		700
Accounts Receivable – net		11,000
Merchandise Inventory		24,000
Office Supplies		600
Prepaid Rent		200
Total Current Assets		$ 41,500
Noncurrent Assets:		
Long-Term Investments		$ 15,000
Property, Plant, and Equipment		
Land		$ 20,000
Buildings	$90,000	
Less: Accumulated Depreciation	(10,000)	80,000
Machinery and Equipment	$70,000	
Less: Accumulated Depreciation	(62,000)	8,000
Property, Plant and Equipment – net		$108,000
Intangible Assets: Franchise – net		$ 4,500
Other Assets		3,100
Total Noncurrent Assets		$130,600
Total Assets		$172,100
Liabilities		
Current Liabilities:		
Accounts Payable		$ 2,700
Short-term Notes Payable		1,000
Current Portion of Long-Term Debt		300
Interest Payable		200
Income Taxes Payable		1,500
Unearned Revenue		400
Total Current Liabilities		$ 6,100
Noncurrent Liabilities:		
Notes Payable		$ 40,000
Bonds Payable		60,000
Total Noncurrent Liabilities		$100,000
Total Liabilities		$106,100
Stockholders' Equity		
Common Stock – at par		$ 20,000
Additional Paid-in Capital		30,000
Retained Earnings		5,000
Accumulated Other Comprehensive Income		11,000
Total Stockholders' Equity		$ 66,000
Total Liabilities and Stockholders' Equity		$172,100

Balance Sheet Presentation: IFRS

IFRS allows an alternative presentation of assets and liabilities by liquidity rather than current and noncurrent groupings so that companies can choose the most effective presentation for financial statement users. Company managers determine the presentation based on their knowledge of the company and its operations.

Asset Presentation: IFRS. IFRS-reporting companies can present either current assets or noncurrent assets first. So, IFRS permits asset presentation in either a decreasing or an increasing order of liquidity. When using an increasing order of liquidity, the least-liquid assets are typically presented first within each balance sheet section. Exhibit 6.4 recasts the Breanne Baking Equipment Company's balance sheet into an IFRS-allowable format by reporting noncurrent assets before current assets and using reverse liquidity ordering.

Liabilities Presentation: IFRS. Similarly to asset presentation, IFRS does not prescribe the ordering of liabilities within each group. In Exhibit 6.4, Breanne Baking Company reports current liabilities before noncurrent liabilities on its balance sheet unlike its presentation of noncurrent assets before current assets.

Balance Sheet Format: IFRS. Under IFRS, aside from the current and noncurrent (or liquidity) presentations, companies have flexibility regarding the format of their balance sheets. For example, Breanne Baking Equipment Company's balance sheet in Exhibit 6.4 includes the total of *net assets*, $66,000 at December 31, 2018. **Net assets**, equal to assets minus liabilities, is another term used for equity. Notice in Exhibit 6.4 that Breanne's total stockholders' equity is also $66,000.

Exhibit 6.4 illustrates the use of the increasing order of liquidity with regard to assets.

Judgment and the Balance Sheet

We introduced earnings management in Chapters 3 and 5 related to reported earnings numbers. Managers also make judgments related to amounts reported as assets and liabilities on the balance sheet. Because managers have incentives to manage the balance sheet, financial statement users should be aware of balance sheet management.

Consider the concepts of liquidity, solvency, and financial flexibility that we discussed earlier. Financial statement users prefer to provide resources to entities with a high level of liquidity, solvency, and financial flexibility. Thus, managers may classify liabilities as noncurrent as opposed to current to enhance the users' perception of the entity's liquidity. As another example, managers have an incentive to classify an item as equity as opposed to debt or not to report a debt on the balance sheet at all in order to enhance the perception of solvency and financial flexibility.

In addition to these incentives, a judgment that results in earnings management in turn results in balance sheet management. For example, if an entity makes a choice not to record warranty expense, then it is simultaneously making the decision not to report a warranty liability, which improves a company's liquidity position.

4 Explain the statement of cash flows and classify common business activities into operating, investing, and financing cash flows.

The Statement of Cash Flows

Cash, one of a company's most important assets, is critical to successful operations and growth. A company needs cash to purchase equipment to manufacture products, to pay employees, and to invest in research. The importance of cash flow merits a separate financial statement devoted to explaining how a company generates cash and indicating where cash is employed. The **statement of cash flows** summarizes a firm's cash inflows and outflows over a period of time.

In this section, we discuss the purpose of the statement of cash flows and the classifications used in the statement. Appendix A presents an overview of the preparation of the statement of cash flows; we revisit this material in more depth in Chapter 22.

EXHIBIT 6.4 IFRS-Acceptable Form Balance Sheet

Breanne Baking Equipment Company Balance Sheet At December 31, 2018	
Assets	
Noncurrent Assets:	
Intangible Assets: Franchise – net	$ 4,500
Property, Plant, and Equipment – net	108,000
Investments	15,000
Other Assets	3,100
Total Noncurrent Assets	$130,600
Current Assets:	
Merchandise Inventory	$ 24,000
Accounts Receivable – net	11,000
Office Supplies	600
Prepaid Rent	200
Trading Securities at fair value	700
Cash	5,000
Total Current Assets	$ 41,500
Total Assets	$172,100
Liabilities	
Current Liabilities:	
Accounts Payable	$ 2,700
Short-term Notes Payable	1,000
Current Portion of Long-term Debt	300
Interest Payable	200
Income Taxes Payable	1,500
Unearned Revenue	400
Total Current Liabilities	$ 6,100
Noncurrent Liabilities:	
Notes Payable	$ 40,000
Bonds Payable	60,000
Total Noncurrent Liabilities	100,000
Total Liabilities	$106,100
Net Assets	$ 66,000
Shareholders' Equity	
Share Capital	$ 20,000
Share Premium	30,000
Reserves	11,000
Retained Profits	5,000
Total Shareholders' Equity	$ 66,000
Total Liabilities and Shareholders' Equity	$172,100

THE CONCEPTUAL FRAMEWORK CONNECTION: Purpose of the Statement of Cash Flows

The statement of cash flows provides information to financial statement users about a firm's cash receipts and cash payments during a period of time. The statement reconciles the change in the cash balance (where cash is defined as cash and cash equivalents) to the cash flows for the period and summarizes the firm's cash flows by *operating, investing,* and *financing activities.* The statement of cash flows enables financial statements users to:

1. Assess the entity's ability to meet its obligations and pay dividends.
2. Determine whether the entity will require external financing.
3. Identify the differences between net income and the associated cash receipts and payments.

The statement of cash flows explains and reconciles many other significant changes in balance sheet items, particularly when it is analyzed with the other financial statements and related footnote disclosures.

Statement of Cash Flows Classifications

The statement of cash flows is divided into three distinct sections: *operating, investing,* and *financing* activities. The statement presents operating activities first, followed by cash flows from investing activities, and finally cash flows from financing activities. The sum of cash inflows or outflows for these three activities results in the net increase or decrease in cash and cash equivalents for the period. The next step is reconciling this change in cash and cash equivalents to the beginning and ending cash and cash equivalents balances. Therefore, the change in cash and cash equivalents on the statement of cash flows plus the beginning cash and cash equivalents balance equals the ending cash and cash equivalents balance as depicted in Exhibit 6.5.

EXHIBIT 6.5 Statement of Cash Flows Classifications

	Net Cash Provided (Used) by Operating Activities
Plus (Minus)	Net Cash Provided (Used) by Investing Activities
Plus (Minus)	Net Cash Provided (Used) by Financing Activities
Equals	Net Increase (Decrease) in Cash and Cash Equivalents
Plus	Beginning Cash and Cash Equivalents
Equals	Ending Cash and Cash Equivalents

Operating Activities. **Operating activities** include cash receipts and disbursements related to the production and delivery of goods and services that are reported on an accrual basis on the statement of net income. A firm must have a positive net cash flow related to operating activities over the long run in order to sustain its operations. Analyzing cash flows from operating activities enables financial statement users to assess the firm's ability to generate future cash flows from its normal earnings cycle.

Cash flows from operating activities primarily include:

1. Cash receipts from customers.
2. Cash receipts from interest and dividends.
3. Cash payments for the purchase of goods for resale or for use in production.
4. Cash payments to suppliers and employees.
5. Cash payments for taxes.
6. Cash payments for interest.

From Exhibit 6.6, ***Golden Enterprises, Inc.,*** a food company making Gold Flake brand snack foods, net cash provided by operating activities was $7,135,855 for the year ended June 3, 2016.

EXHIBIT 6.6 Statement of Cash Flows, ***Golden Enterprises***, Financial Statements, June 3, 2016

GOLDEN ENTERPRISES, INC. AND SUBSIDIARY
CONSOLIDATED STATEMENTS OF CASH FLOWS
For the Fiscal Years Ended June 3, 2016 and May 29, 2015

	2016	2015
Cash flows from operating activities		
Cash received from customers	$136,289,283	$131,980,056
Miscellaneous income	97,108	88,918
Cash paid to suppliers and employees for cost of goods sold	(66,550,001)	(63,720,473)
Cash paid for suppliers and employees for selling, general and administrative	(61,224,782)	(61,947,388)
Income taxes	(1,140,191)	(1,839,759)
Interest expense	(335,562)	(458,184)
Net cash provided by operating activities	7,135,855	4,103,170
Cash flows from investing activities		
Purchases of property, plant and equipment	(1,182,854)	(2,725,450)
Proceeds from sale of property, plant and equipment	56,446	284,806
Net cash used in investing activities	(1,126,408)	(2,440,644)
Cash flows from financing activities		
Change in line of credit	(2,823,477)	294,966
Debt (repayments) proceeds	(824,435)	1,698,505
Principal payments under capital lease obligation	(30,970)	–
Purchases of treasury shares	–	(2,204,375)
Cash dividends paid	(1,496,160)	(1,452,803)
Net cash used in financing activities	(5,175,042)	(1,663,707)
Net increase (decrease) in cash and cash equivalents	834,405	(1,181)
Cash and cash equivalents at beginning of year	1,159,449	1,160,630
Cash and cash equivalents at end of year	$ 1,993,854	$ 1,159,449

Supplementary Cash Flow information:

In the period ending June 3, 2016 the Company entered into capital leases totaling $239,382.

Source: Golden Enterprises, Inc. Statement of Cash Flows, June 3, 2016. https://www.sec.gov/Archives/edgar/data/42228/000114420416120097/v447241_10ka.htm#a_014

Investing Activities. Cash flows from **investing activities** relate to acquiring and disposing of productive property, investing in debt and equity securities, and making and collecting loans. Cash flows from investing activities primarily include:

1. Cash receipts from the collection or sale of notes receivable from lending to others.
2. Cash receipts from the sale of debt and equity securities of other entities.
3. Cash receipts from the sale of productive assets (e.g., property, plant, and equipment).
4. Cash payments for extending credit to others.
5. Cash payments for investments in the debt and equity securities of other entities.
6. Cash payments for property, plant, and equipment, and other productive assets.

From Exhibit 6.6, ***Golden Enterprises'*** net investing cash flows were $(1,126,408) for the year ended June 3, 2016. Its investing cash outflows include cash payments for items such as the acquisition of property, plant, and equipment whereas its investing cash inflows are from the sale of property, plant, and equipment.

Financing Activities. **Financing activities** involve the cash receipts and payments from debt and equity financing. Cash flows from financing activities primarily include:

1. Cash receipts from issuing equity to owners.
2. Cash receipts from borrowing through bonds and notes or other debt instruments.
3. Cash payments to repurchase equity from owners.
4. Cash payments for principal on debt.
5. Cash payments for dividends.

Golden Enterprises' net financing cash flows for the year ended June 3, 2016, were $(5,175,042) as Exhibit 6.6 illustrates. The company's financing cash outflows primarily include cash payments for lines of credit, debt, and dividends. Exhibit 6.7 summarizes common cash inflows and outflows by operating, investing, and financing activities.

EXHIBIT 6.7 Common Cash Inflows and Outflows: Operating, Investing, and Financing Activities

	Cash Receipts	Cash Payments
Operating	• Receipts from customers • Receipts from interest and dividends	• Payments for the purchase of goods for resale or for use in production • Payments to suppliers and employees • Payments for taxes • Payments for interest
Investing	• Receipts from the collection or sale of notes • Receipts from the sale of investments in debt and equity securities • Receipts from the sale of productive assets (e.g., property, plant, and equipment)	• Payments for extending credit to others • Payments for investments in debt and equity securities • Payments for property, plant, and equipment, and other productive assets
Financing	• Receipts from issuing equity to owners • Receipts from borrowing through bonds, notes, or other debt instruments	• Payments to repurchase equity from owners (e.g., treasury stock) • Payments for principal on debt • Payments for dividends

Classification of Dividends, Interest, and Taxes: IFRS

IFRS differs from U.S. GAAP in the classification of the following items:

1. Cash receipts from interest and dividends
2. Cash payments for taxes
3. Cash payments for interest
4. Cash payments for dividends

As shown in Exhibit 6.8, U.S. GAAP requires companies to report the preceding items in operating cash flows except for the payment of dividends. IFRS grants companies discretion in classifying these items as operating, investing, or financing activities as Exhibit 6.8 illustrates.

EXHIBIT 6.8 Classification of Dividends, Interest, and Taxes

	Standard	
Activities	**U.S. GAAP**	**IFRS**
Cash receipts from interest and dividends	Operating	Operating or Investing
Cash payments for taxes	Operating	Operating activities, unless they can be specifically identified with Financing or Investing activities.
Cash payments for interest	Operating	Operating or Financing
Cash payments for dividends to owners	Financing	Operating or Financing

5 Explain the direct and indirect formats of the statement of cash flows.

Format for Cash Flows from Operating Activities

There are two acceptable formats for cash flows from operating activities:

- The *indirect method* (or the reconciliation format)
- The *direct method* (or the income statement format)

The only difference between the statement of cash flows under the direct and indirect methods is reporting cash flows from operating activities: The investing and financing sections of the direct and indirect reporting formats are the same. The FASB prefers the direct method, but it is the least popular in practice—it is used by only 1% of U.S. companies.[13] What explains this disconnect? Companies generally indicate that they do not have systems in place to provide them with the needed information to prepare a statement of cash flows under the direct format.[14]

We begin our discussion by presenting operating activities under the indirect method. Appendix A presents additional detail on the different formats for cash flows from operating activities; we examine the preparation of the statement of cash flows in more depth in Chapter 22.

The Indirect Method of Reporting Cash Flows from Operating Activities. The **indirect method** (also referred to as the reconciliation format) begins with net income from the income statement and then reconciles the net income to net cash generated from operating activities. Reconciling items are separated into two groups:

- Adjustments for noncash items
- Changes in operating assets and liabilities

Exhibit 6.9 lists a few of the common adjustments or reconciling items.

[13] AICPA, *Accounting Trends and Techniques* – 2012 (New York, NY: AICPA, 2012).

[14] For example, see pages 12 through 15 of the comment letter from the Financial Executives International to the FASB concerning the discussion paper on Financial Statement Presentation. This letter can be found at http://www.fasb.org/cs/BlobServer?blobkey=id&blobwhere=1175818489075&blobheader=application%2Fpdf&blobcol=urldata&blobtable=MungoBlobs

EXHIBIT 6.9 Reconciling Items for the Indirect Method

ADDITIONS:

Additions—Noncash Transactions

- Depreciation, depletion, and amortization expense
- Bad debt expense
- Loss on sale of long-term assets
- Unrealized losses on investment trading securities and certain other investments

Additions—Changes in Operating Assets and Liabilities

- Decreases in current assets (accounts receivable, inventory, prepaid expenses)
- Increases in current liabilities (accounts payable, accrued liabilities)

DEDUCTIONS:

Deductions—Noncash Transactions

- Gain on sale of long-term assets
- Unrealized gains on investment trading securities and certain other investments

Deductions—Changes in Operating Assets and Liabilities

- Increases in current assets (accounts receivable, inventory, prepaid expenses)
- Decreases in current liabilities (accounts payable, accrued liabilities)

Exhibit 6.10 provides the operating activities section of ***Johnson & Johnson's*** Statement of Cash Flows using the indirect method. Note that the first line in the operating section is net income, followed by the adjustments for noncash items such as depreciation and bad debt expense (referred to in the exhibit as "accounts receivable allowances"). Although depreciation expense and bad debt expense are deducted on the income statement, they are not cash outflows. Thus, ***Johnson & Johnson*** must add them back to net income to arrive at net operating cash flows.

Next, ***Johnson & Johnson*** adjusts for changes in operating assets and liabilities such as accounts receivable and accounts payable. Other common operating asset and liability adjustments are for inventory, prepaid expenses, and accrued liabilities.

EXHIBIT 6.10 Statement of Cash Flows, Operating Activities, ***Johnson & Johnson,*** Financial Statements, for the Year Ended January 1, 2017

JOHNSON & JOHNSON AND SUBSIDIARIES
CONSOLIDATED STATEMENTS OF CASH FLOWS
For Year Ended January 1, 2017

(Dollars in Millions) (Note 1)	2016	2015	2014
Cash flows from operating activities			
Net earnings	$16,540	$15,409	$16,323
Adjustments to reconcile net earnings to net cash flows from operating activities:			
Depreciation and amortization of property and intangibles	3,754	3,746	3,895
Stock-based compensation	878	874	792
Venezuela adjustments	–	122	87
Asset write-downs	283	624	410
Net gain on sale of assets/businesses	(563)	(2,583)	(2,383)
Deferred tax provision	(341)	(270)	441
Accounts receivable allowances	(11)	18	(28)
Changes in assets and liabilities, net of effects from acquisitions and divestitures:			
Increase in accounts receivable	(1,065)	(433)	(247)
Increase in inventories	(249)	(449)	(1,120)
Increase in accounts payable and accrued liabilities	656	287	1,194
Decrease in other current and noncurrent assets	18	65	442
(Decrease)/Increase in other current and noncurrent liabilities	(1,133)	2,159	(1,096)
Net cash flows from operating activities	$18,767	$19,569	$18,710

Source: Johnson & Johnson's Statement of Cash Flows: Operating Activities, 2016. http://files.shareholder.com/downloads/JNJ/3809936545x0xS200406-17-6/200406/filing.pdf

To illustrate changes in operating assets and liabilities, consider accounts receivable. Assume that NRR Company reported accounts receivable of $10,000 and $12,000 at the beginning and end of the year, respectively. The company also reported $55,000 in sales revenue. The increase in accounts receivable indicates that $2,000 of this year's sales were not collected. As a result, NRR collected $53,000 from customers ($55,000 − $2,000). Therefore, NRR subtracts the increase in accounts receivable ($2,000) from net income to arrive at net cash provided by operations.

EXAMPLE 6.1

Operating Cash Flows: Indirect Method

PROBLEM: Walker Welding Company provided you with the following information for the current year:

Income Statement	Amount
Sales	$25,000
Depreciation Expense	(3,000)
Selling, General, and Administrative Expenses	(7,000)
Operating Income	15,000
Tax Expense	(6,000)
Net Income	$ 9,000

Account Changes from the Balance Sheet	
Increase in Accounts Receivable	$6,000
Increase in Accounts Payable	$2,500
Decrease in Income Taxes Payable	$4,000

Compute net cash flow from operating activities for Walker Welding under the indirect reporting format.

SOLUTION: The indirect method requires applying a series of adjustments to net income to arrive at net cash flow from operating activities. We first add back depreciation expense because it is a noncash expense. That is, depreciation is an expense deducted on the income statement reducing net income, but it does not use cash.

Because accounts receivable increased by $6,000 during the year, Walker Welding did not collect all of its sales. As a result, we subtract the increase in accounts receivable from net income to determine the cash collected from customers.

Accrual-basis expense is recognized at the same time that the accounts payable is recognized. However, if accounts payable increase, this indicates that Walker Welding has not yet paid the balance. Therefore, less cash is paid for expenses than reported under the accrual basis on the income statement. So, we add the increase in accounts payable back to net income to reflect the cash paid for these expenses.

The accrual-basis income tax expense is recognized at the same time that the income taxes payable is reported. Because the payable balance decreased, Walker Welding actually paid more for income taxes than it recorded as expense this year. In other words, the company paid all of this year's taxes and the remaining liability from last year. Thus, its cash-basis tax expense was higher than its accrual-basis tax expense, and we deduct the decrease in income tax payable from net income to arrive at operating cash flow.

Walker's operating activities section of the statement of cash flows follows.

Walker Welding Company
Partial Statement of Cash Flows

Operating Activities	Amount
Net Income	$9,000
Add back: Depreciation Expense	3,000
Increase in Accounts Receivable	(6,000)
Increase in Accounts Payable	2,500
Decrease in Income Taxes Payable	(4,000)
Net Cash Provided by Operating Activities	$4,500

Indirect Method: IFRS. Under IFRS, a company can begin its reconciliation to operating cash flows with other income numbers, such as income before taxes or operating income.[15]

The Direct Method of Reporting Cash Flows from Operating Activities. Under the **direct method** (also referred to as the income statement format) for reporting cash flows from operating activities, companies report actual cash inflows and outflows in the operating section of the statement of cash flows. That is, instead of presenting a reconciliation between net income and net operating cash flows, a company converts each individual income statement line item from the accrual to the cash basis.

The FASB prefers the direct method because the cash receipts and cash payments approach is easy to understand.

EXAMPLE 6.2 Operating Cash Flows: Direct Method

PROBLEM: Using the information provided by Walker Welding Company, compute net cash flow from operating activities using the direct reporting format.

SOLUTION: The direct method uses the same adjustments as the indirect method but applies the adjustments to each income statement line item, as illustrated in the following computation.

Income Statement	Accrual Basis Amount	Adjustment	Cash Flow
Sales	$25,000	Increase in Accounts Receivable: ($6,000)	$19,000
Depreciation Expense	(3,000)	Depreciation expenses: +$3,000	0
Selling, General and Administrative Expenses	(7,000)	Increase in accounts payable: +$2,500	(4,500)
Operating Income	15,000		
Tax Expense	(6,000)	Decrease in taxes payable: ($4,000)	(10,000)
Net Income	$ 9,000		$ 4,500

We are now able to prepare the operating activities section under the direct method.

Walker Welding Company Partial Statement of Cash Flows	
Operating Activities	
Cash Collected from Customers	$19,000
Cash Paid to Other Suppliers	(4,500)
Cash Paid for Taxes	(10,000)
Net Cash Provided by Operating Activities	$ 4,500

6 Review the four primary financial statements and financial statement articulation.

Financial Statement Articulation

Financial statement articulation, the relationships among financial statements and financial statement elements, is a critical concept in understanding financial statements. The elements of the four basic financial statements are intrinsically interrelated:

- Firms compute net income and other comprehensive income (OCI) on the statements of net income and comprehensive income. Revenues and gains increase net income and expenses and losses decrease net income.

[15] We provide an in-depth discussion of this difference in the preparation of the statement of cash flows in Chapter 22.

- Both net income and OCI are then included in the stockholders' equity section of the balance sheet and affect the statement of stockholders' equity. Net income is used to arrive at ending retained earnings, and current-year OCI is used to arrive at the ending balance in accumulated OCI.
- Firms report ending retained earnings and ending accumulated OCI in the stockholders' equity section of the statement of financial position.
- Firms use the statement of net income (or the statement of comprehensive income) and the balance sheet to prepare the statement of cash flows. For example, operating cash flows are computed as net income, adjusted for the changes in operating working capital accounts on the balance sheet and noncash revenues and expenses on the statement of net income.

Exhibit 6.11 provides an overview of financial statement articulation.

EXHIBIT 6.11 Financial Statement Articulation

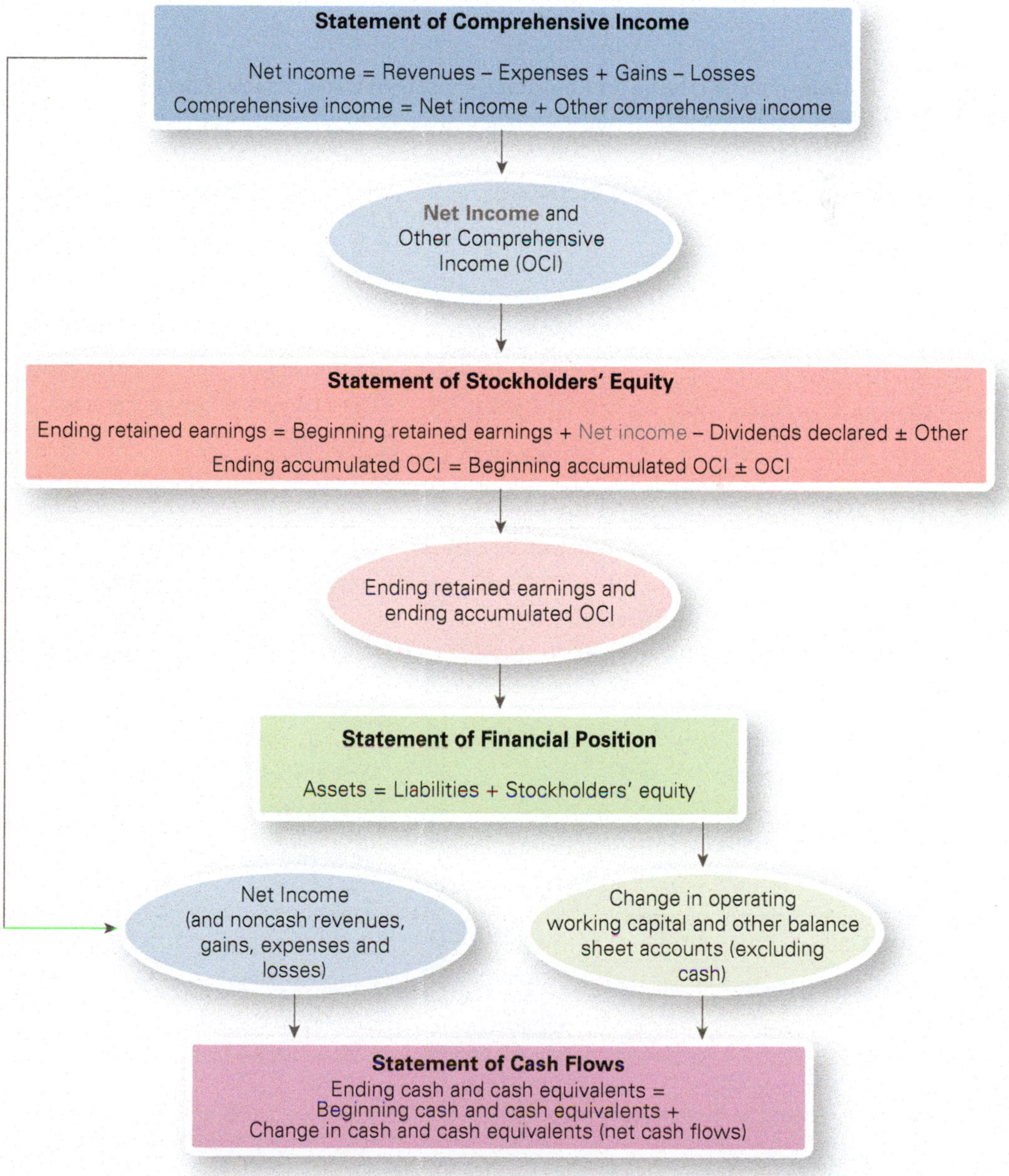

Exhibit 6.12 illustrates financial statement articulation using the 2016 ***Johnson & Johnson*** financial statements.

1. ***Johnson & Johnson*** reported net income of $16,540 million on the statement of comprehensive income (and the statement of net income). This number then flows into the statement of stockholders' equity, resulting in an increase in retained earnings.
2. OCI for the year on the statement of comprehensive income is a loss of $1,736 million, resulting in a decrease in accumulated OCI on the statement of stockholders' equity.
3. ***Johnson & Johnson*** reported the ending retained earnings balance, $110,551 million, and the ending accumulated OCI balance, $(14,901) million, from the statement of stockholders' equity on the balance sheet.
4. Under the indirect method, the cash flow statement begins with net income from the statement of comprehensive income, $16,540 million, and adjusts for changes in various balance sheet accounts such as accounts receivable and inventory.
5. On the cash flow statement, the increase in cash and cash equivalents of $5,240 million reconciles to the change in cash and cash equivalents from the balance sheet, where beginning cash and cash equivalents are $13,732 million and ending cash and cash equivalents are $18,972 million.

EXHIBIT 6.12 ***Johnson & Johnson*** Financial Statement Articulation (in millions), Financial Statements, For Year Ending January 1, 2017

STATEMENT OF COMPREHENSIVE INCOME	
Revenues	
Expenses	
Net Income or Loss	$16,540
Other Comprehensive Income (Loss)	(1,736)
Comprehensive Income	$14,804

STATEMENT OF STOCKHOLDERS' EQUITY	Retained Earnings	Accumulated Other Comprehensive Income (Loss)
Beginning Balance	$103,879	$(13,165)
Net Income	16,540	
Other Comprehensive Income (Loss)		(1,736)
Dividends	(8,621)	
Other	(1,247)	—
Ending Balance	$ 110,551	$(14,901)

STATEMENT OF CASH FLOWS	
Net Income or Loss	$16,540
Net Cash Provided by Operating Activities	
Net Cash Provided by Investing Activities	
Net Cash Provided by Financing Activities	
Increase (Decrease) in Cash and Cash Equivalents	$ 5,240
Add: Beginning Cash and Cash Equivalents	13,732
Ending Cash and Cash Equivalents	$18,972

BALANCE SHEETS	Beginning of Year	End of Year
Cash and Cash Equivalents	$13,732	$18,972
Total Assets		
Total Liabilities		
Stockholders' Equity		
Common Stock		
Additional Paid-in Capital		
Retained Earnings		110,551
Accumulated Other Comprehensive Income (Loss)		(14,901)
Total Liabilities & Stockholders' Equity		

EXAMPLE 6.3 Financial Statement Articulation

PROBLEM: Complete the following financial statement articulation exercises.

a. If net income is \$52,000 and comprehensive income is \$70,000, what is other comprehensive income?
b. If ending retained earnings are \$122,000, beginning retained earnings are \$98,000, and dividends declared are \$20,000, what is net income?
c. If the beginning balance of cash was \$653,000 and the ending balance of cash is \$522,000, what is the net change in cash?

SOLUTION:

a. Other comprehensive income is \$18,000. We use the following relationship to solve for other comprehensive income:

$$\begin{aligned}\text{Comprehensive Income} &= \text{Net Income} + \text{Other Comprehensive Income}\\ 70{,}000 &= 52{,}000 + \text{Other Comprehensive Income}\\ 18{,}000 &= \text{Other Comprehensive Income}\end{aligned}$$

b. The amount of net income is \$44,000. We use the following relationship to solve for net income:

$$\begin{aligned}\text{Ending Retained Earnings} &= \text{Beginning Retained Earnings} + \text{Net Income}\\ &\quad - \text{Dividends Declared} \pm \text{Other}\\ 122{,}000 &= 98{,}000 + \text{Net Income} - 20{,}000 \pm 0\\ 44{,}000 &= \text{Net Income}\end{aligned}$$

c. The amount of net cash flows is a \$131,000 decrease in cash. We use the following relationship to solve for net change in cash:

$$\begin{aligned}\text{Net Change in Cash} &= \text{Ending Cash} - \text{Beginning Cash}\\ \text{Net Change in Cash} &= \$522{,}000 - \$653{,}000\\ \text{Net Change in Cash} &= \$(131{,}000)\end{aligned}$$

7 Explain the purpose of the notes to the financial statements, including the summary of significant accounting policies, subsequent events, going concern uncertainties, and related-party transactions.

Notes to the Financial Statements

The notes (or footnotes) are an integral part of the financial statements that provide descriptive information regarding a company's accounting policies, supplemental disclosures of items not reported on the financial statements, and additional details for transactions reported on the four main financial statements. For example, a company will disclose its depreciation policy for long-lived assets in its financial statement footnotes. A company could also provide additional disclosures on historical cost and accumulated depreciation according to significant types of assets. Notes to the financial statements are typically extensive. For example, in ***Johnson & Johnson's*** 2016 annual report, the financial statements are covered on 5 pages; the notes span 43 pages!

Johnson & Johnson's notes, summarized in Exhibit 6.13, are representative of the information provided by most reporting entities and are typical for an entity of its size and complexity.

Johnson & Johnson's balance sheet refers readers to Notes 1 and 3 for further information on inventories. Note 1 explains that the firm measures inventory with the *lower-of-cost-or-market rule* determined by the *first-in, first-out* method. Note 3, presented in Exhibit 6.14, segregates the \$8,144 million aggregate inventory amount into its components: raw materials and supplies, goods in process, and finished goods.

EXHIBIT 6.13 Notes to the 2016 Financial Statements, *Johnson & Johnson*, Financial Statements, January 1, 2017

Note 1	Summary of Significant Accounting Policies
Note 2	Cash, Cash Equivalents, and Current Marketable Securities
Note 3	Inventories
Note 4	Property, Plant, and Equipment
Note 5	Intangible Assets and Goodwill
Note 6	Fair Value Measurements
Note 7	Borrowings
Note 8	Income Taxes
Note 9	Employee Related Obligations
Note 10	Pensions and Other Benefit Plans
Note 11	Savings Plan
Note 12	Capital and Treasury Stock
Note 13	Accumulated Other Comprehensive Income
Note 14	International Currency Translation
Note 15	Earnings Per Share
Note 16	Rental Expense and Lease Commitments
Note 17	Common Stock, Stock Option Plans, and Stock Compensation Agreements
Note 18	Segments of Business and Geographic Areas
Note 19	Selected Quarterly Financial Data
Note 20	Business Combinations and Divestitures
Note 21	Legal Proceedings
Note 22	Restructuring

Source: Johnson & Johnson Notes to the 2016 Financial Statements. See Johnson & Johnson Company's annual report at http://files.shareholder.com/downloads/JNJ/3809936545x0xS200406-17-6/200406/filing.pdf

EXHIBIT 6.14 Inventory Notes, ***Johnson & Johnson,*** Financial Statements, January 1, 2017

NOTE 3: Inventories

At the end of 2016 and 2015, inventories were comprised of:

(Dollars in Millions)	2016	2015
Raw materials and supplies	$ 952	$ 936
Goods in process	2,185	2,241
Finished goods	5,007	4,876
Total inventories	$8,144	$8,053

Source: See Johnson & Johnson Company's annual report at http://files.shareholder.com/downloads/JNJ/3809936545x0xS200406-17-6/200406/filing.pdf

THE CONCEPTUAL FRAMEWORK CONNECTION: Notes to the Financial Statements

In early 2014, the FASB issued an exposure draft of Chapter 8 of the Conceptual Framework addressing the notes to the financial statements. FASB stated that the notes to the financial statements provide relevant information that is not included in the face of the financial statements and categorized the disclosures into three types:

1. Information about specific line items on the financial statements that amplifies or explains that information more fully.

2. Information about the nature of the entity and its activities along with information about the entities' advantages, disadvantages, restrictions, and privileges.
3. Information about events and circumstances that may affect the entity's future cash flows.

We address the current disclosure requirements for most of the notes to the financial statements in subsequent chapters. In the sections that follow, we describe general disclosures: the summary of significant accounting policies, and disclosures pertaining to *subsequent events*, going concern uncertainties, and *related-party transactions*.

Summary of Significant Accounting Policies. Companies must disclose their significant accounting policies, usually in the first footnote. The **summary of significant accounting policies** note provides the entity's portfolio of GAAP methods used in preparing its financial statements. For example, an entity selects from four methods when measuring the cost of its inventory: *specific identification, weighted average, first-in, first-out,* or *last-in, first-out.* Companies disclose the method used whenever there are acceptable alternatives.

The summary of significant accounting policies—the first footnote in ***Johnson & Johnson's*** annual report—includes definitions, policies, and methods used to account for areas such as cash equivalents; investments; property, plant, and equipment; revenue recognition; inventories; intangible assets and goodwill; financial instruments; product liability; credit risk; research and development; income taxes; and earnings per share. Exhibit 6.15 includes ***Johnson & Johnson's*** significant accounting policies for property, plant, and equipment; inventories; and intangible assets.

EXHIBIT 6.15 Selected Disclosures of Significant Accounting Policies, ***Johnson & Johnson,*** Financial Statements, January 1, 2017

Property, Plant and Equipment and Depreciation

Property, plant and equipment are stated at cost. The Company utilizes the straight-line method of depreciation over the estimated useful lives of the assets:

Building and building equipment	20–30 years
Land and leasehold improvements	10–20 years
Machinery and equipment	2–13 years

The Company capitalizes certain computer software and development costs, included in machinery and equipment, when incurred in connection with developing or obtaining computer software for internal use. Capitalized software costs are amortized over the estimated useful lives of the software, which generally range from 3 to 8 years.

The Company reviews long-lived assets to assess recoverability using undiscounted cash flows. When certain events or changes in operating or economic conditions occur, an impairment assessment may be performed on the recoverability of the carrying value of these assets. If the asset is determined to be impaired, the loss is measured based on the difference between the asset's fair value and its carrying value. If quoted market prices are not available, the Company will estimate fair value using a discounted value of estimated future cash flows.

Inventories

Inventories are stated at the lower of cost or market determined by the first-in, first-out method.

Intangible Assets and Goodwill

The authoritative literature on U.S. GAAP requires that goodwill and intangible assets with indefinite lives be assessed annually for impairment. The Company completed the annual impairment test for 2016 in the fiscal fourth quarter. Future impairment tests will be performed annually in the fiscal fourth quarter, or sooner if warranted. Purchased in-process research and development is accounted for as an indefinite lived intangible asset until the underlying project is completed, at which point the intangible asset will be accounted for as a definite lived intangible asset, or abandoned, at which point the intangible asset will be written off or partially impaired.

Intangible assets that have finite useful lives continue to be amortized over their useful lives, and are reviewed for impairment when warranted by economic conditions. See Note 5 for further details on Intangible Assets and Goodwill.

Source: Johnson & Johnson Company's annual report at http://files.shareholder.com/downloads/JNJ/3809936545x0xS200406-17-6/200406/filing.pdf

Subsequent Events. A **subsequent event** is a significant event that occurs after the date of the fiscal year-end but before the financial statements are issued or available to be issued. Examples of common subsequent events are the sale of a business, the issuance of debt or equity securities, and the settlement of litigation.

Firms either recognize material subsequent events in the financial statements for the preceding year or disclose them in the notes to the financial statements. The recognition versus disclosure decision depends upon whether the event relates to a condition that existed on the balance sheet date (the end of the fiscal year):

1. If the condition existed as of the balance sheet date, the firm should make an adjustment to the financial statements to account for the subsequent event.
2. If the condition did not exist as of the balance sheet date, the entity is required to disclose only the subsequent event as opposed to adjusting the financial statements.

EXAMPLE 6.4

Recognized Subsequent Event

PROBLEM: LAStyles Company is involved in a patent-infringement lawsuit. As of December 31, 2017 (its fiscal year-end), the company recorded an estimated liability related to the lawsuit of $1 million. On January 15, 2018, it settled the lawsuit for $1.2 million.

In addition, on January 15, 2018, a customer fell on the ice in front of one of LAStyles' stores. The customer sued LAStyles the next day, and the suit was settled for $1 million on February 27, 2018.

LAStyles will issue its financial statements on March 1, 2018. Should the company make an adjustment to its financial statements for these lawsuits? Should LAStyles disclose any information regarding these events in the notes to the financial statements?

SOLUTION: With regard to the infringement lawsuit, because the subsequent event (the settlement of the lawsuit) related to a condition that existed as of December 31, LAStyles should make an adjustment to the financial statements by increasing the liability and loss by $0.2 million. A related disclosure is also required in the notes to the financial statements.

With regard to the lawsuit initiated by the customer who fell on the ice, because the subsequent event is related to a condition (i.e., the customer's injury) that did not exist as of December 31, no adjustment is necessary. However, LAStyles should include this information in a footnote disclosure.

In its fiscal 2015 annual report, ***Wal-Mart Stores, Inc. (Walmart)*** reported a subsequent event for dividends declared after year-end (see Exhibit 6.16).

EXHIBIT 6.16 Subsequent Event Disclosure, *Wal-Mart Stores, Inc.*, Financial Statements, January 31, 2016

NOTE 15: Subsequent Event

Dividends Declared

On February 18, 2016, the Board of Directors approved an increase in the annual dividend for fiscal 2017 to $2.00 per share, an increase over the $1.96 per share. For fiscal 2017, the annual dividend will be paid in four quarterly installments of $0.50 per share, according to the following record and payable dates:

Record Date	Payable Date
March 11, 2016	April 4, 2016
May 13, 2016	June 6, 2016
August 12, 2016	September 6, 2016
December 9, 2016	January 3, 2017

Source: http://s2.q4cdn.com/056532643/files/doc_financials/2016/annual/2016-Annual-Report-PDF.pdf

Going Concern Uncertainties. As discussed in Chapter 2, the going concern concept indicates that accountants record transactions and prepare financial statements if the entity will continue to operate for an indefinite period of time unless there is evidence to the contrary. Management must evaluate whether there is substantial doubt as to whether the entity will continue to operate within one year after the financial statements are issued. If substantial doubt does exist, then management must consider any plans it has to mitigate the entity's going concern issue. If it is probable that these plans will be implemented and will alleviate the conditions that raise doubt about the entity's ability to continue operating, then the entity must disclose information about:

- The conditions or events that raised substantial doubt about the entity's ability to continue operations.
- Management's evaluation of the significance of those conditions.
- Management's plans that alleviate substantial doubt about the entity's continued operations.

If conditions exist that raise substantial doubt about the entity's ability to continue as a going concern and this doubt is not alleviated by management's plans, then the entity must disclose that there is substantial doubt about the entity's ability to continue as a going concern within one year from the date that the financial statements are issued (or available to be issued). Additionally, the entity should disclose information about:

- The conditions that raise substantial doubt about the entity's ability to continue operations.
- Management's evaluation of the significance of those conditions.
- Management's plans that are intended to mitigate the conditions or events that raise substantial doubt about the entity's ability to continue as a going concern.

Related-Party Transactions. **Related-party transactions** are transactions that an entity engages in with owners, firm management, affiliated entities, or any other entity that can exert significant influence on the company.[16]

FASB requires disclosure of related-party transactions because it is possible that the transaction was not objective and not completed at market prices. For example, if a corporate officer borrows funds from her employer, she may do so below the market rate of interest. The disclosure of a related-party transaction must include:

1. The nature of the relationship.
2. A description of the transaction.
3. The amount of the transaction.
4. Any amounts due from or to related parties.

Exhibit 6.17 presents part of the disclosure provided by ***Luby's, Inc.,*** the restaurant operator, related to the CEO and CFO's transactions with the company, including owning two ***Luby's*** restaurants.

EXHIBIT 6.17 Related-Party Transaction Disclosure (partial), ***Luby's Inc.,*** Financial Statements, August 31, 2015

NOTE 14: Related Parties

Affiliate Services

The Company's Chief Executive Officer, Christopher J. Pappas, and Harris J. Pappas, a Director of the Company, own two restaurant entities (the "Pappas entities") that may provide services to the Company and its subsidiaries, as detailed in the Master Sales Agreement dated November 8, 2013, among the Company and the Pappas entities.

Under the terms of the Master Sales Agreement, the Pappas entities continue to provide specialized (customized) equipment fabrication primarily for new construction and basic equipment maintenance, including stainless steel stoves, shelving, rolling carts, and chef tables. The total costs under the Master Sales Agreement of custom-fabricated and refurbished equipment in fiscal years 2016, 2015, and 2014 were approximately $2,000, zero, and $4,000, respectively. Services provided under this agreement are subject to review and approval by the Finance and Audit Committee of the Company's Board of Directors.

Source: Luby's Inc., 2016 Annual Report. http://www.lubysinc.com/investors/filings/files/Lubys_083116_Form10K_FiscalYear.pdf

[16]The complete list of related parties can be found in FASB ASC 850-10-20, *Related Party Disclosures – Overall – Glossary.*

IFRS Notes to the Financial Statements. IFRS requires similar information in the notes to the financial statements such as significant accounting policies, subsequent events, going concern uncertainties, and related-party transactions. However, the identification of subsequent events and disclosure of going concern uncertainties and related parties differ slightly. Additionally, IFRS requires disclosure of sources of uncertainty in the measurement of assets and liabilities.

Subsequent Events: IFRS. Under IFRS, a subsequent event must be reported if it occurs after the balance sheet date but before the financial statements have been authorized for issuance.[17] A company must disclose when the financial statements have been authorized and who authorized them. Commonly, a company's board of directors will authorize the financial statements for issuance. The authorization date is usually before the issuance date that U.S. GAAP uses. Therefore, a U.S. GAAP reporter may report a subsequent event that would not be required under IFRS.

EXAMPLE 6.5 **Subsequent Events: IFRS**

PROBLEM: Augsburg Company's board of directors met and authorized its financial statements on February 2. The company plans to make its financial statements available to the public on February 10. On February 8, a flood destroyed Augsburg's major manufacturing facility. Does Augsburg need to report the loss of the manufacturing facility as a subsequent event under IFRS?

SOLUTION: Under IFRS, Augsburg is not required to report the loss of the manufacturing facility as a subsequent event. Augsburg's board authorized the financial statements for issuance before the flood. Therefore, although the event occurred before Augsburg issued the financial statements, Augsburg is not required to report it as a subsequent event under IFRS.

Going Concern Uncertainties: IFRS. IFRS requires disclosures about going concern uncertainties when management is aware of material uncertainties related to conditions that may cause significant doubt about the entity's ability to continue as a going concern. However, under IFRS, the assessment period is at least one year from the financial statement date with no upper time limit.

Related-Party Transactions: IFRS. IFRS defines related-party transactions and requires disclosures similar to U.S. GAAP.[18] However, IFRS also includes specific disclosure requirements on executive compensation in total and by type such as short-term employee benefits, post-employment benefits, other long-term benefits, and share-based payments.

Sources of Estimation Uncertainty: IFRS. Under IFRS, companies are required to disclose information about the assumptions and estimates made at the end of the reporting period.[19] Assumptions and estimates can result in estimation uncertainty about the carrying values reported for assets and liabilities, as discussed in Chapter 3. Given the assumptions and estimates made, companies determine whether there is a significant risk of a material adjustment to the carrying amounts of assets and liabilities within the next financial year. For assets and liabilities, the company reports their nature and their carrying amounts at the end of the reporting period. Exhibit 6.18 presents ***Unilever's*** disclosure to financial statement items where it made significant estimates and assumptions, including pension obligations and deferred taxes, referring to more detail on these items in the specific notes to the financial statements.

[17] See IASC, *International Accounting Standard 10* "Events After the Reporting Period" (London, UK: International Accounting Standards Committee, Revised).

[18] See IASC, *International Accounting Standard 24*, "Related Party Disclosures" (London, UK: International Accounting Standards Committee, Revised).

[19] See Paragraphs 125 through 133 of IASC, *International Accounting Standard 1*, "Presentation of Financial Statements."

MICHAEL COHEN

MANAGING PARTNER, COHNREZNICK »

Michael Cohen

Recently retired, Michael Cohen oversaw all accounting and tax operations for CohnReznick's New Jersey offices. In this capacity, he directed over 400 people, including over 70 partners, and was a member of the firm's Management Committee. Mr. Cohen provided accounting and advisory services to middle market companies in diverse industries that range in size from $1 million to $3 billion.

1 How can financial statement users, most of whom focus on net income, assess a company's ability to create shareholder wealth using the balance sheet?

Assets and liabilities aren't nearly as eye catching to financial statement users as revenue and earnings. While earnings are important, they don't tell the whole story. The balance sheet reflects the financial condition of a company and offers a snapshot of a company's health.

Business owners create shareholder wealth by keeping the cost of capital below the rate of return on investment. By reviewing the balance sheet, a reader should be able to determine the various drivers of shareholders' wealth, including invested capital, cost of capital (including cost of debt), and incremental capital expenditures.

2 How does the information reported in the balance sheet enable a financial statement user to effectively measure a company's liquidity, solvency, and financial stability?

Investors use ratio analysis to measure a company's liquidity, solvency, and financial stability. Typically, they use the current ratio, quick ratio, net working capital, and debt-to-equity ratio, among others, to evaluate whether a company has sufficient resources to satisfy existing obligations in a timely manner. They can also determine whether a company's financial condition allows it to take advantage of potential opportunities and withstand unexpected crises.

3 What are the most critical estimates used in developing information reported in the balance sheet, and how do these estimates affect risk assessment for CohnReznick?

Typically, critical estimates include allowance for bad debts, allowance for inventory obsolescence and slow-moving items, fair value of financial instruments, impairment of long-lived assets and intangible assets, warranty liabilities, contingent liabilities, stock-based compensation, valuation of deferred tax assets, uncertain tax positions, and valuations in business combinations. These are high-risk audit areas because significant judgment is involved in determining estimates. Sometimes management's estimates are not reasonable and require revision. Such estimates must be challenged by auditors, who spend considerable time reviewing critical estimates to ensure that a client's accountants used proper methods and procedures, reasonable inputs, and consistent methods from year to year.

4 Do you believe that the historical cost model is still relevant in today's reporting environment?

The balance sheet does not portray the fair value of the entity as a going concern or its liquidation value. Despite this limitation, the balance sheet provides information useful for assessing future cash flows and near- and long-term liquidity. Using 100% fair value accounting does not currently seem practical for various reasons, including the increased cost involved in determining fair value estimates, the differences in values based upon the methods used to determine fair value, and a lack of expertise in the market place to value all balance sheet items at fair value.

5 How significant are off-balance sheet entities? How do you apply current disclosure requirements to factor in the impact of these off-balance sheet entities when assessing a company's financial condition?

The Enron fraud and bankruptcy revealed how certain companies used off-balance sheet entities to offload debt from their books. The FASB tightened requirements by adopting rules for Special Purpose Entities (SPEs) and Variable Interest Entities (VIEs). If consolidation of SPEs and VIEs is not required under U.S. GAAP, the auditors must review whether the company has contractual obligations to fund the operations of the off-balance sheet entities. The contractual obligations should be disclosed in the notes to the financial statements.

6 What is the role of the balance sheet, when used with the other financial statements, in assessing a company's ability to efficiently use capital and generate future cash flows?

No financial statement, standing by itself, can give a user a clear picture of a company's financial position and/or performance. Users should interrelate the income statement, cash flow statement, and balance sheet in their financial analysis to determine a company's overall financial health.

Discussion Questions

1. Discuss how the balance sheet can be used to project the cash-generating ability of an entity.
2. Discuss the advantages and disadvantages of using fair value to measure the elements reported on the balance sheet. Include specific examples and connect your response to the conceptual framework.

EXHIBIT 6.18 Disclosure of Sources of Estimation Uncertainty, ***Unilever Group***, Financial Statements, December 31, 2016

Financial Statements ***Unilever Group***

NOTE 1: Accounting Information and Policies (Partial)

Information about critical judgements in applying accounting policies, as well as estimates and assumptions that have the most significant risk of causing a material adjustment to the carrying amounts of assets and liabilities within the next financial year, are included in the following notes:

- separate presentation of items in the income statement – note 3;
- measurement of defined benefit obligations – note 4B;
- utilisation of tax losses and recognition of other deferred tax assets – note 6B;
- key assumptions used in discounted cash flow projections for impairment testing of goodwill and intangible assets – note 9;
- likelihood of occurrence of provisions and contingencies, including tax investigations and audits – notes 6A, 19 and 20; and
- measurement of consideration and assets and liabilities acquired as part of business combinations – note 21.

Source: Unilever. https://www.unilever.com/Images/unilever-annual-report-and-accounts-2016_tcm244-498880_en.pdf

8 Identify and describe the typical content of an annual report.

The Annual Report

The financial statements are included in an annual report that provides a comprehensive picture of a company's operations, the risks it faces, and its operating and financial performance. A country's security regulators usually determine the form and content of the annual report. In the United States, the Securities and Exchange Commission (SEC) has the authority to promulgate standards that establish the structure of the annual report called the 10-K.[20] The U.S. annual report contains detailed information on 15 major areas. The financial statements and the notes to the financial statements are included in the 10-K. In addition, we discuss the following areas that are most relevant to the course material:

- Management discussion and analysis
- Auditor's report
- Management's report
- Board of directors

We use the ***Johnson & Johnson*** annual report for fiscal year 2016 ending January 1, 2017, to illustrate the contents of a company's annual report. Companies can also voluntarily provide other disclosures and discussions in a variety of other areas. For example, ***Johnson & Johnson*** prepares a report on sustainability and corporate responsibility that includes areas such as quality and safety of products, climate, water, governance, transparency, and stakeholder engagement. Companies report many of these other items in the investor relations part of their Web sites.

Management Discussion and Analysis

Management's discussion and analysis of the financial condition and results of operations (typically referred to as the *MD&A*) is a required part of the annual report. The MD&A section provides the information necessary to understand the entity's financial condition, changes in financial condition, and results of operations.[21] The SEC specifies the topics discussed including:

1. Liquidity
2. Capital resources

[20] For IFRS reporters, the content of the annual report varies with the country and the regulator in which the company operates. The IASB has issued a statement describing important disclosures in a management commentary that companies can voluntarily follow.

[21] See SEC Rule 240.14a–d(b)(5)(ii), Item 303 of SEC Regulation S-K and SEC Interpretative Guidance.

3. Results of operations
4. Off-balance sheet arrangements
5. Disclosure of contractual obligations
6. Critical accounting policies[22]

The MD&A section focuses on material events and uncertainties known to management that could affect the faithful representation of the financial information reported elsewhere in the annual report. Examples include trends, events, and uncertainties that did not impact the entity in the past but could affect future financial position, operating results, and cash flows. Conversely, the MD&A provides information related to prior trends and events and uncertainties that may not occur in future reporting periods.

The MD&A section allows top management to provide the reader with an extensive analysis related to the firm's future performance. Although the discussion may contain some management bias, auditors are required to read the MD&A to ensure consistency with all the information provided throughout the financial statements. Thus, although it is not part of the audited financial statements and should be viewed with some degree of caution, there are some assurances that the information is accurate.

Johnson & Johnson's MD&A on pages 14 to 32 of its 2016 10-K begins with a description of the company, business segments, and management objectives. The MD&A then reviews the results of operations and provides an analysis of consolidated sales. This analysis addresses multiple dimensions, such as U.S. versus international results, performance by geographic region, and performance across the company's three business segments (consumer, pharmaceutical, and medical devices and diagnostics). The MD&A section also presents a combined discussion of ***Johnson & Johnson's*** liquidity and capital resources with a breakdown of its contractual obligations and commitments.

Critical accounting policies involve estimates and assumptions that could have a material impact on the company's financial condition or operating performance. These are areas with high levels of subjectivity and judgment necessary to account for uncertain matters or matters subject to change. Company disclosure supplements rather than duplicates the description of accounting policies that are already disclosed in the notes to the financial statements. ***Johnson & Johnson*** begins its discussion of critical accounting policies on page 26. ***Johnson & Johnson*** identifies the following critical areas: revenue recognition, income taxes, legal and self-insurance contingencies, valuation of long-lived assets, assumptions used to determine the amounts recorded for pensions, and other employee benefit plans and accounting for stock-based awards.

Auditors' Report

An audit is an examination of the financial statements (including the footnote disclosures) and the internal controls over the systems that generate the financial statements and notes. Auditors then attest to the fairness of the financial statements. For public companies, the auditors must also test the internal controls and attest to their effectiveness. The SEC requires all public companies to conduct an annual audit of their financial statements and footnote disclosures. Many private companies also choose to have an annual audit.

The format of most auditors' reports is nearly identical because the report must be in compliance with standards set forth by the Public Company Accounting Oversight Board (PCAOB).[23]

Typically, companies will receive an unqualified opinion, but other opinions are sometimes found in practice. Exhibit 6.19 summarizes the types of auditors' opinions.

The firm may issue the auditors' report on the effectiveness of the internal controls as a separate report within the annual report or include it with the opinion regarding the presentation of the financial statements within the annual report.

[22]Item 303 of SEC Regulation S-K requires that these topics be discussed but does not mandate the level of detail to be provided within each topic.

[23]The PCAOB sets the standards for public company audits, whereas the AICPA sets the standards for private company audits.

EXHIBIT 6.19 Auditors' Opinions

Type of Auditors' Opinion	Issued When . . .
Unqualified opinion (also referred to as a clean opinion)	The financial statements are presented fairly and are in compliance with GAAP. All required financial statements are included, the audit was performed in compliance with appropriate audit standards, the financial statements are in conformity with GAAP, and there are no additional circumstances that require an explanatory paragraph.
Unqualified opinion with an explanatory paragraph	Additional explanation is needed. Some of the most common are: 1. GAAP is not consistently applied. 2. Concern that the company might not continue in existence. 3. A particular matter may need to be emphasized (such as significant subsequent events).
Qualified opinion	1. The auditor concludes that the financial statements are fairly presented, but the scope of the audit was subject to significant limitations or 2. The financial statements are not in compliance with GAAP.
Adverse opinion	The auditor determines that the financial statements are not fairly presented.
Disclaimer opinion	The auditor is either not independent or is unable to form an opinion.

Johnson & Johnson's auditors prepared a combined report, as presented on page 84 of its 10-K filing. The first paragraph of the report states that ***Johnson & Johnson*** received an unqualified opinion; it goes on to state that the auditors believe that ***Johnson & Johnson's*** internal controls are effective.

Financial statement users should always read the auditors' report. The statements should be used with caution if a company receives anything other than a clean opinion on its financial statements.

Management Report

The management of a publicly traded entity is required to provide two letters in the annual report: a letter stating its responsibility for the financial statements and a letter providing an assessment of the effectiveness of the internal controls over the financial reporting process.[24]

Management's Responsibility for the Financial Statements. The management of a firm is ultimately responsible for the preparation and presentation of the financial statements. In order to emphasize this point and hold management accountable, the annual report or Form 10-K of a publicly traded entity must include certifications from the firm's management that include:

- A statement that the officers have reviewed the financial report.
- A statement that the financial statements do not contain any material omissions or untrue or misleading statements.
- A statement that the financial statements fairly present the financial condition and results of the entity.
- A statement that the officers are responsible for and have evaluated the internal controls.
- A list of all deficiencies in the internal controls.
- Information on any fraud that involves employees who are involved with internal activities.
- A discussion of any significant changes in internal controls that could have a negative impact on the internal controls.[25]

[24]The letter of management responsibility for the financial statements and the management assessment of internal controls letter can be combined.

[25]Section 302 of the Sarbanes-Oxley Act.

Johnson & Johnson includes the certifications in Exhibits 31(a) and 31(b) of its Form 10-K.

Management's Report on Internal Control over Financial Reporting. Annual reports of publicly traded entities must also include a letter that provides an assessment of the company's internal controls. In this letter, management is required to provide a statement:

- On management's responsibility for establishing and maintaining adequate internal control over financial reporting for the company.
- On management's assessment of the effectiveness of the company's internal control over financial reporting.
- Identifying the framework used by management to evaluate the effectiveness of the company's internal control over financial reporting.
- That the registered public accounting firm that audited the company's financial statements included in the annual report has issued an attestation report on management's assessment of the company's internal control over financial reporting.[26]

Johnson & Johnson's letter, presented on page 85 of its 10-K filing, states that management has assessed the effectiveness of internal controls and concluded that the internal controls over financial reporting are effective. As is the case with the management responsibility letter for the financial statements, this letter is signed by the CEO and the CFO.

Board of Directors

Public entities must provide a disclosure of the members of its **board of directors**, a body that oversees the activities of the company. Companies are also required to provide the principal occupations of their board members. This disclosure includes the names and the principal business activities of the entities employing the members of the board.

Johnson & Johnson's 10 directors, including the CEO and Chairman, approved the corporation's annual report. A number of its Board members are retired CEOs from other large corporations.

Summary by Learning Objectives

In the following, we summarize the main points by learning objective. Throughout the chapter, we discuss the accounting and reporting of U.S. GAAP and IFRS side by side. The following table also highlights the major similarities and differences between the standards.

1 Discuss the usefulness and limitations of the statement of financial position, including its use in understanding liquidity, solvency, and financial flexibility.

Summary	Similarities and Differences between U.S. GAAP and IFRS
The balance sheet: 1. Summarizes the economic resources and obligations. 2. Aids in assessing the rate of return. 3. Aids in an assessment of the riskiness of the entity. The balance sheet consists of permanent accounts with cumulative balances that are carried forward period to period and accumulate over the life of the firm.	Similar under U.S. GAAP and IFRS.

[26]Section 404 of the Sarbanes-Oxley Act.

Summary by Learning objectives, continued

2 Provide an overview of classifications on the statement of financial position for typical assets, liabilities, and stockholders' equity.

Summary	Similarities and Differences between U.S. GAAP and IFRS

The three primary classifications on the balance sheet are assets, liabilities, and stockholders' equity. Within each, typical accounts are
 	
Assets:
• Current assets
  • cash and cash equivalents
  • short-term investments
  • accounts receivable
  • inventory
  • prepaid expenses
• Long-term investments
• Property, plant, and equipment
• Intangible assets
• Other assets
	➤ Similar under U.S. GAAP and IFRS except that IFRS requires reporting certain assets, liabilities, and equity at a minimum.
	
	IFRS further considers current assets as assets that are held primarily for trading and cash and cash equivalents *unless* they are restricted for use.

Liabilities:
• Current liabilities
  • accounts payable
  • short-term notes payable
  • current maturities of long-term debt
  • accrued liabilities
  • unearned revenues
• Noncurrent liabilities
 	
Equity:
• Contributed capital
• Retained earnings
• Accumulated other comprehensive income
• Noncontrolling interest
 	
One of the primary distinctions is current versus noncurrent. Current assets include resources that are expected to be converted to cash or consumed
• within the next year or
• within the *operating cycle*, whichever is longer.
 	
Current liabilities are obligations that are expected to be liquidated through
• the use of current assets or
• the creation of other current liabilities
	➤ IFRS also considers current liabilities as liabilities that are held primarily for trading or liabilities that a company does not have the right to defer settling beyond the current year.
	
	IFRS refers to accumulated other comprehensive income as reserves. IFRS also refers to common stock as share capital, paid-in capital in excess of par as share premium, and retained earnings as retained profits.

Summary by Learning objectives, continued

3 Explain the presentation of current and noncurrent assets and liabilities on the statement of financial position and name the common statement formats.

Summary	Similarities and Differences between U.S. GAAP and IFRS
Current assets (liabilities) are presented before noncurrent assets (liabilities). Within current and noncurrent, assets are ordered by liquidity while liabilities are arranged by maturity. Two common balance sheet formats are the 1. Account format, which lists assets on the left side and liabilities and stockholders' equity on the right side of the statement. 2. Report format, which lists liabilities and stockholders' equity directly below assets on the same page.	➤ IFRS allows companies discretion in presenting current assets (liabilities) before or after noncurrent assets (liabilities). Within current and noncurrent, companies also have the choice of how they want to order each component. If more informative, companies can present assets and liabilities by liquidity rather than by current and noncurrent. Aside from the current and noncurrent (or liquidity) presentations, companies have flexibility in how to format their balance sheets.

4 Explain the statement of cash flows and classify common business activities into operating, investing, and financing cash flows.

Summary	Similarities and Differences between U.S. GAAP and IFRS
The statement of cash flows summarizes cash inflows and outflows for a firm over a period of time by operating, investing, and financing activities. Operating activities: 1. Cash receipts from customers 2. Cash payments for the purchase of goods for resale or for use in production 3. Cash payments to suppliers and employees 4. Cash payments related to taxes 5. Cash receipts related to interest and dividend income 6. Cash payments of interest Investing activities: 1. Cash receipts from the collection or sale of loans made by the entity 2. Cash receipts from the sale of debt and equity securities of other entities 3. Cash receipts from the sale of productive assets (e.g., property, plant, and equipment) 4. Cash payments for extending credit to others 5. Cash payments for investments in debt and equity securities of other entities 6. Cash payments for property, plant, and equipment and other productive assets Financing activities: 1. Cash receipts from issuing equity to owners 2. Cash receipts from borrowing through bonds or notes or other instruments 3. Cash payments to repurchase equity from owners 4. Cash payments for principal on debt 5. Cash payments for dividends	➤ Similar under U.S. GAAP and IFRS, except companies have choices in where to classify interest paid, dividends paid, and taxes paid, as well as interest received and dividends received, under IFRS.

Summary by Learning objectives, continued

❺ Explain the direct and indirect formats of the statement of cash flows.

Summary	Similarities and Differences between U.S. GAAP and IFRS
The indirect method (also referred to as the reconciliation format) begins with net income from the income statement and reconciles it to net cash generated from operating activities. The direct method (also referred to as the income statement format) reports cash receipts and payments for all activities. The investing and financing sections of the direct and indirect statement of cash flows are the same. The only difference is how cash flows are reported in the operating activities section.	➤ Similar under U.S. GAAP and IFRS except that IFRS does not specify the income line item that must begin the reconciliation of operating cash flows under the indirect method.

❻ Review the four primary financial statements and financial statement articulation.

Summary	Similarities and Differences between U.S. GAAP and IFRS
The main financial statements are: – Statements of Net Income and Comprehensive Income (Alternatively, both statements can be replaced with the Statement of Comprehensive Income) – Statement of Stockholders' Equity – Statement of Financial Position – Statement of Cash Flows Financial statement articulation makes clear the interaction among assets, liabilities, and equity elements with revenues and expenses. Common relationships are: <u>Statements of Net Income and Comprehensive Income</u> Net income = Revenues − Expenses + Gains − Losses Comprehensive Income = Net Income + Other Comprehensive Income <u>Statement of Stockholders' Equity</u> Ending Retained Earnings = Beginning Retained Earnings + Net income − Dividends Declared ± Other Ending Accumulated OCI = Beginning Accumulated OCI ± OCI <u>Statement of Financial Position</u> Assets = Liabilities + Stockholders' Equity <u>Statement of Cash Flows</u> Net Change in Cash = Ending Cash − Beginning Cash	Similar under U.S. GAAP and IFRS.

Summary by Learning objectives, continued

7 Explain the purpose of the notes to the financial statements, including the summary of significant accounting policies, subsequent events, going concern uncertainties, and related-party transactions.

Summary	Similarities and Differences between U.S. GAAP and IFRS
Notes are an integral part of the financial statements and provide additional information related to the line items presented. The notes both expand on financial information included in the financial statements and provide additional disclosures. Examples of notes that provide additional disclosures include: • Summary of significant accounting policies: Details the methods that the entity has selected in reporting various accounts. • Subsequent events: Describes significant events that occur after the date of the fiscal year-end but before the financial statements are issued or available to be issued. • Going concern uncertainties: Management must evaluate whether there is substantial doubt as to whether the entity will continue to operate within one year after the financial statements are issued. If substantial doubt does exist, disclosures are required. • Related-party transactions: Details transactions that an entity engages in with owners, firm management, affiliated entities, or any other entity that can exert significant influence on the company.	➤ Similar under U.S. GAAP and IFRS except for the following. • Subsequent events: Events that occur after the balance sheet date but before the financial statements have been authorized for issuance must be reported. • Going concern uncertainties: The window of evaluation for IFRS is at least one year from the financial statement date with no upper time limit. • Related-party transactions: IFRS includes specific disclosure requirements on total executive compensation. • Sources of estimation uncertainty: Companies disclose information about the source of estimation uncertainty resulting from assumptions and estimates they made at the end of the reporting period.

8 Identify and describe the typical content of an annual report.

Summary	Similarities and Differences between U.S. GAAP and IFRS
A company's annual report provides insight into its operating performance, financial position, and cash flows. It includes: • The management discussion and analysis. • The auditors' report. • The management report. • Board of directors. • Financial statements. • The footnotes to the financial statements. The U.S. Securities and Exchange Commission determines the content of the annual report, called the 10-K, for publicly traded companies.	➤ A country's security regulator usually determines the content of the annual report. Therefore, the content of the annual report varies for IFRS reporters. The IASB has issued a statement that companies can voluntarily follow describing important disclosures in a management commentary.

MyLab Accounting

Go to **http://www.pearson.com/mylab/accounting** for the following Questions, Multiple-Choice Questions, Brief Exercises, Exercises, and Problems. They are available with immediate grading, explanations of correct and incorrect answers, and interactive media that acts as your own online tutor.

6 Statements of Financial Position and Cash Flows and the Annual Report

Questions

1 **Q6-1.** What are the limitations of the balance sheet?

1 **Q6-2.** What does a firm's liquidity measure?

1 **Q6-3.** What does a firm's solvency measure?

2 **Q6-4.** What are the four major components of stockholders' equity? Explain each component.

2 **Q6-5.** What items are included in cash and cash equivalents? How would financial statement preparers report these items on the balance sheet?

2 **Q6-6.** When can a liability be classified as current?

2 **Q6-7.** Where is accumulated other comprehensive income reported on the financial statements? Why?

3 **Q6-8.** How do firms report assets on the balance sheet?

3 **Q6-9.** How do firms report assets on the balance sheet under IFRS?

3 **Q6-10.** What are the two main balance sheet formats? Explain both formats.

4 **Q6-11.** Why is the cash flow statement useful to the users of the financial statements?

4 **Q6-12.** What is the purpose of the cash flow statement?

5 **Q6-13.** What are the two formatting options for reporting the operating activities section of the statement of cash flows? Explain both formats.

6 **Q6-14.** What is financial statement articulation?

6 **Q6-15.** How is net income closed? Is the closing entry the same for other comprehensive income? Explain.

7 **Q6-16.** Why are the notes to the financial statements an integral part of the financial statements?

7 **Q6-17.** What is included in the summary of significant accounting policies disclosure?

7 **Q6-18.** What is a subsequent event?

7 **Q6-19.** What is a subsequent event under IFRS?

7 **Q6-20.** How do firms report a material subsequent event on the financial statements?

7 **Q6-21.** Over what period must management assess the entity's ability to continue as a going concern under U.S. GAAP?

7 **Q6-22.** Over what period must management assess the entity's ability to continue as a going concern under IFRS?

7 **Q6-23.** What is a related-party transaction? Why does the FASB require disclosure of related parties?

8 **Q6-24.** How does the role of the FASB differ from that of the Securities and Exchange Commission with regard to the establishment of accounting standards?

8 **Q6-25.** What information is provided in the Management's Discussion and Analysis section of the financial statements?

8 **Q6-26.** What do auditors attest to in an audit report?

8 **Q6-27.** What does it mean when an auditor issues an adverse opinion on the financial statements?

8 **Q6-28.** Explain the five different types of auditor's opinions.

8 **Q6-29.** Where do auditors include their report on the effectiveness of a firm's internal controls? Explain.

8 **Q6-30.** What is management's responsibility for the financial statements?

8 **Q6-31.** What information is included in the annual report letter written by managers of publicly traded companies?

8 **Q6-32.** Who is responsible for designing and implementing a company's system of internal controls? Where is this policy stated?

B **Q6-33.** What is the difference between liquidity and solvency?

B **Q6-34.** What are the two key measures of liquidity? Explain each measure.

B **Q6-35.** What does the debt-to-equity ratio measure for a company?

B **Q6-36.** What does a high current ratio indicate about a company?

B **Q6-37.** Is it useful to compare working capital among companies in the same industry to determine relative liquidity? Explain.

Multiple-Choice Questions

4 MC6-1. Sykes Corporation's comparative balance sheets at December 31, Year 2 and Year 1, reported accumulated depreciation balances of $800,000 and $600,000, respectively. Property with a cost of $50,000 and a carrying amount of $40,000 was the only property sold in Year 2. Depreciation charged to operations in Year 2 was:

a. $190,000 b. $200,000 c. $210,000 d. $220,000

4 MC6-2. During Year 1, Brianna Company had the following transactions related to its financial operations:

Payment for the retirement of long-term bonds payable (carrying value $740,000)	750,000
Distribution in Year 1 of cash dividend declared in Year 0 to preferred shareholders	62,000
Carrying value of convertible preferred stock of Brianna converted into common shares	120,000
Proceeds from sale of treasury stock (carrying value at cost $86,000)	95,000

On its Year 1 statement of cash flows, net cash used in financing activities should be:

a. $717,000 b. $716,000 c. $597,000 d. $535,000

4 MC6-3. Which of the following items would *not* be included in the operating activities section of an entity's statement of cash flows under U.S. GAAP?

a. Interest received
b. Proceeds from the sale of trading securities
c. Dividends paid
d. Income taxes paid

4 MC6-4. Kong Co. purchased a three-month U.S. Treasury bill. Kong's policy is to treat as cash equivalents all highly liquid investments with an original maturity of three months or less when purchased. How should this purchase be reported in Kong's statement of cash flows?

a. As an outflow from operating activities
b. As an inflow from investing activities
c. As an outflow from financing activities
d. Not reported

4 MC6-5. Bales Company is preparing a statement of cash flows. Which of the following would be shown on the statement?

a. Stock dividend
b. Stock split
c. Appropriation of retained earnings
d. None of the answer choices is correct

5 MC6-6. Big Dollars Corporation's comparative financial statements included the following amounts for the current year:

Net income	$650,000
Depreciation expense	93,000
Equity in earnings of unconsolidated affiliate	61,000
Gain on sale of fixed assets	4,000
Increase in accounts receivable	25,000
Decrease in inventory	(57,000)
Decrease in fixed assets	38,000
Increase in accounts payable	42,000
Decrease in notes payable (nontrade)	(75,000)

On its current-year statement of cash flows, what is Big Dollars' net cash provided by operating activities?

a. $677,000 b. $714,000 c. $752,000 d. $790,000

5 MC6-7. In its year-end income statement, Black Knights Company reported cost of goods sold of $450,000. Changes occurred in several balance sheet accounts during the year as follows:

Inventory	$160,000	decrease
Accounts payable-suppliers	40,000	decrease

What amount should the Black Knights Company report as cash paid to suppliers in its cash flow statement prepared under the direct method?

a. $250,000 b. $330,000 c. $570,000 d. $650,000

5 MC6-8. On its current year income statement, Vegas Parties, Inc. reported sales revenue of $945,000. Changes occurred in several balance sheet accounts, including the following:

Accounts receivable:	90,000	decrease
Unearned revenue:	$75,000	increase

What amount should Vegas report as cash received from customers in its current year statement of cash flows prepared using the direct method?

a. $780,000 b. $930,000 c. $960,000 d. $1,110,000

Brief Exercises

1 **BE6-1. Advantages of the Statement of Financial Position.** List and explain the three primary advantages of the statement of financial position.

1 **BE6-2. Disadvantages of the Statement of Financial Position.** List and explain the three primary disadvantages of the statement of financial position.

2 **BE6-3. Account Classification: Current and Noncurrent Assets and Liabilities, Equity.** Classify the following accounts as current assets, noncurrent assets, current liabilities, noncurrent liabilities, contributed capital, or accumulated other comprehensive income.

Account	Balance Sheet Classification
Current portion of long-term debt	______________
Property, plant, and equipment – net	______________
Investments in affiliate companies (noncurrent)	______________
Accounts receivable	______________
Investments at fair value held for immediate sale	______________
Accounts payable	______________
Additional paid-in capital	______________
Dividends payable	______________
Equipment under capital lease	______________
Intangible assets – net	______________
Merchandise inventory	______________
Income taxes payable	______________
Bonds payable, due in 10 years	______________
Common stock, $1 par value	______________
Cash	______________
Notes payable due in 90 days	______________
Obligations under capital leases	______________
Obligations under pension plans	______________

2 **BE6-4. Account Classification: Current and Noncurrent Assets and Liabilities, Equity.** Classify the following accounts as current assets, noncurrent assets, current liabilities, noncurrent liabilities, or stockholders' equity.

Account	Balance Sheet Classification
Property, plant, and equipment – net	______________
Accounts receivable	______________
Accounts payable	______________
Additional paid-in capital	______________
Dividends payable	______________
Intangible assets – net	______________
Merchandise inventory	______________
Income taxes payable	______________
Bonds payable, due in 10 years	______________
Common stock, $1 par value	______________
Cash	______________
Notes payable (36-month term)	______________

3 **BE6-5. Classified Balance Sheet.** Armstrong Associates provided the following balance sheet for its current year ended December 31.

Armstrong Associates
Balance Sheet
At December 31

Assets	***Amount***
Cash	$ 255,000
Receivables	1,390,000
Prepaid Assets and Supplies	722,000
Property, Plant, and Equipment – net	2,075,000
Total Assets	$4,442,000
Liabilities	
Payables and Accrued Expenses	$1,040,500
Income Taxes Payable	316,750
Notes Payable, due in 5 years	1,007,000
Total Liabilities	$2,364,250
Stockholders' Equity	
Contributed Capital	$1,855,000
Retained Earnings	222,750
Total Stockholders' Equity	$ 2,077,750
Total Liabilities and Stockholders' Equity	$4,442,000

The following account analyses were made during the company's recent year-end audit.

Receivables	
Accounts Receivable	$ 450,000
Indefinite-life Intangible Assets	940,000
Receivables	$1,390,000
Prepaid Assets and Supplies	
Merchandise Inventory	$ 641,000
Prepaid Rent	81,000
Prepaid Assets and Supplies	$ 722,000
Payables and Accrued Expenses	
Accounts Payable	$ 519,000
Accrued Expenses	521,500
Payables and Accrued Expenses	$1,040,500
Contributed Capital	
Common Stock, $1 par value	$ 815,000
Additional Paid-in Capital	1,040,000
Contributed Capital	$1,855,000

Required »

Prepare a corrected classified balance sheet.

3 **BE6-6. Classified Balance Sheet, Report Format.** Martell Manufacturing Incorporated provided the following list of account balances for the current year ended December 31.

Account	Debit	Credit
Accounts receivable	$ 300,000	
Bonds payable, due in 20 years		$ 400,000
Investments at fair value (trading)	58,000	
Accounts payable		175,000
Additional paid-in capital		587,000
Accumulated other comprehensive loss	165,300	
Current portion of long-term debt		25,000
Property, plant, and equipment – net	1,264,500	
Dividends payable		135,000
Merchandise inventory	254,000	
Income taxes payable		65,800
Cash	145,000	
Notes payable, due in 5 years		138,500
Retained earnings		625,500
Common stock, $1 par value	—	35,000
Totals	$2,186,800	$2,186,800

Prepare a classified balance sheet for the current year using the report format.

3 **BE6-7. Classified Balance Sheet, Account Format.** Using the information provided in BE6-6, prepare a classified balance sheet using the account format.

3 **BE6-8. Classified Balance Sheet, Report Format.** Bowe Company provided the following list of accounts.

Account	Debit	Credit
Accumulated other comprehensive loss	$ 14,900	
Current portion of long-term debt		$ 45,600
Property, plant, and equipment – net	876,500	
Accounts receivable	50,000	
Bonds payable, due in 20 years		125,000
Accounts payable		76,500
Additional paid-in capital		345,000
Dividends payable		1,200
Merchandise inventory	200,000	
Income taxes payable		32,500
Cash	15,325	
Notes payable, due in 10 years		9,000
Retained earnings		400,900
Common stock, $1 par value	—	121,025
Totals	$1,156,725	$1,156,725

Prepare a classified balance sheet using the report format.

3 **BE6-9. Classified Balance Sheet, Account Format.** Using the information provided in BE6-8, prepare a classified balance sheet using the account format.

4 5 **BE6-10. Classification as Operating, Investing, or Financing Activity on the Statement of Cash Flows.** A list of cash receipts and cash payments for Exis Communications follows. Classify each amount as operating, investing, or financing. Use the direct method.

Cash Receipt or Payment	Classification
Cash payments for extending credit to others	________
Cash payments to repurchase equity from owners	________
Cash payments to suppliers and employees	________
Cash payments for taxes	________
Cash receipts from the collection or sale of loans made by the entity	________

4 5 **BE6-11. Classification as Operating, Investing, or Financing Activity on the Statement of Cash Flows.** A list of cash receipts and cash payments for Mexis Communications follows. Classify each amount as operating, investing, or financing. Use the direct method.

Cash Receipt or Payment	Classification
Cash receipts from borrowing through bonds, notes, or other instruments	________
Cash payments for debt and equity securities of other entities	________
Cash payments for the purchase of goods for resale or for use in production	________
Cash receipts from dividends	________
Cash payments for dividends	________

4 5 **BE6-12. Classification as Operating, Investing, or Financing Activity on the Statement of Cash Flows.** A list of cash receipts and cash payments for Axis Communications follows. Classify each amount as operating, investing, or financing. Use the direct method.

Cash Receipt or Payment	Classification
Cash receipts from interest	________
Cash payments for principal on debt	________
Cash receipts from customers	________
Cash payments for property, plant, and equipment and other productive assets	________
Cash receipts from the sale of debt and equity securities of other entities	________

4 5 **BE6-13. Classification as Operating, Investing, or Financing Activity on the Statement of Cash Flows.** A list of cash receipts and cash payments for Bexis Communications follows. Classify each amount as operating, investing, or financing. Use the direct method.

Cash Receipt or Payment	Classification
Cash receipts from issuing equity to owners	________
Cash payments for interest	________
Cash receipts from the sale of productive assets (e.g., property, plant, and equipment)	________
Cash receipts from customers	________
Cash payments to suppliers and employees	________

4 5 **BE6-14. Classification as Operating, Investing, or Financing Activity on the Statement of Cash Flows, IFRS.** A list of cash receipts and cash payments for Exis Communications follows. Classify each amount as operating, investing, or financing, assuming that Exis Communications reports under IFRS. Use the direct method.

Cash Receipt or Payment	Classification
Cash payments for extending credit to others	________
Cash payments to repurchase equity from owners	________
Cash payments to suppliers and employees	________
Cash payments for taxes	________
Cash receipts from the collection or sale of loans made by the entity	________

4 5 **BE6-15. Classification as Operating, Investing, or Financing Activity on the Statement of Cash Flows, IFRS.** A list of cash receipts and cash payments for Mexis Communications follows. Classify each amount as operating, investing, or financing, assuming that Mexis Communications reports under IFRS. Use the direct method.

Cash Receipt or Payment	Classification
Cash receipts from borrowing through bonds, notes, or other instruments	________
Cash payments for debt and equity securities of other entities	________
Cash payments for the purchase of goods for resale or for use in production	________
Cash receipts from dividends	________
Cash payments for dividends	________

4 5 **BE6-16. Classification as Operating, Investing, or Financing Activity on the Statement of Cash Flows, IFRS.** A list of cash receipts and cash payments for Axis Communications follows. Classify each amount as operating, investing, or financing, assuming that Axis Communications reports under IFRS. Use the direct method.

Cash Receipt or Payment	Classification
Cash receipts from interest	________
Cash payments for principal on debt	________
Cash receipts from customers	________
Cash payments for property, plant, and equipment and other productive assets	________
Cash receipts from the sale of debt and equity securities of other entities	________

4 5 **BE6-17. Classification as Operating, Investing, or Financing Activity on the Statement of Cash Flows, IFRS.** A list of cash receipts and cash payments for Bexis Communications follows. Classify each amount as operating, investing, or financing, assuming that Bexis Communications reports under IFRS. Use the direct method.

Cash Receipt or Payment	Classification
Cash receipts from issuing equity to owners	________
Cash payments for interest	________
Cash receipts from the sale of productive assets (e.g., property, plant, and equipment)	________
Cash receipts from customers	________
Cash payments to suppliers and employees	________

4 5 **BE6-18. Statement of Cash Flows, Direct Method.** A list of cash receipts and cash payments for Tucson Telecommunications follows. Compute cash flows from operating activities under the direct reporting format.

Cash Receipts and Payments	Amount
Cash collected from customers	$1,971,300
Cash paid to suppliers	$860,740
Cash receipts from borrowing	445,000
Cash paid to purchase equipment	347,000
Cash paid for taxes	244,300
Cash receipts from issuing equity	236,900
Cash payments for property, plant, and equipment	145,600
Cash payments for loans made	56,096
Cash payments on principal on debt	50,700
Cash payments for dividends	6,500
Cash paid for interest	4,300
Cash receipts from interest	480

5 **BE6-19. Statement of Cash Flows, Indirect Method.** Identify whether each of the following items is added or subtracted from net income to compute cash flows from operating activities under the indirect method.

Item	Add or Subtract from Net Income to Compute Cash Flows from Operating Activities
a. Depreciation expense	________
b. Decrease in taxes payable	________
c. Increase in accounts receivable	________
d. Gain on the sale of equipment	________
e. Increase in accounts payable	________
f. Decrease in prepaid rent	________

6 **BE6-20. Financial Statement Articulation.** Complete the following financial statement articulation exercises.

a. If net income is $40,000 and comprehensive income is $32,000, what is other comprehensive income (loss)?
b. If ending retained earnings is $76,000, beginning retained earnings is $42,000, and net income is $40,000, what is the amount of dividends declared?
c. If ending retained earnings is $34,000, beginning retained earnings is $42,000, and dividends declared is $3,000, what is net income (loss)?
d. If ending retained earnings is $76,000, net income is $40,000, and dividends declared is $10,000, what is the amount of beginning retained earnings?
e. If the beginning balance of cash was $96,000 and the ending balance of cash is $128,000, what is the net change in cash?
f. If the beginning balance of cash was $128,000 and the ending balance of cash is $96,000, what is the net change in cash?

7 **BE6-21. Subsequent Events.** The Junebug Corporation is preparing its annual financial statements and needs to determine which of the following events are subsequent events. If the event is a subsequent event, identify whether it should be recognized or disclosed in the financial statements. For all scenarios, assume Junebug has a December 31 year-end and issues its financial statements on February 10.

Scenario	Subsequent Event	Disclosed or Recognized
a. On January 25, an earthquake caused $1.2 million in damages to the company's manufacturing facility.	________	________
b. The company hired a new chief executive officer on February 1.	________	________

Scenario	Subsequent Event	Disclosed or Recognized
c. On February 8, a judge ruled against the company and found it liable for $500,000 in a case that had been ongoing for the last year.	________	________
d. On January 18, the company settled a lawsuit for $275,000 that had been ongoing for the last year.	________	________
e. On February 9, the company settled a lawsuit for $0.7 million arising from an accident in its manufacturing plant on January 2.	________	________
f. On February 12, a severe blizzard caused $450,000 in damages to the company's manufacturing facility.	________	________
g. On January 6, the company acquired a medium-sized competitor for $207 million.	________	________

7 **BE6-22. Related Parties.** The Firefly Company is preparing its annual financial statements and needs to identify all its related parties. Which of the following would be related parties of the Firefly Company?

Party	Related Party (Yes or No)
a. A member of Firefly's board of directors	________
b. A shareholder who owns 25% of Firefly's shares	________
c. A shareholder who owns two shares of Firefly's stock	________
d. Firefly's chief executive officer	________
e. The husband of Firefly's chief financial officer	________
f. Firefly's pension trust fund	________
g. A company in which Firefly owns 40% of its stock	________
h. A company in which Firefly owns 100 shares, less than 1% of its stock	________

8 **BE6-23. Contents of the Annual Report.** Match each annual report section with its description.

Annual report sections:

a. Management's discussion and analysis
b. Auditors' report
c. Management's responsibility for the financial statements
d. Management's report on internal control over financial reporting
e. Board of directors

Description:

________ Statement of independent opinion on whether the financial statements are presented fairly and in compliance with U.S. GAAP.

________ Description of the body that oversees the activities of the company and its members.

________ Statement from the chief executive officer and chief financial officer that they are in charge of the preparation and presentation of the financial statements.

________ Description of significant aspects of the company's financial condition and results of operations, including liquidity, capital resources, results of operations, off-balance sheet arrangements, and contractual obligations.

________ Statement from the chief executive officer and chief financial officer that they have assessed the processes used in preparing the financial reports.

A **BE6-24. Statement of Cash Flows, Direct Method.** Identify and compute the cash flow related to each item on the following income statement. Use the direct method.

	Balance Sheet Accounts		Income Statement Accounts	
	Beginning Balance	Ending Balance		
a. Accounts Receivable	$1,035	$1,123	Sales	$35,678
b. Prepaid Insurance	400	514	Insurance Expense	1,346
c. Inventory	5,461	6,723	Cost of Goods Sold	34,762
d. Accounts Payable	4,312	5,125		
e. Taxes Payable	3,009	2,400	Tax Expense	45,098

A **BE6-25. Statement of Cash Flows, Indirect Method.** Tennis Emporium provided the following information for the current year.

Tennis Emporium Statement of Net Income for the Current Year Ended	Amount
Sales	$767,000
Depreciation Expense	(52,000)
Selling, General, and Administrative Expenses	(688,000)
Operating Income	27,000
Tax Expense	(6,000)
Net Income	$ 21,000

Changes in Balance Sheet Accounts	
Increase in Accounts Receivable	$10,000
Increase in Accounts Payable (Related to Selling, General, and Administrative Expenses)	$ 5,000
Decrease in Income Taxes Payable	$ 3,000

Compute the net cash flow from operating activities for Tennis Emporium under the indirect reporting format.

A **BE6-26. Statement of Cash Flows, Direct Method.** Use the information from BE6-25 to compute the net cash flow from operating activities for Tennis Emporium under the direct reporting format.

B **BE6-27. Ratio Analyses.** Identify whether the following measures are indicators of liquidity, solvency, or profitability.

Measure	Indicator of
a. Current Ratio	________
b. Debt-to-Equity Ratio	________
c. Profit Margin	________
d. Interest Coverage Ratio	________
e. Return on Assets	________
f. Working Capital	________
g. Return on Stockholders' Equity	________

B **BE6-28. Ratio Analyses.** Green Grasshopper Incorporated is interested in assessing the following scenarios on its indicators of liquidity, solvency, and profitability. Solve each scenario independently.

a. Green Grasshopper's debt-to-equity ratio is 40%. It is considering issuing $13 million in bonds that would increase its total liabilities to $68 million. What would Green Grasshopper's debt-to-equity ratio be if it issued the bonds?

b. Green Grasshopper's current ratio is 1.45. It is considering issuing $30 million in bonds to purchase a new manufacturing facility. Its current liabilities are $28 million, but the new debt would increase the current portion of its long-term debt payable by $3.2 million. What would Green Grasshopper's current ratio be if it issued the bonds and used the proceeds to purchase the facility?

Exercises

❷ **E6-1. Classification of Assets and Liabilities.** Darin Development Company engaged in the following transactions during the current year.

a. Borrowed $400,000 from Pleasantville Community Bank at the beginning of the year. The terms of the note call for annual payments of $50,000. The first annual payment has not been paid as of the end of the current year. (Ignore any interest payable.)
b. Made sales for the current year amounting to $2,900,000 with 40% collected during the current year.
c. Acquired inventory costing $345,000 on account.
d. Incurred taxes due on the current year's income of $76,000.
e. Paid $60,000 for a three-year insurance policy in advance on January 1 of the current year.
f. Acquired new equipment costing $890,000 by borrowing the full amount at the end of the current year. The loan is due in 5 years.

Required »

Identify and classify the noncash assets and liabilities resulting from the current-year transactions. Assume that your classification is made as of the end of the current year.

❷ **E6-2. Classification of Assets, Liabilities, and Equity.** Classify each of the following accounts as an asset, liability, or stockholders' equity. In the case of the assets, further classify them as current assets; long-term investments; property, plant, and equipment; intangible assets; or other assets. In the case of liabilities, further classify the accounts as current or noncurrent.

Account	Asset, Liability, or Stockholders' Equity	Classification
Accounts payable	________	________
Trademark	________	________
Cash	________	________
Income taxes payable	________	________
Tractors	________	________
Common stock	________	________
Accounts receivable	________	________
Retained earnings	________	________

❷ **E6-3. Classification of Assets, Liabilities, and Equity.** Classify each of the following accounts as an asset, liability, or stockholders' equity. In the case of the assets, further classify them as current assets; long-term investments; property, plant, and equipment; intangible assets; or other assets. In the case of liabilities, further classify the accounts as current or noncurrent.

Account	Asset, Liability, or Stockholders' Equity	Classification
Notes payable – due in 10 years	________	________
Preferred stock	________	________
Investments held for immediate trading	________	________
Accumulated other comprehensive income	________	________
Accrued salaries payable	________	________
Factory building	________	________
Notes payable due in 6 months	________	________
Inventory	________	________

❷ **E6-4. Classification of Assets, Liabilities, and Equity.** Classify each of the following accounts as asset, liability, or stockholders' equity. In the case of the assets, further classify them as current assets; long-term investments; property, plant, and equipment; intangible assets; or other assets. In the case of liabilities, further classify the accounts as current or noncurrent.

Account	Asset, Liability, or Stockholders' Equity	Classification
Unearned revenues – related to services to be performed within the next year	______	______
Cash equivalents	______	______
Investment in debt instrument – held for long-term appreciation	______	______
Interest payable	______	______
Patent	______	______
Additional paid-in capital	______	______
Current maturity of long-term debt	______	______
Prepaid expenses	______	______

❸ **E6-5. Prepare Balance Sheet.** Blackburn Building Products Company provided the following information for the current year ended December 31.

Account	Debit	Credit
Cash	$ 645,235	
Notes payable, due in 5 years		$ 190,900
Retained earnings		857,735
Obligations under capital leases (noncurrent)		575,000
Obligations under pension plans		301,250
Deferred tax liability (noncurrent)		35,500
Accumulated other comprehensive loss	356,700	
Current portion of long-term debt		356,800
Property, plant, and equipment – net	2,745,600	
Investments in affiliate companies (noncurrent)	567,500	
Accounts receivable	450,000	
Bonds payable, due in 10 years		1,890,750
Investments at fair value (trading)	235,000	
Accounts payable		500,000
Additional paid-in capital		710,300
Dividends payable		55,000
Equipment under capital lease	1,511,750	
Intangible assets – net	205,700	
Merchandise inventory	665,750	
Income taxes payable		40,000
Common stock, $1 par value		1,870,000
Totals	$7,383,235	$7,383,235

Required »

a. Prepare the current-year classified balance sheet using the report format.
b. Prepare the current-year classified balance sheet using the account format.

3 **E6-6. Prepare Balance Sheet.** Lake Company provided the following information for the current year ended December 31.

Account	Debit	Credit
Bonds payable, due in 10 years		$ 200,975
Investments at fair value (current)	$ 25,000	
Accounts payable		135,000
Additional paid-in capital		400,000
Dividends payable		3,200
Equipment under capital lease	856,800	
Intangible assets – net	207,000	
Merchandise inventory	667,500	
Income taxes payable		32,525
Cash	12,750	
Accumulated other comprehensive income		20,000
Current portion of long-term debt		100,000
Property, plant, and equipment – net	1,098,000	
Investments in affiliate companies (noncurrent)	43,000	
Accounts receivable	60,000	
Notes payable, due in 5 years		300,000
Retained earnings		701,735
Obligations under capital leases		210,500
Obligations under pension plans		185,400
Deferred tax liability (noncurrent)		16,000
Common stock, $1 par value		664,715
Totals	$2,970,050	$2,970,050

Required »

a. Prepare the current-year classified balance sheet using the report format.
b. Prepare the current-year classified balance sheet using the account format.

5 **E6-7. Statement of Cash Flows, Indirect Method.** Tulsa Corporation provided you with the following information for the current year.

Tulsa Corporation
Statement of Net Income
for the Current Year Ended

Sales	$45,700
Depreciation Expense	(1,800)
Selling, General, and Administrative Expenses	(21,000)
Loss on Sale of Equipment	(3,000)
Other Income	400
Income before Taxes	20,300
Tax Expense	(6,090)
Net Income	$14,210

Changes in Balance Sheet Accounts	Amount
Decrease in Accounts Receivable	$ 2,300
Increase in Accounts Payable	900
Increase in Income Taxes Payable	1,600

Compute the net cash flow from operating activities under the indirect reporting format.

5 **E6-8. Statement of Cash Flows, Direct Method.** Using the information from E6-7, compute net cash flow from operating activities for Tulsa Corporation under the direct reporting format.

5 **E6-9. Statement of Cash Flows, Indirect Method.** Compute the net cash flow from operating activities for Bernadino Company under the indirect reporting format. Bernadino Company provided you with the following information for the current year. Accounts Payable relate to Selling, General and Administrative Expenses.

Bernadino Company
Statement of Net Income
for the Current Year Ended

Sales	$ 39,000
Depreciation Expense	(5,700)
Selling, General, and Administrative Expenses	(32,400)
Gain on Sale of Equipment	1,400
Other Expenses	(4,100)
Income before Taxes	(1,800)
Tax Benefit	540
Net Loss	$ (1,260)

Account Changes from the Balance Sheet	**Amount**
Decrease in Accounts Receivable	$ 1,600
Decrease in Accounts Payable	700
Increase in Wages Payable	2,800

Compute net cash flow from operating activities under the indirect reporting format.

5 **E6-10. Statement of Cash Flows, Direct Method.** Using the information from E6-9, compute the net cash flow from operating activities for Bernadino Company under the direct reporting format.

5 **E6-11. Statement of Cash Flows, Indirect Method.** Compute cash flows from operating activities for Edwards Company under the indirect reporting format. Edwards Company provided you with the following information for the current year. Accounts Payable relate to Selling, General and Administrative Expenses.

Edwards Company
Statement of Net Income
for the Ended December 31, 2019

Sales	$ 347,000
Depreciation Expense	(35,000)
Selling, General, and Administrative Expenses	(117,000)
Gain on Sale of Equipment	7,400
Other Expenses	(8,200)
Income before Taxes	194,200
Tax Expense	(58,260)
Net Income	$135,940

	December 31,	
Select Balance Sheet Accounts	**2018**	**2019**
Cash	$ 40,000	$ 37,400
Investments (noncurrent)	25,000	35,800
Prepaid Rent	248,200	280,200
Accounts Payable	116,400	136,000
Income Taxes Payable	4,300	5,900
Long-Term Debt	189,600	176,300
Common Stock	248,900	305,600

Compute net cash flow from operating activities under the indirect reporting format.

6 **E6-12. Financial Statement Articulation.** Use the information presented below to complete the following table. Scenarios A, B, and C are independent scenarios. Assume that there are no dividends declared in any of the scenarios.

Item	A	B	C
Net Income (Loss)	$100,000	$ (d)	$45,000
Other Comprehensive Income (Loss)	(a)	5,300	(4,000)
Retained Earnings – Ending Balance	(b)	19,000	94,000
Retained Earnings – Beginning Balance	49,000	49,000	49,000
Accumulated Other Comprehensive Income – Ending Balance	2,000	(e)	(g)
Accumulated Other Comprehensive Income – Beginning Balance	4,000	4,000	4,000
Cash – End of Year	24,000	(f)	8,600
Cash – Beginning of Year	(c)	37,000	6,700
Increase (Decrease) in Cash	3,000	(5,000)	(h)

7 **E6-13. Subsequent Events.** For each of the following subsequent event financial statement disclosures, determine whether the treatment is proper. The fiscal year-end is December 31 in each scenario. The financial statements are issued on February 7, 2019.

a. On January 21, 2019, the Company settled a product liability lawsuit for $4.5 million. The Company had previously recorded a liability for $3.0 million related to this lawsuit. No additional liability and loss are recorded on January 21, 2019.

b. On February 15, 2019, the Company announced that it had entered into an agreement to acquire the Snap Cracker Company for approximately $1.7 billion, which it expects to fund by issuing approximately $1.5 billion of long-term debt. The transaction is subject to customary conditions, including the receipt of regulatory approval. The Company expects the transaction to close in fall 2019. The company did not record a journal entry or prepare a footnote.

c. On February 2, 2019, an earthquake destroyed the Company's pasta manufacturing facility in Italy, causing $2.6 million in losses that reduced its 2018 net income.

8 **E6-14. Contents of the Annual Report.** Use ***Johnson & Johnson's*** 2016 Annual Report, 10-K, to answer the following questions. You can locate ***Johnson & Johnson's*** financial statements on its Web site, the Securities and Exchange Commission's Web site of company reports, or the accompanying textbook Web site.

a. From Item 1, Business, how does the management describe ***Johnson & Johnson's*** business? What are ***Johnson & Johnson's*** main business segments?

b. In Item 7, Management Discussion and Analysis, on the top of page 15, ***Johnson & Johnson*** decomposed its annual change in sales into three factors. What are these three factors?

c. In Item 7, Management Discussion and Analysis, starting on page 23, ***Johnson & Johnson*** provides an analysis of Income Before Tax by Segment. Which business segment or segments show increasing income before tax?

d. In Item 7, Management Discussion and Analysis, on page 24, ***Johnson & Johnson*** begins to discuss Liquidity and Capital Resources. From the first paragraph in Liquidity and Capital Resources, what are ***Johnson & Johnson's*** primary sources and uses of cash?

e. In Item 7, Management Discussion and Analysis, on pages 26–27, ***Johnson & Johnson*** discusses its Critical Accounting Policies and Estimates. What accounting topics does it discuss?

f. How many footnotes are in ***Johnson & Johnson's*** financial statements?

g. What accounting firm performed ***Johnson & Johnson's*** independent audit?

h. Who signed ***Johnson & Johnson's*** Management's report on internal control over financial reporting?

A **E6-15. Statement of Cash Flows, Indirect Method.** Use the following information Hockey Apparel Providers, Inc. provided for the current year to compute net cash flow from operating activities under the indirect reporting format.

Hockey Apparel Providers, Inc.
Statement of Net Income
for the Current Year Ended

	Amount
Sales	$2,452,000
Cost of Goods Sold	(1,251,000)
Depreciation Expense	(178,000)
Selling, General, and Administrative Expenses	(558,000)
Operating Income	465,000
Tax Expense	(145,000)
Net Income	$ 320,000

Changes in Balance Sheet Accounts	**Amount**
Decrease in Accounts Receivable	$ 29,000
Decrease in Inventory	43,000
Increase in Prepaid Expenses	9,000
Decrease in Accounts Payable	34,000
Increase in Income Taxes Payable	32,000

A **E6-16. Statement of Cash Flows, Direct Method.** Use the information from E6-15 that Hockey Apparel Providers, Inc. provided for the current year to compute net cash flow from operating activities under the direct reporting format.

B **E6-17. Liquidity Analyses.** Use the following excerpt of Dragonfly Corporation's asset balances to compute Dragonfly's working capital and current ratio for 2019 and 2018. Comment on Dragonfly's liquidity and changes in liquidity from 2018 to 2019. Dragonfly's current liabilities are $89,754 million and $82,271 million in 2019 and 2018, respectively.

Assets (dollars in millions)	**2019**	**2018**
Current assets		
Cash and cash equivalents	$ 13,420	$ 19,355
Marketable securities	7,623	2,394
Accounts receivable trade – net	22,120	20,872
Inventories	47,415	45,630
Prepaid expenses and other receivables	1,312	1,264
Total current assets	91,890	89,515
Property, plant, and equipment – net	67,045	65,762
Other assets	3,773	3,770
Total assets	$162,708	$159,047

B **E6-18. Solvency Analyses.** The following items are from the financial statements of Tall Oak Company.

Item	**2019**	**2018**
Total liabilities	$450,000	$414,000
Total stockholders' equity	634,000	621,000
Net income	63,000	61,000
Tax expense	18,900	18,300
Interest expense	13,500	12,420
Interest paid	12,100	13,660

Compute Tall Oak's debt-to-equity ratio and interest coverage ratio for 2018 and 2019. Comment on Tall Oak's solvency and changes in solvency from 2018 to 2019.

Problems

❸ **P6-1. Prepare Balance Sheet.** Larkin Corporation provided the following account balances prepared at December 31 of the current year.

Account	Debit	Credit
Additional paid-in capital		$ 891,500
Dividends payable		10,000
Equipment under capital lease	$ 375,000	
Intangible assets – net	324,500	
Merchandise inventory	877,185	
Income taxes payable		200,800
Cash	630,000	
Notes payable, due in 10 years		725,000
Accumulated other comprehensive loss	235,000	
Current portion of long-term debt		345,000
Property, plant, and equipment – net	3,245,000	
Investments in affiliate companies (noncurrent)	123,543	
Accounts receivable	240,007	
Bonds payable, due in 20 years		1,000,000
Investments at fair value (current)	678,590	
Accounts payable		500,500
Retained earnings		1,250,750
Obligations under capital leases		240,000
Obligations under pension plans		609,575
Deferred tax liability (noncurrent)		330,700
Common stock, $1 par value		625,000

Required »

a. Prepare the balance sheet at December 31st using the report format.
b. Prepare the balance sheet at December 31st using the account format.

❸ **P6-2. Prepare Balance Sheet.** Using the information provided by Larkin Corporation in P6-1, restructure the balance sheet for December 31 of the current year using the report format with the following change in assumptions:

1. The investments at fair value are held in a noncurrent asset fund created for the purpose of liquidating long-term debt.
2. The firm will use the earnings on fund investments to pay the current portion of long-term debt each year.

❸ **P6-3. Prepare Balance Sheet.** Jennings Incorporated provided the following account balances at December 31 for the current year.

Account	Debit	Credit
Investments at fair value (trading)	$ 340,000	
Accounts payable		$324,560
Additional paid-in capital		700,000
Dividends payable		35,400
Equipment under capital lease	670,000	
Intangible assets – net	123,000	
Merchandise inventory	890,125	
Income taxes payable		65,000
Cash	187,000	

Account	Debit	Credit
Notes payable, due in 10 years		800,000
Retained earnings		713,000
Obligations under capital leases (noncurrent)		640,000
Obligations under pension plans		325,675
Deferred tax liability (noncurrent)		25,000
Accumulated other comprehensive income		235,750
Current portion of long-term debt		76,000
Property, plant, and equipment – net	1,567,500	
Investments in affiliate companies (noncurrent)	493,960	
Accounts receivable	450,000	
Bonds payable, due in 20 years		606,700
Common stock, $1 par value		174,500

Required »

a. Prepare the balance sheet at December 31 using the report format.
b. Prepare the balance sheet at December 31 using the account format.

3 **P6-4. Prepare Stockholders' Equity Section of Balance Sheet.** Delaney Products, Inc. provided the following information from its current-year trial balance.

Account	Debit	Credit
Gain on disposal of plant assets		$ 890
Dividends	$ 125	
Cost of goods sold	25,000	
Selling expenses	5,000	
Dividend income		866
Advertising expense	7,000	
Office salaries expense	6,700	
Depreciation expense	8,250	
Systems consulting fees expense	350	
Loss on asset impairment	467	
Unrealized gain on trading investments		200
Accounting and legal fees expense	300	
Loss on discontinued operations before tax	1,000	
Office supplies expense	2,000	
Interest income		4,000
Gain on uninsured flood damage before tax		5,600
Unrealized loss on available-for-sale bonds before tax	933	
Amortization expense	5,500	
Interest expense	900	
Sales salaries expense	2,100	
Sales		400,000
Retained earnings: beginning balance		750,000
Accumulated other comprehensive income: beginning balance		210,000
Common stock – no par: beginning balance		82,000

Delaney issued $55,000 of no-par common stock on October 1 of the current year. The company also repurchased $13,500 of its shares at the end of the reporting period. The company is subject to a 40% income tax rate.

Required »

Prepare the stockholders' equity section of the balance sheet at December 31 of the current year. Round to the nearest dollar.

3 **P6-5. Prepare Stockholders' Equity Section of Balance Sheet.** Society Teas, Inc. provided the following information from its current-year trial balance.

Account	Debit	Credit
Loss on disposal of plant assets	$ 740	
Dividends	790	
Cost of goods sold	548,450	
Selling expenses	70,515	
Dividend income		$ 65
Advertising expense	39,175	
Office salaries expense	6,268	
Depreciation expense	94,020	
Loss on asset impairment	3,250	
Accounting and legal fees	15,600	
Interest income		712
Unrealized loss on available-for-sale bonds before tax	450	
Interest expense	9,600	
Sales		783,500
Retained earnings: beginning balance		368,900
Accumulated other comprehensive loss: beginning balance	5,700	
Common stock – no par: beginning balance		85,800

Society Teas issued $5,400 of no-par common stock on April 1 of the current year.

Required »

Prepare the stockholders' equity section of the balance sheet at December 31 of the current year. Ignore taxes.

3 **P6-6. Prepare Classified Balance Sheet.** Centre Company provided the following listing of the current year's post-closing account balances.

Account	Debit	Credit
Cash	***Solve***	
Notes payable, due in 10 years		$12,000
Treasury stock at cost	$ 5,600	
Accumulated other comprehensive income		1,000
Current portion of long-term debt		500
Property, plant, and equipment – net	46,500	
Investments in affiliate companies (noncurrent)	3,000	
Accounts receivable	8,000	
Bonds payable, due in 20 years		20,000
Common stock, $1 par value		15,000
Investments at fair value (available-for-sale) (noncurrent)	2,100	
Accounts payable		6,200
Additional paid-in capital		14,800
Dividends payable		300
Intangible assets – net	4,000	
Merchandise inventory	5,800	
Income taxes payable		1,500
Retained earnings		6,800

Centre reported net income of $3,200 and declared dividends amounting to $600. Unrealized losses on the company's available-for-sale portfolio amounted to $400 for the current year. There are no other events that affect stockholders' equity.

Required »

Prepare a classified balance sheet at December 31 of the current year.

6 **P6-7. Financial Statement Articulation.** Use the *Foot Locker, Inc.'s* 2015 financial statements found in its 2015 annual report to complete the following financial statement articulation worksheets. You can locate *Foot Locker's* financial statements on its Web site or the Securities and Exchange Commission's Web site of company reports.

STATEMENT OF COMPREHENSIVE INCOME

Revenues:	
Expenses:	
Net Income or Loss	***(A)***
Other Comprehensive Income	***(B)***
Comprehensive Income	

STATEMENT OF STOCKHOLDERS' EQUITY

	Retained Earnings	Accumulated Other Comprehensive Loss
Beginning Balance		
Net Income	***(A)***	
Other Comprehensive Income		***(B)***
Dividends		
Ending Balance	***(C)***	***(D)***

STATEMENT OF CASH FLOWS

Operating Activities:	
Net Income or Loss	***(A)***
Investing Activities:	
Financing Activities:	
Increase (Decrease) in Cash and Cash Equivalents	***(G)***
Add: Beginning Cash and Cash Equivalents	***(E)***
Ending Cash and Cash Equivalents	***(F)***

BALANCE SHEETS

	Beginning of Year	End of Year
Assets		
Current Assets		
Cash and Cash Equivalents	***(E)***	***(F)***
Noncurrent Assets		
Total Assets		
Liabilities		
Current Liabilities		
Noncurrent Liabilities		
Stockholders' Equity		
Capital Stock		
Additional Paid-in Capital		
Retained Earnings		***(C)***
Accumulated Other Comprehensive Income		***(D)***
Total Liabilities & Stockholders' Equity		

7 8 **P6-8. Contents of the Annual Report, Financial Statement Notes.** Use the 2015 Annual Report, 10-K, of *Foot Locker, Inc.*, to answer the following questions. You can locate *Foot Locker's* financial statements on its Web site or the Securities and Exchange Commission's Web site of company reports.

a. What sections are included in the 10-K?
b. From Item 1, Business, how does management describe *Foot Locker, Inc.'s* business?
c. From Item 6, Selected Financial Data, how many years of information does *Foot Locker* provide? What are the four main areas for which *Foot Locker* provides data?
d. From Item 7, Management's Discussion and Analysis, *Foot Locker* provides an "Overview of Consolidated Results." What are the main income statement numbers highlighted?
e. From the Management's Discussion and Analysis starting on the page numbered 24 of *Foot Locker's* 10-K in its Annual Report, *Foot Locker* discusses "Liquidity and Capital Resources." What are *Foot Locker's* primary sources of liquidity? What are *Foot Locker's* primary uses of cash?
f. What accounting firm performed *Foot Locker's* independent audit? What type of opinion did *Foot Locker* receive?
g. How many notes accompany *Foot Locker's* financial statements? Does *Foot Locker* report any subsequent events? Does *Foot Locker* report any related parties or related-party transactions?

A **P6-9. Statement of Cash Flows, Operating Activities Section, Direct Method.** Snail Company provided the following balance sheet and income statement for the current year. Prepare the operating activities section of the cash flow statement using the direct method. Accrued expenses relate to Selling, General and Administrative Expenses.

Snail Company
Balance Sheet
At December 31

Assets	**Ending**	**Beginning**
Current Assets		
Cash	$ 1,000	$ 5,000
Accounts Receivable	5,500	7,000
Merchandise Inventory	4,000	1,800
Total Current Assets	$10,500	$13,800
Noncurrent Assets		
Investments in Bonds	$30,000	$ 6,000
Property, Plant, and Equipment – net	$50,000	$60,000
Total Noncurrent Assets	$80,000	$66,000
Total Assets	$90,500	$79,800
Liabilities		
Current Liabilities		
Accounts Payable	$ 3,200	$ 4,400
Accrued Expenses	6,700	6,550
Income Taxes Payable	1,500	450
Total Current Liabilities	$11,400	$11,400
Noncurrent Liabilities		
Notes Payable	$35,000	$30,000
Total Noncurrent Liabilities	$35,000	$30,000
Total Liabilities	$46,400	$41,400
Stockholders' Equity		
Common Stock, $1 Par Value	$10,000	$ 9,000
Additional Paid-in Capital	15,334	12,000
Retained Earnings	18,766	17,400
Total Stockholders' Equity	$44,100	$38,400
Total Liabilities and Stockholders' Equity	$90,500	$79,800

Snail Company
Income Statement
For the year ended December 31

Sales	$56,000
Cost of Goods Sold	33,600
Gross Profit	$22,400
Selling, General, and Administrative Expenses	$ 11,600
Depreciation Expense	6,000
Total Operating Expenses	$ 17,600
Income Before Interest and Taxes	$ 4,800
Interest Expense	$ (2,100)
Income Before Tax	$ 2,700
Income Tax Expense	(1,334)
Net Income	$ 1,366

Ⓐ **P6-10. Statement of Cash Flows, Operating Activities Section, Indirect Method.** Repeat the requirements of P6-9 under the indirect method.

Ⓐ **P6-11. Statement of Cash Flows, Direct Method.** Prepare the statement of cash flows under the direct method for the Snail Company using the information from P6-9 and the following cash flow information:

Description	Cash Inflow (Outflow)
Cash receipt from sale of property, plant, and equipment	$ 4,000
Cash payment to acquire investment securities	(24,000)
Cash receipt from issuance of common stock	4,334
Cash receipt from issuance of loan	5,000

Ⓐ **P6-12. Statement of Cash Flows, Indirect Method.** Prepare the statement of cash flows under the indirect method for Snail Company using the information from P6-10 and the following cash flow information:

Description	Cash Inflow (Outflow)
Cash receipt from sale of property, plant, and equipment	$ 4,000
Cash payment to acquire investment securities	(24,000)
Cash receipt from issuance of common stock	4,334
Cash receipt from issuance of loan	5,000

Ⓐ **P6-13. Statement of Cash Flows, Operating Activities Section, Direct Method.** Easthoff, Incorporated provided the following balance sheets and income statement for the current year. Prepare the operating activities section of the cash flow statement using the direct method. Accrued expenses relate to Selling, General, and Administrative Expenses.

Easthoff, Incorporated
Balance Sheet
At December 31

Assets	Ending	Beginning
Current Assets		
Cash	$ 7,000	$ 3,500
Accounts Receivable	8,500	8,000
Merchandise Inventory	2,300	4,000
Prepaid Expenses	1,700	2,200
Total Current Assets	$ 19,500	$ 17,700
Noncurrent Assets		
Investments	$ 12,000	$ 24,300
Property, Plant, and Equipment – net	75,000	58,000
Total Noncurrent Assets	$ 87,000	$ 82,300
Total Assets	$106,500	$100,000
Liabilities		
Current Liabilities		
Accounts Payable	$ 4,500	$ 1,000
Accrued Expenses	9,800	5,120
Income Taxes Payable	6,000	4,850
Total Current Liabilities	$ 20,300	$ 10,970
Noncurrent Liabilities		
Notes Payable	$ 31,000	$ 42,630
Total Noncurrent Liabilities	31,000	42,630
Total Liabilities	$ 51,300	$ 53,600
Stockholders' Equity		
Common Stock, $1 par value	$ 10,000	$ 9,000
Additional Paid-In Capital	24,700	20,000
Retained Earnings	20,500	17,400
Total Stockholders' Equity	$ 55,200	$ 46,400
Total Liabilities and Stockholders' Equity	$106,500	$100,000

Easthoff, Incorporated
Income Statement
For the year ended December 31

Sales	$80,085
Cost of Goods Sold	48,051
Gross Profit	32,034
Selling, General, and Administrative Expenses	10,700
Depreciation Expense	2,400
Total Operating Expenses	13,100
Income Before Interest and Taxes	18,934
Interest Expense	(4,000)
Income Before Tax	14,934
Income Tax Expense	(7,334)
Net Income	$ 7,600

A **P6-14. Statement of Cash Flows, Operating Activities Section, Indirect Method.** Repeat the requirements in P6-13 using the indirect method.

A **P6-15. Statement of Cash Flows, Direct Method.** Prepare the statement of cash flows under the direct method for Easthoff, Incorporated using the information from P6-13 and the following cash flow information:

Description	**Cash Inflow (Outflow)**
Cash received on common stock issue	$ 5,700
Cash payments for dividends	(4,500)
Cash payment for acquisition of property, plant, and equipment	(19,400)
Cash receipt from the sale of investment securities	12,300
Cash payments for repayment of notes	(11,630)

A **P6-16. Statement of Cash Flows, Indirect Method.** Prepare the statement of cash flows under the indirect method for Easthoff, Incorporated using the information from P6-14 and the following cash flow information:

Description	**Cash Inflow (Outflow)**
Cash received on common stock issue	$ 5,700
Cash payments for dividends	(4,500)
Cash payment for acquisition of property, plant, and equipment	(19,400)
Cash receipt from the sale of investment securities	12,300
Cash payments for repayment of notes	(11,630)

Excel Project

Autograded Excel Project available in **MyLab Accounting**

CASES

Judgment Cases

Judgment Case 1: Balance Sheet Management

The CFO of First Things Computing, Inc. (FTC) prepared the following balance sheet as of December 31, 2019.

First Things Computing, Inc.
Balance Sheet
As of December 31, 2019

Assets	
Current Assets:	
Cash	$ 5,000
Trading Securities at Fair Value	700
Accounts Receivable – net	11,000
Merchandise Inventory	24,000
Office Supplies	600
Prepaid Rent	200
Total Current Assets	$ 41,500
Noncurrent Assets:	
Investments	$ 15,000
Property, Plant, and Equipment	
Land	20,000
Buildings	80,000
Machinery and Equipment	70,000
Less: Accumulated Depreciation	(62,000)
Total Property, Plant, and Equipment – net	108,000
Deferred Tax Asset	5,000
Intangible Assets: Franchise – net	4,500
Other Assets	3,100
Total Noncurrent Assets	$135,600
Total Assets	$ 177,100
Liabilities	
Current Liabilities:	
Accounts Payable	$ 2,700
Short-term Notes Payable	1,000
Current Portion of Long-term Debt	300
Interest Payable	200
Income Taxes Payable	1,500
Unearned Revenue	5,400
Total Current Liabilities	$ 11,100
Noncurrent Liabilities:	
Notes Payable, due 10 years	$ 40,000
Bonds Payable, due 20 years	60,000
Total Noncurrent Liabilities	100,000
Total Liabilities	$ 111,100
Stockholders' Equity	
Common Stock – at par	$ 20,000
Additional Paid-in Capital	30,000
Retained Earnings	5,000
Accumulated Other Comprehensive Income	11,000
Total Stockholders' Equity	$ 66,000
Total Liabilities and Stockholders' Equity	$ 177,100

For the sake of simplicity, assume that FTC does not incur income tax expense. Thus, the impact on equity can be computed as the combination of the impact on assets and the impact on the liabilities.

The CFO must make the following adjustments before finalizing the financial statements:

1. FTC will need to record some amount of bad debt expense. The offset will be a reduction in accounts receivable. This adjustment is a matter of judgment, and reasonable estimates range between $1,000 and $3,000.
2. FTC will need to write down its inventory (i.e., reduce the reported value of inventory). The offset will be to cost of goods sold. This adjustment is a matter of judgment, and reasonable estimates range between $2,500 and $3,750.
3. FTC may need to record an impairment loss on its PPE (i.e., reduce the reported value of PPE). The offset will be an impairment loss reported on the statement of net income. This adjustment is a matter of judgment, and reasonable estimates range between $0 and $5,000.
4. FTC may need to record an impairment loss on its noncurrent investments (i.e., reduce the reported value of noncurrent investments). The offset will be an impairment loss reported on the statement of net income. This adjustment is a matter of judgment, and reasonable estimates range between $250 and $750.
5. FTC may need to record a litigation contingency (i.e., it may need to record a liability for an unresolved lawsuit). The offset is to litigation expense. The lawsuit is expected to be settled in 2020. FTC's attorneys believe that they can provide a point estimate of amount for which FTC will be liable. The estimate will either be $2,000 or $10,000.
6. FTC may need to reduce the reported amount of its deferred tax asset. The amount by which the asset needs to be reduced is highly judgmental and ranges from $0 to $5,000. The offset to this adjustment is income tax expense. Assume the deferred tax asset is noncurrent.
7. FTC currently has unearned revenue on its balance sheet of $5,400. Up to $5,000 of this amount could possibly be recognized as revenue in 2019. However, this amount is a matter of judgment.

Required »

a. If FTC makes the most conservative choices for all these adjustments that will result in the lowest net income number, what is the impact on assets and liabilities in terms of absolute dollar impact and percentage change?

b. If FTC makes the least conservative choices for all these adjustments that will result in the highest net income number, what is the impact on assets and liabilities in terms of absolute dollar impact and percentage change?

c. What is the impact on the current ratio and the debt-to-equity ratio of these choices if management makes the most conservative choices? What is the impact on these ratios if management makes the least conservative choices?

d. Do you think that the management of FTC will care very much about the choices related to these adjustments?

Financial Statement Analysis Case

Financial Statement Analysis Case 1: Liquidity, Solvency, and DuPont Analysis of *Foot Locker*

Use ***Foot Locker, Inc.'s*** balance sheet and other information provided on the next page to answer the following questions.

a. Compute ***Foot Locker's*** working capital in 2015 and 2014.

b. Compute ***Foot Locker's*** current ratio in 2015 and 2014.

c. Comment on what the working capital and current ratio indicate about ***Foot Locker*** in 2015 and 2014.

d. Compute ***Foot Locker's*** debt-to-equity ratio for 2015 and 2014. Comment on what the debt-to-equity ratio indicates about ***Foot Locker*** in 2015 and 2014.

e. Use DuPont analysis to decompose ***Foot Locker's*** return on equity into return on assets and financial leverage. ***Foot Locker's*** net income in 2015 was $541 million. Comment on the effect of financial leverage on return on equity.

Foot Locker, Inc.

CONSOLIDATED BALANCE SHEETS

	2015	2014
	(in millions)	
ASSETS		
Current Assets		
Cash and cash equivalents	**$1,021**	$ 967
Merchandise inventories	**1,285**	1,250
Other current assets	**300**	239
Total Current Assets	**2,606**	2,456
Property and Equipment – net	**661**	620
Deferred Taxes	**234**	221
Goodwill	**156**	157
Other Intangible Assets – net	**45**	49
Other Assets	**73**	74
Total Assets	**$3,775**	$3,577
LIABILITIES AND SHAREHOLDERS' EQUITY		
Current Liabilities		
Accounts payable	**$ 279**	$ 301
Accrued and other liabilities	**420**	393
Current portion of capital lease obligations	**1**	2
Total Current Liabilities	**700**	696
Long-Term Debt and Obligations under Capital Leases	**129**	132
Other Liabilities	**393**	253
Total Liabilities	**1,222**	1,081
Total Shareholders' Equity	**2,553**	2,496
Total Liabilities and Shareholders' Equity	**$3,775**	$3,577

Source: Foot Locker. http://www.footlocker-inc.com/ns/annual-report-2015

Surfing the Standards Cases

Surfing the Standards Case 1: Liquidation Accounting

Techy Corporation, a calendar-year company, manufactures innovative technological equipment. Techy began experiencing extensive financial difficulties in the current fiscal year due to the entrance of several competitors into the industry. On December 31, Techy's Board of Directors approved a plan for liquidation. The Board has the authority to make this decision and there are no other parties that could block the plan.

The balance sheet for Techy is on the next page followed by additional information. Using the codification as a guide, prepare a statement of net assets in liquidation for Techy Corporation for December 31 of the current year. Provide a discussion for each additional item of information that explains any necessary adjustments or why an adjustment is not necessary.

Techy Corporation Balance Sheet
As of December 31

Assets	
Current Assets:	
Cash	$ 95,000
Trading Securities at fair value	7,200
Accounts Receivable – net	154,500
Merchandise Inventory	99,000
Other Current Assets	15,800
Total Current Assets	$ 371,500
Noncurrent Assets:	
Investments at fair value	$ 98,000
Property, Plant, and Equipment	
Land	550,000
Buildings	789,000
Machinery and Equipment	351,000
Less: Accumulated Depreciation	(395,400)
Total Property, Plant, and Equipment – net	1,294,600
Total Noncurrent Assets	$1,392,600
Total Assets	$1,764,100
Liabilities	
Current Liabilities:	
Accounts Payable	$ 37,000
Short-term Notes Payable	6,500
Current Portion of Long-term Debt	25,000
Accrued Liabilities	6,400
Unearned Revenue	5,400
Total Current Liabilities	$ 80,300
Noncurrent Liabilities:	
Notes Payable	$ 320,000
Bonds Payable	570,000
Total Noncurrent Liabilities	$ 890,000
Total Liabilities	$ 970,300
Stockholders' Equity	
Common Stock – at par	$ 140,000
Additional Paid-in Capital	275,000
Accumulated Other Comprehensive Income	35,000
Retained Earnings	343,800
Total Stockholders' Equity	$ 793,800
Total Liabilities and Stockholders' Equity	$1,764,100

1. Techy has a backorder on one of its products that it plans on fulfilling for 100 units at a selling price of $1,500 per unit. Techy expects to incur payroll costs of $45,000 related to this back order.
2. Techy's investments and trading securities are all investments in entities that are traded in highly liquid markets. Techy typically incurs brokerage fees of 1% to trade these securities.
3. Techy has discussed selling its accounts receivable to another party. The potential buyer has indicated that it will purchase the receivables at a 10% discount. Techy does not anticipate any significant costs to this transaction.
4. Techy plans on selling its remaining merchandise inventory to a competitor. The competitor will purchase the inventory at Techy's cost.

5. Techy does not anticipate that it will have the ability to sell any of its other current assets, which are mostly prepaid items.
6. Although the fair value of the property, plant, and equipment is close to $2 million, Techy management does not believe that it will be able to receive this much from property due to the speed with which it will need to be disposed. Management estimates that the property, plant, and equipment will sell for $1.5 million. They anticipate costs associated with the disposal of 6% of consideration received.
7. Techy anticipates that it will receive special terms from the bank that holds its note and will most likely need to repay only 80% of the balance. It is likely that the other liabilities of the firm will be paid off as originally scheduled.
8. Techy holds several patents that are not reported on its balance sheet. Management expects to sell these patents for $550,000. They anticipate incurring costs of disposal of $27,000.

Surfing the Standards Case 2: True and Fair Override

IFRS has a feature commonly referred to as the *true and fair override.* Read *International Accounting Standard 1*, paragraphs 19 through 24.

1. What is the true and fair override, and should it be used frequently?
2. When can an entity use the true and fair override and what should management consider in deciding whether to use the true and fair override?

Basis for Conclusions Cases

Basis for Conclusions Case 1: Liquidation Accounting

If liquidation is imminent for an entity, then the company must use the liquidation basis of accounting. The rules for the liquidation basis of accounting were set forth in ASU 2013-07 and subsequently incorporated into the codification.

When the FASB was deliberating on the issue of the liquidation basis of accounting, the board addressed when the entity should start applying liquidation accounting. Originally, prior to issuing an exposure draft, FASB had decided that liquidation would be considered imminent when the plan for liquidation had been approved by the parties that had the authority to do so.

1. What problem did the FASB discover with this approach? What did it then conclude should be done?

Later, the FASB issued an exposure draft on the liquidation basis of accounting. Many of the respondents to the exposure draft expressed a concern with the definition of "imminent."

2. What concern did the respondents express? What was the board's response?

Other issues related to the liquidation basis of accounting involve the measurement bases used. The recognition bases under liquidation accounting are generally inconsistent with the measurement used in general-purpose financial statements.

3. How did the FASB respond to this contradiction within its own framework?

The FASB concluded that in measuring assets under the liquidation basis of accounting, the entity should measure the assets based on the amounts it expects to receive.

4. Why did the FASB not just state that the measurement should be based on fair value? Is it correct that fair value is the same as the amounts the entity expects to receive in liquidation?

The FASB also concluded that liabilities should not be written down until the entity is legally released from them.

5. What was FASB's reasoning for this conclusion?

Basis for Conclusions Case 2: Notes to the Financial Statements

On March 4, 2014, the FASB issued an exposure draft on *Conceptual Framework for Financial Reporting - Chapter 8: Notes to Financial Statements*. The purpose of this project is to identify a broad range of possibilities for the board to consider when it makes disclosure rules related to particular topics.

1. An issue arose in deliberations of this exposure draft related to whether the FASB should require disclosure of alternative measures. For example, an entity would record the historical cost of an asset on the face of the balance sheet but be required to disclose its fair value. What are the pros and cons of requiring alternative disclosures in some circumstances? What did the FASB decide?
2. Another issue in the deliberations related to whether future-oriented information should be included in the disclosures to the financial statements. Why were some respondents opposed to including this information in the notes to the financial statements? What did the FASB decide?

APPENDIX A

Overview of the Preparation of the Statement of Cash Flows

We outlined the purpose of the statement of cash flows and its classifications in the chapter. In this appendix, we provide an overview of the preparation of the statement.[27]

Reporting Cash Flows from Operating Activities: Indirect Method

The indirect method begins with net income from the income statement and then reconciles the net income to net cash provided by operating activities. Reconciling items are separated into two groups:

- Adjustments for items such as depreciation expense and unrealized gains and losses.
- Changes in operating assets and liabilities such as increases in accounts payable or decreases in inventory.

Exhibit 6A.1 shows the effects of changes in specific common current assets and current liabilities.

EXHIBIT 6A.1 The Effect of Changes in Current Assets and Current Liabilities

Current Asset/ Liability	Increase/ Decrease	Effect on Cash Flow	Rationale	Action
Trade Receivables	Increase	Decrease	An increase in trade receivables represents uncollected sales.	Deduct the amount of the increase from net income to adjust sales to the amount of cash collected from customers.
	Decrease	Increase	A decrease in trade receivables indicates that all of this year's sales as well as a portion of prior years' sales were collected.	Add the amount of the decrease back to net income to adjust sales to the amount of cash collected from customers.
Inventory	Increase	Decrease	An increase in inventory indicates the company acquired inventory to cover the cost of goods sold and increased inventory held in the warehouse. The increase in warehouse inventory results in additional cash outflow to pay for this inventory.	Deduct the amount from net income to adjust cost of goods sold to cash paid for purchases.
	Decrease	Increase	A decrease in inventory indicates that of the cost of inventory sold this year, some of the units sold were purchased in prior years.	Add the amount back to net income to adjust the cost of goods sold to the cash paid for inventory.
Prepaid Expenses	Increase	Decrease	An increase in prepaid expenses is a cash outflow that appears on the balance sheet and does not affect net income. However, the cash is paid as part of cash outflow from operations.	Deduct the increase in prepaid expense from net income to adjust to the amount of cash paid for operating expenses.

[27]We provide an in-depth discussion of the preparation of the statement of cash flows in Chapter 22.

Current Asset/ Liability	Increase/ Decrease	Effect on Cash Flow	Rationale	Action
Prepaid Expenses	Decrease	Increase	A decrease in prepaid expenses represents a cash outflow made in a previous period that is reflected as an expense on the income statement in the current period.	Add the decreased amount back to net income to arrive at cash paid for operating expenses.
Accounts Payable	Increase	Increase	An accounts payable increase represents invoices for inventory not paid in the current year.	Add the increase in accounts payable to net income to adjust cost of goods sold to cash paid for inventory acquired.
	Decrease	Decrease	If accounts payable decreases, the current invoices as well as a portion of last year's invoices were paid.	Deduct this decrease from net income to adjust cost of goods sold to arrive at cash paid for inventory acquired.
Accrued Expenses Payable	Increase	Increase	An accrued expense increase represents operating expenses not paid in the current year.	Add the increase in accrued expenses to net income to adjust operating expenses to cash paid to suppliers.
	Decrease	Decrease	Decreases in accrued expenses indicate that this year's operating expenses as well as a portion of prior years' expenses were paid in cash.	Deduct the decrease in accrued expenses from net income to adjust operating expenses to cash paid to suppliers.

Example 6A.1 provides a comprehensive illustration of the preparation of the operating activities section of the statement of cash flows under the indirect method.

EXAMPLE 6A.1

Operating Cash Flows: Indirect Method

PROBLEM: Aries Endoscope, Inc. presents the following income statement and select balance sheet accounts. Prepare the operating cash flows section of the cash flow statement using the indirect method.

Aries Endoscope, Inc.
Statement of Net Income
For the Current Year Ended

Sales Revenue	$1,345,000
Cost of Goods Sold	852,000
Gross Profit	493,000
Wage Expense	54,000
General and Administrative Expenses	112,000
Depreciation Expense	27,000
Operating Income	300,000
Interest Expense	10,000
Income before Taxes	290,000
Income Tax Expense	87,000
Net Income	$ 203,000

Additional information:

Select Balance Sheet Accounts

Account	Beginning	Ending
Accounts Receivable	$ 20,000	$ 15,250
Inventory	543,400	575,300
Prepaid Expenses	12,450	10,590
Accounts Payable	55,670	52,000
Wages Payable	5,400	6,700
Interest Payable	2,250	2,000

SOLUTION: We begin with net income and adjust for noncash expenses. From the income statement and additional information, we identify depreciation expense of $27,000 as a noncash expense. We add this noncash expense back to net income. There are no noncash revenues to include in the adjustments.

We then adjust for changes in the current assets and liabilities, according to Exhibit 6A.1. The following table identifies the balance sheet accounts, the change in each account, and how the change is presented in the operating cash flow section of the statement of cash flows.

Account	Ending Balance	Beginning Balance	Change	Action	Rationale
Accounts Receivable	$ 15,250	$ 20,000	$(4,750)	Add decrease	A decrease in trade receivables indicates that all of this year's sales as well as a portion of prior years' sales were collected.
Inventory	575,300	543,400	31,900	Subtract increase	An increase in inventory indicates the company acquired inventory to cover the cost of goods sold and increased inventory held in the warehouse. The increase in warehouse inventory results in additional cash outflow to pay for this inventory.
Prepaid Expenses	10,590	12,450	(1,860)	Add decrease	A decrease in prepaid expenses reduces net income but no cash is paid, so the decrease is added to net income.
Accounts Payable	52,000	55,670	(3,670)	Subtract decrease	If accounts payable decreases, the current invoices as well as a portion of last year's invoices were paid.
Wages Payable	6,700	5,400	1,300	Add increase	An increase in wages payable represents operating expenses not paid in the current year.
Interest Payable	2,000	2,250	(250)	Subtract decrease	Decreases in interest payable indicate that this year's interest expense as well as a portion of last years' interest expense was paid in cash.

The completed operating activities section of the statement of cash flows under the indirect method follows.

Aries Endoscope, Inc.
Statement of Cash Flows (Partial)
For the Current Year Ended

Operating Activities:	
Net Income	$203,000
Adjustments to reconcile net income to net cash provided by operating activities:	
Depreciation Expense	27,000
Changes in Operating Working Capital Accounts:	
Decrease in Accounts Receivable	4,750
Increase in Inventory	(31,900)
Decrease in Prepaid Expenses	1,860
Decrease in Accounts Payable	(3,670)
Increase in Wages Payable	1,300
Decrease in Interest Payable	(250)
Net Cash Provided by Operating Activities	$202,090

The Indirect Statement of Cash Flows: IFRS. IFRS does not specify the income level to use as the first line in the reconciliation of income to operating cash flows. As a result, a company can begin the reconciliation with net income or operating income.[28]

Reporting Cash Flows from Operating Activities: Direct Method

Under the direct method, companies report actual cash inflows and outflows in the operating section of the statement of cash flows by converting each income statement line item from the accrual basis to the cash basis.

Cash Collected from Customers

To compute cash collected from customers, examine the activity in accounts receivable, which increases with sales revenue and decreases with collections.

Accounts Receivable

From Balance Sheet	Beginning Balance		
From Income Statement	Sales Revenue	**Cash Collected**	*Computed*
From Balance Sheet	Ending Balance		

This approach focuses on the change in the receivables balance. An increase in accounts receivable indicates that the firm has recorded more revenue than the amount of cash it received. A decrease in accounts receivable indicates that it has recorded less revenue than the amount of cash received.

Cash Collected from Customers:

Sales Revenue
Less: Increase in Net Accounts Receivable
OR
Add: Decrease in Net Accounts Receivable
Cash Collected from Customers

[28]We provide an in-depth discussion of this difference in the preparation of the statement of cash flows in Chapter 22.

Cash Paid for Merchandise

The computation of cash paid for merchandise requires two steps. First, determine the purchases on an accrual basis. Second, determine how much cash the firm spent on these purchases.

To determine the purchases on an accrual basis, examine the activity in inventory.

Inventory

From Balance Sheet	Beginning Balance		
Computed ⟶	**Purchases**	Cost of Goods Sold	*From Income Statement*
From Balance Sheet	Ending Balance		

Next, review the activity in accounts payable because purchases are usually made on account. Use the purchases computed above to obtain cash paid for merchandise.

Accounts Payable

		Beginning Balance	*From Balance Sheet*
Computed ⟶	**Cash Paid**	**Purchases**	*From Inventory*
		Ending Balance	*From Balance Sheet*

The beginning and ending balances are obtained from the balance sheet, and cost of goods sold is reported on the income statement.

Again, we focus on the changes in the balance sheet accounts to determine the cash flow related to acquiring merchandise. If inventory increases, purchases are higher than cost of goods sold. If inventory decreases, purchases are lower than cost of goods sold. In other words, a decrease in inventory indicates that some of the units sold this year were purchased and possibly paid for in prior years.

An increase in accounts payable represents invoices for inventory not paid in the current year. A decrease in accounts payable represents invoices for inventory paid for in the current year but not purchased in the current year.

Cash Paid for Merchandise:

Cost of Goods Sold
Add: Increase in Inventory
OR
Less: Decrease in Inventory
Purchases on the Accrual Basis
Less: Increase in Accounts Payable
OR
Add: Decrease in Accounts Payable
Cash Paid for Merchandise

Cash Paid to Employees and Cash Paid for Other Accrued Expenses, Including Interest and Taxes

To compute cash paid for accrued expenses, examine the activity in related payable accounts, which increases with the expense and decreases with the cash paid. Let's use cash paid to employees and wages payable as an example:

Wages Payable

		Beginning Balance	*From Balance Sheet*
Computed	**Cash Paid**	Wage Expense	*From Income Statement*
		Ending Balance	*From Balance Sheet*

Focusing on the change in the payables balance, note that:

- An increase in the payable indicates that the firm has recorded more expense under the accrual system than the amount of cash paid out.
- A decrease in the payable indicates that the firm has recorded less expense under the accrual system than the amount of cash paid out.

Following are the computations of cash paid for wages and other accrued expenses, interest, and income taxes.[29]

Cash Paid to Employees for Wages and Other Accrued Expenses

Wage Expense
Add: Decrease in Wages Payable
OR
Less: Increase in Wages Payable
Cash Paid to Employees for Wages

Cash Paid for Interest:

Interest Expense
Add: Decrease in Interest Payable
OR
Less: Increase in Interest Payable
Cash Paid for Interest

Cash Paid for Income Taxes:

Income Tax Expense
Add: Decrease in Income Taxes Payable
OR
Less: Increase in Income Taxes Payable
Cash Paid for Income Taxes

Cash Paid for Other Operating Costs, Including Insurance and Other Prepaid Expenses

To compute cash paid for insurance and other prepaid expenses, we review the activity in the related prepaid asset account, which increases with cash paid and decreases with the expense.

	Prepaid Insurance		
From Balance Sheet	Beginning Balance		
Computed	**Cash Paid**	Insurance Expense	*From Income Statement*
From Balance Sheet	Ending Balance		

We use the changes in the prepaid balances to determine the amount and direction of cash flow related to prepaid insurance. A decrease in prepaid expenses represents a cash outflow made in a previous period that is reflected as expense on the income statement in the current period. Thus, subtract it from the accrual-basis expense to arrive at cash paid for operating expenses.

An increase in prepaid expenses is a cash outflow that appears on the balance sheet and does not affect net income. However, because the firm paid cash as part of operations, add the increase in prepaid expense to the accrual-basis expense to adjust to the amount of cash paid for operating expenses.

[29]This formula for income taxes paid is simplified because it does not consider balances in the deferred tax accounts.

Cash Paid for Insurance and Other Prepaid Expenses:

Insurance Expense	
Add: Increase in Prepaid Insurance	
OR	
Less: Decrease in Prepaid Insurance	
Cash Paid for Insurance	

EXAMPLE 6A.2

Operating Cash Flows: Direct Method

PROBLEM: Aries Endoscope, Inc. presents the following income statement and select balance sheet accounts. Prepare the operating cash flows section of the cash flow statement using the direct method.

Aries Endoscope, Inc.
Statement of Net Income
For the Current Year Ended

Sales Revenue	$1,345,000
Cost of Goods Sold	852,000
Gross Profit	493,000
Wage Expense	54,000
General and Administrative Expenses	112,000
Depreciation Expense	27,000
Operating Income	300,000
Interest Expense	10,000
Income before Taxes	290,000
Income Tax Expense	87,000
Net Income	$ 203,000

Select Balance Sheet Accounts

Account	**Beginning**	**Ending**
Accounts Receivable	$ 20,000	$ 15,250
Inventory	543,400	575,300
Prepaid Expenses	12,450	10,590
Accounts Payable	55,670	52,000
Wages Payable	5,400	6,700
Interest Payable	2,250	2,000

SOLUTION: Under the direct method, we compute each line item separately, as follows.

Cash Received from Customers	
Sales Revenue	$1,345,000
Add: Decrease in Accounts Receivable	4,750
Cash Received from Customers	$1,349,750

Cash Paid for Merchandise	
Cost of Goods Sold	$ 852,000
Add: Increase in Inventory	31,900
Accrual Basis Purchases	883,900
Add: Decrease in Accounts Payable	3,670
Cash Paid for Merchandise	$ 887,570

Cash Paid to Employees	
Wage Expense	$ 54,000
Deduct: Increase in Wages Payable	(1,300)
Cash Paid to Employees	$ 52,700

Cash Paid to Other Suppliers	
General and Administrative Expenses	$112,000
Deduct: Decrease in Prepaid Expenses	(1,860)
Cash Paid to Other Suppliers	$110,140

Interest Paid	
Interest Expense	$ 10,000
Add: Decrease in Interest Payable	250
Interest Paid	$ 10,250

Aries has no taxes payable. Therefore, taxes paid must equal tax expense.

The operating activities section of the cash flow statement is as follows:

Operating Activities	
Cash Collected from Customers	$1,349,750
Cash Paid for Merchandise	(887,570)
Cash Paid to Other Suppliers	(110,140)
Cash Paid to Employees	(52,700)
Cash Paid for Interest	(10,250)
Cash Paid for Income Taxes	(87,000)
Net Cash Provided by Operating Activities	$ 202,090

Notice that the net cash provided by operating activities under the direct approach ($202,090) is the same as the net cash provided by operating activities under the indirect approach in Example 6A.1.

Reporting Cash Flows from Investing and Financing Activities

As discussed in the text, the statement of cash flows also includes a section showing the cash flows related to investing activities and a section showing the cash flows related to financing activities. Cash flows from investing activities relate to the acquisition and disposition of productive property, investments in debt and equity securities, and making and collecting loans. Financing activities involve the cash receipts and payments from debt and equity financing.

EXAMPLE 6A.3

Investing and Financing Activities

PROBLEM: Consider Aries Endoscope, Inc. from Example 6A.2. In addition to the information presented in that example, Aries also received and paid the following amounts:

Description	Cash Inflow (Outflow)
Cash receipt from sale of property, plant, and equipment	$50,000
Cash payment for acquisition of investment securities	(20,000)
Cash receipt from loan from bank	60,000
Cash payments for repayment of loan amounts	(10,000)

Aries Endoscope had a beginning cash balance of $120,000 and an ending cash balance of $402,090. Prepare the statement of cash flows (using the direct method for the operating activities section) for Aries Endoscope, Inc.

SOLUTION: We have already prepared the operating section of the cash flow statement. We include the cash receipt from the sale of property, plant, and equipment and the cash payment for the acquisition of investment securities in the investing activities section. We include all cash transactions related to the loans in the financing activities section.

Aries Endoscope statement of cash flows is as follows:

Aries Endoscope, Inc.
Statement of Cash Flows
for the Current Year Ended

Operating Activities:	
Cash Collected from Customers	$1,349,750
Cash Paid for Merchandise	(887,570)
Cash Paid to Other Suppliers	(110,140)
Cash Paid to Employees	(52,700)
Cash Paid for Interest	(10,250)
Cash Paid for Income Taxes	(87,000)
Net Cash Provided by Operating Activities	$ 202,090
Investing Activities:	
Sold Property, Plant, and Equipment	$ 50,000
Acquired Investment Securities	(20,000)
Net Cash Provided by Investing Activities	$ 30,000
Financing Activities:	
Issued Loan	$ 60,000
Repaid Loan	(10,000)
Net Cash Provided by Financing Activities	$ 50,000
Increase in Cash for the Year	$ 282,090
Beginning Cash Balance	120,000
Ending Cash Balance	$ 402,090

APPENDIX B
Liquidity and Solvency Analysis

We introduced the importance and usefulness of ratio analysis in Chapter 5. We now continue the discussion with a focus on the key balance sheet ratios of liquidity and solvency and link these concepts through *DuPont Analysis*.

Liquidity

Recall that liquidity measures a company's ability to meet current obligations from short-term resources. Specifically, it measures how quickly a company can convert assets into cash with minimal risk of loss in order to meet its current obligations. Generally, the more liquid a company's assets, the more likely it is that the company can meet its current obligations as they come due. There are two key measures of liquidity:

1. *Working Capital*
2. *Current Ratio*

Working Capital

Working capital is equal to current assets minus current liabilities.

$$\text{Working Capital} = \text{Current Assets} - \text{Current Liabilities} \tag{6B.1}$$

When current assets are higher than current liabilities, this indicates that a company has sufficient current resources to meet its current obligations as they come due. Working capital is expressed in dollars and can vary with company size or growth. For example, the working capital of a large company will likely be higher than that of a small company simply due to the size difference. Therefore, it is important to be able to express working capital in a ratio.

Current Ratio

In contrast to working capital, the **current ratio**, also known as the working capital ratio, expresses liquidity as the ratio of current assets to current liabilities:

$$\text{Current Ratio} = \frac{\text{Current Assets}}{\text{Current Liabilities}} \tag{6B.2}$$

The numerator represents cash and the other current assets the firm expects to convert into cash within one year or operating cycle, whichever is longer. These resources are available to liquidate the short-term obligations due during the same period as the denominator. The current ratio indicates the proportion of current assets to each dollar of current liabilities. A current ratio higher than 1 typically means a company has sufficient current resources to meet its current obligations as they come due.

In practice, too much working capital or too high a current ratio can indicate that a company is forgoing profitable investment opportunities. A complete interpretation of the current ratio requires knowledge of trends and the industry in which the firm operates.

EXAMPLE 6B.1 **Liquidity Analysis of *Johnson & Johnson Company* and *Pfizer***

PROBLEM: Using information from the 2016 balance sheets of ***Johnson & Johnson*** and ***Pfizer***, answer the following questions about each company's liquidity.

a. Compute each company's working capital.
b. Compute each company's current ratio.

c. Based on total assets, which company is larger?

d. Comment on what the working capital and current ratio indicate about each company. Comment on the effect of the size of the companies in this comparison.

Fiscal year 2016 *(in millions)*	***Johnson & Johnson***	***Pfizer***
Total assets	$141,208	$171,615
Current assets	65,032	38,949
Current liabilities	26,287	31,115

SOLUTION:

(a) and (b). The table below computes the working capital and current ratio for each company.

Liquidity Measure	***Johnson & Johnson***	***Pfizer***
Working Capital = Current Assets − Current Liabilities	$65,032 − $26,287 = $38,745	$38,949 − $31,115 = $7,834
Current Ratio = Current Assets/Current Liabilities	$\frac{\$65{,}032}{\$26{,}287} = 2.47$	$\frac{\$38{,}949}{\$31{,}115} = 1.25$

c. Based on total assets, ***Pfizer*** is the larger company, with about 1.22 ($171,615/141,208) times the total assets of ***Johnson & Johnson.***

d. Both ***Johnson & Johnson*** and ***Pfizer*** have positive working capital and a current ratio more than 1. These measures indicate both companies are in a strong liquidity position. ***Johnson & Johnson's*** working capital is higher than ***Pfizer's***. Because ***Pfizer*** is the larger company, it is surprising that its working capital is not higher. However, ***Johnson & Johnson's*** current ratio (2.47) is almost double that of ***Pfizer's*** (1.25).

Solvency

Solvency measures a company's ability to meet its long-term obligations as they come due. A company can finance its operations with debt or equity. When a company decides to use debt, it has to repay the amount borrowed and generally make periodic interest payments. Both creditors and investors need to assess the company's ability to pay off its long-term obligations when due. Creditors are concerned about timely repayment; investors are interested in sharing profits and securing assets in liquidation as the residual claimants. Firms must pay principal and interest on debt before equity investors share in firm profits. If a company has too much debt, there is a risk that the firm will not be able to repay its debt and be forced to declare bankruptcy.

Two common measures of solvency are:

1. *Debt-to-equity ratio*
2. *Interest coverage*

Debt-to-Equity Ratio

Leverage is an indicator of the relative size of financing from creditors versus financing from owners. The **debt-to-equity ratio** is a measure of leverage computed as:

$$\text{Debt-to-Equity Ratio} = \frac{\text{Total Liabilities}}{\text{Total Stockholders' Equity}} \tag{6B.3}$$

A company with high debt must devote significant resources to making interest and principal payments. When operations are strong and the economy is growing, a company is generally able to make its debt payments. However, if sales decline or an economic recession occurs, the company may struggle to make debt payments. Generally, a high debt-to-equity ratio indicates lower solvency and a greater risk of default.

Interest Coverage Ratio

The **interest coverage ratio** measures a company's ability to make payments on, or service, its debt by computing the amount of interest payments that it can make from its operating earnings.[30] Operating earnings are earnings before interest expense and tax expense.[31] Adding both interest expense and tax expense back to net income provides a measure of income that is available to service debt. The interest coverage ratio equation is:

$$\text{Interest Coverage Ratio} = \frac{\text{Net Income} + \text{Interest Expense} + \text{Tax Expense}}{\text{Interest Payments}} \tag{6B.4}$$

The ratio indicates how many times a company can cover its interest charges before taxes. A high interest coverage ratio indicates that a company is able to service its debt—that is, the company has high solvency.

EXAMPLE 6B.2

Solvency Analysis of *Johnson & Johnson Company*, 2016 and 2015

PROBLEM: Using the following information from ***Johnson & Johnson's*** 2016 annual report, compute the debt-to-equity ratio and interest coverage ratio for 2015 and 2016. What does each measure indicate about ***Johnson & Johnson's*** solvency? What do the measures taken together indicate about ***Johnson & Johnson's*** solvency?

(all dollars in millions)

Balance Sheets (excerpts)	**2016**	**2015**
Total liabilities	$70,790	$62,261
Total stockholders' equity	$70,418	$69,752
Statement of Earnings (excerpts)	**2016**	**2015**
Sales to customers	$71,890	$70.074
Interest expense	726	552
Provision for taxes on income	3,263	3,787
Net earnings	$16,540	$15,409
Statement of Cash Flows (excerpts)	**2016**	**2015**
Interest Paid	$ 730	$ 617

SOLUTION: The table on the next page provides the computations of ***Johnson & Johnson's*** debt-to-equity ratio and interest coverage ratio for 2016 and 2015.

Johnson & Johnson's debt-to-equity ratio of 0.893 in 2015 is below 1, indicating that the company obtains more of its financing from shareholders than from creditors. In 2016, its debt-to-equity ratio is 1.005 indicating that the company obtains more of its financing from creditors than from shareholders. The ratio has increased from 2015 to 2016, implying a decrease in solvency.

The interest coverage ratio, which is 32.006 in 2015 and 28.122 in 2016, is higher than 1, indicating that ***Johnson & Johnson*** is able to service its debt from current operations. However, the ratio has decreased from 2015 to 2016, also suggesting a decrease in solvency.

[30]This ratio is also called the *times interest earned ratio.*

[31]Operating earnings are also known as *earnings before interest and taxes* or *EBIT*.

Overall, this ratio analysis suggests that ***Johnson & Johnson*** is in a strong position to meet its long-term obligations.

Solvency Measure	2016	2015
Debt-to-Equity Ratio $= \dfrac{\text{Total Liabilities}}{\text{Total Stockholders' equity}}$	$\dfrac{\$70{,}790}{\$70{,}418} = 1.005$	$\dfrac{\$62{,}261}{\$69{,}752} = 0.893$
Interest Coverage Ratio $= \dfrac{\text{Net Income + Interest Expense + Tax Expense}}{\text{Interest Payments}}$	$\dfrac{\$16{,}540 + \$726 + \$3{,}263}{\$730} = 28.122$	$\dfrac{\$15{,}409 + \$552 + \$3{,}787}{\$617} = 32.006$

Exhibit 6B.1 summarizes the liquidity and solvency ratios.

EXHIBIT 6B.1 Liquidity and Solvency Ratios

Area	Definition	Ratios	Desirable Characteristics	Pitfalls
Liquidity	A company's ability to meet short-term obligations from short-term resources	Working Capital = Current Assets − Current Liabilities	Current assets higher than current liabilities	Cannot compare across companies because of differences in size.
		Current Ratio = Current Assets/Current Liabilities	Ratio of 1 or higher	If the ratio is too high, the company may be forgoing more profitable investment opportunities. Includes assets that are not as liquid, such as inventory.
Solvency	A company's ability to meet long-term obligations as they come due	Debt-to-Equity Ratio $= \dfrac{\text{Total Liabilities}}{\text{Total Stockholders' Equity}}$	Lower ratio is preferred to higher	U.S. companies generally range between 0.8 and 1.2.
		Interest Coverage Ratio $= \dfrac{\text{Net Income + Interest Expense + Tax Expense}}{\text{Interest Payments}}$	Higher ratio is preferred to lower	Net income can include non-recurring items

DuPont Analysis

Profitability enables a company to generate a return for its shareholders. Specifically, the return on equity (ROE) ratio measures the return on shareholders' investment in the company. This return is enhanced by effective use of available resources to increase revenue.

DuPont Analysis is a financial statement analysis tool that separates ROE into components to analyze a company's sources of profitability. We focus on the form of the DuPont Analysis that indicates how a company uses debt financing to increase its return to shareholders.[32]

We begin with ROE, which is net income divided by average stockholders' equity:

$$\text{ROE} = \frac{\text{Net Income}}{\text{Average Stockholders' Equity}} \tag{6B.5}$$

[32]In subsequent chapters, we discuss other forms of the DuPont Analysis to further analyze additional aspects of profitability.

We expand the ratio by dividing net income by average total assets and multiplying by average total assets divided by average stockholders' equity:

$$\text{ROE} = \frac{\text{Net Income}}{\text{Average Total Assets}} \times \frac{\text{Average Total Assets}}{\text{Average Stockholders' Equity}} \quad (6B.6)$$

As noted in Chapter 5, net income divided by average total assets is return on assets (ROA). The second part, average total assets divided by average stockholders' equity, is another leverage ratio, called financial leverage. The lower the ratio, the lower the financing from debt. A higher ratio indicates more debt financing and higher leverage. ROE is also expressed as follows:

$$\text{ROE} = \text{Return on Assets} \times \text{Financial Leverage} \quad (6B.7)$$

From Equation 6B.7, observe that a company with a high ROA can generate a high ROE. High financial leverage also increases ROE. Exhibit 6B.2 illustrates the effect of financial leverage on return on equity. When ROA is constant, a company can increase its ROE by increasing its financial leverage.

EXHIBIT 6B.2 Effect of Financial Leverage on Return on Equity

	Return on Assets	Financial Leverage	Return on Equity
Lower Financial Leverage	10%	0.80	8%
	10%	0.90	9%
	10%	1.00	10%
	10%	1.10	11%
Higher Financial Leverage	10%	1.20	12%

Therefore, shareholders can benefit from increased profitability when a company uses debt financing. However, too much debt can increase a company's risk of bankruptcy.

EXAMPLE 6B.3 DuPont Analysis of *Johnson & Johnson Company*, 2016 and 2015

PROBLEM: In Chapter 5, we computed ***Johnson & Johnson's*** return on equity (ROE) as 23.6% and 21.9% in 2016 and 2015, respectively. Use the DuPont analysis to determine whether this increase in ROE is due to a change in return on assets or financial leverage. The following information is relevant:

(in millions)	2016	2015
Net Income	$ 16,540	$ 15,409
Average Total Assets	$ 137,310	$131,885
Average Stockholders' Equity	$ 70,085	$ 70,451

SOLUTION: Using Equation 6B.6, we compute ROE using the DuPont Analysis as follows:

$$\text{ROE} = \frac{\text{Net Income}}{\text{Average Total Assets}} \times \frac{\text{Average Total Assets}}{\text{Average Stockholders' Equity}}$$

2016	2015
$ROE = \frac{\$16,540}{\$137,310} \times \frac{\$137,310}{\$70,085}$	$ROE = \frac{\$15,409}{\$131,885} \times \frac{\$131,885}{\$70,451}$
$= 12.05\% \times 1.959$	$= 11.68\% \times 1.872$
$= 23.6\%$	$= 21.9\%$

Separating ROE into ROA and financial leverage indicates that ***Johnson & Johnson's*** ROA increased to 12.05% in 2016 from 11.68% in 2015, representing an approximate 3.2% increase from the prior year [(12.05% − 11.68%)/11.68%]. The company's financial leverage also increased to 1.959 in 2016 from 1.872 in 2015. This is approximately a 4.6% increase from the prior year [(1.959 − 1.872)/1.872]. The increase in financial leverage and increase in ROA suggest that ***Johnson & Johnson's*** increase in ROE is due both to the increasing ROA and financial leverage.

7 Accounting and the Time Value of Money

LEARNING OBJECTIVES

1. Explain the time value of money concept, including the calculations of simple and compound interest; define the effective interest rate.
2. Compute solutions to future value and present value of single-sum problems.
3. Compute solutions to future value of ordinary annuity and annuity due problems.
4. Compute solutions to present value of ordinary annuity and annuity due problems.
5. Compute solutions to future value and present value of deferred annuity problems.
6. Apply time value of money concepts to accounting applications involving determining the present value of expected cash flows and valuing bonds.

Iain Masterton/Alamy Stock Photo

Introduction

TO DETERMINE THE VALUE of money you have in the bank today, you simply check the account balance. Yet how would you determine the amount of money you need to save each year in order to purchase a new car in the future? You first need to determine when you want to buy the car. Then, you have to decide when you will start saving. You will also have to estimate how much interest your savings will earn based on the interest rate on your savings account. After you make these estimates, mathematical techniques involving the *time value of money* enable you to compute the total amount you must save to purchase the car.

Companies use time value of money techniques in a variety of areas—from capital budgeting to assessing financing needs to determining pension obligations. Consider ***Adidas,*** the German sports footwear, apparel, and accessories company. In its 2016 annual report, ***Adidas*** stated that it used *present value* techniques to evaluate returns on planned capital expenditures. In its footnotes to the financial statements, ***Adidas*** disclosed that it used present values in accounting for receivables, leases, pensions, and asset impairments. For example, ***Adidas*** reports its receivables and other financial assets at fair value, estimating the fair value as the present value of future cash flows. In financial reporting, time value of money concepts are critical to understanding these areas and others such as long-term liabilities and the valuation of certain types of financial instruments.

This chapter discusses the fundamental concepts needed to work with the time value of money throughout the remainder of this text. We begin with the basics of the time value of money, including *simple* and *compound interest*. We then illustrate several problems involving the *future* and *present values* of a single sum. Next, we cover problems involving the future and present values of *ordinary annuities* and *annuities due*. Finally, we discuss more complex areas such as deferred annuities before highlighting selected accounting applications of the time value of money. «

1 Explain the time value of money concept, including the calculations of simple and compound interest; define the effective interest rate.

Time Value of Money Basic Concepts

The **time value of money** concept means that a dollar received today is worth more than a dollar received at some time in the future. This statement is true because a dollar received today can be invested to provide a return. For example, if you invest $1,000 in a savings account today and the savings account yields 2% annually, then you will have $1,020 one year from today. The $20 earned on the initial investment is your **interest**, the return on money over time.

Time Value of Money in Accounting

The time value of money concept is critical in several areas of accounting, particularly when valuing many of the assets and liabilities reported in the financial statements. For example, measuring assets and liabilities at fair value may require time value of money computations. Time value of money concepts determine the asset's value today based on the future cash flows it will generate. To illustrate, consider a company that leases equipment to a customer. In return, the customer pays the company periodic cash payments in the future for the use of the leased equipment. The value of the net investment in the lease today can be measured using the future cash flows the company will receive and time value of money concepts.

The same approach applies to determining the fair value of a liability. For example, a pension liability today can be measured using time value of money concepts and the future cash outflows a company promises to make to its employees when they retire. The future cash flows depend on many estimates and assumptions such as when the employee will retire, how long the employee will live after retirement, and the inflation rate.

The measurements of many financial statement items such as leases, pensions, and bonds payable are based on estimates of future cash flows and time value of money computations. Exhibit 7.1 illustrates several financial statement items and the type of future cash flows used to measure them.

EXHIBIT 7.1 Examples of Financial Statement Items Measured at the Present Value of Future Cash Flows

Financial Statement Item	Type of Future Cash Flow
Notes Receivable	A company makes a loan today and receives periodic interest payments and a principal payment at the note maturity.
Net Investment in Lease	A company provides the use of a product or property and receives periodic payments from the party to whom it gives the use of the product or property.
Warranty Liability	A company sells some products and promises to maintain, repair, or replace the products, which represent estimated future cash outflows.
Bond Payable	A company receives cash today and promises to make periodic interest payments over time and a principal payment at the bond's maturity.
Leases Obligation	A company receives the use of a product or property and promises to make periodic payments to the party from whom it obtained the use of the product or property.
Pension Obligation	A company promises to pay employees a certain amount after they retire.

We begin our discussion of the time value of money by distinguishing between two types of interest—*simple* and *compound.*

Simple Interest

The term *simple interest* means that interest is computed on only the principal (the initial amount) but is not computed on any interest earned and left on deposit. Thus, **simple interest** is the initial investment multiplied by the stated interest rate for a single period and the amount of time (in terms of the number of periods) the investment is held.

$$\text{Simple Interest} = \text{Principal} \times \text{Interest Rate} \times \text{Time} \tag{7.1}$$

EXAMPLE 7.1

Simple Interest

PROBLEM: Solitude Company borrows $60,000 for 3 years with a stated annual rate of 5%. What is the interest expense incurred by Solitude, assuming that interest is computed as simple interest?

SOLUTION: We use Equation 7.1 to compute the simple interest expense.

$$\text{Interest} = \text{Principal} \times \text{Interest Rate} \times \text{Time}$$
$$\$9{,}000 = \$60{,}000 \times 5\% \times 3 \text{ years}$$

Solitude will pay $3,000 per year in interest for a total of $9,000 at the end of the loan term.

Compound Interest

Interest computed on both the principal and the interest left on deposit is referred to as **compound interest**. Any interest earned is then immediately included in the computation of the next period's interest. The compounding period can be over any time period such as a quarter or a day.

Exhibit 7.2 provides a graphical depiction of compound interest. Assume you invest $100 today for 10 years at an annual interest rate of 10%. Today (Year 0) you have $100. After the first year, you have the original $100 plus an additional $10 ($100 × 10%) of interest. So, you now leave $110 on deposit.

During the second year, that $110 also earns 10% interest or $11 ($110 × 10%). At the end of the second year, your deposit is valued at $121 ($100 + $10 + $11). This pattern continues until the tenth year, when you have a total of $259, which consists of your original deposit or principal of $100 plus $100 of interest earned on the principal ($100 × 10% × 10 years) and $59 of interest earned on the interest left on deposit. If this investment earned only simple interest, your total value at the end of the tenth year would be $200. That is, interest would be earned only on the principal ($100 = $100 × 10% × 10 years), not on the interest left on deposit. Therefore, compounding increases your return by $59 and increases your *effective interest rate*.

EXHIBIT 7.2 Compound Interest

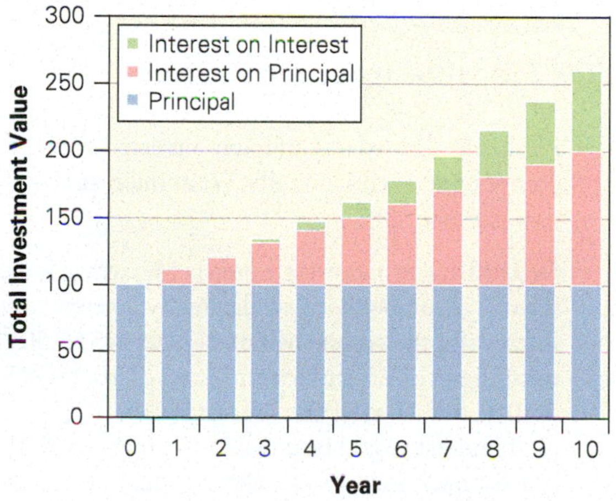

An illustration of compound interest with annual compounding is presented in Example 7.2.

EXAMPLE 7.2 Compound Interest with Annual Compounding

PROBLEM: Solitude Company borrowed $60,000 for 3 years at a 5% interest rate with interest compounded annually. Solitude will repay the entire amount (principal plus interest) at the end of the 3-year period. Thus, it is not paying any interest until the end of the 3 years. How much interest will it pay? Compare this amount of interest to the amount computed in Example 7.1 using the simple interest computation.

SOLUTION: We begin by computing the interest incurred in the first year, which is $3,000 ($60,000 × 5%). We then add this amount to the principal to compute the next period's interest of $3,150 ($63,000 × 5%). We add this amount to the principal plus interest balance at the beginning of the period to get a principal plus interest balance of $66,150 at the end of the second period. Interest in the third period is then $3,308 ($66,150 × 5%), resulting in a principal plus interest balance at the end of 3 years of $69,458.

Year	*Annual Interest*	*Amount Left on Deposit*
1	$60,000 × 5% × 1 = $3,000	$60,000 + $3,000 = $63,000
2	$63,000 × 5% × 1 = $3,150	$63,000 + $3,150 = $66,150
3	$66,150 × 5% × 1 = $3,308	$66,150 + $3,308 = $69,458

Assuming annual compounding, the total interest is equal to $9,458 ($3,000 + $3,150 + $3,308). This total interest is $458 higher than the $9,000 simple interest incurred over the same 3-year period in Example 7.1.

As Example 7.2 shows, if interest is compounded, the total amount of interest earned or paid is higher than if simple interest is used. Likewise, the more frequently the interest is compounded, the more interest is earned. If, for example, interest is compounded monthly, then the computed interest is higher than if interest is compounded annually.

Effective Interest Rates

Many investments earn interest compounded daily (for example, bank accounts). Daily compounding increases the interest earned on the investment. Note that interest rates are always stated as an annual amount. When interest is compounded more than once per year, we determine the interest rate used in computations by dividing the annual rate by the number of compounding periods in a year. If interest is compounded more than once a year, then the **effective interest rate**, which is the amount of interest actually earned, will be higher than the stated interest rate. Example 7.3 illustrates computing an effective interest rate.

EXAMPLE 7.3 Effective Interest Rates

PROBLEM: Crowded Company invested $1,000 for 1 year at a stated rate of 10%. Interest is compounded semiannually. What interest rate is used for the computations? What is the effective interest rate?

SOLUTION: The interest rate used is 5%, which is the stated interest rate of 10% divided by 2 because interest is compounded semiannually. Interest for the first half of the year is $50 ($1,000 × 5%). Interest for the second half of the year is $52.50 ($1,050 × 5%). Thus, total interest is $102.50, resulting in an effective interest rate of 10.25% ($102.50/$1,000). Here, the stated rate of interest is 10%, but the effective interest rate is 10.25%. If interest was compounded annually, then your total interest would be equal to $100 ($1,000 × 10%). In this case, the stated and the effective interest rates are the same and are equal to 10% ($100/$1,000). This example illustrates that more frequent compounding increases the effective interest rate.

Types of Time Value of Money Problems

The first step in most business decision models is to identify the value of the cash flows to be received or paid at two different, terminal time periods. The cash flow values at these two terminal time periods are the *present value* and the *future value*:

1. The **present value** (PV) is the value today of a cash flow or a series of cash flows to be received or paid in the future.
2. The **future value** (FV) is the value at some specified point in the future of a cash flow or a series of cash flows to be paid or received between the current date and the specified point in the future.

A business problem can involve having knowledge of either the PV or the FV and solving for the other using the interest rate and the time period. The process of moving from the PV to the FV is known as **compounding**. The process of moving from the FV to the PV is known as **discounting**. The time period begins at time (t) zero, and ends at some future time (t), which we represent with a capital T. Exhibit 7.3 presents the distinction between compounding and discounting using a timeline.

EXHIBIT 7.3 Compounding and Discounting

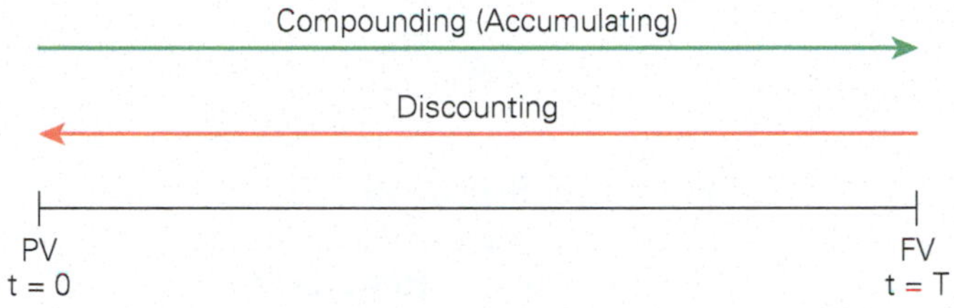

In analyzing the time value of money, there are two types of cash flows to identify: single cash flows and *annuities*. An **annuity** is a series of periodic payments or receipts of equal amounts that occur at equal time intervals between each cash flow.

Annuity payments can occur at the beginning or the end of a period. When payments take place at the beginning of the period, the series of cash flows is called an **annuity due** or an **annuity in advance**. Rent is an example of a payment made at the beginning of a period. If the payments occur at the end of the period, the series of periodic payments is known as an **ordinary annuity** or an **annuity in arrears**. Interest paid at the end of the month on a bank deposit is an illustration of an ordinary annuity.

❷ Compute solutions to future value and present value of single-sum problems.

Single-Sum Problems

We begin our discussion by illustrating applications of compounding and discounting a single sum, usually known as an amount of $1. There are four important variables in a single-sum problem:

1. Present value (*PV*)
2. Future value (*FV*)
3. Interest rate per compounding period (*I/Y*)
4. Time period or number of compounding periods (*N*)

If you know any three of these variables, you can solve for the fourth one. The **interest rate per compounding period** is the annual interest rate (I) divided by the number of times per year that interest compounds (Y). For example, if you are earning 8% interest compounded quarterly, then the interest rate per compounding period is 2% (i.e., 8%/4 quarters). The **number of compounding periods** (N) is the number of times per year that interest compounds multiplied by the total number of years for which a present or future value is computed. For example, if you are holding a 5-year note receivable that pays interest quarterly, then there are 20 compounding periods (i.e., 5 years × 4 quarters).

We begin by solving for the future value and illustrating various techniques to solve each problem. There are a number of techniques available to solve time value of money problems, such as financial calculators, smart phones, and spreadsheets. We illustrate four methods in this chapter:[1]

1. The Formula Solution
2. The Factor Table Solution
3. The Spreadsheet Application Solution
4. The Financial Calculator Solution

Future Value of a Single Sum

For the future value of a single sum, we know the present value of the single cash flow, the interest rate, and the number of periods—and we need to compute the future value. Consider a single bank deposit with $100 left on deposit for 1 year at an 8% rate of interest, as depicted in Exhibit 7.4.

EXHIBIT 7.4 Future Value of a Single Sum

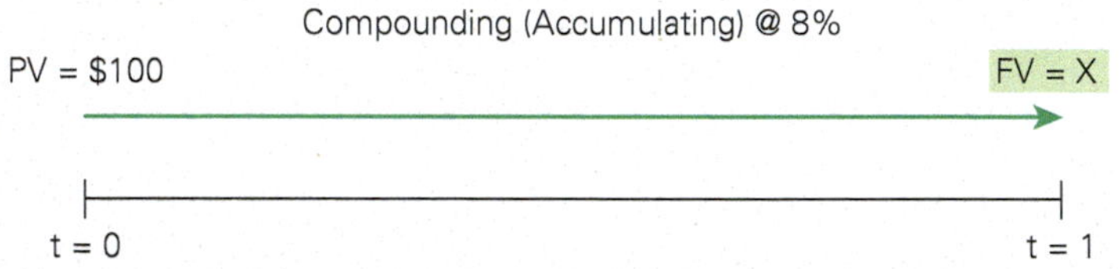

Formula Solution. To compute the future value of a single sum, we compute interest one period at a time and determine the new principal plus interest balance at the end of each period, as in Example 7.2. However, this approach is quite burdensome, particularly for problems involving many periods. A less cumbersome approach is to restate the problem using the time value of money variables defined in the previous section using the following formula:

$$FV = PV \times (1 + I/Y)^N \tag{7.2}$$

where *PV* is the present value, *FV* is the future value, *I/Y* is the interest rate per compounding period, and *N* is the number of compounding periods. Note that the future value (*FV*) is directly related to the rate of interest, *I/Y*, and the period of time, *N*.

We illustrate annual compounding in Example 7.4.

EXAMPLE 7.4 **Future Value of a Single Sum: Annual Compounding**

PROBLEM: Solitude Company invested $10,000 for 10 years at 8% with interest compounded annually. Solitude will receive the entire amount (principal plus interest) at the end of the 10-year period. What is the future value of this single sum using the formula approach?

SOLUTION: We use Equation 7.2 to solve for the future value.

$$FV = PV \times (1 + I/Y)^N$$
$$FV = \$10{,}000 \times (1 + .08)^{10}$$
$$FV = \$10{,}000 \times 2.1589$$
$$FV = \$21{,}589$$

The future value of this single-sum investment is $21,589.

Example 7.5 illustrates a more complex problem.

[1]Note that in all time value of money problems, different approaches may give you slightly different answers due to rounding.

EXAMPLE 7.5 Future Value of a Single Sum: Formula Approach

PROBLEM: Solitude Company invested \$10,000 in a 10-year investment with a stated rate of 8%. Interest is compounded quarterly. Determine the future value of this investment using the formula approach.

SOLUTION: We use Equation 7.2 to solve for the future value. The present value is \$10,000. The relevant interest rate is 2%, which is the stated rate of 8% divided by 4 because there are 4 periods per year. The number of compounding periods is 40 (10 years × 4 periods per year).

$$FV = PV \times (1 + I/Y)^N$$
$$FV = \$10{,}000 \times (1 + .02)^{40}$$
$$FV = \$10{,}000 \times 2.20804$$
$$FV = \$22{,}080.40$$

The future value of the 10-year investment is \$22,080.40.

Factor Table Solution. We can also solve future value problems using *factor* tables. A **factor** is a number derived from a combination of an interest rate and compounding period that can be multiplied by an amount to obtain the value needed. Instead of using the formula, the factor is a short-cut to compute the needed value. To illustrate, let's develop the future value of 1 dollar (\$1) compounding factors using the future value formula from Equation 7.2. If $N = 40$, $I/Y = 2\%$, and $PV = \$1$ as in Example 7.5, then the future value is:

$$FV = PV \times (1 + I/Y)^N \quad (7.2)$$
$$2.20804 = 1 \times (1 + .02)^{40}$$

With a deposit of \$1, the *FV* after 40 periods when the interest rate is 2% is equal to \$2.21 (rounded), as obtained above.

Table 7A.1 in Appendix A presents the complete set of compound interest factors for future value of \$1 factors for solving future value problems. Rows of the table represent the number of compounding periods. Columns have the interest rate per compounding period. The amount presented in the cell for each row and column is computed from Equation 7.2: It is the factor for a future value of \$1 for the given interest rate and number of periods. In the excerpt in Exhibit 7.5, we use the 2% column and then search down to the 40-period row to locate the factor 2.20804 that we derived above using the formula.

EXHIBIT 7.5 Select Future Value of \$1 Factors

$FV = PV \times FACTOR_{7A.1}$

Periods	1%	2%	3%	4%	5%	6%
1	1.01000	1.02000	1.03000	1.04000	1.05000	1.06000
2	1.02010	1.04040	1.06090	1.08160	1.10250	1.12360
3	1.03030	1.06121	1.09273	1.12486	1.15763	1.19102
4	1.04060	1.08243	1.12551	1.16986	1.21551	1.26248
5	1.05101	1.10408	1.15927	1.21665	1.27628	1.33823
10	1.10462	1.21899	1.34392	1.48024	1.62889	1.79085
20	1.22019	1.48595	1.80611	2.19112	2.65330	3.20714
25	1.28243	1.64061	2.09378	2.66584	3.38635	4.29187
30	1.34785	1.81136	2.42726	3.24340	4.32194	5.74349
35	1.41660	1.99989	2.81386	3.94609	5.51602	7.68609
40	1.48886	2.20804	3.26204	4.80102	7.03999	10.28572

The factors in Table 7A.1 illustrate that the future value is directly related to N and I/Y.

We can now use the factors from Table 7A.1 in Equation 7.3 to solve single-sum future value problems:

$$FV = PV \times FACTOR_{7A.1} \quad (7.3)$$

where $FACTOR_{7A.1}$ refers to the factor that can be found in Table 7A.1.

To solve for the future value, find the factor that is in the row for the number of compounding periods and the column for the interest rate per compounding period. Multiply this factor times the present value to obtain the future value. Example 7.6 demonstrates the table approach.

EXAMPLE 7.6

Future Value of a Single Sum: Table Approach

PROBLEM: Solitude Company invested $10,000 in a 10-year investment with a stated rate of 8%. Interest is compounding quarterly. Determine the future value of this investment using the table approach.

SOLUTION: We use Equation 7.3 to solve for the future value. The present value is $10,000. The relevant interest rate is 2%, which is the stated rate of 8% divided by 4 because there are 4 periods per year. The number of compounding periods is 40 (10 years × 4 periods per year). In Table 7A.1, look across columns to find the interest rate of 2% and then go down the rows to find 40 number of periods. The factor in this cell is 2.20804.

$$FV = PV \times FACTOR_{7A.1}$$
$$FV = \$10{,}000 \times 2.20804$$
$$FV = \$22{,}080.40$$

The future value of the 10-year investment is $22,080.40.

Spreadsheet Solution. A spreadsheet application such as Microsoft Excel is another way to solve future value problems. The future value function in a spreadsheet cell follows:

= FV(I/Y,N,PMT,PV,type)

The FV function requires inputting the following variables:

I/Y = interest rate per compounding period
N = number of compounding periods
PMT = amount of periodic payments
PV = present value of single sum
type = 0 if payments are due at the end of the period (ordinary annuity) and 1 if payments are due at the beginning of the period (annuity due)

For the future value of a single sum, we put a 0 in the third position because there are no periodic payments. Because the type defaults to 0, we do not need to include the last variable because we do not have an annuity problem. In the spreadsheet examples, we use the convention of designating borrowing or receiving payments as cash inflows and lending or investing money as cash outflows. In the time value of money spreadsheet computations, cash inflows are positive values and cash outflows are negative values. Example 7.7 illustrates the spreadsheet approach.

EXAMPLE 7.7

Future Value of a Single Sum: Spreadsheet Approach

PROBLEM: Solitude Company invested $10,000 in a 10-year investment with a stated rate of 8%. Interest is compounding quarterly. Determine the future value of this investment using the spreadsheet approach.

SOLUTION: We input N = 40 (4 periods per year for 10 years), I/Y = 2% (8% per year with interest compounding 4 times per year), PV = −10,000, and PMT = 0 because there are no payments in a single-sum problem.

	N	I/Y	PV	PMT	FV	Excel Formula
Given	40	2.00%	−10,000	0		
Solve for FV					**22,080.40**	=FV(0.02,40,0,−10000)

The future value is computed in the spreadsheet as $22,080.40.

Financial Calculator Solution. Finally, we illustrate solving future value problems with a financial calculator. To solve the problem in Example 7.7, enter the following keystrokes.[2]

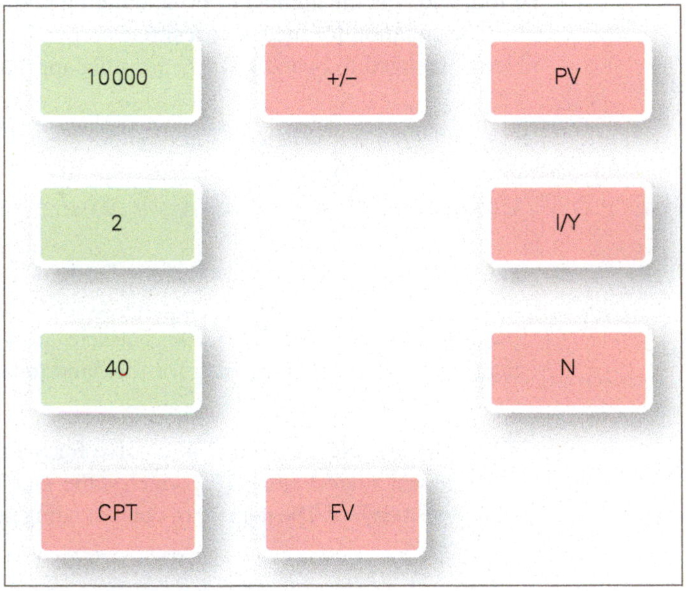

These keystrokes correspond to an outflow of $10,000 today at a 2% interest rate per compounding period and 40 compounding periods. The calculator provides the solution of $22,080.40.

Present Value of a Single Sum

The present value of a single sum is another common time value of money problem found in practice. In this type of problem, we know the future value of the single cash flow, the interest rate, and the number of periods and we need to compute the present value. As an example, assume that you are offered an opportunity to receive $108 at the end of 1 year. You could earn a rate of return of 8% on your next-best alternative investment. How much are you willing to invest today to have the opportunity to receive $108 at the end of 1 year? Exhibit 7.6 graphically analyzes this problem.

EXHIBIT 7.6 Present Value of a Single Sum

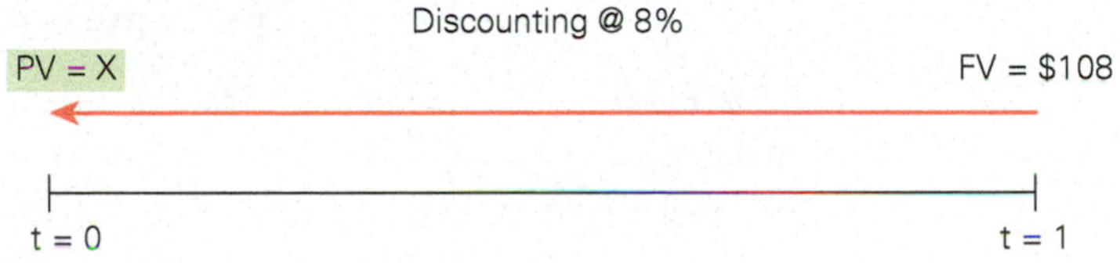

[2]We use Texas Instruments BA II Plus to illustrate keystrokes. Most financial calculators are similar.

As with single-sum future value problems, present value problem solutions may use a formula, table, a spreadsheet, or a financial calculator.

Formula Solution. The present value formula is an algebraic manipulation of Equation 7.2. That is, we start with the equation for the FV of a single sum:

$$FV = PV \times (1 + I/Y)^N \tag{7.2}$$

where *PV* is the present value, *FV* is the future value, *I/Y* is the interest rate per compounding period, and *N* is the number of compounding periods.

Then we can solve for the PV by dividing both sides of the equation by $(1 + I/Y)^N$.

The resulting formula for the present value is presented in Equation 7.4:

$$PV = FV \times 1/(1 + I/Y)^N \tag{7.4}$$

where *PV* is the present value, *FV* is the future value, *I/Y* is the interest rate per compounding period, and *N* is the number of compounding periods.

The equation for the PV of a single sum indicates that it is directly related to the FV and it is inversely related to N and I/Y. The formula approach is shown in Example 7.8.

EXAMPLE 7.8 Present Value of a Single Sum: Formula Approach

PROBLEM: Purple and Orange Fashion Designs, Inc. (P&OFD) has more cash than it currently needs for operations. Accordingly, it is considering investing in a piece of land that it believes it can sell in 5 years for $175,000. The relevant interest rate is 12% with monthly compounding. What should P&OFD pay for this land today (specifically, what is the present value of this investment)?

SOLUTION: We use Equation 7.4 to solve for the present value. The future value is $175,000. The relevant interest rate is 1%, which is the stated rate of 12% divided by 12 because there are 12 periods per year. The number of compounding periods is 60 (5 years × 12 periods per year).

$$PV = FV \times 1/(1 + I/Y)^N$$
$$PV = \$175{,}000 \times 1/(1.01)^{60}$$
$$PV = \$175{,}000 \times 1/1.8167$$
$$PV = \$175{,}000 \times 0.55045$$
$$PV = \$96{,}328.75$$

The present value of the land investment is $96,328.75.

Factor Table Solution. Table 7A.2 presents the factors for solving present value problems. Similar to Table 7A.1, the number of compounding periods is found in rows of the table. Columns have the interest rate per period. The amount presented in the cell for each row and column is computed from the interest component of Equation 7.4. It is the factor for the present value of $1 for the given interest rate and number of periods. Equation 7.5 solves single-sum present value problems using the factors in Table 7A.2.

$$PV = FV \times FACTOR_{7A.2} \tag{7.5}$$

Refer to the factor that is in the row for the number of compounding periods and the column for the interest rate per compounding period. For example, referring to the excerpt in Exhibit 7.7, the factor for a 3% interest rate and 10 periods is 0.74409.

EXHIBIT 7.7 Select Present Value of $1 Factors

$PV = FV \times FACTOR_{7A.2}$

Periods	1%	2%	3%	4%
1	0.99010	0.98039	0.97087	0.96154
2	0.98030	0.96117	0.94260	0.92456
3	0.97059	0.94232	0.91514	0.88900
4	0.96098	0.92385	0.88849	0.85480
5	0.95147	0.90573	0.86261	0.82193
10	0.90529	0.82035	0.74409	0.67556
20	0.81954	0.67297	0.55368	0.45639
25	0.77977	0.60953	0.47761	0.37512
30	0.74192	0.55207	0.41199	0.30832
35	0.70591	0.50003	0.35538	0.25342
40	0.67165	0.45289	0.30656	0.20829
45	0.63905	0.41020	0.26444	0.17120
50	0.60804	0.37153	0.22811	0.14071
60	0.55045	0.30478	0.16973	0.09506

The factors in Table 7A.2 indicate that the PV is inversely related to N and I/Y. Example 7.9 illustrates the table approach.

EXAMPLE 7.9

Present Value of a Single Sum: Table Approach

PROBLEM: Purple and Orange Fashion Designs, Inc. (P&OFD) has more cash than it currently needs for operations. Accordingly, it is considering investing in a piece of land that it believes it can sell in 5 years for $175,000. The relevant interest rate is 12% with monthly compounding. What should P&OFD pay for this land (specifically, what is the present value of this investment)?

SOLUTION: We use Equation 7.5 to solve for the present value. The future value is $175,000. The relevant interest rate is 1%, which is the stated rate of 12% divided by 12 because there are 12 periods per year. The number of compounding periods is 60 (5 years × 12 periods per year). In Table 7A.2, look across the columns to find the interest rate of 1% and then go down the rows to find 60 number of periods. The factor in this cell is 0.55045.

$$PV = FV \times FACTOR_{7A.2}$$
$$PV = \$175{,}000 \times 0.55045$$
$$FV = \$96{,}328.75$$

The present value of the land investment is $96,328.75.

Spreadsheet Solution. Spreadsheet applications such as Microsoft Excel provide a present value function in a spreadsheet cell as follows:

= PV(I/Y,N,PMT,FV,type)

The PV function requires inputting the following variables:

I/Y = interest rate per compounding period
N = number of compounding periods
PMT = amount of periodic payments
FV = future value of single sum
type = 0 if payments are due at the end of the period and 1 if payments are due at the beginning of the period

For the present value of a single sum, we put a 0 in the third position because there are no periodic payments. Because the type defaults to 0, we do not need to include the last variable because this is not an annuity problem.

EXAMPLE 7.10

Present Value of a Single Sum: Spreadsheet Approach

PROBLEM: Purple and Orange Fashion Designs, Inc. (P&OFD) has more cash than it currently needs for operations. Accordingly, it is considering investing in a piece of land that it believes it can sell in 5 years for $175,000. The relevant interest rate is 12% with monthly compounding. What should P&OFD pay for this land (specifically, what is the present value of this investment)?

SOLUTION: We input N = 60 (12 periods per year for 5 years), I/Y = 1% (12% per year with interest compounding 12 times per year), FV = 175,000, and PMT = 0 because there are no payments in a single-sum problem.

	N	I/Y	PV	PMT	FV	Excel Formula
Given	60	1.00%		0	175,000	
Solve for PV			**−96,328.68**			=PV(0.01,60,0,175000)

The present value is computed in the spreadsheet as $(96,328.68).

Financial Calculator Solution. Finally, present value problems can be solved using a financial calculator. To solve the problem in Example 7.10, enter the following keystrokes.

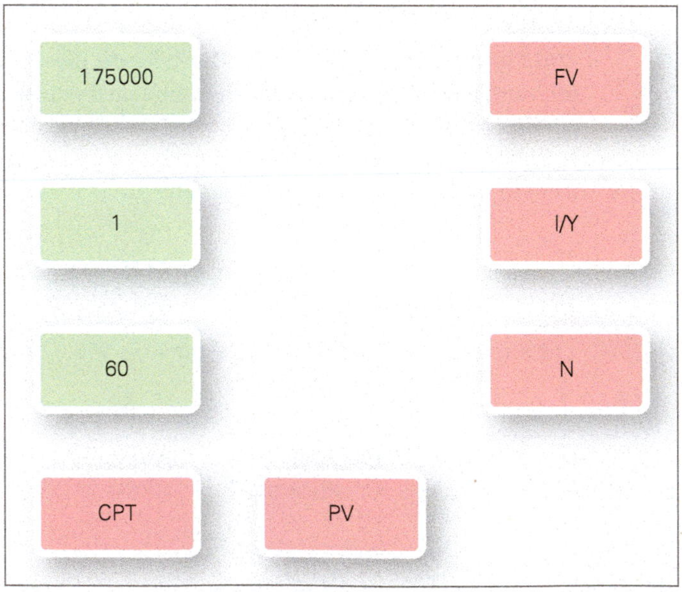

These keystrokes correspond to an inflow of $175,000 in 5 years at a 1% interest rate per compounding period and 60 compounding periods. The calculator shows the present value is $(96,328.68).

Other Single-Sum Problems

As we have discussed, there are four variables in the single-sum problems. Typically, problems either solve for the present value or future value, as discussed above. However, at times the present and future values are known factors and solutions require solving for either the interest rate for the compounding period or the number of compounding periods.

Solving for the Interest Rate. We illustrate solving for the interest rate when we have the other three variables—FV, PV, and N.

To solve for the interest rate with a formula, we rearrange the variables in Equation 7.2 to arrive at Equation 7.6:

$$FV = PV \times (1 + I/Y)^N \quad (7.2)$$

$$FV/PV = (1 + I/Y)^N$$

$$(FV/PV)^{1/N} = 1 + I/Y$$

$$I/Y = (FV/PV)^{1/N} - 1 \quad (7.6)$$

EXAMPLE 7.11 Solving for the Interest Rate in a Single-Sum Problem

PROBLEM: LJ Enterprises borrowed $5,000 from its bank. LJ will repay $6,083 in 5 years. What interest rate did LJ incur on this loan, assuming annual compounding?

SOLUTION: The future value (FV) is $6,083, the present value (PV) is $5,000, and the number of compounding periods is five. We use Equation 7.6 to solve this problem as follows:

$$I/Y = (FV/PV)^{1/N} - 1$$

$$I/Y = (\$6,083/\$5,000)^{1/5} - 1$$

$$I/Y = 1.04 - 1 = 4\%$$

LJ is borrowing at a 4% interest rate.

To use the factor tables, start on the inside cells of the table. Referring to Table 7A.1, we know from Equation 7.3 that the FV equals the PV times the Table 7A.1 factor.

$$FV = PV \times FACTOR_{7A.1} \quad (7.3)$$

To solve for the interest rate, we rearrange as follows:

$$FV/PV = FACTOR_{7A.1} \quad (7.7)$$

Thus, solving for the interest rate involves:

1. Computing the left-hand side of the equation by dividing future value by present value.
2. Searching for the interest rate in the row corresponding to the number of compounding periods.[3]

[3]Finding a factor in the table will depend on interest rates and the number of periods presented. If a factor is not found in a table, use another approach such as the formula or spreadsheet.

EXAMPLE 7.12 Solving for the Interest Rate in a Single-Sum Problem

PROBLEM: LJ Enterprises borrowed \$5,000 from its bank. LJ will repay \$6,083 in 5 years. What interest rate did LJ incur on this loan, assuming annual compounding? Prepare the solution with factor tables.

SOLUTION: We use Equation 7.7 to solve this problem. The future value (FV) is \$6,083, the present value (PV) is \$5,000, and the number of compounding periods is 5.

$$FV/PV = FACTOR_{7A.1}$$
$$6{,}083/5{,}000 = 1.2166$$

The factor is 1.2166, and we know there are 5 compounding periods. We then search in Table 7A.1 for future value of \$1 factors along the row for 5 compounding periods until we find the factor as illustrated here.

TABLE 7A.1 Future Value of \$1

$FV = PV \times FACTOR_{7A.1}$

Periods	1%	2%	3%	4%	5%
1	1.01000	1.02000	1.03000	1.04000	1.05000
2	1.02010	1.04040	1.06090	1.08160	1.10250
3	1.03030	1.06121	1.09273	1.12486	1.15763
4	1.04060	1.08243	1.12551	1.16986	1.21551
5	1.05101	1.10408	1.15927	1.21665	1.27628
6	1.06152	1.12616	1.19405	1.26532	1.34010
7	1.07214	1.14869	1.22987	1.31593	1.40710
8	1.08286	1.17166	1.26677	1.36857	1.47746
9	1.09369	1.19509	1.30477	1.42331	1.55133
10	1.10462	1.21899	1.34392	1.48024	1.62889

In this case, factor 1.21665 is in the 4% column. Thus, the interest rate is about 4%.

We solve for the interest rate variable, I/Y, using the RATE function in a spreadsheet cell as follows:

= RATE(N,PMT,PV,FV,type)

All variables are previously defined. To solve the problem in Example 7.12, enter the following amounts in each cell.

	N	I/Y	PV	PMT	FV	Excel Formula
Given	5		5,000	0	−6,083	
Solve for I/Y		**4.00%**				=RATE(5,0,5000,−6083,0)

The spreadsheet provides the solution, 4.00%.

We can solve interest rate problems using a financial calculator. To solve the problem in Example 7.12, enter the following keystrokes.

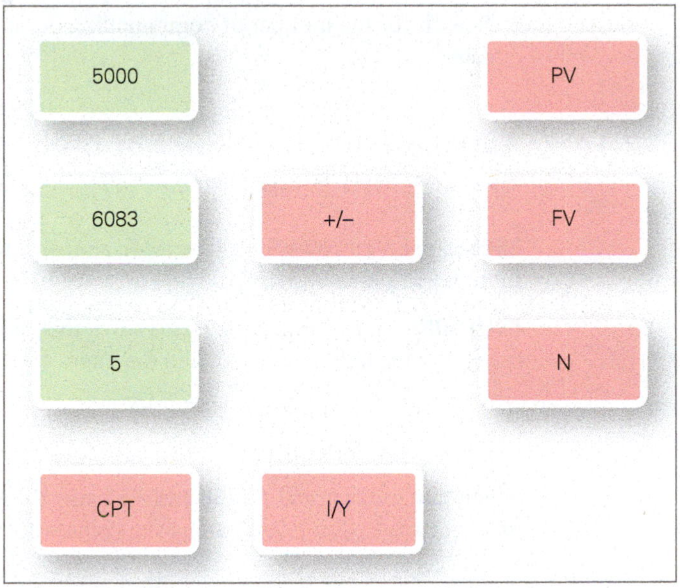

The calculator shows the interest rate is 4%.

Solving for the Number of Periods. We illustrate solving for the number of periods when we have the other three variables—FV, PV, and I/Y.

To solve for the number of periods, we can once again rearrange Equation 7.2 to arrive at Equation 7.8.

$$FV = PV \times (1 + I/Y)^N \tag{7.2}$$

$$(FV/PV) = (1 + I/Y)^N$$

$$\ln(FV/PV) = N \times \ln(1 + I/Y)$$

$$N = \ln(FV/PV)/\ln(1 + I/Y) \tag{7.8}$$

EXAMPLE 7.13 Solving for the Number of Compounding Periods in a Single-Sum Problem

PROBLEM: LJ Enterprises borrowed $5,000 from its bank at a 4% annual interest rate and will repay $6,083. Assume annual compounding. When will LJ repay the loan?

SOLUTION: We use Equation 7.8 to solve this problem. The future value (FV) is $6,083, the present value (PV) is $5,000, and the interest rate is 4%.

$$N = \ln(FV/PV)/\ln(1 + I/Y)$$

$$N = \ln(6{,}083/5{,}000)/\ln(1.04)$$

$$N = 0.1960601/0.0392207$$

$$N = 5 \text{ years}$$

LJ will repay the loan in approximately 5 years.

Alternatively, to use the factor tables, start on the inside of the table, once again using Equation 7.7. To solve for the number of compounding periods:

1. Compute the left-hand side of the equation by dividing future value by present value.
2. Search for the number of compounding periods in the column corresponding to the interest rate.[4]

EXAMPLE 7.14

Solving for the Number of Compounding Periods in a Single-Sum Problem

PROBLEM: LJ borrows $5,000 at a 4% annual interest rate and will repay $6,083. When will LJ repay the loan?

SOLUTION: We use Equation 7.7 to solve this problem. The future value (FV) is $6,083, the present value (PV) is $5,000, and the interest rate is 4%.

$$FV/PV = FACTOR_{7A.1}$$

$$6{,}083/5{,}000 = 1.2166$$

Given that the factor is 1.2166 and we know the interest rate is 4%, search in the future value of $1 factors in Table 7A.1 along the column for a 4% interest rate to find the factor.

TABLE 7A.1 Future Value of $1

$FV = PV \times FACTOR_{7A.1}$

Periods	1%	2%	3%	4%	5%
1	1.01000	1.02000	1.03000	1.04000	1.05000
2	1.02010	1.04040	1.06090	1.08160	1.10250
3	1.03030	1.06121	1.09273	1.12486	1.15763
4	1.04060	1.08243	1.12551	1.16986	1.21551
5	1.05101	1.10408	1.15927	1.21665	1.27628
6	1.06152	1.12616	1.19405	1.26532	1.34010
7	1.07214	1.14869	1.22987	1.31593	1.40710
8	1.08286	1.17166	1.26677	1.36857	1.47746
9	1.09369	1.19509	1.30477	1.42331	1.55133
10	1.10462	1.21899	1.34392	1.48024	1.62889

The factor is 1.21665 in the 5 compounding periods row. Thus, LJ will be repaid in approximately 5 periods because the factor we solved for (1.2166) is close to the factor in the table of 1.21665.

We solve for the number of periods, N, using the NPER function in a spreadsheet cell as follows:

=NPER(I/Y,PMT,PV,FV,type)

[4]Finding a factor in the table will depend on interest rates and numbers of periods presented. If a factor is not found in a table, use another approach such as the formula or spreadsheet.

All variables are previously defined. To solve the problem in Example 7.14, enter the following amounts in each cell.

	N	I/Y	PV	PMT	FV	Excel Formula
Given		4.00%	5,000	0	−6,083	
Solve for N	**5.00**					=NPER(0.04,0,5000,−6083,0)

The spreadsheet provides the solution, which approximates 5 periods.

A number of compounding period problems can be solved using a financial calculator. To solve the problem in Example 7.14, enter the following keystrokes.

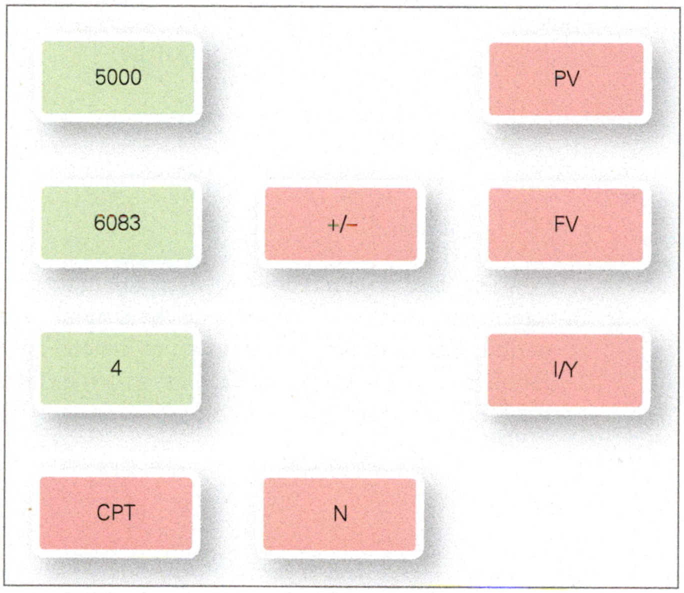

These keystrokes correspond to an inflow of $5,000 today and an outflow of $6,083 at a 4% interest rate per compounding period. Thus, the number of periods is 5.

❸ Compute solutions to future value of ordinary annuity and annuity due problems.

Annuities

As stated earlier in the chapter, an annuity is a series of periodic payments or receipts of equal amounts that occur at equal time intervals between each cash flow. For example, the monthly payments on a car loan are an annuity. The equal cash flows are referred to as **payments** (PMT). There are two types of annuities: an *ordinary annuity* and an *annuity due*.

An **ordinary annuity** is an annuity where the cash flows occur at the end of the interest period. An **annuity due** is an annuity where the cash flows occur at the beginning of the interest period.

Annuity problems can have five variables:

1. Present value (*PV*)
2. Future value (*FV*)
3. Interest rate per compounding period (*I/Y*)
4. Number of compounding periods (*N*)
5. Payments (*PMT*)

We begin our discussion with the computations of the future value of ordinary annuities.

Future Value of Ordinary Annuities

In a future value of an ordinary annuity problem, the payments, the interest rate, and the number of compounding periods are known and we compute the future value. Again, payments occur at the end of the period for an ordinary annuity. For example, assume that an undergraduate accounting student wants to accumulate a sum of money to pay for a master's program to earn the 150 credit hours required for accounting certification. The student will make $10,000 deposits at the end of each year for 3 years and the interest rate is 10%, as depicted by Exhibit 7.8. Interest is compounded annually.

EXHIBIT 7.8 Future Value of an Ordinary Annuity

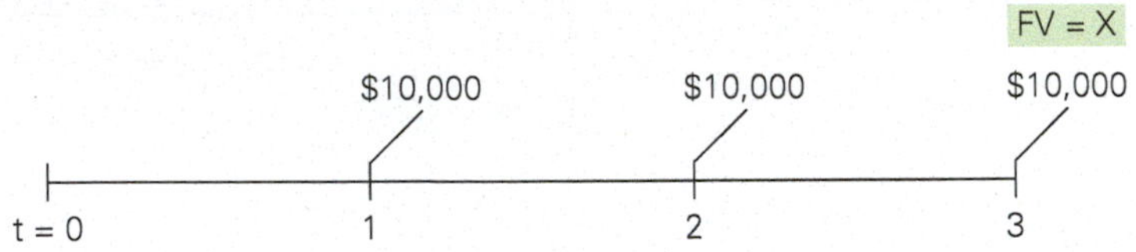

The third payment does not earn any interest. The first payment is on deposit and accumulates interest for two periods, and the second payment accumulates interest for only a single period. The third payment is made at the end and does not accumulate interest. To solve this problem, we can compound each cash flow as three separate single-sum problems as shown in the following table.

Payment	End of Period	Amount	$FACTOR_{7A.1}$	Future Value	Number of Compounding Periods
1st	1	$10,000	1.21	$12,100	2
2nd	2	10,000	1.10	11,000	1
3rd	3	10,000	1.00	10,000	0
Total		$30,000	3.31	$33,100	

The future value of this annuity is therefore $33,100. The difference between the sum of the cash flows ($30,000) and the future value of the cash flows ($33,100) represents the interest earned on the investment, $3,100.

This approach of turning an annuity into a series of single-sum problems is too cumbersome for most annuity problems. Techniques involving a formula, table, spreadsheet, or financial calculator are efficient ways of solving future value of ordinary annuity problems.

Formula Solution. The formula for a future value of an ordinary annuity problem is as follows:

$$FV_{OA} = PMT \times [(1 + I/Y)^{N} - 1]/I/Y \tag{7.9}$$

Where FV_{OA} is the future value of an ordinary annuity, *I/Y* is the interest rate per compounding period, *N* is the number of compounding periods, and *PMT* is the amount of the equal cash flows.

EXAMPLE 7.15

Future Value of an Ordinary Annuity: Formula Approach

PROBLEM: Magoli Company deposits $100,000 every quarter in a savings account (beginning at the end of the current quarter) for the next 4 years so that it can purchase a specialized piece of machinery at the end of the 4years. The interest rate is 12%. How much money will Magoli have at the end of the 4 years?

SOLUTION: We use Equation 7.9 to solve for the future value. There are 16 compounding periods (4 years × 4 periods per year) and the interest rate is 3% (12%/4 periods per year).

$$FV_{OA} = PMT \times [(1 + I/Y)^N - 1]/I/Y$$
$$FV_{OA} = \$100{,}000 \times [1.03^{16} - 1]/0.03$$
$$FV_{OA} = \$100{,}000 \times [0.604706]/0.03$$
$$FV_{OA} = \$100{,}000 \times 20.15688$$
$$FV_{OA} = \$2{,}015{,}688$$

Magoli will have $2,015,688 at the end of the 4 years. Note that the sum of the nominal cash flows is equal to $1,600,000 ($100,000 × 4 quarters × 4 years). Therefore, the interest earned over the life of this investment is $415,688 ($2,015,688 − $1,600,000).

Factor Tables Solution. Table 7A.3 presents the factors for solving future value of an ordinary annuity problems. The amount presented in the cell for each row and column is computed from the interest component in Equation 7.9: It is the factor that is the future value of a $1 annuity for the given interest rate and number of periods. Equation 7.10 solves future value of ordinary annuity problems using the factors in Table 7A.3.

$$FV_{OA} = PMT \times FACTOR_{7A.3} \tag{7.10}$$

We use the factor that is in the row for the number of compounding periods and the column for the interest rate per compounding period. For example, from Exhibit 7.9, the factor for a 5% interest rate and a 7-year period is 8.14201.

EXHIBIT 7.9 Select Future Value of Ordinary Annuity Factors

$FV = PMT \times FACTOR_{7A.3}$

Periods	1%	2%	3%	4%	5%	6%
1	1.00000	1.00000	1.00000	1.00000	1.00000	1.00000
2	2.01000	2.02000	2.03000	2.04000	2.05000	2.06000
3	3.03010	3.06040	3.09090	3.12160	3.15250	3.18360
4	4.06040	4.12161	4.18363	4.24646	4.31013	4.37462
5	5.10101	5.20404	5.30914	5.41632	5.52563	5.63709
6	6.15202	6.30812	6.46841	6.63298	6.80191	6.97532
7	7.21354	7.43428	7.66246	7.89829	8.14201	8.39384
8	8.28567	8.58297	8.89234	9.21423	9.54911	9.89747
9	9.36853	9.75463	10.15911	10.58280	11.02656	11.49132
10	10.46221	10.94972	11.46388	12.00611	12.57789	13.18079

EXAMPLE 7.16

Future Value of an Ordinary Annuity: Table Approach

PROBLEM: Magoli Company deposits $100,000 every quarter in a savings account (beginning at the end of the current quarter) for the next 4 years so that it can purchase a specialized piece of machinery at the end of the 4 years. The interest rate is 12%. How much money will Magoli have at the end of the 4 years?

SOLUTION: We use Equation 7.10 to solve for the future value. There are 16 compounding periods (4 years × 4 periods per year) and the interest rate is 3% (12%/4 periods per year). In Table 7A.3, look across the columns to find the interest rate of 3% and then go down the rows to find 16 number of periods. The factor in this cell is 20.15688.

$$FV_{OA} = PMT \times FACTOR_{7A.3}$$
$$FV_{OA} = \$100{,}000 \times 20.15688$$
$$FV_{OA} = 2{,}015{,}688$$

Magoli will have $2,015,688 at the end of the four years.

Spreadsheet Solution. To calculate the future value of an ordinary annuity using a spreadsheet application such as Microsoft Excel, input the following variables into a spreadsheet cell:

= FV(I/Y,N,PMT,PV,type)

I/Y = interest rate per compounding period
N = number of compounding periods
PMT = amount of periodic payments
PV = present value equals 0 as computing the future value of a series of payments.
type = 0 if payments are due at the end of the period and 1 if payments are due at the beginning of the period

For the future value of an ordinary annuity, do not input a variable into the fifth position, because it is assumed to be zero. Because the type defaults to 0, do not include the last variable when the payment occurs at the end of each period.

EXAMPLE 7.17

Future Value of an Ordinary Annuity: Spreadsheet Approach

PROBLEM: Magoli Company deposits $100,000 every quarter in a savings account (beginning at the end of the current quarter) for the next four years so that it can purchase a specialized piece of machinery at the end of the 4 years. The interest rate is 12%. How much money will Magoli have at the end of the 4 years?

SOLUTION: We input N = 16 (4 periods per year for 4 years), I/Y = 3% (12% per year with interest compounding 4 times per year), PV = 0, and PMT = −100,000.

	N	I/Y	PV	PMT	FV	Excel Formula
Given	16	3.00%	0	−100,000		
Solve for FV					**2,015,688.13**	=FV(0.03,16,−100000,0)

The future value is computed in the spreadsheet as $2,015,688.13.

Financial Calculator Solution. Finally, we solve for the future value of an ordinary annuity using a financial calculator. To solve the problem in Example 7.17, enter the following keystrokes. Note that the default mode for the calculator is "end mode," or it is set to compute an ordinary annuity with cash flows occurring at the end of each period.

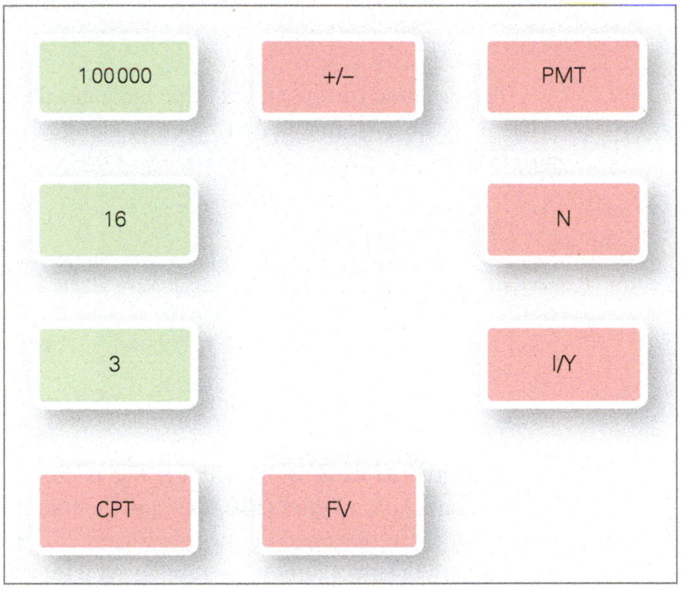

These keystrokes correspond to an outflow of \$100,000 for 16 compounding periods at a 3% interest rate per compounding period. From the calculator, Magoli will have \$2,015,688.13.

Future Value of an Annuity Due

Future values of annuities due differ from future values of ordinary annuities because the payments occur at the *beginning* of the period instead of the end of the period.

For example, assume that an undergraduate accounting student wants to accumulate a sum of money to pay for a master's program to earn the 150 credit hours required for accounting certification. Rather than investing a single amount today that will grow to a future value, she decides to invest \$10,000 a year over the next three years in a savings account paying 10% interest compounded annually. She decides to make the first payment to the bank immediately (specifically, at the beginning of the year). How much will she have available in her account at the end of three years?

Let's compare this annuity due with the ordinary annuity we discussed in the previous section. In the previous section, the student made the deposits at the end of each year; thus, the problem was an ordinary annuity. However, if the student makes the payment at the beginning of each year, it is an annuity due.

The timeline depicts a future value for an annuity due with the payments occurring at the beginning of each period. Note that there are three deposits with three compounding periods. That is, each cash flow earns interest.

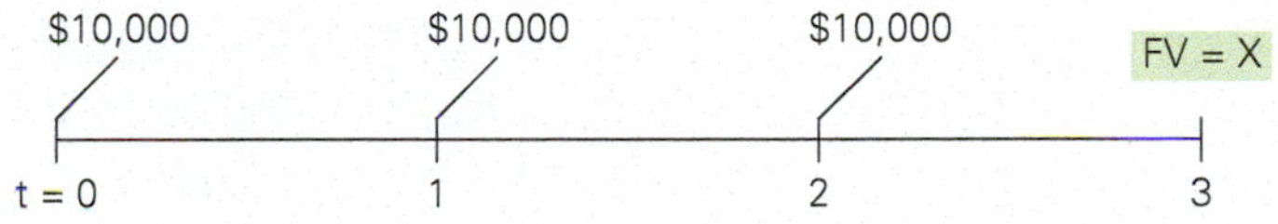

Now compare the annuity due to the ordinary annuity depicted on the following page. There are still three deposits, but now there are only two compounding periods. That is, the last deposit does not earn interest. As a result, the future value of an annuity due is more valuable than a future value of an ordinary annuity.

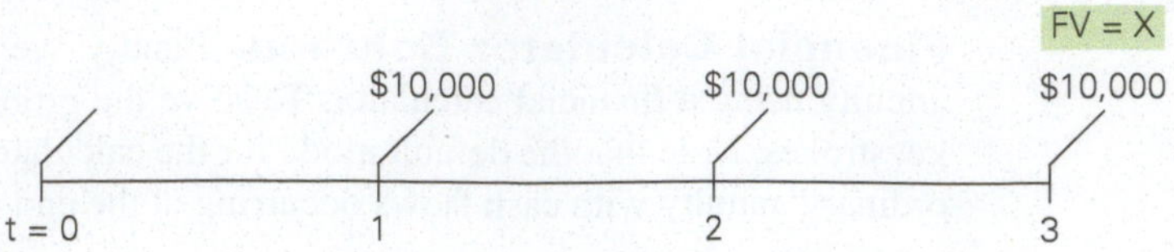

The timeline for the annuity due indicates that there are three cash flows and all three earn interest for at least one period. We can compute the future value using a series of single-sum problems as presented in the following table.

Payment	End of Period	Amount	$FACTOR_{7A.1}$	Future Value	Number of Compounding Periods
1st	1	$10,000	1.331	$13,310	3
2nd	2	10,000	1.210	12,100	2
3rd	3	10,000	1.100	11,000	1
Total		$30,000	3.641	$36,410	

The accumulated value of the annuity due is therefore $36,410. The difference between the sum of the nominal cash flows ($30,000) and the future value of the future cash flows ($36,410) represents the interest earned on the investment, $6,410.

As with ordinary annuities, solving for a future value of an annuity due as a series of single-sum problems is inefficient. Thus, to determine the future value of an annuity due, use a formula, table, spreadsheet, or financial calculator.

Formula Solution. Equation 7.11 shows the formula for a future value of an annuity due problem:

$$FV_{AD} = PMT \times \{[(1 + I/Y)^N - 1]/I/Y\} \times (1 + I/Y) \tag{7.11}$$

Where FV_{AD} is the future value of an annuity due, I/Y is the interest rate per compounding period, N is the number of compounding periods, and PMT is the amount of the equal cash flows.

EXAMPLE 7.18

Future Value of an Annuity Due: Formula Approach

PROBLEM: Magoli Company deposits $100,000 at the beginning of every quarter in a savings account for the next 4 years so that it can purchase a specialized piece of machinery at the end of the 4 years. The interest rate is 12%. How much money will Magoli have at the end of the 4 years?

SOLUTION: We use Equation 7.11 to solve for the future value. The annuity payment of $100,000 is an annuity due because it is made at the beginning of the compounding period. There are 16 compounding periods (4 years × 4 periods per year) and the interest rate is 3% (12%/4 periods per year).

$$FV_{AD} = PMT \times \{[(1 + I/Y)^N - 1]/I/Y\} \times (1 + I/Y)$$
$$FV_{AD} = \$100{,}000 \times \{[1.03^{16} - 1]/0.03\} \times 1.03$$
$$FV_{AD} = \$100{,}000 \times \{0.604706/0.03\} \times 1.03$$
$$FV_{AD} = \$100{,}000 \times 20.7615727$$
$$FV_{AD} = \$2{,}076{,}157.27$$

Magoli Company will have $2,076,157.27 at the end of the 4 years. Note that the sum of the nominal cash flows is equal to $1,600,000 ($100,000 × 4 quarters × 4 years). Therefore, the interest earned over the life of this investment is $476,157.27 ($2,076,157.27 − $1,600,000).

In comparison to the ordinary annuity case, the company has only $2,015,688 at the end of the 4 years and earns $415,688 in interest. This makes the annuity in advance more valuable than an ordinary annuity.

Factor Table Solution. Table 7A.4 presents the factors for solving future value of annuity due problems. We use Equation 7.12 to solve future value of annuity due problems using the factors in Table 7A.4.

$$FV_{AD} = PMT \times FACTOR_{7A.4} \tag{7.12}$$

The pertinent factor is in the row for the number of compounding periods and the column for the interest rate per compounding period. For example, Exhibit 7.10 presents the factor of 6.89829 for a 4% interest rate over 6 periods.

EXHIBIT 7.10 Select Future Value of Annuity Due Factors

$FV = PMT \times FACTOR_{7A.4}$

Periods	1%	2%	3%	4%	5%
1	1.01000	1.02000	1.03000	1.04000	1.05000
2	2.03010	2.06040	2.09090	2.12160	2.15250
3	3.06040	3.12161	3.18363	3.24646	3.31013
4	4.10101	4.20404	4.30914	4.41632	4.52563
5	5.15202	5.30812	5.46841	5.63298	5.80191
6	6.21354	6.43428	6.66246	6.89829	7.14201
7	7.28567	7.58297	7.89234	8.21423	8.54911
8	8.36853	8.75463	9.15911	9.58280	10.02656
9	9.46221	9.94972	10.46388	11.00611	11.57789
10	10.56683	11.16872	11.80780	12.48635	13.20679
11	11.68250	12.41209	13.19203	14.02581	14.91713
12	12.80933	13.68033	14.61779	15.62684	16.71298
13	13.94742	14.97394	16.08632	17.29191	18.59863
14	15.09690	16.29342	17.59891	19.02359	20.57856
15	16.25786	17.63929	19.15688	20.82453	22.65749
16	17.43044	19.01207	20.76159	22.69751	24.84037
17	18.61475	20.41231	22.41444	24.64541	27.13238
18	19.81090	21.84056	24.11687	26.67123	29.53900
19	21.01900	23.29737	25.87037	28.77808	32.06595
20	22.23919	24.78332	27.67649	30.96920	34.71925

EXAMPLE 7.19

Future Value of an Annuity Due: Table Approach

PROBLEM: Magoli Company deposits $100,000 every quarter in a savings account (with the first payment occurring at the beginning of the quarter) for the next 4 years so that it can purchase a specialized piece of machinery at the end of the 4 years. The interest rate is 12%. How much money will Magoli have at the end of the 4 years?

SOLUTION: We use Equation 7.12 to solve for the future value. There are 16 compounding periods (4 years × 4 periods per year) and the interest rate is 3% (12%/4 periods per year). In Table 7A.4, look across the columns to find the interest rate of 3% and then go down the rows to find 16 number of periods. The factor in this cell is 20.76159.

$$FV_{AD} = PMT \times FACTOR_{7A.4}$$
$$FV_{AD} = \$100{,}000 \times 20.76159$$
$$FV_{AD} = 2{,}076{,}159$$

Magoli Company will have $2,076,159 at the end of the four years.

Spreadsheet Solution. To solve for the future value of an annuity due with a spreadsheet application such as Microsoft Excel, input the following variables into a spreadsheet cell:

= FV(I/Y, N,PMT,PV,type)

I/Y = interest rate per compounding period
N = number of compounding periods
PMT = amount of periodic payments
PV = present value equals 0 as computing the future value of a series of payments
type = 0 if payments are due at the end of the period and 1 if payments are due at the beginning of the period

For the future value of an annuity due, we put a 1 in the fifth position because the payments occur at the beginning of each period.

EXAMPLE 7.20

Future Value of an Annuity Due: Spreadsheet Approach

PROBLEM: Magoli Company deposits $100,000 every quarter in a savings account (with the first payment occurring at the beginning of the quarter) for the next 4 years so that it can purchase a specialized piece of machinery at the end of the four years. The interest rate is 12%. How much money will Magoli have at the end of the 4 years?

SOLUTION: We input N = 16 (4 periods per year for 4 years), I/Y = 3% (12% per year with interest compounding 4 times per year), PV = 0, PMT = −100,000, and type = 1.

	N	I/Y	PV	PMT	FV	Excel Formula
Given	16	3.00%	0	−100,000		
Solve for FV					**2,076,158.77**	=FV(0.03,16,−100000,0,1)

The future value is computed in the spreadsheet as $2,076,158.77.

Financial Calculator Solution. Finally, future value of annuity due problems can be solved using a financial calculator. To solve the problem in Example 7.20, enter the following keystrokes.

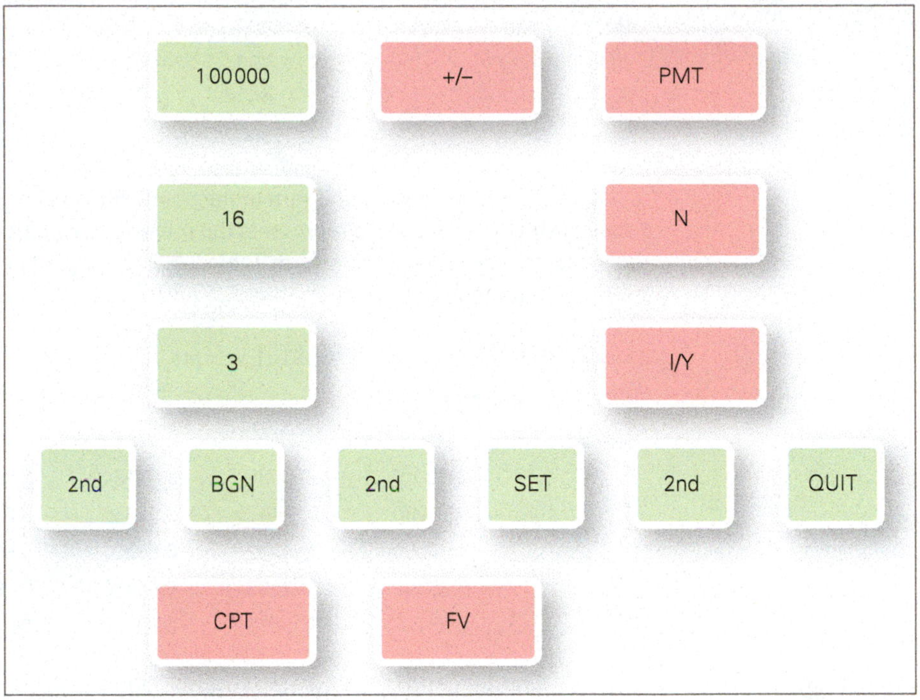

The calculator shows the future value of the annuity due is $2,076,158.77. These keystrokes correspond to an outflow of $100,000 for 16 compounding periods at a 3% interest rate per compounding period. The fourth row of keystrokes adjusts the calculator settings to "beginning mode" because this is an annuity due with the payments occurring at the beginning of the period as opposed to an ordinary annuity (the default mode) where the payments occur at the end of the period.

4 Compute solutions to present value of ordinary annuity and annuity due problems.

Present Value of Ordinary Annuities

In a present value of an ordinary annuity problem (cash flows occur at the end of the period), we know the payments, the interest rate, and the number of compounding periods, and we are asked to compute the present value. For example, assume that you have the opportunity to receive $100 at the end of each of the next three years. Given an interest rate of 8%, how much would you be willing to pay for this investment today? Exhibit 7.11 depicts this scenario graphically.

EXHIBIT 7.11 Present Value of an Ordinary Annuity

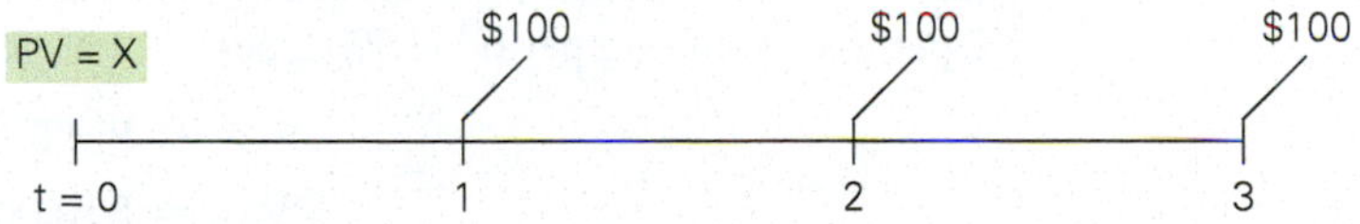

We can solve this problem using a series of single-sum problems as shown in the table on the next page by computing the present value for each of the $100 payments. The present value for the first, second, and third payments, respectively, is $92.59, $85.73, and $79.38. We add these three present values together to get a total present value of $257.70.

Payment	End of Period	Amount	$FACTOR_{7A.2}$	Present Value	Number of Compounding Periods
1st	1	$100	0.92593	$ 92.59	1
2nd	2	100	0.85734	85.73	2
3rd	3	100	0.79383	79.38	3
Total		$300	2.57710	$257.70	

The difference between the sum of the nominal cash flows ($300) and the present value of the future cash flows ($257.70) represents the interest of $42.30 earned on the investment. By using the present value of $1 factors from Table 7A.2 (excerpted next), we can also determine that you would be willing to pay no more than $257.70.

TABLE 7A.2 Present Value of $1 (Excerpt)

$PV = FV \times FACTOR_{7A.2}$

Periods	1%	2%	4%	6%	8%	10%
1	0.99010	0.98039	0.96154	0.94340	0.92593	0.90909
2	0.98030	0.96117	0.92456	0.89000	0.85734	0.82645
3	0.97059	0.94232	0.88900	0.83962	0.79383	0.75131
4	0.96098	0.92385	0.85480	0.79209	0.73503	0.68301
5	0.95147	0.90573	0.82193	0.74726	0.68058	0.62092

Although present value of ordinary annuity problems can be solved using a series of single-sum problems, it is more efficient to solve using a formula, table, spreadsheet, or financial calculator.

Formula Solution. Equation 7.13 is the formula for a present value of an ordinary annuity problem:

$$PV_{OA} = PMT \times [(1 - (1/(1 + I/Y)^N))/I/Y] \quad (7.13)$$

where PV_{OA} is the present value of an ordinary annuity, *I/Y* is the interest rate per compounding period, *N* is the number of compounding periods, and *PMT* is the amount of the equal cash flows.

EXAMPLE 7.21

Present Value of an Ordinary Annuity: Formula Approach

PROBLEM: SAO, Inc. will receive $10,000 semiannually for the next 10 years with the first amount received at the end of the first semiannual period. The interest rate is 10%. What is this stream of future cash flows worth today?

SOLUTION: We use Equation 7.13 to solve for the present value. The annuity payment of $10,000 is an ordinary annuity because it is received at the end of each compounding period. There are 20 compounding periods (10 years × 2 periods per year), and the interest rate is 5% per compounding period (10%/2 periods per year).

$$PV_{OA} = PMT \times [(1 - (1/(1 + I/Y)^N))/I/Y]$$
$$PV_{OA} = \$10,000 \times [(1 - (1/(1.05)^{20}))/0.05]$$
$$PV_{OA} = \$10,000 \times [(1 - 0.37689)/0.05]$$
$$PV_{OA} = \$10,000 \times 12.4622$$
$$PV_{OA} = \$124,622$$

Today's value of this stream of future cash flows is $124,622.

Factor Table Solution. Table 7A.5 presents the factors for solving present value of ordinary annuity problems. Equation 7.14 solves present value of ordinary annuity problems using the factors in Table 7A.5.

$$PV_{OA} = PMT \times FACTOR_{7A.5} \quad (7.14)$$

Refer to the factor that is in the row for the number of compounding periods and the column for the interest rate per compounding period. For example, referring to Exhibit 7.12, the factor associated with four periods and a 2% interest rate is 3.80773.

EXHIBIT 7.12 Select Present Value of Ordinary Annuity Factors

$PV = PMT \times FACTOR_{7A.5}$

Periods	1%	2%	3%	4%	5%	6%
1	0.99010	0.98039	0.97087	0.96154	0.95238	0.94340
2	1.97040	1.94156	1.91347	1.88609	1.85941	1.83339
3	2.94099	2.88388	2.82861	2.77509	2.72325	2.67301
4	3.90197	3.80773	3.71710	3.62990	3.54595	3.46511
5	4.85343	4.71346	4.57971	4.45182	4.32948	4.21236
10	9.47130	8.98259	8.53020	8.11090	7.72173	7.36009
15	13.86505	12.84926	11.93794	11.11839	10.37966	9.71225
20	18.04555	16.35143	14.87747	13.59033	12.46221	11.46992

EXAMPLE 7.22

Present Value of an Ordinary Annuity: Table Approach

PROBLEM: SAO, Inc. will receive $10,000 semiannually for the next 10 years with the first amount received at the end of the first semiannual period. The interest rate is 10%. What is this stream of future cash flows worth today?

SOLUTION: We use the factors from Table 7A.5 to solve for the present value. The annuity payment of $10,000 is an ordinary annuity because it is received at the end of each discounting period. There are 20 discounting periods (10 years × 2 periods per year), and the interest rate is 5% per discounting period (10%/2 periods per year).

$$PV_{OA} = PMT \times FACTOR_{7A.5}$$
$$PV_{OA} = \$10,000 \times 12.46221$$
$$PV_{OA} = \$124,622$$

The stream of future cash flows is worth $124,622 today.

Spreadsheet Solution. To solve the present value of ordinary annuity problems with a spreadsheet application such as Microsoft Excel, input the following variables into a spreadsheet cell:

= PV(I/Y,N,PMT,FV,type)

I/Y = interest rate per compounding period
N = number of compounding periods
PMT = amount of periodic payments
FV = future value, equals 0 as computing the present value of a series of payments
type = 0 if payments are due at the end of the period and 1 if payments are due at the beginning of the period

For the present value of an ordinary annuity, do not input a variable into the fifth position because if it is omitted, it is assumed to be zero. Because the type defaults to 0, do not include the last variable when the payment occurs at the end of each period.

EXAMPLE 7.23 Present Value of an Ordinary Annuity: Spreadsheet Approach

PROBLEM: SAO, Inc. will receive $10,000 every 6 months for the next 10 years with the first amount received in 6 months. Its interest rate is 10%. What is this stream of cash flows worth today?

SOLUTION: We input N = 20 (2 periods per year for 10 years), I/Y = 5% (10% per year with interest compounding 2 times per year), FV = 0, and PMT = 10,000.

	N	I/Y	PV	PMT	FV	Excel Formula
Given	20	5.00%		10,000	0	
Solve for PV			**−124,622.10**			=PV(0.05,20,10000,0)

The present value is computed in the spreadsheet as $(124,622.10).

Financial Calculator Solution. Finally, present value of an ordinary annuity problems can be solved using a financial calculator. To solve the problem in Example 7.23, enter the following keystrokes.

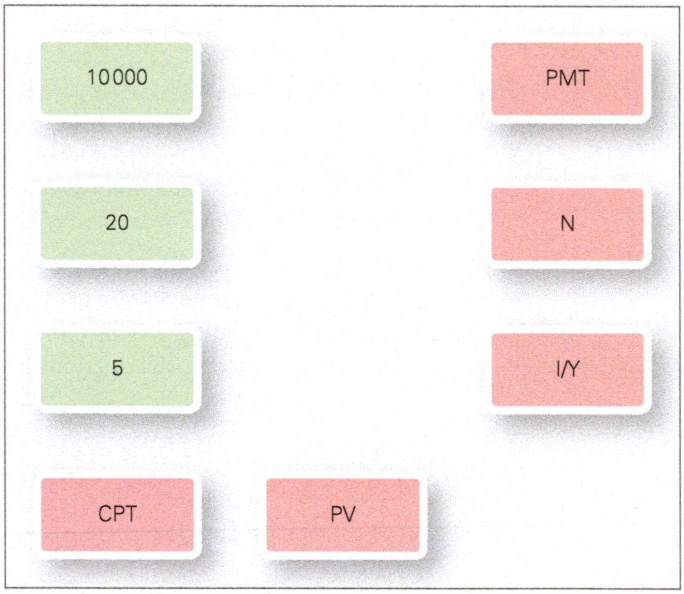

The calculator shows the present value of the annuity is $(124,622.10). These keystrokes correspond to an inflow of $10,000 for 20 compounding periods at a 5% interest rate per compounding period. Note that the calculator defaults to "end mode" for an ordinary annuity because the cash flows occur at the end of each period.

Present Value of an Annuity Due

Present values of annuities due differ from present values of ordinary annuities because the payments occur at the beginning of the period instead of the end of the period. For example, assume that you have the opportunity to receive $100 for the next three years with the first payment occurring today. Given an interest rate of 8%, how much would you be willing to pay for this investment today?

Let's compare this annuity due with the ordinary annuity we discussed in the previous section. In the previous section, the payments occurred at the end of each period and, thus, the problem was an ordinary annuity. However, if the payments are made at the beginning of each period, it is an annuity due.

The following timeline depicts a present value for an annuity due with the payments occurring at the beginning of each period. There are three deposits with only two discount periods. The first cash flow is not discounted and is valued at $100 because it is received today.

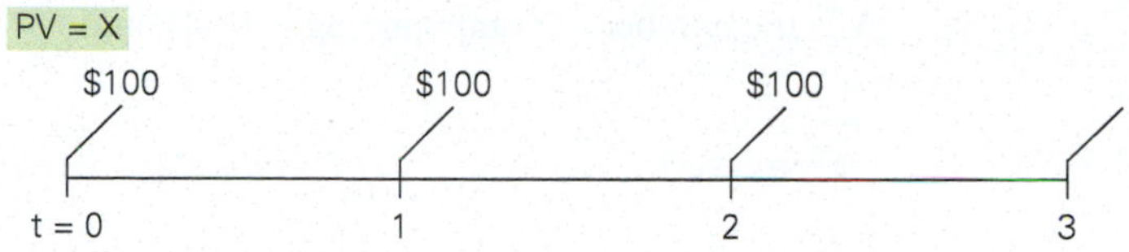

Now compare the annuity due to the ordinary annuity depicted in the following timeline. There are still three deposits, but there are three discount periods. Unlike the annuity due, we have to wait until the end of the period for the first cash flow. As a result, the present value of an annuity due is more valuable than a present value of an ordinary annuity.

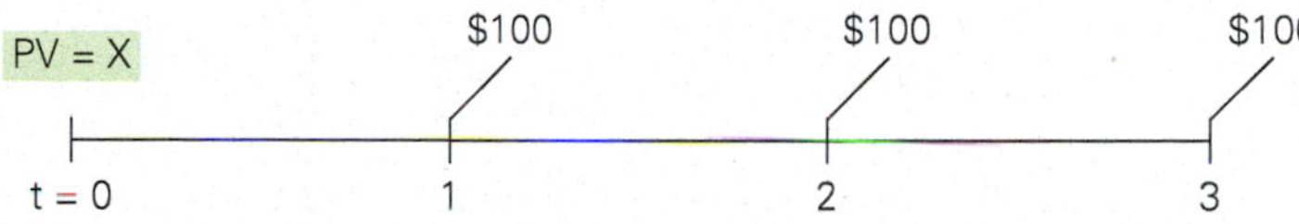

We can solve this problem using a series of single-sum problems as shown in the following table.

Payment	Beginning of Period	Amount	$\text{FACTOR}_{7A.2}$	Present Value	Number of Compounding Periods
1st	1	$100	1.00000	$100.00	0
2nd	2	100	0.92593	92.59	1
3rd	3	100	0.85734	85.73	2
Total		$300	2.78327	$278.32	

By using the present value of $1 factors from Table 7A.2 excerpted next, we can determine that you would be willing to pay no more than $278.32.

TABLE 7A.2 Present Value of $1 (Excerpt)

$PV = FV \times \text{FACTOR}_{7A.2}$

Periods	1%	2%	4%	6%	8%	10%
1	0.99010	0.98039	0.96154	0.94340	0.92593	0.90909
2	0.98030	0.96117	0.92456	0.89000	0.85734	0.82645
3	0.97059	0.94232	0.88900	0.83962	0.79383	0.75131
4	0.96098	0.92385	0.85480	0.79209	0.73503	0.68301
5	0.95147	0.90573	0.82193	0.74726	0.68058	0.62092

The annuity due is more valuable than the ordinary annuity by $20.62 (i.e., $278.32 − $257.70). What causes this difference? The first payment of an annuity due is not discounted whereas all payments are discounted with the ordinary annuity. The difference between the sum of the nominal cash flows ($300) and the present value of the future cash flows ($278.32) represents the interest of $21.68 earned on the investment.

A series of single-sum problems can be used to solve these types of problems, but it is most efficient to solve present value of annuity due problems using a formula, table, spreadsheet, or financial calculator.

Formula Solution. Equation 7.15 is the formula for a present value of an annuity due:

$$PV_{AD} = PMT \times [(1 - (1/(1 + I/Y)^N))/I/Y] \times (1 + I/Y) \quad (7.15)$$

where PV_{AD} is the present value of an annuity due, *I/Y* is the interest rate per compounding period, *N* is the number of compounding periods, and *PMT* is the amount of the equal cash flows.

EXAMPLE 7.24 Present Value of an Annuity Due: Formula Approach

PROBLEM: SAO, Inc. will receive \$10,000 semiannually for the next 10 years with the first amount received at the beginning of the first semiannual period. The interest rate is 10%. What is this stream of future cash flows worth today?

SOLUTION: We use Equation 7.15 to solve for the present value. The cash receipt of \$10,000 is an annuity due because it is received at the beginning of each period. There are 20 discounting periods (10 years × 2 periods per year), and the interest rate is 5% per discounting period (10%/2 periods per year).

$$PV_{AD} = PMT \times [(1 - (1/(1 + I/Y)^N))/I/Y] \times (1 + I/Y)$$
$$PV_{AD} = \$10{,}000 \times [(1 - (1/(1.05)^{20}))/0.05] \times 1.05$$
$$PV_{AD} = \$10{,}000 \times [(1 - 0.37689)/0.05] \times 1.05$$
$$PV_{AD} = \$10{,}000 \times 12.4622 \times 1.05$$
$$PV_{AD} = \$10{,}000 \times 13.0853$$
$$PV_{AD} = \$130{,}853$$

Today's valuation of this stream of future cash flows is \$130,853.

Factor Table Solution. Table 7A.6 presents the factors used to solve present value of annuity due problems. We use Equation 7.16 to solve present value of annuity due problems using the factors in Table 7A.6.

$$PV_{AD} = PMT \times FACTOR_{7A.6} \quad (7.16)$$

Refer to the factor in the row for the number of compounding periods and the column for the interest rate per compounding period. In Exhibit 7.13, the factor for a 6% interest rate over 9 periods is 7.20979.

EXHIBIT 7.13 Select Present Value of Annuity Due Factors

$PV = PMT \times FACTOR_{7A.6}$

Periods	1%	2%	3%	4%	5%	6%
1	1.00000	1.00000	1.00000	1.00000	1.00000	1.00000
2	1.99010	1.98039	1.97087	1.96154	1.95238	1.94340
3	2.97040	2.94156	2.91347	2.88609	2.85941	2.83339
4	3.94099	3.88388	3.82861	3.77509	3.72325	3.67301
5	4.90197	4.80773	4.71710	4.62990	4.54595	4.46511
6	5.85343	5.71346	5.57971	5.45182	5.32948	5.21236
7	6.79548	6.60143	6.41719	6.24214	6.07569	5.91732
8	7.72819	7.47199	7.23028	7.00205	6.78637	6.58238
9	8.65168	8.32548	8.01969	7.73274	7.46321	7.20979
10	9.56602	9.16224	8.78611	8.43533	8.10782	7.80169
20	18.22601	16.67846	15.32380	14.13394	13.08532	12.15812

EXAMPLE 7.25 Present Value of an Annuity Due: Table Approach

PROBLEM: SAO, Inc. will receive $10,000 semiannually for the next 10 years with the first amount received at the beginning of the first semiannual period. The interest rate is 10%. What is this stream of future cash flows worth today?

SOLUTION: We use Equation 7.16 to solve for the present value. The cash receipt of $10,000 is an annuity due because it is received at the beginning of each period. There are 20 discounting periods (10 years × 2 periods per year) and the interest rate is 5% per discounting period (10%/2 periods per year).

$$PV_{AD} = PMT \times FACTOR_{7A.6}$$
$$PV_{AD} = \$10{,}000 \times 13.08532$$
$$PV_{AD} = \$130{,}853.20$$

Today's value of this stream of future cash flows is $130,853.20.

Spreadsheet Solution. To solve present value of annuity due problems with a spreadsheet application such as Microsoft Excel, input the following variables into a spreadsheet cell:

= PV(I/Y,N,PMT,FV,type)

I/Y = interest rate per compounding period
N = number of compounding periods
PMT = amount of periodic payments
FV = future value equals 0
type = 0 if payments are due at the end of the period and 1 if payments are due at the beginning of the period

For the present value of an annuity due, we put a 1 in the fifth position because the payments occur at the beginning of each period. We input a variable of 0 into the fourth position because this is not a future value problem.

EXAMPLE 7.26 Present Value of an Annuity Due: Spreadsheet Approach

PROBLEM: SAO, Inc. will receive $10,000 semiannually for the next 10 years with the first amount received at the beginning of the first semiannual period. The interest rate is 10%. What is this stream of future cash flows worth today?

SOLUTION: We input N = 20 (2 periods per year for 10 years), I/Y = 5% per discount period (10% per year with interest discounted 2 times per year), FV = 0, PMT = 10,000, and type = 1.

	N	I/Y	PV	PMT	FV	Excel Formula
Given	20	5.00%		10,000	0	
Solve for PV			−130,853.21			=PV(0.05,20,10000,0,1)

The present value is computed in the spreadsheet as $(130,853.21).

Financial Calculator Solution. Finally, present value of annuity due problems can be solved using a financial calculator. To solve the problem in Example 7.26, enter the following keystrokes.

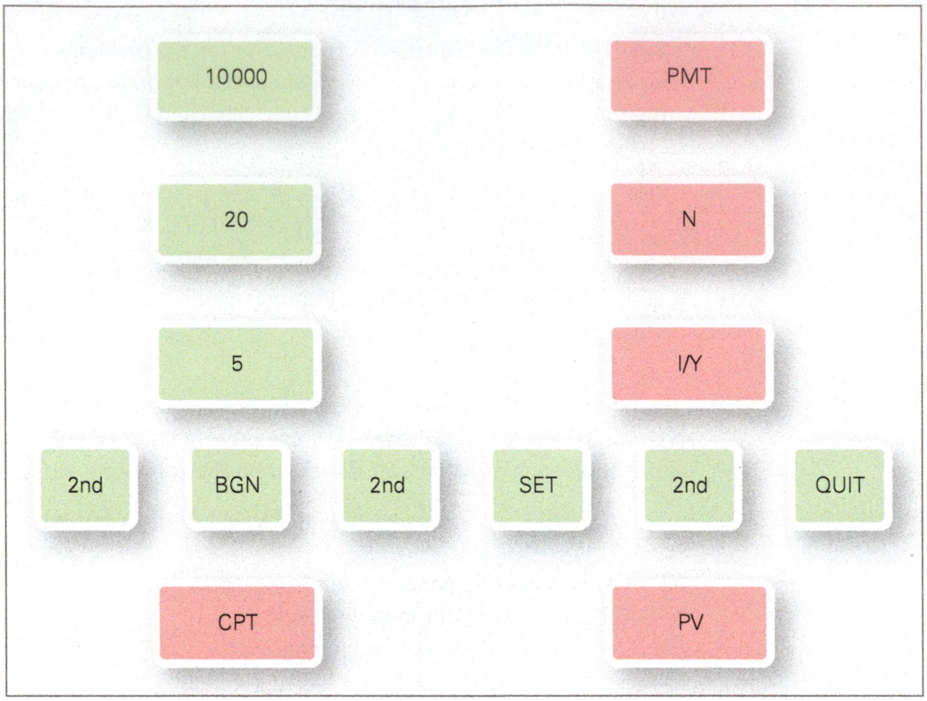

The calculator shows the present value of the annuity due is $(130,853.21). These keystrokes correspond to an inflow of $10,000 for 20 compounding periods at a 5% interest rate per compounding period. The fourth row of keystrokes adjusts the variables to "beginning mode" because this is an annuity due as opposed to an ordinary annuity.

Other Annuity Problems

In the preceding annuity problems, we knew the interest rate, the payments, and the number of compounding periods and solved for either the present value or future value. However, there are times when you will be asked to solve for the interest rate, payments, or number of periods. We discuss these scenarios for ordinary annuities next.[5]

Solving for the Interest Rate. To solve for the interest rate in an ordinary annuity problem, we could use Equation 7.13 and solve for *I/Y*, but that is complex. Therefore, we present the other solution approaches.

Using the factor tables, start on the inside of the table. Referring to the present value of an ordinary annuity factors in Table 7A.5, we know from Equation 7.14 that the PV_{OA} equals the *PMT* times the Table 7A.5 factor. We can rearrange as follows:

$$\text{PV}_{\text{OA}}/\text{PMT} = \text{FACTOR}_{7\text{A}.5} \qquad (7.17)$$

Thus, we compute the left-hand side of the equation and search for the interest rate in the row corresponding to the number of compounding periods.[6]

[5]We discuss only ordinary annuities in this section, but it is straightforward to extrapolate these procedures to the annuity due case.

[6]Finding a factor in the table will depend on interest rates and the number of periods presented. If a factor is not found in a table, use another approach such as the formula or spreadsheet.

EXAMPLE 7.27 Solving for the Interest Rate in an Ordinary Annuity Problem

PROBLEM: You have just won your state's big lottery, the Mega Power Pick-6! The jackpot is \$250,000,000. You have the option of receiving a check for \$12,500,000 at the end of each of the next 20 years. You would receive the first check in a year. The state lottery commission also allows you the option of receiving a one-time payment of \$155,777,629 when you turn in the winning ticket. What interest rate is the state lottery commission using to determine the one-time payment?

SOLUTION: We know that the present value of the series of 20 cash payments of \$12,500,000 over the next 20 years is \$155,777,629. To solve for the interest rate, we use Equation 7.17.

$$PV_{OA}/PMT = FACTOR_{7A.5}$$
$$\$155{,}777{,}629/\$12{,}500{,}000 = 12.46221$$

The factor is 12.46221 and there are 20 compounding periods. We then search in Table 7A.5 (excerpted as follows) along the row for 20 compounding periods until we find the factor 12.46221 in the 5% column. Thus, the state lottery commission is using a 5% interest rate annually to determine the one-time payment.

TABLE 7A.5 Present Value of an Ordinary Annuity (Excerpt)

$PV = PMT \times FACTOR_{7A.5}$

Periods	1%	2%	3%	4%	5%
1	0.99010	0.98039	0.97087	0.96154	0.95238
2	1.97040	1.94156	1.91347	1.88609	1.85941
3	2.94099	2.88388	2.82861	2.77509	2.72325
4	3.90197	3.80773	3.71710	3.62990	3.54595
5	4.85343	4.71346	4.57971	4.45182	4.32948
6	5.79548	5.60143	5.41719	5.24214	5.07569
7	6.72819	6.47199	6.23028	6.00205	5.78637
8	7.65168	7.32548	7.01969	6.73274	6.46321
9	8.56602	8.16224	7.78611	7.43533	7.10782
10	9.47130	8.98259	8.53020	8.11090	7.72173
11	10.36763	9.78685	9.25262	8.76048	8.30641
12	11.25508	10.57534	9.95400	9.38507	8.86325
13	12.13374	11.34837	10.63496	9.98565	9.39357
14	13.00370	12.10625	11.29607	10.56312	9.89864
15	13.86505	12.84926	11.93794	11.11839	10.37966
16	14.71787	13.57771	12.56110	11.65230	10.83777
17	15.56225	14.29187	13.16612	12.16567	11.27407
18	16.39827	14.99203	13.75351	12.65930	11.68959
19	17.22601	15.67846	14.32380	13.13394	12.08532
20	18.04555	16.35143	14.87747	13.59033	12.46221

We solve for the interest rate variable, I/Y, using the RATE function in a spreadsheet cell as follows:

$$= \text{RATE(N,PMT,PV,FV,type)}$$

All variables are previously defined. To solve the problem in Example 7.27, enter the following amounts in each cell.

	N	I/Y	PV	PMT	FV	Excel Formula
Given	20		155,777,629	−12,500,000	0	
Solve for I/Y		**5.00%**				=RATE(20,−12500000,155777629,0,0)

The spreadsheet provides the solution, 5.00%.

We can also solve for the interest rate in an ordinary annuity problem using a financial calculator. To solve the problem in Example 7.27, enter the following keystrokes.

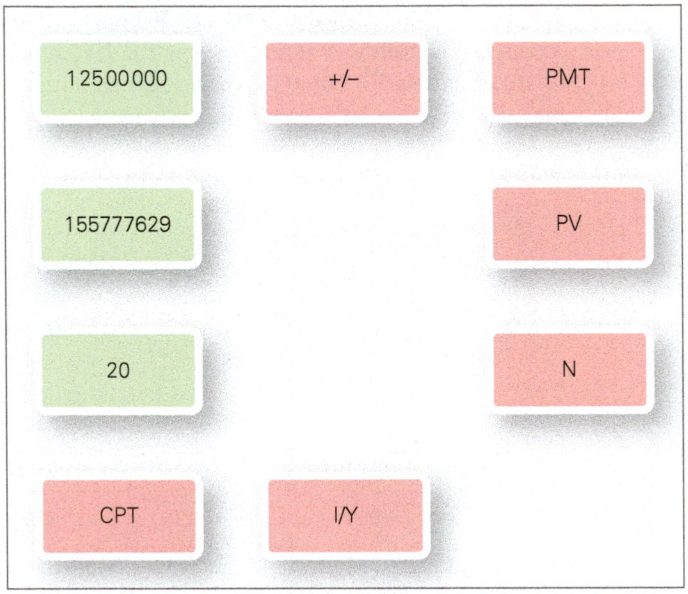

These keystrokes correspond to an annuity with 20 payments of $12,500,000 and a present value of $155,777,629. The calculator provides the solution of 5%.

Solving for the Number of Compounding Periods. Problems may also require solving for the number of compounding periods. Again, we can use the present value of an ordinary annuity factors in Table 7A.5 to solve by using Equation 7.17 to determine the factor and then finding the corresponding number of periods in the factor table.

EXAMPLE 7.28 Solving for the Number of Periods in an Ordinary Annuity Problem

PROBLEM: KW Enterprises borrows $202,772 at an interest rate of 8% today and will repay this amount by making semiannual payments of $25,000. Payments begin at the end of six months. How long will it take for KW to pay off the loan?

SOLUTION: The present value of the series of semiannual cash payments at 8% annual interest is $202,772. To solve for how long it will take KW to pay off the loan, we use Equation 7.17 to determine the table factor.

$$PV_{OA}/PMT = FACTOR_{7A.5}$$
$$\$202{,}772/\$25{,}000 = 8.11088$$

The factor is 8.11088, and the interest rate over the semiannual compounding period is 4%. We then search in Table 7A.5 (excerpted on next page) along the 4% column until we find the factor in the row corresponding to 10 periods. Thus, the loan will be paid off in 10 periods, or 5 years.

TABLE 7A.5 Present Value of an Ordinary Annuity (Excerpt)

PV = PMT × FACTOR$_{7A.5}$

Periods	1%	2%	3%	4%	5%
1	0.99010	0.98039	0.97087	0.96154	0.95238
2	1.97040	1.94156	1.91347	1.88609	1.85941
3	2.94099	2.88388	2.82861	2.77509	2.72325
4	3.90197	3.80773	3.71710	3.62990	3.54595
5	4.85343	4.71346	4.57971	4.45182	4.32948
6	5.79548	5.60143	5.41719	5.24214	5.07569
7	6.72819	6.47199	6.23028	6.00205	5.78637
8	7.65168	7.32548	7.01969	6.73274	6.46321
9	8.56602	8.16224	7.78611	7.43533	7.10782
10	9.47130	8.98259	8.53020	8.11090	7.72173

We solve for the number of periods, N, using the NPER function in a spreadsheet cell as follows:

= NPER(I/Y,PMT,PV,FV,type)

All variables are previously defined. To solve the problem in Example 7.28, enter the following amounts in each cell.

	N	I/Y	PV	PMT	FV	Excel Formula
Given		4.00%	202,772	−25,000	0	
Solve for N	**10**					=NPER(0.04,−25000,202772,0)

The spreadsheet provides the solution, 10 periods.

Financial calculators also facilitate solving for the number of compounding periods. To solve the problem in Example 7.28, enter the following keystrokes.

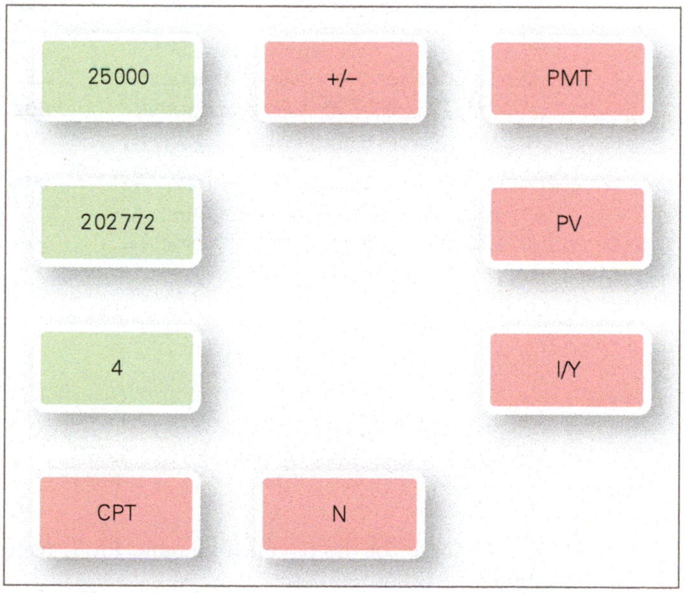

The calculator shows that the number of compounding periods is 10. These keystrokes correspond to an ordinary annuity with payments of $25,000 at a 4% interest rate per compounding period and a present value of $202,772.

Solving for the Payment Amount. Finally, problems may require solving for the amount of the payments.

We will use the present value of ordinary annuity factors in Table 7A.5 to solve for the payment because we know from Equation 7.14 that the PV_{OA} equals the PMT times the Table 7A.5 factor. We can rearrange as follows:

$$PMT = PV_{OA}/FACTOR_{7A.5} \quad (7.18)$$

and use Equation 7.18 to solve for the payment amount.

EXAMPLE 7.29

Solving for the Payment Amount in an Ordinary Annuity Problem

PROBLEM: KW Enterprises borrows $202,772 at an interest rate of 8% today and will repay this amount by making 10 semiannual payments. Payments begin in six months. What is the amount of the payments that KW will need to make?

SOLUTION: The present value of the series of 10 semiannual cash payments at 8% annual interest over 5 years is $202,772. To solve for the payment amount, we use Equation 7.18.

$$PMT = PV_{OA}/FACTOR_{7A.5}$$
$$PMT = \$202{,}772/8.11090$$
$$PMT = \$24{,}999.94$$

KW will need to make $24,999.94 payments.

TABLE 7A.5 Present Value of Ordinary Annuity (Excerpt)

$PV = PMT \times FACTOR_{7A.5}$

Periods	1%	2%	3%	4%	5%
1	0.99010	0.98039	0.97087	0.96154	0.95238
2	1.97040	1.94156	1.91347	1.88609	1.85941
3	2.94099	2.88388	2.82861	2.77509	2.72325
4	3.90197	3.80773	3.71710	3.62990	3.54595
5	4.85343	4.71346	4.57971	4.45182	4.32948
6	5.79548	5.60143	5.41719	5.24214	5.07569
7	6.72819	6.47199	6.23028	6.00205	5.78637
8	7.65168	7.32548	7.01969	6.73274	6.46321
9	8.56602	8.16224	7.78611	7.43533	7.10782
10	9.47130	8.98259	8.53020	8.11090	7.72173

We solve for the payment amount, PMT, using the PMT function in a spreadsheet cell as follows:

= PMT(I/Y,N,PV,FV,type)

All variables are previously defined. To solve the problem in Example 7.29, enter the following amounts in each cell.

	N	I/Y	PV	PMT	FV	Excel Formula
Given	10	4.00%	202,772		0	
Solve for PMT				**(24,999.95)**		=PMT(0.04,10,202772,0,0)

The spreadsheet provides the solution, $(24,999.95).

To solve the problem in Example 7.29 with a financial calculator, enter the following keystrokes.

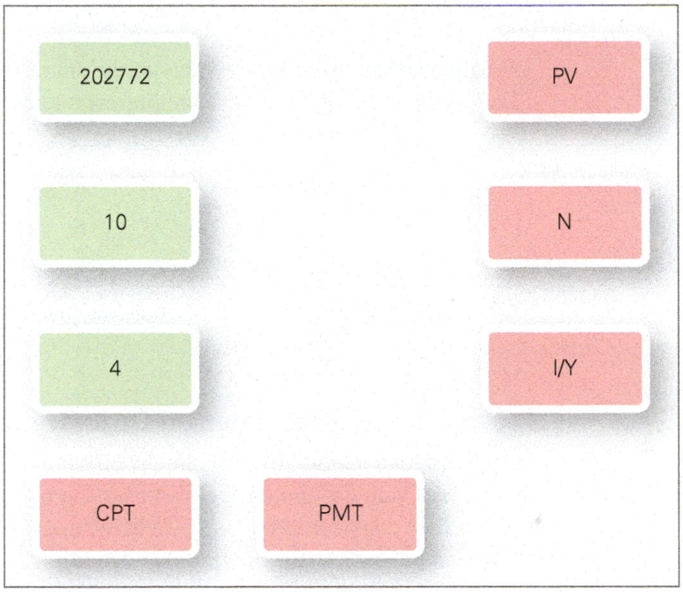

The calculator provides the payment amount of $(24,999.95). These keystrokes correspond to an annuity with 10 payments at a 4% interest rate per compounding period and a present value of $202,772.

5 Compute solutions to future value and present value of deferred annuity problems.

Deferred Annuities

A **deferred annuity** results from a variety of contracts whose payments or receipts are delayed until a future period. For example, a company may receive annual payments of $50,000 for five years, but the payments will not begin until three years from today. Deferred annuities may require calculating the present value or the future value.

Future Value of a Deferred Ordinary Annuity

Computing the future value of a deferred ordinary annuity involves using any of the same methods as when we compute the future value of an ordinary annuity with one difference: We will discount the cash flows only for the number of periods in which the payments occur, not the total period. This is due to the fact that we do not include the deferral period.

EXAMPLE 7.30 **Future Value of a Deferred Ordinary Annuity**

PROBLEM: Short Stack Pancake Company has budgeted $370,000 to build a new factory 10 years from today. Short Stack will finance the project by making seven annual deposits of $45,000 into a savings fund at the end of each year that commences at the end of Year 4. The company's interest rate is 6%. Prepare a timeline that depicts this time value of money problem. Will Short Stack have sufficient funds to pay for the $370,000 factory at the end of the 10-year period?

Continued

SOLUTION: We prepare the timeline as follows. Note that there are three deferral periods in which there are no deposits made into the fund. The deposits begin in Year 4 and end in Year 10, so there are seven deposits in total.

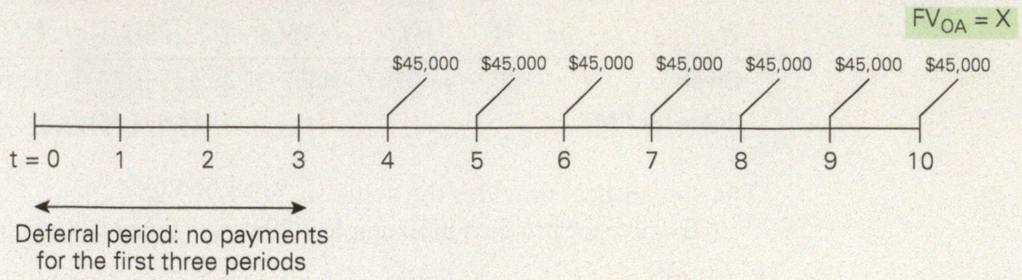

We then compute the future value of the annuity using the future value of an ordinary annuity factors from Table 7A.3 with an interest rate of 6% and seven periods.

$$FV_{OA} = \$45{,}000 \times FACTOR_{7A.3}$$
$$FV_{OA} = \$45{,}000 \times 8.39384$$
$$FV_{OA} = \$377{,}722.80$$

Thus, the company will have sufficient funds to pay for the $370,000 factory at the end of Year 10. Alternatively, we can use a financial calculator, a spreadsheet, or the formula.

Present Value of a Deferred Ordinary Annuity

One alternative method to compute the present value of a deferred ordinary annuity is to determine the present value of the cash flows over the period in which the cash flows occur. This present value is then considered as a lump-sum receipt (FV) received at the end of the deferral period. Discount this FV back to time period 0 to determine the present value of the deferred ordinary annuity.

EXAMPLE 7.31 Present Value of a Deferred Ordinary Annuity

PROBLEM: Barone Contracting Corporation (BCC) is required to pay the pension of one of its unionized employees. According to the terms of the union contract, the employee will retire in 5 years. The employee will receive $25,000 at the end of the consecutive 4 years following retirement. BCC's relevant interest rate is 3%. Prepare a timeline for this problem, and compute the pension obligation that BCC has incurred today.

SOLUTION: This series of cash payments is a deferred annuity with annual compounding. The deferral period consists of the 5 years prior to retirement, and the payment period is 4 years following the employee's retirement date. The timeline follows:

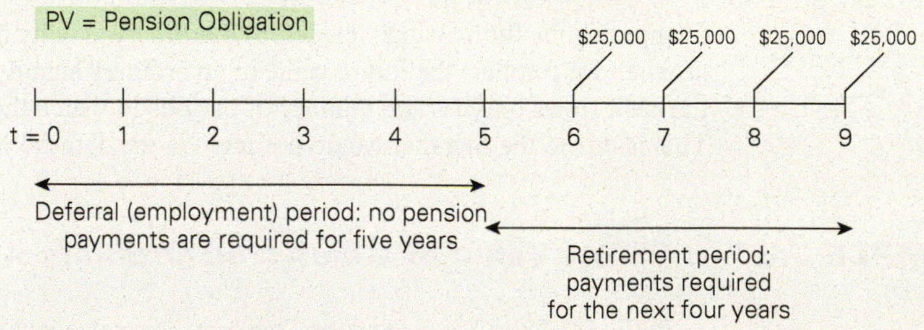

Computing the present value of an ordinary annuity of $25,000 for four payments at an interest rate of 3% gives us the value of the ordinary annuity stream at the beginning of Period 5 in the timeline above. We can use any of the available methods for computing the present value of an ordinary annuity; we will use the table approach here with an interest rate of 3% and 4 periods.

$$PV_{OA} = PMT \times FACTOR_{7A.5}$$
$$PV_{OA} = \$25{,}000 \times 3.71710$$
$$PV_{OA} = \$92{,}927.50$$

This step gives us the value as of time Period 5. This amount ($92,927.50) is now considered a future value of an amount of $1 to be received 5 years from now. We discount $92,927.50 back to the present to estimate BCC's pension obligation. We then must discount this single sum back 5 periods at 3%.

$$PV = FV \times FACTOR_{7A.2}$$
$$PV = 92{,}927.50 \times .86261$$
$$PV = 80{,}160.19$$

BCC has therefore incurred a pension obligation of $80,160.19 today.

6 Apply time value of money concepts to accounting applications involving determining the present value of expected cash flows and valuing bonds.

Time Value of Money Accounting Applications

We summarized several examples of the use of time value of money concepts in accounting. Now that we have discussed time value of money tools, we return to two basic accounting applications in more detail: the present value of expected cash flows and bond valuation.

THE CONCEPTUAL FRAMEWORK CONNECTION
Present Value of Expected Cash Flows

In the conceptual framework, the FASB describes five different methods that can be used to measure assets and liabilities: historical cost, current cost, current market value, net realizable value, and present value of future cash flows. The measurement of asset and liabilities—that is, the amount at which they are reported on the balance sheet—is extremely important in accounting. Because one of the commonly used measures is the present (or discounted) value of future cash flows, time value of money concepts are quite important.

We use present value techniques to measure both assets and liabilities. Assets such as notes receivable; investments in debt and equity securities; property, plant and equipment; and intangible assets may be measured using a discounted future cash flows approach. Likewise, liabilities such as notes payable and bonds payable utilize a present value of future cash flows approach.

PETER BICHÉ

CHIEF FINANCIAL OFFICER, MONUMENTAL SPORTS & ENTERTAINMENT WASHINGTON, DC»

Peter Biché

As CFO of Monumental Sports & Entertainment, Peter Biché oversees the financial operations of the Washington Capitals (hockey), Washington Wizards (basketball), and Washington Mystics (women's basketball) teams, the Verizon Center, George Mason University's Patriot Center, and the Kettler Capitals Iceplex.

1 What are the most common applications of time value of money models used in accounting by your franchise?

In the past, a common application of the time value of money (TVM) in the sports industry was for deferred compensation built into player and staff (e.g., general manager, coach) contracts, using a relatively straightforward net present value calculation to compare the costs and benefits of alternative payment plans. We now rarely enter into deferred payment or front-loaded agreements with either players or our team executives, both by our choice and that of the athlete/staff member. For our teams, collective bargaining agreements and salary cap restrictions have significantly reduced the appeal of such arrangements. Most players and staff realize that tying future payments to a team introduces an element of credit risk (for example, the significant amount the Pittsburgh Penguins owed Mario Lemieux under a deferred-compensation agreement and the team's later bankruptcy). Most players now have relatively sophisticated financial advisors and can arrange a "deferred" payment plan through other means.

The current exception is signing bonuses (up-front payments) with certain athletes. These tend to be relatively small compared to the overall size of the player contract; other considerations such as the player's cash flow needs and commitment to the player take precedence. An athlete might defer the receipt of a payment for several reasons, including if the team agreed to make a sufficiently larger payment or series of payments at a later date or if there were tax advantages (i.e., deferring the payment of taxes to a later date) to doing so. Both of these use time value of money calculations. We also consider time value issues in multi-year business agreements with our suite tenants, corporate sponsors, and media partners.

2 Describe some significant judgments involved when the team estimates the future cash flows used in a time value of money application.

The judgments considered depend on and vary dramatically based on the type of agreement we are entering into. For example, when negotiating a player contract, we compare the upfront payment versus the net present value of the deferred payments and the expected player performance in later years. While not time value of money related, we also consider the payments' impact on the team's current and future salary cap position.

With a capital investment, judgment factors include the potential for increased revenues and the payback period (how long it takes to recover our investment) compared to alternative investments or other requirements. For alternative investments, we modify the discount rate depending on the risk of our target investment and the alternatives. Typically, these investments would include either future revenue generation upside or cost savings. For business agreements, we factor the amount of royalties for merchandising, endorsements, and broadcast revenues into our future revenues and outflows.

3 How do you apply time value of money to capital investments, such as upgrading or renovating a sports venue?

Often a capital investment will generate returns to us (increased revenues and/or decreased costs). For example, if we want to increase ticket revenues by adding luxury boxes or upgrade the food concession facilities, we weigh the expected amount and timing of the returns (higher ticket revenues or concession commissions) against the initial capital outlay for the renovation to determine the attractiveness of the investment. Using time value of money calculations, we compare the costs and benefits to find the difference between the cash inflows and cash outflows for the potential investment. In addition, in an even modestly inflationary environment, we must consider the potential for rising costs if we advance or defer an investment and factor that risk into our analysis by modifying the discount rate.

Discussion Questions

1. Assume that you have been offered an executive position with a major corporation. The company gives you two compensation options: deferred compensation or advance payment. How would you decide which option to select? (Include illustrations to support your response.)
2. In his interview, Peter Biché defines the payback period as the amount of time it takes for a project to recover an investment. How is the payback period computed and what are its advantages and disadvantages?

Present Value of Future Cash Flows

A common method of measuring assets is the present value of expected future cash flows. For example, notes receivable are reported on the balance sheet at the present value of future cash flows, using the market rate of interest as the discount rate in the present value computations. The face value of the note does not matter. The amount reported on the balance sheet is always equal to the present value of the future cash flows.

EXAMPLE 7.32

Present Value of Expected Cash Flows

PROBLEM: Metatech, Inc. accepts a $2,000,000 note on January 1 issued by Totot Corporation. Specifically, Totot will issue a non-interest-bearing note with $2,000,000 due in 10 years in exchange for cash. The current market rate is 10%. Interest is compounded annually. Metatech is a calendar-year firm that prepares financial statements annually. At what amount will Metatech report the notes receivable on January 1?

SOLUTION: We will compute the present value of a lump sum. There are no interest payments because this is a non-interest-bearing note. The interest rate is 10% and there are 10 compounding periods. The future value is the $2,000,000 that Metatech will receive in 10 years.

We can use any method to compute this present value. For simplicity, we will show the formula and the spreadsheet approaches.

$$PV = FV \times 1/(1 + I/Y)^N$$
$$PV = \$2{,}000{,}000 \times 1/(1.10)^{10}$$
$$PV = \$2{,}000{,}000 \times 1/2.593742$$
$$PV = \$2{,}000{,}000 \times 0.3855434$$
$$PV = \$771{,}087$$

The present value of the note receivable is $771,087.

If we use the spreadsheet method, we also get a present value of $771,087.

	N	I/Y	PV	PMT	FV	Excel Formula
Given	10	10.00%		0	2,000,000	
Solve for PV			(771,087)			=PV(0.1,10,0,2000000)

Computing Bond Issue Proceeds

A common application of time value of money concepts is determining the amount of cash received when a company issues a bond to raise capital. With a bond, a company receives cash from a lender today, usually in return for the commitment to pay a fixed amount back at a certain future date when the bond matures, called the *face value*. The company typically also promises to pay periodic interest payments at fixed amounts until that date. The interest payment is based on an interest rate the company agrees to when it issues the bond. We discuss bonds in detail in a later chapter. Here we focus on using the time value of money to determine how much cash a company will receive when it issues a bond.

To determine the amount of cash received, we take the present value of the future cash outflows on the bond. The present value combines the present value of an amount paid when the bond matures and the present value of periodic interest payments. The interest rate used to discount these cash flows is the interest rate at which the company borrows the cash, the market interest rate.

EXAMPLE 7.33 Bond Issue Proceeds

PROBLEM: On January 1, 2016, the Auto-Stop Corporation issued bonds in the amount of $10,000 that will be paid in 3 years. Interest of $400 is payable semiannually each January 1 and July 1 with the first interest payment at the end of the period, on July 1 of the current year. Draw a time line of the bond's cash outflows. If the market rate of interest is 10%, what is the amount of the bond issue proceeds (cash received) when Auto-Stop Corporation issued the bonds?

SOLUTION: To determine the bond issue proceeds, we take the sum of:

- The present value of the future cash outflows of $10,000 in 3 years discounted at the market interest rate of 10%. This is the present value of a single sum.
- The present value of the six interest payments (2 per year times 3 years) of $400 each at the market rate of interest. This is the present value of an ordinary annuity.

The following timeline depicts the bond's cash outflows.

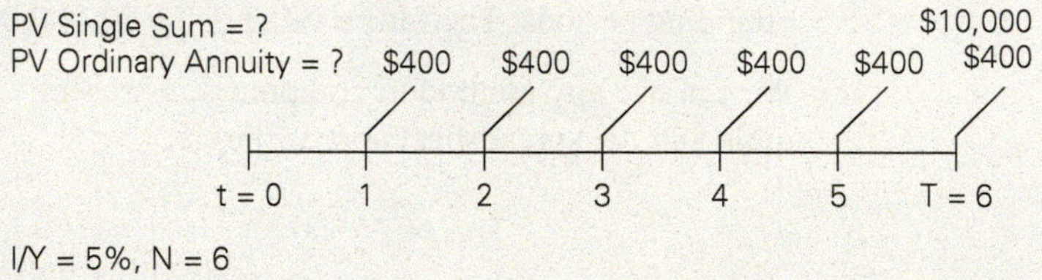

For simplicity, we present the solution using the table approach. All PV factors use the semiannual market rate because the bonds are priced at the market interest rate. Therefore, I/Y = 5% (10%/2), and N = 6 (3 years × 2). For the $10,000 face value payment, we take the present value of a single sum:

$$PV = FV \times FACTOR_{7A.2}$$
$$PV = \$10{,}000 \times 0.74622$$
$$FV = \$7{,}462.20$$

For the interest payments of $400, we take the present value of an ordinary annuity:

$$PV_{OA} = FV \times FACTOR_{7A.5}$$
$$PV_{OA} = \$400 \times 5.07569$$
$$PV_{OA} = \$2{,}030.28$$

Therefore, the bond issue proceeds (cash received) is $9,492.48.

Cash Flows	Present Value
Face Value	$ 7,462.20
Interest Payment	+ 2,030.28
Bond Issue Proceeds (Cash Received)	$ 9,492.48

Exhibit 7.14 summarizes the different types of time value of money problems and related solution techniques from throughout the chapter.

EXHIBIT 7.14 Summary of Time Value of Money Problems

Type of Problem	Formula	Table	Spreadsheet Formula
Future Value of a Single Sum	$FV = PV \times (1 + I/Y)^N$	7A.1	= FV(I/Y,N,0,PV)
Present Value of a Single Sum	$PV = FV \times 1/(1 + I/Y)^N$	7A.2	= PV(I/Y,N,0,FV)
Future Value of an Ordinary Annuity	$FV_{OA} = PMT \times [(1 + I/Y)^N - 1]/I/Y$	7A.3	= FV(I/Y,N,PMT)
Future Value of an Annuity Due	$FV_{AD} = PMT \times \{[(1 + I/Y)^N - 1]/I/Y\} \times (1 + I/Y)$	7A.4	= FV(I/Y,N,PMT,0,1)
Present Value of an Ordinary Annuity	$PV_{OA} = PMT \times [(1 - (1/(1 + I/Y)^N))/I/Y]$	7A.5	= PV(I/Y,N,PMT)
Present Value of an Annuity Due	$PV_{AD} = PMT \times [(1 - (1/(1 + I/Y)^N))/I/Y] \times (1 + I/Y)$	7A.6	= PV(I/Y,N,PMT,0,1)

Summary by Learning Objectives

In the following, we summarize the main points by learning objective. Throughout the chapter, we discuss the accounting and reporting of U.S. GAAP and IFRS. The following table highlights the major similarities and differences between the standards.

1 Explain the time value of money concept, including the calculations of simple and compound interest; define the effective interest rate.

Summary	Similarities and Differences between U.S. GAAP and IFRS
The time value of money concept means that a dollar today is worth more than a dollar at some time in the future because a dollar invested today will grow to a larger amount. Simple interest is computed on the initial amount but is not computed on any interest earned. Compound interest is computed on both the principal and the interest left on deposit. The effective interest rate is the amount of interest actually earned or incurred. It will be higher than the stated interest rate if interest is compounded more than one time a year.	Similar under U.S. GAAP and IFRS.

2 Compute solutions to future value and present value of single-sum problems.

Summary	Similarities and Differences between U.S. GAAP and IFRS
The future value is the value at a future point in time. The present value is the value at the current point in time. There are four variables of importance in a single-sum problem: 1. Present value (*PV*) 2. Future value (*FV*) 3. Interest rate per compounding period (*I/Y*) 4. Time period or number of compounding periods (*N*) If we know three of these variables, we are able to compute the fourth. A formula, factor table, spreadsheet, or financial calculator can be used to compute the future values and present values.	Similar under U.S. GAAP and IFRS.

Summary by Learning Objectives, continued

3 Compute solutions to future value of ordinary annuity and annuity due problems.

Summary	Similarities and Differences between U.S. GAAP and IFRS
An annuity is a series of periodic payments or receipts of equal amounts that occur at equal time intervals between each cash flow. The equal cash flows are referred to as payments (PMT). There are two types of annuities: • An ordinary annuity is an annuity when the cash flows occur at the end of the interest period. • An annuity due is an annuity when the cash flows occur at the beginning of the interest period. The future value of an annuity is the amount that the series of payments will be valued at some future period. A formula, factor table, spreadsheet, or financial calculator can be used to compute the future value of an annuity.	Similar under U.S. GAAP and IFRS.

4 Compute solutions to present value of ordinary annuity and annuity due problems.

Summary	Similarities and Differences between U.S. GAAP and IFRS
The present value of an annuity is the amount that the series of payments is valued at in the current period. A formula, factor table, spreadsheet, or financial calculator can be used to compute the present value of an annuity.	Similar under U.S. GAAP and IFRS.

5 Compute solutions to future value and present value of deferred annuity problems.

Summary	Similarities and Differences between U.S. GAAP and IFRS
A deferred annuity is when payments or receipts are delayed until a future period.	Similar under U.S. GAAP and IFRS.

6 Apply time value of money concepts to accounting applications involving determining the present value of expected cash flows and valuing bonds.

Summary	Similarities and Differences between U.S. GAAP and IFRS
A common method of measuring assets is the present value of expected future cash flows. For example, notes receivable are reported on the balance sheet at the present value of future cash flows, using the market rate of interest as the discount rate. To determine bond issue proceeds, take the present value of the future cash outflows on the bond, the sum of: • Amount paid when the bond matures (face value) and • Periodic interest payments. Use the market interest rate to discount the cash flows.	Similar under U.S. GAAP and IFRS.

MyLab Accounting

Go to **http://www.pearson.com/mylab/accounting** for the following Questions, Multiple-Choice Questions, Brief Exercises, Exercises, and Problems. They are available with immediate grading, explanations of correct and incorrect answers, and interactive media that acts as your own online tutor.

7 Accounting and the Time Value of Money

For the time value of money end-of-chapter exercises and problems, solutions can be computed using formulas, factor tables, a spreadsheet, or a financial calculator.

Questions

1 **Q7-1.** What is interest? Explain.

1 **Q7-2.** Will an investor earn more if interest is compounded semiannually or if the investment pays only simple interest? Explain.

1 **Q7-3.** If interest is compounded more than once a year, will the effective interest rate be higher than the annual stated interest rate? Explain.

2 **Q7-4.** What is the relation between the present value of an investment and time and interest rate? Explain.

2 4 **Q7-5.** Can an ordinary annuity table be used to determine the present value of a three-year investment that pays $100 in the first year, $150 in the second, and $200 in the last year of the contract? Explain.

3 **Q7-6.** Is it possible to convert the future value of an ordinary annuity table to the future value of an annuity due table? Explain.

4 **Q7-7.** Is the present value of an ordinary annuity more valuable than an annuity due? Explain.

4 **Q7-8.** Is it possible to convert a present value of an ordinary annuity table to the present value of an annuity due table? Explain.

Brief Exercises

1 **BE7-1. Simple Interest.** Assume Shafer Corporation borrowed $100,000 for two years with a stated interest rate of 5%. Interest is not compounded. What is the total interest expense?

1 **BE7-2. Compound Interest.** Assume Shafer Corporation borrowed $100,000 for two years with a stated interest rate of 5%. Interest is compounded annually. What is the total interest expense?

2 **BE7-3. Future Value of a Single Sum.** You decide to deposit $500 at a local bank for one year at a 6% rate of interest. What is the future value of your investment? Draw a timeline to illustrate the problem.

2 **BE7-4. Future Value of a Single Sum, Compound Interest.** You decide to deposit $500 at a local bank for three years at a 6% rate of interest. What is the future value of your investment? Draw a timeline to illustrate the problem. Interest is compounded annually.

2 **BE7-5. Present Value of a Single Sum.** You have been offered an opportunity to receive $1,500 at the end of one year. You can earn an 8% rate of return on your next-best alternative investment. How much are you willing to invest/deposit today ($t = 0$) to have the opportunity to receive $1,500 at the end of one year given that your interest rate is 8%? Draw a timeline to illustrate the problem.

2 **BE7-6. Present Value of a Single Sum, Compound Interest.** You have been offered an opportunity to receive $1,500 at the end of two years. You can earn an 8% rate of return on your next-best alternative investment. How much are you willing to invest/deposit today ($t = 0$) to have the opportunity to receive $1,500 at the end of two years, given that your interest rate is 8%? Draw a timeline to illustrate the problem. Interest is compounded annually.

2 **BE7-7. Future Value of a Single Sum, Compound Interest.** Adam Levine invested $100,000 in a fund that earns 8% annual interest compounded annually. How much will his investment be worth in five years? Draw a timeline to illustrate the problem.

2 **BE7-8. Future Value of a Single Sum, Compound Interest Semiannually.** Blake Shelton decides to invest $50,000 in a fund that will earn 8% annual interest compounded *semiannually*. How much will his investment be worth in three years? Draw a timeline to illustrate the problem.

2 **BE7-9. Present Value of a Single Sum, Compounded Interest Quarterly.** A student needs to have $80,000 in four years. What amount must she invest today if her investment earns 12% annual interest compounded quarterly? Draw a timeline to illustrate the problem.

2 **BE7-10. Present Value of a Single Sum, Calculating Annual Interest Rate.** Kenney Chesney decides to invest $43,630 today because he would like to build a guitar factory for $100,000 in 17 years. Interest is compounded annually. What annual interest rate must he receive to reach the required amount?

2 **BE7-11. Present Value of a Single Sum, Calculating Time Period.** Christina Aguilera decides to invest $352,480 today in a fund that will earn 6% annual interest compounded annually. How many years will it take her to earn $500,000?

3 **BE7-12. Future Value of an Ordinary Annuity.** An undergraduate student decides to make $5,000 deposits in a fund each year over the next four years to accumulate enough money to pay for a master's program. The fund will earn 10% annual interest compounded annually. If the first payment occurs at *year-end*, what amount will be in the fund after four years? Draw a timeline to illustrate the problem.

3 **BE7-13. Future Value of an Annuity Due.** Mariah Carey invests $20,000 each year in a fund that earns 8% annual interest compounded annually. If the first payment into the fund occurs *at the beginning of the year*, what amount will be in the fund after eight years? Draw a timeline to illustrate the problem.

3 **BE7-14. Future Value of an Ordinary Annuity: Calculating Payments.** Assume that you need to have $25,000 in four years. How much must you invest at the *end* of each year to reach your goal? You will earn 8% interest compounded annually. Draw a timeline to illustrate the problem.

4 **BE7-15. Present Value of an Ordinary Annuity.** CB Corporation hopes to withdraw $10,000 at the *end* of each year for six years from a fund that earns 5% interest. How much should the corporation invest today? Draw a timeline to illustrate the problem. Interest is compounded annually.

4 **BE7-16. Present Value of an Annuity Due, Semiannual Compounding Interest.** Genius LLP must withdraw $50,000 at the *beginning* of each semiannual period for the next eight years to satisfy its employee pension obligation. Assuming 10% interest with *semiannual* compounding, how much should the corporation invest today? Draw a timeline to illustrate the problem.

4 **BE7-17. Present Value of an Ordinary Annuity, Calculating Interest Rate.** Cee Lo Green decides to borrow $100,000. In order to settle this loan, he plans to make 10 payments of $13,586.79 at the end of each year. Interest is compounded annually. What is the interest rate on this loan?

Exercises

3 4 **E7-1. Ordinary Annuity, Annuity Due, Using Interest Tables.** Indicate which rate and time period you would use in order to select the correct interest factor for the following situations. In addition, indicate the interest factor that would be used.

a. Using PV of an Ordinary Annuity of $1 Table 7A.5:

Annual Rate	Time Period	Compounded Interest
4%	10	Annually
8%	8	Semiannually
12%	5	Quarterly

b. Using FV of an Annuity Due of $1 Table 7A.4:

Annual Rate	Time Period	Compounded Interest
3%	7	Annually
10%	9	Semiannually
16%	4	Quarterly

1 **E7-2 Simple and Compound Interest.** A recent college graduate decides to invest the $8,000 he received for his college graduation in a fund earning 12% annual interest for four years. At the end of the four-year period, he expects to withdraw the money to purchase a reasonably priced used car. Answer the following questions:

a. What amount would the graduate withdraw after four years, if the investment earns *simple interest*?
b. What amount would the graduate withdraw after four years if interest is compounded *annually*?
c. What amount would the graduate withdraw after four years if interest is compounded *semiannually*?
d. What amount would the graduate withdraw after four years if interest is compounded *quarterly*?

2 **E7-3. Future Value and Present Value of a Single Sum.** Using the present value and future value tables, a financial calculator, or a spreadsheet, answer the following questions.

a. $200,000 is to be received five years from today. What is the PV of this cash flow if 6% interest is compounded *annually*?
b. $200,000 is to be received five years from today. What is the PV of this cash flow if 6% interest is compounded *semiannually*?
c. $100,000 is left on deposit for three years. What is the FV of this investment if 6% interest is compounded *semiannually*?
d. $100,000 is left on deposit for three years. What is the FV of this investment if 6% interest is compounded *quarterly*?

3 4 **E7-4. Future Value and Present Value of Annuities.** Using the present value and future value tables, a financial calculator, or a spreadsheet, answer the following questions.

a. $8,000 is to be deposited at the *end* of each year for the next five years. What is the FV of this investment if 8% interest is compounded *annually*?
b. $8,000 is to be deposited at the *beginning* of each semiannual period for the next five years. What is the FV of this investment if 8% interest is compounded *semiannually*?
c. $5,000 is to be received at the *end* of each year for the next six years. What is the PV of this investment if 10% interest is compounded *annually*?
d. $5,000 is to be received at the *beginning* of each semiannual period for the next six years. What is the PV of this investment if 10% interest is compounded *semiannually*?

3 5 **E7-5. Future Value of an Ordinary Annuity, Future Value of Annuity Due, Deferred Annuity.** Using the appropriate future value table, compute the future value of the following amounts received:

a. $10,000 received at the *end* of each year for five years compounded annually at 10%.
b. $3,000 received at the *beginning* of each year for eight years compounded annually at 7%.
c. $15,000 received at the *end* of the fifth, sixth, seventh, and eighth years at 12% compounded annually.

4 5 **E7-6. Present Value of Ordinary Annuity, Present Value of Annuity Due, Deferred Annuity.** Using the appropriate PV table, compute the present value of the following amounts:

a. $25,000 payable at the *end* of each year for 10 years with 6% interest compounded *annually*.
b. $15,000 receivable at the *beginning* of each semiannual period for five years with 6% interest compounded *semiannually*.
c. $5,000 payable at the *beginning* of the seventh, eighth, and ninth years at 7% compounded annually.

4 5 **E7-7. Present Value of Ordinary Annuity, Deferred Annuity.** Calculate the present value of each of the following cash flows at 8% using interest tables, a financial calculator, or a spreadsheet:

a. $15,000 is to be received at the end of each of the next six *semiannual* interest periods plus $20,000 to be received at the end of each of the next four *semiannual* interest periods after that. Interest is compounded semiannually.
b. There are no cash flows to be received at the end of the first eight *semiannual* periods. However, $24,000 is to be received at the end of the next six *semiannual* periods after that (this is known as a *deferred annuity with semiannual compounding*).

3 5 **E7-8. Future Value of an Ordinary Annuity, Future Value of an Annuity Due, Deferred Annuity.** Calculate the future value of each of the following cash flows using a 5% interest rate:

a. Proven Co. agreed to finance a project by making eight annual deposits of $20,000 at the *end* of each year. The deposits will commence three years from today. Interest is compounded annually. Will the company have enough funds to finance the project, which is estimated to cost $200,000?
b. Proven Co. agreed to finance a project by making eight annual deposits of $20,000 at the *beginning* of each year. The deposits will commence three years from today. Interest is compounded annually. Will the company have enough funds to finance the project, which is estimated to cost $200,000?

2 **E7-9. Single Sum, Solving for Other Variables.** Two independent situations follow. Solve for the appropriate variable.

a. Nardo Co. wants to purchase a piece of heavy equipment in seven years for $751,815. The corporation currently has $500,000 to invest for this purpose. Determine the rate of return (assuming annual compounding) required to accumulate sufficient funds to acquire the equipment at the end of the seven-year period.
b. Apollo Inc. decides to pay a one-time bonus of $59,702.50 to its vice president, who is expected to retire within the next few years. Apollo can invest $50,000 at 3% compounded annually. How many years will it take to have the $59,702.50 to pay the bonus?

2 3 4 **E7-10. Ordinary Annuity, Solve for Interest Rate, Financial Calculator.** Two independent situations follow. Interest is compounded annually. Solve for the appropriate interest rate using a financial calculator or a spreadsheet.

a. A college student wishes to purchase a new car. In order to pay for the vehicle, he borrows $15,000 from his parents today (beginning of the current year). Starting at the end of the current year, he must make 15 equal annual payments of $1,200 each. What interest rate is the student paying his parents?
b. A finance professor wishes to invest $50,000 at the end of this year. He wants his investment to grow to $200,000 in 20 years. At what interest rate must the professor invest to reach his goal?

2 4 **E7-11. Present Value, Note Payable Prices.** Wiz Khalifa would like to invest in an $80,000 face value note payable. The note has a 12-year term and pays 10% annual interest, at the end of each year. Interest is compounded annually.

a. What would he pay for the note if he wanted the note to yield 10%?
b. What would he pay for the note if he wanted the note to yield 12%?
c. What would he pay for the note if he wanted the note to yield 20%?

5 **E7-12. Future Value of a Deferred Annuity.** Lenny Shafer Bakery and Co. budgeted $350,000 to build a factory 10 years from today. Shafer will finance the project by making six equal annual deposits of $50,000 at the *end* of each year commencing four years from today. The company can invest in a financial instrument earning 5%. Interest is compounded annually. Will Shafer have sufficient funds to pay for the $350,000 factory at the end of the 10-year period?

5 **E7-13. Present Value of a Deferred Annuity.** Onix Corporation is required to pay the pension cost of one of its unionized employees. According to the terms of the union contract, the employee will retire in eight years and receive $20,000 at the end of the three consecutive years following retirement. Interest is compounded annually. Compute the pension obligation that Onix has incurred today if the discount rate is 4%.

2 4 **E7-14. Present Value of an Ordinary Annuity, Present Value of Annuity Due, Best Alternative.** Bella D'oro wants to open a new factory in New Jersey. The company can either purchase or lease the factory. There are three options available for Bella D'oro:

1. Purchase a factory with a useful life of 20 years today for $500,000 in cash. This factory has no additional space for rent.
2. Lease a factory with annual lease payments of $50,000 for 20 years. Payments are made at the *beginning* of each year.
3. Purchase a factory with a useful life of 20 years today for $550,000. In addition, the company can rent some additional space for annual rent of $5,000. Assume Bella D'oro would receive the rental payments at the end of each year.

Interest is compounded annually. Which option should Bella D'oro choose given a 10% interest rate?

4 **E7-15. Present Value, Present Value of an Annuity Due, Pension Obligation.** Dave the Lying King Inc., a mattress manufacturer, decides to participate in a pension plan commencing on January 1, 2018. The plan requires a pension payment each year following retirement. An actuary provides the following information: On average, employees will retire in 12 years, their expected life following retirement is 8 years, and the required payment made at the end of each year after retirement is $800,000. The interest rate is 6% compounded annually. What is the PV of the pension liability the company should report on its balance sheet?

2 4 5 **E7-16. Future Value, Present Value, Deferred Annuity, Debt Retirement.** Ne-Yo borrowed $500,000 to build a recording studio in his home. The total amount of the debt along with 8% annual interest must be repaid in 15 years. He decides to invest in a debt sinking fund that will be used to retire the debt. The fund earns 10% interest and requires him to pay an equal amount each year (end of each year) starting in Year 5 and lasting through maturity. Interest is compounded annually. What amount must Ne-Yo contribute each year in order to successfully retire the debt in 15 years?

2 3 **E7-17. Future Value of an Annuity Due, Decision Making.** JayZ reports outstanding debt on his balance sheet of $250,603. He has two options to settle the debt: He can either pay $650,000 at maturity in 10 years, or he can make annual payments of $38,500 for 10 years. Payments are due at the *beginning* of each year. Interest is compounded annually. If JayZ is given an interest rate of 10%, which option should he select?

2 3 **E7-18. Future Value of an Ordinary Annuity, Decision Making.** Assume the same facts as E7-17, except that JayZ is required to make the annual payments at the *end* of the year. Would his decision be the same?

6 **E7-19. Expected Cash Flows.** Jannie Company estimates two scenarios of possible future accounts receivable uncollectibles and the probability of each not being collected in the next year. The risk-free rate is 4%. For each of the scenarios, compute the expected cash flow value based on the probabilities given. Compare the expected cash flows on each case.

Scenario 1		Scenario 2	
Estimated Loss	**Probability**	**Estimated Loss**	**Probability**
$52,000	20%	$52,000	30%
55,000	25%	55,000	25%
60,000	25%	60,000	25%
65,000	30%	65,000	20%

6 **E7-20. Expected Cash Flows.** Build-It-Big Company estimates two scenarios of possible future notes receivable uncollectibles and the probability of each not being collected in the next year. The risk-free rate is 5%. For each of the scenarios, compute the expected cash flow value based on the probabilities given. Compare the expected cash flows on each case.

	Scenario 1		Scenario 2	
	Estimated Loss	**Probability**	**Estimated Loss**	**Probability**
	$ 45,000	20%	$ 45,000	5%
	130,000	75%	130,000	75%
	1,250,000	5%	1,250,000	20%

6 **E7-21. Bond Issue Proceeds.** Determine the bond issue proceeds for each of the following bonds payable. All bonds are issued on January 1, 2019.

a. Solmark Corporation issued bonds in the amount of $150,000 that will be paid in five years. Interest of $15,000 is payable annually each December 31 with the first interest payment at the end of the year on December 31, 2019. If the market rate of interest is 8%, what is the amount of the bond issue proceeds?

b. Meltech Corporation issued bonds in the amount of $800,000 that will be paid in 10 years. Interest of $24,000 is payable semiannually each June 30 and December 31 with the first interest payment at the end of the period on June 30, 2019. If the market rate of interest is 8%, what is the amount of the bond issue proceeds?

6 **E7-22. Bond Issue Proceeds.** Determine the bond issue proceeds for each of the following bonds payable. All bonds are issued on January 1, 2019.

a. Belmark Corporation issued bonds in the amount of $1,250,000 that will be paid in 10 years. Interest of $18,750 is payable semiannually each June 30 and December 31 with the first interest payment at the end of the first period on June 30, 2019. If the market rate of interest is 4%, what is the amount of the bond issue proceeds?

b. Tomtech Corporation issued bonds in the amount of $4,000,000 that will be paid in eight years. Interest of $160,000 is payable semiannually each June 30 and December 31 with the first interest payment at the end of the first period on June 30, 2019. If the market rate of interest is 6%, what is the amount of the bond issue proceeds?

Problems

3 4 **P7-1. Present Value of an Ordinary Annuity, Future Value of an Ordinary Annuity.** FA Manufacturers must make several investment decisions related to its business operations. Interest is compounded annually. Analyze the following independent situations to help FA make a profitable investment.

a. FA Manufacturers reported a $150,000 debt that matures in eight years. In order to accumulate sufficient funds to pay for the debt, the company decided to make eight equal annual payments into a fund paying 5% interest. What amount must FA Manufacturers deposit into the fund at the *end* of each year so that the company will be able to liquidate its debt?

b. On January 1, 2019, FA Manufacturers decided to purchase a piece of heavy machinery. FA agreed to pay $50,000 on the date of purchase and would like to pay the remaining balance with six annual installments of $20,000 commencing at the end of 2019. Given an interest rate of 8%, what value should FA give to the machinery?

c. FA purchased a new machine and wants to pay for it using five equal annual installments of $40,000. The payments start in one year. Given an interest rate of 10%, at what amount should FA value the machine?

2 4 **P7-2. Present Value, Present Value of an Ordinary Annuity, Analysis of Alternatives.** Boyne Painting Contractors needs to purchase a new truck. The owner is considering two different truck models that are currently on the market. Boyne's two alternatives are presented here:

Truck A: Boyne can purchase Truck A for $45,000. The truck has a useful life of 12 years and will require annual maintenance costs of $1,500 each year. Boyne expects to sell the truck for $7,000 after 12 years.

Truck B: Boyne can purchase Truck B for $40,000. This truck also has a useful life of 12 years but will have no scrap value. It will require maintenance costs every four years as follows:

Year 4:	$3,000
Year 8:	$6,000
Year 12:	$8,000

Which truck should Boyne purchase given an interest rate of 6% compounded annually? Assume that maintenance costs will be paid at year-end.

2 4 **P7-3. Present Value, Present Value of an Annuity Due, Analysis of Alternatives.** Charlie Sheen hits the $500,000 jackpot at the Palms Casino in Las Vegas. The casino gives him two options for collecting his winnings:

Option A: Sheen can take all of his winnings today. They will be taxed by the federal government at 40%.

Option B: Sheen can receive his winnings on an installment plan. He would receive 15 annual payments of $40,000 beginning today. Each payment will be taxed at a rate of 20%.

Given an interest rate of 7% compounded annually, which option should Sheen choose?

❷❸❹ **P7-4. Future Value, Present Value of an Ordinary Annuity, Solving for Other Variables.** Answer the following independent questions:

a. You borrowed $15,000 from a friend and promised to repay the loan in seven equal annual installments. Installments begin at the end of the first year. What are the annual payments required to pay back your friend, who would like to earn 4% annual interest compounded annually?

b. Stillwell Corporation has an outstanding debt of $89,800. Assume no interest will accrue on the debt. It has $50,000 to invest in a fund earning 5% interest compounded annually. How many years will it take Stillwell to earn enough money to pay back the debt?

c. Zenith & Co. purchases jewelry from a supplier for $60,020.50. Zenith uses a note to pay for the jewelry that requires the company to make seven annual payments of $10,000. Payments begin at the end of the first year. What interest rate is used in this agreement?

d. Your parents wish to accumulate $200,000 to purchase a summerhouse on the Jersey Shore in 10 years. They would like to make deposits into a fund earning 8% interest compounded semiannually. Deposits begin at the end of the first semi-annual period. Determine the semiannual deposits required to purchase the home.

❹❺ **P7-5. Present Value of an Ordinary Annuity, Deferred Annuity.** A 50-year-old employee of IQ Entertainment was asked to select one of three potential early retirement packages.

Package A: $60,000 received today.

Package B: $10,000 to be received each year for the next eight years.

Package C: $40,000 received today and $5,000 per year for five years beginning at age 55.

Which retirement package should the employee select if he can invest funds at 5% compounded annually, assuming all retirement payments are received at the *beginning* of the year?

❹❺ **P7-6. Present Value of an Annuity Due, Deferred Annuities.** Assuming the same facts as P7-5, how would the employee's decision change if all retirement payments are received at the *end* of the year?

❹❺ **P7-7. Present Value of an Ordinary Annuity, Deferred Annuities.** Norton Dog Care Co. wants to finance a new animal shelter by making eight annual deposits into a fund earning 7% compounded annually. The first four deposits are $20,000 each and will be paid at the *end* of the next four years. The last four deposits are $30,000 each and will be paid at the *end* of the last four years. What is the cost of the new animal shelter?

❹❺ **P7-8. Present Value of an Annuity Due, Deferred Annuities.** Norton Dog Care Co. wants to finance a new animal shelter by making eight annual deposits into a fund earning 7% compounded annually. The first four deposits are to be $20,000 each and will be paid at the *beginning* of the next four years. The last four deposits are to be $30,000 each and will be paid at the *beginning* of the last four years. What is the cost of the new animal shelter?

❷❹ **P7-9. Present Value of an Ordinary Annuity, Present Value of an Annuity Due, Lease Payments.** Carfly Barbers decides to lease a second barbershop. The barbershop has a cash price of $200,000. If Carfly borrowed money to purchase the shop, it would incur a 9% interest rate compounded annually. Answer the following questions:

a. What are the lease payments if the agreement requires eight annual payments beginning *today*?

b. What are the lease payments if the agreement requires eight annual payments beginning *one year* from the agreement date?

c. What are the lease payments if the agreement requires eight annual payments beginning *today* and Carfly will be able to buy the barbershop at the end of the eight-year lease paying a $30,000 residual value? (*Hint:* Subtract the PV of the $30,000 residual value from the cash price of the barbershop to determine the payments using present value tables.)

❸❹❺ **P7-10. Future Value of an Ordinary Annuity, Deferred Annuity.** Carfly Barbers wants to have $200,000 in 10 years to build a second barbershop 10 years from today. Commencing two years from today, Carfly will make eight annual deposits of $18,000 at the end of each year. Alternatively, the company can invest in a financial instrument earning 9% compounded annually.

Answer the following questions:

a. Will Carfly have sufficient funds to pay for the $200,000 barbershop at the end of the 10-year period if the deposits are made at the *end* of the year?

b. Will Carfly have sufficient funds to pay for the $200,000 barbershop at the end of the 10-year period if the deposits are made at the *beginning* of each year?

❷❹ **P7-11. Present Value, Present Value of an Ordinary Annuity, Present Value of an Annuity Due, Lease Payments/Various Compounding Periods.** Carfly Barbers decides to lease another barbershop for a 10-year period. The barbershop has a cash price of $200,000. If Carfly borrowed money to purchase the shop, it would have had to pay 12% interest. Answer the following questions:

a. What are the required payments if the lease agreement requires *annual* payments beginning *one year from today*?

b. What are the required payments if the lease agreement requires *semiannual* payments beginning *six months from the agreement date*?

c. What are the required payments if the lease agreement requires *quarterly* payments beginning *today*?

(2)(4) **P7-12. Present Value of an Ordinary Annuity, Purchase or Lease Analysis.** Fata Food Emporium decides to obtain a new refrigerator to store its meat and produce. The refrigerator has a 15-year useful life and can be sold for $15,000 at the end of its useful life. Fata has two options:

a. Purchase the Refrigerator: Purchase the refrigerator in cash for $100,000. Fata would have to pay all maintenance/insurance costs, which would be $3,000 per year.

b. Lease the Refrigerator: Lease the refrigerator for a 15-year period. Annual lease payments amount to $15,000 with the first payment beginning at the *end* of the year. The seller will pay maintenance and insurance costs, and Fata will return the refrigerator to the seller after 15 years.

Assuming that maintenance and insurance costs are paid at year-end and an interest rate of 10% compounded annually, which option should Fata choose?

(2)(4)(6) **P7-13. Present Value, Present Value of an Ordinary Annuity, Investment Analysis.** Jewels Hair Design Studios would like to purchase another hair salon that is being sold in a neighboring town for $500,000. Assume cash flows occur at the end of the year. Based on past volume of sales, Jewels estimates the net cash flows that would be generated by the salon:

Years	Cash Flows
1-3	$60,000
4	70,000
5	80,000
6	60,000

After six years, Jewels can sell the salon for $300,000. If the interest rate on this investment is 8% compounded annually, should Jewels purchase the salon?

(6) **P7-14. Expected Cash Flows.** Hiteck Electronics sells a diagnostic machine to a hospital with a four-year payment plan. The company would like to estimate the bad debt allowance needed to cover the notes outstanding over the next four years. Estimated lost cash flows and the probability of occurrence for each of the next four years are summarized in the following schedule. The risk-free rate is 8%.

Year	Projected Cash Flow Loss from Uncollected Notes	Probability of Loss Occurring
2019	$ 8,000	90%
	18,000	10%
2020	$10,000	15%
	22,000	70%
	45,000	15%
2021	$ 6,000	85%
	14,000	15%
2022	$26,000	50%
	35,000	50%

What is the estimated bad debt allowance at December 31, 2018?

(6) **P7-15. Bond Issue Proceeds.** Make-It-Big Corporation is planning to build a new factory costing $2,000,000. On January 1, 2019, Make-It-Big plans to issue bonds in the amount of $1,800,000 that will be paid in five years. Interest of $45,000 will be paid semiannually each January 1 and July 1 with the first interest payment at the end of the period on July 1, 2019.

Required »

a. If the market rate of interest is 6%, will Make-It-Big raise enough to build the factory?

b. If the market rate of interest is 2%, will Make-It-Big raise enough to build the factory?

Excel Project

Autograded Excel Project available in **MyLab Accounting**

APPENDIX A

Time Value of Money Factor Tables

Here we present the complete factor tables referenced in the chapter for future value, present value, future value of an ordinary annuity, and future value of an annuity due problems.

TABLE 7A.1 Future Value of $1

$FV = PV \times FACTOR_{7A.1}$

Periods	1%	2%	3%	4%	5%	6%	7%	8%	9%	10%	11%	12%	13%	14%	15%	16%	17%	18%	19%	20%
1	1.01000	1.02000	1.03000	1.04000	1.05000	1.06000	1.07000	1.08000	1.09000	1.10000	1.11000	1.12000	1.13000	1.14000	1.15000	1.16000	1.17000	1.18000	1.19000	1.20000
2	1.02010	1.04040	1.06090	1.08160	1.10250	1.12360	1.14490	1.16640	1.18810	1.21000	1.23210	1.25440	1.27690	1.29960	1.32250	1.34560	1.36890	1.39240	1.41610	1.44000
3	1.03030	1.06121	1.09273	1.12486	1.15763	1.19102	1.22504	1.25971	1.29503	1.33100	1.36763	1.40493	1.44290	1.48154	1.52088	1.56090	1.60161	1.64303	1.68516	1.72800
4	1.04060	1.08243	1.12551	1.16986	1.21551	1.26248	1.31080	1.36049	1.41158	1.46410	1.51807	1.57352	1.63047	1.68896	1.74901	1.81064	1.87389	1.93878	2.00534	2.07360
5	1.05101	1.10408	1.15927	1.21665	1.27628	1.33823	1.40255	1.46933	1.53862	1.61051	1.68506	1.76234	1.84244	1.92541	2.01136	2.10034	2.19245	2.28776	2.38635	2.48832
6	1.06152	1.12616	1.19405	1.26532	1.34010	1.41852	1.50073	1.58687	1.67710	1.77156	1.87041	1.97382	2.08195	2.19497	2.31306	2.43640	2.56516	2.69955	2.83976	2.98598
7	1.07214	1.14869	1.22987	1.31593	1.40710	1.50363	1.60578	1.71382	1.82804	1.94872	2.07616	2.21068	2.35261	2.50227	2.66002	2.82622	3.00124	3.18547	3.37932	3.58318
8	1.08286	1.17166	1.26677	1.36857	1.47746	1.59385	1.71819	1.85093	1.99256	2.14359	2.30454	2.47596	2.65844	2.85259	3.05902	3.27841	3.51145	3.75886	4.02139	4.29982
9	1.09369	1.19509	1.30477	1.42331	1.55133	1.68948	1.83846	1.99900	2.17189	2.35795	2.55804	2.77308	3.00404	3.25195	3.51788	3.80296	4.10840	4.43545	4.78545	5.15978
10	1.10462	1.21899	1.34392	1.48024	1.62889	1.79085	1.96715	2.15892	2.36736	2.59374	2.83942	3.10585	3.39457	3.70722	4.04556	4.41144	4.80683	5.23384	5.69468	6.19174
11	1.11567	1.24337	1.38423	1.53945	1.71034	1.89830	2.10485	2.33164	2.58043	2.85312	3.15176	3.47855	3.83586	4.22623	4.65239	5.11726	5.62399	6.17593	6.77667	7.43008
12	1.12683	1.26824	1.42576	1.60103	1.79586	2.01220	2.25219	2.51817	2.81266	3.13843	3.49845	3.89598	4.33452	4.81790	5.35025	5.93603	6.58007	7.28759	8.06424	8.91610
13	1.13809	1.29361	1.46853	1.66507	1.88565	2.13293	2.40985	2.71962	3.06580	3.45227	3.88328	4.36349	4.89801	5.49241	6.15279	6.88579	7.69868	8.59936	9.59645	10.69932
14	1.14947	1.31948	1.51259	1.73168	1.97993	2.26090	2.57853	2.93719	3.34173	3.79750	4.31044	4.88711	5.53475	6.26135	7.07571	7.98752	9.00745	10.14724	11.41977	12.83918
15	1.16097	1.34587	1.55797	1.80094	2.07893	2.39656	2.75903	3.17217	3.64248	4.17725	4.78459	5.47357	6.25427	7.13794	8.13706	9.26552	10.53872	11.97375	13.58953	15.40702
16	1.17258	1.37279	1.60471	1.87298	2.18287	2.54035	2.95216	3.42594	3.97031	4.59497	5.31089	6.13039	7.06733	8.13725	9.35762	10.74800	12.33030	14.12902	16.17154	18.48843
17	1.18430	1.40024	1.65285	1.94790	2.29202	2.69277	3.15882	3.70002	4.32763	5.05447	5.89509	6.86604	7.98608	9.27646	10.76126	12.46768	14.42646	16.67225	19.24413	22.18611
18	1.19615	1.42825	1.70243	2.02582	2.40662	2.85434	3.37993	3.99602	4.71712	5.55992	6.54355	7.68997	9.02427	10.57517	12.37545	14.46251	16.87895	19.67325	22.90052	26.62333
19	1.20811	1.45681	1.75351	2.10685	2.52695	3.02560	3.61653	4.31570	5.14166	6.11591	7.26334	8.61276	10.19742	12.05569	14.23177	16.77652	19.74838	23.21444	27.25162	31.94800
20	1.22019	1.48595	1.80611	2.19112	2.65330	3.20714	3.86968	4.66096	5.60441	6.72750	8.06231	9.64629	11.52309	13.74349	16.36654	19.46076	23.10560	27.39303	32.42942	38.33760
25	1.28243	1.64061	2.09378	2.66584	3.38635	4.29187	5.42743	6.84848	8.62308	10.83471	13.58546	17.00006	21.23054	26.46192	32.91895	40.87424	50.65783	62.66863	77.38807	95.39622
30	1.34785	1.81136	2.42726	3.24340	4.32194	5.74349	7.61226	10.06266	13.26768	17.44940	22.89230	29.95992	39.11590	50.95016	66.21177	85.84988	111.06465	143.37064	184.67531	237.37631
35	1.41660	1.99989	2.81386	3.94609	5.51602	7.68609	10.67658	14.78534	20.41397	28.10244	38.57485	52.79962	72.06851	98.10018	133.17552	180.31407	243.50347	327.99729	440.70061	590.66823
40	1.48886	2.20804	3.26204	4.80102	7.03999	10.28572	14.97446	21.72452	31.40942	45.25926	65.00087	93.05097	132.78155	188.88351	267.86355	378.72116	533.86871	750.37834	1051.66751	1469.77157
45	1.56481	2.43785	3.78160	5.84118	8.98501	13.76461	21.00245	31.92045	48.32729	72.89048	109.53024	163.98760	244.64140	363.67907	538.76927	795.44383	1170.47941	1716.68388	2509.65060	3657.26199
50	1.64463	2.69159	4.38391	7.10668	11.46740	18.42015	29.45703	46.90161	74.35752	117.39085	184.56483	289.00219	450.73593	700.23299	1083.65744	1670.70380	2566.21528	3927.35686	5988.91390	9100.43815
60	1.81670	3.28103	5.89160	10.51963	18.67919	32.98769	57.94643	101.25706	176.03129	304.48164	524.05724	897.59693	1530.05347	2595.91866	4383.99875	7370.20137	12335.35648	20555.13997	34104.97092	56347.51435

TABLE 7A.2 Present Value of $1

$PV = FV \times FACTOR_{7A.2}$

Periods	1%	2%	3%	4%	5%	6%	7%	8%	9%	10%	11%	12%	13%	14%	15%	16%	17%	18%	19%	20%
1	0.99010	0.98039	0.97087	0.96154	0.95238	0.94340	0.93458	0.92593	0.91743	0.90909	0.90090	0.89286	0.88496	0.87719	0.86957	0.86207	0.85470	0.84746	0.84034	0.83333
2	0.98030	0.96117	0.94260	0.92456	0.90703	0.89000	0.87344	0.85734	0.84168	0.82645	0.81162	0.79719	0.78315	0.76947	0.75614	0.74316	0.73051	0.71818	0.70616	0.69444
3	0.97059	0.94232	0.91514	0.88900	0.86384	0.83962	0.81630	0.79383	0.77218	0.75131	0.73119	0.71178	0.69305	0.67497	0.65752	0.64066	0.62437	0.60863	0.59342	0.57870
4	0.96098	0.92385	0.88849	0.85480	0.82270	0.79209	0.76290	0.73503	0.70843	0.68301	0.65873	0.63552	0.61332	0.59208	0.57175	0.55229	0.53365	0.51579	0.49867	0.48225
5	0.95147	0.90573	0.86261	0.82193	0.78353	0.74726	0.71299	0.68058	0.64993	0.62092	0.59345	0.56743	0.54276	0.51937	0.49718	0.47611	0.45611	0.43711	0.41905	0.40188
6	0.94205	0.88797	0.83748	0.79031	0.74622	0.70496	0.66634	0.63017	0.59627	0.56447	0.53464	0.50663	0.48032	0.45559	0.43233	0.41044	0.38984	0.37043	0.35214	0.33490
7	0.93272	0.87056	0.81309	0.75992	0.71068	0.66506	0.62275	0.58349	0.54703	0.51316	0.48166	0.45235	0.42506	0.39964	0.37594	0.35383	0.33320	0.31393	0.29592	0.27908
8	0.92348	0.85349	0.78941	0.73069	0.67684	0.62741	0.58201	0.54027	0.50187	0.46651	0.43393	0.40388	0.37616	0.35056	0.32690	0.30503	0.28478	0.26604	0.24867	0.23257
9	0.91434	0.83676	0.76642	0.70259	0.64461	0.59190	0.54393	0.50025	0.46043	0.42410	0.39092	0.36061	0.33288	0.30751	0.28426	0.26295	0.24340	0.22546	0.20897	0.19381
10	0.90529	0.82035	0.74409	0.67556	0.61391	0.55839	0.50835	0.46319	0.42241	0.38554	0.35218	0.32197	0.29459	0.26974	0.24718	0.22668	0.20804	0.19106	0.17560	0.16151
11	0.89632	0.80426	0.72242	0.64958	0.58468	0.52679	0.47509	0.42888	0.38753	0.35049	0.31728	0.28748	0.26070	0.23662	0.21494	0.19542	0.17781	0.16192	0.14757	0.13459
12	0.88745	0.78849	0.70138	0.62460	0.55684	0.49697	0.44401	0.39711	0.35553	0.31863	0.28584	0.25668	0.23071	0.20756	0.18691	0.16846	0.15197	0.13722	0.12400	0.11216
13	0.87866	0.77303	0.68095	0.60057	0.53032	0.46884	0.41496	0.36770	0.32618	0.28966	0.25751	0.22917	0.20416	0.18207	0.16253	0.14523	0.12989	0.11629	0.10421	0.09346
14	0.86996	0.75788	0.66112	0.57748	0.50507	0.44230	0.38782	0.34046	0.29925	0.26333	0.23199	0.20462	0.18068	0.15971	0.14133	0.12520	0.11102	0.09855	0.08757	0.07789
15	0.86135	0.74301	0.64186	0.55526	0.48102	0.41727	0.36245	0.31524	0.27454	0.23939	0.20900	0.18270	0.15989	0.14010	0.12289	0.10793	0.09489	0.08352	0.07359	0.06491
16	0.85282	0.72845	0.62317	0.53391	0.45811	0.39365	0.33873	0.29189	0.25187	0.21763	0.18829	0.16312	0.14150	0.12289	0.10686	0.09304	0.08110	0.07078	0.06184	0.05409
17	0.84438	0.71416	0.60502	0.51337	0.43630	0.37136	0.31657	0.27027	0.23107	0.19784	0.16963	0.14564	0.12522	0.10780	0.09293	0.08021	0.06932	0.05998	0.05196	0.04507
18	0.83602	0.70016	0.58739	0.49363	0.41552	0.35034	0.29586	0.25025	0.21199	0.17986	0.15282	0.13004	0.11081	0.09456	0.08081	0.06914	0.05925	0.05083	0.04367	0.03756
19	0.82774	0.68643	0.57029	0.47464	0.39573	0.33051	0.27651	0.23171	0.19449	0.16351	0.13768	0.11611	0.09806	0.08295	0.07027	0.05961	0.05064	0.04308	0.03670	0.03130
20	0.81954	0.67297	0.55368	0.45639	0.37689	0.31180	0.25842	0.21455	0.17843	0.14864	0.12403	0.10367	0.08678	0.07276	0.06110	0.05139	0.04328	0.03651	0.03084	0.02608
25	0.77977	0.60953	0.47761	0.37512	0.29530	0.23300	0.18425	0.14602	0.11597	0.09230	0.07361	0.05882	0.04710	0.03779	0.03038	0.02447	0.01974	0.01596	0.01292	0.01048
30	0.74192	0.55207	0.41199	0.30832	0.23138	0.17411	0.13137	0.09938	0.07537	0.05731	0.04368	0.03338	0.02557	0.01963	0.01510	0.01165	0.00900	0.00697	0.00541	0.00421
35	0.70591	0.50003	0.35538	0.25342	0.18129	0.13011	0.09366	0.06763	0.04899	0.03558	0.02592	0.01894	0.01388	0.01019	0.00751	0.00555	0.00411	0.00305	0.00227	0.00169
40	0.67165	0.45289	0.30656	0.20829	0.14205	0.09722	0.06678	0.04603	0.03184	0.02209	0.01538	0.01075	0.00753	0.00529	0.00373	0.00264	0.00187	0.00133	0.00095	0.00068
45	0.63905	0.41020	0.26444	0.17120	0.11130	0.07265	0.04761	0.03133	0.02069	0.01372	0.00913	0.00610	0.00409	0.00275	0.00186	0.00126	0.00085	0.00058	0.00040	0.00027
50	0.60804	0.37153	0.22811	0.14071	0.08720	0.05429	0.03395	0.02132	0.01345	0.00852	0.00542	0.00346	0.00222	0.00143	0.00092	0.00060	0.00039	0.00025	0.00017	0.00011
60	0.55045	0.30478	0.16973	0.09506	0.05354	0.03031	0.01726	0.00988	0.00568	0.00328	0.00191	0.00111	0.00065	0.00039	0.00023	0.00014	0.00008	0.00005	0.00003	0.00002

TABLE 7A.3 Future Value of an Ordinary Annuity

$FV = PMT \times FACTOR_{7A.3}$

Periods	1%	2%	3%	4%	5%	6%	7%	8%	9%	10%
1	1.00000	1.00000	1.00000	1.00000	1.00000	1.00000	1.00000	1.00000	1.00000	1.00000
2	2.01000	2.02000	2.03000	2.04000	2.05000	2.06000	2.07000	2.08000	2.09000	2.10000
3	3.03010	3.06040	3.09090	3.12160	3.15250	3.18360	3.21490	3.24640	3.27810	3.31000
4	4.06040	4.12161	4.18363	4.24646	4.31013	4.37462	4.43994	4.50611	4.57313	4.64100
5	5.10101	5.20404	5.30914	5.41632	5.52563	5.63709	5.75074	5.86660	5.98471	6.10510
6	6.15202	6.30812	6.46841	6.63298	6.80191	6.97532	7.15329	7.33593	7.52333	7.71561
7	7.21354	7.43428	7.66246	7.89829	8.14201	8.39384	8.65402	8.92280	9.20043	9.48717
8	8.28567	8.58297	8.89234	9.21423	9.54911	9.89747	10.25980	10.63663	11.02847	11.43589
9	9.36853	9.75463	10.15911	10.58280	11.02656	11.49132	11.97799	12.48756	13.02104	13.57948
10	10.46221	10.94972	11.46388	12.00611	12.57789	13.18079	13.81645	14.48656	15.19293	15.93742
11	11.56683	12.16872	12.80780	13.48635	14.20679	14.97164	15.78360	16.64549	17.56029	18.53117
12	12.68250	13.41209	14.19203	15.02581	15.91713	16.86994	17.88845	18.97713	20.14072	21.38428
13	13.80933	14.68033	15.61779	16.62684	17.71298	18.88214	20.14064	21.49530	22.95338	24.52271
14	14.94742	15.97394	17.08632	18.29191	19.59863	21.01507	22.55049	24.21492	26.01919	27.97498
15	16.09690	17.29342	18.59891	20.02359	21.57856	23.27597	25.12902	27.15211	29.36092	31.77248
16	17.25786	18.63929	20.15688	21.82453	23.65749	25.67253	27.88805	30.32428	33.00340	35.94973
17	18.43044	20.01207	21.76159	23.69751	25.84037	28.21288	30.84022	33.75023	36.97370	40.54470
18	19.61475	21.41231	23.41444	25.64541	28.13238	30.90565	33.99903	37.45024	41.30134	45.59917
19	20.81090	22.84056	25.11687	27.67123	30.53900	33.75999	37.37896	41.44626	46.01846	51.15909
20	22.01900	24.29737	26.87037	29.77808	33.06595	36.78559	40.99549	45.76196	51.16012	57.27500
25	28.24320	32.03030	36.45926	41.64591	47.72710	54.86451	63.24904	73.10594	84.70090	98.34706
30	34.78489	40.56808	47.57542	56.08494	66.43885	79.05819	94.46079	113.28321	136.30754	164.49402
35	41.66028	49.99448	60.46208	73.65222	90.32031	111.43478	138.23688	172.31680	215.71075	271.02437
40	48.88637	60.40198	75.40126	95.02552	120.79977	154.76197	199.63511	259.05652	337.88245	442.59256
45	56.48107	71.89271	92.71986	121.02939	159.70016	212.74351	285.74931	386.50562	525.85873	718.90484
50	64.46318	84.57940	112.79687	152.66708	209.34800	290.33590	406.52893	573.77016	815.08356	1163.90853
60	81.66967	114.05154	163.05344	237.99069	353.58372	533.12818	813.52038	1253.21330	1944.79213	3034.81640

Periods	11%	12%	13%	14%	15%	16%	17%	18%	19%	20%
1	1.00000	1.00000	1.00000	1.00000	1.00000	1.00000	1.00000	1.00000	1.00000	1.00000
2	2.11000	2.12000	2.13000	2.14000	2.15000	2.16000	2.17000	2.18000	2.19000	2.20000
3	3.34210	3.37440	3.40690	3.43960	3.47250	3.50560	3.53890	3.57240	3.60610	3.64000
4	4.70973	4.77933	4.84980	4.92114	4.99338	5.06650	5.14051	5.21543	5.29126	5.36800
5	6.22780	6.35285	6.48027	6.61010	6.74238	6.87714	7.01440	7.15421	7.29660	7.44160
6	7.91286	8.11519	8.32271	8.53552	8.75374	8.97748	9.20685	9.44197	9.68295	9.92992
7	9.78327	10.08901	10.40466	10.73049	11.06680	11.41387	11.77201	12.14152	12.52271	12.91590
8	11.85943	12.29969	12.75726	13.23276	13.72682	14.24009	14.77325	15.32700	15.90203	16.49908
9	14.16397	14.77566	15.41571	16.08535	16.78584	17.51851	18.28471	19.08585	19.92341	20.79890
10	16.72201	17.54874	18.41975	19.33730	20.30372	21.32147	22.39311	23.52131	24.70886	25.95868
11	19.56143	20.65458	21.81432	23.04452	24.34928	25.73290	27.19994	28.75514	30.40355	32.15042
12	22.71319	24.13313	25.65018	27.27075	29.00167	30.85017	32.82393	34.93107	37.18022	39.58050
13	26.21164	28.02911	29.98470	32.08865	34.35192	36.78620	39.40399	42.21866	45.24446	48.49660
14	30.09492	32.39260	34.88271	37.58107	40.50471	43.67199	47.10267	50.81802	54.84091	59.19592
15	34.40536	37.27971	40.41746	43.84241	47.58041	51.65951	56.11013	60.96527	66.26068	72.03511
16	39.18995	42.75328	46.67173	50.98035	55.71747	60.92503	66.64885	72.93901	79.85021	87.44213
17	44.50084	48.88367	53.73906	59.11760	65.07509	71.67303	78.97915	87.06804	96.02175	105.93056
18	50.39594	55.74971	61.72514	68.39407	75.83636	84.14072	93.40561	103.74028	115.26588	128.11667
19	56.93949	63.43968	70.74941	78.96923	88.21181	98.60323	110.28456	123.41353	138.16640	154.74000
20	64.20283	72.05244	80.94683	91.02493	102.44358	115.37975	130.03294	146.62797	165.41802	186.68800
25	114.41331	133.33387	155.61956	181.87083	212.79302	249.21402	292.10486	342.60349	402.04249	471.98108
30	199.02088	241.33268	293.19922	356.78685	434.74515	530.31173	647.43912	790.94799	966.71217	1181.88157
35	341.58955	431.66350	546.68082	693.57270	881.17016	1120.71295	1426.49102	1816.65161	2314.21372	2948.34115
40	581.82607	767.09142	1013.70424	1342.02510	1779.09031	2360.75724	3134.52184	4163.21303	5529.82898	7343.85784
45	986.63856	1358.23003	1874.16463	2590.56480	3585.12846	4965.27391	6879.29065	9531.57711	13203.42423	18281.30994
50	1668.77115	2400.01825	3459.50712	4994.52135	7217.71628	10435.64877	15089.50167	21813.09367	31515.33633	45497.19075
60	4755.06584	7471.64111	11761.94979	18535.13328	29219.99164	46057.50853	72555.03813	114189.66648	179494.58379	281732.57177

TABLE 7A.4 Future Value of an Annuity Due

$FV = PMT \times FACTOR_{7A.4}$

Periods	1%	2%	3%	4%	5%	6%	7%	8%	9%	10%	11%	12%	13%	14%	15%	16%	17%	18%	19%	20%
1	1.01000	1.02000	1.03000	1.04000	1.05000	1.06000	1.07000	1.08000	1.09000	1.10000	1.11000	1.12000	1.13000	1.14000	1.15000	1.16000	1.17000	1.18000	1.19000	1.20000
2	2.03010	2.06040	2.09090	2.12160	2.15250	2.18360	2.21490	2.24640	2.27810	2.31000	2.34210	2.37440	2.40690	2.43960	2.47250	2.50560	2.53890	2.57240	2.60610	2.64000
3	3.06040	3.12161	3.18363	3.24646	3.31013	3.37462	3.43994	3.50611	3.57313	3.64100	3.70973	3.77933	3.84980	3.92114	3.99338	4.06650	4.14051	4.21543	4.29126	4.36800
4	4.10101	4.20404	4.30914	4.41632	4.52563	4.63709	4.75074	4.86660	4.98471	5.10510	5.22780	5.35285	5.48027	5.61010	5.74238	5.87714	6.01440	6.15421	6.29660	6.44160
5	5.15202	5.30812	5.46841	5.63298	5.80191	5.97532	6.15329	6.33593	6.52333	6.71561	6.91286	7.11519	7.32271	7.53552	7.75374	7.97748	8.20685	8.44197	8.68295	8.92992
6	6.21354	6.43428	6.66246	6.89829	7.14201	7.39384	7.65402	7.92280	8.20043	8.48717	8.78327	9.08901	9.40466	9.73049	10.06680	10.41387	10.77201	11.14152	11.52271	11.91590
7	7.28567	7.58297	7.89234	8.21423	8.54911	8.89747	9.25980	9.63663	10.02847	10.43589	10.85943	11.29969	11.75726	12.23276	12.72682	13.24009	13.77325	14.32700	14.90203	15.49908
8	8.36853	8.75463	9.15911	9.58280	10.02656	10.49132	10.97799	11.48756	12.02104	12.57948	13.16397	13.77566	14.41571	15.08535	15.78584	16.51851	17.28471	18.08585	18.92341	19.79890
9	9.46221	9.94972	10.46388	11.00611	11.57789	12.18079	12.81645	13.48656	14.19293	14.93742	15.72201	16.54874	17.41975	18.33730	19.30372	20.32147	21.39311	22.52131	23.70886	24.95868
10	10.56683	11.16872	11.80780	12.48635	13.20679	13.97164	14.78360	15.64549	16.56029	17.53117	18.56143	19.65458	20.81432	22.04452	23.34928	24.73290	26.19994	27.75514	29.40355	31.15042
11	11.68250	12.41209	13.19203	14.02581	14.91713	15.86994	16.88845	17.97713	19.14072	20.38428	21.71319	23.13313	24.65018	26.27075	28.00167	29.85017	31.82393	33.93107	36.18022	38.58050
12	12.80933	13.68033	14.61779	15.62684	16.71298	17.88214	19.14064	20.49530	21.95338	23.52271	25.21164	27.02911	28.98470	31.08865	33.35192	35.78620	38.40399	41.21866	44.24446	47.49660
13	13.94742	14.97394	16.08632	17.29191	18.59863	20.01507	21.55049	23.21492	25.01919	26.97498	29.09492	31.39260	33.88271	36.58107	39.50471	42.67199	46.10267	49.81802	53.84091	58.19592
14	15.09690	16.29342	17.59891	19.02359	20.57856	22.27597	24.12902	26.15211	28.36092	30.77248	33.40536	36.27971	39.41746	42.84241	46.58041	50.65951	55.11013	59.96527	65.26068	71.03511
15	16.25786	17.63929	19.15688	20.82453	22.65749	24.67253	26.88805	29.32428	32.00340	34.94973	38.18995	41.75328	45.67173	49.98035	54.71747	59.92503	65.64885	71.93901	78.85021	86.44213
16	17.43044	19.01207	20.76159	22.69751	24.84037	27.21288	29.84022	32.75023	35.97370	39.54470	43.50084	47.88367	52.73906	58.11760	64.07509	70.67303	77.97915	86.06804	95.02175	104.93056
17	18.61475	20.41231	22.41444	24.64541	27.13238	29.90565	32.99903	36.45024	40.30134	44.59917	49.39594	54.74971	60.72514	67.39407	74.83636	83.14072	92.40561	102.74028	114.26588	127.11667
18	19.81090	21.84056	24.11687	26.67123	29.53900	32.75999	36.37896	40.44626	45.01846	50.15909	55.93949	62.43968	69.74941	77.96923	87.21181	97.60323	109.28456	122.41353	137.16640	153.74000
19	21.01900	23.29737	25.87037	28.77808	32.06595	35.78559	39.99549	44.76196	50.16012	56.27500	63.20283	71.05244	79.94683	90.02493	101.44358	114.37975	129.03294	145.62797	164.41802	185.68800
20	22.23919	24.78332	27.67649	30.96920	34.71925	38.99273	43.86518	49.42292	55.76453	63.00250	71.26514	80.69874	91.46992	103.76842	117.81012	133.84051	152.13854	173.02100	196.84744	224.02560
25	28.52563	32.67091	37.55304	43.31174	50.11345	58.15638	67.67647	78.95442	92.32398	108.18177	126.99877	149.33393	175.85010	207.33274	244.71197	289.08827	341.76268	404.27211	478.43056	566.37730
30	35.13274	41.37944	49.00268	58.32834	69.76079	83.80168	101.07304	122.34587	148.57522	180.94342	220.91317	270.29261	331.31511	406.73701	499.95692	615.16161	757.50377	933.31863	1150.38748	1418.25788
35	42.07688	50.99437	62.27594	76.59831	94.83632	118.12087	147.91346	186.10215	235.12472	298.12681	379.16441	483.46312	617.74933	790.67288	1013.34568	1300.02703	1668.99450	2143.64890	2753.91433	3538.00937
40	49.37524	61.61002	77.66330	98.82654	126.83976	164.04768	213.60957	279.78104	368.29187	486.85181	645.82693	859.14239	1145.48579	1529.90861	2045.95385	2738.47840	3667.39055	4912.59137	6580.49649	8812.62941
45	57.04589	73.33056	95.50146	125.87057	167.68516	225.50812	305.75176	417.42607	573.18602	790.79532	1095.16880	1521.21764	2117.80603	2953.24387	4122.89773	5759.71774	8048.77006	11247.26098	15712.07483	21937.57193
50	65.10781	86.27099	116.18077	158.77377	219.81540	307.75606	434.98595	619.67177	888.44108	1280.29938	1852.33598	2688.02044	3909.24304	5693.75433	8300.37372	12105.35258	17654.71696	25739.45053	37503.25023	54596.62890
60	82.48637	116.33257	167.94504	247.51031	371.26290	565.11587	870.46681	1353.47036	2119.82342	3338.29803	5278.12308	8368.23805	13291.00327	21130.05194	33602.99038	53426.70990	84889.39461	134743.80644	213598.55470	338079.08612

TABLE 7A.5 Present Value of an Ordinary Annuity

$PV = PMT \times FACTOR_{7A.5}$

Periods	1%	2%	3%	4%	5%	6%	7%	8%	9%	10%	11%	12%	13%	14%	15%	16%	17%	18%	19%	20%
1	0.99010	0.98039	0.97087	0.96154	0.95238	0.94340	0.93458	0.92593	0.91743	0.90909	0.90090	0.89286	0.88496	0.87719	0.86957	0.86207	0.85470	0.84746	0.84034	0.83333
2	1.97040	1.94156	1.91347	1.88609	1.85941	1.83339	1.80802	1.78326	1.75911	1.73554	1.71252	1.69005	1.66810	1.64666	1.62571	1.60523	1.58521	1.56564	1.54650	1.52778
3	2.94099	2.88388	2.82861	2.77509	2.72325	2.67301	2.62432	2.57710	2.53129	2.48685	2.44371	2.40183	2.36115	2.32163	2.28323	2.24589	2.20958	2.17427	2.13992	2.10648
4	3.90197	3.80773	3.71710	3.62990	3.54595	3.46511	3.38721	3.31213	3.23972	3.16987	3.10245	3.03735	2.97447	2.91371	2.85498	2.79818	2.74324	2.69006	2.63859	2.58873
5	4.85343	4.71346	4.57971	4.45182	4.32948	4.21236	4.10020	3.99271	3.88965	3.79079	3.69590	3.60478	3.51723	3.43308	3.35216	3.27429	3.19935	3.12717	3.05763	2.99061
6	5.79548	5.60143	5.41719	5.24214	5.07569	4.91732	4.76654	4.62288	4.48592	4.35526	4.23054	4.11141	3.99755	3.88867	3.78448	3.68474	3.58918	3.49760	3.40978	3.32551
7	6.72819	6.47199	6.23028	6.00205	5.78637	5.58238	5.38929	5.20637	5.03295	4.86842	4.71220	4.56376	4.42261	4.28830	4.16042	4.03857	3.92238	3.81153	3.70570	3.60459
8	7.65168	7.32548	7.01969	6.73274	6.46321	6.20979	5.97130	5.74664	5.53482	5.33493	5.14612	4.96764	4.79877	4.63886	4.48732	4.34359	4.20716	4.07757	3.95437	3.83716
9	8.56602	8.16224	7.78611	7.43533	7.10782	6.80169	6.51523	6.24689	5.99525	5.75902	5.53705	5.32825	5.13166	4.94637	4.77158	4.60654	4.45057	4.30302	4.16333	4.03097
10	9.47130	8.98259	8.53020	8.11090	7.72173	7.36009	7.02358	6.71008	6.41766	6.14457	5.88923	5.65022	5.42624	5.21612	5.01877	4.83323	4.65860	4.49409	4.33893	4.19247
11	10.36763	9.78685	9.25262	8.76048	8.30641	7.88687	7.49867	7.13896	6.80519	6.49506	6.20652	5.93770	5.68694	5.45273	5.23371	5.02864	4.83641	4.65601	4.48650	4.32706
12	11.25508	10.57534	9.95400	9.38507	8.86325	8.38384	7.94269	7.53608	7.16073	6.81369	6.49236	6.19437	5.91765	5.66029	5.42062	5.19711	4.98839	4.79322	4.61050	4.43922
13	12.13374	11.34837	10.63496	9.98565	9.39357	8.85268	8.35765	7.90378	7.48690	7.10336	6.74987	6.42355	6.12181	5.84236	5.58315	5.34233	5.11828	4.90951	4.71471	4.53268
14	13.00370	12.10625	11.29607	10.56312	9.89864	9.29498	8.74547	8.24424	7.78615	7.36669	6.98187	6.62817	6.30249	6.00207	5.72448	5.46753	5.22930	5.00806	4.80228	4.61057
15	13.86505	12.84926	11.93794	11.11839	10.37966	9.71225	9.10791	8.55948	8.06069	7.60608	7.19087	6.81086	6.46238	6.14217	5.84737	5.57546	5.32419	5.09158	4.87586	4.67547
16	14.71787	13.57771	12.56110	11.65230	10.83777	10.10590	9.44665	8.85137	8.31256	7.82371	7.37916	6.97399	6.60388	6.26506	5.95423	5.66850	5.40529	5.16235	4.93770	4.72956
17	15.56225	14.29187	13.16612	12.16567	11.27407	10.47726	9.76322	9.12164	8.54363	8.02155	7.54879	7.11963	6.72909	6.37286	6.04716	5.74870	5.47461	5.22233	4.98966	4.77463
18	16.39827	14.99203	13.75351	12.65930	11.68959	10.82760	10.05909	9.37189	8.75563	8.20141	7.70162	7.24967	6.83991	6.46742	6.12797	5.81785	5.53385	5.27316	5.03333	4.81219
19	17.22601	15.67846	14.32380	13.13394	12.08532	11.15812	10.33560	9.60360	8.95011	8.36492	7.83929	7.36578	6.93797	6.55037	6.19823	5.87746	5.58449	5.31624	5.07003	4.84350
20	18.04555	16.35143	14.87747	13.59033	12.46221	11.46992	10.59401	9.81815	9.12855	8.51356	7.96333	7.46944	7.02475	6.62313	6.25933	5.92884	5.62777	5.35275	5.10086	4.86958
25	22.02316	19.52346	17.41315	15.62208	14.09394	12.78336	11.65358	10.67478	9.82258	9.07704	8.42174	7.84314	7.32998	6.87293	6.46415	6.09709	5.76623	5.46691	5.19515	4.94759
30	25.80771	22.39646	19.60044	17.29203	15.37245	13.76483	12.40904	11.25778	10.27365	9.42691	8.69379	8.05518	7.49565	7.00266	6.56598	6.17720	5.82939	5.51681	5.23466	4.97894
35	29.40858	24.99862	21.48722	18.66461	16.37419	14.49825	12.94767	11.65457	10.56682	9.64416	8.85524	8.17550	7.58557	7.07005	6.61661	6.21534	5.85820	5.53862	5.25122	4.99154
40	32.83469	27.35548	23.11477	19.79277	17.15909	15.04630	13.33171	11.92461	10.75736	9.77905	8.95105	8.24378	7.63438	7.10504	6.64178	6.23350	5.87133	5.54815	5.25815	4.99660
45	36.09451	29.49016	24.51871	20.72004	17.77407	15.45583	13.60552	12.10840	10.88120	9.86281	9.00791	8.28252	7.66086	7.12322	6.65429	6.24214	5.87733	5.55232	5.26106	4.99863
50	39.19612	31.42361	25.72976	21.48218	18.25593	15.76186	13.80075	12.23348	10.96168	9.91481	9.04165	8.30450	7.67524	7.13266	6.66051	6.24626	5.88006	5.55414	5.26228	4.99945
60	44.95504	34.76089	27.67556	22.62349	18.92929	16.16143	14.03918	12.37655	11.04799	9.96716	9.07356	8.32405	7.68728	7.14011	6.66515	6.24915	5.88188	5.55529	5.26300	4.99991

TABLE 7A.6 Present Value of an Annuity Due

$PV = PMT \times FACTOR_{7A.6}$

Periods	1%	2%	3%	4%	5%	6%	7%	8%	9%	10%	11%	12%	13%	14%	15%	16%	17%	18%	19%	20%
1	1.00000	1.00000	1.00000	1.00000	1.00000	1.00000	1.00000	1.00000	1.00000	1.00000	1.00000	1.00000	1.00000	1.00000	1.00000	1.00000	1.00000	1.00000	1.00000	1.00000
2	1.99010	1.98039	1.97087	1.96154	1.95238	1.94340	1.93458	1.92593	1.91743	1.90909	1.90090	1.89286	1.88496	1.87719	1.86957	1.86207	1.85470	1.84746	1.84034	1.83333
3	2.97040	2.94156	2.91347	2.88609	2.85941	2.83339	2.80802	2.78326	2.75911	2.73554	2.71252	2.69005	2.66810	2.64666	2.62571	2.60523	2.58521	2.56564	2.54650	2.52778
4	3.94099	3.88388	3.82861	3.77509	3.72325	3.67301	3.62432	3.57710	3.53129	3.48685	3.44371	3.40183	3.36115	3.32163	3.28323	3.24589	3.20958	3.17427	3.13992	3.10648
5	4.90197	4.80773	4.71710	4.62990	4.54595	4.46511	4.38721	4.31213	4.23972	4.16987	4.10245	4.03735	3.97447	3.91371	3.85498	3.79818	3.74324	3.69006	3.63859	3.58873
6	5.85343	5.71346	5.57971	5.45182	5.32948	5.21236	5.10020	4.99271	4.88965	4.79079	4.69590	4.60478	4.51723	4.43308	4.35216	4.27429	4.19935	4.12717	4.05763	3.99061
7	6.79548	6.60143	6.41719	6.24214	6.07569	5.91732	5.76654	5.62288	5.48592	5.35526	5.23054	5.11141	4.99755	4.88867	4.78448	4.68474	4.58918	4.49760	4.40978	4.32551
8	7.72819	7.47199	7.23028	7.00205	6.78637	6.58238	6.38929	6.20637	6.03295	5.86842	5.71220	5.56376	5.42261	5.28830	5.16042	5.03857	4.92238	4.81153	4.70570	4.60459
9	8.65168	8.32548	8.01969	7.73274	7.46321	7.20979	6.97130	6.74664	6.53482	6.33493	6.14612	5.96764	5.79877	5.63886	5.48732	5.34359	5.20716	5.07757	4.95437	4.83716
10	9.56602	9.16224	8.78611	8.43533	8.10782	7.80169	7.51523	7.24689	6.99525	6.75902	6.53705	6.32825	6.13166	5.94637	5.77158	5.60654	5.45057	5.30302	5.16333	5.03097
11	10.47130	9.98259	9.53020	9.11090	8.72173	8.36009	8.02358	7.71008	7.41766	7.14457	6.88923	6.65022	6.42624	6.21612	6.01877	5.83323	5.65860	5.49409	5.33893	5.19247
12	11.36763	10.78685	10.25262	9.76048	9.30641	8.88687	8.49867	8.13896	7.80519	7.49506	7.20652	6.93770	6.68694	6.45273	6.23371	6.02864	5.83641	5.65601	5.48650	5.32706
13	12.25508	11.57534	10.95400	10.38507	9.86325	9.38384	8.94269	8.53608	8.16073	7.81369	7.49236	7.19437	6.91765	6.66029	6.42062	6.19711	5.98839	5.79322	5.61050	5.43922
14	13.13374	12.34837	11.63496	10.98565	10.39357	9.85268	9.35765	8.90378	8.48690	8.10336	7.74987	7.42355	7.12181	6.84236	6.58315	6.34233	6.11828	5.90951	5.71471	5.53268
15	14.00370	13.10625	12.29607	11.56312	10.89864	10.29498	9.74547	9.24424	8.78615	8.36669	7.98187	7.62817	7.30249	7.00207	6.72448	6.46753	6.22930	6.00806	5.80228	5.61057
16	14.86505	13.84926	12.93794	12.11839	11.37966	10.71225	10.10791	9.55948	9.06069	8.60608	8.19087	7.81086	7.46238	7.14217	6.84737	6.57546	6.32419	6.09158	5.87586	5.67547
17	15.71787	14.57771	13.56110	12.65230	11.83777	11.10590	10.44665	9.85137	9.31256	8.82371	8.37916	7.97399	7.60388	7.26506	6.95423	6.66850	6.40529	6.16235	5.93770	5.72956
18	16.56225	15.29187	14.16612	13.16567	12.27407	11.47726	10.76322	10.12164	9.54363	9.02155	8.54879	8.11963	7.72909	7.37286	7.04716	6.74870	6.47461	6.22233	5.98966	5.77463
19	17.39827	15.99203	14.75351	13.65930	12.68959	11.82760	11.05909	10.37189	9.75563	9.20141	8.70162	8.24967	7.83991	7.46742	7.12797	6.81785	6.53385	6.27316	6.03333	5.81219
20	18.22601	16.67846	15.32380	14.13394	13.08532	12.15812	11.33560	10.60360	9.95011	9.36492	8.83929	8.36578	7.93797	7.55037	7.19823	6.87746	6.58449	6.31624	6.07003	5.84350
25	22.24339	19.91393	17.93554	16.24696	14.79864	13.55036	12.46933	11.52876	10.70661	9.98474	9.34814	8.78432	8.28288	7.83514	7.43377	7.07263	6.74649	6.45095	6.18223	5.93710
30	26.06579	22.84438	20.18845	17.98371	16.14107	14.59072	13.27767	12.15841	11.19828	10.36961	9.65011	9.02181	8.47009	7.98304	7.55088	7.16555	6.82039	6.50983	6.22924	5.97472
35	29.70267	25.49859	22.13184	19.41120	17.19290	15.36814	13.85401	12.58693	11.51784	10.60857	9.82932	9.15656	8.57170	8.05985	7.60910	7.20979	6.85409	6.53557	6.24895	5.98984
40	33.16303	27.90259	23.80822	20.58448	18.01704	15.94907	14.26493	12.87858	11.72552	10.75696	9.93567	9.23303	8.62684	8.09975	7.63805	7.23086	6.86946	6.54682	6.25720	5.99592
45	36.45545	30.07996	25.25427	21.54884	18.66277	16.38318	14.55791	13.07707	11.86051	10.84909	9.99878	9.27642	8.65678	8.12047	7.65244	7.24089	6.87647	6.55174	6.26066	5.99836
50	39.58808	32.05208	26.50166	22.34147	19.16872	16.70757	14.76680	13.21216	11.94823	10.90630	10.03624	9.30104	8.67302	8.13123	7.65959	7.24566	6.87967	6.55389	6.26211	5.99934
60	45.40459	35.45610	28.50583	23.52843	19.87575	17.13111	15.02192	13.36668	12.04231	10.96387	10.07165	9.32294	8.68663	8.13972	7.66492	7.24902	6.88180	6.55524	6.26297	5.99989

8 Revenue Recognition

LEARNING OBJECTIVES

1. Understand basic revenue recognition and measurement issues.
2. Explain how to identify a contract with a customer.
3. Identify the separate performance obligations in a contract, including determining whether there are distinct goods or services.
4. Explain how to determine the transaction price in recognizing revenue.
5. Demonstrate allocating the transaction price to performance obligations when recognizing revenue.
6. Assess whether to recognize revenue when, or as, each performance obligation is satisfied.
7. Describe the accounting for long-term contracts, including implementing the percentage-of-completion method and the completed-contract method.
8. Describe and demonstrate the accounting for special issues in revenue recognition, including right-to-return sales, consignment sales, principal-agent sales, bill-and-hold arrangements, and channel stuffing.
9. Detail required disclosures related to revenue recognition.

Kristoffer Tripplaar/Alamy Stock Photo

Introduction

REVENUE IS THE FIRST LINE item on any company's income statement. Depending on the nature of a company's business, revenue may be called sales revenue, rental revenue, royalty revenue, investment revenue, or service revenue. Some revenues are accounted for easily, such as ***Target*** recording sales revenue for a customer purchase. Other sales transactions are more complex due to timing issues related to when the company should recognize the revenue.

When to record revenue is an important issue in many companies. Consider the purchase of a Kindle from ***Amazon***. A Kindle buyer typically receives the device, wireless access, and software upgrades. That is, the buyer pays one sales price and receives multiple items. What does ***Amazon*** record as a sale—the sale of the Kindle, the wireless service, the software upgrades, or the sum of all three? In practice, ***Amazon*** allocates the sales price to these three items, recording the revenue for each item in different time periods based on when it transfers the good or service. That is, the seller recognizes the revenue related to the device, which is a substantial portion of the sales price on the date of the delivery. ***Amazon*** then recognizes revenues related to wireless access and software upgrades as it provides the services over the average life of the device.

In this chapter, we discuss revenue recognition and the primary accounting issues of determining the timing and amount of revenue recognition. Usually, a company recognizes revenue when it delivers a good or provides a service. Sometimes a company recognizes revenue before the delivery of a good, such as with long-term construction contracts. We also discuss these scenarios and other more complex revenue recognition cases. The revenue recognition standard is fully converged between U.S. GAAP and IFRS. «

1 Understand basic revenue recognition and measurement issues.

Revenue Recognition Overview

Revenue recognition involves issues dealing with both timing (i.e., when revenue is recognized) and measurement (i.e., how much revenue is recognized). With regard to timing, the fundamental principle of revenue recognition is that a company should recognize revenue when it transfers *control* of an asset (either a good or service) to the customer. With regard to measurement, the fundamental principle is that a company should recognize the amount of revenue that it expects to be entitled to receive in exchange for the goods or services. Finally, the company recognizes revenue as it satisfies each performance obligation.

In order to accomplish these objectives of revenue recognition, companies must follow five steps. These five steps are outlined in Exhibit 8.1.

EXHIBIT 8.1 Overview of Five Steps in Revenue Recognition

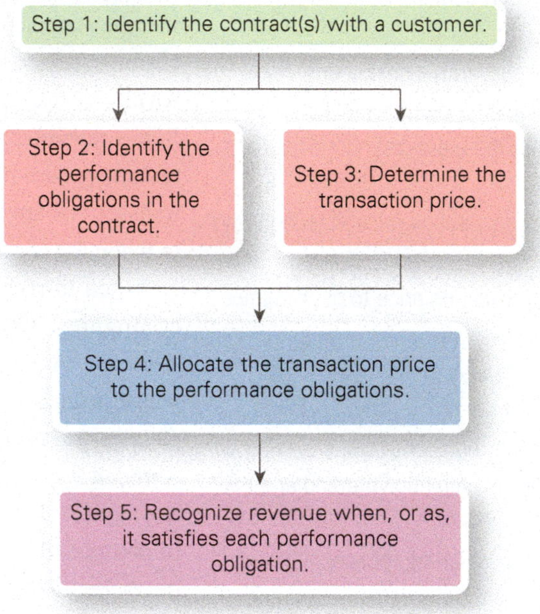

The seller must meet the Step 1 requirement, to identify the contract, in order to continue with the revenue recognition process. Once the contract is identified, the seller must identify both the separate performance obligations (Step 2) and the transaction price (Step 3) in order to continue with Step 4. Step 4 takes the transaction price that is determined in Step 3 and allocates it to the separate performance obligations that are identified in Step 2. Once the seller has identified the separate performance obligations and has a price attached to each, it determines the appropriate timing for the recognition of revenue for each performance obligation separately. Example 8.1 provides a simplified illustration of the five-step approach to provide a conceptual understanding of the steps.

EXAMPLE 8.1

Simplified Example of the Five Steps

PROBLEM: Access Unlimited (AU) sells smartphones and phone service. AU sells phones for $350 each and 12-month service plans for $40 a month. The phones cost AU $150 each. AU also bundles the phones with a 12-month service plan for $750. On January 1, a customer signs a contract with AU to purchase the bundle with the service plan starting immediately. The customer pays in full, and receives the phone on January 1. AU uses the perpetual inventory method. AU prepares financial statements on a quarterly basis. When does AU recognize revenue, and what is the amount of revenue to be recognized?

SOLUTION: In Step 1, AU identifies the contract with the customer. It separates the transaction into two separate performance obligations—the smartphone and the service plan in Step 2. Regarding Step 3, the transaction price is $750.

To complete Step 4, AU will allocate the $750 between the phone and the service plan on a relative sales value basis. (We cover this approach in more detail in our discussion of Step 4). The combination of the separate selling prices for the phone ($350) and service plan ($480) is $830. The phone constitutes 42.2% of the total price ($350/$830), and the service plan is 57.8% of the total price ($480/$830). Thus, AU allocates 42.2% of the transaction price of $750, or $316.50, to the phone and 57.8% of the transaction price of $750, or $433.50, to the service plan.

To complete Step 5, AU will recognize the $316.50 revenue for the phone when the phone is delivered to the customer. It will recognize the $433.50 revenue for the plan over the 12-month service period.

Thus, on January 1, AU will record the cash receipt. Because it delivered the phone on that day, it will record $316.50 of revenue and will record cost of goods sold and reduce its phone inventory.

Account	**January 1**	
Cash	750.00	
Unearned Revenue		433.50
Sales Revenue		316.50
Cost of Goods Sold	150.00	
Inventory		150.00

AU will recognize $108.38 ($433.50/4 quarters) service revenue over each of the following four quarters.

Account	**March 31, June 30, September 30, and December 31**	
Unearned Revenue	108.38	
Service Revenue		108.38

THE CONCEPTUAL FRAMEWORK CONNECTION
Revenue Recognition

The revenue recognition standards discussed in this chapter are new and are effective for public companies with fiscal years beginning after December 15, 2017. They are not completely aligned with the conceptual framework. That is, the revenue recognition standards indicate that the overarching principle of revenue recognition is the notion of the transfer of control of the goods or services. In contrast, the current conceptual framework does not mention transfer of control but rather states that a company recognizes revenue when it meets two conditions:

1. The revenue has been earned, and
2. The revenue is realized or realizable.

Although transfer of control often occurs simultaneously with the culmination of the earning process, there are scenarios in which they do not happen at the same time. How then can the standards and the conceptual framework that both come from the FASB conflict? As we discussed in Chapter 2, the FASB is currently in the process of rewriting the conceptual framework. We expect that the FASB will align the conceptual framework with the new standard when it rewrites the framework.

Next, we cover each of the five steps in the revenue recognition process in depth. Note that we do not actually record a journal entry until the fifth step. The point of the five-step approach is to determine when to recognize revenue and how much revenue to recognize. Thus, we will not know the proper journal entry to record the sale until we complete the entire process.

2 Explain how to identify a contract with a customer.

Step 1: Identify the Contract(s) with a Customer

The first step in the revenue recognition process is to identify the *contract*, or *contracts* with the customer. A **contract** is an agreement between two or more parties that creates enforceable rights and obligations.[1]

Contract Criteria

If the seller meets the following five criteria related to the contract, then it continues through the remaining four steps to determine the timing and measurement of revenue recognition.

1. All parties to the contract have agreed to the contract and are committed to performing under the contract. The approval by the parties can be in writing, provided orally, or implied by an entity's customary business practices.
2. Each party's rights with respect to the goods or services that are being transferred are identifiable.
3. The payment terms for the goods or services that are being transferred are identifiable.
4. The contract has **commercial substance**, meaning that the risk, timing, or amount of the entity's future cash flows is expected to change as a result of the contract.
5. It is probable that the seller will collect the consideration to which it is entitled in exchange for the goods or services. To assess the probability of collection, the seller considers the customer's ability and intention to pay this specific amount of consideration when it is due.

For purposes of the fifth criterion, U.S. GAAP defines probable as "likely to occur." The seller assesses collectability on the expected consideration (the estimated transaction price), not the contract price. For example, if the seller intends to offer a **price concession**, which is a reduction in the contract price, then the estimated transaction price will be less than the contract price.

Also related to the fifth criterion, the company should consider only the amount that is at risk of not being collected, which may be less than the entire consideration. For example, if the customer is required to pay a portion of the consideration before delivery, then the seller would consider only the probability of collecting the amounts due after delivery. Or, if the seller is contractually allowed to stop transferring goods or services should the customer fail to pay, then only the consideration related to the goods or services that would be delivered is considered. Exhibit 8.2 summarizes the five criteria to identify a contract with customers.

EXHIBIT 8.2 Five Criteria to Identify Contracts with Customers

1. All parties agree to the contract and commit to performing.
2. Each party's rights are identifiable.
3. Payment terms are identifiable.
4. The contract has commercial substance.
5. Collection of consideration is probable.

Example 8.2 illustrates the collectability assessment.

[1]FASB ASC 606-10-20 – *Revenue from Contracts with Customers – Overall – Glossary.*

EXAMPLE 8.2

Collectability Assessment

PROBLEM: JC Enterprises manufactures designer cases for tablets and is attempting to enter a new market with its product. To implement this strategy, JC sells 5,000 units to a retailer for a contract price of $75 each. JC is aware that this retailer is struggling financially but is willing to enter into the contract because of its desire to penetrate a new market. Due to the financial instability of its customer, JC believes that it will need to provide a 20% price concession. Does this agreement meet the fifth criterion to determine the existence of a contract?

SOLUTION: Yes, this agreement meets the definition of a contract. Even though it is not probable that JC will receive the full contract price of $375,000 (5,000 units at $75 each), it is probable that JC will collect a portion of the contract price for a transaction price of $300,000 (80% × $375,000).

Failure to Meet Contract Criteria

If a seller does not satisfy all of the five Step 1 criteria, then it should recognize revenue when it has received the consideration and when one or more of the following have occurred:

1. The seller has no remaining obligations to transfer goods or services and substantially all (or all) of the consideration has been received by the seller and is nonrefundable, or
2. The contract has been terminated and any consideration already received from the customer is nonrefundable, or
3. The seller has transferred control of the goods or services, is no longer transferring the goods or services, has no obligation to transfer additional goods or services, and the consideration received is nonrefundable.

If the seller receives cash before the appropriate time to recognize revenue, it should report the consideration as a liability. In addition, the seller should not remove the inventory from its balance sheet. Example 8.3 provides an illustration of the accounting treatment for a transaction in which the five criteria are not met.

EXAMPLE 8.3

Five Criteria Not Met

PROBLEM: SBA Inc., a retail developer, sells a building to Margots Corporation on September 30, 2018. The contract price is $5 million. Margots pays SBA 10% of the contract price on September 30. The remaining 90% will be paid over the following five years with $225,000 due each quarter. The first payment is due on December 31, 2018. The payments are nonrefundable. If Margots defaults, then SBA keeps the payments that it has received up to that point but is not entitled to further compensation. In addition, the building will revert back to SBA.

Margots intends to open a hotel in the building. However, the building is not located in an attractive area. SBA is aware that Margots will have only adequate resources to make the required payments if the hotel is profitable. Accordingly, on September 30, SBA concludes that it is not probable that it will collect the transaction price.

Margots remits the $500,000 deposit and the first two required quarterly payments of $225,000 each to SBA on December 31, 2018, and March 31, 2019, respectively. On June 30, 2019, Margots does not make the required payment and terminates the contract. What are the required journal entries for SBA Inc. from September 30, 2018, through June 30, 2019?

SOLUTION: Because SBA does not consider it probable that it will collect the transaction price from the buyer, this arrangement does not meet the definition of a contract and thus must be accounted for under the alternative method. SBA will not recognize revenue until June 30, 2019,

(continued)

when the contract has been terminated and all consideration it has received to date is nonrefundable. In addition, on September 30, 2018, SBA will not derecognize the building. The journal entries follow.

Account	September 30, 2018	
Cash	500,000	
Unearned Revenue		500,000

Account	December 31, 2018	
Cash	225,000	
Unearned Revenue		225,000

Account	March 31, 2019	
Cash	225,000	
Unearned Revenue		225,000

Account	June 30, 2019	
Unearned Revenue	950,000	
Revenue		950,000

Multiple Contracts

It is not uncommon for vendors to enter into multiple contracts with the same customer. Under certain circumstances, the seller should combine these contracts and account for them as a single contract. Specifically, if one of the following criteria is met, the seller should combine multiple individual contracts into a single contract for purposes of determining the timing and measurement of revenue:

1. The contracts are negotiated as a package and have a single commercial objective.
2. The amount of consideration to be received by the seller related to one contract depends on the price or performance of another contract.
3. The goods or services promised in the separate contracts are all part of one *performance obligation*.[2]

Identify the Contract(s) with Customers: IFRS

When identifying a contract with a customer, IFRS differs from U.S. GAAP in two ways. First, IFRS defines probable as "more likely than not" whereas U.S. GAAP defines probable as "likely to occur" in the fifth criterion that assesses collectability. "More likely than not" implies a probability of more than 50%. "Likely to occur" implies a probability threshold significantly higher than 50%. Although U.S. GAAP does not precisely define "likely to occur," it is often interpreted to be somewhere around 70 or 75%. Thus, U.S. GAAP sets a higher threshold for the assessment of collectability than IFRS. For example, Turro Company makes a sale to Milano Corporation, and Turro determines the probability of collection is 55%. Under IFRS, the 55% probability suggests that it is "more likely than not" that Turro will collect from Milano. Under U.S. GAAP, a probability of 55% does not meet the "likely to occur" threshold. Therefore, the collectability criterion will be met under IFRS but not U.S. GAAP.

If the revenue recognition standard is converged, why is there a different interpretation of probable? The difference is because the FASB and IASB decided to set the threshold at a level consistent with their previous revenue recognition standards and based on the interpretations of "probable" under each set of standards.

[2]We discuss performance obligations in our presentation of Step 2.

The second difference is in determining when to recognize revenue when the five criteria for a contract are not met. IFRS does not explicitly include the third condition that the seller has transferred control of the goods or services, is no longer transferring the goods or services, has no obligation to transfer additional goods or services, and the consideration received is nonrefundable. The FASB added this condition to clarify when to recognize revenue. The IASB did not believe this clarification was needed because the first two conditions should cover these cases. The IASB noted that contracts often specify that a company has the right to terminate a contract if a customer is not paying. However, for any goods or services already transferred, the company has a right to collect payment.

3 Identify the separate performance obligations in a contract, including determining whether there are distinct goods or services.

Step 2: Identify the Performance Obligations in the Contract

A seller needs to identify the various *performance obligations* in a contract to allocate the transaction price to these different performance obligations and to recognize revenue when or as it satisfies each individual one. Conceptually, a **performance obligation** is a promise to transfer a good or service that is distinct. As shown in Exhibit 8.3, a performance obligation is either:

- A promise to transfer a good or service, or a bundle of goods or services, that is distinct, or
- A promise to transfer a series of distinct goods or services that are substantially the same and have the same pattern of transfer to the customer.[3]

EXHIBIT 8.3 Performance Obligation

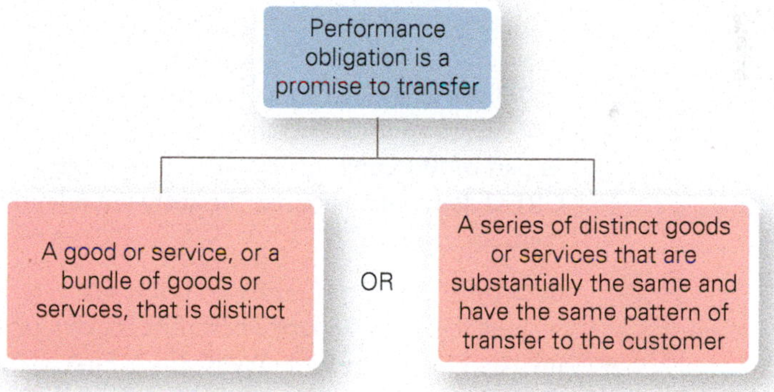

The determination of separate performance obligations starts with identifying the promised goods and services. After identifying the goods or services in the contract, the seller must determine which goods and services are distinct. The notion of "distinct" goods and services is critical to determining separate performance obligations. To be distinct, a good or service must meet two conditions:

1. The customer can benefit from the good or service on its own or in conjunction with other *readily available resources* to the customer, and
2. The promise of the seller to deliver that good or service is separately identifiable from other promises in the contract.

It is often clear that a customer can benefit from the product or service on its own (or in conjunction with other assets). At other times, this determination requires more judgment. If the good or service can be used, consumed, or sold for a nontrivial amount, then it passes the test of being distinct. A good or service is also distinct if the customer can benefit from it in conjunction

[3]A series of goods or services that have the same pattern of transfer if the performance obligation is satisfied over time per FASB ASC 606-10-25-27 and the same method would be used to measure the entity's progress toward satisfaction of the performance obligation according to paragraphs 31 and 32 of FASB ASC 606-10-25. See paragraphs 14 and 15 of FASB ASC 606-10-25 for a discussion of the identification of performance obligations.

with other *readily available resources*. Another resource is considered to be a **readily available resource** if it is sold separately by the seller or another entity, or if the customer already has obtained it from the seller or in some other transaction. For example, consider a set of earbuds packaged with a mobile phone. Because the earbuds can be sold separately and can be used with other electronic devices, the earbuds are a readily available resource.

A promise to deliver a good or service is separately identifiable if it is not highly dependent or interrelated to another promise in the contract to deliver another good or service. Judgment may be involved in the determination of whether the promise to deliver the good or service is separate from other promises. For example, consider a lawn care company that mows the lawn and then blows clippings off the sidewalk and driveway. Blowing the clipping is highly dependent on having the lawn mowed. Without mowing the lawn, there would be no clippings to blow away. So, blowing the clippings is not separately identifiable from the promise to mow the lawn.

At times a seller may provide a "free" good or service with the contract, such as in the telecommunications industry where entities offer free mobile phones with a service agreement. These goods and services should be considered as possible performance obligations even though they are identified in the contract as being free of charge.

Also, the promised good or service does not have to be explicitly identified in the contract. If the customer has a valid expectation that the seller will provide the good or service, then this item should also be assessed as a possible performance obligation.

An entity should aggregate the goods or services promised in a contract until it identifies a bundle of goods or services that is distinct and thus defined as a separate performance obligation. There may be only one performance obligation identifiable in a contract. Example 8.4 illustrates how to identify separate performance obligations.

EXAMPLE 8.4 Separate Performance Obligations

PROBLEM: CRED Corp. contracts with a customer to license and install payroll application software. In addition to the software license, CRED Corp. will provide installation services as part of this contract. The installation service could be performed by other entities because CRED does not customize the software. Identify the separate performance obligations in this contract.

SOLUTION: CRED promises both the software license and installation service. To determine whether these are separate performance obligations, CRED needs to assess whether they meet the two conditions for being distinct. First, CRED assesses whether the customer can benefit from the good or service on its own or in conjunction with other assets that are readily available to the customer. The software license provides a benefit on a standalone basis because it is not dependent upon installation by CRED because the software can be installed by another entity. Therefore, the software license and the installation are not interdependent.

CRED next must assess the second condition of whether its promise to deliver each of these two goods and services is separately identifiable from the other promise in the contract. In this case, because the installation service does not modify the software and could be performed by another entity, the software and installation service are separately identifiable in the contract.

Thus, the software license and the installation service are distinct goods and services and the contract contains two performance obligations.

Modification of this contract will result in a different outcome as seen in Example 8.5.

EXAMPLE 8.5 **One Performance Obligation**

PROBLEM: CRED Corp. contracts with a customer to license and install a payroll software application. In addition to the software license, CRED Corp. will provide installation services as part of this contract. The installation service customizes the software to integrate with other systems that the customer is currently using. Identify the separate performance obligations in this contract.

SOLUTION: Because the installation service will modify the software and the software cannot be used until it is installed, the software and installation service are interdependent and are not separately identifiable in the contract. Therefore, the second condition for being distinct is not met: The promise to deliver the software is not separately identifiable from the promise to install. Thus, the contract contains only one performance obligation—the software license and the installation service combined.

4 Explain how to determine the transaction price in recognizing revenue.

Step 3: Determine the Transaction Price

The third step in the revenue recognition process is to determine the *transaction price*. The **transaction price** is the amount of consideration that the entity expects to be entitled to as a result of providing goods or services to the customer. The transaction price is not necessarily the price stated in the contract—rather, it is the amount the seller *expects* to receive. The transaction price does not include amounts collected that will be remitted to third parties (such as sales tax).

The transaction price is the amount that an entity will ultimately recognize as revenue. Measuring the transaction price can be quite simple in some cases. For example, assume a customer shopping at a retail store selects and pays $100 cash for a new dress. The transaction price is $100. However, with complex transactions, determining the transaction price is involved. Sellers consider the effects of a number of different factors when determining the transaction price, including:

1. *Variable consideration* and constraining estimates of variable consideration
2. Any significant financing component in the contract
3. Noncash consideration
4. Consideration payable to a customer

We discuss each of these factors in the following sections.

Variable Consideration and Constraining Estimates of Variable Consideration

Variable consideration is when the payment received for providing a good or service is not a fixed amount. The amount of consideration may vary from a fixed amount due to price concessions, performance bonuses or penalties, discounts, refunds, rebates, and incentives. Elements of variable consideration may be stated explicitly or implicitly in the contract. For example, a discount for early payment typically offered by a seller is considered an element of variable consideration, even though it may not be specified explicitly in the contract.

If variable consideration is included in the contract, then the entity must estimate the consideration that it expects to receive using one of two acceptable approaches: the *expected-value approach* or the *most-likely-amount approach*. The entity should use the approach that provides the best estimate of the amount of consideration it will receive.

Expected-Value Approach. To compute the expected transaction amount under the **expected-value approach**, the entity sums the probability-weighted amounts in a range of possible consideration amounts. This method is best suited when the entity has a large number of contracts with similar characteristics. This approach is illustrated in Example 8.6.

EXAMPLE 8.6 Estimating Variable Consideration: Expected-Value Approach

PROBLEM: Binco Brass Corp. (BBC) is a wholesaler that sells musical instruments to retailers. On February 1 of the current year, BBC contracts with Music Extravaganza, Inc. (MEI) to sell 1,000 trumpets to MEI with delivery scheduled for the month of February. The contract price is $500 per trumpet. However, the contract includes the possibility of a volume discount if total annual purchases exceed a given amount. These discounts are as follows:

If Total Sales Equal or Exceed	Discount Percentage
$1,000,000	1%
$2,000,000	2%
$5,000,000	5%

These discounts are retroactive—once a volume trigger is met, BBC refunds to MEI amounts on previous purchases. BBC believes that it is 15% likely that it will not contract with MEI again this year. BBC believes the following probability estimates are accurate:

Total Sales	Probability
$ 500,000	15%
$1,000,000	60%
$2,000,000	20%
$5,000,000	5%

Using the expected-value approach, what is the estimate of the consideration amount in this contract?

SOLUTION: In order to determine the transaction price for the contract to sell 1,000 trumpets, BBC sums the probability-weighted amounts in the range of possible consideration amounts. That is, for every possible outcome, BBC multiplies the total consideration for the 1,000 trumpets at $500 each, $500,000, times the probability. It then sums these amounts to arrive at the total consideration amount.

Total Annual Sales	Discount Percentage	Consideration Amount for the 1,000 Trumpets	Probability	Expected Consideration
$ 500,000	0%	$500,000	15%	$ 75,000
$1,000,000	1%	495,000	60%	297,000
$2,000,000	2%	490,000	20%	98,000
$5,000,000	5%	475,000	5%	23,750
				$493,750

Thus, BBC estimates the transaction price as $493,750 for the February 1 sale of 1,000 trumpets. In other words, BBC estimates the discount that MEI will ultimately receive on the 1,000 trumpets to be $6,250.

Most-Likely-Amount Approach. The **most-likely-amount approach** uses the single most likely amount in a range of possible consideration amounts as the estimate. This approach is best suited when there are only two possible outcomes. Example 8.7 illustrates estimating variable consideration under the most likely amount approach.

EXAMPLE 8.7 Estimating Variable Consideration: Most-Likely-Amount Approach

PROBLEM: Consider BBC Corp. and MEI from the previous example. Using the most-likely-amount approach, what is the estimate of the consideration amount in this contract?

SOLUTION: BBC uses the estimated consideration amount that is associated with the highest probability assessment. In this case, BBC assesses that it is 60% likely that the total sales volume with MEI will be between $1 and $2 million. In this case, BBC estimates the consideration amount as $495,000 for the February 1 sale of 1,000 trumpets.

Total Annual Sales	Discount Percentage	Consideration Amount for the 1,000 Trumpets	Probability
$ 500,000	0%	$500,000	15%
$1,000,000	1%	495,000	60%
$2,000,000	2%	490,000	20%
$5,000,000	5%	475,000	5%

Constraining Estimates of Variable Consideration. Entities must also assess the contract to determine if there are any constraints to variable consideration. For the entity to include variable consideration in the estimated transaction price (and thus the amount of revenue recognized), it has to conclude that it is probable that a significant revenue reversal will not occur in future periods. "Probable" is generally interpreted as 70 to 75%. This assessment requires the use of a cumulative probability level to determine if the definition of probable (likely to occur) is met. Example 8.8 provides a case with a constraining estimate of variable consideration.

EXAMPLE 8.8 Constraining Estimate of Variable Consideration

PROBLEM: CallTech Company provides call center services for various software companies. CallTech entered into a contract with a customer in which CallTech will receive a fixed amount equal to $3,000,000 under a one-year contract. In addition, CallTech is eligible for bonus payments if the average annual customer wait time is less than a target number of minutes. The bonus schedule, along with CallTech's probability assessments for each bonus, follow.

Bonus Payment	Average Customer Wait Time	Probability Assessment
$ 0	Over 4 minutes	5%
250,000	Over 3 minutes but 4 minutes or less	20%
500,000	Over 2 minutes but 3 minutes or less	20%
750,000	2 minutes or less	55%
		100%

At what amount should CallTech measure the transaction price for this contract, assuming it uses the most-likely-amount approach for measuring variable consideration?

SOLUTION: The $3,000,000 is part of the transaction price. Next, CallTech will estimate the variable consideration. Because it assesses a 55% probability that its average annual customer wait time will be 2 minutes or less, the estimate of variable consideration is $750,000.

However, CallTech must assess the constraint on variable consideration. CallTech must determine the probability that it will have to reverse any of the $750,000 revenue. It is

(continued)

45% (5% + 20% + 20%) probable that it will receive a bonus of less than $750,000 (and thus reverse part of the $750,000 revenue.) Thus, there is a 55% probability that it will not have to reverse revenue. A probability of 55% is not considered probable (i.e., "likely to occur"), and thus the variable consideration is constrained. Next, CallTech assesses a cumulative probability of 75% (55% + 20%) that it will receive at least $500,000 for call times less than three minutes. Because a cumulative probability of 75% would generally meet the definition of probable (i.e., likely to occur), CallTech will estimate the constrained variable consideration at $500,000 per year. Thus, the estimated transaction price for the one-year contract is $3,500,000 ($3,000,000 fixed amount plus $500,000 for the variable component).

Variable Consideration and Constraining Estimates of Variable Consideration: IFRS. In estimating the constraint on variable consideration, U.S. GAAP uses the term "probable," whereas IFRS uses the term "highly probable." The definitions of "probable" under U.S. GAAP and "highly probable" under IFRS are essentially the same.

Significant Financing Component

In contracts when delivery of the goods or services occurs in advance of the payment, the seller is providing financing to the buyer. Alternatively, in contracts when delivery occurs well after payment, the buyer is providing financing to the seller. When the time lapse between payment and delivery is more than one year, entities are required to separate the revenue generated from the contract from the financing component if the financing component is significant at the individual contract level.

The rationale is that the seller should recognize revenue at the amount that properly reflects the price that a buyer would pay if payment occurred on the same date as delivery. In determining whether a significant financing component exists, the entity considers three factors:

1. The difference between the contract price and the cash selling price of the goods or services.
2. The length of time between delivery and payment.
3. The prevailing interest rate in the market.

Once an entity concludes that there is a significant financing component, it determines the transaction price by using the time value of money:

- If the delivery occurs *before* payment, the entity discounts the promised consideration amount back to the present value, using the same discount rate it would use if it entered into a separate financing arrangement.
- If the delivery occurs *after* the payment, the entity determines the future value of the payment, using the same discount rate it would use if it entered into a separate financing arrangement.

The entity ultimately recognizes the transaction price as sales or service revenue and records the difference between the total contract price and the present or future value as interest revenue if the payment occurs after delivery or interest expense if the payment occurs before delivery.

We present an example of a contract with a significant financing component in Example 8.9.

EXAMPLE 8.9 Significant Financing Component—Delivery before Payment

PROBLEM: KMR Enterprises enters into a sales contract with a new customer. Delivery occurs at the date of contract inception. However, payment of the contract price of $1 million will not occur until two years later. The interest rate charged in similar arrangements in the industry is 10%. Does a significant financing component exist? If so, what amount should KMR record as sales revenue and what amount should KMR record as interest revenue?

SOLUTION: Because there is a time lapse of two years between delivery and payment and the interest rate is 10%, a significant financing component exists. To compute the transaction price (the amount that will ultimately be recognized as sales revenue), KMR must discount the $1 million future value to the present value using a 10% interest rate. We calculate a present value of $826,446 as follows.

	N	I/Y	PV	PMT	FV	Excel Formula
Given	2	10.00%		0	1,000,000	
Solve for PV			(826,446)			=PV(0.1,2,0,1000000)

Thus, KMR ultimately records $826,446 of sales revenue at the date of delivery and $173,554 ($1,000,000 less $826,446) of interest revenue over the two-year period.

Example 8.10 provides an illustration of a scenario in which the delivery occurs after the payment.

EXAMPLE 8.10 Significant Financing Component–Delivery after Payment

PROBLEM: KMR Enterprises enters into a sales contract with a new customer. Payment of the contract price of $1 million occurs at the date of contract inception. However, delivery of the product will not occur until two years later. The interest rate charged in similar arrangements in the industry is 10%. Does a significant financing component exist? If so, what amount should KMR record as sales revenue and what amount should KMR record as interest expense?

SOLUTION: Because there is a time lapse of two years between delivery and payment and the interest rate is 10%, a significant financing component exists. To compute the transaction price (the amount that will ultimately be recognized as sales revenue), KMR must compute the future value of the $1 million using a 10% interest rate. We compute the future value of $1,210,000 as follows:

	N	I/Y	PV	PMT	FV	Excel Formula
Given	2	10.00%	1,000,000	0		
Solve for FV					(1,210,000)	=FV(0.1,2,0,1000000)

Thus, KMR ultimately records $1,210,000 of sales revenue at the date of delivery and $210,000 ($1,210,000 less $1,000,000) of interest expense.

Noncash Consideration

In some contracts, instead of paying cash for the good or service, customers compensate the seller with goods, services, or other noncash items, such as shares of stock in the customer's corporation. In this case, the transaction price should be measured at the fair value at contract inception of the noncash consideration received by the seller. If the seller cannot reasonably estimate the fair value of the noncash consideration received, then she should measure the transaction price at the standalone selling price of the goods or services promised to the customer. Example 8.11 demonstrates accounting for noncash consideration.

EXAMPLE 8.11

Noncash Consideration

PROBLEM: TrueTech provides laptop-related maintenance services to Shemco. In exchange, TrueTech received 100 shares of Shemco no-par common stock. Determine the transaction price in the contract for the following scenarios: (a) 100 shares of Shemco's stock is traded on an active market for $55,000. The standalone value of the maintenance services is $56,000. (b) Shemco is privately held, making it difficult to estimate the fair value of the shares given in exchange for the maintenance services.

SOLUTION: In scenario (a) in which Shemco's stock is publicly traded, the transaction price is the fair value of the noncash consideration (the fair value of the stock). Thus, the transaction price is $55,000.

In scenario (b) in which the stock is not publicly traded and, therefore, does not have a reasonably estimable fair value, TrueTech determines the transaction price as the standalone value of the services provided. The transaction price is $56,000.

Consideration Payable to a Customer

At times, a seller makes payments to a customer if the seller is providing incentives to entice the buyer to purchase, or continue to purchase, its goods. Unless the payment to the customer is in exchange for a distinct good or service transferred to the seller, the seller should deduct the amount of the consideration payable to the customer from the transaction price. Example 8.12 demonstrates this accounting treatment.

EXAMPLE 8.12

Consideration Payable to a Customer

PROBLEM: Clever Company enters into a contract with a customer in which it promises to deliver products for a price of $10 million. The contract also stipulates a slotting fee of $250,000 that Clever Company will pay to the buyer. Manufacturers commonly pay a slotting fee to retailers to have their goods displayed prominently in the retailers' stores. What is the transaction price in this contract?

SOLUTION: In this case, the slotting fees are not a distinct good or service that is provided to Clever Company. Thus, Clever Company should treat the slotting fee as a reduction in the transaction price as opposed to a fee that would be expensed. The transaction price for the contract is $9,750,000 ($10,000,000 less $250,000).

Exhibit 8.4 summarizes determining the transaction price.

EXHIBIT 8.4 Determining the Transaction Price

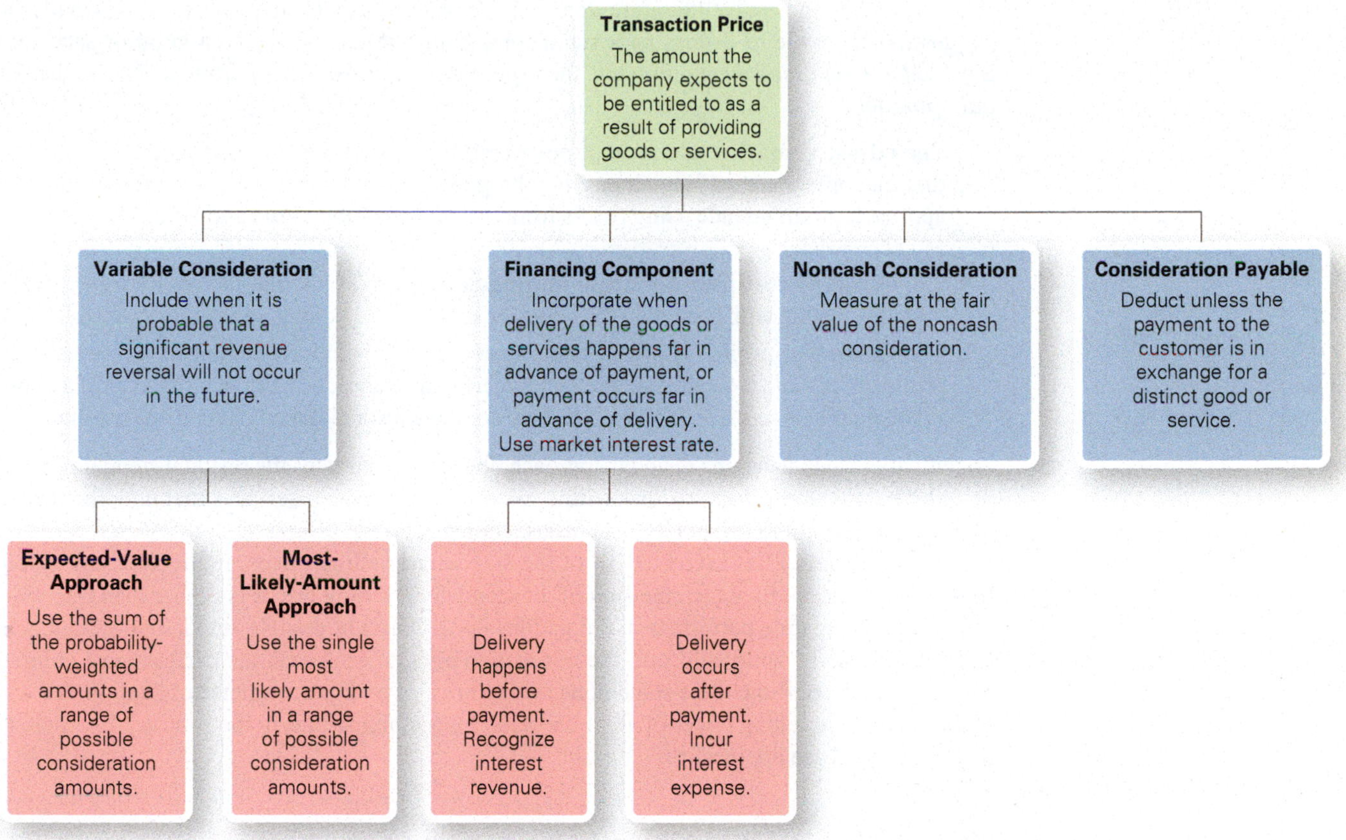

❺ Demonstrate allocating the transaction price to performance obligations when recognizing revenue.

Step 4: Allocate the Transaction Price to the Performance Obligations

The next step in the revenue recognition process is allocating the transaction price determined in Step 3 to the performance obligations determined in Step 2. If the determination from Step 2 is that there is only one performance obligation, then Step 4 is not required.

Standalone Selling Price

To allocate the transaction price, the entity first determines the standalone selling price of the goods or services related to each performance obligation. Then, if the sum of the standalone selling prices is higher than the transaction price, the seller typically allocates the discount to separate performance obligations on the basis of the relative standalone selling prices.

The standalone selling price of each performance obligation is the price the seller would charge for the same goods or services if it sold them on a standalone basis to similar customers under similar circumstances. Companies can often determine the standalone selling price using this method because they typically sell their goods or services on a standalone basis.

However, in practice the seller sometimes does not sell the same goods or services separately. In this case, the seller must estimate the standalone selling price. The authoritative literature does not stipulate an exact method but states that the company should use a method that maximizes the use of observable inputs. Whatever method the entity chooses for estimating the standalone selling price, it should use the same method consistently in similar circumstances.

Standalone Selling Price Estimation Methods

Although the authoritative literature does not specify a particular method, it does provide three suggestions suitable to determine a standalone selling price specific to a good or service: the *adjusted market assessment approach*, the *expected-cost-plus-a-margin approach*, and the *residual approach*.

1. The **adjusted market assessment approach** focuses on the amount that the seller believes that customers are willing to pay for the good or service by evaluating the market. This approach might include using prices from the seller's competitors and adjusting those prices as necessary.
2. The **expected-cost-plus-a-margin approach** focuses on internal factors by forecasting the costs associated with providing the goods or services and adding an appropriate profit margin.
3. The **residual approach** allows an entity to estimate one or more, but not all, of the standalone selling prices and then allocate the remainder of the transaction price, or the residual amount, to the goods or services for which it does not have a standalone selling price estimate.

Specifically, when using the residual approach, the entity estimates the residual standalone selling price by subtracting the standalone selling prices of the goods or services that underlie the other performance obligations from the total transaction price.

Once the entity has estimated all of the standalone selling prices, it allocates any discount (that is, any amount by which the sum of the standalone selling prices is higher than the transaction price) to separate performance obligations on the basis of relative standalone selling prices. In other words, the entity allocates the transaction price to each separate performance obligation based on the proportion of the standalone selling price of each performance obligation to the sum of the standalone selling prices of all of the performance obligations in the contract. Example 8.13 illustrates the three approaches.

EXAMPLE 8.13 Allocation of the Transaction Price to the Separate Performance Obligations

PROBLEM: Bord Industries enters into a contract with a customer to sell three products for a total transaction price of $650,000. Each product is appropriately classified as a separate performance obligation. Bord Industries sells products A and B only on an individual basis, so it must estimate the standalone selling price for product C. Information related to these three products is provided in the following table.

Product	Standalone Selling Price	Market Competitor Prices	Forecasted Cost
A	$175,000	$ 133,000	$ 120,000
B	300,000	312,000	250,000
C	Not available	200,000	130,000
Total		$645,000	$500,000

How should Bord Industries allocate the transaction price to the three products under each of the following three approaches: (a) the adjusted market assessment approach, (b) the expected-cost-plus-a-margin approach, and (c) the residual approach?

SOLUTIONS: We illustrate each method separately.

a. **Adjusted market assessment approach** Bord Industries should estimate the standalone selling prices based on the prices that the customers in the market would be willing to pay, such as competitor prices, and then allocate on a relative basis as follows:

Product	Market Competitor Prices	Percentage of Total	Estimated Standalone Selling Price
A	$ 133,000	20.62%	$134,030
B	312,000	48.37	314,405
C	200,000	31.01	201,565
Total	$ 645,000	100.00%	$650,000

The percentage column is computed as the market competitor price for the individual product divided by the total market competitor prices for all three products. The allocated transaction price for each product is the percentage for that product times the total transaction price.

b. **Expected-cost-plus-a-margin approach** Bord Industries should estimate the standalone selling prices based on forecasted cost with an appropriate margin. Given a total cost of $500,000 and a total transaction price of $650,000, an appropriate margin would be 30% (($650,000 − $500,000) / $500,000). Thus, to determine the allocated transaction price for each product, multiply the forecasted cost for each product by 1.30.

Product	Forecasted Cost	Estimated Standalone Selling Price
A	$120,000	$156,000
B	250,000	325,000
C	130,000	169,000
Total	$500,000	$650,000

c. **Residual approach** Using the residual approach, Bord Industries estimates the standalone selling price for product C by deducting the available standalone selling prices for products A and B from the total transaction price, which results in a residual amount of $175,000 for Product C.

Product	Estimated Standalone Selling Price
Transaction Price	$ 650,000
A	(175,000)
B	(300,000)
C	$ 175,000

Standalone Selling Price Exceptions

Whereas the general rule is that the transaction price should be allocated to the performance obligations based on the relative standalone selling prices, there are two possible exceptions.

- When the contract includes variable consideration.
- When the discount is not related to all of the contract's performance obligations.

Related to the first exception, the seller should allocate variable consideration to one or more, but not all, performance obligations if two criteria are met:

1. The terms of the variable amount relate to one or more, but not all, of the specific performance obligations.
2. Allocating the variable amount entirely to one or more, but not all, of the specific performance obligations is consistent with the objective of performing the allocation in a way that reflects a reasonable allocation of the transaction price on the basis of the standalone selling prices.

Example 8.14 demonstrates a situation in which variable consideration is allocated entirely to one performance obligation.

EXAMPLE 8.14 Allocation of Variable Consideration: Allocated to One Performance Obligation

PROBLEM: Franklin Inventors sells two of its patents in a contract with a retailer that sells toys and other children's products. The first is a patent for a super absorbent diaper and the second is a patent for a new digital toy. Franklin determines that each of these patents comprises a separate performance obligation. The estimated standalone selling prices are $5 million for the diaper patent and $2 million for the digital toy patent. The stated price in the contract for the diaper patent is a fixed payment of $5 million. The stated price for the digital toy patent is 5% of the customer's future sales of the toys. Franklin estimates the variable consideration for this patent to be $2 million. What amount of the transaction price should Franklin allocate to each performance obligation?

SOLUTION: The variable consideration in this example is the 5% of the customer's future sales of the toys related to the toy patent. Franklin meets the two criteria to allocate the variable consideration to just one performance obligation. The variable consideration relates only to the toy patent. Allocating the $2 million entirely to the toy patent is consistent with the objective of a reasonable allocation based on standalone selling prices because the $2 million is equal to the standalone selling price of the patent and therefore considered reasonable variable consideration. Thus, Franklin allocates $5 million of the transaction price to the diaper patent. Franklin allocates the variable consideration solely to the digital patent.

Example 8.15 illustrates a contract whose variable consideration cannot be allocated to just one performance obligation.

EXAMPLE 8.15 Allocation of Variable Consideration: Allocated to All Performance Obligations

PROBLEM: Franklin Inventors sells two of its patents in a contract with a retailer that sells toys and other children's products. The first is a patent for a super absorbent diaper and the second is a patent for a new digital toy. Franklin determines that each of these patents comprises a separate performance obligation. The estimated standalone selling prices are $5 million for the diaper patent and $2 million for the digital toy patent. The stated price in the contract for the diaper patent is a fixed payment of $3.8 million. The price stated for the digital toy patent is 8% of the customer's future sales of the toys. Franklin estimates the variable consideration for this patent as $3.2 million. During the current year, the customer has sales related to the toy patent of $12.5 million, resulting in a $1 million payment to Franklin Inventors and a total consideration of $4.8 million. What amount of the transaction price should Franklin allocate to each performance obligation?

SOLUTION: The variable consideration in this example is the 8% of the customer's future sales of the toys related to the toy patent. Franklin does not meet the two criteria to allocate the variable consideration to only one performance obligation. Although the variable consideration relates only to the toy patent, allocating all of the variable consideration to the toy patent would not satisfy the objective that the allocation reflect a reasonable allocation based on standalone selling prices because the variable consideration of $3.2 million is significantly higher than the standalone selling price of $2 million. Thus, Franklin allocates both the fixed and variable consideration to the two patents on a relative standalone selling price basis.

Patent	Standalone Selling Price (a)	Percentage Standalone Selling Price to Total Price (b)	Allocation of Fixed Consideration (c) = Fixed Consideration × (b)	Allocation of Current Year Variable Consideration (d) = Variable Consideration × (b)	Total Consideration (e) = (c) + (d)
Diaper	$5 million	71.43%	$2,714,340	$ 714,300	$3,428,640
Toy	2 million	28.57%	1,085,660	285,700	1,371,360
	$7 million	100.00%	$3,800,000	$1,000,000	$4,800,000

The second exception to the relative standalone selling price allocation method involves the allocation of a discount measured as the difference between the sum of the standalone selling prices and the transaction price. Typically, any discount should be allocated proportionately to the performance obligations based on the relative standalone selling prices. However, if an entity determines that the discount is not related to all of the performance obligations, it should allocate only the discount to the performance obligations to which it relates. Specifically, if the following three criteria are met, then the seller should allocate the discount to one or more, but not all, of the performance obligations.

1. The entity regularly sells the goods/services in the contract on a standalone basis.
2. The entity regularly sells a bundle of some of these goods/services at a discount to the sum of the standalone selling prices of the separate goods/services.
3. The discount in the bundle of goods/services described in (2) is basically the same as the discount in this contract.

Example 8.16 provides an illustration of a discount that is not proportionally allocated to the performance obligations (that is, the discount does not relate to all performance obligations).

EXAMPLE 8.16 Allocation of a Discount

PROBLEM: GW Company is a wholesaler that sells hockey equipment. It regularly sells the following products separately at the following standalone selling prices:

Equipment	Standalone Selling Price
Sticks	$100
Helmets	75
Skates	300

GW also regularly bundles helmets and skates together for $350. GW signs a contract with Hockey Equipment Retailers to sell 100 sticks, helmets, and skates for $45,000. GW determines that each product is a separate performance obligation. How should GW allocate the transaction price to each product?

SOLUTION: The contract contains a $2,500 discount because the sum of the standalone selling price is $47,500 [($100 per stick + $75 per helmet + $300 per skates) × 100], and the transaction price is $45,000. Because GW regularly sells the three products on a standalone basis and the bundled helmets and skates for $350, it can determine that the discount on the bundled helmets and skates is $25 [($75 per helmet + $300 per skates) − $350 bundled price]. The bundled discount totaling $2,500 ($25 bundled discount × 100) is equal to the discount in the contract, so GW should allocate the contract discount only to the helmets and skates.

(continued)

Thus, GW allocates $10,000 (100 sticks × $100) to the sticks. GW determines the allocation of the remaining $35,000 to the helmets and skates on a proportional basis.

Equipment	Standalone Selling Price	Percentage	Allocation of Transaction Price
Helmets	$ 75	20%	$ 7,000
Skates	300	80%	28,000
	$375	100%	$35,000

Exhibit 8.5 provides a summary of allocating the transaction price.

EXHIBIT 8.5 Allocating the Transaction Price

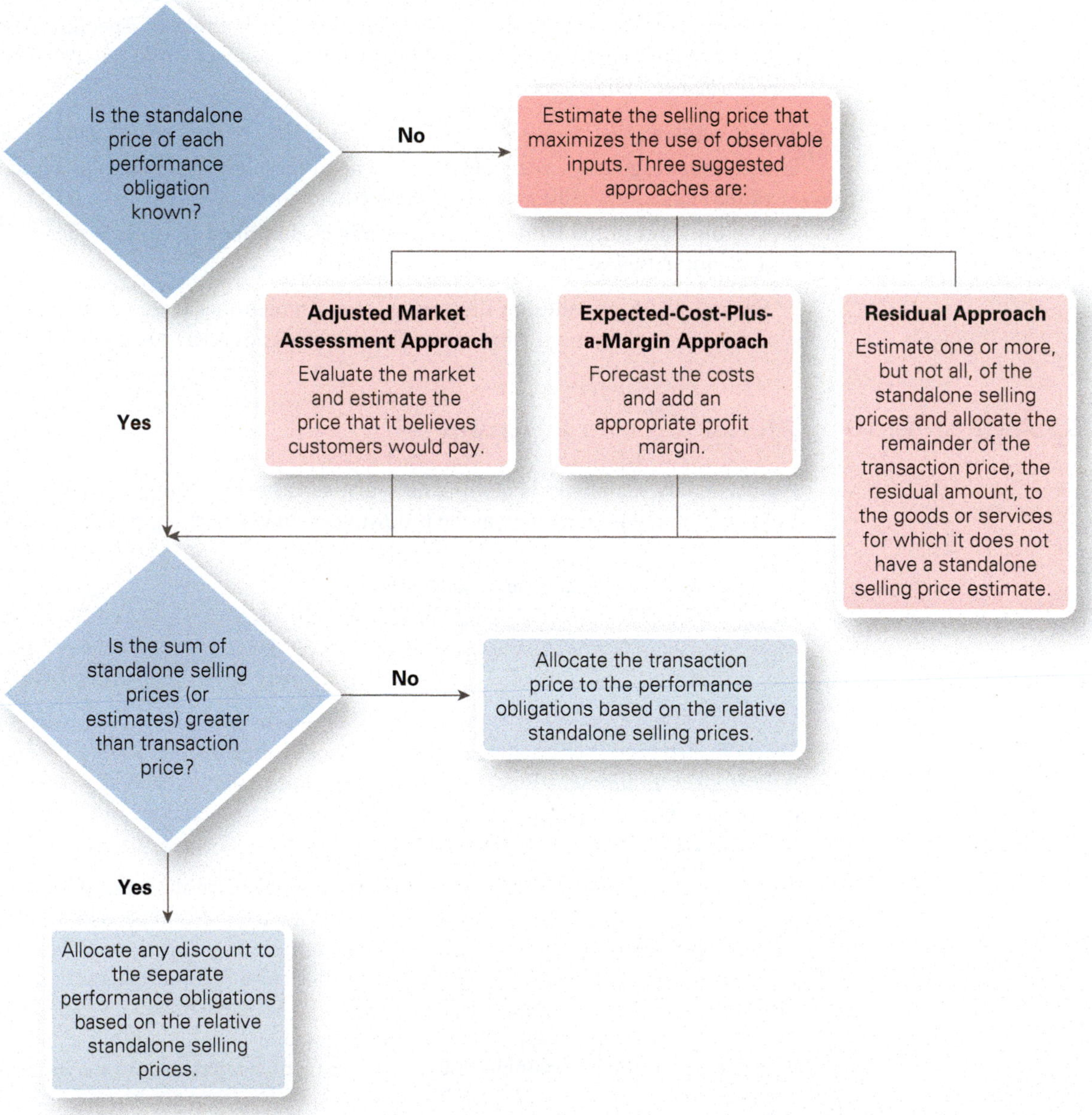

6 Assess whether to recognize revenue when, or as, each performance obligation is satisfied.

Step 5: Recognize Revenue When, or As, Each Performance Obligation Is Satisfied

Companies determine when to recognize revenue in Step 5 based on when the goods or services are transferred to the customer. A good or service is transferred when the customer obtains *control*. A customer has **control** of the asset if it has the ability to direct the use of the asset and receives all (or substantially all) of the remaining benefits of owning the asset.

Transfer over Time

Goods and services may be transferred to the customer over time or at a point in time. If the goods or services are transferred over time, then the seller recognizes revenue over that time period. However, if the goods or services are transferred to the customer at a point in time, then the seller recognizes the revenue at that point in time. Companies must determine whether the goods/services are transferred over time or as of a point in time at the inception of the contract.

Goods or services are transferred over time if the seller meets any one of the following three criteria:

1. The customer receives and consumes the benefits of the goods or services simultaneously (for example, health club memberships and magazine subscriptions).
2. The customer controls the asset as the seller creates it or enhances it over time (for example, software updates).
3. The asset the seller is creating does not have an alternative use to the seller, and the seller has an enforceable right to payment for the performance completed to date.

If a good or service is transferred over time, then the seller recognizes revenue over that same time period, based on the progress that it has made toward completion. However, if the seller does not have a reasonable way to measure its progress toward completion, then it should not recognize *any* revenue until it can reasonably estimate progress. Progress toward completion can be measured using either output methods or input methods. Examples of output methods include units produced or delivered, progress such as floors or miles completed, and time elapsed. Examples of input methods include labor hours expended, machine hours used, and costs incurred.

Example 8.17 illustrates transferring services over time because the customer receives and consumes the benefit simultaneously.

EXAMPLE 8.17

Transfer over Time: Simultaneous Receipt and Consumption of Benefit

PROBLEM: H&L Health Clubs sells annual memberships for $120 each. On January 1, the company sold 100 memberships and received cash. H&L prepares financial statements on a quarterly basis. What journal entries should H&L record during the current year?

SOLUTION: In this case, H&L's customers simultaneously receive and consume the benefits of the membership. Thus, H&L should recognize the revenue over the membership period. H&L initially records the memberships as unearned revenue, but it recognizes one-fourth of the revenue at the end of each quarter.

Account	January 1	
Cash	12,000	
Unearned Revenue		12,000

Account	March 31, June 30, September 30, and December 31	
Unearned Revenue	3,000	
Sales Revenue		3,000

Example 8.18 illustrates a scenario in which the seller recognizes revenue over the service period and the contract meets the second criteria to recognize revenue. Here the customer controls the asset as the seller creates or enhances the item over time.

EXAMPLE 8.18 Transfer over Time: Customer Controls the Asset as the Seller Creates It

PROBLEM: Rand Technology engages in a contract with the federal government to create an IT system for a transaction price of $12 million. Rand receives $2 million from the government at contract inception and the other $10 million upon completion of the project. The government stipulates in the contract that it controls the system during its creation. Rand Technology measures its progress toward completion using labor hours incurred. It estimates that the project will require 25,000 labor hours. During the current year of the contract, Rand spent 15,000 labor hours. During the following year, Rand spent another 10,000 labor hours to finish the project. What journal entries should Rand make over the life of this contract?

SOLUTION: Because Rand's customer controls the IT system as Rand is creating it, Rand can recognize revenue over the service period. Rand recognizes 60% of the revenue in the current year and the remaining 40% in the following year. Rand computes the 60% as 15,000 labor hours divided by the total labor hours of 25,000. The 40% is 10,000 labor hours divided by the total labor hours of 25,000. Computations are presented in the following table.

Year	Labor Hours (a)	Percentage Labor Hours to Total (b)	Revenue (c) = Total Revenue × (b)
1	15,000	60%	$ 7,200,000
2	10,000	40%	4,800,000
Total	25,000	100%	$12,000,000

The journal entry at the contract initiation follows.

Account	At Contract Inception	
Cash	2,000,000	
Unearned Revenue		2,000,000

At the end of the current year, Rand records the following entry to recognize the $7,200,000 revenue earned, reduce the unearned revenue by $2,000,000, and debit accounts receivable for the $5,200,000 uncollected balance due for the current year.

Account	Current Year	
Unearned Revenue	2,000,000	
Accounts Receivable	5,200,000	
Service Revenue		7,200,000

At the end of the second year, the following entry records the $4,800,000 revenue earned, the $10,000,000 cash collection and the reduction of the accounts receivable.

Account	Following Year	
Cash	10,000,000	
Accounts Receivable		5,200,000
Service Revenue		4,800,000

Transfer at a Point in Time

If the seller does not meet the three criteria to recognize revenue over time, then she assumes that the goods or services are transferred at a point in time. It is often straightforward to determine when control is transferred. For example, consider a retailer that sells computers. Control is transferred when a customer purchases a computer at the retailer, takes delivery at the register, and pays for a computer at the point of sale. However, other times it is more difficult to make this determination. In these cases, the entity should consider a number of indicators of the transfer of control to the customer:

1. The seller has a present right to payment for the asset.
2. The customer has legal title to the asset.
3. The seller has transferred physical possession of the asset.
4. The customer has the significant risks and rewards of ownership of the asset.
5. The customer has accepted the asset.

These five conditions indicate that control may have transferred, but any one of them does not determine whether control has actually passed to the customer. The entity should consider all of the facts and circumstances to make this determination. Example 8.19 provides an illustration of goods transferred as of a point in time.

EXAMPLE 8.19 Goods Transferred at a Point in Time

PROBLEM: On April 13, a customer purchased four trees from Hannah Greenhouses for $1,000 on credit. The customer takes immediate delivery of the trees at the greenhouse. The trees cost the greenhouse $650. The company uses the perpetual inventory method. What are the necessary journal entries on April 13 to record the sale and the cost of goods sold?

SOLUTION: Hannah records the accounts receivable and revenue of $1,000 on April 13 because it has transferred control of the trees to the customer.

Account	April 13	
Accounts Receivable	1,000	
Sales Revenue		1,000

The company also records the $650 reduction in inventory and an increase in cost of goods sold for the same amount.

Account	April 13	
Cost of Goods Sold	650	
Inventory		650

Exhibit 8.6 summarizes determining when to recognize revenue.

Summary of the Five-Step Revenue Recognition Process

Now that we have discussed each of the five steps in detail, we illustrate an application in a comprehensive example. Exhibit 8.7 presents a summary of the revenue recognition process in graphical form as a guide for this analysis.

EXHIBIT 8.6 Determining When to Recognize Revenue

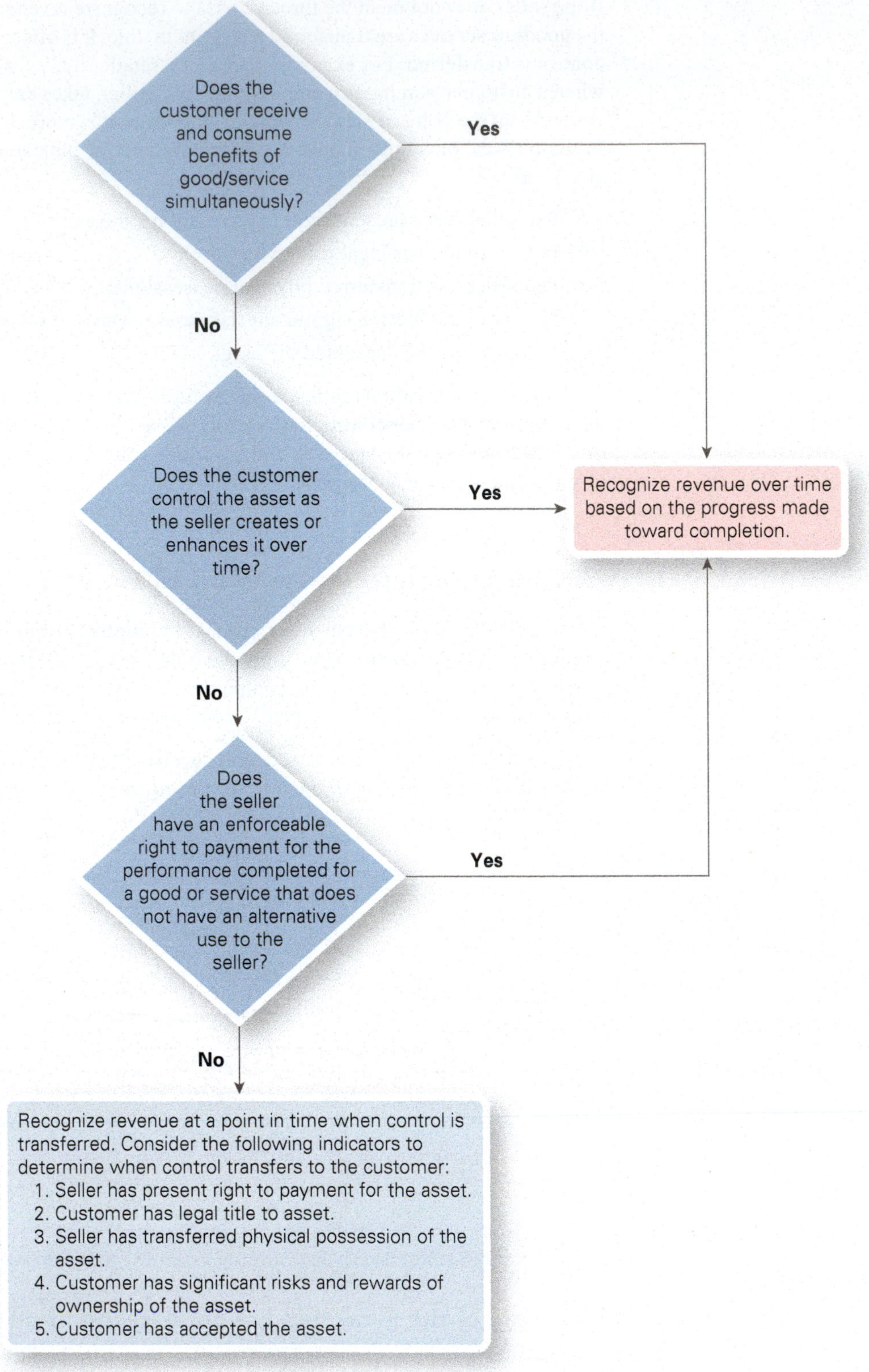

EXHIBIT 8.7 Summary of Five Steps in Revenue Recognition

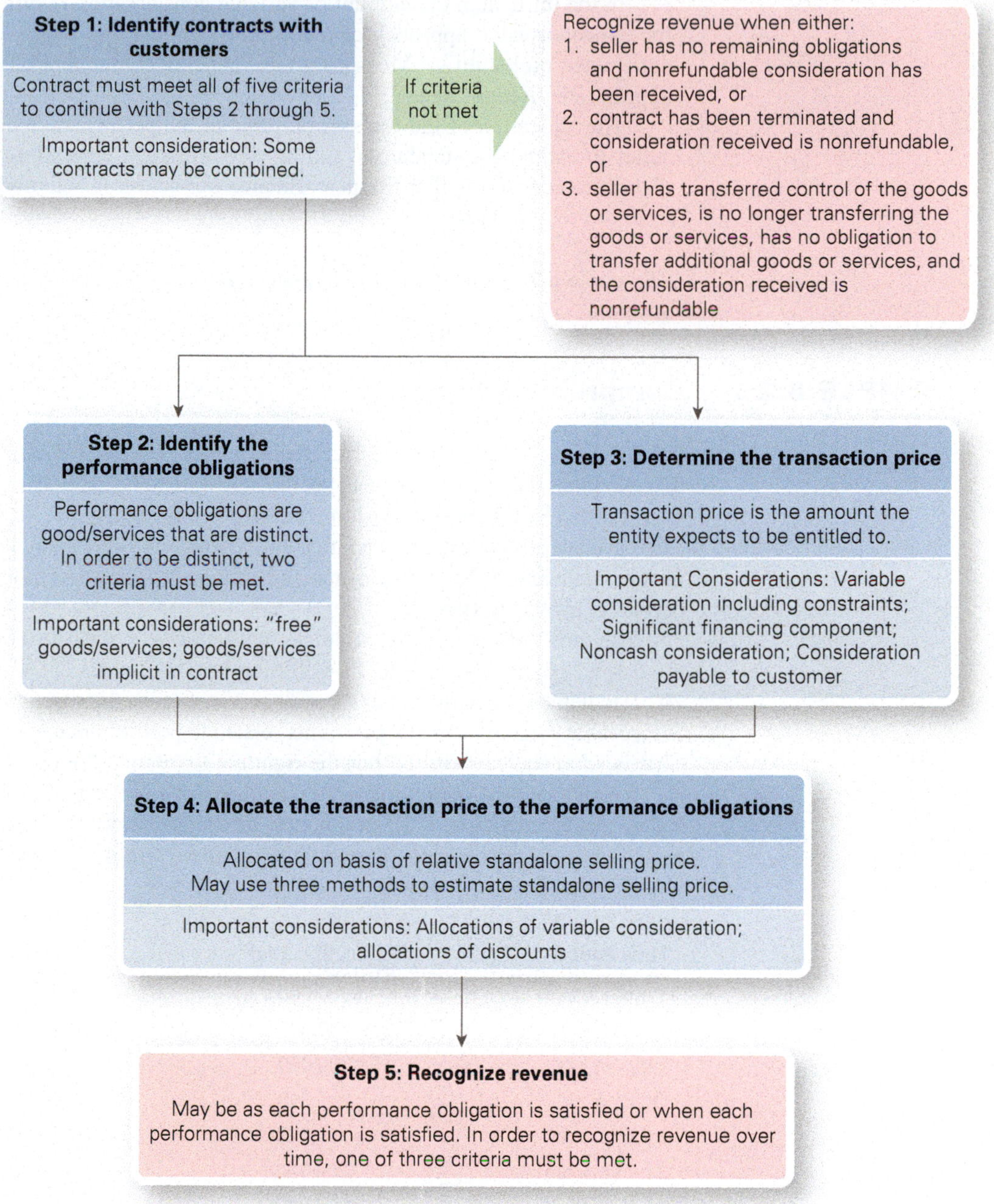

JUDGMENTS IN ACCOUNTING: Revenue Recognition

Companies use extensive judgment when implementing the five steps in the revenue recognition process. When identifying the contract, companies make judgments as to whether it is probable that they will collect the consideration. This may be particularly challenging when an entity may expect to receive partial payment. Is the difference between full payment and the partial payment simply a price concession that affects the transaction price? Or does the lack of a full payment indicate that the transaction price is not collectable? In addition, the determination of whether contracts should be combined may be a matter of judgment.

With regard to the second step, entities may need to exercise judgment to determine if goods or services are distinct. Will a customer benefit from the product or service on a standalone basis? In addition, there may also be judgment involved in determining whether the promise to deliver the good or service is separate from other promises.

In the third step, the amount of variable consideration is often an estimate. Using either the expected-value approach or most-likely-amount approach, entities must estimate their anticipated probabilities. Measuring the financing component also involves estimation of an appropriate discount rate.

The allocation of the transaction price to the performance obligation often requires the seller to estimate a standalone selling price. Finally, depending on the circumstances, the determination of whether the performance obligation is satisfied at a point in time or over time can require judgment.

Example 8.20 summarizes the five-step revenue recognition process with a comprehensive illustration.

EXAMPLE 8.20 Comprehensive Example

PROBLEM: On February 1, 2018, Tide Technologies (TT) and Fab, Inc. signed a written contract that stipulates that TT will deliver specific hardware to Fab and also install and customize software for this hardware. The customized software is highly specific to Fab and would require extensive alterations if used by another entity. Fab is in good financial health and is purchasing the hardware and software to enhance the efficiency of its operations. Both companies use the perpetual inventory system.

The terms of the contract stipulate that Fab will make a $10,000,000 payment to TT at the date of contract inception. TT will then have two years or 24 months (until February 1, 2020) to deliver the hardware and install and customize the software. Furthermore, TT has an enforceable right to keep any payments related to performance to date based on time elapsed. That is, after each month, TT has the right not to refund 1/24 of the payment.

In addition, the contract specifies a bonus/penalty scheme related to the timing of the software customization. If TT completes the project before two years, it will receive a bonus. However, if it completes the project late, it will incur a penalty. The specific amounts, along with TT's probability assessments, are presented next.

Time Period	Bonus (Penalty)	Probability
3 months early	$300,000	7%
2 months early	200,000	40%
1 month early	100,000	30%
On time	0	20%
1 month late	(100,000)	2%
2 months late	(200,000)	1%
3 months late	(300,000)	0%

TT routinely sells the hardware on a standalone basis for $4,000,000. The cost to TT of the hardware is $2,500,000. It does not sell the software and customization on a standalone basis and is not aware of any similar arrangements offered by its competitors. TT anticipates that its costs associated with the software are $2,000,000 and the costs associated with the installation are $4,500,000.

TT delivers the hardware to Fab on December 31, 2019. At this time, Fab accepts the hardware and legal title passes. TT completes the installation on January 2, 2020.

TT has a normal profit margin of 10% and an interest rate of 8%. It allocates interest expense on a straight-line basis. It is a calendar-year company that prepares financial statements annually. It uses time elapsed as its measure of progress for performance obligations that are satisfied over time. It uses the most-likely-amount approach when estimating variable consideration. Perform the five steps in the revenue recognition process. Provide necessary journal entries. You do not need to record costs related to software and installation.

SOLUTION: The five steps of revenue recognition for this contract are analyzed below.

Step 1: Identify the contract

In the first step, TT needs to assess whether this arrangement qualifies as a contract. TT determines whether the contract meets all five of the criteria as follows:

Step 1 Criteria to Identify the Contract	Met?	Explanation
1. All parties to the contract have agreed to the contract and are committed to performing under the contract.	Yes	Both parties signed the contract.
2. Each party's rights with respect to the goods or services that are being transferred are identifiable.	Yes	The provisions of the contract in terms of the transfer of goods and services and the right to payment are all clearly specified.
3. The payment terms for the goods or services that are being transferred are identifiable.	Yes	The up-front payment and bonus/penalty scheme are clearly identified.
4. The contract has commercial substance.	Yes	TT will have increased cash inflows due to the contract and Fab will have decreased cash outflows due to increased efficiencies.
5. It is probable that the seller will collect the consideration to which it is entitled in exchange for the goods or services.	Yes	Fab is in good financial health, so there are no foreseen problems.

Step 2: Identify the performance obligations

The next step is to determine how many performance obligations are included in the contract. There are possibly three: the hardware, software, and installation. However, because the installation involves a significant amount of customization that is useful only to Fab, the software and installation together are one performance obligation. These two items are not distinct from one another and are considered to be interdependent because the installation significantly modifies the software. Thus, this contract contains two performance obligations: the hardware and the combined software/installation.

Step 3: Determine the transaction price

In this case, the stated contract price is $10,000,000. However, the bonus/penalty scheme is an element of variable consideration. In addition, because TT receives the payment two years before the contract will be completed, a significant financing component exists.

With respect to the variable consideration, the most likely amount is a bonus of $200,000 (40% likely).

Time Period	Bonus (Penalty)	Probability	Cumulative Probability
3 months early	$300,000	7%	7%
2 months early	200,000	40%	47%
1 month early	100,000	30%	77%
On time	0	20%	97%
1 month late	(100,000)	2%	99%
2 months late	(200,000)	1%	100%
3 months late	(300,000)	0%	100%

However, this estimate is constrained. Using a cumulative probability measure, TT is 47% likely to receive a bonus of $200,000 or more. But this means that if it records revenue of $200,000, it is only 47% likely that a revenue reversal will not occur and 47% does not qualify as probable. Thus, TT reports variable consideration of $100,000, which is 77% likely on a cumulative probability basis.

In addition, TT considers the financing component. In this case, it is the future value of the consideration. The future value, and thus transaction price, of the $10,000,000 payment is $11,664,000.

(continued)

	N	I/Y	PV	PMT	FV	Excel Formula
Given	2	8.00%	10,000,000	0		
Solve for FV					(11,664,000)	=FV(0.08,2,0,10000000)

Because TT will not receive the estimated bonus until the end of the contract, there is no financing component related to it. Thus, the variable consideration amount is $100,000.

Step 4: Allocate the transaction price to the performance obligations

Next, TT allocates the transaction price to the hardware and software/installation performance obligations. The hardware has a standalone selling price of $4 million. TT can estimate the standalone selling price of the software/installation using the expected cost-plus-a-margin approach. The expected cost of this performance obligation is $6,500,000 ($2,000,000 for the software and $4,5000,000 for the installation). Because TT has a profit margin of 10%, it computes the standalone selling price of the software/installation as $7,150,000 ($6,500,000 × 110%).

In addition, TT must determine how to allocate the variable consideration. Because it applies to only the software/installation performance obligation and allocating it to the software/installation performance obligation is still consistent with the objective of relative standalone selling price allocations, TT allocates the variable consideration exclusively to software/installation.

TT allocates the transaction price as follows:

Performance Obligation	Standalone Selling Price (a)	Percentage of Total (b)	Transaction Price (c)	Allocated Transaction Price–excluding Variable Consideration (d) = (c) × (b)	Allocated Variable Consideration (e)	Total Allocation (d) + (e)
Hardware	$ 4,000,000	35.87%	$11,664,000	$ 4,183,877		$ 4,183,877
Software/ Installation	7,150,000	64.13%	11,664,000	7,480,123	$100,000	7,580,123
TOTAL	$11,150,000	100.00%		$11,664,000	$100,000	$11,764,000

Step 5: Recognize revenue

TT recognizes revenue for the hardware at the point in time it is delivered. Thus, it will recognize $4,183,877 in revenue on December 31, 2019.

Because the software/installation does not have an alternative use to TT, it recognizes revenue for this performance obligation over time as it performs the installation. As stated in the problem, TT uses a time-elapsed method based on the number of months. Thus, TT recognizes 11/24th of the $7,580,123 in 2018, 12/24th in 2019, and 1/24th in 2020.

TT recognizes total interest expense of $1,664,000, which is the difference between the total transaction price of $11,764,000 and the combined estimated payments of $10,100,000. Because TT recognizes interest expense on a straight-line basis, it recognizes 11/24th of the $1,664,000 in 2018, 12/24th in 2019, and 1/24th in 2020.

On February 1, 2018, at the inception of the contract, TT increases cash by $10 million to record the payment from Fab. TT cannot yet recognize revenue so it credits unearned revenue.

Account	February 1, 2018	
Cash	10,000,000	
Unearned Revenue		10,000,000

On December 31, 2018, TT recognizes service revenue for the year ($7,580,123 × 11/24) and interest expense ($1,664,000 × 11/24). The offset to these two transactions is unearned revenue.

Account	December 31, 2018	
Unearned Revenue	2,711,556	
Interest Expense	762,667	
Service Revenue		3,474,223

On December 31, 2019, TT recognizes the appropriate amount of service revenue for the year ($7,580,123 × 12/24) and interest expense ($1,664,000 × 12/24). In addition, it recognizes the $4,183,877 sales revenue related to the hardware because it is delivered as well as the $2,500,000 cost of the hardware. The offset to these transactions is unearned revenue.

Account	December 31, 2019	
Unearned Revenue	7,141,939	
Interest Expense	832,000	
Sales Revenue		4,183,877
Service Revenue		3,790,062
Cost of Goods Sold	2,500,000	
Inventory		2,500,000

On January 2, 2020, TT records the receipt of the $100,000 bonus payment. It credits service revenue for that amount.

Account	January 2, 2020	
Cash	100,000	
Service Revenue		100,000

Finally, on January 31, TT recognizes the remaining service revenue and interest expense and amortizes the remaining unearned revenue.

Account	January 31, 2020	
Unearned Revenue	146,505	
Interest Expense	69,333	
Service Revenue		215,838

7 Describe the accounting for long-term contracts, including implementing the percentage-of-completion method and the completed-contract method.

Accounting for Long-Term Contracts

Long-term contracts are a type of transaction for which firms report revenue, costs, and gross profit over time as opposed to at a point in time. They are prevalent in industries such as communications, homebuilding, software development, aircraft, shipbuilding, and construction. Consider a company that enters into a contract to manufacture or build a product for the customer when the manufacturing process will take a period of time substantially longer than a year. If the firm recognized revenue at a point of time, it would not recognize the revenue (and associated gross profit) attributable to the long-term contract until it completed the product and delivered it to the customer. However, as we discuss next, this approach may not provide the most accurate presentation of the company's financial position and economic performance.

There are two accounting methods for revenue recognition for long-term contracts: the *percentage-of-completion method* and the *completed-contract method*. Total revenue and costs for a long-term contract are the same under both methods. The difference between the two approaches is the timing of revenue and gross profit recognition on the contract: The **percentage-of-completion method** recognizes gross profit over the production period whereas the **completed-contract method** recognizes gross profit only at the end of the contract.

An entity should use the percentage-of-completion method when it meets one of the three criteria for goods and services transferred over time (discussed earlier for transfer of control to the customer), and it can reasonably measure its progress toward completion. If these conditions are met, the financial statements are more accurately presented under the percentage-of-completion method because the entity's economic activities are reported on the income statement. If the contract does not meet any of the three criteria or if the entity cannot reasonably measure progress toward completion, then it uses the completed-contract method. For example, ***General Electric Company*** will use the completed-contract method to account for the revenue from the production of commercial airplane engines because contracts do not transfer control during the manufacturing process.[4] We discuss each of these methods next.

[4]http://www.ge.com/ar2016/assets/pdf/GE_AR16.pdf

THE CONCEPTUAL FRAMEWORK CONNECTION
Revenue Recognition for Long-Term Contracts

Relevance and faithful representation are the two fundamental qualitative characteristics of financial reporting that make information useful. To be relevant, information should have predictive value—that is, the information is an input that should help predict future outcomes. Assume a company is engaged in a 10-year project for which it does not recognize any revenues or costs until completion. Waiting until completion to recognize any revenue could be misleading because the income statement will not report any activity for the first nine years.

Now consider the case in which ***Boeing*** needs five years to develop a new passenger jet. Using point-of-sale accounting would delay revenue and expense recognition until ***Boeing*** manufactures and delivers the jet to the customer. If this were ***Boeing's*** only project in process, the income statement would show no activity in the first four years and recognize the full amount of the transaction in the fifth year. The resulting volatile trend in earnings would distort operating results and not faithfully represent the underlying economic event.

Percentage-of-Completion Method

In this section, we discuss accounting for contracts under the *percentage-of-completion method.* We begin with a discussion of estimating the percentage of completion of a long-term contract. Then, we explain the accounting procedures and introduce accounts specific to accounting for long-term contracts.

Determining the Estimated Percentage of Completion. As discussed earlier in the chapter, firms can estimate the degree of completion by using input measures (for example, costs incurred and direct labor hours used), output measures (for example, miles of highway and the number of cell towers installed), or engineering estimates.

Input Measures. A common method used in practice, the **cost-to-cost approach**, estimates the cumulative percentage of completion by dividing the total cost incurred to date by total estimated costs as follows:

$$\text{Cumulative Percentage Complete} = \frac{\text{Total Costs Incurred to Date}}{\text{Estimated Total Cost of the Project}} \quad (8.1)$$

The estimated total cost of the project equals the total actual costs incurred to date plus the estimated costs to complete the project. The estimated total cost of the project is likely to change throughout the contract period. This does not create a problem because the ratio is computed each period using the current costs to date and estimated total cost.

Determination of Revenue, Costs, and Gross Profit under the Percentage-of-Completion Method. Under the percentage-of-completion method, firms recognize revenues based on the project's stage of completion. Specifically, firms recognize revenue, costs, and gross profit in each year by:

1. Computing cumulative revenue by multiplying the total estimated contract revenue times the percentage complete. Revenue for the current period is cumulative revenue less revenue recognized in all prior periods.
2. Recording actual costs for the current period as incurred.[5]
3. Computing gross profit for the year as the revenue recognized in the current period in (1) less the costs recognized in the period in (2).

If the reported costs exceed the reported revenues in a given year for an otherwise profitable contract, then the gross profit is negative. In this case, the firm credits construction in progress in the journal entry made to record revenues, costs, and gross profit.

Example 8.21 illustrates the computation of revenue and gross profit under the cost-to-cost approach.

[5]This is simplified somewhat. Some costs will actually be capitalized and amortized in a systematic basis consistent with the transfer of the good or service to the customer.

EXAMPLE 8.21 Percentage-of-Completion Method: Cost-to-Cost Approach

PROBLEM: Natalie Networks Incorporated (NNI) accepts a fixed-fee contract to develop and implement a communications network for Summit Sound Systems. NNI accepts a fixed fee of $18,600 and must complete the project within three years. NNI uses the percentage-of-completion method of accounting to determine the percent complete using the cost-to-cost approach. Costs incurred and estimated total costs are summarized in the following table:

	2018	2019	2020
Actual costs incurred during the year	$ 3,000	$ 1,500	$10,000
Actual costs incurred in previous years	0	3,000	4,500
Estimated costs to complete	12,000	5,500	0
Estimated total costs	$15,000	$10,000	$14,500

Determine the amount of gross profit that NNI will report in each of the three years.

SOLUTION: Under the percentage-of-completion method, costs for the period are the actual construction costs incurred. In 2018, actual construction costs are $3,000. The cumulative percent complete is 20% computed as $3,000 actual construction costs divided by $15,000 estimated total costs. Because 20% is completed in 2018, 20% of the estimated revenue is recognized in 2018. Thus, NNI reports $3,720 ($18,600 × 20%) of revenue in 2018 and actual costs of $3,000. It reports gross profit of $720 ($3,720 less $3,000).

The 2019 actual construction costs of $1,500 added to the $3,000 construction costs incurred in prior years results in $4,500 of cumulative construction costs through 2019. Because the estimated costs to complete are $5,500, the estimated total costs are $10,000 ($4,500 actual constructions costs through 2019 plus the $5,500 estimated costs to complete). The cumulative percent complete in 2019 is 45% computed as $4,500 actual construction costs divided by $10,000 estimated total costs. The cumulative revenue recognized through 2019 is $8,370 ($18,600 × 45%). Because $3,720 of revenue was recognized in 2018, NNI recognizes $4,650 in 2019. It recognizes actual costs of $1,500 and gross profit of $3,150 ($4,650 less $1,500).

In the final year of the contract, NNI incurs $10,000 in actual costs, bringing the cumulative construction costs incurred to $14,500. The contract is now 100% complete so that the remaining $10,230 of revenue is recognized ($18,600 total contract price less the cumulative revenue recognized to date of $8,370). The year's gross profit recognized is $230 ($10,230 current year revenue − $10,000 actual costs for the year).

Estimated Total Costs	2018	2019	2020
Actual construction costs incurred during the year	$ 3,000	$ 1,500	$ 10,000
Construction costs incurred in prior years	0	3,000	4,500
Cumulative construction costs incurred to date	$ 3,000	$ 4,500	$ 14,500
Estimated costs to complete	12,000	5,500	0
Estimated total costs	$15,000	$10,000	$ 14,500
Percent Complete			
Actual (cumulative) costs incurred to date	$ 3,000	$ 4,500	$ 14,500
Estimated total costs	$15,000	$10,000	$ 14,500
Cumulative percent complete	20.00%	45.00%	100.00%
Revenue and Gross Profit Recognition			
Contract price	$18,600	$18,600	$ 18,600
Times: Percent complete	20.00%	45.00%	100.00%
Cumulative revenue	$ 3,720	$ 8,370	$ 18,600
Revenue recognized in prior years	0	3,720	8,370
Current year revenue	$ 3,720	$ 4,650	$ 10,230
Less: Actual costs	3,000	1,500	10,000
Gross profit recognized in the current year	$ 720	$ 3,150	$ 230

Output Measures. In addition to the cost-to-cost approach, which is an input measure of the degree of completion, firms also use output measures in practice. Output measure examples include miles of highway completed or square footage completed of a building. Example 8.22 illustrates the use of an output measure to estimate the percent completed.

Percentage-of-Completion Method Accounting Procedures As a company constructs an asset, it accumulates resources used in construction such as raw materials in an inventory account called **construction in progress** (CIP). Long-term construction contracts usually allow a company, also called a contractor, to bill the customer periodically over the contract term. When a company bills the customer, it increases accounts receivable with a debit. The credit is to an account called *billings on construction in progress*. **Billings on construction in progress** is a contra account to the construction-in-progress account and reduces the net carrying value of the asset, CIP. In effect, this entry offsets the physical asset in the CIP (inventory) with a financial asset in billings on CIP (accounts receivable). Using the contra account avoids double counting the total asset value.

As discussed, revenue is based on the progress to date (that is, the percentage of the project that has been completed). Unique to accounting for long-term construction contracts, revenue from long-term contracts is credited, the construction costs account is debited, and the debit to the CIP account is the difference between the revenue and the construction cost (the gross profit). At the end of the project, the company removes the CIP account from the books with a credit and removes the billings on construction in progress account with a debit.

At each balance sheet date, the company reports the balance of accounts receivable and the net amount of the CIP and billings on CIP. If the CIP amount is higher than the billings account, the net amount is an asset called **costs and recognized profits in excess of billings**. If, however, the amount in the billings account is higher than in the CIP account, then the net amount is a liability called **billings in excess of costs and recognized profits**.

The measurement of the net asset or net liability position of each contract has implications for financial statement users:

- If the company reports a net asset position, the contract has unbilled receivables. That is, the contractor has an asset, giving the firm the right to bill the buyer for work performed.
- If the company reports a significant amount of unbilled receivables, the buyer may have little capital at risk and can easily abandon the project.
- If the company reports a significant net liability position, this implies that the contractor has received cash in advance and has the obligation to perform on the contract. However, if the contractor expends cash received for alternative uses, there may be insufficient resources to complete the project.

To summarize, the percentage-of-completion method involves the following accounting procedures:

1. Accumulate resources used in construction such as raw materials by increasing an asset (inventory), construction in progress (CIP).
2. When the contractor sends bills to the customer, increase accounts receivable with a debit and increase billings on CIP with a credit.
3. When the contractor receives cash from the customer, increase cash with a debit and decrease accounts receivable with a credit.
4. Recognize the revenue and the associated costs each year, basing the amount of revenue in a given year on the progress to date (that is, the percentage of the project that has been completed). Credit revenue from long-term contracts, debit the construction costs, and debit the difference between the revenue and the cost of the construction (the gross profit) to the CIP account.
5. At each balance sheet date, report the net amount of the CIP and billings on CIP on the balance sheet. An asset, costs and recognized profits in excess of billings, is reported if the CIP is higher than the billings on CIP. A liability, billings in excess of costs and recognized profits, is reported if the billings on construction in progress amount is higher than the CIP. At the end of the project, remove the CIP account from the books with a credit and remove the billings on construction in progress account with a debit.

As discussed, the company estimates revenue on the contract based on progress toward completion. Example 8.22 illustrates the percentage-of-completion method showing all journal entries.

EXAMPLE 8.22

Percentage-of-Completion Method: Output Measure

PROBLEM: Bronco Builders accepts a contract with Steib Stores to construct a strip mall on Route 3 on January 2, 2018. The builder accepts a fixed fee of $9,300,000 and must complete the project within three years. Costs incurred, estimated total costs, billings, and cash collections are summarized in the following table:

	2018	2019	2020
Actual construction costs incurred during the year	$1,500,000	$7,000,000	$ 500,000
Estimated costs to complete	7,200,000	400,000	0
Progress billings made during the year	4,000,000	3,000,000	2,300,000
Cash collections during the year	3,100,000	3,100,000	3,100,000

The arrangement meets the criteria for recognizing revenue over time, and Bronco Builders uses the percentage-of-completion method of accounting. It determines percent complete using the percentage of the square feet that it has completed. The strip mall will be a total of 40,000 square feet. The following table summarizes the square footage completed each year:

	2018	2019	2020
Cumulative square feet completed	10,000	28,000	40,000

Prepare the journal entries for the three years of the contract and post the journal entries to the appropriate t-accounts. Also prepare a partial income statement and balance sheet for the three years.

SOLUTION: Each year, Bronco follows the percentage-of-completion method procedures by recording:

- Actual construction costs each year with a debit to construction in progress.
- Billings with a debit to accounts receivable and a credit to billings on construction in progress.
- Cash collections with a debit to cash and a credit to accounts receivable.

The journal entries with explanations for these steps follow:

	2018		*2019*		*2020*	
Account	***Debit***	***Credit***	***Debit***	***Credit***	***Debit***	***Credit***
Construction in Progress	1,500,000		7,000,000		500,000	
Cash, Materials Inventory, Supplies Inventory, etc.		1,500,000		7,000,000		500,000
To record construction costs						
Accounts Receivable	4,000,000		3,000,000		2,300,000	
Billings on Construction in Progress		4,000,000		3,000,000		2,300,000
To record billings						
Cash	3,100,000		3,100,000		3,100,000	
Accounts Receivable		3,100,000		3,100,000		3,100,000
To record cash collections						

(continued)

Each year, Bronco must also report revenue, costs, and gross profit on the contract. To determine these amounts, we must first compute the percent completed each year based on the ratio of square feet completed to total square feet.

	2018	2019	2020
Cumulative square feet completed	10,000	28,000	40,000
Total square feet	40,000	40,000	40,000
Percent complete	25%	70%	100%

We then use the percent complete to compute the revenue and cost for each year.

	2018	2019	2020
Estimated total revenue	$9,300,000	$ 9,300,000	$9,300,000
Percent complete (from above)	25%	70%	100%
Cumulative revenue	$2,325,000	$ 6,510,000	$9,300,000
Revenue recognized in prior years	0	2,325,000	6,510,000
Current year revenue	$2,325,000	$ 4,185,000	$2,790,000
Less: Actual costs	1,500,000	7,000,000	500,000
Gross profit (loss) recognized in the current year	$ 825,000	$ (2,815,000)	$2,290,000

The journal entries to record the revenue, costs, and gross profit are presented next followed by the t-accounts.

	2018		*2019*		*2020*	
Account	***Debit***	***Credit***	***Debit***	***Credit***	***Debit***	***Credit***
Construction Costs	1,500,000		7,000,000		500,000	
Construction in Progress	825,000			2,815,000	2,290,000	
Revenue on Long-term Contract		2,325,000		4,185,000		2,790,000
To record revenue, costs and gross profit						
Billings on Construction in Progress					9,300,000	
Construction in Progress						9,300,000
To close completed contract						

Construction in Progress

	Debit	Credit	
2018 Construction Costs	1,500,000		
2018 Gross Profit	825,000		
2018 Balance	2,325,000		
2019 Construction Costs	7,000,000		
		2,815,000	2019 Gross loss
2019 Balance	6,510,000		
2020 Construction Costs	500,000		
2020 Gross Profit	2,290,000		
2020 Balance	9,300,000		
		9,300,000	Close
Final 2020 Balance	0		

Billings on Construction in Progress

		4,000,000	2018 Billing
		3,000,000	2019 Billing
		7,000,000	2019 Balance
		2,300,000	2020 Billing
		9,300,000	2020 Balance
Close	9,300,000		
		0	Final 2020 Balance

Accounts Receivable

2018 Billing	4,000,000	3,100,000	2018 Collections
2018 Balance	900,000		
2019 Billing	3,000,000	3,100,000	2019 Collections
2019 Balance	800,000		
2020 Billing	2,300,000	3,100,000	2020 Collections
2020 Balance	0		

The partial income statement at the end of each year follows. The income statement includes the revenues, costs, and gross profits we just computed.

	2018	2019	2020
Revenue from Long-Term Contracts	$ 2,325,000	$ 4,185,000	$2,790,000
Costs of Construction	1,500,000	7,000,000	500,000
Gross Profit	$ 825,000	$(2,815,000)	$2,290,000

The total profit recognized over the life of the contract is $300,000, which is equal to the total contract price of $9,300,000 less the total costs of $9,000,000.

At year end, the balance sheet reports the assets and liabilities associated with the long-term contract. Prior to closing out the contract, the net asset (liability) related to the costs and billings of the contract are as follows:

	2018	2019	2020
Construction in Progress	$ 2,325,000	$ 6,510,000	$ 9,300,000
Billings on Construction in Progress	4,000,000	7,000,000	9,300,000
Net Asset (Liability)	$ (1,675,000)	$ (490,000)	$ 0

	2018	2019	2020
Assets:			
Accounts Receivable	$ 900,000	$800,000	$0
Costs and Recognized Profits in Excess of Billings			0
Liabilities:			
Billings in Excess of Costs and Recognized Profits	$ 1,675,000	$490,000	$0

Completed-Contract Method

Companies use the completed-contract method only when they do not meet the criteria required to use percentage-of-completion. The timing of revenue and gross profit recognition is the key the completed-contract and percentage-of-completion methods. Under the completed-contract method, a company recognizes revenue each year equal to the actual costs incurred. Thus, the company reports zero gross profit until the project is complete. At the conclusion of the project, the total gross profit is recognized.[6] The completed-contract approach involves the following accounting procedures:

1. Accumulate construction costs by debiting an asset (inventory) account called construction in progress (CIP).
2. Increase accounts receivable with a debit and increase with a credit the account billings on CIP when the contractor bills the customer.
3. Increase cash with a debit and decrease accounts receivable with a credit when the contractor receives cash from the customer.
4. Recognize the actual costs incurred and the same amount of revenue each year. Credit revenue from long-term contracts and debit the construction costs. Record the total gross profit only at the conclusion of the project.
5. Report the net amount of the CIP and billings on CIP on the balance sheet at each balance sheet date. An asset, costs in excess of billings, is reported if the CIP is higher than the billings on CIP. A liability, billings in excess of costs, is reported if the billings on CIP are higher than the CIP. At the end of the project, remove from the books the CIP account with a credit and the billings on construction in progress account with a debit.

The completed-contract method accounting procedures in Steps 1, 2, 3, and 5 are the same as the percentage-of-completion method. The timing of revenue and gross profit recognition in Step 4 is the key difference between the completed-contract and percentage-of-completion methods. Example 8.23 illustrates the completed-contract method.

EXAMPLE 8.23 Completed-Contract Approach

PROBLEM: Bronco Builders accepted a contract with Steib Stores to construct a strip mall on Route 3 on January 2, 2018. The builder accepted a fixed fee of $9,300,000 and must complete the project within three years. Costs incurred, billings, and cash collections are summarized in the following table. The arrangement does not meet any of the three criteria necessary to recognize revenue over time, so Bronco Builders uses the completed-contract method of revenue recognition. Prepare the t-accounts and journal entries for the three years of the contract. Also prepare a partial income statement and balance sheet for the three years.

	2018	2019	2020
Actual construction costs incurred during the year	$1,500,000	$7,000,000	$ 500,000
Progress billings made during the year	4,000,000	3,000,000	2,300,000
Cash collections during the year	3,100,000	3,100,000	3,100,000

SOLUTION: Each year, Bronco follows the completed-contract approach procedures by recording:

- Actual construction costs each year with a debit to construction in progress.
- Billings with a debit to accounts receivable and a credit to billings on construction in progress.
- Cash collections with a debit to cash and a credit to accounts receivable.
- Revenues and costs based on the amount of actual costs incurred.

[6] This approach is slightly different than the U.S. GAAP revenue recognition rules that were effective prior to December 15, 2017. The completed-contract approach used previously did not recognize any costs or revenues until the completion of the project. However, FASB ASC 606-10-25-37 states that revenue should be recognized to the extent of the costs incurred. Also, this new approach is simplified somewhat. Some costs will actually be capitalized and amortized in a systematic basis consistent with the transfer of the good or service to the customer.

We record the gross profit for the entire project in 2020 when Bronco completes the project. The revenue for the project is $9,300,000 as agreed on by the buyer and seller. The costs were $9,000,000, leaving a gross profit (debited to construction in progress) of $300,000 in the final year of the project. Finally, we close the billings on construction in progress and construction in progress accounts.

The journal entries and t-accounts are below.

	2018		2019		2020	
Account	**Debit**	**Credit**	**Debit**	**Credit**	**Debit**	**Credit**
Construction in Progress	1,500,000		7,000,000		500,000	
Cash, Materials Inventory, Supplies Inventory, etc.		1,500,000		7,000,000		500,000
To record construction costs						
Accounts Receivable	4,000,000		3,000,000		2,300,000	
Billings on Construction in Progress		4,000,000		3,000,000		2,300,000
To record billings						
Cash	3,100,000		3,100,000		3,100,000	
Accounts Receivable		3,100,000		3,100,000		3,100,000
To record cash collections						
Construction in Progress					300,000	
Construction Costs	1,500,000		7,000,000		500,000	
Revenue on Long-Term Contract		1,500,000		7,000,000		800,000
To record revenue and costs (and gross profit in 2020)						
Billings on Construction in Progress					9,300,000	
Construction in Progress						9,300,000
To close completed contract						

Construction in Progress

	Debit	Credit	
2018 Construction Costs	1,500,000		
2019 Construction Costs	7,000,000		
2019 Balance	8,500,000		
2020 Construction Costs	500,000		
2020 Gross Profit	300,000		
2020 Balance	9,300,000		
		9,300,000	Close
Final 2020 Balance	0		

Billings on Construction in Progress

	Debit	Credit	
		4,000,000	2018 Billing
		3,000,000	2019 Billing
		7,000,000	2019 Balance
		2,300,000	2020 Billing
		9,300,000	2020 Balance
Close	9,300,000		
		0	Final 2020 Balance

(continued)

Accounts Receivable

	Debit	Credit	
2018 Billing	4,000,000	3,100,000	2018 Collections
2018 Balance	900,000		
2019 Billing	3,000,000	3,100,000	2019 Collections
2019 Balance	800,000		
2020 Billing	2,300,000	3,100,000	2020 Collections
2020 Balance	0		

The partial income statement for each year follows. As is always the case under the completed-contract method, revenue equals costs of construction and the income statement includes zero gross profit for the long-term contract until the year the project is completed. In 2020, the final year, Bronco reports the actual costs incurred of $500,000 and the remaining revenues of $800,000. Thus, Bronco has reported total revenues of $9,300,000 and the total costs of $9,000,000 for the contract.

	2018	2019	2020
Revenue from Long-Term Contracts	$ 1,500,000	$7,000,000	$800,000
Costs of Construction	1,500,000	7,000,000	500,000
Gross Profit	$ 0	$ 0	$300,000

At year end, the balance sheet reports the assets and liabilities associated with the long-term contract. Prior to closing out the contract, we compute the net asset (liability) related to the costs and billings of the contract as follows:

	2018	2019	2020
Construction in Progress	$ 1,500,000	$8,500,000	$ 9,300,000
Billings on Construction in Progress	4,000,000	7,000,000	9,300,000
Net Asset (Liability)	$(2,500,000)	$1,500,000	$ 0

	2018	2019	2020
Assets:			
Accounts Receivable	$ 900,000	$ 800,000	$ 0
Costs in Excess of Billings		1,500,000	
Liabilities:			
Billings in Excess of Costs	$ 2,500,000	$ 0	$ 0

8 Describe and demonstrate the accounting for special issues in revenue recognition, including right-to-return sales, consignment sales, principal-agent sales, bill-and-hold arrangements, and channel stuffing.

Special Issues in Revenue Recognition

We next discuss various special issues in revenue recognition including *right-to-return sales*, *consignment sales*, *principal-agent transactions*, *bill-and-hold transactions*, and *channel stuffing*.[7]

Right-to-Return Sales

When a company makes a **right-to-return sale,** it is providing customers with the ability to return a product that has been transferred to them. The seller is obligated to accept the returned product if the buyer chooses to return it. The right of return does not represent a separate performance obligation but rather is a component of variable consideration affecting the transaction price. The entity recognizes the amount of expected returns as a refund liability, which represents its obligation to the customer to stand ready to receive the returned product and refund the customer's

[7] Warranties are covered in Chapter 13.

consideration (or provide the customer with a credit or a different product). The seller does not recognize revenue for the amount of expected returns until the amounts are no longer subject to the constraint, such as at the end of the return period. In addition to recording a refund liability, the seller must reduce the cost of goods sold by the amount of costs attributable to the products that it expects will be returned. However, the seller should continue to reduce the inventory by the full amount of the cost of sales. The seller recognizes the offset as an asset that it records separately from inventory. Example 8.24 illustrates accounting for a sale with the right of return.

EXAMPLE 8.24 **Revenue Recognition with Right of Return**

PROBLEM: On December 3, Haxbo, Inc. sold merchandise costing $100,000 to a customer for $140,000 cash and anticipated that 10% of the merchandise would be returned. On December 28, Haxbo refunded $10,000 for the return of a portion of the merchandise. The cost of the merchandise returned is $7,143. Assume Haxbo uses the perpetual inventory system. What is the journal entry to record the sale and the sales return?

SOLUTION: On December 3, Haxbo records the sale at 90% of $140,000 and a refund liability for the 10% expected returns.

Account	December 3	
Cash	140,000	
Refund Liability		14,000
Sales Revenue		126,000

Haxbo also records the cost of goods sold at 90% of $100,000 and records a separate inventory asset for the 10% expected return.

Account	December 3	
Cost of Goods Sold	90,000	
Other Assets – Estimated Returns	10,000	
Inventory		100,000

On December 28, Haxbo records the sales return by debiting the refund liability and crediting cash.

Account	December 28	
Refund Liability	10,000	
Cash		10,000

In addition, Haxbo will increase inventory and decrease the estimated return inventory account for $7,143.

Account	December 28	
Inventory	7,143	
Other Assets – Estimated Returns		7,143

Consignment Sales

A **consignment sale** is an arrangement in which a seller (referred to as the consignor) delivers goods to a third party (the consignee), who sells the goods to the customer. A consignment sale is an example of a **principal-agent arrangement** in which one party (the agent) acts on behalf of another party (the principal). In this case, the consignor is the principal and the consignee is the agent.

Consignment sales—for goods such as books, furniture, musical instruments, toys, automobiles, and sporting goods—are quite common in practice. For example, a retailer of musical instruments can hold a piano from a manufacturer that it will sell on a consignment basis. eBay drop-off sites make use of consignment sales.

Determining whether a particular arrangement is a consignment arrangement is based on whether the seller passes control to the other party. If so, then it is a normal sale. If not, then it qualifies as a consignment arrangement. The authoritative literature provides three indicators that an arrangement is a consignment arrangement.

1. The seller controls the product until a specified event occurs, such as the sale to the ultimate consumer.
2. The seller can require that the product be returned to it or sent to another third party.
3. The third party does not have an unconditional obligation to pay for the product.

The parties must use judgment to determine whether control has passed based on these indicators. If an arrangement is classified as a consignment arrangement, the consignee does not record the inventory on its books, and the consignor does not record revenue when the goods are delivered. Rather, on the delivery date, the consignor credits inventory and debits inventory on consignment, and the consignee makes no entry. The consignor records revenue, along with the commission expense and receivable or cash, upon notification that the consignee has sold the inventory. The consignor will also record cost of goods sold and remove the inventory on consignment from its books. When the consignee sells the inventory, it records commissions revenue and an amount that is due to the consignor for the sale. Example 8.25 illustrates recording consignment sales.

EXAMPLE 8.25 Consignment Sales

PROBLEM: Wessel Guitars delivers its products to small musical instrument retailers on consignment. Wessel shipped four guitars with a total cost of $10,000 to Barchester Music Center on February 18 of the current year. Barchester accepted the guitars on consignment. The guitars have a combined retail selling price of $16,000. If Barchester sells the guitars, it will be paid a 20% commission on the total retail price of the products. Barchester sold all four guitars on April 20 for cash. It notified Wessel of the sale and remitted the cash, net of the 20% commission, on April 21. Both companies use the perpetual inventory method. Prepare the journal entries for Wessel and for Barchester to record the consignment transactions.

SOLUTION: Wessel Guitars, the consignor, uses a special inventory account to record the inventory out on consignment. Wessel reclassifies the amount of inventory consigned from its regular inventory account to an account called inventory on consignment. The reclassification entry is made on February 18, the date of delivery.

Account	***February 18***	
Inventory on Consignment	10,000	
Inventory		10,000

Wessel waits until April 21 to record revenue and the commission expense because this is the date of notification that the consignee sold the inventory.

Account	***April 21***	
Cash	12,800	
Sales Commission Expense (20% × $16,000)	3,200	
Sales Revenue		16,000

Wessel also records the cost of goods sold on the date of notification, April 21.

Account	April 21	
Cost of Goods Sold	10,000	
Inventory on Consignment		10,000

Barchester does not make any entry when it receives the inventory. When it sells the inventory on April 20, it records the cash and a liability to the consignor as well as its commission earned.

Account	April 20	
Cash	16,000	
Due to Consignor		12,800
Commissions Revenue		3,200

On April 21, it records the remittance of the cash to Wessel.

Account	April 21	
Due to Consignor	12,800	
Cash		12,800

Other Principal-Agent Transactions

Other common principal-agent transactions—such as travel agency transactions, transactions related to advertisements and mailing lists, and auction transactions—require special accounting. For example, a travel agent can arrange airline tickets, hotel reservations, and car rentals, or travelers can make these arrangements online using a service such as ***Priceline.com***. Whether the arrangements are made in person or online, the agent will recognize some amount of revenue.

To illustrate, let's assume that a travel agent books a flight for a client. Conceptually, there are two options for recognizing the revenue:

1. Record the total amount of the ticket (the gross amount) as revenue and recognize the cost of sales for the amount remitted to the airline. The **gross revenue reporting approach** records the gross amount as revenue and the amount remitted to the supplier of the product in cost of revenues.
2. Record only the net fee—that is, the amount billed to the customer less the amount paid to the airline for the tickets. The **net revenue reporting approach** records only the net amount in revenue.

An entity determines which of these methods to use based on whether it is the principal or the agent in the transaction. If the entity obtains control of the product before passing it to the consumer, it is the principal and should use the gross revenue reporting approach. If it never obtains control, then it is the agent and should use the net revenue reporting approach. For example, ***Priceline.com Incorporated***, the online travel company, uses both methods depending on the types of transactions. For transactions in which ***Priceline*** is the seller of record—that is, it selects suppliers and determines the price it will accept from the customer—it uses the gross revenue reporting approach. In transactions in which customers purchase hotel room reservations or rental car reservations directly from suppliers at disclosed contractual rates, ***Priceline*** recognizes revenue using the net revenue reporting approach.

Gross profit is the same under the gross and net methods—so is the approach used important to the financial statement user? Because companies are often evaluated, at least partially, on their revenues, the implications of the two different approaches can be significant, as illustrated in Example 8.26.

EXAMPLE 8.26 Principal-Agent Arrangement

PROBLEM: Youflywithme.com reports the following income statement information for the current year. All sales result from principal-agent transactions. Compare the financial statement presentation under the gross revenue and net revenue reporting approaches.

Youflywithme.com Incorporated Statement of Net Income For the Year Ended December 31	
Revenues	$ 500,000
Cost of Revenues	380,000
Gross Profit (Loss)	$ 120,000

SOLUTION: The following analysis compares the financial statement presentation under the gross revenue reporting and the net revenue reporting approaches.

	Gross Method	Net Method
Revenues	$ 500,000	$ 120,000
Cost of Revenues	(380,000)	0
Gross Profit	$ 120,000	$ 120,000

The amount of gross profit recognized is the same under either approach. However, reported revenues are significantly higher using the gross method as compared to the net method. If Youflywithme.com controls the product and is the seller of record, then the gross method is correct. If the company acts as an agent for the seller, it must use the net method.

Bill-and-Hold Arrangements

Bill-and-hold arrangements are transactions in which a buyer accepts title and billings but delays the physical receipt of the goods. The buyer may request a delay in delivery for several reasons: a temporary shortage of warehouse space, current excess inventory levels, a significant backlog in the production cycle, or the construction of a new facility.

If the seller has transferred control of the goods to the buyer, then the seller can recognize revenue at the point of sale. The seller determines if it has transferred control by considering the normal indicators of control discussed earlier in the chapter. In addition, the seller must meet all of the following four criteria to claim that it has transferred control to the buyer:

1. The reason for the bill-and-hold must be substantive. An example of this would be that the customer requested the bill-and-hold arrangement.
2. The product must be separately identified as belonging to the customer.
3. The product must be ready for physical transfer to the customer.
4. The seller cannot have the ability to use the product in any way, including delivering it to another customer.

If the seller meets all four of these conditions, it can recognize revenue at the time of sale; otherwise, the seller must wait until it meets the conditions or it delivers the goods to the buyer.

Broadwind Energy, Inc., an alternative energy company, was accused in 2015 of accelerating $3 million in revenues through improper bill-and-hold arrangements. Broadwind shipped products at the end of the month, knowing customers would not accept them until the next month or period. If ***Broadwind*** had not misstated its revenue, it would have been at risk of violating its debt covenants.[8]

[8] https://www.sec.gov/litigation/complaints/2015/comp-pr2015-24.pdf.

Channel Stuffing

Companies often engage in *channel stuffing* selling practices designed to accelerate revenue recognition. **Channel stuffing** (also referred to as **trade loading**) is a practice in which a company induces wholesale distributors to buy more inventory than they can sell in the current period, thus "stuffing" the distribution channel with increased discounts or liberal return policies. If the distributors cannot sell the inventory in the next period, they return the goods to the seller.

Channel stuffing inflates sales in the current period, thus making the seller's financial statements look better. Although this technique allows an entity to recognize increased sales in the current period, it reduces the sales in the next period or increases sale returns significantly.[9] For example, in 2015, ***Diageo PLC,*** a large U.K. beverage company, was investigated for shipping excess inventory to distributors to increase sales to boost the company's results.[10] Channel stuffing caused a buildup of the customers' inventory levels that posed risks to the company's future sales and earnings.

Firms should not recognize revenue from a channel stuffing arrangement because the risks and rewards of ownership have not passed to the buyer given the buyer's ability to return the product. Also, the SEC has explicitly stated that a significant increase in the amount of inventory in the distribution channel is a factor that precludes the ability of the seller to make a reliable estimate of returns, meaning the seller should not recognize the revenue.[11]

Disclosures Related to Revenue Recognition

9 Detail required disclosures related to revenue recognition.

Companies provide extensive revenue recognition disclosures for financial statements users to understand the nature, amount, timing, and uncertainty of revenue and cash flows arising from contracts with customers. Specifically, companies provide both qualitative and quantitative information in two main areas:

- Contracts with customers.
- Significant judgments made, and changes in judgments in applying, the revenue recognition standards.

We discuss each of the two areas next. Additionally, companies must disclose any assets recognized from the costs to obtain or fulfill a contract with a customer.

Contracts with Customers

Companies disclose revenue recognized from a contract with customers separately from other sources of revenue.

Disaggregation of Revenue. Companies provide a detailed disaggregation of their revenues into categories such as revenues by type of goods or services, geographical region, market type of customer, or contract duration. Companies are permitted to choose the approach for disaggregating revenues based on the information about revenue they have presented for other purposes, including earnings releases, annual reports, or investor presentations. Companies should also consider presenting information consistent with what managers regularly review to evaluate the performance of operating segments.

Contract Balances. Quantitative information includes the beginning and ending balances of receivables and unearned revenue from contracts with customers and significant changes in these accounts. Any revenue recognized in the period that was included in the beginning unearned revenue balance should be reported. Further, companies should disclose revenue recognized in the period from performance obligations satisfied (or previously satisfied) in previous periods, such as changes in transaction price. Companies must explain how the timing of satisfaction of their performance obligations relates to the typical timing of payment. In turn, companies should

[9] Sales in the next period may not be affected if channel stuffing can be repeated in the following year.

[10] https://www.wsj.com/articles/sec-investigating-smirnoff-maker-diageo-1437678975

[11] See Securities and Exchange Commission, SAB Topic 13.A.4.b.

discuss how the timing of satisfaction of their performance obligations affect the contract asset and contract liability balances.

Performance Obligations. Companies provide information about performance obligations in contracts with customers, including descriptions of:

- When the company typically satisfies its performance obligations (for example, upon shipment, upon delivery, or as services are rendered, including when performance obligations are satisfied in a bill-and-hold arrangement).
- The significant payment terms, when payment is due, whether there is variable consideration and if it is constrained, whether there is a significant financing component.
- The nature of goods or services that the entity has promised to transfer, highlighting any performance obligations to arrange for another party to transfer goods or services (an entity or acting as an agent).
- Obligations for return, refunds, or similar obligations.
- Types of warranties and related obligations.

Transaction Price Allocated to the Remaining Performance Obligations. Companies disclose the total amount of transaction prices related to any performance obligations that are unsatisfied (or partially satisfied) at the end of the period. Companies also explain when they expect to recognize the amount as revenue. As a practical matter, companies need not provide disclosure if the performance obligation is part of a contract that has an original expected duration of one year or less or there is a right to consideration based on the value of performance to date. Example 8.27 illustrates disclosure of the transaction price allocated to the remaining performance obligations.

EXAMPLE 8.27 Required Disclosures

PROBLEM: On September 1, 2018, Shiney Company enters into two contracts with separate customers to provide services. Each contract has a two-year non-cancellable term. Shiney considers the guidance in each contract to be included in the disclosure of the transaction price allocated to the remaining performance obligations at December 31, 2018.

Contract A. Cleaning services are to be provided over the next two years typically at least once per month. For services provided, the customer pays Shiney an hourly rate of $50.

Contract B. Cleaning services and lawn services are to be provided only as and when needed with a maximum of four visits per month over the next two years. The customer pays Shiney a fixed price of $500 per month for both services. Shiney measures its progress toward complete satisfaction of the performance obligation using the passage of time.

Determine the required disclosures related to the remaining performance obligations in Contract A and Contract B.

SOLUTION: Related to Contract A: Because Shiney bills a fixed amount for each hour of service, it has a right to invoice the customer in the amount corresponding directly with the value of its performance completed to date. Consequently, Shiney has no disclosure as a practical matter because it has the right to consideration based on the value of its performance to date.

Related to Contract B: Shiney discloses the amount of the transaction that has not yet been recognized as revenue in a table that illustrates when the company expects to recognize the revenue. The information for Contract B included in the overall disclosure is as follows:

	2019	2020	Total
Revenue expected to be recognized on this contract as of December 31, 2018	$6,000*	$4,000**	$10,000

*$6,000 = $500 × 12 months estimated
**$4,000 = $500 × 8 months estimated

MICHAEL HALL
PARTNER, KPMG »

Michael Hall

Michael Hall is a Partner in KPMG's National Office. Prior to that, he was a partner in KPMG's Accounting Advisory Practice. Mr. Hall also spent 11 years in KPMG's Audit Practice.

1 Why is revenue so important to financial statement preparers and investors?

Revenue is an important measure of a company's success and trends in performance over time. Investment analysts measure revenue based on different indicators for each industry they follow. Over time, there has been give-and-take in the analysts and financial statement preparers to arrive at a revenue recognition method understandable to the analysts.

2 The FASB and the IASB passed new standards for revenue recognition in May 2014. Why was it important to the Boards to significantly change the revenue recognition standards?

Prior to this project, there was no comprehensive revenue recognition standard adaptable across entities, industries, and capital markets. Prior U.S. GAAP was an amalgamation of revenue recognition standards adopted over time and as industries developed. Individual entities may have chosen accounting policies and approaches that differed from their industry peers. For example, applications of revenue recognition guidelines can vary among large aerospace companies because each can make different judgments on when revenue is recognizable.

Industries also formed their own accounting practices. The original principles of revenue recognition were written well before there was a software industry. Software companies had to promote industry-specific standards. Other industries that developed industry-specific standards over time include building and construction, real estate, telecommunications, and asset management. Thus, the FASB and IASB jointly issued new revenue standards that include a five-step model to remove inconsistencies across entities, industries, and capital markets, replacing almost all existing U.S. GAAP and IFRS guidance.

3 Under the new rules, companies recognize revenue when the seller has passed control of the goods or services to the buyer. What are the objectives of this standard?

The objectives of the standard include (1) removing inconsistencies and weaknesses in the existing requirements to improve comparability, (2) providing more useful information through disclosure requirements, (3) providing a more robust framework for addressing revenue issues, and (4) simplifying financial statements by providing one revenue framework. The new standard provides a logical set of steps to determine whether revenue should be recognized. The lens of control, under the new rules, is intended to be a precise means of evaluating whether revenue is realized (or realizable) or earned.

4 We have seen some notorious frauds related to revenue recognition over the years. Why is revenue a popular place to commit fraud?

Revenue is a common place for fraud because it is a significant measure of a company's success. Fraud relating to revenue recognition can come in two forms—intentional, improper revenue recognition methodology or intentional, improper recording of the transactions. Furthermore, management is often compensated based on the level of sales revenue, which can create an incentive for overstatement.

5 What are some areas in revenue recognition that involve judgment?

The intention of the five-step process is to allow companies to use the same framework when making judgments. The new standards don't eliminate all disparities, and we will still have differences in judgments and circumstances. Companies, even in the same industry, have different types of contracts and contract terms.

For example, assume that Company A sells widgets to Company B. Company A charges one price for both the widgets and shipping and handling. Company A generally provides replacements for widgets damaged during the shipping process. A question arises as to how many performance obligations Company A would have relating to this contract. Judgment would be applied because the potential performance obligations would be sales of widgets, delivery, and potential risk of loss coverage. Then Company A would need to determine whether such performance obligations are separate and distinct or could be bundled together for purposes of allocating the transaction price.

Discussion Questions

1. In his interview, Michael Hall indicates that revenue is a common place for fraud because it is a significant measure of a company's success. Briefly describe two U.S. or international accounting fraud cases related to improper revenue recognition.
2. Discuss areas of judgment that may be needed to apply the five steps of revenue recognition.

Significant Judgments in Revenue Recognition

Companies disclose the judgment and changes in judgments made in applying the revenue recognition guidance. Companies provide a description of the timing of satisfaction of performance obligations, including the methods used to recognize revenue and an explanation of why the methods provide a faithful depiction of the transfer of goods or service. Companies also disclose information about the transaction price and the amounts allocated to performance obligations based on:

- Determining the transaction price, including estimating variable consideration, adjustments for time value of money, and measuring noncash consideration.
- Assessing whether an estimate of variable consideration is constrained.
- Allocating the transaction price, including standalone selling prices and variable consideration.
- Measuring obligations for returns, refunds, or other similar obligations.

FINANCIAL STATEMENT ANALYSIS

Comparison of the Percentage-of-Completion and Completed-Contract Methods

In this section, we highlight the financial statement effects of the percentage-of-completion versus the completed-contract methods. The primary criticism of the completed-contract method is that it does not properly measure economic activity. This criticism is avoided under the percentage-of-completion method.

The total revenues and costs for a long-term contract are the same under the completed-contract and percentage-of-completion methods. However, the timing of revenue and gross profit recognition on the contract differs with the methods. The percentage-of-completion method recognizes gross profit over the production period whereas the completed-contract method recognizes gross profit only at the end of the contract. The following tables based on the Bronco Builders illustrations from Examples 8.22 and 8.23 compare the gross profit recognized and the net asset or net liability reported each year under the two revenue recognition methods.

	Gross Profit (Loss) Recognized	
Year	Percentage of Completion	Completed Contract
2018	$ 825,000	$ 0
2019	(2,815,000)	0
2020	2,290,000	300,000
Total	$ 300,000	$ 300,000

Total gross profit recognized, $300,000, is the same; only the timing of recognition differs. The percentage-of-completion method best measures economic activity as it reports gross profit as production takes place each year.

	Net Asset (Liability) Position	
Year	Percentage of Completion	Completed Contract
2018	$(1,675,000)	$(2,500,000)
2019	(490,000)	1,500,000
2020	0	0

The percentage-of-completion method also best measures the net asset (liability) position of the contractor. The difference in the valuation of the net asset (liability) is due to the recognition of gross profit only under the percentage-of-completion method. Failure to recognize gross profit under the completed-contract method overstates the net liability or understates the net asset. Therefore, financial statement ratios using amounts such as revenue, net income, total assets, liabilities, and equity differ in the two methods.

Financial Statement Analysis, continued

Because the percentage-of-completion method recognizes gross profit over the production process, revenues and net income will typically be higher in early years than under the completed-contract method. Therefore, the profit margin ratio will be higher under the percentage-of-completion method. Under the percentage-of-completion method, assets are generally higher (and liabilities are lower) because the asset construction-in-progress includes a portion of the estimated profits. Equity is also higher under the percentage-of-completion method because profit is recognized. Therefore, the debt-to-equity ratio will generally be lower under the percentage-of-completion method. Exhibit 8.8 summarizes these effects on common ratios.

EXHIBIT 8.8 Select Financial Statement Ratios: Percentage-of-Completion Method versus Completed-Contract Method

Measure	Expectation	Explanation
$\text{Profit Margin} = \dfrac{\text{Net Income}}{\text{Sales}}$	Generally higher under the percentage-of-completion method	Revenues (sales) and gross profit are generally reported earlier with percentage-of-completion. Higher gross profits increase net income. However, it may be lower if there is a loss on the contract.
$\text{Debt-to-Equity Ratio} = \dfrac{\text{Total Liabilities}}{\text{Total Shareholders' Equity}}$	Generally lower under percentage-of-completion method	Liabilities are lower; assets are generally higher because percentage-of-completion includes a portion of estimated profits in construction in progress. Shareholders' Equity is higher when profit is reported. However, the debt-to-equity ratio may be higher if there is a loss on the contract under percentage-of-completion.

Example 8.28 illustrates and compares these financial statement analysis ratios under the percentage-of-completion and completed-contract methods.

EXAMPLE 8.28 Financial Statement Ratios: Percentage-of-Completion and Completed-Contract Methods

PROBLEM: Use the following information related to Bronco Builders based on Examples 8.22 and 8.23 to answer the following questions.

Percentage-of-Completion Method

	For the Year		
Income Statement Information	2018	2019	2020
Revenue from long-term contracts	$2,325,000	$ 4,185,000	$2,790,000
Costs of construction	1,500,000	7,000,000	500,000
Gross profit (loss)	$ 825,000	$(2,815,000)	$2,290,000

	End of Year Balances			
Balance Sheet Information	2017	2018	2019	2020
Assets	$20,000,000	$22,500,000	$18,500,000	$20,300,000
Liabilities	10,000,000	11,675,000	10,490,000	10,000,000
Equity	10,000,000	10,825,000	8,010,000	10,300,000

(continued)

Financial Statement Analysis, continued

Completed-Contract Method

	For the Year		
Income Statement Information	2018	2019	2020
Revenue from long-term contracts	$1,500,000	$7,000,000	$800,000
Costs of construction	1,500,000	7,000,000	500,000
Gross profit	$ 0	$ 0	$300,000

	End of Year Balances			
Balance Sheet Information	2017	2018	2019	2020
Assets	$20,000,000	$22,500,000	$20,000,000	$20,300,000
Liabilities	10,000,000	12,500,000	10,000,000	10,000,000
Equity	10,000,000	10,000,000	10,000,000	10,300,000

a. Compute the profit margins under the percentage-of-completion and completed-contract methods each year. Comment on the differences.

b. Compute the debt-to-equity ratios under the percentage-of-completion and completed-contract methods each year. Comment on the differences.

SOLUTION:

a. The profit margins under the percentage-of-completion and completed-contract methods each year are computed as follows.

	2018	2019	2020
Percentage-of-Completion Method			
Profit Margin $= \frac{\text{Net Income}}{\text{Revenues}}$	$35.5\% = \frac{\$825{,}000}{\$2{,}325{,}000}$	$(67.3)\% = \frac{\$(2{,}815{,}000)}{\$\ 4{,}185{,}000}$	$82.1\% = \frac{\$2{,}290{,}000}{\$2{,}790{,}000}$
Completed-Contract Method			
Profit Margin $= \frac{\text{Net Income}}{\text{Revenues}}$	$0\% = \frac{\$0}{\$1{,}500{,}000}$	$0\% = \frac{\$0}{\$7{,}000{,}000}$	$37.5\% = \frac{\$300{,}000}{\$800{,}000}$

The profit margin under the completed-contract method is 0% in 2018 and 2019 as expected. Under the percentage-of-completion method, profit margin varies with estimated revenues and gross profit. Note also, under both methods, the profit margin on the contract overall is 3.2% (total net income of $300,000 divided by total revenues of $9,300,000).

b. The debt-to-equity ratios under the completed-contract and percentage-of-completion methods each year are computed below.

	2018	2019	2020
Percentage-of-Completion Method			
Debt-to-Equity Ratio $= \frac{\text{Total Liabilities}}{\text{Total Shareholders' Equity}}$	$1.08 = \frac{\$11{,}675{,}000}{\$10{,}825{,}000}$	$1.31 = \frac{\$10{,}490{,}000}{\$\ 8{,}010{,}000}$	$0.97 = \frac{\$10{,}000{,}000}{\$10{,}300{,}000}$
Completed-Contract Method			
Debt-to-Equity Ratio $= \frac{\text{Total Liabilities}}{\text{Total Shareholders' Equity}}$	$1.25 = \frac{\$12{,}500{,}000}{\$10{,}000{,}000}$	$1.0 = \frac{\$10{,}000{,}000}{\$10{,}000{,}000}$	$0.97 = \frac{\$10{,}000{,}000}{\$10{,}300{,}000}$

The debt-to-equity ratio is lower in 2018 under the percentage-of-completion method than the completed-contract method, as expected. In 2019, the debt-to-equity ratio is higher under the percentage-of-completion method because a loss is reported. In the last year of the contract, the debt-to-equity ratio is the same under both methods because the same amounts of net income are earned over the life of the contract.

Summary by Learning Objectives

In the following, we summarize the main points by learning objectives. Throughout the chapter, we discuss the accounting and reporting of U.S. GAAP and IFRS side-by-side. The table below also highlights the major similarities and differences between the standards.

1 Understand basic revenue recognition and measurement issues.

Summary	Similarities and Differences between U.S. GAAP and IFRS
A company should recognize revenue when it transfers control of an asset (either a good or service) to a customer. A company recognizes as revenue the amount it expects to be entitled to receive in exchange for the goods or services. The company recognizes revenue as it satisfies each performance obligation. The five steps in revenue recognition are: 1. Identify the contract(s) with a customer. 2. Identify the performance obligations in the contract. 3. Determine the transaction price. 4. Allocate the transaction price to the performance obligations. 5. Recognize revenue when, or as, each performance obligation is satisfied.	Similar under U.S. GAAP and IFRS.

2 Explain how to identify a contract with a customer.

Summary	Similarities and Differences between U.S. GAAP and IFRS
A contract is an agreement between two or more parties that creates enforceable rights and obligations. A contract must meet the following five criteria: 1. All parties agree to the contract and commit to performing. 2. Each party's rights are identifiable. 3. Payment terms are identifiable. 4. The contract has commercial substance. 5. Collection of consideration is probable. If the five criteria are not met, then the entity recognizes revenue when consideration is received and one of the following occurs: 1. The seller has no remaining obligations to transfer goods or services and substantially all (or all) of consideration has been received by the seller and is nonrefundable, or 2. The contract has been terminated and any consideration already received from the customer is nonrefundable, or 3. The seller has transferred control of the goods or services, is no longer transferring the goods or services, has no obligation to transfer additional goods or services, and the consideration received is nonrefundable. When there are multiple contracts, combine individual contracts into a single contract to determine the timing and measurement of revenue if one of the following criteria is met: 1. The contracts are negotiated as a package and have a single commercial objective. 2. The amount of consideration to be received by the seller related to one contract depends on the price or performance of another contract. 3. The goods or services promised in the separate contracts are part of one performance obligation.	➤ Similar under U.S. GAAP and IFRS except for the following. IFRS defines probable as "more likely than not" whereas U.S. GAAP defines probable as "likely to occur" in the fifth criterion. IFRS does not explicitly include the third condition to evaluate when to recognize revenue when the criteria for a contract are not met.

Summary by Learning Objectives, continued

❸ Identify the separate performance obligations in a contract, including determining whether there are distinct goods or services.

Summary	Similarities and Differences between U.S. GAAP and IFRS
A performance obligation is either: 1. a promise to transfer a good or service, or a bundle of goods or services, that is distinct, or 2. a promise to transfer a series of distinct goods or services that are substantially the same and have the same pattern of transfer to the customer. To be distinct, a good or service must: 1. benefit the customer on its own or in conjunction with other resources that are readily available to the customer, and 2. be separately identifiable from other promises in the contract.	Similar under U.S. GAAP and IFRS.

❹ Explain how to determine the transaction price in recognizing revenue.

Summary	Similarities and Differences between U.S. GAAP and IFRS
The transaction price is the amount of consideration the company expects to be entitled to as a result of providing goods or services to the customer. Consider the following when determining the transaction price: 1. Variable consideration and constraining estimates of variable consideration 2. Significant financing component in the contract 3. Noncash consideration 4. Consideration payable to a customer Variable consideration occurs when the payment received for providing a good or service is not a fixed amount. Estimate variable consideration using one of two acceptable approaches: 1. Expected-value approach uses the sum of the probability-weighted amounts in a range of possible consideration amounts. 2. Most-likely-amount approach uses the single most likely amount in a range of possible consideration amounts. To include variable consideration in the estimated transaction price (and thus revenue), the company has to conclude that it is probable that a significant revenue reversal will not occur in future periods. A significant financing component may occur either when • Delivery of the goods or services happens far in advance of payment. In this case, the seller is providing financing to the buyer. • Delivery occurs well after payment. In this case, the buyer is providing financing to the seller. When the time between payment and delivery is more than one year, separate the contract revenue from the financing component, if significant. When the contract includes noncash consideration, measure the transaction price at the fair value at contract inception of the noncash consideration. Consideration payable is deducted from the transaction price unless the payment to the customer is in exchange for a distinct good or service.	➤ Similar under U.S. GAAP and IFRS except in estimating the constraints on variable consideration. U.S. GAAP uses the term "probable," whereas IFRS uses the term "highly probable." The definitions of "probable" under U.S. GAAP and "highly probable" under IFRS are essentially the same.

Summary by Learning Objectives, continued

5 Demonstrate allocating the transaction price to performance obligations when recognizing revenue.

Summary	Similarities and Differences between U.S. GAAP and IFRS
Determine the standalone selling price of the goods or services that underlie each performance obligation to allocate the transaction price. If the sum of the standalone selling prices is greater than the transaction price, allocate this discount to the separate performance obligations on the basis of the relative standalone selling prices. To determine the standalone selling price of each performance obligation, determine the price the seller would charge for those goods or services if it sold the same goods or services on a standalone basis to similar customers under similar circumstances. When the seller does not sell the same goods or services separately, estimate the selling prices that maximize the use of observable inputs. Three suggested approaches are: 1. Adjusted market assessment approach: Evaluate the market and estimate the price that customers would pay. 2. Expected cost plus a margin approach: Forecast costs associated with providing the goods or services and add an appropriate profit margin. 3. Residual approach: Estimate one or more, but not all, of the standalone selling prices and allocate the remainder of the transaction price, or the residual amount, to the goods or services for which it does not have a standalone selling price estimate.	Similar under U.S. GAAP and IFRS.

6 Assess whether to recognize revenue when, or as, each performance obligation is satisfied.

Summary	Similarities and Differences between U.S. GAAP and IFRS
Recognize revenue when the goods or services are transferred to the customer. A good or service is transferred when the customer obtains control, the ability to direct the use of the asset, and gets all (or substantially all) of the remaining benefits of owning the asset. Goods and services can be transferred over time or at a point in time. Goods or services are transferred over time if any of the following three criteria are met: 1. The customer receives and consumes the benefits of the goods or services simultaneously. 2. The customer controls the asset as the seller creates it or enhances it over time. 3. The asset the seller is creating does not have an alternative use to the seller and the seller has an enforceable right to payment for the performance completed to date. If the transfer is over time, then recognize revenue over that same time period based on the progress that it has made toward completion. If the seller cannot reasonably measure the progress toward completion, then it should recognize revenue when progress is reasonably estimable. Measure progress toward completion using either an output method or input method. If the three criteria to recognize revenue are not met, then assume that the goods or services are transferred at a point in time.	Similar under U.S. GAAP and IFRS.

Summary by Learning Objectives, continued

7 Describe the accounting for long-term contracts, including implementing the percentage-of-completion method and the completed-contract method.

Summary	Similarities and Differences between U.S. GAAP and IFRS
Two common methods are percentage-of-completion and completed contract. Use the percentage-of-completion method when the company meets one of the three criteria for transfer of control and can reasonably measure its progress toward completion. If the contract does not meet any of the three criteria or if the entity cannot reasonably measure progress toward completion, then use the completed-contract method. **Use the percentage-of-completion method when the company is able to make reliable estimates of the degree of completion and the seller meets one of three criteria necessary for goods transferred over time. Use either an input measure (such as costs) or an output measure (such as miles of road paved) to determine the percentage-of-completion. Recognize both revenues and gross profit based on the project's stage of completion by:** 1. Computing cumulative revenue by multiplying the total estimated contract revenue times the percentage complete. Revenue for the period is cumulative revenue less revenue recognized in all prior periods. 2. Actual costs will be given for the period in question. 3. Computing gross profit for the year as the revenue recognized in the period in (1) above less the actual costs recognized in the period in (2) above. The steps to implement the percentage-of-completion method are: 1. Accumulate construction costs in an asset (inventory) account called construction in progress (CIP). 2. Periodically bill the customer. Debit accounts receivable and credit an account called billings on construction in progress. Billings on construction in progress is a contra account to the construction in progress account. The contra account reduces the net carrying value of the asset, CIP. 3. When cash is received from the customer, increase cash and decrease accounts receivable. 4. Each year, recognize the revenue and the associated gross profit. The amount of gross profit that is recognized in a given year is based on the progress to date. Credit revenue from long-term contracts, debit the cost of construction, and debit the CIP account for the difference between the revenue and the cost of the contract (the gross profit). 5. At the end of the project, remove the CIP account and the billings on construction in progress account from the books. The completed-contract approach involves the following accounting procedures: 1. Accumulate construction costs by debiting an asset (inventory) account called construction in progress (CIP). 2. When the contractor sends bills to the customer throughout the project, increase accounts receivable with a debit and increase with a credit the account billings on construction in progress. 3. When the contractor receives cash from the customer, increase cash with a debit and decrease accounts receivable with a credit. 4. Recognize the actual costs incurred and the same amount of revenue each year. Thus, the firm reports no gross profit. Record the total gross profit at the conclusion of the project. 5. At the end of the project, remove from the books the CIP account with a credit and the billings on construction in progress account with a debit. **The timing of revenue and gross profit recognition in Step 4 is the key difference between the completed-contract method and percentage-of-completion methods. The income statement reports revenue equal to costs (until the period in which the project is completed).**	Similar under U.S. GAAP and IFRS.

Summary by Learning Objectives, continued

8 Describe and demonstrate the accounting for special issues in revenue recognition, including right-to-return sales, consignment sales, principal-agent sales, bill-and-hold arrangements, and channel stuffing.

<table>
<tr><th>Summary</th><th>Similarities and Differences between U.S. GAAP and IFRS</th></tr>
<tr><td>
The right of return is a component of variable consideration and thus affects the transaction price. Recognize the amount of expected returns as a refund liability, which represents the seller's obligation to the customer to stand ready to receive the returned product and refund the customers consideration. Recognize revenue when no longer subject to the constraint, such as at the end of the returns period.
A consignment sale is an arrangement in which a seller (the consignor) delivers goods to a third party (the consignee), who attempts to sell the goods to the customer. The consignee does not record sales revenue when the good is sold. Rather, the consignee earns a sales commission fee. The consignor records sales revenue when the consignee sells the goods.
There are two approaches to record revenue for arrangements in which an agent is making a sale of a principal's product:
<ol>
<li>Gross revenue reporting approach: Agent records the total amount of the item sold as revenue and recognizes the cost of sales for the amount remitted to the principal.</li>
<li>Net revenue reporting approach: Only the net fee (the amount billed to the customer less the amount paid to the principal) is recorded.</li>
</ol>
If the company obtains control of the product before passing it to the consumer, it is the principal and should use the gross revenue reporting approach. If the company never obtains control, then it is the agent and should use the net revenue reporting approach.
In a bill-and-hold arrangement, a buyer accepts title and billing but delays the physical receipt of the goods. If the seller has transferred control of the goods to the buyer, then the seller can recognize revenue at the point of sale. To determine whether the seller has transferred control, it should consider the normal indicators of control. In addition, the seller must meet all of the following four criteria to claim that it has transferred control to the buyer:
<ul>
<li>The reason for the bill-and-hold must be substantive.</li>
<li>The product must be separately identified as belonging to the customer.</li>
<li>The product must be ready for physical transfer to the customer.</li>
<li>The entity cannot have the ability to use the product in any way, including delivering it to another customer.</li>
</ul>
Channel stuffing (also referred to as trade loading) is a practice in which a seller induces wholesale distributors to buy more inventory than they can sell in the current period. Firms should not recognize revenue from a channel stuffing arrangement because the risks and rewards of ownership have not really passed given the ability of the buyer to return the product.
</td><td>Similar under U.S. GAAP and IFRS.</td></tr>
</table>

Summary by Learning Objectives, continued

⑨ Detail required disclosures related to revenue recognition.	
Summary	**Similarities and Differences between U.S. GAAP and IFRS**
Related to contracts with customers, companies must disclose: • Disaggregation of revenue. • Contract balances and changes in balances. • Performance obligations. • Transaction price allocated to any remaining performance obligations. **Related to significant judgments and changes in judgments made, companies disclose methods for:** • Determining the transaction price including estimating variable consideration, adjustments for time value of money, measuring noncash consideration. • Assessing constraints on variable consideration. • Allocating the transaction price, including standalone selling prices and variable consideration. • Measuring obligations for returns, refunds, or other similar obligations.	Similar under U.S. GAAP and IFRS.

8 Recognition

Questions

❶ **Q8-1.** What are the primary issues involved in revenue recognition?

❶ **Q8-2.** What is the fundamental principle underlying the timing of revenue recognition?

❶ **Q8-3.** What is the fundamental principle underlying the measurement of revenue?

❶ **Q8-4.** What are the five basic steps in revenue recognition?

❷ **Q8-5.** What is commercial substance?

❸ **Q8-6.** How is a performance obligation defined?

❸ **Q8-7.** What are the two criteria to define a good or service as distinct?

❸ **Q8-8.** What factors may indicate that a promise to deliver a good or service is ***not*** separate from other promises?

❹❺❻ **Q8-9.** What principles regarding timing and measurement determine when, and for how much, firms recognize revenue?

❹ **Q8-10.** What is the transaction price in a contract? What factors determine the transaction price?

❹ **Q8-11.** What is variable consideration and what factors cause it?

❹ **Q8-12.** Describe and contrast the two approaches used to estimate the amount of variable consideration in a contract.

4 **Q8-13.** How does a constraint to variable consideration affect revenue recognition?

4 **Q8-14.** What factors should accountants consider to determine if there is a significant financing component in a contract?

4 **Q8-15.** How does the computation of the financing component differ when delivery is before and after the payment?

4 **Q8-16.** How does a seller account for any consideration paid to a customer?

5 **Q8-17.** What methods allocate the total transaction price to performance obligations?

5 **Q8-18.** What are the two exceptions to the general rule that an entity should allocate the transaction price based on the relative standalone selling prices?

6 **Q8-19.** What are the three criteria required to recognize revenue when goods and services are transferred over time?

6 **Q8-20.** When an entity does not meet the three criteria required to recognize revenue over time, it must determine when the goods and services are transferred to the customer. What are the indicators for determining transfer of control?

7 **Q8-21.** Can firms recognize revenue prior to completion of a long-term contract? Explain.

7 **Q8-22.** Are the percentage-of-completion and completed-contract methods both viable alternatives for a given contract? Explain.

7 **Q8-23.** How does a firm estimate the degree completed under the percentage-of-completion approach?

8 **Q8-24.** Can a firm record inventory out on consignment as revenue when transferred to the consignee? Explain.

8 **Q8-25.** What method do agents in a transaction use to record sales?

8 **Q8-26.** What selling practice do companies fraudulently use to accelerate revenue recognition?

9 **Q8-27.** What qualitative disclosures do the standards require for revenue recognition?

Multiple-Choice Questions

In partnership with: BECKER PROFESSIONAL EDUCATION®

Becker CPA Exam Review multiple-choice questions are available in MyLab Accounting.

2 **MC8-1.** All of the following are elements of a contract except:

a. The contract has commercial substance.
b. The vendor can identify payment terms for the goods or services.
c. It is not approved by both parties to the agreement.
d. The vendor can identify each party's rights.

3 **MC8-2.** A performance obligation is:

a. An enforceable promise in a contract with a customer to transfer a good or service to the customer.
b. An offer to transfer a good or service to the customer.
c. An expectation of a customer for the receipt of a good or service by a vendor.
d. A promise in a contract with a customer to transfer a good or service to the customer.

3 **MC8-3.** Telecom Co. enters into a two-year contract with a customer to provide wireless service (voice and data) for $40 per month. To induce customers, Telecom Co. provides a free phone. Telecom Co. normally sells the phone on a standalone basis for $200. Telecom Co. also charges the customer a one-time activation fee of $35. Which of the following is true?

a. The free phone constitutes a marketing expense.
b. The activation fee is a separate performance obligation.
c. There are two distinct performance obligations: the wireless service and the phone.
d. There are two distinct performance obligations: the voice service and the data service.

4 **MC8-4.** The transaction price must reflect the time value of money if:
a. The vendor expects the period between customer payment and delivery of goods or services will be less than two years.
b. The contract has a financing component that is significant to the contract.
c. The interest rate in the contract is higher than 13%.
d. Consideration would not differ if paid in cash or under normal credit terms.

4 **MC8-5.** Items that may cause variable consideration include:
a. Discounts.
b. An hourly rate for services.
c. A fixed fee.
d. A retainer.

5 **MC8-6.** When allocating the transaction price to separate performance obligations, one must determine the standalone selling price of the goods or services. Which of the following is not an estimation method for determining the standalone selling price?
a. Adjusted market assessment.
b. Expected cost plus a margin.
c. Residual approach.
d. Observable prices when goods or services are sold separately.

6 **MC8-7.** Which of the following indicators is not considered when determining whether performance obligations are satisfied at a point in time?
a. The vendor has a present right to payment for the asset.
b. The customer is likely to reject delivery of the asset.
c. The customer has the significant risks and rewards of ownership of the asset.
d. The customer has legal title to the asset.

7 **MC8-8.** During Year 1, Meriwether Construction Company started a construction job with a contract price of $3,000,000. The job was completed in Year 2, and the company uses the percentage of completion method. The following information is available for Year 1 and Year 2:

	Year 1	Year 2
Cost incurred to date	$ 500,000	$2,400,000
Estimated cost to complete	1,500,000	0
Billings to date	300,000	1,800,000
Collections to date	100,000	1,600,000

What amount of gross profit should Meriwether recognize for this job for Year 2?
a. $250,000 b. $1,000,000 c. $350,000 d. $600,000

8 **MC8-9.** All of the following are indicators that the vendor is acting as an agent instead of as a principal except:
a. The other party is primarily responsible for fulfilling the contract.
b. The vendor has latitude in establishing prices for the other party's goods or services.
c. The vendor does not have inventory risk.
d. The vendor's consideration is in the form of a commission.

8 **MC8-10.** Assume a retailer sells 10 widgets for $2,000 each. The widgets cost $100 and the sale includes a return right for 90 days. The retailer determines that the probability of returns associated with sales of the widgets is 10% based on prior customer behavior. The asset recognized at the point of sale for potential returns should be:
a. $100 b. $900 c. $1,000 d. $20,000

9 **MC8-11.** Disclosures for annual periods of public companies must include all but which of the following with respect to contracts with customers?
a. Identification of the top five largest customers.
b. Disaggregation of reported revenues.
c. Explanations of changes in balances.
d. Information about performance obligations.

Brief Exercises

2 **BE8-1. Identify a Contract with a Customer.** Complete the blanks in the five criteria to identify a contract with a customer.

1. All parties agree to the ________ and commit to ______.
2. Each party's rights with respect to the goods or service being transferred are _____________.
3. Payment terms for the goods or services that are being transferred are ______________.
4. The contract has ______________, meaning that the risk, timing, or amount of the entity's future cash flows is expected to change as a result of the contract.
5. It is _______ that the seller will _______ the consideration to which it is entitled in exchange for the goods or services.

2 **BE8-2. Identify a Contract with a Customer.** Discuss whether the following scenarios would preclude a contract from a customer under the revenue recognition standard.

a. Tarik Company is not certain that it can recognize revenue of sales made to a customer because it has no formal written agreement with the customer.
b. Pipes Plumbing provides services to Help-Out Hands, a not-for-profit organization. Pipes gives Help-Out an estimate for the services. After Pipes completes the services, it sends Help-Out an invoice including the statement "No payment required."

3 **BE8-3. Identifying Performance Obligations.** Perfect Party Company contracts with a customer to provide its birthday party package, including a cake, balloons, and musical entertainment. In addition, Perfect Party will host the event. Perfect Party offers the musical entertainment only when it also hosts the party. It often sells cakes and balloons separately that it delivers before a party. Identify the separate performance obligations in this contract.

3 **BE8-4. Identifying Performance Obligations.** Perfect Party Company contracts with a customer to provide its birthday party package, including a cake, balloons, and musical entertainment. In addition, Perfect Party will host the event. Perfect Party commonly offers the musical entertainment when it hosts the party. However, it will provide the musical entertainment without hosting the party. Perfect Party often sells cakes and balloons separately that it delivers before a party. Identify the separate performance obligations in this contract.

4 **BE8-5. Estimating Variable Consideration.** Gear Garage Inc. enters into a contract to provide services totaling $80,000. The contract includes a potential performance bonus based on when Gear Garage completes the services. Gear Garage estimates the following scenarios for completion. Determine the expected value of the bonus under each scenario. Ignore any constraints on variable consideration.

		Probability		
Complete within	**Bonus**	**Scenario 1**	**Scenario 2**	**Scenario 3**
3 days	$10,000	65%	50%	0%
5 days	$ 6,000	10%	40%	90%
8 days	$ 2,000	25%	10%	10%

4 **BE8-6. Estimating Variable Consideration.** Using the information provided in BE8-5, determine the bonus using the most-likely-amount approach. Ignore any constraints on variable consideration.

4 **BE8-7. Estimating Variable Consideration.** Sellet Billboard Company entered into an agreement to display billboard advertising for Highlife Incorporated for 10 months for a $60,000 fixed fee. The agreement also includes a potential $6,000 bonus based on certain goals. Sellet estimates that it is 70% likely to receive the entire bonus and 30% likely to receive none of the bonus. What approach should Sellet use to estimate variable consideration? What is the estimate of the consideration amount in this contract?

4 **BE8-8. Estimating Variable Consideration.** Sellet Billboard Company entered into an agreement to display billboard advertising for Wynne Incorporated for 10 months for a $60,000 fixed fee. The agreement also includes a potential bonus based on certain goals. Sellet believes the following probability estimates on receiving a bonus are accurate:

Bonus	**Probability**
$8,000	20%
$6,000	58%
$4,000	17%
$2,000	5%

What approach should Sellet use to estimate variable consideration? What is the estimate of the consideration amount in this contract?

4 **BE8-9. Significant Financing Component.** Determine the amount and type of financing component in the following contracts.

a. Payment of $1,500,000 occurs two years after delivery when the interest rate is 8%.
b. Payment of $1,500,000 occurs two years before delivery when the interest rate is 8%.
c. Delivery is three years after payment of $500,000 when the interest rate is 12%.
d. Delivery is three years before payment of $500,000 when the interest rate is 12%.

5 **BE8-10. Allocation of Transaction Price.** Martin Software Developers, Inc. recently signed a contract for $1,600,000 to create a registration, grade report, and transcript system for MacFarlane State University. Each part of the system will be delivered separately and must be fully functional upon installation. The standalone sales value of each performance obligation is reported below.

Description	Standalone Selling Prices
Registration System	$ 500,000
Grade Reporting System	800,000
Transcript System	700,000
Total	$2,000,000

How should Martin allocate the $1,600,000 transaction price across the performance obligations?

5 **BE8-11. Allocation of Transaction Price.** TGW Construction Company enters into a contract to build an office building and detached parking garage for $24 million. TGW determines that the building and parking garage represent separate performance obligations. The standalone price of similar structures would be $21 million for the office building and $7 million for the parking garage. How should TGW allocate the transaction price?

5 **BE8-12. Allocation of Transaction Price.** Sycamore Sidewalk Company enters into a contract with a customer to sell three products for a total transaction price of $15,000. Information related to these three products is provided in the following table.

Product	Standalone Selling Price
Bricks	$6,200
Stones	$8,000
Cement	$3,000

How should Sycamore Sidewalk Company allocate the transaction price to the three products?

5 **BE8-13. Allocation of Transaction Price.** Sycamore enters into a contract with a customer to sell three products for a total transaction price of $15,000. Each product is appropriately classified as a separate performance obligation. Sycamore only sells products A and B on an individual basis, so it must estimate the standalone selling price for cement. Information related to these three products is provided in the following table.

Product	Standalone Selling Price	Market Competitor Prices	Forecasted Cost
Bricks	$6,200	$7,800	$5,500
Stones	$8,000	$8,200	$5,000
Cement	Not available	$4,000	$2,000

How should Sycamore allocate the transaction price to the three products using the adjusted market assessment approach?

5 **BE8-14. Allocation of Transaction Price.** Using the information in BE8-13, indicate how Sycamore should allocate the transaction price to the three products using the expected-cost-plus-a-margin approach.

5 **BE8-15. Allocation of Transaction Price.** Using the information in BE8-13, indicate how Sycamore should allocate the transaction price to the three products using the residual approach.

6 **BE8-16. When to Recognize Revenue.** For each scenario, determine when to recognize revenue.

a. Top Notch Processing, Inc. enters into a contract to provide monthly accounting services to a customer for one year.
b. A customer purchased a motorcycle from Bright Star Cycles for $16,000. The customer takes delivery immediately.

c. A customer purchased a motorcycle from Revup Cycles for $18,000. Prior to delivery, Revup performs a custom paint job on the motorcycle that the customer required as a condition of purchase.
d. Seahawk, Inc. enters into a contract to deliver a customized accounting system to its client for $600,000. Seahawk estimates that it will take 1,000 labor hours to complete. Before completion, the customer cannot use the system.
e. Seahawk, Inc. enters into a contract to deliver an accounting system to its client for $600,000. Seahawk estimates that it will take 1,800 labor hours to complete. The customer has control of the system as it is being created.

7 **BE8-17. Percentage-of-Completion Method.** Vermont Cabin Construction Company uses the percentage-of-completion method on a three-year project with the cost-to-cost method of measuring progress. Compute the percent completed and the amount of revenue and gross profit to be recognized for each year based on the following information.

Contract price	$700,000		
	2018	**2019**	**2020**
Actual construction costs incurred during the year	$140,000	$130,000	$160,000
Estimated total costs	$400,000	$360,000	$430,000

7 **BE8-18. Percentage-of-Completion Method, Current Year.** Cosmo Computer Consultants (CCC) signed a contract in 2018 to develop a computer network system for Platinum Entertainment. Cosmo uses the percentage-of-completion method and determines its measure of progress using the cost-to-cost approach. The firm provided the following information for 2018.

Contract price	$85,000
	2018
Actual construction costs incurred during the year	$12,000
Estimated total costs	60,000
Progress billings made during the year	30,500
Cash collections during the year	25,000

Compute the percentage completed, gross profit recognized, and the amount of the revenue recorded in 2018.

7 **BE8-19. Percentage-of-Completion Method, Journal Entries.** Prepare all journal entries necessary to reflect the use of the percentage-of-completion method in 2018 for CCC in BE8-18.

7 **BE8-20. Completed-Contract Method, Journal Entries.** Spot-On Contractors, Inc. provided the following information for the current year's construction activity.

Contract price	$170,000
	2018
Actual construction costs incurred during the year	$ 24,000
Estimated costs to complete	96,000
Estimated total costs	120,000
Progress billings made during the year	61,000
Cash collections during the year	50,000

Prepare the journal entries required to record Spot-On's construction activity assuming that the company uses the completed-contract method.

8 **BE8-21. Sales with the Right of Return.** Botti Incorporated manufactures and sells professional ski equipment. Botti offers a money-back guarantee for one year after the date of purchase. Cash sales for the current year amounted to $620,000. Botti estimates that 5% of all sales are returned within the one-year period. Cost of goods sold is 75% of sales. The company uses a perpetual inventory system. Record sales and estimated sales returns for the current year.

8 **BE8-22. Sales with the Right of Return.** Using the information provided in BE8-21, prepare the journal entry to record $5,000 of actual sales returns within one year after revenue was recognized by Botti.

8 **BE8-23. Sales Returns.** Historically, about 5% of the merchandise that Thompson Tools, Inc. sells is returned. In the month of March, Thompson Tools sold merchandise costing $546,000 to customers for $712,000. The company uses a perpetual inventory system and all sales are on account. What is the estimated amount of sales returns? What is the journal entry to record this sale and estimated return?

8 **BE8-24. Sales on Consignment.** Hanna Lighting recently transferred $60,000 of electrical supplies to Goshen Supermarkets on consignment. The retail price of the supplies is $81,000. Hanna offers its consignees a 25% fee on the retail price of the inventory sold. Hanna shipped the supplies to Goshen on April 1 and Goshen sold the inventory on June 30. Prepare the journal entries required for Hanna Lighting to record the consignment transaction.

Exercises

3 **E8-1. Determining Performance Obligations.** Pagit Inc, a software development company, enters into a contract with Plato Company to provide computer and hosting services. Pagit will provide a hosted accounting software system that requires Plato to purchase hardware from Pagit. Plato also purchases other computing services from Pagit to migrate historical data and create interfaces with its other existing management systems. Pagit delivers the hardware first followed by other computing services, and finally the online hosting services.

Required »

a. Determine the performance obligations if Pagit commonly sells goods and services separately or as a package.
b. Determine the performance obligations if Pagit never sells the hardware separately but always bundles it with hosting services. It does commonly sell the other goods and services separately.

3 4 **E8-2. Determining Performance Obligations, Estimating Transaction Price.** Shownow Film Company grants a customer the rights to broadcast three films under a single licensing agreement. The arrangement includes a fixed fee of $90,000. The arrangement provides for an even reduction in the film license fee if the third film is not completed and made available for delivery. Shownow determines that it is 80% likely that it will deliver the third film on time.

Required »

a. What are the performance obligations under the licensing agreement?
b. What is the transaction price? (Consider any variable consideration.)

4 **E8-3. Estimating Variable Consideration.** King Rat Pest Control, Incorporated was recently hired to exterminate pests in an office complex for $300,000. King Rat will receive an additional $10,000 based on the success of the extermination. The additional $10,000 will be paid in full if the extermination is fully successful after one month. That amount will be decreased to $8,000 if the extermination is successful after two months and further reduced to $5,000 if successful after three months. Based on past experience with similar contracts, King Rat estimates that there is a 20% probability that the process will be successful with the first month, a 75% probability that it will take two months to be successful, and a 5% probability that the process will be effective after three months.

Required »

a. Determine the transaction price for this contract using the expected value approach.
b. Determine the transaction price for this contract using the most-likely-amount approach

4 **E8-4. Constraining Estimates of Variable Consideration.** Skivoso Incorporated owns and operates high-priced ski resorts in Europe. Skivoso recently entered into a contract to provide lodging for several corporate events and conferences sponsored by JeffCo for a total fee of $10,000,000.

JeffCo agreed to additional fees based on conference participant satisfaction surveys. The fee schedule and the related satisfaction survey scores follow.

Additional Fee	Average Score on Participant Satisfaction Survey
$ 50,000	75%–79%
$ 300,000	80%–84%
$ 700,000	85%–89%
$ 950,000	90%–100%

Using past survey experience, Skivoso estimates the probabilities that it will receive these scores on the JeffCo participant surveys:

Average Score on Participant Satisfaction Survey	Probability Assessment
75%–79%	9%
80%–84%	18%
85%–89%	21%
90%–100%	52%

Required »

Using the most-likely-amount approach for measuring variable consideration, determine the transaction price for this contract.

4 **E8-5. Significant Financing Component, Delivery before Payment.** Shifty Beaver Transmission Company enters into a contract with a major U.S. auto manufacturer to design and produce four-speed transmissions for small SUVs. Under the terms of the contract, Shifty Beaver will deliver the transmission immediately, but the auto manufacturers will defer payment for four years, the end of the life of the base warranty. The contract price is $3,500,000, and the interest rate incurred on similar financing agreements in the industry is 5%.

Required »

a. Is there a significant financing component in this contract?
b. If there is a significant financing component, determine the amount of sales revenue and interest revenue to be recognized by Shifty Beaver.

4 **E8-6. Significant Financing Component: Delivery after Payment.** Smart Cookie Learning Centers enters into a contract to customize and sell its LaLa tutoring software to the Westbro United School District. The contract price is $6,000,000 and must be paid to Smart Cookie immediately. Under the terms of the contract, Smart Cookie must deliver the software at the end of a two-year period. The interest rate incurred on similar financing agreements in the industry is 8%.

Required »

a. Is there a significant financing component in this contract?
b. If there is a significant financing component, determine the amount of sales revenue and interest expense to be recognized by Smart Cookie.

5 **E8-7. Allocation of Variable Consideration.** Green-Up Inc. contracts with a building manager to provide goods and services to enhance energy efficiency. It offers consulting services, including recommending ways to increase energy efficiency and monitor performance. It also provides items such as thermostats and automatic light switches as part of the contract. Green-Up charges 60% of the reduction in energy usage during the first year as a consulting fee. Green-Up determines that the consulting services compose one performance obligation and the items provided are another performance obligation. The estimated standalone selling prices are $180,000 for the consulting services and $100,000 for the items to increase energy efficiency. The stated price in the contract for the items provided is a fixed payment of $100,000. The price stated for the consulting fees is 60% of the customer's reduction in future energy costs. Green-Up estimates the variable consideration for the consulting services to be $180,000. What amount of the transaction price should Green-Up allocate to each performance obligation?

5 **E8-8. Allocation of Variable Consideration.** Green-Up Inc. contracts with a building manager to provide goods and services to enhance the energy efficiency. It offers consulting services, including recommending ways to increase energy efficiency and monitor performance. It also provides items such as thermostats and automatic light switches as part of the contract. Green-Up charges 60% of the reduction in energy usage during the first year as a consulting fee. Green-Up determines that the consulting services compose one performance obligation and the items provided are another performance obligation. The estimated standalone selling prices are $180,000 for the consulting services and $100,000 for the items to increase energy efficiency. The stated price in the contract for the items provided is a fixed payment of $60,000. The price stated for the consulting fees is 60% of the customer's reduction in future energy costs. Green-Up estimates that the customer will reduce its energy usage by $500,000. The customer's actual energy reduction is $550,000. What amount of the transaction price should Green-Up allocate to each performance obligation?

5 **E8-9. Allocation of Variable Consideration, Allocation of Discount.** Perfect Party Company contracts with a customer to provide its birthday party package including a cake, balloons, and musical entertainment. It regularly sells the following products separately at the following standalone selling prices.

Item	Standalone Selling Price
Balloons	$ 70
Cake	40
Musical Entertainment	120
Hosting	100

Perfect Party also regularly bundles musical entertainment and hosting together for $160. Perfect Party signs a contract with a customer to provide balloons, a cake, musical entertainment and to host a party for $270. Perfect Party determines that each product is a separate performance obligation. How should Perfect Party allocate the transaction price to each product?

5 **E8-10. Allocation of Transaction Price.** Gundy Communications Systems signed a contract to develop and install an integrated network for Dwight Auto Dealerships, Inc. in five phases. Each phase is considered a performance obligation. The transaction price, including installation, is $2,600,000. Each phase is fully functional at the point of delivery. Each of the five phases of the total network products has standalone value as follows:

Network Phase	Standalone Sales Value
Phase 1	$ 300,000
Phase 2	760,000
Phase 3	560,000
Phase 4	440,000
Phase 5	940,000
Total	$3,000,000

The contract price is collected in advance, and Phases 1 and 2 are completed during the current year. Gundy expects Phase 3 and 4 to be completed in the next 12 months and Phase 5 in the following year. Ignore implications of any financing component.

Required »

a. Prepare the journal entry to record any revenue to be recognized during the current period. Show all supporting computations.
b. Prepare disclosures related to any remaining performance obligations at the end of the current year.

6 **E8-11. Determination of When to Recognize Revenue.** Far Horizons, Inc. sells mobile phones, wireless plans, and service plan packages. Far Horizons packages the following items for sale.

Package	Amount	Description
Phone	$199.00	Paid when customer purchases the phone.
Wireless Plan per month	40.00	Unlimited calling. Minimum coverage of 12-months. Paid monthly.
Service Plan per month	24.00	12-month coverage. Paid when customer purchases the phone.
Total When Purchased	$263.00	

Far Horizons has determined that each item is a separate performance obligation. A customer purchases a new phone package on September 1. Explain how and when revenue is recognized. Prepare the journal entries for the month of September, assuming that Far Horizons makes adjusting entries on September 30.

7 **E8-12. Percentage-of-Completion Method.** Shemsoft Software Technicians recently accepted a contract to develop an inventory management system for Chez and Company. Shemsoft is required to complete the installation of the new inventory management system in two years. Shemsoft provided the following contract information.

Contract price	$1,500,000	
	2018	**2019**
Actual construction costs incurred during the year	$ 255,000	$ 800,000
Construction costs incurred in prior years	0	255,000
Cumulative construction costs incurred to date	255,000	1,055,000
Estimated costs to complete	382,500	0
Estimated total costs	637,500	1,055,000
Progress billings made during the year	900,000	600,000
Cash collections during the year	750,000	750,000

Prepare the journal entries required for each year of the contract, assuming that Shemsoft uses the percentage-of-completion method and the cost-to-cost approach for measuring progress.

7 **E8-13. Percentage-of-Completion Method.** Gary Construction Associates accepted a contract to build an office building on January 2, 2018. The company will complete the contract within two years. Gary provided the following information related to the revenue, estimated costs, progress billings, and collections over the two-year period.

Contract price	$4,000,000	
	2018	**2019**
Actual construction costs incurred during the year	$2,625,000	$ 900,000
Construction costs incurred in prior years	0	2,625,000
Cumulative construction costs incurred to date	2,625,000	3,525,000
Estimated costs to complete	875,000	0
Estimated total costs	3,500,000	3,525,000
Progress billings made during the year	2,400,000	1,600,000
Cash collections during the year	2,000,000	2,000,000

Prepare the journal entries for each year to record the contract, assuming that Gary uses the percentage-of-completion method with the cost-to-cost approach to measure progress. Show all supporting computations.

7 **E8-14. Completed-Contract Method, Journal Entries.** Using the information provided in E8-13, prepare the journal entries for each year to record the contract, assuming that Gary uses the completed-contract method (show all supporting computations).

7 **E8-15. Percentage-of-Completion Method.** Bailey Builders Corporation accepted a three-year, $1,000,000 fixed-fee contract to renovate a parking deck. Bailey uses the percentage-of-completion method and the cost-to-cost method of measuring progress. Information related to the construction contract follows.

Contract price	$1,000,000		
	2018	**2019**	**2020**
Actual construction costs incurred during the year	$350,000	$ 525,000	$ 50,000
Construction costs incurred in prior years	0	350,000	875,000
Cumulative construction costs incurred to date	350,000	875,000	925,000
Estimated costs to complete	450,000	25,000	0
Estimated total costs	800,000	900,000	925,000
Progress billings made during the year	500,000	300,000	200,000
Cash collections during the year	400,000	350,000	250,000

Prepare the journal entries required in each year to record the contract. Show all supporting computations.

7 **E8-16. Completed-Contract Method.** Using the information provided in E8-15, assume that Bailey uses the completed-contract method. Prepare the journal entries required in each year to record the contract (show all supporting computations).

8 **E8-17. Sales with the Right of Return.** Webster Hall, Inc. is a major publisher of college textbooks. Webster Hall allows college bookstores to return all purchases within two months of delivery. The company shipped $700,000 in textbooks in December 2019 based on orders for the spring 2020 semester. Webster Hall estimates that 35% of the books will be returned. All shipments were on account and unpaid at the time of returns.

Required »

a. Prepare the journal entry to record sales and estimated returns for 2019. Ignore cost of goods sold and inventory.

b. Assume that Webster Hall reports $189,000 in total sales returns in February 2020. Prepare the journal entry required to record the total sales returns.

8 **E8-18. Sales Returns.** Historically, about 8% of all the merchandise Asiago, Inc. sells is returned. On January 4, Asiago sold merchandise costing $40,000 to a customer for $62,000 on account. On January 17, Asiago refunded $3,200 for the return of some of the merchandise. On January 28, Asiago sold merchandise costing $12,000 for $15,000 on account. Assume the company uses a perpetual inventory system and all accounts are unpaid at the time of returns. Prepare the journal entries to record the sales, estimated returns, and the actual return.

8 **E8-19. Sales on Consignment.** Ray's Sporting Goods, Inc. shipped aluminum baseball bats on consignment to Martin Stores on April 6, 2019. The total cost of the bats is $31,000 with a retail value of $50,000. Martin agrees to accept the consigned merchandise and is eligible to receive a 15% commission on all sales. Martin sells the entire shipment to Anoi College and received cash on May 28, 2019, and notifies Ray's Sporting Goods immediately.

Prepare the journal entries to record the consignment sale transactions on both Ray's and Martin's books.

8 **E8-20. Other Principal Agent Transactions, Net Revenue Reporting Method.** ATickets.com sells discount airline tickets online. The company orders the tickets after a customer makes a purchase request. Atickets.com earns a flat fee of 25% of the total ticket price. The company sold $1,000,000 in airline tickets during the current year and had collected $800,500 as of the end of the year. ATickets.com is an agent in this transaction and thus uses the net revenue reporting method of accounting for sales.

Required »

a. Record the sales transactions for the current year.
b. Record the cash collections for the current year.
c. Record the amount remitted to the airlines.

Problems

2 3 4 5 6 **P8-1. Comprehensive Revenue Recognition Problem.** Moran Consulting currently provides tax services to Weiss Inc. Weiss engages Moran to advise it on the sale of one of its subsidiaries. Moran Consulting receives a non-refundable, up-front retainer fee of $100,000. Moran is also entitled to a success fee of 1.5% of the proceeds received when the subsidiary is sold.

Required »

a. Should Moran combine the tax services contract with the advisory contract?
b. Identify the performance obligations in the advisory contract.
c. Determine the transaction price at the inception of the advisory contract.
d. Determine the allocation of the transaction price to the performance obligation.
e. Determine when to recognize revenue.

2 3 4 5 6 **P8-2. Comprehensive Revenue Recognition Problem.** On September 1, 2019, Conboy Construction signed a contract with Venuti Enterprises to construct a new corporate headquarters and parking garage on land that Venuti owns. Conboy determines that control of the building is passed to Venuti as it is constructed, but control of the parking garage will transfer when the garage is completed. Venuti will use the garage for its employees and open it for public parking.

The contract price is $40 million for both the building and the garage, but Venuti includes a price adjustment for early or late completion of the building. For each day before September 1, 2021, that the building is completed, the promised consideration will increase by $30,000. For each day after September 1, 2021, that the building is incomplete, the promised consideration will be reduced by $30,000. Conboy considers it 60% likely that it will complete the building seven days early, 15% likely that it will complete the project on time, and 25% likely that the project will be delayed five days. The building is constructed based on Venuti's specifications and would require extensive alterations if used by another entity. The transaction has commercial substance, and Venuti is in good financial health.

The parties have also agreed that the building will be inspected and assigned a green building certification level. If the building achieves the certification level specified in the contract, Conboy will be entitled to a bonus of $300,000. Conboy has been highly successful in achieving the certification on prior building projects.

The terms of the contract stipulate that Venuti will make a $40,000,000 payment to Conboy at the completion of the project. Conboy will have two years or 24 months (until September 1, 2021) to complete the project. Furthermore, Conboy has an enforceable right to demand payment related to performance to date based on time elapsed.

Conboy has constructed similar buildings and sold them for $30 million but does not have experience in garage construction. Conboy is aware of similar garages constructed by its competitors that were sold for $8 million.

Due to good weather, Conboy is able to complete the building early. Conboy completes the building and garage on August 21, 2021. Venuti receives control and legal title on these dates. The building also receives the required green building certification on August 21, 2021. Venuti pays Conboy any amounts owned on September 1, 2021.

Conboy has a normal profit margin of 15% and an interest rate of 10%. It allocates interest revenue on a straight-line basis. It is a calendar-year company that prepares financial statements annually. It uses time elapsed as its measure of progress for performance obligations that are satisfied over time.

Required»

Perform the five steps in the revenue recognition process. Provide all necessary journal entries.

❷❸❹❺❻ **P8-3. Comprehensive Revenue Recognition Problem.** Casale Products Corporation manufactures and resurfaces bowling pins for commercial and residential use. On January 2 of the current year, Casale signs a contract with Closmeyer Lanes to be the exclusive supplier of pins for its lanes located throughout the United States. Casale initially agreed to deliver 300,000 pins at a price of $15 each (i.e., total revenue $4,500,000). Casale's cost of sales is $10 per pin. Delivery of the pins is scheduled for December 31.

Under the terms of the agreement, Casale will also provide pin refurbishing services (free of charge) that includes recoating the pins as requested by Closmeyer. Pin refurbishment contracts are provided by Casale to other customers for an annual fee of $300,000.

Casale offers volume discounts to its customers. For purposes of this contract, volume discounts will be granted to Closmeyer if total sales to the lanes exceed specified amounts. The discount is related to the total sales and services provided. The volume discount schedule for this contract, which includes the expected probability for each sales level, follows.

Sales Level	Volume Discount Offered	Probability of Reaching the Specified Sales Level
$ 4,500,000	0%	10%
7,000,000	5%	60%
10,000,000	8%	30%

The sales volume discount offer is retroactive in that if a sales level is reached, the refund for the discount is applied to previous sales.

Required»

Perform the five steps in the revenue recognition process, assuming that Casale uses the expected value approach to determine the transaction price and the residual approach to allocate that transaction price. Provide all necessary journal entries to record revenue for the current year.

❺ **P8-4. Allocation of Transaction Price.** On April 7, 2020, McCool Systems signed a contract to develop and install a virtual private network (VPN) for Billy Majors Stores. The transaction price, including installation, is $580,000. The VPN consists of four components: regional offices, corporate office, retail stores, and remote users (for example, buyers). Each component is fully functional at the point of delivery. Each of the four components of the total network is correctly classified as a performance obligation, and each has standalone fair values as follows:

VPN Component	Standalone Sales Value
Regional offices	$130,000
Corporate office	270,000
Retail stores	150,000
Remote users	50,000
Total	$600,000

McCool collects the contract price in advance. McCool completed the regional office and remote user components on December 31, 2020.

Prepare the journal entry to record the contract and to record any revenue to be recognized during the current period. Show all supporting computations.

6 **P8-5. Determining When to Recognize Revenue.** Megrew Building Company is developing a multi-unit residential building complex. Kit Collier enters into a binding sales contract with Megrew for a specified unit that is under construction. Each unit is of a similar size and has a similar floor plan, but other characteristics of the units, such as the location of the unit within the complex, are different.

Scenario 1. Collier pays a deposit of $10,000 that is refundable only if Megrew fails to complete construction of the unit in accordance with the contract. The remainder of the contract price of $240,000 is payable on completion of the contract when Collier obtains physical possession of the unit. If Collier defaults on the contract before completion of the unit, Megrew has only the right to retain the deposit.

Scenario 2. Collier pays a $10,000 nonrefundable deposit upon entering into the contract and will make four progress payments during construction of the unit. The contract includes the following other terms:

- Megrew is precluded from being able to transfer the unit to another customer.
- Collier does not have the right to terminate the contract unless Megrew fails to perform as promised.
- If Collier defaults on its obligations by failing to make the promised progress payments, Megrew would have a right to all of the consideration promised in the contract if it completes the construction of the unit. (The courts have previously upheld similar rights that entitle developers to require the customer to perform subject to the entity meeting its obligations under the contract.)

Scenario 3. Use the same facts as in Scenario 2 except that in the event of Collier's default, Megrew can either require Collier to perform as required under the contract or Megrew can cancel the contract, keep the unit under construction, and impose a penalty on Collier.

Required »

For each scenario, determine whether the performance obligation is satisfied over time or at a point in time.

7 **P8-6. Percentage-of-Completion Method.** Nance Network Consultants, Incorporated uses the percentage-of-completion method to account for its long-term contracts. It uses the cost-to-cost approach to measure progress. During the current year, Nance signed a contract to develop a computer network for an international accounting firm. Information related to the contract follows.

Contract price	$800,000		
	2018	**2019**	**2020**
Actual construction costs incurred during the year	$ 200,000	$300,000	$150,000
Construction costs incurred in prior years	0	200,000	500,000
Cumulative construction costs incurred to date	200,000	500,000	650,000
Estimated costs to complete	400,000	300,000	0
Estimated total costs	600,000	800,000	650,000
Progress billings made during the year	300,000	400,000	100,000
Cash collections during the year	220,000	380,000	200,000

Required »

a. Compute the percentage-of-completion for each year.
b. Compute the gross profit and revenue to be recognized each year of the contract.
c. Prepare the journal entries required for each year of the contract.
d. Prepare the t-accounts for construction in progress, billings on construction in progress, and accounts receivable.
e. Determine the net asset (liability) for each year of the contract on December 31.

7 **P8-7. Percentage-of-Completion Method.** Bigelow Contractors signed a contract to construct a storage facility for RGN Manufacturing, Inc. The fixed-fee contract specifies that the facility is to be completed in three years. Bigelow uses the percentage-of-completion method (cost-to-cost approach) to account for its construction transactions. Information related to this contract is summarized in the following table.

Contract price	$2,000,000		
	2018	**2019**	**2020**
Actual construction costs incurred during the year	$ 900,000	$ 300,000	$ 600,000
Construction costs incurred in prior years	0	900,000	1,200,000
Cumulative construction costs incurred to date	900,000	1,200,000	1,800,000
Estimated costs to complete	600,000	400,000	0
Estimated total costs	1,500,000	1,600,000	1,800,000
Progress billings made during the year	700,000	700,000	600,000
Cash collections during the year	400,000	800,000	800,000

Required »

a. Compute the percentage completed for each year.
b. Compute the gross profit and revenue to be recognized each year of the contract.
c. Prepare the journal entries required for each year of the contract.
d. Prepare the t-accounts for construction in progress, billings on construction in progress, and accounts receivable.
e. Determine the net asset (liability) for each year of the contract on December 31.

7 **P8-8. Completed-Contract Method.** Repeat the requirements of P8-7 assuming Bigelow Contractors uses the completed-contract method to report its long-term contracts. Additionally, compare the reported gross profit and net asset (liability) position reported under the percentage-of-completion method (from P8-7) and the completed-contract method.

7 **P8-9. Percentage-of-Completion Method.** R. Wayne Computer Consultants, Incorporated develops and installs integrated computer systems and networks for large utilities. On January 2, 2018, the company signed a contract to deliver an electricity deployment system for a grid covering three New England states. The contract paid R. Wayne a fixed fee of $18,000,000. Wayne Computer Consultants uses the percentage-of-completion method (cost-to-cost approach) to report its long-term contracts. Other relevant information related to the contract is presented in the following table.

Contract price	$18,000,000		
	2018	**2019**	**2020**
Actual construction costs incurred during the year	$ 4,500,000	$ 6,000,000	$ 5,000,000
Construction costs incurred in prior years	0	$ 4,500,000	$10,500,000
Estimated costs to complete	$10,500,000	$ 2,625,000	0
Estimated total costs	$15,000,000	$13,125,000	$15,500,000
Progress billings made during the year	$ 6,600,000	$ 8,400,000	$ 3,000,000
Cash collections during the year	$ 6,000,000	$ 6,000,000	$ 6,000,000

Required »

a. Compute the gross profit and revenue to be recognized each year of the contract.
b. Prepare the journal entries required for each year of the contract.
c. Prepare the t-accounts for construction in progress, billings on construction in progress, and accounts receivable.
d. Determine the net asset (liability) for each year of the contract on December 31.

7 **P8-10. Completed-Contract Method.** Repeat the requirements of P8-9 assuming Wayne Computer Consultants uses the completed-contract method to report its long-term contracts.

7 **P8-11. Completed-Contract Method.** Bernard Brothers Building (BBB) signed a contract for a fixed fee of $60,000 and used the completed-contract method to account for the contract. BBB provided the following information related to the contract.

Contract price	$60,000		
	2018	**2019**	**2020**
Actual construction costs incurred during the year	$15,000	$20,000	$20,000
Construction costs incurred in prior years	0	15,000	35,000
Cumulative construction costs incurred to date	15,000	35,000	55,000
Estimated costs to complete	5,000	15,000	0
Estimated total costs	20,000	50,000	55,000
Progress billings made during the year	25,000	23,000	12,000
Cash collections during the year	20,000	20,000	20,000

Required »

a. Prepare the journal entries required for each year of the contract.
b. Prepare the t-accounts for construction in progress, billings on construction in progress, and accounts receivable.
c. Determine the net asset (liability) for each year of the contract on December 31.

8 **P8-12. Sales on Consignment.** Pablo Products, Ltd. sells stuffed animals to local convenience stores and small pharmacy chains. All of Pablo's sales are on consignment. The consignee receives a 15% commission for each product sold.

Pablo completed the following consignment-related transactions:

Date	Transaction	Amount
February 2, 2020	Ships merchandise on consignment to Left Aid Pharmacy.	Cost = $400,000 Retail Value = $1,000,000
May 15, 2020	Left Aid Pharmacy sells 75% of the consigned inventory for cash.	$ 750,000
June 1, 2020	Left Aid notifies Pablo about the sale and remits the cash collected to Pablo, net of the 15% commission.	$ 750,000
January 3, 2021	Left Aid sells the remainder of the consigned merchandise for cash.	$ 250,000
January 5, 2021	Left Aid notifies Pablo and remits the cash collected net of the 15% commission.	$ 250,000

Record all journal entries for consignment-related transactions for both the consignor and consignee.

Excel Project

Autograded Excel Project available in **MyLab Accounting**

CASES

Judgment Cases

Judgment Case 1: Judgment in Revenue Recognition

Absco, Inc. is a calendar-year-end clothing manufacturer that sells exclusively to retailers. It engages in a large number of contracts with its customers. Following are some specific contract issues that have arisen this year.

1. Absco signed a contract with Socks Are Us to ship 100,000 pairs of socks on December 27. The contract price is $5 per pair with nonrefundable payment due upon receipt of the socks. Absco immediately delivers the socks to Socks Are Us once the contract is signed by both parties with the socks arriving on December 28. However, Socks Are Us has not remitted payment as of December 31. It is clear to Absco that it will have to offer the customer a price concession in order to receive any payment at all. Absco has not had extensive dealings with Socks Are Us but estimates that it will need to offer a 25% discount. Should Absco recognize any revenue related to this arrangement in the current year? If so, how much?
2. Absco signed a contract with Jeans Are Us to ship 300,000 pair of jeans. The contract price is $20 per pair. These particular jeans are very fashionable at the current time but are not expected to stay in style for a long period of time. Because they are new, Absco has manufactured only 10,000 pairs. The contract specifies that Absco will immediately ship the 10,000 pairs and will then ship the remaining portions of the 290,000 pairs as soon as possible after a specific number of pairs are requested by Jeans Are Us. If Absco has shipped fewer than 300,000 pairs of jeans by the end of the year, it will ship the remaining jeans to fulfill the contract at the end of one year. Because Jeans Are Us is concerned that the demand for these jeans will be heavy, it has provided an incentive in the contract for Absco to expedite production of the jeans. Jeans Are Us will provide a bonus to Absco if it delivers the jeans within a certain period of time of the request. The percentage bonus is as follows:

Delivered within	Percentage Bonus
1 day of request	5%
3 days of request	4%
5 days of request	3%
10 days of request	2%

Absco has never been involved in a transaction that involves bonuses for delivery expediency. In addition, because of the newness of this particular style of jeans on the market, Jeans Are Us is not able to give Absco any idea of when it will request jeans and how many it will request each time.

Absco uses the expected value method of measuring variable consideration. Accordingly, it has determined that the expected value of the bonus consideration is $180,000. However, Absco is quite uncertain how quickly it can manufacture these jeans. What is the total transaction price for this contract? You may want to read paragraphs 11 through 13 of ASC 606-10-32. Explain your answer.

Financial Statement Analysis Case

Financial Statement Analysis Case 1: Comparing Percentage-of-Completion and Completed Contract Methods

Use the information related to Bigelow Contractors from P8-7 and P8-8 to answer the following questions. Assume that Bigelow's total assets were $5,000,000 and its liabilities were $2,000,000 at the beginning of the year.

a. Compute net income under the percentage-of-completion and completed-contract methods for each year. (Ignore income taxes.)
b. Compute the total assets, liabilities, and equity under the percentage-of-completion and completed-contract methods at the end of each year.
c. Compute the profit margins under the percentage-of-completion and completed-contract methods each year. Comment on the differences.
d. Compute the debt-to-equity ratios under the percentage-of-completion and completed-contract methods each year. Comment on the differences.

Surfing the Standards Case

Surfing the Standards Case 1: Contract Changes

On January 2, 2018, JCR Jets, a calendar-year company, accepts a contract with a major airline to build four jets. JCR accepts a fixed fee of $300 million and must complete the project within three years. JCR Jets uses the percentage-of-completion method of accounting. It determines percent complete using the percentage of labor hours incurred relative to expected total labor hours. Management expects that it will take 2 million labor hours to build the three jets. During 2018, JCR incurs actual costs of $112 million and estimates that it will cost an additional $160 million to complete the jets. It incurred 800,000 labor hours during 2018.

On January 3, 2019, JCR Jet agrees with its customer to upgrade the jets. The parties agree that the fixed fee for the four jets will now be $350 million. JCR estimates that this upgrade will require an additional 400,000 labor hours and additional costs of $40 million.

Provide a written analysis and your conclusions of how JCR should account for this contract upgrade, using the Codification for support. Provide any necessary computations.

Basis for Conclusions Case

Basis for Conclusions Case 1: Control

According to ASC 606, an entity should recognize revenue when goods or services are transferred to a customer. Goods and services are transferred to a customer when the customer obtains control. Refer to the Basis for Conclusions section of ASU 2014-09 to answer the following questions.

1. In considering a control-based model for revenue recognition, FASB could have specified that goods and services are considered to be transferred when the seller gives up control as opposed to when the customer receives control. Are these two concepts always the same? If not, why did FASB choose to specify that the transfer occurs when the customer obtains control?
2. Is the control-based approach to revenue recognition new to ASU 2014-09, or has revenue always been recognized when control is transferred? What other approach(s) did FASB consider, and why did it choose the control model?
3. *Control* is defined by FASB as the ability to direct the use of and obtain substantially all of the remaining benefits from the asset. Briefly, and in your own words, describe and explain each component of this definition.
4. There was some disagreement by respondents to the Exposure Draft of ASU 2014-09 about using the notion of transfer of control to determine when revenue should be recognized. The respondents generally felt that the control model would work well for the sale of goods. However, some respondents felt that this model might not work as well for other types of transactions. What type of transactions were the respondents worried about? Why did they think the control model would not work as well for these transactions? How did these respondents think FASB should address this concern? What did FASB choose to do and why?

9 Short-Term Operating Assets: Cash and Receivables

LEARNING OBJECTIVES

1. Define cash and cash equivalents and describe the accounting for restricted cash and compensating balances.
2. Demonstrate the initial measurement and accounting for accounts receivable, including volume, trade, and sales discounts.
3. Understand the subsequent measurement and accounting for accounts receivable, including establishing an allowance for uncollectible accounts.
4. Estimate an allowance for uncollectible accounts using the aging of receivables method and explain the accounting for write-offs and subsequent recoveries.
5. Discuss the use of accounts receivable to generate immediate cash—including pledging or assigning, factoring receivables, and securitization—and demonstrate the accounting for these transactions.
6. Describe accounting for short-term notes receivable when issued and after issuance.
7. Explain the required disclosures for accounts and notes receivable.

Douglas Isaacson/Alamy Stock Photo

Introduction

WOULD A BALANCE SHEET seem complete without cash? Nearly all firms report cash on their balance sheet and view it as a factor in day-to-day operations and growth. However, most companies sell the majority of their goods and services on credit and wait to receive the related cash flows. Why do businesses sell on credit and delay cash collection? The answer is simple: Credit sales increase sales volume, motivating companies to trade off the risk that buyers will not pay against the benefits of increased sales.

Companies do mitigate this risk. For example, ***Levi Straus & Co. (Levi's)***, the global apparel company, analyzes new distributors for creditworthiness before it makes any sales on credit. Some portion of a company's receivables, however, will not be collected. Management must exercise judgment to estimate the losses expected from uncollected accounts receivable. It is impossible, though, to determine the amount of accounts receivable that will ultimately become uncollectible with perfect accuracy.

The financial statements disclose information related to these estimates. ***Levi's*** net accounts receivable from customers were \$479 million, or about 16.0% of its total assets, at the end of fiscal 2016. ***Levi's*** estimated that it would not collect about \$12 million, representing roughly 2.4% of accounts receivable, and reduced its accounts receivable by this amount. ***Levi's,*** like any other company, carefully monitors customers' accounts receivable to improve cash collections and make adjustments to its credit terms and policies.

Cash and receivables are parts of a company's short-term operating assets. As noted in the case of ***Levi's,*** receivables can make up a significant portion of a company's liquidity position. Receivables require proper credit management to ensure that a company can convert sufficient resources into cash needed to liquidate current obligations when they become due. Companies hold short-term operating assets such as inventory, supplies, and prepaid expenses in order to provide goods and services to customers on a timely basis.

In this chapter, we focus on cash and receivables, addressing two important issues: measurement and classification. Proper measurement and classification of cash and receivables enables a financial statement user to accurately assess a company's short-term liquidity position. Cash typically does not pose a significant measurement issue but may not always be available for use in the current operating cycle. Receivables involve both measurement (due to the risk of not collecting the cash) and classification issues (due to the timing of the expected collection). Any significant delay in the collection of receivables can adversely affect a company's operating cycle and liquidity position. «

1 Define cash and cash equivalents and describe the accounting for restricted cash and compensating balances.

Accounting for Cash and Cash Equivalents

We begin our discussion of accounting for cash by reviewing key terminology and introducing concepts such as restricted cash, *compensating balances*, and required disclosures.[1] We discuss internal controls over cash in the chapter appendix.

Review of Cash and Cash Equivalents

Together, transactions involving cash and cash equivalents are part of the firm's overall cash management activities. Companies add cash equivalents to cash in one line entitled "cash and cash equivalents" on the balance sheet. We introduced the statement of cash flows in Chapter 6. In this chapter, we focus on the definition and measurement of cash.

Cash consists of coins, currency, and bank deposits, as well as negotiable instruments such as checks and money orders. Firms generally classify cash as a current asset unless it is restricted from use in the current operating cycle.

Cash equivalents are short-term, highly liquid investments with original maturities of three months or less; examples include Treasury bills, commercial paper, certificates of deposit, and money market funds. Cash equivalents are cash substitutes that companies can easily convert back into cash if needed in the operating cycle. Original maturity is the length of time from the investment's purchase date to its due date. For example, a three-year Treasury instrument acquired with 2 months remaining until its due date qualifies as a cash equivalent because the company will hold it for less than 3 months.

Bank overdrafts occur if a company writes checks in amounts that exceed the balance in its account. That is, the account has a negative balance. Firms typically report bank overdrafts as current liabilities on the balance sheet rather than as "negative assets." If material, firms also must disclose bank overdrafts in the notes or list them separately on the face of the balance sheet.

Restricted Cash and Compensating Balances

Cash is one of the only assets that typically does not involve any questions as to measurement. However, proper classification can be an issue. Two classifications—*restricted cash* and *compensating cash balances*—limit the use of cash in operations.

Restricted Cash. A company classifies cash as a current asset on the balance sheet unless it is restricted from use in the current operating cycle. Cash balances that may involve restrictions on withdrawal include foreign bank accounts, collateral for certain obligations, or cash held by a third party for a specific purpose.[2]

[1]For most of the relevant authoritative literature for this topic, see FASB ASC 305—*Cash and Cash Equivalents* and ASC 210-10—*Balance Sheet—Overall* for U.S. GAAP and IASC, *International Accounting Standard 7*, "Statement of Cash Flows" (London, UK: International Accounting Standards Committee, Revised) for IFRS.

[2]Examples include a long-term debt sinking fund when the third party holds cash to make payments on the company's debt or an escrow account when the third party holds cash to pay the company's real estate taxes or make insurance payments.

When cash is legally restricted from use in the current operating cycle, the company reclassifies the restricted amount from the regular cash line item on the balance sheet into **restricted cash** as follows:

1. If the restriction extends *beyond 1 year* from the balance sheet date, classify the restricted funds account as a noncurrent asset and include it in the other assets section of the balance sheet.
2. If the restriction is for *less than 1 year*, classify the restricted funds account as current, but segregate it from the regular cash line item in the current assets section of the balance sheet.

Compensating Balances. **Compensating balances** are minimum cash balances that debtors are required to keep on deposit as support for existing credit agreements that are either part of a contractual agreement or an informal one. Companies classify legally restricted compensating balances as follows:

1. If the balance is held against short-term debt, reclassify the cash held as a separate current asset.
2. If the balance is held against long-term debt, reclassify the amount of cash held as a noncurrent asset on the balance sheet.

In either case, companies cannot combine the legally restricted compensating balances with regular cash on the balance sheet.

If the compensating balances are not part of a contractual agreement, companies must disclose the amounts, terms, and length of the arrangement in the footnotes to the financial statements. However, a classification out of regular cash on the face of the balance sheet is not required.

Regardless of the accounting treatment, a compensating balance requirement increases the entity's effective cost of borrowing. That is, the entity will have less cash to use but is still required to repay the full amount of the loan. For example, assume that a small business borrows $1,000 at 10% interest. The required cash interest payment is $100 for the year (10% × $1,000). Due to an unsatisfactory credit rating, the creditor requires the business to leave 4% or $40 of the loan on deposit at the lending institution as security. It must keep $40 on deposit and can use only $960 ($1,000 − $40). Given that the annual interest payment is $100 and ignoring the time value of money due to the short-term nature of the loan, the annual cost of borrowing increases from 10% to 10.42% ($100/$960).

Cash and Cash Equivalents: IFRS

Under International Financial Reporting Standards (IFRS), bank overdrafts are permitted to be included in cash and cash equivalents as a reduction if the overdraft balance is part of an integrated cash management strategy. This treatment allows for differences in banking systems and practices across countries. For example, banks in some countries may allow companies to have a negative cash balance that is repayable on demand.

Required Disclosures for Restricted Cash and Cash Equivalents

Accounting standards require separate disclosure for cash and cash equivalents that are restricted from withdrawal or use in operations. Companies describe the provisions of any restrictions in a note to the financial statements. Companies disclose informal compensating balance arrangements in the notes to the financial statements. These disclosures must describe the specific arrangements and the amount involved, if determinable, for the most recent audited balance sheet.

In its 2016 financial statements, ***Tesla, Inc.,*** the electric car designer and manufacturer, included $106 million of restricted cash in current assets and $268 million of restricted cash in noncurrent assets on its balance sheet.[3] Exhibit 9.1 contains ***Tesla, Inc.'s*** footnote disclosure discussion of its restricted cash balance.

[3]Tesla, Inc. reported the amount of restricted cash in note 2 to its financial statements.

EXHIBIT 9.1 Restricted Cash Disclosure, ***Tesla, Inc.***, Annual Report, December 31, 2016

Note 2—Summary of Significant Accounting Policies (excerpt)

RESTRICTED CASH AND DEPOSITS

We maintain certain cash amounts restricted as to withdrawal or use. Current and noncurrent restricted cash as of December 31, 2016, and 2015 was comprised primarily of cash as collateral related to our sales to lease partners with a resale value guarantee and for letters of credit including for our real estate leases, and insurance policies. In addition, restricted cash as of December 31, 2016, includes cash received from certain fund investors that had not been released for use by us, cash held to service certain payments under various secured debt facilities, including management fees, principal and interest payments, and balances collateralizing outstanding letters of credit, outstanding credit card borrowing facilities and obligations under certain operating leases.

Source: Tesla,, Inc.'s annual report. http://ir.tesla.com/sec.cfm?mode=&CompanyCIK=1318605&DocType=Annual&Year=&FormatFilter=

❷ Demonstrate the initial measurement and accounting for accounts receivable, including volume, trade, and sales discounts.

Accounting for Accounts Receivable: Initial Measurement

Accounts receivable (also referred to as trade accounts) are amounts due to an entity from its customers or clients that originated from the sale of goods or services. Accounts receivable do not involve signed contracts, and there is generally no interest charged due to their short-term nature.

Companies generally record accounts receivable at the amount of the sale.[4] The terms of sale—particularly discounts such as *trade discounts, volume discounts,* and *sales discounts*—affect the initial measurement of accounts receivable.[5]

Trade Discounts and Volume Discounts

Trade discounts are reductions of the catalog or list price when a company sells to a reseller in the same industry. A **volume discount** reduces the list price for customers purchasing a large quantity of merchandise. Therefore, both trade and volume discounts lower the amount of the sales revenue and impact the amount initially recorded in accounts receivable. Example 9.1 illustrates accounting for volume discounts. Accounting for trade discounts is similar.

EXAMPLE 9.1

Volume Discounts on Accounts Receivables

PROBLEM: KWH, Inc. sells custom-built kitchen island cabinets and offers a 10% discount to its high-volume customers. JSR Construction, Inc. purchased cabinets on account with a list price of \$132,000 and received a 10% volume discount of the purchase price amounting to \$13,200 (i.e., \$132,000 × 10%). What is the journal entry to record this sale (ignoring the effect on inventory and cost of goods sold)?

SOLUTION: KWH deducts the \$13,200 discount from the list price of \$132,000 to obtain an initial measurement of \$118,800 (\$132,000 × 90%) for the accounts receivable. Thus, the journal entry to record the accounts receivable is as follows:

Account	*Current Year*	
Accounts Receivable	118,800	
Sales Revenue		118,800

[4]Both U.S. GAAP and IFRS allow companies to choose to value most financial assets at fair value. This fair value option is discussed in more detail in Chapter 16.

[5]Sales returns also may impact the initial measurement of accounts receivable. Companies selling products often give the buyer the right to return the product. Returned merchandise is referred to as a sales return. We discuss sales returns in greater depth in Chapter 8.

Sales Discounts

Sales discounts (also called cash discounts) are reductions granted to customers for early cash payment as an incentive to encourage quick invoice payment. Although the seller will collect less total cash, it will have cash earlier for use in current operations. The benefits of improved cash flow and liquidity are greater than the cost of the discount.

Companies usually include sales discounts on customer invoices. A typical sales discount is written as 2/10, n/30, which means the customer will receive a 2% discount if she pays within 10 days of the invoice date; otherwise, the full balance is due within 30 days. ***Kellogg Company,*** the multinational food company, disclosed in its 2015 financial statements that it generally requires payment for goods sold 11 or 16 days subsequent to the date of invoice as 2/10, n/11, 1/15, or n/16 in the United States, but terms can vary around the world and by business type.[6] There are two acceptable approaches to recording sales discounts: the *most-likely-amount method* or the *expected-value method.*

Most-Likely-Amount Method. Under the **most-likely-amount method,** a company initially records accounts receivable at the most-likely amount of cash that it will collect from its customer. If the company anticipates that its customer will not take the discount, then it will record the receivable at the full (gross) sales amount (the gross method).

1. If the customer pays *after* the discount period, it pays the full amount. The amount of cash received is the gross amount of the receivable on the books. No further adjustments are needed to reflect the fact that the customer did not take the discount.
2. If the customer pays *within* the discount period, the journal entry must reflect the discount because the company receives less cash than the gross account receivable on the books. The net amount of cash received is the difference between the gross receivable amount and the discount. The sales discount equals the gross amount of the receivable or invoice times the sales discount percentage. The sales discount is recorded in a contra-revenue account, reducing the amount of revenue recorded on the income statement.

If the company anticipates that the customer will take the sales discount, then it initially records sales and accounts receivable at the net amount (the net method).

1. If the customer pays *within* the discount period, then the journal entry measures the amount of cash received as the net amount of the receivable on the books. No additional adjustments are required to reflect the discount taken.
2. If the customer pays *after* the discount period, the company receives more cash than the net carrying value of the receivable. In this case, the credit to accounts receivable is less than the debit to cash. The seller credits the difference to the sales discounts forfeited account, a revenue account. The sales discounts forfeited can be interpreted as interest revenue on extending credit to the customer.

For most companies, recording accounts receivable at the net amount is more appropriate than recording the receivable at the gross amount because their customers usually take the discount. Thus, recording the receivable at the net amount is considered a more reliable measurement of the current asset. Example 9.2 illustrates accounting for sales discounts using the most-likely-amount method.

EXAMPLE 9.2 Sales Discounts on Accounts Receivable Using the Most-Likely-Amount Method

PROBLEM: Clark and Lewis Wholesalers, Inc. sells hiking boots for $100 per pair. On June 1, the company sold 50 pairs on account to a customer with terms of 2/10, n/30. The customer paid for 20 pairs of boots on June 9 and paid for the remaining 30 pairs on June 29. Provide the necessary journal entries for Clark and Lewis to record these transactions using the most-likely-amount method assuming that the customer will not take the discount. Also, prepare the journal entries assuming that the customer will take the discount. (Ignore the journal entry that would typically be necessary to record the cost of goods sold and the reduction of inventory.) Also provide a comparison of the impact on the income statement for each assumption.

Continued

[6]Source: Kellogg Company's 10-K filing, page 2, https://www.sec.gov/Archives/edgar/data/55067/000162828016011639/k-2015q410xk.htm

SOLUTION: First, Clark and Lewis records the sale. Under the gross method, the company records the full $5,000 of sales revenue (50 pairs of boots × $100 per pair).

Under the net method, the company records the amount net of the discount ($4,900). The net amount is the $5,000 gross amount (50 pairs of boots × $100 per pair) less the discount of $100 ($5,000 × 2%). The journal entries on June 1 are as follows:

Gross Method	Debit	Credit	Net Method	Debit	Credit
Accounts Receivable	5,000		Accounts Receivable	4,900	
Sales		5,000	Sales		4,900

On June 9, Clark and Lewis receives payment of $1,960 from its customer. The net amount per pair of boots is $98, which is the gross amount of $100 less the discount of $2 per pair (i.e., 2% × $100). Thus, the customer pays for 20 pairs of boots or $1,960 (20 pairs of boots × $98 per pair). Under the gross method, although Clark and Lewis receives only $1,960 in cash, we must remove accounts receivable at $2,000, the gross amount of the sale. We apply the $40 (i.e., $2 × 20) to the sales discounts account (a contra-revenue account).

Under the net method, Clark and Lewis originally recorded the accounts receivable at the net amount, so we debit cash and credit accounts receivable for the $1,960. The journal entries on June 9 when the discount is taken follow.

Gross Method	Debit	Credit	Net Method	Debit	Credit
Cash	1,960		Cash	1,960	
Sales Discounts	40		Accounts Receivable		1,960
Accounts Receivable		2,000			

Finally, on June 29, Clark and Lewis receives payment of $3,000 for the remaining gross receivable. The customer did not pay within the discount period, so the discount is not taken. Thus, the journal entry for the gross method requires debiting the cash account for the $3,000 and crediting accounts receivable for the same amount.

Under the net method, the company removes the accounts receivable balance at the net amount of $2,940 ($3,000 less a 2% discount of $60). The $60 ($2 × 30 pairs) discount is recorded by crediting the sales discounts forfeited account, which is a revenue account. The journal entries on June 29 when the discount is not taken follow.

Gross Method	Debit	Credit	Net Method	Debit	Credit
Cash	3,000		Cash	3,000	
Accounts Receivable		3,000	Accounts Receivable		2,940
			Sales Discounts Forfeited		60

The total revenue reported is the same for both methods; only the classification on the income statement may differ.

Income Statement Comparison

Gross Method		Net Method	
Sales	$5,000	Sales	$4,900
Less: Sales discounts	(40)	Add: Sales discounts forfeited	60
Total Revenue	$4,960	Total Revenue	$4,960

Expected-Value Method. Under the **expected-value method,** the entity sums the probability-weighted amounts in a range of possible consideration amounts. For example, if the company thinks it is 30% likely that the customer will take the discount, then it will initially record the accounts receivable at the sum of the gross amount times 70% plus the net amount times 30%. Example 9.3 illustrates accounting for sales discounts using the expected-value method.

EXAMPLE 9.3 Sales Discounts on Accounts Receivable Using the Expected-Value Method

PROBLEM: Clark and Lewis Wholesalers, Inc. sells hiking boots for $100 per pair. On June 1, the company sold 50 pairs on account to a customer with terms of 2/10, n/30. The customer paid for 20 pairs of boots on June 9 and paid for the remaining 30 pairs on June 29. Provide the necessary journal entries for Clark and Lewis to record these transactions using the expected-value method assuming that Clark and Lewis believe that it is 75% likely that the customer will not take the discount. (Ignore the journal entry that would typically be necessary to record the cost of goods sold and the reduction of inventory.) Also provide a comparison of the impact on the income statement for the expected-value method versus the two scenarios under the most-likely-amount method.

SOLUTION: First, Clark and Lewis records the sale. Under the expected-value method, the company records the full accounts receivable and sales at $4,975 [($5,000 × 75%) + ($4,900 × 25%)]. This amount is $99.50 per pair of boots ($4,975/50). The journal entry on June 1 is as follows:

Expected-Value Method	*Debit*	*Credit*
Accounts Receivable	4,975	
Sales		4,975

On June 9, Clark and Lewis receives payment of $1,960 from its customer. The net amount per pair of boots is $98, which is the gross amount of $100 less the discount of $2 per pair (i.e., 2% × $100). Thus, the customer pays for 20 pairs of boots or $1,960 (20 pairs of boots × $98 per pair). Although Clark and Lewis receives only $1,960 in cash, we must remove accounts receivable at $1,990 (20 pairs of boots × $99.50 per pair). We apply the $30 difference to the sales discounts account (a contra-revenue account).

Expected-Value Method	*Debit*	*Credit*
Cash	1,960	
Sales Discounts	30	
Accounts Receivable		1,990

Finally, on June 29 Clark and Lewis receives payment of $3,000 for the remaining gross receivable. The customer did not pay within the discount period, so the discount is not taken. Thus, the company removes the accounts receivable balance at the amount of $2,985 (30 pairs of boots × $99.50 per pair). The $15 discount is recorded by crediting the sales discounts forfeited account, which is a revenue account. The journal entry on June 29 when the discount is not taken follows.

Expected-Value Method	*Debit*	*Credit*
Cash	3,000	
Accounts Receivable		2,985
Sales Discounts Forfeited		15

Continued

The total revenue reported is the same for both the expected-value and mostly-likely-amount methods; only the classification on the income statement may differ.

Income Statement Comparison

Most-Likely-Amount Method (Gross)		*Most-Likely-Amount Method (Net)*		*Expected-Value Method*	
Sales	$5,000	Sales	$4,900	Sales	$4,975
Less: Sales discounts	(40)			Less: Sales discounts	(30)
		Other Revenue: Sales discounts forfeited	60	Net Sales	$4,945
				Other Revenue: Sales discounts forfeited	15
Total Revenue	$4,960	Total Revenue	$4,960	Total Revenue	$4,960

3 Understand the subsequent measurement and accounting for accounts receivable, including establishing an allowance for uncollectible accounts.

Accounting for Accounts Receivable: Subsequent Measurement

Managers understand that selling their products on credit increases total sales because customers prefer to buy on credit. However, there is the risk that the company will not collect the full amount of the receivables. The uncollectible portion of a company's receivables creates a measurement problem for accountants. Accounts receivable must be reported on the balance sheet at *net realizable value*. The term **net realizable value (NRV)** describes the estimated amount that a company reasonably expects to collect from its customers and is measured as the gross accounts receivable less an estimated allowance for uncollectible accounts (a contra-asset account).

Firms report **bad debt expense** on the income statement to reflect the cost of uncollectible accounts. It is not possible to know which specific accounts will ultimately become uncollectible with certainty. Thus, at the end of each reporting period, management must estimate the NRV of accounts receivable and bad debt expense.

THE CONCEPTUAL FRAMEWORK CONNECTION
Accounting for Uncollectible Accounts

A number of concepts in the conceptual framework relate to accounting for uncollectible accounts, including the fundamental characteristics—relevance and faithful representation. Even before knowing which customer will not make payment, a company estimates the amount of receivables that will be uncollectible under accrual accounting. Accountants then record bad debt expense for the year with an adjusting entry. Cash is not affected, but management estimates the amount of the bad debt expense to report on the income statement and the resulting NRV of accounts receivable reported on the balance sheet. The amounts provide predictive value to the users of the financial statements assessing the firm's future cash inflows.

In addition, the accrual of bad debt expense results in a more faithful representation of the financial statements than when using a cash-basis system. A faithful representation of the balance sheet requires consideration of the accounts receivable amounts that will likely not generate a future economic benefit. Likewise, a faithful representation of the income statement requires a reduction in income resulting from bad debts. Management's estimation techniques should match bad debt expense with revenues.[7]

[7]See FASB, *Statement of Financial Accounting Concepts No. 5*, "Recognition and Measurement in Financial Statements of Business Enterprises," Paragraph 86 for a discussion of when the consumption of economic benefits should be recognized.

The Allowance Method

We now focus our presentation on the **allowance method**, which estimates the NRV of accounts receivable and the current period's bad debt expense in the period of the sale. There are two key considerations related to uncollectible accounts:[8]

1. The measurement of accounts receivable on the balance sheet at estimated NRV
2. The inclusion of bad debt expense related to the uncollectible accounts on the income statement in the appropriate period

To illustrate, assume that a company sells a product on credit for $1,000, but it expects that the customer will ultimately pay only $900. As a result, the company will:

1. Report accounts receivable on the balance sheet at $900, computed as follows:

Accounts receivable	$1,000
Less: Allowance for uncollectible accounts	(100)
NRV of accounts receivable	$ 900

2. Record revenue of $1,000 and bad debt expense of $100 in the same period.

In this way, the allowance method measures the receivable at its NRV and reports the cost of selling on credit with the additional revenue generated from extending credit to customers in the same period.

As noted earlier, companies estimating bad debt expense also create an allowance for uncollectible accounts.[9] The allowance account is a contra-asset that reduces accounts receivable so that the NRV of accounts receivable is reported on the balance sheet. Example 9.4 illustrates the allowance for uncollectible accounts. In the year in which a company determines that a specific account is uncollectible, it writes off the account receivable against the allowance without a further reduction of earnings.[10]

EXAMPLE 9.4 Allowance for Uncollectible Accounts

PROBLEM: American Wholesalers sells cereal to a customer for $10,000 on account on December 1. The customer has not paid the balance due as of the end of the year. After an analysis of the customer's account, American Wholesalers estimates that the customer will ultimately pay only $9,000 of the $10,000 that is due. Prepare the journal entries needed to record these transactions. (Ignore the journal entry that would typically be necessary to record the inventory reduction and the cost of goods sold.)

SOLUTION: The December 1 sale is recorded as follows:

Account	December 1	
Accounts Receivable	10,000	
Sales Revenue		10,000

American Wholesalers records the estimated allowance for uncollectible accounts and the bad debt expense of $1,000 on December 31 as follows:

Account	December 31	
Bad Debt Expense	1,000	
Allowance for Uncollectible Accounts		1,000

Continued

[8]An alternative is to report bad debt expense only during the period when an account is determined to be uncollectible. This approach, known as the direct write-off method, is generally not allowed under GAAP.

[9]We also refer to the allowance for uncollectible accounts as the allowance for bad debts or the allowance for doubtful accounts.

[10]We will discuss write-offs later in the chapter.

Consequently, on its December 31 financial statements, American Wholesalers will report $10,000 of revenue and $1,000 of bad debt expense on its income statement with a $9,000 net increase in earnings. On the balance sheet, the company reports the NRV of accounts receivable at $9,000 (i.e., $10,000 gross accounts receivable less the $1,000 allowance for uncollectible accounts).

4 Estimate an allowance for uncollectible accounts using the aging of receivables method and explain the accounting for write-offs and subsequent recoveries.

Uncollectible Accounts Estimates

Managers form estimates of the amount expected to be uncollectible using the *aging of accounts receivable method.*

Aging of Accounts Receivable

Under the **aging of accounts receivable method,** a company estimates the allowance for uncollectible accounts using the following steps:

1. Determine the balance in each aging category by separating the accounts receivable balances based on the age of the receivable (i.e., the amount of time that has passed from the original date of sale to the bad debt estimation date).
2. Multiply the balance in each aging category by an estimated percentage of uncollectible accounts for that specific category.
3. Add the subtotals of each aging category to determine the required balance in the allowance for uncollectible accounts.
4. Record the bad debt expense needed to adjust the allowance for uncollectible accounts to the correct balance.

Commonly, a company bases the percentage of uncollectible accounts in each age category on experience in collecting its accounts receivable and existing economic conditions. Percentages usually increase with the time the receivables are outstanding because collection becomes less likely for older balances.

The aging of accounts receivable illustrated in Example 9.5 is considered a balance sheet approach because companies calculate the ending balance in the allowance account directly and focus on the proper measurement of accounts receivable at NRV. The resulting bad debt expense and the matching of that expense to sales revenue are ignored.

EXAMPLE 9.5

Aging of Accounts Receivable Method

PROBLEM: Stafford Corporation provides the following information regarding accounts receivable during 2018, its second year of operations.

Net credit sales during 2018	$6,525,000
Accounts receivable at December 31, 2018 (end of the year)	1,600,000
Allowance for uncollectible accounts (credit balance), December 31, 2018, unadjusted	120,000

The company performs an aging of accounts receivable in order to estimate its allowance for uncollectible accounts. Stafford uses the following estimated percentages of receivables expected to be uncollectible within each category:

Aging Category	Percentage Estimated to Be Uncollectible
Current	1%
1–30 days past due	5
31–60 days past due	15
61–90 days past due	30
Over 90 days past due	95

Stafford's aged schedule of receivables is as follows:

Stafford Corporation: Aged Schedule of Accounts Receivable

		Past Due				
Customer	**Current**	**1–30 Days**	**31–60 Days**	**61–90 Days**	**Over 90 Days**	**Totals**
Mills Brothers		$200,000	$400,000			$ 600,000
Star Company	$200,000					200,000
Vaughn Monroe, Inc.		100,000	200,000			300,000
Prima Products				$300,000	$200,000	500,000
Totals	$200,000	$300,000	$600,000	$300,000	$200,000	$1,600,000

What is the journal entry to record the bad debt expense for 2018? What is the NRV of accounts receivable balance at the end of the year?

SOLUTION: First, we compute the required balance in the allowance for uncollectible accounts by multiplying the total accounts receivable amount in each category by the relevant percentage. For example, Stafford has $200,000 of accounts receivable in the current category. We multiply this balance by the 1% estimated percentage of uncollectible accounts, yielding a $2,000 allowance. We follow this process for each category of receivable and sum the allowances for each aging category. The complete computation follows.

Stafford Corporation: Aged Schedule of Accounts Receivable

		Past Due				
Customer	**Current**	**1–30 Days**	**31–60 Days**	**61–90 Days**	**Over 90 Days**	**Totals**
Mills Brothers		$200,000	$400,000			$ 600,000
Star Company	$200,000					200,000
Vaughn Monroe, Inc.		100,000	200,000			300,000
Prima Products				$300,000	$200,000	500,000
Totals	$200,000	$300,000	$600,000	$300,000	$200,000	$1,600,000
% Uncollectible	1%	5%	15%	30%	95%	
Allowance Needed	$ 2,000	$ 15,000	$ 90,000	$ 90,000	$190,000	$ 387,000

Based on the analysis of aging, the required allowance account balance at year-end is $387,000. The allowance for uncollectible accounts is a permanent account, and the company reported an existing credit balance of $120,000 at the end of the year. As a result, the company needs to increase the allowance only by the difference of $267,000 (i.e., $387,000 − $120,000). The year-end adjusting entry to record the bad debt expense for 2018 follows.

Account	***Year-End***	
Bad Debt Expense	267,000	
Allowance for Uncollectible Accounts		267,000

The balance in the allowance account is now $387,000 as shown in the following t-account.

Continued

Allowance for Uncollectible Accounts

	120,000	Unadjusted Ending Balance
	267,000	Adjustment
	387,000	Ending Balance

The NRV of accounts receivable at year-end is as follows:

Accounts receivable	$1,600,000
Less: Allowance for uncollectible accounts	(387,000)
NRV of accounts receivable	$1,213,000

Using the aging of accounts receivable method, a company directly estimates the ending balance of the allowance account to determine the NRV of accounts receivable. As a result, the amount for the bad debt expense, which is the change in the allowance account, is "forced" to be set equal to the adjustment needed in the allowance account. The aging of accounts receivable method focuses on the proper balance sheet valuation of the NRV of accounts receivable. However, it may report a bad debt expense that does not match with current-period net sales. This issue is heightened when there is an existing debit balance in the allowance account.[11] Under the aging of accounts receivable method, an existing debit balance would be added to the required allowance to arrive at the necessary journal entry as shown in Example 9.6.

EXAMPLE 9.6 Aging of Accounts Receivable Method with Debit Allowance Balance

PROBLEM: Stafford Corporation provides the following information regarding accounts receivable during 2018.

Net credit sales during 2018	$6,525,000
Accounts receivable at December 31, 2018 (end of the year)	1,600,000
Allowance for uncollectible accounts (debit balance), December 31, 2018, unadjusted	155,000

Based on the analysis of aging, the required allowance account balance at year-end is $387,000. Provide the journal entry to record the bad debt expense for the year.

SOLUTION: Stafford Corporation needs an ending credit balance of $387,000. Thus, as shown in the following t-account, it needs to credit the allowance for $542,000.

Allowance for Uncollectible Accounts

Unadjusted Balance	155,000		
		542,000	Adjustment
		387,000	Ending Balance

[11]The balance in the allowance account could be a debit due to write-offs (which we discuss in the next section) in excess of amounts previously provided.

The adjusting journal entry follows.

Account	Year-End	
Bad Debt Expense	542,000	
Allowance for Uncollectible Accounts		542,000

The NRV of accounts receivable at year-end is as follows:

Accounts receivable	$1,600,000
Less: Allowance for uncollectible accounts	(387,000)
NRV of accounts receivable	$1,213,000

Note that the bad debt expense increases from $267,000 to $542,000 because of the change in assumption regarding the existing balance in the allowance account. Although the NRV of accounts receivable is the same as in Example 9.5, the fact that there is now a debit balance in the allowance account increases the bad debt expense by $275,000. Once again, the use of the aging of accounts receivable method results in a bad debt expense that is "forced" to be set equal to the adjustment needed in the allowance account.

Companies must disclose the method they use to estimate the allowance for doubtful accounts. Exhibit 9.2 presents an example from ***Levi Strauss & Co.*** indicating that the company uses an aging of accounts receivable approach combined with other factors.

EXHIBIT 9.2 Accounts Receivable Disclosure, ***Levi Strauss & Co.***, Annual Report, November 27, 2016

ACCOUNTS RECEIVABLE, NET

The Company extends credit to its customers that satisfy predefined credit criteria. Accounts receivable are recorded net of an allowance for doubtful accounts. The Company estimates the allowance for doubtful accounts based upon an analysis of the aging of accounts receivable at the date of the consolidated financial statements, assessments of collectability based on historic trends, customer-specific circumstances, and an evaluation of economic conditions.

Source: Levi Strauss & Co. Annual Report, 2016. https://www.sec.gov/Archives/edgar/data/94845/000009484517000012/a2016yeform10-k.htm

Uncollectible Account Write-Off

A company *writes off* an account receivable when it no longer expects to collect the amount due from a customer. When it decides to **write off** a specific account, the company reduces or debits the allowance for uncollectible accounts and reduces or credits the accounts receivable.

The write-off under the allowance method has no balance sheet effect related to the NRV of the accounts receivable. There is also no income statement effect from the write-off under the allowance method because the company previously reduced income by the estimated bad debt expense in the year of the sale.

Companies maintain the general ledger account accounts receivable that reflects the amount of the gross accounts receivable reported on the balance sheet. In addition, companies include the specific customer accounts in an accounts receivable subsidiary ledger.

When estimating the NRV of accounts receivable, the company uses the allowance for uncollectible accounts to offset the gross accounts receivable account on the balance sheet as opposed to any specific customer accounts. However, the company removes the individual customer account from the subsidiary ledger when it ultimately writes off the account. The gross accounts receivable and the allowance accounts are also reduced by the amount of the write-off. Example 9.7 provides an example of a write-off.

EXAMPLE 9.7 Write-Off of an Uncollectible Account

PROBLEM: Continuing the Stafford Corporation illustration in Example 9.6, assume that actual bad debts were $85,000 in 2019. Specifically, on January 2, 2019, Stafford determined that Prima Products is unable to pay a portion of its balance due. Stafford uses the aged balance of accounts receivable to estimate its bad debt expense. What is the journal entry necessary to write off this account? What is the NRV of the accounts receivable before the write-off? What is the NRV of the accounts receivable after the write-off?

SOLUTION: When writing off an uncollectible account, a company will always debit the allowance for uncollectible accounts and credit accounts receivable to remove the amount written off from both accounts. The journal entry is as follows:

Account	January 2, 2019	
Allowance for Uncollectible Accounts	85,000	
Accounts Receivable—Prima Products		85,000

The credit to accounts receivable reduces both the gross accounts receivable account on the balance sheet and the individual customer's account balance.

The NRV is not directly affected by the write-off: The NRV of accounts receivable is $1,213,000 both before and after the write-off of the actual uncollectible account as illustrated in the following table.

Description	Before Write-Off	Write-Off	After Write-Off
Accounts receivable	$1,600,000	$ (85,000)	$1,515,000
Less: Allowance for uncollectible accounts	(387,000)	85,000	(302,000)
NRV	$1,213,000	$ 0	$1,213,000

Subsequent Recoveries

A company writes off an account receivable when it no longer expects to collect the amount due from a customer. However, the customer legally still owes money to the company and may eventually pay the amount due. A **recovery** occurs when a company receives payment on an account that it had previously written off. There are two steps to account for the subsequent recovery of accounts previously written off against the allowance account:

1. Reinstate the account receivable and restore the allowance account.
2. Record the cash collection.

Example 9.8 illustrates accounting for the recovery of a write-off.

EXAMPLE 9.8 Subsequent Recovery

PROBLEM: Consider the information provided for Stafford Corporation in Example 9.7. Assume that Stafford subsequently collects the $85,000 due from Prima Products that it has previously written off. What are the required journal entries to record the recovery?

SOLUTION: First, we must reinstate the account receivable and the allowance accounts as follows:

Account	At Recovery	
Accounts Receivable—Prima Products	85,000	
Allowance for Uncollectible Accounts		85,000

This procedure restores the allowance account and reinstates the receivable from Prima Products.

Second, we record the cash collection as follows:

Account	At Recovery	
Cash	85,000	
Accounts Receivable—Prima Products		85,000

JUDGMENTS IN ACCOUNTING
Subsequent Measurements of Accounts Receivable

Management exercises a great deal of judgment and subjectivity in estimating the bad debt expense and the allowance for uncollectible accounts. In a survey of 175 companies, 40% of them indicated that they make estimates and use judgment in reporting their allowance for uncollectible accounts.[12] For example, as presented in Exhibit 9.3, in its 2016 financial statements, ***Thomson Reuters Corporation,*** the mass media and information firm, reported that the balance in its allowance account was 6% of its gross receivables. In other words, the company estimated that it would never collect 6% of the amount it is owed. Also, notice that ***Thomson*** disclosed that changing this estimate by 1% would have a $14 million impact on pre-tax earnings.

EXHIBIT 9.3 Critical Accounting Estimates and Judgments, ***Thomson Reuters Corporation***, December 31, 2016, Financial Statements

NOTE 2: Critical Accounting Estimates and Judgments

The preparation of financial statements requires management to make estimates and judgments about the future. Estimates and judgments are continually evaluated and are based on historical experience and other factors, including expectations of future events that are believed to be reasonable under the circumstances. Accounting estimates will, by definition, seldom equal the actual results. The following discussion sets forth management's:

- most critical estimates and assumptions in determining the value of assets and liabilities; and
- most critical judgments in applying accounting policies.

Critical Accounting Estimates and Assumptions

Allowance for doubtful accounts and sales adjustments

We must make an assessment of whether accounts receivable are collectible from customers. Accordingly, we establish an allowance for estimated losses arising from non-payment and other sales adjustments, taking into consideration customer creditworthiness, current economic trends and past experience. If future collections differ from estimates, future earnings would be affected. At December 31, 2016, the combined allowances were $87 million, or 6%, of the gross trade accounts receivable balance of approximately $1.4 billion. An increase to the reserve based on 1% of accounts receivable would have decreased pre-tax earnings by approximately $14 million for the year ended December 31, 2016.

Source: Thomson Reuters, Inc. https://annual-report.thomsonreuters.com/downloads/annual-report-2016-thomson-reuters.pdf, page 81.

No U.S. GAAP or IFRS standards require a specific estimation method. Companies follow both U.S. GAAP and IFRS in using the allowance method, but these standards do not specify *how* to estimate the bad debt expense. Consequently, companies exercise discretion in the specific method used to estimate the bad debt expense, such as the aging of accounts receivable method.

[12] AICPA, *IFRS Accounting Trends and Techniques—2012* (New York, NY: AICPA, 2012).

Management has flexibility in choosing the percentages for aging categories in the aging of accounts receivable method. The bad debt expense accrual leaves a great deal of room for earnings management activities. Consider that Stafford Corporation in Example 9.5 estimated its bad debts as 15% of accounts receivable 31–60 days past due. A decrease of just one percentage point to 14% would result in a $6,000 decrease in bad debt expense ($90,000 – $84,000) and thus a $6,000 increase in net income.

Both ***PepsiCo, Inc.*** and ***Coca-Cola Company,*** two large beverage companies, disclose that they base allowances and bad debt expense on the aging of accounts and prior customer experience. Exhibit 9.4 compares the accounts receivable measurement practices of the two companies. Even though both companies use the same general approach, the allowances vary due to the judgment used in assessing the NRV of accounts receivable as indicated by the percentages used in Exhibit 9.4. ***PepsiCo's*** 2016 allowance is about 1.0% of gross receivables and ***Coca-Cola's*** is 10.8%. Of course, the allowances also reflect each company's credit-extension policies.

EXHIBIT 9.4 Accounting Policies for Allowance for Uncollectible Accounts

	PepsiCo, Inc. **December 31, 2016**	***Coca-Cola Company,*** **December 31, 2016**
Policy	"We estimate and reserve for our bad debt exposure based on our experience with past due accounts and collectability, the aging of accounts receivable and our analysis of customer data."	"We calculate this allowance based on our history of write-offs, the level of past-due accounts based on the contractual terms of the receivables, and our relationships with, and the economic status of, our bottling partners and customers. We believe our exposure to concentrations of credit risk is limited due to the diverse geographic areas covered by our operations."
(in millions) Allowance for Uncollectible Accounts	$ 37	$ 466
Gross Accounts Receivable	$5,709	$4,322
Percent Allowed For	0.6%	10.8%

Sources: Pepsico, Inc. Annual Report, December 2016. http://www.pepsico.com/Investors/Annual-Reports-and-Proxy-Information and Coca-Cola Company's Annual Report 2016. http://www.coca-colacompany.com/content/dam/journey/us/en/private/fileassets/pdf/investors/2016-AR-10-K.pdf

Exhibit 9.4 indicates the impact of estimated bad debt expense on the amount of earnings reported. For example, ***Coca-Cola*** reported pre-tax income of $8,136 million in 2016. If the company had estimated the allowance a percentage higher at 11.8% of the $4,322 receivable balance, then bad debt expense would have been $44 million higher ($510 – $466), reducing pre-tax income by $44 million, or nearly 0.5% ($44/$8,136). Likewise, if ***Coca-Cola*** had reduced this percentage by 1% to 9.8%, pre-tax income would have increased by $44 million.

5 Discuss the use of accounts receivable to generate immediate cash—including pledging or assigning, factoring receivables, and securitization—and demonstrate the accounting for these transactions.

Financing with Accounts Receivable

In managing short-term operating assets, firms can secure immediate cash from accounts receivable rather than waiting for a customer to remit payment. We address three alternate techniques—*pledging* or *assigning* accounts receivable, *factoring* accounts receivable, and *securitizations*.

A company uses its receivables as collateral for a lending arrangement by *pledging* or *assigning* the receivables. *Factoring* involves selling the receivables to a third party at a discount. *Securitization* involves bundling together and selling an interest in many separate receivables.

Pledging and Assigning Accounts Receivable

Pledging and *assigning* receivables are both forms of collateralized borrowing. When a firm **pledges accounts receivable**, the receivables are collateral for a financing arrangement. When the company **assigns accounts receivable**, specifically designated receivables are collateral for the loan, but the company must use the receipts on collection of the receivables to repay the debt.[13]

When pledging and assigning, the accounts receivable remain on the balance sheet. If the receivables are used as collateral for a short-term loan, they continue to be classified as current assets on the balance sheet. If the liability is long term, then the receivables pledged or assigned are reclassified as noncurrent assets on the balance sheet. Footnotes to the financial statements indicate the contingent liability related to the transfer of the accounts receivable rights to others. Financial statement users should consider the potential adverse effects on liquidity from a default on the debt relating to the receivables pledged or assigned to third parties. Example 9.9 illustrates accounting for assigned accounts receivable.

EXAMPLE 9.9

Assigning Accounts Receivable

PROBLEM: On March 1, Cole Company borrowed $600,000 from Damone Financing Associates by securing a revolving line of credit at a 6% interest rate. Interest is due and payable at the beginning of each month based on the outstanding balance at the beginning of the prior month. Cole assigned $680,000 of its accounts receivable as collateral for the lending arrangement. On April 1, Cole collected $180,000 of the assigned accounts receivable. Prepare the necessary journal entries for these transactions.

SOLUTION: Cole Company makes the following journal entries to record the lending arrangement.

Account	***March 1***	
Cash	600,000	
Notes Payable		600,000
Assigned Accounts Receivable	680,000	
Accounts Receivable		680,000

Cole Company records the cash collected on the receivables.

Account	***April 1***	
Cash	180,000	
Assigned Accounts Receivable		180,000

Then, Cole Company remits cash to Damone Financing each month based on the dollar amount of receivables it collects. Thus, on April 1, Cole will pay Damone Financing the $180,000 plus interest. We compute the interest as $3,000 ($600,000 loan balance × 6% × 1/12).

Account	***April 1***	
Notes Payable	180,000	
Interest Expense	3,000	
Cash		183,000

[13]These borrowing arrangements are often called asset-based lending. Any type of loan backed by assets can be called an asset-based loan. However, asset-based lending is typically used to describe a borrowing arrangement when the collateral is inventory, accounts receivable, or equipment.

Factoring Accounts Receivable

Factoring accounts receivable occurs when a company sells its accounts receivable to a third party, known as a factor, at a discount. In most factoring arrangements, customers are instructed to pay the factor directly. The factoring company discounts or reduces the amount remitted due to the risk of bad debts and the cost of collection.

Accounting for a factoring transaction depends on whether the arrangement qualifies as a sale and whether the sale includes conditions guaranteeing collection of the receivables.

Sales versus Secured Borrowing. When a company factors its receivables, it must first determine whether the transaction meets the requirements to record the transaction as a sale.

Companies must meet all of the following conditions in order to record the transaction as a sale:[14]

1. The receivables are isolated from the selling company. That is, the receivables must be out of the reach of the seller as well as its creditors—even in the case of bankruptcy.
2. The factor has the ability to pledge or exchange the receivables.
3. The selling company does not maintain effective control over the receivables (i.e., there is no continuing involvement by the selling company).

In general, these conditions, summarized in Exhibit 9.5, ensure that the seller does not retain any control of the receivables.

If the company determines that the factoring arrangement is a sale, it derecognizes the receivables (i.e., the company removes the receivables from the balance sheet). If the transaction does not qualify as a sale, the company treats it as a secured borrowing by using the same accounting as if the company had pledged or had assigned the receivables.

EXHIBIT 9.5 Sales versus Secured Borrowing

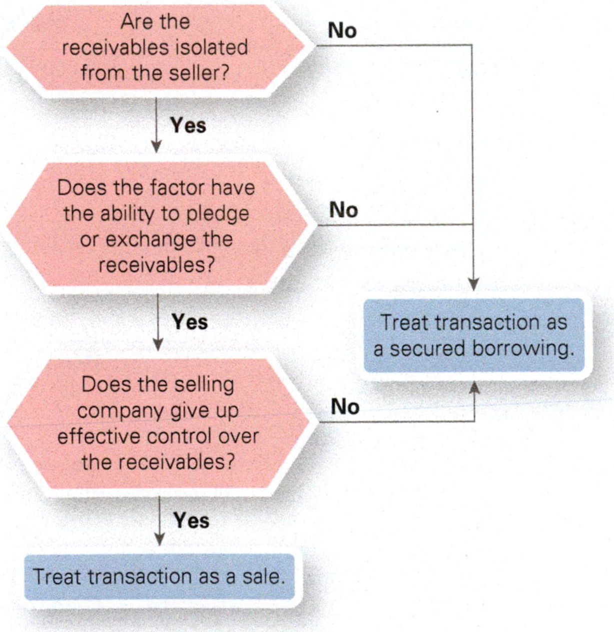

If a transaction meets the conditions to be recorded as a sale, the accounting depends on whether the receivables are sold with or without a **recourse** provision guaranteeing that they will be collected in the factoring contract.

[14]The specific conditions are presented in paragraph 5 of FASB ASC 860-10-40—*Transfers and Servicing – Overall – Derecognition.*

Factoring without Recourse. If the receivables are transferred without a guarantee of collection, the factor assumes the risk of uncollectible accounts and absorbs any credit losses. The customers now pay the buyer or factor. When the seller does not guarantee collectability, the receivables are transferred **without recourse.** When factoring receivables without recourse, the seller company no longer retains any of the risks or rewards of the receivable.

When the sale of accounts receivable is made without recourse, the selling company removes the accounts receivable from its books and records the related gain or loss on the transaction as shown in Example 9.10. The gain or loss is the difference between the proceeds on the sale and the face amount of the receivables factored adjusted for any *hold back*. A **hold back** is an amount of cash that the buyer does not remit to the seller but instead retains as additional security. The seller recognizes the amount of the holdback as a type of receivable on its books. After the receivables are fully collected, the buyer returns the holdback amount to the seller.

EXAMPLE 9.10

Factoring Accounts Receivable without Recourse

PROBLEM: ABJ, Inc. factors $480,000 of its accounts receivable to S&E Lawrence Factors without recourse. The transaction qualifies as a sale. S&E Lawrence charges a fee equal to 8% of the receivables factored and holds back an additional 3% as security. S&E Lawrence Factors will return the hold back to ABJ in full when it collects the receivables. What is ABJ Inc.'s journal entry to record the transaction?

SOLUTION: ABJ removes $480,000 of accounts receivable from the books. ABJ receives cash proceeds of $427,200 on the sale computed as follows:

Accounts receivable	$480,000
Factoring fee ($480,000 × 8%)	(38,400)
Holdback ($480,000 × 3%)	(14,400)
Cash proceeds from factor	$ 427,200

ABJ records the holdback as an asset and records the factoring fee charge as a loss on the sale of receivables. The journal entry is as follows:

Account	Current Year	
Cash	427,200	
Loss on Sale of Receivables	38,400	
Receivable from Factor	14,400	
Accounts Receivable		480,000

Factoring with Recourse. When a seller transfers receivables **with recourse**, the seller guarantees that all or part of the receivables transferred will be collected. The selling company assumes the risk of uncollectability and resulting credit losses. The seller separately recognizes any liability created by the guarantee by recording a recourse liability along with an additional estimated loss for possible losses due to the guarantee. The seller estimates the amount of the recourse liability as the amount that the buying company is not expected to collect. Example 9.11 provides an example of accounting for a factoring with recourse.

EXAMPLE 9.11

Factoring Accounts Receivable with Recourse

PROBLEM: ABJ, Inc. factors $480,000 of its accounts receivable to S&E Lawrence Factors with recourse. The transaction qualifies as a sale. S&E Lawrence charges a fee equal to 6% of the receivables factored and holds back an additional 3% as security. S&E Lawrence Factors will return the hold back to ABJ when it collects the receivables. In addition, the fair value of the recourse liability is estimated at $10,000. What is ABJ, Inc.'s journal entry to record the transaction?

Continued

SOLUTION: ABJ must remove accounts receivable of $480,000 from the books. ABJ will also record the $436,800 cash proceeds received on the sale, computed as follows:

Accounts receivable	$480,000
Factoring fee ($480,000 × 6%)	(28,800)
Hold back ($480,000 × 3%)	(14,400)
Cash collected	$436,800

ABJ records the $14,400 hold back as an asset, records the $10,000 recourse obligation as a liability, and increases the loss on the sale by this same amount. Thus, the total loss is the $28,800 factoring fee plus the $10,000 obligation. The journal entry follows:

Account	Current Year	
Cash	436,800	
Loss on Sale of Receivables ($28,800 Fee + $10,000 Recourse Obligation)	38,800	
Receivable from Factor	14,400	
Recourse Obligation		10,000
Accounts Receivable		480,000

Factoring Accounts Receivable: IFRS. IFRS differs from U.S. GAAP by determining whether a factoring arrangement is a sale based on the transfer of contractual rights to the cash flows.[15] When a company transfers the contractual rights to receive the cash flows from the receivables, it assesses whether it has also transferred all the risks and rewards of ownership. If it has, then the transfer is a sale. If the seller retains substantial risks and rewards of owning the receivable, he still may have a sale, but only if he meets three conditions. A company retaining the contractual rights to receive the cash flows must meet three conditions for the transfer to be considered a sale:

1. The company does not have to pay the factor unless it collects the receivables.
2. The company cannot use the receivables as collateral for other transactions.
3. The company has to pay the factor the cash it collects without a long delay.

Exhibit 9.6 provides a flowchart of the sale versus secured borrowing decision under IFRS. Observe that under U.S. GAAP, isolating the receivables and giving up effective control over the

EXHIBIT 9.6 Sales versus Secured Borrowing under IFRS

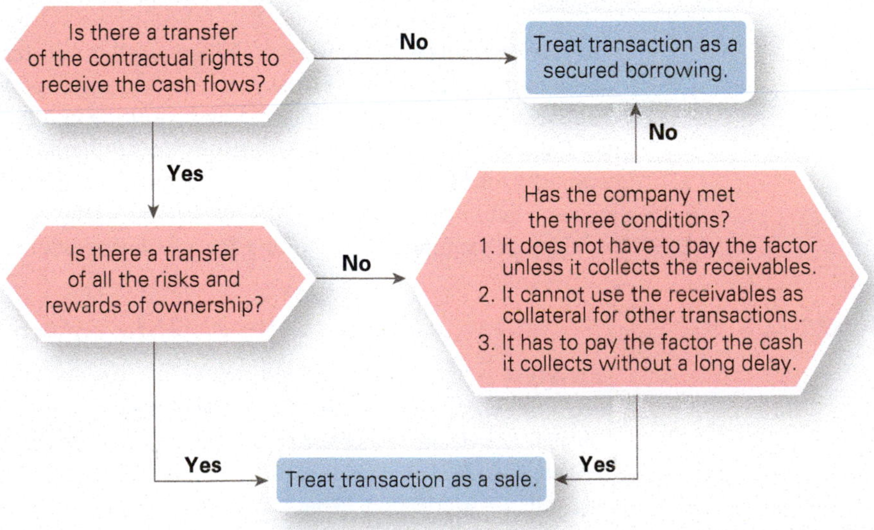

[15] IFRS Requirements for derecognition of financial assets are in Section 3.2 of IASB, *International Financial Reporting Standard 9*, "Financial Instruments" (London, UK: International Accounting Standards Board, 2014, Revised).

receivables are both required for a sale as illustrated in Exhibit 9.5. However, under IFRS, receivables do not have to be isolated and companies do not have to give up effective control as long as they pay out any cash collected on a timely basis to the factor.

Although U.S. GAAP and IFRS use somewhat different criteria in determining whether the transfer is a sale, both standards often arrive at the same conclusion.

At December 31, 2016, ***Fiat Chrysler Automobiles N.V.***, a European car manufacturer and IFRS reporter, had transferred without recourse and derecognized €6,573 million of receivables. ***Fiat Chrysler*** indicates that even though some transactions may be legally viewed as a sale of receivables, it does not substantially transfer the risks and rewards associated with the receivables because of the significant loss guarantees and its continuing exposure. As such, these transactions do not meet the conditions required to record these transactions as sales. The carrying amount of ***Fiat Chrysler's*** transferred receivables not derecognized and the related liabilities total €410 million.[16]

Securitizations

The term **securitization** refers to a financing technique that involves taking many separate, and oftentimes diverse, financial assets and combining them into a single pool or bundle. Investors then purchase interests in the pool of assets rather than buying an individual asset or group of assets.[17]

Securitization allows a company to engage in a collateralized borrowing arrangement with a large number of lenders by issuing debt obligations or equity shares rather than attempting to sell each asset. Securitization also allows a company to obtain financing at a lower cost of borrowing. The pooling of many individual assets diversifies the default risk from each individual asset, thereby enhancing an investor's ability to predict the investment's future cash flows, lowering risk, and thereby lowering the required rate of return.

These benefits are possible because a company can select high-quality assets to collateralize the notes or equity shares. For example, a major telecommunications company can bundle the cell phone accounts of subscribers with the highest credit rating to use as collateral for a series of notes payable. The investors purchasing the notes can rely on the collection of the cell phone receivables to pay interest and cover the note principal at maturity. Rather than attempting to sell the receivables to a single factor, the company has effectively sold the receivables to multiple investors, lowering the cost and the concentration of risk. A company can also bundle diverse types of receivables into the securitization transaction. For example, the credit affiliate of an automobile manufacturer can bundle auto loans and lease receivables as security for a note payable.

Securitization can also have drawbacks. Potential investors do not always have detailed knowledge on the original borrowers or their risk of default. Therefore, a company may have to offer the securities at a lower price. Even when a company can securitize its receivables, there is still the risk of non-collection. For example, securitization of mortgage receivables from borrowers with poor credit histories and higher risks of default led to the subprime mortgage crisis of 2007–2010.

Exhibit 9.7 summarizes ways in which a company can use accounts receivable to provide financing.

EXHIBIT 9.7 Financing with Accounts Receivable

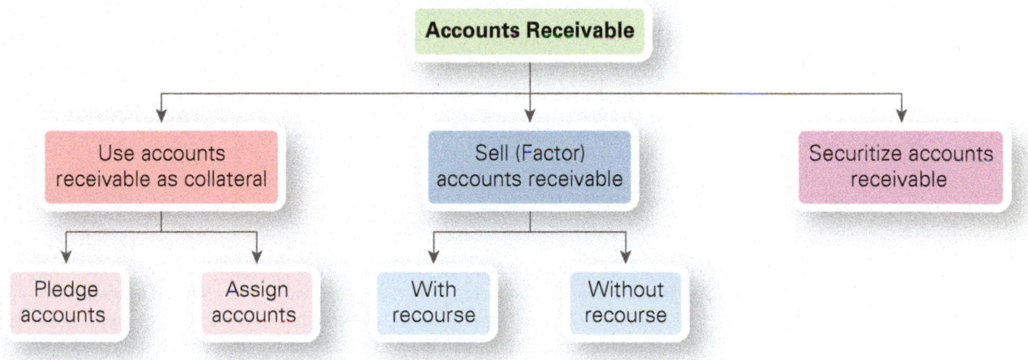

[16]Source: Fiat Chrysler Automobiles N.V.'s 2016 financial statements. https://www.fcagroup.com/en-US/investor_relations/financial_information_reports/annual_reports/annual_reports/FCA_2016_Annual_Report.pdf

[17]Securitized transactions are typically covered in much greater depth in advanced accounting courses.

6 Describe accounting for short-term notes receivable when issued and after issuance.

Accounting for Short-Term Notes Receivable

We introduce the key features of *notes receivable* and review the accounting methods used to record notes receivable, which depend on whether the stated interest rate is at or below the market interest rate.[18]

Basic Features of Notes Receivable

A **note receivable** is a formal, written promise to receive a fixed sum of money at a specified date (or dates) in the future, usually with a *stated interest rate*. The fixed sum of money that will be received at a specified date in the future is the **face value** of the note receivable. Notes receivable are classified as current or noncurrent on the balance sheet based on the expected collection date. Notes originate from either trade or *nontrade* transactions. **Nontrade notes receivable** include loans made to officers or employees and special financing arrangements with customers or vendors. Notes receivable can be *interest bearing* or *non-interest bearing*—but all notes include an interest element. The holder of an **interest-bearing note** receives periodic interest over the loan term. Conversely, the holder of a **non-interest-bearing note** does not receive periodic interest over the term of the note.

When a company accepts a note in exchange for goods and services, the note may have a *stated rate* of interest, may not specify an interest rate, or may have a *stated rate* of interest that is significantly different than the current *market rate*. The **stated rate** is the interest rate that the holder of the note will receive and is expressed as an annual rate. The **market rate** is the interest rate on a similar investment in the market. Regardless of the note's stated interest rate, companies always report the note receivable at the present value of the future cash flows discounted at the market rate on the balance sheet. Similarly, if the note does not specify an interest rate, the note receivable is reported at the present value of the future cash flows discounted at the market rate. Interest is recorded on the note over its life by the amortization of a discount.[19]

Next, we present the accounting for a note receivable with a stated interest rate equal to the market interest rate. Then, we discuss accounting for a note with a stated interest rate that is below the market interest rate.

Stated Interest Rate Equal to the Market Rate

When short-term notes are interest bearing at the current market rate of interest when issued, the face amount of the note is the same as its present value. In this case, the company records the note at its face value and interest accrues over the life of the note as illustrated in Example 9.12.

EXAMPLE 9.12

Note's Stated Rate Equals the Market Rate

PROBLEM: Fitzgerald Associates develops custom computer systems for auto dealers. On March 1, 2018, Fitzgerald installed a $1,200,000 sales and service system for Mel's Auto Mall. Fitzgerald agreed to accept a 4-month, 7% note with interest due at maturity, June 30, 2018. The current market rate is 7%. Fitzgerald prepares financial statements at the end of every calendar quarter. Prepare all journal entries necessary over the term of the note for Fitzgerald.

SOLUTION: Fitzgerald records sales revenue on the date it installs the computer system and it is fully functional. Therefore, the company records the March 1 sale as follows:

Account	***March 1, 2018***	
Notes Receivable	1,200,000	
Sales Revenue		1,200,000

[18] In this chapter, we discuss only notes receivable that are used in operations and are usually short term. Commonly, companies hold long-term notes as investments. Accounting for these notes requires the use of time value money concepts and amortization tables. We provide a detailed discussion of this topic in Chapter 16, Investing Assets.

[19] Management must assess notes receivable for potential uncollectible notes by following the same procedures used for accounts receivable. Firms may also need to record an impairment of notes receivable or report them at fair value using the fair value option. We address both of these issues in a later chapter.

Fitzgerald accrues interest on the note as of March 31 for the quarterly financial statements by recording interest of $7,000 for the 1 month that the note was outstanding (i.e., $1,200,000 × 7% × 1/12).

Account	March 31, 2018	
Interest Receivable	7,000	
Interest Revenue		7,000

When the note is due on June 30, 2018, Fitzgerald will receive four full months' interest. Therefore, the interest received at maturity is $28,000 (i.e., $1,200,000 × 7% × 4/12). Fitzgerald previously recorded $7,000 interest revenue for 1 month with the balance of $21,000 of interest revenue to be recognized this calendar quarter (i.e., $1,200,000 × 7% × 3/12). Fitzgerald collects a total amount of $1,228,000 from Mel's. Fitzgerald's entry to record the collection of the note plus accrued interest on June 30, 2018, follows.

Account	June 30, 2018	
Cash	1,228,000	
Interest Receivable		7,000
Interest Revenue		21,000
Note Receivable		1,200,000

No Stated Interest Rate or Stated Interest Rate Less Than the Market Rate

When there is no interest rate stated or the stated interest rate is less than the market interest rate, the face value of a note receivable no longer provides a valid measure of its present value. In this case, a company records the note at its present value rather than its face value. There are two approaches to measure present value:

- If a company receives the note in exchange for goods or services, assume that the note's present value is the fair value of the goods or services provided. Fair value estimates can be based on the value of comparable goods and services or the market value of the note if it is traded.
- If the company cannot determine the fair value of the goods or services, compute present value as the value of the note discounted at the market rate of interest. Here the market rate of interest is known as the imputed rate of interest.

The difference between the face value of the note and the fair value of the goods and services provided or the present value of the note is a **discount,** which represents the deferred interest revenue to be earned over the note's life. The firm initially records deferred interest revenue as a discount on notes receivable (a contra-asset account) and then amortizes the amount to interest revenue over the loan term. Example 9.13 shows accounting for a note with no stated interest rate.

EXAMPLE 9.13

Note with No Stated Interest Rate

PROBLEM: Fitzgerald Associates develops custom computer systems for auto dealers. On June 1, 2018, Fitzgerald installed a $975,000 sales and service system for Hoola Autos. Fitzgerald agreed to accept a $1,000,000, 3-month, non-interest-bearing note due on September 1, 2018. Fitzgerald prepares financial statements at the end of every calendar year. Prepare all journal entries necessary for the term of the note for Fitzgerald.

Continued

SOLUTION: Although the face value of the note is $1,000,000, its present value is less because the amount is not due for 3 months. The system Fitzgerald installed for Hoola Autos has a current selling price of $975,000. As a result, the company records the note receivable at $975,000, the fair value of the asset sold. Specifically, Fitzgerald records notes receivable of $1,000,000 and a discount on notes receivable (contra asset) of $25,000.

Account	June 1, 2018	
Notes Receivable	1,000,000	
Discount on Notes Receivable		25,000
Sales Revenue		975,000

On September 1, 2018, Fitzgerald records the collection of the note and recognizes interest revenue by amortizing the deferred interest revenue to income.

Account	September 1, 2018	
Cash	1,000,000	
Notes Receivable		1,000,000

Account	September 1, 2018	
Discount on Notes Receivable	25,000	
Interest Revenue		25,000

In this example, Fitzgerald collected the note before the end of its fiscal year. However, if the note is still outstanding when the company prepares financial statements, it must record interest on the loan as shown in Example 9.14.

EXAMPLE 9.14 Note with No Stated Interest and Discount Amortization

PROBLEM: Fitzgerald Associates develops custom computer systems for auto dealers. On November 1, 2018, Fitzgerald installed a $975,000 sales and service system for Hoola Autos. Fitzgerald agreed to accept a $1 million 3-month, non-interest-bearing note due on February 1, 2019. Fitzgerald prepares financial statements at the end of every calendar year. Prepare all journal entries necessary for the term of the note for Fitzgerald.

SOLUTION: Although the face value of the note is $1,000,000, its present value is less because the amount is not due for 3 months. The system Fitzgerald installed for Hoola Autos has a current selling price of $975,000. As a result, the company records the note receivable at $975,000, the fair value of the asset sold. Specifically, Fitzgerald records notes receivable of $1,000,000 and a discount on notes receivable (contra asset) of $25,000.

Account	November 1, 2018	
Notes Receivable	1,000,000	
Discount on Notes Receivable		25,000
Sales Revenue		975,000

On December 31, 2018, Fitzgerald must record 2 months of interest revenue. Total interest revenue will be $25,000 for 3 months, so it will record two-thirds of the total, or $16,667 ($25,000 × 2/3).

Account	December 31, 2018	
Discount on Notes Receivable	16,667	
Interest Revenue		16,667

On February 1, 2019, Fitzgerald records the collection of the note and records interest revenue by amortizing the remaining $8,333 of deferred interest revenue to income ($25,000 × 1/3).

Account	February 1, 2019	
Cash	1,000,000	
Notes Receivable		1,000,000
Discount on Notes Receivable	8,333	
Interest Revenue		8,333

Financing with Notes Receivable. In a manner similar to accounts receivable, companies can sell notes receivable to secure immediate cash. A company sells a note receivable by transferring it to another party before the maturity date. Selling a note receivable is typically referred to as **discounting.** The accounting approach for selling or discounting a note receivable is similar to factoring accounts receivable as illustrated in Example 9.15. If the conditions are met to consider the transaction a sale, the company removes the receivable from the books and reports a gain or loss. One difference in accounting for the sale of a note receivable versus an account receivable is that notes receivable earn interest. Therefore, the company must accrue any interest that has been earned but not received as of the time the note is sold.

EXAMPLE 9.15

Discounting Notes Receivable

PROBLEM: On January 1, Horton's Horse Farms (HHF) sold horses in exchange for a 6-month note with an 8% interest rate. On April 1, HHF discounted the $320,000 note to R&T Factors without recourse. The transaction qualifies as a sale. R&T charges a 10% discount rate. What is HHF's journal entry to record the transaction?

SOLUTION: HHF first must record the interest that has accrued as of April 1 ($320,000 × 8% × 3/12).

Account	April 1	
Interest Receivable	6,400	
Interest Revenue		6,400

HHF then removes the $320,000 note receivable from the books. HHF receives cash proceeds of $324,480 on the sale, computed as follows:

Note receivable	$320,000
Interest received at maturity ($320,000 × 8% × 6/12)	12,800
Cash received at maturity	332,800
Discount fee ($332,800 × 10% × 3/12)	(8,320)
Cash proceeds from factor	$324,480

HHF removes the note and interest receivable from its books and records the cash proceeds and the loss. The $1,920 loss is the difference between the cash received and the value of the assets removed from the books: the note receivable and the interest receivable. The journal entry is as follows:

Account	April 1	
Cash	324,480	
Loss on Sale of Receivables	1,920	
Interest Receivable		6,400
Note Receivable		320,000

7 Explain the required disclosures for accounts and notes receivable.

Disclosures for Accounts Receivable and Notes Receivable

Companies disclose a summary of significant accounting policies relating to accounts receivable and notes receivable in the notes to the financial statements. The disclosures for receivables include accounting policies and the methodology used to estimate the allowance for uncollectible accounts, such as a description of the elements that influence management's judgment and credit risk. Companies also provide a description of the policy for writing off uncollectible receivables.

Companies commonly report net receivables on the balance sheet and disclose gross receivables and the allowance for uncollectible accounts in the notes to the financial statements. For the allowance, companies disclose activity during the year such as:

1. The allowance balance at the beginning and end of each period
2. Current-period bad debt expense
3. Write-offs charged against the allowance
4. Recoveries of amounts previously written-off

When a company has pledged, assigned, or factored any accounts receivable, it must provide detailed disclosures of the amounts, terms, and collateral. Exhibit 9.8 provides an example of ***Kellogg Company's*** accounts receivable disclosures. ***Kellogg*** provides a table showing all its accounts receivables, composed primarily of trade receivables, of $1,106 million and $1,169 million in fiscal 2016 and 2015, respectively. Another table provides the changes from the beginning balance to the ending balance for the allowance for doubtful accounts.

EXHIBIT 9.8 Accounts Receivable Disclosures, ***Kellogg Company***, Financial Statements, December 31, 2016

NOTE 1: Accounting Policies

Accounts Receivable

Accounts receivable consists principally of trade receivables, which are recorded at the invoiced amount, net of allowances for doubtful accounts and prompt payment discounts. Trade receivables do not bear interest. The allowance for doubtful accounts represents management's estimate of the amount of probable credit losses in existing accounts receivable, as determined from a review of past due balances and other specific account data. Account balances are written off against the allowance when management determines the receivable is uncollectible. As of year-end 2016 and 2015, the Company's off-balance sheet credit exposure related to its customers was insignificant.

NOTE 17

SUPPLEMENTAL FINANCIAL STATEMENT DATA

Consolidated Balance Sheet (millions)	**2016**	**2015**
Trade receivables	$ 1,106	$ 1,169
Allowance for doubtful accounts	(8)	(8)
Refundable income taxes	24	27
Other receivables	109	156
Accounts receivable, net	$ 1,231	$1,344

Allowance for doubtful accounts (millions)	**2016**	**2015**	**2014**
Balance at beginning of year	$ 8	$ 7	$ 5
Additions charged to expense	9	4	6
Doubtful accounts charged to reserve	(9)	(3)	(4)
Balance at end of year	$ 8	$ 8	$ 7

Source: Kellogg Company, Annual Report, December 2016. http://investor.kelloggs.com/~/media/Files/K/Kellogg-IR/Annual%20Reports/kellogg-2016-ar-10-k.PDFFinancial Statement Analysis

FINANCIAL STATEMENT ANALYSIS

Operating Cycle Analysis

Financial statement users consider cash management critical to a company's operations and ability to maintain and grow operations. Analyzing a company's cash management involves answering questions such as:

- How long does it take to collect cash?
- How long does it take to convert inventory to cash?
- How long does it take to make payments?
- Does the company have sufficient cash, or does it need additional financing?

Operating Cycle

The **operating cycle** is the length of time it takes a company to generate cash from its operations, thereby providing answers to the questions of how long it takes a company to collect cash and how long it takes to convert inventory to cash. The following diagram illustrates the operating cycle:

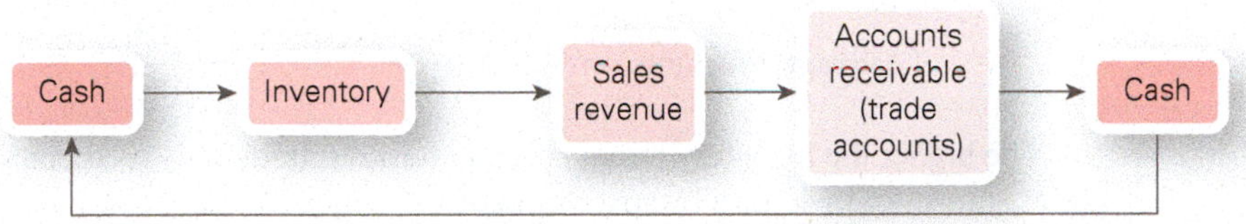

We can use basic financial statement ratios to determine the length of a company's operating cycle. The operating cycle is computed as the number of days between when inventory is acquired and cash is collected on the sale of the inventory:

$$\text{Operating Cycle} = \text{Days Sales Outstanding} + \text{Days Inventory on Hand} \tag{9.1}$$

Financial analysts use the following ratios to compute a company's operating cycle: days sales outstanding and days inventory on hand.

Days Sales Outstanding

To determine the number of days that accounts receivable are outstanding, we start by computing the *accounts receivable turnover ratio*. The **accounts receivable turnover ratio** indicates how many times per year the firm goes from a full receivable balance to complete collection.

$$\text{Accounts Receivable Turnover Ratio} = \frac{\text{Credit Sales}}{\text{Average Accounts Receivable}} \tag{9.2}$$

where

$$\text{Average Accounts Receivable} = \frac{\text{Beginning Accounts Receivable} + \text{Ending Accounts Receivable}}{2} \tag{9.3}$$

The higher the accounts receivable turnover ratio, the more frequently a company collects its receivables. For example, an accounts receivable turnover ratio of 12.0 indicates that a company turns over its receivables 12 times a year, or about once every month. Consider a manufacturer that extends credit and expects payment in 30 days. An accounts receivable turnover ratio of 12.0 would be expected given that there are 12 months in a year and payment is due within 30 days.

The accounts receivable turnover ratio can be used to determine the expected number of days it takes to collect accounts receivable balances. The **days sales outstanding** is the number of days a company takes to collect its receivables from customers. It is calculated by dividing the number of days in a year, 365, by the number of times accounts receivable turns in a year:

$$\text{Days Sales Outstanding} = \frac{365}{\text{Accounts Receivable Turnover Ratio}} \quad (9.4)$$

This ratio is also called the number of days sales in accounts receivable or the collection interval. If a manufacturer has an accounts receivable turnover of 12.0, its days sales outstanding would be 30.4 days, or about a month.

Days Inventory Is on Hand

To estimate the number of days inventory is on hand, we begin by computing the *inventory turnover ratio*. The **inventory turnover ratio** indicates how many times per year the firm goes from a full inventory balance to selling all its inventory:

$$\text{Inventory Turnover Ratio} = \frac{\text{Cost of Goods Sold}}{\text{Average Inventory}} \quad (9.5)$$

$$\text{Average Inventory} = \frac{\text{Beginning Inventory} + \text{Ending Inventory}}{2} \quad (9.6)$$

The higher the inventory turnover ratio, the more frequently a company sells out its inventory. For example, an inventory turnover ratio of 4.0 indicates that a company turns over its inventory every quarter. Consider a clothing store that sells clothes for each season—winter, spring, summer, and fall. An inventory turnover ratio of 4.0 would be expected given the four seasons of clothing the store sells.

The inventory turnover ratio can be used to determine the expected number of days it takes a company to sell inventory. The **days inventory on hand** is the number of days that the company takes to sell its inventory; it is calculated by dividing the number of days in a year, 365, by the number of times that inventory turns over in a year.

$$\text{Days Inventory on Hand} = \frac{365}{\text{Inventory Turnover Ratio}} \quad (9.7)$$

This ratio is sometimes called the number of days inventory held or the holding interval.

Cash Operating Cycle

To better understand a company's cash needs, the *cash operating cycle* assists a financial analyst in determining a company's ability to pay its suppliers when due. The **cash operating cycle** is the period of time it takes a company to pay its suppliers less the time a company takes to collect cash from sales. The cash operating cycle can help answer the question of whether a company has sufficient cash or needs additional financing. The cash operating cycle is also called the firm's cash-to-cash cycle or cash conversion cycle. The following diagram illustrates the cash operating cycle:

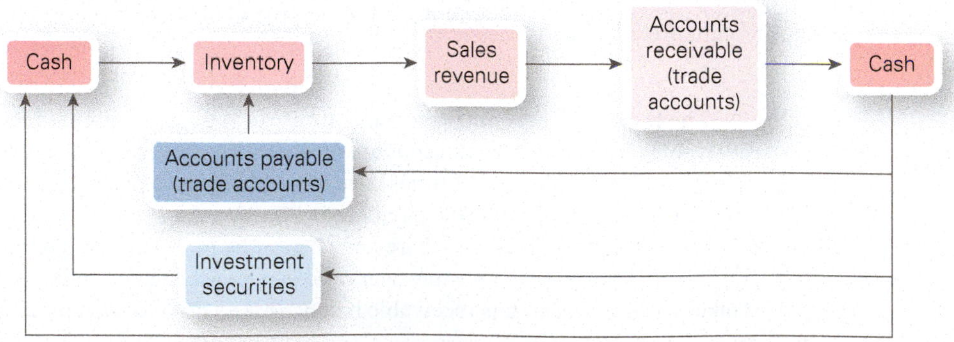

Financial Statement Analysis, continued

Now we need to consider the amount of time the company's suppliers allow it to repay accounts payable. If the accounts payable must be paid before cash is collected, the company may need to borrow or liquidate investments in order to pay the balance due.

The cash operating cycle is computed as:

$$\text{Cash Operating Cycle} = \text{Days Accounts Payable Outstanding} - \text{Operating Cycle} \quad (9.8)$$

A positive cash operating cycle suggests that a company does not need to obtain additional financing to meet its cash needs. That is, excess cash can be used to pay off short-term lines of credit or re-invest in the business. The company is collecting cash sooner than it needs to pay its suppliers. A negative cash operating cycle means a company needs to obtain additional financing. It is collecting cash more slowly than it needs to pay its suppliers. A negative cash operating cycle can indicate that a company has poor cash management or that it is growing. For example, a company with a lenient credit-extension policy could take longer to collect from its customers than to pay its suppliers. Alternatively, if a company is growing, it is likely purchasing more inventory from its suppliers, expecting future sales. Next, we explain the computation of days accounts payable outstanding.[20]

Days Accounts Payable Outstanding

To estimate the number of days that accounts payable are outstanding, first compute the *accounts payable turnover ratio*. The **accounts payable turnover ratio** indicates the number of times per year a company goes from full accounts payable balances to full repayment:

$$\text{Accounts Payable Turnover Ratio} = \frac{\text{Production or Purchases}}{\text{Average Accounts Payable}} \quad (9.9)$$

When we assume that a company's beginning inventory and ending inventory are approximately the same each year, cost of goods sold can be used as a proxy for purchases or production as illustrated by the following example:

Beginning inventory	$ 1,000
Add: Purchases or production	***600***
Cost of goods available for sale	$ 1,600
Less: Ending inventory	(1,000)
Cost of goods sold	**$ 600**

Companies typically use the following ratio to measure accounts payable turnover:

$$\text{Accounts Payable Turnover Ratio} = \frac{\text{Cost of Goods Sold}}{\text{Average Accounts Payable}} \quad (9.10)$$

$$\text{Average Accounts Payable} = \frac{\text{Beginning Accounts Payable} + \text{Ending Accounts Payable}}{2} \quad (9.11)$$

A higher accounts payable turnover ratio indicates that a company is paying off its payables frequently. For example, a company with an accounts payable turnover ratio of 12 pays its suppliers sooner than a company with an accounts payable turnover ratio of 6.

The accounts payable turnover ratio can be used to determine the expected number of days it takes to pay suppliers. The **days accounts payable outstanding**, the number of days a company takes to pay its suppliers, is calculated by dividing the number of days in a year, 365, by the number of times accounts payable turns over in a year:

$$\text{Days Accounts Payable Outstanding} = \frac{365}{\text{Accounts Payable Turnover Ratio}} \quad (9.12)$$

[20] A further refinement is to examine the days payable for accrued liabilities and related expenses.

Financial Statement Analysis, continued

Example 9.16 illustrates computations for operating cycle and cash operating cycle.

EXAMPLE 9.16 Operating Cycle and Cash Operating Cycle

PROBLEM: The following information is from the financial statements of ***L'Oréal,*** the French beauty products company.

Balance Sheet Information

At December 31 (in million euros)	2016	2015	2014
Accounts Receivable	€3,941.8	€3,627.7	€3,297.8
Inventories	2,698.6	2,440.7	2,262.9
Accounts Payable	4,135.3	3,929.0	3,452.8

Income Statement Information

For the Year	2016	2015	2014
Sales (all credit)	€25,837.1	€25,257.4	€22,532.0
Cost of Goods Sold	7,341.7	7,277.4	€6,500.7

Source: L'Oreal Group, Annual Report, December 2016. http://www.loreal-finance.com/_docs/0000000136/LOreal_2016_Annual_Report.pdf

Use ***L'Oréal's*** financial information to answer the following questions:

a. What is ***L'Oréal's*** operating cycle (in days) in 2016 and 2015? Assume that all sales are on credit.

b. What is ***L'Oréal's*** cash operating cycle (in days) in 2016 and 2015?

c. Comment on the change in ***L'Oréal's*** cash operating cycle in 2016 and 2015.

SOLUTIONS:

a. ***L'Oréal's*** operating cycle was 181.06 days and 168.19 days in 2016 and 2015, respectively. In 2016, the company's time from holding inventory to collecting cash increased by 12.87 days (181.06 − 168.19).

b. ***L'Oréal's*** cash operating cycle was 19.49 days and 17.09 days in 2016 and 2015, respectively. These results imply that the company is in a positive cash position. That is, ***L'Oréal*** is collecting cash faster than it is paying its suppliers. A positive cash operating cycle suggests that the company does not need to obtain additional financing to meet its cash needs.

c. The cash operating cycle increased by 2.4 days (19.49 − 17.09) in 2016. The increase is primarily due to an increase in the operating cycle of 12.87 days (181.06 − 168.19). The operating cycle increased due to increases in both days sales outstanding of 3.37 days (53.44 − 50.07) and days inventory on hand of 9.5 days (127.62 − 118.12). The increase in the cash operating cycle implies that the company was generating cash faster than paying cash to suppliers in 2016 when compared to 2015. We present the computations in the following table.

Financial Statement Analysis, continued

Components (In millions of euros)	2016	2015
Accounts Receivable Turnover Ratio $= \frac{\text{Credit Sales}}{\text{Average Accounts Receivable}}$	$6.83 = \frac{€25{,}837.1}{€3{,}784.8}$	$7.29 = \frac{€25{,}257.4}{€3{,}462.8}$
Average Accounts Receivable $= \frac{(\text{Beginning Accounts Receivable} + \text{Ending Accounts Receivable})}{2}$	$€3{,}784.8 = \frac{(€3{,}627.7 + €3{,}941.8)}{2}$	$€3{,}462.8 = \frac{(€3{,}297.8 + €3{,}627.7)}{2}$
Days Sales Outstanding $= \frac{365}{\text{Accounts Receivable Turnover Ratio}}$	$53.44 = \frac{365}{6.83}$	$50.07 = \frac{365}{7.29}$
Inventory Turnover Ratio $= \frac{\text{Cost of Goods Sold}}{\text{Average Inventory}}$	$2.86 = \frac{€7{,}341.7}{€2{,}569.7}$	$3.09 = \frac{€7{,}277.4}{€2{,}351.8}$
Average Inventory $= \frac{(\text{Beginning Inventory} + \text{Ending Inventory})}{2}$	$€2{,}569.7 = \frac{(€2{,}440.7 + €2{,}698.6)}{2}$	$€2{,}351.8 = \frac{(€2{,}440.7 + €2{,}262.9)}{2}$
Days Inventory on Hand $= \frac{365}{\text{Inventory Turnover Ratio}}$	$127.62 = \frac{365}{2.86}$	$118.12 = \frac{365}{3.09}$
Accounts Payable Turnover Ratio $= \frac{\text{Cost of Goods Sold}}{\text{Average Accounts Payable}}$	$1.82 = \frac{€7{,}341.7}{€4{,}032.2}$	$1.97 = \frac{€7{,}277.4}{€3{,}690.9}$
Average Accounts Payable $= \frac{(\text{Beginning Accounts Payable} + \text{Ending Accounts Payable})}{2}$	$€4{,}032.2 = \frac{(€3{,}929.0 + €4{,}135.3)}{2}$	$€3{,}690.9 = \frac{(€3{,}452.8 + €3{,}929.0)}{2}$
Days Accounts Payable Outstanding $= \frac{365}{\text{Accounts Payable Turnover Ratio}}$	$200.55 = \frac{365}{1.82}$	$185.28 = \frac{365}{1.97}$
Operating Cycle = Days Sales Outstanding + Days Inventory on Hand	181.06 = 53.44 + 127.62	168.19 = 50.07 + 118.12
Cash Operating Cycle = Days Accounts Payable Outstanding − Operating Cycle	19.49 = 200.55 − 181.06	17.09 = 185.28 − 168.19

Interview

CHIEF AUDIT OFFICER, MERCK & CO. »

Dalton Smart

Dalton Smart is Chief Audit Officer for Merck & Co., a leading U.S. pharmaceutical company. He leads the company's financial, business integrity assurance and information technology audits, and assurance services.

1 How do industry-specific factors come into play in managing Merck's cash and accounts receivable?

Merck is a major international pharmaceutical company that sells its products through pharmaceutical distributors to different channels, including government, public and private health care institutions, and well-established retail pharmacy chains. So, we must look beyond the distributor to the type of end user to evaluate the conversion of receivables to cash. Although they may pay slowly, governments eventually pay their bills; this reliability reduces our credit risk dramatically. Also, pharmaceuticals are a cash-flow-rich industry in contrast to industries such as manufacturing. A manufacturer selling to hundreds or thousands of small customers faces different credit risk worries than Merck, whose customers are large and more centralized. Merck is less concerned about the ability to pay than the timing of receivables.

2 What significant judgments does Merck use in granting credit?

We start with the type of customer and the quality of information we receive and then assess the potential customer's credit profile, credit rating, and financial statements. We look differently at government-related payors who pay in due course, such as nationalized health care systems, than we do emerging market customers. It's challenging to get good quality data from emerging market customers to assess credit risk. We rely on various sources to determine the speed at which inventory is being consumed so that we record revenue at a speed consistent with the sales of products to end customers. We also watch such factors as days' sales outstanding (DSO) and inventory levels where rising trends may indicate a longer period to receive cash. Finally, we consider market size, growth rates, and our market growth relative to that of our peers.

3 What are the primary factors that Merck considers when estimating the amount needed in the allowance for bad debts?

Consistent with GAAP, Merck applies the allowance method to account for bad debts. Using the allowance method allows us to record revenues and expenses in the same period incurred. There is an inherent risk that customers could default on a payment, so accounts receivable are recorded at their net realizable value. In each monthly accounting period, we calculate the receivable balance and estimate the allowance for bad debt expense. We closely evaluate both a customer's ability to pay, based on financial metrics, and intent to pay, demonstrated through payment history and maintenance of performance ratios. We look for any significant changes in customer circumstances and monitor multiple metrics such as receivable aging and turnover ratios and financial condition changes such as bankruptcy proceedings, litigation, and credit rating downgrades. Once we see gaps in a customer's payment history, we quickly analyze its ability to pay. Then, on a monthly basis, we examine bad debt expense and the number of write-offs as it relates to the overall reasonableness of the allowance for bad debts, adjusting as required.

4 What judgment factors does the company use to determine when an account should be written off?

In addition to analyzing ability and intent to pay, we focus on whether we have exhausted all collection efforts, if there are any disputed balances, and if other public information exists about the customer. Another important factor that comes into play is the type of customer. Merck sells mostly to wholesalers, who then sell to the health care industry's end customers—all with different speeds of receivables collection. We take the payment time frame into account, evaluating customers by type.

5 Does Merck sell receivables to secure immediate cash?

In certain markets, selling receivables works to Merck's advantage. We know that governmental institutions will eventually pay us, but we may want to collect now rather than wait. Our analysis of whether to sell receivables is a financial decision based on the rate we can receive for those receivables and our cost of capital.

Discussion Questions

1. Dalton Smart mentions that Merck monitors factors such as days sales outstanding (DSO) and inventory levels to assess its ability to collect cash quickly from a potential customer. Discuss the financial ratios that a firm can use to measure the time it will take to collect cash from a potential customer on average.
2. Why would a company be willing to sell its accounts receivable at a discounted amount (i.e., the amount received from the buyer is less than the recorded amount)?

Summary by Learning Objectives

Below we summarize the main points by learning objective. Throughout the chapter, we discuss the accounting and reporting of U.S. GAAP and IFRS side-by-side. The table below also highlights the major similarities and differences between the standards.

1 Define cash and cash equivalents and describe the accounting for restricted cash and compensating balances.

Summary	Similarities and Differences between U.S. GAAP and IFRS
Cash consists of coins, currency, and bank deposits as well as negotiable instruments such as checks and money orders. Cash equivalents are short-term, highly liquid investments with original maturities of 3 months or less. Companies report restricted cash and compensating balances separately from cash.	Similar under U.S. GAAP and IFRS.

2 Demonstrate the initial measurement and accounting for accounts receivable, including volume, trade, and sales discounts.

Summary	Similarities and Differences between U.S. GAAP and IFRS
Trade receivables are generally measured at the amount of the sale made. Trade discounts are reductions of the catalog or list price when a company sells to a reseller in the same industry. A volume discount reduces the list price for customers purchasing a large quantity of merchandise. Sales discounts are reductions in the cash received and sales for early payments. A company can use the most-likely-amount or expected-value method to record the receivable initially. • Under the most-likely-amount method, a company records the accounts receivable at the gross amount if it anticipates that the company will not take the discount and at the net amount if it anticipates that the customer will take the discount. • Under the expected-value method, the entity sums the probability-weighted amounts in a range of possible consideration amounts to arrive at the initial measurement of accounts receivable.	Similar under U.S. GAAP and IFRS.

3 Understand the subsequent measurement and accounting for accounts receivable, including establishing an allowance for uncollectible accounts.

Summary	Similarities and Differences between U.S. GAAP and IFRS
Companies report accounts receivable at their net realizable value (NRV), which is the estimated amount a company reasonably expects to collect from its customers. Uncollectible amounts are estimated and reported in the allowance for uncollectible accounts, a contra asset. Bad debt expense increases the allowance. Write-offs decrease the allowance.	Similar under U.S. GAAP and IFRS.

Summary by Learning Objectives, continued

4 Estimate an allowance for uncollectible accounts using the aging of receivables method and explain the accounting for write-offs and subsequent recoveries.

Summary	Similarities and Differences between U.S. GAAP and IFRS
The aging of receivables methods estimates the ending balance of the allowance of uncollectible accounts by dividing accounts receivable into categories by how long they have been past due. When a company determines that a specific account is uncollectible, it writes that account off by reducing accounts receivable and reducing the allowance. If a company subsequently collects a written-off account, it reverses the write-off and records the cash collection.	Similar under U.S. GAAP and IFRS.

5 Discuss the use of accounts receivable to generate immediate cash—including pledging or assigning, factoring receivables, and securitization—and demonstrate the accounting for these transactions.

Summary	Similarities and Differences between U.S. GAAP and IFRS
Pledged accounts receivable are collateral for a financing arrangement. Assigned accounts receivable are also collateral, but collection of the receivables is used to pay down the debt. Companies disclose the arrangements in financial statements. Factoring is the sale of accounts receivable. If the seller transfers the receivables without recourse, the buyer assumes the risk of uncollectible accounts and absorbs any credit losses. If the seller transfers the receivables with recourse, the risk of uncollectability and the resulting credit losses remain with the seller. Securitization refers to a financing technique that involves taking many separate, and often diverse, financial assets and combining them into a single pool or bundle.	➤ While there are some differences in wording, the treatment is generally similar under U.S. GAAP and IFRS except in determining whether a factoring arrangement is a sale. Under IFRS, when a company transfers the contractual rights to receive the cash flows from the receivables, it assesses whether it also transfers all the risks and rewards of ownership. If it has, then the transfer is a sale.

Summary by Learning Objectives, continued

6 Describe accounting for short-term notes receivable when issued and after issuance.

Summary	Similarities and Differences between U.S. GAAP and IFRS
A note receivable is a formal, written promise to receive a fixed sum of money at a specified date in the future, usually with a stated interest rate. To account for notes, identify the: • face value—fixed sum of money that will be received at a specified date in the future • stated rate—interest rate that the holder of the note will receive • market rate—interest rate on a similar investment in the market A company reports a note receivable at the present value of its future cash flows using the market interest rate. Interest is accrued on the note over its life, as appropriate. An interest-bearing note requires periodic interest payments over the loan term. A non-interest-bearing note does not require periodic interest payments over the term of the note. When the stated interest rate is equal to the market rate, the note is recorded at its face value and interest accrues over the life of the note. When the note has no stated rate or the stated interest rate is less than the market rate, two approaches are used to measure present value: a. If the note is in exchange for goods or services, the note's present value is the fair value of the goods or services provided. b. If the fair value of the goods or services cannot be determined, compute the present value as the value of the note discounted at the market rate of interest called the *imputed rate of interest*. Notes receivable can be sold, which is typically referred to as *discounting*. If the conditions are met to consider the transaction a sale, the receivable is removed from the books and a gain or loss is reported.	Similar under U.S. GAAP and IFRS.

7 Explain the required disclosures for accounts and notes receivable.

Summary	Similarities and Differences between U.S. GAAP and IFRS
Common disclosures include the total accounts receivable, the allowance, and changes in the allowance. Companies also describe the elements that influence management's judgment and credit risk when estimating the allowance. Other disclosures include the method used to estimate bad debts and the policy for writing off uncollectible receivables.	Similar under U.S. GAAP and IFRS.

MyLab Accounting

Go to **http://www.pearson.com/mylab/accounting** for the following Questions, Multiple-Choice Questions, Brief Exercises, Exercises, and Problems. They are available with immediate grading, explanations of correct and incorrect answers, and interactive media that acts as your own online tutor.

9 Short-Term Operating Assets: Cash and Receivables

Questions

1 **Q9-1.** What are cash equivalents?

1 **Q9-2.** Do companies always classify cash as a current asset on the balance sheet? Explain.

1 **Q9-3.** How is cash held as a compensating balance reported on the balance sheet?

2 **Q9-4.** Do accountants typically measure accounts receivable by discounting them for the time value of money? Explain.

4 **Q9-5.** Under the allowance method, will the actual write-off of an uncollectible account have a net effect on the financial statements? Explain.

4 **Q9-6.** How does an entity record a subsequent recovery of an account previously written off?

4 **Q9-7.** Does the aging of accounts receivable method of estimating the allowance for uncollectible accounts provide a more accurate measurement of net accounts receivable than bad debt expense? Explain.

5 **Q9-8.** What is the difference between pledging accounts receivable and assigning accounts receivable in a secured borrowing transaction?

5 **Q9-9.** How do companies account for receivables that are factored?

6 **Q9-10.** Is the face value of a note receivable exchanged for goods and services always equal to the sales value of the transaction? Explain.

6 **Q9-11.** What do firms use to record the sales value of a transaction when a note receivable has either an unreasonable rate of interest or no interest rate stated?

A **Q9-12.** Explain why a company must have highly effective internal controls over cash.

Multiple-Choice Questions

1 **MC9-1.** The following are held by YRT Corporation at December 31, Year 1:

Cash in checking account	$15,000
Petty cash	250
Check from customer dated 01/31/Year 2	350
3-month certificate of deposit, due 01/15/Year 2	40,000
12-month certificate of deposit, due 02/28/Year 2	36,000
Cash in bond sinking fund account	60,000

YRT Corporation classifies investments with original maturities of three months or less as cash equivalents. In its December 31, Year 1, balance sheet, what amount should YRT Corporation report as cash and cash equivalents?

a. $ 15,250 b. $ 55,250 c. $ 55,600 d. $ 151,250

3 4 **MC9-2.** Fernandez Company had an accounts receivable balance of $150,000 on December 31, Year 2, and $175,000 on December 31, Year 3. The company wrote off $40,000 of accounts receivable during Year 3. Sales for Year 3 totaled $600,000, and all sales were on account.

The amount collected from customers on accounts receivable during Year 3 was:

a. $575,000 b. $531,000 c. $600,000 d. $535,000

4 **MC9-3.** On its December 31, Year 2, balance sheet, Red Rock Candle Company reported accounts receivable of $855,000 net of an allowance for doubtful accounts of $45,000. On December 31, Year 3, Red Rock's balance sheet showed gross accounts receivable of $922,000, and Red Rock's income statement reported credit sales of $3,000,000. During the year, accounts receivable of $35,000 were written off and $18,000 were recovered.

Based on past experience, 5% of Red Rock's ending accounts receivable are uncollectible. How much should Red Rock report as bad debt expense on its Year 3 income statement?

a. $18,100 b. $35,000 c. $46,100 d. $150,000

5 **MC9-4.** Stanberry Company sold $500,000 of net accounts receivable to Cork Company for $450,000. The receivables were sold outright on a without recourse basis, and Stanberry Company retained no control over the receivables. The journal entries to record the sale would be which of the following?

a.	Cash	500,000	
	Accounts Receivable (net)		500,000
b.	Cash	450,000	
	Loss on Sale of Accounts Receivable	50,000	
	Accounts Receivable (net)		500,000
c.	Cash	450,000	
	Unrealized Loss on Sale of Accounts Receivable	50,000	
	Accounts Receivable (net)		500,000
d.	Cash	450,000	
	Due from Cork Company	50,000	
	Accounts Receivable (net)		500,000

6 **MC9-5.** On November 30, Year 1, Derin Corporation agreed with its customers to change accounts receivable to notes receivable in order to allow a longer payment period. The terms of the notes receivable are that the principal is due on November 30, Year 4, and the interest payments are due annually on November 30 until November 30, Year 4. Derin's customer has made all required payments to date. How should the notes receivable and accrued interest be classified on the balance sheet as of June 30, Year 3?

	Notes Receivable	Accrued Interest
a.	Current	Current
b.	Current	Noncurrent
c.	Noncurrent	Current
d.	Noncurrent	Noncurrent

7 **MC9-6.** Which of the following disclosures about accounts receivable are required?

I. Accounts receivable serving as collateral
II. The percentage used to calculate allowance for doubtful accounts
III. Total allowance for doubtful accounts

a. I only b. I and II c. I and III d. I, II, and III

Brief Exercises

2 **BE9-1. Volume Discounts.** Arc Company sells stone garden statues and offers a 6% discount to its high-volume customers. Sunny Garden Center purchased statues on account with a list price of $54,000 and received a volume discount of 6% of the purchase price. Give the journal entry to record this sale (ignore the effect on inventory and cost of goods sold).

2 **BE9-2. Sales Discounts, Most-Likely-Amount Method.** On July 1, Willette Corp. made a sale of $650,000 to Luc, Inc. on account. Terms of the sale were 2/10, n/30. Luc makes payment on July 9. Willette uses the most-likely-amount method and assumes that the customer will not take the discount when accounting for sales discounts. Ignore cost of goods sold and the reduction of inventory.

a. Prepare all Willette's journal entries.
b. What net sales does Willette report?

2 **BE9-3. Sales Discounts, Most-Likely-Amount Method.** On July 1, Willette Corp. made a sale of $650,000 to Luc, Inc. on account. Terms of the sale were 2/10, n/30. Luc makes payment on July 29. Willette uses the most-likely-amount method and assumes that the customer will not take the discount when accounting for sales discounts. Ignore cost of goods sold and the reduction of inventory.

a. Prepare all Willette's journal entries.
b. What net sales does Willette report?

2 **BE9-4. Sales Discounts, Expected-Value Method.** On July 1, Gillette Corp. made a sale of $650,000 to Huck, Inc. on account. Terms of the sale were 2/5, n/30. Huck makes payment on July 29. Gillette uses the expected-value method assuming that there is an 80% chance that the customer will not take the discount when accounting for sales discounts. Ignore cost of goods sold and the reduction of inventory.

a. Prepare all Gillette's journal entries.
b. What net sales does Gillette report?

2 **BE9-5. Sales Discounts, Most-Likely-Amount Method.** On July 1, Oura Corp. made a sale of $450,000 to Stratus, Inc. on account. Terms of the sale were 2/10, n/30. Stratus makes payment on July 9. Oura uses the most-likely-amount method and assumes that the customer will take the discount when accounting for sales discounts. Ignore cost of goods sold and the reduction of inventory.

a. Prepare all Oura's journal entries.
b. What net sales does Oura report?

2 **BE9-6. Sales Discounts, Most-Likely-Amount Method.** On July 1, Oura Corp. made a sale of $450,000 to Stratus, Inc. on account. Terms of the sale were 2/10, n/30. Stratus makes payment on July 29. Oura uses the most-likely-amount method and assumes that the customer will take the discount when accounting for sales discounts. Ignore cost of goods sold and the reduction of inventory.

a. Prepare all Oura's journal entries.
b. What net sales does Oura report?

4 **BE9-7. Allowance for Uncollectible Accounts, Write-Off.** Grotto Products, Inc. reported an opening balance in the allowance for doubtful accounts of $560,000. During the year, the company determined that a $23,000 receivable due from Zeer Company was uncollectible. Prepare the journal entry to write off the Zeer account assuming that Grotto uses the allowance method.

4 **BE9-8. Allowance for Uncollectible Accounts, Write-Off.** Vince Ventures Company reported an opening balance of $925,000 in its allowance for uncollectible accounts. Vince Ventures determined that a $57,500 account due from Ric Associates was uncollectible. Prepare the journal entry to write off the Ric account assuming that Vince Ventures uses the allowance method.

4 **BE9-9. Allowance for Uncollectible Accounts, Recovery.** Ciano Landscaping Company uses the allowance method to account for its uncollectible accounts. Three years ago, it wrote off a $40,000 account due from Haber Incorporated. Haber paid this account in full on June 30 of the current year. Prepare the journal entries required to record the recovery of the Haber account.

4 **BE9-10. Bad Debt Expense, Journal Entry.** Paul Anchor, Incorporated estimated that bad debt expense would equal 4% of the ending balance of accounts receivable for the current year. This year's ending balance of accounts receivable amounted to $2,500,000. There was a $69,000 credit balance in the allowance for uncollectible accounts prior to the year-end adjustment. Prepare the adjusting journal entry to record bad debt expense for the current year.

4 **BE9-11. Bad Debt Expense, Journal Entry.** Paul Anchor, Incorporated estimated that bad debt expense would equal 4% of the ending balance of accounts receivable for the current year. This year's ending balance of accounts receivable amounted to $2,500,000. There was a $69,000 debit balance in the allowance for uncollectible accounts prior to the year-end adjustment. Prepare the adjusting journal entry to record the bad debt provision for the current year.

4 **BE9-12. Bad Debt Expense, Aging of Accounts Receivable, Journal Entry.** Burl Brothers provided the following information regarding its accounts receivable at the beginning of the current year:

Accounts receivable	$1,320,000
Allowance for doubtful accounts	(320,000)
Net realizable value	$1,000,000

During the year, the company reported net credit sales of $21,000,000 of which it collected $9,900,000. The company wrote off $51,000 of actual bad debts for the year. Burl Brothers estimates the allowance for doubtful accounts at 4% of the ending accounts receivable balance. Prepare the journal entry to record the year-end adjusting entry for the bad debt expense.

4 **BE9-13. Bad Debt Expense, Aging of Accounts Receivable, Journal Entry.** Using the information provided in BE9-12, prepare the journal entry to record the year-end adjusting entry for the bad debt expense assuming that Burl Brothers recovered $12,000 of the $51,000 write-offs during the year.

4 **BE9-14. Allowance for Uncollectible Accounts, Aging of Accounts Receivable.** Banks Corporation estimates its annual provision for uncollectible accounts by analyzing the aged schedule of accounts receivable.

Banks Corporation: Aged Schedule of Accounts Receivable

		Past Due				
	Current	**1–30 Days**	**31–60 Days**	**61–90 Days**	**Over 90 Days**	**Total**
Totals	$237,000	$127,400	$110,000	$56,000	$19,600	$550,000

It is common industry practice to estimate an allowance for uncollectible accounts based on the following estimates

Aging Category	Allowance Provided
Current	2%
1–30 days past due	7
31–60 days past due	20
61–90 days past due	40
Over 90 days past due	100

Prepare the journal entry to record the provision for bad debts assuming that the existing credit balance in the allowance for doubtful accounts is equal to $23,108.

5 **BE9-15. Assigned Receivables.** Kitt Company borrows $800,000 from Neville Capital by issuing an 8-year (96-month), 12% note payable. Interest is due and payable each month based on the outstanding balance at the beginning of the month. Kitt assigns $850,000 of its accounts receivable as collateral for the lending arrangement. Prepare the journal entries to record the financing arrangement on Kitt's books.

5 **BE9-16. Assigned Receivables.** Using the information provided in BE9-15, assume that during the first month after the financing is completed, Kitt collects $250,000 of the assigned accounts receivable. Kitt remits this amount to Neville Capital along with the payment of 1 month's interest. Prepare the journal entries to record the cash collection on the receivables and payment to Neville.

5 **BE9-17. Factoring Receivables without Recourse.** Nicks Incorporated sells $2,450,000 of its accounts receivable to Fairfield Factors (FF) without recourse. FF charges a fee equal to 7% of the receivables factored and holds back an additional 4% as security. FF will return the hold back to Nicks when the receivables are collected. Assuming a sale, prepare the journal entry to record Nicks Incorporated's sale of the accounts receivable to FF.

5 **BE9-18. Factoring Receivables with Recourse.** Using the information provided in BE9-17, prepare the journal entry to record Nicks Incorporated's sale of accounts receivable to FF assuming that the receivables are factored with recourse and can be reported as a sale. The estimated recourse liability is $75,500.

6 **BE9-19. Notes Receivable.** Welk Associates sold a piece of equipment to Convey Company on June 1, 2016, for $800,000. Welk agreed to accept a 7-month, 7% note with interest due on its maturity date, December 31, 2016. Welk prepares financial statements only at its calendar year-end. Prepare the journal entries required to record the sale and the full collection at maturity. Ignore cost of goods sold and inventory.

6 **BE9-20. Notes Receivable with Year-End Interest Accrual.** Using the information provided in BE9-19, prepare the journal entries to record the sale, the accrued interest revenue, and the full collection at maturity assuming that the sale date was September 1, 2016, and the note was due on March 31, 2017.

6 **BE9-21. Notes Receivable with Discount.** Foster Technologies, Inc., provides specialized network solutions for companies in the financial services industry. During the current year, Foster completed a network project for Hextel Communications. The fair value of the project is not determinable. As part of the agreement, on February 1, Foster accepted a $5,000,000, 6-month, zero-coupon note receivable at a time when the current market rate of interest was 5%. Foster prepares financial statements at its calendar year-end only. Prepare the journal entry to record the transaction and the collection at maturity.

7 **BE9-22. Note Disclosure.** Complete the following lettered items representing the disclosures of trade accounts receivables from Cheris Corp.'s notes to the financial statements.

Note 7. Trade Receivables

Year	2017	2016
Trade Receivables	$3,600	e
Allowance	a	195
Trade Receivables, Net	b	$3,705
Allowance for Uncollectible Accounts		
January 1	c	$ 175
Bad Debt Expense	375	f
Write-Off	d	350
December 31	$ 180	g

Ⓐ **BE9-23. Internal Controls.** Identify whether the following internal control procedures relate to cash receipts or cash disbursements.

Internal Control Procedure	Cash Receipt?	Cash Disbursement?
All payments must be made by check except for immaterial payments made from petty cash.	______	______
Checks can be signed only by authorized individuals.	______	______
The summary of checks is sent to the employee in charge of preparing the cash receipts journal.	______	______
The summary of checks is forwarded to the employee responsible for depositing checks.	______	______
Authorization is required prior to preparing a check.	______	______
An employee will receive checks, open the envelopes, and prepare a cash receipts summary. The summary should include the customer name, account number, and the amount of the check.	______	______

Ⓐ **BE9-24. Internal Control.** Identify and discuss at least four features of an effective system of internal controls over cash receipts and disbursements.

Ⓐ **BE9-25. Bank Reconciliation.** The following information pertains to Silver Key Company. Prepare the bank reconciliation at July 31 by determining the correct balances for both book and bank using the following template. Prepare any required journal entries.

Item	Bank	Silver Key
1. Cash balance per bank, $9,136	______	______
2. Cash balance per books, $8,490	______	______
3. July bank service charge not recorded by the depositor, $25	______	______
4. Deposits in transit, July 31, $780	______	______
5. Error made by Silver Key in recording check 1156 to the utility company for $245 instead of $345	______	______
6. Outstanding check, July 31, $1,551	______	______
Correct balances	______	______

Ⓐ **BE9-26. Bank Reconciliation.** The following information pertains to Pewter Cup Company at August 30. Prepare the bank reconciliation for Pewter Cup by determining the correct balances for both book and bank. Prepare any required journal entries.

1. Cash balance per bank, $769
2. August bank service charge not recorded by the depositor, $24
3. Cash balance per books, $1,243
4. Outstanding check, August 30, $87
5. Deposits in transit, August 30, $547
6. Error made by Pewter Cup in recording collection from customer as deposit of $890 for only $880.

Ⓐ **BE9-27. Imprest Petty Cash Fund.** Gem Consulting established a $500 imprest petty cash fund at the beginning of the year. The fund custodian held the cash to be used to pay minor expenditures. During the year, the custodian paid the following expenditures from the petty cash fund:

Meal receipts	$174
Postage	153
Supplies (used up by end of year)	145
Parking and tolls	23

At the end of the year, $7 remained in the fund. The custodian took the petty cash receipts to the controller and requested reimbursement. Prepare the journal entries to record the current year's activity in the petty cash fund.

Ⓐ **BE9-28. Imprest Petty Cash Fund.** Round-up Garden Center established a $200 imprest petty cash fund at the beginning of the year. The fund custodian held the cash to be used to pay minor expenditures. During the year, the following expenditures were paid from the imprest petty cash fund:

Parking and tolls	$36
Meal receipts	98
Postage	63

At the end of the year, $2 remained in the fund. The custodian took the petty cash receipts to the controller and requested reimbursement. At that time, the controller increased the imprest petty cash fund to $250. Prepare the journal entries to record the current year's activity in the petty cash fund.

Exercises

1 **E9-1. Restricted Cash and Compensating Balances.** Eaves Elevators Incorporated provided the following information regarding restrictions placed on its use of cash:

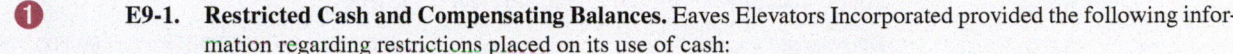

Amount of Cash	Type of Restriction	Purpose of the Restriction	Type of Debt
$128,500	Legally restricted	Compensating balance	Short term
391,450	Legally restricted	Compensating balance	Long term
75,875	Not legally restricted	Insurance obligations	Short term

In addition to these balances, Eaves had $595,825 of unrestricted cash at the end of the year.

Prepare the relevant asset sections to be reported on Eaves' balance sheet at the end of the year.

2 **E9-2. Volume Discounts, Sales Discounts.** Sodesta Company offers volume discounts to its customers. Customers buying more than $100,000 in products receive a 1% discount. Customers buying more than $200,000 in products receive a 3% discount. Sodesta also offers sales discounts with payment terms of 2/10, n/30. Sodesta uses the most-likely-amount method and assumes that the customer will take the discount to account for the sales discounts. On July 2, Sodesta made sales of $220,000 on account to Gridar Company. Gridar paid $150,000 on July 12 and the remaining balance on August 1.

Required »

a. What is the volume discount? What is the sales discount? What is the journal entry when the sale is initially recorded on July 2? Ignore the effect on inventory and cost of goods sold.
b. What is the journal entry on July 12?
c. What is the journal entry on August 1?

3 4 **E9-3. Allowance for Uncollectible Accounts, Journal Entries, Write-Off.** Kelly Klothing Designs started the current year with the following account balances related to its customer accounts:

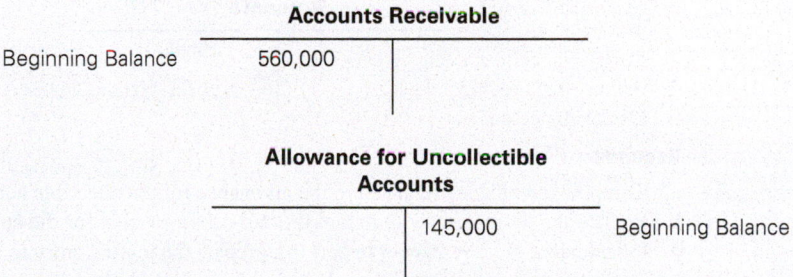

Accounts Receivable

Beginning Balance	560,000	

Allowance for Uncollectible Accounts

	145,000	Beginning Balance

Kelly reported credit sales of $1,211,800 for the current year. The company collected $56,000 on account and determined that a $35,000 account due from Cruze Company was uncollectible.

Required »

Prepare the journal entries required for each of the following events:

a. Credit sales for the current year. Ignore the effects on cost of goods sold and inventory.
b. Cash collections for the year.
c. The write-off of the Cruze Company account.
d. The current year's provision for bad debts assuming that Kelly estimates bad debts at 15% of ending accounts receivable.

4 **E9-4. Bad Debt Expense, Aging of Accounts Receivable, Journal Entry.** Giaraldi Garden Products, Inc. developed an aged schedule of accounts receivable at the end of each year.

Giaraldi Garden Products: Aged Schedule of Accounts Receivable

		Past Due				
Customer	**Current**	**1–30 Days**	**31–60 Days**	**61–90 Days**	**Over 90 Days**	**Totals**
Carey Company				$ 10,000	$ 34,500	$ 44,500
Gibson, Ltd.	$423,000	$ 27,000				450,000
KW Quarterly		33,000	$ 67,000		1,500	101,500
Onix Construction			100,000	45,000	90,500	235,500
Carpenter Lumber	387,000	125,000			500	512,500
Totals	$810,000	$185,000	$167,000	$55,000	$127,000	$1,344,000

The company estimated an allowance for uncollectible accounts based on the following estimates:

Aging Category	**Allowance Provided**
Current	3%
1–30 days past due	6
31–60 days past due	18
61–90 days past due	45
Over 90 days past due	100

Giaraldi reported net credit sales of $18,500,000 for the current year. We present the company's ending balances of accounts receivable and the allowance for uncollectible accounts:

	Accounts Receivable		
Ending Balance	1,344,000		

Allowance for Uncollectible Accounts		
	130,000	Unadjusted Ending Balance

Required »

a. Compute the balance required in the allowance for uncollectible accounts at the end of the year.
b. Prepare the journal entry to record the bad debt provision for the current year.
c. Independent of your answer to part (b), prepare the journal entry to record the bad debt provision for the current year assuming that the allowance for uncollectible accounts had a $30,000 debit balance.

4 **E9-5. Bad Debt Expense, Write-Offs, Journal Entry.** Answer the following questions using the information provided in E9-4.

Required »

Prepare the journal entries required to record each of the following events.

a. Giaraldi's credit management decided to write off all accounts that were more than 90 days past due.
b. A year after the write-offs recorded in part (a), assume that Onix Construction pays the entire balance due.

4 **E9-6. Bad Debt Expense, Aging of Accounts Receivable, Journal Entry.** Sammy's Downtown Properties developed an aged schedule of accounts receivable at the end of each year.

Sammy's Downtown Properties: Aged Schedule of Accounts Receivable

		Past Due				
Customer	**Current**	**1–30 Days**	**31–60 Days**	**61–90 Days**	**Over 90 Days**	**Totals**
Crosby Consultants	$120,000	$45,000	$ 3,000			$168,000
Whitemann Company	4,000		18,500		$ 68,000	90,500
Lite Laser Products		29,500	45,700	$13,900	196,900	286,000
Dual Power Industries				31,800	11,100	42,900
Totals	$124,000	$74,500	$67,200	$45,700	$276,000	$ 587,400

The company estimated an allowance for uncollectible accounts based on the following estimates:

Aging Category	Allowance Provided
Current	4%
1–30 days past due	8
31–60 days past due	10
61–90 days past due	35
Over days past due	50

Sammy's reported net credit sales of $4,500,000 for the current year. We present the company's ending balances of accounts receivable and the allowance for uncollectible accounts:

Accounts Receivable

	Debit	Credit
Ending Balance	587,400	

Allowance for Uncollectible Accounts

Debit	Credit	
	120,000	Unadjusted Ending Balance

Required »

a. Compute the balance required in the allowance for uncollectible accounts.
b. Prepare the journal entry to record the bad debt provision for the current year.
c. Independent of your answer to part (b), prepare the journal entry to record the bad debt provision for the current year assuming that the allowance for uncollectible accounts had a $7,435 debit balance.
d. Using your solution to parts (a) and (b), indicate how Sammy's will report its accounts receivable on the company's year-end balance sheet.

4 **E9-7. Bad Debt Expense, Aging of Accounts Receivable, Journal Entry.** The Klug Group provided the following analysis of its aged schedule of accounts receivable:

Aging Category	Ending Balance	Percent Estimated Uncollectible
Current	$300,000	0%
1–30 days past due	620,000	12
31–60 days past due	122,000	25
61–90 days past due	178,500	70
Over 90 days past due	63,000	90

The allowance for uncollectible accounts had a credit balance of $260,400 at the beginning of the year. During the year, the company wrote off bad debts of $10,650. Klug's net credit sales were $2,900,550.

Required »

a. Prepare all journal entries required to record the bad debt provision for the current year.
b. Repeat part (a) assuming that the allowance for uncollectible accounts had a debit beginning balance of $23,545.

4 **E9-8. Bad Debt Expense, Percentage of Accounts Receivable, Journal Entry.** Using the information provided in E9-7, prepare the journal entries required to record the provision for bad debts for the current year assuming the following.

Required »

Klug estimates its bad debt expense as 4% of ending accounts receivable. For purposes of part (a), assume that there is a $25,000 credit balance in the allowance account before making any year-end adjustments to this account. For purposes of part (b), assume that there is a $25,000 debit balance in the allowance account before making any year-end adjustments to this account.

5 **E9-9. Assigned Receivables.** Michael's Bucket Company borrowed $350,000 from J.R. Malone Capital by issuing a 4-year (48-month), 7% note payable. Interest is due and payable at the beginning of each month based on the outstanding balance at the beginning of the prior month. Michael's assigns $420,000 of its accounts receivable as collateral for the lending arrangement. At the beginning of the next month, Michael's collects $110,000 of the receivables and remits this amount to J.R. Malone plus interest.

Required »

a. Prepare the journal entries to record the lending arrangement.
b. Prepare the journal entries to record the collection of the receivables and the payment to J.R. Malone.
c. Indicate how accounts receivable would be reported on Michael's balance sheet at the end of the year. Assume no additional collections of accounts receivable.

5 **E9-10. Assigning Receivables, Factoring Receivables.** Sawyer's Fence Company borrowed $240,000 from Hannibal Capital by issuing a 3-year (36-month), 6% note payable. Sawyer's uses $270,000 of its accounts receivable as collateral for the lending arrangement, transferring the right to the receivable payments if Sawyer's defaults on the loan. Sawyer's services the accounts receivable, sending bills and collecting the payment from customers. Sawyer's must pay Hannibal $7,500 at the end of the month regardless of the amount of the receivables it collects. At the end of the first month, Sawyer's has collected $7,000 of the receivables that are collateral for the loan and pays $7,500 to Hannibal plus interest.

Required »

a. Determine whether Sawyer's borrowing from Hannibal would be treated as a borrowing or sale under U.S. GAAP. Prepare any journal entries needed at the initiation of the arrangement.
b. Prepare the journal entries to record the collection of the receivables and the payment to Hannibal.

5 **E9-11. Assigning Receivables, Factoring Receivables, IFRS.** Use the same information in E9-10 and now assume that Sawyer's Fence Company reports under **IFRS.**

Required »

a. Determine whether Sawyer's borrowing from Hannibal would be treated as a borrowing or sale under **IFRS.** Prepare any journal entries needed at the initiation of the arrangement.
b. Prepare the journal entries to record the collection of the receivables and the payment to Hannibal.

5 **E9-12. Factoring Receivables with and without Recourse.** Krouse Incorporated sold $1,000,000 of its accounts receivable to Fusilli Factors. Fusilli charges a fee equal to 8% of the receivables factored and holds back an additional 4% as security. Fusilli will return the hold back to Krouse when the receivables are collected. This transaction is to be recorded as a sale.

Required »

a. Prepare the journal entry required to record the sale of receivables assuming that the receivables are factored without recourse.
b. Independent of your answer to part (a), prepare the journal entry required to record the sale of the receivables assuming that the receivables are factored with recourse. The recourse liability is estimated at 2% of the receivables factored.

5 **E9-13. Factoring Receivables without Recourse, Factoring Receivables with Recourse.** Mac Antiques, Inc. sold $15,780,000 of its accounts receivable to Maximum Cash Capital (MCC). MCC charges a fee equal to 5% of the receivables factored and holds back an additional 2% as security. MCC will return the hold back to Mac when the receivables are collected. This transaction is to be recorded as a sale.

Required »

a. Prepare the journal entry required to record the sale of receivables assuming that the receivables are factored without recourse.

b. Independent of your answer to part (a), prepare the journal entry required to record the sale of the receivables assuming that the receivables are factored with recourse. The recourse liability is estimated as $175,000.

5 **E9-14. Factoring Receivables without Recourse, Factoring Receivables with Recourse.** On May 1, Onyx, Inc. factored $600,000 of accounts receivable with Cookie Finance without recourse. Cookie Finance assessed a finance charge of 6% of the total accounts receivable factored and retained an amount equal to 2% (i.e., there is a 2% holdback). Assume that the transaction is a sale.

Required »

a. Prepare the journal entry required on Onyx's books on May 1.
b. Now assume that Onyx factors the $600,000 of accounts receivable with Cookie Finance with recourse. The recourse provision has a fair value of $10,000. Prepare the journal entry required on Onyx's books on May 1.

5 **E9-15. Factoring Receivables with Recourse.** DRB, Inc. enters into an arrangement with Genius Enterprises by which Genius will purchase $100,000 of DRB's receivables and charge a 6% fee. As part of the agreement, Genius will hold back $9,000 as additional security. DRB sold the receivable with recourse, and the estimated recourse liability is $3,000.

Prepare the journal entry to record the agreement assuming that the transaction qualifies as a sale for DRB.

6 **E9-16. Notes Receivable with Year-End Interest Accrual, Sale of Notes Receivable.** On May 1, 2018, Lubin's Heavy Equipment sold a piece of equipment to Perry Products, Inc., at a selling price of $4,850,000. Lubin's agreed to accept a 10-month, 8% note with interest due on its maturity date, March 1, 2019. Lubin's year-end is December 31. Assume that 8% is reasonable when compared to the going market rate of interest for similar financing arrangements.

Required »

Prepare the journal entries to record the following events:

a. The equipment sale on May 1, 2018. Ignore cost of goods sold and the reduction of inventory.
b. The year-end interest accrual on December 31, 2018.
c. The collection of the note receivable on its maturity date of March 1, 2019.
d. Assume that Lubin's sells the note receivable on January 15, 2019, for $5,120,000. Record the journal entry for the sale. Assume that the transaction qualifies as a sale.

A **E9-17. Bank Reconciliation.** The following information is from the books of SunBright Solar Company for the month of March.

Cash Receipts Journal

Date	Cash Received
March 1	$ 50,000
3	98,000
10	125,000
14	6,000
19	9,400
28	125,000
30	15,000

Cash Disbursements Journal

Check Number	Cash Payment
1133	$45,000
1134	16,000
1135	27,500
1136	4,000
1137	150
1138	100
1139	65,000

The balance in SunBright Solar's cash account on March 31 is $313,850. SunBright Solar received the following bank statement from Jefferson Street Bank for the month of March:

Jefferson Street Bank Checking Account

Account Activity Summary			
Beginning balance			**$ 43,200**
Deposits and Other Additions			
Deposits			
March	1	$ 50,000	
	3	98,000	
	10	125,000	
	14	6,000	
	19	9,400	
	28	125,000	
Interest earned this statement period		320	413,720
Checks Written and Other Subtractions			
Checks			
	1133	$ 45,000	
	1134	16,000	
	1136	4,000	
	1137	150	
	1138	100	
Monthly Service Charge		50	(65,300)
Ending Balance on March 31			**$391,620**

Prepare the bank reconciliation for SunBright Solar by determining the correct balances for both book and bank. Record all journal entries required to correct SunBright Solar's cash balance.

A **E9-18. Bank Reconciliation.** The following information is from the books of Towl Ball Company for the month of April.

Cash Receipts Journal

Date	Cash Received
April 2	$2,500
5	2,000
9	1,800
11	1,500
14	2,250
17	1,000
23	3,000
30	2,500
30	1,250

Cash Disbursements Journal

Check Number	Cash Payment	Purpose
3449	$4,000	Payroll
3450	2,850	Suppliers
3451	1,100	Suppliers
3452	56	Postage
3453	27	Supplies
3454	1,450	Utilities
3455	5,400	Payroll
3456	30	Supplies

The balance in Towl Ball's cash account on April 30 is $16,232. Towl Ball received the following bank statement from Independence Day Bank for the month of April:

Independence Day Bank
Checking Account

Account Activity Summary

Beginning balance		**$13,345**
Deposits and Other Additions		
Deposits		
April 2	$2,500	
5	2,000	
9	1,800	
11	1,500	
14	2,250	
17	1,000	
23	3,000	
Interest earned this statement period	28	14,078
Checks Written and Other Subtractions		
Checks		
3449	4,000	
3450	2,850	
3451	1,200	
3452	56	
3454	1,450	
3456	30	
Monthly Service Charge	35	(9,621)
Ending Balance on April 30		**$ 17,802**

Prepare the bank reconciliation for Towl Ball by determining the correct balances for both book and bank. Record all journal entries required to correct Towl Ball's cash balance. Assume that the correct amount of check 3451 is $1,200.

Problems

3 4 **P9-1. Allowance for Uncollectible Accounts, Journal Entries.** Prepare the journal entries required to record the following transactions on the books of Sullivan Stamping Company (assume that the company uses the allowance method).

Required »

a. Writes off an account from Stewart Foods in the amount of $489,000.
b. Records credit sales for the year of $6,679,000. Ignore cost of goods sold and the reduction of inventory.
c. Receives $107,675 (selling price) of merchandise returned by I-Tel Company that had been purchased on credit and not yet paid for. Ignore cost of goods sold and the increase in inventory.
d. Collects $1,283,500 on account.

2 **P9-2. Sales Discounts, Most-Likely-Amount, and Expected-Value Methods Comparison**. Seramin Importers, Inc. sells coffee pots for $80 each. On November 12, the company sold 35 to a customer on account with terms of 1/15, n/30. The customer paid for 25 of the coffee pots on November 27 and paid for the remaining 10 on December 11.

Required »

a. Provide the necessary journal entries for Seramin to record these transactions under both the most-likely-amount and expected-value methods. For the most-likely-amount method, assume both that the customer will take the discount and won't take the discount. For the expected-value approach, assume that the customer is 65% likely to take the discount and ignore any constraints on variable consideration. (Ignore the journal entry that would typically be necessary to record the reduction of inventory and cost of goods sold.) Round to two decimal places.
b. Provide a comparison of the impact on the income statement for each method.

3 4 **P9-3. Allowance for Uncollectible Accounts, Aging of Accounts Receivable, Write-Off.** The partial balance sheets of Williams Iron Works, Inc. follow:

Description	***2019***	***2018***
Accounts Receivable, Net of Allowances for Uncollectible Accounts of $362,600 and $225,000 for 2019 and 2018, Respectively	$8,702,400	$475,000

Additional Information:

- Net credit sales for 2019 amounted to $9,350,000.
- Cash collections for 2019 were $930,000.

Required »

a. Determine the amount of accounts receivable written off during 2019.
b. Compute the amount of bad debt expense recorded for 2019.

4 **P9-4. Bad Debt Expense, Percent of Accounts Receivable.** Paulson Corporation provided the following account analyses for the current year:

Accounts Receivable

Beginning Balance	3,659,000		
Sales	29,900,500	368,960	Write-Offs
		200,364	Sales Returns
		10,750,642	Collections

Allowance for Uncollectible Accounts

		1,097,750	Beginning Balance
Write-Offs	368,960		

Required »

Prepare the journal entry to record the bad debt provision at year-end assuming that Paulson estimates its uncollectible accounts at 5% of its ending accounts receivable balance. Round to the nearest dollar.

4 **P9-5. Bad Debt Expense, Aging of Accounts Receivable, Write-Offs, Journal Entry.** Cho Sportswear, Ltd. develops an aged schedule of accounts receivable at the end of each year.

Cho Sportswear: Aged Schedule of Accounts Receivable

		Past Due				
Customer	**Current**	**1–30 Days**	**31–60 Days**	**61–90 Days**	**Over 90 Days**	**Totals**
Ryoko Design Associates	$ 100,000	$ 23,800				$ 123,800
Marcy Fashions, Inc.	657,000	198,000	$ 76,000			931,000
Conroy Clothing				$ 456,000	$789,412	1,245,412
Lee Womenswear	237,200	10,230	54,570	349,200		651,200
Bauer Brands, Ltd.	100,230	76,770		41,588	19,000	237,588
Totals	$1,094,430	$308,800	$130,570	$ 846,788	$808,412	$3,189,000

The company estimated an allowance for uncollectible accounts based on the following estimates:

Aging Category	**Allowance Provided**
Current	5%
1–30 days past due	9
31–60 days past due	20
61–90 days past due	55*
Over 90 days past due	80*

*The percentages are applied after a specific review of all accounts in these aging categories.

After a specific review of the company's accounts receivable, Cho's credit manager decided to provide a full allowance against all Bauer Brands' balances that are more than 60 days past due. The percentage allowance is applied to the 61–90 days and over 90 days past due aging categories only after deducting the balances due from Bauer Brands.

Cho reported net credit sales of $45,000,000 for the current year. We present the company's ending balances of accounts receivable and the allowance for uncollectible accounts:

Accounts Receivable

	Debit	Credit
Ending Balance	3,189,000	

Allowance for Uncollectible Accounts

Debit	Credit	
	348,810	Unadjusted Ending Balance

Required »

a. Compute the balance required in the allowance for uncollectible accounts at year-end. Round up to the nearest dollar.
b. Prepare the journal entry to record the bad debt provision for the current year.
c. Independent of your answer to part (b), prepare the journal entry to record the bad debt provision for the current year assuming that the allowance for uncollectible accounts had a $331,000 debit balance.
d. In the following year, Cho's credit management decided to write off all accounts that were over 90 days past due. Prepare the journal entry.
e. After the write-offs recorded in part (d), assume that Conroy Clothing pays the entire balance due. Prepare the journal entries required to record the subsequent recovery of the Conroy Clothing receivables.

4 5 **P9-6. Bad Debt Expense, Aging of Accounts Receivable, Factoring, Journal Entry.** Anche Company has organized its accounts receivable by customer and how long each receivable has been outstanding. Anche records bad debt expense based on an analysis of an aged schedule. The following information is as of the end of the year (December 31):

			Days Past Due			
Customer No.	**Total Due**	**Current**	**1–30 Days**	**31–60 Days**	**Over 60 Days**	
10901	$ 70,000	$ 60,000	$ 10,000			
10902	60,000	50,000	10,000			
10903	170,000	150,000	20,000			
10904	30,000		20,000	$ 10,000		
10905	50,000		20,000	10,000	$20,000	
10906	110,000	90,000	20,000			
Totals	$490,000	$350,000	$100,000	$20,000	$20,000	
% uncollectible		2%	5%	30%	95%	

At the beginning of the year, Anche had accounts receivable of $500,000 and a credit balance of $30,000 in its allowance for uncollectible accounts. During the year, it wrote off specific accounts receivable in the amount of $80,000. Assume no recoveries of write-offs during the year.

Required »

a. Compute bad debt expense for the year ending December 31 and the net realizable value of Anche's accounts receivable as of December 31.
b. Prepare the journal entry to record the bad debt expense for the year.
c. Independent of the information used in parts (a) and (b), assume that on January 1 of the current year with the net realizable value of accounts receivable equal to $470,000, the company decided to factor $400,000 of accounts receivable to Gustav Factors, Ltd. Gustav retains 6% of the amount factored as a reserve or hold back. Gustav Factors also charged Anche a 4% financing fee (4% of the total factored amount). As a result, only 90% of the proceeds are remitted.
   i. Prepare the journal entry to record the factoring of $400,000 of accounts receivable assuming that Anche sold the receivables without recourse.
   ii. Prepare the journal entry to record the factoring of $400,000 of accounts receivable assuming that Anche sold the receivables with recourse and the recourse obligation is estimated to be $5,000.

4 **P9-7. Aging of Accounts Receivable, Write-Offs, Journal Entries.** Council Company develops an aged schedule of accounts receivable at the end of each year.

Council Company: Aged Schedule of Accounts Receivable

		Past Due				
Customer	**Current**	**1–30 Days**	**31–60 Days**	**61–90 Days**	**Over 90 Days**	**Totals**
Grey City Products					$ 82,500	$ 82,500
Smokey Industries			$45,780	$168,900	345,000	559,680
Bleak Enterprises		$567,000	500			567,500
Drifter Incorporated	$235,800	34,000	200			270,000
Denti Cosmetic Company	130,700	300	320			131,320
Totals	$366,500	$601,300	$46,800	$168,900	$427,500	$1,611,000

The company estimated an allowance for uncollectible accounts based on the following estimates:

Aging Category	Allowance Provided
Current	5%
1–30 days past due	9%
31–60 days past due	20%
61–90 days past due	55%
Over 90 days past due	100%

Council reported net credit sales of $20,000,000 for the current year. We present the company's ending balances of accounts receivable and the allowance for uncollectible accounts:

Accounts Receivable

	Debit	Credit
Ending Balance	1,611,000	

Allowance for Uncollectible Accounts

Debit	Credit	
	94,800	Unadjusted Ending Balance

Required »

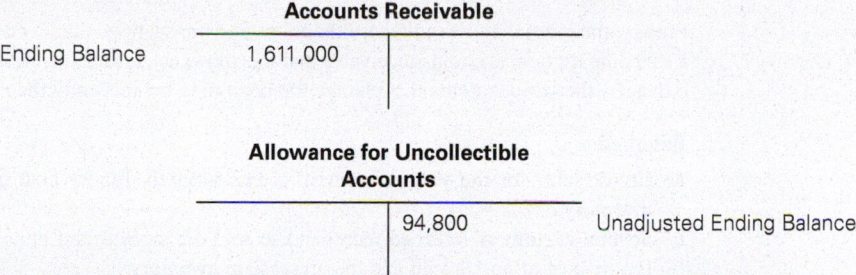

a. Compute the balance required in the allowance for uncollectible accounts.
b. Prepare the journal entry to record the bad debt provision for the current year.
c. Independent of your answer to part (b), prepare the journal entry to record the bad debt provision for the current year assuming that the allowance for uncollectible accounts had a $231,000 debit balance.
d. Provide the necessary journal entry based on Council's credit management deciding to write off all accounts that were over 90 days past due in the following year.
e. Prepare the journal entries required to record the subsequent recovery of Smokey Industries' receivable if, after the write offs recorded in part (d), Smokey Industries pays the entire balance due.

5 **P9-8. Assigned Receivables, Pledged Receivables.** Softa Company borrows $850,000 from Deer Financing Associates by securing a revolving line of credit at a 6% interest rate on April 15. Interest is due and payable at the end of each month based on the outstanding balance at the beginning of the month. Softa assigns $900,000 of its accounts receivable as collateral for the lending arrangement. Assume that accounts receivable are collected at the end of the month and the proceeds are remitted to Deer at the end of the month. The following is a list of payments collected on accounts receivable.

Month	Accounts Receivable Collected
April	$100,000
May	487,000
June	113,000

Required »

a. Compute the balance of notes payable at the end of each month.
b. Prepare the necessary journal entries for these transactions.
c. If the accounts receivable had been pledged as collateral, what entry would be made at April 15?

4 5 **P9-9. Aging of Accounts Receivable, Write-Offs, Factoring with Recourse, Journal Entries.** Astro Carpets Incorporated provided the following accounts related to beginning balances in its accounts receivable and allowance accounts for the current year:

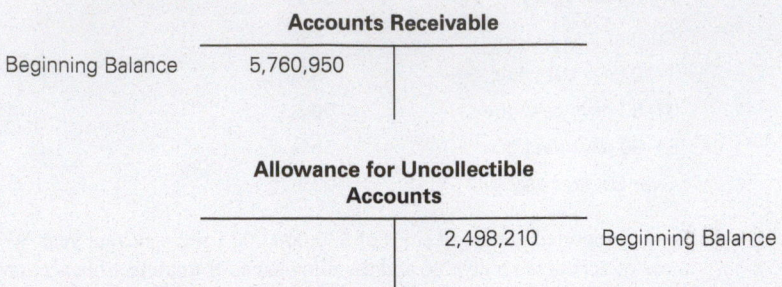

	Accounts Receivable (Debit)	Accounts Receivable (Credit)	
Beginning Balance	5,760,950		

	Allowance for Uncollectible Accounts (Debit)	Allowance for Uncollectible Accounts (Credit)	
		2,498,210	Beginning Balance

Prepare the journal entries to record the following transactions that occurred during the current year. Prepare a schedule for both accounts receivable and the allowance for uncollectible accounts that shows the beginning balances, the various items that change the beginning balance, and the ending balance.

Required »

a. Credit sales for the year amounted to $12,346,976. Ignore cost of goods sold and the reduction of inventory.
b. Several customers returned merchandise sold on account and unpaid, totaling $975,613 (retail value). Ignore cost of goods sold and the increase in inventory.
c. Astro wrote off $567,890 of uncollectible accounts from Jones Inc.
d. Astro sold $1,450,000 of its accounts receivable to Siegal Capital with recourse. Siegal charged a fee equal to 8% of the receivables factored and held back an additional 2% as security. Siegal will return the hold back to Astro when the receivables are collected. The estimated recourse liability is $15,000. This transaction qualifies as a sale.
e. The company recovered $25,675 of accounts receivable written off two years ago from Smith Industries.
f. The company recorded the bad debt expense for the year. Astro estimates its uncollectible accounts at 16% of accounts receivable. Round to the nearest dollar.

4 5 7 **P9-10. Disclosure.** Using the transactions listed in P9-9, prepare a partial balance sheet at December 31 and a partial income statement for the current year.

7 **P9-11. Accounts Receivable Disclosure.** Using ***Kellogg Company's*** accounts receivable disclosures from Exhibit 9.8 in the text and the following information, answer the questions.

(in millions)	2016	2015
Net sales	$13,014	$13,525
Accounts receivable, net	1,231	1,344
Total assets	15,111	15,251

Source: Kellogg Company. Annual Report, December 2016. http://investor.kelloggs.com/~/media/Files/K/Kellogg-IR/Annual%20Reports/kellogg-2016-ar-10-k.PDF

Required »

a. How is the carrying value of accounts receivable determined?
b. What factors influence management's judgment in its estimate of the amount of collectible receivables?
c. What is the percent of trade receivables to total assets at the end of 2016 and 2015?
d. What is the percent of the allowance for uncollectible accounts to total trade receivables in 2016 and 2015? (See Note 19 in 2016 Annual Report.)
e. What were ***Kellogg's*** write-offs of accounts receivable in 2016 and 2015? (See Note 19 in 2016 Annual Report.)

Excel Project

Autograded Excel Project available in **MyLab Accounting**

CASES

Judgment Cases

Judgment Case 1: Allowance for Doubtful Accounts[21]

Wildcat Sporting Goods (WSG) sells athletic shoes and trendy sports apparel to a variety of sporting goods stores in the Northeast and, in 2011, WSG also began direct Internet sales to consumers. WSG's common shares are publicly traded and WSG has a December 31 year-end. WSG has historically received an unqualified opinion from its audit firm.

Selected financial data is provided below:

	2009	2010	2011	2012
Sales	$300,000,000	$360,000,000	$420,000,000	$370,000,000
Credit sales	100%	100%	90%	80%
Internet sales	0%	0%	10%	20%
Accounts receivable	$ 42,000,000	$ 53,000,000	$ 48,000,000	$ 67,000,000
Allowance for doubtful accounts	$ 4,150,000	$ 5,000,000	$ 4,300,000	$ 16,300,000
Allowance/accounts receivable	9.88%	9.43%	8.96%	24.33%
Total assets	$200,000,000	$250,000,000	$300,000,000	$320,000,000
Pretax income	$ 10,000,000	$ 12,000,000	$ 15,000,000	$ 4,000,000*

*2012 pretax income is an estimate

Assume that you are the controller. At year-end, the CFO has asked you to determine the amount of the allowance for doubtful accounts for accounts receivable. The CFO received an accounts receivable allowance analysis (see below) from the new credit manager that estimated an allowance of $16.3 million, which is up significantly from the prior year. The CFO has asked you to scrutinize the attached analysis, as she expects that the allowance balance should not exceed last year's allowance, given that sales are down approximately 12% from the prior year. The aging in the attached analysis indicates the days outstanding since the original sale (e.g., a 30-day-old receivable would indicate the sale occurred 30 days ago and not that the receivable is 30 days past due). The CFO also mentioned that the company's debt covenants require, among other things, pretax earnings of at least $10.0 million.

You had discussions with various personnel this month and have gained the following additional insights.

An economic recession caused WSG's sales to decline in 2012. In an effort to improve its sales, WSG extended more generous credit terms to its customers. Beginning in the fourth quarter of 2012, customers were granted an additional 30 days to pay off their debts, so the credit window has been extended from 30 days to 60 days. Days sales outstanding have increased slightly from approximately 44 days in 2011 to 57 days in 2012.

The Internet sales have little credit risk, because the credit card company must approve the charge before any shipments are made. These sales are settled in less than 30 days. The December 31 receivable balances on Internet sales in the 0–30 aging were $3.0 million and $6.0 million in 2011 and 2012, respectively.

With the exception of a few large customers, the receivables are due from a large group of small, homogenous customers. The estimated allowance for doubtful accounts has been based on general expectations and historical losses for most accounts receivable. The average credit score of customers in 2012 is essentially unchanged from prior years. For those customers with more than a $500,000 balance, a specific analysis of accounts receivable is performed. Estimates of the allowance for doubtful accounts were a bit less than actual losses in 2009 and 2010, and a bit higher than actual losses in 2011. See the attached allowance analysis.

Approximately 22.4% of the accounts receivable balance at December 31, 2012, is over 91 days old.

Based on a discussion with the Senior VP of Sales, the following is a summary of the major customers with balances over $500,000.

- Sports World's accounts receivable from 2011 remains outstanding at December 31, 2012. This customer agreed to pay off this balance by paying $200,000 per month starting in August 2012. The first three monthly payments were made and the balance at December 31, 2012, is $3.0 million. The payments due in November 2012, December 2012, and January 2013 have not been received. The phone

[21]Reprinted from the Ernst & Young Academic Resource Center with permission of the Ernst & Young Foundation.

calls of the credit manager have not been returned. At December 31, 2011, the receivable was 31 to 60 days old and this receivable was reserved at the same level as other receivables in this aging category.

- A new customer in 2011, Slow Pay, has always paid its bills after it sells the product. At December 31, 2012, Slow Pay has an outstanding balance of $10.0 million; $3.0 million is over 120 days old, $2.0 million is 91 to 120 days old, and $5.0 million is 31 to 60 days old. Payments continue to be received and all amounts over 120 days old at December 31, 2012, were collected in January 2013. At December 31, 2011, Slow Pay had an outstanding balance of $4.0 million; $500,000 was over 120 days old, $500,000 was 91 to 120 days old, $2.0 million was 31 to 60 days old, and $1.0 million was 0 to 30 days old. No reserve was provided for this customer's receivables in 2011 and all amounts were collected in 2012.
- New Wave has an outstanding balance of $5.0 million at December 31, 2012; $1.0 million is over 120 days old, $1.5 million is 91 to120 days old, and the $2.5 million balance is 61 to 90 days old. This company was a new start-up in 2012 and, therefore, WSG does not have any credit history for New Wave. WSG has put a hold on additional shipments to New Wave until payments are received. The credit manager said there are rumors that the company might go into bankruptcy. Separately, in December 2012, the Senior VP of Sales spoke to the wealthy owner of New Wave, who personally assured him that New Wave intended to pay its outstanding balance in the coming weeks. In January 2013, the Senior VP of Sales obtained a written personal guarantee of the amounts owed from the owner of New Wave. The personal financial statements of the owner confirmed he has a net worth in excess of $20.0 million.
- High Flyer has an outstanding balance of $1.0 million at December 31, 2012: $500,000 is 61 to 90 days old and the balance is 31 to 60 days old. The owners of High Flyer have just put another company they own in a troubled industry into bankruptcy.
- None of the remaining customer balances is greater than $500,000 at December 31, 2012.
- At December 31, 2011, the only two customers with balances over $500,000 were Sports World and Slow Pay. Prior to 2011, the company did not have any customers whose balance exceeded $500,000 at year-end.

The new credit manager's compensation is, in part, tied to his ability to reduce the write-off rate for sales starting in 2013. Thus, the credit manager has an incentive to justify more significant write-offs in the current year than may be warranted.

Required »

- For December 31, 2012, perform an assessment of the allowance for doubtful accounts receivable.
- Document your judgment in a draft memorandum format that you will provide to the CFO (not to exceed three pages). Use the Codification for support.

Accounts Receivable Allowance Analysis

	0 to 30 Days	31 to 60 Days	61 to 90 Days	91 to 120 Days	Over 120 Days	Total
2009 accounts receivable aging balance	$30,000,000	$ 4,000,000	$ 2,500,000	$4,000,000	$ 1,500,000	$42,000,000
Aging percentage	71.43%	9.52%	5.95%	9.52%	3.57%	
Estimated uncollectible	$ 1,200,000	$ 400,000	$ 550,000	$ 800,000	$ 1,200,000	$ 4,150,000
Estimated uncollectible percentage	4.00%	10.00%	22.00%	20.00%	80.00%	9.88%
Actual uncollectible write-off						$ 4,200,000
Actual write-off percentage						10.00%
2010 accounts receivable aging balance	$35,000,000	$10,000,000	$ 3,000,000	$1,000,000	$ 4,000,000	$53,000,000
Aging percentage	66.04%	18.87%	5.66%	1.89%	7.55%	
Estimated uncollectible	$ 700,000	$ 800,000	$ 900,000	$ 400,000	$ 2,200,000	$ 5,000,000
Estimated uncollectible percentage	2.00%	8.00%	30.00%	40.00%	55.00%	9.43%
Actual uncollectible write-off						$ 5,100,000
Actual write-off percentage						9.62%
2011 accounts receivable aging balance	$30,000,000	$ 8,000,000	$ 4,000,000	$2,000,000	$ 4,000,000	$48,000,000
Aging percentage	62.50%	16.67%	8.33%	4.17%	8.33%	
Estimated uncollectible	$ 300,000	$ 600,000	$ 800,000	$ 800,000	$ 1,800,000	$ 4,300,000
Estimated uncollectible percentage	1.00%	7.50%	20.00%	40.00%	45.00%	8.96%
Actual uncollectible write-off						$ 4,200,000
Actual write-off percentage						8.75%
2012 accounts receivable aging balance	$15,000,000	$ 27,000,000	$10,000,000	$5,000,000	$10,000,000	$ 67,000,000
Aging percentage	22.39%	40.30%	14.93%	7.46%	14.93%	
Estimated uncollectible	$ 600,000	$ 2,700,000	$ 3,000,000	$2,000,000	$ 8,000,000	$16,300,000
Estimated uncollectible percentage	4.00%	10.00%	30.00%	40.00%	80.00%	24.33%

Financial Statement Analysis Case

Financial Statement Analysis Case: *Revlon*

The following information is from the 2016 financial statements of ***Revlon***, the beauty products company.

Balance Sheet Information (in million of dollars)*

At December 31	**2016**	**2015**	**2014**
Accounts Receivable	$ 423.9	$ 244.9	$ 238.9
Inventories	424.6	183.8	156.6
Accounts Payable	296.9	201.3	153.5
Income Statement Information			
For the year	**2016**	**2015**	**2014**
Sales (all credit)	$2,334.0	$1,914.3	$1,941.0
Cost of Goods Sold	917.1	667.8	668.3

Required »

Use ***Revlon's*** financial information to answer the following questions:

a. What is ***Revlon's*** operating cycle (in days) in 2016 and 2015? Comment on the change from year to year.
b. What is ***Revlon's*** cash operating cycle (in days) in 2016 and 2015? Comment on the change from year to year.
c. Use ***Revlon's*** financial information to compare the components of ***Revlon's*** operating cycle and cash operating cycle to ***L'Oréal's*** for 2016. The following table provides the amounts for ***L'Oréal*** from worked Example 9.17 in the text.

Component	**L'Oréal 2016**	**Revlon 2016**
Accounts receivable turnover ratio	6.83	________
Days sales outstanding	53.44	________
Inventory turnover ratio	2.86	________
Days inventory on hand	127.62	________
Accounts payable turnover ratio	1.82	________
Days accounts payable outstanding	200.55	________
Operating cycle	181.06	________
Cash operating cycle	19.49	________

*Source: Revlon, Inc. Financial Statements, December 2016. http://phx.corporate-ir.net/phoenix.zhtml?c=81595&p=irol-reportsannual

Surfing the Standards Cases

Surfing the Standards Case 1: Transfer of Accounts Receivables

Companies sometimes use accounts receivable as collateral in a secured borrowing or sell them to a factor. The accounting method for these types of transactions is governed by ASC 860—*Transfers and Servicing*. Review all of ASC 860-10 to answer the following questions with a focus on the paragraphs that follow:

- ASC 860-10-05 paragraphs 14–15
- ASC 860-10-40 paragraphs 4–6 (not 6a), 7–11, and 15–27
- ASC 860-10-55 paragraphs 18–18B, 26–32, 34–41, and 45–46

1. List the rules that govern the determination of whether these transactions would be viewed as a sale or as a secured borrowing.
2. Hand Computers, Inc. engages in a transaction to transfer its receivables with recourse to JRMH, Inc. Although Hand does have some continuing involvement with the receivables, it does not maintain any control over them, nor does it place any restrictions on the ability of JRMH to pledge or exchange the receivables. Because Hand does not typically engage in the transfer of its receivables, the company did not think to get a true sale opinion from its attorney. However, the company is not concerned about this oversight because the company's probability of bankruptcy is negligible. Should Hand Computers account for this transfer as a sale or as a secured borrowing? Support your answer with references to the applicable standards.
3. Hand Computers, Inc. engages in a transaction to transfer its receivables with recourse to JRMH, Inc. Hand clearly meets the first and third conditions (the isolation and effective control conditions) in ASC 860-10-40-5 to treat this transaction as a sale. Hand also believes that it meets the second condition. However, a clause in the contract does not allow JRMH to pledge its receivables to three specific competitor companies named in the contract. Hand claims that this clause does not constrain JRMH from pledging its receivables because there are a number of other companies with which it can contract. Should Hand Computers account for this transfer as a sale or as a secured borrowing? Support your answer with specific references to the applicable standards.

Surfing the Standards Case 2: Costs Associated with Receivables

ABC Lending signed a loan agreement with AMRO, Inc. on January 2, 2017. AMRO is borrowing $500,000 for 10 years with a stated interest rate of 7%. AMRO will make a payment of $71,188.75 at the end of each year. AMRO paid $10,000 in points to ABC Lending on January 2, 2017.

In connection with this transaction, ABC Lending paid fees to a third party for loan processing. These fees were 0.5% of the loan balance. ABC Lending also paid a bonus to an employee of 1% of the loan balance. Finally, ABC paid advertising costs of $1,500 and incurred expenses of $2,000 related to the preparation of the loan documents.

Prepare a memo to the file regarding the correct accounting treatment for this transaction for ABC Lending. Use the Codification for support.

Basis for Conclusions Case

Basis for Conclusion Case: Transfer of Accounts Receivable

Companies sometimes use accounts receivable as collateral in a secured borrowing or sell them to a factor. The accounting method for these types of transactions is governed by ASC 860—*Transfers and Servicing*, the majority of which derives from SFAS No. 140.

1. Read the Basis for Conclusions, paragraphs 116 and 117 in SFAS No. 140. What issue was the FASB trying to address?
2. Read the Basis for Conclusions, paragraphs 132 through 133, paragraphs 138 through 140, and paragraphs 143 through 146 in SFAS No. 140. What are the two fundamental approaches that the board considered in the treatment of transfers of financial assets? Which did the board choose, and why?

APPENDIX A
Internal Controls over Cash

Internal controls are processes implemented in a company to ensure that key objectives are met, including the objectives of reliable financial reporting, effective and efficient operations, and compliance with regulations. Internal controls over cash must be highly effective because cash is an asset that is highly susceptible to misappropriation.[22]

Cash Control Guidelines

An effective system of internal controls over cash receipts and disbursements:

- Clearly establishes responsibilities
- Ensures proper segregation of duties
- Uses documentation to create proper monitoring over cash movement
- Establishes proper physical control over cash
- Includes independent verification of cash transactions (e.g., preparing monthly bank reconciliations)
- Creates proper controls over human resources, such as conducting background checks, bonding employees handling cash, and requiring that all employees take vacation days

Separation of duties is one of the most critical internal controls to deter theft and misappropriation of cash. Any individuals who have physical custody over cash should not also handle accounting records. Specifically, any employees handling cash should not have access to ledger accounts and bank statements and should not be responsible for reconciling the bank statements to the ledger accounts. Similarly, the responsibility for approving, signing, and mailing checks and handling cash disbursement documents and records should be separate functions.

A typical cash receipts process should include the following steps:

1. An employee receives checks, opens the envelopes, and prepares a cash receipts summary. The summary should include the customer name, account number, and the amount of the check.
2. The summary is then forwarded to the employee responsible for depositing checks.
3. The summary is also sent to the employee in charge of preparing the cash receipts journal.

Control procedures to prevent any misappropriation and irregularities in the cash disbursements process include the following:

1. All cash disbursements except for immaterial payments made from petty cash must be made by check.
2. Authorization is required for all cash disbursements prior to preparing a check. The person preparing the check must have all appropriate documentation, including the vendor invoice; the approved purchase order; the receiving report that verifies that the correct items were received and the proper price was charged; and the signed check request.
3. Checks can be signed only by authorized individuals.

The Sarbanes-Oxley Act of 2002 (SOX) requires that publicly traded U.S. companies maintain an effective system of internal controls. SOX also established the Public Company Accounting Oversight Board (PCAOB), which is responsible for establishing generally accepted auditing standards and overseeing assurance functions for publicly traded companies.

Section 404 of SOX requires the documentation and assessment of internal control systems by publicly traded entities. PCAOB Standard No. 5 requires that auditors issue an opinion on the effectiveness of these systems over financial reporting.[23]

[22]Systems of internal controls will be covered fully in your auditing and accounting information systems courses.

[23]Public Company Accounting Oversight Board, *Auditing Standards No. 5,* "An Audit of Internal Control Over Financial Reporting that is Integrated with an Audit of Financial Statements" (Washington, DC: PCAOB, 2007).

Important internal control procedures for cash include the use of *bank reconciliations* and an *imprest petty cash fund*. We discuss both of these next.

Controlling Cash by Use of a Bank Account

Bank accounts provide a company with several important controls over cash because banks have standing procedures to safeguard cash. For example, key documents used by banks to protect depositors' cash include checks, deposit tickets, signature cards, and bank statements.

Bank Reconciliation

Referring to the bank statement, companies prepare a *bank reconciliation* each month. A **bank reconciliation** compares the bank statement to the amount recorded in the company's general ledger cash account. Any differences between the company's books and the bank statement amounts must be reconciled. The bank reconciliation is a significant part of internal controls over cash: If differences cannot be explained, the company will investigate and determine whether any misappropriation has occurred.

There are four common reconciling items:

1. *Deposits in transit*
2. *Outstanding checks*
3. *Bank charges and credits*
4. *Errors*

Deposits in Transit. **Deposits in transit** reflect a timing difference that occurs when a company makes a bank deposit at the end of the current month and the amount of that deposit is recorded in the company's books. However, that deposit may not be recorded by the bank until the following month.

Outstanding Checks. **Outstanding checks** also result from timing differences. The company will deduct checks written on the books, but the checks may not have cleared the bank in time to be reported on the bank statement.

Bank Charges and Credits. **Bank charges** are fees that depositors pay for services such as check printing, safe deposit box rentals, and other services. There are also charges for nonsufficient funds (NSF checks). The company is usually not aware of the amount of these charges until receiving the bank statement. **Bank credits** are deposits of cash such as interest accrued. The company is not notified regarding any interest earned until it receives the bank statement.

Errors. The company may make one or more **errors**, such as incorrectly recording or omitting a check or deposit. The bank may also make an error, but that is far less common.

When a company learns about bank charges and bank credits or company errors in the preparation of its bank reconciliation, it makes any journal entries required to record these in its accounting system.

Format for the Bank Reconciliation

There are two formats used to construct a bank reconciliation:

- Reconcile bank to book or book to bank.
- Reconcile both bank and book balances to the correct cash balance.

The most common approach used in practice is to reconcile both the bank and book balances to the correct cash balance:

1. Start with the bank balance and add any deposits in transit and subtract any outstanding checks to arrive at the correct balance.

2. Begin with the book balance and subtract any bank charges and add any bank credits.
3. Adjust the book balance for any company errors to arrive at the correct cash balance. The corrected bank and book balances should be identical.

After completing the bank reconciliation, the company makes journal entries to reflect accrued interest revenue, other bank credits, and bank charges because these events were not previously recorded on the company's books. Entries are also required to correct any book errors. Example 9A.1 illustrates a reconciliation of both the bank and book balances to the correct amounts.

EXAMPLE 9A.1

Bank Reconciliation

PROBLEM: The following information is from the books of EM Plumbing Corporation for the month of October.

Date	Cash Received
October 2	$ 5,000
6	7,320
12	6,000
15	900
22	1,230
30	13,500

Cash Disbursements Journal

Check Number	Cash Payment
2120	$10,200
2121	6,080
2122	6,500
2123	5,250
2124	3,945
2125	7,355

The balance in EM Plumbing's cash account on October 31 is $110,500. EM received the bank statement on the following page from Cottage Valley Bank for the month of October:

Cottage Valley Bank
Checking Account

Account Activity Summary

Beginning Balance			$115,880
Deposits and Other Additions			
Deposits*			
October	4	$ 5,000	
	8	7,320	
	14	6,000	
	20	900	
	28	1,230	
Interest Earned This Statement Period		700	21,150
Checks Written and Other Subtractions			
Checks**			
2120		$10,200	
2121		6,800***	
2123		5,250	
NSF Check		1,000	
Monthly Service Charge		80	(23,330)
Ending Balance on October 31			$113,700

*Note that the October 30 deposit recorded in the cash receipts journal is not reflected on the bank statement.
**Note that check numbers 2122, 2124, and 2125 were recorded in the cash disbursements journal but have not yet cleared the bank.
***The correct amount of check number 2121 is $6,800.

The NSF check was received from a customer during the previous month. In addition, EM discovered an error in its cash disbursement journal. Specifically, EM erroneously recorded a cash disbursement for plumbing supplies as $6,080, but the correct amount of check number 2121 is $6,800.

Prepare the bank reconciliation for EM Plumbing by determining the correct balances for both book and bank. Record all journal entries required to correct EM Plumbing's cash balance.

SOLUTION: We begin with the balance per the bank of $113,700 and add the deposits in transit and subtract the outstanding checks. These calculations give the correct cash balance of $109,400. Next, we begin with the cash balance per the books of $110,500, add the interest payment, and subtract the NSF check and the service charge. We also adjust for the error in check number 2121. The bank reconciliation is shown on the next page.

Continued

EM Plumbing Corporation
Bank Reconciliation
October 31

Cottage Valley Bank Statement:		
Balance, October 31		$113,700
Add: Deposit in transit		13,500
		$ 127,200
Less: Outstanding checks:		
Check No.		
2122	$6,500	
2124	3,945	
2125	7,355	(17,800)
Correct bank balance, October 31		$109,400
EM Plumbing's Books:		
Balance, October 31		$110,500
Add: Interest earned for the month		700
		$ 111,200
Less: NSF check	$1,000	
Service charge	80	
Book error—$6,800 check recorded as $6,080	720	
		(1,800)
Correct book balance, October 31		$109,400

Because the correct bank balance is equal to the correct book balance, the reconciliation is complete.

Finally, we need to make four journal entries for items not yet recorded in the books. EM Plumbing records the $700 interest revenue:

Account	October 31	
Cash	700	
Interest Revenue		700

In the second journal entry, EM Plumbing increases accounts receivable by $1,000 for the amount of the NSF check:

Account	October 31	
Accounts Receivable	1,000	
Cash		1,000

The third journal entry records the $80 service charge:

Account	October 31	
Miscellaneous Expense	80	
Cash		80

EM Plumbing decreases accounts payable to correct the $720 error related to check 2121 in the fourth journal entry:

Account	October 31	
Accounts Payable	720	
Cash		720

Petty Cash

Petty cash funds are minor amounts of cash that a company keeps on hand in order to pay for small, miscellaneous expenses such as visitor parking, lunches, and reimbursements for tolls and supplies. It is impractical to issue checks through the company's cash disbursement system to pay for these minor expenses. Therefore, cash is held for these purposes.

An *imprest petty cash system* provides the best internal control over cash on hand. An **imprest petty cash system** involves a cash fund for which a fixed amount of cash is reserved on hand and is then replenished at the end of the period. At any point in time, the sum of cash on hand plus petty cash receipts must equal the fixed amount of the fund. If there is a shortage or overage, the company uses a cash short and over account to record the difference from the imprest amount. Shortage and overage amounts are reported on the income statement as other expenses and revenues, respectively. Example 9A.2 illustrates accounting for an imprest petty cash fund.

EXAMPLE 9A.2

Impress Petty Cash Fund

PROBLEM: Monochrome Printers established a $1,000 imprest fund at the beginning of the year. The fund custodian holds the cash to pay minor expenditures. During the year, the following expenditures were paid from the petty cash fund:

Postage	$560
Parking and tolls	200
Supplies	210
Total petty cash receipts	$970

At the end of the year, there was $20 remaining in the fund. The custodian took the petty cash receipts totaling $970 to the controller and requested reimbursement. Prepare the journal entries to record the current year's activity in the petty cash fund.

SOLUTION: To establish the petty cash fund, we make the following entry:

Accounts	Beginning of the Year	
Petty Cash	1,000	
Cash		1,000

At the end of the year, there should be $30 of cash left in the fund ($1,000 less $970). Because there is only $20 left, the fund is short $10. The journal entry to replenish the fund at the end of the year is as follows:

Accounts	End of the Year	
Postage Expense	560	
Miscellaneous Expense	200	
Supplies Expense	210	
Cash Short or Over	10	
Cash		980

Notice that the only journal entries to the regular cash account are when Monochrome Printers credits the regular cash account to establish the fund and replenish the fund. The petty cash account is not affected when the fund is replenished.

10 Short-Term Operating Assets: Inventory

LEARNING OBJECTIVES

1. Describe the types of inventory and demonstrate accounting under periodic and perpetual inventory systems.
2. Discuss inventory costing, including accounting for goods in transit, consigned goods, costs included in inventory, and purchase discounts.
3. Explain the need for inventory cost-flow assumptions and calculate inventory and cost of goods sold under four inventory allocation methods: specific identification; moving average; last-in, first-out (LIFO); and first-in, first-out (FIFO).
4. Demonstrate an understanding of and illustrate the accounting for the LIFO reserve, the LIFO effect, and LIFO liquidations. Compute inventory and cost of goods sold using the dollar-value LIFO method.
5. Explain the lower-of-cost-or-market (LCM) rule.
6. Calculate inventory and cost of goods sold using the retail inventory method.
7. Explain the gross profit method of estimating inventory.
8. Detail required disclosures for inventory.

Patti McConville/Alamy Stock Photo

Introduction

GO INTO ANY STORE and you will see inventory all around you. Grocery stores are stocked with fresh fruits and vegetables, boxes of cereal, and gallons of milk. Retailers like ***Abercrombie & Fitch*** and ***Old Navy*** sell all types of clothing such as pants, shirts, and sweaters. ***Best Buy*** is stocked with computers, cell phones, and flat-screen televisions. Maintaining sufficient inventory levels is critical to operating a successful business.

Consider ***Foot Locker, Inc.***, the world's leading retailer of athletically inspired footwear and apparel. ***Foot Locker's*** $1.307 billion inventory represented about 34% of its total assets at the end of 2016. ***Foot Locker*** seeks to accurately predict the market for the merchandise in its stores as well as its customers' purchasing habits, which enables it to maintain sufficient inventory levels to increase inventory turnover and merchandise flow. If ***Foot Locker*** accumulates excess inventory, it may be forced to mark down or hold promotional sales to dispose of any excess or slow-moving inventory. Both outcomes could have a materially adverse effect on ***Foot Locker's*** business, financial condition, and results of operations. By analyzing its market and consumer purchasing habits and maintaining sufficient levels of inventory, ***Foot Locker*** increased its gross profit percentage by 0.1% from 33.8% in 2015 to 33.9% in 2016.

In this chapter, we discuss key issues in accounting for inventory. Inventory is a short-term operating asset consisting of goods held for resale for a merchandising company and inventories of raw materials, work-in-process, and finished goods for a manufacturing company. As is the case with ***Foot Locker***, inventory is typically a significant portion of a company's total current assets. The valuation of inventory affects the company's balance sheet and the cost of goods sold on the income statement.

We first cover the *periodic* and *perpetual* methods a company uses to account for inventory. Then, we address costs to include in inventory and present inventory cost-flow assumptions including *specific identification, first-in, first out* (FIFO), *last-in, first-out* (LIFO), and *moving average*. We also consider the issues related to the LIFO cost-flow assumption and the tax and cash flow implications of IFRS not allowing the LIFO inventory cost-flow assumption. Next, we address specific guidelines for reporting inventory with the *lower-of-cost-or-market rule*, including differences between U.S. GAAP and IFRS. Then, we discuss the *conventional retail inventory method*, a technique that **Foot Locker** uses. Finally, we illustrate estimating ending inventory using the gross profit method and detail required disclosures.[1] «

1 Describe the types of inventory and demonstrate accounting under periodic and perpetual inventory systems.

Types of Inventory and Inventory Systems

We begin our discussion of inventory measurement with an overview of the inventory classifications and the two types of inventory systems.[2]

Types of Inventory

Retail, wholesale, and manufacturing firms hold inventory. Retailers and wholesalers typically hold only **merchandise inventory**, which consists of goods purchased to resell without any additional manufacturing. Manufacturing firms generally report three types of inventory based on the stage of the production process:

1. *Raw materials*
2. *Work-in-process*
3. *Finished goods*

Raw materials inventory is composed of inputs that the firm has not yet placed into production. For example, cloth would be included in the raw materials inventory for a clothing manufacturer. The raw materials inventory is increased by purchases and decreased when these items are transferred into *work-in-process inventory*.

Work-in-process inventory, the goods that are currently in the manufacturing process, includes three different types of costs: raw materials, cost of labor, and allocated overhead costs. Overhead includes expenditures made for factory-related costs such as supervisory salaries, utilities, and supplies.

Work-in-process inventory becomes *finished goods* at the end of the production process. **Finished goods inventory** includes those goods for which the manufacturing process is complete. A company charges the value of finished goods to the cost of goods sold account when it sells the inventory. Increases in raw materials and work-in-process inventories are often indicators that a company plans to expand production to meet expected future sales increases.

Exhibit 10.1 summarizes the flow of inventory costs on the balance sheet and income statement from raw materials inventory to work-in-process inventory and finished goods inventory, and finally to cost of goods sold when the inventory is sold.

EXHIBIT 10.1 Cost Flows in a Manufacturing Firm

Inventory Accounts on the Balance Sheet						Income Statement	
Raw Materials Inventory		**Work-in-Process Inventory**		**Finished Goods Inventory**		**Cost of Goods Sold**	
Beg. Balance + Purchases	– Transferred to → Work-in-Process	Beg. Balance + Raw Materials + Labor + Allocated Overhead	– Cost of Units → Completed	Beg. Balance + Cost of Units Completed	– Cost of → Goods Sold	+ Cost of Goods Sold	
End. Balance		End. Balance		End. Balance		End. Balance	

[1]We discuss inventory errors in Chapter 21.

[2]For most of the relevant authoritative literature for this topic, see FASB ASC 330 – *Inventory* for U.S. GAAP and IASC, *International Accounting Standard 2*, "Inventories" (London, UK: International Accounting Standards Committee, Revised) for IFRS.

Exhibit 10.2 shows ***Johnson & Johnson's*** disclosures by types of inventory from its 2016 annual report. Approximately 61% of ***Johnson & Johnson's*** inventories are comprised of finished goods, and the other 39% is made up of raw materials and work-in-process.

EXHIBIT 10.2 Types of Inventories, *Johnson & Johnson*, Financial Statements, January 1, 2017

NOTE 3: Inventories
At the end of 2016 and 2015, inventories were composed of:

	2016	2015
	(Dollars in millions)	
Raw materials and supplies	$ 952	$ 936
Goods in process	2,185	2,241
Finished goods	5,007	4,876
Total inventories	$8,144	$8,053

Source: ***Johnson & Johnson's*** 2016 annual report, http://files.shareholder.com/downloads/JNJ/3995555343x0x934262/A4542599-AECD-43F0-9E4C-99CCE31E5C20/JNJ_2017-0310-ar-bookmarked.pdf, page 31.

Inventory Systems

Companies use either a *periodic* or *perpetual* inventory system.

Periodic Inventory System. Under a **periodic system**, a company determines the inventory balance and cost of goods sold at the end of the accounting period. Each time a sale is made, a company does not reduce inventory and increase cost of goods sold. Rather, a company determines them periodically.

The balance sheet includes the opening balance of inventory. Purchases made during the period increase inventory available for sale. Firms net any purchase returns, allowances, and discounts with purchases made. Firms record purchases in a separate purchases account, a temporary account used to accumulate inventory acquisitions during a period that is closed out at the end of the period. The beginning inventory balance plus the net purchases is the cost of goods available for sale—that is, the total amount of inventory that will either be sold during the period or remain in ending inventory.

The ending inventory balance is based on a physical count of the inventory made by going to manufacturing and storage facilities and actually counting the inventory located at these sites. Firms determine the cost of goods sold at the end of the period using the computation illustrated in Exhibit 10.3.

EXHIBIT 10.3 Computation of Cost of Goods Sold: Periodic Inventory System

	Cost of Goods Sold Computation	*Amount from*
	Beginning Inventory	Known from prior period
+	Net Purchases	Recorded in Purchases Account, Purchase Returns and Allowances Account, and Purchase Discounts Account
=	Cost of Goods Available for Sale	Subtotal
−	Ending Inventory	Physically counted
=	Cost of Goods Sold	Computed

Example 10.1 illustrates accounting under the periodic inventory system.

EXAMPLE 10.1 **Periodic Inventory System**

PROBLEM: CCS Quilting Supplies uses a periodic inventory system. On January 1, 2018, CCS's inventory is $76,000. On March 2, 2018, CCS sells merchandise for $19,000 on account. On June 10, 2018, CCS purchases additional inventory for $22,000 on account. CCS sells

Continued

merchandise for $65,000 on account on August 15, 2018. On December 31, 2018, CCS counts its inventory and determines it has $34,000 of inventory on hand. What is CCS's cost of goods sold in 2018? Provide all journal entries for 2018.

SOLUTION: Using the equation from Exhibit 10.3, the cost of goods sold is:

	Beginning Inventory	$ 76,000
+	Net Purchases	+22,000
=	Cost of Goods Available for Sale	$ 98,000
−	Ending Inventory	−34,000
=	Cost of Goods Sold	$ 64,000

On March 2, CCS records the $19,000 sale. Because CCS uses a periodic system, it does not record the reduction of inventory at the time of sale.

Account	March 2, 2018	
Accounts Receivable	19,000	
Sales Revenue		19,000

On June 10, CCS records the $22,000 purchase into a purchases account.

Account	June 10, 2018	
Purchases	22,000	
Accounts Payable		22,000

On August 15, CCS records the $65,000 sale. Because CCS uses a periodic system, it does not record the reduction of inventory at the time of sale.

Account	August 15, 2018	
Accounts Receivable	65,000	
Sales Revenue		65,000

Finally, on December 31, CCS counts its inventory and adjusts the balance. Because its inventory decreased from $76,000 to $34,000, it credits inventory for $42,000. In this same entry, it also removes the purchases account. CCS credits the purchases account for its $22,000 balance and records the cost of goods sold for $64,000.

Account	December 31, 2018	
Cost of Goods Sold	64,000	
Inventory		42,000
Purchases		22,000

Thus, CCS reports inventory of $34,000 on the December 31, 2018, balance sheet and cost of goods sold of $64,000 on the income statement for the year ended December 31, 2018.

Perpetual Inventory System. In practice, technological advances have made the periodic system obsolete and provided the computer software for firms to use a *perpetual system*. Under a **perpetual system**, firms continually update inventory accounts for each purchase and each sale. A perpetual system is superior to a periodic system because it always provides current information about inventory levels, cost of goods sold, and gross profit.

The following t-account shows the activity in a perpetual system of inventory. Inventory increases with net purchases and is reduced when units are sold. The inventory balance is always current.

Inventory	
Beginning Inventory + Net Purchases	– Cost of Goods Sold
Ending Inventory	

At the end of the period, a company performs a physical count of inventory. The company adjusts for the difference between the actual count and the perpetual records resulting from issues such as theft, breakage, and obsolescence. Example 10.2 illustrates accounting under a perpetual inventory system.

EXAMPLE 10.2 Perpetual Inventory System

PROBLEM: Assume that CCS Quilting Supplies from Example 10.1 now uses a perpetual inventory system. CCS reports an inventory balance of $76,000 on January 1, 2018. On March 2, CCS sells merchandise on account for $19,000 that cost $12,000. CCS purchases additional inventory for $22,000 on account on June 10, 2018. On August 15, 2018, CCS sells merchandise costing $52,000 for $65,000 on account. On December 31, 2018, CCS counts its inventory and determines that it has $34,000 worth of inventory on hand.

a. What is CCS's cost of goods sold in 2018? Provide all journal entries for 2018 under a perpetual inventory system.
b. Are the ending balances of inventory and cost of goods sold different under the periodic and perpetual systems?
c. Now assume that CCS conducts a physical count of inventory and determines that the amount of inventory on hand is $30,000 as opposed to the $34,000 current balance. Provide the necessary journal entry for adjustment of the inventory account.

SOLUTION: On March 2, CCS records the sale.

Account	***March 2, 2018***	
Accounts Receivable	19,000	
Sales Revenue		19,000

Because CCS uses a perpetual system, it records the reduction of inventory when the sale is made.

Account	***March 2, 2018***	
Cost of Goods Sold	12,000	
Inventory		12,000

On June 10, CCS records the $22,000 purchase directly in the inventory account.

Account	***June 10, 2018***	
Inventory	22,000	
Accounts Payable		22,000

On August 15, the company records the sale.

Account	***August 15, 2018***	
Accounts Receivable	65,000	
Sales Revenue		65,000

Because CCS uses a perpetual system, it immediately records the reduction of inventory when the sale is made.

Account	***August 15, 2018***	
Cost of Goods Sold	52,000	
Inventory		52,000

On December 31, CCS has the correct amount of inventory and cost of goods sold reported. The t-accounts for inventory and cost of goods sold follow:

Inventory

	Debit	Credit	
Beginning Balance	76,000		
		12,000	March 2
June 10	22,000		
		52,000	August 15
Ending Balance	34,000		

Cost of Goods Sold

	Debit	Credit
Beginning Balance	0	
March 2	12,000	
August 15	52,000	
Ending Balance	64,000	

Thus, CCS reports inventory of $34,000 on the December 31, 2018, balance sheet and reports cost of goods sold of $64,000 on the income statement for the year ended December 31, 2018. These are the same balances as we computed under the periodic system.

If CCS counted inventory and determined that there was $30,000, instead of $34,000, it would record a $4,000 loss. An adjusting entry is required to credit the inventory account and debit a loss account for $4,000.

Account	***December 31, 2018***	
Loss on Inventory Shortage	4,000	
Inventory		4,000

Inventory

	Debit	Credit	
Beginning Balance	76,000		
		12,000	March 2
June 10	22,000		
		52,000	August 15
Ending Balance	34,000		
		4,000	December 31
Ending Balance (adjusted)	30,000		

❷ Discuss inventory costing, including accounting for goods in transit, consigned goods, costs included in inventory, and purchase discounts.

Inventory Costing: Units and Costs Included

So far, we have focused on the total dollar amount of inventory that the firm reports on its balance sheet. The total dollar amount of inventory is equal to the number of units on hand multiplied by the cost per unit. To illustrate, consider the inventory of sweaters at a clothing store. To assign a value, the firm multiplies the number of sweaters by the cost of each sweater. Although the total inventory value is a straightforward concept, there are four complexities in practice:

1. Determining what goods are included in inventory.
2. Measuring cost per unit.
3. Allocating the cost of the goods purchased or manufactured by the company between the units that remain in inventory at the end of the period and the units that are sold during the period.
4. Accounting for a decrease in the market value of inventory.

We begin by briefly covering the types of goods included in inventory and then address each of the remaining three issues.

Goods Included in Inventory

Ending inventory typically consists of the goods that are in the company's physical possession as well as some *goods in transit* and some goods in consignment arrangements.[3]

Goods in Transit. **Goods in transit** are items that have left the seller's place of business but have not yet been received by the buyer. If inventory is in transit at the end of the reporting period, does the buyer or the seller report these items in inventory? The answer depends on who has title to the goods:

1. If the goods are shipped **f.o.b. (free on board) shipping point**, then title passes from the seller to the buyer when the goods are shipped. Consequently, the buyer reports the goods in its inventory because the buyer obtains title to the goods as soon as they leave the seller's location.
2. If goods are shipped **f.o.b. destination**, then title passes from the seller to the buyer when the goods are received by the buyer. Thus, the seller reports the goods in its inventory while in transit because the seller remains the owner until the goods arrive at the buyer's destination.

Example 10.3 provides an example of determining the title of goods in transit.

EXAMPLE 10.3

Goods in Transit

PROBLEM: Rock Enterprises has inventory of $150,000 in its warehouse as of December 31. It also has two shipments that left the supplier's warehouse by December 31 that it expects to receive on January 2. The first shipment of $15,000 was sold f.o.b. shipping point and the second shipment of $17,000 was sold f.o.b. destination. What inventory amount should Rock report on its balance sheet as of December 31?

SOLUTION: Rock should report $165,000 for inventory as of December 31—the $150,000 of inventory in its possession as well as the $15,000 of inventory in transit that was sold f.o.b. shipping point—because it obtained title to the goods when they were shipped. Rock will not report the $17,000 of goods sold f.o.b. destination because it will not take title of those goods until the merchandise arrives at Rock's location.

Consigned Goods. Recall from the revenue recognition chapter that a company enters into a consignment arrangement when one party (the consignee) agrees to sell a product for another party (the consignor) without taking ownership of the merchandise. In this case, although the consignee has physical possession of the inventory, the inventory is reported on the consignor's balance sheet. For example, Electronics Emporium may ship 100 DVD players to LookVideos, Inc. on consignment. In this case, Electronics Emporium is the consignor and LookVideos is the consignee. Although LookVideos has physical possession of the DVD players, it does not report them as part of its inventory. Electronics Emporium will include the DVD players in its inventory because the company still has control of the inventory.

Costs Included in Inventory

Inventory costs reflect the price paid for the goods to be held for resale or the manufacturing costs incurred in producing the units, including materials, labor, and allocated overhead. The costs initially capitalized into inventory also include expenditures such as **freight-in costs**, the transportation costs incurred to bring the inventory to the appropriate location. Other capitalized costs include packaging and handling costs. These reasonable and necessary expenditures are considered to have asset value because they are required to acquire the inventory. **Freight-out costs**, transportation costs incurred by the seller to move the inventory to the buyer, are expensed as a component of selling, general, and administrative expenses when incurred.

---

[3]Companies selling products often give the buyer the right to return the product. If the company estimates that returns will be a material amount, then it must record the estimated returns. We discuss sales returns in more depth in Chapter 8.

Although the accounting standards specify general rules, there is a great deal of discretion regarding costs to capitalize in inventory and to expense as incurred. For example, in its significant accounting policies footnote in the 2016 financial statements, ***Foot Locker*** explained that it capitalized transportation, distribution center, and sourcing costs in merchandise inventories.[4] The cost of inventory excludes expenditures related to *abnormal costs*. This treatment is based on the theory that abnormal costs are not reasonable and necessary and do not represent asset value. **Abnormal costs** include abnormal spoilage and excess freight, which are costs that exceed the normal costs expected to be incurred.

Purchase Discounts

Finally, inventory costs are reduced by *purchase discounts*. **Purchase discounts** reduce the amount that is due to sellers if the buyer pays within a certain time period. Purchase discounts are related to sales discounts discussed in Chapter 9. The company selling the inventory offers a discount to the buyer. The selling company accounts for the sales discount. The company buying the inventory accounts for the purchase discount. A typical purchase discount is stated as 2/10, n/30, which means the buyer will receive a 2% discount by paying within 10 days; otherwise, the buyer must pay the balance within 30 days. There are two acceptable approaches to recording purchase discounts: the *gross method* and the *net method*.

Gross Method. Under the **gross method**, a company making a purchase initially records the inventory and accounts payable at the full (gross) purchase amount on the invoice.

1. If the buyer pays *after* the discount period, the accounting is simple because the full amount is paid. That is, the amount of cash paid is the gross amount of the payable and inventory on the books.
2. If the buyer pays *within* the discount period, the journal entry must reflect the discount. That is, when a buyer takes a purchase discount, the buyer pays less cash than the gross account payable on the books: The net amount is the difference between the gross amount and the discount. The company still needs to remove the gross amount of the payable because it is no longer owed to the seller, but less cash is needed to liquidate the liability. Under a perpetual system, the buyer credits the inventory account for the difference between the gross payable amount and the net cash paid, reducing the value of the inventory to the net amount.[5]

Net Method. Under the **net method**, the company making the purchase assumes that it will take the discount and initially records the accounts payable and inventory at the net amount.

1. If the buyer pays *within* the discount period, then the journal entry treats the amount of cash paid as the net amount of the payable on the books.
2. If the buyer pays *after* the discount period, the buyer pays more cash than the net payable on the books. The difference is the amount of the discount lost by not paying within the discount period. By not paying on time, the company incurs an additional cost that represents interest accrued on the unpaid balance after the discount period. The buyer debits the difference to interest expense to reflect the fact that this difference is an amount due to the seller for providing financing.

Example 10.4 illustrates accounting for purchase discounts under both the gross and net methods.

[4]Source: https://www.sec.gov/Archives/edgar/data/850209/000085020917000003/fl-20170128x10k.htm, page 44.

[5]We discuss only the perpetual system here. However, a company using a periodic system would credit purchase discounts, a contra account to purchases.

EXAMPLE 10.4 Purchase Discounts Using the Gross and Net Methods

PROBLEM: On June 1, Sure Foot Outfitters, Inc. bought 50 pairs of hiking boots for $100 per pair from a vendor on account with terms of 2/10, n/30. Sure Foot paid for 20 pairs of the boots on June 9 and paid for the remaining 30 pairs on June 29. Provide the necessary journal entries for Sure Foot to record these transactions under both the gross and net methods. Sure Foot uses the perpetual inventory system.

SOLUTION: First, Sure Foot records the purchase. Under the gross method, the company records the full $5,000 (50 pairs of boots × $100 per pair).

Under the net method, the company records $4,900, which is the $5,000 gross amount of the invoice (50 pairs of boots × $100 per pair) less the $100 discount amount ($5,000 × 2%). The journal entries are as follows:

Gross Method	Debit	Credit	Net Method	Debit	Credit
Inventory	5,000		Inventory	4,900	
Accounts Payable		5,000	Accounts Payable		4,900

Under the gross method, on June 9, Sure Foot makes payment of $1,960. The net amount per pair of boots is $98, which is the gross amount of $100 less the discount amount of $2 ($100 × 2%). The discount is granted because the invoice was paid within the 10-day period. Thus, Sure Foot pays $1,960 for 20 pairs of boots (20 pairs of boots × $98 per pair). Although Sure Foot pays only $1,960 in cash, we must remove accounts payable at the gross amount of $2,000 (20 pairs of boots at $100 per pair) and apply the difference to the inventory account.

Under the net method, Sure Foot originally recorded the accounts payable at the net amount, so we debit accounts payable and credit cash for the $1,960. The journal entries are as follows:

Gross Method	Debit	Credit	Net Method	Debit	Credit
Accounts Payable	2,000		Accounts Payable	1,960	
Cash		1,960	Cash		1,960
Inventory		40			

Finally, on June 29, Sure Foot makes full payment of $3,000 for the remaining accounts payable. No discount is applied because Sure Foot did not pay within the discount period. Thus, the journal entry for the gross method requires crediting the cash account for the $3,000 and including an offsetting entry to accounts payable.

Under the net method, Sure Foot must remove the accounts payable balance at the net amount of $2,940 ($3,000 less a 2% discount of $60). The $60 difference represents the discount lost by not paying the invoice within the discount period. The discount lost is a debit to interest expense. The journal entries are as follows:

	Debit	Credit	Net Method	Debit	Credit
Accounts Payable	3,000		Accounts Payable	2,940	
Cash		3,000	Interest Expense	60	
			Cash		3,000

In practice, the net method is more appropriate than the gross method because buyers usually take the discount. Thus, recording the payable at the net amount is likely an accurate portrayal of the amount that the buyer will ultimately pay and therefore minimizes the need for adjustments.

JUDGMENTS IN ACCOUNTING
Inventory Costs

Judgment is crucial in determining the initial measurement of inventory. Deciding what costs to include in inventory is often subjective, as indicated by the Codification's statement that "although principles for the determination of inventory costs may be easily stated, their application . . . is difficult because of the variety of considerations in the allocation of costs and charges."[6] As a simple example, consider the requirement that companies capitalize freight-in costs into the inventory account whereas abnormal freight must be expensed. Deciding what freight cost is normal versus what is abnormal requires subjective judgment. For example, if an auto dealer pays freight for a shipment of vehicles delivered from the factory, it is a normal part of the dealer's business operations. In this case, the freight is considered part of the cost of inventory because it was reasonable and necessary to have the inventory in place and ready for sale. However, if sales begin to slow down and the dealer holds too much inventory, this inventory may have to be shipped to alternate locations. This additional freight may be considered abnormal and expensed because it is not a reasonable and necessary cost and does not represent a part of inventory value.

The decision to use the gross or net method of recording purchase discounts also affects the balance in the inventory account. In Example 10.4, the final balance in the inventory account is $4,960 using the gross method and $4,900 using the net method for the same three transactions. Thus, the inventory balance is impacted by management's choice of the method to account for the discount.

❸ Explain the need for inventory cost-flow assumptions and calculate inventory and cost of goods sold under four inventory allocation methods: specific identification; moving average; last-in, first-out (LIFO); and first-in, first-out (FIFO).

Inventory Cost-Flow Assumptions

A company usually does not track each individual item of inventory in its accounting system as the item is purchased and eventually sold. Rather, a company will choose a **cost-flow assumption** to move the cost of the item from inventory to cost of goods sold in the accounting system.

Consider a store that buys sweaters in different sizes and colors during the year. The cost of each type of sweater varies slightly depending on when it was purchased. If the store does not track each individual sweater, how does the store determine the cost of the sweaters sold and the cost of the sweaters remaining in the store? If the cost of each sweater were always the same, the store would simply multiply the number of sweaters sold and the number of sweaters remaining in ending inventory by the constant cost to determine the cost of goods sold and ending inventory, respectively. But a constant cost is unlikely to occur in practice. Thus, the store must determine which of the sweaters available for sale were sold and which remain in the store.

To make this allocation, the store first determines the cost of the goods that it has available for sale as illustrated in Example 10.5.

EXAMPLE 10.5 Determining the Cost of Goods Available for Sale

PROBLEM: Cowboy Accessories Enterprises began the year with 1,000 cowboy hats in stock with a cost of $20 per hat. On April 22, the company purchased 200 hats at $22 each. Cowboy purchased 350 hats at $25 each on July 2 and acquired an additional 100 hats at $27 each on November 7 as shown in the following table.

Cowboy Accessories has 400 hats in ending inventory.

Beginning inventory	1,000
April 22 purchase	200
July 2 purchase	350
November 7 purchase	100

[6]See FASB ASC 330-10-30-2, *Inventory – Overall – Initial Measurement.*

What is Cowboy Accessories' cost of goods available for sale?

SOLUTION: The cost of goods available for sale for the year is $35,850, which is determined as the cost of the beginning inventory plus all the purchases during the year as follows:

	Units	Price	Total
Beginning inventory	1,000	$20	$20,000
April 22 purchase	200	$22	4,400
July 2 purchase	350	$25	8,750
November 7 purchase	100	$27	2,700
Cost of goods available for sale	1,650		$35,850

Example 10.5 illustrates that allocation complexities result from varying inventory acquisition costs. Cowboy Accessories Enterprises has a total of 1,650 units available for sale with a total cost of $35,850. Allocating the $35,850 cost of goods available for sale between cost of goods sold and ending inventory depends on which hats were sold and which hats remain in inventory. Exhibit 10.4 depicts this allocation issue. Beginning inventory of $20,000 and purchases of $15,850 contribute to cost of goods available for sale of $35,850. Cowboy Accessories must allocate this amount between cost of goods sold and ending inventory. That is, it needs to determine the portion of the $35,850 to include in ending inventory on the balance sheet and how much of the cost of goods available for sale to report as cost of goods sold on the income statement.

EXHIBIT 10.4 The Inventory Allocation Problem

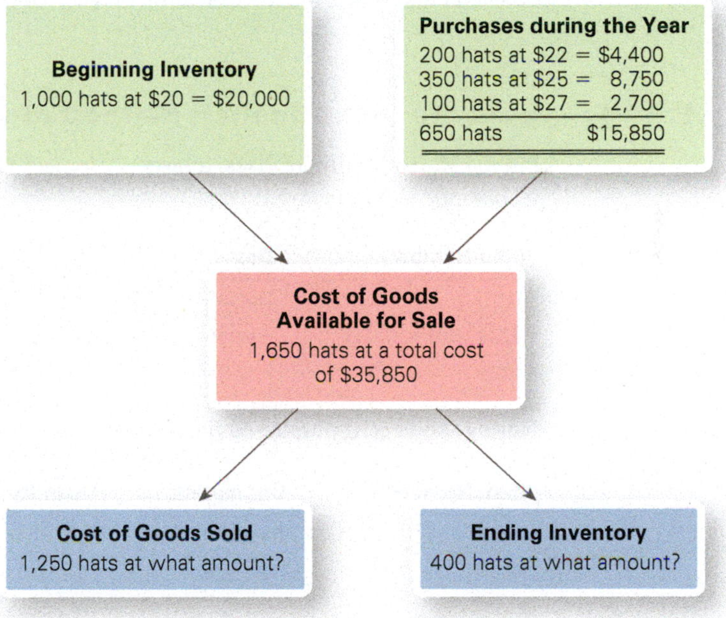

If the cost of hats is constant over time or if Cowboy Accessories can specifically identify the exact cost of the units sold, the allocation is straightforward. However, prices are seldom constant over time, and it is not always practical to specifically identify each unit. In the case of changing prices, firms usually make cost-flow assumptions. Specifically, rather than tracking the cost of each hat purchased and sold, Cowboy can use cost-flow assumptions to allocate the $35,850 total cost of goods available for sale to the 400 hats in ending inventory and the 1,250 hats sold.

Inventory Allocation Methods

There are four common methods to allocate the cost of goods available for sale between ending inventory and cost of goods sold:

1. **Specific identification method**: The company identifies each unit and tracks the cost associated with that specific unit.
2. **Moving-average method**: The company determines an average cost for the units on hand and applies that average unit cost to the next sale to determine the cost of goods sold.
3. **First-in, first-out (FIFO) method**: The company assigns the most recent costs to ending inventory and the oldest costs to cost of goods sold.
4. **Last-in, first-out (LIFO) method**: The company assigns the oldest costs to ending inventory and the most recent costs to cost of goods sold.

It is important to note that a company does not have to sell its inventory in a pattern that resembles its accounting assumptions. For example, a grocery store is likely to sell gallons of older milk first. Yet, it could choose to use a moving-average cost to determine the cost of goods sold because it is easier to implement. We will examine the four methods in depth using a common example to compare and contrast the financial reporting effects.

Each of two other approaches to inventory allocation—the *retail inventory method* and *gross profit method*—approximates the ending inventory balance reported. We discuss the retail inventory method and the gross profit method later in the chapter.

Specific Identification Method

With the specific identification method, a company identifies each unit and tracks its actual cost as illustrated in Example 10.6. This approach is suitable for companies that sell high-dollar products with low sales volume. For example, a truck dealer can identify a vehicle that was available for sale by referencing its vehicle identification number and determining whether it was sold or is still in ending inventory. The method is impractical, however, for most companies. Imagine a grocery wholesaler using specific identification on each of the products it sells!

EXAMPLE 10.6

Specific Identification Method of Cost Allocation

PROBLEM: Horton Enterprises, a farm equipment retailer, had the following units on hand as of January 1 of the current year.

Item Number	Description	Quantity	Cost per Unit
1167	Horse Trailer	2	$50,000
2234	Tractor	1	45,000
4423	Hay Baler	1	25,000

During the year, it purchased the following pieces of equipment:

Item Number	Description	Quantity	Cost per Unit
2288	Tractor	1	$42,000
4467	Hay Baler	1	37,000

During the year, Horton sold all of the units in its beginning inventory except for the Hay Baler (item 4423). It also sold the tractor that was purchased during the year (item 2288). What are Horton's ending inventory and cost of goods sold under the specific identification method?

SOLUTION: Referencing its cost records for each item, Horton computes cost of goods sold and ending inventory as follows:

Item Number	Description	Quantity	Cost per Unit	Cost of Goods Sold	Ending Inventory
1167	Horse Trailer	2	$50,000	$100,000	$ 0
2234	Tractor	1	45,000	45,000	0
2288	Tractor	1	42,000	42,000	0
4423	Hay Baler	1	25,000	0	25,000
4467	Hay Baler	1	37,000	0	37,000
Total				$ 187,000	$62,000

Moving-Average Method

The moving-average method determines an average cost for the units on hand and applies that average unit cost to the next sale to determine the cost of goods sold.[7] The ending inventory is the remaining (unsold) units valued at the average unit cost as shown in Example 10.7. The moving-average method is useful for firms selling a high volume of a homogeneous product (e.g., oil and gas) and is often used for inventory of raw materials and supplies.

EXAMPLE 10.7

Moving-Average Method of Cost Allocation

PROBLEM: Broadway Stores reports the following transactions related to inventory.

Transaction	Units Purchased	Unit Cost	Units Sold	Total Cost
Beginning inventory – 1/1	1,000	$2.00		$ 2,000
Purchase – 3/30	6,000	3.00		18,000
Purchase – 4/16	4,000	4.00		16,000
Sale – 5/11			2,000	
Purchase – 6/13	2,000	4.50		9,000
Sale – 7/1			3,500	
Purchase – 10/5	3,000	5.00		15,000

Broadway sells all products at $7 each. What is Broadway's cost of goods available for sale, cost of goods sold, and ending inventory for the current year using the moving-average method under a perpetual system?

SOLUTION: Under the moving-average method, Broadway determines an average cost for the units. The company computes a new moving-average cost with every purchase by taking the cumulative cost and dividing it by the cumulative units in inventory.

Please refer to the table on the next page. Beginning with 1,000 units in inventory at a cumulative cost of $2,000, the initial moving-average cost is $2.00 per unit. We add the 6,000-unit purchase at $3.00 per unit on March 30 to get cumulative units of 7,000 and a cumulative

Continued

[7]The term moving-average method, is used in a perpetual inventory system. Under a periodic inventory system, this approach is generally referred to as the weighted-average method.

cost of $20,000. The moving-average cost as of March 30 is $2.86 ($20,000 divided by 7,000). Finally, we add the 4,000-unit purchase at $4.00 per unit and get cumulative units of 11,000 and a cumulative cost of $36,000. Thus, the moving-average cost as of April 16 is $3.27 ($36,000 divided by 11,000).

Because Broadway uses a perpetual inventory system, it records the reduction in inventory and the increase in cost of goods sold on May 11 when it sells 2,000 units. It records the cost of goods sold at the current moving-average cost per unit. On May 11, Broadway sells 2,000 units at a cost of $3.27 per unit, resulting in a decrease in the inventory account and an increase in the cost of goods sold account of $6,540.

On June 13, Broadway purchases 2,000 more units at a cost of $4.50 per unit, which increases the cumulative cost to $38,460 with cumulative units of 11,000, resulting in a moving-average cost of $3.50 per unit ($38,460 divided by 11,000 units). On July 1, Broadway sells 3,500 units and records the cost of these sales at the current moving-average cost of $3.50 per unit for a total of $12,250. Finally, Broadway purchases 3,000 more units at a cost of $5.00 per unit, resulting in an ending inventory of 10,500 units and a cumulative cost of $41,210—the ending inventory balance. The average cost per unit at the end of the year is then $3.92 ($41,210 cumulative cost divided by 10,500 units). These inventory transactions are summarized in the following table.

Transaction	Units Purchased (Sold)	Unit Cost	Cumulative Units	Total Cost	Cost of Goods Sold (Cumulative)	Cumulative Cost (Balance in Inventory Account)	Average Cost per Unit
Beginning inventory	1,000	$2.00	1,000	$ 2,000		$ 2,000	$2.00
Purchase – 3/30	6,000	3.00	7,000	18,000		20,000	2.86
Purchase – 4/16	4,000	4.00	11,000	16,000		36,000	3.27
Sale – 5/11	(2,000)	3.27	9,000	(6,540)	6,540	29,460	3.27
Purchase – 6/13	2,000	4.50	11,000	9,000		38,460	3.50
Sale – 7/1	(3,500)	3.50	7,500	(12,250)	18,790	26,210	3.50
Purchase – 10/5	3,000	5.00	10,500	15,000		41,210	3.92

The t-accounts for inventory and cost of goods sold are as follows:

Inventory

Beginning Balance	2,000		
March 30	18,000		
April 16	16,000		
		6,540	May 11
June 13	9,000		
		12,250	July 1
October 5	15,000		
	41,210		

Cost of Goods Sold

Beginning Balance	0	
May 11	6,540	
July 1	12,250	
	18,790	

Therefore, the cost of goods sold for the year is $18,790. We compute cost of goods available for sale as follows:

Transaction	Units Purchased	Unit Cost	Total Cost
Beginning inventory – 1/1	1,000	$2.00	$ 2,000
Purchase – 3/30	6,000	3.00	18,000
Purchase – 4/16	4,000	4.00	16,000
Purchase – 6/13	2,000	4.50	9,000
Purchase – 10/5	3,000	5.00	15,000
Cost of goods available for sale	16,000		$60,000

Broadway allocates this $60,000 cost of goods available for sale between ending inventory ($41,210) and cost of goods sold ($18,790).

First-In, First-Out Method

The first-in, first-out (FIFO) method assigns the most recent costs to ending inventory and the oldest costs to cost of goods sold. Under a perpetual system, the company records the cost of goods sold at the point of each sale.

FIFO is conceptually sound for firms selling products that can perish or are subject to style changes, obsolescence, or rapid technological changes. The FIFO cost-flow assumption accurately portrays the actual flow of goods in most companies. For example, it is logical that a computer manufacturer will attempt to sell its oldest models first because they will certainly be replaced by units with more advanced technology.[8] Example 10.8 illustrates the FIFO method.

EXAMPLE 10.8

FIFO Method of Cost Allocation

PROBLEM: Consider Broadway Stores in Example 10.7. What is Broadway's cost of goods sold and ending inventory for the current year using the FIFO method under a perpetual system?

SOLUTION: Under a perpetual FIFO system, Broadway computes and records cost of goods sold at the time of every sale. Broadway made sales on May 11 and July 1. Thus, on May 11, we must determine the cost to allocate to the 2,000 units sold. Beginning with the first goods purchased, the costs allocated will be $2 for the first 1,000 sold on that day and $3 for the next 1,000. We assume that 5,000 of the units purchased on March 30 are still in inventory. On July 1, Broadway sells 3,500 more units that we assume come from the March 30 purchase because those are the earliest goods still presumed to be in inventory.

Continued

[8]The allocation between cost of goods sold and ending inventory is the same using either the perpetual or the periodic system for the FIFO method. This is not the case for the LIFO and moving-average cost methods.

Transaction	Units Purchased	Unit Cost	Total Cost	Units Sold	Cost of Goods Sold per Unit	Cost of Goods Sold	Inventory Balance
Beginning inventory	1,000	$2.00	$ 2,000				$ 2,000
Purchase – 3/30	6,000	3.00	18,000				20,000
Purchase – 4/16	4,000	4.00	16,000				36,000
Sale – 5/11				2,000	1,000 @ $2 1,000 @ $3	$ 5,000	31,000
Purchase – 6/13	2,000	4.50	9,000				40,000
Sale – 7/1				3,500	3,500 @ $3	$10,500	29,500
Purchase – 10/5	3,000	5.00	15,000				44,500
Goods Available for Sale/Cost of Goods Available for Sale	16,000		$60,000				
Units Sold/Cost of Goods Sold				5,500		$15,500	

The preceding table shows that total cost of goods sold for the year is $15,500. We also compute the goods available for sale and the cost of goods available for sale as 16,000 units and $60,000, respectively. Because Broadway had 16,000 units available for sale and sold 5,500 units, it reports 10,500 units in ending inventory. Under FIFO, we assume that these units are the last units purchased. We compute ending inventory as $44,500 as in the following table.

Latest items purchased are in inventory ....→

Transaction	Units Purchased	Units in Ending Inventory	Unit Cost	Cost in Ending Inventory
Purchase – 10/5	3,000	3,000	$5.00	$15,000
Purchase – 6/13	2,000	2,000	4.50	9,000
Purchase – 4/16	4,000	4,000	4.00	16,000
Purchase – 3/30	6,000	1,500	3.00	4,500
Beginning inventory	1,000	0	2.00	0
Ending inventory		10,500		$44,500

Inventory

Beginning Balance	2,000		
March 30	18,000		
April 16	16,000		
		5,000	May 11
June 13	9,000		
		10,500	July 1
October 5	15,000		
Ending Balance	44,500		

	Cost of Goods Sold
Beginning Balance	0
May 11	5,000
July 1	10,500
Ending Balance	15,500

Broadway allocates the $60,000 cost of goods available for sale between ending inventory ($44,500) and cost of goods sold ($15,500).

Last-In, First-Out Method

The last-in, first-out (LIFO) method assigns the oldest costs to ending inventory and the most recent costs to cost of goods sold as illustrated in Example 10.9. LIFO is conceptually sound for any company that accumulates inventory, sells units from its most recent acquisitions, and maintains a base stock (such as a mining company). However, actual inventory management at most firms does not follow this pattern.

EXAMPLE 10.9

LIFO Method of Cost Allocation

PROBLEM: Consider Broadway Stores in Example 10.7. What is Broadway's cost of goods sold and ending inventory for the current year using the LIFO method under a perpetual system?

SOLUTION: Under a perpetual LIFO system, Broadway computes and records cost of goods sold at the time of every sale. Broadway made sales on May 11 and July 1. Thus, on May 11, we will determine what cost to allocate to the 2,000 units sold. Beginning with the last goods purchased on April 16, the costs allocated will be $4. We assume that 2,000 of the units purchased on April 16 are still in inventory. On July 1, Broadway sells 3,500 units of which 2,000 are assumed to come from the June 13 purchase and 1,500 from the April 16 purchase because those are the most recently purchased goods still assumed to be in inventory.

Transaction	Units Purchased	Unit Cost	Total Cost	Units Sold	Cost of Goods Sold per Unit	Cost of Goods Sold	Inventory Balance
Beginning inventory	1,000	$2.00	$ 2,000				$ 2,000
Purchase – 3/30	6,000	3.00	18,000				20,000
Purchase – 4/16	4,000	4.00	16,000				36,000
Sale – 5/11				2,000	2,000 @ $4.00	$ 8,000	28,000
Purchase – 6/13	2,000	4.50	9,000				37,000
Sale – 7/1				3,500	2,000 @ $4.50 1,500 @ $4.00	$15,000	22,000
Purchase – 10/5	3,000	5.00	15,000				37,000
Goods Available for Sale/Cost of Goods Available for Sale	16,000		$60,000				
Units Sold/Cost of Goods Sold				5,500		$23,000	

Continued

The table on the prior page indicates that total cost of goods sold for the year is $23,000. We also compute the goods available for sale and the cost of goods available for sale as 16,000 units and $60,000, respectively. Because Broadway had 16,000 units available for sale and sold 5,500 units, it reports 10,500 units in ending inventory. Under LIFO, we assume that these units are the first units purchased. We compute ending inventory as $37,000 as follows.

Earliest items purchased are in inventory ....→

Transaction	Units Purchased	Units in Ending Inventory	Unit Cost	Cost in Ending Inventory
Beginning inventory	1,000	1,000	$2.00	$ 2,000
Purchase – 3/30	6,000	6,000	3.00	18,000
Purchase – 4/16	4,000	500	4.00	2,000
Purchase – 6/13	2,000	0	4.50	0
Purchase – 10/5	3,000	3,000	5.00	15,000
Ending inventory		10,500		$37,000

Inventory

	Debit	Credit	
Beginning Balance	2,000		
March 30	18,000		
April 16	16,000		
		8,000	May 11
June 13	9,000		
		15,000	July 1
October 5	15,000		
Ending Balance	37,000		

Cost of Goods Sold

	Debit	Credit
Beginning Balance	0	
May 11	8,000	
July 1	15,000	
Ending Balance	23,000	

Broadway allocates its $60,000 cost of goods available for sale between ending inventory ($37,000) and cost of goods sold ($23,000).

Comparison of the Moving-Average, FIFO, and LIFO Methods

Companies typically use either the moving-average cost, FIFO, or LIFO methods for costing inventory. Although the specific identification method is allowed, virtually no firms use it. Exhibit 10.5 presents the percentage of U.S. companies that use the different cost-flow assumptions for at least part of their inventory.[9] As shown, FIFO is the most popular method.

[9]Note that the percentages do not add to 100% because companies can use different cost assumptions for different inventory items. That is, a company can use more than one cost-flow assumption for its inventory. For example, a company can use FIFO for its merchandise inventory and moving-average cost for miscellaneous inventory such as supplies.

EXHIBIT 10.5 Usage of Cost-Flow Assumptions

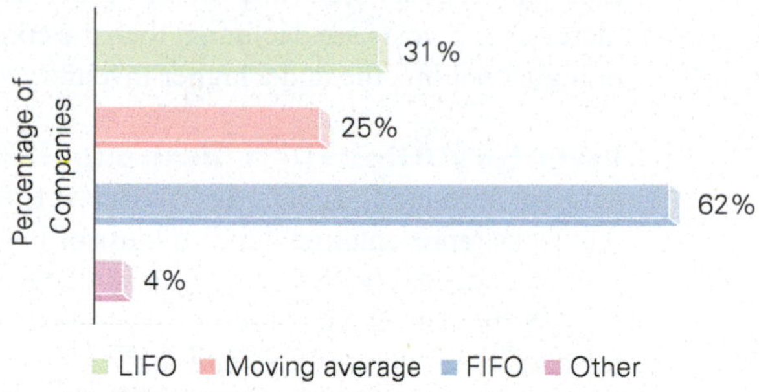

Source: Accounting Trends and Techniques—2011 (AICPA, New York, NY)

Examples 10.7, 10.8, and 10.9 demonstrate that the three primary cost-flow assumptions produce different results for the cost of goods sold reported on the income statement and the valuation of inventory on the balance sheet. The different results can have a significant impact on reported income and several key financial ratios.

The cost-flow assumptions affect only the allocation of ending inventory and cost of goods sold: The choice of inventory valuation method does not affect cash flows directly. However, the **IRS LIFO conformity rule** mandates that a company using LIFO for tax purposes must also use it for financial reporting. The effect of inventory valuation methods on cost of goods sold, and thus net income, and the required book-tax conformity for LIFO lead to possible tax and cash-flow consequences. LIFO generally results in a lower income figure in a period of rising inventory costs. Thus, it is advantageous to use LIFO for tax purposes because its use will increase cash flow by decreasing cash paid for income taxes. Investors and other financial statement users understand that even though using LIFO results in lower net income, using LIFO increases the amount of cash that the company retains and can use in operations. Therefore, investors and other financial statement users do not penalize a company for using LIFO and reporting lower net income.

Exhibit 10.6 summarizes the moving-average, FIFO, and LIFO inventory valuation methods illustrated in Examples 10.7, 10.8, and 10.9, providing important insights:

1. In terms of measuring cost of goods sold and ending inventory, the moving-average method falls between the two extreme approaches, LIFO and FIFO.
2. FIFO will result in the *lowest* measurement of cost of goods sold (and thus the highest reported net income) and the *highest* valuation of inventory on the balance sheet as long as the unit cost of inventory is increasing.
3. LIFO will result in the *highest* cost of goods sold (and thus the lowest reported net income) and the *lowest* valuation of inventory on the balance sheet as long as the unit cost of inventory is increasing.

EXHIBIT 10.6 Cost of Goods Sold and Inventory Valuation; Cost-Flow Method Comparison

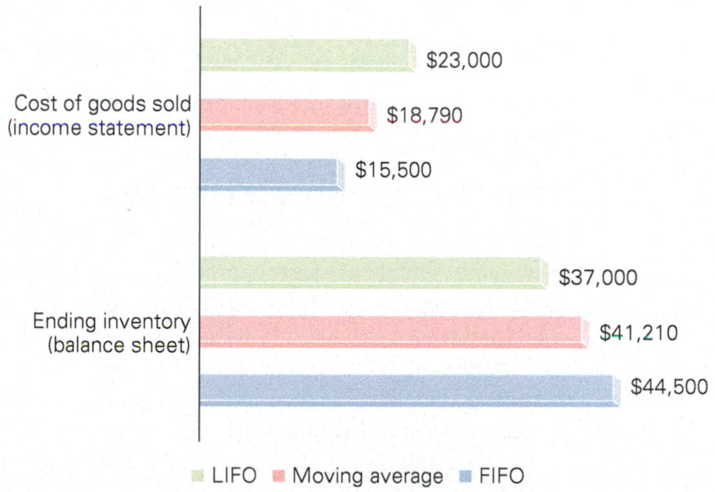

The relationships and rankings between the LIFO and FIFO methods noted in Exhibit 10.6 hold only if costs are rising for inventory acquisitions and if units in inventory are constant or increasing. If costs are declining, then the comparison is exactly the opposite with LIFO resulting in higher net income and a higher inventory valuation.

Inventory Allocation Methods: IFRS. IFRS does not allow the LIFO approach. International accounting standard setters view LIFO as imposing an unrealistic cost flow assumption that lacks representational faithfulness of inventory flows.[10]

The fact that IFRS does not permit the LIFO cost-flow assumption would be a major obstacle for U.S companies if the United States allowed IFRS. There could be significant cash flow effects for companies currently saving taxes as a result of using LIFO. A company ceasing the use of LIFO is obligated to pay the IRS all the tax savings it received from using LIFO over a four-year period. Consider ***Chevron Corporation***, a petroleum company that uses the LIFO cost-flow assumption. By the end of 2016, it had saved more than $1 billion in taxes by using LIFO.

THE CONCEPTUAL FRAMEWORK CONNECTION
Inventory Valuation Methods

Although U.S. GAAP allows LIFO, many argue that this method is generally not a conceptually sound assumption for the cost flow of inventory. It is rare for a company to sell its most recent purchases before its earlier purchases. A concrete plant might use the most recent cement first because it is on the top of the pile—but in reality, few other types of companies would operate this way. IFRS does not permit the use of LIFO for this reason.

FIFO measures inventory on the balance sheet more accurately than LIFO because it values ending inventory using the most recent purchases and thus more closely reflects current costs. Some argue that LIFO better measures the cost of goods sold because it uses the most recent purchases and thus matches these current costs with current selling prices. However, this benefit is not always achieved with the LIFO method in practice.

In addition to being theoretically deficient, LIFO is the most difficult and costly method to implement in practice. So, why do a significant number of U.S. firms continue to use the LIFO method? The primary reason is that LIFO can provide significant tax benefits for a firm. Before the LIFO conformity rule, many firms adopted LIFO for tax purposes while continuing to use FIFO for financial reporting. This dual approach allowed firms to report higher income to their shareholders while reducing income for tax purposes. Congress believed that this was misleading because if LIFO is used for taxes, then LIFO must be viewed by a company to be the proper valuation of inventory. As a result, the IRS LIFO conformity rule requires that if a company wants to maximize tax benefits (i.e., lower taxable income) by using LIFO for tax purposes, it must also adopt LIFO for financial reporting.

As we will discuss in Chapter 17, inventory valued using the LIFO method is one of the few areas where tax and financial reporting methods are required to conform.

4 Demonstrate an understanding of and illustrate the accounting for the LIFO reserve, the LIFO effect, and LIFO liquidations. Compute inventory and cost of goods sold using the dollar-value LIFO method.

The LIFO Cost-Flow Assumption in Detail

The next section of this chapter discusses the issues encountered when using the LIFO method in practice.

The LIFO Reserve and LIFO Effect

Inventory management is important to the operations of a firm, and LIFO does not provide a conceptually sound cost-flow approach to measuring inventory for most companies. Consequently, a firm that reports externally on the LIFO basis will often measure inventory on its trial balance for internal records on another basis, such as FIFO. If costs are increasing, the firm will then use an allowance account, referred to as the **LIFO reserve**, to reduce the inventory to the measurement under LIFO. The balance in the LIFO reserve account is the difference between the inventory measured using FIFO and LIFO. The footnotes to the financial statements disclose the LIFO reserve. Example 10.10 illustrates the conversion from FIFO to LIFO.

[10]IASC, *International Accounting Standard 2*, "Inventories," BC 11, 19.

EXAMPLE 10.10 LIFO Reserve

PROBLEM: Cosmop Enterprises reports externally using LIFO but keeps its inventory records internally using FIFO. On January 1, its inventory was $100,000 measured using FIFO and $92,000 using LIFO. On December 31 of that year, its inventory was $130,000 using FIFO and $119,000 using LIFO. During the year, Cosmop recorded cost of goods sold of $50,000 and purchased new inventory of $80,000. What is the balance in Cosmop's inventory and LIFO reserve accounts as of January 1? What is the balance in the inventory and LIFO reserve accounts as of December 31? What journal entry is required on December 31 to convert to LIFO? What is the LIFO effect for the year?

SOLUTION: At the beginning of the year, the internal inventory account had a $100,000 debit balance using FIFO. Cosmop reports inventory valued at $92,000 under the LIFO method. As a result, the LIFO reserve requires a credit balance of $8,000 (FIFO − LIFO = $100,000 − $92,000). Thus, Cosmop reports inventory on the balance sheet at the net amount of $92,000. On December 31, the internal inventory account had a $130,000 debit balance under FIFO and an inventory measurement of $119,000 using LIFO. The ending LIFO reserve account requires a credit balance of $11,000 (FIFO − LIFO = $130,000 − $119,000).

The partial t-account for the inventory account using FIFO and the LIFO reserve is as follows:

Inventory – FIFO

	Debit	Credit	
January 1	100,000		
		50,000	Cost of Goods Sold
Purchases	80,000		
December 31	130,000		

We know that Cosmop has a beginning balance of $8,000 in the LIFO reserve account and needs an ending balance of $11,000. Thus, we compute the required adjustment as follows:

Ending LIFO reserve needed	$11,000
Beginning balance	(8,000)
Adjustment required	$ 3,000

LIFO Reserve

Debit	Credit	
	8,000	January 1
	3,000	Year-End Adjustment
	11,000	December 31

The adjusting journal entry that follows records a credit of $3,000 to the LIFO reserve account that is offset by a debit of $3,000 to cost of goods sold. The LIFO effect is a decrease to pretax income of $3,000.

Account	***Year-End***	
Cost of Goods Sold	3,000	
LIFO Reserve		3,000

The debit to the cost of goods sold increases that account to $53,000, which reflects the use of the LIFO method ($50,000 FIFO cost of goods sold + $3,000 LIFO effect). The LIFO reserve reduces ending inventory to the proper LIFO valuation of $119,000 ($130,000 FIFO Inventory − $11,000 LIFO reserve).

In the process of recording the LIFO reserve account adjustment, the company will also adjust the cost of goods sold account as shown in Example 10.10. The income statement adjustment in the LIFO reserve account is referred to as the **LIFO effect**, which is the change in the LIFO reserve account during the year and its impact on cost of goods sold.

LIFO Liquidations

As noted earlier, if costs are declining, using LIFO will result in lower cost of goods sold and thus higher net income when compared to FIFO. If inventory unit levels are decreasing and costs are increasing, then using LIFO may also result in higher net income than FIFO.

As a company uses LIFO over time, it builds **LIFO layers**, which are annual increases in the quantity of inventory. When inventory levels decline under the LIFO method and costs are increasing, the company sells older low-cost LIFO layers, reducing cost of goods sold and increasing book (and taxable) income. A decrease in inventory layers under the LIFO method is called a **LIFO liquidation** and is illustrated in Example 10.11. Recall that companies choose LIFO to lower their tax bills. Because of the possibility that a LIFO liquidation decreases cost of goods sold and increases taxable income, companies seek to avoid liquidating their LIFO layers.[11] For example, ***Deere & Company,*** the agriculture and construction equipment company, reported a favorable pre-tax income effect from the liquidation of LIFO inventory during 2016 and 2015 of approximately \$4 million and \$22 million, respectively. For ***Deere,*** the LIFO liquidations were less than a 1% increase in pre-tax income. Exhibit 10.7 presents the disclosure that ***Caterpillar Inc.,*** another leading manufacturer of construction and mining equipment, provided in its 2013 10-K related to a larger LIFO liquidation that resulted in an increase in net income of \$0.12 per share, or about 2.1%.

EXHIBIT 10.7 Excerpt from Inventory Disclosure, ***Caterpillar Inc.,*** Annual 10-K Report, December 31, 2013

> During 2013 inventory quantities were reduced. This reduction resulted in a liquidation of LIFO inventory layers carried at lower costs prevailing in prior years as compared with current costs. In 2013, the effect of this reduction of inventory decreased cost of goods sold by approximately \$115 million and increased profit by approximately \$81 million or \$0.12 per share.

Source: Caterpillar. http://www.caterpillar.com/en/investors/sec-filings.html

EXAMPLE 10.11 LIFO Liquidation

PROBLEM: Poppins Products provided you with the following information regarding its 2018 inventory and sales. The company uses a FIFO perpetual inventory management system for internal purposes and employs a LIFO perpetual system for external reporting and tax.

Data for 2018	FIFO		LIFO	
Description	**Unit Cost × Units**	**Total Cost**	**Unit Cost × Units**	**Total Cost**
Beginning inventory: January 1, 2018				
Layer from 2016	\$3 × 1,000	= \$3,000	\$1 × 3,000	\$ 3,000
Layer from 2017	\$5 × 3,000	= 15,000	\$3 × 1,000	3,000
Beginning inventory: January 1, 2018*	4,000	\$18,000	4,000	\$ 6,000
Purchases during 2018	\$6 × 1,000	= 6,000	\$6 × 1,000	6,000
Cost of goods available for sale	5,000	\$24,000	5,000	\$12,000
Units sold during 2018	(4,500)		(4,500)	
Ending inventory: December 31, 2018	500		500	

*The beginning LIFO reserve is \$12,000 (FIFO − LIFO = \$18,000 − \$6,000)

a. What is Poppins' ending inventory on both a FIFO and a LIFO basis?
b. What is the LIFO reserve balance at end of the year?

[11] A LIFO liquidation will not always result in an increase to net income.

c. What is the LIFO effect for the year? Typically, the LIFO effect decreases income. Is that the case here?

d. What is the journal entry to record the LIFO effect?

SOLUTION: Ending inventory and cost of goods sold computed under the FIFO perpetual basis are as follows:

Description	Units	Unit Cost	Total Cost
FIFO Ending Inventory			
Most recent cost	500	$6	$ 3,000
FIFO Cost of Goods Sold			
Oldest cost	1,000	$3	$ 3,000
Next oldest cost	3,000	5	15,000
Next oldest cost	500	6	3,000
Totals	4,500		$21,000

Under the LIFO perpetual method, Poppins Products has the following ending inventory and cost of goods sold.

Description	Units	Unit Cost	Total Cost
LIFO Ending Inventory			
Oldest cost	500	$1	$ 500
LIFO Cost of Goods Sold			
Most recent cost	1,000	$6	$ 6,000
Next most recent cost	1,000	3	3,000
Next most recent cost	2,500	1	2,500
Totals	4,500		$11,500

The ending LIFO reserve is $2,500, the difference between ending inventory on a LIFO and FIFO basis ($3,000 − $500). The beginning and ending LIFO reserve amounts and the year-end adjustment needed are as follows:

Ending LIFO reserve needed	$ 2,500
Beginning balance	(12,000)
Adjustment required	$(9,500)

LIFO Reserve

	Debit	Credit
January 1, 2018		12,000
Year-End Adjustment	9,500	
December 31, 2018		2,500

A decrease in the LIFO reserve (the LIFO effect) will increase Poppins' inventory and reduce cost of sales. The journal entry to record the LIFO effect is a debit of $9,500 to the LIFO reserve and a credit to the cost of goods sold:

Account	***Year-End***	
LIFO Reserve	9,500	
Cost of Goods Sold		9,500

Notice that the journal entry credits cost of goods sold, thus decreasing cost of goods sold and increasing net income. Because Poppins liquidated LIFO layers, its use of LIFO increased net income.

Dollar-Value LIFO

LIFO computations for each individual product can become extremely time consuming when a firm carries a significant number of different products and product lines. Imagine the work involved in computing LIFO layers for a department store with thousands of stock numbers and multiple product lines. When a company considers only one product at a time to compute a LIFO inventory valuation, the LIFO layers associated with it must all be liquidated if that product becomes obsolete.

Techniques to simplify the LIFO computation aggregate inventory items into groups called **pools** and perform the LIFO computations on the inventory pool as opposed to individual items. The most common technique is the **dollar-value LIFO method**, which pools inventory items and uses the dollar as the common unit of measure of the inventory. Because the unit of measure (the dollar) applies to all inventory items, firms can aggregate multiple items into a single LIFO pool. Dollar-value LIFO offers several advantages:

1. Firms account for dollars, not units. Dollars are a common unit of measure regardless of the specific inventory item. Therefore, an extremely diverse inventory can be made homogeneous by restating the physical units into dollars.
2. It avoids problems when there are changes in product mix. When a firm adds or deletes a product or product line, it simply replaces dollars with other dollars (both products are carried at the same common unit of measure).
3. It can minimize the likelihood of liquidation because the removal of one stock number is not going to liquidate an entire cost pool. Again, dollars are replaced by dollars and the units of measure are the same.

Dollar-Value LIFO Computation. The dollar-value LIFO approach involves computing the pool of inventory on the basis of the dollar, not in terms of units. Consequently, when comparing beginning inventory with ending inventory, the firm determines how much of the change is due to changes in price and how much is due to changes in quantity.[12] Computing the LIFO layers indicates the change in quantity.

There are six steps involved in reporting inventory using the dollar-value LIFO approach. To illustrate, consider Lookout, Inc., which has ending inventory in 2018 (computed under FIFO) of $100,000 and ending inventory in 2019 (under FIFO) of $120,000. The company first adopts dollar-value LIFO in 2018, which is the base year with a price index of 1.00. The relevant price index for 2019 is 1.15. That is, prices generally increased 15% from 2018 to 2019 for the type of products that Lookout buys and sells. Sometimes indices are expressed as, for example, 1.15 or as 115. Both of these imply a 15% price increase.[13]

The six steps are as follows:

1. **Determine the ending inventory stated in terms of base-year prices.** The **base year** is the first year that the company reports under dollar-value LIFO. In Lookout's case, this is 2018. To determine the ending inventory in terms of base-year prices, a company divides the ending inventory at year-end prices by the cumulative price index. That is, Lookout divides $120,000 by the 1.15 index and computes the ending inventory at the base-year price to be $104,348. Ending inventory for 2018 is already at base-year prices of $100,000.
2. **Determine the increase (or decrease) in quantity at base-year prices.** Lookout's 2019 beginning inventory is at the base-year price of $100,000 and ending inventory is at the base-year price of $104,348. The difference measures the increase in quantity. Under dollar-value LIFO, the quantities in the pool are now measured in common units, dollars, and there is no need to track inventory (for LIFO purposes) in terms of physical units. The increase in quantity for Lookout is $4,348 ($104,348 less $100,000) stated in base-year dollar terms.
3. **Determine the increase (or decrease) in quantity at current-year prices.** To determine the increase in quantity at current-year prices, a company takes the increase in the quantity stated in base-year dollars (in the case of Lookout, this was $4,348) and prices it in terms of current

[12]We use the term *price* to represent the unit cost of inventory.

[13]Companies use indices such as the consumer price index (CPI) and various other industry-specific indices for these computations.

(end-of-year) prices by multiplying it by the cumulative price index. Therefore, Lookout multiplies the $4,348 by the 1.15 index to determine an increase in quantity at current-year prices of $5,000.

4. **Add all of the layers together to get the dollar-value LIFO ending inventory.** For Lookout, the layers are as follows:

Year	Layer
2018	$100,000
2019	5,000
Ending inventory under dollar-value LIFO	$105,000

The layers under dollar-value LIFO are the increase in quantity at current-year prices.

5. **Calculate the LIFO reserve.** The LIFO reserve is the difference between the inventory balance computed per the internal books and the LIFO inventory balance. In the case of Lookout, the LIFO reserve at the end of 2019 is $15,000 ($120,000 FIFO less $105,000 dollar value LIFO).
6. **Record the journal entry to make the LIFO adjustment.** Because Lookout did not have a LIFO reserve at the end of the prior year, the entry will record the $15,000 reserve as follows:

Account	*2019 Year-End*	
Cost of Goods Sold	15,000	
LIFO Reserve		15,000

The example of Lookout, Inc. was fairly simple because it involved only one year after the initial adoption of dollar-value LIFO. We now turn to a more complex example, again following the six steps. Example 10.12 provides a multi-year illustration of dollar-value LIFO.

EXAMPLE 10.12 Dollar-Value LIFO

PROBLEM: WJS, Inc. uses a perpetual FIFO-based inventory management system, but it reports externally using dollar-value LIFO. WJS reported the following price indices and FIFO inventory at year-end prices. For each year, provide the LIFO ending inventory, the LIFO reserve balance, and the year-end LIFO adjusting entry.

Year	Ending Inventory at Year-End Prices (FIFO)	Cumulative Price Index
2016	$150,000	1.00
2017	250,000	1.20
2018	260,000	1.25
2019	210,000	1.26

SOLUTION: We will once again work through the six steps. We will work through all years for each step at once. In practice, you will do only one year at a time because you have information for only the current year.

1. **Determine the ending inventory stated in terms of base-year prices.** The base year, the first year that WJS reported under LIFO, is 2016. Note that the cumulative price index in the base year is always 1.00. The ending inventory in terms of base-year prices is the ending inventory at year-end prices divided by the cumulative price index as follows:

Year	Ending Inventory at Year-End Prices (FIFO)	Cumulative Price Index	Ending Inventory at Base-Year Price
2016	$150,000	1.00	$150,000
2017	250,000	1.20	208,333
2018	260,000	1.25	208,000
2019	210,000	1.26	166,667

Continued

2. **Determine the increase (or decrease) in quantity at base-year prices.** To determine the increase in quantity at base-year prices, we compute the change from year to year as follows:

Year	Ending Inventory at Year-End Prices	Cumulative Price Index	Ending Inventory at Base-Year Prices	Change in Quantity at Base-Year Prices	Increase in LIFO layers or Decrease of LIFO layers?
2016	$150,000	1.00	$150,000	$0	
2017	250,000	1.20	208,333	$58,333 = $208,333 − $150,000	Increase
2018	260,000	1.25	208,000	$(333) = $208,000 − $208,333	Decrease
2019	210,000	1.26	166,667	$(41,333) = $166,667 − $208,000	Decrease

Next, we will complete steps 3 through 6 together for each year.

3. **Determine the increase (or decrease) in quantity at current-year prices.**
4. **Add all of the layers together to get the dollar-value LIFO ending inventory.**
5. **Calculate the LIFO reserve.**
6. **Record the journal entry to make the LIFO adjustment.**

The increase in quantity at current-year prices is the increase in the quantity stated in dollars priced in terms of base-year prices multiplied by the cumulative price index. We summarize the FIFO inventory and LIFO inventory and compute the LIFO reserve as the difference.

Next, we build our LIFO layers one year at a time as follows:

2017: The 2017 layer is the increase in inventory at base-year prices $(58,333) multiplied by the cumulative price index in 2017 (1.20), yielding a LIFO layer of $70,000 for 2017. Again, keep in mind that under dollar-value LIFO, the LIFO layer is the increase in quantity stated at current (i.e., end-of-year) prices.

We add the layers together to determine the LIFO ending inventory of $220,000.

	Base-Year Prices	Index	Current-Year Prices
2016 layer and ending balance	$150,000	1.00	$150,000
2017 layer	58,333	1.20	70,000
2017 ending balance	$208,333		$220,000

We now compute the LIFO reserve balance by summarizing the FIFO inventory and LIFO inventory as follows and computing the LIFO reserve as the difference:

Year (a)	Ending Inventory at Year-End Prices (FIFO) (b)	Ending Inventory at Dollar-Value LIFO (c)	LIFO Reserve Balance (Cumulative Balance Sheet Effect) (d) = (b) − (c)	Change in the LIFO Reserve (Specific LIFO Income Statement Effect) (e) = (d) − Prior (d)
2016	$150,000	$150,000	$ 0	$ 0
2017	250,000	220,000	30,000	30,000

WJS begins in 2017 with a zero balance in the LIFO reserve account. Thus, in order to have a $30,000 credit balance in the LIFO reserve, it makes the following journal entry:

Account	2017 Year-End	
Cost of Goods Sold	30,000	
LIFO Reserve		30,000

2018: The computations for 2018 are complex because WJS decreased part of its 2017 layer. We know this because the change in ending inventory at base-year prices was negative (i.e., a decrease in inventory). Thus, WJS has to remove $333 at base-year prices from its 2017 layer. It then recalculates the adjusted 2017 LIFO layer (at 2017 prices) as $69,600. Because it liquidated part of a layer in 2018, it does not build a 2018 layer. Adding up the LIFO layers, WJS has $219,600 in ending inventory under dollar-value LIFO for 2018.

	Base-Year Prices	Index	Current-Year Prices (at Dollar-Value LIFO)
2016 Beginning inventory	$150,000	1.00	$150,000
2017 layer	58,333	1.20	70,000
2018 layer liquidation	(333)	1.20	(400)
2017 adjusted layer	58,000	1.20	69,600
2018 ending inventory	$208,000		$219,600

Liquidating a layer *does not* result in a change to prior inventory balances, so the 2017 inventory of $220,000 does not change. However, the liquidation of a prior layer is priced at the index for that year, meaning that a company liquidates LIFO layers in LIFO order.

We now compute the LIFO reserve balance by summarizing the FIFO inventory and LIFO inventory as follows and computing the LIFO reserve as the difference:

Year (a)	Ending Inventory at Year-End Prices (FIFO) (b)	Ending Inventory at Dollar-Value LIFO (c)	LIFO Reserve Balance (Cumulative Balance Sheet Effect) (d) = (b) − (c)	Change in the LIFO Reserve (Specific LIFO Income Statement Effect) (e) = (d) − Prior (d)
2016	$150,000	$150,000	$ 0	$ 0
2017	250,000	220,000	30,000	30,000
2018	260,000	219,600	40,400	10,400

We begin in 2018 with a credit balance of $30,000 in the LIFO reserve account. Thus, in order to end up with a $40,400 credit balance, WJS makes the following journal entry:

Account	2018 Year-End	
Cost of Goods Sold	10,400	
LIFO Reserve		10,400

2019: In 2019, there is a decrease in inventory at base-year prices of $41,333, signaling a layer liquidation. Thus, WJS has to remove $41,333 at base-year prices from the 2017 layer. It then recalculates the adjusted 2017 LIFO layer (at 2017 prices) as $20,000. Because WJS liquidated a partial layer in 2018 and 2019, it has not built a 2018 or 2019

Continued

layer. Adding up the LIFO layers, there is $170,000 in ending inventory under dollar-value LIFO for 2019.

	Base-Year Prices	Index	Current-Year Prices (at Dollar-Value LIFO)
2016 Beginning inventory	$150,000	1.00	$150,000
2017 layer	58,333	1.20	70,000
2018 layer liquidation	(333)	1.20	(400)
2017 adjusted layer	58,000		69,600
2019 layer liquidation	(41,333)	1.20	(49,600)
2017 adjusted layer	16,667	1.20	20,000
2019 ending inventory	$166,667		$170,000

We now compute the LIFO reserve balance by summarizing the FIFO inventory and LIFO inventory as follows and computing the LIFO reserve as the difference:

Year (a)	Ending Inventory at Year-End Prices (FIFO) (b)	Ending Inventory at Dollar-Value LIFO (c)	LIFO Reserve Balance (Cumulative Balance Sheet Effect) (d) = (b) − (c)	Change in the LIFO Reserve (Specific LIFO Income Statement Effect) (e) = (d) − Prior (d)
2016	$150,000	$150,000	$ 0	$ 0
2017	250,000	220,000	30,000	30,000
2018	260,000	219,600	40,400	10,400
2019	210,000	170,000	40,000	(400)

We begin in 2019 with a credit balance of $40,400 in the LIFO reserve account. Thus, in order to report with a $40,000 credit balance, WJS makes the following journal entry:

Account	***2019 Year-End***	
LIFO Reserve	400	
Cost of Goods Sold		400

In 2019, WJS had a significant decrease in inventory. Consequently, the LIFO effect in 2019 was an increase in income of $400 as opposed to the more common decrease in income expected under LIFO.

JUDGMENTS IN ACCOUNTING
The LIFO Effect

Management determines the cost-flow assumption that the company uses in the financial statements. To allow comparability, firms generally do not change methods. Other than the tax effects, the choice of method does not impact cash flows. That is, whether a company uses LIFO or FIFO has no bearing on what its suppliers will charge it for the inventory nor what it will charge its customers when it sells the inventory. Choosing LIFO or FIFO is just an internal accounting decision. Yet, because each method results in different measurements of ending inventory on the balance sheet and cost of goods sold on the income statement, this decision can be quite critical. Management and financial statement users must have a thorough understanding of the impact of the different methods.

Consider the disclosure in Exhibit 10.8 included in the 10-K filed by **Deere & Company** for the year ended October 31, 2016.

EXHIBIT 10.8 Inventory Disclosure from ***Deere & Company,*** Annual Report, October 31, 2016

NOTE 15: Inventories

Most inventories owned by Deere & Company and its U.S. equipment subsidiaries are valued at cost, on the "last-in, first-out" (LIFO) basis. Remaining inventories are generally valued at the lower of cost, on the "first-in, first-out" (FIFO) basis, or market. The value of gross inventories on the LIFO basis represented 61 percent and 66 percent of worldwide gross inventories at FIFO value at October 31, 2016 and 2015, respectively. The pretax favorable income effects from the liquidation of LIFO inventory during 2016 and 2015 were approximately $4 million and $22 million, respectively. If all inventories had been valued on a FIFO basis, estimated inventories by major classification at October 31 in millions of dollars would have been as follows:

	2016	2015
Raw materials and supplies	$1,369	$1,559
Work-in-process	453	450
Finished goods and parts	2,976	3,234
Total FIFO value	4,798	5,243
Less adjustment to LIFO value	1,457	1,426
Inventories	$3,341	$3,817

Source: Deere & Company. https://s2.q4cdn.com/329009547/files/doc_financials/annual_reports/2016/2016_John-Deere-Annual-Report.pdf

In its October 31, 2016, balance sheet, ***Deere & Company*** reported an inventory valuation of $3,341 million on a LIFO basis. If it had reported under FIFO, inventory would have been $4,798 million, which is a 44% increase. This substantial difference results solely because of a management decision. The LIFO effect of $31 million for the 2016 year is the difference in the beginning and ending LIFO reserve balances, $1,426 less $1,457 (called the "adjustment to LIFO value" in the footnote).

Again, this large effect on income is due to management's accounting choice of inventory cost-flow assumptions. It is not uncommon for there to be a significant impact on income related to this choice.

5 Explain the lower-of-cost-or-market rule.

The Lower-of-Cost-or-Market Rule

After a company has established its method for valuing inventory, it must monitor its inventory over time for business planning and financial reporting purposes to assess its future revenue-generating ability. The **lower-of-cost-or-market rule** requires that if a measure of the market value of inventory falls below its cost basis (as determined by an inventory allocation method), then the company must report inventory at the lower of its cost or market value. Specifically, when the market value of inventory falls below its cost, a company:

1. Reports the difference between the cost basis and the market-based measure as a loss on the income statement (indirect method) or an increase to cost of goods sold (direct method).
2. Carries the inventory at the lower amount on the balance sheet.

For example, technology companies often have short product life cycles that can lead to rapid obsolescence and price erosion. If a company builds its inventories during periods of anticipated growth and that growth does not materialize, the result may be excess or obsolete inventory. For example, ***BlackBerry Limited***, the manufacturer of ***BlackBerry*** smartphones, had to write down inventory by about $1.6 billion in fiscal 2013 when it experienced lower-than-anticipated future demand for certain products. In fiscal 2014 and 2015, Blackberry recorded additional inventory write-downs of $95 million and $36 million, respectively.[14]

[14]Source: http://us.blackberry.com/content/dam/bbCompany/Desktop/Global/PDF/Investors/Governance/Q416_Financial_Statements.pdf

THE CONCEPTUAL FRAMEWORK CONNECTION
Lower of Cost or Market

The conceptual framework defines assets as probable future economic benefits obtained or controlled by a particular company as a result of past transactions or events. The portion of the definition requiring that an asset provide probable future economic benefits is critical to understanding the lower-of-cost-or-market rule. The most relevant inventory method better measures the future economic benefits. If the expected economic benefits are less than the amount that the firm is currently reporting in inventory, then the firm should reduce the amount on the balance sheet.

At times, measuring an asset's value at other than historical cost involves a trade-off between the two fundamental characteristics in the conceptual framework—namely, relevance and faithful representation. When a firm writes down an asset, it must determine a new carrying amount based upon its expectation of future economic benefits. For some assets (such as property, plant, and equipment), the measurement of future economic benefits can be quite subjective and thus not reliable. Fortunately, for most types of inventory, the assessment of a market value is highly reliable because most inventory items are frequently bought and sold in the marketplace.

Lower-of-Cost-or-Market Rule Method

Implementation of the lower-of-cost-or-market rule involves three steps:

1. Determine the market value of inventory.
2. Compare the market value measure to cost as determined using an inventory allocation method.
3. Record the write-down, if necessary.

We discuss each of these steps in turn.

Determination of Market Value. The method that firms use to determine market value depends on their inventory cost-flow assumption. Having two methods complicates the determination of market value and results in inconsistent measures of market value.

Cost-Flow Assumptions Other than LIFO or Retail Inventory. Firms determine market value at *net realizable value (NRV)* if they use a method other than LIFO or the retail inventory method (which we discuss later in the chapter). **Net realizable value (NRV)** is the item's selling price less the cost of disposal. Disposal costs include packaging, shipping, and commissions. Disposal costs are also referred to as the costs of completion and sale.

LIFO or Retail Inventory Cost-Flow Assumption. Firms that use LIFO or the retail inventory method to measure the cost of inventory measure the market value as the amount at which they could currently purchase or reproduce the inventory, known as the **current replacement cost (CRC)**.[15] However, there are two boundaries on the use of CRC:

1. The CRC cannot exceed a **ceiling** equal to NRV. The ceiling prevents overvaluing inventory or using a value above the amount that the firm reasonably expects to realize in cash from the disposal of the item.
2. The CRC cannot fall below a **floor** value of **net realizable value less a normal profit margin (NRV – NP)**. The floor prevents undervaluation of inventory. For example, firms may undervalue inventory and report a large loss on their income statements if they are taking a *big bath*. A big bath occurs when a firm frontloads expenses and losses in one year so that it can look much better, comparatively, in future years. The NRV – NP valuation is the lowest measure of market value at which the firm can carry inventory on its balance sheet.

[15]The lower-of-cost-or-market test is excluded from the fair value measurement provisions of FASB ASC 820. As a result, fair value is not an exit price in the valuation of inventory.

These two boundaries lead us to the three scenarios for computing a measure of market value.

- Scenario 1: CRC lies between NRV and NRV – NP. Market is measured as CRC.
- Scenario 2: CRC lies above the ceiling, NRV. Market is measured as the NRV.
- Scenario 3: CRC lies below NRV – NP. Market is measured as the NRV – NP.

Exhibit 10.9 illustrates the lower-of-cost-or-market rule in valuing inventory.

EXHIBIT 10.9 Lower-of-Cost-or-Market; Inventory Valuation for LIFO or Retail Inventory Method

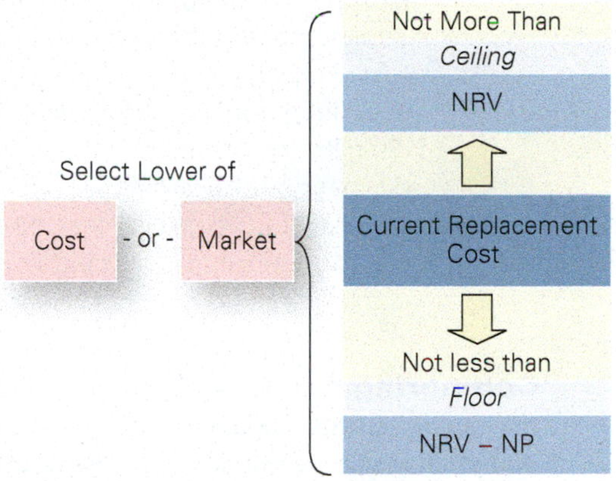

LIFO and retail method firms compare the NRV, CRC, and NRV – NP for each item in inventory to determine that item's market value as illustrated in Example 10.13.

EXAMPLE 10.13 Determination of Market Value

PROBLEM: Jarrod Clothing Wholesalers, Inc. provided you with the following information regarding inventory as of December 31, 2018:

Item (a)	Cost (b)	Selling Price (c)	Dis-posal Costs (d)	Normal Profit Margin (e)	NRV (Ceiling) (f) = (c) − (d)	NRV – NP (Floor) (g) = (f) − (e)	CRC (h)
Shorts – men	$10,000	$36,000	$16,000	$8,000	$20,000	$12,000	$15,000
Jeans – men	20,000	23,000	4,000	2,000	19,000	17,000	18,000
Shirts & blouses	5,000	6,000	3,000	1,000	3,000	2,000	4,000
Skirts	8,000	20,000	5,000	4,000	15,000	11,000	12,000
Jeans – women	15,000	43,000	31,000	1,000	12,000	11,000	9,000

1. Determine the market value that Jarrod will use in its lower-of-cost-or-market rule calculations for each inventory item assuming that Jarrod computes inventory cost using the FIFO method.
2. Determine the market value that Jarrod will use in its lower-of-cost-or-market rule calculations for each inventory item assuming that Jarrod computes inventory cost using the LIFO method.

SOLUTION: If Jarrod uses the FIFO method for computing inventory cost, then the market value of each item is simply equal to its NRV.

Item	Cost	NRV	Market Value
Shorts – men	$10,000	$20,000	$20,000
Jeans – men	20,000	19,000	19,000
Shirts & blouses	5,000	3,000	3,000
Skirts	8,000	15,000	15,000
Jeans – women	15,000	12,000	12,000

Continued

If Jarrod uses LIFO for computing inventory cost, then the computations become more complex. The default market value is the CRC unless it is higher than the NRV ceiling or lower than the NRV – NP floor. The CRCs of the men's shorts, men's jeans, and skirts inventory items all fall between the NRV and NRV – NP, so Jarrod assigns the CRC as the market value for these items. The CRC for the shirts and blouses is above the NRV ceiling, so we use the NRV. The CRC for the women's jeans is below the NRV – NP floor, so we use the NRV – NP. The far-right column of the following table shows the resulting market value from this analysis:

Item	Cost	NRV	CRC	NRV – NP	Market Value
Shorts – men	$10,000	$20,000	$15,000	$12,000	$15,000
Jeans – men	20,000	19,000	18,000	17,000	18,000
Shirts & blouses	5,000	3,000	4,000	2,000	3,000
Skirts	8,000	15,000	12,000	11,000	12,000
Jeans – women	15,000	12,000	9,000	11,000	11,000

Comparing Cost to Market. After determining the market value of the inventory, firms must compare this amount to the cost basis of the inventory determined using an inventory allocation method. This comparison is done the same way, no matter what costing method a firm uses.

Firms can apply the lower-of-cost-or-market rule for inventory to the aggregate inventory, groups of inventory, or individual items in inventory. U.S. GAAP does not specify a preference among these three approaches except that a company should use the approach that best measures income. The individual-item approach is the most common in practice and the most conservative because it results in the largest write-down. Any grouping approach, called a group by group approach, will minimize the amount of the loss as higher market values of some items above cost will offset cases where market is lower than cost. Applying LCM to aggregate inventory, then, results in the lowest loss.

Companies must justify the grouping choice (for example, into product lines or total inventory) based on economic reality or marketing techniques used to distribute a company's products. For example, assume a computer company adds a free printer with the purchase of every laptop computer. Does this mean that the printer has a zero market value and should be completely written off under the LCM rule? The logical approach is to combine the printer and the laptop computer as a single product group and compare the market value of the group to its combined cost. The marketing technique used by the entity typically determines the grouping of products for purposes of the LCM test. Other examples of logical product groups include printers and toner cartridges, razors and blades, and mechanical pencils and lead refills.

If the market value is below the cost basis, the write-down amount is the difference between the two amounts. Example 10.14 provides an illustration of accounting for inventory write-downs.

EXAMPLE 10.14 Computation of Inventory Write-Down

PROBLEM: Continuing with Jarrod Clothing Wholesalers from Example 10.13 and assuming that Jarrod determines inventory cost using the LIFO method, determine the necessary write-down under the assumption that Jarrod uses (1) an individual-item approach, (2) a group approach with men's and women's groups, and (3) an aggregate approach.

SOLUTION: Under an individual-item approach, Jarrod compares cost and market on an item-by-item basis as shown in the following table, leading to the lower-of-cost-or-market rule inventory valuation of $50,000. Because the cost basis is $58,000, Jarrod records an $8,000 write-down.

Item	Cost	Market Value	Lower of Cost or Market
Shorts – men	$10,000	$15,000	$10,000
Jeans – men	20,000	18,000	18,000
Shirts & blouses	5,000	3,000	3,000
Skirts	8,000	12,000	8,000
Jeans – women	15,000	11,000	11,000
TOTAL	$58,000		$50,000

Refer to the following table. Under the product-line approach, Jarrod first computes the cost and market values by group (men's and women's in this case) and then compares these numbers to arrive at the lower-of-cost-or-market rule inventory valuation of $56,000. Because the cost basis is $58,000, Jarrod records a write-down of $2,000.

Item	Cost	Market Value	Group Cost	Group Market Value	Lower of Cost or Market
Shorts – men	$10,000	$15,000			
Jeans – men	20,000	18,000			
MEN'S TOTAL			$30,000	$33,000	$30,000
Shirts & blouses	$ 5,000	$ 3,000			
Skirts	8,000	12,000			
Jeans – women	15,000	11,000			
WOMEN'S TOTAL			$28,000	$26,000	$26,000
TOTAL	$58,000				$56,000

Under the aggregate approach shown in the following table, Jarrod computes total cost ($58,000) and total market value ($59,000) and compares the two. Because cost is lower than market, Jarrod does not need to make a lower-of-cost-or-market rule adjustment.

Item	Cost	Market Value	Lower of Cost or Market
Shorts – men	$10,000	$15,000	
Jeans – men	20,000	18,000	
Shirts & blouses	5,000	3,000	
Skirts	8,000	12,000	
Jeans – women	15,000	11,000	
TOTAL	$58,000	$59,000	$58,000

Recording the Write-Down. Firms can use two methods to write down inventory to market if needed:

1. The **direct method** writes off the loss directly to the inventory account and records that loss in the cost of goods sold reported on the income statement.
2. The **indirect method** reports the loss as a separate line item on the income statement within income from continuing operations and reduces the inventory account by the use of an allowance account.[16] Under the indirect method, when the firm increases the allowance, it reports a loss. When it decreases the allowance, the firm records income.

[16]The direct method is also known as the *cost of goods sold method*, and the indirect method is also known as the *loss method*.

If the write-down is significant, then the indirect method is preferred because it discloses the loss separately from the cost of goods that were actually sold. When a loss is disclosed as an individual line item on the income statement, the financial statement user can easily identify that the loss has taken place and determine its magnitude. The direct method includes the loss in cost of goods sold and therefore is not as transparent to the financial statement user. Recording a write-down is illustrated in Example 10.15.

EXAMPLE 10.15 Recording the Lower-of-Cost-or-Market Rule Write-Down

PROBLEM: Continuing with Example 10.14, assume that Jarrod uses the individual item approach for computing the necessary lower-of-cost-or-market rule adjustment and that Jarrod had a beginning allowance balance of zero.

a. What is the journal entry to record the write-down under the direct method?

b. What is the journal entry to record the write-down under the indirect method?

SOLUTION:

a. Direct Method: The direct method writes inventory down directly and records the loss in cost of goods sold. Thus, the entry to record the write-down from a cost basis of $58,000 to the lower-of-cost-or-market rule basis of $50,000 is as follows:

Account	December 31, 2018	
Cost of Goods Sold	8,000	
Inventory		8,000

b. Indirect Method: The indirect method records the loss on inventory write-down as a separate line item on the income statement and reduces inventory with an allowance account.

Account	December 31, 2018	
Loss on Inventory Write-Down	8,000	
Allowance to Reduce Inventory to Market		8,000

The indirect method can result in a loss amount that is misleading in subsequent years. Because the allowance account is a permanent account, the write-down (and thus the amount of the loss on the inventory write-down) is "forced" to arrive at the correct balance in the allowance account. Example 10.16 illustrates the use of the allowance account in subsequent years.

EXAMPLE 10.16 Recording the Lower-of-Cost-or-Market Rule Write-Down in Subsequent Years

PROBLEM: Continuing the Jarrod Clothing Wholesalers example, assume that in 2019, Jarrod sold all of its beginning inventory having a cost basis of $58,000 and lower-of-cost-or-market rule basis of $50,000. As of December 31, 2019, it had inventory with a cost basis of $120,000. Jarrod computed a lower-of-cost-or-market rule valuation of $108,000.

Using the direct method, what is the write-down journal entry and what is the impact on net income for 2019 and inventory valuation for inventory transactions during 2019? What value does Jarrod report for inventory on the balance sheet at December 31, 2019, under the direct method? Answer these same questions assuming that the indirect method is used.

SOLUTION: Under the direct method, Jarrod records the $12,000 ($120,000 − $108,000) write-down directly to cost of goods sold and inventory.

Account	December 31, 2019	
Cost of Goods Sold	12,000	
Inventory		12,000

The total cost of goods sold will be $62,000, which is the $50,000 recorded throughout the year as Jarrod sold inventory with a cost basis of $50,000 plus the $12,000 write-down. Jarrod reported inventory on the balance sheet of $108,000, which is the cost basis of $120,000 less the lower-of-cost-or-market adjustment of $12,000 made at year-end.

Impact on Balance Sheet:	
Inventory at cost	$120,000
Write-Down to market	(12,000)
Inventory valuation on balance sheet	$108,000

Impact on Income Statement:	
Cost of Goods Sold (from Sales)	$50,000
Write-Down to Market	12,000
Total impact on cost of goods sold and income statement	$62,000

Under the indirect method, Jarrod adjusts its inventory allowance account so that the ending balance is $12,000. The beginning balance of the allowance account is $8,000 and an allowance of $12,000 is needed at the end of the year.

The computation of the year-end adjustment to the allowance account follows:

Ending allowance needed	$12,000
Beginning balance	(8,000)
Adjustment required	$ 4,000

The t-account for the allowance account is as follows:

	Allowance to Reduce Inventory to Market	
January 1, 2019		8,000
Year-End Adjustment		4,000
December 31, 2019		12,000

Thus, Jarrod credits the allowance account for $4,000 and charges the loss to a separate line item on the income statement as follows:

Account	***December 31, 2019***	
Loss on Inventory Write-Down	4,000	
Allowance to Reduce Inventory to Market		4,000

The value of inventory Jarrod reports on the balance sheet is the $120,000 less the $12,000 allowance balance, or $108,000. Jarrod's beginning inventory at cost was $58,000. All of the beginning inventory is sold, therefore the impact on the income statement is the $58,000 reported in cost of goods sold plus the $4,000 loss reported at year-end for a total of $62,000. Jarrod's cost of goods sold does not change under the indirect method. Therefore, its gross profit is higher under the indirect method.

Impact on Balance Sheet	
Inventory at cost	$120,000
Allowance to reduce inventory to market	(12,000)
Inventory valuation on balance sheet	$108,000

Impact on Income Statement:	
Cost of goods sold (from sales)	$ 58,000
Loss on inventory write-down	4,000
Total impact on income statement	$ 62,000

As illustrated by Example 10.16, the direct and indirect methods have the same overall impact on the financial statements. However, the line-item placement of the inventory-related expenses and losses on the income statement differs for the two methods. If management prefers to reflect a higher gross profit ratio, it will use the indirect method.

Lower-of-Cost-or-Market Rule: IFRS

IFRS-reporting firms always measure the market value as net realizable value (NRV) under the lower-of-cost-or market rule. NRV, the estimated selling price less the estimated costs of completion and sale, is the same value under IFRS and U.S. GAAP. Unlike U.S. GAAP, IFRS does not use a different approach to measure market, depending on the inventory costing method.

Determination of Market Value and Cost Comparison. IFRS-reporting firms determine whether a write-down is necessary by comparing the historical cost to the NRV.

Similar to U.S. GAAP, IFRS reporters typically determine the lower-of-cost-or-market value on an individual-item basis but may also use a group basis. It is generally not acceptable, however, to write inventories down based on aggregate inventory. Unlike U.S. GAAP, IFRS inventory write-downs can be reversed later if the value increases.

The various lower-of-cost-or-market tests can lead to differences in the amount of inventory and write-down under IFRS and U.S. GAAP, particularly when U.S. GAAP firms use the LIFO or retail inventory methods for inventory costing.

Reversal of Inventory Write-Downs. Firms can reverse an IFRS inventory write-down when there is clear evidence of an increase in net realizable value. For example, consider inventory that a firm wrote down because its selling price declined. If the inventory is still on hand when its selling price increases, the company will write up the inventory to its new net realizable value. The reversal will increase both inventory and reported income. The amount of the reversal is limited to the amount of the original write-down. We illustrate write-down reversals in Example 10.17.

EXAMPLE 10.17

Reversal of Inventory Write-Down under IFRS

PROBLEM: Zodeo Company, an IFRS reporter, installs swimming pools. At the end of 2018, it made a $5,000 lower-of-cost-or-market adjustment on its inventory group of prefabricated swimming pools because of low demand and decreased selling prices. At the time, the NRV of the inventory group was $45,000. This year, demand and prices have increased. The new NRV of the inventory group is $48,000. What journal entry is required to record the reversal of the write-down on December 31, 2019?

SOLUTION: Zodeo will record a reversal of $3,000 because the net realizable value of the inventory increased by $3,000 ($48,000 new NRV less $45,000 prior NRV) and the increase in value falls within the write-up limitation of $5,000 (the amount of the original write-down). Thus, Zodeo debits the allowance account and credits the recovery of inventory write-down account for $3,000 as follows:

Account	***December 31, 2019***	
Allowance to Reduce Inventory to Market	3,000	
Recovery of Inventory Write-Down		3,000

JUDGMENTS IN ACCOUNTING
The Lower-of-Cost-or-Market Rule

There are several estimates involved in the lower-of-cost-or-market rule computations, although in many cases these judgments are less subjective than in other areas of financial reporting. In a survey of 175 companies, 22% reported making estimates and using significant judgment in reporting their inventory.[17]

Determining NRV, CRC, and the normal profit margin requires judgment. In certain scenarios, these measurements will be clear. For example, imagine a grocery store determining these values for a box of Cheerios. None of these measures should be difficult to determine: The sales price and replacement cost are readily available, and the store should have a long history related to the normal profit margin. However, in the case of a heavy equipment dealer, these values may be much more difficult to estimate for a piece of custom-made equipment.

Exhibit 10.10 presents a disclosure from ***Clicks Group Limited***, a health- and beauty-focused retail and supply group. ***Clicks Group*** reported that it performs estimates and judgments related to the determination of the net realizable value of inventory that have a significant risk of resulting in material adjustment to the carrying amount of inventory.

EXHIBIT 10.10 Critical Accounting Estimates and Judgments Note Excerpt, ***Clicks Group Limited***, Financial Statements, August 31, 2016

Significant Accounting Estimates and Judgments

Estimates and judgments that have a significant risk of causing a material adjustment to the carrying amounts of assets and liabilities within the next financial year are outlined below and disclosed in the relevant notes to the financial statements.

Allowance for Net Realizable Value of Inventories

The group evaluates its inventory to ensure that it is carried at the lower of cost or net realizable value. Provision is made against slow moving, obsolete, and damaged inventories. Damaged inventories are identified and written down through the inventory counting procedures conducted within each business. Allowance for slow moving and obsolete inventories is assessed by each business as part of its ongoing financial reporting. Obsolescence is assessed based on comparison of the level of inventory holding to the projected likely future sales using factors existing at the reporting date.

Source: Clicks Group Limited. http://www.clicksgroup.co.za/IRDownloads/IntegratedAnnualReport2016/Clicks_AFS_2016.pdf, page 15.

In applying the lower-of-cost-or-market rule adjustment, management exercises judgment in choosing an individual, product line, or aggregate basis to which the rule will be applied. In Example 10.14, the inventory valuation ranged from $50,000 to $58,000 solely because a different basis was used in applying the lower-of-cost-or market rule.

[17] AICPA, *Financial Statements: Best Practices in Presentation and Disclosure – 2012* (New York, NY: AICPA, 2012).

Interview

BARBARA J. WIGHT

CHIEF FINANCIAL OFFICER TAYLOR GUITARS »

Barbara J. Wight

Barbara Wight is Chief Financial Officer at Taylor Guitars, an industry-leading guitar manufacturer whose instruments are played by leading musicians worldwide. She directs all financial, information technology, and legal affairs on behalf of the company and oversees various aspects of operations management, multinational manufacturing, acquisitions, and international compliance.

1 What are the primary factors considered by management when selecting an inventory valuation method? Which method does Taylor use?

Taylor uses the FIFO methodology. GAAP does not require that our valuation methodology match the flow of our inventory; however, in our case, FIFO does closely approximate the actual physical flow of our goods. Our primary raw material is wood, and it must be aged and dried before we use it to build a guitar. Therefore, we are always using the oldest wood first.

In addition, our business is not as susceptible to inflation as other businesses might be. For example, the price of the wood we purchase is directly related to supply and demand at a given point in time, and the sales price of our finished guitars is relatively stable over time. Therefore, LIFO would not necessarily provide us a sustainable, consistent tax advantage.

Taylor's inventories (both finished goods and raw materials) are stated at standard cost, which is determined based on expected labor, overhead, and material costs and approximates the lower of actual cost (first-in, first-out) or market.

2 Why would a business use more than one inventory valuation method for its inventory?

Businesses may use more than one inventory valuation method if they have foreign operations because LIFO is not permitted under IFRS. So companies that use LIFO for U.S. operations would use FIFO for international units. Businesses might also apply different methodologies to different types of inventory or different business segments. For example, if a company's different business segments have different underlying raw material market deliveries, it might want to use LIFO for materials subject to inflation and FIFO for materials whose pricing is stable or even in decline.

3 Describe the most common components included in the unit cost of inventory at Taylor.

Taylor states inventories at standard cost based on the expected raw material costs, labor, and overhead. Our primary raw material is wood.

At the beginning of each year, Taylor determines how many total labor hours it will need to build the forecasted number of guitars and allocates overhead (and labor) to each guitar based on the calculated overhead and labor rate. The overhead rate times the number of labor hours per guitar equals overhead applied to each guitar unit. Taylor drives production based on a hybrid model; we build to order and to a sales forecast of specific models to ensure that high-turnover models are in stock at all times.

4 What are the most significant judgments employed in the decision to write inventory down to market when applying the lower-of-cost-or-market rule?

The most significant judgments are the replacement cost, expected selling price, cost of completion and/or disposal, and normal profit. After appropriately calculating these items, we apply the lower-of-cost-or-market rule. Another area that requires judgment is the determination of whether to calculate the lower-of-cost-or-market rule based on total inventory in question, the inventory category, or on an item-by-item basis. The latter is the most conservative approach.

Each quarter Taylor reviews inventory for slow-moving or obsolete items to establish an excess and obsolete (E&O) inventory reserve balance. Finished goods are typically not reserved against and written off. If a guitar model is deemed to be subnormal, or if it is determined that a model needs to be reengineered to improve the quality to the customer, we write off these specifically identified models.

5 Does Taylor use estimated inventory techniques for financial reporting? Why or why not?

One estimated inventory technique is related to how we value our raw wood. It is not practical (and nearly impossible) to accurately and consistently measure raw wood when it is brought in directly from the forest. So, we have a standard process for estimating the value, which has been accepted by our auditing firm.

Discussion Questions

1. Discuss why LIFO is not permitted under IFRS.
2. Although Taylor Guitars makes limited use of estimating inventory, describe some of the reasons why a company may elect to estimate ending inventory and whether it may report estimated inventory on external financial statements.

6 Calculate inventory and cost of goods sold using the retail inventory method.

The Retail Inventory Method

In addition to the inventory allocation methods we have discussed, companies may use the *conventional retail inventory method* to determine the valuation of inventory reported on the balance sheet. The **conventional retail inventory method** approximates the cost of ending inventory balance by taking into consideration the requirement that firms report inventory at lower of cost or market based on the relationship between cost and selling price. Before we cover the conventional retail method, we will discuss the basic retail method and some retail method terminology.

Basic Retail Method

Large retail firms such as ***Target*** and ***Walmart*** cannot track the costs of each sale of inventory. Instead, these companies may use the basic retail method by maintaining information on:

- Beginning inventory and purchases in terms of cost to the company.
- Beginning inventory and purchases in terms of the sales price (retail values).
- Net sales at retail.

The basic retail method does not, however, track information on sales at cost. To estimate both ending inventory at cost and cost of goods sold, the company:

1. Computes its cost-to-retail ratio by dividing the goods available for sale at cost by the goods available for sale at retail.[18]
2. Applies this ratio to ending inventory at retail to obtain ending inventory at cost.
3. Subtracts the computed ending inventory at cost from the cost of goods available for sale to arrive at cost of goods sold.

Example 10.18 illustrates the basic retail method.

EXAMPLE 10.18

Basic Retail Method

PROBLEM: Boxer Sales Corporation provided the following information on its beginning inventory and purchases for the year:

	Cost	Retail
Beginning inventory	$ 23,400	$ 39,000
Purchases	106,400	156,000

In addition, it recorded sales (at retail) of $160,000. What ending inventory and cost of goods sold will Boxer record under the basic retail method?

SOLUTION: Boxer Sales first computes its cost-to-retail ratio using the goods available for sale. The cost of goods available for sale is $129,800, and the retail value of goods available for sale is $195,000.

	Cost	Retail	Cost-to-Retail Ratio
Beginning inventory	$ 23,400	$ 39,000	
Purchases	106,400	156,000	
Goods available for sale	$129,800	$195,000	67%

Continued

[18]Variations in the composition of the cost-to-retail ratio will approximate different inventory methods. The retail method can produce results that approximate FIFO, LIFO, average-cost, and lower-of-cost-or-market methods. Our focus is on the conventional retail method (which approximates LCM). We discuss the LIFO retail inventory method in Appendix A.

The cost-to-retail ratio is 67% ($129,800 divided by $195,000). Because the company had retail sales of $160,000, Boxer's ending inventory at retail is $35,000. Applying the 67% cost-to-retail ratio, the ending inventory at cost is $23,450 ($35,000 × 67%). Subtracting the ending inventory at cost from the cost of goods available for sale leads to a cost of goods sold of $106,350, as illustrated next.

	Cost	Retail
Beginning inventory	$ 23,400	$ 39,000
Purchases	106,400	156,000
Goods available for sale	$129,800	$195,000
Sales		(160,000)
Ending inventory – retail		$ 35,000
Cost-to-retail ratio		× 67%
Ending inventory – cost	23,450	
Cost of goods sold	$106,350	

In its 2016 annual report, ***Foot Locker*** explained that it uses the retail inventory method due to its practicality. ***Foot Locker*** groups its inventory into departments and determines cost by applying a cost-to-retail percentage across groupings of similar items, known as departments. The company then applies the cost-to-retail percentage to ending inventory at its retail value to determine the cost of ending inventory on a department basis.[19]

Retail Method Terminology

Retail selling prices typically fluctuate throughout the year. Therefore, companies must also account for *markups* and *markdowns* of selling price when implementing the retail method as shown in Example 10.19.

- An **initial markup** is the difference between the selling price that the company originally sells the product for and the cost of the product.
- An **additional markup** is the amount by which the firm increases the selling price above the original selling price.
- A **markdown** is the amount by which the firm decreases the original selling price.
- A **markup cancellation** is the amount by which the firm reduces an additional markup but not below the original selling price.
- A **markdown cancellation** is the amount by which the firm reduces a markdown and increases the selling price but not to exceed the original selling price.

EXAMPLE 10.19 Markup and Markdown Terminology

PROBLEM: Holiday Town, Inc. has one product in inventory with an original selling price of $100. The product was initially selling so well that Holiday Town increased the selling price to $110. However, the company carried excess inventory levels and needed to sell more units. To increase sales, Holiday Town decreased the selling price to $108. Later it reduced the price to $97. Finally, Holiday Town increased the selling price to $98. Identify the additional markups, markdowns, markup cancellations, and markdown cancellations in these events.

[19]Source: https://www.sec.gov/Archives/edgar/data/850209/000085020917000003/fl-20170128x10k.htm

SOLUTION: The following table presents the prices changes and descriptions.

Selling Price	Increase (Decrease) in Selling Price	Description
$100		Original selling price
110	$10	Additional markup
108	(2)	Markup cancellation
97	(11)	$8 markup cancellation
		$3 markdown
98	1	Markdown cancellation

The first price change from $100 to $110 is a $10 additional markup. When Holiday Town subsequently lowered the price to $108, there was a markup cancellation of $2. Subsequently, it reduced the price by $11 from $108 to $97. Because Holiday Town initially had an additional markup of $10 and has already "used up" $2 of this, the first $8 of the $11 price reduction is a markup cancellation, but the remaining $3 price reduction is a markdown. The final $1 increase in price is a markdown cancellation.

The Conventional Retail Inventory Method

The basic retail method includes both net markups and net markdowns in the cost-to-retail ratio. The most common retail inventory method, the conventional retail inventory method (also referred to as the approximate LCM method) approximates the lower-of-cost-or-market rule by including net markups but not net markdowns in the cost-to-retail ratio. By including net markups but not net markdowns, the denominator of the cost-to-retail ratio increases, which reduces the ratio. The reduced cost-to-retail ratio results in a lower reported ending inventory. Under the conventional retail method illustrated in Example 10.20, firms deduct net markdowns directly from retail inventory as a write-down reflecting the inventory's loss of utility.

EXAMPLE 10.20

The Conventional Retail Inventory Method

PROBLEM: The Boxer Sales Corporation provided the following data related to its inventory at the end of the current year:

Description	Cost	Retail
Beginning inventory	$ 23,400	$ 39,000
Purchases	106,400	156,000
Additional markups		13,000
Markup cancellations		4,000
Markdowns		15,600
Markdown cancellations		2,600
Sales		160,000

a. What is Boxer Sales' ending inventory and cost of goods sold under the conventional retail method?

b. What is Boxer Sales' ending inventory and cost of goods sold under the basic retail method?

c. Which method provides the lower ending inventory value consistent with the lower-of-cost-or-market method?

Continued

SOLUTION:

a. Under the conventional retail method, we include only markups (no markdowns) in Boxer Sales' cost-to-retail percentage to determine ending inventory and cost of goods sold. To arrive at the cost-to-retail ratio, we add beginning inventory, purchases, and markups in terms of both cost and retail and then compute the ratio. We subtract the retail markdowns to arrive at retail goods available for sale. We subtract the sales at retail from the retail value of goods available for sale to arrive at ending inventory at retail. We then apply the cost-to-retail ratio to get the ending inventory at lower of cost or market.

Description	Cost	Retail	Cost-to-Retail Ratio
Beginning inventory	$ 23,400	$ 39,000	
Purchases	106,400	156,000	
Net markups ($13,000 − $4,000)	0	9,000	
Subtotal	$129,800	$204,000	
Cost-to-retail ratio: $129,800 / $204,000			63.63%
Net markdowns ($15,600 − $2,600)	0	(13,000)	
Goods available for sale	$129,800	$191,000	
Less: Sales at retail		(160,000)	
Ending inventory at retail		$ 31,000	
Ending inventory at lower of cost or market ($31,000 × 63.63%)	$ 19,725		
Cost of goods sold	$ 110,075		

b. Under the basic retail method, ending inventory and cost of goods sold are computed as follows.

Description	Cost	Retail	Cost-to-Retail Ratio
Beginning inventory	$ 23,400	$ 39,000	
Purchases	106,400	156,000	
Net markups ($13,000 − $4,000)	0	9,000	
Net markdowns ($15,600 − $2,600)	0	(13,000)	
Goods available for sale	$129,800	$191,000	
Cost-to-retail ratio: $129,800 / $191,000			67.96%
Less: Sales at retail		(160,000)	
Ending inventory at retail		$ 31,000	
Ending inventory at cost ($31,000 × 67.96%)	$ 21,068		
Cost of goods sold	$108,732		

c. The conventional retail method results in an ending inventory that is less than the basic retail inventory method, thus approximating LCM.

7 Explain the gross profit method of estimating inventory.

Gross Profit Method of Estimating Inventory

The **gross profit method** provides an approximation of the ending inventory balance. Whereas companies perform a physical count of inventory at the end of each fiscal year, there may be circumstances under which a company needs to estimate ending inventory for other purposes, including:

- To determine the balances of ending inventory and cost of goods sold for interim periods without performing a physical inventory count.
- To determine the cost of inventory that has been lost, stolen, or destroyed.
- In auditors' testing of the overall reasonableness of inventory amounts reported by clients.
- For budgeting and forecasting purposes.

Applying the gross profit method involves the following steps:

1. Compute cost of goods available for sale from the inventory records.
2. Determine a historical gross profit percentage based on historical sales and cost of goods sold data. The gross profit percentage is computed as follows:

   Gross Profit Percentage = (Net Sales − Cost of Goods Sold)/Net sales (10.1)

3. Estimate cost of goods sold as follows:

   Estimated Cost of Goods Sold = Net Sales × (1 − Gross Profit Percentage) (10.2)

4. Compute estimated ending inventory as follows:

   Estimated Ending Inventory
   = Cost of Goods Available for Sale − Estimated Cost of Goods Sold (10.3)

Example 10.21 provides an example of the gross profit method.

EXAMPLE 10.21

Gross Profit Method

PROBLEM: In the current year, Boyer Company experienced a major casualty loss due to the destruction of its warehouse and entire inventory by a hurricane. The company began the year with inventory of $800,000. There were net purchases of $4,000,000 and net sales of $5,000,000 during the year prior to the casualty. The company's historical gross profit percentage has averaged 30% over the last 5 years. Estimate the inventory on hand on the date of the casualty.

SOLUTION: We first compute the cost of goods available for sale as follows:

Beginning inventory	$ 800,000
Plus: Net purchases	4,000,000
Cost of goods available for sale	$4,800,000

We know that the average gross profit percentage is 30%. We estimate the cost of goods sold as follows:

Net sales	$5,000,000
× (1 − Gross profit percentage)	70%
Estimated cost of goods sold	$3,500,000

We then estimate ending inventory as follows:

Cost of goods available for sale	$4,800,000
Less: Estimated cost of goods sold	3,500,000
Estimated ending inventory	$1,300,000

8 Detail required disclosures for inventory.

Inventory Disclosures

In the financial statement and footnotes, inventory disclosures include:

- Accounting policies, including the measurement basis upon which amounts are stated with costing methods such as FIFO or LIFO.
- Carrying amounts by type of inventory such as raw materials or finished goods.
- Any inventory financing arrangements.
- Carrying amount of inventories carried at less than cost and the amount of write-downs recognized as expense.
- The use of the LIFO costing method when applicable, including the LIFO reserve (or replacement cost of inventory used to compute the reserve) and effects of any LIFO liquidations.

Exhibit 10.11 illustrates inventory disclosures for ***Foot Locker, Inc.*** from its 2016 annual report. Note 1 indicates that ***Foot Locker*** uses both the LIFO and FIFO cost-flow methods. It uses LIFO primarily in the United States and FIFO outside the United States. The numeric details of inventory accounted for under LIFO and FIFO are included in Note 6. Because the LIFO value of inventory approximates its FIFO cost, ***Foot Locker*** does not report a LIFO reserve.

EXHIBIT 10.11 Inventory Disclosures, ***Foot Locker, Inc.***, Financial Statements, January 28, 2017

From Financial Statement Notes:

NOTE 1: Summary of Significant Accounting Policies

Merchandise Inventories and Cost of Sales

Merchandise inventories for the Company's Athletic Stores are valued at the lower of cost or market using the retail inventory method. Cost for retail stores is determined on the last-in, first-out ("LIFO") basis for domestic inventories and on the first-in, first-out ("FIFO") basis for international inventories. Merchandise inventories of the Direct-to-Customers business are valued at the lower of cost or market using weighted-average cost, which approximates FIFO.

The retail inventory method is commonly used by retail companies to value inventories at cost and calculate gross margins due to its practicality. Under the retail inventory method, cost is determined by applying a cost-to-retail percentage across groupings of similar items, known as departments. The cost-to-retail percentage is applied to ending inventory at its current owned retail valuation to determine the cost of ending inventory on a department basis. The Company provides reserves based on current selling prices when the inventory has not been marked down to market. . . .

NOTE 5: Merchandise Inventories

	2016	2015
	(in millions)	
LIFO inventories	$ 861	$ 847
FIFO inventories	446	438
Total merchandise inventories	$1,307	$1,285

The value of the Company's LIFO inventories, as calculated on a LIFO basis, approximates their value as calculated on a FIFO basis.

Source: Foot Locker, Inc. January 28, 2017 Financial Statement. https://www.sec.gov/Archives/edgar/data/850209/000085020917000003/fl-20170128x10k.htm, pages 44 and 52.

Inventory Disclosures: IFRS. IFRS inventory disclosures are similar to those required under U.S. GAAP. Additionally, IFRS requires firms to report the amount of any LCM reversals.

FINANCIAL STATEMENT ANALYSIS

Conversion from LIFO to FIFO

A company's cost-flow assumption choice impacts the amounts of reported inventory, cost of goods sold, and net income. When costs are increasing and inventory unit levels are stable or increasing, a company will report:

- Higher inventory under FIFO than LIFO.
- Higher cost of goods sold under LIFO than FIFO.
- Lower net income under LIFO than FIFO.

For financial statement users, comparing companies that use different cost-flow assumptions can be difficult. By referencing a company's disclosure of its LIFO reserve, however, users can convert inventory and cost of goods sold (COGS) amounts to FIFO in order to make useful comparisons across companies. Specifically, financial statement users can convert the inventory valuation from LIFO to FIFO on the balance sheet. Similarly, firms can use the change in the LIFO reserve or the LIFO effect to convert the income statement cost of goods sold from LIFO to FIFO.

As previously discussed, the LIFO reserve is the difference between inventory valued under FIFO versus LIFO:

$$\text{LIFO Reserve} = \text{FIFO Inventory Balance} - \text{LIFO Inventory Balance} \qquad (10.4)$$

The change in the LIFO reserve, referred to as the *LIFO effect*, is the impact on cost of goods sold. An increase (credit) in the LIFO reserve results in a debit (increase) to COGS whereas a decrease (debit) in the LIFO reserve results in a credit (decrease) to COGS.

$$\text{Change in LIFO Reserve} = \text{Ending LIFO Reserve} - \text{Beginning LIFO Reserve} \qquad (10.5)$$

If the LIFO reserve increases during the year, COGS will be higher under LIFO than FIFO. The adjustment to increase the LIFO reserve is a credit whereas COGS is debited. An increasing LIFO reserve leads to higher COGS and lower income and taxes.

If the LIFO reserve decreases during the year, COGS will be lower under LIFO than FIFO. The adjustment to decrease the LIFO reserve requires a debit to the reserve account and a credit to COGS. A decreasing LIFO reserve will result in lower COGS and higher income and taxes. The following t-account illustrates the described adjustments to the LIFO reserve.

LIFO Reserve

	Beginning balance
Debit adjustment decreases COGS	Credit adjustment increases COGS
	Ending balance

When the LIFO reserve is increasing, the change in the LIFO reserve multiplied by the company's tax rate estimates the amount of taxes saved during the year by using LIFO. The cumulative balance of the LIFO reserve multiplied by the tax rate estimates the amount of taxes the company has saved over time by using LIFO.

$$\text{Taxes Saved} = \text{LIFO Reserve} \times \text{Tax Rate} \qquad (10.6)$$

The discussion of the cash operating cycle introduced the inventory turnover ratio and days inventory on hand. Example 10.22 examines the effect of a company's choice of a cost-flow assumption on financial statement analysis indicators.

Financial Statement Analysis, continued

EXAMPLE 10.22 LIFO to FIFO Conversion[20]

PROBLEM: ***Hershey Company*** reported the information in Exhibit 10.12 about inventory in its 2016 financial statements and footnotes. Hershey uses LIFO for the majority of its U.S. inventories. During 2016, its cost of goods sold was $4,282,290, and its net sales were $7,440,181. Use this information to answer the following questions:

a. What is the value of ***Hershey's*** ending inventory at December 31, 2016, under LIFO? Determine the LIFO reserve balance at the end of 2016 and 2015.

b. If ***Hershey*** used the FIFO cost-flow assumption to account for its entire inventory, what would the inventory balance be at December 31, 2016, and December 31, 2015?

c. What would ***Hershey's*** cost of goods sold under FIFO have been in 2016?

d. Would ***Hershey's*** gross profit, taxes, and net income in 2016 have been higher or lower under FIFO?

e. If ***Hershey's*** tax rate is 35%, how much has the use of LIFO saved it in taxes paid over time?

f. Compare ***Hershey's*** gross profit percentage, inventory turnover ratio, and days in inventory on hand under LIFO versus FIFO in 2016.

EXHIBIT 10.12 Inventory Disclosure, ***The Hershey Company***, Financial Statements, December 31, 2016

Excerpt from Note 16

NOTE 16: Supplemental Balance Sheet Information

Inventories

The components of certain Consolidated Balance Sheet accounts are as follows:

December 31,	**2016**	**2015**
In thousands of dollars		
Raw materials	$315,239	$353,451
Goods in process	88,490	67,745
Finished goods	528,587	534,983
Inventories at FIFO	932,316	956,179
Adjustment to LIFO	(186,638)	(205,209)
Total inventories	$745,678	$750,970

Source: Securities and Exchange Commission. http://phx.corporate-ir.net/phoenix.zhtml?c=115590&p=irol-sec, page 91.

SOLUTION:

a. Note 16 indicates that ***Hershey*** uses LIFO for a significant portion of its inventory. Its inventory is $745,678 and $750,970 under LIFO at the end of 2016 and 2015, respectively.

The LIFO reserve, called the Adjustment to LIFO in Exhibit 10.12, at the end of 2016 and 2015 is $186,638 and $205,209, respectively.

[20] All numbers used in this illustration are in thousands.

Financial Statement Analysis, continued

b. The amount of inventory before the LIFO reserve is the FIFO inventory of $932,316 and $956,179 at the end of 2016 and 2015, respectively.

c. The difference in cost of goods sold under LIFO and FIFO for 2016 is $18,571, computed as follows:

(In Thousands)	
Ending LIFO reserve needed	$(186,638)
Beginning balance	(205,209)
Decrease in LIFO reserve	$ (18,571)

This adjustment will result in a debit or reduction in the LIFO reserve account and lower cost of goods sold under LIFO as compared to the FIFO method.

	LIFO Reserve	
January 1		205,209
Year-End Adjustment	18,571	
December 31		186,638

This decrease in the LIFO reserve of $18,571 corresponds to an increase in cost of goods sold of $18,571 under FIFO versus LIFO.

(In Thousands)		
LIFO cost of goods sold	$4,282,290	← from income statement
Add: Decrease in LIFO reserve	18,571	
FIFO cost of goods sold	$4,300,861	

d. FIFO cost of goods sold ($4,300,861) is higher than LIFO cost of goods sold ($4,282,290), indicating gross profit, taxes, and net income would have been lower under FIFO than LIFO.

e. Even though ***Hershey's*** net income and taxes would be higher in fiscal 2016 under LIFO, over time, Hershey's has saved approximately $65,323 in taxes by using LIFO through the end of 2016.

$$\text{Taxes Saved} = \text{LIFO Reserve} \times \text{Tax Rate}$$

$$\$65{,}323 = \$186{,}638 \times 35\% \qquad (10.6)$$

f. Under LIFO and FIFO, the gross profit and gross profit percentage are as follows:

(In Thousands)	LIFO	FIFO
Net sales	$7,440,181	$ 7,440,181
Cost of sales	4,282,290	4,300,861
Gross profit	$3,157,891	$3,139,320
Gross profit percentage	42.4%	42.2%

Under FIFO, the gross profit and gross profit percentage are lower as expected given the decrease in the LIFO reserve.

Under LIFO, ***Hershey's*** inventory turnover would be 5.72, which is higher than the 4.55 under FIFO. The average inventory under LIFO is much lower than the average inventory

Continued

Financial Statement Analysis, continued

under FIFO, resulting in a higher inventory turnover ratio under LIFO than FIFO. The number of days inventory on hand under LIFO would be only 63.8, compared to 80.2 under FIFO.

Ratio	LIFO	FIFO
Inventory Turnover Ratio $= \frac{\text{Cost of Goods Sold}}{\text{Average Inventory}}$	$5.72 = \frac{\$4,282,290}{\$748,324}$	$4.55 = \frac{\$4,300,861}{\$944,248}$
Average Inventory $= \frac{\text{Beginning Inventory + Ending Inventory}}{2}$	$\$748,324 = \frac{(\$750,970 + \$745,678)}{2}$	$\$944,248 = \frac{(\$956,179 + \$932,316)}{2}$
Days Inventory on Hand $= \frac{365}{\text{Inventory Turnover Ratio}}$	$63.8 = \frac{365}{5.72}$	$80.2 = \frac{365}{4.55}$

Summary by Learning Objectives

In the following, we summarize the main points by learning objective. Throughout the chapter, we discuss the accounting and reporting of U.S. GAAP and IFRS side-by-side. The following table also highlights the major similarities and differences in the standards.

1 Describe the types of inventory and demonstrate accounting under periodic and perpetual inventory systems.

Summary	Similarities and Differences between U.S. GAAP and IFRS
Merchandise inventory and manufacturing inventory are the two types of inventory. Manufacturing inventory includes: 1. Raw materials 2. Work-in-process 3. Finished goods There are two types of inventory systems: 1. Periodic: The ending inventory balance and cost of goods sold are determined at the end of each accounting period. 2. Perpetual: Inventory accounts are continually updated for purchases. The cost of goods sold is recorded after each sale.	Similar under U.S. GAAP and IFRS.

Summary by Learning Objectives, continued

2 Discuss inventory costing, including accounting for goods in transit, consigned goods, costs included in inventory, and purchase discounts.

Summary	Similarities and Differences between U.S. GAAP and IFRS
Goods in transit are items that have left the seller's place of business but have not yet been received by the buyer. F.o.b. (free on board) shipping point means that title passes to the buyer when the goods are shipped. The seller does not include these goods in inventory after shipment. F.o.b. destination means that title passes to the buyer when the goods are received. The goods remain in the seller's inventory until they arrive at the buyer's destination. A consignment arrangement occurs when one party (the consignee) agrees to sell a product for another party (the consignor) without taking ownership of the merchandise. Freight-in transportation costs are incurred in order to bring the inventory to the appropriate location and are included in the cost of inventory. Freight-out costs consist of transportation costs incurred to move the inventory to the buyer. Freight-out costs are expensed as incurred. Purchase discounts are reductions that companies receive from sellers if they pay for purchases within a certain time period. There are two methods to account for a purchase discount: 1. Gross method: The company initially records the inventory and accounts payable at the full (gross) purchase amount. 2. Net method: The company assumes that it will take the discount and initially records the accounts payable and inventory at the net amount.	Similar under U.S. GAAP and IFRS.

3 Explain the need for inventory cost-flow assumptions and calculate inventory and cost of goods sold under four inventory allocation methods: specific identification; moving average; last-in, first-out (LIFO); and first-in, first-out (FIFO).

Summary	Similarities and Differences between U.S. GAAP and IFRS
Cost-flow assumptions are needed because inventory costs are tracked separately from the physical flow of inventory. There are four common inventory allocation methods: 1. Specific identification method: The company identifies each unit and keeps track of the cost of each one. 2. Moving-average method: The company determines an average cost for the units on hand and applies that average unit cost to the next sale to determine the cost of goods sold. 3. First-in, first-out (FIFO) method: The company assigns the most recent inventory costs to ending inventory and the oldest costs to cost of goods sold. 4. Last-in, first-out (LIFO) method: The company assigns the oldest inventory costs to ending inventory and the most recent costs to cost of goods sold.	➤ Similar under U.S. GAAP and IFRS except that IFRS does not allow the use of the LIFO method.

Summary by Learning Objectives, continued

4 Demonstrate an understanding of and illustrate the accounting for the LIFO reserve, the LIFO effect, and LIFO liquidations. Compute inventory and cost of goods sold using the dollar-value LIFO method.

Summary	Similarities and Differences between U.S. GAAP and IFRS
The LIFO reserve account is the difference between the inventory balance measured using FIFO and LIFO. The LIFO effect is the change in the LIFO reserve account during the year and is the impact on cost of goods sold. As a company uses LIFO over time, it builds LIFO layers, which are increases in the quantity of inventory. When inventory levels decline under the LIFO method and costs are increasing, the company sells the older low-cost LIFO layers, reducing cost of goods sold and increasing book (and taxable) income. A LIFO liquidation is a decrease in inventory layers under the LIFO method. Under the dollar-value LIFO method, firms pool inventory items and the common unit of measure of the inventory is the dollar. The six steps in dollar-value LIFO accounting are to: 1. Determine the ending inventory stated in terms of base-year prices 2. Determine the increase (or decrease) in quantity at base-year prices 3. Determine the increase (or decrease) in quantity at current-year prices 4. Add all of the layers together to find the dollar-value LIFO ending inventory 5. Calculate the LIFO reserve 6. Record the journal entry to make the LIFO adjustments	➤ Not applicable to IFRS because IFRS does not allow the use of the LIFO method.

5 Explain the lower-of-cost-or-market rule.

Summary	Similarities and Differences between U.S. GAAP and IFRS
Under U.S. GAAP, the measurement of the market value depends on what method is used for inventory costing. If the costing method is anything other than LIFO or the retail inventory method, market is measured at the net realizable value (NRV). If the costing method is LIFO or the retail inventory method, market is measured as the amount at which the inventory could currently be purchased or reproduced, known as the current replacement cost (CRC). The CRC cannot exceed a ceiling that is equal to NRV. NRV is the item's selling price less the cost of disposal. CRC cannot fall below a floor value and net realizable value less a normal profit margin (NRV – NP). To calculate a write-down: 1. Determine the market value of the inventory 2. Compare the market value to cost 3. Record the write-down if market value is less than cost	➤ Under IFRS, the market value in the lower-of-cost-or-market rule is always measured as net realizable value (NRV). Under IFRS, reversals of write-downs are permitted up to the original cost.

Summary by Learning Objectives, continued

❻ Calculate inventory and cost of goods sold using the retail inventory method.

Summary	Similarities and Differences between U.S. GAAP and IFRS
The conventional retail inventory method is an allowed approximation of ending inventory that takes into consideration the requirement that inventory be reported at the lower of cost or market. • An initial markup is the difference between the selling price at which the company originally sells the product and the cost paid for the product. • An additional markup is any amount by which the company increases the selling price above the original selling price. • A markdown is the amount by which the company decreases the original selling price. • A markup cancellation is the amount by which a company reduces an additional markup but not below the original selling price. • A markdown cancellation is the amount by which a company reduces a markdown and increases the selling price but not to exceed the original selling price. The conventional retail method approximates the lower-of-cost-or-market rule by including net markups but not markdowns in the cost-to-retail ratio. Net markdowns are deducted from the retail inventory as a write-down reflecting the inventory's loss of utility. Not deducting the net markdowns from the denominator of the cost-to-retail ratio lowers the ratio compared to the presence of markdowns in the calculation, resulting in a lower reported ending inventory.	Similar under U.S. GAAP and IFRS.

❼ Explain the gross profit method of estimating inventory.

Summary	Similarities and Differences between U.S. GAAP and IFRS
The gross profit method estimates ending inventory as cost of goods available for sale less estimated cost of goods sold. Estimated cost of goods sold is based on sales to date multiplied by 1 minus the estimated gross profit percentage.	Similar under U.S. GAAP and IFRS.

❽ Detail required disclosures for inventory.

Summary	Similarities and Differences between U.S. GAAP and IFRS
Required inventory disclosures include: • Accounting policies, including the company's inventory costing method and measurement basis • Carrying amounts by type • Inventory financing arrangements • Carrying amount of inventories carried at an amount less than cost and the amount of write-downs recognized as expense • The use of the LIFO costing method when applicable, including the LIFO reserve (or replacement cost of inventory used to compute the reserve) and effects of any LIFO liquidations	➤ Similar under U.S. GAAP and IFRS except that IFRS requires firms to report the amount of write-down reversals. Reversals of write-downs are not allowed under U.S. GAAP.

MyLab Accounting

Go to **http://www.pearson.com/mylab/accounting** for the following Questions, Multiple-Choice Questions, Brief Exercises, Exercises, and Problems. They are available with immediate grading, explanations of correct and incorrect answers, and interactive media that acts as your own online tutor.

10 Short-Term Operating Assets—Inventory

Questions

1 **Q10-1.** How is inventory tracked under a perpetual inventory system?

1 **Q10-2.** What is the difference between merchandise inventory and manufacturing inventory?

2 **Q10-3.** What costs should be included in the unit cost of an item of inventory?

3 **Q10-4.** When does the inventory allocation problem arise?

3 **Q10-5.** Explain the difference between the FIFO method of inventory valuation and the LIFO method. Which of these methods best approximates the physical flow of units for most companies? Explain.

3 **Q10-6.** Which method of inventory results in an inventory valuation that reflects current costs and provides the best matching of costs with revenues? Explain.

3 4 **Q10-7.** If unit costs are rising and inventory levels are constant or increasing, which method of inventory valuation will result in the lowest net income? Why?

4 **Q10-8.** How can financial statements be converted from the LIFO basis to the FIFO basis of inventory valuation and vice versa?

4 **Q10-9.** Explain the unit of measure under the dollar-value LIFO method of inventory valuation.

5 **Q10-10.** What do firms use as the market value when applying the lower-of-cost-or-market (LCM) rule? Are there any limits on the use of this value? Explain.

5 **Q10-11.** Do U.S. GAAP and IFRS treat inventory write-downs the same way? Explain.

5 **Q10-12.** Under IFRS, how do firms determine lower-of-cost-or-market rule adjustments?

6 **Q10-13.** How does the conventional retail method approximate the lower-of-cost-or-market valuation? What is the impact on ending inventory?

7 **Q10-14.** Why would a company use the gross profit method to estimate ending inventory?

8 **Q10-15.** How are required LIFO disclosures used to compute inventory balances and cost of goods sold under the FIFO cost flow?

A **Q10-16.** How does a company build LIFO layers under the LIFO retail inventory method?

Multiple-Choice Questions

In partnership with: BECKER PROFESSIONAL EDUCATION®

Becker CPA Exam Review multiple-choice questions are available in MyLab Accounting.

4 **MC10-1.** Giddens Company adopted the dollar-value LIFO inventory method on December 31, Year 1. On December 31, Year 1, Giddens' inventory was in a single inventory pool and was valued at $400,000 under the dollar-value LIFO method. Inventory data for Year 2 are as follows:

12/31 Year 2 inventory at year-end prices	$550,000
Price index at 12/31 Year 2 (base year Year 1)	110

Giddens' inventory at dollar-value LIFO at December 31, Year 2 is:

a. $440,000 b. $510,000 c. $500,000 d. $550,000

3 **MC10-2.** The Loyd Company had 150 units of product Omega on hand at December 1, Year 1, costing $400 each. Purchases of product Omega during December were as follows:

Date	Units	Unit Cost
December 7	100	$440
December 14	200	$460
December 29	300	$500

Sales during December were 500 units on December 30. Assume that a perpetual inventory system is used. The cost of inventory at December 31, Year 1, under the LIFO method would be:

a. $100,000 b. $104,000 c. $75,000 d. $125,000

5 **MC10-3.** Simmons, Inc. uses the lower-of-cost-or-market method to value its inventory that is accounted for using the LIFO method. Data regarding an item in its inventory is as follows:

Cost	$26
Replacement cost	20
Selling price	30
Cost of completion and disposal	2
Normal profit margin	7

What is the lower of cost or market for this item?

a. $21 b. $20 c. $28 d. $26

5 **MC10-4.** Simmons, Inc. uses the lower-of-cost-or-market method to value its inventory that is accounted for using the FIFO method. Data regarding an item in its inventory is as follows:

Cost	$26
Replacement cost	20
Selling price	30
Cost of completion and disposal	2
Normal profit margin	7

What is the lower-of-cost-or-market method for this item?

a. $18 b. $26 c. $28 d. $30

3 **MC10-5.** The Loyd Company had 150 units of product Omega on hand at December 1, Year 1, costing $400 each. Purchases of product Omega during December were as follows:

Date	Units	Unit Cost
December 7	100	$440
December 14	200	460
December 29	300	500

Sales during December were 500 units on December 30. Assume that a perpetual inventory system is used. The cost of inventory at December 31, Year 1, under the FIFO method would be closest to:

a. $100,000 b. $104,000 c. $115,000 d. $125,000

3 **MC10-6.** The Loyd Company had 150 units of product Omega on hand at December 1, Year 1, costing $400 each. Purchases of product Omega during December were as follows:

Date	Units	Unit Cost
December 7	100	$440
December 14	200	460
December 29	300	500

Sales during December were 500 units on December 30. Assume that a perpetual inventory system is used. Round per unit costs to two decimal places. The cost of inventory at December 31, Year 1, under the moving-average method would be closest to:

a. $100,000 b. $104,000 c. $115,000 d. $125,000

6 **MC10-7.** On March 1, Year 1, LuxWear Inc. had beginning inventory and purchases at cost of $50,000 and $20,000, respectively. The beginning inventory and purchases had a retail value of $75,000 and $30,000, respectively. The company had sales of $60,000, as well as markups of $6,000 and markdowns of $10,000. What would LuxWear report as the lower of cost or market for its ending inventory on March 31, Year 1, using the conventional (LCM) retail method? (Round the cost-to-retail ratio to two decimal places.)

a. $25,830 b. $27,470 c. $28,290 d. $41,000

Brief Exercises

1 **BE10-1. Types of Manufacturing Inventory.** Complete the following inventory disclosure:

At the end of 2019 and 2018, inventories were composed of:

	2019	2018
Raw materials and supplies	$2,206	$ b.
Goods in process	a.	2,320
Finished goods	3,566	3,490
Total inventories	$8,537	$7,883

1 **BE10-2. Periodic Inventory System.** Emmy Company uses a periodic inventory system. On December 31, 2018, Emmy counts its inventory and determines that it has $72,000 of inventory on hand. On December 31, 2017, inventory was $106,000. Emmy made inventory purchases totaling $78,000 during the year. What is Emmy's cost of goods sold in 2018?

2 **BE10-3. Purchase Discounts Using the Gross Method.** On October 16, Sueco Retailers bought 80 parkas on account at $75 each. Terms of the purchase were 2/10, n/30. It paid for 60 parkas on October 25 and paid for the remaining 20 parkas on November 15. If Sueco uses the gross method to account for its inventory purchases, what is its cash payment and reduction of inventory on October 25? What is the amount of accounts payable after the October 25 payment? Assume that the perpetual inventory system is used.

2 **BE10-4. Purchase Discounts Using the Net Method.** Use the same information for BE10-3 but assume that Sueco Retailers uses the net method to account for its inventory purchases. What is its cash payment and reduction of inventory on October 25? What is the amount of accounts payable after the October 25 payment? Assume that the perpetual inventory system is used.

3 **BE10-5. FIFO, Perpetual Basis.** Spider Incorporated provided the following information regarding its inventory for the current year.

Transaction	Units	Sales in Units	Unit Cost	Total Cost
Beginning inventory 1/1	3,500		$50	$ 175,000
Purchases				
March 30	5,000		65	325,000
July 15	1,000		72	72,000
September 1		6,100		
Total available for sale	9,500			$572,000
Units sold September 1	(6,100)			
Ending inventory	3,400			

Determine Spider's ending inventory and cost of goods sold under the FIFO perpetual basis.

3 **BE10-6. LIFO, Perpetual Basis.** Using the information provided in BE10-5, assume that Spider uses the LIFO method. Determine Spider's ending inventory and cost of goods sold under the LIFO perpetual basis.

3 **BE10-7. Moving-Average Method, Perpetual Basis.** Perry Manufacturing Company provided the following information regarding its inventory transactions for the current year.

Transaction	Units	Sales in Units	Unit Cost	Total Cost
Beginning inventory 1/1	8,000		$16	$128,000
Purchases and Sales				
February 8	4,000		21	84,000
June 24	1,800		23	41,400
Subtotal	13,800			$253,400
September 18		5,500		
December 24	3,000		26	78,000
Total available for sale	16,800			$331,400
Units sold September 18	(5,500)			
Ending inventory	11,300			

Determine the ending inventory and cost of goods sold that Perry should report assuming that the firm uses the moving-average cost method (perpetual basis). Round per unit cost to two decimal places.

4 8 **BE10-8. LIFO Reserve.** Best Stores is considering a change in its inventory valuation method. The company currently uses the FIFO method and may want to change to the LIFO method. Inventory information for the current year follows.

Description	FIFO Cost	LIFO Cost
Beginning inventory: January 1	$11,800	$ 9,600
Ending inventory: December 31	$14,100	$11,150

Cost of goods sold under the LIFO basis is $34,500 for the current year.

Best Stores would like to use LIFO for tax purposes but wants to be sure that its shareholders will be able to convert the LIFO financial statements to a FIFO basis. Provide Best Stores with an illustration of how financial statement users can convert LIFO to the FIFO basis.

3 **BE10-9. LIFO, Perpetual Basis.** Source Enterprises reports the following inventory information for the current year.

	LIFO Inventory	
Description	**Unit Cost × Units**	**Total Cost**
Beginning inventory: January 1		
First layer	$ 9 × 800	$ 7,200
Second layer	$13 × 1,100	14,300
Total beginning inventory	1,900	$21,500
Purchases or production:		
August 31	$ 16 × 700	11,200
Cost of goods available for sale	2,600	$32,700
Units sold on December 1 at $9.60	(2,300)	
Ending inventory: December 31	300	

Compute the ending inventory and the cost of goods sold under the LIFO perpetual basis.

4 **BE10-10. LIFO Liquidation.** Using the information provided in BE10-9, determine whether there is a LIFO liquidation.

4 **BE10-11. Dollar-Value LIFO.** Todgren Incorporated adopted the dollar-value LIFO method last year. Last year's ending inventory was $56,400 with a price index of 1.0. The ending inventory for the current year at year-end (FIFO) costs is $96,000 and the price index is 1.2. Based on this information, compute Todgren's ending inventory for the current year on a dollar-value LIFO basis.

4 **BE10-12. Dollar-Value LIFO, Conversion to FIFO.** Using the information provided in BE10-11, prepare the journal entry required to adjust Todgren's ending inventory from a FIFO to a dollar-value LIFO basis.

5 **BE10-13. Lower of Cost or Market.** Count Clothing Company manufactures two types of raincoats—Regular and Stain Resistant. Information related to both products is presented in the following table.

Group	Current Replacement Cost	Selling Price	Disposal Costs	Normal Profit Margin	Cost
Regular	$120	$190	$20	$70	$118
Stain Resistant	230	250	26	45	240

Determine the ending inventory value per unit and the amount of any write-downs per unit using the lower-of-cost-or-market rule assuming that Count Clothing uses the LIFO costing method and the group-by-group approach to LCM.

5 **BE10-14.** **Lower of Cost or Market.** Using the information in BE10-13, prepare the journal entry to record the write-down to market for the Stain Resistant model under both the direct and indirect methods. Assume that Count Clothing has 3,500 units of the Stain Resistant model in stock.

5 **BE10-15.** **Lower of Cost or Market,** IFRS. Using the information in BE10-13, now assume that Count Clothing is an IFRS reporter. Determine the ending inventory value per unit and the amount of any write-downs per unit using the lower-of-cost-or-market rule assuming that Count Clothing uses the group-by-group approach to LCM. Assume the company uses FIFO.

5 **BE10-16.** **Lower of Cost or Market,** IFRS. Using the information in BE10-15, prepare the journal entry to record the write-down to market for the Stain Resistant model under both the direct and indirect methods. Assume that Count Clothing has 3,500 units of the Stain Resistant model in stock. Assume the company uses FIFO.

5 **BE10-17.** **Lower of Cost or Market, Reversal,** IFRS. Using the facts in BE10-15, assume that Count Clothing has 2,000 units of its Stain Resistant model in stock a year later when the net realizable value has increased to $230. What is the reversal of the inventory write-down, if any? Assume the company uses FIFO.

5 **BE10-18.** **Lower of Cost or Market.** Sarat Boot Company manufactures two types of boots—rain boots and snow boots. Information related to both products is presented in the following table.

Group	Current Replacement Cost	Selling Price	Disposal Costs	Normal Profit Margin	Cost
Rain	$70	$ 95	$24	$12	$60
Snow	84	110	24	15	93

Determine the ending inventory value per unit using the lower-of-cost-or-market rule assuming that Sarat Boot uses LIFO for costing purposes and the group-by-group approach to LCM.

5 **BE10-19.** **Lower of Cost or Market.** Using the information in BE10-18, now assume that Sarat Boot uses FIFO for inventory costing purposes. Determine the ending inventory value per unit using the lower-of-cost-or-market rule assuming that Sarat Boot uses the group-by-group approach to LCM.

5 **BE10-20.** **Lower of Cost or Market,** IFRS. Using the information in BE10-18, now assume that Sarat Boot is an IFRS. reporter. Determine the ending inventory value per unit using the lower-of-cost-or-market rule assuming that Sarat Boot uses the group-by-group approach to LCM. Assume the company uses FIFO.

6 **BE10-21.** **Conventional Retail Inventory Method.** Big B Stores uses the conventional retail method to value its ending inventory. The following information relates to Big B's inventory at both cost and retail for the current year.

Description	Cost	Retail
Beginning inventory	$ 55,000	$ 78,500
Purchases	245,000	325,000
Additional markups		24,000
Markup cancellations		7,000
Markdowns		12,000
Markdown cancellations		3,500
Sales		400,000

Compute Big B's ending inventory for the current year using the conventional retail method (round all percentages to two decimal places).

7 **BE10-22. Gross Profit Method.** Sammi Company needs to determine the amount of inventory in its warehouse at the time that an earthquake destroyed it. Sammi's gross profit percentage averaged 28% over the last three years. Sammi began the current year with inventory of $657,400. Its net purchases were $3,498,000 and net sales were $4,336,000 during the year before the earthquake occurred. Use the gross profit method to estimate the inventory on hand on the date of the earthquake.

7 **BE10-23. Gross Profit Method.** A tornado severely damaged one of Down Town Dig's retail clothing stores, destroying all the inventory in the store. Down Town Dig's ending store inventory last year was $109,500. Its net purchases were $672,600, and net sales were $1,279,800 during the year prior to the tornado. Down Town Dig used the gross profit method to determine that it had $218,988 of the inventory on hand on the date the tornado hit. What is its historical gross profit percentage?

A **BE10-24. LIFO Retail Inventory Method.** Complete the following table to find the ending inventory under the Dollar Value LIFO Retail Inventory Method. Round percentages to two decimal places.

Base-Year price index	1.00		
Current year price index	1.06		
	Cost	**Retail**	**Cost-to-Retail Ratio**
Beginning inventory	$ 15,000	$ 25,000	A
Purchases	83,000	123,000	
Net markups		6,500	
Net markdowns		B	
Current year layer	C	119,500	D
Goods available for sale	E	F	
Less: Sales		114,000	
Ending inventory at retail		G	
Ending Inventory at Base-Year Prices = Ending Inventory at Retail / Price Index	H / I	J	

A **BE10-25. LIFO Retail Inventory Method.** Complete the following table to find the ending inventory under the Dollar Value LIFO retail inventory method. Round percentages to two decimal places.

Base-year price index	1.00		
Current-Year price index	1.03		
	Cost	**Retail**	**Cost-to-Retail Ratio**
Beginning inventory	A	$ 36,400	74.18%
Purchases	102,000	117,110	
Net markups		B	
Net markdowns		(3,600)	
Current year layer	C	132,910	D
Goods available for sale	E	F	
Less: Sales		156,000	
Ending inventory at retail		G	
Ending Inventory at Base-year Prices = Ending Inventory at Retail / Price Index	H / I	J	

Exercises

❸ **E10-1. Moving Average, FIFO, LIFO.** Arthur Lloyd Associates provided the following information regarding its inventory for the current year, its second year of operations.

Transaction	Units	Sales in Units	Unit Cost	Total Cost
Beginning inventory 1/1	10,000		$18	$ 180,000
Purchases				
February 8	23,000		20	460,000
March 15	18,600		22	409,200
Subtotal	51,600			$1,049,200
Units sold – April 2 at $41		49,500		
April 30	37,000		28	1,036,000
July 15	12,400		31	384,400
Subtotal	101,000			$2,469,600
Units sold – September 1 at $47		26,000		
November 9	34,500		29	1,000,500
Total available for sale	135,500			$3,470,100
Total units sold	(75,500)			
Ending inventory	60,000			

Required »

Compute Arthur Lloyd's ending inventory and cost of goods sold under each of the following cost-flow methods assuming that the company uses a perpetual inventory system (round your answer for cost per unit to two decimal places):

a. Moving Average b. FIFO c. LIFO

❸ **E10-2. Moving Average, FIFO, LIFO, Presentation, and Disclosures.** Answer the following questions using the information provided in E10-1:

Required »

a. Prepare a partial income statement and balance sheet for Arthur Lloyd under each of the inventory valuation methods.

b. Assume that the company reported current assets (without inventory) of $2,890,000 at the beginning of the year and $2,100,000 at the end of the year. Also assume that it reports current liabilities of $2,000,150 and $2,450,000 at the beginning and end of the year, respectively. Compute the current ratio and inventory turnover ratio under each of the inventory valuation methods. The inventory turnover ratio is required only for the end of the period.

❸ **E10-3. Moving Average, FIFO, LIFO.** Zoola, Inc. provided the following information regarding its inventory for the current year, its second year of operations.

Transaction	Units	Unit Cost
Beginning inventory 1/1	3,000	$17.00
Purchases, January 23	4,500	16.00
Purchases, February 14	1,200	16.50
Purchases, March 17	2,300	17.00
Units sold – April 13 at $20	9,600	
Purchases, May 5	5,600	15.00
Purchases, July 4	3,200	16.00
Units sold – October 31 at $19	8,700	
Purchases, November 22	1,400	15.00

Compute Zoola's ending inventory and cost of goods sold under each of the following cost-flow methods assuming that the company uses a perpetual inventory system (round your answer for cost per unit to two decimal places):

Required »

a. Moving Average b. FIFO c. LIFO

3 **E10-4. Moving Average, FIFO, LIFO, Presentation and Disclosures.** Answer the following questions using the information provided in E10-3:

Required »

a. Prepare a partial income statement and balance sheet for Zoola, Inc. under each of the inventory valuation methods.
b. Assume that the company reported current assets (without inventory) of $469,801 at the beginning of the year and $480,976 at the end of the year. Also assume that it reports current liabilities of $403,568 and $423,571 at the beginning and end of the year, respectively. Compute the current ratio and inventory turnover ratio under each of the inventory valuation methods. The inventory turnover ratio is required only for the end of the period.

3 4 8 **E10-5. LIFO, Conversion to FIFO.** Inventory transactions for Jack Franklin Stores are summarized in the following table. The company uses the LIFO perpetual method for both financial and tax reporting.

Transaction	Units	Sales in Units	Unit Cost	Total Cost
Beginning inventory: January 1				
Oldest cost	2,000		$ 5	$ 10,000
Next oldest cost	1,750		8	14,000
Total beginning inventory	3,750			$ 24,000
Purchases				
January 20	5,000		9	45,000
February 18	12,500		11	137,500
Subtotal	21,250			$206,500
Units sold on May 1 at $18		19,000		
July 28	18,750		10	187,500
Total available for sale	40,000			$394,000
Total units sold	(19,000)			
Ending inventory	21,000			

The inventory footnote from Jack Franklin Stores' annual report indicates that the difference between the LIFO costs and the current (FIFO) costs of inventory is equal to $0 and $12,750 at the beginning and end of the year, respectively.

Required »

a. Determine the ending inventory and cost of goods sold for the current year.
b. Use the footnote information provided in the question to convert the beginning and ending inventories from a LIFO to a FIFO basis.
c. Convert the cost of goods sold for the current year from the LIFO to the FIFO basis.
d. Compare the inventory turnover ratio for the current year computed under the two methods of inventory valuation.

❸❽ **E10-6. LIFO.** Burke Company uses the LIFO perpetual method for financial reporting and tax purposes. A summary of Burke's inventory for the current year follows.

	LIFO Inventory			
Description	**Units**	**Unit Cost**	**Total Cost**	**Units Sold**
Beginning inventory: January 1				
First layer	10,000	$3.10	$ 31,000	
Second layer	6,000	3.90	23,400	
Total beginning inventory	16,000		$ 54,400	
Units sold on February 20 at $7.05				14,000
Purchases or production:				
March 31	2,000	5.10	10,200	
July 15	8,500	5.60	47,600	
Units sold on December 1 at $7.25				11,000
Cost of goods available for sale	26,500		$112,200	
Total units sold	(25,000)			
Ending inventory: December 31	1,500			

Required »

a. Compute the ending inventory and cost of goods sold for the current year.
b. Prepare a partial income statement showing the gross profit for the current year.

❹ **E10-7. Dollar-Value LIFO, LIFO Reserve.** Total Color, Inc. manufactures and distributes house paints. Total Color uses the dollar-value LIFO method. Information for 2018, 2019, and 2020 is presented in the following table.

Year	**Inventory – FIFO**
2018 – Base year	$356,000
2019	$379,700
2020	$414,000

The cumulative price indices for 2018, 2019, and 2020, respectively are 1.0000, 1.0230, and 1.0537.

Required »

a. Compute the company's ending inventory using dollar-value LIFO for each year. Round to the nearest dollar.
b. Prepare the journal entry required to adjust the LIFO reserve for each year.

❹ **E10-8. Dollar-Value LIFO, LIFO Reserve.** CWB Teleconcepts, Inc. manufactures and distributes three models of handheld devices: the Flame, the Globe, and the HD3. CWB uses the dollar-value LIFO method. Information for 2018, 2019, and 2020 is presented in the following table.

Description	**Base Year: 2018**		**2019**		**2020**	
Inventory	**Units**	**Total FIFO Cost**	**Units**	**Total FIFO Cost**	**Units**	**Total FIFO Cost**
Flame	5,000	$450,000	7,000	$658,000	4,000	$392,000
Globe	6,000	660,000	5,000	580,000	3,000	375,000
HD3	3,000	450,000	5,000	800,000	1,000	170,000

The cumulative price indices for 2018, 2019, and 2020, respectively are 1.00, 1.056, and 1.1155.

Required »

a. Compute the company's ending inventory using dollar-value LIFO for each year. Treat the three models as one group. Round to the nearest dollar.
b. Prepare the journal entry required to adjust the LIFO reserve for each year.

4 **E10-9. Dollar-Value LIFO, No Liquidation.** Joe the Grocer Markets, Inc. (JTGM) adopted the dollar-value LIFO inventory method using 2018 as the base year. JTGM uses FIFO for its internal books. Information related to its inventory is presented in the following table:

Year	Ending Inventory at End-of-Year Prices per Internal Books	Cumulative Price Index
2018	$ 870,000	100
2019	980,000	102
2020	1,050,000	103

Required »

a. Compute JTGM's ending inventory under the dollar-value LIFO method for the years 2018 through 2020.
b. Prepare the journal entries for 2019 and 2020 to adjust inventory to the dollar-value LIFO basis.
c. Determine the ending balance of the LIFO reserve for 2019 and 2020.

4 **E10-10. Dollar-Value LIFO, LIFO Liquidation.** Nicky Bisco Products adopted the dollar-value LIFO method using 2018 as the base year for financial reporting purposes. It uses FIFO for its internal books. Information related to Bisco's inventory follows:

Year	Ending Inventory at End-of-Year Prices per Internal Books	Cumulative Price Index
2018	$495,000	100
2019	588,000	110
2020	612,000	112

Required »

a. Compute Bisco's ending inventory under the dollar-value LIFO method for the years 2018 through 2020.
b. Prepare the journal entries for 2019 and 2020 to adjust inventory to the dollar-value LIFO basis.
c. Determine the ending balance of the LIFO reserve for 2019 and 2020.

5 **E10-11. Lower of Cost or Market.** All-Kinds-of-Cases Company sells cases for smart phones and notepad computers. The company uses the LIFO method for costing inventory. All-Kinds-of-Cases groups inventory by the device manufacturer for which the case is made in its LCM computations. All-Kinds-of-Cases provided the following information regarding inventory at the end of the current year.

Group No.	Manufacturer	CRC	No. of Units	SP	Disposal	NPM	Cost
Smart phone case	General Tech	$ 8	450	$14	$1	$ 6	$ 5
Notepad case	General Tech	14	300	35	2	18	16
Smart phone case	Pacific Base	5	750	8	2	4	7
Notepad case	Pacific Base	12	520	32	2	15	14

Definitions:
CRC = Current Replacement Cost
SP = Selling Price
DISPOSAL = Costs of Completion and Disposal
NPM = Normal Profit Margin

Required »

a. Conduct a lower-of-cost-or-market test for All-Kinds-of-Cases assuming that it uses the total inventory approach for LCM computations.
b. Conduct a lower-of-cost-or-market test for All-Kinds-of-Cases assuming that it uses the individual-item approach for LCM computations.
c. Conduct a lower-of-cost-or-market test for All-Kinds-of-Cases assuming that it uses the group-by-group approach for LCM computations.
d. Prepare the journal entry needed to adjust All-Kinds-of-Cases's inventory to a lower-of-cost-or-market (LCM) basis assuming that LCM is applied to total inventory groups. All-Kinds-of-Cases uses the indirect approach to record any adjustments to LCM.

5 **E10-12. Lower of Cost or Market, IFRS.** Use the same information in E10-11 now assuming that All-Kinds-of-Cases Company is an IFRS reporter. Assume the company uses FIFO.

Required »

a. Conduct a lower-of-cost-or-market test for All-Kinds-of-Cases assuming that it uses the individual-item approach for LCM computations.
b. Conduct a lower-of-cost-or-market test for All-Kinds-of-Cases assuming that it uses the group-by-group approach for LCM computations.
c. Prepare the journal entry needed to adjust All-Kinds-of-Cases's inventory to a lower-of-cost-or-market (LCM) basis assuming that LCM is applied to individual items. All-Kinds-of-Cases uses the indirect approach to record any adjustments to LCM.

5 **E10-13. Lower of Cost or Market.** Printmaster Distributors Company sells laser printers and replacement toner cartridges. Printmaster uses FIFO for inventory costing. It sells two models—black and color laser printers. The black printers and black toner cartridges are in Group 100 and the color printer and color toner cartridges are in Group 200. Printmaster provided the following information regarding inventory at the end of the current year.

Group No.	Model No.	CRC	No. of Units	SP	Disposal	NPM	Cost
No. 100 Black Laser Printer	LP100	$175	2,000	$210	$20	$35	$170
No. 100 Black Toner	BT100	40	1,500	55	10	16	48
No. 200 Color Laser Printer	CP200	200	3,400	235	25	20	185
No. 200 Color Toner	CT200	65	2,750	145	15	25	55

Definitions:
CRC = Current Replacement Cost
SP = Selling Price
Disposal = Costs of Completion and Disposal
NPM = Normal Profit Margin

Required »

a. Conduct a lower-of-cost-or-market test for Printmaster assuming that it uses the total inventory approach for LCM computations.
b. Conduct a lower-of-cost-or-market test for Printmaster assuming that it uses the individual-item approach for LCM computations.
c. Conduct a lower-of-cost-or-market test for Printmaster assuming that it uses the group-by-group approach for LCM computations.
d. Prepare the journal entry needed to adjust Printmaster's inventory to a lower-of-cost-or-market (LCM) basis assuming that LCM is applied to individual items. Printmaster uses the indirect approach to record any adjustments to LCM.

5 **E10-14. Lower of Cost or Market.** Use the information in E10-13 but now assume that Printmaster Distributors Company measures inventory cost using the LIFO method.

Required »

a. Conduct a lower-of-cost-or-market test for Printmaster assuming that it uses the total inventory approach for LCM computations.
b. Conduct a lower-of-cost-or-market test for Printmaster assuming that it uses the individual-item approach for LCM computations.
c. Conduct a lower-of-cost-or-market test for Printmaster assuming that it uses the group-by-group approach for LCM computations.
d. Prepare the journal entry needed to adjust Printmaster's inventory to a lower-of-cost-or-market (LCM) basis assuming that LCM is applied to product groups. Printmaster uses the indirect approach to record any adjustments to LCM.

5 **E10-15. Lower of Cost or Market, Reversal, IFRS.** Use the same information in E10-13 but now assume that Printmaster Distributors Company is an IFRS reporter.

Required »

a. Conduct a lower-of-cost-or-market test for Printmaster assuming that it uses the individual-item approach for LCM computations.

b. Conduct a lower-of-cost-or-market test for Printmaster assuming that it uses the group-by-group approach for LCM computations.
c. Prepare the journal entry needed to adjust Printmaster's inventory to a lower-of-cost-or-market (LCM) basis assuming that LCM is applied to individual items. Printmaster uses the indirect approach to record any adjustments to LCM.
d. Assume that in the following year Printmaster has 1,000 units of BT100 Black Toner still in its inventory. The selling price has increased to $58 dollars. Prepare the journal entry needed to adjust Printmaster's inventory for any reversal of its lower-of-cost-or-market adjustment.

6 **E10-16. Conventional Retail Inventory Method.** Melvin Corporation uses the conventional retail method for financial reporting. The company's inventory records are summarized as follows.

Description	Cost	Retail
Beginning inventory	$ 700,000	$1,015,000
Purchases	1,320,000	1,857,500
Additional markups		72,000
Markup cancellations		12,000
Markdowns		18,500
Markdown cancellations		3,000
Sales		2,740,500

Estimate Melvin's ending inventory using the conventional retail method. (Round percentages to two decimal places.)

7 **E10-17. Gross Profit Method.** A tsunami destroyed Kyoto Company's warehouse and all of its inventory. Kyoto's prior-year balance sheet reported ending inventory totaling $5,097. Kyoto's management believes that last year's gross profit percentage is a good estimate of the gross profit in the current year. Kyoto's sales last year were $48,540 and its cost of goods sold was $27,490. Before the tsunami, Kyoto's net sales were $28,903, and Kyoto purchased $18,005 of inventory. Of the inventory purchased, $45 had not yet been delivered to Kyoto. Round percentages to one decimal place. Use the gross profit method to determine the following:

Required »

a. What is Kyoto's historical gross profit percentage?
b. What is Kyoto's estimated cost of goods sold?
c. What is Kyoto's estimated gross profit?
d. What is Kyoto's estimated ending inventory?

7 **E10-18. Gross Profit Method.** A flood destroyed Addio Company's warehouse and all of its inventory. Addio will use the gross profit method to determine its inventory in the warehouse at the time. Addio's management believes that the average of the last two years' gross profit percentage is a good estimate of the gross profit in the current year. Sales last year were $7,128 and $6,789 in the year before. Its cost of goods sold was $4,946 last year and $4,580 the year before. Addio's prior-year balance sheet reported ending inventory of $437. Before the flood, net sales were $5,702. Addio purchased $3,715 of inventory. Round percentages to one decimal place. Use the gross profit method to determine the following:

Required »

a. What is Addio's historical gross profit percentage?
b. What it Addio's estimated cost of goods sold?
c. What is Addio's estimated gross profit?
d. What is Addio's estimated ending inventory?

A **E10-19. LIFO Retail Inventory Method.** Zimma, Inc. uses the LIFO retail inventory method for costing inventory. It has beginning inventory at a cost of $23,000 and at a cost-to-retail ratio of 58%. During the year, Zimma purchased goods with a cost basis of $78,400 and a retail value of $132,881. It had net markups of $2,400 and net markdowns of $8,900. Zimma has net sales of $124,000. What is Zimma's ending inventory using the LIFO retail method? Round percentages to two decimal places.

A **E10-20. LIFO Retail Inventory Method.** Kiresh, Inc. uses the LIFO retail inventory method for costing inventory. It has beginning inventory at a cost of $57,000 and retail value of $95,000. During the year, Kiresh purchased goods with a cost basis of $136,700 and a retail value of $220,484. It had net markups of $6,700 and net markdowns of $15,400. Kiresh has net sales of $266,400. What is Kiresh's ending inventory using the LIFO retail method? Round percentages to two decimal places.

Ⓐ **E10-21. Dollar-Value LIFO Retail Inventory Method.** Zorinak, Inc. uses the dollar-value LIFO retail inventory method for costing inventory. It has beginning inventory costing $154,000 at a cost-to-retail ratio of 72%. During the year, Zorinak purchased goods with a cost basis of $770,000 and a retail value of $1,100,000. It had net markups of $33,000 and net markdowns of $49,500. Zorinak sold 80% of its goods available for sale during the year. The current-year price index is 1.03. What is Zorinak's ending inventory at cost and retail using the dollar-value LIFO retail method? Round percentages to two decimal places.

Problems

③ **P10-1. Moving Average, FIFO, LIFO.** Morocco Imports provided the following information regarding its inventory for the current year, its second year of operations.

Transaction	Units	Sales in Units	Unit Cost	Total Cost
Beginning inventory January 1	35,000		$3.50	$ 122,500
Purchases				
February 8	45,500		3.60	163,800
March 15	100,250		3.80	380,950
April 10	62,000		4.10	254,200
Subtotal	242,750			$ 921,450
Units sold April 22 at $12		155,000		
May 9	81,000		4.35	352,350
June 19	28,000		4.56	127,680
Subtotal	351,750			$1,401,480
Units sold August 11 at $14		115,500		
September 20	15,000		4.75	71,250
October 30	41,000		4.85	198,850
November 17	8,000		4.90	39,200
Subtotal	415,750			$1,710,780
Units sold December 21 at $16		21,500		
Total available for sale	415,750			
Total units sold	(292,000)			
Ending inventory	123,750			

Compute Morocco's ending inventory and cost of goods sold under each of the following cost-flow assumptions assuming a perpetual inventory system. (Round your answer for cost per unit to two decimal places.)

Required »

a. Moving Average b. FIFO c. LIFO

③ **P10-2. Moving Average, FIFO, LIFO.** Use the information provided in P10-1 for Morocco Imports. For each of the three cost-flow assumptions (moving-average, FIFO, and LIFO methods):

Required »

a. Prepare a partial income statement up to the cost of goods sold section.
b. Compute the gross profit percentage.
c. Comment on the ranking of the gross profit percentages.

③④ **P10-3. LIFO, Conversion to FIFO.** The Outsider Company, Inc. provided the following information regarding its inventory for the year ended December 31, 2019. It made all of the purchases before it had any sales transactions for the year.

Description	LIFO		FIFO	
Beginning inventory: January 1, 2019	8,000 @ $6	$ 48,000	4,000 @ $7	$ 28,000
	8,000 @ $7	56,000	12,000 @ $8	96,000
Total beginning inventory	16,000 units	$ 104,000	16,000 units	$124,000
Purchases	14,000 @ $9	126,000	14,000 @ $9	126,000
Cost of goods available	30,000 units	$ 230,000	30,000 units	$250,000
Ending inventory	6,000 @ $6	36,000	6,000 @ $9	54,000
Cost of goods sold	24,000 units	$ 194,000	24,000 units	$196,000

Required »

a. Compute the LIFO reserve at the beginning of the year (i.e., at December 31, 2018).
b. Compute the LIFO reserve at the end of the year (i.e., at December 31, 2019).
c. Illustrate how the firm can use the LIFO reserve to convert ending inventory from the LIFO to the FIFO basis for both years (i.e., 2018 and 2019).
d. Illustrate how the firm can use the LIFO reserve to convert the LIFO cost of goods sold to the FIFO cost of goods sold for 2019.
e. Describe the conditions that indicate that there is a LIFO liquidation for 2019.

4 **P10-4. Dollar-Value LIFO.** The Happenings Company adopted the dollar-value LIFO inventory method on December 31, 2017, when the price index was 1.00. Ending inventory on the date that it adopted dollar-value LIFO follows.

Item	Number of Units	Total FIFO Cost
MAS1840	280	$ 840
JAS2307	850	5,950
TOTAL		$6,790

Information related to the year-end prices for the two years after the adoption of dollar-value LIFO is summarized in the following table.

	December 31	
Description	**2018**	**2019**
Year-end prices (FIFO) – MAS1840 inventory	$ 2,100	$ 2,639
Year-end prices (FIFO) – JAS2307 inventory	10,080	16,800

The cumulative price index for 2018 is 1.3385, and the cumulative price index for 2019 is 1.4399. Treat both models as one group.

Required »

a. Calculate the ending inventory for 2018 at dollar-value LIFO and determine the LIFO reserve needed, if any. Prepare the journal entry to record the LIFO reserve.
b. Calculate the ending inventory for 2019 at dollar-value LIFO and determine the LIFO reserve needed, if any. Prepare the journal entry to record the LIFO reserve.

4 **P10-5. Dollar-Value LIFO, No Liquidation.** Nat's Toy Stores Limited adopted the dollar-value LIFO inventory method using 2017 as the base year. The cumulative price index for 2018 through 2021 was 1.01, 1.03, 1.04 and 1.06, respectively. Ending inventory according to Nat's Toy Stores' trial balance, using FIFO, is presented in the following table:

Year	Ending Inventory per the Trial Balance
2017	$ 860,000
2018	1,100,000
2019	1,313,000
2020	1,420,000
2021	1,510,000

Required »

a. Compute Nat's ending inventory under the dollar-value LIFO method for the years 2017 through 2021.
b. Prepare the journal entries for 2018 through 2021 to adjust inventory to the dollar-value LIFO basis.
c. Determine the ending balance of the LIFO reserve for 2018 through 2021.

4 **P10-6. Dollar-Value LIFO, LIFO Liquidation.** The following information was provided by Capri Company:

Year	Ending Inventory at Average Cost	Cumulative Price Index
2014	$530,000	100
2015	620,000	105
2016	610,000	110
2017	485,000	111
2018	620,000	115

Capri adopted the dollar-value LIFO method using 2014 as the base year.

Required »

a. Compute Capri's ending inventory under the dollar-value LIFO method for the years 2014 through 2018.
b. Prepare the journal entries for 2015 through 2018 to adjust inventory to the dollar-value LIFO basis.
c. Determine the ending balance of the LIFO reserve for 2015 through 2018.

4 **P10-7. Dollar-Value LIFO, LIFO Liquidation.** Silvio's Taverns, Inc. adopted the dollar-value LIFO Method in 2015. Information related to Silvio's inventory follows:

Year	Ending Inventory at End-of-Year Prices per FIFO	Cumulative Price Index
2015	$505,000	100
2016	612,000	103
2017	645,000	108
2018	487,000	112
2019	610,000	119

Required »

a. Compute Silvio's ending inventory under the dollar-value LIFO method for the years 2015 through 2019.
b. Prepare the journal entries for 2016 through 2019 to adjust inventory to the dollar-value LIFO basis.
c. Determine the ending balance of the LIFO reserve for 2016 through 2019.

5 **P10-8. Lower of Cost or Market.** Framingdale Factories, Inc. manufactures low-cost furniture. The company produces three sizes of wardrobes 4 foot (S), 6 foot (M), and 8 foot (L). Framingdale provided the following data:

Description	4 Foot (S)	6 Foot (M)	8 Foot (L)
Selling price	$100	$120	$145
FIFO cost	84	94	150
Current replacement cost	72	88	125
Disposal cost	22	25	20
Normal profit (% of selling price)	20%	25%	30%
Units in ending inventory	1,000	2,100	900

Required »

a. Determine the inventory carrying value with the lower-of-cost-or-market rule using the individual-item basis.
b. Prepare the journal entry to record any write-down required using the indirect method.
c. Determine the inventory carrying value with the lower-of-cost-or-market rule using the total inventory basis.
d. Prepare the journal entry to record any write-down using the direct method.

5 **P10-9. Lower of Cost or Market.** O'Sullivan Corporation provided the following information regarding its ending inventory for the current year. O'Sullivan manufactures three types of athletic shoes. Selling costs are 10% of the selling price. The company values its ending inventory at the lower of LIFO cost or market.

There are 1,000 units of each product in inventory.

Product	LIFO Cost	Current Replacement Cost	Selling Price	Normal Profit Margin*
Assurant	$210	$225	$260	30%
Biglow	250	220	280	20%
Cartata	170	140	200	15%

*As a percentage of selling price

Required »

a. Compute the amount of write-down, if any, on both an individual and a total inventory basis.
b. Prepare any journal entries necessary to reflect the inventory at lower of cost or market assuming that O'Sullivan uses the indirect method.

c. Repeat requirement (b) assuming that O'Sullivan uses the direct method to record any required write-down to lower of cost or market.

6 **P10-10. Conventional Retail Inventory Method.** John Stevens Corporation uses the conventional retail method for financial reporting. The company's inventory records are summarized here.

Description	Cost	Retail
Beginning inventory	$ 20,000	$ 56,000
Purchases	144,500	198,400
Additional markups		9,000
Markup cancellations		3,000
Markdowns		5,000
Markdown cancellations		1,500
Sales		235,700

Estimate John Stevens' ending inventory using the conventional retail inventory method. (Round percentages to two decimal places.)

6 **P10-11. Conventional Retail Inventory Method.** On January 1, 2017, Goodbye Electronics Outlets adopted the conventional retail method of accounting for its merchandise inventory.

	Cost	Retail
Inventory, 1/1/2017	$ 45,730	$ 68,000
Markdowns		17,850
Additional markups		28,500
Markdown cancellations		6,500
Markup cancellations		3,500
Net purchases	155,500	190,000
Sales		195,500

Determine the company's ending inventory under the conventional retail method. (Round percentages to two decimal places.)

7 **P10-12. Gross Profit Method.** In 2018, Sawyer Company experienced a major casualty loss. The roof of its warehouse collapsed in an ice storm and destroyed its entire inventory. The company began the year with inventory of $598. It made purchases of $2,400 but returned $24 worth of merchandise. Sales prior to the ice storm were $3,945. Sawyer must use the gross profit method to determine inventory on hand on the date of the casualty. Round percentages to one decimal place. The following is an excerpt of its income statement for the last three years.

	2015	2016	2017
Net Sales	$3,404	$3,540	$3,735
Cost of Goods Sold	1,401	1,365	1,424
General and Administrative Expense	243	259	262
Depreciation Expense	302	315	320
Operating Income	$1,458	$1,601	$1,729

Required »

a. Assume that Sawyer uses the most recent three years of net sales and cost of goods sold to determine its historical gross profit. What are estimated cost of goods sold, estimated gross profit, and estimated ending inventory?

b. Assume that Sawyer uses the most recent two years of net sales and cost of goods sold to determine its historical gross profit. What are estimated cost of goods sold, estimated gross profit, and estimated ending inventory?

c. Comment on the differences in estimated cost of goods sold, estimated gross profit, and estimated ending inventory from parts (a) and (b).

6A **P10-13. Basic Retail Inventory Method and Conventional Retail Inventory Methods.** The Monte Sales Company provided the following data related to its inventory at the end of the current year. Round percentages to two decimal places.

Description	Cost	Retail
Beginning inventory	$ 21,800	$ 45,000
Purchases	112,500	132,000
Additional markups		21,000
Markup cancellations		4,200
Markdowns		15,800
Markdown cancellations		2,800
Sales		165,000

Required »

a. What are Monte's ending inventory and cost of goods sold under the conventional retail method?
b. What are Monte's ending inventory and cost of goods sold under the basic retail method?
c. Which method provides the lower ending inventory value consistent with the lower-of-cost-or-market method?

6A **P10-14. Basic Retail Inventory Method and Conventional Retail Inventory Methods.** The Johnny Fruit Company provided the following data related to its inventory at the end of the current year. Round percentages to two decimal places.

Description	Cost	Retail
Beginning inventory	$ 17,800	$ 28,000
Purchases	123,400	213,000
Additional markups		24,000
Markup cancellations		3,200
Markdowns		19,200
Markdown cancellations		2,200
Sales		200,000

Required »

a. What are Johnny Fruit's ending inventory and cost of goods sold under the conventional retail method?
b. What are Johnny Fruit's ending inventory and cost of goods sold under the basic retail method?
c. Which method provides the lower ending inventory value consistent with the lower-of-cost-or-market method?

6 **P10-15. Conventional Retail Inventory Method (LCM).** The Tally Billiard Supply Corporation provided the following data related to its inventory at the end of the current year:

Description	Cost	Retail
Beginning inventory	$ 8,500	$ 38,000
Purchases	153,200	132,000
Additional markups		13,000
Markup cancellations		3,000
Markdowns		14,800
Markdown cancellations		2,700
Sales		146,000

What are Tally Corporation's ending inventory and cost of goods sold under the conventional retail method? Round percentages to two decimal places.

A **P10-16. Conventional Retail Inventory Method, Lower of Cost or Market.** The Wallace Weed Corporation provided the following data related to its inventory at the end of the current year:

Description	Cost	Retail
Beginning inventory	$18,700	$38,000
Purchases	99,400	142,000
Additional markups		12,000
Markup cancellations		4,000
Markdowns		17,800
Markdown cancellations		7,600
Sales		158,000

Required »

a. What is Wallace Weed's ending inventory and cost of goods sold under the conventional retail method? Round percentages to two decimal places.
b. What is the cost to retail ratio under the basic retail method.

Excel Project
Autograded Excel Project available in **MyLab Accounting**

CASES

Judgment Cases

Judgment Case 1: The Choice to Use LIFO

The ***Kroger Co.*** reported cash income taxes paid of $557 million for the year ended January 28, 2017 (fiscal year 2016). In addition, it reported the following:

THE KROGER CO.
CONSOLIDATED BALANCE SHEETS

(In millions)	January 28, 2017	January 30, 2016
ASSETS		
Current assets		
Cash and temporary cash investments	$ 322	$ 277
Store deposits in-transit	910	923
Receivables	1,649	1,734
FIFO inventory	7,852	7,440
LIFO reserve	(1,291)	(1,272)
Prepaid and other current assets	898	790
Total current assets	10,340	9,892
Property, plant and equipment, net	21,016	19,619
Intangibles, net	1,153	1,053
Goodwill	3,031	2,724
Other assets	965	609
Total Assets	$36,505	$33,897

THE KROGER CO.
CONSOLIDATED STATEMENTS OF OPERATIONS

Years Ended January 28, 2017, January 30, 2016, and January 1, 2015

(In millions)	2016 (52 weeks)	2015 (52 weeks)	2014 (52 weeks)
Earnings before income tax expense	$2,914	$3,094	$2,649
Income tax expense*	957	1,045	902
Net earnings including noncontrolling interests	$1,957	$2,049	$1,747

*Cash paid for income taxes in 2016 $557

Source: The Kroger Co. http://ir.kroger.com/Doc/Index?did=40034683

a. What is the LIFO reserve for ***Kroger*** as of January 28, 2017? January 30, 2016?

b. What is the impact of ***Kroger's*** decision to use LIFO on its January 28, 2017 balance sheet in terms of the effect on inventory, current assets, and total assets?

c. What is the amount of the LIFO effect for ***Kroger*** for the year ended January 28, 2017?

d. What is the impact of ***Kroger's*** decision to use LIFO on its income statement for the year ended January 28, 2017, in terms of earnings before taxes?

e. What is the impact of ***Kroger's*** decision to use LIFO on its cash taxes paid for the year ending January 28, 2017, assuming an effective tax rate of 35%?

Judgment Case 2: Inventory Costing

BBS is a calendar-year corporation that manufactures baseballs. BBS produced 9.5 million baseballs in 20X7 and incurred fixed production overhead costs of $2 million. In the past 5 years, it has produced the following number of baseballs:

20X2	9.7 million
20X3	9.7 million
20X4	9.1 million
20X5	10.1 million
20X6	10.1 million

The decline in production in 20X4 was due to an employee strike.

Read ASC 330-10-30 and determine what amount of fixed production overhead costs should be allocated to inventory and what amount should be included in current-period expenses. Outline your thought process as well as the judgment(s) you made in reaching this conclusion.

Judgment Case 3: Lower of Cost or Market

KR Automotives is a calendar-year car dealer that sells cars made by Hoyta. KR uses LIFO and calculates the lower of cost or market using an individual-item basis. The CFO of KR believes that KR will need to write-down its inventory of one particular car.

The Kaminator has historically sold very well at KR. In fact, in recent years, it has sold above its sticker price of $34,000 because of the high demand for the car. The average selling price of the Kaminator in 2014 was $35,000 and the average selling price in 2015 was $36,000. However, in late 2016, a rival car manufacturer produced a car, the Crumbder, that is very similar to the Kaminator. However, the competitor's car received significantly higher ratings from consumer organizations that rate cars for safety and gas mileage among other things. In addition, the Crumbder was rated as a "recommended best buy." Crumbder's entry on the market significantly reduced sales of the Kaminator; sales in December 2016, after the release of the Crumbder, averaged $27,000. The sales force at KR Automotives is convinced that the sales will stagnate even more in 2017.

The CEO of KR is trying to determine what to do with the 200 Kaminators that were left on the lot on December 31, 2016. He has come up with four possibilities:

1. Keep the cars on the lot and try to sell them to retail customers. The sales force is very uncertain what price at which they could ultimately sell these cars. In a similar situation 10 years ago, KR sold the older cars for 25% below sticker.

2. Sell the cars to dealers overseas. One overseas dealer has already offered to buy 20 Kaminators for $19,000 each. This dealer indicated that it may be willing to buy more, depending upon how well the 20 sell.
3. Sell the cars to a used car lot at a much reduced price, likely around 40% below sticker.
4. Put the cars up for auction. KR has not tried this before and has no history of how the cars might sell. There is some limited evidence that indicates that excited buyers might buy the car for sticker price.

The current selling costs are $500 per car and KR uses a 15% profit margin in its LCM computations. KR paid $23,000 per car for the Kaminators that are on the lot. The replacement cost of these cars is $20,000 per car.

What is the most appropriate write-down amount, if any, for the Kaminators? Outline your thought process as well as the judgment(s) you made in reaching this conclusion.

Financial Statement Analysis Cases

Case 1: LIFO to FIFO Conversion and Comparison of Companies

Kimberly-Clark Corporation and ***Procter & Gamble*** Company reported the following information about inventory in their financial statements and footnotes. Use this information to answer the following questions:

a. What cost-flow assumption(s) does ***Kimberly-Clark*** use?
b. What is ***Kimberly-Clark's*** LIFO reserve at the end of 2014, 2015, and 2016?
c. If ***Kimberly-Clark*** used the FIFO cost-flow assumption to account for all of its inventory, what would its balance of ending inventory be in 2014, 2015, and 2016?
d. What would ***Kimberly-Clark's*** cost of goods under FIFO have been in 2015 and 2016?
e. Would ***Kimberly-Clark's*** gross profit, taxes, and net income have been higher or lower under FIFO in 2015 and 2016?
f. Compare ***Kimberly-Clark's*** gross profit percentage, inventory turnover ratio, and days in inventory on hand under LIFO versus FIFO for 2015 and 2016.
g. What cost-flow assumption(s) does ***Procter & Gamble*** use?
h. For fiscal 2016, compare ***Procter & Gamble's*** inventory turnover ratio and days in inventory on hand to those of ***Kimberly-Clark*** under FIFO from part (f).

Kimberly-Clark Corporation

Excerpt from 2016 Annual Report, ***Kimberly-Clark Corporation***

KIMBERLY-CLARK CORPORATION AND SUBSIDIARIES
CONSOLIDATED INCOME STATEMENT

(Millions of dollars)	Years Ended December 31 2016	2015	2014
Net Sales	$18,202	$18,591	$19,724
Cost of products sold	11,551	11,967	13,041
Gross Profit	$ 6,651	$ 6,624	$ 6,683

NOTE 1: Accounting Policies (excerpt)

Inventories and Distribution Costs

Most U.S. inventories are valued at the lower of cost, using the Last-In, First-Out (LIFO) method, or market. The balance of the U.S. inventories and inventories of consolidated operations outside the U.S. are valued at the lower of cost, using either the First-In, First-Out (FIFO) or moving-average cost methods, or market. Net realizable value is the estimated selling prices in the ordinary course of business, less reasonably predictable costs of completion, disposal, and transportation. Distribution costs are classified as cost of products sold.

Excerpt from 2016 Annual Report, ***Kimberly-Clark Corporation***

NOTE 17: Supplemental Data

Summary of Inventories (modified) At the lower of cost, determined on the FIFO or moving-average cost methods, or market (Millions of dollars)	**December 31**		
	2016	**2015**	**2014**
Raw materials	$ 329	$ 397	$ 426
Goods in process	203	203	215
Finished goods	1,030	1,214	1,183
Other	280	278	288
Inventories at FIFO	1,842	2,092	2,112
Adjustment to LIFO	(163)	(183)	(220)
Total inventories	$1,679	$1,909	$1,892

Source: Kimberly-Clark Corporation. http://www.cms.kimberly-clark.com/umbracoimages/UmbracoFileMedia/KMB-2016-10K_umbracoFile.pdf

The Procter & Gamble Company

Statement of Earnings (excerpt) Amounts in millions, Years ended June 30	**2016**	**2015**
Net Sales	$65,299	$70,749
Cost of Sales	32,909	37,056
Gross Profit	$32,390	$33,693
Balance Sheet (excerpt)		
Amounts in millions, June 30	**2016**	**2015**
Materials and supplies	$ 1,188	$ 1,266
Work in process	563	525
Finished goods	2,965	3,188
Total inventories	$ 4,716	$ 4,979

Note 1: Summary of Significant Accounting Policies (excerpt)

Inventory Valuation

Inventories are valued at the lower of cost or market value. Product-related inventories are primarily maintained on the first-in, first-out method. The cost of spare part inventories is maintained using the average-cost method.

Source: P&G 2016 Annual Report. https://www.pg.com/fr_FR/downloads/annual_reports/PG_Annual_Report_2016.pdf

Case 2: Analysis of Inventory Disclosures

PROBLEM: Selected disclosures related to ***Foot Locker*** Company's inventory follow. Use these disclosures to answer the following questions:

a. What percentage of inventory at the end of 2016 is accounted for under each cost-flow assumption that ***Foot Locker*** uses?
b. Why would ***Foot Locker*** use LIFO for domestic U.S. inventories but FIFO for international inventories?
c. How does ***Foot Locker*** apply the retail inventory method?
d. What types of costs are included in the cost of sales?
e. Why does ***Foot Locker*** not report a LIFO reserve?
f. What is ***Foot Locker's*** gross profit percentage in 2014, 2015, and 2016?
g. What is ***Foot Locker's*** inventory turnover ratio and days inventory on hand in 2016?

Foot Locker, Inc.
Consolidated Statements of Operations

	2016	2015 (in millions)	2014
Sales	$7,766	$7,412	$7,151
Cost of sales	5,130	4,907	4,777

From Financial Statement Notes:

NOTE 1: Summary of Significant Accounting Policies (excerpt)

Merchandise Inventories and Cost of Sales

Merchandise inventories for the Company's Athletic Stores are valued at the lower of cost or market using the retail inventory method. Cost for retail stores is determined on the last-in, first-out ("LIFO") basis for domestic inventories and on the first-in, first-out ("FIFO") basis for international inventories. Merchandise inventories of the Direct-to-Customers business are valued at the lower of cost or market using weighted-average cost, which approximates FIFO.

The retail inventory method is commonly used by retail companies to value inventories at cost and calculate gross margins due to its practicality. Under the retail inventory method, cost is determined by applying a cost-to-retail percentage across groupings of similar items, known as departments. The cost-to-retail percentage is applied to ending inventory at its current owned retail valuation to determine the cost of ending inventory on a department basis. The Company provides reserves based on current selling prices when the inventory has not been marked down to market.

Transportation, distribution center, and sourcing costs are capitalized in merchandise inventories. The Company expenses the freight associated with transfers between its store locations in the period incurred. The Company maintains an accrual for shrinkage based on historical rates.

Cost of sales is composed of the cost of merchandise, as well as occupancy, buyers' compensation, and shipping and handling costs. The cost of merchandise is recorded net of amounts received from suppliers for damaged product returns, markdown allowances, and volume rebates, as well as cooperative advertising reimbursements received in excess of specific, incremental advertising expenses. Occupancy includes the amortization of amounts received from landlords for tenant improvements.

NOTE 5: Merchandise Inventories

	2016	2015
	(in millions)	
LIFO inventories	$ 861	$ 847
FIFO inventories	446	438
Total merchandise inventories	$1,307	$1,285

The value of the Company's LIFO inventories, as calculated on a LIFO basis, approximates their value as calculated on a FIFO basis.

Source: https://www.sec.gov/Archives/edgar/data/850209/000085020917000003/fl-20170128x10k.htm

Surfing the Standards Cases

Surfing the Standards Case 1: Inventory in the Agriculture Industry[21]

Tarheel Farm, Inc. (TFI) is a North Carolina corporation involved in agricultural production and has an October 31 fiscal year-end. It is not publicly traded, but it is required to prepare annual financial statements complying with U.S. GAAP for its bank. TFI typically produces four products: beef cattle, corn, winter wheat, and sugar beets. All four of these products have a life cycle of less than 1 year. The following information is available as of October 31:

[21]Reprinted from the Ernst & Young Academic Resource Center with permission of the Ernst & Young Foundation.

- TFI had 400 acres of field corn planted. The corn will not be harvested until next month. The accumulated cost of the corn is $95,000. The estimated selling costs are $4,500. The current market value of land is $5,000 per acre. Although there is no current market value available for land growing a corn crop on it, TFI is certain that this land would sell for more than $2,200,000.
- TFI had 6,000 bushels of winter wheat harvested and stored in its grain bins. The accumulated cost of the wheat is $27,000. The current market price at the local elevator is $6.10 per bushel. The market price of wheat has increased 10 cents per bushel since the wheat was harvested. The transportation costs from the farm to the elevator are about 5 cents per bushel.
- TFI has a herd of cattle, including heifers and steers, that have not yet been weaned. TFI does not anticipate keeping any of the heifers for its breeding herd. The accumulated cost of the heifers and steers is $50,000. The expected selling costs are $2,000. The replacement cost and selling price for these heifers and steers is $70,000.
- Finally, TFI has 200 tons of sugar beets harvested. The accumulated costs are $25 per ton. TFI anticipates selling costs of $3 per ton. Due to the rarity of the production of sugar beets in North Carolina, there is no local market for sugar beets. TFI sold a few tons of sugar beets two months ago for $50 a ton; however, the market is not stable at this time.

Prepare a memo to the file regarding the valuation of TFI's products at year-end. Support your conclusions using the Codification.

Surfing the Standards Case 2: Inventory in the Agriculture Industry – IFRS[22]

Tarheel Farm, Inc. (TFI) is a North Carolina corporation involved in agricultural production and has an October 31 fiscal year-end. It is not publicly traded, but it is required to prepare annual IFRS-complying financial statements for its bank. TFI typically produces four products: beef cattle, corn, winter wheat, and sugar beets. All four of these products have a life cycle of less than 1 year. The following information is available as of October 31:

- TFI had 400 acres of field corn planted. The corn will not be harvested until next month. The accumulated cost of the corn is $95,000. The estimated selling costs are $4,500. The current market value of land is $5,000 per acre. Although there is no current market value available for land growing a corn crop on it, TFI is certain that this land would sell for more than $2,200,000.
- TFI had 6,000 bushels of winter wheat harvested and stored in its grain bins. The accumulated cost of the wheat is $27,000. The current market price at the local elevator is $6.10 per bushel. The market price of wheat has increased 10 cents per bushel since the wheat was harvested. The transportation costs from the farm to the elevator are about 5 cents per bushel.
- TFI has a herd of cattle, including heifers and steers, that have not yet been weaned. TFI does not anticipate keeping any of the heifers for its breeding herd. The accumulated cost of the heifers and steers is $50,000. The expected selling costs are $2,000. The replacement cost and selling price for these heifers and steers is $70,000.
- Finally, TFI has 200 tons of sugar beets harvested. The accumulated costs are $25 per ton. TFI anticipates selling costs of $3 per ton. Due to the rarity of the production of sugar beets in North Carolina, there is no local market for sugar beets. TFI sold a few tons of sugar beets two months ago for $50 a ton; however, the market is not stable at this time.

Prepare a memo to the file regarding the valuation of TFI's products at year-end. Support your conclusions using references to IFRS.

Surfing the Standards Case 3: Time Shares

Treasure Island Corporation (TIC) sells time shares in luxury oceanfront cottages. During the year ended December 31, 2017, TIC completed a project consisting of 100 cottages in a particularly scenic portion of Hawaii. The project cost TIC $110.24 million. During the current year, TIC sold 1,924 weekly time shares in the cottages for $40,000 each.

TIC's sales policy requires a 20% down payment, so TIC received $8,000 for each time share this year. Because TIC's customers consist of only the most wealthy individuals, TIC does not anticipate any uncollectible accounts. Customers that purchased time shares will not make any more payments this year. TIC uses the full accrual method for revenue recognition purposes.

[22]Reprinted from the Ernst & Young Academic Resource Center with permission of the Ernst & Young Foundation.

Prepare a memo for the file discussing how to account for this transaction. Include a discussion of what the account balances should be related to this transaction. (Ignore any interest on the amounts due from customers.) Support your conclusions using the Codification.

Surfing the Standards Case 4: Lower of Cost or Market

More Toys, Inc., a toy retailer that has a calendar year-end and prepares interim financial statements quarterly. As of March 31, 20X4, More Toys has 10,000 Gabriella dolls in stock. The Gabriella dolls are from a recent movie that was showing in the theatres. The dolls cost More Toys, Inc. $20 each, and the replacement cost for each doll is also $20.

The average selling price for the dolls in the fourth quarter of 20X3 was $24. However, due to the fact that the movie was no longer showing in theatres, children were not as interested in the doll. In response, More Toys reduced the price of the dolls and is now selling them for $18 each. More Toys has decided to take the dolls off the shelves and keep them until the third quarter of 20X4 when the movie will begin streaming on Webpix. The management of More Toys believes that they can then sell the Gabriella dolls for $22 per doll.

Should More Toys record a lower-of-cost-or-market write-down for its Gabriella dolls on its March 31, 20X4, interim financial statements? Support your answer using the Codification.

Basis for Conclusions Cases

Basis for Conclusions Case 1: The Use of LIFO, IFRS

Although U.S. GAAP allows LIFO inventory costing, IFRS does not. Read paragraphs BC9 through BC21 of IASC, *International Accounting Standard 2*, "Inventories."

a. Why did the IASB decide not to allow the use of LIFO?
b. Explain why you agree or disagree with the IASB's reasoning.

Basis for Conclusions Case 2: The Lower of Cost or Market – U.S. GAAP, IFRS[23]

Scene 1

Both IFRS and U.S. GAAP require that firms report inventory at the lower of cost or market. What is the basic principle/characteristic behind this standard that results in this "lower" reporting approach (asset write-down)?

Scene 2

Read the objectives for IFRS (IASC, *International Accounting Standard 2*, paragraph 1) and U.S. GAAP (FASB ASC 330-10-10-1).

Based upon what is stated in these objectives, which set of standards is more concerned with the balance sheet presentation of inventories?

Scene 3

Do you think that the reversal of a write-down of inventory does a better job of accurately reflecting the information related to inventory on the balance sheet or on the income statement?

Is the fact that U.S. GAAP disallows the reversal and IFRS allows the reversal consistent with the objectives?

Scene 4

Currently, IFRS is more likely than U.S. GAAP to report assets at fair value (e.g., property, plant, and equipment can be revalued under IFRS but not U.S. GAAP.)

Is the IFRS requirement that prior inventory write-downs be reversed a different way of saying that inventory should be reported at market value under IFRS?

[23]Reprinted from the Ernst & Young Academic Resource Center with permission of the Ernst & Young Foundation.

Scene 5

While neither IASC, *International Accounting Standard 2* nor FASB ASC 330 provides the reasoning for why the reversal of inventory write-downs is allowed or not allowed, the issues surrounding the reversal of write-downs for long-lived assets should be quite similar. Read the basis of conclusions under U.S. GAAP (FASB, *Statement of Financial Accounting Standards No. 144*, paragraph B53) and under IFRS (IASC, *International Accounting Standard 36*, paragraphs BCZ 182 through BCZ 186) that provide a discussion of the reasons the Boards made the decisions that they did.

What are the reasons that one might oppose reversals? What are the reasons that one might support reversals?

Scene 6

Do you believe that companies should be allowed/required to reverse prior inventory write-downs if the market value of the inventory increases in periods subsequent to the initial write-down?

APPENDIX A
LIFO Retail Inventory Method

We discussed both the LIFO method and the retail method earlier in the chapter. Some companies combine these methods to determine the cost basis of their inventory. The LIFO retail method uses cost-to-retail ratios to build the LIFO layers.

Basic LIFO Retail Inventory Method

The first step under the LIFO retail inventory method is computing two cost-to-retail ratios: The first layer is based on beginning inventory, and the second layer is based on the change in the ending inventory at retail. Each year after that, the company builds a new layer based on the change in inventory during the year, including net markups and net markdowns in the inventory layer each year.

Layers are built by multiplying the layer of ending inventory at retail by the appropriate cost-to-retail ratio. The layers at cost are then summed to arrive at ending inventory. Example 10A.1 illustrates this method.

EXAMPLE 10A.1

LIFO Retail Inventory Method

PROBLEM: Absco, Inc. uses the LIFO retail inventory method for inventory costing. It has beginning inventory at a cost of $18,000 with a retail value of $30,000. During the year, Absco purchased goods with a cost basis of $82,000 and a retail basis of $120,000. It had net markups of $5,000 and net markdowns of $10,000. Absco has net sales of $105,000. What is the cost of Absco's ending inventory using the LIFO retail inventory method?

SOLUTION: We begin by computing the cost-to-retail ratio of 60% ($18,000/$30,000) for the beginning inventory layer. We then compute the current-year layer cost-to-retail ratio using the current-year cost ($82,000) and retail value ($115,000) of 71.30% ($82,000/$115,000). The retail value includes net markups and net markdowns. We compute goods available for sale by summing beginning inventory and net purchases. We arrive at ending inventory at retail by subtracting sales from goods available for sale at retail.

	Cost	Retail	Cost-to-Retail Ratio
Beginning inventory	$ 18,000	$ 30,000	60.00%
Purchases	82,000	120,000	
Net markups		5,000	
Net markdowns		(10,000)	
Current year layer	82,000	115,000	71.30%
Goods available for sale	$100,000	145,000	
Sales		(105,000)	
Ending inventory at retail		$ 40,000	

We convert ending inventory at retail to ending inventory at cost using the cost-to-retail ratios. Beginning inventory at retail was $30,000 and ending inventory at retail was $40,000. Thus, the increase (new layer) at retail is $10,000.

Continued

	Ending Inventory at Retail	Ratio	Ending Inventory at LIFO Cost
Beginning inventory	$30,000	60.00%	$18,000
Increase	10,000	71.30%	7,130
Ending inventory	$40,000		$25,130

We compute the beginning layer at cost of $18,000 ($30,000 × 60%) and the current year's layer at cost of $7,130 ($10,000 × 71.3%) This sums to an ending inventory of $25,130 at LIFO cost.

Dollar-Value LIFO Retail Inventory Method

The LIFO retail method implicitly assumes that price levels do not change during the year. In other words, any increase in inventory at retail is assumed to be due to an increase in quantity. However, this is typically not a valid assumption. The dollar-value LIFO retail method relaxes this assumption by adjusting for any changes in the price of goods.

The computations for the dollar-value LIFO retail method are similar to the LIFO retail method:

1. Compute a cost-to-retail ratio for both beginning inventory and the change in the ending inventory at retail.
2. Include net markups and net markdowns in the inventory layer each year.

Before building the layers, ending inventory at retail is adjusted to base-year prices. We then use the cost-to-retail ratio and the price index to build the layer. Example 10A.2 illustrates this method using the facts from Example 10A.1 except that we will now assume that there has been a price-level increase.

EXAMPLE 10A.2

Dollar-Value LIFO Retail Inventory Method

PROBLEM: Absco, Inc. uses the dollar-value LIFO retail inventory method for inventory costing. It has beginning inventory at a cost of $18,000 with a retail value of $30,000. During the year, Absco purchased goods with a cost basis of $82,000 and a retail basis of $120,000. It had net markups of $5,000 and net markdowns of $10,000. Absco has net sales of $105,000. The price index for the current year is 1.10. Absco adopted the dollar-value LIFO retail method at the end of the prior year, which is designated as the base year with a price index of 1.00. What is the cost of Absco's ending inventory using the dollar-value LIFO retail inventory method?

SOLUTION: We begin by computing the cost-to-retail ratio of 60% ($18,000/$30,000) for the beginning inventory layer. We then compute the current-year layer cost-to-retail ratio using the current-year cost ($82,000) and retail value ($115,000) of 71.30% ($82,000/$115,000). The retail value includes net markups and net markdowns. We compute goods available for sale by summing beginning inventory and net purchases. We arrive at ending inventory at retail by subtracting sales from goods available for sale at retail.

	Cost	Retail	Cost-to-Retail Ratio
Beginning inventory	$ 18,000	$ 30,000	60.00%
Purchases	82,000	120,000	
Net markups		5,000	
Net markdowns		(10,000)	
Current-year layer	82,000	115,000	71.30%
Goods available for sale	$100,000	145,000	
Sales		(105,000)	
Ending inventory at retail		$ 40,000	

We then adjust ending inventory at retail to base-year prices by dividing by the price index.

$$\begin{aligned}\text{Ending Inventory at Base-Year Prices} &= \text{Ending Inventory at Retail/Price Index}\\ &= \$40{,}000/1.10\\ &= \$36{,}364\end{aligned}$$

We can now build the layers in terms of base-year prices. Ending inventory at base-year prices is $36,364, and beginning inventory at base-year prices is $30,000. Thus, the current year layer is $6,364. We multiply these layers by their respective cost-to-retail ratios and price indices to arrive at the layers of ending inventory at dollar-value LIFO cost. This sums to an ending inventory cost of $22,991.

	Ending Inventory at Base-Year Prices	Ratio	Price Index	Ending Inventory at LIFO Cost
Beginning inventory	$30,000	60.0%	1.00	$18,000
Increase	6,364	71.3%	1.10	4,991
Ending inventory	$36,364			$22,991

11 Long-Term Operating Assets: Acquisition, Cost Allocation, and Derecognition

LEARNING OBJECTIVES

1. Identify the types of property, plant, and equipment and determine the initial measurement of each; apply the definition of an asset to the decision to expense or capitalize an expenditure.
2. Demonstrate the accounting for property, plant, and equipment subsequent to acquisition, including subsequent expenditures and depreciation.
3. Determine and illustrate the appropriate accounting for asset derecognition of property, plant, and equipment, including sales and abandonments.
4. Identify required disclosures for property, plant, and equipment.
5. Specify the characteristics and types of intangible assets.
6. Determine and illustrate the initial measurement of different types of intangible assets, including internally generated intangibles, intangibles acquired individually or in a group, intangibles acquired in a business combination, and research and development costs.
7. Demonstrate accounting for intangible assets subsequent to acquisition, including amortization and derecognition.
8. Detail required disclosures for intangible assets.

Sam Dao/Alamy Stock Photo

Introduction

EVEN IN TODAY'S HIGH-TECH, wireless communication-dependent economy, a company's long-term operating assets remain critical to its success. Companies require these economic resources to achieve their primary business purposes and generate income and cash flows for an extended period of time. Long-term operating assets—which consist of *tangible fixed assets* (also referred to as *property, plant, and equipment*), *natural resources*, and *intangible assets*—typically have a significant impact on a firm's financial statements. In 2016, companies in the S&P 500 Index reported that, on average, 25% of their total assets were tangible fixed assets and 24% were intangible assets. Depreciation and amortization averaged 7.9% of sales.[1]

For communications giant ***AT&T Inc.***, long-term operating assets represented approximately 87% of total assets on December 31, 2016. ***AT&T*** operates in both wireless and wired-line communications such as voice and data services, handheld devices, and telephone and cable connections. On the balance sheet at December 31, 2016, ***AT&T's*** tangible fixed assets were 36% of all its long-term operating assets; ***AT&T's*** intangible assets made up the remaining 64%.

AT&T's tangible fixed assets are its "bricks-and-mortar" assets, including buildings, equipment, cables, and wires. When was your last dropped cell phone call or the realization that you were in a no-service area? In the competitive communications environment, ***AT&T*** must continually invest in state-of-the-art technology and equipment: Retaining customers requires maintaining the physical capacity to provide services, superior call quality, and extensive coverage. Intangible assets—such as licenses from the FCC to operate wireless systems on certain radio frequencies and ***AT&T's*** trade name—are key resources that have no physical substance. Other intangibles are difficult to

[1] Based on authors' analysis of companies in S&P 500 index for the year-ending in 2016.

measure, such as a superior management team and an innovative business strategy, so ***AT&T*** does not report them as assets.

In this chapter, we discuss the characteristics and types of long-term operating assets, including initial measurement at acquisition, accounting in subsequent accounting periods, disposal and derecognition, and disclosure requirements. We begin our presentation of long-term operating assets with an analysis of property, plant, and equipment and conclude with a discussion of accounting and reporting issues related to intangible assets. Accounting and reporting under U.S. GAAP and IFRS are very similar with just a few differences that we will highlight throughout the chapter. «

1 Identify the types of property, plant, and equipment and determine the initial measurement of each; apply the definition of an asset to the decision to expense or capitalize an expenditure.

Initial Measurement of Property, Plant, and Equipment

Property, plant, and equipment (PPE) also referred to as tangible fixed assets, are assets used in the production of goods and services that the firm sells in order to generate operating income and cash flow. PPE assets are:

1. Tangible in nature
2. Expected to be used for more than 1 year (or more than one operating cycle, whichever is longer)
3. Used in the production and sale of other assets, for rental to others or for administrative purposes

PPE includes land and land improvements; buildings, machinery, and equipment; and furniture and fixtures.[2] PPE also includes natural resources covered in Appendix B. In this section, we will examine how firms report PPE in practice beginning with the measurement of PPE on the date of acquisition.

THE CONCEPTUAL FRAMEWORK CONNECTION
Property, Plant, and Equipment Measurement

Firms measure PPE by determining the amounts to record as an asset or to expense immediately. **Capitalization** is the process of recording an expenditure as an asset. A **capital expenditure** is a cost recorded by a company as an asset rather than an expense. In the U.S. GAAP Conceptual Framework, the definition of an asset includes three essential characteristics:[3]

1. It represents probable future economic benefits.
2. The firm can obtain the benefit of the asset and can also control others' access to it.
3. The transaction or other event giving rise to the entity's right to the benefit or control of the benefit has already occurred.

Firms also require reliable measurement methods to record a cost as an asset.[4]

Identifying an asset involves differentiating between costs with probable future economic benefits and costs that have expired without the ability to generate revenue in subsequent accounting periods. Typically, this distinction is straightforward in practice. For instance, weekly salaries are expensed immediately because they represent payment for past services without future benefit. As another example, assume that a company purchases a new factory building and expects to use the building to provide future economic benefits. It is fairly certain that the company will indeed realize future benefits from the building, so it will capitalize the cost.

[2]For most of the relevant authoritative literature for this topic, see FASB ASC 360 – *Property, Plant, and Equipment* for U.S. GAAP and IASC, *International Accounting Standard 16*, "Property, Plant, and Equipment" (London, UK: International Accounting Standards Committee, Revised) for IFRS.

[3]FASB, *Statement of Financial Accounting Concepts No. 6,* "Elements of Financial Statements," Paragraph 26.

[4]FASB, *Statement of Financial Accounting Concepts No. 5,* "Recognition and Measurement in Financial Statements of Business Enterprises," Paragraph 65.

In other cases, it is difficult to assess the probable future benefits from corporate expenditures. For example, expenditures for advertising or research also have future economic benefits—but these benefits can be difficult to quantify. To illustrate, in 2016, ***Cisco Systems, Inc.,*** which designs and manufactures networking and other products related to communications and information technology, spent $186 million on advertising and $6.3 billion in research and development. Yet, because of the uncertainty of realizing those future benefits, ***Cisco*** expensed these costs as opposed to capitalizing them as assets. That is, these expenditures did not meet the first characteristic of an asset in that the future economic benefits were not probable.

Firms must also consider the cost-benefit trade-off and materiality when measuring PPE. Assume that a firm expects that a $50 expenditure will provide a future economic benefit. The firm can measure the expenditure reliably and the expenditure meets the other characteristics of an asset, so it seems the firm should record it as an asset. However, $50 is an immaterial amount that will not provide useful information to financial statement users. Consequently, the firm would simply record the outlay as an expense to avoid bookkeeping costs because the additional cost of maintaining depreciation records for the $50 expenditure exceeds the expected benefit.

Capitalizing or expensing an expenditure for a fixed asset affects the financial statements differently. When a firm expenses an item, earnings are reduced for the full amount in the first year. When a firm capitalizes an expenditure, assets increase and earnings are reduced only for the depreciation expense in the first year. Therefore, firms may prefer to capitalize expenditures whenever possible in order to avoid the larger decrease in earnings in the first year. Of course, future earnings will decrease but by a lower amount than expensing immediately.

Overview of Initial Measurement

A company determines the amount to capitalize as PPE as the costs that are reasonable and necessary to bring the asset to the location and condition required for its intended use. Consequently, costs such as installation, delivery, special wiring, interest from the financing of constructed assets, closing costs, and sales tax are included in the initial measurement of PPE.

Not all fixed assets are capitalized. In practice, firms develop a **capitalization policy** for PPE, which typically sets guidelines based on the type and/or the magnitude of the cost of the asset acquired. A materiality threshold for capitalization specifies that the firm immediately expense an asset that falls below a predetermined fixed dollar limit (e.g., $1,000) rather than capitalize it as an asset. For example, ***Ford Motor Company's*** 2012 annual report noted that it capitalized new assets that it expected to use for more than 1 year with acquisition costs greater than $2,500.

Firms typically have several subcategories of PPE.

PPE Categories

Land. The cost of land generally includes the purchase price, development costs, legal fees, closing costs, delinquent property taxes, the costs of grading and clearing the land, and a portion of the interest costs incurred during the development process. In addition, firms consider the cost to remove an old structure, net of any proceeds on the sale of scrap materials, as part of the land's acquisition cost because these costs are required to bring the land to the condition necessary for its intended use.

Land Improvements. Firms capitalize land improvements—which include landscaping costs, lighting, fence installations, lawn sprinkler systems, and driveway construction—in a separate land improvements account. A separate account is needed because land improvements are subject to depreciation whereas land is not.

Machinery and Equipment. The cost of machinery and equipment includes the acquisition cost (including any sales tax) plus the cost of shipping, installation, and testing. These costs include any special wiring or modifications to existing structures required to install the asset. Firms expense any costs incurred to repair any damage experienced during installation because these costs have no future economic benefit.

Buildings. The cost of buildings includes any acquisition or construction costs as well as legal and closing costs similar to those incurred in the acquisition of land. In addition, firms may capitalize interest on financing employed during the construction period as part of the building under construction.

Example 11.1 illustrates the allocation of expenditures to assets or expenses.

EXAMPLE 11.1 Allocation of Expenditures to an Asset or an Expense

PROBLEM: Langford, LTD. acquired an assembly machine at an invoice cost of $280,000 during the current year. The delivery cost was $900, and installation costs amounted to $1,890. The machine required a separate electrical line that cost $1,000 to install. During the installation, a negligent employee damaged an exterior wall attached to the assembly shop. The company paid $1,210 to repair the wall. What is the acquisition cost of the assembly machine? Prepare the journal entries to properly account for the expenditures made assuming that Langford paid cash for all expenditures.

SOLUTION: The first step in the solution is to determine the total cost of the machine. The acquisition cost of the assembly machine is as follows:

Invoice price	$280,000
Delivery charges	900
Installation cost	1,890
Electrical fees	1,000
Total cost	$283,790

These costs are reasonable and necessary for the asset to be in its existing condition and location and ready for its intended use.

Langford expenses the $1,210 cost to repair the wall as incurred because it is not necessary for the assembly machine to be in place and ready for production. The repair costs do not have any future economic benefit and do not meet the definition of an asset.

Langford makes the following journal entries on the date of acquisition:

Account	*Current Year*	
Assembly Machine	283,790	
Cash		283,790

Account	*Current Year*	
Repair Expense	1,210	
Cash		1,210

In a **nonmonetary exchange**, a company acquires an asset by exchanging another asset with the seller rather than paying cash. Nonmonetary exchanges are an infrequent way to acquire PPE and are discussed in Appendix A.

Initial Measurement of Basket Purchases

In a **basket purchase**, a firm acquires two or more fixed assets together for a single purchase price. How does a firm assign the lump-sum expenditure to the individual assets acquired? The valuation of assets acquired in a basket purchase includes both **homogeneous assets**, assets that are the same, and **heterogeneous assets**, assets that are dissimilar from one another.

Basket Purchase: Homogeneous Assets. When a firm acquires homogeneous assets, it records the PPE at cost and includes it on the balance sheet, assigning an equal amount to each asset. For example, if a firm acquires five identical laptop computers at a total cost of $5,250, it would value each laptop at $1,050 (i.e., $5,250 / 5) and report the total cost of $5,250 in the office equipment account on the balance sheet.

Basket Purchase: Heterogeneous Assets. In basket purchases involving heterogeneous assets, the firm must properly allocate the total cost to the individual accounts to be reported on the balance sheet (e.g., manufacturing equipment, building, land, and inventory). To illustrate, assume that a firm pays one price for a piece of land that has four buildings on it. At what amounts does the firm initially record the land and each of the four buildings? The **relative fair value method** allocates the total purchase cost to the individual assets acquired in a single transaction by assigning the total cost incurred based on the percentage that each asset's fair value bears to the total fair value of all the assets purchased as illustrated in Example 11.2.

EXAMPLE 11.2 The Relative Fair Value Method for Basket Purchases

PROBLEM: During the current year, Great Belton Company acquired a manufacturing facility at a total acquisition cost of $4,000,000. The acquisition included the factory building, land, and all existing equipment in the facility. The firm estimates the fair value of the assets if acquired separately at a total of $4,300,000 with the fair value of the factory building at $2,150,000, the fair value of the land at $860,000, and the fair value of the equipment at $1,290,000. Determine the capitalized cost of each asset using the relative fair value method and prepare the necessary journal entry to record the acquisition assuming that Great Belton paid cash for the facility.

SOLUTION: To properly value each asset, Great Belton must allocate the total acquisition cost to each account based on relative fair values.

The percentage of fair value for each asset is the fair value for the asset divided by the total fair value of all the assets purchased. For example, the percentage of total fair value for the factory building is 50% ($2,150,000 / $4,300,000). To determine the allocation, we multiply each individual asset's percentage of total fair value by the total cost of the manufacturing facility. For example, the allocated cost of the factory building is 50% × $4,000,000 = $2,000,000. The table below shows the fair value of the individual assets acquired and the resulting allocation.

Asset Type	Fair Value	Percentage of Total Fair Value (a)	Total Cost of Manufacturing Facility (b)	Allocation to Specific Balance Sheet Accounts (a) × (b)
Factory building	$2,150,000	50%	$4,000,000	$2,000,000
Land	860,000	20%	4,000,000	800,000
Equipment	1,290,000	30%	4,000,000	1,200,000
Total	$4,300,000	100%		$4,000,000

The acquisition date journal entry follows:

Account	***Current Year***	
Factory Building	2,000,000	
Land	800,000	
Equipment	1,200,000	
Cash		4,000,000

Initial Measurement with Deferred Payment Arrangements

Firms can acquire PPE by making an immediate cash payment, financing the acquisition by issuing a *note payable*, or some combination of the two. The payment method used impacts the amount of PPE the firm records.

Notes payable are formal credit arrangements between a creditor (lender) and a debtor (borrower) requiring the payment of a stated face amount on a specified maturity date. In a straightforward notes payable issue, the face value of an interest-bearing note is equal to the cash price (i.e., the fair value) of the asset. In this case, for the initial measurement, the firm debits the asset and credits the note payable for that amount. The firm recognizes interest expense each period on the unpaid balance of the debt and pays the debt in full at maturity.

Asset Valuation: Determinable Market Value. In most cases, accounting for deferred payment arrangements are straightforward as noted previously. However, there can be complications in practice. For instance, how do we record the asset when the face amount of a note does not reasonably represent the present value of the consideration given or received in the exchange—that is, today's cash price? The accountant must then determine the proper valuation of the asset. For example, notes payable are sometimes issued with a zero interest rate stated or at a stated rate that is significantly below the market rate of interest. If the asset's fair value is readily determinable or if the note is traded, the firm records the acquired asset at the fair value of the consideration given (the note) or the fair value of the consideration received (the asset), whichever value is more clearly evident. The difference between the face amount of the note and fair value of the property (or the note) is called the discount and represents the amount of interest to be deferred over the loan term. The discount on notes payable, a contra-liability account, reduces the face value of the note payable to its present value. The firm reports the note payable's carrying value—its par or face value less the balance of the unamortized discount—on the balance sheet. Example 11.3 illustrates how we determine an asset's value when the market value is readily determinable.

EXAMPLE 11.3 Asset Valuation: Determinable Market Value

PROBLEM: Smithfield Metals, Inc. acquired a new piece of factory equipment by issuing a zero-interest rate note with a face value of $120,000. The equipment has a reliable fair value of $100,000. What journal entry is necessary to record the asset acquisition?

SOLUTION: Smithfield records the asset at its fair value of $100,000 and a note payable at the face value of $120,000. It also records a $20,000 discount on notes payable, a contra-liability account, which represents the interest deferred over the term of the loan.

Account	*Year of Acquisition*	
Factory Equipment	100,000	
Discount on Notes Payable	20,000	
Notes Payable		120,000

At the date of acquisition, the balance sheet will report the carrying value of notes payable at $100,000 (Face Value − Discount = $120,000 − $20,000).

Asset Valuation: Nondeterminable Market Value. How does the firm value an asset that does not have a comparable market value—for instance, custom machinery, an antique car, or a rare painting—and the note is not publicly traded? When the fair values of the asset or the note are not clearly evident, the firm must compute the present value of the note as an estimate of the asset's fair value. The firm computes the fair value of the asset by discounting the note payable at an implied or **imputed rate of interest** reflecting the market rate of interest that a borrower would incur today under similar terms and conditions. After determining the present value of the note payable, the firm allocates the face value of the note between the asset's acquisition cost (which equals the present value of the note payable) and the discount, which represents the deferred interest expense (i.e., finance charges).

When using the effective interest rate method of amortization, the carrying value of the note payable will always equal the present value of the remaining cash flows discounted at the historical market rate as illustrated in Example 11.4.[5]

EXAMPLE 11.4 Asset Valuation: Nondeterminable Market Value

PROBLEM: JBS, Inc. contracts to buy a specialized machine to crush and sort plastic, glass, and aluminum cans and bottles for recycling. It agrees to make a one-time payment of $310,000 to the manufacturer at the end of 4 years and signs a zero coupon note payable with a face value of $310,000. What journal entry is necessary to record the asset acquisition? Assume that the market rate of interest is 6%.

SOLUTION: The face value of the note payable is $310,000. No interest payments are made on the note. If the market rate of interest is 6%, the present value of the note payable is $245,549, as shown in the following spreadsheet solution.

	N	I/Y	PV	PMT	FV	Excel Formula
Given	4	6.00%		0	−310,000	
Solve for PV			**245,549**			= PV(0.06,4,0−310000)

Thus, JBS records the acquisition cost of the machine at $245,549. The deferred interest is $64,451 (the face value of the note payable of $310,000 less the present value of the note payable $245,549). The net liability is $245,549, which is the note payable balance less the discount balance.

Account	***Date of Acquisition***	
Equipment	245,549	
Discount on Notes Payable	64,451	
Notes Payable		310,000

Separating the asset value from the finance charges is critical for proper expense classification on the income statement. Depreciation affects operating income whereas interest expense is a non-operating expense. Ignoring taxes, combining the finance charge with the acquisition cost overstates the asset's carrying value on the balance sheet. Improper measurement of the asset's cost and the finance charge will also overstate depreciation expense and interest expense on the income statement. Based on the purchase in Example 11.4, the interest expense on the note payable in the first year would be $14,733 ($245,549 times 6%) and depreciation expense for the equipment would be $61,387 ($245,549 divided by 4 years) if the equipment has a 4-year useful life and no residual value. However, if the asset value and finance charges were not separated, the interest expense on the note payable in the first year would be $18,600 ($310,000 times 6%), and depreciation expense for the equipment would be $77,500 ($310,000 divided by 4 years).

Interest Capitalization

A company constructing a long-term operating asset such as a new manufacturing facility may need to finance the costs of construction. When financing by issuing debt, the company must determine whether to add interest costs to the cost of the asset (that is, to capitalize) or to expense the interest costs as incurred. In other words, accountants must determine whether interest is a cost of a constructed plant asset or if it is a financing cost.

[5]We discuss accounting for long-term debt in more detail in Chapter 14.

To properly value the cost of a constructed plant asset, firms capitalize material interest charges incurred in the construction of certain assets. The amount of interest capitalized is the lesser of actual interest incurred and *avoidable interest*. **Avoidable interest** is the interest amount that the firm could have avoided if it had not borrowed funds to construct the plant asset.

There are four major considerations in the application of interest capitalization requirements:

1. Assets that qualify for interest capitalization
2. Expenditures on which the firm should compute interest
3. Rate of interest
4. Period of capitalization

Because capitalized interest increases an asset's cost, depreciation expense on the asset will be higher in the future. However, interest expense is lower in the construction period.

Qualifying Assets. Firms should capitalize interest for assets constructed or otherwise produced for the firm's own use (for example, a public utility's self-constructed power plant). Qualifying assets include assets constructed by others for the firm's use when deposits and progress payments have been made. The manufacture of inventory or other routine production are not qualifying assets. Firms should also capitalize interest on assets intended for sale or lease that they construct or otherwise produce as discrete projects (for example, office buildings and land purchased for development).

Expenditures. As construction occurs, a company records its expenditures in a noncurrent asset account (construction in progress) and computes interest on the *weighted-average accumulated expenditures* for the accounting period in which it is calculating interest capitalization. The **weighted-average accumulated expenditures** are the construction expenditures weighted by the portion of the year that the expenditure is outstanding until the project is complete or the end of the year if the project is not complete. Example 11.5 illustrates calculating the weighted-average accumulated expenditures.

EXAMPLE 11.5 Weighted-Average Accumulated Expenditures

PROBLEM: Hipmo, Inc. is constructing a plant for its use in operations. During the first year of construction, the firm incurred expenditures equal to \$3,000,000. It paid the \$3,000,000 in four equal installments of \$750,000 at the end of each quarter. Compute the weighted-average accumulated expenditures. The plant is not complete at the end of the first year.

SOLUTION: To compute the weighted-average accumulated expenditures, we weight each expenditure by the period of time outstanding in a year.

Date	Actual Expenditures	Weighted-Average Accumulated Expenditures
March 31	\$750,000 × 9/12	\$ 562,500
June 30	750,000 × 6/12	375,000
September 30	750,000 × 3/12	187,500
December 31	750,000 × 0/12	0
Total		\$1,125,000

The computations indicate that if Hipmo used \$750,000 to repay debt each quarter rather than to construct the asset, the company would have saved interest computed on a weighted-average balance of \$1,125,000.

Rate of Interest. Firms use two separate interest rates to determine the amount of interest to capitalize.

1. The interest rate incurred on specific borrowings applies to the portion of the weighted-average accumulated expenditures that is *less than or equal to* the amount borrowed specifically to finance the construction of the asset.
2. The weighted-average interest rate on all other general outstanding debt during the period applies to the amount of the weighted-average accumulated expenditures that is *greater* than the amount borrowed specifically to finance the construction of the asset.[6]

Example 11.6 provides an example of the interest rate to use.

EXAMPLE 11.6 Rate of Interest

PROBLEM: Hipmo, Inc. is constructing a plant for its use in operations. It has weighted-average accumulated expenditures of $1,125,000. It borrowed $900,000 at a 9% interest rate specifically to finance the plant construction. In addition, it has three other general outstanding debt issues that have been outstanding as of the beginning of the year.

Principal	Interest Rate
$500,000	10%
275,000	8%
120,000	11%

What rate of interest should Hipmo use to compute the amount of capitalized interest?

SOLUTION: Hipmo will use the 9% rate for all expenditures less than or equal to the $900,000 specific borrowing. It will compute a weighted-average interest rate for the remaining general outstanding debt to apply to the excess weighted-average accumulated expenditure of $225,000 ($1,125,000 less $900,000). The weighted-average interest rate is:

Principal	Interest Rate	Actual Interest
$500,000	10%	$50,000
275,000	8%	22,000
120,000	11%	13,200
$895,000		$85,200

$$\text{Weighted-Average Interest Rate} = \frac{\text{Total Interest}}{\text{Total Principal}} = \frac{\$85{,}200}{\$895{,}000} = 9.52\%$$

The company will use the 9.52% weighted-average interest rate on indirect debt to compute interest on the excess weighted-average accumulated expenditure of $225,000.

Period of Capitalization. Firms capitalize interest from the time of the initial expenditure to the time the asset is ready for its intended use. When construction is completed but the asset is held idle—envision protesters blocking the operation of a nuclear power plant—the firm must charge interest incurred after the completion of construction to expense.

Computation of Capitalized Interest. Firms compute the amount of avoidable interest as the weighted-average accumulated expenditures times the appropriate interest rate. If the

[6]Specific debt and general outstanding debt are also known as direct and indirect debt, respectively.

computed avoidable interest exceeds the actual interest for the year, the firm capitalizes only the actual interest incurred. In other words, it capitalizes the lesser of the actual interest or the avoidable interest as illustrated in Example 11.7.

How does the firm account for any interest revenue it earns? Companies often invest excess borrowed funds, particularly at the beginning of a construction project, in short-term interest-bearing investments that earn interest revenue. Companies report interest revenue separately rather than netting this interest revenue with their interest costs.

EXAMPLE 11.7 Interest Capitalization with No General Outstanding Debt

PROBLEM: On January 1, 2018, Ryder Retail Associates began constructing its own warehouse. The total estimated cost of the project is $10,000,000. Ryder's year-end is December 31. During the year, it made the following payments to the contractor:

2018 Date	Amount of Payment
February 1	$2,400,000
April 1	100,000
July 1	1,450,000
October 1	250,000
December 1	3,000,000
Total Expenditures	$7,200,000

Ryder borrowed specifically for this project by issuing a $3,500,000, 10% note at SwoboBank on January 1, 2018. Interest is due on December 31. The firm has no other outstanding debt. During the year, Ryder Retail invested the funds and earned interest revenue of $6,000. The project will be completed in 2019. Compute the amount of interest that Ryder should capitalize. Prepare all necessary journal entries.

SOLUTION: On January 1, Ryder borrows money for the project as follows:

Account	January 1, 2018	
Cash	3,500,000	
Note Payable		3,500,000

Each time Ryder makes a payment, the company debits a noncurrent asset account, construction in progress, and credits cash. For example, the journal entry for the first payment on February 1 follows:

Account	February 1, 2018	
Construction in Progress	2,400,000	
Cash		2,400,000

The weighted-average accumulated expenditures for the period are computed next. The weights are the number of months from the date of the expenditure to year-end.

2018 Date	Amount of Payment	Weight	Weighted-Average Accumulated Expenditures
February 1	$2,400,000	× 11/12	$2,200,000
April 1	100,000	× 9/12	75,000
July 1	1,450,000	× 6/12	725,000
October 1	250,000	× 3/12	62,500
December 1	3,000,000	× 1/12	250,000
Total	$7,200,000		$3,312,500

The weighted-average accumulated expenditures ($3,312,500) are less than the amount of the specific borrowing ($3,500,000) for the construction. As a result, to calculate avoidable interest, we multiply the amount of the weighted-average accumulated expenditures by the interest rate on the specific borrowing. The avoidable interest is $331,250, calculated as $3,312,500 × 10%.

The actual interest paid for the year is $350,000 (i.e., 10% × $3,500,000). The interest to be capitalized is the lower of the actual interest or the avoidable interest. So, the interest capitalized is $331,250. The interest expense reported on the income statement is the difference between the interest paid and the interest capitalized.

Account	**December 31, 2018**	
Construction in Progress	331,250	
Interest Expense	18,750	
Cash		350,000

The entry to record interest earned on the borrowed funds follows.

Account	**December 31, 2018**	
Cash	6,000	
Interest Revenue		6,000

Example 11.8 illustrates the calculation of interest capitalization with general outstanding debt.

EXAMPLE 11.8 Interest Capitalization with General Outstanding Debt

PROBLEM: On January 1, 2018, Slyder Retail Associates began constructing its own warehouse. The total estimated cost of the project is $10,000,000. Slyder's year-end is December 31. The project will be completed in 2019. During the year, Slyder made the following payments to the contractor:

2018 Date	**Amount of Payment**
February 1	$2,400,000
April 1	100,000
July 1	1,450,000
October 1	250,000
December 1	3,000,000
Total expenditures	$ 7,200,000

Slyder borrowed specifically for this project by issuing a $3,000,000, 10% note at SwoboBank on January 1, 2018. Interest is due December 31 of each year. During the year, Slyder invested the funds and earned interest revenue of $6,000. Slyder also reports the following general debt with interest due December 31 of each year. All debt has been outstanding as of the beginning of the year.

Interest Rate	**Amount**
8%	$ 700,000
12%	8,550,000
Total	$9,250,000

Continued

Compute the amount of interest that Slyder should capitalize. Prepare all necessary journal entries. Prepare the construction in progress t-account.

SOLUTION: Slyder borrows money for the project as seen here:

Account	January 1, 2018	
Cash	3,000,000	
Note Payable		3,000,000

Each time that Slyder makes a payment, the company debits a noncurrent asset account, construction in progress, and credits cash. For example, the journal entry for the first payment on February 1 follows:

Account	February 1, 2018	
Construction in Progress	2,400,000	
Cash		2,400,000

The weighted-average accumulated expenditures for the period are computed in the following table. The weights are the number of months from the date of the expenditure to year-end.

2018 Date	Amount of Payment	Weight	Weighted-Average Accumulated Expenditures
February 1	$2,400,000	× 11/12	$2,200,000
April 1	100,000	× 9/12	75,000
July 1	1,450,000	× 6/12	725,000
October 1	250,000	× 3/12	62,500
December 1	3,000,000	× 1/12	250,000
Total	$7,200,000		$3,312,500

The weighted-average accumulated expenditures of $3,312,500 exceed the amount of specific debt of $3,000,000 by $312,500. As a result, Slyder must compute the weighted-average interest rate on the general outstanding debt.

Debt Type	Principal	Rate	Actual Interest
Specific	$3,000,000	× 10%	$ 300,000
General outstanding	$ 700,000	× 8%	$ 56,000
General outstanding	8,550,000	× 12%	1,026,000
Total general debt	$9,250,000		$1,082,000

The weighted-average interest rate is 11.7% computed as $1,082,000 / $9,250,000. The total actual interest incurred for the year is equal to $1,382,000. The actual total interest incurred is the sum of interest on the specific debt or $300,000 plus the interest on the general debt of $1,082,000. We compute the amount of avoidable interest in the following table.[7]

Debt Type	Weighted-Average Accumulated Expenditures	Rate	Avoidable Interest
Specific	$3,000,000	× 10.0%	$300,000
General	312,500	× 11.7%	36,563
Totals	$3,312,500		$336,563

[7]In practice, some companies have been using a single weighted-average interest rate on all outstanding debt. In this case, the weighted-average interest rate on all debt is 11.28% ($1,382,000 / $12,250,000) and avoidable interest is computed as follows: $3,312,500 × 11.28% = $373,650.

The maximum interest that Slyder can capitalize is equal to $1,382,000, the actual interest for the year. Because the $336,563 avoidable interest is lower than the maximum interest, Slyder will capitalize the avoidable interest in 2018.

Interest expense reported on the income statement is the difference between the total interest incurred and the amount capitalized. In this case, the interest expense on the income statement is $1,045,437 (i.e., $1,382,000 − $336,563).

Slyder makes the following journal entry assuming that it pays interest only at the end of the year.

Account	December 31, 2018	
Construction in Progress	336,563	
Interest Expense	1,045,437	
Cash		1,382,000

The entry to record interest earned on the borrowed funds follows:

Account	December 31, 2018	
Cash	6,000	
Interest Revenue		6,000

After recording all payments to the contactor and the interest capitalized for the year, the construction in progress account is $7,536,563. This balance is equal to the total accumulated expenditures (i.e., $7,200,000) plus the capitalized interest. The construction in progress account follows.[8]

	Construction in Progress	
February 1, 2018	2,400,000	
April 1, 2018	100,000	
July 1, 2018	1,450,000	
October 1, 2018	250,000	
December 1, 2018	3,000,000	
Subtotal	7,200,000	
Capitalized Interest	336,563	
December 31, 2018	7,536,563	

The company will transfer the balance of construction in progress to the appropriate account in property, plant, and equipment upon completion of the project.

Constructed Assets and Overhead Costs. When a company constructs an asset, it may contribute certain portions of the labor and material toward the completion of the project. For example, a company incurs costs to pay the builders and buy the concrete and steel needed to construct a new headquarters. Firms capitalize direct materials used and direct labor hours expended on the project as part of the acquisition cost of the asset.

Indirect overhead costs (for example, general supervisory salaries and depreciation) are generally accounted for using *full-cost accounting*. Under **full-cost accounting**, the firm allocates a proportionate share of all indirect cost incurred by the company to the construction project.

IFRS Interest Capitalization. Accounting for interest capitalization under IFRS is similar to the U.S. GAAP process for all areas discussed:

1. Assets that qualify for interest capitalization
2. Expenditures on which firms should compute interest
3. Rate of interest
4. Period of capitalization

[8]Note that if a project extends over multiple periods, then the beginning balance of construction in progress is included in the weighted-average accumulated expenditure and weighted as of the beginning of the year.

There are two main differences in U.S. GAAP and IFRS related to the capitalization of interest for specific borrowings. First, IFRS-reporting firms capitalize all borrowing costs related to a loan obtained specifically to acquire or construct the asset because the debt is used directly to finance the construction. Unlike U.S. GAAP, there is no need to use the weighted-average accumulated expenditures to determine interest to capitalize for specific borrowing. The weighted-average accumulated expenditures are used only to determine interest to capitalize for general debt. Second, income from the temporary investment of specific borrowings reduces capitalized borrowing costs.

In Examples 11.9 and 11.10, we revisit the scenarios in Examples 11.7 and 11.8 using IFRS.

EXAMPLE 11.9 IFRS Interest Capitalization with No General Outstanding Debt

PROBLEM: On January 1, 2018, Ryder Retail Associates, an IFRS reporter, began constructing its own warehouse. The total estimated cost of the project is $10,000,000. Ryder's year-end is December 31. During the year, Ryder made the following payments to the contractor:

2018 Date	Amount of Payment
February 1	$2,400,000
April 1	100,000
July 1	1,450,000
October 1	250,000
December 1	3,000,000
Total expenditures	$ 7,200,000

Ryder borrowed specifically for this project by issuing a $3,500,000, 10% note at SwoboBank on January 1, 2018. Interest is due December 31 of each year. Ryder has no other outstanding debt. During the year, Ryder invested the funds and earned interest revenue of $6,000. The project will be completed in 2019. Compute the amount of interest that Ryder should capitalize. Prepare all necessary journal entries.

SOLUTION: Ryder borrows money for the project as seen next:

Account	January 1, 2018	
Cash	3,500,000	
Note Payable		3,500,000

Each time Ryder makes a payment, the company debits a noncurrent asset account, construction in progress, and credits cash. The journal entry for the first payment follows.

Account	February 1, 2018	
Construction in Progress	2,400,000	
Cash		2,400,000

Under IFRS, reporting firms capitalize all borrowing costs related to the debt incurred specifically to acquire the asset. Therefore, capitalized interest is based on the specific debt balance of $3,500,000. The amount of interest capitalized is $350,000, or 10% × $3,500,000. Because the avoidable interest equals actual interest of $350,000, there is no interest expense. However, IFRS requires that firms net any income earned on the funds obtained from the construction loan, if invested, against the interest expense. During the year, Ryder earned $6,000 of interest income. So, Ryder can capitalize interest of $344,000 ($350,000 less $6,000).

Account	December 31, 2018	
Construction in Progress	344,000	
Cash		344,000

For Example 11.10, notice that the capitalized interest under IFRS is lower than under U.S. GAAP due to the different treatment of specific debt and netting interest earned on borrowed funds.

EXAMPLE 11.10 IFRS Interest Capitalization with General Outstanding Debt

PROBLEM: Assume that Slyder Retail Associates in Example 11.8 is an IFRS reporter. Compute the amount of interest that Slyder should capitalize. Prepare all necessary journal entries. Prepare the construction in progress t-account.

SOLUTION: Slyder borrows money for the project as seen here:

Account	January 1, 2018	
Cash	3,000,000	
Note Payable		3,000,000

Each time Slyder makes a payment, the company debits a noncurrent asset account, construction in progress, and credits cash. The journal entry for the first payment follows.

Account	February 1, 2018	
Construction in Progress	2,400,000	
Cash		2,400,000

We must calculate the weighted-average accumulated expenditures. The weights are the number of months from the date of the expenditure to year-end.

2018 Date	Amount of Payment	Weight	Weighted-Average Accumulated Expenditures
February 1	$2,400,000	× 11/12	$2,200,000
April 1	100,000	× 9/12	75,000
July 1	1,450,000	× 6/12	725,000
October 1	250,000	× 3/12	62,500
December 1	3,000,000	× 1/12	250,000
Total	$ 7,200,000		$3,312,500

The weighted-average accumulated expenditures of $3,312,500 exceed the amount of specific debt of $3,000,000 by $312,500. As a result, Slyder must compute the weighted-average interest rate on the outstanding general debt.

Debt Type	Principal	Rate	Actual Interest
Specific	$3,000,000	10%	$ 300,000
General outstanding	$ 700,000	8%	$ 56,000
General outstanding	8,550,000	12%	1,026,000
Total general debt	$9,250,000		$1,082,000

The weighted-average interest rate is 11.7% computed as $1,082,000 / $9,250,000. The total actual interest incurred for the year is equal to $1,382,000. The actual total interest incurred is the sum of interest on the specific debt, or $300,000, plus the interest on the general debt of $1,082,000. We compute the amount of avoidable interest in the following table.

Continued

Debt Type	Weighted-Average Accumulated Expenditures	Rate	Avoidable Interest
Specific	$3,000,000	10.0%	$300,000
General	312,500	11.7%	36,563
Total			$336,563

Because the $336,563 ($300,000 plus $36,563) is lower than total interest expense during the year, Slyder capitalizes this amount in 2018. Under IFRS, the $6,000 of interest earned on the borrowed funds is offset against the amount capitalized. Therefore, the amount of interest capitalized is $330,563, or ($336,563 − $6,000).

Interest expense reported on the income statement is the difference between the net interest expense incurred and the interest capitalized. The net interest expense incurred equals the total actual interest minus the interest revenue earned on excess construction funds. In this case, the interest expense on the income statement is $1,045,437 (i.e., $1,376,000 − $330,563).

Slyder makes the following journal entry assuming that it pays interest only at the end of the year.

Account	***December 31, 2018***	
Construction in Progress	330,563	
Interest Expense	1,045,437	
Cash*		1,376,000

*The credit to cash represents Net Interest Expense Incurred = Interest Expense − Interest Revenue ($1,382,000 − $6,000 = $1,376,000).

After recording all payments to the contactor and the interest capitalized for the year, the construction in progress account would be equal to $7,530,563. This balance is equal to the total accumulated expenditures (i.e., $7,200,000) plus the capitalized interest. The construction in progress account follows.

	Construction in Progress	
February 1, 2018	2,400,000	
April 1, 2018	100,000	
July 1, 2018	1,450,000	
October 1, 2018	250,000	
December 1, 2018	3,000,000	
Subtotal	7,200,000	
Capitalized Interest	330,563	
December 31, 2018	$7,530,563	

The company will transfer the balance of construction in progress to the appropriate account in property, plant, and equipment upon completion of the project.

Exhibit 11.1 provides a comparison of the requirements for interest capitalization under U.S. GAAP and IFRS.

EXHIBIT 11.1 Comparison of Requirements for Interest Capitalization under U.S. GAAP and IFRS

Requirement	U.S. GAAP	IFRS
Assets that qualify for interest capitalization	Assets constructed or otherwise produced for the firm's own use. Qualifying assets include assets constructed by others for the firm's use when deposits and progress payments have been made.	Similar to U.S. GAAP.
Expenditures on which the firm should compute interest	Weighted-average accumulated expenditures for the accounting period in which it is calculating interest capitalization.	Similar to U.S. GAAP.
Rate/amount of interest to use in the computation	Two interest rates are used to determine the amount of interest to capitalize. 1. For specific borrowings: The interest rate incurred on specific borrowings applies to the portion of the weighted-average accumulated expenditures that is less than or equal to the amount of the specific borrowing. 2. For general debt: The weighted-average interest rate of all other outstanding debt during the period applies to the amount of the weighted-average accumulated expenditures that is greater than the amount borrowed specifically to finance the construction of the asset.	➤ The two interest rates are applied differently under IFRS: 1. For specific borrowings: All borrowing costs related to a loan obtained specifically to acquire or construct the asset are capitalized. 2. For general debt: Firms use the weighted-average accumulated expenditures to determine interest to capitalize. Additionally, income from the temporary investment of specific borrowings reduces capitalized borrowing costs.
Period of capitalization	From the time of the initial expenditure to the time the asset is ready for its intended use.	Similar to U.S. GAAP.

JUDGMENTS IN ACCOUNTING:
The Initial Measurement of Property, Plant, and Equipment

Managers exercise judgment with the initial measurement of PPE when deciding whether to expense or capitalize an expenditure. Based on the definition of an asset and other authoritative guidance, firms capitalize the costs related to activities required to bring the asset to the condition and location necessary for use. For example, when a company buys a computer, it receives an invoice including the purchase price, taxes, and shipping charges. All of these costs are required to bring the asset to the condition and location necessary for use—so the firm capitalizes all the costs on the invoice as acquisition costs of the computer.

Now assume that a computer technician spends 3 hours setting up the computer at a user's desk, including adding a printer, a monitor, and all cables. Should the firm capitalize the cost associated with the technician's time as a cost related to an activity required to bring the asset to a condition and location necessary for use? Based on the authoritative literature, the technician's time seems to be a required activity. However, in practice, few companies track the technician's time and capitalize it. Tracking systems are costly, and the benefits of capitalizing the additional cost are viewed as immaterial. Contrast this decision to the purchase of major manufacturing equipment. Installation and testing is often lengthy and costly, so a company will monitor these costs and capitalize them.

The decision to expense or capitalize an expenditure can have significant effects on published financial statements—and many significant accounting failures have involved inappropriate cost capitalization. In a flagrant case of fraudulently capitalizing expenditures that it should have expensed, ***Waste Management, Inc.*** misstated its financial statements for the period from 1992 through 1997 by improperly capitalizing and deferring operating expenses. By deferring the recognition of these expenses, ***Waste Management*** significantly overstated its assets and increased its operating income. The 1997 cumulative earnings restatement amounted to $1.4 billion, covering the 1992 to 1997 period.

With basket purchases, the firm allocates one purchase price to specific assets based on fair values. For some assets, markets may not exist or are not active. When fair values for specific assets are not available, allocations for basket purchases are not possible. Standard setters have not provided extensive rules in this area. Companies often set policies on asset capitalization after considering materiality and cost-benefit criteria. Management must use judgment in forming and applying a capitalization policy, and auditors are required to exercise their professional judgment in assessing the appropriateness of managements' decisions.

2 Demonstrate the accounting for property, plant, and equipment subsequent to acquisition, including subsequent expenditures and depreciation.

Subsequent Measurement of Property, Plant, and Equipment

Accounting for long-term operating assets extends beyond acquisition. New machinery must be maintained, *depreciated* over time, or impaired if its value falls. Several events and transactions affect long-term fixed assets after acquisition, including subsequent expenditures related to the fixed assets, depreciation, and impairments. Impairments, discussed in Chapter 12, are decreases in an asset's carrying value whenever the asset no longer provides the future benefits expected. In this section, we discuss the accounting for subsequent expenditures and depreciation and how they affect measuring the carrying value of the asset.

Subsequent Expenditures

Firms either capitalize or expense expenditures made after acquisition of a fixed asset. Again, the decision to capitalize or expense these costs depends on the definition of an asset.

Firms expense noncapital expenditures, such as ordinary repairs, which are expenditures to maintain the operating efficiency immediately of an asset that do not extend its original useful life. For example, ***AT&T's*** 2016 annual report disclosed that it charged the cost of maintenance and repairs of property, plant, and equipment to operating expenses. Most ordinary repairs are relatively small expenditures that recur on a regular basis, such as a periodic oil change for a vehicle. An oil change does not increase the life of the asset beyond the original estimate, and it does not enhance its output. If an expenditure provides future economic benefit and, therefore, qualifies as an asset (i.e., it is a capital expenditure), the firm capitalizes the cost by adding the cost of the expenditure to the carrying value of the long-term fixed asset. Examples of capital expenditures are major overhauls of existing property, plant, and equipment; extraordinary repairs; and plant expansion. Adding an additional floor to a factory building or installing a refrigeration system in a delivery van would qualify as a capital expenditure. Example 11.11 illustrates accounting for subsequent expenditures.

EXAMPLE 11.11

Subsequent Expenditures

PROBLEM: Cunningham Bakeries needs new racks and a refrigeration unit in its existing delivery van to begin delivering ice cream cakes. It paid the total cost of the asset modification, $15,000, in cash. In addition, Cunningham took its delivery van in for service and paid $60 cash for an oil change and tire rotation. What journal entries are needed to record these two transactions?

SOLUTION: Because the $15,000 expenditure increased delivery capacity and productivity and thus changed the asset's revenue-generating ability, Cunningham will consider it a capital expenditure. The journal entry to record the capital expenditure is:[9]

Account	Current Year	
Delivery Van	15,000	
Cash		15,000

The cost of the oil change and tire rotation is not a capital expenditure, so Cunningham will expense the $60 immediately. The journal entry to record the event is:

Account	Current Year	
Repairs and Maintenance Expense	60	
Cash		60

Depreciation of Tangible Fixed Assets

A company's allocation of the initial cost of the asset to future periods of expected benefit from use of the asset is a critically important aspect of accounting for PPE. **Depreciation** is the systematic and rational allocation of the cost of a long-term plant asset to expense over the asset's expected useful life. As the asset is depreciated, the firm reports depreciation expense on the income statement and reduces the carrying value of the asset on the balance sheet. We will discuss the depreciation process in detail, including the pertinent judgments and methods employed.

THE CONCEPTUAL FRAMEWORK CONNECTION
The Cost Allocation Process

Depreciation is a process of allocating costs to the periods in which the benefits are consumed. Depreciation is therefore consistent with the conceptual framework's guidance for expense recognition.

Firms use tangible fixed assets in the revenue-generating process over an extended period of time. Thus, the loss of asset value through utilization meets the definition of an expense. Similarly, as firms use tangible fixed assets, the future economic benefits they provide to the company generally decline. Consequently, in the cost-allocation process, accountants use depreciation to adjust the acquisition cost of tangible fixed assets to reflect their use.

To illustrate, assume that a florist purchased a delivery truck for $21,000 that he expects to use evenly over 7 years. At the end of the 7 years, he will take the truck to the junk yard. (The truck will have no residual or scrap value.) The florist records the truck as an asset with an acquisition cost of $21,000. Every year for the next 7 years, the florist will reduce the carrying value of the truck by $3,000 ($21,000 / 7 years) and report $3,000 in depreciation expense to the income statement. Consequently, at the end of the 7 years, the carrying value of the truck will be zero and the asset will be scrapped at no gain or loss.

Land is not depreciated because it typically has an unlimited life—generally, it is not consumed in operations. Accordingly, per the conceptual framework, it would not be appropriate to allocate the cost of land over time.

[9]If an expenditure is viewed as extending the useful life of an asset rather than increasing output or capacity, some companies will debit accumulated depreciation instead of the asset account. The asset's book value is the same whether we debit accumulated depreciation or debit the asset account directly.

Overview of the Depreciation Process for Property, Plant, and Equipment. Allocating the cost of a fixed asset through depreciation requires that management estimate the asset's useful life and its *scrap value* and choose the depreciation method.

1. **Estimate useful life.** Management consider a number of different factors in estimating the productive life of a fixed asset. For example, managers may consider experience using this type of asset in prior years, relevant industry practice, maintenance policy, specific firm usage versus normal usage, and the possibility of obsolescence. Useful life varies by type of asset. For instance, ***AT&T*** depreciates its buildings and improvements over 2 to 44 years; office equipment over 3 to 10 years; and cable, wiring, and conduits over 15 to 50 years.
2. **Estimate scrap value.** The **scrap value** (also referred to as residual or salvage value) is the amount the firm expects to realize on disposal of the fixed asset at the end of its productive service to the firm. The scrap value reduces the depreciable base of the asset, so the firm depreciates only the cost less scrap value over the life of the asset. Scrap values are designed to minimize or avoid any gain or loss on disposal. For example, assume that a company sells its fleet of service vans every 5 years. If the dealership allows a trade-in value equal to 10% of original cost, then there is a 10% residual value. If the company depreciates the vans using a 10% residual value, there would never be a gain or loss on the disposal. Management estimates scrap values based on their experience or relevant industry practice. For example, management teams that estimate residual values for fixed assets used in high-tech industries typically assume a zero scrap value due to rapid advances in technology that cause a minimal residual value in a short period of time. As a result, the cost of estimating scrap values is not worth the benefit.
3. **Select depreciation method.** Management also decides which depreciation method to use for the company's fixed assets. The goal is to select a depreciation method reflecting the pattern that most closely articulates with the revenue generated from the use of the asset. Recall that the conceptual framework directs firms to recognize expenses when they consume benefits in revenue-generating activities.

Depreciation Guidelines. Depreciation expense is an end-of-period adjustment that firms include on the income statement in the computation of operating income. Firms generally report depreciation expense as part of selling, general, and administrative expenses.[10]

On the balance sheet, firms reduce the tangible fixed asset by increasing **accumulated depreciation,** a contra-asset account that represents the total depreciation taken over the life of the asset. Firms subtract accumulated depreciation from the original cost of the fixed asset and report **net book value (NBV)**, also referred to as **net fixed assets (NFA)**, in the noncurrent asset section of the balance sheet. The following t-accounts illustrate the changes in the asset's cost and accumulated depreciation accounts.

Fixed Asset Cost

Beginning Balance	− Disposals
+ Purchases	
+ Subsequent Capital Expenditures	
Ending Balance	

Accumulated Depreciation

− Disposals	Beginning Balance
	+ Depreciation Expense
	Ending Balance

Initially, the most objective information regarding a fixed asset's value is its cost. As a result, the accountant preserves the record of historical cost and records the estimated depreciation in the separate accumulated depreciation account. For financial statement purposes, firms report the net book value as a single line item.

Depreciation Methods. Rather than requiring a particular method of depreciation, U.S. GAAP simply states that the method of depreciation should result in a systematic allocation of

[10]For manufacturing firms, depreciation may be included in part of manufacturing overhead (i.e., in inventory as a product cost and charged to cost of sales when sold).

the cost of the asset. Thus, firms employ a number of different depreciation methods in practice. We will focus our presentation on the three most common allocation methods:

1. *Straight-line method*
2. *Units-of-output method*
3. *Double-declining balance approach*[11]

These three methods are used by the vast majority of firms. Note that in recent years, U.S. firms depreciated over 90% of tangible fixed assets using the straight-line method.[12]

1. **Straight-Line (SL) method.** The **straight-line method** applies a constant rate of depreciation against a constant depreciable cost. The firm determines the rate of depreciation by dividing 1 by the useful life of the asset. Depreciable base (also referred to as depreciable cost) is equal to acquisition cost less estimated scrap value. Depreciation expense is the depreciable base divided by the useful life or the depreciable base multiplied by the straight-line rate as shown in the following equation and illustrated in Example 11.12.

$$\text{Depreciable Base} = \text{Acquisition Cost} - \text{Scrap Value} \tag{11.1}$$

$$\text{Straight-Line Depreciation Expense} = \text{Depreciable Base/Useful Life} \tag{11.2}$$

or

$$\text{Straight-Line Rate} = \text{1/Useful Life} \tag{11.3}$$

$$\text{Straight-Line Depreciation Expense} = \text{Depreciable Base} \times \text{Straight-Line Rate} \tag{11.4}$$

EXAMPLE 11.12

Straight-Line Depreciation

PROBLEM: On January 1, Naylor Company acquired a piece of heavy equipment at a total cost of $670,000. The firm estimates that the asset will have a useful life of 5 years and expects a $70,000 scrap value at the end of its useful life. Compute the annual depreciation for Naylor over the life of the asset using the straight-line method and prepare the journal entry that Naylor will record at the end of the first year.

SOLUTION: Using the data provided, Naylor Company's straight-line depreciation is as follows:

$$\text{Depreciation Expense} = \frac{\text{Depreciable Base}}{\text{Useful Life}} = \frac{\$670{,}000 - \$70{,}000}{\text{5 Years}} = \underline{\underline{\$120{,}000/\text{Year}}}$$

or

$$\begin{aligned} \text{Straight-Line Rate} &= \text{1/5 years} = 20\% \\ \text{Depreciation Expense} &= \text{Depreciable Base} \times \text{Straight-Line Rate} \\ &= (\$670{,}000 - \$70{,}000) \times 20\% \\ &= \underline{\underline{\$120{,}000/\text{year}}} \end{aligned}$$

The journal entry at the end of the first year is:

Account	End of First Year	
Depreciation Expense—Equipment	$120,000	
Accumulated Depreciation—Equipment		$120,000

[11]Alternative depreciation methods include the sum-of-the-years digits approach, the 150% declining balance method, group methods, and composite methods.

[12]See surveys reported in AICPA, *Accounting Trends and Techniques*–2012 (New York, NY: AICPA, 2012).

2. **Units-of-Output method.** The **units-of-output method** derives a rate of depreciation per unit produced and applies that rate against the actual number of units produced each period. For example, the number of miles driven could be used to depreciate a delivery truck. Depreciation expense is the depreciable base divided by the estimated total units of output times the actual number of units produced each period. The depreciable base is cost less estimated scrap value.

$$\text{Depreciation Rate per Unit} = \frac{\text{Depreciable Base}}{\text{Estimated Total Units of Output}} \quad (11.5)$$

$$\text{Units-of-Output Depreciation Expense} = \text{Depreciation Rate per Unit} \times \text{Actual Units Produced} \quad (11.6)$$

or

$$\text{Units-of-Output Depreciation Expense} = \text{Depreciable Base} \times \frac{\text{Actual Units of Output}}{\text{Estimated Total Units of Output}} \quad (11.7)$$

Example 11.13 illustrates the units-of-output depreciation method.

EXAMPLE 11.13 Units-of-Output Depreciation

PROBLEM: On January 1, Naylor Company acquired a piece of heavy equipment at a total cost of $670,000. The firm estimates that the asset will have a useful life of 100,000 units of output and expects a $70,000 residual value at the end of its useful life. The company manufactures 30,000, 45,000, and 25,000 units in the first, second, and third year of use, respectively. Compute the annual depreciation for Naylor over the life of the asset using the units-of-output method and prepare the journal entry that Naylor will record at the end of the first year.

SOLUTION: The depreciation rate per unit of output is $6 per unit as computed here:

Depreciable Base/Estimated Total Units of Output = $600,000/100,000 = $6 per Unit

Depreciation Expense = $6 per Unit × Actual Units Produced

The depreciation schedule is as follows:

Year	Units of Output Produced	Depreciable Base / Estimated Total Units of Output	Depreciation Expense
1	30,000	$6	$180,000
2	45,000	$6	270,000
3	25,000	$6	150,000
Total	100,000		$600,000

The journal entry at the end of the first year is:

Account	End of First Year	
Depreciation Expense—Equipment	180,000	
Accumulated Depreciation—Equipment		180,000

3. **Double-Declining balance (DDB) method. Decreasing-charge methods** are depreciation methods that take more depreciation in the early years than in the late years of the asset's useful life. Acceleration of depreciation charges is based on the premise that an asset is often most productive in its early years of service. Thus, decreasing-charge methods match higher depreciation expense with higher related revenues in the early years of the asset's life and match lower depreciation charges against lower related revenues in the later years. Accelerated depreciation generally results in constant total annual usage costs (depreciation expense and repair and maintenance expense) charged against income over the life of the asset. In the early

years of the asset's life, there are high depreciation expenses but low repair and maintenance expenses. When the asset is older, there are high repair and maintenance expenses and low depreciation expenses. Thus, the decreasing-charge methods of depreciation result in a fairly constant level of asset utilization costs over the asset's useful life.

Exhibit 11.2 illustrates a decreasing-charge method of depreciation expense and repair and maintenance costs for a fixed asset with a 5-year useful life. Depreciation expense is higher than repair and maintenance expense in Years 1 and 2 when the asset is most productive. Depreciation expense declines in Years 4 and 5 when the asset is less productive and needs more repairs and maintenance. In this example, the total expenses related to the asset (depreciation and repair and maintenance) decline as the asset's useful life decreases and productivity declines.

EXHIBIT 11.2 Fixed Asset Utilization Costs

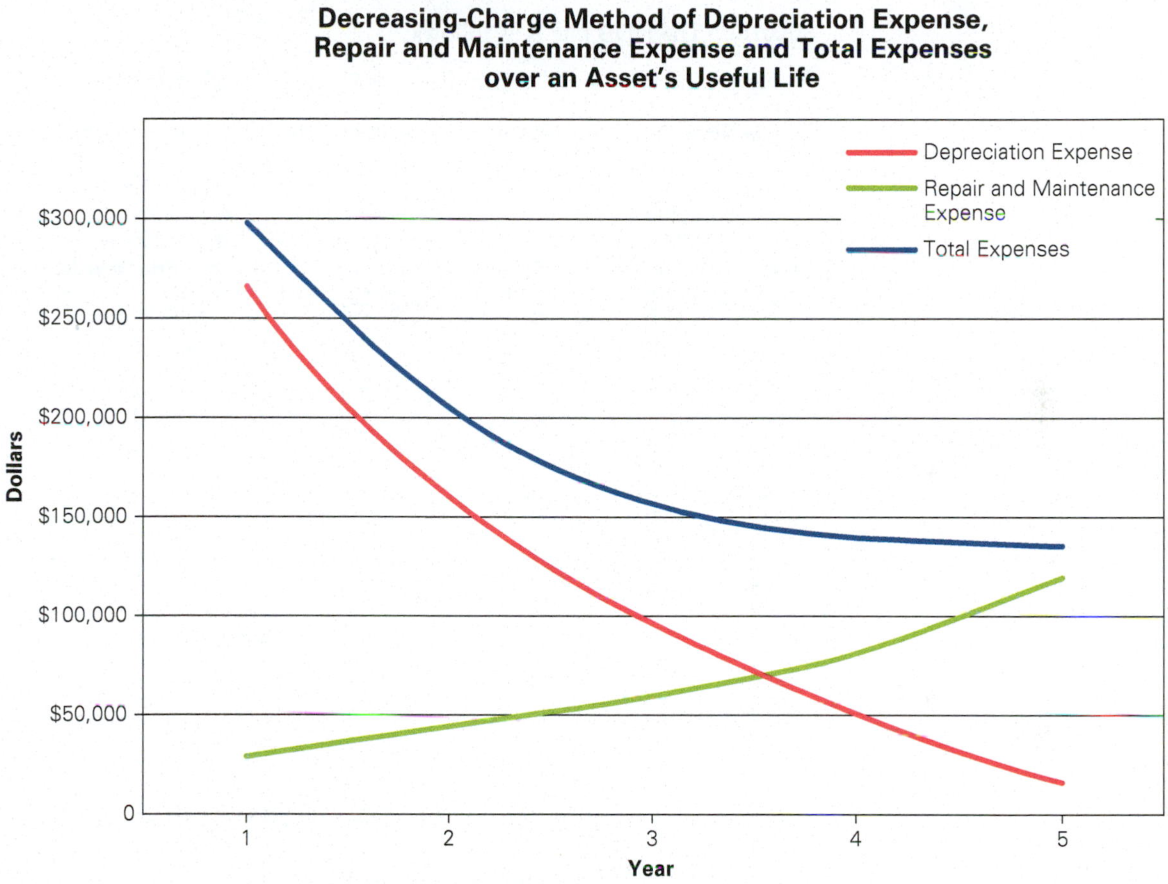

The **double-declining balance (DDB) method** is a decreasing-charge method that applies a constant rate of depreciation against a declining net book value (defined as cost less accumulated depreciation). The constant rate used in declining balance methods is a multiple of the straight-line rate. Note that the asset's net book value is the depreciable base for DDB, not the cost less scrap value. Therefore, DDB does not subtract the scrap value from the depreciable base before computing the annual depreciation expense. Firms compute the DDB rate as twice the straight-line rate—hence the term "double" in the title of the method.[13]

$$\text{DDB Rate} = 2 \times \text{Straight-Line Rate} \quad (11.8)$$

or

$$\text{DDB Rate} = 2 \times 1/\text{Useful Life} \quad (11.9)$$

$$\text{DDB Depreciation Expense} = \text{Net Book Value at Beginning of Period} \times \text{DDB Rate} \quad (11.10)$$

[13]The DDB approach is one of several declining-balance methods. For example, with the "150% declining balance," the constant rate is $1\frac{1}{2}$ times the straight-line rate.

With the DDB approach, the ending net book value is not always equal to the planned scrap value. In this case, the firm reduces the depreciation expense in the last year to the necessary amount to arrive at an ending book value equal to the scrap value. The DDB depreciation method is illustrated in Example 11.14.

EXAMPLE 11.14 Double-Declining Balance Depreciation

PROBLEM: On January 1, Naylor Company acquired a piece of heavy equipment at a total cost of $670,000. The firm estimates that the asset will have a useful life of 5 years and expects a $70,000 residual value at the end of its useful life. Prepare the depreciation schedule for Naylor over the life of the asset using the DDB and prepare the journal entry that Naylor will record at the end of the first year.

SOLUTION: The DDB rate is as follows:

Straight-Line Rate = 1/Useful Life = 1/5 Years = 20% DDB Rate = 2 × 20% = 40%

Double-Declining Balance Method Depreciation Schedule for Naylor Company

Year	Beginning Net Book Value (a)	DDB % (b)	Depreciation Expense (c) = (a) × (b)	End-of-Year Accumulated Depreciation (d) = (c) + Prior Year (d)	End-of-Year Net Book Value (e) = Cost − (d)
1	$670,000	40%	$268,000	$268,000	$402,000
2	402,000	40%	160,800	428,800	241,200
3	241,200	40%	96,480	525,280	144,720
4	144,720	40%	57,888	583,168	86,832
5	86,832		16,832*	600,000	70,000

*Depreciation expense needed to have the ending net book value equal to the $70,000 planned scrap value.

At the end of Year 5, the equipment's net book value is $70,000, its residual value. The journal entry at the end of the first year is:

Account	***End of First Year***	
Depreciation Expense—Equipment	268,000	
Accumulated Depreciation—Equipment		268,000

Exhibit 11.3 compares the straight-line and DDB methods graphically.

EXHIBIT 11.3 Comparison of Depreciation Methods

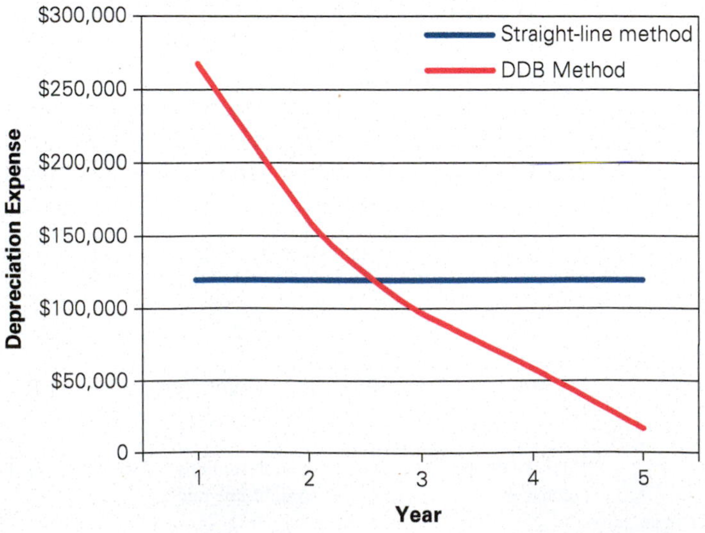

In Example 11.12, we determined that the straight-line method results in a constant $120,000 depreciation expense per year in the Naylor Company example. In contrast, the DDB method results in Naylor depreciating $268,000 and $160,800 in Years 1 and 2, respectively. The differences begin to reverse in Year 3 when the straight-line depreciation expense of $120,000 exceeds the DDB depreciation expense of $96,480.

Partial-Year Depreciation. The depreciation examples thus far have assumed that firms purchased PPE at the beginning of the year. In reality, though, firms purchase PPE throughout the year. If a calendar-year firm purchased a piece of equipment on August 14, it would be inappropriate for the firm to record a full year's depreciation expense. Computing the depreciation based on the number of days the firm held the asset in the year could be a time-consuming approach that costs more than the benefits derived.

In practice, firms employ a large variety of methods to compute partial-year depreciation that assume the firm purchased the asset at certain fixed points during the year. For example, with a **half-year convention**, the firm records a half year of depreciation for an asset acquired during the year of purchase (the assumption is that the firm acquired the asset at the midpoint of the year). The company also records a half-year's depreciation in the final year of the asset's life. For example, for an asset with a 5-year life purchased on May 1, the firm takes a half year of depreciation in Year 1 and Year 6.

Other approaches assume that the firm acquired the asset at the beginning or the middle of the month it was placed in service. Partial-year depreciation using the straight-line method is shown in Example 11.15.

EXAMPLE 11.15 Partial-Year Depreciation: Straight-Line Method

PROBLEM: On May 8, the Naylor Company (a calendar-year firm) acquired a piece of heavy equipment at a total cost of $670,000. Naylor estimates that the asset has a useful life of 5 years. Naylor expects a $70,000 scrap value at the end of its useful life. The company uses a simplifying assumption that all assets are placed in service on the first day of the month in which they were actually placed into service. What is the depreciation expense in the first year using the straight-line method? What is the depreciation schedule using the straight-line method?

SOLUTION: Under Naylor's simplifying assumption, we account for the asset as if it were acquired on May 1. First, we need to calculate depreciation expense for a full year under the straight-line method:

$$\text{Depreciation Expense} = \frac{\text{Cost} - \text{Scrap Value}}{\text{Useful Life}}$$

$$= \frac{\$670{,}000 - \$70{,}000}{5\ \text{Years}} = \underline{\underline{\$120{,}000/\text{Year}}}$$

Second, we develop the depreciation schedule using the straight-line method, applying the partial-period assumption in the first and last years of the asset's useful life. Thus, in the first year, depreciation expense is the full-year amount times 8/12 because we are assuming that Naylor holds the asset for 8 months in the first year. So, the first year's depreciation expense is $80,000.

In the last year, depreciation expense is the full-year amount times 4/12 because we are assuming that Naylor holds the asset for 4 months in the last year. In the last year, depreciation expense is $40,000. The depreciation schedule is shown below:

Year	Depreciation Expense	Original Cost	End-of-Year Accumulated Depreciation	End-of-Year Net Book Value
1	**$120,000 × 8/12 = $ 80,000**	$670,000	$ 80,000	$590,000
2	120,000	670,000	200,000	470,000
3	120,000	670,000	320,000	350,000
4	120,000	670,000	440,000	230,000
5	120,000	670,000	560,000	110,000
6	**$120,000 × 4/12 = 40,000**	670,000	600,000	70,000
Total	$600,000			

Companies that use the double-declining balance method also use partial-year depreciation by allocating the first year's annual DDB depreciation expense on a proportional basis. Example 11.16 illustrates the partial-year depreciation using the double-declining balance method.

EXAMPLE 11.16 Partial-Year Depreciation: Double-Declining Balance (DDB) Method

PROBLEM: On May 8, the Naylor Company (a calendar-year firm) acquires a piece of heavy equipment at a total cost of $670,000. Naylor estimates that the asset has a useful life of 5 years. Naylor expects a $70,000 scrap value at the end of its useful life. The company uses a simplifying assumption that all assets are placed in service on the first day of the month in which they were actually placed into service. What is the depreciation schedule using the DDB method?

SOLUTION: Under Naylor's simplifying assumption, we account for the asset as if it were acquired on May 1. So, we allocate 8/12 of the full first-year DDB depreciation expense to the first year. The following table shows that the first year's depreciation expense is $178,667. We then use the 40% rate for the following years. Depreciation expense in Year 5 is reduced in order to bring the end-of-year net book value to $70,000, the original estimated scrap value.

Year	Beginning Net Book Value (NBV)	DDB %	Depreciation Expense (Income Statement)	End-of-Year Accumulated Depreciation	End-of-Year Net Book Value (NBV)
1	$670,000	40% × 8/12	$178,667	$178,667	$491,333
2	491,333	40%	196,533	375,200	294,800
3	294,800	40%	117,920	493,120	176,880
4	176,880	40%	70,752	563,872	106,128
5	106,128		36,128*	600,000	70,000

*Depreciation expense needed to have the ending net book value equal to the $70,000 planned scrap value.

IFRS Component Depreciation. IFRS requires that firms separately depreciate each part or component of a fixed asset that is significant in relation to the asset's total cost. For example, the purchase of a building would involve a number of different components, such as the foundation and frame, heating and air conditioning systems, and other non-weight-bearing parts. After the firm identifies the components, the methodology to depreciate is identical to our prior discussion.

Although U.S. GAAP allows the components-based approach, it does not require it. Consequently, most firms that report under U.S. GAAP do not separate their depreciable assets into components. Example 11.17 illustrates the component depreciation method.

EXAMPLE 11.17 IFRS Component Depreciation Expense

PROBLEM: FastAir Corporation, an IFRS reporter, identified three major components of its new airplane purchased on January 1 for $10,000,000. It allocates $5,000,000 of the cost to the airframe, $4,000,000 to engines, and $1,000,000 to the interior. The airframe has a useful life of 20 years and $500,000 salvage value. The engines have a 16-year useful life and $200,000 salvage value. The interior has a 5-year useful life and no salvage value. FastAir uses the straight-line method for all components. What is the annual depreciation expense for the first year?

SOLUTION: Annual depreciation expense for the first year is $662,500. For each component, we calculate annual depreciation expense as the component cost less component salvage value divided by component useful life.

Component	Component Cost	Salvage Value	Depreciable Base	Useful Life (in Years)	Annual Depreciation Expense
Airframe	$ 5,000,000	$500,000	$4,500,000	20	$225,000
Engines	4,000,000	200,000	3,800,000	16	237,500
Interior	1,000,000		1,000,000	5	200,000
Total	$10,000,000				$662,500

3 Determine and illustrate the appropriate accounting for asset derecognition of property, plant, and equipment, including sales and abandonments.

Derecognition of Property, Plant, and Equipment

Companies remove or derecognize tangible fixed assets from their accounts when they sell or abandon items of PPE.[14] Derecognition requires that the firm remove all related accounts from the ledger, including the asset's cost and its accumulated depreciation. Before removing the asset from the ledger, the firm must bring the accumulated depreciation up to date at the time of derecognition. Because firms generally make an entry for depreciation expense and accumulated depreciation only when the financial statements are prepared, the firm must recognize any depreciation expense related to the use of the asset from the last financial statement date until the date of derecognition.

Asset Derecognition: Sale

When a firm sells or abandons an asset, it recognizes a gain or loss on the income statement measured as the difference between any cash proceeds received and the carrying value of the asset as illustrated in Example 11.18.

EXAMPLE 11.18

Sale of a Tangible Fixed Asset

PROBLEM: On May 31, 2018, J. Franz Company sold a piece of machinery it had purchased on January 1, 2011, with an original cost of $355,000. The asset had a useful life of 15 years and a scrap value of $67,000. It sold the asset for $265,000 in cash. Franz recorded depreciation through December 31, 2017, using the straight-line method. What was the carrying value of the asset on the date of sale? What is the gain or loss on disposal? Record the journal entry for the sale.

SOLUTION: To properly calculate the gain or loss on disposal, we need to determine the carrying value of the asset when it was sold. The depreciable base equals $288,000 ($355,000 original cost less $67,000 estimated scrap value), and the asset had a useful life of 15 years. Thus, the annual depreciation expense for the machinery is $19,200 ($288,000 / 15). Because Franz had held the asset for 7 years as of December 31, 2017, the accumulated depreciation as of the end of 2017 is $134,400 ($19,200 × 7 years).

We also need to include depreciation expense for the five months in 2018; monthly depreciation is $1,600 ($19,200 / 12). Thus, the additional depreciation up to the date of disposal is $8,000 ($1,600 × 5 months), and the accumulated depreciation up to the date of the disposal is $142,400 (i.e., $134,400 + $8,000). The journal entry to update the depreciation for the current year follows:

Account	*May 31, 2018*	
Depreciation Expense—Machinery	8,000	
Accumulated Depreciation—Machinery		8,000

[14] Companies may also derecognize property, plant, and equipment due to an involuntary conversion, which is the disposal of an asset due to an unexpected event (e.g., a loss due to a fire). Involuntary conversions are not discussed in this chapter.

The carrying value of the asset on the date of the sale is $212,600 (cost of $355,000 less accumulated depreciation of $142,400). There is a gain on disposal of $52,400 (sales proceeds of $265,000 less the asset's carrying value of $212,600).

Because Franz no longer owns the equipment, it removes the balances in all accounts related to the machinery—the machinery and accumulated depreciation accounts. The journal entry to record the sale is as follows:

Account	May 31, 2018	
Cash	265,000	
Accumulated Depreciation—Machinery	142,400	
Machinery		355,000
Gain on Sale of Machinery		52,400

Asset Derecognition: Abandonment

When an asset reaches the end of its productive life or is rendered obsolete, a company may choose to scrap or abandon it. In this case, the company will not receive any significant amount of cash—and it may incur some disposal costs. If the firm does not receive any cash, the loss on abandonment is equal to the asset's net book value on the date of the disposal. Example 11.19 illustrates accounting for the abandonment of operating assets.

EXAMPLE 11.19 Abandonment of Operating Assets

PROBLEM: On May 31, 2018, J. Franz Company decided to scrap a piece of machinery that had an original cost of $355,000 and accumulated depreciation (brought up to the date of the disposal) of $142,400. Therefore, the net book value of the asset is $212,600 (i.e., $355,000 − $142,400) on the disposal date. The company is required to pay $3,000 to have the asset picked up and taken to a city warehouse for proper disposal. What is the gain or loss on abandonment? Record the journal entry for the sale.

SOLUTION: There is a loss on the abandonment of $212,600, which is equal to the carrying value of the machinery. Because Franz no longer has the equipment, it removes the balances in all accounts related to the machinery—the machinery and accumulated depreciation accounts. The company will also recognize the disposal costs as a miscellaneous expense. The journal entry to record the abandonment is as follows:[15]

Account	May 31, 2018	
Miscellaneous Expense	3,000	
Accumulated Depreciation—Machinery	142,400	
Loss on Abandonment of Machinery	212,600	
Cash		3,000
Machinery		355,000

4 Identify required disclosures for property, plant, and equipment.

Disclosures of Property, Plant, and Equipment

Companies commonly report the carrying value of property, plant, and equipment in total or by major class of long-term assets on the balance sheet. Companies are also required to disclose:

- The balances of depreciable assets by major classes at the end of the fiscal year, either on the face of the financial statements or in the footnotes. A major class can be defined either by nature or function of the long-term assets.

[15]Alternatively, Franz could add the disposal costs to the loss on abandonment, bringing the total loss to $215,600.

- The accumulated depreciation on property, plant, and equipment at the end of the fiscal year by major class or in total.
- A general description of the method or methods used in computing depreciation with respect to major classes of depreciable assets.
- The amount of depreciation expense for the period.

Exhibit 11.4 presents a sample fixed asset footnote from ***AT&T Inc.'s*** 2016 annual report. Typically, companies will report the method of depreciation in the accounting policies footnote (Note 1). ***AT&T*** uses the straight-line method, which is the most common method used in practice. The majority of information related to PPE is in a separate footnote (Note 6) in which the company discloses depreciation expense, the balances of depreciable assets by major classes, and the accumulated depreciation on its property, plant, and equipment.

EXHIBIT 11.4 Fixed Asset Accounting Disclosures, ***AT&T Inc.*** Annual Report, December 31, 2016

NOTE 1: Significant Accounting Policies (Excerpt)

Property, Plant and Equipment Property, plant, and equipment is stated at cost, except for assets acquired using acquisition accounting, which are initially recorded at fair value (see Note 6). . . . The cost of additions and substantial improvements to property, plant, and equipment is capitalized and includes internal compensation costs for these projects . . . . The cost of maintenance and repairs of property, plant, and equipment is charged to operating expenses. Property, plant, and equipment costs are depreciated using straight-line methods over their estimated economic lives. Certain subsidiaries follow composite group depreciation methodology. Accordingly, when a portion of their depreciable property, plant, and equipment is retired in the ordinary course of business, the gross book value is reclassified to accumulated depreciation, and no gain or loss is recognized on the disposition of these assets.

NOTE 6: Property, Plant, and Equipment (Excerpt)

Property, plant, and equipment is summarized as follows at December 31:

	Lives (years)	2016	2015
Land	–	$ 1,643	$ 1,638
Buildings and improvements	2–44	35,036	33,784
Central office equipment[1]	3–10	92,954	93,643
Cable, wiring and conduit	15–50	79,279	75,784
Satellites	12-15	2,710	2,088
Other equipment	2–23	88,436	81,972
Software	3–5	14,472	11,347
Under construction	–	5,118	5,971
		319,648	306,227
Accumulated depreciation and amortization		(194,749)	(181,777)
Property, plant, and equipment – Net		$ 124,899	$124,450

[1] Includes certain network software.

Our depreciation expense was $20,661 in 2016, $19,289 in 2015, and $17,773 in 2014. Depreciation expense included amortization of software totaling $2,362 in 2016, $2,660 in 2015, and $1,504 in 2014.

Source: Fixed Asset Accounting Disclosures, AT&T Inc. Annual Report, December 31, 2016. https://www.att.com/Investor/ATT_Annual/2016/downloads/att_ar2016_completeannualreport.pdf Intangible Assets: Characteristics and Types

IFRS Disclosures

IFRS disclosure requirements, while similar, are more comprehensive than U.S. GAAP. For each class of property, plant, and equipment, a company must disclose the historical cost and its accumulated depreciation at the beginning and the end of the period. The company is required to provide a reconciliation of the carrying amount at the beginning of the period to the end of the period. Companies must also disclose the depreciation method and useful lives (or equivalently, the depreciation rate).[16]

[16] A similar footnote is required in the Form 10-K under SEC reporting guidelines.

5 Specify the characteristics and types of intangible assets.

Intangible Assets: Characteristics and Types

The second major long-term operating asset class is *intangible assets.* **Intangible assets** are assets without physical substance that have economic value because of the contractual or legal rights they confer upon the holder. There are two general classes of intangible assets—*finite-life* (also referred to as definite-life) intangible assets and *indefinite-life intangible assets*. The indefinite-life intangible category includes *goodwill* along with other intangible assets such as trademarks and renewable licenses.[17]

Finite-Life Intangible Assets

Finite-life intangible assets are intangible assets that can be individually identified and have limited useful lives. There are six main types of finite-life intangible assets: patents, copyrights, leaseholds, leasehold improvements, customer lists, and limited-term franchises. Due to their limited useful lives, finite-life intangible assets are subject to amortization.

Patents. A **patent** grants the holder an exclusive right to use a formula, product, or process for a fixed period of time, usually 20 years. In the United States, the federal government grants exclusive rights through the U.S. Patent and Trademark Office. For example, Qualcomm holds patents on 4G technology.

Copyrights. A **copyright** is an exclusive right to reproduce and sell an original work—including books, musical scores, advertisements, other works of art, and computer programs—for the creator's life plus 70 years. The federal government grants copyrights.

Leaseholds. A **leasehold** is the right to use a specific piece of property for a fixed period of time in exchange for a certain payment. In order to lease several floors of a large office building in a major city, the owner of the property may require a significant up-front payment before the monthly lease payments begin. The leasehold represents a down payment on the lease and reduces the amount of the monthly rental fee required each period. The cash payment serves as a prepayment of rent: It does not transfer ownership, but it is a requisite payment to complete a lease contract.

Leasehold Improvements. **Leasehold improvements** are permanent betterments made to leased property. Examples include construction of offices, conference rooms, and training facilities in a leased building. Upon termination of the lease, these improvements revert to the owner of the building. As a result, the company leasing the building has the right only to use the improvements: The building owner retains the legal right of ownership of the tangible property.[18]

Customer Lists. A **customer list** consists of information about customers such as their names and contact information. It may be in the form of a database that includes other information about the customers such as their order history and demographic information. Examples of customer lists include depositors at a commercial bank, a CPA firm's clients, and investors engaging in transactions with a broker-dealer. Compiling customer lists is much simpler than valuing them given that there are no reliable markets to determine a value. Because an asset must be measured reliably to be reported on the balance sheet, firms often do not record customer lists as assets. In a business combination, the acquiring company may be willing to pay for the customer list. The merger transaction then provides a value for customer lists to report on the balance sheet. For example, ***AT&T*** reported customer lists and customer relationships from large acquisitions such as ***DIRECTV*** and ***BellSouth***. A customer list is classified as a finite-life intangible asset when the firm expects the relationships to terminate within a specified period of time. Otherwise, it is classified as an indefinite-life intangible asset.

[17]For most of the relevant literature for this topic, see FASB ASC 350 – *Intangibles – Goodwill and Other* and in FASB ASC 805 – *Business Combinations* for U.S. GAAP and IASC, *International Accounting Standard 38*, "Intangible Assets" (London, UK: International Accounting Standards Committee, Revised) and IASB, *International Financial Reporting Standard 3*, "Business Combinations" (London, UK: International Accounting Standards Board, Revised) for IFRS.

[18]Companies will sometimes classify leasehold improvements as property, plant, and equipment.

Franchises. A **franchise** (for example, a ***McDonald's*** restaurant) represents the right or privilege to sell a product or deliver a service of another entity, such as a business or government. The owner of the product or service (the franchisor) enters into a contractual relationship with another person or business (the franchisee) that gives the franchisee the right to conduct business under the franchisor's name in exchange for a fee. The contractual relationship can be limited by time or may be continually renewable. A limited-term franchise agreement is considered a finite-life intangible asset.

Indefinite-Life Intangibles Other than Goodwill

An **indefinite-life intangible asset** has no identifiable legal, regulatory, contractual, or competitive factors that limit the asset's revenue-generating term. As a result, indefinite-life intangible assets are not subject to amortization unless managers determine a finite life in a subsequent accounting period. There are three main categories of indefinite-life intangible assets: customer lists (discussed in the previous section), renewable licenses and permits, and trademarks and trade names. (We discuss *goodwill* separately in the following section.)

Renewable Licenses and Permits. **Renewable indefinite-life intangible assets** are assets subject to renewal on a regular basis whose renewal is reasonably certain, such as renewable broadcast licenses and taxi medallions. ***AT&T*** must renew its Federal Communications Commission (FCC) licenses for certain radio frequencies periodically, generally every 10 years. Renewal is reasonably certain, so ***AT&T*** classifies these licenses as an indefinite-life intangible asset that is not subject to amortization. If the firm does not expect a renewal to occur, it treats a license as a finite-life intangible asset.

Trademarks and Trade Names. A **trademark** (the ***Nike*** swoosh, for example) or **trade name** represents a firm's product or service; the firm has the legal right to protect the trademark and trade name from any unauthorized use by outside parties. This indefinite-life intangible asset can consist of a design, a trade name, a logo, or a symbol. The federal government grants a registered trademark for 10 years initially with an indefinite number of future renewals for 10-year periods. For ***AT&T***, trade names made up about 11% of its intangible assets other than goodwill at December 31, 2016.

Goodwill

Goodwill is an intangible asset created by factors that are typically difficult to identify and measure. For instance, a firm can generate goodwill from its product quality, reputation, ability to generate earnings above the industry average, the quality of its management, preferred physical location, or employee training programs. Because these factors are difficult to reliably measure, accounting standards allow firms to record goodwill as an asset only when a firm is acquired. When one firm buys another firm, the purchase price may be higher than the fair value of the acquired net assets, that is, its assets minus its liabilities. The premium paid at acquisition is **goodwill**, an indefinite-life intangible asset. The purchase transaction provides a reliable measurement of goodwill to report as an asset on the consolidated balance sheet. Because goodwill is tied to the specific business operations acquired and exists as long as these operations continue, it is not subject to amortization.

6 Determine and illustrate the initial measurement of different types of intangible assets, including internally generated intangibles, intangibles acquired individually or in a group, intangibles acquired in a business combination, and research and development costs.

Initial Measurement of Intangible Assets

In this section, we discuss accounting for the initial measurement of an intangible asset beginning with the conceptual framework as a reference point. We discuss the initial measurement of intangible assets according to the method by which they are acquired:

- Internally generated intangibles
- Intangibles acquired individually or with a group of assets
- Intangibles acquired in a business acquisition
- Goodwill
- Research and development costs

To determine whether expenditures incurred to generate an intangible asset qualify for asset recognition, firms (1) assess whether there is an identifiable asset that will generate probable future economic benefits and (2), if so, determine whether they can reliably measure that asset's value.

THE CONCEPTUAL FRAMEWORK CONNECTION
Intangible Asset Measurement

The most important concept underlying the initial valuation of an intangible asset is whether the firm can reliably measure its value. Many firms' measurements of internal expenditures for intangible assets are not faithful representations and thus are not recorded as an asset. For example, many businesses consider their brand names to be assets. However, the value of a brand name is difficult to measure, so brand names are typically not recorded as assets unless purchased externally, for example, as part of a merger or acquisition (i.e., a business combination).[19]

When determining what constitutes an asset, firms must differentiate between costs with probable future economic benefits—the first characteristic of an asset—and costs that have expired without the ability to generate revenue in subsequent accounting periods. Many expenditures, such as those for advertising or research, may have future economic benefits. Yet, because of the uncertainty of those future benefits, firms expense rather than capitalize these expenditures.

Internally Generated Intangibles

It can be difficult to identify and value future related economic benefits for internally generated intangible assets. As a result of this uncertainty, companies generally do not record most expenditures for internally generated intangibles as assets, instead expensing them as incurred. In such cases, firms can recognize some direct costs, including legal fees, as the intangible asset. For example, a company may sue another company for infringing on its patent by using the technology protected by patent without permission. For example, ***Apple*** sued ***Samsung***, alleging that ***Samsung's*** smartphones and tablets copied patented features in the iPhone and iPad. To successfully defend a patent, a company usually incurs legal fees. The company can capitalize legal fees from successfully defending a patent because the patent will generate probable future economic benefits. In contrast, if the patent is not successfully defended, no asset is recorded.

Intangibles Acquired Individually or with a Group of Assets

Companies can purchase intangible assets from an outside party either individually or as a group of assets. The firm recognizes acquired intangibles as assets because they will likely generate future economic benefits and their values are reliably measureable at cost.

When purchasing a group of intangible assets in a basket purchase, a company allocates the cost to the individual assets based on their relative fair values. This approach is identical to our earlier discussion of a basket purchase of PPE.

Intangibles Acquired in a Business Acquisition

When a company purchases another company, it measures all assets and liabilities acquired, including any intangible assets, at fair value. Accountants report these intangible assets at fair value on the consolidated balance sheet because they were acquired and measured in an objective transaction.

Goodwill

Goodwill is an intangible asset with an indefinite life. As discussed earlier, firms include goodwill on the balance sheet only when it is purchased in a business acquisition. Due to the difficulties in identifying and measuring purchased goodwill, firms generally compute it as a residual—specifically, the

[19]The direct costs associated with developing brand names, such as legal fees, can be capitalized. However, these costs are typically a very small percentage of the value of the brand name.

acquisition cost of a business in excess of the fair values of the identifiable net assets acquired (including identifiable intangible assets):

	Acquisition cost
Less:	Fair value of identifiable net assets acquired
Equals:	Goodwill

The acquiring company records goodwill and all other assets and liabilities acquired at their fair values. For instance, ***AT&T*** recorded goodwill of $34.7 billion when it purchased the ***DIRECTV*** in 2015. ***AT&T*** paid $47.4 billion for ***DIRECTV*** when the fair value of its net assets other than goodwill was $12.7 billion. Example 11.20 illustrates how goodwill is determined when one firm acquires another.

EXAMPLE 11.20 Goodwill Acquired in a Business Acquisition

PROBLEM: Buy Company exchanges $140,000 (market value) of its no-par value common stock to acquire 100% of the common stock of Sell Company. Sell Company reports total assets of $500,000 consisting of $40,000 cash, $160,000 inventory, and a $300,000 factory building. Sell Company reports liabilities of $420,000 consisting of $180,000 accounts payable and $240,000 long-term debt. Therefore, the historical cost of the net assets acquired is equal to $80,000 ($500,000 − $420,000). An appraisal of Sell Company's assets and liabilities indicated that Sell Company's factory building, part of its PPE, is undervalued by $40,000. The book values of all other assets and liabilities approximate their fair values. What is the fair value of the identifiable net assets Buy acquires from Sell? What is the amount of goodwill on Buy's acquisition of Sell? What is the journal entry to record Buy Company's purchase of Sell Company?

SOLUTION: The fair value of Sell's identifiable net assets is the difference between the fair value of all its assets and the fair value of all its liabilities. The fair value of the identifiable net assets Buy acquires is equal to $120,000, which is the fair value of its assets of $540,000 less the fair value of liabilities of $420,000.

	Book Value	Fair Value
Cash	$ 40,000	$ 40,000
Inventory	160,000	160,000
Property, Plant, and Equipment	300,000	340,000
Total Assets	$500,000	$540,000
Accounts Payable	$180,000	$180,000
Long-Term Debt	240,000	240,000
Total Liabilities	$420,000	$420,000
Net Assets	$ 80,000	$120,000

Goodwill is $20,000, as computed next.

Calculation of Goodwill

	Acquisition cost	$140,000
Less:	Fair value of the identifiable net assets acquired	(120,000)
Equals:	Goodwill	$ 20,000

Continued

Buy Company prepares the following journal entry to record the purchase of Sell Company:

Account	Acquisition Date	
Cash	40,000	
Inventory	160,000	
Factory Building	340,000	
Goodwill	20,000	
Accounts Payable		180,000
Long-Term Debt		240,000
Common Stock		140,000

Bargain Purchase. A company makes a **bargain purchase** when the fair value of the identifiable net assets in an acquisition exceeds the purchase price, meaning that the buying entity acquired the company for less than its fair value. That is, instead of paying more than the fair value of a company's identifiable net assets and creating goodwill, the price paid for the acquired company is less than the sum of the fair value of each of the identifiable assets less the fair value of liabilities.

A bargain purchase usually occurs when stock prices are depressed. With undervalued share prices, the acquiring company may be able to pay less than the fair values of the net assets acquired. The acquiring firm reports the gain from the bargain purchase as income from continuing operations on the income statement—specifically, it is recognized as an unusual or infrequent item (other gain). For example, ***Retrophin, Inc.,*** a biopharmaceutical company specializing in treatments for rare diseases, recorded an $88.5 million gain when it acquired Cholbaum, a treatment for disorders due to enzyme defects and its pediatric applications, from ***Asklepion Pharmaceuticals, LLC***, in 2015. ***Retrophin*** paid ***Asklepion*** $91.5 million, acquired the fair value of Cholbaum's net assets of $180.0 million, and recorded a gain on the bargain purchase.

Research and Development Costs

Research and development (R&D) is one of the most important investments for industries such as pharmaceuticals and information technology. R&D activity includes laboratory research designed to discover new knowledge, to test to determine process alternatives, to modify product or process design, and to engage in conceptual formulation and design of product or process alternatives. There is a distinction between research- and development-phase costs:

- *Research-phase activities* include an original and planned investigation undertaken with the prospect of gaining new scientific or technical knowledge and understanding.
- *Development-phase expenditures* relate to the application of research findings or other knowledge to a plan or design for the production of new or substantially improved materials, devices, products, processes, systems, or services before the start of commercial production or use.

R&D activity excludes quality control, troubleshooting, and routine and ongoing initiatives designed to refine existing products or processes and the adaptation of existing capabilities.

A company undertakes R&D activities to create new products or processes to generate future revenues. For example, ***Eli Lilly and Company***, a large pharmaceutical manufacturer, disclosed in the management discussion and analysis of its 2016 10-K that it "invest[s] heavily in research and development because we believe it is critical to our long-term competitiveness." It further details its research and development activities, including a focused explanation of the "Phases of New Drug Development," identified as Discovery Research Phase, Early Development Phase, Product Phase, and Submission Phase (***Eli Lilly and Company***, Financial Reports, December 2016). Over the last 3 years, ***Lilly's*** research and development costs averaged about 24% of its sales.

Accounting for Research and Development Costs. Firms must expense almost all R&D costs as incurred.[20] Does the fact that firms expense R&D costs immediately mean that these expenditures have no future economic benefit? R&D expenditures often have a future benefit, but it is difficult to identify and measure. For example, what is the future economic benefit of a patented product? Which R&D costs are going to result in successful products, and which costs will become worthless? Using a cost-benefit justification, standard setters ultimately took the position that almost all R&D expenditures should be expensed as incurred. Expensing all R&D costs, however, potentially understates assets and income. Example 11.21 provides an example of accounting for research and development costs.

EXAMPLE 11.21

Research and Development Costs

PROBLEM: Morrow Pharmaceuticals, Inc. provided you the following information regarding current-year expenditures in its research facility.

Expenditures	Amount
Testing materials used in experimentation	$ 123,000
Salaries of laboratory technicians	434,800
General-purpose testing equipment (acquired on January 1 of the current year: 10-year life)	768,510
Consultant fees for process improvements	33,090
Total expenditures for the current year	$1,359,400

What is the R&D expense? Record all journal entries for the expenditures. Assume that the expenditures are paid in cash.

SOLUTION: Morrow is required to expense the testing materials used, salaries incurred, and the consulting fees paid. However, it can use the general-purpose testing equipment in the laboratory for an extended period of time for several alternative experiments. As a result, Morrow should capitalize and depreciate the equipment over 10 years. Morrow will charge the current-year depreciation and subsequent-period depreciation of this testing equipment to R&D expense.

To record the R&D expense for the year, we include all laboratory expenditures except for the equipment cost. These expenditures include the cost of the materials ($123,000), the salaries ($434,800), and the consultant fees ($33,090) for a total R&D expense of $590,890. The journal entries required to record Morrow's R&D activities for the current year are:

Account	Current Year	
Research and Development Expense	590,890	
Cash		590,890

We capitalize the equipment, which has alternative future uses, as follows:

Account	January 1, Current Year	
Testing Equipment	768,510	
Cash		768,510

Continued

[20] In limited cases, firms can capitalize some R&D costs. R&D costs that are reimbursed under contract (i.e., sold to another firm or through customer-funded R&D) would be capitalized as a receivable or accumulated in an inventory account if reimbursed. Firms can also capitalize R&D equipment and buildings with alternative future uses. In addition, firms can capitalize the cost of R&D in a patent account if the research was purchased from an outside research firm. Finally, certain internally generated software development costs can be capitalized after the company establishes technological feasibility and the software is sold, leased, or marketed to third parties (external users).

We then depreciate the equipment as follows:

Account	December 31, Current Year	
Research and Development Expense	76,851	
Accumulated Depreciation—Testing Equipment		76,851

IFRS Research and Development Cost Accounting. IFRS requires that firms expense costs during a research phase but allows firms to capitalize development-phase costs under certain conditions. Under IFRS, a firm can capitalize development-phase expenditures if it can demonstrate all of the following:[21]

1. The technical feasibility of completing the intangible asset so that it will be available for use or sale
2. Its intention to complete the intangible asset and use or sell it
3. Its ability to use or sell the intangible asset
4. How the intangible asset will generate probable future economic benefits
5. The availability of adequate technical, financial, and other resources to complete the development and to use or sell the intangible asset
6. Its ability to measure reliably the expenditure attributable to the intangible asset during its development

Demonstrating all six conditions increases the likelihood that the expenditures will provide future economic benefit. For example, in its accounting policy for intangible assets in its 2016 financial statements, ***Telefonaktiebolaget LM Ericsson***, the Swedish telecommunications company, stated that it capitalizes costs incurred for the development of products when it has established technical and economic feasibility. Its capitalized expenses are mainly generated internally and include direct labor and directly attributable overhead costs. It then amortizes the capitalized development costs when the product is available for general release. During 2016, ***Ericsson*** capitalized 4.5 million Swedish Krona (SEK) of development costs, representing about 2% of sales. At the end of the year, it reported an intangible asset related to development costs of 8.1 million SEK, or about 2.9% of total assets. Example 11.22 illustrates accounting for research and development costs under IFRS.

EXAMPLE 11.22 IFRS Research and Development Costs

PROBLEM: Morrow Pharmaceuticals, Inc. provided you the following information regarding current-year expenditures in its research facility.

Account	Amount
Testing materials used in experimentation	$ 123,000
Salaries of laboratory technicians	434,800
General-purpose testing equipment (acquired on January 1 of the current year; 10-year life)	768,510
Consultant fees for process improvements	33,090
Total Expenditures for the Current Year	$1,359,400

What is the R&D expense under IFRS? Record all journal entries required for these expenditures. Assume that all expenditures are paid in cash. Assume that development-phase expenditures meet all of the conditions for capitalization and have a useful life of 3 years.

SOLUTION: In the research facility, the cost of the materials ($123,000) and the salaries ($434,800) are not specifically related to development-phase activities. Therefore, these costs, totaling $557,800, are expensed.

[21]IASC, *International Accounting Standard 38*, "Intangible Assets" (London, UK: International Accounting Standards Committee, Revised).

Account	Current Year	
Research and Development Expense	557,800	
Cash		557,800

The testing equipment is used for general purposes and so has alternative uses. Therefore, we capitalize the equipment as follows:

Account	January 1, Current Year	
Testing Equipment	768,510	
Cash		768,510

We also depreciate the equipment over 10 years, as follows:

Account	December 31, Current Year	
Research and Development Expense	76,851	
Accumulated Depreciation—Testing Equipment		76,851

Under IFRS, we consider the process improvements a development-phase activity and capitalize them as a development asset:

Account	January 1, Current Year	
Development Asset	33,090	
Cash		33,090

We then amortize the development asset over 3 years:

Account	December 31, Current Year	
Amortization Expense—Development Asset	11,030	
Accumulated Amortization—Development Asset		11,030

Acquired In-Process Research and Development Costs. Acquiring firms must account for R&D costs purchased in business combination transactions. **Acquired in-process R&D** is an asset obtained in a business combination representing the fair value assigned to in-progress research and development projects that are not yet commercially viable. Companies account for acquired in-process R&D as follows:

1. Record acquired in-process R&D as an indefinite-life intangible asset until the project is completed.
2. If the project is successful, record the intangible asset and amortize it.
3. Write off against earnings if the project is found to be without value in a subsequent period.

All additional R&D expenditures incurred to complete the project follow the accounting for internally generated R&D discussed earlier and are expensed as incurred.[22]

For instance, ***Eli Lilly and Company*** reported in its 2016 financial statements that it capitalized in-process research and development assets acquired as part of the acquisition of a business. ***Lilly*** reported in-process research and development assets of $180.2 million and $177.6 million at December 31, 2016, and 2015, respectively.

[22]An exception to this rule is for technology projects for which technological feasibility has been achieved. In such case, the allocated cost is capitalized and amortized.

JUDGMENTS IN ACCOUNTING
The Measurement of Intangible Assets

Assessing the certainty of future economic benefits involves judgment. If a firm deems the benefits to be probable, it capitalizes the expenditures in an intangible asset account. However, if the benefits are not probable, the firm expenses them as incurred. This assessment can be quite difficult in many instances; as a result, accounting standards limit the types of intangible assets that firms can capitalize.

For example, consider the planned development of a portable charging unit designed to recharge electric cars. This product will be fairly expensive for the ultimate consumer. In order for the costs incurred to acquire this patent provide future economic benefits, electric cars must become more popular and consumers must be willing to pay a substantial cost for the benefit of having access to a portable charger. Management must forecast the demand for electric vehicles as well as the prices that the market will be willing to pay for the charger before recording the costs incurred as an intangible asset.

7 Demonstrate accounting for intangible assets subsequent to acquisition, including amortization and derecognition.

Subsequent Measurement and Derecognition of Intangible Assets

Several factors affect the carrying value of intangible assets, including subsequent expenditures. Firms very rarely capitalize subsequent expenditures related to intangible assets as an asset.[23] The majority of subsequent expenditures related to an intangible asset simply maintain the existing future economic benefits as opposed to enhancing future economic benefits and are expensed as incurred.

Amortization is the systematic and rational allocation of the cost of a finite-life intangible asset to expense over the asset's expected useful life or legal life, whichever is shorter. Firms report amortization expense on the income statement and reduce the carrying value of the finite-life intangible asset on the balance sheet.

THE CONCEPTUAL FRAMEWORK CONNECTION
The Cost-Allocation Process

The conceptual framework treats the principles of cost allocation of finite-life intangible assets and tangible fixed assets in the same way. Finite-life intangible assets consumed in the revenue-generating process over their useful lives meet the definition of an expense. Likewise, as the firm uses these assets, their future economic benefits generally decline. The carrying amount of these assets is reduced to reflect this decline in value and provide an accurate report of total assets on the balance sheet.

As previously discussed, firms do not depreciate land because it has an unlimited life. The same concept applies to certain intangible assets. Specifically, because goodwill as well as the other indefinite-life intangibles have an unlimited life, they are not subject to amortization.

Amortization Method

Only finite-life intangible assets are subject to amortization: Firms do not amortize goodwill and other indefinite-life intangible assets. Firms may include estimated residual values in the computations, although they are rarely used in practice.

To determine estimated useful lives of finite-life intangible assets, firms consider legal, regulatory, contractual, and competitive factors. The expected period of economic benefit of the asset must take into account the effects of obsolescence, demand, and technological advances. Current

[23] Expenditures related to legal fees incurred to successfully defend a patent, copyright, or trademark are typically capitalized into the intangible assets.

accounting standards do not specify either a method of amortization to use or a limit on the useful life. The period of amortization should be either the useful life or legal life, whichever is shorter.

For example, assume that a leading computer manufacturer was granted a patent for a new computer chip with a legal life of 20 years. However, the economic life of the computer chip is only 3 years due to technological advances and the certain obsolescence of the product. As a result, the patent amortization cannot exceed 3 years. Also consider the case of leasehold improvements that will last 10 years but the related lease is only for a 6-year period. The firm must amortize the leasehold improvements over the 6-year lease term, the legal life, because it is shorter than the economic life of the improvement.

The method of amortization should reflect the pattern in which the firm utilizes the asset's economic benefits. If the firm cannot reasonably estimate a revenue stream, it should use the straight-line method. As is the case with PPE, most companies utilize the straight-line method to amortize their finite-life intangible assets. Amortization of finite-life intangible assets is shown in Example 11.23.

EXAMPLE 11.23 Amortization of Finite-Life Intangible Assets

PROBLEM: JJ Inc. currently leases an office building. It initiated the original 20-year lease 15 years ago, so 5 years remain on the lease. On January 1, JJ paid $20,000 to install a new heating and cooling system with a 10-year estimated useful life that it expects to use ratably over the remaining term of the lease. What is the journal entry to record the expenditure? How much amortization will JJ report and for how many years? What is the journal entry for the first year?

SOLUTION: The $20,000 expenditure is for a leasehold improvement, a finite-life intangible asset. The journal entry to record the expenditure made in the current period follows:

Account	***January 1***	
Leasehold Improvements	20,000	
Cash		20,000

We compute the amortization on a straight-line basis because JJ expects the usage of the system to occur ratably. The useful life is 5 years, the remaining life of the lease. Thus, amortization each year is $4,000 (i.e., $20,000 / 5 years). The journal entry made at the end of the current period is as follows:

Account	***December 31***	
Amortization Expense	4,000	
Leasehold Improvements		4,000

Note that the credit in this journal entry is made to the finite-life intangible asset directly. Alternatively, JJ could have credited a contra account, accumulated amortization.

Derecognition of Intangible Assets

Firms remove intangible assets from their books upon disposal or when they expect no further economic benefits from the use of the assets. If the firm sells an intangible asset, it recognizes a gain or loss on the income statement, measured as the difference between the sales proceeds and the carrying value of the asset.

STEPHEN J. COSGROVE

FORMER VICE PRESIDENT, CORPORATE CONTROLLER, AND CHIEF ACCOUNTING OFFICER JOHNSON & JOHNSON, NEW BRUNSWICK, NJ»

Stephen J. Cosgrove

Stephen J. Cosgrove is the Former Vice President, Corporate Controller, and Chief Accounting Officer of Johnson & Johnson, a leading manufacturer of pharmaceuticals, medical devices, and consumer products. He has served on the Financial Accounting Standards Advisory Council and is currently a member of the Financial Executives International Committee on Corporate Reporting.

1 Why are intangible assets one of the most important economic resources on Johnson & Johnson's balance sheet, and why should students understand how to report these assets?

Intangible assets comprise approximately 30% of total assets on the Johnson & Johnson balance sheet. These assets are important economic resources, capable of generating future value for shareholders. They include the goodwill associated with various acquisitions, intellectual knowledge, brand names—Neutrogena®, Listerine®, Acuvue®, and Zyrtec®, to name a few—and the acquired in-process research and development projects that are vital to generating future value. Intangible assets on Johnson & Johnson's balance sheet are often the direct result of acquisitions such as the recent acquisition of Synthes Holdings, AG.

Students who understand how to measure, value, and report intangible assets will be positioned to assist their future employers to communicate the value of these assets to the investor community and customers as well as comply with accounting and tax regulations.

2 How do you measure the economic benefits of an intangible asset?

Johnson & Johnson uses the direct or indirect contribution to cash flows to measure the economic benefits of our intangible assets. We make risk-adjusted estimates of the present value of the forecasted streams of revenues associated with each asset.

3 In-Process Research and Development (R&D) is recorded as an asset upon acquisition of another company. How does a company like Johnson & Johnson measure the potential success of a research and development project?

In-Process R&D assets have a wide range of risk of success associated with individual projects or potential products. In particular, the probability of success of an early-stage pharmaceutical compound can be extremely low. This risk is taken into account when determining the value of each potential opportunity. Factors used to determine risk include success of similar compounds or products, results of clinical studies, and how far a project has progressed through the regulatory process. Ultimate product approval and introduction to the marketplace determine whether the associated intangible asset is amortized over the remaining useful life or expensed if unapproved or abandoned.

4 What factors do you consider when looking for a possible impairment of a capitalized indefinite-life intangible asset?

Johnson & Johnson performs intangible asset reviews on an ongoing basis, especially if any significant factor changes. Some of the factors we consider are management intentions as to the use and funding of the assets, whether there have been any significant changes in the assumptions used in the initial valuation, and any delays in clinical trials or product launches. Other common triggers include a significant decrease in the market price of the asset or losses associated with the use of the asset.

5 Under current U.S. GAAP, firms capitalize a portion of software development costs as an intangible asset while expensing all internally generated research and development costs. Can you justify this divergence in practice?

Johnson & Johnson capitalizes certain internal costs associated with software development, such as coding and testing costs incurred during the projects' application development phase. These software development costs meet the essential characteristics of an asset, because they have probable future economic benefit. For Johnson & Johnson these costs are typically not significant and generally incurred quickly, and the time between capitalization and potential write-off tends to be short.

The opposite is true for internally developed R&D such as the costs of discovery, testing, and developing new products. All internal research and development costs are expensed as incurred. R&D costs can span several years, the costs can be significant, and the probability of successful approval of any one project is low based on industry history. These costs do not meet the definition of an asset, primarily due to the uncertainty of receiving future benefits.

Discussion Questions

1. What are some of the judgments used in estimating the future economic benefit (specifically, measuring the value) of intangible assets?
2. Compare and contrast the accounting for research and development expenditures under U.S. GAAP and IFRS, including the rationale used to justify each accounting treatment. (Do not address in-process R&D.)

8 Detail required disclosures for intangible assets.

Disclosures of Intangible Assets

U.S. GAAP requires significant disclosures for intangible assets by major class of intangibles such as brand names, licenses and franchises, copyrights, patents, and development costs. These disclosures include:

- Amounts of assets with an indefinite and finite useful lives
- If the asset has a finite useful life, whether to use the useful life or the legal life
- The amortization methods used for intangible assets with finite useful lives
- The gross carrying amount and any accumulated amortization at the beginning and end of the period
- The aggregate amortization expense for the current period as well as the estimated aggregate amortization expense for each of the next 5 years
- Any goodwill and the changes in the carrying amount of the goodwill, including goodwill acquired, goodwill impaired, and the goodwill that was included in a disposal of a reporting unit for each period presented.[24]

We present a sample of an intangible assets footnote from ***AT&T Inc.'s*** 2016 annual report in Exhibit 11.5. In Note 1, ***AT&T*** indicated that it amortizes customer lists and relationships using an accelerated (sum-of-the-months-digits) method that reflects the expectation that higher revenues will be generated earlier in the relationships with customers. ***AT&T*** uses the straight-line method for other finite-life intangibles.

In Note 7, ***AT&T*** provides a tabular reconciliation of the changes in goodwill balances. Increases in goodwill are due to acquisitions in both years. Notice that ***AT&T*** acquired $35,517 million and $481 million of the total goodwill in 2015 and 2016, respectively. Decreases are primarily due to the sale of businesses and impairments. ***AT&T*** also includes the gross carrying value (acquisition cost) and accumulated amortization balances for each class of finite-life intangibles (primarily customer lists and relationships). Finally, note that the carrying value of indefinite-life intangibles other than goodwill includes licenses and trade names.

EXHIBIT 11.5 Intangible Asset Disclosures, ***AT&T Inc.***, Annual Report, December 31, 2016

NOTE 1: Significant Accounting Policies

Goodwill and Other Intangible Assets AT&T has five major classes of intangible assets: goodwill; licenses, which include Federal Communications Commission (FCC) licenses and other wireless licenses and orbital slots; other indefinite-lived intangible assets, primarily made up of the AT&T and international DIRECTV trade names including SKY; customer lists and various other finite-lived intangible assets (see Note 7).

Goodwill represents the excess of consideration paid over the fair value of net assets acquired in business combinations. Wireless licenses (including FCC licenses) provide us with the exclusive right to utilize certain radio frequency spectrum to provide wireless communications services. While FCC licenses are issued for a fixed period of time (generally 10 years), renewals of FCC licenses have occurred routinely and at nominal cost. Moreover, we have determined that there are currently no legal, regulatory, contractual, competitive, economic or other factors that limit the useful lives of our wireless licenses. Orbital slots represent the space in which we operate the broadcast satellites that support our digital video entertainment service offerings. Similar to our wireless licenses, there are no factors that limit the useful lives of our orbital slots. We acquired the rights to the AT&T and other trade names in previous acquisitions. We have the effective ability to retain these exclusive rights permanently at a nominal cost.

. . .

Intangible assets that have finite useful lives are amortized over their useful lives (see Note 7). Customer lists and relationships are amortized using primarily the sum-of-the-months-digits method of amortization over the period in which those relationships are expected to contribute to our future cash flows. The remaining finite-lived intangible assets are generally amortized using the straight-line method.

Continued

[24] Accounting for goodwill impairment is discussed in Chapter 12.

NOTE 7: GOODWILL AND OTHER INTANGIBLE ASSETS

The following table sets forth the changes in the carrying amounts of goodwill by segment, which is the same as reporting unit for Business Solutions, Entertainment Group and Consumer Mobility. The International segment has three reporting units: Mexico Wireless, Brazil, and PanAmericana.

	Business Solutions	Entertainment Group	Consumer Mobility	International	Wireless	Wireline	Total
Balance as of December 31, 2014	$ —	$ —	$ —	$ —	$36,469	$ 33,223	$ 69,692
Goodwill acquired		30,839	—	4,672	6	—	35,517
Foreign currency translation adjustments	—	—	—	(638)	—	—	(638)
Allocation of goodwill	45,351	7,834	16,512	—	(36,471)	(33,226)	—
Other	—	—	—	(2)	(4)	3	(3)
Balance as of December 31, 2015	45,351	38,673	16,512	4,032	—	—	104,568
Goodwill acquired	22	380	14	65	—	—	481
Foreign currency translation adjustments	—	—	—	167	—	—	167
Other	(9)	—	—	—	—	—	(9)
Balance as of December 31, 2016	**$45,364**	**$39,053**	**$16,526**	**$4,264**	**$ —**	**$ —**	**$105,207**

Our other intangible assets are summarized as follows:

	December 31, 2016			December 31, 2015		
Other Intangible Assets	**Gross Carrying Amount**	**Currency Translation Adjustment**	**Accumulated Amortization**	**Gross Carrying Amount**	**Currency Translation Adjustment**	**Accumulated Amortization**
Amortized Intangible assets:						
Customer lists and relationships:						
Wireless acquisitions	**$ 942**	**$ —**	**$ 715**	$ 1,055	$ —	$ 679
BellSouth Corporation	**4,450**	—	**4,429**	4,450		4,347
DIRECTV	**19,547**	**(125)**	**5,618**	19,505	(294)	1,807
AT&T Corp.	**33**	—	**26**	33	—	23
Mexican wireless	**506**	**(108)**	**214**	485	(60)	110
Subtotal	25,478	(233)	11,002	25,528	(354)	6,966
Trade name	**2,942**	**(7)**	**1,394**	2,905	—	424
Other	**707**	**(3)**	**283**	686	—	195
Total	**$29,127**	**$(243)**	**$12,679**	$ 29,119	$(354)	$ 7,585
Indefinite-lived intangible assets not subject to amortization:						
Licenses						
Wireless licenses	$ 82,474			$81,147		
Orbital slots	11,702			11,946		
Trade name	6,479			6,437		
Total	$100,655			$99,530		

Source: AT&T Inc., Annual Report, December 31, 2016. https://www.att.com/Investor/ATT_Annual/2016/downloads/att_ar2016_completeannualreport.pdf

IFRS Intangible Asset Disclosure

IFRS requires that a company disclose significant classes of intangible assets. Firms must distinguish between internally generated intangible assets and other intangible assets, including the historical cost and accumulated amortization at the beginning and the end of the period. Further, the company must provide a reconciliation of the carrying amount at the beginning of the period to the end of the period.

For each class, the company should also identify whether the useful lives are indefinite or finite and, if finite, the useful lives and amortization methods used.

FINANCIAL STATEMENT ANALYSIS

Long-Term Fixed Assets

Long-term operating assets generate income and cash flows over many years, making them some of the most significant assets for many companies. Consequently, it is important to understand and analyze a company's investments in long-term fixed assets. In this section, we focus on the analysis of long-term fixed assets.[25]

Analyzing long-term fixed assets requires applying techniques discussed in earlier chapters, such as assessing the percent of long-term fixed assets to total assets or determining the change in long-term fixed assets during the year. Specific ratios for long-term fixed assets include:

- *Average age*
- *Average remaining life*
- *Fixed asset turnover*

The average age and average remaining life of long-term fixed assets provide information useful in evaluating a company's current long-term fixed assets and the need for potential future investments. If a company has older assets, it will likely need to invest to replace them in the near future. Investments in long-term fixed assets decrease future investing cash flows. If the company does not continue to invest in its income-generating assets, then net income and cash flow could decrease in the future.

New fixed assets likely employ the most recent technology and are more efficient than older assets. Consequently, a company with new assets may have a competitive advantage compared to another company that has not invested in new assets. Therefore, it is important for the statement user to be able to estimate the age of a company's plant assets and approximate when replacement becomes necessary.

The *average age* and *average remaining life* provide complementary indicators of a fixed asset's age. The **average age** of a company's assets is computed as the amount of accumulated depreciation divided by depreciation expense. The **average remaining life** is computed as the balance of ending net fixed assets divided by depreciation expense.

$$\text{Average Age} = \frac{\text{Accumulated Depreciation}}{\text{Depreciation Expense}} \tag{11.11}$$

and

$$\text{Average Remaining Life} = \frac{\text{Ending Net Fixed Assets}}{\text{Depreciation Expense}} \tag{11.12}$$

These ratios enable comparisons of a company to itself over time, comparisons of two competing companies, or comparisons of a company to its industry. We can also compare the average age to the average remaining life. A higher average age compared to the average remaining life indicates that more of an asset's productive capacity has been used up than is left to use, suggesting a need to re-invest in long-term fixed assets in the near future.

The *fixed asset turnover ratio* reveals how well a company is using its fixed assets to generate revenues. The **fixed asset turnover ratio** is computed as total revenues divided by a company's average net fixed assets. The ratio provides the amount of revenues generated for each dollar of investment in fixed assets.

$$\text{Fixed Asset Turnover Ratio} = \frac{\text{Total Revenues}}{\text{Average Net Fixed Assets}} \tag{11.13}$$

[25] The main financial statement analysis issue related to intangible assets is potential impairment, which we discuss in the next chapter.

Financial Statement Analysis, continued

Average net fixed assets is used as the base in the denominator under the assumption that the firm earns revenues evenly over the year on the fixed assets it employs. Firms compute average net fixed assets as:

$$\text{Average Net Fixed Assets} = \frac{\text{Beginning Net Fixed Assets} + \text{Ending Net Fixed Assets}}{2} \quad (11.14)$$

A high fixed asset turnover ratio indicates that a company is generating a large amount of revenue for each dollar invested in fixed assets.

There are a number of caveats when using the long-term fixed asset ratios:

1. The age ratios focus on depreciable assets. Net fixed assets, then, should exclude land and construction in process. Fixed asset turnover can include or exclude land and construction in process, so it is important to note whether they are included.
2. Long-term fixed assets are composed of different types of assets, often with different useful lives. However, most companies disclose total depreciation expense, accumulated depreciation, and net fixed assets. Thus, we can analyze only the total amounts. Asset composition changes could lead to differences in the ratios.

Example 11.24 illustrates using these financial statement analysis tools to analyze long-lived assets.

EXAMPLE 11.24 Financial Statement Analysis of Long-Term Fixed Assets

PROBLEM: Use ***AT&T's*** disclosures in Exhibit 11.4 and the following additional information to answer the following questions on ***AT&T's*** long-term fixed assets.

(Dollars in Millions)	2016	2015
Average net fixed assets	$124,675	$118,674
Total assets	403,821	402,672
Total revenues	163,786	146,801

a. What is the percent of ***AT&T's*** long-term fixed tangible assets to total assets in 2016 and 2015? In the definition of long-term fixed tangible assets, include the total of ***AT&T's*** property, plant, and equipment (PPE) – net. Comment on any changes from year to year.

b. Compute average age and average remaining life for 2016 and 2015. Comment on any changes from year to year.

c. Compute fixed asset turnover in 2016 and 2015. In the definition of long-term fixed tangible assets (fixed assets), include the total of ***AT&T's*** property, plant, and equipment (PPE) – net. Comment on any changes from year to year.

SOLUTION:

a. We compute the percent of long-term fixed tangible assets to total assets as follows:

(Dollars in Millions)	2016	2015
PPE – Net	$124,899	$124,450
Total assets	403,821	402,672
Percent PPE – Net to total assets	30.9%	30.9%

The percent of long-term fixed tangible assets to total assets is 30.9% each year.

Financial Statement Analysis, continued

b. We compute average asset age and remaining life as follows:
Average Age:

(Dollars in Millions)	2016	2015
Accumulated Depreciation	$194,749	$181,777
divided by Depreciation Expense	÷ 20,661	÷ 19,289
Average age (in years)	9.4	9.4

Average Remaining Life:

	2016	2015
PPE – Cost	$ 319,648	$306,227
Less: Land	(1,643)	(1,638)
Less: Construction	(5,118)	(5,971)
Subtotal	$ 312,887	$298,618
Less: Accumulated depreciation	(194,749)	(181,777)
PPE (excluding land and construction) – Net	$118,138	$116,841
divided by Depreciation Expense	÷ 20,661	÷ 19,289
Average remaining life (in years)	5.7	6.1

The average age of 9.4 years remained the same in 2016 and 2015. The average remaining life decreased to 5.7 in 2016 from 6.1 and 2015. Also note that the average age is higher than the average remaining life, indicating that more of the assets' productive capacity has been used up than is left to use.

c. We compute the fixed asset turnover ratios as follows:

	2016	2015
Total Revenues	$163,786	$ 146,801
divided by Average Net Fixed Assets	÷ $124,675	÷ $ 118,674
Fixed asset turnover	1.31	1.24

The fixed asset turnover ratios indicate that ***AT&T*** generates $1.31 in revenues for each dollar invested in fixed assets in 2016. The fixed asset turnover ratio increased slightly from 2015 to 2016, indicating that fixed assets are generating increased revenue.

Summary by Learning Objectives

Below we summarize this chapter's main points by learning objective. Throughout the chapter, we discuss the accounting and reporting of U.S. GAAP and IFRS side-by-side. The table below also highlights the major similarities and differences between the standards.

Summary by Learning Objectives, continued

1 Identify the types of property, plant, and equipment and determine the initial measurement of each; apply the definition of an asset to the decision to expense or capitalize an expenditure.

Summary	Similarities and Differences between U.S. GAAP and IFRS
There are three necessary characteristics for property, plant, and equipment: 1. Asset is tangible. 2. Asset is expected to be used for more than 1 year (or more than one operating cycle). 3. Asset is used in the production and sale of other assets, for rental to others, or for administrative purposes. Types of PPE include land, plant, equipment, and buildings. Acquisition cost includes the costs necessary to bring the asset to the location and condition for its intended use. If an expenditure is not necessary to bring the asset to this location and condition, the firm should include the expenditure in expenses. Firms can capitalize interest as part of the acquisition cost on assets constructed or otherwise produced for the firm's own use. The amount of interest capitalized is based on the weighted-average accumulated expenditures for the accounting period.	➤ Similar under U.S. GAAP and IFRS except for the following items relating to interest capitalization.
Two interest rates are used to determine the amount of interest to capitalize. 1. For specific borrowings: The interest rate incurred on specific borrowings. 2. For general debt: The weighted average interest rate of all other outstanding debt during the period applies to the amount of the weighted-average accumulated expenditures that is higher than the amount borrowed specifically to finance the construction of the asset. Interest costs can be capitalized from the time of the initial expenditure to the time the asset is ready for its intended use. Income from the temporary investment of specific borrowings does not reduce capitalized interest.	The two interest rates are applied differently under IFRS: 1. For specific borrowings, all borrowing costs related to a loan obtained specifically to acquire or construct the asset are capitalized. 2. For general debt, firms use the weighted-average accumulated expenditures to determine interest to capitalize. Additionally, income from the temporary investment of specific borrowings reduces capitalized borrowing costs.

2 Demonstrate the accounting for property, plant, and equipment subsequent to acquisition, including subsequent expenditures and depreciation.

Summary	Similarities and Differences between U.S. GAAP and IFRS
Depreciation is the systematic and rational allocation of the cost of a long-term plant asset to expense over the asset's expected useful life. Companies choose a useful life, scrap value, and depreciation method. Common depreciation methods include: • Straight-line – depreciation expense is determined as the asset's depreciable base (cost less salvage value) over its useful life. • Units-of-output – depreciation expense is the depreciable base (cost less salvage value) divided by the estimated total units of output times the actual number of units produced each period. • Double-declining balance – depreciation expense is determined as a constant rate against a declining net book value. The constant rate used in the double- declining balance method is two times the straight-line rate. Companies capitalize subsequent expenditures that provide probable future benefit. Other expenditures are included in net income for the current period.	➤ Similar under U.S. GAAP and IFRS except that IFRS requires firms to apply depreciation to components.

Summary by Learning Objectives, continued

3 Determine and illustrate the appropriate accounting for asset derecognition of property, plant, and equipment, including sales and abandonments.

Summary	Similarities and Differences between U.S. GAAP and IFRS
Companies recognize a gain or loss on the income statement upon sale or abandonment of long-term operating assets. The gain or loss is measured as the difference between sales proceeds received and the carrying value of the asset.	Similar under U.S. GAAP and IFRS.

4 Identify required disclosures for property, plant, and equipment.

Summary	Similarities and Differences between U.S. GAAP and IFRS
Common disclosures include: 1. Balances of depreciable assets by major classes at end of fiscal year 2. Accumulated depreciation on property, plant, and equipment at end of fiscal year 3. A general description of the method or methods the firm used in computing depreciation 4. The amount of depreciation expense for the period	➤ Similar under U.S. GAAP and IFRS except that IFRS has more detailed disclosure requirements, such as reconciliations of beginning to ending account balances.

5 Specify the characteristics and types of intangible assets.

Summary	Similarities and Differences between U.S. GAAP and IFRS
The two general classes of intangible assets are finite life (also referred to as definite life) and indefinite life. Goodwill is an indefinite-life asset.	Similar under U.S. GAAP and IFRS.

6 Determine and illustrate the initial measurement of different types of intangible assets, including internally generated intangibles, intangibles acquired individually or in a group, intangibles acquired in a business combination, and research and development costs.

Summary	Similarities and Differences between U.S. GAAP and IFRS
Intangible assets can be internally generated, acquired individually or with a group of other assets, or acquired in a business acquisition. Initial measurement depends on how the firm acquired the intangible asset. For internally generated intangibles, the firm recognizes only expenditures such as direct costs for legal fees as intangible assets. For acquired intangibles through an asset purchase or business acquisition, the firm capitalizes the intangible.	➤ Similar under U.S. GAAP and IFRS except that U.S. GAAP requires all research and development costs to be expensed. IFRS requires development phase costs to be capitalized.

Summary by Learning Objectives, continued

7 Demonstrate accounting for intangible assets subsequent to acquisition, including amortization and derecognition.	
Summary	**Similarities and Differences between U.S. GAAP and IFRS**
Finite-life intangibles are subject to amortization, similar to depreciation of tangible long-term assets. The most common amortization method is straight line. Companies recognize a gain or loss on the income statement upon disposal of an intangible asset. The gain or loss is measured as the difference between sales proceeds received and the carrying value of the asset.	Similar under U.S. GAAP and IFRS.

8 Detail required disclosures for intangible assets.	
Summary	**Similarities and Differences between U.S. GAAP and IFRS**
Common disclosures include: 1. Amounts of indefinite-life and finite-life intangible assets 2. For intangible assets subject to amortization, the average amortization period in total and by major intangible asset class 3. The carrying amount in total and for each major intangible class at beginning and end of period 4. The aggregate amortization expense for the current period as well as the estimated aggregate amortization expense for each of the next 5 years 5. Changes in the carrying amount of goodwill, including goodwill acquired, goodwill impaired, and goodwill that was included in a disposal 6. Accumulated amortization in total and for each major asset class at beginning and end of period 7. Amortization methods used for finite-life intangible assets	➤ Similar under U.S. GAAP and IFRS except that IFRS has more detailed disclosure requirements, such as reconciliations of beginning to ending account balances.

MyLab Accounting

Go to **http://www.pearson.com/mylab/accounting** for the following Questions, Multiple-Choice Questions, Brief Exercises, Exercises, and Problems. They are available with immediate grading, explanations of correct and incorrect answers, and interactive media that acts as your own online tutor.

11 Long-Term Operating Assets: Acquisition, Cost Allocation, and Derecognition

Questions

1 **Q11-1.** Is an asset required to have a finite life to be classified as a long-term operating asset?

1 **Q11-2.** Do managers capitalize expenditures that they believe have future economic benefits? Why or why not?

1 **Q11-3.** What should the total acquisition cost of a long-lived operating asset include?

1 **Q11-4.** What is included in an asset's acquisition cost?

1 **Q11-5.** Will the expense/capitalization choice impact asset valuation, income measurement, and total cash flows?

1 **Q11-6.** Can firms combine the cost of acquiring land and land improvements in a single "land" account on the balance sheet? Explain.

1 **Q11-7.** Should firms value multiple assets acquired in a lump-sum purchase separately? Explain.

1 **Q11-8.** For a long-lived operating asset acquired by issuing a note payable, do firms measure the initial carrying value of the asset by the face value of the note? Explain.

1 **Q11-9.** Does a firm acquiring a long-lived operating asset by issuing a note payable record the finance charges and asset value separately? Explain.

1 **Q11-10.** Does a firm always measure the amount of interest capitalized by multiplying the weighted-average accumulated expenditures by the firm's weighted-average interest rate? Explain.

1 **Q11-11.** What is the maximum amount of interest to be capitalized?

1 **Q11-12.** What is the maximum amount of interest to be capitalized under IFRS?

1 **Q11-13.** If borrowed funds are idle and invested in income-generating investments, is interest to be capitalized reduced by the amount of interest earned?

1 **Q11-14.** Under IFRS, if borrowed funds are idle and invested in income-generating investments, can firms reduce interest to be capitalized by the amount of interest earned?

1 **Q11-15.** Do assets under construction for a company's own use qualify for interest cost capitalization? Explain.

2 **Q11-16.** Do firms expense all costs incurred after the acquisition of a long-lived operating asset? Why or why not?

2 **Q11-17.** After a firm determines an asset's useful life and salvage value, can they be changed? Explain.

2 **Q11-18.** What is the carrying value of a long-lived asset?

2 **Q11-19.** When using the double-declining balance depreciation method, will the ending net book value of a plant asset equal the planned scrap value? Explain.

2 **Q11-20.** Under IFRS, when depreciating an asset, do managers have to estimate the useful life and salvage value for all components of the asset? Explain.

3 **Q11-21.** Will a firm recognize a loss on the income statement if a plant asset is either abandoned or damaged by a casualty?

3 **Q11-22.** How do you calculate a gain or loss on the sale of a plant asset?

5 **Q11-23.** Does an intangible asset have a finite or indefinite life? Explain.

5 **Q11-24.** Why is the leasehold account an intangible asset?

5 **Q11-25.** Distinguish between a tangible and an intangible asset.

5 **Q11-26.** Differentiate between a leasehold and a leasehold improvement.

5 **Q11-27.** What is an indefinite-life intangible asset?

5 **Q11-28.** What is a finite-life intangible asset?

5 **Q11-29.** What is the intangible-asset goodwill?

6 **Q11-30.** How can intangible assets pose some significant valuation problems? Does the determination of useful life for an intangible asset pose a valuation problem? Explain.

6 **Q11-31.** Do firms initially record internally created intangibles at cost?

6 **Q11-32.** How do firms record the gain from a bargain purchase?

6 **Q11-33.** What is goodwill and how is it recorded?

6 **Q11-34.** When can a company report goodwill?

6 **Q11-35.** When can a company capitalize research and development costs?

6 **Q11-36.** What is acquired in-process research and development and how is it recorded?

7 **Q11-37.** How do companies select the method of amortization for finite-life intangible assets?

7 **Q11-38.** Does legal life take precedence over the economic life when amortizing a finite-life intangible asset? Explain.

7 **Q11-39.** Do all intangible assets require amortization? Why or why not?

8 **Q11-40.** Are all intangibles reported in a single line on the balance sheet? Explain.

A **Q11-41.** In a nonmonetary exchange, does a firm record the new asset acquired at the book value of the asset given up in the transaction? Explain.

A **Q11-42.** When can a firm recognize a gain on a nonmonetary exchange?

A **Q11-43.** When can an IFRS-reporting firm recognize a gain on a nonmonetary exchange?

B **Q11-44.** How does a company record natural resources?

B **Q11-45.** Explain the accounting for exploration costs associated with natural resources.

Multiple-Choice Questions

In partnership with: BECKER PROFESSIONAL EDUCATION

Becker CPA Exam Review multiple-choice questions are available in MyLab Accounting.

1 **MC11-1.** On June 30, Year 1, Bluebird Inc. purchased a $750,000 tract of land for a new regional office. Costs related to purchasing the property and preparing the land for construction included:

Legal fees	$ 32,000
Title guarantee insurance	15,000
Cost to clear timber from land	18,000
Proceeds from sale of timber	7,000
Excavation costs for office building	20,000

In its December 30, Year 1, balance sheet, Boyd should report a balance in the land account of:

a. $797,000 b. $808,000 c. $815,000 d. $828,000

1 **MC11-2.** On January 1, Year 1, Bluebird Inc. borrowed $10 million at a rate of 9% for 5 years and began construction of its new regional office building. Bluebird has no other debt. During Year 1, Bluebird's weighted-average accumulated construction expenditures totaled $3,750,000. What should Bluebird report as interest expense on its income statement for Year 1?

a. $337,500 b. $500,000 c. $562,500 d. $900,000

2 **MC11-3.** Lavery Company purchased a machine that was installed and placed in service on July 1, Year 1, at a cost of $240,000. Salvage value was estimated at $40,000. The machine is being depreciated over 10 years by the double-declining balance method. For the year ended December 31, Year 2, what amount should Lavery report as depreciation expense?

a. $48,000 b. $38,400 c. $32,000 d. $43,200

3 **MC11-4.** Visual Graphics Company sold a printing press for $74,000 on the last day of the reporting period. The printing press had a gross and net amount of $100,000 and $65,000, respectively, reflected on the balance sheet at that date. Which of the following is the journal entry made by the company to reflect this asset sale?

a.	Cash	74,000	
	Printing Equipment		65,000
	Gain on Sale		9,000
b.	Cash	74,000	
	Accumulated Depreciation	35,000	
	Printing Equipment		100,000
	Gain on Sale		9,000
c.	Cash	74,000	
	Printing Equipment		65,000
	Gain on Sale		9,000
d.	Accumulated Depreciation	65,000	
	Printing Equipment		35,000
	Gain on Sale		30,000

6 **MC11-5.** Holly Company incurred research and development costs in Year 1 as follows:

Equipment acquired for use in various R&D projects	$ 400,000
Depreciation on the above equipment	60,000
Materials used	100,000
Compensation costs of personnel	200,000
Fees to outside consulting firms	70,000
Indirect costs appropriately allocated	100,000

The total research and development expense in Holly 's Year 1 income statement under U.S. GAAP should be:
a. $930,000 b. $870,000 c. $530,000 d. $470,000

6 **MC11-6.** Hi-Tech Corp. spent $300,000 on research and development to generate new product lines. Only one of the five product lines resulted in a patented item, and the remaining four were considered unsuccessful. Under U.S. GAAP, how much of the $300,000 should be recognized as an expense?
a. $300,000 b. $240,000 c. $60,000 d. $0

6 **MC11-7.** Hi-Tech Corp. spent $300,000 on research and development to generate new product lines. Only one of the five product lines resulted in a patented item; the remaining four were considered unsuccessful. The cost of the product that was successfully patented included $30,000 in research costs and $40,000 in development costs. Under IFRS, how much of the $300,000 should be recognized as an expense?
a. $300,000 b. $270,000 c. $260,000 d. $230,000

A **MC11-8.** Pate paid $50,000 and gave a plot of undeveloped land with a carrying amount of $320,000 and a fair value of $450,000 to Bizzell Co. in exchange for a plot of undeveloped land with a fair value of $500,000. The land was carried on Bizzell's books at $350,000. The exchange is one that has commercial substance under U.S. GAAP. At what amount is the land received from Pate recorded on Bizzell's books?
a. $370,000 b. $320,000 c. $500,000 d. $450,000

Brief Exercises

1 **BE11-1. Determining Acquisition Cost.** Haply, Inc. incurred the following expenditures when acquiring a new assembly machine:

Price	$175,000
Sales tax	10,500
Delivery charges	1,000
Installation cost	2,500

Additionally, Haply sold its old assembly machine for $500. What is the acquisition cost of the new assembly machine?

1 **BE11-2. Determining Acquisition Cost.** Tarpley, Inc. acquired land for $400,000. The closing costs amounted to $11,000, and the firm paid $7,250 for the current period's property taxes at the end of the year. Tarpley plans to build a new storage facility on the land costing $2,350,000. To prepare for construction on the new facility, Tarpley removed an old storage building at a cost of $23,000 and acquired building permits for $2,500. What is the acquisition cost of the land?

1 **BE11-3. Determining Acquisition Cost in a Basket Purchase.** Holman Enterprises acquired three different pieces of furniture and equipment for its newly renovated office. The bulk purchase from Wonder Technologies, Inc. included the following assets and corresponding retail prices: office furniture, $1,800; an integrated telephone system, $3,700; and a desktop computer system, $4,500. Wonder charged a bulk price of $6,000. Determine the value assigned to each asset.

1 **BE11-4. Determining Acquisition Cost for an Asset Acquired in Exchange for a Note Payable.** Assume that Springfield Foods, Inc. acquired a custom-made refrigeration system by issuing a $1,500,000, 10-year, non-interest-bearing note payable at a time when the market interest rate for similar debt instruments was 5%. The asset and the note do not have a readily determinable fair value. Prepare the journal entry required to record Springfield's purchase of the refrigeration system.

1 **BE11-5. Capitalization of Interest, Specific Debt**. Mariah Corporation is constructing a new wind power-generating facility. Construction began on January 2 and was completed on December 31 of the current year. Mariah made the following expenditures during the year:

Date	Amount
January 2	$ 500,000
August 1	400,000
October 1	1,200,000
December 1	100,000

To specifically finance the project, Mariah issued $2,200,000 of 2-year, 8% notes payable on January 2. Interest is payable annually on December 31 each year. It earned interest income of $3,000 from investing the proceeds of the note during the year. What amount of interest can Mariah capitalize during the year?

1 **BE11-6. Capitalization of Interest, Specific Debt, IFRS.** Repeat BE11-5 assuming that Mariah Corporation reports under IFRS.

2 **BE11-7. Determining Acquisition Cost, Repairs, and Maintenance.** Circle City Transportation made the following expenditures for its fleet during the current year: oil changes, $2,000; filter changes, $5,000; tire rotations, $3,000; engine overhauls, $15,000; and retrofitting vehicles to function as party buses, $40,000. Prepare the journal entry or entries necessary to record Circle's activities. Assume that all expenditures are paid in cash. Assume that the overhauls extend the assets' lives.

2 **BE11-8. Determining Acquisition Cost, Repairs, and Maintenance.** Flowers Corp. owns a delivery truck it acquired for $57,000 last year. During the current year, it added shelving, costing $2,800, to the truck to expand its delivery capacity. It also purchased a new set of tires costing $1,200 and seat covers (replaced annually) for $110. Which current-year costs are capitalized? Which current-year costs are expensed?

2 **BE11-9. Depreciation, Straight-Line Method.** Hermit Associates acquired a machine on January 1 at a cost of $250,000. Hermit estimates that the machine has a useful life of 10 years and a $50,000 residual value. Compute the depreciation expense for the first 2 years and determine the net book value at the end of the second year assuming that the straight-line method is used.

2 **BE11-10. Depreciation, Units-of-Output Method.** Using the data from BE11-9, compute the depreciation expense for the first 2 years and determine the net book value at the end of the second year (assume that Hermit Associates uses the units-of-output depreciation method). The machine's total output is expected to be 100,000 units. Actual output during Year 1 was 12,000 units. Actual output during Year 2 was 8,000 units.

2 **BE11-11. Depreciation, Double-Declining Balance Method.** Using the data from BE11-9, compute the depreciation expense for the first 2 years and determine the net book value at the end of the second year assuming that Hermit Associates uses the double-declining balance method.

2 **BE11-12. Depreciation, Straight-Line Method, Component Method, IFRS.** Using the data from BE11-9, compute the depreciation for the first 2 years and determine the net book value at the end of the second year assuming that Hermit Associates is an IFRS reporter that identifies the casing and engine as significant components of the machine. Attribute $100,000 of the cost to the casing, which has an estimated useful life of 12 years and a $30,000 residual value. Attribute the remaining $150,000 cost to the engine, which Hermit estimates to have a useful life of 8 years and a $20,000 residual value. Assume that the straight-line method is used.

2 **BE11-13. Depreciation, Straight-Line Method, Partial Year.** Kobas Kookies, Inc. acquired an oven for its baking operations on June 10 of the current year at a total cost of $384,000. It estimates that the oven has a 16-year useful life with no scrap value. Assume that Kobas uses the half-month convention by which depreciation expense is taken for one-half of the month regardless of when the asset is purchased during the month. The firm's year-end is December 31. Compute the depreciation expense for the first 2 years using the straight-line method.

3 **BE11-14. Derecognition Due to Abandonment.** Greene Corp. updated its fleet of trucks, scrapping old gas-guzzling trucks for new hybrid vehicles. It took its old trucks to the scrap yard and received $0. The fleet of trucks scrapped originally cost $190,000 and their current carrying value is $24,000. What is the entry to record the abandonment?

5 6 **BE11-15. Types of Intangibles.** For each intangible asset listed below, identify whether it is typically a finite-life intangible asset, an indefinite-life intangible asset, or other.

Intangible Asset	Finite-Life, Indefinite-Life, or Other
Advertising	__________
Copyrights	__________
Customer lists	__________
Development costs	__________
Leasehold improvements	__________
Leaseholds	__________
Limited-Term franchises	__________
Patents	__________
Renewable licenses (broadcasting)	__________
Renewable permits	__________
Research costs	__________
Trade names	__________
Trademarks	__________

6 **BE11-16. Intangibles Acquired in a Group**. Chalko Candy Corporation purchased the trademark for the popular Yummm Candy Bar from the YumYum Company. At the same time, Chalko also purchased YumYum's customer list. Chalko paid the total purchase price of $750,000 in cash. Chalko's valuation consultants independently estimate the value of the trademark to be $312,000 and customer list to be $468,000. What is the journal entry to record the purchase?

6 **BE11-17. Acquired Goodwill.** On January 1, Buckingham Brothers acquired 100% of Julian Systems for $12,000,000. The book value of Julian's net assets on the date of acquisition was $7,000,000. However, a detailed appraisal of Julian's net assets revealed that its net assets were undervalued by $1,000,000. Determine the amount of goodwill or gain from a bargain purchase to be recorded on the acquisition and indicate where it should be reported on the consolidated financial statements.

6 **BE11-18. Bargain Purchase.** Repeat the requirements of BE11-17 assuming that the acquisition cost was $7,000,000.

6 **BE11-19. Research and Development Expenditures.** Dimension Pharmaceuticals paid cash for the following to fund its research activities: testing materials and supplies, $600,000; research consultants, $100,000; planning and design consultants, $135,000; and general-purpose laboratory equipment, $950,000. The equipment has a 10-year useful life and no residual value. Prepare the journal entry required to record Dimension's research expenditures for the year. The equipment was acquired on January 1.

6 **BE11-20. Research and Development Expenditures, IFRS**. Use the same information in BE11-19 and assume that Dimension Pharmaceuticals is an IFRS reporter. Prepare the journal entry required to record Dimension's research expenditures for the year. Assume that projects developed by planning and design consultants meet conditions for capitalization. The equipment was acquired on January 1.

7 **BE11-21. Leasehold Improvements.** At the beginning of its fiscal year, Beau Co. leased office space for a 20-year period. Prior to occupying the office, Beau needed to make renovations costing $750,000 with an expected useful life of 15 years. The renovations are to be recorded as leasehold improvements. Assuming that Beau uses the straight-line method, prepare the journal entry to record the first year's amortization.

Exercises

1 **E11-1. Determining Acquisition Cost.** St. Charles Flooring Company recently purchased a new tile-cutting machine with an invoice price of $215,500. The cost of delivery was $2,000, and installation amounted to $3,550. To test the machine, St. Charles cut 100 tiles that cost $4.50 each. The testing process lasted 2 hours and involved three employees who earn $20 per hour. Management removed the employees from their regular production shifts to engage in the testing. The company held training sessions costing $6,000 for all employees after installing the machine.

Required »

a. Determine the cost of the machine and any expenses incurred during the acquisition.
b. Prepare the journal entries necessary to record the amount of costs capitalized and the costs charged to expense related to the acquisition. Assume that all expenditures were made in cash.

1 **E11-2. Determining Acquisition Cost.** On January 2 of the current year, Vaughn, Inc. acquired land for $2,000,000 to be used to construct a new service and repair center. The closing costs amounted to $110,000, and Vaughn paid $20,000 for the current period's property taxes. There was an existing structure on the land that had been abandoned for several years. Vaughan agreed to remove the building and dispose of any scrap materials. The demolition cost was $67,000, and the company was required to pay $13,800 to remove the debris. Vaughn was able to sell scrap materials for $4,500.

Required »

a. Determine the cost of the land and any expenses incurred during the acquisition.
a. Prepare the journal entries necessary to record the amount of costs capitalized and the costs charged to expense related to the property's acquisition. Assume that all expenditures were made in cash.

1 2 **E11-3. Determining Acquisition Cost in a Basket Purchase, Depreciation.** Sonata Manufacturing Corporation decided to expand its operations and open a new facility in Illinois. Rather than constructing a new plant, Sonata negotiated a contract to purchase an existing facility from a former competitor for a total cost of $5,000,000. The facility included the land, building, machinery and equipment, inventory, and manufacturing supplies. The former competitor was closing its operations and decided to sell the facility at a reduced price as reflected in the fair values of the individual assets acquired.

Description	Fair Value
Building	$3,200,000
Land	1,600,000
Machinery and equipment	864,000
Inventory	183,500
Manufacturing supplies	52,500
Total	$5,900,000

The building has a remaining useful life of 20 years, and Sonata expects the machinery and equipment to be productive for an additional 5 years from the date of acquisition. Sonata uses the straight-line method and does not use residual values when computing depreciation. Sonata accounts for inventory under the FIFO basis and expenses the supplies as consumed in operations.

During the first year after the acquisition, the company sold all inventory acquired for $220,000 in cash and used 60% of the supplies in the production process. Assume that Sonata uses a perpetual inventory system.

Required »

a. Determine the proper allocation of the purchase cost to each of the assets acquired. Round all calculations to two decimal places.
b. Prepare the journal entries necessary to record the acquisition of the assets. Assume that all expenditures were made in cash.
c. Prepare the journal entries necessary to record the depreciation of the building and the machinery and equipment, the sale of inventory, and the use of the manufacturing supplies. Assume that assets were acquired on January 1.

1 **E11-4. Acquiring an Asset with a Note Payable (Deferred Payment Arrangements).** On December 31, 2018, the Clearwater Corporation acquired a custom-made plant asset by issuing a promissory note with a face value of $750,000, a due date of December 31, 2023, and a stated (coupon) rate of interest of 2%. Interest is compounded annually and is payable at the end on each year. The fair value of the customized asset is not readily determinable and the note receivable is not publicly traded. Given the company's incremental borrowing rate and current market conditions, the imputed rate of interest for the note is estimated as 6%.

Determine the present value of the note and prepare the journal entry to record the transaction for Clearwater Corporation.

1 **E11-5. Acquiring an Asset with a Zero Coupon Note Payable (Deferred Payment Arrangements).** Quartech Enterprises manufactures and distributes thermostats for major kitchen appliances. At the beginning of the current year, Quartech decided to expand its operations by acquiring a metal soldering machine. The machine is to be produced by the manufacturer according to Quartech's specifications and does not have a market

outside of this transaction. To finance this purchase, the manufacturer provided Quartech credit and asked the company to issue a 5-year, $800,000 non-interest-bearing note payable. If Quartech borrowed the funds from a commercial bank, it would have incurred a 4% interest rate.

Required »

a. Determine the proper valuation of the machine.
b. Prepare the journal entry to record the acquisition.

1 **E11-6. Capitalization of Interest, Specific and General Debt, Journal Entries.** Rolling Blackout Power Company constructed a new power plant to supply energy to the Northeast Electrical Grid. The construction began on January 2 and ended on December 31 of the current year. On the date of completion, the plant had a total cost of $8,500,000. The weighted-average accumulated expenditures for the year were $4,250,000.

The company had the following debt outstanding for the entire year:

Debt Instrument and Purpose	Amount
8% note payable: Used to finance the power plant construction project	$2,000,000
12% bond payable: Used to finance maintenance of local transmitters	$1,800,000
13% note payable: Used to finance construction of corporate headquarters	$4,200,000

Required »

a. Compute the amount of interest to be capitalized for the current year.
b. Compute the amount of interest to be expensed in the current year.
c. Prepare the journal entry to record the cash interest payments for the current year. Assume that all interest is paid at the end of the year and any interest capitalized is debited to the construction in progress account.

1 **E11-7. Capitalization of Interest, Specific and General Debt, Journal Entries, IFRS.** How would the solution to E11-6 change if Rolling Blackout Power Company was an IFRS reporter and earned $11,000 interest income on investing the excess funds from the construction loan during the year? Prepare the journal entry to record the cash interest payments for the current year.

1 **E11-8. Capitalization of Interest, Specific and General Debt, Computing Weighted-Average Accumulated Expenditures, Journal Entries**. Yawyag Corporation engaged Sir Peter, Inc. to design and construct a manufacturing facility. Construction began on January 2 and was completed on December 31 of the current year. The following payments were made to the contractor during the year:

Date	Amount
January 2	$2,400,000
August 1	1,800,000
October 1	3,600,000
December 1	1,200,000

To specifically finance the project, Yawyag issued $2,800,000 of 3-year, 5% notes payable on January 2. Interest is payable annually on December 31 each year. Prior to the commencement of the latest construction project, Yawyag had other debt in its capital structure. All general debt is outstanding as of the beginning of the current year. The general debt consists of $5,000,000 par value, 6% bonds payable, and a $1,000,000, 9% note payable. Both debt instruments require annual interest payments each December 31.

Required »

a. Compute the weighted-average accumulated expenditures for the current year.
b. Compute the amount of avoidable interest and actual interest cost for the current year.
c. Indicate the amount of total interest to be capitalized and the amount of interest to expense for the year.
d. Prepare the journal entry to record the December 31 interest payments. Assume that the interest is paid in cash and that any interest capitalized is recorded in the Construction in Progress account.

1 **E11-9. Capitalization of Interest, Specific and General Debt, Computing Weighted-Average Accumulated Expenditures, Journal Entries.** Assume that the project in E11-8 was not completed in Year 1. Yawyag was required to make two additional payments to the contractor in Year 2: $900,000 on April 1 and $1,800,000

on August 1 of Year 2. On January 2 of Year 2, Yawyag was required to take out a $2,400,000, 9% line of credit to help finance its operating cycle. The plant was completed on October 1.

Required »

a. Compute the weighted-average accumulated expenditures for the current year.
b. Compute the amount of avoidable interest and actual interest cost for the current year.
c. Indicate the amount of total interest to be capitalized and the amount of interest to expense for the year.
d. Prepare the journal entry to record the December 31 interest payments. Assume that the interest is paid in cash and that any interest capitalized is recorded in the construction in progress account.

❶ **E11-10. Capitalization of Interest, Specific and General Debt, Computing Weighted-Average Accumulated Expenditures, Journal Entries, IFRS.** Assume that the Yawyag Corporation in E11-8 is an IFRS reporter and complete the following:

Required »

a. Compute the weighted-average accumulated expenditures for the current year.
b. Compute the amount of interest related to the construction project and actual interest cost for the current year.
c. Indicate the amount of total interest to be capitalized and the amount of interest expense for the year.
d. Prepare the journal entry to record the December 31 interest payment. Assume that the interest is paid in cash and that any interest capitalized is recorded in the construction in progress account.

❷ **E11-11. Expensing versus Capitalizing Expenditures—Analysis and Journal Entries.** Clave Building Products, Inc. conducts regularly scheduled maintenance of its machinery and equipment every Friday afternoon. The cost of maintenance for the current year amounted to $345,000. The regular maintenance revealed the need to conduct a major overhaul on one of Clave's older pieces of equipment. The firm completed the overhaul this year at a cost of $16,000. In addition, the company installed a new roof on its factory at a total cost of $59,000. Due to increased demand for its products, Clave decided to expand one of its loading docks. The cost of the factory expansion was $187,000. The new roof and overhaul extended the assets' useful lives.

Prepare the journal entry (entries) required to record those transactions. Assume that Clave paid for all expenditures in cash.

❷ **E11-12. Expensing versus Capitalizing Expenditures—Analysis and Journal Entries, IFRS.** Avery Air, Plc, a UK company, conducts regularly scheduled maintenance and improvement of its fleet of airplanes. During the year, it replaced engines at a cost of £2,900,000, upgraded airplane interiors at a cost of £610,000, and spent £1,300,000 on normal repairs and upkeep, including instrument repair and replacement. The new engines will increase an airplane's useful life by 5 years. The new interiors will be used for 3 years before being replaced. Avery depreciates each major airplane component separately.

Prepare the journal entry (entries) required to record those transactions. Assume that all expenditures are paid in cash.

❷❸ **E11-13. Depreciation Methods, Disposal.** Kurtis Koal Company, Inc. purchased a new mining machine at a total cost of $900,000 on the first day of its fiscal year. The firm estimates that the machine has a useful life of 6 years or 6,000,000 tons of coal and a residual value of $60,000 at the end of its useful life. The following schedule indicates the actual number of tons of coal mined with the machine per year:

Year	Tons of Coal
1	700,000
2	1,400,000
3	1,600,000
4	1,000,000
5	750,000
6	550,000

Required »

Prepare the depreciation schedules for the machine assuming that Kurtis Koal used the following methods (each case is independent):

a. Straight-line method.
b. Units-of-output method.
c. Double-declining balance method. (Adjust the depreciation expense in the last year to the necessary amount to arrive at an ending book value equal to the scrap value.)
d. Kurtis Koal sells the mining machine for $450,000 at the end of Year 3. What is the gain or loss on sale under each of the depreciation methods in parts (a)–(c)?

2 3 **E11-14. Depreciation Methods, Disposal, IFRS.** Repeat the requirements in E11-13 assuming that Kurtis Koal Company, Inc. is an IFRS reporter and the mining machine has two components: casing and engine. The amount allocated to the engine is $800,000. The engine has a 6-year useful life and $60,000 salvage value. The amount allocated to the casing is $100,000. The casing has a 10-year useful life and no salvage value. The straight-line method is used.

Required »

a. Prepare the depreciation schedule for the machine.
b. Kurtis Koal sells the mining machine for $450,000 at the end of Year 3. What is the gain or loss on the sale?

2 3 **E11-15. Depreciation Methods, Partial-Year Depreciation.** Repeat the requirements in E11-13 assuming that Kurtis Koal Company, Inc. acquired the asset on August 1 of the current year.

2 3 **E11-16. Depreciation Methods, Partial-Year Depreciation, IFRS.** Repeat the requirements in E11-14 assuming that Kurtis Koal Company, Inc. acquired the asset on August 1 of the current year. Use partial-year depreciation without adopting any of the acceptable conventions that simplify the computation.

2 3 **E11-17. Depreciation Methods.** Ace Manufacturing, Inc. purchased a new piece of manufacturing equipment at a total acquisition cost of $3,000,000 on January 4 of the current year. The firm estimates that the equipment has a useful life of 10 years or 13,250,000 units of output and a residual value of $350,000 at the end of its useful life. The following schedule indicates the actual number of units output with the machine per year:

Year	Units of Output	Year	Units of Output
1	1,600,000	6	1,300,000
2	1,600,000	7	1,200,000
3	1,500,000	8	1,200,000
4	1,500,000	9	1,100,000
5	1,300,000	10	1,100,000

Required »

Prepare the depreciation schedules for the manufacturing equipment assuming that Ace used the following methods (each case is independent):

a. Straight-line method.
b. Units-of-output method.
c. Double-declining balance method. (Reduce the depreciation expense in the last year to the necessary amount to arrive at an ending book value equal to the scrap value.)
d. Ace sells the manufacturing equipment at the end of Year 5 for $1,465,000. What is the gain or loss on sale under each of the depreciation methods in parts (a)–(c)?

2 3 **E11-18. Depreciation Methods, IFRS.** Repeat the requirements in E11-17 assuming that Ace is an IFRS reporter and the manufacturing equipment has two components: computer controls and engine. The amount allocated to the computer controls is $500,000. The computer controls have a 5-year useful life and $0 salvage value. The amount allocated to the engine, which has a 10-year useful life and $250,000 salvage value, is $2,500,000. The straight-line method is used.

Required »

a. Prepare the depreciation schedule for the manufacturing equipment.
b. Ace sells the manufacturing equipment for $1,465,000 at the end of Year 5. What is the gain or loss on the sale?

2 3 **E11-19. Depreciation Methods, Partial-Year Depreciation,** Repeat the requirements in E11-17 assuming that Ace acquired the asset on July 14 of the current year. Use partial-year depreciation assuming that the manufacturing equipment was acquired at the beginning of the month to simplify the computation.

2 3 **E11-20. Depreciation Methods, Partial-Year Depreciation, IFRS.** Repeat the requirements in E11-18 assuming that Ace acquired the asset on July 14 of the current year. Use partial-year depreciation assuming that the manufacturing equipment was acquired at the beginning of the month to simplify the computation.

2 3 **E11-21. Partial-Year Depreciation, Sale of Property, Plant, and Equipment.** The Gemini Group sold one of its plant assets on August 1 of the current year for $200,000. The asset had an original cost of $500,000 and an estimated residual value of $80,000. The firm used the straight-line method of depreciation assuming an estimated useful life of 8 years. The asset was in service for 5 years as of January 1 of the current year.

Required »

a. Prepare the journal entry required to record the depreciation for the current year.
b. Prepare the journal entry required to record the sale of the asset.

2 3 **E11-22. Partial-Year Depreciation, Sale of Property, Plant, and Equipment.** The Aries Group sold one of its plant assets on April 1 of the current year for $250,000. The asset had an original cost of $500,000 and an estimated residual value of $80,000. Aries used the straight-line method of depreciation assuming an estimated useful life of 8 years. The asset was in service for 5 years as of January 1 of the current year.

Required »

a. Prepare the journal entry required to record the depreciation for the current year.
b. Prepare the journal entry required to record the sale of the asset.

4 **E11-23. Disclosure of Property, Plant, and Equipment.** Use the information in E11-13, part (a) to prepare the required footnote disclosure for Kurtis Koal Company, Inc.'s property, plant, and equipment for Years 1 and 2, including a statement of its accounting policy and a table with account balances.

4 **E11-24. Disclosure of Property, Plant, and Equipment, IFRS.** Use the information in E11-14, part (a) to prepare the required footnote disclosure under IFRS for Kurtis Koal Company, Inc.'s property, plant, and equipment for Years 1 and 2, including a statement of its accounting policy and a table with account balances.

6 **E11-25. Goodwill Computation.** On January 2, 2019, Bubba and Company paid $5,000,000 in cash to acquire 100% of the Cire Company's voting common stock. Cire's balance sheet on that date showed the following balances in its accounts:

Cire Company
Balance Sheet
December 31, 2018

Plant and Equipment	$5,574,900
Mortgage Payable	$4,324,900
Stockholders' Equity	1,250,000
Total	$5,574,900

The appraised value of Cire's net assets was $1,400,000 greater than its book value on the date of acquisition.

Required »

a. Compute the amount of goodwill to be recorded on the date of acquisition.
b. How is goodwill accounted for subsequent to the date of acquisition?

6 **E11-26. Research and Development Activities.** During the current year, Carlson Industries, Inc. conducted significant research activities related to the development of a new computer chip. Carlson had the following costs:

Description	Amount
Diagnostic equipment (5-year life, $10,000 residual value, S-L method, purchased January 1)	$ 500,000
Salaries of laboratory technicians	325,000
Testing materials used in experimentation	137,500
Supplies used in the testing process	23,500
Salary for engineer in the design phase of production	87,000
Depreciation expense on research facilities	8,000
Total cost of research activities	$1,081,000

Prepare all journal entries required to record Carlson's R&D activities for the current year.

6 **E11-27. Research and Development Activities, IFRS.** Repeat the requirements in E11-26 assuming that Carlson reports under IFRS. Assume that all the conditions to capitalize development costs have been met and the project is completed on January 1. Capitalized development costs are amortized over 4 years. What is the difference between the research and development expense under U.S. GAAP compared to the expense under IFRS?

6 7 **E11-28.** **Goodwill Computation, Acquisition of Intangibles, Amortization.** Alto Devices acquires Medifast, a small start-up company, by paying $2,170,000 in cash on January 2. Following are the book values and fair values of Medifast on the date of acquisition.

Medifast	Book Value	Fair Value
Cash	$ 36,000	$ 36,000
Receivables	100,437	100,400
Manufacturing equipment	640,275	654,234
Patents (remaining life 10 years)	60,000	854,000
Trademarks	14,652	187,450
Payables	58,902	58,902

Required »

a. What is the amount of goodwill acquired?

b. What intangible assets are acquired? Which of the intangibles have an indefinite life? Which will be amortized? What will the amortization expense be in the year after acquisition?

A **E11-29.** **Exchange of Assets with and without Commercial Substance, Journal Entries.** On January 2, 2018, Temptations Corporation paid $31,500 in cash and exchanged a chocolate mixing machine, which had a fair value of $437,500 and a book value of $500,000 ($1,135,000 historical cost – $635,000 accumulated depreciation brought up to the date of the transaction) for another chocolate mixing machine from Rascals Candy, Inc. The new mixing machine had a fair value of $469,000 and a book value of $380,000 ($1,500,000 – $1,120,000).

Required »

a. Record the journal entry on the books of Temptations Corporation to record the exchange assuming that the transaction altered the economic positions of the parties.

b. Assume that the fair value of the old machine is now estimated at $562,500 and that that new mixing machine had been appraised at $594,000. In addition, the exchange will not materially change the economic positions of the parties to the transaction. Record the journal entry on the books of Temptations Corporation to record the exchange of the machines. All other information remains the same as in part (a).

c. Repeat part (b) on the books of Rascals Candy, Inc.

A **E11-30.** **Exchange of Assets without Commercial Substance, Journal Entries, IFRS.** Assume that Rascals Candy, Inc. reports under IFRS. Repeat the requirement of E11-29, part (c).

A **E11-31.** **Exchange of Plant Assets, Depreciation Adjustment, Journal Entries.** You have been asked to account for a plant asset exchange on the books of the Ecara Video Game Company. On January 1, 2013, Ecara acquired a plastic extruding machine at a cost of $260,000. This machine had an original estimated useful life of 10 years and a scrap value of $20,000. The machine was depreciated using the straight-line method. On August 1, 2018, Ecara exchanged the old machine for a similar asset with a market value of $157,250. Ecara also received cash of $27,750. The estimated fair value of the old machine is $185,000. The old machine was depreciated up to December 31, 2017.

Required »

a. Determine the gain or loss to be recognized on the exchange for Ecara assuming that the exchange has commercial substance after bringing the accumulated depreciation up to the date of the transaction.

b. Prepare all journal entries required on August 1, 2018, for Ecara.

c. Prepare the journal entry for Ecara to record the exchange as if the exchange had lacked commercial substance.

A **E11-32.** **Exchange of Plant Assets, Journal Entries, IFRS.** Assume that the Ecara Video Game Company reports under IFRS. Repeat the requirement of E11-31, part (c).

A **E11-33.** **Exchange with Commercial Substance.** Mercurial Company traded its cutting equipment for the newer air-cooled equipment manufactured by Broad Street Corporation. The air-cooled equipment will increase Mercurial's productivity. The old equipment had a book value of $140,000 (cost of $700,000 less accumulated depreciation of $560,000). Assume that the accumulated depreciation is brought up to the date of the exchange. The old equipment was recently appraised at fair value of $210,000. Mercurial paid Broad Street $602,000 in cash. The new air-cooled equipment had a fair value of $812,000.

Prepare the journal entry to record the exchange on the books of Mercurial Company.

A **E11-34. Exchange Lacks Commercial Substance, Cash Paid.** Doris Company traded a tract of land to Rick's Real Estate for a similar tract of land with no significant effect on future cash flows. The old land had a carrying value of $6,500,000. The land was appraised for $9,000,000. As part of the exchange, Doris paid $3,500,000 in cash.

Prepare the journal entry to record the land exchange on the books of Doris Company.

A **E11-35. Exchange with Commercial Substance: Gain Case.** Clayton Company exchanged a used machine with a book value of $26,000 (cost $54,000 less $28,000 accumulated depreciation) and cash of $8,000 for a delivery truck. The machine is estimated to have a fair market value of $36,000. The cash flows related to the truck will be different from the cash flows generated from the use of the machine.

Prepare the journal entry to record the exchange on the books of Clayton Company.

A **E11-36. Exchange with Commercial Substance: Loss Case.** Clarke Company traded a used mixing machine for a new model. The used machine has a book value of $11,000 (cost $32,000 less $21,000 accumulated depreciation) and a fair market value of $8,000. The new mixing machine has a list price or fair value of $31,000, the seller has allowed a trade-in allowance of $8,000 on the old machine, and Clarke paid the balance, $23,000 ($31,000 − $8,000), in cash.

Prepare the journal entry required to record the exchange on the books of Clarke Company. Assume that the exchange has commercial substance.

A **E11-37. Exchange Lacking Commercial Substance, Cash Paid.** Brown Company contracts with Sebastian Company to exchange refrigerated trucks. Brown Company will trade three SMC trucks for four DROF trucks owned by Sebastian Company. The trucks are approximately the same age and have the same remaining useful lives. The fair value of the SMC trucks is $51,000 with a book value of $38,000 (cost $65,000 − $27,000 accumulated depreciation). The DROF trucks have a fair value of $66,000, and Brown Company gives $15,000 in cash (paid) in addition to the SMC trucks.

Record the transaction on the books of the Brown Company. Assume that the exchange does not have commercial substance.

A **E11-38. Exchanges Lacking Commercial Substance, Cash Received.** Brown Company contracts with Sebastian Company to exchange refrigerated trucks. Brown Company will trade three SMC trucks for four DROF trucks owned by Sebastian Company. The DROF refrigerated trucks have a cost of $100,000 and accumulated depreciation up to the date of the exchange of $52,000. The trucks are approximately the same age and have the same remaining useful lives. The fair value of the SMC trucks is $51,000 with a book value of $38,000 (cost $65,000 less $27,000 accumulated depreciation). The DROF trucks have a fair value of $66,000, and Brown Company gives $15,000 in cash (paid) in addition to the SMC trucks.

Prepare the journal entry to record the exchange on the books of the Sebastian Company. Assume that the exchange does not have commercial substance.

A **E11-39. Exchanges Lacking Commercial Substance, Cash Received, IFRS.** Assume that Sebastian Company from E11-38 reports under IFRS. Prepare the journal entry to record the exchange on the books of Sebastian Company.

B **E11-40. Accounting for Natural Resources, Full-Cost Method.** Ferro Fuel Company (FFC) acquired a tract of land to be used for oil and gas exploration at the beginning of the current year. FFC paid $500,000 to acquire the land, paid $325,000 in development costs, and incurred $130,000 in exploration and evaluation costs for nonproducing wells and $200,000 for a producing well. The asset retirement obligation is estimated at $100,000. The producing well is expected to generate 1,000,000 barrels of oil over its useful life. Assume that all expenditures are paid in cash.

Required »

a. Determine the total cost of the natural resource under the full-cost method.
b. Prepare the journal entries to record the acquisition of the natural resource.
c. Record the depletion of the natural resource at the end of the first year assuming that 145,000 barrels of oil were produced during the first year of operations. Depletion is recorded under the units-of-output method.

B **E11-41. Accounting for Natural Resources, Full-Cost Method.** Repeat the requirements in E11-40 assuming that FFC uses the successful-efforts method.

B **E11-42. Accounting for Natural Resources, Full-Cost Method, Successful-Efforts Method.** Spill Oil Corporation drilled 10 oil wells at the beginning of the current year. The total exploration costs associated with this oil and gas activity amounted to $8,500,000. Only six of the wells were producing; the remaining wells are dry or nonproductive assets. It is estimated that the six successful wells will produce 17,000,000 barrels of oil over their estimated useful life. Assume that all expenditures are paid in cash.

Required »

a. Prepare the journal entry to record the exploration costs assuming that the company uses the full-cost method.
b. Prepare the journal entry to record the exploration costs assuming that the company uses the successful-efforts method.
c. Assuming that 2,000,000 barrels of oil were produced during the current year, prepare the journal entry to record the depletion expense under the units-of-output approach (no residual value) assuming that:
   i. The full-cost method is used.
   ii. The successful-efforts method is used.

Problems

1 **P11-1. Note Payable Exchanged for a Plant Asset (Deferred Payment Arrangement).** Hoppie Products signed a contract with Coleman Manufacturing to design, develop, and produce a specialized plastic molding machine for its factory operations. The machine is not currently sold to the public. Hoppie issued a 3%, 8-year, $690,000 note payable to Coleman to pay for the machine. If Hoppie were required to borrow at a commercial bank to finance the acquisition, it would have incurred the current market rate of 6%. Assume that all transactions occurred at the beginning of the current fiscal year (January 1). Interest is paid at the end of each year.

Required »

a. Prepare the journal entry required to record the asset acquisition.
b. Prepare the amortization table for the note payable.
c. Record the interest expense for the first 2 years.
d. Indicate the effects of these transactions (i.e., the asset acquisition and the interest payment and amortization of discount) on the current year-end balance sheet (ignore cash effects), income statement, and cash flow statement under the direct and indirect methods.
e. Independent of parts (a)–(d), assume that the molding machine is sold to the general public on a regular basis and has a fair value of $560,000. Prepare the journal entry to record the acquisition of the machine from Coleman.

1 **P11-2. Capitalization of Interest, Specific and General Debt, Computing Weighted-Average Accumulated Expenditures, U.S. GAAP.** On January 1, 2018, Union Power and Light commenced construction of a new generating plant to serve the northeast corridor of the state. The total cost of the project is $4,100,000, and it will be completed on June 1, 2019. Scheduled payments to contractors are summarized in the following table.

Date	Amount Paid
January 1, 2018	$ 950,000
April 1, 2018	300,000
July 1, 2018	1,200,000
Total 2018	$2,450,000
February 1, 2019	$1,150,000
April 1, 2019	500,000
Total 2019	$1,650,000
Total expenditures	$4,100,000

To finance the project, Union Power obtained a bank loan on January 1, 2018, for $1,800,000 at 10% interest. Union's other general (or indirect) outstanding debt during 2018 and 2019 includes the following:

General Debt	Amount
7% note	$1,000,000
9% note	3,500,000
6% bonds	2,000,000
Total	$6,500,000

All debt was issued at par and is outstanding for the full year. Interest for all debt is paid on December 31.

Required »

a. Determine the amount of interest to be capitalized and expensed by Union Power Company for both 2018 and 2019.
b. Prepare all journal entries required.
c. Determine the final valuation of the power plant.

❶❷ **P11-3. Acquisition Costs with Multiple Assets.** Mund Manufacturing, Inc. started operations at the beginning of the current fiscal year. The following transactions took place during the year. Assume that the transactions are cash transactions unless indicated as a nonmonetary event.

1. Acquired land at a cost of $5,000,000. In addition, legal fees, closing costs, and delinquent property taxes amounted to $35,000.
2. Paid current-period property taxes on the land, $23,000.
3. Removed existing structure on the land at a cost of $68,000 and sold scrap materials for $6,800.
4. Paid $320,000 for landscaping, lighting, fencing, and driveways.
5. Constructed a factory building at a cost of $35,000,000.
6. Acquired factory equipment at a cost of $985,000. Paid $35,000 for delivery and installation. Installed additional electrical circuits to run two of the machines at a cost of $55,000.
7. Damaged the loading dock during the installation of one piece of equipment; repair cost amounted to $18,500.
8. Acquired three delivery trucks by signing a 5-year note at the dealership with 0% financing. The total market value of the trucks amounted to $121,080. The note carried a face value of $195,000. The current market rate of interest on similar financing is 10%. Trucks are acquired on January 1.
9. Adjusted the entry for interest expense (amortizing discount) at the end of the year.
10. Adjusted depreciation at the end of the year: All assets are depreciated on a straight-line basis with no residual values using a half-year convention taking a half-year depreciation in the year of acquisition and a half-year in the last year of the asset's life. The estimated useful lives are as follows:
    - Buildings, 30 years
    - Equipment, 10 years
    - Vehicles, 8 years
    - Land improvements, 5 years

Required »

a. Prepare the journal entries to record each of the transactions.
b. Indicate the effects of these transactions on the current year-end income statement, balance sheet (exclude effects on the cash balance), and cash flow statement under both the direct and indirect methods.

❷ **P11-4. Depreciation Methods and Depreciation Schedules.** On January 1 of the current year, Minguss Manufacturing Company purchased a metal cutting and polishing machine at a cost of $4,000,000. The installation and delivery costs amounted to $250,000. The firm expects the machine to be productive for a total of 5 years and a residual value of $500,000 at the end of the asset's useful life.

Required »

Prepare the depreciation schedules for the machine assuming that the following methods were used (each case is independent):

1. Straight-line method.
2. Double-declining balance method (DDB). (Reduce the depreciation expense in the last year to the necessary amount to arrive at an ending book value equal to the scrap value.)

❷ **P11-5. Depreciation and Asset Use, Analysis.** Jack Pinno, Vice President of Production at Greco Corporation, is considering changing the company's capital acquisition and use policy. Greco's policy has been to use equipment through its useful life and then to scrap it. Greco uses straight-line depreciation. Pinno has noticed that repair and downtime of equipment dramatically increases in the last few years of the equipment's life, leading to lost sales and higher production costs. He is proposing to use the equipment for a shorter period and then sell it in the used equipment market. He would like to better understand the financial statement effects of changing the policy. He has asked you to analyze the following information and financial statement effects in net income and cash flows. What would your analysis provide?

	Current	Proposed
Estimated cost	$10,000	$10,000
Salvage value	0	$3,000 (based on current price for similar used equipment)
Useful life	10 years	7 years
Annual repairs and maintenance		
Years 1–2	$ 250	$ 250
Years 3–7	325	325
Years 8–10	625	

2 3 **P11-6. Disposals of Long-Term Operating Assets—Analysis, Depreciation, and Journal** Information related to the long-term operating assets of Rivera Retail Distributors, Inc. at December 31, 2018, is as follows:

Balance Sheet Category	Cost	Accumulated Depreciation Through 12/31/2018	Estimated Useful Life (Years)	Estimated Residual Value	Depreciation Method
Equipment	$ 500,000	$ 180,000	10	$ 50,000	Double-declining balance
Machinery	345,500	170,000	8	5,500	Straight line
Vehicles	127,900	75,000	5	2,900	Straight line
Leasehold Improvements	65,400	21,800	3	0	Straight line
Building	12,000,000	3,252,000	20	1,500,000	Straight line
Land	4,560,000	N/A	N/A	N/A	N/A

The fiscal year-end of the company is December 31. The following events occurred during 2019:

1. On February 1, Rivera sold the vehicles to Wholesale Produce, Inc. for $15,000.
2. On March 31, all of Rivera's equipment and machinery was destroyed by a fire in one of its facilities.
3. On May 1, the equipment was replaced at a cost of $625,000, and the machinery cost the company $420,000 to replace. The estimated useful lives and residual values remained the same as specified for the original machinery and equipment. The company paid cash for the new assets.

Required »

a. Prepare the journal entries required to record each of those events and to record depreciation expense at the end of the year.

b. Determine the ending net book value of Rivera's long-term operating assets on its December 31, 2019, balance sheet. Show the balance for each asset individually and in total.

6 **P11-7. Goodwill and Bargain Purchase Computations.** The trial balance for the Dark Horse Company follows:

Description	Debit	Credit
Cash	$ 30,000	
Inventory	100,000	
Property, plant, and equipment – Net	370,000	
Current liabilities		$ 50,000
Common stock – No par		150,000
Retained earnings		300,000
Totals	$500,000	$500,000

Assume that MPL, Inc. offers to acquire Dark Horse at a purchase price of $650,000. A study of Dark Horse's assets revealed that the inventory had a fair market value of $180,000 and the plant assets were undervalued by $50,000.

Required »

a. Given this set of assumptions, calculate the amount of goodwill or bargain purchase gain to be recorded on the acquisition.

b. Assume now that MPL, Inc. offers to acquire Dark Horse at a purchase price of $250,000. Determine the amount of goodwill or bargain purchase gain.

c. Indicate how to account for goodwill and any gain from a bargain purchase in the financial statements.

6 7 **P11-8. Research and Development Expenditures, Amortization.** Greene Motors, Ltd. recently entered the automobile industry by introducing its first fully electric vehicle, the Bolt. The Bolt is the first of many planned vehicles that Greene will produce. In order to expand its product line, Greene requires a state-of-the-art testing facility and a new research and development laboratory. The following transactions are related to Greene's research and development activities:

1. Constructed a new testing facility at a cost of $14,000,000. The facility is estimated to have a 20-year economic life and a $4,000,000 residual value at the end of that time. The facility will be depreciated using the straight-line method.

Within the new facility, Greene made the following expenditures to conduct its research and development (R&D) activities:

2. Purchased R&D equipment for $568,000. The equipment has a 5-year life and no residual value. The equipment will be depreciated using the straight-line method.
3. Acquired testing materials and supplies at a cost of $125,000. Research projects consumed 70% of the materials and supplies in the current year.
4. Developed a prototype for a new battery, the Powerizer. The prototype cost $265,700 for development and testing.
5. Paid $168,500 in salaries and wages for testing activities.
6. Obtained a patent for the Powerizer. The patent application and legal fees to successfully defend the patent amounted to $560,000. The economic life of the patent is 7 years.
7. Acquired Bizet Automotive Suppliers, Inc. at the beginning of the current year. As part of the transaction, Greene acquired in-process R&D for $356,700. Subsequent R&D expenditures for these projects amounted to $120,000. The acquired projects continue in development for 2 more years.
8. Recorded all required depreciation and amortization at the end of the year.

Required »

a. Prepare the journal entries to record each of the transactions assuming that all purchases were made with cash. Assume that the transactions occurred on January 1.
b. Indicate the effects of these transactions on the current year-end balance sheet (excluding the effects on the cash balance), income statement, and cash flow statement under the direct and indirect methods.

6 7 **P11-9. Research and Development Activities, Amortization, IFRS.** Repeat the requirements in P11-8 assuming that Greene Motors, Ltd. reports under IFRS. Assume that all the conditions to capitalize development costs have been met. Any development costs are amortized over 3 years. What is the difference between the research and development expense under U.S. GAAP compared to IFRS?

6 7 **P11-10. Intangible Assets, Amortization.** Hein Technologies conducted the following cash transactions on January 1.

1. Paid $712,000 to fund internal research designed to develop a new digital scanner. The company expects the useful life to be 3 years.
2. Patented a product based on internal research that could be sold to consumers. Before applying for the patent, incurred additional costs of $200,000 to complete product development ensuring that the product was technologically feasible. Paid $13,800 for patent filing costs and legal fees to successfully defend the patent. The company expects the new technology will be profitable for a 3-year period.
3. Leased three floors of office space. The lease was secured by making an advance payment of $300,000. The lease is a 10-year lease with no renewal options.
4. Paid $560,000 to renovate the leased property to prepare the leased floors for intended use. The useful life of the renovations is estimated at 10 years.
5. Paid $45,000 to acquire a franchise to distribute ICC external hard drives for a 9-year period.

Required »

a. Prepare the journal entries to record each of the transactions.
b. Assume that Hein acquired Dolan Development last year. Hein recorded the following intangible assets on the date of acquisition:
   - Goodwill, $1,500,000
   - Dolan Development trademark, $600,000
   - Renewable licenses, $56,000

   Prepare the year-end adjusting entries required for each of Hein's intangible assets. Assume that the straight-line method is used and a full year's amortization is taken in the year of acquisition.
c. Indicate the effects of these transactions on the current year-end income statement, balance sheet (excluding the effect on the cash balance), and cash flow statement using the direct and the indirect methods.

6 7 **P11-11. Intangible Assets, Amortization, IFRS.** Repeat the requirements in P11-10 assuming that Hein Technologies reports under IFRS. Assume that all the conditions to capitalize development costs have been met. What is the difference between the research and development expense under U.S. GAAP compared to that expense under IFRS?

Excel Project

Autograded Excel Project available in **MyLab Accounting**

CASES

Judgment Cases

Judgment Case 1: Property, Plant, and Equipment: Initial Measurement

Bookstores International, a bookstore chain, has been quite successful over the past few decades and is now in expansion mode. It typically approaches opening a new bookstore by first determining the general geographic location for a new store and then identifying three to five possible locations within the broader geographic selection. It then hires two consultants: One consultant performs feasibility studies on the three to five locations, and the other consultant develops detailed building plans, including an assessment of potential building costs, for each of the selected sites. Because the plans for the various sites are not completely independent of each other, the consultant simply charges one fee for the plans for an entire geographic location selection. Based upon the results of the feasibility studies and the predicted building costs, the management of Bookstores International then selects a site and begins the construction process.

Should the fees paid to the consultants be capitalized as part of the new building, or should they be expensed? Support your determination with research at ASC 360-10-30 (*Property, Plant, and Equipment – Overall-Initial Measurement*) and ASC 720-15 (*Other Expenses – Start-Up Costs*).

Judgment Case 2: Intangibles Assets: Subsequent Measurement

Tolls R Us is a company whose primary business activity is operating toll roads. Tolls R Us receives licenses from the government to operate the toll roads that are typically expensed for a specified period of time. The company routinely projects the anticipated tolls per year that it will be able to charge over the period of the license as well as its projected per car toll increases. Often, due to expected growth, the company projects an increasing usage of the toll road over time. These projections have proven to be reliable in the past. What method should Tolls R Us use to amortize the cost of these licenses? Justify your answer.

Financial Statement Analysis Case

Financial Statement Analysis of Long-Term Fixed Assets

Kellogg Company and ***Kraft Heinz Company, Inc.*** are two companies operating in the packaged food industry. You have noticed their products in numerous grocery and convenience stores and are interested in their production process. Your first step is to analyze the information on their productive capacity. Examine the fixed asset disclosures in the two companies' financial statements to address the following issues:

a. What categories of tangible long-lived assets does each company report? What is the useful life of each category? Compare the categories and useful lives disclosed by each company.
b. For each company, what is the percent of long-lived tangible assets to total assets in 2016 and 2015? In the definition of long-lived tangible assets, include the total of property, plant, and equipment (PPE) – net. Comment on any differences between the two companies.
c. Compute average age and average remaining life for 2016 and 2015. Comment on any differences between the two companies.
d. Compute the fixed asset turnover in 2016. In the definition of long-lived tangible assets (fixed assets), include the total property, plant, and equipment (PPE) – net. Comment on any differences between the two companies.

Kellogg Company

NOTE 1: Accounting Policies

Property

The Company's property consists mainly of plants and equipment used for manufacturing activities. These assets are recorded at cost and depreciated over estimated useful lives using straight-line methods for financial reporting and accelerated methods, where permitted, for tax reporting. Major property categories are depreciated over various periods as follows (in years): manufacturing machinery and equipment 5–30; office equipment 4–5; computer equipment and capitalized software 3–7; building components 15–25; building structures 50. Cost includes interest associated with significant capital projects. . . .

NOTE 19: Supplemental Financial Statement Data

	2016	2015
Land	$ 131	$ 142
Buildings	2,020	2,076
Machinery and equipment	5,646	5,617
Capitalized software	366	328
Construction in progress	686	694
Accumulated depreciation	(5,280)	(5,236)
Property, net	$ 3,569	$ 3,621

Additional financial statement information:

(dollars in millions)	2016	2015
Revenues	$ 13,014	$ 13,525
Depreciation Expense	$ 510	$ 526
Total Assets	$ 15,111	$ 15,251
Average Net Fixed Assets	$ 3,595	$ 3,695

Source: Kellogg Company, Annual Report, December 2016. http://investor.kelloggs.com/~/media/Files/K/Kellogg-IR/Annual%20Reports/kellogg-2016-ar-10-k.PDF

Kraft Heinz Company, Inc.

NOTE 1: Summary of Significant Accounting Policies (excerpt)

Property, Plant and Equipment:

Property, plant, and equipment are stated at historical cost and depreciated by the straight-line method over the estimated useful lives of the assets. Machinery and equipment are depreciated over periods ranging from 3 to 20 years and buildings and improvements over periods up to 40 years. . . .

NOTE 5: Property, Plant, and Equipment

Property, Plant, and Equipment

Property, plant, and equipment at December 31, 2016 and January 3, 2016 were (in millions):

(in millions)	December 31, 2016	January 3, 2016
Land	$ 264	$ 297
Buildings and improvements	1,884	1,700
Machinery and equipment	4,770	4,432
Construction in progress	1,600	1,001
	8,518	7,430
Accumulated depreciation	(1,830)	(906)
Property, plant, and equipment, net	$ 6,688	$6,524

Additional financial statement information:

(dollars in millions)	2016	2015
Revenues	$ 26,487	$ 18,338
Depreciation Expense	$ 1,337	$ 740
Total Assets	$120,480	$122,973
Average Net Fixed Assets	$ 6,606	$ 4,445

Source: Kraft Heinz Company, SEC Filing, 2016. https://www.sec.gov/Archives/edgar/data/1637459/000163745917000007/khc201610k.htm

Surfing the Standards Cases

Surfing the Standards Case 1: Nonmonetary Exchanges

On rare occasions, a company will acquire property, plant, or equipment in a nonmonetary exchange in which two entities exchange one nonmonetary asset for another nonmonetary asset.

Read sections 5, 20, and 30 of ASC 845-10. Describe the accounting treatment for a nonmonetary exchange that has commercial substance. Apply the accounting to the following two independent scenarios:

Scenario 1. ALR Sporting Goods, Inc. has four basketball goals it uses for demonstrations. The goals were originally purchased for $750 each. Accumulated depreciation on the four goals is $300. ALR transacts with NPR Sporting Goods, Inc. and exchanges these four goals for one football goalpost. The fair value of each basketball goal is now $700 each. In addition to trading the four basketball goals, ALR pays $500 (net present value—NPR) in cash. What is the journal entry for ALR? Assume that the exchange has commercial substance.

Scenario 2. Assume that instead of ALR trading its basketball goals, the company gives NPR 100 shares of its common stock. The stock has a par value of $10 per share and is currently trading at $35 per share. What is the journal entry for ALR?

Surfing the Standards Case 2: Involuntary Conversion

Ed's Market Company (EMC) grows and sells fresh fruits and vegetables. EMC experienced three different unfortunate events in the current year.

1. In February, the government acquired 20 acres from EMC in an eminent domain case. EMC was carrying the land on its balance sheet at $6,000. The government paid EMC $10,000. EMC purchased an additional 20 acres of land on the other side of its farm for $25,000 in June to compensate for this loss.
2. In July, a fire destroyed one of EMC's barns. The barn had an original cost of $200,000 and accumulated depreciation of $120,000. EMC expected to receive $50,000 in insurance money. EMC received insurance proceeds of $50,000 in November.
3. In December, one of EMC's tractors was stolen. The original cost of the tractor was $45,000 and the accumulated depreciation was $42,500. The tractor was insured, but as of December 31, it had not been determined exactly how much the insurance company would pay EMC, although it is likely to be around $5,000.

Prepare a memo to the file using the Codification for support. Include any necessary journal entries in the conclusion section of the memo.

Surfing the Standards Case 3: Involuntary Conversion, IFRS

Ed's Market Company (EMC) grows and sells fresh fruits and vegetables. EMC is an IFRS reporter. EMC experienced three different unfortunate events in the current year.

1. In February, the government acquired 20 acres from EMC in an eminent domain case. EMC was carrying the land on its balance sheet at $6,000. The government paid EMC $10,000. EMC purchased an additional 20 acres of land on the other side of its farm for $25,000 in June to compensate for this loss.
2. In July, a fire destroyed one of EMC's barns. The barn had an original cost of $200,000 and accumulated depreciation of $120,000. EMC expected to receive $50,000 in insurance money. EMC received insurance proceeds of $50,000 in November.
3. In December, one of EMC's tractors was stolen. The original cost of the tractor was $45,000 and the accumulated depreciation was $42,500. The tractor was insured, but as of December 31, it was not determined exactly how much the insurance company would pay EMC, although it is likely to be around $5,000.

Prepare a memo to the file using the international standards for support. Include any necessary journal entries in the conclusion section of the memo.

Surfing the Standards Case 4: Software Development Costs

Companies sometimes develop software for either external use (for example, to sell to customers) or for internal use. Should a company expense or capitalize software for internal use? U.S. GAAP provides specific guidance regarding software and, furthermore, has separate guidance for software developed for internal use versus software developed for external use.

a. Does U.S. GAAP require that software development costs related to external-use software be expensed or capitalized? Please explain. Use the Codification for support.
b. Does U.S. GAAP require that software development costs related to internal-use software be expensed or capitalized? Please explain. Use the Codification for support.

Surfing the Standards Case 5: Software Development Costs, IFRS

Assume the same information for Case 4. IFRS does not provide specific rules for software; the accounting for software development costs falls under the general guidance for intangible assets.

Does IFRS require that software development costs be expensed or capitalized? Please explain. Use the international authoritative literature for support.

Basis for Conclusions Cases

Basis for Conclusions Case 1: Property, Plant, and Equipment: Subsequent Measurement, IFRS

Consider the Basis for Conclusions in IAS 16, Property, Plant, and Equipment (particularly paragraphs BC26 and BC27). What is the principle underlying component depreciation under IFRS? Although U.S. GAAP does not contain a basis for conclusions for the topic of property, plant, and equipment, what is the most likely principle that would underlie the decision not to require component depreciation?

Basis for Conclusions Case 2: Intangible Assets – Subsequent Measurement

What are the general rules related to the amortization of intangible assets? Read the basis for conclusions in SFAS No. 142, particularly paragraphs B49 through B53. What were the amortization rules for intangibles prior to the passage of SFAS No. 142? In the 1999 Exposure Draft for SFAS No. 142, FASB had suggested that 20 years be a presumptive maximum. That is, a life longer than 20 years could be used only if the longer life is based on legal life or exchangeability of the asset. What did the board conclude with regard to this issue, and why did it reach that conclusion?

APPENDIX A
Nonmonetary Exchanges

In a nonmonetary exchange, a company acquires an asset by exchanging another asset with the seller rather than paying cash. In these exchanges, accountants must determine the proper measurement of the new asset received and the amount of gain or loss (if any) to record. Factors in making these determinations include:

1. Does the transaction have commercial substance?
2. Was cash received on the trade?
3. Did the transaction result in a gain or a loss?

A nonmonetary exchange transaction has **commercial substance** if the future cash flows change as a result of the transaction—that is, if the economic positions of the parties to the transaction change. Commercial substance can result if the exchange involves either similar assets (one truck is exchanged for another) or dissimilar assets (land is exchanged for a building).

There are three possible valuation bases for nonmonetary exchanges, depending on whether the transaction possesses commercial substance, if cash is received, and if a gain or loss results.

Exchanges with Commercial Substance

Firms recognize all gains and losses—computed as the difference between the carrying value and the fair value of the asset given up—on an exchange with commercial substance. The firm records the new asset at fair value of the assets given in the exchange, which is the fair value of the asset given up plus cash paid or minus cash received. If the fair value of the assets given in exchange is not readily determinable, then the fair value of the assets received is used to measure the transaction. Example 11A.1 illustrates accounting for a gain on a nonmonetary exchange with commercial substance.

EXAMPLE 11A.1 Gain on Exchange with Commercial Substance

PROBLEM: Trogg Construction Company exchanged a core drill for a backhoe acquired from Metro Cities Equipment Associates. Trogg also received a cash consideration of $130,000. It expects the future cash flows to change as a result of this transaction and, therefore, the exchange has commercial substance.

The carrying value and fair value of the core drill and backhoe at the date of the exchange are as follows:

Asset	Cost	Accumulated Depreciation	Carrying Value	Fair Value
Core drill (asset given up)	$630,000	$110,000	$520,000	$530,000
Backhoe (asset received)	525,000	165,000	360,000	400,000

Prepare the journal entry to record the transaction for Trogg.

SOLUTION: We value the backhoe (the new asset) at the fair value of the consideration given in the exchange minus the cash received. The new asset's value is equal to the fair value of the old asset given up less the cash received (i.e., $530,000 − $130,000 = $400,000). Trogg will recognize any gain or loss on the exchange because the transaction has commercial substance. In this case, there is a $10,000 gain measured as the difference between the fair value and the carrying value of the asset given up in the exchange (i.e., $530,000 − $520,000 = $10,000).

Continued

The entry to record the transaction by Trogg is as follows:

Account	*Date of the Exchange*	
Equipment – Backhoe (New)	400,000	
Accumulated Depreciation – Core Drill (Old)	110,000	
Cash	130,000	
Equipment – Core Drill (Old)		630,000
Gain on Exchange of Equipment		10,000

Example 11A.2 illustrates accounting for a loss on a nonmonetary exchange with commercial substance.

EXAMPLE 11A.2 Loss on Exchange with Commercial Substance

PROBLEM: Trogg Construction Company exchanged a core drill for a backhoe acquired from Metro Cities Equipment Associates. Trogg Construction Company also received a cash consideration of $130,000. Trogg expects the future cash flows to change as a result of this transaction and, therefore, the exchange has commercial substance.

The carrying value and fair value of the core drill and backhoe at the date of the exchange are as follows:

Asset	Cost	Accumulated Depreciation	Carrying Value	Fair Value
Core drill (asset given up)	$660,000	$110,000	$550,000	$530,000
Backhoe (asset received)	525,000	165,000	360,000	400,000

Prepare the journal entry for Trogg to record the transaction.

SOLUTION: We value the backhoe (the new asset) at the fair value of the consideration given in the exchange minus the cash received. The new asset's value is equal to the fair value of the old asset given up less the cash received (i.e., $530,000 − $130,000 = $400,000). Trogg will recognize any gain or loss on the exchange because the transaction has commercial substance. In this case, there is a $20,000 loss measured as the difference between the fair value and the carrying value of the asset given up in the exchange (i.e., $530,000 − $550,000 = $20,000).

The entry to record the transaction is as follows:

Account	*Date of the Exchange*	
Equipment – Backhoe (New)	400,000	
Accumulated Depreciation – Core Drill (Old)	110,000	
Cash	130,000	
Loss on Exchange of Equipment	20,000	
Equipment – Core Drill (Old)		660,000

Exchanges without Commercial Substance and No Cash Received

If the exchange lacks commercial substance and no cash is received, firms defer any gain by adjusting the carrying value of the new asset. However, due to conservatism, firms must recognize all losses immediately, similar to a transaction with commercial substance as shown in Example 11A.3.

EXAMPLE 11A.3

Gain on Exchange without Commercial Substance and No Cash Received

PROBLEM: Sam's Taxi Company exchanged a fleet of Toyota vehicles for an equal-size fleet of Nissan vehicles from Dave Transportation Group. Sam's Taxi does not expect the future cash flows to change significantly as a result of this exchange and, therefore, the transaction lacks commercial substance. The carrying value and fair value of each fleet of vehicles on the date of the exchange are as follows:

Asset	Cost	Accumulated Depreciation	Carrying Value	Fair Value
Toyota fleet (assets given up)	$1,090,000	$510,000	$580,000	$695,000
Nissan fleet (assets received)	980,000	290,000	690,000	695,000

Prepare the journal entry to record the exchange transaction for Sam's Taxi Company.

SOLUTION: The gain on the transaction is $115,000, which is the fair value of $695,000 less the carrying value of $580,000 of the Toyota fleet given up by Sam's Taxi Company. However, because the transaction lacks commercial substance and Sam's Taxi Company does not receive any cash, no gain is recognized. We record the new automobiles at the carrying value of the assets given up.

Account	***Date of the Exchange***	
Automobiles (Nissan fleet – new)	580,000	
Accumulated Depreciation—Automobiles (Toyota fleet – old)	510,000	
Automobiles (Toyota fleet – old)		1,090,000

Exchanges without Commercial Substance and Cash Received

Firms recognize total or partial gains in a transaction lacking commercial substance if cash is received. If cash is received, the transaction is considered a partial sale with all or a portion of the gain recognized in income. The partial gain recognized is equal to:

$$\text{Percent of Gain Recognized} = \text{Cash Received/Total Consideration Received}$$

$$= \text{Cash Received/(Cash Received + FMV of the Asset Received)}$$

If the percent of the gain recognized is 25% or more, the firm recognizes the total gain even if the transaction lacks commercial substance. If cash is more than 25% of the entire value exchanged, the firm considers the asset to be effectively sold for cash and thus recognizes the full gain. Example 11A.4 illustrates accounting for a gain on a nonmonetary exchange without commercial substance where cash is received.

EXAMPLE 11A.4 Gain on Exchange without Commercial Substance and Cash Received

PROBLEM: Sam's Taxi Company exchanged a fleet of Toyota vehicles for an equal-sized fleet of Nissan vehicles from the Dave Transportation Group. The carrying value and fair value of each fleet of vehicles on the date of the exchange are as follows:

Asset	Cost	Accumulated Depreciation	Carrying Value	Fair Value
Toyota fleet (assets given up)	$1,090,000	$510,000	$580,000	$795,000
Nissan fleet (assets received)	980,000	290,000	690,000	715,500

Sam's Taxi received cash of $79,500 and the Nissan fleet in exchange for the Toyota fleet. Sam's Taxi does not expect the future cash flows to change significantly as a result of this exchange and, therefore, the transaction lacks commercial substance.

Prepare the journal entry to record the exchange transaction for Sam's Taxi Company.

SOLUTION: The total potential gain is equal to $215,000:

$$\text{Fair Value of the Asset Given Up} - \text{Carrying Value of the Asset Given Up}$$
$$= \$795{,}000 - \$580{,}000 = \$215{,}000$$

The percentage of gain to recognize is as follows:

$$\text{Percent of Gain Recognized} = \text{Cash Received / Total Consideration Received}$$
$$= \text{Cash Received / (Cash Received + FMV of the Assets Received)} = \$79{,}500 / (\$79{,}500 + \$715{,}500)$$
$$= \underline{\underline{10.0\%}}$$

We then compute the portion of the gain recognized and the portion deferred:

$$\text{Partial Gain Recognized} = \$215{,}000 \times 10.0\% = \underline{\underline{\$21{,}500}}$$
$$\text{Deferred Gain} = \$215{,}000 - \$21{,}500 = \underline{\underline{\$193{,}500}}$$

Given that the transaction lacks commercial substance, the initial carrying value of the Nissan fleet on Sam's financial statements is the carrying amount of the asset given up (i.e., the Toyota fleet) adjusted by deducting any cash received or adding any cash paid. We add the amount of the recognized gain to the carrying value of the new asset ($580,000 − $79,500 + $21,500 = $522,000). Alternatively, we can reduce the fair value of the asset received by the amount of the deferred gain ($715,500 − $193,500 = $522,000). Note that the deferred gain reduces the carrying value of the new asset received. This lower carrying value reduces future depreciation charges and in effect spreads the gain recognition over the life of the new asset. This gain is deferred to future accounting periods through lower depreciation charges.

The entry recorded by Sam's Taxi is as follows:

Account	***Date of the Exchange***	
Automobiles (Nissan fleet – new)	522,000	
Accumulated Depreciation- Automobiles (Toyota fleet – old)	510,000	
Cash	79,500	
Automobiles (Toyota fleet – old)		1,090,000
Gain on Exchange of Automobiles		21,500

IFRS Accounting for Nonmonetary Exchanges

IFRS accounting for nonmonetary exchanges depends on whether an exchange has commercial substance or lacks commercial substance. Therefore, accounting for nonmonetary exchanges under IFRS is similar to the process under U.S. GAAP for the following cases discussed earlier:

- Exchanges with commercial substance
- Exchanges without commercial substance and no cash received

Under IFRS, if an exchange lacks commercial substance, the accounting is the same whether or not the firm receives cash. Consequently, firms cannot recognize any gain on exchanges that lack commercial substance even if cash is received. Firms recognize losses immediately. Example 11A.5 illustrates accounting for a gain on a nonmonetary exchange without commercial substance where cash is received under IFRS.

EXAMPLE 11A.5

Gain on Exchange without Commercial Substance and Cash Received: IFRS

PROBLEM: Sam's Taxi Company from Example 11A.4 reports under IFRS. Prepare the journal entry to record the exchange transaction.

SOLUTION: Because the transaction is without commercial substance, Sam's Taxi cannot recognize a gain even if cash is received.

Given that the transaction lacks commercial substance, the initial carrying value of the Nissan fleet on Sam's financial statements is the carrying amount of the asset given up (i.e., the Toyota fleet) adjusted by deducting any cash received or adding any cash paid. The initial carrying value of the Nissan fleet is \$500,500 (\$580,000 − \$79,500). Alternatively, we can reduce the fair value of the asset received by the amount of the deferred gain (\$715,500 − \$215,000 = \$500,500). Note that the deferred gain reduces the carrying value of the new asset received. This lower carrying value reduces future depreciation charges and in effect spreads the gain recognition over the life of the new asset. This gain is deferred to future accounting periods through lower depreciation charges.

The entry recorded by Sam's Taxi is as follows:

Account	***Date of the Exchange***	
Automobiles (Nissan fleet – new)	500,500	
Accumulated Depreciation—Automobiles (Toyota fleet – old)	510,000	
Cash	79,500	
Automobiles (Toyota fleet– old)		1,090,000

Exhibit 11A.1 compares U.S. GAAP to IFRS in accounting for nonmonetary exchanges.

EXHIBIT 11A.1 Comparison of Accounting for Nonmonetary Exchanges under U.S. GAAP and IFRS

Type	U.S. GAAP	IFRS
Exchanges with Commercial Substance		
• Gain or • Loss	A firm recognizes all gains and losses immediately. The gain or loss is the difference between the carrying value of the asset given up and the fair value of the asset given up.	Similar to U.S. GAAP.
Exchanges without Commercial Substance		
• Gain – no cash received	If no cash is received, the carrying value of the new asset is the carrying value of the asset given up plus the cash paid. The firm defers any gain.	Similar to U.S. GAAP.
• Gain – cash received	If cash is received, the firm recognizes total or partial gains. The partial gain recognized is equal to: Percent of Gain Recognized $= \frac{\text{Cash Received}}{\text{Total Consideration Received}}$ $= \frac{\text{Cash Received}}{(\text{Cash Received} + \text{FMV of the Asset Received})}$ If the percent of the gain recognized is 25% or more, the firm recognizes the total gain even if the transaction lacks commercial substance.	IFRS does not permit the recognition of a gain even when cash is received. The carrying value of the new asset is the carrying value of the asset given up less cash received plus cash paid, if any.
• Loss	The firm recognizes losses immediately.	Similar to U.S. GAAP.

APPENDIX B
Natural Resources

Natural resources, another category of long-term operating assets, include oil and gas deposits, timberlands, coal and other mineral deposits. Natural resources are initially recorded at cost and then *depleted* over their economic lives. The process of allocating the cost of the natural resource over its useful life is referred to as **depletion**, similar to depreciation for tangible long-lived assets.

Costs Included in Natural Resources

The cost of a natural resource consists of four elements.

1. **Acquisition costs.** The acquisition cost is the price paid to obtain the property or the right to search and explore, including acquisitions accounted for as capitalized leases. Acquisition costs are typically capitalized initially, but not depleted until the exploration is completed. If exploration efforts are successful, the acquisition cost is included in the cost basis of the natural resource and thus depleted over the economic life of the natural resource. However, if exploration efforts are unsuccessful, the company will write off the acquisition cost as a loss.
2. **Exploration and evaluation costs.** Exploration and evaluation costs are costs incurred to find and determine the technical feasibility and commercial viability of extracting the resource. For example, the costs associated with drilling for oil and gas are exploration costs. These costs are either expensed immediately or capitalized into the cost basis of the natural resource, as we discuss later.

3. **Development costs.** *Development costs* include intangible costs (such as grading the land and digging tunnels and shafts) as well as tangible costs (such as heavy equipment needed to extract the natural resource). The intangible and tangible costs are included in the cost basis of the natural resource and are depleted.

   If equipment can be moved to other locations, then it is depreciated separately over its useful life. For instance, a piece of drilling equipment used in multiple locations can be accounted for with other property, plant, and equipment and depreciated separately from the depletion process for the natural resource. If the equipment is not movable, such as offshore oil rigs, then the cost is included in the cost basis of the natural resource and is depleted.
4. **Restoration costs.** Companies may incur substantial costs, referred to as **restoration costs**, to return property to its original condition after the removal of the natural resource. An example would be the costs to restore property used in mining. The fair value of these costs is capitalized into the cost basis of the natural resource and depleted. We discuss these costs, sometimes also referred to as asset retirement obligations, in more depth in Chapter 13.

Exploration Costs

The *full-cost method* and the *successful-efforts method* are two methods of accounting for exploration costs in the oil and gas industry.

The **full-cost method** capitalizes all costs associated with both successful and unsuccessful exploration costs into the natural resource. The full-cost method is justified by considering that the costs of exploring and drilling dry wells are necessary to discover producing wells, so the costs of exploring both successful and unsuccessful wells are spread over the successful wells.

The **successful-efforts method** capitalizes only those costs associated with exploring and developing successful wells and expenses the costs associated with dry wells. The justification for the use of the successful-efforts method is that dry wells do not generate oil and gas and provide no future economic benefit to the company. Therefore, these costs do not meet the definition of an asset and are expensed at the point the well is determined to be nonproductive.

Depletion

As is the case with property, plant, and equipment, companies expense the cost of the natural resource over its economic life.

Depletion is typically computed using the units-of-output method. To determine depletion expense, we first compute the expected depletion cost per unit of output as the cost basis of the natural resource less salvage value (depletion base) divided by the estimated total units of output. The depletion expense is then computed as the units produced during the current period times the rate of depletion per unit.

$$\text{Rate of Depletion per Unit} = \text{Depletion Base}/\text{Estimated Total Units of Output} \qquad (11B.1)$$

$$\text{Depletion Expense} = (\text{Actual Units of Output} \times \text{Rate of Depletion per Unit}) \qquad (11B.2)$$

Example 11B.1 illustrates accounting for natural resources under the full-cost and successful-efforts methods.

EXAMPLE 11B.1 Natural Resources

PROBLEM: On January 1, Percy Petroleum Company (PPC) purchased land for $500,000 to use to explore for oil. On January 1, it purchased heavy equipment costing $55,000 that can be moved from one location to another and has a 10-year expected life with no residual value. PPC also incurred a cost of $150,000 for a non-movable oil rig. PPC incurred $60,000 in exploration and evaluation costs for both productive and dry wells. Producing wells cost the firm $20,000 and the remainder was a result of exploration costs incurred for nonproducing wells.

The successful oil wells are expected to produce 10,000 barrels of oil. No residual value is expected. PPC uses the units-of-output depletion method and the straight-line depreciation method. A total of 2,000 barrels of oil were produced during the current year. Categorize each expenditure into a cost related to acquisition, exploration and evaluation, or development. Assume that PPC pays cash for all expenditures. Provide the journal entries required under both the full-cost and the successful-efforts methods.

SOLUTION: Expenditures categorized by the cost of natural resources:

Purchase of land for $500,000 – acquisition cost
Purchase of heavy equipment for $55,000 – development cost; reclassified as PPE
Purchase of non-movable oil rig for $150,000 – development cost
Incur exploration costs of $60,000 – exploration costs

Full-Cost Method. Under the full-cost method, PPC will capitalize costs of $710,000, which includes the purchase price for the land ($500,000), the cost of the non-movable oil rig ($150,000), and all of the exploration costs ($60,000) into the natural resource, oil, and gas deposit. PPC will capitalize the $55,000 paid for the heavy equipment into the equipment account, classified as property, plant, and equipment.

Account	***January 1***	
Oil and Gas Deposit	710,000	
Cash		710,000

Account	***January 1***	
Equipment	55,000	
Cash		55,000

PPC computes depletion expense and depreciation expense as follows:

$$\text{Rate of Depletion per Unit} = \text{Depletion Base/Estimated Total Units of Output} \quad (11B.1)$$

$$\$71 \text{ per Unit} = \$710{,}000/10{,}000 \text{ Units}$$

$$\text{Depletion Expense} = \text{Actual Units of Output} \times \text{Rate of Depletion per Unit} \quad (11B.2)$$

$$\text{Depletion Expense} = \$142{,}000 = 2{,}000 \text{ Units} \times \$71 \text{ per Unit}$$

Alternatively, depletion expense can be computed as follows:

$$\text{Depletion Expense} = \frac{2{,}000 \text{ Actual Units of Output} \times \$710{,}000 \text{ Depletion Base}}{10{,}000 \text{ Estimated Total Units of Output}} = \$142{,}000$$

$$\text{Depreciation Expense} = \$55{,}000 \text{ Depreciable Base / 10 Years} = \$5{,}500$$

The journal entries for depletion expense and depreciation expense are as follows:

Account	December 31	
Depletion Expense—Oil and Gas Deposit	142,000	
Oil and Gas Deposit (or Accumulated Depletion)		142,000
Depreciation Expense—Equipment	5,500	
Accumulated Depreciation—Equipment		5,500

Successful-Efforts Method. The answer is similar under the successful-efforts method except that only the $20,000 exploration costs related to the successful well are capitalized. The remaining $40,000 is expensed immediately. The journal entries are as follows:

Account	January 1	
Oil and Gas Deposit	670,000	
Unsuccessful Exploration Costs	40,000	
Cash		710,000

Account	January 1	
Equipment	55,000	
Cash		55,000

PPC computes depletion expense and depreciation expense as follows:

$$\text{Rate of Depletion per Unit} = \text{Depletion Base/Estimated Total Units of Output} \quad (11B.1)$$

$$\$67 \text{ per Unit} = \$670{,}000/10{,}000 \text{ Units}$$

$$\text{Depletion Expense} = \text{Actual Units of Output} \times \text{Rate of Depletion per Unit} \quad (11B.2)$$

$$\$134{,}000 = 2{,}000 \text{ Units} \times \$67 \text{ per Unit}$$

$$\text{Depreciation Expense} = \$55{,}000 \text{ Depreciable Base / 10 Years} = \$5{,}500$$

Account	December 31	
Depletion Expense—Oil and Gas Deposit	134,000	
Oil and Gas Deposit (or Accumulated Depletion)		134,000
Depreciation Expense—Equipment	5,500	
Accumulated Depreciation—Equipment		5,500

IFRS Costs Included in Natural Resources

Accounting for natural resources is similar to accounting for other tangible and intangible assets under IFRS.[26]

Compared to U.S. GAAP, however, the following three items related to accounting for natural resources differ:

- IFRS permits the full-cost method during the exploration and evaluation phase. Most companies classify long-lived tangible assets in either of these phases as property, plant, and equipment.
- IFRS requires *impairment testing* for exploration and evaluation assets rather than depletion. (We discuss impairment accounting in the next chapter.)
- IFRS allows companies to retain the policies for the capitalization of exploration and evaluation costs they used before the IFRS accounting standard for natural resources became effective. Therefore, even though IFRS recommends a certain accounting treatment for exploration and evaluation costs, they can be expensed as incurred or capitalized depending on the company's prior policy.

An additional distinction is the determination of the treatment of exploration and evaluation expenditures under IFRS. A company has to determine the "unit" to which these costs should be allocated. For example, in the oil and gas industry, the unit to which exploration and evaluation costs are to be allocated could be an individual well. Within the mining industry, a common approach is to allocate exploration and evaluation costs between areas of interest, primarily different geological areas that are examined and tracked separately.

[26]Accounting for natural resources is found in *IASB, International Financial Reporting Standard 6*, "Exploration for and Evaluation of Mineral Resources" (London, UK: International Accounting Standards Board, Revised), which became effective for years beginning January 1, 2006.

12 Long-Term Operating Assets: Departures from Historical Cost

LEARNING OBJECTIVES

1. Specify the categories of long-term operating assets tested for impairment.
2. Describe and demonstrate the accounting for impairments of property, plant, and equipment and intangible assets with finite lives under U.S. GAAP.
3. Explain and illustrate accounting for impairments of intangible assets with indefinite lives under U.S. GAAP.
4. Explain and illustrate the accounting for goodwill impairments under U.S. GAAP.
5. Describe and demonstrate the accounting for impairments of property, plant, and equipment, finite-life intangible assets, and indefinite-life intangible assets other than goodwill under IFRS.
6. Explain and illustrate the accounting for goodwill impairments under IFRS.
7. Detail required disclosures for impaired assets.
8. Illustrate the accounting for long-term operating assets held for sale or disposal and describe the required disclosures for these assets.

Mark Baynes/Alamy Stock Photo

Introduction

WHEN IS AN ASSET NOT AN ASSET? The question sounds contradictory, but the answer is simple: when it no longer provides a future economic benefit. A company investing in long-lived assets such as buildings and equipment expects them to generate future sales and future cash flows. Consider ***BlackBerry Limited,*** the manufacturer of ***BlackBerry*** smart phones. After investing heavily in only one type of smart phone technology, ***BlackBerry*** lost significant market share to other manufacturers, such as ***Apple*** and ***Samsung,*** that moved to touch-screen technology.

When business conditions deteriorate, a company must determine whether the carrying values of its assets continue to reflect the future economic benefits of its resources. When the demand for ***BlackBerry*** smart phones declined, the company questioned its ability to generate sufficient cash flows to fully recover the current carrying value of its assets. ***BlackBerry*** reported significant *impairment* losses of $2.7 million in 2013.

What happens if the conditions change and the impairment losses reverse? Assume, for example, that sales subsequently increase and future cash-flow predictions are positive. The accounting method for reversing impairment losses depends on whether a company uses IFRS or U.S. GAAP.

In Chapter 11, we discussed the historical cost model of accounting for long-term operating assets. In this chapter, we examine two departures from historical cost accounting: *impairments* and long-term operating assets held for sale. In Appendix A, we also discuss *revaluations under IFRS,* which occur when a company reports a long-term asset at its fair value rather than its historical cost. With both impairments and revaluations, the economic value of a long-term asset differs from its depreciated historical cost (carrying value). For each topic, we will examine the accounting under U.S. GAAP and then IFRS, highlighting differences in the standards and the key judgments managers make. «

❶ Specify the categories of long-term operating assets tested for impairment.

Overview: Impairment of Long-Term Operating Assets

An **impairment** occurs when an asset's total future cash-generating ability falls below its carrying value. To illustrate, suppose you own a commercial building with office space that you rent. The local economy is in a downturn because a major manufacturer closed its factory. To avoid vacancies, you must decrease the rent charged to tenants. The decreased rental income causes future cash flows related to the building to decline. Therefore, the economic value of the building is impaired.

When a long-term operating asset's future economic value is impaired, the firm:

1. Recognizes the decline in value as a loss on the income statement in the period that it determines the impairment occurred.
2. Reduces the asset's carrying value on the balance sheet because its economic value has declined.

The impairment loss is a noncash expense that has no impact on the statement of cash flows.

THE CONCEPTUAL FRAMEWORK CONNECTION
Accounting for Impaired Long-Term Operating Assets

Several concepts underlie the accounting treatment of impairments—the most critical being the need for accounting information to be relevant and asset values (dollar amounts) to be representationally faithful. An asset involves probable future economic benefits, so a firm should measure these benefits using a relevant amount. If the expected economic benefits are less than the asset's carrying value reported on the balance sheet, the firm should reduce the asset's carrying value.

Measuring an impaired asset at a value other than historical cost may involve a trade-off between relevance and faithful representation. When an asset is impaired, the firm must determine a new carrying amount based upon its expectation of future economic benefits. The estimate of expected future benefits can be quite subjective, meaning that an asset balance may not faithfully represent the economic position of the firm with a high degree of accuracy. For example, in order to measure future benefits, a manager may need to estimate the future cash flows expected over the remainder of an asset's 20-year life. The manager's assessment of cash flows 20 years from now is undoubtedly quite subjective.

Although this is a trade-off between relevance and faithful representation, when in doubt, firms should err on the side of not overstating net income and assets. Thus, companies are required to write down assets with reduced future economic benefits.

Categories and Steps Associated with the Impairment of Long-Term Operating Assets

The method of accounting for the impairment of long-term operating assets depends upon the type of asset. We will discuss the following types of assets and their specific treatment in the following sections:[1]

- Property, plant, and equipment and finite-life intangible assets
- Indefinite-Life intangible assets
- Goodwill

[1]The authoritative literature for U.S. GAAP is in three subtopics in the codification: FASB ASC 360-10 – *Property, Plant, and Equipment – Overall,* FASB ASC 350-20 – *Intangibles – Goodwill and Others – Goodwill,* and FASB ASC 350-30 – *Intangibles – Goodwill and Others – General Intangibles Other than Goodwill.*

The key steps related to accounting for impairments of long-term operating assets include the following:

- Asset grouping
- When to test for impairment
- Impairment test
- Measurement subsequent to impairment

We will discuss each of these steps for each type of long-term operating asset.

❷ Describe and demonstrate the accounting for impairments of property, plant, and equipment and intangible assets with finite lives under U.S. GAAP.

Accounting for Impairments: Property, Plant, and Equipment and Finite-Life Intangible Assets

The accounting procedures for the determination of impairment are identical for property, plant, and equipment and finite-life intangible assets.

Asset Grouping

Before testing assets for impairment, a firm must determine whether to assess them as individual assets or in asset groups. An **asset grouping** is the lowest level of identifiable and independent cash flows. So, if cash flows are identifiable and independent for an individual asset such as a delivery truck, the firm can test the delivery truck for impairment. Alternatively, if the delivery truck is part of a fleet of a store's delivery trucks, the delivery fleet could be considered an asset group. The rationale is that the cash flows from an individual truck are dependent on the cash flows from the other trucks in the fleet. Example 12.1 illustrates asset groups.

EXAMPLE 12.1

Asset Group

PROBLEM: Booth Brothers Corporation operates concession stands in several sports and performance venues. It supplies the stands with equipment such as cash registers, refrigerators and freezers, stovetops, and frying machines. Currently, Booth has 14 concession contracts with over 100 stands. Booth Brothers determines that the cash flows from two of the five stands at the Tiger Town Sports Arena are operating at a significant loss and that it will not be able to recover the carrying amounts of the equipment installed in those two stands. The other three stands are profitable individually, and when combining all five stands, they report a net profit. Should Booth Brothers assess impairment for each individual stand? Alternatively, should Booth assess the possible impairment for all stands as a group?

SOLUTION: Booth Brothers has contracted with the arena to provide five stands. Overall, the five stands are profitable. The cash flows generated from the contract and the three profitable stands are not independent of the cash flows of the unprofitable stands. Consequently, Booth Brothers should assess impairment at the group level—combining all five stands relating to the Tiger Town Sports Arena contract.

When to Test for Impairment

After identifying the asset group, the firm then determines if impairment testing is required. If impairment testing is required, it then performs a two-step test to determine whether there is an impairment. If there is an impairment, the firm then computes the amount of the loss.[2]

[2]For the remainder of this chapter, we will often refer to the individual asset, but this may also be an asset group.

Firms conduct an impairment test whenever events and circumstances referred to as **impairment indicators** indicate that an asset may be impaired. Exhibit 12.1 outlines FASB's recommended impairment indicators.

EXHIBIT 12.1 Impairment Indicators

a. A significant decrease in the market price of a long-lived asset (asset group)
b. A significant adverse change in the extent or manner in which a long-lived asset (asset group) is being used or in its physical condition.
c. A significant adverse change in legal factors or in the business climate that could affect the value of a long-lived asset (asset group), including an adverse action or assessment by a regulator
d. An accumulation of costs significantly in excess of the amount originally expected for the acquisition or construction of a long-lived asset (asset group)
e. A current-period operating or cash-flow loss combined with a history of operating or cash-flow losses or a projection or forecast that demonstrates continuing losses associated with the use of a long-lived asset (asset group)
f. A current expectation that, more likely than not, a long-lived asset (asset group) will be sold or otherwise disposed of significantly before the end of its previously estimated useful life. The term more likely than not refers to a level of likelihood that is more than 50%

Source: Financial Accounting Foundation, ASC 360-10-35-21 *"Property, Plant, and Equipment-Overall-Subsequent Measurement-Impairment or Disposal of Long-Lived Assets."* Copyright © 2014.

Firms develop their own impairment indicators based on the guidelines in Exhibit 12.1. Exhibit 12.2 provides ***BlackBerry's*** disclosure of the impairment indicators it employs in its annual report that led to its $2.7 billion impairment loss in 2013.

EXHIBIT 12.2 Disclosure of Impairment Loss Indicators, ***BlackBerry Limited,*** Financial Statements, March 1, 2014

The Company reviews long-lived assets ("LLA") such as property, plant, and equipment and intangible assets with finite useful lives for impairment whenever events or changes in circumstances indicate that the carrying amount of the asset or asset group may not be recoverable. These events and circumstances may include significant decreases in the market price of an asset or asset group, significant changes in the extent or manner in which an asset or asset group is being used by the Company or in its physical condition, a significant change in legal factors or in the business climate, a history or forecast of future operating or cash flow losses, significant disposal activity, a significant decline in the Company's share price, a significant decline in revenues or adverse changes in the economic environment.

Source: Blackberry, Ltd., Financial Statements, March 2014. http://us.blackberry.com/content/dam/bbCompany/Desktop/Global/PDF/Investors/Documents/2014/Q4_FY14_Filing.pdf

Example 12.2 provides an example of assessing impairment indicators.

EXAMPLE 12.2 Assessment of Impairment Indicators

PROBLEM: Viva Enterprises provided you with the following information with respect to its tangible and intangible assets on December 31, 2018.

	Plant and Equipment Asset Group	Radio Broadcast License
Cost	$4,200,000	$780,000
Accumulated depreciation / Amortization	(2,100,000)	(273,000)
Net book value	$2,100,000	$ 507,000

Viva acquired a 10-year term radio broadcast license on July 1, 2015. Viva used the straight-line method of amortization with no residual value expected. The broadcast license is for a fixed term and there is no evidence that ensures renewal, so Viva classified it as a finite-life intangible asset. Viva acquired the plant and equipment on January 1, 2016, and estimated its total useful life as 6 years. The company used the straight-line method of depreciation and amortization with no residual value expected.

During 2018, management reviewed several events and circumstances.

1. Viva uses the plant and equipment to manufacture products that have experienced significant declines in sales. Management expects that the demand for these products will continue to decline for the foreseeable future, resulting in a decline in the value of the company's plant assets.
2. Expanded satellite radio subscriptions, Internet broadcasts, and the use of iPod players have caused the company's radio advertising revenues to decline substantially over the past year.

Do these events and circumstances constitute impairment indicators? Based on this information, will Viva need to determine if there is an impairment loss?

SOLUTION: Based on the decline in demand for the company's products and radio revenues, Viva must proceed with the impairment process for both assets.

Two-Step Impairment Test

If impairment indicators suggest that an asset might be impaired, the firm then performs a two-step test to determine if there is an impairment loss and, if so, the amount of the impairment loss. The two steps are:

1. Assess recoverability
2. Compare the carrying value to fair value, if required[3]

Assess Recoverability. If the impairment indicators suggest an impairment of a long-term operating asset, the firm assesses the asset's *recoverability*. In general, the **recoverability** of an asset refers to the firm's ability to recover the asset's carrying value based on the sum of the undiscounted cash flows from the use and disposal of the asset:

1. If the sum of the undiscounted future cash flows is less than the carrying value of the asset, then the asset is impaired and the company must measure the impairment loss.
2. If the sum of the undiscounted future cash flows exceeds the carrying value of the asset, then the asset is not impaired.

Because ***BlackBerry*** indicates its testing sequence in its footnote on significant accounting policies, it first determines whether the carrying value of the asset is recoverable. ***BlackBerry*** also notes that it considers the company as one asset group. Example 12.3 illustrates determining recoverability of assets.

EXAMPLE 12.3 Determine Recoverability of the Assets

PROBLEM: On December 31, 2018, as determined in Example 12.2, the management of Viva Enterprises needs to estimate the expected future cash flows to be generated from the use of the assets over their remaining useful lives. Again, there are no expected residual values—so the only cash flows expected are related to the use of the assets. The company's cost of capital is 5%. In addition, estimated disposal costs are insignificant. The projected future undiscounted cash flows, projected future discounted cash flows, and fair values are listed on the next page.

Continued

[3]This part of the test is commonly referred to as the "fair value test."

		Plant and Equipment Asset Group	Broadcast License
Cost		$4,200,000	$780,000
Less: Accumulated depreciation / Amortization		(2,100,000)	(273,000)
Carrying value		$2,100,000	$ 507,000
Future cash flows (occurring at the end of each year)			
Remaining Life	**Year**		
1	2019	$ 600,000	$185,000
2	2020	400,000	115,000
3	2021	380,000	100,000
4	2022	0	80,000
5	2023	0	40,000
6	2024	0	20,000
7	2025		0
Total undiscounted future cash flows		$1,380,000	$540,000
Total discounted future cash flows at 5%		$1,262,499	$478,964
Fair value		$1,200,000	$455,000

Based on this information, determine the recoverability of these assets.

SOLUTION: The determination of recoverability is computed as follows.

Step	Plant & Equipment	Broadcast License
Step 1. Assess recoverability	Undiscounted future cash flows of $1,380,000 are less than carrying value of $2,100,000, so go to Step 2. The asset group is impaired.	Undiscounted future cash flows of $540,000 are greater than carrying value of $507,000, so stop. The asset is not impaired.
Step 2. Compare the carrying value to fair value, if required.	*Required: See Example 12.4 on next page*	Not required.

Determine Any Impairment Loss. When the asset's carrying value is more than its fair value, a company reports an **impairment loss** calculated as the carrying value less the fair value. The asset's fair value is the amount that the asset holder will receive from the sale of an asset in a current transaction between willing parties. Because the definition of fair value is based on selling an asset, it is often called an exit price.

Quoted prices in active markets are the best evidence of fair value. If market prices are not available (which is frequently the case), then accountants base fair value estimates on the best information available or use valuation techniques such as market comparables, review of recent transactions, and discounted cash-flow valuation.[4] In the absence of market prices, we use discounted future cash flows in this chapter.

When recording the impairment loss, the firm eliminates the balance in the accumulated depreciation (or accumulated amortization) account and reduces the asset account. Specifically, it recognizes the impairment loss by:

1. Debiting the loss
2. Debiting the accumulated depreciation or accumulated amortization for its entire balance
3. Crediting the asset account for the sum of the loss and the accumulated depreciation or accumulated amortization

[4]We covered the fair value hierarchy in more depth in Chapter 2.

These steps ensure that the asset's carrying value reflects its fair value. That is, after recognizing the impairment, the firm carries the asset at its fair value with no accumulated depreciation or amortization. There is a new basis of accounting as if the asset were just acquired. Calculating an impairment loss is illustrated in Example 12.4.

EXAMPLE 12.4

Calculating the Impairment Loss

PROBLEM: Continuing Example 12.3, Viva Enterprises must measure its impairment loss for plant and equipment. Determine the impairment loss and the revised annual depreciation expense. Prepare any necessary journal entries to record the impairment.

SOLUTION: Viva measures the impairment loss by comparing the fair value of the asset to its carrying value. If the fair value of Viva's assets is less than their carrying value, Viva will record an impairment loss. We have already determined that no impairment is necessary for the broadcast license. Thus, we compute a loss for only the plant and equipment.

The loss for the plant and equipment follows:

Fair value	$1,200,000
Less: Carrying Value	(2,100,000)
Impairment loss	$ (900,000)

The journal entry is:

Accounts	***December 31, 2018***	
Accumulated Depreciation—Plant and Equipment	2,100,000	
Impairment Loss on Plant and Equipment	900,000	
Plant and Equipment		3,000,000

The t-accounts for the asset and related accumulated depreciation are as follows:

Plant and Equipment

	Debit	Credit	
Beginning Balance	4,200,000		
		3,000,000	Impairment
Ending Balance (at fair value)	1,200,000		

Accumulated Depreciation—Plant and Equipment

	Debit	Credit	
		2,100,000	Beginning Balance
Impairment	2,100,000		
Ending Balance	0		

The new cost basis for depreciation is the fair value of $1,200,000. Viva will depreciate this amount on a straight-line basis over the remaining 3-year useful life with no salvage value. This calculation results in an annual depreciation expense of $400,000 per year [i.e. ($1,200,000 − 0)/3 years].

Exhibit 12.3 illustrates the process for determining impairment losses for property, plant, and equipment and finite-life intangible assets.

EXHIBIT 12.3 Determining Impairment Losses on Property, Plant, and Equipment and Finite-Life Intangible Assets

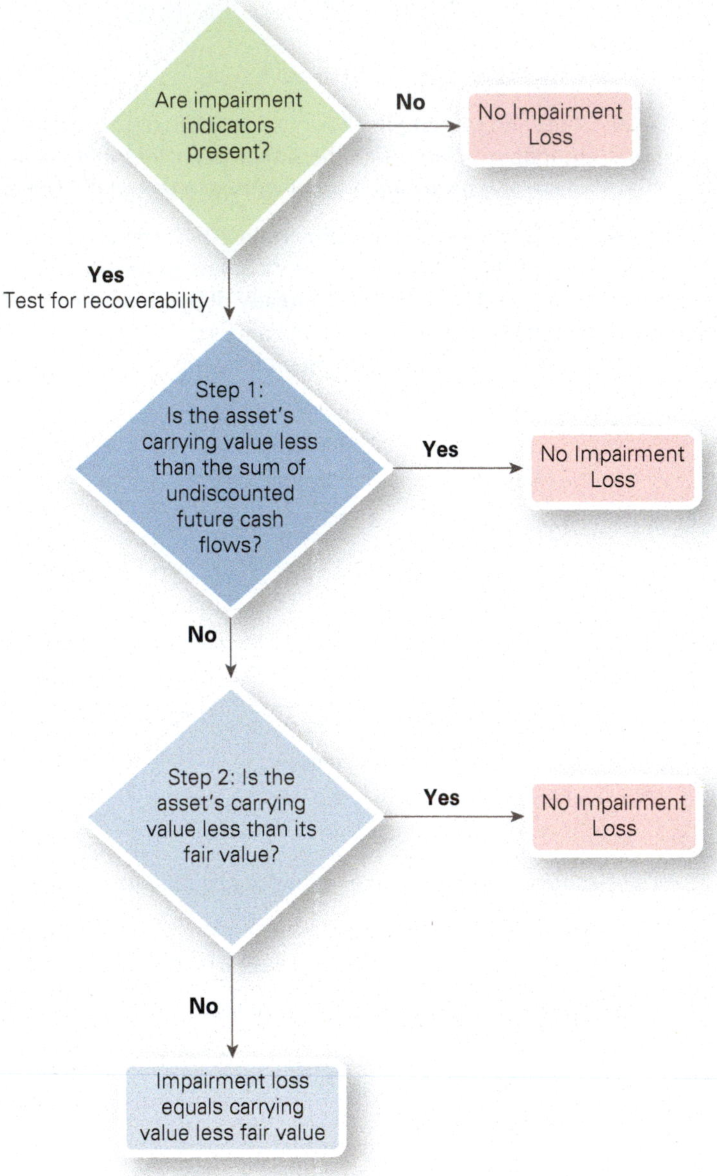

Measurement Subsequent to Impairment

After a write-down, conditions could change and the asset's future cash-generating ability could recover. In this case, the asset's fair value may be higher than its carrying value after the impairment. However, once an impairment loss is taken, U.S. GAAP does not permit subsequent reversals of write-downs for long-term operating assets held for use in operations. For example, if the fair value of Viva's plant and equipment from Example 12.4 increased by \$400,000 to \$1,600,000 from \$1,200,000 after the impairment, Viva cannot write up the carrying value. Whereas the \$1,600,000 fair value may be relevant, allowing impairment reversals questions the reliability of the initial impairment loss and provides an opportunity for managers to opportunistically increase earnings. As noted earlier, the revised carrying value after the write-down becomes the new cost for subsequent depreciation and amortization.

3 Explain and illustrate accounting for impairments of intangible assets with indefinite lives under U.S. GAAP.

Accounting for Impairments: Indefinite-Life Intangible Assets

We now address impairment testing for indefinite-life intangible assets following the same key steps.

Asset Grouping

U.S. GAAP stipulates that firms combine indefinite-life intangibles into an asset grouping if they are operated as a single asset and thus are not separable from each other.

When to Test for Impairment

The firm must consider the possibility of impairment of its indefinite-life intangible assets annually. Firms are allowed two options:

1. Assess qualitative factors annually to determine whether it is necessary to perform the quantitative impairment test. Indefinite-life intangibles are tested annually as opposed to when indicators exist because they are not amortized and thus are more likely to be overstated. If it is "more likely than not" that the asset is impaired, the firm then proceeds to conduct a quantitative assessment of impairment.[5] Qualitative factors could include changes in technology and the marketplace such as consumers preferring touch-screen phones, changes in economic factors such as interest rates that effect present value calculations, or an adverse legal ruling restricting a company's activities.
2. Perform an annual impairment test. The impairment indicators are the same as those identified in Exhibit 12.1.

One-Step Impairment Test

The fair value test determines the impairment loss for an indefinite-life intangible asset as the amount by which the carrying value of the asset exceeds the fair value of the asset.

There is no recoverability test based on future undiscounted cash flows for indefinite-life intangible assets. Many indefinite-life intangible assets easily meet the recoverability test because their cash flows extend many years into the future. The impairment of an indefinite-life intangible asset is illustrated in Example 12.5.

EXAMPLE 12.5

Impairment of an Indefinite-Life Intangible Asset

PROBLEM: Continuing the Viva Enterprises illustration, assume now that the radio broadcast license is renewable at the end of each 10-year term and management has provided evidence that approval of the renewal is highly probable. In this case, the broadcast license qualifies as an indefinite-life intangible asset and is not subject to amortization. Therefore, the firm carries the broadcast license at its original cost of $780,000.

On December 31, 2018, the company noted substantial declines in radio advertising revenues over the past year due to expanded satellite radio subscriptions, Internet broadcasts, and the use of iPod players. Based on the required annual review and consideration of the available impairment indicators, management believes that it is more likely than not that the

Continued

[5]"More likely than not" is measured as a more than 50% chance.

broadcast license may be impaired. Therefore, the company must test the broadcast license for impairment. Similar broadcast licenses have been sold in auctions for $672,000.

Assuming that renewal of the broadcast license is probable for this indefinite-life intangible asset, analyze the accounting for impairment and prepare the journal entries.

SOLUTION: We will address each phase of impairment testing.

Determine When to Test for Impairment

The broadcast license is an indefinite-life intangible asset. Because management believes it is more likely than not that the license is impaired, there is qualitative evidence that the asset is impaired and Viva will conduct a quantitative impairment test.

Determine the Impairment Loss, if Any

To determine the impairment loss, we must compare the carrying value to the fair value.

Carrying value	$ 780,000
Less: Fair value	(672,000)
Impairment loss	$(108,000)

The following journal entry records the impairment loss. This entry differs from the one used to write down a finite-life intangible asset in that there is no accumulated amortization for indefinite-life intangible assets.

Accounts	***December 31, 2018***	
Impairment Loss on Broadcast License	108,000	
Renewable Broadcast License		108,000

The t-account for the broadcast license is as follows:

	Renewable Broadcast License		
Beginning Balance	780,000		
		108,000	Impairment
Ending Balance (at fair value)	672,000		

The $672,000 ending balance is Viva's new basis of reporting for the broadcast license.

Exhibit 12.4 illustrates the process for determining impairment losses for indefinite-life intangible assets.

Measurement Subsequent to Impairment

Similar to accounting for impairment losses on property, plant, and equipment and finite-life intangible assets, U.S. GAAP does not permit subsequent reversals of impairment losses. After the write-down, the firm reports the asset at its revised carrying value.

EXHIBIT 12.4 Determining Impairment Losses on Indefinite-Life Intangible Assets

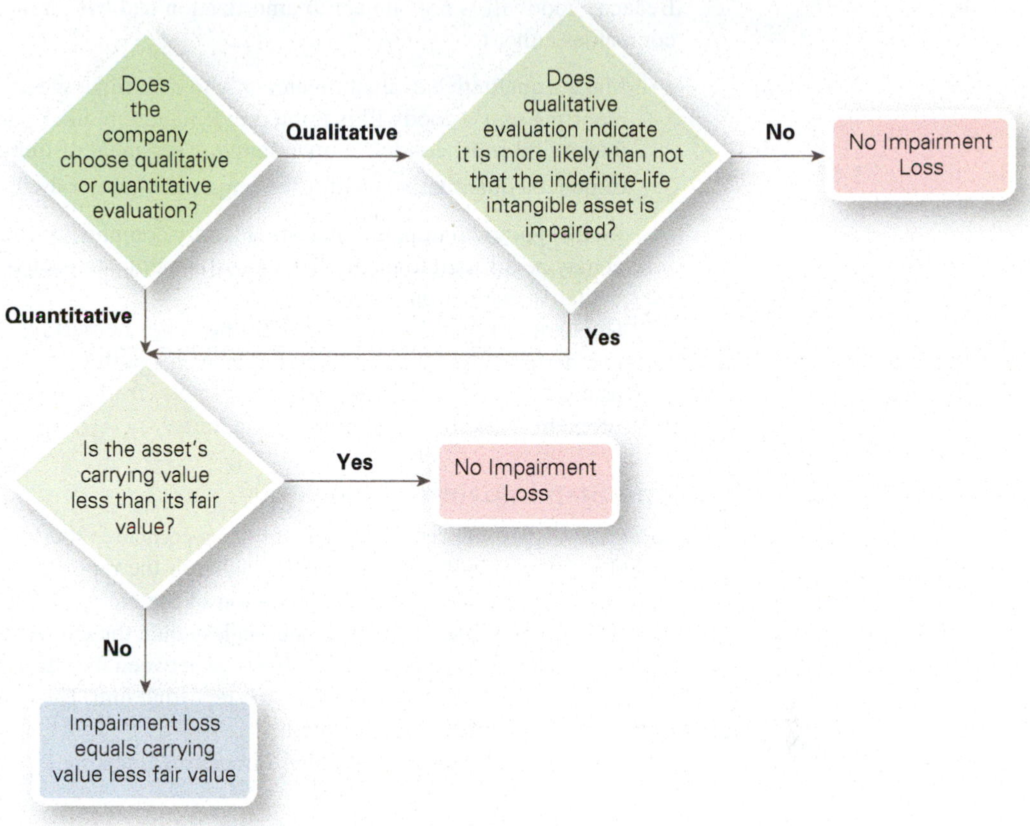

4 Explain and illustrate the accounting for goodwill impairments under U.S. GAAP.

Accounting for Impairments: Goodwill

Impairment testing for goodwill is significantly different from the impairment tests we have discussed thus far. As noted in Chapter 11, goodwill is a unique asset that is not separable from the entity as a whole. Because a firm cannot separate goodwill from a specific set of net assets, it cannot associate goodwill with a specific stream of cash flows as we did for tangible fixed assets and other intangible assets that have value in use.

Asset Grouping

Firms associate goodwill with the group of net assets in the **reporting unit** (**RU**), which is an *operating segment* or one level below an *operating segment*. The Codification defines an **operating segment** as a component of a public entity with the following three characteristics:

1. It engages in business activities from which it may earn revenues and incur expenses.
2. The entity's chief decision maker regularly reviews the performance of the segment.
3. The segment's discrete financial information is available.[6]

[6]See FASB ASC 280-10-50-1 for the complete definition.

When to Test for Impairment

Because goodwill is not subject to amortization and has an uncertain value, U.S. GAAP allows companies either to:

- Make a qualitative evaluation annually to determine whether it is more likely than not that a reporting unit's goodwill is impaired. If it is more likely than not that goodwill is impaired, then a firm must conduct a quantitative assessment of impairment.
- Conduct a quantitative test for the impairment of goodwill at least annually.

Annual goodwill impairment testing is very complex, time consuming, and expensive. Therefore, it may be difficult to justify from a cost-benefit perspective. As a result, U.S. GAAP permits the qualitative evaluation option.

The annual impairment assessment need not be performed at fiscal year-ends. Instead, a firm can perform the fair value measurement for each unit at any time during the fiscal year as long as it uses that measurement date consistently from year to year. A firm can also use different measurement dates for different reporting units.

One-Step Impairment Test

After identifying the reporting unit, the firm compares the fair value of a reporting unit (which includes any goodwill) to the carrying value of the reporting unit, including goodwill. The fair value of the reporting unit is the valuation of the entity as if the company were to be sold in a business combination. If the fair value is less than the carrying value of the reporting unit, then the impairment loss is equal to the difference between the carrying value (including goodwill) and the fair value (including goodwill) of the reporting unit. However, the impairment loss is limited to the carrying value of the goodwill.

Example 12.6 illustrates goodwill impairment testing.

EXAMPLE 12.6 Goodwill Impairment Test: Case 1

PROBLEM: Levi and Peter's Athletic Emporium (LPAE) provided the following information.

Case 1	
Fair value of the reporting unit, including goodwill	$ 1,000
Fair value of the net assets, excluding goodwill	$ 900
Book value of net assets, excluding goodwill	$ 800
Add: Book value of goodwill	300
Book value of the reporting unit, including goodwill	$ 1,100

The qualitative assessment of goodwill is completed and it is more likely than not that goodwill is impaired. Determine whether LPAE needs to record a goodwill impairment loss and prepare any required journal entries.

SOLUTION: We solve the problem based on the following impairment analysis.

Determine When to Test for Impairment
It is more likely than not that LPAE's goodwill is impaired, so we will perform the quantitative test.

One-Step Impairment Test
We compare the fair value of the reporting unit (including goodwill) to its carrying value (including goodwill). The fair value of $1,000 is less than the $1,100 carrying value; thus

LPAE will recognize an impairment loss of $100, which is the difference between the carrying value and fair value. LPAE will make the following journal entry:

Account	Date of Adjustment	
Impairment Loss on Goodwill	100	
Goodwill		100

Example 12.7 illustrates goodwill impairment testing when the impairment loss is limited by the carrying value of the goodwill.

EXAMPLE 12.7 Goodwill Impairment Test: Case 2

PROBLEM: Now assume that LPAE provides the following information.

Case 2	
Fair value of the reporting unit, including goodwill	$500
Fair value of the net assets, excluding goodwill	$400
Book value of net assets, excluding goodwill	$600
Add: Book value of goodwill	300
Book value of the reporting unit, including goodwill	$900

Note that LPAE performs the quantitative test on at least an annual basis. The qualitative assessment of goodwill reveals that it is more likely than not that the goodwill is impaired.

Is there a goodwill impairment loss? Prepare any required journal entries.

SOLUTION: We solve the problem based on the following impairment analysis.

Determine When to Test for Impairment
It is more likely than not that LPAE's goodwill is impaired, so we will perform the quantitative test.

One-Step Impairment Test
We compare the fair value of the reporting unit (including goodwill) to the book value of the reporting unit (including goodwill). Because the carrying value of $900 is more than the fair value of $500, LPAE will recognize an impairment loss. However, it will not recognize the entire $400 difference because the loss is limited to the carrying value of the goodwill. LPAE recognized the impairment loss by making the following journal entry:

Account	Date of Adjustment	
Impairment Loss on Goodwill	300	
Goodwill		300

Exhibit 12.5 illustrates the process for determining impairment losses on goodwill.

EXHIBIT 12.5 Determining Impairment Losses on Goodwill

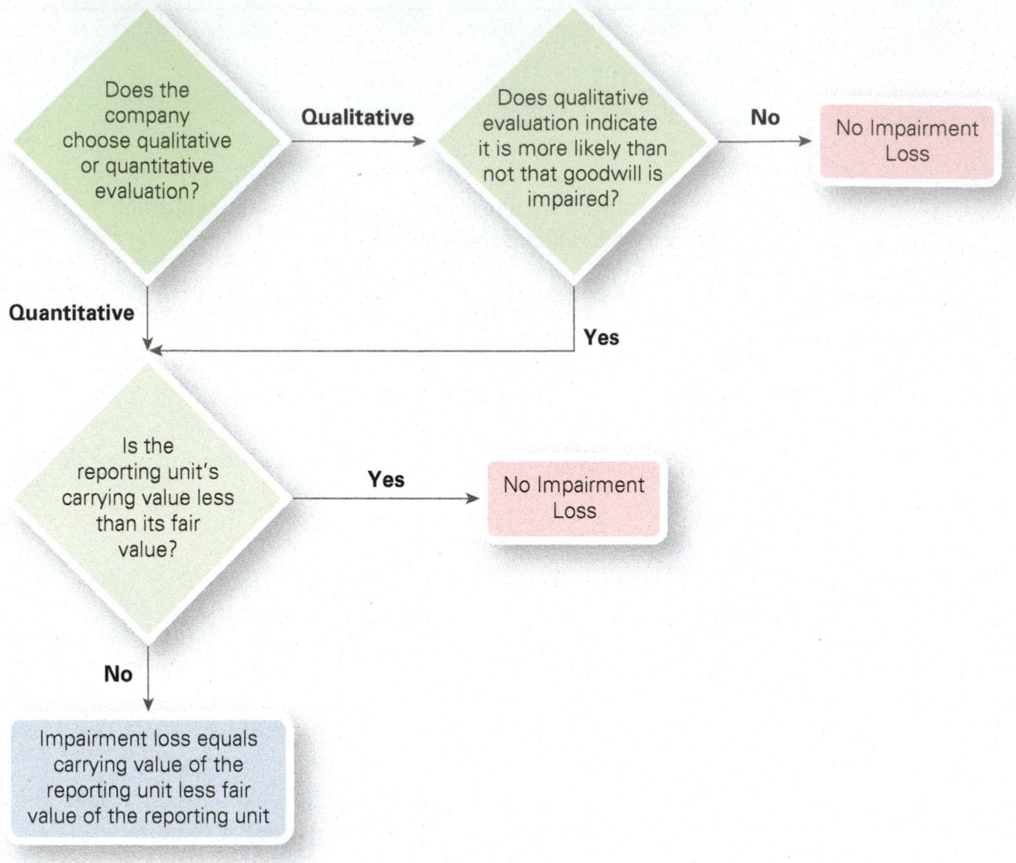

Measurement Subsequent to Impairment

U.S. GAAP does not permit subsequent reversals of goodwill impairment losses. After the write-down, the firm reports goodwill at its revised carrying value.

JUDGMENTS IN ACCOUNTING
For Impaired Long-Term Operating Assets

Managers employ a significant amount of judgment in impairment testing, particularly when determining the inputs used in the impairment process. In fact, in a survey of 175 companies, 51% of these companies reported making estimates and using judgment in estimating their impairments of PPE, if any.[7] Impairment testing is the number one area in the survey where significant judgment is exercised: Seventy-nine percent of companies reported the use of significant judgment in determining their impairments of intangible assets.

Firms determine a new carrying value for an impaired asset based upon an expectation of future economic benefits. But how do they arrive at this new estimate? Common sources include market values of similar assets or a computation of the present value of the future cash flows. In either case, these estimates will often involve a great deal of subjectivity given that the inputs in these computations are based on management judgment.

[7]AICPA, *IFRS Financial Statements: Best Practices in Presentation and Disclosure—2012* (New York, NY: AICPA, 2012).

Consider the facts presented in Example 12.3 related to the possible impairment of the broadcast license (nonrenewable). The carrying value, future cash flows, and fair value were given as follows:

		Broadcast License
Carrying Value		**$507,000**
Future Cash Flows		
Remaining Life	**Year**	
1	2019	$185,000
2	2020	115,000
3	2021	100,000
4	2022	80,000
5	2023	40,000
6	2024	20,000
7	2025	0
Total undiscounted future cash flows		$540,000
Total discounted future cash flows at 5%		$478,964
Fair value		$455,000

We originally concluded that there was no impairment of the broadcast license because the sum of the undiscounted future cash flows was greater than the carrying value. However, Viva's management estimated the future cash flows. How likely is it that management can accurately estimate the cash flows for a broadcast license for the next 6.5 years? Management may be inclined to bias the estimated cash flows in a particular direction either because it would prefer not to record an impairment loss or because it is generally positive about prospects for the company.

Assume that Viva estimated 2019 cash flows at $165,000 (instead of $185,000) and 2020 cash flows at $100,000 (instead of $115,000). The total undiscounted future cash flows would then be $505,000, which is less than the carrying value of $507,000. Viva would then have to move to Step 2 of the impairment test for this finite-life intangible assets. Now, Viva would determine an impairment loss of $52,000, which is the carrying value of $507,000 less the fair value of $455,000.

This illustration shows that the judgment used in estimating future cash flows can make a significant difference in the calculation of impairment losses. Also note that the fair value of an asset is not always reasonably determinable—and fair value estimates and appraisals involve a great deal of judgment.

For example, ***TrueBlue, Inc.,*** a management staffing and outsourcing company, recorded impairment losses on goodwill and intangible assets of $104 million in 2016 resulting in an operating loss of $17 million. If the company had not reported impairment losses, operating income would have been approximately $87 million. ***TrueBlue*** provides a discussion of the many judgments that the company made in order to estimate the impairment. In this discussion of goodwill impairment, ***TrueBlue*** comments "this analysis requires significant estimates and judgments, including estimation of future cash flows, which is dependent on internal forecasts, estimation of the long-term rate of growth for our business, estimation of the useful life over which cash flows will occur, and determination of our weighted average cost of capital, which is risk-adjusted to reflect the specific risk profile of the reporting unit being tested."

5 Describe and demonstrate the accounting for impairments of property, plant, and equipment, finite-life intangible assets, and indefinite-life intangible assets other than goodwill under IFRS.

Accounting for Impairments: Property, Plant, and Equipment, Finite-Life Intangible Assets and Indefinite-Life Intangible Assets: IFRS

We next discuss accounting for impairments under IFRS for long-lived assets other than goodwill. Unlike U.S. GAAP, IFRS impairment testing is similar for all types of long-lived assets other than goodwill. Therefore, we discuss impairments of property, plant, and equipment, finite-life intangible assets, and indefinite-life intangible assets together, and then address goodwill impairment.

Asset Grouping

Asset grouping is similar under U.S. GAAP and IFRS, although there may be some differences in practice. For example, under IFRS, firms will first base impairment on the individual asset. If a firm cannot estimate the recoverable amount of the individual asset, then it groups assets. Under IFRS, the asset group is called a **cash-generating unit (CGU)**, which is the smallest identifiable group of assets that generates cash inflows that are largely independent of the cash inflows from other assets or groups of assets.[8]

When to Test for Impairment

Under IFRS, firms must review the impairment indicators every year to determine whether an impairment test is needed. Similar to U.S. GAAP, a company assesses whether the indicators exist by considering both external factors (such as market interest rates, economic environment, technological breakthrough, or a decline in market capitalization) and internal factors (such as the evidence of obsolescence and restructuring activities in the entity).[9]

Additionally, IFRS requires an annual test for indefinite-life intangibles even in the absence of indicators. For indefinite-life intangible assets, the existence of impairment indicators can prompt more frequent testing. Why are impairment tests more frequent for indefinite-life intangible assets than for PPE and finite-life intangible assets? Because indefinite-life intangible assets are not amortized, there is more risk that firms will overvalue them than with plant and equipment or finite-life intangible assets, which firms carry at net book value.

Impairment Test

IFRS uses a one-step impairment test that has two parts.

- Part 1: Determine the asset's recoverable amount
- Part 2: Compare the asset's recoverable amount to its carrying value

The asset's recoverable amount is the greater of

1. The asset's estimated fair value less costs to sell, or
2. Its **value in use**, the present value of the future cash flows the firm expects to derive from an asset.

Firms then compare the recoverable amount to the carrying value of the asset:

1. If the recoverable amount is *less than* the carrying value of the asset, then the entity is required to measure the impairment loss.
2. If the recoverable amount is *greater than* the carrying value of the asset, then there is no impairment loss.

Under IFRS, the impairment loss is simply the difference between the recoverable amount and carrying value of the asset.[10]

[8]From IASC, *International Accounting Standard 36*, "Impairment of Assets" (London, UK: International Accounting Standards Board, Revised), Paragraph 6.

[9]From IASC, *International Accounting Standard 36*, Paragraph 6.

[10]If assets have been revalued under IFRS, the impairment is treated as a revaluation decrease. We discuss revaluations in Appendix A.

GlaxoSmithKline plc, a large IFRS-reporting pharmaceutical company based in the United Kingdom, discussed recoverability and estimates used in determining value in use in its significant accounting policies footnote, as shown in Exhibit 12.6.

EXHIBIT 12.6 Impairment Accounting Policy, ***GlaxoSmithKline plc***, December 31, 2013, Financial Statements

IMPAIRMENT OF NON-CURRENT ASSETS

The impairment losses principally arise from decisions to rationalise facilities and are calculated based on either fair value less costs of disposal or value in use. The fair value less costs of disposal valuation methodology uses significant inputs which are not based on observable market data, ... These calculations determine the net present value of the projected risk-adjusted, post-tax cash flows of the relevant asset or cash generating unit, applying a discount rate of the Group post-tax weighted average cost of capital (WACC) of 7%, adjusted where appropriate for relevant specific risks. For value in use calculations, where an impairment is indicated and a pre-tax cash-flow calculation is expected to give a materially different result, the test would be re-performed using pre-tax cash flows and a pre-tax discount rate. The Group WACC is equivalent to a pre-tax discount rate of approximately 10%. The impairment losses have been charged to cost of sales £32 million (2012 – £25 million), R&D £14 million (2012 – £9 million) and SG&A £78 million (2012 – £24 million), and include £62 million (2012 – £7 million) arising from the major restructuring programmes.

Source: http://www.gsk.com/content/dam/gsk/globals/documents/pdf/Annual-Report-2013.pdf

The journal entry to record the impairment loss is the same format under both U.S. GAAP and IFRS. When recording the impairment loss, the firm eliminates the balance in the accumulated depreciation or accumulated amortization account and then reduces the asset account. The asset account will reflect its recoverable amount (which is the higher of fair value less costs to sell or value in use). At the date of impairment, the firm records the asset at its recoverable amount. The recoverable amount becomes the new cost of the asset as if it were just acquired, and is subject to depreciation or amortization. Example 12.8 illustrates the impairment calculation under IFRS.

EXAMPLE 12.8

Impairment Calculation: IFRS

PROBLEM: Use the data presented in Example 12.3 and assume that Viva is an IFRS reporter. Based on this information, determine whether these assets are impaired and, if so, compute an impairment loss. Assume no disposal costs.

SOLUTION: We apply the IFRS one-step impairment test as follows.

	Plant and Equipment	**Broadcast License**
1. Determine recoverable amount as the greater of fair value less costs to sell (d) or value in use (c).	Value in use is greater, so recoverable amount is $1,262,499.	Value in use is greater, so recoverable amount is $478,964.
2. Compare carrying value (a) to recoverable amount.	Carrying value greater than recoverable amount.	Carrying value greater than recoverable amount.
	(a) > (c)	(a) > (c)
	$2,100,000 > $1,262,499	$507,000 > $478,964
	Impairment loss is $(837,501).	*Impairment loss is $(28,036).*

PLANT AND EQUIPMENT Under IFRS, plant assets are impaired whenever their recoverable amount is less than the carrying value. Here the plant and equipment's recoverable amount of $1,262,499 is the value in use, which is lower than the plant asset's carrying value ($2,100,000). The impairment loss for the plant and equipment is $837,501.

Continued

Recoverable amount (value in use)	$1,262,499
Less: Carrying value	(2,100,000)
Impairment loss	$ (837,501)

Accounts	December 31, 2018	
Accumulated Depreciation – Plant and Equipment	2,100,000	
Impairment Loss on Plant and Equipment	837,501	
Plant and Equipment		2,937,501

The t-accounts for the asset and related accumulated depreciation are as follows:

Plant and Equipment

	Debit	Credit	
Beginning Balance	4,200,000		
		2,937,501	Impairment
Ending Balance (at value in use)	1,262,499		

Accumulated Depreciation—Plant and Equipment

	Debit	Credit	
		2,100,000	Beginning Balance
Impairment	2,100,000		
Ending Balance	0		

The new cost for depreciation is the value in use of $1,262,499. Viva will depreciate this amount on a straight-line basis over the remaining three-year useful life with no salvage value. This procedure results in an annual depreciation expense of $420,833 per year (i.e., [$1,262,499 − 0]/3 years).

BROADCAST LICENSE The recoverable amount determined under IFRS for the broadcast license also indicates an impairment loss because its recoverable amount ($478,964) is less than the carrying value ($507,000). For the broadcast license, the recoverable amount is the value in use.

Recoverable amount (value in use)	$478,964
Less: Carrying value	(507,000)
Impairment loss	$ (28,036)

Accounts	December 31, 2018	
Accumulated Amortization – Broadcast License	273,000	
Impairment Loss on Broadcast License	28,036	
Broadcast License		301,036

The t-accounts for the asset and related accumulated amortization are as follows:

Broadcast License

	Debit	Credit	
Beginning Balance	780,000		
		301,036	Impairment
Ending Balance (at value in use)	478,964		

Accumulated Amortization—Broadcast License

	Debit	Credit	
		273,000	Beginning Balance
Impairment	273,000		
Ending Balance	0		

The new cost for amortization is the value in use of $478,964. Viva will amortize this amount on a straight-line basis over the remaining 6.5 years of useful life with no salvage value. This procedure results in an annual amortization expense of $73,687 per year (i.e., [$478,964 − 0]/6.5 years).

Example 12.9 illustrates the case of an impairment of an indefinite-life intangible asset.

EXAMPLE 12.9

Impairment of an Indefinite-Life Intangible Asset: IFRS

PROBLEM: Continuing our Viva Enterprises illustration, assume that the radio broadcast license is renewable at the end of each 10-year term and management provided evidence that approval of the renewal is highly likely. The broadcast license qualifies as an indefinite-life intangible asset and is not subject to amortization. Therefore, the firm carries the broadcast license at its original cost of $780,000.

On December 31, 2018, the company noted substantial declines in radio advertising revenues since the past year due to expanded satellite radio subscriptions, Internet broadcasts, and the use of iPod players. Based on the required annual review and consideration of the available impairment indicators, management believes that it should review the broadcast license for impairment. Similar broadcast licenses have been sold in auctions for $672,000. Management estimates the present value of the future cash flows to be $693,000.[11]

Assuming that renewal of the broadcast license is probable for this indefinite-life intangible asset, analyze the accounting for impairment under IFRS and prepare the journal entries. Assume no disposal costs.

SOLUTION: We solve the problem as follows.

Determine When to Test for Impairment

The broadcast license is an indefinite-life intangible asset that Viva must review for impairment on an annual basis under IFRS. In addition, based on the declining radio advertising revenues, the value of Viva's broadcast license may be impaired.

Impairment Test

The following is the determination of impairment under IFRS.

	Broadcast License – Indefinite Life
1. Determine recoverable amount as the greater of fair value less costs to sell or value in use.	Value in use of $693,000 is greater than the $672,000, so recoverable amount is $693,000.
2. Compare carrying value to recoverable amount.	Carrying value of $780,000 is greater than recoverable amount of $693,000.
	Impairment loss is $(87,000).

Continued

[11]This present value estimation is greater than the estimate in Example 12.3 because we are now assuming that the asset has an indefinite life.

To record the impairment loss under IFRS, Viva makes the following journal entry:

Accounts	December 31, 2018	
Impairment Loss on Broadcast License	87,000	
Renewable Broadcast License		87,000

The balance of $693,000 is Viva's new basis of reporting for the broadcast license.

Exhibit 12.7 illustrates the process for determining impairment losses on property, plant, and equipment, finite-life intangible assets, and indefinite-life intangible assets under IFRS.

EXHIBIT 12.7 Determining Impairment Losses on Property, Plant, and Equipment, Finite-Life Intangible Assets and Indefinite-Life Intangible Assets: IFRS

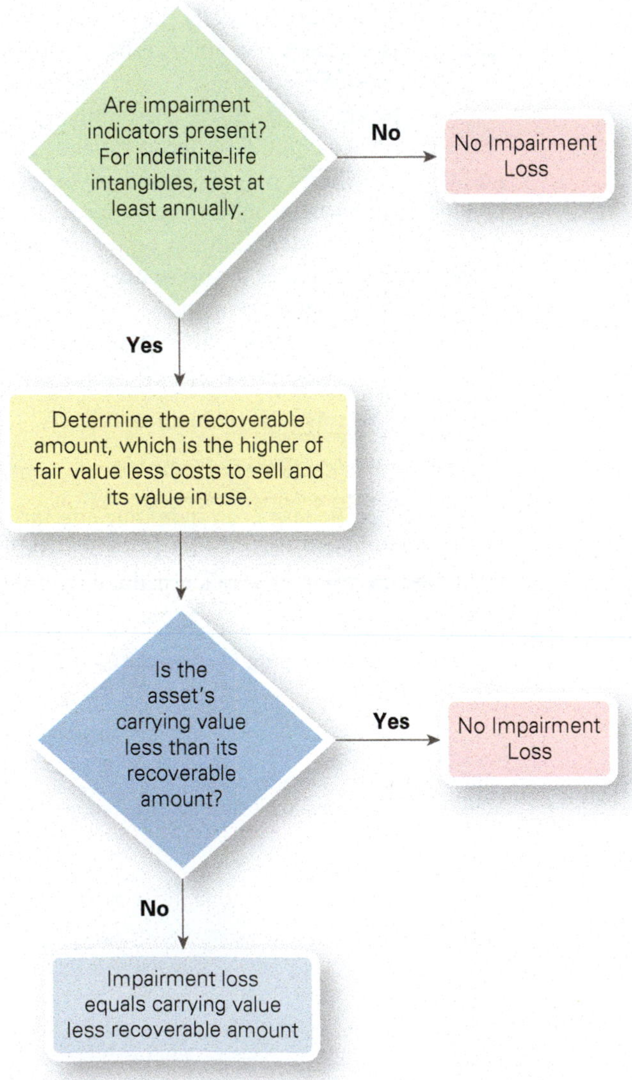

Measurement Subsequent to Impairment. In contrast to U.S. GAAP, IFRS allows firms to reverse impairment loss write-downs on property, plant, and equipment as well as finite-life intangible assets. If the asset's future cash-generating ability improves and its fair value increases, IFRS views the fair value as relevant and reliable information. There are two important constraints:

1. The amount of the write-up (reversal) is limited to the amount of the original impairment loss. The reversal cannot exceed the original impairment loss.
2. The reversal cannot result in a company reporting a value that is higher than what it would be reporting if the asset had never been impaired.

Firms report a reversal of an impairment loss in income.[12] For example, ***GlaxoSmithKline,*** a UK IFRS reporter, reported impairment losses of £289 million and reversals of impairment losses of £97 million on its property, plant, and equipment and intangibles assets in 2016. Impairment reversal is illustrated in Example 12.10.

EXAMPLE 12.10

Impairment Reversal: IFRS Write-Up Limited to Amount of Impairment Loss

PROBLEM: Referring to Example 12.8, assume now that Viva's management found evidence of a reversal of the impairment loss 2 years after it impaired the broadcast license. The value in use of the broadcast license is $340,000 and its fair value is now $350,000. The recoverable amount is the greater of these amounts, which is $350,000. Determine whether Viva can reverse the impairment loss under IFRS and, if so, indicate the maximum amount of the reversal. What is the journal entry to record the reversal? Assume there are no disposal costs.

SOLUTION: We need to compare the current carrying value to the recoverable amount.

Broadcast License	Carrying Value Based on Cost, Adjusted for Impairment
Cost, adjusted for impairment in 2018	$478,964
Less: Accumulated amortization since 2018*	(147,374)
Carrying value (a)	$331,590
Fair value	$350,000
Value in use	$340,000
Recoverable amount (greater of fair value or value in use) (b)	$350,000
Potential reversal of impairment loss (b) – (a)	$ 18,410

*$478,964/6.5 years = $73,687 per year × 2 years

Determining the maximum amount of the reversal that Viva can report in income requires two steps:

Step **1.** Verify that the amount of the reversal is less than the original impairment loss: The $18,410 reversal is less than the original impairment loss of $28,036.

Step **2.** Verify that the newly calculated recoverable amount ($350,000) does not exceed what the original carrying amount, net of amortization, would have been if the license had not been impaired initially. We compute this maximum amount as follows:

Broadcast License	Carrying Value Based on Original Cost
Original Cost	$ 780,000
Less: Accumulated amortization	(429,000)
Carrying value based on original cost	$ 351,000

Continued

[12]For assets revalued under IFRS, we treat an impairment reversal as an increase in a revaluation. We discuss revaluations in Appendix A.

The accumulated amortization is the original cost divided by the 10-year life multiplied by 5.5 years [($780,000/10) × 5.5]. Note that 5.5 years is the total amount of time that has passed since Viva put the broadcast license into use. Because the recoverable amount of $350,000 does not exceed the carrying value ($351,000), based on the original cost less accumulated amortization, Viva can report the impairment reversal of $18,410 in income. The journal entry and t-accounts are as follows:

Accounts	**December 31, 2020**	
Accumulated Amortization – Broadcast License	147,374	
Broadcast License		128,964
Gain on Reversal of Impairment Loss of Broadcast License		18,410

Broadcast License

	Debit	Credit	
Beginning Balance	478,964		
		128,964	Impairment
Ending Balance (at fair value)	350,000		

Accumulated Amortization – Broadcast License

	Debit	Credit	
		147,374	Beginning Balance
Impairment	147,374		
Ending Balance	0		

Example 12.11 illustrates an impairment reversal that is limited to the value that the company would be reporting if the asset had never been impaired.

EXAMPLE 12.11

Impairment Reversal: IFRS Write-Up Limited to Amount of Original Carrying Amount Net of Amortization

PROBLEM: Refer to Example 12.10. Assume that the fair value of Viva's broadcast license is $355,000, instead of $350,000. Thus, the recoverable amount is $355,000, and the potential impairment reversal is $23,410 (Fair value − Carrying value = $355,000 − $331,590). Determine whether Viva can reverse the impairment loss under IFRS and, if so, the maximum amount of the reversal. What is the journal entry to record the reversal?

SOLUTION: The $23,410 reversal is less than the original impairment loss of $28,036. However, the recoverable amount of $355,000 exceeds the amount that the original carrying amount, net of amortization, would have been in the absence of an impairment. This amount, as we computed in Example 12.10, is $351,000. Thus, the impairment reversal can bring the balance for the broadcast license back up only to $351,000. The impairment reversal is therefore equal to $19,410 and is included in net income. The calculation is $23,410 − $4,000 = $19,410. The $4,000 deduction represents $355,000 − $351,000. The journal entry and t-accounts are as follows:

Accounts	**December 31, 2020**	
Accumulated Amortization – Broadcast License	147,374	
Broadcast License		127,964
Gain on Reversal of Impairment Loss of Broadcast License		19,410

Broadcast License

	Debit	Credit	
Beginning Balance	478,964		
		127,964	Impairment
Ending Balance (carrying value based on original cost if no impairment)	351,000		

Accumulated Amortization—Broadcast License

	Debit	Credit	
		147,374	Beginning Balance
Impairment	147,374		
Ending Balance	0		

Notice that after the reversal entry, the carrying value of the broadcast license is equal to what the carrying value would be if Viva had never recorded an impairment (and subsequent reversal).

Exhibit 12.8 shows the impairment testing requirements for long-lived assets other than goodwill under U.S. GAAP and IFRS side by side.

EXHIBIT 12.8 Summary of Impairment Testing for Property, Plant, and Equipment, Finite-Life Intangible Assets, and Indefinite-Life Intangible Assets

U.S. GAAP			IFRS	
Property, Plant, and Equipment and Finite-Life Intangible Assets		**Indefinite-Life Intangible Assets**	**Property, Plant, and Equipment, Finite-Life Intangible Assets, and Indefinite-Life Intangible Assets**	
When to Test for Impairment				
When indicators are present		Firms may opt to: (1) Perform an annual qualitative evaluation to determine whether it is more likely than not that the indefinite-life intangible is impaired. If so, the firm conducts a quantitative assessment of impairment. (2) Conduct a quantitative test at least annually.	Assess existence of impairment indicators annually. For indefinite-life intangibles, test at least annually, even in the absence of indicators.	
Impairment Test				
1. Assess recoverability	Determine whether the asset's carrying value is less than the sum of the future undiscounted cash flows. If no, move to Step 2. If yes, stop.	Compare the carrying value to fair value. If carrying value is less than fair value, no impairment. If carrying value is greater than fair value, impairment loss is the difference between the carrying value and the fair value.	1. Determine recoverable amount	Determine the recoverable amount, which is the greater of fair value less costs to sell and its value in use. Then, move to 2.
2. Compare the carrying value to the fair value (if required)	Compare the carrying value to the fair value. If carrying value is less than fair value, no impairment. If carrying value is greater than fair value, impairment loss is the difference between the carrying value and the fair value.		2. Compare recoverable amount to carrying value	Compare the carrying value to recoverable amount (from 1 above) If carrying value is less than the recoverable amount, no impairment. If carrying value is greater than the recoverable amount, the impairment loss is the difference between the carrying value and the recoverable amount.

Continued

U.S. GAAP		IFRS
Property, Plant, and Equipment and Finite-Life Intangible Assets	**Indefinite-Life Intangible Assets**	**Property, Plant, and Equipment, Finite-Life Intangible Assets, and Indefinite-Life Intangible Assets**
	Loss Reversal (Recovery of Value)	
Not allowed	Not allowed	Allowed up to amount of the original impairment loss. New recoverable amount cannot exceed what the carrying value based on original cost would have been had there not been an impairment.

6 Explain and illustrate the accounting for goodwill impairments under IFRS.

Accounting for Impairments: Goodwill under IFRS

Next, we address accounting for goodwill impairments under IFRS focusing on differences in asset groupings, deciding when to test for impairment, and determining the impairment loss, if any.

Asset Grouping

IFRS associates goodwill with a cash-generating unit (CGU), which is the smallest identifiable group of assets that generates cash inflows that are largely independent of the cash inflows from other assets or groups of assets. After identifying the cash-generating unit, the firm determines the amount of any goodwill impairment.

When to Test for Impairment

IFRS requires an impairment test for goodwill at least annually. The firm can perform the fair value measurement for each unit at any time during the fiscal year as long as it uses the measurement date consistently from year to year. A firm can also use different measurement dates for different units.

IFRS indicates conditions under which a firm may waive the annual goodwill impairment test and instead utilize the prior year's test.[13] In general, these conditions ensure that the makeup of the cash-generating unit has not changed substantially and that the prior test for impairment resulted in a considerable margin between the recoverable amount of the cash-generating unit and the carrying value of the cash-generating unit.

Impairment Test

IFRS uses a one-step impairment test that has two parts to assess goodwill impairment: Part 1—Determine the recoverable amount of the CGU, and Part 2—Compare the recoverable amount of the CGU to the carrying value of the CGU including goodwill.

The firm determines the recoverable amount of a CGU and then compares it with the carrying value of the cash-generating unit, including goodwill. The recoverable amount of the cash-generating unit is the greater of the fair value (less selling costs) of the CGU or the value in use of the cash-generating unit.

The firm reports an impairment loss when the recoverable amount of the cash-generating unit is *less than* the carrying value of the cash-generating unit, including goodwill. If the impairment loss is *greater than* the amount of reported goodwill, the firm first reduces goodwill and then prorates the remaining loss to the unit's other assets based on their carrying value. Goodwill impairment under IFRS is illustrated in Example 12.12.

[13]See IASC, *International Accounting Standard 36*, Paragraph 99 for the specific IFRS conditions.

EXAMPLE 12.12 IFRS Goodwill Impairment: Case 1

PROBLEM: Now assume that Levi and Peter's Athletic Emporium (LPAE) from Example 12.6 is an IFRS reporter and provided the following information.

CASE 1 – IFRS	
Fair value of the CGU	$ 1,000
Value in use of the CGU	$ 650
Book value of net assets of the CGU, excluding goodwill	$ 500
Add: Book value of Goodwill of the CGU	300
Book value of the CGU, including goodwill	$ 800

Based on this information, determine whether there is a goodwill impairment loss under IFRS and prepare any required journal entries. Assume that there are no selling costs associated with the sale of the cash-generating unit.

SOLUTION: We solve the problem using the one-step impairment process.

Determine When to Test for Impairment

IFRS requires firms to test for goodwill impairment at least every year.

Impairment Testing

1. **Assess recoverability.** To determine the recoverable amount, we use the greater of the fair value (less costs to sell) of the CGU or value in use of the cash-generating unit. The recoverable amount is $1,000, the fair value of the cash-generating unit.
2. **Compare the recoverable amount to carrying value.** The recoverable amount of the unit ($1,000) exceeds its total book value ($800), which includes goodwill. LPAE does not have an impairment loss under IFRS.

Example 12.13 illustrates a goodwill impairment under IFRS with an impairment loss.

EXAMPLE 12.13 IFRS Goodwill Impairment: Case 2

PROBLEM: LPAE provided the following information:

CASE 2 – IFRS	
Fair value of the CGU	$700
Value in use of CGU	$650
Book value of the CGU, including $300 goodwill	$800

Is there a goodwill impairment loss under IFRS? Prepare any required journal entries. Assume there are no disposal costs associated with the sale of the cash-generating unit.

SOLUTION: We once again solve the problem with the IFRS one-step impairment process.

Determine When to Test for Impairment

LPAE must test for goodwill impairment at least every year.

Impairment Testing

1. **Assess recoverability.** The recoverable amount is the greater of the fair value (less costs to sell) or value in use of the cash-generating unit. The recoverable amount is $700, the fair value of the cash-generating unit.

Continued

2. **Compare the recoverable amount to carrying value.** The recoverable amount of the unit, $700, is less than its carrying value, $800, indicating there is an impairment loss. The impairment loss is $100 (carrying value of $800 less the $700 fair value).

LPAE recognizes the impairment loss by making the following journal entry:

Account	*Date of Adjustment*	
Impairment Loss on Goodwill	100	
Goodwill		100

Under IFRS, if the impairment loss is greater than the carrying value (book value) of goodwill, the firm reduces the value of other assets of the unit on a prorated basis. Example 12.14 illustrates this scenario.

EXAMPLE 12.14 IFRS Goodwill Impairment: Case 3

PROBLEM: LPAE has a cash-generating unit with a recoverable amount of $400 and a carrying value of $800, which includes goodwill carried at $300. The other assets of the unit are inventory reported at $50 and equipment reported at $450. Should LPAE record a goodwill impairment loss under IFRS? Prepare any required journal entries.

SOLUTION: We solve the problem next.

Determine When to Test for Impairment

LPAE must test for goodwill impairment at least every year.

Impairment Testing

1. **Assess recoverability.** *The recoverable amount of the unit is given to be $400.*
2. **Compare the recoverable amount to carrying value.** Because the $400 recoverable amount of the unit is less than its carrying value of $800, there is an impairment loss. The impairment loss is $400, computed as follows:

CASE 3 – IFRS	
Recoverable amount of the CGU	$ 400
Less: Book value of the CGU, including goodwill	(800)
Impairment loss	$(400)

3. The $400 impairment loss is $100 greater than the amount of goodwill, $300. To record the impairment loss, LPAE reduces the value of the unit's other assets (other than goodwill) by the additional $100 loss. It prorates $10 [$50/($450 + $50) × $100] to inventory and the remaining $90 [$450/($450 + $50] × $100) to equipment. The journal entry is as follows:

Account	*Date of Adjustment*	
Impairment Loss	400	
Goodwill		300
Inventory		10
Equipment		90

Exhibit 12.9 illustrates the process for determining impairment losses on goodwill under IFRS.

EXHIBIT 12.9 Determining Impairment Losses on Goodwill: IFRS

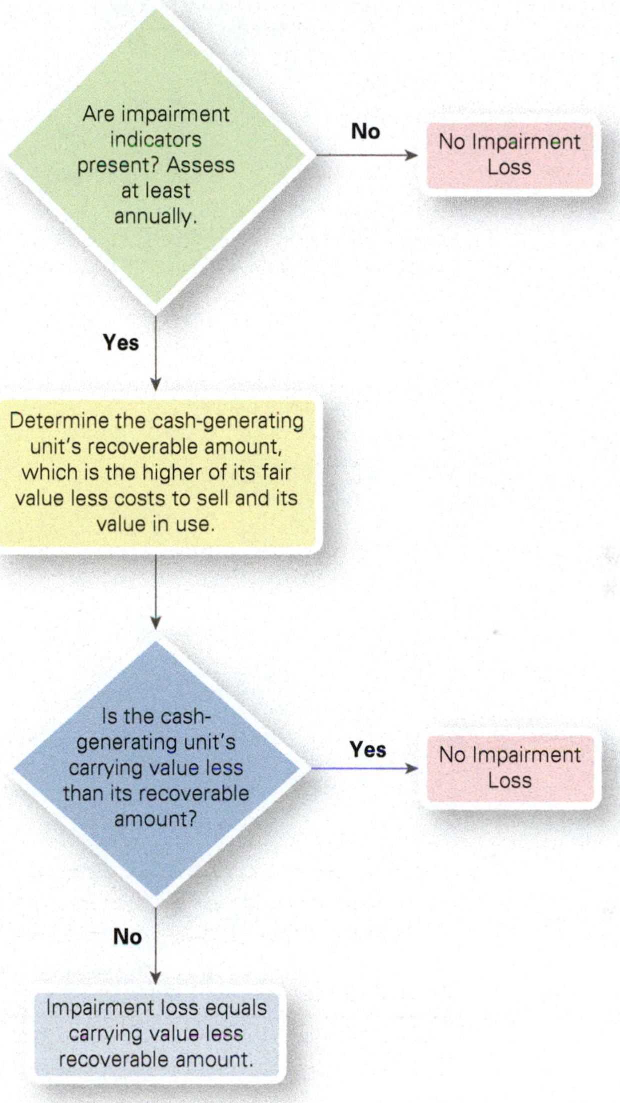

Exhibit 12.10 shows the goodwill impairment testing requirements under U.S. GAAP and IFRS side by side.

EXHIBIT 12.10 Summary of Impairment Testing for Goodwill

U.S. GAAP		IFRS	
When to Test for Impairment			
Firms may opt to: • Make a qualitative evaluation annually to determine whether it is more likely than not that a reporting unit's goodwill is impaired. If it is more likely than not, then a quantitative assessment of impairment must be conducted. —or— • Conduct a quantitative test for goodwill at least annually.		At least annually	
Impairment Test			
1. Compare the carrying value to the fair value	Compare the carrying value of reporting unit (including goodwill) to the fair value of the reporting unit (including goodwill). If carrying value is less than the fair value, no impairment. If carrying value is greater than the fair value, impairment loss is the difference between the carrying value and the fair value. Impairment loss is limited to the carrying value of goodwill.	1. Determine the recoverable amount	Determine the cash-generating unit's recoverable amount, which is the greater of its fair value less costs to sell and its value in use.
		2. Compare the recoverable amount to carrying value	Compare the cash-generating unit's carrying value (including goodwill) to its recoverable amount (from 1 above). If carrying value is less than the recoverable amount, no impairment. If carrying value is greater than the recoverable amount, impairment loss is the difference between the carrying value of the cash-generating unit (including goodwill) and the recoverable amount of the cash-generating unit (including goodwill). Goodwill is first reduced to zero and then the remaining loss is prorated to the unit's other assets.
Loss Reversal (Recovery of Value)			
Not allowed		Not allowed	

7 Detail required disclosures for impaired assets.

Required Disclosures for Asset Impairments

In this section, we detail the required disclosures under U.S. GAAP and IFRS for long-term asset impairments.

Impaired Asset Disclosure Requirements

A firm recognizing an impairment loss on its financial statements should disclose:

1. The asset or asset group that was impaired
2. The events and circumstances that led to the recognition of the impairment (based on the impairment indicators)
3. The amount of the impairment loss in the notes to the financial statements (if the firm does not separately disclose this amount on the income statement)
4. The method or methods used to estimate the fair value of the asset

As introduced earlier, Exhibit 12.2 illustrates ***BlackBerry's*** impairment accounting policies. Exhibit 12.11 presents excerpts from the ***Yahoo's*** fiscal 2016 financial statements illustrating its disclosures related to the impairments of certain intangible assets. Note that the total impairments of $88 million, $4,476 million, and $482 million in the years ended December 31, 2014, 2015, and 2016, respectively, are reported as line items on the income statement. Additional explanation is provided in the financial statement notes. We analyze these disclosures in more detail in the Financial Statement Analysis section later in the chapter.

EXHIBIT 12.11 Impairment Disclosures, ***Yahoo Inc.,*** Annual Report, December 31, 2016

[Excerpt from Income Statement]

For the years ended December 31 (in thousands)	2014	2015	2016
(in thousands, except per share amounts)			
Revenue	$ 4,618,133	$ 4,968,301	$ 5,169,135
Operating expenses:			
Cost of revenue-traffic acquisition costs	217,531	877,514	1,650,786
Cost of revenue-other	1,169,844	1,200,234	1,068,108
Sales and marketing	1,084,438	1,080,718	881,521
Product development	1,156,386	1,177,923	1,055,462
General and administrative	686,272	687,804	650,708
Amortization of intangibles	66,750	79,042	58,302
Gain on sale of patents and land	(97,894)	(11,100)	(121,559)
Asset impairment charge	-	44,381	-
Goodwill impairment charge	88,414	4,460,837	394,901
Intangible assets impairment charge	-	15,423	87,335
Restructuring charges, net	103,450	104,019	88,629
Total operating expenses	4,475,191	9,716,795	5,814,193
Income (loss) from operations	$ 142,942	($4,748,494)	($645,058)

Note 5 Goodwill

The changes in the carrying amount of goodwill for the years ended December 31, 2015 and 2016 were as follows (in thousands):

	Americas(1)	EMEA(2)	Asia Pacific(3)	Total
Net balance as of January 1, 2015	$ 4,322,219	$532,469	$ 297,882	$ 5,152,570
Acquisitions and related adjustments	130,450	21,606	-	152,056
Goodwill impairment charge	(3,929,576)	(531,261)	-	(4,460,837)
Foreign currency translation adjustments	(4,207)	(22,814)	(8,654)	(35,675)
Net balance as of December 31, 2015	$518,886	$ 0	$ 289,228	$ 808,114
Goodwill impairment charge	(394,901)	-	-	(394,901)
Foreign currency translation adjustments	-	-	2,596	2,596
Net balance as of December 31, 2016	$ 123,985	$ -	$ 291,824	$ 415,809

1. Gross goodwill balances for the Americas segment were $4.3 billion as of January 1, 2015 and $4.4 billion as of December 31, 2016. The Americas segment includes accumulated impairment losses of $4.3 billion as of December 31, 2016.
2. Gross goodwill balances for the EMEA segment were $1.2 billion as of January 1, 2015 and December 31, 2016. The EMEA segment includes accumulated impairment losses of $630 million as of January 1, 2016, and $1.2 billion as of December 31, 2016.
3. Gross goodwill balances for the Asia Pacific segment were $457 million as of January 1, 2015 and $451 million as of December 31, 2016. The Asia Pacific segment includes accumulated impairment losses of S159 million as of January 1, 2015 and December 31, 2016.

2016 Impairment Testing

Interim Test.

After recording the goodwill impairment charge for Tumblr during the fourth quarter of 2015, the fair value of the Tumblr reporting unit approximated its carrying value. As such, any significant unfavorable changes in the forecast would result in the fair value being less than the carrying value. During the second quarter of 2016, the Company determined that there were indicators present to suggest that it was more likely than not that the fair value of the Tumblr reporting unit was less than its carrying amount. The significant changes for the Tumblr reporting unit subsequent to the annual goodwill impairment test performed as of October 31, 2015 included a decline in the 2016 and beyond forecasted revenue, operating income and cash flows.

Annual Test.

As of October 31, 2016, the Company conducted its annual impairment test and no additional impairment was identified.

2015 Impairment Testing

In 2015, the estimated fair values of the reporting units for all reporting units identified, except for Tumblr and Latin America, were estimated using a combination of a market approach and an income approach, giving equal weighting to each. This combination is deemed to be the most indicative of the reporting units' estimated fair value in an orderly transaction between market participants and is consistent with the methodology used for the goodwill impairment test in prior years. For the Tumblr reporting unit, the fair value was estimated using an income approach which was deemed to be the most indicative of fair value in an orderly transaction between market participants. For the Latin America reporting unit, the fair value was estimated using the market approach as the income approach yielded negative cash flows and was not deemed to be comparable. The forecast and related assumptions were derived from the most recent annual financial forecast for which the planning process commenced in the fourth quarter of 2015. The estimated fair values of the Company's Taiwan, Hong Kong, and Australia & New Zealand reporting units exceeded their estimated carrying values and therefore goodwill in those reporting units was not impaired. In 2015, the carrying value exceeded the fair value for the following reporting units: U.S. & Canada, Europe, Tumblr and Latin America. . . . The Company recorded goodwill impairment charges of $3,692 million, $531 million, $230 million and $8 million, associated with the U.S. & Canada, Europe, Tumblr, and Latin America reporting units, respectively, for the year ended December 31, 2015. The impairments were a result of a combination of factors, including a sustained decrease in the Company's market capitalization in fourth quarter of 2015 and lower estimated projected revenue and profitability in the near term. The lower estimated projected cash flows and higher discount rates were used to estimate the fair value of each reporting unit affected by such changes.

2014 Impairment Testing

In 2014, as a result of the annual goodwill impairment test, the Company concluded that the carrying value of the Middle East reporting unit, included in the EMEA reportable segment, and the carrying value of the India & Southeast Asia reporting unit included in the Asia Pacific reportable segment both exceeded their respective fair values. . . . Accordingly, the Company recorded a goodwill impairment charge related to the Middle East and India & Southeast Asia reporting units of $79 million and $9 million, respectively, during the quarter ended December 31, 2014 for the difference between the carrying value of the0 goodwill in the reporting unit and its implied fair value with no goodwill remaining in either reporting unit. The impairment resulted from a decline in business conditions in the Middle East and India & Southeast Asia during the latter half of 2014.

Note 6 Intangibles Assets, Net

	Gross Carrying	**Accumulated**	**Impairment**	
December 31, 2015 (in thousands)	**Amount**	**Amortization(*)**	**Charge**	**Net**
Customer, affiliate, and advertiser related relationships	$355,568	$(135,513)		$220,055
Developed technology and patents	170,289	(83,380)		86,909
Trade names, trademarks, and domain names	67,119	(26,814)	-	40,305
Total intangible assets, net	$592,976	$(245,707)	-	$347,269
December 31, 2016				
Customer, affiliate, and advertiser related relationships	$350,896	$(181,451)	$(66,680)	$102,765
Developed technology and patents	128,732	(81,489)	-	47,243
Trade names, trademarks, and domain names	66,631	(34,340)	(20,655)	11,636
Total intangible assets, net	$546,259	$(297,280)	$(87,335)	$161,644

*Cumulative foreign currency translation adjustments, reflecting movement in the currencies of the underlying entities, totaled approximately $18 million and $17 million for the years ended as of December 31, 2015 and 2016, respectively.

Definite-lived intangible assets are carried at cost and are amortized over their estimated useful lives, generally on a straight-line basis, as follows:

- Customer, affiliate, and advertiser related relationships—1 to 6 years;
- Developed technology and patents—3 to 6 years; and
- Trade names, trademarks, and domain names—3 to 7 years.

The Company recognized amortization expense for intangible assets of $132 million, $137 million, and $100 million for 2014, 2015, and 2016, respectively, including $65 million, $58 million, and $42 million, respectively, included in cost of revenue-other. Based on the current amount of intangibles subject to amortization, the estimated amortization expense for each of the succeeding years is as follows: 2017: $76 million; 2018: $55 million; 2019: $30 million; and 2020 and after: $1 million.

Intangibles Impairment Testing

The Company reviews identifiable intangible assets to be held and used for impairment whenever events or changes in circumstances indicate that the carrying value of the assets may not be recoverable. Determination of recoverability is based on the lowest level of identifiable estimated undiscounted cash flows resulting from use of the asset and its eventual disposition. Intangible assets with indefinite useful lives are not amortized but are reviewed for impairment whenever events or changes in circumstances indicate that it is more likely than not that the fair value is less than its carrying amount. If the Company determines that an intangible asset with an indefinite life is more likely than not impaired, a quantitative test comparing the fair value of the indefinite-lived purchased

2016 Testing. During the second quarter of 2016, the Company reviewed its Tumblr asset group for impairment as there were events and changes in circumstances that indicated that the carrying value of the long-lived assets may not be recoverable. As a result, the Company performed a quantitative test comparing the fair value of the Tumblr long-lived assets with the carrying amounts and recorded a partial impairment charge of $87 million associated with its definite-lived intangible assets, which were included within customer, affiliate, and advertiser related relationships and trade names, trademarks, and domain names in the Americas segment. In the fourth quarter of 2016, the Company reviewed its definite-lived intangible assets for impairment. No impairment was identified for definite-lived intangibles.

2015 Testing. In the fourth quarter of 2015, the Company reviewed both definite-lived and indefinite-lived intangible assets for impairment. No impairment was identified for definite-lived intangibles. For indefinite-lived intangibles, the Company performed a quantitative test comparing the fair value of the indefinite-lived intangible assets with their carrying amount and recorded an impairment charge of $15 million related to certain indefinite-lived intangible assets in the EMEA segment. As a result, the entire carrying value of the indefinite-lived intangible assets was fully impaired as of December 31, 2015.

Source: Yahoo Inc., Annual Report, December 31, 2016. http://files.shareholder.com/downloads/YHOO/4381508767x0xS1193125-17-65791/1011006/filing.pdf

Impaired Asset Disclosure Requirements: IFRS

IFRS disclosure requirements are identical to U.S. GAAP with one exception. IFRS also requires disclosure of whether the recoverable amount was fair value less costs to sell or value in use.

Because IFRS allows recoveries of impairment losses, it requires the following additional disclosures by segment:

1. The events and circumstances that led to the recognition of the impairment loss reversal
2. The amount of any impairment loss reversal in income or other comprehensive income
3. The amount of any impairment loss the firm reported in other comprehensive income for assets that it has previously revalued

8 Illustrate the accounting for long-term operating assets held for sale or disposal and describe the required disclosures for these assets.

Long-Term Operating Assets Held for Sale or Disposal

Finally, we address departures from historical cost accounting for long-term operating assets classified as held for sale or disposal. The accounting for assets held for sale or disposal under U.S. GAAP and IFRS is substantially converged.[14] The concepts and judgments that underlie the accounting treatment of assets held for sale are the same as those involved in the accounting treatment of impairments for long-term operating assets.

Recording Long-Term Operating Assets Held for Sale or Disposal

A company selling or disposing of an asset measures the asset at the lower of cost (carrying value) or net realizable value (fair value less selling costs). If a write-down is necessary, then the loss is equal to the difference between the carrying value of the asset and its fair value net of selling costs. If the company writes down the asset in one period and still holds the asset in the next period, then the company can report an increase in value in the subsequent period if the fair value net of selling costs has increased. However, because the asset is held at the lower of cost or fair value less selling costs, the write-up could never result in a carrying value greater than the carrying value of the asset before the write-down or impairment.[15] Exhibit 12.12 illustrates the process of determining a loss on assets held for sale or disposal.

Companies do not depreciate or amortize long-term operating assets while holding them for sale or disposal because they are reporting them at the lower of cost or fair value less selling costs. Companies report the asset as a separate line item on the balance sheet, if material in amount. Accounting for a long-term operating asset is illustrated in Example 12.15.

EXAMPLE 12.15

Long-Term Operating Asset Held for Disposal

PROBLEM: On December 31, 2018, ALR classified one of its plant assets, land, as held for sale. The carrying value of the land as of that date was $2,000,000. The fair value less selling costs on that date was $1,800,000. As of December 31, 2019, the company had not sold the asset, but ALR still classified it as held for sale. The fair value net of selling costs as of December 31, 2019, was $1,950,000. Based on this information, indicate how ALR should report the asset on its December 31, 2018, and December 31, 2019, balance sheets. Prepare any journal entries required.

SOLUTION: ALR makes two journal entries on December 31, 2018. The first is to reclassify the land as held for sale as follows:

Accounts	***December 31, 2018***	
Land Held for Sale	2,000,000	
Land		2,000,000

Then, ALR makes a journal entry to write down the asset as follows:

Accounts	***December 31, 2018***	
Loss on Land Held for Sale	200,000	
Land Held for Sale		200,000

ALR will report the land at $1,800,000, in a separate line on the December 31, 2018, balance sheet, if material in amount. If the plant asset were a depreciable asset, the plant asset would not be depreciated while holding it for disposal.

[14]Under U.S. GAAP, accounting for long-term operating asset impairments and accounting for assets held for sale or disposal are both included in the same set of standards. Under IFRS, a separate standard addresses the accounting for assets held for sale, IASB, *International Financial Reporting Standard 5*, "Non-current Assets Held for Sale and Discontinued Operations" (London, UK: International Accounting Standards Board, Revised).

[15]This accounting is very similar to the lower-of-cost-or-market rule for inventory.

EXHIBIT 12.12 Determining Loss on Assets Held for Sale or Disposal

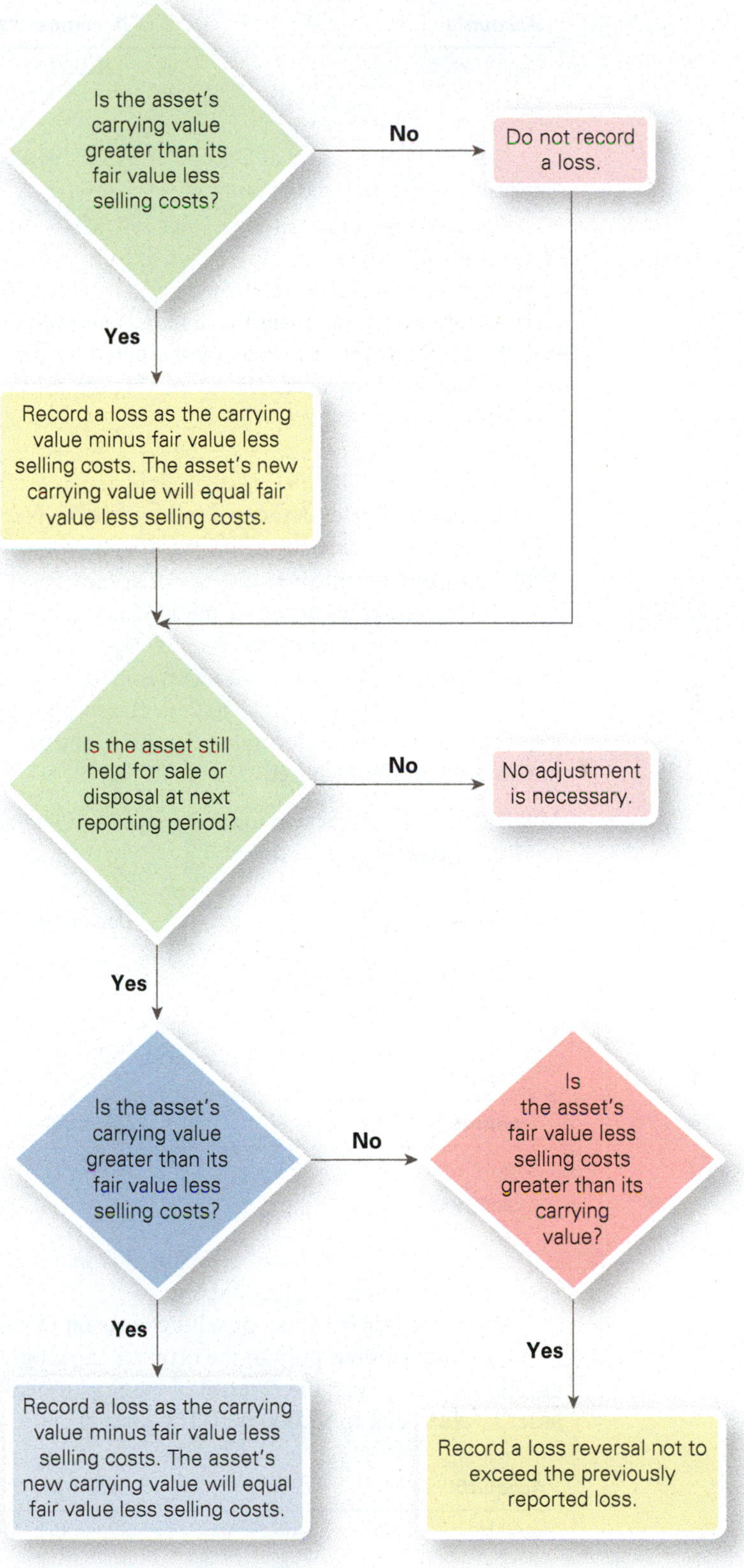

The journal entry to record the market recovery as of December 31, 2019, is as follows.

Accounts	December 31, 2019	
Land Held for Sale	150,000	
Gain on Land Held for Sale		150,000

On the balance sheet at December 31, 2019, ALR will report the land at $1,950,000 on a separate line, if material in amount.

Example 12.16 illustrates that a gain is allowed on the change in the fair value of assets held for disposal. However, the recovery is limited by the carrying value of the asset as of the date it was classified held for sale.

EXAMPLE 12.16 Long-Term Operating Asset Held for Disposal

PROBLEM: On December 31, 2018, ALR, Inc. classified one of its plant assets (land) as held for sale. The carrying value of the land as of that date was $2,000,000. The fair value less selling costs on that date was $1,800,000. As of December 31, 2019, the company had not sold the asset, so it was still classified as held for sale. The fair value net of selling costs as of December 31, 2019, was $2,050,000. Based on this information, indicate how ALR should report the asset on the December 31, 2018, and December 31, 2019, balance sheets. Prepare any journal entries required.

SOLUTION: ALR makes two journal entries on December 31, 2018. First, ALR reclassifies the land as held for sale as follows.

Accounts	December 31, 2018	
Land Held for Sale	2,000,000	
Land		2,000,000

Then ALR writes down the asset as follows:

Accounts	December 31, 2018	
Loss on Land Held for Sale	200,000	
Land Held for Sale		200,000

ALR will report the land at $1,800,000 in a separate line on the December 31, 2018, balance sheet, if material in amount.

Given the fair value net of selling costs on December 31, 2019, of $2,050,000, ALR will write up the asset but only to the original carrying value as of the date it classified the asset as held for sale. Thus, the reversal of the impairment loss is limited to $200,000, bringing the asset's value back to $2,000,000. The journal entry follows:

Accounts	December 31, 2019	
Land Held for Sale	200,000	
Gain on Land Held for Sale		200,000

On the balance sheet at December 31, 2019, ALR will report the land at $2,000,000 on a separate line of the statement, if material in amount.

JACK MARKEY ASSISTANT CONTROLLER, EISAI US, NEW YORK, NEW YORK »

Jack E. Markey

Jack Markey is Assistant Controller at Eisai US, a pharmaceutical company. He serves on the AICPA Financial Reporting Executive Committee.

1 Is a balance sheet more informative for financial statement users if long-term operating assets are stated at fair value rather than at historical cost?

A fair value measurement of long-term operating assets (LTOAs) varies depending on the type of asset, how it is used, the market participants, the asset's highest and best use, and the variables used to compute the asset's fair value (projected cash flows, discount rates, disposal costs, appraised values, etc.). While I favor a mixed attribute model that blends fair value and historical cost, some situations—such as impairments—call for measuring LTOAs at fair value.

While IFRS permits an entity to measure its LTOAs at fair value, the question then becomes what defines a "reliable measurement?" A major concern is that fair value measurement could be the highest possible selling price of the asset—irrespective of its existing use. That can result in a disconnect between the asset's true value and its intended use.

2 How does a revaluation differ from an impairment for long-term operating assets?

An impairment is often caused by an unanticipated event and results in adjusting book value downward. As such, fair value measurements can consider such factors as distressed sales, the entity's liquidity needs, and market volatility. A revaluation applies more of a mark-to-market model and is typically a structured process. This includes regular reassessment of fair value using valuation techniques and measurement models or updated reports from appraisers. As such, its costs might outweigh the benefits.

3 In your opinion, should impairment losses be reflected in current earnings or in other comprehensive income within the stockholders' equity section of the balance sheet?

An impairment loss on a long-lived asset should always be reflected in current earnings. In the absence of an impairment loss, the asset's depreciation or amortization is still reported in earnings. One could argue that the recognition of an impairment loss is a one-time acceleration or "catch-up" of depreciation or amortization that recovers the cost of the asset. If the impairment loss is deferred in Accumulated OCI, the question is what is the appropriate time and circumstances to reclassify the deferred cost into earnings.

4 Given that impairment losses are one-time, non-cash events, many financial statement users may discount the importance of such losses when making future cash-flow projections. Do you agree with this assessment?

It would be a mistake to disregard the importance of impairment losses. Many financial analysts, loan officers, credit rating agencies, and sophisticated investors attempt to model an entity's "cash earnings," often starting with GAAP-based financial statements and working their way back to a cash-based model. By stripping out one-time non-cash events such as impairment losses, analysts supposedly make better earnings forecasts. However, the recognition of an impairment loss indicates that something changed or went wrong within a specific part of the business or management did not foresee an event or condition that led to the impairment charge. Sometimes an impairment may be an early warning for additional problems.

5 What types of judgments do managers make when assessing impairment indicators?

In addition to the impairment indicators within ASC 360-10-35-21, other significant factors in determining whether an impairment exists include:

- How long the asset may be held for sale
- Macroeconomic conditions and the expected time frame to recovery
- Deterioration in market conditions specific to the particular industry
- Cash burn rate and availability of other liquidity sources
- Entity-specific events or circumstances such as changes in management or the core business model, loss of major customer or supplier, and litigation
- Technological obsolescence of the entity's products and/or services and its investment in R&D and new product development.

Discussion Questions

1. Jack Markey indicates that firms currently follow appropriate accounting procedure by reporting impairment losses in current earnings. Provide justification for his assertion and indicate when it may be appropriate to report an unrealized gain or loss in other comprehensive income (OCI).
2. Plant assets are not revalued under U.S. GAAP but revaluation is an option under IFRS. What are some of the benefits of revaluation from the standpoint of a financial statement user?

Required Disclosures of Long-Term Operating Assets Held for Disposal

Companies must disclose the following items when classifying assets as held for sale:

1. The description of the facts and circumstances that led to the expected disposal as well as the expected manner and timing of the disposal
2. The carrying values of the major classes of assets and liabilities included as part of the disposal group (reported either on the face of the financial statements or in the note disclosures)
3. The gain or loss included in net income due to a write-down or write-up (reported either on the face of the income statement or in the note disclosures)
4. The segment, if applicable, that includes the disposal group

FINANCIAL STATEMENT ANALYSIS

Long-Term Operating Assets with Departures from Historical Cost

The quality of earnings is an important issue when analyzing financial statements—and is particularly challenging with long-lived asset impairments and gains or losses on assets held for sale. As noted in Chapter 5, earnings quality captures the degree to which reported income provides financial statement users with useful information in predicting future firm performance.

Permanent earnings—earnings that are likely to continue in the future—are likely to be good indicators of future performance. Impairments are usually viewed as one-time charges unlikely to continue in the future. Therefore, impairment losses are usually not a good predictor of future earnings. However, impairment losses can have implications for future earnings. An impaired asset is no longer likely to generate the originally expected cash flows and future earnings. If assets are impaired, then future earnings are likely to be lower. Similarly, when long-lived assets are held for disposal (or disposed of), future earnings will be lower because the firm is no longer using these productive assets.

In examining impairment charges, a financial statement user should understand and do the following:

- Determine whether the firm has any impaired long-lived assets. If so, determine which assets and the amount of the impairment.
- Identify where impairment losses are reported in the financial statements, such as net income or other comprehensive income. If impairment losses are included in net income, identify the line item in which they are reported.
- Assess performance with and without the impairment losses.

Example 12.17 illustrates the effect of long-lived asset impairments on financial statement analysis.

EXAMPLE 12.17

Financial Statement Analysis of Long-Lived Assets: Departures from Historical Cost

PROBLEM: ***Yahoo Inc.***, the digital information company, reported impairments of long-lived intangible assets of $88 million, $4,476 million, and $482 million in the years ended December 31, 2014, 2015, and 2016, respectively. You are interested in further examining these and any other impairment losses at ***Yahoo*** and have identified the following financial statement excerpts to further analyze. Refer to these financial statements excerpts in Exhibit 12.11 to answer the questions on the next page:

Financial Statement Analysis, continued

Required »

a. What types of intangible assets does ***Yahoo*** report? If ***Yahoo's*** total assets were $45,203,966 thousand and $48,083,079 thousand at December 31, 2015, and December 31, 2016, respectively, how significant are intangible assets to ***Yahoo***?

b. What is the total amount of impairment losses ***Yahoo*** reports in the years ended December 31, 2014, 2015, and 2016? To what types of assets do the impairment losses relate?

c. To what reporting unit(s) does ***Yahoo's*** goodwill impairment loss relate? What was the percentage decline in goodwill due to the impairment loss by reporting segment in 2015, and 2016? Use the beginning balance of goodwill in each year.

d. What is the amount of impairment losses on intangible assets other than goodwill that ***Yahoo*** reports for the years ended December 31, 2015, and 2016? To what type of intangible asset do the losses relate?

e. What would operating income be in 2014, 2015, and 2016 if the impairment losses were excluded? Compare operating income excluding impairment losses to reported operating income for 2014, 2015, and 2016. Comment on how the inclusion or exclusion of impairment losses affects any trend in operating income.

SOLUTIONS:

a. ***Yahoo*** reports intangible assets of customer, affiliate, and advertiser related relationships, developed technology, patents, trade names, trademarks, domain names, and goodwill.

(in thousands)	December 31, 2015	December 31, 2016
Goodwill	$ 808,114	$ 415,809
Intangible Assets, Net	347,269	161,664
Total Intangible Assets	$ 1,155,383	$ 577,473
Total Assets	$ 45,203,966	$ 48,083,079
Percent	2.6%	1.2%

Yahoo's intangible assets compose 2.6% and 1.2% of its total assets at December 31, 2015, and December 31, 2016, respectively. From December 31, 2015, to December 31, 2016, the percent dropped which could be due to intangible asset impairments.

b. On the income statement, we find the total impairment losses and the types of assets impaired in the financial statement notes:

For the Years Ended December (in thousands)	2014	2015	2016
Asset impairment charge	$ -	$ 44,381	$ -
Goodwill impairment charge	88,414	4,460,837	394,901
Intangible assets impairment charge	-	15,423	87,335
Impairment losses	$88,414	$4,520,641	$482,236

The impairment losses relate to goodwill, intangible assets, and originally developed and acquired content.

c. ***Yahoo's*** goodwill impairment loss of $3,929,576 thousand for the year ended December 31, 2015, is related to its Americas reportable segment. ***Yahoo's*** goodwill impairment loss of $394,901 thousand for the year ended December 31, 2016, is related to its Americas reportable segment. The goodwill impairment loss of $531,261 thousand for the year ended December 31, 2015 is due to the EMEA segment. The beginning balance of goodwill in these reportable segments and the decrease due to the impairment losses is presented in the following table.

Financial Statement Analysis, continued

	2015		2016
(in thousands)	**Americas**	**EMEA**	**Americas**
Goodwill, beginning balance	$4,322,219	$532,469	$518,886
Impairment loss	(3,929,576)	(531,261)	(394,901)
Percent decrease due to impairment	(90.9%)	(99.8%)	(76.1%)

d. In 2016, the remaining amount of ***Yahoo's*** impairment loss on intangible assets is due to the impairment of the customer, affiliate, and advertiser related relationships of $66,680 thousand and trade names, trademarks, and domain names of $20,655 thousand.

e. The comparison of the percent change in operating income with and without the impairment losses follow.

Reported			
For the Years Ended December 31 (in thousands)	**2014**	**2015**	**2016**
Operating income	$142,942	$(4,748,494)	$(645,058)
Adjusted to Exclude Long-lived Asset Impairment Losses			
Operating Income	$142,942	$(4,748,494)	$(645,058)
Add back impairment losses from part (b)	88,414	4,520,641	482,236
Adjusted operating income	$231,356	$ (227,853)	$(162,822)

Analyzing ***Yahoo's*** operating income without the impairment losses, we note that the company would have still reported operating losses in 2015 and 2016. Therefore, the other components of operating income contribute to the decline in operating income in 2015 and 2016. These other factors should be given more weight in an analysis because, unlike the impairment losses, the other revenue and expense components are part of the continuing operations of the company.

Source: Yahoo Inc., Annual Report, December 31, 2016. http://files.shareholder.com/downloads/YHOO/4381508767x0xS1193125-17-65791/1011006/filing.pdf

Summary by Learning Objectives

Below we summarize the main points by learning objective. Throughout the chapter, we discuss the accounting and reporting of U.S. GAAP and IFRS side-by-side. The table below also highlights the major similarities and differences between the standards.

1 Specify the categories of long-term operating assets tested for impairment.

Summary	Similarities and Differences between U.S. GAAP and IFRS
Three categories of long-term operating assets are tested for impairment: 1. Property, plant, and equipment and finite-life intangible assets 2. Indefinite-Life intangible assets 3. Goodwill	Similar under U.S. GAAP and IFRS.

Summary by Learning Objectives, continued

2 Describe and demonstrate the accounting for impairments of property, plant, and equipment and intangible assets with finite lives under U.S. GAAP.

Summary	Similarities and Differences between U.S. GAAP and IFRS
Accounting for impairments includes assessing when to test for impairment and computing any impairment loss when impairment indicators are present. Determine whether to recognize an impairment loss using a two-step procedure: Step 1. Assess recoverability by determining whether the asset's carrying value is less than the sum of the future undiscounted cash flows. If no, move to Step 2. If yes, stop. Step 2. If required, compare the carrying value to the fair value. If carrying value is less than fair value, there is no impairment. If carrying value is greater than fair value, impairment loss is the difference between the carrying value and the fair value.	➤ Significant differences are summarized in Learning Objective 5.

3 Explain and illustrate accounting for impairments of intangible assets with indefinite lives under U.S. GAAP.

Summary	Similarities and Differences between U.S. GAAP and IFRS
Accounting for impairments includes assessing when to test for impairment with a qualitative evaluation annually and computing any impairment loss. If it is more likely than not that an asset is impaired, then the firm must conduct a quantitative assessment of impairment. Alternatively, the firm can conduct a quantitative test at least annually. To determine whether to recognize an impairment loss, compare the asset's carrying value to fair value. If the carrying value is less than fair value, there is no impairment. If the carrying value is greater than fair value, the impairment loss is the difference between the carrying value and the fair value.	➤ Significant differences are summarized in Learning Objective 5.

4 Explain and illustrate the accounting for goodwill impairments under U.S. GAAP.

Summary	Similarities and Differences between U.S. GAAP and IFRS
Accounting for impairments includes assessing when to test for impairment and computing any impairment loss. A firm can make a qualitative evaluation annually. If it is more likely than not that the goodwill is impaired, then the firm must conduct a quantitative assessment of impairment. Alternatively, the firm can conduct a quantitative test at least annually. Determine whether to recognize an impairment loss, using a one-step procedure: Compare the reporting unit's (RU's) carrying value with goodwill to its fair value with goodwill. If the carrying value is greater, then the impairment loss equals the carrying value of the reporting unit less the fair value of the reporting unit. The impairment loss is limited to the carrying value of goodwill.	➤ Significant differences are summarized in Learning Objective 6.

Summary by Learning Objectives, continued

5 Describe and demonstrate the accounting for impairments of property, plant, and equipment, finite-life intangible assets, and indefinite-life intangible assets other than goodwill under IFRS.

Summary	Similarities and Differences between U.S. GAAP and IFRS
See Learning Objectives 2 and 3 for summary of U.S. GAAP.	➤ Accounting for impairments includes assessing when to test for impairment and computing any impairment loss. Under IFRS, assess existence of impairment indicators annually. However, for indefinite-life intangible assets, IFRS requires an annual test even in the absence of indicators. Determine whether to recognize an impairment loss using a one-step procedure with two parts: Part 1. Determine the recoverable amount, which is the greater of fair value less costs to sell and its value in use. Part 2. Compare the carrying value to recoverable amount. If the carrying value is less than the recoverable amount, no impairment. If carrying value is greater than the recoverable amount, the impairment loss is the difference between the carrying value and the recoverable amount. Impairment losses can be reversed if the asset's value recovers.

6 Explain and illustrate the accounting for goodwill impairments under IFRS.

Summary	Similarities and Differences between U.S. GAAP and IFRS
See Learning Objective 4 for summary of U.S. GAAP.	➤ Accounting for impairments includes assessing when to test for impairment and computing any impairment loss. Under IFRS, test for goodwill impairments at least annually. The test may be waived if certain conditions are met. Determine whether to recognize an impairment loss using a one-step procedure with two parts: Part 1. Determine the cash-generating unit's recoverable amount, which is the greater of its fair value less costs to sell and its value in use. Part 2. Compare the cash-generating unit's carrying value (including goodwill) to its recoverable amount. If the carrying value is less than the recoverable amount, there is no impairment. If the carrying value is greater than the recoverable amount, the impairment loss is the difference between the carrying value of the cash-generating unit (including goodwill) and the recoverable amount of the cash-generating unit (including goodwill). Goodwill is first reduced to zero and then the remaining loss is prorated to the unit's other assets. The specific procedures are summarized in Exhibit 12.9.

7 Detail required disclosures for impaired assets.

Summary	Similarities and Differences between U.S. GAAP and IFRS
Disclosures include: 1. Asset or asset group that was impaired 2. Events and circumstances that led to the recognition of the impairment 3. Amount of the impairment loss in the notes to the financial statements 4. Method or methods used to estimate the fair value of the asset	➤ In addition to the disclosures required by U.S. GAAP, IFRS requires disclosure of whether the recoverable amount was measured as fair value less costs to sell or value in use as well as additional disclosures by segment.

Summary by Learning Objectives, continued

8 Illustrate the accounting for long-term operating assets held for sale or disposal and describe the required disclosures for these assets.	
Summary	**Similarities and Differences between U.S. GAAP and IFRS**
Firms record long-term operating assets held for disposal at the lower of cost (carrying value) or fair value less selling costs. These assets are not depreciated.	Similar under U.S. GAAP and IFRS.

MyLab Accounting

Go to **http://www.pearson.com/mylab/accounting** for the following Questions, Multiple-Choice Questions, Brief Exercises, Exercises, and Problems. They are available with immediate grading, explanations of correct and incorrect answers, and interactive media that acts as your own online tutor

12 Long-Term Operating Assets: Departures from Historical Cost

Questions

1 2 3 4 **Q12-1.** Is the impairment test for tangible, long-term operating assets identical to the impairment test for intangible assets? Explain.

2 **Q12-2.** Can firms group all property, plant, and equipment for purposes of performing an impairment test? Explain.

1 2 3 4 **Q12-3.** Does recognizing an impairment loss on a long-term operating asset have the same effect on the financial statements as recording depreciation expense and amortization expense? Explain.

2 3 4 **Q12-4.** Is an annual impairment test required for all long-term operating assets? Explain.

2 3 4 **Q12-5.** Do firms follow the same steps for impairment testing of finite- and indefinite-life intangible assets? Explain.

2 3 4 **Q12-6.** When measuring an impairment loss for a long-term operating asset, must firms determine the fair value using a discounted cash-flow model? Explain.

3 **Q12-7.** After recording an impairment of an indefinite-life operating asset, can a firm recover the impairment loss in subsequent accounting periods? Explain.

4 **Q12-8.** Are firms required to test goodwill acquired in a business combination for impairment on an annual basis? Explain.

5 6 **Q12-9.** Under IFRS, if a firm recovers an impairment loss on a long-term operating asset, does it report the asset at its current fair value? Explain.

5 6 **Q12-10.** Under IFRS, when do firms test plant assets and finite-life intangible assets for impairment?

A **Q12-11.** Under IFRS, when revaluing a plant asset to fair value, do firms include all gains and losses in net income? Explain.

A **Q12-12.** Under IFRS, when a firm sells a plant asset that it revalued to fair value, what is the gain or loss on the sale?

Multiple-Choice Questions

2 **MC12-1.** Sumrall Corporation owns machinery that was purchased 20 years ago. The machinery, which originally cost $2,000,000, has been depreciated using the straight-line method using a 40-year useful life and no salvage value and has a current carrying amount of $1,000,000 and a current fair value of $800,000. Sumrall estimates that the machinery has a remaining useful life of 20 years and will provide net cash inflow of $45,000 per year. Sumrall should record an impairment loss associated with the machinery of:

a. $0 since there is no impairment
b. $150,000
c. $100,000
d. $200,000

2 **MC12-2.** On December 31, Year 1, Brown Brothers purchased machine A for $770,000 and machine B for $300,000. The machines are depreciated on the straight-line basis over 10 years with no salvage value. Brown reviews its assets for impairment annually. While doing the U.S. GAAP impairment analysis at year-end of Year 6, Brown determines that the expected future cash flows are $70,000 per year from machine A and $40,000 per year from machine B over the remaining lives of the assets. At December 31, Year 6, the fair values of machines A and B are $300,000 and $180,000, respectively. What amount of impairment loss should Brown report on its Year 6 income statement under U.S. GAAP?

a. $85,000 b. $35,000 c. $50,000 d. $0

2 **MC12-3.** On December 31, an entity analyzed a finite life trademark with a net carrying value of $750,000 for impairment. The entity determined the following:

Fair value	$700,000
Undiscounted future cash flows	$740,000

What is the impairment loss that will be reported on the December 31 income statement under U.S. GAAP?

a. $0 b. $10,000 c. $40,000 d. $50,000

4 **MC12-4.** On December 31, Star Corp. had a reporting unit that had a book value of $950,000, including goodwill of $130,000. As part of the company's annual review of goodwill impairment, Star determined that the fair value of the reporting unit was $890,000. Star assigned $840,000 of the reporting unit's fair value to its assets and liabilities other than goodwill. What is the goodwill impairment loss to be reported on December 31 under U.S. GAAP?

a. $50,000 b. $60,000 c. $80,000 d. $110,000

5 **MC12-5.** Sumrall Corporation owns machinery that was purchased 20 years ago. The machinery, which originally cost $2,000,000, has been depreciated using the straight-line method using a 40-year useful life and no salvage value and has a current carrying amount of $1,000,000 and a current fair value of $800,000. Sumrall estimates that it would incur selling costs of $10,000 if it sold the machine and that the present value of the future cash flows from the machine is $820,000. Under IFRS, Sumrall should record an impairment loss associated with the machinery of:

a. $0 b. $180,000 c. $200,000 d. $210,000

5 **MC12-6.** On December 31, an entity analyzed a finite life trademark with a net carrying value of $750,000 for impairment. The entity determined the following:

Fair value (less costs to sell)	$ 700,000
Present value of future cash flows	710,000

What is the impairment loss that will be reported on the December 31 income statement under IFRS?

a. $0 b. $10,000 c. $40,000 d. $50,000

Brief Exercises

2 **BE12-1. Tangible Asset Groups.** Almonzo's Flower Box, Inc. operates a floral delivery service. The company has three delivery trucks. It recently signed a contract to make deliveries for two local florists. The delivery route for one of the florists has been unprofitable. Are the three trucks considered an asset group for purposes of conducting an impairment test? Assume that all three trucks are used for both florists.

2 **BE12-2. Tangible Asset Impairment.** Fillepeel Manufacturing, Inc. has only one plant asset used in production. The asset had a cost of $500,000 and has been depreciated for 2 full years since the date of acquisition. This accounting resulted in a total accumulated depreciation of $200,000. The firm expects the asset to be productive for an additional 3 years and projects the asset's future cash flows to be $120,000 per year. Information about the company's products indicates that the asset might be impaired. Should the firm record an impairment loss for the current year? (Provide supporting computations.)

2 **BE12-3. Tangible Asset Impairment.** Tank Top Menswear, Ltd. reported net plant and equipment of $1,600,000. These assets cost $2,500,000 with accumulated depreciation taken to date of $900,000. Based on recently assessed negative evidence, Tank Top's management concluded that its plant assets might be impaired. Tank Top estimates total expected future cash flows from the use of the assets as only $1,300,000 and appraises the fair value of the assets at $1,000,000. Are the company's assets impaired? If there is an impairment loss, prepare the journal entry necessary to record the impairment.

2 **BE12-4. Finite-Life Intangible Asset Impairment.** Fredrick Wilson Company determined that one of its finite-life intangible assets is impaired. The asset's net carrying value on the date of the impairment is $905,000. Fredrick Wilson does not use a separate accumulated amortization account. In order to estimate fair value,

Fredrick Wilson must use the discounted cash-flow model. The company projected the asset's future cash flows as follows.

Future Period	Cash-Flow Projection
Year 1	$400,000
Year 2	250,000
Year 3	140,000
Year 4	60,000
Total	$850,000

Assuming a discount rate of 8%, prepare the journal entry to record the impairment loss (show all supporting computations).

3 **BE12-5. Indefinite-Life Intangible Asset Impairment.** Genius Auto Malls recently conducted its annual impairment review of the value of its trademark (an indefinite-life intangible asset), which it currently carries at $2,500,000. Evidence indicates that the trademark may be impaired. Genius estimates the future cash flows related to the trademark for the next 5 years as follows:

Future Period	Cash-Flow Projection
Year 1	$ 800,000
Year 2	700,000
Year 3	460,000
Year 4	140,000
Year 5	100,000
Total	$2,200,000

The company estimates that the fair value of the trademark is $1,700,000. Determine whether the trademark is impaired. If so, what is the amount of the impairment loss?

4 **BE12-6. Goodwill Impairment.** Events and circumstances indicate the need for Lenny Schaeffer Bakeries to undertake quantitative testing of goodwill. The current carrying value of the reported goodwill for the reporting unit is $800,000. The goodwill pertains to the reporting unit. The book value of the net assets of the reporting unit, excluding goodwill, is equal to $1,200,000. The fair value of the reporting unit including goodwill is $2,200,000. Determine whether Schaeffer's goodwill is impaired.

4 **BE12-7. Goodwill Impairment.** Local Craft Designs, Inc. reported goodwill at $600,000 related to its Central Avenue Division. The fair value of Central Avenue is $2,500,000. The carrying value of Central Avenue's net assets, excluding goodwill, is reported at $2,100,000 and appraised at $2,310,000. Determine whether goodwill is impaired and prepare any journal entry necessary to record the impairment loss.

5 **BE12-8. Tangible Asset Groups, IFRS.** Almonzo's Flower Box, Inc., an IFRS reporter, operates a floral delivery service. The company has three delivery trucks. It recently signed a contract to make deliveries for two local florists. The delivery route for one of the florists has been unprofitable. Should it consider the three trucks an asset group for purposes of conducting an impairment test? Assume all three trucks are used for both florists.

5 **BE12-9. Tangible Asset Impairment, IFRS.** Fillepeel Manufacturing, Inc., an IFRS reporter, has only one plant asset used in production. The asset had a cost of $500,000 and was depreciated for 2 full years since the date of acquisition. This accounting resulted in a total accumulated depreciation of $200,000. The firm expects the asset to be productive for an additional 3 years. The asset's value in use is $223,000, and its fair value less costs to sell is $309,000. Information about the company's products indicates that the asset might be impaired. Should the firm record an impairment loss for the current year? (Provide supporting computations.)

5 **BE12-10. Tangible Asset Impairment, IFRS.** Tank Top Menswear, Ltd., an IFRS reporter, reported net plant and equipment of $1,600,000. These assets cost $2,500,000 with accumulated depreciation taken to date of $900,000. Based on recently assessed negative evidence, Tank Top's management concluded that its plant assets might be impaired. Tank Top estimates that the value in use is $1,087,000, based on discounted expected future cash flows from the use of the assets. The fair value of the assets less costs to sell is $1,000,000. Are the company's assets impaired? If there is an impairment loss, prepare the journal entry necessary to record the impairment.

5 **BE12-11. Impairment Reversal, IFRS.** Perlu Products, an IFRS reporter, reported an impairment loss of $65,000 for one of its plant assets on December 31, 2018. At December 31, 2019, the asset's recoverable amount increased by $90,000. The current carrying value is $100,000 less than it would have been if the asset had not been impaired. The recoverable amount does not exceed the original carrying value net of accumulated depreciation as if the asset was not impaired. Can Perlu record a recovery? Prepare the journal entry to record the recovery if it is permitted.

5 **BE12-12. Finite-Life Intangible Asset Impairment, IFRS.** Fredrick Wilson Company, an IFRS reporter, determined that one of its finite-life intangible assets is impaired. The asset's net carrying value on the date of the impairment is $905,000. Fredrick Wilson does not use a separate accumulated amortization account. To measure the impairment loss, the company projected the asset's future cash flows as follows:

Future Period	Cash-Flow Projection
Year 1	$400,000
Year 2	250,000
Year 3	140,000
Year 4	60,000
Total	$850,000

The selling price in the market, less costs to sell, for similar assets is $720,000.

Assuming a discount rate of 8%, prepare the journal entry to record the impairment loss (show all supporting computations).

5 **BE12-13. Indefinite-Life Intangible Asset Impairment, IFRS.** Genius Auto Malls, an IFRS reporter, recently conducted its annual impairment review of the value of its trademark (an indefinite-life intangible), which it currently carries at $2,500,000. Evidence exists that the trademark may be impaired. Genius estimates the future cash flows related to the trademark for the next 5 years as follows:

Future Period	Cash-Flow Projection
Year 1	$ 800,000
Year 2	700,000
Year 3	460,000
Year 4	140,000
Year 5	100,000
Total	$2,200,000
Present value of cash flows	$1,987,722

The company estimated that the fair value less costs to sell the trademark is $1,700,000. Determine whether the trademark is impaired. If so, what is the amount of the impairment loss?

6 **BE12-14. Goodwill Impairment, IFRS.** Lenny Schaeffer Bakeries, an IFRS reporter, is required to test goodwill for impairment each year. The current carrying value of its reported goodwill is $800,000. The goodwill pertains to the cash-generating unit. The book value of the net assets of the cash-generating unit, excluding goodwill, is equal to $1,200,000. The fair value of the cash-generating unit (less costs to sell) is $2,200,000. Its value in use is $2,150,000. Determine whether Schaeffer's goodwill is impaired.

6 **BE12-15. Goodwill Impairment, IFRS.** Local Craft Designs, Inc., an IFRS reporter, reported goodwill at $600,000 related to its Central Avenue Division. The fair value less costs to sell Central Avenue is $2,500,000. Its value in use is $2,550,000. The firm reports Central Avenue's carrying value of the net assets, excluding goodwill, at $2,100,000. Determine whether goodwill is impaired and prepare any journal entry necessary to record the impairment loss.

7 **BE12-16. Tangible Asset Impairment, Disclosure.** Airwave Corporation was required to write down one of its plant assets by $1,650,000 on December 31 of the current year because the asset's technology has been rendered obsolete. It estimated the fair value of the asset using a discounted cash-flow model. It projected future cash flows for the next 5 years and used a 9% cost of capital for this purpose. Prepare the footnote disclosure for the impairment loss.

7 **BE12-17. Tangible Asset Impairment, Disclosure, IFRS.** Airwave Corporation, an IFRS reporter, was required to write down one of its plant assets by $1,650,000 on December 31 of the current year because the asset's technology was rendered obsolete. It used a discounted cash-flow model to estimate the asset's value in use. It projected future cash flows for the next 5 years and used a 9% cost of capital for this purpose. The value in use was greater than the estimated fair value less selling costs. Prepare the footnote disclosure for the impairment loss.

8 **BE12-18. Tangible Asset Held for Disposal.** Perlu Products reported a write-down loss of $65,000 for one of its plant assets on December 31, 2018. The asset is currently held for disposal. At December 31, 2019, the fair value of the asset increased by $90,000. Can Perlu record a recovery? Prepare the journal entry to record the recovery if it is permitted.

8 **BE12-19. Tangible Asset Held for Disposal, IFRS.** Perlu Products, an IFRS reporter, reported a write-down loss of $65,000 for one of its plant assets on December 31, 2018. The asset is currently held for disposal. At December 31, 2019, the fair value of the asset increased by $90,000. Can Perlu record a recovery? Prepare the journal entry to record the recovery if it is permitted.

A **BE12-20. Asset Revaluation, Upwards, IFRS.** Esta Company, an IFRS reporter, has opted to revalue land. The land originally cost €2,000,000 on January 1. At the end of the year, the land is appraised at €2,200,000. Determine the amount of gain or loss on the asset revaluation and indicate where to report this information on the consolidated financial statements.

A **BE12-21. Asset Revaluation, Downward, IFRS.** Esta Company, an IFRS reporter, has opted to revalue land. The land originally cost €2,000,000 on January 1. At the end of the year, the land is appraised at €1,800,000. Determine the amount of gain or loss on the asset revaluation and indicate where to report this information on the consolidated financial statements.

A **BE12-22. Sale of Revalued Assets, IFRS.** Blanc Corporation sold a piece of land for $620,000. The land originally cost $450,000, but Blanc revalued it to $600,000 last year.

a. What is the gain or loss on the sale?
b. What are the journal entries to record the sale?

A **BE12-23. Sale of Revalued Assets, IFRS.** Verde Corporation sold a piece of land for $720,000. The land originally cost $810,000, but 2 years ago Verde had revalued it to $700,000. What is the gain or loss on the sale? What is the journal entry to record the sale?

Exercises

2 **E12-1. Tangible Asset Impairment.** Henne Optical Corporation reported the following information regarding long-term operating assets for its Lens Manufacturing Operations:

Description	Carrying Value	Estimated Fair Value
Factory building (used in several segments)	$10,000,000	
Less: Accumulated depreciation	(4,500,000)	
Net book value	$ 5,500,000	$ 8,900,000
Land	$ 7,000,000	$14,000,000
Lens manufacturing equipment	$ 2,100,000	
Less: Accumulated depreciation	(600,000)	
Net book value	$ 1,500,000	$ 1,100,000
Lens polishing equipment	$ 3,000,000	
Less: Accumulated depreciation	(1,200,000)	
Net book value	$ 1,800,000	$ 1,625,000
General factory equipment (used in several segments)	$ 6,500,000	
Less: Accumulated depreciation	(4,000,000)	
Net book value	$ 2,500,000	$ 2,400,000
Delivery trucks (used in several segments)	$ 1,750,000	
Less: Accumulated depreciation	(300,000)	
Net book value	$ 1,450,000	$ 1,125,000
Total net fixed assets	$19,750,000	

Recent advances in technology have rendered the company's lens manufacturing operations nearly obsolete. Management projects the following future cash flows for its lens manufacturing operations.

Future Period	Cash-Flow Projection
Year 1	$1,200,000
Year 2	750,000
Year 3	400,000
Year 4	350,000
Year 5	300,000
Total	$3,000,000

Required »

a. Determine the asset group for purposes of impairment testing and justify your decision.
b. Compute the impairment loss for the asset group identified in part (a) for the current year, if any.
c. Prepare the journal entry to record the impairment loss, if needed.

❷ **E12-2. Tangible Asset Impairment Loss.** Use the same information from E12-1 except now assume the following cash-flow projections:

Future Period	Cash-Flow Projection
Year 1	$1,450,000
Year 2	850,000
Year 3	400,000
Year 4	400,000
Year 5	250,000
Total	$3,350,000

Required »

a. Compute the impairment loss for the current year, if any.
b. Prepare the journal entry to record the impairment loss, if needed.

❷ **E12-3. Tangible Asset Impairment.** Derrick's Domino Manufacturing Company learned that one of its cutting machines is obsolete. Although the company will continue to use this machinery in the future, management believes that an impairment write-down is required. The following information relates to the cutting machine:

Description	Cutting Machine
Cost	$3,200,000
Accumulated depreciation (up to the date of the impairment test)	$1,280,000
Total estimated future cash flows	$1,225,000
Total discounted future cash flows	$1,060,000
Estimated fair value	$1,050,000
Costs to sell	$ 4,000
Remaining useful life from the impairment date	6 years

The firm estimates that the machine has a useful life of 10 years and it has used it for 4 years. It has no salvage value.

Required »

a. Prepare the journal entry required to record the impairment loss.
b. Assuming that Derrick's uses the straight-line method with no residual value, prepare the journal entry to record the revised depreciation expense for the first year immediately following the impairment.
c. Assume that 2 years following the impairment write-down, the fair value of the asset falls to $725,000. The sum of the undiscounted future cash flows is $745,000. What is the carrying value of the asset at this time? Prepare any journal entry necessary to reflect the change in fair value.

❷❸ **E12-4. Finite-Life and Indefinite-Life Intangible Assets Impairment.** SMC Research Associates reports the following intangible assets on its December 31 balance sheet:

Intangible Asset	Net Carrying Value	Remaining Life
Franchise	$ 850,000	5 years
Patent	400,000	3 years
Trade name	3,950,000	N / A
Total	$5,200,000	

It does not use a separate accumulated amortization account for the intangible assets (i.e., it deducts the amount of amortization directly from the intangible asset account).

Management provided the following information related to intangible assets it obtained during the current year:

- Franchise. Due to current market conditions, products sold under the franchise have experienced significant sales declines from possible obsolescence.
- Patent. SMC is currently involved in litigation that will determine whether the company has the exclusive right to sell the patented product. Legal counsel informed SMC that the value of the patent will likely be reduced.
- Trade name. The company is required to test for impairment of its indefinite-life intangible assets annually.

SMC's cost of capital is 6%. Management estimates the following future cash flows to be generated over the next 5 years from the use of its intangible assets:

Future Period	Franchise	Patent	Trade Name
Year 1	$300,000	$280,000	$ 800,000
Year 2	220,000	90,000	610,000
Year 3	110,000	10,000	590,000
Year 4	45,000	0	510,000
Year 5	25,000	0	365,000
Total	$700,000	$380,000	$2,875,000

Required »

a. Compute the impairment loss (if any) for each intangible asset.
b. Prepare the journal entry necessary to record the impairment loss.
c. Assuming that SMC amortizes its finite-life intangible assets using the straight-line method with no scrap value, prepare the journal entry to record the annual amortization for the first year subsequent to the impairment write-down.

4 **E12-5. Goodwill Impairment.** Brigatti Company pays $1,560,000 to acquire 100% of the common stock of Cornish Incorporated. It assumes that Cornish's plant assets (such as the factory building and land) are undervalued by $40,000. The historical cost of the net assets acquired, excluding goodwill, is equal to $1,500,000. Cornish will be held as a division of Brigatti. The following information is available 1 year after the acquisition of the subsidiary company (i.e., the reporting unit):

Description	Debit	Credit
Cash	$ 200,000	
Inventory	300,000	
Property, plant, and equipment, net	1,500,000	
Goodwill	20,000	
Current liabilities		$ 400,000
Common stock – no par		340,000
Retained earnings		1,280,000
Totals	$2,020,000	$2,020,000

Brigatti estimated the fair (appraisal) value of the division's net assets (excluding goodwill) 1 year after the date of acquisition at $1,605,000.

Required »

a. Compute goodwill recorded on the date of acquisition.
b. Determine whether goodwill is impaired assuming that the fair value of the Cornish Division with goodwill 1 year after acquisition is equal to $2,000,000. Provide the impairment journal entry, if needed.
c. Determine whether goodwill is impaired assuming that the fair value of the Cornish Division with goodwill 1 year after acquisition is equal to $1,608,000. Prepare the impairment journal entry, if needed.

5 **E12-6. Tangible Asset Impairment Loss, IFRS.** Use the same information from E12-1 but now assume that Henne Optical Corporation is an IFRS reporter. Henne Optical's discount rate is 5% and costs to sell any equipment are zero.

Required »

a. Determine the asset group for purposes of impairment testing and justify your decision.
b. Compute the impairment loss for the asset group identified in (a) for the current year, if any.
c. Prepare the journal entry to record the impairment loss, if needed.

5 **E12-7. Tangible Asset Impairment, Potential Reversal, IFRS.** Use the same information from E12-3 but now assume that Derrick's Domino Manufacturing Company is an IFRS reporter.

Required »

a. Prepare the journal entry required to record the impairment loss.
b. Assuming that Derrick's uses the straight-line method with no residual value, prepare the journal entry to record the revised depreciation expense for the first year immediately following the impairment.
c. Assume that 2 years following the impairment write-down, the fair value (less the costs to sell) and value in use of the asset falls to $725,000. Prepare any journal entry necessary to reflect the change in fair value.

5 **E12-8. Finite- and Indefinite-Life Intangible Assets Impairment, IFRS.** Use the same information from E12-4 but now treat SMC Research Associates as an IFRS reporter.

Required »

a. Compute the impairment loss (if any) for each intangible asset.
b. Prepare the journal entry necessary to record the impairment loss.
c. Assuming that SMC amortizes its finite-life intangible assets by using the straight-line method with no scrap value, prepare the journal entry to record the annual amortization for the first year subsequent to the impairment write-down.

6 **E12-9. Goodwill Impairment, IFRS.** Use the same information from E12-5 but now assume that Brigatti Company is an IFRS reporter and that Cornish Division is a cash-generating unit. Assume that costs to sell the unit are zero.

Required »

a. Determine whether goodwill is impaired assuming that the fair value of the Cornish Division with goodwill 1 year after acquisition is equal to $2,000,000 and its value in use 1 year after acquisition was $1,712,000. Provide the impairment journal entry, if necessary.
b. Determine whether goodwill is impaired assuming that the fair value of the Cornish Division with goodwill 1 year after acquisition is equal to $1,608,000 and value in use 1 year after acquisition was $1,612,000. Provide the impairment journal entry, if necessary.

8 **E12-10. Assets Held for Disposal.** Hattie Corporation recently decided to dispose of a significant portion of its plant assets. The assets to be held for disposal are summarized here:

Description	Machinery*	Equipment**
Cost	$696,000	$1,550,000
Accumulated depreciation	(348,000)	(620,000)
Net book value at year end	$348,000	$ 930,000

* Machinery is depreciated by the straight-line method, assuming a 6-year life with no scrap value. The asset was acquired 3 years ago.
** Equipment is depreciated by the straight-line method, assuming a 10-year life with no scrap value. The asset was acquired 4 years ago.

At the time the decision was made to dispose of the assets, the book values of the assets approximated their fair values. Assume that costs to sell the assets are zero. When the assets were held for disposal, the following changes in fair value occurred:

Subsequent Year	Machinery	Equipment
End of Year 1 fair value	$200,000	$900,000
End of Year 2 fair value	$215,000	950,000

Prepare any journal entries necessary to account for the changes in fair value for Years 1 and 2.

A **E12-11. Asset Revaluation, Upwards, IFRS.** Sousa Company revalues equipment with a carrying value of €1,100,000 to its fair value of €1,400,000. The original cost of the equipment is €1,600,000 and accumulated depreciation is €500,000.

Required »

a. What is the revaluation surplus or unrealized loss?
b. Where does the firm report the revaluation surplus or unrealized loss in the financial statements?
c. Provide the journal entries to record the revaluation (assume that Sousa eliminates all prior accumulated depreciation and adjusts the historical cost to fair value)

A **E12-12. Asset Revaluation, Downwards, IFRS.** Lousa Company revalues its equipment with a carrying value of €1,100,000 to its fair value of €950,000. The original cost of the equipment is €1,500,000 and accumulated depreciation is €400,000.

Required »

a. What is the revaluation surplus or unrealized loss?
b. Where does the firm report the revaluation surplus or unrealized loss in the financial statements?
c. Provide the journal entries to record the revaluation (assume that Lousa eliminates all prior accumulated depreciation and adjusts the historical cost to fair value).

Problems

2 **P12-1. Tangible Asset Impairment.** Chrispian Cookies, Inc. is reviewing all available information regarding the future use of its baking equipment, which it intends to use for the foreseeable future. The information indicates that this equipment may be obsolete and could be impaired. Chrispian acquired the equipment 3 years ago at a cost of $9,000,000 and depreciated it using the straight-line method with an estimated residual value of $1,800,000 and an 8-year useful life. At the end of the third year, management estimates the following cash flows from the use of the asset:

Future Period	Cash-Flow Projection
Year 1	$1,800,000
Year 2	1,600,000
Year 3	980,000
Year 4	890,000
Year 5	730,000
Total	$6,000,000

The asset is highly specialized and is not traded in an active market. As a result, the fair value of the asset must be estimated. Chrispian's cost of capital is 6%.

Required »

a. Conduct an impairment test for Chrispian's baking equipment.
b. Prepare the journal entry to record any impairment loss indicated.
c. Compute the amount of the revised depreciation expense at the end of the next year. Assume that management now estimates that there will be no residual value at the end of the asset's life.
d. The estimated fair value at the end of the next year is $4,400,000. The sum of the undiscounted future cash flows exceeds the asset's carrying value. Compare the carrying value of the asset to its fair value. Explain how to treat the difference between the asset's carrying value and fair value.

2 **P12-2. Tangible Asset Impairment.** Cupcakes-R-Us, Inc. is reviewing all available information regarding the future use of its baking equipment, which it intends to use for the foreseeable future. The company has observed a decline in the demand for its products. The information also indicates that this equipment may be obsolete and could be impaired. Cupcakes-R-Us acquired the equipment 2 years ago at a cost of $500,000 and depreciated it using the straight-line method with an estimated residual value of $10,000 and a 7-year useful life. At the end of the second year, management estimates the following cash flows from the use of the asset:

Future Period	Cash-Flow Projection—Estimate 1	Cash-Flow Projection—Estimate 2
Year 1	$120,000	$120,000
Year 2	100,000	100,000
Year 3	70,000	80,000
Year 4	35,000	35,000
Year 5	30,000	30,000
Total	$355,000	$365,000

Required »

a. Compute the carrying value of Cupcakes-R-Us's equipment.
b. Compute the present value of expected cash flows under Estimate 1 and Estimate 2. Assume that the cost of capital is 8%. For each estimate, is the present value of estimated future cash flows higher or lower than the equipment's carrying value?
c. Conduct the impairment tests for Cupcakes-R-Us under Estimate 1 and Estimate 2. If required, prepare the journal entry to record any impairment loss.

2 **P12-3. Tangible Asset Impairment.** Using the same information from P12-2, assume that Cupcakes-R-Us determines that the likelihood of the expected future cash flows under Estimate 1 is 70% and 30% under Estimate 2.

Required »

a. Compute the carrying value of Cupcakes-R-Us's equipment.
b. Compute the expected cash flows given the likelihood of Estimate 1 and Estimate 2. What is the present value of the expected cash flows?
c. Conduct the impairment tests for Cupcakes-R-Us using the results from part (b). If required, prepare the journal entry to record any impairment loss.

23 **P12-4. Finite- and Indefinite-Life Intangible Assets Impairment.** PCG, Ltd. is in the process of assessing the valuation of its intangible assets. At the end of the current year, management reported the following intangible assets:

Description	Trademark	Franchise	Permit
Cost	$600,000	$530,000	$180,000
Accumulated amortization	(0)	(212,000)	(0)
Net book value at year-end	$600,000	$318,000	$180,000

The firm acquired the franchise 2 years ago and estimates that it has a 5-year useful life with no residual value. PCG uses the straight-line depreciation method. The permit is renewable every three years for an indefinite period of time. PCG management is concerned about the value of its franchise. The products sold under the franchise agreement have been experiencing sales declines over the past 2 years, prompting the company to test for impairment. It classifies the trademark and the renewable permit as indefinite-life intangible assets and must test for impairment on an annual basis. Management is unable to determine fair values from the market for the intangibles but provides the following cash-flow projections related to each of its intangible assets:

Future Period	Trademark	Franchise	Permit
Year 1	$300,000	$200,000	$ 60,000
Year 2	260,000	80,000	43,000
Year 3	150,000	20,000	32,000
Year 4	40,000	0	29,000
Year 5	20,000	0	18,000
Total	$770,000	$300,000	$182,000

The company's cost of capital is 5%.

Required »

a. Conduct an impairment test for PCG's intangible assets.
b. Prepare the journal entries required to record the impairment loss, if any.
c. Compute the amount of the annual amortization for the franchise for years subsequent to the impairment test.

234 **P12-5. Goodwill Impairment, Tangible Fixed Assets, and Finite-Life Intangible Assets' Impairments.** Green River Company acquired 100% of the voting stock of the AutoStyle Group on January 1 of the current year for a total acquisition cost of $250,000. The trial balance of AutoStyle on the date of acquisition follows.

Description	Debit	Credit
Investment securities – held to maturity	$ 30,000	
Plant and equipment – net	195,000	
Intangible assets – net	70,000	
Long-term debt		$ 115,000
Contributed capital		60,000
Retained earnings		120,000
Totals	$295,000	$295,000

The AutoStyle Group acquired the intangible assets 3 years ago. It amortizes the assets using the straight-line method with no estimated residual value. The appraisal of the subsidiary's net assets on the date of acquisition indicated that the following adjustments were required:

Description	Book Value	Fair Value	Adjustment
Plant and equipment – net	$195,000	$210,000	$15,000
Customer list	0	50,000	50,000
Long-term debt	(115,000)	(120,000)	(5,000)
Total net assets	$ 80,000	$140,000	$60,000

On December 31 (1 year after the acquisition), Green River's management conducted its annual impairment test for goodwill. Management has also assessed recent events and determined that it should review its plant and equipment and finite-life intangible assets for possible impairment. Management determines AutoStyle to be the reporting unit, which is also the cash-generating unit. Management estimated that the fair value of the unit (AutoStyle) with goodwill 1 year after the acquisition was $300,000; its value in use was $310,000; and the costs to sell were $20,000. The net assets of the unit, excluding goodwill, were appraised at $294,000. Assume that annual depreciation is $5,000, annual amortization for the customer list is $1,000, and the annual amortization for the other intangible assets is $3,500. Green River uses separate accounts for accumulated depreciation and accumulated amortization. Treat the customer list as a finite-life intangible asset.

Management is unable to determine fair values for the reporting unit's assets, but it estimates the following future cash flows for each of the unit's assets with the exception of goodwill. Assume that Green River's cost of capital is 5%.

Future Period	Plant and Equipment	Finite-Life Intangible Assets	Customer List
Year 1	$ 51,500	$11,000	$16,800
Year 2	40,000	10,000	14,200
Year 3	20,500	8,900	10,600
Year 4	14,000	7,700	9,500
Year 5	0	6,500	8,800
Year 6	0	6,000	5,100
Year 7	0	3,900	3,000
Total	$126,000	$54,000	$68,000

Required »

a. Compute the amount of goodwill to be recorded on the date of acquisition.
b. Conduct the impairment test for goodwill at the end of the year, 1 year after the acquisition. Assume no changes in the reporting unit's assets and liabilities except for depreciation and amortization.
c. Conduct the impairment tests indicated for assets other than goodwill at the end of the year, 1 year after the acquisition.
d. Prepare the journal entries required to record any impairment losses computed in parts (b) and (c).

5 **P12-6. Tangible Asset Impairment, Potential Reversal, IFRS.** Use the same information from P12-1 with three modifications:

- Chrispian Cookies, Inc. is an IFRS reporter.
- Similar baking equipment could be sold for $5,100,000.
- Chrispian estimates that costs to sell the baking equipment are $5,000.

Required »

a. Conduct an impairment test for Chrispian's baking equipment.
b. Prepare the journal entry to record any impairment loss indicated.
c. Compute the amount of the revised depreciation expense at the end of the next year. Assume that management now estimates that there will be no residual value at the end of the asset's life.
d. Prepare any journal entry necessary if the estimated fair value less costs to sell at the end of the next year is $5,400,000 and its value in use is $4,900,000.

5 **P12-7. Finite-Life and Indefinite-Life Intangible Assets Impairment, IFRS.** Peter Gordon, Ltd., an IFRS reporter, is in the process of assessing the valuation of its intangible assets. At the end of the current year, management reported the following intangible assets:

Description	Trademark	Franchise	Permit
Cost	$600,000	$530,000	$180,000
Accumulated amortization	(0)	(212,000)	(0)
Net book value at year end	$600,000	$318,000	$180,000

The firm acquired the franchise 2 years ago and estimates that it has a 5-year useful life with no residual value. The permit is renewable every 3 years for an indefinite period of time. Peter Gordon's management is concerned about the value of its franchise. Sales of the products sold under the franchise agreement have declined over the past 2 years, prompting the company to test for impairment. The firm classifies the trademark and the renewable permit as indefinite-life intangible assets and is required to test them for impairment on an annual basis. Management provides the following estimates related to each of its intangible assets:

	Trademark	Franchise	Permit
Fair value	$560,000	$290,000	$181,000
Costs to sell	7,000	5,000	2,000
Fair value less costs to sell	553,000	285,000	179,000
Value in use	580,000	280,000	185,000

Required »

a. Conduct an impairment test for Peter Gordon's intangible assets.
b. Prepare the journal entries required to record the impairment loss, if any.
c. Compute the amount of the annual amortization for the franchise for years subsequent to the impairment test.

5 6 **P12-8. Goodwill Impairment, Tangible and Finite-Life and Indefinite-Life Assets Impairments, IFRS.** Use the same information from P12-5 and the following additional information, now assuming that Green River Company is an IFRS reporter.

The following are estimates of current fair values less costs to sell:

	Plant and Equipment	Finite-Life Intangible Assets	Customer List
Current selling price (less costs to sell)	$134,000	$43,600	$55,700

Required »

a. Compute the amount of goodwill to be recorded on the date of acquisition.
b. Conduct the impairment test for goodwill at the end of the year, 1 year after the acquisition. Assume no changes in the cash-generating unit's assets and liabilities during the year except for depreciation and amortization.
c. Conduct the impairment tests indicated for assets other than goodwill at the end of the year, 1 year after the acquisition.
d. Prepare the journal entries required to record any impairment losses computed in parts (b) and (c).

A **P12-9. Comprehensive Asset Revaluation Problem (Initial Upward Revaluation, Accumulated Depreciation Elimination Method), IFRS.** Hampton Plc. revalues equipment with a carrying value of £715,000 to its fair value of £750,000. The original cost of the equipment was £1,000,000. Hampton uses straight-line depreciation. The equipment has a 10-year useful life and scrap value of £50,000. Assume that Hampton eliminates all prior accumulated depreciation and adjusts the historical cost to fair value.

Required »

a. What is the revaluation surplus or unrealized loss?
b. Where does the firm report the revaluation surplus or unrealized loss in the financial statements?
c. What are the journal entries to record the revaluation?
d. What is the depreciation expense on the equipment after the revaluation?
e. Hampton chooses to take any revaluation surplus to retained earnings over the equipment's remaining useful life. What is the amount of the surplus, if any, taken to retained earnings in the year following the revaluation?

f. If Hampton sells the equipment at the end of the third year after revaluation for £405,000, what are the journal entries?

g. Now assume Hampton holds the equipment at the beginning of the fourth year following revaluation and revalues the equipment again when its fair value is £380,000. What are the journal entries to record the revaluation? Where does the firm report the revaluation surplus or unrealized loss in the financial statements? Ignore part (f).

A **P12-10. Comprehensive Asset Revaluation Problem (Initial Downward Revaluation, Accumulated Depreciation Elimination Method), IFRS.** Essex Plc. is revaluing equipment with a carrying value of £715,000 to its fair value of £673,000. The original cost of the equipment was £1,000,000. The equipment has a 10-year useful life and scrap value of £50,000. Essex uses straight-line depreciation. Assume that Essex eliminates all prior accumulated depreciation and adjusts the historical cost to fair value.

Required »

a. What is the revaluation surplus or unrealized loss?

b. Where does the firm report the revaluation surplus or unrealized loss in the financial statements?

c. What are the journal entries to record the revaluation?

d. What is the depreciation expense on the equipment after the revaluation?

e. Essex chooses to take any revaluation surplus to retained earnings over the equipment's remaining useful life. What is the amount of the surplus, if any, taken to retained earnings in the year after revaluation?

f. If Essex sells the equipment at the end of the third year after revaluation for £415,000, what is the journal entry?

g. Now assume that Essex holds the equipment. At the beginning of the fourth year after revaluation, Essex revalues its equipment again when the fair value is £425,000. What are the journal entries to record the revaluation? Where does the firm report the revaluation surplus or unrealized loss in the financial statements? Ignore part (f).

A **P12-11. Sale of Revalued Property Plant and Equipment, IFRS.** The Taurus Group sold a piece of equipment on December 30 of the current year for $250,000 when the equipment's carrying value was $290,000. Three years ago, the equipment had been revalued to $500,000. At the time of the revaluation, Taurus eliminated all prior accumulated depreciation. It reports a revaluation surplus of $22,000 related to the equipment in accumulated other comprehensive income. Prepare the journal entry required to record the sale of the asset.

Excel Project

Autograded Excel Project available in **MyLab Accounting**

CASES

Judgment Cases

Judgment Case 1: Impairments of PPE under IFRS

Refer to the information in Surfing the Standards Case 1 later in the chapter to answer the following questions.

a. Prepare the calculation of the impairment loss.

b. What items included in the case itself involved issues of judgment? (Include only those that are ultimately relevant in determining the impairment loss.)

c. What judgments/decisions did you still need to make? Why did you make the particular decisions in your responses?

Judgment Case 2: Property, Plant and Equipment: Impairment[16]

Background

Toyda, Inc. (Toyda) is one of the world's leading car manufacturers. It sells cars exclusively in the United States. In recent years, Toyda has begun producing electric cars as well as specialized equipment that is used to charge electric cars. Management of Toyda had been very optimistic about this recent venture. For internal purposes, Toyda projected a growth rate of 40% for the electric car production and for the production of the

[16]Reprinted from the Ernst & Young Academic Resource Center with permission of the Ernst & Young Foundation.

specialized equipment. Management believes that these estimates were conservative. Currently, Toyda is the only U.S. carmaker that is producing electric cars.

In December 2015, a number of oil reserves were discovered in Alaska. These oil reserves are much more significant than any reserves that currently exist. U.S. consumers are euphoric over these discoveries. Accordingly, many automobile manufacturing companies and industry and government analysts believe that the demand for electric cars will decrease substantially.

While the CEO is exceedingly worried about this new turn of events, she is not really worried about the financial statements for the December 31, 2015 year-end. Because Toyda is still in the early stages of producing and selling electric cars, most of the company's current net income is attributable to traditional cars. The current consensus analyst forecast for net income per share is $10.25, which equates to $30.0 million of net income. Although Toyda has not yet finalized its financial statements for 2015, the draft income statement provided to the CEO on February 1, 2016, showed net income of $35 million, an effective tax rate of 20%, and total assets of $500.0 million. Toyda is audited annually.

The CFO at Toyda has been consulting with external valuation specialists since early December to determine if there is a need to impair one or both production facilities. Toyda is not considering a potential sale or an alternative use of its production facilities. The valuation specialists have extensive experience with the global automotive industry, including the electric car industry in Europe. The valuation specialists issued their report on February 3, 2016. The report included an analysis of expected growth rates based on available market data, industry trends, historical results, and other pertinent data. The report indicated that Toyda will be able to maintain its expected growth rates for two more years, until the newly discovered oil reserves are ready to begin production. Beginning in 2018, Toyda would expect growth rates between 15% and 19% for the specialized equipment facility and the car production facility. The valuation specialists anticipate that Toyda will be able to dispose of the production facility for electric cars in 20 years, with proceeds of $500,000. Likewise, the production facility for the specialized equipment could be disposed of in 10 years with proceeds of $10,000. The valuation specialists also believe that the highest and best use of the facility is its current use and an expected present value technique (i.e., expected cash flows) would be the most appropriate method to make a fair value determination. The CFO has been heavily involved in the preparation and review of the valuation specialists' report, and she believes it is a balanced and fair assessment.

The table below provides data on the two facilities.

Asset Group: Production Facilities	Carrying Value December 31, 2015	Remaining Life in Years	Actual Data					
			Operating Cash Flows			Operating Income		
			2013	2014	2015	2013	2014	2015
Electric cars	$25,000,000	20	$45,000	$77,000	$98,000	$32,000	$ 43,000	$ 57,000
Electric car chargers	4,000,000	10	5,000	19,000	25,000	(8,000)	(15,000)	(12,000)

The following table provides the annual yield on the risk-free rate expected over the next 20 years obtained from the U.S. Department of the Treasury. The CFO has engaged in discussions with investment bankers to determine what the appropriate risk premium would be for these facilities (analyzed and supported based on market data available for comparable companies). Based on these discussions, she believes that a risk premium of 8% to 12% should be added to the risk-free rate to reflect a current discount rate.

Year	1	2	3	4	5	6	7	8	9	10	11	12	13	14	15	16	17	18	19	20
Yield (%)*	0.12	0.27	0.40	0.62	0.89	1.12	1.41	1.67	1.81	1.97	2.05	2.11	2.25	2.32	2.45	2.50	2.59	2.62	2.65	2.67

*This represents the annual yield to maturity for each time period. Thus, for example, an investment held for 10 years would yield a 1.97% return per year.

As the junior accountant, the CFO has asked you to provide her an analysis of the need for an impairment of the production facilities and the amount of impairment loss to be recorded, if any.

Required »

For December 31, 2015, using your judgment, perform an analysis of the need for an impairment of the production facilities and the amount of impairment loss to be recorded, if any. In performing your analysis, you should use an Excel spreadsheet to support any calculations. Document your judgment to provide to the

CFO (not to exceed three pages). Be sure to include specific references to the applicable guidance and quote the applicable guidance. Also attach your Excel spreadsheet with your calculations.

Judgment Case 3: Goodwill Impairment[17]

Background

AKS Company's common shares are publicly traded and it files with the SEC. AKS has a single reporting unit, which sells high-end consumer electronics. AKS has a March 31 fiscal year-end.

Fiscal 2021 data

On April 1, 2020, AKS acquired a competitor, BMN, for $20.0 million. The purchase price was approximately 10 times BMN's projected fiscal 2022 income. After completing the purchase price allocation, the goodwill from this acquisition was recorded at $10.0 million.

In compliance with ASC 350, AKS was required to perform a goodwill impairment test. The goodwill impairment test identifies potential impairment by comparing the fair value of a reporting unit with its carrying amount, including goodwill. AKS decided they would perform this test annually in January. The company determined that there was one reporting unit (AKS in total) at which the goodwill would be tested for impairment.

In January 2021, as directed by the CFO, the controller of AKS initiated the process to determine whether there was any impairment of the goodwill. Because this was a new process, the controller decided to hire a certified specialist in the valuation business to prepare the valuation. Below is information available regarding the valuation process:

- The valuation specialist used the income approach using a discounted cash flow model to derive the fair value.
- The weighted-average cost of capital (WACC) to AKS was 7%.
- Revenue growth attributed to BMN in the cash flow model was 10% in fiscal 2022 and 15% in fiscal 2023.
- Income projections prepared as part of the acquisition work indicated expected growth in AKS' consolidated income of 10%, to $22.0 million, in fiscal 2022 and 15%, to $25.3 million, in fiscal 2023 from BMN.
- Expenses other than for cost of goods sold were budgeted to remain flat for the next two years.

Based on the valuation, the fair value of the reporting unit exceeded its carrying amount by 20%. AKS concluded that based on this quantitative analysis; there was no goodwill impairment in fiscal 2021.

Fiscal 2022 data

In January 2017, ASU 2017-04, *Intangibles – Goodwill and Other (Topic 350) – Simplifying the Test for Goodwill Impairment,* was issued. This ASU was issued in response to concerns about the cost and complexity of performing the two step goodwill impairment test. Topic 350 still provides management the option to first assess qualitative factors to make a determination of whether it is more likely than not that the fair value of a reporting unit is less than its carrying amount. If, after a full qualitative assessment, an entity determines it is more likely than not that the fair value of a reporting unit is more than its carrying amount, then performing the quantitative assessment is unnecessary.

In January 2022, you have assumed the role of the controller. You are now responsible for performing the annual impairment testing for goodwill. The CFO believes that there is no impairment issue given that a valuation was just performed in the prior year, which indicated a fair value 20% over carrying value and also because the fiscal results for 2022 have remained stable so far. He has advised you to take advantage of the option to use the qualitative approach in an effort to eliminate the $100,000 appraisal fee incurred in the prior year. The CFO believes this approach will be simple and should reduce the accounting department's workload.

You had discussions with the AKS executive team early this month and have gained the following insights:

- The BMN acquisition has been successful and there are no intentions to sell any portion of the business. The BMN management team remains intact and is still operating under a non-compete agreement for another year. The executive team for AKS is also expected to remain consistent.
- The price of AKS' stock has been stable this year and is not expected to change significantly in the fourth quarter. The stock prices of AKS' public competitors have also been fairly stable.

[17]Reprinted from the Ernst & Young Academic Resource Center with permission of the Ernst & Young Foundation.

At December 31, 2021, AKS had total assets of $100 million and net equity of $10.0 million. The following additional financial information is based on actual results for the first three quarters of fiscal 2022, ended December 31, 2021, and projected results for the fourth quarter ended March 31, 2022. Auditors of AKS have performed reviews of quarterly results to date for fiscal 2022. There have been no restatements.

- Revenues are projected to increase by 18%. This increase is primarily driven by the acquisition of BMN (approximately 11% of the increase); the addition of three large customers, which were taken away from competitors (approximately 5% of the increase); and the balance is the result of increased demand for AKS' products.
- The demand for AKS' products was very strong in the first six months. During the second half of the year, the economy softened and the demand for AKS' products began to drop. The forecasted decrease in units sold for the last six months is estimated to be 3% to 4%.
- In the fourth quarter, AKS began offering pricing concessions to maintain sales. The price concessions offered so far in the fourth quarter have been in the range of 2% to 3%, and have helped mitigate the decline in units sold.
- Income for the year is forecasted to be $24.0 million.
- The WACC for AKS is expected to remain at 7%.
- Expenses other than for cost of goods sold increased by 1%.
- The S&P 500 index has dropped 5% since the prior year. The S&P index for public companies within AKS' industry are down on average 1%.

Required »

a. For fiscal 2022, perform the qualitative assessment.

b. Document your judgment related to the qualitative assessment in a draft memorandum format that you will provide to the CFO (not to exceed three pages). Be sure to include specific references and quotes to applicable guidance.

Financial Statement Analysis Case

Financial Statement Analysis Case 1: Long-Lived Asset Impairments

BlackBerry Limited, the smartphone manufacturer, reported a $2,748 million impairment loss on its income statement during the year ended March 1, 2014. You are interested in further examining this and any other impairment losses at ***BlackBerry*** and have identified the financial statement excerpts on the following pages to further analyze. Refer to these financial statements excerpts and Exhibit 12.2 in the text to answer the following questions:

Required »

a. What types of long-lived assets does ***BlackBerry*** report? What is the dollar amount and percent change in total and by each type of long-lived asset from March 2, 2013, to March 1, 2014? What are long-lived assets in total and by type as a percent of total assets at March 1, 2014, and March 2, 2013?

b. What is the total amount of impairment losses ***BlackBerry*** reported in the years ended March 1, 2014, March 2, 2013, and March 3, 2012? To what types of assets do the impairment losses relate?

c. What is the amount of impairment losses on intangible assets that ***BlackBerry*** reported for the years ended March 1, 2014, March 2, 2013, and March 3, 2012? To what type of intangible asset do the losses relate?

d. Compute the percent change in operating income for all years. What would the percent change in operating income be excluding the impairment losses? Comment on how the inclusion or exclusion of impairment losses affects the percentage change in operating income and the trend in operating income.

BlackBerry Limited
Incorporated under the Laws of Ontario
(United States dollars, in millions)

Consolidated Balance Sheets

	At	
	March 1, 2014	**March 2, 2013**
Assets		
Current		
Cash and cash equivalents	$1,579	$ 1,549
Short-term investments	950	1,105
Accounts receivable, net	972	2,353
Other receivables	152	272
Inventories	244	603
Income taxes receivable	373	597
Other current assets	505	469
Deferred income tax asset	73	139
Assets held for sale	209	354
	5,057	7,441
Long-term investments	129	221
Property, plant and equipment, net	942	2,073
Intangible assets, net	1,424	3,430
	$7,552	$13,165

BlackBerry Limited
(United States dollars, in millions, except per share data)
Consolidated Statements of Operations

	For the Year Ended		
	March 1, 2014	**March 2, 2013**	**March 3, 2012**
Revenue			
Hardware and other	$ 3,880	$ 6,902	$14,031
Service and software	2,933	4,171	4,392
	6,813	11,073	18,423
Cost of sales			
Hardware and other	6,383	7,060	11,217
Service and software	473	579	631
	6,856	7,639	11,848
Gross margin	(43)	3,434	6,575
Operating expenses			
Research and development	1,286	1,509	1,556
Selling, marketing and administration	2,103	2,111	2,600
Amortization	606	714	567
Impairment of long-lived assets	2,748	—	—
Impairment of goodwill	—	335	355
Debentures fair value adjustment	377	—	—
	7,120	4,669	5,078
Operating income (loss)	$(7,163)	$ (1,235)	$ 1,497

5. Consolidated Balance Sheets Details

Impairment of long-lived assets

During fiscal 2014, the Company recorded the LLA Impairment Charge of approximately $2.7 billion, of which $852 million of the charge was applicable to property, plant, and equipment and $1.9 billion was applicable to intangible assets.

Intangible assets, net

Intangible assets were comprised of the following:

	At March 1, 2014		
	Cost	Accumulated Amortization	Net Book Value
Acquired technology	$ 387	$ 284	$ 103
Intellectual property	2,176	855	1,321
	$2,563	$1,139	$1,424

	At March 2, 2013		
	Cost	Accumulated Amortization	Net Book Value
Acquired technology	$ 432	$ 257	$ 175
Intellectual property	4,382	1,127	3,255
	$4,814	$1,384	$3,430

During fiscal 2014, the additions to intangible assets primarily consisted of payments relating to amended or renewed licensing agreements, as well as agreements with third parties for the use of intellectual property, software, messaging services and other BlackBerry related features.

Source: Blackberry, Ltd., Financial Statements, 2014. http://us.blackberry.com/content/dam/bbCompany/Desktop/Global/PDF/Investors/Documents/2014/Q4_FY14_Filing.pdf

Surfing the Standards Cases

Surfing the Standards Case 1: Impairments of PPE under IFRS

A&N, Inc. is a manufacturer and retailer of specialized office equipment. It currently operates in two countries, both of which follow IFRS for their financial reporting. For the sake of simplicity, assume that both countries have the same currency, the dollar. During its annual impairment assessment of PPE, A&N determined that one of its factories presents with various impairment indicators. Facts related to this factory follow:

1. The estimated future life of the factory is 20 to 25 years, and it has a current carrying value of $1,200,000.
2. A&N has no sales agreement for the factory, nor does an active market exist. It did sell a similar factory several years ago in another country for $1,000,000. The costs to sell the factory were $67,000.
3. A&N has a similar factory in the other country in which it currently operates. Due to differences in the market for their products in the two countries, the cash flow streams will not be similar.
4. The table on the next page presents the projected cash inflows for the factory based on the most recent budgets approved by management.
5. Although management can demonstrate that its short-term projects tend to be reasonably accurate, there is some uncertainty as to the projected cash flows. Management assesses that there is a range on either side of the projected cash inflows: The cash inflows could be as much as 10% lower than projected or 5% greater than projected. While the most likely amount is included in the following schedule presented, the probabilities associated with each amount are unknown.
6. The table on the next page also presents the total projected cash outflows for overhead as well as specific projected outflows for maintenance of the factory. Generally, 25% of overhead is allocable to the use of the factory.
7. The increase in projected cash inflows in Year 4 is related to a planned overhaul of the factory. The estimated cash outflow for the overhaul is $50,000 (which is included in the table's Other Projected Cash Outflows column). The anticipated increase in cash inflow is $10,000 a year.
8. The cash-flow amounts presented are net of the corporate tax rate of 20%.
9. A&N anticipates a steady long-term growth rate of 3%. Its historical growth rate has been 0.5%.
10. Management anticipates that it will ultimately sell the factory for $1,000,000 because that is the amount of the last factory sale and that disposal costs will be similar to those incurred for the last sale. Because this anticipated sale is far off in time, the confidence range on this transaction is 50% less and 25%

greater than these estimates. Although management finds it 60% likely that it will obtain the sales price of $1,000,000 (and disposal costs of $67,000), the firm believes that the bottom of the range and the top of the range are each 20% likely.

11. All cash flows are presented in nominal terms as opposed to real terms.
12. A&N's pre-tax weighted cost of capital is currently 8%. Management expects this amount to increase in Year 4 to 9% due to a change in the term structure of interest rates. These rates include an expectation for general inflation.
13. The operations in the particular country in which this factory is located are a bit riskier due to political unrest than in the other country in which A&N operates. Management believes that this increased risk would translate into a 1% increase in the appropriate discount rate for the factory itself.

Read IAS 36, *Impairment of Assets,* paragraphs 18 through 57 as well as paragraphs A1 through A21 in its Appendix A. Provide answers to the following questions based upon this reading.

1. Because the determination of the amount of the impairment loss involves the use of the fair value (net of disposal costs), does A&N have to use the $933,000 net selling price of its other factory to approximate the fair value less disposal costs even though this number may not be very solid?
2. What adjustments does management need to make to the projected cash inflows presented in the following table in order to reflect projected cash inflows that are consistent with the requirements in IAS 36 for determining value in use?
3. What adjustment does management need to make to the projected cash outflows presented in the following table in order to reflect projected cash outflows that are consistent with the requirement in IAS 36 for determining value in use?
4. How should A&N include the expectations about the anticipated sale of the factory in the computation of value in use?
5. What discount rate should A&N use to compute value in use?

Original Projections by Management

Year	Projected Cash Inflows	Total Projected Overhead	Other Projected Cash Outflows	Total Cash Outflows
1	$70,000	$8,000	$2,500	$10,500
2	$73,000	$8,040	$2,500	$10,540
3	$72,000	$8,080	$2,500	$10,580
4	$83,000	$8,121	$52,500	$60,621
5	$84,000	$8,161	$2,500	$10,661
6	$86,520	$8,202	$2,500	$10,702
7	$89,116	$8,243	$2,500	$10,743
8	$91,789	$8,284	$2,500	$10,784
9	$94,543	$8,326	$2,500	$10,826
10	$97,379	$8,367	$2,500	$10,867
11	$100,300	$8,409	$2,500	$10,909
12	$103,309	$8,451	$2,500	$10,951
13	$106,409	$8,493	$2,500	$10,993
14	$109,601	$8,536	$2,500	$11,036
15	$112,889	$8,579	$2,500	$11,079
16	$116,276	$8,621	$2,500	$11,121
17	$119,764	$8,665	$2,500	$11,165
18	$123,357	$8,708	$2,500	$11,208
19	$127,058	$8,751	$2,500	$11,251
20	$130,869	$8,795	$2,500	$11,295
21	$134,795	$8,839	$2,500	$11,339
22	$138,839	$8,883	$2,500	$11,383
23	$143,004	$8,928	$2,500	$11,428
24	$147,295	$8,972	$2,500	$11,472
25	$151,713	$9,017	$2,500	$11,517

Surfing the Standards Case 2: Goodwill Impairment in Private Companies

Kraker, Inc. is a calendar-year private company that is not required to register with the SEC. It operates five different restaurant chains, two of which are fast-food chains and three of which provide higher-end dining experiences. On January 2, 2017, Kraker engaged in a business combination that resulted in its recording goodwill of $1 million. At that time, Kraker made the accounting policy elective provided in ASC 350-20-15-4 to utilize the accounting alternative. Kraker also elected to test for goodwill impairment at the entity level and estimated the useful life of the goodwill to be 10 years. Kraker does not utilize the option to do a qualitative assessment of goodwill as part of its impairment testing.

During 2019, there was a general downturn in the economy. Although the downturn did not have a significant effect on the fast-food chains, the revenues, net income, and cash flows from the three higher-end chains have declined dramatically. Thus, the financial performance of the firm as a whole has experienced a significant downturn.

The carrying value of the net assets of Kraker, excluding goodwill, is $15 million as of December 31, 2019. The fair value of the entity (including goodwill) is $14.8 million as of December 31, 2019.

Prepare a memo to the file related to Kraker's goodwill as of December 31, 2019. Use the Codification for support.

Basis for Conclusions Cases

Basis for Conclusions Case 1: Property, Plant, and Equipment Subsequent Measurement

Consider the Basis for Conclusions in IAS 16, Property, Plant and Equipment (particularly paragraph BC25) as well as the legacy U.K. standard on tangible fixed assets Financial Reporting Standard (FRS) 15 (particularly Appendix IV, paragraphs 17 and 29 through 34).

Both IFRS and legacy U.K. GAAP allow firms to revalue PPE, whereas U.S. GAAP does not.

Required »

a. Does either the discussion in IAS 16 or in FRS 15 provide any insight as to why PPE revaluations were/are allowed?

b. Why, according to FRS 15, are upward revaluations treated differently than downward revaluations with respect to where firms report the unrealized gains and losses in the financial statements?

Basis for Conclusions Case 2: Intangible Assets – Subsequent Measurement

Under certain circumstances, IFRS allows some intangible assets to be revalued, whereas U.S. GAAP does not allow revaluation. Read the Basis for Conclusions in IAS 38, *Intangible Assets*, particularly paragraphs BC76 and BC77. Does the IASB provide any insight as to why it decided to allow the revaluation of some intangible assets?

Basis for Conclusions Case 3: Goodwill Impairment for Private Companies

FASB issued ASU 2014-02 in January 2014 to allow private companies an alternative to testing goodwill for impairment.

1. Please provide a discussion of why FASB issued the standard.
2. What are the primary differences in this standard for private companies and the accounting for goodwill impairments for public companies?
3. Explain why FASB chose to allow each of these differences.

APPENDIX A

Revaluation Model in IFRS Accounting for Certain Long-Term Operating Assets

In this appendix, we address the *revaluation* of certain long-term operating assets as an alternative to historical cost methods available under IFRS. A **revaluation** occurs when a company reports a long-term asset at its fair value rather than its historical cost. Thus, the revaluation can increase or decrease the carrying value of an asset:

1. If an asset's fair value is *more than* its carrying value, the firm increases the carrying value of the asset.
2. If an asset's fair value is *less than* its carrying value, the firm decreases the carrying value of the asset.

Under the revaluation model, a company can choose to report a class of property, plant, or equipment or an intangible asset at its fair value rather than reporting it based on historical cost. IFRS allows (but does not require) the revaluation model; it is not permissible under U.S. GAAP.[18]

To illustrate, assume that a company owns a commercial building that it holds for rental purposes. The local economy is now booming, and several major employers have moved into the area. Demand for office space is high, and the company is able to increase rent, generating higher expected future cash flows from the use of the building. Revaluation accounting permits a write-up of the building's carrying value to reflect the increased economic value.

THE CONCEPTUAL FRAMEWORK CONNECTION: Revaluation

Measuring an asset at current fair value versus cost involves a trade-off between relevance and faithful representation. The cost basis provides a high level of faithful representation—it represents the price paid to acquire the asset. However, it is not necessarily very relevant. The current fair value better reflects the future economic benefits that the asset will provide to the company relative to the cost basis. For example, assume that a company reports land acquired 50 years ago on its balance sheet. The original cost of the land was $100,000, and the current fair value is $500,000. Under the historical cost approach, the company will report the land at $100,000 whereas under a fair value approach, the company would report it at $500,000. Whereas the $100,000 amount is a faithful representation of the historical cost, it is not particularly relevant for financial statement users' decision making. However, the $500,000 amount, while relevant, may not be a highly faithful representation of fair value because the fair value may be difficult to measure.

Managers must also keep in mind the cost-benefit constraint. Ideally, managers would obtain a professional appraisal for each asset for the periodic assessments of valuation. The costs related to periodic assessments of the valuation of certain types of property, plant, and equipment and intangible assets could be prohibitive.

The Revaluation Model

There are four steps involved in revaluing long-term operating assets under IFRS:

1. Measure the fair value.
2. Record the revaluation.
3. Compute the revised depreciation expense.
4. Determine the treatment of the revaluation surplus, if any.

[18] AICPA, *IFRS Financial Statements: Best Practices in Presentation and Disclosure 2 – 012* reports that 7.4% of companies included in its survey of 175 companies revalue at least one asset class.

Measure Fair Value

A firm must be able to measure the fair value of the asset—property, plant, and equipment or intangible assets—to implement the revaluation model. Fair value is the amount at which knowledgeable and willing parties would exchange for an asset in an arm's-length transaction. The fair value is usually determined by an appraisal based on market values and current market conditions. To revalue property, plant, and equipment, IFRS requires that a company can reliably measure fair value; for an intangible asset, IFRS requires that an active market exists for that intangible. Perhaps due to this active market restriction, firms rarely, if ever, revalue intangible assets under IFRS.[19] Consequently, we address only property, plant, and equipment.

How does a firm determine the fair value of property, plant, and equipment for revaluation purposes when there is no active market? Consider a highly specialized piece of equipment with no active market. In such cases, the firm estimates fair value using projected income or replacement cost.

A company revaluing assets makes revaluations when the asset's carrying amount differs materially from its current fair value at the end of the reporting period. If a company chooses to revalue one asset, then it must revalue every other asset in that class.[20] After determining the fair value, the company reports the asset at its fair value on the date of the revaluation. Under the **accumulated depreciation elimination method,** a company eliminates all prior accumulated depreciation and adjusts the historical cost of the asset to fair value.[21]

Record the Revaluation

The firm recognizes the difference between the revalued amount and carrying value either in net income or in other comprehensive income. The choice depends on the revaluation's impact on the asset's carrying value:

1. If the revaluation initially *increases* the asset's carrying value, the firm records the difference between the carrying value and the fair value (the unrealized gain) in the **revaluation surplus** account, a specific account in other comprehensive income (OCI) in the statement of comprehensive income. If the asset's fair value decreases in subsequent accounting periods, the firm reduces the revaluation surplus. If the decrease is more than the amount of the revaluation surplus, the firm reports the excess as an unrealized loss on the income statement. It cannot reduce the revaluation surplus below zero (that is, there cannot be a debit balance).
2. If the revaluation initially *decreases* the asset's carrying value, the firm reports the difference between the carrying value and fair value as an unrealized loss on the income statement. If the asset's fair value increases in subsequent accounting periods, the firm reports the unrealized gain on the income statement, but only to the extent of previously recognized losses. If the unrealized gain exceeds the previously recognized losses, then the excess is credited to the revaluation surplus.

Compute New Depreciation Expense

After recording the revaluation, the firm must recalculate subsequent depreciation based on the revised carrying value of the asset. The company then carries the asset on the balance sheet at the revalued amount less accumulated depreciation.

[19]AICPA, IFRS *Financial Statements: Best Practices in Presentation and Disclosure – 2012* reports that of 175 companies surveyed, none revalued intangible assets.

[20]IFRS does not define a class of assets in this context.

[21]Another way to record a revaluation adjusts the gross carrying amount. For example, the gross carrying amount may be restated based on observable market data or it may be restated proportionately to the change in the carrying amount. The accumulated depreciation is then adjusted to equal the difference between the gross carrying amount and the carrying amount of the asset. The new carrying value of the asset and depreciation expense after the revaluation will be the same as under the accumulated depreciation elimination method.

Determine Treatment of Revaluation Surplus, if Any

A company has two options when accounting for the revaluation surplus:

1. Reclassify the revaluation surplus into retained earnings over the asset's remaining useful life: The amount reclassified to retained earnings is the difference between the original depreciation expense and the new depreciation expense. Selecting this option decreases the revaluation surplus with a debit and increases retained earnings with a credit.
2. Retain the balance of the revaluation surplus until the asset is sold: If the company sells or abandons the asset, it may debit any balance in the revaluation surplus and close to retained earnings (i.e., credit or increase retained earnings).

The company may choose either of these options.

Exhibit 12A.1 summarizes the initial and subsequent accounting treatment of upward and downward revaluations.

EXHIBIT 12A.1 Subsequent Accounting Treatment: Upward and Downward Revaluations

Revaluation	Upward Revaluation	Downward Revaluation
Initial revaluation	Credit to equity (revaluation surplus in other comprehensive income) *See Example 12A.1*	Debit to unrealized loss, reported on the income statement *See Example 12A.3*
Subsequent revaluation	(When credit balance in revaluation surplus)	(When no revaluation surplus)
Upward	Credit to equity (revaluation surplus in other comprehensive income) *Similar to Example 12A.1*	Credit to unrealized gain reported on income statement up to the amount of any unrealized loss previously reported. Then, credit to equity (revaluation surplus in other comprehensive income). *See Example 12A.4*
Downward	Debit equity up to the amount of the revaluation surplus (in other comprehensive income) then debit unrealized loss reported on the income statement. *See Example 12A.2*	Debit to unrealized loss, reported on the income statement. *Similar to Example 12A.3*

We provide examples of each of these scenarios starting with Example 12A.1 that illustrates an initial upward revaluation.

EXAMPLE 12A.1

Initial Upward Revaluation: IFRS

PROBLEM: After 3 full years of use, the Rite-Up Company revalues equipment with a carrying value of €980,000 to its fair value of €1,200,000 using the accumulated depreciation elimination method. The original cost of the equipment is €1,400,000 and the equipment has a useful life of 10 years with no scrap value. Rite-Up depreciates under the straight-line method. Therefore, the annual depreciation expense is €140,000 per year (€1,400,000 / 10 years). The accumulated depreciation up to the date of the revaluation is €420,000 (€140,000 × 3 years).

Use the four-step process to address the following questions. What is the new carrying value of the asset? What is the increase or decrease in the carrying value of the asset, and where does Rite-Up report any unrealized gain or loss in the financial statements? What is the new annual depreciation expense after the revaluation? What amount would Rite-Up transfer from any revaluation surplus to retained earnings?

Continued

SOLUTION: We use the four-step revaluation model to illustrate the solution to the problem.

Step 1. **Measure the fair value.** The fair value is given at €1,200,000, which will be the new carrying value of the asset.

Step 2. **Record the revaluation.** The revaluation of the asset increases its carrying value by €220,000 (the fair value of €1,200,000 less the carrying value of €980,000). Because this initial revaluation increases the asset value, Rite-Up reports the revaluation surplus as other comprehensive income on the statement of comprehensive income and accumulated other comprehensive income in the stockholders' equity section of the statement of financial position (balance sheet). The balance in the revaluation surplus is €220,000 after the first revaluation.

Under the accumulated depreciation elimination method, Rite-Up must first eliminate all prior accumulated depreciation. The elimination of the accumulated depreciation account results in an asset balance of €980,000 solely in the equipment account. Then, Rite-Up increases the value of the equipment by €220,000 to its fair value. The balance in the equipment account is then equal to its fair value of €1,200,000. We summarize these adjustments in the following table.

Summary: Initial Upward Revaluation Accumulated Depreciation Elimination Method

	Equipment	Accumulated Depreciation	Net Carrying Value
Beginning balance	€1,400,000	€ 0	€1,400,000
Accumulated depreciation	0	420,000	(420,000)
Balance before revaluation	1,400,000	420,000	980,000
Accumulated depreciation elimination	(420,000)	(420,000)	0
Balance	980,000	0	980,000
Initial revaluation	220,000	0	220,000
Balance after revaluation	€1,200,000	€ 0	€1,200,000

The journal entries are:

Account	*End of Year, Current Year*	
Accumulated Depreciation – Equipment	420,000	
Equipment		420,000
Equipment	220,000	
Revaluation Surplus – Equipment (OCI)		220,000

Step 3. **Compute new depreciation.** The original life was 10 years, but 3 years have already passed. Consequently, the new annual depreciation expense will be €171,429, which is the new carrying value of €1,200,000 divided by 7 years.

Account	*End of Year, Each Year after Revaluation*	
Depreciation Expense – Equipment	171,429	
Accumulated Depreciation – Equipment		171,429

Step 4. **Determine treatment of revaluation surplus, if any.** Rite-Up chooses to transfer the revaluation surplus to retained earnings. It will reduce the surplus by €31,429, the difference between the new depreciation expense of €171,429 and the original depreciation expense of €140,000. The journal entry is as follows:

Account	End of Year, Each Year after Revaluation	
Revaluation Surplus – Equipment (OCI)	31,429	
Retained Earnings		31,429

Example 12A.2 is an extension of Example 12A.1 that illustrates a subsequent revaluation.

EXAMPLE 12A.2

Subsequent Revaluation after an Initial Upward Revaluation: IFRS

PROBLEM: It is 2 years later, and Rite-Up Company from Example 12A.1 is revaluing its equipment again. The fair value is €600,000. The revaluation surplus account in stockholders' equity reflects a balance of €157,142 [€220,000 − (€31,429 × 2 years)]. The accumulated depreciation is now €342,858 (i.e., revised depreciation expense of €171,429 multiplied by 2 years). Determine the increase or decrease in the carrying value of the asset and indicate where Rite-Up should report any unrealized gain or loss in the financial statements.

SOLUTION: With a subsequent revaluation, we typically follow the same four-step process. However, this problem asks us to perform only Steps 1 and 2.

Step 1. **Measure the fair value.** The fair value is given to be €600,000.

Step 2. **Record the revaluation.** With the accumulated depreciation elimination method, Rite-Up must first eliminate the balance in accumulated depreciation. After 2 years, that balance is now equal to €342,858 (i.e., the recomputed annual depreciation of €171,429 × 2 years). Rite-Up also decreases the value of the equipment by €257,142 to its fair value of €600,000. Of the €257,142 decrease, it applies €157,142 against the €157,142 credit balance in the revaluation surplus. The remaining €100,000 (i.e., €257,142 − €157,142) is an unrealized loss that Rite-Up includes in net income.

The following table summarizes the effect of the second revaluation under the accumulated depreciation elimination method.

Summary: Subsequent Revaluation

	Equipment	Accumulated Depreciation	Net Carrying Value
Beginning balance	€1,200,000	€ 0	€1,200,000
Accumulated depreciation	0	342,858	(342,858)
Balance before revaluation	1,200,000	342,858	857,142
Accumulated depreciation elimination	(342,858)	(342,858)	0
Balance	857,142	0	857,142
Subsequent revaluation	(257,142)	0	(257,142)
Balance after revaluation	€ 600,000	€ 0	€ 600,000

Continued

The journal entry to eliminate the accumulated depreciation is as follows:

Account	End of Year, Current Year	
Accumulated Depreciation – Equipment	342,858	
Equipment		342,858

The journal entry to decrease the equipment follows:

Account	End of Year, Current Year	
Revaluation Surplus – Equipment (OCI)	157,142	
Unrealized Loss – Equipment (NI)	100,000	
Equipment		257,142

The next series of examples illustrate initial downward revaluations followed by subsequent revaluations. Example 12A.3 illustrates an initial downward revaluation.

EXAMPLE 12A.3

Initial Downward Revaluation: IFRS

PROBLEM: After 3 full years of use, the Rite-Down Company revalues equipment with a carrying value of €980,000 to its fair value of €900,000 using the accumulated depreciation elimination method. The original cost of the equipment is €1,400,000 and the equipment has a useful life of 10 years with no scrap value. Rite-Down depreciates under the straight-line method. Therefore, the annual depreciation expense is €140,000 per year (€1,400,000 / 10 years). The accumulated depreciation up to the date of the revaluation is €420,000 (€140,000 × 3 years).

Use the four-step revaluation process to address the following questions: What is the new carrying value of the asset? What is the increase or decrease in the carrying value of the asset and where will Rite-Down report any unrealized gain or loss in the financial statements? What is the new annual depreciation expense after revaluation? What amount would Rite-Down transfer from any revaluation surplus to retained earnings?

SOLUTION: We use the four-step revaluation model to illustrate the solution.

Step 1. **Measure the fair value.** The fair value is given to be €900,000, which will be the new carrying value.

Step 2. **Record the revaluation.** The downward revaluation is equal to €80,000 (carrying value of €980,000 less the fair value of €900,000). Because this initial revaluation of the asset decreases the asset value, Rite-Down includes the unrealized loss on the revaluation in net income.

With the accumulated depreciation elimination method, Rite-Down eliminates all prior accumulated depreciation, resulting in an asset balance of €980,000 solely in the equipment account. Rite-Down also decreases the value of the equipment's net carrying value by €80,000. The balance in the equipment account is then equal to the fair value of €900,000. As noted in the table on the next page, the asset's cost is reduced by a total of €500,000. We summarize the effects of the initial revaluation using the accumulated depreciation elimination method in the table on the next page.

Summary: Initial Downward Revaluation: Accumulated Depreciation Elimination Method

	Equipment	Accumulated Depreciation	Net Carrying Value
Beginning balance	€1,400,000	€ 0	€1,400,000
Accumulated depreciation	0	420,000	(420,000)
Balance before revaluation	1,400,000	420,000	980,000
Accumulated depreciation elimination	(420,000)	(420,000)	0
Balance	980,000	0	980,000
Initial revaluation	(80,000)	0	(80,000)
Balance after revaluation	€ 900,000	€ 0	€ 900,000

The journal entry to eliminate the accumulated depreciation follows:

Account	***End of Year, Current Year***	
Accumulated Depreciation – Equipment	420,000	
Equipment		420,000

The journal entry to decrease the equipment follows:

Account	***End of Year, Current Year***	
Unrealized Loss – Equipment (NI)	80,000	
Equipment		80,000

Step 3. **Compute new depreciation.** The original life was 10 years, but 3 years have already passed. Consequently, the new annual depreciation expense will be €128,571, which is €900,000 divided by 7 years.

Account	***End of Year, Each Year after Revaluation***	
Depreciation Expense – Equipment	128,571	
Accumulated Depreciation – Equipment		128,571

Step 4. **Determine treatment of revaluation surplus, if any.** There is no surplus.

Example 12A.4 builds on Example 12A.3 to illustrate a subsequent revaluation.

EXAMPLE 12A.4

Subsequent Revaluation after an Initial Downward Revaluation: IFRS

PROBLEM: The Rite-Down Company from Example 12A.3 is responsible for monitoring fair values for its assets in subsequent accounting periods and must revalue in cases when there is a significant difference between the asset's carrying value and its fair value. The company revalued its equipment again 2 years later when its fair value is €725,000. The balance in the accumulated depreciation account is €257,142 (i.e., the recomputed annual depreciation of €128,571 × 2 years). What are the entries to reflect the revaluation on the company's financial statements?

Continued

SOLUTION: With a subsequent revaluation, we typically follow the same four-step procedure. However, we need to perform only steps 1 and 2 in this illustration.

Step 1. **Measure the fair value.** The fair value is given at €725,000.

Step 2. **Record the revaluation.** Under the accumulated depreciation elimination method, Rite-Down first eliminates the balance in accumulated depreciation. The balance in the accumulated depreciation account is €257,142, which is two times the recomputed annual depreciation of €128,571. The carrying value of the equipment was €900,000 after the initial revaluation, so the current carrying value is €642,858 (€900,000 − €257,142 in accumulated depreciation). Rite-Down now increases the value of the equipment by €82,142 to its fair value of €725,000. Because it originally recorded a loss of €80,000 for this asset, it reports €80,000 of the unrealized gain in net income. Rite-Down includes the remaining or excess gain of €2,142 in other comprehensive income by crediting the revaluation surplus account.

We summarize the effects of the subsequent revaluation using the accumulated depreciation elimination method in the following table.

Summary: Subsequent Revaluation – Accumulated Depreciation Elimination Method

	Equipment	Accumulated Depreciation	Net Carrying Value
Balance after revaluation	€900,000	€ 0	€900,000
Accumulated depreciation	0	257,142	(257,142)
Balance before revaluation	900,000	257,142	642,858
Accumulated depreciation elimination	(257,142)	(257,142)	0
Balance	642,858	0	642,858
Subsequent revaluation	82,142	0	82,142
Balance after revaluation	€725,000	€ 0	€725,000

The journal entries are:

Account	End of Year, Current Year	
Accumulated Depreciation – Equipment	257,142	
Equipment		257,142
Equipment	82,142	
Unrealized Gain – Equipment (NI)		80,000
Revaluation Surplus – Equipment (OCI)		2,142

Derecognition after a Revaluation

Under IFRS, if a company is derecognizing an asset that it has revalued upward, then it should eliminate both the asset's net carrying value (cost less accumulated depreciation) and the balance in revaluation surplus that relates to that asset. The related revaluation surplus account should be eliminated against retained earnings. An example of the derecognition of a revalued asset is provided in Example 12A.5.

EXAMPLE 12A.5

Derecognition of Previously Revalued Asset: IFRS

PROBLEM: On May 31, 2018, J Franz Company sold a piece of equipment for $410,000. After bringing the depreciation up to date, the carrying value of the equipment was $400,000. Specifically, the asset had an original cost of $545,000 and the accumulated depreciation balance up to the date of the sale was $145,000. The related revaluation surplus account balance was $53,000. What are the entries to account for the derecognition of the equipment given a balance in the revaluation surplus?

SOLUTION: First, we remove the revaluation surplus account from the books by debiting the account for $53,000 and crediting retained earnings as follows:

Account	***May 31, 2018***	
Revaluation Surplus – Equipment	53,000	
Retained Earnings		53,000

The gain on the sale of the equipment is $10,000, which we compute as the $410,000 cash proceeds less the $400,000 net book value. The journal entry required to record the sale follows:

Account	***May 31, 2018***	
Cash	410,000	
Accumulated Depreciation – Equipment	145,000	
Equipment		545,000
Gain on Sale of Equipment		10,000

JUDGMENTS IN ACCOUNTING
Revaluation under IFRS

The revaluation of long-term operating assets involves judgment regarding whether to revalue various assets. Managers must think carefully about the trade-off between relevance and faithful representation when choosing a measurement method (that is, to revalue or report at historical cost). Financial statement users should examine the company's accounting policies to determine whether the company has revalued any of its noncurrent assets.

Companies that report under IFRS and choose to revalue their PPE or intangible assets also exercise judgment in the determination of fair value. The fair value of certain assets—for example, investments in securities for which there is a liquid market and quoted market prices—are readily available and objective. In contrast, the fair value of long-term operating assets, particularly intangible assets, can be highly subjective. Thus, management must exercise discretion in determining the value to report on the balance sheet.

To illustrate, consider the Rite-Down Company presented in Example 12A.3. In that example, we were given the carrying value of €980,000 and the fair value of €900,000. As a result, the unrealized loss included in net income was €80,000 (€980,000 carrying value – the €900,000 fair value). But how did management measure fair value in the case of PPE? Sometimes, there is a market price available for that exact piece of equipment—of identical age and same condition. For instance, if the asset in question were a car, then blue book values are available that would provide a close estimate of fair value. However, what if the equipment is not as generic as a car? In fact, what if it is a specialized piece of equipment? In such cases, the estimate of fair value involves a great deal of subjectivity. For Rite-Down, if the fair value was €880,000 instead of €900,000, the unrealized loss included in net income would be €100,000, as opposed to €80,000.

Required Disclosures for Revaluation of Long-Term Operating Assets

Under IFRS, if a company reports any class of PPE at revalued amounts, it must include changes in asset values in the reconciliation of the beginning to ending balances. IFRS requires additional disclosures relating to revaluations, including:

1. The date of the revaluation
2. Whether an independent appraiser was involved
3. The methods and significant assumptions used in estimating fair values
4. The extent to which the company determined fair values directly in an observable, active market; used recent market transactions on arm's length terms; or estimated using other valuation techniques

For each class of revalued asset, the company must report the carrying amount it would have reported as if it had carried the assets under the historical cost model. Finally, companies must disclose the revaluation surplus.

Exhibit 12A.2 contains excerpts from the significant accounting policies and the property, plant, and equipment footnotes of ***Sasini Limited,*** a major tea and coffee producer based in Kenya that reports under IFRS. These disclosures illustrate the accounting policies and disclosures for asset revaluations. ***Sasini*** revalues assets using market values obtained from independent appraisers. At the end of fiscal 2016, net revaluations in 2016 increased the value of its property by 5,517 million Kenyan shillings, representing about 66% of total shareholders' equity.

EXHIBIT 12A.2 Revaluation Accounting Policy, ***Sasini Limited,*** Financial Statement, September 30, 2016

NOTE 3: Significant Accounting Policies (excerpt)

(g) Property, plant, & equipment and depreciation

Property, plant, and equipment are measured at cost or revalued amounts less accumulated depreciation and any impairment losses. Cost includes expenditures that are directly attributable to the acquisition of the asset.

Revaluation increases arising on the revaluations are recognised in other comprehensive income and accumulated in the revaluation reserve in equity, except to the extent that it reverses a revaluation decrease for the same asset previously recognised as an expense, in which case the increase is credited to profit or loss to the extent of the decrease previously charged. A decrease in carrying amount arising out of revaluation is charged as an expense to the extent that it exceeds the balance, if any, held in the revaluation reserve relating to a previous revaluation of that asset.

An annual transfer from the asset revaluation reserve to retained earnings is made for the difference between depreciation based on the revalued amount of the asset and the original cost. Additionally, accumulated depreciation at the revaluation date is eliminated against the gross carrying amount of the asset and the net amount is restated to the revalued amount of the asset. Upon disposal, any surplus remaining in the revaluation reserve relating to the particular asset being sold is transferred to retained earnings.

Revaluations are done with sufficient regularity to ensure that the carrying amount does not differ materially from that which would be determined using fair value at the end of the reporting period.

. . . . .

NOTE 18: Property, Plant, and Equipment (excerpt)

The Group's building and freehold land was revalued on 30 September 2014 by Knight Frank Valuers Limited, a firm of registered independent valuers, on the market value existing use basis.

The Group's plant, equipment, machinery, furniture and fittings were revalued on 30 September 2016 by Knight Frank Valuers Limited, registered valuers, on the market value existing use basis.

The carrying values of the property, plant, and equipment were adjusted to the revaluations and the resultant surplus and deferred tax effect, was recognised in other comprehensive income and accumulated in equity as at that date.

Source: Sasini Limited, Financial Statement, September 30, 2016. http://sasini.co.ke/investor-center/

13 Operating Liabilities and Contingencies

LEARNING OBJECTIVES

1. Define and demonstrate accounting for operating liabilities, including accounts payable, trade notes payable, unearned revenues, gift cards, deposits, sales taxes payable, and compensated absences.
2. Discuss and illustrate the accounting for asset retirement obligations and required disclosures.
3. Describe the accounting for gain and loss contingencies, including recognition and disclosures related to loss contingencies.
4. Demonstrate the accounting for common loss contingencies involving litigation, warranties, and premiums.

Introduction

MANUFACTURERS AND RETAILERS depend on suppliers for the materials and inventory needed to produce and sell their goods. Consider ***GameStop Corporation,*** a Fortune-500 company known as the world's largest video game and software retailer with over 6,500 retail stores worldwide. ***GameStop*** sells many popular products such as ***Microsoft's*** Xbox One, ***Nintendo's*** Wii, and ***Sony's*** PlayStation. Manufacturers often target new releases of these game systems for the winter holiday season—and gaming devotees will line up for special deals and first access to newly released systems. When supplier delays cause these video game systems to be out of stock or available in limited quantity, resellers such as ***GameStop*** may experience lost sales. For this reason, ***GameStop's*** 2016 annual report discloses that overall sales of video game systems or game software could be reduced if any supplier issues occur such as delivery delays or insufficient quantities.

John Greim/Contributor/Getty Images

Businesses also rely on supplier relationships for short-term financing through accounts payable. Instead of using cash to pay ***Microsoft*** for Xbox inventory, ***GameStop*** can delay the cash payment until it receives the inventory and sells it to its customers. ***GameStop's*** 2016 annual report notes that it depends significantly upon such supplier business arrangements, including payment terms, competitive prices, return policies, and advertising allowances. These arrangements provide short-term financing, allowing ***GameStop*** to offer products to customers at competitive prices. ***GameStop's*** balance sheet shows the extent to which it relies on suppliers for credit: at the end of fiscal 2016, ***GameStop's*** accounts payable of $616.6 million was one of its largest liabilities, representing about 35% of current liabilities and 23% of total liabilities.

In this chapter, we focus on accounting for the complexities of business-supplier relationships. We begin with the general *operating liabilities* that companies rely on to conduct day-to-day functions and to finance growth in sales and profits. We then discuss a unique operating liability—*asset retirement obligations*. Accounting for operating liabilities and asset retirement obligations is similar under U.S. GAAP and IFRS.

Finally, we examine accounting for *contingencies*, which are potential obligations that the entity may or may not have to pay in the future. Because of the uncertainties related to the amount and probability of incurring an obligation, companies need to determine whether to report contingencies as liabilities. The determination of a contingent liability differs under U.S. GAAP and IFRS. «

❶ Define and demonstrate accounting for operating liabilities, including accounts payable, trade notes payable, unearned revenues, gift cards, deposits, sales taxes payable, and compensated absences.

Operating Liabilities

The conceptual framework defines **liabilities** as "probable future sacrifices of economic benefits arising from present obligations of a particular entity to transfer assets or provide services to other entities in the future as a result of past transactions or events."[1] This definition includes three characteristics:

1. The entity will probably need to make a future sacrifice to satisfy the obligation (for example, disburse cash).
2. The entity has little or no option to avoid a future sacrifice.
3. The transaction or event giving rise to the obligation has already occurred.

Operating liabilities are obligations arising from the firm's primary business operations, including short-term obligations such as accounts payable, trade notes payable, accrued liabilities such as advance collections, sales and payroll taxes payable, and income tax payable. We discuss operating liabilities in this chapter and financing liabilities in the chapter that follows.

We begin with the following operating liabilities:

- Accounts payable and trade notes payable
- Unearned revenues
- Gift cards
- Deposits
- Sales taxes payable
- Income taxes payable
- Compensated absences

We cover payroll taxes payable in the Appendix A to this chapter.

Accounts Payable and Trade Notes Payable

Accounts payable are amounts owed for goods, supplies, or services purchased on open account, meaning that the invoice is the only formal documentation for the credit agreement. **Trade notes payable** are formal, written promises to pay a certain sum of money on a specified date in the future that arise from the purchase of goods, supplies, or services. Trade notes payable typically specify a stated rate of interest. Firms usually classify both accounts payable and trade notes payable as current liabilities because these obligations are generally due within 1 year (or one operating cycle, if longer).

Companies usually recognize both types of payables when title passes. Example 13.1 illustrates the acquisition of inventory with an open accounts payable.

EXAMPLE 13.1 **Accounts Payable**

PROBLEM: On May 5, Ivan Brick Company orders 1,000 pallets of red bricks at a cost of $245 per pallet from Yang Grew Foundries on an open account. The shipping terms are f.o.b. destination. Ivan Brick receives the bricks on May 12. It uses the perpetual inventory method. Prepare the journal entry to record the receipt of the bricks.

SOLUTION: Ivan Brick records the following journal entry on May 12, which is the date that the goods are received and title passes to the buyer.

Account	***May 12***	
Inventory (1,000 × $245)	245,000	
Accounts Payable		245,000

[1] FASB, Statement of *Financial Accounting Concepts No. 6*, "Elements of Financial Statements," Paragraph 35.

The accounting for trade notes payable is very similar with the exception that notes payable generally involve interest as Example 13.2 illustrates.

EXAMPLE 13.2

Trade Notes Payable

PROBLEM: Templeton Graphics, Inc. purchased production materials on October 1 of the current year using a trade note payable for $10,000. The 4-month note is due on February 1 of the following fiscal year. The short-term note carries a 6% annual interest rate. Templeton's fiscal year-end is December 31. Prepare the journal entries required to record the notes payable transaction for both the current and the following year.

SOLUTION: Templeton makes the following journal entry on the date that it signs the note.

Account	October 1, Current Year	
Raw Materials Inventory	10,000	
Notes Payable		10,000

Three months' interest has accrued by December 31 and Templeton must record the $150 interest expense ($10,000 × 6% × 3/12) and the liability for unpaid interest. The year-end adjusting entry for the accrued interest follows.

Account	December 31, Current Year	
Interest Expense	150	
Interest Payable		150

Templeton pays the interest in the following year on the due date of the note. The total interest due is $200 ($10,000 × 6% × 4/12). Of the $200 total interest, $150 was incurred in the prior year, and the $50 balance is expensed on the due date of February 1 of the following year ($10,000 × 6% × 1/12). The entry to pay the principal and interest due on February 1 follows.

Account	February 1, Following Year	
Notes Payable	10,000	
Interest Payable	150	
Interest Expense	50	
Cash		10,200

Unearned Revenues

Unearned revenues (also known as deferred credits or deferred revenues) are advance collections from customers for goods and services to be provided at some future date. The liability arises from the obligation to deliver goods or provide the agreed-upon services. The seller recognizes revenue when it delivers the goods or provides the service. In some cases, such as insurance premiums collected in advance, the seller earns revenue evenly over the term of the contract based on the passage of time. In other cases, revenue recognition is tied to actual delivery. For example, ***GameStop Corporation*** initially reports subscriptions to the company's PowerUp Rewards loyalty program and magazines as unearned revenues. ***GameStop*** then recognizes subscription revenue on a straight-line basis over the subscription period as the magazines are delivered.

Unearned revenues are most often classified as a current liability. When ***Delta Air Lines, Inc.***, sells air travel tickets to its customers, ***Delta*** initially records an unearned revenue, called air traffic liability. ***Delta*** recognizes revenue when it provides transportation to the customers. Because the travel is expected to be taken within the next 12 months, ***Delta*** reports its air traffic liability as a current liability. At the end of 2016, ***Delta*** reported an air traffic liability of $4,626 million, or about 30% of its current liabilities. However, if the company did not expect to deliver the good or service until after 1 year (or operating cycle, if longer), it would then classify the unearned revenue as a noncurrent liability. Unearned revenues may be divided into a current and a noncurrent portion, if appropriate.

Example 13.3 illustrates unearned revenues related to the advance collection of insurance premiums.

EXAMPLE 13.3 Unearned Revenues

PROBLEM: Midwest Insurance collects $36,000 for a 3-year casualty policy on June 1 of the current year. Coverage begins on June 1. Midwest has a December 31 year-end. Prepare the journal entries for the current year. What is the balance in the unearned revenue account at December 31 of the current year? What does Midwest report as a current liability on the balance sheet at December 31 of the current year?

SOLUTION: Midwest Insurance makes the following journal entry on the date it collects the insurance premium.

Account	June 1, Current Year	
Cash	36,000	
Unearned Revenue		36,000

Because the insurance coverage is based on time, Midwest earns revenue evenly over the life of the policy. Specifically, Midwest will recognize $1,000 in revenue each month (i.e., $36,000 / 36 months). At the end of the fiscal year, Midwest will have earned 7 months of insurance premiums, or $7,000 ($1,000 per month × 7 months) based on the time period for which it has provided coverage. The adjusting entry to record the income earned in the current period follows.

Account	December 31, Current Year	
Unearned Revenue	7,000	
Insurance Revenue		7,000

The t-account for unearned revenue is presented next.

Unearned Revenue

	Debit	Credit	
		36,000	June 1
December 31	7,000		
		29,000	Ending Balance

On December 31, the balance in the unearned revenue account is $29,000 ($36,000 collected in advance less the $7,000 earned). Of this $29,000, the current liability is $12,000 ($1,000 × 12 months), representing the insurance coverage to be provided to the customer over the next 12 months. The remaining $17,000 ($29,000 − $12,000) is a noncurrent liability because the insurance coverage will be provided in a period longer than 1 year from the balance sheet date.

Gift Cards

Although used for decades, *gift cards* have become quite popular in recent years. A **gift card** is a certificate allowing the holder to receive goods or services of a specified value from the issuer. Customers appreciate gift cards for their convenience, and companies benefit from the sale of gift cards when receiving cash upon issuance. In addition, gift card recipients often spend more than the gift card amount, resulting in an increased sales volume for the company. Finally, a percentage of the company's total gift card sales referred to as **breakage** is never redeemed.

Initial Sale and Redemption. The accounting for the initial sale and the redemption of the gift card is straightforward. The company:

1. Records the transaction as unearned revenue when issuing the gift card by debiting cash and crediting a liability for the unearned revenue on the date it sells the cards.
2. Maintains a liability on the balance sheet until the gift card is redeemed and then recognizes sales revenue earned upon redemption with a corresponding reduction of the liability.

For example, at the end of fiscal 2016, the ***Target Corporation*** reported a gift card liability of $693 million, or about 5.5% of its current liabilities.[2] When gift cards are redeemed, ***Target*** debits the unearned revenue and credits sales revenue. Example 13.4 illustrates accounting for gift cards.

EXAMPLE 13.4 Gift Card Sale and Redemption

PROBLEM: Rohl's Department Stores, Inc. records $120,000 in gift card sales and receives cash in Year 1. Customers used 25% of the gift cards to purchase merchandise in Year 2. Cost of sales is 40% of total sales. Rohl's uses the perpetual inventory system. Record the sale and redemption of the gift cards in Years 1 and 2, respectively.

SOLUTION: In the year of the sale, Rohl's records cash and the unearned revenue for $120,000.

Account	At Time of Sale of Gift Cards – Year 1	
Cash	120,000	
Unearned Revenue – Gift Cards		120,000

The gift cards are partially redeemed in the second year and, as a result, the company recognizes $30,000 of revenue ($120,000 × 25%). The journal entry follows.

Account	At Time of Redemption – Year 2	
Unearned Revenue – Gift Cards	30,000	
Sales Revenue		30,000

Rohl's also recognizes cost of goods sold of $12,000 ($30,000 × 40%) at the point the cards are redeemed and sales revenue is recorded.

Account	At Time of Redemption – Year 2	
Cost of Goods Sold	12,000	
Inventory		12,000

Breakage. Breakage introduces complexity in accounting for gift cards. Given that not all gift cards will be redeemed, when can the company remove the liability from its books and recognize revenue? If the company expects to be entitled to a breakage amount and it can be estimated, then it should use the *proportional method* to account for breakage. Otherwise, it should use the *remote method.*

The **remote method** requires the seller to reliably estimate the amount of breakage. The company recognizes revenue from gift card breakage and removes the liability for the advance collection (unearned revenue) only when the probability of redemption becomes remote. For example, ***Lululemon Athletica Inc.,*** the athletic apparel company, sells gift cards that generally do not have expiration dates. ***Lululemon*** recognizes revenue from gift cards when either the customer redeems the gift card or the likelihood of the customer redeeming the gift card is

[2] ***Source:*** Annual financial statement, footnote 18. https://www.sec.gov/Archives/edgar/data/27419/000002741917000008/tgt-20170128x10k.htm#s1B7D75BDA162E9BAE0AD72260A437BA8

remote. ***Lululemon*** estimates gift card breakage based on historical redemption patterns. In fiscal 2016, ***Lululemon*** recognized $4.5 million of revenue from unredeemed gift cards.[3]

Under the **proportional method**, breakage revenue is recognized ratably as actual card redemptions occur. To use this method, the company must have reliable estimates of breakage and the time period of actual gift card redemption. The proportional method requires the company to pool together all gift cards sold over a certain time period. The company estimates the breakage percentage of these cards as well as the time period over which these cards will be redeemed. The company then recognizes the estimated breakage revenue (and derecognizes the liability) over the estimated time period of redemption. For example, ***Target Corporation*** sells gift cards that do not expire. ***Target*** estimates breakage in proportion to actual gift card redemptions based on historical redemption rates.[4] The proportional method is shown in Example 13.5.

EXAMPLE 13.5 Breakage: Proportional Method

PROBLEM: Elliot Electronics Company offers gift cards to its customers. Elliot reported $400,000 in gift card sales in Year 1, and received cash. The company reliably estimates the amount of breakage at 15% and the time period of redemption as 2 years. Elliot uses the proportional method to account for breakage. Customers redeemed $180,000 in gift cards in Year 1. Elliot's cost of goods sold percentage is 35%. Elliot uses the perpetual inventory system. Provide the journal entries for Year 1.

SOLUTION: In Year 1, Elliot records the cash received and the performance obligation to redeem the gift cards (i.e., unearned revenue).

Account	***Sale of Gift Cards***	
Cash	400,000	
Unearned Revenue – Gift Cards		400,000

Elliot also records the redemption of $180,000 of gift cards.

Account	***Redemption of Gift Cards***	
Unearned Revenue – Gift Cards	180,000	
Sales Revenue		180,000

Elliott also records the related cost of goods sold of $63,000 ($180,000 × 35%).

Account	***Redemption of Gift Cards***	
Cost of Goods Sold	63,000	
Inventory		63,000

In addition, Elliot recognizes a proportion of breakage revenue. It estimates total breakage as $60,000 ($400,000 × 15%). Because 53% [$180,000 / ($400,000 − $60,000)] of the estimated cards to be redeemed were redeemed in Year 1, Elliot recognizes 53% of the estimated breakage revenue in Year 1 for a total of $31,800 ($60,000 × 53%).

Account	***December 31, Year 1***	
Unearned Revenue – Gift Cards	31,800	
Breakage Revenue		31,800

[3] ***Source:*** Financial statement footnote 1. http://files.shareholder.com/downloads/LULU/4387429514x0xS1397187-17-8/1397187/filing.pdf

[4] ***Source:*** Annual, financial statement footnote 2. https://www.sec.gov/Archives/edgar/data/27419/000002741917000008/tgt-20170128x10k.htm#s1B7D75BDA162E9BAE0AD72260A437BA8

Deposits

Businesses often require buyers to pay a **deposit** for goods or services, which is an amount a buyer remits to a seller that will be returned to the buyer at some point in time when a specific event occurs. For example, deposits are often required by companies (such as chemicals manufacturers) that deliver their products in returnable containers. If the containers are not returned, the company keeps the deposit and the customer forfeits that amount. In leasing arrangements, most apartment owners require a security deposit from tenants that the landlord will return to the tenant when the apartment is vacated. If the apartment is damaged, then the landlord will deduct the cost of repairs from the deposit and return the balance to the tenant. The tenant forfeits the amount of the deposit retained.

When an entity receives the deposit, it credits a liability account. The accounting for deposits depends upon the amount the entity returns upon completion of the transaction:

1. **Returns the entire deposit.** The entity simply debits the same liability account and credits cash.
2. **Returns part of the deposit.** The entity debits the entire liability account, and the credit will depend upon the reason for the forfeiture of the deposit.
3. **Deposits are not returned.** The entity credits a revenue account and debits the liability account. If repairs to the property are required such as rental property, the entity credits cash as repairs are made.

Example 13.6 demonstrates accounting for deposits.

EXAMPLE 13.6 Deposits

PROBLEM: Stubben Chemicals collected a $500 deposit for 10 containers used to deliver inventory to a major pharmaceutical company. The cost of each container is $40. The company uses the perpetual inventory method. What journal entries are required if the containers are returned to Stubben? What journal entries are required if the containers are damaged and the customer forfeits the deposit?

SOLUTION: Stubben reports the $500 deposit as a liability when it delivers the inventory to the customer.

Account	*Inventory Delivered to the Customer*	
Cash	500	
Deposit Liability		500

If the containers are returned to Stubben and the deposit is refunded to the customer, then Stubben will make the following journal entry.

Account	*Containers Returned*	
Deposit Liability	500	
Cash		500

If the customer damages the containers and does not return them to Stubben, then Stubben removes the liability and recognizes revenue and the cost of sales related to the containers.

Account	*Containers Not Returned*	
Deposit Liability	500	
Container Sales Revenue		500

The cost of each container is $40, so with 10 not being returned and the deposit forfeited, the total cost of sales is $400 (10 × $40).

Account	*Containers Not Returned*	
Cost of Goods Sold	400	
Container Inventory		400

Sales Taxes Payable

Sales taxes payable is a liability (typically classified as current) resulting from the seller's obligation to collect sales taxes from customers and remit these taxes to the appropriate taxing jurisdiction. Sales taxes are not an expense for the seller. The company acts as a conduit for the government by simply collecting and remitting the tax. The seller collects sales taxes from customers when making sales and incurs the obligation to remit the tax to the government. The seller credits a sales tax payable account when the taxes are collected from the customer and derecognizes this liability when it remits the sales tax to the government as illustrated in Example 13.7.

EXAMPLE 13.7 Sales Taxes Payable

PROBLEM: Gobble Stores operates in Chester County. The state sales tax rate is 8.375%. The company sells $180,000 in merchandise for the month of March. The company uses a periodic inventory system. How much sales tax did Gobble collect and what is the journal entry to record the sale and the remittance to the state government?

SOLUTION: Gobble collected $15,075 in sales taxes (i.e., $180,000 × 8.375%). Gobble's customers paid a total of $195,075, which is the sum of the merchandise sales value plus the sales taxes (i.e., $180,000 + $15,075). The company makes the following journal entry to record its March sales.

Account	***March 31***	
Cash (or Accounts Receivable)	195,075	
Sales		180,000
Sales Tax Payable		15,075

The entry to remit the sale taxes collected to the appropriate government agency follows.

Account	***March 31***	
Sales Tax Payable	15,075	
Cash		15,075

Income Taxes Payable

Most countries impose a tax on corporate income. In addition, most states within the United States also impose an additional income tax, and some local governmental units may impose a separate income tax. These jurisdictional taxes result in a liability (typically classified as current) on corporate balance sheets. The tax payable that a company reports on its balance sheet represents the amount that is owed to the governmental units.[5]

Compensated Absences

Compensated absences are employer-paid time off for vacation, illness, holidays, military service, jury duty, and maternity leave. Employees accrue these benefits over time as they work and get paid when they take the time off in the future.[6]

An employer must meet four criteria to report an expense and accrue a liability for future paid absences:

1. The obligation for future payment is a result of services already performed by the employee.
2. The benefits to be paid either vest or accumulate.
3. The future payment must be probable.
4. The future payment must be reasonably estimable.

[5]We discuss the computation of taxes payable in depth in Chapter 17.

[6]For the relevant authoritative literature for this topic, see FASB ASC 710-10-25 – *Compensation – General – Overall – Recognition* for U.S. GAAP and IASC, *International Accounting Standard 19*, "Employee Benefits," (London, UK: International Accounting Standards Committee, Revised), Paragraphs 8-16 for IFRS.

Vested versus Accumulated Benefits. Accounting for compensated absences depends on whether the benefits *vest* or *accumulate*. **Vested rights** exist whenever an employer has the obligation to make compensation payments if it terminates the employee. So, with vested compensated absences, rights to the benefits are not dependent on future employment. That is, firms pay vested compensation benefits even if they terminate the employee. As a result, vested compensation benefits should be accrued.

Accumulated rights permit an employee to carry forward unused benefits to future periods. So, employees can carry accumulated compensated absences forward past the current period in which they are earned and use them in future periods. In contrast, employees cannot carry non-accumulated compensated absences forward beyond the current period.

If the benefits accumulate but are not vested, then the accounting treatment must address the probability of payment. Assume the likelihood that the company will pay the benefits is low or very uncertain. Because the accumulated compensated absences do not meet the definition of a liability of being a probable future sacrifice, the firm would not accrue them.

With non-vested accumulated compensated absences, accountants must consider the employer's prior practices. Does the employer permit employees to accumulate sick days when they are not used? If so, a customary practice would justify the accrual of compensation expense. Accountants may also adjust the amount accrued for estimated forfeitures because these benefits are not vested and may not be fully utilized. Absences due to holidays, military leave, maternity leave, and time off for jury duty typically do not accumulate and should not be accrued.

Current versus Estimated Future Compensation Rates. After determining that a compensated absence should be accrued, the company next determines the rate of compensation to use: current or future rates. Typically, companies measure the obligation at the current rate rather than estimating the future salary or wage rate expected to be in effect when the employee uses the compensated absence. This approach is theoretically correct when the future rate is uncertain. However, when future rates are known, as in the case of a union contract signed with increased wage rates beginning in the next period, the employer should use the future wage rates in the accrual. If compensation rates change in the period of actual payment, the company debits the difference between the new, higher rate and the lower, accrued rate to compensation expense in the year it pays the compensated absence.

Accrual of Sick Days. As noted earlier, the accrual of non-vested sick days is not mandatory due to the high degree of uncertainty of incurring the obligation. Future sick day payment is dependent on illness, which fortunately is not a certain event. Again, accountants must consider customary practices used in corporations. For example, many companies pay the accumulation of sick days upon retirement. Some employers convert sick days into personal days if the employer specifies a fixed number of sick days to be awarded regardless of illness. In these cases, the company measures and accrues the compensated absences in the year the employee earns them.

Accounting for compensated absences is shown in Example 13.8.

EXAMPLE 13.8 Accounting for Compensated Absences

PROBLEM: Alberto Motors, Inc. employs 1,000 hourly employees. During the current year, employees earned 2,250 weeks of vacation, but 400 employees elected to carryover a total of 850 vacation weeks to the following year. Employees took the remaining 1,400 weeks of vacation during the current year.

Alberto typically follows a policy that all accum ulated vacation days are lost by the employee either upon termination or at retirement. Using an average wage rate of $900 per week, prepare the journal entries required to record Alberto's vacation accrual.

SOLUTION: Alberto records the compensation expense of $1,260,000 related to the 1,400 vacation weeks (at $900 per week) taken during the current year as follows:

Account	Current Year	
Vacation Wage Expense	1,260,000	
Cash		1,260,000

To record the compensation expense related to the 850 vacation weeks carried over to future periods, Alberto records vacation wage expense of $765,000 (850 × 900) in the current year.

Account	Current Year	
Vacation Wage Expense	765,000	
Liability for Compensated Absences		765,000

Alberto makes the next entry in the following year when employees take the vacation days:

Account	Following Year	
Liability for Compensated Absences	765,000	
Cash		765,000

A company can also base the accrual on its experience regarding the amount of vacation employees actually take. If the employer compensates employees for weeks taken, its accrual is generally based on the likelihood that the vacation time is taken. As Example 13.9 demonstrates, both the liability and expense change when assuming that some vacation time is not used.

EXAMPLE 13.9 Accounting for Compensated Absences with Partial Accrual

PROBLEM: Using the information for Alberto Motors, Inc. from the previous example, now assume that experience indicates that employees do not take 20% of accrued vacations. What is the journal entry to record the vacation accrual?

SOLUTION: The entry to accrue vacation pay would include a debit to wage expense and a credit to liability for compensated absences only for the portion expected to be paid. We estimate the amount as the number of weeks of vacation times the pay per week multiplied by the probability that the vacation will be taken. So, in this case, the expense and liability are $612,000 (850 weeks × $900 per week × 80%).

Account	Current Year	
Vacation Wage Expense	612,000	
Liability for Compensated Absences		612,000

Differences in Actual and Estimated Wage Rates. In the year when employees take the vacation time related to the accrued vacation liability, net earnings is typically not affected. That is, the company debits the expense in the prior year when employees provide services. An exception occurs when the actual wage rate in effect when the compensation is paid differs from the estimated rate used to accrue the compensated absence. In this case, the company reports the difference between the actual and estimated wage rates as an increase in compensation expense in the period when the compensated absence is taken. Example 13.10 illustrates accounting for differences in actual and estimated wage rates.

EXAMPLE 13.10 **Differences in Actual and Estimated Wage Rates**

PROBLEM: When Alberto Motors Inc.'s employees from Example 13.8 take the carried-over vacation days, the actual wage rate is $950, not the estimated $900 we used in the prior-year accrual. Recalculate the liability for compensated absences based on this information and prepare the journal entry to pay the accrued liability and to recognize the wage rate increase.

SOLUTION: Alberto Motors should charge the excess to expense in the year the employees take the vacations. The following journal entry assumes the wage rate increased by $50:

Account	***Following Year***	
Vacation Wage Expense [850 weeks × ($950 − $900)]	42,500	
Liability for Compensated Absences	765,000	
Cash		807,500

Compensated Absences: IFRS. Accounting for compensation absences is similar under IFRS except that IFRS specifies that firms should recognize the expense based on the expected cost to the entity. Thus, if the company can estimate future compensation rates, it will record the liability and expense based on the future rates. This difference can result in a higher liability under IFRS than under U.S. GAAP when a current cost estimate is used.

Footnote Disclosures: Operating Liabilities

On the balance sheet, companies generally provide totals of accounts payable and accrued liabilities. In the footnote disclosures, companies may provide additional detail on the specific types of operating liabilities. Exhibit 13.1 presents ***Target's*** footnote disclosure of accrued and other current liabilities from its 2016 annual report. Accrued and other current liabilities include liabilities such as wages and benefits, taxes payable, and gift card liability. The accounts payable of $7,252 million plus accrued and other current liabilities of $3,737 million represent about 42% of ***Target's*** total liabilities at January 28, 2017.

EXHIBIT 13.1 Disclosure of Accrued and Other Current Liabilities, ***Target Corporation***, Financial Statements, January 28, 2017

NOTE 18: Accrued and Other Current Liabilities

Accrued and Other Current Liabilities *(millions)*	**January 28, 2017**	**January 30, 2016**
Wages and benefits	$ 812	$ 884
Gift card liability, net of estimated breakage	693	644
Real estate, sales and other taxes payable	571	574
Dividends payable	334	337
Straight-line rent accrual[a]	271	262
Income tax payable	158	502
Workers' compensation and general liability[b]	141	146
Interest payable	71	76
Other	686	811
Total	$ 3,737	$ 4,236

[a] Straight-line rent accrual represents the amount of rent expense recorded that exceeds cash payments remitted in connection with operating leases.

[b] We retain a substantial portion of the risk related to general liability and workers' compensation claims. Liabilities associated with these losses include estimates of both claims filed and losses incurred but not yet reported. We estimate our ultimate cost based on analysis of historical data and actuarial estimates. General liability and workers' compensation liabilities are recorded at our estimate of their net present value.

Source: https://www.sec.gov/Archives/edgar/data/27419/000002741917000008/tgt-20170128x10k.htm Asset Retirement Obligations

2 Discuss and illustrate the accounting for asset retirement obligations and required disclosures.

Asset Retirement Obligations

Asset retirement obligations (AROs) are long-term legal obligations to dismantle and scrap assets or to restore property used for business purposes. For example, companies may be obligated to restore property by dismantling oil and gas facilities, decommissioning nuclear power plants, and closing mining operations and landfills.[7]

Accounting for Asset Retirement Obligations

Accounting for an ARO requires estimating the fair value that the company would have to pay to retire the asset in today's market.[8] Whereas the amount may appear to be straightforward to estimate, AROs are often related to very specific, unique assets. As a result, developing an ARO estimate may involve a substantial amount of judgment.

A company recognizes the amount of the ARO as a liability and records *accretion expense* over the life of the obligation using the effective interest rate method of amortization.[9] **Accretion expense** is the expense, reported in operating income, resulting from the increase in the carrying amount of the liability. Companies capitalize the ARO liability amount as part of the initial carrying amount of the related asset: It is not a separate asset because there is no future economic benefit associated with the cost itself. The total cost of the related asset is increased by the ARO because of the requirement to restore the property upon project completion. A company depreciates the total cost of the asset, including the capitalized amount for the ARO, over its life. For example, in its 2016 financial statement, ***Ford Company*** disclosed that it reported asset retirement obligations of $186 million in its other liabilities.

When retiring the asset, the company incurs the anticipated environmental remediation costs. If the actual costs are less than the balance in the ARO account, then the company will record a gain. If the actual costs are greater than the balance in the ARO account, the company will record a loss. Example 13.11 illustrates accounting for AROs.

EXAMPLE 13.11 **Asset Retirement Obligations**

PROBLEM: FuelCo built a gas station with underground tanks and put them in service on January 1, 2019, at a cost of $500,000. The company estimates that the fuel tanks will have a useful life of 15 years and that the fair value of the costs to remove the fuel tanks will be $75,000 at the end of 15 years. Further, the company assumes a 10% discount rate and depreciates the fuel tanks using the straight-line method with no residual value. In the fifteenth year, FuelCo closes the gas station, incurring environmental remediation costs of $77,000. What is the amount of the ARO that the company should recognize in the current year? What are the necessary journal entries for 2019? What are the necessary journal entries to remove the gas station from FuelCo's books?

SOLUTION: FuelCo initially records the liability for the asset retirement at its present value and adds this same amount to the carrying value of the asset. During the life of the asset, FuelCo will record depreciation expense as well as accrue accretion expense on the obligation. When it closes the gas station, FuelCo will remove the asset and liability from its books and record any gain or loss, as necessary.

[7]For most of the relevant authoritative literature for this topic, see FASB ASC 410 – *Asset Retirement and Environmental Obligations* for U.S. GAAP. Under IFRS, reference to asset retirement obligations is made in IAS 16, *Accounting for Property, Plant and Equipment,* and further guidance is given in IFRIC 1, *Changes in Existing Decommissioning, Restoration and Similar Liabilities,* and IFRIC 5, *Rights to Interests Arising from Decommissioning, Restoration and Environmental Funds.*

[8]The FASB ASC 820 hierarchy is used to measure fair value and rank the reliability of fair value estimates from quoted market prices, market comparables, and management estimates and assumptions (e.g., discounted cash flow analysis).

[9]Accretion expense functions in the same way as interest expense.

We estimate the fair value of the ARO as the present value of the future removal costs. The present value of $75,000 in 15 years at a 10% discount rate is $17,954:

	N	I/Y	PV	PMT	FV	Excel Formula
Given	15	10.00%		0	−75,000	
Solve for PV			**17,954**			= PV(0.1,15,0,−75000)

The journal entry at the completion of construction is as follows:

Account	***January 1, 2019***	
Gas Station	517,954	
Asset Retirement Obligation		17,954
Cash		500,000

Each year, FuelCo will record depreciation of $34,530 ($517,954 / 15 years) as well as accretion expense on the obligation.

Account	***December 31, 2019***	
Depreciation Expense – Gas Station	34,530	
Accumulated Depreciation – Gas Station		34,530

The first year's accretion expense is $1,795 ($17,954 × 10%).

Account	***December 31, 2019***	
Accretion Expense	1,795	
Asset Retirement Obligation		1,795

After these entries are made, the new ARO balance is $19,749 ($17,954 + $1,795).

In the second year through fifteenth year, FuelCo will again record depreciation and accretion expenses. Thus, by the end of the gas station's life, the balance in the ARO account will be $75,000 (the future value of the present value of $17,954) and the balance in the accumulated depreciation account will be $517,954 ($34,530 × 15 years, including rounding of $4).

FuelCo is responsible for removing the fuel tanks. The total costs of removal are $77,000 and, as a result, the company incurs a $2,000 loss to settle the ARO (i.e., $75,000 − $77,000) because it costs more to liquidate the obligation than its carrying value. When FuelCo closes the site, the company must remove balances related to the gas station and record the settlement of the ARO as follows:

Account	***End of 15th Year***	
Accumulated Depreciation – Gas Station	517,954	
Gas Station		517,954

Account	***End of 15th Year***	
Asset Retirement Obligation	75,000	
Loss on Settlement of Asset Retirement Obligation	2,000	
Cash		77,000

Footnote Disclosures: Asset Retirement Obligations

An entity is required to disclose all of the following information about its asset retirement obligations:

1. A general description of the asset retirement obligations and the associated long-lived assets.
2. The fair value of assets that are legally restricted for purposes of settling asset retirement obligations.

3. A reconciliation of the beginning and ending aggregate carrying amount of asset retirement obligations showing separately the changes attributable to the following components when there is a significant change in any of them during the reporting period:

   - Liabilities incurred in the current period
   - Liabilities settled in the current period
   - Accretion expense
   - Revisions in estimated cash flows

If a company cannot reasonably estimate the fair value of an asset retirement obligation, it must disclose this fact and the reasons why it cannot make a reliable estimate.

Exhibit 13.2 illustrates ***Ford Motor Company's*** disclosure of its ARO for its long-lived assets, such as buildings. ***Ford's*** AROs relate to the estimated costs for asbestos abatement and the removal of other regulated building materials. Notice that ***Ford*** includes the estimated ARO in the carrying value of its assets and reports a related liability.

EXHIBIT 13.2 Disclosure of Asset Retirement Obligations, ***Ford Motor Company,*** Financial Statements, December 31, 2016

[Excerpt from Ford Motor Company's 2016 Annual Report]

NOTE 11: Net Property and Lease Commitments:

Conditional Asset Retirement Obligations

Conditional asset retirement obligations relate to legal obligations associated with the retirement, abandonment, or disposal of tangible long-lived assets. Estimates of the fair value liabilities for our conditional asset retirement obligations that are recorded in *Other liabilities and deferred revenue* in the non-current liabilities section of our consolidated balance sheet at December 31 were as follows (in millions):

	December 31, 2015	December 31, 2016
Beginning balance	$228	$216
Liabilities settled	(6)	(2)
Revisions to estimates	(6)	(28)
Ending balance	$216	$186

Source: Excerpt from Ford Motor Company's 2016 Annual Report. http://shareholder.ford.com/~/media/Files/F/Ford-IR/annual-report/2016-annual-report.pdf

Asset Retirement Obligations: IFRS

Accounting for AROs under IFRS differs in three main ways from U.S. GAAP:

- An obligation to restore property can be a legal obligation similar to U.S. GAAP accounting or an economic obligation. Therefore, AROs may be reported more frequently under IFRS.
- The obligation is estimated based on the costs rather than fair value of dismantling and removing any items or restoring the site.
- Estimated costs are discounted using a pre-tax interest rate and the risks specific to the liability. So, the analyses do not require the company to perform other detailed calculations on taxes. A pre-tax interest rate is higher than an after-tax interest rate, so the present value of the obligation would be lower. The accretion expense is referred to as interest expense.

Under IFRS, AROs are considered loss contingencies, which we discuss next.

3 Describe the accounting for gain and loss contingencies, including recognition and disclosures related to loss contingencies.

Gain and Loss Contingencies

Typically, companies are certain about the future amounts and timing of the cash disbursements required to liquidate their obligations. However, with *contingencies*, the amount and timing of future obligations are uncertain. A **contingency** is an existing condition, situation, or set of circumstances involving uncertainty that will ultimately be resolved when one or more future events occur or fail to occur.[10]

Although *loss contingencies* are most common, a *gain contingency* is also possible. We discuss both gain and loss contingencies in the remaining sections of this chapter.[11]

The recognition of a contingent gain results in the recognition of an asset as well as the recognition of a gain (or revenue). Thus, by recording a contingent gain, a company recognizes revenue before it is realized. Firms typically disclose contingent gains in the footnotes only when there is high certainty of realization. As a result, contingent gains are often not recognized or disclosed in the financial statements due to conservatism.[12]

Gain Contingency

A **gain contingency** is an existing condition, situation, or set of circumstances involving uncertainty as to possible gain to an entity that will ultimately be resolved when one or more future events occur or fail to occur.[13] A company serving as the plaintiff in a lawsuit that could receive a judgment in its favor is an example of a gain contingency. A gain contingency is often referred to as a *contingent asset* because recognition of a gain contingency results in an increase in an asset account.[14]

Loss Contingency

A **loss contingency** is an existing condition, situation, or set of circumstances involving uncertainty as to possible loss to an entity that will ultimately be resolved when one or more future events occur or fail to occur.[15] Examples include a company that is a defendant in a pending lawsuit as well as warranties, premiums, coupons, and environmental remediation liabilities. A loss contingency is also referred to as a *contingent liability*. Recognition of a contingent liability either increases an obligation or reduces the carrying value of an asset.

While loss contingencies are a type of liability, they differ from other liabilities because they involve a substantial degree of uncertainty. Consider a company facing pending litigation. The event that gave rise to the liability has already occurred, but until the lawsuit is resolved, there is uncertainty as to the amount, timing, and the requirement to pay damages. That is, it is uncertain whether the company will be required to disburse any amounts and the amount of this payment.

---

[10]These elements are similar under U.S. GAAP, FASB ASC 450-10-20 – *Contingencies – Overall – Glossary,* and IFRS, IASC, *International Accounting Standard 37*, "Provisions, Contingent Liabilities and Contingent Assets" (London, UK: International Accounting Standards Committee, Revised), Paragraph 10.

[11]For most of the relevant authoritative literature for this topic, see FASB ASC 450 – *Contingencies* for U.S. GAAP and IASC, *International Accounting Standard 37* for IFRS.

[12]An exception to this is certain income tax contingencies, such as net operating loss carryforwards and other income tax credit carryforwards. In these cases, companies typically recognize a tax asset and decrease income tax expense. Accruals and disclosures for income tax impacts of carryforwards are frequently reported by companies. We discuss this topic in greater detail in Chapter 17.

[13]FASB ASC 450-10-20.

[14]Tax loss carryforwards are another type of gain contingency discussed in Chapter 17.

[15]FASB ASC 450-10-20.

THE CONCEPTUAL FRAMEWORK CONNECTION
Loss Contingencies

Should a company report a loss contingency on the balance sheet? Specifically, is a contingent liability an actual obligation? The conceptual framework is a useful reference point for answering these questions. The three characteristics of a liability defined in the conceptual framework and noted earlier in the chapter are:

1. The entity will probably be required to make a future sacrifice to satisfy the obligation (for example, to disburse cash).
2. The entity has little or no option to avoid a future sacrifice.
3. The transaction or event giving rise to the obligation has already occurred.

In the case of loss contingencies, the second and third characteristics are met. The entity may indeed have no choice but to make a future sacrifice, and the event giving rise to the contingency has already occurred. The first condition is most difficult to measure and recognize because liabilities involve *probable* future sacrifices. Thus, the ability to recognize the contingency depends on the likelihood of required future disbursements. That is, the company must determine how "probable" is the need to make future payments and accrue a loss contingency only in cases when it is fairly certain that it will make a future sacrifice. In cases where it is not likely that the company will be required to make a future sacrifice, it will not accrue the contingency. Clearly, there is a significant degree of uncertainty regarding the decision whether or not to accrue the contingency.

Exhibit 13.3 presents the results of a survey of 500 U.S. companies. It demonstrates that loss contingencies are disclosed far more often than are gain contingencies.[16]

EXHIBIT 13.3 Percentage of Companies Reporting Contingencies

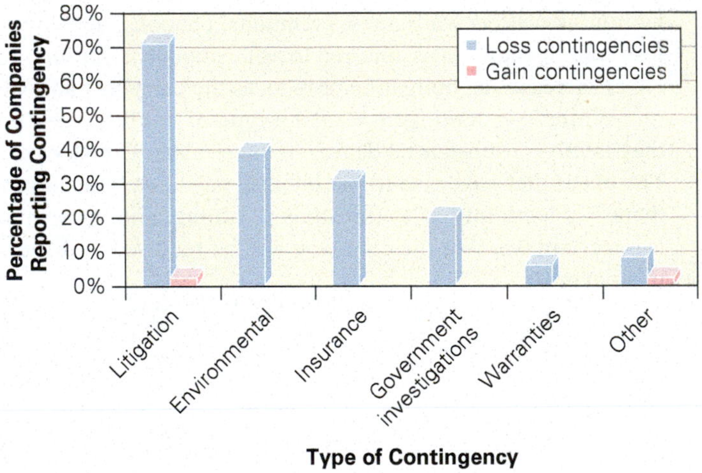

Source: AICPA, *U.S. GAAP Financial Statements: Best Practices in Presentation and Disclosure* – 2012 (New York, New York: AICPA, 2012).

Recognition and Measurement of Loss Contingencies

The criteria for determining how to treat a loss contingency are based on two factors:

1. The probability that the company will ultimately incur a loss.
2. The ability to reasonably estimate the amount of the potential loss.

The loss contingency must relate to an event that occurred in either the current or prior periods.

[16]The exhibit excludes contingencies related to income taxes. These types of gain contingencies are frequently disclosed by companies.

To assess whether a company will ultimately incur a loss, management must assess the likelihood of occurrence. That is, management must determine whether the loss *is probable, remote*, or *reasonably possible*:

- **Probable**. If the loss is likely to occur, it is considered probable. U.S. GAAP does not specify a probability level at which the loss becomes probable. However, "likely to occur" is a significantly higher threshold than "more likely than not."
- **Remote**. The probability of occurrence is only slight.
- **Reasonably possible**. The probability of occurrence is less than likely but more than remote.

A company is able to make a reasonable estimate when it can measure the potential loss. Reasonable estimation can be a single-point estimate or a range of possible estimates.

Accounting for Loss Contingencies

Based on the company's assessment of the probability of a loss and its ability to reasonably estimate the amount, there are three possible accounting alternatives for contingencies:

1. **Accrue a loss contingency.** Recognize the event in the current financial statements with adequate footnote disclosure.
2. **Disclose a loss contingency.** Include a footnote disclosure, but do not accrue the contingency.
3. **Do not recognize or disclose a contingency.** Do not accrue the contingency, and do not disclose the contingency in the footnotes.

We will discuss each of these three accounting alternatives in detail.

Accrue a Loss Contingency. A company records (accrues) the contingent loss only if, prior to issuing financial statements, it meets the following two conditions:

1. There is evidence that it is probable that the company has incurred a liability (or an asset has been impaired) as of the date of the financial statements.
2. The company can reasonably estimate the amount of the loss.

Often management can estimate a range for the loss but cannot identify a single most likely outcome within that range. In this case, it accrues the minimum point of the range. Companies can also discount contingent liabilities to their present value when the amount of the liability and the timing of the payments are fixed or reliably determinable.

Disclose a Loss Contingency. A company is generally required to disclose a loss contingency even if it does not meet the two criteria required to accrue the loss.

Disclosure of the loss contingency is required in two cases:

1. If a loss is probable but not reasonably estimable.
2. The loss is reasonably possible even if the amount is not reasonably estimable.

Do Not Recognize or Disclose a Loss Contingency. Firms do not disclose (or record) an estimated loss if the probability of occurrence is remote. However, to provide financial statement users with complete information, a company might make some disclosure of the event. For example, a footnote can include a description of the event and a statement that the company does not expect the loss to have a material effect on the financial statements.

Exhibit 13.4 summarizes the accounting and disclosures requirements for loss contingencies.

EXHIBIT 13.4 Loss Contingency Accounting and Disclosures

Probability of the Occurrence	*Amount of the Loss*	
	Can Be Reasonably Estimated	**Cannot Be Reasonably Estimated**
Probable	Liability accrued with adequate footnote disclosure	Footnote disclosure only
Reasonably possible	Footnote disclosure only	Footnote disclosure only
Remote	No footnote disclosure required	No footnote disclosure required

Accounting for Contingencies: IFRS

The terminology used for contingencies is somewhat different under IFRS than under U.S. GAAP. Under IFRS, a contingency is called a **provision** when a company reports it as an obligation or an asset. The terms *contingent loss* and *contingent gain* refer to uncertainties only that a firm discloses, not recognizes.[17] Despite the difference in terminology, the accounting for loss contingencies under IFRS is similar to U.S. GAAP, except for the following three differences:

- **Definition of probable.** Where U.S. GAAP defines probable as "likely," IFRS defines probable as "more likely than not," which is greater than 50% probable. Thus, some contingencies that would not be reported on the balance sheet under U.S. GAAP will be reported under IFRS.
- **Estimate in a range.** When a company can estimate a range for the loss, but cannot identify a single most-likely outcome within that range, IFRS requires that it accrue the midpoint of the range rather than the minimum as under U.S. GAAP.
- **Discounting.** IFRS reporters take into account the time value of money when evaluating contingent liabilities and discount the liability, when material. Recall that U.S. GAAP reporters can discount contingent liabilities to their present value when the amount of the liability and the timing of the payments are fixed or reliably determinable.

EXHIBIT 13.5 U.S. GAAP versus IFRS: Accounting for Loss Contingencies

	Definition of Probable	Estimate in a Range	Discounting
U.S. GAAP	Likely to occur	Minimum in range	Generally not measured at present value, but discounting is not prohibited.
IFRS	More likely than not, which is 50% or more	Midpoint in range	Measure the liability at its present value, if material.

Exhibit 13.5 summarizes the key significant differences between U.S. GAAP and IFRS in accounting for contingencies.

Under IFRS, unless the possibility of loss is remote, a company discloses the contingency. As with U.S. GAAP, an IFRS reporter's footnote disclosure should include a description of the nature of the contingency and an estimate of the possible loss, an estimated range of the loss, or a statement that it cannot make an estimate of the loss.

4 Demonstrate the accounting for common loss contingencies involving litigation, warranties, and premiums.

Loss Contingencies: Litigation, Warranties, and Premiums

Now that we have a basic understanding of loss contingencies, we will examine some common examples: accounting for litigation, *warranties*, and *premiums*.

Accounting for Litigation

It is common for companies to record or disclose a loss contingency related to litigation. For example, ***DuPont***, the large chemical company, agreed in 2017 to settle for $671 million a lawsuit related to litigation alleging health problems after a chemical used to make Teflon got into drinking water. At the end of 2016, ***DuPont*** had accrued a contingent liability of $117 million related to this litigation.

The rules for litigation-related loss contingencies are the same as for other contingencies. That is, a company accrues the contingent litigation liability only when, prior to issuing financial statements, there is evidence that it is probable that it has incurred a liability as of the date of the financial statements and, in addition, the company can reasonably estimate the amount of the loss.

[17] IASC, *International Accounting Standard 37*, "Provisions, Contingent Liabilities and Contingent Assets."

In order to accrue the liability, the event(s) giving rise to the lawsuit must have occurred before the company's year-end. However, it is not necessary for the company to be aware of the pending litigation at year-end—yet it must be aware of the litigation before issuing the financial statements. Example 13.12 illustrates accounting for a loss contingency.

EXAMPLE 13.12

Accrual of a Loss Contingency

PROBLEM: In June of 2018, a customer at Oh So Good Restaurant slipped on a wet floor and broke a hip. The customer sued the corporation in July 2018. The company's attorneys believe that it is 99% likely that Oh So Good will lose this case and estimate that the loss will range between $500,000 and $800,000. There is no best estimate in this range of possible losses. What is the journal entry to record the contingent liability on the December 31 financial statements?

SOLUTION: Oh So Good will record a contingent liability of the $500,000 minimum point in the range. Thus, the journal entry is as follows:

Account	December 31, 2018	
Litigation Loss	500,000	
Contingent Litigation Liability		500,000

Oh So Good must disclose details regarding the potential loss due to litigation in the footnotes to the financial statements.

It was probable that the loss would occur in Example 13.12. If the loss is not probable, then it cannot be accrued but can be disclosed in the footnotes to the financial statements as Example 13.13 illustrates.

EXAMPLE 13.13

Disclosure or Accrual of a Loss Contingency

PROBLEM: In June 2018, a customer at Oh So Good Restaurant slipped on a wet floor and broke a hip. The customer sued the corporation in July, 2018. The company's attorneys believe that it is 55% likely that Oh So Good will lose this case. Management concludes that the 55% likelihood of incurring the loss is less than probable. The attorneys estimate that the loss will range between $500,000 and $800,000. There is no best estimate in this range of possible losses. How should Oh So Good report the loss contingency in its financial statements?

SOLUTION: Oh So Good will not record a contingent liability because the 55% likelihood of incurring the loss is less than probable. While the 55% is not probable, it is reasonably possible. Therefore, Oh So Good must disclose details regarding the potential loss due to litigation in the footnotes to the financial statements. An example of this footnote might read as follows:

Note 5: Litigation

The company is currently the defendant in a lawsuit for an injury claim by one of our customers. Based on consultation with legal counsel, we believe that it is not likely that we will be found responsible for such a claim. However, the range of possible losses is between $500,000 and $800,000.

Accounting for Litigation: IFRS

IFRS reporters follow the same rules for litigation-related loss contingencies as for other contingencies as summarized in Exhibit 13.5. Example 13.14 applies the IFRS criteria to determine the accounting for the lawsuits from Examples 13.12 and 13.13.

EXAMPLE 13.14

Accrual of a Loss Contingency: IFRS

PROBLEM: A customer at Oh So Good Restaurant slipped on a wet floor and broke a hip in June 2018. The customer sued the corporation in July 2018. The attorneys estimate that the loss will range between $500,000 and $800,000. There is no best estimate in this range of possible losses. What is the journal entry to record the contingent liability under IFRS in the December 31 financial statements if the company's attorneys believe that it is 99% likely that Oh So Good will lose this case? What is the journal entry to record the contingent liability under IFRS in the December 31 financial statements if the company's attorneys believe that it is 55% likely that Oh So Good will lose this case?

SOLUTION: Oh So Good will record a contingent liability under IFRS under both the 99% and 55% likely scenarios as both probabilities are greater than 50%. Under IFRS, it will record the midpoint in the range. The midpoint is $650,000, computed as ($500,000 + $800,000)/2. Thus, the journal entry under both scenarios is as follows:

Account	December 31, 2018	
Litigation Loss	650,000	
Litigation Provision		650,000

Oh So Good must disclose details regarding the potential loss due to litigation in the footnotes to the financial statements under IFRS.

Accounting for Warranty Costs

A **warranty** is a company's promise or guarantee to repair or replace any defective goods for a specified period of time after the date of purchase. There are two types of warranties: *assurance-type warranties* and *service-type warranties*. An **assurance-type warranty** (also referred to as a *base warranty*) does not provide an additional good or service to the customer. The seller is merely providing a guarantee of quality. A **service-type warranty** (also referred to as an *extended warranty*) exists if the customer has the option to purchase the warranty separately or if the warranty provides a service to the customer beyond the period covered by the assurance-type warranty.

At times, it is difficult to determine whether a warranty is an assurance-type or a service-type warranty. Accordingly, the authoritative literature provides three factors that companies should consider when making this determination:

1. If the warranty is required by law, it is more likely to be an assurance-type warranty because such laws exist to protect customers from purchasing defective products.
2. Warranties that cover longer time periods are more likely to be service-type warranties because they are more likely to provide a service beyond a guarantee of quality.
3. If the nature of the promised tasks entails specific tasks to provide assurance that a product complies with certain standards, then it is more likely that the warranty is an assurance-type warranty.

We discuss the accounting treatment for each type of warranty.

Assurance-Type Warranty. An assurance-type warranty is the manufacturer's promise to repair or replace the product free of charge to the customer if product failure occurs within a specified period of time (such as 1 year from the date of purchase). For example, ***Ford Motor Company*** offers warranties on its cars. During 2016, ***Ford*** reported warranty expense of $3,686 million and made warranty claim payments of $3,286 million. At the end of 2016, ***Ford's*** warranty liability was $4,960 million, or about 11.8% of current liabilities in its automotive segment.

The repair costs covered by the seller's warranty include both parts and labor. The time period for coverage under an assurance-type warranty depends on the type of product. For instance, the typical laptop computer warranty is usually for a 1-year period whereas an automobile warranty is usually for 3 years or a mileage limit, whichever comes first.

Ideally, firms account for assurance-type warranties by using an accrual-basis approach. With the accrual-basis approach, the firm matches the cost of providing the warranty with sales revenue. Specifically, the firm expenses the estimated expenditures related to providing the repairs or product replacement in the year of the sale and accrues the estimated liability for repair costs in the year of the sale. Customer claims under warranty (in the year the actual repair takes place) satisfy the liability without charging any additional expenses. So, the firm recognizes the expense in the year of the sale, not in the year the repairs take place. Example 13.15 shows the accrual-basis approach.

EXAMPLE 13.15 Assurance-Type Warranty: Accrual-Basis Approach

PROBLEM: Lark Associates manufactures and distributes component parts for car audio systems. Lark's assurance-type warranty covers all repair costs, including parts and labor, for 2 years after the date of sale. During the current year, Lark sold $4,000,000 of component parts to several manufacturers of car audio systems. Ignore cost of goods sold. The company estimates that warranty costs will be 4% of sales. Lark did not make any repairs in the year of the sale. However, during the following year, the company incurred $56,000 in warranty claims. The repair costs include $32,000 in parts and $24,000 in labor (unpaid). Lark uses the accrual basis to account for its assurance-type warranty costs. What journal entries are necessary to record these transactions?

SOLUTION: Under the accrual method, Lark records an estimated warranty expense of $160,000 ($4,000,000 × 4%) in the year of sale. In this way, Lark matches the warranty expense with revenue in the year of the sale. There is no additional warranty expense recognized when the actual repairs take place. When the products are repaired, Lark credits any cash disbursed, parts used, labor incurred, and such, and debits the warranty liability account. That is, the actual repair represents the performance required to liquidate the warranty obligation.

Lark makes the following entries in the year of the sale and in the period in which it makes the actual repairs.

Account	***Year of the Sale***	
Cash (or Accounts Receivable)	4,000,000	
Sales Revenue		4,000,000
Warranty Expense	160,000	
Contingent Warranty Liability		160,000

Account	***Year of Actual Repair***	
Contingent Warranty Liability	56,000	
Parts Inventory		32,000
Wages Payable		24,000

Companies use the cash-basis approach to account for assurance-type warranties when the amount of the repair cost is not subject to reasonable estimation. Under the cash-basis approach, companies charge warranty costs to expense only in the period when the related repairs take place (that is, not in the year of the sale). In addition, companies do not record any liability for future repairs using a cash basis. This approach is theoretically deficient because it fails to report cost and revenues in the year of the sale. An example of the cash-basis approach is provided in Example 13.16.

EXAMPLE 13.16 Base Warranty: Cash-Basis Approach

PROBLEM: Lark Associates manufactures and distributes component parts for car audio systems. Lark's assurance-type warranty covers all repair costs, including parts and labor, for 2 years after the date of sale. During the current year, Lark sold $4,000,000 of component

Continued

parts to several manufacturers of car audio systems. Ignore cost of goods sold. The company cannot estimate the future warranty costs. Lark did not make any repairs in the year of the sale. However, during the following year, the company incurred $56,000 in actual warranty claims. The repair costs included $32,000 in parts and $24,000 in labor (unpaid). Lark uses the cash-basis to account for its assurance-type warranty costs. What are the necessary journal entries related to these transactions?

SOLUTION: Lark does not make any journal entries for the warranties in the year of sale under the cash-basis approach and instead only records the sale as follows:

Account	Year of Sale	
Cash (or Accounts Receivable)	4,000,000	
Sales Revenue		4,000,000

Lark makes the following entry in the year of the actual repairs:

Account	Year of Actual Repair	
Warranty Expense	56,000	
Parts Inventory		32,000
Wages Payable		24,000

Note that Lark charges the expense in a year subsequent to the sale and fails to match the warranty costs with current period sales revenue.

Service-Type Warranty. A service-type warranty is essentially an insurance policy that covers the repair of the product purchased for a period beyond the assurance-type warranty time limit. The service-type warranty is often sold separately from the product. The time period for service-type warranties varies greatly because they are product and provider specific.

When a company sells the warranty contract, it accounts for the warranty as an advance collection and records a liability for unearned revenue.[18] As time passes and warranty coverage is provided, the company earns the revenue and records it on the income statement. Companies usually amortize the unearned revenue for service-type warranty contracts by using the straight-line method unless some other pattern of revenue recognition is considered more appropriate under the circumstances. For example, ***GameStop Corporation*** sells product replacement plans, a service-type warranty. ***GameStop*** recognizes revenue on the product replacement plans on a straight-line basis over the coverage period. Example 13.17 demonstrates the accounting for a service-type warranty.

EXAMPLE 13.17 Service-Type Warranty

PROBLEM: Good Buys, Inc. offers a 1-year assurance-type warranty on each television sold. The company also sells a 3-year service-type warranty contract for its televisions. On January 1, 2019, Good Buys sold $300,000 of service-type warranties and received cash. The service-type warranty contracts are effective immediately and cover the period from January 1, 2019, through December 31, 2021. Good Buys incurred costs of $78,000 in 2020 related to the warranties; $50,000 of this cost was for parts, and the remaining $28,000 was for labor (unpaid). Provide the necessary journal entries to account for the service-type warranty contract over the January 1, 2019, through December 31, 2021, period.

[18]If the warranty is sold in a package with the product, then the warranty is considered a separate performance obligation and a portion of the transaction price is allocated to the warranty based on the standalone selling prices of the product and the warranty. See Chapter 8 for more discussion of the allocation of a transaction price to separate performance obligations.

SOLUTION: At the time of sale, Good Buys records the sale of service-type warranty contracts as unearned revenue. The journal entry is as follows:

Account	January 1, 2019	
Cash	300,000	
Unearned Warranty Revenue		300,000

Once the warranty period begins (January 1, 2019), Good Buys recognizes one-third of the unearned revenue as revenue earned each year. Revenue recognition is based on the warranty coverage provided. Thus, Good Buys makes the following adjusting journal entry at the end of each year in 2019 through 2021.

Account	December 31, 2019, 2020, and 2021	
Unearned Warranty Revenue	100,000	
Warranty Revenue		100,000

Finally, Good Buys records the actual expenses incurred in 2020. Note that unlike the assurance-type warranty, costs incurred under a service-type warranty contract are charged to warranty expense because an estimated contingent liability is not established in the year of the sale.

Account	During 2020	
Warranty Expense	78,000	
Parts Inventory		50,000
Wages Payable		28,000

Warranty Accounting in Practice. If you had a choice between two alternative products, one with a warranty and another without, which one would you buy? Most people would prefer to purchase the warranty-backed product. As a result, offering assurance-type warranty coverage increases product sales. For example, to increase sales volume, automobile manufacturers extend the period of warranty coverage they offer. An increased warranty coverage period can be as effective a sales incentive as lower interest rates or cash rebates.

As noted earlier, the cash-basis approach is theoretically deficient because it does not address the effect of an assurance-type warranty on increasing sales volume. That is, it mismatches costs and revenue by recording the warranty expense in a period other than the year of the sale. Because the warranty increases sales, the seller should recognize the expense of providing that warranty in the year of sale. The matching principle supports this approach in the same way that a company recognizes the bad debt expense in the year of the sale under the allowance method. The theoretical deficiencies of the cash-basis approach make the accrual-basis approach preferable in practice.

Exhibit 13.6 illustrates a disclosure from ***Deere & Company,*** the manufacturer of agricultural machinery, of the warranty coverage it offers on its products. Notice ***Deere's*** 2016 reconciliation of warranty liability with an ending balance of $1,226 million of which $447 million is related to service-type warranties (referred to as extended warranties in the disclosure).

Accounting for Premiums

Loss contingencies also result when companies offer *premiums* to stimulate sales. **Premiums** are promotional items such as toys, t-shirts, coffee mugs, or other collectables featuring a brand name that a company offers to buyers of specific products. Typically, the buyer will need to mail in box tops or redeem codes online to obtain the premium.[19] Using the accrual basis of accounting, firms account for premiums in the same way as other contingency liabilities. That is, they estimate the

[19]Companies may also offer coupons or cash rebates. Customers can redeem coupons when purchasing the product and thus receive a discount on the selling price. In some cases, a company may use mail-in rebates. Customers must mail in a copy of the sales receipt and a rebate form to receive cash back on the purchase. Cash rebates are cash awards that companies offer to buyers of certain products.

EXHIBIT 13.6 Warranty Disclosure, ***Deere & Company,*** Financial Statements, October 31, 2016

[Excerpt from ***Deere & Company's*** 2016 Annual Report]

NOTE 22: Commitments and Contingencies

The company generally determines its warranty liability by applying historical claims rate experience to the estimated amount of equipment that has been sold and is still under warranty based on dealer inventories and retail sales. The historical claims rate is primarily determined by a review of five-year claims costs and current quality developments.

The premiums for the company's extended warranties are primarily recognized in income in proportion to the costs expected to be incurred over the contract period. The unamortized extended warranty premiums (deferred revenue) included in the following table totaled $447 million and $454 million at October 31, 2016 and 2015, respectively.

A reconciliation of the changes in the warranty liability and unearned premiums in millions of dollars follows:

	Warranty Liability/ Unearned Premiums	
	2016	**2015**
Beginning of year balance	$ 1,261	$1,234
Payments	(783)	(779)
Amortization of premiums received	(202)	(161)
Accruals for warranties	758	810
Premiums received	181	209
Foreign exchange	11	(52)
End of year balance	$1,226	$1,261

***Source*:** Financial Statements from Deere & Company's 2016 Annual Report. https://s2.q4cdn.com/329009547/files/doc_financials/annual_reports/2016/2016_John-Deere-Annual-Report.pdf

costs associated with the incentive plans and record these costs along with the contingent liability related to the future obligation in the accounting period when the sales revenue is recognized. An example is ***Johnson & Johnson's*** reported promotion expense of $1,908 million and an accrued promotions liability in its consumer segment of $358 million at the end of 2016. Accounting for premiums is illustrated in Example 13.18.

EXAMPLE 13.18 Accounting for Premiums

PROBLEM: Full of Sugar, Inc. offered its customers a free toy dog in exchange for 10 box tops from its cereal. During 2018, Full of Sugar purchased 15,000 stuffed dogs at $2 each and sold 1 million boxes of cereal at $4 each. The company recorded cereal inventory at a cost of $3 per box. Full of Sugar did not receive any box tops during 2018, but the company anticipated that 20% of its consumers would redeem box tops. In 2019, consumers mailed 120,000 box tops to Full of Sugar for redemption. The company uses the perpetual inventory system. Provide all necessary journal entries for these transactions.

SOLUTION: In the current year, Full of Sugar needs to record the cereal sales as well as the purchase of the stuffed dog inventory. The company records revenue of $4,000,000 ($4 × 1,000,000 boxes) and cost of goods sold of $3,000,000 ($3 × 1,000,000 boxes).

Account	***Year of the Sale (2018)***	
Cash (or Accounts Receivable)	4,000,000	
Sales Revenue		4,000,000

Account	Year of the Sale (2018)	
Cost of Goods Sold	3,000,000	
Cereal Inventory		3,000,000

It records the purchase of the stuffed dog inventory of $30,000 ($2 × 15,000 units).

Account	Year of the Sale (2018)	
Stuffed Dog Inventory	30,000	
Cash (or Accounts Payable)		30,000

It also accrues the contingent liability related to this premium offer. We compute the premium liability and expense as follows:

Boxes of cereal sold	1,000,000
Expected redemption	20%
Estimate of box tops redeemed	200,000
Number of box tops per dog	÷ 10
Estimated stuffed dogs required	20,000
Cost per stuffed dog	× $2
Contingency to be Accrued	$40,000

Account	Year of the Sale (2018)	
Premium Expense	40,000	
Contingent Premium Liability		40,000

In 2019, Full of Sugar records the redemption of the 120,000 box tops. Because customers were required to send in 10 box tops for each stuffed dog, Full of Sugar will ship and deliver 12,000 stuffed dogs (120,000 box tops / 10 box tops per premium) at a cost of $2 per dog.

Account	2019	
Contingent Premium Liability	24,000	
Stuffed Dog Inventory		24,000

Kellogg Company, the leading cereal maker, discussed the estimates required in accounting for premiums (promotional expenditures) in its 2016 annual report as shown in Exhibit 13.7. ***Kellogg*** also commented on the size of the premiums (0.4% of net sales, or about $52 million) and potential effect of changes in these estimates.

EXHIBIT 13.7 Disclosure of Estimates Required in Accounting for Premiums, ***Kellogg Company,*** Financial Statements, December 31, 2016

Promotional Expenditures

Our promotional activities are conducted either through the retail trade or directly with consumers and include activities such as in-store displays and events, feature price discounts, consumer coupons, contests, and loyalty programs. The costs of these activities are generally recognized at the time the related revenue is recorded, which normally precedes the actual cash expenditure. The recognition of these costs therefore requires management judgment regarding the volume of promotional offers that will be redeemed by either the retail trade or consumer. These estimates are made using various techniques including historical data on performance of similar promotional programs. Differences between estimated expense and actual redemptions are normally insignificant and recognized as a change in management estimate in a subsequent period. On a full-year basis, these subsequent period adjustments represent approximately 0.4% of our company's net sales. However, our company's total promotional expenditures (including amounts classified as a revenue reduction) are significant, so it is likely our results would be materially different if different assumptions or conditions were to prevail.

***Source*:** Financial Statements from Kellogg Company's Annual Report, December 31, 2016. http://investor.kelloggs.com/~/media/Files/K/Kellogg-IR/Annual%20Reports/kellogg-2016-ar-10-k.pdf

JUDGMENTS IN ACCOUNTING
For Contingencies

Proper accounting for contingencies involves a significant amount of judgment skills. In a survey of 175 companies, 46% reported making estimates and using judgment in reporting their contingent liabilities.[20]

U.S. GAAP does not define "probable," lending additional complexity to the issue. Therefore, management, with the help of attorneys, must assess both the probability of a future disbursement and whether that probability qualifies as "probable." Making a quantitative assessment of an event that may or may not occur in the future is more art than science. Contingencies such as warranties are fairly easy to estimate. A future disbursement will be necessary and past product performance serves as a guide. However, a potential loss involving litigation is far less clear. Whereas attorneys may be able to assess the probability of the potential loss, the ultimate outcome of many lawsuits is quite difficult to predict.

Once management has assessed that a future obligation is probable, they must estimate the amount of the potential loss. In many cases, the estimate is very subjective—and the amounts in consideration can be substantial. As an example, consider the 2016 annual report from ***DuPont,*** the large chemical company. ***DuPont's*** disclosure related to litigation contingencies is four pages long. The company reports on litigation and contingent liabilities accrued including the $117 million related to a chemical used at various sites including one in West Virginia. In early 2017, ***DuPont*** settled related lawsuits in West Virginia and Ohio for $671 million. Exhibit 13.8 presents an excerpt from ***DuPont's*** footnote disclosure on its contingencies in its 2016 financial statements.

EXHIBIT 13.8 Contingencies, Commitments, and Guarantees Disclosure, ***Dupont,*** Financial Statements, December 31, 2016

NOTE 15: Commitments and Contingencies

The company is subject to various legal proceedings arising out of the normal course of its business including product liability, intellectual property, commercial, environmental and antitrust lawsuits. It is not possible to predict the outcome of these various proceedings. Although considerable uncertainty exists, management does not anticipate that the ultimate disposition of these matters will have a material adverse effect on the company's results of operations, consolidated financial position or liquidity. However, the ultimate liabilities could be material to results of operations in the period recognized.

PFOA

DuPont used PFOA (collectively, perfluorooctanoic acids and its salts, including the ammonium salt), as a processing aid to manufacture some fluoropolymer resins at various sites around the world including its Washington Works plant in West Virginia. At December 31, 2016, DuPont has an accrual balance of $117 related to the PFOA matters. . . .

Source: Financial statements from American International Group, Inc., Annual Report, 2016. http://www.aig.com/content/dam/aig/america-canada/us/documents/investor-relations/2017/aig-2016-annual-report.pdf, page 265.

[20] AICPA, *IFRS Financial Statements: Best Practices in Presentation and Disclosure—2012* (New York, New York: AICPA, 2012).

CATHY ENGELBERT

CHAIRMAN AND CEO, DELOITTE & TOUCHE LLP»

Catherine Engelbert

Cathy Engelbert is Chairman and Chief Executive Officer of Deloitte & Touche LLP, the U.S. accounting, auditing, and risk advisory subsidiary of Deloitte LLP. She leads the Audit practice. During her 28-year career, including the past 16 years as a partner, she has a distinguished record working with several of Deloitte's largest and most complex global clients. She has served as the lead partner at several large global life sciences companies.*

1 What are some of the most critical issues facing an auditor when assessing the likelihood of a loss contingency?

Some critical issues that are inherent to the assessment of loss contingencies relate to the evaluation of the available audit evidence and include:

1. Evaluating whether management's controls, policies, and procedures are sufficient to identify, evaluate, and account for litigation, claims, and assessments.
2. Understanding and testing the assumptions management uses to evaluate the likelihood and amount of a loss contingency.
3. Evaluating limitations in legal responses, including the potential to limit the scope of the audit.
4. Determining whether management has the ability to assess the likelihood of a loss contingency.

2 What common cost elements are included in the amount of a loss contingency to either accrue or disclose?

As an example, consider litigation, a common form of loss contingency. The primary cost element is the probable payment(s) required to settle the litigation. The legal fees that an entity has incurred or are likely to incur are an additional cost component. Companies should disclose their policy for accruing legal costs—and should identify whether they record legal costs "as incurred" or within the overall accrual for the related loss contingency, as well as where they classified these costs in the statement of operations.

3 What types of estimates determine whether the estimated loss or range of possible losses is reasonable?

The types of estimates that determine a reasonable estimate of loss, or range of loss, are based on the facts and circumstances surrounding the loss contingency. However, the Codification provides a framework of factors to consider, including:

- The nature of the litigation, claim, or assessment
- The progress of the matter
- The opinions or views of legal counsel and other advisers
- The experience of the entity in similar cases
- The experience of other entities
- Any decision of the entity's management as to how the entity intends to respond to the lawsuit, claim, or assessment

4 What specific factors can a client use to justify its decision not to disclose an amount for a loss contingency or range of losses?

For a loss contingency, the Codification requires an entity to disclose an estimate of the possible loss, or range of loss, or to provide a statement that such an estimate cannot be made, which may lead the staff of the U.S. Securities and Exchange Commission (SEC) to request supplemental information. The inability to determine a possible loss, or range of loss, is based on the specific facts and circumstances surrounding the contingency. For example, an entity might cite early-stage litigation as a significant factor for concluding that it cannot determine a loss for disclosure. The SEC considers the case facts and circumstances.

5 Under what circumstances can a client disclose a gain contingency?

Many factors, including judgment, fact, and circumstance assessment, help determine whether an entity discloses a gain contingency. The Codification states that "adequate disclosure shall be made of a contingency that might result in a gain, but care shall be exercised to avoid misleading implications as to the likelihood of realization." (ASC 450-30-50-1) In addition, the resolution of a gain contingency after the balance sheet date, but before issuance of the financial statements, should be considered a nonrecognized subsequent event that may need to be disclosed.

Discussion Questions

1. Cathy Engelbert indicates several issues that auditors face when assessing the probability of a contingent loss and a range of possible losses. Discuss the ways in which U.S. GAAP and IFRS estimates of contingent losses can differ.
2. Cathy Engelbert mentions several circumstances that could result in the disclosure of a gain contingency. Discuss the advantages and disadvantages of disclosing gain contingencies for a financial statement user.

*As used in this document, "Deloitte" means Deloitte & Touche LLP, a subsidiary of Deloitte LLP. Please see www.deloitte.com/us/about for a detailed description of the legal structure of Deloitte LLP and its subsidiaries. Certain services may not be available to attest clients under the rules and regulations of public accounting. Member of Deloitte Touche Tohmatsu Limited.

Required Disclosures for Contingencies

We discuss the required disclosures for contingencies in this section of the chapter.

Loss Contingency Accruals. A company that accrues a loss contingency should disclose the nature of the accrual. In some circumstances, it may be necessary for the entity to disclose the amount accrued to avoid misleading financial statement users. The firm must also include a disclosure indicating that it is at least reasonably possible that the estimate of the probable liability could change in the near term.

Unrecognized Contingencies. A company must disclose a contingency if it is at least reasonably possible that it may have incurred a loss (or an additional loss) that did not meet the conditions for the recognition of a loss contingency (i.e., both probable and subject to reasonable estimation). In other words, contingencies should not be accrued but should be disclosed if they are either (1) probable, but not estimable, or (2) reasonably possible. Exhibit 13.4 summarized the accrual and disclosure scenarios for contingent losses.

The disclosure should include:

1. The nature of the contingency
2. An estimate of the possible loss or range of loss or a statement that such an estimate cannot be made

Companies should disclose any loss contingency that is probable or reasonably possible but is not accrued because they cannot reasonably estimate the amount of loss.

In general, disclosure is not required for a loss contingency involving an unasserted claim if the potential claimant has not made the company aware of the possible claim. However, if it is probable that a claim will be asserted or there is a reasonable possibility that the outcome will be unfavorable, then the contingency should be disclosed.

Gain Contingencies. When the probability of occurrence is nearly certain, companies typically disclose a gain contingency in order to avoid any misleading implications as to the likelihood of realization.

Required Disclosures for Contingencies: IFRS

Under IFRS, companies must also disclose the following for each type of contingency accrued:

- The carrying amount at the beginning and end of the year
- Additional amounts expensed during the year
- Amounts used during the year
- Unused amounts reversed during the year
- Any increase during the year in the discounted amount due to passage of time and the effect of any change in the discount rate

FINANCIAL STATEMENT ANALYSIS

More on Liquidity

We introduced the importance and usefulness of liquidity analysis in Appendix B of Chapter 6. Liquidity is a company's ability to meet current obligations from short-term resources. We now extend the discussion with a focus on refinements of key balance sheet liquidity ratios.

In Chapter 6, we indicated that working capital and the current ratio are two basic measures of liquidity. Working capital is current assets less current liabilities. The higher the working capital, the more current resources the firm has to meet its current obligations as they come due. The current ratio is current assets divided by current liabilities.

Using total current assets in these measures assumes that firms can quickly convert all current assets to pay obligations when due. In practice, this is not always feasible. For example, inventory is a current asset that must be sold before the firm collects cash. Further, firms often sell inventory on account, so the accounts receivable would also have to be collected. Three additional liquidity ratios address this limitation:

1. *Quick or acid test ratio*
2. *Cash ratio*
3. *Defensive interval ratio*

The **quick or acid test ratio** modifies the current ratio by including only the current assets that the firm expects to convert into cash quickly. As a result, the numerator normally includes only cash and cash equivalents, short-term marketable securities, and accounts receivable.

$$\text{Quick or Acid Test Ratio} = \frac{\text{Cash and Cash Equivalent} + \text{Short-term Marketable Securities} + \text{Accounts Receivable}}{\text{Current Liabilities}} \quad (13.1)$$

The quick ratio is always lower than the current ratio. Similar to the current ratio, a quick ratio of more than 1 typically indicates that a company has sufficient resources to meet its current obligations. If the ratio is too high, however, the company might be holding too much cash or short-term securities and forgoing more profitable investment opportunities.

The cash ratio includes only cash and cash equivalents and highly liquid short-term marketable securities in the numerator. It is a conservative measure of liquidity, representing a company's ability to immediately meet current obligations.

$$\text{Cash Ratio} = \frac{\text{Cash and Cash Equivalents} + \text{Short-term Marketable Securities}}{\text{Current Liabilities}} \quad (13.2)$$

A high cash ratio indicates great liquidity. Short-term marketable securities are measured at fair value. If a company maintains relatively constant levels of cash and cash equivalents and current liabilities, changes in the fair value of the marketable securities could cause this ratio to vary. For example, if the stock markets are performing poorly and security values decline, then the cash ratio will be lower.

Finally, the **defensive interval ratio** gauges liquidity based on current resources available to meet current cash expenditures.

$$\text{Defensive Interval Ratio} = \frac{\text{Cash and Cash Equivalents} + \text{Short-term Marketable Securities} + \text{Accounts Receivable}}{\text{Daily Cash Expenditures}} \quad (13.3)$$

$$\text{Daily Cash Expenditures} = \frac{\text{Cost of Goods Sold} + \text{Selling, General, and Administrative Expenses} + \text{Research and Development Expenses} - \text{Depreciation and Amortization Expense}}{\text{Number of Days in Period}} \quad (13.4)$$

The defensive interval ratio measures the number of days a company can operate without receiving additional cash inflows. Daily cash expenditures is the total cash expenditures for a period divided by the number of days in the period. To estimate daily cash expenditures, first sum the income statement expenses: cost of goods sold; selling, general, and administrative expenses: and research and development expenses. From this sum, then subtract any noncash expenses included such as depreciation and amortization. The longer a company can operate given its current resources, the more liquid it is.

When using any ratio—including current liabilities—beware of the existence of contingent liabilities. Depending on the probability, ability to estimate a contingent liability, and expected payment timeframe, a contingent liability may or may not be included in current liabilities. Financial statements users can also consider contingencies that are disclosed but not reported on the balance sheet in analyzing a company's liquidity. A liquidity analysis of ***Johnson & Johnson*** is shown in Example 13.19.

EXAMPLE 13.19 Liquidity Analysis of *Johnson & Johnson*

PROBLEM: Using information from ***Johnson & Johnson's*** 2015 and 2016 financial statements, answer the following questions about the company's liquidity.

a. Compute ***Johnson & Johnson's*** quick ratio for each year.
b. Compute ***Johnson & Johnson's*** cash ratio for each year.
c. Compute ***Johnson & Johnson's*** defensive interval ratio for each year.
d. Comment on changes in ***Johnson & Johnson's*** liquidity from 2015 to 2016 based on the ratios computed.

Johnson & Johnson

Fiscal Year *(in millions)*	2015	2016	Percent Change
Total assets	$133,411	$141,208	5.8%
Cash and cash equivalents	13,732	18,972	38.2
Short-term marketable securities	24,644	22,935	(6.9)
Accounts receivable	10,734	11,699	9.0
Current assets	60,210	65,032	8.0
Current liabilities	27,747	26,287	(5.3)
Cost of goods sold	21,536	21,685	0.7
Selling, general, and administrative expenses	21,203	19,945	(5.9)
Research and development expense	9,046	9,095	0.5
Depreciation and amortization	3,746	3,754	0.2
Working capital	32,463	38,745	19.4
Current ratio	2.17	2.47	13.8

SOLUTION:

(a), (b), and (c). The table on the next page computes ratios for ***Johnson & Johnson*** for each year.

Financial Statement Analysis, continued

Liquidity Measure			2015	2016
Quick Ratio	$= \frac{\text{Cash and Cash Equivalents} + \text{Short-Term Marketable Securities} + \text{Accounts Receivable}}{\text{Current Liabilities}}$	(13.1)	$1.77 = \frac{\$13{,}732 + \$24{,}644 + \$10{,}734}{\$27{,}747}$	$2.04 = \frac{\$18{,}972 + \$22{,}935 + \$11{,}699}{\$26{,}287}$
Cash Ratio	$= \frac{\text{Cash and Cash Equivalents} + \text{Short-Term Marketable Securities}}{\text{Current Liabilities}}$	(13.2)	$1.38 = \frac{\$13{,}732 + \$24{,}644}{\$27{,}747}$	$1.59 = \frac{\$18{,}972 + \$22{,}935}{\$26{,}287}$
Defensive Interval Ratio	$= \frac{\text{Cash and Cash Equivalents} + \text{Short-Term Marketable Securities} + \text{Accounts Receivable}}{\text{Daily Cash Expenditures}}$	(13.3)	$373.15 = \frac{\$13{,}732 + \$24{,}644 + \$10{,}734}{\$131.61}$	$416.55 = \frac{\$18{,}972 + \$22{,}935 + \$11{,}699}{\$128.69}$
Daily Cash Expenditures	$= \frac{\text{Cost of Goods Sold} + \text{Selling, General, and Administrative Expenses} + \text{Research and Development Expenses} - \text{Depreciation and Amortization Expense}}{\text{Number of Days in Period}}$	(13.4)	$\$131.61 = \frac{\$21{,}536 + \$21{,}203 + \$9{,}046 - \$3{,}746}{365}$	$\$128.69 = \frac{\$21{,}685 + \$19{,}945 + \$9{,}095 - \$3{,}754}{365}$

d. All three ratios have increased from 2015 to 2016, indicating increased liquidity. The increases are likely attributable to the 38.2% increase in cash and cash equivalents.

Examining each ratio also indicates strong liquidity overall. The quick ratio is 2.04 in 2016. The cash ratio is higher than 1, which indicates that ***Johnson & Johnson*** has enough cash and cash equivalents plus short-term marketable securities to pay off all current liabilities immediately. However, the likelihood of having to pay off all current liabilities immediately is very low. Finally, ***Johnson & Johnson's*** defensive interval ratio indicates that the company has over 416 days of current resources available to cover daily cash expenditures.

Source: Financial statements from Johnson & Johnson Company's Annual Report, 2015, 2016.

Summary by Learning Objectives

Below we summarize the main points by learning objective. Throughout the chapter, we discuss the accounting and reporting of U.S. GAAP and IFRS side-by-side. The table below also highlights the major similarities and differences between the standards.

Summary by Learning Objectives, continued

1 Define and demonstrate accounting for operating liabilities, including accounts payable, trade notes payable, unearned revenues, gift cards, deposits, sales taxes payable, and compensated absences.

Summary	Similarities and Differences between U.S. GAAP and IFRS
Companies initially record current liabilities at the amounts owed for goods or services. Accounts payable are amounts owed to suppliers. Trade notes payable are formal, written promises to pay a certain sum of money on a specified date in the future. These arise from the purchase of goods, supplies, or services and usually accrue interest. Unearned revenues are payments received in advance of a company providing some good or service. Companies will earn the unearned revenues when they provide the goods or services. A gift card is a certificate allowing the holder to receive goods or services of a specified value from the issuer. The seller debits cash and credits a liability for the unearned revenue when selling the cards. When redeemed, it debits the unearned revenue and credits sales revenue. Breakage is the percentage of the gift card sales not redeemed. Companies should recognize breakage using the proportional method. If the entity is unable to estimate the breakage amount, the remote method is used. A company collects sales taxes on sales and remits them to taxing authorities. Sales taxes are not a seller's expense. Deposits are amounts a buyer pays that will be paid back at the point in time a specific event occurs. For instance, a company can require a deposit to be held against some potential future loss or damage. All or part can be repaid, depending on the need to pay for any loss or damage. Compensated absences are employer-paid time off for vacation, illness, holidays, military service, jury duty, and maternity leave. They can be vested or unvested. Accumulated compensated absences carry over into future periods; non-accumulated ones do not. Four common conditions exist that dictate whether an employer reports an expense and accrues a liability for future paid absences: 1. The obligation for future payment is a result of services already performed by the employee. 2. The benefits to be paid either vest or accumulate. 3. The future payment must be probable. 4. The future payment must be reasonably estimable. The compensation expense is adjusted for changes in estimates when they are made.	Similar under U.S. GAAP and IFRS except for compensated absences. ➤ Should recognize expense for compensated absences based on expected future cost.

2 Discuss and illustrate the accounting for asset retirement obligations and required disclosures.

Summary	Similarities and Differences between U.S. GAAP and IFRS
Asset retirement obligations (AROs) are long-term legal obligations to dismantle and scrap assets or restore property used for business purposes. When acquiring an asset, a company estimates the ARO liability as the discounted fair value it will have to pay to retire the asset. The present value amount increases the reported asset. Over the life of the ARO, the company accrues accretion expense and increases the liability to its fair value when disposing the asset. An entity is required to disclose all of the following information about its asset retirement obligations: a. A general description of the asset retirement obligations and the associated long-lived assets. b. The fair value of assets that are legally restricted for purposes of settling asset retirement obligations. c. A reconciliation of the beginning and ending aggregate carrying amount of asset retirement obligations.	➤ Similar under U.S. GAAP and IFRS except for the following: • An obligation to restore property can be a legal or economic obligation. • The obligation is estimated based on the costs, rather than fair value of dismantling and removing the asset, or restoring the site. • Estimated costs are discounted using a pre-tax interest rate and the risks specific to the liability. • The accretion expense is referred to as interest expense.

Summary by Learning Objectives, continued

3 Describe the accounting for gain and loss contingencies, including recognition and disclosures related to loss contingencies.

<table>
<tr><th>Summary</th><th>Similarities and Differences between U.S. GAAP and IFRS</th></tr>
<tr><td>A contingency has three key elements:
1. It is an existing condition, situation, or set of circumstances.
2. It involves uncertainty as to possible gain (gain contingency) or loss (loss contingency).
3. The uncertainty will ultimately be resolved when one or more future events occur or fail to occur.
Gain contingencies are not recognized in the financial statements and are disclosed only in the footnotes when there is high certainty of realization in the future.
Loss contingency accounting centers on two issues:
1. The probability that the company will ultimately incur a loss.
2. Whether the company can reasonably estimate the amount of the potential loss.
To assess whether the company will ultimately incur a loss, it determines whether the loss is probable, reasonably possible, or remote:
• Probable: likely to occur.
• Remote: the probability of occurrence is only slight.
• Reasonably possible: the probability of occurrence is less than likely but more than remote.
When a loss contingency is both probable and can be reasonable estimated, companies accrue it as a liability.
When a loss contingency is either probable or can be reasonably estimated, companies disclose it in a footnote.
Firms disclose the nature of a loss contingency accrual and in some circumstances the amount accrued to avoid misleading financial statement users.
The firm must disclose that it is at least reasonably possible that the entity's estimate of its probable liability could change in the near term.
Firms must disclose unrecognized contingencies if there is at least a reasonable possibility that it incurred a loss (or an additional loss) and did not make an accrual for a loss contingency because the following conditions for recognition were not met:
a. No evidence that it is probable that the company incurred a liability.
b. An estimate of the possible loss or range of loss or a statement that such an estimate cannot be made.
Companies make adequate disclosure of a contingency that might result in a gain if there is a high certainty of realization.</td><td>➤ Similar under U.S. GAAP and IFRS except for areas noted below.
IFRS terminology is somewhat different. Under IFRS, a contingency is called a provision when a company reports it as an obligation or an asset. The terms contingent loss and contingent gain refer only to uncertainties that a firm discloses, not recognizes.
Under U.S. GAAP, probable is defined as "likely." Under IFRS, probable is defined as "more likely than not," which is greater than 50% probable.
In the case of a range of estimates under U.S. GAAP, a company accrues the minimum point of the range. Under IFRS, it accrues the midpoint of the range.
Under U.S. GAAP, companies can discount contingent liabilities when the amount of the liability and the timing of the payments are fixed or reliably determinable. Under IFRS, contingent liabilities should take into account the time value of money and be discounted, when material.
Under IFRS companies additionally disclose for each accrued contingency:
• The carrying amount at the beginning and end of the year
• Additional provisions
• Amounts used
• Unused amounts reversed
• The increase during the year in the discounted amount due to the passage of time and the effect of any change in the discount rate</td></tr>
</table>

Summary by Learning Objectives, continued

❹ Demonstrate the accounting for common loss contingencies involving litigation, warranties, and premiums.	
Summary	**Similarities and Differences between U.S. GAAP and IFRS**
For pending litigation, follow the guidance for a loss contingency discussed in Learning Objective 3. A warranty is a promise or guarantee to repair or replace any defective goods for a specified period of time. Warranties can be of two types: an assurance-type warranty or a service-type warranty. The assurance-type warranty comes with the product and provides the promise to repair or replace the product without additional cost. When the liability is probable and companies can estimate expenses under the warranty, companies use the accrual-basis approach, which reports warranty expense and accrues warranty liability in the year of the sale. If the liability is not probable or accountants cannot estimate expenses, companies use the cash-basis approach, which expenses warranty costs when incurred. A service-type warranty is sold separately from the sale of the product. When selling a service-type warranty contract, the firm records a liability for unearned revenue. As time passes, the firm earns the unearned revenue. Companies estimate the cost of premiums—such as cash rebates, goods, or coupons—and report a liability.	Similar under U.S. GAAP and IFRS except for areas discussed in Learning Objective 3.

MyLab Accounting

Go to **http://www.pearson.com/mylab/accounting** for the following Questions, Multiple-Choice Questions, Brief Exercises, Exercises, and Problems. They are available with immediate grading, explanations of correct and incorrect answers, and interactive media that acts as your own online tutor.

13 Operating Liabilities and Contingencies

Questions

❶ **Q13-1.** When is a liability classified as current?

❶ **Q13-2.** How are unearned revenues classified?

❶ **Q13-3.** Are advance collections from customers considered liabilities? Explain.

❶ **Q13-4.** Do sellers recognize sales taxes as expenses on their income statement? Explain.

❶ **Q13-5.** Why are all compensated absences accrued as long as the obligation for future payment is due to services already performed by the employee and the benefits to be paid vest?

❶ **Q13-6.** Are there any significant differences in accounting for compensated absences if the rights to the future benefits are vested versus accumulated? Explain.

❶ **Q13-7.** How do companies accrue compensated absences?

❸ **Q13-8.** What is a gain contingency? Is it accrued and recorded in the financial statements? Explain.

❸ **Q13-9.** Do firms always accrue and record loss contingencies in the financial statements? Explain.

❸ **Q13-10.** Under IFRS, do firms always accrue and record loss contingencies in the financial statements? Explain.

❸ **Q13-11.** If the probability of a loss contingency is remote, is it necessary for a firm to accrue or disclose it? Explain.

❸ **Q13-12.** What must firms use when estimating the amount of a loss contingency in a range of estimates to report in the financial statements?

3 **Q13-13.** Under IFRS, what must firms use when estimating the amount of a loss contingency in a range of estimates to report in the financial statements?

4 **Q13-14.** Are all warranty costs accounted for under the accrual basis of accounting? Explain.

2 **Q13-15.** When does a company record an asset retirement obligation?

A **Q13-16.** Does an employer recognize payroll taxes as expenses on its income statement? Explain.

Multiple-Choice Questions

3 4 **MC13-1.** In June, Year 1, Westchase Corporation became involved in product litigation. As a result of this litigation, it is probable that Westchase will have to pay $900,000. In August, a competitor commenced a suit against Westchase alleging violation of antitrust laws seeking damages of $100,000,000. Westchase denies the allegations, and the likelihood that it will pay any damages is remote. In September, Harris County brought action against Westchase for $9,000,000 for polluting. It is reasonably possible that Harris County will be successful, but the amount of damages Westchase will have to pay is not reasonably determinable. Westchase's tax rate is 40%. What amount, if any, should be accrued by a charge to income in Year 1?

a. $109,900,000 b. $109,000,000 c. $9,900,000 d. $900,000

3 4 **MC13-2.** Far Out Producers is involved in two product liability lawsuits and a third lawsuit that the company brought against a competitor for patent infringement. At December 31, Year 1, the company's attorneys informed management of the following:

- It is probable that Far Out will lose one of the product liability lawsuits, although the actual settlement could be as low as $800,000 and as high as $2,000,000.
- It is possible that the company could lose $1,000,000 in the second product liability lawsuit.
- It is probable that Far Out will win $500,000 in the patent infringement case.

What should Far Out report on its December 31, Year 1, balance sheet for these contingencies?

a. $300,000 contingent liability b. $800,000 contingent liability
c. $1,800,000 contingent liability d. $3,000,000 contingent liability

4 **MC13-3.** Specialty Appliances and More, Inc. (SAM) has a 3-year warranty on its solar refrigerators for defects. Warranty costs are estimated at 2% of sales in Year 1 (the year of the sale) and 5% of sales in each of the following 2 years. The warranty expires at the end of the third year. Annual sales and actual warranty repair costs were as follows:

	Sales	Actual Warranty Cost
Year 1	$ 275,000	$ 27,500
Year 2	350,000	17,500
Year 3	425,000	30,000
	$1,050,000	$75,000

What total amount should SAM record as warranty expense in the first 3 years?

a. $51,000 b. $75,000 c. $93,000 d. $126,000

A **MC13-4.** Medical Services Inc. allows employees at the end of the year to carry forward up to 40 hours of paid time off at their current salary. James is a full-time employee who has unused vacation time of 80 hours, and Marcia, also a full-time employee, has unused vacation time of 48 hours. How much should Medical Services Inc. record as a liability for the unpaid vacation time at the end of the year?

Employee	Hourly Rate
James	$14.00
Marcia	16.00

a. $1,200 b. $1,328 c. $1,760 d. $1,888

Brief Exercises

1 **BE13-1.** **Trade Notes Payables.** On February 1, Seville Sales, Inc. purchased inventory costing $450,000 using a 6-month trade note payable. The note carries an annual interest rate of 9%. Seville has a December 31 year-end. Prepare the journal entries required. The company uses the perpetual inventory system. What is interest expense during the current year?

1 **BE13-2.** **Unearned Revenues.** On June 1 of the current year, Tedesco Publishers collected $432,000 for 4-year online subscriptions to its *Houston Style Magazine*. Tedesco has a December 31 year-end. Prepare the journal entries required on the date Tedesco collects the subscriptions and at year-end. What revenue is earned in the current year? What is the balance in the unearned revenue account at December 31 of the current year?

1 **BE13-3.** **Unearned Revenues.** GoSnow Inc. provides snow removal services for its customers in the months of November, December, January, February, and March. On November 1, GoSnow's customers prepay a $315 fee for the winter; the company currently has 116 customers. GoSnow recognizes revenue evenly over the months it provides the snow removal services. If GoSnow's year-end is December 31, what is the balance in unearned revenues at December 31? Prepare the journal entries required on the date GoSnow collects the fees and at year-end.

1 **BE13-4.** **Gift Cards.** Coral Boutique sold $1,400 of gift cards and received cash on May 25. On June 29, customers redeemed $800 of the gift cards, purchasing merchandise that cost Coral $425. The store uses a perpetual inventory system. Prepare the journal entries to record the activities related to the gift cards.

1 **BE13-5.** **Accounting for Deposits.** Evergreen Waste Company provides weekly trash collection services to small companies. Evergreen collected a $1,000 deposit from each of 12 new customers for large trash dumpsters. The cost of each dumpster is $700. The company uses a perpetual inventory system. What journal entries are required when 10 dumpsters are returned to Evergreen? What journal entries are required if two of the dumpsters are damaged and the customer forfeits the deposit?

1 **BE13-6.** **Sales Taxes Payable.** Roth Tile and Carpets, Incorporated operates in Blue Bay, Wisconsin, where sales taxes are 6% of sales. Roth's sales this month amounted to $2,560,500. The company uses a periodic inventory system. Prepare the journal entry to record sales for the current month.

1 **BE13-7.** **Sales Taxes Payable.** Kloth Fabric Store operates in Philadelphia, Pennsylvania, where sales taxes are 7% of sales. Kloth collected $27,860 on sales made this month, including the sales price and sales taxes. The company uses a periodic inventory system. Prepare the journal entry to record sales for the current month. What is the amount of sales taxes Kloth will remit to taxing authorities?

1 **BE13-8.** **Compensated Absences, Journal Entries.** Magro Machinery allows its employees 10 paid sick days per year. If the employees do not take the sick days in any given year, the days accumulate. If an employee either leaves or is terminated, he or she will be paid in cash for the sick days. During the current year, 20 employees took all 10 sick days, and 5 employees did not use any of their days. The current wage rate for all of Magro's employees is $200 per day. Prepare the journal entry to record compensated absences for the current year.

1 **BE13-9.** **Compensated Absences, Journal Entries.** Colorado Closets, Inc. employs 50 employees earning an average of $1,000 per week. The company awards each employee two weeks of vacation per year. Vacation days neither accumulate nor vest if not taken in the year earned. During the current year, 45 of Colorado's employees took their 2 full weeks while the other 5 employees were unable to take any vacation this year. Prepare the journal entry necessary to record Colorado's vacation pay.

1 **BE13-10.** **Compensated Absences, Journal Entries.** The employees of Wilson Lumber are allowed to take 5 sick days per year. The sick days vest and are paid at the current rate of $150 per day. Wilson employs 70 employees. Employees took 80% of the sick days in the current year and carried over the remainder of the days to take next year. Prepare the journal entry necessary in the next year to record the payment of the sick days carried over assuming that the wage rate increases to $165 per day.

2 **BE13-11.** **Asset Retirement Obligation at Acquisition.** On January 1, Pollison Energy Group, Inc. acquired an oil processing plant at a total cost of $13,560,000 and paid cash. The estimated cost to dismantle the plant and restore the property at the end of the plant's 10-year life is $2,100,000. Pollison's cost of capital is 5%. Pollison depreciates the asset over its useful life by using the straight-line method with no salvage value. Prepare the journal entries required to record the acquisition of the plant asset.

2 **BE13-12.** **Asset Retirement Obligation Subsequent to Acquisition.** Using the information provided in BE13-11, prepare the journal entries to record the first year's depreciation and accretion accrual.

BE13-13. Asset Retirement Obligation, Disposal. Buckner Chemical Products reported the following information on its latest balance sheet dated December 31 of the current year. The relevant t-accounts follow.

Plant Asset

	Debit	Credit
Cost	12,000	
ARO	3,000	
	15,000	

Accumulated Depreciation – Plant Asset

Debit	Credit
	4,500
	4,500

Asset Retirement Obligation

Debit	Credit	
	3,000	Beginning
	900	Accretion
	3,900	

On January 1 of the following year, Buckner sold the plant asset for $9,000 and incurred $6,200 in disposal costs. Prepare the journal entries required to record the disposal of the asset and the settlement of the asset retirement obligation.

[3] [4] **BE13-14. Accrual of a Loss Contingency.** In August 2018, a customer at TU Bank slipped on a wet floor and broke an arm. The customer sued the bank in September 2018. As of TU Bank's December 31 year-end, the company's attorneys believe that it is 80% likely that TU will lose this case. The attorneys estimate that the loss will range between $200,000 and $350,000. What is the journal entry?

[3] [4] **BE13-15. Accrual of a Loss Contingency, IFRS.** Use the information from BE13-14 and now assume that TU Bank is an IFRS reporter. What is the journal entry under IFRS?

[4] **BE13-16. Warranty Liability, Assurance-Type Warranty, Cash Basis.** Landau Manufacturing Company manufactures and distributes small power tools. Landau offers an assurance-type warranty that covers all repair costs, including parts and labor, for 2 years after the date of sale. During the current year, the company sold $8,000,000 in power tools to major retail stores. The company estimates that warranty costs will be 6% of sales. Landau made no repairs in the year of the sale. However, during the following year, the company incurred $182,000 in actual warranty claims. The repair costs included $132,000 in parts and $50,000 in labor (unpaid). Prepare the journal entries necessary to record the base warranty in the year of the sale and the actual repairs incurred during the following year assuming that Landau uses the cash basis.

[4] **BE13-17. Warranty Liability, Assurance-Type Warranty, Accrual-Basis Approach.** Using the information provided in BE13-16, prepare the journal entries necessary to record the assurance-type warranty in the year of the sale and the actual repairs incurred during the following year assuming that Landau uses the accrual basis.

[4] **BE13-18. Warranty Liability, Assurance-Type Warranty, Service-Type Warranty.** Michael and Sons, Ltd. sells lawn and garden products for home use. The company offers an assurance-type warranty that covers all repair costs, including parts and labor, for 1 year after the date of sale of lawn tractors. Michael also sells a service-type warranty contract that covers all parts and labor for 5 years after the date of sale of lawn tractors. In the year in which it sold the products, the company sold 8,000 service-type warranties at a price of $175 per contract and received cash. Michael and Sons sold the contracts at the end of the year and did not recognize warranty revenue in the year of the sale. Michael and Sons did not make any actual repairs in the year of the sale during the base warranty period. During the following year, the company incurred $98,100 in actual warranty claims that are now covered only under the service-type warranty contract. The repair costs included $61,000 in parts and $37,100 in labor (unpaid). Prepare the journal entries required to record the effects of offering the service-type warranty contract in the year of the sale and during the following year.

[A] **BE13-19. Payroll Taxes Payable.** Romero Brothers Contracting reports a $1,200,000 biweekly payroll. Romero and its employees must pay Social Security (federal insurance contribution act (or FICA)) taxes, and none of the employees has exceeded the wage base for FICA taxes or the minimum amount that triggers the additional Medicare tax. Income taxes withheld average 30% for federal and 8% for state and local taxes. The state unemployment tax rate is 5.4%, but Romero gets an experience credit of 4%. The state unemployment wage base is $7,000 per employee. Only $100,000 of the total payroll applies to wages that fall under this cap. Prepare the journal entries required to record the biweekly salary accrual and payment. Also record the journal entry for payroll tax expense.

A **BE13-20.** **Payroll Taxes Payable.** Paragon Stores Company's weekly payroll amounts to $400,000. Paragon is responsible for paying its share of Social Security tax. The company is also responsible for federal and state unemployment taxes. The state unemployment tax rate is 4.7%, but Paragon receives a 3.7% credit. The state unemployment wage base is $10,000. No employee has earned over $7,000 this year. Prepare the employer's entry to record the payroll tax expense incurred. Assume the employees do not exceed the wage base for FICA taxes or meet the minimum amount that triggers the additional Medicare tax.

Exercises

1 **E13-1.** **Trade Notes Payable.** On November 1, Barcelona Sales, Inc. purchased inventory costing $589,000 using a 5-month trade note payable. The note carries an annual interest rate of 10%. Barcelona has a December 31 year-end. The company uses a perpetual inventory system.

Required »

a. What is interest expense during the current year? What is the interest expense the following year?
b. Prepare all required journal entries.

1 **E13-2.** **Unearned Revenues.** On May 1 of the current year, Interstate Home and Casualty, Inc. collected $720,000 for 3-year insurance policies. Coverage begins on May 1. Interstate has a December 31 year-end.

Required »

a. Prepare the journal entries required on the date that Interstate collects the insurance premiums.
b. Prepare the year-end adjusting entry for the current year.
c. Prepare the journal entries required for the next 3 years.

1 **E13-3.** **Gift Cards.** Diamond Depot sold $57,000 of gift cards during the current year and received cash. Diamond uses the proportional method for accounting for gift card breakage. Based on historical experience, it estimates a breakage percentage of 12% of its gift card sales. During the year, customers redeemed $46,300 of gift cards, purchasing inventory costing $28,000. The company uses a perpetual inventory system.

Required »

a. Prepare the journal entries required to record the gift card activity.
b. What is the end-of-year liability for gift cards if the liability for them was $15,500 at the beginning of the year?

1 **E13-4.** **Sales Taxes Payable.** Eaton Technology operates retail stores throughout the tristate area. The company's sales are subject to a 7% sales tax payable to the state and county government. At the end of the current year, Eaton reported accounts receivable of $5,617,500 for credit sales, which includes the sales value of the merchandise sold plus the sales taxes.

Required »

a. Prepare the journal entry required to record the sales for the current year. The company uses a periodic inventory system.
b. Prepare the journal entry to record the sales taxes Eaton remitted to the state and county taxing jurisdictions.

1 **E13-5.** **Compensated Absences, Journal Entries.** Bristol Stamping Company provides its 100 employees with a comprehensive benefits package. As part of this package, Bristol allows each of its 100 employees 12 paid sick days per year. The average wage rate for the current year is $140 per day. If employees do not take the sick days in the current year, the days carry over indefinitely and will be paid to the employee upon termination. Employees took 60% of the days during the current year and carried over the remaining sick days to the next year.

Required »

a. Prepare the journal entry required to record the sick days for the current year.
b. Prepare the journal entry required to record the payment of the sick days in the following year assuming that employees take all remaining days at that time.
c. Independent of your answers to parts (a) and (b), prepare the journal entry to record the sick days taken in the next year assuming that the wage rate increased to $147 per day. Employees take all remaining days at that time.

2 **E13-6. Asset Retirement Obligation.** On January 1, Evergreen Utilities Company acquired a power plant at a total cost of $23,500,000 and paid cash. The estimated cost to dismantle the plant and restore the property at the end of the plant's 20-year life is $4,850,000. Evergreen's cost of capital is 8%. Evergreen will depreciate the asset over its useful life using the straight-line method. The asset has no residual value.

Required »

a. Prepare the journal entries required to record the acquisition of the plant asset.
b. Prepare the journal entry to record the first year's depreciation and accretion accrual.
c. Prepare the journal entries required to record the disposal of the asset and the settlement of the asset retirement obligation at the end of the fifth year after acquisition. Evergreen sold the asset for $17,000,000, and the costs of dismantling the plant and restoring the property totaled $5,400,000.

2 **E13-7. Asset Retirement Obligation.** On January 1, Tritrua Auto Company built a new manufacturing facility at a total cost of $15,000,000 and paid cash. To dismantle the plant and restore the property at the end of the plant's 25-year life, the estimated cost is $850,000. Tritrua will depreciate the asset over its useful life using the straight-line method. The asset has no residual value. Tritrua's cost of capital is 6%.

Required »

a. Prepare the journal entries required to record the acquisition of the plant asset.
b. Prepare the journal entry to record the first year's depreciation expense and accretion expense.
c. Prepare the journal entries required to record the disposal of the asset and the settlement of the asset retirement obligation at the end of the seventh year after acquisition. Tritrua sold the asset for $11,000,000, and the costs of dismantling the plant and restoring the property totaled $310,000.

3 4 **E13-8. Accrual of a Loss Contingency.** In January 2018, a customer filed a lawsuit against Fireen's Boutique. The customer fell on an icy patch in the store's parking lot and broke an ankle in December. Fireen's fiscal year-end is January 31. The company's attorneys believe that it is reasonably possible that Fireen's will lose this case, with a 60% probability. The attorneys estimate that the loss will range between $400,000 and $500,000, which is material to Fireen's.

Required »

a. Explain how the lawsuit should be reported.
b. Prepare any journal entries required.

3 4 **E13-9. Accrual of a Loss Contingency, IFRS.** Using the same information from E13-8, assume that Fireen's reports under IFRS.

Required »

a. Explain how the lawsuit should be reported under IFRS.
b. Prepare any journal entries required.

4 **E13-10. Warranty Liability, Assurance-Type Warranty, Accrual- and Cash-Basis Approach.** Cole Electronics, Inc. manufactures and distributes LCD televisions. Every television manufactured by Cole carries an assurance-type warranty covering all parts and labor to protect against defects for a 2-year period. During the current year, Cole's sales amounted to $10,000,000. Cole estimates that the total costs of providing the assurance-type warranty will be 4% of sales. Actual repair costs for the first year after the sale were $218,000 with $150,000 for parts and $68,000 for labor (paid). During the second year, the company incurred $230,000 in total repairs with $148,000 for parts and $82,000 for labor (paid).

Required »

a. Prepare the journal entries for each year under the warranty assuming that Cole uses the cash basis.
b. Independent of your answer to part (a), prepare the journal entries required to record the events related to the warranty using the accrual basis.

4 **E13-11. Warranty Liability, Service-Type Warranty.** Genius Computers sells computers and offers an assurance-type warranty that covers all repair costs, including parts and labor, for 1 year after the date of purchase. Genius also sells a service-type warranty contract that covers all parts and labor for 3 years after the base warranty expires. The company estimates that the service-type warranty will be used 40% in the first year, 35% in the second, and 25% in the third year of the contract. In the year in which the computers were sold, the company also sold 10,000 service-type warranties at a price of $200 per contract and received cash. Genius sold the contracts at the end of the year and did not recognize any warranty revenue in the year of the sale. The firm did not make any actual repairs in the year of the sale covered by the assurance-type warranty. During the following year, the company incurred $45,000 in actual warranty claims that are now covered

only under the service-type warranty contract. The repair costs included $31,000 in parts and $14,000 in labor (unpaid).

Prepare the journal entries required to record the effects of offering the service-type warranty contract in the year of the sale and during the following year.

4 **E13-12. Accounting for Premiums.** Supergreen Grocers, Inc. offered its customers a free baking pan in exchange for 100 green stickers. Customers earn 1 green sticker for each $10 of groceries purchased at Supergreen during 2018. During 2018, Supergreen purchased with cash 1,100 baking pans at $8 each and sold $3.2 million of groceries. Supergreen expects about 38% of its customers to redeem the stickers. In 2019, consumers redeemed 105,000 stickers. Provide all necessary journal entries related to the baking pan offer.

A **E13-13. Payroll Taxes Payable.** Neumann Consulting Group reports a $1,200,000 biweekly payroll. Payroll income taxes average 20% for federal and 4% for state and local taxes. The company is also responsible for federal and state unemployment taxes. The federal unemployment tax rate is 1.6%. The state unemployment tax rate is 4.4% on a wage base of $7,000, but Neumann gets a 3.2% credit. Neumann has not paid any employee more than $7,000. None of the employees has exceeded the income base for FICA tax, nor have any employees earned enough to trigger the additional Medicare tax.

Required»

a. Prepare the journal to record the biweekly payroll.
b. Prepare the journal entry to pay the liability for accrued salaries.
c. Prepare the journal entry necessary to record Neumann's payroll tax expense for the biweekly payroll.

A **E13-14. Payroll Taxes Payable, Pay Exceeds Wage Base.** Elyctric Company reports a $2,850,000 monthly payroll. Payroll income taxes average 20% for federal and 4% for state and local taxes. The company is also responsible for federal and state unemployment taxes. The federal unemployment tax rate is 1.6%. The state unemployment tax rate is 4.4% on a wage base of $7,000, but Elyctric gets a 3.2% credit. Payroll for employees who have exceeded the $7,000 wage base was $2,140,000. Payroll for employees who have exceeded the income base for federal insurance contribution act (FICA) tax is $247,000. Payroll for employees who have exceeded the minimum amount to be subject to the additional Medicare taxes is $180,000.

Required »

a. Prepare the journal to record the monthly payroll.
b. Prepare the journal entry to pay the liability for accrued salaries.
c. Prepare the journal entry necessary to record Elyctric payroll tax expense for the monthly payroll.

Problems

1 **P13-1. Current Operating Liabilities.** James Stores, Inc. completed the following transactions during the current year, the company's first year of operations. James Stores has a December 31 year-end.

1. January 16: Purchased $546,000 of merchandise inventory from various suppliers on account (no discount for early payment offered).
2. February 1: Sold merchandise that cost $100,000 for $120,500 on account. The sales tax rate is 8%.
3. February 10: Paid half of the January 16 purchases.
4. February 16: Paid the remaining balance of accounts payable from the January 16 purchase.
5. March 1: Paid the sales taxes recorded on February 1.
6. June 1: Sold merchandise that cost $212,000 for $300,000 on account. The sales tax rate is 8%.

Required »

a. Prepare the journal entries required to record the transactions in the preceding list. Assume that a perpetual inventory system is used.
b. Prepare a partial income statement for the current fiscal year.

1 **P13-2. Current Operating Liabilities.** Sukulo Stores, Inc. completed the following transactions during the current year, the company's first year of operations. Sukulo Stores has a December 31 year-end.

1. September 2: Purchased $65,000 of merchandise inventory from Texrex Company using a trade note payable. The note is due in 3 months and carries an 8% annual interest rate.
2. September 21: Purchased $391,000 of inventory from various suppliers on account.
3. October 12: Sold merchandise that cost $80,000 for $128,000 on account.
4. October 16: Sold $4,000 of gift cards and received cash.

5. November 16: Paid for all the items purchased on September 21.
6. December 2: Paid off the trade note payable plus interest.
7. December 15: Redeemed gift cards totaling $3,500 from customers who purchased merchandise costing $2,188.
8. December 31: Used the proportional method to account for breakage. Its estimated breakage rate is 8%.

Required »

a. Prepare the journal entries required to record the transactions in the preceding list. Assume that a perpetual inventory system is used.
b. Prepare a partial income statement for the current fiscal year.

2 **P13-3. Asset Retirement Obligation.** On January 1 of the current year, Wright Oil invested $7,500,000 to construct an offshore oil platform and paid cash. As part of its offshore drilling agreement, Wright is responsible for dismantling and removing the platform at the end of its 15-year useful life. Wright depreciates the platform by using the straight-line method with no residual value expected at the end of its useful life. The asset did not have a reasonably determinable quoted market price, and market comparables are not available. As a result, Wright decided to use a probability-based estimate of the cost of dismantling and removing the platform to estimate the fair value of the retirement obligation. The probability-based estimate employs the expected cash flows needed to comply with the offshore drilling agreement based on costs of dismantling and removal. The estimated values are as follows:

Estimated Future Cash Flows	Probability of Occurrence
$ 675,000	62%
890,000	30
1,021,100	8

The company's estimated cost of capital is 6%.

Required »

a. Prepare the journal entries required to record the investment in the offshore oil platform.
b. Prepare the journal entry to record the first year's depreciation and accretion accrual.
c. Prepare the journal entries required to record the disposal of the asset and the settlement of the asset retirement obligation at the end of the eighth year after acquisition. Wright sold the asset for $980,000, and the costs of dismantling and removing the offshore oil platform totaled $1,200,000.

2 **P13-4. Asset Retirement Obligation.** On January 1 of the current year, ListenUp Telecommunication invested idle cash of $12,500,000 in transmission towers and $9,000,000 in poles and lines to improve service to its customers. ListenUp is responsible for dismantling and removing the towers, poles, and lines at the end of their useful lives under each city's and town's removal and restoration requirements. The towers have a 10-year useful life, and the poles and lines have a 15-year useful life. ListenUp uses the straight-line method for depreciation with no residual value expected at the end of the useful lives of the assets. ListenUp estimates the cost to dismantle and restore property related to the towers at $950,000.

Even though the poles and line method of transmission has been used for many years, ListenUp is installing these in numerous cities and towns. Recently, cities and towns have been increasing their standards for removal and restoration. Therefore, the costs to remove and restore the poles and lines do not have a reasonably determinable quoted market price, and market comparables are not available. As a result, ListenUp decided to use a probability-based estimate. The probability-based estimate employs the expected cash flows needed for the costs of dismantling and removal. The estimated values are as follows:

Estimated Future Cash Flows	Probability of Occurrence
$ 50,500	5%
350,000	35
790,000	40
985,000	20

The company's estimated cost of capital is 5%.

Required »

a. Prepare the journal entries required to record the acquisition of each asset.
b. Prepare the journal entry to record the first and second year's depreciation and accretion accrual for each asset.
c. What is the carrying value of each asset at the end of the second year? What is the carrying value of the ARO at the end of the second year?

3 4 **P13-5. Contingency Problem.** Exwella Pharmaceuticals, Inc. is involved in various lawsuits regarding product liability, commercial liability, and other matters that arise from time to time in the ordinary course of business. The lawsuits pending at the beginning of the year and those filed in the current years follow.

Pending Lawsuits at the Beginning of the Year

1. Product liability lawsuit related to Nowaya, a pharmaceutical drug, in which claimants seek substantial damages. Exwella's attorneys assess the likelihood of losing the lawsuit as reasonably possible at 60%. At the beginning of the year, the estimated loss ranged from $500,000 to $1,500,000. At the end of the year, the attorney's assessment of the loss increased to a range between $750,000 and $2,000,000.
2. A personal injury lawsuit in which a claimant seeks substantial damages. Exwella's attorneys assess the likelihood of losing the lawsuit as probable at 95%. At the beginning of the year, Exwella reported a contingent liability of $750,000 for the lawsuit. At the end of the year, the attorney's assessment of the loss increased to a range between $900,000 and $3,000,000.

New Pending Lawsuits

3. A new product liability lawsuit was filed related to the drug Dontacit. Exwella's attorneys assess the likelihood of losing the lawsuit as remote at 10%. The attorney's assessment of the loss increased to a range between $10,000,000 and $15,000,000.
4. A new product liability lawsuit was filed related to the drug Noapproval. Exwella's attorneys assess the likelihood of losing the lawsuit as probable. The attorney's assessment of the loss increased to a range between $2,000,000 and $4,000,000.

Required »

a. Explain how each of the lawsuits is accounted for under U.S. GAAP.
b. Prepare any journal entries required at the end of the year.

3 4 **P13-6. Contingency Problem, U.S. GAAP, IFRS.** Using the information from P13-5, assume that Exwella Pharmaceuticals, Inc., reports under IFRS.

Required »

a. Explain how each lawsuit is accounted for under IFRS. Prepare any journal entries required. Under IFRS, Exwella has a contingent liability of $1,000,000 at the beginning of the year related to Nowaya in P13-5.
b. Compare the litigation loss and contingency liability at the end of the year under U.S. GAAP from P13-5 and IFRS.

4 **P13-7. Warranty Liability, Assurance-Type and Service-Type Warranties.** Packard Products manufactures wireless routers for home use. The company reported total sales on account of $11,200,000 during the current year. The cost of the merchandise sold was $5,000,000. Packard offers an assurance-type warranty that covers all repair costs, including parts and labor, for 1 year after the date of sale. The company estimates that warranty costs will amount to 4% of total sales. In the year in which it sold the products, the company also sold 45,000 service-type warranties at a price of $85 per contract and received cash. Packard sold the contracts at the end of the year and did not recognize any warranty revenue in the year of the sale. The service-type warranty covers all parts and labor for 3 years after the expiration of the assurance-type warranty. The company estimates that the service-type warranty will be used 70% in the first year of the contract, 18% in the second year, and 12% in the third year. During the year of the sale, customers made warranty claims of $286,500 against the assurance-type warranty. Of this amount, $197,500 was paid for parts, and the $89,000 balance was incurred for labor (unpaid). During the following year, the company incurred $185,000 in actual warranty claims that are now covered only under the service-type warranty contract. The repair costs included $101,000 in parts and $84,000 in labor (unpaid).

Required »

Part 1. Prepare the journal entries required to record the following:

a. Router sales for the current year. The company uses the perpetual inventory system.
b. Accrual for the estimated warranty costs for the current year.
c. Actual repairs for the current year.
d. Service-type warranty contract sales for the current year.
e. Recognition of contract revenue for 3 years subsequent to the sale of the service-type contracts.
f. Actual repairs for the first year under the service-type warranty contracts.

Part 2. How does Packard classify the liability for the assurance-type warranty and the unearned revenue under the service-type warranty contract on the balance sheet at the end of the year in the year of the sale?

Part 3: Record the journal entry necessary to record the estimated liability under the assurance-type warranty for the next year (i.e., the year following the current year), assuming that total sales amounted to $15,675,000. Assume that no warranty claims were made in Year 2.

A **P13-8. Payroll Taxes Payable.** Jackson Corporation employs 45 production workers and pays them all the same salary. Jackson employs 10 administrative staff personnel and pays them all the same salary. The following annual information is available for each employee group.

Description	Production	Administrative
Salaries and wages	$4,500,000	$1,050,675
Federal income tax rate	18%	22%
State and local income tax rate	6%	9%
Federal unemployment tax rate – effective	2.5%	2.5%
State unemployment tax – effective (wage cap per employee = $7,000)	1.5%	1.5%

Required »

a. Prepare the journal entry to record the annual payroll.
b. Prepare the journal entry to pay the liability for accrued salaries.
c. Prepare the journal entry necessary to record Jackson's payroll tax expense for the annual payroll.

Excel Project
Autograded Excel Project available in **MyLab Accounting**

CASES

Judgment Cases

Judgment Case 1: Contingencies

Generics, Inc. is a U.S. GAAP reporter that manufactures and sells generic drugs and has a December 31 year-end. On March 1, 2018, it began selling a drug, Anocyn, which is a generic of Dicital. Dicital was patented by the pharmaceutical company Pharma, Inc. The patent period on Dicital has not expired, but Generics believes that the patent is invalid because the drug currently patented is not sufficiently different from the original drug that Pharma developed, patented, and sold.

As soon as Generics began marketing Anocyn, Pharma sued for patent infringement. As of December 31, 2018 the case was still in the early stages. Generics' attorneys believe that they will likely win the case, yet they cannot provide an estimated asset as of December 31, 2018. By December 31, 2019, the case had progressed. At this point, Generics' attorneys believe that Pharma has a viable case. They can estimate only a very broad range for the potential liability of between $1 million and $3 million. By December 31, 2020, the case has gone to court. Now Generics' attorneys believe that it is likely that they will lose the case. They currently estimate the loss at $4 million.

1. Do you think Generics should accrue the contingency, only disclose the contingency, or not report the contingency at all in its December 31, 2018, financial statements?
2. How should it report the contingency at December 31, 2019, if at all?
3. How should it report the contingency at December 31, 2020, if at all?

Judgment Case 2: Contingencies, IFRS

Use the information in Judgment Case 1 and assume that Generics, Inc. reports under IFRS.

1. Do you think Generics should accrue the contingency, only disclose the contingency, or not report the contingency at all in its December 31, 2018, financial statements?
2. How should it report the contingency at December 31, 2019, if at all?
3. How should it report the contingency at December 31, 2020, if at all?

Judgment Case 3: Asset Retirement Obligations

PDC Coal, Inc. received a mining permit to strip mine 1,000 acres of land in West Virginia on January 5 of the current year. Prior to receiving the permit, PDC submitted a legally-binding plan that included a timetable for the full reclamation process. PDC anticipates operating the mine for 5 to 7 years. Once it has closed the mine, PDC will restore the ground to its original contour. It will then reclaim the ground cover and provide reforestation. PDC will also engage in activities designed to minimize the air and water pollution created by the strip mining process. Finally, PDC has committed to a process for restoring the pre-existing wildlife to the area.

PDC makes the following estimates regarding the ultimate cost of the asset retirement obligation.

1. Labor costs related to the reclamation of the soil, ground cover, and reforestation are currently $20 per hour. However, PDC is certain that the costs will increase between 5 and 15% in the next 5 to 7 years. PDC believes it is most likely that the percentage increase will be somewhere in the middle of this range, but there is some possibility that the increase will be only 5% or as much as 15%.
2. PDC estimates that it will take between 8 and 10 hours per acre related to the soil, ground cover, and tree reclamation. It does not have any better estimates.
3. PDC estimates allocated equipment and overhead costs as 75% of labor costs.
4. PDC estimates that grass seed will cost $600 per acre and the seedlings will cost $500 per acre.
5. PDC estimates that it will take between $400,000 and $600,000 to reclaim the damages done by the air and water pollution created by the strip mining process. It does not have any better estimates.
6. PDC has not previously made any attempts to restore the wildlife to an area that has been strip mined. Its best guess is that the costs will range from $150,000 to $500,000.
7. No signification inflation is anticipated during this time period.
8. All of the reclamation work will be done within 1 year of when the strip mine is closed.

The risk-free rate on January 5 is 2%. If a contractor were going to lock in a price today to provide the reclamation services, it would typically charge a 3% premium.

What amount do you think PDC should recognize related to its asset retirement obligation? Support your answer with computations and explanations. You may find ASC 410-20 – *Asset Retirement and Environmental Obligations – Asset Retirement Obligations* helpful.

Financial Statement Analysis Case

You are interested in further analyzing and comparing the liquidity of ***Pfizer Inc.***, and ***Johnson & Johnson Company***. In an earlier analysis in Appendix B of Chapter 6, you found the current ratios of both companies at the end of fiscal year 2016 were above the threshold of 1 at 1.25 for ***Pfizer*** and 2.47 for ***Johnson & Johnson***. In the Chapter 13 Financial Statement Analysis case, you assessed additional measures of ***Johnson & Johnson's*** liquidity, which follow. Using information from the 2015 and 2016 financial statements for ***Pfizer***, answer the following questions about the company's liquidity and then compare the two companies.

a. Compute ***Pfizer's*** quick ratio for each year.
b. Compute ***Pfizer's*** cash ratio for each year.
c. Compute ***Pfizer's*** defensive interval ratio for each year.
d. Comment on changes in ***Pfizer's*** liquidity from 2015 to 2016 based on the ratios computed.
e. Compare the changes in ***Pfizer's*** liquidity from 2015 to 2016 to those computed in Example 13.19 in the text for ***Johnson & Johnson***. The following tables are included for the comparison.

Pfizer Inc.*

Fiscal Year *(in millions)*	**2015**	**2016**	**Percent Change**
Total assets	$167,381	$171,615	2.5%
Cash and cash equivalents	3,641	2,595	(28.7)
Short-term marketable securities	19,649	15,255	(22.4)
Accounts receivable	8,176	8,225	0.6
Current assets	43,804	38,949	(11.1)
Current liabilities	29,399	31,115	5.8

Pfizer Inc.*

Fiscal Year *(in millions)*	**2015**	**2016**	**Percent Change**
Cost of goods sold	9,648	12,329	27.8
Sales, marketing and administrative expenses	14,809	14,837	0.2
Research and development expense	7,690	7,872	2.4
Depreciation and amortization	5,157	5,757	11.6
Working capital	14,405	7,834	(45.6)
Current ratio	1.49	1.25	(16.1)

* ***Source***: Financial data from Pfizer PLC. Annual Reports, 2015, 2016. http://investor.Pfizer.com/phoenix.zhtml?c=207592&p=irol-reportsannual

Johnson & Johnson Company**
(from Example 13.19 in text)

	2015	**2016**	**Percent Change**
Working capital	$32,463	$38,745	19.4%
Current ratio	2.17	2.47	13.8
Quick or acid test ratio	1.77	2.04	15.3
Cash ratio	1.38	1.59	15.2
Defensive interval ratio	373.1	416.6	11.6

** ***Source***: Financial data from Johnson & Johnson Company's Annual Reports, 2015, 2016. http://files.shareholder.com/downloads/JNJ/2719746024x0x733042/DDD2ABD5-2CC6-41D2-8ACB-EC2A967727E4/ar2016_JNJ.pdf

Surfing the Standards Cases

Surfing the Standards Case 1: Environmental Remediation Costs

Environmental remediation costs have become increasingly prevalent in the last few decades. Read paragraphs 4 through 7, paragraph 15, and paragraph 25 of ASC 410-30-05. Also read paragraphs 1 through 13 of ASC 410-30-25.

1. Briefly explain the following terms:
   a. Environmental remediation liability
   b. Superfund
   c. Potentially responsible parties
2. Are environmental remediation liabilities a type of contingent liability?
3. Are the rules governing the accrual of environmental remedial liabilities the same as those governing the accrual of other contingent liabilities?
4. Based on your review of the literature, respond to the following questions.
   a. What factors do firms consider in the estimation of environmental remediation liabilities?
   b. What does an entity do if it can only reasonably estimate some of the components of the liability?
   c. What should be done if the entity can only estimate a range for the obligation?
   d. What should be done if there are uncertainties about the share of the obligation the entity will bear?

Surfing the Standards Case 2: Severance Pay for Factory Workers

The managers of Axbo Company, a private company whose bank requires it to follow U.S. GAAP, have decided to close one of its factories. The managers made this decision on July 16 of the current year and communicated this plan to their workers on August 1. All 200 workers will receive $1,250 per month for 12 months if they stay at work until the factory closes on March 1 of the following year. The first of these payments will occur 1 month after the factory closes. The managers estimate that 90% of the workers will remain long enough to receive their severance pay. The workers will receive no additional severance benefits of any kind beyond the severance pay. Axbo uses a 6% discount rate when computing fair values.

The factory closing will not qualify as a discontinued operation, and it is highly unlikely that any changes will be made to the plan. Also, Axbo management has the authority to approve this plan without board approval.

The management of Axbo is unsure how to account for the severance pay, including the impact on the financial statements and when it will show up on the financial statements. They are not concerned with required disclosures. Prepare a memo to the file using the Codification for support.

Basis for Conclusions Cases

Basis for Conclusions Case 1: Provisions and Contingencies[1]

Note: In the following exercise, you are required to review the Basis for Conclusions (BCs) for the standard(s) that provide the accounting guidance for this topic. Because the BCs is generally not included in the codification and thus is not authoritative, it will most likely be necessary for you to research it through review of the pre-codified standards. Appropriate references have been provided to allow you to do so. Pre-codified standards are accessible on the FASB website or through the American Accounting Association's Academic Accounting Access program, if your school participates in this program.

Scene 1:

Read IAS 37, paragraphs 10 and 11.

- What makes a provision different from the other types of current liabilities reported on a company's balance sheet?

Scene 2:

Read ASC 450-20-05-01 and ASC 450-20-05-03.

- How do the definitions of a provision under IFRS and a contingency under U.S. GAAP differ? How do the definitions of provisions and contingencies differ from other liabilities?
- Why is it important that provisions be separately identified in an entity's financial statements rather than being included with other accrued liabilities?

Scene 3:

To determine the proper accounting treatment for contingent liabilities (loss contingencies), both U.S. GAAP and IFRS require management to assess the likelihood that a contingency will be ultimately paid. Both standards provide guidance to assist management when making these decisions. The interpretation of the guidance and the judgment management uses are very important because they determine how a contingent liability will be presented in the financial statements.

ASC 450-20-20 provides the following definitions:

Probable: The future event or events are likely to occur.

Reasonably possible: The chance of the future event or events occurring is more than remote but less than likely.

Remote: The chance of the future event or events occurring is slight.

IAS 37, paragraph 23, provides two distinctions:

[1]Reprinted from the Ernst & Young Academic Resource Center with permission of the Ernst & Young Foundation.

Probable: The event is more likely than not to occur.

Remote (no definition provided.)

- What probabilities (percentages) would you assign to each category under U.S. GAAP and IFRS?
- Why are probabilities not used in the standards rather than the expressions that are subject to interpretation?
- Do you consider the guidance provided for loss contingencies under U.S. GAAP to be rules based or principles based? Why? Is the guidance under IFRS more principles based than the U.S. GAAP guidance?

Scene 4:

Read IAS 37, paragraph 25, and paragraph 59 in the BCs of SFAS No. 5.

- Both of these paragraphs reflect the views of the different boards with respect to estimating loss contingencies. Do you consider one view to be more liberal than another? Why or why not?

Scene 5:

- Under which standard would you expect to see more disclosure in the financial statements?

Scene 6:

Read SFAS No. 5 BCs, paragraphs 82 through 84 and paragraph IN4 of IAS 37.

- Should the concept of "conservatism" be considered when determining whether to recognize a contingency?
- Are the standards at odds with the concept of conservatism because they do not require contingent losses to be recognized unless they are probable and can be reasonably estimated?
- Should the concept of conservatism be a guiding principle as the boards continue to develop accounting standards?

APPENDIX A
Payroll Taxes Payable

Payroll taxes payable are liabilities that companies incur related to the payment of employee salary and wages. Payroll taxes include:

- Social Security taxes
- Unemployment taxes
- Income taxes withheld

Both employers and employees bear the responsibility for payroll taxes. In addition to an employee's salary, an employer is responsible for paying certain taxes, such as unemployment taxes and a portion of Social Security taxes. These payroll taxes are considered part of the company's wage expense in addition to the employee's salary.

Employees also pay taxes—such as a portion of Social Security and income taxes—that the employer deducts from their gross wages and remits to the appropriate taxing jurisdictions and agencies. That is, the employer collects the tax for the government agencies imposing the tax and has an obligation to remit the amounts withheld but does not incur an expense.

We will discuss each tax separately and then provide a comprehensive payroll example.

Social Security Taxes

Social Security taxes are divided into two parts:

1. Federal insurance contribution act tax (FICA tax)
2. Medicare tax[21]

FICA primarily provides funds for old-age benefits: Employees (and their employers) contribute to the plan when they are working, and then employees receive benefits upon retirement. The tax is 12.4% with half (6.2%) paid by the employer and half (6.2%) paid by the employee.[22] Employers remit the full 12.4% of wages to the government up to a maximum *wage base* of $127,200.[23] A **wage base** is the maximum salary or wages on which taxes are levied; earnings exceeding the wage base are not subject to the tax.

The Medicare tax rate is 2.9%, again split evenly between employee and employer (1.45% each).[24] Unlike FICA, Medicare does not have a maximum wage base, so all earnings are fully taxable. In addition to the 2.9% Medicare rate, there is an additional Medicare tax of 0.9% that is paid only by the employee. This rate is effective on all wages over $200,000 for individuals, $250,000 for couples filing a joint tax return, and $125,000 for married couples filing separate returns.

Unemployment Taxes

Employers also pay unemployment taxes, which are levied by the federal and state governments to provide funding for unemployment insurance.

The federal tax, referred to as the Federal Unemployment Tax Act (FUTA), is applicable to most businesses. The rate is 6% on the first $7,000 paid to each employee during the year. However, the employer receives a credit for up to 5.4% of unemployment taxes paid to the state. So, if an employer pays a state rate of 5.4% or more, it is subject to only a 0.6% FUTA rate (6.0% less 5.4%).

[21] FICA is also referred to as the Old Age, Survivor, and Disability Insurance (OASDI), and Medicare is also referred to as the federal hospital insurance tax.
[22] These tax rates are from the U.S. Social Security Administration (http://www.ssa.gov/oact/progdata/taxRates.html).
[23] This wage base is effective for 2017.
[24] Ibid 4.

Unemployment tax rates and laws vary by state with state-specific rates and wage ceilings. However, all states provide reductions in the maximum rate based on employer-specific experience. Consider a company that has paid state unemployment taxes for a number of years. The state will grant a reduced rate if the company has only a low number of former employees who have sought unemployment compensation. Even with the reduced state unemployment tax rate, the employer will still get full credit against its FUTA rate at the maximum state rate. To illustrate, assume the maximum state rate is 5.4% and the employer gets an experience-rate reduction of 3%. The company will pay a 2.4% state rate and a 0.6% federal rate (6.0% − 5.4%).

Income Taxes Withheld

Federal laws and most state laws require that employers withhold income taxes from employee paychecks. The amount of withholding is based on a number of factors such as income level, marital status, and number of dependents. The tax is on the employee, not the employer. Again, the employer is merely serving as an intermediary, collecting the tax from the employee and remitting it to the government. Example 13A.1 provides a comprehensive illustration of payroll accounting.

EXAMPLE 13A.1

Comprehensive Payroll Example

PROBLEM: e-Grant, Inc. has a $400,000 monthly payroll that covers 100 employees who are each paid $48,000 per year. The company pays each employee $4,000 ($400,000 total monthly payroll/100 employees) per month. Information regarding relevant payroll taxes and rates follows:

- Federal payroll income taxes average 21%.
- State and local payroll income taxes average 4%.
- The state in which e-Grant operates has a state unemployment rate of 6% with a wage base of $7,000. However, the state gives e-Grant an experience credit of 5%.

Compute the amount of taxes that e-Grant will withhold from the employees and the amount of payroll tax expense that the company will incur. What are the journal entries to record the payroll for the first 2 months of the year?

SOLUTION: We begin by computing the taxes that e-Grant will withhold from its employees, as well as the amount for which the company will be responsible to pay. Because the monthly salary is $4,000 per employee, the FICA wage base will not be reached. Thus, the tax applies to the total payroll of $400,000. The tax is $24,800 ($400,000 × 6.2%) for both employee and employer each month.

Medicare is always 1.45% of the wage base for both employer and employee. Federal taxes are 21% and state taxes are 4%. The additional Medicare tax does not apply to these employees because their salaries are below the amount at which the additional Medicare becomes applicable.

In the first month, the unemployment wage base has not been reached. However, in the second month, only $3,000 per employee is subject to the federal and state unemployment taxes because the $7,000 maximum is reached at this point. Therefore, with 100 employees paid $4,000 per month, the total unemployment wage base is $400,000 in the first month but only $300,000 in the second month.

	First Month	Second Month	Total
Employee 1	$4,000	$3,000	$7,000
Employee 2	4,000	3,000	7,000

The following table presents the tax computations.

	First Month		Second Month	
	Employer	Employee	Employer	Employee
Social Security Taxes:				
FICA				
Wage base	$ 400,000	$400,000	$ 400,000	$ 400,000
Tax rate	× 6.2%	× 6.2%	× 6.2%	× 6.2%
FICA taxes payable	$ 24,800	$ 24,800	$ 24,800	$ 24,800
Medicare				
Wage base	$ 400,000	$400,000	$ 400,000	$ 400,000
Tax rate	× 1.45%	× 1.45%	× 1.45%	× 1.45%
Medicare taxes payable	$ 5,800	$ 5,800	$ 5,800	$ 5,800
Federal Income Taxes				
Wage base		$ 400,000		$ 400,000
Tax rate		× 21%		× 21%
Federal income tax payable		$ 84,000		$ 84,000
State Income Taxes				
Wage base		$ 400,000		$ 400,000
Tax rate		× 4%		× 4%
State income tax payable		$ 16,000		$ 16,000
FUTA				
Wage base	$ 400,000		$ 300,000	
Tax rate	× 0.6%		× 0.6%	
FUTA payable	$ 2,400		$ 1,800	
State unemployment:				
Wage base	$ 400,000		$ 300,000	
Tax rate	× 1%		× 1%	
State unemployment tax payable	$ 4,000		$ 3,000	

The journal entry for the payroll taxes for which e-Grant is responsible in the first month follows.

Account	***End of First Month***	
Payroll Tax Expense	37,000	
FICA Taxes Payable		24,800
Medicare Taxes Payable		5,800
FUTA Payable		2,400
State Unemployment Tax Payable		4,000

The journal entry for the payroll withholdings from the employees' wages in the first month follows.

Account	End of First Month	
Wage Expense	400,000	
FICA Taxes Payable		24,800
Medicare Taxes Payable		5,800
Federal Income Tax Payable		84,000
State Income Tax Payable		16,000
Cash		269,400

In the second month, the journal entry for the payroll taxes for which e-Grant is responsible follows.

Account	End of Second Month	
Payroll Tax Expense	35,400	
FICA Taxes Payable		24,800
Medicare Taxes Payable		5,800
FUTA Payable		1,800
State Unemployment Tax Payable		3,000

Additionally, in the second month, the journal entry for the payroll withholdings from the employees' wages follows.

Account	End of Second Month	
Wage Expense	400,000	
FICA Taxes Payable		24,800
Medicare Taxes Payable		5,800
Federal Income Tax Payable		84,000
State Income Tax Payable		16,000
Cash		269,400

14 Financing Liabilities

LEARNING OBJECTIVES

1. Describe and illustrate accounting for notes payable.
2. Explain the common features of bonds payable and discuss the initial recognition at par value, at a discount, and at a premium.
3. Demonstrate accounting for bonds issued at par or at a discount or premium, including computation of the bond issue price, interest expense, and amortization of the discount or premium using the effective interest rate method.
4. Explain and illustrate accounting for bonds issued between interest payment dates.
5. Discuss and illustrate the accounting for bond issue costs.
6. Determine the accounting for bonds payable at early retirement.
7. Explain and illustrate the accounting for convertible bonds.
8. Describe and illustrate the accounting for warrants, including those that are detachable and nondetachable.
9. Explain the reclassification of financing liabilities for current maturities of long-term debt, short-term debt expected to be refinanced, and callable obligations.
10. Discuss and illustrate the fair value option in accounting for financing liabilities.
11. Detail required disclosures for financing liabilities.

Xinhua/Alamy

Introduction

COMPANIES SEEK CAPITAL FOR A VARIETY OF PURPOSES: investing in new facilities, replacing existing equipment, acquiring other companies, or funding general business activities. Companies commonly use debt financing to raise capital for these purposes by borrowing cash with the obligation to repay it, usually with interest, at some point in the future. Consider ***Tesla, Inc.***, the manufacturer and seller of high-performance fully electric vehicles, and solar and energy storage systems, which reported approximately $8.1 billion and $3.1 billion in debt outstanding at the end of its 2016 and 2015 fiscal years, respectively. This outstanding debt represented about 33% of its total assets at the end of fiscal 2016 and 2015. During 2016, ***Tesla's*** debt increased by more than $2.8 billion, primarily as the result of issuing bonds to fund its operations and capital expenditures. ***Tesla's*** debt also increased by about $3.6 billion when it acquired ***SolarCity***. Then in 2016, ***Tesla's*** debt decreased by about $1.8 billion because of net repayments.

Companies monitor the amount of debt carried on their balance sheets to ensure that they can repay the debt and have continued access to capital markets in the future. ***Tesla's*** 2016 annual report explained to investors that its ability to make debt payments depends on its future performance, which is subject to economic, financial, competitive, and other factors beyond its control. ***Tesla*** cautioned that its business may not continue to generate cash flow from operations in the future sufficient to satisfy its obligations and any future indebtedness it may incur and to make necessary capital expenditures. If Tesla is unable to generate such cash flow, it may be required to reduce or delay investments or capital expenditures, sell assets, refinance, or obtain additional equity capital on terms that may be unfavorable. Its ability to refinance existing or future indebtedness will depend on the capital markets and its financial condition at such time. Firms also use long-term debt capital to extinguish short-term liabilities, including accounts payable, accrued liabilities, and short-term notes payable.

In this chapter, we discuss several types of financing liabilities. After discussing notes payable, including installment loans, we address accounting for bonds payable, starting with the straightforward case of issuing a bond at its face value and progressing to the more complex cases of issuing bonds at a discount or premium. We then explain other issues in accounting for bonds, such as issuing bonds between interest payment dates and the accounting for bond issue costs related to legal fees and banking fees. We complete our discussion of bonds by illustrating the accounting for the early retirement of debt. We also explain accounting for debt with an equity feature, including convertible bonds and bonds issued with warrants. Next, we discuss special issues such as short-term debt expected to be refinanced and debt that becomes callable by the creditor. Before we cover required disclosures, we also revisit the fair value option by applying this methodology to the valuation of liabilities. «

1 Describe and illustrate accounting for notes payable.

Notes Payable

Recall that notes payable are formal credit arrangements between a creditor (lender) and a debtor (borrower) that require the payment of a specified face amount, the **principal**, at a fixed maturity date. The principal is also referred to as the face, par, or maturity value of the note. Typically, interest is payable at a specified percentage of the principal balance. Notes payable are most often long term, but entities sometimes use them for short-term borrowing. In this section of the chapter, we discuss both short- and long-term notes payable.

Short-Term Notes Payable

Companies report short-term notes payable on the balance sheet as current liabilities because they are due and payable within 1 year from the balance sheet date or operating cycle, whichever is longer. Short-term notes require the use of current assets or creation of other current liabilities in their liquidation. Companies borrow by issuing short-term notes for several reasons:

1. The short-term debt can fill a temporary gap when cash flows from operations are insufficient to meet current liquidity needs.
2. The term of short-term notes matches well with a firm's operating cycle. That is, companies expect that inventory sales and collection of accounts receivable will generate the cash needed to liquidate the short-term obligations when due.
3. Short-term debt typically carries a lower interest rate than long-term notes and can represent the least costly financing alternative for the firm.
4. Small businesses or firms with low credit ratings may not be able to obtain financing on a long-term basis, making the short-term note the only alternative available to raise capital.

In 2012, because of varying short-term financing needs, ***Kellogg*** issued $779 million of notes payable with maturities less than or equal to 90 days and $724 million of notes payable with maturities greater than 90 days. ***Kellogg*** also issued $1,727 million of long-term debt that was primarily notes payable, a portion related to its acquisition of Pringles.

A company typically records a notes payable with a debit to cash and a credit to the appropriate liability account. The company records interest expense by debiting the expense account and crediting cash if it is paying the interest or crediting interest payable if it is accruing it at year-end. When the company pays off the note, it debits the liability and credits cash. Proceeds on issue and repayment of the principal are generally reported as financing activities on the statement of cash flows. Interest payments are classified as cash flows from operating activities. Example 14.1 illustrates accounting for a short-term note.

EXAMPLE 14.1 Short-Term Notes Payable and Accrued Interest

PROBLEM: Auso Company recently experienced a temporary delay in cash collections and needed to borrow $100,000 on November 1 of the current year to pay trade accounts payable. The 6-month, 6% note and interest are due on May 1 of the following year. Auso has a December 31 fiscal year-end. What are the required journal entries to record the issuance of the note, accrued interest, and the payment of principal and interest at maturity?

SOLUTION: Auso records the issuance of the note by making the following journal entry:

Account	***November 1***	
Cash	100,000	
Short-Term Note Payable		100,000

On December 31, Auso must make an adjusting entry to record the accrued interest payable. The monthly interest on the loan is $500 [$100,000 × (6%/12)]. Two months of interest, or $1,000 ($500 × 2 months), has accrued as of December 31. The adjusting journal entry is as follows:

Account	***December 31***	
Interest Expense	1,000	
Interest Payable		1,000

On May 1, the due date of the note, Auso will record the remaining 4 months of interest expense of $2,000 ($500 × 4 months) and derecognize the note payable and interest payable.

Account	***May 1***	
Interest Expense	2,000	
Interest Payable	1,000	
Short-Term Note Payable	100,000	
Cash		103,000

Long-Term Notes Payable: Term Loans

Companies report long-term notes payable on the balance sheet as noncurrent liabilities because they are due and payable within a period greater than 1 year from the balance sheet date or operating cycle, whichever is longer. Long-term notes can be *term loans* or *installment loans*.

Term Loan. A **term loan** typically requires the borrower to pay interest each period with the principal due only at maturity. Firms preparing financial statements between interest payment dates accrue interest with a debit to expense and a credit to interest payable as shown in Example 14.2.

EXAMPLE 14.2 Note Payable: Term Loan

PROBLEM: Salada Corporation borrowed $500,000 by issuing a term loan on February 1, 2018. The note agreement specifies that the company will pay interest every 3 months (April 30, July 31, October 31, and January 31) at 10%, and the principal will be due on January 31, 2023. Salada has a December 31 year-end and prepares quarterly financial statements. What journal entries will Salada make on February 1, 2018, at the end of each calendar quarter, at each interest payment, and on January 31, 2023?

SOLUTION: Salada records the long-term note on the date of issuance as follows:

Account	February 1, 2018	
Cash	500,000	
Long-Term Notes Payable		500,000

Salada accrues interest expense at the end of each calendar quarter. Quarterly interest is $12,500 per quarter ($500,000 × 10%/4 quarters). Monthly interest is one-third of this amount, or $4,167. Thus, on March 31, June 30, September 30, and December 31, Salada will accrue 2 months of interest.

Account	March 31, 2018 (and Every Quarter through December 31, 2022)	
Interest Expense	8,333	
Interest Payable		8,333

At each interest payment date, Salada will record the cash payment of $12,500, remove the interest payable of $8,333 because the company no longer owes that interest, and record 1 month of interest expense.

Account	April 30, 2018 (and Every Three-Month Payment through January 31, 2023)	
Interest Expense	4,167	
Interest Payable	8,333	
Cash		12,500

At maturity, Salada pays the note principal and removes it from the balance sheet.

Account	January 31, 2023	
Long-Term Notes Payable	500,000	
Cash		500,000

Long-Term Notes Payable: Installment Loans

An **installment loan** requires a fixed payment each period that includes both principal and interest. Although the payment is the same each period, the amount applied to principal and interest varies. Installment notes are used in auto loans and home mortgages.[1]

Computing the required payment involves using the time value of money techniques from Chapter 7 by first computing the payment and then preparing an amortization table to assist in

[1]Because installment loans typically require some payments to be made within the next year, a portion of these notes payable will be classified as a current liability. We discuss this classification issue later in the chapter.

preparing the journal entries. The amortization table includes columns for the date, the interest, principal, total payment, and the note's carrying value. The interest is the beginning note balance multiplied by the periodic interest rate. Interest is recorded as a debit to interest expense. The principal payment, the difference between the total payment and the interest payment, is recorded as a debit to the note payable. The ending balance of the note payable is the beginning balance less the principal payment. Example 14.3 illustrates the accounting for an installment loan.

EXAMPLE 14.3 Note Payable with Amortization Table: Installment Loan

PROBLEM: AS&K, Inc. borrowed $250,000 by issuing an 8%, 3-year note on January 1, 2018. AS&K must make payments every 6 months, beginning June 30, 2018. The note will be fully paid at maturity on December 31, 2020. AS&K prepares annual financial statements. Prepare the amortization table for this note along with any necessary journal entries. Also prepare the t-account for the notes payable account.

SOLUTION: We first compute the semiannual payment.

	N	I/Y	PV	PMT	FV	Excel Formula
Given	6	4.00%	250,000		0	
Solve for PMT				**(47,690)**		= PMT(0.04,6,250000,0)

We then prepare the amortization table. Interest for each period is the beginning balance of the note payable times the 4% periodic interest rate. The principal payment is the total payment of $47,690 less the interest payment. The ending note balance is the beginning balance of the note payable less the principal payment.

Period	Date	Total Payment (a)	Interest Payment (b) = 4% × Prior (d)	Principal Payment (c) = (a)−(b)	Carrying Value (d) = Prior (d) − (c)
					$250,000
1	June 30, 2018	$47,690	$10,000	$37,690	212,310
2	December 31, 2018	47,690	8,492	39,198	173,112
3	June 30, 2019	47,690	6,924	40,766	132,346
4	December 31, 2019	47,690	5,294	42,396	89,950
5	June 30, 2020	47,690	3,598	44,092	45,858
6	December 31, 2020	47,690	1,832*	45,858*	0

* Adjusted due to rounding errors.

AS&K makes the following journal entry at inception:

Account	January 1, 2018	
Cash	250,000	
Long-Term Notes Payable		250,000

AS&K uses the information contained in the amortization table to record the semiannual payments. The payments made for an installment loan contain principal plus interest. AS&K makes the following journal entries to record the payments in 2018:

Account	June 30, 2018		December 31, 2018	
Interest Expense	10,000		8,492	
Long-Term Notes Payable	37,690		39,198	
Cash		47,690		47,690

Continued

The journal entries in 2019 follow.

Account	June 30, 2019		December 31, 2019	
Interest Expense	6,924		5,294	
Long-Term Notes Payable	40,766		42,396	
Cash		47,690		47,690

The journal entries in 2020 follow.

Account	June 30, 2020		December 31, 2020	
Interest Expense	3,598		1,832	
Long-Term Notes Payable	44,092		45,858	
Cash		47,690		47,690

The t-account for the notes payable account is as follows:

Long-Term Notes Payable		
January 1, 2018		250,000
June 30, 2018	37,690	
December 31, 2018	39,198	
June 30, 2019	40,766	
December 31, 2019	42,396	
June 30, 2020	44,092	
December 31, 2020	45,858	
		0

The timing of a note payable may be such that the company will need to accrue interest before it prepares financial statements. Example 14.4 modifies Example 14.3 to illustrate an installment loan with a year-end interest accrual.

EXAMPLE 14.4

Note Payable with Amortization Table: Installment Loan with Interest Accrual

PROBLEM: AS&K, Inc. borrowed $250,000 by issuing an 8%, 3-year note on March 1, 2018. AS&K must make payments every 6 months beginning August 31, 2018. The note will be fully paid at maturity on February 28, 2021. AS&K prepares annual financial statements. Prepare the amortization table for this note. Prepare the journal entries for 2018 and the first interest payment in 2019.

SOLUTION: We computed the total payment amount as $47,690 in Example 14.3. We can refer to the amortization table from that example and change the dates for the payments.

Date	Total Payment (a)	Interest Payment (b) = 4% × Prior(d)	Principal Payment (c) = (a) − (b)	Carrying Value (d) = Prior (d) − (c)
				$250,000
August 31, 2018	$47,690	$10,000	$37,690	212,310
February 28, 2019	47,690	8,492	39,198	173,112
August 31, 2019	47,690	6,924	40,766	132,346
February 28, 2020	47,690	5,294	42,396	89,950
August 31, 2020	47,690	3,598	44,092	45,858
February 28, 2021	47,690	1,832*	45,858*	0

* Adjusted due to rounding errors.

Again, AS&K makes the following journal entry at inception:

Account	**March 1, 2018**	
Cash	250,000	
Long-Term Notes Payable		250,000

AS&K records the first interest payment using the information in the amortization table.

Account	**August 31, 2018**	
Interest Expense	10,000	
Long-Term Notes Payable	37,690	
Cash		47,690

Because AS&K prepares financial statements before the next interest payment, we need to accrue interest for 4 months (September through December) at year-end. The total interest for the second period is $8,492; thus, we accrue 4 / 6 of this, or $5,661.

Account	**December 31, 2018**	
Interest Expense	5,661	
Interest Payable		5,661

On February 28, 2019, AS&K records the second interest payment, removing the interest payable from the year-end accrual.

Account	**February 28, 2019**	
Interest Expense	2,831	
Interest Payable	5,661	
Long-Term Notes Payable	39,198	
Cash		47,690

Long-Term Notes Payable: Stated Rate Less than Market Rate

Companies sometimes borrow with a loan that has no interest rate stated (a non-interest-bearing note) or a stated interest rate that is less than the market interest rate. In this case, the note is measured as the present value of the note discounted at the market rate of interest.

The difference between the *face value* and the present value of the note is called the discount and represents some of the interest expense to be incurred over the life of the note. The company uses the *effective interest method* to subsequently amortize the discount on notes payable (a contra-liability account) to interest expense over the loan term.

There are two primary effects of the discount amortization. Discount amortization:

1. Increases the interest expense so that the corporation's *effective interest rate* is brought up to the higher market rate
2. Reduces the discount and increases the carrying value of the note payable until the carrying value is brought up to its *face value* at the maturity date

Discount amortization is recorded at the end of each period. In reality, the discount is paid only at maturity. However, with accrual accounting, the company must recognize the additional interest each period by amortizing the discount.

The amortization table for below-market-rate installment notes starts with the computation of the present value of the note. The cash payment each period is the *face value* of the note multiplied by the periodic stated interest rate. The interest expense each period is the beginning carrying value of the note multiplied by the periodic historical market rate. The amount of discount that is amortized each period into interest expense is the difference between the cash interest paid and the computed effective interest expense. Finally, the change in the carrying value of the note payable is the amount of the discount amortization. An example of accounting for a note payable with a stated rate less than the market rate is provided in Example 14.5.

EXAMPLE 14.5 Note Payable with a Stated Rate Less than the Market Rate

PROBLEM: JN Min Corporation, a calendar-year company, borrowed $1,000,000 on August 15, 2018. The note specifies an 8% interest rate and is due in 3 years. Interest is paid quarterly. The fiscal year ends on December 31. The current market rate is 12%. Interest is compounded quarterly. JN Min prepares quarterly financial statements. Prepare the amortization table for the note and the journal entries for 2018.

SOLUTION: The first step is to compute the present value of the note, which is $900,460.

	N	I/Y	PV	PMT	FV	Excel Formula
Given	12	3.00%		−20,000	−1,000,000	
Solve for PV			**900,460**			=PV(0.03,12,−20000,−1000000)

The amortization table follows. We use the stated rate of 2% per quarter to compute the cash interest and the market rate of 3% per quarter to compute the effective interest.

Date	Cash Interest (2%) (a)	Effective Interest (b) = 3% × Prior (d)	Discount Amortized (c) = (b) − (a)	Carrying Value (d) = Prior (d) + (c)
At issuance				$ 900,460
November 15, 2018	$20,000	$27,014	$7,014	907,474
February 15, 2019	20,000	27,224	7,224	914,698
May 15, 2019	20,000	27,441	7,441	922,139
August 15, 2019	20,000	27,664	7,664	929,803
November 15, 2019	20,000	27,894	7,894	937,697
February 15, 2020	20,000	28,131	8,131	945,828
May 15, 2020	20,000	28,375	8,375	954,203
August 15, 2020	20,000	28,626	8,626	962,829
November 15, 2020	20,000	28,885	8,885	971,714
February 15, 2021	20,000	29,151	9,151	980,865
May 15, 2021	20,000	29,426	9,426	990,291
August 15, 2021	20,000	29,709	9,709	1,000,000

The journal entry to record the note payable and the discount is as follows:

Account	*August 15, 2018*	
Cash	900,460	
Discount on Note Payable	99,540	
Long-Term Note Payable		1,000,000

At this point, the carrying value of the note payable on the balance sheet is $900,460, which is the balance in the note payable account ($1,000,000) less the balance in the discount account ($99,540).

On September 30, 2018, JN Min prepares financial statements. Thus, it will accrue interest from August 15 through September 30. The interest for the first period is $27,014 per the amortization table. However, JN Min will accrue interest expense for one-half of that amount. Specifically, the period from August 15 to September 30 is 1.5 months, or exactly one-half of the quarter. As a result, JN Min will amortize one-half of the discount and record interest payable of $10,000, which is one-half of the anticipated interest payment.

Account	September 30, 2018	
Interest Expense	13,507	
Discount on Note Payable		3,507
Interest Payable		10,000

On November 15, 2018, JN Min makes a $20,000 interest payment. It records the following journal entry.

Account	November 15, 2018	
Interest Payable	10,000	
Interest Expense	13,507	
Discount on Note Payable		3,507
Cash		20,000

Finally, on December 31, 2018, JN Min will accrue interest for one-half of the second period as follows (November 15 to December 31 is also one and one-half months, representing one-half of a quarter):

Account	December 31, 2018	
Interest Expense	13,612	
Discount on Note Payable		3,612
Interest Payable		10,000

❷ Explain the common features of bonds payable and discuss the initial recognition at par value, at a discount, and at a premium.

Overview of Bonds Payable

A **bond payable** is a debt instrument typically issued for a period greater than a year to raise capital that requires the debtor to repay the principal balance at a specified date in the future, referred to as the maturity date. Bonds usually involve interest payments at fixed time intervals (for example, quarterly).

When a company issues a bond, it becomes the debtor, and the purchaser of the bond is the creditor. Bonds are offered to the public and can usually be traded in the secondary market: A company issues bonds to a large number of lenders in the market, and each lender extends credit to the corporation. This feature contrasts with a note payable where there is one debtor and one creditor that transact directly.

Credit Ratings

Creditors seek a return on each lending arrangement and, as such, are concerned about a debtor's ability to repay principal and interest when due. A company's creditworthiness is determined by many factors, including its profitability, existing level of debt, net asset position, earnings, and cash flows. Yet, it is often difficult and time consuming for an individual investor to assess these factors. Consequently, credit rating agencies such as ***Standard & Poor's*** and ***Moody's*** rate corporate debt by examining a company's creditworthiness and giving an opinion on the company's credit quality. The rating is expressed as a letter grade, such as "AAA" for the companies with a strong capacity to repay their debt. Exhibit 14.1 presents the credit ratings used by ***Standard & Poor's*** and their general meaning. Other rating agencies use different scales.

EXHIBIT 14.1 ***Standard & Poor's*** **Credit Ratings**

The general meaning of our credit rating opinions is summarized below.

AAA	Extremely strong capacity to meet financial commitments. Highest Rating.
AA	Very strong capacity to meet financial commitments.
A	Strong capacity to meet financial commitments, but somewhat susceptible to adverse economic conditions and changes in circumstances.
BBB	Adequate capacity to meet financial commitments, but more subject to adverse economic conditions.
BBB−	Considered lowest investment grade by market participants.
BB+	Considered highest speculative grade by market participants.
BB	Less vulnerable in the near-term but faces major ongoing uncertainties to adverse business, financial and economic conditions.
B	More vulnerable to adverse business, financial and economic conditions but currently has the capacity to meet financial commitments.
CCC	Currently vulnerable and dependent on favorable business, financial and economic conditions to meet financial commitments.
CC	Currently highly vulnerable.
C	Currently highly vulnerable obligations and other defined circumstances.
D	Payment default on financial commitments.

Note: Ratings from "AA" to "CCC" may be modified by the addition of a plus (+) or minus (−) sign to show relative standing within the major rating categories.
Source: From Standard & Poor. Copyright © Standard & Poor's Financial Services LLC. http://www.standardandpoors.com/ratings/definitions-and-faqs/en/us

The ability to score a high credit rating is important for two reasons:

- The better the credit rating, the easier it is for a company to issue debt.
- Higher credit ratings are usually associated with a lower cost of debt.

In 2016, ***Johnson & Johnson***, an S&P 500 pharmaceutical and consumer products company, had a "AAA" debt rating. ***Johnson & Johnson*** maintained its financial discipline during the global recession in 2007–2009 and held its "AAA" credit rating. As an "AAA"-rated company, it was able to carry out a $1.1 billion debt offering in 2010 at the lowest interest rate for long-term corporate debt in history at the time.[2]

Bond Indenture

The **bond indenture** contract between the corporation and the bondholders (represented by a trustee) protects the rights of multiple creditors by outlining the *debt covenants*, enforcement, and the type and terms of the bond.

[2]See www.investor.jnj.com/2010annualreport/pdf/2010-annual-report.pdf, p. 3. Johnson & Johnson sold $550 million of 2.95%, 10-year notes, and the same amount of 4.5%, 30-year bonds.

Debt covenants are debt compliance agreements that place restrictions on the corporation to protect the bondholders' interest and ensure that cash is available for repayment of the debt. Common debt covenants include restrictions such as holding *compensating cash balances*, maintaining specified retained earnings levels, maintaining set ratios or working capital levels, and limiting future borrowings or dividend payments. **Compensating cash balances** are restricted deposits that a debtor is required to maintain to support existing lending arrangements.

A **technical default** occurs when a debtor violates one or more terms of its debt covenants. When a debtor misses interest and/or principal payments, it is known as an **actual default**. In the event of either technical or actual default, the bond indenture provides information regarding the enforcement of the contract between the debtor and creditors.

There are numerous types of bonds, such as:

- **Secured bonds**, which use specific assets as collateral
- **Debenture bonds**, which are unsecured bonds (that is, there is no collateral backing)
- **Serial bonds**, which have multiple maturity dates
- **Term bonds**, which have a single maturity date
- **Callable bonds**, which can be called at the corporation's option at specified dates
- **Convertible bonds**, which bondholders may convert into capital stock
- **Bonds with stock warrants attached**, which are bonds that also include long-term options to acquire common stock

Bond indentures detail the terms of the future cash payments to the lender, including:

- **Face value** (also referred to as par value or principal), the amount that the company will pay the bondholder at maturity. Bonds typically have a face value of $1,000.
- **Stated interest rate** (also referred to as the nominal, coupon, or face rate), the amount of interest that the bond issuer will pay in cash expressed as an annual rate.
- **Interest payment period**, the frequency with which cash interest payments are made to the bondholders. Common interest periods are quarterly, semiannually, and annually.
- **Maturity date**, the specified date when the bond issuer must pay the face value of the bonds to the bondholders.

Bond Pricing

Corporations can issue bonds at:

- Their face value
- A **discount**, a price below face value
- A **premium**, a price above face value

The discount or premium is determined by the difference between the stated or face rate of interest and the current market rate. The bond purchaser makes the investment in order to earn the current *market rate* of interest for an amount of comparable risk. The **market rate**, or **yield**, is the actual return that the investors will receive. We also call the actual return the **effective interest rate**.

Stated Interest Rate versus Market Rate. The market rate often differs from the bond's stated interest rate because of a time lag caused by the delay in issuing bonds while bonds are printed, indentures are prepared, and the bonds are sold to an underwriter. Therefore, whether a company issues bonds at their face value, a discount, or a premium depends on the relation between the bonds' stated interest rate and the market rate of interest for a similar bond.

1. **Bonds issued at par or face value.** When the stated interest rate is equal to the market rate, the bonds will sell at par value. The company is paying the interest rate demanded by the market, so its bonds are equivalent to any other debt security available.

2. **Bonds issued at a discount.** When the stated interest rate is less than the market rate of interest, the bonds will sell at a discount (i.e., the issue price is less than the face value). Investors are demanding a higher rate of interest than the company is offering, so investors will not pay the full face value. When an investor pays an amount less than face value, the effective return for the investor equals the higher market rate. The effective cost of borrowing for the corporation increases because the company has less cash to use and must repay the full amount at maturity. For example, if a corporation sells a $1,000 par bond with a stated interest rate of 5% for $900, the corporation receives only $900 but must repay the $1,000 at maturity. The $100 discount represents additional interest resulting in a higher effective cost of borrowing in excess of 5%. The investor's rate of return increases because only $900 is invested with $1,000 returned at maturity.
3. **Bonds issued at a premium.** When the stated interest rate is more than the market rate of interest, the company issues the bonds at a premium (i.e., the issue price is greater than the face value). The company is paying a higher rate of interest than investors are demanding, so it will sell the bond for more than its face value. By paying more than face value, the effective return for the investor equals the lower market rate. The effective cost of borrowing for the corporation also decreases because the company has more cash to use over the bond term and has to repay only the face value. For example, if a $1,000 par bond with a stated interest rate of 5% is sold for $1,100, the corporation receives $1,100 but has to repay only $1,000 at maturity. The additional cash received reduces the effective cost of borrowing to a rate below 5%. The investor also earns less than 5% because he pays $1,100 but receives only $1,000 at maturity.

There is an inverse relationship between current market rates and bond prices as illustrated by Exhibit 14.2.

EXHIBIT 14.2 Bond Issues: The Relationship between Stated Rates and Market Rates

Stated rate	=	Market rate	Bonds issued at	Par
Stated rate	<	Market rate	Bonds issued at	Discount
Stated rate	>	Market rate	Bonds issued at	Premium

Bond Price Quotes. Bond prices are often quoted as a percentage of face or par value. The quoted price of a bond issued at par value is 100%. The quote for a bond issued at a discount is less than 100%, and the quote for a bond issued at a premium is greater than 100%.

Exhibit 14.3 presents an excerpt from ***Johnson & Johnson's*** January 1, 2017, debt footnote disclosure in which it reported $24,146 million in long-term debt, including $1,704 million payable currently. Excluding the debt paid or newly issued, when comparing the carrying values of the debt issues from 2015 to 2016, there are only minor differences, indicating that the outstanding debt was issued at close to its face value. The changes in carrying values from 2015 to 2016 indicate that ***Johnson & Johnson*** issued debt at a discount or premium, and the changes are due to the amortization of discount or premium.

For each bond issue, ***Johnson & Johnson*** discloses the stated rate at the beginning of each debt issue, the year of maturity, the current carrying value, and the effective interest rate at issuance. For example, the fifth issue listed refers to notes with a stated rate of 1.125%, maturing in 2017. The effective interest rate at issuance was 1.15%.

EXHIBIT 14.3 Long-Term Debt Disclosure, ***Johnson & Johnson***, Financial Statement, January 1, 2017

NOTE 7: Borrowings [Excerpt]
The components of long-term debt are as follows:

(Dollars in Millions)	2016	Effective Rate %	2015	Effective Rate %
2.15% Notes due 2016	$ —	—	$ 900	2.22
3 month LIBOR+0.07% FRN due 2016	—	—	800	0.48
0.70% Notes due 2016	—	—	398	0.74
5.55% Debentures due 2017	1,000	5.55	1,000	5.55
1.125% Notes due 2017	699	1.15	700	1.15
5.15% Debentures due 2018	899	5.18	899	5.15
1.65% Notes due 2018	600	1.70	602	1.70
4.75% Notes due 2019 (IB Euro 1.0449)(2)/(IB Euro 1.0882)(3)	1,041(2)	5.83	1,085(3)	5.83
1.875% Notes due 2019	499	1.93	502	1.93
0.89% Notes due 2019	299	1.20	—	—
1.125% Notes due 2019	699	1.13	—	—
3% Zero Coupon Convertible Subordinated Debentures due 2020	84	3.00	137	3.00
2.95% Debentures due 2020	546	3.15	545	3.15
3.55% Notes due 2021	447	3.67	448	3.67
2.45% Notes due 2021	348	2.48	349	2.48
1.65% Notes due 2021	997	1.65	—	—
0.250% Notes due 2022 (IB Euro 1.0449)(2)	1,041(2)	0.26	—	—
6.73% Debentures due 2023	249	6.73	250	6.73
3.375% Notes due 2023	807	3.17	811	3.17
2.05% Notes due 2023	497	2.09	—	—
0.650% Notes due 2024 (750 MM Euro 1.0449)(2)	779(2)	0.68	—	—
5.50% Notes due 2024 (500MM GBP 1.2237)(2)/(500 MM GBP 1.4818)(3)	605(2)	6.75	737(3)	6.75
2.45% Notes due 2026	1,989	2.47	—	—
1.150% Notes due 2028 (750 MM Euro 1.0449)(2)	775(2)	1.21	—	—
6.95% Notes due 2029	296	7.14	297	7.14
4.95% Debentures due 2033	497	4.95	500	4.95
4.375% Notes due 2033	857	4.24	864	4.24
1.650% Notes due 2035 (1.5B Euro 1.0449)(2)	1,549(2)	1.68	—	—
3.55% Notes due 2036	987	3.59	—	—
5.95% Notes due 2037	990	5.99	996	5.99
5.85% Debentures due 2038	695	5.85	700	5.86
4.50% Debentures due 2040	537	4.63	540	4.63
4.85% Notes due 2041	296	4.89	298	4.89
4.50% Notes due 2043	495	4.52	499	4.52

Continued

(Dollars in Millions)	2016	Effective Rate %	2015	Effective Rate %
3.70% Notes due 2046	1,970	3.74	—	—
Other	77	—	104	—
Subtotal	**24,146**[(4)]	**3.33%**[(1)]	**14,961**[(4)]	**4.06**[(1)]
Less current portion	1,704		2,104	
Total long-term debt	**$22,442**		**$12,857**	

(1) Weighted average effective rate.

(2) Translation rate at January 1, 2017.

(3) Translation rate at January 3, 2016.

(4) The excess of the fair value over the carrying value of debt was $1.6 billion in 2016 and $1.7 billion in 2015.

Source: Financial statements from Johnson & Johnson Company's Annual Report, 2016. http://files.shareholder.com/downloads/JNJ/3809936545x0xS200406-17-6/200406/filing.pdf

3 Demonstrate accounting for bonds issued at par or at a discount or premium, including computation of the bond issue price, interest expense, and amortization of the discount or premium using the effective interest rate method.

Accounting for the Initial and Subsequent Measurement of Bonds Payable

We first discuss the accounting for bonds issued at par value followed by accounting for bonds issued at a premium or discount.

Bonds Issued at Par

Accounting for bonds issued at par is straightforward: When issuing the bonds, the corporation increases both the liability account and the cash account. Throughout the life of the bond, the corporation records the interest payments and, if necessary, makes adjusting entries to record interest accruals. At the maturity of the bond, the corporation records the payment of the face value of the bond and removes the liability from its accounts. Example 14.6 illustrates accounting for a bond payable issued at face value.

EXAMPLE 14.6 Accounting for Bond Payable: Face Value

PROBLEM: On January 1, 2018, Ruffin Corporation issued $40,000 par value, 4%, 4-year bonds that mature on December 31, 2021. Ruffin will pay interest quarterly on March 31, June 30, September 30, and December 31. The company's fiscal year ends on December 31. What is the issue price of this bond assuming that the market rate of interest is 4%? What is the journal entry to record the bond issue? What are the journal entries to record the first year's interest? What entry is made at maturity?

SOLUTION: Because the stated interest rate on the bond equals the market rate when the bonds are issued, Ruffin sells the bonds at the $40,000 par value.

At maturity, Ruffin will pay bondholders the face value of the bond, $40,000. Ruffin will also make the interest payment to bondholders every March 31, June 30, September 30, and December 31 over the 4-year period. We calculate the interest payment as:

$$\text{Interest Payment} = \text{Face Value} \times \text{Annual Interest Rate} \times \text{Time Period}$$
$$= \$40,000 \times 4\% \times 1/4 = \$400$$

The journal entry to record the bond issuance is as follows:

Account	***January 1, 2018***	
Cash	40,000	
Bonds Payable		40,000

Interest for the first year is recorded as follows:

Account	March 31, June 30, September 30, and December 31, 2018	
Interest Expense	400	
Cash		400

The entries required at maturity on December 31, 2021, follow. The journal entry to record the last interest payment and interest expense on December 31, 2021, also follows.

Account	December 31, 2021	
Interest Expense	400	
Cash		400

The entry to record the full repayment of principal follows.

Account	December 31, 2021	
Bonds Payable	40,000	
Cash		40,000

Overview of Bonds Payable Issued at a Discount or Premium

A bond's issue price always equals the sum of the present value of the future cash flows related to the bond discounted at the market rate of interest. Specifically, the bond issue price is the sum of:

- The present value of the par value (the present value of an amount of $1)
- The present value of the interest payments (the present value of an ordinary annuity)

Interest expense, the cost of borrowing for the period, composes both the cash interest payments and the amortization of any bond premium or discount. Because a bond discount occurs when the market interest rate is greater than the stated interest rate, the discount represents *increased* interest expense for the corporation over the life of the bond. In the case of a bond premium, the market interest rate is lower than the stated rate, so the premium represents *decreased* interest expense over the life of the bond.

To summarize, there are two primary effects of amortization.

1. Discount (premium) amortization increases (decreases) the interest expense so that the corporation's effective cost of borrowing is brought up to (brought down to) the higher (lower) market rate.
2. Discount (premium) amortization reduces the discount (premium) and increases (decreases) the carrying value of the bonds until the carrying value is brought up to (brought down to) the par value at the maturity date.

For example, if a company issues bonds with a par value of $10,000 for $8,000, it would record a discount of $2,000. The $2,000 discount represents an increased interest expense for the corporation over the life of the bond. In other words, the corporation borrows and has the use of $8,000 today, but it must repay the full $10,000 at maturity. At maturity, the company reports the bond at its face value.

There are two methods of amortization: the *effective interest method* and the *straight-line method*. We discuss the effective interest method next and the straight-line method in Appendix A.

The Effective Interest Rate Method of Amortization

The **effective interest rate method** computes interest expense by multiplying the *historical market interest rate* by the beginning balance of the debt. The **historical market interest rate** is the market interest rate in effect on the date the bonds are issued determined based on the price received for the bond. The effective interest rate method is theoretically correct for two reasons:

1. The interest expense properly reflects the effective cost of borrowing at the market rate in effect when the company originally issued the debt (i.e., at the historical market rate).
2. At any point in time, the carrying value of the debt is equal to the present value of the remaining future cash flows discounted at the historical market rate of interest.

The cash or coupon interest payments are the face value of the bond multiplied by the stated interest rate. The amount of discount or premium amortized or allocated to each period is the difference between the effective total interest and the cash interest.

The effective interest rate method of amortization equations are:

$$\text{Effective Interest Expense} = \text{Historical Market Rate} \times \text{Carrying Value of the Bond at the Beginning of the Period} \quad (14.1)$$

$$\text{Discount/Premium Amortization} = \text{Effective Interest Expense} - \text{Cash Interest Paid} \quad (14.2)$$

Accounting for Bonds Payable Issued at a Premium

In the case of a premium, the company:

- Records the increase in cash and the increase in the bond payable account when issuing the bonds.
- Credits the bond premium (an adjunct account to the bond payable account).
- Records the interest expense for every interest payment and reduces the bond premium account.

Example 14.7 illustrates issuing bonds at a premium using the effective interest rate method of amortization.

EXAMPLE 14.7

Accounting for Bonds Payable Issued at a Premium: Effective Interest Method

PROBLEM: On January 1, 2018, Ruffin Corporation issued $40,000 par value, 4%, 4-year bonds that mature on December 31, 2021. Ruffin will pay interest semiannually on June 30 and December 31. The company's fiscal year ends on December 31. What is the issue price of this bond assuming that the market rate of interest is 2%? What is the journal entry to record the issuance? Prepare an amortization table using the effective interest rate method. What journal entries are required to record interest expense for the first year? Prepare the journal entry to record the maturity of the bonds. Prepare the t-accounts for the bond payable and bond premium accounts for the life of the bond.

SOLUTION: Because the stated interest rate is higher than the market rate when the bonds are issued, Ruffin issued the bonds at a premium. The terms to compute the future payments to bondholders are:

- **Face value** = $40,000
- **Stated annual interest rate** = 4%
- **Historical market annual interest rate** = 2%

- **Interest payment period** = semiannually on June 30 and December 31
- **Maturity date** = December 31, 2021

At maturity, Ruffin will pay bondholders the face value of the bond, $40,000. Every June 30 and December 31 for 4 years, Ruffin will also make the interest payment to bondholders. We calculate the interest payment as:

$$\text{Interest Payment} = \text{Face Value} \times \text{Annual Interest Rate} \times \text{Time Period}$$
$$= \$40{,}000 \times 4\% \times 1/2 = \$800$$

We next determine the bond issue price, which is equal to the sum of the present value of the future cash flows. The present value includes the maturity amount of $40,000 as well as the semiannual interest payments of $800. We use the semiannual market rate of 1% (2% / 2) and N = 8 (4 years × 2).

	N	I/Y	PV	PMT	FV	Excel Formula
Given	8	1.00%		−800	−40,000	
Solve for PV			**43,061**			= PV(0.01,8,−800,−40000)

The bond issue price is $43,061 and, thus, the premium is $3,061 ($43,061 − $40,000). The journal entry includes a premium account to record the bond issuance as follows:

Account	***Entry at Issuance (January 1, 2018)***	
Cash	43,061	
Bonds Payable		40,000
Premium on Bonds Payable		3,061

We next prepare the amortization table with the effective interest rate method using Equations 14.1 and 14.2 to compute the effective interest expense and the premium amortization, respectively.

Amortization Table under the Effective Interest Rate Method

Date	**2% Cash Interest (a)**	**1% Effective Interest (b) = 1% × Prior (d)**	**Premium Amortization (c) = (a) − (b)**	**Carrying Value (d) = Prior (d) − (c)**
January 1, 2018				$43,061
June 30, 2018	$ 800	$ 431	$ 369	42,692
December 31, 2018	800	427	373	42,319
June 30, 2019	800	423	377	41,942
December 31, 2019	800	419	381	41,561
June 30, 2020	800	416	384	41,177
December 31, 2020	800	412	388	40,789
June 30, 2021	800	408	392	40,397
December 31, 2021	800	403*	397*	40,000
TOTALS	$6,400	$3,339	$3,061	

* Adjusted due to rounding errors.

We present the journal entry to record the first semiannual interest payment on June 30, 2018.

Account	***June 30, 2018***	
Interest Expense	431	
Premium on Bonds Payable	369	
Cash		800

Continued

We present the journal entry to record the second semiannual interest payment on December 31, 2018.

Account	December 31, 2018	
Interest Expense	427	
Premium on Bonds Payable	373	
Cash		800

Note that the cash interest paid exceeds the effective interest. The amount of the premium amortized reduces the carrying value of the debt rather than increasing interest expense.

Ruffin pays for the bonds at maturity and makes the following entry.

Account	December 31, 2021	
Bonds Payable	40,000	
Cash		40,000

The t-accounts for the bond payable and bond premium accounts are as follows:

Bond Payable			Premium on Bond Payable		
January 1, 2018		40,000	January 1, 2018		3,061
			June 30, 2018	369	
			December 31, 2018	373	
			June 30, 2019	377	
			December 31, 2019	381	
			June 30, 2020	384	
			December 31, 2020	388	
			June 30, 2021	392	
December 31, 2021	40,000		December 31, 2021	397	
Balance		0			0

Accounting for Bonds Payable Issued at a Discount

In the case of a discount, the company:

- Records the increase in cash and the increase in the bond payable account when issuing the bonds
- Debits the bond discount (a contra-account to the bond payable account)
- Records the interest expense for every interest payment and reduces the bond discount account

Example 14.8 illustrates this process.

EXAMPLE 14.8 Accounting for Bonds Payable Issued at a Discount: Effective Interest Method

PROBLEM: On January 1, 2018, Ruffin Corporation issued $40,000 par value, 4%, 4-year bonds that mature on December 31, 2021. Ruffin will pay interest semiannually on June 30 and December 31. On the date that Ruffin issued the bonds, the market rate of interest was 6%. The company's fiscal year ends on December 31. What is the issue price of this bond? Prepare the journal entry to record the issuance. Prepare an amortization schedule over the 4-year period using the effective interest rate method. Prepare the journal entries to record the interest entries for the first year, the journal entry to record the payment of the bonds at maturity, and the t-accounts for the bond payable and bond discount accounts for the life of the bond.

SOLUTION: Because the stated interest rate was lower than the market rate when Ruffin issued the bonds, the bonds were sold at a discount. The terms to compute the future payments to bondholders are:

- **Face value** = \$40,000
- **Stated annual interest rate** = 4%
- **Historical market annual interest rate** = 6%
- **Interest payment period** = semiannually on June 30 and December 31
- **Maturity date** = December 31, 2021

At maturity, Ruffin will pay bondholders the face value of the bond, \$40,000. Ruffin will also make the interest payment to bondholders semiannually every June 30 and December 31, for the next 4 years. The semiannual interest payment is computed as follows:

$$\text{Interest Payment} = \text{Face Value} \times \text{Annual Interest Rate} \times \text{Time Period}$$
$$= \$40{,}000 \times 4\% \times {}^{1}/_{2} = \$800$$

We next determine the bond issue price. This present value includes both the face amount of \$40,000 and the semiannual interest payments of \$800. We use the semiannual market rate because the bonds are priced to yield the market. Therefore, I/Y = 3% (6%/2) and N = 8 (4 years × 2).

	N	I/Y	PV	PMT	FV	Excel Formula
Given	8	3.00%		−800	−40,000	
Solve for PV			**37,192**			=PV(0.03, 8, −800, −40000)

The bond issue price is \$37,192 and, thus, the discount is \$2,808 (\$40,000 − \$37,192). The journal entry to record the bond issuance includes a discount account as follows:

Account	***Entry at Issuance (January 1, 2018)***	
Cash	37,192	
Discount on Bonds Payable	2,808	
Bonds Payable		40,000

To prepare an amortization table, we start with the bond issue price and use the effective interest rate method. Refer to Equations 14.1 and 14.2 for the effective interest expense and the discount amortization, respectively.

Amortization Table under the Effective Interest Rate Method

Date	**2% Cash Interest (a)**	**3% Effective Interest (b) = 3% × Prior (d)**	**Discount Amortization (c) = (b) − (a)**	**Carrying Value (d) = Prior (d) + (c)**
January 1, 2018				\$ 37,192
June 30, 2018	\$ 800	\$ 1,116	\$ 316	37,508
December 31, 2018	800	1,125	325	37,833
June 30, 2019	800	1,135	335	38,168
December 31, 2019	800	1,145	345	38,513
June 30, 2020	800	1,155	355	38,868
December 31, 2020	800	1,166	366	39,234
June 30, 2021	800	1,177	377	39,611
December 31, 2021	800	1,189*	389*	40,000
TOTALS	\$6,400	\$9,208	\$2,808	

* Adjusted due to rounding errors.

Continued

Next we present the journal entry to record the first semiannual interest payment during 2018 from the amortization table.

Account	June 30, 2018	
Interest Expense	1,116	
Cash		800
Discount on Bonds Payable		316

The journal entry to record the second semiannual interest payment during 2018 from the amortization table follows.

Account	December 31, 2018	
Interest Expense	1,125	
Cash		800
Discount on Bonds Payable		325

Note that the effective interest expense exceeds the cash interest paid. The difference is the amortization of the bond discount, which increases the carrying value of the debt.

Ruffin pays for the bonds at maturity and makes the following entry.

Account	December 31, 2021	
Bonds Payable	40,000	
Cash		40,000

The t-accounts for the bond payable and bond discount accounts are as follows:

Bond Payable			
		January 1, 2018	40,000
December 31, 2021	40,000		
		Balance	0

Discount on Bond Payable			
January 1, 2018	2,808		
		June 30, 2018	316
		December 31, 2018	325
		June 30, 2019	335
		December 31, 2019	345
		June 30, 2020	355
		December 31, 2020	366
		June 30, 2021	377
		December 31, 2021	389
			0

Interest Accrual. Often the cycle of interest payments does not correspond to the issuer's year-end. In that case, the company must accrue interest before preparing financial statements as shown in Example 14.9.

EXAMPLE 14.9 Accounting for Bonds Payable Issued at a Discount: Effective Interest Method with Interest Accrual

PROBLEM: On August 1, 2018, QuarterPound Corporation issued $100,000 par value, 6%, 3-year bonds that mature on July 31, 2021. QuarterPound will pay interest annually on July 31. On the date that QuarterPound issued the bonds, the market rate of interest was 8%. The company's fiscal year ends December 31. What is the issue price of this bond? Prepare the journal entry to record the issuance. Prepare an amortization schedule over the 3-year period using the effective interest rate method. Prepare the journal entries to record the bonds through July 31, 2019.

SOLUTION: Because the stated interest rate is lower than the market rate when QuarterPound issued the bonds, the bonds were sold at a discount. The terms to compute the future payments to bondholders are:

- **Face value** = $100,000
- **Stated annual interest rate** = 6%
- **Historical market annual interest rate** = 8%
- **Interest payment period** = annually on July 31
- **Maturity date** = July 31, 2021

At maturity, QuarterPound will pay bondholders the face value of the bond, $100,000. QuarterPound will also make the interest payment to bondholders annually every July 31 for the next 3 years. The annual interest payment is computed as follows:

$$\text{Interest Payment} = \text{Face Value} \times \text{Annual Interest Rate} \times \text{Time Period}$$
$$= \$100{,}000 \times 6\% \times 1 = \$6{,}000$$

To determine the bond issue price, take the present value of the face amount and the annual interest payments. We use the annual market rate because the bonds are priced to yield the market. Therefore, I/Y = 8% and N = 3.

	N	I/Y	PV	PMT	FV	Excel Formula
Given	3	8.00%		−6,000	−100,000	
Solve for PV			**94,846**			= PV(0.08,3,−6000,−100000)

The bond issue price is $94,846 and, thus, the discount is $5,154 ($100,000 − $94,846). The journal entry to record the bond issuance includes a discount account as follows:

Account	***Entry at Issuance***	
Cash	94,846	
Discount on Bonds Payable	5,154	
Bonds Payable		100,000

To prepare an amortization table, we start with the bond issue price and use the effective interest rate method. Refer to Equations 14.1 and 14.2 for the effective interest expense and the discount amortization, respectively.

Amortization Table under the Effective Interest Rate Method

Date	**6% Cash Interest (a)**	**8% Effective Interest (b) = 8% × Prior (d)**	**Discount Amortization (c) = (b) − (a)**	**Carrying Value (d) = Prior (d) + (c)**
At issuance				$ 94,846
July 31, 2019	$ 6,000	$ 7,588	$1,588	96,434
July 31, 2020	6,000	7,715	1,715	98,149
July 31, 2021	6,000	7,851*	1,851*	100,000
TOTALS	$18,000	$23,154	$5,154	

* Adjusted due to rounding errors.

Because QuarterPound will prepare financial statements on December 31 of each year, it will accrue interest and amortize the discount on that date. On December 31, 2018,

Continued

QuarterPound will record interest expense of $3,162 for 5 months ($7,588 × 5/12) and interest payable of $2,500 for 5 months ($6,000 × 5/12). The entry will also reduce the discount account by $662 for 5 months of amortization ($1,588 × 5/12).

Account	December 31, 2018	
Interest Expense	3,162	
Interest Payable		2,500
Discount on Bonds Payable		662

At the first interest payment on July 31, 2019, QuarterPound will remove the interest payable and record interest expense of $4,426 for the 7 months in the current year ($7,588 × 7/12) and amortization of the discount of $926 for 7 months ($1,588 × 7/12). It will also record the $6,000 cash payment.

Account	July 31, 2019	
Interest Expense	4,426	
Interest Payable	2,500	
Discount on Bonds Payable		926
Cash		6,000

Zero-Coupon Bonds. **Zero-coupon bonds** are bonds that do not pay cash interest because the coupon rate, or stated rate, is zero. Although there is no cash interest, the holder will receive the face value at maturity. The difference between the issue price and the face value represents interest expense over the life of the bond. Zero-coupon bonds are typically issued at significant discounts because the market interest rate is always higher than the zero-coupon rate. Accounting for these bonds is a special case of bonds issued at a discount as shown in Example 14.10.

EXAMPLE 14.10 Accounting for Bonds Payable: Zero-Coupon Bond

PROBLEM: Assume that Ceros Company issued a $100,000 face value, 5-year, zero-coupon bond on January 1 of the current year. The current market interest rate is 4%. What is the bond issue price? Prepare an amortization table using the effective interest rate method. What are the journal entries to record the issuance and interest for the first year?

SOLUTION: The bond issue price equals the present value of the future cash flows. The only cash flow is the face amount of $100,000. Compounding is annual; therefore, I/Y = 4% and N = 5.

	N	I/Y	PV	PMT	FV	Excel Formula
Given	5	4.00%		0	−100,000	
Solve for PV			**82,193**			=PV(0.04,5,0,−100000)

The journal entry to record the bond issuance includes a discount account as follows:

Account	Entry at Issuance	
Cash	82,193	
Discount on Bonds Payable	17,807	
Bonds Payable		100,000

Ceros accrues interest expense of 4% of the carrying value each year. We show the Cash Interest column in the following amortization table to highlight the fact that no interest payments are made and to be consistent with other amortization tables.

Year	0% Cash Interest (a)	4% Effective Interest (b) = 4% × Prior (d)	Discount Amortization (c) = (b) − (a)	Carrying Value (d) = Prior (d) + (c)
At issuance				$ 82,193
Year 1	$0	$3,288	$3,288	85,481
Year 2	0	3,419	3,419	88,900
Year 3	0	3,556	3,556	92,456
Year 4	0	3,698	3,698	96,154
Year 5	0	3,846	3,846	100,000
	0			

We present the following journal entry to record the first year's interest expense from line 1 of the amortization table.

Account	*December 31*	
Interest Expense	3,288	
Discount on Bonds Payable		3,288

Recording Bonds Payable: IFRS

IFRS prefers using the *net method* to record bonds payable. Under the **net method**, the discount is subtracted from the face value or the premium is added to the face value without using a separate discount or premium account. This method results in the same carrying value for bonds payable as under the U.S. GAAP.

4 Explain and illustrate accounting for bonds issued between interest payment dates.

Bonds Issued between Interest Dates

Bonds are not always sold on their interest payment dates; market interest rate fluctuations or a depressed bond market can delay the bond issue. When bonds are sold between interest dates, the buyer must pay the issuer the amount of accrued interest from the prior interest date or date on the bonds to the date of the bond issue. The issuer then returns this amount to the buyer when paying the full interest on the next interest date.

To illustrate, assume that a company sold a bond dated January 1, 2018, on May 1, 2018. The bond pays $12,000 interest every January 1 and June 30. Because the company sold the bond on May 1, the bondholders have earned only 2 months' interest by the first interest payment on June 30, 2018. However, because of the significant number of bondholders, the company will not allocate interest to individual investors who acquired the bonds on different dates. As an alternative, the company collects the accrued interest on the issue date from the purchaser and then pays the full 6 months' interest on the next interest payment date. The investor will pay the corporation 4 months' interest, or $8,000, on the date of purchase, May 1 ($12,000 × 4/6). However, on June 30, the bondholder will receive the full 6 months' interest of $12,000. As a result, the bondholder earns interest equal to $4,000, which represents the earnings over the 2 months she held the bond ($12,000 × 2/6). That is, she paid $8,000 but received $12,000 for a net interest income of $4,000. Example 14.11 illustrates accounting for bonds sold between interest dates at par.

EXAMPLE 14.11 Bonds Sold between Interest Dates at Par

PROBLEM: Nelson Company issued $400,000 par value, 5-year, 3% bonds on June 1, 2018. The bonds are dated January 1, 2018, and pay interest semiannually each June 30 and December 31. The bonds are sold at par plus accrued interest because they are sold between interest dates. The company's fiscal year ends on December 31. Prepare the journal entries required to issue the bonds on June 1, 2018, and record the first interest payment on June 30, 2018.

SOLUTION: The semiannual interest is $6,000 computed as follows:

$$\$400{,}000 \times 3\% \times {}^{1}/_{2} = \$6{,}000$$

On the date of the bond issue, there are 5 months of accrued interest from the date of the bonds (January 1) to the date of sale (June 1). As a result, there is $5,000 accrued interest on the issue date ($6,000 × 5/6). The bonds are issued at par plus accrued interest or $405,000 ($400,000 par + $5,000 accrued interest).

Account	**June 1, 2018**	
Cash	405,000	
Bonds Payable		400,000
Interest Payable		5,000

Nelson makes the following journal entry on the first interest date:

Account	**June 30, 2018**	
Interest Expense	1,000	
Interest Payable	5,000	
Cash		6,000

The interest expense for the corporation is $1,000, or 1 month's interest for the period in which the bond is outstanding (i.e., $6,000 × 1/6). Although the corporation paid $6,000 on June 30, it received $5,000 from the investor on the date of sale.

Example 14.12 illustrates accounting for bonds issued at a discount between interest dates.

EXAMPLE 14.12 Bonds Sold between Interest Dates at a Discount

PROBLEM: Martino Motors Company issued $800,000 par value, 6%, 5-year bonds dated January 1, 2018. The bonds pay interest semiannually each June 30 and December 31. Because of an unusual increase in market rates of interest, Martino delayed the bond issue until March 1, 2018, when the market rate of interest was 8%. Determine the bond issue price on March 1, 2018. Prepare an amortization table for the bond issue using the effective interest rate method. Prepare the journal entries required on the date of issue and on the first two interest dates in 2018, June 30 and December 31.

SOLUTION: The bonds are sold between interest dates and, as a result, the buyer will pay the seller the accrued interest from the date of the bonds to the day the bonds are sold. In this case, Martino delayed the bond issue for 2 months (January 1 to March 1).

$$\text{Interest Payment} = \$800{,}000 \times 6\% \times {}^{1}/_{2} = \$24{,}000 \text{ Semiannually}$$

The monthly interest payment is $4,000 ($24,000 / 6). As a result, the buyer will pay 2 months' interest, or $8,000, on the date of purchase. Then, on June 30, the first interest payment date, the buyer will receive the full $24,000. The difference, $16,000, is the net interest paid by the corporation for the 4 months the bonds are outstanding (March 1 to June 30).

To determine the bond issue price, we must first compute the value on June 30, 2018, and then discount this amount back to March 1, 2018, the date of issue.

To determine the present value of the bonds on June 30, discount the relevant cash flows for 9 periods. Because June 30 is the first interest period of the 10 semiannual interest periods (5 years × 2), only 9 remain. The semiannual market rate is 4% (8%/2).

	N	I/Y	PV	PMT	FV	Excel Formula
Given	9	4.00%		−24,000	−800,000	
Solve for PV			**740,517**			=PV(0.04,9,−24000,−800000)

On June 30, the bonds will also pay the investor 4 months' interest, or $16,000 ($4,000×4 months). Therefore, the total cash flow to be received on June 30 is $756,517 ($740,517 + $16,000). We discount this amount back to the date of issue to determine the selling price. Consider the $756,517 as a future value and discount it back to March 1, 2018. Treat the 4-month period as a single period to determine an interest rate for it. That rate is 2.667% computed as follows:

Interest Rate for a 4-Month Period = 4% × 4 Months/6 Months = 2.667%

The present value of the bonds on the date of issue is $736,865.

	N	I/Y	PV	PMT	FV	Excel Formula
Given	1	2.667%		0	756,517	
Solve for PV			**(736,865)**			=PV(0.02667,1,0,756517)

The bonds are issued at a discount:

Par value	$ 800,000
Bond issue price	(736,865)
Discount on bonds payable	$ 63,135

The buyer will also pay the seller the $8,000 accrued interest on the date of purchase. So, the total cash received by the corporation on the date of issue is $744,865 ($736,865 + $8,000).

The amortization table for the bond issue follows. Note that Period 1 is a single period from March 1 to June 30.

Date	3% Cash Interest (a)	4% Effective Interest (b) = 4% × Prior (d)	Discount Amortization (c) = (b) − (a)	Carrying Value (d) = Prior (d) + (c)
March 1, 2018				$736,865
June 30, 2018	$ 16,000[(a)]	$ 19,650[(b)]	$ 3,650	740,515
December 31, 2018	24,000	29,621	5,621	746,136
June 30, 2019	24,000	29,845	5,845	751,981
December 31, 2019	24,000	30,079	6,079	758,060
June 30, 2020	24,000	30,322	6,322	764,382
December 31, 2020	24,000	30,575	6,575	770,957
June 30, 2021	24,000	30,838	6,838	777,795
December 31, 2021	24,000	31,112	7,112	784,907
June 30, 2022	24,000	31,396	7,396	792,303
December 31, 2022	24,000	31,697*	7,697*	800,000
TOTAL	$232,000	$ 295,135	$ 63,135	

* Adjusted due to rounding errors.

(a) The first period's interest is for 4 months and is computed as follows: $24,000 × 4/6 = $16,000.

(b) The effective interest for the first period is computed as follows: 4% × 4/6 × $736,865 = $19,650.

Continued

The remainder of the table is constructed as a normal amortization table. For example, the second interest period is equal to $740,515 × 4% = $29,621.

On the date of the bond issue, there are 2 months' accrued interest from the date of the bonds (January 1) to the date of sale (March 1). As a result, there is $8,000 accrued interest on the issue date ($4,000 per month × 2 months). The bonds are issued at a discount plus accrued interest, or $744,865 ($800,000 par − $63,135 discount + $8,000 accrued interest).

Account	March 1, 2018	
Cash	744,865	
Discount on Bonds Payable	63,135	
Bonds Payable		800,000
Interest Payable		8,000

Martino Motors makes the following journal entry on the first interest period:

Account	June 30, 2018	
Interest Expense	19,650	
Interest Payable	8,000	
Discount on Bonds Payable		3,650
Cash		24,000

Note that the interest expense for the first period (March 1 to June 30) is $19,650. Martino Motors makes the following journal entry on the second interest payment date:

Account	December 31, 2018	
Interest Expense	29,621	
Discount on Bonds Payable		5,621
Cash		24,000

5 Discuss and illustrate the accounting for bond issue costs.

Bond Issue Costs

When seeking to raise capital via bond issues, companies must consider costs related to printing, accounting fees, legal fees, and underwriting. Under both U.S. GAAP and IFRS, bond issue costs are deducted from the carrying value of the bond payable (by increasing the discount or decreasing the premium) and are included when determining the effective interest rate on the debt. The accounting treatment recognizes that bond issue costs reduce a company's cash proceeds, effectively decreasing the carrying value of the bonds, which means that borrowing costs are higher. Accounting for bond issue costs is illustrated in Example 14.13.

EXAMPLE 14.13 Bond Issue Costs

PROBLEM: On January 1, 2018, Compex Corp. issued $1,000,000 par value, 6%, 3-year bonds when the market rate of interest was 7%. Interest is payable annually each December 31. Compex incurred bond issue costs of $24,000. What is the journal entry when Compex issued the bonds? Prepare the amortization table for the bonds.

SOLUTION: Because the stated interest rate is less than the market interest rate, Compex issued the bonds at a discount. The present value of the bonds is $973,757.

	N	I/Y	PV	PMT	FV	Excel Formula
Given	3	7.00%		−60,000	−1,000,000	
Solve For PV			**973,757**			=PV(0.07,3,−60000,−1000000)

The bond issue costs increase the discount by an additional $24,000. Thus, the total discount is the discount attributable to the difference in the stated and effective interest rates ($26,243) and the issue costs ($24,000). The journal entry follows:

Account	***January 1, 2018***	
Cash	949,757	
Discount on Bonds Payable	50,243	
Bonds Payable		1,000,000

	N	I/Y	PV	PMT	FV	Excel Formula
Given	3		949,757	−60,000	−1,000,000	
Solve For RATE		**7.9478%**				=RATE(3,−60000,949757,−1000000)

We then use the 7.9478% interest rate to prepare the amortization table.

	6.0% Cash Interest (a)	**7.9478% Effective Interest (b) = 7.9478% × Prior (d)**	**Discount Amortization (c) = (b)−(a)**	**Carrying Value (d) = Prior (d) + (c)**
January 1, 2018				$ 949,757
December 31, 2018	$ 60,000	$ 75,485	$15,485	965,242
December 31, 2019	60,000	76,716	16,716	981,958
December 31, 2020	60,000	78,042*	18,042*	1,000,000
TOTAL	$180,000	$230,243	$50,243	

* Adjusted due to rounding errors.

6 Determine the accounting for bonds payable at early retirement.

Early Retirement of Bonds Payable

As noted earlier, derecognition of bonds payable involves removing the debt from an entity's balance sheet. A company derecognizes its debt when it pays the bonds at maturity, retires the debt early (before maturity), restructures an existing debt agreement, or converts the bonds into common or preferred stock. We have illustrated derecognition at maturity several times throughout this chapter. In this section, we examine the accounting for bond derecognition upon early retirement.

Companies often *extinguish* debt before maturity to take advantage of lower market rates of interest. In this case, the debtor retires high-cost debt and replaces or refinances this debt with lower-cost obligations. Alternatively, a company in an excess cash position may lower interest costs by using the excess cash to retire debt. When a company retires bonds early, it is referred to as a **debt extinguishment**. The accounting is more complex for extinguishments than it is for debt derecognized at maturity.[3] Debt retirement generally results in a gain or loss on early retirement. A company determines the gain or loss by taking the difference between the net carrying value of the debt and the retirement price as shown in Equation 14.3.

$$\text{Gain (Loss) on Early Extinguishment} = \text{Net Carrying Value of the Debt} - \text{Retirement Price} \quad (14.3)$$

There is a gain if the retirement price is less than the net carrying value and a loss if the company pays more than the net carrying value to retire the debt.

[3]For most of the relevant authoritative literature for this topic, see FASB ASC 470-50-45, *Debt – Modifications and Extinguishments* for U.S. GAAP and IASB, *International Financial Reporting Standard 7*, "Financial Instruments: Disclosures" (London, UK: International Accounting Standards Board, Revised), Paragraph 10, for IFRS.

Before computing the gain or loss on the early extinguishment, the company must amortize any discount or premium up to the retirement date. It includes any fees incurred in retiring the debt in the computation of the gain or loss. Example 14.14 provides an example of accounting for the early extinguishment of bonds.

EXAMPLE 14.14 Early Extinguishment of Bonds

PROBLEM: As noted in Example 14.8, on January 1, 2018, Ruffin Corporation issued $40,000 par value, 4%, 4-year bonds that mature on December 31, 2021. The market rate of interest was 6%. Ruffin pays interest semiannually on June 30 and December 31. Assume that Ruffin decides to retire the debt on December 31, 2019, for $36,000. What gain or loss should Ruffin report in its 2019 financial statements? What is the journal entry to record the derecognition?

SOLUTION: We can use the amortization table in Example 14.8 to determine the present value of $38,513 for the bonds as of December 31, 2019.

The gain or loss on early retirement is then computed as follows:

Present value at retirement date (net carrying value)	$ 38,513
Retirement price	(36,000)
Gain on early retirement of debt	$ 2,513

There is a gain on early retirement because the company paid less than the net carrying value to retire its debt.

Ruffin makes the following journal entry to record the early retirement of debt.

Account	Entry at Early Retirement	
Bonds Payable	40,000	
Discount on Bonds Payable		1,487
Gain on Early Retirement of Debt		2,513
Cash		36,000

The balance in the discount on bonds payable account is computed as the par value ($40,000) less the present value of $38,513.

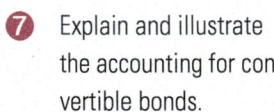

7 Explain and illustrate the accounting for convertible bonds.

Convertible Bonds

Convertible bonds are financial instruments that enable the holder to convert the bonds into a specified number of shares of common stock or preferred shares. When the bondholder elects to convert bonds into common or preferred stock, the company derecognizes the debt. The number of equity shares received on conversion is based on the exchange ratio included in the bond indenture (e.g., each bond converts into 25 shares of common stock). Convertible bonds are one type of **hybrid security**, which is a security that possesses characteristics of both debt and equity.[4]

Corporations issue convertible bonds as a vehicle to ultimately raise equity capital in a practice called back-door equity financing when equity prices are temporarily depressed and the firm needs to raise a required amount of capital. For example, assume that a company needs to raise $30,000,000 in new financing. If the current market price of the company's equity is $6 per share, the company would have to issue an additional 5,000,000 shares of stock (i.e., $30,000,000/$6 per share = 5,000,000 shares). As an alternative, the company could raise

[4]For most of the relevant authoritative literature for this topic, see FASB ASC 470-20, *Debt with Conversion and Other Options* for U.S. GAAP and IASC, *International Accounting Standard 32,* "Financial Instruments: Presentation," Paragraphs 28–32, for IFRS.

$30,000,000 by issuing 30,000 of $1,000 par value convertible bonds with each bond convertible into 45 shares of the company's common stock. If the company's share price increases, bondholders are likely to convert the debt to stock and only 1,350,000 new shares would be issued (i.e., 30,000 bonds × 45 shares per bond = 1,350,000 shares).[5] By raising capital with convertible bonds, the company issues fewer shares of stock and is less likely to significantly dilute its share price and earnings per share.

Convertible bonds are also attractive to investors. That is, in the immediate term, the bondholders get a fixed interest payment. In the long term, bondholders have the potential to convert their investment into an equity investment.

THE CONCEPTUAL FRAMEWORK CONNECTION
Convertible Bonds

Convertible bonds possess characteristics of both debt and equity securities. Should companies classify these financial instruments as debt *or* equity? To examine this question, we refer to the conceptual framework.

Liabilities involve probable future sacrifices of economic benefits. In the case of convertible bonds, there are probable future sacrifices in the form of interest and potentially principal repayment if the bondholders do not convert to equity. Equity is the residual interest in the assets after deducting the liabilities. Specifically, equity represents the ownership interest in the entity. Conceptually, part of the amount paid for a convertible bond is for an equity stake in the firm.

Because of the hybrid nature of convertible bonds, it is not conceptually sound to record a convertible bond entirely as a liability or entirely as equity. Rather, firms should separate the convertible security into two components: debt and equity.

Faithful representation in the conceptual framework requires that financial reporting depict the substance of an economic phenomenon completely, neutrally, and without material error.[6] Thus, a faithful representation of a convertible bond includes the separation of the issue price into liability and equity.

Accounting for Convertible Bonds

Because of the difficulty of measuring the debt and equity components, U.S. GAAP usually treats an entire convertible bond issue as debt.[7] The accounting for convertible debt is the same as straight debt. Specifically, companies amortize the convertible bonds throughout their life as if they were not convertible.[8] The only difference is the accounting at conversion.

When convertible bonds are converted to equity, the company removes the bonds payable along with any unamortized premium or unamortized discount from the balance sheet. The company also recognizes common stock (or preferred stock) and any additional paid-in capital. The company does not record a gain or loss; rather, it includes this amount in additional paid-in capital. There is no gain or loss to recognize because this is a capital transaction—that is, an exchange involving the entity's own equity. Gains and losses by definition are not permitted when the transaction involves the entity's own equity shares.[9] Example 14.15 illustrates accounting for convertible bonds.

[5] The company usually has a call option attached to convertible debt. With it, the company can call in the debt to force conversion. The call price can be at par or above par. If the call price is above par, the excess over par is known as a call premium.

[6] FASB, *Statement of Financial Accounting Concepts No. 8*, "Chapter 1, The Objective of General Purpose Financial Reporting," and Chapter 3, "Qualitative Characteristics of Useful Financial Information."

[7] An exception to this is when a beneficial conversion option exists. We discuss beneficial conversion options in the next section.

[8] See the Basis for Conclusions cases at the end of the chapter for more discussion of this issue.

[9] This approach is called the book value method. An alternative method known as the market value method values the shares on the bond conversion at the fair value of the shares issued or the bonds converted, whichever is more clearly evident. The difference between the fair value used and the carrying value of the bonds is recorded as a gain or loss on conversion. The conversion is viewed as a constructive early retirement of debt.

EXAMPLE 14.15 **Convertible Bonds**

PROBLEM: On January 1, 2018, Tarco Company issued $500,000, par value, 8%, 4-year convertible bonds. Each $1,000 bond is convertible into 30 shares of Tarco's $1 par common stock. Tarco received $572,598 for the bonds when issued; consequently, the effective interest yield is 4%. Interest is payable annually each December 31. The bonds were converted on December 31, 2019, when the carrying value was $537,722.[10] Assume the bonds do not have a beneficial conversion option. What journal entry does Tarco record at the issue of the bonds? What is the journal entry to record the conversion?

SOLUTION: Tarco records the bonds with a $72,598 premium. Recording a convertible bond issue is no different from that of the sale of a non-convertible bond. The journal entry is as follows:

Account	January 1, 2018	
Cash	572,598	
Bonds Payable		500,000
Premium on Bonds Payable		72,598

At conversion, Tarco removes the bonds payable of $500,000 and the remaining premium account of $37,722. In addition, there are 500 bonds in this issue ($500,000 / $1,000 par) so that 15,000 shares will be issued on conversion (i.e., 500 bonds × 30 shares per bond on conversion). Upon conversion, Tarco credits common stock at par value for $15,000 (500 bonds × 30 shares per bond × $1 par value per share). The remaining credit will be to additional paid-in-capital. The journal entry is as follows:

Account	December 31, 2019	
Bonds Payable	500,000	
Premium on Bonds Payable	37,722	
Common Stock – Par Value		15,000
Additional Paid-in Capital in Excess of Par – Common		522,722

At the end of fiscal 2016, ***Tesla*** had convertible notes with a carrying value of $2.957 billion. ***Tesla*** estimates that the fair value of the convertible debt would be $3.206 billion with the difference between the carrying value and fair value primarily attributed to the conversion feature on the debt.

Beneficial Conversion Options

Accounting standards require companies to separate the debt and equity values of convertible bonds if a *beneficial conversion option* exists at issuance. A **beneficial conversion option** is an option to convert the debt to equity that is *in the money*. The conversion option is **in the money** if the market price of the stock exceeds the implied exercise price. At the date of issue, the beneficial conversion option is measured at its **intrinsic value**, the market price of the stock less the implied exercise price. Accounting for bonds issued with a beneficial conversion option is illustrated in Example 14.16.

[10]We can compute the effective yield using the internal rate of return function in a spreadsheet. The amortization table is then straightforward based on the stated rate of 8% and a yield of 4%.

EXAMPLE 14.16 Convertible Bonds with Beneficial Conversion Options

PROBLEM: Ayden Alexander Associates (AAA) issues a 10-year, 4%, $1,000 par value convertible bond at par. The $1,000 bond converts into 20 shares of $1 par value common stock at the option of the bondholder beginning 2 years after the date of issue. There are no bond issue costs. Bond interest is paid annually. The market price of the common stock was $65 per share. Prepare the journal entry to record the issuance of AAA's convertible debt. Compute the effective interest rate on the bond.

SOLUTION: To determine whether the debt and equity features of this financial instrument can be separated, we must first identify whether the market price of the shares exceeds the implied exercise price of the stock on the commitment date, indicating a beneficial conversion option.

The implied exercise price is the par value of the bond divided by the number of shares to be issued at conversion. In this case, the implied exercise price is $50 per share ($1,000/ 20 shares). The market price of the common stock less the exercise price is the intrinsic value of the option, $15 per share ($65 − $50). Because the market price of the stock exceeds the implied exercise price, the bonds are issued with a beneficial conversion option. The value of the beneficial conversion option is $300 ($15 intrinsic value × 20 shares). The bond is valued at $700 ($1,000 on issue proceeds less $300 beneficial conversion option).

The journal entry to record the bond issue with a beneficial conversion option follows:

Account	***Entry at Issue Date***	
Cash	1,000	
Discount on Bonds Payable	300	
Bonds Payable		1,000
Additional Paid-in Capital – Beneficial Conversion Option		300

We compute the effective interest rate or yield as 8.59% using the Excel spreadsheet.

	N	I/Y	PV	PMT	FV	Excel Formula
Given	10		700	−40	−1,000	
Solve for RATE		**8.59%**				= RATE (10,−40,700,−1000)

Any discount on the bonds is amortized using the effective interest rate. In Example 14.17, the effective interest rate is 8.59%.

When the bonds are converted, the company removes the carrying value of the bonds and the additional paid-in capital related to the beneficial conversion option amount and replaces them with equity. The fair value of the equity issued is not taken into account. Example 14.17 illustrates the accounting at the conversion of the debt to equity.

EXAMPLE 14.17 Convertible Debt at Conversion: Beneficial Conversion Option

PROBLEM: Continuing our previous illustration for Ayden Alexander Associates (AAA), assume that the bond converts after 2 years. The balance of the discount at the date of conversion is $258. The bond converts into 20 shares of $1 par value common stock. The balance of additional paid-in capital – beneficial conversion option is $300. Prepare the journal entry to record the bond conversion.

Continued

SOLUTION: AAA accounts for the bond conversion by removing the carrying value of the bonds and the additional paid-in capital related to the beneficial conversion option and replacing it with the common stock at par and additional paid-in capital. The carrying value of the bonds at the date of conversion is $742 ($1,000 face value − $258 remaining discount). The amount of additional paid-in capital related to the beneficial conversion option is $300. The carrying value of the new equity issued is equal to the book value of the debt and the additional paid-in capital for the beneficial conversion option, $1,042 ($742 + $300). The common stock par value is $1 per share and 20 shares are issued, so AAA credits common stock at par $20.

Account	On the Date of Conversion	
Bond Payable	1,000	
Additional Paid-in Capital – Beneficial Conversion Option	300	
Discount on Bonds Payable		258
Common Stock (at Par)		20
Additional Paid-in Capital in Excess of Par – Common		1,022

Accounting for Convertible Bonds: IFRS

IFRS follows the conceptually sound approach of separately classifying the convertible bond's debt and equity components. Separating, or bifurcating, the convertible bond's debt and equity components is consistent with the conceptual framework definitions of these elements. Whereas U.S. GAAP separates the debt and equity components only for bonds with beneficial conversion options, IFRS requires separating the debt and equity components for all convertible bonds. Additionally, IFRS uses market values to measure the debt component. IFRS determines the debt and equity components as follows:

- The debt component is the present value of future cash flows at the market rate at the time of issuance.
- The equity component is the bond issue price less the amount of the debt component. This amount is recorded in an equity account referred to as other capital reserves.[11]

Exhibit 14.4 compares accounting for convertible bonds under U.S. GAAP and IFRS.

EXHIBIT 14.4 Comparison of Accounting for Convertible Bonds under U.S. GAAP and IFRS

	U.S. GAAP	IFRS
Separate debt and equity components?	No, except for convertible bonds with a beneficial conversion option.	Yes.
Measuring debt and equity components.	Allocate full amount to debt except for convertible bonds with a beneficial conversion option. The beneficial conversion option is measured at its intrinsic value, the market price of the stock less the implied exercise price.	Measure the debt component as the present value of future cash flows at the market rate at the time of issuance. The equity component is the bond issue price less the amount of the debt component.

Example 14.18 illustrates the issuance and conversion of convertible bonds under IFRS.

[11]Under IFRS, companies divide bond issue costs into debt and equity based on the initial percentages of the debt and equity components at issuance.

EXAMPLE 14.18 Issuance and Conversion of Convertible Bonds: IFRS

PROBLEM: Assume now that Tarco is an IFRS reporter. On January 1, 2018, it issued $500,000 of 8%, 4-year bonds. Interest is payable annually each December 31. The market rate of interest on January 1, 2018, the date of issue, for similar nonconvertible bonds was 6%. Each $1,000 bond is convertible into 30 shares of Tarco's $1 par common stock. The company received $572,598 for the bonds on the issue date. All of the bonds were converted on December 31, 2019, when the carrying value was $518,334. What journal entries does Tarco record at the issue and conversion of the bonds?

SOLUTION: We begin with the journal entry at issuance. Under IFRS, Tarco must first determine the debt component by computing the present value of all future cash flows at the market rate of interest.

	N	I/Y	PV	PMT	FV	Excel Formula
Given	4	6.00%		−40,000	−500,000	
Solve for PV			**534,651**			= PV (0.06,4,−40000,−500000)

Tarco records this amount as a liability ($500,000 as bonds payable and $34,651 as a premium). The equity component is the difference between the $572,598 bond issue price and the $534,651 debt component, or $37,947. Tarco records the $37,947 as equity, other capital reserves, as follows:

Account	***January 1, 2018***	
Cash	572,598	
Other Capital Reserves		37,947
Bonds Payable		534,651

At conversion, Tarco removes the carrying value of bonds payable and other capital reserves. It replaces the carrying value of the bonds and other capital reserves with the par value and additional paid-in capital of the equity shares issued. On December 31, 2019, the carrying value of the bond payable is $518,334, which is the present value of remaining cash flows at the 6% market rate.

Account	***December 31, 2019***	
Bonds Payable	518,334	
Other Capital Reserves	37,947	
Share Capital – Par Value		15,000
Share Premium		541,281

JUDGMENTS IN ACCOUNTING
Convertible Bonds

Convertible bonds have characteristics of both debt and equity, so the ideal accounting would involve splitting the proceeds in some way between debt and equity and reporting both components on the balance sheet. IFRS accounts for convertible bonds this way, even if the bonds do not contain a beneficial conversion option, to present a faithful representation of the financial position of the company.[12]

However, under U.S. GAAP, convertible bonds are not divided into the debt and equity components (unless they have a beneficial conversion option). FASB's approach is not based on conceptual grounds. Rather, FASB is concerned that separating the security into debt and equity components is too complex and difficult to measure.[13] In other words, FASB chose not to require (or allow) the security to be separated because of the significant judgment involved.

[12] See IASC, *International Accounting Standard 32,* Paragraphs 28 through 32.

[13] See FASB, *Statement of Financial Accounting Standards No. 150,* Paragraph B53.

Because of the current accounting treatment under U.S. GAAP, accounting for convertible bonds without a beneficial conversion option does not require extensive judgment. Companies record the face value as bonds payable and record any difference between the issue price and the face value as a premium or discount. However, under IFRS, significant judgment may be involved. Consider a difference between the issue price and the face value. Is the difference because the market rate for the bonds, exclusive of the conversion option, varies from the stated rate? Or is the difference because the market is paying an extra amount for the conversion option?

The correct market rate is the one a company with an identical credit risk would use to issue identical bonds on the same day. The only difference is that these bonds would not have a conversion feature. Of course, it is highly unlikely that the same firm would go to the market with two bond issues in one day! Thus, management of the issuing firm must make an informed decision as to what the market rate will be. Consider Example 14.18. What if management concluded that the market rate was 7% instead of 6%? In this case, the present value of the bonds would be $516,936, lower than the amount of $534,651 from Example 14.18, and the journal entry would be:

Account	**January 1, 2018**	
Cash	572,598	
Other Capital Reserves		55,662
Bonds Payable		516,936

Judgments about the market rate affect a company's reported debt. A company concerned about the amount of its debt could select a higher interest rate to report less debt. Unlike many other management decisions, this judgment does not have an immediate impact on income: It simply increases the amount included in other capital reserves and decreases any premium paid, thus reducing the bond's carrying value. However, because companies ultimately amortize the premium paid as a reduction in interest expense, this decision will impact income by making interest expense higher and income lower.

Bayer AG, the German healthcare and agricultural products company, is an example of a company required to estimate the debt and equity components of convertible debt. ***Bayer*** raised €4,000 million when it issued convertible bonds with a face value of €500 million in fiscal 2016. As an IFRS reporter, ***Bayer*** separated the debt and equity components of the convertible debt. After adjusting for €48 million bond issue costs and €191 million deferred taxes, ***Bayer*** estimated the equity related to the conversion features of the bonds at €3,491 million. ***Bayer*** reported the debt at €652 million, implying that the debt was issued at par. Although IFRS requires that the convertible debt be separated, management uses judgment to estimate the amounts to be reported as debt versus equity.

8 Describe and illustrate the accounting for warrants, including those that are detachable and nondetachable.

Bonds with Stock Warrants

Bonds are sometimes issued with **stock warrants**, which are long-term options to acquire a stated number of shares of common stock for a stated price. Stock warrants with bonds may make investing attractive if the interest rate is lower or make borrowing feasible for a company wishing to issue debt.

When firms issue stock warrants with bonds, the warrants can either be *nondetachable* or *detachable*. **Detachable warrants** can be removed by the holder and sold separately on the secondary market whereas **nondetachable warrants** cannot be.

Accounting for Stock Warrants

If the warrants are nondetachable, then the total debt proceeds received are typically assigned to the debt issue and there is no allocation between debt and equity.[14]

[14]This section assumes that the hybrid instrument does not have an embedded beneficial conversion option.

If the warrants are detachable, then the firm allocates the proceeds to both the debt and equity components using one of the following methods:

- **Proportional method.** Allocate based on the relative fair values of the bond without the warrants and the warrants on a standalone basis at the time of issuance.
- **Incremental (or residual) method.** If the fair value of the bonds or the warrants is not readily determinable, allocate the portion of the proceeds to the instrument based on the readily available fair value and allocate the residual amount to the other instrument.

The issuance of bonds with warrants is illustrated in Example 14.19.

EXAMPLE 14.19 Issuance of Bonds with Stock Warrants

PROBLEM: CPW Company issued 2,000 of its $1,000 par value bonds for $1,450, providing total cash proceeds of $2,900,000. It sold each bond with 40 warrants. Each warrant provides the holder with the right to acquire one share of the company's $2 par value, common stock for $25 per share. CPW has existing bonds outstanding that trade without warrants at $1,200. Other CPW warrants outstanding trade for $25 each. What is the journal entry to record the issuance of the 2,000 bonds if the warrants are nondetachable? What is the journal entry to record the issuance of the 2,000 bonds if the warrants are detachable? Finally, what is the journal entry to record the bond issue if the warrants are detachable but do not have a readily determinable fair value?

SOLUTION: If the warrants are nondetachable, then CPW records the entire proceeds as a liability as follows:

Account	At Issuance	
Cash	2,900,000	
Bonds Payable		2,000,000
Premium on Bonds Payable		900,000

If the warrants are detachable, then CPW allocates the proceeds between debt and equity using the proportional method.

Component	Number of Units	Market Value of Existing Units	Total Market Value	Proportion for Allocation
Bonds	2,000	$1,200	$2,400,000	54.55%
Warrants	80,000	25	2,000,000	45.45
			$4,400,000	100%

Allocation to bonds: $2,900,000 × 54.55% = $1,581,950
Allocation to warrants: $2,900,000 × 45.45% = $1,318,050

The bonds are now issued at a $418,050 discount (i.e., $2,000,000 − $1,581,950).

Account	At Issuance	
Cash	2,900,000	
Discount on Bonds Payable	418,050	
Bonds Payable		2,000,000
Additional Paid-in Capital – Stock Warrants		1,318,050

If the warrants are detachable but do not have a readily determinable fair value, then CPW allocates the fair value to the bonds and the residual of the total issue price to the warrants

Continued

using the incremental method. Assuming that the warrants do not have a readily determinable fair value, CPW determines the allocation of the issue price as follows:

Allocation to bonds: 2,000 × \$1,200 = \$2,400,000.

Allocation to warrants: \$2,900,000 − \$2,400,000 = \$500,000

The bonds are now issued at a \$400,000 premium (i.e., \$2,400,000 − \$2,000,000).

Account	At Issuance	
Cash	2,900,000	
Bonds Payable		2,000,000
Premium on Bonds Payable		400,000
Additional Paid-in Capital – Stock Warrants		500,000

When exercising the warrants, the firm removes the additional paid-in capital-stock warrants account, credits common stock for the par value, and credits the remainder to additional paid-in capital as shown in Example 14.20.

EXAMPLE 14.20 Exercise of Stock Warrants

PROBLEM: CPW Company issued 2,000 of its \$1,000 par value bonds for \$1,450, providing total cash proceeds of \$2,900,000. It sold each bond with 40 detachable warrants. Each warrant provides the holder with the right to acquire one share of the company's \$2 par value, common stock for \$25 per share. CPW has existing bonds outstanding that trade without warrants at \$1,200. There are other CPW warrants outstanding that trade for \$25 each. What is the journal entry to record the exercise of the warrants?

SOLUTION: Based on information in Example 14.19, we know that the balance in the additional paid-in capital account is \$1,318,050. Thus, CPW debits this account for its balance as well as the cash account for the cash proceeds of \$2,000,000 (80,000 warrants × \$25 exercise price per warrant). It credits the common stock account for the \$2 par value per share multiplied by the 80,000 shares. CPW credits the remainder to additional paid-in capital.

Account	At Exercise	
Cash	2,000,000	
Additional Paid-in Capital – Stock Warrants	1,318,050	
Common Stock		160,000
Additional Paid-in Capital in Excess of Par – Common		3,158,050

Accounting for Stock Warrant: IFRS

Similar to accounting for convertible bonds and consistent with the conceptual framework, IFRS separates the convertible bond's debt and equity components. When ***Siemens AG***, the German engineering and electronics company, issued about \$3 billion of bonds with detachable warrants in 2012, it allocated roughly \$21.7 million to the value of the warrants.

9 Explain the reclassification of financing liabilities for current maturities of long-term debt, short-term debt expected to be refinanced, and callable obligations.

Reclassifications of Financing Liabilities

There are a number of scenarios under which a company will change the classification of notes and bonds payable between long term and short term.

Current Maturities of Long-Term Debt

When a long-term obligation becomes payable within the next year (or operating cycle, if longer), it meets the definition of a current liability. In this case, the firm will liquidate the long-term obligation through the use of current assets or the creation of other current liabilities. In such cases, the firm reclassifies the obligation from long-term to short-term as illustrated in Example 14.21.

EXAMPLE 14.21

Current Maturity of Long-Term Debt

PROBLEM: Backo, Inc. issued $750,000 of bonds on December 15, 2018, when the market rate of interest was 5%. The 5-year bonds pay interest annually at 5%. Backo has a December 31 fiscal year-end. Prepare the journal entries to record the issuance of the bonds and the reclassification of the bonds on December 31, 2022.

SOLUTION: Backo's journal entry when issuing the bonds is as follows:

Account	*December 15, 2018*	
Cash	750,000	
Bonds Payable (long-term)		750,000

On December 31, 2022, the bonds payable are no longer long term because they mature within the next year (December 15, 2023). Thus, Backo must reclassify the bonds from long term to short term.

Account	*December 31, 2022*	
Bonds Payable (long term)	750,000	
Current Maturities of Bonds Payable		750,000

Short-Term Debt Expected to Be Refinanced

Under certain conditions, a company can reclassify short-term debt as long-term.[15] For example, a company could:

- Reclassify short-term debt expected to be refinanced as long-term debt
- Refinance a short-term note to extend payment due dates or to take advantage of lower interest rates, particularly if cash is needed beyond the original maturity date of the short-term loan

A company would want to reclassify debt as long term to improve its liquidity ratios.

Short-Term Debt Reclassification. A company can reclassify short-term debt as long-term debt if the short-term debt is expected to be (1) extended or replaced by debt that will be due beyond 1 year from the balance sheet date or (2) replaced or refinanced with equity securities.

In either case, the obligation will no longer require the use of current assets or the creation of other current liabilities in its liquidation. Therefore, the obligation no longer meets the definition of

[15]For most of the relevant authoritative literature for this topic, see FASB ASC 470-10-45, *Debt–Overall–Other Presentation Matters* for U.S. GAAP and IASC, *International Accounting Standard 1, "Presentation of Financial Statements,"* Paragraphs 72–73, for IFRS.

a current liability so that the firm must reclassify it as long-term debt, providing adequate footnote disclosure with details of the refinancing.[16]

U.S. GAAP sets forth two criteria that firms must meet to exclude a short-term obligation from current liabilities and reclassify it as long-term debt:

1. Management must intend to refinance on a long-term basis *and*
2. Management must demonstrate the ability to consummate the refinancing.

Management demonstrates its ability to refinance by either:

1. Completing an actual refinancing during the post-balance sheet period, *or*[17]
2. Demonstrating the existence of a firm agreement that permits refinancing on a long-term basis with readily determinable terms.[18]

The reclassification of short-term debt is an important issue when preparing the balance sheet. For example, a firm that has short-term debt at the balance sheet date could meet the two criteria to reclassify the debt as long term before issuing the financial statements to the public. If the firm meets the two criteria before the financial statements are issued, it would classify the debt as long term on its balance sheet. An example of the reclassification from short-term to long-term debt is provided in Example 14.22.

EXAMPLE 14.22 **Reclassification from Short-Term to Long-Term Debt**

PROBLEM: Barbero Building Products Company reported a $478,000 short-term note payable on its December 31, 2018, trial balance. The note is due on March 23, 2019. On February 2, 2019, Barbero extended the term of the loan for $300,000 of the balance, changing the due date to March 23, 2020. Barbero finalized the loan extension on February 2, 2019, and it is not subject to any modifications. Barbero released financial statements on February 16, 2019. How should Barbero classify the $478,000 note payable on the December 31, 2018, balance sheet? Provide any necessary journal entries.

SOLUTION: Because the refinancing is for $300,000, Barbero reclassifies only that amount as long-term debt. Barbero should still classify the remaining $178,000 as a current liability. Because the refinancing occurs on February 2, 2019, which is during the post-balance sheet period, it can reclassify the short-term debt as long-term debt as of year-end, December 31, 2018. The journal entry for this reclassification follows:

Account	***December 31, 2018***	
Short-Term Notes Payable	300,000	
Long-Term Notes Payable		300,000

Short-Term Debt Reclassification: IFRS. Similar to U.S. GAAP, when an IFRS-reporting company completes a refinancing on a long-term basis prior to the financial statement date, it can record the debt as long term under IFRS. Unlike U.S. GAAP, if the company completes the refinancing after the financial statement date, it must report the debt as short-term

[16]The firm must first refinance (obtain the additional financing) and then liquidate the short-term obligation. If this sequence of events were reversed, the firm would be using cash from the current operating cycle and the liability would still be classified as current.

[17]The post-balance sheet period is the time between the fiscal year-end and the date that the financial statements are issued.

[18]An agreement including a material adverse change clause would violate this criterion. A material adverse change clause can be included in lending arrangements to protect the lender against any significant adverse changes in market conditions or the financial position of the borrowing company from the date of the loan commitment until the date the loan is executed. In addition, an agreement including a provision that states that the refinancing is dependent on an increase in income over the subsequent 3 months would violate this agreement.

debt. The IFRS requirement seeks to report the underlying economic condition that exists at the balance sheet date. Even though events after the balance sheet date can occur that then change the classification, IFRS does not allow a future event to change the reporting of a contractual obligation that the company had at a point in time.

However, even if a company has not completed a refinancing before the financial statement date, it can reclassify short-term debt as long term when it both:

- Expects to refinance the debt within the next 12 months, and
- Has the ability to refinance the debt for at least 12 months after the reporting period under an *existing* arrangement to provide refinancing.

If a company expects to refinance the debt, it does not intend to use working capital to pay it off. Importantly, the second condition requires that the company has an existing arrangement under which it can refinance on a long-term basis. That is, the company has a current agreement with the debtholder to refinance and does not have to rely on some future event dependent on a future agreement of a debtholder, which is not certain. When a company has an existing arrangement to provide for refinancing in the next 12 months, it has the ability to defer the payment beyond the short term. Example 14.23 presents a scenario in which the refinancing occurs after the balance sheet date.

EXAMPLE 14.23

Reclassification from Short-Term to Long-Term Debt: IFRS

PROBLEM: Now assume that Barbero Building Products Company is an IFRS reporter. Barbero reported a $478,000 short-term note payable on its December 31, 2018, trial balance. The note is due on March 23, 2019. On February 2, 2019, Barbero extended the term of the loan for $300,000 of the balance, changing the due date to March 23, 2020. Barbero finalized the loan extension on February 2, 2019, and it is not subject to any modifications. Barbero released financial statements on February 16, 2019. How should Barbero classify the $478,000 note payable on the December 31, 2018, balance sheet? Provide any necessary journal entries.

SOLUTION: Because the refinancing occurs on February 2, 2019, which is after the balance sheet date, Barbero must report the debt as short-term debt under IFRS. It cannot reclassify to long term.

Example 14.24 presents an example in which the company has the intent and ability to refinance.

EXAMPLE 14.24

Reclassification from Short-Term to Long-Term Debt: IFRS

PROBLEM: Barbero Building Products Company, an IFRS reporter, reported a $478,000 short-term note payable on its December 31, 2018, trial balance. The note is due on March 23, 2019. It expects to refinance the full amount of the note payable and has an existing credit arrangement under which it could refinance on a long-term basis. How should Barbero classify the $478,000 note payable on the December 31, 2018, balance sheet? Provide any necessary journal entries.

SOLUTION: Because Barbero has the intent and ability to refinance, it can reclassify the short-term debt as long term as of its year-end, December 31, 2018. The journal entry for this reclassification follows:

Account	December 31, 2018	
Short-Term Notes Payable	478,000	
Long-Term Notes Payable		478,000

Exhibit 14.5 illustrates the classification of short-term debt expected to be refinanced under U.S. GAAP and IFRS.

EXHIBIT 14.5 Short-Term Debt Expected to Be Refinanced

U.S. GAAP		IFRS	
When Refinanced	**Classification**	**When Refinanced**	**Classification**
Before year-end	Long term	Before year-end	Long term
After financial statement date but before financial statements issued	Long term	After financial statement date but before financial statements issued	Short term
Expected after financial statements date when the company both • Intends to refinance the debt on a long-term basis. • Demonstrates the ability to consummate the refinancing with either long-term debt or with equity securities.	Long term	Expected after financial statements date when the company both • Expects to refinance the debt within the next 12 months. • Has the ability to refinance the debt for at least 12 months after the reporting period under an *existing* arrangement.	Long term

Obligations Callable by Creditor

Callable obligations are liabilities for which the creditor can require immediate payment when specified conditions exist. For example, debt can be called at the creditor's option on fixed dates specified in loan agreements.

Reclassification of Obligations Callable by Creditor. Debtors in technical default may be required to reclassify long-term debt as short-term debt in certain situations.[19] Specifically, reclassification should occur if either:

1. The debtor violated a provision of the debt agreement, making the debt callable at the balance sheet date, *or*
2. The debtor violated a debt agreement that, if not addressed within a specified grace period, will make the obligation callable.

The debtor may continue to classify the callable obligation as long term if it meets one of the following conditions:

1. The creditor waives or loses the right to demand payment (for example, the time period to exercise the call expires), *or*
2. The obligation will not become callable because it is probable that the debtor will address the violation within the grace period. For example, the debtor may be able to restore working capital to the level required in the restrictive debt covenant.

A creditor may waive the right to call in a loan that is in technical default if the debtor is otherwise making payments when due and the loan carries an interest rate higher than the current market rate. In addition, the call may result in additional financial distress for the debtor, which in turn may lead to bankruptcy. The event of bankruptcy can reduce the probability of collection for the creditor.

The timing of when the creditor grants a waiver is important. A creditor can grant a waiver until the time the debtor releases the financial statements, allowing the firm to continue classifying the debt as long term. Example 14.25 provides an example when the debtor violates a debt covenant.

[19] For the relevant authoritative literature, see FASB ASC 470-10- 45, *Debt – Overall – Other Presentation Matters* for U.S. GAAP and IASC, *International Accounting Standard 1,* "Presentation of Financial Statements," Paragraphs 74–76, for IFRS.

EXAMPLE 14.25

Reclassification of Callable Debt

PROBLEM: Renee Realty reported a $560,000 long-term note payable on its year-end balance sheet. As part of the loan agreement, Renee is required to maintain a compensating balance of 10% of the loan principal, or $56,000. Working capital deficiencies forced Renee to draw down the compensating balance and thereby violate the restrictive debt covenants of the loan agreement. The loan became callable by the creditor on December 31 of the current year. How should Renee classify the $560,000 note payable on the December 31 balance sheet? Provide any necessary journal entries.

SOLUTION: Assuming that the creditor will not waive his right to call the loan and Renee will not address the violation, Renee must reclassify the debt as short term. The following journal entry is required because the loan is now callable:

Account	***December 31***	
Long-Term Notes Payable	560,000	
Short-Term Notes Payable		560,000

Classification of Obligations Callable by Creditor: IFRS. When debt is in technical default, IFRS allows debtors to continue classifying the debt as long term only if they receive a waiver prior to year-end. So, if a call is waived after year-end but before the firm issues financial statements, the firm reclassifies the debt as short-term debt. Under U.S. GAAP, however, it would remain as long-term debt. Similar to short-term debt reclassification under refinancing, the IFRS requirement seeks to report the underlying economic condition that exists at the balance sheet date.

⑩ Discuss and illustrate the fair value option in accounting for financing liabilities.

The Fair Value Option to Value Liabilities

Under the **fair value option**, companies can elect to value most types of financial assets and obligations at fair value.[20] The fair value option improves financial reporting by enabling entities to offset volatility in reported earnings. Consider a company that has an asset and a liability that are related. If the liability is reported at fair value but the asset is not, the company will report an earnings stream that is more volatile than if both the asset and liability (whose fair values are correlated) are reported at fair value. Electing the fair value option allows management to report both the asset and liability at fair value.[21]

Fair Value Option Accounting at Initial Recognition

A company can choose the fair value option for some liabilities without choosing it for all liabilities. Typically, the company must elect the fair value option at the time it borrows the money or issues the debt. After a company elects the fair value option, it is generally irrevocable.

When electing the fair value option at initial recognition, the company

1. Reports the liability on the balance sheet at fair value
2. Reports unrealized gains and losses not related to changes in instrument-specific credit risk in net income
3. Reports unrealized gains and losses related to changes in the *instrument-specific credit risk* in other comprehensive income. **Instrument-specific credit risk** relates to the risk of the specific security, not general market risk or interest rate risk.

[20]Most financial instruments are eligible for the fair value option under U.S. GAAP. Paragraphs 4 and 5 of FASB ASC 825-10-15 outline the specific requirements. For example, financial instruments that are not eligible for the fair value option include pension assets and liabilities, obligations related to deferred compensation arrangements, financial assets and liabilities related to leasing transactions, and investments in subsidiaries or variable interest entities that the company is required to consolidate.

[21]For the relevant authoritative literature, see FASB ASC 825-10, IASC, *Financial Instruments – Overall* for U.S. GAAP and IASC, *International Accounting Standard 39,* "Financial Instruments: Recognition and Measurement" for IFRS.

Companies initially measure the liability at its fair value at inception and use a fair value adjustment account when remeasuring the liability to its fair value. Companies net the fair value adjustment account with the liability account and report the net amount on the balance sheet. In Example 14.26, we use the information from Example 14.8 to illustrate the fair value option.

EXAMPLE 14.26 **Fair Value Option**

PROBLEM: On January 1, 2018, Ruffin Corporation issued $40,000 of par value, 4%, 4-year bonds that mature on December 31, 2021. The market rate of interest was 6% when Ruffin issued the bonds. The company uses the effective interest method to amortize any bond premium or discount. Interest is payable semiannually each June 30 and December 31. Ruffin elects the fair value option for these bonds and prepares financial statements only annually. Changes in fair value relate only to the change in interest rates. On December 31, 2018, the fair value of the bonds is $41,325. What is the journal entry to record the fair value?

SOLUTION: As noted in Example 14.8, Ruffin issued the bonds for $37,192. Our solution to Example 14.8 showed that the carrying value of the bonds on December 31, 2018, is $37,833. Because the fair value of the debt is greater than its carrying value, Ruffin has an unrealized loss of $3,492 ($41,325 fair value − $37,833 carrying value). Specifically, if the company were to retire its debt today, it would have to pay a fair value that exceeds the carrying value of the debt and incur a loss. The journal entry follows:

Account	December 31, 2018	
Unrealized Loss on Bonds Payable – Net Income	3,492	
Fair Value Adjustment on Bonds Payable		3,492

Ruffin reports the unrealized holding loss as part of net income because it is the result of the change in interest rates, not a change in instrument-specific credit risk. The company adds the credit balance in the fair value adjustment account to the bonds payable account that it reports on the balance sheet at the gross amount.

Fair Value Option: IFRS

Similar to U.S. GAAP, IFRS allows a company to use the fair value option for liabilities.[22] IFRS additionally stipulates that a company can use the fair value option for financial assets when doing so results in more relevant information because either:

- A company has a documented risk management or investment strategy prescribing that it will manage and evaluate its performance on the fair values and changes in fair values of its financial assets and/or liabilities.
- The fair value option ensures consistently measuring liabilities or assets and their associated gains or losses on the same bases. That is, the fair value option eliminates or significantly reduces accounting mismatches from measuring liabilities or assets (and their associated gains and losses) on different bases.

11 Detail required disclosures for financing liabilities.

Disclosures for Financing Liabilities

We conclude the chapter with the disclosure requirements for financing liabilities. Companies disclose a detailed list and description of each significant debt issue, including the:

- Type of borrowing
- Outstanding balance
- Interest rate

[22] IFRS requires companies to separate the change in the liabilities' fair value into changes attributable to own credit risk and other changes in fair value. Changes in fair value because of a company's own credit risk generally are presented in other comprehensive income, not net income.

- Payment terms
- Maturity date

Next, we discuss more specific disclosure requirements for certain types of debt.

Short-Term Debt Expected to Be Refinanced

Disclosures for short-term debt expected to be refinanced include a description of the agreement and terms of the new obligation incurred or expected to be incurred or any equity issued or expected to be issued. Firms disclose the conditions and circumstances that avoid calling the debt in a footnote.

Long-Term Debt

Disclosures for long-term debt include the total amount of maturities and any *sinking fund* requirements for each of the next 5 years. A **sinking fund** is cash or other assets held in a separate account that is used to repay debt at maturity. These disclosures provide financial statement users with the expected future cash payments based on current debt commitments. The disclosures also include a description of the rights and privileges of the various classes of outstanding debt securities and any guarantees. ***Johnson & Johnson*** disclosed the debt payable in each of the next 5 years as shown in Exhibit 14.6. Notice that the majority of the debt is due in more than 5 years, after 2021.

EXHIBIT 14.6 Long-Term Debt Disclosure, ***Johnson & Johnson***, Note, January 1, 2017

NOTE 7: Borrowings

Aggregate maturities of long-term obligations commencing in 2017 are:

(Dollars in Millions) 2017	2018	2019	2020	2021	After 2021
$1,704	1,561	2,538	629	1,795	15,919

Source: Financial statements from Johnson & Johnson Company's Annual Report, 2016. http://files.shareholder.com/downloads/JNJ/3809936545x0xS200406-17-6/200406/filing.pdf

Convertible Debt

Disclosures for debt with conversion and other options include detailed information about the terms of convertible debt instruments and the manner in which convertible securities affect the financial statements.

Separate disclosures are required for the debt and equity components of hybrid securities that are separated on the balance sheet. For the liability component, the entity must disclose the principal amount, the unamortized premium or discount, the net carrying amount of the debt, the number of shares to be delivered upon conversion, the effective interest rate, the cash interest, and the interest adjustment from the premium or discount amortization.

Fair Value Disclosures

For financial liabilities reported at fair value, companies disclose the valuation methods used and any assumptions made to arrive at the fair value. For financial liabilities reported at carrying value, companies provide disclosures of their fair values, including the methods used and assumptions made. We can use these disclosures to further assess the amount of a company's debt.

In Exhibit 14.3, we examined ***Johnson & Johnson's*** financial statement note disclosure of long-term debt issues. ***Johnson & Johnson*** discloses the fair value of its debt in footnote 4 to the table in that exhibit, stating that the fair value is higher than the carrying value by $1.6 billion in 2016 and $1.7 billion in 2015.

FINANCIAL STATEMENT ANALYSIS

Credit Risk

As discussed earlier in the chapter, credit rating agencies such as Standard & Poor's (S&P) and Moody's rate corporate debt. A company with a high credit rating can usually access credit markets when needed and raise capital at a low cost. Creditors also rely on these ratings when making decisions to invest in a company's debt.

Rating agencies identify key factors that determine a company's creditworthiness, assess these factors for it, and give an opinion on its credit quality. Although these agencies do not reveal the detailed process they use, S&P has periodically provided information about its criteria to rate corporate debt. Among the many factors it considers, S&P assesses a company's business risk and financial risk profile. The assessment of business risk includes analyzing a company's:

- Country risk
- Industry factors
- Competitive position
- Profitability/Peer group comparisons

The assessment of financial risk includes examining a company's

- Governance/Risk tolerance/Financial policies
- Accounting
- Cash flow adequacy
- Capital structure/Asset protection
- Liquidity/Short-term factors

Exhibit 14.7 describes how the assessment of business risk and financial risk map into the credit ratings. For example, a company that has an excellent business risk profile could receive a lower credit rating of "BBB−/BB+" if it is highly leveraged.

EXHIBIT 14.7 Business Risk and Financial Risk in Credit Ratings

Combining the Business and Financial Risk Profiles

	Financial Risk Profile					
Business Risk Profile	**1 (minimal)**	**2 (modest)**	**3 (intermediate)**	**4 (significant)**	**5 (aggressive)**	**6 (highly leveraged)**
1 (excellent)	AAA/AA+	AA	A+/A	A−	BBB	BBB−/BB+
2 (strong)	AA/AA−	A+/A	A−	BBB	BB+	BB
3 (satisfactory)	A/A−	BBB+	BBB/BBB−	BB+	BB	B+
4 (fair)	BBB/BBB−	BBB−	BB+	BB	BB−	B
5 (weak)	BB+	BB+	BB	BB−	B+	B/B
6 (vulnerable)	BB−	BB−	BB−	B+	B	B−

Sources: From Standard & Poor. Copyright © Standard & Poor's Financial Services LLC. Standard & Poor's, Request for Comment: Corporate Criteria, 2013. http://www.standardandpoors.com/spf/upload/Ratings_US/RfC_Corporate_Criteria.pdf

Financial statement analysis provides a key input into assessing financial risk as a primary source of information to analyze a company's financial condition and financial performance. For example, S&P identifies certain "core" ratios, such as funds from operations (FFO) over debt and debt over earnings before interest, taxes, depreciation and amortization (EBITDA), that it uses to assess financial risk as illustrated in Exhibit 14.8.

Financial Statement Analysis, continued

The FFO / debt and debt / EBITDA ratios are indicators of the liquid resources a company has available relative to its debt. S&P gives ranges for each of these ratios. For example, when a company's FFO / debt is greater than 60, its financial risk is considered minimal. These indicators of a company's financial risk can provide contradictory information—but they enhance the credit analyst's determination of overall financial risk.

EXHIBIT 14.8 Select Financial Risk Measures in Credit Ratings

Cash Flow Leverage Analysis Ratios—Standard Volatility [Excerpt]*

	Core Ratios	
	FFO / Debt (%)	**Debt/EBITDA(×)**
Minimal	60+	Less than 1.5
Modest	45–60	1.5–2
Intermediate	30–45	2–3
Significant	20–30	3–4
Aggressive	12–20	4–5
Highly leveraged	Less than 12	5+

* S&P uses a company's industry and country risk to determine its volatility category as either standard or low. Here we present the ratios for the standard volatility category.

Sources: From Standard & Poor. Copyright © Standard & Poor's Financial Services LLC. Standard & Poor's, Request for Comment: Corporate Criteria, 2013. http://www.standardandpoors.com/spf/upload/Ratings_US/RfC_Corporate_Criteria.pdf

Exhibit 14.9 shows the equations used to compute the FFO / debt and debt / EBITDA ratios and their desirable characteristics.

EXHIBIT 14.9 Select Indicators of Financial Risk

Indicator	**Definition**		**Desirable Characteristics**
FFO/Debt	$= \frac{\text{Operating Income from Continuing Operations after Tax + Depreciation and Amortization + Deferred Income Tax Expense + Other Major Recurring Noncash Items}}{\text{Short- and Long-Term Debt}}$	(14.4)	Higher ratio is preferred to lower.
Debt/EBITDA	$= \frac{\text{Short- and Long-Term Debt}}{\text{Operating Profits before Interest Income, Interest Expense, Income Taxes + Depreciation and Amortization + Asset Impairment}}$	(14.5)	Lower ratio is preferred to higher.

Sources: From Standard & Poor. Copyright © Standard & Poor's Financial Services LLC. Standards & Poor's, Corporate Ratings Criteria, 2008. http://www.standardandpoors.com/ratings/criteria/en/us/?filtername=General
Standard & Poor's, Request for Comment: Corporate Criteria, 2013. http://www.standardandpoors.com/spf/upload/Ratings_US/RfC_Corporate_Criteria.pdf

Credit rating agencies periodically update and change their rating criteria. The analysis of financial risk, however, usually uses financial statement information as a starting point. Sometimes analysts adjust for accounting classifications and choices made by companies. For example, debt might be defined to include a company's pension or lease obligations. Example 14.27 illustrates using these indicators of financial risk.

EXAMPLE 14.27 Credit Ratings

PROBLEM: In May 2017, ***Johnson & Johnson's*** credit rating was "AAA." ***Teva Pharmaceutical Industries Limited***, a pharmaceutical company based in Israel and a U.S. GAAP reporter, had debt rated as "BBB." From the companies' latest annual financial statements, you locate the information on the following page:

Financial Statement Analysis, continued

Fiscal 2016 ($ in millions)	Johnson & Johnson	Teva
Income (loss) from continuing operations after tax	$16,540	$ 311
Operating profit (loss) before interest income, interest expense, and income taxes	20,161	2,154
Depreciation and amortization	3,754	1,524
Deferred income tax expense (income)	(341)	15
Asset impairment	283	1,645
Major noncash charges	0	0
Short-Term debt	4,684	3,276
Long-Term debt	22,442	32,524
Equity	70,418	34,993

Compute funds from operations over debt and debt / EBITDA for ***Johnson & Johnson*** and ***Teva***. Using the benchmarks from Exhibit 14.8, assess the financial risk of each company for these indicators. How would you categorize each company's business risk given its credit rating?

SOLUTION: We compute the financial risk for ***Johnson & Johnson*** as follows:

Ratios	Definition	Johnson & Johnson
Funds from Operations over Debt	$= \dfrac{\text{Operating Income from Continuing Operations after Tax + Depreciation and Amortization + Deferred Income Tax Expense + Other Major Recurring Noncash Items}}{\text{Short- and Long-Term Debt}}$	$0.746 = \dfrac{\$16{,}540 + \$3{,}754 + \$(341) + \$283 + 0}{\$4{,}684 + \$22{,}442}$
Debt to EBITDA	$= \dfrac{\text{Short- and Long-Term Debt}}{\text{Operating Profits before Interest Income, Interest Expense, Income Taxes + Depreciation and Amortization + Asset Impairment}}$	$1.121 = \dfrac{\$4{,}684 + \$22{,}442}{\$20{,}161 + \$3{,}754 + \$283}$

Based on the indicators of financial risk, ***Johnson & Johnson's*** financial risk is minimal. Its funds from operations over debt, at 74.6, is greater than the minimal benchmark of 60 from Exhibit 14.8, and its debt to EBITDA at 1.121 is less than the 1.5 minimal benchmark. Given that all of ***Johnson & Johnson's*** indicators indicate minimal financial risk and ***Johnson & Johnson's*** credit rating is "AAA," its business risk is likely considered excellent based on information in Exhibit 14.7.

Ratios	Definition	Teva
Funds from Operations over Debt	$= \dfrac{\text{Operating Income from Continuing Operations after Tax + Depreciation and Amortization + Deferred Income Tax Expense + Other Major Recurring Noncash Items}}{\text{Short- and Long-Term Debt}}$	$0.098 = \dfrac{\$311 + \$1{,}524 + \$15 + \$1{,}645 + \$0}{\$3{,}276 + \$32{,}534}$
Debt to EBITDA	$= \dfrac{\text{Short- and Long-Term Debt}}{\text{Operating Profits before Interest Income, Interest Expense, Income Taxes + Depreciation and Amortization + Asset Impairment}}$	$6.727 = \dfrac{\$3{,}276 + \$32{,}534}{\$2{,}154 + \$1{,}524 + \$1{,}645}$

Based on the indicators of financial risk, ***Teva's*** financial risk is highly leveraged. The amount of funds from operations over debt, at 9.8, is below the highly leveraged benchmark of 12 and its Debt / EBITDA at 6.727 is above the highly leveraged benchmark of 5. Given that these indicators of financial leverage are in the highly leveraged range and its credit rating is "BBB," ***Teva's*** business risk is likely "excellent" based on information in Exhibit 14.7.

Sources: Financial statements from Teva Pharmaceuticals' Annual Report, 2016. http://ir.tevapharm.com/phoenix.zhtml?c=73925&p=irol-sec

Financial statements from Johnson & Johnson Company's Annual Report, 2016. http://files.shareholder.com/downloads/JNJ/3809936545x0xS200406-17-6/200406/filing.pdf

CAROLYN SLASKI

MANAGING PARTNER, NORTHEAST REGION ASSURANCE, ERNST & YOUNG LLP»

Carolyn Slaski

Carolyn Slaski is the Northeast Region Assurance Managing Partner at Ernst & Young LLP responsible for managing all strategic, client service, quality, and operational matters. She works closely with the firm's Assurance Leaders on the ongoing development and execution of the firm's market strategy, client service delivery model, and key matters impacting audit methodology and quality.

1 What are the advantages of debt financing over equity financing for your clients? How do capital market conditions affect a corporation's choices?

A company decides to finance with debt versus equity based on a thorough understanding of its business and industry, target capital structure, economic environment, and capital markets. When these conditions call for debt financing, the advantages include lower after-tax capital costs and a more optimal, shareholder-friendly capital structure. An additional benefit of issuing debt is that it generally does not provide the investor with control of the issuer through equity voting rights (e.g., the ability to vote on decisions regarding activities that are significant to the issuer).

2 Why is an announcement that a client will issue debt a positive signal regarding its future performance?

Investors interpret debt issuance positively when they believe the underlying business is stable and predictable enough to support regular interest and principal payments. If they view the company as underleveraged, additional debt moves the company to a more optimal capital structure. On the other hand, if investors believe management is allocating too much capital to R&D, capital expenditures, mergers and acquisitions, or excess working capital—or the cost structure is too high—an increase in debt to raise dividends or repurchase shares could be viewed as imposing more discipline on capital allocation processes.

3 What are some reasons why a client would elect to retire outstanding debt before maturity?

Companies choose to retire outstanding debt for a number of reasons. They may be able to refinance at a lower interest rate or with less restrictive terms. A company that wishes to rebalance its capital structure may retire debt so that it can issue equity. If a company has a debt obligation that is trading below its face value, it may wish to retire it to receive a tax deduction for the "loss."

4 Are companies electing to use the fair value option to value their debt obligations and, if so, why?

In practice, mainly financial institutions (rather than corporations) have elected the fair value option (FVO) for their debt. This choice may be a result of the limitations of hedge accounting in reducing the volatility of their debt. The FVO addresses both simplification and cost-benefit considerations; for example, accounting for hybrid debt instruments (such as convertible debt) at fair value can eliminate the potential need to separately account for the embedded derivative features from their debt host.

5 How does the use of the fair value option to value debt enhance information provided to the users of financial statements?

The FVO reflects economic events in earnings, such as credit quality and interest rates, on a timely basis. It also contributes to simplification of reporting because it negates the need for cumbersome disclosures required for complex financial instruments.

6 Ernst & Young is an international accounting firm. How do U.S. accounting standards differ from those issued under IFRS with respect to the separation of the debt and equity features of hybrid debt securities?

Both sets of accounting standards require identification of the same hybrid instrument's contractual features for analysis, although frequently there will be differences in the resulting classification. Under U.S. GAAP, the mind-set is more "instrument based," whereas IFRS is more "feature based." IFRS concentrates more on the substance rather than legal form of the instrument.

Discussion Questions

1. Explain how the use of the fair value option for investments in debt securities can mitigate volatility in reported earnings caused by measuring related assets and liabilities differently without applying complex hedge accounting provisions.
2. Discuss the benefits to financial statement users when accountants separate the debt and equity features of hybrid debt securities.

Summary by Learning Objectives

Below we summarize the main points by learning objective. Throughout the chapter, we discuss the accounting and reporting of U.S. GAAP and IFRS side by side. The table below also highlights the major similarities and differences between the standards.

1 Describe and illustrate accounting for notes payable.

Summary	Similarities and Differences between U.S. GAAP and IFRS
Notes payable are initially recognized at their fair value. Most notes include specified principal amount, specified interest rate, and maturity date. Short-term (long-term) notes payable are current (noncurrent) liabilities because they are due and payable within 1 year (within a period greater than 1 year) from the balance sheet date or operating cycle, whichever is longer. Interest expense is the carrying value of the note payable times the interest rate. An installment note requires a fixed payment each period that includes both principal and interest. The interest portion of the payment is the note balance at the beginning of the period times the interest rate. The principal portion of the payment is the total payment less the interest portion. When a loan has no interest rate stated (a non-interest-bearing note) or the stated interest rate is less than the market interest rate, the present value is measured as the value of the note discounted at the market rate of interest.	Similar under U.S. GAAP and IFRS.

2 Explain the common features of bonds payable and discuss the initial recognition at par value, at a discount, and at a premium.

Summary	Similarities and Differences between U.S. GAAP and IFRS
Bonds payable are contractual obligations under which a company commonly pays a face value at maturity and periodic interest payments until maturity. Bonds are issued at: • Par value when the stated interest rate on the bond equals the market rate. • A discount when the stated interest rate is lower than the market rate. • A premium when the stated rate is greater than the market rate. Credit rating agencies help creditors and investors assess a company's credit quality. The better the credit rating, the stronger is a company's capacity to repay its debt.	Similar under U.S. GAAP and IFRS.

Summary by Learning Objectives, continued

3 Demonstrate accounting for bonds issued at par or at a discount or premium, including computation of the bond issue price, interest expense, and amortization of the discount or premium using the effective interest rate method.

Summary	Similarities and Differences between U.S. GAAP and IFRS
Bonds payable issued at par are recorded at their face value. Interest expense is incurred over the periods that a bond is outstanding at the bond's stated (coupon) rate. The bond issue price is the present value of future cash flows. For bonds that make interest payments, the future cash flows are: • The periodic interest payments. • The principal payment at maturity. Firms use the market rate to discount the cash flows. Bonds are carried at the present value after issuance. Any bond discount or premium is amortized over the life of the bond. Under the effective interest rate method, interest expense is the carrying value of the bond at the beginning of the period times the market interest rate. The computation is: Equation (14.1): Effective Interest Expense = Historical Market Rate × Carrying Value of Bond at the Beginning of the Period The discount or premium amortization under the effective interest rate method is: Equation (14.2): Discount/Premium Amortization = Effective Interest Expense − Cash Interest Paid A zero-coupon bonds whose stated rate is zero and no interest is paid to bondholders is a special case of bonds issued at a discount.	➤ Similar under U.S. GAAP and IFRS except that IFRS prefers the net method to record bonds on initial recognition.

4 Explain and illustrate accounting for bonds issued between interest payment dates.

Summary	Similarities and Differences between U.S. GAAP and IFRS
When bonds are issued between interest payment dates, the purchasers pay any interest accrued.	Similar under U.S. GAAP and IFRS.

5 Discuss and illustrate the accounting for bond issue costs.

Summary	Similarities and Differences between U.S. GAAP and IFRS
Bond issue costs reduce the carrying value of the bond and require that a new effective interest rate be computed.	Similar under U.S. GAAP and IFRS.

Summary by Learning Objectives, continued

6 Determine the accounting for bonds payable at early retirement.

Summary	Similarities and Differences between U.S. GAAP and IFRS
Mature bonds are retired when the company pays the principal payment to the bondholders. If a bond is paid off before maturity, a company recognizes a gain or loss on early extinguishment. Equation (14.3): Gain (Loss) on Early Extinguishment = Net Carrying Value of the Debt − Retirement Price	Similar under U.S. GAAP and IFRS.

7 Explain and illustrate the accounting for convertible bonds.

Summary	Similarities and Differences between U.S. GAAP and IFRS
Convertible bonds are financial instruments that enable the holder to convert the bonds into a specified number of shares of common stock or preferred shares. Even though convertible bonds contain debt and equity components, they are accounted for as debt under U.S. GAAP. At conversion, the company removes the bonds payable along with any unamortized premium or unamortized discount from the balance sheet. The company also recognizes stock and any additional paid-in capital for the amount of the derecognized bond. If a beneficial conversion option exists at bond issuance, it is measured at its intrinsic value on the date of issue and reported as equity, additional paid-in capital. When the bonds are converted, the carrying value of the bonds and the additional paid-in capital related to the beneficial conversion option amount are removed and replaced with equity.	➤ Under IFRS, the debt and equity components of convertible debt are accounted for separately. The debt component is the present value of the bond's future cash flows at the market rate. The equity component is the issue price less the debt component. At conversion, the company removes the bonds payable, any unamortized premium or discount, and the equity recorded at issuance.

8 Describe and illustrate the accounting for warrants, including those that are detachable and nondetachable.

Summary	Similarities and Differences between U.S. GAAP and IFRS
Warrants are long-term options to acquire a stated number of shares of common stock for a stated price. Stock warrants may be issued with bonds and can either be: • Detachable: Removable by the holder and sellable separately on the secondary market. • Nondetachable: Not separable from the bond. For nondetachable warrants, the total debt proceeds are typically assigned to the debt issue. For detachable warrants, the proceeds are allocated to the debt and equity components using one of the following methods: • Proportional method: When fair values of both the bonds and warrants are known, the allocation is on the relative fair values. • Incremental (or residual) method: If the fair value of the bonds or the warrants is not readily determinable, allocate the portion of the proceeds to the instrument with the readily available fair value and allocate the residual amount to the other instrument.	➤ Under IFRS, the debt and equity components are accounted for separately. The debt component is the present value of the bond's future cash flows at the market rate. The equity component is the issue price less the debt component.

Summary by Learning Objectives, continued

9 Explain the reclassification of financing liabilities for current maturities of long-term debt, short-term debt expected to be refinanced, and callable obligations.

Summary	Similarities and Differences between U.S. GAAP and IFRS
The portion of a long-term obligation that becomes payable within the next year (or operating cycle, if longer) is reclassified to current liabilities. Short-term debt expected to be refinanced on a long-term basis can be classified as noncurrent debt when management intends and has the ability to refinance. Long-term debt may be reclassified to short-term debt when the creditor can call the debt, usually because of the violation of a provision of the debt agreement. If a creditor waives the provision or offers a grace period, the debt may remain classified as long term.	➤ Similar under U.S. GAAP and IFRS except when callable debt can remain classified as long-term debt. Under U.S. GAAP, a creditor can grant a waiver until the time the financial statements are released to be able to continue to classify the debt as long term. IFRS allows long-term debt to continue to be classified as long term if a waiver is received prior to year-end. Short-term debt expected to be refinanced can be classified as noncurrent debt when management intends and has the discretion to refinance the debt for at least 12 months after the reporting period under an existing arrangement to provide refinancing.

10 Discuss and illustrate the fair value option in accounting for financing liabilities.

Summary	Similarities and Differences between U.S. GAAP and IFRS
Companies can choose to report their financial liabilities at fair value subsequent to initial recognition. Changes in fair value unrelated to instrument-specific risk are taken to net income. Changes in fair value related to changes in the instrument-specific credit risk are taken to other comprehensive income.	➤ Similar under U.S. GAAP and IFRS except that IFRS is more restrictive than U.S. GAAP regarding when a company can choose the fair value option. Under IFRS, a company can choose the fair value option in one of two circumstances: • When the information presented is more relevant. • When fair value consistently measures liabilities or assets and gains or losses on them on the same bases.

11 Detail required disclosures for financing liabilities.

Summary	Similarities and Differences between U.S. GAAP and IFRS
Companies disclose a detailed list and description of each significant debt issue, including the: • Type of borrowing • Outstanding balance • Interest rate • Payment terms • Maturity date Other specific disclosures depend on the type of debt.	Similar under U.S. GAAP and IFRS.

MyLab Accounting

Go to **http://www.pearson.com/mylab/accounting** for the following Questions, Multiple-Choice Questions, Brief Exercises, Exercises, and Problems. They are available with immediate grading, explanations of correct and incorrect answers, and interactive media that acts as your own online tutor.

14 Financing Liabilities

Questions

1 2 **Q14-1.** What conditions or terms does a note payable contain?

2 **Q14-2.** If the market rate of interest exceeds the face or stated rate on a long-term debt obligation, will the company issue the debt at a discount or premium? Explain.

5 **Q14-3.** What is included in bond issue costs and how should a company account for them?

3 **Q14-4.** What method of amortization must companies use to amortize a bond discount or premium when reporting?

3 **Q14-5.** When a bond is issued at a discount, will its periodic interest expense be greater or less than the interest payment? Explain.

6 **Q14-6.** If a company opts to retire debt before maturity, will it report a gain or loss in net income? Explain.

7 **Q14-7.** What is convertible debt and how do firms account for it?

7 **Q14-8.** Under IFRS, how do firms account for convertible debt?

8 **Q14-9.** Debt issued with warrants is considered a hybrid security that possesses both debt and equity characteristics. Will accountants always separate the total proceeds into debt and equity on the balance sheet? Explain.

9 **Q14-10.** Can companies reclassify short-term debt expected to be refinanced on a long-term basis after the balance sheet date as long-term debt? Explain.

9 **Q14-11.** Under IFRS, can companies reclassify short-term debt expected to be refinanced on a long-term basis during the post-balance sheet period as long-term debt? Explain.

9 **Q14-12.** Do companies always reclassify long-term debt that becomes callable by the creditor as a short-term obligation? Explain.

10 **Q14-13.** Can a company choose the fair value option for any long-term financial liability? Explain.

10 **Q14-14.** Can a company choose the fair value option for any long-term financial liability under IFRS? Explain.

10 **Q14-15.** If a company elects the fair value option for long-term liabilities, can it report unrealized gains and losses in other comprehensive income? Explain.

11 **Q14-16.** Does a company have to disclose the total amount of debt that matures each year for all long-term debt? Explain.

Multiple-Choice Questions

In partnership with: BECKER PROFESSIONAL EDUCATION®

Becker CPA Exam Review multiple-choice questions are available in **MyLab Accounting**.

1 **MC14-1.** During the fourth quarter ended December 31, Year 1, Lighting Fixtures Inc. (LFI) had average outstanding revolving bank loans of $1.2 million. Assume that the quarterly interest charges associated with these loans was $7,500. If LFI makes the interest payment to the banks on January 15, Year 2, what is the journal entry (if any) made by the company on December 31 to reflect this information?

a. Accrued Interest Payable	7,500	
Interest Expense		7,500
b. Interest Expense	7,500	
Accrued Interest Payable		7,500
c. Interest Expense	7,500	
Loan Payable		7,500
d. No journal entry necessary.		

3 **MC14-2.** On July 1, Year 1, Cobb Company issued 9% bonds in the face amount of $1,000,000 that mature in 10 years. The bonds were issued for $939,000 to yield 10%, resulting in a bond discount of $61,000. Cobb uses the effective interest method of amortizing bond discount. Interest is payable annually on June 30.

At June 30, Year 3, Cobb's unamortized bond discount should be:

a. $52,810 b. $57,100 c. $48,800 d. $43,000

3 **MC14-3.** On July 1, Year 1, Planet Corporation sold Ken Company 10-year, 8% bonds with a face amount of $500,000 for $520,000. The market rate was 6%. The bonds pay interest semiannually on June 30 and December 31. For the 6 months ended December 31, Year 1, what amount should Planet report as bond interest expense and long-term liability in the balance sheet and income statement for Year 1?

Balance Sheet	Income Statement
a. $511,200	$31,200
b. $500,000	$20,000
c. $504,400	$ 4,400
d. $515,600	$15,600

3 **MC14-4.** On November 1, Year 1, Dixon Corporation issued $800,000 of its 10-year, 8% term bonds dated October 1, Year 1. The bonds were sold to yield 10% with total proceeds of $700,000 plus accrued interest. Interest is paid every April 1 and October 1. What amount should Dixon report for interest payable in its December 31, Year 1, balance sheet?

a. $17,500 b. $16,000 c. $11,667 d. $10,667

3 **MC14-5.** On January 1, Year 1, Congo.com issued $1,000,000 of its 10-year, 9% bonds (interest paid annually) to yield 8%. The present value of $1 at 9% for 10 years is 0.4224, and the present value of an ordinary annuity of $1 at 9% for 10 years is 6.4177. The present value of $1 at 8% for 10 years is 0.4632, and the present value of an ordinary annuity of $1 at 8% for 10 years is 6.7101. Which of the following is closest to the selling price of the bond?

a. $920,000 b. $1,000,000 c. $1,040,800 d. $1,067,100

6 **MC14-6.** Clothes Horse Corp. (CHC) issued $500,000 bonds due in 10 years on January 1, Year 1, at a premium for $567,105. On January 1, Year 6, when the carrying value of the bond was $539,940, CHC redeemed the bonds at 102. What amount of gain should CHC record related to the redemption?

a. $10,000 b. $29,940 c. $39,940 d. $0

7 **MC14-7.** Walco Manufacturing Inc. holds 500 convertible bonds from Indwell Semiconductor that it purchased on January 1, Year 1, for $518,110. The face amount of each bond is $1,000. Each bond is convertible into one share of Indwell common stock. The par value of Indwell's stock is $55. On January 2, Year 1, Walco converted half of the bonds to common stock. Indwell uses the book value method to record the conversion. In the journal entry to record the conversion, what amount will Indwell debit to the premium on bond payable?

a. $0 b. $9,055 c. $13,750 d. $18,110

7 **MC14-8.** On July 1, Year 1, after recording interest and amortization, Wake Company's shareholders converted $1,000,000 of its 10% convertible bonds into 50,000 shares of its $1 par value common stock. On the conversion date, the carrying amount of the bonds was $1,500,000, the market value of the bonds was $1,400,000, and Wake's common stock was publicly trading at $40 per share. Assume there is no beneficial conversion option. Using the book value method, what amount of additional paid-in capital should Wake record as a result of the conversion?

a. $500,000 b. $1,500,000 c. $1,950,000 d. $1,450,000

8 **MC14-9.** On December 30, Year 1, Wayne Corporation issued 1,000 of its 10-year, 8%, $1,000 face value bonds with detachable stock warrants at par. Each bond carried a detachable warrant for one share of Wayne's common stock at a specified option price of $25 per share. Immediately after issuance, the market value of the bonds without the warrants was $1,080,000, and the market value of the warrants was $120,000. In its December 31, Year 1 balance sheet, what amount should Wayne report as bonds payable?

a. $1,080,000 b. $1,000,000 c. $900,000 d. $1,200,000

8 **MC14-10.** Use the information provided in MC14-9 except that immediately after issuance, the market value of each warrant was $120. In its December 31, Year 1, balance sheet, what amount should Wayne report as the book value of bonds payable?

a. $880,000 b. $900,000 c. $1,000,000 d. $1,120,000

5 **MC14-11.** On June 30 of the current year, Huff Corp. issued 1,000 of its 8%, $1,000 bonds at 99. The bonds were issued through an underwriter to whom Huff paid bond issue costs of $35,000. On June 30 of the current year, Huff should report the bond liability on its balance sheet at:

a. $955,000 b. $965,000 c. $990,000 d. $1,000,000

Brief Exercises

1 **BE14-1. Notes Payable**. Scudder Products, Inc. borrowed $600,000 by issuing a 6-month note on September 1 of the current fiscal year. The note is due on March 1 of the following fiscal year. The short-term note carries a 5% annual interest rate with interest due at maturity. The company's fiscal year ends on December 31. Prepare the journal entries on September 1 and December 31 of the current year.

1 **BE14-2. Notes Payable**. Using the information provided in BE14-1, prepare the journal entry required to record Scudder's full payment of the note at maturity.

1 **BE14-3. Long-Term Notes Payable**. Andy Corporation borrowed $1,500,000 on January 1, 2016. The note agreement specifies that it will pay interest quarterly at 8% on March 31, June 30, September 30 and December 31. The principal will be due on December 31, 2021. The company's fiscal year ends on December 31. What journal entry will Andy Corporation make on January 1, 2016? What journal entry will Andy Corporation make at the end of each quarter? What journal entries will Andy Corporation make on December 31, 2021?

1 **BE14-4. Short-Term Notes Payable**. Sallie Corporation borrowed $700,000 on November 1, 2016. The note agreement specifies that it will pay interest quarterly at 6% and the principal will be due on October 31, 2017. The company's fiscal year ends December 31. What journal entry will Sallie make on November 1, 2016? What journal entry will Sallie make on December 31, 2016?

1 **BE14-5. Installment Loans, Long Term**. For each case, provide the missing information. Assume that payments occur at the end of each period.

	(1)	(2)	(3)	(4)
Amount borrowed	(a)	$675,000	$456,000	$750,000
Interest rate	4%	4%	6%	12%
Number of periodic payments per year	4	2	1	4
Maturity (in years)	10	10	(c)	4
Periodic payment	$10,354.90	(b)	$81,685.57	(d)

1 **BE14-6. Installment Loans, Long Term**. Ironbound, Inc. borrows $150,000 by issuing a 12%, 4-year note on January 1, 2016. Ironbound must make payments of principal and interest every 3 months, beginning March 31, 2016. The note will be fully paid at maturity on December 31, 2019. The company's fiscal year ends on December 31. Prepare the journal entries at January 1, 2016, and March 31, 2016.

2 **BE14-7. Bond Terminology**. Match each term with its definition or explanation. Terms can be used more than once.

Term	Definition/Explanation
a. Face value	______ Frequency with which cash interest payments are made to the bondholders
b. Premium	______ Nominal rate
c. Maturity date	______ Principal
d. Discount	______ Occurs when a bond issue is priced below par value
e. Interest payment period	______ Occurs when the effective interest rate is higher than the stated interest rate
f. Stated interest rate	______ Par value
g. Market rate	______ Occurs when a bond issue is priced above par value
	______ Amount of interest that the bond issuer will pay in cash expressed as an annual rate
	______ Occurs when the effective interest rate is lower than the stated interest rate
	______ Face rate
	______ Actual return that the investors will receive
	______ Specified date when the bond issuer must pay the face value of the bonds to the bondholders
	______ Coupon rate
	______ The amount that the company will pay the bondholder at maturity

2 **BE14-8. Bond Pricing.** Fill in the missing items for each of the cases below:

	(1)	(2)	(3)	(4)
Face value	$100,000	(d)	$250,000	$1,980,000
Stated rate	5%	5%	6%	(i)
Interest payment period	Quarterly	Semiannually	Quarterly	Quarterly
Interest payment	(a)	$13,250	$3,750	$34,650
Maturity (in years)	10 years	5 years	3 years	4 years
Market rate	4%	(e)	8%	4%
Bond issue price	(b)	(f)	(g)	(j)
(Discount) / Premium	(c)	($19,216)	(h)	(k)

3 **BE14-9. Bond Issue Price.** Jorge Corporation issued $100,000 par value, 6%, 4-year bonds (i.e., there were 100 of $1,000 par value bonds in the issue). Interest is payable semiannually each January 1 and July 1 with the first interest payment due at the end of the period on July 1. Determine the issue price of the bonds if the market rate of interest is 8%.

3 **BE14-10. Bond Issue Price.** Using the information from BE14-9, determine the issue price of the bonds assuming that the market rate of interest is 4%.

3 5 **BE14-11. Bond Issue, Bond Issue Costs.** On January 1, Plum Company issued $800,000 par value, 8%, 5-year bonds (i.e., there were 800 of $1,000 par value bonds in the issue). Interest is payable semiannually each January 1 and July 1 with the first interest payment due at the end of the period on July 1. Plum paid $9,000 in underwriting fees. Determine the issue price of the bonds with a 12% market rate of interest and prepare the journal entry to record the bond issue.

3 5 **BE14-12. Bond Issue, Bond Issue Costs.** Using the information from BE14-11, determine the issue price of the bonds assuming that the market rate of interest is 6%, and prepare the journal entry to record the bond issue.

3 5 **BE14-13. Bond Issue, Bond Issue Costs.** West Fork Corporation issued $100,000 par value, 6%, 4-year bonds (i.e., there were 100 of $1,000 par value bonds in the issue). Interest is payable annually with the first interest payment made at the end of the period. West Fork paid $1,800 in underwriting fees. Determine the issue price of the bonds assuming that the market rate of interest is 8%. Prepare the journal entry to record the bond issue.

3 **BE14-14. Bond Issue, Effective Interest Rate Method, Amortization Table.** On January 1, 2018, Stark Incorporated issued $1,500,000 par value, 5%, 7-year bonds (i.e., there were 1,500 of $1,000 par value bonds in the issue). Interest is payable semiannually each January 1 and July 1 with the first interest payment due at the end of the period on July 1. Determine the issue price of the bonds based on an 8% market rate of interest. Prepare the amortization table for the first 2 years assuming that Stark uses the effective interest rate method.

A **BE14-15. Bond Issue, Straight Interest Rate Method, Amortization Table.** Using the information provided in BE14-14, prepare the amortization table for the first 2 years assuming that Stark uses the straight-line method.

3 **BE14-16. Bond Issue, Effective Interest Rate Method, Amortization Table.** Using the information provided in BE14-14, determine the issue price of the bonds assuming that the market rate of interest is 4%, and prepare the amortization table for the first 2 years assuming that Stark uses the effective interest rate method.

A **BE14-17. Bond Issue, Straight Interest Rate Method, Amortization Table.** Using the information provided in BE14-14, prepare the amortization table for the first 2 years assuming that Stark uses the straight-line method.

3 **BE14-18. Bonds Retired at Maturity.** Balsam Associates issued $600,000 par value, 10-year bonds on January 1, 2018, with a 2% stated interest rate. It will make interest payments semiannually each June 30 and December 31 with the first interest payment at the end of the period on June 30, 2018. The market rate of interest on the date of the bond issue was 4%. On what date do the bonds mature? Prepare the journal entry when the bonds mature (you do not need to include an entry for the interest payment).

4 **BE14-19. Bonds Issued between Interest Payment Dates.** For each of the following scenarios, compute the accrued interest and cash received when the bond is issued.

Scenario	**1**	**2**	**3**	**4**
Face value	$850,000	$250,000	$650,000	$350,000
Stated interest rate	5%	3%	5%	6%
Interest payments	Semiannually	Quarterly	Semiannually	Quarterly
Interest payment date	July 1	March 31	January 1	June 30
Issue date	September 30	May 1	May 1	August 31
Bond issue proceeds	$863,200	$197,500	$623,000	$357,000
Accrued interest	________	________	________	________
Cash received	________	________	________	________

6 **BE14-20. Early Bond Retirement.** On January 1, Todd Manufacturing issued $4,500,000 par value 8%, 5-year bonds (i.e., there were 4,500 of $1,000 par value bonds in the issue). Interest is payable semiannually each January 1 and July 1 with the first interest payment due at the end of the period on July 1. The market rate of interest was 10% on the date that Todd issued the bonds. Todd retired the bonds at $4,000,000 with an open market purchase at the end of the first year. Prepare the journal entry to record the derecognition of the obligation. Todd uses the effective interest rate method.

6 **BE14-21. Early Bond Retirement.** Dott Manufacturing retired its $6,000,000 par value, 7%, 10-year bonds early on February 28, 2018, for $6,720,408, including accrued interest of $70,000. The carrying value of the bonds at retirement was $6,330,956. What is the gain or loss on early retirement? Prepare the journal entry to record the derecognition of the obligation.

7 **BE14-22. Convertible Bonds.** Lee Equipment Company issued 200 of 8-year, 6% convertible bonds for $227,200. Each bond had a par value of $1,000. Each $1,000 bond converts into eight shares of $1 par value common stock at the option of the bondholder beginning 2 years after the date of issue. The market price of the common stock on the commitment date was equal to $120 per share, and the market rate of interest was 6% at issuance. Prepare the journal entry to record the bond issue.

7 **BE14-23. Convertible Bonds, Conversion.** Using the information from BE14-22, prepare the journal entry to record the bond conversion assuming that the balance of the unamortized premium on the date of conversion is $14,660.

7 **BE14-24. Convertible Bonds, IFRS.** Using the information from BE14-22, prepare the journal entry to record the bond issue assuming that Lee Equipment Company is an IFRS reporter.

7 **BE14-25. Convertible Bonds, Conversion, IFRS.** Using the information from BE14-22, prepare the journal entry to record the bond conversion assuming that Lee Equipment Company is an IFRS reporter.

7 **BE14-26. Convertible Bonds.** Walsh Beverages has outstanding convertible debt with a book value of $325,700 at the end of the current year. The bonds have a total par value of $300,000 and an unamortized premium of $25,700. Each $1,000 bond is convertible into 20 shares of $1 par value common stock. Prepare the journal entry required to record the bond conversion. Assume the bonds do not have a beneficial conversion option.

7 **BE14-27. Convertible Bonds Beneficial Conversion Option.** Determine whether each of the following convertible bonds has a beneficial conversion option. Each bond has a $1,000 face value and is issued at par.

a. Eight-year, 5% convertible bond converts to 50 shares of common stock. The market price of the common stock is $23 per share.
b. Five-year, 8% convertible bond converts to 100 shares of common stock. The market price of the common stock is $11 per share.
c. Five-year, 8% convertible bond converts to 25 shares of common stock. The market price of the common stock is $38 per share.

8 **BE14-28. Warrants.** Crow Company issued 6,000 of its $1,000 par value bonds for $1,580, providing total cash proceeds of $9,480,000. The market price of Crow's common shares on the date that it issued the bonds was $20 per share. It sold the bonds with 240,000 detachable warrants to acquire 240,000 shares of the company's $1 par value common stock for $20 per share. That is, each bond carried 40 warrants × 6,000 bonds = 240,000 shares. Crow had existing bonds outstanding that trade without warrants at $1,310. There were other Crow Company warrants outstanding that traded for $20 each. Prepare the journal entry to record the issuance of the bonds assuming that the proportional method is used.

8 **BE14-29. Warrants.** Using the information provided in BE14-28, prepare the journal entry to record the issuance of the bonds assuming that the incremental method is used and the market value of the warrants is not reasonably determinable.

9 **BE14-30.** **Short-Term Debt Expected to Be Refinanced, U.S. GAAP.** Saxon Woods, Inc. has a fiscal year-end of December 31, 2017. The company reported $124,500 in short-term notes payable due on April 1, 2018, on its year-end balance sheet. Saxon Woods extended the due date for this debt to January 31, 2019, during the post-balance sheet period. The bank agreed to extend the debt term for $100,000 of the total amount of the loan; $24,500 is due on its original due date. Prepare the journal entry required on December 31, 2017, to reflect the refinancing agreement under U.S. GAAP.

9 **BE14-31.** **Short-Term Debt Expected to Be Refinanced, IFRS.** Using the information provided in BE14-30, prepare the journal entry required on December 31, 2017, to reflect the refinancing agreement under IFRS.

9 **BE14-32.** **Callable Debt, U.S. GAAP.** Braylon Brands, Inc. borrowed $2,000,000 from Home Town Bank. The note payable had a term of 5 years and carried a 6% coupon interest. Because of an inadequate credit score, Braylon Brands agreed to several restrictive debt covenants. The debt agreement requires the company to maintain a 3-to-1 working capital ratio. Home Town Bank's review of the company's year-end financial statements indicated that Braylon achieved a working capital ratio of only 2 to 1. As a result, Home Town Bank will call in the loan within 3 months of the balance sheet date. Prepare the journal entry to record the call on the debtor's financial statements under U.S. GAAP.

9 **BE14-33.** **Callable Debt, IFRS.** Using the information provided in BE14-32, prepare the journal entry to record the effect of the call on the debtor's financial statements under IFRS.

9 **BE14-34.** **Callable Debt, U.S. GAAP.** Megga Brands, Inc. borrowed $1,500,000 from Telcity Bank. The note payable has a term of 15 years and carries a 4% coupon interest. Because it had an inadequate credit score, Megga Brands agreed to several restrictive debt covenants. The debt agreement requires the company to maintain a compensating balance of $150,000. On December 15, Megga was forced to draw down on the compensating balance to meet working capital requirements. The loan became callable by Telcity on December 31 of the current year. On January 15, Telcity granted Megga a waiver and opted not to call its debt. Megga will release its annual financial statements to shareholders on February 15. How should Megga classify the $1,500,000 note payable on the December 31 balance sheet? Provide any necessary journal entries under U.S. GAAP.

9 **BE14-35.** **Callable Debt, IFRS.** Using the information provided in BE14-34, how should Megga classify the $1,500,000 note payable on the December 31 balance sheet under IFRS? Provide any necessary journal entries.

10 **BE14-36.** **Fair Value Option.** Saratoga Company issued bonds with a face value of $200,000 on January 1, 2018, for $202,716. Saratoga uses the fair value option to measure the bonds. At the end of 2018, the carrying value of the bonds is $201,403, and their fair value is $203,780. The change in fair value relates to a change in interest rate. What is the entry to record the fair value adjustment?

10 **BE14-37.** **Fair Value Option.** Saratoga Company issued bonds with a face value of $300,000 on January 1, 2018, for $306,000. Saratoga uses the fair value option to measure the bonds. At the end of 2018, the carrying value of the bonds is $304,702 and their fair value is $301,600. Half of the fair value change relates to instrument-specific credit risk. What is the entry to record the fair value adjustment?

11 **BE14-38.** **Financial Statement Disclosure.** Use the following excerpt from the financial statements of Fixet Company's debt footnote (from Fixet Company's 2018 annual report) to answer these questions:

a. At December 31, 2018, what is the amount of the current portion of long-term debt?
b. How much debt will mature over the next 5 years?
c. What would be the difference in liabilities if Fixet reported the debt at fair values?

Fixet Company
Note 9—Long-Term Debt [Excerpt]

Long-term debt net of unamortized premiums and discounts and swap fair value adjustments is comprised of the following:

In millions of U.S. dollars	December 31, 2018
5.66% Corporate bond, payable July 23, 2020	$ 27.0
5.4% Corporate bond, payable August 7, 2020	16.1
4.7% Corporate bond, payable October 1, 2021	50.0
5.15% Corporate bond, payable December 15, 2023	110.4
4.3% Japanese yen note, payable June 26, 2025	117.7
1.52125% Japanese yen note, payable February 14, 2020	55.1
Total	376.3
Less current maturities	7.4
Non-Current Portion	$368.9

The scheduled maturity of long-term debt in each of the years ending December 31, 2019, through 2023, is $7.4 million, $172.1 million, $57.4 million, $47.4 million, and $7.3 million at face value, respectively.

The Company's long-term debt is recorded at adjusted cost, net of amortized premiums and discounts. The fair value of long-term debt is estimated based upon quoted prices for similar instruments. The fair value of the Company's long-term debt, including the current portion, was approximately $403 million at December 31, 2018.

Source: Financial statements from Fixet Company's 2018 annual report.

Exercises

1 **E14-1. Notes Payable.** Gardiner Manufacturing, Inc. borrowed $950,000 by issuing an 8-month note on July 1 of the current year. The note is due on March 1 of the following fiscal year. The short-term note carries a 6% annual interest rate with interest due at maturity. The company's fiscal year ends on December 31.

Required »

a. Prepare the journal entry to record the issuance of the note payable.
b. Prepare the journal entry required at year-end to record the interest accrual.
c. Prepare the journal entry to record the payment of the note at maturity.

1 **E14-2. Note Payable with Amortization Table.** EA&Y, Inc. borrowed $350,000 on January 1, 2018, with a 6% interest rate. It will make a payment of $101,007 annually (beginning December 31, 2018) until the note is paid off on December 31, 2021. The company's fiscal year ends on December 31. The payment includes interest and principal.

Required »

a. Prepare the journal entry to record the issuance of the note payable.
b. Prepare the amortization table for the note.
c. What is the journal entry at December 31, 2018?

1 **E14-3. Installment Loans, Long-Term.** Broad Street Company borrows $975,050 by issuing an 8%, 7-year note on January 1, 2018. Broad Street must make payments of principal and interest every 6 months beginning June 30, 2018. The note will be fully paid at maturity on December 31, 2024. The company's fiscal year ends on December 31.

Required »

a. Prepare the journal entry to record the issuance of the note payable.
b. Prepare an amortization table.
c. Prepare the journal entry to record payments for the first year.
d. What is the amount of the note payable on the balance sheet at December 31, 2018? What is the interest expense for the year?

1 **E14-4. Note Payable with Amortization Table.** On March 31, 2018, Vine Company issued a $487,000, 2%, 3-year note payable when the market rate was 8%. Interest is due on each March 31, beginning March 31, 2019. The company's fiscal year ends on December 31.

Required »

a. Prepare the journal entry to record the issuance of the note payable.
b. Prepare an amortization table.
c. Prepare the journal entry to record interest expense at December 31, 2018.
d. Prepare the journal entry required on March 31, 2019.

3 **E14-5. Bond Issue, Interest Payments, Effective Interest Rate Method, Amortization Table.** On January 1, 2018, Mill Road Corporation issued $300,000 par value, 5%, 5-year bonds. Interest is payable semiannually each January 1 and July 1 with the first interest payment due at the end of the period on July 1, 2018. The market rate of interest on the date of the bond issue was 8%. The company's fiscal year ends on December 31.

Required »

a. Determine the issue price of the debt.
b. Prepare the amortization table for the bond issue assuming that Mill Road uses the effective interest rate method of amortization.
c. Prepare the journal entries to record the bond issue, the first interest entry, and payment of the bonds at maturity. Assume that the company uses a premium or discount account if needed.

3 **E14-6. Bond Issue, Interest Payments, Effective Interest Rate Method, Amortization Table.** On January 1, 2018, the Landon Capital Partners issued $600,000 par value, 6%, 6-year bonds. Interest is payable semiannually

each January 1 and July 1 with the first interest payment due at the end of the period on July 1, 2018. The market rate of interest on the date of the bond issue was 4%.

Required »

a. Determine the issue price of the debt.
b. Prepare the amortization table for the bond issue assuming that Landon uses the effective interest rate method of amortization.
c. Prepare the journal entries to record the bond issue, the first interest entry, and payment of the bonds at maturity. Assume that the company uses a premium or discount account, if needed.

3 **E14-7. Zero-Coupon Bond Issue, Interest Payments, Effective Interest Rate Method.** On January 1, 2018, McMillan Corporation issued $100,000 par value, 5-year, zero-coupon bonds. The market rate of interest on the date of the bond issue was 6%. The company's fiscal year ends on December 31.

Required »

a. Determine the issue price of the debt.
b. Prepare the amortization table for the bond issue assuming that McMillan uses the effective interest rate method of amortization.
c. Prepare the journal entries to record the bond issue, the amortization entry on December 31, 2018, and payment of the bonds at maturity. Assume that the company uses a premium or discount account if needed.

3 **E14-8. Bond Issue, Interest Payments, Effective Interest Rate Method.** On January 1, 2018, Faxico, Inc. issued $4,500,000 par value, 8%, 5-year bonds. Interest is payable semiannually each January 1 and July 1 with the first interest payment due at the end of the period on July 1, 2018. The market rate of interest on the date of the bond issue was 10%.

Required »

a. Determine the issue price of the debt.
b. Prepare the amortization table for the bond issue assuming that the effective interest rate method of amortization is used.
c. Prepare the journal entries to record the bond issue and the first interest entry. Assume that the company uses a premium or discount account if needed.

4 **E14-9. Bond Sold between Interest Payment Dates, Sold at Par.** Takedo Company issued $600,000 par value, 10-year, 5% bonds on February 1, 2018. The bonds are dated January 1, 2018, and pay interest quarterly each March 31, June 30, September 30, and December 31. The bonds are sold at par plus accrued interest because the bonds are sold between interest dates. Prepare the journal entries required to issue the bonds on February 1, 2018, and record the first interest payment on March 31.

4 **E14-10. Bond Sold between Interest Payment Dates, Sold at Discount.** Briscoe Company issued $700,000 par value, 5-year, 4% bonds on April 30, 2018. The bonds are dated January 1, 2018, and pay interest semiannually on June 30 and December 31. The bonds are sold at $703,455, including accrued interest, because they are sold between interest dates. Prepare the journal entries required to issue the bonds on April 30, 2018, and record the first interest payment on June 30, 2018. The market rate of interest on the date of sale of the bonds was 4.2%.

4 **E14-11. Bond Sold between Interest Payment Dates, Sold at Premium.** Teter Company issued $700,000 par value, 5-year, 3% bonds on November 30, 2018. The bonds are dated July 1, 2018, and pay interest semiannually on June 30 and December 31. The bonds are sold at $723,807, including accrued interest, because they are sold between interest dates. The market rate of interest on the date of sale was 2.5%. Prepare the journal entries required to issue the bonds on November 30, 2018, and record the first interest payment on December 31, 2018.

6 **E14-12. Early Bond Retirement, Effective Interest Rate Method.** On January 1, 2018, Faxico, Inc. issued $4,500,000 par value 8%, 5-year bonds. Interest is payable semiannually on January 1 and July 1 with the first interest payment on July 1, 2018. The market rate of interest on the date of the bond issue was 10%. Faxico retired the debt early at the end of the third year for $4,000,000.

Required »

a. Determine the carrying value of the bond at retirement.
b. Prepare the journal entry to record the early retirement of the debt at the end of the third year.

7 **E14-13. Convertible Bonds, Conversion.** On January 1, 2018, Mobile Technology, Incorporated issued $850,000 of $1,000 par value, 6%, 6-year bonds. Interest is payable semiannually each January 1 and July 1 with the first interest payment due at the end of the period on July 1, 2018. The market rate of interest for similar non-convertible bonds on the date of the bond issue was 10%. However, because these bonds are

convertible, the effective rate is 8%. Each bond is convertible into 20 shares of Mobile Technology's $2 par value common stock. Assume there is no beneficial conversion option.

Required »

a. Determine the issue price of the debt.
b. Prepare the amortization table for the bond issue assuming that Mobile Technology uses the effective interest rate method of amortization.
c. Prepare the journal entry when Mobile Technology issued the bonds.
d. Prepare the journal entry to record the first interest payment.
e. The bonds converted on January 1, 2021. Prepare the journal entry to record the bond conversion.

7 **E14-14. Convertible Bonds, Conversion.** Using the information provided in E14-13, complete the following requirements assuming that the effective rate of interest for convertible bonds is 4% on the date of issue.

Required »

a. Determine the issue price of the debt.
b. Prepare the amortization table for the bond issue assuming that Mobile Technology uses the effective interest rate method of amortization.
c. Prepare the journal entry when Mobile Technology issued the bonds.
d. Prepare the journal entry to record the first interest payment.
e. The bonds converted on January 1, 2021. Prepare the journal entry to record the bond conversion.

7 **E14-15. Convertible Bonds, Conversion, IFRS.** Using the information provided in E14-13, complete the following requirements assuming that Mobile Technology reports under IFRS.

Required »

a. Determine the present value of bond cash flows.
b. Prepare the amortization table for the bond issue assuming that Mobile Technology uses the effective interest rate method of amortization.
c. Prepare the journal entry when the bonds are issued.
d. The bonds converted on January 1, 2021. Prepare the journal entry to record the bond conversion.

7 **E14-16. Convertible Bonds Beneficial Conversion Option.** Marly, Inc., issues 1,000 of 6-year, 3% convertible bonds at par of $1,000. Each $1,000 bond converts into 10 shares of no-par value common stock at the option of the bondholder beginning 3 years after the date of issue. There were no bond issue costs. The market price of the common stock when the bonds are issued is $116 per share. Interest is paid annually. Prepare the journal entry to record the issuance of Marly's convertible debt. What is the effective interest rate on the bonds?

7 **E14-17. Convertible Bonds Beneficial Conversion Option, Conversion.** Use the information from E14-16 and assume that all bonds convert after 3 years. The carrying value of the bonds at the conversion date is $913,000. Prepare the journal entry at conversion.

8 **E14-18. Warrants.** Randolph Company issued 4,500 of its $1,000 par value bonds for $1,440, providing total cash proceeds of $6,480,000. There are no bond issue costs. The market price of Randolph's common shares on the date that the bonds were issued was $40 per share. The bonds were sold with 90,000 warrants to acquire 90,000 shares of the company's $1 par value common stock for $50 per share. That is, each bond carries 20 warrants. Randolph has existing bonds outstanding that currently trade without warrants at $1,160. There are other Randolph warrants outstanding that trade for $35 each. Assume that the fair value of the bonds is more reliable than the market value of the warrants.

Required »

a. Prepare the journal entry to record issuance of the bonds assuming that the warrants are nondetachable.
b. Prepare the journal entry to record the issuance of the bonds assuming that the warrants are detachable using the proportional method.
c. Prepare the journal entry to record the issuance of the bonds assuming that the warrants are detachable using the incremental method.
d. Assuming that the incremental method is used, prepare the journal entry required to record the exercise of all warrants.

8 **E14-19. Warrants.** DHC Associates issued 2,100 of its $1,000, 8%, 5-year par value bonds. There are no bond issue costs. Interest is paid annually. The market rate on the date of issue was 9%. The market price of DHC common shares on the date that the bonds are issued is $50 per share. The bonds were sold with 50,000 warrants to acquire 50,000 shares of the company's $1 par value common stock for $40 per share. That is, each bond carries 25 warrants. DHC has existing bonds outstanding that trade without warrants at $920. There are other DHC warrants outstanding that trade for $40 each.

Required »

a. Determine the issue price of the bonds.

b. Prepare the journal entry to record issuance of the bonds assuming that the warrants are nondetachable.
c. Prepare the journal entry to record the issuance of the bonds assuming that the warrants are detachable using the proportional method.
d. Prepare the journal entry to record the issuance of the bonds assuming that the warrants are detachable using the incremental method. Assume that the fair value of the bonds is more reliable.
e. Assuming that the incremental method is used, prepare the journal entry required to record the exercise of all warrants.

10 **E14-20. Fair Value Option.** On January 1, 2018, McMillan Corporation issued $86,000 par value, 6-year bonds with a 0% stated interest rate. The discount on the bonds is amortized annually each December 31. The market rate of interest on the date of the bond issue was 3.25%. Fair value changes are not the result of instrument-specific credit risk. The amortization table for the bond follows. Assume that McMillan elected the fair value option on the date of issue.

Amortization Table under Effective Interest Rate Method

Period	0% Cash Interest	3.25% Effective Interest	Discount Amortization	Carrying Value	Fair Value
0				$70,984	$70,984
1	0	$ 2,307	$ 2,307	73,291	72,500
2	0	2,382	2,382	75,673	76,817
3	0	2,459	2,459	78,132	78,002
4	0	2,539	2,539	80,671	80,880
5	0	2,622	2,622	83,293	83,325
6	0	2,707	2,707	86,000	86,000
Total	$0	$15,016	$15,016		

Required »

Prepare the entry required to adjust the balance of the debt to fair value at the end of the first, second, and third years.

10 **E14-21. Fair Value Option.** On January 1, 2018, Sohape Corporation issued $100,000 par value, 5-year bonds with a 3% stated interest rate. Interest is paid annually each December 31. The market rate of interest on the date of the bond issue was 2.5%. The amortization table for the bond follows. Assume that Sohape elected the fair value option on the date of issue. Fair value changes are not the result of instrument-specific credit risk.

Amortization Table under Effective Interest Rate Method

Period	3% Cash Interest	2.50% Effective Interest	Premium Amortization	Carrying Value	Fair Value
0				$102,323	$102,323
1	$ 3,000	$ 2,558	$ 442	101,881	102,970
2	3,000	2,547	453	101,428	102,160
3	3,000	2,536	464	100,964	102,099
4	3,000	2,524	476	100,488	102,067
5	3,000	2,512	488	100,000	100,000
Total	$15,000	$12,677	$2,323		

Required »

Prepare the entry required to adjust the balance of the debt to fair value at the end of the first, second, and third years.

Problems

1 **P14-1. Long-Term Notes Payable with Amortization Table.** On January 1, 2017, Antonia Lee Stores, Inc., borrowed $700,000 and immediately received the full amount. The note carried a 7% interest rate and requires annual payments of $146,857 beginning on December 31, 2017. The note matures on December 31, 2022. The company's fiscal year ends on December 31. The payment includes interest and principal.

Required »

a. Prepare the journal entry to record the issuance of the note payable.
b. Prepare the amortization table for the note.
c. Prepare the journal entry required to record the first payment on December 31, 2017.
d. What is the balance of the note on December 31, 2021, after the payment?
e. Prepare the journal entry to record the payment of the note at maturity.

1 **P14-2. Long-Term Notes Payable, Semiannual Interest, Amortization Table.** On January 1, 2018, Priolo Builders Company borrowed $650,000 by issuing 4%, 5-year notes. The full amount of the cash was received immediately. Under the terms of the loan agreement, Priolo must make principal and interest payments every 6 months, beginning June 30, 2018. The note matures on December 31, 2022. The company's fiscal year ends on December 31.

Required »

a. Prepare the journal entry to record the issuance of the note payable.
b. Determine the semi-annual payment required under the loan agreement.
c. Prepare an amortization table.
d. Prepare the journal entry to record payments for the first year.
e. What is the amount of the note payable on the balance sheet at December 31, 2020, after the semiannual payment? What is the interest expense for the year?
f. Prepare the journal entry to record the final payment at maturity.

1 **P14-3. Note Payable Issued at a Discount with Amortization Table.** On September 30, 2018, Laurino Landscaping Company issued a 6-year, 3%, $800,000 note payable. The note was issued on a date when the market rate was 5%. Interest at 3% is due annually every September 30, beginning September 30, 2019. The full amount of the principal amount is due and payable at maturity. The company's fiscal year ends on December 31.

Required »

a. Determine the present value of the note and the discount on the note payable.
b. Prepare the journal entry to record the issuance of the note payable.
c. Prepare an amortization table.
d. Prepare the journal entry to record an accrued interest expense on December 31, 2018.
e. Prepare the journal entry required on September 30, 2019.
f. Prepare the journal entries required at maturity.

3 5 6 **P14-4. Bond Issue, Zero-Coupon Bond, Effective Interest Rate Method, Early Retirement, Bond Issue Costs.** Freiberg Associates issued $700,000 par value, 4-year, zero-coupon bonds on January 1, 2018. The market rate of interest on the date of the bond issue was 4%. Bond issue costs are $3,600. The company's fiscal year ends on December 31.

Required

a. Determine the issue price of the debt.
b. Find the effective interest rate after considering bond issue costs. Prepare the amortization table for the bond issue assuming that Freiberg uses the effective interest rate method of amortization.
c. Prepare the journal entries to record the bond issue and the entry on December 31, 2018. Assume that the company uses a discount or premium account if needed.
d. Describe the income statement, balance sheet, and cash flow statement effects in 2018 of the bond issue and the amortization of discount.
e. The bonds are retired early on November 30, 2019, for $655,000. Prepare the journal entry.

3 5 **P14-5. Bond Issue, Interest Payments, Effective Interest Rate Method, Bond Issue Costs.** On January 1, 2018, Tara Clothing Corporation issued $900,000 par value, 5%, 6-year bonds. Interest is payable semiannually each January 1 and July 1 with the first interest payment due at the end of the period on July 1, 2018. The market rate of interest on the date of the bond issue was 8%. Bond issue costs are $72,725. The company's fiscal year ends on December 31.

Required »

a. Determine the issue price of the debt and the amount of the bond discount or premium.
b. Find the effective interest rate after considering bond issue costs. Prepare the amortization table for the bond issue assuming that Tara uses the effective interest rate method of amortization.
c. Prepare the journal entries necessary to account for the bonds for the first year (January 1, 2018, through January 1, 2019). Assume that the company uses a premium or discount account if needed.
d. Prepare the journal entries to record the interest accrual and amortization for year three.
e. Prepare the journal entry to record payment of the bonds at maturity.

3 6 **P14-6. Bond Issue, Interest Payments, Effective Interest Rate Method, Early Retirement.** On January 1, 2018, Organic Products issued $1,200,000 par value, 7%, 5-year bonds. Interest is payable semiannually at the end of the period. The market rate of interest on the date of the bond issue was 6%.

Required »

a. Determine the issue price of the debt.
b. Prepare the amortization table for the bond issue assuming that Organic Products uses the effective interest rate method of amortization.
c. Prepare the journal entry to record the bond issue. Assume that the company uses a premium or discount account if needed.
d. Prepare the journal entry to record the early retirement of the bonds at the end of the third year (December 31, 2020) for $1,265,000.

4 6 **P14-7. Bonds Sold between Interest Dates at a Discount, Bond Issue Proceeds, Retirement.** Summa Manufacturing Company issued $900,000 par value, 5%, 5-year bonds dated January 1, 2018. The bonds pay interest semiannually each June 30 and December 31. Summa issued the bonds on April 30, 2018, when the market rate of interest was 6%.

a. Determine the bond issue price including accrued interest on April 30, 2018.
b. Prepare an amortization table for the bond issue using the effective interest rate method.
c. Prepare the journal entries required on the date of issue and on the first two interest dates in 2018, June 30, and December 31.
d. The bonds are retired on June 30, 2020, for $891,000. Prepare the journal entries at retirement.

4 5 **P14-8. Bonds Sold between Interest Dates at a Discount, Bond Issue Costs, IFRS.** Tyka Manufacturing Company, an IFRS reporter, issued $900,000 par value, 5%, 5-year bonds dated January 1, 2018. The bonds pay interest semiannually each June 30 and December 31. Tyka received cash of $863,825 when the bonds were issued, excluding accrued interest and bond issue costs, on April 30, 2018, to yield an effective interest rate of 7.742%. Bond issue costs were $59,000.

Required »

a. Discuss the treatment of bond issue costs under IFRS. What is the discount or premium on the bond?
b. Prepare an amortization table for the bond issue using the effective interest rate method.
c. Prepare the journal entries required on the date of issue and on the first two interest dates in 2018 of June 30 and December 31.

7 **P14-9. Convertible Bonds, Conversion.** On January 1, 2018, Super View Video, Incorporated issued $1,550,000 of $1,000 par value, 8%, 6-year bonds. Interest is payable semiannually each January 1 and July 1 with the first interest payment due at the end of the period on July 1, 2018. The market rate of interest for similar non-convertible bonds on the date of the bond issue was 10%. The bonds were sold for $1,704,287, yielding an effective rate of 6%. Each bond is convertible into 20 shares of Super View's $1 par value common stock. Assume that there is no beneficial conversion option.

Required »

a. Prepare the amortization table for the bond issue assuming that Super View uses the effective interest rate method of amortization.
b. Prepare the journal entry to record the bond issue.
c. Prepare the journal entry to record the first interest payment.
d. The bonds converted on January 1, 2021. Prepare the journal entry to record the bond conversion.

7 **P14-10. Convertible Bonds, Conversion, IFRS.** Using the information provided in P14-9, complete the following requirements assuming that Super View Video is an IFRS reporter.

Required »

a. Prepare the journal entry to record the bond issue.
b. Prepare the amortization table.
c. Prepare the journal entry to record the first interest payment.
d. The bonds converted on January 1, 2021. Prepare the journal entry to record the bond conversion.

5 7 **P14-11. Convertible Bonds, Bond Issue Costs, Conversion.** On January 1, 2018, Mesa Machinery Corporation issued 75 of 12-year, 12% convertible bonds at par. Each bond had a par value of $1,000 and pays interest annually on December 31. Because the bonds were issued at par, the yield on the bond is also equal to 12%. Each $1,000 bond converts into 25 shares of $1 par value common stock at the option of the bondholder beginning 2 years after the date of issue. Bond issue costs are $480. The market price of the common stock on the issue date was equal to $60 per share. Any discount is amortized using the effective interest rate method.

Required »

a. Prepare the journal entry to record the bond issuance.
b. Find the effective rate of interest after considering bond issue costs. Prepare the amortization table using the new effective rate of interest and the effective interest rate method.
c. Prepare the journal entries to record the interest payment for the first 3 years.
d. Prepare the entry to record the bond conversion assuming that all bonds convert at the end of the third year.

8 **P14-12. Warrants.** Davis Company issued 11,250 of its $1,000 par value bonds for $1,310, providing total cash proceeds of $14,737,500. Davis did not incur any bond issue costs. Bond interest is paid annually. The market price of Davis's common shares on the date that the bonds were issued was $125 per share. The bonds were sold with 22,000 warrants to acquire 22,000 shares of the company's $1 par value common stock for $125 per share. Davis has existing bonds outstanding that trade without warrants at $1,200. There are other Davis warrants outstanding that trade for $87.50 each. The market value of the company's bonds is considered more reliable than the trading price of the warrants.

Required »

a. Prepare the journal entry to record issuance of the bonds assuming that the warrants are nondetachable.
b. Prepare the journal entry to record the issuance of the bonds assuming that the warrants are detachable using the proportional method.
c. Prepare the journal entry to record the issuance of the bonds assuming that the warrants are detachable using the incremental method.
d. Assuming that the proportional method is used, prepare the journal entry required to record the exercise of all warrants.
e. Assuming that the incremental method is used, prepare the journal entry required to record the exercise of all warrants.

8 **P14-13. Warrants.** Tutte Company issued 3,000 of its 9%, 5-year, $1,000 par value bonds. Bond interest is paid annually on December 31. The market rate on the date of issue was 15%. The market price of Tutte common shares on the date that the bonds were issued was $60 per share. The bonds were sold with 18,000 warrants to acquire 18,000 shares of the company's $1 par value common stock for $60 per share. Tutte has existing bonds outstanding that trade without warrants at $750. There are other Tutte warrants outstanding that trade for $60 each. The market value of the warrants is considered to be more reliable than the fair value of the company's outstanding bonds.

Required »

a. Determine the issue price of the bonds.
b. Prepare the journal entry to record issuance of the bonds assuming that the warrants are nondetachable.
c. Prepare the journal entry to record the issuance of the bonds assuming that the warrants are detachable using the proportional method.
d. Prepare the journal entry to record the issuance of the bonds assuming that the warrants are detachable using the incremental method.
e. Assuming that the proportional method is used, prepare the journal entry required to record the exercise of all warrants.
f. Assuming that the incremental method is used, prepare the journal entry required to record the exercise of all warrants.
g. Compare the financial statement effects of the bonds and detachable warrants using the proportional versus the incremental methods.

CASES

Judgment Cases

Judgment Case 1: Debt or Equity[23]

Background

Companies normally obtain financing for operations from three sources:

1. Borrowing funds (debt)
2. Issuing shares (equity)
3. Using internally generated capital (from retained profits)

Sometimes, deciding how to present and classify these sources of financing in the financial statements is easily determined. For example, common stock is considered equity and issued bonds are considered debt. However, certain instruments have mixed attributes of debt and equity. Consider the following examples:

- Preferred stock
- Redeemable preferred stock
- Convertible bonds
- Bonds with detachable warrants

Required »

a. Establish a list of criteria that differentiate debt from equity (e.g., debt pays interest whereas equity pays dividends). For purposes of this part, assume that the debt is a secured loan and that the equity is common stock.

b. For each of the four instruments noted above, make a list of debt and equity attributes.

c. For each of the four instruments, discuss and provide your opinion about which instruments should be classified (for financial statement presentation purposes) as a long-term liability and which should be classified as equity. Indicate whether you believe this classification is really important and give your opinion as to why or why not.You may want to obtain copies of the FASB's 2007 Preliminary Views, *Financial Instruments with Characteristics of Equity* and the IASB's 2008 *Discussion Paper, Financial Instruments with Characteristics of Equity.*

Judgment Case 2: Jillian Limited: The Debt Equity Dilemma[24]

Background

Jillian Limited (JL) issued a financial instrument with the following terms:

- A face value of $100.
- Not secured by any assets of the entity (unsecured).
- Redeemable in cash at the option of the issuer.
- Pays 5% of face value annually.
- The 5% doubles in five years (to 10%) if the financial instrument is not redeemed. In 10 years, the annual payments double again if not redeemed by that time.

Other information to consider:

- Current interest rates are 4%. Rates are expected to remain stable or decline in the short to midterm.
- JL currently has a loan outstanding with the bank. Under the terms of the loan agreements, the debt-to-equity ratio may not exceed 2:1. Currently, before accounting for the new instrument, the debt-to-equity ratio is 2:1.

Required »

a. Discuss how JL should account for the financial instrument on the balance sheet (debt or equity) assuming that that JL reports under U.S. GAAP.

---

[23]Reprinted from the Ernst & Young Academic Resource Center with permission of the Ernst & Young Foundation. Copyright 2014. All rights reserved.

[24]Reprinted from the Ernst & Young Academic Resource Center with permission of the Ernst & Young Foundation. Copyright 2014. All rights reserved.

Judgment Case 3: Jillian Limited: The Debt Equity Dilemma: IFRS[25]

Background

Jillian Limited (JL) issued a financial instrument with the following terms:

- A face value of $100.
- Not secured by any assets of the entity (unsecured).
- Redeemable in cash at the option of the issuer.
- Pays 5% of face value annually.
- The 5% doubles in five years (to 10%) if the financial instrument is not redeemed. In 10 years, the annual payments double again if not redeemed by that time.

Other information to consider:

- Current interest rates are 4%. Rates are expected to remain stable or decline in the short to midterm.
- JL currently has a loan outstanding with the bank. Under the terms of the loan agreements, the debt-to-equity ratio may not exceed 2:1. Currently, before accounting for the new instrument, the debt-to-equity ratio is 2:1.

Required »

Discuss how JL should account for the financial instrument on the balance sheet (debt or equity) assuming that JL reports under IFRS. Discuss any ramifications of this classification.

Financial Statement Analysis Case

Financial Statement Analyses Case: Credit Ratings

Grifols, S.A. is a Spanish pharmaceutical company focusing on the development, manufacturing, and sale of therapeutic products. At the end of 2016, ***Grifols*** was rated "BB" by Standard & Poor's and considered to have a stable business risk profile.

	December 31	
Grifols, S.A. **(€ in thousands)**	**2016**	**2015**
Operating income from continuing operations after tax	€ 544,543	€ 531,441
Operating profits before interest income, interest expense, and income taxes	939,408	970,370
Depreciation and amortization	201,869	189,755
Deferred income tax expense	(40,161)	24,357
Asset impairment	(88)	125
Major noncash charges (gains)	(1,218)	37,221
Short-term debt	230,065	262,497
Long-term debt	4,712,071	4,597,654
Equity	3,727,978	3,301,390

Source: Financial statements taken from https://www.grifols.com/documents/10192/23539299/cons-2016-en/8f9148c9-dc4f-490a-8866-bf2044cb9e8bhttp://www.grifols.com/documents/10192/243545/ia-2013-en/7e4105bb-2bd2-4459-9e89-73350789a4f3, http://www.grifols.com/documents/10192/30795/cons-2012-en/8e6ff3ad-41e3-4985-9010-a5dc7c6d2ec4

Required »

a. What is a credit rating and why would a potential investor in bonds be interested in a company's credit rating?
b. What factors does a credit rating agency consider in rating a company?
c. Compute funds from operations over debt and debt to EBITDA for 2015 and 2016 using the selected financial statement information.
d. Using the benchmarks from Exhibit 14.8, assess the financial risk of the company using these indicators. Assess its financial risk profile at the end of 2016. How does the financial risk in 2016 compare to that in 2015?

Surfing the Standards Cases

Surfing the Standards Case 1: Fair Value Option Disclosures

Under U.S. GAAP, firms may choose to report most financial assets and financial liabilities at fair value, using the fair value option. The rules related to the fair value option are included in ASC 825-10 *Financial*

[25]Reprinted from the Ernst & Young Academic Resource Center with permission of the Ernst & Young Foundation.

Instruments—Overall. When an entity chooses the fair value option for a financial instrument, a number of disclosures are required.

1. What are the principal objectives of these disclosures?
2. What are the expectant results of the disclosures?

Surfing the Standards Case 2: Bonds with Detachable Warrants

Companies sometimes issue bonds with detachable warrants entitling the bondholder to buy the stock of the company at a fixed price. The U.S. GAAP rules related to the issue of these bonds are included in ASC 470-20, *Debt with Conversion and Other Options*. Read paragraphs 2 and 3 of section 5, paragraphs 2 and 3 of section 25, and paragraphs 1 and 2 of section 30.

1. Why do companies sometimes issue bonds with detachable warrants?
2. Does U.S. GAAP treat bonds with detachable warrants as debt or equity?
3. How are the proceeds of the issue allocated to the financial statement components?

Doxy, Inc. issued $1,000,000 par value, 5%, 10-year bonds with detachable warrants on April 1 for $1,100,000. (April 1 is also the commitment date.) Interest is payable quarterly at the end of each quarter. Doxy can reliably determine that the market rate of interest that would be applicable to the bond issue without warrants is 6%. It can also reliably determine that the fair value of the warrants, if they were detached from the bonds, would be $200,000.

4. Provide the journal entry to record the issuance on April 1.
5. Provide the journal entry to record the first interest payment on June 30.

Basis for Conclusions Cases

Basis for Conclusions Case 1: Long-Term Debt Violation at the Balance Sheet Date[26]

Note: In the following exercise, you are required to review the Basis for Conclusions (BCs) for the standard(s) that provide the accounting guidance for this topic. As the BCs are generally not included in the codification and thus are not authoritative, it will most likely be necessary for you to research them through review of the pre-codified standards. Appropriate references have been provided to allow you to do so. Pre-codified standards are accessible on the FASB website or through the American Accounting Association's Academic Accounting Access program, if your school participates in this program.

Scene 1

At December 31, 2012, the Gray Mountain Company (GMC), a rain-making eco-friendly company, has a five-year note payable to a large bank. The underlying note agreement contains certain restrictive covenants (minimum capital requirements, total debt-to-equity ratio, working capital ratio, and minimum cash balance requirements) that could accelerate the immediate payment of the debt if GMC does not meet these covenants each quarter-end (March 31, June 30, September 30, and December 31). GMC was not in compliance with two of the ratios at December 31, 2012, but received a waiver from the bank for these two debt covenant violations on January 31, 2013, which was retroactive to December 31, 2012, and through January 1, 2014.

Please read the following:

FASB ASC 470-10-45-13 through 21 and Statement of Financial Accounting Standards No. 6, *Classification of Short Term Debt Obligations Expected to be Refinanced*, paragraphs 1 through 6 and Appendix A—Basis for Conclusion, paragraphs 18 through 31.

International Accounting Standard 1, *Presentation of Financial Statements*, paragraphs 69, 71, 74, and 75 and the BCs in IAS 1, paragraphs BC 39 through BC 48.

- Determine how the debt would be classified in GMC's balance sheet at December 31, 2012, under both U.S. GAAP and IFRS.
- Discuss and articulate the rationale and thought that the FASB and IASB went through in reaching their decisions in the accounting for debt balance sheet classification if a debt covenant violation was cured near the balance sheet date.

[26]Reprinted from the Ernst & Young Academic Resource Center with permission of the Ernst & Young Foundation.

APPENDIX A
The Straight-Line Method of Amortization

The *straight-line method* of amortization can be used when the results are not significantly different from the effective interest rate method. The **straight-line method** amortizes a constant amount of discount or premium each period, leading to a constant interest expense.

$$\text{Straight-Line Discount or Premium Amortization} = (\text{Discount or Premium})/\text{Number of Interest Payments} \quad (14A.1)$$

The straight-line method is theoretically deficient because it results in a variable cost of borrowing and the carrying value of the debt is not equal to the present value of the remaining cash flows discounted at the historical market rate.

Example 14A.1 presents an illustration of the straight-line method of amortization for a bond issued at a discount.

EXAMPLE 14A.1

Straight-Line Bond Discount Amortization

PROBLEM: Consider Ruffin Corporation from Example 14.8. On January 1, 2018, Ruffin Corporation issued $40,000 par value, 4%, 4-year bonds that mature on December 31, 2021. The market rate on the date of issue is 6%. Ruffin will pay interest semiannually on June 30 and December 31. Prepare the journal entry on January 1, 2018. Prepare an amortization schedule over the 4-year period using the straight-line method of amortization. Prepare the journal entries for June 30 and December 31, 2018. Prepare the t-accounts for the bond payable and bond discount accounts. Compare the interest expense computed under the straight-line method and the effective interest rate method from Example 14.8.

SOLUTION: Because the stated interest rate is lower than the market rate when Ruffin issued the bonds, the bonds were issued at a discount. The terms to compute the future payments to bondholders are:

- **Face value** = $40,000
- **Stated annual interest rate** = 4%
- **Historical market annual interest rate** = 6%
- **Interest payment period** = semiannually on June 30 and December 31
- **Maturity date** = December 31, 2021

At maturity, Ruffin will pay bondholders the face value of the bond, $40,000. Ruffin will also make the interest payment to bondholders semiannually every June 30 and December 31 for the next 4 years. The semiannual interest payment is computed as follows:

$$\begin{aligned}\text{Interest Payment} &= \text{Face Value} \times \text{Annual Interest Rate} \times \text{Time Period} \\ &= \$40{,}000 \times 4\% \times {}^{1}/_{2} = \$800\end{aligned}$$

We next determine the bond issue price. This present value includes both the face amount of $40,000 and the semiannual interest payments of $800. We use the semiannual market rate because the bonds are priced to yield the market. Therefore, I/Y = 3% (6%/2) and N = 8 (4 years × 2).

	N	I/Y	PV	PMT	FV	Excel Formula
Given	8	3.00%		−800	−40,000	
Solve for PV			37,192			=PV(0.03,8,−800,−40000)

The bond issue price is $37,192; thus, the discount is $2,808 ($40,000 − $37,192).

The journal entry to record the bond issuance includes a discount account as follows:

Account	January 1, 2018	
Cash	37,192	
Discount on Bonds Payable	2,808	
Bonds Payable − Face Value		40,000

Under the straight-line method, we divide the discount by the number of interest payments to compute amortization each period. For this bond, Ruffin makes eight interest payments (4 years × 2 semiannual interest payments per year). So, using Equation 14A.1, the discount amortization for each of the eight semiannual periods is $351 ($2,808 discount / 8 interest payments). This amortization is the same over the life of the bond. The $1,151 interest expense each period is the sum of the cash interest ($800) plus the discount amortization ($351).

Amortization Table under the Straight-Line Method

Date	2% Cash Interest (a)	Straight-Line Interest (b) = (a) + (c)	Discount Amortization Initial Discount / Number of Periods (c)	Carrying Value (d) = (d) + (c)
				$37,192
June 30, 2018	$ 800	$ 1,151	$ 351	37,543
December 31, 2018	800	1,151	351	37,894
June 30, 2019	800	1,151	351	38,245
December 31, 2019	800	1,151	351	38,596
June 30, 2020	800	1,151	351	38,947
December 31, 2020	800	1,151	351	39,298
June 30, 2021	800	1,151	351	39,649
December 31, 2021	800	1,151	351	40,000
TOTALS	$6,400	$9,208	$2,808	

We present the journal entry to record the first semiannual interest payment during 2018 with a discount account.

Account	June 30, 2018	
Interest Expense	1,151	
Cash		800
Discount on Bonds Payable		351

The journal entry to record the second semiannual interest payment during 2018 with a discount account follows.

Account	December 31, 2018	
Interest Expense	1,151	
Cash		800
Discount on Bonds Payable		351

In the amortization table, the interest expense and the discount amortization are the same each 6-month period.

The t-accounts for the bond payable and bond discount accounts are as follows:

	Bond Payable			Discount on Bond Payable	
January 1, 2018		40,000	January 1, 2018	2,808	
			June 30, 2018		351
			December 31, 2018		351
			June 30, 2019		351
			December 31, 2019		351
			June 30, 2020		351
			December 31, 2020		351
			June 30, 2021		351
December 31, 2021	40,000		December 31, 2021		351
Balance		0			0

We next compare the interest expense computed under the effective interest rate method from Example 14.8 and the straight-line method. In the early (later) periods, the interest expense is higher (lower) under the straight-line method.

Period	Interest Expense under the Straight-Line Method from This Example	Interest Expense under the Effective Interest Method from Example 14.8	Difference [Straight Line Greater than (Less than) the Effective Interest Method]
June 30, 2018	$1,151	$ 1,116	$ 35
December 31, 2018	1,151	1,125	26
June 30, 2019	1,151	1,135	16
December 31, 2019	1,151	1,145	6
June 30, 2020	1,151	1,155	(4)
December 31, 2020	1,151	1,166	(15)
June 30, 2021	1,151	1,177	(26)
December 31, 2021	1,151	1,189	(38)
TOTALS	$9,208	$9,208	$ 0

The total interest expense over the life of the bond is the same under both the effective interest method and the straight-line method: Only the timing of when interest expense is reported differs.

Exhibit 14A.1 presents a graph of the difference in interest expense for Ruffin under the straight-line (Example 14A.1) and the effective interest rate (Example 14.8) methods. These interest expense differences also lead to differences in the effective interest rates computed from the amounts presented in the amortization tables and financial statements. Computing the interest rate each period as the reported interest expense divided by the beginning outstanding balance of debt yields a constant interest rate of 3% in each of 6 months under the effective interest rate method. This constant rate represents the actual interest rate incurred on the debt.

Under the straight-line-method, the interest rate varies. In the first period, it is 3.09% ($1,151 / $37,192). In the second period, the computed interest rate is 3.07% ($1,151 / $37,543). These interest rates under the straight-line method are only approximations of the actual interest rates and decline as the carrying value of the debt increases in the later years of the bond term.

EXHIBIT 14A.1 Comparison of Computed Interest Rate under the Straight-Line Method and the Effective Interest Rate Method

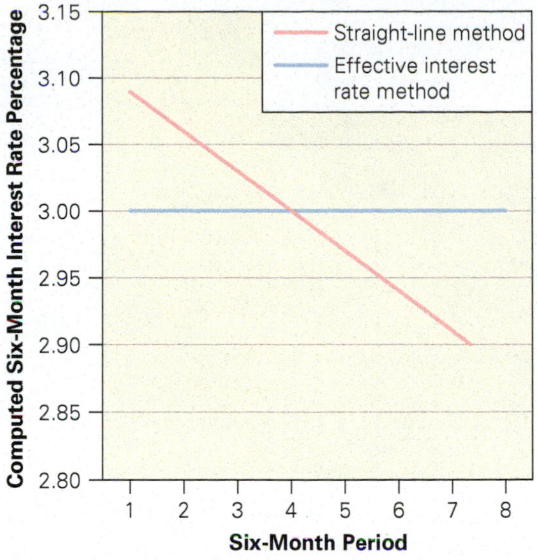

Straight-Line Amortization: IFRS

IFRS does not allow the use of the straight-line method. Both U.S. GAAP and IFRS typically require the effective interest method of amortization. However, under U.S. GAAP, the straight-line method is permitted if the results are not significantly different from the effective interest rate method.

15 Accounting for Stockholders' Equity

LEARNING OBJECTIVES

1. Describe stockholders' equity and its main components.
2. Explain and illustrate the accounting for common stock, including share issuance, issue costs, and stock splits.
3. Record treasury stock transactions, including repurchases, reissuance under the cost method, and retirement.
4. Describe preferred stock and its features; demonstrate the accounting for issuance, dividends, and consideration of potential debt features of preferred stock.
5. Explain the accounting for retained earnings, including dividends and prior-period adjustments.
6. Describe the components of other comprehensive income and accumulated other comprehensive income.
7. Detail required disclosures for stockholders' equity.

Introduction

RAISING CAPITAL IN PUBLIC EQUITY MARKETS for the first time via an initial public offering (IPO) is a major milestone for a company. In recent years, several U.S. Internet companies—***Facebook***, ***Snap***, and ***trivago***—deliberated the pros, cons, and potential timing for their IPOs. A company decides to go public for many reasons: to raise capital for business expansion, provide liquidity for current owners, or initiate the possibility for raising future equity capital. ***Facebook Inc.***, the Internet social networking company, went public in May 2012, selling stock at $38 per share. It sold about 180 million shares valued at approximately $6.76 billion to new investors in its IPO and used this capital to fund expansion and growth. Another $9.1 million was allocated to the company's other pre-IPO shareholders who sold about 241 million of their shares in the public market on the IPO date. At the end of 2016, a share of ***Facebook***'s stock was priced at about $115 per share.

Shannon Stapleton/Thomson Reuters (Markets) LLC

Raising capital by issuing shares is a type of a transaction that a company can engage in with its owners. In this chapter, we focus on accounting for *stockholders' equity*, the owners' interest in the company. As the company operates and generates earnings, net income increases equity. A company can also decide to distribute dividends to owners or repurchase shares in the capital markets. We discuss accounting for these equity transactions, the types of equity securities a company can issue, and the presentation of equity and changes in equity that assist investors in their assessment of a company's performance. «

1 Describe stockholders' equity and its main components.

Overview of Stockholders' Equity

Stockholders' equity (also referred to as shareholders' equity) is the sum of all residual claims against the net assets of the firm and is measured as the difference in the assets and the liabilities of the entity. Stockholders' equity is also called the **net assets** or the book value of the firm. It represents the interests held by the owners. Shareholders can assert their claims only after the company has satisfied the senior claims of creditors. Thus, stockholders' equity is a claim against net assets, not a claim against any specific asset(s).[1]

Components of Stockholders' Equity

Stockholders' equity has three major components that we will examine in detail in the remaining sections of the chapter:

1. *Contributed capital*
2. *Retained earnings*
3. *Accumulated other comprehensive income*

We begin our discussion with an overview of these three major components.

Contributed Capital. **Contributed capital** includes the amounts paid in by *common* and *preferred* shareholders. **Common shareholders** are the residual claimants of the firm who receive dividend distributions after the company has paid all other providers of capital their return on investment. Common shareholders can be individuals, other corporations, or institutions (such as mutual funds). **Preferred shareholders** are investors holding shares in a company that have preferential rights over common shares. We discuss a number of types of preferred shares later in the chapter.

Contributed capital includes the *par value* of common and preferred shares as well as *additional paid-in capital in excess of par or stated value*. The face or stated value on the share certificate is its **par value**, which is an arbitrary value that corporate organizers assigned to each class of stock. **Additional paid-in capital in excess of par or stated value** represents the amounts that common and preferred shareholders contribute in excess of the par or stated value. For example, if Farnon Company issued 1,000 shares of its $2 par value common stock for $10 per share, it would record $2,000 in the common stock account at par and record the excess over par ($8,000) as additional paid-in capital in excess of par.

Retained Earnings. **Retained earnings** are a firm's cumulative earnings or losses that it has not distributed as dividends. Events other than dividends, net income, or net loss can also impact retained earnings.[2] However, as discussed later in the chapter, net income or loss less dividends declared account for the majority of changes in retained earnings.

Accumulated Other Comprehensive Income. **Accumulated other comprehensive income** includes the cumulative amount of items such as unrealized gains and losses on available-for-sale debt investment securities, foreign currency translation adjustments, and certain pension cost adjustments. Recall from Chapter 5 these items are reported in other comprehensive income, not net income.

Exhibit 15.1 on the next page presents an overview of the topics that we cover in this chapter.

---

[1]For most of the relevant authoritative literature for this topic, see FASB ASC 505—*Equity* for U.S. GAAP and IASC, *International Accounting Standard 1*, "Presentation of Financial Statements" (London, UK: International Accounting Standards Committee, Revised, 2016), for IFRS.

[2]As discussed in a subsequent section of this chapter, treasury stock transactions and prior-period adjustments also affect retained earnings.

EXHIBIT 15.1 Overview of Stockholders' Equity Coverage

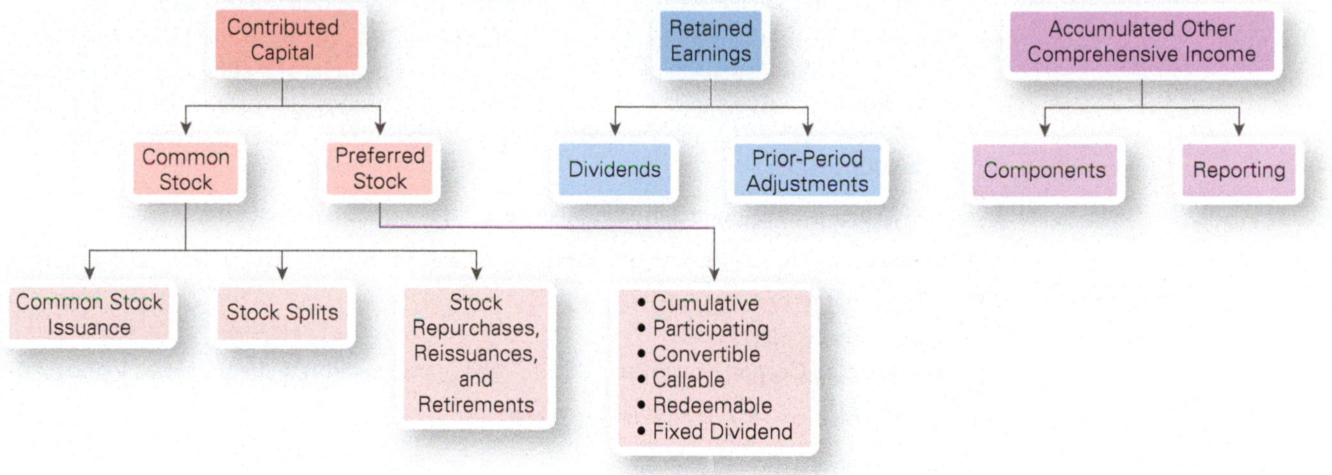

Stockholders' Equity Terminology: IFRS. IFRS uses different terminology than U.S. GAAP to refer to the stockholders' equity components as indicated in Exhibit 15.2.

EXHIBIT 15.2 Stockholders' Equity Terminology: U.S. GAAP and IFRS

U.S. GAAP	IFRS
Contributed capital, paid-in capital, common stock	Share capital
Additional paid-in capital	Share premium
Retained earnings	Retained profit, accumulated profit and loss
Accumulated other comprehensive income	Reserves, other reserves

Source: International Financial Reporting Standards (IFRS).

❷ Explain and illustrate the accounting for common stock, including share issuance, issue costs, and stock splits.

Accounting for Common Stock

We begin our discussion of the components of stockholders' equity by discussing key terms and relevant legal issues surrounding common stock and outlining the accounting for common stock issuances and stock splits.[3]

Overview of Common Stock

Several terms are important to understand when discussing common stock: *authorized*, *issued*, *unissued*, *treasury*, and *outstanding shares.*[4]

- **Authorized shares** refer to the total number of shares that the firm can legally issue. Typically, the attorney general in the state of incorporation approves the authorization. The firm includes the number of authorized shares in the articles of incorporation filed with the state.
- **Issued shares** refer to the number of shares sold or otherwise distributed to shareholders.
- **Unissued shares** are shares authorized but not issued.

[3]This section discusses the issuance of common stock in the primary market. That is, we address only transactions involving the initial sale or issuance of common stock to the market. We illustrate transactions involving two market participants (secondary market transactions) in the chapter on accounting for investments.

[4]These terms are the same for common and preferred shares.

- **Treasury shares** are the corporation's own shares that it repurchased and holds for some future use (for example, to be distributed to satisfy the terms of an employee stock option plan). Reacquired shares can also be retired rather than held in the treasury.
- **Outstanding shares** refer to the number of shares still in the hands of the stockholders and are computed as issued shares less treasury shares. Financial statistics such as earnings per share and book value per share use the number of outstanding shares for calculation purposes. In addition, cash dividends are paid only on outstanding shares, and only outstanding shares have voting rights.

Example 15.1 illustrates the relationship between these common stock terms.

EXAMPLE 15.1 Common Stock Terminology

PROBLEM: Retgo Corporation presents the following information in the footnotes to the financial statements:

Authorized shares	75,000
Issued shares	58,000
Shares held in the treasury	16,000

How many shares are outstanding? How many shares are unissued?

SOLUTION: Retgo has 42,000 shares outstanding—the 58,000 issued shares less 16,000 treasury shares. It has 17,000 shares unissued—the 75,000 authorized shares less 58,000 issued.

Legal Issues: Par and Stated Values

Several legal requirements impact the accounting for common stock. When a corporation is formed, the organizers designate the stock's par value, usually setting an immaterial amount such as 1 cent per share. The concept of par value dates back to when all firms were required to maintain a minimum amount of capital that they could not distribute to shareholders. Maintaining assets equal to the par value of its shares protected creditors in the event of liquidation. So, an original purchaser of the company's shares could be liable for any amounts contributed below par value in the event of corporate liquidation.

Although many states have repealed the minimum legal capital laws and permit the issuance of no-par stock, other states still require some form of legal capital. For example, legal capital can be par value, the total proceeds on original issue, or the **stated value**, which is an amount specified by the board of directors.[5] In states requiring legal capital, a firm cannot distribute the amount designated as legal capital until it has settled all prior creditor claims.

Although the designation of par values is no longer required in some states, many currently outstanding common shares that were issued in previous years have a par value associated with them. As a result, firms continue to allocate the proceeds from a stock issuance to the stock's par value and any additional capital paid-in.

Accounting for Common Stock Issuances

While firms normally issue common stock for cash, it can also be issued for noncash consideration. We discuss the accounting for both types of issuances on the next page.[6]

[5]A stated value can be designated for no-par stock by resolution of the board of directors. The stated value is not as formal as par value and can be changed with another resolution by the board of directors. A change in stated value does not require shareholder approval and filings with the state as would be the case if par value were changed. Stated value functions in the same way as par value when accounting for the issuance of new equity shares.

[6]Firms can also issue common stock for stock subscriptions that are arrangements under which the corporation and future shareholders enter into a contract by which the corporation agrees to issue a fixed number of shares at a future specified date in exchange for a fixed or specified price.

Common Stock Issued for Cash. When issuing stock for cash, firms allocate the total proceeds to the par or stated value and the additional paid-in capital (that is, the amount paid in excess of par or stated value). If the shares have no par or stated value, firms record the total proceeds in the common stock account. For instance, ***Snap Inc.*** sold 160.3 million new shares of $0.00001 par value common stock for $17 per share at its initial public offering. ***Snap*** therefore allocated $1,603 (160.3 million shares times $0.00001 par value) to par value.[7] The remaining amount increased additional paid-in capital. Example 15.2 illustrates accounting for the issuance of common stock with no par value.

EXAMPLE 15.2 Common Stock (with No Par Value) Issued for Cash

PROBLEM: Piper Products decided to raise additional financing by issuing common stock. The company received $4,000 in exchange for 1,000 shares of its no-par stock. What is the necessary journal entry to record this transaction?

SOLUTION: Because Piper's shares have no par value, it records the issuance of capital stock entirely in the common stock account.

Account	Current Year	
Cash	4,000	
Common Stock – No Par		4,000

Next, let's assume that Piper's common stock has a par value in Example 15.3.

EXAMPLE 15.3 Common Stock (with Par Value) Issued for Cash

PROBLEM: Piper Products decided to raise additional financing by issuing common stock. The company received $4,000 in exchange for 1,000 shares of $1 par value common stock. What is the necessary journal entry to record this transaction?

SOLUTION: Piper allocates the $4,000 total cash proceeds to the par value and the additional paid-in capital in excess of par – common. The 1,000 shares have a total par value of $1,000 ($1 × 1,000 shares), and the additional paid-in capital in excess of par – common is $3,000. The following journal entry records the stock issue.

Account	Current Year	
Cash	4,000	
Common Stock – $1 par		1,000
Additional Paid-in Capital in Excess of Par – Common		3,000

Piper would make the same entry if the shares had a $1 stated value.

Stock Issue Costs. In order to issue stock, companies typically incur costs related to legal and underwriting fees. Attorneys assist in the filing process with the SEC and the state of incorporation. Companies pay underwriting fees to investment banks or other financial institutions for the risk assumed by purchasing the securities directly from the issuing corporation. The underwriter buys the shares from the issuer net of the fee and then sells the shares in the market.

[7] Snap Inc. reports its financial statements in thousands of dollars. Therefore, it showed $2,000 allocated to the par value of common stock, which is the $0.00001 par value times 160.3 million shares rounded to the nearest thousand.

Firms treat these issue costs as a reduction of additional paid-in capital in excess of par. ***Facebook***'s fees were about $81 million on its initial stock issue. The firm sold its shares in the market for $6.84 billion; the fees of $81 million reduced ***Facebook***'s proceeds to $6.76 billion. Therefore, ***Facebook*** increased its equity by the $6.76 billion net proceeds. Accounting for stock issue costs is illustrated in Example 15.4.

EXAMPLE 15.4 Common Stock Issue Costs

PROBLEM: Piper Products decided to raise additional financing by issuing common stock. The company received $4,000 in exchange for 1,000 shares of $1 par value common stock. Piper paid an underwriter $200 in stock issue costs. What is the necessary journal entry to record this transaction?

SOLUTION: The $200 of issue costs reduces Piper's cash received from the sale of the stock. Thus, it records the cash received at the net amount of $3,800, which is the $4,000 total proceeds less the $200 stock issue costs. The issue costs also reduce the additional paid-in capital in excess of par—common by $200. The journal entry follows.

Account	Current Year	
Cash	3,800	
Common Stock – $1 par		1,000
Additional Paid-in Capital in Excess of Par – Common		2,800

Common Stock Issued for Noncash Consideration. Firms also issue common stock in exchange for noncash consideration. For example, an attorney could exchange legal services for common stock of the corporation that is receiving the service. In this case, how does the corporation determine the value of the shares issued to pay for the noncash consideration it receives in exchange?

Theoretically, the corporation should value the goods and services received at the fair value of the consideration given up in the exchange. The value given in exchange would be the fair value of the stock issued in the transaction that the firm "gave up" (its cost) to acquire the goods or services. In other words, the fair value of the shares issued is the cost of the goods and services received in exchange. Therefore, the corporation records the noncash assets or services at the fair value of the stock issued in the exchange. However, if the stock does not have a reliable fair value, the corporation uses the fair value of the consideration received—that is, the goods or services received—to value the shares issued. Example 15.5 provides an example of issuing common stock for noncash consideration.

EXAMPLE 15.5 Common Stock Issued for Noncash Consideration

PROBLEM: Bordeaux Pharmaceuticals issues common stock in exchange for legal services received. The common stock has a fair value of $2,000 and a par value of $600. What is the necessary journal entry to record this transaction?

SOLUTION: Because the fair value of the stock is known, Bordeaux debits the noncash consideration for $2,000. It allocates the credit to the equity accounts of $2,000 to common stock for $600 par value and to $1,400 additional paid-in capital in excess of par – common for the remainder ($2,000 − $600). The journal entry follows.

Account	Current Year	
Legal Fees Expense	2,000	
Common Stock		600
Additional Paid-in Capital in Excess of Par – Common		1,400

The determination of fair value in a transaction exchanging common stock for noncash consideration involves management's judgment. In some cases, the fair value of the stock or the noncash consideration is apparent. However, in many situations it is not. For example, if the company issuing the stock is not publicly traded, the fair value of the stock may not be easily and reliably determined. Then we use the fair value of the services provided. If the services are provided on a regular basis, such as legal services, then the fair value is probably easy to determine by using the rate charged to other clients of the law firm. However, if the services provided are more customized, it may be difficult to determine a fair value. In these cases, management exercises judgment to determine an appropriate fair value at which to record the transaction.

Stock Splits

A **stock split** results in a proportionate increase in the number of equity shares and a proportionate decrease in the share's par value per share if the shares have a par value. For example, in a 2-for-1 split, a company gives an additional share of stock to a shareholder for each share held. If a shareholder held 100 shares of $2 par value stock before a split, after the split, the shareholder would have 200 shares of $1 par value stock. That is, the shareholder now has two shares after the split for every one share held before. When ***Netflix, Inc.***, the worldwide Internet television network, split its common stock 7 for 1, its number of shares increased seven times to about 426.3 million from 60.6 million.[8] Exhibit 15.3 presents a timeline depicting a 2-for-1 stock split.

EXHIBIT 15.3 Stock Split Timeline

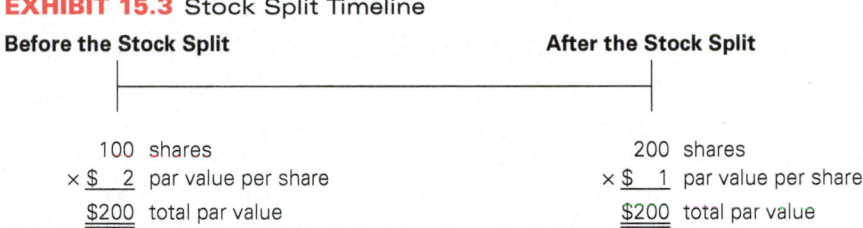

Before the Stock Split	After the Stock Split
100 shares	200 shares
× $ 2 par value per share	× $ 1 par value per share
$200 total par value	$200 total par value

A company typically issues a stock split when it believes that its shares are trading at a price that is too high to attract a wider ownership base. Absent other reasons for the stock price to move, a 2-for-1 split would cause the new stock price to be one-half of the pre-split price.[9] For example, if one share of a company's stock was trading for $150 per share before a 2-for-1 split, then after the split, two shares will trade at $75 per share ($150 / 2 shares). Note that the shareholder, now owning two shares, still holds stock valued at $150. The day before the ***Netflix*** 7-for-1 stock split, its stock was trading at $702.60 per share. The day of the split, ***Netflix*** stock opened trading at about one-seventh the price per share at $99.97 per share. A ***Netflix*** stockholder who held one share of stock before the split was holding seven shares of stock after the split with a total value of $699.79.[10] The total value is slightly lower likely due to new information about the company's future performance being priced.

A stock split affects the disclosures for stockholders' equity, but the firm does not record anything in the accounts. A memorandum (verbal) entry can be entered into the journal to note the stock split and the changes to the number of shares and par value per share. As noted earlier, if the stock has a par value, there is also a proportionate decrease in the par value of the stock at the individual share level. Example 15.6 illustrates the effects of a stock split on the number of shares outstanding, par value, and the book value of equity.

[8] Netflix stock split was effective on July 15, 2015.

[9] Note that management's decision to enact a stock split itself provides information to the market, thus typically causing a movement in stock price.

[10] A reverse stock split is used to increase share prices. For example, a 1-for-2 reverse split requires the investor to surrender two shares of common stock for one share of the new common equity security. An investor who originally paid $1,250 per share for the two shares would now have one share with a cost of $2,500. Companies may use a reverse stock split to raise the market price of their shares to avoid being delisted from a stock exchange or removed from a stock index. A reverse split can also be used to raise stock prices to avoid the market perception that the company's shares are "cheap" or "penny" stock.

EXAMPLE 15.6 Stock Split

PROBLEM: ASG Corporation issued 400,000 shares of $2 par value stock. The book value of ASG's common stockholders' equity is equal to $60 million. ASG implements a 2-for-1 stock split. What is the total number of shares outstanding after the stock split? What is the par value per share after the split? What is the book value of equity after the split?

SOLUTION: After the stock split, the total number of shares outstanding is 800,000, or 400,000 shares before the split times 2. The new par value is $1 per share, or $2 per share before the split divided by 2. There would be no change in the total book value of the firm. However, the stock split reduced the book value per share proportionately. Before the split, the book value per share is $150 per share ($60,000,000 / 400,000 shares), which is reduced to $75 per share after the split. We summarize the effects of the stock split as follows:

Description	Before the 2-for-1 Split	After the 2-for-1 Split
Shares outstanding	400,000 shares	800,000 shares
Total par value	$ 800,000	$ 800,000
Par value per share	2	1
Total book value	60,000,000	60,000,000
Book value per share	150	75

3 Record treasury stock transactions, including repurchases, reissuance under the cost method, and retirement.

Accounting for Share Repurchase Transactions

Share repurchase transactions also impact stockholders' equity. When a company repurchases its shares, the company can hold these shares in treasury for future use or it can retire the shares. A treasury share is a corporation's own stock that is authorized, issued, and previously outstanding that the corporation buys back. Treasury shares are still considered issued shares. Retired shares are similar except that these shares are no longer considered issued, a topic we will revisit later in the chapter.

THE CONCEPTUAL FRAMEWORK CONNECTION
Share Repurchase Transactions

The stockholders' equity topics in this chapter relate to FASB's conceptual framework's definitions of financial statement elements. Equity is "the residual interest in the assets of an entity that remains after deducting its liabilities."[11] The conceptual framework identifies investments by owners and distributions to owners as transactions that impact the equity of the firm directly. As a result, when a company purchases and sells treasury shares for amounts above and below cost, it does not report these "gains" and "losses" on the income statement. Rather, it reports them in the stockholders' equity section of the balance sheet because they are considered capital transactions.

Purpose of Share Repurchases

Usually, corporations intend to reissue treasury shares for some specific purpose. Some of the purposes of purchasing treasury shares follow.

- Treasury shares are used in stock option plans, stock bonus plans, and employee stock purchase plans.
- Treasury shares are used in exchange for another firm's voting shares in a merger or acquisition.
- Repurchase transactions are used to support the market price of the stock. By buying shares back from the market, there are fewer shares outstanding, raising the price per share and the earnings per share.
- Repurchase transactions are used to prevent takeover attempts. When shares are repurchased, the market price of the stock rises, increasing the cost of a takeover. In addition, if a sufficient number of shares are reacquired, major shareholders may have enough voting rights to control the corporation and directly prevent a takeover.

[11]FASB, *Statement of Financial Accounting Concepts No. 6,* "Elements of Financial Statements" (Norwalk, CT: FASB, 1985).

- Repurchase transactions distribute cash to shareholders without formally increasing the cash dividend. A formal dividend increase would have to be continued in the future to avoid adverse stock price effects from the market's negative reaction to a cut in dividends. Rather than increasing dividends, a company can use share repurchases to distribute cash to shareholders.

For example, ***Microsoft Corporation*** uses share repurchases to obtain shares to be issued to satisfy stock option plan requirements and to distribute cash to shareholders. In fiscal 2016, ***Microsoft*** purchased 294 million of its shares for $14.8 billion.

Accounting for Treasury Stock Transactions

Firms typically record treasury stock in a contra-stockholders' equity account and report treasury stock as a reduction of total stockholders' equity on the balance sheet. As noted earlier, the treasury shares reduce the number of shares outstanding. In addition, treasury shares do not have voting rights and cannot receive cash dividends. However, treasury shares do split and can receive stock dividends in some states.

The two methods of accounting for treasury stock are the *cost method* and the *par value method*. The **cost method** records the acquisition of treasury shares at the cost of the repurchased shares. The **par value method** records the acquisition at the par value of the repurchased shares. The cost method is the most popular method used in practice and will be covered in this chapter.[12]

Cost Method: Acquisition of Treasury Shares. Under the cost method, when a firm repurchases shares, it debits the treasury stock account for the cost of the repurchased shares. The repurchase of shares does not change the common stock account or the additional paid-in capital in excess of par – common account. The repurchased shares are still considered issued, but they are no longer outstanding.

Cost Method: Reissuance of Treasury Shares. A firm holding treasury stock usually reissues these shares at a selling price that is different from the acquisition cost. If the company sells the treasury shares at a price above cost, it classifies the excess over cost as additional paid-in capital from treasury stock transactions. Although this excess is similar to a gain, it should not be reported on the income statement because it results from a capital transaction.

To illustrate, we begin with a hypothetical example involving a company transacting with only one shareholder in Example 15.7.

EXAMPLE 15.7

Acquisition and Sale of Treasury Stock above Cost

PROBLEM: Small Corp. repurchases shares from a shareholder for $1,000. Three months later, the shareholder buys the same shares back at $1,100. What journal entries are required to record these transactions?

SOLUTION: The journal entry on the date of acquisition records the shares at cost in the treasury stock account.

Account	*Date of Acquisition*	
Treasury Stock	1,000	
Cash		1,000

The journal entry to record the resale of the stock removes the treasury stock account and records the excess of the sales price over the cost in the additional paid-in capital from treasury stock transactions account.

Continued

[12]AICPA, *U.S. GAAP Financial Statements Best Practices in Presentation and Disclosure – 2012* (New York, NY: AICPA, 2012) reports that less than 2% of companies that have treasury stock use the par value method. Note that the par value method is nearly identical to accounting for share retirements, which we cover in the next section.

Account	Date of Reissue	
Cash	1,100	
Treasury Stock		1,000
Additional Paid-in Capital from Treasury Stock Transactions		100

At the end of 3 months, the shareholder owns the same number of shares held prior to these transactions but paid $100 more. This $100 is simply additional paid-in-capital provided to Small Corp. by its shareholder and is not accounted for as a gain on sale.

Below-Cost Treasury Stock Reissue. Firms can also reissue treasury shares at a price that is below cost. In this case, the firm first reduces additional paid-in capital from treasury stock transactions by the amount that is below cost. If the firm has no additional paid-in capital from treasury stock transactions or its balance is less than the amount below cost, the remaining amount reduces retained earnings. This treatment is logical because additional paid-in capital cannot have a negative (or debit) balance. Although similar to a loss, this accounting does not affect the income statement because it results from a capital transaction as illustrated in Example 15.8. In substance, the difference between the cost and the reissue price is a cash distribution to stockholders similar to a dividend.

EXAMPLE 15.8 Sale of Treasury Stock below Cost

PROBLEM: Consider Small Corp. from Example 15.7. Now assume that at the end of 3 months, the shareholder buys the same shares back at $800. Small Corp. has a zero balance in its additional paid-in capital from treasury stock transactions account. What is the journal entry to record this transaction?

SOLUTION: The journal entry to record the resale of the stock reduces treasury stock by its cost and records the excess of the cost over the resale price as a reduction to the retained earnings account.

Account	Date of Reissue	
Cash	800	
Retained Earnings	200	
Treasury Stock		1,000

At the end of 3 months, the shareholder owns the same number of shares held prior to these transactions but now has $200 in additional cash. This transaction is essentially a distribution to the shareholder.

Exhibit 15.4 outlines the process for accounting for the reissuance of treasury stock.

EXHIBIT 15.4 Accounting for the Reissuance of Treasury Stock

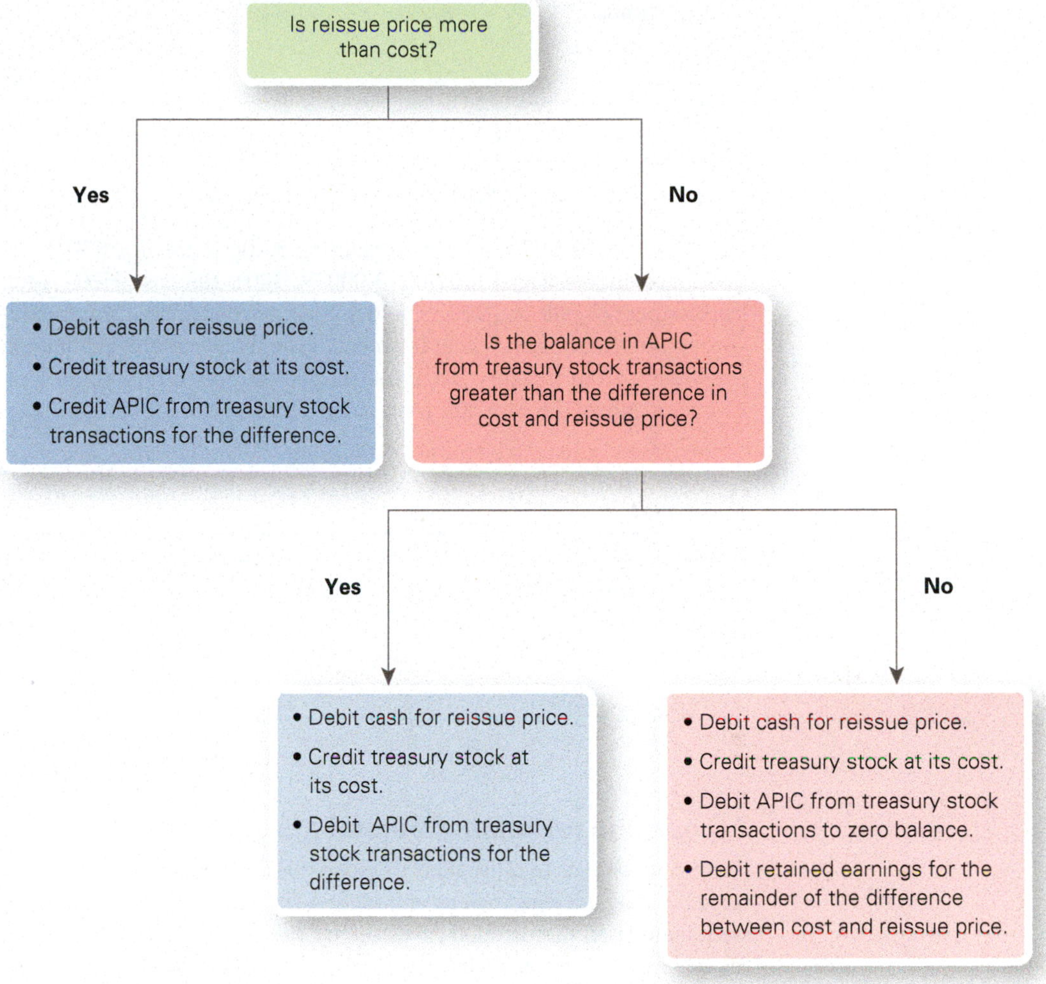

Example 15.9 provides a comprehensive illustration of accounting for treasury stock transactions under the cost method.

EXAMPLE 15.9 Comprehensive Illustration: Treasury Stock

PROBLEM: On February 16, Hollie Home Goods, Incorporated (HHG) acquired 5,000 shares of its own shares at a cost of $40 per share. On April 29, HHG sold 2,000 of the 5,000 shares of its treasury stock for $65 per share. On June 4, HHG sold the remaining 3,000 shares of treasury stock for $10 per share. What are the necessary journal entries to record these transactions?

SOLUTION: At acquisition, HHG records the shares at cost (5,000 × $40) as shown in the following entry.

Account	*February 16*	
Treasury Stock	200,000	
Cash		200,000

Continued

On April 29, HHG sells the 2,000 shares for $130,000 (2,000 × $65). The cost of these shares was $80,000 (2,000 × $40). Because HHG sold the shares for $50,000 above cost [2,000 shares × ($65 − $40)], we increase additional paid-in capital from treasury stock transactions.

Account	April 29	
Cash	130,000	
Treasury Stock		80,000
Additional Paid-in Capital from Treasury Stock Transactions		50,000

On June 4, HHG sold the remaining 3,000 shares for $30,000 (3,000 × $10). The cost of these shares was $120,000 (3,000 × $40). Because HHG sold the shares for $90,000 below cost [3,000 × ($10 − $40)], we first reduce additional paid-in capital from treasury stock transactions and then, if needed, retained earnings. The balance in the additional paid-in capital from treasury stock transactions is only $50,000, so we first reduce this account to zero. Next, the $40,000 remainder decreases retained earnings. The journal entry is as follows:

Account	June 4	
Cash	30,000	
Additional Paid-in Capital from Treasury Stock Transactions	50,000	
Retained Earnings	40,000	
Treasury Stock (3,000 shares at $40 cost)		120,000

Accounting for Share Retirements

Firms may choose to retire their treasury shares. In this case, the shares are still considered authorized but now are classified as unissued. A firm accounts for a share retirement as if it were a final settlement with the original investors by removing the number of common shares retired from the accounts at par and eliminating the average additional paid-in capital related to the retired shares from the balance sheet. The sum of the par value and the average additional paid-in capital represents the original issue proceeds.

If the repurchase price is less than the original amount paid in, the firm credits the difference to additional paid-in capital – retired shares. Conversely, if the repurchase price is greater than the original issue's proceeds, the firm debits additional paid-in capital – retired shares. If this account is reduced to zero, the firm debits the remainder to retained earnings. For example, ***Papa John's International***, the worldwide pizza company, retired $530.1 million of stock it held as treasury stock during fiscal 2013. ***Papa John's*** decreased common stock at par by $0.3 million, additional paid-in-capital in excess of par by $156.4 million, and retained earnings by $373.4 million. The debit to retained earnings indicates that the repurchase price was greater than the original proceeds and that there is an insufficient balance in additional paid-in capital – retired shares. Exhibit 15.5 outlines the process for accounting for share retirements.

EXHIBIT 15.5 Accounting for Share Retirements

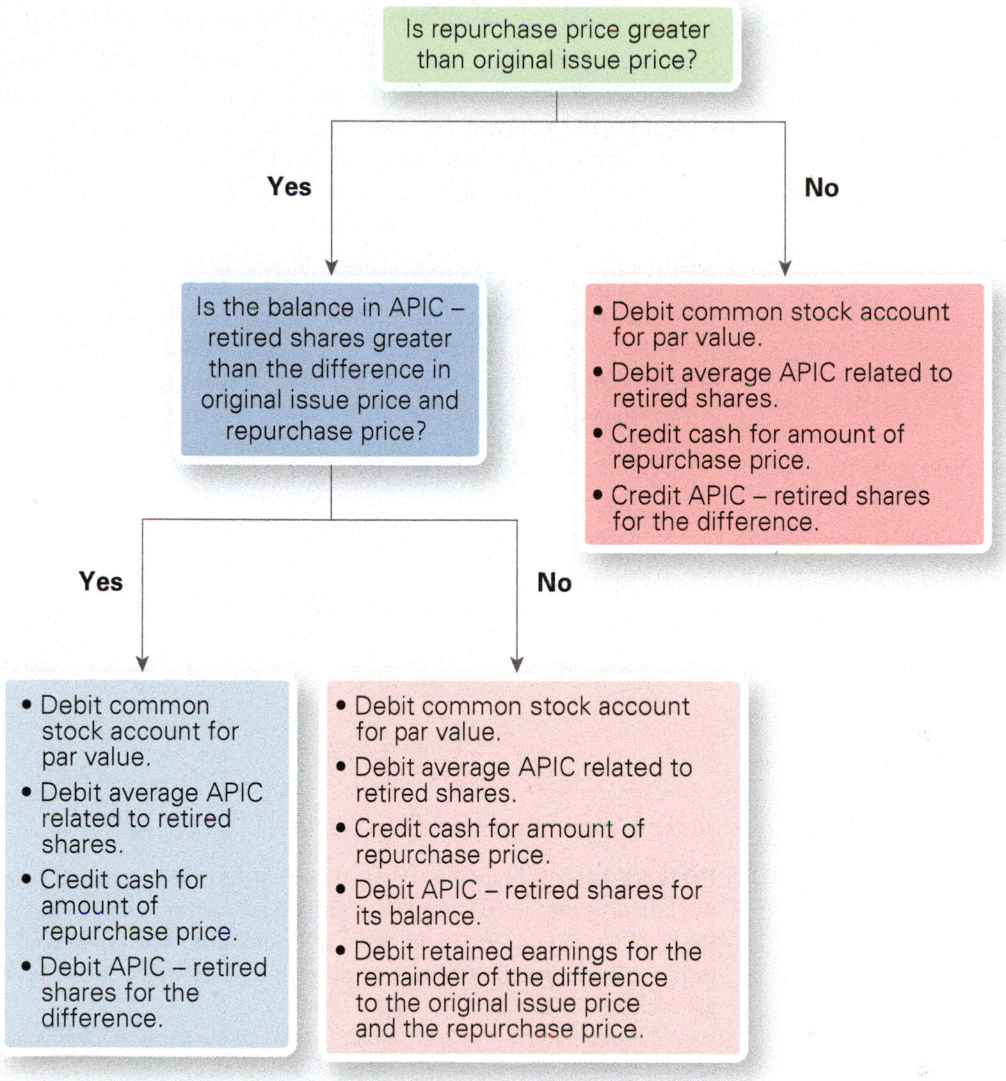

Although the amount paid below (above) the original issue proceeds is similar to a gain (loss), these amounts are generated from capital transactions and, as a result, firms do not report them on the income statement. Rather, the amount paid above or below the original issue proceeds flows through the stockholders' equity section of the balance sheet. Example 15.10 illustrates accounting for share retirements.

EXAMPLE 15.10 Retired Shares

PROBLEM: Neon Rainbow Company provides the following information regarding its most recent balance sheet.

Stockholders' Equity	
Common stock, $2 par value, 500,000 shares authorized, 172,500 shares issued and outstanding	$ 345,000
Additional paid-in capital in excess of par – common	1,207,500
Additional paid-in capital – retired shares	98,500
Retained earnings	1,249,000
Total stockholders' equity	$2,900,000

Continued

Neon Rainbow acquired 20,000 shares of common stock in the open market at $15 per share and retired the shares. What is the journal entry to record this transaction?

SOLUTION: The common shares have a $2 par value and a $7 average additional paid-in capital value (i.e., $1,207,500 / 172,500 shares). So, we measure the original issue proceeds as $9 per share (i.e., $2 par value per share plus $7 average additional paid-in-capital per share). Note that Neon Rainbow currently has a balance of $98,500 in additional paid-in capital – retired shares.

In order to record this transaction, we remove the 20,000 shares from the common stock account at $2 par value per share as well as the average additional paid-in capital in excess of par at $7 per share. There is a $120,000 "loss" on the retirement because the company paid $300,000 to retire shares that generated only $180,000 in cash at the time they were originally issued. Because the amount below cost is generated in a capital transaction, we cannot record the "loss" on the income statement. Rather, the amount below cost must be reported in the stockholders' equity section of the balance sheet. Therefore, we first use the "loss" to reduce the balance of additional paid-in capital—retired shares ($98,500) and charge the $21,500 remainder ($120,000 − $98,500) to retained earnings.

Account	***Date of Repurchase***	
Common Stock	40,000	
Additional Paid-in Capital in Excess of Par – Common	140,000	
Additional Paid-in Capital – Retired Shares	98,500	
Retained Earnings	21,500	
Cash		300,000

4 Describe preferred stock and its features; demonstrate the accounting for issuance, dividends, and consideration of potential debt features of preferred stock.

Accounting for Preferred Stock

Preferred stock is an equity security that has two common preferences over common stock. Specifically, preferred stock has priority over common shares in terms of receiving dividends and the right to claim assets in the event of liquidation. Most preferred stock is nonvoting. In this section, we examine the features of preferred stock, also called preferred shares, and discuss the accounting for this class of equity security.

THE CONCEPTUAL FRAMEWORK CONNECTION
Preferred Stock

The distinction between debt and equity is an important concept underlying the accounting for preferred stock. The codification defines debt as " . . . a contractual obligation to pay money on demand or on fixed or determinable dates. . . ."[13] However, hybrid securities that are financial instruments with characteristics of both debt and equity exist in practice but do not fit this formal definition of debt. For example, consider preferred shares, which are legally equity but offer the holder a fixed dividend, similar to debt interest. Are the preferred shares equity or a liability considering that these securities typically require payment of a fixed amount of dividends? As discussed later, this differentiation can often be quite complex. U.S. GAAP and IFRS offer differing interpretations regarding the proper classification of certain types of preferred shares on the balance sheet.

Overview of Preferred Stock

With a dividend preference, the firm must pay preferred shareholders before declaring any dividends to common shareholders. However, preferred shareholders have no right to dividends if the firm does not declare dividends for a given period. There is never a legal liability for the corporation to pay dividends unless the board of directors declares a dividend.

[13]From ASC Glossary, Financial Accounting Standards Board.

Preferred Stock versus Debt Financing. As noted earlier, preferred stock is generally nonvoting and pays a fixed dividend. The fixed dividend payment and the absence of voting rights make preferred shares similar to debt securities. Preferred stock provides certain advantages over debt and common equity financing for a corporation:

- Corporations that are held by only a few shareholders commonly issue nonvoting preferred shares to raise private equity capital without giving up control of the corporation.
- Preferred stock is less risky than debt for an issuing corporation because the corporation is not required to issue dividends to preferred shareholders, but interest payments to debt holders are mandatory to avoid default.

Nonetheless, preferred stock is not always advantageous with respect to taxation. Dividends paid to preferred shareholders are generally not tax deductible whereas debt interest is tax deductible for the corporation. Thus, corporations lose a valuable tax deduction when they issue preferred shares instead of debt.

Preferred Stock Par Values. Preferred stock par values can be significant, such as $100 par value per share. The par values are higher than those used for common shares because firms usually pay preferred dividends as a fixed percentage of par value. For example, a 5% preferred share with a $100 par value would pay an annual dividend of $5. What if a preferred stock has no par value? Dividends in this case would be a fixed dollar amount per share. In the example above, no-par preferred shares could state a dividend as $5 per share.

Accounting for the issuance of preferred stock is the same as accounting for common stock. Here, the firm separates the total cash proceeds received on issuance of preferred stock to par value and additional paid-in capital in excess of par – preferred as shown in Example 15.11.

EXAMPLE 15.11 Preferred Stock Issuance and Dividends

PROBLEM: On January 1, 2018, Koro Company issued 1,000 shares of 6%, $100 par value preferred stock for $130,000. The board of directors declared dividends on December 30, 2018. Koro paid the dividends on January 30, 2019. What journal entries are necessary to record these transactions?

SOLUTION: At the date of issuance, Koro records the preferred stock in equity in the same manner as a common stock issuance. That is, the company separates the total proceeds received to par value and additional paid-in capital in excess of par – preferred. The journal entry is as follows:

Account	*January 1, 2018*	
Cash	130,000	
Preferred Stock – 6%, $100 Par		100,000
Additional Paid-in Capital in Excess of Par – Preferred		30,000

The dividend is 6% of the preferred stock par value or $6,000 (6% × $100,000 par value). The journal entries to record the declaration and payment of the dividends are as follows:

Account	*December 30, 2018*	
Dividends – Preferred	6,000	
Dividends Payable – Preferred		6,000

Account	*January 30, 2019*	
Dividends Payable – Preferred	6,000	
Cash		6,000

Features of Preferred Shares

Preferred stock may possess a number of different features. The most common features include the following:

- *Cumulative*
- *Participating*
- *Convertible*
- *Callable*
- *Redeemable*
- *Fixed dividend*

We discuss each of these features next.

Cumulative Preferred Shares. **Cumulative preferred shares** contain a provision stipulating that if the board of directors does not declare a dividend, the dividends accumulate. The accumulated dividends are referred to as **dividends in arrears**. The firm cannot pay dividends to common shareholders until it has paid all preferred dividends in arrears plus the current-year preferred dividends. However, corporations do not include dividends in arrears as a liability on the balance sheet because the dividends become a legal liability of the corporation only when they are declared. Because a corporation must pay dividends in arrears before paying dividends on common shares, it must disclose any arrearage in the financial statements. This important disclosure enables the common stockholders and potential investors in common stock to determine that they will not be entitled to dividends until all dividends in arrears are distributed to the preferred shareholders. Example 15.12 illustrates accounting for cumulative preferred shares.

EXAMPLE 15.12 Cumulative Preferred Shares

PROBLEM: On January 1, 2017, Koro Company issued 1,000 shares of 6%, $100 par value, cumulative preferred stock for $130,000. The board of directors did not declare dividends on these shares until December 16, 2021, at which time it declared dividends of $30 per share. Therefore, dividends in arrears had accumulated since 2017. Koro paid the dividends in arrears and the regular preferred dividend for the current year on January 10, 2022. What journal entries and footnote disclosures are necessary to record these transactions?

SOLUTION: At the date of issuance, Koro records the preferred shares in equity in the same manner as a common share issuance. The journal entry is as follows:

Account	*January 1, 2017*	
Cash	130,000	
Preferred Stock – 6%, $100 Par		100,000
Additional Paid-in Capital in Excess of Par – Preferred		30,000

Every year that the board of directors does not declare a dividend, the amount of dividends in arrears increases by $6 per share, or a total of $6,000 per year. Thus, Koro reports dividends in arrears in its footnote disclosures as follows:

Year	Dividends in Arrears Reported (Cumulative)
2017	$ 6,000
2018	12,000
2019	18,000
2020	24,000

In 2021, Koro cannot distribute common dividends and the regular preferred dividend of $6 per share until it pays the $24,000 of dividends in arrears. Koro must disclose this fact to current and potential investors. Again, the amount of dividends in arrears is not a legal liability until the board of directors declares dividends. The current-year preferred dividend is $6,000 so that the total dividend distribution is $30,000 in 2021, the $24,000 dividends in arrears plus the $6,000 current-year dividend.

The journal entries to record the declaration and payment of the dividends are as follows:

Account	**December 16, 2021**	
Dividends – Preferred	30,000	
Dividends Payable – Preferred		30,000

Account	**January 10, 2022**	
Dividends Payable – Preferred	30,000	
Cash		30,000

Participating Preferred Shares. **Participating preferred shares** contain a provision requiring preferred shareholders to share ratably in distributions with common shareholders. The additional dividends distributed from the participation occur most often when dividends to common shareholders exceed the percentage stated for the preferred shares.[14] For example, assume that a company has 6% participating preferred shares. If the company pays common shareholders dividends that are 8% of common par value, it must also distribute an additional dividend to the preferred shareholders equal to 2% of preferred par.

Convertible Preferred Shares. **Convertible preferred shares** allow the shareholder to convert its shares to common shares at a predetermined rate or exchange ratio. Convertible preferred shareholders carry the same preferences as non-convertible preferred stock; however, they may also convert to common shares. The conversion feature enables preferred shareholders that convert to common stock to participate in voting rights, not to be limited to the fixed dividend return of preferred shares.

U.S. GAAP accounts for the issuance of convertible shares in the same way as non-convertible preferred shares. Accounting for convertible preferred shares is illustrated in Example 15.13.

EXAMPLE 15.13 Convertible Preferred Shares

PROBLEM: On January 1, 2017, Koro Company issued 1,000 shares of $70 par value, convertible preferred shares for $100,000. Each preferred share is convertible into one share of $1 par common stock. On June 15, 2019, all preferred shareholders converted their shares into common stock. What are the necessary journal entries to record these transactions?

SOLUTION: We treat the preferred share issuance as any issue of equity shares by separating the proceeds to par value of $70,000 ($100,000 × $70 par value per share) and to additional paid-in capital in excess of par – preferred of $30,000 ($100,000 − $70,000 preferred stock at par).

Account	**January 1, 2017**	
Cash	100,000	
Convertible Preferred Stock – Par		70,000
Additional Paid-in Capital in Excess of Par – Preferred		30,000

Continued

[14]There are other types of participation provisions. For example, preferred shares can be partially or fully participating. Partial participation places a ceiling on the amount of sharing whereas full participation allows the preferred stock to share an equal percentage of par value with common stock. Alternatively, preferred shares can receive their fixed dividend and then share the remaining dividend amount with common shareholders based on the ratio of par value or some other allocation method.

When the shares are converted, Koro removes the accounts related to the preferred shares and credits the common stock account for par value and additional paid-in capital in excess of par – common for the remainder.

Account	June 15, 2019	
Convertible Preferred Stock	70,000	
Additional Paid-in Capital in Excess of Par – Preferred	30,000	
Common Stock – Par		1,000
Additional Paid-in Capital in Excess of Par – Common		99,000

The debits to the convertible preferred stock and additional paid-in-capital in excess of par-preferred accounts remove the book value of the preferred shares whereas the credits to common stock and the additional paid-in-capital in excess of par – common represent the transfer of the preferred book value into the common stock accounts.

Immediately prior to its initial public offering, preferred shareholders at ***LinkedIn*** converted about 45.6 million preferred shares carried at \$103,827,000 to common shares. ***LinkedIn*** decreased preferred stock by \$103,827,000 and increased its common stock par value by \$5,000 with the remaining \$103,822,000 increasing additional paid-in capital.

Callable Preferred Shares. **Callable preferred shares** are shares for which the issuing entity has the right to call (in essence, buy back) the shares at a specified price and future date. Firms account for callable preferred shares in the same way as they do non-callable preferred shares. When the firm calls the shares, it must pay any dividends in arrears to the preferred shareholders. The company has the right to call the shares, so callable preferred shares are classified as equity. That is, because the payment is under the control of the issuing corporation, callable preferred shares are not classified as debt. Accounting for callable preferred shares is illustrated in Example 15.14.

EXAMPLE 15.14 Callable Preferred Shares

PROBLEM: On January 1, 2018, Koro Company issued 1,000 shares of \$70 par callable preferred shares for \$100,000. According to the preferred share agreement, Koro has the right to call these preferred shares on January 1, 2020, for \$100 per share. On January 1, 2020, Koro calls the shares. What are the necessary journal entries to record these transactions?

SOLUTION: Koro records the preferred share as a regular issue of shares by separating the proceeds to par value and additional paid-in capital in excess of par – preferred.

Account	January 1, 2018	
Cash	100,000	
Preferred Stock – Par		70,000
Additional Paid-in Capital in Excess of Par – Preferred		30,000

When Koro calls the shares, it removes the accounts related to the preferred shares and credits cash for the \$100,000 paid to call the shares.

Account	January 1, 2020	
Preferred Stock – Par	70,000	
Additional Paid-in Capital in Excess of Par – Preferred	30,000	
Cash		100,000

Mandatorily Redeemable Preferred Shares. Shareholders can redeem **redeemable preferred shares** at certain dates or upon the occurrence of certain events. Redeemable preferred shares can be *mandatorily redeemable* or *non-mandatorily redeemable*. **Mandatorily redeemable preferred shares** are preferred shares for which redemption is certain at a specified price on a specified date. The certain event that causes mandatory redemption can be the passage of time or the occurrence of a specific event, such as the death of a corporate officer.

U.S. GAAP treats mandatorily redeemable shares as a liability. The definition of a liability is a probable future sacrifice of economic benefits arising from present obligations of a particular entity to transfer assets or provide services to other entities in the future as a result of past transactions or events. Mandatorily redeemable shares contain a contractual obligation to disburse cash resulting from the right of the holder to demand payment and the fact that the exercise of that right is certain to occur. The requirement to disburse cash is outside the control of the issuing corporation, making these securities debt, not equity. Example 15.15 illustrates accounting for mandatorily redeemable preferred shares.

EXAMPLE 15.15 Mandatorily Redeemable Preferred Shares

PROBLEM: Tortoise Company issues 5,000 shares of $80 par preferred stock for $420,000. Tortoise must buy back the preferred stock in 5 years. Should Tortoise classify this preferred stock as a liability or equity? What is the required journal entry?

SOLUTION: Tortoise classifies this preferred stock as a liability because it contains a contractual obligation to disburse cash.

Account	At Issuance	
Cash	420,000	
Obligation Related to Mandatorily Redeemable Preferred Shares		420,000

Non-mandatorily redeemable preferred shares are preferred shares that can be redeemed at the option of the shareholder, but that option may not be exercised with certainty. For example, in the case of non-mandatorily redeemable preferred shares with an option to convert into common stock, the preferred shareholders may convert into common stock before the possible redemption dates. U.S. GAAP reports non-mandatorily redeemable preferred shares as equity because the preferred shares may not be redeemed as illustrated in Example 15.16.

EXAMPLE 15.16 Non-Mandatorily Redeemable Preferred Shares

PROBLEM: Porpoise Company issues 7,000 shares of $60 par preferred stock for $450,000. It is not required to buy back the preferred stock. However, the preferred stock includes a redemption feature that gives the holder the option to redeem the shares for cash at specified dates. Should Porpoise classify this preferred stock as a liability or equity?

SOLUTION: Because the preferred shares give the holder the option to redeem, they are not mandatorily redeemable. Therefore, Porpoise classifies the preferred stock as equity.

Fixed-Dividend Preferred Shares. **Fixed-dividend preferred shares** are preferred shares whose dividend is fixed and payment is required. The fixed dividend is a contractual obligation to pay cash (or some other asset) to the holder. Even though fixed-dividend preferred shares have characteristics of both debt and equity, firms do not separately evaluate the accounting for the shares and dividends: The entire proceeds are treated as equity at issuance. Dividends are a reduction of equity. Example 15.17 illustrates accounting for fixed-dividend preferred shares.

EXAMPLE 15.17 Fixed-Dividend Preferred Shares

PROBLEM: Doug Hunt Company issued $10,000,000 of preferred stock at par on January 1, 2018. The preferred stock has a 6% fixed annual cash dividend and no maturity date. Doug Hunt can repay the preferred shares at any time. The current market interest rate is 6%. What is the journal entry when the firm issues the preferred shares?

SOLUTION: Because Doug Hunt can repay the preferred shares at any time, the preferred shares are not mandatorily redeemable. Therefore, Doug Hunt classifies the entire proceeds as equity with the following journal entry.

Account	January 1, 2018	
Cash	10,000,000	
Preferred Stock (Equity)		10,000,000

Accounting for Preferred Shares: IFRS. U.S. GAAP and IFRS account for certain types of preferred stock differently. The differences primarily relate to preferred stock with features of equity and debt. Under IFRS, firms separate the debt features and report them as a liability. We discuss the areas of differences next.

1. *Convertible preferred shares.* IFRS classification depends on the terms of the conversion feature. If there is a fixed number of shares to be delivered upon conversion, the shares are classified as equity. Otherwise, the shares are classified as debt.
2. *Non-Mandatorily redeemable preferred shares.* Under IFRS, when the preferred stockholder has the option to require redemption, the firm reports redeemable preferred shares as a liability. Here, the company may not be able to avoid paying cash, so it reports the preferred stock as a liability. In this case, the possible requirement to distribute cash is not under the control of the issuing corporation.
3. *Fixed-Dividend preferred shares.* Under IFRS, the shares are classified as a liability because there is a contractual obligation and a fixed payment is required.

Example 15.18 illustrates accounting for non- mandatorily redeemable preferred shares under IFRS.

EXAMPLE 15.18 Non-Mandatorily Redeemable Preferred Shares—IFRS

PROBLEM: Porpoise Company issues 7,000 shares of $60 par preferred stock for $450,000. Porpoise is not required to buy back the preferred stock. However, the preferred stock includes a redemption feature that gives the holder the option to redeem the shares for cash at specified dates. Should Porpoise classify this preferred stock as a liability or equity under IFRS?

SOLUTION: IFRS classifies the preferred stock as a liability because Porpoise has a contractual obligation to pay cash upon the shareholders' request. Although not mandatorily redeemable, the company is obligated by contract to pay cash at the shareholders' option.

TD Bank, a Canadian bank and IFRS reporter, has issued both mandatorily and non-mandatorily redeemable preferred stock. ***TD Bank*** reported a 27 million Canadian dollar (CAD) liability for the mandatorily redeemable preferred stock that is convertible at the holder's option on its fiscal 2013 balance sheet. ***TD Bank*** also reported CAD$3,395 million of preferred stock in equity related to its preferred stock that is not mandatorily redeemable or convertible.

Exhibit 15.6 on the next page summarizes the various features of preferred stock and accounting for them under U.S. GAAP and IFRS.

EXHIBIT 15.6 Features of Preferred Stock and Accounting: U.S. GAAP and IFRS

		Accounting under	
Type of Preferred Shares	**Description**	**U.S. GAAP**	**IFRS**
Cumulative	Preferred shares with a provision stipulating that if the board of directors does not declare a dividend, the dividends accumulate.	Track the amount of dividends in arrears. Any dividend declared first goes to reduce the amount of dividends in arrears.	Similar to U.S. GAAP.
Participating	Preferred shares with a provision requiring that preferred shareholders share ratably in distributions with common shareholders.	Any dividend declared first goes ratably to preferred shareholders.	Similar to U.S. GAAP.
Convertible preferred shares	These preferred shares allow shareholders to convert their shares to common shares at a predetermined rate or exchange ratio.	Classified as equity.	If there are a fixed number of shares to be delivered, classify as equity. Otherwise, classify as debt.
Callable preferred shares	Preferred shares for which the issuing entity has the right to call (buy back) the shares at a specified price and future date.	Classified as equity.	Similar to U.S. GAAP.
Mandatorily redeemable	Preferred shares that shareholders will redeem at certain dates or upon the occurrence of certain events.	Classified as liability.	Similar to U.S. GAAP.
Non-Mandatorily redeemable	Preferred shares that can be redeemed at the option of the shareholder. That option may not be exercised with certainty.	Classified as equity.	Classified as liability when the holder has the option to redeem the shares.
Fixed-Dividend preferred shares	Preferred shares with the dividend fixed and the payment required.	Classified as equity.	Classified as liability.

5 Explain the accounting for retained earnings, including dividends and prior-period adjustments.

Accounting for Retained Earnings

We now address retained earnings, the second component of stockholders' equity, which represents the cumulative earnings of the firm that it has not distributed as dividends. Thus, retained earnings are amounts *earned* by the firm, as opposed to contributed capital, which are amounts *invested* by the equity holders of the firm.

Net income (loss) and dividends are the most common events that affect retained earnings. However, other transactions, such as the sale of treasury stock below cost, can affect retained earnings. In this section, we discuss the impact of accounting for dividends on retained earnings. In addition, we discuss *prior-period adjustments*, which affect retained earnings and current-period income and dividends.

Types of Dividends

Dividends represent a return to shareholders on their investment in the corporation. **Cash dividends**, distributions that firms make to the shareholders in cash, are the most common type of dividend. However, there are other types of dividends, namely *stock dividends*, *property dividends*, and *liquidating dividends*.

- **Stock dividends** are distributions in the form of the firm's own equity shares.
- **Property dividends** are distributions of any asset other than cash (e.g., inventory or investments in shares of other entities) that firms make. Cash, stock, and property dividends are all distributed from retained earnings.
- **Liquidating dividends** are any distribution that the firm pays from contributed capital instead of retained earnings.

Because of the rarity in practice of property and liquidating dividends, we focus on cash and stock dividends in this chapter.[15]

[15]Of 500 surveyed companies, only 1 distributed property dividends, and 2 distributed stock dividends. From AICPA, *U.S. GAAP Financial Statements Best Practices in Presentation and Disclosure – 2012* (New York, NY: AICPA, 2012).

Accounting for Cash Dividends

There are four key dates involved with a cash dividend:

1. *Declaration date*
2. *Record date*
3. *Ex-Dividend date*
4. *Payment date*

On the **declaration date**, the date on which the board of directors declares the dividend and the firm records a legal liability for the dividend, the company records the dividend with a debit to the dividends account and a credit to dividends payable. The dividends account is closed to the retained earnings account at the end of the period when the company prepares financial statements. On the **record date**, the firm determines the registered stockholders, and only these stockholders receive the cash dividend. No formal accounting entry is made on the date of record.

The **ex-dividend date**, which is determined by the relevant stock exchange once the company has announced the record date, is generally set as 2 business days before the record date. An investor who purchases the stock on its ex-dividend date or after will not receive the dividend. This 2-day difference between record date and ex-dividend date allows time for stock transactions to clear and settle. Again, no formal accounting entry is made on the ex-dividend date. Finally, the **payment date** is the date that the firm actually distributes the dividend. The company removes the dividends payable account from the books at this time and credits cash for the amount of the payment. Example 15.19 illustrates accounting for a cash dividend.

EXAMPLE 15.19 Cash Dividend

PROBLEM: Collins, Inc. declared a cash dividend of $3,000 on June 1, 2018. It sets the record date as June 17, 2018, the ex-dividend date as June 15, 2018, and the payment date as July 7, 2018. What journal entries are necessary to record this dividend?

The timeline related to the cash dividend declaration and payment follows.

Date of Declaration June 1, 2018	Ex-dividend Date June 15, 2018	Date of Record June 17, 2018	Payment Date July 7, 2018
Legal liability incurred	Stock bought on this date or later will not receive the dividend	Ownership determined at the close of business	Liability paid

SOLUTION: On the declaration date, Collins must record a liability for the dividend because it is then legally obligated to distribute the $3,000 amount to shareholders. Collins reduces retained earnings by this amount via the dividends – common account because firms distribute all dividends (except liquidating dividends) from retained earnings. The journal entry is as follows:

Account	*June 1, 2018*	
Dividends – Common	3,000	
Dividends Payable		3,000

There are no formal accounting entries on the date of record and the ex-dividend date. On the date of payment, Collins records the dividend payment in the same way as the payment of other liabilities by debiting the payable and crediting cash.

Account	*July 7, 2018*	
Dividends Payable	3,000	
Cash		3,000

Johnson & Johnson regularly pays quarterly cash dividends. In the third quarter on October 20, 2016, its board declared dividends of $0.80 per share. The ex-dividend date was November 18, and date of record was November 22. ***Johnson & Johnson*** paid the dividend on December 6.[16] In fiscal 2016, ***Johnson & Johnson*** paid cash dividends of $3.15 per share totaling $7.8 billion.

Accounting for Stock Dividends

Instead of a cash dividend, a company may declare a stock dividend to provide a return to shareholders. Stock dividends can also be used to supplement a cash dividend without increasing cash dividends. Unlike cash dividends, when a board of directors declares a stock dividend, it is not under any legal obligation to distribute the dividend. Thus, firms do not increase a liability account when declaring a stock dividend.

Stock dividends affect the components of stockholders' equity but do not change the total equity balance. Retained earnings are decreased and contributed capital is increased by the amount of the stock dividend. Thus, the stock dividend permanently capitalizes retained earnings by transferring amounts from retained earnings to contributed capital. The amount of the transfer from retained earnings to contributed capital depends on the size of the dividend.

Small (Ordinary) Stock Dividend. A stock dividend is considered a **small stock dividend** if the number of shares issued does not exceed 20% to 25% of the previously outstanding shares. Unless there is evidence to the contrary, the accountant assumes that a dividend of this size would not have a material, negative effect on the market price per share of the stock when the additional shares are distributed. Accounting for small stock dividends involves the following steps:

1. Value the dividend at the market price at the date of declaration.
2. On the date of declaration, increase the dividends account by the dividend at market value, which will ultimately be closed to retained earnings.
3. Increase the common stock dividends distributable account for the par value of the stock dividend. This account is a capital stock account.
4. Increase the additional paid-in-capital in excess of par – common account for the difference between the market value and the par value of the stock to be distributed.
5. When the dividend is distributed, remove the common stock dividends distributable account with a debit and credit the common stock account.

At the end of the period, the dividends account is closed to retained earnings. An example of accounting for a small stock dividend is provided in Example 15.20.

EXAMPLE 15.20

Small Stock Dividend

PROBLEM: Wallace Company reported the following stockholders' equity section in its most recent balance sheet.

Stockholders' Equity	Balance
Common Stock ($1 par, 2,000,000 shares authorized, 1,345,000 shares issued, 1,300,000 shares outstanding)	$ 1,345,000
Additional Paid-in Capital in Excess of Par – Common	12,105,000
Total Contributed Capital	$13,450,000
Retained Earnings	12,550,000
Total Contributed Capital and Retained Earnings	$26,000,000
Less: Cost of Treasury Stock (45,000 shares)	(1,800,000)
Total Stockholders' Equity	$24,200,000

Wallace Company declared a stock dividend of 195,000 shares on a date when the firm's common stock was selling for $15 per share. The shares issued to satisfy the stock dividend

Continued

[16]See http://www.investor.jnj.com/divhistory.cfm for Johnson & Johnson's dividend history.

are newly issued shares, not treasury shares, and the treasury shareholders are not entitled to the stock dividend. Provide the journal entries at the declaration date and the issue date. Prepare the stockholders' equity section of the balance sheet after the issuance of the dividend.

SOLUTION: Wallace accounts for this stock dividend as a small dividend because it is 15% of outstanding shares computed as follows.

Common shares issued	1,345,000
Less: Treasury shares	(45,000)
Common shares outstanding	1,300,000
Shares issued	195,000
Divided by: Common shares outstanding	1,300,000
Percentage	15%

Thus, Wallace will transfer the $2,925,000 market value of the stock (195,000 shares × $15 per share) from retained earnings to contributed capital. Wallace makes the following journal entries to account for the stock dividend. Keep in mind that the dividends account will be closed to retained earnings at year-end.

Account	***Date of Declaration***	
Dividends	2,925,000	
Common Stock Dividends Distributable		195,000
Additional Paid-in-Capital in Excess of Par – Common		2,730,000

On the distribution date, Wallace makes the following entry:

Account	***Date of Distribution***	
Common Stock Dividends Distributable	195,000	
Common Stock – Par		195,000

The stockholders' equity section after the declaration and issuance of the small stock dividend follows.

Stockholders' Equity	**Balance**
Common Stock ($1 par, 2,000,000 shares authorized, 1,540,000 shares issued, and 1,495,000 shares outstanding)*	$ 1,540,000
Additional Paid-in Capital in Excess of Par – Common**	14,835,000
Total Contributed Capital	$ 16,375,000
Retained Earnings***	9,625,000
Total Contributed Capital and Retained Earnings	26,000,000
Less: Cost of Treasury Stock (45,000 shares)	(1,800,000)
Total Stockholders' Equity	$24,200,000

*Common stock increased by $195,000.
**Additional paid-in capital increased by $2,730,000.
***Retained earnings decreased by $2,925,000.

Large Stock Dividend. A stock dividend is considered a **large stock dividend** if the number of shares issued is more than 20% to 25% of the previously outstanding shares. Unless there is evidence to the contrary, the accountant assumes that a dividend of this size would materially reduce the market price per share of the stock when the additional shares are distributed. Therefore, the value given to the shareholder is not known, but the dividend cannot be accounted for at below minimum legal capital. As a result, the dividend is accounted for at the par value of the stock.[17]

[17] Large stock dividends are sometimes accounted for as a stock split. For example, a 50% stock dividend would be treated the same as a 3-for-2 split.

Accounting for large-stock dividends involves the following steps:

1. When declaring a large stock dividend, debit dividends for the par value of the stock.
2. Credit common stock dividends distributable, an equity account, for the par value of the stock.
3. When distributing the stock dividend, reduce the common stock dividends distributable and increase common stock at par.

As dividends are closed out to retained earnings, a large stock dividend also permanently transfers retained earnings to contributed capital. Example 15.15 shows the accounting for a large stock dividend.

EXAMPLE 15.21 Large Stock Dividend

PROBLEM: Wallace Company reported the following stockholders' equity section in its most recent balance sheet.

Stockholders' Equity	Balance
Common Stock ($1 par, 2,000,000 shares authorized, 1,345,000 shares issued, 1,300,000 shares outstanding)	$ 1,345,000
Additional Paid-in Capital in Excess of Par – Common	12,105,000
Total Contributed Capital	$13,450,000
Retained Earnings	12,550,000
Total Contributed Capital and Retained Earnings	$26,000,000
Less: Cost of Treasury Stock (45,000 shares)	(1,800,000)
Total Stockholders' Equity	$24,200,000

Wallace Company declared a stock dividend of 390,000 shares on a date when the firm's common stock was selling for $15 per share. The shares issued to satisfy the stock dividend are newly issued shares, not treasury shares, and the treasury shares are not entitled to the stock dividend. Provide the journal entries at the declaration date and the issue date. Prepare the stockholders' equity section of the balance sheet after the issuance of the dividend.

SOLUTION: Wallace accounts for this stock dividend as a large dividend because it is 30% of outstanding shares.

Common shares issued	1,345,000
Less: Treasury shares	(45,000)
Common shares outstanding	1,300,000
Shares issued	390,000
Divided by: Common shares outstanding	1,300,000
Percentage	30%

Thus, Wallace will transfer the $390,000 par value of the stock (390,000 shares × $1 par value per share) to common stock at par. Wallace makes the following journal entries to account for the stock dividend. Keep in mind that the dividends account will be closed to retained earnings at year-end.

Account	Date of Declaration	
Dividends	390,000	
Common Stock Dividends Distributable		390,000

Continued

Account	Date of Distribution	
Common Stock Dividends Distributable	390,000	
Common Stock – Par		390,000

The stockholders' equity section after the declaration and issuance of the large stock dividend follows.

Stockholders' Equity	Balance
Common Stock ($1 par, 2,000,000 shares authorized, 1,735,000 shares issued, 1,690,000 shares outstanding)*	$ 1,735,000
Additional Paid-in Capital in Excess of Par – Common	12,105,000
Total Contributed Capital	$13,840,000
Retained Earnings**	12,160,000
Total Contributed Capital and Retained Earnings	$26,000,000
Less: Cost of Treasury Stock (45,000 shares)	(1,800,000)
Total Stockholders' Equity	$24,200,000

*Common stock increased by $390,000.
**Retained earnings decreased by $390,000.

JUDGMENTS IN ACCOUNTING
Stock Dividends

Because FASB does not specify an exact percentage cutoff to distinguish small stock dividends from large stock dividends, there is some room for judgment in accounting for stock dividends. The difference in accounting for small stock dividends and large stock dividends affects the balance in the retained earnings account and, thus, investors may be influenced by the accounting treatment. In addition, possible violation of restrictive debt covenants can occur if retained earnings fall below a specified level, resulting in technical default.

Consider Wallace Company from Examples 15.20 and 15.21. Assume the stock dividends in Examples 15.20 and 15.21 did not occur. Now assume that Wallace Company declared a stock dividend of 300,000 shares, which represents 23% of the current outstanding shares. If Wallace accounts for this transaction as a small stock dividend, it makes the following entries:

Account	Date of Declaration	
Dividends	4,500,000	
Common Stock Dividends Distributable		300,000
Additional Paid-in Capital in Excess of Par – Common		4,200,000

Account	Date of Distribution	
Common Stock Dividends Distributable	300,000	
Common Stock – Par		300,000

Thus, after closing its books, Wallace will have a retained earnings balance of $8,050,000 ($12,550,000 beginning balance less dividends of $4,500,000).

If Wallace accounts for the transaction as a large stock dividend, it will make the following entries:

Account	Date of Declaration	
Dividends	300,000	
Common Stock Dividends Distributable		300,000

Account	Date of Distribution	
Common Stock Dividends Distributable	300,000	
Common Stock – Par		300,000

Thus, after closing its books, Wallace will have a retained earnings balance of $12,250,000 ($12,550,000 beginning balance less dividends of $300,000). Consequently, Wallace reports a retained earnings balance that is $4,200,000 larger under the large dividend approach than under the small dividend approach. This difference is substantial because this involves only a financial reporting choice, not a difference in the underlying transaction.

Prior-Period Adjustments

From time to time, companies uncover errors in their financial statements. If the company discovers the error *before* releasing the financial statements, the correction is straightforward: The company makes the correction prior to release of the financial statements. However, if a company finds an error *after* releasing the financial statements, it must determine whether corrections to past years' financial statements are necessary. This correction of prior-period financial statements is called a **prior-period adjustment**.

Firms are only required to report material errors that would influence the economic decisions of financial statements users. Errors corrected using a prior-period adjustment include mathematical mistakes and incorrect application of accounting standards.[18] For instance, a company could make a mathematical error in the calculation of its bad debt expense.

The accounting method used to correct an error depends on when the firm made the error. Companies commonly report 1 or 2 years of prior years' financial statements to enhance comparability. For example, in the 2019 annual report, a company provides income statements for 2019, 2018, and 2017 and balance sheets for 2019 and 2018. If the error was made in one of these prior-year financial statements (2018 or 2017) that are presented with the current-year financial statements, the firm retroactively changes relevant financial statement line items and includes a disclosure in the footnotes explaining the error in the 2019 annual report. A **retroactive adjustment** correctly recognizes, measures, and provides disclosures as if the error never occurred. Correcting financial statements in this way is also referred to as a restatement.

If the error occurred in any year that is not included in the comparative statements in the annual report, the firm makes a prior-period adjustment by:

1. Correcting the appropriate balance sheet accounts in the earliest balance sheet presented.
2. Reporting any income effects in retained earnings, net of tax, as of the beginning of the first period presented in the comparative statements.
3. Reporting correct balance sheet amounts in the current and all future periods.

For example, assume that a company discovers in 2019 that it failed to record depreciation expense on its trucks in 2016. To make the prior-period adjustment in 2019, the company reports comparative balance sheets for 2018 and 2019. So, it adjusts the 2018 beginning balances of its fixed assets and retained earnings, which will then affect the beginning balances of these accounts for fiscal 2019.

Stein Mart, Inc., a large U.S. retailer, made a prior-period adjustment for errors made with regard to inventory markdowns, leasehold improvement costs, compensated absences (paid vacation), and other items in fiscal 2012. ***Stein Mart*** reported 3 years of income and changes in stockholders' equity, so it adjusted fiscal 2010 and 2011 income and the beginning retained earnings of fiscal 2010. The prior-period adjustment decreased 2010 beginning retained earnings by $17 million, or about 9%. The adjustment increased ***Stein Mart's*** 2010 and 2011 earnings by $0.1 million and $7.9 million, respectively. Example 15.22 illustrates accounting for a prior-period adjustment.

[18]For the relevant authoritative literature for prior-period adjustments, see FASB ASC 250, *Accounting Changes and Error Corrections* for U.S. GAAP and IASC, *International Accounting Standard 8*, "Accounting Policies, Changes in Accounting Estimates and Errors" (London, UK: International Accounting Standards Committee, Revised, 20XX) for IFRS.

EXAMPLE 15.22 Prior-Period Adjustment

PROBLEM: As Merrilee Fashions was preparing its 2018 financial statements, it discovered an error in its 2015 financial statements: Merrilee had not recorded a $50,000 sale on both its books and tax returns. As a result, the firm understated sales and accounts receivable in 2015. Merrilee never collected the receivable but is seeking payment from the customer. Merrilee has a constant tax rate of 40% and reports 3 years of comparative income statements and 2 years of comparative balance sheets with its financial reports. What is the necessary journal entry to record the prior-period adjustment, and how should Merrilee report its accounts receivable and retained earnings balances in these financial statements?

SOLUTION: The effect on 2015 income would have been $30,000 higher had Merrilee discovered the error in that year. The $30,000 net income effect consists of the $50,000 increase in income due to the sales revenue less the related tax expense of $20,000 ($50,000 times 40%). Consequently, Merrilee records a prior-period adjustment increasing retained earnings by $30,000. It also increases accounts receivable by $50,000. Finally, it records the $20,000 of taxes owed to the government related to the sales revenue when filing amended tax returns.

The journal entry to record the prior-period adjustment on December 31, 2018, follows.

Account	December 31, 2018	
Accounts Receivable	50,000	
Retained Earnings – Prior-Period Adjustment		30,000
Income Tax Payable		20,000

Merrilee will report these adjustments in the opening balances on the first balance sheet it presents, the December 31, 2017 balance sheet.

6 Describe the components of other comprehensive income and accumulated other comprehensive income.

Accounting for Other Comprehensive Income

Firms do not include the effects of certain events and transactions in net income. For example, unrealized gains and losses on adjusting the carrying value of debt investments to fair value are not always reported in net income. Because some changes in equity bypass net income, companies report **comprehensive income**, which is a measure of changes in a company's equity that result from recognized transactions and all economic events of the period other than transactions with owners.[19] Reporting comprehensive income assists investors, creditors, and others in assessing a company's activities and the timing and magnitude of a company's future cash flows.[20]

Components of Comprehensive Income

Comprehensive income includes all changes in equity during a period from all sources except those resulting from investments by owners and distributions to owners. Comprehensive income is composed of two major components: net income and other comprehensive income. Other comprehensive income (OCI) is the portion of comprehensive income that is not included in net income. The elements of net income are revenues, expenses, gains, and losses.

The primary elements of OCI are:

- Unrealized gains and losses from the available-for-sale portfolio of debt investment securities and derivatives classified as cash flow hedges[21]

[19]For the relevant authoritative literature for U.S. GAAP, see FASB ASC 220, *Comprehensive Income*. For IFRS, IASC, *International Accounting Standard 1*, "Presentation of Financial Statements" (London, UK: International Accounting Standards Committee, Revised, 2016) is the relevant authoritative literature.

[20]We also discuss other comprehensive income in Chapter 5.

[21]We cover investment securities in more detail in Chapter 16.

- Foreign currency translation adjustments
- Unrecognized pension costs and benefits[22]

Exhibit 15.7 presents graphically the components of comprehensive income.

EXHIBIT 15.7 Components of Comprehensive Income

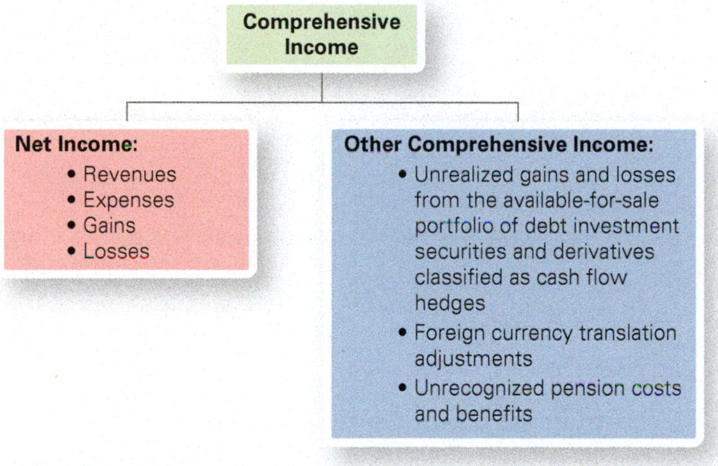

THE CONCEPTUAL FRAMEWORK CONNECTION
Other Comprehensive Income

The elements of other comprehensive income create changes in equity that are not related to investor transactions. Why, then, do firms not report them on the income statement? There is no clear conceptual reason for reporting certain transactions in other comprehensive income. There are three reasons, however, that support the presentation of other comprehensive income separate from net income:

1. OCI items have a low probability of cash flow realization in the short term and therefore should not be included in net income. Including these items would further remove net income from the underlying cash flows of the firm.
2. The temporary nature of OCI items would create earnings volatility (when these temporary events reverse) if included in net income.
3. OCI events are not part of normal business operations, so they should not be included in net income.

Reporting Other Comprehensive Income

A company has two options for reporting OCI:

1. Include components of OCI after net income on one continuous statement summing to comprehensive income. The statement is the statement of comprehensive income.
2. Present a separate statement of other comprehensive income that begins with net income on the first line and details the components of OCI. This approach results in presenting two statements, one displaying the details of net income and the other displaying the details of other comprehensive income. The statements are the statement of net income and the statement of comprehensive income.

Facebook, Inc., the online social media company, uses the second approach, as illustrated in Exhibit 15.8. In 2016, ***Facebook***'s comprehensive income was $248 million lower than its net income because of other comprehensive income items.

---

[22]We cover pensions in more detail in Chapter 19.

EXHIBIT 15.8 Statement of Comprehensive Income, ***Facebook, Inc.***, Financial Statements, December 31, 2016

Facebook, Inc.
Consolidated Statements of Comprehensive Income
(In millions)

	Year Ended December 31		
	2016	**2015**	**2014**
Net income	$10,217	$3,688	$2,940
Other comprehensive income (loss):			
Change in foreign currency translation adjustment, net of tax	(152)	(202)	(239)
Change in unrealized gain/loss on available-for-sale investments, net of tax	(96)	(25)	(3)
Comprehensive income	$ 9,969	$3,461	$2,698

Source: Facebook, Inc. Annual Report. http://www.annualreports.com/HostedData/AnnualReports/PDF/NASDAQ_FB_2016.pdf

Accumulated Other Comprehensive Income

Accumulated other comprehensive income, the aggregation of OCI over the years, is the third component of stockholders' equity. Firms report accumulated other comprehensive income on the balance sheet in the stockholders' equity section, along with contributed capital and retained earnings.

7 Detail required disclosures for stockholders' equity.

Stockholders' Equity Disclosures

For stockholders' equity required disclosures, companies commonly report the classes of stock, any par values, and the number of shares authorized, issued, and outstanding in the equity section of the balance sheet.

Exhibit 15.9 presents an excerpt from ***Facebook***'s 2016 statement of stockholders' equity. Note that the columns across the top include both the number of shares and amounts for common stock. Other columns are additional paid-in capital, accumulated other comprehensive income, retained earnings, and the total stockholders' equity column. Down the rows, there are several issuances of common stock during the year, increasing the number of shares and amount of additional paid-in capital. During 2016, ***Facebook*** issued 3 million shares of common stock when stock options were exercised for employee services and compensation. The loss from other comprehensive income of $248 million decreased accumulated other comprehensive income. Net income of $10,217 million increased retained earnings. The cumulative-effect adjustment relates to the adoption of a new accounting update, which we discuss in Chapter 21.

In the notes to the financial statements, companies provide details about the rights and privileges of each class of capital stock. The notes also detail terms and provisions of callable, convertible, and redeemable securities; stock options; and other contingent shares or potentially dilutive securities. Information regarding potentially dilutive securities is essential to current and potential investors because the issuance of additional shares on conversion will reduce the ownership share of current equity holders and dilute EPS.

We summarize the common disclosure requirements by the type of security in the following sections.

Rights and Privileges of Classes of Stock

The disclosures for stockholders' equity must include the pertinent rights and privileges of the various securities outstanding. Examples of disclosed information are dividend and liquidation preferences, participation rights, call prices and dates, conversion or exercise prices or rates and pertinent dates, sinking-fund requirements,[23] unusual voting rights, and significant terms of contracts to issue additional shares. An entity must also disclose the number of shares issued upon conversion, exercise, or satisfaction of required conditions.

EXHIBIT 15.9 Statement of Stockholders' Equity, ***Facebook, Inc.***, Financial Statements, December 31, 2016

Facebook, Inc.
Consolidated Statements of Stockholders' Equity
(In millions)

	Class A and Class B Common Stock		Additional Paid-in Capital	Accumulated Other Comprehensive (Loss) Income	Retained Earnings	Total Stockholders' Equity
	Shares	Par Value				
Balances at December 31, 2015	2,845	—	$34,886	$ (455)	$ 9,787	$44,218
Cumulative-effect adjustment from adoption of ASU 2016-09	—	—	39	—	1,666	1,705
Issuance of common stock for cash upon exercise of stock options	3	—	16	—	—	16
Issuance of common stock related to acquisitions	1	—	74	—	—	74
Issuance of common stock for settlement of restricted stock units (RSUs)	43	—	—	—	—	—
Shares withheld related to net share settlement	—	—	(6)	—	—	(6)
Share-based compensation related to employee share-based awards	—	—	3,218	—	—	3,218
Other comprehensive income (loss)	—	—	—	(248)	—	(248)
Net income	—	—	—	—	10,217	10,217
Balances at December 31, 2016	2,892	$ —	$38,227	$(703)	$21,670	$59,194

Source: Facebook, Inc. Annual Report. http://www.annualreports.com/HostedData/AnnualReports/PDF/NASDAQ_FB_2016.pdfForm 10-K (Annual). United States Securities and Exchange Commission. EDGAR Online, Inc. Source: http://files.shareholder.com/downloads/AMDA-NJ5DZ/3272447189x0xS1326801-14-7/1326801/filing.pdf

[23]A sinking fund is a separate account consisting of cash and other liquid assets used to repay debt or redeemable preferred stock when they are due.

Interview

ROBERT LAUX

NORTH AMERICAN LEAD INTERNATIONAL INTEGRATED REPORTING COUNCIL»

Robert Laux

Robert Laux is the North American Lead for the International Integrated Reporting Council (IIRC). The IIRC is a global coalition of regulators, investors, companies, standard setters, the accounting profession and NGOs promoting communication about value creation as the next step in the evolution of corporate reporting.

1 Why are the extensive disclosures for stockholders' equity important for the financial statement user?

The detailed stockholders' equity disclosures provide critical information, in particular returns to stockholders, that may not be readily apparent from other financial information such as the income statement, balance sheet, or statement of cash flows. For instance, the stockholders' equity statement clearly shows the amount of dividends that have been paid and the amount of stock repurchased, both of which are returns to stockholders. In addition, detailed disclosures also give users information on how a company may be diluting stockholders' interests, either by issuing additional stock or providing stock-based compensation to employees. They also provide users important information on Board of Director-approved stock repurchase plans and how much of the authorized amount is still available for stock repurchases.

2 What is the most common method of accounting for stock repurchases, and what accounts for its popularity?

Under ASC 505, Equity, a corporation has two alternatives to account for stock retirements or repurchases. It may allocate an excess of repurchase price over par or stated value between additional paid-in capital and retained earnings, or it may charge the excess entirely to retained earnings. While practice is mixed, many companies allocate the excess of repurchase price between additional paid-in capital and retained earnings. This approach accurately reflects return of capital to stockholders. The amount allocated to additional paid-in capital reflects the additional paid-in capital originally received when the shares were sold, while the remainder of the repurchase price depicts the return of retained earnings to stockholders.

3 What common items do firms include in other comprehensive income on its financial statements? How does disclosing the components of accumulated other comprehensive income assist financial statement users in assessing an entity's financial position, operating results, and cash flows?

Common items included in other comprehensive include unrealized gains/(losses) on derivatives, unrealized gains/(losses) on investments, translation adjustments and actuarial gains and losses. The unrealized gains/(losses) on derivatives include gains/(losses) on cash flow hedges. The unrealized gains/(losses) on investments are from the impact of market movements on certain securities. Translation adjustments arise from remeasurement of foreign subsidiaries from their functional currency to the U.S. dollar. Certain actuarial gains and losses from pension plans are charged directly to other comprehensive income. In general, the disclosing of the components of accumulated other comprehensive income assist financial statement users understand the impact of certain changes in fair value that are not included in the calculation of net income.

4 Why do corporations decide to acquire and/or retire their own shares?

Corporations repurchase shares to provide a return to investors and also to reduce weighted-average shares outstanding. It is important to note that some companies have a broad-based employee stock compensation plan with a large amount of stock awarded to employees as part of their compensation. In order to avoid a transfer of wealth from shareholders to employees, a company may have an aggressive stock repurchase plan that offsets the impact of issuing shares to employees as part of their compensation.

5 Under what circumstances would an entity implement a share split or reverse share split?

Opinions differ on whether share splits (or reverse share splits) really produce any economic affects. If a company's stock price reached a certain level, the company may consider a stock split in the belief that a lower stock price may attract more individuals to their stock.

Discussion Questions

1. Robert Laux indicated that items included in other comprehensive income enables financial statement users to understand the impact of certain changes in fair value that are not included in the computation of net income. Discuss the usefulness of including other comprehensive income (OCI) in the financial statements by elaborating on Robert Laux's assessment.
2. Robert Laux stated that corporations repurchase shares to provide a return to investors, to reduce the weighted-average number of shares outstanding, or for use in employee compensation plans. Elaborate on these uses and discuss some other reasons why an entity will repurchase its own shares.

Preferred Shares and Liquidation Preferences

A company with preferred shares (or other senior equity securities) outstanding that has a preference in involuntary liquidation considerably in excess of the par or stated value of the shares must disclose the liquidation preference of the stock.[24] In addition, an entity must disclose both of the following either on the face of the statement of financial position or in the notes to the financial statements:

- The aggregate or per share amounts at which preferred stock may be called or are subject to redemption through sinking-fund operations or otherwise.
- The aggregate and per share amounts of dividends in arrears on cumulative preferred shares.

Convertible Equity Securities

The company must provide adequate disclosure regarding the significant terms of the conversion features of a contingently convertible security. This information enables financial statement users to understand the circumstances of the contingency and the potential impact of conversion. The disclosures include all of the following:

1. Events or changes in circumstances that would cause the contingency to be met
2. Any significant features necessary to understand the conversion rights and the timing of those rights (e.g., the periods in which the contingency might be met and the securities that may be converted if the contingency is met)
3. The conversion price and the number of shares into which a security is potentially convertible
4. Events or changes in circumstances, if any, that could adjust or change the contingency, conversion price, or number of shares, including significant terms of those changes
5. The manner of settlement upon conversion and any alternative settlement methods (e.g., cash, shares, or a combination)

Redeemable Preferred Shares

If a company issues redeemable preferred stock, it must disclose the amount of redemption requirements, separately by issue or combined, for all issues of capital stock that are redeemable at fixed or determinable prices on fixed or determinable dates in each of the 5 years following the date of the latest statement of financial position presented.

Changes in Stockholders' Equity Accounts

A company must disclose changes in the separate accounts comprising stockholders' equity (in addition to retained earnings) and of the changes in the number of shares of equity securities. As we discussed in Chapter 5, firms can present the disclosure of these changes in a separate statement of stockholders' equity or in the notes to the basic financial statements.

Disclosures: IFRS

Most disclosure requirements under U.S. GAAP and IFRS are similar. Additionally, IFRS requires a company to disclose information that enables users to assess its objectives, policies, and processes for managing capital. In the United States, the SEC has similar requirements for publicly traded companies.

[24]When preferred shares have a liquidation premium, in the event of liquidation, the preferred shareholder is entitled to par plus an amount over par after creditors are paid but before any distributions are made to common shares. So, preferred shares with \$100 par value may have a liquidation preference, and each share would receive \$110 in liquidation after all creditor claims have been satisfied. The \$10 difference is called the liquidation premium (\$110 − \$100).

FINANCIAL STATEMENT ANALYSIS

Valuation Ratios

Stockholders' equity represents an accounting measure of owners' interest in a company. The valuation of stockholders' equity—total assets less total liabilities—depends on how each asset and each liability is measured on the balance sheet. For example, the carrying value of a building purchased 20 years ago would generally be lower than its fair value today. Because of conventions such as historical cost accounting, the total amount of stockholders' equity on the balance sheet is often not representative of the value of the company to its stockholders.

Another measure of owners' interest in a company is its *market value*. The total **market value** of a company (also called market capitalization) whose stock is traded on a public stock exchange is the number of common shares outstanding multiplied by the price per share at which the stock is currently trading. Investors continually assess a company's expected profitability to determine its market value. As their assessment changes with new or updated information, the company's market value also changes. For example, when a pharmaceutical company receives regulatory approval to sell a new drug, the company's future sales will likely increase. Investors will incorporate the news of the drug approval and increasing future sales by raising the company's market value.

Investors also rely on accounting information in determining a company's market value. Common valuation ratios such as the *price-to-earnings (P/E) ratio* and *price-to-book (P/B) ratio* are also useful in making investment decisions and comparing companies.

The **P/E ratio** expresses the relationship between the company's market value and its net income as shown in the following equation.[25]

$$\text{Price to Earnings Ratio (P/E)} = \frac{\text{Market Value of Common Stock}}{\text{Net Income}} \tag{15.1}$$

The P/E ratio indicates how much an investor is willing to pay for a company per dollar of its earnings. In general, the higher the P/E ratio, the greater the expectation of a company's future profitability. For example, a P/E ratio of 15 indicates an investor is valuing the company at 15 times its net income. For a given amount of earnings, a P/E ratio of 15 implies that a company's future profitability is expected to be better than a company with a P/E ratio of 10.

Because the P/E ratio has net income in the denominator, this ratio can be sensitive to one-time items such as impairments or gains on the disposal of a business. Therefore, when a company has unusually high or low net income, the P/E ratio is not as useful a valuation ratio. For example, if a company has a large impairment leading to unusually low net income, its P/E ratio will be high simply because of the low net income amount in the denominator of the ratio.

The P/B ratio expresses the company's market value to its book value as shown in the following equation:

$$\text{Price-to-Book (P/B) Ratio} = \frac{\text{Market Value of Common Stock}}{\text{Book Value of Common Stockholders' Equity}} \tag{15.2}$$

A benchmark for a P/B ratio is 1.

- A P/B ratio of 1 indicates that the market is valuing a company's net assets 1 for 1.
- A P/B ratio greater than 1 indicates that the market is valuing a company at more than its book value.
- A P/B ratio greater than 1 indicates that the market expects strong future profitability and growth.

Companies that have unrecorded intangible assets such as brands or customer relationships would likely have a P/B ratio greater than 1. However, P/B ratios are generally somewhat greater than 1 because of the use of historical cost accounting. For example, under historical cost accounting, the value of a long-lived asset such as land is often less than its current market value at any point in time.

A P/B ratio lower than 1 can occur for three main reasons:

1. The market believes the asset values are overstated.
2. A company has off-balance sheet liabilities such as leases.
3. The company is earning a very low return on its assets.

[25] The P/E ratio is also computed as price per share divided by earnings per share.

Financial Statement Analysis, continued

Because book value is usually more stable than net income, the P/B ratio can be useful in evaluating a company when its earnings are volatile.

Exhibit 15.10 summarizes the computation of each valuation ratio, desirable characteristics, and pitfalls when assessing these ratios.

EXHIBIT 15.10 Summary of Valuation Ratios

Ratio	Desirable Characteristics	Pitfalls
$\text{Price to Earnings (P/E) Ratio} = \frac{\text{Market Value of Common Stock}}{\text{Net Income}}$	Higher P/E ratio indicates higher expected profitability.	When net income is unusually high or low, the P/E ratio is not as useful.
$\text{Price to Book (P/B) Ratio} = \frac{\text{Market Value of Common Stock}}{\text{Book Value of Common Stockholders' Equity}}$	Higher P/B ratio indicates higher expected profitability and growth.	P/B ratios are often higher when a company has unrecorded intangibles.

Example 15.23 illustrates financial statement analysis using the valuation ratios.

EXAMPLE 15.23

Valuation Ratios

PROBLEM: The following table presents net income for the year, book value of total stockholders' equity, and market value of total stockholders' equity at the end of each fiscal year for five global pharmaceutical companies. Using this information, complete the following items.

- Compute the price-to-earnings (P/E) ratios and price-to-book (P/B) ratios for each company for each year.
- Compute an average price-earnings (P/E) ratio and price-to-book (P/B) ratio for all the companies in each year.
- Comment on each company's P/E ratio over time. Are there any unusually high or low P/E ratios? If so, why? Comment on the average over time.
- Why would the P/B ratios in the pharmaceutical industry generally be greater than 1? Comment on each company's P/B ratio over time. Comment on the average over time.

		Fiscal Year		
Company and Location	**Measure (U.S. dollars in millions)**	**2014**	**2015**	**2016**
Johnson & Johnson – U.S.	Net income	$ 16,323	$ 15,409	$ 16,540
	Book value of common stockholders' equity	69,752	71,150	70,418
	Market value of common stock	292,703	284,220	313,432
Merck & Co – U.S.	Net income	11,920	4,442	3,920
	Book value of common stockholders' equity	48,647	44,676	40,088
	Market value of common stock	161,901	147,555	162,313
Pfizer Inc. – U.S.	Net income	9,135	6,960	7,215
	Book value of common stockholders' equity	71,301	64,720	59,544
	Market value of common stock	196,265	199,281	197,100

Continued

Financial Statement Analysis, continued

Company and Location	Measure (U.S. dollars in millions)	Fiscal Year 2014	2015	2016
Sanofi – France	Net Income	$ 5,354	$ 4,660	$ 4,957
	Book value of common stockholders' equity	68,620	63,272	60,762
	Market value of common stock	122,438	115,546	104,491
Novartis AG – Switzerland	Net Income	10,210	17,783	6,712
	Book value of common stockholders' equity	70,766	77,046	74,832
	Market value of common stock	252,441	234,710	190,852

SOLUTION: The following table shows the P/E and P/B ratios for each company and each year.

	Fiscal Year 2014	2015	2016
P/E Ratios			
Johnson & Johnson	17.93	18.45	18.95
Merck & Co	13.58	33.22	41.41
Pfizer Inc.	21.48	28.63	27.32
Sanofi	22.87	24.80	21.08
Novartis AG	24.72	13.20	28.43
Average	20.12	23.66	27.44
P/B Ratios			
Johnson & Johnson	4.20	3.99	4.45
Merck & Co	3.33	3.30	4.05
Pfizer Inc.	2.75	3.08	3.31
Sanofi	1.78	1.83	1.72
Novartis AG	3.57	3.05	2.55
Average	3.13	3.05	3.22

Johnson & Johnson's and ***Merck's*** P/E ratios are increasing over time, indicating that the market expects continued high profitability. ***Pfizer's*** and ***Sanofi's*** P/E ratios increased from 2014 to 2015 and then decreased in 2016. ***Novartis'*** P/E ratio decreased in 2015, likely because of high net income in 2015. The average P/E ratios for the group of companies increased from 2014 to 2016, indicating an increase in expected industry profitability.

P/B ratios in the pharmaceutical industry are greater than 1, likely because of unrecorded intangible assets such as drug patents, brands, or customer relationships. The P/B ratios for ***Johnson & Johnson, Merck,*** and ***Pfizer*** increased from 2014 to 2016, indicating expected future profitability and growth. The increase in the average P/B ratios from 2014 to 2016 suggests high future profitability and growth. ***Johnson & Johnson's*** and ***Merck's*** P/B ratios exceeded the average in all years.

Summary by Learning Objectives

In the following, we summarize the main points by learning objective. Throughout the chapter, we discuss the accounting and reporting of U.S. GAAP and IFRS side by side. The following table also highlights the major similarities and differences between the standards.

1 Describe stockholders' equity and its main components.

Summary	Similarities and Differences between U.S. GAAP and IFRS
Stockholders' equity represents the residual claims against the assets of the firm. It has three main components: 1. Contributed capital: Amounts paid in by common and preferred stockholders. It is often separated into a par value and additional paid-in capital in excess of par. 2. Retained earnings: Cumulative earnings of the firm that have not been distributed as dividends. 3. Accumulated other comprehensive income: Includes unrealized gains and losses on debt investment securities, foreign currency translation adjustments, and certain pension cost adjustments.	➤ Similar under U.S. GAAP and IFRS except for some differences in terminology: 1. Share capital and share premium are commonly used terms for par value and additional paid-in capital. 2. Accumulated profit and loss is used instead of retained earnings. 3. Reserves and other reserves are used instead of accumulated other comprehensive income.

2 Explain and illustrate the accounting for common stock, including share issuance, issue costs, and stock splits.

Summary	Similarities and Differences between U.S. GAAP and IFRS
Firms report common stock at the amount paid in by owners. The capital raised is recorded as par value, if any is specified, and additional paid-in capital in excess of par – common. Issue costs reduce additional paid-in capital in excess of par. Stock splits proportionately change any par value. No journal entry is required for recording stock splits.	Similar under U.S. GAAP and IFRS.

3 Record treasury stock transactions, including repurchases, reissuance under the cost method, and retirement.

Summary	Similarities and Differences between U.S. GAAP and IFRS
Treasury stock is a reduction of equity that firms record at cost. When reissued above cost, additional paid-in capital from treasury stock transactions increases by the amount above cost. When reissued below cost, additional paid-in capital from treasury stock transactions decreases by the amount below cost. If there is no additional paid-in capital from treasury stock or paid-in capital from treasury stock is reduced to zero, retained earnings is reduced by the remainder of the amount sold below cost. When retiring treasury stock, firms remove the number of common shares retired from the accounts at par and reduce the average additional paid-in capital in excess of par – common.	Similar under U.S. GAAP and IFRS.

Summary by Learning Objectives, continued

❹ Describe preferred stock and its features; demonstrate the accounting for issuance, dividends, and consideration of potential debt features of preferred stock.	
Summary	**Similarities and Differences between U.S. GAAP and IFRS**
Common features of preferred stock include cumulative, participating, convertible, callable, redeemable, and fixed dividends. Preferred stock is reported at the amount paid in by stockholders. The capital raised is recorded as par value, if any is specified, and additional paid-in capital in excess of par – preferred. Dividends are recorded when declared. Cumulative preferred dividends in arrears, if any, are disclosed. Mandatorily redeemable preferred stock is reported as a liability.	➤ Similar under U.S. GAAP and IFRS except that (1) on convertible preferred stock, the classification as debt or equity depends on the terms of the conversion feature under IFRS, (2) non-mandatorily redeemable preferred stock when the holder has the option to redeem is reported as equity under U.S. GAAP and a liability under IFRS, and (3) IFRS reports preferred stock with fixed dividends as a liability, not equity.

❺ Explain the accounting for retained earnings, including dividends and prior-period adjustments.	
Summary	**Similarities and Differences between U.S. GAAP and IFRS**
Retained earnings increases (decreases) with net income (loss). Dividends decrease retained earnings when declared. Prior-period adjustments are corrections of errors made in years before the current-year financial statements. Firms correct the beginning amounts in the balance sheet for the earliest year presented.	Similar under U.S. GAAP and IFRS.

❻ Describe the components of other comprehensive income and accumulated other comprehensive income.	
Summary	**Similarities and Differences between U.S. GAAP and IFRS**
Other comprehensive income includes income items that bypass the income statement: unrealized gains and losses from the available-for-sale portfolio of debt investment securities and derivatives classified as cash flow hedges, foreign currency translation adjustments, and unrecognized pension costs and benefits. Comprehensive income is net income plus other comprehensive income. Other comprehensive income can be shown on the income statement after net income or in a separate statement of comprehensive income. Firms report other comprehensive income in accumulated other comprehensive income in stockholders' equity.	Similar under U.S. GAAP and IFRS.

Summary by Learning Objectives, continued

7 Detail required disclosures for stockholders' equity.

Summary	Similarities and Differences between U.S. GAAP and IFRS
Disclosures for stockholders' equity include details on the rights and privileges of each class of capital stock and details on terms and provisions of callable, convertible, and redeemable securities, stock options, and other contingent shares or potentially dilutive securities.	➤ Similar under U.S. GAAP and IFRS. Under IFRS, additional disclosures are required regarding the management of capital.

MyLab Accounting

Go to **http://www.pearson.com/mylab/accounting** for the following Questions, Multiple-Choice Questions, Brief Exercises, Exercises, and Problems. They are available with immediate grading, explanations of correct and incorrect answers, and interactive media that acts as your own online tutor.

15 Accounting for Stockholders' Equity

Questions

1 **Q15-1.** What is stockholders' equity?

1 **Q15-2.** What are the retained earnings of a firm?

2 **Q15-3.** Do firms capitalize stock issue costs as intangible assets on the balance sheet? Explain.

2 **Q15-4.** How do firms measure the value of the shares issued in a nonmonetary exchange?

3 **Q15-5.** Does an entity have to legally dissolve treasury stock shortly after acquiring the shares? Explain.

3 **Q15-6.** What are the two available methods used to account for treasury stock transactions? Explain each method.

4 **Q15-7.** Are preferred shares hybrid financial instruments? Explain.

4 **Q15-8.** Is mandatorily redeemable preferred stock classified as equity? Explain.

4 Q15-9. Does IFRS classify mandatorily redeemable preferred stock as equity? Explain.

4 **Q15-10.** Is non-mandatorily redeemable preferred stock classified as equity? Explain.

4 **Q15-11.** Are dividends in arrears on cumulative preferred shares a legal liability of the corporation? Explain.

5 **Q15-12.** Do firms often use stock dividends to avoid providing a cash return to shareholders? Explain.

5 **Q15-13.** How do firms record prior-period adjustments?

6 **Q15-14.** What is included in other comprehensive income?

6 **Q15-15.** Is a specific format required for reporting comprehensive income? Explain.

7 **Q15-16.** Do current accounting standards require extensive shareholders' equity disclosures? Explain.

Multiple Choice Questions

5 **MC15-1.** Boone Corporation's outstanding capital stock on December 15 consisted of the following:

- 30,000 shares of 5% cumulative preferred stock, par value $10 per share, fully participating as to dividends. No dividends were in arrears.
- 200,000 shares of common stock, par value $1 per share.

On December 15, Boone declared dividends of $100,000. What was the amount of dividends payable to Boone's common stockholders?

a. $10,000 b. $34,000 c. $47,500 d. $40,000

3 **MC15-2.** At its date of incorporation, McCarty Company issued 100,000 shares of its $10 par common stock at $11 per share. During the current year, McCarty acquired 30,000 shares of its common stock at $16 per share and accounted for them using the cost method. Subsequently, these shares were reissued at a price of $12 per share. There have been no other issuances or acquisitions of its own common stock. What effect does the reissuance of the stock have on the following accounts?

Retained Earnings	Additional Paid-in Capital
a. Decrease	Decrease
b. No effect	Decrease
c. Decrease	No effect
d. No effect	No effect

7 **MC15-3.** On September 1, Year 1, Royal Corp., a newly formed company, had the following stock issued and outstanding:

- Common stock, no par, $1 stated value, 5,000 shares originally issued for $15 per share.
- Preferred stock, $10 par value, 1,500 shares originally issued for $25 per share.

Royal's September 1, Year 1, statement of stockholders' equity should report:

Common Stock	Preferred Stock	Additional Paid-in Capital
a. $5,000	$15,000	$92,500
b. $5,000	$37,500	$70,000
c. $75,000	$37,500	$ 0
d. $75,000	$15,000	$22,500

4 **MC15-4.** Classic Cars Corp. has 50,000 shares of $10 par common stock and 20,000 shares of $15 par fully participating 10% cumulative preferred stock. If the company declares cash dividends of $100,000 during the current year and there are no dividends in arrears, what will be the total dividend payment to preferred shareholders?

a. $37,500 b. $42,500 c. $57,500 d. $62,500

3 **MC15-5.** On January 1, Year 1, Black Dog Corp. began operations and issued 30,000 shares of $5 par common stock for $9 per share. On June 30, the company bought back 10,000 shares for $8 per share. Then, on September 15, the company resold 5,000 shares for $12 per share. What amount of total additional paid-in capital should Black Dog report on its December 31, Year 1, balance sheet if Black Dog uses the cost method to account for its treasury stock?

a. $20,000 b. $120,000 c. $140,000 d. $165,000

5 **MC15-6.** Backdoor Inc. had 200,000 shares of $5 par common stock outstanding. The company declared a stock dividend of 30,000 shares when the market price was $25. By how much did additional paid-in capital increase when the dividend was declared?

a. $0 b. $600,000 c. $150,000 d. $750,000

5 **MC15-7.** Backdoor Inc. had 200,000 shares of $5 par common stock outstanding. The company declared a stock dividend of 100,000 shares when the market price was $25. By how much did additional paid-in capital increase when the dividend was distributed to the shareholders?

a. $0　b. $500,000　c. $1,000,000　d. $2,500,000

Brief Exercises

1 **BE15-1. Stockholders' Equity.** ABC Toy Company earned $357 million of net income in 2019 and paid $45 million in dividends. It issued no new stock. Complete the stockholders' equity section for ABC Toy Company:

	December 31	
(in millions)	**2018**	**2019**
Common Stock, Par Value	$ 100	C
Additional Paid-in Capital in Excess of Par – Common	1,245	D
Retained Earnings	A	1,104
Accumulated other comprehensive income (loss)	B	53
Total Stockholders' Equity	$1,717	E

1 **BE15-2. Stockholders' Equity Terminology, U.S. GAAP, IFRS.** Match the U.S. GAAP term with the IFRS term. There may be more than one match, and responses may be repeated.

U.S. GAAP

A. Contributed capital

B. Additional paid-in capital

C. Retained earnings

D. Accumulated other comprehensive income

E. Common stock

IFRS	Answer
Reserves	________
Accumulated profit and loss	________
Share premium	________
Other reserves	________
Share capital	________

2 **BE15-3. Common Stock Issuance, No Par Value.** Perdido Products, Inc. issues 2,500 shares of its no-par common stock. The issue price of the stock is $24 per share. Prepare the journal entry required to record the issuance of the shares.

2 **BE15-4. Common Stock Issuance, Stated Value.** Perdido Products, Inc. issued 2,500 shares of its common stock. The common stock has a stated value of $10 per share and was issued at $24 per share. Prepare the journal entry required to record the issuance of the shares.

2 **BE15-5. Common Stock Issuance, Par Value.** At the beginning of the current year, Niles Corporation issued 1,600 shares of its own $2 par value common stock for $19 per share. Prepare the journal entry required to record the issuance of the shares.

2 **BE15-6. Common Stock Issuance, Par Value, Issue Costs.** Carlos Company decided to raise additional capital in the equity market. It engaged an underwriter to float a new common share issue. The issue consisted of 5,000 shares of $3 par value common stock. Carlos paid the underwriter 2% of the total issue price and issued the shares at $16 per share. Prepare the journal entry required to record the issuance of the shares assuming that the stock issue costs are not capitalized.

❷ **BE15-7. Common Stock Issuance, Exchange for Services.** Wonder Spring Water Company recently employed a consultant to revise its production and distribution procedures. In order to compensate the consultant, Wonder issued 1,000 shares of its $1 par value common stock. Those shares are not publicly traded, but the board of directors has estimated their value at $45 per share. The consulting firm billed other clients $34,500 for similar services in recent transactions. Prepare the journal entry required to record the transaction.

❷ **BE15-8. Stock Split.** Assume that Cornish Corporation has 2,500,000 shares of $3 par value common stock issued and outstanding. The company is authorized to issue 10 million shares. Due to increased share prices, the corporation decided to implement a 2-for-1 stock split. Prepare the journal entries required on the declaration and distribution of the stock split.

❸ **BE15-9. Treasury Stock Transactions.** Ginger Spice Distributors acquired 14,500 shares of its own common shares at a cost of $64 per share. After 6 months, Ginger sold half of the shares in the open market at $70 per share. Prepare the journal entries to record the acquisition and sale of the treasury shares.

❸ **BE15-10. Treasury Stock Transactions.** On March 15, Chief Company acquired 20,000 shares of its own $2 par value common shares at a cost of $17 per share. Chief had originally issued the shares at $12 per share. On July 5, Chief sold 7,000 of the shares in the open market at $20 per share. On October 19, Chief sold the remaining shares at $8. Prepare the journal entries to record the acquisition and sale of the treasury shares.

❸ **BE15-11. Treasury Stock Transactions, Retirement.** Using the information provided in BE15-10, assume that Chief Company retired all of the shares on July 5 (rather than holding shares in the treasury and reissuing them). Prepare the journal entries to record the acquisition and retirement of the treasury shares. Assume that the par value of additional paid-in capital – retired shares is $0.

❺ **BE15-12. Dividends.** Sterzel Company declared its quarterly cash dividend on March 31 of the current year. The dividend of $.75 per share was to be paid on May 1 to the shareholders of record as of April 18. The company reported 120,000 shares issued with 15,500 shares held in the treasury. Prepare the journal entries required to record the cash dividend for the quarter on the dates of declaration, record, and payment.

❺ **BE15-13. Prior-Period Adjustment.** In its audit of Oz Lollypop Company, Able and Ready, CPAs, discovered in 2018 that the firm had not recorded a $975,000 expense in 2014 (for both book and tax purposes). Oz never paid this amount due on the invoice it received. Assuming a constant tax rate of 35%, prepare the journal entry required to record the correction of the error.

❺ **BE15-14. Prior-Period Adjustment.** Using the information provided in BE15-13 and the following stockholders' equity section of Oz Lollypop Company, adjust the balance sheet for the correction of the error.

Stockholders' Equity

Contributed Capital	
Common Stock, at par	$ 1,000,000
Additional Paid-in Capital in Excess of Par – Common	15,500,000
Total Contributed Capital	$ 16,500,000
Retained Earnings	$ 32,797,400
Total Stockholders' Equity	$ 49,297,400
Additional information:	
Retained earnings on 1/1/2018 as previously reported	$23,670,000
Net income for the year ended 12/31/2018	9,452,000
Dividends declared for year ended 12/31/2018	324,600

Exercises

❷ **E15-1. Common Stock Issuance, Stated Value, Issue Costs.** Pergolesi Products, Inc. recently issued 5,000 shares of no-par common stock. The shares carry a $2 per share stated value. The market price of the shares on the date of issue was $35 per share. The company paid $12,000 in underwriting fees to issue the shares. Prepare the entry to record the new stock issue.

2 **E15-2. Common Stock Issuance, Par Value, Issue Costs, Disclosure.** Advanced Computer Systems reported the following shareholders' equity section as of the beginning of the current year:

Stockholders' Equity	
Contributed Capital:	
Common Stock, $.50 par value, 850,000 shares authorized, 225,000 shares issued, and 201,375 shares outstanding	$ 112,500
Additional Paid-in Capital in Excess of Par – Common	9,900,000
Total Contributed Capital	$ 10,012,500
Retained Earnings	$20,346,563
Accumulated Other Comprehensive Income (Loss)	(453,800)
Less: Treasury Stock (23,625 common shares at cost)	(945,000)
Total Stockholders' Equity	$28,960,263

Advanced Computer issued 125,000 shares of its $.50 par common stock during the year. The market price of the shares on the date of issue was $51 per share. The company paid $88,000 in underwriting fees to issue the shares. Advanced reported $6,789,000 in net income for the year and declared and paid dividends of $4 per share at year-end.

Required »

a. Prepare the entry to record the new stock issue.
b. Prepare the journal entries required to record the declaration and payment of the cash dividend.
c. Prepare the stockholders' equity section of the balance sheet at the end of the year.

2 **E15-3. Common Stock Issuance, Exchange for Goods, Par Value, Issue Costs.** Liberty Associates recently hired Gervin Brothers to develop an online sales system for its consumer products division. The customized online system does not have a readily determinable market value. Gervin wanted to be paid in Liberty common shares. As a result, Gervin accepted 10,000 shares of Liberty Associates' $8 par value common shares. On the date the online system was fully functional, the contract was satisfied and Liberty issued the shares to Gervin. Liberty shares were not publicly traded but were valued at $132 per share on that date by an investment bank. Because the shares are privately placed, there are no stock issue costs. Prepare the journal entry to record the development of the online system.

2 **E15-4. Common Stock Issuance, Exchange for Goods, Par Value, Issue Costs.** Using the information provided in E15-3, prepare the journal entry to record the acquisition of the new computer system assuming that the system is a standardized product with a current retail value of $1,470,000.

3 5 7 **E15-5. Treasury Stock Transactions, Disclosure.** The following shareholders' equity section was taken from the books of Aubry Corporation at the beginning of the current year:

Common Stock, $10 par value, 1,000,000 shares authorized, 98,950 shares issued and outstanding	$ 989,500
Additional Paid-in Capital in Excess of Par – Common	120,000
Additional Paid-in Capital from Treasury Stock Transactions	0
Retained Earnings	1,545,000

Required »

a. Prepare the journal entries required to record each of the following events:
   - Aubry acquired 15,000 shares of common stock to be held in the treasury at a cost of $16 per share.
   - Aubry sold 4,800 shares of treasury stock at $19 per share.
   - Aubry sold 7,200 shares of treasury stock at $8 per share.
   - Aubry reported a net loss of $367,540 for the year.
   - The company declared and paid a $2 per share cash dividend at year-end.

b. Prepare the shareholders' equity section at the end of the year.

3 7 **E15-6. Treasury Stock Transactions, Retirement, Disclosure.** Using the information provided in E15-5, prepare the journal entries to record the acquisition of the treasury stock assuming that it is immediately retired. Also, prepare the journal entries to record the loss and the dividend transactions as well as the shareholders' equity section of the balance sheet at the end of the year. Round per share prices to four decimal places.

3 7 **E15-7. Treasury Stock Transactions, Disclosure.** The stockholders' equity section of DRB plc's balance sheet at December 31, 2018, was as follows:

Common Stock – $3 par (2,000,000 shares authorized, 1,000,000 shares issued and outstanding)	$ 3,000,000
Additional Paid-in Capital in Excess of Par – Common	7,000,000
Retained Earnings	24,700,000
Total Stockholders' Equity	$34,700,000

Required »

a. Prepare the journal entry required on January 9, 2019, if on that date DRB repurchased 50,000 shares of treasury stock for $750,000.
b. On March 23, 2019, DRB sold 10,000 of the treasury shares for $36 per share. Prepare the journal entry to record this transaction.
c. Prepare the journal entry required on June 30, 2019, assuming that the firm sold 30,000 of the treasury shares for $25 per share.
d. Prepare the stockholders' equity section of DRB's balance sheet on December 31, 2019, assuming that the company reported net income of $16,000,000 and declared and paid a cash dividend of $1.75 per share at year-end.

3 **E15-8. Treasury Stock Transactions.** Several years ago, Indirect Bookie Company issued 10,000 shares of $2 par value common stock for $24 per share. Since that time, the company entered into several treasury stock transactions. Assume that additional paid-in capital from treasury stock transactions is zero.

Required »

Record the following treasury stock transactions using the cost method.
a. Purchased 5,000 shares of common shares as treasury stock at $28.
b. Sold 2,000 shares of treasury stock for a total of $42,000.
c. Sold the remaining 3,000 shares of treasury stock for a total $90,000.

3 **E15-9. Treasury Stock Transactions.** Samuel Company has the following accounts in its shareholders' equity section at the beginning of the current year:

Common Stock ($1 par, 1,000,000 shares authorized, 600,000 shares issued and outstanding)	$ 600,000
Additional Paid-in Capital in Excess of Par – Common	1,800,000
Retained Earnings	2,000,000

Required »

Prepare the journal entries required to record the following share buyback transactions assuming that Samuel Company holds the shares in the treasury using the cost method:
- Reacquired 20,000 shares to hold as treasury stock, paying $8.25 per share.
- Sold 10,000 of the shares for $11.50 per share.
- Reissued the remaining 10,000 shares for $4.10 per share.

3 **E15-10. Treasury Stock Transactions, Retirement.** Repeat the requirements of E15-9 and assume that the shares are retired rather than held in the treasury.

3 5 7 **E15-11. Treasury Stock Transactions, Dividends, Disclosure.** The stockholders' equity section of Bellwood Brands' 2017 balance sheet follows:

Stockholders' Equity

Common Stock – no par, 100,000 shares authorized, 1,000 shares issued and outstanding	$ 90,000
Retained Earnings	360,000
Less: Cost of Treasury Stock	0
Total Stockholders' Equity	$450,000

During 2018, Bellwood completed the following transactions:

- November 9: Purchased 200 shares of its own stock to be held in the treasury. The cost was $90 per share.
- November 17: Declared and paid a cash dividend of $5 per share.
- November 30: Sold 100 treasury shares for $80 per share.
- December 31: Reported $50,000 net income for the year.

Required »

a. Prepare the journal entries necessary to record those transactions.
b. Based on the information provided, prepare the statement of stockholders' equity and the stockholders' equity section of the balance sheet for Bellwood Brands at December 31, 2018.

3 5 **E15-12. Treasury Stock Transactions, Dividends.** Pavane Company recorded the original issuance of its $10 par value common shares as follows:

Account	Debit	Credit
Cash	8,750,000	
Common Stock		1,950,000
Additional Paid-in Capital in Excess of Par – Common		6,800,000

Required »

Provide the journal entries for the following transactions.

a. Pavane bought 95,000 shares of common stock as treasury shares at $55. It used the cost method to account for treasury transactions.
b. Pavane declared a $5 per share cash dividend.
c. Pavane sold 22,000 shares of treasury stock at $76.
d. Pavane sold 61,500 treasury shares at $38.
e. Pavane paid the cash dividend.

4 7 **E15-13. Preferred Stock Issuance, Dividends, Disclosure.** Rory Storm Roofing and Siding, Inc. reported the following shareholders' equity section as of the beginning of the current year:

Stockholders' Equity

Contributed Capital:	
Common Stock, $2 par value, 2,350,000 shares authorized and 745,000 shares issued, and 691,500 shares outstanding	$ 1,490,000
Additional Paid-in Capital in Excess of Par – Common	20,115,000
Total Contributed Capital	$21,605,000
Retained Earnings	$ 7,658,450
Accumulated Other Comprehensive Income (Loss)	897,945
Less: Treasury Stock (53,500 common shares at cost)	(1,070,000)
Total Stockholders' Equity	$29,091,395

Rory Storm also issued 823,000 shares of its $5 par value preferred stock. There is a 6% dividend rate on the preferred shares that Rory Storm issued at $11 per share. The company paid $180,000 in underwriting fees to issue the shares. It reported $2,633,000 in net income for the year and declared and paid dividends of $1 per share on its common shares and 6% of par for the preferred shares. The company has 1,000,000 shares authorized for preferred stock.

Required »

a. Prepare the journal entry required to record the preferred stock issue.
b. Prepare the journal entries required to record the declaration and payment of the cash dividends.
c. Prepare the stockholders' equity section of the balance sheet at the end of the year.

4 **E15-14. Callable Preferred Shares.** On January 1, 2018, Gato Company issued 1,000 shares of $80 par callable preferred shares for $200,000. Gato can call these preferred shares on January 1, 2019, for $200 per share. On June 1, 2019, Gato calls the shares.

Required »

a. What is the journal entry to record the issuance of the preferred shares?
b. What is the journal entry when Gato calls the preferred shares?

4 **E15-15. Fixed Dividend Preferred Shares.** Fontlyn Inc. issued $20 million of $10 par preferred stock on February 1, 2018. The company issued 1 million shares. The preferred stock has a 4% fixed annual cash dividend and no maturity date. Assume that the holder of the preferred shares has the option to require redemption.

a. How would Fontlyn account for the preferred stock dividends?
b. What is the journal entry when the firm issued the preferred shares?

4 **E15-16. Fixed Dividend Preferred Shares, IFRS.** Use the same information from E15-15, assume that Fontlyn is an IFRS reporter. Prepare the journal entry for Fontlyn's issue of the preferred shares.

5 7 **E15-17. Dividends, Disclosure.** Dentquity Corporation has the following capital structure at the beginning of the current year:

8% Preferred Stock, $10 par value, 520,000 shares authorized, issued, and outstanding	$ 5,200,000
Common Stock, $4 par value, 1,870,000 shares authorized, 625,000 shares issued and outstanding	2,500,000
Additional Paid-in Capital in Excess of Par – Common	4,000,000
Total Contributed Capital	$11,700,000
Retained Earnings	912,050
Total Stockholders' Equity	$12,612,050

Required »

a. Prepare the journal entries (including closing entries) to record each of the following transactions affecting shareholders' equity during the current year. There are separate accounts for dividends payable for common stock and preferred stock. Assume that there are no preferred dividends in arrears.
   - Declared a total cash dividend of $880,000 on common and preferred stock.
   - Had net income for the year of $40,000.
b. Prepare the stockholders' equity section of the balance sheet at the end of the current year.

5 **E15-18. Prior-Period Adjustment.** In 2018, Meg Inc. discovered an error in its 2015 financial statements. The firm recorded $11,000,000 of depreciation expense on its equipment instead of recording $10,000,000. Meg has a constant tax rate of 40% and reports 3 years of comparative income statements and 2 years of comparative balance sheets with its financial reports. Assume that Meg uses the same depreciation method for tax and financial reporting. Retained earnings and accumulated depreciation as of December 31, 2017, were $12,075,000 and $5,400,000, respectively.

Required »

a. What is the necessary journal entry to record the prior-period adjustment?
b. How would Meg report its accumulated depreciation and retained earnings balances in the restated balance sheet dated December 31, 2017?

5 **E15-19. Prior-Period Adjustment.** In 2018, Thom Inc. discovered an error in its 2015 financial statements. The firm recorded $8,500,000 of depreciation expense on its equipment instead of recording $9,500,000. Thom has a constant tax rate of 40% and reports 3 years of comparative income statements and 2 years of comparative balance sheets with its financial reports. Assume that Thom uses the same depreciation method for tax and financial reporting. Retained earnings and accumulated depreciation as of December 31, 2017, were $12,075,000 and $4,600,000, respectively.

Required »

a. What is the necessary journal entry to record the prior-period adjustment?
b. How would Thom report its accumulated depreciation and retained earnings balances in the restated balance sheet dated December 31, 2017?

6 **E15-20. Other Comprehensive Income.** Neddle Corporation reported net income of $176,000 for the current year. It had unrealized gains on available-for-sale debt investment securities of $5,000 after tax and a foreign currency translation loss of $8,000 after tax. The beginning balance of its accumulated other comprehensive income was a credit of $100.

Required »

a. What is other comprehensive income for the current year?
b. What is comprehensive income for the current year?
c. What is the ending balance of accumulated other comprehensive income?

6 **E15-21.** **Other Comprehensive Income.** Saddle Corporation reported comprehensive income of $14,000 for the current year. It had unrealized losses on available-for-sale debt investment securities of $750 after tax and a foreign currency translation gain of $3,500 after tax. The beginning balance of its accumulated other comprehensive income was a debit of $2,000.

Required »

a. What is other comprehensive income for the current year?
b. What is net income for the current year?
c. What is the ending balance of accumulated other comprehensive income?

7 **E15-22.** **Disclosure.** On January 1, 2018, Queens Company reported the following stockholders' equity:

Common Stock, $5 par (300,000 shares authorized, 100,000 shares issued and outstanding)	$ 500,000
Additional Paid-in Capital in Excess of Par – Common	200,000
Retained Earnings	700,000
Total Stockholders' Equity	$1,400,000

On January 4, the company purchased 10,000 shares of its own stock at $25 per share to be held as treasury stock. On June 30, the company declared a $2 per share cash dividend to be paid on July 7. Net income for the year ended December 31 amounted to $280,000.

Prepare the stockholders' equity section of Queens Company's balance sheet at December 31, 2018.

Problems

2 **P15-1.** **Common Stock Issuance, No Par Value, Stock Split, Disclosure.** The stockholders' equity section of Five Voices Music, Inc.'s balance sheet at December 31, 2017, follows:

Stockholders' Equity	
Common Stock – no par, 10,000 shares authorized, 1,000 shares issued and outstanding	$ 90,000
Retained Earnings	360,000
Total Stockholders' Equity	$450,000

During 2018, Five Voices Music completed the following transactions:

- May 24: Issued 200 no-par common shares for cash amounting to $16,000.
- December 1: Implemented a 2-for-1 stock split.
- December 31: Announced net income of $50,000 for the year ended December 31, 2018.

Based on the information provided, prepare the stockholders' equity section for Five Voices Music at December 31, 2018.

2 3 4 5 7 **P15-2.** **Common Stock Issuance, Treasury Stock, Dividends, Disclosure.** Sanmartini Van Lines, Ltd. began operations at the beginning of the current year and engaged in the following transactions affecting the stockholders' equity section of its current balance sheet. The company has 1,000,000 shares authorized for each common and preferred stock.

1. Issued 500,000 shares of its $2 par value common stock at $64 per share. The underwriter charged a 1% fee for issuing the shares.
2. Issued 100,000 shares of $4.50 par value, 7% preferred stock at $120 per share. These shares were privately placed and Sanmartini did not pay any stock issue costs.
3. Purchased 120,000 shares of common stock at $70 per share.
4. Declared a $75,000 dividend for the first half of the year. (The declarations should be recorded separately for the common and the preferred shares.)
5. Sold 45,000 of the treasury shares at $60 per share.

6. Paid the cash dividends.
7. Declared a $75,000 cash dividend for the second half of the year. (The declarations should be recorded separately for the common and the preferred shares.)
8. Reported net income of $9,879,455 for the current year.
9. Closed out all dividends accounts.

Required »

a. Prepare all journal entries required to record those transactions.
b. Construct the shareholders' equity section for the year-end balance sheet and the relevant t-accounts.

②③④⑤⑦ **P15-3. Common Stock Issuance, Preferred Stock Issuance, Convertible Stock Issuance, Retirement, Dividends, Disclosure.** Shore Town Suites, Ltd. began operations at the beginning of the current year and engaged in the following transactions affecting the stockholders' equity section of its current balance sheet. The company has 1,000,000 shares authorized for each common and preferred stock.

1. Issued 200,000 shares of its $1 par value common stock at $26 per share. The underwriter charged a 1% fee for issuing the shares.
2. Issued 100,000 shares of its $1 par value common stock to a major investor who contributed a new headquarters building to Shore Town. At the time, Shore Town's stock price was $27 per share.
3. Issued 10,000 shares of 2%, $28 par value, convertible preferred shares for $290,000. Each preferred share is convertible into one share of $1 par common stock.
4. Purchased 12,000 shares of common stock at $28 per share and immediately retired the shares.
5. Declared a $82,000 dividend for the year. (The declarations should be recorded separately for the common and the preferred shares.)
6. Paid the cash dividends.
7. Issued 5,000 shares of $30 par value, 5% mandatorily redeemable preferred stock for $200,000.
8. Related to Transaction 3, all preferred shareholders converted their shares into common stock.
9. Reported net income of $865,300 for the current year.
10. Closed out all dividends accounts.

Required »

a. Prepare all journal entries required to record those transactions.
b. Construct the shareholders' equity section for the year-end balance sheet and the relevant t-accounts.

②③④⑤⑥⑦ **P15-4. Common Stock Issuance, Treasury Stock, Preferred Stock, Dividends, Comprehensive Income, Disclosure.** Castleline, Inc. reported the following shareholders' equity section as of the beginning of the current year:

Stockholders' Equity

Contributed Capital:	
Common Stock, $1 par value, 3,850,000 shares authorized, 905,000 shares issued, and 821,500 shares outstanding	$ 905,000
Additional Paid-in Capital in Excess of Par – Common	22,625,000
Total Contributed Capital	$ 23,530,000
Retained Earnings	$ 8,957,450
Accumulated Other Comprehensive Income	1,057,600
Less: Treasury Stock (83,500 common shares at cost)	(1,670,000)
Total Stockholders' Equity	$ 31,875,050

During the current year, Castleline engaged in the following transactions affecting the stockholders' equity section of its current balance sheet.

1. Issued 400,000 shares of its $1 par value common stock at $31 per share. The underwriter charged a 3% fee for issuing the shares. The stock issue costs are not capitalized.
2. Issued 500,000 shares of $10 par value 6% preferred stock (2,550,000 authorized) at $40 per share. These shares were privately placed and Castleline did not pay stock issue costs.
3. Purchased 220,000 shares of common stock at $32 per share.
4. Declared a $450,000 dividend for the first half of the year. (The declarations should be recorded separately for the common and the preferred shares.)
5. Sold 105,000 of the treasury shares at $44 per share. (The 83,500 treasury shares on hand at the beginning of the year are considered sold first. The company paid $20 per share for these shares of treasury stock).
6. Paid the cash dividends.

7. Reported net income of $3,180,500 for the current year.
8. In addition to the net income, Castleline incurred an $801,000 unrealized loss on an available-for-sale debt investment.
9. Declared a $450,000 cash dividend for the second half of the year. (The declarations should be recorded separately for the common and the preferred shares.)
10. Closed out all dividends and other comprehensive income accounts.

Required »

a. Prepare all journal entries required to record those transactions.
b. Construct the shareholders' equity section for the year-end balance sheet and the relevant t-accounts.

3 5 6 7 **P15-5. Common Stock Issuance, Treasury Stock, Dividends, Comprehensive Income, Disclosure.** The stockholders' equity section of Siri Stores, Inc.'s balance sheet at December 31, 2017, follows:

Stockholders' Equity

Common Stock: no-par, $3 stated value, 80,000 shares authorized, 50,000 shares issued, and 40,500 shares outstanding	$ 150,000
Additional Paid-in Capital in Excess of Stated Value – Common	300,000
Retained Earnings	940,000
Less: Cost of Treasury Stock (9,500 shares)	(199,500)
Total Stockholders' Equity	$1,190,500

During 2018, Siri completed the following transactions:

- November 9: Purchased 3,000 shares of its own stock to be held in the treasury. The cost per share was $21.
- November 17: Declared and paid a cash dividend of $6 per share.
- November 30: Sold 1,800 treasury shares for $15 per share. Assume FIFO is used.
- December 31: Declared and paid a cash dividend of $6 per share.
- December 31: Wrote down an available-for-sale debt investment by $23,500.
- December 31: Reported $50,000 net income for the year and closed net income, other comprehensive income, and dividend accounts.

Required »

a. Prepare the journal entries required to reflect those transactions.
b. Based on the information provided, prepare the stockholders' equity section for Siri at December 31, 2018, and the relevant t-accounts.

2 3 5 6 **P15-6. Common Stock Issuance, Treasury Stock, Dividends, Comprehensive Income.** Royal Hill Companies provided the following information regarding its stockholders' equity section of the balance sheet for the 3-year period ending December 31, 2018.

Stockholders' equity:

(In millions, except for share amounts)	2018	2017	2016
Common Stock, no par value	$ 229.20	$ 229.20	$ 229.20
Additional Paid-in Capital from Treasury Stock Transactions	99.24	99.24	119.09
Retained Earnings	2,089.68	1,809.72	2,217.50
Accumulated Other Comprehensive Income (Loss) – Unrealized Debt Investment Gain (Loss)	(0.24)	(0.36)	0
Treasury Stock, at Cost; 56,071,000 and 32,835,000 shares, in 2018 and 2017 respectively	(1,717.92)	(1,031.28)	(1,237.97)
Total Stockholders' Equity	$ 699.96	$1,106.52	$1,327.82

Required »

Prepare the summary journal entries for 2017 and 2018 to reflect the changes in the shareholders' equity accounts included in the statement provided above. Royal Hill did not pay any dividends in these years and made no prior-period adjustments. Assume that the treasury stock transactions did not affect retained earnings.

P15-7. Information from the shareholders' equity footnote for Mendes Manufacturing follows.

Additional Paid-in Capital from Treasury Stock Transactions	**2018**	**2017**	**2016**
Balance at January 1	$ 20,996	$20,746	$20,032
Increase in equity on treasury stock sales	5,538	250	714
Decrease in equity on treasury stock sales	0	0	0
Balance at December 31	$ 26,534	$20,996	$20,746

Retained Earnings	**2018**	**2017**	**2016**
Balance at January 1	$ 99,823	$90,851	$82,570
Net earnings	20,183	18,283	17,000
Dividends	(10,313)	(9,311)	(8,719)
Balance at December 31	$109,693	$99,823	$90,851

Common Stock Held in Treasury	**2018**	**2017**	**2016**
Balance at January 1	$ 29,516	$31,952	$32,299
Purchases	2,270	1,412	3,421
Sales	(16,472)	(3,848)	(3,768)
Balance at December 31	$ 15,314	$29,516	$31,952

Required »

Prepare the journal entries for 2017 and 2018 to reflect the treasury stock transactions included in the preceding footnote information.

P15-8. Preferred Stock Issuance, Dividends in Arrears. On January 1, 2016, Pollo Company issued 1,000 shares of 4%, $100 par cumulative preferred stock for $110,000. On December 26, 2017, the board of directors declared dividends of $6,000, which were paid on December 31, 2017. The board of directors did not declare dividends again until December 24, 2020, at which time they declared dividends of $20,000. Pollo paid the dividends on December 27, 2020. Any dividends declared beyond what is due to the preferred stockholders go to the common stockholders.

Required »

a. What is the journal entry to record the issuance of preferred stock?
b. What is the journal entry to record the declaration and payment of stock dividends in 2017? What footnote disclosures are necessary for dividends in arrears in fiscal year 2017?
c. What footnote disclosures are necessary for dividends in arrears in fiscal year 2019?
d. What is the journal entry to record the declaration and payment of stock dividends in 2020?

P15-9. Prior-Period Adjustment. When preparing its financial statements at the end of 2018, Thorn Retail Inc. discovered an error in accounting for inventory. When Thorn started to purchase merchandise from a new supplier, it expensed all transportation costs rather than capitalizing them as a cost of the inventory. It estimated that a portion of the transportation costs was erroneously expensed in 2017 and 2018. Transportation costs were $326,367 and $333,784 in fiscal 2017 and 2018, respectively. The company expensed all of the transportation costs in the year incurred when it should have capitalized a portion of the costs as ending inventory. Thorn determined that 90% of the inventory purchased in 2017 was sold in 2017 and 92% of the inventory purchased in 2018 was sold in 2018. Assume that all inventory on hand at the beginning of the year is sold during the year. Assume no tax implications. Round to the nearest dollar. The information from Thorn's financial statements before any adjustment follows:

Not Restated	**2016**	**2017**	**2018**
Net income	$ 250,000	$ 287,000	$ 302,000
Cost of goods sold	5,006,000	5,320,000	5,575,360
Inventory, 12/31	470,564	256,684	267,324
Retained earnings, 12/31	4,750,103	5,008,403	5,021,903

Required »

a. Would net income have been higher or lower in 2017 and by how much? What will Thorn report as net income in 2018?
b. What would Thorn report as its inventory and retained earnings balances at the beginning of 2018 and at December 31, 2018?
c. Prepare the retained earnings portion of the statement of stockholders' equity for 2018.
d. What is the necessary journal entry to record the prior-period adjustment in 2018?

Excel Project

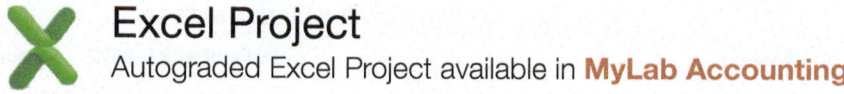

Autograded Excel Project available in **MyLab Accounting**

CASES

Judgment Cases

Judgment Case 1: Treasury Stock

TUFA, Inc. is a calendar-year, nonpublic company that follows U.S. GAAP. TUFA uses the cost method to account for repurchases of treasury stock. Recently, TUFA repurchased 10,000 shares of its common stock from a key shareholder at $55 per share. This particular shareholder had initiated a lawsuit against TUFA. Thus, a settlement of this lawsuit was included in the repurchase agreement. Because TUFA is not publicly traded, it does not have an established market price. It repurchased shares last year at $35 per share. However, TUFA has increased performance each year for the past 5 years in terms of operating cash flow and earnings. Net income last year was $1.67 per share. This year it was $2 per share.

Provide the journal entry(ies) that TUFA should make when it reacquires the shares. Use the Codification to provide support for your response.

Judgment Case 2: Impact of Judgment in Accounting for Stock Dividends

On June 6, 2012, ***Universal Bioenergy, Inc.*** declared a 20% stock dividend. Because it is a 20% dividend, it had the flexibility to account for this as a small or large stock dividend. Its common stock was trading at $0.01 per share at that time. Excerpts from its 10-K follow the questions.

1. What journal entry did ***Universal Bioenergy*** record on June 6? What journal entry did it record on July 20? Did ***Universal Bioenergy*** account for this stock dividend as a small or large stock dividend? You may find ASC 505-20-30-5 helpful in understanding this entity's approach.
2. What would be the impact on the accounts if ***Universal Bioenergy*** did not use the alternative treatment permitted for closely held entities?

What would be the impact on the accounts if ***Universal Bioenergy*** did not use the alternative treatment permitted for closely held entities and chose a different basic treatment? That is, if the company recorded it as a small stock dividend, how would the accounts change?

Discussion of the stock dividend included in ITEM 1 in the 10-K

*Approval of Stock Dividend**

On June 6, 2012, our Board of Directors passed a resolution and declared a stock dividend to distribute to all registered shareholders of record on or before July 13, 2012, on a 10 for 2 basis. On July 20, 2012, our transfer agent issued 78,161,209 shares of common stock to all registered shareholders of record in accordance with the resolution and declaration.

Excerpts from financial statements:

UNIVERSAL BIOENERGY, INC.
CONSOLIDATED BALANCE SHEETS

Assets:	December 31, 2012	December 31, 2011
Current Assets:		
Cash	$ 2,274	$ 3,706
Accounts receivable	4,800,967	10,004,123
Other loans	600	—
Total current assets	4,803,841	10,007,829
Property and Equipment – net	6,989	8,951

**Universal Bioenergy* uses the phrase "10 for 2 basis" in its financial statements when describing the stock dividend—that is, the company issued 2 shares for every 10 shares held.

UNIVERSAL BIOENERGY, INC.
CONSOLIDATED BALANCE SHEETS

Assets:	**December 31, 2012**	**December 31, 2011**
Other Assets:		
Accounts receivable – other	10,050	10,050
Investments	2,919,500	889,500
Intangible assets	250,000	250,000
Deposit	7,453	46,516
Total other assets	3,187,003	1,196,066
Total Assets	$7,997,833	$11,212,846
Liabilities and Stockholders' Equity (Deficit):		
Current Liabilities:		
Accounts payable	$ 4,983,318	$ 10,099,502
Other accounts payable and accrued expenses	185,422	208,848
Accrued interest payable	468,572	101,860
Line of credit	7,942	7,850
Current portion of long-term debt	248,395	172,560
Derivative liability	350,237	—
Advances from affiliates	4,250	4,250
Total current liabilities	6,248,136	10,594,870
Long-term Debt		
Notes payable	$ 2,261,406	$ 131,086
Notes payable- related parties	934,729	191,000
Total Long-term Debt	3,196,135	322,086
Total Liabilities	9,444,270	10,916,956
Preferred stock, $.001 par value, 10,000,000 shares authorized. Preferred stock Series A, zero issued and outstanding shares	—	—
December 31, 2012 and December 31, 2011, respectively		
Preferred stock Series B, 232,080 issued and outstanding shares December 31, 2012 and December 31, 2011, respectively	232	232
Common stock, $.001 par value, 3,000,000,000 shares authorized; 673,521,813 and 199,969,927 issued and outstanding as of December 31, 2012 and December 31, 2011, respectively	673,522	199,970
Additional paid-in capital	20,546,023	19,111,601
Noncontrolling interest	(263,836)	(125,543)
Accumulated deficit	(22,402,379)	(18,890,370)
Total stockholders' equity (deficit)	(1,466,438)	295,890
Total Liabilities and Stockholders' Equity	$ 7,997,832	$ 11,212,846

The accompanying notes are an integral part of these consolidated financial statements.

Note: Mathematical errors in 10K. Total assets sum to $7,997,833 but the company reports total assets as $7,997,832. Total long-term debt sums to $3,196,135, but the company reports total long-term debt of $3,196,134.

UNIVERSAL BIOENERGY, INC.
CONSOLIDATED STATEMENTS OF CHANGES IN STOCKHOLDERS' EQUITY (DEFICIT)
FOR THE YEARS ENDED DECEMBER 31, 2012 AND 2011

			Common Stock		Preferred A		Preferred B			
	Total	Accumulated Deficit	Shares	Amount	Shares	Amount	Shares	Amount	Additional Paid-in Capital	Non-controlling Interest
Balances at December 31, 2011	$ 295,890	$(18,890,370)	199,969,927	$199,970		-	232,080	$ 232	$19,111,602	$(125,543)
Common stock issued for debt conversion	1,533,668		382,262,752	382,263					1,151,405	
Common stock issued for officer compensation	118,280		13,127,925	13,128					105,152	
Beneficial conversion feature of convertible notes payable	247,321								247,321	
Common stock issued for dividend	-		78,161,209	78,161					(78,161)	
Noncontrolling interest	(138,293)									(138,293)
Net (Loss)	(4,916,502)	$ (4,916,502)								
Balances at December 31, 2012	(2,859,636)	(23,806,872)	673,521,813	$673,522		-	232,080	$ 232	$20,537,319	$(263,836)

Excerpt from the notes to the financial statements follow:

NOTE 4: Equity

On December 26, 2012, the Company amended its Articles of Incorporation, and increased the authorized shares of common stock from 1,000,000,000 to 3,000,000,000 shares at $.001 par value. There are 673,521,813 shares of common stock issued and outstanding as of December 30, 2012.

On June 6, 2012, our Board of Directors passed a resolution and declared a stock dividend to distribute to all registered shareholders of record on, or before, July 13, 2012, on a 10 for 2 basis. On July 20, 2012, our transfer agent issued 78,161,209 shares of common stock to all registered shareholders of record in accordance with the resolution and declaration.

The Company has authorized a total of 10,000,000 shares of Preferred Stock with a par value of $0.001 per share. On September 29, 2008, the Company authorized 100,000 Series A Preferred shares and 232,080 Series B Preferred Shares of stock. As of December 31, 2012, there were no Series A preferred shares issued and outstanding, and a total of 232,080 Series B preferred shares issued and outstanding.

Source: Financial Statements from Universal Bioenergy, Inc.'s 2013 Annual Report. https://www.sec.gov/Archives/edgar/data/1320729/000126493113000230/R10.htm

Financial Statement Analysis Case

With declining demand and sales, the last several years have been challenging in the global auto industry. You are interested in better understanding the performance and valuation of major global companies in the industry. The following table presents net income for the year and shareholders' equity and market value at the end of each fiscal year for four global auto companies.

		Fiscal Year		
Company	**Measure (U.S. dollars in millions)**	**2014**	**2015**	**2016**
Ford Motor Company – U.S.	Net income	$ 1,231	$ 7,373	$ 4,596
	Book value of common stockholders' equity	24,438	28,642	29,170
	Market value of common stock	58,556	54,920	47,342
General Motors Company – U.S.	Net income	3,949	9,687	9,427
	Book value of common stockholders' equity	35,457	39,871	43,836
	Market value of common stock	56,090	52,926	53,199
Honda Motor Company – Japan	Net income	6,074	4,241	3,059
	Book value of common stockholders' equity	61,600	59,184	60,032
	Market value of common stock	64,003	58,863	49,632
Daimler AG – Germany	Net income	8,940	9,157	8,975
	Book value of common stockholders' equity	53,250	58,218	61,000
	Market value of common stock	89,984	90,215	79,641

Sources: Data taken from Annual Reports 2014–2016 of Ford Motor Company, General Motors, Inc., Honda Motors, and Daimler AG.

http://shareholder.ford.com/~/media/Files/F/Ford-IR/annual-report/2016-annual-report.pdf
http://corporate.ford.com/doc/ar20122015-20122015%20Annual%20Report.pdf
https://www.gm.com/content/dam/gm/en_us/english/Group4/InvestorsPDFDocuments/10-K.pdf
http://www.gm.com/annualreport/downloads/20132016_GM_Annual_Report.pdf
http://world.honda.com/content/dam/site/world/investors/cq_img/library/annual_report/FY201603_annual_report_e_01.pdf
http://world.honda.com/investors/library/annual_report/20132016/honda20132016ar-all-e.pdf
https://www.daimler.com/documents/investors/reports/annual-report/daimler/daimler-ir-annualreport-2016.pdf
http://www.daimler.com/Projects/c2c/channel/documents/2432177_Daimler_20132016_Annual_Report.pdf

Required »

a. Comment on changes in net income and book values of each year.
b. Compute the price-earnings (P/E) ratios and price-to-book (P/B) ratios for each year.
c. Compute an average of price-earnings (P/E) ratios and price-to-book (P/B) ratios for each year.
d. Comment on the companies' P/E ratios over time. Are there any unusually high or low P/E ratios? If so, why? Comment on the average over time.
e. Why would the P/B ratios in the automotive industry generally be higher than 1? Are there any unusually high or low P/B ratios? If so, why? Comment on the companies P/B ratios over time. Comment on the average over time.
f. Compare the average P/E and P/B ratios for the pharmaceutical companies from Example 15.23 in the text with those in the auto industry.

Surfing the Standards Cases

Surfing the Standards Case 1: Preferred Dividends

Toofles Company, a publicly traded entity, issued nonredeemable preferred stock on January 1, 2018, Toofles issued 1,000 shares of $100 par value shares for $82,425. On January 1, 2015, the market rate of interest for preferred stock with the same characteristics was 6%. The preferred shares will not pay any dividends in 2015 or 2016. In 2017, they will pay 1% of par. In 2018, they will pay 3% of par. In 2019 and thereafter, the shares will pay 6% of par.

Management would like to know how to account for these shares both at issuance and thereafter. Prepare a memo to the file using the Codification for support. Include any relevant journal entries. Assume that dividend payments occur at the end of the year.

Basis for Conclusions Cases

Basis for Conclusions Case 1: Bifurcation[26]

Many financial instruments include characteristics of both a liability and equity. Read ASC 480-10-15, paragraphs 3 and 4, and ASC 480-10-25, paragraph 1. Also read International Accounting Standard 32, paragraphs 28 through 32. In addition, read the relevant paragraphs in the Basis for Conclusions in Statement of Financial Accounting Standards No. 150, paragraphs B50 through B54, as well as the relevant paragraphs in the Basis for Conclusions in International Accounting Standard 32, paragraphs BC22 through BC31.

a. How does U.S. GAAP treat these instruments? How does IFRS treat these instruments?
b. Provide a discussion of the rationale each standard-setting body used to arrive at their conclusions.
c. Based on the thoughts of the boards, it appears that there is a trade-off with respect to the bifurcation decision. What is this trade-off and which view do you prefer?

Basis for Conclusions Case 2: Capital Structure Disclosures

In January 1996, FASB issued an exposure draft of a standard that would address both the computation of earnings per share and the disclosure of information about a firm's capital structure. However, the board divided these topics into two standards. *Statement of Financial Accounting Standards No. 128* was issued to address earnings per share issues and *Statement of Financial Accounting Standards No. 129* was issued to address information related to the capital structure of firms. Read *Statement of Financial Accounting Standards No. 129* and answer the following questions.

Required »

a. Why did FASB decide to split the exposure draft into two final standards?
b. Why did FASB make SFAS No. 129 applicable to nonpublic entities?
c. Why did FASB include securities that do not impact the computation of earnings per share in these disclosure requirements?

[26]Reprinted from the Ernst & Young Academic Resource Center with permission of the Ernst & Young Foundation.

16 Investments in Financial Assets

LEARNING OBJECTIVES

1. Describe debt and equity investments, the two main types of investment securities that companies hold, and the key issues in accounting for them, including cost and fair value accounting.
2. Describe and illustrate accounting for investments in debt securities—including held-to-maturity, trading, and available-for-sale securities—at initial recognition and subsequent to acquisition.
3. Discuss and demonstrate accounting for investments in equity securities when the investor has no significant influence at initial recognition and subsequent to acquisition, including accounting for investments without readily determinable fair values.
4. Explain and illustrate accounting for investments in equity securities when the investor has significant influence over the investee company.
5. Explain and demonstrate the accounting for long-term notes receivable.
6. Discuss and illustrate the fair value option in accounting for investments in financial assets.
7. Detail required disclosures for investments in financial assets.

Tim Graham/Alamy Stock Photo

Introduction

COMPANIES HOLD INVESTMENTS IN FINANCIAL ASSETS for many reasons, such as facilitating liquidity, earning investment income and/or realizing capital gains, or forming strategic alliances with other companies. To facilitate liquidity, a company holds investments on a temporary basis and sells them when it needs cash in the operating cycle. In other cases, the company may hold the investment as a source of ongoing dividend and interest income. Selling an investment may also yield a capital gain.

Financial service entities such as banks and insurance companies usually hold a large amount of investments from which they intend to earn investment income and/or realize capital gains. For example, about one-third of ***Citigroup Inc.****'s* $1,792 billion of assets at the end of 2016 were investment securities. ***Citigroup*** actively intended to trade about 41% of its investment assets and held the rest to generate investment income.

To form a strategic alliance with another company, an entity purchases a sufficient number of voting shares, thereby enabling it to exert significant influence over the other company. Consider ***Starbucks Corporation***, a premier roaster, marketer, and retailer of specialty coffee operating in over 75 countries. ***Starbucks'*** products are available to consumers throughout the world through its own stores or through a network of affiliated companies. ***Starbucks*** owns most of its U.S. retail stores and is a major investor in the companies that operate other stores, primarily outside of the United States. ***Starbucks*** maximizes the strength and efficiency of its worldwide distribution and marketing capabilities by making significant investments in the equity of companies operating in China, Japan, Korea, and Taiwan that represented about 3% of its total assets at the end of 2016. ***Starbucks*** exercises significant influence over the operating and financial policies of these affiliate companies. ***Starbucks*** holds other investments in corporate bonds and government securities, comprising about 8% of its total assets, to fund domestic and international operations, provide liquidity, or earn a return.

In this chapter, we cover accounting for different types of debt and equity securities. We first discuss debt investments. In the accounting and valuation for these investments, we demonstrate the importance of understanding whether the company intends to hold a debt investment until maturity, whether it intends to actively trade the securities, or whether it is holding these securities as a source of liquidity to sell if cash is needed in the operating cycle. This section is followed by a discussion about equity investments when the investor does not have significant influence over the investee. Accounting for equity investments when a company has significant influence over the investee is covered next. We also discuss long-term notes receivable and explain the fair value option. We conclude the chapter with an overview of required disclosures. We discuss the impairment of investment assets in Appendix A.

Throughout the chapter, we also discuss differences in accounting for investments under U.S. GAAP and IFRS, including the accounting for different types of investments in debt and equity securities as well as impairment testing.«

1 Describe debt and equity investments, the two main types of investment securities that companies hold, and the key issues in accounting for them, including cost and fair value accounting.

Overview of Investments in Debt and Equity

Firms measure some investments in financial assets at cost, some at amortized cost, and some at fair value. For those measured at fair value, firms must report unrealized gains and losses in either net income or other comprehensive income. Each different type of investment in a financial asset may be accounted for differently.

We begin our discussion of the different types of investments held by companies and each type's accounting treatment with an introduction to investments in debt and equity securities.

Investments in Debt Securities

Debt securities are investments in the notes or bonds payable issued by another company. A bond, or promissory note, is a form of borrowing by which a company raises capital today in exchange for a contractual obligation to pay bondholders (the lenders) the principal amount (face value) and interest in the future. Corporations invest in bonds in order to receive periodic interest payments and a final payment of the principal amount (face value). Firms usually issue bonds with a face value (also referred to as *par value*) indicating the amount that the issuer will pay the bondholder at maturity. Bonds also typically have a stated interest rate, which determines the amount of interest that bondholders will receive in cash. Bonds are usually sold in an issue (for example, a $5,000,000 bond issue consists of 5,000 of $1,000 par value bonds).

Bonds can be purchased at their par value, at a discount (a price below par), or at a premium (a price above par). In all cases, bonds are priced such that their *yield* will be the same as the market rate of interest, which is also called the *effective interest rate*, for a similar amount of risk. **Yield** is the actual return that the investors will receive.

Investments in Equity Securities

Investments in equity securities are investments in the common or preferred shares of another company. The investor (the party purchasing the equity security) may receive returns in the form of dividends, which are distributions (most often cash) that the investee (the party that issued the equity security) pays to the investor. In addition, the investor could eventually sell the investment for an amount higher than its purchase price and earn a gain on disposal.

THE CONCEPTUAL FRAMEWORK CONNECTION: Fair Value versus Cost

When a company purchases an investment, it typically reports the investment at its cost on the date of acquisition. Several questions arise after the date of acquisition.

- If the value of the investment changes, should the company continue to report the asset at its cost, similar to land, or should it report the asset at its current fair value?
- If a company uses fair value to measure the investment, how does the company obtain the fair value, and what if there is no readily available fair value?
- If a company uses fair value to measure the investment, should it report the change in fair value in net income or in other comprehensive income?

The answers to these questions are not always clear. In fact, accounting standard setters have debated the issue of fair value versus cost for decades. Firms measured assets on the balance sheet at cost almost exclusively 25 years ago. In today's mixed-attribute balance sheets, firms report some items—such as certain investments—at fair value and other items—such as land—at cost.

The standard setters' requirements for cost or fair value accounting involve a trade-off between the two fundamental qualitative characteristics in the conceptual framework: relevance and faithful representation. The cost-basis method of valuation clearly provides a faithful representation of an asset's value. That is, it represents what it is intended to represent with a very high degree of accuracy. However, it is often not very relevant. Fair value is highly relevant in that it reflects the future economic benefits associated with the asset. However, in many cases, the fair value is subjective and thus may not provide a faithful representation.

To illustrate, assume that ReadWrite Corporation purchased an equity investment in MathSkills', Inc. 20 years ago for $100,000. MathSkills' equity shares are not publicly traded, but management estimates a fair value of $900,000. The $100,000 acquisition price faithfully represents the cost. The $900,000 fair value may be a good estimation of the fair value, but it is only an estimate. Thus, it is not as faithfully representative as the cost basis. However, the $900,000 is much more relevant for decision-making purposes than the cost basis of $100,000 because if management decides to sell the investment, the amount received on the sale will be closer to $900,000 than to the original cost of $100,000.

The fair values of publicly traded financial assets provide representational faithfulness in addition to being relevant because these amounts result from objectively determined quoted market prices. In fact, the first balance sheet items that the FASB required firms to report at fair value were debt investments and equity investments with readily determinable fair values.

Key Questions for Investments in Debt and Equity Securities

Accounting for investments in debt and equity securities involves addressing four key questions:

1. Is the investment a debt security or an equity security?
2. If the investment is a debt security, how long does management intend to hold the investment?
3. If the investment is an equity security, how much control does the investor have over the investee company?
4. If the investment is an equity security, is the fair value readily determinable?

Although the answer to the first question of whether an investment is a debt or equity security is straightforward, it is important because companies account for equity security investments differently than debt security investments. We discuss the second question on classification of debt securities based on management intent in the next section and cover the last two questions later in the chapter.

2 Describe and illustrate accounting for investments in debt securities—including held-to-maturity, trading, and available-for-sale securities—at initial recognition and subsequent to acquisition.

Investments in Debt Securities

Companies classify and account for debt securities in one of three ways, depending on management intent and ability to hold the investments.[1]

Classification of Debt Securities

Accounting for debt securities depends on management's reason for purchasing the securities. Management classifies debt securities into one of three portfolio categories at acquisition: *held-to-maturity securities*, *trading securities*, and *available-for-sale securities*.

1. **Held-to-maturity securities.** A company classifies a debt security as a **held-to-maturity investment** if it has both the positive intent and ability to hold a debt investment until it matures. Positive intent is not just the absence of the intent to sell: The company must actually plan on holding the debt security to maturity. If the company's intent to hold the instrument is uncertain, then it should not classify the security as held to maturity.
2. **Trading securities.** A **trading security** is a debt investment that a company intends to hold only for the short term.[2] A company generally classifies securities as trading when it plans to actively buy and sell securities with the objective of generating a gain on the sale.
3. **Available-for-sale securities.** If a debt security is not classified as held to maturity or trading, then it is classified as an **available-for-sale security**.

Investments in debt securities commonly change in fair value. The portfolio classification determines:

- The valuation of the security on the balance sheet (at amortized cost or fair value)
- If carried at fair value, where changes in fair value are reported (in earnings or other comprehensive income)

If the company actually sells the securities, then the change in fair value results in a **realized gain or loss**. If the company holds the securities, then the change in fair value is an **unrealized gain or loss**.

Management may transfer securities from one category to another. We discuss portfolio transfers later in the chapter.

Held-to-Maturity Debt Securities

Initial Valuation of Held-to-Maturity Debt Securities. Companies record held-to-maturity (HTM) debt security investments at cost when purchased. The process for determining a HTM debt security's purchase price is identical to determining the initial price of a bond.[3] A bond's purchase price will always equal the present value of the cash flows related to the bond, discounted at the market rate of interest. Thus, the bond's purchase price is equal to the sum of the present value of the face or par value (the present value of a lump sum) plus the present value of the interest payments (the present value of an ordinary annuity). When the purchase price is less than the face value, the company purchases the bonds at a discount. When the purchase price is greater than face value, the company purchases the bonds at a premium. When the company purchases bonds, it typically does not record separate accounts for the bond discount or premium. Rather, the company records the asset at the purchase price—the face value of the bond, net of the discount or premium.

---

[1]For the relevant authoritative literature, see FASB ASC 320 –10 – *Investments – Debt Securities – Overall* for U.S. GAAP and IASB, *International Financial Reporting Standard 9*, "Financial Instruments" (London, UK: International Accounting Standards Board, 2014).

[2]FASB ASC 320-10, *Investments – Debt Securities – Overall* defines trading securities more thoroughly as follows. "Securities that are bought and held principally for the purpose of selling them in the near term and therefore held for only a short period of time. Trading generally reflects active and frequent buying and selling, and trading securities are generally used with the objective of generating profits on short-term differences in price."

[3]We cover the treatment of a bond issue from the issuer's perspective in Chapter 14.

Examples 16.1 and 16.2 illustrate the computation of the purchase price of a bond. First, we examine the case of a bond purchased at a discount.

EXAMPLE 16.1 Determining the Purchase Price of a Bond—Discount

PROBLEM: On January 1, 2018, the Coley Corporation purchased $400,000 par value 4% bonds that mature on December 31, 2021. The company has the positive intent and ability to hold the bonds until they mature. The market rate of interest was 6% when Coley purchased the bonds. Coley receives interest on the bonds semiannually each June 30 and December 31. What future cash inflows will Coley receive on this investment? What is the purchase price of the bonds? Did Coley purchase the bonds at a discount or premium? Prepare the journal entry to record the acquisition of the bonds.

SOLUTION: We know that Coley will receive semi-annual interest payments on the bonds and payment of the face value ($400,000) when the bonds mature. Each semi-annual receipt is $8,000, computed as follows:

$$\$400{,}000 \times 4\% \times 1/2 = \$8{,}000$$

The bond purchase price is equal to the present value of the future cash flows. This present value includes the face value of $400,000 as well as the semi-annual interest payments. All present value inputs are at the semi-annual market rate because the bonds are priced to yield the market. Therefore, $I/Y = 3\%$, (6%/2), and $N = 8$ (4 years × 2).

	N	I/Y	PV	PMT	FV	Excel Formula
Given	8	3.00%		8,000	400,000	
Solve for PV			**(371,921)**			=PV(0.03,8,8000,400000)

Coley purchased the bonds at a discount of $28,079 because the $371,921purchase price is less than their $400,000 face value. The journal entry to record the acquisition is as follows:

Account	***January 1, 2018***	
Held-to-Maturity Debt Investments – Cost	371,921	
Cash		371,921

Example 16.2 illustrates the same bond purchased at a premium when the market rate is lower than the stated rate.

EXAMPLE 16.2 Determining the Purchase Price of a Bond—Premium

PROBLEM: Referring to Example 16.1, now assume the same bonds were issued when the market rate of interest is 2%. What future cash inflows will Coley receive on this investment? What is the purchase price of the bonds? Did Coley purchase the bonds at a discount or premium?

SOLUTION: We know that Coley will receive semi-annual interest payments on the bonds and payment of the face value ($400,000) when the bonds mature. Each semi-annual receipt is $8,000, computed as follows:

$$\$400{,}000 \times 4\% \times 1/2 = \underline{\underline{\$8{,}000}}$$

The bond purchase price is equal to the present value of the future cash flows. This present value includes the face value of $400,000 as well as the semi-annual interest payments. All present value inputs are at the semi-annual market rate because the bonds are priced to yield the market. Therefore, $I/Y = 1\%$, (2%/2), and $N = 8$(4 years × 2).

	N	I/Y	PV	PMT	FV	Excel Formula
Given	8	1.00%		8,000	400,000	
Solve for PV			**(430,607)**			=PV(0.01,8,8000,400000)

Coley purchased the bonds at a premium of $30,607 because the $430,607 purchase price is greater than their $400,000 face value. The journal entry to record the acquisition is as follows:

Account	***January 1, 2018***	
Held-to-Maturity Debt Investments – Cost	430,607	
Cash		430,607

When purchasing bonds between interest payment dates, the purchaser pays the seller any accrued interest on the bonds. Because the interest payment is a part of the bond agreement, the issuing corporation pays the full interest payment to the current bondholder on the payment date regardless of how long the bondholder held the bond. To ensure that the purchaser receives the cash related to the interest revenue earned over the period the bonds were held, the seller requires the purchaser to pay for the interest accrued up to the purchase date.

For example, on October 1, a company purchases bonds that pay interest annually on December 31. Nine months of interest have accrued on the bonds at October 1. On December 31, the company purchasing the bonds will receive an interest payment representing the full 12 months of interest, but it held the bonds for only 3 months. When buying the bond on October 1, the purchaser must also pay the seller for the 9 months of accrued interest as Example 16.3 illustrates.

EXAMPLE 16.3 Bonds Purchased with Accrued Interest

PROBLEM: On October 1, 2018, Foley Corporation purchased $500,000 par value 5% bonds that mature on December 31, 2021, for $500,000 plus accrued interest. The company has the positive intent and ability to hold the bonds until maturity. The bonds pay interest annually on December 31. What is the amount of accrued interest on the bond? What is the journal entry at acquisition? What is the amount of the interest payment that Foley receives on December 31?

SOLUTION: Foley pays $18,750 for 9 months of accrued interest when it purchases the bonds, computed as follows:

$$\$500,000 \times 5\% \times 9/12 = \underline{\underline{\$18,750}}$$

The journal entry at acquisition includes interest receivable of $18,750.

Account	***October 1, 2018***	
Held-to-Maturity Debt Investments – Cost	500,000	
Interest Receivable	18,750	
Cash		518,750

On December 31, Foley receives the annual interest payment on the bonds of $25,000, computed as follows:

$$\$500,000 \times 5\% = \underline{\underline{\$25,000}}$$

Therefore, Foley's net interest revenue earned at December 31, 2018, is $6,250 ($25,000 − $18,750). This amount represents the interest earned for the 3 months the bonds were held ($6,250 = 5% × 3/12 × $500,000).

Subsequent Valuation of Held-to-Maturity Debt Securities. After purchase, companies report HTM debt security investments at *amortized cost*. **Amortized cost** is original cost less the unamortized amount of the premium or discount. Any discount or premium is amortized to income subsequent to the date of acquisition and over the bond term. Amortized cost is a more relevant value than fair value for securities held until maturity. That is, fair values are not relevant if management does not intend to sell the debt investment before maturity.

In accounting for the debt investment, companies usually combine any discount or premium with the debt's face value. The debtor uses a separate premium or discount account when accounting for bonds payable; however, the investor typically combines these accounts into a single investment account. Using separate premium and discount accounts for investments is acceptable, but it is not typically found in practice.

Companies recognize interest revenue on HTM debt investments using the *effective interest method* of amortization. The **effective interest method** computes interest revenue by multiplying the *historical market rate* of interest by the carrying value of the debt investment at the beginning of the period. The **historical market rate** is the interest rate used to value the investment at the date of acquisition.

$$\text{Effective Interest Revenue} = \text{Historical Market Rate} \times \text{Carrying Value of Debt Investment at the Beginning of the Period} \quad (16.1)$$

When reporting interest revenue, companies also amortize the discount or premium. The amount amortized is the difference between the effective interest revenue and the cash interest received:

$$\text{Discount/Premium Amortization} = \text{Effective Interest Revenue} - \text{Cash Interest Received} \quad (16.2)$$

Example 16.4 illustrates the accounting for HTM debt securities.

EXAMPLE 16.4 Held-to-Maturity Debt Securities

PROBLEM: Cornish Associates acquired $4,000,000 par value, 5%, 4-year bonds of Mendes Manufacturing on January 1 of the current year for investment purposes. Interest is payable semiannually each June 30 and December 31. The market rate on the date of acquisition was 8%. The investment is classified as held to maturity because Cornish has a positive intent and ability to hold the bonds until maturity. What are the journal entries for the current year and the journal entry to record the maturity of the debt investment?

SOLUTION: First, we determine the bond purchase price, which is equal to the sum of the present value of the future cash flows. All present value inputs are at the semi-annual market rate because the bonds are priced to yield the market. Therefore, $I/Y = 4\%$ (8%/2), and $N = 8$ (4 years $\times$ 2).

	N	I/Y	PV	PMT	FV	Excel Formula
Given	8	4.00%		100,000	4,000,000	
Solve for PV			**(3,596,035)**			=PV(0.04,8,100000,4000000)

Cornish purchased the bonds at a discount of $403,965 because the $4,000,000 face value is greater than the $3,596,035 purchase price. Cornish makes the following entry on the date of acquisition.

Account	***Acquisition***	
Held-to-Maturity Debt Investments – Mendes Bonds	3,596,035	
Cash		3,596,035

Continued

To determine the interest revenue each period, we construct an amortization table using the effective interest rate method as follows.

Period	Cash Interest at 2.5% (a)	Effective Interest at 4% (b) = 4% × Prior (d)	Discount Amortization (c) = (b) − (a)	Amortized Cost (d) = Prior (d) + (c)
0				$3,596,035
1	$100,000	$ 143,841	$ 43,841	3,639,876
2	100,000	145,595	45,595	3,685,471
3	100,000	147,419	47,419	3,732,890
4	100,000	149,316	49,316	3,782,206
5	100,000	151,288	51,288	3,833,494
6	100,000	153,340	53,340	3,886,834
7	100,000	155,473	55,473	3,942,307
8	100,000	157,693*	57,693*	4,000,000
Total	$800,000	$1,203,965	$403,965	

*Adjusted due to rounding errors.

The cash interest received each period ($100,000) is the face value ($4,000,000) multiplied by the stated interest rate per semi-annual period of 2.5% (5%/2). The effective interest (Column 3) is the amortized cost at the beginning of the period multiplied by the 4% market interest rate. For example, the effective interest for Period 1 is computed as $3,596,035 × 4%. The amount of discount amortization is the difference between the cash interest received and the effective interest. The ending amortized cost is the beginning amortized cost plus the discount amortization. In the case of a bond premium, the ending amortized cost is the beginning amortized cost less the premium amortization.

The entries to record interest revenue for the first year (first two interest periods) follow.

Account	***June 30***		***December 31***	
Cash	100,000		100,000	
Held-to-Maturity Debt Investments – Mendes Bonds	43,841		45,595	
Interest Revenue		143,841		145,595

Every 6 months, Cornish records interest revenue and increases the carrying value of the investment according to the amortization table. Thus, when the debt matures, the investment account will reach $4,000,000 at maturity. The journal entry to record the collection of face value at maturity is as follows:

Account	***Maturity***	
Cash	4,000,000	
Held-to-Maturity Debt Investments – Mendes bonds		4,000,000

Trading Debt Securities

A company holds trading debt securities with the intent to actively and frequently trade them. An investor reports changes in fair value of trading securities in net income. Reporting the changes in fair value in net income accurately portrays the way a company manages its operations and economic activity, resulting in relevant financial information for shareholders. When the company sells the securities, it also reports any realized gains or losses in net income.

Revaluing a debt investment to its current fair value requires a separate fair value adjustment account to reflect the difference between the fair value and the amortized cost of the investment. The fair value adjustment account captures fair value fluctuations each reporting period and avoids excessive changes in the investment account. The fair value adjustment account can have a debit or credit balance depending on whether the company recognizes unrealized gains or losses, respectively:

- If the fair value at the end of the year is *greater than* the amortized cost of the debt investment, the fair value adjustment account will have a debit balance.
- If the fair value at the end of the year is *less than* the amortized cost of the debt investment, the fair value adjustment account will have a credit balance.

For balance sheet reporting, the company combines the investment and fair value adjustment accounts. In addition to recording fair value adjustments, the company must amortize any discount or premium, similar to accounting for HTM debt investments. However, because of the short-term nature of trading securities, this amortization becomes much less significant than with long-term, HTM debt securities.

Example 16.5 illustrates accounting for a single investment classified as a trading security. The examples in this section focus on fair value adjustments and assume debt securities are purchased at face value. Therefore, there is no discount or premium to amortize.

EXAMPLE 16.5 Trading Debt Securities

PROBLEM: Phoneex Company, a calendar year-end firm, invested in a debt security with a face value of $450,000 on October 1, 2018, that it properly classified as a trading security. Phoneex paid $450,000 for the debt security. On December 31, 2018, the investment paid interest of $4,500 and had a fair value of $442,000. Phoneex sold the security on January 1, 2019, for $441,000. Phoneex had not purchased any other trading securities before October 1, 2018, and it did not purchase any additional debt securities after the sale on January 1, 2019. What journal entries should Phoneex prepare to record these transactions?

SOLUTION: On October 1, Phoneex records the purchase of the securities as follows.

Account	***October 1, 2018***	
Trading Debt Investments	450,000	
Cash		450,000

Because the acquisition cost is equal to the face value, there is no discount or premium. On December 31, Phoneex records the interest revenue from the security.

Account	***December 31, 2018***	
Cash	4,500	
Interest Revenue		4,500

On December 31, Phoneex makes the entry to adjust the securities to fair value. Because the fair value of the security has decreased, Phoneex records an $8,000 unrealized loss and credits the fair value adjustment account by $8,000. The unrealized loss is reported in other income or investment income on the income statement.

Account	***December 31, 2018***	
Unrealized Loss – Net Income	8,000	
Fair Value Adjustment – Trading Debt Investments		8,000

Continued

After recording the fair value adjustment, the carrying value of the investments is $442,000, as the t-accounts illustrate:

	Trading Debt Investments		+	Fair Value Adjustment – Trading Debt Investments		
Cost, 10/1	450,000					
					8,000	Fair Value Adjustment, 12/31
Balance, 12/31	450,000				8,000	= $442,000

Phoneex reports the investment on the balance sheet as a single amount: $442,000 fair value = $450,000 investment at cost – $8,000 fair value adjustment account.

In the following year, Phoneex records the sale of the trading securities as follows:

Account	January 1, 2019	
Cash	441,000	
Realized Loss – Net Income	9,000	
Trading Debt Investments		450,000

Note that the realized gain or loss on sale is computed by subtracting the carrying value (using the original cost basis) from the selling price. We do not consider the fair value adjustment account on the sale of the securities.

At year-end, Phoneex holds no other trading securities but still has a balance in its fair value adjustment account that it must remove:

Account	December 31, 2019	
Fair Value Adjustment – Trading Debt Investments	8,000	
Unrealized Gain – Net Income		8,000

After this entry, Phoneex has a zero balance in its fair value adjustment account as well as a net loss of $1,000 reported on its 2019 income statement. In summary, Phoneex reports a loss of $8,000 in 2018 and a loss of $1,000 in 2019, resulting in a total loss of $9,000 over the life of the investment.

Available-for-Sale Debt Securities

A company reports available-for-sale securities at fair value and includes unrealized gains or losses in other comprehensive income. Reporting changes in fair value in other comprehensive income rather than net income reduces any volatility in earnings that could occur due to dramatic changes in the securities' fair value. Because a company holds the securities with the intent to have them available for sale (rather than to trade), the earnings volatility would not reflect the way it manages its business nor the impact of economic events on performance. Consequently, a company defers unrealized gains or losses by including them in accumulated other comprehensive income on the balance sheet. When the company sells the securities, it reports any realized gains or losses in net income.

Similar to trading securities, the company debits or credits a fair value adjustment account for the difference between the asset's fair value and its amortized cost. In addition, the company amortizes any discount or premium using the effective interest rate method.

Consider ***Starbucks Corporation's*** short-term and long-term investments in available-for-sale securities. ***Starbucks*** reported $65.7 million of short-term securities and $1,141.7 million of long-term securities accounted for as available for sale, including investments in corporate debt, at the end of fiscal 2016. ***Starbucks*** reported unrealized holding gains of $2.4 million (net of tax) during the year on its available-for-sale investments in other comprehensive income.

Example 16.6 illustrates the accounting for available-for-sale debt securities.

EXAMPLE 16.6 Available-for-Sale Debt Securities

PROBLEM: Littock, Inc. purchased JJR Company's $400,000 par value, 5%, 4-year bonds on January 1, 2018, for $359,604 and classified this investment as available for sale. The market rate on the date of issue was 8%. Interest is payable semiannually each June 30 and December 31. On December 31, 2018, the fair value of the investment was $350,000 and on December 31, 2019, was $360,050. Littock sold the investment on January 2, 2020, for $365,000. Littock did not invest in any additional available-for-sale securities in 2020. Prepare the journal entries for 2018 through 2020 and reconcile the gains and losses reported in other comprehensive income over the life of the investment.

SOLUTION: Littock makes the following entry on the date of acquisition.

Account	***January 1, 2018***	
Available-for-Sale Debt Investments	359,604	
Cash		359,604

To determine the interest revenue each period, we construct an amortization table using the effective interest rate method as follows.

Date	**Cash Interest at 2.5% (a)**	**Effective Interest at 4% (b) = 4% × Prior (d)**	**Discount Amortization (c) = (b) − (a)**	**Amortized Cost (d) = Prior (d) + (c)**
January 1, 2018				$359,604
June 30, 2018	$10,000	$14,384	$ 4,384	363,988
December 31, 2018	10,000	14,560	4,560	368,548
June 30, 2019	10,000	14,742	4,742	373,290
December 31, 2019	10,000	14,932	4,932	378,222
June 30, 2020	10,000	15,129	5,129	383,351
December 31, 2020	10,000	15,334	5,334	388,685
June 30, 2021	10,000	15,547	5,547	394,232
December 31, 2021	10,000	15,768*	5,768*	400,000
Total	$80,000	$120,396	$40,396	

*Adjusted due to rounding errors.

The entries to record interest revenue for the first year (first two interest periods) follow.

Account	***June 30, 2018***		***December 31, 2018***	
Cash	10,000		10,000	
Available-for-Sale Debt Investments	4,384		4,560	
Interest Revenue		14,384		14,560

Based on the amortization table, the carrying value of the investment on December 31, 2018, is $368,548. The fair value is $350,000.

Continued

As of	Fair Value (a)	Amortized Cost (b)	Fair Value Adjustment Account Balance Debit (Credit) (c) = (b) − (a)	
December 31, 2018	$350,000	$368,548	$(18,548)	← This is the balance needed in the fair value adjustment account at *December 31, 2018*
Existing balance in the fair value adjustment account			0	
Amount of adjustment needed			$(18,548)	

Thus, Littock needs a credit balance in the fair value adjustment account of $18,548. Because there is currently a zero balance in the account, Littock will credit the full amount.

Account	***December 31, 2018***	
Unrealized Loss – Other Comprehensive Income	18,548	
Fair Value Adjustment – Available-for-Sale Debt Investments		18,548

After the fair value adjustment, the balance of AOCI related to unrealized gains and losses on securities is a debit of $18,548 at December 31, 2018 (beginning balance $0 plus $18,548 unrealized loss), and the carrying value of the investment is at its fair value of $350,000 as the t-accounts illustrate:

	Available-for-Sale Debt Investments (Debit)	Available-for-Sale Debt Investments (Credit)	+	Fair Value Adjustment – Available-for-Sale Debt Investments (Debit)	Fair Value Adjustment – Available-for-Sale Debt Investments (Credit)	
Balance, 12/31/18	368,548					
					18,548	← Fair value adjustment, 12/31/18
Balance, 12/31/18	368,548				18,548	= $350,000

The balance sheet will reflect the $368,548 investment's amortized cost less the fair value adjustment at December 31, 2018, of $18,548. As a result, Littock reports the net asset amount of $350,000 on the balance sheet. The unrealized loss, reported in other comprehensive income, is closed out to accumulated other comprehensive income (AOCI) in stockholders' equity.

In 2019, Littock will first record the interest received and discount amortization on June 30 and December 31.

Account	***June 30, 2019***		***December 31, 2019***	
Cash	10,000		10,000	
Available-for-Sale Debt Investments	4,742		4,932	
Interest Revenue		14,742		14,932

Based on the amortization table, the carrying value of the investment on December 31, 2019, is $378,222. The fair value is $360,050.

As of	Fair Value (a)	Amortized Cost (b)	Fair Value Adjustment Account Balance Debit (Credit) (c) = (b) − (a)	
December 31, 2019	$360,050	$378,222	$(18,172)	← This is the balance needed in the fair value adjustment account at December 31, 2019
Existing balance in the fair value adjustment account			$(18,548)	
Amount of adjustment needed			$ 376	

Thus, Littock needs a credit balance in the fair value adjustment account of $18,172. Currently, the account has a credit balance of $18,548. As a result, Littock must reduce the fair value adjustment account by $376. The company will debit the fair value adjustment account and credit an unrealized gain in other comprehensive income for $376.

Account	***December 31, 2019***	
Fair Value Adjustment – Available-for-Sale Debt Investments	376	
Unrealized Gain – Other Comprehensive Income		376

After the fair value adjustment, the balance of AOCI related to unrealized gains and losses on securities is a debit of $18,172 at December 31, 2019 (beginning balance $18,548 minus $376 unrealized gain), and the carrying value of the investments is $360,050 as the t-accounts illustrate:

	Accumulated Other Comprehensive Income (Debit)	(Credit)
Balance, 12/31/18	18,548	
Adjustment		376
Balance, 12/31/19	18,172	

	Available-for-Sale Debt Investments (Debit)	(Credit)	+	**Fair Value Adjustment – Available-for-Sale Debt Investments** (Debit)	(Credit)	
Balance, 12/31/18	368,548				18,548	12/31/18
Amortization	4,742					
Amortization	4,932					
Balance, 12/31/19	378,222				18,548	Balance, 12/31/19
			Fair value adjustment, 12/31/19	376		
Balance, 12/31/19	378,222				18,172	= $360,050

The balance sheet will reflect the $378,222 investment's amortized cost less the fair value adjustment at December 31, 2019, of $18,172. As a result, Littock reports the fair value of the investment as the net asset amount of $360,050 on the balance sheet. The unrealized gain, reported in other comprehensive income, is closed out to AOCI in stockholders' equity.

Continued

Littock records the sale of the securities on January 2, 2020. The journal entry to record the sale removes the investment from the balance sheet and reports a realized loss for the difference in the proceeds and the investment's amortized cost.

Account	January 2, 2020	
Cash	365,000	
Realized Loss	13,222	
Available-for-Sale Debt Investments		378,222

To compute the realized gain or loss on sale, we subtract the amortized cost (using the original cost basis) from the selling price. We do not consider the fair value adjustment account on the sale.

Sales price		$365,000
Original cost	$359,604	
Discount amortized to face value of investment	18,618*	
Amortized cost		(378,222)
Loss on sale of investment		$ (13,222)

*$4,384 + $4,560 + $4,742 + $4,932 discount amortization from amortization table.

Finally, Littock must assess the fair value adjustment account at year-end. Because Littock does not have any available-for-sale debt investments remaining as of December 31, 2020, it adjusts the balance to zero, as follows.

Account	December 31, 2020	
Fair Value Adjustment – Available-for-Sale Debt Investments	18,172	
Unrealized Gain – Other Comprehensive Income		18,172

The $13,222 represents the realized loss from the sale of the investment and is recorded on the income statement in other expenses. However, Littock reported $18,172 of net unrealized losses ($18,548 − $376) in other comprehensive income in prior periods. Assuming that there are no other available-for-sale investments, the fair value adjustment account is no longer needed and should be removed. As a result, Littock reverses the fair value adjustment account at December 31, 2020. This entry also records a $18,172 unrealized gain. If Littock did not make the reversal entry, the total loss on the investment would be $31,394, which understates other comprehensive income ($18,548 unrealized loss in 2018 less $376 unrealized gain in 2019 plus $13,222 realized loss in 2020).

The following table reconciles the total gains and losses recognized in comprehensive income for the security:

	Reported in Other Comprehensive Income		Reported in Net Income	
Date	Unrealized Gain	Unrealized Loss	Realized Loss	Total Effect on Comprehensive Income
12/31/18: FV adjustment		$(18,548)		$(18,548)
12/31/19: FV adjustment	$ 376			376
01/02/20: Sale			$(13,222)	(13,222)
12/31/20: FV adjustment	18,172			18,172
Totals	$18,548	$(18,548)	$(13,222)	$(13,222)

Exhibit 16.1 is an excerpt from ***Coca-Cola Company's*** accounting policies footnote for investments in debt securities from the 2016 financial statements. In the note, ***Coca-Cola*** explains its accounting for the three categories of debt investments we have just discussed. ***Coca-Cola's*** investment footnote (not disclosed here) further indicates that it classified the majority of its debt investments, with a fair value of $4,758 million and cost of $4,700 million, as available-for-sale securities in 2016.

EXHIBIT 16.1 Accounting Policy for Investments in Debt Securities, ***Coca-Cola Company,*** Financial Statements, December 31, 2016

NOTE 1: Business and Summary of Significant Accounting Policies

Investments in Equity and Debt Securities [Excerpt]

Our investments in debt securities are carried at either amortized cost or fair value. Investments in debt securities that the Company has the positive intent and ability to hold to maturity are carried at amortized cost and classified as held to maturity. Investments in debt securities that are not classified as held to maturity are carried at fair value and classified as either trading or available for sale.

Source: Financial Statements from Coca-Cola Company's 2016 Annual Report. http://www.coca-colacompany.com/our-company/company-reports

Exhibit 16.2 summarizes the accounting treatment for investments in debt securities.

EXHIBIT 16.2 Summary of Accounting Treatment for Investments in Debt Securities under U.S. GAAP

Management Intent	Portfolio Classification	Balance Sheet Treatment	Income Statement Treatment
Positive intent and ability to hold to maturity	Held-to-maturity	Amortized cost	Only realized gains and losses are recognized in net income. Unrealized gains and losses are not recognized. Interest revenue is recognized using the effective interest method; thus, discounts and premiums are amortized.
Acquired to sell	Trading	Fair value	Unrealized gains and losses are reported in net income.
Neither held to maturity nor short-term trading	Available for sale	Fair value	Unrealized gains and losses are reported in other comprehensive income.

Presentation of Other Comprehensive Income: Reclassification Adjustments for Available-for-Sale Debt Investments

A company classifying debt securities as available for sale reports unrealized gains and losses in other comprehensive income. It reports realized gains and losses in net income. When using fair values to measure the carrying amount of securities on the balance sheet, the company determines unrealized gains and losses at the end of each reporting period and again when realized on disposal of the investment. Consequently, a company might double count gains and losses in comprehensive income in the year it sells an investment. A reclassification adjustment avoids double counting by separating the change in the unrealized gains and losses from the realized gains and losses reported in net income.

Example 16.7 illustrates the reclassification adjustment.

EXAMPLE 16.7 Presentation in Other Comprehensive Income

PROBLEM: Consider the investments made by Littock, Inc. in Example 16.6. Specifically, consider the gains and losses reported in 2020. Assume that Littock reported net income before including any realized gains and losses of $2,300,000 in 2020. It had no other items included in net income that year. Recall that Littock reported the following gains and losses in 2018 through 2020.

	Carrying Value	Fair Value	Cumulative Unrealized Gain (Loss)	Realized Gain (Loss)
1/1/18 (purchase date)	$359,604			
12/31/18	368,548	$350,000	($18,548)	
12/31/19	378,222	360,050	(18,172)	
1/2/20 (sale date)	378,222	365,000		($13,222)
12/31/20			18,172	

Prepare the partial statement of comprehensive income that relates to available-for-sale debt securities on December 31, 2020.

SOLUTION: Littock's statement of comprehensive income *without a reclassification* is as follows:

Littock, Inc.
Partial Statement of Comprehensive Income
For the Year Ended December 31, 2020

Operating Income		$2,300,000
Other Loss:		
Realized Loss on Available-for-Sale Investments		(13,222)
Net Income		$2,286,778
Other Comprehensive Income:		
Unrealized Gain on Available-for-Sale Investments	$18,172	
Other Comprehensive Income		$ 18,172
Comprehensive Income		$ 2,304,950

However, this statement is misleading. Littock did not have an unrealized gain this year. The $18,172 is a reversal of prior unrealized losses. Thus, the correct presentation for Littock for 2020 is as follows:

Littock, Inc.
Partial Statement of Comprehensive Income
For the Year Ended December 31, 2020

Operating Income		$2,300,000
Other Loss:		
Realized Loss on Available-for-Sale Investments		(13,222)
Net Income		$2,286,778
Other Comprehensive Income:		
Unrealized Gain on Available-for-Sale Investments	$ 0	
Plus: Reclassification of Gains on Available-for-Sale Investments Included in Net Income	18,172	
Other Comprehensive Income		$ 18,172
Comprehensive Income		$2,304,950

The ***Coca-Cola Company*** disclosed its reclassification adjustments in its financial statements for the year ended December 31, 2016. ***Coca-Cola*** reported $17 million of net unrealized gains on available-for-sale securities in other comprehensive income in 2016. In its financial statement notes, ***Coca-Cola*** disclosed that $96 million was unrealized gains (net of taxes) that arose during the year and $79 million was a reclassification adjustment for realized gains reported in net income.

JUDGMENTS IN ACCOUNTING
For Debt Investments

Financial statement reporting depends upon management intent when applying the accounting rules for debt investments. Whether a company reports the investment at fair value and whether it includes unrealized gains and losses in net income versus other comprehensive income is completely dependent upon managerial judgment in applying the accounting standards. If management states that debt investments will be held to maturity, then the financial statements will not include any unrealized gains or losses because held-to-maturity securities are valued at amortized cost, not at fair value. However, if management states that the debt investment will be sold in the short term and classifies them as trading, then the company values the trading securities at fair value and reports unrealized gains and losses on the income statement.

How can management know with certainty if they will hold or sell the investment and when it will be sold? This subjectivity can affect the financial statements. Consider Example 16.5. Because Phoneex Company classified the securities as trading, it reported a $8,000 loss in net income in 2018. However, if it had classified the securities as available for sale, then net income would not have been affected. Rather, the $8,000 would flow through other comprehensive income, where it is often overlooked by market participants. Alternatively, if these were debt securities classified as held to maturity, then Phoneex would not report a loss in the financial statements because they would be carried at amortized cost.

As another example, consider ***Citigroup Inc***. As of December 31, 2016, it had investments in securities classified as held-to-maturity debt securities with a carrying value of $45,667 million. This same portfolio had a fair value of $45,555 million. Thus, at some point in time, ***Citigroup*** experienced net unrealized losses of $112 million. However, because these securities were classified as held to maturity, ***Citigroup*** did not report these losses on the statement of comprehensive income. ***Citigroup*** also classified debt investments with a fair value of $299,033 million at December 31, 2016, as available for sale. During the year ended December 31, 2016, ***Citigroup*** recorded unrealized gains on investment securities of $108 million in other comprehensive income.[4]

Given the judgment and flexibility allowed under the accounting standards, it is prudent for financial statement users to carefully review the footnote disclosures related to debt investments and consider the financial statement implications of possible management changes in the classifications.

Transfers between Classifications

Management typically does not transfer securities from one portfolio classification (trading, available for sale, and held to maturity) to another. However, portfolio transfers may be implemented on occasion. All transfers between portfolios are accounted for at fair value on the date of the transfer to prevent managers from transferring securities to held to maturity to avoid fair value reporting.

Generally, any unrealized gains or losses are treated according to the rules associated with the portfolio to which the security is being transferred. In other words, if a company transfers a security into available for sale from held to maturity, then it reports the unrealized gains or losses in other comprehensive income.

[4]http://www.citigroup.com/citi/investor/quarterly/2016/ar15c_en.pdf

However, if the company is transferring from the trading portfolio, then no adjustment is necessary because the adjustment should have already occurred and been reported in net income. This treatment assumes that the transfer occurs at the end of the reporting period (annual or quarterly). For a transfer from available for sale to held to maturity, the company does not report the unrealized gain or loss at the time of transfer. Instead, it carries the unrealized gain or loss in accumulated other comprehensive income and amortizes the unrealized gain or loss to net income over the remaining life of the investment.

Exhibit 16.3 summarizes the accounting treatment for transfers of securities.

EXHIBIT 16.3 Accounting Treatment for Transfers of Securities

Transfer From	Transfer To	Unrealized Gain or Loss from Transfer at Fair Value
Available for sale	Trading	Recognize in net income.
Available for sale	Held to maturity	Unrealized gains and losses are not reported in income; they are carried in accumulated other comprehensive income and amortized to net income over the remaining life of the security.
Held to maturity	Trading	Recognize in net income.
Held to maturity	Available for sale	Recognize in other comprehensive income.
Trading	Held to maturity	Already recognized in net income; no adjustment is necessary.
Trading	Available for sale	Already recognized in net income; no adjustment is necessary.

Accounting for Debt Investments under IFRS

Similar to U.S. GAAP, debt investments may be measured at amortized cost, fair value with unrealized gains and losses reported in net income, or fair value with unrealized gains and losses reported in other comprehensive income under IFRS. However, the determination of which measure to use and when to use each measure differs under IFRS.

IFRS considers two tests to determine which measure to use: the *contractual cash flow characteristics test* and the *business model test*. The **contractual cash flow characteristics test** is passed if cash flows from the debt investment are solely payments of principal and interest on the outstanding principal balance. This test is referred to as the SPPI test (solely payments of principal and interest).

The **business model test** assesses management's intent in holding the investment. Management can intend to hold an investment to obtain cash flows for three reasons:

- Collecting contractual cash flows
- Selling the financial asset
- Both collecting contractual cash flows and selling the financial asset

If a debt investment passes the SPPI test and management's intent is to hold the asset to collect contractual cash flows, the investment is measured at amortized cost. If a debt investment passes the SPPI test and management's intent is to generate cash flows from the investment by both collecting contractual cash flows and selling the asset, the asset is measured at fair value with unrealized gains and losses reported in other comprehensive income. This treatment is similar to available-for-sale securities under U.S. GAAP. If managements intends to sell the debt investment or it does not pass the SPPI test, then the debt investment is measured at fair value with unrealized gains and losses reported in net income, similar to trading securities under U.S. GAAP. Exhibit 16.4 presents the measurement of debt investments under IFRS.

EXHIBIT 16.4 IFRS Measurement of Debt Investments and Comparison to U.S. GAAP

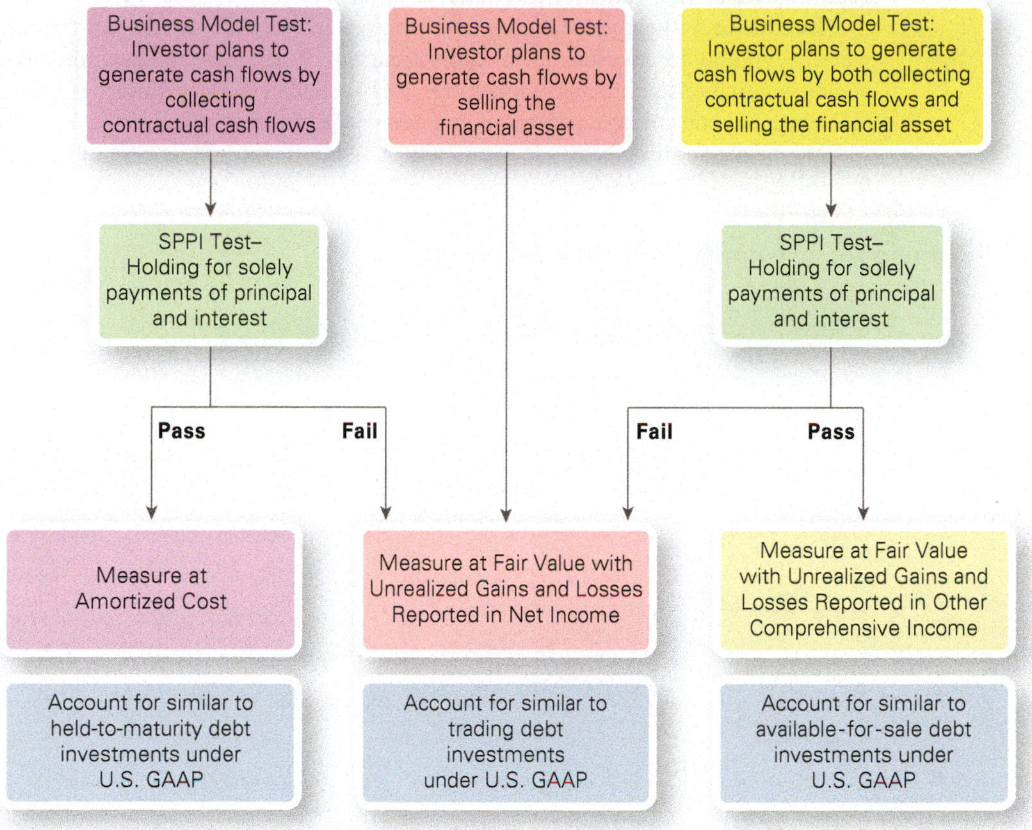

❸ Discuss and demonstrate accounting for investments in equity securities when the investor has no significant influence at initial recognition and subsequent to acquisition, including accounting for investments without readily determinable fair values.

Investments in Equity Securities: No Significant Influence

The appropriate accounting method for equity investments depends on the investor's level of influence over the investee company. There are three possible levels of influence:

1. **No significant influence.** The investor lacks the ability to participate in the decisions of the investee company.[5]
2. **Significant influence.** The investor company has the ability to exert influence over operating and financial policy decisions of the investee company even though it does not legally control the investee company, generally holding 20 to 50% of the investee's stock.
3. **Control.** Typically gained by an investor company holding more than 50% of the voting shares of the investee company.

Other factors that determine the level of influence that the investor can exert over the investee company include controlling membership on the investee's board of directors, interchanging management or technology, and interdependent inventory supply relationships.

We will first discuss the case in which the investor does not have significant influence followed by a discussion of accounting for investments in equity securities when the investor has

[5]For the relevant authoritative literature, see FASB ASC 321 – 10 – *Investments – Equity Securities – Overall* for U.S. GAAP and IASB, *International Financial Reporting Standard 9*, "Financial Instruments" (London, UK: International Accounting Standards Board, 2014).

significant influence but not legal control.[6] We must also consider whether there is a readily determinable market value for an equity security.

Exhibit 16.5 illustrates the key considerations in determining the appropriate method to use when accounting for investments in equity securities. When there is no significant influence, companies generally use fair value accounting. They use the equity method when there is significant influence and consolidation accounting applies when there is control.

We begin by discussing securities with no significant influence and readily determinable fair values.

EXHIBIT 16.5 Accounting for Investments in Equity Securities

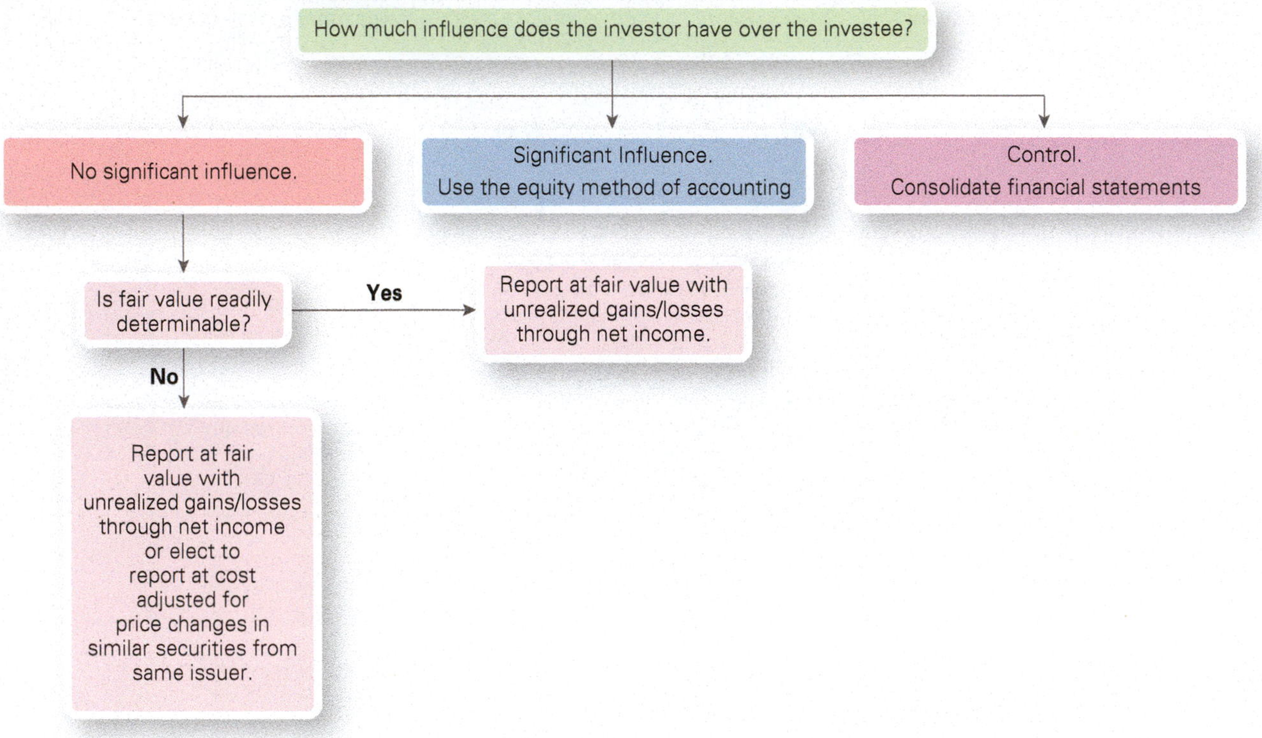

Equity Investments With No Significant Influence: Readily Determinable Fair Value

Companies report an equity investment with no significant influence and a readily determinable fair value at its fair value.Generally, an equity security has a readily determinable fair value if the sales price is currently available on a securities exchange that is registered with the SEC, or in the over-the-counter market, provided that those prices or quotations for the over-the-counter market are publicly reported by the National Association of Securities Dealers Automated Quotations systems or by OTC Markets Group Inc.[7] Each reporting period, the company revalues the investment to its current fair value and reports unrealized gains or losses in net income. The company also reports realized gains and losses in net income when it sells the securities. Both realized and unrealized gains and losses reported in earnings are classified as other income (expense) on the income statement. Any dividends received are reported as dividend income. Example 16.8 illustrates accounting for a portfolio of equity securities with readily determinable fair values.

---

[6]Companies use consolidation accounting for investments when the investor has legal control; this topic is covered in advanced accounting textbooks and courses.

[7]See ASC 321-10-20 for more detail.

EXAMPLE 16.8 Equity Securities with No Significant Influence and Readily Determinable Fair Values

PROBLEM: Easy as Pie, Incorporated purchased equity securities during 2018 and 2019. Easy as Pie does not have significant influence over the investees. The securities all have readily determinable fair values. It had not purchased any equity securities before this time and did not make any additional investments after its purchase of Security D. Information on the purchase, fair value, and selling price of the securities is presented in the following table.

Security	Purchase Date	Purchase Price	Fair Value – December 31, 2018	Fair Value – December 31, 2019	Date Sold	Selling Price
A	November 29, 2018	$500,000	$480,000	N/A	January 5, 2019	$470,000
B	December 10, 2018	120,000	125,000	N/A	January 21, 2019	124,000
C	December 5, 2019	54,000	N/A	$ 51,000	January 3, 2020	53,500
D	December 22, 2019	135,000	N/A	134,000	January 5, 2020	134,500

Prepare the journal entries to account for the events related to each investment. Reconcile the gains and losses reported in comprehensive income each year.

SOLUTION: Easy as Pie records the purchase of the 2018 investments (Securities A and B) as follows:

Account	November 29, 2018		December 10, 2018	
Equity Investments – Cost	500,000		120,000	
Cash		500,000		120,000

The total portfolio fair value as of December 31, 2018, is $605,000 ($480,000 + $125,000). The portfolio fair value decreased by $15,000 from the original purchase price of $620,000. Thus, Easy as Pie records an unrealized loss in net income and uses the fair value adjustment account to decrease the carrying value of the investment.

Account	December 31, 2018	
Unrealized Loss – Net Income	15,000	
Fair Value Adjustment – Equity Investments		15,000

After the fair value adjustment, the carrying value of the investments is $605,000 as the t-accounts illustrate:

	Equity Investments		+	Fair Value Adjustment – Equity Investments		
Balance, 12/31/17	0				0	
2018 entries	620,000				15,000	
Balance, 12/31/18	620,000				15,000	= $605,000

In January 2019, Easy as Pie records the sale of Securities A and B as follows:

Account	January 5, 2019		January 21, 2019	
Cash	470,000		124,000	
Realized Loss – Net Income	30,000			
Realized Gain – Net Income				4,000
Equity Investments – Cost		500,000		120,000

Continued

In December 2019, Easy as Pie records the purchase of Securities C and D.

Account	***December 5, 2019***		***December 22, 2019***	
Equity Investments – Cost	54,000		135,000	
Cash		54,000		135,000

On December 31, 2019, Easy as Pie must adjust the fair value adjustment account to properly reflect the fair value of the investments on the balance sheet. The fair value of the portfolio on December 31, 2019, is $185,000 ($51,000 + $134,000) and consists of Securities C and D. The cost of the portfolio is $189,000 ($54,000 + $135,000). We compute the adjustment as follows.

As of	**Fair Value (a)**	**Cost (b)**	**Fair Value Adjustment Account Balance Debit (Credit) (c) = (b) – (a)**
December 31, 2019	$185,000	$189,000	$ (4,000)
Existing balance in the fair value adjustment account (credit)			(15,000)
Amount of adjustment needed			$11,000

Easy as Pie will reduce the credit balance in the fair value adjustment account in this case because there is a $15,000 credit balance in the account, and it needs only a $4,000 credit balance. Consequently, it needs to debit the account by $11,000.

Easy as Pie debits the fair value adjustment account for $11,000 and recognizes a gain on the income statement for the same amount.

Account	***December 31, 2019***	
Fair Value Adjustment – Equity Investments	11,000	
Unrealized Gain – Net Income		11,000

After the fair value adjustment, the carrying value of the investments is $185,000 as the t-accounts illustrate:

	Equity Investments		+	**Fair Value Adjustment – Equity Investments**		
Balance, 12/31/17	0				0	
2018 entries	620,000				15,000	
Balance, 12/31/18	620,000				15,000	= 605,000
Sale		620,000				
Purchase	189,000					
Fair value Adjustment				11,000		
Balance, 12/31/19	189,000				4,000	= 185,000

In January 2020, Easy as Pie records the sale of the securities as follows:

Account	***January 3, 2020***		***January 5, 2020***	
Cash	53,500		134,500	
Realized Loss – Net Income	500		500	
Equity Investments – Cost		54,000		135,000

As of December 31, 2020, Easy as Pie does not hold any investments in equity securities, and thus the balance in the fair value adjustment account should be zero. Easy as Pie makes the following entry:

Account	***December 31, 2020***	
Fair Value Adjustment – Equity Investments	4,000	
Unrealized Gain – Net Income		4,000

The following tables reconcile the total gains and losses for the security. First, we compute the amount of total gains and losses that flowed through the gain and loss accounts:

	Reported in Net Income				
Date	**Unrealized Gain**	**Unrealized Loss**	**Realized Gain**	**Realized Loss**	**Total Effect on Comprehensive Income**
12/31/18: FV adjustment		$(15,000)			$(15,000)
2019 sale			$4,000	$(30,000)	(26,000)
12/31/19: FV adjustment	$11,000				11,000
2020 sale				(1,000)	(1,000)
12/31/20: FV adjustment	4,000				4,000
Totals	$15,000	$(15,000)	$4,000	$(31,000)	$(27,000)

Second, we compare the total gain(loss) to the difference between the purchase price and the selling prices for all of the securities:

Security	**Purchase Date**	**Purchase Price**	**Selling Price**	**Gain (Loss)**
A	November 29, 2018	$500,000	$470,000	$(30,000)
B	December 10, 2018	120,000	124,000	4,000
C	December 5, 2019	54,000	53,500	(500)
D	December 22, 2019	135,000	134,500	(500)
TOTAL		$809,000	$782,000	$(27,000)

The computations show that the total loss on Easy as Pie's investing activities was $(27,000).

Equity Investments With No Significant Influence: No Readily Determinable Fair Values

For certain equity investments with no significant influence, a readily determinable fair value is not available. Consider an investment in a private company—because the company is not publicly traded, no market price exists. Alternatively, a company could have more than one class of equity security available but only one class is publicly traded.

Generally, companies report no significant influence securities with no readily determinable fair values at estimated fair value with unrealized gains and losses in net income.[8] Realized gains and losses on disposal are also reported in net income. However, a company can elect, on a security-by-security basis, to report an equity security without a readily determinable fair value at cost with an adjustment for changes resulting from observable price changes for similar (or identical) securities of the same issuer. The amount of the adjustment should account for any differences in the two securities. The adjustment is reported in net income along with any realized gains and losses.

[8]Companies use inputs specified in Level II and Level III of the fair value hierarchy to estimate fair value for these investments. Chapter 2 provides a more in-depth discussion of the fair value hierarchy.

Example 16.9 provides an illustration of the election available for equity securities with no readily determinable fair value.

EXAMPLE 16.9

Equity Investments with No Significant Influence and No Readily Determinable Fair Value

PROBLEM: Tekky Corporation purchased 10,000 shares of preferred stock – Class A in Hui Zu, Ltd. on December 15 for $100,000 and sold it the following June 22 for $114,000. Tekky does not have significant influence over the investee, Hui Zu, Ltd. This class of preferred stock is not actively traded and it does not have a readily determinable fair value. However, Hui Zu, Ltd. has another issue of preferred stock (Class B) outstanding that is nearly identical to the stock that Tekky holds except that it is publicly traded. The price of the Class B stock increased 10% between December 15 and December 31.

Tekky chooses to use the exception provided in the authoritative literature to measure the investment at adjusted cost. What journal entries are required to record these transactions?

SOLUTION: Tekky records the purchase at cost as follows:

Account	***December 15, Current Year***	
Equity Investments	100,000	
Cash		100,000

At year-end, Tekky will adjust the equity investment in the Class A shares for the 10% observable price increase in the Class B stock.

Account	***December 31, Current Year***	
Fair Value Adjustment – Equity Investments	10,000	
Unrealized Gain – Net Income		10,000

When Tekky sells the investment during the following year, it recognizes the realized gain of $14,000 on the income statement computed as the difference between the $114,000 selling price and the $100,000 original cost. The entry to record the disposal of the investment follows:

Account	***June 22, Following Year***	
Cash	114,000	
Gain on Sale of Equity Investment		14,000
Equity Investments		100,000

As of December 31 of the following year, Tekky does not hold any investments in equity securities, and thus the balance in the fair value adjustment account should be zero. Tekky makes the following entry:

Account	***December 31, Following Year***	
Unrealized Loss – Net Income	10,000	
Fair Value Adjustment – Equity Investments		10,000

JUDGMENTS IN ACCOUNTING:
Equity Investments with No Significant Influence and No Readily Determinable Fair Values

Determining the measurement for investments in equity securities with no readily determinable fair value requires a great deal of judgment. If a company does not make the election to report the investment at adjusted cost, then the company must determine a fair value of an investment that does not have a readily determinable fair value. Doing so requires an estimation technique.

But even if the company makes the election, it still needs to make a variety of estimates. For example, is the other security of that issuer "similar" enough to the investment that the company holds? The authoritative literature does not indicate just how similar the two instruments have to be. The authoritative literature does say that the company should consider the different rights and obligations, such as voting rights, distribution rights and preferences, and conversion features of the securities. However, the standard setters do not provide any specific guidance on how many differences can exist between the security that the company holds as an investment and the comparison security.

Once a company does decide that the comparison security is similar to the investment, it then must make adjustments to the observable price change of the comparison security to account for differences such as voting rights and conversion features before applying that price change to the measurement of its investment.

Accounting for Equity Investments with No Significant Influence under IFRS

Unlike U.S. GAAP, IFRS does not distinguish between no significant influence investments with and without a readily determinable value. Accounting for equity investments can differ under U.S. GAAP and IFRS. Under IFRS, these investments are typically measured at fair value with unrealized gains and losses reported in net income similar to U.S. GAAP. However, under certain circumstances, a company can elect to report gains and losses in other comprehensive income, called fair value through other comprehensive income (FVOCI). If the company makes this election, then all gains and losses—both realized and unrealized—are reported in other comprehensive income. A company can make this election under two circumstances, specifically, when the equity investment is:

- Not held for trading
- Not part of contingent consideration in a business combination when it could possibly be given as additional payment on the purchase of a business after it is acquired

This election to designate an equity investment as FVOCI is irrevocable and is made on an investment-by-investment basis. Example 16.10 illustrates accounting for equity investments using the FVOCI under IFRS.

EXAMPLE 16.10

IFRS Accounting for Equity Investments – Fair Value through Other Comprehensive Income

PROBLEM: Dobigs Company, an IFRS reporter, purchased equity securities on November 29, 2018, for $25,000. Dobigs does not have significant influence in the investee and elects to report this investment at fair value through other comprehensive income. The fair value of the investment was $23,500 on December 31, 2018, and $26,000 on December 31, 2019. Dobigs sold the investment on January 22, 2020, for $26,250.

Prepare the journal entries to account for the events related to this investment.

SOLUTION: Dobigs records the purchase of the security:

Account	*November 29, 2018*	
Equity Investment – FVOCI	25,000	
Cash		25,000

Dobigs records the 2018 year-end fair value adjustment, reducing the equity investment – FVOCI account as follows:

Account	*December 31, 2018*	
Unrealized Loss – Other Comprehensive Income	1,500	
Equity Investment – FVOCI		1,500

Continued

Dobigs records the 2019 year-end fair value adjustment by increasing the investment account and reporting the gain in other comprehensive income.

Account	December 31, 2019	
Equity Investment – FVOCI	2,500	
Unrealized Gain – Other Comprehensive Income		2,500

On January 22, 2020, Dobigs records the disposal of the security, recording the realized gain in other comprehensive income.

Account	January 22, 2020	
Cash	26,250	
Equity Investment – FVOCI		26,000
Realized Gain – Other Comprehensive Income		250

Dividends on equity investments designated at FVOCI are normally reported in net income. However, dividends that represent a return of the cost of the investment are reported in OCI. Determining whether dividends represents a return of the cost of the investment is a matter of judgment. For example, an unusually large dividend could represent a return of the cost of the investment rather than a distribution of earnings.

4 Explain and illustrate accounting for investments in equity securities when the investor has significant influence over the investee company.

Investments in Equity Securities: Significant Influence

When an investor has significant influence over the investee but does not have control, companies use the *equity method* of accounting for the investment.[9] Significant influence is the power to participate in the financial and operating decisions of the company but not to control those policies. An investor is generally presumed to have significant influence at 20% or more ownership unless it can be clearly demonstrated that this is not the case.[10] Significant influence changes to control when ownership exceeds 50%.

Under the **equity method**, the investor recognizes the increases and decreases in the economic resources of the investee. The investor initially reports the investment account at cost and thereafter reports any events that affect the book value of the investee's retained earnings in the carrying value of its investment account and financial statements.

During 2016, ***Starbucks*** used the equity method to account for its 50% ownership of companies in China, India, Korea, and Taiwan and a 50% partnership with ***Pepsi-Cola Company*** in North America. If ***Starbucks***' equity investments in these companies were any larger than 50%, its influence would be considered a controlling interest rather than a significant influence as shown in Exhibit 16.6, and its accounting would change.

The Equity Method

When a company acquires an equity investment that provides significant influence over the investee company, it initially reports the investment at its cost. The investor company subsequently adjusts the investment's carrying amount for changes in the retained earnings of the investee company. The subsequent adjustments depend on whether:

- The book value of net assets of the investee *equals* its fair value at the date of the acquisition
- The book value of net assets of the investee *is different from* its fair value at the date of the acquisition.

A company's net assets are its equity, which is why this method is called the *equity method*.

[9]For the relevant authoritative literature for this topic, see FASB ASC 323-10, *Investments – Equity Method and Joint Ventures – Overall* for U.S. GAAP and IASC, *International Accounting Standard 28*, "Investments in Associates" (London, UK: International Accounting Standards Committee, 1989, Revised) for IFRS.

[10]For the relevant authoritative literature for this topic, see FASB ASC 323-10, *Investments – Equity Method and Joint Ventures – Overall* for U.S. GAAP and IASC, *International Accounting Standard 28*, "Investments in Associates," for IFRS, Paragraph 6.

Investee's Net Assets Equal Fair Value. A company's net assets increase when it earns net income and decrease when it declares dividends or incurs a net loss. So, the investor's investment account increases by its share of the investee's net income. If the investee has a net loss, then the investor's investment account decreases by its share of the net loss. The investor decreases the investment account by its share of the dividends declared by the investee company.[11]

Dividends reduce the investment account and are not recorded as income for several reasons:

1. Dividends received on investments accounted for under the equity method are a return *of* an investment, not a return *on* investment.
2. The decision to distribute investee dividends is influenced by the investor. As a result, this is not an objective transaction, and the investor should not recognize this event as income.
3. Because the investor recognizes its share of investee's net income or loss on the income statement, recognizing dividends as income would double count a portion of the investee's earnings on the investor's income statement.

When the book value of the net assets of the investment equals its fair value at acquisition, the increases and decreases to the investment account under the equity method are as follows.

Investment – Equity Method

Purchase Price	– Percent of Investee's Net Loss
+ Percent of Investee's Net Income	– Percent of Investee's Dividends Declared
= Ending Balance	

Example 16.11 illustrates the equity method when the book value of the investee's net assets equals their fair value.

EXAMPLE 16.11

Equity Method: Net Assets Equal Fair Value

PROBLEM: Krieger Krisp Donuts, Inc. acquired 40% of the voting common shares of Delevan Bakers Corporation on January 1, 2018, at a total cost of $2,535,000. At acquisition, the reported book value of Delevan Bakers' net assets equaled its fair value. This investment allows Krieger to exert significant influence over Delevan's operating and financing policies. At the end of 2018, Delevan reported $769,500 in net income and declared and paid $123,475 in dividends for the period. At the end of 2019, Delevan reported a net loss of $432,000. No dividends were declared in 2019. What journal entries should Krieger record related to its investment in Delevan Bakers? What is the amount of the investment in Delevan Bakers at December 31, 2018? At December 31, 2019?

SOLUTION: Krieger initially records the investment at cost as follows:

Account	***January 1, 2018***	
Investment in Delevan Bakers Corporation (Equity method)	2,535,000	
Cash		2,535,000

At the end of 2018, Krieger records its share of net income ($769,500 × 40% = $307,800) and declared dividends ($123,475 × 40% = $49,390) as follows.

	December 31, 2018	
Investment in Delevan Bakers Corporation (Equity method)	307,800	
Income from Investment		307,800

Continued

[11]If the investor pays more (or less) than the book value of the investee, then there are additional accounting considerations that we will discuss in a subsequent example.

Account	December 31, 2018	
Cash	49,390	
Investment in Delevan Bakers Corporation (Equity method)		49,390

At the end of 2019, Krieger records its share of net loss ($432,000 × 40%).

Account	December 31, 2019	
Loss on Investment	172,800	
Investment in Delevan Bakers Corporation (Equity method)		172,800

Notice in the following t-account that Krieger's investment in Delevan Bakers is $2,793,410 and $2,620,610 at the end of 2018 and 2019, respectively. The t-account for the equity method investment follows.

Investment in Delevan Bakers Corporation

	Debit	Credit	
1/1/18 Purchase Price	2,535,000		
40% of 2018 Net Income	307,800	49,390	40% of 2018 Dividends Declared
12/31/18 Balance	2,793,410		
		172,800	40% of 2019 Investee's Net Loss
12/31/19 Balance	2,620,610		

Investee's Net Assets Do Not Equal Fair Value. An investee's fair value often does not equal the reported book value of its net assets at the date of acquisition for a variety of reasons, including:

- Differences between the fair values and book values of assets such as inventory or property, plant, and equipment
- Unreported intangible assets such as brands that can be identified
- Unreported goodwill

The investor will make additional adjustments for any items that would affect net income. For example, consider the case when the book value of the investee's net assets are less than its fair value because the fair value of an investee's equipment is higher than its book value. The investee computes depreciation expense based on the equipment's book value. However, the purchase price is based on the equipment's fair value. In this case, the investor needs to adjust the income from the investment for additional depreciation expense on the difference between the equipment's fair value and its book value. Example 16.12 provides an illustration.

EXAMPLE 16.12 Equity Method: Net Assets Not Equal to Fair Value

PROBLEM: Krieger Krisp Donuts, Inc. acquired 40% of the voting common shares of Delevan Bakers Corporation on January 1, 2018, at a total cost of $2,785,000, when its fair value was $6,962,500. At acquisition, the reported book value of Delevan Bakers' net assets was $6,337,500. The difference between Delevan's fair value and the book value of its net assets is due to the fair value of equipment that is higher than its book value. The equipment has a 20-year remaining useful life. This investment allows Krieger to exert significant influence over the operating and financing policies of Delevan. At the end of 2018, Delevan reported $769,500 in net income and declared and paid $123,475 in dividends for the period. What journal entries should Krieger record related to its investment in Delevan Bakers? What is the amount of the investment in Delevan Bakers at December 31, 2018?

SOLUTION: Krieger initially records the investment at cost as follows:

Account	January 1, 2018	
Investment in Delevan Bakers Corporation (Equity method)	2,785,000	
Cash		2,785,000

At the end of 2018, Krieger records its share of net income (\$769,500 × 40% = \$307,800) and declared dividends (\$123,475 × 40% = \$49,390) as follows:

Account	December 31, 2018	
Investment in Delevan Bakers Corporation (Equity method)	307,800	
Income from Investment		307,800

Account	December 31, 2018	
Cash	49,390	
Investment in Delevan Bakers Corporation (Equity method)		49,390

The fair value of Delevan's net assets is \$625,000 higher than its book value (\$6,962,500 less \$6,337,500) because the fair value of its equipment is higher than its book value. Krieger adjusts its income for the investment by its share of the additional depreciation expense computed as follows:

(\$625,000 Difference/20-year Useful Life) × 40% Ownership = \$12,500

The additional depreciation expense reduces income from the investment and the investment. The journal entry is as follows:

Account	December 31, 2018	
Income from Investment	12,500	
Investment in Delevan Bakers Corporation (Equity method)		12,500

In the following t-account, notice that Krieger's investment in Delevan Bakery is \$3,030,910 at the end of 2018.

Investment – Equity Method

	Debit	Credit	
1/1/18 Purchase Price	2,785,000		
40% of 2018 Net Income	307,800	49,390	40% of 2018 Dividends Declared
		12,500	40% of Additional Depreciation Expense
12/31/18 Balance	3,030,910		

Exhibit 16.6 presents an excerpt from ***Starbucks Corporation's*** 2016 financial statement footnote on equity and cost investments. ***Starbucks*** uses the equity method for equity investments when the investor has significant influence over the investee company—and ***Starbucks'*** significant influence over its investee companies is evidenced by the levels of ownership ranging from 39.6% to 50% of the voting shares held. At October 2, 2016, ***Starbucks'*** investments accounted for under the equity method were about \$354.5 million, or about 2.5% of its \$14,329.5 million in total assets. ***Starbucks'*** income from these investments during fiscal year 2016 was about \$318.2 million, or about 7.6% of its operating income.

EXHIBIT 16.6 Accounting for Equity Investments, ***Starbucks Corporation,*** Financial Statements, October 2, 2016

NOTE 6: Equity and Cost Investments *(in millions)*

Equity Method Investments [Excerpt]

As of October 2, 2016, we had a 50% ownership interest in each of the following international equity method investees: President Starbucks Coffee (Shanghai); Starbucks Coffee Korea Co., Ltd.; President Starbucks Coffee Corporation (Taiwan) Company Limited; and Tata Starbucks Limited (India). These international entities operate licensed Starbucks® retail stores.

We also license the rights to produce and distribute Starbucks-branded products to our 50% owned joint venture, The North American Coffee Partnership with the Pepsi-Cola Company, which develops and distributes bottled Starbucks® beverages, including Frappuccino® coffee drinks, Starbucks Doubleshot® espresso drinks, Starbucks Refreshers® beverages, and Starbucks® Iced Espresso Classics.

Our share of income and losses from our equity method investments is included in income from equity investees on the consolidated statements of earnings. Also included in this line item is our proportionate share of gross profit resulting from coffee and other product sales to, and royalty and license fee revenues generated from, equity investees.

Source: Financial Statements from Starbucks Corporation's 2016 Annual Report. http://s21.q4cdn.com/369030626/files/doc_financials/2016/Annual/FY16-Annual-Report-on-Form-10-K.pdf

Exhibit 16.7 summarizes the accounting methods for equity investments under U.S. GAAP and IFRS.

EXHIBIT 16.7 Summary of Accounting Treatment for Equity Investments under U.S. GAAP and IFRS

	Investments in Equity Securities			
	No Significant Influence		**Significant Influence**	**Control**
	Fair Value Readily Determinable	**Fair Value Not Readily Determinable**	**With or without a Readily Determinable Fair Value.**	**With or without a Readily Determinable Fair Value**
U.S. GAAP	Fair value with unrealized gains/losses reported in net income.	Fair value with unrealized gains/losses reported in net income. Entities can also elect to report at cost adjusted for observable price changes in similar securities of the same entity.	Measured initially at cost and subsequently adjusted for the investor's share of income, dividends, and excess depreciation.	The investor reports consolidated financial statements.
IFRS	Fair value with unrealized gains/losses reported in net income. Entities can elect, under certain circumstances to report at fair value with unrealized gains/losses and realized gains/losses reported in other comprehensive income.		Measured initially at cost and subsequently adjusted for the investor's share of income, dividends, and excess depreciation.	The investor reports consolidated financial statements.

JUDGMENTS IN ACCOUNTING: For Equity Investments

When measuring an equity investment at fair value on the balance sheet, the investor typically holds less than 20% of the voting shares of the investee company. Conversely, when accounting for equity investments using the equity method, typically the investor holds less than a controlling share but 20% or more of the voting shares of the investee company.

Are these guidelines strict standards? No, the percentages are general guidelines—and the primary trigger to use the equity method is whether the investor can exert significant influence on the investee. Holding 20% or more of investee voting stock is presumed to be an indicator of influence but only in the absence of information to the contrary.[12] Thus, the decision as to whether the investor has significant influence is a matter of managerial judgment. Some indicators of significant influence include:

1. Controlling representation on the company's board of directors
2. Participation in policy-making processes, including participation in decisions about dividends or other distributions
3. Material transactions with the company
4. Interchange of managerial personnel
5. Provision of essential technical information[13]

Managers and auditors analyze and consider these indicators to determine the level of influence. For example, assume that an investor holds 25% of the voting stock of the investee corporation but was rejected controlling membership on the investee's board of directors. The investor likely does not have effective control over the investee. Now consider an investor holding only 15% of the voting stock of the investee corporation that has controlling membership on the investee's board of directors, is the major supplier or customer of the investee, and exchanges management with the investee. This investor likely possesses significant influence. Nonetheless, the degree of control is not always clear in practice.

Starbucks Corporation's 2016 financial statements provide strong evidence to justify its use of the equity method. Equity investments amount to 49% to 50% of the voting shares of investee companies. Further, Starbucks generates significant sales, royalty, and license fee revenues from its equity investees. Starbucks Corporation has also guaranteed the repayment of certain Japanese bank loans of its equity investee, Starbucks Japan.

The accounting method used can have a significant impact on the financial statements. An investor who does not have significant influence reports unrealized gains and losses through net income and reports the investment asset on the balance sheet at fair value. In contrast, an investor who does have significant influence will use the equity method and include its portion of the investee's income or loss in its income statement.

5 Explain and demonstrate the accounting for long-term notes receivable.

Long-Term Notes Receivable

As we discussed in Chapter 9, a note receivable is a formal, written promise to receive a fixed sum of money at a specified date (or dates) in the future with a stated interest rate. We now address **long-term notes receivable**, which are notes receivable with a maturity date longer than a year from the balance sheet date (or one operating cycle, if longer). Companies initially measure long-term notes receivable at the present value of future cash flows at the historical market rate of interest when issued. Subsequently, they report long-term notes receivable at amortized cost on the balance sheet. We begin with a discussion of notes with stated interest rates equal to the market rate and then move to notes with stated rates less than the market rate.

[12]For the relevant authoritative literature for this topic, see FASB ASC 323-10, *Investments – Equity Method and Joint Ventures – Overall* for U.S. GAAP and IASC, *International Accounting Standard 28*, "Investments in Associates," for IFRS, Paragraph 7.

[13]See FASB ASC 323-10-15-6 for a complete list.

Stated Interest Rate Equal to the Market Rate

When a note's interest rate is the same as the market rate, the face value of the note equals its present value, and periodic payments are computed using the time value of money techniques. After computing the periodic payments, an amortization table assists in the preparation of journal entries with columns for the date, the interest earned (effective interest), principal reduction, total payment, and the note balance. The computation for each column is presented in Exhibit 16.8.

EXHIBIT 16.8 Computations for Amortization Table When Stated Rate Equals Market Rate

Column	Computation	Impact on Journal Entry
Effective Interest	Beginning Note Balance × Market Interest Rate	Credit to interest revenue
Principal Reduction	Total Periodic Payment Received – Effective Interest	Credit to note receivable
Payment Received	Computed as the payment using time value of money techniques	Debit to cash
Note Balance	Beginning Balance – Principal Reduction	

Example 16.13 illustrates a note receivable with a stated rate equal to the market rate.

EXAMPLE 16.13 Note Amortization and Journal Entries

PROBLEM: AN, Inc. accepts a $300,000, 12% note from Paulino Products on January 1, 2018, and lends money to Paulino. AN will receive periodic, equal payments every 6 months, beginning June 30. The loan matures in 3 years (on December 31, 2020), and the interest rate equals the market rate of 12%. AN is a calendar-year firm and prepares financial statements annually. Prepare the amortization table and the journal entries for the first year.

SOLUTION: Using Excel, the periodic payment is $61,009.

	N	I/Y	PV	PMT	FV	Excel Formula
Given	6	6.00%	(300,000)			
Solve for PV				**61,009**		= PMT(0.06,6,–300000,0)

The amortization table is as follows:

Date	Effective Interest (6%) (a) = Prior (d) × 6%	Principal Reduction (b) = (c) – (a)	Payment Received (c)	Note Balance (d) = Prior (d) – (b)
At inception				$300,000
June 30, 2018	$18,000	$43,009	$61,009	256,991
December 31, 2018	15,419	45,590	61,009	211,401
June 30, 2019	12,684	48,325	61,009	163,076
December 31, 2019	9,785	51,224	61,009	111,852
June 30, 2020	6,711	54,298	61,009	57,554
December 31, 2020	3,455*	57,554*	61,009	0

*Adjusted due to rounding errors.

During 2018, AN will first record the receipt of the note receivable:

Account	January 1, 2018	
Notes Receivable	300,000	
Cash		300,000

On June 30 and December 31, AN records the cash received, interest earned, and reduction in the note receivable balance:

Account	June 30, 2018		December 31, 2018	
Cash	61,009		61,009	
Interest Revenue		18,000		15,419
Note Receivable		43,009		45,590

A company may also initially recognize notes receivable with interest payment dates that do not coincide with a company's fiscal year-end. When this occurs, the company needs to accrue any interest receivable before preparing financial statements as shown in Example 16.14.

EXAMPLE 16.14 Note Receivable with Accrued Interest

PROBLEM: AN, Inc. accepts a $300,000, 12% note from Paulino Products on February 1, 2018, and lends money to Paulino. AN will receive periodic, equal payments every six months, beginning July 31. The loan matures in 3 years (on January 31, 2021) and the interest rate equals the market rate of 12%. AN is a calendar-year firm and prepares quarterly financial statements. Prepare the journal entries from February 1 through July 31, 2018.

SOLUTION: The amortization table is the same as we computed in Example 16.13, except that the dates change.

Date	Effective Interest (6%) (a) = Prior (d) × 6%	Principal Reduction (b) = (c) − (a)	Payment Received (c)	Note Balance (d) = Prior (d) − (b)
At inception				$300,000
July 31, 2018	$18,000	$43,009	$61,009	$256,991
January 31, 2019	15,419	45,590	61,009	211,401
July 31, 2019	12,684	48,325	61,009	163,076
January 31, 2020	9,785	51,224	61,009	111,852
July 31, 2020	6,711	54,298	61,009	57,554
January 31, 2021	3,455*	57,554*	61,009	0

*Adjusted due to rounding errors.

During 2018, AN first records the receipt of the note receivable:

Account	February 1, 2018	
Notes Receivable	300,000	
Cash		300,000

Because AN prepares quarterly financial statements on March 31 and June 30, it accrues interest on the note receivable. As of March 31, it has earned interest for the first 2 months of the note. The semi-annual interest earned for the first 6-month interest period is $18,000, or

Continued

$3,000 per month ($18,000 / 6 months). Thus, we compute the accrued interest for 2 months ended March 31 as $6,000 ($3,000 × 2). As of June 30, AN has earned 3 more months of interest from March 31, or $9,000 ($3,000 per month × 3 months). The journal entries to accrue interest for the first 2 quarters of 2018 follow:

Account	March 31, 2018		June 30, 2018	
Interest Receivable	6,000		9,000	
Interest Revenue		6,000		9,000

An additional 1-month's interest is earned as of the July 31 payment date. The entry to record the first note payment follows. The first note payment records the collection of $18,000 of interest and $43,009 of the principal.

Account	July 31, 2018	
Cash	61,009	
Interest Receivable ($6,000 + $9,000)		15,000
Interest Revenue		3,000
Notes Receivable		43,009

Stated Interest Rate Less than the Market Rate

When there is no interest rate stated (a non-interest-bearing note) or the stated interest rate is less than the market interest rate, the face value of a note receivable will not equal its present value.

Because the stated rate is less than the market rate, the difference between the note's face value and its present value is a discount on the note. The note's present value is therefore the value of its future cash flows discounted at the market rate of interest.[14] The discount represents deferred interest revenue to be earned over the life of the note. Companies amortize the discount to interest revenue over the loan term using the effective interest method.

There are two primary effects of the discount amortization:

1. Increases the interest revenue so that the corporation's effective rate of return is brought up to the higher market rate.
2. Reduces the discount and increases the carrying value of the note receivable until the carrying value is brought up to its face value at the maturity date.

The amortization table for notes with a stated rate less than the market rate starts with the computation of the present value of the note. The table includes columns for the date, the interest received, the effective interest, the discount amortization and the note balance. The computation for each column is presented in Exhibit 16.9.

EXHIBIT 16.9 Computations for Amortization Table When Stated Rate Is Less than the Market Rate

Column	Computation	Impact on Journal Entry
Interest Received	Face Value of the Note × Stated Interest Rate	Debit to cash
Effective Interest	Beginning Note Balance × Historical Market Interest Rate	Credit to interest revenue
Discount Amortized	Effective Interest − Interest Received	Debit to discount on notes receivable
Note Balance	Beginning Balance + Discount Amortized	

[14]If a company receives the note in exchange for goods or services, then we assume that the note's present value is the fair value of the goods or services provided if the fair value is determinable.

The cash interest received each period is the face value of the note multiplied by the stated interest rate. The effective interest revenue is computed each period as the beginning carrying value of the note multiplied by the historical market rate. The amount of discount that is amortized each period into interest revenue is the difference between the interest received and the computed interest revenue (effective interest). Finally, the change in the carrying value of the note receivable is the amount of the discount amortization.

Example 16.15 illustrates accounting for a non-interest-bearing note receivable.

EXAMPLE 16.15 Non-Interest-Bearing Note Receivable

PROBLEM: Amsterdam Sports Company accepts a $1,000,000 note on January 1 issued by NJ Max Corporation, a major real estate developer. Specifically, NJ Max will issue a non-interest-bearing note due in 7 years in exchange for cash. The current market rate is 10%. Interest is compounded annually. Amsterdam is a calendar-year firm that prepares financial statements annually. Prepare the amortization table for the note and the journal entries for the first year.

SOLUTION: The first step is to compute the present value of the note:

	N	I/Y	PV	PMT	FV	Excel Formula
Given	7	10.00%		0	1,000,000	
Solve for PV			**(513,158)**			=PV(0.1,7,0,1000000)

The discount amount is then $486,842 ($1,000,000 less $513,158).

The amortization table follows.

Date	Interest Received (0%) (a)	Effective Interest (10%) (b) = Prior (d) × 10%	Discount Amortized (c) = (b) − (a)	Note Balance (d) = Prior (d) + (c)
At inception	-	-	-	$ 513,158
Year 1	0	$ 51,316	$ 51,316	564,474
Year 2	0	56,447	56,447	620,921
Year 3	0	62,092	62,092	683,013
Year 4	0	68,301	68,301	751,314
Year 5	0	75,131	75,131	826,445
Year 6	0	82,645	82,645	909,090
Year 7	0	90,910*	90,910*	1,000,000
Total	0	$486,842	$486,842	

*Adjusted due to rounding errors.

The journal entry to record the note receivable and discount is as follows:

Account	***January 1***	
Notes Receivable	1,000,000	
Discount on Notes Receivable		486,842
Cash		513,158

At this point, the carrying value of the note receivable on the balance sheet is $513,158, which is the balance in the note receivable account ($1,000,000) less the balance in the discount account ($486,842). Note that in the case of the investment, the discount is a contra-asset account.

Continued

The entry to record the discount amortization for Year 1 follows.

Account	December 31	
Discount on Notes Receivable	51,316	
Interest Revenue		51,316

After the first period's amortization, the carrying value of the note receivable on the balance sheet is $564,474, which is the balance in the note receivable account ($1,000,000) less the balance in the discount account ($435,526).

Example 16.16 illustrates a note receivable that is interest bearing, but the stated rate is below the market rate. We also include accrued interest revenue.

EXAMPLE 16.16 Note Receivable: Stated Rate Less than the Market Rate

PROBLEM: Helsinki Sports Company, a calendar-year company, accepts a $1,000,000, 8% note on August 15, 2018, issued by JN Min Corporation, a major real estate developer. In exchange, Helsinski lends JN Min money. Specifically, JN Min will issue a note due in 3 years. The current market rate is 12%. Interest is paid quarterly, beginning on November 15. Helsinki prepares quarterly financial statements and is a calendar-year company. Prepare the amortization table for the note and the journal entries for 2018.

SOLUTION: The first step is to compute the present value of the note:

	N	I/Y	PV	PMT	FV	Excel Formula
Given	12	3.00%		20,000	1,000,000	
Solve for PV			(900,460)			=PV(0.03,12,20000,1000000)

The amortization table follows.

Date	Interest Received (2%) (a)	Effective Interest (3%) (b) = Prior (d) × 13%	Discount Amortized (c) = (b) − (a)	Note Balance (d) = Prior (d) + (c)
At inception				$ 900,460
November 15, 2018	$20,000	$27,014	$7,014	907,474
February 15, 2019	20,000	27,224	7,224	914,698
May 15, 2019	20,000	27,441	7,441	922,139
August 15, 2019	20,000	27,664	7,664	929,803
November 15, 2019	20,000	27,894	7,894	937,697
February 15, 2020	20,000	28,131	8,131	945,828
May 15, 2020	20,000	28,375	8,375	954,203
August 15, 2020	20,000	28,626	8,626	962,829
November 15, 2020	20,000	28,885	8,885	971,714
February 15, 2021	20,000	29,151	9,151	980,865
May 15, 2021	20,000	29,426	9,426	990,291
August 15, 2021	20,000	29,709	9,709	1,000,000

The journal entry to record the note receivable and discount is as follows:

Account	August 15, 2018	
Notes Receivable	1,000,000	
Discount on Notes Receivable		99,540
Cash		900,460

At this point, the carrying value of the note receivable on the balance sheet is $900,460, which is the balance in the note receivable account ($1,000,000) less the balance in the discount account ($99,540).

On September 30, 2018, Helsinki prepares quarterly financial statements. Thus, it accrues interest from August 15 through September 30. This is one and one-half months or one-half of the quarter. The total interest for the first period is $27,014 per the amortization table. Helsinki accrues interest revenue for half of that amount (for half the quarter, or $27,014/2) and amortizes half of the discount ($7,014/2). It records interest receivable of $10,000, which is half of the anticipated interest receipt.

Account	September 30, 2018	
Interest Receivable	10,000	
Discount on Notes Receivable	3,507	
Interest Revenue		13,507

On November 15, 2018, Helsinki receives a $20,000 interest payment. At this point, the company must accrue the additional interest for one-half of the quarter and amortize the other half of the discount. It will also recognize the collection of the interest receivable accrued on September 30. Therefore, the company records the following journal entry.

Account	November 15, 2018	
Cash	20,000	
Discount on Notes Receivable	3,507	
Interest Receivable		10,000
Interest Revenue		13,507

Finally, on December 31, 2018, Helsinki accrues interest for one-half the second period. Again, this is a period of one and one-half months from November 15 to December 31. This accrual is based on the amortization table; the company will recognize interest revenue of $13,612 for one-half of the quarter ($27,224/2) and amortize one-half of the discount of $3,612 ($7,224/2). The required journal entry on December 31 follows:

Account	December 31, 2018	
Interest Receivable	10,000	
Discount on Notes Receivable	3,612	
Interest Revenue		13,612

IFRS Accounting for Note Receivable

Under IFRS, a company is likely to classify and account for a note receivable at amortized cost. Similar to determining the accounting for a debt investment at amortized cost, the note receivable must meet two criteria: (1) be held within a business model whose objective is to hold it to collect contractual cash flows and (2) satisfy the SPPI contractual cash flow characteristics test.

6 Discuss and illustrate the fair value option in accounting for investments in financial assets.

The Fair Value Option for Reporting Investments

Under the fair value option, companies can elect to value most types of financial assets and obligations at fair value.[15] The fair value option improves financial reporting by enabling entities to offset volatility in reported earnings. Consider a company that has an asset and a liability whose fair values are related to one another. If the liability is reported at fair value but the asset is not, then the company will report an earnings stream that is more volatile than if both the asset and liability (whose fair values are negatively correlated) are reported at fair value. Thus, in this case, the fair value option allows management to report both the asset and liability at fair value.[16]

A company can choose the fair value option for some assets without choosing it for all assets. Typically, the company must elect the fair value option at the time it acquires the asset. After a company elects the fair value option, it is typically irrevocable.

When electing the fair value option at initial recognition, the company reports the asset on the balance sheet at fair value and reports all unrealized gains and losses in net income. Trading debt securities and equity investments without significant influence are also reported at fair value with gains and losses reported in net income, so the fair value option does not change the reporting for these investments.[17] The accounting for held-to-maturity and available-for-sale debt investments as well as equity investments with significant influence will change substantially if a company elects the fair value option. For example, instead of using the equity method for an investment for which the investor has significant influence, the company will adjust the asset account by making an entry to a fair value adjustment account and then use this account to increase or decrease the investment account on the balance sheet. Example 16.17 demonstrates accounting under the fair value option.

EXAMPLE 16.17

Fair Value Option

PROBLEM: On May 2 of the current year, Alex Associates acquired an equity investment in a start-up company, Ayden Enterprises, for $200,000. Alex has significant influence over Ayden Enterprises. Alex elected to report its investment in Ayden using the fair value option. Due to Ayden Enterprises' tremendous growth opportunities and the efforts it put into development activities, the fair value of Alex's investment at the end of the year increased to $475,000. Prepare the journal entry to record the investment using the fair value option.

SOLUTION: Alex Associates records the investment on May 2 at cost:

Account	***May 2, Current Year***	
Equity Investment in Ayden Enterprises	200,000	
Cash		200,000

Alex records the fair value adjustment on December 31 as follows:

Account	***December 31, Current Year***	
Fair Value Adjustment – Fair Value Option	275,000	
Unrealized Gain on Equity Investment – Fair Value Option (Net income)		275,000

[15]Most financial instruments are eligible for the fair value option under U.S. GAAP. Paragraphs 4 and 5 of FASB ASC 825-10-15 outline the specific requirements. For example, financial instruments that are not eligible for the fair value option include pension assets and liabilities, obligations related to deferred compensation arrangements, financial assets and liabilities related to leasing transactions, and investments in subsidiaries or variable interest entities that the company is required to consolidate.

[16]For the relevant authoritative literature, see FASB ASC 825-10, *Financial Instruments – Overall* for U.S. GAAP and IASC, *International Accounting Standard 39*, "Financial Instruments: Recognition and Measurement" (London, UK: International Accounting Standards Committee, Revised) for IFRS.

[17]Some equity investments without significant influence are held at adjusted cost because the company elects to do so. The company would not make both this election and the fair value option election.

Fair Value Option: IFRS

Similar to U.S. GAAP, IFRS allows a company to use the fair value option with the exception of investments under the equity method. IFRS additionally stipulates that a company can use the fair value option for financial assets when doing so results in more relevant information because either:

- A company has a documented risk management or investment strategy that prescribes it will manage and evaluate its performance on the fair values and changes in fair values of its financial assets and/or liabilities.
- The fair value option ensures consistently measuring liabilities or assets and gains or losses on them on the same bases. That is, the fair value option eliminates or significantly reduces accounting mismatches from measuring liabilities or assets (and the gains and losses on them) on different bases.

7 Detail required disclosures for investments in financial assets.

Disclosures for Investments in Financial Assets

In general, companies provide qualitative and quantitative disclosures of investments in financial assets. Qualitative disclosures include the nature and extent of risks arising from financial assets. For each significant category of investments in financial assets, companies disclose a detailed list, description, and carrying value of each significant type of investing asset, including classification as trading, available-for-sale, or held-to-maturity debt securities. Major security types are based on the nature and risks of the security.

Next we discuss specific requirements for equity investments when the investor does not have the ability to exercise influence over the investee company. Then, we discuss disclosures related to equity method investments, notes receivable, and fair values. Disclosures under IFRS are similar except where noted.

Debt Securities

A company discloses major security types based on the nature and risks of the security. For investment in debt securities, a company considers the following factors in determining whether to disclose more detail by security type:

- Business sector
- Age of any debt
- Geographic concentration
- Credit quality
- Economic characteristic

We discuss additional disclosures related to the type of debt investment next.

Held-to-Maturity Debt Securities. For securities classified as held to maturity, companies disclose the following by major security type:

- Amortized cost basis
- Aggregate fair value
- Total unrealized gains (losses) for securities with net gains (losses) in accumulated other comprehensive income
- Information about the maturity of debt securities
- Any impairment loss and where reported

For any sales of or transfers from securities classified as held to maturity, a company discloses all of the following:

- Net carrying amount of the sold or transferred security
- Net gain or loss in accumulated other comprehensive income for any derivative that hedged the forecasted acquisition of the held-to-maturity security
- Related realized or unrealized gain or loss
- Circumstances leading to the decision to sell or transfer the security.

Available-for-Sale Debt Securities. For securities classified as available for sale, companies disclose the following by major security type:

- Amortized cost basis
- Aggregate fair value
- Total unrealized holding gains (losses)
- Net carrying amount
- Information about the maturity of debt securities

Related to earnings during the period, a company also discloses the following items:

- Proceeds from sales of available-for-sale securities and the gross realized gains and gross realized losses that have been included in earnings as a result of those sales
- Basis on which the cost of a security sold or the amount reclassified out of accumulated other comprehensive income into earnings was determined (that is, specific identification, average cost, or other method used)
- Gross gains and gross losses included in earnings from transfers of securities from the available-for-sale category into the trading category
- Amount of the net unrealized holding gain or loss on available-for-sale securities for the period that has been included in accumulated other comprehensive income and the amount of gains and losses reclassified out of accumulated other comprehensive income into earnings for the period

Exhibit 16.10 provides ***Adobe Systems'*** quantitative disclosures of its available-for-sale debt investments of $3,749 million, or about 30% of its total assets, at December 2, 2016. There were both unrealized gains and losses on the debt securities in 2016. ***Adobe Systems*** reported all unrealized gains and losses on its available-for-sale debt securities in other comprehensive income.

Trading Debt Securities. A company discloses the portion of unrealized gains and losses for the period that relates to trading securities still held at the reporting date.

EXHIBIT 16.10 Disclosure of Investment Securities, ***Adobe Systems Incorporated,*** Financial Statements, December 2, 2016

NOTE 3: Cash, Cash Equivalents and Short-term Investments [Excerpt]

We classify all of our cash equivalents and short-term investments as "available-for-sale." In general, these investments are free of trading restrictions. We carry these investments at fair value, based on quoted market prices or other readily available market information. Unrealized gains and losses, net of taxes, are included in accumulated other comprehensive income (loss), which is reflected as a separate component of stockholders' equity in our Consolidated Balance Sheets. Gains and losses are recognized when realized in our Consolidated Statements of Income. When we have determined that an other-than-temporary decline in fair value has occurred, the amount of the decline that is related to a credit loss is recognized in income. Gains and losses are determined using the specific identification method.

. . . short-term investments consisted of the following as of December 2, 2016 (in thousands):

	Amortized Cost	Unrealized Gains	Unrealized Losses	Estimated Fair Value
Short-term fixed income securities:				
Asset-backed securities	$ 111,009	$ 95	($ 190)	$ 110,914
Corporate bonds and commercial paper	2,464,769	3,135	(9,554)	2,458,350
Municipal securities	134,710	37	(525)	134,222
U.S. agency securities	39,538	42	—	39,580
U.S. Treasury securities	1,008,195	194	(1,470)	1,006,919
Total short-term investments	$3,758,221	$3,503	($11,739)	$3,749,985

. . . short-term investments consisted of the following as of November 27, 2015 (in thousands):

	Amortized Cost	Unrealized Gains	Unrealized Losses	Estimated Fair Value
Short-term fixed income securities:				
Asset backed securities	$ 83,449	$ 11	($ 146)	$ 83,314
Corporate bonds and commercial paper	1,890,253	2,273	(5,612)	1,886,914
Foreign government securities	1,276	—	(8)	1,268
Municipal securities	137,280	101	(49)	137,332
U.S. agency securities	130,397	85	(14)	130,468
U.S. Treasury securities	873,400	101	(1,273)	872,228
Total short-term investments	$3,116,055	$2,571	($7,102)	$3,111,524

***Source*:** Financial Statements from Adobe Systems Incorporated 2016 Annual Report. http://wwwimages.adobe.com/content/dam/Adobe/en/investor-relations/PDFs/ADBE-10K-FY16-FINAL-CERTIFIED.PDF

Equity Securities with No Significant Influence

A company reports the fair value of equity securities with no significant influence on the balance sheet and discloses the portion of unrealized gains and losses on equity securities held at the reporting date. The portion of unrealized gains and losses for the period related to equity securities still held at the reporting date is computed as net gains and losses recognized during the period less net gains or losses on equity securities sold during the period.

Equity Method Investments

For investments accounted for under the equity method, companies disclose:

- The name of the investee and percentage of ownership
- Investments held with less than 20% ownership that are accounted for under the equity method and why
- Investments held with greater than 20% ownership that are not accounted for under the equity method and why
- The difference, if any, between the carrying value of the investment and the amount of underlying equity in net assets
- The fair value for those investments with a quoted market price
- Whether the conversion of convertible securities of the investee would have significant effect on the reported income from the investment

Refer to Exhibit 16.6 for selected equity method disclosures for ***Starbucks***, including the ownership percentage held for each equity method investment.

Disclosures of Equity Method Investments: IFRS. IFRS additionally requires disclosure of summarized financial information of the investee, including the amounts of total assets, total liabilities, revenues, and net income (loss).

Notes Receivable

Disclosures related to notes receivable are similar to those for accounts receivable, including a summary of significant accounting policies relating to notes receivable, receivables by customer group and significant customers, and information on an allowance for uncollectible accounts.

Fair Value Measurement Disclosures

For investments in financial assets reported at fair value, companies disclose information to enable users to assess the fair value estimates and reasonableness of assumptions made in determining fair values. Companies report securities based on a fair value hierarchy that reflects the reliability of significant inputs used in making fair value measurements. Level 1 is the most reliable estimates of inputs used, and Level 3 fair value input estimates require the most judgment:

- **Level 1.** Fair values are determined based on quoted prices in active markets for identical assets.
- **Level 2.** Fair values are determined using significant other observable inputs. Other observable input could include securities dealer quotes or prices based on similar assets in other markets.
- **Level 3.** Fair values are determined using significant unobservable inputs. For instance, fair values in this group could be estimated based on pricing models such as discounted cash flows.

Fair Value Disclosures

For financial assets not reported at fair values, companies provide disclosures of their fair values, including the methods used and assumptions made.

Exhibit 16.11 contains an excerpt from ***Coca-Cola Company's*** fair value measurement disclosures in 2016. Note its description of each of the three levels in the hierarchy. At December 31, 2016, 27.3% of ***Coca-Cola's*** fair value securities were classified in Level 1 for which the fair value estimate was based on a quoted price in an active market. ***Coca-Cola's*** holdings of Level 3 securities for which there is no active market amounted to 2.1% of its investments.

EXHIBIT 16.11 Fair Value Measurement Disclosure, ***Coca-Cola Company,*** Financial Statements, December 31, 2016

[Excerpts from Annual Report]

NOTE 16: Fair Value Measurements

Accounting principles generally accepted in the United States define fair value as the exchange price that would be received for an asset or paid to transfer a liability (an exit price) in the principal or most advantageous market for the asset or liability in an orderly transaction between market participants at the measurement date. Additionally, inputs used to measure fair value are prioritized based on a three-level hierarchy. This hierarchy requires entities to maximize the use of observable inputs and minimize the use of unobservable inputs. The three levels of inputs used to measure fair value are as follows:

- Level 1 — Quoted prices in active markets for identical assets or liabilities.
- Level 2 — Observable inputs other than quoted prices included in Level 1. We value assets and liabilities included in this level using dealer and broker quotations, certain pricing models, bid prices, quoted prices for similar assets and liabilities in active markets, or other inputs that are observable or can be corroborated by observable market data.
- Level 3 — Unobservable inputs that are supported by little or no market activity and that are significant to the fair value of the assets or liabilities. This includes certain pricing models, discounted cash flow methodologies and similar techniques that use significant unobservable inputs.

Source: Financial Statements from Coca-Cola Company's 2016 Annual Report. http://www.coca-colacompany.com/our-company/company-reports

Interview

THOMAS ANGELL PARTNER, WITHUMSMITH + BROWN »

Thomas Angell

Thomas Angell is an audit partner in the Financial Services Group at WithumSmith + Brown's New York office. Tom has more than 30 years' experience providing audit, tax, and consulting services to private equity and venture capital funds and investment advisors on all aspects of private equity and venture capital transactions.

1 What specific steps should an auditor use to determine whether an investment in debt securities is properly classified as trading, held to maturity, or available for sale?

Auditors must first determine (1) the "type" of investment held by the reporting entity and (2) the reporting entity's ability and intent to hold the investment to maturity. Then they must determine whether past and present security classifications corroborate the reporting entity's intended classification, follow up on any securities classification changes, and verify that held-to-maturity securities will in fact be kept until the end of the debt term. Furthermore, a reporting entity cannot classify debt securities as held to maturity if certain financial or market conditions indicate management's inability or intent to hold the investment to maturity (liquidity demands, availability, or yield of alternative investments, etc.).

2 What qualitative factors determine whether an investment asset should be considered impaired?

Some common qualitative factors of impairment include situations when fair value is significantly below cost; the decline in fair value can be attributed to adverse conditions related to the security or specific industry or geographic conditions; the decline in fair value has existed for an extended period of time; a rating agency has downgraded a debt security's rating; the security issuer's financial condition has deteriorated; scheduled interest payments on debt securities have not been made; or equity dividends have been reduced or eliminated.

3 How do fair value measurements help a financial statement user to assess an entity's future operating performance and cash flows?

FASB's ASC 820, *Fair Value Measurement and Disclosure*, provides a uniform framework for measuring fair value and assists financial statement users in making informed decisions about asset and liability values. For publicly traded securities, determining fair value is easier than for illiquid securities when fair value measurement is based on forward-looking assumptions of company growth and risk. For financial statement users, fair value provides a better measure of an entity's true value than historical cost. It shows the current value of the entity's assets and liabilities and helps predict future cash flows based on current values.

4 How effective is the fair value hierarchy disclosure in assessing the reliability of the inputs used in determining fair value?

The recently adopted three-level fair value hierarchy and the required detailed financial statement disclosures provide greater transparency and comparability of fair value measurements and disclosures among other reporting entities. For example, there is enhanced transparency into valuation assumptions such as expected growth rates, trends in profitability, future cash flow requirements, and potential risk factors that allows financial statement users to assess the future operating performance and cash flows of an entity.

5 What critical issues face the accounting profession from the expanded use of fair value measurements?

The more fair value measurement is used in financial reporting, the greater the accounting profession's risk, especially relating to illiquid investments and the increased use of unobservable inputs in determining fair value. Unobservable inputs reflect the reporting entity's own asset pricing assumptions. Examples include choice of discount rate, EBITDA multiple, and weighted average cost of capital. Fair value reporting requires a company to report significant swings in asset and liability values from one period to the next. In 2008–2010, the U.S. capital market experienced significant illiquidity and volatility, creating challenging conditions for fair value assessments. Many financial services companies were adversely affected by the new fair value measurement standard and had to significantly write down impaired assets. Some people even argue that the implementation of fair value accounting was a major contributor to the 2008 financial crisis.

Discussion Questions

1. Equity securities may not always have a readily determinable fair value. How are equity securities measured if fair values are not readily determinable?
2. How would the following items be classified in the fair value hierarchy?
   a. Asset retirement obligations
   b. Equity securities without readily determinable fair values

FINANCIAL STATEMENT ANALYSIS

Investments in Debt Securities and Equity Securities with No Significant Influence

Given management's choices to purchase debt and equity investments and its ability to choose how to classify the debt investment securities, understanding a company's investment securities is an important area when analyzing financial statements. For debt securities, the accounting depends on management's intent. Assessing a company's portfolio of held-to-maturity, trading, and available-for-sale debt securities is the starting point for such an analysis.

When a company records its debt or equity investments at fair value, the balance sheet is up-to-date with the most current values. However, the estimates and judgments involved in determining fair values make this area challenging to analyze. Understanding the models used to estimate fair values and the assumptions required is especially critical.

To analyze investment securities, begin by doing the following:

- Identify the types of investments.
- Determine the amount of debt investments in the firm's portfolio: held-to-maturity, trading, and available-for sale securities.
- Identify whether the firm has any investment securities reported at fair value (no significant influence equity investments, trading debt securities, available-for-sale debt securities, or investments accounted for under the fair value option).
- Evaluate the footnote disclosure of the fair value hierarchy of investments.
- Assess the types and amount of investments in each level in the hierarchy.
- Evaluate the reasonableness of valuation methods used.
- Examine any assumptions and estimates used in valuation.
- Determine the effect of changes in fair value on net income and other comprehensive income. Consider the effects of the portfolio classification on net income.

The types of investments a company holds vary by industry. Many manufacturers and retailers hold investments. Given the nature of the industries, few actively trade investments. On the other hand, financial service companies, such as banks and insurance companies, more commonly hold trading portfolios. Therefore, the net income of a financial services company can vary more in line with debt and equity markets than other types of companies.

An example of financial statement analysis of investment securities is provided in Example 16.18.

EXAMPLE 16.18 Financial Statement Analysis of Investment Securities

PROBLEM: Use the following information with Exhibit 16.10 to analyze ***Adobe Systems'*** investment securities.

At or for the Year Ended ($ thousands)	December 2, 2016	November 27, 2015
Total assets	$12,707,114	$11,726,472
Net income	1,168,782	629,551

Financial Statement Analysis, continued

CONSOLIDATED STATEMENTS OF COMPREHENSIVE INCOME

	Year Ended		
(thousands)	**December 2, 2016**	**November 27, 2015**	**November 28, 2014**
Net income	$1,168,782	$629,551	$268,395
Other comprehensive income (loss), net of taxes:			
Available-for-sale securities:			
Unrealized gains/losses on available-for-sale securities	(1,618)	(9,226)	2,315
Reclassification adjustment for recognized gains/losses on available-for-sale securities	(1,895)	(2,955)	(3,928)
Net increase (decrease) from available-for-sale securities	(3,513)	(12,181)	(1,613)
Derivatives designated as hedging instruments:			
Unrealized gains/losses on derivative instruments	35,199	29,795	41,993
Reclassification adjustment for recognized gains/losses on derivative instruments	(16,425)	(55,535)	(18,705)
Net increase (decrease) from derivatives designated as hedging instruments	18,774	(25,740)	23,288
Foreign currency translation adjustments	(19,783)	(123,065)	(75,872)
Other comprehensive income (loss), net of taxes	(4,522)	(160,986)	(54,197)
Total comprehensive income, net of taxes	$1,164,260	$468,565	$214,198

Source: Financial Statements from Adobe Systems Incorporated 2016 Annual Report. http://www.adobe.com/content/dam/Adobe/en/investor-relations/PDFs/ADBE-10K-FY16-FINAL-CERTIFIED.PDF

Address the following questions:

1. What types of investments does ***Adobe Systems*** hold in 2016 and 2015? What percentage of total assets do its investments compose? Use fair value.
2. How are ***Adobe Systems'*** investments reported on the balance sheet? Which investment securities does ***Adobe Systems*** report at fair value? What is the difference between fair value and cost?
3. Determine the effect of changes in fair value on net income and other comprehensive income. If unrealized gains and losses on available-for-sale securities were reported in net income rather than other comprehensive income, what would be the effect on net income?

SOLUTION:

1. From Exhibit 16.10, ***Adobe Systems*** held $3,749,985 thousand and $3,111,524 thousand of short-term investments at the end of 2016 and 2015, respectively. From the captions, these are debt investments. ***Adobe*** values these investments at fair value. In fiscal 2016 and 2015, the ***Adobe Systems'*** investments are a percentage of total assets of 29.5% ($3,749,985 / $12,707,114) and 26.5% ($3,111,524 / $11,726,472), respectively.

Financial Statement Analysis, continued

2. ***Adobe Systems*** reported its available-for-sale debt securities at fair value. At the end of 2016 and 2015, the amortized cost of the debt investments was higher than their fair value. Thus, the company had net unrealized losses on these debt investments. The difference between amortized cost and fair value is ($8,236,000) and ($4,531,000) in 2016 and 2015, respectively.

Total short-term investments	Amortized Cost	(in thousands) Estimated Fair Value	Difference
December 2, 2016	$3,758,221	$3,749,985	($8,236)
November 27, 2015	$3,116,055	$3,111,524	($4,531)

3. The Statement of Comprehensive Income indicates that ***Adobe Systems*** had $1,618 thousand of net unrealized losses in 2016 and $9,226 thousand of net unrealized losses in 2015 on available-for-sale securities reported in other comprehensive income. From the statement of comprehensive income, $1,895 thousand of losses and $2,995 thousand of losses were realized and reported in net income in 2016 and 2015, respectively. If ***Adobe Systems*** had reported the unrealized losses on available-for-sale securities in net income, net income would have been $1,167,164 thousand ($1,168,782 thousand net income less unrealized losses of $1,618 thousand), or about 0.1% lower in 2016. If ***Adobe Systems*** had reported the unrealized losses on available-for-sale securities in net income, net income would have been $620,325 thousand ($629,551 thousand net income minus unrealized losses of $9,226 thousand), or about 1.5% lower in 2015.

Summary by Learning Objectives

In the following, we summarize the main points by learning objective. Throughout the chapter, we discuss the accounting and reporting of U.S. GAAP and IFRS side-by-side. The following table also highlights the major similarities and differences between the standards.

1 Describe debt and equity investments, the two main types of investment securities that companies hold, and the key issues in accounting for them, including cost and fair value accounting.

Summary	Similarities and Differences between U.S. GAAP and IFRS
A debt investment is an investment in another company's bonds. An equity investment is an investment in another company's stock. Accounting at cost or fair value involves a trade-off between the two fundamental qualitative characteristics in the conceptual framework: relevance and faithful representation.	Similar under U.S. GAAP and IFRS.

Summary by Learning Objectives, continued

2 Describe and illustrate accounting for investments in debt securities—including held-to-maturity, trading, and available-for-sale securities—at initial recognition and subsequent to acquisition.

Summary	Similarities and Differences between U.S. GAAP and IFRS
Companies classify investments into three categories based on their intent in holding the security: • Held to maturity: debt securities that the company plans to hold to maturity (has both positive intent and ability to hold until maturity). These investments are reported at amortized cost on the balance sheet. Interest income is recorded using the effective interest rate method. • Trading securities: debt securities that a company plans to hold short term. They are reported at fair value on the balance sheet. All unrealized gains or losses are reported in net income. • Available for sale: debt securities that a company plans neither to hold to maturity nor to trade. They are reported at fair value on the balance sheet. All unrealized gains or losses are reported in other comprehensive income.	➤ Under IFRS, companies classify debt investments using two tests: 1. Contractual cash flow characteristics test–passed if cash flows from the debt investment are solely payments of principal and interest (SPPI) on the outstanding principal balance. 2. Business model test–based on how the company plans to generate cash flows from the investment: • collect contractual cash flows • sell the financial asset • both collect contractual cash flows and sell the financial asset. Debt investments are measured at • Amortized cost when the company holds to collect contractual cash flows and the SPPI test is passed. • Fair value with unrealized gains and losses reported in net income when the company holds to sell. • Fair value with unrealized gains and losses reported in other comprehensive income when the company holds to collect contractual cash flows and to sell. The SPPI test also must be passed.

3 Discuss and demonstrate accounting for investments in equity securities when the investor has no significant influence at initial recognition and subsequent to acquisition, including accounting for investments without readily determinable fair values.

Summary	Similarities and Differences between U.S. GAAP and IFRS
Equity investments in which a company does not have significant influence—typically ownership less than 20%—are generally reported at fair value on the balance sheet. All unrealized gains or losses are reported in net income. When an equity investment does not have a readily determinable fair value, it is still reported at fair value, although the company can elect to report it at cost adjusted for observable price changes in similar securities of the same issuer. Changes in fair value are taken to net income.	➤ Under IFRS, equity investments are typically measured at fair value with unrealized gains and losses reported in net income similar to U.S. GAAP. Under certain circumstances, a company can elect to report unrealized and realized gains and losses in other comprehensive income, called fair value through other comprehensive income (FVOCI). A company can make this election when the equity instrument is: • Not held for trading • Not part of contingent consideration in a business combination when it could possibly be given as additional payment on the purchase of a business after it is acquired.

4 Explain and illustrate accounting for investments in equity securities when the investor has significant influence over the investee company.

Summary	Similarities and Differences between U.S. GAAP and IFRS
Equity investments in which a company has significant influence are accounted for using the equity method. Generally, these are investments in which a company holds between 20% and 50% of equity. Equity investments with significant influence are initially reported at cost. The investor subsequently adjusts the carrying amount of the investment for changes in the net assets of the investee company. The investment is increased by the company's share of the investee's net income. If the investee has a net loss, then the investor's investment account is decreased by its share of the net loss. The investment account is decreased by dividends declared by the investee company.	Similar under U.S. GAAP and IFRS.

Summary by Learning Objectives, continued

5 Explain and demonstrate the accounting for long-term notes receivable.

Summary	Similarities and Differences between U.S. GAAP and IFRS
Long-term notes receivable are reported at the present value of their future cash flows using the historical market rate of interest when issued. Subsequently, a note receivable is reported at amortized cost with any discount or premium amortized to interest revenue.	➤ Similar under U.S. GAAP and IFRS because a note receivable is likely to be classified and accounted for at amortized cost under IFRS. However the note receivable must meet two criteria: (1) be held within a business model whose objective is to hold it to collect contractual cash flows and (2) meet the SPPI contractual cash flow characteristics test.

6 Discuss and illustrate the fair value option in accounting for investments in financial assets.

Summary	Similarities and Differences between U.S. GAAP and IFRS
Companies have the option to value most types of financial assets at fair value, which is referred to as the fair value option. A company can choose the fair value option for some assets without choosing it for all assets. Typically, the fair value option must be chosen at the time the asset is acquired. If the fair value option is used, the asset is reported on the balance sheet at fair value and all unrealized gains and losses are reported in net income.	➤ Similar to U.S. GAAP except that IFRS places additional conditions under which a company can use the fair value option for financial assets. Specifically, it can be used for financial assets when doing so results in more relevant information. IFRS does not allow the fair value option for equity method investments.

7 Detail required disclosures for investments in financial assets.

Summary	Similarities and Differences between U.S. GAAP and IFRS
Companies provide qualitative and quantitative disclosures of investments in financial assets. Qualitative disclosures include the nature and extent of risks arising from financial assets such as credit risk, liquidity risk, and market risk. For each significant category of investment securities, companies disclose a detailed list, description, and carrying value of each significant type of investment in financial assets, including classification as trading, available for sale, held to maturity, no significant influence, and significant influence. Unrealized holding gains and losses on available-for-sale securities included in other comprehensive income are reported. Unrealized gains and losses on trading securities included in net income are reported.	Similar under U.S. GAAP and IFRS.
Disclosure for equity-method investments include the name of the investee and percentage of ownership; disclosure of investments held with ownership less (more) than 20% that are (not) accounted for under the equity method and why; the difference, if any, between the carrying value of the investment and the amount of underlying equity in net assets; the fair value for those investments with a quoted market price; whether the conversion of convertible securities of the investee would have significant effect on the reported income from the investment. For investments measured at fair value, companies disclose three levels to allow users to assess the fair value estimates and reasonableness of assumptions made in determining fair values. • Level 1: Fair values are determined based on quoted prices in active markets for identical assets. • Level 2: Fair values are determined using significant other observable inputs. Other observable inputs could include securities dealer quotes or prices based on similar assets in other markets. • Level 3: Fair values are determined using significant unobservable inputs. For instance, fair values in this group could be estimated based on pricing models such as discounted cash flows. Companies must disclose fair values of those investments in financial assets *not* reported at fair values on the balance sheet.	➤ Under IFRS, companies must also disclose financial information of the investee including its total assets, total liabilities, revenue, and net income (loss).

MyLab Accounting

Go to **http://www.pearson.com/mylab/accounting** for the following Questions, Multiple-Choice Questions, Brief Exercises, Exercises, and Problems. They are available with immediate grading, explanations of correct and incorrect answers, and interactive media that acts as your own online tutor.

16 Investments in Financial Assets

Questions

1 **Q16-1.** Are debt investments classified as current or non-current investments? Explain.

1 **Q16-2.** Is reporting an investment at its cost considered relevant? Explain.

1 **Q16-3.** Is the fair value of an investment subjective? Explain.

2 **Q16-4.** What categories can managers use to classify debt investments?

3 **Q16-5.** How does a company account for equity investments in which it has significant influence?

2 3 **Q16-6.** Do entities report unrealized gains and losses on fair value adjustments to both debt and equity security investments in earnings? Explain.

3 **Q16-7.** What categories can managers use to classify equity investments?

4 **Q16-8.** When is the equity method of accounting for investments required?

6 **Q16-9.** Does the fair value option enable firms to offset earnings volatility in financial reporting? Explain.

6 **Q16-10.** Can companies apply the fair value option to all financial instruments? Explain.

7 **Q16-11.** What is the fair value hierarchy for investment securities?

7 **Q16-12.** Do companies generally disclose the amounts of debt investment by classification: held to maturity, trading, or available for sale? Explain.

A **Q16-13.** How do companies report impairment losses on debt investments measured at amortized cost?

A **Q16-14.** How do companies report impairment losses on equity investments?

A **Q16-15.** Is there a difference in how companies report impairment losses on debt investments under IFRS compared to U.S. GAAP?

A **Q16-16.** Is there a difference in how companies report impairment losses on equity investments under U.S. GAAP and IFRS?

A **Q16-17.** Are companies required to assess whether their equity investments are impaired? Explain.

Multiple-Choice Questions

2 **MC16-1.** Deutsch Imports has three securities in its available-for-sale debt investment portfolio. Information about these securities is as follows:

		Market Value	
Security	**Amortized Cost**	**12/31/Year 1**	**12/31/Year 2**
NCB	$78,000	$ 93,600	$100,000
TRR	$ 17,000	$120,000	0
Enson	$58,500	$ 53,300	$ 50,700

TRR was sold in Year 2 for $127,400.

Which of the following statements is correct?

i. On its 12/31/Year 2 balance sheet, Deutsch should report the NCB debt investment at its fair value of $100,000.
ii. On its 12/31/Year 2 balance sheet, Deutsch should report an unrealized holding gain on the NCB debt investment of $22,000 in stockholders' equity.
iii. On its income statement for the year ending December 31, year 2, Deutsch should report an unrealized holding gain on the NCB debt investment of $22,000.

a. I only is correct.
b. I and II only are correct.
c. I and III only are correct.
d. None of the listed answers is correct.

2 **MC16-2.** The following data pertains to Tyne Co.'s investments in marketable debt securities:

	Amortized Cost	Market Value 12/31/Y2	12/31/Y1
Trading	$150,000	$155,000	$100,000
Available-for-sale	150,000	130,000	120,000

What amount should Tyne report as net unrealized loss on available-for-sale marketable debt securities at December 31, year 2, in accumulated other comprehensive income on the balance sheet?

a. $0 b. $10,000 c. $15,000 d. $20,000

2 **MC16-3.** Merlin Enterprises sold the following debt investment on September 30, year 2:

	Amortized Cost	Market Value 12/31/Y1	9/30/Y2
Beard Inc.	$67,000	$59,000	$71,000

What is the amount of the realized gain or loss on Merlin's Year 2 income statement, assuming that the investment in Beard Inc. is classified as a trading debt security?

a. $0 b. $(8,000) c. $4,000 d. $12,000

2 **MC16-4.** Merlin Enterprises sold the following debt investment on September 30, Year 2:

	Amortized Cost	Market Value 12/31/Y1	9/30/Y2
Beard Inc.	$67,000	$59,000	$71,000

What is the amount of the realized gain or loss on Merlin's Year 2 income statement, assuming that the investment in Beard Inc. is classified as an available-for-sale debt security?

a. $0 b. $(8,000) c. $4,000 d. $12,000

2 **MC16-5.** Money for Nothing Enterprises ("MNE") held the following available-for-sale debt securities during year 2:

	Amortized Cost	Market Value 12/31/Y1	Sales Price	Market Value 12/31/Y2
Alpha Corp.	$50,000	$53,000	$57,000	—
Beta Corp.	$35,000	$30,000		$38,000
Omega Corp.	$21,000	$27,000		$24,000

What will MNE report as unrealized gain on available-for-sale debt securities on its Year 2 statement of comprehensive income (ignore taxes)?

a. $2,000 b. $3,000 c. $6,000 d. $8,000

2 **MC16-6.** Money for Nothing Enterprises ("MNE") held the following available-for-sale debt securities during Year 2:

	Amortized Cost	Market Value 12/31/Y1	Sales Price	Market Value 12/31/Y2
Alpha Corp.	$50,000	$53,000	$57,000	—
Beta Corp.	$35,000	$30,000		$38,000
Omega Corp.	$21,000	$27,000		$24,000

What will MNE report as accumulated other comprehensive income on its 12/31/Y2 balance sheet (ignore taxes)?

a. $2,000 b. $3,000 c. $6,000 d. $8,000

4 **MC16-7.** On January 2, year 1, Kean Co. purchased a 30% interest in Pod Co. for $250,000. On this date, Pod's stockholders' equity was $500,000. The carrying amounts of Pod's identifiable net assets approximated their fair values, except for land, whose fair value exceeded its carrying amount by $200,000. Pod reported net income of $100,000 for year 1, and paid no dividends. Kean accounts for this investment using the equity method.

In its December 31, Year 1, balance sheet, what amount should Kean report as investment in subsidiary?

a. $210,000 b. $220,000 c. $270,000 d. $280,000

Brief Exercises

2 **BE16-1. Debt Investments, Held to Maturity.** Sills Products acquired $2,960,000 face value, 5% bonds as a held-to-maturity investment on January 1 of the current year when the market rate of interest was 10%. Interest is paid annually each December 31. Sills purchased the bonds, which mature in 6 years, for $2,315,421. Sills amortizes the discount using the effective interest method. The fair value of the bonds at the end of the year is $2,185,455. Prepare the journal entries required on the date of acquisition and at the end of the first year after acquisition.

2 **BE16-2. Debt Investments, Available for Sale.** Kuban Company acquired $3,500,000 face value, 8% bonds as an available-for-sale investment on January 1 of the current year when the market rate of interest was 10%. Interest is paid annually each December 31. Kuban purchased the bonds, which mature in 12 years, for $3,023,042. Kuban amortizes the discount using the effective interest rate method. The fair value of the bonds at the end of the year is $3,000,000. Prepare the journal entries required on the date of acquisition and at the end of the first year after acquisition.

2 **BE16-3. Debt Investments, Trading.** Using the information provided in BE16-2, prepare the entry to record the fair value adjustment if Kuban classified this investment as a trading security.

2 **BE16-4. Debt Investments, IFRS.** Gills Products, an IFRS reporter, acquired $2,960,000 face value, 5% bonds on January 1 of the current year when the market rate of interest was 10%. Gills plans to hold the bonds to generate cash flows by collecting contractual cash flows only, and it passes the SPPI test. Interest is paid annually each December 31. Gills purchased the bonds, which mature in 6 years, for $2,315,421. Gills amortizes the discount using the effective interest method. The fair value of the bonds at the end of the year is $2,185,455. Prepare the journal entries required on the date of acquisition and at the end of the first year after acquisition.

2 **BE16-5. Debt Investments, IFRS.** Ruban Company, an IFRS reporter, acquired $3,500,000 face value, 8% bonds on January 1 of the current year when the market rate of interest was 10%. Ruban plans to hold the bonds to generate cash flows by collecting contractual cash flows but could sell them if needed, and it passes the SPPI test. Interest is paid annually each December 31. Ruban purchased the bonds, which mature in 12 years, for $3,023,042. Ruban amortizes the discount using the effective interest rate method. The fair value of the bonds at the end of the year is $3,000,000. Prepare the journal entries required on the date of acquisition and at the end of the first year after acquisition.

2 **BE16-6. Debt Investments, IFRS.** Using the information provided in BE16-5, prepare the entry to record the fair value adjustment if Ruban plans to hold the bonds to generate cash flows by selling the bonds.

3 **BE16-7. Equity Investments, Readily Determinable Fair Value.** Turner Tires, Inc. acquired 40,000 shares of Fenwick Corporation stock at a price of $35 per share during 2016. This investment does not allow Turner to participate in the decision making of Fenwick, and the company therefore does not have the ability to exert significant influence over the investee company. The market value of the shares at December 31, 2016, is $41 per share. Prepare the journal entries required on the date of acquisition and at the end of the year.

3 **BE16-8. Equity Investments, Readily Determinable Fair Value, IFRS.** Using the information provided in BE16-7, prepare the entries assuming that Turner Tires, Inc. is an IFRS reporter and elects to report these securities at fair value through other comprehensive income. Turner is not holding the investment for trading, nor is it part of contingent consideration in a business combination. Prepare the journal entries required on the date of acquisition and at the end of the year.

3 **BE16-9. Equity Investments, Readily Determinable Fair Value, IFRS.** Using the information provided in BE16-7, prepare the entries assuming that Turner Tires, Inc. is an IFRS reporter. Turner plans to trade the securities. Prepare the journal entries required on the date of acquisition and at the end of the year.

3 **BE16-10. Equity-Investments, Readily Determinable Fair Value with Partial Disposal of Shares, IFRS.** Prepare the journal entry needed to record the partial sale of the investment acquired in BE16-9. Assume that Turner sold 12,800 of the Fenwick shares for $47 per share in 2017 and the fair value of the remaining shares is $41 per share on December 31, 2017. Prepare the journal entry on December 31, 2017.

4 **BE16-11. Equity Investments, Equity Method.** On January 1, Jefferson Company acquired 25% of the outstanding voting shares of Tremont Corporation at a cost of $1,340,000 by acquiring 20,000 of the total 80,000 outstanding shares at a cost of $67 per share. During the year, Tremont reported $875,000 in net income and declared and paid $3.75 per share dividends. At acquisition, Tremont's market value equaled the book value of its net assets. Prepare the journal entries required to record these events assuming that Jefferson uses the equity method to account for its investment in Tremont.

4 **BE16-12. Equity Investments, Equity Method.** On January 1, Newman acquired a 30% interest in the common shares of MultiGram Entertainment at a cost of $4,295,000. During the year, MultiGram reported a net loss of $630,000 and paid no dividends. At acquisition, MultiGram's market value equaled the book value of its net assets. Prepare the journal entries required to record these events assuming that Newman uses the equity method to account for its investment in MultiGram.

5 **BE16-13. Notes Receivable.** Natale Enterprises, a major real estate developer, recently accepted a $10,000,000, 5-year, 2% note receivable in exchange for products sold. Interest is paid annually. The current market rate of interest is 6%. The note is not publicly traded. Prepare the journal entry to record the sale. Ignore cost of goods sold.

5 **BE16-14. Notes Receivable.** Aaron Anatole accepted a $250,000, 4-year, non-interest-bearing note receivable upon a sale. The current market rate of interest is 8%. The note is not publicly traded. Prepare the journal entry to record the sale. Ignore cost of goods sold.

6 **BE16-15. Debt Investments Classified as Held to Maturity, Fair Value Option.** Thornwood Consultants, Ltd. adopted the fair value option for a recent acquisition of debt investment securities that were originally classified as held to maturity. Thornwood acquired bonds of Wicker Enterprises at a cost of $1,100,000. The year-end fair value of the debt held by Thornwood is $1,300,000. Prepare the journal entries on the date of acquisition and at year-end to adjust Thornwood's investments to fair value.

7 **BE16-16. Disclosures, Fair Value Hierarchy.** Fill in the blanks in the following statements:

a. Level 1: Fair values are determined based on ____________ for identical assets.

b. Level 2: Fair values are determined using ____________. Other observable inputs could include ____________ based on similar assets in other markets.

c. Level 3: Fair values are determined using ____________. For instance, fair values in this group could be estimated based on ____________, such as discounted cash flows.

A **BE16-17. Debt Investments, Impairments.** For each debt investment in the following table, compute the impairment loss, if any, and determine whether the loss is reported in net income. All of the investments were purchased in the current year. Assume that the investor is not expected to sell the investments prior to full recovery of the decline in fair value except for Investment d.

	U.S. GAAP Classification	Significant Increase in Credit Risk?	12-Month Default Rate	Lifetime Default Rate	Carrying Value	Fair Value	Present Value of Future Cash Flows	Impairment Loss	Loss Reported in Net Income (NI) or Other Comprehensive Income (OCI)?
a.	Held to maturity	Yes	2%	10%	$10,000	$ 9,000	$ 9,300	________	________
b.	Trading	No	3	15	10,000	9,000	9,300	________	________
c.	Available for sale	No	1	2	10,000	11,000	10,300	________	________
d.	Available for sale	Yes	1	8	10,000	9,000	9,300	________	________

A **BE16-18. Debt Investments, Impairments, IFRS.** For each debt investment in BE16-17, compute the impairment loss, if any, and determine whether the loss is reported in net income or other comprehensive income under IFRS. The available-for-sale investments are classified as fair value through other comprehensive income investments under IFRS.

A **BE16-19. Debt Investments, Impairments.** For each debt investment in the following table, compute the impairment loss, if any, and determine whether the loss is reported in net income. Assume that the investor is not expected to sell the investments prior to full recovery of the decline in fair value.

	Classification	Carrying Value	Fair Value	Present Value of Future Cash Flows	Impairment Loss	Loss Reported in Net Income (NI) or OCI?
a.	Trading	$11,000	$ 10,300	$9,000	______	______
b.	Available for sale	11,000	8,000	11,000	______	______
c.	Available for sale	11,000	6,000	9,000	______	______

Exercises

2 **E16-1. Debt Investments, Held to Maturity.** The Davis Group acquired $4,500,000 par value, 4%, 20-year bonds on their date of issue, January 1 of the current year. The market rate at the time of issue was 6%, and interest is paid annually on December 31. Davis will use the effective interest rate method to account for this investment. Davis intends to hold the investment until the bonds mature, and has the ability to do so.

Required »

a. Determine the purchase price of the investment in bonds.
b. Prepare the journal entry to record the acquisition of the bond investment.
c. Prepare the journal entry to record the interest income for the first year.

2 **E16-2. Debt Investments, Available for Sale.** John Quinn Associates acquired $7,550,000 par value, 6%, 20-year bonds on their date of issue, January 1 of the current year. The market rate at the time of issue is 10%, and interest is paid semiannually on June 30 and December 31. Quinn uses the effective interest rate method to account for this investment. It does not intend to hold the investment until maturity, nor will it actively trade the bonds. The fair value of the bonds at the end of the year of acquisition is $5,197,500.

Required »

a. Determine the purchase price of the investment in bonds.
b. Prepare the journal entry to record the acquisition of the bond investment.
c. Prepare the journal entries to record the interest income for the first year.
d. Prepare the journal entry required to adjust the investment's carrying amount to fair value at year-end, if necessary.

2 **E16-3. Debt Investments, Available for Sale.** Using the information provided in E16-2, prepare the fair value adjustment journal entries at the end of the second and third years after the acquisition of the investment assuming that the fair value of the bonds is equal to $5,100,000 at the end of Year 2 and $4,905,750 at the end of Year 3. Prepare the amortization table for six semi-annual interest payments.

3 **E16-4. Equity-Investments, Fair Value is Readily Determinable.** Barney Equipment Corporation acquired the following equity investments at the beginning of Year 1. Barney does not have significant influence over the investees. Both companies are publicly traded.

Description	Boris Company	Monterey Group
Number of shares	10,550	8,355
Market price per share	× $42	× $87
Share acquisition price	$443,100	$726,885

Share prices at the end of Years 1 and 2 follow.

Fair Value	Boris Company	Monterey Group
End of Year 1	$48	$78
End of Year 2	$43	$83

Required »

a. Prepare the journal entry to record the acquisition of the investments.
b. Prepare the journal entry to record the end of Year 1 fair value adjustment.
c. Assume that Barney sells 5,000 Boris Company shares for $50 per share at the beginning of Year 2. Prepare the journal entry required to record the sale. Barney does not correct the fair value adjustment account at this time.
d. Prepare the journal entry to record the end of Year 2 fair value adjustment.

3 **E16-5. Equity-Investments, Fair Value Is Readily Determinable, IFRS.** Using the same information from E16-4, assume that Barney Equipment Corporation is an IFRS reporter and the company would like to elect to report these investments at fair value through other comprehensive income if it qualifies for this treatment. Barney is not holding the investment for trading, nor is it part of contingent consideration in a business combination.

3 **E16-6. Equity-Investments, Fair Value Is Readily Determinable.** Armonico Capital Partners, Ltd. acquired the following equity investments at the beginning of Year 1. Armonico does not have significant influence over the investees.

Description	Finelli Brothers	MBW Company
Number of shares	15,500	20,000
Market price per share	× $25	× $18
Share acquisition price	$387,500	$360,000

Share prices at the end of Years 1 and 2 follow.

Fair Value	Finelli Brothers	MBW Company
End of Year 1	$19	$22
End of Year 2	23	28

Required »

a. Prepare the journal entry to record the acquisition of the investments.
b. Prepare the journal entry to record the end of Year 1 fair value adjustment.
c. Assume that Armonico sells 15,000 MBW Company shares for $16 per share at the beginning of Year 2. Prepare the journal entry required to record the sale. Armonico does not correct the fair value adjustment account at this time.
d. Prepare the journal entry to record the end of Year 2 fair value adjustment.
e. What is the effect of these investments on earnings in Years 1 and 2?

3 **E16-7. Equity-Investments, Fair Value Is Not Readily Determinable.** Using the information provided in E16-6, satisfy the following requirements assuming that the equity securities held by Armonico Capital do not have a readily determinable fair value because neither company is publicly traded. Armonico elects to carry both securities at cost and to adjust the cost basis for changes in observable price changes for similar securities of the same investee. Assume that both companies have Class B common shares that are publicly traded and are similar to the securities held by Armonico. The market price of the Class B shares increased by 5% and 8% for Finelli and MBW, respectively.

Required »

a. Prepare the journal entry to record the acquisition of the investments.
b. Prepare the journal entry to record the end of Year 1 fair value adjustment.
c. Assume that Armonico sells 15,000 MBW Company shares for $16 per share at the beginning of Year 2 to a private investor. Prepare the journal entry required to record the sale. Armonico does not adjust the fair value adjustment account at this time.
d. Prepare the journal entry to record the sale of the remaining shares in the total portfolio for $496,500 to a private investor in at the end of Year 2.
e. Prepare a table that compares the income effects over the 2-year period of the two methods (fair value through net income and adjusted cost).

2 3 **E16-8. Debt and Equity Investments, Available-for-Sale Debt and Equity with Fair Values Readily Determinable.** Greenburg Company reported the following investment activity occurring at January 1 of the current year. Greenburg does not have significant influence over the investees.

Description	Amount Paid	Portfolio
Investment in bonds ($5,600,000 par value, 7% coupon, annual interest paid on December 31, 15 years to maturity, 9% effective yield)	$4,697,203	Held to maturity
Investment in publicly traded common stock (100,000 shares, $33 per share acquisition price)	3,300,000	
Investment in publicly traded preferred stock (25,000 shares, $10 par, $10,000 annual dividend, $18 per share acquisition price)	450,000	

Required »

a. Prepare the journal entry required to record the acquisition of the investments at the beginning of the current year.
b. Prepare the journal entries to record interest and dividend income at year-end assuming that Greenburg receives the dividends on the preferred shares.
c. Prepare the journal entries required to adjust the carrying amount of the investments to their fair values at the end of the first year: bonds, $4,595,425; common stock, $38 per share; and preferred stock, $12 per share.

2 3 **E16-9.** **Debt and Equity Investments, Available-for-Sale Debt and Equity with Fair Values Readily Determinable, IFRS.** Repeat E16-8 assuming that Greenburg Company is an IFRS reporter and the company would like to elect to report the investment at fair value through other comprehensive income if it qualifies for this treatment. Greenburg is holding the investment in common stock for trading. Greenburg is not holding the investment in preferred stock for trading, nor is it part of contingent consideration in a business combination.

3 **E16-10.** **Equity Investments without a Readily Determinable Fair Value.** Tekky Corporation purchased an equity investment in Hui Zu, Ltd. on December 15 for $100,000. Tekky accounts for the equity investment by using market comparables. Hui Zu, Ltd.'s equity is not actively traded, and it does not have a readily determinable fair value, but fair value is estimated at $105,000 on December 31. Tekky does not have significant influence over the investee. The investment is sold on June 22 of the next year for $114,000. What are the necessary journal entries?

3 **E16-11.** **Equity Investments without a Readily Determinable Fair Value, IFRS.** Repeat E16-10 assuming that Tekky is an IFRS reporter. Tekky accounts for the investment as a fair value through other comprehensive income investment because the corporation does not intend to trade it nor is holding it as contingent consideration. Prepare the journal entries to record the purchase and sale of the investment assuming that Tekky is an IFRS reporter.

4 **E16-12.** **Equity Investments, Equity Method, Book Value of Net Assets Equal to Fair Value.** On January 1, Chloe Mikenzie Incorporated acquired 32% of the outstanding voting shares of Mannin Company at a cost of $2,196,000 by acquiring 72,000 of the company's total 225,000 outstanding shares at a cost of $30.50 per share. During the year, Mannin reported $1,238,000 in net income and declared and paid $1.15 per share dividends. At the time of acquisition, the book value of Mannin's net assets equaled its market value.

Required »

a. Prepare the journal entry required to record the acquisition of the investment in Mannin Company.
b. Prepare the journal entry required to record Chloe Mikenzie's share of the investee's net income.
c. Prepare the journal entry required to record the receipt of the cash dividends.
d. What is the carrying value of Chloe Mikenzie's investment in Mannin Company at the end of the year?

4 **E16-13.** **Equity-Investments, Equity Method, Book Value of Net Assets Equal to Fair Value.** Smart Cookie Corporation purchased 40% of the 320,000 outstanding shares of JT's Fine Foods, Inc. on January 1 of the current year. Smart Cookie acquired the shares at a price of $3.20 per share. JT's Fine Foods, Inc. reported net income of $64,000 and declared and paid cash dividends of $25,600 during the current year. At the time of acquisition, the book value of JT's Fine Foods' net assets equaled its market value.

Prepare all journal entries necessary to account for this investment in JT's on Smart Cookie's books under the equity method.

4 **E16-14.** **Equity-Investments, Equity Method, Book Value of Net Assets Equal to Fair Value.** On January 1, Douglas Stores, Incorporated acquired 30% of Kirk Shoe Company. Douglas is acquiring the affiliate to secure a reliable source of supply. Douglas acquired 195,000 shares of the 650,000 shares of the investee company at a cost of $2,540,000. At the time of acquisition, the book value of Kirk's net assets equaled its market value. Kirk reported $8,136,700 net income and declared and paid dividends of $2,275,000 at the end of the year of acquisition.

Required »

a. Prepare the journal entry required to record the acquisition of the investment in Kirk Shoe.
b. Prepare the journal entry required to record Douglas's share of the investee's net income.
c. Prepare the journal entry required to record the receipt of the cash dividends.
d. What is the carrying value of Douglas's investment in Kirk Shoe at the end of the year?

4 6 **E16-15.** **Equity Method Investments, Fair Value Option.** Using the information provided in E16-14, assume that Douglas elected the fair value option on the date of acquisition. At the end of the year of acquisition, Kirk's shares are trading for $18 per share.

Required »

a. Prepare the journal entry required to record the acquisition of the investment in Kirk Shoe.
b. Prepare the journal entry required to record the receipt of the cash dividends.
c. Prepare the journal entry required to adjust the investment balance to fair value.
d. Prepare an analysis comparing the pre-tax income and cash flows relating to the investment under the equity method and the fair value method.
e. Prepare an analysis comparing the pre-tax income and cash flows relating to the investment under the equity method and the fair value method, assuming that Douglas sold the investment for $5,000,000 on January 1 of the year after acquisition.

4 6 **E16-16. Equity Method Investments, Fair Value Option.** On January 1, Clayton Incorporated acquired 32% of the outstanding voting shares of Kola Company at a cost of $2,196,000 by acquiring 72,000 of the total 225,000 outstanding shares at a cost of $30.50 per share. Clayton elected the fair value option. During the year, Kola reported $1,238,000 in net income and declared and paid $1.15 per share dividends. At the end of the year, the fair value of the investment is $2,109,000.

Required »

a. Prepare the journal entry to record the acquisition of the investment securities.
b. Prepare the journal entries at year-end to record the fair value adjustment at the end of the year of acquisition.
c. Prepare the journal entry to record the sale of 65% of the Kola common shares for $1,675,000 on January 1 of the year following the acquisition.

5 **E16-17. Notes Receivable.** Each of the following three columns refers to an independent case. All data represent amounts as of January 1, the date on which the long-term notes receivable were issued except for the interest income, which is for the life of the note. Assume annual interest payments. Fill in the missing information identified by the letters A through I.

Item	Case 1	Case 2	Case 3
Notes receivable, face value	$900,000	$1,000,000	$2,000,000
Initial carrying value	A	$ 901,819	G
Market rate	B	8%	H
Stated rate	8%	7%	10%
Term of notes (in years)	20 years	D	5 years
Note receivable discount	(153,244)	E	I
Interest income over the note's term	C	F	1,200,000

5 **E16-18. Notes Receivable.** On January 1, 2018, Racine Company accepted a 10% note, dated January 1, 2018, with a face amount of $2,400,000 in exchange for cash. The note is due in 10 years. For notes of similar risk and maturity, the market interest rate is 12%. Interest is paid each December 31.

Required »

a. Determine the present value of the note at January 1, 2018.
b. Prepare the journal entry at the issuance of the note.
c. Prepare the journal entry to record the interest revenue for the first 2 years.

A **E16-19. Debt Investment, Held to Maturity, Impairments.** Gretta Company purchased a debt investment on June 15, 2017, and classified it as held to maturity. On December 31, 2017, the investment had a carrying value of $8,500 and a fair value of $8,000. On that date, the present value of the future cash flows from the debt investment is $8,100. On December 31, 2018, the carrying value, fair value, and present value of the future cash flows from the investment are $7,900, $7,800, and $7,800, respectively. What is the amount of the impairment loss/gain in 2017 and 2018? Where does Gretta report the impairment loss/gain?

A **E16-20. Debt Investment, Impairments, IFRS.** Repeat E16-19 assuming that Gretta Company reports under IFRS and measures the debt security at amortized cost. Gretta determines that there has not been a significant increase in credit risk in 2017 or 2018. In 2017, Gretta determines that the probability of default is 1% over the next 12 months and 3% over the life of the investment. In 2018, Gretta determines that there is a .75% probability of default over the next 12 months and a 2% probability over the lifetime of the investment.

A **E16-21. Debt Investment, Available for Sale, Impairments.** Gretta Company purchased a debt investment on June 15, 2016, and classified it as available for sale. On December 31, 2016, the investment had a carrying value of $8,500 and a fair value of $8,000. On that date, the present value of the future cash flows from the debt investment is $8,100. On December 31, 2017, the carrying value, fair value, and present value of the investment are $7,900, $7,800, and $7,800, respectively. Gretta does not anticipate selling the investment before it recovers. What is the amount of the impairment loss/gain in 2016 and 2017? Where does Gretta report the impairment loss/gain?

A **E16-22. Debt Investment, Impairments, IFRS.** Repeat E16-21 assuming that Gretta measures the debt security at fair value through OCI. Assume for simplicity that the carrying value is not reduced by amortization during 2017; thus, the carrying value on December 31, 2017, is $8,000 (accounting for the prior year write-down). Gretta determines that there has not been a significant increase in credit risk in 2016 and 2017. In 2016, Gretta determines the probability of default is 1% over the next 12 months and 3% over the the life of the investment. In 2017, Gretta determines that the probability of default is 0.75% over the next 12 months and 2% over the lifetime of the investment.

A **E16-23. Equity Investment with No Readily Determinable Fair Value, Impairments.** Regal Inc., a U.S. GAAP reporter, holds an equity investment with a carrying value of $107,250. This investment is not publicly traded and Regal has elected to carry it at adjusted cost. At December 31, 2016, the fair value of the investment is $98,000, which was estimated by using a discounted cash flow valuation. Assume that Regal determines that the investment is impaired. What is the amount of the impairment? Where does Regal report the impairment loss?

A **E16-24. Equity Investment with No Readily Determinable Fair Value Impairments, IFRS.** Repeat E16-23 assuming that Regal Inc. reports under IFRS.

A **E16-25. Debt Investment, Impairments, IFRS.** Bronze Company, an IFRS reporter, holds a debt investment measured at fair value through OCI with a carrying value of $45,000. The current fair value of the investment is $38,000, and the appropriate expected credit loss is $1,000. There has not been a significant increase in credit risk in the current year.

Required »

a. Determine whether an impairment loss exists.
b. If an impairment exists, what amount of loss will Bronze report in net income? What amount of loss will it report in other comprehensive income? What is the journal entry for the impairment loss if needed?

Problems

2 **P16-1. Debt Investments, Held to Maturity.** Capitol Corporation acquired $6,735,000 par value, 6%, 5-year bonds on their date of issue, January 1 of the current year. The market rate at the time of issue was 10%, and interest is paid semiannually on June 30 and December 31. Capitol will use the effective interest rate method to account for this investment. Capitol intends to hold the investment until the bonds mature, and has the ability to do so.

Required »

a. Determine the purchase price of the investment in bonds.
b. Prepare the journal entry to record the acquisition of the bond investment.
c. Prepare an amortization table for the investment using the effective interest rate method.
d. Prepare the journal entry to record the interest income for the first year.
e. Prepare the journal entry to record the sale of the bonds at the end of the third year for $6,100,000.

2 **P16-2. Debt Investments, Trading.** Freder Software Group acquired $1,550,000 par value, zero coupon, 5-year bonds on their date of issue, January 1 of the current year. The market rate at the time of issue was 6%, and interest is compounded annually. Freder uses the effective interest rate method to account for this investment. The company classifies the investment as a trading security. The fair value of the bonds at the end of the year of acquisition is $1,097,500.

Required »

a. Determine the purchase price of the investment in bonds.
b. Prepare the journal entry to record the acquisition of the bond investment.
c. Prepare an amortization table assuming that Freder uses the effective interest rate method.
d. Prepare the journal entry to record the interest income for the first 2 years.
e. Prepare the journal entry required to adjust the investment's carrying amount to fair value at the end of the first year.
f. Prepare the journal entry to record the sale of the investment on January 2 of Year 2 for a net price of $987,150.

2 **P16-3. Debt Investments, Trading.** Sabran Corporation, a calendar year-end firm, invested in three debt securities on December 15, 2016, and classified them as trading securities. Sabran sold all three securities on January 1, 2017. The following table provides the purchase price, fair values, annual interest amounts, and selling prices for all three securities. All securities were acquired at face value and pay interest annually each December 31.

Security	Purchase Price	Fair Value at December 31, 2016	Annual Interest Amount	Selling Price
A	$50,000	$45,000	$350	$46,000
B	25,000	32,000	125	34,000
C	10,000	9,000	175	8,000
Total	$85,000	$86,000	$650	$88,000

Sabran had not purchased any other trading securities before January 1, 2016, and it did not make any additional investments subsequent to the sale on January 1, 2017. What journal entries are required to properly record these events?

❸ **P16-4. Equity Investments, Readily Determinable Fair Value.** DeNault Aircraft Corporation acquired the following equity investments at the beginning of Year 1 to be held in a portfolio. DeNault does not have significant influence over the investees.

Description	Revere Group	Belton Brothers	Yan-Co Associates	Lopes Company
Number of shares	100,100	98,000	45,000	69,500
Market price per share	× $23	× $11	× $16	× $68
Share acquisition price	$2,302,300	$1,078,000	$720,000	$4,726,000

Share prices at the end of Years 1 and 2 follow.

Fair Value	Revere Group	Belton Brothers	Yan-Co Associates	Lopes Company
End of Year 1	$26	$9	$21	$59
End of Year 2	$18	$6	$25	$51

Required »

a. Prepare the journal entry to record the acquisition of the investments.
b. Prepare the journal entry to record the end of Year 1 fair value adjustment for the portfolio.
c. Assume that DeNault sells 35,000 Yan-Co shares for $23 per share at the beginning of Year 2. Prepare the journal entry required to record the sale. DeNault does not adjust the fair value adjustment account at this time.
d. Prepare the journal entry to record the Year 2 fair value adjustment.

❸ **P16-5. Equity-Investments, Readily Determinable Fair Value, IFRS.** Repeat P16-4 assuming that DeNault Aircraft Corporation is an IFRS reporter and would like to elect to report the investments at fair value through other comprehensive income if it qualifies for this treatment. DeNault is not holding the investments for trading nor is it part of contingent consideration in a business combination.

❷❸ **P16-6. Debt Investment, Equity Investments.** K&Z Potato Chip Company, a U.S. GAAP reporter, provides you with the following information regarding its investments in equity securities during the current year.

Date	Description
January 1 **(Beginning Balance: No entry required)**	K&Z is currently holding 8,500 of Faithful Corporation common shares (publicly traded). The Faithful shares cost $20 per share. There is a debit balance of $17,000 in the fair value adjustment account. K&Z does not have a significant influence over the investee.
January 23	K&Z purchased 1,700 shares of Lawrence Company common stock for $155 per share. Lawrence Company is publicly traded. K&Z does not have a significant influence over the investee.
February 4	K&Z acquired 136,000 of the 340,000 outstanding shares of Zombie, Inc. for a total cost of $1,020,000.
March 23	Faithful Corporation paid a $3.40 per share cash dividend.
June 30	Zombie, Inc. reported $1,850,000 in net income for the year. Zombie also declared and paid a cash dividend of $2.55 per share.
October 15	K&Z purchased 340 bonds of the Pierre Nardo Group (PNG) at $1,000 par and intends to hold the debt investment to maturity.
December 31	K&Z accrued interest on the PNG bonds amounted to $42,500.
December 31	The year-end market values of the Faithful Corporation and Lawrence shares are $30.60 and $170 per share, respectively. The PNG bonds were trading at $1,700 at the end of the current period, and Zombie was trading at $10 per share.

Required »

Prepare all journal entries necessary to record K&Z's investment transactions for the year. Show all computations.

3 **P16-7. Equity Investments, Readily Determinable Fair Value.** Bullet Bob Company has the following securities in its portfolio on December 31 of Year 1. Bullet Bob Company does not have a significant influence over the investees. All securities are purchased during Year 1:

Description	Cost	Fair Value
Dolt Corporation common stock: 15,000 shares	$ 345,000	$ 259,000
Single JA common stock: 200,000 shares	1,000,000	1,800,500
Portfolio totals	$1,345,000	$2,059,500

Bullet Bob acquired and sold securities from this portfolio during Year 2. Specifically, on June 3, the company sold 7,500 shares of Dolt Corporation stock for $20 per share. On November 9, Bullet Bob acquired 4,000 shares of FOAH Stores' common stock for $81 per share.

Bullet Bob Company's portfolio of equity securities on December 31 of Year 2 follows.

Description	Cost	Fair Value
Dolt Corporation common stock: 7,500 shares	$ 172,500	$ 157,000
Single JA common stock: 200,000 shares	1,000,000	1,400,850
FOAH common stock: 4,000 shares	324,000	344,000
Portfolio totals	$1,496,500	$1,901,850

Bullet Bob does not elect the adjusted cost method for any of its equity investments.

Required »

a. Prepare the entry to record the acquisition of the investments in Year 1.
b. Prepare the journal entry to adjust the portfolio to fair value at the end of Year 1.
c. Prepare the journal entry to record the sale of the Dolt Corporation common shares.
d. Prepare the journal entry to record the acquisition of the FOAH common stock.
e. Prepare the journal entry to adjust the portfolio to fair value at the end of Year 2.

3 **P16-8. Equity Investments, Readily Determinable Fair Value.** Pugh Company purchased 1,800 shares of the Kramer Group common stock for $64,800 (i.e., $36 per share) at the beginning of the current year. There were 36,000 outstanding Kramer shares on the date of acquisition. Total stockholders' equity of Kramer Company is $1,080,000 on the date of acquisition. Kramer reported $360,000 in net income and declared and paid $1.44 per share cash dividends at year-end.

Required »

a. Prepare the journal entry to record the purchase of the Kramer shares.
b. Prepare the journal entries necessary to reflect Pugh's share of Kramer's dividends.
c. Prepare the journal entry required to adjust Pugh's investment to its fair value of $54 per share at year-end.
d. Prepare the journal entry necessary to record the sale of 900 Kramer shares for $63 per share at the beginning of the next year.

3 **P16-9. Equity Investments, Readily Determinable Fair Value, IFRS.** Repeat P16-8 assuming that Pugh Company is an IFRS reporter and would like to elect to report the investment at fair value through other comprehensive income if it qualifies for this treatment. Pugh is not holding the investments for trading, nor is it part of contingent consideration in a business combination.

3 4 **P16-10. Equity Investments, Equity Method.** Dale Corporation acquired a 35% interest in Roger Inc. for $300,000 on January 1 of the current year. Specifically, Dale acquired 68,250 of the 195,000 voting common shares outstanding. Roger reported net income of $120,000 at the end of the current year and paid cash dividends of $36,000 during the current year. At the time of acquisition, the book value of Roger's net assets equaled its market value. Roger's shares were selling for $6 per share at the end of the current year.

Required »

a. Prepare all journal entries required to record the transactions indicated assuming that Dale uses the equity method.
b. Determine the carrying value of the investment at the end of the current year assuming that Dale uses the equity method.
c. Prepare the journal entries required to account for Dale's investment in Roger assuming that the investment does not permit Dale to exercise significant influence over Roger.

4 **P16-11. Equity Investments, Equity Method, Net Assets Not Equal to Market Value.** Smart Cookie Corporation purchased 40% of the 320,000 outstanding shares of JT's Fine Foods, Inc. on January 1 of the current year. Smart Cookie acquired the shares at a price of $3.20 per share. The following additional data were available for JT's Fine Foods, Inc. on the date of acquisition.

Description	Book Values	Fair Values
Current assets	$256,000	$256,000
Depreciable assets (10-year remaining life/straight-line depreciation)	192,000	230,400
Total Assets	$448,000	$486,400
Liabilities	$ 32,000	$ 32,000
Contributed Capital (Common Stock and Additional Paid-in Capital)	$320,000	$320,000
Retained Earnings	96,000	134,400
Total Shareholders' Equity	$416,000	$454,400
Total Liabilities and Stockholders' Equity	$448,000	$486,400

JT's Fine Foods, Inc. reported net income of $64,000 at the end of the current year and declared and paid cash dividends of $25,600 during the current year.

Required »

a. Compute the amount of goodwill implied on Smart Cookie's acquisition of JT's Fine Foods shares.
b. Prepare all journal entries necessary to account for this investment in JT's under the equity method.

4 6 **P16-12. Equity Investments, Equity Method, Fair Value Option, Net Assets Not Equal to Market Value.** Jacob Corporation paid $536,200 for a 30% share of Gardner Enterprises on January 1 of the current year. Gardner reported net assets at a book value of $1,414,000 on the date of acquisition. On the date of acquisition, it was determined that Gardner's plant assets were undervalued by $118,000. Gardner's plant assets have a 10-year remaining life and are depreciated by the straight-line method with no residual value. Gardner reported net income of $224,000 and declared and paid cash dividends of $182,000 during the current year. Finally, Gardner's common shares are valued at $1,737,667 at the end of the current year.

Required »

a. Compute the amount of goodwill on the exchange, if any, assuming that the equity method is used to account for the investment.
b. Prepare all journal entries indicated on the books of the Jacob Corporation under the fair value option and equity methods.
c. Assume that Jacob Corporation sold the investment for $540,000 on January 1 of the next year. Prepare the journal entries required to record the sale of the investment under both the fair value option and the equity methods.
d. Prepare a schedule that compares the amount and timing of revenue recognition for the fair value option and the equity methods.

4 6 **P16-13. Equity Investments, Equity Method, Fair Value Option.** Jacob Corporation paid $536,200 for a 30% share of Gardner Enterprises on January 1 of the current year. Gardner reported net income of $224,000 and declared and paid cash dividends of $182,000 during the current year. At the time of acquisition, the book value of Gardner's net assets equaled its market value. Finally, Gardner's common shares are valued at $1,737,667 at the end of the current year.

Required »

a. Prepare all journal entries indicated on the books of the Jacob Corporation under the fair value option and the equity method.
b. Assume that Jacob sells the investment for $540,000 on January 1 of the next year. Prepare the journal entries required to record the sale of the investment under both the fair value option and the equity method.

c. Prepare a schedule that compares the amount and timing of revenue recognition for the fair value option and the equity method.

P16-14. Debt Investment, Held to Maturity, Impairments. Melia Company purchased a debt investment in 2016 and classified it as held to maturity. The carrying value on December 31, 2016, is $250,000. At December 31, 2016, the fair value of the investment is $238,000, and the present value of the future cash flows from the debt investment is $241,000. Melia does not intend to sell the investment, but it does deem it more likely than not that it will have to sell the investment before the market recovers.

Required »

a. If there is an impairment, what amount of loss will Melia report in net income? What amount of loss will Melia report in other comprehensive income?
b. Prepare the journal entry for the impairment loss if needed.

P16-15. Debt Investment, Impairments, IFRS. Griffin Company, an IFRS reporter, holds a debt investment measured at amortized cost of $250,000. The debt security is investment grade. The current fair value of the investment is $238,000, and the present value of the future cash flows from the debt investment is $241,000. The 12-month expected credit loss is $1,250, and the lifetime expected credit loss is $4,000. There has not been a significant increase in credit risk during the current year.

Required »

a. If impairment exists, what amount of loss will Griffin report in net income? What amount of loss will it report in other comprehensive income?
b. Prepare the journal entry for the impairment loss if needed.

P16-16. Debt Investment, Available for Sale, Impairments. Potter Company holds an available-for-sale debt investment with a carrying value of $95,000 that it purchased in the current year. The current fair value of the investment is $87,000 and the present value of the future cash flows from the debt investment is $90,000. Potter does not intend to sell the investment; however, it does deem it more likely than not that it will be able to hold the investment until the market recovers.

Required »

a. If impairment exists, what amount of loss will Potter report in net income? What amount of loss will it report in other comprehensive income?
b. What is the journal entry for the impairment loss if needed?

P16-17. Debt Investment, Impairments, IFRS. Use the same information as in problem P16-16 except now assume that Potter Company is an IFRS reporter and carries the debt at fair value through OCI. Also, assume that the present value accurately measures the difference between the carrying value and the expected credit loss. There has not been a significant increase in credit risk during the current year.

Required »

a. If impairment exists, what amount of loss will Potter report in net income? What amount of loss will it report in other comprehensive income?
b. What is the journal entry for the impairment loss if needed?

P16-18. Equity Investment, No Readily Determinable Fair Value, Impairments. Mulligan Company carries an equity investment of a privately held company. Mulligan elected to measure this equity security without a readily determinable fair value at adjusted cost. The current carrying value of the equity shares is equal to $326,400. Mulligan uses market comparables to estimate the current fair value of the investment at $315,000. A qualitative assessment indicates that impairment does exist.

Required »

a. If impairment exists, what amount of loss will Mulligan report in net income? What amount of loss will it report in other comprehensive income?
b. What is the journal entry for the impairment loss if needed?

P16-19. Equity Investment, Impairments, IFRS. Repeat P16-18 assuming Mulligan Company reports under IFRS.

Excel Project

Autograded Excel Project available in **MyLab Accounting**

CASES

Judgment Cases

Judgment Case 1: Impairment Decisions: U.S. GAAP

Refer to Exhibit 16A.1, which presents a decision tree for impairments of investments in financial assets under U.S. GAAP. Detail the decisions and judgments that you must make when determining whether an investing asset has been impaired and, if so, the amount of impairment. Provide explanations as necessary. Is the area of investing asset impairments more of an objective or subjective area of financial reporting?

Judgment Case 2: Impairment Decisions: IFRS

Refer to Exhibit 16A.2, which presents a decision tree for impairments of investments in financial assets under IFRS. Please detail the decisions and judgments that you must make when determining whether an investing asset has been impaired and, if so, the amount of impairment. Provide explanations as necessary. Is the area of investing asset impairments more of an objective or subjective area of financial reporting?

Financial Statement Analysis Case

Cisco Systems, Inc., the leading Internet protocol-based networking equipment company, has significant holdings of investment securities. Use the financial statement information provided to analyze ***Cisco's*** holdings and answer the following questions and complete the following requirements:

1. What types of investments are in the firm's portfolio in fiscal 2016 and 2015? What percentage of total assets do its investments compose? Comment on changes in the composition and percentage of investments to total assets from year to year. Use fair value.
2. Which investment securities did ***Cisco*** report at fair value in fiscal 2016 and 2015? What is the difference between fair value and cost?
3. Determine the effect of changes in fair value on net income and other comprehensive income in fiscal 2016, 2015, and 2014. If unrealized gains and losses on available-for-sale securities were reported in net income rather than other comprehensive income, what would be the effect on net income in fiscal 2016, 2015, and 2014?
4. For its investment securities, determine the types and amount of investments in each level in the hierarchy in fiscal 2016.

At or for the Year Ended *(in millions)*	July 30, 2016 (Fiscal 2016)	July 25, 2015 (Fiscal 2015)	July 26, 2014 (Fiscal 2014)
Total Assets	$121,652	$113,373	$105,070
Net Income	$ 10,739	$ 8,981	$ 7,853

Statement of Comprehensive Income (excerpt)

Year Ended	July 30, 2016 (Fiscal 2016)	July 25, 2015 (Fiscal 2015)	July 26, 2014 (Fiscal 2014)
Net income	$10,739	$8,981	$7,853
Available-for-sale investments:			
Change in net unrealized gains (losses), net of tax of $(49), $14, and $(146) for fiscal 2016, 2015, and 2014, respectively	$ 92	$ (12)	$ 233
Net (gains) losses reclassified into earnings, net of tax expense (benefit) of $0, $57, and $111 for fiscal 2016, 2015, and 2014, respectively	1	(100)	(189)
Total	$ 93	($ 112)	$ 44

Selected Excerpts of Cisco Systems, Inc. Financial Statements and Annual Report

Note 2: Summary of Significant Accounting Policies [Excerpt]

(b) Available-for-Sale Investments The Company classifies its investments in both fixed income securities . . . as available-for-sale investments. Fixed income securities primarily consist of U.S. government securities, U.S. government agency securities, non-U.S. government and agency securities, corporate debt securities, and U.S. agency mortgage-backed securities. These available-for-sale investments are primarily held in the custody of a major financial institution. A specific identification method is used to determine the cost basis of fixed income and public equity securities sold. These investments are recorded in the Consolidated Balance Sheets at fair value. Unrealized gains and losses on these investments, to the extent the investments are unhedged, are included as a separate component of accumulated other comprehensive income (AOCI), net of tax. The Company classifies its investments as current based on the nature of the investments and their availability for use in current operations.

(k) Fair Value Fair value is defined as the price that would be received from selling an asset or paid to transfer a liability in an orderly transaction between market participants at the measurement date. When determining the fair value measurements for assets and liabilities required or permitted to be either recorded or disclosed at fair value, the Company considers the principal or most advantageous market in which it would transact, and it also considers assumptions that market participants would use when pricing the asset or liability.

The accounting guidance for fair value measurement requires an entity to maximize the use of observable inputs and minimize the use of unobservable inputs when measuring fair value. The standard establishes a fair value hierarchy based on the level of independent, objective evidence surrounding the inputs used to measure fair value. A financial instrument's categorization within the fair value hierarchy is based upon the lowest level of input that is significant to the fair value measurement. The fair value hierarchy is as follows:

Level 1 applies to assets or liabilities for which there are quoted prices in active markets for identical assets or liabilities.

Level 2 applies to assets or liabilities for which there are inputs other than quoted prices that are observable for the asset or liability such as quoted prices for similar assets or liabilities in active markets; quoted prices for identical assets or liabilities in markets with insufficient volume or infrequent transactions (less active markets); or model-derived valuations in which significant inputs are observable or can be derived principally from, or corroborated by, observable market data.

Level 3 applies to assets or liabilities for which there are unobservable inputs to the valuation methodology that are significant to the measurement of the fair value of the assets or liabilities.

Note 8. Investments

(a) Summary of Available-for-Sale Investments
The following tables summarize the Company's available-for-sale investments (in millions):

	Amortized Cost	Gross Unrealized Gains	Gross Unrealized Losses	Fair Value
July 30, 2016				
Fixed income securities:				
U.S. government securities	$26,473	$ 73	$ (2)	$26,544
U.S. government agency securities	2,809	8	–	2,817
Non-U.S. government and agency securities	1,096	4	–	1,100
Corporate debt securities	24,044	263	(15)	24,292
U.S. agency mortgage-backed securities	1,846	22	–	1,868
Total fixed income securities	$56,268	$370	$(17)	$56,621

	Amortized Cost	Gross Unrealized Gains	Gross Unrealized Losses	Fair Value
July 25, 2015				
Fixed income securities:				
U.S. government securities	$29,904	$41	$ (6)	$29,939
U.S. government agency securities	3,662	2	(1)	3,663
Non-U.S. government and agency securities	1,128	1	(1)	1,128
Corporate debt securities	15,802	34	(53)	15,783
U.S. agency mortgage-backed securities	1,456	8	(3)	1,461
Total fixed income securities	$51,952	$86	$(64)	$51,974

(b) Gains and Losses on Available-for-Sale Investments

The following table presents the gross realized gains and gross realized losses related to the Company's available-for-sale investments (in millions):

Years Ended	July 30, 2016	July 25, 2015	July 26, 2014
Gross realized gains	$ 152	$221	$341
Gross realized losses	(153)	(64)	(41)
Total	$ (1)	$157	$300

	JULY 30, 2016			
	FAIR VALUE MEASUREMENTS			
	Level 1	Level 2	Level 3	Total Balance
Available-for-sale				
U.S. government securities	$ –	$26,544	$ –	$26,544
U.S. government agency securities	–	2,817	–	2,817
Non-U.S. government and agency securities	–	1,100	–	1,100
Corporate debt securities	–	24,292	–	24,292
U.S. agency mortgage-backed securities	–	1,868	–	1,868

Source: Financial Statements from Cisco Corporation's 2016 Annual Report. http://www.cisco.com/c/dam/en_us/about/annual-report/2016-annual-report-full.pdf

Surfing the Standards Case

Surfing the Standards Case: Partnership Investment

GTI Corporation acquired a 15% interest in DDA Partnership on February 15 of the current year. GTI is preparing its financial statements for the first quarter and needs to determine how to report the investment. GTI realizes that it will either report at cost, fair value, or under the equity method. Auditors have pointed the corporation to ASC 323 *Investments – Equity Method and Joint Ventures* and ASC 825-10-25 *Financial Instruments – Overall – Recognition*. Based on your review of the pertinent codification, how should GTI report its investment in DDA Partnership?

Basis for Conclusions Cases

Basis for Conclusions Case 1: Reasons for the Fair Value Option

ASC 825-10 *Financial Instruments – Overall* permits (but does not require) the option to report most financial assets at fair value. Read paragraph A3 of the Basis for Conclusions in *Statement of Financial Accounting Standards No. 159.* Briefly explain the four reasons the board decided to allow the fair value option.

Basis for Conclusions Case 2: Electing the Fair Value Option

ASC 825-10 *Financial Instruments – Overall* permits (but does not require) the option to report most financial assets at fair value. Read paragraphs A12 – A19 of the Basis for Conclusions in *Statement of Financial Accounting Standards No. 159.*

1. When must entities make the fair value option election? Why did the board decide that?
2. ASC 825-10 allows the election of the fair value option on an instrument-by-instrument basis. What were the main concerns expressed by the respondents to the Exposure Draft to this approach? Why did the FASB decide to allow the instrument-by-instrument approach?

APPENDIX A
Impairments of Investment Securities

Firms must assess every asset on the balance sheet to ensure that all provide future economic benefit to the firm at an amount commensurate with the amount reported on the balance sheet. An **impairment** occurs when an asset's total future cash-generating ability falls below its carrying value.

The approach to testing and reporting impairments depends on the way that each type of investing asset, absent impairment, is measured. Accounting for increases or decreases in the fair value of investments varies for trading, available-for-sale, and held-to-maturity debt securities and equity securities with and without readily available fair values:

- For trading debt securities, companies account for changes in fair value through net income.
- For available-for-sale debt securities, companies account for changes in fair value through other comprehensive income.
- For held-to-maturity debt securities, companies do not report changes in fair value because they carry these investments at amortized cost, not at fair value.
- For equity securities with readily determinable fair values, companies reports changes in fair value through net income.
- For equity securities without readily determinable fair values, companies either report changes in fair value through net income or elect to report at cost with adjustments for price changes in similar securities of the same entity.

How does management account for impaired investment securities? When impairment occurs, companies reduce the value of the asset on the balance sheet and report this change in the carrying value of securities in income. The exact procedure depends on the type of investment. In the case of trading debt securities and equity securities with readily determinable fair values, companies do not need to perform an impairment assessment because they are already reported at fair value with the unrealized gains and losses reported in net income. We next discuss impairments of held-to-maturity and available-for-sale debt securities followed by equity securities without readily determinable fair values.[18]

Accounting for Impairments of Debt Investments Measured at Amortized Cost

Here we discuss the steps used to evaluate and measure impairments of debt investments that are measured at amortized cost such as held-to-maturity debt securities and notes receivable. U.S. GAAP and IFRS differ in several ways, as we address later.

We use an expected loss model to account for an impairment of a debt investment measured at amortized cost. A firm should report the asset on the balance sheet at the amount it expects to collect. Impairing debt investments measured at amortized cost involves the following steps.

Step 1. Compute the Expected Amount to Be Collected

At the end of every reporting period, the company should compute the expected amount that will be collected. The authoritative literature does not specify a particular method to use, and there are many approaches used in practice.[19] However, whatever method the firm chooses must be consistently applied.

[18]Most of the U.S. GAAP relevant authoritative literature for this topic is found in FASB ASC 320-10, *Investments – Debt and Equity Securities – Overall* , ASC 321-10, *Investments – Equity Securities – Overall*, and ASC 326, *Financial Instruments – Credit Losses*. For IFRS the authoritative literature is found in IFRS 9, *Financial Instruments*.

[19]Examples of common methods are loss rate, roll rate, aging, and probability of default

We will focus on the discounted cash flow method, which requires discounting all expected future cash flows to the present value at the balance sheet date, using the effective interest rate of the financial asset.

Step 2. Compute an Allowance for Credit Loss

The allowance for credit loss is a contra-asset account. It measures the difference between the amortized cost of the investment and the amount expected to be collected. The account balance of the allowance for credit loss must be presented separately on the balance sheet.

Step 3. Report the Change in the Allowance for Credit Loss in Net Income

Any change in the allowance for credit loss is recognized through net income. When the amount that is expected to be collected falls below amortized cost for the first time, the firm reports an unrealized loss. In subsequent periods, the firm may report additional unrealized losses. Alternatively, if the security recovers, the firm can report a reversal of a prior unrealized loss in net income. However, these reversals cannot exceed the initial unrealized loss (that is, the allowance for credit loss can have only a credit balance).

Example 16A.1 illustrates accounting for the impairment of a held-to-maturity debt investment.

EXAMPLE 16A.1

Impairment of a Held-to-Maturity Debt Investment

PROBLEM: On January 1 of Year 1, Silver Company purchased a bond and classified it as held to maturity. The 5-year bond has a face value of $1,000,000, pays interest annually on December 31, and has a stated and effective interest rate of 5%. Silver receives the first two payments on December 31, Year 1 and Year 2, respectively. On December 31 of Year 2, Silver determines that the investment's expected collections have dropped below the contractual amounts. Silver anticipates that the remaining three payments will be $45,000 instead of $50,000. Silver does anticipate that the principal balance will be received in full.

On December 31, Year 3, Silver reassesses the investment and anticipates that the remaining two payments will be $48,000 each. Prepare the journal entry for the impairment loss and recovery on December 31 of Year 2 and Year 3.

SOLUTION: To determine whether an impairment loss exists, we follow the steps of impairment testing. We begin with Year 2.

STEP 1: COMPUTE THE EXPECTED AMOUNT TO BE COLLECTED

Silver expects to collect $45,000 interest over the next 3 years and the $1,000,000 principal at the end of the last year. The present value of this stream of cash flows at 5% is $986,384.

	N	I/Y	PV	PMT	FV	Excel Formula
Given	3	5.00%		45,000	1,000,000	
Solve For PV			**(986,384)**			=PV(0.05,3,45000,1000000)

STEP 2: COMPUTE AN ALLOWANCE FOR CREDIT LOSS

The allowance is the difference between the amortized cost and the expected amount to be collected. The amortized cost is $1,000,000. Because the bond was purchased at par value, there is no premium or discount amortization; thus, the cost basis remains at $1,000,000. The expected amount to be collected is $986,384 as determined in Step 1. Thus, the balance in the allowance for credit loss account should be $13,616.

Continued

STEP 3: REPORT THE CHANGE FOR THE ALLOWANCE FOR CREDIT LOSS IN NET INCOME

The journal entry is:

Account	December 31, Year 2	
Impairment Loss – Net Income	13,616	
Allowance for Credit Loss: Held-to-Maturity Debt Investment		13,616

We continue with Year 3.

STEP 1: COMPUTE THE EXPECTED AMOUNT TO BE COLLECTED

Silver expects to collect $48,000 interest over the next 2 years, and the $1,000,000 principal at the end of the last year. The present value of this stream of cash flows at 5% is $996,281.

	N	I/Y	PV	PMT	FV	Excel Formula
Given	2	5.00%		48,000	1,000,000	
Solve For PV			**(996,281)**			=PV(0.05,2,48000,1000000)

STEP 2: COMPUTE AN ALLOWANCE FOR CREDIT LOSS

The allowance is the difference between the amortized cost and the expected amount to be collected. The amortized cost is $1,000,000. Because the bond was purchased at par value, there is no premium or discount amortization; thus, the cost basis remains at $1,000,000. The expected amount to be collected is $996,281 as determined in Step 1. Thus, the balance in the allowance for credit loss account should be $3,719.

STEP 3: REPORT THE CHANGE FOR THE ALLOWANCE FOR CREDIT LOSS IN NET INCOME

Silver has a beginning balance in the allowance for credit loss account of $13,616. At the end of Year 3, it needs a balance of $3,719. Thus, it will debit the allowance account for $9,897 and record a loss recovery in net income, which increases net income.

The journal entry is:

Account	December 31, Year 3	
Allowance for Credit Loss: Held-to-Maturity Debt Investment	9,897	
Recovery of Impairment Loss: Held-to-Maturity Debt Investment		9,897

Accounting for Impairments of Available-for-Sale Debt Investments

Recall that available-for-sale debt securities are measured at fair value with unrealized gains and losses reported in other comprehensive income even in the absence of an impairment. However, with an impairment, the portion of the difference between the carrying value and the fair value that is due to the credit loss is reported net income. We next discuss the steps used to evaluate and measure impairments of available-for-sale debt investments. U.S. GAAP and IFRS differ in several ways, as we address later.

Step 1. Compute the Present Value of Expected Future Cash Flows

To correctly account for changes in the value of available-for-sale debt securities, we need to know the present value of expected future cash flows of the investment as well as the fair value. To compute the present value, we use the effective interest rate implicit in the security at the date of acquisition.

Step 2. Compute the Balance in the Allowance for Credit Loss and the Security Fair Value Adjustment Account

We divide changes in the value of available-for-sale debt investments into two components:

- Credit loss component
- Non-credit loss component.

We report the credit loss in the allowance for credit loss (a contra-asset account) and the non-credit loss in the security fair value adjustment account. The allowance for credit loss is measured as the difference between the present value of future cash flows and the amortized cost. The security fair value adjustment account is measured as the difference between the present value of future cash flows and the fair value. Non-credit loss relates to all factors, such as market illiquidity and market interest rate fluctuations, that cause the debt security's fair value to be below its present value.

The allowance for credit loss cannot be higher than the difference between the amortized cost and the fair value of the asset. In other words, the credit loss portion of the impairment is limited to the amount by which the amortized cost exceeds the fair value. The account balance of the allowance for credit loss along with the amortized cost must be presented parenthetically on the balance sheet.

Step 3. Report the Impairment Loss in Other Comprehensive Income

Any change in the allowance for credit loss is reported in net income. Any change in the security fair value adjustment account is reported in other comprehensive income.

When a firm reports a credit loss on an asset for the first time, it reports an unrealized loss. In subsequent periods, the firm may report additional unrealized credit losses. Alternatively, if the security recovers, the firm can report a reversal of prior unrealized credit losses in net income. However, these reversals cannot exceed the initial unrealized credit loss (that is, the allowance for credit loss can have only a credit balance).

Accounting for the impairment of an available-for-sale debt investment is illustrated in Example 16A.2.

EXAMPLE 16A.2

Impairment of an Available-for-Sale Debt Investment

PROBLEM: On January 1 of Year 1, Palladium Converters, Inc. purchased a bond and classified it as available for sale. The 5-year bond has a face value of $1,000,000, pays interest annually on December 31, and has a stated and effective interest rate of 5%. Palladium receives the $50,000 interest payment on December 31, Year 1. On December 31, Year 1, the bond has a fair value of $975,000. Palladium anticipates that it will receive only $46,000 for each of the next four interest payments. However, it does believe it will receive the full principal amount at the end of the fifth year. Provide the journal entry to record the credit loss in Year 1.

SOLUTION: To determine the credit loss, we follow the steps of impairment testing.

STEP 1. COMPUTE THE PRESENT VALUE OF FUTURE CASH FLOWS

Palladium expects to collect $46,000 interest over the next 4 years and the $1,000,000 principal at the end of the last year. The present value of this stream of cash flows at 5% is $985,816.

	N	I/Y	PV	PMT	FV	Excel Formula
Given	4	5.00%		46,000	1,000,000	
Solve For PV			**(985,816)**			=PV(0.05,4,46000,1000000)

STEP 2. COMPUTE THE BALANCE IN THE ALLOWANCE FOR CREDIT LOSS AND THE SECURITY FAIR VALUE ADJUSTMENT ACCOUNT

The total loss is the difference between the amortized cost and the fair value. The credit loss is the difference between the amortized cost and the present value of expected cash flows. The non-credit loss is the portion of the total loss that is not included in the credit loss.

Continued

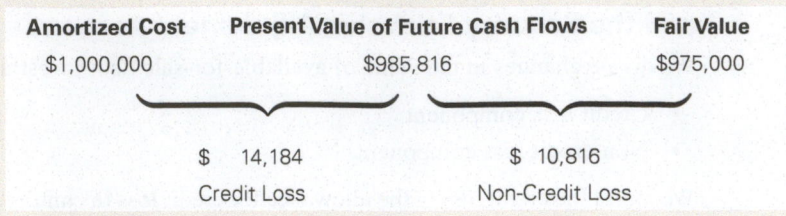

Amortized Cost	Present Value of Future Cash Flows	Fair Value
$1,000,000	$985,816	$975,000
	$ 14,184 Credit Loss	$ 10,816 Non-Credit Loss

Palladium's allowance for credit loss is $14,184.

STEP 3. REPORT THE IMPAIRMENT LOSS IN COMPREHENSIVE INCOME

Palladium reports the credit loss in net income and the non-credit loss in other comprehensive income.

Account	*December 31, Year 1*	
Credit Loss – Net Income	14,184	
Allowance for Credit Loss: Available-for-Sale Debt Investments		14,184
Non-Credit Loss – OCI	10,816	
Fair Value Adjustment–Available-for-Sale Debt Investments		10,816

If the investor plans on selling the investment or if it is more likely than not that the investor will be required to sell the asset before it recovers the amortized cost, then the investment is written down to its fair value with the entire amount reported in net income. This new basis becomes the investment's amortized cost and thus cannot be reversed through net income if the investment recovers in value. Example 16A.3 illustrates accounting for the impairment of an available-for-sale debt investment when the investor is required to sell.

EXAMPLE 16A.3 **Impairment of an Available-for-Sale Debt Investment—Investor Required to Sell**

PROBLEM: Consider the previous example of Palladium Converters, Inc. How would the December 31, Year 1, journal entry change if Palladium concluded that it was more likely than not that it would need to sell the investment before recovering the amortized cost?

SOLUTION: In this case, Palladium will need to record the entire loss in net income and reduce the amortized cost basis of the asset. The total loss is $25,000 ($14,184 credit loss plus $10,816 non-credit loss). Because Palladium is reducing the amortized cost basis of the asset, it credits the asset itself as opposed to an allowance account.

Account	*December 31, Year 1*	
Impairment Loss – Net Income	25,000	
Available-for-Sale Debt Investments		25,000

Accounting for Impairments of Equity Securities with No Readily Determinable Fair Value

Here we discuss the steps in evaluating and measuring impairments of equity securities with no readily determinable fair value. If a company has elected to measure an equity security without a readily determinable fair value at adjusted cost, it uses the following steps to assess and possibly record the impairment of an equity security.

Step 1. Determine Whether There Is an Impairment Loss for the Asset

Under U.S. GAAP the equity investment is impaired if the following apply to it:

- The fair value of the investment is less than its carrying value.
- A qualitative assessment indicates that the investment is impaired.

When making the qualitative assessment, companies should consider all of the following along with any other indicators that could be relevant.

- A significant deterioration in the earnings performance, credit rating, asset quality, or business prospects of the investee
- A significant adverse change in the regulatory, economic, or technological environment of the investee
- A significant adverse change in the general market condition of either the geographical area or the industry in which the investee operates
- A legitimate offer to purchase, an offer by the investee to sell, or a completed auction process for the same or similar investment for an amount less than the carrying amount of that investment
- Factors that raise significant concerns about the investee's ability to continue as a going concern, such as negative cash flows from operations, working capital deficiencies, or noncompliance with statutory capital requirements or debt covenants.[20]

Step 2. Measure the Impairment Loss

The impairment loss for an equity security with no readily determinable fair value is the difference between the carrying value and the estimated fair value.

Step 3. Report the Impairment Loss in Net Income

For equity securities with no readily determinable fair value, companies report the impairment loss in net income. Example 16A.4 illustrates accounting for the impairment of a held-to-maturity debt investment with no readily determinable fair value.

EXAMPLE 16A.4

Impairment of an Equity Investment with No Readily Determinable Fair Value

PROBLEM: Platinum Plating Company holds an equity investment in Silver Metal Company with a carrying value of $80,000. The investment does not have a readily determinable fair value. The current fair value of the investment is $56,000. Silver Metal Company has experienced financial difficulty to the extent that it is now questionable as to whether it will even remain in business. Does impairment exist? If so, what amount of loss will Platinum report in net income? What amount of loss will it report in other comprehensive income? What is the journal entry for the impairment loss, if needed?

SOLUTION: To determine whether an impairment loss exists, we follow the steps of impairment testing.

STEP 1. DETERMINE WHETHER THERE IS AN IMPAIRMENT LOSS FOR THE ASSET

We base our determination on two parts.

1. Comparing the $80,000 carrying value to the $56,000 fair value indicates an impairment loss of $24,000.
2. Because Silver Mining Company is experiencing significant financial difficulties, the qualitative assessment indicates that the investment is impaired.

STEP 2. MEASURE THE IMPAIRMENT LOSS

The impairment loss is the carrying value of $80,000 less the fair value of $56,000. Platinum should record an impairment loss of $24,000.

STEP 3: REPORT THE IMPAIRMENT LOSS IN NET INCOME

Platinum reports the impairment loss of $24,000 in net income because it is an equity security.

The journal entry is:

Account	December 31, Current Year	
Impairment Loss – Income	24,000	
Equity Investment		24,000

Exhibit 16A.1 presents a decision tree for the impairment of investments in financial assets under U.S. GAAP.

[20] ASC 321-10-35-3.

EXHIBIT 16A.1 Investments in Financial Assets: Impairment Decision Tree, U.S. GAAP

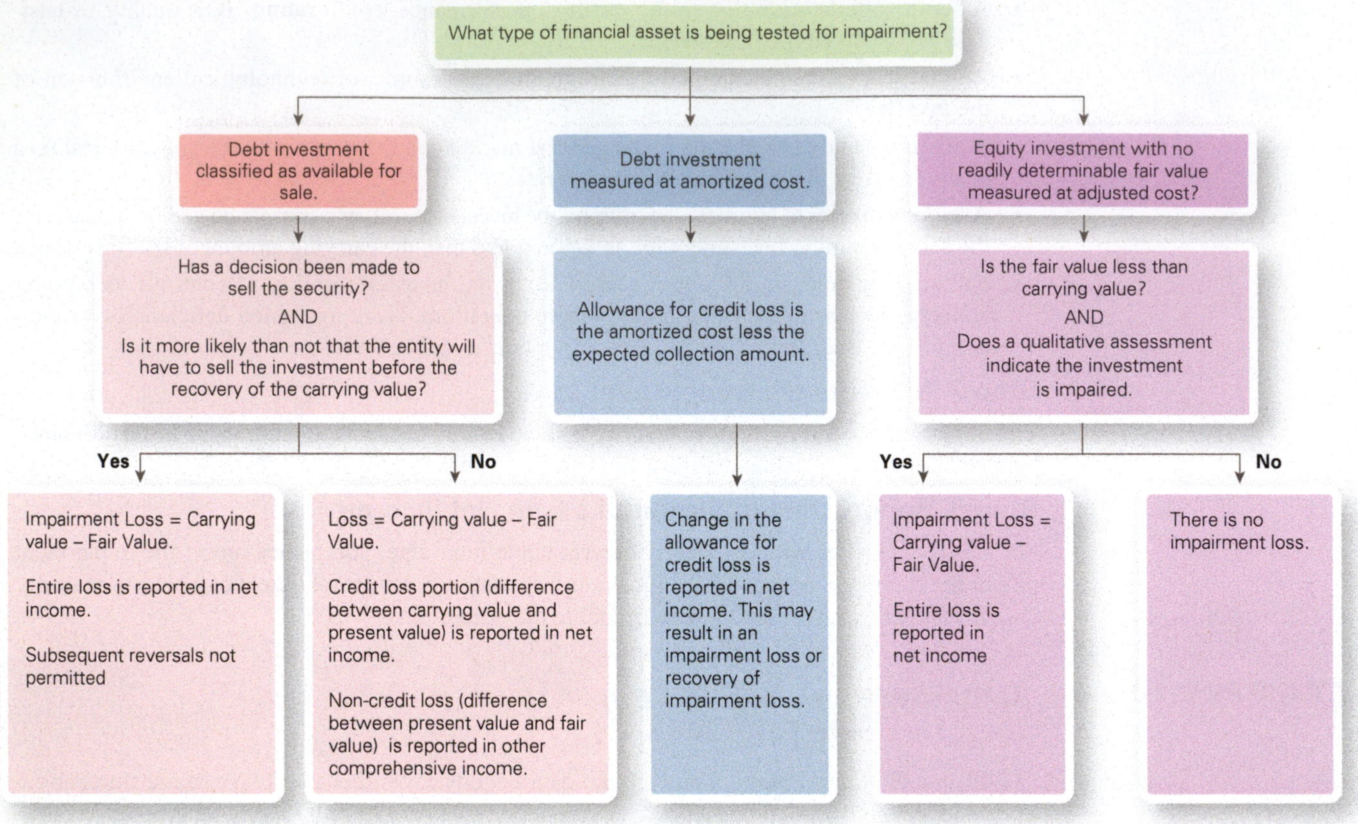

Accounting for Impairments: IFRS

Next, we discuss accounting for impairments of debt securities under IFRS, which differs from the U.S. GAAP approach to impairment. Under IFRS, equity securities are not tested for impairment. This is true even for the equity securities for which a company has elected to report unrealized gains and losses through other comprehensive income.

Accounting for Impairments under IFRS: Debt Securities Reported at Amortized Cost or Fair Value through Other Comprehensive Income

The computation of the impairment loss under IFRS is the same for debt investments measured at amortized cost and debt investments measured at fair value with unrealized gains and losses recognized in other comprehensive income. Although debt investment impairments are always based on an expected credit loss model, in accounting for debt investment impairments under IFRS, we must differentiate between two possible scenarios.

Scenario 1. The *credit risk* of the instrument has not significantly increased since initial recognition.

Scenario 2. The *credit risk* of the instrument has significantly increased since initial recognition. Thus, the accounting for impairments depends on the **credit risk**, which refers to the chance that the borrower will not repay the principal and/or interest. If the credit risk has not significantly increased since initial recognition of the instrument, then the computation of the expected credit loss is based on losses that would be incurred as a result of default events that are possible within the next 12 months.[21] If the credit risk has significantly increased since initial recognition, then the computation of the expected credit loss is based on losses that are expected over the remaining life of the investment.[22]

In the case of debt investments measured at amortized cost, an allowance is computed as the expected credit loss. The change in the allowance is recognized in net income. Example 16A.5 illustrates accounting for the impairment of a debt investment measured at amortized cost under IFRS.

EXAMPLE 16A.5

Impairment of a Debt Investment Measured at Amortized Cost: IFRS

PROBLEM: On January 2, 2018, Bronze Company purchased a debt investment for $100,000 and measures it at amortized cost. The debt has an interest rate of 5% over its contractual term of 10 years and has a 5% effective interest rate. On December 31, 2018, the fair value of the debt instrument has decreased to $95,000 as a result of changes in market interest rates. Bronze determines that there has not been a significant increase in credit risk since initial recognition and that expected credit losses should be measured at an amount equal to 12-month expected credit losses, which amounts to $3,000. What amount of loss, if any, will Bronze report in net income? What amount of loss will Bronze report in other comprehensive income? Prepare the journal entry for the impairment loss, if needed.

SOLUTION: Because the investment is measured at amortized cost, we are not concerned with the decrease in fair value. However, Bronze will recognize the allowance that is measured as the expected credit loss ($3,000).

The journal entry is:

Account	December 31, 2018	
Impairment Loss – Net Income	3,000	
Allowance for Impairment Loss		3,000

For debt investments reported at fair value through OCI, an impairment loss is reported in net income; however, an allowance account is not utilized. In this case, IFRS-reporting firms report the change in fair value in other comprehensive income. Example 16A.6 illustrates accounting for the impairment of a debt investment measured at fair value through OCI under IFRS.

EXAMPLE 16A.6

Impairment of a Debt Investment Measured at Fair Value through OCI: IFRS

PROBLEM: On January 2, 2018, Bronze Company purchased a debt investment for $100,000 and measures it at fair value through other comprehensive income. The debt has an interest rate of 5% over its contractual term of 10 years and has a 5% effective interest rate. On December 31, 2018, the fair value of the debt instrument has decreased to $95,000 as a result of changes in market interest rates. Bronze determines that there has not been a significant increase in credit risk since initial recognition and that expected credit losses should be measured at an amount equal to 12-month expected credit losses, which amounts to $3,000. What amount of loss, if any, will Bronze report in net income? What amount of loss will Bronze report in other comprehensive income? Prepare the journal entry for the impairment loss, if needed.

[21]The authoritative literature provides a useful simplification for investment grade instruments. In this case, the company can assume that there is not a significant increase in credit risk and thus compute only a 12-month expected credit loss.

[22]If the asset is credit impaired, interest revenue is computed using the effective interest rate and the net carrying amount (gross carrying amount less the allowance for impairment losses). Otherwise, interest revenue is computed using the effective interest rate and the gross carrying amount.

SOLUTION: Bronze separates the $5,000 decline in fair value into a $3,000 impairment credit loss reported in net income and the $2,000 unrealized loss reported in other comprehensive income.

The journal entry is:

Account	December 31, 2018	
Impairment Loss – Net Income	3,000	
Unrealized Loss – Other Comprehensive Income	2,000	
Debt Investment – FVOCI		5,000

Exhibit 16A.2 presents a decision tree for the impairment of investments in financial assets under IFRS.

EXHIBIT 16A.2 Investments in Financial Assets: Impairment Decision Tree, IFRS

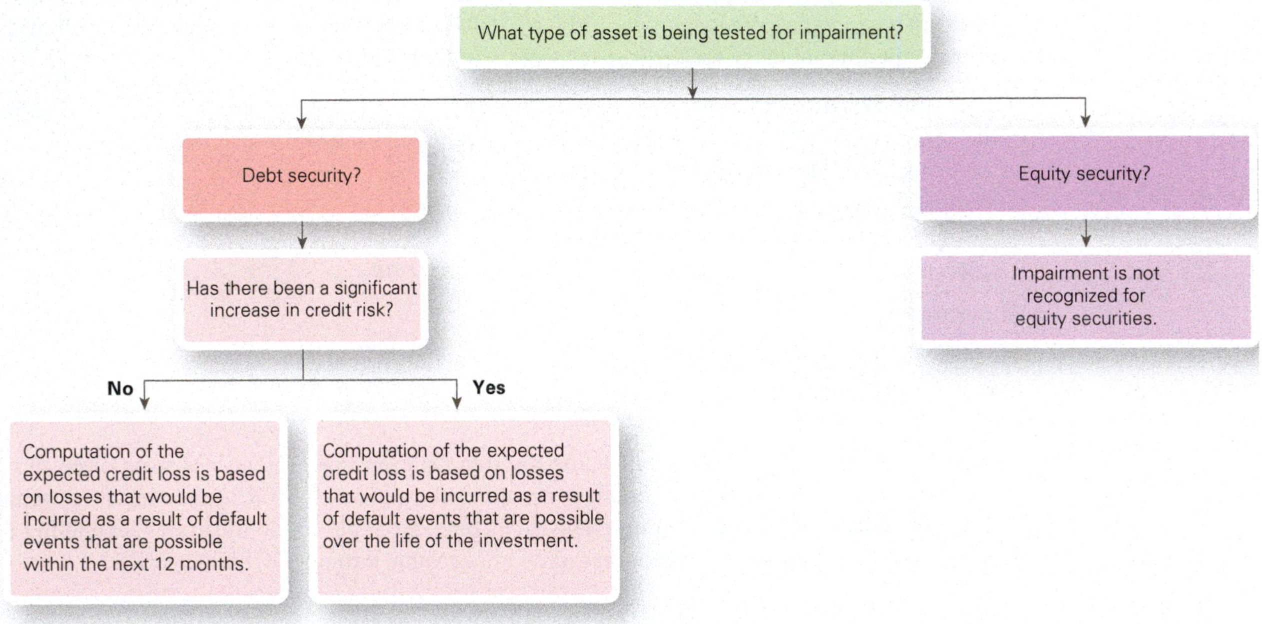

JUDGMENTS IN ACCOUNTING: Impairments of Investments in Financial Assets

Assessing whether an asset has been impaired involves a great deal of judgment, particularly when there is not an objectively determined fair value. Specifically, determining an asset's fair value involves judgments when estimating the inputs into the measurement process.

In the case of equity securities, is there evidence to support a fair value higher than (or equal to) the carrying value? In the case of some debt investments, is management going to sell, or is it more likely than not that they will have to sell the investment before recovery? These decisions cannot be predicted with certainty. How will management know whether they will have to sell the investment before the market recovers?

In the case of debt investments, management may also need to estimate the present value of future cash flows. But again, it is not possible to provide management an accurate estimate of future cash flows.

Exhibit 16A.3 presents a disclosure in ***Citigroup Inc.'s*** 2016 annual report. The disclosure indicates that management must make estimates related to fair value measurements and that current market conditions increase the risk and complexity of these judgments.

EXHIBIT 16A.3 Summary of Significant Accounting Policies Note, ***Citigroup Inc.,*** Financial Statements, December 31, 2016 [Excerpt]

Use of Estimates

Management must make estimates and assumptions that affect the Consolidated Financial Statements and the related Notes to the Financial Statements. Such estimates are used in connection with certain fair value measurements. See Note 24 to the Consolidated Financial Statements for further discussions on estimates used in the determination of fair value . . . . While management makes its best judgment, actual amounts or results could differ from those estimates. Current market conditions increase the risk and complexity of the judgments in these estimates.

Source: Financial Statements from Citigroup, Inc. Company's 2016 Annual Report. http://www.citigroup.com/citi/investor/quarterly/2017/ar16_en.pdf?ieNocache=759

A recent government debt crisis in Greece illustrates how judgment is used by managers to make valuation decisions. In 2011, a number of European banks such as France's ***BNP Paribas SA*** and Germany's ***Deutsche Bank AG*** made different accounting choices as to how they valued impaired Greek government bonds. Some banks valued the debt at its market value, which was about half of its face value, and then recorded an impairment charge against earnings to write down the other half. This approach resulted in a 100% write off of the investment on the balance sheet. Others asserted there was no active market for the debt, so they used their own valuation models. France's ***BNP Paribas*** reported impairment charges of 21% of its Greek debt. The U.K.'s ***Royal Bank of Scotland Group PLC***, however, impaired similar Greek government debt by 50%. Among these banks, the amount of the impairment write-down for the same debt instrument ranged from 21 to 100%. These accounting choices highlight the subjectivity of impairments based on judgments related to the inputs used in developing the estimated fair value of investment securities.

17 Accounting for Income Taxes

LEARNING OBJECTIVES

1. Define book income and taxable income; compute income tax expense and income taxes payable when there are no book-tax differences.
2. Discuss permanent differences and calculate income tax expense and income taxes payable when there are permanent differences.
3. Explain temporary differences and illustrate the balance sheet approach of accounting for deferred tax assets and deferred tax liabilities.
4. Explain and demonstrate how to assess and report the realizability of deferred tax assets.
5. Illustrate the effects of a change in tax rates.
6. Determine the accounting for net operating losses (NOLs), including NOL carrybacks and carryforwards and the valuation of related deferred tax assets.
7. Explain and demonstrate accounting for uncertain tax positions.
8. Describe the financial statement presentation of the income tax accounts.
9. Detail required disclosures for income taxes.

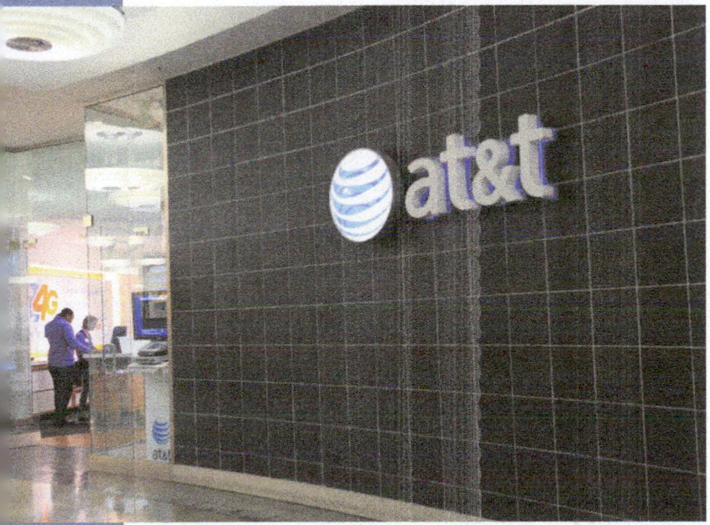

Sam Dao/Alamy Stock Photo

Introduction

WHY DID ***T-MOBILE US INC.*** report income tax expense of $867 million in 2016, but pay only $25 million in income taxes? How could ***AT&T*** report income tax expense of $6,479 million, but pay only $3,721 million in income taxes in 2016?

The differing objectives of financial reporting and tax reporting provide insight into these questions. The primary objective of financial reporting is to provide useful financial information. In contrast, taxing authorities at federal, state, and local levels implement tax codes to raise revenues, achieve economic objectives, or promote social objectives.

The different accounting methods for financial reporting and income taxation cause a company to pay income taxes that are not equal to the income tax expense reported on the income statement under financial reporting standards. Financial reporting and tax reporting differ because the amount of income taxes currently owed to the taxing authority is determined by rules and regulations set forth by tax law whereas accounting standards determine the income tax expense reported on the income statement. For example, governments allow companies to depreciate long-lived assets faster than financial reporting permits in order to spur economywide investment. The higher depreciation expense incurred for tax purposes lowers companies' taxable income. This in turn decreases the amount of cash paid to the government and frees up cash to invest in plant assets or to hire additional employees. To promote social objectives, governments encourage donations to nonprofit organizations by allowing tax deductions for charitable contributions. Similarly, the federal government does not tax interest income from investments in state and local bonds to help finance municipal projects and infrastructure.

The timing of revenue and expense recognition differs for book and tax purposes. For example, when deducting accelerated depreciation for taxes, a company postpones paying taxes in the current year that it will eventually owe in future years. So, the company has a *deferred tax liability* for financial reporting purposes. ***AT&T's*** deferred tax liability related to depreciation was $44.9 million at the end of 2016, meaning that it paid $44.9 million less in taxes over time because of accelerated tax depreciation deductions. ***AT&T*** benefitted by keeping more cash in the company in the short term.

Retiree pension and health care benefit expense requires companies to pay more taxes today than the company recognizes under financial reporting. The government allows a tax deduction only when the actual benefits are paid to the retired employees. For financial reporting purposes, firms accrue an estimated retiree pension and health care benefit expense during the time the employees work and earn the retirement benefits. In the case of advance tax payments, the company reports a *deferred tax asset* that will provide a future tax benefit. ***AT&T*** reported a $10.0 million deferred tax asset from retiree pension and health care benefits at the end of 2016.

Accounting for income taxes is not the same as tax return preparation. In fact, we rarely refer to preparing income tax returns in this chapter. Our focus is on reporting income tax expense and income taxes payable in the financial statements. We begin with a basic case in which book income—that is, income for financial reporting purposes—and taxable income are the same and then discuss differences between the book and taxable income. Some of these differences will create *deferred tax assets* and others will result in *deferred tax liabilities*. When evaluating deferred tax assets, companies must consider their ability to realize the future tax benefits. Because governments change tax rates, we will also address how to account for tax rate changes in terms of the effects of the changes on the measurement of income tax expense, income tax payable, and deferred income taxes. Next, we discuss two complex areas of tax accounting: *net operating losses* and *uncertain tax positions*. Finally, we conclude the chapter with discussions of disclosures and financial statement presentation of deferred tax assets and liabilities.[1] «

1 Define book income and taxable income; compute income tax expense and income taxes payable when there are no book-tax differences.

No Differences between Book and Tax Reporting

Computing income tax expense and income taxes payable is straightforward when *book income* and *taxable income* are identical. **Book income** is the amount of income that a company reports in its financial statements. **Taxable income** is the amount of income that a company reports on its tax return. In this case, the **basis**, or carrying value, of assets and liabilities, as well as the income of the entity, are the same for book and tax reporting. That is, the amount a company records as income tax expense will equal the income taxes payable to the government as illustrated in Example 17.1.

EXAMPLE 17.1

No Difference between Book and Tax Reporting

PROBLEM: Otis Optics, Inc. began business in 2018 and billed but did not collect $500,000 in revenue. Assume that Otis did not incur any expenses during the year. This sales transaction is treated identically for both book and income tax purposes. The tax rate is 35%, and Otis will pay any income taxes due in 2019. What journal entries are required to record both the revenues and the related income tax expense in 2018? What accounts and amounts will Otis report on its balance sheet?

SOLUTION: Otis Optics reports revenue of $500,000 on its GAAP-based income statement for 2018. The company recognizes income tax expense of $175,000 ($500,000 × 35%).

[1]For most of the relevant authoritative literature for this topic, see FASB ASC 740—*Income Taxes* for U.S. GAAP and IASC, *International Accounting Standard 12*, "Income Taxes" (London, UK: International Accounting Standards Committee, Revised, 2016) for IFRS.

Otis Optics will also pay income taxes of \$175,000 (\$500,000 × 35%) to the government because book income is the same as taxable income. On its 2018 year-end balance sheet, Otis reports an accounts receivable of \$500,000 and income taxes payable of \$175,000. Because net income increases stockholders' equity, Otis Optics now has equity of \$325,000. The journal entries are as follows:

Account	**2018**	
Accounts Receivable	500,000	
Sales Revenue		500,000

Account	**December 31, 2018**	
Income Tax Expense	175,000	
Income Taxes Payable		175,000

❷ Discuss permanent differences and calculate income tax expense and income taxes payable when there are permanent differences.

Permanent Differences between Book and Tax Reporting

We now consider transactions for which the book and tax treatment differs. These differences fall into two categories: *permanent differences* and *temporary differences*. We address *permanent differences* in this section.

Permanent differences in book income and taxable income result from transactions that are included:

1. In the computation of taxable income but never in book income.
2. In the computation of book income but never in taxable income.

Exhibit 17.1 presents several examples of permanent differences. Notice that permanent differences can cause book income to be greater or less than taxable income.

EXHIBIT 17.1 Permanent Book-Tax Differences under the U.S. Tax Code

Differences Resulting in Book Income Being *Greater* Than Taxable Income

1. Municipal interest income: Tax-free interest is reported on the financial statements as income, but it is not taxable.
2. Dividend received deduction: Corporations can deduct all or a portion of inter-corporate dividends received for tax purposes. However, all of the dividends received are reported as income on the financial statements.
3. Life insurance death proceeds for key officers or employees: Officers' life insurance proceeds received are reported as income on the financial statements but are not taxable.
4. Domestic production activities deduction: This is a tax deduction that provides incentives for businesses to produce most of their goods or services in the U.S., but it is not recognized as an expense on the financial statements.

Differences Resulting in Book Income Being *Less* Than Taxable Income

1. Fines and penalties: Fines and penalties are reported as expenses on the income statement but are not tax deductible.
2. Certain meals and entertainment expenses: Meals and entertainment costs are reported as expenses on the income statement but are not fully tax deductible.
3. Life insurance premiums paid for key officers or employees: Officers' life insurance is an expense subtracted on the income statement, but this cost cannot be deducted for tax purposes.
4. Expenses incurred in securing tax-exempt income: These expenses are subtracted from earnings on the income statement but are not deductible for tax purposes.

Accounting for Permanent Differences

When there are permanent differences, companies record both income tax expense and income tax payable on the financial statements based on the tax rules. For example, companies include municipal interest income in book revenues, but the U.S. federal government does not include municipal interest in taxable income. Therefore, a company does not pay taxes on this income and excludes the income from its computation of income tax expense as illustrated in Example 17.2.

EXAMPLE 17.2

Permanent Differences

PROBLEM: Modifying Example 17.1, assume that Otis Optics, a U.S. GAAP reporter, began business in 2018 and billed, but did not yet collect, $500,000 in revenue. In addition to its 2018 sales revenue, Otis Optics received $40,000 of municipal bond interest revenue. Otis Optics did not incur any expenses during the year. The company is subject to a 35% income tax rate. What journal entries are required to record the revenues and the related income tax for the year?

SOLUTION: Otis Optics's book income before income taxes is $540,000 ($500,000 in sales and $40,000 of municipal bond interest), and its taxable income is $500,000 (the $40,000 municipal bond interest is not taxable). The company will never be taxed on the $40,000 of municipal bond interest revenue, so we compute the income tax expense as follows:

Income before income taxes	$540,000
Less: Permanent differences	$(40,000)
Taxable income	$500,000
Tax rate	× 35%
Income tax expense	$175,000

Income taxes payable is computed as follows:

Taxable income	$500,000
Tax rate	× 35%
Income tax payable	$175,000

The journal entries to record these transactions follow:

Account	2018	
Accounts Receivable	500,000	
Sales Revenue		500,000

Account	2018	
Cash	40,000	
Interest Revenue		40,000

Account	December 31, 2018	
Income Tax Expense	175,000	
Income Taxes Payable		175,000

Permanent Differences and Effective Tax Rates

Permanent differences result in an *effective tax rate* that is different than the *statutory tax rate*. The **statutory tax rate** is the legally imposed rate in a given taxing jurisdiction. The **effective tax rate (ETR)** is income tax expense divided by book income before taxes. In Example 17.1 where book and taxable income are the same, the ETR is 35% ($175,000 / $500,000). In Example 17.2 where there is a permanent difference, the ETR is lower—specifically, 32.4% ($175,000 / $540,000). The company, Otis Optics, received tax-free income, so its tax rate on total income is lower than the 35% statutory income tax rate.

U.S. GAAP requires companies to reconcile the federal statutory income tax rate to the effective tax rate shown in either percentages of book income, dollars, or both. The required reconciliation for Example 17.2 follows.

Description	Dollars	Percentage
Income tax at the statutory tax rate	$189,000*	35.0%
Tax savings from municipal interest	(14,000)**	(2.6%)***
Tax at the effective rate	$175,000	32.4%****

* $540,000 × 35%
** $40,000 × 35%
*** $14,000 / $540,000
**** $175,000 / $540,000

Exhibit 17.2 illustrates the required reconciliation of a 35% statutory tax rate to 21.1%, 16.8%, and 19.3% effective tax rate for ***Google*** in fiscal 2014, 2015, and 2016, respectively. Its parent company is ***Alphabet Inc. Google*** provided the reconciliation of percentages from the statutory rate to its effective tax rate. Foreign tax rate differentials and federal research credits are permanent differences that reduce ***Google's*** tax rate.

EXHIBIT 17.2 Reconciliation of Statutory Tax Rate to Effective Tax Rate, ***Google's*** Annual Report, December 31, 2016

The reconciliation of federal statutory income tax rate to our effective income tax rate is as follows:

	Year Ended December 31,		
	2014	2015	2016
U.S. federal statutory tax rate	35.0%	35.0%	35.0%
Foreign rate differential	(12.2)%	(13.4)%	(11.0)%
Federal research credit	(1.8)%	(2.1)%	(2.0)%
Stock-based compensation expense	0.1%	0.3%	(3.4)%
Other adjustments	0.0%	(3.0)%	0.7%
Effective tax rate	21.1%	16.8%	19.3%

Source: Alphabet's Inc. 2016 Annual Report. United States Securities and Exchange Commission. Form 10K. https://abc.xyz/investor/pdf/2016_google_annual_report.pdf, page 72.

3 Explain temporary differences and illustrate the balance sheet approach of accounting for deferred tax assets and deferred tax liabilities.

Temporary Differences between Book and Tax Reporting

Temporary differences occur when the book treatment and the tax treatment for a given transaction are different in a given year but will be the same over the life of the firm. Specifically, the tax basis of an asset or liability differs from its book basis, resulting in taxable or deductible amounts in future years. Temporary differences occur because of events that have been recognized in the financial statements and will result in taxable or deductible amounts in future years or events that are taxable or deductible before they will be recognized in the financial statements.[2] Example 17.3 illustrates differences in book and tax carrying values.

EXAMPLE 17.3 Temporary Differences: Book and Tax Carrying Values

PROBLEM: Azorca Company uses straight-line depreciation for financial accounting and accelerated depreciation for tax accounting. No salvage value is used for either book or tax purposes. The company purchased equipment for $100,000 and depreciated it over 4 years for book purposes ($100,000/4 years = $25,000 per year). For tax purposes, the asset depreciates for 3 years: $40,000 the first year and $30,000 in each of the following 2 years. Thus, the total depreciation under both systems is $100,000.

Determine the book carrying value and the tax basis of the asset over its 4-year useful life.

SOLUTION: Using different book and tax depreciation methods will result in a different book carrying value and tax basis until the asset is fully depreciated as illustrated in the following tables:

Book Depreciation

Year	Straight-Line Depreciation Expense per Books	Accumulated Depreciation per Books	Carrying Value per Books ($100,000 – Accumulated Depreciation)
1	$ 25,000	$ 25,000	$75,000
2	25,000	50,000	50,000
3	25,000	75,000	25,000
4	25,000	100,000	0
Total	$100,000		

Tax Depreciation

Year	Accelerated Depreciation Deduction per Tax	Accumulated Depreciation per Tax	Tax Basis ($100,000 – Accumulated Depreciation)
1	$ 40,000	$ 40,000	$60,000
2	30,000	70,000	30,000
3	30,000	100,000	0
4	0	100,000	0
Total	$100,000		

The following table illustrates the difference in the equipment's carrying value per books and tax basis.

Year	Carrying Value per Books—Book Basis	Carrying Value per Tax—Tax Basis	Book-Tax Difference
1	$75,000	$60,000	$15,000
2	50,000	30,000	20,000
3	25,000	0	25,000
4	0	0	0

The differences between book income and taxable income originate in Years 1 through 3 and reverse (are reduced) in Year 4. At the end of the life of the asset, there are no differences between book income and taxable income and all differences are fully reversed.

[2] See FASB ASC 740-10-20 for a full definition of temporary differences.

Accounting for Temporary Differences

Companies use a *balance sheet approach* to account for temporary differences. The **balance sheet approach**, also referred to as the **asset and liability method**, focuses on the differences between book carrying values and tax bases of a firm's assets and liabilities.[3]

In Example 17.3, in Year 1 the book basis of the equipment is $75,000 and the tax basis is $60,000. The $15,000 difference between the book basis and tax basis of the equipment represents $15,000 less in current-year taxable income for the company and less tax currently payable. There is $15,000 less taxable income because more depreciation is deducted for tax purposes resulting in the lower tax basis relative to book. However, at the future point when the equipment is fully depreciated, the company will pay taxes on this $15,000 both for book and tax purposes. At a 35% tax rate, there is an additional $5,250 in future taxes payable ($15,000 × 35%). In effect, the company will owe this $5,250 tax, but it does not need to pay it at this time.

Deferred Tax Assets and Liabilities

Temporary differences create either *deferred tax liabilities* or *deferred tax assets*. The $5,250 tax liability from Example 17.3 is an example of a *deferred tax liability*. A **deferred tax liability** represents additional income taxes payable that will be due in future years. In other words, less tax is paid today, but that tax will be paid at some point in the future. Conversely, a **deferred tax asset** represents a future reduction in income taxes payable. That is, more tax is paid today, but the company will experience tax savings at some point in the future.

Under the balance sheet approach, deferred tax assets and deferred tax liabilities are computed by multiplying the income tax rate by the difference between the book carrying value and the tax basis of a company's assets and liabilities.

We discuss the four possible scenarios that create deferred tax assets or liabilities.

Scenario 1: Tax Basis of Asset Greater Than Book Basis of Asset. A deferred tax asset results when the tax basis of assets is greater than the book basis of assets. For example, consider inventory that a firm writes down for obsolescence under U.S. GAAP but not for tax purposes. If the firm has obsolete inventory, the tax basis of inventory will be higher than the book basis. When the firm eventually sells the inventory at a loss (or disposes of it), it receives a tax benefit because the transaction creates a tax deduction. Thus, until the temporary difference reverses (that is, until it sells or disposes of the inventory), the firm will report a deferred tax asset on its books representing this future tax benefit.

Scenario 2: Book Basis of Asset Greater Than Tax Basis of Asset. A deferred tax liability occurs when the book basis of assets is greater than the tax basis of assets. For example, a company typically depreciates fixed assets at a faster rate for tax purposes than it does for book purposes. Thus, in earlier years, the book basis in these assets is greater than the basis under income tax reporting. In future years, tax deductions for depreciation related to these assets will decrease, in turn increasing the company's income tax payment to the government.

Scenario 3: Tax Basis of Liability Greater Than Book Basis of Liability. There is a deferred tax liability when the tax basis of liabilities is greater than their book basis. This scenario is rare because it is far more likely that liabilities are accrued for book purposes before they are paid. When this scenario is found in practice, it involves complex transactions.

Scenario 4: Book Basis of Liability Greater Than Tax Basis of Liability. A deferred tax asset is created when the book basis of a liability is greater than the tax basis of the liability. For example, under book reporting, a firm will recognize a warranty expense and record an estimated liability for future warranty costs when it is both estimable and probable. However,

[3]Whereas it can be tempting to think of these transactions in terms of differences between book and taxable income, according to the authoritative guidance, this approach is not correct. In fact, in some more complex transactions, a computation approach that is based on income statement differences can yield incorrect results.

the company cannot deduct the estimated warranty cost under tax reporting until the warranty repairs actually take place. Thus, the book basis of the liability is greater than the tax basis. Because the firm has not yet deducted the cost of product repair under warranty, there will be a future tax benefit at the time the deduction occurs. As a result, a company will record a deferred tax asset for the future tax benefit when it records an estimated warranty liability for book purposes. Exhibit 17.3 summarizes these four scenarios.

EXHIBIT 17.3 Four Scenarios for Creating Deferred Tax Assets and Liabilities

Situation	Balance Sheet Elements	
	Assets	**Liabilities**
Tax basis > Book basis	Scenario 1. Deferred tax asset	Scenario 3. Deferred tax liability
Book basis > Tax basis	Scenario 2. Deferred tax liability	Scenario 4. Deferred tax asset

Exhibit 17.4 presents common examples of temporary differences based on U.S. GAAP and the U.S. tax laws. The first column, Differences That Lead to Deferred Tax Liabilities, identifies the item giving rise to the deferred tax. The second column lists which of the four scenarios the item usually falls under. The third column, Balance Sheet Effect, describes the difference in the book versus tax basis of the item resulting in the deferred tax. The fourth column explains the tax treatment accounting, and the fifth column explains the GAAP accounting. For example, *installment sales* generally fall under Scenario 2 in which the book basis of installment sales

EXHIBIT 17.4 Examples of Temporary Book-Tax Differences

Differences That Lead to Deferred Tax Liabilities	Scenario	Balance Sheet Effect	Tax Treatment	Book Treatment
1. **Installment sales**	Scenario 2: Deferred tax liability	Installment sales receivable is higher for book than for tax	Recognize revenue only when cash is received	Recognize revenue and installment sales receivable when the product is sold
2. **Depreciation**	Scenario 2: Deferred tax liability	Carrying value of property, plant, and equipment is higher for book than for tax	Use accelerated method to calculate depreciation expense	Record depreciation expense using straight line
3. **Goodwill**	Scenario 2: Deferred tax liability	Goodwill is higher for book than for tax	Generally amortize to expense over 15 years	Test for impairment and expense only if impaired
4. **Equity method investment**	Scenario 2: Deferred tax liability	Equity method investment (asset) is higher for book than for tax	Do not record share of investee's net income	Record share of investee's net income

Differences That Lead to Deferred Tax Assets	Scenario	Balance Sheet Effect	Tax Treatment	Book Treatment
1. **Unearned revenues (advance receipts)**	Scenario 4: Deferred tax asset	Unearned revenues higher for book than for tax	Recognize revenues when cash is received	Recognize revenue and decrease liability when earned
2. **Contingent liabilities**	Scenario 4: Deferred tax asset	Contingent liabilities higher for book than for tax	Deduct the loss only when amounts are known	Recognize the loss and liability when it is probable and estimable
3. **Bad debt expense**	Scenario 1: Deferred tax asset	Net accounts receivable lower for book than for tax	Deduct the bad debt expense only when specific account is written off	Deduct the bad debt expense and record a contra-asset in the period of the sale
4. **Warranty liability**	Scenario 4: Deferred tax asset	Warranty liability higher for books than for tax	Deduct only when the warranty service is performed	Expense the estimated cost of repair and record a liability when the product is sold

receivable is higher than the tax basis. For taxes, an **installment sale** is generally recognized as revenue only when cash is received. Therefore, the tax basis of the receivable is zero. Under GAAP, revenue is often recognized when the product is sold. So, there is usually an installment sales receivable under GAAP and higher book basis than tax basis of the receivable.

Exhibit 17.5 presents ***Target Corporation's*** tax footnote disclosing the components of deferred tax assets and liabilities from its January 2017 balance sheet. Note the allowance for accruals and reserves not currently deductible such as the doubtful accounts led to a deferred tax asset of $328 million on January 28, 2017. Bad debts are written off only when the account is determined to be uncollectible for tax purposes. ***Target*** used the allowance method for book purposes when recording the bad debt expense in the year of the sale. In this case, the net accounts receivable is lower for book purposes than for tax purposes. That is, there is a lower carrying value of accounts receivable for books that resulted in a deferred tax asset. Property and equipment cost created a deferred tax liability of $1,822 million at January 28, 2017. For it, ***Target*** used accelerated depreciation for tax purposes and the straight-line method for books. It reported fixed assets at a higher carrying value for financial reporting than for tax. The higher book carrying value for the fixed assets results in a deferred tax liability.

EXHIBIT 17.5 Components of Deferred Tax Assets and Liabilities, ***Target Corporation,*** Annual Financial Statements, January 28, 2017

Net Deferred Tax Asset/(Liability) (millions)	**January 28, 2017**	**January 30, 2016**
Gross deferred tax assets:		
Accrued and deferred compensation	$ 455	$ 476
Accruals and reserves not currently deductible	328	323
Self-insured benefits	178	199
Prepaid store-in-store lease income	258	270
Other	62	90
Total gross deferred tax assets	$ 1,281	$ 1,358
Gross deferred tax liabilities:		
Property and equipment	$(1,822)	$(1,790)
Inventory	(182)	(190)
Other	(102)	(168)
Total gross deferred tax liabilities	(2,106)	(2,148)
Total net deferred tax asset/(liability)	$ (825)	$ (790)

Source: Target Corporation, Annual Reports. 2016 Annual Report. https://corporate.target.com/_media/TargetCorp/annualreports/2016/pdfs/Target-2016-Annual-Report.pdf?ext=.pdf

Example 17.4 provides a detailed illustration of accounting for temporary differences.

EXAMPLE 17.4

Scenario 2: Book Basis of Assets Greater Than Tax Basis Resulting in a Deferred Tax Liability

PROBLEM: Otis Optics, Inc. began business during 2018 and billed but did not collect $500,000 in revenue. Otis Optics also sold $60,000 of merchandise on installment sales. None of the installment sales is collected during the current year. Installment sales are considered revenue and installment sales receivable for book purposes but not for tax purposes. Otis will recognize revenue on installment sales for tax purposes only when it collects cash. Ignore cost of goods sold. Assume no operating expenses during the year. Assume also that the company did not incur any expenses during the year. In addition, Otis did not report any permanent differences.

Continued

The company's tax rate is 35%. What is Otis's income tax expense and income taxes payable? Show the difference in the book carrying value and the tax basis of the receivable from installment sales and compute the deferred tax liability. What journal entries are required for the year to record both the revenues and the related income tax?

SOLUTION: The book carrying value of the installment sales receivable is $60,000 greater than the tax basis of zero. The tax basis is zero because the installment sale is not recorded as revenue or a receivable for tax purposes. Exhibit 17.3 indicates that when the book basis of an asset is greater than its tax basis, the company reports a deferred tax liability. The deferred tax liability is the difference in the basis of the asset times the statutory tax rate. Thus, we compute the deferred tax liability as follows:

	Book (GAAP) Basis	Tax Basis	Difference
Installment sales receivable	$60,000	$0	$60,000
Tax rate			× 35%
Deferred tax liability			$21,000

Income tax expense is the tax rate multiplied by book income adjusted for permanent differences. Otis's book income is $560,000, which is the sum of its regular sales and installment sales ($500,000 + $60,000). There are no permanent differences in this example, so income tax expense is equal to $196,000 ($560,000 × 35%). Taxable income is only $500,000 because it excludes the revenue from the installment sale. Income tax payable, the amount that Otis Optics owes the government this year, is $175,000 ($500,000 × 35%). These computations are presented in the following table.

Computation of Income Tax Expense		Computation of Income Tax Payable	
Sales revenue	$500,000	Sales revenue	$500,000
Installment sales revenue	$ 60,000	Installment sales revenue	0
Income before income taxes	$560,000	Taxable income	$500,000
Tax rate	× 35%	Tax rate	× 35%
Income tax expense	$196,000	Income taxes payable	$175,000

The difference between Otis's income tax expense of $196,000 and income taxes payable of $175,000 results from the difference in the book and tax treatments for installment sales receivable.

The journal entries follow:

Account	2018	
Accounts Receivable	500,000	
Sales Revenue		500,000

Account	2018	
Installment Sales Receivable	60,000	
Installment Sales Revenue		60,000

Account	December 31, 2018	
Income Tax Expense	196,000	
Deferred Tax Liability		21,000
Income Taxes Payable		175,000

Temporary Difference Reversal

Example 17.4 provided an analysis of the initial creation of a deferred tax liability account. When a deferred tax account is created and continues to increase, we say that it originates. What accounting is required when Otis collects the installment sales receivable and the temporary difference *reverses*? In general, a temporary difference **reverses** when a company either:

1. Has to pay the taxes it previously recorded as a deferred tax liability or
2. Receives the benefits of reduced taxes originally reported as a deferred tax asset.

The reversal reduces the deferred tax account in both cases. To illustrate, Example 17.5 presents the reversal of the deferred tax liability created by Otis Optics in Example 17.4.

EXAMPLE 17.5

Temporary Difference Reversal—Scenario 2: Book Basis of Assets Greater Than Tax Basis

PROBLEM: Continuing with Example 17.4, assume that Otis Optics collected the $60,000 of installment sales receivable in 2019. This amount is taxable income because it is collected in cash. Otis already had recorded book income for installment sales in 2018 along with the related installment sales receivable, so no book income is recognized in the year of cash collection. In addition, Otis recorded $200,000 of regular sales on account during 2019. Ignore cost of goods sold. Assume no operating expenses in 2019. Determine the difference in the book carrying value and tax basis of the account receivable from the installment sale and compute the deferred tax liability. What is the journal entry to record income taxes for the year?

SOLUTION: Once Otis collects the $60,000, both the book basis and tax basis of the related installment sales receivable is zero.

	Installment Sales Receivable—Book Basis	Installment Sales Receivable—Tax Basis	Difference	Tax Rate (%)	Deferred Tax Liability
Beginning balance	$60,000	$0	$60,000	35%	$21,000
Change	(60,000)	0	(60,000)	35	(21,000)
Ending balance	$ 0	$0	$ 0	35%	$ 0

So, the ending balance of the deferred tax liability is also equal to zero. The deferred tax liability of $21,000 has fully reversed during the year as illustrated in the t-account that follows.[4]

Deferred Tax Liability

	Debit	Credit	
		21,000	Prior Year–Origination
Following Year–Reversal	21,000		
		0	End of Year

We decrease the deferred tax liability for the reversal with a debit of $21,000. When a deferred tax liability reverses, income taxes become currently payable. Therefore, we increase income taxes payable. The computation of income tax expense and income tax payable is presented on the next page.

Continued

[4]Although the book tax differences completely reverse, there is a tax benefit by paying less tax in Year 1 based on the time value of money. However, the time value of money is not considered in accounting for income taxes.

Computation of Income Tax Expense		Computation of Income Tax Payable	
Sales revenue	$200,000	Sales revenue	$200,000
Installment sales revenue	0	Installment sales revenue	60,000
Income before income tax	$200,000	Taxable income	$260,000
Tax rate	× 35%	Tax rate	× 35%
Income taxes expense	$ 70,000	Income tax payable	$ 91,000

The journal entries follow:

Account	***2019***	
Accounts Receivable	200,000	
Sales Revenue		200,000

Account	***2019***	
Cash	60,000	
Installment Sales Receivable		60,000

Account	***December 31, 2019***	
Income Tax Expense	70,000	
Deferred Tax Liability	21,000	
Income Taxes Payable		91,000

Note that Otis will pay $91,000 for income taxes this year. The payment consists of two parts: $70,000 for income generated from current economic activity and $21,000 to pay the liability deferred in the prior year and owed currently.

Examples 17.6 and 17.7 illustrate accounting for the origination of a deferred tax asset and its subsequent reversal.

EXAMPLE 17.6 Scenario 4: Book Basis of Liabilities Greater Than Tax Basis Resulting in a Deferred Tax Asset

PROBLEM: Otis Optics reported sales on account of $500,000 in 2018 and no permanent differences. The company also recorded an estimated product warranty liability and the related warranty expense of $110,000 for book purposes. There were no additional expenses in 2018. Under tax law, Otis cannot deduct the estimated warranty expense and does not create a tax liability for these amounts until it actually provides the services by repairing the product. Ignore cost of goods sold. Assume no operating expenses during the year. The company's tax rate is 35%. What is Otis's income tax expense and income taxes payable? Show the difference between the book carrying value and the tax basis of the warranty liability. In addition, compute the deferred tax asset. What journal entries are required for the year to record the revenues, warranty expense, and the related income tax?

SOLUTION: The book basis of the firm's liabilities is greater than the tax basis because Otis does not create a liability for the warranty for tax purposes until the product is actually repaired. From Exhibit 17.3, we know that when the book basis of a liability is greater than its tax basis, the company will report a deferred tax asset. We compute the deferred tax asset as follows:

	Book (U.S. GAAP)	Tax	Difference
Warranty liability	$110,000	$0	$110,000
Tax rate			× 35%
Deferred tax asset			$ 38,500

The income tax expense is the tax rate times book income adjusted for permanent differences. Otis's book income is $390,000 computed as revenues less the estimated warranty expense ($500,000 − $110,000). There are no permanent differences, so income tax expense is equal to $136,500 ($390,000 × 35%). Taxable income is equal to total revenues of $500,000 because the warranty expense is not tax deductible until actual repairs are made. Income tax payable, the amount that Otis Optics owes the government this year, is $175,000 ($500,000 × 35%). Income tax expense and income tax payable are computed as follows:

Computation of Income Tax Expense		Computation of Income Taxes Payable	
Sales revenue	$500,000	Sales revenue	$500,000
Warranty expense	$(110,000)	Warranty expense	0
Income before income taxes	$390,000	Taxable income	$500,000
Tax rate	× 35%	Tax rate	× 35%
Income tax expense	$ 136,500	Income taxes payable	$175,000

The difference between Otis's income tax expense and income taxes payable results from the difference in book and tax treatments of the warranty expense.

The journal entries to record the transactions for the year follow:

Account	2018	
Accounts Receivable	500,000	
Sales Revenue		500,000

Account	December 31, 2018	
Warranty Expense	110,000	
Warranty Liability		110,000

Account	December 31, 2018	
Income Tax Expense	136,500	
Deferred Tax Asset	38,500	
Income Taxes Payable		175,000

In our next example, we account for a deferred tax asset and its reversal when the book basis of liabilities exceeds the tax basis. Example 17.7 demonstrates the creation of a deferred tax asset from an underlying difference in the book and tax basis of a warranty liability account. After the warranty liability is satisfied by making actual repairs, it is reduced to zero for book purposes, and the deferred tax asset reverses.

EXAMPLE 17.7 Temporary Difference Reversal—Scenario 4: Book Basis of Liabilities Greater Than Tax Basis

PROBLEM: Continuing Example 17.6, assume that Otis Optics made actual warranty repairs at a total cost of $110,000 in 2019. The company also reported $300,000 in sales revenue on account and did not incur any additional expenses for the year. The company is subject to a 35% income tax rate and does not report any permanent differences. Ignore cost of goods sold. Show the difference in the book and tax bases of the warranty liability and compute the deferred tax asset. What journal entries are required to record this year's sales and the income tax provision for the year?

SOLUTION: Because Otis satisfied the warranty liability by making the actual product repairs, both the book and tax basis of the liability is zero. As a result, Otis can remove the deferred tax asset associated with this temporary difference (i.e., the book-tax difference reverses).

	Warranty Liability—Book Basis	Warranty Liability—Tax Basis	Difference	Tax Rate (%)	Deferred Tax Asset
Beginning balance	$110,000	$0	$110,000	35%	$38,500
Change	(110,000)	0	(110,000)	35	(38,500)
Ending balance	$ 0	$0	$ 0	35%	$ 0

The ending balance of the deferred tax asset is zero because the beginning balance of $38,500 fully reversed during the year. The t-account for the deferred tax asset follows.

	Deferred Tax Asset		
Prior Year–Origination	38,500		
		38,500	Following Year–Reversal
End of Year	0		

We decrease the deferred tax asset with a credit of $38,500. Reversing a deferred tax asset lowers currently payable income taxes.

Computation of Income Tax Expense		Computation of Income Taxes Payable	
Sales revenue	$300,000	Sales revenue	$300,000
Warranty expense	(0)	Warranty expense	(110,000)
Income before income taxes	$300,000	Taxable Income	$190,000
Tax rate	× 35%	Tax rate	× 35%
Income tax expense	$105,000	Income taxes payable	$ 66,500

The journal entries to record transactions for the year are as follows:

Account	*2019*	
Accounts Receivable	300,000	
Sales Revenue		300,000

Account	*2019*	
Warranty Liability	110,000	
Cash		110,000

Account	December 31, 2019	
Income Tax Expense	105,000	
Deferred Tax Asset		38,500
Income Taxes Payable		66,500

Otis pays $66,500 in tax rather than the income tax expense of $105,000 recorded on the income statement because it had paid the difference of $38,500 in the prior year. The taxes paid in the prior year provided future economic benefit and were recorded as a deferred tax asset (i.e., Otis deferred realization of the benefit of the asset until the year it actually made the warranty repair).

Examples 17.4 through 17.7 presented the origination and reversal of one book-tax difference without the existence of permanent differences. The chapter Appendix provides a comprehensive example of multiple temporary and permanent book-tax differences.

Temporary Differences and Tax Rates

In Examples 17.4 and 17.6, the effective tax rate is 35% as shown in the following, which is the same as the starting statutory rate.

Income Statement (GAAP or Book)	Example 17.4	Example 17.6
Income tax expense	$196,000	$136,500
Income before tax	$560,000	$390,000
Effective tax rate	35%	35%

Temporary differences do not cause the effective tax rate to vary from the statutory tax rate and do not change amounts that ultimately become taxable or become tax deductible. Temporary differences affect only the timing of revenue and expense recognition. Only permanent differences result in an effective rate that is different than the statutory rate, because permanent differences change the amounts that are ultimately taxable or tax deductible.

THE CONCEPTUAL FRAMEWORK CONNECTION
Temporary Differences

Preparers and users of financial statements have debated the merits of the current approach to accounting for temporary differences for years. The accounting standards used in accounting for income taxes are quite complex, leading some to question their necessity. Key areas questioned include the following:

1. Should companies base income tax expense reported on the income statement on book income after adjusting for permanent differences, or should they instead record income tax expense based on taxable income?
2. Should companies record deferred tax assets and deferred tax liabilities? In other words, are deferred tax assets and deferred tax liabilities *real* assets and liabilities?

The basics of financial reporting as presented in the conceptual framework provide insight into these questions. First, the framework states that "[a]ccrual accounting attempts to record the financial effects on an entity of transactions and other events and circumstances that have cash consequences for the entity in the periods in which those transactions, events, and circumstances occur rather than only in the periods in which cash is received or paid by the entity."[5]

[5] Financial Accounting Standards Board, *Statement of Financial Accounting Concepts No. 6, "Elements of Financial Statements,"* Paragraph 139.

Thus, under accrual accounting, income tax expense cannot simply be the amount that the firm pays to the government: That approach would occur only under a cash-basis system. Instead, firms should record expenses based on principles of the conceptual framework. The framework states "expenses are generally recognized when an entity's economic benefits are consumed. . . ."[6]

Consider Example 17.4 involving installment sales. Otis recorded revenues and installment sales receivable for book purposes. It did not record these items on its tax returns. Because Otis recorded revenue in its books, it also recognized income tax expense related to that revenue. So Otis recognized income tax expense on its books even though there was no income tax currently payable. With an accrual system, the entity will eventually receive cash for *the transaction that has already occurred* and will pay income taxes on installment sales revenue only when cash is received. Otis earned revenue from the installment sales, and the fact that the company did not collect cash in the year the sales were made is not relevant for financial reporting.

Whether firms should record a deferred tax asset or liability is related to the question involving income tax expense. The conceptual framework defines assets as "probable future economic benefits obtained or controlled by a particular entity as a result of past transactions or events. . . ."[7] Liabilities are "probable future sacrifices of economic benefits arising from present obligations of a particular entity to transfer assets or provide services to other entities in the future as a result of past transactions or events."[8] Thus, for example, Otis will eventually receive cash and will be required to pay taxes for the previously deferred liability related to the installment sales. Because the transaction has already occurred, the deferred income taxes are a true liability.[9]

4 Explain and demonstrate how to assess and report the realizability of deferred tax assets.

Realizability of Deferred Tax Assets: Assessing and Reporting

When a firm records a deferred tax asset, it is required to consider the likelihood that it will actually receive economic benefit from that asset. That is, the firm must consider whether it will ever realize a reduction in its income taxes paid to the government.

Consider the balance of accounts receivable reported on the balance sheet. A company will assess this balance for possible uncollectible accounts and use an allowance account to reduce the balance of accounts receivable to its net realizable value. The same assessment is required to arrive at the proper valuation of deferred tax assets. A company assesses deferred tax assets for future realization, and if it expects all or a portion of the future benefits to be unrealized, it uses an allowance account to reduce the deferred tax asset to its net realizable value. The reduction of the deferred tax asset increases income tax expense. We discuss the use of a *valuation allowance* to reduce the carrying value of a deferred tax asset in this section.

Treatment of Deferred Tax Assets

U.S. GAAP specifies that if it is "more likely than not" that the firm will not realize some portion of the deferred tax asset, the firm must reduce the deferred tax asset to its net realizable value. U.S. GAAP defines "more likely than not" as a likelihood of slightly more than 50%.

[6]Financial Accounting Standards Board, *Statement of Financial Accounting Concepts No. 5, "Recognition and Measurement in Financial Statements of Business Enterprises,"* Paragraph 65.

[7]Financial Accounting Standards Board, *Statement of Financial Accounting Concepts No. 6, "Elements of Financial Statements,"* 1985, Paragraphs 25 and 35.

[8]Ibid.

[9]For a further examination of this issue, see the Basis for Conclusions Cases at the end of the chapter.

Assessing Realizability. Because deferred tax assets produce future tax deductible amounts, income is needed in order to realize these tax benefits. Firms must use reasonable estimates of future income sources to assess the realizability of a deferred tax asset. U.S. GAAP lists four possible sources of taxable income that firms should consider:

1. Future reversals of existing taxable temporary differences
2. Future taxable income exclusive of reversing temporary differences and *carryforwards*
3. Taxable income in prior *carryback* year(s) if carryback is permitted under the tax law
4. Tax-planning strategies that would, if necessary, be implemented[10]

Management must examine all available evidence, both positive and negative, to determine whether it is more likely than not that all or a portion of the future tax benefits of a deferred tax asset will not be realized. Positive evidence would include any of the four sources of taxable income in addition to other forms of evidence, such as:

1. Existing contracts or firm sales backlog
2. An excess of appreciated asset value over the tax basis of the entity's net assets
3. A strong earnings history exclusive of the loss that created the future deductible amount[11]

Some examples of negative evidence to be considered when assessing the need to reduce the net realizable value of a deferred tax asset are:

1. Cumulative losses in recent years
2. A history of operating loss or tax credit carryforwards expiring unused
3. Unsettled circumstances that could adversely affect future operations
4. A *carryback* or *carryforward* period that is so brief that it could limit realization of tax benefits[12]

Reporting Realizability. U.S. GAAP uses a two-step approach to record the net realizable amount:

1. Record the full amount of the deferred tax asset
2. Assess the deferred tax asset for realizability

If the firm determines that all or a portion of the deferred tax asset is not realizable, it uses a *valuation allowance* to reduce the balance of the deferred tax asset. The **valuation allowance** is a contra-asset to the deferred tax asset account on the balance sheet. Thus, the company reports a net deferred tax asset on its balance sheet measured as the deferred tax asset net of the valuation allowance.

Anytime a firm increases or decreases its valuation allowance to decrease or increase its deferred tax asset, there is a corresponding increase or decrease in income tax expense. As a result, there is a change in the firm's effective tax rate.

If the valuation allowance is increased (reducing the net realizable value of the deferred tax asset), income tax expense also increases. Conversely, when the valuation allowance is decreased (increasing the net realizable value of the deferred tax asset), there is a decrease in income tax expense (an increase to the *income tax benefit*). The **income tax benefit** is a reduction of income tax expense and thus increases income. Although temporary differences do not cause the ETR to differ from the statutory rate, a change in the assessment of deferred tax assets' realizability result in a change in the ETR. For example, ***Luby's Inc.,*** the restaurant operator, increased its valuation allowance by $6.9 million in 2016, lowering its ETR by 128.3%. Example 17.8 illustrates assessing and reporting the realizability of deferred tax assets.

[10]This list can be found in FASB ASC 740-10-30-18.
[11]This list can be found in FASB ASC 740-10-30-22.
[12]This list can be found in FASB ASC 740-10-30-21.

EXAMPLE 17.8 Assessing and Reporting the Realizability of Deferred Tax Assets

PROBLEM: Consider Otis Optics from Example 17.6. Otis recorded $500,000 in sales revenue in 2018. The company is subject to a 35% tax rate. Otis recorded a deferred tax asset of $38,500 in 2018 because of a $110,000 basis difference in warranty liabilities ($110,000 × 35%). Based on its assessment of all positive and negative evidence associated with this deferred tax asset, management has assessed that it is more likely than not that it will not realize 40% of the deferred tax asset. Ignore cost of goods sold. What are the necessary journal entries to record the deferred tax asset and valuation allowance? Prepare a partial 2018 income statement and balance sheet for Otis Optics and compare it with the financial statements from Example 17.6 that do not include a valuation allowance. What is the effective tax rate in the two examples? Provide the footnote reconciliation of the federal statutory income tax rate to the effective tax rate in both dollars and percentages, incorporating the use of the valuation allowance.

SOLUTION: Management needs to record a 40% valuation allowance for the $38,500 deferred tax asset, or $15,400 ($38,500 × 40%). The journal entries required to record the 2018 transactions follow:

Account	2018	
Accounts Receivable	500,000	
Sales Revenue		500,000

Account	December 31, 2018	
Warranty Expense	110,000	
Warranty Liability		110,000

Account	December 31, 2018	
Income Tax Expense	136,500	
Deferred Tax Asset	38,500	
Income Taxes Payable		175,000

Account	December 31, 2018	
Income Tax Expense	15,400	
Valuation Allowance for Deferred Tax Asset		15,400

After recording the valuation allowance, Otis Optics has a net deferred tax asset of $23,100 ($38,500 − $15,400) and income tax expense of $151,900 ($136,500 plus $15,400). The comparison of the partial income statements shows that when a firm recognizes a valuation allowance, its net income decreases (by increasing income tax expense). Otis's net income is decreased from $253,500 to $238,100 in this case. A comparison of the partial balance sheets shows that when a firm recognizes a valuation allowance, it decreases assets (by decreasing the net deferred tax asset balance). In this case, Otis's assets were decreased from $538,500 to $523,100.

	Without Valuation Allowance	With Valuation Allowance
Partial Income Statement		
Sales Revenue	$500,000	$500,000
Warranty Expense	(110,000)	(110,000)
Income before Income Taxes	390,000	390,000
Income Tax Expense	(136,500)	(151,900)
Net Income	$253,500	$238,100
Effective Tax Rate	35%	38.9%
Partial Balance Sheet		
Assets:		
Accounts Receivable	$500,000	$500,000
Deferred Tax Asset—Net of Valuation Allowance	38,500	23,100
TOTAL	$538,500	$523,100
Liabilities and Stockholders' Equity:		
Warranty Liability	$ 110,000	$ 110,000
Income Taxes Payable	175,000	175,000
Stockholders' Equity	253,500	238,100
TOTAL	$538,500	$523,100

The ETR before recording a valuation allowance is 35% ($136,500 / $390,000). The effective tax rate after recording the valuation allowance increases to 38.9% ($151,900 / 390,000). The higher ETR is a result of the increase in income tax expense caused by the use of a valuation allowance.

The required footnote reconciliation after recognizing the valuation allowance follows.

Description	Dollars	Percentage
Income tax at the statutory tax rate	$136,500*	35.0%
Increase in the valuation allowance	15,400	3.9%**
Tax at the effective rate	$151,900	38.9%***

* $390,000 × 35%
** $15,400 / $390,000
*** $151,900 / $390,000

Treatment of Deferred Tax Assets: IFRS

IFRS uses the term "probable" when defining the portion of a deferred tax asset that the firm will not realize. IFRS guidance views "probable" as a likelihood greater than 50%. Although the terms that U.S. GAAP and IFRS use differ, the amount determined to be realizable should be the same. IFRS uses a one-step approach under which the company assesses the realizability of the deferred tax asset before recording it. Firms then report only the realizable portion of the deferred tax asset. IFRS does not use a valuation allowance. Because the assessment of the realizability should result in the same amount under IFRS and U.S. GAAP, the reported net deferred tax asset should be the same under both.

Companies evaluate the realizable amount of deferred tax assets every time they prepare financial statements. Thus, for example, if at the end of 2019 Otis Optics judged that there is more than a 50% chance that it will realize the entire deferred tax asset, it would remove the valuation allowance from its books and decrease the income tax expense.

Exhibit 17.6 summarizes the U.S. GAAP and IFRS approaches to valuing deferred tax assets.

EXHIBIT 17.6 U.S. GAAP and IFRS: Assessing and Recording the Realizability of Deferred Tax Assets

	U.S. GAAP	IFRS
Assessment of realizability [chance that the entity will not realize some portion of the deferred tax asset (DTA)]	"More likely than not" likelihood of more than 50%	"Probable" likelihood of more than 50%
Recording realizable deferred tax asset	Two steps: 1. Record full amount of deferred tax asset. 2. Assess deferred tax asset for realizability and establish a valuation allowance account, if needed.	One step: Assess realizability and record net deferred tax asset. A separate valuation allowance account is not used under IFRS.

Source: International Financial Reporting Standards (IFRS).

In Example 17.9, we revisit Example 17.8 under IFRS.

EXAMPLE 17.9 Assessing and Reporting the Realizability of Deferred Tax Assets: IFRS

PROBLEM: Otis Optics is an IFRS reporter. The firm earned revenues of $500,000 and incurred warranty expense for book purposes of $110,000. Otis estimates a deferred tax asset of $38,500 because of a basis difference in warranty liabilities. Management has assessed that it is probable that it will not realize 40% of the deferred tax asset. What is the necessary journal entry to record the deferred tax asset? Prepare a simplified 2018 income statement and balance sheet for Otis Optics and compare it with the financial statements from Example 17.8 that do not include a valuation allowance. What is the effective tax rate in the two examples?

SOLUTION: Management records the deferred tax asset it expects to realize, which is 60% of the $38,500 deferred tax asset, or $23,100. It does not expect to collect $15,400 (40% of $38,500). The journal entry is as follows:

Account	***December 31, 2018***	
Income Tax Expense	151,900	
Deferred Tax Asset	23,100	
Income Taxes Payable		175,000

Otis Optics now has a deferred tax asset of $23,100 and income tax expense of $151,900 ($136,500 plus $15,400 increase in expense because of a reduction of the deferred tax asset). The comparison of the simplified income statement shows that when a firm reduces a deferred tax asset because it assesses that the asset cannot be fully realizable, its net income decreases (by increasing tax expense). In this case, net income is decreased from $253,500 to $238,100. A comparison of the simplified balance sheet shows that Otis's assets are also decreased (by decreasing the net deferred tax asset balance). In this case, assets were decreased from $538,500 to $523,100.

Otis's ETR before recording a valuation allowance is 35% ($136,500 / $390,000). Its ETR after recording the valuation allowance increases to 38.9% ($151,900 / 390,000) because of the increase in the tax expense.

	Without Assessing Realizability of Deferred Tax Asset	With Assessing Realizability of Deferred Tax Asset
Simplified income statement		
Sales revenue	$500,000	$500,000
Warranty expense	(110,000)	(110,000)
Income before income taxes	$390,000	390,000
Income tax expense	(136,500)	(151,900)
Net income	$253,500	$238,100
Balance sheet		
Asset:		
Accounts receivable	$500,000	$500,000
Deferred tax asset	38,500	23,100
TOTAL	$538,500	$523,100
Liabilities and stockholders' equity		
Warranty liability	$ 110,000	$ 110,000
Income taxes payable	175,000	175,000
Stockholders' equity	253,500	238,100
TOTAL	$538,500	$523,100
Effective tax rate	35%	38.9%

JUDGMENTS IN ACCOUNTING
Temporary Book-Tax Differences

Accounting for income taxes requires much judgment. In fact, 74% of 175 companies surveyed reported making estimates and using judgment in estimating their tax accounts.[13] This area is the number two area, second only to impairments of goodwill and other intangibles, for which significant judgment is exercised, according to the survey.

Determining whether a valuation allowance account is needed to offset the deferred tax assets and, if so, the amount of the valuation allowance requires significant judgment. Making these determinations entails an assessment of future events, which are difficult to forecast.

Decisions regarding changes to the realizable value of deferred tax assets, including changes to the valuation allowance, directly impact earnings. Because of this impact on earnings, there is a potential for managers to manipulate earnings. Consider Example 17.8. Otis Optics recorded a deferred tax asset of $38,500. Management concluded that it was more likely than not that it would not realize 40% of this deferred tax asset and thus recorded a valuation allowance of $15,400. However, the reliability of this estimate is difficult to determine. Although managers carefully analyze these assessments and provide documentation for their decisions, there is still subjectivity involved. Exhibit 17.7 demonstrates the effect of different non-realizability estimates for deferred tax assets on income tax expense, net income, and the effective tax rate for this example.

Note that the impact on earnings varies from zero if Otis determines that the entire deferred tax asset is realizable, and to $38,500 if Otis determines that none of the deferred tax asset is realizable. In addition, as management changes its estimated valuation allowance from year to year, there can be a significant impact on income tax expense and net income. Finally, changes

[13]AICPA, *IFRS Financial Statements: Best Practices in Presentation and Disclosure – 2012* (New York: AICPA, 2012).

EXHIBIT 17.7 Effects of Different Non-Realizability Estimates of Deferred Tax Assets for Otis Optics

Assessment of Non-Realizable Deferred Tax Asset (%)	0%	20%	40%	80%	100%
Income before tax	$390,000	$390,000	$390,000	$390,000	$390,000
Income tax expense–no valuation allowance	$136,500	$136,500	$136,500	$136,500	$136,500
Increase in income tax expense from the estimated valuation allowance	0	7,700	15,400	30,800	38,500
Income tax expense—with valuation allowance	$136,500	$144,200	$151,900	$ 167,300	$175,000
Net income	$253,500	$245,800	$238,100	$222,700	$215,000
Effective tax rate	35.0%	37.0%	38.9%	42.9%	44.9%

in the estimated valuation allowance result in volatility in the effective tax rate: Otis's effective tax rate ranges from 35.0% to 44.9% in this illustration.

Exhibit 17.8 presents part of the income tax footnote for ***Luby's, Inc.'s*** 2016 10-K. In this portion of the footnote disclosure, ***Luby's*** provides information regarding the judgments it used to determine the realizability of certain deferred tax assets, including future operational performance and taxable income, that have a direct effect on income tax expense and net income.

EXHIBIT 17.8 Discussion of Evaluation of the Valuation Allowance, ***Luby's, Inc.***, Annual 10-K Report, August 31, 2016

The Company had deferred tax assets, excluding liabilities, at August 31, 2016 of approximately $12.1 million, the most significant of which include the Company's general business tax credits carryovers to future years of approximately $10.5 million. This item may be carried forward up to twenty (20) years for possible utilization in the future. The carryover of general business tax credits,beginning in fiscal 2002, will begin to expire at the end of fiscal 2022 through 2036, if not utilized by then.

. . .

Collectively, the available evidence supports an assertion that our deferred tax assets will be realized, but with the exception of a certain portion of the Company's general business and foreign tax credit carryovers that are not likely at this time to be realized, and on which the Company has established a valuation allowance. The general business credits and foreign tax credit carryovers generally expire if unused within twenty (20) years and ten (10) years, respectively. We have, as a result of the foregoing assessment, established a $6.9 million valuation allowance for deferred tax assets pertaining to general business and foreign tax credit carryforward balances that are not likely to be realized prior to their expiration.

Source: Luby's Inc. 2016 Annual Report. http://www.annualreports.com/HostedData/AnnualReports/PDF/NYSE_LUB_2016.pdf

5 Illustrate the effects of a change in tax rates.

Change in Tax Rates

Changes in income tax rates directly affect the valuation of deferred tax assets and liabilities. In this section, we examine the accounting for these changes in tax rates and their impact on deferred tax accounts.

Accounting for Changes in Tax Rates

Properly valuing deferred tax assets and deferred tax liabilities requires measuring deferred tax accounts at the statutory income tax rate expected to be in effect at the future reversal date. The expected future income tax rate is the current rate if there is no change in tax rates or a tax rate enacted into law that will take effect in the future period. The standards view deferred taxes based on a future tax rate enacted into law as a faithful representation of the amount of deferred taxes. Companies remeasure deferred tax accounts whenever there is a change in the statutory income tax rate. Example 17.10 illustrates the use of future enacted tax rates to value deferred tax accounts.

EXAMPLE 17.10

Future Income Tax Rates

PROBLEM: Lands Canoes recorded book income of $100,000 in 2018. The company did not have any permanent differences; the company's only temporary difference relates to a $30,000 warranty expense that it recorded on the income statement but cannot deduct for tax purposes until actual repairs are made. Lands Canoes anticipates satisfying the warranty liability equally over the next 3 years. The current enacted tax rate is 40%. The enacted tax rates for 2019, 2020, and 2021 are 35%, 30%, and 30%, respectively. Determine the value of the deferred tax asset to be recorded for this temporary book-tax difference.

SOLUTION: Because the book basis of the warranty liability is higher than the tax basis of the liability, Lands Canoes records a deferred tax asset. However, in order to properly measure the deferred tax asset, the company must apply the appropriate income tax rate to the amounts reversing each year. As a result, Lands Canoes needs to prepare a schedule to determine the years the reversals will occur.

	2019	2020	2021	Total
Amount of difference reversing each year	$10,000	$10,000	$10,000	$30,000
Relevant income tax rate	× 35%	× 30%	× 30%	
Deferred tax asset	$ 3,500	$ 3,000	$ 3,000	$ 9,500

By taking into consideration the different tax rates in the years of reversal, Lands computes a total deferred tax asset of $9,500 in 2018.

Effect of Tax Rate Changes on Deferred Tax Accounts

Firms must adjust the balance of the deferred tax accounts in the year of tax rate change to reflect the change in tax rate. The adjustment is considered a change in estimate accounted for on a prospective basis, so there is no impact on prior-period financial statements from the adjustment. The adjustments needed to remeasure the balance of deferred tax accounts do, however, impact income tax expense and the effective tax rate. The effect on income tax expense results in a difference between the statutory income tax rate and the effective tax rate.

EXAMPLE 17.11

Effect of a Change in Tax Rates

PROBLEM: Whitewater Rafts, Inc. reported a net deferred tax asset balance of $137,000 resulting from an estimated warranty expense accrual for book purposes. The total book-tax difference related to the bases of the estimated warranty liability is $391,429. The enacted statutory tax rate related to this balance changed from 35% to 30%, effective immediately. What journal entry does Whitewater Rafts need to make to adjust for this change in tax rates?

SOLUTION: Whitewater Rafts computed the current deferred asset balance of $137,000 at a 35% tax rate. The adjusted deferred tax asset balance from the change in tax rate is $117,429 ($391,429 × 30%). Because tax rates decreased, the future tax deductions taken are less valuable. Consequently, Whitewater Rafts will reduce its deferred tax asset balance by $19,571 ($137,000 − $117,429).[14] The deferred tax asset is now expected to provide less future benefit, thereby increasing income tax expense and the effective tax rate, as reflected in the following journal entry:

Continued

[14]The tax rate change adjustment can also be computed by multiplying the cumulative book tax difference by the change in the tax rates: $391,429 × (35% − 30%) = $19,571.

Account	Current Year	
Income Tax Expense	19,571	
Deferred Tax Asset		19,571

Accounting for Tax Rate Changes: IFRS

U.S. GAAP and IFRS definitions of the expected statutory tax rate differ. Under IFRS, the expected rate is the tax rate that has been substantively—but not necessarily fully—enacted.[15]

Example 17.11 would be the same under U.S. GAAP and IFRS because the future tax rates are enacted. Next, we look at Example 17.12 where the rates are substantively enacted to illustrate the differences under U.S. GAAP and IFRS.

EXAMPLE 17.12 Future Tax Rates: Substantively Enacted: U.S. GAAP/IFRS Comparison

PROBLEM: Sea Crafts recorded book income of $250,000 in 2018. The company does not have any permanent differences; the company's only temporary difference relates to a $45,000 installment sale that it recorded for book purposes. Sea Crafts anticipates receiving payments equally over the following 3 years. The current enacted tax rate in 2018 is 40%. The substantively enacted tax rates for the following 3 years are 35%, 30%, and 30%, respectively. What deferred tax amount should Sea Crafts record for this temporary difference under U.S. GAAP and IFRS?

SOLUTION: Because the book basis of the installment receivable from the installment sales is higher than the tax basis of the asset, Sea Crafts records a deferred tax liability.

Under U.S. GAAP, Sea Crafts uses the enacted tax rate of 40%. The deferred tax liability is $18,000 (40% of $45,000). Under IFRS, Sea Crafts uses the substantively enacted tax rate. We need to schedule out the reversal to take into account the changing tax rates under IFRS.

	2019	2020	2021	Total
Amount of difference reversing each year	$15,000	$15,000	$15,000	$45,000
Relevant tax rate	× 35%	× 30%	× 30%	
Deferred tax liability	$ 5,250	$ 4,500	$ 4,500	$ 14,250

Taking into consideration the substantively enacted tax rates in the years of reversal, the total deferred tax liability is $14,250 in 2018 under IFRS and is lower than the $18,000 deferred tax liability recognized under U.S. GAAP.

[15]Under IFRS, the point at which legislation is substantively enacted will vary from country to country based on the country's legal procedures. Typically, tax legislation requires the approval of the head of state before it can become law. However, the head of state in some jurisdictions has executive power whereas in other jurisdictions, the head of state plays only a ceremonial role. Thus, in the first case where the head of state has executive power, a tax rate is not substantively enacted until it has been actually approved by the head of state. In the latter case, the tax rate has been substantively enacted before it reaches the head of state.

JUDGMENTS IN ACCOUNTING
Changing Tax Rates

Predicting the expected reversal dates of temporary book-tax differences can require judgment. In contrast, the reversal dates of some deferred tax accounts are known with near certainty. For example, deferred tax liabilities arising from differences in the basis of equipment resulting from different depreciation methods can be estimated with a high degree of accuracy.

However, the reversal of other book-tax differences cannot be known with such certainty. Consider, for example, a deferred tax asset that has arisen from a lawsuit in which a company accrues a litigation liability for book purposes, but cannot recognize this obligation for tax purposes until the liability is paid.

Example 17.13 illustrates accounting for uncertainty in the timing of the reversal of a deferred tax asset.

EXAMPLE 17.13 Uncertainty in the Timing of the Reversal of a Deferred Tax Account

PROBLEM: In 2018, several customers at Maydew Restaurants, Inc. presented with cases of food poisoning and subsequently sued Maydew. Maydew reported a $5 million contingent liability on its December 31, 2018, financial statements. The tax rate for 2018 is 35%. However, the enacted tax rates for 2019, 2020, 2021, and thereafter are 34%, 32%, and 30%, respectively. What amount should Maydew record for the deferred tax asset related to the contingency?

SOLUTION: Maydew needs to record a deferred tax asset computed as the book-tax basis difference in the contingent liability times the tax rate that will be in effect at the time of the reversal. The problem is that this deferred tax asset won't reverse until Maydew settles the case or the case works its way through the court system. If we assume that the case will not be resolved until after 2021, the deferred tax asset will be measured at $1.5 million ($5 million × 30%). However, if we believe that the case will be resolved in 2019, the deferred tax asset will be measured at $1.7 million ($5 million × 34%).

6 Determine the accounting for net operating losses (NOLs), including NOL carrybacks and carryforwards and the valuation of related deferred tax assets.

Accounting for Net Operating Losses

A **net operating loss** (NOL) is a net loss for tax purposes that occurs when tax-deductible expenses exceed taxable revenues. When a company reports a tax loss, it has no income taxes currently payable. However, many countries allow corporations experiencing an NOL to recover past income taxes paid or reduce future income taxes payable by applying the current year's loss to offset prior or future taxable income.

Carrybacks and Carryforwards under U.S. Tax Law

Under the U.S. tax law, companies with NOLs can elect to *carryback* or *carryforward* a tax loss. The **carryback** allows a company to offset the current tax loss against prior years' taxable income and claim a refund for taxes previously paid on the amount offset. The **carryforward** permits a company to offset the current tax loss against future taxable income, thereby reducing future taxable income and lowering the amount of tax due in the year of the offset.

NOL carrybacks and carryforwards provide a means of smoothing taxable income for companies that have a more volatile earnings stream as compared with those with a steady stream of income. To illustrate, consider two companies with a 35% tax rate that have taxable income of $1 million over a 2-year period. Company B earns $500,000 each year, and Company A has taxable income of $1.5 million in Year 1 and a loss of $500,000 in Year 2. Without any special provisions, Company B will pay taxes of $175,000 ($500,000 × 35%) each year for a total of $350,000.

Company A will pay taxes in Year 1 of $525,000 ($1.5 million × 35%) and no taxes in Year 2 for a total of $525,000. But if Company A is able to carryback a loss and offset prior taxable income, it will incur the same tax liability as Company B, for example:

Company	Description	Year 1	Year 2	Total
A	Taxable income	$1,500,000	$(500,000)	$1,000,000
	Carryback loss	$ (500,000)	0	
	Taxable income	$1,000,000	$(500,000)	$1,000,000
	Tax rate	× 35%	N/A	× 35%
	Tax liability	$ 350,000	$ 0	$ 350,000
B	Taxable income	$ 500,000	$ 500,000	$1,000,000
	Tax rate	× 35%	× 35%	× 35%
	Tax liability	$ 175,000	$ 175,000	$ 350,000

U.S. GAAP allows companies to carry back a tax loss against prior taxable income for the previous 2 years and/or carry forward taxable income for 20 years or until the tax loss is fully utilized. Under current law, any unused carryforward deductions expire after 20 years. For example, a company with a taxable loss of $100,000 in 2018 has two options:

1. Carryback the NOL into 2016 and 2017 in that order. The NOL must be carried back to the earliest year first. If taxable income for the prior 2 years is less than the NOL, it can carry forward the remainder of the NOL for up to 20 years.
2. Carryforward the NOL for up to 20 years if it does not have sufficient taxable income in the carryback period or if it elects not to carry back the tax loss.[16]

Accounting for an NOL Carryback

When a company carries back the entire NOL, it records a refund receivable for income taxes previously paid and reduces its income tax expense by the amount of the anticipated refund. The tax refund receivable and the related tax benefit are recognized in the year of the loss because it is measurable and currently realizable in that year. Example 17.14 illustrates accounting for an NOL carryback.

EXAMPLE 17.14 Net Operating Loss Carryback

PROBLEM: Lawson Enterprises experienced an NOL of $567,000 in 2018. The company reported taxable income of $434,000 in 2016 and $327,000 in 2017. The tax rate for all years is 40%. Lawson elects to carryback the NOL. What is the necessary journal entry to record the NOL carryback in the year of the loss? Prepare a partial income statement for the year of the loss.

SOLUTION: Lawson Enterprises first carries back the loss to 2016, the earliest possible year to which the loss can be applied. If any of the loss remains, the company can carry back that amount to 2017. Lawson reported taxable income of $434,000 in 2016, so the company can carry back that amount to 2016. The remaining NOL of $133,000 ($567,000 − $434,000) is a carryback to 2017. Therefore, Lawson has sufficient taxable income in the 2 years before the year of the NOL to carry back the entire amount of the NOL.

[16]Generally, companies carry back losses if possible, but under certain conditions, they can choose not to carry back even if taxable income is available in the carryback period. For example, a company can expect higher future income and/or increased income tax rates in future periods. As a result, the carryforward can provide more tax benefit than the carryback.

Description	2016	2017	Year of the Loss 2018	Total NOL Carryback
Taxable income (loss)	$434,000	$327,000	$(567,000)	
Carryback				
Carried back first to 2016 and then remaining amount to 2017	(434,000)	(133,000)		(567,000)

Income Tax Benefit Computation	2016	2017	Total
Carryback (from above)	$(434,000)	$(133,000)	$(567,000)
× Tax rate	× 40%	× 40%	× 40%
Income tax benefit	$(173,600)	$ (53,200)	$(226,800)

Lawson carries back $434,000 to 2016 and fully offsets 2016 taxable income. The company can also carry back the remaining $133,000 ($567,000 − $434,000) to 2017. Given the 40% income tax rate in both years, Lawson can claim a refund for $226,800 (see table above). In addition, Lawson will have $194,000 (original taxable income of $327,000 – $133,000 used) remaining from 2017 that could be used to offset an NOL in 2019.

The journal entry to record the NOL carryback is presented follows:

Account	*December 31, 2018*	
Income Tax Refund Receivable	226,800	
Income Tax Benefit		226,800

The partial income statement is presented next. Note that Lawson reports an income tax benefit as opposed to income tax expense, which reduces its net loss after tax.

Partial Income Statement	
Net loss before tax benefit	$ (567,000)
Income Tax Benefit	226,800
Net loss after tax benefit	$(340,200)

The income tax benefit reduces Lawson's net loss by $226,800.

Accounting for an NOL Carryforward

When a company does not have sufficient taxable income in prior years to fully utilize an NOL, it can carryforward the unused amount of the NOL. Alternatively, a company can simply forgo the carryback option and carryforward the entire NOL instead. The NOL carryforward gives rise to a deferred tax asset. A deferred tax asset provides a future reduction in income taxes payable. When a company reports positive earnings for tax purposes, it can reduce its taxable income by the NOL carryforward and pay less tax in the carryforward year. Accounting for a net operating loss carryforward is illustrated in Example 17.15.

EXAMPLE 17.15

Net Operating Loss Carryforward: Year of the NOL

PROBLEM: Piewares, Inc. began business in 2018 and reported sales revenue of $500,000 and expenses of $600,000, resulting in a $100,000 net loss for the current year. Assume that Piewares has not yet received cash for its sales, nor has it paid cash for its expenses incurred during the year. It has no permanent or temporary differences; thus, its taxable loss equals its book loss of $100,000. Because it began business in 2018, the carryback option is not

Continued

available, so Piewares must carry forward its $100,000 NOL. The tax rate is 35%, and a valuation allowance is not required. What is the necessary journal entry to record the impact of the NOL carryforward on the company's financial statements? Prepare a partial 2018 income statement and balance sheet for Piewares.

SOLUTION: Piewares records a deferred tax asset of $35,000 ($100,000 × 35%) and a related income tax benefit of $35,000. The company does not owe any taxes, nor will it record any income taxes payable for the current year.

	Year of the Loss 2018
Taxable income (loss)	$(100,000)
NOL carryforward	(100,000)
Tax rate	× 35%
Income tax benefit	$ 35,000

The journal entry is as follows:

Account	***December 31, 2018***	
Deferred Tax Asset	35,000	
Income Tax Benefit		35,000

The partial income statement and balance sheet follow. Note that Piewares reports an income tax benefit as opposed to income tax expense, which reduces its net loss after tax.

Partial Income Statement	
Sales Revenue	$ 500,000
Operating Expenses	(600,000)
Net Loss before Tax Benefit	$(100,000)
Income Tax Benefit	35,000
Net Loss after Tax Benefit	$ (65,000)
Balance Sheet	
Assets:	
Accounts Receivable	$ 500,000
Deferred Tax Assets	35,000
TOTAL	$ 535,000
Liabilities and Stockholders' Equity:	
Accounts Payable	$ 600,000
Stockholders' Equity	(65,000)
TOTAL	$ 535,000

When a company carries forward an NOL, it realizes the benefits of a deferred tax asset in future periods when taxable income is earned. In the period that it reports future income, the company will compute income tax expense based on current-year book income. However, its income tax payable will be reduced because of the realization of the NOL carryforward benefit. Example 17.16 illustrates the realization of NOL carryforward benefits in the profitable years following the loss.

EXAMPLE 17.16 Net Operating Loss Carryforward: Years Following the Year of the NOL

PROBLEM: In Example 17.15, we determined that Piewares has a deferred tax asset of $35,000 related to the $100,000 NOL in 2018. In 2019, the company generates revenues of $500,000 and incurs operating expenses of $200,000. Again, there are no temporary or permanent differences, meaning that book income is equal to taxable income. So, Piewares reports taxable income of $300,000 before considering the effect of its NOL. The company's tax rate is 35%. What is the tax-related journal entry for 2019?

SOLUTION: Piewares' 2019 tax expense is $105,000 ($300,000 × 35% tax rate). Piewares will apply the $100,000 NOL carryforward to reduce taxable income to $200,000 ($300,000 − $100,000 NOL). Therefore, income tax payable is only $70,000 (35% × $200,000).

	2018	2019	Total NOL Carryforward
Taxable income (loss)	$(100,000)	$ 300,000	
Carryforward: Carryforward NOL to 2019		$(100,000)	$(100,000)
Taxable income after carryforward		$ 200,000	

Income Tax Benefit Computation	2019
Carryforward (from above)	$(100,000)
× Tax rate	× 35%
Income tax benefit realized	$ (35,000)

Applying the NOL results in an income tax payable of $70,000 ($200,000 × 35%). The $35,000 difference between its tax expense and income taxes payable is the benefit from realization of the deferred tax asset. So, Piewares also reduces its deferred tax asset because it fully utilizes the NOL carryforward benefits in 2019.

The journal entry is as follows:

Account	*December 31, 2019*	
Income Tax Expense	105,000	
Income Tax Payable		70,000
Deferred Tax Asset		35,000

Note that Piewares still has $200,000 of taxable income from 2019 that can be used to offset an NOL occurring in 2020 or 2021.

It is not uncommon that a company carries back an NOL to the preceding 2 years but will not be able to fully offset the loss. In this case, the company can then carry forward the remainder as illustrated in Example 17.17.

EXAMPLE 17.17 Net Operating Loss Carryback and Carryforward

PROBLEM: Backus Inc. reported a loss of $500,000 in 2018. The company reported taxable income of $125,000 in 2016 and $230,000 in 2017. It has no permanent or temporary differences, and its tax rate is 35%. What is the necessary journal entry for 2018? Backus reported taxable income of $250,000 in 2019. What is the necessary journal entry for 2019?

SOLUTION: Backus first carries back the loss to 2016, the earliest possible year in which it can apply the loss, and then to 2017. Backus reported taxable income of $125,000 in 2016, so the company can carry back that amount to 2016. It reported taxable income of $230,000 in 2017, so it carries back that amount also. Thus, the total carryback is $355,000, leaving $145,000 available as a carryforward.

Description	2016	2017	Year of the Loss 2018
Taxable income (loss)	$ 125,000	$ 230,000	$(500,000)
Carryback	(125,000)	(230,000)	(355,000)
Carryforward			$(145,000)

Computation Income Tax Benefit from the NOL	2016	2017	Total
Carryback (from above)	$125,000	$230,000	$355,000
× Tax rate	× 35%	× 35%	× 35%
Income tax benefit	$ 43,750	$ 80,500	$124,250

Because Backus did not have enough taxable income in the preceding 2 years to fully offset the current year's loss, it has an NOL carryforward of $145,000 ($500,000 − $355,000). This carryforward results in a deferred tax asset of $50,750 ($145,000 × 35%). We compute the total tax benefit as follows:

Tax benefit of NOL carryback	$124,250
Tax benefit of NOL carryforward	50,750
Total tax benefit	$175,000

Note that the $175,000 tax benefit can also be computed as the total loss ($500,000) multiplied by the tax rate of 35%.

Backus records a tax benefit of $175,000, a tax refund receivable of $124,250 related to the carryback, and a deferred tax asset of $50,750 related to the carryforward.

Account	*December 31, 2018*	
Income Tax Refund Receivable	124,250	
Deferred Tax Asset	50,750	
Income Tax Benefit		175,000

In 2019, Backus generates enough taxable income to fully utilize its available NOL carryforward. We compute the impact on the tax accounts as follows:

	2019	Tax Rate (%)	Impact on Tax Accounts	Specific Account
Taxable income before carryforward (also book income before taxes)	$ 250,000	35%	$ 87,500	Tax Expense
Carryforward	$(145,000)	35%	$(50,750)	Deferred Tax Asset
Taxable income after carryforward	$ 105,000	35%	$ 36,750	Tax Payable

The journal entry is as follows:

Account	December 31, 2019	
Income Tax Expense	87,500	
Income Tax Payable		36,750
Deferred Tax Asset		50,750

Assessing NOL Carryforward Realizability

An important consideration when accounting for NOLs is the firm's ability to realize the tax benefit from a deferred tax asset. If a firm has an NOL carryforward, there is a possibility that it will not generate sufficient taxable income before the carryforward expires. Thus, the firm must assess the probability that it will be able to benefit from the NOL carryforward. If the firm determines that it is more likely than not that it will not benefit from some or all of the NOL carryforward, it will recognize a valuation allowance to reflect the deferred tax asset at its reduced net realizable value. Example 17.18 illustrates assessing the realizability of a net operating loss carryforward.

EXAMPLE 17.18 Net Operating Loss Carryforward: Assessing Realizability

PROBLEM: Refer to information for Piewares, Inc. from Example 17.15. In 2018, the company experienced a $100,000 net operating loss and recorded a deferred tax asset of $35,000 in 2018. Now assume that Piewares decides that it is more likely than not that it will be able to generate only $60,000 of taxable income during the carryforward period. As a result, without generating an additional $40,000 of future taxable income, it will not be able to fully realize the NOL carryforward benefit. What is the journal entry necessary to record the net deferred tax asset in 2018? Prepare a partial income statement and balance sheet for Piewares.

SOLUTION: Piewares will report a net deferred tax asset of $21,000 [($100,000 − $40,000) × 35%]. The company reports a deferred tax asset of $35,000 ($100,000 × 35%) and records a valuation allowance of $14,000 ($40,000 × 35%). Piewares' income tax benefit will decrease by $14,000, and its net deferred tax asset will decrease by $14,000 because of the need for the valuation allowance.

The journal entries follow:

Account	December 31, 2018	
Deferred Tax Asset	35,000	
Income Tax Benefit		35,000

Account	December 31, 2018	
Income Tax Benefit	14,000	
Valuation Allowance for Deferred Tax Asset		14,000

Continued

The income statement and balance sheet follow. Note that the deferred tax asset is reported at its net value of $21,000 and the income tax amount is a net benefit of $21,000.

Partial Income Statement	
Sales revenue	$ 500,000
Operating expenses	(600,000)
Net Loss before income tax benefit	$(100,000)
Income tax benefit	21,000
Net Loss after tax benefit	$ (79,000)
Balance Sheet	
Assets:	
Accounts receivable	$ 500,000
Deferred tax assets	21,000
Total	$ 521,000
Liabilities and stockholders' equity:	
Accounts payable	$ 600,000
Stockholders' equity	(79,000)
Total	$ 521,000

Assessing NOL Carryforward Realizability: IFRS

As discussed earlier, IFRS reporters also assess the realizably of deferred tax assets. However, a valuation allowance is not used under IFRS.

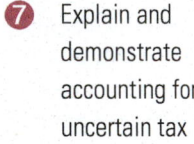

7 Explain and demonstrate accounting for uncertain tax positions.

Uncertain Tax Positions

In many cases, tax authorities can disallow all or a portion of a particular position taken by a company on its tax return. For example, a company can classify a certain transaction as tax exempt. These positions are known as **uncertain tax positions**, which typically result from aggressive tax positions taken by companies when preparing tax returns. These tax positions can result in the company reporting a tax-related liability referred to as a **tax contingency** on its balance sheet.

Examples of uncertain tax positions include:

- A decision not to file a tax return
- A shift of income across jurisdictions
- A decision to exclude potentially taxable income from a tax return
- A choice to treat a transaction as tax-exempt[17]

To illustrate, consider a company that takes an aggressive tax position on its U.S. federal tax return to reduce income tax payable by $100,000. It is possible that the Internal Revenue Service will ultimately require the company to pay at least some of this amount in the future. How much of the $100,000 should the company record as a tax liability from the uncertain tax position, and how much should it record as a tax benefit?[18] The tax benefit is simply the reduction in the reported tax expense and liability as the result of the uncertain tax position.

[17]These examples are taken from FASB ASC 740-10-20.

[18]Firms rarely report the liability from uncertain tax positions on the face of the balance sheet. However, disclosure standards (discussed later in the chapter) require that firms report the balance of the liability for uncertain tax positions in the footnotes.

Accounting for Uncertain Tax Positions

U.S. GAAP uses a two-step approach, recognition and measurement, to account for uncertain tax positions. In general, accounting under U.S. GAAP is intended to be a "principles-based" methodology requiring significant judgment by management, attorneys, and auditors.

Step 1: Recognition: To account for uncertain tax positions, the company first determines whether it should recognize any benefits from its tax position. To do so, it must decide if it is more likely than not that it will sustain the tax position after examination by the taxing authority, assuming that the taxing authority has full knowledge of all relevant information. In concrete terms, after the taxing authority examines all available evidence (both positive and negative), the company must determine whether there is slightly more than a 50% chance that it will sustain the tax position. If the company expects that it will sustain the position, it can recognize a benefit and measure the tax benefit as determined in Step 2.

Step 2: Measurement: If a tax position meets the more-likely-than-not threshold, the company measures the amount of tax benefit to be recognized in the financial statements. The tax benefit is the largest amount of benefit that is greater than 50% likely of being realized upon ultimate settlement. This measurement system is based on cumulative probability computations without considering the time value of money. In other words, a tax benefit should be measured as the largest amount of benefit that is cumulatively greater than 50% likely to be realized.

Exhibit 17.9 illustrates ***AT&T's*** disclosure related to its uncertain tax position. Note the discussion of the more-likely-than-not likelihood of realization upon settlement explained in Step 2. At December 31, 2016, ***AT&T*** disclosed that approximately $3,701 million of estimated liabilities for uncertain tax positions would be realized if such liabilities were actually incurred.

EXHIBIT 17.9 Uncertain Tax Position Disclosures, ***AT&T Inc.***, Financial Statements, December 31, 2016

Note 11: Income Taxes

We recognize the financial statement effects of a tax return position when it is more likely than not, based on the technical merits, that the position will ultimately be sustained. For tax positions that meet this recognition threshold, we apply our judgment, taking into account applicable tax laws, our experience in managing tax audits and relevant GAAP, to determine the amount of tax benefits to recognize in our financial statements. For each position, the difference between the benefit realized on our tax return and the benefit reflected in our financial statements is recorded on our consolidated balance sheets as an unrecognized tax benefit (UTB). We update our UTBs at each financial statement date to reflect the impacts of audit settlements and other resolutions of audit issues, the expiration of statutes of limitation, developments in tax law and ongoing discussions with taxing authorities.

Source: AT&T, Inc. AT&T Inc. Annual Report. https://www.att.com/Investor/ATT_Annual/2016/downloads/att_ar2016_completeannualreport.pdf

Example 17.19 considers an expansive example of a tax contingency.

EXAMPLE 17.19 **Recognition and Measurement of an Uncertain Tax Position**

PROBLEM: Hush Sound Systems, Inc. took an aggressive tax position on its current-year tax return. The taxing jurisdictions have challenged the deduction claimed in prior years upon examining the returns of other firms in the industry. Hush reported $600,000 in taxable income after the $500,000 deduction in question. In other words, the company earned $1,100,000 in taxable income before the $500,000 deduction. Hush is subject to a 34% tax rate and has no book-tax differences.

Based on a careful analysis, management believes that it is more likely than not that the position will be sustained upon examination. Therefore, the potential tax benefit will be recognized. The company will assess the following probabilities corresponding to possible tax deduction outcomes in order to measure the potential tax benefit:

Possible Estimated Outcome (i.e., amount allowed as a tax deduction)	Individual Probability of Occurring (%)
$500,000	5%
380,000	30
300,000	25
210,000	15
190,000	25

What journal entry is required to record the current year's income tax expense, income tax payable, and tax liability for the uncertain tax position?

SOLUTION: The first step is to determine whether management can report any benefit from this tax position. If they cannot recognize any tax benefit—that is, if the $500,000 tax deduction is not recognized—taxable income is $1,100,000 ($600,000 + 500,000). If none of the deduction is recognized, the company debits income tax expense for $374,000 ($1,100,000 × 34%) and credits income tax payable for the same amount. However, because it is more likely than not that the position will be sustained upon examination, the company is allowed to recognize some amount of benefit. In other words, Hush will not be required to record the full $374,000 of income tax expense.

With the more-likely-than-not threshold being satisfied, the next step is to measure the amount of the income tax benefit that Hush will recognize. The amount of the benefit recognized equals the largest amount of income tax benefit that is likely to be realized at a greater than 50% cumulative probability upon final settlement by the taxing authorities. The largest amount of the tax benefit is $102,000 ($300,000 × 34%) because it represents the largest amount of benefit that is cumulatively more than 50% likely to occur as determined in the following table:

Possible Estimated Outcome (i.e., amount allowed as a tax deduction)	Individual Probability of Occurring (%)	Cumulative Probability of Occurring (%)
$500,000	5%	5%
380,000	30	35
300,000	***25***	***60***
210,000	15	75
190,000	25	100

Thus, Hush multiplies the remaining $200,000 of the tax position by the tax rate and records a $68,000 liability for the uncertain tax position [($500,000 − $300,000) = $200,000 × 34% = $68,000]. It records income taxes payable of $204,000, which is the reported taxable income of $600,000 multiplied by the 34% tax rate. So, Hush's income tax expense is $272,000, the sum of its current income tax payable of $204,000 plus the liability of $68,000 for the uncertain tax position.

Observe that Hush's income tax expense of $272,000 is the $374,000 full tax expense less the largest amount of the benefit allowed, $102,000.

The journal entry to record the current year's tax provision and the liability for the uncertain tax position follows:

Description	*December 31, Current Year*	
Income Tax Expense	272,000	
Income Tax Payable		204,000
Tax Contingency		68,000

Accounting for Uncertain Tax Positions: IFRS

IFRS does not specifically address uncertain tax positions. Rather, it requires firms to measure tax assets and tax liabilities at the amount expected to be paid. So, IFRS reporters rely on standards for accounting for contingencies as guidance.[19] Under this guidance, the company:

1. Assesses whether it has a present obligation as a result of a past event
2. Determines whether it is probable that it will use resources to settle the obligation and whether it can reliably estimate the obligation

Example 17.20 illustrates accounting for uncertain tax positions under IFRS.

EXAMPLE 17.20

Recognition and Measurement of an Uncertain Tax Position: IFRS

PROBLEM: Use the same information from Example 17.19 but assume that Hush Sound Systems, Inc., reports using IFRS. Determine the income tax liability that Hush should recognize in its financial statements under IFRS.

SOLUTION: Under IFRS, Hush Sound Systems needs to recognize the amount expected to be paid. However, there is no specific guidance on determining the amount to be recognized. Assuming a 34% income tax rate, the total possible liability related to this tax deduction is \$170,000 (\$500,000 × 34%). Because it is likely Hush would settle for less than the full amount of the entire position, it should recognize some amount of contingent liability less than \$170,000. The exact amount of the liability to be recognized is highly subjective and requires further analysis to determine with certainty.

JUDGMENTS IN ACCOUNTING
Uncertain Tax Positions

Accounting for uncertain tax positions is based on management's decisions regarding difficult-to-predict projections of future events—and these decisions impact both income tax expense and reported net income. In order to record a liability for an uncertain tax position under U.S. GAAP, management must assess the probabilities that some portion of the position will be sustained upon examination by the taxing authorities.

In Example 17.19, Hush Sound Systems, Inc. recorded an aggressive \$500,000 tax deduction on its tax return constituting an uncertain tax position. The company reported \$600,000 in taxable income after the deduction. Consequently, Hush will record income taxes payable of \$204,000 (\$600,000 × 34%). How much income tax expense should Hush record? What is the amount of the liability for the uncertain tax position?

In Example 17.19, management provided the following schedule of estimated probabilities for the amounts of possible tax deductions allowed.

Possible Estimated Outcome (i.e., amount allowed as a tax deduction)	Individual Probability of Occurring (%)	Cumulative Probability of Occurring (%)
\$500,000	5%	5%
380,000	30	35
300,000	***25***	***60***
210,000	15	75
190,000	25	100

[19] IASC, *International Accounting Standard 37*, "Provisions, Contingent Liabilities and Contingent Assets" (London, UK: International Accounting Standards Committee, Revised, 2001).

Because these projections and estimated probabilities are highly subjective, the company could have used a different set of probabilities. For example, assume that management provided the following table as an alternative set of estimated outcomes and related probabilities:

Possible Estimated Outcome (i.e., amount allowed as a tax deduction)	Individual Probability of Occurring (%)	Cumulative Probability of Occurring (%)
$500,000	15%	5%
480,000	***40***	***55***
300,000	5	60
210,000	15	75
190,000	25	100

The company projects that it will sustain a deduction of $480,000. Thus, Hush will report a liability for an uncertain tax position of $6,800 [($500,000 − $480,000) × 34%] and tax expense of $210,800 [($1,100,000 − $480,000) × 34%]. This $210,800 income tax expense is significantly less than the income tax expense recognized in the original example in which Hush's reported income tax expense of $272,000.

The amounts that firms could potentially report as liabilities related to uncertain tax positions can be quite large. For example, ***AT&T's*** reported unrecognized tax benefit (i.e., potential liability for uncertain tax positions) of $3,701 million in the notes to its financial statements for the year ended December 31, 2016, is shown in Exhibit 17.10.

EXHIBIT 17.10 Reconciliation of the Unrecognized Tax Benefits, ***AT&T Inc.***, Financial Statements, December 31, 2016

NOTE 11: Income Taxes

A reconciliation of the change in our UTB balance from January 1 to December 31 for 2016 and 2015 is as follows:

Federal, State and Foreign Tax (in millions)	2016	2015
Balance at beginning of year	$6,898	$4,465
Increases for tax positions related to the current year	318	1,333
Increases for tax positions related to prior years	473	660
Decreases for tax positions related to prior years	(1168)	(396)
Lapse of statute of limitations	(25)	(16)
Settlements	50	10
Current year acquisitions	-	864
Foreign currency effects	(30)	(22)
Balance at end of year	6,516	6,898
Accrued interest and penalties	1,140	1,138
Gross unrecognized income tax benefits	7,656	8,036
Less: Deferred federal and state income tax benefits	(557)	(582)
Less: Tax attributable to timing items included above	(3,398)	(3,460)
Less: UTBs included above that relate to acquisitions that would impact goodwill if recognized during the measurement period	-	(842)
Total UTB that, if recognized, would impact the effective income tax rate as of the end of the year	$3,701	$3,152

Source: AT&T, Inc. AT&T Inc. Financial Review 2016. https://www.att.com/Investor/ATT_Annual/2016/downloads/att_ar2016_completeannualreport.pdf

8 Describe the financial statement presentation of the income tax accounts.

Financial Statement Presentation

There are a number of important issues to consider in the financial statement presentation of the income tax accounts on the balance sheet and the income statement.

Balance Sheet Presentation

Companies report several income tax accounts on the balance sheet. For example, companies typically present income taxes payable in the current liabilities section. Income tax payable can be disclosed as a separate line item, or it can be combined with other short-term payables. In addition to income taxes payable, companies report the income tax contingency as a liability on the balance sheet.

The deferred tax account is the result of many book-tax differences. Some of these differences will give rise to deferred tax liabilities and others will result in deferred tax assets. Under both U.S. GAAP and IFRS, deferred tax liabilities and deferred tax assets should be netted as long as the right to offset exists. For example, netting is permitted only if the amounts are payable and receivable from the same taxing jurisdiction. For simplicity, all deferred tax assets and liabilities are reported as noncurrent. Example 17.21 illustrates the netting of deferred tax assets and liabilities.

EXAMPLE 17.21 **Netting of Deferred Tax Assets and Liabilities**

PROBLEM: Weiss Company has two deferred tax assets and two deferred tax liabilities at the end of the year as shown in the following table. How should Weiss report its deferred tax accounts on its balance sheet?

Deferred Tax Account	Amount
Deferred tax asset from Germany	$ 80,000
Deferred tax liability from Brazil	320,000
Deferred tax asset from Brazil	8,000
Deferred tax liability from the Germany	62,000

SOLUTION: Weiss should net all of its deferred tax accounts from Germany and then all of its deferred tax accounts from Brazil.

Germany	
Deferred tax asset	$ 80,000
Deferred tax liability	(62,000)
Net deferred tax asset	$ 18,000
Brazil	
Deferred tax liability	$320,000
Deferred tax asset	(8,000)
Net deferred tax liability	$312,000

Thus, Weiss will report a deferred tax asset of $18,000 and a deferred tax liability of $312,000. On the balance sheet, the deferred tax asset will be classified as a noncurrent asset. The deferred tax liability will be classified as a noncurrent liability.

Income Statement Presentation

Companies report income tax expense (or income tax benefit) on the income statement. Typically, firms report a line item for income tax expense immediately before income from continuing operations. The amount of income tax expense reported consists of both current and deferred income tax expense.

Note, however, that the amount of total income tax expense reported as a line item on the face of the income statement does not necessarily include the firm's entire income tax expense. Discontinued operations are reported net of income tax expense following income from continuing operations on the income statement.

Companies also report taxes related to other comprehensive income items on the comprehensive statement of income. Other comprehensive income is reported net of tax.[20] For example, income tax expense related to unrealized gains or losses from available-for-sale debt investments is reported in other comprehensive income as opposed to net income. The allocation of income tax expense to different sections of the comprehensive income statement is referred to as **intraperiod tax allocation**. Example 17.22 illustrates intraperiod tax allocation.

EXAMPLE 17.22 Intraperiod Tax Allocation

PROBLEM: Planet Entertainment, Inc. reported income from continuing operations before taxes of $575,000 and income from discontinued operations of $150,000. Planet also reported $72,000 of unrealized gains from available-for-sale debt investments recorded as other comprehensive income. The company is subject to a 40% tax rate and reports no permanent differences. What is Planet's total income tax expense for the year? How much income tax expense does Planet report as a line item directly below Income from Continuing Operations before Taxes? Prepare a partial comprehensive income statement for Planet Entertainment.

SOLUTION: Planet Entertainment reports total comprehensive income before tax of $797,000 ($575,000 continuing operations before taxes + $150,000 discontinued operations + $72,000 other comprehensive income). The company's total tax expense is $318,800 ($797,000 × 40%) and its after-tax comprehensive income is $478,200 ($797,000 − $318,800). However, because of intraperiod tax allocation, Planet will not report the entire $318,800 in the line item Income Tax Expense. Planet reports income from continuing operations, income from discontinued operations, and other comprehensive income, net of tax, as presented in the table below.

Income Statement Component	Gross Amount	Tax	Net of Tax Amount
Income from continuing operations before taxes	$575,000	$230,000	$345,000
Discontinued operations	150,000	60,000	90,000
Other comprehensive income	72,000	28,800	43,200
Total comprehensive income	$ 797,000	$318,800	$478,200

Planet's partial statement of comprehensive income follows:

Income from continuing operations before taxes	$575,000
Income tax expense	(230,000)
Income from continuing operations	$345,000
Discontinued operations – Net of $60,000 tax	90,000
Net Income	$435,000
Other comprehensive income – Net of $28,800 tax	43,200
Comprehensive income	$478,200

[20] The cumulative effect of accounting changes is also reported in the stockholders' equity section of the balance sheet net of income tax expense.

9 Detail required disclosures for income taxes.

Income Tax Financial Statement Disclosures

We discuss the required financial statement disclosures related to income taxes in this section.

Income Tax Expense and Income Taxes Paid

Firms disclose the portion of their income tax expense that is current and the portion that is noncurrent. The firm's current income tax expense represents the amount of expense that is attributable to current-year taxable income. The noncurrent portion of income tax expense, known as the *deferred provision*, is attributable to items that give rise to deferred taxes. These taxes are reported according to jurisdiction, commonly federal, state, and international.

Exhibit 17.11 illustrates ***Google's*** 2016 disclosure of its current and deferred taxes according to federal, state, and international jurisdictions. In 2016, its total tax expense is $4,672 million, of which $4,792 million is current and $(120) million is deferred. The negative deferred amount indicates the reversal of net deferred tax assets.

In addition, firms must disclose the amount of income tax expense that they allocate to financial statement elements that are not part of income from continuing operations.

To provide information on cash flows, companies are also required to disclose the amount of income taxes paid. For example, ***Google*** disclosed that it paid $1,643 million in income taxes in fiscal 2016.

EXHIBIT 17.11 Current and Deferred Income Tax Expense, ***Google,*** Financial Statements, December 31, 2016

Provision for Income Taxes (millions)	2014	2015	2016
Current:			
Federal	$2,716	$3,235	$3,520
State	157	(397)	306
Foreign	774	723	966
Total current	$3,647	$3,561	$4,792
Deferred:			
Federal	$ 29	$ (198)	$ (70)
State	6	(43)	—
Foreign	(43)	(17)	(50)
Total deferred	$ (8)	$ (258)	$ (120)
Total provision	$3,639	$3,303	$4,672

Source: Alphabet Inc. Annual Report. 2016 Annual Report. https://abc.xyz/investor/pdf/2016_google_annual_report.pdf

Tax Rate Reconciliation

Firms must provide a reconciliation of the domestic federal statutory tax rate to their effective tax rate as illustrated for ***Google*** in Exhibit 17.2. The firm must disclose any significant reconciling items.[21] Some of the major categories of differences in the effective tax rate and the federal statutory rate are significant permanent book-tax differences. As discussed earlier in this chapter, permanent differences cause the effective tax rate to fluctuate from the statutory rate.

Other items cause the reported effective tax rate to differ from the statutory rate, such as state, local, and foreign tax rates that differ from the U.S. statutory rate. These items are not differences in book and tax income, so they are not permanent differences. Most often, they are differences in the tax rates in the various jurisdictions in which a company operates.

[21] Securities and Exchange Commission, *Regulation S-X Rule 4–08(h)* indicates that significant is considered 5% of the statutory rate.

Deferred Tax Liabilities and Deferred Tax Assets

A company must disclose the individual components of its deferred tax liabilities and deferred tax assets if significant. Firms typically report these amounts on the balance sheet on a net basis and separately on an individual basis in the footnotes as illustrated for ***Target*** in Exhibit 17.5.

With regard to deferred tax assets, companies disclose the amount and expiration of carryforwards for net operating losses and unused tax credits. Companies must also report the amount of the valuation allowance for deferred tax assets and disclose any change in the valuation allowance because of a change in circumstances.

Uncertain Tax Positions

Finally, reporters are required to provide extensive disclosures related to uncertain tax positions, including both qualitative and quantitative information. For example, the qualitative disclosures must include the specific tax positions that management expects will change within 1 year from the balance sheet date. The quantitative disclosures require, among other things, a roll-forward reconciliation of worldwide, aggregated unrecognized tax benefits (UTB) from uncertain positions. The roll-forward, illustrated for ***AT&T*** in Exhibit 17.10, includes:

- The beginning balance
- The additions to the balance because of new tax positions
- The additions to the balance because of increases from adjustments of previously recorded positions
- A list of the reductions to the balance because of settlements
- A list of balance reductions from adjustments to previously recorded positions
- A list of balance reductions because of the lapse of the relevant statute of limitations

Income Statement Disclosures: IFRS

Disclosures under U.S. GAAP and IFRS are similar. However, under IFRS, a firm can begin the reconciliation to the effective tax rate with a statutory rate that aggregates domestic rates in various jurisdictions. U.S. GAAP reporters begin the rate reconciliation with the U.S. statutory tax rate.

Interview

LAURIE WAX

TAX PARTNER, RSM US LLP, NEW YORK, NY »

Laurie Wax

Laurie Wax is a tax partner at RSM US LLP, the leading provider of audit, tax, and consulting services focused on the middle market. It is the U.S. member firm of RSM International, a global network of independent audit, tax, and consulting firms. Her areas of expertise include compliance and advising on corporate income tax accounting issues, including stock compensation and business combinations related to SEC filings along with IFRS preparation for tax accounting.

1 Do your clients have difficulty with the concept of deferred accounting for taxes? Why?

Although our clients can understand the mechanics of recording tax deferrals, often they do not understand *why* we have deferrals. Recording deferrals informs the financial statement user of the company's future tax situation, not just today's. Tax laws differ in general from the more conservative GAAP approach, necessitating a way for accountants to disclose and record the differences between the two very different systems. Deferrals represent this difference: a holding place to define the discrepancy between tax and GAAP accounting.

2 In what ways are deferred tax assets and deferred tax liabilities considered to be "real" economic resources and obligations in terms of future cash flows?

Deferrals are not just debits and credits—they are very real from a cash flow perspective. Deferred tax assets represent deductions in the future and thus provide a cash tax deduction on a future tax return. Cash planners must also factor in deferred tax liabilities, which represent higher taxes that the company must pay in the future. Therefore, deferrals affect a firm's day-to-day cash flow.

3 Are disclosures for uncertain tax positions (UTPs) informative in terms of scope and content? How do decision makers use these disclosures?

UTPs arise when a taxpayer believes its interpretation of earnings recognition or deductions can be less strong than the those of the IRS and therefore records a reserve in an audited financial statement. Companies must disclose any increases/decreases for uncertain tax positions. The financial statements show a dollar figure with the details given in the footnotes. If there *is* a UTP, there must be a liability for it. Lenders and the informed investment community look at UTP disclosures to evaluate the magnitude and materiality of the liability as would someone buying the business. Typically, executives do not review UTPs but are involved in deciding whether to record one.

4 What factors does RSM US LLP consider in determining whether a client has created an adequate valuation allowance against a deferred tax asset?

As an audit firm, RSM US LLP would request that the client provide us an analysis that would evaluate the positive and negative evidence of a company's situation before asking management to include a valuation allowance. For example, 3 consecutive years of losses provides negative evidence that the client would need a valuation allowance against its deferred tax assets. We then work with the company to determine what the valuation allowance should be. A company with consistent tax losses will be reporting that most of its deferred tax assets result from net operating loss carryforwards. If the company does not expect to use the tax benefits from the net loss carryforwards, the deferred tax asset will be reduced by a valuation allowance. We can also find positive signs indicating that a valuation allowance is not necessary. These can include tax-planning strategies, significant deferred revenue, and property with built-in gains.

5 What are some common reasons given by your clients for not carrying back net operating losses?

We rarely have a client who does not want to carry back net operating losses so that it can apply for a refund of prior paid taxes. Occasionally, clients realize that they have not paid in enough taxes for the current year so they could want to carry the losses forward to avoid possible exposures to penalties in the current year. Some clients think doing so will trigger an audit; however, carrying back a loss typically does not cause an audit.

6 How do tax rate changes affect your clients' deferred tax assets and deferred tax liabilities?

Once a new rule is enacted, we recalculate the accounts with the applicable tax rates at that time. Any changes in tax expense are absorbed in the financial statement period when the law takes effect. This rate change usually affects the amount of projected cash taxes in the future. «

Discussion Questions

1. Laurie Wax mentions that most of her clients elect to carryback a net operating loss (NOL) but provides several reasons why her clients elect to carry a loss forward rather than elect the carryback-carryforward option. Provide several other reasons why an entity would elect the NOL carryforward-only option, not the carryback loss.
2. How can the use of a valuation allowance against a deferred tax asset impact or smooth reported earnings?

FINANCIAL STATEMENT ANALYSIS

Accounting for Income Taxes

Companies have conflicting incentives when reporting taxes. On the one hand, a company wants to maximize net income, which usually implies higher taxes. On the other hand, a company seeks to minimize the amount of taxes it actually pays. Taxes paid are cash outlays, so the lower amount of taxes paid, the more cash a company can keep to use in its business operations.

The tax code provides opportunities for companies to pay lower taxes while maintaining book income. Permanently sheltering income from taxes—such as investing in tax-exempt securities—decreases a company's income tax expense and cash taxes paid. Another way to decrease tax paid is to defer income taxes paid, such as through the use of accelerated depreciation for tax purposes and straight-line depreciation for financial reporting purposes. This strategy would also increase a company's deferred tax liabilities.

However, an increase in deferred tax liabilities (or decrease in deferred tax assets) could indicate to financial statement users that a company is making income-increasing accounting choices as opposed to increasing its income from operations. For example, assume that a company extends the useful life or increases the salvage value of its depreciable long-lived assets to increase its reported net income. The deferred tax liability related to differences in depreciation accounting would increase. Or consider a case in which a company decreases its warranty expense to increase its net income. The deferred tax asset related to the warranty liability also decreases. It is important to note, however, that neither of these income-increasing accounting decisions indicates an increase in income from the company's operations—they are merely accounting strategies used to increase the net income line on the income statement.

The **conservatism ratio** is the ratio of a company's aggressiveness in financial reporting compared with tax reporting. The lower the ratio, the more conservative the company. The higher the ratio, the more aggressive the company.

$$\text{Conservatism Ratio} = \frac{\text{Reported Income before Taxes}}{\text{Taxable Income}} \quad (17.1)$$

Companies are not required to disclose taxable income, so this amount must be estimated. We can estimate taxable income as:[22]

$$\text{Taxable Income} = \frac{\text{Current Tax Expense}}{\text{Effective Income Tax Rate}} \quad (17.2)$$

When reported income before taxes is high relative to taxable income, a company pays less in taxes in the short term. A high conservatism ratio, then, usually indicates that the company will have to pay higher taxes in the future relative to the present. Example 17.24 provides an example of the financial statement analysis of income taxes.

EXAMPLE 17.24 Financial Statement Analysis—Accounting for Income Taxes

PROBLEM: To further understand income tax reporting at ***AT&T***, use the following information to address the questions after the note.

Note 11: Income Taxes

A reconciliation of income tax expense (benefit) and the amount computed by applying the statutory federal income tax rate (35%) to income from continuing operations before income taxes is as follows:

[22]One potential problem with using the current tax expense to estimate taxable income is that the income tax expense reported on the income statement does not include all of the income tax expense. As noted earlier, certain items, such as income from discontinued operations and other comprehensive income, are reported net of tax after income from continuing operations.

Financial Statement Analysis, continued

(in millions)	2016	2015	2014
Taxes computed at federal statutory rate	**$6,934**	$7,242	$3,624
Increases (decreases) in income taxes resulting from:			
State and local income taxes – net of federal income tax benefit	**416**	483	(113)
Connecticut wireline sale	**—**	—	350
Loss of foreign tax credits in connection with América Móvil sale	**—**	—	386
Mexico restructuring	**(471)**	—	—
Other – net	**(400)**	(720)	(628)
Total	**$6,479**	$7,005	$3,619
Effective Tax Rate	**32.7%**	33.9%	34.9%

Other information follows:

(in millions)	2016	2015	2014
Provision for Income Taxes			
Current	$ 3,532	$ 2,888	$ 1,671
Deferred	2,947	4,117	1,948
Total provision	$ 6,479	$ 7,005	$ 3,619
Net Income before Taxes	$19,812	$20,692	$10,355

Source: https://www.att.com/Investor/ATT_Annual/2016/downloads/att_ar2016_completeannualreport.pdf

a. What is ***AT&T's*** effective tax rate each year? What is the difference between ***AT&T's*** effective tax rate and the statutory rate? Detail the items making up this difference.

b. Compute ***AT&T's*** conservatism ratio for each year. Comment on any changes in the ratio over the years. Would you characterize ***AT&T*** as a conservative or aggressive tax reporter? Round to three decimal places.

SOLUTION:

a. ***AT&T's*** effective tax rate is 32.7%, 33.9%, and 34.9% in fiscal 2016, 2015, and 2014, respectively. In each year, the statutory tax rate is 35%. Therefore, ***AT&T's*** effective tax rate is lower than the statutory tax rate in all years. The effective tax rate is lower because of permanent tax differences such as state and local income taxes and Mexico restructuring costs.

b. To compute the conservatism ratio, we first have to estimate taxable income. Then, we use the taxable income in the computation of the conservatism ratio.

	2016	2015	2014
Taxable Income $= \dfrac{\text{Current Tax Expense}}{\text{Effective Income Tax Rate}}$	$\$10{,}801 = \dfrac{\$3{,}532}{32.7\%}$	$\$8{,}519 = \dfrac{\$2{,}888}{33.9\%}$	$\$4{,}788 = \dfrac{\$1{,}671}{34.9\%}$
Conservatism Ratio $= \dfrac{\text{Reported Income before Taxes}}{\text{Taxable Income}}$	$1.834 = \dfrac{\$19{,}812}{\$10{,}801}$	$2.429 = \dfrac{\$20{,}692}{\$8{,}519}$	$2.163 = \dfrac{\$10{,}355}{\$4{,}788}$

AT&T's conservatism ratio is highest in fiscal 2015 at 2.429. A conservatism ratio of 2.429 indicates that ***AT&T's*** reported income before taxes is 2.429 times greater than its taxable income. Therefore, ***AT&T*** is deferring taxes to be paid in future periods. ***AT&T's*** conservatism ratio decreased from 2.163 to 1.834 from 2014 to 2016, respectively, indicating that ***AT&T's*** tax reporting has become somewhat more conservative. Yet in 2016, the conservatism ratio is still greater than 1.

Summary by Learning Objectives

In the following, we summarize the main points by Learning Objective. Throughout the chapter, we discuss the accounting and reporting of U.S. GAAP and IFRS side-by-side. The following table also highlights the major similarities and differences between the standards.

1 Define book income and taxable income; compute income tax expense and income taxes payable when there are no book-tax differences.

Summary	Similarities and Differences between U.S. GAAP and IFRS
Income tax expense is based on book income. Income tax payable is based on taxable income. When book income and taxable income are equal, there is tax conformity and income tax expense equals income tax payable.	Similar under U.S. GAAP and IFRS.

2 Discuss permanent differences and calculate income tax expense and income taxes payable when there are permanent differences.

Summary	Similarities and Differences between U.S. GAAP and IFRS
A permanent difference arises when book income and taxable income differ because either (1) an item is included in the computation of taxable income but never in book income or (2) an item is included in the computation of book income but never in taxable income. When there are permanent differences, companies record both income tax expense and income tax payable on the financial statements based on the tax rules.	Similar under U.S. GAAP and IFRS.

3 Explain temporary differences and illustrate the balance sheet approach of accounting for deferred tax assets and liabilities.

Summary	Similarities and Differences between U.S. GAAP and IFRS
Temporary differences occur when the book treatment and the tax treatment for a given transaction are different in a given year but will be the same over the life of the firm. Specifically, a temporary difference exists when the tax basis of an asset or liability differs from the book basis of that asset or liability. This difference results in taxable or deductible amounts in future years. Temporary differences give rise to deferred tax assets or deferred tax liabilities.	Similar under U.S. GAAP and IFRS.

4 Explain and demonstrate how to assess and report the realizability of deferred tax assets.

Summary	Similarities and Differences between U.S. GAAP and IFRS
Firms assess deferred tax assets for realizability and report them on the balance sheet at the amount they expect to realize. U.S. GAAP uses a two-step process: (1) Record the full amount of the deferred tax asset and (2) assess the deferred tax asset for realizability and set up a valuation allowance account if needed.	➤ U.S. GAAP uses the criterion "more likely than not" to assess realizability. IFRS uses "probable." Both imply the likelihood of more than 50%. IFRS assesses realizability and records the net deferred tax asset without using a valuation allowance.

Summary by Learning Objectives, continued

5 Illustrate the effects of a change in tax rates.

Summary	Similarities and Differences between U.S. GAAP and IFRS
Firms use future tax rates to calculate their deferred tax assets and liabilities. When tax rates change, the company remeasures its deferred tax assets and liabilities. Any differences are recorded as income tax expense or income tax benefit in the year of remeasure.	➤ U.S. GAAP uses enacted tax rates. IFRS allows substantively enacted tax rates.

6 Determine the accounting for net operating losses (NOLs), including NOL carrybacks and carryforwards, and the valuation of related deferred tax assets.

Summary	Similarities and Differences between U.S. GAAP and IFRS
A net operating loss (NOL) is a net loss for tax reporting purposes. A company offsets the current tax loss against prior taxable income with a carryback. A company can also offset the current tax loss against future taxable income with a carryforward. A carryforward gives rise to a deferred tax asset. The deferred tax asset is assessed for realizability as detailed in Learning Objective 4.	➤ IFRS assesses the realizability of deferred tax assets but does not use a valuation allowance.

7 Explain and demonstrate accounting for uncertain tax positions.

Summary	Similarities and Differences between U.S. GAAP and IFRS
Tax contingencies (also referred to as *uncertain tax positions* or *tax cushions*) are liabilities that represent the amount that a company determines that it will owe the government upon completion of a tax audit related to the use of aggressive tax positions on its tax return. U.S. GAAP uses a two-step approach in which companies first recognize and then measure any contingencies. A threshold of greater than 50% likelihood is used.	➤ IFRS has no specific guidance for tax contingencies, so IFRS reporters refer to general guidance on accounting for contingencies.

8 Describe the financial statement presentation of the income tax accounts.

Summary	Similarities and Differences between U.S. GAAP and IFRS
On the balance sheet, firms net deferred tax assets and liabilities, as long as the right to offset exists. On the income statement, firms report a line item for income tax expense that is related to income before tax. Firms report discontinued operations net of tax expense. Tax expense related to items in other comprehensive income is included in other comprehensive income.	Similar under U.S. GAAP and IFRS.

Summary by Learning Objectives, continued

9 Detail required disclosures for income taxes.

Summary	Similarities and Differences between U.S. GAAP and IFRS
Footnote disclosures include: 1. Current and deferred portions of tax expense. 2. Tax expense that is not included in income from continuing operations. 3. Reconciliation of the federal statutory tax rate to the effective tax rate. 4. Individual components of deferred tax assets and liabilities. 5. Amount of and any changes in the deferred tax asset valuation allowance. 6. Disclosures related to tax contingencies.	➤ Similar under U.S. GAAP and IFRS except that under IFRS, a firm can also provide a reconciliation to the effective tax rate with a statutory rate that aggregates domestic rates in various jurisdictions. U.S. GAAP reporters begin the reconciliation with the U.S. statutory tax rate.

MyLab Accounting

Go to **http://www.pearson.com/mylab/accounting** for the following Questions, Multiple-Choice Questions, Brief Exercises, Exercises, and Problems. They are available with immediate grading, explanations of correct and incorrect answers, and interactive media that acts as your own online tutor.

17 Accounting for Income Taxes

Questions

1 **Q17-1.** Do the objectives of GAAP accounting and tax accounting methods differ?

1 **Q17-2.** When will income tax expense and income taxes payable be equal?

2 **Q17-3.** Will permanent differences cause the effective tax rate to be lower than the statutory rate?

2 **Q17-4.** When do permanent differences arise?

3 **Q17-5.** How are deferred tax assets and deferred tax liabilities created?

3 **Q17-6.** How does the balance sheet approach measure deferred taxes?

3 **Q17-7.** When do deferred tax liabilities occur?

4 **Q17-8.** When can firms recognize net deferred tax assets on the balance sheet?

4 **Q17-9.** Does the requirement that a firm must assess its deferred tax assets every period for realizability and adjust the valuation allowance as necessary create volatility in the entity's effective tax rate? Explain.

4 **Q17-10.** How does a firm determine the need for a valuation allowance against a deferred tax asset in the more-likely-than-not test?

5 **Q17-11.** Do firms measure deferred tax accounts at the statutory tax rate expected to be in effect at the future reversal date to properly value the deferred tax asset and deferred tax liability?

5 **Q17-12.** When do firms adjust for the cumulative effect of changes in future tax rates affecting income?

6 **Q17-13.** Does accounting for a net operating loss (NOL) carryback require less judgment than accounting for the NOL carryforward?

7 **Q17-14.** How does an entity account for uncertain tax positions?

7 **Q17-15.** Do U.S. GAAP and IFRS have similar approaches to accounting for tax contingencies?

8 **Q17-16.** How do firms classify deferred tax accounts?

8 **Q17-17.** Do U.S. GAAP and IFRS classify deferred tax accounts in the same manner?

9 **Q17-18.** Are extensive disclosures required for deferred taxes?

Multiple-Choice Questions

3 **MC17-1.** Cavan Company prepared the following reconciliation between book income and taxable income for the current year

Pretax accounting	$1,000,000
Taxable income	(600,000)
Difference	$ 400,000
Differences	
Interest on municipal income	$ 100,000
Lower financial depreciation	300,000
Total	$ 400,000

Cavan's effective income tax rate for Year 1 is 30%. The depreciation difference will reverse equally over the next 3 years at enacted tax rates as follows:

Year	Tax Rate (%)
Year 2	30%
Year 3	25
Year 4	25

In Cavan's Year 1 income statement, the current portion of its provision for income taxes should be:
a. $300,000 b. $250,000 c. $180,000 d. $150,000

❸❺ **MC17-2.** Cavan Company prepared the following reconciliation between book income and taxable income for the current year

Pretax accounting	$1,000,000
Taxable income	(600,000)
Difference	$ 400,000
Differences	
Interest on municipal income	$ 100,000
Lower financial depreciation	300,000
Total	$ 400,000

Cavan's effective income tax rate for Year 1 is 30%. The depreciation difference will reverse equally over the next 3 years at enacted tax rates as follows:

Year	Tax Rate (%)
Year 2	30%
Year 3	25
Year 4	25

In Cavan's Year 1 Income Statement, the deferred portion of its provision for income taxes should be:
a. $120,000 b. $80,000 c. $100,000 d. $90,000

❸ **MC17-3.** Two independent situations are described below. Each involves future deductible amounts and/or future taxable amounts produced by temporary differences:

Situation	1	2
Taxable income	$40,000	$80,000
Amounts at year-end		
Future deductible amounts	5,000	10,000
Future taxable amounts	0	5,000
Balances at beginning of year		
Deferred tax asset	$ 1,000	$ 4,000
Deferred tax liability	0	1,000

The enacted tax rate is 40% for both situations. Determine the deferred tax asset balance at year-end.

Situation 1	Situation 2
a. $5,000	$10,000
b. $3,000	$ 8,000
c. $1,000	$ 3,000
d. $2,000	$ 4,000

3 **MC17-4.** Two independent situations are described here. Each situation has future deductible amounts and/or future taxable amounts produced by temporary differences:

Situation	**1**	**2**
Taxable income	$40,000	$80,000
Amounts at year-end		
Future deductible amounts	5,000	10,000
Future taxable amounts	0	5,000
Balances at beginning of year		
Deferred tax asset	$ 1,000	$ 4,000
Deferred tax liability	0	1,000

The enacted tax rate is 40% for both situations. Determine the income tax expense for the year.

Situation 1	**Situation 2**
a. $16,000	$32,000
b. $15,000	$33,000
c. $11,000	$30,000
d. $20,000	$28,000

4 6 8 **MC17-5.** At the end of Year 6, the tax effects of temporary differences reported in Maple Company's year-end financial statements were as follows:

	Deferred tax assets (liabilities)
Accelerated tax depreciation	$(120,000)
Warranty expense	80,000
NOL carryforward	200,000
	$ 160,000

A valuation allowance was not considered necessary. Maple anticipates that $40,000 of the deferred tax liability will reverse in Year 7, that actual warranty costs will be incurred evenly in Years 8 and 9, and that the NOL carryforward will be used in Year 7. On Maple's December 31, Year 6, balance sheet, what amount should be reported as a noncurrent deferred tax asset under U.S. GAAP? Assume all deferred accounts are from the same taxing jurisdiction.

a. $160,000 b. $200,000 c. $240,000 d. $280,000

3 5 6 **MC17-6.** The pretax financial income and taxable income of Zeus Corporation were the same for the following years (i.e., there were no permanent or temporary differences):

	Income	**Tax Rate (%)**
Year 4	$ 20,000	30%
Year 5	15,000	25
Year 6	(100,000)	25
Year 7	70,000	40

What amount of income tax benefit will Zeus Corporation record in Year 6 under U.S. GAAP, assuming that Zeus elects to use the 2-year carryback/20-year carryforward option? Assume that the Year 7 tax rate is known in Year 6 and is enacted at the beginning of Year 7.

a. $25,000 b. $26,000 c. $35,750 d. $37,750

5 6 **MC17-7.** The pretax financial income and taxable income of Zeus Corporation were the same for the following years (i.e., there were no permanent or temporary differences):

	Income	Tax Rate (%)
Year 4	$ 20,000	30%
Year 5	15,000	25
Year 6	(100,000)	25
Year 7	5,000	40

What amount of income tax benefit will Zeus Corporation record in Year 6 under U.S. GAAP, assuming that Zeus elects to use the 2-year carryback/20-year carryforward option and that it is more likely than not that there will be no taxable earnings after Year 7? Assume the Year 7 tax rate is known in Year 6.

a. $9,750 b. $11,750 c. $24,000 d. $26,000

Brief Exercises

1 **BE17-1. Income Taxes Payable.** Immox Company has conformity between its taxable income and income before taxes. If Immox's taxes payable are $140,000, and its tax rate is 40%, what is its net income?

1 **BE17-2. Income Taxes Payable.** Limmox Company has conformity between its taxable income and income before taxes. Limmox Company's net income after taxes is $195,000, and its tax rate is 35%. What is its taxes payable?

2 **BE17-3. Permanent Differences**. Simmox Company's income before taxes is $290,000, and its tax rate is 35%. Note that $40,000 is nontaxable interest income from its investment in municipal bonds and is included in $290,000. There are no other book-tax differences. What are Simmox's tax expense and taxes payable? What is its net income?

2 **BE17-4. Permanent Differences.** Plimmox Company's income before taxes is $410,000, and its tax rate is 35%. Plimmox included $60,000 in nondeductible fines in the $410,000. There are no other book-tax differences. What are its tax expense and taxes payable? What is its net income?

2 9 **BE17-5. Permanent Differences, Reconciliation of Statutory Tax Rate to Effective Tax Rate.** Simmox Company's income before taxes is $290,000, and its tax rate is 35%. Note that $40,000 is nontaxable interest income from its investment in municipal bonds and is included in the $290,000. There are no other book-tax differences. Prepare a reconciliation of Simmox's statutory tax rate to its effective tax rate.

2 9 **BE17-6. Permanent Differences, Reconciliation of Statutory Tax Rate to Effective Tax Rate.** Plimmox Company's income before taxes is $410,000, and its tax rate is 35%. Plimmox included $60,000 in nondeductible fines in the $410,000. There are no other book-tax differences. Prepare a reconciliation of Plimmox's statutory tax rate to its effective tax rate.

3 **BE17-7. Temporary Differences, Deferred Tax Liability.** Marlena Group uses straight-line depreciation for financial reporting purposes and accelerated depreciation on its tax returns. The company reported $40,000 in income before tax and depreciation for book purposes. The equipment has an original cost of $20,000. Straight-line depreciation is $2,000, and accelerated depreciation amounts to $6,000 for the asset's first year of utilization. There are no other book-tax differences.

Required »

a. What is the book basis of the equipment at the end of the first year?
b. What is the tax basis of the equipment at the end of the first year?
c. Compute the deferred tax liability, income tax payable, and income tax expense for the current year assuming that Marlena is subject to a 40% tax rate.

3 **BE17-8. Temporary Differences, Deferred Tax Asset.** Mathus, Inc. reported income before tax of $180,000, and taxable income was $200,000. This $20,000 difference resulted from unearned revenues that the firm recorded as revenue for tax purposes but as a liability for book purposes. Mathus is subject to a 35% tax rate.

Required »

a. What is the book basis of the unearned revenue?
b. What is the tax basis of the unearned revenue?
c. What are Mathus's deferred tax asset, income tax payable, and income tax expense for the current year?
d. Prepare the journal entry to record the tax provision for the current year.

3 **BE17-9. Temporary Differences, Deferred Tax Liability.** The Block Company uses the accrual basis to account for all sales transactions. Total sales for the current year amounted to $450,000. Of this amount, $120,000 is from sales on installment. The firm uses the installment method (i.e., cash basis) to account for the installment sale for tax purposes. Operating expenses are $180,000 for both GAAP and tax reporting.

Required »

a. What is the book basis of the installment sales receivable?
b. What is the tax basis of the installment sales receivable?
c. Assuming a 40% tax rate, compute income tax payable, the deferred tax provision, and income tax expense for the current year.

3 **BE17-10. Temporary Differences, Deferred Tax Asset.** Hondell Industries offers a 3-year basic warranty on all its products. At the beginning of the current year, the estimated warranty liability had a balance of $110,000. Actual repairs cost $35,000, and the company accrued an additional $60,000 for the current year. Hondell reported $380,000 in total sales this year for both GAAP and tax purposes. The company reported $90,000 in other operating expenses for both GAAP and tax purposes.

Assuming a 40% tax rate, determine the balance of the deferred tax account, the amount of income tax expense, and the income tax payable.

3 **BE17-11. Temporary Differences, Deferred Tax Liability.** Bobby James Puppet Company acquired a new plastic molding machine at the beginning of the current year at a cost of $420,000. The asset has a 6-year useful life for financial reporting purposes and is depreciated on a straight-line basis with no residual value expected at the end of its useful life. The company uses the double-declining balance method on its income tax returns. The company is subject to a 34% tax rate.

Compute the deferred tax portion of the income tax expense for the first 2 years.

3 **BE17-12. Temporary Differences, Deferred Tax Asset.** Reflections Mirrors, Ltd. offers a 3-year warranty on all its products. In Year 1, the company reported income before warranty expense of $620,000 and estimated that warranty repairs would cost the company $150,000 over the 3-year period. Actual repairs for the year amounted to $50,000. Reflections Mirrors' tax rate is 40%.

Prepare the journal entries required to record the tax provision for Year 1.

3 **BE17-13. Temporary Differences, Deferred Tax Asset.** Using the information for Reflections Mirrors, Ltd. provided in BE17-12, prepare the journal entries required to record the tax provision for Year 2 assuming that Reflections reported income before warranty costs and taxes of $200,000 and incurred actual repair costs of $40,000. Assume that the firm did not accrue additional warranty costs in Year 2.

2 3 **BE17-14. Temporary Differences, Deferred Tax Liability, Permanent Differences.** Wells Junior Apparel Incorporated reported pre-tax book income of $825,000 for the current year. The change in the difference in the basis of plant assets is $210,000, and the book basis is higher than the tax basis. Wells invested in tax-free bonds and earned $78,000 in nontaxable interest income (included in the $825,000 pre-tax income).

Prepare the journal entry required to record the tax expense for the current year assuming a 40% income tax rate.

4 **BE17-15. Realizability of Deferred Assets.** Maves, Inc. booked a deferred tax asset of $45,000 resulting from a basis difference in warranty liabilities. Management has assessed that it is more likely than not that the firm will not realize 30% of the deferred tax asset. Provide the necessary journal entries to record the deferred tax asset, and what is the valuation allowance?

4 **BE17-16. Realizability of Deferred Assets, IFRS.** Use the same information as in BE17-15 but now assume that Maves is an IFRS reporter. What is the journal entry to record the deferred tax asset?

5 **BE17-17. Change in Tax Rates.** Finer Shoes Company recorded book income of $120,000 in 2016. It does not have any permanent differences, and the only temporary difference relates to a $60,000 installment sale that it recorded for book purposes. Finer Shoes anticipates collecting the installment sales equally over the following 2 years. The current enacted tax rate is 40%. The substantively enacted tax rates for the following 3 years are 42%, 45%, and 45%, respectively. What deferred tax amount should Finer Shoes record for this temporary difference under U.S. GAAP?

5 **BE17-18. Change in Tax Rates, IFRS.** Use the same information as in BE17-17, but now assume that Finer Shoes Company is an IFRS reporter. What deferred tax amount should the company record for this temporary difference under IFRS?

5 **BE17-19. Change in Tax Rates.** Errol Toys, Inc. recorded book income of $240,000 in 2016. It does not have any permanent differences, and the only temporary difference relates to a $12,000 warranty expense that it recorded for book purposes. Errol Toys anticipates fulfilling half of the warranties in the following year and then the rest equally over the next 2 years. The current enacted tax rate is 40%. The enacted tax rates for the following 3 years are 32%, 25%, and 25%, respectively. What deferred tax amount should Errol Toys record for this temporary difference?

6 **BE17-20. Net Operating Losses.** W. Pickett Fence Company incurred a net loss for Year 3. The firm does not have any book-tax differences. We present the results of operations for the first 3 years of the company's operations:

Year	Income (Loss) before Tax	Tax Rate (%)
1	$300,000	40%
2	200,000	35
3	(450,000)	35

Future tax rates are expected to be 35%. W. Pickett always elects the carryback/carryforward option, There are no uncertainties regarding realization of future tax benefits.

Prepare the journal entry(s) required to record the Year 3 net operating loss.

6 **BE17-21. Net Operating Losses.** How would your answer to BE17-20 change if Year 1 income were equal to $100,000?

7 **BE17-22. Tax Contingencies.** Terrell Toy Company uses an acceptable tax method that provided a $10,000 tax deduction for the current year. Book income and taxable income before considering this tax deduction are equal to $245,000 (i.e., there are no book-tax differences). Terrell is subject to a 35% income tax rate. Tax authorities have challenged this type of tax deduction in the past, and Terrell is now concerned about the realizability of this tax deduction in the future. However, management believes that it is more likely than not that the firm will sustain the tax benefits upon examination by tax authorities. Terrell provides the following analysis regarding the probabilities of sustaining the tax deduction:

Amount Sustained	Probability (%)
$10,000	30%
8,000	15
6,000	10
2,000	45

Prepare the journal entry required to record the tax provision for the current year assuming that Terrell is subject to a 35% tax rate.

7 **BE17-23. Tax Contingencies, IFRS.** Using the data from BE17-22, now assume that Terrell Toy Company is an IFRS reporter. What amount should Terrell Toy report as a tax contingency?

8 **BE17-24. Deferred Tax Classification.** Following is a list of CCS Company's deferred tax assets and liabilities.

Item	Amount	Asset/Liability	Jurisdiction
Receivable–Installment sales	$ 55,000	Liability	1
Equipment–Depreciation expense	64,000	Liability	2
Warranty liability–Warranty expense	2,000	Asset	1
Net operating loss–carryforward	120,000	Asset	2

What will CCS report on its balance sheet?

2 9 **BE17-25. Deferred Tax Disclosure.** Bell Junior Apparel Incorporated reported pre-tax book income of $825,000 for the current year. The change in the difference in the basis of plant assets is $210,000; the book basis is higher than the tax basis. Bell invested in tax-free bonds and earned $90,000 in nontaxable interest income (included in the pre-tax income of $825,000). Its income tax rate is 40%. Prepare the footnote to reconcile the federal tax rate to the firm's effective income tax rate. Present the reconciliation in both dollars and percentages.

Exercises

3 **E17-1. Temporary Differences, Deferred Tax Liability.** Farris Casinos recently acquired a newly built hotel and casino in Atlantic City. The cost of the complex was $6,000,000 with a 6-year useful life and no residual value expected. Farris depreciates its buildings using the straight-line method for financial reporting and an accelerated method for tax purposes. The tax depreciation percentages for the first 2 years are 20% and 32%, respectively. Farris is subject to a 40% income tax rate.

Required »

a. Assuming that Year 2 income before tax and depreciation is $3,700,000, determine the Year 2 income tax payable, the deferred tax provision, and income tax expense.

b. Compute the deferred tax account on the balance sheet at the end of Year 2 and indicate whether the balance represents a deferred tax asset or a deferred tax liability.

3 **E17-2. Temporary Differences, Deferred Tax Liability.** Andre Company reported a $192,640 balance in its deferred tax liability account at the beginning of Year 5. The deferred tax liability was the result of using the straight-line method on its books and an accelerated depreciation method for tax purposes. The plant asset has 2 years of useful life remaining. At the beginning of Year 5, the plant asset had a book basis of $1,000,000 and a tax basis of $518,400. We present depreciation expense and income before tax and depreciation for Years 5 and 6 in the following table.

Year	Tax Depreciation	GAAP Depreciation	Income before Tax and Depreciation
5	$345,600	$500,000	$850,000
6	172,800	500,000	925,000

Assuming a tax rate of 40%, prepare the journal entries required to record the tax provision for Years 5 and 6.

2 3 **E17-3. Temporary Differences, Deferred Tax Liability, Permanent Differences.** Synthia Manufacturing Corporation reported pre-tax book income of $3,250,000 for the current year.

- The change in the difference in the basis of plant assets is $430,000. The book basis is higher than the tax basis.
- Of the Synthia's pre-tax book income, $12,000 is nontaxable income from municipal bonds.
- At the beginning of the current year, Synthia's estimated warranty liability had a balance of $67,000. Actual repairs cost $55,000, and the company accrued an additional $72,000 for the current year.
- Synthia paid fines of $100,000 to the federal government for not complying with relevant regulations. Fines were included in pre-tax book income.

Prepare the journal entry required to record the tax expense for the current year assuming a 40% income tax rate.

3 **E17-4. Temporary Differences, Deferred Tax Liability.** Blue Collar Clothing, Inc. acquired a new fabric-cutting machine at the beginning of the current year. The machine cost $600,000 with no residual value expected. Blue Collar uses the straight-line method for financial reporting assuming a 6-year useful life. The firm classifies the equipment as 5-year MACRS property for tax purposes using the following percentages.

Year	MACRS (%)
1	20.00%
2	32.00
3	19.20
4	11.52
5	11.52
6	5.76

The company is subject to a 40% income tax rate and has no other book-tax differences. We present Blue Collar's income before tax and depreciation:

Year	Income before Tax and Depreciation
1	$ 850,000
2	900,000
3	930,000
4	1,100,000
5	1,400,000
6	1,850,000

Required »

(Show all supporting computations.)

a. Prepare all journal entries required to record Blue Collar's income tax provision for Years 3 and 4.
b. What is the balance of the deferred tax account at the end of Year 3?
c. What is reported net income for Years 3 and 4?

③ **E17-5. Temporary Differences, Deferred Tax Assets and Liabilities.** Oliver Starshine Group provided the following income information from its first 3 years of operation.

	Year 1		Year 2		Year 3	
Account	**GAAP**	**Tax**	**GAAP**	**Tax**	**GAAP**	**Tax**
Sales	$1,100	$1,100	$1,250	$1,250	$1,420	$1,420
Operating expenses	(600)	(600)	(720)	(720)	(833)	(833)
Estimated warranty cost	(110)	0	(125)	0	(142)	0
Actual warranty repairs	0	0	0	(200)	0	(177)
Income before tax	$ 390		$ 405		$ 445	
Taxable income		$ 500		$ 330		$ 410
Tax rate		× 40%		× 40%		× 40%
Tax payable		$ 200		$ 132		$ 164

Oliver offers a 1-year warranty on its commercial floor polishing system. The company estimates its warranty cost at 10% of sales.

Required »

a. Compute the deferred tax expense and the balance of the deferred tax account for each year.
b. Prepare all journal entries required to record Oliver's income tax provision for all 3 years.

③ **E17-6. Temporary Differences, Deferred Tax Assets and Liabilities.** Fortunes Hotel Associates reported the following income information for the current year:

	Current Year	
Account	**GAAP**	**Tax**
Sales	$500,000	$500,000
Operating expenses	(280,000)	(280,000)
Depreciation expense	(70,000)	(100,000)
Estimated warranty cost	(30,000)	0
Actual warranty repairs	0	(10,000)
Income before tax	$120,000	
Taxable income		$ 110,000
Tax rate		× 35%
Tax payable		$ 38,500

Required »

a. Prepare the journal entry to record the tax provision for the current year.
b. Are there any differences between the federal income tax rate and Fortunes' effective tax rate? Explain.

②③ **E17-7. Temporary Differences, Deferred Tax Assets and Liabilities, Reconciliation of Statutory Tax Rate and Effective Tax Rate.** J.W. Jones Markets, Inc. accepts prepaid grocery orders for home and commercial delivery. This year, the company collected $160,000 in advance orders and delivered $48,000 of the advance orders. The company paid $15,000 in insurance premiums for a policy covering the life of its founder and CEO. Income before considering any revenue recognized on the delivered groceries and the insurance expense is $800,000. J.W. Jones is subject to a 40% income tax rate.

Required »

a. Prepare the journal entry to record the current-year income tax provision.
b. Prepare the footnote, in dollars and percentages, to reconcile the company's federal income tax rate to its effective (actual) tax rate.

③ **E17-8. Temporary Differences, Deferred Tax Liabilities.** Meyer-Swift Construction Equipment Manufacturers engaged in an installment sale with one of its major customers. The firm negotiated the terms of the installment sale for a specialized piece of equipment; full payment is required within 3 years. We present information related to Meyer-Swift's first 3 years of operation:

	Year 1		Year 2		Year 3	
Account	**GAAP**	**Tax**	**GAAP**	**Tax**	**GAAP**	**Tax**
Sales	$5,000	$5,000	$6,200	$6,200	$7,800	$ 7,800
Gross profit on installment sales	3,200	0	0	0	0	0
Taxable portion of cash collected on installment sales		700		1,500		1,000
Operating expenses	(500)	(500)	(620)	(620)	(780)	(780)
Income before tax	$7,700		$5,580		$7,020	
Taxable income		$5,200		$ 7,080		$8,020
Tax rate		× 35%		× 35%		× 35%
Tax payable		$1,820		$2,478		$2,807

Required »

a. Prepare the journal entries required to record the tax expense for all 3 years.
b. Determine the net income reported on the income statement for the 3 years.

2 5 9 **E17-9. Change in Tax Rates, Permanent Difference, Reconciliation of Statutory Tax Rate to Effective Tax Rate.** Using the same information provided in E17-8, assume that Meyer-Swift invested in tax-free municipal bonds. The bonds pay interest of $1,000 each year. In addition, a new tax law enacted at the beginning of Year 2 reduced the corporate tax rate to 30%.

Required »

a. Prepare the journal entries required to record the tax provision for all 3 years, as well as the journal entry needed to record the effect of the tax rate change on any deferred tax accounts.
b. Determine the net income reported on the income statement for all 3 years.
c. Prepare the footnote, in dollars and percentages, required to reconcile the company's federal statutory income tax rate with its effective tax rate.

4 **E17-10. Deferred Tax Assets and Valuation Allowance.** Flex Mirrors, Ltd. offers a 3-year warranty on all its products. In Year 1, the company reported income before warranty expense of $600,000 and estimated that warranty repairs would cost the company $115,000 over the 3-year period. Actual repairs for the current year amounted to $40,000. Flex Mirrors' tax rate is 40%. After reviewing all available evidence, management determines that only 75% of the deferred tax asset will ultimately result in tax-deductible expenses over the warranty period.

Prepare the journal entries required to record the tax provision and valuation allowance for Year 1.

5 **E17-11. Change in Tax Rates.** Turnabout Enterprises provided the following information regarding book-tax differences for its first year of operations:

Source of Book-Tax Difference	**GAAP**	**Tax**
Installment sales: Income recognized	$500,000	$100,000
2-year warranty costs: Warranty expense	60,000	40,000
Depreciation expense	80,000	120,000

Installment sales are a normal part of Turnabout's operations. The depreciation expense is related to a building costing $1,600,000. Income before including any of the book-tax differences is $920,000. Deferred tax assets are expected to be fully realized and, as a result, no allowance account is needed. Turnabout is subject to a 40% income tax rate.

Prepare the journal entry(ies) necessary to record the effects of a tax-rate reduction from 40% to 34% effective the beginning of Year 2.

6 9 **E17-12. Net Operating Loss, Carryback.** Phlash Photo Labs, Ltd. provided you the following information for the 3 years ended December 31.

Year	**Income (Loss) before Tax**	**Tax Rate (%)**
1	$120,000	34%
2	70,000	25
3	(280,000)	40

Required »

a. Assuming no book-tax differences and no uncertainty regarding the realization of the tax benefits of the net operating loss carryforward, prepare the journal entry to record the tax expense for each of the 3 years presented. The company always elects the carryback/carryforward option. Future tax rates are expected to remain unchanged.
b. Prepare a partial income statement for Year 3.

6 8 9 **E17-13. Net Operating Loss, Carryforward.** Loggins Lumber Company experienced net losses during the first 2 years of its operations. Year 3 was the company's first profitable year. Loggins uses the same accounting methods for financial reporting and its tax returns. The company always elects the carryback/carryforward option. Management examined all available evidence, both positive and negative, and has determined that it is more likely than not that all of the carryforward tax benefits are fully realizable. The following information is taken from the company's financial records for the first 4 years of its operations:

Year	Income (Loss) before Tax	Tax Rate (%)
1	$(380,000)	34%
2	(135,000)	34
3	425,000	34
4	585,000	34

Required »

a. Prepare the journal entries needed to record the tax provision for Years 3 and 4.
b. Prepare partial income statements for all 4 years.
c. What is the balance of the deferred tax account at the end of Year 3?

6 9 **E17-14. Net Operating Loss, Carryback, Valuation Allowance.** Aurora Incorporated provided the following information:

Year	Income (Loss) before Tax	Tax Rate (%)
1	$405,000	34%
2	220,000	34
3	(975,000)	34

Aurora reported no book-tax differences and elected the carryback/carryforward option for its Year 3 loss. Future tax rates are not expected to change.

Required »

a. Prepare any necessary journal entries needed to record the Year 3 tax provision assuming that Aurora expects only $200,000 in future taxable income over the carryforward period.
b. Prepare a partial income statement for Year 3.

6 **E17-15. Net Operating Loss, Carryforward, Valuation Allowance, Disclosure.** Use the same information provided in E17-14. Now assume that in Year 4, taxable income is $280,000. This amount is higher than anticipated by management, and they now believe that they will be able to utilize the entire NOL carryforward.

Required »

a. Prepare the journal entries needed to record Aurora's income tax provision for Year 4.
b. Prepare the footnote in dollars and percentages required to reconcile the federal statutory income tax rate to the company's effective income tax rate.

2 5 6 9 **E17-16. Net Operating Loss, Carryforward, Tax Rate Change.** Hamilton Container Company reported the following income (loss) information for the first 4 years of its operations:

Year	Income (Loss) before Tax	Tax Rate (%)
1	$(400,000)	40%
2	100,000	34
3	230,000	34
4	620,000	42

There are no uncertainties about the realization of the net operating loss benefits. All tax rate changes were enacted as of the beginning of the year. All tax rate changes are not known until the year of change.

Required »

a. Prepare the journal entry(ies) needed to record the annual tax provision for Years 1 through 4.
b. Prepare a partial income statement for each year.
c. Prepare the footnote in both dollars and percentages required to reconcile Hamilton's federal tax rate to its effective income tax rate each year.

2 6 9 **E17-17. Net Operating Losses, Carrybacks, Carryforwards.** DiVito Imported Provisions, Inc. reported pre-tax accounting income equal to its taxable income as follows:

Year	Income (Loss) before Tax	Tax Rate (%)
1	$60,000	35%
2	82,000	40
3	58,000	40
4	(300,000)	40
5	50,000	35
6	45,000	35
7	80,000	35
8	(250,000)	40
9	20,000	38
10	30,000	38

All tax changes are enacted into law as of the beginning of the year. No tax rate changes are known until the year of change. DiVito elects the carryback/carryforward option for all net operating losses. For the losses noted, management concluded that it is more likely than not that the benefits of the net operating losses will be fully realizable in the future.

Required »

a. Prepare the journal entries necessary to record the tax provisions for Years 4 through 8.
b. Prepare a partial income statement for Years 4 through 8.
c. Compute the effective tax rate for Years 4 through 8.

2 6 9 **E17-18. Net Operating Losses, Carrybacks, Carryforwards.** Using the information provided in E17-17, assume that in Year 8, DiVito determined that it is more likely than not that it will earn only $50,000 in the future to be used to offset the net operating loss carryforward.

Required »

a. Prepare the journal entries necessary to record the tax provision for Years 8 through 10.
b. Prepare the footnote in both dollars and percentages required to reconcile DiVito's federal tax rate to its effective income tax rate for Years 8 through 10.

7 **E17-19. Uncertain Tax Positions.** Lewis Eagle Corporation concluded that it was able to exclude $2,500,000 in income from its current tax return. Income before the exclusion is $6,000,000. There are no book-tax differences. This income is subject to a 30% tax rate. Based on its technical merits, Lewis Eagle determined that it is more likely than not that the exclusion would be sustained upon examination by tax auditors. The possible outcomes and their related probabilities follow.

Filed Amount of the Exclusion That Management Expects to Maintain	Likelihood That the Tax Position Will Be Sustained at This Level (%)
$2,500,000	10%
2,000,000	20
1,500,000	25
1,000,000	35
880,000	10

Determine the amount of tax benefit from the exclusion that Lewis Eagle should recognize in its tax provision for the current year and prepare the journal entry needed to record the tax provision for the current year.

7 **E17-20. Uncertain Tax Positions.** Based on the information provided in E17-19, assume that Lewis Eagle Corporation reported the following income levels for both book and tax purposes for the following year.

Description	Amount
Income before exclusion	$8,000,000
Tax exclusion	(3,000,000)
Income before tax	$5,000,000

Assume that Lewis Eagle passed the more-likely-than-not test. Based on an analysis of the estimated cumulative probabilities, Lewis Eagle should recognize a tax benefit of $1,950,000. Assuming a tax rate of 30%, prepare the journal entry(ies) needed to record the tax provision for the current year.

Problems

2 3 **P17-1. Temporary Differences, Deferred Tax Liabilities, Reconciliation of Statutory Tax Rate to Effective Tax Rate.** Bradley Manufacturing uses long-term installment contracts to market its building products. It uses the accrual basis for financial reporting and the cash basis for tax purposes. The company also sells several products without offering installment contracts. We present the results of operations for the last 5 years.

	Year 1		Year 2		Year 3		Year 4		Year 5	
Account	**GAAP**	**Tax**	**GAAP**	**Tax**	**GAAP**	**Tax**	**GAAP**	**Tax**	**GAAP**	**Tax**
Sales	$3,200	$3,200	$4,000	$4,000	$4,400	$4,400	$4,750	$4,750	$5,100	$5,100
Gross profit on installment sales	2,500	0	3,100	0	1,500	0	1,550	0	2,000	0
Taxable portion of cash collected on installment sales	0	1,340	0	2,800	0	2,325	0	1,600	0	2,585
Operating expenses	1,500	1,500	1,800	1,800	2,100	2,100	2,250	2,250	1,900	1,900
Income before tax	$4,200		$5,300		$3,800		$4,050		$5,200	
Taxable income		$3,040		$5,000		$4,625		$4,100		$5,785
Tax rate		× 40%		× 40%		× 40%		× 40%		× 40%
Tax payable		$1,216		$2,000		$1,850		$1,640		$2,314

Required »

a. Determine the balance of the deferred tax account at the end of each of the 5 years.
b. Prepare the journal entries to record the tax for the 5 years. Show the effective tax rate for each year.

3 5 **P17-2. Temporary Differences, Deferred Tax Liabilities, Change in Tax Rate.** Simm-Mills Incorporated (SMI) acquired a piece of equipment at a total cost of $4,200,000. SMI uses the straight-line method for financial reporting and an accelerated method for tax purposes. The asset has a 6-year life for book and tax purposes. There is no estimated scrap value. SMI is subject to a 40% tax rate. We present the income and depreciation summary for both tax and GAAP.

Year	Income before Tax and Depreciation	Tax Depreciation	GAAP Depreciation
1	$ 920,000	$ 840,000	$ 700,000
2	1,600,000	1,344,000	700,000
3	1,780,000	806,400	700,000
4	2,100,000	483,840	700,000
5	1,750,000	483,840	700,000
6	1,200,500	241,920	700,000
Totals		$4,200,000	$4,200,000

Required »

a. Determine the balance of the deferred tax account at the end of each year.
b. Prepare the journal entries to record the tax provision for each year.
c. Prepare the journal entry to record the effect of a 35% income tax rate that is enacted into law effective as of the beginning of Year 4.

3 **P17-3. Temporary Differences, Deferred Tax Liabilities.** Early in 2018, Bicycle Messenger Service Corporation (BMSC) purchased a multiline/multifunction telephone system at a cost of $50,000. At that time, BMSC estimated that the system had a useful life of 5 years with no salvage value expected at the end of that time. The company elected to use the straight-line method for financial reporting with a half-year depreciation taken in the first and last years of the asset's life.

For tax purposes, the company depreciates the system using the following percentages:

Year	MACRS (%)
2018	20.00%
2019	32.00
2020	19.20
2021	11.52
2022	11.52
2023	5.76

There were no permanent differences during both 2018 and 2019. Income before tax and depreciation is $120,000 in 2018 and $200,000 in 2019. The company is subject to a 40% tax rate.

Required »

a. Prepare a schedule comparing book and tax depreciation and show the deferred tax provision and the cumulative balance of the deferred tax account.
b. Compute income tax expense and income taxes payable for 2018 and 2019.
c. What is the balance in the deferred tax account at December 31, 2019?
d. What is the firm's reported net income for 2018 and 2019?

3 4 5 **P17-4. Temporary Differences, Deferred Tax Assets and Liabilities, Realizability of Deferred Assets, Change in Tax Rate.** The following information is available for the first 4 years of operations for Shooting Star Corporation:

Year	Taxable Income (incorporates all information presented)	Enacted Tax Rate (%)
2018	$200,000	40%
2019	132,000	40
2020	110,000	40
2021	120,000	40

On January 2, 2018, the firm acquired heavy equipment costing $200,000 in a cash transaction. The equipment had a useful life of 5 years and no scrap value. The firm used the straight-line method of depreciation for book purposes; see the following for the tax depreciation taken each year:

Tax Depreciation				
2018	**2019**	**2020**	**2021**	**Total**
$66,000	$90,000	$30,000	$14,000	$200,000

On January 2, 2019, the firm collected $120,000 in advance for rental of a building for a 3-year period. The firm reported the entire $120,000 as taxable income in 2019, but $80,000 of the advance collection was unearned at December 31, 2019. The $80,000 was earned evenly over the next 2 years (i.e., 2020 and 2021).

Required »

a. Determine the balance of the deferred tax accounts at the end of 2021.
b. Repeat requirement (a) assuming that a newly enacted tax law increased the corporate tax rate to 43%, effective the beginning of 2019.

c. Prepare the journal entries for 2018 and 2019 in requirement (b).
d. Prepare the journal entries for 2019 and 2020 in requirement (b) assuming that based on all available evidence, it is more likely than not that half of the deferred tax asset will not be realized. Reverse out the allowance for the realized portion of the deferred tax asset in 2020.

3 5 **P17-5. Temporary Differences, Deferred Tax Liabilities, Change in Tax Rates.** Kimm-Mills Incorporated (KMI) acquired a piece of equipment at a total cost of $5,400,000. KMI uses the straight-line method of depreciation for financial reporting purposes and an accelerated method for tax purposes. The asset has a 6-year life for book purposes and for tax purposes. There is no estimated scrap value. KMI is subject to a 40% tax rate. We present the income and depreciation summary for both tax and GAAP.

Year	Income before Tax and Depreciation	Tax Depreciation	GAAP Depreciation
1	$1,200,000	$1,080,000	$ 900,000
2	1,880,000	1,728,000	900,000
3	1,980,000	1,036,800	900,000
4	2,100,000	622,080	900,000
5	1,750,000	622,080	900,000
6	1,200,500	311,040	900,000
Totals		$5,400,000	$5,400,000

Required »

a. Determine the balance of the deferred tax account at the end of each year.
b. Prepare the journal entries to record the tax provision for each year.
c. Prepare the journal entry to record the effect of a 35% income tax rate that is enacted into law effective as of the beginning of Year 4.

6 **P17-6. Net Operating Loss, Carryback, Carryforward.** Andrew, Inc. provides DJ services for corporate parties. Andrew reported a net operating loss of $750,000 on its 2018 tax return. During the 3 preceding years, Andrew had taxable income and paid taxes at various tax rates as follows:

Year	Taxable Income	Income Tax Rate (%)
2015	$300,000	34%
2016	100,000	25
2017	50,000	15

Although Andrew had a net operating loss in 2018, it was because of an unusual event. Andrew's management has substantial evidence to indicate that the company will be profitable over the foreseeable future and will incur a 34% tax rate for each of those years. In fact, during 2019, Andrew reported a profit before tax of $800,000. Andrew does not report any book-tax differences.

Required »

a. Prepare the journal entries to account for the NOL carryback and NOL carryforward in 2018.
b. Compute reported net income (loss) after tax for 2018.
c. Prepare the journal entries to account for income taxes in 2019.
d. Compute reported net income after tax for 2019.

4 6 **P17-7. Net Operating Loss, Carryback, Carryforward, Realizability of Deferred Assets.** Michael's Incorporated reported the following tax information for its first 3 years of operations.

Year	Taxable Income or Loss	Income Tax Rate (%)
2017	$ 400,000	34%
2018	(900,000)	36
2019	1,200,000	40

Assume that in 2018, there are no uncertainties regarding the realization of the NOL carryforward benefits. All tax rates were enacted at the beginning of the year. No tax rate changes are known until the year of change.

Required »

Based on the information provided,

a. Determine the amount of any refund receivable from the 2018 NOL. In addition, indicate the amount of the tax benefits related to the NOL carryforward. Prepare any journal entries required in the year of the loss.
b. What is the after-tax net income or loss reported on the 2018 income statement?
c. Compute the amount of any tax due in 2019
d. Determine the balance of the NOL carryforward benefits remaining at the end of 2019.
e. Determine the income tax expense reported for 2019 and prepare the journal entry needed to record the 2019 tax provision.
f. Repeat parts (a) and (b) assuming that management has negative evidence indicating that the firm will realize only 70% of the NOL carryforward benefits over the carryforward period.

❷❹❻❾ **P17-8. Net Operating Loss, Carryforward, Realizability of Deferred Tax Assets, Reconciliation of Statutory Tax Rate to Effective Tax Rate.** In 2018, its first year of operations, Genius Corp. had a $700,000 net operating loss when the tax rate was 30%. There are no differences between book (GAAP) income and taxable income. In 2018, the management of Genius Corp. determined that it was more likely than not that it would not realize the loss carryforward in the near future because the company had been in operations for only one year. In 2019, Genius had $300,000 taxable income and the tax rate remained 30%.

Required »

a. What are the journal entries in 2018 to record the tax loss carryforward?
b. What journal entries should Genius make in 2019 to record the current and deferred income taxes and to recognize the loss carryforward?
c. Assume that in 2018, management believes that the maximum amount of taxable income available for realization of the NOL carryforward is $400,000. Therefore, $300,000 of the NOL carryforward is expected to remain unrealized in the future. What journal entries are required to record the 2018 and 2019 tax provisions?
d. Based on your answer to part (c), prepare the footnote in dollars and percentages to reconcile the federal tax rate to the firm's effective (actual) income tax rate for each year presented.

❻ **P17-9. Net Operating Loss, Carryback, Carryforward.** CPF Corporation reported the following results for its first 3 years of operation:

Description	Amount
2018 income (before income taxes)	$ 80,000
2019 loss (before income taxes)	(620,000)
2020 income (before income taxes)	800,000

There were no permanent or temporary differences during these 3 years. Assume a corporate tax rate of 46% for 2018, 40% for 2019, and 34% for 2020. CPF elects to use the carryback-carryforward provision. All tax rates were enacted at the beginning of the year. No tax rate changes are known until the year of change.

Required »

a. What income (loss) should CPF report in 2019? (Assume that any deferred tax asset recognized is more likely than not to be realized.)
b. Prepare the journal entry(ies) to record the tax provision for 2019.
c. Prepare the journal entry or entries to record the tax provision for 2020.
d. Independent of your answer to part (a), assume now that CPF elects to use the carryforward-only provision, not the carryback provision. What income (loss) does CPF report in 2019?
e. Using the assumptions made in part (d), prepare the journal entry entries for 2019.
f. Using the assumptions made in part (d), prepare the journal entry entries for 2020.

❼❾ **P17-10. Uncertain Tax Position, Disclosure.** Assume that Kenne Diagnostics, Inc. makes an $800,000 capital investment and elects an immediate expense deduction for tax purposes. Management designated this treatment to be an uncertain tax position. The uncertainty of this tax position is whether the capital expenditure qualifies as eligible property for an immediate deduction. The equipment is capitalized for financial reporting purposes and is depreciated over a 10-year useful life using the straight-line basis with no residual value, resulting in depreciation expense of $80,000 per year.

Based on an analysis of prior tax cases, the most likely sustainable position would be to use MACRS depreciation for 5-year property resulting in a first-year depreciation expense of $160,000 (i.e., 20% × $800,000).

The entity reports $1,960,000 of income before tax and depreciation (or taking any Section 179 deductions) and is subject to a 40% tax rate. Managements' analysis of the likelihood of sustainability of this deduction under examination by the taxing authorities is presented below.

"As Filed" Amount of the Tax Benefit That Management Expects to Sustain	Percentage Likelihood That the Tax Position Will Be Sustained at This Level
$800,000	5%
340,000	30
160,000	20
110,000	45

Required »

a. Prepare the journal entry to record the tax provision for the current year.
b. Kenne's unrecognized tax benefits at the beginning of the year amounted to $120,000. Of this amount, $44,500 was settled during the year. Based on this information, prepare the roll forward reconciliation for Kenne's unrecognized tax benefits.

3 9 **P17-11. Deferred Taxes, Classification of Deferred Tax Accounts, Financial Statement Presentation.** Graham Department Stores reported the following year-end balances on its current balance sheet. Graham is subject to a 40% tax rate.

Account	GAAP Carrying Value	Tax Basis
Accounts Receivable–Net	$ 105,500	$ 125,000
Installment Sales Receivable	75,000	0
Estimated Warranty Liability	32,000	0
Unearned Subscription Revenue	120,000	0
Inventory	650,000	500,000
Plant and Equipment–Net	1,350,500	1,100,000
Investment in Affiliate Company (equity method)	675,000	500,000

The beginning cumulative balances of the deferred tax accounts are as follows:

Account	Beginning Balance
Deferred Tax Asset—Total	$ 41,000
Deferred Tax Liability—Total	$300,000

Taxable income is $2,500,000 and book income is $2,331,500. Assume installment sales, warranties, and subscriptions are 1-year contracts.

Required »

a. Compute the ending balances of the total deferred tax asset and total deferred tax liability.
b. Compute the deferred tax provision for the current year.
c. Prepare the journal entry to record the tax provision for the current year.

2 3 8 9 **P17-12. Permanent Differences, Temporary Differences, Reconciliation of Statutory and Effective Tax Rate, Financial Statement Presentation.** The following information is from the financial statements of the Core Products Group for the first 3 years of its operations.

	Year 1		Year 2		Year 3	
Account	**GAAP**	**Tax**	**GAAP**	**Tax**	**GAAP**	**Tax**
Revenue from Product Sales	$300,000	$300,000	$380,000	$380,000	$525,000	$525,000
Revenue from Subscriptions	30,000	0	20,000	0	25,500	0
Cash Collected on Subscriptions	0	15,500	0	28,000	0	32,000
Installment Sales	230,000	0	128,500	0	195,000	0
Taxable Portion on Installment Sales Collections	0	145,500	0	198,000	0	210,000
Tax-Free Interest Income	42,000	0	42,000	0	42,000	0
Total Revenues	$602,000	$461,000	$570,500	$606,000	$787,500	$767,000

	Year 1		Year 2		Year 3	
Account	**GAAP**	**Tax**	**GAAP**	**Tax**	**GAAP**	**Tax**
Cost of Sales	$120,000	$180,000	$150,000	$195,000	$180,000	$75,000
Estimated Warranty Expense	60,000	0	62,000	0	98,000	0
Actual Repair Costs	0	20,000	0	80,000	0	120,000
Operating Expenses	80,000	80,000	140,000	140,000	170,000	170,000
Insurance Expense: Officers' Life	20,000	0	20,000	0	20,000	0
Depreciation Expense	90,000	135,000	90,000	90,000	90,000	45,000
Total Expenses	$370,000	$415,000	$462,000	$505,000	$558,000	$410,000
Income before Tax	$232,000		$108,500		$229,500	
Taxable Income		$ 46,000		$101,000		$357,000
Tax Rate		× 40%		× 40%		× 40%
Tax Payable		$ 18,400		$ 40,400		$142,800

Required »

a. Identify all book-tax differences and classify each difference as temporary or permanent.
b. Prepare the footnote in percentages and dollars to reconcile the company's federal tax rate to its effective (actual) tax rate for the 3 years presented.
c. Determine the net income reported on the income statement for each year.

❷❸❺❾ **P17-13. Permanent Differences, Temporary Tax Differences, Change in Tax Rates, Reconciliation of Statutory Tax Rate to Effective Tax Rate, Classification of Deferred Tax Accounts, Disclosure.** Simply Syrup Incorporated, a maple syrup maker, reported the following events causing differences between pretax accounting income and taxable income during its first full year of operations:

- In 2018, Simply Syrup purchased equipment costing $440,000 (with a useful life of 4 years and no salvage value) that it will depreciate on a straight-line basis for financial reporting purposes. Simply Syrup will use an accelerated method for tax purposes and depreciate $200,000 in the first year and $80,000 in the following 3 years (i.e., 2019 through 2021).
- On December 31, 2018, Simply Syrup collected $70,000 for future delivery of 3,500 cases of its Maple Light Syrup. It is scheduled to deliver 2,100 cases in 2019 and the remainder in 2020.
- Simply Syrup invests in U.S. government securities to earn tax-free interest. In 2018, the company reported $8,000 of interest income from this investment on its income statement.
- Simply Syrup makes a promise to its customers: "We will give you a full refund if you are hospitalized after eating our syrup on your pancakes." Based on past experience, the company estimates that this warranty will cost 10% of sales. Sales of syrup in 2018 amounted to $100,000, and the firm recorded an accrued warranty expense of $10,000. The warranties expire in 1 year.
- In 2018, Simply Syrup insured the life of its president, Hill L. Minimon. The premiums paid amounted to $5,000. The company is the beneficiary.

Simply Syrup has a 40% tax rate and reported income before tax of $500,000 under GAAP for 2018.

Required »

a. Compute income tax payable in 2018.
b. Determine the deferred tax asset and liability at the end of 2018.
c. Determine income tax expense for 2018 and prepare the journal entry or entries necessary to record the tax provision for the year. Record deferred tax assets and deferred tax liabilities separately.
d. Compute the 2018 effective tax rate and reconcile it to the statutory federal rate of 40% in both percentages and dollars.
e. Prepare the entry necessary in 2018 based on having obtained information that Simply Syrup will not realize one-half of the deferred tax asset over the reversal period.
f. Assume that the 2020 Congress enacts a new law on January 1, 2020, reducing the tax rate to 36% effective January 1, 2020. Assume also that Simply Syrup has no further warranty accruals and no warranty claims in 2019. Prepare the journal entry necessary on January 1, 2020, to reflect this tax rate change. Record any deferred tax assets and deferred tax liabilities separately and ignore any allowance account for a deferred tax asset. Assume that planned reversals of deferred accounts were recorded in 2019.

CASES

Judgment Cases

Judgment Case 1: Permanently Reinvested Earnings

[*Note:* Complete the "Permanently Reinvested Earnings" Surfing the Standards Case before making the judgments in this case.]

Mini Golf Corporation is a fully owned foreign subsidiary of Fun Parks, Inc. Mini Golf operates in a foreign jurisdiction with a tax rate of 15% whereas Fun Parks, Inc. is a U.S. corporation that has a 35% tax rate. Mini Golf has earnings of $2,000,000 this year, and there are no book-tax differences. The firm is subject to taxation at 15% in its home country. When it eventually distributes the earnings back to Fun Parks (which will not happen in the current year), it will have to pay the additional 20% tax (the U.S. tax rate of 35% – the foreign rate of 15%).

Typically, Fun Parks (a U.S. GAAP reporter) does not use the exception for recording its tax accrual found in FASB ASC 730-30-25-17. Thus, it would typically record the tax expense in the current year at $700,000. However, this year it has decided to take advantage of the exception and report tax expense of only $300,000. If you were the auditor, what other pieces of information would you like to evaluate before signing off on the company's tax accrual?

Judgment Case 2: Valuation Allowance

Fashion Designs, Inc. (FD) is a manufacturer of high-end women's clothing. The firm is involved in the manufacture and design of the clothing. FD has been in this business for many years and has historically reported strong earnings. However, its earnings have been declining in recent years. In the 2 years prior to the current year, it reported only a very small net income. In the current year, it incurred a $10,000,000 loss resulting from several factors:

- The economy as a whole was in a slump.
- There is a general consensus among buyers that FD's designs are becoming dated and are not appealing to the new generation of consumers.

However, a few buyers still like the designs by FD. In fact, FD currently has nearly completed the negotiations for a large contract with one of its primary buyers.

The management of FD has begun an overhaul of the business to address buyer concerns. Unfortunately, this process will take some time, possibly several years. And, of course, there is uncertainty about the feasibility of any turnaround plan for the business. To make matters worse, FD is facing a discrimination lawsuit that could ultimately result in a large payout.

FD is a U.S. GAAP reporter and has no book-tax differences. Because the firm incurred a net operating loss this year and had very little net income in the two preceding years, it will record a deferred tax asset for the NOL carryforward.

Based upon your judgment, should FD record a valuation allowance to offset its deferred tax asset? If so, should it record a full valuation allowance (i.e., the valuation allowance amount would equal the deferred tax asset amount) or just a partial valuation allowance? If a partial allowance, what percentage of the deferred tax asset should it offset with the allowance? Justify your answer. (Consider consulting paragraphs 21 and 22 of FASB ASC 740-10-30.)

Financial Statement Analysis Case

Case: Accounting for Income Taxes

You have been tasked with understanding income tax reporting at ***T-Mobile US, Inc.*** and comparing it to that of ***AT&T***. Use the following information from ***T-Mobile*** to address the questions.

NOTE 10: Income Tax

Income tax expense is summarized as follows:

	Fiscal Years		
(Amounts in millions)	**2016**	**2015**	**2014**
Current tax expense (benefit)			
Federal	$ (66)	$ (30)	$ –
State	29	2	6
Puerto Rico	(10)	17	38
Total current tax expense (benefit)	(47)	(11)	44
Deferred tax expense (benefit)			
Federal	804	281	79
State	96	(37)	40
Puerto Rico	14	12	3
Total deferred tax expense	914	256	122
Total income tax expense	$867	$245	$166

Effective Income Tax Rate Reconciliation

The reconciliation between the U.S. federal statutory income tax rate and our effective income tax rate is as follows:

	Year Ended December 31,		
	2016	**2015**	**2014**
Federal statutory income tax rate	35.0%	35.0%	35.0%
State taxes, net of federal benefit	4.0	(1.1)	(8.8)
Puerto Rico taxes, net of federal benefit	—	3.3	5.0
Change in valuation allowance	1.0	(3.2)	18.8
Permanent differences	0.6	1.6	1.4
Federal tax credits, net of reserves	(0.5)	(9.5)	(10.6)
Equity-based compensation	(2.2)	—	—
Other, net	(0.6)	(1.0)	(0.6)
Effective income tax rate	37.3%	25.1%	40.2%

Fiscal Year (in millions)	**2016**	**2015**	**2014**
Income before Taxes	$2,327	$978	$413

Source: http://investor.t-mobile.com/Cache/1001223313.PDF?O=PDF&T=&Y=&D=&FID=1001223313&iid=4091145

Required »

a. What is ***T-Mobile's*** effective tax rate each year? What is the difference between ***T-Mobile's*** effective tax rate and the statutory rate? Detail the items making up the difference.

b. Compare ***AT&T's*** effective tax rate for 2016, 2015, and 2014 from Example 17.24 in the text with the rate for ***T-Mobile***.

c. Compute ***T-Mobile's*** conservatism ratio for each year. Comment on any changes in the ratio over the years. Would you characterize ***T-Mobile*** as a conservative or aggressive tax reporter?

d. Compare ***AT&T's*** conservatism ratio from Example 17.24 in the text with the ratio for ***T-Mobile***.

Surfing the Standards Cases

Surfing the Standards Case 1: Tax Rates Dependent upon Distribution[23]

In certain countries, the tax rate applied in a company's tax return depends on whether the profits for the period are distributed or undistributed. Amounts are initially taxed at a higher rate, but a tax credit is received when amounts are distributed. Therefore, companies need to determine what rate (distributed versus undistributed) should be applied when measuring the amount of current and deferred taxes.

Multinational Corporation (Multinational) is a U.S. company that owns and operates a consolidated subsidiary in a foreign jurisdiction, where income taxes are payable at a higher rate on undistributed profits than on distributed earnings. For the year ending December 31, 2015, Multinational's foreign consolidated subsidiary's taxable income was $150,000. Multinational's foreign consolidated subsidiary also had net taxable temporary differences amounting to $50,000 for the year, thus creating the need for a deferred tax liability. The tax rate on distributed profits is 40% and the rate on undistributed profits is 50%; the difference results in a credit if profits are later distributed. As of the date of the balance sheet, no distributions have been proposed or declared. On March 31, 2016, Multinational's foreign consolidated subsidiary distributed dividends of $75,000.

Required »

a. Obtain and review the measurement guidance related to anticipated future tax credits in sections 25 and 30 of FASB ASC 740-10, *Income Taxes–Overall.*
b. Review and discuss the general rules for this type of situation.
c. Provide the necessary journal entries for 2015 and 2016.

Surfing the Standards Case 2: Tax Rates Dependent upon Distribution: IFRS[24]

Using the information in the Surfing the Standards Case 1, now assume that Multinational Corporation (Multinational) is an IFRS reporter.

Required »

a. Obtain and review the measurement guidance related to anticipated future tax credits in *International Accounting Standard 12*, "Income Taxes."
b. Review and discuss the general rules for this type of transaction using IFRS.
c. Provide the necessary journal entries for 2015 and 2016 under IFRS.

Surfing the Standards Case 3: Permanently Reinvested Earnings

Mini Golf Corporation is a fully owned foreign subsidiary of Fun Parks, Inc. Mini Golf operates in a foreign jurisdiction with a tax rate of 15% whereas Fun Parks, Inc. is a U.S. corporation that has a 35% tax rate. Mini Golf has earnings of $2,000,000 this year and there are no book-tax differences. The firm is subject to taxation at 15% in its home country. When Mini Golf eventually distributes the earnings back to Fun Parks (which will not happen in the current year), it will have to pay the additional 20% tax (the U.S. tax rate of 35% – the foreign rate of 15%).

1. What is your intuition as to how to handle this tax accrual? Specifically, for what amount should taxes payable be credited? For what amount should tax expense be debited? If these two numbers are not the same, what other account should be debited or credited and for how much? Why?
2. Read FASB ASC 740-30-25-3. Based upon this paragraph, what is the journal entry to record the tax provision in the current year?
3. Read FASB ASC 740-30-25-17. Are there any circumstances in which the company would not have to record the incremental tax expense and the deferred tax liability? If so, what would the journal entry be to record the tax provision in the current year?

---

[23]Reprinted from the Ernst & Young Academic Reousrce Center with permission of the Ernst & Young Foundation.

[24]Reprinted from the Ernst & Young Academic Resource Center with permission of the Ernst & Young Foundation.

4. Does the exception in (3) make sense to you? Please explain.
5. IFRS contains the same general rule that is included in U.S. GAAP in FASB ASC 740-30-25-3. IFRS also has an exception to this rule. Read *International Accounting Standard 12*, "Income Taxes," paragraph 39. Is the exception under IFRS the same as the exception under U.S. GAAP? Explain.

Basis for Conclusions Cases

[*Note:* In the following exercise, you are required to review the Basis for Conclusions (BCs) for the standard(s) that provide the accounting guidance for this topic. Because the BCs is generally not included in the Codification and thus is not authoritative, it will most likely be necessary for you to research it by reviewing the pre-codified standards. Appropriate references have been provided to allow you to do so. Pre-codified standards are accessible on the FASB website at www.fasb.org, or, in the event that your school participates in the American Accounting Association's *Academic Accounting Access* program, they can be found there as well.]

Basis for Conclusions Case 1: Is it *really* a liability?[25]

Scene 1: The concept of the deferred tax liability (which is reported under both U.S. GAAP and IFRS) has been at the root of disagreement among financial statement users for quite some time. While some do believe that it is truly a liability, others do not. The following is an excerpt from "The Valuation of Deferred Taxes," by Eli Amir, Michael Kirschenheiter and Kristen Willard, published in *Contemporary Accounting Research*, Vol. 14, No. (4 (Winter 1997), pages 597–622.

> Financial statement users often disagree as to the most appropriate method for valuing a firm that has deferred tax assets and liabilities on its balance sheet. Some claim that net deferred taxes represent obligations to pay taxes in the future, and hence, should be regarded as financial liabilities. As such, these liabilities should be offset against the firm's other long-term net financial assets. Proponents of this method often argue that if the temporary differences, which gave rise to the deferred tax liabilities, are not expected to reverse (settle) in the near future, these liabilities should be discounted similar to other long-term financial obligations, taking into account the expected time to achieve reversal and the cost of borrowing.
>
> Others argue that many deferred tax liabilities (e.g., deferred taxes resulting from depreciation and temporary amortization differences) are never settled; hence, net deferred tax liabilities should be added to (and net deferred tax assets should be subtracted from) the firm's book value of shareholders' equity. Consistent with this approach, *Statement of Standard Accounting Practice (SSAP) No. 15* issued by the Accounting Standards Committee in the United Kingdom (ASC 1985) requires companies to adopt a partial interperiod tax allocation method, that is, to recognize only those deferred taxes that are expected to materialize in the foreseeable future (3–5 years). This partial recognition effectively regards long-term temporary differences as part of equity.

Read paragraphs 75 through 79 in the BCs of FASB's *Statement of Financial Accounting Standards No. 109*, "Income Taxes." Does the FASB believe that the deferred tax liability is really a liability? How does it support this position?

Scene 2: Do you agree with the FASB's position and its supporting arguments? Please explain and support your position.

Scene 3: IFRS Consistent with the discussion above, some financial statement users believe that the deferred tax liability account should be discounted, or that a partial interperiod tax allocation method should be allowed. Read *International Accounting Standard 12*, "Income Taxes,"

[25]Reprinted from the Ernst & Young Academic Resource Center with permission of the Ernst & Young Foundation.

paragraphs 16, 53, and 54. Also, read paragraphs 198, 199, 203, 204, and 205 in the BCs of FASB's *Statement of Financial Accounting Standards No. 109*, "Income Taxes."

a. Do the boards allow deferred tax liabilities to be discounted?
b. Do the boards allow the use of a partial interperiod allocation method?
c. How do the boards support their position on discounting?
d. How does the FASB support its position related to interperiod tax allocation?

Basis for Conclusions Case 2: Uncertain Tax Positions and Examination Risk[26]

Scene 1: Current guidance on uncertain tax positions requires that when an entity is making its assessment as to whether a tax position is more likely than not to be sustained, it must assume that the position will be examined by the relevant taxing authority and that the taxing authority has all the relevant knowledge and information (FASB ASC 740-10-25-6 and FASB ASC 740-10-25-7). There is some controversy over this decision. Read paragraphs B17 through B22 in the BCs in FASB's *Interpretation No. 48*.

What are the arguments of the opponents of this rule?

Scene 2: What are the arguments of the proponents of this rule?

Scene 3: Which position do you support? Explain.

[26]Reprinted from the Ernst & Young Academic Resource Center with permission of the Ernst & Young Foundation.

APPENDIX A

Comprehensive Book-Tax Difference Problem

Example 17A.1 this Appendix provides a comprehensive illustration of accounting for deferred taxes over a 3-year period.

EXAMPLE 17A.1 Comprehensive Book-Tax Difference Problem

PROBLEM: Homeward Products, Inc. provided the following information about its first 3 years of operations.

- In its first year of operations, the company used installment sales to promote its products. The company reported $4,000 in installment sales for the period. It did not have any installment sales for the next 2 years. Homeward received cash of $600, $1,000, and $2,400 for installment sales in Years 1, 2, and 3, respectively.
- Homeward uses MACRS (an accelerated depreciation system) for tax purposes and straight-line depreciation for book purposes. It recorded $10,000 in depreciation expense each year for book purposes. For tax purposes, it recorded $17,000, $12,000, and $9,000 in Years 1, 2, and 3, respectively.
- Homeward uses the allowance method to recognize bad debt expense for book purposes and the direct write-off method for tax purposes. Under the allowance method, Homeward recognized $5,000, $7,000, and $6,500 of bad debt expense in Years 1, 2, and 3, respectively, for book purposes. It recognized $0, $4,600, and $6,000 of bad debt expense in Years 1, 2, and 3, respectively, for tax purposes.
- Homeward recorded a $5,000 contingent litigation liability in Year 2 for book purposes.
- In each year, the firm received municipal interest of $1,000.
- Homeward operates only in one taxing jurisdiction, and its statutory tax rate is 35%. The firm assesses that it will not need a valuation allowance for any deferred tax assets.

Follows are the partial income statements and selected balance sheet accounts for both book and tax reporting purposes for each of the 3 years.

	Year 1		Year 2		Year 3	
Description	**GAAP**	**Tax**	**GAAP**	**Tax**	**GAAP**	**Tax**
Sales Revenue	$50,000	$50,000	$61,300	$61,300	$72,000	$72,000
Installment Sales Revenue	4,000	600	0	1,000	0	2,400
Total Revenue	54,000	50,600	61,300	62,300	72,000	74,400
Depreciation Expense	10,000	17,000	10,000	12,000	10,000	9,000
Bad Debt Expense	5,000	0	7,000	4,600	6,500	6,000
Litigation Expense	0	0	5,000	0	0	0
Other Operating Expenses	22,000	22,000	27,000	27,000	30,000	30,000
Total Operating Expenses	37,000	39,000	49,000	43,600	46,500	45,000
Operating Income	$ 17,000	$11,600	$12,300	$18,700	$25,500	29,400
Municipal Interest Revenue	1,000	0	1,000	0	1,000	0
Income before Tax	$18,000	11,600	$13,300	18,700	$26,500	$29,400

Continued

	Year 1		Year 2		Year 3	
	GAAP	Tax	GAAP	Tax	GAAP	Tax
ASSETS						
Accounts Receivable–Regular Sales	$ 17,000	$ 22,000	$ 9,000	$16,400	$12,500	$20,400
Receivable–Installment Sales	3,400	0	2,400	0	0	0
Property, Plant and Equipment–Net	115,000	108,000	105,000	96,000	95,000	87,000
LIABILITIES AND EQUITY						
Litigation Contingency	$ 0	$ 0	$ 5,000	$ 0	$ 5,000	$ 0

What is Homeward's income tax provision for each of the 3 years? Prepare the journal entries required to record the income tax provision for the first 3 years of operation.

SOLUTION: In order to prepare the journal entries to record the income tax provisions for the 3 years, we need to perform several computations. First, we compute the balances in Homeward's deferred tax accounts by comparing the tax basis of the underlying assets and liabilities to the book carrying values. Second, we determine the change in the deferred tax asset or liability balance. We also compute the income taxes payable based on taxable income and the income tax expense based on book income, adjusted for permanent differences.

We compute the balances in the deferred tax accounts as follows:

1. Installment sales create a difference in the book and tax bases of receivables. Because the book basis of the receivable is greater than the tax basis of the asset in all 3 years, there is a deferred tax liability (Scenario 2 from Exhibit 17.3).

Installment Sales Receivable	**Year 1**	**Year 2**	**Year 3**
Book basis	$ 3,400	$ 2,400	$ 0
Tax basis	0	0	0
Difference	$ 3,400	$ 2,400	$ 0
Tax rate	× 35%	× 35%	× 35%
Deferred tax liability	$ 1,190	$ 840	$ 0

2. Depreciation creates a difference in the book and tax bases of property, plant, and equipment (PP&E). Because the book basis of PP&E is greater than the tax basis of the asset, there is a deferred tax liability (Scenario 2 from Exhibit 17.3).

Property, Plant, and Equipment (Depreciation)	**Year 1**	**Year 2**	**Year 3**
Book basis	$115,000	$105,000	$95,000
Tax basis	108,000	96,000	87,000
Difference	7,000	9,000	8,000
Tax rate	× 35%	× 35%	× 35%
Deferred tax liability	$ 2,450	$ 3,150	$ 2,800

3. Bad debt expense accounting causes a difference in the book and tax bases of accounts receivable. Because the book basis of accounts receivable is less than the tax basis of the asset, there is a deferred tax asset (Scenario 1 from Exhibit 17.3).

Accounts Receivable (Bad Debts)	**Year 1**	**Year 2**	**Year 3**
Book basis	$17,000	$ 9,000	$12,500
Tax basis	22,000	16,400	20,400
Difference	5,000	7,400	7,900
Tax rate	× 35%	× 35%	× 35%
Deferred tax asset	$ 1,750	$ 2,590	$ 2,765

4. Litigation expense creates a difference in the book and tax bases of contingent liabilities. Because the book basis of a contingent liability is greater than the tax basis of the liability, there is a deferred tax asset (Scenario 4 from Exhibit 17.3).

Contingencies Liability	Year 1	Year 2	Year 3
Book basis	$ 0	$5,000	$5,000
Tax basis	0	0	0
Difference	$ 0	$5,000	$5,000
Tax tate	× 35%	× 35%	× 35%
Deferred tax asset	$ 0	$ 1,750	$1,750

We summarize the four temporary book-tax differences to determine the following net deferred tax balance in each of the 3 years (deferred liabilities are in parentheses):

Summary of Deferred Taxes	Year 1	Year 2	Year 3
Installment sales	$(1,190)	$ (840)	$ 0
Depreciation	(2,450)	(3,150)	(2,800)
Total deferred tax liabilities	$(3,640)	$(3,990)	$(2,800)
Change in deferred tax liabilities	(3,640)	(350)	1,190
Bad debts	$ 1,750	$ 2,590	$ 2,765
Contingencies	0	1,750	1,750
Total deferred tax assets	$ 1,750	$ 4,340	$ 4,515
Change in deferred tax assets	$ 1,750	$ 2,590	$ 175
Change in net amount			
(deferred tax expense)	$(1,890)	$ 2,240	$ 1,365

The journal entry for the deferred tax provision records the changes in the accounts. Thus, for Year 1, Homeward records a deferred tax liability of $3,640 and a deferred tax asset of $1,750. In Year 2, it records a deferred tax liability for $350 and a deferred tax asset for $2,590. In Year 3, Homeward records a deferred tax asset of $175 and reduces (debits) the deferred tax liability by $1,190.

The taxes payable based on taxable income are as follows:

Computation of Taxes Payable	Year 1	Year 2	Year 3
Taxable income	$11,600	$18,700	$29,400
Tax rate	× 35%	× 35%	× 35%
Taxes payable	$ 4,060	$ 6,545	$10,290

Finally, we compute the tax expense that Homeward will record on its income statement.

Computation of Tax Expense	Year 1	Year 2	Year 3
Income before Income Taxes	$18,000	$13,300	$26,500
Less: Permanent Differences	(1,000)	(1,000)	(1,000)
	$ 17,000	$12,300	$25,500
Tax Rate	× 35%	× 35%	× 35%
Tax Expense	$ 5,950	$ 4,305	$ 8,925

Based upon these computations, the tax accrual journal entries are as follows:

Account	December 31, Year 1	
Deferred Tax Asset	1,750	
Income Tax Expense	5,950	
Deferred Tax Liability		3,640
Income Taxes Payable		4,060

Account	December 31, Year 2	
Deferred Tax Asset	2,590	
Income Tax Expense	4,305	
Deferred Tax Liability		350
Income Taxes Payable		6,545

Account	December 31, Year 3	
Income Tax Expense	8,925	
Deferred Tax Liability	1,190	
Deferred Tax Asset	175	
Income Taxes Payable		10,290

18 Accounting for Leases

LEARNING OBJECTIVES

1. Understand the basic concepts of lease accounting and identify the advantages and disadvantages of leasing.
2. Understand lease contracts and determine how to separate lease and nonlease components and how to allocate contract consideration to the various components.
3. Classify leases as operating, finance, direct financing, and sales-type.
4. Demonstrate the accounting for an operating lease for both the lessee and the lessor.
5. Demonstrate lessee accounting for a finance lease.
6. Illustrate lessor accounting for sales-type leases.
7. Illustrate lessor accounting for direct financing leases.
8. Detail the required lease disclosures.

Introduction

A *LEASE* IS ONE OF THE most common means by which companies obtain the use of long-term operating assets. In a lease, a company acquires the use of an asset—such as a copy machine, office space, or even an airplane—by financing it directly through the asset's owner. In the airline industry, about one-third of airplanes are leased.[1] Airlines decide to lease versus buy assets for a variety of reasons, including the ability to obtain financing, reduced risk of obsolescence, or operating flexibility. For example, small, recently established airlines, which may have difficulty obtaining capital to buy large airplanes, lease planes to exploit new routes. At the end of fiscal 2016, the operating fleet of ***Spirit Airlines*** consisted of 95 airplanes of which 38% were owned and 62% were leased. ***Spirit*** also leases most of its land and buildings that it occupies, such as its aircraft maintenance base as well as various computers, cargo, flight kitchens, and training facilities. On your next trip to the airport, consider that airlines lease the ticket counter and other terminal space, operating areas, and air cargo facilities in most of the airports that they serve.

Carlos Yudica.Shutterstock

Is there a difference in the economic substance of acquiring a long-term operating asset (such as an airplane) by issuing long-term debt or acquiring the use of an asset by signing a lease contract? In most cases, there is no real substantial difference in leasing and purchasing. The form of the contract is different, but the substance of these transactions is the same.

A lease typically results in obtaining the use and control of a long-term asset and the recognition of a long-term financing liability. Accounting for the liability requires similar accounting procedures as used in accounting for a long-term debt instrument. Because the lease will involve the use and control of an asset, we also discuss accounting for long-term operating assets.

We begin the chapter with an overview of leases and their advantages and disadvantages. Then, we discuss how to determine whether a lease exists, how to separate lease and nonlease components, and how to allocate consideration among these components. We then consider the proper

[1] "Aircraft Leasing: Buy or Rent?: The Steady Rise of Airlines with No Passengers," *The Economist*, January 21, 2012.

classification of leases and illustrate lease accounting from the perspective of both parties: the company obtaining the use of the asset (the lessee) and the company providing the asset for use (the lessor). Finally, we review required lease disclosures and then explore the possible financial statement effects of the lease accounting alternatives. ❮❮

1 Understand the basic concepts of lease accounting and identify the advantages and disadvantages of leasing.

Leases: Overview

A **lease** gives the *lessee* the right to control and use the property, plant, or equipment legally owned by the *lessor* for a specified period of time in return for periodic payments or rentals made by the lessee. The owner of the asset is called the **lessor**. The party acquiring the use of the asset is the **lessee**. The lease contract conveys only the right to use the asset—it typically does not result in a transfer of ownership of the asset. This property right has economic value to the lessee and, in substance, represents the purchase of an asset with a corresponding obligation.

Advantages of Leasing for the Lessee

What accounts for the popularity of leasing? Leasing provides multiple advantages over buying.

Complete Financing. Many leases allow the lessee to enter into a lease agreement with little or no money down and with no security deposit. The lessee maintains its cash and other assets, resulting in 100% financing for the leased asset.

Lessor Bears the Risk of Obsolescence. The risk of obsolescence is borne by the owner of the asset, the lessor, and is reflected in high lessee monthly rental payments. However, the lessee is willing to pay this premium when leasing an asset that is subject to rapid technological obsolescence. A lessee company upgrading to the latest technology maintains its competitive advantage. For example, consider leased photocopy equipment, which is one of the most common types of leased assets. Over time, technology has improved the features in photocopiers with options such as scanning, emailing, and remote copying. A company that owns its copier would need to buy a new copy machine to obtain these features. A company that leases a photocopier can easily upgrade when new features become available.

Business and Financial Flexibility. Leases can offer many business options for the lessee. For example, the lessee can upgrade the asset, return the asset, continue the lease with extended terms, modify rental amounts, or exercise a purchase option. The lease may also provide financial flexibility by permitting the lessee to obtain an additional source of financing without affecting existing lines of credit.

Tax Benefits. When a company purchases equipment by issuing a long-term note, the interest element of the payment is tax deductible. However, if the company leases equipment, the *entire* lease payment may be tax deductible. In addition, in a purchase of real estate, only the building but not the land is depreciable. If a company leases a building (on the land), the total lease payment may be fully tax deductible as rent expense.

Disadvantages of Leasing for the Lessee

Although there are multiple advantages to leasing, there are a few disadvantages.

Overall Cost of the Asset. In general, the costs of the asset over the life of the lease are higher than had the lessee purchased the asset. The lease payments must compensate the lessor for the use of the asset, financing costs, and the risk of ownership.

Lack of Ownership. Unless the lease arrangement includes a transfer of ownership or a purchase option that is exercised, the asset does not belong to the lessee at the end of the lease.

Understanding the Basics of Lease Accounting

Lease accounting is complex and detailed. However, the basic concepts behind lease accounting are straightforward. Let's start with these basic concepts before examining the details of lease accounting.

An important concept to understand is that the substance of a typical lease transaction is similar to the purchase of an asset on credit. In a lease transaction, the lessor obtains the right to use the leased asset in return for payments made to the lessor. So, this is similar to the lessee purchasing an asset from the lessor with the lessor providing the financing. Although there are some differences in a lease transaction and a purchase financed by the seller, there are more similarities than differences.

Thus, the accounting treatment follows the substance of the transaction. As in the case of a purchase financed by the seller, a lease transaction typically results in the leased asset on the lessee's balance sheet. In addition, the lessee reports a long-term obligation. Consistent with accounting for long-term debt and long-term operating assets, the lessee records both interest expense and amortization on its income statement.[2]

The lessor often (although not always) removes the leased asset from its balance sheet and instead recognizes a financial asset that represents the amounts that are receivable from the lessee. The lessor also records interest revenue on its income statement related to the financing component of the transaction. In addition, the lessor may report revenue and cost of goods sold related to what is, in substance, a sales transaction.

2016 Lease Standards. This chapter is based on the lease standards issued by FASB and the IASB in 2016, which are effective beginning in 2019. Prior to the release of these standards, lessees did not report all leases on the balance sheet. These new standards accomplish the standard setters' primary goal of requiring lessees to report the leased asset and lease liability on their balance sheets.

Key Steps in Lease Transactions. This chapter addresses the key steps in the flow of a lease transaction.

Step 1. Identify a lease contract.

Step 2. Identify lease and nonlease components and allocate costs to each component.

Step 3. Classify the lease.

Step 4. Recognize and initially measure the lease transaction.

Step 5. Determine subsequent measurement of the lease transaction.

Within each step, lessees and lessors make many judgments in applying lease accounting. Exhibit 18.1 presents these steps.

EXHIBIT 18.1 Steps in Accounting for Leases

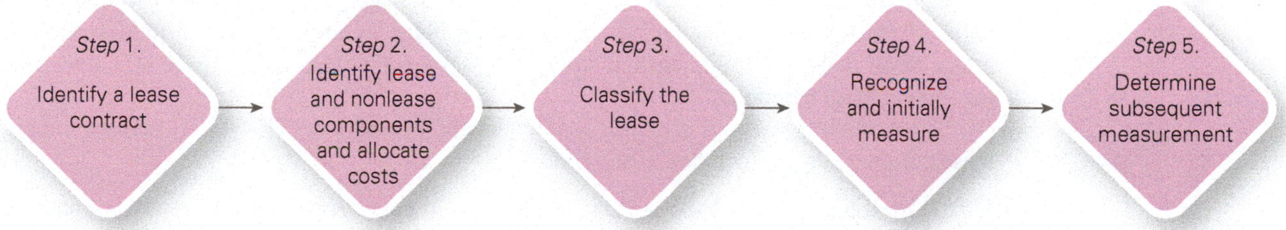

[2] We use the word "amortization" rather than "depreciation" for leased assets because the lessee does not own the physical asset but has the right to use it.

❷ Understand lease contracts and determine how to separate lease and nonlease components and how to allocate contract consideration to the various components.

Lease Contracts, Lease Components, and Contract Consideration

The first step in lease accounting for both the lessee and the lessor is to determine whether a contract contains a lease. A company makes this determination at the inception of a contract. An agreement could be a separate lease contract, or a lease contract could be embedded in another agreement, such as a contract for services. The determination of whether a contract contains a lease is generally clear, but there can be cases in which it is much more complex.[3]

Lease contracts often contain multiple *components* that may be lease or nonlease components. A **component** of a contract is an item or activity that transfers a good or service to the lessee. Both the lessee and lessor are required to identify and separate the various lease and nonlease components. After identifying the lease and nonlease components, the lessor and lessee will be able to allocate consideration to these components.

Companies include only lease components when accounting for the lease transaction. Any nonlease components are accounted for under other areas of the authoritative literature as appropriate. Examples of nonlease components in a lease agreement include goods or services such as maintenance services or supplies.

Separating Components in a Lease Contract

Prior to allocating any consideration, a company has to identify the components in the contract.

Lease Components. When lease contracts contain the right to use several assets, the company must identify each right-of-use asset. For example, a company that leases a building can also have the right to use the building's adjacent parking lot. Typically, the right to use these multiple assets is considered a single lease component. However, if both of the following criteria are met, the right to use an asset is considered a separate lease component:

1. The lessee can benefit from the right of use of the asset either on its own or together with other resources that are readily available to the lessee.
2. The right of use is neither highly dependent on nor highly interrelated with the other rights to use the underlying assets in the contract.

In the case of the building and parking lot, the parking lot is highly interrelated to the building. The lessee would have no use for the parking lot if it were not also leasing the building.

Land. The right to use land is considered a separate lease component unless the impact on the financial statements of not separating the land from the other asset(s) is insignificant.

Example 18.1 illustrates identifying lease and nonlease components.

EXAMPLE 18.1 **Identification of Lease and Nonlease Components**

PROBLEM: Bassey Seafood Company leased a warehouse from the Gilli Group for a term of 10 years to store its products. The warehouse includes refrigeration units. The warehouse lease includes the use of forklifts, pallets, and conveyer belts. In addition, Gilli provides maintenance of all items of equipment included in the agreement. The maintenance is included in the annual lease payments.

What are the lease and nonlease components of the contract? How many lease and nonlease components are included in the contract?

SOLUTION: Bassey receives the use of warehouse storage, refrigeration units, and warehouse equipment. It also gets the use of maintenance services. The warehouse and the refrigeration units cannot be separated because they are interdependent. That is, the warehouse cannot be

[3] We do not discuss identifying lease contracts in depth in this chapter. See Surfing the Standards Case 1 for a more in-depth analysis of this issue.

used to store seafood without proper refrigeration. However, the warehouse equipment (forklifts, pallets, and conveyer belts) function independently and can be used separately in any warehouse. Therefore, this contract contains two lease components: the warehouse (with refrigeration) and the equipment. Maintenance is an additional nonlease component of the contract.

In total, the contract contains three components: two lease and one nonlease.

Lease Components	Nonlease Component
Warehouse with refrigeration	Maintenance
Equipment	

Allocating Consideration in a Lease Contract

After identifying the lease and nonlease components of the contract, lessees and lessors must then allocate the total contract consideration to the components. Although the approach to allocating consideration across the components is similar for lessees and lessors, there are some differences. Let's examine the lessee and lessor requirements separately.

Lessee Allocation Procedures. To separate the lease and nonlease components, the lessee allocates the contract consideration on a relative *standalone price* basis. The lessee first determines the **standalone price** of each component, which is the price at which it would purchase a component of a contract separately. The lessee then computes for each component the percentage of the component's standalone price to the sum of the standalone prices for all components. Then, to determine the amount of consideration allocated to a particular component, the lessee multiplies the percentage by the total consideration.

Ideally, the lessee uses the observable standalone prices. However, if observable prices are not available, the lessee can estimate the standalone prices. When estimating standalone prices, the lessee should maximize the use of observable inputs.

In cases in which the standalone price is highly variable or uncertain, the lessee may use a *residual method* of determining the standalone price. The **residual method** subtracts the other standalone prices from the total contract consideration and assigns the remaining amount as the estimated standalone price of the remaining component.[4]

Initial direct costs are incremental costs that the lessee would not have incurred if he had not obtained the lease, such as commissions, legal fees resulting from the execution of the lease, costs to prepare documents after the execution of the lease, and payments to existing tenants to move out of a facility. The lessee allocates initial direct costs to the separate lease components on the same basis as the lease payments. We discuss the accounting treatment for initial direct costs in more detail later in the chapter.

Lessor Allocation Procedures. The lessor allocates the lease transaction price to the separate components in accordance with the revenue recognition guidance discussed in Chapter 8. The lessor allocates the total consideration in the contract to each individual lease and nonlease component using the relative standalone selling price allocation. If there is not an observable standalone selling price, the lessor must use an estimate of the standalone selling price and allocate it based on any of the following methods:

1. Adjusted market assessment approach
2. Expected-cost-plus-a-margin approach
3. Residual approach[5]

[4]The lessee can make an election not to allocate the lease and nonlease components separately. This choice simplifies the accounting for the lease because the lessee allocates all of the contract consideration to this single component.

[5]These methods are discussed in detail in Chapter 8.

In all cases, the lessor must use observable data when possible. The lessor allocates any initial direct costs to the separate lease and nonlease components to which the costs relate. Example 18.2 illustrates the allocation of consideration to separate lease and nonlease components.

EXAMPLE 18.2 **Allocating Consideration to the Components**

PROBLEM: Consider Bassey Seafood Company from Example 18.1. We determined three components in the lease agreement: (1) the warehouse and refrigeration, (2) the equipment, and (3) the maintenance services. The total consideration in the contract is a $450,000 lease payment per year. Bassey identifies the following standalone prices:

Component	Standalone Price
Warehouse and refrigeration	$275,000
Equipment	150,000
Maintenance	75,000
Total	$500,000

How should Bassey allocate the consideration?

SOLUTION: Because the total consideration in the contract is not equal to the sum of the standalone prices, Bassey uses the relative standalone prices to allocate the total consideration to each component. Bassey allocates the $450,000 total consideration as follows:

Component	Standalone Price	Percentage	Allocated Consideration
Warehouse and refrigeration	$275,000	55%	$ 247,500
Equipment	150,000	30	135,000
Maintenance	75,000	15	67,500
Total	$500,000	100%	$450,000

The next step in accounting for a lease transaction is to classify the lease. So far, we have identified the lease and its lease and nonlease components. At this point, we have to determine whether the lease transfers control of the asset in order to determine the proper lease classification.

3 Classify leases as operating, finance, direct financing, and sales-type.

Lease Classifications

Before discussing the procedures for lease accounting, we need to clearly classify the lease. The lease classification determines the lease's proper accounting treatment. Lessees classify all leases as either *operating leases* or *finance leases*. Lessors classify leases as *operating*, *sales type*, or *direct financing*.

Before examining the classification criteria, we first need to distinguish the *lease inception* date from the *lease commencement* date. The **lease inception** is the date the lease agreement is signed. The **lease commencement** is the date on which the lessee is allowed to begin using the leased asset.

Criteria for Classification

Parties involved in a lease transaction consider two groups of criteria to classify leases. The Group I criteria, which apply to both lessees and lessors, provide guidance on which party to the lease effectively "owns" and controls the asset. The Group II criteria, which apply only to lessors, determine the extent to which the lessor will absorb the credit risk related to the lease contract.

Group I Criteria. Group I criteria provide guidance to operationalize the concept of ownership and control of an asset. Both the lessor and lessee use the Group I criteria. To meet the Group I conditions, a transaction needs only to *meet one of the five criteria*:

1. The lease transfers ownership of the leased asset to the lessee at the end of the *lease term*. If the lease transfers ownership, the lessee firm has in essence purchased the asset.
2. The lessee is given an option to purchase the asset that the lessee is reasonably certain to exercise. For example, it might be reasonably certain that the lessee would exercise a purchase option if the specified purchase price is well lower than the expected value of the leased asset at the completion of the lease term.
3. The *lease term* is for a major part of the economic life of the asset.[6] If the *lease term* provides the lessee the use and control over substantially all of the asset's useful life, the agreement should be considered equivalent to purchasing the asset.

   The **lease term** begins at the lease commencement date and includes the noncancellable period for which a lessee has the right to use the leased asset. The lease term also includes periods covered by an option to renew the lease if the lessee is reasonably certain to renew. The lessee is likely to renew if the lease payments over the renewal period are substantially lower than the fair value rental amount. If the lessor controls the option to renew the lease, the renewal period is included in the lease term.

   If a lease agreement contains an option to terminate and the lessee is reasonably likely to exercise that option, the lease term ends on the earliest date that the lease can be terminated. If the lessor has the option not to terminate the lease then, the lease term is the total lease period and will not terminate early.
4. The present value of the sum of the *lease payments* and any *residual value* the lessee guarantees to pay (that is not otherwise included in the lease payments) is equal to substantially all of the asset's fair value. In this case, the lessor is able to recover the cost of the asset. The present value computation includes lease payments in the renewal periods, if any. Meeting this criterion implies that the lessee is providing the lessor compensation that is equivalent to the purchase of the asset.
5. The leased asset is of a *specialized nature*. An asset with a **specialized nature** has no alternative use to the lessor at the end of the lease term. Because the asset has no alternative use to the lessor, its specialized nature implies that the lessor must have transferred control over the asset to the lessee.

Group II Criteria. Group II criteria apply to the lessor only. To meet the Group II criteria, a transaction must meet both criteria.

1. The present value of the sum of the lease payments and any residual value the lessee or a third party guarantees to pay (that is not otherwise included in the *lease payments*) is equal to substantially all of the asset's fair value.
2. It is probable that the lessor will collect the *lease payments* plus any amount necessary to satisfy a residual value guarantee.

Many of the Group I and Group II criteria depend highly on judgment. FASB does give some implementation guidance, and we discuss that in the judgment section later in the chapter. However, even with this limited guidance, much judgment is needed.

Lessee Classification. The classification is fairly straightforward for lessees. If the lease transaction meets any one of the five Group I criteria, the lessee classifies the lease as a **finance lease**. If none of the Group I criteria is met, the lessee classifies the lease as an **operating lease**. The Group II criteria are not used by the lessee.

[6] This criterion is not used for classification if the lease commencement date falls at or near the end of the life of the underlying asset.

Exhibit 18.2 presents lease classification for the lessee with the Group I criteria.

EXHIBIT 18.2 Lessee Classification of an Operating and Finance Lease

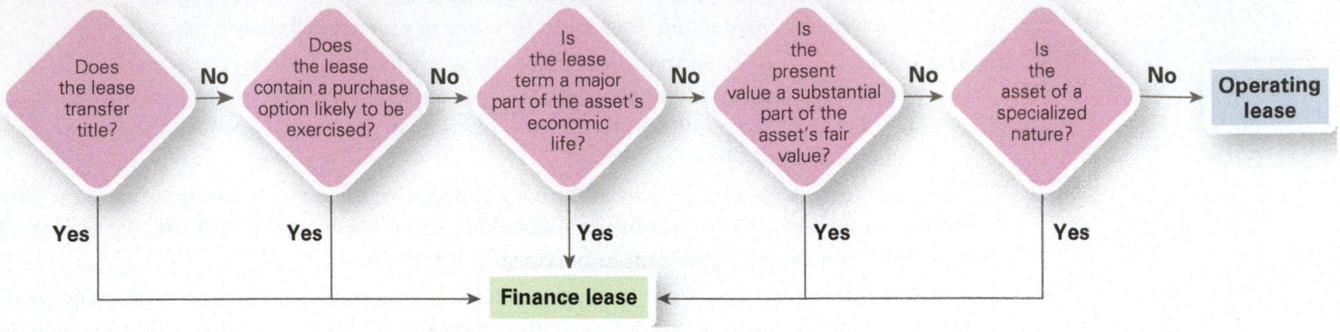

Lessor Classification. The classification for the lessor is a bit more complex than for the lessee. If the lessor meets any one of the five Group I criteria, the lessor classifies the lease as a **sales-type lease**. If the lessor meets both of the Group II criteria but none of the Group I criteria, the lessor classifies the lease as a **direct financing lease**. If the transaction does not meet either the Group I or Group II criteria, the lessor classifies the lease as an **operating lease**.

Exhibit 18.3 presents an illustration of lease classification for the lessor.

EXHIBIT 18.3 Lessor Classification of Operating, Sales-Type, and Direct Financing Leases

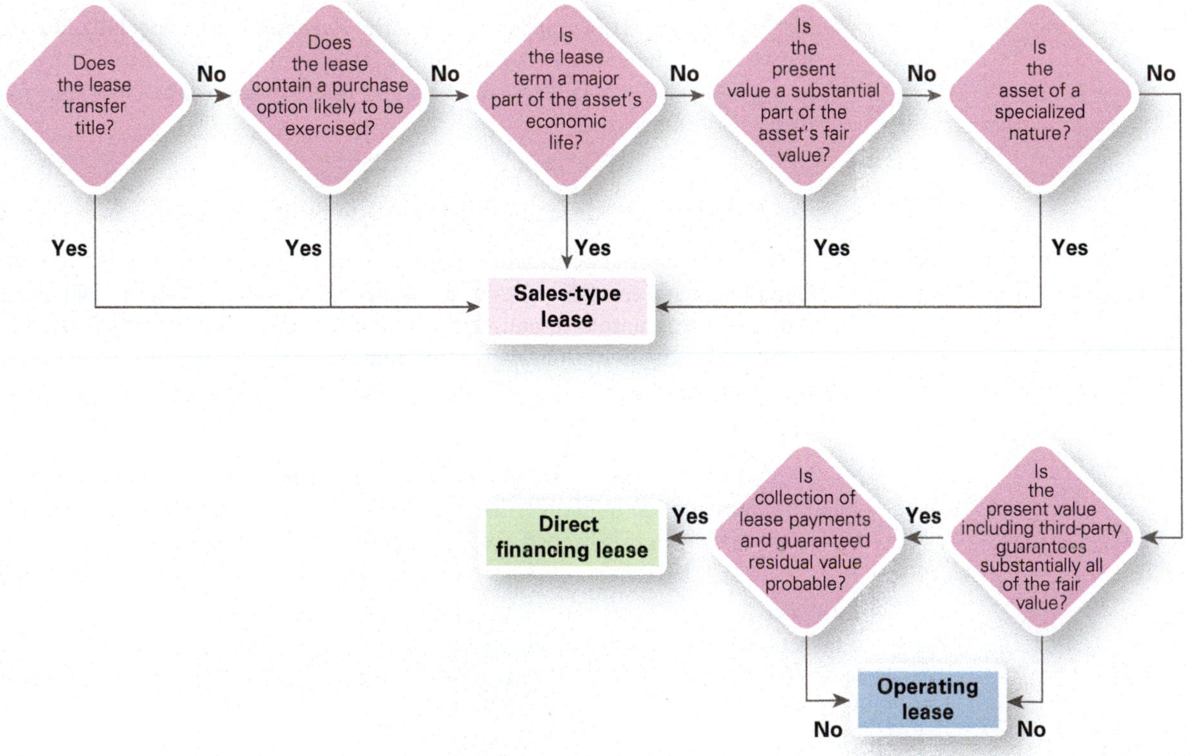

Exhibit 18.4 summarizes the lease classification decision.

EXHIBIT 18.4 Lease Classification Summary

Criteria	Lessee	Lessor	
Group I met	Finance	Sales-Type	
Group I not met	Operating	& Group II met	Direct-Financing
Group I not met		& Group II not met	Operating

Lease Payments and Discount Rates

In order to analyze the lease classification, we need to clearly define what is included in *lease payments* and what is the appropriate discount rate to use.

Lease Payments. The definition of a **lease payment** includes six elements. In any given lease arrangement, it is not likely that all six elements would be present. The six elements are:

1. Fixed payments less any *lease incentives* paid or payable to the lessee.[7]
2. Variable lease payments that depend on a rate or index (such as the consumer price level index or a market rate of interest) using the rate or index in effect at the lease commencement date.
3. The exercise price of an option to purchase the asset if the lessee is reasonably certain to exercise the option.
4. Penalty payments for lease termination if the lessee exercises an option to terminate the lease.
5. Fees paid by the lessee to the owners of a special-purpose entity for structuring the transaction. However, these fees are not included in the fair value of the leased asset.[8]
6. For a lessee only, the amounts that are probable of being owed by the lessee under *residual value guarantees*. Note that this component does not include any *unguaranteed residual assets* or any *residual value guarantees* made by a third party.

Lease incentives are payments the lessor makes to the lessee to provide an incentive to enter into a lease agreement. For example, the lessor may agree to pay IT system installation charges at a new location to give the lessee incentive to lease the new facility. As another example, the lessor may agree to pay the lessee's remaining rentals on another lease so the lessee can terminate that lease.

A **residual value guarantee** is a guarantee or assurance made to the lessor that he will receive a fixed dollar amount for the leased asset at the end of the lease. The lessee or a third party may provide this guarantee. If the fair value of the asset at the end of the lease is less than the residual value guarantee, the guarantor will make a payment to the lessor for the difference in the residual value guarantee and the fair value of the asset.

An **unguaranteed residual asset** is an amount the lessor expects to derive from the leased asset at the end of the lease term. This amount is simply the lessor's expectation; the lessee or a third party does not guarantee the residual value.

Discount Rates. Now that we have established the elements of lease payments, we discuss the determination of the appropriate discount rate to use in our lease computations. To compute the present value of the lease payments, both the lessor and the lessee have to determine the appropriate discount rate at the commencement of the lease. The lessor uses the *implicit rate*, which is a rate that is determined implicitly based on the equation in Exhibit 18.5.

The **implicit rate** is the rate of interest that sets the present value of the lease payments plus the present value of the amount that a lessor expects to obtain from the leased asset at the end of the lease term equal to the sum of the fair value of the leased asset and any deferred initial direct

[7]This includes any in-substance fixed payments These types of payments are discussed in more depth in Surfing the Standards Case 2.

[8]These fees are not explicitly included by IFRS in the lease payments.

costs incurred by the lessor. Exhibit 18.5 presents the equality used in the computation of the implicit rate.

EXHIBIT 18.5 Implicit Rate

Present value of lease payments + Present value of guaranteed and unguaranteed residual asset = Fair value of leased asset + Deferred initial direct costs of lessor

Because the lessor has to incur initial direct costs to obtain the lease, they are also included in determining the implicit rate of return on the lease. Note that the initial direct costs can either be deferred or expensed and if deferred, the initial direct costs are included in the computation of the implicit rate. The lessor may expense initial direct costs rather than defer these costs at the lease commencement. We discuss the rules that determine whether initial direct costs are expensed initially or deferred later in the chapter.

The lessee also uses the implicit rate unless it cannot determine the implicit rate. In that case, the lessee uses the **incremental borrowing rate**, which is the rate of interest that a lessee would have to pay to borrow an amount equal to the lease payments on a collateralized basis over a similar term to the lease in a similar economic environment. Example 18.3 illustrates determining the implicit rate.

EXAMPLE 18.3 Rate Implicit in the Lease

PROBLEM: JPAX Company, a lessor, enters into a 4-year lease transaction with payments due at the beginning of each year.

- The lease payments are $48,000 per year.
- The fair value of the leased asset is $260,000.
- The lessor's deferred initial direct costs are equal to $12,000.
- The lessor's estimate of the unguaranteed residual asset is $115,000.

What is the implicit rate in the lease for the lessor?

SOLUTION: JPAX solves for the implicit rate using the following equality:

Present Value of Lease Payments + Present Value of Estimated Residual Value
= Fair Value of Asset + Deferred Initial Direct Costs

JPAX applies time value of money concepts to identify the terms needed to solve for the implicit rate: the present value, *PV*; the number of periods, *N*; the payments per period, *PMT*; and the future value, *FV*. Because the payments are due at the beginning of the period, this is a present value of an annuity due problem. The present value, *PV*, is the present value of the lease payments plus the expected residual value which equals the fair value of the leased asset plus the deferred initial direct costs:

Present Value of Lease Payments + Present Value of Estimated Residual Value
= $260,000 Fair Value of Leased Asset + $12,000 Initial Direct Costs = $272,000

The number of periods, *N*, is 4 years. The payments each period, *PMT*, are $48,000. The future value, *FV*, is the residual value of $115,000.We use the spreadsheet application from Chapter 7 to determine the implicit rate as 5.22%:

	N	I/Y	PV	PMT	FV	Excel Formula
Given	4		−272,000	48,000	115,000	
Solve for RATE		**5.22**				=RATE(4,48000,−272000,115000,1)

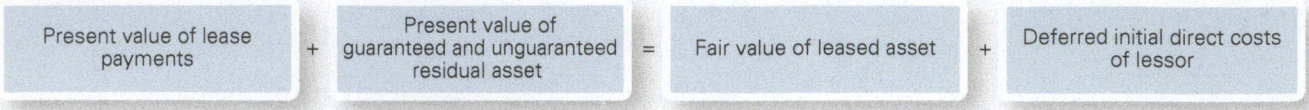

After determining the lease payments and discount rates, we can now classify the lease as shown in Example 18.4.

EXAMPLE 18.4 Lease Classification

PROBLEM: On January 1, 2019, Sturge Manufacturing leased a piece of machinery for use in its North American operations from Borko Bank. The machinery is not specialized and, therefore, could also be leased to other parties. The 9-year, noncancellable lease requires lease payments of $13,000 due at the beginning of each year. The present value of the lease payments is $77,579. The lease agreement does not transfer ownership of the machinery and it does not contain a purchase option. Sturge has not guaranteed a residual value, but a third party has provided a guarantee with a present value of $18,031. The machinery has a fair value of $95,455 and an estimated life of 10 years. Borko views it highly probable that the bank will collect the lease payments from Sturge and the third-party residual value guarantor. Determine whether Sturge should report the lease as an operating or finance lease. Determine whether Borko should classify the lease as operating, direct financing, or sales type.

SOLUTION: The following table presents an analysis of the indicators to assess.

Group I Criteria	Met?	Explanation
Transfer of ownership?	No	
Purchase option likely to be exercised?	No	
Lease term major part of economic life?	Yes	The lease term is 90% (9 years / 10 years) of economic life.
Present value substantial part of fair value?	Uncertain	The present value of the lease payments of $77,579 is 81% of the $95,455 fair value of the machinery.
Asset is specialized?	No	

Group II Criteria	Met?	Explanation
Present value including third-party guarantees substantially all of fair value?	Yes	The present value of the lease payments plus the third-party guaranteed residual value of $95,610 is 100.16% of the $95,455 fair value of the machinery.
Lease payments and guaranteed residual value collection probable?	Yes	

To determine whether Sturge, the lessee, should classify the lease as an operating or a finance lease, we need only to assess the Group I criteria. Sturge should classify the lease as a finance lease because the lease term is 90% of the life of the asset. Whereas this is an area requiring judgment, 90% likely meets the "major part" criterion. For purposes of end-of-chapter exercises and problems, we will assume the cutoff for the third criterion is 75% and 90% for the fourth criterion.

To determine whether Borko Bank should classify the lease as operating, direct financing, or sales type, we assess the Group I first. The lease meets Group I criteria because the lease term is a major part of the economic life. Because the lease meets Group I criteria, Borko Bank will classify the lease as a sales-type lease. Borko does not need to assess the Group II criteria, but include them here to demonstrate the calculations involved.

IFRS Lease Classification

Lease classification is different under U.S. GAAP and IFRS.

In the case of the **lessee,** IFRS does not classify leases as operating and financing and does not distinguish two types of leases. Rather, lessee accounting treatment is the same for all leases under IFRS. All leases are recorded with leased assets and lease liabilities.

In the case of the **lessor**, IFRS includes only one group of criteria. If the criteria are met, the lease is classified as a finance lease; otherwise, the lease is classified as an operating lease. The goal of the IFRS classification standards for lessors is to determine whether the risks and rewards of ownership have been transferred to the lessee. IFRS does not distinguish between sales-type and direct financing leases.

The first five IFRS criteria are the same as U.S. GAAP Group I criteria for the lessor. However, IFRS does not specify that if one of the criteria is met, the lease is a finance lease. Rather, IFRS takes the approach that these scenarios are indicators that the lease is a finance lease for the lessor.

IFRS also identifies three additional indicators that individually or in combination could lead to classifying a lease as a finance lease. The terms of the lease imply a finance lease if:

1. The lessee bears the lessor's losses if the lessee cancels the lease.
2. The lessee absorbs the gains or losses from fluctuations in the fair value of the residual value of the asset.
3. The lessee may extend the lease for a secondary period at a rent substantially below the market rent in a renewal option.

An example of lease classification under IFRS is presented in Example 18.5.

EXAMPLE 18.5 IFRS Finance Lease: Lessor

PROBLEM: On January 1, 2019, Sturge Manufacturing, an IFRS reporter, leased a piece of machinery for use in its North American operations from Borko Bank. The 9-year, noncancellable lease requires lease payments of $14,000 due at the beginning of each year. The machinery built to Sturge's specifications would require significant modifications for another manufacturer to use it. The present value of the lease payments, including payments during the renewal period, is $77,519. The lease agreement does not transfer ownership of the machinery, and it does not contain a purchase option. Sturge can renew the lease for $500 a year for 10 additional years and expects these terms to be lower than the market rent on the renewal date. The machinery has a fair value of $95,455 and an estimated life of 20 years. Determine whether Borko Bank should report the lease as an operating or finance lease under IFRS.

SOLUTION: Borko Bank classifies this as a finance lease because the lease is for the major part of the machinery's economic life and at an amount representing a substantial portion of its fair value. Because the lease is noncancellable and the machinery is specialized, Sturge assumes the risks of ownership. The following table analyzes the situations and indicators of situations that Borko must assess. This analysis suggests that the lease transfers the risks and rewards of ownership. Therefore, Borko should classify the lease as a finance lease.

IFRS Criteria	Met?	Explanation
1. Transfer of ownership?	No	
2. Purchase option likely to be exercised?	No	
3. Lease term major part of economic life?	Yes	The lease term is 95% (19 years / 20 years) of economic life. Based on the IFRS criterion, it is likely that 95% would be considered a major part of the asset's economic life.
4. Present value substantial part of fair value?	Uncertain	The present value of $77,519 is 81% of the $95,455 fair value. Based on the IFRS criterion, it is likely that 81% would be considered substantially all of the fair value of the leased asset. Cutoffs for IFRS are lower than for U.S. GAAP.
5. Asset is specialized?	Yes	The problem states that major modifications would have to be made.

IFRS Criteria	Met?	Explanation
Additional IFRS Indicators		
1. Does the lessee bear the lessor's losses if the lessee cancels the lease?	Uncertain	This issue is not addressed.
2. Does the lessee absorb the gains or losses from fluctuations in the fair value of the residual value of the asset?	Uncertain	This issue is not addressed.
3. May the lessee extend the lease for a secondary period at a rent payment substantially lower than the market rental?	Yes	The decrease in rent from $14,000 to $500 implies that rent in the renewal would be substantially lower than the market rental.

CONCEPTUAL FRAMEWORK CONNECTION
Lease Classification

Prior to 2019, lessees did not include an asset and liability for operating leases on their balance sheets. Both FASB and IASB issued new standards that, with few exceptions, will require lessees to report an asset and liability on their balance sheets when they engage in a lease transaction. This accounting results in a more faithful representation of the rights and obligations arising from leases.

However, the FASB carried over the classification criteria from the previous standard in a way that does not always seem logical. The Group I criteria were originally designed to determine whether the lessee held the risks and rewards of the leased asset's ownership. For example, a purchase option that is likely to be exercised would indicate that the risks and rewards of ownership had been transferred to the lessee. The Group I criteria were effective in evaluating the transfer of risk and rewards. Because all leased assets and lease liabilities are now on the balance sheet, the current Group I criteria are no longer logical; that is, requiring the lessee to report all leased assets and lease liabilities on the balance sheet seems to answer the question of who holds the risks and rewards—the lessee.

In reality, the Group I criteria are now used to determine the subsequent accounting for operating and finance leases for the lessee. As we discuss later in the chapter, when the amount the expenses are reported and where on the income statement they are reported differs for an operating lease and a finance lease. Yet, the Group I criteria are not related to the leased asset's subsequent use and cannot be used to explain the differences in expense reporting. Whereas the U.S. GAAP standard initially results in a faithful representation of the leased asset and liability on the balance sheet, the subsequent treatment on the income statement is more difficult to justify from a conceptual standpoint. The IFRS model—for which there is no distinction in operating and finance leases for a lessee—is much more conceptually sound.

Likewise, it is challenging to understand the objective of the Group II criteria. Under the prior standards, U.S. GAAP distinguished a sales-type lease from a direct financing lease based on whether a profit existed. Now the distinction is based on whether there is a third-party guaranteed residual value. Presumably, FASB did not want lessors to recognize a profit at lease commencement from non-operating lease treatment due solely to a third-party residual value guarantee. But the Group II criteria seem like a highly complex way to achieve this reporting outcome.

Finally, there is a disconnect for lessee and lessor accounting under both U.S. GAAP and IFRS. Under both standards, the lessee always recognizes the leased asset and the lease liability (unless he meets one of the limited exceptions that we discuss later in the chapter). However, in the case of the operating lease, the lessor continues to recognize the asset on its balance sheet. If the risks and returns of ownership have truly passed to the lessee, causing the lessee to recognize the leased asset and lease liability on the balance sheet, then why wouldn't the lessor derecognize the asset? This is a question that the current standards do not answer.

4 Demonstrate the accounting for an operating lease for both the lessee and the lessor.

Accounting for Operating Leases: Lessee and Lessor

We now examine the details of lease accounting related to initial and subsequent measurement. Our discussion begins with operating leases of both lessee and lessor accounting.

Initial Measurement of an Operating Lease: Lessee

As noted earlier in this chapter, in the case of an operating lease, the lessee should report the leased asset and the related liability on its balance sheet. The lease transaction is similar to a purchase transaction in which the lessor provides financing. The lease liability reflects the fact that the lessee is obligated to make future lease payments whereas the leased asset, which we refer to as the **right-of-use asset**, indicates that the lessee then has the right to control the leased asset.

Measuring the Lease Liability. The lessee measures a lease liability on the lease commencement date as the present value of the remaining lease payments discounted at the implicit rate in the lease (or the incremental borrowing rate if the implicit rate is not readily determinable) plus the guaranteed residual value (if the lessee provides the guarantee).

The lease payments used to measure the lease are generally the same as those used in the Group I criteria to classify the lease. However, the lessee uses all payments (including payments made before the lease commencement date) to classify the lease whereas it uses only the remaining lease payments to measure the lease liability.

Measuring the Right-of-Use Asset. The right-of-use asset is initially measured to reflect the lessee's net cash outflows related to the lease. The lessee capitalizes all of the costs associated with the lease into the right-of-use asset account so that it includes all of the lease payments along with any initial direct costs incurred. In addition, if the lessee receives lease incentives (a cash inflow), then he reduces the right-of-use asset by this amount. Specifically, the right-of-use asset includes the following components:

1. The lease liability determined as the present value of the remaining lease payments as of the commencement date.
2. Lease payments the lessee makes to the lessor at or before the commencement date. These payments are prepayments made prior to the lease commencement date, often on the lease inception date. The lessee initially reports them as prepaid assets and then reclassifies them to right-of-use assets on the lease commencement date.
3. Any initial direct costs the lessee incurs. Lessees initially report initial direct costs as prepaid assets and then reclassify these costs to increase the right-of-use asset on the lease commencement date.
4. A reduction for any lease incentives the lessee receives. Lessees initially report lease incentives as liabilities and then reclassify these incentives to reduce the right-of-use asset on the lease commencement date.

The asset could have an initial measurement that differs from the liability because of the lease payments made before the lease commencement date, lease incentives, and initial direct costs. Exhibit 18.6 presents the initial measurement of the right-of-use asset.

EXHIBIT 18.6 Initial Measurement of the Right-of-Use Asset

	Right-of-Use Asset
	Lease liability defined as the present value of the remaining lease payments
+	Prepaid lease payments
+	Lessee's initial direct costs
−	Lease incentives

Example 18.6 illustrates the lessee's initial measurement of the lease liability and the right-of-use asset for an operating lease.

EXAMPLE 18.6

Initial Measurement of an Operating Lease: Lessee

PROBLEM: Mac Sullivan Company leases nonspecialized medical equipment with a fair value of $195,000 from RehabCo. The lease term is for 5 years and commences on January 1, 2019. The estimated economic life of the equipment is 10 years. Mac Sullivan prepaid the first rental payment of $20,000 on December 15, 2018 (the inception date) and received $28,800 from RehabCo on the inception date to terminate a lease from another lessor. Mac Sullivan must pay five additional rental fees of $20,000 each year beginning on January 1, 2019. The second payment is due on December 31, 2019. Thereafter, each payment is due on December 31. The implicit rate in the lease is 4%. Mac Sullivan incurred initial direct costs prior to the lease commencement of $3,500 that it originally recorded as prepaid initial direct costs. The lease agreement does not contain a transfer of ownership or a purchase option. Mac Sullivan has determined that none of the Group I criteria are met, so the company classifies the lease as an operating lease. How would the lessee measure and record the lease liability and the right-of-use asset?

SOLUTION: Mac Sullivan measures the lease liability as the present value of all remaining lease payments on the commencement date. The present value of the annuity due of the five lease payments of $20,000 at a discount rate of 4% is $92,598.

	N	I/Y	PV	PMT	FV	Excel Formula
Given	5	4.00%		−20,000	0	
Solve for PV			**92,598**			=PV(0.04,5,−20000,0,1)

Mac Sullivan measures the right-of-use asset as the sum of the initial lease liability measurement, prepayments net of lease incentives, and initial direct costs:

Initial measurement of the lease liability	$92,598
Add: Prepayments Mac Sullivan made to the lessor prior to the lease commencement date	20,000
Subtract: Lease incentives Mac Sullivan receives	(28,800)
Add: Mac Sullivan's initial direct costs	3,500
Initial measurement of the right-of-use asset	$87,298

The following entry records the payment Mac Sullivan made to the lessor RehabCo prior to the lease commencement date as an asset.

Account	**December 15, 2018**	
Prepaid Lease Payment	20,000	
Cash		20,000

The lessee receives $28,800 from the lessor as an incentive to sign the lease. Mac Sullivan records this lease incentive as a liability.

Account	**December 15, 2018**	
Cash	28,800	
Liability for Lease Incentive		28,800

The lessee also paid initial direct costs and records that payment as a prepaid asset.

Account	**Prior to January 1, 2019**	
Prepaid Initial Direct Costs	3,500	
Cash		3,500

At December 31, 2018, the liability for the lease incentive, the prepaid initial direct costs and the prepaid lease payment appear on Mac Sullivan's balance sheet.

Continued

On the lease commencement date, Mac Sullivan records the right-of-use asset and the lease liability. In addition, it reclassifies the lease incentive and the initial direct costs. It also removes the prepaid lease payment. Mac Sullivan makes the following entry on January 1:

Account	January 1, 2019	
Right-of-Use Asset	87,298	
Liability for Lease Incentive	28,800	
Prepaid Lease Payment		20,000
Prepaid Initial Direct Costs		3,500
Lease Liability		92,598

In addition to the initial measurement of the lease liability and right-of-use asset, Mac Sullivan also records the first annual lease payment as follows:

Account	January 1, 2019	
Lease Liability	20,000	
Cash		20,000

Subsequent Measurement of an Operating Lease: Lessee

After the lease commences, the lessee subsequently adjusts the balances of the lease liability and the right-of-use asset and recognizes the lease expense. The lease expense is composed of interest on the lease liability and amortization of the right-of-use asset. We adopt a simplified, practical approach to subsequent measurement.[9]

The practical approach for subsequent measurement for an operating lease involves a five-step methodology:

Step 1: Determine the total payments to be made by the lessee from the lease inception date to the termination date, including prepayments and initial direct costs incurred by the lessee, net of any incentives received.

Step 2: Determine the amount of lease expense to be recognized each year by dividing the total payments computed in Step 1 by the lease term.

Step 3: Compute the periodic interest expense on the lease liability by using the effective interest rate method.

Step 4: Compute the reduction in the lease liability each period as the payment made that period less the interest computed in Step 3.

Step 5: Determine the amortization of the right-of-use asset, which is measured as the difference in the straight-line lease expense and the interest expense from Step 3.[10]

[9]The authoritative literature provides an approach to subsequent measurement that involves remeasuring the asset and liability, with the lease expense recognized on a straight-line basis. While the step-by-step method is different than that implied in the Codification, the end result, in terms of journal entries and financial statement impact is the same. See Surfing the Standards Case 3 for a more in-depth analysis of the Codification on this issue.

[10]The terminology for the systematic reduction of the carrying value of leased assets is slightly different than that used for other fixed assets. Normally, we refer to the periodic reduction in the asset balance as depreciation. However, in the case of a leased asset, we use the word *amortization*.

This approach is illustrated in Example 18.7.

EXAMPLE 18.7 Subsequent Measurement of an Operating Lease: Lessee

PROBLEM: Consider Mac Sullivan Company from the Example 18.6. Provide all necessary journal entries for Mac Sullivan over the lease term.

SOLUTION: As noted in Example 18.6, this is an operating lease. Also recall that we initially measured the lease liability at $92,598 and the right-of-use asset at $87,298. Given this information from the prior example, we now illustrate subsequent measurement using the five steps.

Step 1. Total Payments

In the first step, we sum all of the payments that Mac Sullivan will make and reduce this by any incentives it receives.

Annual payments ($20,000 × 5 years)	$100,000
Lease payment on December 15, 2018	20,000
Lease incentive	(28,800)
Initial direct costs	3,500
Total payments	$ 94,700

Step 2. Straight-Line Expense

In the second step, we allocate the total payments computed in Step 1 on a straight-line basis across the life of the lease to arrive at the annual lease expense.

Total Payments	$94,700
Divided by years	5
Annual lease expense	$18,940

We include this lease expense on the income statement each year on one line in operating income.

Steps 3 and 4. Periodic Interest and Reduction in the Liability

We next compute the periodic interest using the effective interest method. Each period the interest is computed as the beginning lease liability balance multiplied by the effective interest rate (the implicit rate if the lessee knows it). We can then compute the periodic reduction in the lease liability by subtracting the interest portion from the total payment.

Date	Payment (a)	Interest (b) = Prior-Period Balance × 4% Step 3	Reduction in Lease Liability (c) = (a) − (b) Step 4	Balance (d) = Prior-period balance – (c)
Lease Commencement – January 1, 2019				$92,598
January 1, 2019	$20,000	0	20,000	72,598
December 31, 2019	20,000	2,904	17,096	55,502
December 31, 2020	20,000	2,220	17,780	37,722
December 31, 2021	20,000	1,509	18,491	19,231
December 31, 2022	20,000	769	19,231	0
		$7,402	$92,598	

Continued

Step 5: Amortization of the Right-of-Use Asset

Finally, we compute the portion of the annual lease expense that is attributable to the asset amortization. This amount is computed as the annual lease expense (computed in Step 2) less the interest portion that we computed in Step 3.

Date	Lease Expense (a)	Interest Column (b) of Preceding Table	Amortization of Right of Use Asset (c) = (a) − (b) Step 5
December 31, 2019	$18,940	2,904	$16,036
December 31, 2020	18,940	2,220	16,720
December 31, 2021	18,940	1,509	17,431
December 31, 2022	18,940	769	18,171
December 31, 2023	18,940	0	18,940
	$94,700	$7,402	$87,298

The journal entries draw on the information provided in the previous tables.

Account	December 31, 2019	
Lease Expense	18,940	
Lease Liability	17,096	
Accumulated Amortization—Right-of-Use Asset		16,036
Cash		20,000

Account	December 31, 2020	
Lease Expense	18,940	
Lease Liability	17,780	
Accumulated Amortization—Right-of-Use Asset		16,720
Cash		20,000

Account	December 31, 2021	
Lease Expense	18,940	
Lease Liability	18,491	
Accumulated Amortization—Right-of-Use Asset		17,431
Cash		20,000

Account	December 31, 2022	
Lease Expense	18,940	
Lease Liability	19,231	
Accumulated Amortization—Right-of-Use Asset		18,171
Cash		20,000

Account	December 31, 2023	
Lease Expense	18,940	
Accumulated Amortization—Right-of-Use Asset		18,940

Account	December 31, 2023	
Accumulated Amortization—Right-of-Use Asset	87,298	
Right-of-Use Asset		87,298

The t-accounts for the right-of-use asset, accumulated amortization, and lease liability reflect this activity.

Right-of-Use Asset

	Debit	Credit	
January 1, 2019	87,298	87,298	December 31, 2023

Accumulated Amortization—Right-of-Use Asset

	Debit	Credit	
		16,036	December 31, 2019
		16,720	December 31, 2020
		17,431	December 31, 2021
		18,171	December 31, 2022
		18,940	December 31, 2023
December 31, 2023	87,298	87,298	December 31, 2023

Lease Liability

	Debit	Credit	
		92,598	January 1, 2019
January 1, 2019	20,000		
December 31, 2019	17,096		
December 31, 2020	17,780		
December 31, 2021	18,491		
December 31, 2022	19,231		
		0	

Operating Lease with Residual Values: Lessee Guaranteed Residual Value

Accounting for the lease is slightly more complex when the lessee makes a residual value guarantee. Residual value guaranteed by the lessee is included in the lease payments. If the residual value is guaranteed by a third party, or is unguaranteed, it does not impact the lessee accounting treatment.

Example 18.8 illustrates an operating lease when the lessee provides a residual value guarantee.

EXAMPLE 18.8

Initial Measurement of an Operating Lease with a Residual Value: Lessee

PROBLEM: Consider Mac Sullivan Company from Example 18.6. Assume that Mac Sullivan enters into the same lease agreement except that Mac Sullivan guarantees a residual value of $25,000.[11] The company has determined that none of the Group I criteria have been met, so Mac Sullivan classifies the lease as an operating lease. Provide the journal entries for 2018 and January 1, 2019.

SOLUTION: Mac Sullivan determines the initial measurement of the lease liability as the present value of an annuity due of the lease payments that have not been made as of the lease commencement date. The present value of an annuity due of the five lease payments of $20,000 and the guaranteed residual value of $25,000 at a discount rate of 4% is $113,146.

	N	I/Y	PV	PMT	FV	Excel Formula
Given	5	4.00%		−20,000	−25,000	
Solve for PV			**113,146**			=PV(0.04,5,−20000,−25000,1)

Continued

[11]Note that the lessor would likely require lower annual lease payments if the lessee guarantees a residual value because the lessor requires a certain rate of return.

Mac Sullivan measures the right-of-use asset as the sum of the initial lease liability measurement, prepayments net of lease incentives, and initial direct costs.

Initial measurement of the lease liability	$113,146
Add: Prepayments Mac Sullivan made to the lessor prior to the lease commencement date	20,000
Subtract: Lease incentives Mac Sullivan receives	(28,800)
Add: Mac Sullivan's initial direct costs	3,500
Initial measurement of the right-of-use asset	$107,846

The following journal entry records the payment Mac Sullivan made to the lessor prior to the lease commencement date as an asset.

Account	**December 15, 2018**	
Prepaid Lease Payment	20,000	
Cash		20,000

The lessee receives $28,800 from the lessor as an incentive to sign the lease. Mac Sullivan records this incentive as a liability.

Account	**December 15, 2018**	
Cash	28,800	
Liability for Lease Incentive		28,800

The lessee also paid initial direct costs and records that payment as a prepaid asset.

Account	**Prior to January 1, 2019**	
Prepaid Initial Direct Costs	3,500	
Cash		3,500

At December 31, 2018, the liability for the lease incentive, the prepaid initial direct costs, and the prepaid lease payment appear on Mac Sullivan's balance sheet.

On the lease commencement date, Mac Sullivan records the right-of-use asset and the lease liability. In addition, it reclassifies the lease incentive and the initial direct costs. It also removes the prepaid lease payment. Mac Sullivan makes the following entry on January 1:

Account	**January 1, 2019**	
Right-of-Use Asset	107,846	
Liability for Lease Incentive	28,800	
Prepaid Lease Payment		20,000
Prepaid Initial Direct Costs		3,500
Lease Liability		113,146

Short-Term Policy Election: Lessee

When a lease term is 12 months or less, the lessee can make a policy election not to record the lease liability and the right-of-use asset. The FASB included this exemption based on the cost constraint. That is, the costs of measuring and reporting the lease liability and the right-of-use asset outweigh the benefits of reporting these amounts on the lessee's balance sheet for a lease with a term of 1 year or less.

When a lessee makes the short-term lease policy election, it records rent expense based on the rent payments. Example 18.9 illustrates accounting for a short-term lease when the lessee makes a policy election not to record the lease liability and the right-of-use asset.

EXAMPLE 18.9

Lessee: Short-Term Lease Policy Election

PROBLEM: Inwood Floor Care rents wood-scraping machinery from Elliot Manufacturing on January 1, 2019. Under the terms of the agreement, Inwood will pay rentals of $2,000 per month for an 8-month period at the first day of every month, beginning on January 1, 2019. Inwood elects to apply the exemption for short-term leases. That is, Inwood makes a policy election not to record the lease liability and the right-of-use asset. What journal entry will Inwood make each month to record the rental payments?

SOLUTION: The monthly journal entry follows:

Account	First Day of Each Month	
Prepaid Rent	2,000	
Cash		2,000

At the end of each month, Inwood will record rent expense and reduce the prepaid asset account.

Account	Last Day of Each Month	
Rent Expense	2,000	
Prepaid Rent		2,000

Rent expense could be debited directly.

Operating Lease: Lessor Accounting

We discuss lessor accounting for operating leases in this section. In an operating lease, the lessor continues to report the leased asset on the lessor's balance sheet. It may also record depreciation expense if it classifies the asset as property, plant, and equipment. The lessor does not record depreciation if it holds the asset as part of inventory.

After the commencement date, the lessor will record rental revenue composed of the following:

a. Total lease payments, recognized on a straight-line basis
b. Variable payments not included in the lease payments[12]

The lessor expenses initial direct costs over the lease term, typically on a straight-line basis. Any residual value, whether guaranteed or unguaranteed, does not affect the lessor's accounting treatment for operating leases. Example 18.10 illustrates the lessor's accounting for an operating lease.

EXAMPLE 18.10

Operating Lease: Lessor

PROBLEM: On January 1, 2019, Joseph Botti AutoWorld, Inc. leases a SUV that it carries in its inventory to Cava Company. The lease term is 4 years with no renewal options, and the economic life of the SUV is 7 years. The fair value of the automobile is $45,000, and Joseph Botti's cost or carrying value is also $45,000. There are no lease incentives. The lease requires monthly payments of $600 at the end of each month. Botti incurs initial direct costs of $2,400 on January 1, 2019. The implicit rate in the lease is 5%. There is no transfer of ownership at the end of the lease term. Lease payment collection is probable. How should the lessor classify the lease? Provide the journal entries for January 2019 and February 2019 for the lessor.

Continued

[12]If the collectability of lease payments and residual value guarantees is not probable, then revenue is limited to the lesser of (1) the amounts in (a) and (b) and (2) the lease payments and variable payments already received.

SOLUTION: To determine whether Botti, the lessor, should classify the lease as operating, direct financing, or sales type, we assess both Group I and Group II criteria.

We have information to assess all of the criteria except for the fourth criterion of Group I. The present value of an ordinary annuity of the 48 remaining lease payments of $600 at a discount rate of 0.4167% per period (5%/12) is $26,054.

	N	I/Y	PV	PMT	FV	Excel Formula
Given	48	0.4167%		600	0	
Solve for PV			**(26,054)**			=PV(0.004167,48,600,0)

The following table presents an analysis of the indicators.

Group I Criteria	Met?	Explanation
Transfer of ownership?	No	
Purchase option likely to be exercised?	No	
Lease term major part of economic life?	No	The lease term is 57% (4 years / 7 years) of economic life.
Present value substantial part of fair value?	No	The present value of $26,054 is 58% of the $45,000 fair value.
Asset is specialized?	No	

Group II Criteria	Met?	Explanation
Present value including third-party guarantees substantially all of fair value?	No	The present value of $26,054 is 58% of the $45,000 fair value.
Lease payment collection probable?	Yes	

The lease does not meet Group I or both of the Group II criteria and thus is an operating lease.

On January 1, 2019, Botti paid for initial direct costs, which it capitalizes as an asset.

Account	January 1, 2019	
Prepaid Initial Direct Costs	2,400	
Cash		2,400

Botti does not remove the asset from its books. However, because the SUV is included in inventory, it is not depreciated. Each period Botti records revenue for the lease payments and expense for the initial direct costs ($2,400/48 months = $50 per month).

Account	January 31, 2019	
Cash	600	
Initial Direct Cost Expense	50	
Rent Revenue		600
Prepaid Initial Direct Costs		50

Account	February 28, 2019	
Cash	600	
Initial Direct Cost Expense	50	
Rent Revenue		600
Prepaid Initial Direct Costs		50

(5) Demonstrate lessee accounting for a finance lease.

Accounting for Finance Leases: Lessee

Next, we discuss the lessee's initial and subsequent measurement of a finance lease. We then explain the accounting treatment for a finance lease when there is a residual value.

Initial and Subsequent Measurement of Finance Leases: Lessee

The initial measurement for a finance lease is the same as for an operating lease. That is, the lessee records a right-of-use asset and a liability on the lease commencement date. However, the subsequent measurement differs.

Unlike subsequent measurement in an operating lease, under a finance lease, the lessee reduces the right-of-use asset by recording amortization expense on a straight-line basis. Companies generally amortize leased assets over the term of the lease because the asset will be returned at the end of the lease. However, if the lease contract includes an ownership transfer or a purchase option that is likely to be exercised, the company amortizes the asset over the expected life of the asset because the lessee will ultimately own the asset.

The lessee also remeasures the lease liability, reducing it by a portion of each lease payment. The lessee computes interest expense on the lease obligation using the effective interest rate method. The lessee allocates lease payments first to cover the interest and then to reduce the lease obligation. This remeasurement of the lease liability is the same as it is under an operating lease. However, recall that in the case of an operating lease, the interest and asset amortization are combined into a single, straight-line lease expense.

For a finance lease, the lessee records a lease expense each period of the lease that includes the following:

1. Use of the appropriate discount rate to compute the present value of the liability at the lease commencement date. Interest expense on the lease liability is computed under the effective interest rate method of amortization.
2. Variable lease payments not included in the lease liability in the period in which the obligation for the variable payments is incurred.
3. Changes in variable lease payments that depend on an index or rate.[13]

Exhibit 18.7 summarizes the subsequent measurement of a finance lease.

EXHIBIT 18.7 Subsequent Measurement of a Finance Lease

Lease Liability	Right-of-Use Asset	Lease Expense*
Present value of the remaining lease payments** Compute interest using the effective interest rate method. Allocate lease payment first to interest, and any remaining amount then reduces the lease liability.	Record amortization expense on a straight-line basis	Interest expense on the lease liability using the effective interest rate method Variable lease payments not included in the measurement of the lease liability Changes in the variable lease payments that depend on an index or rate

* The lease expense also includes any impairment of the right-of-use asset.

** Use the implicit rate at the commencement date if known. Otherwise, use the incremental borrowing rate at the commencement date.

[13]The lease expense also includes any impairment of the right-of-use asset.

Example 18.11 illustrates the lessee's accounting for a finance lease that does not contain a residual value guarantee.

EXAMPLE 18.11 Finance Lease: Lessee

PROBLEM: On January 1, 2019, Berg Manufacturing leased a nonspecialized piece of machinery for use in its North American operations from Borko Bank. The lease agreement was signed on January 1 and the equipment was provided to Berg on the same day. The 9-year, noncancellable lease requires annual lease payments of $12,000, beginning January 1, 2019, and at each December 31 thereafter through 2026. The lease agreement does not transfer ownership of the machinery, nor does it contain a purchase option. The machinery has a fair value of $75,000 and an estimated life of 10 years. Borko Bank's implicit rate is not known to Berg. Berg's incremental borrowing rate is 11%. Berg incurs initial direct costs of $3,000 on January 1, 2019. Analyze the lease classification criteria to determine whether the lease is an operating or finance lease for Berg. Provide the journal entries for Berg for 2019.

SOLUTION: We use the Group I criteria to determine whether this lease should be classified as a finance lease for the lessee. We have information to assess all of the Group I criteria except for the fourth criterion on the present value as a substantial part of the fair value. The present value of an annuity due of the nine remaining lease payments of $12,000 at a discount rate of 11% is $73,753.

	N	I/Y	PV	PMT	FV	Excel Formula
Given	9	11.00%		−12,000	0	
Solve for PV			**73,753**			=PV(.011,9,−12000,0,1)

This lease is a finance lease because it meets both Criteria 3 and 4. The lease term is 90% of the life of the asset, which is a major part. Also, the present value of the lease payments is 98.3% of the asset's fair value, a substantial part.

Group I Criteria	Met?	Explanation
Transfer of ownership?	No	
Purchase option likely to be exercised?	No	
Lease term major part of economic life?	Yes	Lease term is 90% (9 years / 10 years of economic life).
Present value substantial part of fair value?	Yes	The present value of $73,753 is 98.3% of the $75,000 fair value.
Asset is specialized?	No	

The initial direct costs are paid on January 1, 2019.

Account	*January 1, 2019*	
Prepaid Initial Direct Costs	3,000	
Cash		3,000

Because this is a finance lease, Berg records the liability at the lease commencement as the present value of the lease payments not yet paid and removes the prepaid initial direct costs. Berg records the right-of-use asset at the amount of the lease liability plus the initial direct costs.

Account	*January 1, 2019*	
Right-of-Use Asset	76,753	
Prepaid Initial Direct Costs		3,000
Lease Liability		73,753

To account for the lease as a finance lease, Berg computes interest on the lease using the effective interest rate method. Interest each period is the beginning lease balance times the interest rate (Column b) as seen in the following table. Berg allocates each lease payment of $12,000 first to interest and any remaining amount then reduces the lease liability (Column c). The amount that reduces the lease liability decreases the lease liability balance (Column d). The amortization table follows.

Date	Payment (a)	Interest (b) = Prior-Period Balance × 11%	Reduction in Lease Liability (c) = (a) − (b)	Balance (d) = Prior-Period Balance − (c)
Lease Commencement – January 1, 2019				$73,753
January 1, 2019	$12,000	$ 0	$12,000	61,753
December 31, 2019	12,000	6,793	5,207	56,546
December 31, 2020	12,000	6,220	5,780	50,766
December 31, 2021	12,000	5,584	6,416	44,350
December 31, 2022	12,000	4,879	7,121	37,229
December 31, 2023	12,000	4,095	7,905	29,324
December 31, 2024	12,000	3,226	8,774	20,550
December 31, 2025	12,000	2,261	9,739	10,811
December 31, 2026	12,000	1,189	10,811	0

Notice that Berg allocates the first payment entirely to principal because interest accrues only with the passage of time.

The journal entry for the first lease payment on January 1, 2019, is as follows:

Account	***January 1, 2019***	
Lease Liability	12,000	
Cash		12,000

At the end of the year, Berg records the following entry. As shown in the amortization table, Berg allocates the second payment on December 31, 2019, to interest expense of $6,793 and reduction of the lease liability of $5,207.

Account	***December 31, 2019***	
Lease Liability	5,207	
Interest Expense	6,793	
Cash		12,000

Berg amortizes the leased asset on a straight-line basis over the lease term. Amortization expense is computed as $8,528: the right-of-use asset of $76,753 divided by the 9-year lease term.

Account	***December 31, 2019***	
Amortization Expense—Right-of-Use Asset	8,528	
Accumulated Amortization—Right-of-Use Asset		8,528

Exhibit 18.8 summarizes the accounting treatment for lessees.

EXHIBIT 18.8 Summary of Lessee Accounting Treatment

	Operating Lease	Finance Lease
Classification	Group I criteria not met	Group I criteria met
Initial measurement—Lease liability	Present value of the remaining lease payments*	
Initial measurement—Right-of-Use asset	Lease liability Plus Prepayments Initial direct costs incurred by the lessee Less Lease incentives received by lessee	
Subsequent measurement—Lease liability	Present value of the remaining lease payments*	Present value of the remaining lease payments* Compute interest using the effective interest rate method. Allocate lease payment first to interest and any remaining amount then reduces the lease liability.
Subsequent measurement—Right-of-Use asset	Lease liability Plus Prepaid lease payments Unamortized initial direct costs Less Accrued lease payments Remaining balance—Incentives Impairments	Record amortization expense on a straight-line basis
Measurement of the lease expense**	1. A single lease cost (which includes the amortization of the right-of-use asset) calculated so that the remaining cost of the lease is allocated over the remaining lease term on a straight-line basis.*** 2. Variable lease payments not included in the measurement of the lease liability. 3. Changes in variable lease payments that depend on an index or rate	1. Interest expense on the lease liability using the effective interest rate method 2. Variable lease payments not included in the measurement of the lease liability. 3. Changes in the variable lease payments that depend on an index or rate

* Use the implicit rate at the commencement date if known. Otherwise, use the incremental borrowing rate at the commencement date.

** The lease expense for both operating and finance leases also includes any impairment of the right-of-use asset.

*** The remaining cost of the lease is calculated as total lease payments (including those previously paid and those not yet paid) plus total lessee initial direct costs less any lease cost recognized in prior periods.

Finance Lease with Residual Values: Lessee

If a lease provides a residual value guarantee, the lessee includes the present value of the residual value guarantee in the initial measurement of the lease liability. Similar to an operating lease, if the residual value is guaranteed by a third party or is unguaranteed, then the residual value does not impact the lessee's accounting treatment.

Example 18.12 illustrates a finance lease with a residual value guarantee.

EXAMPLE 18.12

Finance Lease with Residual Value: Lessee

PROBLEM: Consider Berg Manufacturing from Example 18.11. Assume that the lease agreement is the same except that Berg has guaranteed a residual value of $15,000.[14] Berg has determined that the lease meets both Group I Criteria 3 and 4, so Berg classifies the lease as a finance lease. Provide the journal entries for Berg for 2019. Provide the journal entry for 2027, assuming that Berg is required to pay Borko Bank the full $15,000 residual value. Also provide the journal entry for 2027 assuming that Berg is not required to pay Borko Bank any of the residual value.

SOLUTION: The initial direct costs of $3,000 are paid on January 1, 2019.

Account	January 1, 2019	
Prepaid Initial Direct Costs	3,000	
Cash		3,000

Because this is a finance lease, Berg records the liability at the lease commencement as the present value of the lease payments not yet paid. The present value of an annuity due of the nine remaining lease payments of $12,000 and the present value of the guaranteed residual value of $15,000 at a discount rate of 11% is $79,617 computed as follows:

	N	I/Y	PV	PMT	FV	Excel Formula
Given	9	11.00%		−12,000	−15,000	
Solve For PV			**79,617**			=PV(0.11,9,−12000,−15000,1)

Berg also removes the prepaid initial direct costs. It records the asset at the amount of the lease liability plus the initial direct costs.

Account	January 1, 2019	
Right-of-Use Asset	82,617	
Prepaid Initial Direct Costs		3,000
Lease Liability		79,617

To account for the lease as a finance lease, Berg allocates each lease payment to reduce the lease debt and cover the interest expense for the period. Berg allocates the $12,000 payment to interest and principal using the effective interest rate method of amortization.

Continued

[14]Note that the lessor would likely require lower annual lease payments if the lessee guarantees a residual value because the lessor requires a certain rate of return.

Date	Payment (a)	Interest (b) = Prior-Period Balance × 11%	Reduction in Lease Liability (c) = (a) − (b)	Balance (d) = Prior-Period Balance – (c)
Lease Commencement – January 1, 2019				$79,617
January 1, 2019	$12,000	$ 0	$12,000	67,617
December 31, 2019	12,000	7,438	4,562	63,055
December 31, 2020	12,000	6,936	5,064	57,991
December 31, 2021	12,000	6,379	5,621	52,370
December 31, 2022	12,000	5,761	6,239	46,131
December 31, 2023	12,000	5,074	6,926	39,205
December 31, 2024	12,000	4,313	7,687	31,518
December 31, 2025	12,000	3,467	8,533	22,985
December 31, 2026	12,000	2,528	9,472	13,513
December 31, 2027	15,000*	1,487**	13,513	0

* The lease liability is fully paid upon realization of the residual value.
** Adjusted due to rounding errors.

Notice that Berg allocates the first payment entirely to principal because interest accrues only with the passage of time.

Account	*January 1, 2019*	
Lease Liability	12,000	
Cash		12,000

Berg amortizes the asset on a straight-line basis over the lease term. Amortization expense is computed as $7,513: the right-of-use asset of $82,617 minus the guaranteed residual value of $15,000 divided by the 9-year lease term.

Account	*December 31, 2019*	
Amortization Expense—Right-of-Use Asset	7,513	
Accumulated Amortization—Right-of-Use Asset		7,513

As shown in the amortization table, Berg allocates the second payment on December 31, 2019, to interest of $7,438 and principal of $4,562.

Account	*December 31, 2019*	
Lease Liability	4,562	
Interest Expense	7,438	
Cash		12,000

At December 31, 2027, the lease termination date, the balance of the lease liability is $13,513. Assuming that Berg must pay the $15,000 to cover the guaranteed residual value, Berg will make the following entry:

Account	*December 31, 2027*	
Lease Liability	13,513	
Interest Expense	1,487	
Accumulated Amortization—Right-of-Use Asset	67,617	
Loss on Lease	15,000	
Right-of-Use Asset		82,617
Cash		15,000

If Berg does not have to pay the $15,000, it will make the following entry because it must remove the liability from its balance sheet:

Account	December 31, 2027	
Lease Liability	13,513	
Accumulated Amortization—Right-of-Use Asset	67,617	
Interest Expense	1,487	
Right-of-Use Asset		82,617

IFRS Accounting for Operating and Finance Leases: Lessee

The primary difference in IFRS and U.S. GAAP related to lessee accounting is that IFRS does not distinguish operating from finance leases in the same way that U.S. GAAP does. Under IFRS, lessees use the same accounting treatment for both types of leases. Specifically, IFRS uses the U.S. GAAP accounting for finance leases for both operating and finance leases. Thus, under IFRS, lessees report interest expense and amortization expense on all leases.

In addition to the short-term policy election to account for a lease as a rental agreement, IFRS makes an exception for leased assets that have low values. IFRS reporters may account for leased assets with original costs of less than $5,000 as rental agreements. For example, assume that a company leases a $4,800 computer for 2.5 years. Under U.S. GAAP, the company records a right-of-use asset and a lease liability because the lease term is greater than 1 year. Under IFRS, the company does not need to record the leased asset and lease liability because the original cost of the leased asset is less than $5,000, and it is a simple rental agreement.

6 Illustrate lessor accounting for sales-type leases.

Accounting for Sales-Type Leases: Lessor

For the lessor, a sales-type lease meets at least one of the Group I criteria. Meeting any one of the five Group I criteria implies that the lessor no longer possesses the right to control the leased asset. That is, the lessor has sold the right to control the asset to the lessee. Thus, the lessor removes the leased asset from its books and instead reports a financial asset that represents its right to receive payments from the lessee. In addition, the lessor reports both revenue and cost of goods sold related to the leased asset.

Initial Measurement of a Sales-Type Lease

For a sales-type lease, a lessor recognizes revenue on the sale and records the asset *net investment in lease – sales-type*. It also removes the leased asset from its accounts and records the cost of goods sold.

Revenue for a sales-type lease is the lower of (1) the fair value of the leased asset and (2) the sum of the *lease receivable* plus any lease payments received before the lease commencement date. Cost of goods sold for a sales-type lease is equal to the carrying value of the leased asset less the present value of any unguaranteed residual asset plus any deferred initial direct costs paid by the lessor.

The **net investment in the lease for a sales-type lease** (NIL-ST) reflects the assets related to the lease transaction and is composed of:

1. The lease receivable
2. The present value of any unguaranteed residual asset

The **lease receivable** is the present value of the payments the lessor will receive plus the present value of any residual value guarantees when the guarantee can be provided by either the lessee or a third party. The lessor earns interest revenue on the lease receivable.

The lessor includes the present value of any unguaranteed residual value in the NIL-ST to reflect the value of the leased asset at the end of the lease. The guaranteed residual value is included in the lease receivable, whereas the unguaranteed residual asset is not part of the receivable.

The lessor expenses initial direct costs if the fair value of the leased asset is not equal to the carrying value. If the fair value equals the carrying value, the initial direct costs are deferred and included in the NIL-ST. However, the lessor does not need to explicitly add the initial direct costs to the NIL-ST. These costs are captured in the computation of the implicit rate. Recall that the implicit rate is the rate at which the present value of the lease payments plus the present value of the amount that a lessor expects to obtain from the leased asset at the end of the lease term equals the fair value of the leased asset plus deferred initial direct costs of the lessor.

Exhibit 18.9 depicts this relationship.

EXHIBIT 18.9 Implicit Rate

Present value of lease payments + Present value of guaranteed and unguaranteed residual values = Fair value of leased asset + Deferred initial direct costs of lessor

If we have deferred initial direct costs, the implicit rate will be set such that the present value of the payments and any residual values will include the deferred initial direct costs. Thus, the NIL-ST will include the deferred initial direct costs through the implicit rate.

Example 18.13 demonstrates how deferred initial direct costs are included in the NIL-ST.

EXAMPLE 18.13 Inclusion of Deferred Initial Direct Costs in the NIL-ST

PROBLEM: Hobnob Company leased a piece of machinery to Cutter, Inc. on January 1, 2019. The lease is correctly classified as a sales-type lease. Hobnob will receive three annual lease payments of $19,000 with the first one received on January 1, 2019. There is no guaranteed or unguaranteed residual value. The fair value of the machine is $50,000, and Hobnob incurs initial direct costs of $5,000. Compute the implicit rate and the NIL-ST assuming that the initial direct costs are expensed. Compute the implicit rate and the NIL-ST assuming that the initial direct costs are deferred.

SOLUTION: First, we compute the implicit rate, assuming that the initial direct costs are expensed. Setting the present value of the payments equal to the fair value of the machine, the implicit rate is 14.72%.

	N	I/Y	PV	PMT	FV	Excel Formula
Given	3		−50,000	19,000	0	
Solve for RATE		**14.72%**				=RATE(3,19000,−50000,0,1)

The NIL-ST is measured as the lease receivable, which is the present value of the payments because there are no residual values. Thus, the NIL-ST equals $50,000.

Now, if we assume that the initial direct costs are deferred, we compute an implicit rate by setting the present value of the lease payments equal to the fair value of the machine plus the deferred initial direct costs (i.e., $55,000 = $50,000 + 5,000).

	N	I/Y	PV	PMT	FV	Excel Formula
Given	3		−55,000	19,000	0	
Solve for RATE		**3.68%**				= RATE(3,19000,−55000,0,1)

The implicit rate is 3.68% and the NIL-ST is (by construction) $55,000, which is the present value of the lease payments and is equal to the lease receivable in this case. Note that we do not separately add in the initial direct costs; they are included in the lease receivable because they are automatically included in the present value of the lease payments through the computation of the implicit rate.

In addition to recording the NIL-ST, the lessor records revenue and cost of goods sold. Revenue for a sales-type lease is the lower of (1) the fair value of the leased asset and (2) the sum of the *lease receivable* plus any lease payments received before the lease commencement date. Cost of goods sold for a sales-type lease is the carrying value of the leased asset less the present value of any unguaranteed residual asset plus any deferred initial direct costs of the lessor.[15]

Exhibit 18.10 illustrates the key terms associated with accounting for a sales-type lease.

EXHIBIT 18.10 Key Sales-Type Terminology for Lessors

Net Investment in: Lease—Sales Type	Lease Receivable	Revenue	Cost of Goods Sold
Lease receivable	Present value of payments to be received	Lower of: Fair value of leased asset OR	Carrying value of the leased asset
Plus: Present value of any unguaranteed residual asset	Plus: Present value of residual value guarantees	Lease receivable plus lease payments received before the lease commencement	Less: present value of unguaranteed residual asset Plus: Deferred initial direct cost of the lessor

Example 18.14 shows the lessor's accounting for the initial measurement of a sales-type lease.

EXAMPLE 18.14 Initial Measurement of a Sales-Type Lease: Lessor

PROBLEM: On January 1, 2019, Carney Brothers Equipment Manufacturers agreed to lease a piece of heavy equipment to Greenbaum Shipping Associates. The equipment is not specialized and was delivered on January 1, 2019. Carney Brothers paid $800,000 to produce the machine and carries it at this amount in inventory. Carney Brothers incurred initial direct costs of $5,000. The lease terms follow:

- Annual rental payments of $188,692 are due on January 1, 2019, and December 31 of every year from 2019 through 2023.
- Lease term is 6 years.
- There is no transfer of the asset at the end of the lease term and no purchase option.
- The economic life of the asset is 6 years.
- Carney Brothers' implicit rate is 9%.
- Collectability of rental payments is probable.
- The fair value (current selling price) of the machine is $922,638.
- There is no residual value guarantee, nor does Carney anticipate a residual value for the asset.

Continued

[15]If collectability is not probable at the lease commencement date, the underlying asset is not derecognized. The net investment in the lease and profit are not recognized. Lease payments received are recorded as a deposit liability.

How does Carney Brothers, the lessor, classify this lease? What journal entries does it make on January 1, 2019?

SOLUTION: This lease is a sales type because it meets both Criteria 3 and 4 of the Group I conditions. The lease term is 100% of the life of the asset, which is a major part of its economic life. Also, the present value of the lease payments is 100% of the asset's fair value. The present value of an annuity due of the six remaining lease payments of $188,692 at a discount rate of 9% is $922,638 computed as follows:

	N	I/Y	PV	PMT	FV	Excel Formula
Given	6	9.00%		188,692	0	
Solve for PV			**(922,638)**			=PV(0.09,6,188692,0,1)

The following table presents an analysis of the indicators.

Group I Criteria	Met?	Explanation
Transfer of ownership?	No	
Purchase option likely to be exercised?	No	
Lease term major part of economic life?	Yes	The lease term is 100% (6 years / 6 years) of its economic life.
Present value substantial part of fair value?	Yes	The present value of $922,638 is 100% of the $922,638 fair value.
Asset is specialized?	No	

Because the Group I criteria are met, we do not need to assess the Group II criteria.

At the commencement of the lease, Carney records the sales revenue and NIL-ST. It also removes the machine from its accounts and records the cost of goods sold. The lease receivable is equal to the net investment in the lease because there is no unguaranteed residual value. The NIL-ST is the present value of the lease payments ($922,638). The sales revenue is $922,638, which is the fair value of the leased asset and the lease receivable. Cost of goods sold includes only the carrying value of the machinery because there is no unguaranteed residual value or deferred initial direct costs. The difference in the $922,638 sales revenue and the $800,000 cost of goods sold is a gross profit (selling profit) of $122,638.

Account	*January 1, 2019*	
Net Investment in Lease – Sales-Type	922,638	
Cost of Goods Sold	800,000	
Sales Revenue		922,638
Inventory of Machinery		800,000

Carney expenses the initial direct costs because the fair value is not equal to the carrying value of the leased asset.

Account	*January 1, 2019*	
Initial Direct Costs Expense	5,000	
Cash		5,000

Carney allocates the first payment to principal by reducing the net investment in the lease because interest accrues only with the passage of time.

Account	*January 1, 2019*	
Cash	188,692	
Net Investment in Lease – Sales Type		188,692

Subsequent Measurement of a Sales-Type Lease

After the lease commencement date, the lessor remeasures the NIL-ST each period and computes interest revenue using the effective interest rate method. The lessor allocates lease payments first to cover the interest and then to reduce the NIL-ST. The interest revenue, which is reported on the income statement, is the amount that produces a constant periodic discount rate on the remaining balance of the NIL-ST.

The lessor records the following items in net income if they are part of the lease agreement:

1. Interest revenue on the NIL-ST
2. Any variable payments received that were not included in the NIL-ST
3. Any changes in variable lease payments that depend on an index or rate in the period of the change[16]

Example 18.15 shows the lessor's accounting for the subsequent measurement of a sales-type lease.

EXAMPLE 18.15 Subsequent Measurement of a Sales-Type Capital Lease: Lessor

PROBLEM: Consider Carney Brothers Equipment Manufacturers from Example 18.14. What journal entries are required for 2019 and 2020 after January 1, 2019?

SOLUTION: We first prepare the amortization table as follows:

Date	Payment (a)	Interest (b) = Prior-Period Balance × 9%	Reduction in Lease Liability (c) = (a) − (b)	NIL-ST Balance (d) = Prior Period Balance − (c)
Lease Commencement – January 1, 2019				$922,638
January 1, 2019	$188,692	$ 0	$188,692	733,946
December 31, 2019	188,692	66,055	122,637	611,309
December 31, 2020	188,692	55,018	133,674	477,635
December 31, 2021	188,692	42,987	145,705	331,930
December 31, 2022	188,692	29,874	158,818	173,112
December 31, 2023	188,692	15,580	173,112	0

As shown in the amortization table, Carney allocates $66,055 of the second lease payment to interest revenue and $122,637 to a reduction of the net investment in lease.

Account	December 31, 2019	
Cash	188,692	
Interest Revenue		66,055
Net Investment in Lease – Sales Type		122,637

On December 31, 2020, Carney allocates $55,018 of the third lease payment to interest revenue and $133,674 to a reduction of the net investment in the lease.

Account	December 31, 2020	
Cash	188,692	
Interest Revenue		55,018
Net Investment in Lease – Sales Type		133,674

[16]Any credit losses on the NIL-ST are also included in the lessor's net income.

Residual Values in a Sales-Type Lease

A guaranteed residual value is included in the lease receivable and thus the net investment in the lease. This is true whether the guarantee is from the lessee or from a third party. An unguaranteed residual asset is explicitly included in the measurement of the net investment in the lease, but it is not part of the lease receivable.

Including residual values has two implications for lease accounting. First, it changes the implicit rate in the lease, which is defined as the interest rate at which the present value of the lease payments plus the present value of the amount that a lessor expects to derive from the leased asset at the end of the lease term equals the sum of the asset's fair value plus any deferred initial indirect costs of the lessor.

Second, the cost of goods sold is affected only by an unguaranteed residual value. Specifically, the cost of goods sold is defined as the carrying value of the leased asset less the present value of any unguaranteed residual asset plus any deferred initial direct costs of the lessor. As a result, the inclusion of a residual value guarantee does not impact cost of goods sold; only the inclusion of an *unguaranteed* residual asset reduces cost of goods sold.

Example 18.16 illustrates a sales-type lease with both a guaranteed and unguaranteed residual value.

EXAMPLE 18.16

Residual Values in a Sales-Type Lease

PROBLEM: Consider Carney Brothers Equipment Manufacturers from Example 18.15. Assume that the lease agreement is the same except that Carney now estimates a residual value of $60,000. The lessee guarantees $25,000 of the $60,000, so $35,000 of the residual value is still not guaranteed. What journal entries are required for 2019?[17] Prepare the amortization table for the NIL-ST.

SOLUTION: Because the lease contains a residual value, we must compute a new implicit rate such that the present value of the lease payments and any additional residual values equal the sum of the fair value of the leased asset plus any deferred initial direct costs. Carney expensed initial direct costs, so the present value of the payments plus the residual value must equal the fair value of $922,638. We compute the implicit rate as 10.76867%.

	N	I/Y	PV	PMT	FV	Excel Formula
Given	6		−922,638	188,692	60,000	=RATE(6,188692, −922638,60000,1)
Solve for RATE		**10.76867%**				

Carney also needs to compute the lease receivable, which is the present value of the lease payments plus the present value of any guaranteed residual values:

	N	I/Y	PV	PMT	FV	Excel Formula
Given	6	10.76867%		188,692	25,000	= PV(0.1076867,6, 188692,25000,1)
Solve for PV			**(903,690)**			

At the commencement of the lease, Carney records the net investment in the lease, removes the machine from its accounts, and records the gross profit. The net investment in the lease is the present value of the lease payments plus the present value of the lessee-guaranteed residual value plus the present value of the unguaranteed residual value at the implicit rate ($922,638). The sales revenue is $903,690, which is the lower of the fair value of the leased asset ($922,638) and the lease receivable ($903,690). Cost of goods sold is the carrying value

[17]Note that the lessor would likely require lower annual lease payments if the lessee guarantees a residual value because the lessor requires a certain rate of return.

of the machinery, $800,000, less the present value of the $35,000 unguaranteed residual asset, $18,948, at the implicit rate that is computed next:

	N	I/Y	PV	PMT	FV	Excel Formula
Given	6	10.76867%		0	35,000	
Solve for PV			**(18,948)**			= PV(0.1076867,6,0,35000,0)

The difference in the $903,690 sales revenue and the $781,052 cost of goods sold results in a gross profit of $122,638.

Account	***January 1, 2019***	
Net Investment in Lease – Sales Type	922,638	
Cost of Goods Sold	781,052	
Sales Revenue		903,690
Inventory of Machinery		800,000

Carney expenses the initial direct costs because the fair value is not equal to the carrying value.

Account	***January 1, 2019***	
Initial Direct Cost Expense	5,000	
Cash		5,000

Carney allocates the first payment to principal because interest accrues only with the passage of time.

Account	***January 1, 2019***	
Cash	188,692	
Net Investment in Lease – Sales Type		188,692

We can then prepare the amortization table as follows:

Date	**Payment (a)**	**Interest (b) = Prior-Period Balance × 10.76867%**	**Reduction in Lease Liability (c) = (a) − (b)**	**NIL-ST Balance (d) = Prior-Period Balance – (c)**
Lease Commencement – January 1, 2019				$922,638
January 1, 2019	$188,692	$ 0	$188,692	733,946
December 31, 2019	188,692	79,036	109,656	624,290
December 31, 2020	188,692	67,228	121,464	502,826
December 31, 2021	188,692	54,148	134,544	368,282
December 31, 2022	188,692	39,659	149,033	219,249
December 31, 2023	188,692	23,610	165,082	54,167
December 31, 2024	60,000*	5,833	54,167	0

* The net investment in the lease is fully recovered upon realization of the residual value.

As shown in the amortization table, Carney allocates the second payment to interest of $79,036 and principal of $109,656.

Account	***December 31, 2019***	
Cash	188,692	
Interest Revenue		79,036
Net Investment in Lease – Sales Type		109,656

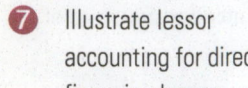

7 Illustrate lessor accounting for direct financing leases.

Accounting for Direct Financing Leases: Lessor

A direct financing lease meets both of the Group II but not the Group I criteria. Because none of the Group I criteria is met, the lessor continues to possess the right to control the leased asset, yet the lessee expects to recover the leased asset's value through the lease agreement. A direct financing lease may give rise to a profit, which is deferred and recognized over the term of the direct financing lease. Any loss is recognized on the lease commencement date. A lessor is often willing to incur a loss at commencement because it will recognize interest revenue on the lease receivable over the lease term that will be greater than the initial loss.

A lessor can classify a lease as a direct financing lease only when there is a residual value guaranteed by a third party. In this situation, none of the Group I criteria is met, but both Group II criteria must be met. The fourth Group I criterion is that the present value of the sum of the lease payments and any residual value guaranteed by the lessee, which is not otherwise included in the lease payments, is equal to substantially all of the fair value of the asset. Group II contains the criterion that the present value of the sum of the lease payments and any residual value guarantee (from both the lessee and a third party in combination) that is not otherwise included in the lease payments is equal to substantially all of the fair value of the asset. Note that the Group I criterion includes only a lessee's guarantee but that the Group II criterion includes a third-party guarantee. Therefore, the Group II criteria may be met while those of the Group I are not met if there is a third-party guarantee.

Initial Measurement of a Direct Financing Lease

For a direct financing lease, the lessor removes the leased asset from its balance sheet and records the net investment in the lease as an asset at the commencement of the lease. The **net investment in the lease for a direct financing lease** (NIL-DF) is composed of

1. The lease receivable
2. The present value of any unguaranteed residual asset
3. A reduction for any deferred profit

In a direct financing lease, all of the initial direct costs are deferred. Similar to the treatment of deferred initial direct costs in a sales-type lease, those costs are automatically included in the NIL-DF because of the way the implicit rate is defined.

Exhibit 18.11 compares and contrasts the measurement of the net investment in the lease for sales-type and direct financing leases.

EXHIBIT 18.11 Initial Measurement of the New Investment in the Lease

Sales-Type Lease*	Direct Financing Lease*
Lease receivable	Lease receivable
Plus: Present value of unguaranteed residual asset	Plus: Present value of unguaranteed residual asset
	Less: Deferred profit

* All deferred initial direct costs are implicitly included in the NIL.

Revenue and cost of goods sold are defined in the same way in a direct financing lease as they are for a sales-type lease. Revenue for a direct financing lease is the lower of (1) the fair value of the leased asset or (2) the sum of the *lease receivable* and any lease payments received before the lease commencement date. Cost of goods sold for a direct financing lease is equal to the carrying value of the leased asset less the present value of any unguaranteed residual asset plus any deferred initial direct costs. The lessor presents revenue and cost of goods sold when it realizes value from goods that it also would sell without providing lease financing. If the lessor uses the lease to provide financing only, the lessor nets revenue and cost of goods sold to present profit or less in a single line. In the examples of direct-financing leases, we show revenue and cost of goods sold separately, except in the case of deferred profit. When there is deferred profit, revenue and cost of goods sold will not be reported at the commencement of the lease.

Example 18.17 provides the lessor's accounting for the initial measurement of a direct financing lease.

EXAMPLE 18.17

Initial Measurement of a Direct Financing Lease

PROBLEM: On January 1, 2019, Flores Fitness Centers leases nonspecialized exercise equipment from Wright-Fit Equipment. The equipment is delivered on January 1. The lease term is 3 years with no renewal or purchase options, and title to the leased asset is retained by the lessor at the end of the lease term. The lease requires annual fixed rental payments of $12,600 per year beginning on January 1, 2019, and then December 31 of each year starting on December 31, 2019. The fair value of the equipment is $50,098 and has a carrying amount on Wright-Fit's books of $55,000. The equipment has a remaining life of 6 years. The estimated residual value of the equipment is $20,804. The lessee does not guarantee the residual value, but Wright-Fit secured an unrelated third party to guarantee $20,804; collection of this guaranteed residual value and lease payments is reasonably certain. The rate implicit in the lease is 10%.

There are no prepaid rentals, and neither party to the agreement pays initial direct costs.

Analyze the lease classification criteria to determine the lessor's classification of this agreement. Provide the journal entries on January 1, 2019.

SOLUTION: We use the Group I and Group II criteria to determine the lessor's lease classification. We have information to assess all of the Group I criteria except for the fourth criterion. The present value of the annuity due of the three remaining lease payments of $12,600 at a discount rate of 10% is $34,468. Note that we do not include the residual value guarantee made by a third party in the lease payments when implementing the Group I conditions.

	N	I/Y	PV	PMT	FV	Excel Formula
Given	3	10.00%		12,600	0	
Solve for PV			**(34,468)**			=PV(0.1,3,12600,0,1)

For the Group II criteria, we compute the present value of the lease payments plus the residual value guaranteed by the third party as $50,098:

	N	I/Y	PV	PMT	FV	Excel Formula
Given	3	10.00%		12,600	20,804	
Solve for PV			**(50,098)**			=PV(0.1,3,12600,20804,1)

The lease does not meet the Group I criteria. The agreement does not include a purchase option or a transfer of ownership. The lease term is for only 50% of the life of the asset. Because we do not include third-party guarantees in the present value computation for Group I, the present value is only 69% of the fair value.

The lease does, however, meet Group II criteria. For Group II, we compute the present value of the lease payments, including third-party guarantees. Thus, the present value is 100% of the fair value. Because the lease meets Group II, but not Group I, criteria, Wright-Fit classifies it as a direct financing lease.

Group I Criteria	Met?	Explanation
Transfer of ownership?	No	
Purchase option likely to be exercised?	No	
Lease term major part of economic life?	No	The lease term is 50% (3 years / 6 years) of economic life.
Present value substantial part of fair value?	No	The present value of $34,468 is 69% of the $50,098 fair value.
Asset is specialized?	No	

Group II Criteria	Met?	Explanation
Present value including third-party guarantees substantially all of fair value?	Yes	The present value of $50,098 is 100% of the $50,098 fair value.
Lease payment collection probable?	Yes	

At the commencement of the lease, Wright-Fit records the net investment in the lease and removes the machine from its accounts.

The sales revenue is $50,098, which is both the fair value of the leased asset and the lease receivable. Cost of goods sold is $55,000, the carrying value of the machinery, because there are no initial direct costs and no unguaranteed residual value. Thus, Wright-Fit recognizes the loss of $4,902 on the lease transaction.

The net investment in the lease is defined as the lease receivable plus the present value of any unguaranteed residual value less any deferred profit. The lease receivable includes the present value of both the lease payments to be received and the residual value guaranteed by the third party. We just computed this amount as $50,098. Thus, the NIL-DF is $50,098 because there is no unguaranteed residual asset and no deferred profit.

Account	January 1, 2019	
Net Investment in Lease – Direct Financing	50,098	
Cost of Goods Sold	55,000	
Revenue		50,098
Inventory of Machinery		55,000

Wright-Fit allocates the first payment to principal because interest accrues only with the passage of time.

Account	January 1, 2019	
Cash	12,600	
Net Investment in Lease – Direct Financing		12,600

Subsequent Measurement of a Direct Financing Lease

After the lease commencement date, the lessor remeasures the NIL-DF each period. The lessor computes interest revenue using the effective interest rate method. The lessor allocates lease payments first to cover the interest and then to reduce the NIL-DF. The interest revenue, which is reported on the income statement, is the amount that produces a constant periodic discount rate on the remaining balance of the NIL-DF. The lessor records the following items in net income if they are part of the lease agreement:

1. Interest revenue on the NIL-DF, which includes interest on the lease receivable, interest on the accretion of any unguaranteed residual asset, and amortization of any deferred profit
2. Variable payments not included in the NIL-DF
3. Change in variable lease payments that depend on an index or rate[18]

Example 18.18 provides an example of the lessor's accounting for the subsequent measurement of a direct financing lease.

[18] Any credit losses on the NIL-DF are also included in net income.

EXAMPLE 18.18 Subsequent Measurement of a Direct Financing Lease: Lessor

PROBLEM: Consider Wright-Fit from Example 18.17. What journal entries are required for 2019 and 2020 after January 1, 2019?

SOLUTION: The amortization table follows. Note that the "payment" listed for December 31, 2021, is not an annual lease payment but rather is the realization of the guaranteed residual value of the asset.

Date	Payment (a)	Interest (b) = Prior-Period Balance × 10%	Reduction in Lease Liability (c) = (a) − (b)	NIL-DF Balance (d) = Prior-Period Balance (d) − (c)
Lease Commencement – January 1, 2019				$50,098
January 1, 2019	$12,600	$ 0	$12,600	37,498
December 31, 2019	12,600	3,750	8,850	28,648
December 31, 2020	12,600	2,865	9,735	18,913
December 31, 2021	20,804*	1,891	18,913	0

* The net investment in the lease is fully recovered upon realization of the residual value.

As shown by the amortization table, Wright-Fit allocates $3,750 of the second lease payment to interest revenue and $8,850 to a reduction of the net investment in lease.

Account	December 31, 2019	
Cash	12,600	
Interest Revenue		3,750
Net Investment in Lease – Direct Financing		8,850

On December 31, 2020, Wright-Fit allocates $2,865 of the third lease payment to interest revenue and $9,735 to a reduction of the net investment in lease.

Account	December 31, 2020	
Cash	12,600	
Interest Revenue		2,865
Net Investment in Lease – Direct Financing		9,735

Exhibit 18.12 presents a summary of lessor accounting treatment for operating, sales-type, and direct financing leases.

EXHIBIT 18.12 Summary of Lessor Accounting Treatment

	Operating Lease	Sales-Type Lease	Direct Financing Lease
Classification	Neither Group I or Group II criteria met	Group I criteria met	Group II criteria met, Group I criteria not met
Initial measurement—net investment in lease*	None recorded	Lease receivable** Plus: Present value of unguaranteed residual asset	Lease receivable** Plus: Present value of unguaranteed residual asset Less: Deferred profit
Initial measurement—net investment in lease	None recorded	Reduced by payment Increased to record interest revenue***	
Measurement of revenue at lease commencement	None recorded	Lessor of: Fair value of leased asset Lease receivable + Lease payments received before the lease commencement	
Measurement of cost of goods sold at lease commencement	None recorded	Carrying value of the leased asset Less: Present value of unguaranteed residual asset Plus: Deferred initial direct costs of lessor	
Measurement of profit or loss at commencement	None recorded	Profit or loss equal to revenue less cost of goods sold is reported.	If cost of goods sold is greater than revenue, then full loss is reported.
Impact on income statement	Record rental revenue composed of: 1. Total lease payments recognized on a straight-line basis 2. Variable payments not included in the lease payments	Record revenue over the lease term composed of: 1. Interest revenue on the NIL 2. Variable payments not included in the NIL 3. Change in variable lease payments that depend on an index or rate 4. Credit losses on the NIL	

* The NIL for both a sales-type and a direct financing lease implicitly includes any deferred initial direct costs.

** Includes the present value of the payments to be received plus the present value of residual value guarantees. Use the implicit rate at the commencement date.

*** Computed as the amount that produces a constant periodic discount rate on the remaining balance of the NIL. Note that the computation will be different for sales-type leases and direct financing leases because the initial measurement of the NIL is different.

IFRS Accounting for Leases: Lessor

Unlike U.S. GAAP, IFRS does not distinguish sales-type leases from direct financing leases. IFRS classifies leases based on whether the risks and rewards of ownership have been transferred to the lessee. If the risks and rewards have been transferred, IFRS classifies the lease as a finance lease (see the IFRS lease classification discussion earlier in the chapter).

The lessor's accounting for IFRS finance leases is similar to the U.S. GAAP accounting for sales-type leases. There are two types of lessors under IFRS: (1) manufacturers and dealers and (2) everyone else. Under IFRS, at the lease commencement manufacturers and dealers report a profit computed the same way as lessors compute profit under U.S. GAAP. Manufacturers and dealers always immediately expense initial direct costs. All other lessors do not recognize a profit at lease commencement and defer initial direct costs.

JUDGMENTS IN ACCOUNTING
For Leases

Throughout the chapter, we have explored the criteria to classify leases. There is a great deal of subjectivity in implementing the criteria under both U.S. GAAP and IFRS.

We begin this section by reviewing the Group I and Group II criteria reproduced in Exhibit 18.13.

EXHIBIT 18.13 U.S. GAAP Lease Classification Criteria

Group I

1. The lease transfers ownership to the lessee at the end of the lease term.
2. The lessee is given an option to purchase the asset that is reasonably certain to be exercised.
3. The lease term is for a major part of the economic life of the asset.
4. The present value of the sum of the lease payments and any residual value guaranteed by the lessee that is not otherwise included in the lease payments is equal to substantially all of the fair value of the asset.
5. The leased asset is of a specialized nature.

Group II

1. The present value of the sum of the lease payments and any residual value guarantee (from both the lessee and a third party in combination) that is not otherwise included in the lease payments is equal to substantially all of the fair value of the asset.
2. It is probable that the lessor will collect the *lease payments* plus any amount necessary to satisfy a residual value guarantee.

Most of the Group I criteria include some aspect of judgment. The purchase option in the second criterion must be "reasonably certain to be exercised." How likely is reasonably certain? The third criterion requires an estimate of the economic life of the property. In addition, the third criterion uses the phrase "major part." What exactly would a "major part" be? FASB has indicated that 75% would be a reasonable cutoff to use, but it has not required that specific percentage as a definition of major part.

The fourth Group I criterion and the first Group II criterion requires the estimation of a fair market value. How subjective is the determination of fair market value for some assets? In addition, both of these criteria use the imprecise phrase "substantially all." FASB has indicated that 90% would be a reasonable definition of substantially all, but it has not required that cutoff.

The Group II criteria also require assessments of collectability, which is again quite subjective. Lessees may prefer to use the judgment afforded by the accounting standards to classify leases as operating leases because expenses are typically recognized more slowly under an operating lease (see the financial statement analysis section for examples).

Conversely, the lessor would most likely prefer a direct financing or sales-type lease to an operating lease. Non-operating lease treatment would permit a financial service company lessor to remove heavy machinery and equipment, jet airlines, oceangoing vessels, and such from its balance sheet and replace it with the net investment in the lease, a financial asset compatible with the nature of its business. In addition, the non-operating lease results in the recognition of interest income rather than rent revenue. Interest income is a source of revenue consistent with a financial service company's normal operations.

For a dealer or manufacturer lessor, the use of a non-operating lease is also preferred because it recognizes financing income and accelerates revenue recognition in the form of the gross profit on the sale in the year of commencement. Under an operating lease treatment, the lessor records only rental income each year, spreading the revenue flow over the lease term.

CHAD SOARES

PARTNER, TRANSACTION SERVICES, PRICEWATERHOUSECOOPERS LLP »

Chad Soares

Chad Soares has more than 20 years of experience advising a variety of clients in the United States and overseas on complex transactions, including leasing. His clients typically need deep knowledge of not only lease accounting, but also related areas such as consolidation, revenue recognition, and joint venture accounting.

1. What is an embedded lease, and what are some of the difficulties in identifying an embedded lease?

An embedded lease is one contained within another type of agreement, such as IT outsourcing, logistics, or contract manufacturing arrangements. These leases exist if there is an explicit or implicit asset in the contract and the customer controls use of the asset. The new FASB leasing standard requires that companies report virtually all leases, including embedded ones, on the balance sheet. Ensuring that you capture all potential embedded leases is critical. Once you've done so, separating the original contract into lease and nonlease components, allocating consideration to each, and classifying each lease as an operating or finance lease would follow. Allocating consideration in the contract to components is not always straightforward. Contracts often include a combination of fixed and variable payments as well as optional purchases, adding complexity to this exercise. Getting it right is critical since it affects balance sheet measurement as well as classification and disclosure.

2. How will a lessee obtain standalone prices needed to allocate payments to lease and nonlease components? What if standalone prices are not available?

Judgment is often required to allocate payments to lease and nonlease components. For example, payments for highly integrated service offerings, such as contract manufacturing or outsourced activities, may not be based on market observable data related to specific components. The Board appears to have anticipated these concerns and allows estimation provided preparers " . . . maximize the use of observable information" and develop such estimates consistently.

3. What are the key conditions that differentiate a sales-type from a direct financing lease for the lessor?

The key distinction in a sales-type lease and a direct financing lease is whether the lease arrangement transfers control from the lessor to the lessee. When control is transferred to the lessee, it represents an in-substance financed sale of an asset. When control doesn't transfer (e.g., when only the "substantially all" criterion is met as a result of third-party residual value insurance), the arrangement is a direct financing lease. Either model requires recognition of the net investment in the lease and derecognition of the underlying asset. However, only a sales-type lease permits up-front revenue and profit recognition.

4. How do we identify variable payments that are classified as in-substance fixed payments?

Variable lease payments may be based on a rate or index, usage of the underlying asset, or other factors. Some payments appear to be variable but are in fact unavoidable, such as a lease that provides the lessee an option about *which* payments it makes, but does not permit a lessee to *avoid* payment (e.g., a take or pay contract). Two examples are usage-based payments that specify a penalty payment if minimums are not achieved and rent payments based on movements in an index such as CPI and subject to a ceiling that is highly likely to be met. Assume that a 10-year lease includes a rent increase in year six, calculated as five times the change in the CPI over the prior 5-year period and capped at 5%. Assume also that a 5% rent increase commencing in the sixth year of the lease term is unavoidable. Therefore, the lessee and lessor should include the 5% rent increase in lease payments.

5. What are the fundamental differences between GAAP and IFRS when classifying lease arrangements?

The most notable difference between IFRS and GAAP is the single income statement model required of all IFRS lessees. Under IFRS all leases (other than short-term or small-ticket leases) will reflect interest expense and amortization similar to any other financing. Under GAAP, only finance leases follow this pattern, and many leases are likely to continue to present lease expense in the income statement similar to operating leases today.

Discussion Questions

1. Prior to the current lease standard, companies were able to structure a significant number of leases in order to keep them off-balance sheet. They did not report the asset and liability on the balance sheet; instead, rent expense was recorded each period without any impact on assets or liabilities. Discuss financial statement effects of the new standard's requirement that lessees record the leased asset and lease liability on the balance sheet for almost all lease transactions.
2. Discuss the factors that determine whether an entity should lease or purchase an asset.

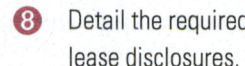

8 Detail the required lease disclosures.

Lease Disclosures

The objective of lease-disclosure requirements is to enable users of financial statements to assess the amount, timing, and uncertainty of cash flows arising from lease agreements. Generally, lease disclosures vary by the type of lease and whether the lessee or lessor is making the disclosures. Both lessees and lessors disclose the significant judgments made in accounting for leases, including:

- The determination of whether a contract contains a lease
- The separation of lease and nonlease components
- The discount rate

Lessees and lessors also provide a description of the leases and amounts recognized in the financial statements. In the disclosures, lessees and lessors consider the level of detail necessary to satisfy the disclosure objective and how much emphasis to place on each of the various requirements. A lessee can aggregate or disaggregate disclosures so that useful information is not obscured by including a large amount of insignificant detail or by aggregating items that have different characteristics.

Lessee-Disclosure Requirements

The lessee's disclosures provide the user with the following information about the nature of the lease:

- Determination of variable lease payments
- Existence, terms, and conditions of options to extend or terminate the lease
- Existence, terms, and conditions of residual value guarantees
- Restrictions or covenants imposed by leases such as limits on dividends or the incurrence of additional financial obligations

Lessees disclose the following amounts relating to total lease costs and cash flows so that financial statement users can better understand the costs from a company's leases:

- Finance lease cost, separated into the amortization expense of the right-of-use assets and interest expense on the lease liabilities
- Operating lease costs
- Short-term lease costs
- Variable lease costs
- Sublease income disclosed on a gross basis separately from the finance or operating lease expense
- Net gain or loss recognized from sale and leaseback transactions
- Amounts for finance and operating leases for the following items:
    - Cash paid for amounts included in the measurement of lease liabilities segregated into operating and financing cash flows
    - Supplemental noncash information on lease liabilities arising from the acquisition of right-of-use assets
    - Weighted-average remaining lease term
    - Weighted-average discount rate

To help financial statement users assess the extent of future cash flows related to leases, lessees provide a maturity analysis of finance lease liabilities and operating lease liabilities separately. Lessees disclose the undiscounted cash flows on an annual basis for a minimum of 5 years and in total for the remaining years. Lessees reconcile the undiscounted cash flows to the finance lease liabilities and operating lease liabilities recognized on the statement of financial position.

Furthermore, the lessee discloses leases that have not yet commenced but that create significant rights and obligations for the lessee, including the nature of any involvement with the construction or design of the leased asset.

Lessees that elect the practical expedient of not separating lease components from nonlease components disclose this accounting policy election and the leased assets to which the election applies.

Lessor-Disclosure Requirements

Lessor disclosures are also quite extensive. The lessor's disclosures provide the user with the following information about the nature of its leases:

- Existence, terms, and conditions of options to extend or terminate the lease
- Existence, terms, and conditions of residual value guarantees
- Leased asset's residual value

To provide further information on income from leases, lessors disclose a table presenting lease income for sales-type leases and direct financing leases:

- Profit or loss recognized at the commencement date
- Interest income either in aggregate or separated by components of the net investment in the lease

For operating leases, lessors disclose lease income relating to lease payments and variable lease payments not included in the measurement of all types of lease receivables.

Related to balance sheet amounts, a lessor discloses the components of net investment in sales-type and direct financing leases. The components are the carrying amount of its lease receivables, its unguaranteed residual assets, and any deferred selling profit on direct financing leases. Lessors also explain significant changes in the balances of their unguaranteed residual assets and deferred selling profit on direct financing leases.

Lessors disclose information about how they manage risk associated with the residual value of leased assets. In particular, a lessor should disclose all of the following:

- Its risk management strategy for residual assets
- The carrying amount of residual assets covered by residual value guarantees
- Any other means by which the lessor reduces its residual asset risk (e.g., buyback agreements or variable lease payments for use in excess of specified limits)

Similar to disclosures for lessees, lessors provide a maturity analysis of operating, sales-type, and direct financing lease liabilities separately. Lessors disclose the undiscounted cash flows on an annual basis for a minimum of 5 years and in total for the remaining years. Lessors reconcile the undiscounted cash flows to the lease receivables recognized in the statement of financial position. Lessors also disclose the amount of leased assets under operating leases.

IFRS-Specific Lessee Disclosure Requirements. IFRS disclosures are similar to those of U.S. GAAP. However, because lease classifications are different, IFRS reporters provide disclosure related to the types of leases they have. For example, the lessee discloses costs related to low-value leases. The lessor's maturity analysis includes its finance leases and operating leases.

FINANCIAL STATEMENT ANALYSIS

Operating Leases versus Finance Leases for the Lessee

All leases result in a lessee reporting a right-of-use asset and a lease liability, but the financial statement effects of operating and finance leases differ. Net income and total assets under finance leases are generally lower in the early years of the lease. Because the lease liability is the present value of future payments, it is generally the same under both types of leases. Companies, then, have the incentive to report a lease as an operating lease to report higher net income and higher total assets.

Within the income statement, however, operating income for a finance lease will be higher. Under a finance lease, amortization of the right-of-use asset reduces operating income but interest expense is reported under non-operating income (or financial income). Under an operating lease, lease cost reduces only operating income. Because lease costs are usually higher than the asset amortization expense in the early years of a lease, operating income will be higher under a finance lease. Similarly, within the statement of cash flows, cash flows from operating activities for a finance lease will be higher. All lease payments for an operating lease reduce cash flows from operating activities. For a finance lease, only interest payments reduce cash flows from operating activities. The reduction in the lease obligation is classified as a cash outflow from financing. Total cash outflows will be the same because the lease payments are the same. Exhibit 18.14 summarizes the financial statement effects of lease classification.

EXHIBIT 18.14 Comparison of Financial Statement Effects of Operating versus Finance Leases in the Early Years of a Lease: Lessee Effects

	Operating Lease		Finance Lease	
	Includes	**Effect**	**Includes**	**Effect**
Income Statement				
Net income	Lease costs	Higher	Amortization expense Plus: Interest expense	Lower
Operating income	Lease costs	Lower	Amortization expense	Higher
Statement of Cash Flows	Lease payment	Same	Lease payment	Same
Cash flows from operating activities	Lease payment	Lower	Interest payment only	Higher
Cash flows from financing activities	None	Higher	Reduction of lease obligation	Lower
Balance Sheet				
Right-of-Use asset balance	Right-of-Use asset amortized less early on	Higher	Right-of-Use asset amortized straight line	Lower
Lease obligation	Lease obligation reduced to present value	Same	Lease obligation reduced to present value	Same

Example 18.19 illustrates the financial statement effects of accounting for the same lease as operating versus financing. Because IFRS accounts for all leases as finance leases, the example also illustrates the financial statement differences in U.S. GAAP and IFRS.

Financial Statement Analysis, continued

EXAMPLE 18.19 Financial Statement Effects of an Operating versus a Finance Lease

PROBLEM: You have been tasked with analyzing the financial statement effects of a lessee accounting for a lease as an operating lease versus finance lease. The lease payments are $600,000 with the first lease payment due on January 1, Year 1, at the commencement of the 5-year lease. The next lease payment is due on December 31, Year 1. The remaining three lease payments are due on December 31 of Years 2 through 4. The lessee's discount rate is 11%, and the present value of the lease payments is $2,461,467. Compare the differences in expenses, operating income, net income, total assets, and cash flows from operating activities of accounting for the lease as an operating lease and finance lease. We assume that the first payment is made at the beginning of Year 1. We ignore the rules that guide the determination of whether a lease is an operating lease or a finance lease so that we can focus on the financial statement effects. The lessee amortizes the right-of-use asset on a straight-line basis under a finance lease. Ignore income taxes.

SOLUTION: First, we need to determine the reporting for the lease as an operating lease. At commencement, the measurement of the right-of-use asset and obligation is $2,461,467. We compute the interest expense and reduction of the lease obligation in the following table.

Date	Payment (a)	Interest (b) = Prior period balance (d) × 11%	Reduction in Lease Liability (c) = (a) − (b)	Balance (b) = Prior-Period balance (d) – (c)
Lease Commencement – January 1, Year 1				$2,461,467
January 1, Year 1	$600,000	$ 0	$600,000	1,861,467
December 31, Year 1	600,000	204,761	395,239	1,466,228
December 31, Year 2	600,000	161,285	438,715	1,027,513
December 31, Year 3	600,000	113,026	486,974	540,539
December 31, Year 4	600,000	59,461	540,539	0

Next, we compute the portion of the annual lease expense that is attributable to the asset amortization. This amount is computed as the annual lease expense less the interest portion as computed.

Date	Lease Expense (a)	Interest in Previous Table Column (b)	Amortization of Right of Use Asset (c) = (a) − (b)
Year 1	$ 600,000	$204,761	$ 395,239
Year 2	600,000	161,285	438,715
Year 3	600,000	113,026	486,974
Year 4	600,000	59,461	540,539
Year 5	600,000	0	600,000
	$2,400,000	$538,533	$2,461,467

The lease expense for the operating lease is $600,000 per year. For a finance lease, the right-of-use asset is amortized on a straight-line basis at $492,293 per year ($2,461,467 / 5 years). Interest expense is the same as the expense we computed for the operating lease. A comparison of the lease costs for the operating lease and finance lease is presented in the following table.

Financial Statement Analysis, continued

Observe that total expenses are higher under a finance lease in the early years of the lease. Therefore, net income will be lower under a finance lease in the early years. Total expenses over the life of the lease are the same. Because the lease cost for the operating lease is reported in operating income whereas only the amortization expense is for the finance lease, operating income is lower for the operating lease.

	Operating Lease	Finance Lease			
Year	**Lease Expense**	**Amortization Expense**	**Interest Expense**	**Total Expense**	**Difference**
	Operating Income	Operating Income	Non-Operating Income		
Year 1	$ 600,000	$ 492,293	$204,761	$ 697,054	$ 97,054
Year 2	600,000	492,293	161,285	653,578	53,578
Year 3	600,000	492,293	113,026	605,319	5,319
Year 4	600,000	492,293	59,461	551,754	(48,246)
Year 5	600,000	492,295*	0	492,295	(107,705)
Total	$3,000,000	$2,461,467	$538,533	$3,000,000	$ 0

* Adjusted due to rounding errors.

On the balance sheet, total assets are lower for the finance lease early on because the amortization on the right-of-use asset is higher in the early years. The amortization on the right-of-use asset increases for the operating lease over time.

	Right-of-Use Asset Balance		
	Operating Lease	**Finance Lease**	**Difference**
January 1, Year 1	$2,461,467	$2,461,467	$ 0
December 31, Year 1	2,066,228	1,969,174	97,054
December 31, Year 2	1,627,513	1,476,881	150,632
December 31, Year 3	1,140,539	984,588	155,951
December 31, Year 4	600,000	492,295	107,705
December 31, Year 5	0	0	0

On the statement of cash flows, the total lease payment reduces cash flow from operating activities for the operating lease. Only the interest portion reduces operating cash flows under the finance lease. Therefore, cash flows from operating activities are higher when a lease is classified as a finance lease each year and in total.

	Cash Outflows from Operating Activities		
	Operating Lease	**Finance Lease**	**Difference**
January 1, Year 1	$ 600,000	$ 0	$ 600,000
December 31, Year 1	600,000	204,761	395,239
December 31, Year 2	600,000	161,285	438,715
December 31, Year 3	600,000	113,026	486,974
December 31, Year 4	600,000	59,461	540,539
Total	$3,000,000	$538,533	$2,461,467

Summary by Learning Objectives

In the following, we summarize the main points by learning objective. Throughout the chapter, we discuss the accounting and reporting of leases under U.S. GAAP and IFRS. The following table also highlights the major similarities and differences in the standards.

1 Understand the basic concepts of lease accounting and identify the advantages and disadvantages of leasing.

Summary	Similarities and Differences between U.S. GAAP and IFRS
A lease is a contract between the owner of an asset (lessor) and the party acquiring the use of the asset (lessee). Advantages of leasing include complete financing, the lessor bears the risk of obsolescence, business and financial flexibility, and tax benefits. Disadvantages of leasing include the overall cost of the asset and the loss of ownership.	Similar under U.S. GAAP and IFRS.

2 Understand lease contracts and determine how to separate lease and nonlease components and how to allocate contract consideration to the various components.

Summary	Similarities and Differences between U.S. GAAP and IFRS
The first step in lease accounting for both the lessee and the lessor is to determine whether a contract contains a lease. A company makes this determination at the inception of a contract. The right to use a leased asset is a separate lease component if 1. The lessee can benefit from the right-of-use of the asset either on its own or together with other resources that are readily available to the lessee and 2. The right-of-use is neither highly dependent on nor highly interrelated with the other rights to use the leased assets in the contract. Nonlease components are agreements to purchase other goods or services such as maintenance services or supplies. Lessee consideration allocation: Allocate contract consideration to lease components on a relative standalone price basis. Lessor consideration allocation: Allocate consideration based on revenue recognition guidance.	Similar under U.S. GAAP and IFRS.

Summary by Learning Objectives, continued

3 Classify leases as operating, finance, direct financing, and sales-type.

Summary	Similarities and Differences between U.S. GAAP and IFRS
Lessees classify leases as operating or finance. Lessors classify leases as operating, direct financing, or sales type. Both use the following Group I criteria: 1. The lease transfers ownership. 2. The lease contains a purchase option that the lessee is reasonably certain to exercise. 3. The lease term is a major part of the asset's economic life. 4. The present value of lease payments and residual value guaranteed by the lessee is a substantial part of the asset's fair value. 5. The asset is of a specialized nature. If any one of the Group I criteria is met, the lessee classifies the lease as a finance lease. Otherwise, the lease is an operating lease. Lessors also consider the following Group II criteria: 1. The present value of lease payments including third-party guarantees is a substantial part of the asset's fair value. 2. Lease payment and guaranteed residual value collection are probable. If none of the Group I or II criteria is met, the lessor classifies the lease as an operating lease. If the Group I criteria are met, the lessor classifies the lease as a sales-type lease. If none of the Group I criteria is met but both Group II criteria are met, the lessor classifies the lease as a direct financing lease. Lease payments include six components. 1. Fixed payments less any lease incentives paid or payable to the lessee. 2. Variable lease payments that depend on a rate or index using the rate or index in effect at the lease commencement date. 3. The exercise price of an option to purchase the leased asset if the lessee is reasonably certain to exercise the option. 4. Payments for penalties for terminating the lease if the lease term reflects the lessee exercising an option to terminate the lease. 5. Fees paid by the lessee to the owners of a special-purpose entity for structuring the transaction. 6. For a lessee only, the amounts probable of being owed by the lessee under residual value guarantees. The lessor uses the rate implicit in the lease, which is the rate of interest that causes the present value of the lease payments plus the present value of the amount that a lessor expects to obtain from the leased asset at the end of the lease term to equal the sum of the fair value of the leased asset and any deferred initial direct costs of the lessor. The lessee's discount rate is the rate implicit in the lease unless that rate cannot be readily determined. In that case, the lessee uses the lessee's incremental borrowing rate.	➤ Lessees do not classify leases under IFRS. All leases are treated the same. Lessees treat all leases as U.S. GAAP finance leases. Lessors classify leases into operating and finance leases. If any one of the Group I criteria is met, the lease is classified as a finance lease. IFRS also includes three additional indicators that individually or in combination could lead to classifying a lease as a finance lease: 1. The lessee bears the lessor's losses if the lessee cancels the lease. 2. The lessee absorbs the gains or losses from fluctuations in the fair value of the residual value of the asset. 3. The lessee may extend the lease for a secondary period at a rent substantially below the market rent in a renewal option. For the lessor, IFRS does not distinguish between direct financing and sale-type leases. IFRS does not use the Group II criteria.

Summary by Learning Objectives, continued

❹ Demonstrate the accounting for an operating lease for both the lessee and the lessor.

Summary	Similarities and Differences between U.S. GAAP and IFRS
Lessee: Initially, the lessee recognizes a lease liability and a right-of-use asset on the lease commencement date. The lease liability is measured as the present value of the remaining lease payments. The right-of-use asset includes the following components: • The present value of all lease payments—the lease liability amount. • Lease payments the lessee makes to the lessor at or before commencement date. • Lease incentives the lessee receives, which reduce the right-of-use asset. • Any initial direct costs the lessee incurs. Subsequently, the liability is remeasured to the present value of remaining lease payments. Subsequently, the right-of-use asset is the sum of the following components: • The present value of lease payments • Prepaid or accrued lease payments • The remaining balance of any lease incentives received • Unamortized initial direct costs • Impairments of the right-of-use asset The lease cost is the remaining lease cost allocated over the remaining lease term on a straight-line basis. The remaining cost of the lease is calculated as total lease payments (including those previously paid and those not yet paid), net of any incentives received plus total lessee initial direct costs less any lease cost recognized in prior periods. Additional lease expenses are any variable lease payments, changes that depend on an index or rate, or impairments. When a lease term is 12 months or less, the lessee can make a policy election not to record the lease liability and the right-of-use asset. Lessor: The lessor records rental revenue, which includes the total lease payments recognized on a straight-line basis and any variable payments not included in the lease payments. The lessor's initial direct costs are expensed over the lease term, typically on a straight-line basis. The lessor records depreciation expense on the leased asset if it classifies the asset as property, plant, and equipment but not if it holds the asset as part of inventory.	➤ Under IFRS, the lessee accounts for both operating and finance leases in the same way that finance leases are accounted for under U.S. GAAP. See Learning Objective 6 summary. Lessor accounting for an operating lease is similar under IFRS and U.S. GAAP.

❺ Demonstrate lessee accounting for a finance lease.

Summary	Similarities and Differences between U.S. GAAP and IFRS
For a finance lease, the lessee records a right-of-use asset and a liability measured the same way that an operating lease is. The lessee records amortization expense on the right-of-use asset and interest expense on the liability using the effective interest rate method. Additional lease expenses are any variable lease payments, changes in variable lease payments that depend on an index or rate, or impairments.	➤ Under IFRS, the lessee accounts for both operating and finance leases in the same way that finance leases are accounted for under U.S. GAAP. ➤ Optional election: Leased assets with original costs less than $5,000 can be treated as rental agreements.

Summary by Learning Objectives, continued

6 Illustrate lessor accounting for sales-type leases.

Summary	Similarities and Differences between U.S. GAAP and IFRS
Initially, the lessor reports the net investment in a lease–sales-type (NIL-ST). The NIL-ST is the sum of the lease receivable and any unguaranteed residual value. The lessor also records revenue and cost of goods sold and removes the asset's carrying value from its books. Revenue is the lower of (1) the fair value of the leased asset and (2) the lease receivable plus lease payments received before the lease commencement. Cost of goods sold is the carrying value of the leased asset less the present value of any unguaranteed residual asset plus any deferred initial direct costs. Subsequently, the lessor earns interest revenue on the lease receivable. The lessor expenses initial direct costs if the fair value of the leased asset is not equal to the carrying value. If the fair value equals the carrying value, the initial direct costs are deferred and included in the NIL-ST by computation of the implicit rate.	➤ IFRS does not distinguish sales-type from direct financing leases. All are treated similar to U.S. GAAP sales-type leases. There are two types of lessors under IFRS: (1) manufacturers and dealers and (2) everyone else. Under IFRS, manufacturers and dealers report a profit at the lease commencement, computed the same as lessors compute profit under U.S. GAAP. Manufacturers and dealers always immediately expense initial direct costs. All other lessors do not recognize a profit at lease commencement and they defer initial direct costs.

7 Illustrate lessor accounting for direct financing leases.

Summary	Similarities and Differences between U.S. GAAP and IFRS
Initially, the lessor recognizes the net investment in lease–direct financing (NIL-DF), which is composed of: • The lease receivable • The present value of any unguaranteed residual asset • A reduction for any deferred profit The lessor also records revenue and cost of goods sold and removes the asset's carrying value from its books. Revenue and cost of goods sold are defined the same way they are in a direct financing lease as they are for a sales-type lease. Subsequently, the interest revenue is the amount that produces a constant periodic discount rate on the remaining balance of the NIL-DF. The lessor records the following items in net income, if they are part of the lease agreement: • Interest revenue on the NIL-DF, which includes interest on the lease receivable, interest on the accretion of any unguaranteed residual asset, and amortization of any deferred profit. • Variable payments not included in the NIL-DF. • Change in variable lease payments that depend on an index or rate. • Credit loss on the NIL-DF. • All initial direct costs are deferred, and expensed over the lease term.	➤ IFRS does not distinguish sales-type from direct financing leases. There are two types of lessors under IFRS: (1) manufacturers and dealers and (2) everyone else. Under IFRS, manufacturers and dealers report a profit at the lease commencement computed the same as lessors compute profit under U.S. GAAP. Manufacturers and dealers always immediately expense initial direct costs. All other lessors do not recognize a profit at lease commencement, and they defer initial direct costs.

Summary by Learning Objectives, continued

8 Detail the required lease disclosures.	
Summary	**Similarities and Differences between U.S. GAAP and IFRS**
Both lessees and lessors disclose the significant judgments made in accounting for leases, including the determination of whether a contract contains a lease, the separation of lease and nonlease components, and the discount rate. Lessees and lessors also provide a description of the leases by type and amount of • Assets and liabilities recognized on the balance sheet • Costs and revenues on the income statement • Related cash flows Both lessees and lessors provide a maturity analysis of leases by type including annual undiscounted cash flows for a minimum of 5 years and for remaining years in total, and they reconcile undiscounted cash flows to amounts on the balance sheet. Both disclose options to extend or terminate the lease and any residual value guarantees. Lessees also disclose: • The determination and amount of variable lease payments • Weighted-average remaining lease term • Any election of the practical expedient of not separating lease components from nonlease components Lessors also disclose: • The leased asset's residual value • Profit or loss recognized at the commencement date • Components of the carrying amount of its lease receivables, its unguaranteed residual assets, and any deferred selling profit on direct financing leases • An explanation of significant changes in the balances of its unguaranteed residual assets and deferred selling profit on direct financing leases • Risk management strategy for residual assets • The carrying amount of residual assets covered by residual value guarantees.	Disclosures are similar under U.S. GAAP and IFRS. ➤ IFRS provides disclosures pertaining to types of leases reported such as low-value leases.

MyLab Accounting

Go to **http://www.pearson.com/mylab/accounting** for the following Questions, Multiple-Choice Questions, Brief Exercises, Exercises, and Problems. They are available with immediate grading, explanations of correct and incorrect answers, and interactive media that acts as your own online tutor.

18 Accounting for Leases

Questions

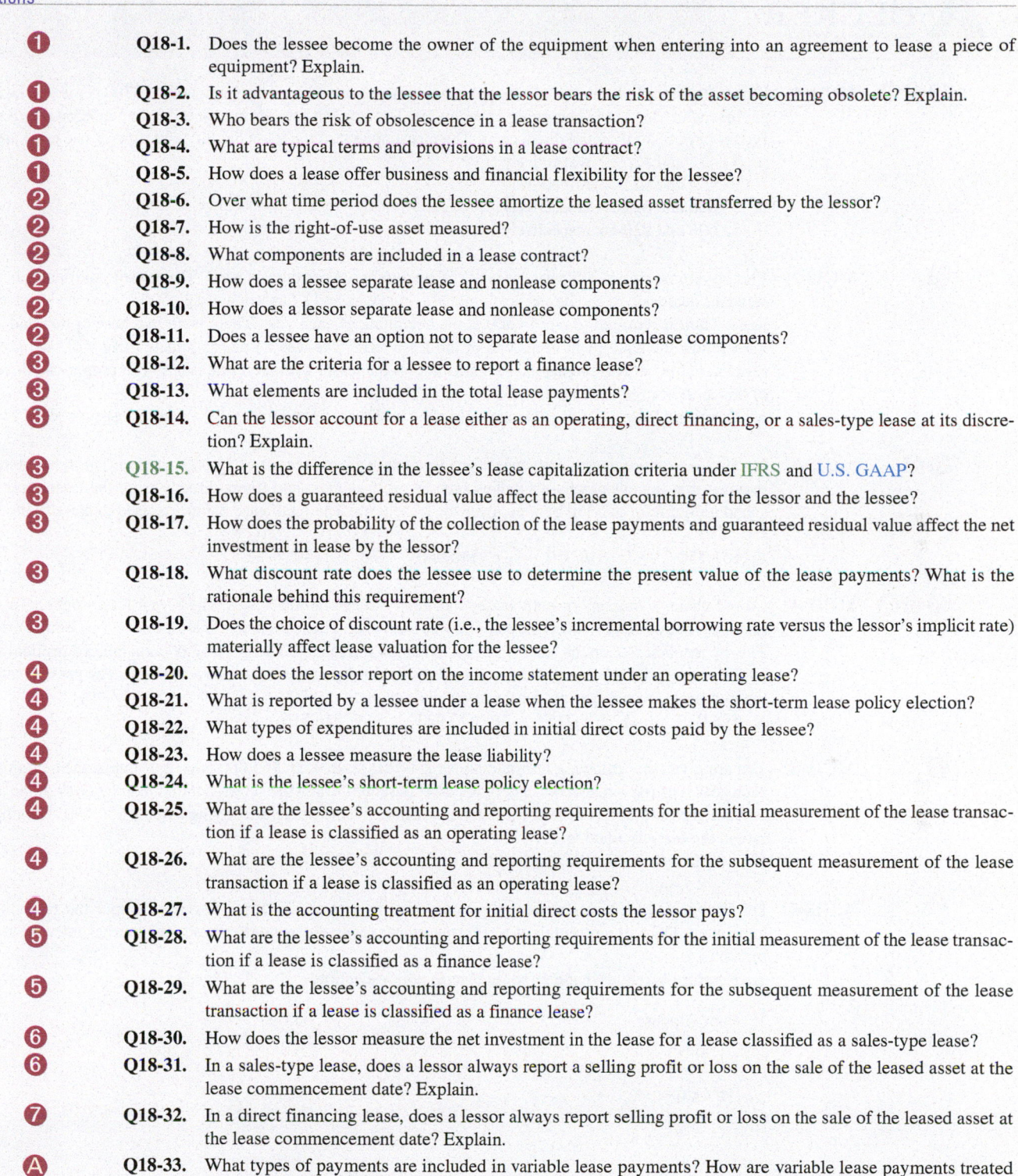

1 **Q18-1.** Does the lessee become the owner of the equipment when entering into an agreement to lease a piece of equipment? Explain.

1 **Q18-2.** Is it advantageous to the lessee that the lessor bears the risk of the asset becoming obsolete? Explain.

1 **Q18-3.** Who bears the risk of obsolescence in a lease transaction?

1 **Q18-4.** What are typical terms and provisions in a lease contract?

1 **Q18-5.** How does a lease offer business and financial flexibility for the lessee?

2 **Q18-6.** Over what time period does the lessee amortize the leased asset transferred by the lessor?

2 **Q18-7.** How is the right-of-use asset measured?

2 **Q18-8.** What components are included in a lease contract?

2 **Q18-9.** How does a lessee separate lease and nonlease components?

2 **Q18-10.** How does a lessor separate lease and nonlease components?

2 **Q18-11.** Does a lessee have an option not to separate lease and nonlease components?

3 **Q18-12.** What are the criteria for a lessee to report a finance lease?

3 **Q18-13.** What elements are included in the total lease payments?

3 **Q18-14.** Can the lessor account for a lease either as an operating, direct financing, or a sales-type lease at its discretion? Explain.

3 Q18-15. What is the difference in the lessee's lease capitalization criteria under IFRS and U.S. GAAP?

3 **Q18-16.** How does a guaranteed residual value affect the lease accounting for the lessor and the lessee?

3 **Q18-17.** How does the probability of the collection of the lease payments and guaranteed residual value affect the net investment in lease by the lessor?

3 **Q18-18.** What discount rate does the lessee use to determine the present value of the lease payments? What is the rationale behind this requirement?

3 **Q18-19.** Does the choice of discount rate (i.e., the lessee's incremental borrowing rate versus the lessor's implicit rate) materially affect lease valuation for the lessee?

4 **Q18-20.** What does the lessor report on the income statement under an operating lease?

4 **Q18-21.** What is reported by a lessee under a lease when the lessee makes the short-term lease policy election?

4 **Q18-22.** What types of expenditures are included in initial direct costs paid by the lessee?

4 **Q18-23.** How does a lessee measure the lease liability?

4 **Q18-24.** What is the lessee's short-term lease policy election?

4 **Q18-25.** What are the lessee's accounting and reporting requirements for the initial measurement of the lease transaction if a lease is classified as an operating lease?

4 **Q18-26.** What are the lessee's accounting and reporting requirements for the subsequent measurement of the lease transaction if a lease is classified as an operating lease?

4 **Q18-27.** What is the accounting treatment for initial direct costs the lessor pays?

5 **Q18-28.** What are the lessee's accounting and reporting requirements for the initial measurement of the lease transaction if a lease is classified as a finance lease?

5 **Q18-29.** What are the lessee's accounting and reporting requirements for the subsequent measurement of the lease transaction if a lease is classified as a finance lease?

6 **Q18-30.** How does the lessor measure the net investment in the lease for a lease classified as a sales-type lease?

6 **Q18-31.** In a sales-type lease, does a lessor always report a selling profit or loss on the sale of the leased asset at the lease commencement date? Explain.

7 **Q18-32.** In a direct financing lease, does a lessor always report selling profit or loss on the sale of the leased asset at the lease commencement date? Explain.

A **Q18-33.** What types of payments are included in variable lease payments? How are variable lease payments treated in accounting for leases?

Multiple-Choice Questions

❷❸❹ **MC18-1.** Baxter Brothers, Inc. enters into a four-year equipment lease with annual payments of $700 per year. The lease payments are due at the beginning of each year. The implicit rate of interest is 5% and is known to Baxter. Baxter pays $250 in initial direct costs. The measurement of the lease liability and right of use asset are:

a. $2,482 and $2,782, respectively
b. $2,482 and $2,232, respectively
c. $2,606 and $2,856, respectively
d. $2,606 and $2,356, respectively

❸ **MC18-2.** Zhou Systems signed a 5-year lease at the beginning of the current year. The leased equipment is from standard dealer stock and has an economic life of 8 years and a fair value of $21,500. Under the terms of the lease, Zhou is required to pay $4,500 at the beginning of each year. There is no purchase option and Zhou must return the equipment at the end of the lease term. The lessor does anticipate there will be a positive residual value but it is unguaranteed. Zhou knows the lessor's implicit rate is 6%. The proper classification of this lease for the lessee is:

a. Operating lease b. Finance lease c. Direct financing lease d. Sales-type lease

❸Ⓐ **MC18-3.** Insight Corporation leases equipment for 5 years with annual rentals of $2,000 per year. The agreement also requires that Insight purchase supplies such as oil, fasteners, and filters directly from the lessor and must spend a minimum of $350 per year over the lease term. The total lease payments used to classify the lease are:

a. $11,750 b. $10,350 c. $10,000 d. $1,750

❸❺Ⓐ **MC18-4.** Lowe Leasing Company recently leased machinery to Amina Associates. The 8-year lease contract requires rental payments of $11,000 at the beginning of each year. The lease meets at least one of the Group I criteria. The 4% implicit rate on the lease is known to Amina Associates. There is a $3,000 guaranteed residual value by the lessee, which is equal to the expected residual value at the end of the lease term. The present value of the minimum lease payments for the lessor are equal to:

a. $98,029 b. $79,215 c. $77,023 d. $56,016

❸ **MC18-5.** You are given the following information for a 4-year lease, with $65,000 payments due at the beginning of each year. The fair value of the underlying asset is $250,000 and the deferred initial indirect costs of the lessor amounted to $15,592. The lessor's estimated residual value in the underlying asset is $50,000. The implicit rate in the lease is equal to:

a. 5.89% b. 8.33% c. 8.85% d. 12.77%

❹ **MC18-6.** DC Products, Inc. leases several copy machines from Avenue Office Services. Under the terms of the agreement, DC will pay rentals of $1,000 per month for an eight-month period. The journal entry made each month is:

a. No entry is required under the short-term policy election.

b. Rent Expense	1,000	
Cash		1,000
c. Rent Expense	8,000	
Cash		8,000
d. Prepaid rent	8,000	
Cash		8,000

❹ **MC18-7.** **Frankel Forges**, Inc., an IFRS reporter, leases a high-capacity forge from Bleake Metal Works Company for total lease payments of $4,200, which is the fair value of the asset. Under the terms of the agreement, Frankel will make equal payments over the 42-month rental period. The journal entry made each month by Frankel is:

a. Rent Expense	100	
Cash		100
b. Rent Expense	4,200	
Cash		4,200
c. Prepaid rent	4,200	
Cash		4,200
d. Leased Asset	100	
Cash		100

❷ **MC18-8.** Bischoff Enterprises leases office space from Kally-Mack Properties for a term of 30 years. The office space that is available will permit the use of existing office equipment and computer equipment. In addition, Kally-Mack will deliver all maintenance services for all items of equipment, including the maintenance of the building (elevator service, window cleaning, and copy machine repairs). The maintenance is included in the annual lease payments. The lease components in this agreement are:

a. Office space
b. Office space and all equipment (office and computer)
c. Office space, office equipment and computer equipment
d. Office space, office equipment, computer equipment and maintenance.

Brief Exercises

❷ **BE18-1.** **Identifying Lease and Nonlease Components.** Deane Company leases office space from Blossom Building Associates for a term of 20 years in order to expand its operations into the southern region of the state. The office space includes the use of office equipment and computer equipment. In addition, Blossom will provide maintenance of all items of equipment included in the agreement and basic repairs and maintenance of the office as needed (e.g., air conditioning, cleaning services, and elevator repairs). The maintenance is included in the annual lease payments. How many lease components are included in the contract and specifically, what are they?

❸ **BE18-2.** **Classification as Finance or Operating Lease, Lessee.** Scott Manufacturing is considering a lease to acquire new equipment. The useful life of the asset is 10 years. Scott can lease the equipment from New City Bank for $1,000 per year over an 8-year period. The lease does not contain a purchase option. There is no transfer of ownership clause in the contract. Should Scott account for this lease as an operating or a finance lease?

❸ **BE18-3.** **Classification as Finance or Operating Lease, Lessee.** Dial Digital Solutions signed a 3-year lease at the beginning of the current year. The leased equipment has an economic life of 5 years and a fair value of $1,450. Under the terms of the lease, Dial is required to pay $500 on January 1 of each year. There is no purchase option, and Dial must return the equipment at the end of the lease term. Dial does not know the lessor's implicit rate but recently borrowed at 5% under a 3-year loan agreement. Should Dial account for this lease as an operating or a finance lease?

❸ **BE18-4.** **Classification as Finance or Operating Lease, Lessee, Discount Rate.** Using the information provided in BE18-3, determine whether this lease is a finance or an operating lease if Dial Digital knows that the lessor's implicit rate is 6%.

❸ **BE18-5.** **Classification as Finance or Operating Lease, Lessee.** Iman Iron Works signed a lease on January 1 with Borko Bank for an iron-stamping machine. The equipment is not specialized in nature. The lease has a 12-year term with no purchase option or transfer of ownership. Under the terms of the contract, Iman must pay $3,500 on January 1 of each year. Borko Bank's implicit rate is 12%. The iron-stamping machine has an economic life of 25 years and a fair value of $35,000. If Iman borrowed at Borko Bank, the loan would carry an interest rate of 14%. The lessee knows the implicit rate. Is this contract an operating or a finance lease for the lessee?

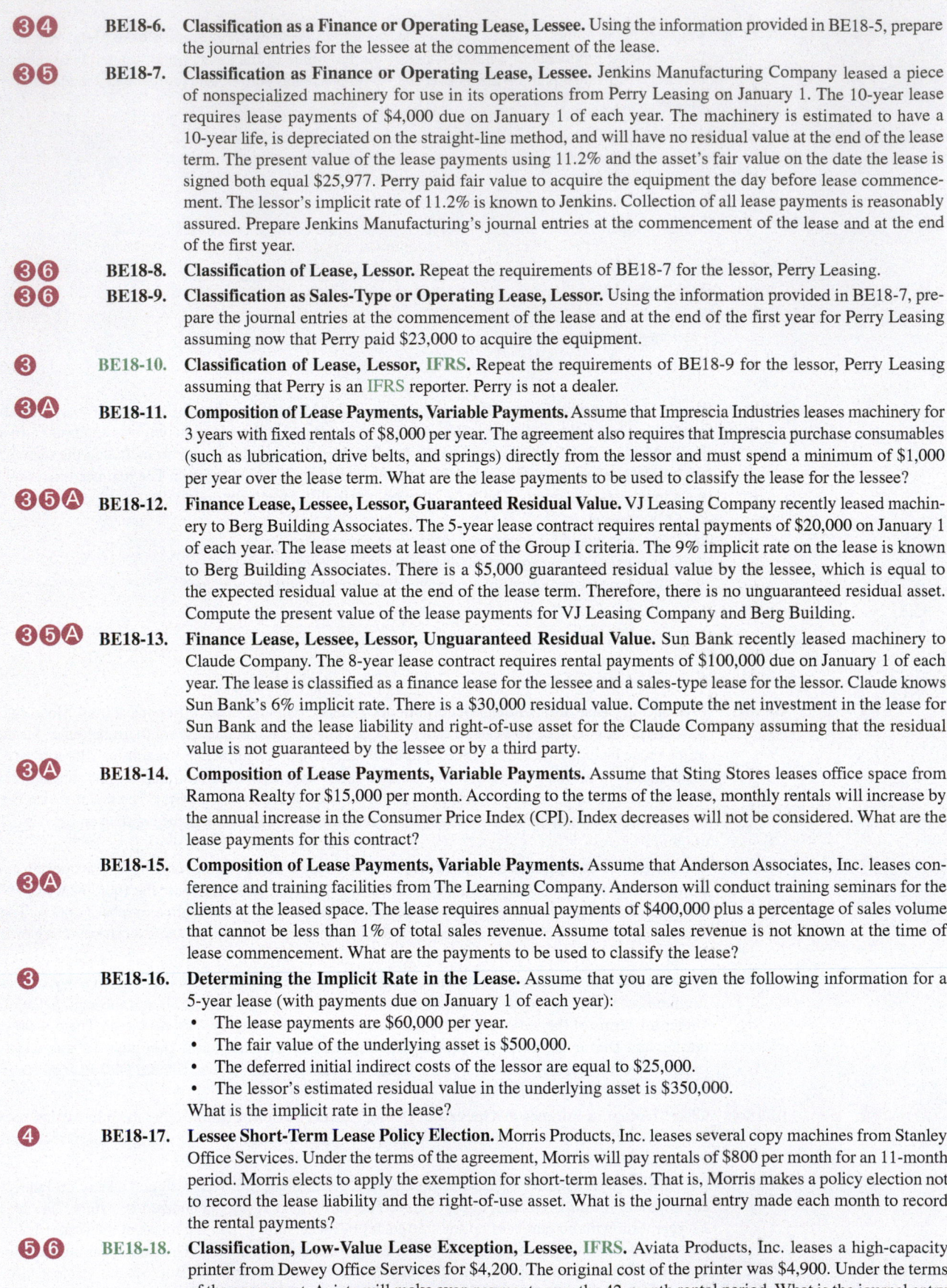

3 4 **BE18-6. Classification as a Finance or Operating Lease, Lessee.** Using the information provided in BE18-5, prepare the journal entries for the lessee at the commencement of the lease.

3 5 **BE18-7. Classification as Finance or Operating Lease, Lessee.** Jenkins Manufacturing Company leased a piece of nonspecialized machinery for use in its operations from Perry Leasing on January 1. The 10-year lease requires lease payments of $4,000 due on January 1 of each year. The machinery is estimated to have a 10-year life, is depreciated on the straight-line method, and will have no residual value at the end of the lease term. The present value of the lease payments using 11.2% and the asset's fair value on the date the lease is signed both equal $25,977. Perry paid fair value to acquire the equipment the day before lease commencement. The lessor's implicit rate of 11.2% is known to Jenkins. Collection of all lease payments is reasonably assured. Prepare Jenkins Manufacturing's journal entries at the commencement of the lease and at the end of the first year.

3 6 **BE18-8. Classification of Lease, Lessor.** Repeat the requirements of BE18-7 for the lessor, Perry Leasing.

3 6 **BE18-9. Classification as Sales-Type or Operating Lease, Lessor.** Using the information provided in BE18-7, prepare the journal entries at the commencement of the lease and at the end of the first year for Perry Leasing assuming now that Perry paid $23,000 to acquire the equipment.

3 **BE18-10. Classification of Lease, Lessor, IFRS.** Repeat the requirements of BE18-9 for the lessor, Perry Leasing assuming that Perry is an IFRS reporter. Perry is not a dealer.

3 A **BE18-11. Composition of Lease Payments, Variable Payments.** Assume that Imprescia Industries leases machinery for 3 years with fixed rentals of $8,000 per year. The agreement also requires that Imprescia purchase consumables (such as lubrication, drive belts, and springs) directly from the lessor and must spend a minimum of $1,000 per year over the lease term. What are the lease payments to be used to classify the lease for the lessee?

3 5 A **BE18-12. Finance Lease, Lessee, Lessor, Guaranteed Residual Value.** VJ Leasing Company recently leased machinery to Berg Building Associates. The 5-year lease contract requires rental payments of $20,000 on January 1 of each year. The lease meets at least one of the Group I criteria. The 9% implicit rate on the lease is known to Berg Building Associates. There is a $5,000 guaranteed residual value by the lessee, which is equal to the expected residual value at the end of the lease term. Therefore, there is no unguaranteed residual asset. Compute the present value of the lease payments for VJ Leasing Company and Berg Building.

3 5 A **BE18-13. Finance Lease, Lessee, Lessor, Unguaranteed Residual Value.** Sun Bank recently leased machinery to Claude Company. The 8-year lease contract requires rental payments of $100,000 due on January 1 of each year. The lease is classified as a finance lease for the lessee and a sales-type lease for the lessor. Claude knows Sun Bank's 6% implicit rate. There is a $30,000 residual value. Compute the net investment in the lease for Sun Bank and the lease liability and right-of-use asset for the Claude Company assuming that the residual value is not guaranteed by the lessee or by a third party.

3 A **BE18-14. Composition of Lease Payments, Variable Payments.** Assume that Sting Stores leases office space from Ramona Realty for $15,000 per month. According to the terms of the lease, monthly rentals will increase by the annual increase in the Consumer Price Index (CPI). Index decreases will not be considered. What are the lease payments for this contract?

3 A **BE18-15. Composition of Lease Payments, Variable Payments.** Assume that Anderson Associates, Inc. leases conference and training facilities from The Learning Company. Anderson will conduct training seminars for the clients at the leased space. The lease requires annual payments of $400,000 plus a percentage of sales volume that cannot be less than 1% of total sales revenue. Assume total sales revenue is not known at the time of lease commencement. What are the payments to be used to classify the lease?

3 **BE18-16. Determining the Implicit Rate in the Lease.** Assume that you are given the following information for a 5-year lease (with payments due on January 1 of each year):

- The lease payments are $60,000 per year.
- The fair value of the underlying asset is $500,000.
- The deferred initial indirect costs of the lessor are equal to $25,000.
- The lessor's estimated residual value in the underlying asset is $350,000.

What is the implicit rate in the lease?

4 **BE18-17. Lessee Short-Term Lease Policy Election.** Morris Products, Inc. leases several copy machines from Stanley Office Services. Under the terms of the agreement, Morris will pay rentals of $800 per month for an 11-month period. Morris elects to apply the exemption for short-term leases. That is, Morris makes a policy election not to record the lease liability and the right-of-use asset. What is the journal entry made each month to record the rental payments?

5 6 **BE18-18. Classification, Low-Value Lease Exception, Lessee, IFRS.** Aviata Products, Inc. leases a high-capacity printer from Dewey Office Services for $4,200. The original cost of the printer was $4,900. Under the terms of the agreement, Aviata will make even payments over the 42-month rental period. What is the journal entry made each month if Aviata elects to use the low-value lease exception to record the rental payments?

Exercises

❷Ⓐ **E18-1. Allocation of Total Payments to Lease and Nonlease Components and Variable Consideration.** SouthSide Services leases several computer servers from Sharpe Computing Company. The lease agreement includes consulting and training updates. The standalone prices charged by Sharpe for each separate component are $850,000 for the servers and $150,000 for the consulting and training. The lease is for 5 years with fixed payments of $300,000 per year. There are also variable payments required amounting to $7,000 per year on average based on the metered usage of the servers. There is no minimum charge included in the contract.

Required »

Assuming that SouthSide allocates consideration based on relative standalone selling prices, determine the allocation of the total consideration to the computer servers and the consulting and training updates.

❷Ⓐ **E18-2. Allocation of Total Payments to Lease and Nonlease Components and Variable Consideration.** Using the same facts as included in E18-1, now assume that the variable payments cannot be less than $2,000 per year.

Required »

Assuming that SouthSide allocates consideration based on relative standalone selling prices, determine the allocation of the total consideration to the computer servers and the consulting.

❷❸❹ **E18-3. Operating Lease, Nonlease Components, Lessee.** BabyClothing (BC) Enterprises leases digital imaging equipment from Sally Systems Leasing. The lease term is for 3 years and the economic life of the equipment is 5 years. The lease contract does not contain a purchase option and title will not be transferred at the end of the lease term. The fair value of the equipment is $5,500 and there is no guaranteed residual value. Sally Systems does not offer any incentives to the lessee to enter the lease. BC paid $550 in initial direct costs on the lease commencement date. BC's incremental borrowing rate is 4% and is used to measure the present value because the lessor's implicit rate is not readily determinable. The annual lease payments (due on January 1 of each year) are $990, which includes technological consulting over the lease term. The digital imaging equipment is typically leased for $900 per year and the consulting is provided at a price of $450 per year. BC has not made the election to account for each separate lease component along with nonlease components as a single lease component. As a result, the components must be separated.

Required »

a. Classify the lease for BC Enterprises.
b. Prepare the journal entries for the lessee and supporting amortization tables to account for this agreement over the lease term.
Hint: To record amounts that would be shown as "interest expense" on the amortization schedule, use the account name "Accrued Lease Payable".

❷❸❹Ⓐ **E18-4. Operating Lease, Rate or Index, Effect of Variable Lease Payments, Lessee.** Caye Comfort, Inc. manufactures a complete line of beds, cots, and futons. Caye Comfort leases a spring fabricating machine from Stein Spring Company for 3 years with no renewal or purchase options. The equipment has a fair value of $10,000 and title will be retained by the lessor at the end of the lease term. The economic life of the equipment is 6 years. The implicit rate in the lease is 5%. The lessee pays all maintenance to a third party, and there are no initial direct costs.

There are no incentives offered by the lessor. The first annual payment is $1,300 (due January 1, Year 1), and the payment increases each year by an amount equal to $1,300 multiplied by the Producers Price Index (PPI). The PPI on the lease commencement date is 1.00 and is forecast to increase by 4% each year. The increases in the payments will be at least 4% per year. The remaining lease payments are due on December 31, Year 1 and December 31, Year 2.

Required »

a. Determine the proper classification of the lease for the lessee.
b. Prepare the journal entries and supporting amortization tables to account for this agreement for the lessee over the lease term.

❷❸❺ **E18-5. Classification as Finance or Operating Lease, Lessee, Journal Entries, Nonlease Components.** On January 1, 2019, Holt National Bank (HNB) acquired a fleet of trucks to be leased to J Rivers Company. HNB paid $105,000 to acquire the vehicles, which is also the fair value of the fleet. The lease terms follow.

- Annual rental payments of $36,272 are due on January 1 of each year.
- Lease term is 3 years.
- There is no residual value and no purchase option.
- The economic life of the asset is 3 years.
- The lessee's incremental borrowing rate is 5%; the lessor's implicit rate is not known to J Rivers Company.

- Included in the rental payments are annual sales taxes and maintenance. Annual sales taxes equal $500 paid to the lessor on January 1 of the year and represent a lease component. Annual maintenance is $800 and is paid to the lessor at the beginning of the year. The maintenance is a nonlease component, and the lessee elected not to allocate the consideration to the lease and nonlease components due to immateriality. The lessee has elected to account for each separate lease and nonlease component as a single component.
- HNB has no material uncertainties regarding future costs to be incurred under the lease, and collectability is reasonably assured. J Rivers depreciates similar vehicles that it owns using the straight-line method.

Required »

a. Classify the lease as either a finance lease or an operating lease for J Rivers Company, the lessee.
b. Prepare the journal entries for the first year of the lease for J Rivers Company, the lessee.

2 3 5 **E18-6. Classification as Finance or Operating Lease, Lessee, Journal Entries, Nonlease Components.** Fontana Company enters into a lease agreement on January 1, 2017, for nonspecialized equipment leased by Mindbender Insurance Company. The following data are relevant to the lease agreement:

- The term of the lease is 4 years with no renewal or purchase options. Annual lease payments of $148,000 are due on January 1 of each year and include all applicable taxes.
- The fair value of the equipment on January 1, 2017, and the cost to Mindbender is $450,000. The equipment has an economic life of 4 years with no salvage value.
- Fontana depreciates similar machinery that it owns using the straight-line method.
- The lessee payments to the lessor include a charge for maintenance. The lessor sells a similar maintenance agreement for $25,000 when purchased without a lease contract. The machinery is leased for $150,000 per year, including taxes, when lessees do not accept the maintenance contract.
- Fontana's incremental borrowing rate is 10% per year. The lessee does not know the implicit rate used in the lease computations.
- Mindbender indicates that collection from Fontana is reasonably certain.
- Fontana does not make a policy election not to separate the lease and nonlease components.

Required »

a. Indicate the type of lease Fontana Company has entered into and what accounting treatment is applicable. Round percentages to the two decimal places.
b. Prepare an amortization schedule for the entire lease term.
c. Prepare the journal entries on Fontana's books that relate to the lease agreement for the first year of the lease term.

3 4 **E18-7. Classification as Finance or Operating Lease, Lessee, Journal Entries, Amortization Tables, Unguaranteed Residual Asset, Annuity Due.** On January 1, Gump Sales Company entered into an agreement to lease a piece of machinery for a period of 5 years from Smokey Boy Equipment (SBE). The machine is not specialized for Gump's business needs, has a sales price of $70,000, and its useful life is 7 years with no guaranteed residual value. The $15,000 annual rentals are due on January 1 of each year. The lease does not contain a transfer of ownership or a purchase option. Assume that there are no initial direct costs associated with this lease. There are also no nonlease components. SBE's implicit rate is not known to Gump whose incremental borrowing rate is 13%. The carrying value of the equipment to SBE is $70,000, its fair value. Assume that collectability of all lease payments is reasonably assured. Gump's fiscal year ends on December 31.

Required »

a. Determine the lease classification for Gump Sales.
b. Prepare the journal entries over Years 1–3 for Gump Sales based on your answer to part (a).
   Hint: To record amounts that would be shown as "interest expense" on the amortization schedule, use the account name "Accrued Lease Payable".
c. Include an amortization table for the lease liability and right-of-use asset.

3 6 7 **E18-8. Classification as Finance or Operating Lease, Lessor, Journal Entries, Guaranteed Residual Value.** Using the same information presented in E18-7, complete the following requirements:

Required »

a. Prepare the entries for the lessor, SBE, for the first year of the lease. Determine the implicit rate.
b. Would the accounting for the lessor change if a third party guarantees a residual value of $20,000 and collection of this amount is probable?
c. Prepare the amortization tables needed (if any) to account for the lease using the part (b) assumptions.

❸❹❺ **E18-9. Initial Measurement of the Lease Liability and the Right-of-Use Asset.** Assume that Bergamini Builders leases medical equipment from Saint Martin's Machine Company. The lease term is for 7 years, and Bergamini must pay seven annual rentals of $40,000 beginning on January 1, 2019, of the current year and every January 1 afterward. The implicit rate in the lease is 3.5%. Bergamini prepaid Saint Martin's Machine Company the first payment of $40,000 on December 31, 2018 (the date the lease is executed, which is prior to the lease commencement date). Bergamini received $15,000 from Saint Martin's Machine Company on the commencement date as an incentive to enter the lease agreement. Bergamini incurred initial direct costs of $5,000 that were originally recorded as prepaid initial direct costs on December 31, 2018. The equipment has no residual value.

Required »

a. Determine the lessee's initial measurement of the lease liability and the right-of-use asset. Note that the initial measurement is the same for both operating and finance leases.
b. Prepare all journal entries necessary in order for Bergamini to record the transactions described in the facts provided.

❸❺ **E18-10. Classification as Finance or Operating Lease, Lessee, Journal Entries.** On January 1, 2018, Temple Leasing Company (TLC) acquired a fleet of stock vehicles to be leased to Delaware River Company. TLC paid $275,000 to acquire the vehicles, which is also the fair value of the fleet. The lease terms follow.

- Annual rental payments of $57,900 are due on January 1 of each year, beginning on January 1, 2018. The lease agreement does not include any nonlease components.
- The lease term is 5 years.
- There is no residual value and no purchase option.
- The economic life of the asset is 5 years.
- The lessee's incremental borrowing rate is 5% and the lessee does not know the lessor's implicit rate.

TLC indicates that collectability of all lease payments is reasonably assured. Delaware Rivers depreciates similar vehicles that it owns using the straight-line method.

Required »

a. Classify the lease as either a finance lease or an operating lease for Delaware River Company, the lessee.
b. Prepare the journal entries at lease commencement and the first lease payment for the lessee.
c. Prepare an amortization table for the lease.
d. Prepare the journal entries at the end of the first year and for the second lease payment for Delaware River Company, the lessee.

❸❺ **E18-11. Classification as Finance or Operating Lease, Lessee, Journal Entries.** On January 1, 2018, Lima Leasing Company (LLC) acquired an airplane to be leased to LA Sky Company. LLC paid $950,000 to acquire the plane, which is also its fair value. The lease terms follow.

- Annual rental payments of $190,000 are due January 1 of each year, beginning on January 1, 2018. There are no nonlease payments.
- The lease term is 6 years.
- There is neither a residual value or a purchase option.
- The economic life of the asset is 8 years, and the airplane is not specialized in nature.
- The lessee's incremental borrowing rate is 8%, and the lessee does not know the lessor's implicit rate.

LLC indicates that collectability of lease payments is reasonably assured. LA Sky depreciates similar vehicles it owns using the straight-line method.

Required »

a. Classify the lease as either a finance lease or an operating lease for LA Sky Company, the lessee.
b. Prepare the journal entries at lease commencement and the first lease payment for the lessee.
c. Prepare an amortization table for the lease.
d. Prepare the journal entries at the end of the first year and for the second lease payment for LA Sky Company, the lessee.

❸❺ **E18-12. Classification as Finance or Operating Lease, Lessee, Journal Entries, Discount Rates, Lease Inception in Middle of Year.** Vanity Jewelers Incorporated signed a lease agreement on July 1, 2020, to lease diamond-polishing equipment from Whitehead Industries. The following information is relevant to the lease agreement.

- The term of the lease is 7 years with no renewal option. Payments of $45,500 are due on July 1 of each year (at the beginning of each period).
- The fair value of the equipment at July 1, 2020, is $300,000. The equipment has an economic life of 10 years.

- Vanity Jewelers depreciates similar equipment that it owns using the straight-line method over the economic life of the property.
- Vanity Jeweler's incremental borrowing rate is 5%. Whitehead's implicit rate on the lease is not known to Vanity Jewelers.
- There are no nonlease components related to this lease.

Required »

a. Determine the type of lease that Vanity Jewelers, the lessee, should record on its books.
b. Prepare all journal entries necessary on the books of Vanity Jewelers for 2020 and 2021. Vanity Jewelers has a December 31 year-end.

3 4 5 **E18-13. Classification as Finance or Operating Lease, Lessee, Sales-Type Lease, Journal Entries, Annuity Due.** Seal Container Corporation (SCC) signed a lease agreement on January 1, 2018, to lease new forklift equipment. The terms of the lease follow.

- The lease has a term of 10 years. There are no purchase or renewal options.
- SCC makes the annual lease payments of $70,000 on January 1 of each year, beginning on January 1, 2018.
- The fair value of the equipment at the commencement of the lease is $567,548.
- The equipment has an economic life of 15 years.
- The lease terms do not include a guaranteed residual value clause.
- The cost of the equipment to the lessor, Cirella Manufacturing Company, is $500,000.
- SCC depreciates the forklifts that it currently owns on a straight-line basis over the economic life of the property.
- SCC's incremental borrowing rate is 5%, and the lessor's implicit rate in the lease is not known to SCC.
- The lessee paid $7,452 in initial direct costs related to this lease on the lease commencement date.
- The lessor is reasonably certain as to collection of the lease payments.

Required »

a. Classify this lease as operating or finance for the lessee.
b. Prepare an amortization table for the lessee from 2018 through 2020 using the effective interest rate method of amortization.
c. Prepare all of SCC's journal entries for the first full year of the lease.
d. Prepare the journal entries and the lease amortization schedule required for SCC in the first year of the lease if it classifies the lease as an operating lease.
   Hint: To record amounts that would be shown as "interest expense" on the amortization schedule, use the account name "Accrued Lease Payable".

3 5 **E18-14. Finance Lease, Purchase Option, Lessee, Amortization Schedules, Journal Entries.** Carrie-Ann Fashions, Inc. entered into a 5-year lease with Reese Rentals to occupy an office building. The economic life of the building is 30 years. The building had a fair value of $8,500,000 and Carrie-Ann has an option to purchase the building at the end of the lease term for $5,500,000, which is expected to be considerably below fair value at lease termination. The annual lease payments are $842,500 and are due on January 1 with the first one due at lease commencement on January 1, 2019. The implicit rate in the lease is 6% and is known by Carrie-Ann. There is no guaranteed residual value specified. The lessor did not offer any incentives to sign the lease. Carrie-Ann did not incur any initial indirect costs. The lease commencement date is January 1. All payments are due on January 1.

Required »

a. Classify this lease for Carrie-Ann Fashions (the lessee).
b. Prepare the journal entries necessary to record this transaction on the lease commencement date.
c. Prepare the lease amortization schedule and prepare the journal entries for the first year.

3 5 6 **E18-15. Classification as Finance or Operating Lease, Lessee, Lessor, Journal Entries, Sales-Type Lease, Discount Rates, Annuity Due, Nonlease Components.** On January 1, 2019, Kane Kite Company leased a nonspecialized fabric-cutting machine from Stewart Standard, Inc. Under the terms of the lease, Kane Kite must pay $200,000 on January 1 of each year, starting in 2019, over a 9-year term. The lease terms do not contain a transfer of ownership, and there is no purchase option. There is also no residual value specified in the contract. The cutting machine has a useful life of 9 years and Kane Kite depreciates similar equipment that it owns using the straight-line method. Kane Kite's incremental borrowing rate is 9%, and the implicit rate of 8% in the lease is known to Kane Kite. The machine cost Stewart Standard $1,300,000 to manufacture, and it has a selling price of $1,349,328. Stewart indicates that collection of the annual lease payments is reasonably certain. Kane is required to pay $5,600 at the end of each year for maintenance to independent third parties, which it records as general and administrative expenses. Neither party to the lease incurs initial indirect costs.

Required »

a. What type of lease is this for both the lessee and lessor?
b. Prepare the lease amortization table for the lease term.
c. Prepare the journal entries necessary for Stewart Standard on January 1, 2019, and on December 31, 2019.
d. Prepare the journal entries necessary for Kane Kite Company on January 1, 2019, and on December 31, 2019.

3 5 6 **E18-16. Classification as Finance or Operating Lease, Lessor, Journal Entries, Discount Rates, Annuity Due, Nonlease Components, IFRS.** Using the information provided in E18-15, assume now that Stewart Standard and Kane Kite are IFRS reporters.

Required »

a. Determine the lessor's classification of the lease.
b. Measure the right-of-use asset and the lease liability at January 1, 2019 and prepare the lessee's amortization table.
c. Prepare the journal entries for Stewart Standard for 2019.

3 5 6 **E18-17. Classification as Finance or Operating Lease, Lessee, Lessor, Lessee Journal Entries, Lease Commencement in the Middle of Year, Annuity Due.** Mr. Kay Food Mart Inc., as lessee, enters into a lease agreement on July 1, 2018, to lease nonspecialized mobile refrigeration equipment from Pollet Products. The cost of the equipment to Pollet is $180,000. The following information is relevant to the lease agreement.

- The term of the lease is 5 years with no renewal options and there is no transfer of title. Payments of $44,880 are due beginning on July 1, 2018, and every July 1 thereafter.
- The fair value of the equipment at July 1, 2018, is $196,898. The equipment has an economic life of 5 years with no residual value.
- Mr. Kay Food Mart depreciates similar equipment that it owns on the straight-line basis over the economic life of the property.
- Mr. Kay Food Mart's incremental borrowing rate is 8%, and the lessor's implicit rate in the lease is not known.
- There are no nonlease components related to this lease.
- Collectability of all lease payments is reasonably assured.

Required »

a. Determine the type of lease that Mr. Kay Food Mart, the lessee, should record on its books.
b. Prepare all journal entries necessary on the books of Mr. Kay Food Mart for 2018 and 2019. Mr. Kay's year-end is December 31.
c. How should Pollet Products classify this lease contract?

3 4 **E18-18. Operating Lease, Lessor.** True Image Copier Company leases a multifunction copier to Fabach Incorporated. The lease term is 4 years with no renewal options; the economic life of the copier is 7 years. The fair value of the copier is $14,000, and True Image Company's equipment carrying value is also $14,000. The residual value expected at the end of the lease term is $5,000 and is not guaranteed. There are no lease incentives and no initial direct costs paid by either party to the lease. Fabach can acquire title to the copier by paying fair value at the end of the lease term. The lease calls for monthly payments of $200 due on the first day of each month. Fabach pays for maintenance to an independent third party. The implicit rate in the lease is 5%. There is no transfer of ownership at the end of the lease term.

Required »

a. Classify the lease for True Image Copier Company.
b. Provide the journal entries required over the lease term assuming that True Image prepares financial statements monthly. Provide all supporting computations.

3 4 **E18-19. Operating Lease, Lessee, Amortization Schedules, Journal Entries.** Cardillo Capital enters into a lease agreement with Vincent Motors to lease a delivery van with a fair value of $55,000 under a 36-month (3-year) lease. The van has an estimated useful life of 8 years. No initial direct costs are incurred by the lessor. Cardillo has an option to purchase the van at the end of the lease for its fair value. Monthly payments are $775 per month (payable on the first day of each month) with no cash down at inception, and there are no lease incentives. Cardillo does not know the rate implicit in the lease and will use its annual incremental borrowing rate of 5%. There is no transfer of title. Cardillo does not guarantee a residual value at the end of the lease term and pays all insurance and maintenance independently of the lease contract to a third party. Any sales tax charged is included in the lease payments. Cardillo paid $900 in initial direct costs on the lease commencement date. Cardillo has a fiscal year end of December 31, and prepares monthly financial statements. The lease starts on January 1.

ment date. Cardillo has a fiscal year end of December 31, and prepares monthly financial statements. The lease starts on January 1.

Required »

a. Classify the lease for Cardillo Capital.
b. Determine the initial measurement of the lease liability and right-of-use asset.
c. Prepare the partial amortization schedules needed to amortize the lease debt and the right-of-use asset for the first 3 months of the lease agreement.
d. Prepare the journal entries for the first 3 months of the lease.
Hint: To record amounts that would be shown as "interest expense" on the amortization schedule, use the account name "Accrued Lease Payable".

3 4 **E18-20. Operating Lease, No Lessee Guaranteed Residual Value, Lessee.** Beachmont Restaurants, Inc. enters into a lease for standard stoves and grills. The lease term is 3 years with no renewal or purchase options. There is no residual value guarantee, and the lease terms do not provide for a transfer of title. The economic life of the asset is 10 years. According to the terms of the lease contract, Beachmont is required to pay rentals of $700 for the first year with payments increasing by 15% per year for Years 2 and 3. All lease payments are made on January 1. The implicit rate in the lease is 6%. The fair value of the asset is $9,000. Beachmont knows the lessor's implicit rate. Beachmont's fiscal year ends on December 31.

Required »

a. Determine the classification of the lease for the lessee.
b. Measure the right-of-use asset and the lease liability and prepare the lessee's amortization tables.
c. Prepare the journal entries over the lease term.
Hint: To record amounts that would be shown as "interest expense" on the amortization schedule, use the account name "Accrued Lease Payable".

3 5 **E18-21. Finance Lease with a Lessee Guaranteed Residual Value.** Using the information provided in E18-20, assume now that Beachmont provides a guarantee of the residual value of $7,000 that will cover any unrecovered fair value by the lessor.

Required »

a. Determine the classification of the lease for the lessee.
b. Measure the right-of-use asset and the lease liability and prepare the lessee's amortization table.
c. Prepare the journal entries over the lease term. Assume the leased asset has a fair value of $7,000 at the end of the lease term.

3 4 7 **E18-22. Classification as Finance or Operating Lease, Lessee, Lessor, Journal Entries, Direct Financing Lease, Annuity Due, Lessee Initial Direct Costs, Third-Party Guaranteed Residual Value.** Plash Photo Company leased a digital reproduction machine on January 1, 2019. The following information was obtained from the lease contract:

- The lease carries a term of 5 years. There is no renewal option and there is no transfer of ownership.
- The rental payments of $120,000 per year are due each January 1 with the first payment due at lease commencement.
- The fair value of the equipment on the date the lease is signed is $650,000. The equipment has an economic life of 8 years. The lessor paid fair value to acquire the asset. On January 1, 2019, the carrying value is $650,000.
- There is a guaranteed residual value of $100,000 provided by a third party. This guaranteed residual value is equal to the expected residual value so that there is no unguaranteed residual asset expected at the end of the lease term.
- Plash Photo depreciates similar machinery that it owns on a straight-line basis.
- The lessee pays initial direct costs of $10,000 at the lease commencement date.
- Plash Photo's incremental borrowing rate is 10% per year. Plash does not know the lessor's implicit rate.
- The lessor is reasonably certain regarding the collection of the lease payments, and it is probable that the lessor will collect the lease payments plus any amount necessary to satisfy a residual value guarantee.

Required »

a. Classify the lease for both the lessor and the lessee. Find the lessor's implicit rate.
b. Prepare the journal entries for Plash Photo (the lessee) for the first year of the lease (i.e., January 1 and December 31).
Hint: To record amounts that would be shown as "interest expense" on the amortization schedule, use the account name "Accrued Lease Payable".
c. Prepare the journal entries for the lessor for the first year of the lease (i.e., January 1 and December 31).

Problems

❷❸❺❻Ⓐ **P18-1. Classification as Finance or Operating Lease, Lessor, Journal Entries, Discount Rates, Sales-Type Lease, Annuity Due, Executory Costs, Guaranteed Residual Value.** Locatelli Partners (LP) agreed to lease a piece of heavy equipment to Sonata Company on January 1. LP paid $195,100 to produce the machine and carried it at this amount in its inventory. This machine is routinely produced by LP and is part of its standard stock in inventory. The fair value (current selling price) of the machine is $210,001. The lease terms follow. Annual rental payments of $46,466 are due on January 1 of each year. These rental payments do not include any other lease components.

- Lease term is 7 years.
- There is a purchase option that is reasonably expected to be exercised to acquire the asset at the end of 5 years for $20,000.
- The lessor expects to recover the guaranteed residual value of $30,000 at the termination of the lease. The lessee guarantees the residual value.
- The economic life of the asset is 8 years.
- Sonata Company knows the lessor's implicit rate.
- The lessee's incremental borrowing rate is 12%.
- Annual maintenance is $8,000 and annual training is $9,500. The lessee pays both at the end of the year to an independent third party.
- LP indicates that the collection of the lease payments is reasonably assured and the recovery of the residual value is probable.
- Sonata depreciates (amortizes) similar machinery that it owns using the straight-line method.

Required »

a. Compute the implicit rate.
b. Classify this lease agreement for both the lessor and the lessee.
c. Prepare an amortization table for the lease.
d. Prepare the journal entries for the lessor and the lessee during the first year of the contract.

❸❹❺❻ **P18-2. Classification as Finance or Operating Lease, Lessor, Journal Entries, Discount Rates, Sales-Type Lease, Nonlease Components, Guaranteed Residual Value.** On January 1, 2018, the lease commencement date, Curran Manufacturing Corporation (CMC) agreed to lease a piece of nonspecialized, heavy equipment to Oates Products, Inc. CMC paid $900,000 to manufacture the machine and carries it at this amount in its inventory. The fair value (current selling price) of the machine is $929,049. The relevant lease terms follow.

- Annual rental payments of $240,000 are due on December 31 of each year. However, the first payment is due at the commencement of the lease. The lease payments do not include any other lease components such as insurance or sales taxes.
- Lease term is 4 years.
- There is no purchase option.
- The lessee guarantees a residual value of $60,000 at the termination of the lease. This amount is equal to the expected residual value and there is no unguaranteed residual asset.
- The economic life of the asset is 7 years.
- The lessor's 6% implicit rate is known to Oates Products, Inc.
- The lessee's incremental borrowing rate is 8%.
- Annual maintenance is $10,000 and annual training is $7,700. The lessee pays both at the end of the year to an independent third-party vendor. The lessee classifies these costs as general and administrative expenses.
- CMC indicates that collectability of all lease payments is reasonably assured, and it is probable that the residual value will be fully recovered.
- Oates depreciates (amortizes) similar equipment using the straight-line method.

Required »

a. Determine whether this is an operating or a finance lease for the lessee and an operating, sales-type, or direct financing lease for the lessor.
b. Prepare the amortization table for the entire lease term.
c. Prepare the lessee's journal entries required for each year of the lease term assuming that the equipment is returned with a fair value of $60,000.
d. Prepare the lessor's journal entries required for each year of the lease term assuming that the equipment is returned with a fair value of $60,000.
e. Prepare the December 31, 2021, journal entry for the lessee assuming that the equipment is returned with a fair value of $45,000.
f. Prepare the December 31, 2021, journal entry for the lessor assuming that the equipment is returned with a fair value of $45,000.

❸❺❻ **P18-3. Classification as Finance, Sales-Type, or Operating Lease, Lessee, Lessor, Journal Entries, Unguaranteed Residual Value.**
Florida Energy Restoration, Ltd. (FER) enters into a lease agreement on January 1, 2018, to lease standard power generators from R&R Electric, Inc. The terms of the lease follow.

- The term of the lease is 7 years with no renewal option. The seven annual lease payments of $300,000 will be made on January 1 of each year.
- The fair value of the equipment at January 1, 2018, is $1,700,479. The equipment has an economic life of 10 years with no salvage value expected at that time. The cost of the equipment to the lessor, R&R, is $1,500,000.
- FER depreciates similar equipment that it owns on a straight-line basis over the economic life of the property.
- FER's incremental borrowing rate is 10%, and the lessor's 9% implicit rate on the lease is known to FER.
- There are no nonlease components related to this lease.
- Neither party to the lease pays initial direct costs.
- The lessor indicates that the collection of the lease payments are reasonably certain.
- There is no guaranteed residual value in the lease contract; however, the lessor, R&R, expects the asset to be worth $100,000 at the end of the lease term.

Required »

a. Provide justification for classifying this as a finance lease for the lessee.
b. Prepare a partial amortization table for 2018 through 2020 for the lessee using the effective interest rate method of amortization.
c. Prepare all of FER's journal entries for 2018 and 2019.
d. Prepare the journal entries required for 2018 and 2019 for FER if this were an operating lease.
Hint: To record amounts that would be shown as "interest expense" on the amortization schedule, use the account name "Accrued Lease Payable"
e. What type of lease is this for the lessor? Justify your answer.

❸❺❻ **P18-4. Classification as Finance or Operating Lease, Lessor, Journal Entries, Sales-Type Lease, Annuity Due.** On January 1, 2018, JLOU Company leases a fleet of stock delivery vehicles from Dolt Motors, Inc. Under the terms of the lease, JLOU must pay $65,000 on January 1 of each year, beginning on January 1, 2018, over a 4-year term. The delivery vehicles have a useful life of 4 years. JLOU depreciates similar vehicles that it owns using the straight-line method. JLOU's incremental borrowing rate is 12%, and the 8% implicit rate in the lease is known to the lessee. The vehicles cost Dolt Motors $200,000 and have a fair value of $232,511. Dolt has no uncertainties as to future costs and collection. The lease terms do not contain a transfer of ownership, and there is no purchase option. There is also no residual value specified in the contract because no residual value is expected at the end of the lease term by the lessor. Assume that there are neither initial direct costs nor nonlease components related to the lease agreement.

Required »

a. Classify this lease agreement for both the lessor and the lessee.
b. Prepare the lease amortization table for the entire lease term.
c. Prepare the journal entries necessary for Dolt Motors on January 1, 2018, and on December 31, 2018.
d. Prepare the journal entries necessary for JLOU Company on January 1, 2018, and on December 31, 2018.

❸❺❻Ⓐ **P18-5. Classification as Finance or Operating Lease, Lessor, Journal Entries, Sales-Type Lease, Guaranteed Residual Value.** Using the same information as found in P18-4, assume that the lease contains a guaranteed residual value of $15,000. The lessee guarantees the residual value.

Required »

a. Compute the annual rent payment needed to ensure that the lessor company recovers the fair value of the vehicles.
b. Compute the present value of the lease payments using this new payment (exclude the guaranteed residual value from this part of the problem).
c. Prepare the amortization table required for the entire term. Use the new payment and guaranteed residual value.

❸❺❻Ⓐ **P18-6. Classification as Finance or Operating Lease, Lessor, Journal Entries, Discount Rates, Sales-Type Lease, Executory Costs, Unguaranteed Residual Value.** On January 1, 2018, Moorecraft Finance Company agreed to lease a piece of machinery to Ward Construction Products, Inc. Moorecraft paid $1,554,516 to acquire the machine from the manufacturer and carries it at this amount in its financial statements. The fair value (current selling price) of the machine is $1,554,516. The relevant lease terms follow.

- Annual rental payments are $263,516. The first payment is made on January 1, 2018, and all subsequent payments are due on December 31 of each year starting on December 31, 2018. These payments do not include any executory costs.
- Lease term is 6 years.

- There is no purchase option.
- The lessor expects to recover the unguaranteed residual value of $280,000 at the termination of the lease.
- The economic life of the asset is 7 years.
- The lessor's implicit rate is known to Ward Construction.
- Annual maintenance is $20,000, and annual property tax is $12,500. The first payment is made on January 1, 2018, and all subsequent payments are due on December 31 of each year starting on December 31, 2018. The property taxes are included in the payment made by the lessee to the lessor.
  Hint: The lessor credits maintenance costs payable when receiving the cash from the lessee for the maintenance costs.
- The lessor has no material uncertainties regarding future costs to be incurred under the lease, and collectability of lease payments is reasonably assured.
- Ward depreciates similar machinery that it owns using the straight-line method.
- The fiscal year ends on December 31 for both companies.

Required »

a. Determine the implicit rate.
b. Determine the lease classification for both the lessor and the lessee.
c. Prepare the amortization table for the entire lease term for the lessor.
d. Prepare the amortization table for the entire lease term for the lessee.
e. Prepare the lessee's journal entries required for each year of the lease term assuming that the equipment is returned with a fair value of $280,000.
f. Prepare the lessor's journal entries required for each year of the lease term assuming that the equipment is returned with a fair value of $280,000.

3 5 6 A **P18-7. Classification as Finance or Operating Lease, Lessee, Lessor, Journal Entries, Discount Rates, Sales-Type Lease, Purchase Option.** On May 1, 2018, Gia Equipment Manufacturers (GEM) agreed to lease nonspecialized machinery to Jason Associates. GEM paid $2,000,000 to produce the machine and carries it at this amount in its inventory. The fair value (current selling price) of the machine is $2,104,317. The lease terms follow.

- Annual rental payments of $345,000 are due beginning on May 1, 2018, and every year on May 1.
- The lease term is 8 years.
- There is a purchase option to acquire the asset at the end of 6 years for $700,000. It is reasonably certain that Jason Associates will exercise this purchase option.
- The economic life of the asset is 10 years.
- The lessor's 9% implicit rate is known to Jason Associates.
- The lessee's incremental borrowing rate is 12%.
- Annual maintenance is $20,000, and annual training is $35,000. The lessee pays both December 31 to independent third parties and charges these payments to general and administrative expenses.
- GEM indicates that collection of all lease payments is reasonably assured.
- Jason depreciates similar machinery that it owns using the straight-line method over 10 years. Jason's and GEM's fiscal years end on December 31.

Required »

a. Determine the lease classification for both the lessor and lessee.
b. Prepare the amortization table for the entire lease term.
c. Prepare the journal entries for the lessee during 2018.
d. Prepare the journal entries for the lessor during 2018.

3 6 **P18-8. Sales-Type Lease, Unguaranteed Residual Value, Lessor.** Barisi Equipment Company leases nonspecialized cutting machinery to Bastone, Inc. over a 4-year term. The lease commencement date is January 1, 2019. The first payment is due on January 1, 2019. The remaining payments are due on December 31, 2019, December 31, 2020, and December 31, 2021. The equipment has a fair value of $18,000 and an economic life of 10 years. Barisi carries the underlying asset at a cost of $15,500. The lease has no renewal or purchase options, and title to the underlying asset remains with Barisi at the end of the lease term. The annual lease payments are $4,500 per year with an estimated residual value of $1,200 upon lease termination. The residual value is not guaranteed by the lessee, and a third-party guarantee is not obtained by Barisi. There are no lease incentives offered, and the lessee pays for all maintenance to third parties. There are no initial direct costs.

Required »

a. Determine the implicit rate in the lease.
b. Classify the lease for Barisi Equipment Company.
c. Prepare the journal entries for the lessor over the lease term and provide all supporting computations. The machine has a fair value of $1,200 at lease termination.

3 6 **P18-9. Finance Lease, Purchase Option, Lessor, Amortization Schedules, Journal Entries.** Lori-Ann Fashions, Inc. entered into a 5-year lease with Krishnan Rentals to use equipment. The economic life of the equipment is 30 years. The equipment had a fair value of $8,500,000. Lori-Ann has an option to purchase the equipment at the end of the lease term for $5,500,000, which is likely to be exercised. The annual lease payments are $983,199 and are due on January 1 of each year. The first payment is due on the lease commencement date of January 1, 2019. The implicit rate in the lease is known by Lori-Ann. There is no guaranteed residual value specified. The lessor did not offer any incentives to sign the lease. Lori-Ann did not incur any initial indirect costs. The company's fiscal year ends on December 31. The carrying value of the equipment is $6,500,000.

Required »

a. Compute the implicit rate.
b. Classify this lease for Krishnan Rentals.
c. Prepare the journal entry necessary for Krishnan Rentals to record this transaction on the lease commencement date.
d. Prepare the lease amortization schedule and prepare the journal entries through January 1, 2020, for Krishnan Rentals.

3 5 **P18-10. Finance Lease, Purchase Option, Lessee, Amortization Schedules, Journal Entries.** Use the information from P18-9 to complete the following requirements.

Required »

a. Compute the implicit rate.
b. Classify this lease for Lori-Ann Fashions.
c. Prepare the journal entry necessary for Lori-Ann Fashions to record this transaction on the lease commencement date.
d. Prepare the lease amortization schedule and prepare the journal entries through January 1, 2020, for Lori-Ann Fashions.

3 7 A **P18-11. Direct Financing Lease, Deferred Selling Profit, Lessor, Amortization Schedules, Journal Entries.** Walker Power Washing Services, Inc. leases nonspecialized equipment from McCoy Equipment. The lease term is 3 years with no renewal or purchase options, and title to the underlying asset is retained by the lessor at the end of the lease term. The lease requires annual fixed rental payments of $25,200 per year on July 1 of each year. The first payment occurs on July 1, 2019, at the lease commencement. The fair value of the equipment is $108,000 and had a carrying amount on McCoy's books of $86,400. The equipment has a remaining life of 6 years. The estimated residual value of the equipment is $41,610. The lessee does not guarantee the residual value, but McCoy secured an unrelated third party guarantee of $30,000, and the collection of this guaranteed residual is probable. The rate implicit in the lease is 5%. McCoy's fiscal year ends on December 31.There are no prepaid rentals, and neither party to the agreement pays initial direct costs.

Required »

a. Classify this lease for the lessor, McCoy Equipment.
b. Provide all journal entries for the lessor for 2019 and 2020. Show all supporting computations.

3 7 A **P18-12. Direct Financing Lease, Deferred Selling Profit, Lessor, Amortization Schedules, Journal Entries.** Crabtree Products, Inc. leases machinery to Beane Poll Enterprises. The machinery is not specialized. The lease is for 3 years requiring payments of $22,500 at the beginning of each lease year (April 1). The equipment has a fair value of $82,833 and is carried in Crabtree's inventory at $72,833. The expected residual value for the asset is $25,000. Crabtree obtains a third-party residual value guarantee in the amount of $15,000. Therefore, the unguaranteed residual value is $10,000. Crabtree pays $2,000 in sales commissions related to the lease transaction. This lease is classified as a direct financing lease. Crabtree has a December 31 year-end.

Required »

Prepare the journal entries for the lessor to account for this transaction over the 3-year period, and provide all supporting computations and amortization tables. Assume the machine has a fair value of $0 at the end of the lease.

Excel Project
Autograded Excel Project available in **MyLab Accounting**

CASES

Judgment Cases

Judgment Case 1: Comparison of Lease Classification Rules

The lease rules discussed in this chapter have an effective date for fiscal years beginning after December 15, 2018. Under U.S. GAAP, the classification rules that were effective before that date are a bit different. Specifically, the Group I rules were as follows:

1. The lease transfers ownership of the property to the lessee at the end of the *lease term*.
2. The lease contains a **bargain purchase option**, which allows the lessee to acquire the property at a price specified at the inception of the lease that is substantially lower than the expected fair market value of the property at the date the option can be exercised.
3. The *lease term* is greater than or equal to 75% of the estimated economic life of the property.
4. The present value of the *minimum lease payments* is greater than or equal to 90% of the fair market value of the property at the inception of the lease.

Required »

a. Compare and contrast the old rules to the new rules.
b. Which set of rules require the most judgment?
c. What are the advantages and disadvantages of the old classification rules versus the new classification rules?
d. Which do you prefer? Explain your answer.

Judgment Case 2: Lease Classification

On January 1, 2019, Lessee Company leased a piece of machinery from Lessor Bank. The machinery could also be used by other parties. The 14-year lease requires payments of $250,000 due at the beginning of each year. The lease agreement does not transfer ownership of the machinery nor does it contain a purchase option. Lessor Bank anticipates that the asset will have a residual value at the end of the lease term, but this value is not guaranteed by Lessee or a third party. The machinery has a fair value of $2,628,000 and an estimated life of 19 years. Lessor Bank's implicit rate is 7% and is known by Lessee Company.

Do you think Lessee should classify this as an operating lease or a finance lease? Explain your answer.

Financial Statement Analysis Case

Financial Statement Analysis Case

You are reviewing the financial statements of Trident Incorporated and observed that Trident entered into a significant operating lease for office equipment at the end of the current year. Because of the nature of items leased and the length of the lease, you question the classification of the leases as operating. You are interested in assessing the income statement effect of classifying the lease as an operating versus a finance lease. Trident disclosed the following schedule of its lease payments:

Year	Future Lease Payments
2019	$ 750,000
2020	750,000
2021	750,000
2022	750,000
2023	750,000
Thereafter	3,750,000
Total lease payments	7,500,000
Less imputed interest	2,891,575
Present value of future lease payments	$4,608,425

Given that lease payments in each of the next 5 years total $750,000, you assume that lease payments going forward are also $750,000 per year. To determine the lease term, you divide the total payments of $3,750,000 after 2023 by $750,000 per year to compute an additional 5 years of lease payments after 2023. Therefore, the total lease term is 10 years. You also determine that Trident's discount rate is 10%.

Use Trident's information to determine its expenses in 2019, 2020, and 2021 related to its operating lease. Determine what the lease expense would be if Trident classified the lease as a finance lease. Assume lease payments occur at the end of each year.

Surfing the Standards Cases

Surfing the Standards Case 1: Lease Contracts

Consider each of the following scenarios and determine whether a lease contract exists for each scenario. Support your conclusions with Topic 842 in the Codification and provide appropriate citations to the Codification.

1. Guitar World Company (GWC) sells musical instruments online. It purchases acoustic guitars from several manufacturers in large volume and needs storage space for its distribution system. To secure storage space, GWC enters into an agreement with Safe Storage Inc. to deliver 500 acoustic guitars per month to Safe Storage's primary location, which is the closest location to GWC. GWC can retrieve the guitars from the storage facility whenever it chooses. Safe Storage can move the guitars anywhere within the storage facility or move some of this inventory to a location in another city that it owns. Safe Storage may want to move the inventory if it can obtain a higher rental rate from another customer for the primary location.
2. Guitar World Company (GWC) sells musical instruments online. It purchases acoustic guitars from several manufacturers in large volume and needs storage space for its distribution system. To secure storage space, GWC enters into an agreement with Safe Storage Inc. to deliver 500 acoustic guitars per month to Safe Storage's primary location, which is the closest location to GWC. GWC can retrieve the guitars from the storage facility whenever it chooses. Because GWC has a policy that all of its acoustic guitars must be kept in a facility that maintains humidity at 48%, the agreement between GWC and Safe Storage required the guitars to be stored at 48% humidity. To accommodate this requirement, Safe Storage modified a section in its primary location to maintain the humidity level at 48%.
3. Johnston Power Company (JPC) recently entered into contract with Spin Move Wind Associates (SMWA) to utilize a particular power-generating facility. JPC is seeking to obtain a backup power source and believes that SMWA can provide the electricity when needed. JPC will give SMWA advance notice as to when and how much additional power is needed up to SMWA facility's full capacity. Because SMWA agrees to provide electricity on demand, it runs the risk of having idle capacity during less-than-peak demand periods.
4. Johnston Power Company (JPC) recently entered into contract with Spin Move Wind Associates (SMWA) to utilize a particular power-generating facility. JPC is seeking to obtain a backup power source and believes that SMWA can provide the electricity needed. JPC agrees to buy all of it power from SPWA on a full-time basis.
5. DataCo enters into an agreement with UtilityCo to use 40% of the capacity UtilityCo's fiber optic cable that runs from Chicago to an outlying suburb. This is the only cable that DataCo will use in this area. DataCo makes the decisions about the use of the fibers (in terms of determining what data and how much data will be transported). UtilityCo can substitute cables but only if the original cables become damaged.
6. Farms, Inc. enters into a 10-year agreement with Land Lovers Company to farm 1,000 acres of Land Lovers' land. The exact plot of land is specified in the contract. Farms will likely use the land to grow corn but may rotate to soybean production every few years. Land Lovers included a clause in the contract that allows Land Lovers to specify operating procedures each year around the fertilization of the soil, depending upon annual soil tests.

Surfing the Standards Case 2: Lease Payments

On January 1, 2019 (lease inception date), Tofootles Company leases a piece of equipment from ABC Leasing Company. The lease term is for 4 years with the first payment of $1,000 due on January 1, 2019. The remaining three payments of $1,000 each are due on January 1, 2020, 2021, and 2022.

In addition to the $1,000 base annual payment, the lease contract specifies an annual adjustment that is $50 for every point that the Consumer Price Index is above 250. The CPI on January 1, 2019, was 250. However, the annual adjustment is limited to a 2% increase. The implicit rate (known by the lessee) in the lease is 8%.

Using Topic 842 in the Codification for support as necessary, determine the present value of the lease payments.

Surfing the Standards Case 3: Subsequent Measurement of Operating Leases

In the text, we discussed the practical, step-by-step approach for the subsequent measurement of an operating lease for the lessee. However, that exact approach is not specified by the Codification. Consider the following lease scenario.

Baldwin Brokerage enters into a lease agreement with Hoyt Motors to lease an automobile with a fair value of $45,000 under a 5-year lease on December 20, 2018. The lease commences on January 1, 2019, and Baldwin will return the automobile to Hoyt on December 31, 2023. The automobile has an estimated useful life of 7 years. Baldwin made a lease payment of $5,000 on December 20, 2018. The lease agreement stipulates the following annual payments in addition to the December 20 payment:

Date	Amount
December 31, 2019	$6,000
December 31, 2020	5,000
December 31, 2021	4,000
December 31, 2022	3,000

The implicit rate of the lease is 9% and is known by Baldwin. There are no purchase option, no lease incentives, no residual value guarantees, and no transfer of ownership. Baldwin incurs initial direct costs of $2,000 prior to lease commencement. Determine whether Baldwin should classify the lease as an operating or finance lease. Provide all journal entries to be recorded by Baldwin (the lessee) over the lease term.

Required »

a. Provide the journal entries that would be made over the lease term using the step-by-step approach provided in the text.

b. Research the Codification (Topic 842) and provide an analysis (with citations) as to what the Codification specifies as the approach to subsequent measurement.

c. Reconcile your answer in (a) to the approach specified in Topic 842 in the Codification.

Basis for Conclusions Cases

Basis for Conclusions Case 1: Operating Lease Treatment versus Finance Lease Treatment

The lease rules discussed in this chapter have an effective date for fiscal years beginning after December 15, 2018. Under U.S. GAAP, the accounting treatment of operating leases for the lessee were quite different than these new rules. Under the old rules, lessees did not include an asset or a liability on their balance sheets related to the lease.

Required »

a. Basing your answers on the Basis for Conclusions for ASU 2016-02, *Leases* (and including citations), explain FASB's reasoning behind changing the accounting treatment for lessee's operating leases.

b. Do you think that the right-of-use asset and the lease liability should be included on the lessee's balance sheet in an operating lease? Justify your answer.

Basis for Conclusions Case 2: Measurement of Lease Expense and the Right-of-Use Asset in an Operating Lease

IFRS accounts for all leases in the same way (for the lessee), but U.S. GAAP measures lease-related expenses and the right-of-use asset for operating leases (lessee) differently than for finance leases.

Required »

a. Explain the subsequent measurement differences in operating leases and finance leases (lessee).

b. Explain the FASB's reasoning for requiring different subsequent measurement treatment for operating and finance leases. Base your explanation on the Basis for Conclusions for ASU 2016-02, *Leases*.

c. Explain FASB's reasoning related to whether or not to just report one single lease cost for operating leases. Base your explanation on the Basis for Conclusions for ASU 2016-02, *Leases*.

d. What do you think they should do? Which is better? Justify your answer.

Basis for Conclusions Case 3: Lease Classification

In deliberating on ASU 2016-02, *Leases*, the Board debated several methods for lease classification. What did the Board decide and why? What other methods did they consider and why did they not choose those methods? Provide citations to the Basis for Conclusions of ASU 2016-02.

APPENDIX A

Complexities in Accounting for Lease Transactions (with a Comprehensive Problem)

In the text, we discussed the accounting treatment for basic lease transactions. However, a number of additional considerations often arise, including the accrual of interest on leases, leasehold improvements, executory costs, purchase options, variable lease payments, deferred initial direct costs, and deferred profit.

Accruing Interest on Leases

The prior examples involved transactions in which the lease commencement occurred at the beginning of a year and the subsequent payments occurred at the end of the year. In reality, the company's year-end often occurs between payment dates, requiring the lessee to accrue the interest expense and the lessor to accrue interest revenue as adjusting entries at the end of the year. After making the payment, the lessee removes the interest payable. After receiving the lease payment, the lessor removes interest receivable.

Example 18A.1 illustrates accruing interest on leases.

EXAMPLE 18A.1

Finance Lease: Interest Accrual

PROBLEM: On January 1, 2019, Berg Manufacturing leased a nonspecialized piece of machinery for use in its North American operations from Borko Bank. The lease agreement was signed on January 1, and the equipment was provided to Berg on the same day. The 9-year, noncancellable lease requires annual lease payments of $12,000 beginning January 1, 2019, and at each January 1 thereafter through 2027. The lease agreement does not transfer ownership of the machinery, nor does it contain a purchase option. The machinery has a fair value of $75,000 and an estimated life of 10 years. Borko Bank's implicit rate of 11% is known to Berg. Berg incurs initial direct costs of $3,000 on January 1, 2019, and debited them to Prepaid Initial Direct Costs. Berg's year-end is December 31. Prepare the journal entries for Berg through January 1, 2020.

SOLUTION: We conclude that this is a finance lease because the lease term is 90% (9 years / 10 years) of the economic life. The present value is $73,753.

	N	I/Y	PV	PMT	FV	Excel Formula
Given	9	11.00%		−12,000	0	
Solve For PV			**73,753**			=PV(0.11,9,−12000,0,1)

Thus, Berg records the lease liability at the lease commencement at the present value of the lease payments. Berg records the right-of-use asset at the amount of the lease liability plus the initial direct costs.

Account	***January 1, 2019***	
Right-of-Use Asset	76,753	
Prepaid Initial Direct Costs		3,000
Lease Liability		73,753

We once again use the amortization table prepared in Example 18.11 and repeat the first few payments.

Date Date	Payment (a)	Interest (b) = Prior-Period Balance from (d) × 11%	Reduction in Lease Liability Principal (c) = (a) − (b)	Balance (d) = Prior-Period balance – (c)
Lease Commencement – January 1, 2019				$73,753
January 1, 2019	$12,000	$ 0	$12,000	61,753
January 1, 2020	12,000	6,793	5,207	56,546
January 1, 2021	12,000	6,220	5,780	50,766

Berg allocates the first payment entirely to principal because interest accrues only with the passage of time.

Account	January 1, 2019	
Lease Liability	12,000	
Cash		12,000

The leased asset is subject to amortization. Berg amortizes $8,528 each year ($76,753 right-of-use asset divided by 9-year lease term).

Account	December 31, 2019	
Amortization Expense—Right-of-Use Asset	8,528	
Accumulated Amortization—Right-of-Use Asset		8,528

As shown in the amortization table, Berg allocates the second payment to interest of $6,793 and principal of $5,207. However, because the payment does not occur until January 1, 2020, Berg must accrue the interest expense on December 31, 2019.

Account	December 31, 2019	
Interest Expense	6,793	
Interest Payable		6,793

On January 1, 2020, Berg records the payment. Because it has already recorded the interest expense, Berg removes the interest payable balance and does not record any additional interest expense.

Account	January 1, 2020	
Lease Liability	5,207	
Interest Payable	6,793	
Cash		12,000

Leasehold Improvements

Lessees typically make **leasehold improvements**, which are improvements made to leased property that are not movable and revert to the lessor when the lease expires. For example, the lessee might construct a building on leased land or make modifications to an existing building such as installing new light fixtures, partitioning rooms, or replacing windows.

Lessees capitalize expenditures for leasehold improvements into a leasehold improvement account reported on the balance sheet under property, plant, and equipment. The lessee depreciates leasehold improvements over the shorter of the life of the improvements or the lease term. If the lease term is shorter than the life of the improvements, the lease term is used as the depreciation period because the leasehold improvement will not benefit the lessee after the leased asset reverts back to the lessor. Example 18A.2 provides an example of accounting for leasehold improvements.

EXAMPLE 18A.2

Leasehold Improvement

PROBLEM: Tweetie Enterprises is currently leasing land with a lease that expires in 20 years. On January 1 of the current year, Tweetie built a barn on the land costing $15,000 that is expected to last for 50 years. Tweetie depreciates its assets using the straight-line method. What is the entry to record the leasehold improvement? What is the journal entry to record the depreciation for the barn every year?

SOLUTION: Tweetie includes the barn in the leasehold improvement account.

Account	*January 1*	
Leasehold Improvement	15,000	
Cash		15,000

Tweetie depreciates the barn over 20 years, which is shorter than the life of the asset and the life of the lease. Thus, it depreciates $750 per year ($15,000 / 20).

Account	*December 31*	
Depreciation Expense—Leasehold Improvement	750	
Accumulated Depreciation—Leasehold Improvement		750

Executory Costs

Lessees often incur costs related to the ownership of a leased asset. These costs, referred to as **executory costs**, include items such as sales and property taxes, insurance, and maintenance. Accounting for these costs depends on the item. Payments related to maintenance such as snow removal and common area cleaning and maintenance are nonlease components. As noted earlier, contract consideration is allocated to the lease component and the nonlease component. Accounting treatment for each specific nonlease component is not included in the authoritative literature that covers leases. Typically, maintenance costs such as these are expensed as incurred.

The treatment of costs related to taxes and insurance depends on whether the payments are fixed or variable. In some cases, the costs are variable. That is, the lessee simply pays the taxes or insurance at whatever amount the government and/or insurance agency charges. In this case, these costs are considered variable lease payments that do not depend on an index or rate. Thus, these costs are excluded from the computation of the lease payments and are included in net income when the obligation is incurred.

Executory costs related to taxes and insurance can be fixed. These costs may be included in the fixed payments that the lessor charges the lessee. In this case, the fixed costs are included in the computation of the lease payments and, thus, the lease obligation.

Example 18A.3 illustrates accounting for executory costs.

EXAMPLE 18A.3

Finance Lease with Executory Costs

PROBLEM: On January 1, 2019, Mapits, Inc. leased a floor of a building for use in its North American operations from Borko Bank. The 9-year, noncancellable lease requires annual lease payments of $15,000, beginning January 1, 2019, and at each December 31 thereafter through 2026.

The lease payment includes costs related to property taxes of $3,000. It also includes payments for common area maintenance. The observable standalone price for the lease (including the property taxes) is $14,000, and the observable standalone price for the common area maintenance is $2,000.

In addition, Mapits agrees to pay insurance on the floor of the building. It pays the insurance each year when it receives an invoice from Borko Bank for the insurance amount. On December 15, 2019, Mapits was billed and paid $1,500 for this insurance.

The lease agreement does not transfer ownership, nor does it contain a purchase option. The leased floor of the building has a fair value of $75,000 and an estimated remaining life of 10 years. Borko Bank's implicit rate of 11% is known to Mapits. Identify the items for which the contract includes executory costs and determine their accounting treatment. Provide Mapits's journal entries for the first year of the lease.

SOLUTION: The contract includes executory costs for property taxes, maintenance, and insurance. The insurance is a variable payment that is not dependent on an index or rate. Thus, insurance is not included in the computation of the lease payments and the lease liability. Insurance is recognized when Mapits becomes obligated to pay. Costs related to property taxes are included in the single lease component and the lease obligation. The common area maintenance is a nonlease component.

Items for Which the Contract Includes Executory Costs	Fixed or Variable?	Included in Lease or Nonlease Contract Consideration?	Accounting Treatment
Property Taxes	Fixed	Lease	Is included in lease payment component when allocating consideration.
Maintenance	Fixed	Nonlease	Allocate consideration from lease payment. Expense separately.
Insurance	Variable	Not included in lease payment	Expense as incurred.

So, Mapits allocates the contract consideration to the lease and nonlease components as follows:

Component	Standalone Price	Percentage	Allocated Consideration
Lease	$14,000	87.5%	$13,125
Nonlease (maintenance)	2,000	12.5	1,875
Total	$16,000	100.0%	$15,000

The present value of the lease is $80,668:

	N	I/Y	PV	PMT	FV	Excel Formula
Given	9	11.00%		−13,125	0	
Solve for PV			**80,668**			=PV(0.11,9,−13125,0,1)

We then determine whether the lease is an operating lease or a finance lease.

Group I Criteria	Met?	Explanation
Transfer of ownership?	No	
Purchase option likely to be exercised?	No	
Lease term major part of economic life?	Yes	The lease term is 90% (9 years / 10 years) of economic life.
Present value substantial part of fair value?	Yes	The present value of $80,668 is more than 100% of the $75,000 fair value.
Asset is specialized?	No	

Based on this analysis, it is a finance lease. Because this is a finance lease, Mapits records the liability at the lease commencement as the present value of the lease payments. Mapits records the asset at the amount of the lease liability.

Account	January 1, 2019	
Right-of-Use Asset	80,668	
Lease Liability		80,668

Mapits allocates the $13,125 payment to interest and principal using the effective interest rate method of amortization.

Date	Payment (a)	Interest (b) = Prior-Period Balance × 11%	Reduction in Lease Liability (c) = (a) − (b)	Balance (d) = Prior-Period Balance − (c)
Lease Commencement – January 1, 2019				$80,668
January 1, 2019	$13,125	$ 0	$13,125	67,543
December 31, 2019	13,125	7,430	5,695	61,848
December 31, 2020	13,125	6,803	6,322	55,526
December 31, 2021	13,125	6,108	7,017	48,509
December 31, 2022	13,125	5,336	7,789	40,720
December 31, 2023	13,125	4,479	8,646	32,074
December 31, 2024	13,125	3,528	9,597	22,477
December 31, 2025	13,125	2,472	10,653	11,824
December 31, 2026	13,125	1,301	11,824	0

Notice that Mapits allocates the first payment to principal and common area maintenance of $1,875.

Account	January 1, 2019	
Lease Liability	13,125	
Maintenance Expense	1,875	
Cash		15,000

On December 15, 2019, Mapits records the expense related to the insurance.

Account	December 15, 2019	
Insurance Expense	1,500	
Cash		1,500

The leased asset is subject to amortization. Mapits amortizes $8,963 ($80,668 / 9) each year.

Account	December 31, 2019	
Amortization Expense—Right-of-Use Asset	8,963	
Accumulated Amortization—Right-of-Use Asset		8,963

As shown by the amortization table, Mapits allocates the second payment to interest of $7,430 and principal of $5,695. On December 31, 2019, we debit Prepaid Maintenance Expense because the maintenance expense for 2019 was recorded on January 1, 2019.

Account	December 31, 2019	
Lease Liability	5,695	
Interest Expense	7,430	
Prepaid Maintenance Expense	1,875	
Cash		15,000

Purchase Options

Our discussion of the lease classification criteria included the purchase option, which gives the lessee the opportunity to acquire the leased property at the date of the option exercise. If at the lease commencement date, it is likely that the lessee will exercise the purchase option, the amount of the purchase option is included in the computation of the lease payments. Thus, the lessee's lease obligation and the lessor's net investment in the lease include the present value of the purchase option.

Some lease contracts allow the lessee to exercise the purchase option before lease termination. If the lessee is likely to exercise the purchase option before lease termination, the lease term ends on the date that the option can be exercised. In this case, the lease term will be shorter because it ends on the earlier exercise date. Because the lessee will eventually acquire the asset, the lessee amortizes the asset over the asset's life under a finance lease, not over the lease term. Example 18A.4 illustrates the accounting for a lease with a purchase option that the lessee is likely to exercise.

EXAMPLE 18A.4

Purchase Option

PROBLEM: On January 1, 2019, DeFeo Brothers Moving and Storage, Inc. entered into an 8-year lease with Firefall Leasing Company to occupy a warehouse. The economic life of the warehouse is 25 years. The warehouse had a fair value of $2,500,000, and DeFeo has an option to purchase the warehouse at the end of the lease term for $1,200,000, which is expected to be substantially lower than the fair value at the end of the lease. The annual lease payments are $248,703 with the first due on January 1, 2019, and the rest on December 31 of each year. The implicit rate in the lease is 5% and is known by DeFeo. There is no guaranteed residual value specified. The lessor did not offer any incentives to sign the lease. DeFeo did not incur any initial indirect costs.

Determine the lessee's lease obligation and the lessor's NIL. Prepare the lease amortization table. How much should DeFeo record as amortization expense each year?

SOLUTION: The lessee's lease obligation and the lessor's NIL is the present value of two components: (1) the annuity due using an 8-year life and a 5% interest rate and (2) the $1,200,000 single-sum purchase option.

The present value of the annuity due is $1,687,791 as follows:

	N	I/Y	PV	PMT	FV	Excel Formula
Given	8	5.00%		−248,703		
Solve for PV			**1,687,791**			= PV(0.05,8,−248703,0,1)

The $1,687,791 is the amount of the lessor's investment recovered through the lease payments.

The present value of the $1,200,000 lump-sum purchase option is $812,207 computed as follows:

	N	I/Y	PV	PMT	FV	Excel Formula
Given	8	5.00%		0	−1,200,000	
Solve for PV			**812,207**			= PV(0.05,8,0,−1200000,0)

The $812,207 is the lessor's investment that is to be recovered by the collection of the purchase option.

Thus, the total present value is $2,499,998 ($1,687,791 + $812,207), which is 100% of the fair value of the machinery. Thus, the lease meets the Group I criteria and is classified as a finance lease for the lessee and a sales-type lease for the lessor.

The lessee records a right-of-use asset and a lease liability of $2,499,998, and the lessor records a NIL-ST of $2,499,998.

The following amortization table applies to both the lessor and the lessee.

Date	**Payment (a)**	**Interest (b) = Prior-Period Balance × 5%**	**Reduction in Lease Liability (c) = (a) − (b)**	**Balance (d) = Prior-Period Balance − (c)**
Lease Commencement – January 1, 2019				$ 2,499,998
January 1, 2019	$ 248,703	$ 0	$ 248,703	2,251,295
December 31, 2019	248,703	112,565	136,138	2,115,157
December 31, 2020	248,703	105,758	142,945	1,972,212
December 31, 2021	248,703	98,611	150,092	1,822,120
December 31, 2022	248,703	91,106	157,597	1,664,523
December 31, 2023	248,703	83,226	165,477	1,499,046
December 31, 2024	248,703	74,952	173,751	1,325,295
December 31, 2025	248,703	66,265	182,438	1,142,857
December 31, 2026	1,200,000	57,143	1,142,857	0

The lease obligation is fully paid with the remittance of the $1,200,000 purchase option.

DeFeo amortizes the right-of-use asset over the asset's economic life. Thus, amortization each year is $100,000 ($2,499,998 / 25 years).

Deferred Profit in Direct Financing Leases

As discussed earlier in the chapter, lessors are required to defer profit in a direct financing lease.

When a direct financing lease contains deferred profit, we need to compute a new effective interest rate. We use the lease's implicit rate to compute the lease receivable and the present values of any residual value guarantees, unguaranteed residual assets, and purchase options. Once we determine these present values and the initial measurement of the net investment in the lease, we compute the new effective interest rate that results in a constant periodic discount rate to amortize the balance in the NIL account.

Example 18A.5 illustrates a direct financing lease with deferred profit.

EXAMPLE 18A.5 Direct Financing Lease with Deferred Profit

PROBLEM: Correll Company leases machinery to Borelli Fabricating, Inc. Both the lease inception and commencement occur on January 1, 2019. It is a 3-year lease requiring payments of $10,500 with the first payment on January 1, 2019, the second on December 31, 2019, and the last on December 31, 2020. The equipment has a fair value of $40,000 and is carried in Correll's inventory at $36,000. The implicit rate in the lease is 6.4368%. The guaranteed residual value (guaranteed by a third party) for the asset is $12,500. The collection of lease payments and the guaranteed residual value is probable. Correll correctly classifies the lease as a direct financing lease.

Prepare Correll's journal entries needed to account for this transaction for 2019 and 2020.

SOLUTION: For a direct financing lease, we first determine any profit or loss. Revenue is the lower of the leased asset's fair value and the sum of the lease receivable plus any prepaid lease payments. Because there are no lease prepayments, we compute the lease receivable as follows:

	N	I/Y	PV	PMT	FV	Excel Formula
Given	3	6.4368%		**10,500**	12,500	
Solve for PV			**(40,000)**			= PV(0.064368,3,10500,12500,1)

Because the fair value is also $40,000, we measure the revenue as the $40,000.

Correll's cost of goods sold is the asset's carrying value less the present value of any unguaranteed residual asset plus deferred initial direct costs. Because we do not have an unguaranteed residual value or initial direct costs, cost of goods sold is $36,000.

The profit is equal to $4,000, which is the revenue of $40,000 less the cost of goods sold of $36,000.

Revenue	$40,000
Less: Cost of goods sold	36,000
Profit	$ 4,000

Correll must defer the profit because this is a direct financing lease. The net investment in the lease (NIL) of $36,000 is equal to the lease receivable of $40,000, less the deferred profit, $4,000.

Lease receivable	$40,000
Less: Deferred profit	(4,000)
Net investment in lease	$36,000

When a firm defers profits, it recalculates the effective interest rate to obtain a constant periodic discount rate on the balance of the net investment in the lease. In Correll's case, the interest rate equates the NIL of $36,000 with the present value of future lease payments of $10,500 plus the present value of the guaranteed residual asset value of $12,500 over the 3-year lease term. The appropriate discount rate is 14.5146%:

	N	I/Y	PV	PMT	FV	Excel Formula
Given	3		−36,000	10,500	12,500	
Solve for RATE		**14.5146%**				= RATE(3,10500,−36000,12500,1)

For the $36,000 net investment in lease, we then compute an amortization table using the new effective interest rate of 14.5146% as follows:

Date	Payment (a)	Interest (b) = Prior-Period Balance × 14.5146%	Reduction in Lease Liability (c) = (a) − (b)	Balance (d) = Prior-Period Balance – (c)
Lease Commencement – January 1, 2019				$36,000
January 1, 2019	$10,500	$ 0	$10,500	25,500
December 31, 2019	10,500	3,701	6,799	18,701
December 31, 2020	10,500	2,714	7,786	10,915
December 31, 2021	12,500	1,585*	10,915	0

* Adjusted for rounding errors.

On January 1, 2019, Correll recognizes the NIL of $36,000 and derecognizes the machinery at its carrying value of $36,000.

Account	January 1, 2019	
Net Investment in Lease – Direct Financing	36,000	
Machinery		36,000

Correll records the receipt of the first lease payment as follows.

Account	January 1, 2019	
Cash	10,500	
Net Investment in Lease – Direct Financing		10,500

On December 31, 2019, Correll records receipt of the second lease payment as follows:

Account	December 31, 2019	
Cash	10,500	
Interest Revenue		3,701
Net Investment in Lease – Direct Financing		6,799

On December 31, 2020, Correll records receipt of the third lease payment as follows:

Account	December 31, 2020	
Cash	10,500	
Interest Revenue		2,714
Net Investment in Lease – Direct Financing		7,786

Variable Lease Payments

As noted earlier, certain variable lease payments are included in the computation of the lease payments and some are not. Specifically, variable lease payments that depend on a rate or index are included in the lease payments using the rate or index in effect at the lease commencement date. For example, payments are sometimes tied to the Consumer Price Index (CPI), a measure indicating the purchasing power based on the weighted average of a basket of consumer goods and services, to protect the lessor against inflation. Other variable payments are not included in the lease payments. Thus, lessees recognize other variable payments and changes in variable payments that depend on an index or rate in expense at the lease payment date when they incur the obligation. Lessors recognize these same amounts in revenue.

Example 18A.6 illustrates variable payments.

EXAMPLE 18A.6 Variable Lease Payments

PROBLEM: Chief Manufacturing Company (CMC) signs a lease agreement on December 10, 2019, to lease nonspecialized equipment with a fair value of $85,000 and a 10-year economic life from TDR Inc. The lease commences on January 1, 2020. CMC will make five payments with the first one on January 1, 2020, and every year thereafter on December 31. These payments will be $10,000 plus an amount based on the Consumer Price Index (CPI). For every point that the CPI is above 230, CMC will pay an extra 1% on the $10,000. For example, if the CPI is equal to 235, or 5 points above the 230 benchmark, CMC would make a lease payment of $10,500 ($10,000 + 5% of $10,000) The CPI as of January 1, 2020, is 240. The implicit rate is 7% and is known by CMC.

CMC correctly classifies the lease as an operating lease. Prepare the journal entries for 2020 through 2022. Assume that the CPI is 242 as of December 31, 2020, and 245 as of December 31, 2021.

SOLUTION: CMC measures the lease payments using the CPI at the lease commencement date. Thus, the lease payments are $11,000, which is $10,000 plus 10% of $10,000. We use 10% because the CPI is 240 on January 1, 2020, and is 10 points higher than the 230 specified in the lease agreement.

CMC determines the initial measurement of the lease liability ($48,259) as the present value of the lease payments that it has not made as of the lease commencement date.

	N	I/Y	PV	PMT	FV	Excel Formula
Given	5	7.00%		−11,000	0	
Solve for PV			**48,259**			= PV(0.07,5,0,−11000,0,1)

CMC measures the right-of-use asset as the sum of the initial lease liability measurement plus prepayments less lease incentives plus initial direct costs. Because there are no prepayments, lease incentives, or initial direct costs, the right-of-use asset is also $48,259.

On the lease commencement date, CMC records the right-of-use asset and the lease liability:

Account	***January 1, 2020***	
Right-of-Use Asset	48,259	
Lease Liability		48,259

Given that each lease payment is $11,000, the straight-line annual lease expense is $11,000 per year.

We prepare the amortization table to determine the reduction in the liability each period.

Date	Payment (a)	Interest (b) = Prior-Period Balance × 7%	Reduction in Lease Liability (c) = (a) − (b)	Balance (d) = Prior-Period Balance − (c)
Lease Commencement – January 1, 2020				$48,259
January 1, 2020	$11,000	$ 0	$11,000	37,259
January 1, 2021	11,000	2,608	8,392	28,867
January 1, 2022	11,000	2,021	8,979	19,888
January 1, 2023	11,000	1,392	9,608	10,280
January 1, 2024	11,000	720	10,280	0

CMC records the first payment of $11,000 on January 1, 2020.

Account	January 1, 2020	
Lease Liability	11,000	
Cash		11,000

CMC records the second payment on December 31, 2020. It makes a cash payment of $11,200, which is the stated amount in the contract of $10,000 times 1.12. We use the multiplier of 1.12 because the CPI is 12 points above the 230 level stated in the lease agreement.

CMC records the $8,392 decrease in the lease liability and the same decrease in the right-of-use asset. It expenses the additional $200 cash payment. This is a change in a variable lease payment that is based on an index.

Account	December 31, 2020	
Lease Expense	11,000	
Lease Expense – Change in Variable Payment	200	
Lease Liability	8,392	
Accumulated Amortization—Right-of-Use Asset		8,392
Cash		11,200

On December 31, 2021, CMC again records a payment. At this date, the CPI is 245. Thus, the payment amount is $10,000 times 1.15, or $11,500. CMC records the $8,979 decrease in the lease liability and the same decrease in the right-of-use asset. It expenses the additional $500 cash payment. This is a change in a variable lease payment that is based on the index.

Account	December 31, 2021	
Lease Expense	11,000	
Lease Expense – Change in Variable Payment	500	
Lease Liability	8,979	
Accumulated Amortization—Right-of-Use Asset		8,979
Cash		11,500

Exhibit 18.A1 summarizes the complex issues in lease accounting by lessee–lessor treatment.

EXHIBIT 18.A1 Summary of Complex Issues in Lease Accounting

Issue	Description	Lessor	Lessee
Lease commencements occurring in the middle of the year	Lease agreement is entered into during the middle of the year.	Accrues interest revenue and interest receivable as an adjusting entry. After the lease payment is received, removes the interest receivable and records the current-period interest revenue.	Accrues the interest expense and interest payable as an adjusting entry at the end of the year. After the payment is made, removes the interest payable and records the current period interest expense.
Leasehold improvements	Lessee makes expenditures for modifications to leased properties that remain with the leased properties after the lease term ends.		Expenditures are capitalized and depreciated over the shorter of the life of the improvement or the life of the lease.
Executory costs	Executory costs are the property tax, insurance, maintenance, and other costs associated with the ownership of the leased asset.	Fixed payments related to insurance and taxes are included in the computation of lease payments if the lessee pays the lessor.	Payments related to maintenance are nonlease components. Variable payments related to insurance and taxes are variable lease payments that don't depend on an index or rate. These costs are excluded from the computation of lease payments. Fixed payments related to insurance and texes are included in the computation of lease payments if the lessee pays the lessor.
Purchase options	Option allowing the lessee to acquire the property at a price specified at the inception of the lease.	Include present value of purchase option in present value computations, and thus in the NIL balance.	Include present value of purchase option in present value computations and thus in the lease obligation balance.
Deferred profits	Direct financing lease: lessors always defer any profit.	Compute a new interest rate for the amortization table that results in a constant periodic discount rate to amortize the balance in the NIL account.	
Variable lease payments	Payments made to the lessor by the lessee that are not a fixed amount.	Variable lease payments that depend on a rate or index are included in the lease payments using the rate or index in effect at the lease commencement date. Other variable payments are not included in the lease payments. Lessors recognize these amounts in revenue.	Variable lease payments that depend on a rate or index are included in the lease payments using the rate or index in effect at the lease commencement date. Other variable payments are not included in the lease payments. Thus, lessees recognize other variable payments and changes in variable payments that depend on an index or rate in expense when they incur the obligation.

Comprehensive Problem: Leasing Complexities

Example 18A.7 is a comprehensive problem that incorporates many of the complexities discussed in this section.

EXAMPLE 18A.7

Comprehensive Problem

PROBLEM: On July 1, 2019, Phipps Motors, a calendar year–end company, leased a piece of nonspecialized machinery from Williams, Inc. Williams is also a calendar year–end company. Williams manufactured the machinery earlier that year for $500,000. It incurred commission fees of $4,000 related to the lease agreement. The lease terms are:

- Annual rental payments of $113,000 due on July 1 each year. The first payment is due at the commencement of the lease and the last payment will be made on July 1, 2023.
- The lease term is effective through June 30, 2024.
- There is no transfer of the asset at the end of the lease term and no purchase option.
- The economic life of the asset is 6 years.
- Williams' implicit rate is not known by Phipps Motors. Phipps' incremental borrowing rate is 14%.
- Collectability of lease payments and residual value is reasonably assured.
- The fair value (current selling price) of the machine is $500,000.
- Phipps Motors will incur insurance costs of $2,500 each year with the first payment due on July 1, 2019. These payments are in addition to the $113,000 payments, and are paid to the lessor.
- Although the lease contract guarantees a residual value of $10,000, Williams expects a $40,000 residual value at the termination of the lease contract. The lessee guarantees a residual value of $10,000.

For both the lessee and lessor, analyze the lease criteria to determine whether the lease is an operating, finance, direct financing, or sales-type lease. What journal entries will both Phipps Motors and Williams make in 2019 and 2020?

SOLUTION

Phipps Motors (Lessee)

We begin with the lessee, Phipps Motors. It will classify this lease as a finance lease because it meets at least one of the Group I criteria. Because the executory costs are fixed and are for insurance, we include these in the lessee's lease payments.

Group I Criteria	Met?	Explanation—Lessee
Transfer of ownership?	No	
Purchase option likely to be exercised?	No	
Lease term major part of economic life?	??	Lease term is 83.3% (5 years / 6 years of economic life).
Present value substantial part of fair value?	Yes	The present value of $457,227 (five payments of $115,500 plus the guaranteed residual value of $10,000 discounted at 14%) is 91.4% of the $500,000 fair value.
Asset is specialized?	No	

Phipps Motors records the asset and the liability at the commencement of the lease. The present value of the lease is $457,227. Phipps only recognized $10,000 of the residual value because the remaining $30,000 is unguaranteed.

	N	I/Y	PV	PMT	FV	Excel Formula
Given	5	14.00%		−115,500	−10,000	
Solve for PV			457,227			= PV(0.14,5,−115500,−10000,1)

The lessee's journal entry at lease commencement follows.

Account	July 1, 2019	
Right-of-Use Asset	457,227	
Lease Liability		457,227

Phipps' amortization table is as follows:

Date	Payment (a)	Interest (b) = Prior-Period balance(d) × 14%	Reduction in Lease Liability (c) = (a) − (b)	Balance (d) = Prior-Period Balance − (c)
July 1, 2019				$457,227
July 1, 2019	$115,500	$ 0	$115,500	341,727
July 1, 2020	115,500	47,842	67,658	274,069
July 1, 2021	115,500	38,370	77,130	196,939
July 1, 2021	115,500	27,571	87,929	109,010
July 1, 2022	115,500	15,261	100,239	8,771
June 30, 2023	10,000	1,229*	8,771	0

* Adjusted for rounding errors.

Phipps records the first payment on July 1, 2019, and attributes it entirely to principal because no time has elapsed.

Account	July 1, 2019	
Lease Liability	115,500	
Cash		115,500

Phipps needs to accrue interest on December 31 computed as 6 / 12 of the $47,842 amount, or $23,921.

Account	December 31, 2019	
Interest Expense	23,921	
Interest Payable		23,921

Phipps also records a half-year of amortization expense. Annual amortization expense is $89,445[($457,227 − $10,000) / 5]. Therefore, Phipps records one-half of $89,445, or $44,723.

Account	December 31, 2019	
Amortization Expense—Right-of-Use Asset	44,723	
Accumulated Amortization—Right-of-Use Asset		44,723

As shown by the preceding table, Phipps allocates the second payment on July 1, 2020, to interest of $47,842 and principal of $67,658. Phipps has already reported interest expense of $23,921 so that the remaining $23,921 is to be expensed in 2020.

Account	July 1, 2020	
Lease Liability	67,658	
Interest Expense	23,921	
Interest Payable	23,921	
Cash		115,500

At year end of 2020, the company once again accrues interest for the last 6 months of the year. Because total interest expense for the second year of the lease, July 1, 2020, to June 30, 2021, is $38,370, Phipps accrues $19,185.

Account	December 31, 2020	
Interest Expense	19,185	
Interest Payable		19,185

Phipps also records amortization for the full year.

Account	December 31, 2020	
Amortization Expense—Right-of-Use Asset	89,445	
Accumulated Amortization—Right-of-Use Asset		89,445

Williams Incorporated (Lessor)

Our first step is to determine the lessor's implicit rate. The implicit rate equates the present value of the payments plus the present value of the residual value (guaranteed and unguaranteed) to the fair value of the leased asset plus deferred initial direct costs. The fair value is $500,000. Initial direct costs are deferred in this case because the fair value equals the carrying value. Thus, we compute the implicit rate as 10.2727%.

	N	I/Y	PV	PMT	FV	Excel Formula
Given	5		**−504,000**	115,500	40,000	
Solve for RATE		**10.2727%**				= RATE(5,115500,−504000,40000,1)

The next step for the lessor is to classify the lease. It is a sales-type lease for Williams because it meets the Group I criteria. (The lease also meets the Group II criteria, but that is not relevant for a sales-type lease. Group II criteria are relevant if a lessor meets Group II criteria and does not meet the Group I criteria.)

Group I Criteria	Met?	Explanation—Lessor
Transfer of ownership?	No	
Purchase option likely to be exercised?	No	
Lease term major part of economic life?	Uncertain	Lease term is 83.3% (5 years / 6 years of economic life).
Present value substantial part of fair value?	Yes	The present value of $485,601 (five payments of $115,500 plus the guaranteed residual value of $10,000 discounted at 10.2727%) is 97.1% of the $500,000 fair value.
Asset is specialized?	No	

At the commencement of the lease, Williams records the net investment in the lease, removes the machine from its accounts, and reports the gross profit by recording sales revenue and cost of goods sold. The net investment in the lease is $504,000—the present value of the payments and the residual value.

	N	I/Y	PV	PMT	FV	Excel Formula
Given	5	10.2727%		115,500	40,000	
Solve for PV			(504,000)			= PV(0.102727,5,115500,40000,1)

The cost of goods sold is the carrying value of the machinery ($500,000) less the present value of the unguaranteed residual value ($18,399) plus the deferred initial direct costs ($4,000), or $485,601.

	N	I/Y	PV	PMT	FV	Excel Formula
Given	5	10.2727%		0	30,000	
Solve for PV			(18,399)			= PV(0.102727,5,0,30000,0)

Williams will report revenue of $485,601, which is the lower of the fair value of the machine and the lease receivable.

	N	I/Y	PV	PMT	FV	Excel Formula
Given	5	10.2727%		115,500	10,000	
Solve for PV			(485,601)			= PV(0.102727,5,115500,10000,1)

Williams will also derecognize the machinery and reduce cash for the initial direct costs.

Account	*July 1, 2019*	
Net Investment in Lease – Sales Type	504,000	
Cost of Goods Sold	485,601	
Sales Revenue		485,601
Inventory of Machinery		500,000
Cash		4,000

Williams prepares the following amortization table:

Date	Payment (a)	Interest (b) = Prior-Period Balance × 10.2727%	Reduction in Lease Liability (c) = (a) − (b)	Balance (d) = Prior-Period Balance (d) − (c)
July 1, 2019				$504,000
July 1, 2019	$115,500	$ 0	$115,500	388,500
July 1, 2020	115,500	39,909	75,591	312,909
July 1, 2021	115,500	32,144	83,356	229,553
July 1, 2022	115,500	23,581	91,919	137,634
July 1, 2023	115,500	14,139	101,361	36,273
June 30, 2024	40,000	3,727*	36,273	0

* Adjusted for rounding errors.

As shown in the table, the first payment is entirely principal because interest accrues only with the passage of time.

Account	*July 1, 2019*	
Cash	115,500	
Net Investment in the Lease – Sales Type		115,500

On December 31, 2019, Williams accrues 6 months of interest ($39,909 × 6/12).

Account	December 31, 2019	
Interest Receivable	19,955	
Interest Revenue		19,955

On July 1, 2020, it records the second lease payment.

Account	July 1, 2020	
Cash	115,500	
Net Investment in Lease – Sales-Type		75,591
Interest Receivable		19,955
Interest Revenue		19,954

Finally, on December 31, 2020, Williams accrues interest for the first 6 months of the lease term, July 1, 2020, through June 31, 2021. It computes the interest receivable (and revenue) by multiplying $32,144 by 6 / 12.

Account	December 31, 2020	
Interest Receivable	16,072	
Interest Revenue		16,072

19 Accounting for Employee Compensation and Benefits

LEARNING OBJECTIVES

1. Describe the characteristics and types of stock-based compensation.
2. Explain and illustrate the initial and subsequent measurement of equity-classified stock-based compensation.
3. Describe and demonstrate the initial and subsequent measurement of liability-classified stock-based compensation.
4. Discuss accounting for stock appreciation rights, restricted stock plans, and employee stock purchase plans.
5. Detail required disclosures for stock plans.
6. Describe the characteristics of defined-contribution and defined-benefit pension plans.
7. Demonstrate the measurement of pension costs and the related liability or asset under defined-benefit plans, including remeasurement due to changes in actuarial assumptions.
8. Detail required disclosures for pension plans.

Introduction

ATTRACTING, DEVELOPING, AND RETAINING talented employees is essential to a company's ability to operate successfully, grow, and compete in the marketplace. ***Unilever PLC***, the global consumer products company, highlighted this fact in its 2016 annual report's risk management discussion. ***Unilever's*** compensation awards structure is a critical element in retaining key talent and grooming future leaders.

BMProductions/Shutterstock

Employees are compensated in a variety of ways for services, including salary, bonus, vacation time, retirement benefits, or stock options. The forms of compensation serve different purposes. Cash provides resources needed to pay for everyday living expenses. Bonuses reward employees for achieving a performance goal, such as a sales or earnings target. Stock-based compensation, including stock options, seeks to align employees' interests with those of the company's shareholders. *Pensions* and other post-retirement benefits encourage employees to build a long-term career with a company, thus providing a stable, reliable workforce. Over time, an employee's compensation mix can change.

At ***Unilever***, employee compensation was about €6.5 billion, amounting to 12.4% of sales of €52.7 billion in 2016. For its 169,000 worldwide employees, cash and other short-term benefits represented about 91% of total compensation, pensions about 6%, and stock-based compensation about 3%. For the senior managers, the compensation mix shifted toward share-based compensation in line with the objective of better aligning managers' and shareholders' interests. Senior manager compensation was about 33% share-based compensation, 65% cash and other short-term benefits, and 2% pension.

Although adequately rewarding employees is critical to a company's success, many companies identify meeting promised pension obligations as a major risk. Because pensions are paid over many years, even decades, there is uncertainty regarding the future payments and cash needs. In recent years, companies such as ***Verizon***, ***Sears***, and ***IBM*** have frozen or cut pension benefits to reduce costs in order to remain competitive.

In this chapter, we examine stock-based compensation and pension benefits.[1] Employees earn these benefits in the periods that they provide services, but the benefits are paid in future periods. Accrual accounting requires the estimation of the benefits that employees have earned so that the company reports the cost of providing these benefits in the same period in which the services are provided regardless of when the employee is actually paid.

The two major accounts related to employee compensation and benefits—expenses and liabilities—are based on the definitions of elements of the financial statements. In the case of stock-based compensation, employees are paid for services rendered. Thus, the employer recognizes an expense and reports it on the income statement over the period that the employee provides the services. Some types of pension plans obligate the employer to pay a fixed or a defined amount to retired employees. These *defined-benefit* pension plans result in liabilities representing the future amount for which the employer will be responsible. «

1 Describe the characteristics and types of stock-based compensation.

Overview of Stock-Based Compensation

Stock-based compensation is a significant portion of total compensation for many employers. In a survey of 500 companies, 488 of the companies disclosed offering stock option plans.[2] Exhibit 19.1 shows the types of compensation plans used by these 488 companies. **Employee stock options**, the most prevalent form of compensation plans, are financial instruments that give an employee the right to purchase shares of the company's stock directly from the company at a fixed price over a specified period of time. The stock awards category ranks as the second most popular. It includes restricted stock awards, performance awards, and bonuses paid by issuing stock. In this section, we examine the initial and subsequent accounting for stock-based compensation.[3]

EXHIBIT 19.1 Use of Compensation Plans at 500 Companies

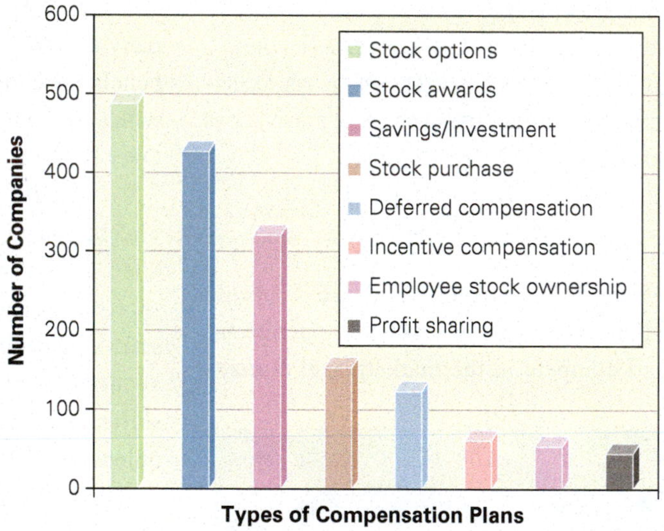

Source: Data taken from (AICPA, New York, NY). Accounting Trends and Techniques—2010 (AICPA, New York, NY).

Stock Option Terminology

Let's begin our discussion of stock-based compensation by reviewing the terminology. Employee stock options are a restricted form of a *call option*. A **call option** gives an investor the right (but not

[1] We covered compensated absences and payroll taxes in Chapter 13.

[2] AICPA, *Accounting Trends and Techniques—2010* (New York, NY: AICPA, 2010).

[3] We focus our discussion on stock option plans because they are the most commonly used in practice. Research cases in the end-of-chapter material address other types of plans.

the obligation) to purchase a security at a fixed price over a specified period of time. Employees are given the right to purchase the employer's equity shares but there is no obligation to do so. Accounting for stock-based compensation plans requires an understanding of the following terms:

1. The **exercise price** or **strike price** is the fixed amount paid to acquire a share of stock based on the terms of the option plan.
2. The **vesting period** or **service period** is the time the employee must remain with the company before exercising the options.
3. The **expiration date** is the point at which the employee can no longer exercise the options.
4. The **compensation arrangement** specifies the number of options granted, the exercise price, the vesting period, and the expiration date.

Stock options seek to align the interests of employees with those of company owners and to motivate employees to work to increase the company's market value. Consequently, companies usually set the exercise price equal to the market price of the stock on the day the company grants the options.[4] For example, ***Johnson & Johnson*** grants options at the average of the stock's high and low price on the date of grant. The employee is motivated to perform in order to increase the market price of the company's stock above the exercise price. The vesting period ensures that the employee works for a certain period of time before being entitled to the benefits. For example, ***Johnson & Johnson*** disclosed in its 2016 annual report that its stock option awards vest over service periods ranging from 6 months to 4 years. Additionally, the employee is usually the only one who can exercise the options. Stock options cannot be sold or transferred in the market.

Upon exercise, the employee turns in the option and pays the fixed cash (exercise) price to the employer. In return, the employer provides stock valued at the current market price. An employee exercises his or her option only when the current market price of the stock exceeds the fixed exercise price. When the market price is higher than the exercise price of the company's stock, the options are "in the money." If there are no restrictions on disposal, the employee may then sell the shares in the market at a gain.

The company can issue new shares of stock or treasury stock to employees exercising options.[5] For example, ***Johnson & Johnson*** settles employee stock option exercises and stock issuances with treasury shares, usually replenishing the number of shares used over the year. An employee leaving the company before completing the vesting period and exercising the options usually forfeits them. However, there may be a forfeiture even if the employee is fully vested in the case of termination. That is, the options are available to the employee only when the employee remains with the company throughout the vesting period and even after the vesting period in certain cases.

THE CONCEPTUAL FRAMEWORK CONNECTION
Stock-Based Compensation

The major conceptual issue in accounting for stock-based compensation accounting is determining whether to recognize an expense on the income statement. When a company exchanges stock for services rendered, has it incurred an expense? The FASB requires companies to record stock compensation as an expense. This requirement, however, is contentious. Companies usually set the exercise price equal to the stock's market price on the day of the option grant. As a result, the stock's **intrinsic value**—the market price of the stock less the option's exercise price—is usually zero. Management at many companies that use stock-based compensation have asserted that because the intrinsic value is zero on the date of the grant, there is no compensation expense to accrue. However, FASB believes that options should be measured at fair value and the expense be based on fair value, not intrinsic value.

[4]There are also tax benefits to setting the exercise price equal to the market price on the grant date.

[5]Shares do not actually have to change hands because a net settlement is possible. That is, when the employee presents the option to the company, he or she receives the difference between the current market price and the exercise price. In all illustrations, we assume that the employee purchases newly issued shares from the corporation when the options are exercised.

The effect on net income of expensing stock-based compensation can be quite significant. For example, ***Microsoft*** reported stock option expense in 2016 that was 13.5% of its pre-tax income. Not surprisingly, one academic research study found strong evidence of an association between the use of stock options for top management compensation and the likelihood that a company opposed the FASB opinion that stock options should be expensed.[6]

Although financial statement preparers may not want to report stock option expense on their income statements, the conceptual framework clearly supports treating employee stock options as an expense. Expensing stock-based compensation at fair value is consistent with all other forms of nonmonetary exchanges. For example, assume that a consultant is paid in shares of stock. The company would measure the amount charged by the consultant at the fair value of the consideration given, the fair value of the stock, the fair value of the consideration received, or the value of the consulting services provided based on which is more clearly evident. The company would then expense this amount on the income statement.

Expensing employee stock options is also comparable to the treatment of other forms of employee compensation such as cash salaries. Therefore, expensing stock options is required to create comparable financial statements. For example, assume that one company pays its executives $10 million in cash and another company pays its executives in stock options with a fair value of $10 million. If stock-based compensation is not expensed, then the first company would report an expense of $10 million, but the second company would not report any compensation expense. Under that scenario, the two sets of financial statements would not be comparable—and comparability is one of the enhancing qualitative characteristics specified in the conceptual framework.

Finally, some accountants have challenged whether the use of employee stock options meets the definition of an expense. According to FASB's *Statement of Financial Accounting Concepts No. 6*, expenses are "outflows or other using up of assets or incurrences of liabilities (or a combination of both) from delivering or producing goods, rendering services, or carrying out other activities that constitute the entity's ongoing major or central operations."[7] The argument questions whether employee options meet this definition by incurring liabilities or using up assets. Standard setters agree that employee stock option transactions do not incur liabilities. However, they maintain that the transactions use up assets. Specifically, the acquisition of the asset (in this case, services) and the use of that asset occur simultaneously. Thus, the company does not record an asset and instead debits an expense account.[8]

Despite the controversy, there is no question that the appropriate accounting treatment is to record an expense for stock options; compensation plans are clearly an expense to the company and should be presented as such. Companies classify the cost of stock-based compensation as an operating expense on the income statement.

Estimates in Accounting for Stock-Based Compensation

Companies expense stock-based compensation in the income statement at fair value.[9] In general, the accounting treatment for stock-based compensation is quite similar under U.S. GAAP and IFRS.

Fair Value Estimate. The first step in measuring compensation expense from granting employee stock options is determining the fair value on the date of the grant. The fair value is based on the market price of the options or similar options if a value is available. Because these values are frequently not available, companies estimate the fair value using either an option-pricing model such as the Black-Scholes option-pricing model (most commonly used in practice)

---

[6]Patricia Dechow, Amy Hutton, and Richard Sloan, "Economic Consequences of Accounting for Stock-Based Compensation," *Journal of Accounting Research* (Supplement 1996): 1–20.

[7]Financial Accounting Standards Board, *Statement of Financial Accounting Concepts No. 6*, "Elements of Financial Statements," Paragraph 80.

[8]See footnote 43 of FASB's *Statement of Financial Accounting Standards No. 6* for a discussion of the simultaneous acquisition and use of an asset.

[9]For the relevant authoritative literature for this topic, see FASB ASC 718-10 – *Compensation – Stock Compensation – Overall* for U.S. GAAP and IASB, *International Financial Reporting Standard 2*, Share-Based Payments (London, UK: International Accounting Standards Board, Revised, 2016) for IFRS.

or a binominal or lattice model (preferred but not required by the FASB).[10] Option-pricing models require inputs such as the

- Stock price
- Time to expiration
- Exercise value
- Risk-free discount rate
- Volatility of the stock
- Probability that the options will vest

After determining the fair value of the stock options, the company allocates this amount to compensation expense over the vesting period.[11] The straight-line amortization method is used to allocate the compensation expense over the vesting period.

Forfeiture Estimate. When the vesting period has ended, an employee's right to receive the stock-based compensation generally no longer depends on continued employment. However, if the employee is terminated or leaves the entity before the vesting period is over, the options are forfeited. The value of the forfeited options reduces total compensation expense. A company can choose either to adjust the amount of compensation expense that it allocates for an estimate of the percentage of options that it expects to be forfeited or to account for actual forfeitures as they occur.

❷ Explain and illustrate the initial and subsequent measurement of equity-classified stock-based compensation.

Equity-Classified Stock-Based Compensation

The accounting for stock-based compensation depends on whether the employee receives equity or some other form of compensation based on the value of the company's equity. In the case of **equity-classified awards**, employees have the right to receive shares.

Issuance of Equity-Classified Awards

To account for the issuance of an equity-classified award, a company first computes the fair value of the award. If the company chooses to adjust for the estimated forfeiture rate, it expenses the adjusted fair value of the award on a straight-line basis over the vesting period. If the company does not adjust for the estimated forfeiture rate, it accounts for forfeitures when they occur. In this case, the company expenses the fair value of the awards on a straight-line basis over the vesting period and adjusts this expense each year for actual forfeitures. Example 19.1 illustrates accounting for equity-classified awards assuming that the company adjusts for estimated forfeitures.

EXAMPLE 19.1

Equity-Classified Award – Estimating Forfeitures

PROBLEM: Davis Enterprises, Inc. granted employee stock options on January 2, 2018, to acquire 60,000 shares of $1.20 par value common stock with an exercise price of $5.10 per share. The market price on January 2, 2018, was also $5.10 per share, so there is no intrinsic value on the date of the grant. Employees must complete a 2-year service (vesting) period in order to exercise the options. The options will expire after a 5-year (total option) period. The estimated fair value of the options using the Black-Scholes option-pricing model is $9.60 per option for a total of $576,000 (60,000 options × $9.60 per option). The company estimates that 10% of the options will be forfeited. The number of options forfeited in 2018 was 2,500 and in 2019 was 28,000. The options are equity-classified awards. Assume that Davis chooses to adjust the fair value for the estimated forfeitures. Determine the amount and allocation of the stock-based compensation expense for the years 2018 and 2019, and prepare the necessary journal entries.

Continued

[10] Both the Black-Scholes option-pricing model and binominal model are based on similar theoretical foundations and require similar assumptions. A key difference is that the binominal model can incorporate the early exercise of an option into its pricing whereas Black-Scholes cannot.

[11] The service period is assumed to be the vesting period unless specified otherwise.

SOLUTION: We measure total compensation expense at the fair value of the options adjusted for estimated forfeitures. The total expense is the fair value of $576,000 multiplied by 90% because the forfeiture rate is 10%, or the probability of vesting is 90%. The 2-year service period requires that Davis Enterprises allocate the expense equally in 2018 and 2019, recognizing $259,200 of expense in each year.

Description	December 31, 2018	December 31, 2019
Total compensation expense at fair value	$576,000	$576,000
Percentage of options expected to vest	× 90%	× 90%
Expected compensation expense	$518,400	$518,400
Cumulative rate of amortization	× 1/2	× 2/2
Cumulative compensation expense	$259,200	$518,400
Less: Expense recognized in prior years	(0)	(259,200)
Compensation expense: Current year	$259,200	$259,200

The entries to recognize compensation expense over the 2-year amortization (service) period follow.

Account	December 31, 2018		December 31, 2019	
Compensation Expense	259,200		259,200	
Additional Paid-in Capital (APIC) – Stock Options		259,200		259,200

Example 19.2 uses the same facts but provides an example of accounting for forfeitures when they occur.

EXAMPLE 19.2 Equity-Classified Award – Accounting for Forfeitures When They Occur

PROBLEM: Use the facts from Example 19.1 but assume that Davis chooses to adjust for forfeitures when they occur. Determine the amount and allocation of the stock-based compensation expense for the years 2018 and 2019 and prepare the necessary journal entries.

SOLUTION: We measure total compensation expense at the fair value of the options, adjusted for actual forfeitures. The total expense over the life of the options is the fair value of the options still outstanding at the end of the period. Each year, the cumulative expense recognized should be the fair value of the options still outstanding times the percentage of the vesting period that has passed.

Description	December 31, 2018	December 31, 2019
Number of options	60,000	60,000
Actual forfeitures	2,500	30,500
Number of options outstanding	57,500	29,500
Fair value	$ 9.60	$ 9.60
Fair value outstanding	552,000	283,200
Number of years in vesting period	2	2
Cost per year	276,000	141,600
Years into the vesting period	1	2
Cumulative expense	276,000	283,200
Amount expensed to date	0	(276,000)
Current year expense	$276,000	$ 7,200

The entries to recognize compensation expense over the 2-year amortization (service) period follow.

Account	December 31, 2018		December 31, 2019	
Compensation Expense	276,000		7,200	
Additional Paid-in Capital—Stock Options		276,000		7,200

Each year's expense is justified by the fact that the allocation is designed to match compensation expense against increased employee productivity over the vesting period. For example, ***Unilever*** awarded about 7 million shares of equity-classified awards with a fair value of €244 million during fiscal 2016. ***Unilever*** expensed the fair value of its awards over 3 years. During 2016, ***Unilever's*** expense related to equity-classified awards was €198 million.

Change in the Fair Value of Equity-Classified Awards

Companies value an equity-classified award based on the market price of the options measured on the date of the grant. How, then, does the accounting change when the fair value of the options changes due to fluctuations in stock price or changes in other inputs to a valuation model after the grant date? Companies do not modify the compensation expense for these changes: The fair value at the grant date is the compensation agreed on by both the company and the employee. Thus, the company should use the fair value at the time it negotiated the compensation with the employees.

Change in the Estimated Forfeiture Rate

If the company chooses to adjust the fair value for the estimated forfeiture rate instead of accounting for actual forfeitures when they occur, it revalues equity-classified awards when there is a change in the estimated percentage of options that will be forfeited. So, the expense related to each option is not adjusted as the fair value changes, but the total expense is adjusted for changes in the number of options expected to be exercised. This is shown in Example 19.3. ***Unilever's*** forfeited shares were 7.5% of outstanding share awards in fiscal 2016 but 11.1% in fiscal 2015, illustrating the difficulty in estimating forfeitures and how it can change over time.

EXAMPLE 19.3 Equity-Classified Award—Forfeiture Change

PROBLEM: Using the information provided in Example 19.1 through 2018, assume that on December 31, 2019, Davis Enterprises estimated that employees will exercise only 40% of the options. What is the journal entry to reflect the change in the vesting probability in 2019? What is the journal entry to record the compensation expense in 2019? What are the balances in the relevant t-accounts after making the adjustment and recording compensation expense in 2019?

SOLUTION: We first compute the compensation expense for 2019, updating the forfeiture estimate to 60%.

Description	December 31, 2018	December 31, 2019
Total compensation expense at fair value	$576,000	$576,000
Percentage of options expected to vest	× 90%	× 40%
Expected compensation expense	$518,400	$230,400
Cumulative rate of amortization	× 1/2	× 2/2
Cumulative compensation expense	$259,200	$230,400
Less: Expense recognized in prior years	(0)	(259,200)
Compensation expense (income): Current year	$259,200	$ (28,800)

Continued

The journal entry to record the compensation expense for 2018 is the same as in Example 19.1

Account	December 31, 2018	
Compensation Expense	259,200	
Additional Paid-in Capital – Stock Options		259,200

Account	December 31, 2019	
Additional Paid-in Capital – Stock Options	28,800	
Compensation Expense		28,800

The t-accounts after posting the 2019 adjustments follow:

	Additional Paid-in Capital – Stock Options	
2018		259,200
2019	28,800	
2019 Balance		230,400

	Compensation Expense	
2018	259,200	
Close to Retained Earnings		259,200
2018 Balance	0	
2019		28,800
Close to Retained Earnings	28,800	
2019 Balance	0	

Exercise of Equity-Classified Awards

Employee stock options will either be exercised or expire. If the employee exercises the option, the company records the issuance of new shares and removes the amount included for the options for those shares in the APIC – stock option account. Thus, the company will record the increase in cash for the amount received from the exercise and the increase in stock at par along with the decrease in the APIC – stock option account. The company will use the APIC in excess of par account to account for the remaining credit needed. This is illustrated in Example 19.4.

EXAMPLE 19.4 Accounting for an Option Exercise

PROBLEM: Davis Enterprises granted employee stock options on January 2, 2018, for 60,000 shares of $1.20 par value common stock with an exercise price of $5.10 per share. Davis chooses to adjust the fair value for the estimated forfeitures. The estimated forfeiture rate was 10%, so there is a 90% vesting probability throughout the 2-year vesting period. The options will expire after a 5-year period (total option period). The estimated fair value of the options using the Black-Scholes option-pricing model is $9.60 per option for a total of $576,000 (60,000 options × $9.60 per option). The options are equity-classified awards. Employees exercised 100% of the options on January 2, 2020. What is the journal entry to record the option exercise? Ignore all tax benefits at exercise.

SOLUTION: Because employees exercised the options, the options must be in the money—that is, the stock price must be greater than $5.10 per share. Since 100% of the options are exercised, instead of 90%, Davis has a change in estimate whereby additional compensation expense must be recorded. The company issues new shares measured at $882,000 separated into common stock at par and additional paid-in capital in excess of par. The $882,000 is computed as the sum of the APIC – stock options balance ($576,000) and the cash received upon exercise ($5.10 × 60,000 = $306,000). Davis measures the common stock at $72,000 (60,000 shares × $1.20 par value) and the additional paid-in capital in excess of par is the difference between the total value of the new shares and the par value of the common stock ($882,000 − $72,000 = $810,000). The total amount of $882,000 is compensation expense of $576,000 (60,000 × $9.60), the value of employee services rendered plus cash received of $306,000 (the $5.10 exercise price per option times 60,000 options exercised).[12] Davis reverses the APIC – Stock Options by $576,000 with a debit and increases cash by $306,000.

Account	January 2, 2020	
Compensation Expense	57,600	
Additional Paid-in Capital – Stock Options		57,600

Account	January 2, 2020	
Cash	306,000	
Additional Paid-in Capital – Stock Options	576,000	
Common Stock		72,000
Additional Paid-in Capital in Excess of Par – Common		810,000

Expiration of Equity-Classified Awards

Companies account for expired options by reclassifying them from APIC – stock options into APIC – expired stock options. The contributed capital from expired options reflects the employee-provided services the company received without providing any compensation. Thus, the contributed capital is a form of donated capital measured at fair value. Accounting for expired options is illustrated in Example 19.5.

EXAMPLE 19.5 Accounting for Expired Options

PROBLEM: In Example 19.1, Davis Enterprises granted employee stock options on January 2, 2018, for 60,000 shares of $1.20 par value common stock with an exercise price of $5.10 per share and an estimated forfeiture rate of 10%. Assume that on January 2, 2023, which is the end of the 5-year total option period, the options are out of the money (i.e., the market price is less than the exercise price). All of the options will expire unexercised. What is the journal entry to record the expiration of the options?

SOLUTION: Because the market price is now less than $5.10 per share, the journal entry to record the expiration is as follows:

Account	January 2, 2023	
Additional Paid-in Capital – Stock Options	518,400	
Additional Paid-in Capital – Expired Stock Options		518,400

Equity-Classified Awards: IFRS

Under IFRS, accounting for equity-classified awards is similar to that under U.S. GAAP except that companies are not allowed the option to adjust for actual forfeitures. Companies must adjust for an estimate of the percentage of the options that are expected to be forfeited.

[12]We assume that the entity issues new shares to satisfy the requirements of the option plan. In practice, it is more common for companies to use treasury shares to satisfy employee stock options. However, we avoid using treasury shares here because doing so creates complications that obscure the key points of accounting for stock options.

3 Describe and demonstrate the initial and subsequent measurement of liability-classified stock-based compensation.

Liability-Classified Stock-Based Compensation

For a **liability-classified award**, an employee receives cash or some other company resource based on the value of the shares in the stock-based compensation. Employee compensation is classified as a liability in the following situations:

1. The option is granted for the acquisition of securities classified as liabilities, such as redeemable preferred stock.
2. The employee can sell back the acquired shares to the employer corporation at the exercise price within a reasonable period of time (such as 6 months). Here the employee does not absorb any risk.
3. The compensation is in the form of **cash-settled stock appreciation rights** with the employee receiving cash for the amount of the increase in a company's share price over a fixed period of time.

Issuance of Liability-Classified Awards

To account for liability-classified awards, the company recognizes the compensation expense on a straight-line basis over the vesting period. As is the case with equity-classified awards, the company can choose to adjust the fair value of the award by an estimated forfeiture rate, or it can choose to account for actual forfeitures when they occur. As with equity-classified awards, if the company chooses to adjust for the estimated forfeiture rate, it revalues the awards when the estimated percentage of options that will be forfeited changes. When the company records the expense, it also accrues a liability. Example 19.6 illustrates accounting for liability-classified awards when the company estimates forfeitures.

EXAMPLE 19.6 **Liability-Classified Awards – Estimating Forfeitures**

PROBLEM: ALR Enterprises, Inc. granted employee stock options on January 2, 2018, for 100,000 shares of $1 par value common stock with an exercise price of $25 per share. The market price of a share of stock on January 2, 2018, was also $25 per share, so there is no intrinsic value on the date of the grant. Employees must complete a 2-year service (vesting) period in order to exercise the options. The options will expire after a 5-year period (total option period). The estimated fair value of the options using the Black-Scholes option-pricing model is $30 per option, or $3,000,000, in total. The employees have the right to sell the shares back to ALR within 3 months of the exercise. The company estimates that there will be 5% forfeitures of the options. The actual number of forfeited options is 2,000 in 2018 and 3,000 in 2019. What journal entry does ALR make for compensation expense in 2018 and 2019 assuming that it adjusts the fair value for estimated forfeitures?

SOLUTION: ALR classifies the award as a liability because employees can sell the shares back to ALR within 3 months of the exercise. ALR allocates the $2,850,000 fair value of the award over the 2-year service period, resulting in compensation expense in each year of $1,425,000 recorded as follows:

Description	*December 31, 2018*	*December 31, 2019*
Total compensation expense at fair value	$3,000,000	$3,000,000
Percentage of options expected to vest	95%	95%
Expected total compensation expense	2,850,000	2,850,000
Cumulative rate of amortization	0.5000	1.0000
Cumulative compensation expense	1,425,000	2,850,000
Expense recognized in prior years	0	1,425,000
Current-year compensation expense	$1,425,000	$1,425,000

The journal entries are as follows:

Account	*December 31, 2018*		*December 31, 2019*	
Compensation Expense	1,425,000		1,425,000	
Liability for Stock-Based Compensation		1,425,000		1,425,000

Example 19.7 uses the same facts but provides an example of accounting for forfeitures when they occur.

EXAMPLE 19.7

Liability-Classified Award – Accounting for Forfeitures as They Occur

PROBLEM: Use the facts from Example 19.6 but assume that ALR chooses to adjust for forfeitures when they occur. What journal entry does ALR make for compensation expense in 2018 and in 2019?

SOLUTION: ALR measures total compensation expense at the fair value of the options adjusted for actual forfeitures. The total expense is the fair value of the options still outstanding at the end of the period. Each year, the cumulative expense recognized should be the fair value of the options still outstanding multiplied by the percentage of the vesting period that has passed.

Description	***December 31, 2018***	***December 31, 2019***
Number of options	100,000	100,000
Actual forfeitures	2,000	5,000
Number of options outstanding	98,000	95,000
Fair value	$ 30	$ 30
Fair value outstanding	2,940,000	2,850,000
Number of years in vesting period	2	2
Cost per year	1,470,000	1,425,000
Years into the vesting period	1	2
Cumulative expense	1,470,000	2,850,000
Amount expensed to date	0	(1,470,000)
Current year expense	$1,470,000	$1,380,000

The journal entries are as follows:

Account	***December 31, 2018***		***December 31, 2019***	
Compensation Expense	1,470,000		1,380,000	
Liability for Stock-Based Compensation		1,470,000		1,380,000

Fair Value Adjustments

At each balance sheet date, companies remeasure the liability and compensation expense to fair value until the award is settled. This treatment is different than the treatment of fair value changes for equity-classified awards. For liability-classified awards, the liability is remeasured because the obligation is actually changing with the change in the fair value. Thus, companies adjust liability-classified awards each year for any changes in the fair value of the options. These adjustments impact the compensation expense recognized in the period of adjustment, leading companies to remeasure the liability account accordingly. Example 19.8 illustrates accounting for liability-classified awards when the fair value changes.

EXAMPLE 19.8

Liability-Classified Award—Change in Fair Value

PROBLEM: Using the information provided in Example 19.6, assume that ALR Enterprises, Inc. reports that the fair value of the award as of December 31, 2018, is $3,200,000 and its fair value as of December 31, 2019, is $3,125,000. What are the journal entries required to record compensation expense in 2018 and 2019?

Continued

SOLUTION: Compensation expense is based on the fair value of the liability-classified award. In 2018, the compensation expense is $1,520,000, which is the total fair value of $3,200,000 adjusted for the vesting probability of 95% and divided by the vesting period of 2 years. In 2019, the fair value of the award is $3,125,000. ALR again adjusts for the vesting probability of 95%. So, over the 2 years, the total compensation expense is $2,968,750. Because ALR expensed $1,520,000 in the prior year, the compensation expense recognized in 2019 is $1,448,750, or $2,968,750 less the $1,520,000 previously expensed. The compensation expense for 2018 and 2019 is as follows:

Description	December 31, 2018	December 31, 2019
Total fair value	$3,200,000	$3,125,000
Vesting probability	× 95%	× 95%
Expected compensation expense	$3,040,000	$2,968,750
Cumulative rate of amortization	× 1/2	× 2/2
Cumulative compensation expense	$1,520,000	$2,968,750
Less: Expense recognized in prior years	(0)	(1,520,000)
Compensation expense (income): Current year	$1,520,000	$1,448,750

Thus, the journal entries to record compensation expense for 2018 and 2019 are as follows:

Account	December 31, 2018		December 31, 2019	
Compensation Expense	1,520,000		1,448,750	
Liability for Stock-Based Compensation		1,520,000		1,448,750

Exercise of Liability-Classified Awards

The accounting treatment for the exercise of a liability-classified award is similar to the exercise of an equity-classified award. The company records any cash received, removes the liability, and records the stock issuance in the common stock at par and additional paid-in capital in excess of par – common accounts as shown in Example 19.9.

EXAMPLE 19.9 Liability-Classified Award Exercise

PROBLEM: In Example 19.6, ALR granted employee stock options on January 2, 2018, for 100,000 shares of $1 par value common stock with an exercise price of $25 per share. The options are liability-classified awards. The employees exercise the stock options on January 2, 2020. What is the journal entry to record the exercise of 100% of the options? Ignore all tax benefits at exercise.

SOLUTION: ALR records the cash receipt of $2,500,000 (100,000 shares × $25 per share) and removes the $2,850,000 liability. It also records common stock at par of $100,000 (100,000 shares × $1 par value) and credits the remainder to additional paid-in capital.

Account	January 2, 2020	
Cash	2,500,000	
Liability for Stock-Based Compensation	2,850,000	
Common Stock		100,000
Additional Paid-in Capital in Excess of Par – Common		5,250,000

Expiration of Liability-Classified Awards

If a liability-classified award expires, the company removes the liability account and records the amount in APIC – expired stock options as shown in Example 19.10.

EXAMPLE 19.10

Liability-Classified Award Expiration

PROBLEM: In Example 19.6, the company granted employee stock options on January 2, 2018, for 100,000 shares of $1 par value common stock with an exercise price of $25 per share. On January 2, 2023, the end of the 5-year total option period, the options are out of the money (meaning the market price is less than the exercise price). All of the options will expire unexercised. What is the journal entry to record the expiration of the options?

SOLUTION: Because the market price is now less than $25 per share, the journal entry to record the expiration is as follows:

Account	*January 2, 2023*	
Liability for Stock-Based Compensation	2,850,000	
Additional Paid-in Capital – Expired Stock Options		2,850,000

Exhibit 19.2 summarizes the treatment of adjustments to compensation expense.

EXHIBIT 19.2 Summary of Adjustments to Compensation Expense

	Adjustment of Compensation Expense for	
Award	**Changes in Vesting Probability**	**Changes in Fair Value**
Equity classified	Yes	No
Liability classified	Yes	Yes

Liability-Classified Awards: IFRS

Under IFRS, accounting for liability-classified awards is similar to that under U.S. GAAP except that companies must adjust for an estimate of the percentage of the options that are expected to be forfeited. IFRS reporters cannot choose to adjust for actual forfeitures of options.

4 Discuss accounting for stock appreciation rights, restricted stock plans, and employee stock purchase plans.

Other Types of Stock-Based Compensation

In this section, we discuss three other common types of stock-based employee compensation:

- Stock appreciation rights
- Restricted stock plans
- Employee stock purchase plans

Stock Appreciation Rights

A stock appreciation right (SAR) is a form of compensation that gives an employee the right to receive an amount equal to the appreciation in a company's stock from the award date to the exercise date. SARs are similar to a bonus tied to the company's stock price because SARs compensate the employee for the increase in the company's stock price. As a result, the employee benefits only if the stock price increases. Unlike stock options, the employee is not required to purchase shares.

A company can grant SARs that give the employee the right to receive cash or shares of stock at the exercise date. To account for SARs, a company records compensation expense based on the SAR's fair value.[13] If the plan specifies that the employee will be compensated with cash, the SARs are liability classified.

If the plan specifies that the employee will be compensated with shares of stock, the SARs will be equity classified to the account additional paid-in capital—stock options. At the end of each period, the company remeasures the liability (or equity) to the SAR's current fair value. Accounting for SARs is illustrated in Example 19.11.

EXAMPLE 19.11 Stock Appreciation Rights

PROBLEM: Spitfire Motor Company initiated a share-appreciation rights plan on January 1, 2018, by granting 30,000 rights to its key executives. The vesting period is 3 years, and the SARs cannot be exercised before January 1, 2021. The plan also expires on January 1, 2022. The closing fair values of the SARs for the years ended December 31, 2018, through 2020 are presented in the following table.

Date	Fair Value
December 31, 2018	$4
December 31, 2019	7
December 31, 2020	5
January 1, 2021	5

The SARs are all exercised on January 1, 2021, when the market price of a share of common stock is $30.

Required »

a. Prepare the journal entries necessary to record the SAR plan assuming that the executives receive cash.

b. Prepare the journal entries as if the plan specified that the SARs would be settled with its $1 par value common stock.

SOLUTION: The computation of the fair value of the SARs at each date is computed:

Date	Fair Value	Total Fair Value (30,000 Rights)	Percent Vested	Cumulative Expense to Be Accrued	Expense Accrued in Current Year
December 31, 2018	$4	$120,000	33.333%	$ 40,000	$ 40,000
December 31, 2019	7	210,000	66.667	140,000	100,000
December 31, 2020	5	150,000	100	150,000	10,000
January 1, 2021	5	150,000	100	150,000	0

a. The journal entries for the scenario in which we assume that the SARs are settled in cash follow. Note that in 2020 the compensation expense and the related liability are both reduced.

Account	***December 31, 2018***	
Compensation Expense	40,000	
Obligation under SAR Plan		40,000

[13]ASC 718-30-35-4 permits a nonpublic entity to measure the compensation expense at either fair value or intrinsic value.

Account		December 31, 2019
Compensation Expense	100,000	
Obligation under SAR Plan		100,000

Account		December 31, 2020
Compensation Expense	10,000	
Obligation under SAR Plan		10,000

Spitfire makes the following entry when the executives exercise the SARs and it pays the obligation:

Account		January 1, 2021
Obligation under SAR Plan	150,000	
Cash		150,000

b. If the SARs were settled with stock, then the journal entries would be as follows:

Account		December 31, 2018
Compensation Expense	40,000	
Additional Paid-in Capital—Stock Options		40,000

Account		December 31, 2019
Compensation Expense	100,000	
Additional Paid-in Capital—Stock Options		100,000

Account		December 31, 2020
Compensation Expense	10,000	
Additional Paid-in Capital—Stock Options		10,000

When the executives exercise the SARs, Spitfire is required to compensate them with 5,000 shares of common stock ($150,000 value of the SARs divided by $30 market price). Spitfire makes the following entry when the executives exercise the SARs:

Account		January 1, 2021
Additional Paid-in Capital—Stock Options	150,000	
Common Stock		5,000
Additional Paid-in Capital in Excess of Par— Common		145,000

Restricted Stock Plans

Under a **restricted stock plan**, a company awards actual shares in the name of a specific employee, resulting in an allocation of restricted shares to the designated employee. Restricted stock plans are therefore not stock options. The restrictions attached to the awarded shares often include the following provisions:

- The employee must remain with the employer for a specified number of years (a vesting period) before selling the awarded shares.
- The employee is not taxed on the award, nor may the employer take a tax deduction for compensation expense until the restrictions expire.

These restrictions create incentives for the employee to remain employed at the company and to increase productivity to enhance the value of the shares awarded. Restricted stock plans are beneficial to the employee. If the market price falls below the strike price of an option, the employee option is worthless. However, a restricted stock plan always has value as long as the underlying shares trade at a non-zero price. Because the restricted shares are expected to have some value, fewer shares are needed as an incentive for employees, making restricted stock plans less dilutive than stock option plans.

On the grant date, deferred compensation on the restricted shares is measured as the fair value of the unrestricted shares multiplied by the number of restricted shares issued. The company amortizes the total deferred compensation evenly over the vesting period for financial reporting purposes. For example, ***Johnson & Johnson*** granted about 7.1 million shares of restricted stock units in fiscal 2016 at an average fair value of $92.45. The units vest over 3 years, so ***Johnson & Johnson*** will amortize them to compensation expense over that period. ***Johnson & Johnson*** ignores subsequent changes in the fair value of the stock for purposes of computing the compensation expense.

When an employee fully vests in the restricted stock plan, no additional entries are required because the shares have already been issued. The company modifies footnote disclosures to indicate that it has removed the restrictions on the shares. Example 19.12 illustrates accounting for restricted stock plans.

EXAMPLE 19.12 Restricted Stock Plan

PROBLEM: On January 1, 2018, Newton Fig Factories, Inc. issued 10,000 shares of $1 par value, restricted stock to one of its key executives, Wayne Smith. Newton's unrestricted shares have a market value of $30 per share on the date of issue. The restricted shares require a vesting period of 3 years. Prepare the journal entries required for 2018 through 2020. Newton's year-end is December 31.

SOLUTION: Newton makes the following entry on the date of the grant of the restricted shares, January 1, 2018. The debit to deferred compensation is a negative or contra-shareholders' equity account that Newton will amortize over the 3-year vesting period.

Account	***January 1, 2018***	
Deferred Compensation – Restricted Stock	300,000	
Common Stock (10,000 shares × $1 par value)		10,000
Additional Paid-in Capital in Excess of Par – Common		290,000

Newton amortizes deferred compensation on a straight-line basis over the 3-year vesting period by debiting compensation expense and crediting deferred compensation for $100,000 per year (i.e., $300,000 / 3 years). Newton makes the following entry each December 31.

Account	***December 31, 2018, 2019, and 2020***	
Compensation Expense	100,000	
Deferred Compensation – Restricted Stock		100,000

If an employee terminates employment prior to vesting, the company reverses the share issue, derecognizes the deferred compensation, and reverses the expense recognition to date by crediting compensation expense. The credit to compensation expense increases income. Accounting for employee termination in restricted stock plans is shown in Example 19.13.

EXAMPLE 19.13 Restricted Stock Plan with Employee Termination

PROBLEM: Continuing with Example 19.12, assume that on January 1, 2019, Wayne Smith leaves Newton Fig Factories 1 year after the restricted shares are issued. At this point, $100,000 was expensed and $200,000 remains in deferred compensation. Prepare the journal entry needed to record the forfeiture of the restricted stock award.

SOLUTION: The entry to record the forfeiture follows:

Account	January 1, 2019	
Common Stock	10,000	
Additional Paid-in Capital in Excess of Par – Common	290,000	
Deferred Compensation – Restricted Stock		200,000
Compensation Expense		100,000

Employee Stock Purchase Plans

To encourage employee loyalty and to increase incentives, many employers offer *employee stock purchase plans*. An **employee stock purchase plan** offers employees the opportunity to purchase the company's shares, usually at a discount and without incurring transactions costs (i.e., brokerage fees). The accounting depends on whether these plans are compensatory or non-compensatory:

- In non-compensatory plans, the company records the issuance of shares purchased by employees in the same way as issuing shares in the open market.
- In compensatory plans, the company records the amount of the discount below the regular market purchase as compensation expense.

An employee stock purchase plan is non-compensatory if it meets the following three conditions:

1. The plan is made available to substantially all employees.
2. After the plan is established, there is a maximum 1-month period to elect to participate in the plan.
3. The discount is not larger than 5% of the open market price or, if a greater discount is offered, the discount can be justified.

Example 19.14 illustrates accounting for employee stock purchase plans.

EXAMPLE 19.14 Employee Stock Purchase Plans

PROBLEM: Milo Cookie Company offers all its employees the opportunity to purchase its \$2 par value common stock at a 3% discount (meaning that the employee pays 97% of the market price). The employees have 2 weeks to elect to participate in the plan. The current market price of the stock is \$30 per share. Employees purchased a total of 10,000 shares after 2 weeks of establishing the purchase plan and setting the discount. What journal entry will Milo make on the date the employees purchase the shares? What journal entry would Milo make if it offered the employee purchase plan only to its full-time, salaried employees?

SOLUTION: Based on the original terms, the plan is determined to be non-compensatory. Thus, Milo does not record compensation expense. It records cash of \$291,000 (\$30 × 97% × 10,000) for the employee purchase. It records common stock of \$20,000 (\$2 par × 10,000 shares) and the remainder in additional paid-in capital in excess of par – common.

Description	Date of Employee Purchase	
Cash	291,000	
Common Stock		20,000
Additional Paid-in Capital in Excess of Par – Common		271,000

If Milo offers the plan only to select employees, the plan is deemed to be compensatory, and Milo must charge the discount to salary expense. Milo records cash

Continued

of $291,000 ($30 × 97% × 10,000) for the employee purchase and salary expense of $9,000 ($30 × 3% ×10,000). It records common stock of $20,000 ($2 par × 10,000 shares) and the remainder in additional paid-in capital in excess of par – common.

Description	Date of Employee Purchase	
Cash	291,000	
Salary Expense	9,000	
Common Stock		20,000
Additional Paid-in Capital in Excess of Par – Common		280,000

5 Detail required disclosures for stock plans.

Stock-Based Compensation Disclosures

Minimum required disclosures for stock-based compensation are fairly extensive to provide financial statement users with enough information to understand:

1. The nature and terms of the stock-based compensation plans that existed during the periods covered by the financial statements
2. The methods used to estimate the required fair values, including models and assumptions used in valuing options
3. The income statement effect of the compensation cost arising from the entity's stock-based compensation plans
4. The effect of the stock-based compensation plans on the entity's cash flow

The description of the nature and terms of stock-based compensation plans include the service period and other vesting requirements, the maximum service period over which the shares are available or liability exists, the number of shares authorized for awards, and those exercisable at the end of the period. Companies must also disclose the policy choice as to whether it recognizes estimated forfeitures or actual forfeitures as incurred. In addition, companies also provide details on the number and weighted-average exercise prices of share options (or units) at the beginning and ending of the year and changes during the year including those related to grants, exercises (or conversion), forfeitures, and expirations. Commonly, this information provides a reconciliation of beginning and ending amounts. Companies disclose information separately for vested and non-vested shares. While stock compensation is accounted for at fair values, companies are also required to disclose the intrinsic values of outstanding stock and options granted.

Exhibit 19.3 illustrates selected stock-based compensation disclosures provided by ***Pfizer Inc.***, a global pharmaceutical company, in its 2016 annual report. For example, ***Pfizer*** disclosed that the income statement effect of the various types of stock-based compensation was $486 million, net of tax, in 2016. ***Pfizer*** disclosed that its stock options expire 10 years from the date of grant and vest after 3 years. ***Pfizer*** uses a variation of the Black-Scholes option-pricing model to value the options, making the required assumptions. The company provided a reconciliation of shares outstanding and the weighted-average exercise price from the beginning to the end of the year. Additionally, it included a table with the outstanding and exercisable shares by the exercise price range.

EXHIBIT 19.3 Selected Footnote Disclosure of Stock-Based Compensation Disclosures, ***Pfizer Inc.'s*** Financial Statements, December 31, 2016

NOTE 13: SHARE-BASED PAYMENTS

Our compensation programs can include share-based payments, in the form of Restricted Stock Units (RSUs), stock options, Portfolio Performance Shares (PPSs), Total Shareholder Return Units (TSRUs) and Performance Share Awards (PSAs).

A. Impact on Net Income

The following table provides the components of share-based compensation expense and the associated tax benefit:

(Millions of Dollars)	Year Ended December 31 2016	2015	2014
Restricted Stock Units	$299	$306	$270
Portfolio Performance Shares	135	147	96
Total Shareholder Return Units	134	36	37
Stock Options	106	165	150
Performance Share Awards	13	11	30
Directors' compensation	4	4	3
Share-based payment expense	691	669	586
Tax benefit for share-based compensation expense	(205)	(198)	(179)
Share-based payment expense, net of tax	$486	$471	$407

B. Restricted Stock Units (RSUs)

RSUs are awarded to select employees and, when vested, entitle the holder to receive a specified number of shares of ***Pfizer*** common stock, including shares resulting from dividend equivalents paid on such RSUs. For RSUs granted during the periods presented, in virtually all instances, the units vest after three years of continuous service from the grant date.

We measure the value of RSU grants as of the grant date using the closing price of ***Pfizer*** common stock. The values determined through this fair value methodology generally are amortized on a straight-line basis over the vesting term into *Cost of sales, Selling, informational and administrative expenses,* and *Research and development expenses*, as appropriate.

The following table summarizes all RSU activity during 2016:

	Shares (Thousands)	Weighted-Average Grant Date Fair Value Per Share
Nonvested, December 31, 2015	29,135	$31.53
Granted	10,581	30.74
Vested	(9,630)	27.41
Reinvested dividend equivalents	1,093	32.56
Forfeited	(1,574)	32.18
Nonvested, December 31, 2016	29,605	$32.59

The following table provides data related to all RSU activity:

(Millions of Dollars)	Year Ended December 31 2016	2015	2014
Total fair value of shares vested	$293	$371	$401
Total compensation cost related to nonvested RSU awards not yet recognized, pre-tax	$262	$279	$255
Weighted-average period over which RSU cost is expected to be recognized (years)	1.7	1.8	1.8

C. Stock Options

Stock options are awarded to select employees and, when vested, entitle the holder to purchase a specified number of shares of ***Pfizer*** common stock at a price per share equal to the closing market price of ***Pfizer*** common stock on the date of grant.

Beginning in 2016, only a limited set of overseas employees received stock option grants. No stock options were awarded to senior and other key management in any period presented; however, stock options were awarded to certain other employees. In virtually all instances, stock options granted since

Continued

2005 vest after three years of continuous service from the grant date and have a contractual term of ten years. In most cases, stock options must be held for at least one year from the grant date before any vesting may occur. In the event of a sale of business or plant closing or restructuring, options held by employees are immediately vested and are exercisable for a period from three months to their remaining term, depending on various conditions.

We measure the value of stock option grants as of the grant date using, for virtually all grants, the Black-Scholes-Merton option-pricing model. The values determined through this fair value methodology generally are amortized on a straight-line basis over the vesting term into *Cost of sales, Selling, informational and administrative expenses*, and *Research and development expenses*, as appropriate.

The following table summarizes all stock option activity during 2016:

	Shares (Thousands)	Weighted-Average Exercise Price Per Share	Weighted-Average Remaining Contractual Term (Years)	Aggregate Intrinsic Value[a] (Millions)
Outstanding, December 31, 2015	232,554	$26.41		
Granted	1,371	30.59		
Exercised	(42,550)	24.03		
Forfeited	(2,949)	33.18		
Expired	(1,750)	28.55		
Outstanding, December 31, 2016	186,676	26.86	5.7	$1,138
Vested and expected to vest[b], December 31, 2016	184,537	26.77	5.6	1,138
Exercisable, December 31, 2016	105,862	$21.85	4.1	$1,126

[a] Market price of underlying Pfizer common stock less exercise price.

[b] The number of options expected to vest takes into account on estimate of expected forfeitures.

The following table summarizes data related to all stock option activity:

(Millions of Dollars, Except Per Stock Option Amounts)	Year Ended December 31 2016	2015	2014
Weighted-average grant date fair value per stock option	$ 3.89	$ 4.30	$ 4.40
Aggregate intrinsic value on exercise	$ 389	$ 666	$ 458
Cash received upon exercise	$1,019	$1,263	$1,002
Tax benefits realized related to exercise	$ 112	$ 187	$ 131
Total compensation cost related to nonvested stock options not yet recognized, pre-tax	$ 58	$ 159	$ 147
Weighted-average period over which stock option compensation cost is expected to be recognized (years)	1.1	1.8	1.8

Source: Selected Footnote Disclosures from Pfizer Inc.'s 2016 Financial Statements. http://www.pfizer.com/investors/sec_filings

THE CONCEPTUAL FRAMEWORK CONNECTION
Stock-Based Compensation

Accountants make two important judgments related to stock-based compensation: measurement of the options at fair value and the probability of forfeiture. Option-pricing models determine the fair value for recording the amount of expense for the options in the income statement. However, even good models provide only an *estimate* of the fair value. Thus, similar to many items reported in the financial statements, the expense related to employee stock options is a judgment-based estimate.

Consider Davis Enterprises, Inc. from Example 19.1. Davis estimated the fair value of its stock options at $9.60 per share. Management could have also estimated an amount higher or lower than $9.60 per share. For example, assume that they used an estimate of $11 per share. Then, instead of reporting compensation expense of $259,200 in 2018 and 2019, the company would report an expense of $297,000, thus reducing net income by an additional $37,800 in each year. There can be incentives for management to use a lower estimate of fair value to result in a lower charge to net income.

Estimating how many options will ultimately be exercisable also relies on judgment related to the probability that employees will exercise their options. Employees forfeit their options if they terminate employment before the option vesting date. Companies record only the amount of expense related to the estimate of options that will not be forfeited. Again, that determination is purely a matter of judgment, and the resulting measure of expense is an estimate.

There was a 10% forfeiture rate in Example 19.1. However, that forfeiture rate is only an estimate based on predictions of future events. What if Davis had instead estimated a 25% forfeiture rate? In that case, the fair value of $576,000 would have been multiplied by 75% and the compensation expense for 2018 and 2019 would be reduced from $259,200 per year to $216,000 per year. Providing a relatively high estimate of the forfeiture rate to decrease expense recognized would directly increase net income, benefiting management.

6 Describe the characteristics of defined-contribution and defined-benefit pension plans.

Overview of Pensions

Employees are often entitled to receive benefits such as pension plans, healthcare plans, and life insurance coverage following retirement. Post-retirement benefits recognize years of service provided by employees. Because an employee will likely work for many years before retiring, the benefits owed to the employee are usually noncurrent liabilities. Our focus is on pensions, which are the most significant post-employment benefits provided to retired employees.[14] After establishing the key background details on pensions, we will examine the accounting process.

Pension Plan Administration

Pension plans can be either *contributory* or *noncontributory*. **Contributory plans** require employees to fund some or all pension benefit costs and allow employees to make additional contributions to voluntarily increase their retirement benefits. In **noncontributory** plans, the employer is responsible for funding the total cost of the plan.

A company (referred to as the sponsor company) sets aside funds for future pension benefits and transfers these assets to a separate legal entity called a **pension trust**. The trust accumulates the pension fund assets and makes payments to retirees. Our focus is on the impact of pension plans on the financial statements of the sponsor company. We do not consider accounting issues related to the pension trust.[15]

Types of Pension Plans

There are two main types of pension arrangements: *defined contribution* and *defined benefit*. According to the *Employee Benefits Survey* for 2016 conducted by the Bureau of Labor Statistics, 8% of businesses offered a defined-benefit retirement plan and 46% offered a defined-contribution plan. We discuss the accounting treatment for both types of plans next.

Defined-Contribution Plans. In a **defined-contribution plan**, the employer contributes a fixed amount each period based on a formula that is typically a percentage of the employee's salary. The employer is not responsible for the value of the pension fund assets.

[14]Because the accounting for non-pension post-retirement benefits (for example, health insurance for retired employees) is very similar to the accounting for pensions, we do not discuss other post-retirement benefits in this text.

[15]The pension trust is a separate legal entity with its own set of financial statements. The pension trust follows unique accounting standards that are not covered in this text.

Employees determine the types of investments held in their plans that ultimately determine the rate of return on the assets and, therefore, the employees bear the risk of loss on their pension fund assets.

Accounting for defined-contribution plans involves recording contributions as expenses and is similar to recording any type of compensation expense. Specifically, when the employee provides services and earns the pension, the company records the pension expense. The company may pay cash into the plan at that time or have a payable to the plan. Example 19.15 illustrates accounting for defined-contribution plans.

EXAMPLE 19.15 Defined-Contribution Plans

PROBLEM: ADF Company pays wages of $1,000,000 this period and has a defined-contribution pension plan that requires the company to contribute 5% of total wages into the plan. What is the journal entry to record ADF's pension expense?

SOLUTION: The following entry records ADF Company's pension expense of $50,000 ($1,000,000 × 5%).

Account	***Current Year***	
Pension Expense	50,000	
Cash		50,000

Under a defined-contribution plan, the employer's annual cost is the amount that it is obligated to contribute to the pension trust. If it makes the contribution in full each year, then there is no pension asset or liability on the balance sheet. If the company contributes more (less) than the formula amount, then a pension asset (liability) results.

Defined-Benefit Plans. A **defined-benefit plan** specifies a predetermined amount of benefits that the employee will receive at the time of retirement. The employer, who bears the risk of loss, is therefore concerned with the rate of return earned on the assets invested in the pension trust. In a defined-contribution plan, the contribution is fixed, but the benefits can vary. In a defined-benefit plan, the contributions can vary, but the benefits are fixed.

The defined-benefit formula is usually a function of a predetermined percentage, salary level, and credits granted for the number of years of service. The defined benefit is calculated as follows:

$$\text{Defined Benefit} = \% \times \text{Salary Level} \times \text{Credits for Years of Service}$$

The defined benefit due each year is a deferred future payment, so it is a liability. Because the quantitative complexity of the information required by the defined-benefit pension plan, *actuaries* handle the actual and projected plan measurements. An **actuary** is an individual skilled in mathematics, statistics, and finance who analyzes the financial consequences of risk based on probability assessments. Actuaries assist in determining the amount of pension plan funding and the costs to service the plan. Actuaries forecast key variables required in pension computations such as turnover rates, life expectancies, future salary levels, interest rates, and retirement patterns.

Measures of the Actuarially Determined Defined-Benefit Pension Obligation

Based on key variables, a company estimates its liability for the future benefits promised under a defined-benefit plan as the present value of the defined benefits. The following timeline depicts the sequence of events for the pension.

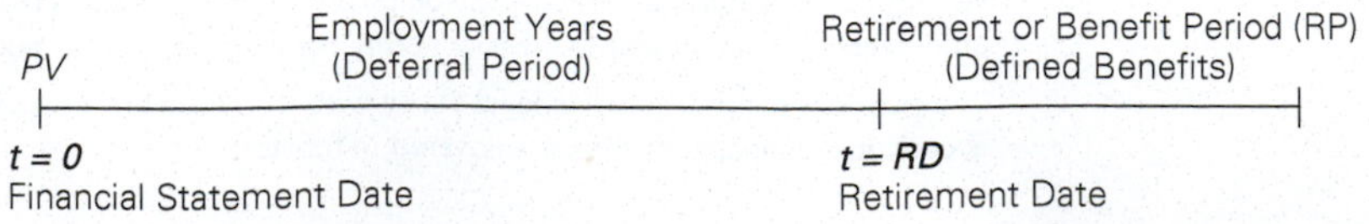

At the financial statement date, the defined-benefit obligation is the present value of the benefit payments to be made after employees retire. While the employees are working, the benefits are deferred. Therefore, the defined-benefit obligation is simply a deferred annuity. The deferral or waiting period is represented by the years of employment.

The defined-benefit payments begin on the retirement date (RD) and extend over a designated retirement period (RP). The length of the retirement period can be based on life expectancy, or it can be specified by the employment contract. For example, the contract may allow the employee to take a lump-sum payment at retirement, receive payments over a fixed term, or base the distribution period on life expectancy.

There are three distinct methods for measuring a company's pension obligation to its employees:

1. Vested benefit obligation (VBO)
2. Accumulated benefit obligation (ABO)
3. Projected benefit obligation (PBO)

The three measures of obligations are equal to the present value of the promised benefit payments with the benefits defined differently depending on whether the employee is vested or not and the salary levels used.

Vested Benefit Obligation. The **vested benefit pension obligation** (VBO) bases the defined-benefit obligation on the vested benefits that accrue to current employees. *Vesting*, as explained, means that an employee's right to pension benefits is not contingent on any future employment with the company. The employer computes the VBO using current salary levels and includes only vested benefits. Because the vested benefits must be paid even if the plan is discontinued or the employees are terminated, the VBO is considered a termination-basis obligation.

Accumulated Benefit Obligation. The **accumulated benefit obligation** (ABO) estimates the pension obligation based on years of service performed by all employees, both vested and non-vested, under the plan considering current salary levels. The ABO is partially a going-concern obligation because it considers all employees. However, it is sometimes considered a minimum obligation because it reflects only current salaries and does not factor in projected increases in compensation.

Projected Benefit Obligation. The **projected benefit obligation** (PBO) considers all employees, both vested and non-vested, using estimated future salary levels. The PBO is usually the largest estimate of the pension obligation because it uses projected future salary levels. The PBO is considered a going-concern obligation because it considers all employees and future compensation rates. FASB requires this obligation for use in pension computations.

Assuming inflation and no salary reductions, Exhibit 19.4 illustrates the expected ranking of the actuarially determined pension obligations.

EXHIBIT 19.4 Measures of the Pension Obligation

Pension Obligation	Benefits Included for Vested Only or Vested and Unvested?	Benefits Computed Using Current Salaries or Future Salaries?	Amount of Pension Benefit Obligation
Vested benefit obligation	Vested only	Current	
Accumulated benefit obligation	Vested and unvested	Current	
Projected benefit obligation	Vested and unvested	Future	

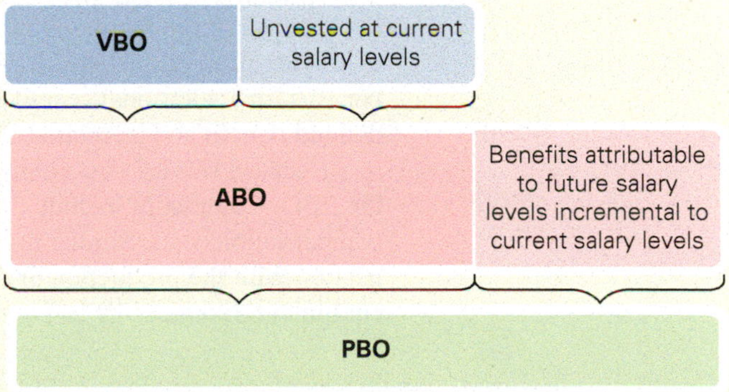

The PBO provides the largest pension obligation of the three methods. The differences in the rankings are explained as follows:

1. The ABO exceeds the VBO by the present value of the difference between the service credits earned by all employees versus vested employees.
2. The PBO exceeds the ABO by the present value of the difference between estimated future and current salary levels.

The remainder of the chapter discusses the complexities of accounting for defined-benefit pension plans.

7 Demonstrate the measurement of pension costs and the related liability or asset under defined-benefit plans, including remeasurement due to changes in actuarial assumptions.

Defined-Benefit Pension Plan Accounting

There are seven key factors in accounting for defined-benefit pension plans. To provide a clear understanding of the financial statement effects of each factor, we consider each factor separately and present the related conceptual journal entry.[16] Note, however, that companies make a single, combined journal entry at the end of the reporting period to account for defined-benefit pension plans. We conclude our discussion by summarizing the seven factors with a combined entry. Before examining each factor in depth, we use the conceptual framework as a starting point.

THE CONCEPTUAL FRAMEWORK CONNECTION
Defined-Benefit Pension Plans

On the balance sheet, two primary accounts are involved in accounting for defined-benefit plans: pension plan assets and pension plan obligations. Companies use an account for pension plan assets because the sponsor company invests funds into the pension plan. A defined-benefit pension plan results in a projected benefit obligation liability. Companies report the difference between the pension plan asset account and the projected benefit obligation on the balance sheet as either a net pension asset or a net pension liability. This amount is called the *funded status of the plan*. If the plan assets exceed the PBO, the plan is overfunded; if the plan assets are less than the PBO, the plan is underfunded.

On the income statement, defined-benefit plans result in pension costs for the company. Consistent with the conceptual framework's definition of expense, the provision of retirement benefits results in either the outflow of assets (cash) or the creation of a liability related to the entity's major operations. In general, the current accounting treatment for pensions ensures that companies properly allocate pension costs in the income statement to the period that the employees provide services to the company.

Next we examine each factor in depth.

Factor 1: Service Cost

Service cost is the increase in the projected benefit obligation resulting from one additional year of service from employees. It is measured as the present value of the cost of providing pension benefits for 1 additional year of service using all employees and estimated future salary rates. The defined benefit and its related obligation increase with additional years of service.

Because service costs obligate a company to increase benefits to its retirees, they increase the PBO. Companies include the service cost in operating income in the same line item as other compensation costs. Similar to other compensation costs, service costs can be capitalized in connection with the production or construction of an asset such as inventory or property, plant, and equipment. Example 19.16 provides an example of accounting for service costs.

[16] For the relevant authoritative literature, see FASB ASC 715-30 – *Compensation – Retirement Benefits – Defined-benefits Plans – Pensions* for U.S. GAAP and IASC, *International Accounting Standard 19*, "Employee Benefits" (London, UK: International Accounting Standards Committee, Revised, 2013) for IFRS.

EXAMPLE 19.16

Service Cost

PROBLEM: Prepare the entry to reflect KMR Bookstore's service cost of $167,000 (as determined by its actuary) in the current year.

SOLUTION: The entry to record service costs is as follows:

Account	Current Year		
Service Cost	167,000		(1)
Projected Benefit Obligation		167,000	

Use the numbered label to the right of the individual journal entry as a guide to understanding the combined entry at the end of the section.

Factor 2: Prior Service Costs

Prior service costs represent service benefits provided to current employees on the initial adoption or amendment of an existing defined-benefit pension plan. For example, assume that an employer amends a union pension plan to increase the defined-benefit rate from 4% to 6% of final salary levels for each year of service. The 2% increase is a retroactive benefit for all prior years of service. The prior service costs represent the present value of these retroactive benefits.

Prior service costs increase the liability balance. Because employers grant these plan amendments to both compensate and motivate employees in future periods, they do not include this additional cost in pension expense on the date of the amendment.[17] Instead, employers defer the prior service cost in other comprehensive income and amortize it to pension expense over future periods. Prior service costs are deferred in other comprehensive income because income is not affected until subsequent periods. When recognized in income, prior service costs are an other pension expense.

U.S. GAAP allows two methods for allocating the amortization:

1. Determine a cost per service year by dividing the prior service cost by the number of future periods of service for each employee active at the date of the amendment who is expected to receive benefits under the plan. The amortization each year after that is the cost per service year multiplied by the actual number of service years performed.
2. Use a straight-line method over the average remaining service period of the employees that are expected to receive the plan benefits. Accounting for prior service costs is shown in Example 19.17.

EXAMPLE 19.17

Prior Service Costs

PROBLEM: KMR Bookstores amends its defined-benefit pension plan, resulting in prior service costs of $55,000. The company will amortize the prior service costs on a straight-line basis over 5 years. What is the journal entry?

SOLUTION: The entry to record this change is as follows:

Account	Current Year		
Other Comprehensive Income – Prior Service Costs	55,000		(2)
Projected Benefit Obligation		55,000	

Continued

[17]Employee compensation increases when an employer enhances pension benefits. Management expects that this increase in compensation will improve employee motivation and productivity in the future. As a result, companies defer the cost of providing increased pension benefits and amortize to future periods of benefit. This approach effectively matches the cost of providing additional compensation with the economic benefits received.

The company amortizes prior service costs over 5 years on a straight-line basis. So, KMR recognizes $11,000 in pension expense each year ($55,000 total prior service costs divided by 5 years). The entry to record the amortization is as follows:

Account	Current Year		
Pension Expense	11,000		(2a)
Other Comprehensive Income – Prior Service Costs		11,000	

Factor 3: Interest on the PBO

Defined-benefit pension plans create a liability (the PBO) computed as the present value of future cash outflows for the defined-benefit payments. As with any deferred-payment arrangement, companies use the effective interest rate method of amortization. The obligation increases by the accrued interest on the obligation each year. Similarly a company's other pension expense increases by this same amount.

The amount of interest is an appropriate interest rate multiplied by the balance of the PBO at the beginning of the year.[18] An actuary determines the **settlement rate**, which is the interest rate used to compute the interest on the PBO.[19] For example, ***Johnson & Johnson's*** settlement rate in fiscal 2016 was 3.78%, resulting in an interest cost of $927 million on its pension obligation. Companies add the interest cost to the pension expense in operating income and increase the PBO by the same amount as shown in Example 19.18.

EXAMPLE 19.18

Interest on the PBO

PROBLEM: KMR Bookstores has a beginning PBO balance of $789,000 and a settlement rate of 10%. What is the entry to record interest expense on the pension obligation?

SOLUTION: The entry to record the PBO interest is as follows (10% × $789,000).

Account	Current Year	
Pension Expense	78,900	
Projected Benefit Obligation		78,900

When a plan amendment increases the PBO, interest costs are also computed on the additional prior service costs. The prior service costs are added to the PBO from the date the amendments are effective as illustrated by Example 19.19.

EXAMPLE 19.19

Interest on the PBO with Prior Service Costs during the Year

PROBLEM: KMR Bookstores has a beginning PBO balance of $789,000 and a settlement rate of 10%. KMR amended its defined-benefit pension plan on January 1 of the current year. The prior service cost related to this amendment is $55,000. What is the entry to record interest expense on the pension obligation?

[18] In determining interest expense, the accountant assumes that all prior service cost adjustments are effective as of the beginning of the year of initial adoption or amendment of the plan. So, companies add the full amount of the prior service cost to the beginning balance of the PBO to compute interest on the projected benefit obligation.

[19] The settlement rate is the rate of return needed to cover all retirement benefits if an annuity contract is purchased today using the current balance of plan assets. Companies can also use the market rate on high-quality Aa corporate bonds for this purpose.

SOLUTION: Interest expense is now $84,400, which is 10% of the beginning PBO of $789,000 plus the $55,000 prior service costs. The entry to record the PBO interest is as follows:

Account	Current Year		
Pension Expense	84,400		(3)
Projected Benefit Obligation		84,400	

This calculation of interest will be used later in the chapter in the calculation of pension expense.

Factor 4: Expected Return on Pension Plan Assets

The sponsor corporation provides assets for the plan in order to pay its obligations when retirements take place. The invested plan assets earn interest, dividends, and capital gains upon sale. Every plan has an **expected return on plan assets**, which is the return based on expectations for interest, dividends, and fluctuations in the market value of the fund assets.

With pension accounting, companies include expected return on plan assets rather than the actual return in the pension cost. The expected return is the beginning plan assets at fair value multiplied by an expected rate of return.[20] Reporting the *expected* return as opposed to the *actual* return as part of pension expense smooths volatility in the pension cost.[21]

Remember that companies set aside plan assets to fulfill the pension obligation when it comes due. Because a company pays the retirement benefits over many years, the obligation decreases as the company pays retirees.

In addition, because of the long-term nature of the pension obligation, any current deviations between the actual and expected return on plan assets should offset over that time. To illustrate, assume that a plan holds only equity securities and the historical rate of return on equity is 15%. The expected return is the beginning plan assets multiplied by the expected rate of 15%. The actual return could be greater or less than 15%. The difference between the actual and expected return is known as the **unexpected return**, a topic that we return to in more detail later. As time passes, the amount of unexpected return above and below the expected return should approximately offset, causing the expected return to approximate the actual return.

Exhibit 19.5 graphs expected and actual average rates of return on pension plan assets for the S&P 500 companies per year from fiscal 2007 to 2016. The expected return on plan assets is fairly

EXHIBIT 19.5 Expected and Actual Rates of Return on Plan Assets, 2007 through 2016

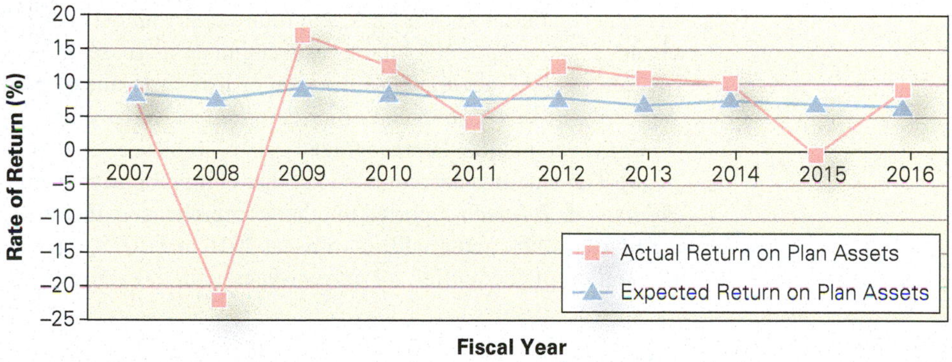

* Based on S&P 500 Companies.
Source: Data taken from Compustat Pension Annual File.

[20] U.S. GAAP specifies using the market-related value of the plan assets, which is a 5-year moving average of the portfolio value. For simplicity, we assume that fair value and the market-related value are the same.

[21] The expected return is also computed on assets contributed during the year. For simplicity, we assume that all funding into the plan takes place at the end of each year. In this way, the beginning balance takes into account all contributions made during the previous year.

constant over this time, around 7% to 9%. For example, ***Johnson & Johnson's*** expected return on plan assets was 8.55% in 2016. The actual return varies with market conditions. Note the large loss on actual plan assets in 2008 consistent with the drop in the stock market.

Expected returns reduce other pension expense and expected losses increase other pension expense. Example 19.20 illustrates accounting for the expected return on plan assets.

EXAMPLE 19.20 Expected Return on Plan Assets

PROBLEM: KMR Bookstores has beginning pension plan assets of $654,000 and the expected return is 9%. What is the entry to record the expected return on plan assets?

SOLUTION: The expected return on plan assets is the beginning balance of pension plan assets multiplied by the expected rate of return. So, KMR will report an expected return on plan assets of $58,860 ($654,000 beginning pension plan assets × 9% expected rate of return). The entry to record the expected return on plan assets is as follows:

Account	***Current Year***		
Pension Plan Assets	58,860		(4)
Pension Expense – Expected Return		58,860	

Factor 5: Current-Year Net Gains and Losses

The current year's net gains and losses arise from two sources:

1. The difference between the expected return on plan assets (factor 4) and the actual return.
2. Changes in actuarial assumptions related to the projected benefit obligation.

Sources of Current-Year Net Gains and Losses. Plan assets change with the actual return on investments—but accountants include the expected return on plan assets in the pension expense. If the actual return is greater than the expected return, the unexpected return is positive. In this case, plan assets have increased *more* than expected and there is a net actuarial gain. If the actual return is less than the expected return, the unexpected return is negative. In this case, plan assets have increased *less* than expected and there is a net actuarial loss. The actual return on the plan assets is the sum of the expected return and unexpected return.

Actuarial gains and losses also result from changes in assumptions related to the projected benefit obligation. Pension obligations are based on actuarial assumptions such as retirement rates, life expectancies, turnover rates, and future salary amounts. Modifying these actuarial assumptions changes the pension obligation, resulting in an increase or a decrease to the PBO.

U.S. GAAP accumulates the gain or loss from unexpected returns and changes in actuarial assumptions in accumulated other comprehensive income and amortizes it over future periods when the accumulated unrecognized gain or loss exceeds a materiality level (discussed on the next page). The amounts accumulated in other comprehensive income can be quite large. For example, ***Johnson & Johnson*** reported in other comprehensive income a $2,302 million actuarial gain and a $1,578 million actuarial loss in fiscal 2016 and 2015, respectively. Example 19.21 provides an illustration of accounting for current-year actuarial gains and losses.

EXAMPLE 19.21 Current-Year Actuarial Gains and Losses

PROBLEM: KMR Bookstores reports an actual return on plan assets of $75,000. Its expected return on plan assets was $58,860. Changes to its actuarial assumptions also resulted in an increase in the PBO of $4,300. What is the entry to record the unexpected return on plan assets? What is the entry to adjust the PBO for changes in actuarial assumptions?

SOLUTION: First, because KMR's actual return on plan assets of $75,000 was higher than the expected return of $58,860, KMR records a gain of $16,140 representing the unexpected return for the period. The entry to record the gain of $16,140 related to plan assets includes a debit to the asset account with a credit to other comprehensive income:

Account	Current Year		
Pension Plan Assets	16,140		(5)
Other Comprehensive Income – Actuarial Gains/Losses		16,140	

Second, because actuarial assumptions have changed, KMR has to increase its obligation. The entry to record the effect on the PBO from the change in actuarial assumption includes a credit to the PBO account and a debit to other comprehensive income.

Account	Current Year		
Other Comprehensive Income – Actuarial Gains/Losses	4,300		(5a)
Projected Benefit Obligation		4,300	

The Corridor Approach. After a company records the net actuarial gains and losses in other comprehensive income, it may amortize them into pension expense over future periods. There is no typical, systematic basis for allocating the unamortized net actuarial gain or loss to future periods. Rather, companies amortize the accumulated amount of the net actuarial gain or loss only if it exceeds a materiality level known as the *corridor*.

The **corridor** is defined as 10% of the higher of the beginning balance of the projected benefit obligation or the beginning balance of the plan assets at market-related value. Key considerations for applying the corridor follow.

1. A company amortizes the net accumulated gain or loss only when the beginning accumulated unamortized balance of the net gain or loss exceeds the corridor. Companies only amortize the excess over the corridor.
2. Although companies may use any acceptable method of amortizing the excess, the amortized amount cannot be less than the amount computed using the straight-line method of amortization.
3. Commonly, the company allocates the amortization over the average remaining service life of its employee base.
4. The corridor test uses the absolute value of the accumulated net gain or loss.

For example, ***Johnson & Johnson*** exceeded the corridor and had to amortize a portion of its accumulated actuarial losses into pension costs, which increased pension costs by $496 million and $745 million in fiscal 2016 and 2015, respectively.

We present Example 19.22 in which there is no amortization required. Note that this example does not use KMR Bookstores. We return to KMR in Example 19.23.

EXAMPLE 19.22 Corridor Approach, No Amortization

PROBLEM: A&N Athletic Equipment, Inc. reports a beginning PBO balance of $944,000 and a beginning balance in plan assets of $852,000 (market-related value). The company has a net actuarial gain at the beginning of the period of $74,200. The A&N employee base has an average remaining service life of 10 years. What is the corridor? What is the required amortization of actuarial gains or losses in the current year for A&N Athletic?

SOLUTION: The corridor is 10% of the greater of the beginning PBO or plan assets. Because the PBO balance is greater than the plan assets, the corridor is 10% of $944,000, or $94,400. The beginning balance related to net actuarial gains and losses is a credit of $74,200, which is less than the $94,400 corridor. So, no amortization is required.

Example 19.23 provides an illustration requiring amortization.

EXAMPLE 19.23

Corridor Approach with Amortization

PROBLEM: KMR Bookstores reports a beginning PBO balance of $789,000 and a beginning balance in plan assets of $654,000 (market-related value). The company has a net actuarial gain at the beginning of the period of $83,500. The KMR employee base has an average remaining service life of 10 years. What is the corridor? What is the required amortization of actuarial gains or losses in the current year?[22]

SOLUTION: The corridor is 10% of the greater of the beginning PBO or plan assets. Because the PBO balance is greater than the plan assets, the corridor is 10% of $789,000, or $78,900. The $83,500 balance of net actuarial gains exceeds the corridor of $78,900. So, KMR amortizes the $4,600 difference between the accumulated net actuarial gain balance ($83,500) and the corridor ($78,900) over the remaining service life (10 years). The amortization is $460 ($83,500 less $78,900 divided by 10). The journal entry is as follows:

Account	***Current Year***		
Other Comprehensive Income – Actuarial Gains/Losses	460		(5b)
Pension Expense		460	

If KMR had a beginning balance in accumulated other comprehensive income related to actuarial losses of $83,500, the amortization would still have been $460. The debit, however, would be to pension expense and the credit to other comprehensive income – actuarial gains/losses.

The amount of amortization is generally not the same each year under the straight-line method. In fact, there may be no amortization in the next year or the amount could be different depending on the results of the corridor test in that year. Therefore, when applying the corridor approach, it is important to note that:

- Companies test the need for amortization only at the beginning of each year. Thus, if in its first year of operations a company experiences an actuarial gain or loss, no corridor test is necessary and no amortization results because there is no beginning net balance in actuarial gains/losses in accumulated other comprehensive income.
- The test can result in no amortization in any given year if the net balance in actuarial gains/losses in accumulated other comprehensive income is less than the corridor.

Factor 6: Funding the Plan

The company funds the pension plan by contributing assets into the fund. As the company contributes cash into the fund, the pension plan assets increase. An example of accounting for plan funding is provided in Example 19.24.

EXAMPLE 19.24

Plan Funding

PROBLEM: KMR Bookstores contributes $100,000 into the fund this year. What is the entry to record its contribution?

SOLUTION: The journal entry is as follows:

Account	***Current Year***		
Pension Plan Assets	100,000		(6)
Cash		100,000	

[22]This example assumes the balance in its beginning accumulated OCI relates to actuarial gains.

Factor 7: Payments to Retirees

Payments made to retirees, the last factor, reduce the plan assets and the PBO. The plan assets decrease as the company uses them to make payments to the retirees on its liability, thus reducing the projected benefit obligation. This process is comparable to a company paying off any debt. Example 19.25 shows the accounting for payments to retirees.

EXAMPLE 19.25

Payments to Retirees

PROBLEM: The retirees of KMR Bookstores receive payments of $72,000 in the current year. Provide the necessary entry to record this payment.

SOLUTION: Because the pension trust, not the sponsor corporation (KMR) pays the cash to the retirees, KMR Bookstores does not need to credit cash in this transaction. The journal entry is as follows:

Account	Current Year		
Projected Benefit Obligation	72,000		(7)
Pension Plan Assets		72,000	

Summary: Accounting Effects of Defined-Benefit Pension Plans

We now combine the KMR Bookstores examples to summarize the income, balance sheet, and off-balance sheet effects in Exhibit 19.6. The total pension cost included in net income is $203,080. Additional prior service costs and actuarial gains included in other comprehensive income are $32,620. On the balance sheet in Exhibit 19.6, the ending PBO is $1,027,700 and plan assets of $757,000 net to a liability of $270,700. Because the beginning PBO was $789,000 and the beginning plan assets were $654,000, the beginning net pension liability was $135,000. The increase in the net pension liability from the beginning balance of $135,000 to the ending balance of $270,700 is $135,700, a credit in the pension journal entry. Finally, KMR credits cash for contributions to the pension fund of $100,000. The summary journal entry made in Exhibit 19.6 is similar to the actual entry made in practice. Because service cost is reported in compensation expense in operating income, the service cost of $167,000 is separated from other pension expenses. Other pension expenses of $36,080 are reported in non-operating income. KMR's footnotes to the financial statements would include the components of pension costs, impact on accumulated other comprehensive income, the PBO, and the plan assets. We provide a comprehensive example in Appendix A.

Accounting for Defined-Benefit Pension Plans: IFRS

Accounting for defined-benefit plans under IFRS differs from U.S. GAAP in the following areas:

- Factor 2: expensing prior service costs
- Factors 3 and 4: measuring the return on plan assets and interest expense
- Factor 5: reporting current-year net actuarial gains and losses

Additionally, IFRS renames the projected benefit obligation under a defined-benefit pension plan the **present value of the defined-benefit obligation** (PVDBO).[23] We illustrate the IFRS differences in the context of the KMR Bookstores example.[24]

[23]For simplicity, we will use the term "PBO" throughout the rest of the chapter.

[24]Under IFRS, a company may be limited in the amount of the net pension asset it reports, called the "asset ceiling." IFRS requires reporting the lower of the net pension asset or the present value of any refunds from the plan or reductions in future contributions to the plan.

EXHIBIT 19.6 Income and Balance Sheet Summary for KMR Bookstore, Pension Journal Entry *(Credits and credit balances reported in parentheses)*

Summary of KMR		Comprehensive Income			Balance Sheet			
Entry	**Description**	**NI – Pension Expense**	**OCI – Prior Service Costs**	**OCI – Actuarial Gains/Losses**	**PBO**	**Plan Assets**	**AOCI – Prior Service Costs**	**AOCI – Actuarial Gains/Losses**
	Beginning balance				$ (789,000)	$ 654,000		$ (83,500)
(1)	Service cost	$167,000			(167,000)			
(2)	Prior service cost		$ 55,000		(55,000)		55,000	
(2a)	Amortization of PSC	11,000	(11,000)				(11,000)	
(3)	Interest on PBO	84,400			(84,400)			
(4)	Expected return on plan assets	(58,860)				58,860		
(5)	Unexpected return on plan assets			$(16,140)		16,140		(16,140)
(5a)	Change in actuarial assumptions			4,300	(4,300)			4,300
(5b)	Amortization of actuarial gains	(460)		460				460
(6)	Funding					100,000		
(7)	Payments to retirees				72,000	(72,000)		
	Pension costs – Net income	$203,080						
	Other comprehensive income		$ 44,000	$(11,380)				
	Ending balances				$(1,027,700)	$ 757,000	$44,000	$(94,880)
	Ending net liability on balance sheet					$(270,700)		

KMR Journal Entry

Service Cost	167,000		
Other Pension Expense	36,080		
OCI – Prior Service Costs	44,000		
OCI – Actuarial Gains/Losses		11,380	
Cash (contributions)		100,000	
Net Pension Liability		135,700	(change from beginning net liability of $135,000 to ending net liability of $270,700)

Factor 2: Prior Service Costs. Accounting for service costs is the same under U.S. GAAP and IFRS. However, the accounting for prior service costs differs. IFRS reporters expense prior service costs when the plan amendments are made. Under U.S. GAAP, these costs are amortized over time. Additionally, IFRS refers to *prior service costs* as *past service costs*.[25] Example 19.26 illustrates that all past service costs are expensed in the current year under IFRS.

[25]For simplicity, we will use the term "prior service costs" throughout the rest of the chapter.

EXAMPLE 19.26 Past Service Costs: IFRS

PROBLEM: KMR Bookstores amends its defined-benefit pension plan, resulting in past service costs of $55,000. What is the entry under IFRS?

SOLUTION: The entry to record this change under IFRS is as follows:

Account	Current Year		
Other Pension Expense – Past Service Costs	55,000		(2 – IFRS)
Projected Benefit Obligation		55,000	

Factors 3 and 4: Interest on the PBO and Expected Return on Pension Plan Assets. Under IFRS, the computation of the interest on the PBO and the expected return on plan assets are combined into *net interest on the net defined benefit liability (asset)*. Under U.S. GAAP, companies can use one interest rate to determine interest expense and another one to determine the expected return on plan assets. IFRS requires applying one interest rate to both the obligation and asset.[26] The view under IFRS is that the plan assets should grow over time in the same way that the pension obligation grows. Therefore, using one rate to determine both interest expense and interest income is appropriate. This approach also recognizes that the pension is being financed by the employees of the company over the time they work for the company. IFRS specifies that a company should determine the interest rate based on market yields at the end of the reporting period on high-quality corporate bonds.[27]

Under U.S. GAAP, companies add the interest cost and deduct expected return from the pension expense in non-operating income. IFRS allows companies the choice to report the net interest on the net defined benefits liability (asset) in operating or financing income. Example 19.27 illustrates accounting for net interest under IFRS.

EXAMPLE 19.27 Net Interest on the Net Defined Benefit Liability (Asset): IFRS

PROBLEM: KMR Bookstores has a beginning PBO balance of $789,000 and beginning pension plan assets of $654,000. The interest rate based on market yields at the end of the reporting period on high-quality corporate bonds is 10%. KMR amended its defined-benefit pension plan on January 1 of the current year. The past service cost related to this amendment is $55,000. What is KMR's interest expense? What is the expected return on plan assets? What is its net defined benefit liability (asset)? What is the net interest expense on the net defined benefit liability (asset)? What is the journal entry?

SOLUTION: Interest expense is $84,400, which is 10% of the beginning PBO of $789,000 plus the $55,000 past service costs. KMR's expected return on plan assets is $65,400 ($654,000 plan assets × 10%). KMR's net defined benefit liability (asset) is $190,000, $844,000 PBO less $654,000 plan assets. Its net interest on the net defined benefit liability (asset) is $19,000, which is 10% of the net defined benefit liability of $190,000, or $84,400 interest expense less $65,400 return on plan assets.

[26] IFRS specifies use of the fair value of the plan assets to determine the expected return on plans assets whereas U.S. GAAP specifies using the market-related value of the plan assets.

[27] In countries where there is a limited market in high-yield corporate bonds, a company can use the market yields on government bonds.

KMR presents two entries separately emphasizing the interest on the PBO and the return on the plan assets that combined represent the net interest on the net defined benefit liability (asset).[28]

Account	Current Year		
Pension Expense or Interest Expense	84,400		(3)
Projected Benefit Obligation		84,400	

Account	Current Year		
Pension Plan Assets	65,400		(4 – IFRS)
Pension Expense or Interest Expense		65,400	

Similar to U.S. GAAP, IFRS reporters add past service costs to the PBO from the date the amendments are effective. Under IFRS, a company accounts for any changes in the plan assets held during the period as a result of contributions and benefit payments in determining the interest expense.

Factor 5: Current-Year Net Gains and Losses. Under IFRS, a company reports all current-year actuarial gains or losses in other comprehensive income.[29] The accounting for current-year actuarial gains and losses is shown in Example 19.28. Therefore, in contrast to U.S. GAAP, actuarial gains and losses are not amortized under IFRS.

EXAMPLE 19.28

Current-Year Actuarial Gains and Losses: IFRS

PROBLEM: KMR Bookstores reports an actual return on plan assets of $75,000. Its expected return on plan assets was $65,400. Changes to its actuarial assumptions also resulted in an increase in the PBO of $4,300. What is the entry to record the unexpected return on plan assets under IFRS? What is the entry to adjust the PBO for changes in actuarial assumptions under IFRS?

SOLUTION: First, because KMR's actual return on plan assets of $75,000 was higher than the expected return of $65,400, KMR records a gain of $9,600. This $9,600 gain is the unexpected return for the period. The entry under IFRS to record the gain of $9,600 related to plan assets includes a debit to the asset account and a credit to other comprehensive income:

Account	Current Year		
Pension Plan Assets	9,600		(5 – IFRS)
Other Comprehensive Income – Actuarial Gains/Losses		9,600	

Second, because actuarial assumptions have changed, KMR has to increase its obligation. The IFRS entry to record the effect on the PBO of the change in actuarial assumption includes a credit to the PBO account and a debit to other comprehensive income.

Account	Current Year		
Other Comprehensive Income – Actuarial Gains/Losses	4,300		(5a – IFRS)
Projected Benefit Obligation		4,300	

[28]If a company debits (credits) pension expense, it reports the amount in operating expenses. Alternatively, when a company debits (credits) interest expense, it reports it as part of financing expense.

[29]Companies currently have the option under both IFRS and U.S. GAAP to report actuarial gains and losses immediately in income. That is, the corridor method results in the minimum amortization and larger amounts can be written off at the option of the reporting entity. However, few companies choose this option, so we do not discuss it further.

Summary: Accounting Effects of Defined-Benefit Pension Plan. Exhibit 19.7 shows the pension worksheet for KMR Bookstore under IFRS.

The total pension costs included in net income is $241,000. We assume that KMR reports services costs of $167,000 in operating income and all other pension expense of $74,000 in non-operating income. Other pension income included in other comprehensive income is $5,300, which is a credit in the pension journal entry.

On the balance sheet, the ending PBO of $1,027,700 and the ending plan assets of $757,000 net to a liability of $270,700. The increase in the net pension liability from the beginning balance of $135,000 to the ending balance of $270,700 is $135,700, a credit in the pension journal entry. Finally, KMR credits cash contributions in the pension journal entry for $100,000.

EXHIBIT 19.7 IFRS Income and Balance Sheet Summary for KMR Bookstore with Pension Journal Entry
(Credits and credit balances reported in parentheses)

	Summary of KMR	Comprehensive Income		Balance Sheet	
Entry	Description	NI—Pension Expense	OCI – Actuarial Gains/Losses	PBO	Plan Assets
	Beginning balance			$ (789,000)	$ 654,000
(1)	Service cost	$ 167,000		(167,000)	
(2 – IFRS)	Past service cost	55,000		(55,000)	
(3)	Interest on PBO	84,400		(84,400)	
(4 – IFRS)	Interest income/Expected return on plan assets	(65,400)			65,400
(5 – IFRS)	Unexpected return on plan assets		$(9,600)		9,600
(5a – IFRS)	Change in actuarial assumptions		4,300	(4,300)	
(6)	Funding				100,000
(7)	Payments to retirees			72,000	(72,000)
	Pension Costs – Net Income	$241,000			
	Other Comprehensive Income		$(5,300)		
	Ending balances			$(1,027,700)	$ 757,000
	Ending net liability on balance sheet				$(270,700)
KMR Journal Entry					
	Service Cost	167,000			
	Other Pension Expense	74,000			
	OCI – Actuarial Gains/Losses		5,300		
	Cash (contributions)		100,000	(change from beginning net liability of $135,000 to ending net liability of $270,700)	
	Net Pension Liability		135,700		

Exhibit 19.8 highlights the key differences between GAAP and IFRS related to defined-benefit pension plans.

EXHIBIT 19.8 Comparison of Accounting for Defined-Benefit Pension Plans under U.S. GAAP and IFRS

Pension Factor	U.S. GAAP	IFRS
Factor 1: Service Cost	Increases PBO. Increases pension cost.	Similar under IFRS.
Factor 2: Prior Service Costs	Increases PBO. Report initially in other comprehensive income and amortize to pension cost over future periods.	Increases plan obligation. Increases pension cost. Called *past service cost.*
Factor 3: Interest on the PBO	Compute as beginning PBO plus prior service costs times settlement rate. Increases PBO. Increases pension cost.	Compute net interest as interest on PBO less expected return on plan assets. Compute interest cost as beginning PBO plus past service costs times the market yield on high-quality corporate bonds. Interest cost increases PBO. Compute expected return on plan assets as beginning plan assets times the market yield on high-quality corporate bonds. Expected return on plan assets increases plan assets. Net interest cost increases pension cost.
Factor 4: Expected Return on Pension Plan Assets	Compute as beginning plan assets times expected rate of return on plan assets. Increases plan assets. Decreases pension cost.	
Factor 5: Current-Year Net Actuarial Gains and Losses	Report initially in other comprehensive income. Amortize to pension cost based on corridor approach.	Report in other comprehensive income.Do not amortize actuarial gains and losses.
Factor 6: Funding the Plan	Increases plan assets	Similar under IFRS.
Factor 7: Payments to Retirees	Reduces PBO and plan assets	Similar under IFRS.

JUDGMENTS IN ACCOUNTING
Defined-Benefit Pension Plans

Accounting for pension plans involves extensive use of judgment. The pension liability measurement should reflect the present value of the company's obligation to provide future retirement benefits to its employees. Given that many of these payments will be made far into the future for any given company, there is a great deal of uncertainty regarding the accuracy of the estimates used in pension computations. In a survey of 175 companies, 49% reported making estimates and using judgment in reporting amounts related to employee benefits.[30]

Consider, for example, the benefits provided to a 25-year-old employee. What amount should be recognized in the liability account today to result in a $1 payment, for example, 40 years in the future? When will that employee retire? What will his salary level be 40 years from now? Once he retires, how long will he live? Actuaries must estimate all of these amounts before the company records the pension expense and liability.

To illustrate the effects of judgment in the pension area on the financial statements, let's consider some of our earlier examples. In Example 19.16, the service costs for KMR were $167,000. But this number was developed by actuaries who estimated factors such as life expectancies, turnover rates, and future salary levels among others. What would be the effect if the actuaries returned with an estimate of the service costs of $207,000? KMR would report net income that is $40,000 lower. Similarly, in Example 19.17, the actuary estimated prior service costs of $55,000. Any change in these estimates will directly affect net income.

Actuaries must also estimate interest rates and expected return on assets. In Example 19.18, the actuary estimated a settlement rate of 10%. What if he had estimated 13% instead? Instead of increasing pension expense by $78,900, KMR would have increased pension expense by $102,570. Again, the estimate has a direct impact on net income. Also, a higher settlement rate results in a lower PBO.

In Example 19.20, the actuary estimated an expected return of 9%. A change in this estimate would directly impact net income. Virtually every component of pension accounting is highly subjective and requires extensive judgments. Undoubtedly, the only reason that more than 49% of companies do not indicate that they used estimates and judgment in reporting amounts related to employee benefits is because many companies do not have a defined-benefit pension plan. Financial statement users should be aware of the subjectivity that surrounds pension accounting. Required disclosures reveal the nature and extent of the estimates used to measure pension expense and the pension asset or liability.

[30] AICPA, *IFRS Financial Statements: Best Practices in Presentation and Disclosure—2012* (New York, NY: AICPA, 2012).

8 Detail required disclosures for pension plans.

Defined-Benefit Pension Plan Disclosure Requirements

Pension accounting standards require detailed disclosure requirements for pension benefits, including a reconciliation of the beginning and ending balances of the projected benefit obligation and plan assets at fair value. The difference represents the funded status of the plan reported on the balance sheet. Disclosures also provide information about the:

1. Estimated future amount of amortization of net gains and losses and prior service cost
2. Unamortized net actuarial gain or loss
3. Five elements of pension cost
   a. Service cost
   b. Interest cost
   c. Expected return on plan assets
   d. Amortization of prior service cost
   e. Amortization of actuarial gains/losses
4. Assumptions used on a weighted-average basis (for example, discount rate, rate of increase in compensation, expected return on plan assets)

The pension footnote also provides amounts and types of securities held by the employer and related parties included in plan assets as well as any alternative methods used to amortize prior service costs and unamortized gains or losses. Under U.S. GAAP, companies report the service cost component of pension expense in operating income. The service cost is included in the same line item as other compensation costs. All other pension costs are reported in non-operating income. If these components are not reported as a separate line item, they must be disclosed. Pension footnotes also disclose target and actual allocation of plan assets within various asset categories—equity securities, debt securities, real estate, and such—and management's investment strategy. In addition, the disclosures must include a detailed schedule of management's best estimate of the cash requirements for the company (that is, the expected funding needs) and the future benefit payments required by the plan for all its pension plans and other benefit plans over each of the next 5 years and the following 5 years in aggregate.

Nonpublic entities are not required to separately disclose the components of net periodic benefit cost.

Exhibit 19.9 includes sample disclosures based on the KMR Bookstore example, including the required financial statement disclosures for KMR Bookstores under U.S. GAAP.

EXHIBIT 19.9 Sample Disclosures for KMR Bookstores, a U.S. GAAP Reporter

Notes to the Financial Statements

Pension Benefits. KMR Bookstores has a funded, noncontributory defined-benefit plan that covers substantially all of its employees. The plan provides defined benefits based on years of service and final average salary level.

Obligations and Funded Status (credit balances and liabilities are noted in parentheses)

At December 31	Current Year
Change in projected benefit obligation	
Projected benefit obligation at the beginning of the year	$ (789,000)
Adjustment for prior service cost granted at the beginning of the year	(55,000)
Adjusted beginning balance of the projected benefit obligation	$ (844,000)
Service cost	(167,000)
Interest on adjusted beginning balance of projected benefit obligation	(84,400)
Benefits paid during the year	72,000
Actuarial loss (from changes in actuarial assumptions) at year-end	(4,300)
Projected benefit obligation at the end of the year	$ (1,027,700)

Continued

At December 31	Current Year
Change in plan assets	
Fair value of plan assets at the beginning of the year	$ 654,000
Actual return on plan assets	75,000
Employer contributions made during the year	100,000
Benefits paid during the year	(72,000)
Fair value of plan assets at the end of the year	$ 757,000
Funded status at the end of the year	$(270,700)

Amounts recognized in the statement of financial position consist of:

	Pension Benefits
Noncurrent assets	$ 0
Current liabilities	$ 0
Noncurrent liabilities	$ (270,700)

Amounts recognized in accumulated other comprehensive income related to pensions consist of:

	Pension Benefits
Net actuarial gain	$ 94,880
Prior service cost	44,000
Total	$138,880

The accumulated benefit obligation for all defined-benefit pension plans was $950,000 at December 31. Accumulated benefit obligation exceeded the fair value of plan assets by $193,000 at December 31.

Information for pension plans with an accumulated benefit obligation in excess of plan assets:

	December 31
Projected benefit obligation	$1,027,700
Accumulated benefit obligation	950,000
Fair value of plan assets	757,000

Components of net periodic benefit cost recognized in net income:

	Current Year Pension Benefits
Service cost	$ 167,000
Interest cost	84,400
Expected return on beginning plan assets	(58,860)
Amortization of prior service costs	11,000
Amortization of actuarial gain	(460)
Net periodic benefit cost	$203,080

Other changes in plan assets and benefit obligations recognized in other comprehensive income:

	Current Year
Net actuarial gains	$ 11,380
Prior service cost	(55,000)
Amortization of prior service cost	11,000
Total recognized in other comprehensive income	$ (32,620)
Net periodic benefit cost (above)	203,080
Total recognized in net periodic benefit cost and other comprehensive income	$170,460

The estimated net loss and prior service cost for the defined-benefit pension plans that will be amortized from accumulated other comprehensive income into net periodic pension cost over the next fiscal year are $0 and $11,000, respectively.

Defined-Benefit Pension Disclosures: IFRS. IFRS disclosures and reporting for defined-benefit pension plans are similar to those under U.S. GAAP except that companies can choose where they classify pension cost components on the income statement and need to disclose where they report the components of pension expense. Most IFRS reporters classify the service cost component in operating income as it relates to employee services received in the current year.

Under IFRS, companies can report interest costs and the expected return on plan assets either in operating income or non-operating (financing) income. Providing a pension can also be viewed as borrowing from employees to be repaid after retirement. Therefore, IFRS allows companies to classify interest costs and the expected return on plan assets in non-operating (financing) income consistent with borrowing from employees.

FINANCIAL STATEMENT ANALYSIS

Defined-Benefit Pension Plan

The measurement and reporting of defined-benefits plans is complex: A company makes many assumptions and estimates in determining the present value of the future benefits it has promised employees. Financial statement users seek to analyze three main areas in a company's defined benefit-pension plans:

- Funded status
- Settlement rate and return on plan asset assumptions
- Actuarial gains/losses in other comprehensive income

The funded status of the pension is the pension obligation less pension plan assets. When pension obligations exceed plan assets, the plan is underfunded. When plan assets exceed the pension obligation, the plan is overfunded. In some countries, such as the United States, companies are required to fund a certain portion of their pension obligation. Yet, the majority of U.S. plans are underfunded. An underfunded pension plan increases a company's liabilities and thus its leverage. An underfunded pension plan also indicates that a company will either have to increase its contributions or earn greater income to meet its pension obligations as they come due.

The settlement rate and the expected return on plan assets estimates are critical in the computation of pension obligation and pension cost. In general, these rates are based on, and vary with, broad factors such as changes in interest rates and stock market performance. Company-specific factors such as creditworthiness and investment strategy also play a role in determining the settlement rate and expected return on plan assets.

The settlement rate is used to discount the future estimated cash payments to retirees. As with any discounting, the computed obligation is lower when the discount rate is higher. A higher discount rate will also lead to higher reported interest expense.

Financial Statement Analysis, continued

The expected return on plan assets, a component of pension costs, reduces pension costs. A higher expected return on plan assets results in a lower reported pension cost. Any difference between the expected return and the actual return on plan assets bypasses the income statement and is deferred in other comprehensive income. Pension cost is affected only when the difference combined with other actuarial gains or losses on the pension obligation exceeds the corridor. Even when the amount exceeds the corridor, the amortization into pension costs is usually not significant.

If actuarial gains or losses and the difference between the expected return and actual return were taken directly into net income, earnings would be more volatile. Therefore, deferring these gains and losses in accumulated other comprehensive income and subsequently amortizing them to pension expense tends to smooth earnings. For instance, when the stock market is performing well, a company's actual return on plan assets could be higher than its expected return. If the actual return was included in the pension cost, net income would be higher. The opposite is true when the stock market is down. Over the long term, these fluctuations in actuarial gains and losses naturally cancel out and therefore bypass net income. However, when actuarial gains and losses exist, the funded status changes. Example 19.29 illustrates the financial statement analysis of ***Johnson & Johnson's*** defined-benefits pension plan.

EXAMPLE 19.29 Financial Statement Analysis of Defined-Benefit Pension Plans

PROBLEM: You are interested in better understanding ***Johnson & Johnson's*** defined-benefits pension plan, including its pension costs and liability. The following table presents select data about ***Johnson & Johnson's*** defined benefits pension plan; use this information to answer the questions that follow.

At the end of fiscal years			
(Dollars in millions)	**2016**	**2015**	**2014**
Pension Accounts (select)			
Pension benefit obligation	$ 28,116	$25,855	$26,889
Plan assets	23,633	22,254	22,575
Pension Cost			
Service cost	$ 949	$ 1,037	$ 882
Interest cost	927	988	1,018
Expected return on plan assets	(1,962)	(1,809)	(1,607)
Amortization of prior service (credit)	1	2	7
Recognized actuarial losses	496	745	460
Other	11	8	(17)
Net periodic benefit cost	$ 422	$ 971	$ 743
Pension-related Other Comprehensive Income (before Tax)			
Actuarial gain (loss) amortization during period	$ 496	$ 745	$ 460
Actuarial gain (loss) – current year	(2,302)	1,578	(5,395)
Assumptions			
Discount rate on benefit obligation	3.78%	4.11%	3.78%
Return on plan assets	8.55%	8.53%	8.46%

Financial Statement Analysis, continued

At the end of fiscal years			
(Dollars in millions)	**2016**	**2015**	**2014**
Other Financial Statement Information			
Total assets	$141,208	$133,411	$130,358
Total liabilities	$ 70,790	$ 62,261	$ 60,606
Net income	$ 16,540	$ 15,409	$ 16,323

Required »

a. What is ***Johnson & Johnson's*** pension cost in 2016, 2015, and 2014? What are the components of its pension cost? What are pension costs after taxes as a percentage of net income? Comment on any changes in pension costs after taxes as a percentage of net income. Assume a 35% tax rate.

b. What is the funded status of ***Johnson & Johnson's*** defined-benefit pension plans in 2016, 2015, and 2014, respectively? How has the funded status changed over time? What is the percent of the net pension liability to total liabilities in 2016, 2015, and 2014, respectively?

c. How have the settlement rate and expected return on plan assets changed from 2014 to 2016? How does the change in the settlement rate affect the pension obligation and pension cost? How does the change in the expected return on plan assets affect the pension cost?

d. If ***Johnson & Johnson*** had reported all actuarial gains and losses in net income rather than other comprehensive income, what would its pension cost have been in 2016, 2015, and 2014, respectively? Comment on the changes in its pension cost.

SOLUTION:

a. ***Johnson & Johnson*** reported pension costs of $422 million, $971 million, and $743 million in 2016, 2015, and 2014, respectively. Its pension costs included the following components: service cost, interest costs, expected return on plan assets, amortization of prior service costs, recognized actuarial losses, and other.

To find the pension cost as a percentage of net income, we first must compute the pension cost after taxes. The following shows the computations. Pension cost as a percentage of net income varies each year at 1.7% of net income in 2016, 4.1% in 2015, and 3.0% in 2014. Pension expense also varies each year. Examining the components of pension costs indicates that the interest costs declined each year whereas the expected return on plan assets increased each year. Both service costs and recognized actuarial losses peaked in 2015, while net income was lower. Both changes contributed to the highest ratio of pension costs to net income in 2015.

Fiscal Year	2016	2015	2014
Pension cost	$ 422	$ 971	$ 743
Pension cost adjusted for tax (1 − 0.35)	$ 274	$ 631	$ 483
Net income	$16,540	$15,409	$16,323
Percentage of adjusted pension cost to net income	1.7%	4.1%	3.0%

Financial Statement Analysis, continued

b. We compute the funded status next. Each year the defined benefit pension plan is underfunded. Although the pension benefit obligation and plan asset increased from 2014 to 2016, the increase in pension benefit obligation leads to the slightly higher underfunding in 2016. The funded status as a percentage of liabilities also decreased in 2016 from 2014 despite the total liabilities increasing.

Fiscal Year (in millions)	2016	2015	2014
Pension benefit obligation	$28,116	$25,855	$26,889
Plan assets	23,633	22,254	22,575
Funded status – Underfunded	$ 4,483	$ 3,601	$ 4,314
Funded status – Underfunded	$ 4,483	$ 3,601	$ 4,314
Total liabilities	$70,790	$62,261	$60,606
Percentage of funded status to total liabilities	6.3%	5.8%	7.1%

c. The expected return on plan assets increased from 2014 to 2016 consistent with the increase in ***J&J's*** assumption on the increasing rate of return on plan assets. The discount rate also increased in 2015 but then declined in 2016. A decline in the discount rate increases the pension obligation but decreases the interest expense component of the pension cost. An increase in the expected return on plan assets would increase the pension cost as a smaller expected return is subtracted, ignoring any change in the amount of plan assets. The trend in both these areas has an opposite effect on pension cost.

d. The table below adjusts pension costs as if ***Johnson & Johnson*** had reported all actuarial gains and losses in net income rather than other comprehensive income. We start with the reported pension cost, subtract the recognized actuarial losses (which would have been reported in an earlier period), and add the actuarial losses reported in other comprehensive income after adjusting for taxes.

Fiscal Year	2016	2015	2014
Pension cost	$ 422	$ 971	$ 743
Subtract: Actuarial losses included in pension cost	(496)	(745)	(460)
Add (Subtract): Current year actuarial loss (gain)	2,302	(1,578)	5,395
Adjusted net periodic benefit cost (income)	$ 2,228	$(1,352)	$ 5,678
Increase (Decrease) in net periodic benefit cost	$ 1,806	$(2,323)	$ 4,935

In 2015, the pension cost would actually be pension income if the actuarial gain were reported in the income statement rather than deferred in other comprehensive income. In 2016, the $2,302 million actuarial loss is greater than the pension costs. In 2016, the pension cost would have increased dramatically if ***Johnson & Johnson*** had reported the actuarial losses on the income statement.

PETER SAYRE
SENIOR VICE PRESIDENT AND CORPORATE CONTROLLER PRUDENTIAL INSURANCE »

Peter Sayre

Prudental Peter Sayre is Senior Vice President and Corporate Controller at Prudential Insurance where he has served as Chief Tax Officer as well as Principal Accounting Officer in charge of companywide financial reporting and planning.

1 What significant assumptions does Prudential use in determining the projected benefit obligation (PBO) and the fair market value (FMV) of plan assets?

The most important economic assumption in the PBO is the discount rate we choose. Key demographic assumptions are actuarial and include the plan participants' termination rate (when they will leave Prudential), retirement, and mortality. Prudential states plan assets at fair market value and therefore there are no economic or demographic assumptions used in the asset values.

2 How sensitive are income statement amounts to changes in the expected return on assets (EROA) and discount rate on the liability?

EROA sensitivity is a function of the level of plan assets and the EROA. The effect of a change in EROA—say, from 5% to 5.5%—depends on the size of the asset balances. The 50 basis point change is material if the plan assets are $1 billion, less so for a $10 million plan. The discount rate affects the PBO, which affects the amount of actuarial gains or losses in equity and therefore its amortization. The PBO's sensitivity to discount rate is largely a function of the PBO's duration. If the duration is 12 years, a 1% change in the discount rate causes the PBO to change by 12%. The discount rate also affects P&L components (service cost and interest cost) in the subsequent year. Interest cost sensitivity is governed by PBO duration and how quickly the discount rate changes. We include these sensitivities in our annual report.

3 Do the EROA assumption and discount rate affect the level of plan assets?

The EROA does not affect the level of plan assets ultimately reported on the balance sheet. As mentioned previously, plan assets are ultimately recorded at fair value. Because the discount rate is used to calculate the present value of the expected cash flows associated with the PBO, it affects the PBO. PBO sensitivity to the discount rate is expressed in the PBO's duration.

4 What conditions are needed in order to report pension income rather than pension expense in the income statement?

Pension income statement activity is the net of expense items (service cost and interest cost), an income item (expected return on plan assets), and items that can either be expense items or income items (amortization of prior service cost/credit and amortization of actuarial gain or loss). Generally, an overfunded plan results in pension income; an underfunded plan, in pension expense. In an overfunded plan, the expected return on plan assets is likely to exceed the other expense items and vice versa for an underfunded plan.

5 How does Prudential Financial determine the amount of pension funding required each year?

One of our pension plans is significantly overfunded. Consequently, employer funding is not required. Rules are set by law for underfunded plans (e.g., the discount rate used to determine the PBO and hence the level of underfunding as well as the time period time during which to correct any underfunding). Companies with underfunded plans work with an actuary to determine the appropriate amount to fund each year based on the governing rules.

6 How can a deferred tax asset result from accounting for employee benefits?

This occurs in an underfunded plan (a plan in a net liability position). This situation arises when an expense has been taken per the books and the tax return has not yet taken a deduction. An examples of plans in a liability position that would give rise to a deferred tax asset is underfunded or unfunded pension plan or an underfunded or unfunded post-retirement plan.

7 How frequently are the estimates used in pension accounting reviewed and possibly changed?

We review our assumptions annually. Changes to economic assumptions—discount rate, salary scale—occur annually. Changes to demographic assumptions are based upon an actuarial assumption study conducted every 5 years. However, if at the third year in the cycle experience deviates more than 20%, we would change the assumption accordingly. «

Discussion Questions

1. Explain why accountants following U.S. GAAP use the expected return on assets (EROA) and the market-related asset value of plan assets rather than the actual return on plan assets and the closing fair value of plan assets, respectively.
2. In his interview, Peter Sayre notes that one of his company's pension plans is significantly overfunded and, therefore, employer contributions are not required. Discuss the factors that an entity considers when deciding on the amount to contribute to its defined benefit pension plan (i.e., funding).

Summary by Learning Objectives

In the following, we summarize the main points by learning objective. Throughout the chapter, we discuss the accounting and reporting of U.S. GAAP and IFRS side-by-side. The following table also highlights the major similarities and differences in the standards.

1 Describe the characteristics and types of stock-based compensation.

Summary	Similarities and Differences between U.S. GAAP and IFRS
Stock-based compensation includes restricted stock awards, performance awards, and bonuses paid by issuing stock. Employee stock option plans are the most prevalent type of stock-based compensation in the United States. Employee stock options are financial instruments that give an employee the right to purchase shares of the company's stock directly from the company at a fixed price over a specified period of time. Stock-based compensation is classified as either equity-classified awards, to which employees have the right to receive shares, or as liability-classified awards, from which an employee receives cash or some other company resource based on the value of the shares.	Similar under U.S. GAAP and IFRS.

2 Explain and illustrate the initial and subsequent measurement of equity-classified stock-based compensation.

Summary	Similarities and Differences between U.S. GAAP and IFRS
Equity-classified stock-based options are initially recorded at fair value as a component of equity. The fair value of equity-classified awards is based on the market price of the shares measured on the date of the grant and is not subsequently remeasured for changes in market prices. Companies choose whether to adjust compensation expense for changes in the estimated percentage of options that will be forfeited or to account for actual forfeitures when they occur.	➤ Similar under U.S. GAAP and IFRS except that under IFRS, companies must adjust for an estimate of the percentage of the options that are expected to be forfeited.

3 Describe and demonstrate the initial and subsequent measurement of liability-classified stock-based compensation.

Summary	Similarities and Differences between U.S. GAAP and IFRS
Liability-classified stock-based options are initially recorded at fair value as a liability. Companies remeasure the liability and compensation expense to fair value at each balance sheet date until the award is settled. Companies choose whether to adjust compensation expense for changes in the estimated percentage of options that will be forfeited or to account for actual forfeitures when they occur.	➤ Similar under U.S. GAAP and IFRS except that under IFRS, companies must adjust for an estimate of the percentage of the options that are expected to be forfeited.

Summary by Learning Objectives, continued

4 Discuss accounting for stock appreciation rights, restricted stock plans, and employee stock purchase plans.

Summary	Similarities and Differences between U.S. GAAP and IFRS
With stock appreciation rights (SARs), an employee is compensated for the increase in stock price over a pre-established price. To account for SARs, companies record compensation expense and either a SAR-related liability (if cash settled) or equity, additional paid-in-capital – stock options, if the SAR will be settled with shares of stock. The liability or equity is measured as the fair value of the SARs. Under restricted stock plans, actual shares are awarded in the name of a specific employee. Compensation expense on the restricted shares is the fair value of the restricted shares times the number of restricted shares issued; it is amortized evenly over the vesting period. An employee stock purchase plan offers employees the opportunity to purchase the company's shares, usually at a discount and without incurring transaction costs. The accounting depends on whether these plans are compensatory or non-compensatory: • Non-compensatory plans: The issuance of shares purchased by employees is recorded in the same way as is issuing shares in the open market. • Compensatory plans: The amount of discount over a regular market purchase is recorded as compensation expense.	Similar under U.S. GAAP and IFRS.

5 Detail required disclosures for stock plans.

Summary	Similarities and Differences between U.S. GAAP and IFRS
Disclosures must provide financial statement users with enough information to understand the nature and terms of the stock-based compensation plans, the methods used to estimate the fair values, and the income statement and cash flow effects.	Similar under U.S. GAAP and IFRS.

6 Describe the characteristics of defined-contribution and defined-benefit pension plans.

Summary	Similarities and Differences between U.S. GAAP and IFRS
Pension plans are contributory or non-contributory. • Contributory plans require employees to cover some or all pension benefit costs and allow employees to make additional contributions to increase their retirement benefits. • Non-contributory plans are plans in which the employer is responsible for funding the total cost of the plan. The two main types of plans are defined contribution and defined benefit. In a defined-contribution plan, the employer contributes a fixed amount each period based on a formula that is often a percentage of the employee's salary. A defined-benefit plan specifies the benefits that the employee will receive at the time of retirement.	Similar under U.S. GAAP and IFRS.

Summary by Learning Objectives, continued

7 Demonstrate the measurement of pension costs and the related liability or asset under defined-benefit plans, including remeasurement due to changes in actuarial assumptions.

Summary	Similarities and Differences between U.S. GAAP and IFRS
For defined-contribution plans, the company records the pension expense when employees provide services and earn their pensions. For defined-benefit plans, the three main accounts are pension plan obligations, pension plan assets, and pension expense. The pension plan obligation is the present value of estimated future benefits promised to employees. Plan assets are available to pay the pension benefits. The net of the pension plan obligation and plan assets is reported on the balance sheet. The pension expense includes service cost, current-period prior service costs, interest on the PBO, and the expected return on plan assets. It may also include actuarial gains or losses. Actuarial gains/losses arise on remeasuring the pension plan obligation. Expected gains or losses reflect the difference between the actual and expected return on plan assets. Any net actuarial gains or losses are taken directly to other comprehensive income. Companies report them in income only as a component of pension expense when the cumulative amount exceeds the corridor. The corridor is 10% of the greater of the beginning pension plan obligation or pension plan assets.	➤ There are significant differences in recognizing and reporting defined-benefit plans under IFRS, as follows: • Net interest expense is the sum of interest expense of the pension obligation less expected interest income on plan assets. Both interest expense and expected interest income are computed using the market yield at the end of the reporting period on high-quality corporate bonds. • All actuarial gains or losses are reported in other comprehensive income and are never reported in net income. • All past service costs are reported in pension expense. They are not amortized. • Pension liability is called Present Value of Defined-Benefit Obligation.

8 Detail required disclosures for pension plans.

Summary	Similarities and Differences between U.S. GAAP and IFRS
Detailed disclosures include a reconciliation of the beginning and ending balances of the benefit obligation and plan assets at fair value, with the difference representing the funded status of the plan reported on the balance sheet. Companies must report components of pension expense, including where they are classified on the income statement. Pension footnotes also disclose target and actual allocation of plan assets within various asset categories—equity securities, debt securities, real estate—and management's investment strategy.	➤ Similar under U.S. GAAP and IFRS except that IFRS allows companies to classify interest costs and the expected return on plan assets in non-operating (financing) income.

19 Accounting for Employee Compensation and Benefits

Questions

1 2 **Q19-1.** What is the allocation period used to expense stock-based compensation?

2 3 **Q19-2.** How do companies account for stock-based compensation?

2 3 **Q19-3.** Do companies with equity-based compensation plans make adjustments for changes in the market price of the stock?

2 3 4 **Q19-4.** When accounting for employee stock options, will a reduction of compensation expense or compensation "income" occur in future periods?

6 7 **Q19-5.** Does the employee always absorb the total risk of loss on pension plan assets?

6 7 **Q19-6.** Does the going-concern concept justify the use of the projected benefit obligation in all pension calculations?

6 7 **Q19-7.** The corridor method requires computing the amortization of net actuarial gains and losses under the straight-line method. Will the amortization be the same each year?

6 7 **Q19-8.** Does a company report the funded status of the defined-benefit plan as calculated by an actuary on the financial statements?

6 7 **Q19-9.** Do corporations report the projected benefit obligation and the plan assets as individual accounts on the sponsor corporation's balance sheet?

7 8 **Q19-10.** Does aggregating the five components of pension cost always results in a reduction in income?

Multiple Choice Questions

In partnership with: BECKER PROFESSIONAL EDUCATION®

Becker CPA Exam Review multiple-choice questions are available in MyLab Accounting.

2 **MC19-1.** On January 1, Year 1, Sweeney Company granted an employee options to purchase 100 shares of Sweeney's common stock at $40 per share. The options became exercisable on December 31, Year 1, after the employee had completed 1 year of service and were exercised on that date. Market prices of the stock and fair values of the options were as follows:

	Market Price of Stock	Fair Value of Options
January 1, Year 1	$50	$61
December 31, Year 1	$65	$75

What amount should Sweeney recognize as compensation cost for Year 1?

a. $6,100 b. $2,100 c. $4,000 d. $0

2 **MC19-2.** Gregory's on Ormond, Inc. grants its president 2,000 stock options on January 1, Year 1, that give him rights to purchase shares of the company for $40 per share on December 31, Year 2. At the time the options were granted, the fair value of the options totaled $20,000. At December 31, Year 1, the company's stock sold for $45 per share and at December 31, Year 2, the selling price of the stock was $55 per share. In its Year 2 financial statements, Gregory's on Ormond would recognize compensation expense relative to the options of:

a. ($10,000) b. $0 c. $15,000 d. $10,000

7 **MC19-3.** The following information pertains to Burnel Corporation's defined benefit pension plan for Year 1:

Service cost	$160,000
Actual and expected gain on plan assets	35,000
Unexpected loss on pension plan assets related to a Year 1 disposal of a subsidiary	40,000
Amortization of unrecognized prior service cost	5,000
Annual interest on pension obligation	50,000

What amount should Burnel report as total pension expense in Year 1?
a. $250,000 b. $220,000 c. $210,000 d. $180,000

7 **MC19-4.** Do It Right, Inc.'s actuary provided the company with the following information regarding its defined benefit pension plan for the year ended December 31, Year 7:

Fair value of plan assets	$5,580,000
Accumulated benefit obligation	3,400,000
Projected benefit obligation	4,930,000
Unrecognized prior service cost	400,000
Unrecognized net gain	140,000
Expected benefit obligation – Year 8	250,000

The company reported net periodic pension cost of $310,000 on its income statement and made a $500,000 contribution to the pension plan during Year 7. The company's effective tax rate is 40%. What amount should Do It Right report in accumulated other comprehensive income related to its pension plan on its December 31, Year 7, balance sheet?
a. $156,000 b. $400,000 c. $260,000 d. $240,000

7 **MC19-5.** The following information applies to Babydoll Company's defined benefit pension plan:

Projected benefit obligation, December 31, Year 7	$2,000,000
Projected benefit obligation, December 31, Year 8	2,220,000
Fair value of plan assets, December 31, Year 7	1,750,000
Fair value of plan assets, December 31, Year 8	2,025,000
Unrecognized prior service cost, December 31, Year 7	500,000
Year 8 service cost	200,000
Expected benefits payable – Year 9	400,000
Discount rate	6%
Expected rate of return on plan assets	8%

The company's employees have an average remaining service life of 10 years. The company has no unrecognized net gains or losses. What is Babydoll's net periodic pension cost for Year 8?
a. $208,000 b. $221,200 c. $230,000 d. $243,200

7 **MC19-6.** Giant Jobs, Inc. amended its overfunded pension plan on December 31, Year 7, resulting in the recognition of prior service cost of $700,000. On December 31, Year 7, Giant Job's employees had an average remaining service life of 20 years. The company has an effective tax rate of 30%. How should the prior service cost be reported in the December 31, Year 7, financial statements?
a. $490,000 increase in net periodic pension cost
b. $490,000 decrease in comprehensive income
c. $700,000 decrease in net income
d. $700,000 increase in pension benefit asset

7 **MC19-7.** The following information relates to the pension plan for the employees of Neal Co.:

	Jan. 1, Year 4	**Dec. 31, Year 4**	**Dec. 31, Year 5**
Accumulated benefit obligation	$4,400,000	$4,600,000	$6,000,000
Projected benefit obligation	4,650,000	4,980,000	6,670,000
Fair value of plan assets	4,250,000	5,200,000	5,740,000
Market-related value of assets	4,100,000	5,160,000	5,650,000
Unrecognized net (gain) or loss	0	(720,000)	(800,000)
Settlement rate (for year)	11%		11%
Expected rate of return (for year)	8%	7%	

Neal estimates that the average remaining service life is 16 years. Neal's contribution was $315,000 in Year 5 and benefits paid were $235,000.

The amount of unrecognized net gain amortized in Year 5 is:
a. $12,750 b. $12,500 c. $9,688 d. $8,314

8 **MC19-8.** The following information applies to Babydoll Company's defined benefit pension plan at December 31, Year 8:

Projected benefit obligation, December 31, Year 7	$2,000,000
Projected benefit obligation, December 31, Year 8	2,220,000
Fair value of plan assets, December 31, Year 7	1,750,000
Fair value of plan assets, December 31, Year 8	2,025,000
Unrecognized prior service cost, December 31, Year 7	500,000
Year 8 service cost	200,000
Expected benefits payable – year	400,000
Discount rate	6%
Expected rate of return on plan assets	8%

The company's employees have an average remaining service life of 10 years. The company has no unrecognized net gains or losses. What is the funded status of Babydoll's pension plan at December 31, Year 7?

a. $195,000 underfunded.
b. $195,000 overfunded.
c. $250,000 underfunded.
d. $250,000 overfunded.

Brief Exercises

1 2 3 4 **BE19-1. Stock Compensation Terminology.** Match the type or form of stock compensation with its definition.

Form or Type

a. Option
b. Equity-classified awards
c. Liability-classified award
d. Stock appreciation rights
e. Restricted stock plans
f. Employee stock purchase plan

Type or Form	Definition
____________	An employee receives cash or some other company resource based on the value of the shares.
____________	An employee receives cash for the amount of the increase in share value over a pre-established price over a fixed period of time.
____________	An employee has the right to purchase a security at a pre-established price.
____________	An employee has the opportunity to purchase the company's shares usually at a discount and without incurring transaction costs.
____________	An employee has the right to receive shares.
____________	A specific employee is awarded actual shares.

2 **BE19-2. Employee Stock Options, Equity-Classified Awards, Journal Entries at Grant Date.** Vince Pickwick Company awarded 1,000 options to acquire 1,000 shares of its common stock. The options have a fair value of $12 each. The market price and the exercise price were both equal to $6 per share on the date of the grant. Prepare the journal entry to record the options on the date of the grant.

2 **BE19-3. Employee Stock Options, Equity-Classified Awards, Journal Entries after Grant Date.** B-Boy Jeans, Inc. awarded 2,000 options to acquire 2,000 shares of its common stock. The options have a fair value of $30 each and cannot be exercised until employees complete a 3-year service period. The market price and the exercise price were both equal to $17 per share on the date of the grant. Prepare the journal entry required at the end of the first year after the options are granted.

2 **BE19-4. Employee Stock Options, Equity-Classified Awards, Journal Entries.** Hillview Homes, Ltd. granted options at the beginning of the current year to all its salaried employees. At the grant date, the options had a

fair value of $900,000 and can be exercised only over a 3-year vesting period. At the end of the year, Hillview charged $300,000 to expense, assuming that all employees would vest. Prepare the journal entry to record the compensation expense for Year 2 assuming that Hillview expects only 35% of employees to vest. Assume that Hillview chooses to adjust the fair value for the estimated forfeitures.

2 **BE19-5. Employee Stock Options, Equity-Classified Awards, Journal Entries at Exercise.** On-the-Fly Limousine Services granted 5,000 options to acquire 5,000 shares of its $1 par value common stock. At the grant date, the fair value of the options is $100,000 and the exercise price per option is $8 each. Assuming that employees exercise all the options at the end of the service period, prepare the journal entry necessary to record the exercise of the options.

2 **BE19-6. Employee Stock Options, Equity-Classified Awards, Journal Entries at Exercise.** Prepare the necessary journal entry assuming that all the options granted by On-the-Fly in BE19-5 expired and were not exercised by any of the company's employees.

3 **BE19-7. Employee Stock Options, Liability-Classified Awards, Journal Entries after Grant Date.** The Goldwick Company awarded 1,000 options to acquire 1,000 shares of its common stock, which can be sold back to the company. The options vest over 3 years. The market price and the exercise price were both equal to $12 per share on the date of the grant. At the grant date, the options have a fair value of $15 each. Prepare the journal entry at the end of the first year, assuming that the fair value does not change during the year.

3 **BE19-8. Employee Stock Options, Liability-Classified Awards, Journal Entries after Grant Date.** Tommi-Boy Jeans, Inc. awarded 4,000 options to acquire 4,000 shares of its preferred stock that can be sold back to the company. At the grant date, the options have a fair value of $12 each and cannot be exercised until employees complete a 2-year service period. The market price and the exercise price were both equal to $8 per share on the date of the grant. Prepare the journal entry required at the end of the first year after the options are granted assuming that the fair value does not change during the year.

4 **BE19-9. Stock Appreciation Rights.** Togo Incorporation started a share appreciation plan on January 1, 2018, when it granted 50,000 rights to its executives. The vesting period is 2 years. The stock appreciation rights are settled for cash. The plan expires on January 1, 2020. The fair value of Togo's SARs for the years ended December 31, 2018 and 2019, are as follows:

Date	Fair Value
December 31, 2018	$6
December 31, 2019	$7

All rights are exercised on January 1, 2020, when their fair value is $7 and the market price of the stock is $35 per share. What is the compensation expense in 2018 and in 2019? Prepare the journal entries to record the SAR plan.

4 **BE19-10. Stock Appreciation Rights.** Using the information from BE19-9, now assume that the stock appreciation rights are settled for stock. Prepare the journal entries to record the SAR plan. The par value of common stock is $1 per share. What journal entry will the company make on the date the employees purchase the shares?

4 **BE19-11. Stock Appreciation Rights.** Kogo Incorporation started a share appreciation plan on January 1, 2017, when it granted 100,000 rights to its executives. The vesting period is 2 years. The stock appreciation rights are settled for cash. The plan expires on January 1, 2019. The fair value of Kogo's SARs for the years ended December 31, 2017 and 2018, are as follows:

Date	Fair Value
December 31, 2017	$4
December 31, 2018	$3

All rights are exercised on January 1, 2019, when the fair value is $5. What is the compensation expense in 2017 and in 2018?

4 **BE19-12. Restricted Stock.** Samsong Company issued 100,000 shares of $1 par value, restricted stock to its top five key employees on January 1, 2017. The market value of Samsong's shares is $45 per share on the date of issue. The restricted shares require a vesting period of 4 years. Prepare the journal entries for the first year.

4 **BE19-13. Employee Stock Purchase Plans, Non-Compensatory.** Siry Company offers all its employees the opportunity to purchase its $2 par value common stock at a 5% discount. The employees have 3 weeks to elect to participate in the plan. The current market price of the stock is $80 per share. Employees purchased a total of 200,000 shares. What journal entry will the company make on the date the employees purchase the shares?

4 **BE19-14. Employee Stock Purchase Plans, Compensatory.** Using the information from BE19-13, now assume that Siry Company offers the plan only to top executives. What journal entry will the company make on the date the employees purchase the shares?

4 **BE19-15. Employee Stock Purchase Plans, Compensatory.** Tash Company offers select executives the opportunity to purchase its $1 par value common stock at a 10% discount. The employees have 2 weeks to elect to participate in the plan. The current market price of the stock is $40 per share. Employees purchased a total of 100,000 shares. What journal entry will the company make on the date the employees purchase the shares?

6 **BE19-16. Defined-Contribution Pension Plan, Journal Entries.** Jen and Benny's Ice Cream offers a defined-contribution plan to its employees. Under the terms of the plan, Jen and Benny must contribute 2% of its employees' salaries. Prepare the journal entry required to record the cost of this plan assuming that total salaries for the year are equal to $875,000 and that the sponsor corporation contributes the full amount due under the plan.

7 **BE19-17. Defined-Benefit Pension Plan, Corridor, Journal Entries.** Northhead Equipment offers its unionized employees a defined-benefit plan. The company determines that the beginning balance of its unamortized net actuarial gain is equal to $136,000. A recent report from the pension plan indicates that the beginning balances of the projected benefit obligation and the plan assets at fair value (the same as the market-related asset value) are equal to $1,150,000 and $1,278,000, respectively.

Required »

a. Compute the current year's amortization required by the corridor method assuming that the average remaining service life of Northhead's employees is 20 years.
b. Prepare the journal entry.

7 **BE19-18. Defined-Benefit Pension Plan, Pension Costs.** Chester West Shoes, Inc., provided the following information regarding its defined-benefit pension plan: service cost, $257,000; interest on the beginning PBO, $121,000; expected return on plan assets, $56,000; amortization of prior service costs related to unvested employees, $24,000; and amortization of net actuarial gain, $87,000. Based on this information, compute the total pension cost for the year.

7 **BE19-19. Defined-Benefit Pension Plan, Pension Costs, IFRS.** Chester West Shoes, Inc., provided the following information regarding its defined-benefit pension plan: service cost, $257,000; interest on the PVDBO, $121,000; expected return on plan assets, $56,000; past service costs of $24,000, and net actuarial gain, $87,000. Based on this information, compute the total pension cost for the year under IFRS.

7 **BE19-20. Defined-Benefit Pension Plan, Journal Entries.** Bidell Builders reported $500,000 of pension cost for the current year. In making this computation, Bidell informs you that the actual return on plan asset in excess of expected returns in the current year is a $231,000 net gain. In addition, the amortization of prior service costs for unvested employees at the end of the year is $79,000. Bidell contributed $100,000 into the plan during the current year. Service cost for the year was $95,000. Prepare the journal entry to record the pension cost for the current year.

7 **BE19-21. Defined-Benefit Pension Plan, Journal Entries, IFRS.** Bidell Builders, an IFRS reporter, has $500,000 of pension cost for the current year. In making this computation, Bidell informs you that the current-year actual return on plan asset in excess of expected returns is a $231,000 net actuarial gain. In addition, past service costs are $79,000 (not included in $500,000 pension cost). Bidell contributed $100,000 into the plan during the current year. Service cost for the year was $95,000. Bidell reports service cost as an operating expense and all other pension expenses as non-operating. Prepare the journal entry to record the pension cost for the current year.

7 **BE19-22. Defined-Benefit Pension Plan, Pension Benefit Obligation Computation.** Armando Hernandez Fashions, Inc. sponsors a defined-benefit pension plan for its employees. The company's pension trust provided the following information: fair value of beginning plan assets, $569,000; projected benefit obligation at the beginning of the year, $678,000; service cost, $54,000; interest on beginning PBO, $56,900; actual loss on plan assets, $35,800 composed of expected gains of $50,000 and unexpected losses of $85,800; actuarial gains because of assumptions about PBO, $98,543; benefit payments made to retirees, $29,780; and contributions made by the sponsor corporation, $86,500. There is no amortization necessary under the corridor approach. Compute the ending balance of the projected benefit obligation.

7 **BE19-23. Defined-Benefit Pension Plan, Plan Asset Computation.** Using the data provided in BE19-22, determine the ending balance of the plan assets and indicate the funded status of the plan at the end of the year.

7 **BE19-24. Defined-Benefit Pension Plan, Pension Benefit Obligation Computation, IFRS.** Silva Blanca Fashions, Inc. sponsors a defined-benefit pension plan for its employees. The company's pension trust provided the following information: fair value of beginning plan assets, $569,000; projected benefit obligation at the beginning of the year, $678,000; service cost, $54,000; interest on PVDBO, $56,900; actual loss on plan assets, $35,800; actuarial gains due to changes in assumptions about PVDBO, $98,543; benefit payments made to retirees, $29,780; and contributions made by the sponsor corporation, $86,500. Compute the ending balance of the PVDBO under IFRS.

7 **BE19-25. Defined-Benefit Pension Plan, Plan Asset Computation, IFRS.** Using the data provided in BE19-24, determine the ending balance of the plan assets and indicate the funded status of the plan at the end of the year under IFRS.

7 **BE19-26. Defined-Benefit Pension Plan, Pension Benefit Obligation Computation.** The following information is provided regarding a company's defined benefit pension plan. The projected benefit obligation (PBO) was $600,000 at the beginning of the current year. During the year, pension benefits paid were $165,000, service cost for the year was $210,000, and a plan amendment retroactive to the beginning of the year increased the PBO by $50,000. The settlement rate for the plan for the year was estimated at 4%. Determine the ending balance of the PBO for the current year.

7 **BE19-27. Defined-Benefit Pension Plan, Plan Asset Computation.** OZ Leasing Associates provides you with the following information for the current year:

Beginning projected benefit obligation	$900,000
Settlement rate	5%
Service costs for the current year	350,000
Pension benefits paid	210,000
Contributions into the plan	85,000
Beginning plan assets at fair value (equal to the market related asset value)	865,000
Actual return on plan assets (equal to the expected return)	100,000

Determine the pension asset or liability to be reported on the balance sheet of OZ Leasing Associates at the end of the year.

7 **BE19-28. Defined-Benefit Pension Plan, Pension Asset, Liability Computation.** At December 31, 2019, the following information was provided by the Oscar Group:

Fair value of plan assets	$850,000
Vested benefit obligation	495,500
Accumulated benefit obligation	700,100
Projected benefit obligation	795,000

Determine the pension asset or liability that will be reported on Oscar's balance sheet on December 31, 2019.

Exercises

2 **E19-1. Employee Stock Options, Equity Classified Awards, Journal Entries.** The following information is from the books of OZP Farms, Inc. regarding its employee stock options. The firm granted options on January 2, 2018, that permit employees to acquire 100,000 shares of $1.20 par value common stock at an exercise price of $4.80 per share. The market price of the company's shares on January 2, 2018, was also $4.80 per share, so there is no intrinsic value on the date of the grant. Employees must complete a 2-year service (vesting) period in order to exercise the options. The options will expire after a 5-year period (total option period). At the grant date, the estimated fair value of the options using the Black-Scholes option-pricing model is $850,000 (i.e., 100,000 shares × $8.50 per share). The firm assumes that the initial vesting probability is 100%. The option plan qualifies as an equity-classified award. Assuming no changes in vesting probability, prepare the journal entries required to record compensation expense over the vesting period.

2 **E19-2. Employee Stock Options, Equity-Classified Awards, Journal Entries.** Max Ferguson Cosmetics compensates its key employees by offering stock options as part of total compensation. On January 1 of the current year, Max Ferguson granted 10,000 options to acquire 10,000 shares of its $2 par value common stock at an

exercise price of $18 per share. The market price on the date of the grant is also $18 per share, so there is no intrinsic value. At the grant date, the fair value of the options is $250,000, or $25 per option. The initial vesting probability is assumed to be 100%. The option plan qualifies as an equity-classified award. Each executive is required to complete a 2-year service period in order to exercise the options.

Required »

a. Assuming no changes in vesting probability, prepare the journal entries required to record compensation expense over the vesting period.
b. Prepare all journal entries required in Year 2 assuming that the vesting probability is reduced to 60% in Year 2. Assume that the company chooses to adjust the fair value for the estimated forfeitures.
c. Using the information computed from part (b), prepare the journal entry required to record the expiration of all options.
d. Prepare all journal entries in Year 1 and Year 2 assuming that 20% of the options are forfeited in Year 1 and another 20% are forfeited in Year 2. Assume that the company accounts for forfeitures when they occur.

2 **E19-3. Employee Stock Options, Equity-Classified Awards, Journal Entries.** Davidson Company compensates its key employees by offering stock options as part of total compensation. On January 1 of the current year, Davidson granted 80,000 options to acquire 80,000 shares of its $1 par value common stock at an exercise price of $37 per share. The market price on the date of the grant is also $37 per share, so there is no intrinsic value. At grant date, the fair value of the options is $4,000,000, or $50 per option. The initial vesting probability is assumed to be 60%. The option plan qualifies as an equity-classified award. There is a 2-year vesting period required before employees can purchase the shares.

Required »

a. Assuming no changes in vesting probability, prepare the journal entries required to record compensation expense over the vesting period.
b. Prepare all journal entries required in Year 2 assuming that the vesting probability increases to 80% in Year 2. Assume that the company chooses to adjust the fair value for the estimated forfeitures.
c. Assume that employees exercise 80% of the options expected to vest from part (b) and the other 20% expire. Prepare any journal entries required to record the exercise and expirations.
d. Assume that 20% of the options are forfeited in Year 1 and another 20% are forfeited in Year 2. Assume that the company accounts for forfeitures when they occur. Prepare all journal entries in Year 1 and Year 2, including the journal entry to record the exercise of the options.

E19-4. Employee Stock Options, Liability-Classified Awards, Journal Entries. Max Ferguson Cosmetics compensates its key employees by offering stock options as part of total compensation. On January 1 of the current year, Max Ferguson granted 10,000 options to acquire 10,000 shares of its $2 par value common stock at an exercise price of $18 per share. The market price on the date of the grant is also $18 per share, so there is no intrinsic value. At the grant date, the fair value of the options is $250,000, or $25 per option. The initial vesting probability is assumed to be 100%. The option plan qualifies as a liability-classified award. Each executive is required to complete a 2-year service period in order to exercise the options. The fair value of the options does not change over the vesting period.

3

Required »

a. Assuming no changes in vesting probability, prepare the journal entries required to record compensation expense over the vesting period.
b. Prepare all journal entries required in Year 2 assuming that the vesting probability is reduced to 60%. Assume that the company chooses to adjust the fair value for the estimated forfeitures.
c. Using the information computed from part (b), prepare the journal entry required to record the expiration of all options.
d. Prepare all journal entries in Year 1 and Year 2 assuming that 20% of the options are forfeited in Year 1 and another 20% are forfeited in Year 2. Assume that the company accounts for forfeitures when they occur.

4 **E19-5. Stock Appreciation Rights.** eGear Company started a share appreciation plan on January 1, 2018, when it granted 200,000 rights to its executives. The vesting period is 2 years. The plan expires on January 1, 2020. The fair value of eGear's SARs for the years ended December 31, 2018 and 2019, are as follows:

Date	Fair Value
December 31, 2018	$6
December 31, 2019	$5

Employees exercise all SARs on January 1, 2020, when their fair value is $5.

Required »

a. Prepare all journal entries to record the SAR plan assuming that the rights are settled with cash.
b. Prepare all journal entries to record the SAR plan assuming that the rights are settled with the company's $1 par value common stock. On the date of exercise, the market price per share is $20.

4 **E19-6. Stock Appreciation Rights.** NR Enterprises, Inc. granted stock appreciation rights to its key employees on January 2, 2018. These SARs allow the employees to receive cash at the end of the vesting period for the difference between the market price of the stock on the exercise date and the pre-established price of $55. NR granted 200,000 of these SARs. Employees must complete a 3-year service (vesting) period in order to receive the cash. The fair value of the SARs on December 31, 2018, is $7 per SAR. The fair value on December 31, 2019, is $13 per SAR, and the fair value on December 31, 2020, is $11 per SAR. The company estimates that there will not be any forfeitures of the rights.

Required »

a. How much compensation expense, if any, should NR recognize in 2018, 2019, and 2020?
b. What are the journal entries to record this compensation expense?

4 **E19-7. Stock Appreciation Rights, IFRS.** NR Enterprises, Inc., an IFRS reporter, granted stock appreciation rights to its key employees on January 2, 2018. These SARs allow the employees to receive cash at the end of the vesting period for the difference between the market price of the stock on the exercise date and the pre-established price of $55. NR granted 200,000 of these SARs. Employees must complete a 3-year service (vesting) period in order to receive the cash. The fair value of the SARs on December 31, 2018, is $7 per SAR. The fair value on December 31, 2019, is $13 per SAR and the fair value on December 31, 2020, is $11 per SAR. The company estimates that there will not be any forfeitures of the rights.

Required »

a. How much compensation expense, if any, should NR recognize in 2018, 2019, and 2020?
b. What is the journal entry to record this compensation expense?

4 **E19-8. Restricted Stock Plan, Termination.** Hwang Company issued 50,000 shares of $1 par value, restricted stock to each of its five key executives on January 1, 2018. Each executive receives 10,000 shares. Hwang's shares have a market value of $28 per share on the date of issue. The restricted shares require a vesting period of 4 years. Hwang's year-end is December 31.

Required »

a. Prepare the journal entries required for 2018 through 2021.
b. Independent of (a), prepare all journal entries for 2018 through 2021 assuming that three of the executives leave the company at January 1, 2020.

7 **E19-9. Defined-Benefit Pension Plan, Comprehensive.** Crystal Glass Works, Ltd. provided you with the following information regarding its defined-benefit pension plan.

Required »

- Beginning plan assets at fair value (market-related value), $600,000
- Beginning projected benefit obligation (PBO), $558,000
- Service cost for the year, $125,800
- Settlement rate, 12%
- Expected return on plan assets, 9%
- Actual return on plan assets, $30,100 loss
- Contributions for the year, $45,700
- Benefit payments for the year, $97,440
- Beginning accumulated other comprehensive income, $42,000 (due to unamortized net actuarial gains)
- Prior service costs awarded during the year (not effective as of the beginning of the year) for vested employees, $19,690
- Amortization of prior service costs, $7,000
- Decrease in the ending projected benefit obligation due to changes in actuarial assumptions (i.e., actuarial gain), $8,000
- Average remaining service life of the employee base, 15 years

Required »

a. Prepare the separate "conceptual" journal entries for the preceding relevant information.
b. Compute the total pension cost for the year.

c. Determine the ending balances of the plan assets and the projected benefit obligation and indicate the funded status of the plan.
d. Prepare the journal entry to record the current year's pension cost.

7 **E19-10. Defined-Benefit Pension Plan, Comprehensive, IFRS.** Redo E19-9, assuming that Crystal Glass Works, Ltd. is an IFRS reporter and the expected return on plan assets is the same as the settlement rate. Crystal Glass reports service cost as an operating expense and all other pension expenses as non-operating.

7 **E19-11. Defined-Benefit Pension Plan, Comprehensive.** Season Tyme Tea Company provided the following information related to its defined-benefit pension plan.

Beginning plan assets at fair value (equal to the market-related asset value)	$ 954,500
Beginning projected benefit obligation (PBO)	1,020,340
Service cost for the year	81,500
Settlement rate	10%
Expected return on plan assets	16%
Actual return on plan assets	123,400
Contributions for the year	67,480
Benefit payments for the year	47,440
Beginning accumulated other comprehensive income related to prior service costs (debit balance)*	65,840
Amortization of prior service costs	15,500
Increase in the ending projected benefit obligation due to changes in actuarial assumptions (i.e., actuarial loss)	78,625
Average remaining service life (ARSL) of employee base	10 years

*There is no AOCI related to actuarial gains/losses as of the beginning of the year.

Required »

a. Compute the total pension cost for the year.
b. Determine the ending balances of the plan assets and the projected benefit obligation and indicate the funded status of the plan.
c. Determine the ending balance for accumulated other comprehensive income.
d. Prepare the journal entry to record the current year's pension cost.
e. Reconcile the ending balance in accumulated other comprehensive income.

7 **E19-12. Defined-Benefit Pension Plan, Comprehensive.** Technique Technologies, Inc. started a defined-benefit plan this year. As part of the union agreement, it provided $560,000 in retroactive benefits to all employees for their prior years' service. The company amortized $15,600 of these benefits during the current year. At the end of the year, the actuary provided you with the following information related to the plan:

- Service cost for the year, $915,590
- Contributions for the year, $345,700
- Expected return on plan assets, 10%
- Settlement rate, 10%
- No retirement benefits paid during the year

Required »

a. Compute the total pension cost for the year.
b. Determine the ending balances of the plan assets and the projected benefit obligation and indicate the funded status of the plan.
c. Prepare the journal entry to record the current year's pension cost.
d. Reconcile the ending balance in accumulated other comprehensive income.

7 **E19-13. Defined-Benefit Pension Plan, Comprehensive.** Desmond Group provided the following information related to its defined-benefit plan for the current year:

Description	Current Year	Prior Year
Beginning plan assets at fair value (equal to the market-related asset value)	*Solve*	$806,160
Beginning projected benefit obligation	*Solve*	965,270

Description	Current Year	Prior Year
Service cost	$73,800	60,000
Settlement rate	10%	10%
Expected return on plan assets	8%	8%
Actual return on plan assets	40,320	40,000
Contributions for the year	106,080	65,760
Benefits paid during the year	28,800	34,560
Amortization of prior service cost	9,200	25,200
Beginning balance of accumulated other comprehensive income due to		
Unamortized prior service cost	*Solve*	38,580*
Unamortized net actuarial losses	*Solve*	95,047*
Average remaining service life of employees	10 years	10 years

*These amounts are included in the beginning balance of the PBO.

Required »

a. Compute the total pension cost for the current year.
b. Determine the ending balances of the plan assets and the projected benefit obligation and indicate the funded status of the plan.
c. Reconcile the ending balance in accumulated other comprehensive income and indicate the amounts attributable to unamortized prior service cost and unamortized net actuarial losses.
d. Prepare the journal entry to record the current year's pension cost.

7 **E19-14. Defined-Benefit Pension Plan.** McDonald-Johnson Engineering Associates offers its employees a defined-benefit pension plan. The company asked you to assess the impact of the following events on its annual pension cost, the balance of accumulated other comprehensive income, and its net pension obligation:

- The pension plan trustee reports actuarial gains and unexpected positive returns on the plan assets.
- The pension plan trustee reports actuarial losses and unexpected negative returns on the plan assets.
- The plan is amended when the plan trustee informs the company of the amount of prior service costs incurred.
- The company's accountant amortizes the balance of the unamortized actuarial gains.
- The company's accountant amortizes the balance of the unamortized actuarial losses.
- The company's accountant amortizes the balance of the unamortized prior service cost.

Required »

Prepare a table indicating the effect of each of the above events on each of the accounts indicated.

7 **E19-15. Defined-Benefit Pension Plan.** The following information relates to the defined benefit pension plan of Murry Corp. for the year ended December 31, 2019:

Prior service cost for a plan amendment during the year	$ 800,000
Projected benefit obligation – beginning balance	945,000
Fair value of plan assets at the beginning of the year	1,000,500
(equal to the market related asset value)	
Service cost	400,000
Interest on projected benefit obligation at 5.4155%	*Solve*
Amortization of prior service cost	80,000
Expected and actual return on plan assets	82,500
Contributions into the plan	300,000
Beginning funded status ($1,000,500 – $945,000)	55,500*

* = overfunded so that there a pension asset on the balance sheet at the beginning of the year.

There were no benefit payments for the year.

Required: (Round all computations to the nearest dollar)

a. Compute the total pension expense.
b. Prepare the journal entry to record pension expense for the year.
c. Determine the ending balances of the projected benefit obligation, plan assets, the pension asset or liability reported on the balance sheet, and accumulated other comprehensive income related to the pension plan.

7 **E19-16. Defined-Benefit Pension Plan.** Welsa Manufacturing, Inc. offers a noncontributory, defined-benefit pension plan to its employees. The average remaining service life of employees is 10 years. The company provides you with the following information for the year ended December 31, 2019:

Employer's contribution at end of year	$1,600,000
Service cost	600,000
Projected benefit obligation – beginning of the year	6,043,200
Plan assets (at fair value market-related value) beginning of the year	4,000,000
Expected return on plan assets	9%
Settlement rate	8%
Actual return on plan assets	$360,000
Cost of plan amendment retroactive to January 1	400,000

There were no benefits were paid during the year.

Required: »

a. Compute the total pension expense recognized in 2019. Assume the prior service cost is amortized over the average remaining service life of the employees.
b. Prepare the journal entry to record pension expense for the year ended December 31, 2019.
c. Indicate the amounts that are reported on the income statement and the balance sheet for 2019.

Problems

2 **P19-1. Employee Stock Options, Equity-Classified Awards – Comprehensive.** The board of directors of Simon Art Supplies Company approved a plan to grant 150,000 options to its key executives to acquire 150,000 shares of no-par common stock at an exercise price of $20 per share. The effective date of the grant is January 1 of Year 1. Simon granted the options on a date when the company's shares are trading for $24 per share. On the grant date, the Black-Scholes option-pricing model estimates the fair value of the options at $66 each. A 3-year service period is required to exercise the options and all options expire at the end of a 5-year period. Management estimates a vesting probability of 100%.

Required »

a. Determine the compensation expense for Year 2.
b. Determine the compensation expense for Year 3 assuming that 25% of Simon's key executives left the company at the beginning of Year 3 and prior to vesting. Prepare the required journal entry. Assume that the company chooses to adjust the fair value for the estimated forfeitures.
c. Prepare the journal entry required to record the exercise of the options by the remaining key executives.

2 **P19-2. Employee Stock Options, Equity-Classified Awards – Comprehensive.** On January 1 of the current year, Brendan B Fashions granted 100,000 stock options to its division managers. The options are equity-classified awards. The plan permits the division managers to acquire the shares at an exercise price of $12 per share. Each option permits the purchase of one share of the company's $2 par value common stock. The options vest in 2 years and expire if they are unexercised at the end of 5 years. On the grant date, the fair value of the options, estimated by an accepted option-pricing model, is equal to $45 each.

Required »

a. Compute the total compensation cost to be recognized by Brendan B Fashions assuming that the company initially expects no forfeitures to occur.
b. Record the journal entries over the vesting period.
c. Prepare the journal entries required to record the actual exercise assuming that:
   - The market price of the stock on the date of exercise is equal to $35 per share.
   - The market price of the stock on the date of exercise is equal to $16 per share.

d. Repeat part (b), assuming that the estimated amount of forfeitures changed to 20% at the beginning of the second year. Assume that the company chooses to adjust the fair value for the estimated forfeitures.

e. Independent of your answers to parts (b), (c), and (d), prepare the journal entry required if 25% of the options expire unexercised. Assume that the company chooses to adjust the fair value for the estimated forfeitures.

2 3 **P19-3. Employee Stock Options, Equity-Classified Awards, Liability-Classified Awards – Comprehensive.** Eagle Builders, Inc. initiated a stock option plan for its employees on January 1 of the current year. The terms of the plan grant each employee 10 options to acquire 10 shares of the company's $1 par value, common stock at an exercise price of $45 per share. The market price on the date of the grant is also $45 per share. On the grant date, a binominal model estimated the fair value of the options at $83 per share. The option plan permits exercise only after 3 years of service and all options expire after 6 years. On the date of the grant, Eagle employed 1,200 employees. The options are equity-classified awards.

Required »

a. Assuming that the initial vesting probability is 100%, prepare the journal entries necessary:
   - To record the recognition of compensation expense each year assuming that the fair value of the options was as follows:
     - $75 per share at the end of the year of the grant.
     - $69 and $81 per share at the end of Year 2 and Year 3, respectively, following the year of the grant.

b. Assume that the company chooses to adjust the fair value for the estimated forfeitures. Repeat the requirements in part (a), assuming that the estimated vesting probabilities are:
   - 80% at the beginning of Year 1
   - 65% at the beginning of Year 2
   - 75% at the beginning of Year 3

c. Repeat the requirements in part (a) assuming that Eagle grants the options to acquire the company's redeemable preferred shares rather than its common stock.

4 **P19-4. Stock Appreciation Rights.** Fiar Company started a share appreciation plan on January 1, 2018, when it granted 100,000 rights to its executives. The vesting period is 3 years. The rights are settled for cash. The plan expires on January 1, 2021. The SARs fair value for the years ended December 31, 2018, through 2020 are as follows:

Date	Closing Market Price
December 31, 2018	$2.00
December 31, 2019	3.00
December 31, 2020	1.60
January 1, 2021	1.00

All SARs are exercised on January 1, 2021, when the fair value is $1.

Required »

a. What is the compensation expense in 2018, 2019, and 2020?

b. Prepare the journal entries to record the plan.

7 **P19-5. Defined-Benefit Pension Plan – Comprehensive.** Tony Joe Restaurants, Inc., provided the following information related to its defined-benefit plan for the current year:

Description	Current Year	Prior Year
Beginning plan assets at fair value (equal to the market-related asset value)	*Solve*	$6,000
Beginning projected benefit obligation	*Solve*	$4,800
Service cost	$ 128	$263
Settlement rate	12%	12%
Expected return on plan assets	10%	10%
Actual return on plan assets	$320	$500
Contributions for the year	$180	$760
Benefits paid during the year	$800	$560
Amortization of prior service cost	$240	$200

Description	Current Year	Prior Year
Beginning balance of accumulated other comprehensive income due to		
Unamortized prior service cost	Solve	$580
Unamortized net actuarial losses	Solve	$247
Average remaining service life of employees	5 years	5 years

Required »

(*Hint*: You must analyze prior-year results in full to complete the following requirements.)

a. Compute the total pension cost for the current year.
b. Determine the ending balances of the plan assets and the projected benefit obligation.
c. Determine the ending balance in accumulated other comprehensive income related to unamortized prior service cost and unamortized net actuarial losses.
d. Prepare the journal entry to record the current year's pension cost.

7 **P19-6. Defined-Benefit Pension Plan, Comprehensive.** Bruce-West Advertising, Inc., initiated a defined-benefit pension plan 5 years ago. All prior service costs are for vested employees. The beginning balances related to the company's pension plan follow:

Description	Current Year (000s omitted)
Beginning plan assets at fair value (market-related value)	$8,010
Beginning projected benefit obligation	9,133
Service cost	1,827
Settlement rate	8%
Expected return on plan assets	4%
Actual return on plan assets	570
Contributions for the year	1,060
Benefits paid during the year	900
Amortization of prior service cost	670
Beginning balance of	
Unamortized prior service cost	2,020
Unamortized net actuarial gains	3,012
Average remaining service life of employees	5 years

Required »

a. Compute the total pension cost for the year.
b. Determine the ending balances of the plan assets and the projected benefit obligation and indicate the funded status of the plan.
c. Reconcile the ending balance in accumulated other comprehensive income and indicate the amounts attributable to unamortized prior service cost and unamortized net actuarial gains/losses.
d. Prepare the journal entry to record the current year's pension cost.

7 **P19-7. Defined-Benefit Pension Plan – Comprehensive, IFRS.** Repeat P19-6 now assuming that Bruce-West Advertising, Inc. follows IFRS and expected a return on plan assets equal to its settlement rate. Assume that there are no past service costs. Bruce-West reports service cost as an operating expense and all other pension expenses as non-operating.

Required »

a. Compute the total pension cost for the year. Ignore past service costs.
b. Determine the ending balances of the plan assets and the present value of defined-benefit obligation and indicate the funded status of the plan.
c. Determine the net pension liability (or asset) reported on the ending balance sheet.
d. Prepare the journal entry to record the current year's pension cost.

7 **P19-8. Defined-Benefit Pension Plan – Comprehensive.** Roweburry Blanket Company offers all employees a defined-benefit pension plan. At the end of the current year, Roweburry's pension plan trustee reported the

following information regarding the changes in the PBO, the plan assets at fair value, and the funded status of the plan.

Projected Benefit Obligation

Benefits paid to retirees	48,672	1,043,692	Beginning balance
Actuarial gain	0	84,744	Prior service cost
		58,084	Service cost
		135,680	Interest on beginning PBO
		152,316	Actuarial loss
		1,425,844	Ending balance

Plan Assets

Beginning balance	1,006,902	0	Actual return (loss)
Contributions (funding)	92,612	48,672	Benefits paid to retirees
Actual return (gain)	84,500		
Ending balance	1,135,342		

Funded Status = PBO − Plan Assets = \$1,425,844 − \$1,135,342 = \$290,502 Net Liability

Roweburry's management confirmed that the market-related asset value of the plan assets is equal to its fair value. The company uses a 9% expected rate of return. The company amortized its unamortized prior service cost at a rate of 20% for the current year. The prior service costs are for employees who are not vested. The beginning balance in the accumulated other comprehensive income account was \$18,252 due to accumulated net actuarial losses. To date, there has been no required amortization of actuarial gains or losses. The accumulated benefit obligation on the pension plan trustee's report is equal to \$1,245,000 at the end of the current year.

Required »

a. Compute the total pension cost for the current year.
b. Prepare a t-account for the accumulated other comprehensive income account.

7 **P19-9. Defined-Benefit Pension Plan – Comprehensive, IFRS.** Botburry Sheet Company offers all employees a defined-benefit pension plan. At the end of the current year, Botburry's pension plan trustee reported the following information regarding the changes in the PVDBO, the plan assets at fair value, and the funded status of the plan.

Present Value of Defined-Benefit Obligation

Benefits paid to retirees	48,672	1,043,692	Beginning balance
Actuarial gain	0	84,744	Past service cost
		58,084	Service cost
		93,932	Interest on PVDBO
		152,316	Actuarial loss
		1,384,096	Ending balance

Plan Assets

Beginning balance	1,006,902	0	Actual return (loss)
Contributions (funding)	92,612	48,672	Benefits paid to retirees
Actual return (gain)	84,500		
Ending balance	1,135,342		

Funded Status = PVDBO − Plan Assets = \$1,384,096 − \$1,135,342 = \$248,754 Net Liability

The beginning balance in the accumulated other comprehensive income account was \$18,252 due to accumulated net actuarial losses. Botburry Sheet reports service cost as an operating expense and all other pension expenses as non-operating. The expected rate of return is 9%.

Required »

a. Compute the total pension cost for the current year.
b. Compute pension-related other comprehensive income for the current year.

8 **P19-10. Defined-Benefit Pension Plan, Disclosure.** Prepare the footnote required for Roweburry Blanket Company in P19-8 for the current year that includes the following components of the pension disclosure:

Required »

a. The plan obligations, the plan assets, and the funded status of the plan at the end of the year.
b. Amounts recognized in the statement of financial position at the end of the year.
c. Ending balance of accumulated other comprehensive income.
d. Information for pension plans with an accumulated benefit obligation in excess of plan assets.
e. Components of Net Periodic Benefit Cost and Other Amounts Recognized in Net Income.
f. Other Changes in Plan Assets and Benefit Obligations Recognized in Other Comprehensive Income.

8 **P19-11. Defined-Benefit Pension Plan, Disclosure, IFRS.** Prepare the footnote required for Botburry Sheet Company in P19-9 for the current year that includes the following components of the pension disclosure:

Required »

a. The plan obligations, the plan assets, and the funded status of the plan at the end of the year.
b. Amounts recognized in the statement of financial position at year-end.
c. Reconciliation of funded status from part (a) to amounts reported in the balance sheet from part (b).
d. Components of net periodic benefit cost and other amounts recognized in net income and other comprehensive income.

7 **P19-12. Defined-Benefit Pension Plan – Comprehensive Three Years.** Penn Manufacturing Company offers a defined-benefit pension plan to its salaried employees. The following information summarizes events related to the Penn pension plan for 2018 through 2020.

Description	2018	2019	2020
Plan assets at the beginning of the year (at fair value, which is assumed to equal the market-related asset value)	$680,000	*Solve*	*Solve*
Projected benefit obligation (PBO) at the beginning of the year	$680,000	*Solve*	*Solve*
Service cost for the year	38,880	$40,320	$41,760
Settlement rate	8%	8%	8%
Expected return on plan assets	6%	6%	6%
Actual return on plan assets	$ 42,000	$37,500	$30,240
Contributions for the year	$ 36,000	$40,000	$45,000
Benefit payments for the year	$ 25,000	$30,000	$32,000
Prior service costs granted on 1/1/2018	$ 10,000	$ 0	$ 0
Amortization of prior service costs	$ 2,000	$ 2,000	*Solve*
Decrease in the ending projected benefit obligation due to changes in actuarial assumptions (i.e., actuarial gain)	$ 0	$97,600	$ 0
Average remaining service life of employee base	5 years	5 years	5 years

Required »

a. Provide the necessary computations and journal entries for Penn Manufacturing for 2018, 2019, and 2020.
b. Prepare the worksheet that summarizes the income statement and balance sheet activity and the pension journal entries for 2018, 2019, and 2020.

CASES

Judgment Cases

Judgment Case 1: Anticipated Forfeitures in Employee Stock Option Grants

Jones Automotives granted employee stock options on January 2, 2018, to acquire 100,000 shares of common stock. The exercise price was $25 per share and the vesting period is 4 years. The estimated fair value of the options is $20 per share.

In 2018, Jones experienced a turnover rate of 1.25%. In 2017 and 2016, it experienced a turnover rate of 2% and 3%, respectively. Jones is using an expected forfeiture rate of 12% to calculate the expense for employee stock options. The managers believe that 12% is the most accurate estimate given the current economic environment in the automotive industry as well as the nature of the current pool of employees.

Jones' EPS for 2018 excluding consideration of these employee stock options is $2.75 per share. The current consensus analyst forecast of EPS for Jones Automotives is $2.15. Jones has 750,000 shares outstanding at the end of 2018.

You are the auditor for Jones Automotives. Will you sign off on the company's 2018 financial statements to report its stock option expense as currently reported? Why or why not? If not, what case will you make to management to support your view?

Financial Statement Analysis Cases

Financial Statement Analysis Case 1: Analysis of Defined-Benefit Pensions Plans

Eli Lilly and Company, a global pharmaceutical company, offers defined-benefit plans to its employees. The following table presents select data about ***Eli Lilly's*** defined-benefits pension plan. ***Eli Lilly*** reports under U.S. GAAP. Use this information to answer the questions that follow regarding ***Eli Lilly's*** defined-benefits pension plan, including its pension costs and liability.

At December 31, or for the year ended December 31 (Dollars in millions)	**2016**	**2015**	**2014**
Pension Accounts (select)			
Pension benefit obligation	$12,455.9	$11,719.2	$12,012.4
Plan assets	$10,179.7	$ 9,995.6	$ 9,835.7
Pension Cost			
Service cost	$ 277.7	$ 315.7	$ 240.9
Interest cost	420.8	476.8	472.6
Expected return on plan assets	(752.1)	(782.3)	(756.6)
Amortization of prior service costs	11.8	10.4	3.6
Recognized actuarial losses	285.6	383.2	282.3
Net periodic benefit cost	$ 243.8	$ 403.8	$ 242.8
Pension-Related Other Comprehensive Income			
Actuarial gain (loss) amortization during period	$ (285.6)	$ (383.2)	$ (282.3)
Actuarial gain (loss)- current year	(725.2)	120.4	(1,939.3)
Assumptions			
Discount rate for benefit obligation	3.9%	4.3%	4.0%
Expected rate of return on plan assets	7.4%	7.4%	8.1%
Other Financial Statement Information			
Total Assets	$38,805.9	$35,568.9	$37,178.2
Total Liabilities	24,725.4	20,978.6	21,790.1
Net Income	2,737.6	2,408.4	2,390.5

Source: Selected Footnote Disclosures from Eli Lilly Inc.'s 2016 Financial Statements. https://investor.lilly.com/annuals.cfm

a. What is ***Eli Lilly's*** pension cost in 2016, 2015, and 2014? What are the components of its pension cost? What are pension costs after taxes as a percentage of net income? Comment on any changes in pension costs after taxes as a percentage of net income. Consider the growth in net income compared to the growth in pension costs after taxes. Assume a 35% tax rate.

b. What is the funded status of ***Eli Lilly's*** defined-benefit pension plans in 2016, 2015, and 2014? How has the funded status changed over time? What is the percent of the net pension liability to total liabilities in 2016, 2015, and 2014?

c. How have the settlement rate and expected return on plan assets changed from 2015 to 2016? How does the change in the settlement rate affect the pension obligation and pension cost? How does the change in the expected return on plan assets affect the pension cost?

d. If ***Eli Lilly*** had reported all actuarial gains and losses in net income rather than other comprehensive income, what would its pension cost have been in 2016, 2015, and 2014? Comment on the changes in its pension cost.

e. From Example 19.29 in the text, compare pensions at ***Eli Lilly*** to those at ***Johnson & Johnson***. Specifically, compare the pension costs after taxes as a percentage of net income and the net pension obligation as a percentage of liabilities.

Financial Statement Analysis Case 2: Analysis of Stock-Based Compensation Disclosures

Pfizer Inc., a global pharmaceutical company, offers several different types of stock-based compensation to its employees. ***Pfizer*** reports under U.S. GAAP. Use the disclosures provided in Exhibit 19.3 to answer the following questions.

Required »

a. What types of stock compensation plans does ***Pfizer*** offer?

b. What was the total expense related to these plans in 2016, 2015, and 2014? What is the expense related to stock-based compensation as a percentage of net income? ***Pfizer's*** net income was $7,125, $6,960, and $9,135 million in 2016, 2015, and 2014, respectively.

c. How many shares of restricted stock units were granted in 2016? What is the vesting period? What is amount of compensation expense that will be recognized over the vesting period? If the restricted stock units were granted on January 1, 2016, what is the deferred compensation expense related to restricted stock units in 2016? How many shares were forfeited?

d. Are the stock options awards equity or liability classified? How many options were granted in 2016? What is the entry when the grant is made? What is the vesting period? How many options were forfeited and expired? If ***Pfizer's*** average stock price during the year was $32.82 per share, can you give a reason why the options expired? What is the compensation expense related to stock options at the end of 2016 Ignore forfeitures.

Surfing the Standards Cases

Surfing the Standards Case 1: Share-Based Payments – Graded Vesting

On January 1, 2018, Western Wear, Inc. granted 100,000 stock options to its employees. Of these options, 30% will vest on December 31, 2018, 30% will vest on December 31, 2019, and the remaining 40% will vest on December 31, 2020. The fair value of the options was $15.34 per share using a weighted-average expected life. The fair value of the 30,000 shares that vest in 2018 is $14.67 per share. The fair value of the 30,000 shares that vest in 2019 is $15.38 per share and the fair value of the remaining options is $16.30 per share in 2020. Western records stock-based compensation by adjusting for estimated forfeitures. However, Western does not expect any forfeitures for these options.

Prepare a memo to the file addressing Western Wear's compensation expense for 2018 through 2020. Use the Codification for support.

Surfing the Standards Case 2: Share-Based Payments – Graded Vesting – IFRS

On January 1, 2018, Western Wear, Inc. granted 100,000 stock options to its employees. Of these options, 30% will vest on December 31, 2018, 30% will vest on December 31, 2019, and the remaining 40% will vest on December 31, 2020. The fair value of the options was $15.34 per share using a weighted-average expected life. The fair value of the 30,000 shares that vest in 2018 is $14.67 per share. The fair value of the 30,000 shares that vest in 2019 is $15.38 per share and the fair value of the remaining options is $16.30 per share in 2020. Western does not expect any forfeitures. Western Wear is an IFRS reporter.

Prepare a memo to the file addressing Western Wear's compensation expense for 2018 through 2020. Use the international authoritative literature for support.

Basis for Conclusions Cases

Basis for Conclusions Case 1: Are Employee Stock Options Really an Expense?

U.S. GAAP did not require companies to expense employee stock options through the income statement prior to 2005. Paragraphs B2 through B11 in the *Statement of Financial Accounting Standards No. 123(R)* basis for conclusions indicate that reaching an agreement to require employee stock option expensing was a long journey. Companies made a number of arguments opposing reporting this expense on their income statements, as laid out in the basis for conclusions in SFAS No. 123(R) (paragraphs B16 through B20 and B27 through B32). Provide a brief explanation of each of the arguments, a summary of the response from the standard setters, and your assessment of the appropriateness of the standard setting boards' responses.

Basis for Conclusions Case 2: Recognition versus Disclosure

Prior to 2005, firms did not have to recognize an expense for all employee stock options but could disclose the effect of the options in the footnotes. The concept of recognition versus disclosure in the context of employee stock options is discussed in the basis for conclusions in *Statement of Financial Accounting Standards No. 123(R)* (paragraphs B22 through B26).

a. What is the standard setters' view on the ability of disclosure to substitute for recognition in the financial statements?

b. What reasons do they give for holding this view?

c. Do you agree or disagree? Why?

APPENDIX A

Comprehensive Illustration of Accounting for Defined-Benefit Pension Plans

This Appendix provides a comprehensive problem to thoroughly illustrate pension accounting over 3 years.

EXAMPLE 19A.1 Comprehensive Example of Accounting for Defined-Benefit Pension Plans

PROBLEM: Footos Candy Company offers a defined-benefit pension plan to its salaried employees. The following information summarizes events related to the Footos pension plan for 2018 through 2020. Provide the necessary computations and journal entries for Footos for 2018 through 2020.

Description	2018	2019	2020
Plan assets at the beginning of the year (at fair value, which is assumed to equal the market-related asset value)	$540,000	*Solve*	*Solve*
Projected benefit obligation (PBO) at the beginning of the year	$540,000	*Solve*	*Solve*
Service cost for the year	$32,400	$33,600	$34,800
Settlement rate	9%	9%	9%
Expected return on plan assets	7%	7%	7%
Actual return on plan assets	$37,800	$50,000	$33,600
Contributions for the year	$38,400	$54,800	$88,400
Benefit payments for the year	$20,400	$28,800	$24,000
Prior service costs granted on 1/1/2019	$0	$50,400	$0
Amortization of prior service costs	$0	$21,000	$25,200
Increase in the ending projected benefit obligation due to changes in actuarial assumptions (i.e., actuarial loss)	$0	$90,000	$0
Average remaining service life of employee base	10 years	10 years	10 years

SOLUTION: We provide the computations and conceptual journal entries for each factor next. We first work through each factor for 2018 and then prepare the comprehensive journal entry for 2018 followed by 2019 and 2020.

Factor 1: Service Cost

	2018		2019		2020	
Service Cost	32,400		33,600		34,800	
Projected Benefit Obligation		32,400		33,600		34,800

Factor 2: Prior Service Costs

Recording prior services costs:

	2018		2019		2020	
OCI – Prior Service Costs	0		50,400		0	
Projected Benefit Obligation		0		50,400		0

Continued

Amortizing prior service costs

	2018		2019		2020	
Pension Expense	0		21,000		25,200	
OCI – Prior Service Costs		0		21,000		25,200

Factor 3: Interest on PBO

Computation:

	2018	2019	2020
PBO – Beginning of year	$540,000	$ 600,600	$804,390
Plus: Prior service costs	0	50,400	0
Subtotal	540,000	$ 651,000	$804,390
Times: Settlement rate	9%	9%	9%
Interest on PBO	$ 48,600	$ 58,590	$ 72,395
Computation of PBO – End of Year			
PBO – Beginning of year	$540,000	$ 600,600	$ 804,390
Plus: Prior service costs	0	50,400	0
Plus: Increase in the ending projected benefit obligation due to changes in actuarial assumptions (i.e., actuarial loss)	0	90,000	0
Plus: Service costs	32,400	33,600	34,800
Less: Benefit payments for the year	(20,400)	(28,800)	(24,000)
Plus: Interest cost	48,600	58,590	72,395
PBO – End of year	$600,600	$ 804,390	$ 887,585

	2018		2019		2020	
Pension Expense	48,600		58,590		72,395	
Projected Benefit Obligation		48,600		58,590		72,395

Factor 4: Expected Return on Pension Plan Assets

Computation:

	2018	2019	2020
PPA – Beginning of year	$540,000	$595,800	$671,800
Expected rate of return	7%	7%	7%
Expected return on PPA	$ 37,800	$ 41,706	$ 47,026

Computation of PPA – End of Year			
PPA – Beginning of year	$540,000	$595,800	$671,800
Expected rate of return	7%	7%	7%
Expected return on PPA	$ 37,800	$ 41,706	$ 47,026
PPA – Beginning of year	$540,000	$595,800	$671,800
Plus: Actual return on plan assets	37,800	50,000	33,600
Plus: Contributions for the year	38,400	54,800	88,400
Less: Benefit payments for the year	(20,400)	(28,800)	(24,000)
PPA – End of year	$595,800	$671,800	$769,800

	2018		2019		2020	
Pension Plan Assets	37,800		41,706		47,026	
Pension Expense		37,800		41,706		47,026

Factor 5: Gains and Losses

Difference between Expected Return and Actual Return on Plan Assets Computation:

	2018	2019	2020
Actual return	$ 37,800	$ 50,000	$ 33,600
Less: Expected return (from factor 4)	37,800	41,706	47,026
Actuarial gain (Loss)	$ 0	$ 8,294	$(13,426)

	2018		2019		2020	
Pension Plan Assets	0		8,294			
OCI – Actuarial Gains/Losses		0		8,294		
OCI – Actuarial Gains/Losses					13,426	
Pension Plan Assets						13,426

Change in Actuarial Assumptions

	2018		2019		2020	
OCI – Actuarial Gains/Losses	0		90,000		0	
Projected Benefit Obligation		0		90,000		0

Amortization of Gains and Losses Computation:

	2018*	2019*	2020
PBO – Beginning of year			$ 804,390
PPA – Beginning of year			671,800
Greater of PBO or PPA			804,390
Corridor percentage			10%
Corridor			80,439
Accumulated OCI – Actuarial gains (losses) – beginning balance			(81,706)**
Amount to amortize			(1,267)
Average remaining service life			10 years
Gain (Loss) amortization			$ (127)

* The beginning balance of the accumulated OCI actuarial gains (losses) is zero, so we do not perform the corridor computation.

** This consists of the prior year's change in actuarial assumptions ($90,000 debit) and the prior year's unexpected return on plan assets ($8,294 credit).

	2018		2019		2020	
Pension Expense	0		0		127	
OCI – Actuarial Gains/Losses		0		0		127

Continued

Factor 6: Funding the Plan

	2018		2019		2020	
Pension Plan Assets	38,400		54,800		88,400	
Cash		38,400		54,800		88,400

Factor 7: Payment to Retirees

	2018		2019		2020	
Projected Benefit Obligation	20,400		28,800		24,000	
Pension Plan Assets		20,400		28,800		24,000

After completing the analyses, Footos prepares one single journal entry for each year, as presented in Exhibit 19A.1.

EXHIBIT 19A.1 Income and Balance Sheet Summary of Pension Journal Entries *(Credits and credit balances reported in parentheses)*

	2018	Comprehensive Income			Balance Sheet			
Factor	Description	NI – Pension Expense	OCI – Prior Service Costs	OCI – Actuarial Gains/Losses	PBO	Plan Assets	AOCI – Prior Service Costs	AOCI – Actuarial Gains/Losses
	Beginning Balance				$(540,000)	$540,000	$ 0	$ 0
(1)	Service Cost	$32,400			(32,400)			
(2)	Prior Service Cost							
(2)	Amortization of PSC							
(3)	Interest on PBO	48,600			(48,600)			
(4)	Expected Return on Plan Assets	(37,800)				37,800		
(5)	Unexpected Return on Plan Assets							
(5)	Change in Actuarial Assumptions							
(6)	Funding					38,400		
(7)	Payments to Retirees				20,400	(20,400)		
	Pension Costs – Net Income	$43,200						
	Other Comprehensive Income		$ 0	$ 0				
	Ending Balances				$(600,600)	$595,800	$ 0	$ 0
	Ending Net Liability on Balance Sheet					$ (4,800)		

Comprehensive Journal Entry	Debit	Credit	
Service Cost	32,400		
Other Pension Expense	10,800		
Cash (contributions)		38,400	
Net Pension Liability		4,800	(Change from beginning net liability of $0 to ending net liability of $4,800)

2019		Comprehensive Income			Balance Sheet			
Factor	Description	NI – Pension Expense	OCI – Prior Service Costs	OCI – Actuarial Gains/Losses	PBO	Plan Assets	AOCI – Prior Service Costs	AOCI – Actuarial Gains/Losses
	Beginning Balance				$(600,600)	$ 595,800	$ 0	$ 0
(1)	Service Cost	$33,600			(33,600)			
(2)	Prior Service Cost		$50,400		(50,400)		50,400	
(2)	Amortization of PSC	21,000	(21,000)				(21,000)	
(3)	Interest on PBO	58,590			(58,590)			
(4)	Expected Return on Plan Assets	(41,706)				41,706		
(5)	Unexpected Return on Plan Assets			$(8,294)		8,294		(8,294)
(5)	Change in Actuarial Assumptions			90,000	(90,000)			90,000
(6)	Funding					54,800		
(7)	Payments to Retirees				28,800	(28,800)		
	Pension Costs – Net Income	$71,484						
	Other Comprehensive Income		$29,400	$81,706				
	Ending Balances				$(804,390)	$ 671,800	$29,400	$81,706
	Ending Net Liability on Balance Sheet					$(132,590)		

Comprehensive Journal Entry	Debit	Credit	
Service Cost	33,600		
Other Pension Expense	37,884		
Other Comprehensive Income–Prior Service Costs	29,400		
Other Comprehensive Income–Actuarial Gains/Losses	81,706		
Cash (contributions)		54,800	
Net Pension Liability		127,790	(Change from beginning net liability of $4,800 to ending net liability of $132,590)

Continued

Factor	2020 Description	Comprehensive Income NI – Pension Expense	OCI – Prior Service Costs	OCI – Actuarial Gains/Losses	Balance Sheet PBO	Plan Assets	AOCI – Prior Service Costs	AOCI – Actuarial Gains/Losses
	Beginning Balance				$(804,390)	$671,800	$29,400	$81,706
(1)	Service Cost	$34,800			(34,800)			
(2)	Prior Service Cost							
(2)	Amortization of PSC	25,200	$(25,200)				(25,200)	
(3)	Interest on PBO	72,395			(72,395)			
(4)	Expected Return on Plan Assets	(47,026)				47,026		
(5)	Unexpected Return on Plan Assets			$13,426		(13,426)		13,426
(5)	Change in Actuarial Assumptions	127		(127)				(127)
(6)	Funding					88,400		
(7)	Payments to Retirees				24,000	(24,000)		
	Pension Costs – Net Income	$85,496						
	Other Comprehensive Income		$(25,200)	$13,299				
	Ending Balances				$ (887,585)	$769,800	$ 4,200	$95,005
	Ending Net Liability on Balance Sheet					$(117,785)		

Comprehensive Journal Entry	Debit	Credit	
Service Cost	34,800		
Other Pension Expense	50,696		
Other Comprehensive Income – Actuarial Gains/Losses	13,299		
Net Pension Liability	14,805		(Change from beginning net liability of $132,590 to ending net liability of $117,785)
Other Comprehensive Income – Prior Service Costs		25,200	
Cash (contributions)		88,400	

20 Earnings per Share

LEARNING OBJECTIVES

1. Compute basic earnings per share, including the necessary adjustments to the earnings per share numerator and the effect of stock splits and stock dividends on the denominator.
2. Calculate diluted earnings per share, including adjustments to income in the numerator and shares in the denominator for potentially dilutive securities such as convertible debt, convertible preferred stock, and employee options.
3. Determine the effect of antidilutive securities on the earnings or loss per share computation.
4. Describe required disclosures for earnings per share.

Introduction

MOST COMPANIES REPORT their financial statements in thousands, millions, even billions of dollars. So, you could find it surprising that CEOs, shareholders, and analysts care about pennies—that is, when those pennies are in *earnings per share*. Earnings per share (EPS), a measure of earnings available to each common shareholder in a company, is the single most often quoted financial statistic in the business media. Business news channels consider every financial quarter "earnings season" and report earnings per share releases for numerous corporations. Commentators compare a company's current-quarter EPS to analysts' estimates. If actual EPS exceeds analysts' expectations, there is typically a positive impact on share prices. Conversely, if actual EPS is lower than analysts' forecasts, then the stock price will often decline.

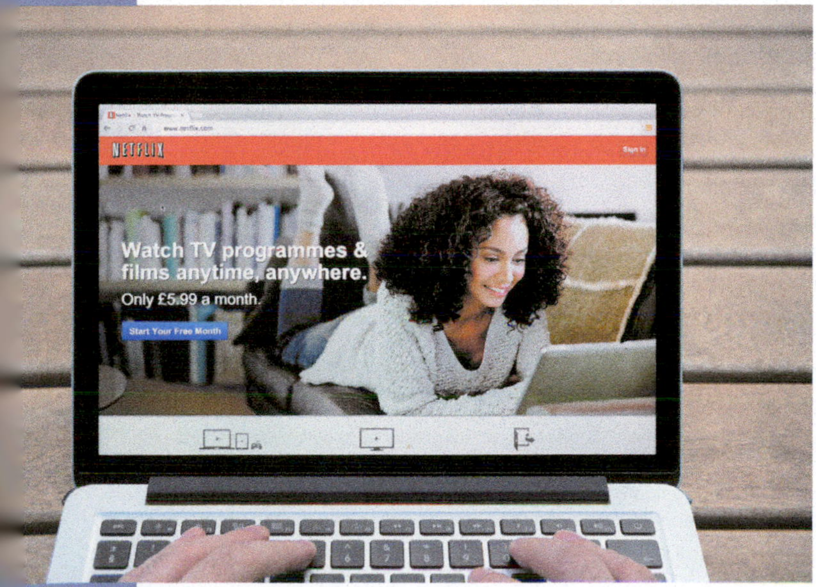

M4OS Photos/Alamy Stock Photo

Consider ***Netflix, Inc.***, the subscription service company that provides movies and TV episodes over the Internet. ***Netflix*** reported a second-quarter EPS of $1.15 per share in July 2014, an increase of $0.66 per share from a year earlier. During the quarter, its revenues were $1.34 billion, an increase of 25% from a year earlier. Yet, ***Netflix*** missed analysts' expected EPS of $1.16 per share by *one* penny and its stock price dropped by 5% on the earnings announcement.

We have discussed revenue and expense measurement and recognition issues throughout this text, working through several illustrations of how the choice of accounting methods can affect bottom-line net income or net loss. Net income or loss and its key subclassifications such as gross profit and operating income enable financial analysts to assess an entity's future earnings and cash flows. These measures often fail to satisfy the information needed by many financial statement users. EPS, the seemingly simple financial ratio of net income divided by the number of common shares, is often the most critical disclosure reported on the income statement.

EPS figures guide potential investors and the market in general in estimating the value of a company. In addition, companies estimate the impact on EPS from new capitalization, initial public offerings, and merger and acquisition activity.

This chapter provides the details of constructing the earnings per share ratio. We begin with an overview of EPS and its importance to shareholders. We then move to the calculation of EPS (both *basic EPS* and *diluted EPS*), focusing on the income and shares used in different measures of earnings per common share. Throughout the discussion, we carefully integrate many topics from stockholders' equity, employee options, convertible securities, and long-term debt. We also present required footnote disclosures for earnings per share. U.S. GAAP and IFRS are fully converged in the areas of EPS we discuss in the chapter. «

1 Compute basic earnings per share, including the necessary adjustments to the earnings per share numerator, and the effect of stock splits and stock dividends on the denominator.

Basic Earnings per Share

We begin our discussion with **basic earnings per share**, which is a measure of the earnings per share available to common shareholders that does not consider the potentially dilutive effects of convertible securities and employee options. We first discuss the conceptual underpinnings of EPS and then consider the components of the numerator and the denominator of basic EPS.[1]

THE CONCEPTUAL FRAMEWORK CONNECTION
Earnings per Share

According to the conceptual framework, the objective of financial reporting is to provide financial information useful to debt and equity investors for making investment decisions. Standard setters require that companies present EPS as a measure of an entity's performance for the reporting periods presented. EPS provides an easily understood snapshot of the performance of the firm in terms of each share of stock that investors own.

EPS is highly relevant to investors because it measures the overall performance of the firm. Specifically, EPS provides both predictive value for assessing the likely future performance of the firm as well as confirmatory value in evaluating prior predictions about the firm.

Basic EPS Numerator

The numerator for basic EPS is **net income available to common shareholders**, which is net income less preferred dividend requirements. Net income is the bottom line reported on the income statement.[2] We subtract preferred dividend requirements from net income to calculate the earnings that are available to common shareholders. That is, the calculation deducts any amounts paid, or required to be paid, to preferred shareholders.

The preferred dividend requirements include both dividends declared on preferred stock during the year and the current-year dividends in arrears on cumulative preferred stock.[3] The prior years' EPS computations incorporated all past dividends in arrears, so it is not necessary to include the total balance of dividends in arrears. For example, ***Kimberly-Clark Corporation*** has no preferred stock, so its net income of $2,166 million in 2016 is the numerator in the basic EPS computation. ***Procter & Gamble Company***, on the other hand, has preferred stock and subtracted $255 million of preferred stock dividends from its net income of $10,508 million in the numerator of the basic EPS computation in 2016.

The numerator of the ratio is called net income available to common shareholders because the calculation excludes preferred shareholder claims. If there is a net loss, loss per share increases by the amount of preferred dividend requirements. The exclusion of preferred dividends clearly emphasizes the fact that EPS applies only to common shares.

[1]For the relevant authoritative literature, see FASB ASC 260-10 – *Earnings per Share – Overall* for U.S. GAAP and IASC, *International Accounting Standard 33*, "Earnings per Share" (London, UK: International Accounting Standards Committee, Revised, 2003) for IFRS.

[2]EPS is reported on several different components of the income statement (e.g., EPS from income from continuing operations and EPS from income from discontinued operations). We will address these variations later in this chapter.

[3]As discussed in Chapter 15, cumulative preferred stock is a class of preference shares that accumulates undeclared dividends. If dividends are not declared on cumulative preferred shares, they go into arrears. Dividends in arrears must be paid before current-year preferred dividends and before any dividends can be paid to common shareholders. EPS computations deduct only the increase in dividends in arrears for the current year, not the total accumulated amount.

Basic EPS Denominator

The denominator for basic EPS is the weighted-average number of shares outstanding. Calculations of the weighted-average number of common shares include only outstanding shares. Outstanding shares are equal to issued shares less any treasury shares held by the company. The basic EPS denominator includes all classes of common stock. If an entity has two classes of common stock, it adds the shares outstanding for the two classes for basic EPS computations.[4]

The Importance of the Weighted Average. The weighted average is based on the amount of time that shares are outstanding. The numerator, net income, is a flow variable, and the denominator, number of outstanding shares, is a static or stock variable. Using the weighted-average number of common shares offers two advantages:

1. It creates a denominator that is consistent with the net income flow.
2. It matches the number of shares with the income generated from the economic resources provided by the shares issued.

The weighted-average computation uses the number of shares outstanding at different share-related events during the year and weights the shares by the percentage of the total year the shares are outstanding. The outstanding shares are weighted from the event date—such as the beginning balance date, issue date, conversion date, or exercise date—to year-end. For example, ***Netflix's*** weighted-average number of shares outstanding used in its basic EPS was 428.8 million in 2016. At the beginning of the year, ***Netflix*** had 427.9 million shares outstanding and at the end of the year, 430.1 million shares were outstanding. During the year, ***Netflix*** issued shares for stock-based executive compensation and upon the conversion of notes, both increasing the number of shares.

Equation 20.1 calculates basic EPS as follows:

$$\text{Basic EPS} = \frac{\text{Net Income Available to Common Shareholders}}{\text{Weighted-Average Number of Common Shares Outstanding}}$$

$$= \frac{\text{Net Income} - \text{Preferred Dividend Requirements}}{\text{Weighted-Average Number of Common Shares Outstanding}} \tag{20.1}$$

Example 20.1 illustrates the computation of the weighted-average number of common shares.

EXAMPLE 20.1 Computation of Weighted-Average Number of Common Shares Using Changes in Shares Outstanding

PROBLEM: Storace Storage Corporation had $170,000 net income and declared $10,000 of preferred dividends in the current year. Storace begins the current year with 15,000 common shares outstanding. The company issued additional shares of 7,500 and 9,000 on May 1 and October 1, respectively. In addition, Storace purchased 1,500 shares of treasury stock on July 1. The firm's year-end is December 31. What is Storace's basic EPS?

SOLUTION: The numerator in Storace's basic EPS computation is $160,000 computed as the $170,000 net income less the $10,000 preferred dividends declared.

Storace computes the weighted-average outstanding shares by defining weights as the percentage of the year from the event date to year-end. In the first row of the following table,

Continued

[4]Companies can issue several classes of common stock. For example, a company could have both Class A and Class B common stock that trade off voting rights for dividends. Class A can have more voting rights and a lower dividend payment than Class B. Nonetheless, both classes are combined for purposes of the EPS computation.

we assign the beginning balance, which is outstanding from January 1 to December 31, a weight of 12 / 12, or 100%. Similarly, the shares issued on May 1 are outstanding for 8 months from May 1 through December 31; the event date is May 1, so that the weight is 8/12. The following table shows the computation of the weighted-average number of common shares outstanding for the current year.

Date	Event	Number of Shares Outstanding	Weight by Number of Months Shares Outstanding	Weighted-Average Shares Outstanding
January 1	Balance	15,000	12 / 12	15,000
May 1	New issue	7,500	8 / 12	5,000
July 1	Treasury stock purchase	(1,500)	6 / 12	(750)
October 1	New issue	9,000	3 / 12	2,250
December 31	Balance	30,000		21,500

Storace has 30,000 outstanding shares at year-end and 21,500 weighted-average shares.

Storace's basic EPS is $7.44 computed as $160,000 divided by the 21,500 weighted shares outstanding.

Stock Splits and Stock Dividends. Stock splits and stock dividends also impact the computation of weighted-average common shares outstanding. For example, when ***Nike Inc.*** split its stock at the end of 2015, the number of shares outstanding doubled from 678 million to 1,356 million. Therefore, to calculate EPS, the company needed to divide its net income available to common stockholders by a greater number of shares outstanding after the split.

The accounting assumes that a stock split or stock dividend occurs at the *beginning of the year* for shares that were outstanding as of the beginning of the year. For share issuances that occur before the split or dividend, the **retroactive assumption** assumes that the split or dividend occurred at the *time of the issuance*. The retroactive assumption is a sound approach for several reasons:

1. In contrast to new issues and treasury share purchases, stock dividends and stock splits do not change cash or net assets. That is, stock dividends and stock splits do not change the economic resources available to generate income. As a result, including the additional shares on a retroactive basis does not mismatch the numerator and denominator of the EPS fraction.
2. Applying the retroactive assumption results in stating the number of shares before and after a stock dividend or split on the same basis. Financial statement users can therefore compare changes in EPS over time.
3. The retroactive assumption prevents management manipulation of EPS by the timing of stock dividends and stock splits. There are many economic reasons that affect the timing of stock dividends and stock splits, and the decision is not solely based on financial reporting results. However, the retroactive assumption prevents managers from timing the splits and dividends to occur later in the year, resulting in less weight, a smaller number for weighted-average shares outstanding, and thus a larger EPS. For example, if all shares are outstanding as of the beginning of the year, a company would weight the additional shares issued due to the stock split or stock dividend by 100%, regardless of the actual date of the split or dividend.[5]

Example 20.2 illustrates the effect of a stock split on the weighted-average number of common shares outstanding.

[5]The retroactive assumption also applies to stock dividends and stock splits that are distributed after the balance sheet date but before the company issues financial statements.

EXAMPLE 20.2 Computation of Weighted-Average Number of Common Shares with a Stock Split

PROBLEM: Sports Emporium, Inc. began the year with 15,000 common shares outstanding. The firm issued an additional 7,500 shares on May 1 and another 1,500 shares on November 1. In addition, it implemented a 2-for-1 stock split on July 1. The firm's year-end is December 31. What are the weighted-average numbers of common shares outstanding for the year?

SOLUTION: Sports Emporium weights the beginning balance of 15,000 shares outstanding by 12/12 for the full year. We weight the 7,500 shares issued on May 1 by 8/12 because they are outstanding for 8 months (May through December). Multiplying the number of shares outstanding on May 1 by 2 reflects the effect of the 2-for-1 stock split on a retroactive basis.

We weight the stock issuance on November 1 by 2/12 because it is outstanding for 2 months. There is no adjustment of this amount for the stock split because it occurs after the split. The following table illustrates the computation of the weighted-average number of common shares outstanding for the current year. There are 40,250 weighted-average common shares and 46,500 outstanding shares at year-end.

Date	Event	Number of Shares Outstanding	Weight by Number of Months Shares Outstanding	Weighted-Average Shares Outstanding
January 1	Balance	15,000	12/12	15,000
May 1	New issue	7,500	8/12	5,000
	Subtotal before the stock split	22,500		20,000
July 1	2-1 stock split	× 2	Retroactive application	× 2
	Subtotal after the stock split	45,000		40,000
November 1	New issue	1,500	2/12	250
December 31	Balance	**46,500**	***Weighted Average***	**40,250**

JUDGMENTS IN ACCOUNTING
Presentation of EPS

At first glance, the EPS computation seems mechanical—just enter numbers into a fixed formula. However, any judgment that affects income also affects EPS. In fact, managers can make decisions for the sole purpose of impacting EPS. As noted earlier, ***Netflix*** missed its second-quarter earnings forecasts in 2014 by only 1 cent per share and its stock price fell by 5%. Managers are incentivized to manage EPS to meet analysts' estimates and avoid the adverse effect on share prices from missing EPS forecasts. Managers are also motivated to manage the company's EPS in order to increase their own compensation when bonus plans or other compensation schemes are based on net income or stock price.

Many of the judgments that we have already discussed throughout this text impact EPS. For example, consider estimating the bad debt expense in a given year (discussed in Chapter 9). Any decisions that affect this accrual will also impact earnings and ultimately EPS. As another example, a decision to record a larger impairment loss will decrease net income and reduce EPS. Many decisions that a firm makes impact net income and thus EPS. Exhibit 20.1 outlines some of the judgments that we have discussed in this book and their impact on EPS.

EXHIBIT 20.1 Summary of Judgments

		Impact of Judgment on	
Chapter	**Issue**	**Statement of Net Income Account**	**Balance Sheet Account**
8	Various issues related to the five steps of revenue recognition	Revenue	Accounts Receivable and others
9	Measurement of bad debt expense and allowance for bad debts	Bad Debt Expense	Allowance for Bad Debts (netted with Accounts Receivable)
10	Initial measurement of inventory	Cost of Goods Sold	Inventory
10	Choice of inventory cost flow assumptions	Cost of Goods Sold	Inventory
11	Initial measurement of PPE*	Depreciation Expense	Accumulated Depreciation (netted with PPE)
12	Measurement of impairments of PPE	Impairment Loss	PPE
13	Initial measurement of ARO**	Depreciation Expense and Accretion Expense	ARO
13	Recognition and measurement of contingencies	Various expense accounts	Contingent Liabilities
14	Bifurcation of debt and equity components of hybrid securities	Interest Expense	Various Liability and Equity accounts
16	Classification of investments	Unrealized Gains/Losses and/or Investee's Portion of Income	Investments
16	Measurement of impairments of investments	Impairment Loss	Investments
17	Determination of valuation allowance	Income Tax Expense	Valuation Allowance (netted with Deferred Tax Asset)
17	Determination of tax contingency	Income Tax Expense	Deferred Tax Liability
18	Classification of lease types	Rental, Amortization, Lease, and Interest Expense, Rental and Interest Revenue	PPE and Lease Obligation
19	Measurement of stock-based compensation	Compensation Expense	APIC-Stock Options, Liability for Stock-Based Compensation
19	Measurement of the pension obligation	Pension Expense	Net Pension Asset or Liability

* Property, plant, and equipment
** Asset retirement obligation

❷ Calculate diluted earnings per share, including adjustments to income in the numerator and shares in the denominator for potentially dilutive securities such as convertible debt, convertible preferred stock, and employee options.

Diluted Earnings per Share

A company's **capital structure** indicates its sources of funds from debt and equity issuances used to finance overall operations and capital expenditures. The previous discussion focused on companies with *simple* capital structures that issue only common and nonconvertible preferred shares. That is, these companies have no **potentially dilutive securities**, which are securities that are not currently common shares but could become common stock through conversion or exercise.

Companies with *complex* capital structures issue potentially dilutive securities, including convertible debt, convertible preferred stock, employee options, and stock warrants.[6] Potentially dilutive securities can increase the number of common shares outstanding when exercised or converted into common shares, thus reducing or diluting EPS. For example, ***Johnson & Johnson's*** earnings per share footnote disclosure in its 2016 financial statements noted that its outstanding convertible debt and stock options could potentially dilute its EPS.

The **diluted EPS** computation incorporates the effects of potentially dilutive securities. In this section, we examine three potentially dilutive securities that commonly impact diluted EPS: convertible debt, convertible preferred stock, and options.[7]

[6]Stock warrants are essentially long-term options and are usually satisfied from new share issues rather than from treasury shares.

[7]Contingent share arrangements are contracts or agreements that could result in firms issuing additional shares upon the satisfaction of certain future conditions. Firms typically include these shares in the computation of EPS when the condition has been met.

If-Converted Assumption

The *if-converted assumption* is used to incorporate potentially dilutive securities in the EPS computation. Under the **if-converted assumption**, a company assumes that both hypothetical and actual conversions of potentially dilutive securities occur:

1. At the *beginning of the year* if the potentially dilutive security is outstanding as of the beginning of the year
2. At the *issue date of the dilutive security* if the potentially dilutive security is issued during the year

This conservative approach maximizes the number of shares that reduce diluted EPS by assuming that events that increase the number of common shares outstanding and reduce EPS occur at the earliest possible point during the year. For example, if an actual bond conversion occurs on July 1 but the bonds were outstanding as of January 1, the company assumes that the conversion occurred at the beginning of the year. In this case, the shares will receive a full 12-month weight when computing the number of weighted-average common shares outstanding rather than using only the actual 6-month weight. As a result, the denominator is larger than if the actual event date is used to weight the shares.

Convertible Debt

Convertible debt is an obligation with an option that permits the debtholder to convert the debt into common stock. We discussed convertible debt extensively in Chapter 14. Calculating diluted EPS for a company with outstanding convertible debt requires adjusting both the numerator and the denominator.

Diluted EPS Numerator. The if-converted assumption places the conversion of all convertible debt into common stock at the earliest possible point during the year. This assumption affects the treatment of interest expense for convertible debt in two ways:

1. The firm avoids the interest expense on convertible debt for the period of the year the debt was assumed to be converted into common stock. For debt issued at a discount or premium, the firm uses the effective interest rate to compute interest expense. By assuming conversion, the firm avoids the amount of interest expense deducted in the computation of net income under the accrual basis and instead adds it back to net income.
2. Interest on debt is generally tax deductible. Therefore, the firm adjusts the net income in the numerator of the diluted EPS for the reduced interest expense, net of tax.

Johnson & Johnson added back $2 million of interest on its convertible debt when computing its diluted EPS in 2016. Example 20.3 demonstrates the effect of convertible debt on the diluted EPS numerator.

EXAMPLE 20.3 Effect of Convertible Debt on the Diluted EPS Numerator

PROBLEM: Cincinnati Crafters reported $100,000 in interest expense for convertible bonds issued several years ago. The company is subject to a 40% effective tax rate. There were no actual conversions during the current year. What adjustment is needed to the company's diluted EPS numerator?

SOLUTION: Using the if-converted assumption, the company assumes that debtholders converted the bonds as of the beginning of the current year and as a result, Cincinnati Crafters would not incur the $100,000 interest expense before tax. The interest tax deduction saves the company $40,000 in taxes paid (40% × $100,000). Therefore, the after-tax cost of interest is $60,000 ($100,000 − $40,000). As a result, net income in the numerator increases by $60,000 computed as follows:

Interest expense	$100,000
Tax deduction (based on a 40% effective tax rate)	(40,000)
Assumed after-tax interest savings on bond conversion	$ 60,000

Diluted EPS Denominator. Firms increase the diluted EPS ratio denominator by the number of shares assumed to be issued upon conversion, weighting the additional shares from the beginning of the year or from the date of issue, if the convertible debt was issued during the year. To illustrate, consider a company that reports debt outstanding from the *beginning* of the year and the debt is convertible to 1,000 shares of common stock. The company increases the weighted-average number of common shares outstanding by 1,000 shares when computing diluted EPS (1,000 shares × 12/12). Alternatively, if the firm issued the convertible debt *midyear* on July 1 and assumed converted, then the company would increase the number of weighted-average common shares outstanding by 500 shares (1,000 × 6/12) when computing diluted earnings per share.

In ***Johnson & Johnson's*** calculation of diluted EPS, it added 1.3 million shares in the denominator related to the dilutive effect of convertible debt in 2016. Exhibit 20.2 illustrates the numerator and denominator adjustments in the diluted EPS computation. Example 20.4 provides an example of the computation of diluted EPS when a company has convertible debt.

EXHIBIT 20.2 Computation of Diluted EPS with Convertible Debt

$$\text{Diluted EPS} = \frac{\text{Net Income Available to Common Shareholders} + \text{Interest Expense} \times (1 - \text{Tax Rate})}{\text{Weighted-Average Number of Common Shares Outstanding} + \text{Weighted Common Shares on Debt Conversion}} \tag{20.2}$$

$$\text{Diluted EPS} = \frac{\text{Net Income} - \text{Preferred Dividend Requirements} + \text{Interest Expense} \times (1 - \text{Tax Rate})}{\text{Weighted-Average Number of Common Shares Outstanding} + \text{Weighted Common Shares on Debt Conversion}} \tag{20.3}$$

EXAMPLE 20.4 Convertible Debt Outstanding for a Full Year with No Actual Conversions

PROBLEM: Dayton Builders began the current year with 800,000 common shares outstanding and issued an additional 300,000 shares on September 1. Dayton also reported $2,300,000 par value, 3% nonconvertible, noncumulative preferred stock outstanding. The preferred shares were outstanding for a full year, and Dayton declared dividends for the current year. In addition, the firm has $20,000,000, 5% convertible bonds outstanding for a full year. Dayton issued the bonds at face value. Therefore, the company incurs $1,000,000 of interest expense per year (i.e., 5% × $20,000,000). The bonds are convertible into 450,000 shares of common stock. Debtholders did not convert any of the bonds during the current year. The company is subject to a 40% effective tax rate and reported net income of $7,000,000 for the current year. What are basic and diluted EPS for Dayton Builders?

SOLUTION: We begin by computing basic EPS for Dayton Builders.

$$\begin{aligned}\text{Numerator} &= \text{Net Income Available to Common Shareholders}\\ &= \text{Net Income} - \text{Preferred Dividend Requirements}\\ &= \$7{,}000{,}000 - (\$2{,}300{,}000 \times 3\%)\\ &= \$7{,}000{,}000 - \$69{,}000\\ &= \$6{,}931{,}000\end{aligned}$$

The weighted-average number of common shares outstanding for the denominator is as follows:

Date	Event	Number of Shares Outstanding	Weight by Number of Months Shares Outstanding	Weighted-Average Shares Outstanding
January 1	Balance	800,000	12/12	800,000
September 1	New issue	300,000	4/12	100,000
December 31	Balance	1,100,000		900,000

There are 900,000 weighted-average common shares at year-end. Thus, basic EPS is:

$$\textbf{Basic EPS} = \frac{\$6{,}931{,}000}{900{,}000} = \underline{\underline{\$7.70}}$$

To compute diluted EPS, we need to adjust the numerator and the denominator. First, we compute the after-tax interest adjustment to the numerator as follows:

Interest expense	$1,000,000
Tax deduction (based on a 40% effective tax rate)	(400,000)
Assumed after-tax interest savings on bond conversion	$ 600,000

We add back $600,000 of after-tax interest so that the adjusted numerator is $7,531,000 ($7,000,000 net income minus preferred dividends of $69,000 plus the $600,000 interest adjustment).

Second, the adjusted denominator is 1,350,000, which consists of the 900,000 shares computed for the basic EPS plus the 450,000 additional shares that Dayton Builders would have outstanding upon assumed conversion of the debt. Diluted EPS is therefore:

$$\textbf{Diluted EPS} = \frac{(\$6{,}931{,}000 + \$600{,}000)}{(900{,}000 + 450{,}000)}$$

$$= \frac{\$7{,}531{,}000}{1{,}350{,}000} = \underline{\underline{\$5.58}}$$

Diluted EPS is $5.58 in comparison to Dayton's basic EPS of $7.70.

Convertible Debt Outstanding with Conversion. Firms still use the if-converted assumption if debtholders actually convert the debt during the year. For example, if all of Dayton Builders' bonds in Example 20.4 convert on October 1, then the 450,000 shares are actually issued for 3 months and receive a 3/12 weight in basic EPS. Dayton therefore includes 112,500 shares on the actual conversion to the weighted-average shares used for basic EPS (i.e., 450,000 shares × 3/12). Applying the if-converted assumption for diluted EPS, Dayton includes shares as of the beginning of the year. This requires an additional 9/12 weight or 337,500 shares included in the weighted-average number of shares used for diluted EPS (i.e., 450,000 shares × 9/12). The total weighted-average shares used in diluted EPS are 450,000 (i.e., 112,500 shares actually issued and 337,500 if-converted shares). This is the same number of weighted-average shares as in the case in which there are no actual conversions. Adjustments to the numerator of EPS will also be made for interest.

Example 20.5 illustrates a similar scenario to Example 20.4, but now all bondholders actually convert their convertible debt into common stock during the year.

EXAMPLE 20.5 Convertible Debt Outstanding with Actual Conversion During the Year

PROBLEM: Use the same information presented in Example 20.4 for Dayton Builders but now assume that all bonds actually converted on March 1 of the current year. Because of the actual bond conversion, 10 months' interest is avoided and Dayton's net income increased by $500,000 to $7,500,000. Dayton incurs interest for only 2 months rather than a full year because the bondholders convert on March 1. The difference in income is due to the after-tax interest savings, as computed as follows.

Description	Computations	Interest Expense
Debt interest for a full year	$20,000,000 × 5% × (1 − .4) × 12/12	$600,000
Debt interest for 2 months	$20,000,000 × 5% × (1 − .4) × 2/12	(100,000)
Increase in income		$500,000

Continued

What are basic and diluted EPS for Dayton Builders?

SOLUTION: We first compute basic EPS. Net income is $7,500,000 and preferred dividend requirements are $69,000 ($2,300,000 × 3%). Thus, the numerator or net income available to common shareholders is $7,431,000 (i.e., $7,500,000 − $69,000). The denominator will not be the same as in Example 20.4 because of the debt conversion on March 1. We compute the weighted-average number of common shares outstanding as follows:

Date and Event	Number of Shares Outstanding	Weight by Number of Months Shares Outstanding	Weighted-Average Shares Outstanding
1/1: Balance	800,000	12/12	800,000
3/1: Actual bond conversion	450,000	10/12	375,000
9/1: New issue	300,000	4/12	100,000
12/31: Balance	**1,550,000**		**1,275,000**

There are 1,275,000 weighted-average shares and 1,550,000 shares outstanding at year-end. Basic EPS is $5.83 per share determined as follows:

$$\textbf{Basic EPS} = \frac{\$7{,}431{,}000}{1{,}275{,}000\text{ shares}} = \underline{\underline{\$5.83}}$$

We now compute the diluted EPS, first determining the numerator adjustment. In Example 20.4, Dayton computed an adjustment to the numerator of $600,000. However, now the debt is outstanding for only 2 months as opposed to 12 months, and the after-tax interest savings from the assumed conversion as of the beginning of the year is $100,000 ($600,000 × 2/12).

Next, we compute the adjustment to the denominator. According to the if-converted assumption, we assume that Dayton converted the bonds at the beginning of the year instead of March 1. Thus, we need to weight the 450,000 converted shares by an additional 2/12 for an adjustment of 75,000 shares. Note that the weighted-average number of common shares for basic EPS captures the 10-month period from the date of conversion to year-end using a 10/12 weight and that the other 2/12 of the year is included in diluted earnings per share. As a result, a full year is included in diluted EPS, which is the same as the case in which the convertible debt was outstanding as of the beginning of the year.

Diluted EPS is computed as follows:

$$\textbf{Diluted EPS} = \frac{\$7{,}500{,}000 - \$69{,}000 + \$100{,}000}{(1{,}275{,}000 + 75{,}000)}$$

$$= \frac{\$7{,}531{,}000}{1{,}350{,}000} = \underline{\underline{\$5.58}}$$

Diluted EPS is $5.58 in comparison to Dayton's basic EPS of $5.83.

Diluted EPS is $5.58 in both Examples 20.4 and 20.5. Therefore, diluted EPS is the same whether there are actual or hypothetical events.

Convertible Debt Issued during the Year. Convertible debt was outstanding as of the beginning of the year in our prior illustrations. What adjustments are required if convertible debt is issued during the year? The firm adjusts the numerator by the interest amount computed from the date of issue until the end of the year and computes the denominator based on the assumption that the bonds are converted when issued. Example 20.6 illustrates computing diluted EPS when convertible debt is issued during the year.

EXAMPLE 20.6 Convertible Debt Issued During the Year

PROBLEM: Using the information from Example 20.4, now assume that Dayton Builders issued convertible debt on February 1 so that the debt is outstanding for only 11 months. With the convertible debt issued during the year, net income of $7,050,000 is $50,000 higher than in Example 20.4. The difference in net income resulting from after-tax interest savings is computed as follows:

Description	Computations	Interest Expense
Debt interest for a full year	$20,000,000 × 5% × (1 − .4) × 12/12	$600,000
Debt interest for 11 months	$20,000,000 × 5% × (1 − .4) × 11/12	(550,000)
Increase in income		50,000

There are no actual conversions during the year. What are basic and diluted EPS for Dayton Builders?

SOLUTION: We first determine basic EPS. Net income is $7,050,000 and preferred dividend requirements are equal to $69,000 ($2,300,000 × 3%). Thus, the numerator or net income available to common shareholders is $6,981,000 ($7,050,000 − $69,000). The weighted-average number of common shares outstanding is as follows:

Date	Event	Number of Shares Outstanding	Weight by Number of Months Shares Outstanding	Weighted-Average Shares Outstanding
January 1	Balance	800,000	12/12	800,000
September 1	New issue	300,000	4/12	100,000
December 31	Balance	**1,100,000**		**900,000**

There are 900,000 weighted-average shares at year-end. We compute basic EPS as $7.76 per share as follows:

$$\textbf{Basic EPS} = \frac{\$6,981,000}{900,000} = \underline{\underline{\mathbf{\$7.76}}}$$

In order to compute diluted EPS, we need to adjust the numerator and the denominator. First, we compute the after-tax interest adjustment to the numerator. Dayton Builders incurred pre-tax interest expense of $916,667 ($20,000,000 × 5% × 11/12) related to the convertible debt. We adjust the numerator for the after-tax interest savings from the assumed bond conversion as follows:

Interest expense	$916,667
Tax deduction (based on a 40% effective tax rate)	(366,667)
Assumed after-tax interest savings on bond conversion	$550,000

Adding back $550,000 of after-tax interest savings, the adjusted numerator is $7,531,000 ($7,050,000 net income minus $69,000 preferred dividend plus the $550,000 interest adjustment).

Second, we adjust the denominator for the assumed conversion. Because Dayton Builders did not issue the convertible bonds until February 1, we can assume conversion only as of that point. Therefore, we weight the 450,000 additional shares by 11/12 to arrive at the 412,500 weighted shares issued on assumed conversion (i.e., 450,000 shares × 11/12).

$$\textbf{Diluted EPS} = \frac{\$7,050,000 - \$69,000 + \$550,000}{900,000 + 412,500}$$

$$= \frac{\$7,531,000}{1,312,500} = \underline{\underline{\mathbf{\$5.74}}}$$

Diluted EPS is $5.74 in comparison to Dayton's basic EPS of $7.76.

Convertible Preferred Stock

As defined in Chapter 15, convertible preferred shares are securities that can be converted to a fixed number of shares of common stock at the option of preferred shareholders. Conversion of preferred stock requires adjustments to both the numerator and the denominator of the EPS equation from applying the if-converted assumption:

1. If the firm issues the preferred stock during the year: Assume that conversion occurs at the issue date.
2. If convertible preferred shares were outstanding as of the beginning of the year: Assume that conversion occurs at the beginning of the year.

Diluted EPS Numerator. Firms adjust the numerator of basic EPS for the preferred dividends avoided if the preferred shares are assumed to convert into common stock. The firm subtracts any preferred dividends declared as well as the current-year increase in dividends in arrears on cumulative preferred stock to determine income available to common shareholders in the computation of basic EPS. Applying the if-converted assumption avoids the dividends associated with the convertible preferred shares. As a result, firms can ignore the preferred dividends and therefore eliminate the effect of the preferred dividend requirements related to the convertible preferred shares. Because dividends are not generally tax deductible, tax effects are not applicable. Cumulative preferred dividends are weighted by the number of months the preferred stock is outstanding in any given year.

Diluted EPS Denominator. As is the case with convertible debt, the firm adjusts the diluted EPS ratio denominator for the impact of the assumed conversion of convertible preferred stock by increasing the denominator by the number of shares issued on assumed conversion. The firm weights the number of shares from the beginning of the year or from the date of issue if it issued the preferred stock during the year.

Exhibit 20.3 illustrates the numerator and denominator adjustments in the diluted EPS computation.

EXHIBIT 20.3 Computation of Diluted EPS with Convertible Preferred Stock

$$\text{Diluted EPS} = \frac{\text{Net Income Available to Common Shareholders} + \text{Preferred Dividends Avoided on Convertible Preferred Stock}}{\text{Weighted-Average Number of Common Shares Outstanding} + \text{Weighted Common Shares on Preferred Stock Conversion}} \quad (20.4)$$

$$\text{Diluted EPS} = \frac{\text{Net Income} - \text{Preferred Dividend Requirements} + \text{Preferred Dividends Avoided on Convertible Preferred Stock}}{\text{Weighted-Average Number of Common Shares Outstanding} + \text{Weighted Common Shares on Preferred Stock Conversion}} \quad (20.5)$$

Example 20.7 illustrates the adjustments for convertible preferred stock in the computation of diluted EPS.

EXAMPLE 20.7 Convertible Preferred Stock

PROBLEM: Hammond Aeronautics has 400,000 shares of common stock and 150,000 shares of noncumulative, convertible preferred stock outstanding throughout the year. Hammond declared $100,000 in dividends on the preferred shares. The preferred stock is convertible into common stock at a rate of one share of preferred stock for each share of common stock. Hammond's net income for the year was $700,000. What are basic and diluted EPS for Hammond Aeronautics?

SOLUTION: We compute the basic EPS as follows:

$$\textbf{Basic EPS} = \frac{\text{Net Income Available to Common Shareholders}}{\text{Weighted-Average Common Shares Outstanding}}$$

$$\textbf{Basic EPS} = \frac{\text{Net Income} - \text{Preferred Dividend Requirements}}{\text{Weighted-Average Common Shares Outstanding}}$$

$$= \frac{\$700{,}000 - \$100{,}000}{400{,}000} = \mathbf{\$1.50}$$

To compute diluted EPS, we assume that all preferred shares convert into common stock as of the beginning of the year. Net income available to common shareholders will increase by the amount of the preferred dividends avoided on assumed conversion. As a result, we need to (1) add back the preferred dividends avoided to the numerator (no tax effects and not weighted) and (2) add the assumed-if converted weighted shares to the denominator as follows:

$$\textbf{Diluted EPS} = \frac{\$700{,}000 - \$100{,}000 + \$100{,}000}{400{,}000 + 150{,}000} = \mathbf{\$1.27}$$

Hammond's diluted EPS is $1.27, in comparison to basic EPS of $1.50.

Options and Warrants

Stock options and warrants are financial instruments that give the holder the right but not the obligation to acquire equity shares from the issuing corporation over a fixed time period and at a specified price. The options are often employee stock options granted by the company to its employees as a form of compensation.[8] A company with any options or warrants outstanding must consider the effects of these potentially dilutive securities on EPS. The if-converted assumption does not usually impact the EPS numerator because there is typically no impact on net income available to common shareholders when the options or warrants are exercised.

Diluted EPS Denominator. There are two key factors to consider for the adjustment to the denominator:

1. The increase in common shares outstanding due to the assumed option/warrant exercise of in-the-money instruments.
2. The cash proceeds the company receives from the assumed exercise of the options or warrants.

The diluted EPS denominator adjustment assumes that the company uses the proceeds to buy its own shares in the market. Subtracting the treasury shares assumed to be repurchased from the total number of shares issued on the assumed exercise determines the number of **incremental shares** remaining in the market. The incremental shares are in the denominator of diluted EPS assuming that the options or warrants were exercised under an approach generally known as the *treasury stock method*.[9]

Treasury Stock Method. The **treasury stock method** assumes that firms use the proceeds from the hypothetical exercise of in-the-money options or warrants to purchase treasury stock at the average market price of the common stock for the period.[10] The average market price should

---

[8]We discussed employee stock options in depth in Chapter 19.

[9]We use all outstanding options for this computation. Outstanding options include both vested (exercisable) and non-vested (non-exercisable) options.

[10]The period of the earnings per share computation can be annual or quarterly. The period of the earnings per share computation is critical because firms make a unique EPS computation for each quarter. As a result, options can be dilutive for 1 quarter and not for another. Similarly, the options can be dilutive for a certain quarter but not for the year-end EPS disclosure. Consequently, EPS cannot be added across quarters, and the annual EPS number is not the sum of those for the 4 quarters' EPS. U.S. GAAP requires that the incremental shares used in the EPS computation for the annual period is equal to the weighted average of the incremental shares reported in the 4 quarters.

represent a meaningful average. Yet what is a meaningful average? In theory, the calculation should include every market transaction for the period in the computation. In practice, a daily or weekly average price is used for companies that are actively traded. However, in cases where shares are not actively traded and there are no significant changes in capital structure, this approach might not be practical or cost effective, so a simple average annual price can be used. If there is little fluctuation in share price during the year, the closing price is considered a meaningful average.

Johnson & Johnson applied the treasury stock method to determine the dilutive effect of its employee stock options in its 2016 financial statements. In 2016, ***Johnson & Johnson*** increased the number of shares over those in its basic EPS by about 3.3% for the dilutive effect of options.

Exhibit 20.4 illustrates the denominator adjustment in the diluted EPS computation for options and warrants assuming no convertible securities.

EXHIBIT 20.4 Computation of Diluted EPS with Options or Warrants

$$\text{Diluted EPS} = \frac{\text{Net Income Available to Common Shareholders}}{\text{Weighted-Average Number of Common Shares Outstanding} + \text{Incremental Common Shares on Option or Warrant Exercise}} \quad (20.6)$$

$$\text{Diluted EPS} = \frac{\text{Net Income} - \text{Preferred Dividend Requirements}}{\text{Weighted-Average Number of Common Shares Outstanding} + \text{Incremental Common Shares on Option or Warrant Exercise}} \quad (20.7)$$

Example 20.8 shows the effect of options on diluted EPS.

EXAMPLE 20.8 Effect of Options on Diluted EPS

PROBLEM: The Edwards Group's current-year net income is $9,000,000. The company reported 5,400,000 common shares outstanding for the year, and the average price per common share for the year is $72. In addition, Edwards has 1,800,000 options outstanding all year with an exercise price of $54 per share. Compute basic and diluted EPS for Edwards Group. Each option can be exercised for one share of common stock.

SOLUTION: The basic EPS for the year is simply the net income ($9,000,000) divided by the weighted-average number of common shares outstanding (5,400,000), or $1.67 per share.

$$\textbf{Basic EPS} = \frac{\text{Net Income} - \text{Preferred Dividend Requirements}}{\text{Weighted-Average Common Shares Outstanding}}$$

$$= \frac{\$9{,}000{,}000}{5{,}400{,}000} = \mathbf{\$1.67}$$

The diluted EPS computation takes into account the potential dilutive effects of the assumed option exercise. First, we consider the 1,800,000 shares associated with the options because these shares would be outstanding if the options were exercised as of the beginning of the year. Second, we consider the number of shares that could be purchased in the market with the cash proceeds from the assumed option exercise. Edwards computes the number of treasury shares that it could purchase as follows:

Number of shares issued from assumed exercise	1,800,000	1,800,000
Times exercise price	× $54	
Proceeds that would be received from assumed exercise	$97,200,000	
Divided by average market price per share	÷ $72	
Number of treasury shares from assumed purchase		(1,350,000)
Adjustment to denominator: Incremental shares		450,000

Thus, we increase the denominator by the 450,000 incremental shares. There is no numerator effect for the assumed exercise of options, so diluted EPS is computed as follows:

$$\textbf{Diluted EPS} = \frac{\$9{,}000{,}000 + 0}{5{,}400{,}000 + 450{,}000} = \underline{\underline{\textbf{\$1.54}}}$$

Edwards Group's diluted EPS is $1.54 in comparison to basic EPS of $1.67.

Exhibit 20.5 summarizes numerator and denominator adjustments to basic EPS for the three types of dilutive securities covered.

EXHIBIT 20.5 Summary of EPS Adjustments for Dilutive Securities

	Adjustments to Basic EPS Computation	
Dilutive Security	***Numerator***	***Denominator***
Convertible debt	Add back after tax interest expense	Add additional weighted shares on debt conversion
Convertible preferred stock	Add back preferred dividends on convertible preferred stock	Add additional weighted shares on preferred stock conversion
Options or warrants	No numerator effect	Add weighted incremental shares on option or warrant exercise using the if-converted assumption

Diluted Earnings per Share: IFRS

The computation of diluted EPS is similar under U.S. GAAP and IFRS except for the assumption related to the conversion of convertible bonds that can also be settled for cash. For example, a company could have the option to pay off convertible bonds rather than issue shares. U.S. GAAP assumes that all of the securities will be settled in shares unless evidence is provided to the contrary. In this case, IFRS assumes that all of these securities will be settled in shares.[11] Therefore, diluted EPS can be lower under IFRS because more shares would be included in the denominator.

3 Determine the effect of antidilutive securities on the earnings or loss per share computation.

Antidilutive Securities

An **antidilutive effect** occurs if EPS increases or loss per share decreases when assuming the conversion of securities or exercising options and warrants. Firms exclude the effects of all antidilutive securities in the EPS computation per the standard setters' intention that diluted EPS be the most conservative measure of EPS. In this section, we overview the process for treating antidilutive convertible securities and options and warrants. Antidilution is tested at the income from continuing operations level.

Antidilutive Convertible Securities

Convertible securities can have either a dilutive or antidilutive effect because they impact both the numerator and the denominator of the EPS ratio. Firms determine whether a security is antidilutive by computing the incremental income per share effect of the assumed conversion and comparing it to basic EPS. If the incremental income per share effect is higher than basic EPS, then the security is antidilutive. Example 20.9 demonstrates the antidilutive effect of a single convertible security.

[11] Another minor difference between U.S. GAAP and IFRS relates to incremental share computation under the treasury stock method. In the computation of the number of incremental shares under the treasury stock method, U.S. GAAP requires the incremental shares to be computed as the weighted average of the incremental shares reported in the 4 quarters. IFRS does not have a similar requirement.

EXAMPLE 20.9 Antidilutive Effect of a Single Convertible Security

PROBLEM: Hammond Aeronautics has 400,000 shares of common stock and 150,000 shares of noncumulative, convertible preferred stock outstanding for the year. Hammond declared $100,000 in dividends on the preferred shares; net income for the year is $700,000. The preferred stock is convertible at a rate of one common share for three shares of preferred stock. Are the convertible preferred shares antidilutive?

SOLUTION: Hammond's basic EPS is $1.50, as computed:

$$\textbf{Basic EPS} = \frac{\text{Net Income Available to Common}}{\text{Weighted-Average Common Shares Outstanding}}$$

$$\textbf{Basic EPS} = \frac{\text{Net Income} - \text{Preferred Dividend Requirements}}{\text{Weighted-Average Common Shares Outstanding}}$$

$$= \frac{\$700{,}000 - \$100{,}000}{400{,}000} = \textbf{\$1.50}$$

Hammond calculates the number of incremental shares using the 3-to-1 conversion ratio, weighting the additional shares by 12/12 because the preferred stock was outstanding for the year (1/3 × 150,000 preferred shares = 50,000 common shares × 12/12). The incremental income per share effect of the preferred shares is determined as follows:

$$\begin{array}{c}\text{Incremental Income}\\ \text{per Share Effect}\end{array} = \frac{\$100{,}000 \text{ Add Back of Preferred Dividends}}{50{,}000 \text{ Common Shares}} = \textbf{\$2.00}$$

When eliminating the effect of preferred dividends, the $2.00 incremental income per share effect is greater than the $1.50 basic EPS, indicating that this security is antidilutive. Therefore, Hammond should not include these convertible preferred shares in the diluted EPS computation.

In a simple example with only one potentially dilutive security, firms can compute diluted EPS by making the adjustments to the numerator and the denominator of the EPS formula. Example 20.10 illustrates adjusting EPS for the antidilutive effect of convertible securities.

EXAMPLE 20.10 Antidilutive Effect of Convertible Securities—Adjusting the EPS Formula

PROBLEM: Consider the information in Example 20.9. Determine whether the convertible preferred stock is antidilutive by making the adjustments to the EPS formula.

SOLUTION: Hammond's diluted EPS is computed as follows:

$$\textbf{Diluted EPS} = \frac{\$700{,}000 - \$100{,}000 + \$100{,}000}{400{,}000 + 50{,}000} = \textbf{\$1.56}$$

If all convertible preferred shareholders convert into common stock, the dividends on the convertible preferred shares are avoided. As a result, the dividends on the related convertible preferred shares are eliminated and diluted EPS ($1.56) is higher than the basic EPS ($1.50). Therefore, the convertible preferred shares are antidilutive and cannot be included in the diluted EPS computation. In this case, Hammond reports both basic and diluted EPS at $1.50 per share.

Antidilutive Options and Warrants

When considering the effects of options and warrants on diluted earnings per share, the security must be in the money—that is, the exercise price must be less than the market price—to assume exercise. An investor would not exercise out-of-the-money securities if it were less expensive to purchase securities in the market. In-the-money securities result in incremental shares; out-of-the-money securities result in negative incremental shares and are antidilutive. With out-of-the-money securities, the issuing company has received more funds than it needs to buy back the issued shares and is able to acquire more shares than it issued. The number of outstanding shares will decrease, and EPS will increase as illustrated in Example 20.11.

Standard setters do not allow firms to include out-of-the-money options in the diluted EPS computation. For example, ***Procter & Gamble's*** diluted EPS excluded 55 million, 8 million, and 9 million shares related to options in 2016, 2015, and 2014, respectively, because the exercise price of the options was greater than their average market value. Positive incremental shares are required for dilution to take place.

EXAMPLE 20.11

Antidilutive Effect of Options on Diluted EPS

PROBLEM: Consider information for the Edwards Group from Example 20.8. Assume that the company reported net income of $9,000,000 for the current year. There are 5,400,000 common shares outstanding for the entire year, and the average market price per common share for the year is $72. In addition, Edwards has 1,800,000 options outstanding all year. The exercise price is now $80 per share. Compute basic and diluted EPS for the Edwards Group. Each option can be used to purchase one share of common stock.

SOLUTION: The basic EPS for the year is the net income ($9,000,000) divided by the weighted-average number of common shares outstanding (5,400,000), or $1.67.

Because the $72 market price is lower than the $80 exercise price, the out-of-the-money options are antidilutive. Edwards cannot include the options and will report basic and diluted EPS as $1.67.

We can also compute the antidilutive effect of out-of-the-money options on the denominator of the diluted EPS as follows:

Number of shares issued from assumed exercise	1,800,000	1,800,000
Times exercise price	× $80	
Proceeds that would be received from assumed exercise	$144,000,000	
Divided by average share price	÷ $72	
Number of treasury shares from assumed purchase		(2,000,000)
Adjustment to denominator: Incremental shares		(200,000)

There are negative incremental shares (fewer shares in the market) because the options are out of the money. Thus, Edwards must *decrease* the denominator by the 200,000, resulting in diluted EPS as follows:

$$\textbf{Diluted EPS} = \frac{\$9{,}000{,}000}{5{,}400{,}000 - 200{,}000} = \textbf{\$1.73}$$

Note that the $1.73 diluted EPS is more than the $1.67 basic EPS because these options are antidilutive. These out-of-the-money options would not be included in the diluted EPS reported to stockholders.

Antidilution Sequencing

How does a firm compute diluted EPS if it has more than one potentially dilutive security? A security could appear to be dilutive when computing its incremental income per share effect individually, but it could actually be antidilutive when including it in combination with other securities.

Testing for antidilution requires considering the issuance of potentially dilutive securities in sequence from the most dilutive to the least dilutive. That is, firms include the potential common shares with the lowest incremental income per share effect in the diluted EPS computation before those with higher incremental income per share effects. The test for dilution includes only the incremental income per share effects on income from continuing operations. This procedure, known as **antidilution sequencing**, results in including potentially dilutive securities in rank order from the most dilutive to the least dilutive. The comprehensive example later in the chapter includes antidilution sequencing.

Antidilution with a Net Loss from Continuing Operations

EPS is negative when a firm has a net loss from continuing operations. As a result, EPS always results in antidilutive per share effects when including potentially dilutive securities in the computation. Therefore, no potentially dilutive securities should be included in the computation of diluted EPS when there is a loss from continuing operations. Consequently, securities that would be dilutive when the company reports net income are antidilutive if the same company reports a net loss and vice versa. Example 20.12 demonstrates antidilution with a net loss from continuing operations.

EXAMPLE 20.12 Antidilution with a Net Loss from Continuing Operations

PROBLEM: PJS Company has 20,000 common shares outstanding with no preferred shares in its capital structure. PJS has outstanding in-the-money options that will result in 10,000 incremental shares. The current income statement indicates the following:

Loss from Continuing Operations	$(600,000)
Income from Discontinued Operations (net of tax)	500,000
Net Loss	$ (100,000)

What are basic and diluted earnings per share?

SOLUTION: Basic and diluted EPS are computed in the following table.

Loss from continuing operations	$ (600,000)
Income from discontinued operations (net of tax)	500,000
Net loss	$ (100,000)
Basic EPS (20,000 shares):	
• Loss from continuing operations $(600,000)/20,000	$ (30.00)
• Income from discontinued operations $500,000/20,000	25.00
• Net loss $(100,000)/20,000	$ (5.00)
Diluted EPS (30,000 shares):	
• Loss from continuing operations $(600,000)/30,000	$ (20.00)
• Income from discontinued operations $500,000/30,000	16.67
• Net loss $(100,000)/30,000	$ (3.33)

In this case, diluted EPS from continuing operations exceeds basic EPS: $(20) is greater than $(30). As a result, PJS cannot include the options in its EPS disclosures. It will report the same amounts for basic and diluted EPS:

Basic and Diluted EPS	
• Loss from continuing operations $(600,000)/20,000	$ (30.00)
• Income from discontinued operations $500,000/20,000	25.00
• Net loss $(100,000)/20,000	$ (5.00)

4 Describe required disclosures for earnings per share.

Earnings per Share Presentation and Disclosures

Standard setters require that firms present basic EPS on the income statement for all periods for which they provide financial data. In addition, if a company has a complex capital structure for any one of the periods reported in the financial statements, it must also show diluted EPS on the income statement for all periods presented. Standard setters stipulate that firms report EPS numbers for continuing operations, discontinued operations, and net income.[12]

For example, in its 2016 annual report, ***Procter & Gamble*** reported both basic and diluted earnings per share for earnings from continuing operations, earnings from discontinued operations, and net earnings. ***Procter & Gamble's*** 2016 EPS disclosure on the income statement is presented in Exhibit 20.6.

EXHIBIT 20.6 Earnings per Share from the Income Statement, ***Procter & Gamble Company***, Financial Statements, June 30, 2016

Procter & Gamble Company
Consolidated Statements of Earnings

Amounts in millions except per share amounts: Years ended June 30	2016	2015	2014
BASIC NET EARNINGS PER COMMON SHARE:[(1)]			
Earnings from continuing operations	$3.59	$2.92	$3.78
Earnings (Loss) from discontinued operations	0.21	(0.42)	0.41
BASIC NET EARNINGS PER COMMON SHARE	$3.80	$2.50	$4.19
DILUTED NET EARNINGS PER COMMON SHARE:[(1)]			
Earnings from continuing operations	$3.49	$2.84	$3.63
Earnings (Loss) from discontinued operations	0.20	(0.40)	0.38
DILUTED NET EARNINGS PER COMMON SHARE	$3.69	$2.44	$4.01
DIVIDENDS PER COMMON SHARE	$2.66	$2.59	$2.45

[(1)] Basic net earnings per common share and diluted net earnings per common share are calculated on net earnings attributable to Procter & Gamble.

Source: From the Income Statement, The Procter & Gamble Company, Financial Statements, June 30, 2016. http://www.pginvestor.com/Cache/1500090608.PDF?O=PDF&T=&Y=&D=&FID=1500090608&iid=4004124

In addition to the presentation on the income statement, firms must disclose a number of items in the footnotes to the financial statements such as per share data for discontinued operations. The company can also include this information on the face of the income statement.

Other required footnote disclosures for EPS include:

1. A discussion of adjustments to the numerator for preferred dividends
2. A reconciliation of both the numerator and denominator of the basic EPS to the numerator and denominator of the diluted EPS for income from continuing operations
3. A discussion of antidilutive securities that were excluded from the computation of diluted EPS
4. Any transactions that occurred after the close of the period that would have materially impacted the denominator of the EPS calculations (such as a new stock issue)

Procter & Gamble's earnings per share footnote from its 2016 annual report is presented in Exhibit 20.7. ***Procter & Gamble's*** income used in the basic EPS computation of $10,508 million excludes $255 million of preferred stock dividends in 2016. ***Procter & Gamble's*** weighted-average number of shares in the diluted EPS computation of 2,844.4 million includes 103.9 million shares for the conversion of preferred shares and 41.6 million shares for exercise of options and other unvested equity awards in 2016.

[12]Firms should restate prior-period EPS for any stock splits or stock dividends.

EXHIBIT 20.7 Earnings per Share Note Disclosure, ***Procter & Gamble Company***, Financial Statements, June 30, 2016

NOTE 6: Earnings Per Share

Net earnings attributable to *Procter & Gamble* less preferred dividends (net of related tax benefits) are divided by the weighted-average number of common shares outstanding during the year to calculate basic net earnings per common share. Diluted net earnings per common share are calculated to give effect to stock options and other stock-based awards (see Note 7) and assume conversion of prefered stock (see Note 8).

Net earnings attributable to *Procter & Gamble* and common shares used to calculate basic and diluted net earnings per share were as follows (in millions):

Years ended June 30	2016			2015			2014		
CONSOLIDATED AMOUNTS	**Continuing Operations**	**Discontinued Operations**	**Total**	**Continuing Operations**	**Discontinued Operations**	**Total**	**Continuing Operations**	**Discontinued Operations**	**Total**
Net earnings/(loss)	**$10,027**	**$ 577**	**$10,604**	$ 8,287	$(1,143)	$ 7,144	$10,658	$ 1,127	$11,785
Net earnings attributable to noncontrolling interests	**(96)**	**—**	**(96)**	(98)	(10)	(108)	(120)	(22)	(142)
Net earnings/(loss) attributable to P&G (Diluted)	**9,931**	**577**	**10,508**	8,189	(1,153)	7,036	10,538	1,105	11,643
Preferred dividends, net of tax	**(255)**	**—**	**(255)**	(259)	—	(259)	(253)	—	(253)
Net earnings/(loss) attributable to P&G available to common shareholders (Basic)	**$ 9,676**	**577**	**$10,253**	$ 7,930	$(1,153)	$ 6,777	$10,285	$ 1,105	$11,390
SHARES IN MILLIONS									
Basic weighted average common shares outstanding	**2,698.9**	**2,698.9**	**2,698.9**	2,711.7	2,711.7	2,711.7	2,719.8	2,719.8	2,719.8
Add: Effect of dilutive securities									
Conversion of preferred shares[1]	**103.9**	**103.9**	**103.9**	108.6	108.6	108.6	112.3	112.3	112.3
Impact of stock options and other unvested equity awards[2]	**41.6**	**41.6**	**41.6**	63.3	63.3	63.3	72.6	72.6	72.6
Diluted weighted average common shares outstanding	**2,844.4**	**2,844.4**	**2,844.4**	2,883.6	2,883.6	2,883.6	2,904.7	2,904.7	2,904.7
PER SHARE AMOUNTS									
Basic net earnings/(loss) per common share[3]	**$ 3.59**	**$ 0.21**	**$ 3.80**	$ 2.92	$ (0.42)	$ 2.50	$ 3.78	$ 0.41	$ 4.19
Diluted net earnings/(loss) per common share[3]	**$ 3.49**	**$ 0.20**	**$ 3.69**	$ 2.84	$ (0.40)	$ 2.44	$ 3.63	$ 0.38	$ 4.01

[1] Despite being included currently in diluted net earnings per common share, the actual conversion to common stock occurs when the preferred shares are sold. Shares could only be sold after being allocated to the ESOP participants pursuant to the repayment of the ESOP's obligations through 2035.

[2] Approximately 55 million in 2016 . . . of the Company's outstanding stock options were not included in the diluted net earnings per share calculation because the options were out of the money or to do so would have been antidilutive (i.e., the total proceeds upon exercise would have exceeded the market value of the underlying common shares).

[3] Basic net earnings per common share and diluted net earnings per common share are calculated on net earnings attributable to Procter & Gamble.

Source: From the Income Statement, The Procter & Gamble Company, Financial Statements, http://www.pginvestor.com/Cache/1500090608.PDF?O=PDF&T=&Y=&D=&FID=1500090608&iid=4004124

Let's apply the presentation and disclosure requirements for EPS to the information for Dayton Builders from Example 20.4. We assume that $1,000,000 of net income was from discontinued operations. Exhibit 20.8 shows the presentation of EPS on the income statement for Dayton Builders.

EXHIBIT 20.8 Dayton Builders EPS Disclosure

Income Statement	***For the Current Year***
Income from Continuing Operations	$6,000,000
Income from Discontinued Operations (net of tax)	1,000,000
Net Income	$ 7,000,000
Basic Earnings per Common Share	
Income from Continuing Operations	$ 6.59
Income from Discontinued Operations*	1.11
Net Income	$ 7.70
Diluted Earnings per Common Share	
Income from Continuing Operations	$ 4.84
Income from Discontinued Operations**	.74
Net Income	$ 5.58

* Basic EPS from Discontinued Operations = $1,000,000/900,000 shares = $1.11
** Diluted EPS from Discontinued Operations = $1,000,000/1,350,000 shares = $.74

In addition, Dayton includes a reconciliation of the numerator and denominator of the basic and diluted EPS computations for income from continuing operations as shown in Exhibit 20.9. This reconciliation ties the numbers used in the EPS computation back to the financial statements.

EXHIBIT 20.9 Dayton Builders EPS Reconciliation Using Income from Continuing Operations

	For the Current Year		
Description	***Income (Numerator)***	***Shares (Denominator)***	***Per Share Amount***
Income from continuing operations	$6,000,000		
Less: Preferred dividend requirements	(69,000)		
Basic EPS			
Income available to common shareholders	$5,931,000	900,000	$6.59
Effect of Dilutive Securities			
5% Convertible Debt	600,000	450,000	
Diluted EPS			
Income available to common shareholders including the effect of assumed conversions	$6,531,000	1,350,000	$4.84

Comprehensive Example: EPS Calculation, Antidilution Sequencing, and Disclosures

As a conclusion to the chapter, Example 20.13 provides a comprehensive example illustrating all steps in EPS calculations and disclosures.

EXAMPLE 20.13 Dario Company's EPS Calculations and Disclosure

PROBLEM: Dario Company reported net income of $570,000 for the current year. The company's net income consisted of income from continuing operations of $1,000,000 and a $430,000 loss from discontinued operations, net of tax. The company is subject to a 40% tax rate. Dario provided the following common share information:

Event and Date	Number of Shares
1/1 Beginning balance	150,000
6/1 New share issue	240,000
8/1 Two-for-one stock split	390,000
10/1 New share issue	390,000
12/1 Treasury stock acquisition	(48,000)

The company granted 120,000 stock options on January 1 that allow employees to acquire 120,000 common shares at $18 per share. The average market price of the company's common shares is $24 per share. As of the beginning of the year, $500,000 of 6% convertible debt is outstanding. Each $1,000 face value bond converts into eight shares of the company's common stock. The company's shareholders' equity section also indicates that there are $140,000 par value, 4%, noncumulative, convertible preferred shares outstanding for the current year. The board of directors declared the annual dividend of $5,600 on these shares ($140,000 × 4%). The preferred shares can convert into 10,000 shares of common stock. There were no actual exercises or conversions during the year. The bonds were issued at par value.

What are basic and diluted EPS for Dario Company? Provide the required income statement presentation and the reconciliation from basic to diluted EPS for income from continuing operations.

SOLUTION: We begin by computing the weighted-average number of common shares outstanding for basic EPS:

Date and Event	Number of Shares Outstanding	Weight by Number of Months Shares Outstanding	Weighted-Average Shares Outstanding
1/1 Balance	150,000	12/12	150,000
6/1 New issue	240,000	7/12	140,000
Subtotal	390,000		290,000
8/1 Two-for-one split	390,000	Retroactive application	× 2
Subtotal	780,000		580,000
10/1 New issue	390,000	3/12	97,500
12/1 Treasury stock	(48,000)	1/12	(4,000)
Total	1,122,000		673,500

Using the 673,500 weighted-average shares, basic EPS related to net income is as follows:

$$\textbf{Basic EPS for net income} = \frac{\text{Net Income} - \text{Preferred Dividends}}{\text{Weighted-Average Common Shares Outstanding}}$$

$$= \frac{\$570{,}000 - \$5{,}600}{673{,}500} = \textbf{\$0.84}$$

Again using the 673,500 weighted-average shares, basic EPS for income from continuing operations is as follows:

$$\textbf{Basic EPS for Income from Continuing Operations} = \frac{\text{Income from Continuing Operations} - \text{Preferred Dividend Requirements}}{\text{Weighted-Average Common Shares Outstanding}}$$

$$= \frac{\$1{,}000{,}000 - \$5{,}600}{673{,}500} = \mathbf{\$1.48}$$

We make three adjustments to arrive at diluted EPS. All weights used are 12/12 because all potentially dilutive securities are outstanding for a full year.

1. Determine the number of additional shares to include in the denominator for the stock options using the treasury stock method: The options are dilutive because the average market price per share is higher than the exercise price (that is, the options are in the money).

Number of shares from assumed exercise	120,000	120,000
Times exercise price	× $18	
Proceeds that would be received from assumed exercise	$2,160,000	
Divided by average market price per share	÷ $24	
Number of shares from assumed purchase		(90,000)
Adjustment to denominator: incremental shares		30,000

2. Determine the incremental income per share effect of the convertible preferred stock: The numerator effect would be $5,600, which is the preferred dividend requirement avoided if the assumed conversion takes place ($140,000 par × 4% dividend). The denominator effect is the 10,000 common shares that would exist if the preferred shares were converted. Thus, the incremental income per share effect is $0.56 ($5,600 / 10,000).

3. Determine the incremental income per share effect of the convertible debt: The numerator effect is the after-tax interest savings on assumed conversion of $18,000 [$500,000 × 6% × (1 − .40)]. The denominator effect is the number of shares assumed on conversion, which totals 4,000 shares ($500,000/$1,000 = 500 bonds and each bond converts into eight shares of common stock). Thus, the incremental income per share effect is $4.50 ($18,000 / 4,000 shares).

We now consider the sequencing of the three potentially dilutive securities. First, we show the earnings per incremental share effect for each potentially dilutive security. The incremental income per share effect is the increase in the numerator divided by the increase in the denominator of the EPS ratio, if conversion or exercise is assumed. Next, we rank the incremental income per share effects from low to high for each entry of potentially dilutive security into the EPS computation.

Determination of Incremental Income per Share

Potentially Dilutive Security	**Increase in Income**	**Increase in the Number of Common Shares**	**Incremental Income per Share***	**Rank: Order of Entry into the EPS Computation**
Employee options	$ 0	30,000	$0.00	***1st***
6% convertible bonds	18,000	4,000	$4.50	***3rd***
Convertible preferred stock	5,600	10,000	$0.56	***2nd***

* *Equal to the Increase in income / Increase in the number of common shares.*

Second, we test for dilution at the income from continuing operations level using antidilution sequencing. The potential common shares with the lowest incremental income per share effect are included in the diluted EPS computation before those with higher incremental income per share effects.

Computation of Diluted Earnings per Share using Antidilution Sequencing

Description	Income Available to Common Shareholders	Common Shares	Per Share	
Income from continuing operations	$ 1,000,000			
Preferred dividend requirements	(5,600)			
Net income available to common	$ 994,400	673,500	$1.48	Basic EPS
1st: Employee options	0	30,000		
	$ 994,400	703,500	$1.41	***Dilutive***
2nd: Convertible preferred stock	5,600	10,000		
	$ 1,000,000	713,500	$1.40	***Dilutive***
3rd: Convertible bonds	18,000	4,000		
	$ 1,018,000	717,500	$1.42	***Antidilutive***

We exclude the convertible bonds from the EPS computation because their effects are antidilutive. Thus, diluted EPS on income from continuing operations is $1.40.

We have tested for dilution and antidilution on the continuing operations level, but Dario Company must report EPS on net income as well. These basic and diluted EPS amounts are computed as follows.

$$\textbf{Basic EPS for Net Income} = \frac{\$570{,}000 - \$5{,}600}{673{,}500} = \textbf{\$0.84}$$

$$\textbf{Diluted EPS for Net Income} = \frac{\$570{,}000 - \$5{,}600 + \$5{,}600 + 0}{673{,}500 + 10{,}000 + 30{,}000} = \textbf{\$0.80}$$

Exhibit 20.10 shows Dario Company's presentation of EPS on the income statement and the related disclosures.

EXHIBIT 20.10 Dario Company EPS Disclosure

Partial Income Statement		
Income from Continuing Operations, net of tax	$	1,000,000
Loss from discontinued operations, net of tax		(430,000)
Net income	$	570,000
Basic net earnings per common share: (673,500 shares)		
Income from continuing operations	$	1.48
Loss on discontinued operations $(430,000)/673,500 shares		(.64)
Net income	$	0.84
Diluted net earnings per common share: (713,500 shares)		
Income from continuing operations	$	1.40
Loss on discontinued operations $(430,000)/713,500 shares		(.60)
Net income	$	0.80

Footnote Disclosure

Reconciliation of EPS Using Income from Continuing Operations

	For the Current Year		
Description	**Income (Numerator)**	**Shares (Denominator)**	**Per Share Amount**
Income from continuing operations	$1,000,000		
Less: Preferred dividend requirements	(5,600)		
Basic EPS			
Income available to common shareholders	$ 994,400	673,500	$1.48
Effect of Dilutive Securities			
Stock options	0	30,000	
Preferred shares	5,600	10,000	
Diluted EPS			
Income available to common shareholders including the effect of assumed conversions	$1,000,000	713,500	$1.40

FINANCIAL STATEMENT ANALYSIS

EPS

EPS is perhaps the most widely known financial statement ratio. Because EPS depends on the number of shares a company has, it cannot be compared across companies. Analyzing EPS values for one company over time is informative, however. For example, a financial statement user can examine whether EPS increased this year from last year or this quarter from the same quarter in the previous year. In addition, comparing the price per share to the earnings per share is a way of determining the price-earnings ratio.

In general, investors prefer higher EPS over lower EPS. Each investor has a greater return on a per share basis when EPS is higher. Investors also prefer growth in EPS over time because growing EPS means that an investor's return is increasing.

Increasing earnings is one way to elevate EPS. Managers can boost earnings through operating activities such as increasing sales or decreasing expenses. Financial statement analysis can alert users to managers' opportunistically managing earnings in an attempt to report an increase in EPS or to meet and beat analysts' forecasts. For example, a company close to the analysts' EPS forecast can reduce expenses such as research and development or advertising to meet the forecast. Reducing the number of shares outstanding by purchasing treasury stock is another way for a company to increase EPS.

To illustrate, assume that a company has $1,000,000 of earnings and 1,000,000 common stock shares outstanding at the beginning of the year. If the company has no transactions in shares, the weighted-average number of shares outstanding during the year would be 1,000,000 and EPS would be $1.00 per share. If the company repurchased 10,000 shares on July 1, its weighted-average shares outstanding during the year would be reduced to 995,000 [1,000,000 − (10,000 × $^1/_2$)]. The company's EPS would then be $1.01 per share ($1,000,000 / 995,000)—an increase of 1 cent, or 1%. Because the shares are reduced on a weighted-average basis over the fiscal year, a company cannot use share repurchases at the end of the fiscal year to increase EPS significantly.

Companies report EPS to the penny. Because the EPS computation involves many calculations, companies round up to the nearest penny. The usual convention is to round up when the thousandths decimal place is greater than 5 and down when it is less than 5. For example, when we computed the new EPS with share repurchases mentioned above, we rounded $1.005 ($1,000,000/995,000) up to the nearest penny to obtain the reported EPS of $1.01. If the company had repurchased only 8,800 shares instead of 10,000, the EPS to the thousandths would be $1.004 and would not be rounded up, remaining at $1.00. In both the numerator and denominator amounts, companies can take advantage of rounding to increase EPS.

Financial Statement Analysis, continued

As we have discussed, a company with dilutive securities reports two main EPS ratios—basic EPS and diluted EPS. The difference between these ratios relates to a company's securities that entitle the holder the option to exchange the potentially dilutive securities for common stock. Therefore, understanding the effect of the potentially dilutive securities is important. The greater the difference between basic EPS and diluted EPS, the lower the potential return to current shareholders. This is due to the fact that if the potentially dilutive securities actually result in additional shares outstanding, an investor's market price per share will decline. Example 20.14 examines ***Procter & Gamble's*** EPS disclosures.

EXAMPLE 20.14 EPS Financial Statement Analysis

PROBLEM: Use the footnote disclosures in Exhibit 20.7 to answer the following questions regarding ***Procter & Gamble's*** EPS.

a. ***Procter & Gamble*** presents EPS from continuing operations and discontinued operations. Why do standard setters require companies to report both EPS amounts?
b. In the income statement, ***Procter & Gamble's*** net income is not the same as net income available to common stockholders used in basic earnings per share. What does the fact that the two amounts are not the same suggest?
c. Is there a difference between ***Procter & Gamble's*** basic income used for basic EPS and diluted income used for diluted EPS? If so, what types of securities create the difference between the company's basic income and diluted income?
d. Is there a difference between ***Procter & Gamble's*** basic shares used for basic EPS and diluted shares used for diluted EPS? If so, what types of securities create the difference between ***Procter & Gamble's*** basic shares and diluted shares?
e. Comment on the changes in basic income from continuing operations, basic EPS for income from continuing operations, and diluted EPS for income from continuing operations over the 3 years.
f. What is the percentage difference in basic EPS for income from continuing operations and diluted EPS for income from continuing operations over time? Comment on changes over time.
g. If you were an analyst, what further information would you want to have to assess changes in EPS over time?

SOLUTIONS: Solutions to each question follow.

a. EPS from continuing operations relates to those activities that a company will continue to operate in the following year. Therefore, EPS from continuing operations is a basis on which to predict future EPS. EPS from discontinued operations relates to those activities that the company will not continue into the future. Therefore, EPS from discontinued operations should not be used to predict future EPS. Recall from Chapter 5, that companies report income from continuing operations and income from discontinued operations separately on the income statement. The presentation of the two EPS amounts follows the income statement.
b. The fact that net income on the income statement and net income available to common stockholders used in the computation of basic EPS are not the same suggests that ***Procter & Gamble*** has preferred stock. From the footnote disclosures, ***Procter & Gamble*** subtracts dividends on preferred stock of $255 million, $259 million, and $253 million, in 2016, 2015, and 2014, respectively. Net income available for common shareholders is then lower than reported net income.

Financial Statement Analysis, continued

c. According to the footnote disclosures, the difference between basic income and diluted income is due to preferred dividends on convertible preferred stock. If ***Procter & Gamble*** had convertible notes or bonds, it would have had to adjust the basic income for interest expense, amortization of discount, and other changes in income or loss that would result from the assumed conversion.

d. Yes, there is a difference between ***Procter & Gamble's*** basic shares and diluted shares. For example, in 2016, basic weighted-average common shares outstanding were 2,698.9 million whereas diluted weighted-average common shares outstanding were higher at 2,844.4 million. Convertible preferred stock, stock options, and other unvested equity awards create the difference between basic shares and diluted shares. As ***Procter & Gamble*** states, the diluted shares assume that these securities are converted or exercised.

e. Calculations for income from continuing operations, basic EPS, and diluted EPS over the 3 years follow.

	2016	2015	2014
Basic income from continuing operations	$9,676	$7,930	$10,285
Basic EPS for income from continuing operations	$3.59	$2.92	$3.78
Diluted EPS for income from continuing operations	$3.49	$2.84	$3.63
Percentage changes			
Basic income from continuing operations	22.02%	(22.90%)	
Basic EPS for income from continuing operations	22.95%	(22.75%)	
Diluted EPS for income from continuing operations	22.89%	(21.76%)	

The changes in basic EPS and diluted EPS mirror the changes in income from continuing operations. The change in income from continuing operations is positive in 2016 and negative in 2015. The percentage increase in basic and diluted EPS is greater than the percentage increase in basic income from continuing operations in 2016. These different relations imply that understanding the adjustments to income and shares are important when assessing the changes in EPS.

f. Percentage differences in basic EPS and diluted EPS for income from continuing operations follows.

	2016	2015	2014
Basic EPS for income from continuing operations	$3.59	$2.92	$3.78
Diluted EPS for income from continuing operations	$3.49	$2.84	$3.63
Difference	$0.10	$0.08	$0.15
Percentage of basic EPS	2.8%	2.7%	4.0%

The difference between basic and diluted EPS is lower in 2016 and 2015 than in 2014. One reason for the difference is the number of additional shares from dilution is decreasing, lowering the difference between the two.

g. An analyst would be interested in assessing the variability in net income by examining whether components of net income changed from year to year because both net income and EPS amounts vary from year to year. Additionally, it would be informative to understand the significance of the decrease in dilutive options, a decrease in the number of shares outstanding, or being out of the money.

Interview

MICHAEL H. DOLAN
MANAGING DIRECTOR, DUFF & PHELPS, LLC »

Michael H. Dolan

Michael H. Dolan, a Managing Director and the New York Office City Leader for Duff & Phelps, LLC, has performed numerous valuations for financial and tax reporting in addition to merger and acquisition needs. He has valued companies' businesses and related assets, including patents, technological items, trademarks, and licenses across a broad spectrum of industries.

1 How is the earnings per share (EPS) ratio used at Duff & Phelps to determine the value of equity shares?

Duff & Phelps compiles projected EPS estimates for selected public companies deemed comparable to the company being valued (the Subject) that are sourced primarily from analyst research consensus. With these EPS estimates, we perform economic comparisons with respect to expected earnings growth, profitability, and return from the equity investor's point of view.

2 How do earnings per share affect a proposed merger or a company's financing plans?

Mergers have an *accretive* effect on EPS when they are expected to increase consolidated EPS for the Subject. Conversely, a merger that is expected to reduce the combined EPS has a *dilutive* effect. In the case of financing, projecting the EPS helps determine how much the proposed financing will increase or decrease current EPS based on the added cost of financing relative to the expansion of earnings it will provide. As an example, debt financing can help finance new earnings initiatives for the Subject, potentially producing levered returns to equity holders, or it can be used to help recapitalize and potentially increase the Subject's levered equity return and thus result in a positive effect on future EPS.

3 What role does judgment play in determining whether one company is of higher value than another if both report the same earnings per share?

First, you must understand the computation of basic or dilutive weighted-average shares outstanding and how this affects EPS. Although companies can have the same EPS, a share's pro rata entitlement of the company's earnings has a bearing on the observed price. Placing that aside, the investment community often prices companies with identical EPS and share counts differently because of perceived risk based on each company's historical EPS trends and future expectation of EPS trends. A prudent investor would price a company with consistent, positive performance trends above one with more volatile earnings from either a growth or profitability perspective.

4 What judgments affect EPS, thereby determining the quality of earnings per share?

Evaluating the quality of earnings involves differentiating between recurring earnings generated from a company's normal operating activities and nonrecurring activities that are one-time or non-operational. Nonrecurring profit and loss items should be excluded from EBITDA[13] on a normalized basis. These items include but are not limited to gains/losses on asset sales, out-of-period reserve reversal, litigation settlements, and changes in accounting methodology. However, you should consider these non-operating or nonrecurring items to understand a company's true earnings per share.

5 Most accountants consider diluted earnings per share the key statistic on the income statement. Do basic earnings per share have a role in valuation?

Because the basic earnings per share figure is calculated on the base of shares *prior* to expected dilution, it helps determine the realized return on equity employed. Prospective earnings would likely incorporate the effects of their expected dilution from such events as the vesting of restricted stock. Prudent investors would incorporate these effects into estimates of future equity returns when pricing equity investments.

6 Do earnings surprises always affect share prices?

In my review of recent studies on the subject, earnings surprises or material events often have an effect on real-time pricing of widely held, liquid equities that have in-depth analyst coverage. However, it is important to keep in mind that share prices reflect cash flow potential in both the short and long term and that to the extent that earnings surprises affect the risk perception of achieving long-term cash returns for shareholders, the effect is positively correlated.

Discussion Questions

1. Identify possible causes of accretion and dilution of EPS in a proposed merger.
2. Discuss the possible impact of managerial judgment and market transactions on reported EPS.

[13]EBITDA is the abbreviation for earnings before tax, depreciation, and amortization expenses.

Summary by Learning Objectives

In the following, we summarize the main points by learning objective. Throughout the chapter, we discuss the accounting and reporting of U.S. GAAP and IFRS side-by-side. The following table also highlights the major similarities and differences between the standards.

1 Compute basic earnings per share, including the necessary adjustments to the earnings per share numerator and the effect of stock splits and stock dividends on the denominator.

Summary	Similarities and Differences between U.S. GAAP and IFRS
Earnings per share (EPS) is a measure of the earnings that are available to common shareholders. Basic earnings per share is net income less preferred dividends divided by the weighted-average number of shares outstanding. ***Basic EPS Equation:*** $$\text{Basic EPS} = \frac{\text{Net Income Available to Common Shareholders}}{\text{Weighted-Average Number of Common Shares Outstanding}}$$ $$\text{Basic EPS} = \frac{\text{Net Income} - \text{Preferred Dividends Requirements}}{\text{Weighted-Average Number of Common Shares Outstanding}} \quad (20.1)$$ The weighted-average number of shares is adjusted for all stock splits and stock dividends assuming that the split or dividend occurred at the beginning of the year or as of the date common shares were issued.	Similar under U.S. GAAP and IFRS.

2 Calculate diluted earnings per share, including adjustments to income in the numerator and shares in the denominator for potentially dilutive securities such as convertible debt, convertible preferred stock, and employee options.

Summary	Similarities and Differences between U.S. GAAP and IFRS
A firm has a simple capital structure if it issues only common and nonconvertible preferred stock. If a firm has potentially dilutive securities, it has a complex capital structure. The numerator and denominator effect of all potentially dilutive securities is important in the calculation of diluted EPS. • For convertible debt, add the after-tax interest expense back to the numerator and add the shares potentially issued to the denominator. • For convertible preferred stock, add the preferred dividends back to the numerator and add the common shares potentially issued to the denominator. • For options, add the number of incremental shares needed (using the treasury stock method) to the denominator. The treasury stock method assumes that a company uses all proceeds received from the exercise of in-the-money options and warrants to buy back the company's stock at current market prices. So, the increase in shares from conversion is net of total shares needed for the exercise of the options or warrants less those that could be repurchased.	➤ Similar under U.S. GAAP and IFRS except when convertible securities can be settled for cash. U.S. GAAP assumes that all of the securities will be settled in shares unless evidence is provided to the contrary. IFRS assumes that all of these securities will be settled in shares.

2 Calculate diluted earnings per share, including adjustments to income in the numerator and shares in the denominator for potentially dilutive securities such as convertible debt, convertible preferred stock, and employee options.

Summary	Similarities and Differences between U.S. GAAP and IFRS
Diluted EPS Equations: *With Convertible Debt* Diluted EPS = $\dfrac{\text{Net Income} - \text{Preferred Dividends} + \text{Interest Expense} \times (1 - \text{Tax Rate})}{\text{Weighted-Average Number of Common Shares Outstanding} + \text{Weighted Common Shares on Debt Conversion}}$ *With Convertible Preferred Stock* Diluted EPS = $\dfrac{\text{Net Income} - \text{Preferred Dividends} + \text{Preferred Dividends Avoided on Convertible Preferred Stock}}{\text{Weighted-Average Number of Common Shares Outstanding} + \text{Weighted Common Shares on Preferred Stock Conversion}}$ *With Options or Warrants* Diluted EPS = $\dfrac{\text{Net Income} - \text{Preferred Dividends}}{\text{Weighted-Average Number of Common Shares Outstanding} + \text{Incremental Common Shares on Option or Warrant Exercise}}$	➤ Similar under U.S. GAAP and IFRS except when convertible securities can be settled for cash. U.S. GAAP assumes that all of the securities will be settled in shares unless evidence is provided to the contrary. IFRS assumes that all of these securities will be settled in shares.

3 Determine the effect of antidilutive securities on the earnings or loss per share computation.

Summary	Similarities and Differences between U.S. GAAP and IFRS
When a potentially dilutive security increases EPS, it is not included in the calculation of diluted EPS.	Similar under U.S. GAAP and IFRS.

4 Describe required disclosures for earnings per share.

Summary	Similarities and Differences between U.S. GAAP and IFRS
Firms must report basic EPS on the face of their financial statements. If a firm has potentially dilutive securities, it must also report diluted EPS on the face of the financial statements. Firms must present per share information for income from continuing operations, discontinued operations, and net income. Footnote disclosures for EPS include: 1. Adjustments made in the numerator for preferred dividends 2. Reconciliation of basic EPS to diluted EPS for income from continuing operations 3. Discussion of antidilutive common shares not included in the computation of diluted EPS 4. Transactions that occurred after the close of the period that would have materially impacted the denominator of the EPS calculations.	Similar under U.S. GAAP and IFRS.

20 Earnings per Share

Questions

1 **Q20-1.** **Understanding EPS.** How do financial statement analysts use earnings per share information?

1 **Q20-2.** **Preferred Dividends.** Do firms adjust the numerator of the EPS ratio for preferred dividends if the dividends are declared?

2 **Q20-3.** **If-Converted Method.** Does the if-converted assumption apply only to diluted earnings per share?

2 **Q20-4.** **Diluted EPS.** If all potentially dilutive securities are dilutive (as opposed to antidilutive), will diluted earnings per share be the same whether there are actual or hypothetical conversions of potentially dilutive securities?

2 **Q20-5.** **Diluted EPS.** Can diluted earnings per share on bottom-line net income or net loss exceed basic earnings per share?

2 **Q20-6.** **Diluted EPS, Convertible Debt, and Preferred Stock.** Does a company with dilutive convertible debt and dilutive convertible preferred shares have to add the after-tax interest and after-tax preferred dividends back to net income in the numerator computation of diluted EPS?

2 **Q20-7.** **Diluted EPS and Convertible Debt.** Does the after-tax interest add-back for convertible debt require the amount of the coupon interest paid for the period of the earnings per share computation?

2 **Q20-8.** **Treasury Stock Method.** When can firms use the treasury stock method?

3 **Q20-9.** **Antidilution.** When is a potentially dilutive security antidilutive?

4 **Q20-10.** **EPS Disclosures.** Is an entity required to present earnings per share on income from continuing operations and earning per share on discontinued operations on the face of its financial statements?

4 **Q20-11.** **EPS Disclosures.** Do earnings per share disclosures include a reconciliation of the numbers used in the computation of EPS to the information provided in the financial statements?

Multiple-Choice Questions

In partnership with:

BECKER PROFESSIONAL EDUCATION®

Becker CPA Exam Review multiple-choice questions are available in MyLab Accounting.

2 **MC20-1.** Hutchins Company had 200,000 shares of common stock, 50,000 shares of convertible preferred stock, and $2,000,000 of 10% convertible bonds outstanding during the entire year. The preferred stock was convertible into 40,000 shares of common stock.

During the current year, Hutchins paid dividends of $1.00 per share on the common stock and $2.00 per share on the preferred stock. Each $1,000 bond was convertible into 50 shares of common stock. The net income for the year was $1,000,000, and the income tax rate was 30%.

Basic earnings per share for the current year was (rounded to the nearest penny):

a. $5.00 b. $4.50 c. $4.30 d. $4.55

1 **MC20-2.** Burken Co. has one class of common stock outstanding and no other securities that are potentially convertible into common stock. During Year 10, 100,000 shares of common stock were outstanding. In Year 11, two distributions of additional common shares occurred: On April 1, 20,000 shares of treasury stock were sold, and on July 1, a 2-for-1 stock split was issued. Net income was $410,000 in Year 11 and $350,000 in Year 10. What amounts should Burken report as earnings per share in its Year 11 and Year 10 comparative income statements?

Year 11	Year 10
a. $1.78	$3.50
b. $2.34	$3.50
c. $2.34	$1.75
d. $1.78	$1.75

1 **MC20-3.** Alvarado Company had the following common stock balances and transactions during the current year:

January 1	Common stock outstanding	60,000
March 1	Issue of a 10% common stock dividend	6,000
May 1	Issue of common stock	9,000
November 1	Issue of common stock for cash	3,000
December 31	Common stock outstanding	78,000

What was the number of Alvarado's current-year weighted-average shares outstanding for basic EPS?
a. 78,000 b. 73,250 c. 72,500 d. 71,500

1 2 **MC20-4.** Anson Company had 8,000,000 shares of common stock outstanding on December 31, Year 11. Anson issued an additional 1,200,000 shares of common stock on April 1, Year 12, and 1,000,000 more on July 1, Year 12. On October 1, Year 12, Anson issued 50,000 of $1,000 face value 4% convertible bonds. Each bond is convertible into 20 shares of common stock. No bonds were converted into common stock in Year 12. What is the number of shares to be used in computing basic earnings per share and diluted earnings per share, respectively, in Year 12?
a. 8,000,000 and 8,000,000
b. 9,400,000 and 9,400,000
c. 9,400,000 and 9,650,000
d. 7,500,000 and 8,500,000

2 **MC20-5.** Refer to the information about Hutchins Company in MC20-1.
Diluted earnings per share for the current year was (rounded to the nearest penny):
a. $5.00 b. $3.35 c. $3.53 d. $3.06

2 **MC20-6.** In determining earnings per share, interest expense net of applicable income taxes on convertible debt that is dilutive should be:
a. Added back to net income for diluted earnings per share and ignored for basic earnings per share.
b. Added back to net income for both basic earnings per share and diluted earnings per share.
c. Deducted from net income for basic earnings per share and ignored for basic diluted earnings per share.
d. Deducted from net income for both basic earnings per share and diluted earnings per share.

Brief Exercises

1 4 **BE20-1. Compute Basic EPS.** Molino Motors, Inc. reported net income equal to $1,200,000, which includes a $650,000 after-tax loss from discontinued operations. Molino has 700,000 common shares outstanding for the entire year. Prepare a partial income statement beginning with income from continuing operations and include the earnings per share disclosures.

1 **BE20-2. Compute Basic EPS with Preferred Stock.** Rainbow Company reported $239,000 net income for the current year. It has 100,000 shares of common shares outstanding for the entire year and another 50,000 shares of 3% nonconvertible, cumulative, $10 par value preferred shares outstanding for the entire year. The board of directors did not declare dividends in the current year. Compute basic earnings per share for the current year.

1 2 **BE20-3. Computing Income for Basic EPS.** Russo Watches, Ltd. reported $1,625,000 net income for the current year. Russo has $5,000,000, 6% convertible debt issued at par and $320,000 par value, 4% nonconvertible, noncumulative preferred shares outstanding. The firm declared dividends for the current year. Russo issued the bonds on April 1, and the preferred shares were outstanding for the entire year. Based on this information, determine net income available to common shareholders for basic earnings per share.

1 **BE20-4. Computing Income for Basic EPS.** Jackson Pet Food Suppliers reported $7,000,000 net income for the current year. The company indicated that it has $450,000 par value, 6% nonconvertible, cumulative preferred shares outstanding. The firm did not declare dividends for the current year. The preferred shares were outstanding for the entire year. Based on this information, determine net income available to common shareholders for basic earnings per share.

1 **BE20-5. Compute Weighted-Average Number of Shares Outstanding.** Elmwood Excavation Consultants began the current year with 30,000 common shares outstanding. It issued additional shares of 15,000 and 18,000 on March 1 and August 1, respectively. The company also purchased 3,000 shares of treasury stock on November 1. The firm's year-end is December 31. Based on this information, determine the weighted-average number of common shares outstanding for the year.

1 **BE20-6. Compute Weighted-Average Number of Shares Outstanding with a Stock Dividend.** Using the information provided in BE20-5, compute the weighted-average number of common shares outstanding for Elmwood Excavation Consultants assuming that the company implemented a 10% stock dividend on December 1.

1 **BE20-7. Compute Weighted-Average Number of Shares Outstanding with a Stock Split.** Bee-Boy Honey Products began the current year with 5,000 common shares outstanding. The firm issued additional shares of 1,500 and 1,800 on February 1 and June 1, respectively. In addition, the firm purchased 600 shares of treasury stock on September 1. The firm's year-end is December 31. In addition, Bee-Boy implemented a 3-for-1 stock split on May 1. Compute the weighted-average shares outstanding.

2 **BE20-8. Simple and Complex Capital Structure.** Fill in the following chart to indicate the capital structure type—simple or complex—for a company holding only this type of security.

Type of Security	Simple Capital Structure	Complex Capital Structure
Common stock	________	________
Preferred stock	________	________
Convertible preferred stock	________	________
Stock options	________	________
Debt	________	________
Convertible debt	________	________
Class A and Class B common stock	________	________

2 **BE20-9. Computing Income Available to Common Shareholders, Basic, and Diluted EPS.** Ardmore Pet Food Suppliers reported $7,000,000 net income for the current year. The company indicated that it has $6,000,000, 5% convertible debt issued at par and $450,000 par value, 6% nonconvertible, cumulative preferred shares outstanding. The firm did not declare dividends for the current year. It issued the bonds on May 31, and the preferred shares were outstanding for the entire year. Based on this information, determine the numerator of the earnings per share fraction for both basic earnings per share and diluted earnings per share. Assume that all financial instruments described are dilutive. The tax rate is 40%.

2 **BE20-10. Computing Diluted EPS, Employee Options.** Crowe Interior Designs of Santa Monica granted 300,000 qualified employee options on June 1 of the current year. The options allow employees to exchange each option for 36 shares of the company's common stock at an exercise price of $20 per share. The average market price of Crowe's common shares is $18 per share. Based on this information, compute the incremental shares to include in the denominator of the diluted earnings per share ratio.

2 **BE20-11. Computing Diluted EPS, Employee Options.** Nickelfront Welders, Inc. granted 300,000 employee options on July 1 of the current year. Employees can exercise each option and receive two shares of the company's common stock at an exercise price of $15 per share. The average market price of Nickelfront's common shares is $18. Based on this information, compute the incremental shares to include in the denominator of the diluted earnings per share ratio.

2 **BE20-12. Computing Basic and Diluted EPS, Options.** Nick's Liquidators reported 450,000 shares of common stock outstanding for the year. The company also had stock options outstanding all year that will result in 125,000 incremental shares upon exercise. The company reported a net loss of $680,000 for the year, but income from continuing operations was equal to $1,500,000. Compute basic and diluted earnings per share for the year for both income from continuing operations and net loss.

2 3 **BE20-13. Computing Diluted EPS, Convertible Debt.** Axelon Enterprises has asked you to determine whether its proposed issue of convertible debt will have dilutive effects on earnings per share. If the convertible bonds prove to be dilutive, the company might consider an alternate vehicle to finance the $10,000,000 construction cost of a new plant facility. Currently, Axelon's basic earnings per share is equal to $14 per share after factoring in the after-tax interest expense on the proposed bond issue. The convertible debt will be issued on April 1 at $10,000,000 par value, pays interest at a rate of 6%, and is convertible to 200,000 common shares. Axelon's tax rate is 25%. Will the convertible debt be dilutive? Provide a brief explanation and all computations needed to support your conclusion.

Exercises

❶ **E20-1. Computing Basic and Diluted EPS, Preferred Stock.** Start Stamping began the current year with 450,000 common shares outstanding. The firm has $1,150,000 par value, 3% nonconvertible, noncumulative preferred stock outstanding. The preferred shares were outstanding for a full year and the firm declared preferred dividends for the current year. The company's net income is $3,500,000. Based on this information, compute basic earnings per share for the current year.

❶ **E20-2. Computing Weighted-Average Number of Common Shares Outstanding with a Stock Split.** Thomas Company began the year with 150,000 common shares outstanding. The firm issued an additional 75,000 shares on May 1 and 15,000 shares on November 1. In addition, Thomas implemented a 2-for-1 stock split on July 1. The firm's year-end is December 31. Determine the weighted-average number of common shares outstanding for the year.

❷ **E20-3. Computing Weighted-Average Number of Shares, Basic and Diluted EPS.** Assume that Jarden Associates began the year with 75,000 outstanding shares and implemented a 7% stock dividend on January 1 of the current year. Jarden employees held 90,000 options that were granted on April 1. If exercised, there would be 18,000 incremental shares. On July 1, Jarden implemented a 3-for-1 stock split. Finally, on November 1, the company purchased 135,000 shares to be held in the treasury. Compute the denominator for basic and diluted earnings per share. Assume that the stock split also applies to the options.

❷ **E20-4. Computing Basic and Diluted EPS, Convertible Bonds, Preferred Stock.** Stewart Stamping began the current year with 400,000 common shares outstanding and issued an additional 150,000 shares on September 1. The firm has $10,000,000, 2.5% convertible bonds outstanding for a full year (i.e., $250,000 coupon interest per year), which are convertible into 325,000 shares of common stock. The firm issued the bonds at par and did not convert any during the current year. It also had $1,150,000 par value, 3% nonconvertible, noncumulative preferred stock outstanding for the full year and declared dividends for the current year. The company is subject to a 40% effective tax rate, and net income is $3,500,000. Based on this information, compute basic and diluted earnings per share for the current year.

❷ **E20-5. Computing Basic and Diluted EPS, Convertible Bonds Issued during the Year, Preferred Stock.** Use the same information in E20-4 except assume that the company issued $10,000,000, 2.5% convertible bonds on June 30 (i.e., $250,000 coupon interest annually), which are convertible into 325,000 shares of common stock. Based on this information, compute basic and diluted earnings per share for the current year.

❶❷ **E20-6. Computing Basic and Diluted EPS, Convertible Bonds Issued during the Year, Preferred Stock Issued during the Year.** On January 1, Bright Star Inc. had 600,000 common shares outstanding. The company issued an additional 200,000 shares on March 1. Bright Star also issued $1,000,000 par value, 2% nonconvertible, noncumulative preferred stock on October 1 and declared dividends for the current quarter. On April 30, the firm issued $5,000,000, 3% convertible bonds outstanding (i.e., $150,000 coupon interest per year) that are convertible into 90,000 shares of common stock. The firm issued all bonds at par and did not convert any during the current year. The company is subject to a 40% effective tax rate, and net income is $6,700,000. Based on this information, compute basic and diluted earnings per share for the current year.

❷ **E20-7. Computing Basic and Diluted EPS, Convertible Bonds Converted during the Year.** Topher Company began the current year with 1,600,000 common shares outstanding. It also reported $800,000 par value, 2% convertible bonds outstanding all year. The bonds were issued at par and can be converted to 800,000 shares of common stock. Topher made interest payments at the end of each quarter. The company is subject to a 40% effective tax rate and reported net income of $950,000 for the current year.

Required »

a. What are basic and diluted EPS for Topher Company?
b. Assume that the bonds were converted on October 1. What are basic and diluted EPS for Topher Company?

❷❹ **E20-8. Computing Basic and Diluted EPS, Convertible Bonds, Preferred Stock.** Assume that the $3,500,000 net income reported by Stewart Stamping in E20-4 includes a $780,000 loss from discontinued operations, net of tax.

Required »

a. Based on this information, compute basic and diluted earnings per share for the current year.
b. Prepare the earnings per share disclosure on the income statement beginning with income from continuing operations.

❷❹ **E20-9. Computing Basic and Diluted EPS, Options, Warrants, Preferred Stock, Disclosures.** You are computing annual earnings per share and required disclosures for Tracy Fencing based on company-provided information. Net income is $4,500,000. The weighted-average number of shares is 2,700,000. The year-end balance of outstanding shares is also 2,700,000. There are options outstanding all year to acquire 1,200,000 shares of common stock at $27 per share. The average price of the company's common stock is $36 per share. The firm has 90,000 shares of $50 par value nonconvertible, noncumulative preferred stock outstanding as of the beginning of the year. The dividend rate is $1.80 per share. The board of directors declared the annual dividend. The company is subject to a 40% tax rate.

Required »

a. Based on this information, compute basic and diluted earnings per share for the current year.
b. Prepare the earnings per share disclosure on the income statement beginning with net income.

❷❸❹ **E20-10. Computing Basic and Diluted EPS, Convertible Bonds, Options, Convertible Preferred Stock, Antidilution, Disclosures.** Archangelo Company provided the following information for the current year. Net income is $8,112,600, and the company is subject to a 40% tax rate. For the entire year, there are 1,020,300 shares of outstanding common stock with an average market price of $32 per share.

The company had three potentially dilutive securities outstanding for the full year. There are qualified employee options to acquire 98,000 shares of common stock at an exercise price of $20 per share. The stockholders' equity section of the balance sheet includes 85,200 shares of convertible preferred stock. The board of directors declared preferred dividends of $6.50 per share for the year. Each preferred share is convertible into 1 share of common stock. Finally, the company issued $6,500,000 face value, 9% convertible bonds at par value on January 1. Each $1,000 par value bond is convertible into 80 shares of common stock.

Required »

a. Based on the information provided, compute basic and diluted earnings per share for the current year. Include all computations related to the application of antidilution sequencing.
b. Prepare the required income statement disclosures beginning with net income.

❷❸❹ **E20-11. Computing Basic and Diluted EPS, Convertible Bonds, Options, Convertible Preferred Stock, Antidilution, Disclosures.** We present Gamba Incorporated's current-year partial income statement:
Gamba is subject to a 35% income tax rate.

Partial Income Statement	Current Year
Income from Continuing Operations	$1,250,990
Discontinued operations—Income, net of tax	533,060
Net Income	$1,784,050

A partial balance sheet for the current year follows.

Partial Balance Sheet	Current Year
Liabilities:	
5% Convertible Debt – Issued at $1,000 par*	$8,113,000
Stockholders' Equity:	
Common Stock, no par (1,032,000 shares issued and outstanding)**	$5,160,000
$3 Convertible Preferred Stock, $100 par value (42,500 shares issued and outstanding)***	4,250,000
Additional Paid-in Capital—Stock Options (employee options to acquire 167,500 shares)****	(1,842,500)

Footnotes to the Balance Sheet:

* Each bond is convertible into 80 shares of common stock. The bonds are outstanding all year.
** The number of shares issued and outstanding did not change throughout the year.
*** Each preferred share is convertible into eight shares of common stock. The firm declared preferred dividends. The preferred stock was outstanding all year.
**** The options are exercisable at $21 per share, and the average market price of the company's stock for the year is $35. The options were outstanding all year.

Required »

a. Based on the information provided, compute basic and diluted earnings per share for the current year. Include all computations related to the application of antidilution sequencing if needed.
b. Prepare the income statement disclosures required beginning with income from continuing operations.

❷❸❹ **E20-12. Computing Basic and Diluted EPS, Convertible Bonds, Options, Convertible Preferred Stock, Antidilution, Net Loss, Disclosures.** Refer to the income statement for Gamba Incorporated from E20-11, noting the following modifications:

Partial Income Statement	Current Year
Loss from Continuing Operations, net of tax	$(1,250,990)
Discontinued Operations—Income, net of tax	3,035,040
Net Income	$ 1,784,050

All other information from E20-11 is unchanged.

Required »

a. Based on the information provided, compute basic and diluted earnings per share for the current year. Include all computations related to the application of antidilution sequencing if needed.
b. Prepare the required income statement disclosures beginning with loss from continuing operations.

Problems

❶❷❹ **P20-1. Computing Basic and Diluted EPS, Convertible Bonds, Preferred Stock, Disclosures.** Kollins Kids, Ltd. began the current year with 320,000 common shares outstanding and issued an additional 120,000 shares on August 1. The firm has $8,000,000, 5% convertible bonds outstanding at the beginning of the year (i.e., $400,000 coupon interest per year), which are convertible into 180,000 shares of common stock. The firm issued the bonds at their par value and converted them on April 1. Kollins Kids also has $920,000 par value, 4% convertible, noncumulative preferred stock outstanding. The preferred shares can convert into 10,000 shares of common stock and were outstanding for a full year. The firm declared dividends for the current year. There were no actual conversions of the preferred stock during the year. Kollins is subject to a 40% effective tax rate, and net income is $2,800,000. Assume that all convertible securities are dilutive.

Required »

a. Based on this information, compute basic and diluted earnings per share for the current year.
b. Prepare the earnings per share disclosure on the income statement beginning with net income.

❷❹ **P20-2. Computing Basic and Diluted EPS, Convertible Bonds, Preferred Stock, Disclosures.** Assume that Kollins issued the convertible bonds described in P20-1 on February 1. Using the other information from P20-1, complete the following.

Required »

a. Compute basic and diluted earnings per share for the current year.
b. Prepare the earnings per share disclosure on the income statement beginning with net income.

❶❷❹ **P20-3. Computing Basic and Diluted EPS, Convertible Bonds, Convertible Preferred Stock, Disclosures.** Daphne Company provided the following share information for the current year.
Daphne reported income from continuing operations of $1,100,000 and a $450,000 loss from discontinued operations, net of tax. The company is subject to a 40% tax rate.

Event and Date	Number of Shares
1/1 Beginning balance	150,000
5/1 New share issue	345,000
7/1 Two-for-one stock split	
10/1 New share issue	300,000
12/1 Treasury stock acquisition	(120,000)

Daphne has $400,000, 3% convertible debt outstanding as of the beginning of the year. The debt was issued at par. Each $1,000 par value bond converts into 20 shares of the company's common stock. The company's shareholders' equity section indicates that the firm also holds $140,000 par value, 4% convertible preferred shares outstanding for the entire year. The board of directors declared the annual dividend. The preferred shares can convert into 10,000 shares of common stock. There were no actual exercises or conversions during the year.

Required »

a. Compute basic and diluted earnings per share for income from both continuing operations and net income. Show all computations.
b. Prepare all required disclosures beginning with income from continuing operations.

❶❷❹ **P20-4. Computing Basic and Diluted EPS, Options, Convertible Preferred Stock, Disclosures.** Baroke Bank, NA started the year with 600,000 common shares outstanding and issued 48,000, 840,000, and 72,000 shares on February 1, May 1, and September 1, respectively. Baroke acquired 12,000 treasury shares on March 1. The company has employee options outstanding all year that enable employees to acquire 358,000 shares of stock at an exercise price of $15 per share. Baroke's shares traded at an annual average price of $10 per share. Employees did not exercise any options during the year.

Baroke also reported convertible preferred shares that can be used to acquire 465,000 shares of common stock outstanding as of the beginning of the year. The firm reported preferred stock at $1,567,000 par value. The preferred shares are cumulative and carry an 8% dividend rate. The board of directors declared the annual dividend.

The following is a partial income statement for the current year. Baroke is subject to a 35% income tax rate.

Partial Income Statement	For the Current Year
Income from Continuing Operations, net of tax	$4,005,320
Loss from Discontinued Operations, net of tax	(1,218,120)
Net Income	$ 2,787,200

Required »

a. Compute basic and diluted earnings per share. Show all computations.
b. Prepare all required disclosures beginning with income from continuing operations.

❶❷❹ **P20-5. Computing Basic and Diluted EPS, Convertible Bonds, Disclosures.** Note the following partial income statement for Cassie Corporation for the current year.

Partial Income Statement	For the Current Year
Income from Continuing Operations	$3,650,000
Income from Discontinued Operations, net of tax	325,200
Net Income	$3,975,200

The company is subject to a 40% tax rate. We present share information for the current year in the following table.

Event and Date	Number of Shares
1/1 Beginning balance	1,890,000
3/1 New share issue	240,000
11/1 Treasury stock acquisition	(90,000)

Cassie had 360,000 options outstanding all year at an exercise price of $25 per share. The average market price per share of the company's shares for the current year is $40. The company issued 7%, $6,500,000 convertible debt on April 1 of the current year at par value. Each $1,000 par value bond converts into 25 shares of the company's common stock. All debt converted into common stock on October 1. Assume that the bonds are antidilutive. Each option is exercisable for one share of common stock.

Required »

a. Compute basic and diluted earnings per share for income from continuing operations and net income. Show all computations.
b. Prepare all required disclosures beginning with income from continuing operations.

❶❷❸❹ **P20-6. Computing Basic and Diluted EPS, Convertible Bonds, Options, Convertible Preferred Stock, Antidilution, Disclosures.** Merion Company provided the following share information for the current year.

Event and Date	Number of Shares
1/1 Beginning balance	150,000
6/1 New share issue	240,000
8/1 Two-for-one stock split	
10/1 New share issue	390,000
12/1 Treasury stock acquisition	(48,000)

Merion reported income from continuing operations of $1,000,000 and a $430,000 loss from discontinued operations, net of tax. The company is subject to a 40% tax rate.

The company granted 120,000 employee options on January 1 that allow employees to acquire 120,000 common shares at $18 per share. The options have an estimated fair value of $10 per share. The average market price of the company's common shares is $24 per share. Merion has $500,000, 6% convertible debt outstanding as of the beginning of the year. Each $1,000 par value bond converts into eight shares of the company's common stock. Merion also has $140,000 par value, 4% convertible preferred shares outstanding for the entire year. The board of directors declared the annual dividend. The preferred shares can convert into 10,000 shares of common stock. There were no actual exercises or conversions during the year.

Required »

a. Compute the weighted-average number of common shares outstanding for basic earnings per share.
b. Determine whether any securities are antidilutive, and compute basic and diluted earnings per share. Show all computations.
c. Prepare all required disclosures beginning with income from continuing operations.

❶❷❸❹ **P20-7. Computing Basic and Diluted EPS, Convertible Bonds, Options Preferred Stock, Disclosures, Antidilution, Net Loss.** The following is a partial income statement for City Line Enterprises for the current year.

Partial Income Statement	For the Current Year
Loss from Continuing Operations	$ (621,000)
Income from Discontinued Operations, net of tax	3,256,000
Net Income	$2,635,000

The company is subject to a 40% tax rate. Share information for the current year follows.

Event and Date	Number of Shares
1/1 Beginning balance	2,000,000
5/1 New share issue	360,000
8/1 New share issue	120,000
12/1 Two-for-one split	2,480,000

City Line provided the following information about its capital structure. The company had employee options to acquire 500,000 shares at an exercise price of $7 per share. The average market price of the company's shares for the current year is $10 per share. The company issued 3%, $1,500,000 convertible debt 2 years ago at par value. Each $1,000 par value bond converts to five shares of the company's common stock. City Line has $800,000 par value, 6% cumulative preferred shares outstanding for the entire year. The preferred shares are nonconvertible. There were no actual exercises or conversions during the year.

Required »

a. Compute the weighted-average number of common shares outstanding for basic earnings per share.
b. Determine whether any securities are antidilutive, and compute basic and diluted earnings per share. Show all computations.
c. Prepare all required disclosures beginning with income from continuing operations.

❶❷❸❹ **P20-8. Computing Basic and Diluted EPS, Convertible Bonds, Options, Convertible Preferred Stock, Antidilution, Disclosures.** Teek Bank, NA started the year with 600,000 common shares outstanding and issued 48,000, 840,000, and 72,000 shares on February 1, May 1, and September 1, respectively. Teek acquired 12,000 treasury shares on March 1.

The company has employee stock options outstanding all year that enable employees to acquire 358,000 shares at an exercise price of $15 per share. Teek's shares traded at an annual average price of $10 per share. Employees did not exercise any options during the year.

Teek also reported convertible debt and convertible preferred shares. The convertible debt securities the firm issued at par on August 1 for $15,000,000 pay interest at 4% per year. Each $1,000 par value bond converts into six shares of the company's common stock at the debtholder's option. Convertible preferred shares available to acquire 465,000 shares of common stock were outstanding as of the beginning of the year. Teek reported the preferred stock at a $1,567,000 par value. The preferred shares are cumulative and carry an 8% dividend rate.

The following is a partial income statement for the current year. Teek is subject to a 35% income tax rate.

Partial Income Statement	For the Current Year
Income from Continuing Operations	$4,005,320
Loss from Discontinued Operations, net of tax	(1,218,120)
Net Income	$ 2,787,200

Required »

a. Compute the weighted-average number of common shares outstanding for basic earnings per share.
b. Determine whether any securities are antidilutive, and compute basic and diluted earnings per share. Show all computations.
c. Prepare all required disclosures beginning with income or loss from continuing operations.

①②③④ **P20-9. Computing Basic and Diluted EPS, Convertible Bonds, Preferred Stock, Disclosures, Net Loss.** The following is a partial income statement for Sonata Enterprises for the current year.

Partial Income Statement	For the Current Year
Loss from Continuing Operations	$ (621,000)
Income from Discontinued Operations, net of tax	3,256,000
Net Income	$ 2,635,000

The company is subject to a 40% tax rate. Share information for the current year follows.

Event and Date	Number of Shares
1/1 Beginning balance	2,000,000
5/1 New share issue	360,000
8/1 New share issue	120,000
12/1 Two-for-one split	

Sonata provided you the following information about its capital structure:

- It issued 3%, $1,500,000 convertible debt 2 years ago at par value.
- Each $1,000 par value bond converts into five shares of the company's common stock.
- It has $800,000 par value, 6% cumulative, nonconvertible preferred shares outstanding for the entire year.
- There were no actual exercises or conversions during the year.

Required »

a. Compute basic and diluted earnings per share for income from continuing operations and net income. Show all computations.
b. Prepare all required disclosures beginning with income from continuing operations.

CASES

Judgment Case

Judgment Case 1: Earnings Management

The CFO of Last Things Computing, Inc. (LTC) prepared the following balance sheet and statement of net income for the year ended December 31, 2018.

Last Things Computing, Inc.
Balance Sheet
At December 31, 2018

Assets	
Current Assets:	
Cash	$ 7,000
Trading Securities at Fair Value	900
Accounts Receivable – net	9,500
Merchandise Inventory	67,000
Office Supplies	550
Prepaid Rent	400
Total Current Assets	$ 85,350
Noncurrent Assets:	
Investments	$ 17,000
Property, Plant, and Equipment	
Land	45,000
Buildings	275,000
Machinery and Equipment	60,000
Less: Accumulated Depreciation	(112,000)
Total Property, Plant, and Equipment – net	$268,000
Deferred Tax Asset	$ 7,500
Intangible Assets: Franchise – net	4,500
Other Assets	2,100
Total Noncurrent Assets	$299,100
Total Assets	$384,450
Liabilities	
Current Liabilities:	
Accounts Payable	$ 22,600
Short-Term Notes Payable	2,000
Current Portion of Long-Term Debt	750
Interest Payable	300
Income Taxes Payable	2,000
Unearned Revenue	5,400
Total Current Liabilities	$ 33,050
Long-Term Liabilities:	
Notes Payable	$ 55,000
Bonds Payable	160,000
Total Long-Term Liabilities	$215,000
Total Liabilities	$248,050
Stockholders' Equity	
Common Stock – at par	$ 15,000
Additional Paid-in Capital	34,500
Retained Earnings	77,900
Accumulated Other Comprehensive Income	9,000
Total Stockholders' Equity	$136,400
Total Liabilities and Stockholders' Equity	$384,450

Last Things Computing, Inc.
Statement of Net Income
For the Year Ended December 31, 2018

Revenues and Gains		
Sales	$578,540	
Interest Income	25,000	
Dividend Income	2,500	
Income from Associates	9,000	
Gain on Disposal of Plant Assets	5,800	
Total Revenues and Gains		$ 620,840
Expenses and Losses		
Cost of Goods Sold	$172,000	
Selling Expenses and Salaries	48,000	
Office Supplies Expense	40,000	
Advertising Expense	21,000	
Office Salaries Expense	11,000	
Depreciation Expense	5,500	
Interest Expense	3,500	
Loss on Asset Impairment	2,000	
Total Expenses and Losses		$ 303,000
Income before Taxes		$ 317,840
Income Tax Expense		(111,244)
Income from Continuing Operations		$ 206,596
Discontinued Operations		
Income from Operations of Discontinued Segment, net of tax of $4,000	$ 10,000	
Loss from Disposal of Discontinued Segment, net of tax of $3,000	(9,800)	$ 200
Net Income		$ 206,796
Earnings per Share:		
Income from Continuing Operations		$ 13.77
Income from Discontinued Operations		0.02
Earnings per Share		$ 13.79

LTC had 15,000 common shares outstanding for the entire year. It had no preferred stock or dilutive securities. Assume that LTC records income tax expense at 35% of income from continuing operations before income taxes.

The CFO will make the following adjustments before finalizing the financial statements.

1. LTC needs to record some amount of bad debt expense. The offset will be a reduction in accounts receivable. This adjustment is a matter of judgment; reasonable estimates range between $1,000 and $3,000.
2. LTC needs to write down its inventory (i.e., reduce the reported value of inventory). The offset will be to cost of goods sold. This adjustment is a matter of judgment; reasonable estimates range between $2,500 and $3,750.
3. LTC could need to impair its PPE (that is, reduce the reported value of PPE). The offset will be an impairment loss reported on the statement of net income. This adjustment is a matter of judgment and reasonable estimates range between $0 and $5,000.
4. LTC could need to impair its noncurrent investments by reducing the reported value of noncurrent investments. The offset will be an impairment loss reported on the statement of net income. This adjustment is a matter of judgment; reasonable estimates range between $250 and $750.
5. LTC could need to record a litigation contingency by recording a liability for an unresolved lawsuit. The offset is to litigation expense. The lawsuit is expected to be settled in 2019. Reasonable estimates of the amount that LTC could be liable for are $2,000 or $10,000.

6. LTC could need to reduce the reported amount of its deferred tax asset. The amount by which the asset needs to be reduced is highly judgmental and ranges from $0 to $5,000. The offset to this adjustment is income tax expense.
7. LTC currently has unearned revenue on its balance sheet of $5,400. However, up to $5,000 of this amount could possibly be recognized as revenue in 2018. The amount is a matter of judgment.

Required »

a. If LTC makes the most conservative choices for all these adjustments that will result in the lowest net income number, what is the impact on assets and liabilities in terms of absolute dollar impact and percentage change? What is the impact on net income and earnings per share?

b. If LTC makes the least conservative choices for all these adjustments that will result in the highest net income number, what is the impact on assets and liabilities in terms of absolute dollar impact and percentage change? What is the impact on net income and earnings per share?

c. What is the impact on the current ratio of these choices if management makes the most conservative choices? What is the impact on this ratio if management makes the least conservative choices?

d. Do you think that the management of LTC will care very much about the choices related to these adjustments?

Financial Statement Analysis Case

Financial Statement Analysis Case 1: EPS Analysis of NCR Corporation

You are asked to analyze ***NCR Corporation's*** EPS. ***NCR*** is a business solution company manufacturing automated teller machines (ATMs), point of sale (POS) terminals and devices, and self-service kiosks. Use the footnote disclosure to answer the questions that follow the disclosure.

***NCR Corporation*, December 31, 2016, Financial Statements (excerpt)**

NCR Corporation

NOTE 1. Basis of presentation and significant accounting policies

Earnings Per Share

The components of basic earnings (loss) per share are as follows:

	Twelve months ended December 31		
	2016	**2015**	**2014**
	In millions, except per share amounts		
Income (loss) from continuing operations	**$ 283**	$ (154)	$ 181
Series A convertible perferred stock dividends	**(49)**	(4)	—
Numerator—from continuing operations	**234**	(158)	181
Loss (income) from discontinued operations, net of tax	**(13)**	(24)	10
Numerator—total	**$ 221**	$ (182)	$ 191
Denominator			
Basic weighted average number of shares outstanding	**125.6**	167.6	167.9
Basic earnings (loss) per share:			
From continuing operations	**$ 1.86**	$ (0.94)	$ 1.08
From discontinued operations	**(0.10)**	(0.15)	0.06
Total basic earnings (loss) per share	**$ 1.76**	$ (1.09)	$ 1.14

The components of diluted earnings (loss) per share are as follows:

	Twelve months ended December 31		
	2016	2015	2014
	In millions, except per share amounts		
Income (loss) from continuing operations	**$ 283**	$ (154)	$ 181
Series A convertible perferred stock dividends	—	(4)	—
Numerator—from continuing operations	**283**	(158)	181
Income (loss) from continuing operations	$ 283	$ (154)	$ 181
Loss from discontinued operations, net of tax	**(13)**	(24)	10
Series A convertible preferred stock dividends	**(49)**	(4)	—
Numerator—total	$ 221	$ (182)	$ 191
Basic weighted average number of shares outstanding	**125.6**	167.6	167.9
Dilutive effect of as-if Series A Convertible Preferred Stock	**28.2**	—	—
Dilutive effect of employee stock options and restricted stock units	**3.6**	—	3.3
Denominator—from continuing operations	**157.4**	167.6	171.2
Basic weighted average number of shares outstanding	**125.6**	167.6	167.9
Dilutive effect of employee stock options and restricted stock units	**3.6**	—	3.3
Denominator—total	**129.2**	167.6	171.2
Diluted earnings (loss) per share:			
From continuing operations	**$ 1.80**	$ (0.94)	$ 1.06
From discontinued operations	**(0.10)**	(0.15)	0.06
Total diluted earnings (loss) per share	**$ 1.71**	$ (1.09)	$ 1.12

Source: From December 31, 2016, Financial Statements, NCR Corporation. http://investor.ncr.com/phoenix.zhtml?c=83840&p=irol-reportsannual_pf

Required »

a. ***NCR's*** net income on the income statement is the same as net income available for common stockholders in earnings per share in 2014 but not 2015 and 2016. What does the fact that the two amounts are not the same in 2015 and 2016 suggest?

b. What types of securities create the difference between ***NCR's*** basic income from continuing operations and diluted income from continuing operations? What is the difference between ***NCR's*** basic income and diluted income each year?

c. What types of securities create the difference between ***NCR's*** basic shares and diluted shares? What is the difference between ***NCR's*** basic shares and diluted shares each year?

d. What are the percentage differences in income from continuing operations, basic EPS for income from continuing operations, and diluted EPS for income from continuing operations from 2014 to 2016? Comment on the changes.

e. What are the percentage differences in basic and diluted EPS for income from continuing operations and the weighted-average number of shares for income from continuing operations used for basic and diluted EPS? Comment on changes over time.

f. If you were an analyst, what further information would you want to assess changes in EPS over time?

Surfing the Standards Case

Surfing the Standards Case 1: Contingently Issuable Shares

On March 1 of the current year, Johanne Stores acquired 100% of the voting shares of Ferry Furniture Company. Johanne reports only annually on a calendar basis. As part of the merger agreement, Johanne agreed to distribute 0.2 additional shares for each share of outstanding stock to its current stockholders if, by the end of the current fiscal year, five new Ferry outlets are opened. On December 31, Johanne provided you the following information:

- Net income for the year is $4,500,000.
- There are 1,000,000 outstanding common shares for the entire year.
- There are 200,000 contingently issuable shares (i.e., $0.2 \times 1{,}000{,}000$).
- Seven new Ferry outlets were opened by December 31 with the fifth store opened on November 1.
- Johanne had $3,000,000 par value, 5% cumulative, nonconvertible preferred shares outstanding for the full year.

Required »

a. Provide a general discussion of the effect of contingently issuable shares on basic earnings per share.
b. Provide a general discussion of the effect of contingently issuable shares on diluted earnings per share.
c. Compute basic earnings per share for Johanne Stores.
d. Compute diluted earnings per share for Johanne Stores.

Basis for Conclusions Cases

Basis for Conclusions Case 1: Antidilutive Securities

Read paragraphs 95 through 99 in Appendix B: Background information and basis for conclusions in FASB's *Statement of Financial Accounting Standards No. 128.*

Required »

a. Why did the Board decide to require an antidilution sequence that considers securities in the order of most dilutive to least dilutive?
b. What line items could appear on an income statement after income from continuing operations, but before net income? Note that when *Statement of Financial Accounting Standards No. 128* was written, companies reported extraordinary items and the effect of changes in accounting principles on the income statement after income from continuing operations. This is no longer true.
c. The FASB chose income from continuing operations as the number that should be used to determine whether securities are dilutive or antidilutive. Why did it choose income from continuing operations as opposed to net income?
d. Did the constituents who wrote comment letters about the exposure draft of *Statement of Financial Accounting Standards No. 128* agree with the use of income from continuing operations as opposed to net income as the control number for the determination of which securities are dilutive?

Basis for Conclusions Case 2: Treasury Stock Method

Read paragraphs 105 through 107 in Appendix B: Background information and basis for conclusions in FASB's *Statement of Financial Accounting Standards No. 128.*

Required »

a. Why did the Board decide to continue to use the treasury stock method?
b. What were the Board's primary concerns with the treasury stock method?
c. Why did the Board choose to use the average stock price to determine the number of treasury shares assumed purchased?

21 Accounting Changes and Error Analysis

LEARNING OBJECTIVES

1. Provide an overview of the types of accounting changes, including the difference between the retrospective and prospective methods.
2. Describe and demonstrate the accounting for a change in accounting principle.
3. Explain and illustrate the accounting for a change in an accounting estimate.
4. Explain the accounting for a change in the reporting entity.
5. Discuss common types of errors and error analysis and demonstrate how to correct errors.

Introduction

MANAGEMENT'S ASSESSMENT OF OPERATIONS drives a company's accounting policies and its financial reporting assumptions and estimates. Managers continually examine their choices, adjusting accounting policies when a financial accounting policy no longer faithfully represents the firm's underlying economics or information lacks sufficient transparency for financial statement users.

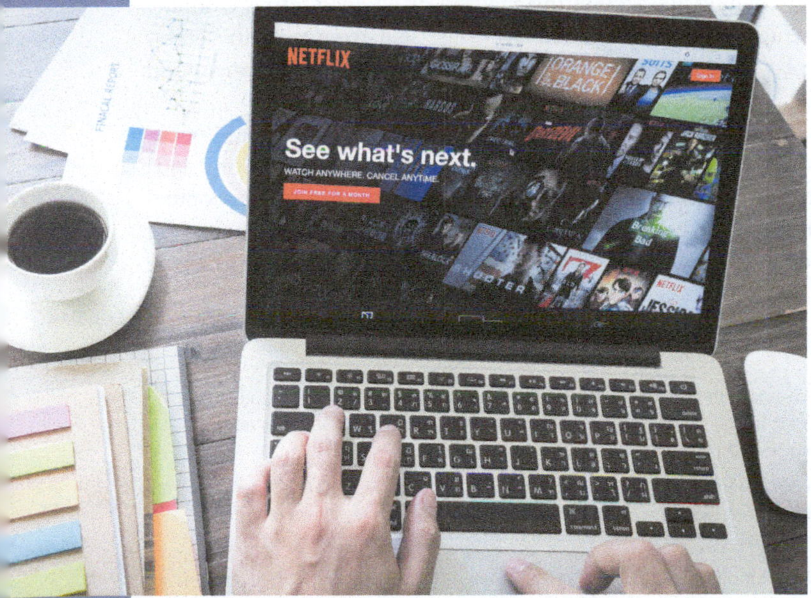

sitthiphong/Shutterstock

Consider ***Netflix, Inc.***, the subscription service company that provides movies and TV episodes over the Internet, such as *House of Cards* and *Orange Is the New Black*, totaling $10.9 billion at the end of 2016. ***Netflix*** amortizes the costs of its streaming content assets over the shorter of each title's estimated period of use or its contractual window of availability. For content when ***Netflix*** expects more upfront viewing from additional merchandising or marketing efforts, the amortization is on an accelerated basis. ***Netflix***'s management reviews factors impacting the amortization of the content assets on a regular basis. Estimates related to these factors require considerable management judgment. In the third quarter of 2016, ***Netflix*** changed the amortization of certain content given changes in estimated viewing patterns of these content assets. The effect of this change in estimate was a $19.8 million decrease in operating income and a $12.3 million decrease in net income. The effect on both basic earnings per share and diluted earnings per share was a decrease of $0.03 for 2016. ***Netflix*** noted that changes in estimates could have a significant impact on its future results of operations.

In this chapter, we discuss accounting changes related to accounting principle (method), accounting estimate, and reporting entity. Managers and investors alike expect these changes as businesses develop or modify overall strategy and expand into diverse markets. It is important to know the reason for the accounting change, the nature of the change, and its effect on the financial statements.

We illustrate the two methods for accounting for a change: the *retrospective* and the *prospective* methods. Firms generally account for and report changes in accounting principle on a *retrospective* basis and changes in accounting estimate on a *prospective* basis. A company's disclosure of both a change in principle and estimate must enable the financial statement user to compare the year of the change with all prior periods. Finally, we examine error analysis because companies must correct mistakes in the financial statements. The method of correction depends on what financial statement is in error and when the company discovers the error. Throughout the chapter, the accounting treatment is similar under U.S. GAAP and IFRS. «

1 Provide an overview of the types of accounting changes, including the difference between the retrospective and prospective methods.

Overview of Accounting Changes

In this section, we describe the three types of accounting changes and two methods that companies use for reporting them.

Types of Accounting Changes

There are three main types of accounting changes:

- **Changes in accounting principle**, which are changes from one generally accepted accounting method to another generally accepted accounting method
- **Changes in accounting estimate**, which involve revisions of estimates used in accounting
- **Changes in the reporting entity**, which occur when a company reports financial statements that are, in effect, financial statements for a different reporting entity[1]

All accounting changes make the financial statements inconsistent from period to period. Consequently, the standards permit accounting changes only when companies provide adequate disclosures to assist financial statement users in restoring comparability with prior-years financial information.[2]

THE CONCEPTUAL FRAMEWORK CONNECTION
Changes in Accounting Principles and Estimates

Comparability, one of the conceptual framework's enhancing qualitative characteristics, enhances the usefulness of relevant and faithfully represented information by helping users to identify and understand the similarities and differences in items reported. Changing accounting principles and estimates from period to period detracts from comparability.

Consistency refers to the firm's use of the same accounting methods for the same transactions from period to period. Although the conceptual framework does not specify consistency as a qualitative characteristic of useful financial information, it does help achieve the goal of comparability. When a company changes its accounting method or an accounting estimate for a particular transaction, its financial statements are not consistent from year to year—and financial statements that are not comparable from year to year violate the conceptual framework.

Whereas accounting standards allow changes in accounting principle, they should occur infrequently, and companies should make adequate disclosures. Changes in accounting estimates are more common than changes in accounting principles. As discussed in the conceptual framework, "financial reports are based on estimates, judgments, and models rather than exact depictions."[3] Consequently, companies commonly change estimates as additional information becomes available.

[1] An additional category, correction of an error made in previously issued financial statements, or prior-period adjustments, will also results in changes in the financial statements. Although not specifically classified as an accounting change, prior-period adjustments will require similar accounting procedures.

[2] For the relevant authoritative literature, see FASB ASC 250 –10, *Accounting Changes and Error Corrections – Overall* for U.S. GAAP and IASC, *International Accounting Standard 8*, "Accounting Policies, Changes in Accounting Estimates and Errors" (London, UK: International Accounting Standards Committee, Revised, 2013) for IFRS.

[3] Financial Accounting Standards Board, *Statement of Financial Accounting Concepts No. 8 Chapter 1, "The Objective of General Purpose Financial Reporting,"* Paragraph OB11.

Methods for Reporting Accounting Changes

There are two approaches for reporting accounting changes—the *retrospective* and *prospective methods*. Examples later in the chapter illustrate applying these methods to account for the three types of accounting changes.

Retrospective Change. Companies reporting an accounting change with the **retrospective method** restate all prior-year financial statements presented in the annual report as if the newly adopted principle had always been used. **Restated financial statements** adjust opening balance sheet accounts for the cumulative effect of applying the new principle in all prior years and present all subsequent financial statements as if the policy had always been used. Specifically, companies adjust:

1. Assets and liabilities as of the beginning of the first period presented to reflect the cumulative effect of the change on periods prior to those presented
2. Retained earnings (or other appropriate components of equity) for the beginning of the first period presented to reflect the cumulative effect of the change on reported income for periods prior to those presented
3. Financial statements for each period presented to reflect the effects of the change

Prospective Change. Companies using the **prospective method** to report an accounting change make the change in the current year (that is, the year of the change) and all future years. They do not make adjustments to previously issued financial statements: The prospective method treats information for all prior years as final and does not change previously issued financial information.

❷ Describe and demonstrate the accounting for a change in accounting principle.

Changes in Accounting Principle

In this section, we examine how firms report a change in accounting principle using the retrospective and prospective methods with related disclosures. Changes in accounting principle can be voluntary or mandatory. Newly issued accounting standards are mandatory accounting changes; voluntary changes occur when a firm decides to change accounting methods. For example, a change in a firm's inventory costing system from FIFO to LIFO or in revenue recognition methods from completed contract to percentage of completion would constitute a change in accounting principle. A firm should voluntarily change accounting principles only if it can justify use of the new principle on the basis that it more accurately portrays its financial position and performance.

The adoption of a new principle in recognition of events that have occurred for the first time is not considered a change in accounting principle. For example, assume that a company begins selling a new product and adopts the average-cost method for this inventory item while continuing to account for all other inventory items under the LIFO basis. The use of the average-cost method for the newly acquired inventory item is not a change in accounting principle.

Reporting a Change in Accounting Principle

Generally, firms are required to report all changes in accounting principle under the retrospective approach. There are two exceptions:

1. In the case of a mandatory change required by a new accounting standard, an entity should follow the specific transition requirements provided within the new standard. The new standard could specify retrospective or prospective application. If no such requirements exist, the firm should follow the retrospective approach.
2. If it is impractical to use the retrospective approach for any one of the following three conditions, the entity should use the prospective approach. The use of the retrospective method is impractical if:

   - The financial statement effects of the retrospective application are not determinable.
   - Retrospective application requires assumptions about management's intent in a prior period.
   - Retrospective application requires significant estimates for a prior period and the availability of the necessary information to determine these estimates cannot be objectively verified.

An entity meeting any one of these three conditions cannot implement a retrospective application but must apply the change in accounting principle prospectively. A change to the LIFO method is an example of an impractical change in accounting principle. For example, determining LIFO inventory base layers at prior-years unit costs is impractical if the firm did not track prior-year costs.

Consider ***Google,*** whose parent company is ***Alphabet, Inc.,*** as an example of a mandatory change required by a new accounting standard. In 2016, ***Google*** adopted a new FASB standard on accounting for employee share-based payments that we discussed in Chapter 19. ***Google*** used the retrospective method when it changed its method of accounting for forfeitures of stock-based compensation awards from estimating expected forfeitures to accounting for forfeitures as they occur. ***Google's*** cumulative adjustment was a decrease of $133 million in beginning 2015 retained earnings.

Direct and Indirect Effects

Changes in accounting principle can have both *direct* and *indirect effects*. **Direct effects** are changes necessary to implement the change in accounting principle. For example, if a firm changes its method of costing inventory, there would be direct effects to the inventory and retained earnings balances. The direct effects could also include necessary changes to the tax accounts. Firms always apply direct effects retrospectively unless it is impractical to do so.

Indirect effects are changes to current or future cash flows that result from the change in accounting principle. The impact on cash flows related to profit sharing and bonus plans or from violating restrictive debt covenants are indirect effects. Firms apply indirect effects only prospectively; retrospective treatment is not permitted for indirect effects of a change in accounting principle. Exhibit 21.1 summarizes direct and indirect effects and the corresponding accounting method.

EXHIBIT 21.1 Summary of Direct and Indirect Effects

	Direct Effects	Indirect Effects
Definition	Changes necessary to implement the change in accounting principle	Changes to current or future cash flows that result from the change in accounting principle
Accounting Method	Retrospective unless it is impractical to do so	Prospective
Example	A change in the accounting method for revenue recognition would impact the revenue account and possibly the unearned revenue and the tax accounts	A change in the accounting method for revenue recognition could impact the bonus plans related to management's compensation

Retrospective Method Illustration

We examine the retrospective method for changes in an accounting principle in Example 21.1 to highlight the key elements involved in applying this approach.

EXAMPLE 21.1 Change in Accounting Principle: Retrospective Method

PROBLEM: Topeka Tile Company began operations on January 1, 2017. At the beginning of 2121, the company elected to change from the FIFO method to the average-cost method for financial reporting purposes. It did not change methods for tax purposes. The company has maintained adequate records to apply the retrospective method. The company is subject to a 40% tax rate and has not declared or paid any dividends. As is typical, in its December 31, 2121, annual report, it presents income statements and statements of stockholders' equity for the years ended December 31, 2019, 2020, and 2121. It reports balance sheets at December 31, 2020 and 2121.

Cost of goods sold under both methods follows.

Year	Cost of Goods Sold FIFO Method	Cost of Goods Sold Average-Cost Method
2017	$7,000	$9,000
2018	5,000	6,000
2019	6,000	7,400
2020	4,000	6,200
2121	2,000	4,700

Topeka's schedule of revenues, operating expenses, and purchases is presented here.

Year	Revenues	Operating Expenses	Purchases
2017	$33,333	$10,000	$20,000
2018	30,000	8,000	10,000
2019	31,000	9,000	10,000
2020	32,000	11,000	5,000
2121	20,000	7,000	15,000

Topeka's balance sheet line items for December 31, 2020, as reported, follows.

Account	Balance
Cash	$31,800
Inventory	23,000
Liabilities	5,000
Common Stock	10,000
Retained Earnings	39,800

As of December 31, 2121, Topeka had a cash balance of $25,400. The balances in liabilities and common stock have not changed since December 31, 2020.

Topeka reported a retained earnings balance of $20,000 as of December 31, 2018. Prepare the financial statements that will be included in the 2121 annual report and prepare the journal entry to implement the change.

SOLUTION: Topeka reports the change using the retrospective method because it is not impractical to do so.

Effect on Income

Cost of goods sold is higher under the new method, resulting in a decrease in net income. In order to compute the decrease in net income for each year, we multiply the difference in the cost of goods sold under the two methods by 1.0 minus the tax rate, or 0.6 (1.0 − 0.4).

Year	Cost of Goods Sold FIFO Method (a)	Cost of Goods Sold Average-Cost Method (b)	Decrease in Net Income Pre-Tax (a) − (b)	Decrease in Net Income (Net of Tax) [(a) − (b)] × 0.6	Cumulative Decrease in Net Income (Net of Tax)
2017	$7,000	$9,000	$2,000	$1,200	$1,200
2018	5,000	6,000	$1,000	600	1,800
2019	6,000	7,400	$1,400	840	2,640
2020	4,000	6,200	$2,200	1,320	3,960
2121	2,000	4,700	$2,700	1,620	5,580

Continued

The comparative income statements after implementing the change in accounting principle follow. Note that the cost of goods sold is presented using the average-cost method (the new method).

Statements of Income

	2121	2020 (As Adjusted)	2019 (As Adjusted)
Revenues	$20,000	$ 32,000	$31,000
Cost of Goods Sold	(4,700)	(6,200)	(7,400)
Operating Expenses	(7,000)	(11,000)	(9,000)
Net Income before Tax	$ 8,300	$ 14,800	$14,600
Income Tax Expense (net income before tax × 40%)	(3,320)	(5,920)	(5,840)
Net Income	$ 4,980	$ 8,880	$ 8,760

Statement of Stockholders' Equity

Topeka begins the retained earnings portion of its statement of stockholders' equity with the balance as of December 31, 2018. The company originally reported a balance of $20,000. Topeka reduces the balance by the cumulative decrease in net income ($1,800), resulting in an ending balance of $18,200.

	Retained Earnings
Balance: December 31, 2018 (as previously reported)	$20,000
Cumulative effect of a change in accounting principle	(1,800)
Balance: December 31, 2018 (as adjusted)	$18,200
Adjusted net income, 2019	8,760
Balance: December 31, 2019 (as adjusted)	$26,960
Adjusted net income, 2020	8,880
Balance: December 31, 2020 (as adjusted)	$35,840
Net income, 2121	4,980
Balance: December 31, 2121	$40,820

Journal Entry

We can analyze the effect of the change on the inventory account by building the inventory accounts under both methods using the purchases and cost of goods sold information provided. Purchases will be the same under any inventory valuation technique. The general ledger inventory accounts under both the FIFO (old) and average cost (new) methods are as follows:

2017		FIFO (Old Method)	Average Cost (New Method)
	Beginning Inventory	$ 0	$ 0
	Purchases	20,000	20,000
	Cost of Goods Available for Sale	20,000	20,000
	Less: Cost of Goods Sold	(7,000)	(9,000)
	Ending Inventory	$13,000	$ 11,000
2018			
	Beginning Inventory	$13,000	$ 11,000
	Purchases	10,000	10,000
	Cost of Goods Available for Sale	23,000	21,000
	Less: Cost of Goods Sold	(5,000)	(6,000)
	Ending Inventory	$18,000	$ 15,000

		FIFO (Old Method)	Average Cost (New Method)
2019			
	Beginning Inventory	$18,000	$ 15,000
	Purchases	10,000	10,000
	Cost of Goods Available for Sale	28,000	25,000
	Less: Cost of Goods Sold	(6,000)	(7,400)
	Ending Inventory	$22,000	$ 17,600
2020			
	Beginning Inventory	$22,000	$ 17,600
	Purchases	5,000	5,000
	Cost of Goods Available for Sale	27,000	22,600
	Less: Cost of Goods Sold	(4,000)	(6,200)
	Ending Inventory	$23,000	$16,400
2121			
	Beginning Inventory	$23,000	$ 16,400
	Purchases	15,000	15,000
	Cost of Goods Available for Sale	38,000	31,400
	Less: Cost of Goods Sold	(2,000)	(4,700)
	Ending Inventory	$36,000	$26,700

Topeka makes the journal entry to record the change in accounting principle to impact the balances as of January 1, 2121, because it has already closed the books for 2020. Topeka decreases the inventory account by $6,600, which is the difference between FIFO inventory ($23,000) and the average-cost inventory ($16,400). The cumulative decrease in net income up to December 31, 2020, is $3,960 (see preceding analysis). This amount represents the after-tax cumulative effect on retained earnings. This difference of $3,960 is also determined as 60% of the total change in inventory ($6,600 × 60%). The remaining 40% ($2,640 = $6,600 × 40%) is attributable to the tax impact. Topeka records a deferred-tax asset: If it used the average-cost method for book purposes and FIFO for tax purposes, the book carrying value of the asset inventory is less than its tax basis, creating future deductible amounts for tax (that is, a deferred-tax asset). The journal entry to record the retrospective change in accounting principle follows. Note that the amounts represent the cumulative adjustments up to, but not including, the year of the change.

Account	***January 1, 2121***	
Retained Earnings	3,960	
Deferred Tax Asset	2,640	
Inventory		6,600

Balance Sheets

We begin with the balance sheet for December 31, 2020. Cash, liabilities, and common stock were not affected by the accounting change. As a result, Topeka continues to report them as originally presented. We have already determined the new ending inventory balance of $16,400 and the ending retained earnings balance of $35,840 ($39,800 as originally reported less $3,960 cumulative effect of the change). Topeka reports a deferred-tax asset of $2,640 on the balance sheet.

The balances in cash, liabilities, and common stock as of December 31, 2121, are not affected by the change in inventory methods. We have already determined the new ending inventory balance of $26,700 and the ending retained earnings balance of $40,820. Topeka increases its deferred-tax asset balance by $1,080 to $3,720. The increase in the deferred-tax

Continued

asset is attributable to 40% of the $2,700 ($4,700 − $2,000) difference in the inventory tax basis under the FIFO method and the inventory carrying value under the average-cost method.

Topeka includes the following balance sheets in its annual report for December 31, 2121:

	December 31, 2121	December 31, 2020 (Adjusted)
Cash	$25,400	$31,800
Inventory	26,700	16,400
Deferred Tax Asset	3,720	2,640
Total Assets	$55,820	$50,840
Liabilities	$ 5,000	$ 5,000
Common Stock	10,000	10,000
Retained Earnings	40,820	35,840
Total Liabilities and Equity	$55,820	$50,840

Abercrombie & Fitch Co. used the retrospective method when it changed its inventory accounting method to the weighted-average cost method from the retail method in fiscal 2012. ***Abercrombie's*** cumulative adjustment was an increase of $47.3 million, about 2%, in beginning retained earnings of the first period presented in its financial statements.[4] This adjustment to retained earnings is shown in the line "Cumulative restatement for change in inventory accounting . . . " in the excerpt of ***Abercrombie's*** statement of stockholders' equity in Exhibit 21.2. The adjustment for the change in inventory method also increased ***Abercrombie's*** beginning inventory by $73.6 million, or about 11%, with the difference between the retained earnings and inventory adjustments going to deferred taxes.

All amounts presented in the financial statements related to the change in the inventory method are adjusted from the beginning of the year of the change and all future periods. The third line in the statement of stockholders' equity reports restated net income, which has been adjusted for the change in inventory method.

Prospective Method Illustration

In Example 21.2, we examine a change in an accounting principle under the prospective method.

EXHIBIT 21.2 Retrospective Method Cumulative Adjustment, ***Abercrombie & Fitch Co***., Financial Statements, February 2, 2013

Abercrombie & Fitch, Co.
Consolidated Statements of Stockholders' Equity (Excerpt)
(Thousands, except per share amounts)

	Common Stock					Treasury Stock		
	Shares Outstanding	Par Value	Paid-In Capital	Retained Earnings	Other Comprehensive (Loss) Income	Shares	At Average Cost	Total Stockholders' Equity
Balance, January 30, 2010	87,986	$ 1,033	$ 339,453	$ 2,183,690	$ (8,973)	15,314	$ (687,286)	$ 1,827,917
Cumulative restatement for change in inventory accounting (See Note 4)				47,341				47,341
Restated Net Income	—	—	—	155,709	—	—	—	155,709

Source: Retrospective Method Cumulative Adjustment, Abercrombie & Fitch Co., Financial Statements, February 2, 2013.

[4]In its fiscal 2012 financial statements, ***Abercrombie & Fitch Co.*** presented its income statement and its statement of stockholders' equity for 3 years: fiscal 2012, 2011, and 2010. Therefore, the beginning of fiscal 2010 is January 30, 2010, and retained earnings on this date are adjusted.

EXAMPLE 21.2

Change in Accounting Principle: Prospective Application

PROBLEM: Assume that Topeka Tile Company from Example 21.1 does not have sufficient information to report the change retrospectively. Prepare the financial statements that Topeka will include in its annual report for 2021.

SOLUTION: Because it is impractical for Topeka Tile to report the change in inventory costing retrospectively, it will report the change prospectively. Thus, the change will not affect prior financial statements. Instead, Topeka will use the FIFO inventory as of December 31, 2020, as its opening inventory balance for 2021 and commence the average-cost method in 2021.

Topeka computes its cost of goods sold for 2021 as follows:

Beginning inventory (FIFO – Old Method)	$23,000
Purchases	15,000
Cost of goods available for sale	38,000
Less: Ending inventory (Average Cost – New Method)	(26,700)
Cost of goods sold	$ 11,300

Topeka's income statements for 2019 and 2020 are as originally reported. Topeka reports cost of goods sold for 2021 as computed above.

Statement of Net Income

	2021	2020 (As Previously Reported)	2019 (As Previously Reported)
Revenues	$ 20,000	$ 32,000	$ 31,000
Cost of goods sold	(11,300)	(4,000)	(6,000)
Operating expenses	(7,000)	(11,000)	(9,000)
Net income before tax	$ 1,700	$ 17,000	$ 16,000
Income tax expense	(680)	(6,800)	(6,400)
Net income	$ 1,020	$ 10,200	$ 9,600

Topeka does not adjust the statement of retained earnings for the average-cost method.

	Statement of Retained Earnings
Balance: December 31, 2018	$20,000
Net income, 2019	9,600
Balance: December 31, 2019	$29,600
Net income, 2020	10,200
Balance: December 31, 2020	$39,800
Net income, 2021	1,020
Balance: December 31, 2021	$40,820

Finally, Topeka's balance sheet for 2020 remains as originally reported. The 2021 balance sheet is identical to the one prepared under the retrospective approach.

	December 31, 2021	December 31, 2020
Cash	$25,400	$31,800
Inventory	26,700	23,000
Deferred Tax Asset	3,720	0
Total Assets	$55,820	$54,800
Liabilities	$ 5,000	$ 5,000
Common Stock	10,000	10,000
Retained Earnings	40,820	39,800
Total Liabilities and Equity	$55,820	$54,800

Required Disclosures for a Change in Accounting Principle

For any change in accounting principle, firms must provide the following footnote disclosures in the year of the change:

1. Description of the nature of the change: An example of this disclosure is "effective January 1, 2019, the company changed its method of accounting for inventory from the FIFO method to the average-cost method."
2. Management's justification for the change, which indicates why the new method is preferable: An example of this disclosure is "management believes that the new method of accounting for inventory valuation will better reflect the company's operations."
3. The method of applying the change: The company specifies the retrospective or prospective method.
4. A description of any adjusted prior-period information.
5. The effect of the change on income from continuing operations, net income, per share amounts, and any other affected line item.
6. The cumulative effect of the change on retained earnings for the first balance sheet presented.

Disclosures: IFRS. IFRS additionally requires a company to report 3 years of balance sheets and 2 years of the other financial statements when reporting a change in accounting principle. IFRS requires these minimum number of years so that financial statement users can better compare changes in a company's financial information from year-to-year as if the company had always applied the new accounting principle.

3 Explain and illustrate the accounting for a change in an accounting estimate.

Changes in Accounting Estimates

Accounting changes due to revisions of underlying estimates involve areas such as bad debt expense, depreciation expense, inventory obsolescence, and pensions. Estimates are natural parts of the accounting process: Changes in estimates are expected, particularly as management becomes more experienced and as new information becomes available.

Prospective Method Illustration

Firms must report changes in accounting estimates using the prospective method. That is, firms implement the new estimate in the year of the change and in all future years as appropriate. Prior-years financial statements are not affected. ***Netflix's*** decrease in net income of $12.3 million in 2016 resulting from changes in estimated viewing patterns is an example of a change in accounting estimate using the prospective method. Example 21.3 illustrates accounting for a change in an estimate.

EXAMPLE 21.3 **Change in Accounting Estimate**

PROBLEM: Adelaide Manufacturing Company acquired a plant asset for $1,000 on January 1, 2013, and depreciated the equipment using the straight-line basis over a 10-year period with no scrap value. On January 1, 2019, after using the asset for 6 full years, Adelaide's management believes that the asset will be productive for an additional 8 years (as opposed to 4 years). The increase in useful life results from an improved maintenance program initiated 2 years ago. How should Adelaide report this change in estimate?

SOLUTION: Annual depreciation is $100 per year ($1,000/10 years) before the change in estimate. After 6 years, when the asset's net book value is $400 ($1,000 − $600), the company believes that the asset will be productive for another 8 years. Therefore, the revised depreciation is $50 per year ($400/8 years). Adelaide will use the revised depreciation from the year of the change (2019) to the date of disposal.

Adelaide does not make any changes to prior financial statements.

Change in Accounting Estimate Effected by a Change in Accounting Principle

It is often difficult to differentiate between a change in accounting estimate and a change in accounting principle. A **change in accounting estimate effected by a change in accounting principle** is a change in estimate that is inseparable from the effect of a related change in accounting principle. For example, a change in depreciation method is based on a change in the estimate regarding the future economic benefits to be derived from the use of the asset. Firms account for a change in accounting estimate effected by a change in accounting principle the same way as a change in accounting estimate—that is, under the prospective method. Accounting for a change in accounting estimate effected by a change in accounting principle is illustrated in Example 21.4.

EXAMPLE 21.4 Change in Accounting Estimate Effected by a Change in Accounting Principle

PROBLEM: Cayo Horizons purchased a piece of equipment on January 1, 2017, for $100,000. Cayo depreciated the asset using the straight-line method over 5 years with no residual value. On January 1, 2019, Cayo decided that the units-of-output method would be a more accurate method of computing depreciation on this equipment than the straight-line method. Management believes that the equipment has 5,000 units remaining as of January 1, 2019. During 2019, Cayo used the equipment to produce 1,000 units. How should Cayo report the change in depreciation methods? What depreciation expense should Cayo report in 2019?

SOLUTION: Because Cayo switched from using the straight-line method to the units-of-output method for depreciating the equipment, this is a change in accounting estimate effected by a change in accounting principle. Thus, Cayo accounts for it prospectively. On January 1, 2019, the book value of the equipment was $60,000 [$100,000 cost less $40,000 for 2 years of depreciation expense ($100,000/5 × 2)]. Cayo uses a depreciation rate of $12 per unit ($60,000 book value divided by 5,000 units remaining) under the new depreciation method. Accordingly, Cayo records $12,000 ($12 per unit × 1,000 units) depreciation expense in 2019.

JUDGMENTS IN ACCOUNTING
Changes in Accounting Estimates

Financial statement users understand that the statements contain many estimates. Judgments are pervasive in accounting for estimates and changes in estimates. We have demonstrated how firms estimate the balances for almost all the line items on a balance sheet to some degree throughout the book. For example, in order to measure accounts receivable, accountants must estimate the amount of uncollectible accounts. In the case of inventory, accountants make assumptions about the flow of inventory in order to estimate the cost of inventory. They also make judgments related to the need to write down inventory to market. Property, plant, and equipment are estimated because depreciation is simply a forecast of future usage.

Accountants use their best judgment to estimate and record these items as accurately as possible. However, as new information becomes available, estimates change—and the adjusted estimates are still estimates.

As an example of the importance of estimates, consider a company that purchased a factory building for $30 million and depreciated it using the straight-line method. What useful life should be used to depreciate the building? The company might be able to reliably estimate that the life will be between 30 and 50 years. But this is a wide range of possible useful lives. If the company chooses 30 years, then the annual depreciation expense will be $1 million. Alternatively, if management decides to depreciate the asset over a 50-year period, the annual depreciation expense will be $600,000. This $400,000 difference has a direct impact on net income.

Disclosure of a Change in Accounting Estimate

Companies should disclose the effect of a change in estimate on income from continuing operations, net income, and related per share amounts of the current period if a change in estimate affects several periods. Consider a change in the service lives of depreciable assets. Firms must provide footnote disclosure indicating why the new estimate is justifiable.

Companies are not required to disclose changes in accounting estimates made as part of normal operations, such as bad debt allowances or inventory obsolescence, unless those changes are material. When a company changes an accounting estimate effected by a change in accounting principle, the disclosure requirements for a change in accounting principle are required.

Exhibit 21.3 shows a sample disclosure for the Adelaide Manufacturing Company from Example 21.3. This disclosure assumes a 40% tax rate.

EXHIBIT 21.3 Change in Accounting Estimate Disclosure

> After several years of implementing significant improvements in the Company's repair and maintenance policies, management has determined that the useful lives of its major plant assets have increased. Therefore, the Company extended the estimated useful lives of its plant assets effective January 1, 2019. The effect of this change in estimate is to reduce depreciation expense from $100 to $50 for the year ended December 31, 2019. Income from continuing operations after tax increased by $30 as a result of the change in estimate for the year ended December 31, 2019.

Honda Motor Co. Ltd., the Japanese automobile manufacturer that reports under U.S. GAAP, changed its method for accounting for depreciation in fiscal 2012. ***Honda*** changed to the straight-line method from the declining-balance method because management believed the straight-line method better reflected the future economic benefit from the use of plant and equipment. ***Honda*** used the prospective method to account for the change. As a result of the change, ***Honda's*** net income increased by ¥35,746 million, or about 11%.

4 Explain the accounting for a change in the reporting entity.

Change in the Reporting Entity

The final type of accounting change that a company may report is the *change in the reporting entity*. A **change in the reporting entity** occurs when a company reports financial statements that are, in effect, financial statements for a different reporting entity. A change in the reporting entity primarily involves:

1. Presenting consolidated or combined financial statements instead of individual financial statements
2. Changing the specific subsidiaries that make up the group of entities for which consolidated financial statements are presented
3. Changing the entities included in combined financial statements

The acquisition of a business is not considered a change in the reporting entity.

Firms account for a change in the reporting entity using the retrospective method by adjusting all financial statements presented from prior periods to reflect the change. For example, ***Sara Lee Corporation***, a manufacturer of consumer food products, announced that its board had agreed to divide the company into two separate publicly traded companies in 2012. The two new companies would be separate reporting entities—so ***Sara Lee*** restated prior financial statements to reflect the two new entities.

Disclosure of a Change in the Reporting Entity

Changes in reporting entity disclosures are essential in restoring comparability and offsetting the violation of consistency resulting from an accounting change. The financial statements for the year of the change should disclose the nature of the change and the reason for the change. Also, firms disclose the effect of the change on income from continuing operations, net income, other comprehensive income, and related per share amounts for all periods presented.[5]

Exhibit 21.4 summarizes the types of accounting changes.

EXHIBIT 21.4 Types of Accounting Changes

Type of Change	Example	Accounting Treatment	Disclosures
Change in accounting principle	Switch from FIFO to LIFO for inventory costing	Retrospective unless a mandatory change required by a new standard does not call for a retrospective transition or if the retrospective method is impractical	1. Description of the nature of the change 2. Management's justification for the change, which indicates why the new method is preferable 3. The method of applying the change: The company specifies the retrospective or prospective method 4. A description of any adjusted prior-period information 5. The effect of the change on income from continuing operations, net income, per share amounts, and any other affected line item 6. The cumulative effect of the change on retained earnings for the first balance sheet presented
Change in accounting estimate	Change in the estimate of the allowance for bad debts	Prospective	1. Companies should disclose the effect of a change in estimate on income from continuing operations, net income, and related per share amounts of the current period if a change in estimate affects several periods 2. Firms must provide a footnote disclosure indicating why the new estimate is justifiable 3. Companies are not required to disclose changes in accounting estimates made as part of normal operations, such as bad debt allowances or inventory obsolescence, unless such changes are material
Change in accounting estimate effected by a change in accounting principle	Change in depreciation method	Prospective	Same as change in accounting principle
Change in the reporting entity	Present consolidated statements instead of individual statements	Retrospective	1. The financial statements for the year of the change should disclose the nature of the change and the reason for it 2. Also, firms disclose the effect of the change on income from continuing operations, net income, other comprehensive income, and related per share amounts for all periods presented

5 Discuss common types of errors and error analysis and demonstrate how to correct errors.

Errors and Error Analysis

When an accountant discovers an *error* that is material in amount, the error must be corrected. An **error** is an unintentional mistake often due to an incorrect application of an accounting policy or incorrect mathematical computation. Do not confuse an accounting error with fraud: An error is unintentional, whereas fraud is considered an intentional misrepresentation.

Firms account for error corrections with the retrospective method and classify all changes affecting retained earnings as prior-period adjustments. We addressed the accounting for prior-period adjustments extensively in Chapter 15. In this section, we discuss common types of errors, their potential effects on the financial statements, and methods for correcting them.

[5]Changes in the reporting entity are covered more extensively in advanced accounting courses.

THE CONCEPTUAL FRAMEWORK CONNECTION
Errors

For financial information to be a faithful representation—one of the fundamental qualitative characteristics—of the underlying position and performance of the firm, it must be free from error. However, it is nearly impossible for accountants to make no errors in the financial reporting process. In fact, the conceptual framework states that "perfection is seldom, if ever, achievable."[6]

Consequently, the framework states that financial information can provide a faithful representation even if it is not perfectly accurate. Information is considered to be free from error when the process used to produce the information is selected and applied with no errors and the description of the transaction is free from error. Financial statements will undoubtedly contain some oversights and errors, but the financial information faithfully represents the position and performance of the firm.

As stated earlier, if a company discovers a material error, it must correct it. Accounting errors can impact the balance sheet, income statement, or both.

Balance Sheet Errors

Balance sheet errors, which affect only asset, liability, and equity accounts, are typically the result of a misclassification of accounts in the recording of a transaction. For example, assume a firm recorded a long-term note receivable as a short-term receivable. After discovering a balance sheet error, the accountant should reclassify the item, and the company should also restate any comparative financial statements. Example 21.5 illustrates correcting balance sheet errors.

EXAMPLE 21.5 Balance Sheet Errors

PROBLEM: Douglas Designs, Incorporated incorrectly recorded a $450,000 note issued by Phillips Bank, NA in 2017 by debiting cash but crediting accounts payable. The note is due in 5 years with no principal payments due until maturity. Interest accruals were recorded correctly. Douglas Designs' auditors discovered the error in 2019. Provide the correcting journal entry.

SOLUTION: The correcting journal entry is a simple reclassification correction. Douglas Designs records the $450,000 as a long-term liability and as a result will debit accounts payable and credit notes payable.

Account	***2019 Correcting Entry***	
Accounts Payable – Phillips Bank	450,000	
Long-Term Notes Payable – Phillips Bank		450,000

Douglas updates the 2018 comparative balance sheet to reflect the correction on a retrospective basis.

Income Statement Errors

Income statement errors, which affect only revenue, gain, expense, and loss accounts, are also commonly caused by misclassification mistakes. For example, a firm could improperly record interest expense as cost of goods sold or a gain from the sale of equipment as sales revenue. Income statement errors do not affect the balance sheet and might not affect net income.

[6]Financial Accounting Standards Board, *Statement of Financial Accounting Concepts No. 8 Chapter 3, "Qualitative Characteristics of Useful Financial Information,"* Paragraph QC12.

If accountants discover income statement errors in the year the error occurred, they must be corrected. However, if accountants discover income statement errors after financial statements have been prepared, no correcting entry is made. However, the company should restate the incorrect amounts from the financial statements that have already been issued in any future comparative financial statements. An example of correcting income statement errors is provided in Example 21.6.

EXAMPLE 21.6

Income Statement Errors

PROBLEM: Begg Incorporated sold a piece of machinery during 2019 for a $35,000 gain. It incorrectly recorded the gain as sales revenue. Begg discovered the error in the same year as the transaction before closing the books. Prepare the correcting entry for 2019. If Begg had already closed its books before discovering the error, what would it need to do? Ignore the impact of income taxes.

SOLUTION: The error affects only the income statement. The correction involves a reclassification out of the sales revenue account and into the gain on sale of equipment account.

Account	*2019 Correcting Entry*	
Sales Revenue	35,000	
Gain on Sale of Equipment		35,000

If the books were already closed, a correcting entry would not be necessary because retained earnings is correctly stated. However, Begg must correct the income statement before issuing financial statements by moving the $35,000 out of sales revenue and reclassifying it as a gain on sale of equipment.

Errors Affecting the Income Statement and the Balance Sheet

Some errors affect both the income statement and the balance sheet—and these errors might or might not correct themselves. A balance sheet error typically is not self-correcting. Consequently, the firm must make a correcting entry to reclassify the item it incorrectly recorded. Most other errors will eventually correct themselves. However, the correction often takes many years. Consider a company that purchases equipment for $100,000 with a 10-year life. Instead of depreciating the asset over 10 years, the company immediately expensed it. The error will eventually correct after the 10th year; however, the financial statements will be incorrect over the 10-year life of the asset. Because of the possible lengthy period until correction, **self-correcting errors** are classified as errors that will self-correct within 2 years.

Self-Correcting Errors. The primary issues in analyzing self-correcting errors that will be offset or corrected over two accounting periods are:

1. Whether the error is discovered in the first year or the second year
2. Whether the books have been closed for the fiscal year

Consider the following specific scenarios:

- If the firm discovers the error after closing the books for the second year, no entry is needed. The error has already self-corrected, the books are closed, and, therefore, retained earnings is correctly stated. Thus, the permanent accounts are all correctly stated.
- If the firm discovers the error after the books are closed for the first year but before the books are closed for the second year, an entry is needed to correct beginning retained earnings and other balance sheet accounts as well as to make any necessary adjustments to the accounts for the second year.
- If the firm discovers the error in the first year and the books have not been closed, it must correct accounts for the first year.

Firms must adjust comparative financial statements retrospectively in all cases (regardless of whether they make correcting entries).

A misstatement of ending inventory, a common type of self-correcting error, has a direct effect on net income. If a firm understates ending inventory because it counted incorrectly, cost of goods sold will be overstated. Recall that ending inventory plus cost of goods sold equals cost of goods available for sale. If cost of goods available for sale is correct and ending inventory is understated, then cost of goods sold is overstated. Thus, net income will be understated. Once the books are closed in the first year, inventory and retained earnings will be understated. If ending inventory is understated, net income, and ultimately retained earnings, will be understated.

Inventory errors are self-correcting within two accounting periods. If ending inventory in the following year is recorded correctly, the original error will have the opposite effect in the second year. If ending inventory was understated in the first year, then cost of goods sold is overstated and net income is understated. In the second year, last year's ending inventory is then the beginning inventory and will be understated, causing cost of goods available for sale to be understated. Because ending inventory is correct in the second year, cost of goods sold is understated, causing net income to be overstated in the second year. However, once the books are closed after the second year, the errors in net income balance out and retained earnings is stated correctly.

Exhibit 21.5 illustrates the effects of an understatement of ending inventory in Year 1. The balance sheet and the income statement are incorrect in Year 1. However, the Year 2 balance sheet is correctly stated. Assuming no additional errors in inventory, accountants know that the income statement will be correct in the third year.

EXHIBIT 21.5 Analysis of a Self-Correcting Inventory Error

	Year 1	Year 2
Beginning inventory	Correct	Understated
+ Purchases	Correct	Correct
= Cost of goods available for sale	Correct	Understated
− Ending inventory	Understated	Correct
= Cost of goods sold	Overstated	Understated
Net income	Understated	Overstated
Retained earnings (after closing)	Understated	Correct
Balance sheet		
Assets (inventory)	Understated	Correct
Liabilities	Correct	Correct
Equity (retained earnings)	Understated	Correct

Example 21.7 analyzes a self-correcting inventory error.

EXAMPLE 21.7 Self-Correcting Inventory Error

PROBLEM: Fazon Associates incorrectly recorded inventory in 2018. Rather than recording ending inventory as $250,000, Fazon's accounting manager entered $280,000, overstating ending inventory by $30,000. An inventory summary for 2018 and 2019 as actually recorded by the company follows. This summary includes the error in ending inventory in 2018.

2018		2019	
Beginning inventory	$ 100,000	Beginning inventory	$ 280,000
+ Purchases	300,000	+ Purchases	300,000
= Cost of goods available for sale	$ 400,000	= Cost of goods available for sale	$ 580,000
− Ending inventory	(280,000)	− Ending inventory	(450,000)
= Cost of goods sold	$ 120,000	= Cost of goods sold	$ 130,000

If this error goes undetected, what is the impact on the income statements and balance sheets for 2018 and 2019? What must Fazon do to correct this error if it is found (1) after the books are closed for 2019, (2) after the books are closed for 2018 but before the books are closed for 2019, and (3) before the books are closed in 2018? Ignore the impact of income taxes.

SOLUTION: The following schedule summarizes the analysis of the inventory error:

	2018		2019	
	As Reported	**Correct**	**As Reported**	**Correct**
Beginning inventory	$ 100,000	$ 100,000	$ 280,000	$250,000
+ Purchases	300,000	300,000	300,000	300,000
= Cost of goods available for sale	$ 400,000	$ 400,000	$ 580,000	$550,000
− Ending inventory	(280,000)	(250,000)	(450,000)	(450,000)
= Cost of goods sold	$ 120,000	$ 150,000	$ 130,000	$100,000
Net income	Overstated $30,000		Understated $30,000	
Retained Earnings (after closing)	Overstated $30,000		Correct	
Balance sheet:				
Assets (inventory)	Overstated $30,000		Correct	
Liabilities	Correct		Correct	
Equity (retained earnings)	Overstated $30,000		Correct	

As noted in the preceding schedule, the inventory error self-corrects after the 2-year period is completed.

1. If Fazon discovers the error later than 2019 (after closing the books for 2019), the error has already been self-corrected and no correcting entry is needed. Any comparative financial statements for 2018 or 2019 should be restated to report the correct balances for cost of goods sold, inventory, and retained earnings.
2. If Fazon discovers the error before closing the books for 2019 but after issuing 2018 statements, it will debit the retained earnings account instead of the cost of goods sold account because cost of goods sold has already been closed to retained earnings.

Account	***2019 Correcting Entry***	
Retained Earnings – Prior-Period Adjustment	30,000	
Inventory		30,000

Fazon will report cost of goods sold of $150,000 on its 2018 comparative income statement when it issues the annual report for 2019.

3. If Fazon discovers the error before closing the books in 2018, then it will simply correct the error by decreasing inventory and increasing cost of goods sold.

Account	***2018 Correcting Entry***	
Cost of Goods Sold	30,000	
Inventory		30,000

Errors That Do Not Self-Correct. If the error is not self-correcting within two accounting periods, correcting entries are always needed regardless of whether the closing entries for the period have been recorded. Again, firms must correct comparative financial statements on a retrospective basis. Example 21.8 examines a non-self-correcting error that is discovered while the books are still open.

EXAMPLE 21.8

Non-self-correcting Error Discovered while Books Are Open

PROBLEM: Underwood Computer Company acquired a circuit board stamping machine for $700,000 on December 31, 2019. The general accountant incorrectly coded the invoice as repair expense. The equipment would normally be depreciated straight-line over 10 years with no salvage value. The error was discovered later on December 31, 2019, before the books were closed. Prepare the correcting entry for this transaction, ignoring income taxes.

SOLUTION: This error will not self-correct within two accounting periods: It will only reverse out at the end of the asset's life. Because the books have not yet been closed, the general accountant simply reclassifies the accounts by debiting machinery and crediting repair expense as shown in the following entry. There was no depreciation taken because the asset was acquired on the last day of the fiscal year.

Account	***December 31, 2019 (Correcting Entry)***	
Machinery	700,000	
Repair Expense		700,000

Example 21.9 examines a non-self-correcting error discovered after the books are closed.

EXAMPLE 21.9

Non-self-correcting Error Discovered after the Books Are Closed

PROBLEM: Underwood Computer Company acquired a circuit board stamping machine for $700,000 on December 31, 2019. The general accountant incorrectly coded the invoice as repair expense. The equipment would normally be depreciated straight-line over 10 years with no salvage value. Underwood discovered the error in 2020 after closing the books for 2019. Prepare the correcting entry for this transaction, ignoring income taxes.

SOLUTION: In this case, the repair expense had already been closed out to retained earnings. As a result, Underwood Computer records machinery and corrects retained earnings. Underwood Computer would also record depreciation expense of $70,000 at December 31, 2020.

Account	***2020 Correcting Entry***	
Machinery	700,000	
Retained Earnings – Prior-Period Adjustment		700,000

The 2019 financial statements should be corrected when they are presented as comparative statements in future years.

Example 21.10 presents an illustration of a non-self-correcting error that was discovered several years after the error was made.

EXAMPLE 21.10

Non-self-correcting Error Discovered in a Period after the Error Was Made

PROBLEM: Underwood Computer Company acquired a circuit board stamping machine for $700,000 on December 31, 2016. The general accountant incorrectly coded the invoice as repair expense. The equipment would normally be depreciated straight-line over 10 years with no salvage value. Underwood discovered the error on December 31, 2019, before closing the books for 2019. Prepare the correcting entry for this transaction, ignoring income taxes.

SOLUTION: In this case, the error affects the amount of expense recorded in the year the error was made (overstating expenses), and it results in a failure to record depreciation on the equipment for the 3 years after the acquisition of the equipment (understating expenses).

The annual depreciation expense should have been $70,000 per year ($700,000/10). Depreciation should have been recorded for 2017 and 2018 as well as 2019. Because 2017 and 2018 have already been closed, Underwood has overstated retained earnings by $140,000 because it did not record depreciation expense. Recording a repair expense in 2016 understated retained earnings by $700,000. Thus, the correcting entry involves a credit to retained earnings of $560,000 ($700,000 − $140,000). Underwood should record machinery of $700,000. The company also needs to record depreciation for 2019. Finally, Underwood records accumulated depreciation of $210,000 ($70,000 × 3 years). The entry to record the error correction follows.

Account	*December 31, 2019 (Correcting Entry)*	
Machinery	700,000	
Depreciation Expense – Machinery	70,000	
Accumulated Depreciation – Machinery		210,000
Retained Earnings – Prior-Period Adjustment		560,000

Underwood also restates any comparative financial statements for 2016 through 2018 that are presented with current-period annual reports.

Exhibit 21.6 summarizes accounting for error corrections. Note that in addition to any necessary correcting entries, firms should correctly state financial statements (both current year and comparative).

EXHIBIT 21.6 Summary of Error Corrections

	Error Self-Corrects within Two Accounting Periods	*Error Does Not Self-Correct within Two Accounting Periods*
Books closed in year of error	No entry needed if the error has already self-corrected Entry needed to adjust retained earnings and other affected balance sheet accounts if the error has not yet self-corrected	Correcting entry needed to adjust retained earnings and other affected balance sheet accounts
Books not closed in year of error	Entry needed to correct the current-year income statement and balance sheet accounts	Correcting entry needed to adjust income statement and balance sheet accounts

JUDGMENTS IN ACCOUNTING
Error Corrections

What makes an error material enough to correct? If an error is immaterial, the company does not need to apply the processes we have just discussed. Materiality is a matter of judgment: The conceptual framework states that financial information is material if omitting it or misstating it would impact a user's decisions.

Consequently, there is no formal specification of a quantitative materiality threshold for all firms and all transactions. Rather, companies must consider materiality in the context of the nature and magnitude of the transaction as well as the context of the financial reports. Different managers' judgment of the level of materiality varies. For example, consider a company with annual revenues of $200 million and assets of $700 million. An error of $100,000 would not typically be considered material for this company. However, a company with annual revenues of $5 million and assets of $7 million might consider a $100,000 error to be material. When judging materiality, qualitative and quantitative factors are relevant. Consider the first company that reports $200 million in annual revenue. Although $100,000 is not a particularly large number comparatively, if correcting the error would result in reporting a net loss instead of a net profit, the company would most likely consider this item to be material because a user would view a net profit much differently than a net loss.

FINANCIAL STATEMENT ANALYSIS

Accounting Changes

Accounting changes, whether changes in a principle or an estimate, can occur in almost every topic we have discussed in the text, from accounts receivable to long-lived assets to pensions. Management makes these changes for various reasons. For example, standard setters can mandate companies to make a change in an accounting principle such as requiring previously off-balance sheet pension assets and obligations to be reported on the balance sheet. Management can also decide to change accounting methods such as switching from the retail inventory method to the weighted-average method. Management, though, almost always initiates changes in estimates such as those used in determining the allowance for bad debts.

In analyzing accounting changes, understanding the reason for the change is important. A company can make a change because it is required as the result of a change in accounting standards, of changing business or macroeconomic conditions, or a shift in its operating strategy. For changes management initiates, it is especially important to consider the effect on earnings and earnings quality. If the change increases earnings, is management acting opportunistically? That is, changing an accounting method or estimate can show an increase in earnings without a change in the underlying economic performance.

In examining accounting changes, a financial statement user should understand and assess the following:

- Whether the company has any changes in accounting principles or estimates. If so, determine the reason for the change. For changes in accounting principle, determine whether the standard setters required the changes or the changes were initiated by management.
- When the changes in accounting principle or estimate are reported in the financial statements, such as the accounts affected on the balance sheet and income statement. For changes in accounting principle, determine whether the reporting is retrospective or prospective.
- Assess the effects of the change on the income statement and balance sheet.

Example 21.11 illustrates the financial statement analysis of the effect of a change in accounting principle.

EXAMPLE 21.11 Financial Statement Analysis of an Accounting Change

PROBLEM: ***Abercrombie & Fitch, Company*** disclosed an inventory accounting change in the notes of its 2012 financial statements presented in Exhibit 21.7.

Financial Statement Analysis, continued

EXHIBIT 21.7 Accounting Change Disclosures, ***Abercrombie & Fitch, Co.***, Financial Statements, February 2, 2013

NOTE 4: Change in Accounting Principle

The Company elected to change its method of accounting for inventory from the lower of cost or market utilizing the retail method to the weighted average cost method effective February 2, 2013. In accordance with generally accepted accounting principles, all periods have been retroactively adjusted to reflect the period-specific effects of the change to the weighted average cost method. The Company believes that accounting under the weighted average cost method is preferable as it better aligns with the Company's focus on realized selling margin and improves the comparability of the Company's financial results with those of its competitors. Additionally, it will improve the matching of cost of goods sold with the related net sales and reflect the acquisition cost of inventory outstanding at each balance sheet date. The cumulative adjustment as of January 30, 2010, was an increase in its inventory of $73.6 million and an increase in retained earnings of $47.3 million.

Source: Accounting Change Disclosures, Abercrombie & Fitch, Co., Financial Statements, February 2, 2013. www.abercrombie.com/anf/investors/investorrelations.html

When ***Abercrombie*** announced its 2012 earnings, the company also prepared additional information on the accounting change, including the following information.

For the Year Ended February 2, 2013 (fiscal 2012)

Line Item – Unaudited (in thousands)	Weighted-Average Cost Method	Retail Method
Net sales	$4,510,805	$4,510,805
Gross profit	2,816,709	2,861,855
Tax expense	132,749	151,715
Net income	241,603	267,783
EPS diluted	2.90	3.22

Source: www.abercrombie.com/anf/investors/investorrelations.html

Use the excerpt from ***Abercrombie's*** financial statement note in Exhibit 21.7, the effects of this change on stockholders' equity in Exhibit 21.2, and the additional disclosures on the accounting change to answer the following questions:

a. What accounting policy did ***Abercrombie*** change?
b. What reason(s) did ***Abercrombie*** give for making this change?
c. What method did ***Abercrombie*** use to account for this change?
d. How did the change affect cost of goods sold, gross profit, tax expense, net income, and earnings per share (EPS) in 2012? What would net income have been in 2012 if ***Abercrombie*** had not made this change?

SOLUTION:

a. ***Abercrombie*** changed its method of accounting for inventory. Prior to fiscal 2012, ***Abercrombie*** used the retail method. In fiscal 2012, ***Abercrombie*** changed to the weighted-average cost method.

Continued

Financial Statement Analysis, continued

b. ***Abercrombie*** provides four reasons for the change in accounting method in the notes to its financial statements. It states that the weighted-average cost method is preferable because it:

1. Better aligns with the company's focus on realized selling margin
2. Improves the comparability of the company's financial results with those of its competitors
3. Improves the matching of cost of goods sold with the related net sales
4. Reflects the acquisition cost of inventory outstanding at each balance sheet date

c. ***Abercrombie*** used the retrospective method to account for this change in accounting method by adjusting the assets, liabilities, and retained earnings as of the beginning of first period presented, fiscal 2010, as shown in Exhibit 21.2. ***Abercrombie*** adjusted the financial statements for each period presented afterward to reflect the effects of the change of accounting method.

d. From the additional information that ***Abercrombie*** presented, the change in accounting method had the following changes on income statement items.

Line Item – Unaudited (in thousands)	Weighted-Average Cost Method	Retail Method	Difference	Percentage of Difference
Net Sales	$ 4,510,805	$ 4,510,805	$ 0	
Cost of goods sold (computed)	1,694,096	1,648,950	$ 45,146	2.7%
Gross profit	$ 2,816,709	$2,861,855	$(45,146)	(1.6%)
Tax expense	$ 132,749	$ 151,715	$(18,966)	(12.5%)
Net income	$ 241,603	$ 267,783	$(26,180)	(9.8%)
EPS diluted	$ 2.90	$ 3.22	$ (0.32)	(9.9%)

Abercrombie's change in accounting for inventory increased its cost of goods sold, which decreased its gross profit, tax expense, net income, and EPS. If Abercrombie did not make the change in inventory method, net income in 2012 would have been $267,783,000.

LAWRENCE STEENVOORDEN

VICE PRESIDENT & GLOBAL CONTROLLER, SIEMENS HEALTHCARE DIAGNOSTICS, TARRYTOWN, NY »

Lawrence Steenvoorden

Lawrence Steenvoorden joined Siemens after 4 years in public accounting. He has held various roles in corporate accounting, reporting, and finance both in the United States and abroad in addition to his involvement with conversions from U. S. GAAP to IFRS. In his current role, he is responsible for global business performance controlling for Siemens Healthcare Diagnostics with worldwide revenues of more than $4 billion.

1 What primary factors would Siemens consider to determine whether a change in accounting method or estimate is appropriate?

One key consideration is whether the new method or estimate reflects actual business performance. For accounting methods, does the new principle better reflect how the business operates? With regard to an estimate, what facts and circumstances changed that should be reflected in the financial statements? The Siemens Healthcare Diagnostics division evolved from three separate acquisitions, and upon review of an updated business plan in 2010, management reassessed growth prospects to reflect delays in technology, product development, and increased competition. The cash flow projection changes resulted in a goodwill write-off in excess of $1 billion. Another consideration is how material the change is to our balance sheet or income statements. IFRS and U.S. GAAP are similar, both providing limited guidance to make this assessment.

2 Why are changes in accounting method given retrospective treatment and changes in accounting estimates given a prospective application?

Comparability is essential for both preparers and users of financial statements. When new standards are pronounced, a retrospective approach that restates all years presented best shows comparability over the periods, "as-if" it were enacted from the first year. We base estimates on management judgment at a certain point in time with the best knowledge available. Hindsight is always "20/20," but management should not be burdened with restating financial statements because certain assumptions have changed. This is not practical and would misrepresent facts and circumstances at the financial statement date.

3 How would Siemens use accounting change disclosures to restore consistency and comparability of the financial information reported in comparative financial statements?

Siemens provides extensive disclosures with a view toward transparency for shareholders, investors, and regulators. We must communicate any changes clearly and, if necessary, present both views to maintain financial statement comparability. Disclosures are critical to explain the underlying story behind the numbers.

4 What are some key judgments involved when making an accounting change?

A cost-benefit analysis is important to consider before making accounting changes. How material is the change to the financial statements? What are the implementation costs? How are other companies also dealing with accounting changes? Once a decision is made to implement an accounting change, it must reflect business performance and be practical to apply. For example, implementing new revenue recognition standards is likely to be expensive and they may drive new business models or even change language in customer contracts.

5 What are the major costs that Siemens incurs when there is a change in accounting principle (either voluntary or mandatory)?

Often changes in accounting principles look simple on paper, but implementation can be quite complex. A global company like Siemens has to consider both local GAAP and IFRS in implementing new accounting principles. In the migration from U.S. GAAP to IFRS, significant costs were incurred for both internal and external resources—for example, to change IT system configurations. Training costs can also be significant to ensure that accounting principles are applied consistently in every country where we operate.

6 In your experience, what are the most common areas subject to accounting changes?

Revenue recognition tops the lists when it comes to accounting changes. Revenue standards can be quite complex, and Siemens operates in various industries, generating sales under many different types of business models. We are now preparing for a new revenue recognition standard that focuses more on a "control" concept than an "ownership" or transfer of title view. Accruals for termination benefits, restructuring, derivatives, and income taxes are other complex areas that tend to have more accounting changes.

Discussion Questions

1. In his interview, Lawrence Steenvoorden mentions some of the costs of implementing an accounting change. Discuss some other possible costs of changing accounting methods.
2. Discuss why disclosures are important whenever there is a change in accounting method or estimate.

Summary by Learning Objectives

In the following, we summarize the main points by learning objective. Throughout the chapter, we discuss the accounting and reporting of U.S. GAAP and IFRS side-by-side. The following table also highlights the major similarities and differences between the standards.

1 Provide an overview of the types of accounting changes, including the difference between the retrospective and prospective methods.

Summary	Similarities and Differences between U.S. GAAP and IFRS
Accounting changes include: • Changes in accounting principles • Changes in accounting estimates • Changes in the reporting entity The retrospective method presents all prior-year financial statements in the annual report as if the newly adopted principle had always been used. Restated financial statements adjust opening balance sheet accounts for the cumulative effect of applying the new principle in all prior years and all subsequent financial statements presented as if the policy had always been used. The prospective method presents an accounting change in the current year and all future years.	Similar under U.S. GAAP and IFRS.

2 Describe and demonstrate the accounting for a change in accounting principle.

Summary	Similarities and Differences between U.S. GAAP and IFRS
A change in accounting principle involves a change from one generally accepted accounting method to another generally accepted accounting method. Changes in accounting principle may be voluntary or mandatory. Generally, all changes in accounting principle are required to be reported under the retrospective approach. There are two exceptions: 1. In the case of a mandatory change required by a new accounting standard, an entity should follow the specific transition requirements provided within the new standard. 2. It is impractical to use the retrospective approach. Application of the retrospective approach is impractical if any one of the following three conditions exists: • Financial statement effects are not determinable. • Application requires assumptions about management's intent in a prior period. • Application requires significant estimates for a prior period and the availability of the necessary information to determine these estimates cannot be objectively verified.	➤ Similar under U.S. GAAP and IFRS except that IFRS requires a company to report 3 years of balance sheets and 2 years of the other financial statements when reporting a change in accounting principle.

Summary by Learning Objectives, continued

3 Explain and illustrate the accounting for a change in accounting estimate.

Summary	Similarities and Differences between U.S. GAAP and IFRS
A change in accounting estimate involves revisions of estimates used in accounting for areas such as the bad debt expense, depreciation, inventory obsolescence, and pensions. The prospective method is used to account for a change in an accounting estimate.	Similar under U.S. GAAP and IFRS.

4 Explain the accounting for a change in the reporting entity.

Summary	Similarities and Differences between U.S. GAAP and IFRS
A change in the reporting entity occurs when a company reports financial statements that are, in effect, financial statements of a different reporting entity. A change in the reporting entity primarily involves the following changes: 1. Presenting consolidated or combined financial statements instead of individual financial statements. 2. Changing the specific subsidiaries that make up the group of entities for which consolidated financial statements are presented. 3. Changing the entities that are included in combined financial statements. Firms account for a change in the reporting entity using the retrospective method.	Similar under U.S. GAAP and IFRS.

5 Discuss common types of errors and error analysis and demonstrate how to correct errors.

Summary	Similarities and Differences between U.S. GAAP and IFRS
Balance sheet errors affect only asset, liability, and equity accounts. These errors are typically the result of a misclassification. Income statement errors affect only revenue, gain, expense, and loss accounts. Misclassification mistakes are a common cause of income statement errors. Some errors affect both the income statement and the balance sheet. Errors are of two types: 1. Self-correcting errors (errors that will self-correct within 2 years) 2. Errors that do not self-correct	Similar under U.S. GAAP and IFRS.

MyLab Accounting

Go to **http://www.pearson.com/mylab/accounting** for the following Questions, Multiple-Choice Questions, Brief Exercises, Exercises, and Problems. They are available with immediate grading, explanations of correct and incorrect answers, and interactive media that acts as your own online tutor.

21 Accounting Changes and Error Analysis

Questions

1 **Q21-1.** Are accounting changes permitted in financial statements?

1 **Q21-2.** How do firms report accounting changes under the retrospective method?

1 2 **Q21-3.** Explain the two approaches that firms use to report accounting changes.

1 3 **Q21-4.** How do firms account for changes in accounting estimates and changes in accounting principles?

2 **Q21-5.** What are the direct and indirect effects of changes in accounting principle on the financial statements?

2 3 **Q21-6.** How do firms account for a change in depreciation method?

2 3 **Q21-7.** What type of change would a change from LIFO to FIFO be considered?

4 **Q21-8.** When does a change in reporting entity occur?

5 **Q21-9.** Do accounting errors that self-correct within two accounting periods require correcting entries?

5 **Q21-10.** Does a firm need to correct an error that misclassifies equipment as inventory if total assets are correct?

Multiple-Choice Questions

In partnership with: BECKER PROFESSIONAL EDUCATION®

Becker CPA Exam Review multiple-choice questions are available in MyLab Accounting.

2 **MC21-1.** On December 31, Year 10, Brown Company changed its inventory valuation method from the weighted-average method to FIFO for financial statement purposes. The change will result in an $800,000 decrease in the beginning inventory at January 1, Year 10. The tax rate is 30%.
The cumulative effect of this accounting change for the year ended December 31, Year 10, in the statement of retained earnings is:
a. $0 b. $800,000 c. $240,000 d. $560,000

2 **MC21-2.** The proper accounting treatment to account for a change in inventory valuation from FIFO to LIFO under U.S. GAAP is:
a. Prospective application
b. Retrospective application
c. Retroactive approach
d. Ignored

2 **MC21-3.** On August 31 of the current year, Harvey Co. decided to change from the FIFO periodic inventory system to the weighted-average periodic inventory system. Harvey uses U.S. GAAP, is on a calendar-year basis, and does not present comparative financial statements. The cumulative effect of the change is determined:
a. During the current year by a weighted average of the purchases
b. During the 8 months ending August 31, by a weighted average of the purchases
c. As of August 31 of the current year
d. As of January 1 of the current year

2 **MC21-4.** On August 31 of the current year, Harvey Co. decided to change from the FIFO periodic inventory system to the weighted-average periodic inventory system. Harvey uses IFRS and is on a calendar-year basis. The cumulative effect of the change is shown as an adjustment to beginning retained earnings on the balance sheet for:
a. August 31 of the current year
b. December 31 of the current year
c. January 1 of the current year
d. January 1 of the prior year

❸ **MC21-5.** Gonzales Company purchased a machine on January 1, Year 1, for $600,000. On the date of acquisition, the machine had an estimated useful life of 6 years with no salvage value. The machine was being depreciated on a straight-line basis. On January 1, Year 4, Gonzales determined that the machine had an estimated life of 8 years from the date of acquisition. An accounting change was made in Year 4.

What is the amount of the depreciation expense that should be recorded for the year ended Year 4?

a. $75,000 b. $100,000 c. $60,000 d. $0

Brief Exercises

❶ **BE21-1. Accounting Changes, Retrospective, and Prospective Methods.** For each of the following events, indicate the type of change and the proper accounting treatment (retrospective or prospective).

Event	Type of Change	Accounting Method
Change in the useful life for a plant asset	___________	___________
Change in accounting for long-term contracts	___________	___________
Adoption of the FIFO method for a new product line	___________	___________
Change from the average-cost method to the LIFO method	___________	___________
Change from the straight-line method to the declining-balance method	___________	___________
Switching to an aging of accounting receivables to compute bad debt expense and the allowance for bad debts instead of using a percentage of sales	___________	___________

❷ **BE21-2. Change in Accounting Principle, Inventory.** Mills Abrams Manufacturing Company changed its method of accounting for inventory from the average-cost method to the LIFO basis as of January 1 of the current year. It still uses the average-cost method for tax purposes. The company is subject to a 40% tax rate. Cumulative cost of goods sold reported prior to the current year is $140,000 under the average-cost method and it would have been $300,000 if Mills had always used the LIFO method. Prepare the journal entry to record the change in method.

❷ **BE21-3. Change in Accounting Principle, Inventory, Disclosure.** Draft a footnote to disclose the accounting change implemented by the Mills Abrams Manufacturing Company using the information provided in BE21-2. Assume that pre-tax income for the current year is $230,000 under the LIFO method but would have been $455,000 under the prior average-cost method. Use the caption "Note F: Change in Method of Accounting for Inventory Valuation."

❷ **BE21-4. Change in Accounting Principle, Long-Term Construction Contracts.** Serat Construction Company elected to change its method of accounting from the percentage-of-completion method to the completed-contract method. Prior-years income (cumulative) would have been $300,000 lower if Serat had always used the completed contract method. The company is subject to a 35% tax rate. Prepare the journal entry to record the change in method.

❷ **BE21-5. Change in Accounting Principle, Long-Term Construction Contracts.** Cole Construction Company elected to change its method of accounting from the completed-contract method to the percentage-of-completion method. Prior-years income (cumulative) would have been $550,000 higher if Cole had always used the percentage-of-completion method. The company is subject to a 35% tax rate. Prepare the journal entry to record the change in method.

❷ **BE21-6. Change in Accounting Principle, Long-Term Construction Contracts, Direct and Indirect Effects.** Assume now that Cole Construction Company from BE21-5 compensates its management team by offering a base salary and a 2% bonus based on reported earnings before tax. The bonus plan requires adjustment for changes in accounting methods that includes prior bonus awards. Compute the effect of the accounting change on management compensation, indicating whether it is a direct or indirect effect of the accounting change and how Cole should report it in the financial statements.

❸ **BE21-7. Change in Estimate, Depreciation.** Enko Incorporated has one plant asset. The asset's original cost was $750,000. There is a $50,000 expected residual value and the estimated useful life is 20 years. On January 1 of the current year, following 10 full years of depreciation, the company determined that the asset will be useful for only another 5 years and reduced the expected residual value to $30,000. The change in estimate is needed to reflect advanced technology used in newer equipment currently available on the market. Enko uses the straight-line method of depreciation. Prepare the journal entry to record the change in estimate, ignoring any tax effects.

3 **BE21-8. Change in Estimate, Depreciation, Disclosure.** Using the information in BE21-7, prepare the footnote to disclose the change in accounting estimate for Enko Incorporated.

3 **BE21-9. Change in Estimate, Depreciation.** Natalie Charles Designs elected to change its method of depreciation from the double-declining balance method to the straight-line method. Cumulative depreciation up to—but not including—the year of the change would have been $345,000 lower had the company always used the straight-line method. Depreciation expense in the year of the change is $30,000 under the straight-line method. Prepare the journal entry to record the change in depreciation method, ignoring any income tax effects.

5 **BE21-10. Error Correction, before Books Closed.** Wilson Incorporated acquired a leather-cutting machine for $200,000 on December 31, 2018. The general accountant incorrectly coded the invoice as Miscellaneous Expense. The general accountant discovered the error in 2018 before the books were closed. The transaction was correctly recorded for tax purposes and all taxes were paid. Prepare the correcting entry for this transaction.

5 **BE21-11. Error Correction, Self-correcting Error, after Books Closed.** Using the data from BE21-10 for Wilson Incorporated, assume now that the general accountant discovered the error in 2019 when the books had already been closed for 2018. Prepare the correcting entry for this transaction.

5 **BE21-12. Error Correction, Self-Correcting Error, before Books Closed.** Barin Retail Outlets incorrectly recorded inventory in 2016. Rather than recording ending inventory as $960,000, Barin's accounting manager entered $690,000, understating ending inventory by $270,000. Barin's controller discovered the error in 2018. Prepare the journal entry necessary to correct the inventory error, ignoring any income tax effects.

5 **BE21-13. Error Correction, after Books Closed.** Using the information from BE21-12, prepare the journal entry necessary to correct the inventory error, assuming that Barin's controller discovered the error in 2017 after the books had been closed for 2016. Ignore any income tax effects.

5 **BE21-14. Error Correction, after Books Closed.** Tyrion Retailers, Inc. incorrectly recorded inventory in 2016. Rather than recording ending inventory as $570,000, Tyrion's accounting manager entered $750,000. Tyrion's controller discovered the error in 2017. Prepare the journal entry necessary to correct the inventory error, ignoring any income tax effects.

Exercises

2 **E21-1. Change in Accounting Principle, Inventory.** Massi Pharmacies, Inc. started operations on January 1, 2014. The company initially used the average-cost method to value its inventory for both book and tax purposes. Effective January 1, 2018, Massi elected to change its inventory valuation method to the FIFO basis for financial reporting purposes. Massi still uses the average-cost method on the company's tax returns. Massi is subject to a 35% tax rate.

The following information is available for net income after tax for both the FIFO and the average-cost methods.

	Net Income	
Year Ended	**Average Cost**	**FIFO**
December 31, 2014	$235,000	$310,000
December 31, 2015	300,000	376,000
December 31, 2016	310,000	400,500
December 31, 2017	425,500	535,000
December 31, 2018	500,000	585,000

Required » (Round to the nearest whole dollar)

a. Prepare the journal entry required to record the accounting change on January 1, 2018.
b. Prepare the partial comparative income statements for the 3 years ending December 31, 2018.
c. Prepare the footnote to disclose the change from the average cost to the FIFO basis. Designate the note as "Note A: Change in Method of Accounting for Inventory Valuation."

2 **E21-2. Change in Accounting Principle, Long-Term Construction Contracts.** Arlen Technology Solutions, Inc. adopted the percentage-of-completion method when it began operations on January 1, 2016. The company elected to change to the completed-contract method on January 1, 2018, due to a change in the size of its computer network contracts. Net income under both methods for the first 3 years of the company's operations is presented in the following table. Ignore income tax effects.

	Net Income	
Year Ended	Percentage of Completion	Completed Contract
December 31, 2016	$168,000	$147,000
December 31, 2017	112,000	98,000
December 31, 2018	231,000	210,000

Required » (Round to the nearest whole dollar)

a. Prepare the journal entry required to record the accounting change on January 1, 2018.
b. Prepare the footnote to disclose the change from the percentage-of-completion to the completed-contract method. Designate the note as "Note A: Change in Method of Accounting for Computer Network Contracts."

2 **E21-3. Change in Accounting Principle, Inventory.** Sumner Stores began operations on January 1, 2014, and adopted the average-cost method of accounting. In 2017, it is considering a change to the FIFO basis. Sumner provided the following information to assist in deciding whether to change inventory valuation techniques.

	Ending Inventory		Cost of Sales		Retained Earnings	
Year Ended	Average Cost	FIFO	Average Cost	FIFO	Average Cost	FIFO
12/31/2014	$10,000	$12,000	$76,000	$74,000	$23,400	$24,600
12/31/2015	16,000	19,500	82,000	78,500	48,300	51,600
12/31/2016	24,000	28,000	95,000	91,000	72,300	78,000
12/31/2017	32,000	35,600	108,000	90,000	95,100	111,600

Sumner Stores reported the following income statement information:

Account	2017	2016	2015	2014
Sales revenue	$200,000	$175,000	$160,000	$145,000
Selling, general, and administrative expenses	$ 54,000	$ 40,000	$ 36,500	$ 30,000
Income tax rate	40%	40%	40%	40%

Required »

a. Prepare the income statements under both methods for the years ended December 31, 2014, through December 31, 2016.
b. Assume that Sumner Stores changes to the FIFO basis effective January 1, 2017. Prepare the comparative income statements for the 3 years ended December 31, 2017.
c. Prepare the retained earnings column of the statement of stockholders' equity for the year ended December 31, 2017, assuming that Sumner does not present comparative statements. Sumner does not declare dividends in 2014–2017.

2 **E21-4. Change in Accounting Principle, Inventory.** Winthur Stores began operations on January 1, 2014, and adopted the FIFO method of accounting for its inventory for book and tax purposes. In 2017, it is considering a change to the average-cost method basis for book purposes only. Winthur provided the following information to assist in deciding whether to change inventory valuation techniques.

	Ending Inventory		Cost of Sales		Retained Earnings	
Year Ended	FIFO	Average Cost	FIFO	Average Cost	FIFO	Average Cost
12/31/2014	$12,000	$10,000	$74,000	$ 76,000	$ 24,600	$23,400
12/31/2015	19,500	16,000	78,500	82,000	51,600	48,300
12/31/2016	28,000	24,000	91,000	95,000	78,000	72,300
12/31/2017	35,600	32,000	90,000	108,000	111,600	95,100

Winthur Stores reported the following income statement information:

Account	2017	2016	2015	2014
Sales revenue	$200,000	$175,000	$160,000	$145,000
Selling, general, and administrative expenses	$54,000	$40,000	$36,500	$30,000
Income tax rate	40%	40%	40%	40%

Required »

a. Prepare the income statements under both methods for the years ended December 31, 2014, through December 31, 2016.
b. Assume that Winthur Stores changes to the average-cost method effective January 1, 2017. Prepare the comparative income statements for the 3 years ended December 31, 2017.
c. Prepare the retained earnings column of the statement of stockholders' equity for the year ended December 31, 2017, assuming that Winthur does not present comparative statements. Winthur does not declare dividends in 2014–2017.

3 **E21-5. Change in Estimate, Depreciation.** Cornnuto Equipment Manufacturers, Inc. (CEM) reported the net book value of a plant asset at $2,600,000 on January 1 of the current year. There is a $500,000 expected residual value, and the estimated useful life is 25 years. On January 1 of the current year, following 10 full years of depreciation, the company determined that the asset will be useful for only another 10 years and reduced the expected residual value to $100,000. The change in estimate is needed to reflect extended usage and running the factory above normal capacity to meet increased demand. CEM uses the straight-line method of depreciation. The company is subject to a 40% tax rate.

Required »

a. Determine the original cost of CEM's plant asset.
b. Compute the annual depreciation expense for the first 10 years of the asset's life.
c. Prepare the journal entry to record the change in estimate.
d. Prepare the footnote disclosure for the accounting change.

3 **E21-6. Change in Estimate, Depreciation.** Hi-Lo Corporation elected to change its method of depreciation from the double-declining balance method to the straight-line method on January 1, of the current year. It acquired the equipment 2 years ago on January 1 for $300,000. The original estimated useful life was 5 years with an original scrap value of $18,000. The company is subject to a 40% income tax rate.

Required »

a. Prepare the journal entry to record the change in depreciation method.
b. Draft a footnote disclosure for the change in depreciation method.

5 **E21-7. Error Analysis and Correction.** Feinstein and Company completed an internal audit of its bookkeeping system that uncovered several errors. It discovered the errors on December 31 before the books were closed.

a. A $45,000 payment for advertising was recorded as an asset in the account deferred advertising expense.
b. Payroll for the two weeks ending November 11 amounted to $123,500 but was never recorded. Payroll taxes withheld for this pay period were $8,500.
c. A 3-year insurance policy for $90,000 acquired on April 1 of the current year was recorded by debiting insurance expense.
d. Sales tax was not recorded separately during the year. The company is required to collect 2% sales tax on its sales. The company's credit sales amounted to $2,500,000 for the current year; there were no cash sales.

Required »

Prepare the journal entries needed to correct the errors listed.

5 **E21-8. Error Analysis and Correction.** Lombardo Lumber Company incorrectly recorded inventory in 2017. Rather than recording ending inventory as $500, Lombardo's accounting manager entered $560, overstating ending inventory by $60.

An inventory summary for 2017 and 2018 as actually recorded by the company follows.

2017		2018	
Beginning inventory	$ 200	Beginning inventory	$ 560
Purchases	+600	Purchases	+600
Available	$ 800	Available	$1,160
Ending inventory	(560)	Ending inventory	(900)
Cost of goods sold	$ 240	Cost of goods sold	$ 260

Required »

a. Prepare an analysis of this error over the 2-year period, recommend any correcting entries required to correct the inventory error, and comment on the effect of the error on gross profit. Assume that Lombardo discovered the error in 2018 before closing the books.

b. What correcting entries are necessary if Lombardo discovered the error in 2019 after closing the books for 2018?

5 **E21-9. Error Analysis and Correction.** Tuscany Timber Company incorrectly recorded inventory in 2017. Rather than recording ending inventory as $2,200, Tuscany's accounting manager entered $2,500. An inventory summary for 2017 and 2018 follows.

	2017	2018
Beginning inventory	$1,400	$2,500
Purchases	2,200	3,600
Ending inventory	2,500	3,800

Required »

a. Prepare an analysis of this error over the 2-year period, recommend any correcting entries required to correct the inventory error, and comment on the effect of the error on gross profit. Assume that Tuscany discovered the error in 2018 before closing the books.

b. What correcting entries are necessary if Tuscany discovered the error in 2019 after closing the books for 2018?

5 **E21-10. Error Analysis and Correction.** Greer Incorporated discovered the following errors on the books at the beginning of 2017:

a. Maintenance expense on account was overstated by $20,000 in 2015 and understated by $30,000 in 2016. The payables for both years are still unpaid.

b. Depreciation expense was overstated by $55,000 in 2015 and understated by $70,000 in 2016.

c. Ending inventory was understated by $120,000 in 2015 and overstated by $178,000 in 2016.

Required »

Prepare the entry required to correct these entries in 2017 when they are discovered, assuming that books have been closed for both 2015 and 2016. Greer does not prepare comparative statements.

Problems

2 **P21-1. Change in Accounting Principle, Inventory.** Second Thought Products (STP) began operations on January 1, 2017, and adopted the FIFO method of inventory valuation at that time. Management elected to change its inventory method to the average-cost method effective January 1, 2020. The new method more fairly presents the company's financial position and results of operations. The following information is available for the years ended December 31, 2017, through December 31, 2020. STP is subject to a 40% income tax rate. The company still uses the FIFO method for income tax reporting.

	Cost of Goods Sold Under	
Year	**Average Cost Method**	**FIFO Method**
2017	$176,400	$201,600
2018	117,600	134,400
2019	252,000	277,200
2020	285,600	260,400

Required »

a. Compute the cumulative effect, net of tax, for the 3-year period needed to record a change from the FIFO method to the average-cost method.
b. Prepare the journal entry to record the change in accounting for inventory valuation.
c. Indicate where STP should report the net of tax cumulative effect, assuming that the first balance sheet presented is for the year ended December 31, 2019.
d. Indicate the cost of goods sold reported on the income statement for 2017, 2018, 2019, and 2020.
e. Assume that this change in principle is considered to be impractical. Indicate the cost of goods on the income statement for 2017, 2018, 2019, and 2020.

2 **P21-2. Change in Accounting Principle, Inventory.** J&S Arnez Company began operations in 2017 and initially adopted the weighted-average method for inventory valuation. In 2019, in accordance with the inventory valuation policies followed by other companies in its industry, Arnez changed its inventory pricing to the FIFO method. The company still uses the weighted-average method of inventory valuation for income tax purposes. Arnez has a 30% tax rate. The pretax income data is reported as follows.

Year	Weighted Average	FIFO
2017	$518,000	$553,000
2018	546,000	602,000
2019	574,000	630,000

Required »

a. What is J&S Arnez's net income in 2019?
b. Compute the cumulative effect on retained earnings from the change in accounting principle from weighted average to FIFO pricing (up to but not including the year of the change).
c. Show condensed, comparative income statements for J&S Arnez Company, beginning with income before taxes, as presented on the 2019 income statement.

2 **P21-3. Change in Accounting Principle, Inventory.** Welsh, Inc. began operations January 1, 2017. During 2019, management changed its method of accounting for inventories from the average-cost method to the first-in, first-out (FIFO) method. This change is effective as of January 1, 2019.

If cost of goods sold had been determined under each of these two methods for all years of operation, the results would have been:

Cost of Goods Sold	2019	2018	2017
Average cost	$142,500	$120,000	$129,000
FIFO	90,000	72,000	78,000

The company's income statements as reported under average cost before implementing the accounting change for 2019, 2018, and 2017 follow. The income tax rate for Welsh is 40%. Welsh will continue to use average cost for income tax reporting.

Welsh, Inc.
Comparative Income Statements
For the Years Ended December 31

	2019	2018	2017
Sales	$ 525,000	$450,000	$ 420,000
Cost of Goods Sold	(142,500)	(120,000)	(129,000)
Operating Expenses	(67,500)	(49,500)	(28,500)
Income before Tax	$ 315,000	$280,500	$ 262,500
Tax Expense (40%)	(126,000)	(112,200)	(105,000)
Net Income after Tax	$ 189,000	$168,300	$ 157,500

Required »

a. Prepare the comparative income statements for Welsh after the change to FIFO.
b. Determine the after-tax cumulative effect in the retained earnings balance for the first balance sheet presented (i.e., at December 31, 2018). Welsh presents comparative balance sheets.

❷ **P21-4. Change in Accounting Principle, Leases.** Romer Corporation began operations on January 1, 2015. The company decided to lease all plant assets rather than purchase them. Romer used the operating method for all leased assets in 2015 and 2016. On January 1, 2017, a new accountant joined the company and determined that the assets should be accounted for as finance leases following U.S. GAAP. Assume that this is a correction of an error. Income before tax and lease-related expenses in 2015, 2016, and 2017 are $580,000, $600,000, and $720,000, respectively. The tax rate is 40%.

Lease-related expenses under the two methods follow:

Year	Finance Lease	Operating Lease
2015	$165,500	$118,000
2016	140,000	118,000
2017	129,000	118,000

Required »

a. Determine the amount of the prior-period adjustment in the year of the correction.
b. Prepare partial comparative income statements for the years ended December 31, 2015 through 2017.

❷ **P21-5. Change in Accounting Principle, Long-Term Construction Contracts.** Porco Construction Company initiated operations on January 1, 2016. At that time, Porco's management used the percentage-of-completion method to account for its contracts. The estimates used indicated that the contracts would generate income equally each year; the projects were 4 years in duration and were 25% complete each year. On January 1, 2019, the company switched to the completed-contract method to better reflect the company's shift in contract length. Contracts are shorter in duration and are not as material in terms of total value. Relevant income information for both methods follows. Porco is subject to a 40% income tax rate. Assume that Porco can use the percentage-of-completion method for tax purposes and on the company's tax returns after the change for financial reporting purposes.

Year	Percentage-of-Completion Method (Old Method)	Completed-Contract Method (New Method)
2016	$88,560	$ 0
2017	88,560	0
2018	88,560	0
2019	88,560	354,240

Required »

a. Compute the cumulative effect after tax.
b. Prepare the journal entry to record the change in method effective January 1, 2019.
c. Prepare the accounting change footnote in the financial statements for the year of the change.

❷❸ **P21-6. Change in Estimate, Inventory, Bad Debt Expense.** Rocket Man, Incorporated provided the following financial statement information for 2018:

Credit sales	$2,500,000
Retained earnings, January 1, 2018	1,600,000
Sales	3,000,000
Selling and administrative expenses	480,000
Restructuring gain (pretax)	720,000
Cash dividends declared	190,000
Cost of goods sold	1,755,000
Error correction: 2013 rent was unpaid and unrecorded	40,000
Interest income	480,000
Interest expense	820,000
Gain on sale of investments (pre-tax)	500,000

- On January 1, 2018, Rocket Man changed its plant and equipment accounting for depreciation from the double-declining balance method to the straight-line method. Rocket Man purchased the assets on January 1, 2017 for $600,000; they had no scrap value and useful lives of 10 years. The balance in the accumulated depreciation account at January 1, 2018 amounted to $120,000. Rocket Man recorded the straight-line depreciation expense of $53,333 in 2018 and included it in the $480,000 reported for selling and administrative expenses. Depreciation expense would have been $96,000 if Rocket Man still used the double-declining balance method.
- Bad debt expense for 2018 of $50,000 is included in selling, general, and administrative expenses on the income statement. Rocket Man uses the percentage of accounts receivable method of estimating bad debt expense. The estimated percentage was 5% in both 2016 and 2017 but changed to 10% in 2018. At December 31, 2018, the Accounts Receivable balance is $600,000, and the Allowance for Uncollectible Accounts (before adjustment) was $10,000 credit balance.

Required »

a. Assuming a tax rate of 40%, prepare the multiple-step income statement for Rocket Man for the year ended December 31, 2018.
b. Compute the cumulative effect of the accounting changes made in 2018.
c. Prepare the journal entries to record the accounting changes made in 2018.
d. Prepare the footnote disclosures required for the accounting changes made in 2018.
e. Prepare the retained earnings column of the statement of stockholders' equity for the year ended December 31, 2018.

❷❸ **P21-7. Change in Accounting Principle, Change in Estimate.** Jupiter Electric Company provided the following financial statement information for 2018 before considering the accounting changes that follow:

Retained earnings, January 1, 2018	$ 49,540
Sales	308,000
Selling and administrative expenses	54,000
Cash dividends declared	15,000
Cost of goods sold (weighted-average cost)	182,000
Interest income	3,300
Interest expense	8,200

- The company failed to record $7,000 interest expense on a zero-coupon bond in 2014. The bonds are still outstanding.
- The company changed its accounting method to FIFO from the weighted-average method in 2018. Beginning inventory would have been $3,000 higher and cost of goods sold would have been $3,000 lower in 2018 using FIFO.
- Bad debt expense is included in selling and administrative expenses on the income statement. Jupiter uses the percentage of accounts receivable method of estimating bad debt expense. At December 31, 2018, the Allowance for Uncollectible Accounts is $5,280 (credit balance), based on the estimates of uncollectible accounts for the quarterly financial statements. At December 31, 2018, the company now believes the quarterly estimates were too high and the Allowance for Uncollectible Accounts should be $2,640 with a credit balance.
- Jupiter's tax rate is 40%.

Required »

a. Prepare the journal entries to record the accounting changes made in 2018.
b. Compute the cumulative effect of the accounting changes made in 2018.
c. Prepare the multiple-step income statement for Jupiter for the year ended December 31, 2018.
d. Prepare the footnote disclosures required for the accounting changes made in 2018.
e. Prepare the retained earnings column of the statement of stockholders' equity for the year ended December 31, 2018.

Excel Project

Autograded Excel Project available in **MyLab Accounting**

CASES

Judgment Case

Judgment Case: Materiality and Error Corrections

SAB Topic 1.M., *Assessing Materiality*, found in FASB ASC 250-10-S99-1, presents the SEC's views on the issue of materiality in the financial statements. Based on this document, indicate whether each of the following errors is material and thus should be corrected.

1. Talky Solutions discovered several large errors. One error overstates inventory and understates cost of goods sold by 8% of uncorrected net income. The other error understates sales revenue and understates accounts receivable by 8.5% of uncorrected net income. Consequently, the two errors combined result in a slight understatement of net income.
2. Net income for the current year for Walker Electric is $1,500,000. It has discovered an error that affects its contingent liability account in the amount of $35,000. The error understates the liability account and overstates net income. Walker has also discovered an error that affects its accounts payable account in the amount of $35,000. The error understates the liability account and overstates net income.
3. Net income for CoCo Corporation is $7,000,000 in the current year. CoCo has a simple capital structure with 1,000,000 shares outstanding, so earnings per share is $7.00 per share. Earnings per share was $6.94 last year and $6.90 the year before that. Analyst forecasts for CoCo's earnings per share this year will be $6.98. CoCo discovered an error of $40,000 that affects its inventory accounts and overstates net income.
4. Net income for Soda, Inc. is $5,000,000 in the current year. Soda has a simple capital structure with 1,000,000 shares outstanding, so earnings per share is $5 per share. Earnings per share was $4.95 last year and $4.93 the year before that. Soda discovered an error of $20,000 in its estimate of bad debts that overstates income.

Financial Statement Analysis Case

Financial Statement Analysis Case

The 2013 financial statements of ***Lexmark International, Inc***., a leading developer, manufacturer, and supplier of printing, imaging, and device management, indicated that it reported an accounting policy change. Use the following information and excerpts from its financial statements to analyze the change and its effect on the financial statements.

a. What accounting policy did ***Lexmark*** change?
b. What reason(s) does ***Lexmark*** give for making this change?
c. What method did ***Lexmark*** use to account for this change?
d. What was ***Lexmark's*** net income in 2013, 2012, and 2011 under the new accounting policy? If Lexmark did not change its accounting policy, what would its 2013, 2012, and 2011 net income have been? Comment on the difference.
e. What was ***Lexmark's*** difference in pension expense in 2013, 2012, and 2011 under the two accounting policies? Using the new policy, is pension expense higher or lower in 2013, 2012, and 2011? Did ***Lexmark*** experience net actuarial gains or losses in 2013, 2012, and 2011?

Accounting Change, ***Lexmark Communications, Inc.,*** Financial Statements, December 31, 2013

NOTE 2: Significant Accounting Policies (excerpt)

The Company's significant accounting policies are an integral part of its financial statements.

Change in Accounting Policy for Pension and Other Postretirement Plans

During the fourth quarter of 2013, Lexmark changed its accounting methodology for recognizing costs for all of its company sponsored U.S. and international pension and postretirement benefit obligations. Previously, the Company recognized the net actuarial gains and losses as a component of stockholders' equity within the Consolidated Statements of Financial Position. On an annual basis the net gains and losses . . . were amortized into operating results (to the extent that they exceeded 10% of the higher of the market-related value of plan assets or the projected benefit obligation of each respective plan) over the average future service period of active employees within the related plans. . . .

Under the new accounting method, Lexmark immediately recognizes the change in the fair value of plan assets and net actuarial gains and losses in pension and other postretirement benefit plan costs annually in the fourth quarter of each year and in any quarter during which a remeasurement is triggered. The remaining components of net periodic benefit cost, primarily net service cost, interest cost and the expected return on plan assets, are recorded on a quarterly basis as ongoing benefit costs. . . . While Lexmark's historical policy of recognizing pension and other postretirement benefit plan asset and actuarial gains and losses was considered acceptable under U.S. GAAP, the Company believes that the new policy is preferable as it eliminates the delay in recognizing changes in the fair value of plan assets and actuarial gains and losses within operating results. This change also improves transparency within Lexmark's operating results by immediately recognizing the effects of economic and interest rate trends on plan investments and assumptions in the year these gains and losses are actually incurred. This change in accounting policy has been applied retrospectively, adjusting all prior periods presented.

Source: Accounting Change, Lexmark Communications, Inc., Financial Statements, December 31, 2013. http://investor.lexmark.com/phoenix.zhtml%3Fc%3D92369%26p%3Dirol-reportsannual

The following summarizes the impact of all adjustments made to the financial statements presented (amounts in millions):

For the year ended December 31 (in millions)		Previous Policy	New Policy
2013	Earnings before income taxes	$252.7	$368.4
	Net earnings	190.6	261.8
2012	Earnings before income taxes	158.0	162.4
	Net earnings	106.3	107.6
2011	Earnings before income taxes	413.6	338.4
	Net earnings	320.0	275.2

Surfing the Standards Case

Surfing the Standards: Change in Accounting Principle

1. Read FASB ASC 250-10-S99 to respond to the following question. ASCO Recordings has decided to change its inventory system from the LIFO method to the FIFO method for the 2015 fiscal year. Because it does not carry much inventory, the change in principle does not have a material effect on the financial statements of prior periods. Accordingly, it plans not to adjust comparative financial statements presented but rather to report the cumulative effect of the change through retained earnings as of the beginning of the 2015 fiscal year. Is this approach permissible? If not, how must ASCO Recordings report this change in principle?
2. Read FASB ASC 250-10-45 to respond to the following question. Basty Needleworks, a calendar-year firm, has decided to change its inventory system from the FIFO method to the LIFO method. It made

this decision in July 2015, and thus plans to report under LIFO for the first time in its third quarter of 2015 filings. Based on the impracticability rules associated with retrospective application, it plans to use the prospective method of reporting for the change in principle beginning in the third quarter. Is this approach permissible? If not, how must Basty report this change in principle?

Basis for Conclusions Case

Basis for Conclusions: Change in Accounting Principle

Read the Basis for Conclusions (paragraphs B1 through B38) in FASB's *Statement of Financial Accounting Standards No. 154* to respond to the following questions.

1. When debating the issues of FASB's "Accounting Changes and Error Corrections," *Statement of Financial Accounting Standards No. 154*, the Board concluded that the retrospective method is the correct approach to use for changes in accounting principles. Why did FASB reach this conclusion?
2. Changes in accounting principle can have both direct and indirect effects. The direct effects are the impact on the related balance sheet and income statement accounts. Firms always apply direct effects retrospectively unless it is impractical to do so. Indirect effects are changes to current or future cash flows that result from the change in accounting principle. Firms apply indirect effects only prospectively. There is some disagreement as to whether indirect effects should be applied retrospectively or prospectively. What are the arguments for each reporting method?

22 The Statement of Cash Flows

LEARNING OBJECTIVES

1. State the purpose of the statement of cash flows and define cash and cash equivalents.
2. Describe the format of the statement of cash flows, including classification of activities into operating, investing, and financing sections; the reconciliation of cash and cash equivalents; and the disclosure of significant noncash investing and financing transactions.
3. Understand and use the conceptual model based on the accounting equation to prepare the statement of cash flows.
4. Explain and prepare the operating cash flows section of the statement of cash flows using the indirect and direct methods.
5. Describe and illustrate the investing cash flows section of the statement of cash flows.
6. Describe and illustrate the financing cash flows section of the statement of cash flows.
7. Discuss and illustrate the reporting of complex transactions in determining cash flows.
8. Detail required disclosures related to the statement of cash flows.

Bloomberg/Contributor/Getty Images

Introduction

CASH, ONE OF A COMPANY'S most important assets, is critical to successful operations and growth. Although cash is only one line on the balance sheet, a separate financial statement—the statement of cash flows—is devoted to explaining a company's sources and uses of cash.

Chapter 6 explained that the statement of cash flows summarizes changes in a firm's cash inflows and outflows over a period of time for operating, investing, and financing activities. Thus, the statement of cash flows plays a pivotal role in completing the financial reporting cycle and enhancing the articulation among the financial statements.

The statement of cash flows explains and reconciles net income to net cash provided by operating activities and reconciles significant changes in balance sheet items. To illustrate, consider ***Alphabet Inc***., the parent company of ***Google***. In 2016, its statement of cash flows indicated that it had generated $36,036 million of net cash from operations. Yet, ***Alphabet's*** net income of $19,478 million was lower than its net cash provided by operating activities. ***Alphabet's*** statement of cash flows indicates that the difference between the net income and net cash provided by operating activities was due mainly to noncash expenses such as depreciation and amortization expenses and stock-based compensation expense. It is common for a growing business to earn lower or no income but to generate positive operating cash flows as is the case with ***Alphabet***. The company used this cash to purchase property and equipment, invest in securities, and acquire other businesses.

Throughout this chapter, we briefly revisit the topics covered in Chapter 6's discussion of the statement of cash flows, including its purposes; classification of cash flows into operating, investing, and financing activities; and the direct and indirect methods of reporting cash flows. We also discuss additional details focusing on the preparation of the statement of cash flows. We develop a conceptual model based on the accounting equation that provides the logic underlying the preparation of the statement of cash flows. Then, we examine the cash flow statement effects on complex topics we have discussed throughout the text and conclude by addressing disclosure requirements for the cash flow statement.

In general, preparation of the statement of cash flows under IFRS and U.S. GAAP is quite similar. We identify significant differences between U.S. GAAP and IFRS when appropriate. «

1 State the purpose of the statement of cash flows and define cash and cash equivalents.

Overview of the Statement of Cash Flows

The statement of cash flows summarizes a firm's cash inflows and outflows over a period of time. Reconciling the change in the cash balance (where cash is defined as cash, cash equivalents, restricted cash, and restricted cash equivalents) to the cash flows for the period enhances the articulation among the financial statements. The statement is also useful in explaining and reconciling many other significant changes in balance sheet items, particularly when the statement is used in conjunction with the other financial statements and related footnote disclosures.

THE CONCEPTUAL FRAMEWORK CONNECTION
Statement of Cash Flows

The conceptual framework's financial reporting objective is to provide existing and potential investors, lenders, and creditors with useful information to help them assess an entity's future net cash flows. Investment decisions by market participants in a company depend on the expected risks and returns. Consequently, it is important for investors to have information about an entity's cash flows. Information in the statement of cash flows explains how the entity obtains and uses cash, including information about debt issuances, repayments, and distributions to equity investors. This information helps market participants understand the operations of the entity and evaluate its liquidity and solvency.

Purposes of the Cash Flow Statement

The primary purpose of the statement of cash flows is to provide information about a firm's cash receipts and cash payments from its operating, investing, and financing activities over a period of time. The statement of cash flows assists financial statement users in:

1. Assessing the ability of the firm to generate future cash flows, particularly related to its operating activities
2. Evaluating the ability of the entity to meet its obligations and pay dividends
3. Determining the entity's need for external financing
4. Understanding the differences between net income and the associated cash receipts and payments
5. Identifying the entity's investing and financing transactions during the period

Cash and Cash Equivalents

The cash flow statement explains the change in cash and *cash equivalents* (including restricted cash and equivalents) during the period.[1] Cash equivalents are short-term, highly liquid investments with original maturities of 3 months or less when acquired. The acquisition and disposal of short-term investments in cash and cash equivalents is part of the firm's overall cash management activities. Exhibit 22.1 provides a description of both cash and cash equivalents.

[1]For the remainder of this chapter, we assume that cash and cash equivalents includes both restricted and non-restricted cash and cash equivalents.

EXHIBIT 22.1 Cash and Cash Equivalents

Item	Description
Cash	Coins, currency, and bank deposits as well as negotiable instruments such as checks and money orders
Cash Equivalents	Short-term, highly liquid investments with original maturities of 3 months or less, including: • Treasury bills • Commercial paper • Money market funds

Original maturity is the length of time between the investment's purchase date by the firm and the date of maturity. For example, a 3-year Treasury instrument purchased with 1 month left until maturity qualifies as a cash equivalent whereas a 3-year Treasury instrument acquired at issuance (with 3 years left until maturity) is not a cash equivalent. Exhibit 22.2 illustrates ***Alphabet's*** disclosure of its definition of cash and cash and equivalents from its 2016 annual report.

EXHIBIT 22.2 Cash and Cash Equivalents Disclosure (excerpt), ***Alphabet Inc.***, Financial Statements, December 31, 2016

Cash, Cash Equivalents, and Marketable Securities

We invest our excess cash primarily in debt investments including those of the U.S. government and its agencies, debt instruments, corporate debt securities, agency mortgage-backed securities, money market and other funds, municipal securities, time deposits, asset backed securities, and debt instruments issued by foreign governments.

We classify all investments that are readily convertible to known amounts of cash and have stated maturities of three months or less from the date of purchase as cash equivalents and those with stated maturities of greater than three months as marketable securities.

Source: Alphabet Inc., Cash and Cash Equivalents Disclosure Excerpt, Financial Statements, December 31, 2016. https://abc.xyz/investor/pdf/2016_google_annual_report.pdf

Cash Equivalents under IFRS

The U.S. GAAP and IFRS definitions of cash equivalents are similar with the exception of *bank overdrafts*. A **bank overdraft** occurs when the balance in a bank account falls below zero. U.S. GAAP does not specifically address bank overdrafts, although they are typically considered to be liabilities. So, a company cannot report a negative cash balance on the asset side of the balance sheet under U.S. GAAP.

Under IFRS, firms include bank overdrafts as cash and cash equivalents and net them against the positive balances included in cash and cash equivalents.

2 Describe the format of the statement of cash flows, including classification of activities into operating, investing, and financing sections; the reconciliation of cash and cash equivalents; and the disclosure of significant noncash investing and financing transactions.

Format of the Cash Flow Statement

Before examining the preparation of the statement of cash flows, we outline the key sections and classifications used in the statement of cash flows.

Sections in the Statement of Cash Flows

The statement of cash flows is divided into three sections.

1. Classification of cash flows by three major activities:
   - Operating activities, which include cash flows that relate to the production and delivery of goods and services
   - Investing activities, which include cash flows that relate to the acquisition and disposal of noncurrent assets, such as plant and equipment and long-term investments, and from the acquisition and disposal of short-term investments not classified as cash equivalents

- Financing activities, which include cash flows that relate to the cash receipts and payments of principal from the short- and long-term debt and equity financing. Financing activities also include dividend distributions to owners.

2. Reconciliation of cash flows during the period to the change in cash and cash equivalents
3. Disclosure of interest paid and taxes paid for cash flow statements prepared under the indirect method and significant noncash investing and financing transactions

In ***Alphabet's*** statement of cash flows in Exhibit 22.3, divisions of the statement of cash flows into cash from operating, investing, and financing activities are in bold print. The line items in each section are added together with net cash flows from operating, investing, and financing activities, summing to $36,036, $(31,165), and $(8,332) (all in millions), respectively, in the year ended December 31, 2016. The total of cash flows from these three major activities (plus exchange rate effects) decreases cash and cash equivalents by $3,631 million in 2016. Next, ***Alphabet*** presents the reconciliation of cash and cash equivalents balances during the period. Adding the beginning cash and cash equivalents of $16,549 million to the $3,631 million decrease in cash and cash equivalents during the year results in the ending cash and cash equivalents balance of $12,918 million. Of course, $12,918 million is the amount of cash and cash equivalents ***Alphabet*** reports on its December 31, 2016, balance sheet.

After the reconciliation, ***Alphabet*** discloses supplemental cash flow information, including cash paid for taxes of $1,643 million and cash paid for interest of $84 million.

Statement of Cash Flows Classifications

Next, we discuss in detail the classifications used in the statement of cash flows. The classifications into operating, investing, and financing activities indicate the source and use of each cash flow, enabling financial statement users to assess the firm's ability to repay principal and interest and to pay dividends in the future. For example, cash generated from operating activities is of higher quality than cash generated from borrowed funds because it is more likely to recur in future periods. Firms disclose significant investing and financing activities that do not involve cash as supplemental information.

Exhibit 22.4 summarizes cash inflows and outflows from operating, investing, and financing activities.

Classification of Dividends, Interest, and Taxes

Companies classify the following items relating to dividends, interest, and taxes in operating cash flows:

1. Cash receipts from interest and dividends
2. Cash payments for taxes
3. Cash payments for interest

Cash payments for dividends to owners are classified as financing activities.

IFRS Classification of Dividends, Interest, and Taxes. In contrast to U.S. GAAP, recall from Chapter 6 that IFRS allows companies discretion in classifying some items as operating, investing, or financing activities. Exhibit 22.5 compares the classification options under U.S. GAAP and IFRS.

EXHIBIT 22.3 Statement of Cash Flows, ***Alphabet Inc.***, Financial Statements, December 31, 2016

Alphabet Inc.
Consolidated Statements of Cash Flows
(In millions)

	Year Ended December 31		
	2014	**2015**	**2016**
Operating activities			
Net income	$14,136	$16,348	$19,478
Adjustments:			
Depreciation and amortization of property and equipment	3,523	4,132	5,267
Amortization of intangible and other assets	1,456	931	877
Stock-based compensation expense	4,279	5,203	6,703
Excess tax benefits from stock-based award activities			
Deferred income taxes	(104)	(179)	(38)
Gain on divestiture of businesses	(740)	0	0
(Gain) loss on marketable and non-marketable investments, net	(390)	334	275
Other	192	212	174
Changes in assets and liabilities, net of effects of acquisitions:			
Accounts receivable	(1,641)	(2,094)	(2,578)
Income taxes, net	591	(179)	3,125
Prepaid revenue share, expenses and other assets	459	(318)	312
Accounts payable	436	203	110
Accrued expenses and other liabilities	757	1,597	1,515
Accrued revenue share	245	339	593
Deferred revenue	(175)	43	223
Net cash provided by operating activities	23,024	26,572	36,036
Investing activities			
Purchases of property and equipment	(11,014)	(9,950)	(10,212)
Proceeds from disposals of property and equipment	55	35	240
Purchases of marketable securities	(56,310)	(74,368)	(84,509)
Maturities and sales of marketable securities	51,315	62,905	66,895
Purchases of non-marketable equity investments	(1,440)	(2,326)	(1,109)
Maturities and sales of non-marketable investments	213	154	494
Cash collateral related to securities lending	1,403	(350)	(2,428)
Investments in reverse repurchase agreements	(775)	425	450
Proceeds from divestiture of businesses	386	0	0
Acquisitions, net of cash acquired, and purchases of intangibles and other assets	(4,888)	(236)	(986)
Net cash used in investing activities	(21,055)	(23,711)	(31,165)
Financing activities			
Net payments related to stock-based award activities	(2,069)	(2,375)	(3,304)
Adjustment Payment to Class C capital stockholders	0	(47)	0
Repurchases of capital stock	0	(1,780)	(3,693)
Proceeds from issuance of debt, net of costs	11,625	13,705	8,729
Repayments of debt	(11,643)	(13,728)	(10,064)
Net cash used in financing activities	(2,087)	(4,225)	(8,332)
Effect of exchange rate changes on cash and cash equivalents	(433)	(434)	(170)
Net increase (decrease) in cash and cash equivalents	(551)	(1,798)	(3,631)
Cash and cash equivalents at beginning of period	18,898	18,347	16,549
Cash and cash equivalents at end of period	$ 18,347	$16,549	$12,918
Supplemental disclosures of cash flow information			
Cash paid for taxes	$ 3,138	$ 3,651	$ 1,643
Cash paid for interest	$ 86	$ 96	$ 84

***Source*:** Alphabet Inc., Statement of Cash Flows, Financial Statements, December 31, 2016. https://abc.xyz/investor/pdf/2016_google_annual_report.pdf

EXHIBIT 22.4 Cash Flows from Operating, Investing, and Financing Activities

Cash Receipts (Inflows)	Cash Payments (Outflows)
Operating Activities	
From the sale of goods and services	To suppliers for inventory, utilities, services, etc.
From interest and dividend income	To employees for services
	To government agencies for taxes
	To creditors for interest paid
Investing Activities	
From the sale of property, plant, and equipment	For acquiring property, plant, and equipment
From the sale of debt and equity security investments[2]	For acquiring debt or equity security investments
	For extending credit to others
From the collection of principal payments from loans made to others	
Financing Activities	
From the issuance of debt securities	To redeem or retire debt
From the issuance of common and preferred stock	To purchase treasury stock or retire capital stock
From the resale of treasury stock	To make dividend distributions to shareholders

EXHIBIT 22.5 Classification of Dividends, Interest, and Taxes

	Standard	
Activities	**U.S. GAAP**	**IFRS**
Cash receipts from interest and dividends	Operating	Operating or investing
Cash payments for taxes	Operating	Operating unless they can be specifically identified with financing or investing activities
Cash payments for interest	Operating	Operating or financing
Cash payments for dividends to owners	Financing	Operating or financing

Reconciliation of Cash and Cash Equivalents

A firm adds the net cash inflow or outflow from operating, investing, and financing activities to obtain the net increase/decrease in cash and cash equivalents for the period. It then reconciles the net increase/decrease in cash and cash equivalents for the period to the ending cash and cash equivalents balance for the period, using a format similar to the following:

	Net Cash Provided (Used) by Operating Activities
Plus	Net cash provided (used) by investing activities
Plus	Net cash provided (used) by financing activities
Equals	Net increase (decrease) in cash and cash equivalents
Plus	Beginning cash and cash equivalents
Equals	Ending cash and cash equivalents

[2]Cash payments and receipts related to investments in debt securities that are classified as trading securities can be classified as operating or investing activities based on management's intent.

Firms present the reconciliation at the end of the cash flow statement. Exhibit 22.3 shows the reconciliation section of ***Alphabet's*** statement of cash flows. In 2016, ***Alphabet's*** net decrease in cash and cash equivalents was $(3,631) million (including foreign exchange effects), which it adds to beginning cash and cash equivalents of $16,549 million to arrive at the ending cash and cash equivalents of $12,918 million.

IFRS Reconciliation of Cash and Cash Equivalents. IFRS also requires a reconciliation of the net increase (decrease) in cash and cash equivalents for the period to the ending balance of cash and cash equivalents. However, IFRS does not require that the increase or decrease in cash and cash equivalents explained in the statement of cash flows agree to a single line item in the balance sheet because cash management practices and banking arrangements differ around the world. If a company uses a different cash and cash equivalents amount, it must provide a reconciliation of the components of cash and cash equivalents to the amounts presented on the statement of financial position.

Significant Noncash Investing and Financing Transactions

A firm generally engages in many significant investing and financing transactions that do not have immediate cash flow consequences. For example, the acquisition of a plant asset financed by the issuance of long-term debt does not involve the receipt or disbursement of cash. These noncash items are not incorporated in the statement of cash flows. Instead, firms disclose them in a footnote or a separate schedule (if material). Other common significant noncash investing and financing activities include:

- Stock dividends
- Conversion of bonds into capital stock
- Finance lease commencement
- Plant asset exchanges and other nonmonetary exchanges

A company can report significant noncash investing and financing transactions at the end of its statement of cash flows or in a note to the financial statements. For example, ***Amazon.com Inc.*** reported about $4 billion as a significant noncash investing and financing transaction from the investment in property and equipment that was financed through finance leases in a noncash transaction.

❸ Understand and use the conceptual model based on the accounting equation to prepare the statement of cash flows.

Conceptual Model for the Statement of Cash Flows

In the remainder of the chapter, we explain how to prepare a statement of cash flows. We begin with a conceptual model for the statement of cash flows and follow with a discussion of each section of the cash flows statement.

Firms can prepare the cash flows statement based on changes in balance sheet accounts. We begin with the accounting equation in Equation 22.1.

$$\text{Assets} = \text{Liabilities} + \text{Stockholders' Equity} \tag{22.1}$$

Next in Equation 22.2, we disaggregate each element of the balance sheet equation into its main components.[3] The restated balance sheet equation is as follows:

$$\text{Cash} + \text{OCA} + \text{NCA} = \text{CL} + \text{NCL} + \text{CS} + \text{RE} \tag{22.2}$$

OCA = Other Current Assets
NCA = Noncurrent Assets
CL = Current Liabilities
NCL = Noncurrent Liabilities
CS = Capital Stock
RE = Retained Earnings

[3]For simplicity, we do not include accumulated other comprehensive income as a component of stockholders' equity.

Subtracting OCA and NCA from both sides of the equation solves for cash as in Equation 22.3.

$$\text{Cash} = \text{CL} + \text{NCL} - \text{OCA} - \text{NCA} + \text{CS} + \text{RE} \quad (22.3)$$

Taking the changes in each equation component creates a model for the statement of cash flows.

$$\Delta\text{Cash} = \Delta\text{CL} + \Delta\text{NCL} - \Delta\text{OCA} - \Delta\text{NCA} + \Delta\text{CS} + \Delta\text{RE} \quad (22.4)$$

Equation 22.4 indicates that the change in cash is based on the changes in all balance sheet accounts. For example, consider accounts payable, a current liability (CL). If accounts payable increase, there is a positive effect on cash flows. Conversely, cash flows decrease by the acquisition (increase) of a noncurrent asset.

For each account, the firm identifies whether the change relates to operating, investing, or financing activities. For example, accounts receivable and accounts payable relate to operating activities. Bonds payable and treasury stock relate to financing activities. Some changes in account balances can relate to more than one activity, and other changes may relate to noncash adjustments as we discuss later in the chapter along with additional complexities.[4]

4 Explain and prepare the operating cash flows section of the statement of cash flows using the indirect and direct methods.

Operating Cash Flows

There are two acceptable formats for the operating section in the statement of cash flows: the indirect method and the direct method. The two methods report the same amount of net cash provided by operating activities using different approaches. Standard setters prefer the direct method, but it is currently less popular in practice than the indirect method.

The Indirect Method

Under the indirect method (also referred to as the reconciliation format), firms reconcile net income to net cash provided by operating activities by making two types of adjustments:

1. Adjustments for noncash revenues, expenses, and other gains and losses
2. Adjustments for changes in current assets and current liabilities

To adjust net income to net cash provided by operating activities, firms add noncash expenses and losses back to net income. Conversely, firms subtract any noncash revenues or gains from net income to arrive at net cash provided by operating activities.[5]

Equation 22.4 illustrated the effects of changes in current assets and liabilities:

1. Increases in current liabilities cause operating cash flows to be higher than accrual-basis income.
2. Decreases in current liabilities cause operating cash flows to be lower than accrual-basis income.
3. Increases in current assets cause operating cash flows to be lower than accrual-basis income.
4. Decreases in current assets cause operating cash flows to be higher than accrual-basis income.

Exhibit 22.6 shows the effects on operating cash flows under the indirect method of changes in specific common current assets and current liabilities.

[4]The change in accumulated other comprehensive income does not actually enter into the preparation of the cash flow statement because OCI transactions are noncash, and we begin the preparation of the cash flow statement with net income, not OCI.

[5]The adjustments needed for gains and losses on sales of noncurrent assets and the cash flow effects of these adjustments will be discussed later in the chapter.

EXHIBIT 22.6 The Effects of Changes in Current Assets and Current Liabilities

Current Asset/ Liability	Increase/ Decrease	Effect on Cash Flows	Rationale	Action
Trade receivables	Increase	Decrease	An increase in trade receivables represents uncollected sales.	Deduct the amount of the increase from net income to adjust sales to the amount of cash collected from customers.
	Decrease	Increase	A decrease in trade receivables indicates that all current-year sales were collected as well as a portion of prior-years sales.	Add the amount of the decrease back to net income to adjust sales to the amount of cash collected from customers.
Inventory	Increase	Decrease	An increase in inventory indicates that the company acquired inventory to cover the cost of goods sold and increased inventory held in the warehouse. The increase in warehouse inventory results in additional cash outflow to pay for this inventory.	Deduct the amount from net income to adjust cost of goods sold to cash paid for purchases of inventory.
	Decrease	Increase	A decrease in inventory indicates that of the cost of inventory sold this year, some of the units sold were purchased in prior years.	Add the amount back to net income to adjust the cost of goods sold to the cash paid for inventory.
Prepaid expenses	Increase	Decrease	An increase in prepaid expenses is a cash outflow that appears on the balance sheet and does not affect net income. However, the cash is paid as part of operations.	Deduct the increase in prepaid expenses from net income to adjust to the amount of cash paid for operating expenses.
	Decrease	Increase	A decrease in prepaid expenses represents a cash outflow made in a previous period that is reflected as an expense on the income statement in the current period.	Add the decreased amount back to net income to arrive at cash paid for operating expenses.
Accounts payable	Increase	Increase	An accounts payable increase represents invoices for inventory not paid in the current year.	Add the increase in accounts payable to net income to adjust cost of goods sold to cash paid for inventory acquired.
	Decrease	Decrease	If accounts payable decreases, the current invoices as well as a portion of last year's invoices were paid.	Deduct this decrease from net income to arrive at cash paid for inventory acquired.
Accrued expenses	Increase	Increase	An accrued expense increase represents operating expenses not paid in the current year.	Add the increase in accrued expenses to net income to adjust operating expenses to cash paid to suppliers.
	Decrease	Decrease	Decreases in accrued expenses indicate that this year's operating expenses were paid in cash as well as a portion of prior years' expenses.	Deduct the decrease in accrued expenses from net income to adjust operating expenses to cash paid to suppliers.

Example 22.1 demonstrates preparing the operating cash flows section of the cash flow statement.

EXAMPLE 22.1 Operating Cash Flows: Indirect Method

PROBLEM: Uniform Direct, Inc. presented the following income statement and selected balance sheet accounts. Prepare the operating cash flows section of the cash flow statement using the indirect method.

Uniform Direct, Inc.
Income Statement

Sales Revenue	$1,345,000
Cost of Goods Sold	852,000
Gross Profit	493,000
Selling Expenses*	57,000
General and Administrative Expenses	112,000
Depreciation Expense	27,000
Operating Income	297,000
Interest Expense	10,000
Interest Revenue	6,000
Income before Taxes	293,000
Income Tax Expense	85,000
Net Income	$ 208,000

*Includes $23,000 expense for stock-based compensation and $34,000 of wage expense.

Selected Balance Sheet Accounts

	Ending	Beginning
Accounts Receivable, net	$ 15,250	$ 20,000
Interest Receivable	200	1,000
Inventory	575,300	562,400
Prepaid Expenses	11,590	12,450
Accounts Payable	52,000	55,670
Wages Payable	5,600	5,400
Interest Payable	2,000	2,250
Income Taxes Payable	35,500	43,200
Accrued Liabilities	15,330	13,830

SOLUTION: We begin with net income and adjust for noncash expenses. From the income statement and additional information, there are the following noncash expenses:

- Depreciation expense of $27,000
- Stock-based compensation expense of $23,000

We add these noncash expenses back to net income because although they reduce income, they do not generate a cash outflow. There are no noncash revenues to include in the adjustments.

We then adjust for changes in the current assets and liabilities according to Equation 22.4 and Exhibit 22.6. The following table identifies the balance sheet accounts, the change in each account, the parts of Equation 22.4 relating to the account, and how the change is presented in the operating cash flow section of the statement of cash flows.

Account	Ending Balance	Beginning Balance	Increase (Decrease) in Account Balance	Equation 22.4	Effect on Statement
Accounts Receivable, net	$ 15,250	$ 20,000	$ (4,750)	ΔCASH = − ΔOCA	Increase
Interest Receivable	200	1,000	(800)	ΔCASH = − ΔOCA	Increase
Inventory	575,300	562,400	12,900	ΔCASH = − ΔOCA	Decrease
Prepaid Expenses	11,590	12,450	(860)	ΔCASH = − ΔOCA	Increase
Accounts Payable	52,000	55,670	(3,670)	ΔCASH = ΔCL	Decrease
Wages Payable	5,600	5,400	200	ΔCASH = ΔCL	Increase
Interest Payable	2,000	2,250	(250)	ΔCASH = ΔCL	Decrease
Income Taxes Payable	35,500	43,200	(7,700)	ΔCASH = ΔCL	Decrease
Accrued Liabilities	15,330	13,830	1,500	ΔCASH = ΔCL	Increase

The operating activities section of the statement of cash flows follows.

Uniform Direct, Inc.
Statement of Cash Flows (Partial)

Operating Activities	
Net Income	$208,000
Adjustments to Reconcile Net Income to Net Cash Provided by Operating Activities	
Depreciation Expense	27,000
Compensation Expense – Stock Options	23,000
Changes in Operating Working Capital Accounts	
Decrease in Accounts Receivable	4,750
Decrease in Interest Receivable	800
Increase in Inventory	(12,900)
Decrease in Prepaid Expenses	860
Decrease in Accounts Payable	(3,670)
Increase in Wages Payable	200
Decrease in Interest Payable	(250)
Decrease in Income Taxes Payable	(7,700)
Increase in Accrued Liabilities	1,500
Net Cash Provided by Operating Activities	$241,590

The Indirect Method under IFRS. IFRS does not specify the income items to reconcile to operating cash flows. Where U.S. GAAP requires that firms reconcile net income to operating cash flows, IFRS allows reporters to choose the income starting point. For example, a company can begin the reconciliation under IFRS with operating income (instead of net income).

An IFRS reporter choosing to reconcile operating income to operating cash flows adjusts for cash inflows and outflows related to all items that are presented after operating income on the income statement. For example, items commonly reported after operating income are taxes paid, interest paid, and interest received. For these items, the actual cash flows are included in the operating cash flows section. Example 22.2 illustrates the operating section of the indirect method with operating income as the starting point.

EXAMPLE 22.2 Operating Cash Flows: IFRS Indirect Method

PROBLEM: Uniform Direct, Inc. presented the following income statement and select balance sheet accounts. Prepare the operating cash flows section of the cash flow statement assuming that Uniform is an IFRS reporter that begins its operating section of the cash flows statement with operating income. Uniform uses the indirect method and treats interest expense, interest revenue, and tax expense as operating activities.

Uniform Direct, Inc.
Income Statement

Sales Revenue	$1,345,000
Cost of Goods Sold	852,000
Gross Profit	493,000
Selling Expenses*	57,000
General and Administrative Expenses	112,000
Depreciation Expense	27,000
Operating Income	297,000
Interest Expense	10,000
Interest Revenue	6,000
Income before Taxes	293,000
Income Tax Expense	85,000
Net Income	$ 208,000

*Includes $23,000 expense for stock-based compensation and $34,000 of wage expense.

Selected Balance Sheet Accounts

	Ending	Beginning
Accounts Receivable – net	$ 15,250	$ 20,000
Interest Receivable	200	1,000
Inventory	575,300	562,400
Prepaid Expenses	11,590	12,450
Accounts Payable	52,000	55,670
Wages Payable	5,600	5,400
Interest Payable	2,000	2,250
Income Taxes Payable	35,500	43,200
Accrued Liabilities	15,330	13,830

SOLUTION: We begin with operating income and adjust for noncash expenses. There are no noncash revenues to include in the adjustments. The following items are reported after operating income: interest expense, interest revenue, and income tax expense. For each item, we compute cash flows from the income statement items and changes in balance sheet accounts using t-accounts.

Interest Receivable

	Debit	Credit	
Beginning Balance	1,000		Solve for
Interest Revenue	6,000	6,800	Interest Received
Ending Balance	200		

Interest Payable

Solve for		2,250	Beginning Balance
Interest Paid	10,250	10,000	Interest Expense
		2,000	Ending Balance

Income Taxes Payable

Solve for		43,200	Beginning Balance
Income Taxes Paid	92,700	85,000	Income Tax Expense
		35,500	Ending Balance

We then adjust for noncash items and changes in the other current assets and liabilities, similar to the process in Example 22.1.

Uniform Direct, Inc.
Statement of Cash Flows (Partial)

Operating Activities	
Operating income	$ 297,000
Adjustments to reconcile operating income to net cash provided by operating activities	
Depreciation Expense	27,000
Compensation Expense – Stock Options	23,000
Changes in Operating Working Capital Accounts	
Decrease in Accounts Receivable	4,750
Increase in Inventory	(12,900)
Decrease in Prepaid Expenses	860
Decrease in Accounts Payable	(3,670)
Increase in Wages Payable	200
Increase in Accrued Liabilities	1,500
Cash from Operating Activities before Financial Items and Tax	337,740
Interest Received	6,800
Interest Paid	(10,250)
Income Taxes Paid	(92,700)
Net Cash Provided by Operating Activities	$241,590

As illustrated in Exhibit 22.7, the IFRS reporter ***A.P. Møller (Maersk Group)***, a global Danish company operating in the transportation and energy sectors, began its 2016 cash flow statement under the indirect method in the operations section with profit (loss) before financial items. In 2016, this amount was $(226). On its income statement (not provided), ***Maersk*** reported several items *after* its profit before financial items, including financial income of $989, financial expenses of $1,606, and tax expense of $1,054. On the statement of cash flows, the corresponding items are the cash flows of $77 of financial income received, $694 of financial expenses paid, and $1,155 of taxes paid (all amounts are in millions).

EXHIBIT 22.7 Cash Flows from Operating Activities, ***A.P. Møller (Maersk Group)***, Financial Statements, December 31, 2016

A.P. Møller (Maersk Group), Consolidated Cash Flow Statement Amounts in US$ million		
	2016	**2015**
Profit (Loss) before financial items	$ (226)	$ 1,870
Depreciation, amortisation and impairment losses, net	7,265	7,944
Gain on sale of non-current assets, etc, net	(90)	(451)
Share of profit/loss in joint ventures	(149)	(165)
Share of profit/loss in associated companies	55	(97)
Change in working capital	(265)	382
Change in provisions and pension obligations, etc.	(855)	(99)
Other noncash items	131	130
Cash flow from operating activities before financial items and tax	5,866	9,514
Dividends received	232	155
Financial income received	77	50
Financial expenses paid	(694)	(277)
Taxes paid	(1,155)	(1,473)
Cash flow from operating activities	$ 4,326	$ 7,969

***Source*:** Cash Flows from Operating Activities, A.P. Moller (Maersk Group), Financial Statements, December 31, 2016. www.maersk.com/en/the-maersk-group/press-room/press-release-archive/2017/2/annual-report-2016

The Direct Method

The direct method (also referred to as the income statement format) prepares the statement of cash flows by disaggregating the income statement and adjusting each line item to convert from the accrual basis to the cash basis. In substance, the firm prepares a cash-basis income statement. The firm applies similar adjustments as under the indirect method except that the adjustments apply to *individual* items of revenue and expense rather than against aggregate net income.

At a minimum, the direct method requires the following line items in the cash flow from operating activities calculation:

- Cash collected from customers, lessees, licensees, etc.
- Cash collected for interest and dividends
- Cash paid for merchandise
- Cash paid to employees and cash paid for other accrued expenses, including interest and taxes
- Cash paid for other operating costs, including insurance and other prepaid expenses

Golden Enterprises, Inc., a manufacturer and distributer of snack items, uses the direct method to prepare the operating cash flow section of its statement of cash flows. As illustrated in Exhibit 22.8, ***Golden*** reported actual cash receipts and payments rather than reconcile net income to net cash provided by operating activities in its 2016 financial statements. For example, ***Golden*** reported the following items that *increased* cash from operating activities: cash received from customers of $136,289,283 and miscellaneous income received of $97,108. ***Golden*** reported items that *decreased* cash from operating activities, including cash paid to suppliers and employees for cost of goods sold of $66,550,001; cash paid for suppliers and employees for selling, general, and administrative of $61,224,782; income taxes of $1,140,191; and interest paid of $335,562. The direct method statement of cash flows does not refer to net income. The income statement (not provided) shows that ***Golden's*** net income was $3,184,803, which is lower than net cash provided by operating activities of $7,135,855.

EXHIBIT 22.8 Direct Method of Reporting Cash Flows from Operating Activities, ***Golden Enterprises, Inc.***, Financial Statements, June 3, 2016

Golden Enterprises, Inc. and Subsidiary Consolidated Statement of Cash Flows For the Fiscal Years Ended June 3, 2016 and May 29, 2015		
	2016	**2015**
CASH FLOWS FROM OPERATING ACTIVITIES		
Cash received from customers	$136,289,283	$131,980,056
Miscellaneous income	97,108	88,918
Cash paid to suppliers and employees for cost of goods sold	(66,550,001)	(63,720,473)
Cash paid for suppliers and employees for selling, general and administrative	(61,224,782)	(61,947,388)
Income taxes	(1,140,191)	(1,839,759)
Interest expense	(335,562)	(458,184)
Net cash provided by operating activities	7,135,855	4,103,170
CASH FLOWS FROM INVESTING ACTIVITIES		
Purchases of property, plant and equipment	(1,182,854)	(2,725,450)
Proceeds from sale of property, plant and equipment	56,446	284,806
Net cash used in investing activities	(1,126,408)	(2,440,644)
CASH FLOWS FROM FINANCING ACTIVITIES		
Change in line of credit	(2,823,477)	294,966
Debt (repayments) proceeds	(824,435)	1,698,505
Principal payments under capital lease obligation	(30,970)	–
Purchases of treasury shares	–	(2,204,375)
Cash dividends paid	(1,496,160)	(1,452,803)
Net cash used in financing activities	(5,175,042)	(1,663,707)
NET INCREASE (DECREASE) IN CASH AND CASH EQUIVALENTS	834,405	(1,181)
CASH AND CASH EQUIVALENTS AT BEGINNING OF YEAR	1,159,449	1,160,630
CASH AND CASH EQUIVALENTS AT END OF YEAR	$ 1,993,854	$ 1,159,449

***Source*:** Direct Method of Reporting Cash Flows from Operating Activities, Golden Enterprises, Inc., Financial Statements, June 3, 2016. www.sec.gov/Archives/edgar/data/42228/000114420416116506/v444550_10k.htmt_013

Next, we explain how to convert each of the key line items on the income statement into cash flows.

Cash Collected from Customers. To compute cash collected from customers, start with the accrual-basis revenue and (1) subtract an increase in accounts receivable or (2) add a decrease in accounts receivable to arrive at cash-basis revenue or cash collected from customers. An increase in accounts receivable indicates that the firm has recorded more revenue under the accrual system than the amount of cash it received. A decrease in accounts receivable indicates that the firm recorded less revenue under the accrual system than the amount of cash it received.

Cash Collected from Customers:

Sales Revenue

Less: Increase in Net Accounts Receivable

OR

Add: Decrease in Net Accounts Receivable

Cash Collected from Customers

Cash Collected for Interest and Dividends. To compute cash collected for interest or dividends, start with the accrual-basis revenue and (1) subtract an increase in interest or dividend receivable or (2) add a decrease in interest or dividends receivable to arrive at cash-basis revenue. An increase in the receivable indicates that the firm has recorded more revenue under the accrual system than the amount of cash it received. A decrease in the receivable indicates that the firm has recorded less revenue under the accrual system than the amount of cash it received.

Cash Collected for Interest (Dividends):

Interest (Dividend) Revenue

Less: Increase in Net Interest (Dividend) Receivable

OR

Add: Decrease in Net Interest (Dividend) Receivable

Cash Collected for Interest (Dividends)

Cash Paid for Merchandise. The computation of cash paid for merchandise requires two steps:

1. Determine the purchases on an accrual basis.
2. Determine how much cash the firm expended for these purchases.

To determine the purchases on an accrual basis, start with cost of goods sold and adjust for changes in inventory. If inventory increases, purchases are greater than cost of goods sold. That is, the company purchased enough inventory to cover its sales and also increased inventory in its warehouse. If inventory decreases, purchases are less than cost of goods sold. In this case, the company sold all inventory purchased as well as some of the beginning inventory to cover units sold in the current period.

Firms adjust the accrual-basis purchases for the change in accounts payable related to inventory. An increase in accounts payable represents invoices for inventory not paid in the current year. Subtract the increase in accounts payable from purchases to arrive at cash paid for inventory acquired. A decrease in accounts payable represents invoices for inventory paid for in the current year but not purchased in the current year. Add the decrease in accounts payable from purchases to adjust to cash paid for inventory acquired.

Cash Paid for Merchandise:

Cost of Goods Sold

Add: Increase in Inventory

OR

Less: Decrease in Inventory

Purchases on the Accrual Basis

Add: Decrease in Accounts Payable related to Inventory

OR

Less: Increase in Accounts Payable related to Inventory

Cash Paid for Merchandise

Cash Paid to Employees and Cash Paid for Other Accrued Expenses Including Interest and Taxes. To compute cash paid to employees and other vendors, subtract the increase in the relevant payable account from the accrual-basis expense to arrive at the cash-basis expense. An increase in the payable indicates that the firm has recorded more expense under the accrual system than the amount of cash paid. Add the decrease in the relevant payable account from the accrual-basis expense to arrive at the cash-basis expense. A decrease in the payable indicates that the firm has recorded less expense under the accrual system than the amount of cash paid.[6]

Cash Paid to Employees for Wages and Other Accrued Expenses:

Wage Expense

Add: Decrease in Wages Payable

OR

Less: Increase in Wages Payable

Cash Paid to Employees for Wages

Cash Paid for Interest:

Interest Expense

Add: Decrease in Interest Payable

OR

Less: Increase in Interest Payable

Cash Paid for Interest

Cash Paid for Income Taxes

Income Tax Expense

Add: Decrease in Income Taxes Payable

OR

Less: Increase in Income Taxes Payable

Cash Paid for Income Taxes

Cash Paid for Other Operating Costs Including Insurance and Other Prepaid Expenses. To compute the cash paid for expenditures included in prepaid expenses, subtract the decrease in the relevant prepaid account from the accrual-basis expense to arrive at the cash-basis expense. A decrease in prepaid expenses represents a cash outflow made in a previous period that is reflected as an expense on the income statement in the current period. Thus, subtract it from the accrual-basis expense to arrive at cash paid for operating expenses.

Add the increase in the relevant prepaid account to the accrual-basis expense to arrive at the cash-basis expense. An increase in prepaid expenses is a cash outflow in the current period that appears on the balance sheet as an asset but does not affect net income. Because the firm paid cash as part of operations, add the increase in prepaid expense to the accrual-basis expense to adjust to the amount of cash paid for operating expenses.

Cash Paid for Insurance and Other Prepaid Expenses:

Insurance Expense

Add: Increase in Prepaid Insurance

OR

Less: Decrease in Prepaid Insurance

Cash Paid for Insurance

[6] This formula for income taxes paid is simplified because it does not consider balances in the deferred tax accounts. We cover these accounts later in this chapter.

Example 22.3 illustrates preparing the operating cash flows section of the cash flow statement using the direct method.

EXAMPLE 22.3 Operating Cash Flows, Direct Method

PROBLEM: Uniform Direct, Inc. presented the following income statement and select balance sheet accounts. Prepare the operating cash flows section of the cash flow statement using the direct method. Assume that accrued liabilities pertain to general, and administrative expenses.

Uniform Direct, Inc.
Income Statement

Sales Revenue	$1,345,000
Cost of Goods Sold	852,000
Gross Profit	493,000
Selling Expenses*	57,000
General and Administrative Expenses	112,000
Depreciation Expense	27,000
Operating Income	297,000
Interest Expense	10,000
Interest Revenue	6,000
Income before Taxes	293,000
Income Tax Expense	85,000
Net Income	$ 208,000

*Includes $23,000 expense for stock-based compensation and $34,000 of wage expense.

Selected Balance Sheet Accounts

	Ending	Beginning
Accounts Receivable – net	$ 15,250	$ 20,000
Interest Receivable	200	1,000
Inventory	575,300	562,400
Prepaid Expenses	11,590	12,450
Accounts Payable	52,000	55,670
Wages Payable	5,600	5,400
Interest Payable	2,000	2,250
Income Taxes Payable	35,500	43,200
Accrued Liabilities	15,330	13,830

SOLUTION: We compute each line item separately, as follows.

Cash Received from Customer	
Sales Revenue	$1,345,000
Add: Decrease in Accounts Receivable	4,750
Cash Received from Customers	$1,349,750
Interest Received	
Interest Revenue	$ 6,000
Add: Decrease in Interest Receivable	800
Interest Received	$ 6,800

Cash Paid for Merchandise	
Cost of Goods Sold	$852,000
Add: Increase in Inventory	12,900
Accrual Basis Purchases	864,900
Add: Decrease in Accounts Payable	3,670
Cash Paid for Merchandise	$868,570
Cash Paid to Employees	
Wage Expense	$ 34,000
Deduct: Increase in Wages Payable	(200)
Cash Paid to Employees	$ 33,800
Cash Paid to Other Suppliers	
General and Administrative Expenses	$112,000
Deduct: Decrease in Prepaid Expenses	(860)
Deduct: Increase in Accrued Liabilities	(1,500)
Cash Paid to Other Suppliers	$109,640
Interest Paid	
Interest Expense	$ 10,000
Add: Decrease in Interest Payable	250
Interest Paid	$ 10,250
Income Taxes Paid	
Income Tax Expense	$ 85,000
Add: Decrease in Income Taxes Payable	7,700
Income Taxes Paid	$ 92,700

The operating activities section of the cash flow statement follows:

Uniform Direct, Inc.
Statement of Cash Flows (Partial)

Operating Activities:	
Cash Collected from Customers	$1,349,750
Cash Received for Interest	6,800
Cash Paid for Merchandise	(868,570)
Cash Paid to Employees	(33,800)
Cash Paid to Other Suppliers	(109,640)
Cash Paid for Interest	(10,250)
Cash Paid for Income Taxes	(92,700)
Net Cash Provided by Operating Activities	$ 241,590

5 Describe and illustrate the investing cash flows section of the statement of cash flows.

Investing Cash Flows

Although operating cash flows are presented on a net basis (for example, the change in accounts receivable), investing and financing cash flows are reported on a gross basis. Consequently, firms must report both the cash receipts and cash payments related to a particular account—such as property, plant, and equipment—separately.

The gross amount of cash receipts and payments is more informative than the net receipts and payments. Why, then, are operating cash flows presented on the net basis? The turnover of these items is quick, the amounts are large, and the maturities are short. Thus, knowledge of the gross cash receipts and payments is not necessary to understand the company's activities.

Firms compute cash flows from investing activities using a direct method approach. As noted in Exhibit 22.4, investing cash flows include transactions involving property, plant, and equipment; debt and equity investments; and notes receivable. Consequently, the investing section of the cash flow statement includes line items such as:

- Acquisitions of property, plant, and equipment
- Proceeds from the sale of property, plant, and equipment
- Purchase of investments
- Proceeds from the sale of investments
- Lending cash
- Proceeds from collection of notes receivable

Firms report increases and decreases separately in the investing section of the cash flow statement. Therefore, the acquisitions and disposals of property, plant, and equipment are separate line items rather than a net change in cash from these activities. The investing cash flows section is based on an analysis of the balance sheet accounts for property, plant, and equipment; investments; and long-term receivables as illustrated in Example 22.4.

EXAMPLE 22.4

Investing Cash Flows

PROBLEM: Prepare the investing section of Zatota, Inc.'s cash flow statement based on the following transactions:

- Purchased equipment this year costing $20,000 using cash. There were no equipment disposals during the period.
- Sold a building for $50,000.
- Purchased stock in Todla, Inc. for $10,000.
- Sold its investment in Lutka, Inc. for $8,000.
- Loaned $3,000 to an unrelated party.

SOLUTION: Zatota reports each investing amount separately on the statement of cash flows as follows:

Zatota, Inc.
Statement of Cash Flows (Partial)

Investing Activities:	
Acquisition of Equipment	$(20,000)
Proceeds from Sale of Building	50,000
Acquisition of Equity Investments	(10,000)
Proceeds from Sale of Equity Investments	8,000
Accepted Notes Receivable	(3,000)
Net Cash Provided by Investing Activities	$ 25,000

6 Describe and illustrate the financing cash flows section of the statement of cash flows.

Financing Cash Flows

Firms also compute cash flows from financing activities using a direct method approach. Exhibit 22.4 indicates that financing cash flows include transactions involving the company's own debt and equity. Consequently, the financing section of the cash flow statement includes line items such as:

- Proceeds from the issuance of capital stock
- Purchase of treasury stock
- Proceeds from bond issues
- Dividends paid
- Payment of principal on debt
- Sale of treasury stock

As is the case with investing cash flows, firms report increases and decreases from financing cash flows separately in the financing section of the cash flow statement. The financing cash flows section is based on an analysis of the debt and equity balance sheet accounts as shown in Example 22.5.

EXAMPLE 22.5 Financing Cash Flows

PROBLEM: Campano, Inc. issued 1,000 shares of common stock for $89 each and 500 shares of preferred stock for $74 each. The company issued bonds at their face value of $200,000 and, in addition, it retired bonds at a cost of $154,300. Campano distributed cash dividends to its shareholders totaling $5,400. Prepare the financing section of Campano's cash flow statement.

SOLUTION: Campano reports the issuance of the common ($89,000) and preferred stock ($37,000) as well as the issuance of bonds ($200,000) as cash inflows. It reports the bond retirement $(154,300) and the dividend distribution $(5,400) as cash outflows. Campano calculates its financing cash flows as follows:

Campano, Inc.
Statement of Cash Flows (Partial)

Financing Activities	
Issuance of Common Stock	$ 89,000
Issuance of Preferred Stock	37,000
Issuance of Bonds	200,000
Retirement of Bonds	(154,300)
Dividends Paid	(5,400)
Net Cash Provided by Financing Activities	$166,300

Note that the issuance and retirement of bonds are shown on a gross change basis and are not netted on the statement of cash flows.

Illustration of the Statement of Cash Flows

Example 22.6 reviews the basic issues involved in preparing the three sections of the statement of cash flows, setting the stage for our discussion of the advanced topics that follow.

EXAMPLE 22.6 Comprehensive Illustration

PROBLEM: Leif Corporation provided the following financial statements and additional information for the year ended December 31, 2019.

Leif Corporation
Statement of Income
For the Year Ended December 31, 2019

Sales		$1,250
Less: Cost of Goods Sold		(950)
Gross Profit		$ 300
Operating Expenses		
Selling, General, and Administrative Expenses	$(75)	
Depreciation Expense	(55)	(130)
Operating Income		170
Interest Expense	$(75)	
Interest Revenue	50	(25)
Income before Taxes		145
Income Tax Expense		(53)
Net Income		$ 92

Continued

Leif Corporation
Balance Sheets
December 31, 2019 and 2018

	2019	2018
ASSETS		
Cash and Cash Equivalents	$ 150	$ 212
Accounts Receivable – net	238	175
Inventory	750	300
Prepaid Expenses	350	225
Plant Assets	485	638
Accumulated Depreciation	(248)	(250)
Total Assets	$1,725	$1,300
LIABILITIES AND STOCKHOLDERS' EQUITY		
Accounts Payable	$ 132	$ 125
Taxes Payable	125	75
Long-Term Debt	555	250
Capital Stock	750	750
Retained Earnings	163	100
Total Liabilities and Stockholders' Equity	$1,725	$1,300

During 2019, Leif paid $263 in cash for new equipment and financed an additional $55 in plant asset acquisitions, borrowing the full amount by issuing a note payable using the equipment dealer's finance subsidiary. Therefore, total capital expenditures are equal to $318. Leif sold plant assets for their book value in a cash transaction. It did not repay any debt during the current year. All dividends declared by the company were cash dividends. Prepare the cash flow statement using both the direct and indirect methods.

SOLUTION: First, we compute the changes in the balance sheet accounts. Second, we classify each account into operating, investing, or financing activities. We describe accounts related to more than one activity in notes ** and ***.

Analysis and Classification of Changes in Balance Sheet Items

	2019	2018	Change*	Activity
ASSETS				
Cash and Cash Equivalents	$ 150	$ 212	$(62)	
Accounts Receivable – net	238	175	63	***Operating***
Inventory	750	300	450	***Operating***
Prepaid Expenses	350	225	125	***Operating***
Plant Assets	485	638	(153)	***Investing***
Accumulated Depreciation	(248)	(250)	(2)	**
Total Assets	$1,725	$1,300		
LIABILITIES AND EQUITIES				
Accounts Payable	$ 132	$ 125	$ 7	***Operating***
Taxes Payable	125	75	50	***Operating***
Long-Term Debt	555	250	305	***Financing***
Capital Stock	750	750	0	***Financing***
Retained Earnings	163	100	63	***
Total Equities	$1,725	$1,300		

**This column includes the account change, not necessarily the change in cash.*

***Accumulated depreciation is changed by depreciation expense (operating) and plant asset disposals (investing).*

****Retained earnings is changed by net income or loss (operating) and dividends declared (financing).*

Next, we will address the items for the operating, investing, and financing sections.

Operating Cash Flows Section

For the indirect method, we take the changes in working capital accounts. These are:

Working Capital Accounts	2019	2018	Change	Impact on Cash Flows
Accounts Receivable – net	$238	$175	$ 63	Subtract increase
Inventory	750	300	450	Subtract increase
Prepaid Expenses	350	225	125	Subtract increase
Accounts Payable	132	125	7	Add increase
Taxes Payable	125	75	50	Add increase

For the direct method, we need to compute the actual cash flows for these accounts.

Cash Collected from Customers during the Year	
Sales	$1,250
Less: Increase in Accounts Receivable	(63)
Cash Collected from Customers	$1,187

Cash Paid for Merchandise	
Cost of Goods Sold	$ 950
Add: Increase in Inventory	450
Purchases (accrual basis)	$1,400
Less: Increase in Accounts Payable	(7)
Cash Paid for Merchandise	$1,393

Cash Paid to Other Suppliers	
Selling, General, and Administrative Expenses	$ 75
Add: Increase in Prepaid Expenses	125
Cash Paid to Other Suppliers	$ 200

Cash Paid for Income Taxes	
Income Tax Expense	$ 53
Less: Increase in Taxes Payable	(50)
Cash Paid for Income Taxes	$ 3

Cash Paid for Interest	
Interest Expense	$ 75
Adjust: Change in Interest Payable	0
Cash Paid for Interest	$ 75

Continued

Investing and Financing Cash Flows Sections

Presenting investing and financing activities requires analyzing each balance sheet account with changes and reconciling all changes in account balances using t-accounts as follow. We solve for missing information identified with an "X".

Plant Assets

	Debit	Credit
Beginning Balance	638	
Acquisitions	318	
X = Assets Sold		471
Ending Balance	485	

Retained Earnings

	Debit	Credit
Beginning Balance		100
Net Income		92
X = Dividends Declared	29	
Ending Balance		163

Accumulated Depreciation – Plant Assets

	Debit	Credit
Beginning Balance		250
Depreciation Expense		55
X = Assets Sold	57	
Ending Balance		248

Long-Term Debt

	Debit	Credit
Beginning Balance		250
Equipment Purchase		55
X = Additional Borrowing		250
Ending Balance		555

The net book value of the asset sold is $414 (Cost – Accumulated Depreciation = $471 – $57). Because Leif sold the asset for its book value, there is no gain or loss on the income statement.

All dividends declared are paid because there are no dividends payable on the balance sheet. (If there were dividends payable and they had increased/decreased during the period, we would subtract/add the change from dividends declared to obtain cash dividends paid.)

With all changes in the balance sheet accounts explained, we proceed to prepare the cash flow statement. The statement of cash flows under the direct and indirect methods follows.

Leif Corporation
Statement of Cash Flows (Direct Method)
For the Year Ended December 31, 2019

Operating Activities		
Cash Received from Customers	$1,187	
Cash Interest Received	50	
Cash Paid for Merchandise	(1,393)	
Cash Paid to Other Suppliers	(200)	
Interest Paid	(75)	
Income Taxes Paid	(3)	
Net Cash Used by Operating Activities		$(434)
Investing Activities		
Proceeds from the Sale of Plant Asset	$ 414	
Purchase Equipment	(263)	
Net Cash Provided by Investing Activities		$ 151
Financing Activities		
Proceeds from Issuance of Long-Term Debt	$ 250	
Cash Dividends Paid	(29)	
Net Cash Provided by Financing Activities		$ 221
Net Decrease in Cash and Cash Equivalents		$ (62)
Cash and Cash Equivalents, Beginning of Year		212
Cash and Cash Equivalents, End of Year		$ 150

Noncash Investing and Financing Activity: Acquisition of plant asset with note payable $55.

Leif Corporation
Statement of Cash Flows (Indirect Method)
For the Year Ended December 31, 2019

Operating Activities		
Net Income	$ 92	
Adjustments to Reconcile Net Income to Net Cash Provided by Operating Activities		
Depreciation Expense	55	
Changes in Operating Working Capital Accounts		
Increase in Accounts Receivable	(63)	
Increase in Prepaid Expenses	(125)	
Increase in Inventory	(450)	
Increase in Taxes Payable	50	
Increase in Accounts Payable	7	
Net Cash Used by Operating Activities		$(434)
Investing Activities		
Proceeds from the Sale of Plant Asset	$ 414	
Purchase Equipment	(263)	
Net Cash Provided by Investing Activities		$ 151
Financing Activities		
Proceeds from Issuance of Long-Term Debt	$ 250	
Cash Dividends Paid	(29)	
Net Cash Provided by Financing Activities		$ 221
Net Decrease in Cash and Cash Equivalents		$ (62)
Cash and Cash Equivalents, Beginning of Year		212
Cash and Cash Equivalents, End of Year		$ 150

Noncash Investing and Financing Activity: Acquisition of plant asset with note payable $55.

JUDGMENTS IN ACCOUNTING
Impacts on the Statement of Cash Flows

Many decisions that managers make impact net income and thus earnings per share (EPS). It is possible that managers make decisions for the sole purpose of impacting earnings per share. Exhibit 20.1 provided a summary of the most significant types of judgments covered throughout this textbook. The earnings management discussions thus far focused on accruals management. That is, the judgments relate to the timing and measurement of certain accounts on the financial statements. For example, the choice of the amount of bad debt expense to report in a particular period impacts the net accounts receivable balance reported on the balance sheet as well as the bad debt expense reported on the income statement. However, this decision does not impact cash flows. Accruals earnings management could help a firm avoid a loss, exceed analysts' forecasts, or increase management compensation.

In contract, real earnings management occurs when decisions regarding a company's cash flows and earnings for the period impact a firm's actual operations. For example, management could increase price discounts in an effort to increase sales. If sales increase, then this decision has a positive impact on both earnings and cash flows. Management could engage in real earnings management for the same reasons that explain the use of accruals management. Other examples of real earnings management are decreases in discretionary spending, decreases in research and development expenditures, and altering the timing of

Continued

dispositions of long-term operating assets and investment assets. While these activities might improve current performance, they are likely to have a negative long-term impact on the firm.

In addition to real earnings management, firms could engage in activities that impact operating cash flows but not earnings. Investors focus on operating cash flows, so management could take certain actions to move cash inflows out of investing or financing activities and into operating cash flows. Or they could move cash outflows out of operating activities and into financing or investing activities. As an example, judgment is involved in determining whether to capitalize or expense certain costs. The decision has an immediate impact on net income and on operating cash flows. Typically, if an expenditure is capitalized, the firm reports the associated cash outflow in cash flows from investing activities. If the cost is expensed immediately, the firm typically reports the cash flows in operating activities. There is no effect on the total net income reported over the life of the transaction because the asset is ultimately depreciated or amortized and the same total expense is charged against income and retained earnings. However, because depreciation and amortization expenses are added back to determine operating cash flow, the cumulative impact on operating cash flow is zero. Other examples of moving cash flows on the statement are investing in purchased research and development (investing outflow) as opposed to internally generated research and development (operating cash outflow) and factoring receivables (operating cash inflows because of the decrease in receivables).

Accelerating customer payments, reducing inventory, and postponing payments to vendors also impact operating cash flows. While all of these actions may be considered a part of cash management, they will have only a one-time impact on operating cash flows. Also, some companies engage in these activities simply to increase operating cash flows. The ultimate business impact, however, could be to create poor relationships with customers and vendors.

7 Discuss and illustrate the reporting of complex transactions in determining cash flows.

Complexities in Determining Cash Flows

Several issues increase the complexity of the cash flow statement preparation:

1. Acquisition and disposition of long-term assets
2. Deferred income taxes
3. Net accounts receivable and bad debt expense
4. Unrealized gains and losses on fair value adjustments
5. Equity method investments
6. Share-based compensation
7. Pension adjustments
8. Amortization of bond discounts and premiums

We analyze each of these issues in detail.

Acquisition and Disposition of Long-Term Assets

Firms must accurately report the gain or loss on the sale of long-term assets. The gain or loss by itself does not provide or use cash. The cash inflow, the amount of cash received on disposal, is reported as an investing activity on the cash flow statement. The gain or loss on disposal is the difference between the cash received and the carrying value of the asset at the time of sale. Thus, firms include any cash proceeds in the investing cash flows section, and the gain or loss is reported in the operating section of the cash flow statement under the indirect method.

Under the indirect method, firms treat gains and losses as adjustments to net income (deducting gains and adding losses) and report the cash proceeds in the investing activities section. Under the direct method, firms include all of the cash proceeds from the sale of property, plant, and equipment in the investing section of cash flows, with no adjustment needed in operating activities. Example 22.7 demonstrates how the sale of property, plant, and equipment is reported on the cash flow statement.

EXAMPLE 22.7 Sale of Property, Plant, and Equipment

PROBLEM: Aline Corporation sold equipment with a net book value of $10,000 for $12,000. The equipment had an original cost of $50,000, and accumulated depreciation taken as of the date of sale was $40,000. Aline reported a $2,000 gain $(12,000 − $10,000). The company also purchased debt securities for $7,000. Net income for the year was $15,000. There were no other transactions conducted during the period. Using the indirect method, what are the operating and investing cash flows for Aline?

SOLUTION: Aline reports net operating cash flows of $13,000:

Net income	$15,000
Less: Gain on sale of plant assets	(2,000)
Net cash provided by operating activities	$13,000

Aline reports net investing cash flows of $5,000:

Acquisition of debt securities	$ (7,000)
Proceeds from the disposal of property, plant, and equipment	12,000
Net cash provided by investing activities	$ 5,000

The investing section of the cash flow statement separates changes in property, plant, and equipment into cash outflows from acquisitions and cash inflows from dispositions. Specifically, firms separately identify the changes in net plant assets as depreciation, additions, and disposals as illustrated in Example 22.8.

EXAMPLE 22.8 Effects of the Changes in the Property, Plant, and Equipment Accounts on the Statement of Cash Flows

PROBLEM: Bline Corporation had the following balances in its property, plant, and equipment accounts:

	End of Year	Beginning of Year
Equipment	$113,000	$100,000
Accumulated Depreciation – Equipment	(41,000)	(32,000)
Buildings	100,000	125,000
Accumulated Depreciation – Buildings	(76,000)	(82,000)
Land	95,000	100,000
Total Property, Plant, and Equipment	$191,000	$211,000

Continued

It reported depreciation expense as follows:

Account	Amount of Depreciation Expense
Equipment	$ 9,000
Building	$12,000

It recorded a gain on the sale of a building of $3,000.

During the year, Bline acquired one new piece of equipment for $13,000 and paid cash and did not sell any equipment. It also acquired land costing $20,000 and paid cash in the current year. Bline did not acquire any buildings during the year. What should Bline report in its investing cash flows related to property, plant, and equipment?

SOLUTION: We begin with an analysis of the equipment account. It increased by $13,000 (from $100,000 to $113,000). Also, the increase in the accumulated depreciation of $9,000 (from $32,000 to $41,000) reconciles with the depreciation expense reported. Thus, Bline reports a cash outflow of $13,000 for acquisition of equipment.

Bline's building account decreased by $25,000 this year from $125,000 to $100,000. Because Bline did not acquire any buildings this year, this total change amount results from the sale of a building. The following analysis of the accumulated depreciation account for buildings uses a t-account to input the beginning and ending balances as well as the credit from depreciation expense for the year. This analysis indicates that the debit needed to balance the account is $18,000 and is likely because of disposals.

Accumulated Depreciation – Building

	Debit	Credit	
		82,000	Beginning Balance
		12,000	Depreciation Expense
X = Disposition of Building	18,000		
		76,000	Ending Balance

Cost of building sold	$25,000
Accumulated depreciation on building sold	(18,000)
Net book value of building sold	$ 7,000
Gain on sale of building	3,000
Cash proceeds on the sale of the building	$10,000

Thus, Bline records a cash inflow of $10,000 from the sale of the building.

Finally, we analyze the land account by using a t-account.

Land

	Debit	Credit	
Beginning Balance	100,000		
Acquisition	20,000		
		25,000	X = Disposition
Ending Balance	95,000		

The land disposition must be $25,000 in order to reconcile the beginning balance of $100,000 and the $20,000 acquisition to the ending balance of $95,000. As noted earlier, investing and financing activities are reported on a gross change basis so that Bline records the cash inflow from the disposition of land of $25,000 separately from the cash outflow of $20,000 for the acquisition of land.

Deferred Income Taxes

The earlier discussion of the computation of income taxes paid reported in operating cash flows did not consider the deferred income tax accounts.

Direct Method Deferred Income Taxes. Under the direct method, firms include deferred taxes in the computation of cash paid for taxes with the following adjustments:

Cash Paid for Income Taxes

Income Tax Expense (Accrual Basis)

Add: Decrease in Income Taxes Payable

OR

Less: Increase in Income Taxes Payable

AND

Add: Decrease in a Deferred Tax Liability or Increase in a Deferred Tax Asset

OR

Less: Increase in a Deferred Tax Liability or Decrease in a Deferred Tax Asset

Cash Paid for Income Taxes

1. An increase in a deferred tax liability represents an amount that is included in tax expense but is not a cash expenditure in the current year. As a result, firms deduct it from the accrual-basis tax expense to arrive at cash-basis tax expense.
2. A decrease in a deferred tax liability represents an amount that a firm previously recorded as an accrual-basis expense but paid in the current period. Therefore, the firm adds it to the accrual-basis expense to arrive at cash-basis expense.
3. An increase in a deferred-tax asset represents amounts the firm paid this period but will not expense until future periods. So, the firm must add the increase to accrual-basis income tax expense to arrive at cash-basis expense.
4. A decrease in a deferred tax asset represents amounts that the firm paid out in previous periods but expensed in the current period. Thus, the firm subtracts this amount from accrual-basis tax expense to arrive at the cash-basis tax expense because it did not use cash in the current period.

Indirect Method Deferred Income Taxes. Under the indirect method, the firm treats adjustments needed for changes in the deferred tax accounts as any asset or liability change—with noncash adjustments rather than part of operating working capital. That is, the firm adds (subtracts) increases (decreases) in deferred-tax liabilities or decreases (increases) in deferred-tax assets back to net income in operating activities. Increases in deferred tax liabilities represent an amount of taxes not paid in the current period. Decreases in deferred tax assets reflect the amortization of the deferred-tax asset to tax expense. This treatment, illustrated in Example 22.9, is the same as any type of depreciation or amortization and is treated as a noncash expense.

EXAMPLE 22.9 Cash Paid for Income Taxes

PROBLEM: D'Antona Delivery Service prepared the following journal entry to record its tax provision for the current year.

Account	*Current Year*	
Income Tax Expense	1,500	
Deferred Tax Asset	500	
Income Tax Payable		800
Cash		1,200

Continued

Recompute the amount of cash paid for income taxes under the direct method by reconciling income tax expense to cash paid. What would D'Antona report in the operating section of the cash flow statement under the indirect method?

SOLUTION: We compute the cash paid for taxes under the direct method as follows:

Cash Paid for Income Taxes	
Income tax expense (accrual basis)	$ 1,500
Less: Increase in income taxes payable	(800)
Add: Increase in a deferred tax asset	500
Cash paid for income taxes	$ 1,200

Under the indirect method, to arrive at operating cash flow, D'Antona will:

- Subtract the $500 increase in the deferred tax assets from net income.
- Add the $800 increase in income taxes payable to net income.

Net Accounts Receivable and Bad Debt Expense

Firms typically report the change in net accounts receivable in operating cash flows. The reporting approach varies under the indirect and direct methods:

- As an adjustment to net income under the indirect method
- As an adjustment to sales revenue to arrive at cash collected from customers under the direct method

The indirect method approach does not address the fact that bad debt expense is a noncash expense. Therefore, it is more accurate to separate the changes in net accounts receivable from bad debt expense for the year from the changes from increased sales and customer payments. Example 22.10 demonstrates the treatment of a change in accounts receivable.

EXAMPLE 22.10 Change in Accounts Receivable

PROBLEM: Horton Industries reported net income of $120,000 for the current year. The balances in its accounts receivable and allowance for bad debts accounts follow. In addition, the company recorded $2,000 of bad debt expense and wrote off $1,500 of uncollectible accounts. Prepare the operating section of the cash flow statement under the indirect method.

	End of Year	**Beginning of Year**
Accounts Receivable	$27,000	$20,000
Allowance for Bad Debts	$ 4,500	$ 4,000

SOLUTION: The net receivables balance increased from $16,000 to $22,500. Thus, in total, Horton subtracts the increase of $6,500 from net income to arrive at operating cash flows.

	End of Year	**Beginning of Year**	**Change**
Accounts Receivable	$ 27,000	$20,000	
Less: Allowance for Bad Debts	4,500	4,000	
Net Accounts Receivable	$22,500	$16,000	$6,500

To separate the overall change in net accounts receivable, we examine the following t-accounts.

Accounts Receivable

	Debit	Credit
Beginning Balance	20,000	
Write-off (given)		1,500
Change excluding Write-off (computed)	8,500	
Ending Balance	27,000	

Allowance for Bad Debts

Debit	Credit	
	4,000	Beginning Balance
	2,000	Bad Debt Expense (given)
1,500		Write-off (given)
	4,500	Ending Balance

Thus, Horton has

- A decrease in net receivables of $2,000 from bad debt expense
- An increase in net accounts receivables of $8,500 from customer sales

Note that the write-off does not affect the net receivables balance because it decreases both the allowance and the gross accounts receivable balance.

Under the indirect method, the operating section of the cash flow statement is as follows:

Net Income	$120,000
Add: Bad Debt Expense	2,000
Less: Increase in Accounts Receivable	(8,500)
Net Cash Provided by Operating Activities	$ 113,500

Unrealized Gains and Losses on Fair Value Adjustments

When adjusting investments and other financial instruments to fair value, the treatment of the unrealized gain or loss varies depending on the classification of the security. For example, if the firm classifies a debt investment as a trading security or uses the fair value option, it reports the unrealized gains and losses in net income. If the firm classifies a debt investment as available for sale, it reports the unrealized gains and losses in other comprehensive income.

The adjustment for unrealized gains and losses reported through other comprehensive income does not have any cash flow effects. The write-up or write-down to fair value changes the carrying value of the investment with the unrealized gain or loss reported in accumulated other comprehensive income in the equity section of the balance sheet. With the exception of disclosure, there are no implications for the cash flow statement.

Conversely, if the firm reports unrealized gains and losses through net income, it needs to adjust net income under the indirect method:

1. Unrealized gains are noncash revenues deducted from net income in the operating activities section of the statement of cash flows.
2. Unrealized losses are noncash expenses added back to net income in operating activities.

Example 22.11 demonstrates the reporting of unrealized gains and losses from debt investments on the statement of cash flows.

EXAMPLE 22.11

Unrealized Gains and Losses From Debt Investments

PROBLEM: Investors, Inc. had net income of $875,000 in the current year. The company reported net unrealized gains from available-for-sale debt investments of $120,000 in other comprehensive income and net unrealized losses from trading debt investments of $80,000 in net income. Prepare the operating section of the cash flow statement.

SOLUTION: To prepare the operating section, we add back the unrealized losses that Investors reported in net income.

Net Income	$875,000
Add: Unrealized Losses From Trading Debt Investments	80,000
Net Cash Provided by Operating Activities	$955,000

We do not adjust for the unrealized gains reported in other comprehensive income because they have no effect on net income or operating cash flows.

Equity Method Investments

In preparing the operating section of the cash flow statement under the indirect method, firms adjust net income for investments accounted for under the equity method. Under the equity method, the investor company reports its share of the investee's net income in its own income statement. However, this is a noncash event, and only the dividends received by the investee should be reported as cash flows. Thus, the operating activities section is affected by the difference between the equity income or loss recognized by the investor company and the cash dividends received from the investee.[7]

When equity income exceeds the amount of cash dividends received, the investor company deducts the excess from net income in operating activities to reflect the dividends received in cash. When cash dividends exceed equity income or if there is a loss from the equity investment, the investor company adds this amount back in the operating activities section. Example 22.12 provides an example of reporting income from equity method investments on the cash flow statement.

EXAMPLE 22.12

Income from Equity Method Investments

PROBLEM: Green Robin Enterprises holds a 40% share of Zito, Incorporated. Zito reported $50,000 in net income and paid $12,500 in cash dividends in the current year. Green Robin recognized its 40% share of the investee company's net income ($20,000) on the income statement as equity income. Green Robin received $5,000 in cash dividends (40% × $12,500). It reported net income of $900,000, including the equity method income. Prepare the operating activities section of the cash flow statement under the indirect method.

SOLUTION: Green Robin reports $20,000 of net equity income in net income but received only $5,000 in cash. Thus, Green Robin decreases net income by the difference of $15,000 to arrive at operating cash flows. A partial cash flow statement follows.

Net Income	$ 900,000
Less: Equity Method Income in Excess of Cash Distributions	(15,000)
Net Cash Provided by Operating Activities	$ 885,000

Share-Based Compensation

Employee compensation paid in equity shares is a noncash expense. Similar to all noncash expenses, firms add back the amount of share-based compensation cost recognized on the income statement to net income in the operating activities section of the statement of cash flows under the indirect method.

[7] Distributions received by an entity reporting the investment under the equity method can be classified as operating or investing, depending on several different factors. For simplicity, we assume that these distributions are reported as operating activities.

Pension Adjustments

The financial reporting standards for defined-benefit pensions require that firms report a pension expense in the income statement. This expense consists of a variety of factors, including service cost, amortization of prior service costs, interest on the projected benefit obligation, and the expected return on plan assets. However, pension expense is a noncash expense. The cash flow related to pension obligations is simply the amount funded or paid into the plan during the current year.

As is the case with equity method investments, under the indirect method, firms adjust net income for the difference between the expense reported and the cash used to fund the plan:

- If the expense is greater than the amount funded, the adjustment is added back to net income.
- If the expense reported is less than the amount funded, the adjustment is deducted from net income.

Example 22.13 illustrates adjusting operating cash flows for defined-benefit pension plans.

EXAMPLE 22.13

Defined-Benefit Pension Plan

PROBLEM: McCrae Associates determined that its pension expense for the year is $71,500 and contributed $55,000 into its pension plan during the year. It reported net income for the year of $567,000. Prepare the operating activities section of the cash flow statement under the indirect method.

SOLUTION: McCrae expensed $16,500 more than it funded ($71,500 of expense less $55,000 in contributions). McCrae adds the difference back to net income to arrive at operating cash flows.

Net Income	$ 567,000
Add: Excess of Pension Expense over Pension Funding	16,500
Net Cash Provided by Operating Activities	$583,500

Amortization of Bond Premiums and Discounts

The amortization of bond discounts and premiums results in a difference between the interest expense reported in net income and the interest paid. When a firm records an interest payment for bonds, it debits interest expense, credits cash, and debits (credit) the bond premium (discount). As a result:

1. The amortization of a bond discount results in more interest expense than cash paid.
2. The amortization of a bond premium results in less interest expense than cash paid.

When computing cash interest paid under the direct method, firms subtract any bond discount amortization to reduce cash paid for interest and add back any bond premium amortization to increase the amount of cash interest paid. The indirect method begins with net income, so firms add any bond discount amortization to and subtract any bond premium amortization from net income to arrive at operating cash flows. Firms include these adjustments with the noncash items as shown in Example 22.14.

EXAMPLE 22.14

Bond Premium Amortization

PROBLEM: McDoodle Industries reported net income in the current year of $150,300. The company reported interest expense of $20,000. The balances of all accounts related to its bonds follow. Compute the cash paid for interest if McDoodle presented its cash flow statement using the direct method. Prepare the operating activities section of the cash flow statement using the indirect method.

	End of Year	Beginning of Year
Interest Payable	$ 5,000	$ 2,000
Bonds Payable	400,000	400,000
Bond Premium	5,800	7,000

Continued

SOLUTION: Under the direct method, we subtract the increase in interest payable and add the premium amortization to interest expense to compute the amount of cash paid for interest.

Cash Paid for Interest	
Interest Expense	$20,000
Less: Increase in Interest Payable	(3,000)
Add: Amortization of Bond Premium	1,200
Cash Paid for Interest	$18,200

Under the indirect method, we subtract the premium amortization from net income and add the increase in interest payable to net income to compute operating cash flows.

Net Income	$150,300
Less: Bond Premium Amortization	(1,200)
Add: Increase in Interest Payable	3,000
Net Cash Provided by Operating Activities	$152,100

Overview of Indirect Method Adjustments

Now that we have discussed the various complexities involved with preparing the cash flow statement, Exhibit 22.9 presents a summary of the most common reconciling items in the indirect method of presenting cash flows from operating activities.

EXHIBIT 22.9 Indirect Method Reconciling Items

ADDITIONS

Noncash Expenses and Losses

- Depreciation, depletion, and amortization expense
- Impairment loss
- Bad debt expense
- Stock-based compensation expense
- Amortization of bond discounts
- Increase in the deferred tax liability or decrease in the deferred tax asset
- Losses recognized on investments under the equity method plus distributions in excess of income
- Loss on the sale of long-term assets
- Unrealized losses on trading debt investments reported through net income
- The excess of pension costs reported over pension funding

Changes in Operating Working Capital Accounts

- Decreases in current assets (receivables, inventory, prepaid expenses)
- Increases in current liabilities (accounts payable, accrued liabilities)

DEDUCTIONS

Noncash Revenues and Gains

- Amortization of bond premiums
- Decrease in the deferred tax liability or increase in the deferred tax asset
- Income recognized on investments under the equity method in excess of distributions
- Gain on the sale of long-term assets
- Unrealized gains on trading debt investments reported through net income
- The excess of pension funding over pension costs reported

Changes in Operating Working Capital Accounts

- Increases in current assets (receivables, inventory, prepaid expenses)
- Decreases in current liabilities (accounts payable, accrued expenses)

8 Detail required disclosures related to the statement of cash flows.

Cash Flow Statement Disclosures

There are five key disclosure items for the statement of cash flows. Specifically, the standards require that an entity disclose its policy regarding cash equivalents, all significant noncash investing and financing activities, interest and dividends paid when the indirect method is used, a reconciliation of net income to net cash flows from operating activities if the direct method is used, and information about cash restrictions. We summarize these disclosure requirements in this section.

Cash Equivalents Policy: Direct and Indirect Methods

An entity is required to disclose its policy for determining which items it treats as cash equivalents. Any change to that policy is a change in accounting principle, requiring that the firm restate financial statements for earlier years for comparative purposes.

Noncash Investing and Financing Activities: Direct and Indirect Methods

Cash flow statement disclosures must include information about any of an entity's investing and financing activities during a period that affect assets or liabilities on the balance sheet but that do not result in cash receipts or cash payments in the period. These disclosures can be either in a footnote or in a separate schedule. Some transactions are part cash and part nonmonetary: The firm reports only the cash portion in the statement of cash flows and reports the noncash amount of the transaction in the notes. In cases when there are only a few noncash events, an entity can provide a summary schedule following the statement of cash flows.

Interest and Income Taxes Paid: Indirect Method Only

If the firm uses the indirect method, it must disclose amounts of interest paid (net of amounts capitalized) and income taxes paid during the period.

Reconciliation of Net Income to Net Cash Provided by Operating Activities: Direct Method Only

When the firm uses the direct method, it must provide a separate schedule that reconciles accrual-basis net income to net cash provided by operations. This is effectively the operating activities section under the indirect method.

Restrictions on Cash and Cash Equivalents: Direct and Indirect Methods

A firm is required to disclose information related to any restricted cash and cash equivalents it has. The firm must provide a discussion of the nature of any restrictions it has on its cash balance.

Cash Flow Statement Disclosures under IFRS

IFRS does not require a reconciliation of net income to net cash provided by operations under the direct method, but it has additional disclosure requirements. IFRS requires that companies disclose any cash balances that are held but not available for use. For example, a company may operate a subsidiary in a country where there are foreign exchange controls or other legal restrictions prohibiting the conversion of cash.[8] IFRS also requires that the entity provide adequate disclosure to explain changes in financing liabilities arising from both cash and noncash changes. Finally, IFRS encourages management to comment on any additional information that could be relevant to users in understanding a company's financial position and its liquidity, such as available borrowing arrangements and cash flows by business segments.

Comprehensive Cash Flow Problem

Example 22.15 presents a comprehensive problem that includes the complexities discussed previously and requires preparation of a firm's statement of cash flows and related disclosures.

[8]IASC, *International Accounting Standard 7*, "Statement of Cash Flows" (London, UK: International Accounting Standards Committee, Revised, 2001), Paragraph 49.

EXAMPLE 22.15 Comprehensive Cash Flow Problem Including Complexities

PROBLEM: KaseyKraft Company's balance sheets and income statement follow.

KaseyKraft Company
Balance Sheets
At December 31

	December 31	
Assets	**Current Year**	**Prior Year**
Current Assets		
Cash	$ 30,000	$ 5,000
Trading Debt Investments	108,500	25,000
Accounts Receivable – net	182,500	68,500
Merchandise Inventory	400,000	402,500
Total Current Assets	$ 721,000	$ 501,000
Noncurrent Assets		
Investments in Affiliate Companies	$ 785,600	$ 620,000
Property, Plant, and Equipment – net	4,075,000	3,214,460
Equipment under Finance Lease	300,000	0
Intangible Assets – net	825,500	900,500
Total Noncurrent Assets	$5,986,100	$4,734,960
Total Assets	$ 6,707,100	$5,235,960
Liabilities		
Current Liabilities		
Current Portion of Long-Term Debt	$ 56,000	$ 68,500
Accounts Payable	100,580	125,020
Income Taxes Payable	187,500	200,000
Total Current Liabilities	$ 344,080	$ 393,520
Noncurrent Liabilities		
Bonds Payable	$2,500,000	$2,500,000
Less: Discount on Bonds	(325,600)	(360,600)
Notes Payable	1,270,880	1,301,450
Obligations under Finance Lease	300,000	0
Deferred Tax Liability	52,000	31,000
Net Obligations under Pension Plans	90,500	61,500
Total Noncurrent Liabilities	$ 3,887,780	$3,533,350
Total Liabilities	$4,231,860	$3,926,870
Shareholders' Equity		
Common Stock, $1 par value	$ 500,500	$ 100,000
Additional Paid-in Capital in Excess of Par – Common	670,000	154,000
Additional Paid-in Capital – Stock Options	11,500	0
Retained Earnings	1,000,000	555,550
Accumulated Other Comprehensive Income	293,240	499,540
Total Shareholders' Equity	$2,475,240	$1,309,090
Total Liabilities and Shareholders' Equity	$ 6,707,100	$5,235,960

KaseyKraft Company
Income Statement
For the Current Year Ended December 31

Sales	$2,457,693
Cost of Goods Sold	1,474,616
Gross Profit	$ 983,077
Selling, General, and Administrative Expenses	$ 25,000
Pension Expense	120,000
Bad Debt Expense	6,500
Depreciation Expense	90,500
Amortization Expense	8,000
Total Operating Expenses	$ 250,000
Operating Income	$ 733,077
Interest Expense	$ (38,800)
Unrealized Gains on Investments	$ 14,000
Investment Income	19,690
Equity Earnings from Affiliate Companies	256,200
Income before Tax	$ 984,167
Income Tax Expense	(393,667)
Net Income	$ 590,500

KaseyKraft provided the following additional information:

- It sold trading investments acquired at a cost of $55,000 for $57,550 and acquired additional trading securities during the year.
- Investment income includes interest income received and the gain on the sale made during the year.
- The company acquired a new plant in a cash transaction; it did not dispose of any property, plant, and equipment.
- It sold one of its franchises for cash: There was no gain or loss on the sale.
- The selling, general, and administrative expenses include stock-based compensation expense of $11,500.
- Pension funding for the year was $297,300.
- The company had no additional borrowings.
- The company leased a fleet of heavy vehicles on December 31 with no cash paid at inception.
- All changes in common stock and additional paid-in capital in excess of par – common result from a new share issue for cash.
- Treat the trading securities as investing activities.

Prepare KaseyKraft's cash flow statement, including disclosures, for the current year under both the indirect and direct reporting formats.

SOLUTION: We prepare the indirect statement of cash flows first and then apply the direct method.

Indirect Method

We begin by computing the changes in the balance sheet accounts. Next, we classify each account into operating, investing, or financing activities. Some accounts relate to more than one classification under the indirect method as noted in the table on the next page.

Analysis of Balance Sheet Changes and Cash Flow Classification

Balance Sheet Item	Ending	Beginning	Change*	Classification**	Notes for Indirect Method
Cash	$ 30,000	$ 5,000	$ 25,000	Answer	
Trading Debt Investments	108,500	25,000	83,500	I, O	Purchases and sales are in investing. Unrealized gain/losses are noncash adjustments in operating.
Accounts receivable – net	182,500	68,500	114,000	O	Bad debt expense is a noncash adjustment in operating.
Merchandise inventory	400,000	402,500	(2,500)	O	
Investments in affiliate companies	785,600	620,000	165,600	I, O	Purchases and sales are in investing. Undistributed equity earnings are noncash adjustments in operating.
Property, plant, and equipment – net	4,075,000	3,214,460	860,540	I, O	Acquisitions and disposals are in investing. Depreciation expense is a noncash adjustment in operating.
Equipment under finance lease	300,000	0	300,000	NC	
Intangible assets – net	825,500	900,500	(75,000)	I, O	Acquisitions and disposals are in investing. Amortization expense is a noncash adjustment in operating.
Current portion of long-term debt	56,000	68,500	(12,500)	F	
Accounts payable	100,580	125,020	(24,440)	O	
Income taxes payable	187,500	200,000	(12,500)	O	
Bonds payable	2,500,000	2,500,000	0	F	
Less: Discount on bonds	(325,600)	(360,600)	(35,000)	NC, O	Amortization is a noncash adjustment in operating.
Notes payable	1,270,880	1,301,450	(30,570)	F	
Obligations under finance leases	300,000	0	300,000	NC	
Deferred tax liability	52,000	31,000	21,000	O	
Net Obligations under pension plans	90,500	61,500	29,000	O	Difference between pension expense and funding is a noncash adjustment in operating.
Common stock, $1 par value	500,500	100,000	400,500	F	
Additional paid-in-capital in excess of par – common	670,000	154,000	516,000	F	
Additional paid-in capital – stock options	11,500	0	11,500	O	Stock-based compensation expense is a noncash adjustment in operating.
Retained earnings	1,000,000	555,550	444,450	O, F	Net income or loss begins the operating section. Dividends paid are in financing.
Accumulated other comprehensive income	293,240	499,540	(206,300)	NA	

**This column includes the account change but not necessarily the change in cash.*
***O = Operating, I = Investing, F = Financing, NC = Noncash, NA = Not applicable.*

Next, we analyze the items to be included in the operating, investing, and financing sections of the cash flow statement.

Operating Cash Flows Section

For the indirect method, we take the changes in all working capital accounts except accounts receivable for which we must consider the noncash bad debt expense. The working capital accounts include:

Working Capital Account	Ending	Beginning	Change	In Statement and Balance Increase or Decrease
Accounts Receivable	$182,500	$ 68,500	$114,000	Separate change and bad debt expense.
Merchandise Inventory	400,000	402,500	(2,500)	Add decrease.
Accounts Payable	100,580	125,020	(24,440)	Subtract decrease.
Income Taxes Payable	187,500	200,000	(12,500)	Subtract decrease.

The balance sheet provides information only about net accounts receivable. Therefore, we solve for the change (excluding any write-off) from the net account. We obtain the balances from the balance sheet and identify items obtained from the income statement with "IS." We must solve for missing information identified with an "X." Notice that a write-off has zero effect on the net accounts receivable, so we do not need to know its amount.

Accounts Receivable, Net

	Debit	Credit	
Beginning Balance	68,500		
		6,500	Bad Debt Expense from IS
X = Change excluding Write-off	120,500		
Ending Balance	182,500		

We add the bad debt expense of $6,500 to net income as a noncash adjustment and subtract the increase in the accounts receivable balance of $120,500.

Investing and Financing Cash Flows Sections

We need to analyze each balance sheet account with changes and reconcile all changes in account balances in order to present investing and financing activities using t-accounts as follows. This approach determines the noncash adjustments for the operating section using the indirect method. We identify these adjustments as each account is solved, but we also determine the amount of depreciation expense, amortization expense, share-based compensation expense, and bond discount amortization deduced on the income statement.

Trading Debt Investments

Debit	Credit	
25,000		Beginning Balance
14,000		Fair Value Adjustment Unrealized Gains from IS
	55,000	Sales*
124,500		X = Purchased
108,500		Ending Balance

Bond Discount

Debit	Credit	
360,600		Beginning Balance
	35,000	Amortization from IS
325,600		Ending Balance

*Related to the sale, we compute any gain/loss as a noncash adjustment in the operating section.

Sales Proceeds − Cost = $57,550 − $55,000 = $2,550 Gain

Continued

Property, Plant, and Equipment – Net

Debit	Credit	
3,214,460		Beginning Balance
	90,500	Depreciation Expense from IS
951,040		X = Purchased
4,075,000		Ending Balance

Notes Payable

Debit	Credit	
	1,301,450	Beginning Balance
30,570		X = Payments
	1,270,880	Ending Balance

Intangible Assets – Net

Debit	Credit	
900,500		Beginning Balance
	8,000	Amortization Expense from IS
	67,000	X = Franchise Sold
825,500		Ending Balance

Common Stock

Debit	Credit	
	100,000	Beginning Balance
	400,500	X = Stock Issue
	500,500	Ending Balance

Investments in Affiliate Companies

Debit	Credit	
620,000		Beginning Balance
256,200*		Equity Income
	90,600*	X = Cash Dividends
785,600		Ending Balance

*Undistributed earnings = $256,200 − $90,600 = $165,600.

Additional Paid-In Capital in Excess of Par – Common

Debit	Credit	
	154,000	Beginning Balance
	516,000	X = Stock Issue
	670,000	Ending Balance

Current Portion of Long-Term Debt

Debit	Credit	
	68,500	Beginning Balance
12,500		X = Payments
	56,000	Ending Balance

Retained Earnings

Debit	Credit	
	555,550	Beginning Balance
	590,500	Net Income from IS
146,050		X = Dividends Declared
	1,000,000	Ending Balance

Bonds Payable

Debit	Credit	
	2,500,000	Beginning Balance
	2,500,000	Ending Balance

Additional Paid-In Capital – Stock Options

Debit	Credit	
	0	Beginning Balance
	11,500	Share-based Compensation Expense from IS
	11,500	Ending Balance

For the obligations under pension plans, we do not have information to complete all changes in the account. However, the firm reported that the amount funded was $297,300. From the income statement, we know that the pension expense is $120,000. Therefore, we subtract the noncash adjustment for the excess of the funding over the expense of $177,300 from net income.

The cash flow statement under the indirect method is presented be follows.

Indirect Method

KaseyKraft Company
Cash Flow Statement—Indirect Method
For the Year Ended December 31

Operating Activities	
Net Income	$ 590,500
Adjustments to Reconcile Net Income to Net Cash Provided by Operating Activities	
Depreciation Expense	90,500
Amortization Expense	8,000
Undistributed Equity Earnings	(165,600)
Unrealized Gain on the Trading Portfolio	(14,000)
Increase in Deferred Tax Liability	21,000
Pension Contributions in Excess of Pension Expense	(177,300)
Stock-Based Compensation Expense	11,500
Gain on Sale of Investments	(2,550)
Amortization of Discount on Bonds Payable	35,000
Bad Debt Expense	6,500
Changes in Operating Working Capital Accounts	
Increase in Accounts Receivable	(120,500)
Decrease in Inventory	2,500
Decrease in Accounts Payable	(24,440)
Decrease in Taxes Payable	(12,500)
Net Cash Provided by Operating Activities	$ 248,610
Investing Activities	
Trading Debt Securities Acquired	$ (124,500)
Trading Debt Securities Sold	57,550
Purchase of Plant	(951,040)
Sale of Franchise	67,000
Net Cash Used by Investing Activities	$ (950,990)
Financing Activities	
Payment of Note	$ (43,070)
Cash Dividends Paid	(146,050)
Common Stock Issue	916,500
Net Cash Provided by Financing Activities	$ 727,380
Increase in Cash	$ 25,000
Beginning Cash Balance	5,000
Ending Cash Balance	$ 30,000

Finally, we prepare necessary disclosures under the indirect method. The company needs to disclose its significant noncash investing activities, its accounting policy for the definition of

Continued

cash equivalents, the amounts of cash paid for taxes, and the cash paid for interest. We compute the cash payments for taxes and interest as follows.

Cash Paid for Income Taxes	
Income Tax Expense	$393,667
Less: Increase in Deferred Tax Liability	(21,000)
Add: Decrease in Income Taxes Payable	12,500
Cash Paid for Income Taxes	$385,167

Cash Paid for Interest	
Interest Expense	$ 38,800
Less: Discount Amortization	(35,000)
Cash Paid for Interest	$ 3,800

Cash Flow Disclosures for the Indirect Method

Significant Noncash Investing and Financing Activities. The company leased equipment on December 31 of the current year during which it made no payments. Leased equipment and a lease obligation of $300,000 were recognized on the balance sheet.

Accounting Policy for Definition of Cash Equivalents. For purposes of the statement of cash flows, the company considers all highly liquid debt instruments purchased with maturities of 3 months or less to be cash equivalents.

Cash Paid for Taxes and Interest

Cash Paid for Taxes	$385,167
Cash Paid for Interest	$ 3,800

Direct Method

We determine the individual line items in operating activities under the direct method as follows.

Cash Collected from Customers	
Sales	$2,457,693
Less: Increase in Accounts Receivable	(114,000)
Less: Bad Debt Expense	(6,500)
Cash Collected from Customers	$ 2,337,193

Interest Received	
Investment Income	$ 19,690
Less: Gain on Sale of Investments	(2,550)
Cash Interest Received	$ 17,140

Cash Paid for Merchandise	
Cost of Goods Sold	$1,474,616
Less: Decrease in Inventory	(2,500)
Purchases (accrual basis)	$1,472,116
Add: Decrease in Accounts Payable	24,440
Cash Paid for Merchandise	$1,496,556

Cash Paid to Other Suppliers and Employees	
Selling, General, and Administrative Expenses	$ 25,000
Less: Stock-Based Compensation	(11,500)
Add: Cash Paid for Pension Funding	297,300
Cash Paid to Other Suppliers and Employees	$310,800

Cash paid for income taxes of $385,167 and cash paid for interest of $3,800 are the same as computed under the indirect method on page 1344. The dividends received on equity investments are calculated on page 1342. The investing and financing sections are the same as under the indirect method from page 1343.

The cash flow statement under the direct method follows.

KaseyKraft Company
Cash Flow Statement—Direct Method
For the Year Ended December 31

Operating Activities	
Cash Collected from Customers	$ 2,337,193
Dividends Received	90,600
Interest Received	17,140
Cash Paid for Merchandise	(1,496,556)
Cash Paid to Other Suppliers and Employees	(310,800)
Cash Paid for Interest	(3,800)
Cash Paid for Taxes	(385,167)
Net Cash Provided by Operating Activities	$ 248,610
Investing Activities	
Trading Debt Securities Acquired	$ (124,500)
Trading Debt Securities Sold	57,550
Purchase of Plant	(951,040)
Sale of Franchise	67,000
Net Cash Used by Investing Activities	$ (950,990)
Financing Activities	
Payment of Note	$ (43,070)
Cash Dividends Paid	(146,050)
Common Stock Issue	916,500
Net Cash Provided by Financing Activities	$ 727,380
Increase in Cash	$ 25,000
Beginning Cash Balance	5,000
Ending Cash Balance	$ 30,000

Finally, we prepare necessary disclosures under the direct method.

Cash Flow Disclosures for the Direct Method

Significant Noncash Investing and Financing Activities. The company leased equipment on December 31 of the current year during which it made no payments. Leased equipment and a lease obligation of $300,000 were recognized on the balance sheet.

Accounting Policy for Definition of Cash Equivalents. For purposes of the statement of cash flows, the company considers all highly liquid debt instruments purchased with maturities of 3 months or less to be cash equivalents.

Continued

Reconciliation of Net Income to Net Cash Provided by Operating Activities

Operating Activities	
Net Income	$590,500
Adjustments to Reconcile Net Income to Net Cash Provided by Operating Activities	
Depreciation Expense	90,500
Amortization Expense	8,000
Undistributed Equity Earnings	(165,600)
Unrealized Gain on the Trading Portfolio	(14,000)
Increase in Deferred Tax Liability	21,000
Pension Contributions in Excess of Pension Expense	(177,300)
Stock-based Compensation Expense	11,500
Gain on Sale of Investments	(2,550)
Amortization of Discount on Bonds Payable	35,000
Bad Debt Expense	6,500
Changes in Operating Working Capital Accounts	
Increase in Accounts Receivable	(120,500)
Decrease in Inventory	2,500
Decrease in Accounts Payable	(24,440)
Decrease in Taxes Payable	(12,500)
Net Cash Provided by Operating Activities	$248,610

Interview

CHRISTINA LOEBACH

VICE PRESIDENT, GLOBAL FINANCE NCH MARKETING SERVICES, DEERFIELD, IL»

Christina Loebach

As NCH Marketing's Vice President, Global Finance, Christina Loebach is responsible for strategic financial planning, accounting, and financial controls for businesses located throughout North America and Europe. Prior to joining NCH Marketing, she was an associate director at Kraft and a senior manager in KPMG's Economic & Valuation Services practice.

1 Why is the indirect method of reporting operating activities more popular with U.S. companies than the direct method?

The indirect method, the method currently used by a majority of companies, starts with net income (from the income statement) and adjusts for noncash items, including changes in the balance sheet. Companies prefer this method because it easily relates back to the income statement, which is usually the first financial statement investors review.

In addition, the direct method typically requires more information to prepare. You must separately track all transactions on a cash basis, rather than an accrual basis, to arrive at cash flow from operations. Under the indirect method, you can complete most of the cash flow statement by relying on the income statement and balance sheet.

2 What are the most common uses of the statement of cash flows by investors and creditors?

Investors generally seek a certain return on a potential investment. The value of a company is usually directly correlated to the discounted value of its future cash flows. The more cash generated (and the sooner), the higher the value of a company. Evaluating a company's cash position and the riskiness in its ability to generate cash flow helps investors determine the potential value of a company—and therefore their potential return on investment.

Creditors focus on a company's ability to repay debt. Assessing liquidity through a review of cash flow enables lenders to decide whether to issue a loan to a company and, if so, the rate, which is normally tied to the assessed risk of repayment.

Looking at a company's balance sheet, stakeholders can determine whether the company maintains sufficient liquidity to pay its obligations.

3 What incremental information is provided by the statement of cash flows to supplement balance sheet and income statement data?

The investing section of the cash flow statement shows how much the company spent on capital expenditures; those are not separately disclosed in the balance sheet or income statement. Comparing capital expenditures to depreciation (in the operating section of the cash flow statement) gives investors an understanding of whether the business is investing significantly in future growth. A high-growth company generally reports higher capital spending than depreciation.

The financing section of the cash flow statement provides information on how cash is returned to stakeholders (i.e., dividends, share repurchase, and debt repayment). A high dividend yield could signal that a company expects to have very stable cash flow. Companies tend to be penalized heavily (through stock price declines) for lowering dividend payments. Significant treasury stock purchases also can indicate that a company has limited investment alternatives or that it is supporting its earnings per share.

4 Companies are required to use the accrual, rather than cash, basis of accounting. Why, then, is the cash flow statement important to complete the financial reporting cycle?

With accrual-based accounting, significant differences can occur between a company's earnings and its cash flow. Bonus payments are a good example of an accrual difference. A company may pay a bonus once a year—even though that bonus relates to the company's/employee's performance over the course of the year. Under accrual-based accounting, one-twelfth of the estimated bonus expense is recognized in earnings each month. However, the cash bonus payment will not appear in the cash flow statement until it is ultimately paid, sometimes not even in the same year it was expensed.

Capital expenses also could have a significant impact on a company's cash flow but not its income statement. An asset is depreciated over its life with only a portion of the expense hitting the income statement each year. However, the full amount of the cash spent to purchase the asset is reflected in cash flow.

Thus, cash flow reporting allows stakeholders to reconcile differences between earnings and cash flow. Cash flow may be a better indication of the health of a company.

Discussion Questions

1. Christina Loebach discussed why the indirect method is the most popular format for the operating activities section of the statement of cash flows in the United States. Although the indirect method is the most popular, the direct method is preferred by the FASB. Discuss some of the reasons why the direct method could have advantages over the indirect reporting format.
2. Beginning with the response provided by Christina Loebach, discuss the specific, expected results (positive or negative) on each activity (operating, investing, and financing) during the four stages of a company's life cycle: rapid growth phase, sustained growth phase, mature phase, and decline phase.

FINANCIAL STATEMENT ANALYSIS

Operating Cash Flow

Operating cash flow is a measure of a company's cash flows generated from operations. A company needs to generate sufficient cash to meet its obligations and operational needs. Operating cash flow is a gauge of how effectively a company translates its operating activities into cash. Here we present two tools for the financial statement analysis of operating cash flow: cash coverage ratios and *free cash flow*.

Cash Coverage Ratios

Cash coverage ratios measure a company's operating cash flows relative to specific items such as obligations, dividends, and sales. Common cash coverage ratios include the following:

- Short-term debt coverage
- Debt coverage
- Dividend coverage
- Sales coverage
- Operating cash flows (OCF) to income ratio

Both the short-term debt and debt coverage ratios are indicators of a company's ability to pay its debts from operating activities.

$$\text{Short-Term Debt Coverage} = \frac{\text{Operating Cash Flows}}{\text{Short-Term Debt}} \tag{22.5}$$

$$\text{Debt Coverage} = \frac{\text{Operating Cash Flows}}{\text{Total Debt}} \tag{22.6}$$

The higher the cash flows relative to debt, the better able a company is to pay off its debt as it comes due and to seek additional financing if needed. Short-term debt includes short-term borrowings, the current portion of finance leases, and the current portion of long-term debt. Total debt is the sum of short-term debt, long-term debt, and finance leases. This debt coverage ratio indicates a company's ability to pay its debt from the cash it generates from operations. Low debt coverage ratios can indicate that a company has a high amount of debt or insufficient cash flows.

The dividend coverage ratio indicates the ability of a company to continue to pay its current level of dividends.

$$\text{Dividend Coverage} = \frac{\text{Operating Cash Flows}}{\text{Cash Dividends}} \tag{22.7}$$

The dividend coverage ratio can assist financial statement users in determining whether the firm can sustain current levels of dividends through operations. The higher the dividend coverage ratio, the better able the firm is to maintain dividends. Large and mature companies often pay large and consistent dividends. On the other hand, growth companies usually keep cash on hand for expansion purposes rather than paying out high dividends.

The sales coverage ratio, also called the cash return on sales ratio, compares a company's operating cash flows to its net sales or revenues. This ratio indicates a company's ability to convert sales into cash.

$$\text{Sales Coverage} = \frac{\text{Operating Cash Flows}}{\text{Net Sales (Revenues)}} \tag{22.8}$$

The higher the sales coverage ratio, the greater the company's ability to generate cash from sales.

The OCF to income ratio highlights the difference between net income and cash flows from operations.

$$\text{OCF to Income Ratio} = \frac{\text{Operating Cash Flows}}{\text{Net Income}} \tag{22.9}$$

Financial Statement Analysis, continued

The higher the OCF to income ratio, the greater the company's ability to generate cash from its operations and activities. An OCF to income ratio greater than 1 indicates that a company is able to generate greater cash flows than net income. The ratio would be greater than 1 when noncash expenses such as depreciation lower a company's income or working capital changes boost cash flows such as increases in accounts payable.

Free Cash Flow

To maintain and increase its ability to continue to generate operating cash flows, a company needs to invest in its productive capacity. That is, a company needs to make capital expenditures to maintain its facilities, whether manufacturing plants or retail stores, that are used to generate the cash flows. **Free cash flow** (FCF) is another measure of cash flows that adjusts for a company's capital expenditures.

$$\text{Free Cash Flow} = \text{Operating Cash Flow} - \text{Capital Expenditures} \tag{22.10}$$

The "free" in free cash flow indicates that cash is available for further expansion and acquisition, repayment of debt, or payment to owners as dividends. The free cash flow to operating cash flow ratio measures the relationship between free cash flow and operating cash flow.

$$\text{Free Cash Flow to Free Cash Flow Ratio} = \frac{\text{Operating Cash Flow} - \text{Capital Expenditure}}{\text{Operating Cash Flow}} \tag{22.11}$$

A higher ratio of free cash flow to operating cash flow suggests a stronger and more flexible cash position. Example 22.16 illustrates the analysis of operating cash flows.

EXAMPLE 22.16 Analysis of Operating Cash Flow

PROBLEM: You are interested in analyzing ***Johnson & Johnson's*** operating cash flows. Use ***Johnson & Johnson's*** statement of cash flows in Exhibit 22.10 and the additional information to address the questions that follow:

Additional Information

For the Year Ended, or at the Year-End (in millions)	2016	2015	2014
Sales	$71,890	$ 70,074	$74,331
Net Income	16,540	15,409	16,323
Short-Term Debt	4,684	7,004	3,638
Long-Term Debt	22,442	12,857	15,122

a. What is ***Johnson & Johnson's*** net cash flow from operations each year? What were the change and percentage of change in ***Johnson & Johnson's*** net cash flow from operations each year? Compare the changes in net cash flow from operations to the changes in net income.

b. What are the major adjustments for noncash expenses and losses? What are the major adjustments for noncash revenues and gains?

c. Compute the following cash coverage ratios for each year and comment on them:
   - Short-term debt coverage
   - Debt coverage
   - Dividend coverage
   - Sales coverage
   - OCF to income ratio

d. Compute ***Johnson & Johnson's*** free cash flows for each year and comment on them. Compare ***Johnson & Johnson's*** free cash flows to its operating cash flows for each year.

Continued

Financial Statement Analysis, continued

EXHIBIT 22.10 Statement of Cash Flows, ***Johnson & Johnson***, Financial Statements, Fiscal Year 2016

Johnson & Johnson and Subsidiaries
Consolidated Statements of Cash Flows
(Dollars in Millions)

	2016	2015	2014
Cash Flows from Operating Activities			
Net Earnings	$16,540	$ 15,409	$ 16,323
Adjustments to Reconcile Net Earnings to Cash Flows from Operating Activities:			
Depreciation and Amortization of Property and Intangibles	3,754	3,746	3,895
Stock Based Compensation	878	874	792
Venezuela Currency Devaluation	-	122	87
Asset Write-downs	283	624	410
Net Gain on Equity Investment Transactions	(563)	(2,583)	(2,383)
Deferred Tax Provision	(341)	(270)	441
Accounts Receivable Allowances	(11)	18	(28)
Changes in Assets and Liabilities, Net of Effects from Acquisitions:			
Increase in Accounts Receivable	(1,065)	(433)	(247)
Increase in Inventories	(249)	(449)	(1,120)
Increase in Accounts Payable and Accrued Liabilities	656	287	1,194
Decrease in Other Current and Non-current Assets	18	65	442
(Decrease)/Increase in Other Current and Non-current Liabilities	(1,133)	2,159	(1,096)
Net Cash Flows from Operating Activities	**$18,767**	**$ 19,569**	**$ 18,710**
Cash Flows from Investing Activities			
Additions to Property, Plant and Equipment	$(3,226)	$ (3,463)	$ (3,714)
Proceeds from the Disposal of Assets	1,267	3,464	4,631
Acquisitions, Net of Cash Acquired	(4,509)	(954)	(2,129)
Purchases of Investments	(33,950)	(40,828)	(34,913)
Sales of Investments	35,780	34,149	24,119
Other (Primarily Intangibles)	(123)	(103)	(299)
Net Cash Used by Investing Activities	**$ (4,761)**	**$ (7,735)**	**$(12,305)**
Cash Flows from Financing Activities			
Dividends to Shareholders	$ (8,621)	$(8,173)	$(7,768)
Repurchase of Common Stock	(8,979)	(5,290)	(7,124)
Proceeds from Short-term Debt	111	2,416	1,863
Retirement of Short-term Debt	(2,017)	(1,044)	(1,267)
Proceeds from Long-term Debt	12,004	75	2,098
Retirement of Long-term Debt	(2,223)	(68)	(1,844)
Proceeds from the Exercise of Stock Options/Excess Tax Benefits	1,189	1,005	1,543
Other	(15)	(57)	-
Net Cash Used by Financing Activities	**$ (8,551)**	**$ (11,136)**	**$(12,499)**
Effect of Exchange Rate Changes on Cash and Cash Equivalents	$ (215)	$ (1,489)	$ (310)
Increase/(Decrease) in Cash and Cash Equivalents	5,240	(791)	(6,404)
Cash and Cash Equivalents, Beginning of Year (Note 1)	13,732	14,523	20,927
Cash and Cash Equivalents, End of Year (Note 1)	**$18,972**	**$ 13,732**	**$ 14,523**

Sources: Johnson & Johnson Subsidiaries Consolidated Statements of Cash Flows, Financial Statements, January 1, 2017. http://files.shareholder.com/downloads/JNJ/3809936545x0xS200406-17-6/200406/filing.pdf

Financial Statement Analysis, continued

SOLUTION:

a. The following table presents ***Johnson & Johnson's*** net cash flow from operations, the change, and the percentage of change each year. Net cash flow from operations is obtained from the operating section of the statement of cash flows. Net cash flow from operations was positive each year. The table also presents ***Johnson & Johnson's*** net income as well as the change and the percentage of change each year. Net income is obtained from the top line of ***Johnson & Johnson's*** indirect method operating section. Net cash flow from operations increased in 2015 but decreased in 2016 whereas net income decreased in 2015 but increased in 2016. The directions of the changes in net cash flow from operations are opposite to the changes in net income. In all years, net cash flow from operations was higher than net income. Part (b) explores reasons for the difference between net cash flow from operations and net income.

	2016	2015	2014
Net Cash Flow from Operations (in millions)	$18,767	$ 19,569	$ 18,710
Change	$ (802)	$ 859	
Percentage of Change	(4.1%)	4.6%	
Net Income (in millions)	$16,540	$ 15,409	$ 16,323
Change	$ 1,131	$ (914)	
Percentage of Change	7.3%	(5.6%)	

b. Major adjustments for noncash expenses and losses are depreciation and amortization of property and intangibles (2014–2016) and stock-based compensation (2014–2016). Major adjustments for noncash revenues and gains are the net gain on equity investment transactions (2014–2016) and the deferred tax provision (2015–2016).

c. The following table provides the computation of the cash coverage ratios.

Ratio		2016	2015	2014
Short-Term Debt Coverage =	Operating Cash Flow / Short-Term Debt	4.01 = $18,767 / $4,684	2.79 = $19,569 / $7,004	5.14 = $18,710 / $3,638
Debt Coverage =	Operating Cash Flow / Total Debt	0.69 = $18,767 / ($4,684 + $22,442)	0.99 = $19,569 / ($7,004 + $12,857)	1.00 = $18,710 / ($3,638 + $15,122)
Dividends Coverage =	Operating Cash Flow / Cash Dividends	2.18 = $18,767 / $8,621	2.39 = $19,569 / $8,173	2.41 = $18,710 / $7,768
Sales Coverage =	Operating Cash Flow / Net Sales	0.26 = $18,767 / $71,890	0.28 = $19,569 / $70,074	0.25 = $18,710 / $74,331
OCF to Income Ratio	Operating Cash Flow / Net Income	1.13 = $18,767 / $16,540	1.27 = $19,569 / $15,409	1.15 = $18,710 / $16,323

With a ratio greater than 1.00 each year, the short-term debt coverage ratio indicates that the company generated enough operating cash flows each year to cover its short-term debt obligations. The debt coverage ratio indicates that operating cash flows each year were high relative to all debt outstanding. In 2015 and 2014, the company had almost enough operating cash flow to pay for all its debt. The debt coverage ratio decreased each year and was the lowest in 2016 when long-term debt increased.

The dividend coverage ratio of more than 2.1 each year shows that the company had over twice as much operating cash as necessary to cover its dividends. The company appears to have used more than 46% ($8,621 dividends divided by $18,767 operating cash flow in 2016) of its operating cash flows for dividends.

Continued

Financial Statement Analysis, continued

The sales coverage ratio indicates that for each dollar of sales, the company generated between 25 and 28 cents in operating cash flow between 2014 and 2016. The OCF to income ratio was greater than 1.00 each year, indicating that ***Johnson & Johnson*** was generating more cash from operations than net income.

d. The following table shows the computations of free cash flow and free cash flow over operating cash flow.

Ratio		2016	2015	2014
Free Cash Flow =	Operating Cash Flow less Capital Expenditures	$15,541 = $18,767 − $3,226	$16,106 = $19,569 − $3,463	$14,996 = $18,710 − $3,714
Free Cash Flow to Operating Cash Flow =	Free Cash Flow / Operating Cash Flow	0.83 = $15,541 / $18,767	0.82 = $16,106 / $19,569	0.80 = $14,996 / $18,710

The company's free cash flow was positive, indicating that it could replace existing productive capacity through capital expenditures using internally generated cash without the need to borrow. The ratio of free cash flow to operating cash flow, ranging from 0.80 to 0.83, implies that the company had about 80 cents of each dollar of operating cash flow available for use in expanding the business, acquiring new companies, or making investments even after it had replaced its productive capacity.

Summary by Learning Objectives

In the following, we summarize the main points by learning objective. Throughout the chapter, we discuss the accounting and reporting of U.S. GAAP and IFRS side-by-side. The following table also highlights the major similarities and differences between the standards.

1 State the purpose of the statement of cash flows and define cash and cash equivalents.

Summary	Similarities and Differences between U.S. GAAP and IFRS
The statement of cash flows provides information about a firm's cash receipts and cash payments during a period of time. It summarizes the firm's cash flows by category: operating, investing, and financing activities.	➤ Similar under U.S. GAAP and IFRS except that IFRS allows bank overdrafts to be reported as reductions of cash and cash equivalents.
Operating activities include producing and delivering goods and services.	
Investing activities relate to the acquisition and sale of property, plant, and equipment; long-term investments; short-term investments not classified as cash equivalents; and intangible assets.	
Financing activities include borrowing from creditors and repaying them, obtaining resources from owners, and providing owners with a return on their investment.	
Cash consists of coins, currency, and bank deposits as well as negotiable instruments such as checks and money orders.	
Cash equivalents include short-term, highly liquid investments with original maturities of 3 months or less when acquired.	
Bank overdrafts are usually classified as liabilities.	

Summary by Learning Objectives, continued

2 Describe the format of the statement of cash flows, including classification of activities into operating, investing, and financing sections; the reconciliation of cash and cash equivalents; and the disclosure of significant noncash investing and financing transactions.

Summary	Similarities and Differences between U.S. GAAP and IFRS
The statement of cash flows summarizes cash inflows and outflows for a firm over a period of time by category: operating, investing, and financing activities. Operating activities include: 1. Cash receipts from customers 2. Cash payments for the purchase of goods for resale or for use in production 3. Cash payments to suppliers and employees 4. Cash payments related to taxes 5. Cash receipts related to interest and dividend income 6. Cash payments of interest Investing activities include: 1. Cash receipts from the collection or sale of notes receivable 2. Cash receipts from the sale of debt and equity securities of other entities 3. Cash receipts from the sale of productive assets (for example, property, plant, and equipment) 4. Cash payments for loans made by the entity 5. Cash payments for debt and equity securities of other entities 6. Cash payments for property, plant, and equipment and other productive assets Financing activities include: 1. Cash receipts from issuing equity to owners 2. Cash receipts from borrowing through bonds, notes, or other instruments 3. Cash payments to repurchase equity from owners 4. Cash payments for principal on debt 5. Cash payments of dividends The statement of cash flows provides a reconciliation of the change in cash during the period. Firms must disclose significant noncash investing and financing transactions on the statement of cash flows.	➤ Similar under U.S. GAAP and IFRS except that: • IFRS allows companies choices in how to classify interest received, interest paid, dividends received, dividends paid, and taxes paid. • IFRS does not require that the increase or decrease in cash and cash equivalents explained in the statement of cash flows agree to a single line item on the balance sheet. If a different amount is used, companies must provide a reconciliation schedule.

3 Understand and use the conceptual model based on the accounting equation to prepare the statement of cash flows.

Summary	Similarities and Differences between U.S. GAAP and IFRS
The cash flow statement is built from changes in balance sheet accounts. We derive a model for the statement of cash flows by converting the accounting equation into a cash equation: Assets = Liabilities + Stockholders' Equity (22.1) $\Delta CASH = \Delta CL + \Delta NCL - \Delta OCA - \Delta NCA + \Delta CS + \Delta RE$ (22.4)	Similar under U.S. GAAP and IFRS.

Summary by Learning Objectives, continued

4 Explain and prepare the operating cash flows section of the statement of cash flows using the indirect and direct methods.

Summary	Similarities and Differences between U.S. GAAP and IFRS
The operating cash flows section reports cash flows relating to operating activities. The indirect method (also referred to as the reconciliation format) begins with net income from the income statement and reconciles it to net cash provided by operating activities. The direct method (also referred to as the income statement format) reports cash receipts and payments for all operating activities. The investing and financing sections of the direct and indirect statement of cash flows are the same: The only difference between the two methods is how cash flows are reported in the operating activities section.	➤ Similar under U.S. GAAP and IFRS except that IFRS does not specify the income line item that must begin the reconciliation of operating cash flows under the indirect method.

5 Describe and illustrate the investing cash flows section of the statement of cash flows.

Summary	Similarities and Differences between U.S. GAAP and IFRS
The investing section reports cash receipts and payments for all investing activities.	Similar under U.S. GAAP and IFRS.

6 Describe and illustrate the financing cash flows section of the statement of cash flows.

Summary	Similarities and Differences between U.S. GAAP and IFRS
The financing section reports cash receipts and payments for all financing activities.	Similar under U.S. GAAP and IFRS.

7 Discuss and illustrate the reporting of complex transactions in determining cash flows.

Summary	Similarities and Differences between U.S. GAAP and IFRS
The more complex topics reviewed in this chapter include: 1. Acquisitions and dispositions of long-term assets 2. Deferred income taxes 3. Accounts receivable: net and bad debt expense 4. Unrealized gains and losses on fair value adjustments 5. Equity method investments 6. Share-based compensation 7. Pension adjustments 8. Amortization of bond discounts and premiums For each of these, any noncash adjustments and cash inflows or outflows must be computed from the relevant income statement and balance sheet information.	Similar under U.S. GAAP and IFRS.

Summary by Learning Objectives, continued

8 Detail required disclosures related to the statement of cash flows.

Summary	Similarities and Differences between U.S. GAAP and IFRS
A company is required to disclose: • Its policy regarding cash equivalents. • All significant noncash investing and financing activities. • Interest and taxes paid when using the indirect method. • A reconciliation of net income to net cash flows from operating activities when using the direct method. • The nature of any restrictions on its cash balance.	➤ Similar under U.S. GAAP and IFRS except that under IFRS: • A company does not have to prepare a reconciliation of net income to net cash flows from operating activities if using the direct method. • IFRS requires that companies disclose any cash balances that are held but not available for use. • IFRS also encourages management's comment on any additional information that may be relevant to users in understanding a company's financial position and liquidity. • IFRS requires the entity to provide adequate disclosure to explain changes in financing liabilities arising from cash and noncash changes.

MyLab Accounting

Go to **http://www.pearson.com/mylab/accounting** for the following Questions, Multiple-Choice Questions, Brief Exercises, Exercises, and Problems. They are available with immediate grading, explanations of correct and incorrect answers, and interactive media that acts as your own online tutor.

22 The Statement of Cash Flows

Questions

❶ **Q22-1.** What is the cash flow statement?

❶ **Q22-2.** What is the primary purpose of the cash flow statement?

❶ ❷ **Q22-3.** To what does the total cash flow computed on the statement of cash flows reconcile?

❷ **Q22-4.** Does a firm classify the acquisition of a plant asset by common stock issuance as both an investing and a financing activity on the cash flow statement in the year of acquisition?

❹ **Q22-5.** What are the two different reporting formats for preparing the operating activities section of the statement of cash flows?

❷❺ **Q22-6.** How do firms reclassify gains and losses on the disposal of property, plant, and equipment? Why is this reclassification appropriate?

❷ **Q22-7.** How do firms classify interest paid and interest received on the statement of cash flows under IFRS?

❹ **Q22-8.** Does the direct reporting format provide complete flexibility in terms of the line items to report in operating activities?

❷ **Q22-9.** How does a firm classify the acquisition of a plant asset by issuing common stock?

❸ **Q22-10.** Does the accounting equation explain the change in cash during the period?

❹ **Q22-11.** Under the indirect method, do companies using IFRS begin the operating section with net income?

❹❺❻ **Q22-12.** What approach is used in preparing the operating activities, investing activities, and financing activities sections of the statement of cash flows?

❹❼ **Q22-13.** Under the indirect method, do firms subtract bond discount amortization from net income to determine operating cash flows?

❹❼ **Q22-14.** Do firms subtract pension expense from net income to determine operating cash flows?

❽ **Q22-15.** Are cash flow disclosure requirements the same for both the direct and indirect reporting formats?

❽ **Q22-16.** Can financial analysts use the required disclosure of interest and taxes paid under the indirect reporting format to offset the inconsistent classification of interest expense and tax paid within the operating activities section of the cash flow statement?

Multiple-Choice Questions

In partnership with: BECKER PROFESSIONAL EDUCATION

Becker CPA Exam Review multiple-choice questions are available in MyLab Accounting.

❷❹ **MC22-1.** Oscar Company is preparing its financial statements for the current year. Which of the following statements is/are correct?

I. A main difference between the income statement and the statement of cash flows is that the income statement is based on the accrual method of accounting and the statement of cash flows is based on the cash basis of accounting.

II. Depreciation is added back to net income in a direct method statement of cash flows because it is a source of cash.

III. Investing and financing activities that do not affect cash do not require disclosure in the financial statements.

IV. Allowing a client company to buy on credit is a use of cash to the client company.

a. I only is correct.

b. I and II only are correct.

c. I and III only are correct.

d. I, II, III, and IV are correct.

4 **MC22-2.** In its year-end income statement, Black Knights Company reports cost of goods sold of $450,000. Changes occurred in several balance sheet accounts during the year as follows:

Inventory	$160,000 decrease
Accounts Payable – Suppliers	40,000 decrease

What amount should the Black Knights Company report as cash paid to suppliers in its cash flow statement prepared under the direct method?

a. $250,000 b. $330,000 c. $570,000 d. $650,000

4 **MC22-3.** Big Dollars Corporation's comparative financial statements included the following amounts for the current year:

Net income	$ 650,000
Depreciation expense	$ 93,000
Equity in earnings of unconsolidated affiliate	$ 61,000
Gain on sale of fixed assets	$ 4,000
Increase in accounts receivable	$ 25,000
Decrease in inventory	$ (57,000)
Decrease in fixed assets	$ 38,000
Increase in accounts payable	$ 42,000
Decrease in notes payable	$ (75,000)

On its current year statement of cash flows, what is Big Dollars' net cash provided by operating activities?

a. $677,000 b. $714,000 c. $752,000 d. $790,000

4 **MC22-4.** Which of the following items would *not* be included in the operating activities section of an entity's statement of cash flows under U.S. GAAP?

a. Interest received
b. Proceeds from the sale of trading securities
c. Dividends paid
d. Income taxes paid

4 5 **MC22-5.** The Year 11 balance sheet of Cool Tools, Inc. reported the following fixed asset balances:

	Year 11	Year 10
Fixed assets	$160,000	$128,000
Accumulated depreciation	(53,000)	(41,000)
Fixed assets – net	$107,000	$ 87,000

On January 1, Year 11, Cool Tools purchased fixed assets for $50,000 and sold fixed assets with an original cost of $18,000 and a book value of $6,000 for $10,000. Cool Tools made no other long-term asset purchases or sales during Year 11. What are the company's (1) net cash used in investing activities and (2) the amount of the depreciation adjustment to the operating section of its statement of cash flows prepared using the indirect method?

Net Cash Used in Investing Activities	Depreciation Adjustment in Operating Section
a. $32,000	$12,000
b. $32,000	$24,000
c. $40,000	$12,000
d. $40,000	$24,000

5 **MC22-6.** Sykes Corporation's comparative balance sheets at December 31, Year 2 and Year 1, reported accumulated depreciation balances of $800,000 and $600,000, respectively. Property acquired at a cost of $50,000 and a carrying amount of $40,000 was the only property sold in Year 2. Depreciation charged to operations in Year 2 was:

a. $190,000 b. $200,000 c. $210,000 d. $220,000

6 **MC22-7.** During Year 1, Brianna Company had the following transactions related to its financing operations:

Payment for the retirement of long-term bonds payable (carrying value $740,000)	$ 750,000
Distribution in Year 1 of cash dividend declared in Year 0 to preferred shareholders	$ 62,000
Carrying value of convertible preferred stock of Brianna converted into common shares	$ 120,000
Proceeds from sale of treasury stock (carrying value at cost $86,000)	$ 95,000

On its Year 1 statement of cash flows, net cash used in financing activities should be:

a. $717,000 b. $716,000 c. $597,000 d. $535,000

8 **MC22-8.** Which of the following supplemental disclosures to the statement of cash flows is *not* required when the indirect method is used?

a. Income taxes paid
b. Reconciliation of net income to net cash provided by operating activities
c. Interest paid
d. Noncash investing and financing activities

Brief Exercises

2 **BE22-1. Classification as Operating, Investing, or Financing Activity on the Statement of Cash Flows**. Classify each item in the following list of cash receipts and cash payments as operating, investing, or financing.

Cash Receipt or Payment	Classification
Cash payments to suppliers and employees	________
Cash payments for principal on debt	________
Cash receipts from customers	________
Cash payments for property, plant, and equipment	________
Cash receipts from the sale of available-for-sale investment securities	________
Cash receipts from interest	________
Cash receipts from issuing equity to owners	________
Cash payments for interest	________
Cash receipts from the sale of property, plant, and equipment	________
Cash payment of dividends	________
Cash receipts of dividends from investments	________

2 **BE22-2. Classification as Operating, Investing, or Financing Activity on the Statement of Cash Flows, IFRS.** Classify each item in the following list of cash receipts and cash payments as operating, investing, or financing under IFRS.

Cash Receipt or Payment	Classification – IFRS
Cash payments to suppliers and employees	________
Cash payments for principal on debt	________
Cash receipts from customers	________
Cash payments for property, plant, and equipment	________
Cash receipts from the sale of investment securities	________
Cash receipts from interest	________
Cash receipts from issuing equity to owners	________
Cash payments for interest	________
Cash receipts from the sale of property, plant, and equipment	________
Cash payment of dividends	________
Cash receipts of dividends from investments	________

3 4 **BE22-3. Operating Activities Section, Indirect Method.** State whether a firm would add or subtract the following items from income to compute cash flows from operations under the indirect method.

Items	Added or Subtracted
Increase in prepaid expense	__________
Decrease in income taxes payable	__________
Decrease in accounts receivable	__________
Increase in inventory	__________
Decrease in the current portion of long-term debt	__________
Increase in accounts payable	__________

3 4 **BE22-4. Operating Activities Section, Indirect Method.** State whether a firm would add or subtract the following items from income to compute cash flows from operations under the indirect method.

Items	Added or Subtracted
Depreciation expense	__________
Increase in income taxes payable	__________
Gain on sale of equipment	__________
Decrease in inventory	__________
Impairment loss	__________
Increase in salaries payable	__________
Bond premium amortization	__________

4 **BE22-5. Operating Activities Section, Direct Method.** Larry's Luggage Company provided the following balance sheet and income statement for the current year. Prepare the operating activities section of the cash flow statement using the direct method. Assume that accrued expenses relate to selling, general, and administrative expenses.

Larry's Luggage Company
Balance Sheets
At December 31

Assets	**Ending**	**Beginning**
Cash	$ 1,000	$ 5,000
Accounts Receivable – net	5,500	3,000
Merchandise Inventory	4,000	1,800
Total Current Assets	$10,500	$ 9,800
Noncurrent Assets		
Investments in Bonds	$30,000	$10,000
Property, Plant, and Equipment – net	50,000	60,000
Total Noncurrent Assets	$80,000	$70,000
Total Assets	$90,500	$79,800
Liabilities		
Current Liabilities		
Accounts Payable	$ 3,200	$ 4,400
Accrued Expenses	6,700	6,550
Income Taxes Payable	1,500	2,450
Total Current Liabilities	$11,400	$13,400
Noncurrent Liabilities		
Notes Payable	$35,000	$28,000
Total Noncurrent Liabilities	$35,000	$28,000
Total Liabilities	$46,400	$41,400

Larry's Luggage Company
Balance Sheets
At December 31

Shareholders' Equity	**Ending**	**Beginning**
Common Stock, $1 par value	$10,000	$ 9,000
Additional Paid-in Capital in Excess of Par–Common	15,000	12,000
Retained Earnings	19,100	17,400
Total Shareholders' Equity	$44,100	$38,400
Total Liabilities and Shareholders' Equity	$90,500	$79,800

Larry's Luggage Company
Income Statement
For the Year Ended December 31

Sales	$56,000
Cost of Goods Sold	33,600
Gross Profit	$22,400
Selling, General, and Administrative Expenses	$11,600
Depreciation Expense	6,000
Total Operating Expenses	$ 17,600
Operating Income	$ 4,800
Interest Expense	$ (2,100)
Investment Income	634
Income before Tax	$ 3,334
Income Tax Expense	(1,334)
Net Income	$ 2,000

4 **BE22-6. Operating Activities Section, Indirect Method.** Repeat the requirements of BE22-5 under the indirect method.

4 **BE22-7. Operating Activities Section, Indirect Method, IFRS.** Repeat the requirements of BE22-5 under the indirect method assuming that Larry's Luggage Company reports under IFRS and begins the reconciliation to operating cash flows with operating income. Larry's Luggage classifies interest paid, interest received, and taxes paid as operating activities.

4 **BE22-8. Operating Activities Section, Indirect Method, IFRS.** Repeat the requirements of BE22-5 under the indirect method assuming that Larry's Luggage Company reports under IFRS and it begins the reconciliation to operating cash flows with operating income. Larry's Luggage classifies interest paid as a financing activity and interest received as an investing activity.

6 **BE22-9. Financing Activities Section, IFRS.** Using the information provided in BE22-5, prepare the financing activities section of Larry's Luggage Company's cash flow statement assuming that Larry's Luggage reports under IFRS. Larry's Luggage classifies interest paid as a financing activity and interest received as an investing activity. Larry's Luggage made payments of $2,000 on its notes payable.

4 **BE22-10. Operating Activities Section, Direct Method.** Rodent World Exotic Pet Shops, Incorporated reported the following comparative balance sheets and income statement for the current year. Prepare the operating activities section of the statement of cash flows using the direct method. Assume that accrued expenses relate to selling, general, and administrative expenses.

Rodent World Exotic Pet Shops, Incorporated Balance Sheets
At December 31

Assets	Ending	Beginning
Current Assets		
Cash	$ 7,000	$ 3,500
Accounts Receivable – net	8,500	8,000
Merchandise Inventory	2,300	4,000
Prepaid Insurance	1,700	2,200
Total Current Assets	$ 19,500	$ 17,700
Noncurrent Assets		
Investments	$ 12,000	$ 24,300
Property, Plant, and Equipment – net	75,000	58,000
Total Noncurrent Assets	$ 87,000	$ 82,300
Total Assets	$106,500	$100,000
Liabilities		
Current Liabilities		
Accounts Payable	$ 4,500	$ 1,000
Accrued Expenses	9,800	5,120
Income Taxes Payable	6,000	4,850
Total Current Liabilities	$ 20,300	$ 10,970
Noncurrent Liabilities		
Notes Payable	$ 31,000	$ 42,630
Total Noncurrent Liabilities	$ 31,000	$ 42,630
Total Liabilities	$ 51,300	$ 53,600
Shareholders' Equity		
Common Stock, $1 par value	$ 9,000	$ 9,000
Additional Paid-in Capital in Excess of Par–Common	20,000	20,000
Retained Earnings	26,200	17,400
Total Shareholders' Equity	$ 55,200	$ 46,400
Total Liabilities and Shareholders' Equity	$106,500	$100,000

Rodent World Exotic Pet Shops Income Statement
For the Year Ended December 31

Sales	$ 80,085
Cost of Goods Sold	48,051
Gross Profit	$ 32,034
Selling, General, and Administrative Expenses	$ 10,700
Depreciation Expense	2,400
Total Operating Expenses	$ 13,100
Operating Income	$ 18,934
Interest Expense	$ (4,000)
Interest Revenue	3,400
Income before Tax	$ 18,334
Income Tax Expense	(7,334)
Net Income	$ 11,000

4 **BE22-11. Operating Activities Section, Indirect Method.** Repeat the requirements in BE22-10 using the indirect method.

4 **BE22-12. Operating Activities Section, Direct Method.** Polly's Imported Goods, Ltd. recently issued its annual report for the current year. Its comparative balance sheets for the current year follow. Prepare the operating activities section of the statement of cash flows using the direct method. Assume that accrued expenses relate to selling, general, and administrative expenses.

Polly's Imported Goods, Ltd.
Balance Sheets At December 31

Assets	**Ending**	**Beginning**
Current Assets		
Cash	$ 26,000	$ 35,000
Accounts Receivable – net	30,000	50,000
Merchandise Inventory	18,900	41,200
Prepaid Rent	10,100	1,800
Total Current Assets	$ 85,000	$128,000
Noncurrent Assets		
Property, Plant, and Equipment – net	$100,000	$ 75,000
Indefinite-Life Intangible Assets	55,000	40,000
Total Noncurrent Assets	$155,000	$115,000
Total Assets	$240,000	$243,000
Liabilities		
Current Liabilities		
Accounts Payable	$ 21,000	$ 19,000
Accrued Expenses	17,000	21,500
Income Taxes Payable	15,750	16,750
Total Current Liabilities	$ 53,750	$ 57,250
Noncurrent Liabilities		
Notes Payable	$ 85,250	$ 107,000
Total Noncurrent Liabilities	$ 85,250	$ 107,000
Total Liabilities	$139,000	$164,250
Shareholders' Equity		
Common Stock, $1 par value	$ 15,000	$ 8,000
Additional Paid-in Capital in Excess of Par–Common	40,000	30,000
Retained Earnings	46,000	40,750
Total Shareholders' Equity	$101,000	$ 78,750
Total Liabilities and Shareholders' Equity	$240,000	$243,000

Polly's Imported Goods, Ltd.
Income Statement
For the Year Ended December 31

Sales	$137,710
Cost of Goods Sold	82,626
Gross Profit	$55,084
Selling, General, and Administrative Expenses	$23,584
Depreciation Expense	8,000
Total Operating Expenses	$31,584
Operating Income	$23,500
Interest Expense	$ (6,000)
Income before Tax	$ 17,500
Income Tax Expense	(7,000)
Net Income	$ 10,500

4 **BE22-13. Operating Activities Section, Indirect Method.** Prepare the operating activities section of the statement of cash flows for Polly's Imported Goods in BE22-12 using the indirect method.

4 **BE22-14. Operating Activities Section, Indirect Method, IFRS.** Prepare the operating activities section of the statement of cash flows for Polly's Imported Goods in BE22-12 using the indirect method assuming that Polly reports under IFRS. Polly begins the operating activities section with operating income. It reports interest paid in the financing activities section and interest received in the investing activities section.

4 **BE22-15. Operating Activities Section, Indirect Method.** Simons Products, Inc. reports the following comparative balance sheets and income statement for the current year.

Simons Products, Inc.
Comparative Balance Sheets
At December 31

	Current Year	Prior Year
Cash	$ 221	$ 156
Accounts Receivable – net	247	208
Inventory	312	260
Prepaid Insurance	26	52
Total Current Assets	$ 806	$ 676
Plant, and Equipment – net	468	364
Total Assets	$1,274	$1,040
Accounts Payable	$ 390	$ 351
Income Tax Payable	65	52
Total Current Liabilities	$ 455	$ 403
Long-Term Debt	195	156
Total Liabilities	$ 650	$ 559
Capital Stock	$ 286	$ 221
Retained Earnings	338	260
Total Shareholders' Equity	$ 624	$ 481
Total Liabilities and Equity	$1,274	$1,040

Simons Products, Inc.
Income Statement
For the Current Year Ended December 31

Sales		$1,300
Operating Expenses		
Cost of Goods Sold	$ 780	
Depreciation	65	
Insurance	39	
Gain on Sale of Equipment	(26)	
Other Expenses	195	(1,053)
Income before Tax		$ 247
Provision for Income Tax		104
Net Income		$ 143

During the year, Simons Products purchased new equipment for $195 and sold equipment with a net book value of $26 for $52. Both events were cash transactions. It paid any dividends declared. Simons made no repayments of debt during the year. Prepare the operating activities section of the statement of cash flows using the indirect method.

4 **BE22-16. Operating Activities Section, Direct Method.** Using the information provided in BE22-15, prepare the operating activities section of the statement of cash flows using the direct method.

4 **BE22-17. Statement of Cash Flows, Indirect Method.** Soccer Emporium provided the following information for the current year.

Simplified Income Statement	Amount
Sales	$ 567,000
Depreciation Expense	(52,000)
Selling, General, and Administrative Expenses	(488,000)
Operating Income	27,000
Tax Expense	(8,000)
Net Income	$ 19,000

Account Changes from the Balance Sheet	
Increase in Accounts Receivable	$ 9,000
Decrease in Prepaid Expenses	$ 8,000
Increase in Accounts Payable	$ 11,000
Decrease in Income Taxes Payable	$ 3,000

Compute cash flows from operating activities for Soccer Emporium under the indirect reporting format.

4 **BE22-18. Statement of Cash Flows, Indirect Method, IFRS.** Use the information from BE22-17 assuming that Soccer Emporium is an IFRS reporter that reconciles operating income to operating cash flows. Compute cash flows from operating activities for Soccer Emporium under the indirect reporting format.

4 **BE22-19. Statement of Cash Flows, Direct Method.** Soccer Emporium provides the following information for the current year.

Simplified Income Statement	Amount
Sales	$ 567,000
Depreciation Expense	(52,000)
Selling, General, and Administrative Expenses	(488,000)
Tax Expense	(8,000)
Net Income	$ 19,000

Account Changes from the Balance Sheet	
Increase in Accounts Receivable	$ 9,000
Decrease in Prepaid Expenses	$ 8,000
Increase in Accounts Payable	$ 11,000
Decrease in Income Taxes Payable	$ 3,000

Compute cash flows from operating activities for Soccer Emporium under the direct reporting format.

5 **BE22-20. Investing Activities Section, Direct Method.** Using the information provided in BE22-15, prepare the investing activities section of Simons Products' cash flow statement.

6 **BE22-21. Financing Activities Section, Direct Method.** Using the information provided in BE22-15, prepare the financing activities section of Simons Products' cash flow statement.

7 **BE22-22. Complex Transactions, Acquisitions and Dispositions of Long-Term Assets.** During the year, Solar Corporation sold equipment with a net book value of $6,000 for $9,000. It also purchased equity securities for $8,000. Net income for the year is $22,000. There were no other transactions conducted during the period.

Required »

a. What is the gain or loss on the sale of equipment?
b. What are Solar's operating and investing cash flows? Use the indirect method.

7 **BE22-23. Complex Transactions, Acquisitions and Dispositions of Long-Term Assets.** During the year, Big Ben Corporation sold equipment for $2,000. The equipment's cost was $25,000 and accumulated depreciation was $18,000. There were no other transactions conducted during the period. Big Ben also purchased a new building for $44,000 and paid cash. Net income for the year was $53,000.

Required »

a. What is the gain or loss on the sale of equipment?
b. What are the operating and investing cash flows for the company? Use the indirect method.

7 **BE22-24. Complex Transactions, Cash Paid for Income Taxes.** Roadster Car Service reported a decrease in income taxes payable of $4,500 during the year and an increase in deferred-tax liability of $3,000. Its income tax expense was $2,300.

Required »

a. What is cash paid for income taxes?
b. What would Roadster report in the operating section of the cash flow statement under the indirect method?

7 **BE22-25. Complex Transactions, Cash Paid for Income Taxes.** During the year, Zurry Coach Service reported an increase in income taxes payable of $1,400 during the year and a decrease in deferred-tax asset of $2,000. Its income tax expense was $5,700.

Required »

a. What is cash paid for income taxes?
b. What would Zurry report in the operating section of the cash flow statement under the indirect method?

7 **BE22-26. Complex Transactions, Change in Accounts Receivable.** Donegal Industries reported net income of $67,000 for the current year. The balances and activity in its accounts receivable accounts follow. In addition, the company recorded $3,300 of bad debt expense and wrote off $2,800 of uncollectible accounts.

Accounts	**End of Year**	**Beginning of Year**
Accounts Receivable	$39,000	$43,000
Allowance	3,500	3,000
Activity		
Bad Debt Expense	$ 3,300	
Write-Offs	2,800	

Required »

Prepare the operating section of the cash flow statement under the indirect method.

7 **BE22-27. Complex Transactions, Unrealized Gains and Losses, Equity Method Investments, Pension Expense, Bond Premiums.** Salat, Inc. has net income of $78,800 in the current year. Pertinent company information follows.

- Salat experiences net unrealized gains on investment securities of $6,200 reported in net income and net unrealized losses of $2,200 reported in other comprehensive income.
- Salat reports $8,300 in income from investments that it accounts for under the equity method and $2,500 in cash dividends received from these investments.
- Salat determines that its pension expense for the year is $5,500 and contributes $3,700 into its plan during the year.
- Salat has amortized $500 of bond premium.

Prepare the operating section of the cash flow statement under the indirect method.

7 **BE22-28. Complex Transactions, Unrealized Gains and Losses, Equity Method Investments, Pension Expense, Equity Compensation, Bond Discount.** Mirat, Inc. has net income of $49,400 in the current year. Additional information for the year follows:

- It experienced net unrealized losses on investment securities of $4,900 reported in net income and net unrealized losses of $2,200 reported in other comprehensive income.
- Mirat reported $7,300 in income from investments for which it accounts under the equity method. It received $1,900 in cash dividends from these investments.
- The firm determined that its pension expense for the year is $6,000 and contributed $6,100 into its plan during the year.
- Mirat expensed $3,400 of employee compensation paid in equity shares (a noncash expense).
- Mirat amortized $500 of bond discount.

Prepare the operating section of the cash flow statement under the indirect method.

Exercises

4 **E22-1. Prepare Statement of Cash Flows, Indirect and Direct.** Hockey Apparel Providers, Inc. provided the following information for the current year.

Simplified Income Statement	Amount
Sales	$ 2,452,000
Cost of Goods Sold	(1,251,000)
Depreciation Expense	(178,000)
Selling, General, and Administrative Expenses	(558,000)
Income Before Taxes	465,000
Tax Expense	(145,000)
Net Income	$ 320,000

Account Changes from the Balance Sheet	
Decrease in Accounts Receivable	$ 29,000
Decrease in Inventory	43,000
Increase in Prepaid Expenses	9,000
Decrease in Accounts Payable	34,000
Increase in Income Taxes Payable	32,000

Required »

a. Compute cash flows from operating activities for Hockey Apparel Providers under the indirect reporting format.

b. Compute cash flows from operating activities for Hockey Apparel Providers under the direct reporting format.

4 **E22-2. Prepare Statement of Cash Flows, Indirect, IFRS.** Use the information from E22-1 assuming that Hockey Apparel Providers, Inc. is an IFRS reporter. Compute cash flows from operating activities for the firm under the indirect reporting format assuming that Hockey reconciles income before taxes to operating cash flows.

4 **E22-3. Operating Activities Section, Indirect Method.** Acerler Fixtures, Inc. reported the following comparative balance sheets and income statement for the current year.

Acerler Fixtures, Inc.
Comparative Balance Sheets
At December 31

	Current Year	Prior Year
Cash	$1,091	$ 155
Accounts Receivable – net	212	175
Inventory	260	229
Prepaid Insurance	53	34
Total Current Assets	$1,616	$ 593
Plant and Equipment – net	1,392	1,348
Total Assets	$3,008	$1,941
Accounts Payable	$ 436	$ 351
Other Payables	543	600
Income Tax Payable	65	52
Total Current Liabilities	$1,044	$1,003
Long-Term Debt	456	308
Total Liabilities	$1,500	$1,311
Capital Stock	$ 523	$ 400
Retained Earnings	985	230
Total Shareholders' Equity	$1,508	$ 630
Total Liabilities and Equity	$3,008	$1,941

Acerler Fixtures, Inc.
Income Statement
For the Current Year Ended December 31

Sales		$4,540
Operating Expenses:		
Cost of Goods Sold	$2,539	
Depreciation	169	
Insurance	49	
Gain on Sale of Equipment	(23)	
Other Expenses	687	3,421
Income before Tax		$1,119
Provision for Income Tax		280
Net Income		$ 839

Acerler Fixtures purchased new equipment for $258 and sold equipment with a net book value of $45. Both events were cash transactions. It paid any dividends declared. It repaid $25 of long-term debt during the year.

Required »

a. Prepare the operating activities section of the statement of cash flows using the indirect method.
b. Prepare the operating activities section of the statement of cash flows using the direct method.

4 **E22-4. Operating Activities Section, Indirect Method.** Sansa Accessories, Inc. reported the following comparative balance sheets and income statement for the current year.

Sansa Accessories, Inc.
Comparative Balance Sheets
At December 31

	Current Year	Prior Year
Cash	$ 29	$ 459
Accounts Receivable – net	568	368
Inventory	850	730
Prepaid Insurance	5	12
Total Current Assets	$ 1,452	$ 1,569
Plant and Equipment – net	2,710	2,380
Total Assets	$ 4,162	$ 3,949
Accounts Payable	$ 436	$ 442
Salaries Payable	540	710
Income Tax Payable	65	68
Total Current Liabilities	$ 1,041	$ 1,220
Long-Term Debt	2,090	1,830
Total Liabilities	$ 3,131	$ 3,050
Capital Stock	$ 2,460	$ 2,460
Retained Earnings	(1,429)	(1,561)
Total Shareholders' Equity	$ 1,031	$ 899
Total Liabilities and Equity	$ 4,162	$ 3,949

Sansa Accessories, Inc.
Income Statement
For the Current Year Ended December 31

Sales		$7,915
Operating Expenses		
Cost of Goods Sold	$6,620	
Depreciation	298	
Salaries Expense	687	
Insurance	24	
Loss on Sale of Equipment	90	7,719
Income before Tax		$ 196
Provision for Income Tax		49
Net Income		$ 147

Sansa Accessories purchased new equipment for $948 and sold equipment with a net book value of $320. Both events were cash transactions. It paid any dividends declared and repaid $120 of long-term debt during the year.

Required »

a. Prepare the operating activities section of the statement of cash flows using the indirect method.
b. Prepare the operating activities section of the statement of cash flows using the direct method.

4 5 6 7 8 **E22-5. Statement of Cash Flows, Indirect Method, Disclosures.** SuperView Company's comparative balance sheets and its current income statement follow.

SuperView Company
Balance Sheets
At December 31

Assets	Current Year	Prior Year
Current Assets		
Cash	$ 98,840	$ 75,890
Accounts Receivable – net	200,500	189,750
Merchandise Inventory	450,000	300,000
Total Current Assets	$ 749,340	$ 565,640
Noncurrent Assets		
Property, Plant, and Equipment – net	$2,185,000	$1,500,000
Intangible Assets – net	205,000	168,750
Deferred Tax Asset – net	200,000	0
Total Noncurrent Assets	$2,590,000	$1,668,750
Total Assets	$3,339,340	$2,234,390
Liabilities		
Current Liabilities		
Current Portion of Long-Term Debt	$ 75,000	$ 50,000
Accounts Payable	386,750	190,000
Income Taxes Payable	0	80,000
Total Current Liabilities	$ 461,750	$ 320,000
Noncurrent Liabilities		
Notes Payable	$ 504,425	$ 303,750
Total Noncurrent Liabilities	$ 504,425	$ 303,750
Total Liabilities	$ 966,175	$ 623,750

SuperView Company
Balance Sheets
At December 31

	Current Year	Prior Year
Shareholders' Equity		
Common Stock, $1 par value	$ 969,375	$ 608,875
Additional Paid-in Capital in Excess of Par–Common	1,980,000	750,000
Retained Earnings	210,340	600,000
Total Shareholders' Equity	$3,159,715	$1,958,875
Less: Treasury Stock at Cost	(786,550)	(348,235)
Total Liabilities and Shareholders' Equity	$3,339,340	$2,234,390

SuperView Company
Income Statement
For the Current Year Ended December 31

Sales	$1,875,000
Cost of Goods Sold	1,125,000
Gross Profit	$ 750,000
Selling, General, and Administrative Expenses	$ 998,500
Bad Debt Expense	65,500
Depreciation Expense	200,000
Amortization Expense	30,000
Total Operating Expenses	$1,294,000
Operating Loss	$ (544,000)
Interest Expense	(75,110)
Franchise Fees	8,950
Loss from Continuing Operations before Tax	$ (610,160)
Income Tax Benefit (Expense)	$ 244,064
Increase in Valuation Allowance	(44,064)
Net Tax Benefit	$ 200,000
Loss from Continuing Operations	$ (410,160)
Discontinued Operations – net of tax	20,500
Net Loss	$ (389,660)

Additional Information »

- SuperView did not sell any plant or intangible assets during the current year. It acquired equipment and a new franchise during the year using cash.
- SuperView reports accounts receivable net of the allowance for bad debts.
- The deferred-tax asset is caused by a net operating loss; SuperView reports it net of a valuation allowance estimated at $44,064.
- Because of its net operating loss, the company is not able to declare and pay dividends this year.
- The company made no debt payments this year.
- Because of the net operating loss, there are no taxes due and payable for the current year. The company did pay the amount of taxes payable from the prior year.
- SuperView reports the income from discontinued operations net of tax as a cash transaction.

Required »

Prepare the company's cash flow statement for the current year under the indirect method and present required disclosures.

4 5 6 8 **E22-6. Statement of Cash Flows, Direct Method, Disclosures.** Using the information provided in E22-5, prepare the cash flow statement for SuperView Company using the direct method. Provide all required disclosures.

4 5 6 8 **E22-7. Statement of Cash Flows, Indirect Method, Disclosures.** Michael Hart Associates closed its books for the current year. The firm provided the following comparative balance sheets and income statement.

Michael Hart Associates
Balance Sheets
At December 31

Assets	**Ending**	**Beginning**
Current Assets		
Cash	$ 18,869	$ 44,400
Held-to-Maturity Debt Investments	30,988	0
Accounts Receivable – net	24,975	27,750
Merchandise Inventory	46,250	37,000
Prepaid Expenses	25,000	15,000
Total Current Assets	$ 146,082	$ 124,150
Noncurrent Assets		
Land	$ 900,000	$ 725,000
Property, Plant, and Equipment	1,684,638	1,684,638
Accumulated Depreciation	(342,000)	(320,000)
Indefinite-Life Intangible Assets	0	22,575
Total Noncurrent Assets	$2,242,638	$ 2,112,213
Total Assets	$2,388,720	$2,236,363
Liabilities		
Current Liabilities		
Accounts Payable	$ 74,062	$ 39,688
Dividends Payable	22,200	0
Income Taxes Payable	18,000	10,000
Total Current Liabilities	$ 114,262	$ 49,688
Noncurrent Liabilities		
Notes Payable	$ 107,208	$ 453,610
Total Noncurrent Liabilities	$ 107,208	$ 453,610
Total Liabilities	$ 221,470	$ 503,298
Shareholders' Equity		
Common Stock, $1 par value	$ 685,000	$ 500,750
Additional Paid-in Capital in Excess of Par – Common	890,250	733,000
Additional Paid-in Capital – Stock Options	37,000	0
Retained Earnings	555,000	499,315
Total Shareholders' Equity	$ 2,167,250	$1,733,065
Total Liabilities and Shareholders' Equity	$2,388,720	$2,236,363

Michael Hart Associates
Income Statement
For the Current Year Ended December 31

Sales	$795,000
Cost of Goods Sold	477,000
Gross Profit	$318,000
Selling, General, and Administrative Expenses	$ 83,250
Bad Debt Expense	8,000
Depreciation Expense	22,000
Total Operating Expenses	$113,250
Operating Income	$204,750
Interest Expense	$ (7,369)
Interest Income	1,650
Income before Tax	$199,031
Income Tax Expense	(79,612)
Net Income	$119,419

Additional Information »

The company sold its indefinite-life intangible assets at their carrying value. Cash was used to acquire land. The debt investments were purchased on December 31.

Required »

Prepare the company's cash flow statement for the current year under the indirect method. Present any required disclosures.

4 5 6 8 **E22-8. Statement of Cash Flows, Direct Method, Disclosures.** Prepare the cash flow statement under the direct format for Michael Hart Associates using the data provided in E22-7.

4 5 6 8 **E22-9. Operating Activities Section, Indirect Method, IFRS.** Prepare the operating activities section of the statement of cash flows for Michael Hart Associates in E22-7 using the indirect method assuming that Michael Hart Associates reports under IFRS. Hart begins the operating activities section with operating income. It reports interest and dividends paid in the financing activities section and interest received in the investing activities section.

4 5 6 8 **E22-10. Statement of Cash Flows, Indirect Method, Disclosures.** Starland Corporation provided the following comparative balance sheets and income statement.

Starland Corporation
Balance Sheets
At December 31

Assets	**Current Year**	**Prior Year**
Current Assets		
Cash	$ 270,001	$ 145,847
Accounts Receivable – net	268,363	255,368
Merchandise Inventory	381,358	268,363
Prepaid Expenses	55,000	75,000
Total Current Assets	$ 974,722	$ 744,578
Noncurrent Assets		
Property, Plant, and Equipment – net	$3,854,542	$4,323,471
Total Noncurrent Assets	$3,854,542	$4,323,471
Total Assets	$4,829,264	$5,068,049
Liabilities		
Current Liabilities		
Current Portion of Long-Term Debt	$ 125,622	$ 360,877
Accounts Payable	528,252	446,695
Income Taxes Payable	185,877	165,255
Total Current Liabilities	$ 839,751	$ 972,827
Noncurrent Liabilities		
Notes Payable	$ 730,854	$ 635,597
Total Noncurrent Liabilities	$ 730,854	$ 635,597
Total Liabilities	$1,570,605	$1,608,424
Shareholders' Equity		
Common Stock, $1 par value	$ 381,358	$ 381,358
Additional Paid-in Capital in Excess of Par – Common	1,129,950	1,129,950
Retained Earnings	2,287,351	2,083,317
Total Shareholders' Equity	$3,798,659	$3,594,625
Less: Treasury Stock at Cost	(540,000)	(135,000)
Total Liabilities and Shareholders' Equity	$4,829,264	$5,068,049

Starland Corporation
Income Statement
For the Current Year Ended December 31

Sales	$1,875,050
Cost of Goods Sold	1,125,030
Gross Profit	$ 750,020
Selling, General, and Administrative Expenses	$ 205,000
Bad Debt Expense	4,394
Depreciation Expense	39,525
Total Operating Expenses	$ 248,919
Operating Income	$ 501,101
Loss on Disposal of Equipment	$ (50,000)
Interest Expense	(12,500)
Income before Tax	$ 438,601
Income Tax Expense	(175,440)
Net Income	$ 263,161

Additional Information »

- Starland did not acquire any additional plant assets during the current year.
- Starland sold equipment with a carrying value of $429,404 at a $50,000 loss.
- The company borrowed additional funds by issuing a long-term note. Any debt payments made during the year reduced the current portion of long-term debt.

Required »

Prepare the cash flow statement for Starland Corporation for the current year using the indirect method. Provide all required disclosures.

4 5 6 8 **E22-11. Statement of Cash Flows, Direct Method, Disclosures.** Complete the requirements of E22-10 using the direct method.

4 5 6 **E22-12. Statement of Cash Flows, Indirect Method.** Ferragosto Services, Ltd. provided the following comparative balance sheets and income statement for the current year.

Ferragosto Services, Ltd.
Balance Sheets
At December 31

Assets	Current Year	Prior Year
Current Assets		
Cash	$ 317,400	$ 93,150
Accounts Receivable – net	312,225	265,305
Supplies Inventory	807,250	603,750
Prepaid Expenses	25,875	23,460
Total Current Assets	$1,462,750	$ 985,665
Noncurrent Assets		
Held-to-Maturity Debt Investments	$ 69,000	$ 120,750
Land	320,850	207,000
Property, Plant, and Equipment	990,150	841,800
Accumulated Depreciation	(120,750)	(44,850)
Total Noncurrent Assets	$1,259,250	$1,124,700
Total Assets	$2,722,000	$2,110,365
Liabilities		
Current Liabilities		
Accrued Liabilities	$ 310,500	$ 289,800
Accounts Payable	393,300	217,350
Total Current Liabilities	$ 703,800	$ 507,150

Ferragosto Services, Ltd.
Balance Sheets
At December 31

	Current Year	Prior Year
Noncurrent Liabilities		
Notes Payable	$ 531,250	$ 207,000
Total Noncurrent Liabilities	$ 531,250	$ 207,000
Total Liabilities	$1,235,050	$ 714,150
Shareholders' Equity		
Common Stock, no par value	$ 345,000	$ 345,000
Retained Earnings	1,193,700	1,078,815
Total Shareholders' Equity	$1,538,700	$1,423,815
Less: Treasury Stock at Cost	(51,750)	(27,600)
Total Liabilities and Shareholders' Equity	$2,722,000	$2,110,365

Ferragosto Services, Ltd.
Income Statement
For the Current Year Ended December, 31

Service Revenue	$ 707,475
Selling, General, and Administrative Expenses	(280,100)
Depreciation Expense	(75,900)
Bad Debt Expense	(20,000)
Operating Income	$ 331,475
Interest Expense	(25,000)
Income before Tax	$306,475
Tax at 40%	(122,590)
Net Income	$ 183,885

Additional Information »

- Ferragosto included the $24,150 loss on disposal of investments in selling, general, and administrative expenses on the income statement.
- Accrued liabilities relate to selling, general, and administrative expenses.
- All dividends declared are paid in cash.
- All interest and taxes are paid in cash.
- Acquisitions of land and property, plant, and equipment used cash only.
- There was no amortization of the held-to-maturity debt investments. There were no adjustments to fair value.

Required »

Prepare Ferragosto's cash flow statement for the current year under the indirect method. Assume that accrued liabilities relate to selling, general, and administrative expenses.

4 5 6 **E22-13. Statement of Cash Flows, Direct Method, Disclosures.** Using the information provided in E22-12, prepare the statement of cash flows for Ferragosto Services, Ltd. under the direct method.

4 5 6 8 E22-14. **Statement of Cash Flows, Direct Method, IFRS, Disclosures.** Using the information provided in E22-12, prepare the statement of cash flows for Ferragosto Services, Ltd. under the indirect method. Use operating income as the starting point. Assume that interest expense and dividends paid are financing activities and that taxes are an operating activity.

4 5 6 **E22-15. Statement of Cash Flows, Indirect Method, Disclosures.** Cuthbert Cookware Distributors, Inc. is a wholesale distributor of brand-name cookware products. The company's current-year comparative balance sheets and income statement follow.

Cuthbert Cookware Distributors, Inc.
Balance Sheets
At December 31

	Current Year	Prior Year
Current Assets		
Cash	$ 107,500	$ 600,000
Accounts Receivable – net	975,000	525,000
Inventory	900,000	1,125,000
Total Current Assets	$1,982,500	$2,250,000
Noncurrent Assets		
Held-to-Maturity Debt Investments	$ 0	$ 300,000
Total Assets	$1,982,500	$2,550,000
Liabilities		
Current Liabilities		
Accrued Liabilities	$ 375,000	$ 600,000
Accounts Payable	393,300	217,350
Total Current Liabilities	$ 768,300	$ 817,350
Noncurrent Liabilities		
Notes Payable	$ 350,000	$ 500,000
Total Noncurrent Liabilities	$ 350,000	$ 500,000
Total Liabilities	$1,118,300	$ 1,317,350
Shareholders' Equity		
Common Stock, no par value	$ 625,000	$ 625,000
Retained Earnings	512,500	750,000
Total Shareholders' Equity	$ 1,137,500	$1,375,000
Less: Treasury Stock at Cost	(273,300)	(142,350)
Total Liabilities and Shareholders' Equity	$1,982,500	$2,550,000

Cuthbert Cookware Distributors, Inc.
Income Statement
For the Current Year Ended December 31

Sales Revenue	$ 2,800,000
Cost of Goods Sold	(1,875,000)
Selling, General, and Administrative Expenses	(885,000)
Depreciation Expense	0
Bad Debt Expense	(10,000)
Loss on Sale of Investments	(37,500)
Interest Expense – net	(5,000)
Loss before Tax	$ (12,500)
Tax at 40%	0
Net Loss	$ (12,500)

Additional information »

- All dividends declared are paid in cash.
- All interest and taxes are paid in cash.
- There was no amortization of the held-to-maturity debt investments.

Required »

Prepare the statement of cash flows using the indirect reporting format. Assume that accrued liabilities relate to selling, general, and administrative expenses.

4 5 6 **E22-16.** **Statement of Cash Flows, Direct Method, Disclosures.** Using the information provided in E22-15, prepare Cuthbert's current-year statement of cash flows under the direct reporting format.

Problems

4 **P22-1. Prepare Statement of Cash Flows, Direct Method.** Shark Company provided the following balance sheet and income statement for the current year. Prepare the operating activities section of the cash flow statement using the direct method. Assume that accrued expenses relate to selling, general, and administrative expenses.

Shark Company
Balance Sheet
At December 31

Assets	Ending	Beginning
Current Assets		
Cash	$ 1,000	$ 5,000
Accounts Receivable – net	5,500	3,000
Merchandise Inventory	4,000	1,800
Total Current Assets	$10,500	$ 9,800
Noncurrent Assets		
Investments in Bonds	$30,000	$10,000
Property, Plant, and Equipment – net	$50,000	$60,000
Total Noncurrent Assets	$80,000	$70,000
Total Assets	$90,500	$79,800
Liabilities		
Current Liabilities		
Accounts Payable	$ 3,200	$ 4,400
Accrued Expenses	6,700	6,550
Income Taxes Payable	1,500	2,450
Total Current Liabilities	$11,400	$13,400
Noncurrent Liabilities		
Notes Payable	$35,000	$28,000
Total Noncurrent Liabilities	$35,000	$28,000
Total Liabilities	$46,400	$41,400
Shareholders' Equity		
Common Stock, $1 par value	$10,000	$ 9,000
Additional Paid-in Capital in Excess of Par – Common	15,334	12,000
Retained Earnings	18,766	17,400
Total Shareholders' Equity	$44,100	$38,400
Total Liabilities and Shareholders' Equity	$90,500	$79,800

Shark Company
Income Statement
For the Year Ended December 31

Sales	$56,000
Cost of Goods Sold	33,600
Gross Profit	$22,400
Selling, General, and Administrative Expenses	$11,600
Depreciation Expense	6,000
Total Operating Expenses	$ 17,600
Operating Income	$ 4,800
Interest Expense	$ (2,100)
Income before Tax	$ 2,700
Income Tax Expense	(1,334)
Net Income	$ 1,366

4 **P22-2. Prepare Statement of Cash Flows, Indirect Method.** Repeat the requirements of P22-1 under the indirect method.

4 **P22-3. Prepare Statement of Cash Flows, Direct Method.** Westhoff, Incorporated provided the following balance sheets and income statement for the current year. Prepare the operating activities section of the cash flow statement using the direct method. Assume that accrued expenses relate to selling, general, and administrative expenses. All acquisitions of property, plant, and equipment were made using cash.

Westhoff, Incorporated
Balance Sheet
At December 31

Assets	**Ending**	**Beginning**
Current Assets		
Cash	$ 7,000	$ 3,500
Accounts Receivable – net	8,500	8,000
Merchandise Inventory	2,300	4,000
Prepaid Insurance	1,700	2,200
Total Current Assets	$ 19,500	$ 17,700
Noncurrent Assets		
Investments	$ 12,000	$ 24,300
Property, Plant, and Equipment – net	75,000	58,000
Total Noncurrent Assets	$ 87,000	$ 82,300
Total Assets	$106,500	$100,000
Liabilities		
Current Liabilities		
Accounts Payable	$ 4,500	$ 1,000
Accrued Expenses	9,800	5,120
Income Taxes Payable	6,000	4,850
Total Current Liabilities	$ 20,300	$ 10,970
Noncurrent Liabilities		
Notes Payable	$ 31,000	$ 42,630
Total Noncurrent Liabilities	$ 31,000	$ 42,630
Total Liabilities	$ 51,300	$ 53,600
Shareholders' Equity		
Common Stock, $1 par value	$ 9,000	$ 9,000
Additional Paid-in Capital in Excess of Par – Common	20,000	20,000
Retained Earnings	26,200	17,400
Total Shareholders' Equity	$ 55,200	$ 46,400
Total Liabilities and Shareholders' Equity	$106,500	$100,000

Westhoff, Incorporated
Income Statement
For the Year Ended December 31

Sales	$80,085
Cost of Goods Sold	48,051
Gross Profit	$32,034
Selling, General, and Administrative Expenses	$10,700
Depreciation Expense	2,400
Total Operating Expenses	$13,100
Operating Income	$18,934
Interest Expense	$ (4,000)
Interest Revenue	3,400
Income before Tax	$18,334
Income Tax Expense	(7,334)
Net Income	$11,000

4 **P22-4. Prepare Statement of Cash Flows, Indirect Method.** Repeat the requirements in P22-3 using the indirect method.

4 5 6 7 8 **P22-5. Statement of Cash Flows, Indirect Method, Complex Accounts, Disclosures.** The Khan Group provided its balance sheet and income statement as of December 31 of the current year.

The Khan Group
Balance Sheets
At December 31

Assets	**Current Year**	**Prior Year**
Current Assets		
Cash	$ 15,000	$ 12,000
Trading Debt Investments	36,000	30,000
Accounts Receivable – net	65,000	35,000
Merchandise Inventory	105,000	115,000
Total Current Assets	$ 221,000	$ 192,000
Noncurrent Assets		
Investments in Affiliate Companies	$ 161,500	$ 100,500
Property, Plant, and Equipment – net	1,533,050	1,128,580
Intangible Assets – net	95,200	88,000
Total Noncurrent Assets	$1,789,750	$ 1,317,080
Total Assets	$2,010,750	$1,509,080
Liabilities		
Current Liabilities		
Current Portion of Long-Term Debt	$ 6,000	$ 4,500
Accounts Payable	87,500	92,500
Dividends Payable	5,000	0
Income Taxes Payable	28,500	30,000
Total Current Liabilities	$ 127,000	$ 127,000
Noncurrent Liabilities		
Bonds Payable	$ 425,000	$ 425,000
Less: Discount on Bonds	(87,500)	(100,250)
Notes Payable	52,500	10,000
Deferred Tax Liability	3,750	1,250
Net Obligations under Pension Plans	45,000	22,630
Total Noncurrent Liabilities	$ 438,750	$ 358,630
Total Liabilities	$ 565,750	$ 485,630
Shareholders' Equity		
Common Stock, $1 par value	$ 60,000	$ 50,000
Additional Paid-in Capital in Excess of Par – Common	132,100	122,100
Additional Paid-in Capital – Stock Options	2,900	0
Retained Earnings	1,175,000	781,850
Accumulated Other Comprehensive Income	75,000	69,500
Total Shareholders' Equity	$1,445,000	$1,023,450
Total Liabilities and Shareholders' Equity	$2,010,750	$1,509,080

The Khan Group
Income Statement
For the Current Year Ended December 31

Sales	$2,212,040
Cost of Goods Sold	1,327,224
Gross Profit	$ 884,816
Selling, General, and Administrative Expenses	$ 43,000
Unrealized Losses on Trading Portfolio	$ 3,600
Pension Expense	210,500
Bad Debt Expense	1,500
Depreciation Expense	17,700
Amortization Expense	6,750
Total Operating Expenses	$ 283,050
Operating Income	$ 601,766
Interest Expense	$ (50,100)
Investment Income (includes gain on sale)	50,000
Equity Earnings from Affiliate Companies	118,500
Income before Tax	$ 720,166
Income Tax Expense	(288,066)
Net Income	$ 432,100

Additional Information »

- The company classifies its current investments as trading securities. During the current year, it sold trading securities that had been acquired for $34,500. Treat the trading securities as an investing activity.
- The company reported accounts receivable net of the allowance for bad debts.
- The company acquired equipment during the year and made no disposals. Paid cash.
- The company acquired intangible assets during the year and made no disposals. Paid cash.
- The company included a $40,500 gain on the sale of trading investments in investment income on the income statement.
- The change in accumulated other comprehensive income is the result of pension adjustments.
- There were no additional investments in affiliate companies during the year.
- The company issued long-term debt of $44,000.

Required »

Prepare the company's cash flow statement for the current year under the indirect method. Provide all required disclosures.

4 5 6 7 8 **P22-6.** **Statement of Cash Flows, Direct Method, Complex Accounts, Disclosures.** Using the data provided in P22-5, prepare the statement of cash flows for The Khan Group using the direct method. Provide all required disclosures.

4 5 6 7 8 **P22-7.** **Statement of Cash Flows, Indirect Method, Complex Accounts, Disclosures.** Norwich Manufacturing, Inc. provided you with the following comparative balance sheets and income statement.

Norwich Manufacturing, Inc.
Balance Sheets
At December 31

Assets	Current Year	Prior Year
Current Assets		
Cash	$ 45,000	$ 22,000
Available-for-Sale Debt Investments	58,000	82,000
Accounts Receivable – net	95,000	55,000
Merchandise Inventory	135,000	95,000
Total Current Assets	$ 333,000	$ 254,000

Norwich Manufacturing, Inc.
Balance Sheets
At December 31

	Current Year	Prior Year
Noncurrent Assets		
Investments in Affiliate Companies	$ 265,000	$ 100,500
Property, Plant, and Equipment – net	1,364,500	1,530,500
Intangible Assets – net	87,500	125,000
Total Noncurrent Assets	$ 1,717,000	$1,756,000
Total Assets	$2,050,000	$2,010,000
Liabilities		
Current Liabilities		
Current Portion of Long-Term Debt	$ 25,000	$ 65,800
Accounts Payable	187,000	128,500
Dividends Payable	75,000	55,000
Income Taxes Payable	65,800	58,500
Total Current Liabilities	$ 352,800	$ 307,800
Noncurrent Liabilities		
Bonds Payable	$ 400,000	$ 400,000
Less: Discount on Bonds	(128,500)	(145,000)
Notes Payable	225,500	225,000
Deferred Tax Liability	62,500	72,500
Net Obligations under Pension Plans	80,000	60,000
Total Noncurrent Liabilities	$ 639,500	$ 612,500
Total Liabilities	$ 992,300	$ 920,300
Shareholders' Equity		
Common Stock, $1 par value	$ 135,000	$ 135,000
Additional Paid-in Capital in Excess of Par – Common	351,500	351,500
Additional Paid-in Capital – Stock Options	16,500	0
Retained Earnings	685,000	523,700
Accumulated Other Comprehensive Income	(130,300)	79,500
Total Shareholders' Equity	$ 1,057,700	$1,089,700
Total Liabilities and Shareholders' Equity	$2,050,000	$2,010,000

Norwich Manufacturing, Inc.
Income Statement
For the Current Year Ended December 31

Sales	$2,433,244
Cost of Goods Sold	1,459,946
Gross Profit	$ 973,298
Selling, General, and Administrative Expenses	$ 59,800
Pension Expense	260,510
Bad Debt Expense	1,650
Depreciation Expense	19,470
Amortization Expense	7,425
Total Operating Expenses	$ 348,855
Operating Income	$ 624,443
Interest Expense	$ (55,110)
Investment Income (includes gain on sale)	55,000
Equity Earnings from Affiliate Companies	164,500
Income before Tax	$ 788,833
Income Tax Expense	(301,873)
Net Income	$ 486,960

Additional Information »

- Norwich sold available-for-sale investments that had been acquired for $55,000 at a gain of $40,500. It included this gain in investment income on the income statement.
- The company acquired additional shares as investments to be carried at fair value. It accounted for all investments, except for investments carried under the equity method, as available-for-sale securities. It recorded a $9,000 unrealized loss for the current year.
- It reported accounts receivable net of the allowance for bad debts.
- It sold equipment at book value.
- It did not increase its percentage ownership of its equity investee (affiliate company).
- It sold one of its franchises at book value.
- It signed a $100,000 promissory note issued by an equipment dealer in the acquisition of a plant asset.
- It did not borrow additional cash funds during the year.

Required »

Prepare Norwich Manufacturing's cash flow statement for the current year using the indirect method. Present required disclosures.

4 5 6 7 8 **P22-8. Statement of Cash Flows, Direct Method, Complex Accounts, Disclosures.** Prepare the cash flow statement for Norwich Manufacturing, Inc. under the direct method using the information provided in P22-7. Provide all required disclosures.

4 5 6 7 8 **P22-9. Statement of Cash Flows, Indirect Method, Complex Accounts, Disclosures.** Orlando Incorporated provided the following comparative balance sheets and the results of operations for the current year.

Orlando Incorporated
Balance Sheets
At December 31

Assets	**Current Year**	**Prior Year**
Current Assets		
Cash	$ 60,750	$ 69,700
Available-for-Sale Debt Investments	78,300	110,700
Accounts Receivable – net	128,250	74,250
Merchandise Inventory	182,250	128,250
Total Current Assets	$ 449,550	$ 382,900
Noncurrent Assets		
Investments in Affiliate Companies	$ 357,750	$ 135,675
Property, Plant, and Equipment – net	1,842,075	2,066,175
Intangible Assets – net	118,125	168,750
Total Noncurrent Assets	$ 2,317,950	$2,370,600
Total Assets	$ 2,767,500	$2,753,500
Liabilities		
Current Liabilities		
Current Portion of Long-Term Debt	$ 33,750	$ 88,830
Accounts Payable	252,450	213,475
Dividends Payable	101,250	74,250
Income Taxes Payable	88,830	78,975
Total Current Liabilities	$ 476,280	$ 455,530
Noncurrent Liabilities		
Bonds Payable	$ 540,000	$ 540,000
Less: Discount on Bonds	(173,475)	(195,750)
Notes Payable	304,425	303,750
Deferred Tax Liability	84,375	97,875
Net Obligations under Pension Plans	108,000	81,000
Total Noncurrent Liabilities	$ 863,325	$ 826,875
Total Liabilities	$1,339,605	$1,282,405

Orlando Incorporated
Balance Sheets
At December 31

	Current Year	Prior Year
Shareholders' Equity		
Common Stock, $1 par value	$ 182,250	$ 182,250
Additional Paid-in Capital in Excess of Par – Common	474,525	474,525
Additional Paid-in Capital – Stock Options	22,275	0
Retained Earnings	924,750	706,995
Accumulated Other Comprehensive Income	(175,905)	107,325
Total Shareholders' Equity	$ 1,427,895	$1,471,095
Total Liabilities and Shareholders' Equity	$ 2,767,500	$2,753,500

Orlando Incorporated
Income Statement
For the Current Year Ended December 31

Sales	$2,342,000
Cost of Goods Sold	1,405,200
Gross Profit	$ 936,800
Selling, General, and Administrative Expenses	$ 66,500
Pension Expense	200,150
Bad Debt Expense	2,835
Depreciation Expense	25,500
Amortization Expense	9,000
Total Operating Expenses	$ 303,985
Operating Income	$ 632,815
Loss on Disposal of Equipment	$ (35,000)
Interest Expense	(75,110)
Investment Income (includes loss on sale)	5,000
Equity Earnings from Affiliate Companies	330,350
Income from Continuing Operations before Tax	$ 858,055
Income Tax Expense	(343,222)
Income from Continuing Operations	$ 514,833
Loss from Discontinued Operations – net of tax	(16,478)
Net Income	$ 498,355

Additional Information »

- Orlando sold available-for-sale investments that had been acquired for the cost of $74,250 at a loss of $14,250. It included this loss in investment income on the income statement.
- It acquired additional shares as investments to be carried at fair value. Orlando accounted for all investments, except for investments carried under the equity method, as available-for-sale securities. It recorded a $6,000 unrealized loss for the current year.
- It reported accounts receivable net of the allowance for bad debts.
- It did not acquire additional plant and equipment during the year but sold a piece of equipment with a book value of $198,600.
- It did not increase its percentage ownership of its equity investee (affiliate company).
- It sold one of its franchises at book value.
- It signed a $675 promissory note.
- It reported the loss from discontinued operations net of tax and as a cash transaction.

Required »

Prepare the current-year cash flow statement for Orlando Incorporated under the indirect method. Present required disclosures.

④⑤⑥⑦⑧ **P22-10. Statement of Cash Flows, Indirect Method, Complex Accounts, Disclosures.** Using the information provided in P22-9, prepare the cash flow statement for Orlando Incorporated using the direct method. Provide all required disclosures.

④⑤⑥⑦⑧ **P22-11. Statement of Cash Flows, Indirect Method, Complex Accounts, Disclosures.** Barry's Clothing Stores, Inc. released its annual report for the current year and included the following comparative balance sheets and income statement.

Barry's Clothing Store, Inc.
Balance Sheets
At December 31

Assets	Current Year	Prior Year
Current Assets		
Cash	$ 94,164	$ 108,035
Available-for-Sale Debt Investments	121,365	171,585
Accounts Receivable – net	198,788	115,088
Merchandise Inventory	282,488	198,788
Total Current Assets	$ 696,805	$ 593,496
Noncurrent Assets		
Investments in Affiliate Companies	$ 554,513	$ 210,296
Property, Plant, and Equipment – net	2,855,216	3,202,571
Intangible Assets – net	183,094	261,563
Total Noncurrent Assets	$3,592,823	$3,674,430
Total Assets	$4,289,628	$4,267,926
Liabilities		
Current Liabilities		
Current Portion of Long-Term Debt	$ 52,313	$ 137,687
Accounts Payable	391,298	330,886
Dividends Payable	156,938	115,088
Income Taxes Payable	137,687	122,411
Total Current Liabilities	$ 738,236	$ 706,072
Noncurrent Liabilities		
Bonds Payable	$ 837,000	$ 837,000
Less: Discount on Bonds	(268,886)	(303,413)
Notes Payable	471,859	470,813
Deferred-Tax Liability	130,781	151,706
Net Obligations under Pension Plans	167,400	125,550
Total Noncurrent Liabilities	$1,338,154	$1,281,656
Total Liabilities	$2,076,390	$1,987,728
Shareholders' Equity		
Common Stock, $1 par value	$ 282,488	$ 282,488
Additional Paid-in Capital in Excess of Par – Common	735,514	735,514
Additional Paid-in Capital – Stock Options	34,526	0
Retained Earnings	1,833,363	1,195,842
Accumulated Other Comprehensive Income	(272,653)	166,354
Total Shareholders' Equity	$2,613,238	$2,380,198
Less: Treasury Stock at Cost	(400,000)	(100,000)
Total Liabilities and Shareholders' Equity	$4,289,628	$4,267,926

Barry's Clothing Stores, Inc.
Income Statement
For the Current Year Ended December 31

Sales	$3,630,100
Cost of Goods Sold	2,178,060
Gross Profit	$1,452,040
Selling, General, and Administrative Expenses	$ 103,075
Pension Expense	310,233
Bad Debt Expense	4,394
Depreciation Expense	39,525
Amortization Expense	13,950
Total Operating Expenses	$ 471,177
Operating Income	$ 980,863
Loss on Disposal of Equipment	$ (54,250)
Interest Expense	(116,421)
Investment Income (including loss on sale)	7,750
Equity Earnings from Affiliate Companies	512,043
Income from Continuing Operations before Tax	$1,329,985
Income Tax Expense	(531,994)
Income from Continuing Operations	$ 797,991
Discontinued Operations – net of tax	(25,541)
Net Income	$ 772,450

Additional Information »

- Barry's sold available-for-sale investments that had been acquired for the cost of $115,088 at a loss of $22,088. It included this loss in investment income on the income statement.
- The firm acquired additional shares as available-for-sale investments to be carried at fair value. It accounted for all investments, except for those carried under the equity method, as available-for-sale securities. Barry's recorded a $9,300 unrealized loss for the current year.
- Barry's reported accounts receivable net of the allowance for bad debts.
- The company did not acquire any plant and equipment during the year but sold a piece of equipment with a carrying value of $307,830.
- Barry's did not increase its percentage ownership of its equity investee (affiliate company).
- The company sold one of its franchises at book value.
- Barry's reported the loss from discontinued operations net of tax and as a cash transaction.
- The company is not required to make payments on long-term debt other than the current portion.
- The company borrowed an additional $1,046 by issuing a long-term note at the end of the year.
- The company repurchased treasury stock at a cost of $300,000.

Required »

Prepare the current-year cash flow statement for Barry's Clothing Stores, Inc. under the indirect method. Present required disclosures.

4 5 6 7 8 **P22-12. Statement of Cash Flows, Direct Method, Complex Accounts, Disclosures.** Prepare the cash flow statement and all required disclosures for Barry's Clothing Stores, Inc. from P22-11 using the direct method.

4 5 6 7 8 **P22-13. Statement of Cash Flows, Indirect Method, Complex Accounts, Disclosures.** American Safety Products, Inc. provided the following comparative balance sheets and income statement for the current year.

American Safety Products, Inc.
Balance Sheets
At December 31

Assets	**Current Year**	**Prior Year**
Current Assets		
Cash	$ 1,379,568	$ 378,122
Trading Debt Investments	424,778	600,548
Accounts Receivable – net	695,756	302,806
Merchandise Inventory	988,706	695,756
Prepaid Expenses	647,500	385,000
Total Current Assets	$ 4,136,308	$ 2,362,232
Noncurrent Assets		
Investments in Affiliate Companies	$ 1,940,794	$ 736,037
Held-to-Maturity Debt Investments	542,500	351,750
Property, Plant, and Equipment – net	9,993,257	11,208,999
Equipment under Finance Lease – net	2,800,000	2,975,000
Intangible Assets – net	640,828	915,469
Deferred Tax Asset – net	195,300	143,500
Total Noncurrent Assets	$ 16,112,679	$16,330,755
Total Assets	$20,248,987	$18,692,987
Liabilities		
Current Liabilities		
Current Portion of Long-Term Debt	$ 183,096	$ 481,903
Accounts Payable	1,369,541	1,058,102
Dividends Payable	549,281	402,806
Income Taxes Payable	481,903	428,439
Total Current Liabilities	$ 2,583,821	$ 2,371,250
Noncurrent Liabilities		
Bonds Payable	$ 2,929,500	$ 2,929,500
Add: Premium on Bonds	941,102	1,061,944
Notes Payable	1,651,506	1,647,844
Obligations under Finance Leases	3,500,875	3,850,000
Deferred Tax Liability	457,734	530,972
Net Obligations under Pension Plans	585,900	439,425
Total Noncurrent Liabilities	$10,066,617	$10,459,685
Total Liabilities	$12,650,438	$12,830,935
Shareholders' Equity		
Common Stock, $1 par value	$ 1,338,706	$ 988,706
Additional Paid-in Capital in Excess of Par – Common	3,274,298	2,574,298
Additional Paid-in Capital – Stock Options	120,842	0
Retained Earnings	6,416,769	4,185,448
Accumulated Other Comprehensive Income (AOCI)	(954,285)	582,238
Total Shareholders' Equity	$10,196,330	$ 8,330,690
Less: Treasury Stock at Cost	(2,597,781)	(2,468,638)
Total Liabilities and Shareholders' Equity	$20,248,987	$18,692,987

American Safety Products, Inc.
Income Statement
For the Current Year Ended December 31

Sales	$ 9,458,700
Cost of Goods Sold	5,460,300
Gross Profit	$ 3,998,400
Selling, General, and Administrative Expenses	$ 360,763
Pension Expense	1,085,814
Bad Debt Expense	15,380
Depreciation Expense	138,338
Amortization Expense – finance leases	175,000
Amortization Expense – intangible assets	48,825
Total Operating Expenses	$ 1,824,120
Operating Income	$ 2,174,280
Loss on Disposal of Equipment	$ (189,875)
Interest Expense	(407,472)
Interest Revenue	789,250
Realized Loss on Trading Securities	(65,500)
Equity Earnings from Affiliate Companies	1,792,149
Income before Tax	$ 4,092,832
Income Tax Expense	(1,493,853)
Net Income	$ 2,598,979

Additional Information:

- American Safety Products sold trading securities at a loss.
- The company sold one of its franchises at book value.
- The company sold plant assets with a carrying value of $1,077,404 for a loss of $189,875.
- The company made debt payments to reduce the current portion of long-term debt and finance lease obligations. American Safety Products borrowed an additional $3,662 by issuing a long-term note.
- The change in AOCI is the result of adjustments required for the company's defined-benefit pension plan.
- American Safety Products acquired additional securities classified as held to maturity. It did not purchase any other investments during the year.
- It did not reissue any treasury stock.
- Treat the trading securities as an investing activity.
- Ignore the amortization of the held-to-maturity investment.
- Assume no adjustments to fair value for trading investments.

Required »

Prepare the cash flow statement for American Safety Products for the current year using the indirect method. Provide all required disclosures.

4 5 6 7 8 **P22-14.** **Statement of Cash Flows, Direct Method, Complex Accounts, Disclosures.** Using the information provided in P22-13, prepare the cash flow statement and all required disclosures for American Safety Products using the direct method.

Excel Project
Autograded Excel Project available in **MyLab Accounting**

CASES

Judgment Case

Judgment Case 1: Operating Cash Flows

Consider KaseyKraft Company from Example 22.15 in the text. As discussed, its operating cash flow (OCF) for the year is $248,610. Because this is much lower than operating income of $733,077, KaseyKraft would like to report a higher OCF figure. What decisions could KaseyKraft make to increase its OCF?

How much would KaseyKraft's operating cash flow increase if it factored one-half of its receivables, reduced its inventory by one-third, and postponed its payment to vendors so that it did not pay off an additional $50,000 of accounts payable?

Financial Statement Analysis Case

Financial Statement Analysis Case 1: Analysis of Operating Cash Flows

Your assignment is to analyze ***Pfizer's Inc.*** operating cash flows and compare it to that of ***Johnson & Johnson***. Use ***Pfizer's*** statement of cash flows and the following information to address these questions:

a. What is ***Pfizer's*** net cash provided by operating activities each year? What was the change and percentage of change in ***Pfizer's*** net cash provided by operating activities each year? Compare the changes in net cash provided by operating activities to the changes in net income.

b. What are ***Pfizer's*** major adjustments for noncash expenses and losses? What are the major adjustments for noncash revenues and gains?

c. For each year, compute and comment on the following cash coverage ratios for ***Pfizer***:

- Short-term debt coverage
- Debt coverage
- Dividend coverage
- Sales coverage
- OCF to income ratio

d. For each year, compute and comment on ***Pfizer's*** free cash flows. Compare its free cash flows to its operating cash flows.

e. Using ***Johnson & Johnson's*** information from Example 22.16 in the text, compare ***Pfizer*** and ***Johnson & Johnson's*** cash coverage ratios and free cash flows.

Additional Information »

For the Year-Ended or at the Year-End (in millions)

	2016	2015	2014
Sales	$52,824	$48,851	$49,605
Short-Term debt	$10,688	$10,159	$ 5,141
Long-Term debt	$31,398	$28,740	$31,541

Pfizer Inc. and Subsidiary Companies
Consolidated Statements of Cash Flows
Year Ended December 31, 2016, 2015, and 2014

(millions)	**2016**	**2015**	**2014**
Operating Activities			
Net income before allocation to noncontrolling interests	$7,246	$6,986	$9,168
Adjustments to reconcile net income before allocation to noncontrolling interests to net cash provided by operating activities:			
Depreciation and amortization	5,757	5,157	5,537
Asset write-offs and impairments	1,613	1,119	531
Foreign currency loss related to Venezuela	—	806	—
Gain/(loss) on disposal of discontinued operations	—	6	(51)
Write-down of HIS net assets to fair value less estimated costs to sell	1,712	—	—
Deferred taxes from continuing operations	(700)	(20)	320
Deferred taxes from discontinued operations	—	2	(3)
Share-based compensation expense	691	669	586
Benefit plan contributions in excess of expense	(712)	(617)	(199)
Other adjustments, net	209	(160)	(430)
Other changes in assets and liabilities, net of acquisitions and divestitures:			
Trade accounts receivable	(134)	21	148
Inventories	365	(199)	175
Other assets	(60)	236	1,161
Trade accounts payable	871	254	297
Other liabilities(a)	(223)	664	(650)
Other tax accounts, net	(734)	(235)	492
Net cash provided by operating activities	15,901	14,688	17,084
Investing Activities			
Purchases of property, plant and equipment	(1,823)	(1,397)	(1,199)
Purchases of short-term investments	(15,957)	(28,581)	(50,954)
Proceeds from redemptions/sales of short-term investments	29,436	40,064	47,374
Net (purchases of)/proceeds from redemptions/sales of short-term investments with original maturities of three months or less	(4,218)	5,768	3,930
Purchases of long-term investments	(8,011)	(9,542)	(10,718)
Proceeds from redemptions/sales of long-term investments	11,254	6,929	6,145
Acquisitions of businesses, net of cash acquired	(18,368)	(16,466)	(195)
Acquisitions of intangible assets	(176)	(99)	(384)
Other investing activities, net	51	344	347
Net cash used in investing activities	(7,811)	(2,980)	(5,654)
Financing Activities			
Proceeds from short-term borrowings	7,472	5,557	13
Principal payments on short-term borrowings	(5,102)	(3,965)	(10)
Net proceeds from/(payments on) short-term borrowings with original maturities of three months or less	(3,084)	2,717	(1,841)
Proceeds from issuance of long-term debt	10,976	—	4,491
Principal payments on long-term debt	(7,689)	(2,990)	(2,110)
Purchases of common stock	(5,000)	(6,160)	(5,000)
Cash dividends paid	(7,317)	(6,940)	(6,609)
Proceeds from exercise of stock options	1,019	1,263	1,002
Other financing activities, net(a)	(196)	109	(123)
Net cash used in financing activities	(8,921)	(10,409)	(10,187)
Effect of exchange-rate changes on cash and cash equivalents	(215)	(1,000)	(83)
Net increase/(decrease) in cash and cash equivalents	(1,046)	298	1,160
Cash and cash equivalents, beginning	3,641	3,343	2,183
Cash and cash equivalents, end	$ 2,595	$ 3,641	$ 3,343

***Source*:** Financial Statements, Pfizer Inc. December 31, 2016. https://investors.pfizer.com/financials/annual-reports/default.aspx

Surfing the Standards Cases

Surfing the Standards Case 1: Classification in the Statement of Cash Flows

Refer to the Codification to determine the correct classification in the statement of cash flows (operating, investing, or financing) for the following transactions:

1. Cash contributions to charities
2. Proceeds from insurance on a building that was destroyed
3. Cash payments made to settle an asset retirement obligation
4. Payment for costs of debt issuance
5. Receipts from the sale of securities that were acquired specifically for resale
6. Cash payments to settle lawsuits
7. Interest paid that is capitalized into the cost of a building

Surfing the Standards Case 2: Cash Flow per Share

Refer to FASB ASC 230-10 and the Basis for Conclusions in FASB's *Statement of Financial Accounting Standards No. 95* to answer the following questions:

1. Are companies permitted to report cash flow per share on their financial statements?
2. What was FASB's rationale for making this decision?

Basis for Conclusions Cases

Basis for Conclusions Case 1: Classification of Interest and Dividends on the Statement of Cash Flows

U.S. GAAP and IFRS differ in the classifications of dividends and interest on the statement of cash flows. U.S. GAAP requires firms to classify cash receipts from interest and dividends and cash payments for interest as operating cash flows. However, IFRS allows entities to report these items in any of the three categories—operating, investing, or financing. Read the basis for conclusions in "Statement of Cash Flows," *FASB Statement of Financial Accounting Standards No. 95*, Paragraphs 88 through 90.

1. Where did certain respondents think these cash receipts and payments should be classified? What was their reasoning?
2. What was the Board's reasoning for requiring that firms include these items in operating cash flows?

Basis for Conclusions Case 2: Indirect versus Direct Method of Presenting Operating Cash Flows

Currently, U.S. GAAP allows entities to present their operating cash flows either under the direct or the indirect method.

1. Briefly describe each method's approach.
2. What is the primary advantage of each method?
3. Discuss which participants in the financial reporting process preferred each of the methods and why.
4. Why did the Board decide to allow both methods?

Glossary/Index

A Combined Glossary/Subject Index

Note: Headings in bold indicate defined terms.

A

abandonment of assets, 614

Abercrombie & Fitch, 507, 1272, 1284–1286

account. An individual record of increases and decreases in specific asset, liability, and stockholder equity items, 98

account format. A balance sheet presentation that lists assets on the left side and liabilities and stockholders' equity on the right side of the statement, 242

accounting cycle. Describes the process by which a company records business *transactions* and ultimately aggregates and summarizes them in the financial statements, 91–169
- adjusted trial balance preparation in, 113–115
- adjusting journal entries in, 106–113
- alternative treatment of expenses and revenues in, 159–161
- analysis of transactions in, 92–97
- closing temporary accounts in, 117–118
- comprehensive example of, 119–134
- definition of, 92
- financial statement preparation in, 115–117
- introduction to, 91
- journalizing transactions in, 97–104
- post-closing trial balance preparation in, 118–119
- reversing entries in, 168–169
- review of, 140–158
- unadjusted trial balance preparation in, 105
- using a worksheet in, 161–167

accounting equation. An equation which illustrates the relationship among assets, liabilities, and stockholders' equity as follows: Assets = Liabilities + Stockholders' Equity or A = L + E, 92–97
- definition of, 92
- definition of terms in, 93
- expanded, 95–97

accounting policies footnote. Part of the financial statements that describes the portfolio of accounting choices. It is typically one of the first notes to the financial statements, 57–58

Accounting Principles Board (APB), 9

Accounting Research Bulletins (ARBs), 9

accounting standards
- conceptual framework in setting, 24–25
- global process for, 12, 14–15
- history of, 9–10
- international, 8
- political process of setting, 15
- process for setting, 9–12, 14–17
- role of standard setters in, 8
- trends in, 15–17

Accounting Standards Codification. (Often referred to as the Codification) The single source of GAAP in the United States and includes all pronouncements issued by any of the standard-setting bodies that have not been superseded, 10
- as authoritative literature in research, 64–67
- Herz on, 68
- referencing, 66
- structure of, 65–66
- topic groupings in, 65

accounting standard setters. Organizations that develop and promulgate accounting concepts, rules, and guidelines that provide information that is relevant and faithfully represents the economic performance and the financial position of the reporting entity, 6
- role of, 8

Accounting Standards Update (ASU), 10, 12, 64

accounts payable. Amounts owed for goods, supplies, or services purchased on open account, meaning that the invoice is the only formal documentation for the credit agreement, 239, 736–737

accounts payable turnover ratio. The number of times per year a company goes from full accounts payable balances to full repayment, 471

accounts receivable. Amounts owed to the entity resulting from the sale of goods or services to customers on credit. Also called trade receivables, 238, 446
- aging of, 452–455
- cases on, 495–499
- disclosures for, 468
- factoring, 460–463
- financing with, 458–463
- initial measurement of, 446–450
- pledging and assigning, 459
- subsequent measurement of, 450–452
- uncollectible, 450–458

accounts receivable turnover ratio. Indicates how many times per year the firm goes from a full receivable balance to complete collection, 469

accretion expense. The expense, reported in operating income, resulting from the increase in the carrying amount of the liability, 746

accrual basis of accounting. A system of accounting that recognizes revenues according to the revenue recognition concept and recognizes expenses according to the expense recognition concept, regardless of when they receive or pay cash, 42
- in adjusting journal entries, 42

B

C

D

E

F

G

J

M

T

Y

Z